The Decades of Henry Bullinger

The Decades of Henry Bullinger

Volume 1

Edited by Thomas Harding

With new introductions by
George Ella and Joel R. Beeke

Reformation Heritage Books
Grand Rapids, Michigan

Reformation Heritage Books
3070 29th St. SE
Grand Rapids, MI 49512
616-977-0889
orders@heritagebooks.org
www.heritagebooks.org

Printed in the United States of America
23 24 25 26 27/11 10 9 8 7 6 5 4 3

ISBNs
978-1-892777-38-6 (vol. 1)
978-1-892777-39-3 (vol. 2)
978-1-60178-827-6 (2 vol. set)

This reprint is photolithographed from the 4-volume Parker Society edition (1849–1852), edited by Thomas Harding, and published by the University Press at Cambridge. Volumes 1 (the first and second Decades) and 2 (the third Decade) of the Parker Society edition are printed as volume 1 of this edition. Volumes 3 (the fourth Decade) and 4 (the fifth Decade) of the Parker Society edition are printed as volume 2 of this edition.

For additional Reformed literature, request a free book list from Reformation Heritage Books at the above regular or email address.

Preface

Henry Bullinger is one of the greatest unsung heroes of the Reformation. Happily, 2004, the 500th anniversary of his birth, has stimulated several books about Bullinger in various languages as well as conference addresses on him and his work in various countries. We are grateful to bring back into print his *Decades*, the most influential of all his writings, to coincide with this anniversary.

This reprint is photolithographed from the 4-volume Parker Society edition (1849-1852), edited by Thomas Harding, and published by the University Press at Cambridge. The only changes made are that we have printed the four volumes in two and have added two lengthy introductions, one by Dr. George Ella on Bullinger's life and the other by myself with the assistance of Dr. Ella on his *Decades*.

—JRB

CONTENTS OF NEW INTRODUCTIONS

Henry Bullinger (1504-1575): Shepherd of the Churches

George Ella

Henry Bullinger's *Decades*

Joel R. Beeke with George Ella

Henry Bullinger (1504-1575): Shepherd of the Churches

CHAPTER I
The Importance of Henry Bullinger

The Reformation's Neglected Heroes

It has long been my conviction that not half of the story of the Reformation has been told. Happily, great men and women of God who were true pioneers and upholders of reform are now being rediscovered, causing a radical alteration in our knowledge and even convictions concerning how the true faith was revived after centuries of papal superstition. Since the 1950s, however, the attention of the Reformed churches has centered on the so-called Puritan Age, often called the Second Reformation, which emphasizes the testimony of men and women of God who graced this earth in the seventeenth century. Since the nineteenth century the comparatively little research that has been done on the earlier Reformers has almost exclusively concentrated on the pioneering influence of Luther and the consolidating influence of Calvin. Luther, however, sadly set himself against much of the work of more consistent Reformers, and Calvin was a second-generation Reformer who built on the work of a number of spiritual giants who are now overshadowed by Calvin's subsequent fame.

The result is that the bulk of pioneer Reformers from the twelfth to the sixteenth centuries, such as Robert Greathead, Thomas Bradwardine, John Wycliffe, John Colet, Miles Coverdale, Martin Bucer, Thomas Lever, John Jewel, and Edmund Grindal, are still vague names and shadows to most modern Christian readers. Indeed, many of these Reformers had an international reputation and influence which was wider than most of the later Puritans. The immediate freshness and spontaneity of these early contenders for hitherto lost truths provides us with a glorious witness second to none. Knowledge of their experimental heart-religion at the dawn of the Reformation when the churches again discovered their first love to Christ is important for our own present-day growth in grace. In seeing how God has worked in the past, we learn to trust Him all the more for the future.

The Folly of Ignoring Bullinger

Perhaps no Reformer has been neglected in modern times as much as Swiss-born Henry Bullinger, whose birth 500 years ago is being celebrated this year. Yet Bullinger was once rightly called "the common shepherd of all Christian churches" and had an international reputation which, in his day, nearly equalled Luther's and may have surpassed Calvin's. This fact, which should no longer be ignored, has moved Fritz Blanke and Immanuel Leuschner,[1] renowned Bullinger experts, to go so far as to call Bullinger "the father of the Reformed Church." Today, few seem to know that Bullinger produced far more Christian writings of equal character than Luther, Calvin, and Zwingli combined. Yet, by the nineteenth century, his star had sadly waned. In 1828, in commemoration of the Bernese Reformation, Johannes Friedrich Franz was commissioned to write a *Denkschrift* (memorial report) which he entitled *Remarkable features in the life of the Zürich Superintendent Henry Bullinger as also his travel instructions to his eldest son Heinrich, student at Strasburg and Wittenburg.* The address was dedicated to the student population of Bern, and Franz confessed that though most of our Reformation heroes have been remembered through biographies and their services were continually being praised by posterity, worthy Bullinger's life has been totally neglected.

As a result Professor Felix Nüscheler, who had just completed a biography of Zwingli, started to write a life of Bullinger but found the Zürich Reformer's theology too "Reformed" for his liking and broke off the enterprise. The first major Bullinger biography was written as late as 1858 by the Zürich pastor Carl Pestalozzi, and few have followed. Bullinger, however, compares most favorably with Luther and Calvin, and is one of our best sources for their lives. We would know far less about both of them were it not for Bullinger's

diaries and histories of the Reformation. So, too, our bio-
graphical knowledge of Zwingli is almost entirely through
Bullinger's writings on him and his diligence in printing
Zwingli's works. Indeed, as Bullinger was in close contact with
most of the great ecclesiastical and political men of the Reformation and corresponded daily with his fellow Reformers, he
presents us with a day to day overview of God's work on the
Continent and in England, which is provided by no other
writer. Thus, it is foolish to neglect Bullinger.

Sadly, Bullinger's works are still unknown to the bulk of
English-speaking Christian readers. Great as Luther's and
Calvin's works are, a careful student will note that Bullinger
is in no way inferior to them and often proves to be the most
balanced teacher. Luther often has an aggressive, intolerant
faith which, as in his teaching on the Lord's Supper, displays
much of Rome and even superstition. Much of Luther is also
lost to the modern scholar because he is invariably viewed
through the eyes of Philip Melanchthon (1497-1560) who
misinterpreted Luther on justification and predestination
and turned a movement of the Spirit into a well-organized
church institution. Also the over-influential Hamburg pastor
Joachim Westphal (1511-1574) almost destroyed the original
Lutheran piety with his inquisitorial temper and theological
narrow-mindedness.

On the other hand, Calvin's works, good as they are,
nevertheless, prove at times to be too defensive. They also
frequently leave the pastoral for the philosophical and legal.
So, too, Calvin lacked Bullinger's consistency. Thus it is
possible for Louis Berkof in his *Systematic Theology* to place
Calvin in the supralapsarian camp which, today, is tantamount to calling him a Hyper-Calvinist, whereas present-
day writers such as Dr. Allan Clifford claim that Calvin was
a thorough-going Amyraldian. This, for some modern
Reformed Christians, is tantamount to calling Calvin an
Arminian. The theological and pastoral quality of Calvin's
earlier works is greatly inferior to his later writings. Thus,
where Luther is strong and authoritative positively on
justification and negatively on the Lord's Supper, Calvin's
teaching on justification is somewhat lost in his personal
animosities against Osiander, and his teaching on the Lord's

Supper at times opens up problems which he does not solve. Luther's negative treatment of Zwingli is paralleled by Calvin's negative treatment of Strasburg Reformer Valerand Poullain. Bullinger, however, always remains clearly Bullinger, and there is a didactic, objective clarity in his works which amazes those who turn to him with an open mind. His patience with Geneva's ever-changing views on the Lord's Supper was due to his respect for Calvin, his love for unity, and his tolerance over minor points.

Bullinger the Mediator
Bullinger was thus as well-balanced in his character as in his writings and so he was able to compose clear, precise theological statements without emotional overtones and without giving the impression that he had an axe to grind. Because of such outstanding characteristics, he was far more able than both Luther and Calvin to referee in theological debates and maintain good contact with both sides, without compromising his own views. This is shown by Bullinger's sound testimony in his disputations with the Catabaptists, his work in bringing the Lutherans and the Reformed together concerning the Lord's Supper, and his mediation between the Precisians[2] and Anglicans in England on the vestment controversy.

It appears to be a forgotten fact among modern students of the Reformation that Calvin's reconciliation with Geneva after his exile from the city in 1538 was, to a large extent, due to Bullinger's pouring oil on troubled waters. He also made sure that Calvin was given a warm welcome in Strasburg during his exile. Thus, where Luther and Calvin made enemies, Bullinger lived at peace with all men of Reformed persuasion.

The Length of Bullinger's Activity Compared with Calvin's
It must also be remembered that Bullinger was converted to the Reformed faith some ten years before Calvin; he had received a reputation as a Reformed teacher and writer over ten years before Calvin took up his pen to defend the Reformed faith. Indeed, by 1532, Bullinger was an internationally recognized authority on the Reformation when Calvin's interests were still centered in furthering the

philosophy of Seneca and reading humanists' works. Dating Calvin's conversion is not easy, but it appears that he must have renounced Rome shortly before 1534.[3] Apart from a small work on soul-sleep, Calvin's first Reformed work was published in 1536. This was a "wee booklet," as Calvin called it, measuring approximately two and a half by four and a half inches of type per page, composed of six chapters, entitled *Christianae Religionis Institutio*. It was originally sent as a letter written to Francis I of France in defense of the persecuted Protestants. Much in the brief work, published in Basel, was borrowed from Zwingli, who had also sent a similar letter to Francis I in 1525, and other parts are obviously taken from Martin Bucer (1491-1551). Calvin was to rely heavily on Bucer's works in subsequent editions of the *Institutes*.[4] Thus older writers such as Gustav Anrich claim that it was Bucer who was the father of Calvinism and not Calvin.[5] Sadly, Martin Bucer's great reforming theology is as lost today, as is Bullinger's.

Until 1536, Calvin was quite unknown in Reformed circles; he did not reach the international eye until a full decade later. Furthermore, few scholars have taken the trouble to compare Calvin's *Institutes* with Bullinger's works. Walter Hollweg, in his *Heinrich Bullingers Hausbuch*, devotes an entire chapter to Bullinger's influence on Calvin's *Institutes*, in particular the 1550 version, and the Heidelberg Catechism.[6] He states that Calvin is not guilty of plagiarism but leaves the impression that Calvin often reworded Bullinger; at times, Calvin includes not only Bullinger's themes and scriptural proofs, but even the examples Bullinger gives to illustrate them. Gillian Lewis has obviously little to say about Bullinger's influence as Calvin is his subject. As soon as Calvin died, however, Lewis turns his gaze on Bullinger and, not surprisingly, but rather critically, says that Bullinger sat like a spider in the center of the web of the Reformation.[7]

It is also important to note that Bullinger outlived Calvin by twelve years. Bullinger's 124 books, not counting his thousands of tracts and letters, were initially in greater demand than Calvin's, though Calvin's popularity grew in the early seventeenth century largely through the impact of his

Institutes, and Bullinger's waned throughout the period of the Great Rebellion (1642-60). Bullinger had allied himself too much with the Church of England in the opinion of many Presbyterians, Independents, and Dissenters, who then traditionally turned to Calvin rather than Bullinger.

Two doctrines of Bullinger, however, remained fundamental to the Puritan cause: his teaching on the covenant and his identification of Sunday with the Old Testament Sabbath. Immanuel Leuschner relates in his *Bullinger's Wirken in Zürich* how neither Zwingli's nor Luther's nor Calvin's teaching concerning the covenant is as central to their theology as is Bullinger's to his. It is primarily Bullinger's covenant teaching that has survived in Calvinist churches.[8] It must also not be forgotten that Bullinger's works were widely circulated in England some thirty to thirty-five years before Calvin's,[9] and during the sixteenth century there were well over fifty European printers turning out hundreds of editions of Bullinger's reforming works in at least five languages. Within a hundred years, at least 400 editions of Bullinger's works had been printed in Switzerland alone and some 230 editions in other countries, including England. Indeed, throughout the sixteenth century, Bullinger was the most read Continental Reformer in England. By the 1550s, he was frequently referred to as "that famouse clerke," as if everyone would know who was meant. The English editor of his *Decades* ended his introductory preface to the 1587 edition with the words:

These sermons of master Bullinger's are such as, whether they be used privately or read publicly, whether of ministers of the word or other God's children, certainly there will be found in them such light and instruction for the ignorant, such sweet and spiritual comfort for consciences, such heavenly delights for souls, that as perfumes, the more they are chafed, the better they smell; and as gold mines, the deeper ye dig them, the more riches they shew.

The *Decades* have not been reprinted in English since the 1850s, so English-speaking Christians are now greatly indebted to Dr. Joel Beeke for making these priceless treasures once again available through Reformation Heritage Books. I trust that now the man Henry Bullinger and his heavenly message will become as well known in the New World as they were in the Old Europe of the sixteenth century. But first a few words about the life and further writings of this great pastor of souls.

CHAPTER II

From Birth to New Birth

Son of a Roman Catholic Parish Priest

Heinrich Bullinger started his earthly pilgrimage in the tiny Swiss town of Bremgarten in the Aargau on July 18, 1504. Bremgarten had then a population of 800 and the house in which he was born had been in the family's possession for some sixty years. For some now unknown reason, the house was called "The Wild Man,"[10] and such a figure decorated the Bullinger coat of arms. Though built in the Middle Ages, the house is still standing in Market Street,[11] but the sign of the wild man has been substituted by the less eye-catching number 66.

Bullinger was the youngest of seven children, five boys and two girls, born to Heinrich Bullinger and Anna Wiederkehr in their common law marriage. This alliance is worthy of particular note as Heinrich Senior was a former organist and deacon who had been appointed parish pastor by the popular vote of the congregation. Church historians have suggested that Heinrich Senior must have regularly bribed the church authorities to allow him to live in wedlock as a priest, but this is mere speculation. Switzerland was ruled democratically in a way otherwise unknown in Europe; neither the church authorities appointed ministers nor the city magistrates, but the local parishioners chose Bullinger Senior because of his obvious abilities. Bullinger's famous contemporaries Leo Judd and Felix Manz were also sons of parish priests.

On May 12, 1509, young Henry, to use his English name, was enrolled as a pupil at the town's Latin school. He was still not five years of age and the specified entrance age was seven. The rules for entrance stipulated fluency in speaking Swiss-German, but Johann and Abraham Schatt, the two teachers at the school, considered Henry able to hold his own in speech and intelligence with children over two years his senior. Henry's entire education up to his twelfth year was limited to reading and writing Latin compositions and liturgical singing. The children were not allowed to communicate in any other language than Latin during school hours. The only religious education Henry received was through the singing lessons.

Singing for His Supper

Henry was sent to further his education in November 1516 to far away Emmerich on the German-Dutch border, a town built on the right-hand shore of the river Rhine. Emmerich was in the county of Cleves, known to the English through Henry VIII's brief marriage to Anne of Cleves. The only reason for his parents' decision appears to be that an eight-year older brother, Johannes Reinhart, was already a pupil there. Henry's quite affluent father told his twelve-year-old son that his accommodation and clothing would be provided by his parents, but for food and other necessities of life he would have to go begging from door to door. This was so he might learn to understand the position of those who live perpetually in poverty. As Henry had a good voice, like Tommy Tucker in the nursery rhyme, he literally "sang for his supper" for the next three years.

At Emmerich, the papal religion was seen as the major educational impulse and Henry soon decided that he would become a Carthusian monk. Humanism had made some inroads in the school, but did not seem to have influenced Henry. When only fifteen, Bullinger matriculated at Cologne University. There he was faced more and more with the teaching of Erasmus and those who placed the Scriptures over Aristotelian logic and ethics. Cologne was the largest city in Germany and the center of Rome's power. Here the slaves of papist superstition kept the supposed bones of the Three Wise Men in a large golden casket behind the High Altar. This alone made the citizens of Cologne feel that their city was the most heavenly on earth. One could not move more than a few yards in Cologne without viewing a church, chapel, or monastery, and without seeing priests go hurrying by in their full regalia. The German mystics under the leadership of Meister Eckart and Johannes Tauler had also settled in large numbers in Cologne, as had Albert the Great and Thomas Aquinas. Here, too, Scotsman John Duns Scotus had breathed his last and was buried. Thus there were mystical features in Cologne's religion and a permanent strife went on between Aquinians, who claimed that religion was a matter of logic, and Scotians, who made religion a product of the will.

Finding the Truth as it is in Jesus

On Henry's arrival at Cologne, he found an increasing number who were teaching that religion is neither a matter of man's logic nor man's will, but of God's will revealed in Scripture. Nevertheless, Cologne became the first and only German university to condemn publicly Luther's writings. Erasmus of Rotterdam, now at Cologne, used his influence to curb the university's anti-Reformed reaction and gained a wide following. This became clear to the Roman Catholic authorities when Hieronymus Alexander, the pope's inquisitor, was sent to Germany in October, 1520, with his bag of papal bulls. His first stop was Cologne, otherwise called "Germany's Rome." He had expected to be received there as a conquering hero, but to his amazement, few took notice of him. Instead, he saw anti-papal posters hung all over the city; the university, city authorities, and clergy had stopped persecuting the Lutherans. Erasmus, however, soon gave in to Rome's pressure and Cologne once again followed him blindly. Luther's works were again burned on November 15, the very day on which sixteen-year-old Bullinger received his Bachelor of Arts degree.

Bullinger now decided to study Luther's position. He had had no theological training and knew nothing of Rome's dogmas. Studying literally day and night, although it was not in his Master of Arts curriculum, Bullinger read as much as he could find on Roman Catholic theology. He discovered that the Roman Catholic writers claimed their authority came from the Church Fathers and so he made a careful study of the sermons and expository works of the earliest Christian saints, especially John Chrysostom, Origen, Ambrose, and Augustine. He found that they appealed to Scripture, so Bullinger bought his first New Testament. He discovered that not only did the Church Fathers teach in full opposition to Rome's sixteenth-century novelties, but that the Scriptures presented the faith and fellowship of Christians in a radically more spiritual and far less legal and "churchy" manner than Rome. Soon, Bullinger was reading that justification is by God-given faith alone and that salvation is by God's good grace and not man's dubious "good works." All ideas of becoming a monk vanished and Bullinger experienced faith in the Lord Jesus Christ and in His saving, redemptive work alone. Bullinger, now seventeen years of age, gained his Master of Arts and returned home to Bremgarten after an absence of almost six years.

All Doors in Bremgarten Found Open

How would his father, a Roman priest, take the news of his conversion? How would the church authorities in his canton accept him as the teacher he now wished to be? Bullinger realized that as a witness for Christ, he could not hide his faith. He resolved to tell one and all of his new life in Christ.

Bullinger was warmly received by his family without a word of reproach. His father even allowed Bullinger to study biblical, Reformed theology at home and at his leisure for some eight months. Then the Cistercian abbot of Kappel, Wolfgang Joner, invited Bullinger to take over the abbey school. The eighteen-year-old visited Joner, gave him his testimony and told him that he could not possibly take the monk's oath, put on a monk's clothing, or attend mass, and he must be free to maintain his own testimony of faith. The abbot accepted all his conditions and made him superintendent of the abbey school on the spot! Bullinger then drew up a new curriculum and the tiny school grew and flourished. For the next six years, the young Reformer expounded through 21 of the 27 New Testament books at the monastery. He found that the monks could hardly understand a word of Latin and thus preached regularly in Swiss-German. He also invited the secular workers, servants, and the entire town to hear his preaching.

The Reformation in Kappel and Bremgarten

Changes made at Kappel were enormous and swift. By 1524 the images had been removed from the abbey church. The mass was abolished in 1525, and by 1526 the entire order of monks were meeting at the Lord's Table in the Reformed manner. On the day of the first Reformed communion meal, all the monks, including the abbot, discarded their robes and renounced their monkish oaths. Though some monks left to become Christian craftsmen and farmers, many stayed on to be further educated by Bullinger.

From 1526 on, what had been a Roman Catholic monastery now became a seminary for Reformed pastors. Parallel to these reforms at Kappel, Huldrich Zwingli was pressing ahead at Zürich in a similar way, though he was meeting more opposition, possibly because he lacked the tact and communication abilities that were so very much Bullinger's.

Zwingli was also provoking the Fünf Orte (a union of five Roman Catholic districts) to war and had allied with Bern to cut off their supplies of food.[12] Actually, Zwingli had protested that Bern's aggressive policy did not go far enough and he was for an all-out war at once. The papists had not yet begun to persecute the Reformed people as it was left to the public vote which community should become Reformed or not. When the Roman Catholic powers eventually decided to put down the Reformation by force, it was not the cities of Bern and Zürich that they aimed to destroy first, but the work of true Reformation at Kappel.

Anna Adischwyler
Many of the Kappel monks, including the abbot, now married and these men assured Bullinger that a wife would be a great support to his ministry. In 1527, Joner gave Bullinger leave of absence from the school to find a bride. During this search, Bullinger visited the former Dominican nunnery at Oetenbach where the nuns had accepted the Reformed faith and disbanded. Two ladies had remained to carry on a Christian witness. One of these was Anna Adischwyler, the daughter of the Lord Mayor's cook, who was a year younger than Bullinger. The Reformer recognized Anna as his future wife and wrote to her, asking her to be his bride, though he scarcely knew her. Bullinger's letter was as scriptural and business-like as could be. He outlined all the advantages and disadvantages of single life, and then did the

same regarding married life. He confessed that he only
received board and lodgings at the school and did not have a
penny to his name. He admitted that he would have some
little fortune to inherit at his father's death, but this would
probably be in a very distant future. Anna replied "yes"
within a few days. They planned to be married, as the custom
was, within two weeks of their engagement.

The two weeks were to become two years. Anna's
mother wanted her daughter to be her companion at home
and only marry after her own death. She had thus agreed to
the engagement which legally bound Anna to Henry but then
refused to allow her daughter to marry him, binding her
daughter to herself and making it impossible for Anna to
marry anyone. Anna continued to press her mother to allow
her to marry, but her mother said she would only relent if
Anna found a rich man. Anna said that it would be Bullinger
or nobody. Mrs. Adischwyler then said that it would have to
be nobody. As public opinion was outraged at Mrs.
Adischwyler's selfish act and put pressure on her, the lady
looked for legal backing. Anna and Bullinger had become
engaged without a witness and a new law passed in Zürich
had ruled that no engagement was to take place without a
witness. Mrs. Adischwyler then argued that her daughter
had never been legally engaged. Happily, witnesses were
called who had been privy to the written correspondence of
the couple regarding their engagement and the court
decided in the couple's favor. But still Mrs. Adischwyler
refused to unbind her daughter. Even the personal
intervention of Zwingli was no help. Two years later, Mrs.
Adischwyler died and the couple were speedily married on
August 17, 1529.

Anna Bullinger must have been a woman of great
strength and courage. When her husband was banned from
Bremgarten by the papist troops, Anna was refused permission to leave the town to join her husband in Zürich. One
night, she tried by stealth to leave the town, carrying her two
babies with her. She was stopped by a guard at the town-gate
and was commanded to return home. Anna overpowered the
armed man, took the key from him, opened the gate, and
after a ten mile walk through the night, was reunited with

her thankful husband. Meanwhile, Bullinger had found lodgings at Werner Steiner's house, the man for whom Bullinger had written *Studiorum ratio* some four years before.

Anna and Henry had eleven children, not counting those they adopted. These were in order of age: Anna, Margareta, Elizabeth, Heinrich, Hans Rudolf, Christoph, Hans, Diethelm, Veritas, Dorothea, and Felix. Diethelm died as an infant, but all the others lived to maturity which was quite an exception in those days. Christoph and Hans probably did not marry, but the other brothers and sisters all married into the families of leading Reformers and Senators. It is said that all Bullinger's sons became pastors.

CHAPTER III
Triumphs and Setbacks

Father and Son Together in the Faith

In February of the same year Heinrich Bullinger Senior, now sixty years of age, announced to his congregation that he had accepted the Reformed faith. On December 31, he officially married his beloved wife of almost forty years, according to the new Reformed rites.

As soon as the elder Bullinger announced his conversion, he received the backing of most of his congregation; however, the city authorities, fearful of Roman Catholic threats to the security of the town, had him ousted. He found a new church, but his old congregation strove democratically to be given Reformed status and, by the summer of that year, were successful. The Bremgarten parish then called Gervasius Schuler to their pastorate, but his implementation of the Reformation was too slow for many in the parish. They therefore unanimously called the younger Bullinger to the joint pastorate. Joner urged Bullinger to accept the offer. He came, now aged almost twenty-five, and preached his first sermon at his home church in May 1529, before a large congregation. His subject was worshipping God in spirit and in truth. There was a tremendous spiritual reaction among the church-goers. After the service the images and altar were removed from the church building and the united congregation dedicated themselves to God and the new faith.

Besides Schuler's dedicated ministry, the Bremgarten congregation heard Bullinger preach every Sunday afternoon, as well as Monday, Tuesday, and Wednesday mornings. He held a well-attended Bible study every day at 3:00 p.m. In the less than three years that Bullinger remained in Bremgarten, he preached through the entire New Testament; this period was often called the Spring Time of the Bremgarten Reformation. During this time Bullinger also translated thirty Psalms from the Hebrew into Latin and Swiss-German and wrote commentaries on both New Testament and Old Testament books. He also wrote a history of the Reformation in Switzerland. Meanwhile, the elder Bullinger was doing pioneer work in the Roman Catholic communities; soon, Muri (1529) and Hermetschwil (1530) adopted the Reformed faith by the votes of the parish members.

Bullinger and Zwingli: Their Differences
From around 1523, Bullinger rode over to Zürich at least once a year to meet with Zwingli and Leo Jud. Most church historians incorrectly label Bullinger as Zwingli's protégé, but Bullinger was fully Zwingli's equal—if not superior—in Reformation matters. Distinctions between Zwingli's and Bullinger's witness are important. Bullinger trained and sent out Reformed preachers some two years before Zwingli, meeting far less opposition. When Bullinger wished to publish his views on the Lord's Supper in 1524, Zwingli asked him to wait because he himself was not ready. Indeed, Zwingli told Bullinger that if and when he was ready, he would publish on the subject, not Bullinger. Zwingli wavered long, slowly coming to a merely commemorative view. Bullinger taught that the Lord's real presence was to be experienced in the Supper because wherever two or three are gathered in His Name, He is in their midst. Nevertheless, Bullinger rejected transubstantiation and consubstantiation—indeed, any view that implied Christ's corporal presence in the elements. Zwingli's and Bullinger's debates on the Lord's Supper show how difficult it was for the Reformers to reach an exact agreement. Both Bullinger and Zwingli confessed that they agreed with the Waldensians on the matter of the Supper, but they interpreted their agreement differently. Four years later Zwingli published his views on the Lord's Supper in opposition to Luther's position, but only after considerable consultations with Bullinger on the subject.

Zwingli was a supralapsarian in his views of election, teaching that God elected some men to salvation and some to reprobation irrespective of the Fall. Bullinger taught that God ordains some of sinful mankind to eternal life and some He passes by—that is, He allows their reprobation. Zwingli never developed a clear, Reformed doctrine of imputation, whereas Bullinger taught both the imputation of Adam's sin to all mankind and the imputation of Christ's righteousness to all the elect. Zwingli could not accept the book of Revelation as the Word of God; Bullinger not only accepted it, but preached from it. Zwingli held to a rigid church discipline and order as a mark of the true church; Bullinger emphasized experimental heart-religion. He believed that order and discipline should be flexible according to the church's situation. Bullinger was a man of peace; thus, Zwingli often asked Bullinger to mediate on the difficult situations in which he often found himself. Bullinger disagreed with Zwingli concerning his involvement in the Kappeler Wars and his trust in Bern's militant "Reformation" policies.

Bullinger and Zwingli: Their Harmony
Bullinger had developed much of his Reformed thinking before meeting Zwingli, but when he read Zwingli's *Auslegung und Begründung der Schlussreden*[13] in the summer of 1523, he was mightily impressed by Zwingli's testimony, and confessed that *Auslegung und Begründung* had greatly strengthened his faith. Zwingli soon became aware of Bullinger's extraordinary abilities and asked him to take down the minutes of his debates with the Catabaptists, Manz, Grebel, and Röubli, and encouraged him to publish his comparisons of ancient and modern heresies in 1525, albeit under the pseudonym of Octavius Florens. When Vadian asked Zwingli what he thought of Florens, he replied that he was a young man very learned both in secular and godly works, but he kept Bullinger's identity secret. It was through Zwingli that Bullinger gained the acquaintance of Konrad Pellikan, from whom he learned Hebrew, and Johannes Rhellikan, Rudolf Collin, and Johann Jakob Ammann, through whom he improved his Greek.

In 1527, Bullinger received permission from Joner to spend five months in Zürich. Bullinger requested that he take his best student, Johannes Fry, with him, to encourage him along the Reformation path; Bullinger himself wished to deepen his Old Testament studies. Thus from June to November, Bullinger attended the lectures of Zwingli, Pellikan, and Ammann. Bullinger received no wages for his work at Kappel, but the monastery owned a small inn on the outskirts of Zürich where he and Fry could live and be fed. The Zürich Senate became so impressed with Bullinger's learning that they asked him to join Zwingli in representing them at the 1528 Bern Disputation. There, Bullinger met many leading Reformers and quickly became a close friend of Martin Bucer's from Strasburg, who was to become so influential in the development of Swiss and Anglican theology.

From this time on, it became evident that Zwingli, twenty years Bullinger's senior, had come to love his friend as a younger brother, if not as a son, and realized that he must decrease and Bullinger must increase. So we find Zwingli gradually writing to friends and, in 1531, even including in publications, that he was giving over his theological responsibilities to Bullinger. The Zürich Synod ordained Bullinger as a preacher under their jurisdiction and asked Bullinger to accompany Zwingli to the now· famous Marburg Colloquy of 1529. This was Zwingli's opportunity to allow Bullinger to stand as an equal with himself, Luther, Bucer, and the other Continental Reformed leaders. Bullinger was only twenty-five at the time. However, this major début was not to be. The Bremgarten Council complained that Bullinger had taken enough leave of absence, and should stick to his teaching and preaching responsibilities. Instead of Bullinger, Zwingli took Oecolampadius from Bern and Collin from Zürich.

The Kappel War

By 1531, Zwingli, at 57 years of age, realized that his time of departure had come. This is the only explanation for the moving scene in August, 1531, when he visited Bullinger's home at Bremgarten. He held secret talks throughout the night with ambassadors from Bern. Early in the morning, Zwingli departed from the house and Bullinger accompanied him to the next village of Zufikon. The two men said farewell twice along the way but still walked on together. Then, Zwingli burst into tears. He embraced his young friend for the third time and said, "God's grace be upon thee, my dear Henry. May God preserve thee. Be true to our Lord Jesus Christ and His Church." Then he turned and departed, a very sad and troubled man. The two friends were never to meet again this side of glory. On October 11, 1531, Zwingli put on his armor and rode into a rather senseless and unnecessary war. His cleaved helmet is still on display in Zürich to show how Zwingli died.

The background of this tragedy is quickly told. On May 15, 1531, the Fünf Orte, goaded by the embargoes on food enforced on them by Protestant Bern and Zürich and Zwingli's claim of military power, decided to use violence themselves. Bullinger and Bremgarten protested against the un-Christian measures of the two Protestant Senates, but the Roman Catholics placed the blame for this merciless persecution on the true upholders of the Reformed faith at Bremgarten, not on the inane politics of the two cities. Bern and Zürich quickly formed a large army, promising to defend Bremgarten. Faithful Christians told Zwingli that it was senseless to defend God's Word with chariots and horsemen. Bern and Zwingli took no heed, and Bern placed Sebastian von Diesbach at the head of their forces. The pope had duped Zwingli and his military allies; Von Diesbach was an avowed opponent of the Reformation! When the Roman Catholic army reached Bremgarten, von Diesbach withdrew his "Reformed" troops and left Zwingli with his smaller army of Zürich men to perish. Zwingli was struck down and handed over to the public executioner who had him drawn, quartered, and then burned to ashes. Immediately, the new masters in Bremgarten forced the town back under Rome's yoke and annulled Zwingli's *Burgrecht* (citizen's rights). As Zwingli had given them no rights, they felt that they were free to do the same with the Protestants.

Bullinger Invited as Zwingli's Successor
Meanwhile, Zwingli's warring nature and Bern's inhumane politics had greatly weakened the Protestant cause. The Roman faction again became very strong. This moved Zürich's faithful to ask Bullinger to become their shepherd. They did not want a man who would build a state on supposedly Christian law, but one who would bring in a time of grace. Thus it is said that Zwingli rescued a people from Rome, but it was Bullinger who made them into a church.

The Senate also welcomed Bullinger, but being suspicious of his friendship with Zwingli, asked him to promise not to follow his predecessor's politics. This was a promise which Bullinger could gladly give.

CHAPTER IV
Establishing the Reformed Church in Switzerland

Settling Down in Zürich

Bullinger soon discovered that leading the Zürich churches was fraught with difficulties. Bern, realizing what a strong leader Bullinger was, painted a bleak picture of Zürich in order to tempt him over to them. Indeed, many of the Zürich magistrates had become so used to the often heroic, but equally often tactless, stubbornness of Zwingli that they thought milder Bullinger was a second-best substitute. Furthermore, the Fünf Orte had been so stung by Zwingli's less than Christian statesmanship when representing Zürich's interests, that they came close to declaring war on the city again, thinking that Bullinger had taken up Zwingli's mantle rather than put on his own. This mistrust came to a head in 1532 when the corporation demanded that Bullinger draw up a *Glaubensmandat* (Mandate of Faith) in the name of the city, proclaiming that the Reformation had come to stay and condemning Rome in no uncertain terms. Bullinger questioned the magistrates' policy but complied. Sadly, the authorities thought Bullinger's resulting declaration was too mild and voted through a more militant version; the surrounding Roman Catholic districts viewed this as not only a breach of the Kappeler Peace, but also a provocation to war. The corporation's act was also timed to coincide with Charles V's Reichstag at Regensburg. Charles was striving to find some sort of mutual tolerance between Roman Catholics, Lutherans, and Reformed, and the *Glaubensmandat* appeared to threaten the Emperor's policy. Ennio Filonardi, the papal legate, promised the Swiss Roman Catholics help from Rome should war become inevitable. The Five Districts asked Zürich to withdraw the Mandate as it went beyond the Kappeler Peace, which stated that each canton should democratically follow the religion of their choice without interfering with other cantons. Bern, who had proved a dubious ally in the Kappeler Wars, urged Zürich to maintain their militant position. In May, 1533, Bullinger and his fellow pastors called a Synod to work out a solution. Bullinger was elected spokesman to tell the corporation that they could not prescribe for Roman Catholic-ruled areas what they should believe; on the contrary, they should allow the Zürich pastors to preach the Word of God and allow the Spirit to work as He will. The Mandate had been too bold, too negative, and most un-diplomatic. The corporation withdrew the Mandate and further war was averted.

Ferdinand I and the papal legate still pressed for military action against the Protestants, but Bullinger had many allies in Upper Germany, both in the Lutheran states and among those cities who had accepted Bucer's *Tetrapolitana* (Four Cities) Confession (Strasburg, Constance, Memmingen, and Lindau) which had influenced the Swiss Reformers. Furthermore, the Lutheran princes had formed the Smalcald League in December 1530 to protect their territories from a Roman Catholic takeover by the Counter-Reformation and they were anxious to extend the League to include the Swiss. Bucer, the great mediator and diplomat wrote, thinking of Zürich: "It would be contrary to brotherly love to pledge ourselves to show no favor to anyone who acknowledges the common Christ with us, even though he should not be at one with us in regard to some article, more in the letter than the spirit."[14]

Protestant Bern, however, remained militant and a threatened breach with Protestant Zürich occurred over a triviality. Bern had no printing press, so they approached Zürich printer Christopher Froschauer (also written Froschover), who served the English Reformers so well, requesting that he print a Bernese Protestant Declaration of Faith for them, illustrating it with Bern's symbol, a bear. The bear that Froschauer printed, however, had its claws withdrawn and looked quite amiable (or so the Bernese thought). Militant Bern took this as an affront to their pride and complained bitterly. Through contact with Berchtold Haller of Bern, who was of a less fiery spirit than the city dignitaries, Bullinger prevented a major break between the two cantons, though Bern never dealt with Froschauer again.

Bullinger's Relationship to Calvin

It is through Bern, however, that Calvin enters our story. Bern, in defiance of Charles of Savoy, cleared French-speaking Geneva of his troops and began to dominate the city's affairs. Through Bern and Freiburg's influence William Farel, Antony Froment, and Peter Viret began to evangelize Geneva, and on May 21, 1536, the Citizens' Assembly declared Geneva to be Protestant. In October of that year, Farel and Viret took Calvin with them to the Lausanne Disputation and eventually persuaded him in early 1537 to settle in Geneva to help Farel. Calvin then authored a catechism which he entitled *Instruction et confession de foy dont on use en l'église Genève*.[15] This catechism was the most severe theological document Calvin ever penned on predestination and reprobation. When this is compared with Calvin's *Catechismus Genevensis* of 1545, written after the trouble his *Instruction et confession* had caused, we can clearly see how Calvin had learned from his mistakes.

Bullinger sent a number of sound men over to help Calvin gain footing in the Swiss churches, and also help him become known outside of Geneva. Among these were the English intellectuals and Reformers John Butler, Nicholas Partridge, Nicholas Eliot, and Bartholomew Traheron, who were furthering their education under Bullinger. These fine, godly men were able to link Calvin with the budding English Reformation. Sadly, however, Calvin got off to a bad start and quarrelled with church and state in an effort to press through reforms which were thought too radical in Geneva. Indeed, he sought to bring the political authorities under his leadership. He further claimed that all who would not accept his still budding theology under oath should be exiled from the city state. Those who dissented from his catechism would have to undergo severe penalties. He then proposed the setting up of an ecclesiastical force to control the morals of the citizens and enforce discipline. At every communion service, the names of the outcasts were to be read publicly. Soon there were strong cries of protest against Calvin's methods in which church, people, and Senate all took to the streets in anti-Calvin demonstrations. By September 1537, whole districts had refused to bow to Calvin's demands. Early in 1538, the Council deposed Calvin and Farel and told them to leave Geneva within seventy-two hours. Farel fled to Neuchâtel and Calvin was invited to Strasburg by Bucer. Largely through negotiations led by Bullinger, Calvin was reaccepted in Geneva in 1541. He had learned much from Bucer and Capito in Strasburg, and now sought to guide his flock in a more pastoral way, building his doctrines and order of service on Strasburg models. On arriving at Geneva, this time without Farel, who stayed in Neuchâtel, Calvin submitted his *Ordonnances ecclésiatiques*[16] to the Council who altered it a little for form's sake. On November 20, 1541, Calvin took up his new preaching and pastoral duties, greatly humbled. He was, however, still struggling for a better understanding of the Lord's Supper. Calvin's powers were now greatly curtailed. He was not allowed to sit on any of the councils and was repeatedly refused Genevan citizenship until 1559, eighteen years after returning from Strasburg and only five years before his death.

Coming to a Consensus on the Lord's Supper at Zürich

Calvin had criticized other Reformers' views of the Lord's Supper, including Bullinger's, before he came to a stable interpretation himself. In May 1549, Calvin visited Bullinger and asked him to help him with his difficulties. Bullinger read through Calvin's writings on the Lord's Supper and reduced them to twenty-four articles, leaving out points which he found unacceptable and adding those which he felt represented the fullness of the Reformed doctrine. Bullinger then asked Calvin if he could use this formulation as a basis for union. Calvin asked leave to make a few minor alterations, and then the two men put aside their differences and drew up their *Consensus Tigurinus*.[17] This allowed for joint participation in the Lord's Supper between Zürich and Geneva. Happily, all the Protestant districts and cities, after a great deal of hesitation from Bern and Basel, signed the Zürich Consensus.

The signing of the consensus was a major step in Calvin's personal development, as he was thus placed in fellowship with the major Swiss Reformers. Ulrich Gäbler comments, "The Zürich Consensus brought a rapprochement between the Geneva and Zürich churches and allowed

Calvin to find his place within the Swiss Reformed Church."[18] In this and other ways, Bullinger led and encouraged Calvin. One notable outcome of the Zürich conference was the birth of the term "Reformierte Kirche,"[19] distinguishing the Swiss Protestant churches from the Roman Catholic system. This is why Blanke and Leuschner call Bullinger "Vater der Reformierten Kirche"[20] in their joint biography of the Reformer.[21] A. G. Dickens comments, "By the Zürich Agreement of 1549 on the Lord's Supper and by the Second Helvetic Confession of 1566, Bullinger united the forces of Zwinglianism and Calvinism into one Reformed religion, a faith able to conquer lands which Zwingli never knew."[22]

Many of Bullinger's and Calvin's friends were not at all pleased when the two Reformers signed the *Consensus Tigurinus*. Theodore Beza, who joined Calvin at this time, believed that Geneva should now lead the Swiss churches and the Waldensians and speak for them. He thus gave out a new declaration concerning the Lord's Supper which approximated the Lutheran position and minimized the points of difference. This caused protests from Bullinger, Berthold Haller, and Peter Martyr, and great embarrassment for Calvin, who was too indebted to Bullinger and their joint aim of uniting the Swiss churches to go it alone. Lutheran Reformers then attacked Bullinger's *Decades* on the grounds that his teaching on the Supper was at variance with Beza's, which they had recommended.[23] Zürich and Geneva never succeeded in keeping to exactly the same path, which is often explained by the French mentality of Geneva and the German mentality of Zürich. This theory does not fit the facts. Calvin leaned heavily on German-speaking Zwingli regarding predestination and was nearer to Wittenberg than Zürich regarding the Lord's Supper. The fact that Calvin's church and ministerial colleagues were rarely one hundred percent behind him often bound his hands where Bullinger was quite free to lead. We know from Calvin's letters, *Institutes,* and *Tracts* that he would have willingly incorporated a number of the English reforms, such as Confirmation, the laying on of hands, and taking the Lord's Supper to the sick, but his church would not allow him. Indeed, John Whitgift's major defense of the Reformed Church of

England against the criticisms of Thomas Cartwright, who claimed to be a Calvinist, was that Calvin stood far closer to the Church of England than Cartwright who rejected a number of Calvin's views. Not only Cartwright had difficulty understanding Calvin; Carter Lindberg points out that Calvin was often misunderstood by second-generation Lutherans who invariably interpreted his moves toward Luther as signs that he was moving toward Zwingli.[24]

Bullinger and Calvin versus Westphal

Joachim Westphal, the Lutheran fiery spirit, also played an indirect part in spreading the reputations of Bullinger and Calvin. He seemed to fear the Swiss Reformers more than all the papist cardinals together. Westphal became especially alarmed when Melanchthon and other Lutherans showed an eagerness to sign the Zürich Consensus; he realized that the Upper German states, Hessen and the Palatine, who supported Martin Bucer's more Reformed views, were moving away from Lutheranism towards a "Zürich" interpretation.[25] Westphal's aggressive methods of preserving Lutheranism against Reformed encroachments brought about a total break between the two groups of churches with the Philippists (followers of Melanchthon) on one side, and the Gnesio-Lutherans (so-called Real Lutherans or the ultra-orthodox) on the other. Now the Gnesio-Lutherans regarded Bullinger and Calvin as their major opponents, primarily because they were the fathers of the *Consensus Tigurinus*. Westphal himself persecuted the Reformed Christians with the ardor of Mary I, calling the Reformers she martyred 'the devil's martyrs.' Indeed, when the English and foreign Reformers fled from England to the Continent on Mary's coming to the throne, Westphal moved the authorities all along the German and Danish coasts to refuse them anchorage in the middle of winter storms, hoping they would either be wrecked at sea or starve. Westphal wrote work after work against the Swiss Reformers, answered ably by Bullinger and Calvin. This united the Reformed churches against a common enemy, but Westphal did not give up his aggression until the Reformers decided simply to ignore him. After Westphal's attacks, however, no one doubted that Bullinger and Calvin led the Continental Reformation.

CHAPTER V

Tackling Switzerland's Problems

Combating False Rumors

One great challenge for Bullinger was rescuing Zwingli's good Christian testimony from his more dubious reputation. The papists had made much of Zwingli's militancy and spread the false rumor that the blood of 5,000 Zürich citizens who had died in the Kappel Wars was on Zwingli's hands. Bullinger made a detailed study of the fallen and published the 512 names of the true casualties. Sadly, Luther took the exaggerated papal protests against Zürich as the truth and a sign that Zwingli's theology was as objectionable as his behavior. He even claimed that Zwingli was an Enthusiast (*Schwärmer*) and a Catabaptist, and had sinned against the Holy Ghost. Now Bullinger, who had been against Zwingli's militant policy and represented a more mature theology, had both the papists and the Lutherans against him. Bullinger soon found out that Zwingli's critics knew little of Zwingli's overall pioneering theological position and even less concerning the Kappel Wars; thus, he wrote a systematic account of his predecessor's faith and a history of the wars, which helped to allay much criticism, though not Luther's. The German Reformer advised Markgraf Duke Albrecht von Brandenburg to ban all those holding the Zürich faith from his realms. Thus one Protestant became the persecutor of other Protestants while Rome looked smugly on.

Luther's Tragic Break with the Swiss Reformers

Luther's criticism of Bullinger, whom he accused of standing on Zwingli's shoulders, is sad, indeed tragic. Bullinger was most impressed by Luther's works, especially his *Babylonian Captivity of the Church*, his *Freedom of the Christian*, and his *Treatise on Good Works*. He recognized Luther as the greatest pioneer of the Continental Reformation. However, he felt that Luther had stopped the Reforming process prematurely; by 1523, Bullinger had set out on the path of a continuing Reformation, including ecclesiastical renewal. The Waldensian teaching on the Lord's Supper helped him gain an understanding of the ordinance which was quite different from Luther's. Bullinger, at this early date, had optimistically believed that what he had experienced would also be the lot of the Lutherans as they progressed along the Reformed path. After the Marburg Colloquy between Zwingli and Luther, which the Bremgarten magistrates forbade Bullinger to attend, the Lutherans hardened in their doctrine of consubstantiation. Rather than acknowledge that their doctrine was more Roman than Reformed, they accused Bullinger and Zwingli of being betrayers of Christ's sacrament and enemies of the Reformation. In 1534, Bullinger drew up a statement regarding the Supper which emphasized the real presence of Christ in the celebration but that the elements themselves were symbols, signs, and witnesses of the Lord's presence with believers. He offered the Lutherans the right hand of fellowship but told them that he could not accept the idea that Christ's actual flesh and blood were in the elements; rather, one fed on Christ in a spiritual manner through faith. Yet Bullinger argued that Lutherans and Reformed could celebrate the Lord's Supper together, each understanding the ordinance as his heart led. Luther rejected this offer of fellowship in several writings.

In 1536, Bullinger then drew up the First Helvetic Confession with Myconius and Grynäus, which was sent to Luther as a peace treaty, again pleading for fellowship around the Lord's Table for all Protestants. This time, Luther responded in June 1538 with a friendly letter congratulating the Swiss on their efforts to bring unity and concord to the churches. After this Bullinger and Luther corresponded amiably on the issue of church unity for some time. This correspondence was suddenly broken off by Luther, who could not get rid of his hate for Zwingli and his suspicion that Bullinger and his friends were all Zwinglis in disguise. As an excuse for breaking with the Swiss, he complained that Zwingli was responsible for the Turkish menace which was threatening Europe. In his commentary on Genesis, published in 1544, he called Zwingli a most inappropriate negative name, as if he had been the greatest heretic the churches had seen.

Bullinger replied by reprinting Zwingli's works so that the world could see that Luther was fighting windmills. This caused Luther to attack Zürich more violently in his writings. The positive outcome of this controversy was that Calvin was moved to approach Bullinger in November 1544, in order to come to an understanding of the Lord's Supper with him that would leave the Luther-Zwingli conflict behind. Thus the Zürich Consensus mentioned above came into being.

The Problem of Swiss Mercenaries

One of Bullinger's greatest problems at Zürich was dealing with revenues in Switzerland which came from dubious sources. The high standard of the military forces in Switzerland had caused other countries to recruit mercenaries among the Swiss; this exporting of men trained to kill had become a lucrative method of financing the cantons. At the beginning of Bullinger's ministry in Zürich, it was estimated that 12,000 Swiss mercenaries from Roman Catholic cantons were serving in France alone and were being used to eliminate Protestant citizens. The massacre of the Waldensians in 1545 after Francis I occupied the Savoy was sadly due to the use of Swiss mercenaries. Indeed, the pope regarded the Swiss hirelings as part of his personal army against the Reformation. Even today, the pope's bodyguard and private army is composed almost entirely of Swiss mercenaries. The French King pushed the Swiss into the fiercest battles, not caring about their lives, as they were merely regarded as imported commodities. For instance, of the 10,000 sent out to serve the French King in 1570, 6,000 soon lost their lives. Switzerland was thus losing the bulk of her young men. Bullinger protested to the cantons supplying the troops and also to the French King and his ambassadors without success. Indeed, the pope placed a bull on him and Emperor Charles V declared him to be a *persona non grata;* furthermore, the French King told Bullinger that he had no business interfering with French policy. This was because Bullinger had dared to tell them, "It is not just for a man to let himself to hire, to kill those who have done him no injury."

Needless to say, Bullinger moved the Zürich magistrates to forbid the exporting of mercenaries from the city and its rural districts and happily, as usual, the Protestant cantons followed Zürich's move. The Roman Catholics then filled the breach, thus making even more money but ruining the future of their own dear country. When Francis II, husband of Mary Queen of the Scots, came to the French throne at age sixteen, Bullinger sent him a statement of faith, outlining what the French Protestants believed and how they were law-abiding citizens, but the carnage continued with the Swiss mercenaries to the fore. This was one of the few occasions in Bullinger's diplomatic service for his Master in which he gained a mere partial triumph.

Bullinger and the Catabaptists[26]

Another problem Bullinger faced was that of the Catabaptists, with whom he quickly entered into dialogue. These Catabaptists are often confused with present day Baptists, but the similarities are not compelling. Most Catabaptists were not even "Dippers" at this time, as their records show that they clearly baptized by pouring. Bullinger reckoned that within less than a decade they had split up into no less than thirteen different movements, some of which were extremely violent and went about well-armed. In next to no time we see Catabaptist (later called Anabaptist) movements going by the names of Swiss, Sabbaths, Austerlitzers, Hoferists, Münsters, Hutterites, etc., treating one another as enemies of the truth. Balthazer Hubmaier, for instance, condemned Hans Hut for allegedly spreading sedition and political revolt and Hans Spittelmaier condemned the "schismatics" from his young movement for refusing to carry weapons. He called them *Stäbler,* or Staff-bearers, in scorn. The Anabaptist sect of the sword bearers formed the *Schwertler Baptists.* Later Anabaptists looked on their Swiss fathers in the faith as "misanthropes" and the Swiss looked upon the spiritual children they had fostered in other lands as "false brethren."[27]

Zwingli, fearing that the Catabaptists were plotting to overthrow the Zürich administration by armed force, became their persecutor. He had pulled Bullinger into the violent controversies by asking him to take part in his debates with the Catabaptists and take down the minutes, some of which have been preserved. However, in spite of the many hundreds of letters extant between Bullinger and the Catabaptists on the subject of baptism, there is still much to be done before the full scope of Bullinger's understanding of the movement can be outlined. Heinold Fast, who has done tremendous work in this field,[28] believes that nobody has influenced an understanding of the history of the Baptists more than Bullinger. However, he compares this influence to a flaming torch which could give more light, but also be used to kindle the flames of persecution. That Bullinger did not kindle such flames becomes apparent when studying his leadership in Zürich until his death in 1575. During this period forty Catabaptists were executed for their faith in Bern in spite of Haller's and Bullinger's protests, but none were executed in Zürich.[29] Indeed, Bullinger surprised all by helping the Catabaptists legally to maintain their citizens' rights against discrimination. A number of debtors had, for instance, decided they could borrow from Catabaptists and need not pay them back as they were heretics!

Tolerant but also Discerning

This does not mean that Bullinger was friendly to the Catabaptist cause. He maintained that their view of baptism was unbiblical as it was purely founded on the often vague[30] testimony of faith of the one to be re-baptized. Baptism, Bullinger argued, was the pictorial gospel of Christ's salvation offered to members of His covenant. It was a display of God's love to sinners and a means of calling the weary and heavy-laden to Him. In other words, the message of baptism was Christ's call to sinners and not the believer's response after heeding the call. Bullinger told the Catabaptists that they misused and misinterpreted the New Testament because they had lost sight of the unity of Scripture and the progression of revelation. They had rejected the Old Testament and thus severed the gospel branches from their roots in history and revelation. The Catabaptists retorted that the baptism administered by the rich, worldly, unbelieving clergy was of no avail. Bullinger replied that dissent was not the correct way to discipline worldly clergy and that the idea that baptism was only valid if the one who baptized had a special spiritual standing before God smacked of Rome. The Catabaptists argued that sinners were not to be baptized, but saints. Bullinger responded by teaching that all saints were sinners and the Catabaptist view of baptism for the pure only was against Scripture and common sense. The gospel call came to those who needed a physician, not to the already healthy. Furthermore, Catabaptist baptism re-introduced the old question of sins committed after baptism, which according to many Catabaptists, left the sinner without salvation or providing a ground for a further baptism after further repentance. Bullinger avoided this confusion by teaching that baptism was God's gift to us and not our gift to God, and that the rite demonstrated Christ's response to man's sin, not man's response to Christ's salvation. The Catabaptists accused Bullinger of confusing state with church but Bullinger argued that it was in the interest of common order that a democratic system was preserved. He pointed out that the Catabaptists held radically different views among themselves concerning taxation, government, and church discipline and order, and if they were all given a free rein, chaos would ensue. It was part of the Christian's testimony to be leaven in the world and not merely in a dissenting body of ever-splitting, temporarily like-minded separatists.

Bullinger regarded the Catabaptists as most unstable citizens, and showed apparent harshness towards them by having them banned from ecclesiastical, military, administrative and legal posts. Actually, this was a concession to the Catabaptists as they strongly renounced such positions themselves. Thus Bullinger made their withdrawal from public life legal. Bullinger diplomatically disciplined the Catabaptists in the eyes of the magistrates but, in reality, allowed the Catabaptists to follow their consciences. He also refused to forbid the Catabaptists freedom of worship and it was not unusual at this time to find groups of two to three hundred Catabaptists gathered for worship even in remote country districts. Bullinger was nevertheless convinced that the Catabaptists wished to establish a society of chaos and superstition, diametrically opposed to the rule of Scripture and apostolic practice.

One outcome of the Catabaptist debate was that Bullinger turned to foreign countries for help in resolving the problems and found allies in Strasburg, Geneva, and London. He was particularly influenced on the question of baptism by Martin Bucer of Strasburg. Sadly, from Luther's side, apart from a short respite, he received only adverse criticism as Luther now ranked the Swiss Reformed churches with the Catabaptists, seeing little, if any, difference.

CHAPTER VI
Teaching the Churches

International Renown as an Educator

After the Kappel Wars, Zürich was left with immense debts; the public blamed the church, arguing that it was Zwingli who had driven them to war. Because the church was the cause of the trouble, they maintained, she should pay off the city's debts. As usual, Bullinger worked out a way to pacify all sides and used church grants to found schools and training institutions which would be a benefit to the entire canton and beyond. He authored a church constitution which defined exactly what relationship the church had to the state,[31] and this was accepted by the Senate. He trained and recruited hundreds of new teachers and authored curricula and examination regulations. The educational policies and standards of Zürich soon won international acclaim; especially the English during the reigns of Henry VIII, Edward VI, Mary I, and Elizabeth willingly sent their young people to be trained by Bullinger. In later years, these students told their congregations, children, and grandchildren of the heavenly times sitting at Bullinger's feet in his private home, listening to Bullinger expounding Isaiah.

Bullinger built a new college, turned nunneries into schools and reduced the number of prebendaries, abolished pluralities and used canonry funds to pay the wages of teachers and pastors and provide grants for students, so relieving the city treasury. Students who made themselves notable through high academic and spiritual attainments were also sent on grants to other cantons, the German, Dutch, and Belgian states, and to Britain where Richard Cox and later Edmund Grindal took care of them. Cox called Bullinger "the pillar of the Church of Christ"[32] and "a second Elijah." Once back home, those students who had sat under Bullinger not only distributed Bullinger's works in England and the Zwingli works Bullinger made available, but also arranged for British businessmen to do business with the Zürich

Senate. This gave the Zürich traders less cause to accuse the church of spending money rather than earning it for the good of the canton. For instance, wood from the Zürich area was in great demand in England, as it was most suitable for making bows and staves. This led John Butler and his close friends to initiate transactions which proved lucrative for the Senate and helpful for England.

The relatively large number of children orphaned by the war and the plague was a strain on public funds, so Bullinger encouraged his colleagues to adopt the orphans. Though he had a large family himself, he set an example by adopting at least two youngsters. One of these, Rudolf Gualter, eventually married Zwingli's daughter and became Bullinger's successor. Both Bullinger, Gualter, and their fellow ministers also opened their homes to the English who were persecuted under Henry VIII and Bloody Mary.

An Exchange Student Testifies

One of Bullinger's exchange students, John ab Ulmis, originally from Thurgau, studied at Oxford until he received his Master of Arts degree and even became a Fellow of the university. A large number of letters signed "your most attached pupil" have been preserved; they show how avidly Bullinger sought news of the English situation and how eagerly Ulmis told him of all that was happening among the Reformers. Judging by the many greetings Ulmis sent from leading churchmen, there must have been few men and women of the English Reformation who did not think it important to be on good terms with Bullinger. Writing in 1548, Ulmis states that England

is adorned and enlightened with the word of God: and that the number of the faithful is daily increasing in vast multitudes more and more. The mass, that darling of the papists, is shaken and in many places its condition corresponds with its name; that is by the best of rights, namely a divine right, it is condemned, and with a safe conscience entirely abolished. The images too are extirpated root and branch in every part of England; nor is there left the least trace which can afford a hope or handle to the papists for confirming their error respecting images, and for leading the people away from the Saviour. Holy wedlock, too, is now free to the clergy, and sanctioned by the king himself.[33]

Ulmis[34] wrote in Latin and his pun on the mass's condition corresponding to its name is not directly translatable into English. The term *missa*, apart from meaning the mass, can also mean "dismissed." Concerning university life at Oxford, Ulmis writes, "It everywhere abounds with excellent and most agreeable writers, and is adorned with great numbers of men who are most distinguished in every kind of learning; and as to myself; that I can enjoy in this place to my heart's content both sacred and profane studies, with the entire liberty of a most delightful and honourable leisure." Foremost in Ulmis' praise of his teachers is Richard Cox, the university High Chancellor, who he finds Reformed in every single doctrine. It is easy to read between the lines and see that Cox is especially favoring Ulmis because of their mutual love and respect for Bullinger. Indeed, if we are to believe Ulmis, and he supports all he says with a good deal of evidence, Bullinger was looked on at Oxford as being absent in the body but everywhere present in the spirit. Ulmis also testifies to the fact that Bullinger's books were being rapidly translated into English. Concerning Hooper, Ulmis says that he never heard or saw anyone who "spoke more piously and with greater kindness respecting Switzerland, and especially your church." When Ulmis comes to praise Peter Martyr, then a professor at Oxford, it almost seems as if he is giving himself a little too much importance as he writes to Bullinger:

> I must tell you that I am most intimate with Peter Martyr, not as a pupil, but as a son; for as I delight to hear him, so I ardently love his peculiar suavity. I pass whole hours with him, so that I have henceforth no occasion for any introduction. If you desire to read any of the lectures or disputations of Peter Martyr, I will send them to you; for I have them all written out, and with Martyr's own corrections.[35]

Further Influence of Educational Policies

Sadly, the French students who trained under Bullinger left Zürich in 1552 and fell into the hands of French King Henry II's inquisitors, who quickly had them burned at the stake. Bullinger heard similar threats from Italy, namely, that the pope's legate had publicly condemned him and had his books burned in public. Even Bullinger's Dutch students were told that they were not welcome in the Dutch states and, under pressure from Emperor Charles V, Bullinger's books were burned at Löwe. The Hungarian, Rumanian, and Bulgarian students were in particular danger, as Protestants were attacked on the one flank by the pope and on the other by the Turks. Here, Bullinger's influence became great; through his teaching and writing he was able to help build a church there which covered a vast area. He also carried out a written ministry to the Hungarian prisoners in Turkish camps in Thrace and along the Aegean coast. Here he was supported by Hungary's ambassadors abroad, such as Johannes Féjertóy, who was a Hungarian diplomat in Vienna. Sandwiched between Rome and the Turks, the Hungarians asked Bullinger whether they should flee the country, but Bullinger urged them to keep up their witness in Hungary. To build them up in the faith, he sent them a "letter" of fifty chapters covering the faith, hope, and love necessary in Christian witness. This document became the Confession of Faith of the Hungarian Church and was the forerunner of the Second Helvetic Confession.

Studiorum Ratio: A Study Guide

Bullinger's letters to his own sons who studied abroad have been preserved and are full of wise, Christian, and pedagogic advice regarding both humanistic and theological studies. Though Luther was less than respectful towards Bullinger, the latter sent at least one son to study under him and Melanchthon. Bullinger had, however, begun to do research into educational methods and curricula as soon as he took over the abbey school at Kappel, and by 1527, at the early age of twenty-three, he had compiled his famous *Studiorum ratio* or Study Guide, originally written for the private use of a friend, Werner Steiner (Wernherus Lithonius). It was later published in a shortened form by Pellikan, and then in its full length years later by one of Zwingli's sons in 1594. Although Erasmus and Zwingli wrote on the subject of education and curricula, there do not appear to be signs of their influence on Bullinger. However, in 1525, Bullinger had prepared a work for the printers entitled *De propheta libri duo,* which was never published; modern scholars such as Susi Hausammann find in this work the forerunner of Bullinger's *Studiorum ratio.*

The lengthy thesis is divided into thirty-three chapters and roughly two parts. The first covers the entire realm of humanistic learning of the age, including philosophy, poetry, rhetoric, and history. Bullinger, however, adds a guide to understanding mathematics and the natural sciences. This part is accompanied by a list of textbooks and literature to be carefully studied. The second part, starting with chapter 15, deals with the critical analysis of literature; in particular it covers that which cultivates a deeper understanding of the Scriptures. Bullinger deals in detail with the entire canon and emphasizes the importance of learning Hebrew and Greek and being open to the illuminating work of the Holy Spirit. Here, Bullinger outlines his doctrine of the covenant as the central axis of the Scriptures and God's revealed will to mankind. In this comprehensive work, Bullinger maintains that thinking comes from reading, and the more one digs into the literary past, the more one is able to think in a way which will solve the problems of the future. In short, he who will not read about the past and understand the *genres* of literature cannot possibly think in any way useful to the education and advancement of mankind, whether in natural or spiritual knowledge. Bullinger thus sees the minister as the teacher and foreseer of the future, who, through his exegetical work, acquaints the reader and hearer with the thoughts of God and the way to God, as well as prepares him for his future life with God. The structure of Bullinger's work is typically humanistic and thus follows a pattern common to Bullinger's age. The originality of the work is found in its application of known literary methods of analysis to Biblical literature, and its emphasis that the qualified student can only be truly such if he is at least as versed in the Scriptures as he is in secular literature. It is obvious that Bullinger thinks that the process of learning how to think and how to study are more important than merely learning by rote.

CHAPTER VII
Shepherding the Churches

Bullinger's Further Works and Correspondence

Contemporary catalogues of Bullinger's works run into many hundreds of pages,[36] so it is only possible to deal with a few of his major works in this brief introduction. Two of Bullinger's earliest extant Reformed works were his lectures on Romans (1525), in which he emphasized the faithfulness of God in the life of the believer and the differences between law, nature, and grace, and his lectures on Hebrews (1526-27), in which he stresses the uniqueness of Christ and the right usage of biblical typology. During this early period, Bullinger published works on the Lord's Supper (1528), against images (1529), and on the Catabaptists (1531). Three years later, he wrote his *Von dem einen und ewigen Testament oder Bund Gottes*,[37] emphasizing the one covenant of grace in the entire Bible against the Catabaptist teaching which rejected the Old Testament. Today, Covenant Theology is widely thought, especially among Presbyterians, to be a development of Calvin's theology; however, Bullinger's covenant teaching is more meticulously developed than Calvin's and much is attributed to the Geneva Reformer which was actually Bullinger's work. During the 1530s and 40s, Bullinger published commentaries on separate books; his New Testament commentary came out in 1554, complete except for Revelation, which was supplied in the 1561 edition. These works were all printed in Latin so they could be used throughout Europe.

Bullinger's first published work outlining his doctrine of the Scriptures, entitled *Ueber die Autorität der Heilige Schrift*,[38] came out in 1538 and a further work on the subject, *Gründlicher Bericht über die Hoheit, Würde und Vollkommenheit der Heiligen Schrift*[39] followed in 1572. However, in 1991, Hans-Georg vom Berg, Bernd Schneider, and Endre Zsindely published a number of hitherto unpublished works of Bullinger's from the 1520s, such as *De scripturae negotio*,[40] showing that Bullinger was one of the very earliest

Reformers to develop the understanding of the Scriptures now shared by Reformed Christians all over the world. We also have Bullinger's earliest thoughts on the Lord's Supper, which Zwingli told him not to publish at the time because they were so innovative.[41] From 1549-51, Bullinger published his *Decades*, called such as the four volumes were divided into five collections of ten books each. This collection of sermons on the doctrines of the Christian Church was translated into German in 1558 and then quickly into English, French, and Dutch.

As Christians were being persecuted all over Europe, Bullinger published his *Der Rechte Vollkommenheit der Christen*[42] as a plea to the secular powers for tolerance. In 1559, he published a manual for persecuted Christians, helping them deal with questions put to them by their persecutors.[43]

Accepting Revelation as a worthy member of the New Testament canon, contrary to the view of several notable Reformers, Bullinger published a collection of sermons entitled *100 Predigten zur Offenbarung*[44] in 1557. The latter work went quickly through 20 editions and was translated into German, English, French, and Dutch. In the same year, he published an eschatological work *Ueber das Ende des Weltzeitalters und das künftige Gericht unserns Herrn Jesus Christus* in 1557.[45]

Bullinger's International Correspondence
Letter writing was considered a form of art in sixteenth-century Europe and was a main feature of Renaissance life and the humanism that developed from it. Erasmus had written his *De conscribendis epistolis*[46] in 1522, classifying letters into their various types and giving advice as to how a letter should reflect its topic and the character of the writer. He laid great stress on the correct form of salutation, greeting and ending, and emphasized the importance of correctly dating and addressing letters. The Reformers took over the art of letter writing and used it to spread the gospel. Bullinger, in keeping with Luther, Melanchthon, Zwingli, Bucer, Calvin, and others, certainly wrote letters with a view to collecting them later and publishing them in book form to

heighten and further their usage. Thus we find Bullinger making copies of letters and re-acquiring letters after the decease of correspondents. Thus many of Bullinger's letters do not contain the usual personal problems and joys of everyday life with comments on health and the weather, but are often theological theses which were obviously meant for a wide readership. Either Bullinger was the greatest letter-writer known to the Reformation, or the great mass of the letters of other Reformers have perished. Of Erasmus' own letters, only 3,100 have been preserved and 4,200 each of Luther's and Calvin's. There are, however, 12,000 letters from Bullinger's correspondence in the Zürich archives alone, and known collections in many other state and city archives hold at least 3,000 more. Editors of Bullinger's correspondence, such as Fritz Büsser, confess that there is still much research to be done in this field.[47] As Bullinger corresponded with people ranging from students to kings throughout Switzerland, Germany, Holland, Belgium, France, Italy, Poland, Austria, Hungary, Rumania, Bulgaria, Denmark, and England, one can imagine that these countries might still have many of Bullinger's literary and spiritual gems in their possession. In the nineteenth century, the Parker Society printed a large number of letters between Bullinger and his English correspondents as well as a number addressed to important Continental Reformers such as Calvin. His English correspondents included giants of the Reformation, such as Archbishops Cranmer and Grindal, Foxe, Hales, the Hoopers, Humphrey, Lever, Jewel, Sampson, Traheron, Parkhurst, Pilkington, Ponet, Coverdale, Horne, Sandys, Cheke, Cox, Lady Jane Grey, and King Edward VI, besides many lesser known men and women.[48] It is because of this massive Europe-wide pastoral witness that Bullinger received the title "Shepherd of the Churches."

The Second Helvetic Confession

Bullinger's most popular and widespread work, the Second Helvetic Confession (1566), or *Confessio helvetica posterior* as it was originally called, was translated into almost all European languages and used as a standard of orthodoxy throughout East and West Europe and in regions of North

America. The First Helvetic Confession of 1536 was a Swiss-Strasburg confession of which Bullinger was only one of several esteemed authors. The confession was initially merely drawn up as a basis for cooperation with the Lutherans—a plan which, as outlined above, came to nought. The Second Helvetic Confession was solely the work of Bullinger; it was designed initially as Bullinger's own statement of faith. Indeed, it was completed during the Black Death of 1564 and placed with Bullinger's will as he, struck by the plague, prepared for his death. He did, however, recover.

Friedrich III, the Elector of the Palatine, left the Lutheran Church and approached Bullinger as a leading Continental theologian to draw up a creed showing that the Reformed faith was the true, apostolic belief. Bullinger sent him his own declaration of faith. Friedrich found the confession ideal and had it translated into German, printed and distributed. It thus came to the notice of all the Swiss churches, the most prominent being Bern, Zürich and Geneva, and was adopted as a pan-Swiss confession. It was quickly translated into French by Beza, and adopted by the French Swiss and Protestants of France. It probably reached Scotland in its French form, where it was accepted as a standard creed by the Scottish Reformed churches in 1567. In 1571, the Hungarian Reformed Church adopted the confession, then the Poles and Czechs. Indeed, next to the Heidelberg Catechism which developed from it, Bullinger's confession of faith became the most generally recognized in the Reformed Church. On reading through the confession, one is immediately struck by its relevance to the theological problems of today. Here one finds the faults of Arminianism dealt with alongside the errors of Antinomianism. Those who build their faith around Old Testament case-law will find their bubbles burst in the confession, but so will those moderns who reject the Old Testament or say that Christ did not put Himself under the law for the sake of His elect. Modern New Covenant teaching of the John Reisinger school, which is so different from the old Reformed teaching, could be put into better shape by consulting Bullinger's confession. On dealing recently with those who say that God does not use means to convert people, not even the preaching of the gospel, but regenerates the soul directly through inward revelation, this author was struck by the clear answer Bullinger gives to such people in his very first chapter entitled *Of the Holy Scriptures Being the True Word of God*. Of such people Bullinger says:

> Inward illumination does not eliminate external preaching. For he that illuminates inwardly by giving men the Holy Spirit, the same one, by way of commandment, said unto his disciples, "Go into all the world, and preach the Gospel to the whole creation" (Mark 16:15). And so in Philippi, Paul preached outwardly to Lydia, a seller of purple goods; but the Lord inwardly opened the woman's heart (Acts 16:14). And the same Paul, after a beautiful development of his thought, in Rom. 10:17 at length comes to the conclusion, "So faith comes from hearing, and hearing from the Word of God by the preaching of Christ."
>
> At the same time we recognize that God can illuminate whom and when he will, even without the external ministry, for that is in his power; but we speak of the usual way of instructing men, delivered unto us from God, both by commandment and example.

Preaching "Outside of the Temple"

Apart from his theological works, Bullinger wrote works on caring for the sick and dying as well as a number of books on the history of Switzerland, the papacy, and the Reformation. He also kept a journal from his youngest days to his death, outlining family news and commenting on current events. Like the English Reformers, such as John Foxe, Bullinger believed that the gospel could be preached *profanus* (outside the temple) in the form of drama; so, from his early twenties on, Bullinger, amid his vast theological writing, composed several stage plays which reached national and international renown. Lucretia and Brutus is the most well-known. In order to impress on his audiences the Christian responsibility of every man great or small, rich or poor, Bullinger tells the story of Lucretia, a happily married woman who is raped by Sextus, the son of the tyrant king, Tarquinius. Lucretia, in her shame, commits suicide before her gathered family. The people elect Lucretia's husband, Collatinus, and Brutus as consuls, depose the tyrant, and proclaim a republic. Tarquinius strives to regain control through bribing Brutus' two sons. Throughout the play, one is reminded of Schiller's *William Tell*, which is thought to have been inspired by Bullinger's much earlier work. Tragically, Brutus is forced by law to sentence his traitor sons to death. The moral is that countries can only be happy if they are ruled by the people, for the people, and only in such a social order can peace reign and the gospel be preached freely.

CHAPTER VIII
The Problem of Michael Servetus
(1511-1553)

Servetus Used to Discredit the Reformation

The brutal execution of the anti-trinitarian and Anabaptist Spaniard Michael Servetus has historically been used by Rome, who paradoxically condemned Servetus to death themselves, and a number of anti-Reformed churches, to denigrate the entire Reformation movement. As Bullinger took a very strong line against Servetus, even stronger than Calvin, it is necessary to look into this matter briefly. First of all, it must be said that there was not a country or state in Europe at the time in which the denial of the Trinity and blasphemy were not capital crimes. German Lutheran Melanchthon, for instance, urged the Swiss not to show any leniency whatsoever regarding Servetus; he must be put to death. Furthermore, the major blame given to Calvin for the burning of Servetus has no historical backing. The Geneva magistrates had initially asked Calvin to give his opinion of Servetus, obviously under pressure from Bern and Basel to take action against the blasphemer. Calvin replied that he had little hope of bringing Servetus to his senses and that he needed to learn humility. This was hardly a view which would help the Senate condemn anyone to death.

Some time later, Servetus strove to discredit Calvin and Christianity in general in his *Restitutio Christianismi*, a parody on Calvin's *Institutes*. It was this work which caused the papists to arrest Servetus and condemn him to be burned. Even in the papist prison in Vienna, however, Servetus condemned Calvin in the strongest terms, calling him a dealer in magic and a sycophant, and demanded that the Geneva Senate should punish him to the uttermost. Servetus, however, escaped from prison and was invited to Geneva by very influential citizens, such as Perrin and Berthelier, who obviously wished to set up Servetus against Calvin, whom they detested.

Calvin Ignored in the Servetus Trial

Here we must deal with another myth. It is commonly thought that Calvin had full control over the Geneva magistrates. This was by no means the case. Calvin did not have the backing of the Senate and was often in danger of being expelled. Furthermore, the opposition party in Geneva was extremely anti-Calvin. Both the Senate and opposition wanted more state and less church; Calvin wanted more church and less state. Calvin was actually forced by the Senate into exile between 1538-41, when he sought asylum in Strasburg. During the period of Servetus' influence in Geneva, Calvin was again threatened with expulsion as we know from his correspondence with Bullinger, who begged him to remain firm and keep up his witness. There were, however, anti-Calvin riots in the city. Such happenings caused August Lang to write in his *Zwingli und Calvin*, "The years 1552 and 1553 were the most bitter and saddening in Calvin's turbulent life. He experienced disparagement and even contempt."[49]

On hearing of Servetus' criticisms of Calvin and the city authorities' suspicion of him, Bullinger assured Calvin of his support, remarking that Servetus was no common heretic but a dangerous deceiver of men who was beyond correction, and that the Geneva magistrates ought to deal with him under the full power of their laws. Bullinger also told Calvin that the Zürich Senate believed that Geneva should "put a stop to this pestilence," that is, put Servetus on trial and pronounce the death penalty.[50] It is obvious from the context that Bullinger was in full agreement with his Senate. As Calvin was seriously considering leaving Geneva himself, whatever the magistrates decided, Bullinger quoted Acts 18:9-10 to him: "Be not afraid, but speak, and hold not thy peace: For I am with thee, and no man shall set on thee: for I have much people in the city," and begged Calvin not to give up the good work he had begun at Geneva. It is, however, at this moment of weakness on Calvin's part, and at a time when he was in danger of reaping the anger of the magistrates, that his critics would have us believe that Calvin ruled Geneva!

On August 13, 1553, Servetus was recognized in Geneva

by several citizens who applied for his arrest. Actually thinking himself secure, Servetus had sat in the congregation of Magdalena Church where Calvin was scheduled to preach! He was quickly put on trial, but the magistrates became nervous because of the pro-Servetus lobby. Rigot, Director of Public Prosecutions, was a member of the opposition party and an avowed opponent of Calvin. Calvin's opinions were of little interest to the court, but the majority also refused to be put under pressure by the influential minority who supported Servetus. Not daring to judge Servetus alone, they gave up their responsibility as an independent court and told Servetus that they would hand him over to the Roman Catholic authorities who had already condemned him to death. Servetus begged with tears to remain in Geneva. Then the Geneva Senate suggested appealing to all the Protestant cantons, promising they would abide by their decision. Servetus and his defenders agreed at once. Calvin protested against this move, but the Senate ignored him completely. He thus wrote to Bullinger on September 7, 1553:

> Our Council will, on an early day, send the opinions of Servetus to your city, to obtain your judgment regarding them. Indeed, they cause you this trouble, despite our remonstrances, but they have reached such a pitch of folly and madness, that they regard with suspicion whatever we say to them. So much so, that were I to allege that it is clear at mid-day, they would forthwith begin to doubt of it.

Protestant Switzerland Unanimous on Servetus
Basel told Geneva that if Servetus did not repent, they must use the powers God gave them to rid the world of one who was so dangerous to the Church. Bern, always critical of Calvin's leniency, told Geneva to eradicate the plague which had settled down among them and burn Servetus at the stake. Bullinger's Zürich reply was, "No severity is too great to punish this outrage." The other cantons gave similar judgements. Bullinger wrote to Theodore Beza privately on August 30, 1553, saying, "But what is your most honourable

senate of Geneva going to do with that blasphemous wretch
Servetus? If they are wise, and do their duty, they will put
him to death, that all the world may perceive that Geneva
desires the glory of Christ to be maintained inviolate."[51]

The Senate thus sentenced Servetus to death by
burning. Calvin pleaded that the sentence should be changed
to death by beheading, which was thought more merciful.
But the Senate took no notice of Calvin. Even Bullinger,
whose friendship with Calvin was stable, could not help
telling his Geneva friend that he had made a mess of things
and had not spoken up against Servetus when he should
have. Referring to Calvin's written refutation of Servetus in
late 1553, in which Calvin had quoted a private letter from
Bullinger without consulting his friend on the matter,
Bullinger tells Calvin that he fears that his book will make
little impact because of its brevity and obscurity and the
weightiness of the subject. He also tells Calvin that his style
is too perplexing, and adds, "I know that you will kindly take
this freedom of mine; for I love you from my heart."[52] It is
thus obvious that the Swiss Protestant cantons were united
in condemning Servetus for his blasphemy and godless religion; the most doubt as to how to pursue was shown by
Geneva who, we must not forget, had the responsibility of
actually dealing with Servetus. Of the Reformers, Calvin was
certainly not the most vigorous in condemning Servetus,
possibly because he was in no position to say much in the city
at all. Indeed, Bullinger sat far more firmly in the Zürich
saddle than Calvin did in Geneva, and was thus able to view
the matter more objectively as he was not directly and
personally involved in the controversy as was Calvin. If any
one man can be given the responsibility of Servetus death, it
must be Bullinger, who strongly influenced the cantons by
his antagonism to Servetus. Thus, the idea that it was
Calvin's iron rule of the Geneva Senate which forced them to
burn Servetus, a myth critics of the Reformation love to
affirm, is without historical backing.

Old prejudices die hard. For instance, although August
Land says that Calvin's influence in Geneva at this time was
the lowest that it had ever been, he still gives Calvin full responsibility for Servetus' burning. He accuses the Genevan

Reformer of not being man enough to confess that he was behind Servetus' arrest and execution, but he brings no evidence whatsoever to support his theory.[53] One thing is certain: after Servetus' execution, Calvin's star began once again to ascend in Geneva. It was, however, Bullinger's strong testimony against Servetus which put off many a writer such as Professor Felix Nüscheler from attempting a biography of Bullinger.

CHAPTER IX
Bullinger's Vast Importance for the English Reformation

Bullinger's Early Contacts with England

When dealing with Calvinism in England during 1558-1640, Patrick Collinson, the acclaimed expert on the Elizabethan Age, states, "If we were to identify one author and one book which represented the center of theological gravity of the Elizabethan Church it would not be Calvin's *Institutes* but the *Common Places of Peter Martyr*, described by his translator, Anthony Marten, as 'a verie Apostle.' And at least equally influential was Bullinger."[54] This is all the more interesting, as Martyr had served in England for a number of years. Bullinger had never set foot in England but was still considered as sharing the top rung of the ladder of fame with him. Bullinger's importance to the English Reformation can scarcely be exaggerated, and there are many good reasons for this. Exiles from the persecutions of Cardinal Wolsey and Henry VIII's notorious Six Articles found shelter in Switzerland; a number lodged in Bullinger's private house, including John Hooper the martyr, who stayed two years in Bullinger's home with his entire family. These refugees were deeply influenced by the beautiful character and plain but profound teaching of the young Reformer. Writing to Bullinger in January, 1546, Hooper said:

> These singular gifts of God exhibited by you to the world at large, I was unwilling to neglect, especially as I perceived them seriously to affect the eternal salvation and happiness of my soul: so that I thought it well worth my while, night and day, with earnest study, and an almost superstitious diligence, to devote my entire attention to your writings.[55]

It is thus not surprising to find Bullinger's commentaries appearing in English in the 1530s. An undated letter from this period written by Nicolas Eliot is extant,[56] in which

Bullinger's English friend and pupil thanks him for his works. Among many compliments, Eliot says:

> Not only the church of Zürich, but all other churches which are in Christ, bear witness to the skill, and purity, and simplicity of faith, with which you have expounded the whole Bible, and especially the epistles of St. Paul. And how great weight all persons attribute to your commentaries, how greedily they embrace and admire them, (to pass over numerous other arguments) the booksellers are most ample witnesses, whom by the sale of your writings alone, from being more destitute than Irus and Codrus, you see suddenly becoming as rich as Croesus. May God therefore give you the disposition to publish all your writings as speedily as possible, whereby you will not only fill the coffers of the booksellers, but will gain over very many souls to Christ, and adorn his church with more precious jewels.[57]

On hearing that Henry VIII had broken with the pope, Bullinger wrote his *The Authority, the Certitude, the Stability and the Absolute Perfection of Holy Scripture and The Institution and the Function of Bishops* which he dedicated to the King; he sent copies to the King, Thomas Cranmer, and Thomas Cromwell via former students Nicolas Eliot and Nicolas Partridge. Both the King and Cranmer requested that the Latin works should be translated into English and Eliot wrote:

> Your books are wonderfully well received, not only by our king, but equally so by the Lord Crumwell, who is keeper of the king's privy seal and vicar general of the church of England . . . but your writings have obtained for you a reputation and honour among the English, to say nothing of other nations, beyond what could possibly be believed.[58]

One of the most famous of the English exiles in Germany and Switzerland was Miles Coverdale, commonly called by his contemporaries "Superintendent-At-Large of the Reformation." Coverdale was a brilliant linguist and pastored a

German-speaking church himself during his Marian exile. His first known translation of Bullinger's works was *Der alt glaub,* or *The Old Faith,* published in 1541. This work was a summary of the Old and New Testaments and the faith once committed to the saints. It proved very popular and was reprinted and modernized by Coverdale a number of times, and revised and retranslated in the seventeenth century. Also in 1541, Coverdale translated and published Bullinger's work on Christian marriage, which begins, "The Christen statye of Matrimonye. The orygenall of holy wedlock: whan where how and of whom it was instituted & ordeyned: what it is: how it ought to proceade: what be the occasions fruit and commodities thereof." By the early forties, Bullinger was so loved in England that even single letters anyone received were quickly snapped up, translated, printed, and distributed in tract form.

The great kindness shown by Bullinger and the Zurich Senate to former exiles caused Edward VI, on coming to the throne, to write to him, thanking him as a personal friend and saying, "In addition to which, there is also a mutual agreement between us concerning the Christian religion and true godliness which ought to render this friendship of ours, by God's blessing, yet more intimate."[59] This more intimate friendship was to make itself apparent when Edward died amid rumors of being poisoned by the papists, and when his half-sister Mary drove the Lord's people who had escaped martyrdom by the thousands out of England. Many of these exiles kept close contact with Bullinger, not only because of his own person but also because in Zürich, he had access to Christopher Froschauer's printing press. Froschauer stood with Bullinger at the side of the English exiles, making sure that Reformed works in English were smuggled into Britain.

A Good Friend of England's in Persecution and Revival
So, too, in the days of Bloody Mary, Bullinger kept an open home for the English and exercised his pan-European influence, enabling the English refugees to set up churches throughout the Continent. He gave advice on who should pastor them, how to get along with the state authorities, and how to defend the faith when placed under pressure to

renounce Christ. The largest Continental English church during 1554-1559 was in Frankfurt, where Charles V had given the English the freedom of the city. Bullinger sent Thomas Lever there with the recommendation that he should pastor the church, so Lever was elected to the office. It was through Lever's diplomacy and moderation and his keeping to sound Reformed principles in the face of several "fiery spirits" which enabled the so-called *Liturgy of Compromise* to be drawn up; this document subsequently united the conflicting parties and became the basis for English worship throughout Germany and Switzerland.

The letter that Lever and eleven of his friends sent to Bullinger and the Zürich magistrates in 1554, requesting asylum in Zürich, has been preserved in the Parker Society's *Original Letters* and reads:

> Forasmuch as we are exiled, most honourable magistrates, from England, our beloved country, and for the sake of that light of divine truth by which she was lately distinguished, we humbly request of your worthiness, that we may be permitted to sojourn in this most famous city, relying upon and supported by your sanction, decree and protection against the violence of those, should any such be found, who would oppose and molest us. The Lord knoweth, for whose sake we have left our all, that we seek for nothing besides himself. And for this reason chiefly we have unanimously and with ready minds come to this place, where he is most sincerely preached and most purely worshipped. This being the case, we entertain the hope that, as you are most zealous defenders of the true Christian religion, so you will protect us by your authority, who by reason of the same are exiled and homeless. May the Lord Jesus long preserve you and this your industrious state in safety and prosperity! Your most humble petitioners, Robert and Margery Horne, James Pilkington, Thomas Lever, John Mullins, Thomas Bentham, Richard Chambers, Thomas Spencer,

Henry Cockraft, Michael Reniger, Laurence Humphrey, William Cole.[60]

These twelve saints were given the best of hospitality and it is said that they lived in Zürich "with great glee." The hospitality of these Zürich believers was enormous. Printer Froschauer took all twelve into his own home, as most of the other Reformers' houses such as Pellikan's were already filled with English refugees. The homeless saints for whom they opened their doors were to become the pillars of the Reformation under Elizabeth, filling important places in church, state, and the universities. Queen Elizabeth, on her coming to power, wrote to Bullinger and the Zürich church, conveying her thanks and sending them a gigantic silver cup in token of her friendship. When the pope "excommunicated" Elizabeth, Bullinger wrote his *Refutatio Bullae papisticae contra Angliae Reginam Elizabetham*[61] in which Bullinger defended the "true Christian Queene, and of the whole Realme of England."

Through correspondence with one of the English exiles, Edwin Sandys, Bullinger first heard of Bloody Mary's death. Sandys had settled down on the Continent, taken out Frankfurt citizenship with his friend John Ponet and had dropped thoughts of ever returning to England as Mary was relatively young. He was having dinner with John Foxe and Peter Martyr when news of Mary's death reached the Reformed friends. Sandys, who had been imprisoned under Mary, refused to return, complaining that he had experienced enough misery in England; Grindal, who also had grown to love Germany and was ever after termed "Germanical," persuaded him to return and help build up the Protestant church in England. Sandys thought it his duty to inform Bullinger immediately of Mary's death and wrote to him in his usual jovial manner:

We yesterday received a letter from England, in which the death of Mary, the accession of Elizabeth, and the decease of cardinal Pole[62] is confirmed. That good cardinal, that he might not raise any disturbance, or impede the progress of the gospel, departed this life the day after his friend Mary. Such was the love and harmony between them, that not even death itself could separate them. We have nothing therefore to fear from Pole, for *dead men do not bite*.[63]

Bishops Horne and Grindal, both old friends of Bullinger's, wrote to him requesting help in restoring the Reformed Church of England. They were particularly interested in the relationship of the Christian to civil laws and the wider problems of state-Church relationships. Above all, however, they were eager to have Bullinger's advice concerning the vestment controversy which was threatening to split the Reformers. Several of the exiles were striving to introduce new forms of clerical wear which they claimed were marks of a truly Reformed Church. Bullinger responded with his *Epistola ad Episcopos et fraters in Anglia* in which he declared that the Church of England was correct in her understanding of the vestments. Bullinger, Gualter, Beza, and Calvin all wrote to the rebel Precisians,[64] telling them that they had misinterpreted the Swiss Reformation, misinformed their Swiss advisors as to the state of the English Church, and were misusing Switzerland's good name by insisting on forcing Continental externals onto the English Church.

Now the Continental Reformers, especially the Church of Geneva, looked to Bullinger to lead them in their renewed association with England. Beza, after taking over from Calvin, was rather worried how Elizabeth would view him, as it was rumored that Calvin had supported Knox and Goodman in their criticism of the English Royal line in general, and rule by women in particular. Calvin denied such support when Lord Cecil challenged him, though the Knox party insisted that he had given it to them. Beza wrote to Bullinger on September 3, 1566, asking for his cooperation in sending a peace delegation from the Zürich and Geneva churches to patch up old quarrels with Elizabeth and the Reformed Church of England. Beza, addressing Bullinger as "my father," told him that he alone in Switzerland had the authority and ability to deal with the English Queen and the English Church. Such sentiments led Adolf Keller to say, "Bullinger was the oracle of the Elizabethan bishops."[65]

Actually, the difficulties had only been on the Geneva side and Bullinger had maintained a spotless witness to and support of the English Reformation. The positive result was that Geneva's wish to have stronger ties with the English Church drew the Swiss churches, well-known for their bickering, gradually together. Beza had been upset to find that Queen Elizabeth had not acknowledged a work of his and concluded that he was considered "hateful" to her. He told Bullinger:

> The reason for her dislike is two-fold: one, because we are accounted too severe and precise, which is very displeasing to those who fear reproof; the other is, because formerly, though without our knowledge, during the lifetime of Queen Mary two books were published here in the English language, one by master Knox against the government of women, the other by master Goodman on the rights of the magistrate. As soon as we learned the contents of each, we were much displeased, and their sale was forbidden in consequence: but she notwithstanding cherishes the opinion she has taken into her head. If therefore you think the present cause worthy of being undertaken by us, it would seem the most suitable plan, and most useful to the brethren, that someone should be chosen from your congregation, if not by the express authority, at least with the permission or connivance of your magistrates, to proceed to England on this special business, and openly solicit from the queen and bishops a remedy for these evils. This would be indeed an heroic action, worthy of your city, and, as I think, very acceptable to God, even though it should not altogether succeed according to our wish.[66]

Bullinger put in a good word for Geneva. Such an amiable fellowship ensued between the Church of England and the Geneva Church that when Beza became bankrupt, Archbishop Whitgift supported him from his own pocket; furthermore, when Geneva's funds sank accordingly, the Church of England took up a generous collection, against the

Queen's express wishes, to help the needy city state protect herself from a Roman Catholic takeover.

As soon as Thomas Lever returned to England, he informed Bullinger that he had contacted the underground church which had become weaker and weaker under Mary's reign of terror, but was now seeing times of revival. He continued:

> Some of us preachers, who had returned to England from Germany, being much affected with these things, and considering that the silence imposed for a long and uncertain period was not agreeable to the command and earnest injunction of Paul, to preach the word of God in season and out of season, having been requested to do so, forthwith preached the gospel in certain parish churches, to which a numerous congregation eagerly flocked together. And when we solemnly treated of conversion to Christ by true repentance, many tears from many persons bore witness that the preaching of the gospel is more effectual to true repentance and wholesome reformation, than any thing that the whole world can either imagine or approve. ... Now popery is at length abolished by authority of Parliament and the true religion of Christ restored.[67]

Reformers such as Thomas Lever earnestly supported the distribution of Bullinger's books in England. One of Bullinger's most popular works was his collection of sermons on Revelation, a book hardly ever dealt with by English and Swiss commentators at this time. When the English translation appeared in 1561, English Bishop Parkhurst ordered all the clergy in his large diocese of Suffolk and Norfolk to purchase and study either the Latin or English text. However, no single work affected the English as much as Bullinger's *Decades*. Single sermons and component parts of the *Decades* had appeared in English since the early forties and the complete German version was being used by students in England by 1566,[68] but the full work was probably not translated until 1577 when an "H. I. student in Diuinite"[69] had the five books printed in three volumes by

"Ralphe Newberrie dwelling in Fleete-streate a little aboue the Conduite." They immediately became the standard work in England on "the chiefe and principall pointes of Christian Religion." The English version of the *Decades* was reprinted in full in 1584 and 1587, but the Latin version was regularly printed in England from 1551 on. Froschauer's versions were also widely distributed in England.

The Special Importance of Bullinger's *Decades*
In 1586 the Archbishop of Canterbury, John Whitgift, drew up instructions for those called to the ministry, which he entitled *Orders for the better increase of learning in the inferior Ministers.* Junior clergymen and those wishing to be licensed as public preachers who did not have a theological education were told to procure a Bible, a copy of Bullinger's *Decades,* and a blank-paged exercise book. The Archbishop told the candidates that they must read a chapter of the Bible every day, making notes of what they had learned in their exercise book. Each week, they should read through one of Bullinger's books and make appropriate notes on what they had learned; then, once a quarter, they met with their tutor to discuss their reading and notes and receive his further instructions.

Over Fifty Years of Earthly Ministry Ended
Upon recovering from the Black Death of 1564-65, Bullinger was left an old man with acute kidney trouble. His dear wife Anna caught the disease while looking after him, and soon died. Friends advised Bullinger, now sixty, to marry again quickly and even scolded him when he said that there could not be a second Anna. Then his daughters Margaretha, Elizabeth, and Anna, and several of their children died within a year. In the same year, one by one, Bullinger's dearest friends and pillars of the Reformation followed one another back to their Maker. Blarer, Gessner, Froschauer, Bibliander, Farel, and Calvin left Bullinger, supported by his adopted son Rudolf Gualter, to live on for another decade. On August 26, 1575, Bullinger, who was looked after by his youngest daughter Dorothea, realized that his pilgrimage was over, and called all the ministers, professors, and

teachers in Zürich to his study for his last admonition, teaching, and farewell. In a long, well-prepared speech, he exhorted his friends and brethren to keep the unity of the Spirit and remain faithful to their testimony, calling, and ministry. He then sent a fitting admonition to the magistrates ending with the words: "The grace of the Father and the blessing of Jesus Christ with the power of the Holy Spirit be with you and gracefully preserve your city and state, your honor, persons and possessions under His divine care and keeping and shield you from all evil."

When friends told Bullinger that they were praying for his full restoration to health, the worn-out spiritual warrior said:

If the Lord will make any further use of me and of my ministry in his church, I shall willingly obey him; but if he shall please (as I much desire) to take me out of this miserable life, I shall exceedingly rejoice; as I shall be delivered from a wretched age, to go to my Saviour Christ. Socrates was glad when his death approached; because, as he thought, he should go to Homer, Hesiod, and other learned men, whom he supposed he should meet with in the other world. How much more do I rejoice, who am sure that I shall see my Saviour Christ, the saints, patriarchs, prophets, apostles, and all the holy men, who have lived from the beginning of the world. Since, I say, I am sure to see them, and partaker of their joys, why should I not willingly die, to be a sharer in their eternal society and glory?[70]

Bullinger fell asleep peacefully in the Lord on September 17, and was buried at the side of his beloved Anna. He was seventy-one years of age and had been in fulltime Christian service for over fifty-five years, forty-three of them as a minister of the gospel. His adopted son, Rudolf Gualter, was almost immediately appointed to succeed him. The choice had been Bullinger's own, and, as usual, his choice could not have been better. Seldom has there been such a great man who made so few mistakes.

FOOTNOTES

Chapter I

[1] See Blanke's and Leuschner's *Heinrich Bullinger: Vater der Reformierte Kirche*; and Blanke's editorial work in *Exegetische Schriften aus den Jahren 1525-1526; Briefe der Jahre 1524-1531; Briefe des Jahres 1532; Briefe des Jahres 1533* and *Beschreibendes Verzeichnis der Literatur über Heinrich Bullinger*, all available from the Theologischer Verlag Zürich.

[2] A radical protest group within the Church of England, sometimes known as "Ultra-Puritans," a number of whom were Separatists.

[3] See François Wendel's *Calvin* for a lengthy discussion concerning Calvin's conversion.

[4] Calvin's enormous dependence on Bucer for the contents of his *Institutes*, especially the editions after 1539 has been outlined in Lang's "The Sources of Calvin's Institutes," *Evangelical Quarterly*, 1936, and Wendel's *Calvin*, 1963.

[5] *Martin Bucer*, Strassburg, 1914, 143-44.

[6] See Chapter 3, "Der Einfluss des Buches auf die Institutio Calvins und den Heidelberger Katechismus."

[7] *International Calvinism*, 67.

[8] See Blanke and Leuschner, *Heinrich Bullinger: Vater der Reformierten Kirche*, 279, and extensive footnote on 323.

[9] See Benjamin Warfield's fine essay entitled "On the Literary History of the Institutes" for Calvin's reception in England, Works, Vol. V, *Calvin and Calvinism*.

Chapter II

[10] Zum Wildenmann.

[11] Marktgasse 66.

[12] Bern was more for the blockade than Zwingli who opted for war. The compromise led to the war in which he perished.

Chapter III

[13] Usually translated as *Analysis and Reasons for the Concluding Statements* but this work, Zwingli's longest, appeared in English under various titles and versions, though some twenty years later, for instance, *The Rekenynge and Declaration of the Fayth and Belefe of Huldrike Zwyngly* (1543).

Chapter IV

[14] Quoted in Wilhelm Moeller's *History of the Christian Church*, Vol. III, 118 from Baumgarten, *Karl V. und die deutsche Reformation*, 65 ff.

[15] Instruction and Confession of Faith as used in the Church of Geneva.

[16] Church Ordinances.

[17] Tiguria was also the English name for Zürich at the time.

[18] *Huldrych Zwingli: His Life and Work* (Fortress Press, 1986), 159.

[19] Reformed Church.

[20] Father of the Reformed Church.

[21] Blanke's work on the young Bullinger was first published in 1942 and this life was completed by Leuschner in 1990 by his adding the story of Bullinger's life in Zürich.

[22] *Reformation and Society*, 124.

[23] See Hollweg's discussion of this problem in Chapter 4 of his *Heinrich Bullinger's Hausbuch*.

[24] See also Horton Davies on *The Worship of the English Puritans* for further sources on this subject as also the Parker Society's volumes of Whitgift's works, Lindberg's *The European Reformations*, and my own *The Troublemakers at Frankfurt*.

[25] Actually, it was Bucer who radically influenced Swiss theology but I am stating the case as Westphal saw it. Westphal's theological understanding was strictly limited, for instance, he thought Calvin was a pupil of Zwingli's whereas, as François Wendel says in his *Calvin*, p. 136, Calvin ridiculed Zwingli's prestige and "Zwingli must have remained completely foreign to Calvin."

Chapter V

[26] The term Catabaptist was formerly used by such as fourth century Gregory of Nazianzus for those who rejected baptism. It was first taken up during the Swiss Reformation by Oecolampadus from whom Zwingli gained it and popularized it. Zwingli appears to have used the term (so Lang, etc.) to indicate either Counter-baptism or Anti-baptism. In Swiss-German the word for "again" and "against" (wider) is the same. Nowadays the term is often replaced by Anabaptism which means re-baptism and thus the original meaning of Catabaptism has been lost. Technically speaking, Catabaptism means drowning or immersing by baptism rather than re- or anti-baptism. The Catabaptists, I believe, never called themselves such. Oecolampadus believed that it was more correct to use Catabaptist than Anabaptist and told Zwingli so. He thought Zwingli used the term in too broad a manner and insisted that *Widertäufer* (Catabaptists) if consistent with their theology, must be "drowners" and not baptizers.

[27] See Werner O. Packull, *Hutterite Beginnings*, (John Hopkins University Press, 1995).

[28] See, for instance, his *Heinrich Bullinger und die Täufer*, published by the Mennonite Historical Society in the Palatine (Pfalz, 1959).

[29] The four Catabaptists executed at Zürich were sentenced under Zwingli.

[30] Often candidates were immediately baptized on their answering such questions as "Do you wish to live righteously?" or "Do you wish to receive all God's blessings?" in the affirmative.

[31] *Pradikanten- und Synodalordnung.*

Chapter VI

[32] *Zürich Letters*, First Series, 286 and 317. Hollweg and others quote Cox as saying "the strongest pillar," but the Parker Society English and Latin versions have merely "pillar."

[33] *Original Letters*, Vol. II, 377.

[34] Ab Ulmis' son of the same name took on the name of Ulmer. He, too, studied at Oxford.

[35] Ibid, 410.

Chapter VII

[36] See *Heinrich Bullinger Werke*, Erste Abteilung, Bibliographie, Band I and II.

[37] On the One, Eternal Testament or Covenant of God.

[38] On the Authority of the Holy Scriptures.

[39] *Thorough Report of the Sovereignty, Dignity, and Perfection of the Holy Scriptures.*

[40] On the Unity of Scripture.

[41] *Heinrich Bullinger Theologische Schriften*, Dritte Abteilung, Band 2, Unveröffentlichte Werke der Kappeler Zeit, TVZ.

[42] *The True Perfection of Christians*, initially written as a plea to Henry II not to persecute the French Protestants.

[43] *Anleitung, wie die Verfolgten antworten sollen.*

[44] One Hundred Sermons on Revelation.

[45] *On the End of the World's Epoch and the Future Judgement of Our Lord Jesus Christ.*

[46] On Writing Letters.

[47] See Büsser's introductory essay to *Heinrich Bullinger Werke*, Zweite Abteilung, Briefwechsel, Band I, Briefe der Jahre 1524-1531, Theologischer Verlag Zürich, 1973.

[48] *Zürich Letters* (2 vols.), 1842 and *Original Letters* (2 vols.), 1846.

Chapter VIII

[49] Bielefeld und Leipzig, 1913, 127.

[50] *Original Letters*, Vol. II., 742.

[51] Ibid, Vol. II, 741-42.

[52] Ibid, Vol. II, 743-47. See also Calvin's letter to Bullinger dated

December 30, 1553 in which Calvin tells Bullinger of his anti-Servetus work.

53 *Zwingli und Calvin*, 130-31.

Chapter IX

54 *International Calvinism 1541-1715*, 214-15.

55 *Original Letters*, Vol. I, Parker Society, 1846.

56 Probably written in 1537.

57 Ibid, Vol. II, 620.

58 Ibid, Vol. II. 618.

59 Ibid, 1.

60 Ibid, Vol. II, 751-52.

61 Refutation of the Papal Bull Against Elizabeth Queen of England.

62 Mary's relation and henchman and fellow-persecutor of the saints. Mary had made Pole Archbishop to replace Cranmer whom she had burned at the stake.

63 *Zürich Letters*, Vol. I, 3.

64 Radical critics of the Elizabethan Settlement. See my discussion of this strategy on the Precisians' part in my *The Troublemakers at Frankfurt*, especially 306-309. See also the above named Swiss Reformers correspondence with Sampson, Turner, Humphrey, Horn, and Grindal in Zürich Letters. Beza's letter *To certain Brethren of the English Churches, upon some Controversies in the English Polity* is found in Book 1, *Of Original Papers*, 37, bound with the 1710 edition of Strype's *The Life and Acts of Archbishop Grindal.*

65 Dynamis. *Formen und Kräfte des amerikanischen Protestantismus*, 1922, 30.

66 *Zürich Letters*, Second Series, 131.

67 Ibid, 28.

68 "Letter from John Abel to Bullinger dated London, June 6, 1566," ibid, 117.

69 The Latin version gives "impensis Radulphi Newberii et Hugonis Jaksonii," so possibly Hugh Jackson was the translator.

70 Quoted in Middleton's *Biographia Evangelica*, Vol. II, 169-70.

Henry Bullinger's *Decades*

CHAPTER I
Bullinger as a Preacher

Henry Bullinger (1504-1575) was one of the most widely esteemed leaders of the sixteenth-century Reformation. His book *The Decades* was the most famous of hundreds of treatises and manuscripts that he wrote. *The Decades* derives its name from being a series of fifty theological sermons, which are divided into five groups or "decades" of ten sermons each. Each sermon is a helpful, detailed exposition of an important doctrine. Combined, they encompass the field of Reformation theology in a readable form for the typical layperson. These sermons became more popular than Calvin's *Institutes* in England. They have now been reprinted in English for the first time since 1850. In this introduction, we will first consider Bullinger as a preacher (Chapter I) and then examine the history (Chapter II) and the contents (Chapter III) of *The Decades*.[1]

Preaching was of central importance in the Reformation. T.H.L. Parker wrote, "In the Reformation preaching occupied a position which it had not held since the fifth century. The Gospel [in the Reformation] is a return through Augustine to the New Testament; the form [of the sermon] is a return to the homily of the Fathers."[2]

Preaching was recognized early in the Reformation as the primary task of the ministry. In fact, the entire office of the ministry became defined by the act of preaching. Reformation pastors were often designated simply as "Minister of the Word" or "Preacher of the Gospel."[3] The pulpit returned to the front and center of church sanctuaries, becoming the most significant piece of furniture in the church. There could be preaching without the sacraments, but not the reverse. At times, Reformed services were called "preachings" or "sermons." People asked each other, "Did you go to the sermon? Did you attend the preaching?"

The Reformation church was grounded in preaching. Preaching was regarded as the primary means whereby God edifies saints, nurtures faith, saves sinners, and calls the unsaved to flee from the wrath to come. In preaching, God's saving grace and love breaks into a sinner's consciousness.[4] Preaching prompts either reconciliation or condemnation. To be genuinely Reformed means to allot preaching a high and central place.

Since many people could not read, preached sermons often served as the arbiter of doctrinal beliefs and opinions. For those who could, written sermons played a similar role, particularly in places preachers could not easily reach.

Henry Bullinger upheld this high view of preaching and was himself one of the most outstanding of the great Reformation preachers. Two events of his life in critical situations underscore this.

The First Event: Preaching in Bremgarten

When Bullinger's father, the dean of Bremgarten, openly acknowledged his evangelical faith from the pulpit early in 1529, the congregation reacted so negatively that the elder Bullinger was deposed from his office and had to take refuge in Zürich. Within months, however, the evangelical party regained the upper hand. Many people then asked to have Bullinger's son serve as preacher. On May 16, 1529, Bullinger, age twenty-four, preached in his large home church for the first time. His subject was worshiping God in Spirit and in truth. Churchgoers reacted to the powerful message by tearing down images in the church. The next day they burned those images in the church yard and demolished the altars. Then the entire congregation dedicated themselves to God and the new faith, instituted a strict course of discipline against all transgressors of the divine commandments, and declared themselves to be a Reformed church.

On May 18, the church council formally asked Bullinger to bring the Reformation to the town. Bullinger, however, informed the council that he was under oath to the Zürich council and could not take a step without its permission. The Bremgarten council quickly dispatched one of its members to Kappel and then to Zürich to plead before its council to release Bullinger from his duty to them. The Zürich council voted to allow Bullinger to take up the new post. On May 22, the congregation called Bullinger by unanimous consent to be co-pastor with Gervasius Schuler, who had been Zwingli's assistant.[5] Bullinger accepted the post with great freedom of conscience. He said farewell to his colleagues and friends at Kappel and Zürich, then took his new calling June 1, 1529.

Bullinger preached for the Bremgarten congregation every Sunday afternoon and Monday, Tuesday, and Wednesday mornings. He also led a daily Bible study. On June 30, Bullinger began to organize the feeding and clothing of the poor, just as he had done at Kappel, and started up an itinerant ministry to the surrounding districts. During his Bremgarten years, Bullinger preached through the entire New Testament.

The Second Event: Preaching in Zürich
People in Zürich were complaining that the clergy had created problems by taking over the city's political leadership. Popular, ribald songs were being written and sung openly, lampooning the Reformation and Zwingli. Haller in Bern was quick to respond to this criticism, but most people in subdued Zürich did not dare. However, some Zürichers responded by composing a number of heartfelt serious hymns of lament and repentance. Many said the enemy without (the Roman Catholics) was not weakening the city as much as Protestants from within. Numerous citizens who had professed Protestantism for the sake of their livelihood said they no longer felt it was advantageous to speak about it. Some Protestant leaders, including Leo Jud, went into hiding.

According to rumor, some Reformed pastors were seriously thinking of reverting back to Roman Catholicism or fleeing the city. Peter Füessli, a member of the Greater Council, had already begun to attend mass again. The Romanist faction in the city was becoming stronger. Füsseli did not fear criticism as the council had begun to remove those councilmen who had voted for war. Berchtold Haller, now greatly alarmed, wrote to Bullinger from Bern to ask if the rumor was true that Zürich was to reinstate the mass.

To make matters worse, the Zürich senate had signed the Peace Treaty of November 20, which stipulated tolerance for Reformed ministers but only after publicly acknowledging that the Roman Catholic cantons possessed "the true, undoubted Christian faith." Bullinger was not concerned about his own safety, but he was worried about that of Gervasius Schuler and his wife and two daughters. So Bullinger wrote to his friend, Ambroseius Blaarer, minister in Upper Germany, asking him to take Gervasius on as a curate. In the political turmoil, Schuler, a German, would be better off outside of Switzerland. Bullinger ended his letter to Blaarer with the words, "Farewell and pray for our poor Switzerland."

In 1531, when Zwingli was killed in battle at Kappel and the Zürichers were defeated, Bullinger and his two evangelical colleagues were compelled to leave Bremgarten. Bullinger came to Zürich as a refugee. He found the church there weak and frightened because of the continual threats of her enemies. Oswald Myconius, then a teacher in Zürich, wrote: "How can the preachers of God's Word fulfil their office? So many threats surround them, so many daggers and swords, that a power without equal would be necessary, a veritable apostolic courage, who, like Paul, lets nothing stop him from preaching the Lord Jesus and from disciplining the godless."

Bullinger had received a call from Bern, but when Johannes Oecolampadius died November 24, 1531, Basel also asked Bullinger to become its pastor. Bullinger's friends assumed that Bullinger would leave Zürich and take one of those calls. Bullinger, however, felt that he was too young and inexperienced for those large assignments and said he would seek a pastorate similar to Bremgarten, now sadly in the papists' hands.

The Zürich church and senate had only Leo Jud to turn to, but Jud had backed Zwingli in his plans for war and was judged too close to some of the Anabaptists and too politically minded for the Zürich councilors. Besides, Jud was battling depression and said that he was unfit for the task. Jud also had strong views, later modified through consultations with Bullinger, about the absolute separation of church and state, meaning that the church would become a state within a state.

The main pulpits in the city were thus empty. On November 23, the young Bullinger, who had not lost his credentials as a Zürich minister, was asked to preach to the defeated and confused congregation. Myconius relates the effect of Bullinger's preaching: "Bullinger thundered out such a sermon that many believed that Zwingli was not dead but, like the phoenix, has been again raised to life." Myconius added that Bullinger was only a guest in the city, thinking that he would not stay. The sermon had so awakened the city, however, that Bullinger was asked to preach again. On December 9, 1531, both church and senate unanimously voted to ask Bullinger to be preacher in the Grossmünster and to lead the Zürich churches. Bullinger, now age twenty-seven, accepted the call.[6]

Bullinger's first sermons at Bremgarten and Zürich showed his gift to bear witness to the congregation "in demonstration of the Spirit and of power" in critical situations (1 Cor. 2:4). But Bullinger also knew how to preach to workers and ordinary folk, who were his major concern. That was somewhat embarrassing to members of the senate who wished to show off their superintendent to visiting foreign dignitaries. Bullinger was well-known as a scholar and student of the ancient languages, but when noblemen and church dignitaries were given a place of honor in the gallery appointed for prominent people, they invariably heard Bullinger preaching in the local dialect. On one occasion, a prominent guest from Germany who wanted to hear Bullinger preach was given a prominent pew in the gallery. Looking down from his vantage point, the German saw what appeared to be a peasant in everyday clothing, speaking in an uncouth language. Afterwards he complained that Bullinger was a simple country preacher and decided to tell him so. Bullinger listened to the criticism, then said to the German, "Did not Your Grace look down from above and see the filled and cramped pews full of rough caps and old wives' headscarves? I preach for them and not for great lords and learned scholars."[7]

The great Swedish Reformer and professor of Hebrew and Greek, Konrad Pellikan, said that Bullinger had one of

the greatest minds of his age, yet was the simplest of preachers. Pellikan had visited almost all the universities of Europe
and taught at the best of them so he knew of what he spoke.
He wrote in his *Chronikon* that Bullinger was the best and
most important preacher that he had ever heard. Pellikan
went on to say that there was no difficult passage in Scripture that Bullinger could not master exegetically by studying
the original texts, then making that knowledge comprehensible to the simplest minds so that people never complained
that they could not follow the preacher.[8] Pellikan credited this
to Bullinger's immense industry and careful, ongoing study.
For example, despite all his responsibilities, Bullinger attended
Professor Theodor Bibliander's lectures on the canon of Scripture year after year so as to stay fresh in his studies.

Calvin himself approved of Bullinger's approach to
preaching. When explaining how his predecessors had helped
him write his commentary on Romans, Calvin credited
Melanchthon with the light he had shed on the epistle, then
continued, "Then comes Bullinger, who also received much
praise; and that rightly, because he has combined simplicity
with learning, and for this he has been highly approved."
Calvin rejected the accusation that he was entering into
"odious rivalry" with his mentors, saying that Melanchthon
merely kept to essentials and left much out; Bullinger was
simpler, though learned; and Bucer was too learned and
complex, though "by his tireless labours has just about said
the last word."

Like other preachers, Bullinger had his critics. Once while
clerking at a synod, Bullinger was criticized for his preaching.
The mild-mannered Reformer duly recorded the criticism of
himself in the minutes: "Mr. Bullinger is too gentle in his
preaching, should be somewhat bolder, rougher, and harder,
especially in relation to the procedures of the council."[9]

Like most Reformers, Bullinger preached often. In the
first six years of his Zürich ministry, he preached six or
seven times a week. When Caspar Megander (Grossmann)
was called to Zürich in 1538 to assist Bullinger, Bullinger cut
back his preaching to about four times a week. In 1542, the
frequency was reduced to twice on Sundays and once on
Friday mornings.

Happily, Bullinger's record of the Biblical books he preached through has survived. He preached through 53 books at least once, the exceptions being Leviticus, Numbers, Ruth, 1 and 2 Chronicles, Ezra, Nehemiah, Esther, Job, Proverbs, Ecclesiastes, Song of Solomon, and Ezekiel. Twice Bullinger preached through Isaiah, Daniel, Hosea, Amos, and Nahum. Three times he preached through Joel, Obadiah, Jonah, Habakkuk, Zephaniah, Haggai, Zechariah, and Malachi. He preached twice through the gospels of Matthew and Mark, the Pauline epistles, and 2 Peter; three times through the gospels of Luke and John, Acts, 1 Peter, and 1 John; and four times through Hebrews.

Bullinger was also a prodigious writer. His writings show how diligent he was in exegesis. From 1532 to 1546, Bullinger published thirteen commentaries that covered the entire New Testament except for the book of Revelation. In the late 1540s he published several volumes of sermons as well as *The Decades* (1549-1551). In 1557, he published one hundred sermons on Revelation and, the following year, eighteen sermons for the Christian feast days. Next, he published sermons on Old Testament books: 170 sermons on Jeremiah (1557-1561), 66 sermons on Daniel (1565), and 190 sermons on Isaiah (1567). Over the years he also published at least twenty-four miscellaneous sermons. In all, Bullinger published at least 618 sermons. Yet none of his sermons became as popular as those in *The Decades*.[10]

In addition to preaching and writing, Bullinger corresponded with hundreds of people all over the world, and he entertained a never-ending stream of guests. This tremendous activity worried his friends, who warned Bullinger that he should take care of himself. Philipp Galicius wrote to Bullinger on January 7, 1556: "I ask you on behalf of all Christians to listen to your body and spare yourself; preach and study less that Christendom may have you longer as a precious jewel and a beautiful light."

The workload did tax Bullinger's strength, especially as he grew older. On March 27, 1562, Bullinger wrote to Fabricius in Char: "I would ask the Lord for rest if it were not contrary to His commandment."[11]

CHAPTER II
History of *The Decades*

Printed sermons often served a dual function in the mid-sixteenth century Reformation. They popularized Reformed theology among the educated laity, and they were often read by ministers who were not qualified to prepare effective sermons by themselves.

Origin

The Decades were written to meet both needs. Originally, Bullinger intended to publish six "decades" of sermons, but in the end he settled for five. As he began writing, the sermons tended to increase in length, which may explain why he cut back on the number, since there appear to be no gaps in the content. Bullinger wrote to a close friend in Basel, Oswald Myconius, on July 26, 1549: "I have decided to publish three volumes; the first I have already done, and I am already at work on the second. Each one will be presented in two decades so that in the end there will be six. If you had read the order and sequence, you could have anticipated the subjects. They will take the place of *loci communes*. May the Lord give me sufficient strength to finish what I have begun."[12]

By designing his book to "take the place of *loci communes*" (i.e., "common places" or chief topics of theology, the sixteenth-century term for "systematic theology"), Bullinger was saying that he hoped this unique set of sermon books would also serve as a theological compendium. His earnest desire was to teach systematic theology to the laity through these sermons.

Bullinger's work on *The Decades* stressed him a great deal. Late in 1549 he wrote to Myconius, "I have been unable to write to you for two months because of my many activities. I am working on my *Decades* but not getting very far. My duties are so manifold and numerous, yes, even more arduous than I can bear. At times I am exhausted; at other times, I am simply overwhelmed."[13]

The first edition of *The Decades* was printed in Latin by Christopher Froschauer in Zurich (1549-1551). The first and second decades were combined into one volume, the title page of which says: "Two Decades of Sermons, Concerning the Most Important Heads of True Religion of Which the Catalog Shows, by Henry Bullinger, author. The preface of the work declares the sure manner in which God, being angered by our sins, can be pleased. It likewise makes available the creeds of the ancient Councils and orthodox church fathers."

The third and fourth decades were published in two parts. The title pages are nearly identical: "Third (or Fourth) Decade of Sermons – of Matters Which You Find to be Examined at End, to the Most Serene King of England Edward VI, by Henry Bullinger, author."

Bullinger found the strength to finish the last volume of *The Decades* early in 1551. Due to the polemical notes he felt obligated to include, especially in relation to the sacraments, Bullinger knew that this volume would provoke Roman Catholics more than any of his other writings. But his goal was deeper than interacting with Rome; Bullinger was hoping that these sermons would resolve intramural debates among Protestants. When he sent Myconius his fifth decade on March 6, 1551, Bullinger wrote, "I know that you will not be displeased with this volume. I know, too, that quite a few will now be able to judge us more fairly who previously condemned us as sacramentarians. I hope I have not labored in vain by writing four sermons on the sacraments."[14]

Christopher Froschauer, one of the great Protestant printers of the sixteenth century, published twenty-seven editions of the full Bible and sixteen of the New Testament. Most of Bullinger's books were printed in Froschauer's shop.

The printer's friendship with Bullinger is evidenced by the generous gift he bequeathed to Bullinger when he died. "Mr. D. Christopher Froschauer died April 1, 1564," Bullinger wrote in his diary. "He left me 700 pounds in his will—very thankful." After Froschauer's death, his nephew, who was his namesake, continued on as Bullinger's printer.

The nephew died in 1585, at which time the business went to John Wolf, who republished some of Bullinger's writings, including *The Decades.*

Unlike Calvin's *Institutes*, which changed and grew over decades, Bullinger's work remained unaltered in size, order, and content. One reason may be that Calvin was only twenty-six years old when he published the first edition of *The Institutes*, whereas Bullinger was at the mature age of forty-five when *The Decades* was published. Unlike Calvin, Bullinger was publishing the ripe fruit of his knowledge and experience.

The Decades sold well from the beginning. The first complete reprint of *The Decades* appeared in a 1552 Latin folio, only one year after the first printing was completed. The title page presented what came to be the standard title: *Five Decades of Sermons, Concerning the Most Essential Heads of the Christian Religion, Digested in Three Volumes, by Henry Bullinger, Minister of the Church of Zurich with a copious index.* Other than the title, the second edition was identical to the first, except that the two parts dedicated to Edward VI appeared as one, and the indices of all the volumes were combined. Bullinger wrote to Wolfgang Salet in Chur January 22, 1552, "Froschauer is now printing my Five Decades in a book in folio, and although this is the second printing, I have added nothing and taken nothing away, nor have I changed anything as so many do nowadays." In later years, Bullinger often directed people to particular sections in his *Decades* when they sought his advice in doctrinal matters.

Further editions of the Latin text appeared from Froschauer in folio form in 1557, 1562, 1569, 1577, and 1582. In 1587, Henry Middleton from England published a Latin text as well. Several Latin editions were cordially received and widely distributed.[15]

Dedications[16]

Bullinger wrote *The Decades* at a critical time in the Reformation. When Luther died in 1546, German Protestantism was about to face momentous problems. The emperor's power had reached its apex because of the desertion of

Maurice of Saxony and the Schmalkald War. The Augsburg Interim, with its fearful results, was a burden on evangelical lands. The apparent goal of Charles V was to name the Spanish prince, Philip, as Emperor. The cause of the Reformation, which was bound in the chains of the Interim, was in great jeopardy. The historian J. H. Kurtz said the Reformation was like a delinquent facing the death sentence.[17] Bullinger's *Decades* addressed many of the needs of Protestants of that time.

Bullinger dedicated the first two decades of his book to his fellow pastors, whom he calls "my dear brothers and fellow workers." According to the church order that Bullinger established, the Zurich church was divided into eight districts, each headed by a dean, whose job was to make sure that the church order was followed and that regular visitations of the churches were held.[18]

Bullinger dedicated the first part of *The Decades* to each of his eight deans as well as to all the preachers of the Zurich church. Referring to the seriousness of the times, he wrote to his colleagues: "The just Lord is angry at our sins, and punishes them also; nay, he is preparing far heavier calamities to pour out on the heads of the impenitent. Our duty is then to watch for the Lord's flock, and upon the approach of the sword to give timely warning to all the sheep committed to our trust, that the blood of those who perish be not required at our hands."

Compelled to show church leaders how to exercise their office in those fearful times, Bullinger wrote: "Cleansing from sin means confessing it, then forsaking it by faith and conversion; that is the only way to go. Sins are certainly to be rebuked, but then in the right way, not by scolding, but with the goal that the sinner confesses them, humbles himself, and believes that all his sins are forgiven for Christ's sake. Such faith does not make folk careless and vicious, but awakens men to prayer and good works. Patience and hope are also needed so that we do not fall away. Whoever exercises the office of the ministry in this way has the promise of great reward. Therefore, we should ask the Lord for His Holy Spirit for true and fruitful office-bearing." Thus, one more reason Bullinger wrote this classic was to help his brothers in the ministry.

Though the emperor's power was strong in Germany and increasingly directed against Protestants, England was becoming more evangelical. The eyes of the Protestants were upon young King Edward VI and his work of reformation. Many Reformation writers dedicated books to this king: John Calvin dedicated his commentary on the Catholic epistles to King Edward in 1551, Peter Paul Vergerie dedicated two works to the king in 1550, and Martin Bucer wrote his second great work on the kingdom of Christ for the king. It is not surprising, then, that Bullinger dedicated the third and fourth decades to King Edward VI. He dedicated the fifth to his trusted counselor, Henry Grey, the Marquis of Dorset.

Bullinger had another reason to honor Edward VI and Lord Grey. Bullinger had received a plea for help from groups in England who were trying to renew the church. One of the most zealous workers there was John Hooper, who later became known as the planter of Puritanism in England. Hooper was appointed Bishop of Gloucester in 1550, then of Worcester. Hooper suggested that the Reformation would be furthered if Bullinger would dedicate one of his books to the king and to his counselor, Lord Grey. In a letter from London dated March 27, 1550, Hooper wrote, "I wish you would dedicate your work either to the king or to the Marquis."[19]

Previously, John of Ulm, a pupil of Bullinger's, had made the same request, so Bullinger acquiesced to the wishes of his English friends. He chose a theme for his dedication that was particularly timely; wanting to speak to the king about the true cause of happiness for all kings and kingdoms, he wrote, "Kings are happy who offer themselves and their whole kingdom to Jesus Christ, the King of kings, and the Lord of lords, and who submit to Him with the confession that He is the highest Prince and King and that they are His vassals and servants, likewise, who follow and govern not according to their own notions but only the laws of the highest and eternal King and improve all things according to the rule of the Word of God alone."

Bullinger's second preface to Edward VI dealt with something he found deeply troubling. The preface of the fifth decade, dedicated to Henry Grey, dealt with this concern at even greater length. One of the main goals of the emperor at that time was to hold a general council that would end the ecclesiastical strife in Germany. At the diet that met in Augsburg on September 1, 1547, the estates of Germany agreed to recognize a general council as the highest and most decisive court in church matters. When the pope opposed that decision, the emperor put through an interim measure, which, as the name suggests, meant "a declaration concerning the state of religion in the Holy Roman Empire until the holding of a General Council." The emperor did not abandon his plans for a council. Those plans became more of a reality when a new pope, formerly chairman of the Council of Trent, ascended the papal throne as Julius III. On November 14, 1550, the new pope issued an order for a new session of the council on May 1, 1551. At the emperor's urging, the Protestant estates expressed willingness to attend the council at the diet meeting in Augsburg in February 1551.[20]

Bullinger was concerned that all of this political activity would negatively impact the evangelical cause. He wrote his preface of August 1550 and March 1551 to warn King Edward VI, his counselor, and his readers about the dangers of what was happening in Germany. Bullinger knew that some people would say, "Don't be so hasty to proceed by your own authority; in difficult matters of religion, the decision of a general council must be awaited." However, Bullinger argued that the prophets and apostles do not refer us to councils but to the Word of God. He said a council summoned by the pope would consist of those who felt they must support the pope; consequently, little scriptural reform would take place. Bullinger pleaded with Lord Grey, "Continue to reform what needs to be reformed."

Bullinger's trusted friends in England received *The Decades* with gratitude. Martin Micronius wrote to Bullinger that John Hooper received the beautifully bound book on April 22, 1550, and three days later gave it to the king via William Parr, brother of Queen Catherine Parr. Hooper told Bullinger that the king "received it in a gracious and friendly manner and not without many expressions of thanks; he asked after you and the welfare of your church."

Lord Henry Grey was highly honored by the dedication of Bullinger's work. His daughter, Jane Grey, had a particularly close relationship with Bullinger. She is best known in history for her appointment by Edward VI to be his successor, but Mary Tudor ended up obtaining England's throne instead of her. Mary had Jane, age eighteen, her husband, and his father, executed. On July 12, 1551, Jane Gray wrote to Bullinger: "My most noble father would have written to you to thank you both for the important labours in which you are engaged, and also for the singular courtesy you have manifested by inscribing your fifth Decade with his name and publishing it under his auspices, had he not been summoned by most weighty business in his Majesty's service to the remotest parts of Britain. But as soon as public matters afford him some leisure, he is determined, he says, to write to you with all diligence."[21]

Six months later, Lord Grey expressed his thanks to Bullinger: "For the book which you have published under the auspices of my name, I thank you not only for my sake but for the sake of the whole church of Christ. I acknowledge God's goodness towards His church, and as Paul says, 'the love of God to man' that He has chosen to adorn and illuminate His church with such lights, so that we who are less enlightened may follow such guides in the beaten path of true religion. For not only by reason of the gifts they have received of God, but also for the love of the brethren, such leaders are willing to point out the path by which we must go. It would be all over for us had God not given such pillars to support his church, or it would surely have collapsed."[22]

Bullinger sought to further the cause of the gospel by dedicating the various parts of his book to men of authority and influence. But this was only one of his goals in writing; his main goal was to serve his brethren in the ministerial office.

Twofold Purpose for Ministers

Bullinger wrote to his ministerial colleagues in his introduction to *The Decades*: "A good pastor must carefully consider the circumstances of the people entrusted to him and give them what is most necessary, keeping in mind edification, true faith, godliness, love, and innocence. He must teach and exhort the congregation in which God has placed us to be godly and holy. Therefore, I am presenting these sermons as patterns to serve those who for years have asked me for this." Bullinger wrote to Calvin March 15, 1550, "I have completed this work for the profit of students and ministers of the Word."[23]

Bullinger had high expectations with regard to the character and the professional qualifications of preachers. He wrote, "Not just anyone should be ordained, but carefully chosen, pious men, who possess many different talents, are well instructed in the Bible, have a firm grasp of the mystery of the faith, are bold and constant, industrious, intelligent, watchful, thoughtful, and live a pious and respectable life so that the ministry may not fall into disrepute because of the evil manners and bad reputation of some who destroy by evil living what has been built up by sound doctrine." Later, he stressed the importance of selecting a minister: "This matter is not to be taken lightly. The well-being of the congregation depends upon it. If an unworthy and uneducated man is put into office, the whole congregation, as a rule, is neglected, confused, and destroyed."[24]

To understand why Bullinger insisted on a ministry that exemplified godliness, we must understand what was going on in the world of the Reformers. Maurice Ritter, a nineteenth-century historian, once described these early years of Protestantism as "ecclesiastical anarchy." Think of the educational state of the clergy prior to and during the Reformation. The monastic schools had largely disappeared, and Roman Catholic universities were unsuitable for training Protestant ministers. Where and how were preachers to be trained?

Protestant churches had to deal with poorly educated clergy. For example, in 1554, Gillius Faber, the well-known preacher of Emden, demanded that his ruler, Countess Anna, depose forty pastors who hardly knew the Ten Commandments and were living disorderly lives. Such problems were common in East Friesland as well as other places. In 1566, Michael Diller, court preacher to Frederick III, stated that if seven able ministers from the Rhenish Palatinate were sent to convert the Upper Palatine Lutherans to the Reformed faith, the former would be deprived of all the good men that it possessed.[25] In 1574, there were only one hundred preachers in Scotland for a thousand parishes, and a fair number of these ministers were neither gifted nor qualified.[26]

The need for good ministers was great even in Switzerland. In 1553, Philip Gallicius, minister of Chur, wrote, "We have preachers among us who never saw the inside of a school, and who know how to read an Italian sermon, but not a word of Latin or German." Gallicius was particularly disturbed that some ministers defended their lack of education on the basis of scriptural texts that described the disciples as "unlearned and ignorant men" (Acts 4:16), and spoke against higher learning because "the letter killeth, but the spirit giveth life" (2 Cor. 3:6).

Former Roman Catholic priests also were a problem because many of them were not able to edify churches or dioceses that converted to Protestantism with them. H. Schokking says this problem was still evident more than fifty years after the Reformation. When the ministers of Classis Neder-Veluwe met in Arnhem, the Netherlands, in 1597 to examine ten former priests who had converted to the Reformed cause, they could not approve any of them.

In response to the dire need for qualified Protestant clergy, Luther had begun work on his *Kirchenpostille [Church Postils]*. A *postil* was a short exposition of a Bible passage that contained theological and moral teaching. Lutheran preachers often based their sermons on a passage being expounded in the assigned daily postils, or based their messages heavily on the postil itself, borrowing freely from it. Sometimes they simply read the postil in its entirety as their sermon. In his *German Mass and Order of Service* (1526), Luther wrote, "It would be best to read the postils of the day in their entirety to the people, not only for the sake of the preachers who cannot proclaim the gospel any better, but also to guard against zealots and sects, as one can often see and feel in the morning homilies. Otherwise, where spiritual understanding is lacking and the Spirit Himself does not speak through the preacher, a sermon takes on a will of its own and comes to the hearers from out of the blue instead of presenting the gospel and its explanation in a scriptural way. This is one reason why we retain the Epistles and Gospels as they are ordered in the postils, because there are few inspired preachers who are able to expound a complete Gospel or another book in a powerful and useful way."[27]

The English church also realized the need to educate preachers. Shortly before Bullinger published *The Decades*, Thomas Cranmer, Ridley, and others published the *Book of Homilies* (1547). These homilies were to be read aloud in the churches by clergy, thereby restricting "free preaching."

Calvin wrote *The Institutes*, and Bullinger, *The Decades*, to fill the same need. Sermons were necessary, not so much as template messages, but as collections of subject matter from which educated preachers could draw and which unlearned clergy could read aloud from the pulpit.[28]

Such emergency measures would present dangers of their own if continued after the number of properly trained ministers substantially increased. But at that time, Reformed Protestantism had no schools suitable for training preachers thoroughly. In France and the Netherlands, Reformed movements were annihilated with fire and sword. England swung between affection and hatred for evangelical movements. Where should the congregations of embattled churches then find preachers who were capable of caring for them? The renewal of a Protestant-minded university finally took place in Heidelberg in 1558. The following year Calvin succeeded in opening the Geneva Academy. The famous Dutch university of Leiden, founded explicitly for providing well-educated ministers, was not founded until 1575. Similarly, the Johannea, a university in Herborn, was established in 1584 "for the preservation of our Reformed faith." But none of these institutions existed when Bullinger published *The Decades*. His book was therefore intended to help prospective and established preachers.[29]

Both Luther and Bullinger realized that there was some danger in allowing preachers to rely on printed sermons. In his foreword to Johann Spangenberg's postils, Luther reprimanded "quite a few lazy ministers and preachers who rely on this or other good books from which they can pull their sermons; they don't pray, they don't study, they don't read, they don't endeavor to write, as if they don't have to read the Bible because they have the postils."[30]

Bullinger was more optimistic. In the foreword to the first *Decades*, he wrote: "I do not pay much attention to the false accusations of those who say that my ministerial brothers will become lazy through such sermons, as it happened in times past when the sermons of Discipulus and Pelbartus were read. I have on my side the example of the most distinguished teachers and bishops in the parish, who have themselves, and that not without great advantage, written sermons and homilies."

Apparently Bullinger viewed *The Decades* as paralleling the sermon collections written by Discipulus and Pelbartus, which were highly valued by Roman Catholic preachers and congregations from the late Middle Ages through the sixteenth century. The author of the first collection was Johann Herolt (d. 1468), lector and prior of the Dominican cloister in Nürnberg. Herolt became known as Discipulus because of a closing comment in his book: "The collected sermons present subject matter from various words of saints and several books. They are titled 'sermons of the student (*discipulus*),' for these sermons do not consist of subtleties written at a master's level, but simple things composed at a student's level." Herolt's *Sermones de sanctis et de tempore* [Sermons on Sacred Matters and the Times] went through 46 editions by 1500, making it the second most popular work of its day. Its practical approach made it extremely successful. Wort Walthers said, "Herolt's wisdom could be heard from the pulpit by thousands of preachers for half a century."[31]

A collection of sermons similar to Herolt's was published by the Hungarian Franciscan, Oswald Pelbartus of Themesvar, who lived around 1500. In the introduction to *Sermones pomarii de tempore et de sanctis* [Fruitful Sermons on Temporal and Sacred Matters], Pelbartus noted that he was providing four sermons to be read for every Sunday of the year so that "ministers who work for many years in the same area will be able to preach a different sermon each year, for if they use the same sermons each year the congregation will grow weary of them."[32]

Both of these Roman Catholic collections were intended to provide subject matter for sermons (*stoffsammlungen*), even though in many places they were simply read aloud without any changes. Since Bullinger modeled *The Decades* after these books, we may tentatively conclude that he viewed his work primarily as a collection of subject matter for sermons and secondarily as a collection of reading sermons. This two-fold purpose set a pattern for many preachers in the late sixteenth and seventeenth centuries.[33]

The Reformed church also recognized the danger of postils for preachers. The *Kurfürstlichen Pfaltz Kirchen-Rats Ordnung de Anno 1564* [Pfaltz Church Order of 1564] noted, "Many ministers have increasingly abused the postils by relaxing during the week or busying themselves with other work; this has had negative consequences for the churches. When they have to preach, they first take a postil, read through it, and use what appeals to them, reciting it to the people without any personal zeal or meditation. This results in hearts not being kindled; people are not incited to listen to and comprehend the divine word."[34]

Dangers notwithstanding, it is astonishing that Bullinger's *Decades* was the only major Reformed collection of doctrinal sermons published by the mid-sixteenth century. In that sense, Bullinger's collection was the forerunner of a plethora of doctrinal sermon books that would follow from the pens of Puritans.

The Language

Bullinger first published *The Decades* in Latin, the recognized academic language of scholars that was understood internationally. Bullinger was proficient in Latin; at his funeral, one preacher said, "He used the Latin language—the most widely used and known language everywhere in the world—as easily as native peoples use their own language, regardless of whether he had to speak formally or off the cuff."[35]

Until the seventeenth century, many preachers wrote their sermons in Latin. Luther published his postils first in Latin, then in 1525 began publishing postils in German.

Martin Bucer, encouraged by Luther, began translating Luther's German postils into Latin so that they could be read around the world. Later, as we shall see, that situation reversed itself with Bullinger's *Decades*. A variety of translations in the vernacular appeared soon after the Latin publication.[36]

Sermon Length

Bullinger's sermons became lengthier as *The Decades* progressed. The first decade of sermons in the English edition averages sixteen pages per sermon; the last decade averages fifty-two pages. G. Oorthuys said these later sermons are simply too long to have been preached as they were written.[37]

Whether that is true or not has not been resolved. Both Reformed and Lutheran church orders of the sixteenth century regarded one hour to be a normal sermon length. Jan Laski's *Forma at ratio* [Forms and Method](London, 1550), which deals with the order of worship, argued that expositions from the Old or New Testament should cover as much as the minister "can expound and reasonably explain in one hour."[38] The Lutheran *Teckenburg Church Order* (1588) said Sunday "exposition should not extend beyond more than an hour."[39] Calvin preached for no more than an hour, while his friends Farel and Viret preached longer.[40] Olevianus typically preached for ninety minutes in Heidelberg.[41]

Lengthy sermons became a problem as people began to complain. Calvin felt compelled to write to Farel in 1552, "I hear that your exceedingly long sermons give many people reason to complain. You have often admitted to us that you yourself see this as an error which you would like to correct. To prevent hostile whispering from becoming a rebellious cry, I implore you to force yourself to preach shorter sermons so that you do not give Satan the occasion he desires."[42]

Other Reformers faced stiffer rebukes. In 1553, a synod accused Martin Bucer of preaching too long.[43] In 1574, the Dutch provincial synod at Dordrecht declared that "the minister is admonished not to burden his audience with long sermons; he should strive, as much as possible, not to stretch sermons beyond an hour."[44]

It seems an official statement on the length of sermons was needed by some preachers. Achelis wrote, "In sixteenth and seventeenth century Germany, it was not unusual for a minister to preach two or even three hours."[45] In East Friesland, ministers did not consider their introduction and concluding applications as part of the sermon; therefore, they could preach for two hours without—in their estimation—violating the one-hour guideline.[46]

We do not know whether Bullinger preached lengthy sermons. We do know that he was aware of the increasing length of his written sermons. In his preface to King Edward VI in his third decade, Bullinger cautioned, "I have written long sermons and dealt with subject matter in such a way that several sermons could be developed from each of these sermons. With their insight, the pastors should be able to understand what is necessary and particularly useful for a congregation." This is perhaps the best proof that Bullinger did not merely intend these sermons to be read as written.

Bullinger wanted to expound the truths of Scripture richly from all sides so that every pastor who used his book could select what might best fit the needs of his own congregation. Other remarks made by Bullinger, however, show that he was stretching the endurance of his audience for receiving spiritual truths. At the end of the seventh sermon of the first decade, Bullinger said, "I would add to these the fifth article, but that the hour is now already spent."[47] But at the end of the second sermon of the second decade, he wrote: "I cannot now again recapitulate, because an hour and a half is already spent."[48] At the end of the ninth sermon of the second decade, Bullinger hoped that burdening his audience for almost two hours was not in vain. At the end of the last sermon of the third decade, Bullinger also apologized for having spoken more than two hours.[49]

How could Bullinger get away with speaking so long? We must remember the intense level of interest in Reformed truths that existed during its first years. People were hungry to hear the Word preached and doctrines explained, so they tolerated longer messages, particularly in the form of stated lectures or addresses.[50]

Topical Sermons

All fifty sermons in Bullinger's *Decades* are topical; none is confined to a single text. This raises the issue of sermons that don't expound a particular text. In the Middle Ages, a sermon without a text was considered perfectly appropriate. R. Cruel said of the German sermon in the Middle Ages, "When you look at the form, a 'homily' always refers to a sermon, which essentially is an exposition of a text, while a 'sermon' discusses a certain topic with or without an accompanying text."[51] Reformation sermons, however, were generally expositions of a specific text, though topical messages were not uncommon. Either way, however, love for the Word was too great not to have Scripture receive the center of attention; thus, either a specific text was used or topical messages were preached that covered a goodly number of texts.

Luther and many of his friends preached through numerous books of the Bible. Eventually, preaching from the pericopes (*Perikopenpredigt*) on specific passages from the Bible manifested itself as the typical form of a Lutheran sermon, while preaching through Bible books consecutively (*lectio continua*) became typically Calvinistic or Reformed. Nevertheless, sermons without specific texts remained fairly common in both branches of the Protestant movement. When Luther traveled from Wartburg to Wittenberg during the fasting season in 1522 to suppress the unrest caused by Karlstadt, he preached eight sermons that did not expound particular texts.[52] Of the 192 Sermons of Martin Luther preached in Wittenberg from 1528 to 1532 (published by Georg Buchwald), forty-four have no particular text. The Unpublished *Sermons of Martin Luther, 1537-1540* (Buchwald, 1905) contain ninety-nine sermons with texts and twenty-one without. None of the few sermons Zwingli published are based on a specific text.

After the Heidelberg Catechism was published, most Reformed congregations followed the custom of preaching on one Lord's Day each Sabbath. Some ministers offered a text with their catechetical preaching; others did not; and still others varied their approach, offering texts only on occasion. The Remonstrants were not happy with catechism preaching that was not based on a particular text; they accused the Zeeland ministers who did that of placing the catechism on a par with the Scriptures. The issue was discussed at the National Synod of Dordt (1618-19), where Ritsius Lucas, a preacher from Emden, remarked that it was more important to teach the catechism, which embraces a goodly number of texts, than to preach from a specific text of Scripture.[53]

Though Bullinger did not limit himself to a single text in his *Decades* sermons, all of his messages were grounded in the Scriptures. His desire to proclaim truths based on a variety of Scriptures shows us that choosing one specific text is not an indispensable criterion for a sermon. We must also remember that Bullinger's sermons were published after he had written a commentary on the entire New Testament, with the exception of Revelation. Good Reformation preaching teaches us that the expository sermon that depends on a single scriptural passage must never lose sight of the whole truth of Scripture, and that the topical sermon which covers all of what Scripture says about a subject must not lose sight of what individual texts offer at different junctures in preaching. Bullinger's preaching without a text did not betray the essence of evangelical preaching.[54]

The Audience

Were Bullinger's *Decades* preached as ordinary sermons to his own congregation, then published afterwards? E. Egli, who published Heinrich Bullinger's diary, which contains an overview of Bullinger's preaching activities, claims there is no conclusive evidence that the sermons of *The Decades* were actually preached in Zürich.

Yet *The Decades* themselves abound with literary devices that suggest these messages were spoken. We have already seen that Bullinger often referred to the length of his sermons near the end of his messages. Such comments are meaningless if these sermons were not delivered to a live audience. Furthermore, the second sermon of the first decade begins with a review of the content of the first sermon, then continues: "Now I am come again, and, by God's favour and the help of your prayers, I will declare unto you, beloved, to whom and to what end, the word of God is revealed."[55] At the end of the first sermon of the second decade, Bullinger said his explanations must be sufficient for "the attentive and faithful hearers, who at their coming home do more diligently think of every point by themselves."[56] Such comments make clear that Bullinger preached these messages to a live audience.

On the other hand, Bullinger never addresses his audience as a congregation. Rather, he frequently calls his audience "brothers," "honorable brothers," and "honorable brothers in the Lord." So who was the audience? Bullinger is apparently speaking to preachers and/or theologians. For example, he says: "We must also let these things affect us *and our congregations.*" An audience of theologians is also assumed when he says that he had already sent out literature on the old faith and on the only and eternal testament of God, adding, "and I know quite well, that they are widely known among you." Hollweg concluded that comments like these prove that these sermons were warm, pastoral lectures to a group of pastors and theologians.

A forum for such sermons called *Prophezei* or gatherings was established by Zwingli. With the exception of Fridays and Saturday, ministers, theologians, and theological students gathered at 8 A.M. in the Zürich cathedral to study exegetical, theological, and practical concerns. Addresses were usually given in Latin. It was not unusual for important theological works to evolve from these sessions. Hollweg suggests that Bullinger may have preached his *Decades* in a similar context.[57]

Simplified Versions

In 1556, Bullinger published *Summa christlicher religion* [Summary of the Christian Religion] as a detailed summary of *The Decades* to serve as a textbook for Zürich students in the higher grades.[58] This shorter work played an essential role in communicating Bullinger's thinking to his contemporaries. In the sixteenth century, five German and five Latin editions were published as well as three Dutch editions and one English edition. The English edition was published by George Byshop under the title, *Commonplaces of Christian*

Religion compendiously written (1572). The translator, John Stockwood, minister in Battle, dedicated the work to Henry, earl of Huntingdon. Bullinger's original treatise was dedicated to William, landgrave of Hesse.

Upon the request of the ministers of Zürich, Bullinger published a catechism to pave the way from basic religious principles to the more theological discussions of *Summa*. The book was titled *Catechesis pro adultioribus scripta, de his potissimum capitibus: De Principis religionis Christianae* (1559) [Instruction Written for Older Persons, chiefly on these heads: The first things of the Christian Religion]. In these writings, Bullinger provided material that the congregations of that time needed for instruction in their families, schools, and worship services.[59]

Their Reception

The Decades was received warmly by Bullinger's contemporaries. When John Calvin sent some of his own books to Bullinger, Bullinger responded by sending Calvin the first twenty sermons of *The Decades*, asking Calvin to receive these "little gifts as a token of gratitude."[60] When Bullinger sent his third decade to Calvin, he wrote, "I send you, honorable and most precious brother in the Lord, Calvin, for your truly golden gifts and your most educated books, a hardly worthy gift: the third decade of my sermons. I am certain of the truth of the doctrine they contain, but doubt if I have presented all these truths in a clear and fitting manner. Yet I did what I could, frequently supporting my work with your writings. May God give that the students and preachers of the Word gain abundant fruit from what I have provided for their use."[61]

When Bullinger sent Calvin the last volume of *The Decades*, he said he did not send these packages because "I would want to teach you through my books, for I claim that more can be learned from your books, but I want to show my heartfelt devotion to you."[62] Calvin responded, "You wrote in an apologetic manner that you did not send your books to me so that I could learn from them, but since I desire that my efforts may be profitable to all believers, I, in turn, happily profit from the writings of others. It is true brotherly communion when we acknowledge that the gifts of the Spirit are so divided among us that no one believes that he can do anything on his own. Therefore your gift was welcome to me."[63]

Peter Martyr responded to the gift he received from Bullinger, writing, "I have received and read the decade of your sermons that you sent me as a present; it has so commended itself to me, that I am anxiously desirous for you to proceed as far as possible in that department of labor. You are by this means providing most useful materials for ecclesiastical preachers, which if they will always keep them ready at hand, as they ought, they will be able to instruct the people abundantly and profitably."[64]

Other lesser-known theologians also responded well to Bullinger's *Decades*. For example, Johannes Hospinianus of Basel wrote to Bullinger, "Who would not read with great joy your clear and comforting sermons about the most important principles of our true faith? Truly, I speak without flattery, that as soon as I saw the title of the book, I found myself only tolerating your enterprise, but when I began to read, first the preface and then the sermons themselves and began to understand your arrangement, I have loaded them with praise." Hospinianus said he found the numerous quotations from the Church Fathers to be helpful, "since many have neither the courage to read the thoughts of the holy Fathers, nor the means to buy them."[65]

Because the Reformed movement in Graubünden had been supervised by Zürich since the time of Zwingli, Bullinger had a close relationship with many of the Graubünden preachers. Several of these men communicated to Bullinger their deep appreciation for *The Decades*. Agostino Meinardi, a seasoned Italian pastor, wrote, "They are as precious to me as gold and gems."[66] Petrus Parisiotus, preacher of Samaden, called the book "a truly golden book and a very great treasure," and added, "You have written many good books which bring you immortal praise and much profit to the whole church of Jesus Christ."[67]

The reviews in England were also positive. In response to Bullinger's gift of *The Decades*, Richard Cox, a member of the royal household and former teacher of the king, wrote, "When reading your book I could not stop thinking of you and storming heaven with my prayers that God may preserve your church for a very long time and fill it increasingly with the Holy Spirit."[68] Jon Abel, an Englishman who fled to Strassburg for the faith, wrote to Bullinger in 1566 after reading the *Second Helvetic Confession*: "This book exceedingly pleases me and many believing hearts. But I am even happier with your *Decades*. In this book, all articles of our Christian faith are explained and presented extensively, and it is comforting, encouraging, and profitable to read it."[69]

Reformers such as Thomas Lever, who spent time in exile under Bullinger's roof, supported the distribution of Bullinger's books in England. No single work affected the English as much as *The Decades*. Single sermons and various parts of the *Decades* had appeared in English since the early 1540s, and the complete German version was being used by students in England by 1566, but the full work was not translated until 1577, when a "H. I. student in Diuinite" had the five books printed in three volumes by "Ralphe Newberrie dwelling in Fleete-streate a little aboue the Conduite." These volumes became the standard work in England on "the chiefe and principall pointes of Christian Religion." The English version of the *Decades* was reprinted in full in 1584 and 1587.

A weekly study of a Bullinger sermon from the *Decades* helped improve the theology in English parishes in the late sixteenth century. In 1586, the Archbishop of Canterbury, John Whitgift, presented these instructions for those called to the ministry, titled *Orders for the better increase of learning in the inferior Ministers:*

> I. Every minister having cure, and being under the degrees of master of arts, and batchelors of law, and not licensed to be a public preacher, shall before the second day of February next provide a Bible, and Bullinger's *Decads* in Latin or English, and a paper book, and shall every day read over one chapter of the holy scriptures, and note the principal contentes thereof briefly in his paper booke, and shall every week read over one sermon in the said *Decads*, and

note likewise the chief matters therein contained in the said paper; and shall once in every quarter (viz. within a fortnight before or after the end of the quarter) shewe his said note to some preacher nere adjoyninge to be assigned for that purpose.

II. Item, The bishop, archdeacons, or other ordinary, being a publick preacher, shall appoint certaine grave and learned preachers, who shall privately examine the diligence, and view the notes of the said ministers, assigninge sixe or seaven ministers, as occasion shall require, to every such preacher, that shall be next adjoyning to him, so as the ministers be not driven to travell for the exhibitinge of their notes above sixe or seaven miles (if it may be), and the said preacher shall by lettres or otherwise, trulie certifie to the archdeacons, or other ordinarye of the place, themselves being publick preachers, and resiant within, or nere to their jurisdiction, and for want thereof, to the bisshop himself, who do performe the said exercises, and how they have profited therein, and who do refuse or neglecte to perform the same; the archdeacons and others receiving the said certificates, shall signifye the same, once in the yere, to the busshope, and that about Michalmas.

III. Item, Such as shall refuse to perform the exercises, or shall be negligent therein, and shall not after admonition by the bishop, archdeacon, or other ordinary aforesaid, reform himself, if he be beneficed, shall be compelled thereunto by ecclesiasticall censures; if he be a curate, he shall be inhibited to serve within the jurisdiction.

VIII. It is concluded that the exercises above written, and no other, shall be henceforth publicly or privately used within any parts of this province.

Later, Whitgift asked for prayer regarding his plans to build the education of the lower clergy around Bullinger's *Decades*. He then reminded all the clergy to do their duty as

outlined above. From that point on in Whitgift's administration, bishops and clergy were admonished to keep up the
training system, which rapidly began to mold the teaching of
the Church of England. In this, Whitgift was following the
spirit of his predecessor, Thomas Cranmer, who had invited
theologians from outside England, such as Martin Bucer, Jan
Laski, and Peter Martyr, to come to England with the
express purpose of forming a church whose confession re-
flected the entire European Reformation.

By the time Whitgift died, the educational level of the
clergy in the Church of England had markedly improved. By
1601, half of the parish clergy were licensed to preach, and
half of those had received a university education (compared
with less than 10 percent a century earlier). Doctrinal knowledge had also greatly increased, due in part to hundreds of
ministers regularly studying Bullinger's *Decades*.

Some English editions of the *Decades* included letters of
Bullinger to Laurence Humphreys, Thomas Sampson,
Robert Horn, John Parkhurst, and Edmund Grindal under
the title *Epistles concerning the Apparell of Ministers and
other indifferent things*. That was a response to some
Precisianists in England who had written to Bullinger and
Gualter, complaining that some ministers of the Reformed
Church of England were officiating at the Lord's Table in
popish regalia. Bullinger wrote back, condemning such
practices. The Precisianists published the letter. On making
enquiries, the Swiss Reformers found out that they had been
misinformed; the ministers critiqued for their popish dress
had only worn hats regularly used in Switzerland and white
surplices. Bullinger wrote again, explaining his views to
Sampson and Humphrey who were against priestly
vestments but who would not join the militant Puritans.
Bullinger also wrote to the three bishops Horn, Grindal, and
Parkhurst, all of whom were moderates of great influence in
the Church of England. In short, Bullinger criticized both
those who made vestments their religion and those who
made the destruction of order their religion.

The English preface to *The Decades* blamed the need to
use a foreign manual of instruction on British bishops who
had been less than diligent in educating candidates for the

ministry or had prescribed the works of Calvin, Gualter, Musculus, Peter Martyr, and Marlorat, which were too complicated for a theological novice. Bullinger, the writer explained, had neither Calvin's obscurity nor Musculus's scholastical subtlety but was able to pack much sound doctrine into comparatively little space, making it interesting to read and easy to remember. The writer also said those who denounced catechisms and instructive reading other than the Bible were like physicians who forbad their patients the very diet that did them good. He added that they did not yet have the clergy to undertake a comprehensive teaching ministry for students.

When the Act of Uniformity was passed in 1559, Bullinger was hailed as the hero of the day. T. M. Lindsay wrote, "This was the end for which they (the Reformers) had been striving, the goal placed before them by their friend and adviser, Henry Bullinger of Zürich. Their letters are full of jubilation." The leading English Reformer, John Jewel, who called Bullinger "the only light of our age," wrote to him, "Religion is again placed on the same footing on which it stood in King Edward's time; to which event, I doubt not, but that your own letters and exhortations, and those of your republic, have powerfully contributed."[70]

Praise for *The Decades* also came from theologians who had formerly worked in England. Jan Laski, who formerly preached at the Walloon church in London, wrote to Bullinger: "I have not been able to read your fifth decade in its entirety, but what I have read pleases me much, and I thank God for the gifts given to you." The Dutchman Martin Micron said that he and others "experience more than normal help in the building of the church of Christ" from *The Decades*.

In Germany, Michael Maler, chancellor of Duke Georg of Württemberg, the brother of the reigning duke and a personal acquaintance of Bullinger, praised the Decades for its order, clarity, and faithfulness to Scripture. Even David Chytraeus, a renowned Lutheran theologian and descendant of Melanchthon, wrote, "With much desire I look forward to your *Decades*, hoping that you will complete this effort to unfold faithfully and clearly the full scope of heavenly doctrine for the sake of the church and for the aid of

students." He compared Bullinger's writings with Melanchthon's *Exposition of the Nicene Creed* (a nearly complete
exposition of Christian doctrine, published in 1550), and
stated: "Your writings are more instructive and deal with
more controversies; I read them with more interest."[71]
Ursinus and Olevianus, who had been students of Bullinger,
acknowledged they leaned on Bullinger's *Decades* in writing
the Heidelberg Catechism.[72] They assisted the Palatine
Elector who wrote to Bullinger for advice and eventually
received the Second Helvetic Confession.[73]

Bullinger's *Decades* sold well among scholars and
theologians and became a bestseller among laypeople.
People eagerly awaited the publication of each volume. On
July 20, 1550, the bookseller, Johannes Birkmann of
Cologne, wrote to Bullinger: "With impatience we await the
book of Doctor Bibliander about the doctrine and life of
Peter; but with more longing we await your remaining
sermons, for nothing sells like these." That was true not only
in Germany; the same bookseller wrote to Bullinger from
London on May 3, 1551, saying, "Your fifth decade is being
snatched out of our hands by all believers."[74]

Within a few years, Bullinger's *Decades* were translated
into many languages. It became such a standard manual for
instruction in Christian doctrine, piety, and conduct for
Reformed households that it was given the title "house book"
(*Hausbuch*) in the German and Dutch translations.[75] Walter
Hollweg details in 116 pages how Bullinger's *Decades* affected
thinking in Switzerland, Germany, France, the Netherlands,
England, Italy, and Spain.[76] In many areas of Reformed
Protestantism, no book had such a wide influence. Those who
read this long overdue reprint will understand why.

CHAPTER III

Contents of *The Decades*

Following an introduction on the ancient creeds, Bullinger's *Decades* are divided into four major sections:

• The Word of God and Faith (First Decade)
• Ethics (Second and Third Decades)
• The Doctrine of God (Fourth Decade)
• The Doctrine of the Church (Fifth Decade)[77]

The sermons on these major truths are, at times, divided somewhat unevenly, with priority given to critical issues of Bullinger's day. For example, there is a long justification of civil government under the sixth commandment.

Here is a more detailed outline of the sermons in *The Decades:*

Sermon Content	Decade (I-V)	Sermon Number
I. Presuppositions		
A. The Word of God	I	1-3
B. Faith		4-5
C. Justification by faith		6
D. The Apostles' Creed		7-9
E. The commandments of Jesus		10
II. The Law of God		
A. The Ten Commandments	II-III	1-10; 1-4
B. Ceremonial law		5-6
C. Judicial law and the two testaments		7
D. The use, fulfillment, and abrogation of the law		8
E. Christian liberty		9
F. Sin		10
III. The Nature of God		
A. Grace and repentance	IV	1-2
B. God, providence, and predestination		3-5
C. The Son of God		6-7

Ancient Creeds

Like all Reformers, Bullinger was concerned to relate Reformed doctrines to the Ancient Church. That is why he regularly cited Latin and Greek fathers. That is also why he opened his first series of instructions from a historical perspective, outlining the ancient creeds and the first four General Councils held at Nicea (325 A.D.), Constantinople (384 A.D.), Ephesus (431 A.D.), and Chalcedon (451 A.D.).

Bullinger said he did this because papists were claiming that the Reformers had departed from the historic Christian faith. Bullinger wished to demonstrate that the Reformed faith was that of the early church, from which Rome had seriously departed. Almost as soon as Bullinger began to teach in Kappel, he demonstrated that Rome on the one side and the Anabaptists on the other had departed from the true, historic faith. In one of his first publications in the 1520s, *A Comparison Between the Old Heresies and those of Our Times and A Friendly Admonishment to Justice,* Bullinger showed how the Reformed faith was the true and ancient Christian faith. So, too, in 1552, he published *The Evangelical Church is Neither Heretical nor Schismatic but Purely and Simply the Orthodox, Catholic Church of the Lord Jesus Christ.* Edward Dowey concludes that Bullinger's emphasis on the antiquity of the Christian faith and upon the catholicity of the Reformation in defending the ancient faith is a pervasive conviction that runs throughout his writings.[78]

The First Decade

It is fitting that Bullinger's first sermon (*Decades* I:1; hereafter, the format I:1 will be used) deals with the authority of the Word of God, since this was the means by which the church was to be reformed. Bullinger explains how God's special revelation was passed orally from man to man through chosen witnesses. He then demonstrates the reliability of the oral tradition by a careful computation of the genealogies, deducing from the longevity of the patriarchs that only seven witnesses were required to cover the 2,368 years from Adam to Moses.[79]

Moses was inspired to write the Pentateuch as the Spirit directed, Bullinger says. Moses' authority was confirmed by miracles, the testimony of Jesus, and the punishment of those who opposed him.[80] After Moses, the Word of God was taught by prophets, whose authority was underscored by their accurate foretelling of future events.[81] Ultimately, the final and total revelation of God was in Jesus, who taught that He is the way to God. Jesus proved His authority by miracles. Jesus chose twelve apostles and Paul, who were inspired to write what they had seen. Like Old Testament revelation, these New Testament writings have been preserved uncorrupted in the church. Bullinger concludes that the books of Scripture comprehend "the full doctrine of godliness" and are "the very word of the true, living, and eternal God."[82]

Bullinger's second sermon (I:2) outlines the correct way to respond to God's Word. The Scriptures are universal in application; both the prophets and the apostles spoke to Gentiles as well as their own people. Bullinger opposes the Anabaptists when he says that Christians could not refuse what Jesus and Paul accepted, though the temporary Old Testament ceremonial laws, which are fulfilled in Christ, must be distinguished from the eternal.[83]

The Scriptures are all-sufficient because they contain instruction adequate for every good work. Thus the Scriptures should be received reverently and with much prayer for light and guidance. Those whose attitude is evil will inevitably misapply that Word.[84]

Bullinger's third sermon focuses on hermeneutics—how to rightly interpret the Word of God. Understanding the form of the Scriptures, the imagery, and use of other languages demands much skill. Jesus Himself provided examples of sound hermeneutics in the synagogue at Nazareth (Luke 4:16-21) and on the road to Emmaus (Luke 24:15-17). To avoid inappropriate personal interpretation, Bullinger stresses the need for hermeneutical principles, e.g., no exposition should ever run "contrary to charity towards God and our neighbour."[85]

Bullinger then deals (I:4-5) with true faith, which comes through understanding the Scriptures rightly applied and with the illuminating grace of the Holy Spirit. Such faith is "most firmly grounded in the mind" as a gift of God's planting. Ultimately, faith depends on God who in the Incarnate Son has offered all His benefits to man. God sends His Spirit through the ministry of the Word to work saving faith in a sinner's heart, even as the sinner prays fervently that his own obduracy will be overcome. True faith produces marvelous effects, such as true wisdom and true happiness. True faith is inseparable from forgiveness, union with God, and justification.[86]

Next, Bullinger deals with justification by faith alone (I:6), apart from the works of the law. This is a masterly exposition of a doctrine that is now being challenged, even in supposedly evangelical, Reformed circles. Sadly, many professing Christians today fail to understand the true Reformed doctrine of justification by faith alone. Bullinger teaches that justification is a *status* given us by grace through Christ's righteousness imputed to us, but this does not exclude the new *state* that this status brings with it. The new state is that we were once lost but we have been found, and that we were sinners but now all our sins are covered. We now are children of God instead of children of the devil. So Bullinger teaches, "To justify is as much to say as to quit from judgment and from the denounced and uttered sentence of condemnation." He adds, "It signifieth to remit offences, to cleanse, to sanctify, and to give inheritance of life everlasting."

Bullinger sees justification as the proof of Christ's intercession for His elect, drawing our condemnation upon Himself and transferring His own guiltless state before God to us. For Bullinger, justification is not only the passive forgiveness of sins but the active adoption of the forgiven as sons of God. The word used by Bullinger, which is translated "sanctification," is *beatificatio*. That links the state and status of one whose sins are covered, i.e., one who was cursed but is now made blessed. Bullinger is emphatic that God has not only freed us from punishment, but has also made us guilt-free in justification and heirs of the glory that is in Christ. This means that the sinner is not merely declared just, but he is also made just to remain just and act justly.

Though justification is solely by faith given by God, justification results in what Bullinger calls "post faith," i.e., faith, once it is given, is never alone but accompanied by the fruits of justification in our lives because we are now God's "workmanship, created in Christ Jesus unto good works, which God hath before ordained that we should walk in them" (Eph. 2:10). Therefore justification comes to sinners without respect to just works, which sinners cannot perform anyway, but justification does not leave the sinner without just works. Justification then, for Bullinger, encompasses being re-created for the good works that God performs through His justified ones. Only in this sense is "true faith the well-spring and root of all virtues and good works," and "all that is born of God overcometh the world: and this is the victory that vanquisheth the world, even your faith."[87]

Bullinger next explains The Apostles' Creed (I:7-9) in three sermons, dividing the twelve articles into four parts: one on each of the three persons of the Trinity and one on the fruits of faith. Bullinger gives much authority to the Creed as representing the substance and matter of true faith, but he stops short of subscribing to the tradition of Cyprian, who held that the creed came directly from the twelve apostles and is to be regarded as having scriptural authority, since it was given to form the church rather than proceeding from the church's development and councils.[88] Most of Bullinger's exposition is basic Reformed truth, with the exception of his treatment of Christ's descent into hell. Bullinger says Christ went to hell to preach to those already dead, be they condemned or faithful.[89]

The first book of decades closes with a sermon on the commandments stressed by Christ as the most important of all: love towards God and our neighbor. Bullinger says Scripture must always be interpreted to fit the law of love. Love is a gift from heaven by which believers delight in God as a response to His outpoured love. What this involves is expounded in the first four commandments of the moral law, while the complementary love of our neighbor is covered in the other six (Exod. 20:1-17; Deut. 5:1-21).[90]

The Second and Third Decades

After affirming that the love of God and our neighbor summarizes all law, Bullinger discusses particular commandments and laws in the twenty sermons of the second and third decades. Bullinger accepts Cicero's description of the function of law to command the right and forbid the evil, then makes a distinction between the laws of men and the laws of God. The second decade of sermons deals with law in general: first, natural law (i.e., implanted in man but corrupted by sin, though still somewhat effective through the conscience); second, human law (i.e., laws made by man for societal good); third, divine law (i.e., as recorded in the Ten Commandments, and more broadly, in the Pentateuch). Bullinger focuses mostly on the Ten Commandments and on planning civil law within a biblical framework.

Bullinger believes natural law contains two basic principles: "The first is, Acknowledge God, and worship him: the second is, Keep or maintain society and friendship among men."[91] Concerning the first law, the wonders of nature are sufficient to teach man about God. The second law is found in the principle of Matthew 7:12, "All things whatsoever ye would that men should do to you, do ye even so to them." Bullinger concludes that natural law is only valid when it is answerable to the written law.

Bullinger disposes of human laws under the rubrics of political and ecclesiastical laws and human traditions. These laws must not contradict divine law, and they must serve to define the good and to restrain evil. Ecclesiastical laws, which relate to the good order of the church, should have their principles drawn from Scripture, while mere human traditions, such as compulsory celibacy, were condemned by Jesus.

For the remainder of Book II, Bullinger focuses on the first seven commandments. In Book III, he completes his series on the Ten Commandments in four sermons (covering the eighth to the tenth) before dealing with the ceremonial and judicial laws of God in three more sermons. The eighth sermon is on the use, fulfillment, and abrogation of the law; the ninth, on Christian liberty, works, and merits; and the tenth on sin.

Bullinger's 350-page exposition of the Ten Commandments is too lengthy to comment on at length in this introduction. Suffice it to say that it is solidly Reformed in its ethics and thoroughly practical, ranging from issues such as the keeping of the Sabbath to "the punishment of wrongdoers, war, the raising of children, respect between generations, the relationship of the Christian with rich and poor, and usury, to name but a few."[92] Most notable is Bullinger's lengthy, four-sermon exposition of the sixth commandment (though he had intended to offer only one). The sermons, which cover ninety-five pages, provide an important summary of Reformed political thought. The last sermon was printed separately as a pamphlet titled *A Treatise or Sermon of Henry Bullinger, much fruitfull and necessarye for this tyme, concernynge magistrates and obedience of subjectes* (London, 1549).

Bullinger's goal in these sermons is to combine civil and private ethics based on the proposition that nothing in this life is as valuable as the life of man. After dealing with the ban on killing, Bullinger discusses the nature of the magistracy. Magistrates are necessary to preserve what is good and right, for even if a group is blessed by God, disputes can still arise among them, he says. Magistrates must be respected as God's agents since they receive their authority from Him. The magistrate's office is sacred at all times, even when a particular magistrate is an evil man. Thus, when believers face persecution, they should first consider whether it is deserved. If so, they must repent. If necessary, they should seek the reformation of the system, always remembering that God is able to change the hearts of princes. In all cases, however, people should be wary of overthrowing tyrants, lest greater evils ensue.

Bullinger discusses the responsibilities of the magistrate's office, especially in relation to religion and the duties of judgment and punishment. He opposes the claims of the papacy and its agents to order the affairs of the church, yet he establishes a degree of authority for the magistrate in religion. Bullinger believed that ministers should work in harmony with city councils. The magistrate's power must be limited, since the ruler is subject to the Word of God. Hence, the ruler cannot make laws that alter doctrine, worship, the sacraments, or basic principles of justice and morality.[93] The magistrate is to make good laws to preserve honesty and peace.

A clear separation must be made between judgment and punishment, Bullinger says. Judgment is forming a just opinion in disputes between two parties. As for punishment, the subject Bullinger treated most extensively in his next sermon (II:8), it must be meted out commensurate to the crime. Good laws are of no use if magistrates do not enforce them. Harsh punishment is to be avoided, but that is still better than disorder. The magistrate should pray fervently before deciding on clemency or rigor.

Bullinger then proposes a Christian attitude to war. He says rulers must be clear before going to war that the causes for it make it a just war. Bullinger says legitimate causes for war include the relief of beleaguered garrisons and the destruction of what is incurably evil, including wars of religion. Subjects should obey the magistrate when he commands them to go to war so long as the cause is just.

Finally, Bullinger concludes this series of sermons by arguing against Anabaptist critics who say it is not legitimate for Christians to serve as magistrates. Since God ordained the office of magistrate for man's safety, a Christian should accept the office if he is called to it, Bullinger says.[94]

David Keep concludes, "These four sermons give a picture of a strict and sober regime, just according to the *lex talonis* and supported by devout prayer. There was no room for the gracious anarchy of the Kingdom of God sought by some sectaries, but rather a political system which might be compared with that of Machiavelli or Hobbes, except that for Bullinger the peace of Jerusalem was the first concern of ruler and ruled."[95]

Regarding the ceremonial laws (III:5-6), Bullinger distinguishes between those of the Old Testament, given to sustain the law and to prefigure Christ, and those of the New

Testament, which apply to all men. The ceremonial laws of Israel were given to help people worship God. These laws required a priesthood, a place, and a time. The major rites are still of value today where they can be applied typologically to the church.[96]

Buried in III:6 on God's ceremonial laws is Bullinger's only significant treatment of the covenant in the *Decades*. Covenant may be a "submerged theme," as J. Wayne Baker claims, but it certainly was not a dominant theme; Bullinger does not even allot one sermon specifically to expounding the covenant. Notwithstanding the fact that Bullinger did treat the covenant more extensively in other works, such as *De Testamento* (1534), in a manner more concise and systematic than Zwingli, so that *De Testamento* can justly be called "the first extended exposition of the covenant of grace," it is quite possible to make more of the covenant theme in Bullinger than Bullinger himself made of it. Andrew Woolsey points out that Bullinger appears to have made the most of covenant theology in his polemical works, written primarily in the 1530s. "This being the case," Woolsey notes, "Bullinger would be expected, in view of the Anabaptist bifurcation of the Testaments and increasing tendency towards antinomianism, to stress the unity and eternity of the covenant and its bilateral nature; and in view of continuing Catholic hostility, to show that justification by grace through faith alone was the way in which men were, and always had been, reconciled with God."[97]

Judicial or civil laws (III:7), the shortest group of Mosaic laws, were God's judicial code for Israel. They covered such concerns as the care of widows and the poor, witnesses and oaths, the control of property, and theft and restitution. They became the basis of all later legal systems. Bullinger says that judges should examine cases and pronounce sentences according to the principles of these laws.[98]

Bullinger then addresses the use, fulfillment, and abrogation of the law (III:8). He begins by examining three functions of the law: to convict of sin, to serve as a pattern of life, and to control those who rebel against that pattern. Since all men are disobedient by nature, Christ had to die to fulfill the demands of the law. His perfect righteousness is imputed to believers who are granted faith to believe this and love to keep His commandments. In this way, God's heavy demands become light for believers. In Christ, the curse of the law is abrogated, but the believer must still obey the law of God to serve God in this world.[99]

The two concluding sermons of the third decade deal with matters that depend on the law but are not contained in it. In III:9, Bullinger explains Christian liberty, works, and merits. He makes clear that Christ delivers sinners from the spiritual bondage of the law but not from its civil or social obligations. Christian liberty coincides with deliverance from the power of sin; it gives the believer certain freedoms in external matters like food, drink, and clothing. Liberty is abused, however, by those who use it as an excuse for indulging their lusts or escaping from obligations. Believers must avoid offending others that might cause them to sin; at the same time, they realize that they do not honor God merely by adhering to external customs. The remainder of this sermon (III:9) sets forth the standard Reformed treatment of the doctrine of good works.[100]

The final sermon (III:10) in Bullinger's long discussion of the law is a succinct, 75-page treatment of the doctrine of sin. Original and actual sin, sins of commission and omission, the sin against the Holy Ghost, and the inevitability of just punishment are all expounded.[101]

The Fourth Decade
The first sermon in Book IV deals with the gospel of salvation. Bullinger links salvation with preaching, grace, repentance, and justification. After stressing the divine nature of preaching, Bullinger explains grace as God's manifest love for sinners. Sinners are justified by grace — by Christ's merit alone, not their own.[102]

Bullinger then considers who are to be saved. All who hear the gospel are called to repentance and salvation. Repentance (IV:2) involves changing one's mind, and with it, one's whole purpose and outlook on life. It involves a genuine returning to the Lord in response to the preaching of His goodness. Man must be moved by the Spirit of God to genuine repentance, similar to that of Peter after he denied

Jesus. The Spirit can use the fear and grief that follow evil actions, as well as love for God, but true repentance must be accompanied by faith, not simply the dread of God's wrath. God is willing to receive all who turn to Him in genuine repentance.

Bullinger concludes IV:2 by showing what confession of sin involves and by describing what is meant by the terms *the old and new man*. Repentance is the process of transforming the old man into the new, Bullinger says. This is a gradual process, for the fleshly inclinations of the believer are never totally eradicated in this life; hence, we should always hasten to repent.[103]

Bullinger dealt with the life and work of the church in earlier sermons before he now comes to its faith. In the third, fourth, and fifth sermons of the fourth decade, he finally reaches the basic, central doctrine of God, which he presupposes throughout his entire series of sermons. The third sermon deals with man's knowledge of God; the fourth, with God's work in creation, predestination, and providence; the fifth, with man's response in serving God.

Throughout these sermons, Bullinger affirms the received teaching of the western church on the nature of God, the Trinity, and the interrelationship between the three persons of the Godhead. No inequality, division, or separation within the Trinity exists, though there is order and distinction according to each divine person's unique characteristics or properties (*proprietates*).[104]

A man can only rightly know God if he thoughtfully and prayerfully contemplates God's Word (IV:3), Bullinger says. God makes Himself known in His names, His appearances, the incarnation and death of Jesus, creation, analogies of His power, and the words spoken through the prophets. These ways of knowing God are validated when they lead us to the doctrine of the Trinity.[105]

Bullinger turns in his fourth sermon to God's purpose in creating and ordering the world. He considers God's providence, including His good will to His people and their election. As interpretations of this doctrine caused much strife in the sixteenth century, it will be instructive to examine Bullinger's views on the subject.

Bullinger titles Sermon IV in Book IV *That God is the Creator of all things, and governeth all things by His Providence: Where mention is also made of the goodwill of God to usward, and of predestination.* In this sermon, Bullinger explains why God created the earth and made it the realm of man's stewardship under His dominion. Bullinger sees the providence of God in His good will to His creation, including mankind, whom He has fashioned to be its steward. Though man is earth's steward, God is earth's governor, and has given man strict, though benevolent, rules on how to govern creation. Every man is obliged to trust in God's benevolence and just government in providence. Whoever appeals merely to God's providence in the form of benevolence for His gospel and excludes His providence in the form of His justice preaches a false gospel.

According to Bullinger, it is erroneous to work out one's gospel of salvation without taking into account man's pre-fall duties in a benevolent creation and how he failed to fulfil them. It is equally erroneous to conceive of a gospel of salvation without respect to God's just government of creation and how man was damned by it. Bullinger believed that Calvin was in danger of forgetting this Biblical view of God in creation in his doctrine of predestination; to Bullinger, the very idea that God would send a man to hell irrespective of his failure as God's steward and irrespective of God's governing justice in creation was unthinkable. Furthermore, he saw election stemming from the elects' union with Christ and His vicarious work for them so that any doctrine of election based on the mere *a priori* idea that God can do as He likes is ignoring the Scripture's doctrine of election. Scripture tells us not what God may do if He likes, which is beyond our comprehension, but what God has done for His elect in Christ. There is thus no dichotomy between God's providence and God's justice, and any doctrine of predestination and election must be centered in God's original plan for mankind as a just steward and his restoration to a higher Eden in Christ.

The doctrine of election, according to Bullinger, is a saving doctrine and thus applicable to fallen men. Election is not attained through a direct belief in God's Person; no man can attain such a belief. Rather, election is realized from belief in the Lord Jesus Christ, the only way, the truth, and the life. Thus the two sides of predestination truth in Bullinger's favorite evangelistic text, Philippians 2:12-13, are always apparent in his teaching that God works so that His salvation can be appropriated. The two sides of his banner of truth are that God adds to the church daily who should be saved and as many as are appointed by Him will by faith surely believe the gospel.[106]

Predestination to salvation has parallels with providence, Bullinger says. Predestination is God working out His eternal purposes in a world whose time flow is before Him from the beginning to the end. He has foreordained who are to be saved and who are to be condemned, but the end of that foreordination is Christ, who becomes the Savior of those who are foreordained to salvation. Therefore God's predestination or foreordination can only be known in Christ, and it is futile to speak of predestination apart from Christ. Indeed, for Bullinger, it is futile to speak of either providence or predestination in Christ without seeing the one in the other.

Bullinger comforts those who have been frightened away from the gospel by thoughts about a God who elects some and condemns others, without considering a Savior who calls not the righteous but sinners to repentance. Bullinger says no one has cause to despair if he seeks Christ but does not immediately find mature faith. Those who hear Christ's voice calling them to salvation will be saved, but their faith will grow only gradually to maturity (Mark 4:28). Faith comes little by little as we pray, "Lord, I believe; help thou mine unbelief" (Mark 9:24), and as we follow the scriptural advice, "Ask, and it shall be given you; seek, and ye shall find; knock and it shall be opened unto you" (Matt. 7:7). Nobody who asks God for bread will be given stones.

Bullinger preaches election and predestination within the framework of the doctrines of God and of the gospel. Cornelis P. Venema notes, "Though Bullinger follows the tradition by treating predestination within the doctrine of God, his actual development of the doctrine suggests that it might just as well have been placed within the doctrine of Christ or the application of his saving work."[107] After defining predestination as including a twofold ordination to save and to destroy, Bullinger hastens to emphasize that the doctrines of predestination and providence merge and center in Christ. He emphasizes that God's providence, the covenant, and Christ's priestly work are all communication channels of God's grace. Thus, in Bullinger's teaching, providence is the story of God's patience with man.

Bullinger never views God's decrees in isolation from the way God chose to effect them, namely, in the person and work of Christ. Christ is both the *means* by which God executes His eternal decree and the *end* of that decree. We are chosen in Christ, by Christ, and through Christ, to the glory of Christ. It is in Christ that we see God's saving and electing decrees to man, and it is through God-given faith in Christ that election is made known. We are never called to believe in decrees for salvation but to believe in Him who fulfils God's decrees, the Lord Jesus Christ.[108] Faith is the most assuring proof that we are elected of God, for faith communes with Christ and the very question of personal election should be formulated in terms of such communion. Personal doubts of election, therefore, are best dealt with by considering Christ and communing with Him.[109]

The fifth sermon of the fourth decade is on worshiping and serving God. Genuine worship involves adoration, invocation, prayer, and service. It requires a right attitude in mind and spirit and body. Without the work of the Holy Spirit, our worship of God and our service is mere hypocrisy.[110]

The sixth and seventh sermons deal with the Godhood, manhood, royalty, and priesthood of Christ, and what the name of a Christian signifies. Sermon eight is an exposition of the person and work of the Holy Spirit. The ninth sermon is on good and evil spirits, and the tenth sermon is on the soul of man and the salvation of those who die in the Lord after the death of the body. All of these sermons are helpful, succinct, standard Reformed treatments.[111]

The Fifth Decade

The fifth decade addresses the most controversial doctrines in Bullinger's day. The first sermon is a basic study of the nature of the church, while the second defends the unity of the church. Bullinger is particularly helpful on the inward marks of the church. He shows that the church is built up by God's Word, is bonded together by love, and is joined to Christ by His Spirit.

Bullinger maintains that though the church is holy in Christ, it can still err on this side of glory. The misuse of excommunication shows how the church can wrongly use the key of discipline. Because of its fallibility, the church has been given limited power to ordain, to regulate doctrine, and to manage its affairs, such as removing an evil minister and judging matrimonial offenses. Absolute power, however, remains in the hands of Christ. Therefore the church may not add to revelation and make new laws. Its duty is to worship God, preserve Christians in the faith, and maintain unity and concord. Finally, Bullinger answers objections that Protestants were schismatic heretics for breaking with Roman Catholicism by arguing that no one whose doctrines were pure could be a heretic.[112]

To rightly understand the church, one needs a correct doctrine of the ministry; consequently, V:3 and V:4 are concerned with the nature of the ministry and the proper method of calling, ordaining, and disciplining pastors. The calling of a minister must be public and through the congregation. The laying on of hands was traditional for ordaining a pastor, but what mattered more was that a candidate for the ministry be blameless in conduct and sound in scholarship. Ministers are to govern the church and feed the flock by example. Preaching is the key to the kingdom of heaven. So ministers are called to preach the Bible accurately, preserve true doctrine, catechize the youth, care for the poor, and visit the sick and imprisoned. They depend on the prayers of God's people as they strive to serve as blameless lights in society. Hirelings fail, but God keeps faithful shepherds in His service throughout all generations.[113]

The last six sermons of the decades cover the means of grace: prayer, the sacraments, and the church's institutions. Together, these sermons cover nearly four hundred pages. Bullinger follows Zwingli in adhering to Augustine's definition of prayer as "the lifting up of the heart to God in prayer" by faith.[114] Bullinger divides prayer into invocation, which includes petition and intercession, and thanksgiving, which includes the use of Psalms. Though prayer should be regularly offered in private, believers need the encouragement of public intercession. There is no scriptural sanction for intermediary prayers except those of Christ. The Spirit's role is to stimulate prayer. Prayer should accent spiritual and heavenly matters of heaven; it should be disciplined by fasting and be filled with love.

Bullinger devotes two long sermons (V:6-7, amounting to 125 pages) to the nature of the sacraments. In keeping with Reformed theology, Bullinger maintains that the physical and spiritual natures remain separate in the sacraments. Without faith, sinners partake of the elements with no benefit, just as they hear sermons in vain. Though sacraments do not convey grace in and of themselves, they do have profitable functions. Determined not to be accused of the Zwinglian view that tended to limit the Lord's Supper to a memorial, Bullinger stresses that Christ is received spiritually in the sacraments. The sacraments confirm believer's rights more effectively than any sealed charter.[115]

With regard to the controversial words of the sacrament, "this is my body," Bullinger argues that not every word in the Bible can be taken literally. Jesus could not have held Himself, so the bread must be a symbol of His body. Christ was using sacramental language; hence He must be received sacramentally by faith. Bullinger is not saying that God was not sufficiently powerful to transform the elements. Rather, he says that our senses are not able to ascertain that the elements have changed. The Bible teaches that Jesus departed from His disciples—His body is in heaven, and hence is not ubiquitous. God does not contradict nature. The presence of Christ in the Lord's Supper is spiritual.[116]

Bullinger's final sermon addresses the church's institutions, including such matters as schools, finances, buildings, discipline, and matrimony. Theological schools are necessary, Bullinger says. They existed in Egypt before Moses. The prophets, Christ, and the apostles all started schools. Theological schools have been corrupted by theologians and philosophers such as Lombard, Magnus, and Aquinas, who abandoned the plain teaching of the Scriptures. Correct study should begin with the Scriptures and the catechism and proceed through them to "tongues" or languages and "good arts."[117]

Conclusion

Edward Dowey concludes that "the Bullinger of the *Decades* is Bullinger himself, more truly than in any other major writing." He writes, "Bullinger's *Decades*, a major Reformation classic, is unchallengeable as his most full-bodied and comprehensive theological work, containing the richness of his scholarship, gathering together themes of all his major writings up to that time, and exhibiting the churchly purpose of being a theological source book for pastors to aid them in the preparation of sermons."[118]

Bullinger concludes *The Decades* by declaring, "I trust that in these fifty sermons I have, as shortly and conveniently as might be, comprehended the whole matter of faith, godliness or true religion, and also the church."[119] It is clear that Bullinger aims for comprehensiveness and unity of thought.

Bullinger departed from the Aristotelian method of demonstrating a whole by showing its parts. He is not a systematic theologian in the modern sense of the word, but is always eager to present the whole gospel to the whole man. This is one advantage of *The Decades* over many other volumes of doctrine; it makes Bullinger more clear than many other writers for the ordinary Christian. Modern scholars often try to make a systematic theologian out of Bullinger, then say he does not compare well with Calvin. However, at times one quite loses the whole picture in Calvin, which has led many scholars to have different opinions about what Calvin's position was as a whole. Recent literature places this confusion on Bullinger as scholars study his views on predestination, justification, and other cardinal doctrines apart from his understanding of Scripture, the gospel, and Christ's covenant work. *The Decades*, when rightly understood, show us that Bullinger must be studied first and foremost as a pastoral preacher and teacher who has in view at the heart of his teaching, as Opitz says, "to preach reconciliation in Christ and to bring the penitent to the Word of God. The demand, 'listen to him' was Bullinger's message. For the *Decades* it meant that this message could not be reduced to a system of *loci* rigorously organized. Rather, each sermon must be understood as a piece of the circle that has as its center point Christ and his message."[120]

At times the modern reader may be frustrated that Bullinger does not address many of the burning issues of our day. It is critical, therefore, that we remember to understand Bullinger within his historical context. What is impressive about the *Decades* is not what Bullinger does not cover, but how contemporary he does sound on so many issues and how readable he still is more than 450 years after he wrote these sermons. Even today, Bullinger sure-footedly guides us intellectually, experientially, and practically through the truths of Reformed doctrine that set us free and enable us to grow in the grace and knowledge of the Lord Jesus Christ.

FOOTNOTES

Chapter I

[1] This introduction is heavily dependent on the work of others. The bulk of the first two sections is a condensed summary and adapted translation of Walter Hollweg's definitive work, *Heinrich Bullingers Hausbuch: Eine Untersuchung über die Anfänge der reformerten Predigtliteratur* (Neukirchen: Neukirchen Verlag der Buchhundlung des Erziehungsvereins, 1956), 18-68 [hereafter, Hollweg]. Peter Opitz's *Heinrich Bullinger als Theologe: Eine Studie zu den "Dekaden"* (Zürich: TVZ, 2004) is Switzerland's contemporary answer to superintendent Hollweg's (Emden) fine work. The major source in English on *The Decades* is David J. Keep, "Henry Bullinger and the Elizabethan Church: A Study of the Publication of His 'Decades,' His letter on the Use of Vestments and His Reply to the Bull Which Excommunicated Elizabeth," 2 vols. (Ph.D. dissertation, University of Sheffield, 1970) [hereafter, Keep]. Keep also leans heavily on Hollweg for much of his historical material. Some of the last section of this introduction is a condensed version of Keep's exposition of *The Decades.* I also wish to express my indebtedness to George Ella who gave me freedom to use some very helpful material that he had compiled on *The Decades;* hence the inclusion of his name in the authorship. Thanks, too, to Charles Krahe, Bill Thies, and Arjen Vreugdenhil for assistance in translating various German materials.

[2] T. H. L. Parker, *The Oracles of God, an Introduction to the Preaching of John Calvin* (London: Lutterworth Press, 1947), 20; cf. Edwin Charles Dargan, *A History of Preaching* (Grand Rapids: Baker, 1:366), and Hughes Oliphant Old, *The Reading and Preaching of the Scriptures in the Worship of the Christian Church, volume 4: The Reformation* (Grand Rapids: Eerdmans, 2001).

[3] Wilhelm Pauck, *The Ministry in Historical Perspectives*, 116.

[4] Cf. Heidelberg Catechism, Q. 65.

[5] Carl Pestalozzi, *Heinrich Bullinger: Leben und ausgewählte Schriften der Väter und Begründer der reformirten Kirche* (Elberfeld, Germany: R. I. Friderichs, 1858), 55-58. This is the standard biography on Bullinger.

[6] Hollweg, 18-19.

[7] Pestalozzi, 71f.

[8] Konrad Pellikan, *Das Chronikon* (Basel: B. Riggenbach, 1877), 125, 136.

[9] Cited in Hollweg, 21.

[10] For a complete bibliography of Bullinger's published writings, see Joachim Staedtke, ed., *Heinrich Bullinger Werke. Pt. 1, Bibliographie. Vol. 1, Beschreibendes Verzeichnis der Gedruckten Werke von Heinrich Bullinger* (Zürich: Theologischer Verlag, 1972). Volume 2, edited by Erland Herkenrath (1977), lists about 2,000 items of secondary literature on Bullinger. For a recent update of work on Bullinger, see Bruce Gordon, "Heinrich Bullinger," in *The Reformation Theologians*, ed. Carter Lindberg (Oxford: Blackwell, 2002), 170-83.

[11] Hollweg, 22-23.

Chapter II

[12] Ibid., 24; taken from a letter in the Zürich State Archives under the signature E II 342, No. 210.

[13] Pestalozzi, *Heinrich Bullinger*, 476.

[14] *Ioannis Calvini Opera Quae Supersunt Omni*, ed. Wilhelm Baum, Eduard Cunitz, and Eduward Reuss (Brunswick: C. A. Schwetschke and Sons, 1863-1900), XIV, Sp. 66, No. 1458 [hereafter CO].

[15] Hollweg, 25-32.

[16] Ibid., 33ff.

[17] J. H. Kurtz, *Lehrbuch der Kirchengeschichte* (Leipzig: A Neuman, 1906), 2:82.

[18] Pestalozzi, *Heinrich Bullinger*, 132-40; E. Bloesch, *Geschichte der Schweizerisch-Reformerten Kirchen* (Bern, 1899), 1:65ff.

[19] *Original Letters relative to the English Reformation, 1537-1558*, trans. and ed. Hastings Robinson (Cambridge: Parker Society, 1846), 1:82. See also W. M. S. West, "A Study of John Hooper: With Special Reference to his Contacts with Henry Bullinger" (Ph.D. dissertation, Universität Zürich, 1953).

[20] Fr. Von Bezold, *Geschichte der deutschen Reformation* (Berlin: G. Grote, 1890), 805-810, 817, 821.

[21] *Original Letters*, 1:7.

[22] Ibid., 1:3f.

[23] CO XIII, 546.

[24] Hollweg, 42.

[25] Traugott Schiess, *Bullingers Korrespondenz mit den Graubündnern* (Basel, 1904), 1:219.

[26] Aart Arnout van Schelven, *Het Calvinisme gedurende zijn bloeitijd* (Amsterdam: W. Ten Have, 1951), 2:22.

[27] *D. Martin Luthers Werke*, ed. J.C. F. Knaake, et al. (Weimar: Herman Bohlaus, 1954), 19:95 [hereafter: WA].

[28] Cf. H. Werdermann, *Luthers Wittenberger Gemeinde wiederhergestellt aus seinen Predigten* (1929), 216.

[29] Hollweg, 46. In January 1523, Bullinger did introduce a rather

extensive training program at a little theological school in Kappel similar to the *Prophezei* that wouldn't be realized in Zürich until two years later. For the content of Bullinger's remarkable breadth of theological lessons, see Kurt Jakob Rüetschi, "Bullinger and the Schools," in *Architect of Reformation: An Introduction to Heinrich Bullinger, 1504-1575*, ed. Bruce Gordon and Emidio Campi (Grand Rapids: Baker, 2004), 219-20. Richard Diethelm describes the *Prophezei* as "the Zürich pedagogical institution ... which since 1525 was the heart of the Zürich Reformation. That the *Prophezei* was originally a theological school and the 'spiritual centre and political heart of the theocracy' has long been established" ("Bullinger and Worship: 'Thereby Does One Plant and Sow the True Faith," in *Architect of Reformation*, 137-39). It appears, however, that neither of these institutions was able at this early stage to sustain the kind of thorough seminary training that Bullinger had established in Kappel from 1523-29.

[30] WA, 53:218.

[31] Wort Walther, "Das 6. Gebot in Johann Herolts Predigten," *Neue kirchliche Zeitschrift* (1903), 485-99.

[32] Cf. R. Cruel, *Geschichte der deutschen Predigt im Mittelalter* (1879), 451ff.

[33] Hollweg, 47-48.

[34] A. L. Richter, *Die Evangelischen Kirchenordnungen des 16. Jahrhunderts* (1846), 2:276-77.

[35] Hollweg, 49.

[36] Ibid., 49-50.

[37] G. Oorthuys, *Anastasius' "Wechwyser," Bullingers "Huysboeck," en Calvyns "Institutie" Vergeleken in Hun Leer Von God en Mensch* (Leiden: Brill, 1919), 19.

[38] Richter, 2:99ff.

[39] Ibid., 2:477.

[40] E. Mülhaupt, *Die Predigt Calvins* (Berlin: W. de Gruyter, 1931), 16f.

[41] A. Bonnard, *Thomas Eraste* (Lausanne, 1894), 77.

[42] H. Kaajan, *De groote Synode van Dordrecht 1618-1619* (Amsterdam: N. V. Standaard, 1918).

[43] G. Anrich, *Martin Bucer* (Strassburg, 1914), 137.

[44] J. Reitsma and S. D. van Veen, *Acta der provinciale en particuliere Synoden* (Groningen: J. B. Wolters, 1892), 2:135.

[45] E. Chr. Achelis, *Lehrbuch der praktischen Theologie* (1898), 1:774.

[46] E. Kochs, *Grondlinien der Ostfriesischen Kirchengeschichte seit der Reformation*, 44.

[47] *Decades*, I:139.

[48] Ibid., II:237.

[49] Ibid., III:432.

[50] Hollweg, 51-53.

[51] R. Cruel, *Geschichte der deutschen Predigt des Mittelalters*, 2.

[52] WA, 60.3.1ff.

[53] G. Brandt, *Historie der Reformatie en andre kerkelyke geschiedenissen in en ontrent de Nederlanden* (Rotterdam, 1704), 3:56.

[54] Hollweg, 54-56.

[55] *Decades*, I:57.

[56] Ibid., I:209.

[57] Hollweg, 58-59.

[58] Pestalozzi, *Heinrich Bullinger*, 386, 414.

[59] Hollweg, 59-60.

[60] CO XIII, 222, No. 1165.

[61] CO XIII, 546, No. 1355.

[62] CO XIII, 54, No. 1453.

[63] CO XIV, 74, No. 1463.

[64] *Original Letters*, 1:497-98.

[65] Hollweg, 62.

[66] Schiess, *Bullingers Korrespondenz mit den Graubündnern*, 1:145.

[67] Ibid., 1:444.

[68] CO XIV, 118, No. 1492.

[69] *The Zurich Letters, Comprising the Correspondence of Several English Bishops and Others, with Some of the Helvetian Reformers, During the Early Part of the Reign of Queen Elizabeth*, trans. and ed. Hastings Robinson (Cambridge: Parker Society, 1845), 2:118.

[70] Cf. Frank Gulley, "The Influence of Heinrich Bullinger and the Tigurine Tradition upon the English Church in the Sixteenth Century" (Ph.D. dissertation, Vanderbilt, 1961).

[71] The State Archives of Zürich, E. II 356, 107.

[72] David J. Keep, "Henry Bullinger, 1504-75: A sketch of his life and work, with special reference to recent literature," *London Quarterly & Holborn Review* 191 (1966):144.

[73] Personal correspondence from George Ella, November 7, 2004.

[74] The State Archives of Zürich, E. II 338, 1492.

[75] Peter Opitz, "Bullinger's *Decades*: Instruction in Faith and Conduct," in *Architect of Reformation*, 101. Cf. Antonius Johannes van't Hooft, *De Theologie van Heinrich Bullinger in betrekking tot de Nederlandsche Reformatie* (Amsterdam: I. de Hoogh, 1888).

[76] Hollweg, 69-185.

Chapter III

[77] For a study of Bullinger's theology when he was young (through 1528), see Joachim Staedtke, *Die Theologie des jungen Bullinger* (Zürich, Zwingli Verlag, 1962).

[78] Edward Dowey, "Heinrich Bullinger as Theologian: Thematic, Comprehensive, and Schematic," in *Architect of Reformation*, 36.

[79] *Decades* I:39-42.

[80] Ibid., I:45-48.

[81] Ibid., I:49-51.

[82] Ibid., I:53-56.

[83] Ibid., I:58.

[84] Ibid., I:63-66.

[85] Ibid., I:70-80.

[86] Ibid., I:81-104.

[87] Ibid., I:104-121.

[88] Ibid., I:122-23.

[89] Ibid., I:138-39.

[90] Ibid., I:180-92.

[91] Ibid., II:196.

[92] Peter Opitz, "Bullinger's *Decades*: Instruction in Faith and Comfort," in *Architect of Reformation*, 106.

[93] *Decades*, II:333-34.

[94] Ibid., II:298-393.

[95] Keep, 202.

[96] *Decades*, III:125-217.

[97] Andrew Woolsey, "Unity and Continuity in Covenantal Thought: A Study in Reformed Tradition to the Westminster Assembly" (Ph.D. dissertation, University of Glasgow, 1988), 1: 278-79. Interestingly, Woolsey points out that Bullinger's commentaries place more emphasis on the unilateral nature of the covenant than do his polemical works. Cf. David C. Steinmetz, *Reformers in the Wings* (Philadelphia: Fortress Press, 1971), 133-42; D. A. Stoute, "The Origin and Development of The Reformed Idea of the Covenant" (Ph.D. dissertation, Cambridge University, 1979), 156ff.; Robert Letham, "Saving Faith and Assurance in Reformed Theology: Zwingli to the Synod of Dort" (Ph.D. dissertation, University of Aberdeen, 1979), 1:45-48; Mark W. Karlberg, "Reformed Interpretation of the Mosaic Covenant," *Westminster Theological Journal* 43 (1980):11; J. Wayne Baker, *Heinrich Bullinger and the Covenant: The Other Reformed Tradition* (Athens: Ohio University Press, 1980); Charles S. McCoy and J. Wayne Baker, *Fountainhead of Federalism: Heinrich Bullinger and the Covenantal Tradition* (Louisville: Westminster/John Knox Press, 1991); Peter A. Lillback, *The Binding of God: Calvin's Role in the Development of Covenant Theology* (Grand Rapids: Baker, 2001).

[98] *Decades*, III:217-36.

[99] Ibid., III:236-300.

[100] Ibid., III:300-357.

101 Ibid., III:358-432.

102 Ibid., IV:1-55.

103 Ibid., IV:55-114.

104 Mark Taplin, "Bullinger on the Trinity: '*Religionis Nostrae Caput et Fundamentum*'," in *Architect of Reformation*, 74-75.

105 *Decades*, IV:123-73.

106 Pieter Walser argues that Bullinger came to a double predestinarian formula by the 1550s, but he can find no developed concept of reprobation in Bullinger's thought (*Die Prädestination bei Heinrich Bullinger im Zusammenhang mit seiner Gotteslehre* [Zürich: Zwingli Verlag, 1957]).

107 Cornelis P. Venema, *Heinrich Bullinger and the Doctrine of Predestination: Author of "the Other Reformed Tradition"?* (Grand Rapids: Baker, 2002), 43.

108 *The Decades*, IV:173-94. For a confessional summary of Bullinger's views of election and predestination, see the Second Helvetic Confession (1566), Chapter X (*Reformed Confessions Harmonized*, ed. Joel R. Beeke and Sinclair B. Ferguson [Grand Rapids: Baker, 1999], 28, 30, 32).

109 Venema, *Heinrich Bullinger and the Doctrine of Predestination*, 45.

110 *The Decades*, IV:194-238.

111 Ibid., IV:238-408.

112 Ibid., V:3-93. Pamela Biel, *Doorkeepers at the House of Righteousness: Heinrich Bullinger and the Zurich Clergy, 1535-1575* (Bern: Peter Lang, 1990) argues that Bullinger's concept of the relationship between church and state became normative in Zürich as he elevated the office of the minister above other governmental offices, thereby giving the ministry a special status. This theory, however, is built on the false idea that Zwingli's politics lived on in Bullinger. Bullinger insisted that preachers should not play the role of politicians; unlike Calvin, he taught that the Christian community, including preachers, should be subject to the rule of the Christian magistracy. This view of the single sphere of the Christian community gave Bullinger leverage against the Anabaptists (J. Wayne Baker, "Heinrich Bullinger," in *Oxford Encyclopedia of the Reformation* [Oxford: Oxford University Press, 1996], 1:229). Because of his influence and enormous abilities, however, Bullinger had been granted the right to appear before the Council in the Town Hall as often as he thought fit (which was not often) and say what the ministers thought. He was also invited to draw up certain mandates by the council. He insisted that both he and his fellow-ministers were servants and that they should not be considered in any way superior to any other citizens and especially not superior to magistrates. There were a few ministers,

however, who thought otherwise and even scolded Bullinger for not usurping authority over the magistrates. Cf. Bruce Gordon, *Clerical Discipline and the Rural Reformation in Zürich, 1532-1580* (Berne: Peter Lang, 1992); Daniel Bolliger, "Bullinger on Church Authority: The Transformation of the Prophetic Role in Christian Ministry," in *Architect of Reformation*, 159-77; Kurt Jakob Rüetschi, "Bullinger and the Schools," in *Architect of Reformation*, 221-22; Andreas Mühling, "Heinrich Bullinger as Church Politician," in *Architect of Reformation*, 243-53.

[113] *Decades*, V:93-163.

[114] Bruce Gordon, "Bullinger's Vernacular Writings: Spirituality and the Christian Life," in *Architect of the Reformation*, 128-29.

[115] *Decades*, V:316; cf. 226-351. For a helpful, succinct treatment of Bullinger's theology on the sacraments, see Robert C. Walton, "Heinrich Bullinger," in *Shapers of Religious Traditions in Germany, Switzerland, and Poland, 1560-1600*, ed. Jill Raitt (New Haven: Yale, 1981), 78-81.

[116] Ibid., V:401-478. For a study of the differences between Bullinger and Calvin on the Lord's Supper, their negotiations, and their eventual agreement in the Consensus Tigurinus, see Paul Rorem, *Calvin and Bullinger on the Lord's Supper* (Nottingham, England: Grove Books, 1989).

[117] *Decades*, V:479-86.

[118] Dowey, "Heinrich Bullinger as Theologian: Thematic, Comprehensive, and Schematic," 49-50, 62.

[119] *Decades*, V:526.

[120] Peter Opitz, "Bullinger's *Decades*: Instruction in Faith and Comfort," in *Architect of Reformation*, 115.

CONTENTS.

ADVERTISEMENT.

ONE of the Parker Society's objects, as stated in the first of its Laws, is "the printing, as may appear desirable, of some of the Early English translations of the Foreign Reformers." Accordingly, the re-publishing of the English Version of the Decades of Bullinger was announced, as in the contemplation of the Council of the Society, in a List which was appended to the Second Annual Report; and the first volume is now, at length, presented to the subscribers. The edition, which is here reprinted, is that of 1587, which scarcely differs at all, in any material respects, from the former edition of 1584, and very little from that of 1577; but any important variations between the translation and the original Latin are carefully specified in the notes. The Version was made, as stated in the title-page, "by H. I. Student in Divinitie,"—" a person," according to Strype's testimony, " of eminency in the Church[1]."

These Decades, it is conceived, possess a peculiar claim on the regard of the members of the Church of England. For not only was Bullinger " well-deserving of this nation for his kind entertainment and harbour of our divines and scholars that fled abroad in Queen Mary's reign, and of note for that friendship and correspondence ever after maintained between him and them[2];" but several of his writings, as they became known here, were eminently appreciated by our theologians and religious persons of the era of the Reformation[3].

[1] Strype, Ann. book II. chap. 10, p. 145, Vol. II. part 2. ed. Oxf. 1824.

[2] Strype, Ann. ibid. p. 144. See also Strype, Mem. II. 1, pp. 531, 532, and Zurich Letters, Parker Soc. ed. pp. 41, 111, 127, 205, &c. 2nd ed.

[3] See Original Letters, Parker Soc. ed. pp. 5, 9, 54, 70, 618, 620, &c. Zurich Letters, 2nd ed. pp. 39, 110, 205, 468. Strype, Ann. chap. 21, p. 383, Vol. I. part 1, and part 2. chap. 46, p. 195, and chap. 48, p. 221. Jewel styled Bullinger, " *oraculum ecclesiarum.*" Zurich Letters, No. LXX. 1st series, p. 156. The University of Oxford, also, selected Bullinger's Catechism, as one of those books which the Tutors there were required to use, for the purpose of imparting sound religious principles to their pupils:—" ad informandum in vera reli-

And, above all, in the Convocation of the province of Canterbury, held in 1586, among the " Orders for the better increase of learning in the inferior Ministers," introduced by Whitgift, Archbishop of Canterbury, the following direction stands foremost :—" Every minister having cure, and being under the degrees of master of arts, and batchelors of law, and not licensed to be a public preacher, shall before the second day of February next provide a Bible, and Bullinger's Decads in Latin or English, and a paper book, and shall every day read over one chapter of the Holy Scriptures, and note the principal contentes thereof briefly in his paper booke, and shall every weeke read over one Sermon in the said Decads, and note likewise the chief matters therein contained in the said paper ; and shall once in every quarter (viz. within a fortnight before or after the end of the quarter) shewe his said note to some preacher nere adjoyninge to be assigned for that purpose[1]." And, agreeably with this order, it is recorded by Strype, Dr. Theophilus Aylmer, Archdeacon of London, acted in his visitation in the early part of the year 1587,— " the Bishop's pious and painful son[2]."

Although a Memoir of Bullinger (together with indexes to the whole work) will be given in the last volume, it may be useful here to state briefly, that he was born at Bremgarten, near Zurich, on July 18, 1504 ; commenced his studies at the University of Cologne in 1519; began to unite himself to the divines of the Reformation in the course of 1524 ; was chosen pastor of Zurich, on the decease of Œcolampadius, in the close of 1531 ; dedicated to Rodolph Gualter and others his first volume of the Decades, March 1, 1549 ; and died September 17, 1575, in the 71st year of his age[3].

N.B. The editing of these Decades having been commenced by the Rev. STEUART A. PEARS, the notes which have the initial (P) affixed to them, are due to his research.

gione juventutem." Wood. Hist. et Ant. Univ. Oxon. Lib. I. p. 296. quoted in Preface, p. iv. to "Sermons on the Sacraments by Henry Bullinger." Cambridge, 1840.

[1] Cardwell's Synodalia, Vol. II. p. 562. Oxf. 1842. Strype's Whitgift, Vol. III. p. 194. App. No. 32. Oxf. ed.

[2] Strype's Aylmer, p. 83. Oxf. ed.

[3] See Adami Vit. Germ. Theol. in vita Bullingeri; and "Bullinger," in Chalmers' Biograph. Dict.

FIFTY SERMONS

DIVIDED INTO

FIVE DECADES.

[BULLINGER.]

FIFTIE
GODLIE AND LEARNED
SERMONS, DIVIDED INTO
FIVE DECADES CONTAINING THE
chiefe and principall points of Christian Religi-
on, written in three severall Tomes or Sections,
by HENRIE BVLLINGER *Minister*
of the Church of TYGVRE *in*
Swicerland.

WHEREVNTO ARE ADDED CER-
TAINE EPISTLES OF THE SAME
Author concerning the Apparell of
Ministers and other indiffe-
rent things.

WITH A TRIPLE OR THREE-FOLD
Table verie fruitfull and ne-
cessarie[1].

Translated out of Latine into English, by
H. I. *Student in Diuinitie.*

MATTHEW. 17.
This is my beloued Sonne in whom I am well pleased : Heare him.

Imprinted at London by Ralph Newberie, dwelling
in Fleete street a little aboue the Conduit,

Cum gratia & priuilegio Regiæ Maiestatis.

1587.

[1 N.B. Notwithstanding what is here stated, the edition of 1587
has not this Table prefixed to it.]

A PREFACE

THAT just cause there is that all spiritual shepherds, and specially these of our time, should see carefully to the feeding of the flocks committed to their charge, may easily appear to him that shall but a little stay his consideration upon this matter. For first, the commandments of the Almighty touching this thing are very earnest, the authority of which should greatly enforce. Secondly, the rewards which he proposeth to vigilant and careful pastors are large and bountiful, the sweetness of which should much allure. Thirdly, the plagues and heavy judgments, which he denounceth against slothful and careless shepherds, are grievous and importable[1], the terror whereof should make afraid. Then the nature and condition of the sheep over whom they watch, the vigilancy of the wolf against whom they watch, the conscience in taking the fleece for which they watch, and this time and age wherein they watch, being rightly considered, will give them to understand sufficiently, that they have good occasion to watch.

How earnestly God commandeth, appeareth, Esay lviii. where he saith, "Cry aloud, spare not, lift up thy voice like a trumpet, shew my people their transgressions, and the house of Jacob their sins." And Esay lxii. "I have set watchmen upon thy walls, O Hierusalem, which all the day and all the night continually shall not cease: ye that are mindful of the Lord, keep not silence." And John xxi. "Feed my lambs, feed my sheep, and if ye love me, feed." And 2 Tim. iv. "Preach the word: be instant in season, out of season, improve[2], rebuke, exhort, &c." How sweetly with rewards he allureth, doth appear in the xii. of Daniel: "They that be wise shall shine as the brightness of the firmament, Isai. lviii.

Isai. lxii.

John xxi.

2 Tim. iv.

Dan xii.

[1 i. e. unsupportable: "importable power."—Spenser. P.]
[2 i. e. reprove.]

1—2

and they that turn many to righteousness shall shine as the
1 Tim. iv. stars for ever and ever." And 1 Tim, iv. "Take heed to
thyself and to doctrine; in them occupy thyself continually.
For in so doing thou shalt save thyself and them which hear
thee." How fiercely also he urgeth and driveth on the
sluggish and careless shepherds with terrible plagues and
whips threatened unto them, appeareth, Ezechiel iii., where
Ezek. iii. he saith, "Son of man, I have made thee a watchman unto
the house of Israel: therefore hear the word of my mouth,
and give them warning from me: when I shall say unto the
wicked, thou shalt surely die, and thou givest him not warning, nor speakest to admonish the wicked of his wicked way
that he may live; the same wicked man shall die in his iniquity, but his blood will I require at thy hand." And
Jer. i. Ieremie i. ver. 17: "Thou therefore, truss up thy loins, and
arise, and speak unto them all that I command thee: be not
afraid of their faces, lest I destroy thee before them." And
1 Cor. ix. 1 Cor. ix. ver. 16: "Though I preach the gospel, I have
nothing to rejoice of[1]; for necessity is laid upon me, and woe
is unto me, if I preach not the gospel: for if I do it willingly,
I have a reward: but if I do it against my will, notwithstanding the dispensation is committed unto me."

Now the sheep, whereof spiritual shepherds have undertaken charge, are not beasts, but men: the very images of
God himself endued with everliving souls, citizens with the
saints and blessed angels, clothed with God's livery, beautified
with his cognizance and all the badges of salvation, admitted
to his table, and to no meaner dishes than the body and blood
of the undefiled Lamb Christ Jesus; bought also and redeemed
out of the wolf's chawes[2] with no less price than of that same
blood more precious than any gold or silver. Sheep also of
that nature they are, that, being carefully fed and discreetly
ordered, they prove gentle and loving towards their shepherds,
and serviceable towards the chief Shepherd Jesus Christ: but
being neglected and left to themselves, they degenerate into
bloody wolves, watching ever opportunity when they may
rent in pieces their shepherds, and all other sheep which are
not degenerated into their wolfish nature.

As for the spiritual wolf, against whom they watch, which

[1 So Tyndale's Versions, and Cranmer's Bible, 1539.]
[2 Chawes: jaws. P.]

is Satan, "He," as the apostle Peter witnesseth, 1 Epistle, 1 Pet. v.
cap. v. "never resteth, but as a roaring lion walketh about,
seeking ever whom he may devour." And for that cause also
is he called, Apoc. xx. ver. 2, "a dragon," which beast is Rev. xx.
naturally very malicious crafty, and watchful : so then, if the
spiritual shepherd must watch whiles the spiritual wolf doth
wake, he can promise unto himself no one moment of security,
wherein he may be careless.

God by his prophet Ezechiel, cap. xxxiv. saith : "Woe Ezek. xxxiv.
be unto the shepherds of Israel that feed themselves: should
not the shepherds feed the flocks? Ye eat the fat, and ye
clothe you with the wool; ye kill them that are fed, but ye
feed not the sheep." This sentence should awake the sleepy
and careless consciences of many shepherds. For as the priest
that serveth the altar is worthy to live upon the offerings,
and the soldier that ventureth is worthy his wages, and the
husbandman that toileth is worthy the harvest, and the
shepherd that feedeth the flock is worthy to be fed with
the milk, and clothed with the wool; so, questionless, the
priest that serveth not is worthy no offerings, the soldier
that fighteth not is worthy no wages, the husbandman that
loitereth is worthy of weeds, and the shepherd that feedeth
not can with no good conscience require either the milk or
the fleece : but his due reward and just recompence is punishment, for that through his default the sheep are hunger-
starved and destroyed of the wolf.

But let the ministers of our time well weigh the condition
and manner of the time; and then, no doubt, they shall see
that it is high time to bestir them to the doing of their
duties. This time succeedeth a time, wherein was extreme
famine of all spiritual food, so that the sheep of this time can
never recover themselves of that feebleness whereinto they
were brought, but by some great and extraordinary diligence.
This time succeedeth a time, wherein the multitude of wolves
and ravenous beasts was so great, and their rage and fury so
fell in every sheepfold, that the good shepherds were either
put to flight, or pitifully murdered; so that the sheep, being
committed to wolves, did either perish, or degenerate into
wolves : so that to regenerate them again into sheep requireth
no small labour. The church in this time is like land that
hath lain, time out of mind, unmanured, uncompassed, untilled;

by reason whereof it is so out of heart, that it requireth arms of iron and legs of brass to recover it again: or like a ship so worn with winds and tempests, so rent with rocks, so crackt and utterly decayed, that it seemeth a rare piece of cunning to make her take the seas again.

No remedy, then, but the ministry of this time, if there be any love or fear of God in them, if they would not have all things run to ruin, if they regard either God, themselves, or their brethren, must forthwith, without further delay, set themselves to feed their flocks, to teach, to exhort, to strengthen, to bind up, to build, to plant, to water, to set, to graff, to leave nothing undone that appertaineth to the feeding and fatting of the Lord's flocks, to the planting of the Lord's paradise, tilling of the Lord's husbandry, dressing of the Lord's vineyard, raising and rearing up of the Lord's temple. What great want there is in many to discharge their duties in this behalf, is very lamentable, and by some means (as much as is possible) to be supplied and remedied, rather than to be made a common theme and argument of railing, which at this day many do: wherein they shew themselves like unto those which find fault at other men's garments, not for that they love them, or mind to give them better, but for that they are proud of their own, and would scornfully shame and vex other. The cause of this great want needs not here to be disputed: but in very deed, any man may judge how unpossible it was for so populous a kingdom, abounding with so many several congregations, to be all furnished with fit and able pastors; and that, immediately after such a general corruption and apostasy from the truth. For unless they should have suddenly come from heaven, or been raised up miraculously, they could not have been. For the ancient preachers of king Edward's time, some of them died in prison, many perished by fire, many otherwise; many also fled into other countries, of whom some there died, and a few returned, which were but as an handful to furnish this whole realm. The universities were also at the first so infected, that many wolves and foxes crept out, who detested the ministry, and wrought the contempt of it everywhere: but very few good shepherds came abroad[1]. And whereas, since that

[1 See Zurich Letters, reign of Q. Elizabeth, 2nd ed. Parker Soc. pages 24, 38, 42, 55, 61, 101, 104, 115, 427.]

time, now eighteen years, the universities being well purged, there was good hope, that all the land should have been overspread and replenished with able and learned pastors; the devil and corrupt patrons have taken such order, that much of that hope is cut off: for patrons now-a-days search not the universities for a most fit pastor; but they post up and down the country for a most gainful chapman. He that hath the biggest purse to pay largely, not he that hath the best gifts to preach learnedly, is presented. The bishops bear great blame for this matter, and they admit (say they) unworthy men. See the craft of Satan, falsely to charge the worthiest pillars of the church with the ruin of the church, to the end that all church-robbers, and caterpillars of the Lord's vineyard, may lie unespied. There is nothing that procureth the bishops of our time more trouble and displeasure, than that they zealously withstand the covetousness of patrons in rejecting their unsufficient clerks. For it standeth them upon of all other, that the church of God doth prosper, in the decay and fall whereof they cannot stand, but perish. But howsoever it cometh to pass, certain it is, that many are far behind in those gifts which are necessary for their function; and small likelihood is there yet that the church shall be served with better, but rather with worse: for it seemeth not that patrons hereafter will bate one penny, but rather more and more raise the market.

The case standing thus, their labour surely is not worst bestowed, neither do they promote the glory of God or profit the church least, which to that end apply their endeavour, that the ministry which now is in place may come forward, and be better able to do their duties: I mean such as either set forth godly and learned treatises, or expositions of the holy scriptures, compiled by themselves in our mother tongue; or else such as translate the worthy works of the famous divines of our time. Both these sorts of men, no doubt, do much edify the godly, and do greatly help forward all those ministers which either not at all, or very meanly, understand the Latin tongue: so that amongst them are found many, which, by painful industry and diligent reading of such books, do God good service in the church; and so might all the rest of them do also, if sloth and worldly affairs did not hinder them. Some of that sort complain, that Calvin's manner of writing in his Institutions[1] is over deep and profound for them: Musculus also, in his Common Places, is very scholastical; the Commentaries of Marlorat[2] upon John, of Peter Martyr upon the Judges, of Gualter upon the small Prophets, and other many are translated and extant[3]; which altogether do handle most points of christian doctrine excellently well: but this sort of ministers for the most part are so bare bitten of their patrons[4], that to buy them all would deeply charge them. Therefore, questionless, no writer yet in the hands of men can fit them better than master Bullinger in these his Decades; who in them amendeth much Calvin's obscurity with singular perspicuity, and Musculus' scholastical subtlety with great plainness and even popular facility. And all those points of christian doctrine, which are not to be found in one, but handled in all, Bullinger packeth up all, and that in good order, in this one book of small quantity. And whereas divers of the ministry which lack knowledge, and some also which have knowledge but yet lack order, discretion, memory, or audacity, cannot, by reason of their wants, either expound, or exhort, or otherwise preach, but only read the order of service; the Decades of master Bullinger in this respect may do more good than shall perhaps at the first be conceived. For in very deed this book is a book of sermons; sermons in name, and in nature; fit to be read out of the pulpit unto the simplest and rudest people of this land: the doctrine of them very plain, without ostentation, curiosity, perplexity, vanity, or superfluity; very sound also, without popery, Ana-

[1 An English translation of this work, The Institution of the Christian Religion, appeared for the first time in 1561. See Introductory Notice to Calvin's Institutes, ed. Calv. Soc. p. lii.]

[2 Marlorat was a Protestant minister born in Lorraine: he wrote commentaries on Genesis, Psalms, Isaiah, and the New Testament, and was executed at Rouen by order of the Duke of Guise in 1562.—Moreri. P.]

[3 Cf. Zurich Letters, Second Series, Parker Soc. ed. p. 148.]

[4 "Burton similarly complained, in his odd way, that if our greedy patrons hold us to such hard conditions as commonly they do, they will make most of us work at some trade, as Paul did; at last turn taskers, maltsters, costermongers, grasiers, sell ale, as some have done, or worse."—Anatomy of Melancholy, Preface, quoted in Sermons on the Sacraments, by Henry Bullinger, Preface, p. v. note 6. Cambridge, 1840.]

baptism, Servetianism[5], or any other heresy; and in number fifty, every Decade containing (as the word importeth) ten; so that they may easily be so divided as there may be for every Sunday in the year one. Neither is it material what those fanatical fellows say, which can away with no homilies or sermons, be they never so sound, pithy, and effectual, to be read in churches. They are like physicians which forbid their patients all those meats which they may have and would do them good; and appoint them only such, as by no means they can obtain: for it will not yet be, that every parish shall have a learned able preacher resident and abiding in it. And in the mean time it cannot be denied, but that an homily or sermon, penned by some excellent clerk, being read plainly, orderly, and distinctly, doth much move the hearers, doth teach, confirm, confute, comfort, persuade, even as the same pronounced without the book doth.

Perhaps some hearers, which delight more to have their eyes fed with the preacher's action, than their hearts edified with his sermon, are more moved with a sermon not read: but to a good christian hearer, whose mind is most occupied on the matter, there is small odds. Better is a good sermon read than none at all. But nothing (say they) must be read in the open congregation, but the very canonical scriptures[6]. That rule is somewhat strait and precise. Then may not either the creed, called the Apostles' creed, or the Nicene creed, or the creed called Athanasius' creed, or any prayers which are not word for word contained in the canon of the scriptures, nor any contents of chapters, be read in the congregation. The church and congregation of the Colossians were enjoined by St Paul, Col. iv. ver. 16, to read amongst them the epistle written from Laodicea; which epistle (as Calvin thinketh[7]) was not written by Paul, but by the church of Laodicea, and sent to Paul, and is not contained in the canon of the scriptures. The church of Corinth also, and other churches of the godly, soon after the apostles' times (as

[5 Michael Servetus published his heretical work on the Trinity in 1531; he was burnt at Geneva in 1553. P.]

[6 See Hooker's Eccles. Pol. book v. § 20.]

[7 Falso putarunt a Paulo scriptam esse. Non dubito quin epistola fuerit ad Paulum missa.—Calvin. Comment. in loc.]

appeareth out of Eusebius, Lib. IV. cap. 23[1], and the writers
of the Centuries[2], Cent. II. cap. 10) did use to read openly,
for admonition sake, certain epistles of Clement, and of Dionysius, bishop of Corinth. Master Bucer, in his Notes upon
the Communion Book in king Edward's time, writeth thus:
" It is better, that where there lacks to expound the scriptures unto the people, there should be godly and learned
homilies read unto them, rather than they should have no
exhortation at all in the administration of the supper[3]." And
a little after he saith: "There be too few homilies, and too
few points of religion taught in them : when, therefore, the
Lord shall bless this kingdom with some excellent preachers,
let them be commanded to make more homilies of the principal points of religion, which may be read to the people by
those pastors that cannot make better themselves[4]." And
that worthy martyr, doctor Ridley, bishop of London, speaking of the church of England that was in the reign of king
Edward (as he is reported by master Foxe, in his book of
Acts and Mon., To. II. page 1940) saith thus[5]: " It had also
holy and wholesome homilies in commendation of the principal virtues which are commended in scripture, and likewise
other homilies against the most pernicious and capital vices
that use, alas! to reign in this church[6] of England." So long,

[1 Ἐν αὐτῇ δὲ ταύτῃ (ἐπιστολῇ) καὶ τῆς Κλήμεντος πρὸς Κορινθίους
μέμνηται (Διονύσιος) ἐπιστολῆς, δηλῶν ἀνέκαθεν ἐξ ἀρχαίου ἔθους ἐπὶ τῆς
ἐκκλησίας τὴν ἀνάγνωσιν αὐτῆς ποιεῖσθαι. Λέγει γοῦν· Τὴν σήμερον οὖν
κυριακὴν ἁγίαν ἡμέραν διηγάγομεν, ἐν ᾗ ἀνέγνωμεν ὑμῶν τὴν ἐπιστολήν.
—Euseb. Hist. Eccles. Lib. IV. cap. 23. ed. Burton.]

[2 Hæc in multis etiam ecclesiis palam ac publice jam olim, et
apud nos quoque legi cognovimus.—Cent. 1. Lib. II. 10. This is given
as a quotation from Eusebius, Lib. III. cap. 16.]

[3 Præstat quidem, dum desunt qui scripturas populo viva voce rite
explicent, recitari populis pias et doctas homilias, quam ut nulla ei
doctrina atque exhortatio in administranda S. cœna exhibeatur.—Bucer. Script. Anglic. Bas. 1577, p. 465.]

[4 Est etiam nimis exiguus homiliarum numerus, paucique loci religionis nostræ his docentur. Cum itaque Dominus regnum hoc donarit
aliquot pereximiis concionatoribus, demandandum illis esset, ut Homilias plures, atque de præcipue necessariis locis componerent, quæ populis ab iis recitarentur pastoribus, qui ipsi meliores non possent
afferre.—Ibid. p. 466.]

[5 Vol. VII. 554, ed. 1838.]

[6 realm, Foxe.]

therefore, as none are read in the church but such as are sound, godly, and learned, and fit for the capacity of the people; and whiles they are not thrust into the church for canonical scriptures, but are read as godly expositions and interpretations of the same; and whiles they occupy no more time in the church than that which is usually left and spared, after the reading of the canonical scriptures, to preaching and exhortation; and whiles they are used, not to the contempt, derogation, or abandoning of preaching, but only to supply the want of it; no good man can mislike the use of them, but such contentious persons as defy all things which they devise not themselves.

And if it be said, there be already good homilies, and those also authorised, and likewise wholesome expositions of sundry parts of scripture to the same purpose: I grant there be so. But store is no sore. And as in meats, which are most dainty, if they come often to the table, we care not for them; so in sermons which are most excellent, if the same come often to the pulpit, they oftentimes please not: others are desired.

But, to end: these sermons of master Bullinger's are such as, whether they be used privately or read publicly, whether of ministers of the word or other God's children, certainly there will be found in them such light and instruction for the ignorant, such sweetness and spiritual comfort for consciences, such heavenly delights for souls, that as perfumes, the more they are chafed, the better they smell; and as golden mines, the deeper ye dig them, the more riches they shew; so these: the more diligently ye peruse them, the more delightfully they will please; and the deeper ye dig with daily study in their mines, the more golden matter they will deliver forth to the glory of God: to whom only be praise, for ever and ever. Amen.

OF THE

FOUR GENERAL SYNODS OR COUNCILS[1].

SINCE the time of the apostles, many councils have been celebrated in sundry provinces. Those (councils) then were synods or assemblies of bishops and holy men, meeting together to consult for keeping the soundness of faith, the unity of doctrine, and the discipline and peace of the churches. Some of which sort the epistles of the blessed martyr Cyprian have made us acquainted withal[2].

The Nicene council.

The first general or universal synod, therefore, is reported to have been called by that most holy emperor Constantine in the city of Nice, the year of our Lord 324[3], against Arius and his partners, which denied the natural deity of our Lord Jesus Christ. And thither came there out of all nations under heaven two hundred and eighteen[4] bishops and excellent learned men, who wrote the Creed commonly called the Nicene Creed.

Hitherto the creed of the Apostles sufficed, and had been sufficient to the church of Christ even in the time of Constantine: for all men confess that all the churches used no other creed than that of the Apostles (which we have made mention of and expounded in the first Decade), wherewith they were content throughout the whole world. But

[1 In his Latin Preface, Bullinger states that he prefixed to his Decades these Creeds of the most ancient councils and orthodox Fathers, that it might manifestly appear that the doctrine and faith of the Protestant churches, which was by many ill-reported of and most undeservedly condemned as heretical, was perfectly agreeable with the teaching of the apostles and of the primitive church.]

[2 viz. Councils at *Rome* and *Carthage* principally, in the matters of Novatus and Novatian, and concerning receiving back the lapsed into the communion of the church, and the validity of baptism by heretics.]

[3 More correctly, A.D. 325.—Mosheim, Eccles. Hist. Vol. I. p. 386, n. 1. ed. Soames, 1845.]

[4 The number should be 318: see Mosheim, ibid.; and Grier's Epit. of Gen. Councils, p. 33.]

for because in the days of Constantine the Great that wicked blasphemer Arius sprang up, corrupting the pureness of christian faith, and perverting the simple truth of doctrine taught by the apostles; the ministers of the churches were compelled of very necessity to set themselves against that deceiver, and in publishing a creed to shew forth and declare out of the canonical scriptures the true and ancient[5] confession of faith, condemning those novelties brought in of Arius. For in the creeds set forth by the other three general councils presently following neither was any thing changed in the doctrine of the apostles, neither was there any new thing added, which the churches of Christ had not before taken and believed out of the holy scripture: but the ancient truth, being wisely made manifest by confessions made of faith, was profitably and godly set against the new corruptions of heretics. Yet were the writings of the prophets and apostles the spring, the guide, the rule, and judge in all these councils; neither did the fathers suffer any thing to be done there according to their own minds[6]. And yet I speak not of every constitution and canon, but namely[7] of those ancient confessions alone, to which we do attribute so much as is permitted by the canonical scripture, which we confess to be the only rule how to judge, to speak, and do.

The second general council was held in the royal city Constantinople, under Gratian the emperor, in the year of our Lord 384. There were assembled in that synod (as witnesseth Prosperus Aquitanicus[8]) one hundred and eighty fathers or bishops, which condemned Macedonius and Eudoxius denying the Holy Ghost to be God[9]. The council of Constantinople.

And about the year of our Lord 434, in the very same The council of Ephesus.

[5 Veram, id est veterem.—Lat.]

[6 See Goode's Divine Rule of Faith and Practice, Vol. I. pp. 141-156, and Vol. II. pp. 327-360.]

[7 specially; Lat. significanter.]

[8 Synodus Patrum CLXXX apud Constantinopolim celebrata est contra Macedonium, Spiritum-sanctum Deum esse negantem.—Prosper. Aquit. Chron. Opp. Par. 1711, col 735.]

[9 This Second General Council was assembled, A.D. 381, by the Emperor Theodosius the Elder, and was attended by 150 bishops, &c. —Mosheim, Eccles. Hist. Vol. I. p. 404. For the heresies of Macedonius and Eudoxius, see Routh, Scrip. Eccles. Opuscul. Vol. I. p. 417, &c.; and Hammond's Canons of the Church, p. 53.]

year that the blessed father Augustine died, when that godly prince Theodosius the Great was emperor, there came together at Ephesus the third synod, of two hundred priests or thereabouts, against Nestorius[1], which tare the mystery of the incarnation and taught that there were two Sons, the one of God, the other of man : whom this council condemned, together with the Pelagians[2], helpers of this doctrine as cousin to their own.

The council of Calcedon.

The fourth general council was assembled at Chalcedon, in the year of our Lord 454, under the emperor Martian; where six hundred and thirty fathers were gathered together, who according to the scriptures condemned Eutyches, which confounded the natures in Christ for the unity of the person[3].

Beda de ratione temporum[4], and many other writers, do join with these four universal councils two general synods more, the fifth and the sixth, celebrated at Constantinople. For the fifth was gathered together when Justinian was emperor, against Theodorus and all heretics, about the year of our Lord 552[5]. The sixth came together under Constantine the son of Constantius, in the year of our Lord 682. And there were assembled two hundred and eighty-nine bishops[6] against the Monothelites. But there was nothing determined in these synods, but what is to be found in the four first councils: wherefore I have noted nothing out of them.

[1] This council of Ephesus was held, A.D. 431, under Theodosius the Younger (not the Great).—Mosheim, Vol. I. p. 472; Grier, p. 74. For the heresy of Nestorius, see Hooker's Eccles. Pol. Book v. § 52. Augustine died August 28, 430.—Mosheim, Vol. I. p. 338, Soames' note.]

[2] una cum multis Pelagianis.—Lat.]

[3] The year of the assembling of this council was 451.—Mosheim, Vol. I. p. 481. For the heresy of Eutyches, see Hooker, Book v. § 52-54.]

[4] Bedæ de Sex Ætatibus Mundi, sive Chronicon, libellus. Opp. Tom. III. p. 116. Col. Agrip. 1612.]

[5] The year was 553.—Mosheim, Vol. II. p. 45; Hammond's Canons of the church, p. 113. "Contra Theodorum, et omnes hæreticos," are the words of Bede.]

[6] This council was held A.D. 680, under the Emperor Constantine Pogonatus. The number of attending bishops increased to near 200. —Mosheim, Vol. II. p. 101; Hammond's Canons, p. 125.]

THE NICENE CREED TAKEN OUT OF THE ECCLESI-
ASTICAL AND TRIPARTITE HISTORY.

We believe in one God, the Father Almighty, maker of of all things visible and invisible. And in one Lord Jesus Christ, the Son of God, the only-begotten Son of the Father, that is, of the substance of the Father; God of God, light of light, very God of very God; begotten, not made, being of the same essence and substance with the Father; by whom all things were made, which are in heaven, and which are in earth: who for us men and for our salvation came down, was incarnate and manned (was made man). He suffered, and rose again the third day, he ascended into heaven, and shall come to judge the quick and the dead. And (we believe) in the Holy Ghost. As for those that say, it was sometime when he was not, and before he was born he was not; and which say, because he was made of things not being (of nothing) or of another substance, that therefore the Son of God is either created, or turned, or changed, them doth the holy catholic and apostolic church curse or excommunicate[3].

[7 Πιστεύομεν εἰς ἕνα Θεὸν, Πατέρα παντοκράτορα, πάντων ὁρατῶν τε καὶ ἀοράτων ποιητήν. Καὶ εἰς ἕνα Κύριον Ἰησοῦν Χριστὸν, τὸν Υἱὸν τοῦ Θεοῦ, γεννηθέντα ἐκ τοῦ Πατρὸς, μονογενῆ, τουτέστιν ἐκ τῆς οὐσίας τοῦ Πατρός· Θεὸν ἐκ Θεοῦ, φῶς ἐκ φωτὸς, Θεὸν ἀληθινὸν ἐκ Θεοῦ ἀληθινοῦ· γεννηθέντα, οὐ ποιηθέντα· ὁμοούσιον τῷ Πατρί· δι' οὗ τὰ πάντα ἐγένετο, τά τε ἐν τῷ οὐρανῷ, καὶ τὰ ἐν τῇ γῇ· τὸν δι' ἡμᾶς τοὺς ἀνθρώπους καὶ διὰ τὴν ἡμετέραν σωτηρίαν κατελθόντα, καὶ σαρκωθέντα, ἐνανθρωπήσαντα, παθόντα καὶ ἀναστάντα τῇ τρίτῃ ἡμέρᾳ, ἀνελθόντα εἰς τοὺς οὐρανούς· ἐρχόμενον κρῖναι ζῶντας καὶ νεκρούς. Καὶ εἰς τὸ Πνεῦμα τὸ Ἅγιον. Τοὺς δὲ λέγοντας ἦν ποτὲ ὅτε οὐκ ἦν, ἢ οὐκ ἦν πρὶν γεννηθῆναι, ἢ ἐξ οὐκ ὄντων ἐγένετο, ἢ ἐξ ἑτέρας ὑποστάσεως ἢ οὐσίας φάσκοντας εἶναι, ἢ κτιστὸν, ἢ τρεπτὸν ἢ ἀλλοιωτὸν, τὸν Υἱὸν τοῦ Θεοῦ, τούτους ἀναθεματίζει ἡ καθολικὴ καὶ ἀποστολικὴ τοῦ Θεοῦ Ἐκκλησία.—Socr. Hist. Eccl. Lib. I. c. 8. ed. Reading. Cantab. 1720. P.]

THE CREED OF THE COUNCIL HELD AT CONSTANTIN-OPLE, TAKEN OUT OF A CERTAIN COPY WRITTEN IN GREEK[1] AND LATIN[2].

I BELIEVE[3] in one God, the Father Almighty, maker of heaven and earth, and of all things visible and invisible. And in one Lord Jesus Christ, the only-begotten Son of God, born of his Father before all worlds, light of light, very God of very God, begotten, not made, being of the same sub-

[1 Πιστεύομεν εἰς ἕνα Θεόν, Πατέρα παντοκράτορα, ποιητὴν οὐρανοῦ καὶ γῆς, ὁρατῶν τε πάντων καὶ ἀοράτων. Καὶ εἰς ἕνα Κύριον Ἰησοῦν Χριστὸν, τὸν Υἱὸν τοῦ Θεοῦ τὸν μονογενῆ, τὸν ἐκ τοῦ Πατρὸς γεννηθέντα πρὸ πάντων τῶν αἰώνων· φῶς ἐκ φωτὸς, Θεὸν ἀληθινὸν ἐκ Θεοῦ ἀληθινοῦ· γεννηθέντα οὐ ποιηθέντα, ὁμοούσιον τῷ Πατρί· δι᾽ οὗ τὰ πάντα ἐγένετο· τὸν δι᾽ ἡμᾶς τοὺς ἀνθρώπους καὶ διὰ τὴν ἡμετέραν σωτηρίαν κατελθόντα ἐκ τῶν οὐρανῶν, καὶ σαρκωθέντα ἐκ Πνεύματος Ἁγίου, καὶ Μαρίας τῆς παρθένου, καὶ ἐνανθρωπήσαντα· σταυρωθέντα τε ὑπὲρ ἡμῶν ἐπὶ Ποντίου Πιλάτου, καὶ παθόντα, καὶ ταφέντα, καὶ ἀναστάντα τῇ τρίτῃ ἡμέρᾳ κατὰ τὰς γραφάς· καὶ ἀνελθόντα εἰς τοὺς οὐρανοὺς, καὶ καθεζόμενον ἐκ δεξιῶν τοῦ Πατρός· καὶ πάλιν ἐρχόμενον μετὰ δόξης κρῖναι ζῶντας καὶ νεκρούς· οὗ τῆς βασιλείας οὐκ ἔσται τέλος. Καὶ εἰς τὸ Πνεῦμα τὸ Ἅγιον, τὸ Κύριον, καὶ τὸ ζωοποιὸν, τὸ ἐκ τοῦ Πατρὸς ἐκπορευόμενον, τὸ σὺν Πατρὶ καὶ Υἱῷ συμπροσκυνούμενον, καὶ συνδοξαζόμενον, τὸ λαλῆσαν διὰ τῶν προφητῶν· εἰς μίαν ἁγίαν καθολικὴν καὶ ἀποστολικὴν ἐκκλησίαν· ὁμολογοῦμεν ἓν βάπτισμα εἰς ἄφεσιν ἁμαρτιῶν· προσδοκῶμεν ἀνάστασιν νεκρῶν, καὶ ζωὴν τοῦ μέλλοντος αἰῶνος. Ἀμήν. P.]

[2 Credimus in unum Deum Patrem omnipotentem, factorem cœli et terræ, visibilium omnium et invisibilium: Et in unum Dominum Jesum Christum, Filium Dei, natum ex Patre ante omnia secula, Deum verum de Deo vero, natum, non factum, consubstantialem Patri: per quem omnia facta sunt, qui propter nos homines et salutem nostram descendit de cœlis, et incarnatus est de Spiritu Sancto ex Maria virgine, et inhumanatus est, et crucifixus est pro nobis sub Pontio Pilato, et sepultus est, et resurrexit tertia die, ascendit in cœlos, sedet ad dexteram Patris, iterum venturus est cum gloria judicare vivos et mortuos, cujus regni non erit finis: Et in Spiritum Sanctum, Dominum et vivificantem, ex Patre procedentem, cum Patre et Filio adorandum et conglorificandum, qui loquutus est per sanctos prophetas: Et unam sanctam catholicam et apostolicam ecclesiam: confitemur unum baptisma in remissionem peccatorum; exspectamus resurrectionem mortuorum, vitam futuri seculi. Amen.—Routh, Scriptor. Eccles. Opuscul. Vol. I. pp. 398, 9. Oxon. 1840.]

[3 Bullinger's copy reads Credo; confiteor; and exspecto; and Spiritum Sanctum Dominum vivificatorem.]

stance with the Father, by whom all things were made : who for us men, and for our salvation, came down from heaven, and was incarnate by the Holy Ghost and the virgin Mary, and was made man. He was also crucified for us under Pontius Pilate. He suffered and was buried: and he rose the third day, according to the scriptures. And he ascended into heaven, and sitteth on the right hand of God the Father : and he shall come again with glory to judge the quick and the dead; whose kingdom shall have no end. And (I believe) in the Holy Ghost, the Lord and giver of life, who, proceeding from the Father, is to be worshipped and glorified together with the Father and the Son; who spake by the prophets : in one catholic and apostolic church. I confess one baptism for the remission of sins. I look for the resurrection of the dead; and the life of the world to come.

THE CONFESSION OF FAITH MADE BY THE SYNOD AT EPHESUS.

INASMUCH as because here I note all things briefly, I could not in writing place with these that large synodal epistle written by St Cyril to Nestorius[4], wherein is contained the full consent of the general council held at Ephesus. I have therefore rather chosen out of the 28th epistle of the same Cyril a short confession sent to the synod, and allowed by the whole council. Before the confession are set these words : " Even as in the beginning we have heard out of the divine scriptures, and the tradition of the holy fathers; so will we briefly speak, not adding any thing at all to the faith set forth by the holy fathers in Nice. For that doth suffice as well to all knowledge of godliness, as also to the utter forsaking of any heretical overthwartness."

And a little after this, the confession is set down in these words : " We acknowledge our Lord Jesus Christ, the only-begotten Son of God, to be perfect God and perfect man, of a reasonable soul and body ; born of the Father according to his Godhead before the worlds, and the very same according to his humanity born in the latter times of the virgin Mary

[4 See Routh, Scriptor. Eccles. Opusc. Vol. II. p. 17, &c. The epistle was written A.D. 430.]

[BULLINGER.]

for us, and for our salvation : for there was made an uniting of the two natures. Wherefore we confess both one Christ, one Son, and one Lord. And according to this understanding of the unconfounded unity, we acknowledge the holy virgin to be the mother of God, because that God the Word was incarnate and made man, and by the very conception gathered to himself a body taken of her. But for the speeches uttered by the evangelists and apostles touching the Lord, we know that the divines do by reason of the two natures divide them, so yet as that they belong to one person ; and that they do refer them, some, because they are more agreeable to the Divinity, to the Godhead of Christ, and other some, (because they are) base, to his humanity."

To this confession Cyril addeth these words : " When we had read these holy words of yours (even in the synod to which the confession was sent), and did perceive that we ourselves were of the same opinion (for there is one Lord, one faith, and one baptism), we glorified God the ̣ Saviour of all (men), rejoicing together in ourselves, for that the churches both ours and yours do believe agreeably to the scriptures of God and tradition of the holy fathers[1]."

[1 .... ὡς ἄνωθεν ἔκ τε τῶν θείων γραφῶν ἔκ τε τῆς παραδόσεως τῶν ἁγίων πατέρων παρειληφότες ἐσχήκαμεν, διὰ βραχέων ἐροῦμεν, οὐδὲν τὸ συνόλον προστιθέντες τῇ τῶν ἁγίων πατέρων τῶν ἐν Νικαίᾳ ἐκτεθείσῃ πίστει· ὡς γὰρ ἔφθημεν εἰρηκότες, πρὸς πᾶσαν ἐξαρκεῖ καὶ εὐσεβείας γνῶσιν, πάσης καὶ αἱρετικῆς κακοδοξίας ἀποκήρυξιν.... Ὁμολογοῦμεν τοιγαροῦν τὸν Κύριον ἡμῶν Ἰησοῦν Χριστὸν, τὸν Υἱὸν τοῦ Θεοῦ τὸν μονογενῆ, Θεὸν τέλειον καὶ ἄνθρωπον τέλειον ἐκ ψυχῆς λογικῆς καὶ σώματος· πρὸ αἰώνων μὲν ἐκ τοῦ Πατρὸς γεννηθέντα κατὰ τὴν Θεότητα, ἐπ' ἐσχάτων δὲ τῶν ἡμερῶν τὸν αὐτὸν δι' ἡμᾶς καὶ διὰ τὴν ἡμετέραν σωτηρίαν ἐκ Μαρίας τῆς παρθένου κατὰ τὴν ἀνθρωπότητα· ὁμοούσιον τῷ Πατρὶ τὸν αὐτὸν κατὰ τὴν Θεότητα, καὶ ὁμοούσιον ἡμῖν κατὰ τὴν ἀνθρωπότητα· δύο γὰρ φύσεων ἕνωσις γέγονε· διὸ ἕνα Χριστὸν, ἕνα Υἱὸν, ἕνα Κύριον ὁμολογοῦμεν. Κατὰ ταύτην τὴν τῆς ἀσυγχύτου ἑνώσεως ἔννοιαν, ὁμολογοῦμεν τὴν ἁγίαν παρθένον Θεοτόκον, διὰ τὸ τὸν Θεὸν Λόγον σαρκωθῆναι, καὶ ἐνανθρωπῆσαι, καὶ ἐξ αὐτῆς τῆς συλλήψεως ἑνῶσαι ἑαυτῷ τὸν ἐξ αὐτῆς ληφθέντα ναόν. Τὰς δὲ εὐαγγελικὰς καὶ ἀποστολικὰς περὶ τοῦ Κυρίου φωνὰς, ἴσμεν τοὺς θεολόγους ἄνδρας τὰς μὲν κοινοποιοῦντας, ὡς ἐφ' ἑνὸς προσώπου, τὰς δὲ διαιροῦντας ὡς ἐπὶ δύο φύσεων· καὶ τὰς μὲν θεοπρεπεῖς κατὰ τὴν Θεότητα τοῦ Χριστοῦ, τὰς δὲ ταπεινὰς κατὰ τὴν ἀνθρωπότητα αὐτοῦ παραδιδόντας.—Ταύταις ὑμῶν ἐντυχόντες ταῖς ἱεραῖς φωναῖς, οὕτω τε καὶ ἑαυτοὺς φρονοῦντας εὑρίσκοντες, (εἷς γὰρ Κύριος, μία πίστις, ἐν βάπτισμα,) ἐδοξάσαμεν τὸν τῶν ὅλων Σωτῆρα Θεόν· ἀλ-

A CONFESSION OF FAITH MADE BY THE COUNCIL OF CHALCEDON, TAKEN OUT OF THE BOOK OF ISIDORE.

AFTER the rehearsal of the creeds set forth by the synods of Nice and Constantinople, with a few words put between, straightway the holy council of Chalcedon doth prescribe (their confession) in these words[2].

" We therefore, agreeing with the holy fathers, do with one accord teach to confess one and the same Son, our Lord Jesus Christ, and him (to be) perfect God in the Deity, and the same also very man of a reasonable soul and body: touching his Godhead (being) of one nature with his Father; and the same, as touching his manhood, of one nature with us, like to us in all things except sin: touching his Godhead, born of his Father before the worlds; and the same in the latter days made man for us and for our salvation. (We teach) to consider, that he is one and the same Christ, the Son, (our) Lord, the only-begotten Son, in two natures, neither

λήλοις συγχαίροντες, ὅτι ταῖς θεοπνεύστοις γραφαῖς καὶ τῇ παραδόσει τῶν ἁγίων ἡμῶν πατέρων συμβαίνουσαν ἔχουσι πίστιν αἵ τε παρὰ ἡμῖν καὶ αἱ παρὰ ὑμῖν ἐκκλησίαι.—Cyril. Alex. Opp. Par. 1638, Tom. v. P. 2, p. 106.]

[2 Ἑπόμενοι τοίνυν τοῖς ἁγίοις πατράσιν, ἕνα καὶ τὸν αὐτὸν ὁμολογεῖν υἱὸν τὸν Κύριον ἡμῶν Ἰησοῦν Χριστὸν συμφώνως ἅπαντες ἐκδιδάσκομεν, τέλειον τὸν αὐτὸν ἐν Θεότητι, καὶ τέλειον τὸν αὐτὸν ἐν ἀνθρωπότητι, Θεὸν ἀληθῶς καὶ ἄνθρωπον ἀληθῶς τὸν αὐτὸν ἐκ ψυχῆς λογικῆς καὶ σώματος· ὁμοούσιον τῷ Πατρὶ κατὰ τὴν Θεότητα, καὶ ὁμοούσιον τὸν αὐτὸν ἡμῖν κατὰ τὴν ἀνθρωπότητα, κατὰ πάντα ὅμοιον ἡμῖν, χωρὶς ἁμαρτίας· πρὸ αἰώνων μὲν ἐκ τοῦ Πατρὸς γεννηθέντα κατὰ τὴν Θεότητα, ἐπ᾽ ἐσχάτων δὲ τῶν ἡμερῶν τὸν αὐτὸν δι᾽ ἡμᾶς καὶ διὰ τὴν ἡμετέραν σωτηρίαν ἐκ Μαρίας τῆς παρθένου τῆς Θεοτόκου κατὰ τὴν ἀνθρωπότητα, ἕνα καὶ τὸν αὐτὸν Χριστὸν, Υἱὸν, Κύριον, μονογενῆ, ἐκ δύο φύσεων ἀσυγχύτως, ἀτρέπτως, ἀδιαιρέτως, ἀχωρίστως γνωριζόμενον· οὐδαμοῦ τῆς τῶν φύσεων διαφορᾶς ἀνῃρημένης διὰ τὴν ἕνωσιν, σωζομένης δὲ μᾶλλον τῆς ἰδιότητος ἑκατέρας φύσεως, καὶ εἰς ἕν πρόσωπον καὶ μίαν ὑπόστασιν συντρεχούσης, οὐκ εἰς δύο πρόσωπα μεριζόμενον ἢ διαιρούμενον, ἀλλ᾽ ἕνα καὶ τὸν αὐτὸν Υἱὸν καὶ μονογενῆ, Θεὸν, Λόγον, Κύριον Ἰησοῦν Χριστόν· καθάπερ ἄνωθεν οἱ προφῆται περὶ αὐτοῦ, καὶ αὐτὸς ἡμᾶς ὁ Κύριος Ἰησοῦς Χριστὸς ἐξεπαίδευσε, καὶ τὸ τῶν Πατέρων ἡμῖν παραδέδωκε σύμβολον. Τούτων τοίνυν μετὰ πάσης πανταχόθεν ἀκριβείας τε καὶ ἐμμελείας παρ᾽ ἡμῶν διατυπωθέντων, ὥρισεν ἡ ἁγία καὶ οἰκουμενικὴ σύνοδος, ἑτέραν πίστιν μηδενὶ ἐξεῖναι προφέρειν, ἢ γοῦν συγγράφειν, ἢ συντιθέναι, ἢ φρονεῖν, ἢ διδάσκειν ἑτέροις. —Labb. Conc. Par. 1671. Tom. iv. fol. 566, 7. P.]

2—2

confounded, nor changed, nor divided, nor separated; and that the difference of the natures is not to be taken away because of the unity, but rather, the property of both (his) natures remaining whole and meeting together in one person and one substance, that he is not parted or divided into two persons, but is one and the same Son, the only-begotten Son, God, the Word, (our) Lord Jesus Christ: even as the prophets from the beginning (have witnessed) of him, as he himself hath instructed us, and the confession of the fathers hath taught us. These things therefore being ordered by us with all care and diligence, the holy and universal synod doth determine, that it should not be lawful for any man to profess any other faith, or else to write, to teach, or speak to the contrary."

THAT THE DECREE OF THE SYNOD OF CHALCEDON IS NOT CONTRARY TO THE DOCTRINE OF THE BLESSED BISHOP CYRIL, TAKEN OUT OF THE FIFTH BOOK OF THE HOLY MARTYR VIGILIUS AGAINST EUTYCHES[1].

But now let us consider the last article in the decree of the synod of Chalcedon: "We confess that Christ our Lord,

[1 Sed jam ultimum decreti capitulum videamus ex decreto synodi Chalcedonensis: "Unum eundemque Christum Dominum unigenitum (confitemur) in duabus naturis inconfuse, inconvertibiliter, indivise, inseparabiliter cognoscendum, nusquam duarum naturarum diversitate evacuata propter unionem, salva magis proprietate utriusque naturæ, in unam personam atque substantiam convenientibus, non ut in duas personas divisum aut segregatum, sed unum eundemque unigenitum Filium Deum Verbum Dominum Jesum Christum." In hoc capitulo hoc eis displicet, cur dixerint, "Salva proprietate utriusque naturæ;" vel, "Non evacuata naturarum differentia:" quæ ut firma esse perdoceant, consueta verborum prolixitate et inani assertione utentes, multa de Cyrilli capitulis interponunt testimonia, quibus ille non duas in Christo negat naturas, sed unam docet esse personam. Ne igitur soli eos nostra disputatione refutemus, Cyrilli etiam nos verba ponamus; ut quomodo Cyrillo teste nituntur, Cyrillo teste vincantur. Ex synodicis Cyrilli ad Nestorium literis hæc sunt: "Non enim dicimus," inquit, "quod divina natura conversa vel immutata facta sit caro, nec quod in totum hominem, quod ex anima est et corpore, transformata sit; sed illud magis, quod carnem animatam rationabile sibi copulaverit Verbum substantialiter, ineffabiliter et indeprehensibiliter factus sit homo, et nuncupatus sit etiam Filius hominis, non nudæ tantummodo voluntatis, sed

the only-begotten Son, is to be understood to be one and the self-same in (his) two natures, neither confounded, nor changed, nor divided, nor separated, not making void the difference of the two natures because of the unity, but keeping sound the property of both natures coming together into one person and substance, not as being divided or separated, but (as being) one and the same only-begotten Son, God, the Word, (our) Lord Jesus."

In this article this displeaseth them, because they said, "The property of both natures remaining sound;" or, "The difference of the natures not being made void." And that they may persuade us that those things (which they mislike) are assuredly so, they, using their accustomed largeness of words and vain assertions, do bring in many testimonies out of the articles of Cyril, wherein he denieth not the two natures in Christ, but teacheth that there is but one person. To the intent therefore that we may not confute them with our disputation alone, let us set down also the words of Cyril, that even as they lean to the testimony of Cyril, so by the testimony of Cyril they may be overcome. In the synodal epistles of Cyril to Nestorius thus it is (written) : "For we do not affirm," saith he, "that the divine nature is turned or changed into flesh, nor yet that it is transformed into the

nec assumptione sola personæ, sed quod diversæ et quodammodo naturæ in unum convenerint. Unus tamen ex ambabus Christus et Filius, non evacuata aut sublata diversitate naturarum per conjunctionem; sed quia simul nobis effecerunt unum Dominum et Christum et Filium, id est, Divinitas et Humanitas per arcanam illam ineffabilemque copulationem ad unitatem." Quid hoc manifestius? quid clarius ad consonantiam synodici decreti Chalcedonensis ex literis Cyrilli potuit demonstrari? Ecce nec dicta dictis, nec sententiæ sententiis adversantur; sed sicut uno fidei sensu, ita iisdem pene usi sunt verbis. Dixit sancta synodus, Nusquam duarum naturarum diversitate evacuata: dixit beatus Cyrillus, Non evacuata aut sublata diversitate naturarum per conjunctionem. Dixit sancta synodus, Utrisque naturis in una persona convenientibus: dixit beatus Cyrillus, Non nudæ tantummodo voluntatis, sed nec assumptione sola personæ, sed quod diversæ quodammodo naturæ in unum convenerint. Dixit sancta synodus, Non in duas personas divisum, sed unum eundemque Christum: dixit beatus Cyrillus, Unus tamen ex ambabus, id est, naturis Christus Filius. Et iterum, Sed quia simul nobis effecerunt unum Dominum Christum et Filium, id est, Divinitas et Humanitas, &c.—Vigilius contra Eutychen. Tigur. 1539. p. 97.]

whole man, which consisteth of the body and soul; but we say rather, that the reasonable soul hath coupled to itself the substance of living flesh, that it is unspeakably and unconceivably made man, and is also called the Son of man, not of bare will alone, nor by the only taking on of the person, but because the two natures do after a certain manner come together in one, so that there is one Christ, and one Son of both (the natures) by joining them in one, not in making void or taking away the difference of the natures, but because they, that is, the Godhead and the manhood together, by that hidden and unspeakable knitting to the unity, have made to us one Lord, and (one) Christ, and (one) Son." What could be spoken more plainly than this? What could be shewed more clearly out of the epistles of Cyril to agree with the determination of the council of Chalcedon? For see, neither are words to words, nor sentence to sentence any thing contrary: but even as they had one meaning of faith, so use they in a manner the self-same words.

The holy synod said, "The difference of the two natures being no where made void;" St Cyril said, "The difference of the natures not being made void, or taken away, by joining them together." The holy synod said, "Both the natures meeting together in one person;" St Cyril saith, "Not of a bare will only, nor yet by the only taking on of a person, but because the two natures after a sort do meet together in one." The holy synod said, "Not being divided into two persons, but being one and the same Christ;" St Cyril said, "So that of two, that is to say (of two) natures in one Christ the Son;" and again, "Because they, that is, the Godhead and the manhood together, have made to us one Lord, (one) Christ, and (one) Son," &c.

THE CREED OF THE FIRST COUNCIL HELD AT TOLEDO, WHEN HONORIUS AND ARCADIUS WERE EMPERORS, TAKEN OUT OF THE BOOK OF ISIDORE[1].

About the year of our Lord 400.

WE believe in one very God, the Father Almighty, and the Son, and the Holy Ghost, maker of things visible and

[1 Credimus in unum Deum Patrem, et Filium et Spiritum Sanctum, visibilium et invisibilium factorem, per quem creata sunt omnia in

invisible, by whom all things were made in heaven and in earth. We believe, that there is one God and one Trinity of the divine substance. And that the Father himself is not the Son, but that he hath a Son, which is not the Father. That the Son is not the Father, but that the Son of God is of the nature of the Father. And also that the Holy Ghost is the Comforter, which neither is the Father himself, nor the Son, but proceeding from the Father and the Son. The Father therefore is unbegotten, the Son begotten, the Comforter not begotten but proceeding from the Father and the Son. The Father is he from whom this voice was heard out of heaven, " This is my beloved Son, in whom I am well pleased: hear him." The Son is he which said, " I went out from the Father, and came from God into the world." The Comforter is the Holy Ghost, of whom the Son said, " Unless I go away to the Father, the Comforter shall not

coelo et in terra: hunc unum Deum et hanc unam esse divinæ substantiæ Trinitatem: Patrem autem non esse ipsum Filium, sed habere Filium qui Pater non sit: Filium non esse Patrem, sed Filium Dei de Patris esse natura: Spiritum quoque Paracletum esse, qui nec Pater sit ipse nec Filius, sed a Patre Filioque procedens. Est ergo ingenitus Pater, genitus Filius, non genitus Paracletus sed a Patre Filioque procedens. Pater est, cujus vox hæc est audita de coelis, *Hic est Filius meus, in quo mihi bene complacui: ipsum audite.* Filius est qui ait, *Ego a Patre exivi, et a Deo veni in hunc mundum.* Paracletus Spiritus est, de quo Filius ait, *Nisi abiero ego ad Patrem, Paracletus non veniet ad vos.* Hanc Trinitatem personis distinctam, substantia unitam, virtute et potestate et majestate indivisibilem, indifferentem; præter hanc nullam credimus divinam esse naturam, vel angeli, vel spiritus vel virtutis alicujus, quæ Deus esse credatur. Hunc igitur Filium Dei, Deum natum a Patre ante omne omnino principium, sanctificasse uterum Mariæ Virginis, atque ex ea verum hominem sine virili generatum semine suscepisse, duabus duntaxat naturis, id est, Deitatis et carnis, in unam convenientibus omnino personam, id est, Dominum nostrum Jesum Christum: nec imaginarium corpus aut phantasmatis alicujus in eo fuisse, sed solidum atque verum: hunc et esurisse et sitisse et doluisse et flevisse et omnes corporis injurias pertulisse: postremo a Judæis crucifixum et sepultum tertia die resurrexisse: conversatum postmodum eum discipulis suis, et quadragesima post resurrectionem die ad coelum ascendisse. Hunc Filium hominis etiam Dei Filium dici. Filium autem Dei Dominum Filium hominis appellamus. Resurrectionem vero futuram humanæ credimus carnis, animam autem hominis non divinam esse substantiam, aut Dei parem, sed creaturam dicimus divina voluntate creatam.—Labb. Concil. Par. 1671. Tom. II. col. 1227. P.]

come." We believe in this Trinity differing in persons (but) all one in substance, not divided nor differing in strength, power and majesty; (and) we believe, that beside this there is no divine nature, either of angel, or of spirit, or any power, which may be believed to be God.

We therefore believe, that this Son of God, being God begotten of his Father altogether before all beginning, did sanctify the womb of the virgin Mary, and that of her he took upon him very man, begotten without the seed of man, the two natures only, that is, of the Godhead and manhood, coming together into one person only, that is, our Lord Jesus Christ. Neither (do we believe) that there was in him an imagined or any phantastical body, but a sound and very (body), and that he both hungered, and thirsted, and taught[1], and wept, and suffered all the damages of the body: last of all, that he was crucified of the Jews, and was buried, and rose again the third day, and afterward was conversant with his disciples, and the fortieth day after his resurrection ascended into heaven. This Son of man, and also the Son of God, we call both the Son of God and the Son of man.

We believe verily, that there shall be a resurrection of the flesh of mankind; and that the soul of man is not of the divine substance, or of God the Father, but is a creature created by the will of God.

THE CREED OF THE FOURTH COUNCIL KEPT AT TOLEDO, TAKEN OUT OF THE BOOK OF ISIDORE[2].

As we have learned of the holy fathers, that the Father, and the Son, and the Holy Ghost are of one Godhead and

---

[1 "Docuisse" for "doluisse" is read in the Latin of Bullinger, by mistake: it ought to be "sorrowed."]

[2 Secundum divinas scripturas, doctrinam quam a sanctis patribus accepimus, Patrem et Filium et Spiritum Sanctum unius Deitatis atque substantiæ confitemur: in personarum diversitate Trinitatem credentes, in Divinitate unitatem prædicantes: nec personas confundimus, nec substantiam separamus. Patrem a nullo factum vel genitum dicimus: Filium a Patre non factum sed genitum asserimus: Spiritum vero Sanctum non creatum, nec genitum, sed procedentem ex Patre et Filio profitemur. Ipsum autem Dominum nostrum Jesum Christum, Dei Filium et Creatorem omnium, ex substantia Patris ante secula

substance, (so) is our confession, believing the Trinity in the difference of persons, and openly professing the unity in the Godhead; neither confound we the persons, nor divide the substance.   We say, that the Father is made or begotten of none: we affirm, that the Son is not made, but begotten of the Father : and we profess that the Holy Ghost is neither created nor begotten, but proceeding from the Father and the Son. And (we confess) that the Lord himself Jesus Christ the Son of God, and the maker of all things, begotten of the substance of his Father before all the worlds, came down from his Father in the latter times for the redemption of the world, who (nevertheless) never ceased to be with the Father. For he was incarnate by the Holy Ghost and the glorious virgin Mary the holy mother of God, and of her was born alone the same Lord Jesus Christ, one in the Trinity, being perfect (man) in soul and body, taking on man without sin, being still what he was, taking to him what he was not: touching his Godhead equal with the Father, (and) inferior to his Father touching his manhood, having in one person the property of two natures.   For (there are) in him two natures, God and man: and yet not two Sons or two Gods, but the same (God and man) one person in both natures, who

genitum, descendisse ultimo tempore pro redemptione mundi a Patre, qui nunquam desiit esse cum Patre.   Incarnatus est enim ex Spiritu Sancto, et sancta gloriosa Dei genitrice Virgine Maria, et natus ex ipsa, solus autem Dominus Jesus Christus; unus de sancta Trinitate, anima et carne perfectum sine peccato suscipiens hominem, manens quod erat, assumens quod non erat: æqualis Patri secundum Divinitatem, minor Patre secundum humanitatem: habens in una Persona duarum naturarum proprietatem: naturæ enim in illo duæ, Deus et homo, non autem duo Filii et Dei duo, sed idem una Persona in utraque natura, perferens passionem et mortem pro nostra salute, non in virtute Divinitatis, sed infirmitate humanitatis.   Descendit ad inferos, ut sanctos qui ibidem tenebantur erueret: devictoque mortis imperio resurrexit: assumptus deinde in cœlum, venturus est in futurum ad judicium vivorum et mortuorum: cujus nos morte et sanguine mundati remissionem peccatorum consecuti sumus: resuscitandi ab eo in die novissima in ea qua nunc vivimus carne: et in ea qua resurrexit idem Dominus forma percepturi ab ipso, alii pro justitiæ meritis vitam æternam, alii pro peccatis supplicii æterni sententiam.   Hæc est catholicæ ecclesiæ fides: hanc confessionem conservamus atque tenemus: quam quisquis firmissime custodierit, perpetuam salutem habebit.
—Labb. Concil. Par. 1671. Tom. v. 1703. P.]

suffered grief and death for our salvation, not in the power of his Godhead, but in the infirmity of his manhood. He descended to them below to draw out by force the saints which were held there. And he rose again, the power of death being overcome. He was taken up into the heavens, from whence he shall come to judge the quick and the dead. By whose death and blood we being made clean have obtained forgiveness of (our) sins, and shall be raised up again by him in the last day in the same flesh wherein we now live, (and) in that manner wherein the same (our) Lord did rise again, (and) shall receive of him, some in reward of their well-doing life everlasting, and some for their sins the judgment of everlasting punishment. This is the faith of the catholic church, this confession we keep and hold, which whosoever shall keep stedfastly, he shall have everlasting salvation.

A DECLARATION OF THE FAITH OR PREACHING OF THE EVANGELICAL AND APOSTOLICAL TRUTH, BY THE BLESSED MARTYR IRENÆUS, TAKEN OUT OF THE THIRD CHAPTER OF HIS FIRST BOOK "CONTRA VALENT."

About the year of our Lord 185.

THE church, dispersed through the whole world even to the ends of the earth, hath of the apostles and their disciples received the belief, which is in one God the Father Almighty, which made heaven and earth, the sea, and all that in them is. And in one Jesus Christ the Son of God, (who was) incarnate for our salvation. And in the Holy Ghost, who by the prophets preached the mystery of the dispensation, and the coming of the beloved Jesus Christ our Lord, with his nativity of the virgin, and his passion, and resurrection from the dead, and his ascension in the flesh into the heavens, and his coming again out of the heavens in the glory of the Father to restore all things, and to raise up again all flesh of mankind : so that to Christ Jesus our Lord, both God, and Saviour, and King, according to the will of the invisible Father, every knee may bow, of things in heaven, and things in earth, and things under the earth, and that every tongue may praise him, and that he may judge rightly in all things, and that he may cast the spirits of naughtiness, with the angels which transgressed and became rebels, and wicked, unjust, mischievous,

and blasphemous men, into eternal fire : and that to the just
and holy ones, and such as have kept his commandments and
remained in the love of him, partly from the beginning and
partly by repentance, he may grant life, bestow immortality,
and give glory everlasting. The church, although it be dispersed throughout the whole world, having obtained, as I
have said, this confession and this faith, doth, as it were
dwelling together in one house, diligently keep them, and
likewise believe them, even as if it had one soul and the
same heart; and doth preach, teach, and agreeably deliver
these things, even as if it had all one mouth. For in the
world the tongues are unlike, but the force of teaching is
one and the same. Neither do the churches, whose foundation
is laid in Germany, believe otherwise, or teach to the contrary : neither those in Spain, nor those in France, nor those
in the east, nor those in Egypt, nor those in Libya, nor those
which are in the world (beside) : but even as the sun, (which
is) the creature of God, is one and the self-same in all the
world; so also the preaching of the truth shineth every where,
and giveth light to all men, which are willing to come to the
knowledge of the truth. And neither shall he, which among
the chief overseers of the church is able to say much, speak
contrary to this; for no man is above his master : neither
shall he, which is able to say little, diminish this doctrine any
whit at all. For seeing that faith is all one and the same,
neither doth he, which is able to say much of it, say more
than should be said : neither doth he, which saith little, make
it ever a whit the lesser [1].

[1] Ἡ μὲν γὰρ ἐκκλησία, καίπερ καθ᾽ ὅλης τῆς οἰκουμένης ἕως περάτων
τῆς γῆς διεσπαρμένη, παρὰ δὲ τῶν ἀποστόλων καὶ τῶν ἐκείνων μαθητῶν πα-
ραλαβοῦσα τὴν εἰς ἕνα Θεὸν Πατέρα παντοκράτορα, τὸν πεποιηκότα τὸν οὐρανὸν, καὶ τὴν γῆν, καὶ τὰς θαλάσσας, καὶ πάντα τὰ ἐν αὐτοῖς, πίστιν· καὶ
εἰς ἕνα Χριστὸν Ἰησοῦν, τὸν Υἱὸν τοῦ Θεοῦ, τὸν σαρκωθέντα ὑπὲρ τῆς ἡμετέρας σωτηρίας· καὶ εἰς Πνεῦμα Ἅγιον, τὸ διὰ τῶν προφητῶν κεκηρυχὸς τὰς
οἰκονομίας, καὶ τὰς ἐλεύσεις, καὶ τὴν ἐκ παρθένου γέννησιν, καὶ τὸ πάθος, καὶ
τὴν ἔγερσιν ἐκ νεκρῶν, καὶ τὴν ἔνσαρκον εἰς τοὺς οὐρανοὺς ἀνάληψιν τοῦ
ἠγαπημένου Χριστοῦ Ἰησοῦ τοῦ Κυρίου ἡμῶν, καὶ τὴν ἐκ τῶν οὐρανῶν ἐν τῇ
δόξῃ τοῦ Πατρὸς παρουσίαν αὐτοῦ, ἐπὶ τὸ ἀνακεφαλαιώσασθαι τὰ πάντα, καὶ
ἀναστῆσαι πᾶσαν σάρκα πάσης ἀνθρωπότητος, ἵνα Χριστῷ Ἰησοῦ τῷ Κυρίῳ
ἡμῶν, καὶ Θεῷ, καὶ Σωτῆρι, καὶ Βασιλεῖ, κατὰ τὴν εὐδοκίαν τοῦ Πατρὸς τοῦ
ἀοράτου, πᾶν γόνυ κάμψῃ ἐπουρανίων καὶ ἐπιγείων καὶ καταχθονίων, καὶ
πᾶσα γλῶσσα ἐξομολογήσηται αὐτῷ, καὶ κρίσιν δικαίαν ἐν τοῖς πᾶσι ποιή-

Read further in the fourth chapter of his third book *Contra Valent.* and you shall perceive that by the term of apostolical tradition he meaneth the Creed of the Apostles.

A RULE OF FAITH, AFTER TERTULLIAN, TAKEN OUT OF HIS BOOK "DE PRÆSCRIPTIONIBUS HÆRETI-CORUM[1]."

About the year of our Lord 210.

THE rule of faith is, that we out of hand profess openly what our belief is; which is that indeed whereby we believe

σηται· τὰ μὲν πνευματικὰ τῆς πονηρίας, καὶ ἀγγέλους παραβεβηκότας καὶ ἐν ἀποστασίᾳ γεγονότας, καὶ τοὺς ἀσεβεῖς, καὶ ἀδίκους, καὶ ἀνόμους, καὶ βλασφήμους τῶν ἀνθρώπων εἰς τὸ αἰώνιον πῦρ πέμψῃ· τοῖς δὲ δικαίοις, καὶ ὁσίοις, καὶ τὰς ἐντολὰς αὐτοῦ τετηρηκόσι, καὶ ἐν τῇ ἀγάπῃ αὐτοῦ δια-μεμενηκόσι, τοῖς ἀπ᾽ ἀρχῆς, τοῖς δὲ ἐκ μετανοίας, ζωὴν χαρισάμενος ἀφθαρ-σίαν δωρήσηται, καὶ δόξαν αἰωνίαν περιποιήσῃ. Τοῦτο τὸ κήρυγμα παρει-ληφυῖα, καὶ ταύτην τὴν πίστιν, ὡς προέφαμεν, ἡ ἐκκλησία, καίπερ ἐν ὅλῳ τῷ κόσμῳ διεσπαρμένη, ἐπιμελῶς φυλάσσει, ὡς ἕνα οἶκον οἰκοῦσα· καὶ ὁμοίως πιστεύει τούτοις, ὡς μίαν ψυχὴν καὶ τὴν αὐτὴν ἔχουσα καρδίαν, καὶ συμφώνως ταῦτα κηρύσσει, καὶ διδάσκει, καὶ παραδίδωσιν, ὡς ἓν στόμα κεκτημένη· καὶ γὰρ αἱ κατὰ τὸν κόσμον διάλεκτοι ἀνόμοιαι, ἀλλ᾽ ἡ δύναμις τῆς παραδόσεως μία καὶ ἡ αὐτή· καὶ οὔτε αἱ ἐν Γερμανίαις ἱδρυμέναι ἐκ-κλησίαι ἄλλως πεπιστεύκασιν, ἢ ἄλλως παραδιδόασιν, οὔτε ἐν ταῖς Ἰβηρίαις, οὔτε ἐν Κελτοῖς, οὔτε κατὰ τὰς ἀνατολὰς, οὔτε ἐν Αἰγύπτῳ, οὔτε ἐν Λιβύῃ, οὔτε αἱ κατὰ μέσα τοῦ κόσμου ἱδρυμέναι· ἀλλ᾽ ὥσπερ ὁ ἥλιος τὸ κτίσμα τοῦ Θεοῦ ἐν ὅλῳ τῷ κόσμῳ εἷς καὶ ὁ αὐτός, οὕτω καὶ τὸ κήρυγμα τῆς ἀληθείας πανταχῆ φαίνει, καὶ φωτίζει πάντας ἀνθρώπους τοὺς βουλομένους εἰς ἐπί-γνωσιν ἀληθείας ἐλθεῖν. Καὶ οὔτε ὁ πάνυ δυνατὸς ἐν λόγῳ τῶν ἐν ταῖς ἐκκλησίαις προεστώτων ἕτερα τούτων ἐρεῖ· (οὐδεὶς γὰρ ὑπὲρ τὸν διδάσκα-λον·) οὔτε ὁ ἀσθενὴς ἐν τῷ λόγῳ ἐλαττώσει τὴν παράδοσιν· μιᾶς γὰρ καὶ τῆς αὐτῆς πίστεως οὔσης, οὔτε ὁ πολὺ περὶ αὐτῆς δυνάμενος εἰπεῖν ἐπλεό-νασεν, οὔτε ὁ τὸ ὀλίγον ἠλαττόνησε.—Iren. adv. Hæres. Lib. I. cap. 3. ed. Grabe. Oxon. 1702.]

[1 Regula est autem fidei, ut jam hinc, quid defendamus, profitea-mur, illa scilicet qua creditur: Unum omnino Deum esse, nec alium præter mundi conditorem, qui universa de nihilo produxerit per Verbum suum primo omnium emissum. Id Verbum Filius ejus appellatum, in nomine Dei, varie visum patriarchis, in prophetis semper auditum, postremo delatum ex Spiritu Patris Dei et virtute in Virginem Mariam, carnem factum in utero ejus, et ex ea natum, egisse Jesum Christum: exinde prædicasse novam legem, et novam promissionem regni cœ-lorum: virtutes fecisse: fixum cruci: tertia die resurrexisse: in cœlos ereptum sedere ad dexteram Patris: misisse vicariam vim Spiritus Sancti, qui credentes agat: venturum cum claritate ad sumendos sanctos in vitæ æternæ et promissorum cœlestium fructum, et ad pro-

that there is one God only, and not any other beside the maker of the world, which by his Word, sent out first of all, brought forth all things of nothing. That Word, being called his Son, being seen after sundry sorts of the patriarchs, being always heard in the prophets, and lastly by the Spirit and power of God the Father being brought into the virgin Mary, being made flesh in that womb and born of her, became Jesus Christ, (which) afterward preached the new law and the new promise of the kingdom of heaven, wrought miracles, sat at the right hand of the Father, was nailed to the cross, rose again the third day, was taken into the heavens, sitteth at the right hand of the Father, sent the power of the Holy Ghost to govern the believers in his own stead, shall come with glory to take the saints into the joy of eternal life and heavenly promises, and to condemn the wicked to everlasting fire, when both the parties are raised up and have their flesh restored again.

This rule, as it shall be proved, being ordained by Christ, hath among us no doubts at all, but those which heresies bring in, and which make men become heretics.

THE CREED OF THE BLESSED ATHANASIUS, BISHOP OF ALEXANDRIA, TAKEN OUT OF HIS BOOKS[2].

WHOSOEVER will be saved : before all things it is necessary that he hold the catholic faith.

About the year of our Lord 333.

fanos judicandos igni perpetuo, facta utriusque partis resuscitatione cum carnis restitutione. Hæc regula, a Christo, ut probabitur, instituta, nullas habet apud nos quæstiones, nisi quas hæreses inferunt, et quæ hæreticos faciunt.—Tertul. Opp. de Præsc. Hær. cap. 13. ed. Semler. Tom. II. p. 13.]

[2 The best and latest critics, who have examined the thing most exactly, make no question but that this creed is to be ascribed to a Latin author, Vigilius Tapsensis, an African bishop, who lived in the latter end of the fifth century, in the time of the Vandalic Arian persecution: first, because this creed is wanting in almost all the manuscripts of Athanasius's works: secondly, because the style and contexture of it does not bespeak a Greek, but a Latin, author: thirdly, because neither Cyril of Alexandria, nor the council of Ephesus, nor pope Leo, nor the council of Chalcedon, have ever so much as mentioned it in all that they say against the Nestorian or Eutychian heresies: fourthly, because this Vigilius Tapsensis is known to have published

Which faith except every one do keep holy[1] and unde-filed: without doubt he shall perish everlastingly.

And the catholic faith is this: that we worship one God in Trinity, and Trinity in Unity.

Neither confounding the persons: nor dividing the sub-stance.

For there is one person of the Father, another of the Son, and another of the Holy Ghost.

But the Godhead of the Father, of the Son, and of the Holy Ghost, is all one: the glory equal, the majesty co-eternal.

Such as the Father is, such is the Son: and such is the Holy Ghost.

The Father uncreate, the Son uncreate: and the Holy Ghost uncreate.

The Father incomprehensible, the Son incomprehensible: and the Holy Ghost incomprehensible.

The Father eternal, the Son eternal: and the Holy Ghost eternal.

And yet there are not three eternals: but one eternal.

As also there be not three incomprehensibles, nor three uncreated: but one uncreated, and one incomprehensible.

So likewise the Father is almighty, the Son is almighty: and the Holy Ghost almighty.

And yet are they not three almighties: but one almighty.

So the Father is God, the Son is God: and the Holy Ghost is God.

And yet they are not three Gods: but one God.

So likewise the Father is Lord, the Son Lord: and the Holy Ghost Lord.

And yet not three Lords: but one Lord.

For like as we be compelled by the christian verity: to acknowledge every person by himself to be God and Lord.

So are we forbidden by the catholic religion: to say there be three Gods or three Lords.

several other of his writings under the borrowed name of Athanasius, —with which this creed is commonly joined.—Bingham's Antiquities, ed. 1840. Vol. III. 372. See also, for a full discussion of the question, Waterland's works. P.]

[1 So also in the two Liturgies of Edward VI. See Parker Society's edition, pages 38 and 229. The Latin is *integram*.]

The Father is made of none : neither created, nor begotten.

The Son is of the Father alone : not made, nor created, but begotten.

The Holy Ghost is of the Father and of the Son : neither made, nor created, nor begotten, but proceeding.

So there is one Father, not three Fathers : one Son, not three Sons : one Holy Ghost, not three Holy Ghosts.

And in this Trinity none is afore or after other : none is greater or less than other.

But the whole three persons be coeternal together : and coequal.

So that in all things, as is aforesaid : the Unity in Trinity, and the Trinity in Unity is to be worshipped.

He therefore that will be saved, must thus think of the Trinity.

Furthermore it is necessary to everlasting salvation : that he also believe rightly[2] in the incarnation of our Lord Jesus Christ.

For the right faith is, that we believe and confess : that our Lord Jesus Christ, the Son of God, is God and man.

God of the substance of the Father, begotten before the worlds : and man of the substance of his mother born in the world.

Perfect God and perfect man : of a reasonable soul, and human flesh subsisting.

Equal to the Father as touching his Godhead : and inferior to the Father touching his manhood.

Who although he be God and man : yet he is not two, but one Christ.

One, not by the conversion of the Godhead into flesh : but by taking of the manhood into God.

One altogether, not by confusion of substance : but by unity of person.

For as the reasonable soul and flesh is one man : so God and man is one Christ.

Who suffered for our salvation, descended into hell, rose again the third day from the dead.

He ascended into heaven, he sitteth on the right hand of

[2 fideliter, Lat.]

the Father, God Almighty: from whence he shall come to judge the quick and the dead.

At whose coming all men shall rise again with their bodies: and shall give account for their own works.

And they that have done good, shall go into life everlasting: and they that have done evil, into everlasting fire.

This is the catholic faith: which except a man believe faithfully[1], he cannot be saved.

THE CREED OF THE BLESSED DAMASUS, BISHOP OF ROME, TAKEN OUT OF THE SECOND TOME OF S. HIEROME HIS WORKS[1].

About the year of our Lord 376.

WE believe in one God the Father Almighty, and in one Jesus Christ our Lord the Son of God, and in the Holy Ghost.

[1 fideliter firmiterque, Lat.]

[2 Credimus in unum Deum, Patrem omnipotentem, et in unum Dominum nostrum Jesum Christum, Filium Dei, et in Spiritum Sanctum. Deum, non tres Deos; sed Patrem, et Filium, et Spiritum Sanctum, unum Deum colimus et confitemur: non sic unum Deum, quasi solitarium; nec eundem, qui ipse sibi Pater sit, ipse et Filius: sed Patrem esse qui genuit, et Filium esse qui genitus sit: Spiritum vero Sanctum non genitum neque ingenitum, non creatum neque factum, sed de Patre Filioque procedentem, Patri et Filio coæternum et coæqualem et cooperatorem: quia scriptum est, Verbo Domini cœli firmati sunt, id est, a Filio Dei, et spiritu oris ejus omnis virtus eorum. Et alibi: Emitte spiritum tuum, et creabuntur, et renovabis faciem terræ. Ideoque in nomine Patris et Filii et Spiritus Sancti unum confitemur Deum, quod nomen est potestatis, non proprietatis. Proprium nomen est Patri Pater; et proprium nomen est Filio Filius; et proprium nomen Spiritui Sancto Spiritus Sanctus. In hac Trinitate unum Deum colimus, quia ex uno Patre quod est unius cum Patre naturæ est, unius substantiæ, et unius potestatis. Pater Filium genuit, non voluntate, nec necessitate, sed natura. Filius ultimo tempore ad nos salvandos et ad implendas scripturas descendit a Patre, qui nunquam desiit esse cum Patre. Et conceptus est de Spiritu Sancto, et natus ex virgine: carnem et animam et sensum, hoc est, perfectum suscepit hominem; nec amisit quod erat, sed cœpit esse quod non erat; ita tamen, ut perfectus in suis sit, et verus in nostris. Nam qui Deus erat, homo natus est; et qui homo natus est, operatur ut Deus; et qui operatur ut Deus, ut homo moritur; et qui ut homo moritur, ut Deus resurgit. Qui, devicto mortis imperio, cum ea carne, qua natus et passus et mortuus fuerat, et resurrexit, ascendit ad Patrem, sedetque

We worship and confess God, not three Gods, but the Father, the Son, and the Holy Ghost, one God : one God, not so as though he were alone, nor as one which is himself Father to himself, and Son himself also ; but him to be the Father which begot, and (him) to be the Son which was begotten; but the Holy Ghost to be neither begotten, nor created, nor made, but proceeding from the Father and the Son, co-eternal, co-equal, and working together with the Father and the Son : because it is written, " By the word of the Lord the heavens were established," that is, by the Son of God, " and by the breath of his mouth all the powers thereof;" and in another place, " Send forth thy breath, and they shall be created, and thou shalt renew the face of the earth."   And therefore under the name of the Father, of the Son, and of the Holy Ghost, we confess one God, which is the name of the power, and not of the property.   The proper name of the Father is the Father : and the proper name of the Son is the Son : and the proper name of the Holy Ghost is the Holy Ghost.   In this Trinity of persons we worship one God (in substance), because that which is of one father is of one nature with the father, of one substance, and one power.   The Father begat the Son, not by will or necessity, but by nature.

The Son in the last time came down from the Father to save us and to fulfil the scriptures, who (nevertheless) never ceased to be with the Father.   And he was conceived by the Holy Ghost, and born of the virgin : he took upon him flesh, and soul, and sense ; that is, he took on him very man, neither lost he what he was, but began to be what he was not; so yet that, in respect of his own properties, he is perfect God ; and in respect of ours, he is very man.   For he which was God is born man ; and he which is born man, doth work miracles as God; and he that worketh miracles as God, doth die as a man ; and he that dieth as man, doth rise again as God : who in the same flesh, wherein he was born and suf-

ad dexteram ejus in gloria, quam semper habuit et habet.   In hujus morte et sanguine credimus emundatos nos; et ab eo resuscitandos die novissimo in hac carne qua nunc vivimus.   Et habemus spem nos consecuturos præmium boni meriti, aut pœnam pro peccatis æterni supplicii.   Hæc lege, hæc crede, hæc retine; huic fidei animam tuam subjuga ; et vitam consequeris et præmium a Christo.—Hieronym. Opp. ed. Par. 1693-1706. Tom. v. col. 122.]

fered and died and rose again, did ascend to the Father, and sitteth at his right hand in the glory which he always had, and yet still hath. By whose death and blood we believe that we are cleansed; and that at the latter day we shall be raised up again by him in this flesh wherein we now live. And we hope that we shall obtain a reward for our good deeds; or else the pain of everlasting punishment for our sins. Read this, believe this, hold this, submit thy soul to this faith, and thou shalt obtain life and a reward at Christ's hand.

Peter, bishop of Alexandria. St Peter, bishop of Alexandria, taught and believed the very same with the blessed Athanasius and Damasus, as it may be gathered out of the thirty-seventh chapter of the seventh book, and the fourteenth chapter of the eighth book, of the Tripartite history[1].

THE IMPERIAL DECREE FOR THE CATHOLIC FAITH[2], TAKEN OUT OF THE TRIPARTITE HISTORY. Lib. IX. Cap. 7.

THE noble emperors, Gratian, Valentinian, and Theodosius, to the people of the city of Constantinople. We will all people, whom the royal authority of our clemency doth rule, to be of that religion, which the religion brought in by (Peter) himself doth at this time declare that St Peter the apostle did teach to the Romans, and which it is evident that bishop Damasus, and Peter the bishop of Alexandria, a man of apostolical holiness, do follow: that is, that, according to the discipline of the apostles and doctrine of the evangelists, in the equality of the majesty and in the holy **Catholics.** Trinity we believe that there is (but) one Godhead of the Father, of the Son, and of the Holy Ghost. Those which keep this law, we command to have the name of catholic Christians: but for the other, whom we judge to be mad and **Hereticks.** out of their wits, (we will) that they, sustaining the infamy

[1 Is (Petrus) Athanasii sudoribus particeps fuit.—Hist. Eccles. Tripart. Lib. VII. cap. 37, p. 317. Petro revertente de Roma cum literis Damasi Romanæ urbis Antistitis, confirmantis consubstantialitatis fidem, et Petri Episcopi roborantis ordinationem.—Ibid. Lib. VIII. cap. 14. Cassiodor. Opp. p. 329. Rotomag. 1679.]

[2 circa annum Domini, 382, Lat.]

of heretical doctrine, be punished first by God's vengeance, and after that by punishment according to the motion of our minds, which we, by the will of God, shall think best of.

> Given the third of the Calends of March,
> at Thessalonica; Gratian the Fifth,
> Valentinian, and Theo-
> dosius, Aug.
> Coss[3].

FINIS.

[3 Impp. Gratianus, Valentinianus, et Theodosius, Augg. ad populum urbis Constantinopolitanæ. Cunctos populos, quos Clementiæ nostræ regit temperamentum, in tali volumus religione versari, quam divinum Petrum apostolum tradidisse Romanis religio usque nunc ab ipso insinuata declarat; quamque Pontificem Damasum sequi claret, et Petrum Alexandriæ episcopum, virum apostolicæ sanctitatis: hoc est, ut secundum apostolicam disciplinam evangelicamque doctrinam, Patris et Filii et Spiritus Sancti unam Deitatem sub pari majestate et sub pia Trinitate credamus. Hanc legem sequentes, Christianorum catholicorum nomen jubemus amplecti: reliquos vero, dementes vesanosque judicantes, hæretici dogmatis infamiam sustinere, divina primum vindicta, post etiam motus nostri, quem ex cœlesti arbitrio sumpserimus, ultione plectendos. Data III. Kalend. Martias. Thessalonicæ. Gratiano quinto et Theodosio Augg. Coss.—Hist. Eccles. Tripart. Lib. IX. cap. 7. ap. Cassiodor. Opp. Rotomag. 1679. p. 334.]

THE

FIRST DECADE OF SERMONS,

WRITTEN BY

HENRY BULLINGER.

OF THE WORD OF GOD; THE CAUSE OF IT; AND HOW, AND BY WHOM, IT WAS REVEALED TO THE WORLD.

THE FIRST SERMON.

ALL the decrees of Christian faith, with every way how to live rightly, well, and holily, and finally, all true and heavenly wisdom, have always been fetched out of the testimonies, or determinate judgments, of the word of God; neither[1] can they, by those which are wise men indeed, or by the faithful and those which are called by God to the ministry of the churches, be drawn, taught, or, last of all, soundly confirmed from elsewhere, than out of the word of God. Therefore, whosoever is ignorant what the word of God, and the meaning of the word of God is, he seemeth to be as one blind, deaf, and without wit, in the temple of the Lord, in the school of Christ, and lastly, in the reading of the very sacred scriptures. But whereas[2] some are nothing zealous, but very hardly drawn to the hearing of sermons in the church; that springeth out of no other fountain than this, which is, because they do neither rightly understand, nor diligently enough weigh, the virtue and true force of the word of God. That nothing therefore may cause the zealous desirers of the truth and the word of God to stay on this point[3]; but rather that that estimation of God's word, which is due unto it, may be laid up in all men's hearts; I will (by God's help) lay forth unto you, dearly beloved, those things which a godly man ought to think and hold, as concerning the word of God. And pray ye earnestly and continually to our bountiful God, that it may please him to give

[1 hodie, Lat.; at this time of day.]
[2 imo quod, Lat.; Yea, and that.]
[3 Ne quid remoretur, Lat.]

to me his holy and effectual power to speak, and to you the opening of your ears and minds, so that in all that I shall say the Lord's name may be praised, and your souls be profited abundantly.

First, I have to declare what the word of God is. *Verb-* *um* in the scriptures, and according to the very property of the Hebrew tongue, is diversely taken. For it signifieth what thing soever a man will; even as among the Germans the word *ding* is most largely used. In St Luke, the angel of God saith to the blessed virgin: "With God shall no word[4] be unpossible;" which is all one as if he had said, all things are possible to God, or to God is nothing unpossible. *Verbum* also signifieth a word uttered by the mouth of man. Sometime it is used for a charge, sometime for a whole sentence, or speech, or prophecy: whereof in the scriptures there are many examples. But when *verbum* is joined with any thing else, as in this place we call it *verbum Dei*, then[5] is it not used in the same signification. For *verbum Dei*, "the word of God," doth signify the virtue and power of God: it is also put for the Son of God, which is the second person in the most reverend Trinity. For that saying of the holy evangelist is evident to all men, "The word was made flesh[6]." But in this treatise of ours, the word of God doth properly signify the speech of God, and the revealing of God's will; first of all uttered in a lively-expressed voice by the mouth of Christ, the prophets and apostles; and after that again registered in writings, which are rightly called "holy and divine scriptures." The word doth shew the mind of him out of whom it cometh: therefore the word of God doth make declaration of God. But God of himself naturally speaketh truth; he is just, good, pure, immortal, eternal: therefore it followeth that the word of God also, which cometh out of the mouth of God, is true, just, without deceit and guile, without error or evil affection, holy, pure, good, immortal, and everlasting. For in the gospel saith the Lord, "Thy word is truth[7]." And the apostle Paul saith, "The word of God is not tied[8]." Again, the scripture everywhere crieth: "The word of the Lord endureth for ever[9]." And

Margin notes:
Verbum, what it is.

In English, a thing.

The word of God, what it is.

---

[4] πᾶν ῥῆμα.—Luke i. 37.   omne verbum, Lat. and Vulg.]
[5] etiam sic, Lat.]
[6] John i. 14.]   [7] John xvii. 17.]
[8] 2 Tim. ii. 9.]   [9] Isai. xl. 8; 1 Pet. i. 25.]

Salomon saith: "Every word of God is purely cleansed. Add thou nothing to his words, lest peradventure he reprove thee, and thou be found a liar[1]." David also saith: "The sayings of the Lord are pure sayings, even as it were silver cleansed in the fire, and seven times fined from the earth[2]."

Of the causes and beginnings of the word of God. This you shall more fully perceive, dearly beloved, if I speak somewhat more largely of the cause or beginning, and certainty, of the word of God. The word of God is truth: but God is the only well-spring of truth: therefore God is the beginning and cause of the word of God. And here indeed God, since he hath not members like to mortal men, wanteth also a bodily mouth: yet nevertheless, because the mouth is the instrument of the voice, to God is a mouth attributed. For he spake to men in the voice of a man, that is, in a voice easily understood of men, and fashioned according to the speech usually spoken among men. This is evidently to be seen in the things wherein he dealt with the holy fathers, with whom, as with our parents Adam and Eva, Noe, and the rest of the fathers, he is read to have talked many and oftentimes. In the mount Sina the Lord himself preached to the great congregation of Israel, rehearsing so plainly, that they might understand those ten commandments, wherein is contained every point of godliness. For in the fifth of Deuteronomy thus we read: "These words," meaning the ten commandments, "spake the Lord with a loud voice, from out of the midst of the fire, to the whole congregation[3]." And in the fourth chapter: "A voice of words you heard, but no similitude did you see beside the voice[4]." God verily used oftentimes the means of angels, by whose ministry he talked with mortal men. And it is very well known to all men, that the Son of God the Father, being incarnate, walked about in the earth; and, being very God and man, taught the people of Israel almost for the space of three years[5]. But in times past, and before that the Son of God was born in the world, God, by little and little, made himself acquainted with the hearts[6] of the holy fathers, and after that with the

[1 Prov. xxx. 5, 6.]　　　　[2 Psalm xii. 6.]
[3 Deut. v. 22.]　　　　[4 Deut. iv. 8.]
[5 The duration of our Lord's ministry is now usually admitted to have been three years and a half.—See Greswell's Harmon. Evang., and Dr Robinson's Harmony of the Gospels.]
[6 insinuavit se Deus animis, Lat.]

minds of the holy prophets; and last of all, by their preaching and writings, he taught the whole world. So also Christ
our Lord sent the Holy Ghost, which is of the Father and
the Son, into the apostles, by whose mouths, words, and
writings he was known to all the world. And all these ser- The word of
God revealed
vants of God, as it were the elect vessels of God, having with to the world
by men.
sincere hearts received the revelation of God from God him-
self, first of all, in a lively expressed voice delivered to the
world the oracles and word of God which they before had
learned; and afterward, when the world drew more to an
end, some of them did put them in writing for a memorial to
the posterity. And it is good to know how, and by whom,
all this was done: for by this narration the true cause,
certainty, and dignity of the word of God doth plainly
appear.

There are not extant to be seen the writings of any man,
from the beginning of the world, until the time of Moses,
which are come to our knowledge; although it be likely that
that same ancient and first world was not altogether without
all writings. For by St Jude, the apostle, and brother of St
James, is cited the written prophecy of our holy father Enoch,
which is read to have been the seventh from our father
Adam[7]. Furthermore, the writing, or history, of Job
seemeth to have been set forth a great while before. But
howsoever it is, all the saints in the church of God give to
Moses, the faithful servant of God, the first place among the
holy writers.

From the beginning therefore of the world, God, by his How and by
whom the
Spirit and the ministry of angels, spake to the holy fathers; word of God
hath been re-
and they by word of mouth taught their children, and chil- vealed from
the begin-
dren's children, and all their posterity, that which they had ning of the
world.
learned at the mouth of God; when they verily had heard it,
not to the intent to keep it close to themselves, but also to
make their posterity partakers of the same. For God oftentimes witnesseth, that "he will be the God of the fathers
and of their seed for evermore[8]." This is most plainly to be
seen in the history of Adam, Noe, and Abraham, the first
and great grandfathers[9]. In the eighteenth of Genesis, verily,
we read, that the angel of God, yea, and that more is, that

[7 Jude, 14, 15.]   [8 Gen. xvii. 7.]
[9 genearcharum, Lat.]

Abraham.   even the Lord himself, did say to Abraham : " And shall I
hide from Abraham what I mind to do? since of Abraham
shall come a great and mighty people, and all the nations of
the earth shall be blessed in him? And this I know, that
he will command his children and his posterity after him, to
keep the way of the Lord, and to do justice, judgment[1]," and
the rest. Abraham therefore, a faithful and zealous worshipper of God, did not (even as also those old fathers of the
first world did not) wax negligent at all herein, but did diligently teach men the will and judgments of God : whereupon
of Moses, yea, and of God himself, he is called a prophet[2].
That devout and lively tradition of the fathers, from hand to
hand, was had in use continually, even from the beginning of
the world until the time of Moses.

  Moreover, God of his goodness did provide that no age at
any time should be without most excellent lights, to be wit-
The clearest   nesses of the undoubted faith, and fathers of great authority.
lights of the
first world.   For the world before the deluge had in it nine most excellent,
most holy, and wise men; Adam, Seth, Enos, Kenam, Malaleel,
Adam and   Jared, Enoch, Methusalem, and Lamech. The chief of these,
Methusalem.
Adam and Methusalem, do begin and make an end of all the
sixteen hundred and fifty-six years[3] of the world before the
deluge. For Adam lived nine hundred and thirty years[4]: he
dieth therefore the seven hundred and twenty-sixth year before
the flood. And Methusalem lived nine hundred and sixty-
nine years[5]: he dieth in the very same year that the flood did
overflow ; and he lived together with Adam two hundred and
forty-three years, so that of Adam he might be abundantly
enough instructed as concerning the beginning of things, as concerning God, the falling and restoring again of mankind, and all
things else belonging to religion, even as he was taught of God
himself. These two fathers, with the rest above named, were
able sufficiently enough to instruct the whole age in the true
salvation and right ways of the Lord.

  After the deluge God gave to the world again excellent
men, and very great lights. The names of them are Noe, Sem,
Arphaxad, Sale, Heber, Palec, Reu, Saruch, Nachor, Thare,

[1 Gen. xviii. 17-19.]   [2 Gen. xx. 7.]
[3 Cf. Bullinger's Treatise, The Old Faith, translated in Coverdale's
writings, &c. Parker Soc. ed. pp. 32, 36.]
[4 Gen. v. 5.]   [5 Gen. v. 27.]

Abraham, Isaac, and Jacob.   Here have we thirteen most excellent patriarchs, among whom the first two, Noe and Sem, are Noe. the chief; next to whom Abraham, Isaac, and Jacob, were more notable than the rest.   Noe lived nine hundred and fifty years in all.   He was six hundred years old when the flood drowned the world[6].   He therefore saw and heard all the holy fathers of the first world before the deluge, three only excepted, Adam, Seth, and Enos.   And also he lived many years together with the other, which had both seen and heard them; so that he could be ignorant in no point of those things which Adam had taught.   Noe dieth (which is marvel to be told, and yet very true) in the forty-ninth year of Abraham's age[7].   Sem, the Sem. son of Noah, lived many years with his father; for he lived in all six hundred years.   He was born to Noah about ninety-six years before the deluge.   He saw and heard, therefore, not only his father Noe and his grandfather Lamech, but also his great grandsire Methusalem, with whom he lived those ninety-six years before the deluge.   Of him he might be informed of all those things which Methusalem had heard and learned of Adam and the other patriarchs.   Sem dieth, after the death of Abraham, in the fifty-second year of Jacob, which was thirty-seven years after the death of Abraham, in the year one hundred and twelve of Isaac's age : so that Jacob, the patriarch, might very well learn all the true divinity of Sem himself, even as he had heard it of Methusalem, who was the third witness and teacher from Adam.   Furthermore, Jacob the patriarch delivered to his children that which he Jacob. received of God[8] to teach to his posterity.   In Mesopotamia there is born to Jacob his son Levi, and to him again is born Kahad[9], which both saw and heard Jacob.   For Kahad lived no small number of years with his grandfather Jacob; for he is rehearsed in the roll of them which went with Jacob down into Egypt[10]: but Jacob lived seventeen years with his children in Egypt.   This Kahad is the grandfather Kahad.
Amram.
Moses.

[6 Gen. vii. 6.]

[7 There is some great miscalculation here; for Abraham, if born at all before Noah's death, could only have been in his infancy.   Yet Calvin also says, that "Abraham was nearly *fifty* years old, when his ancestor Noe died."—Comment. in Gen. cap. ix. 28.   But see note, p. 42.]

[8 a Deo per patres accepit.—Lat.]

[9 Kohath.—Vulg. Caath.]

[10 Gen. xlvi. 11.]

of Moses, the father of Amram, from whom Moses did perfectly draw that full and certain tradition by hand, as concerning the will, commandments, and judgments of God, even as Amram his father had learned them of his father Kahad, Kahad of Jacob, Jacob of Sem, Sem of Methusalem and of Adam the first father of us all: so now that Moses is from Adam the seventh witness in the world. And from the beginning of the world to the birth of Moses are fully complete two thousand three hundred and sixty-eight years of the world. And whosoever shall diligently reckon the years, not in vain set down by Moses in Genesis and Exodus, he shall find this account to be true and right[1].

The chief contents of the holy fathers' lively tradition. Now also it behoveth us to know those chief principles of that lively tradition, delivered by the holy fathers at the appointment of God, as it were from hand to hand, to all the posterity. The fathers taught their children that God, of his natural goodness, wishing well to mankind, would have all men to come to the knowledge of the truth, and to be like in nature to God himself, holy, happy, and absolutely blessed: and therefore that God, in the beginning, did create man to his own similitude and likeness, to the intent that he should be good, holy, immortal, blessed, and partaker of all the good gifts of God; but that man continued not in that dignity and happy state; but by the means of the devil, and his own proper fault, fell into sin, misery, and death, changing his likeness to God into the similitude of the devil. Moreover, that God here again, as it were, of fresh began the work of salvation, whereby mankind, being restored and set free from all evil, might once again be made like unto God; and that he meant to bring this mighty and divine work to pass by a certain middle mean, that is, by the Word incarnate. For as, by this taking of flesh, he joined man to God; so, by dying in the flesh, with sacrifice he cleansed, sanctified, and delivered

---

[1 It is scarcely necessary to observe that the system of chronology here used differs considerably from the received system according to Usher. Bullinger followed the vulgar Jewish chronology, upon which the arrangements of Scaliger, Petavius, and Usher were afterwards founded. See Hales's Chronology, Vol. I. The difference does not materially affect the argument. P.—The line of the patriarchal tradition may be seen traced in Gray's Key to the Old Testament, pp. 80, 81. ed. 1797. Lond.]

mankind; and, by giving him his Holy Spirit, he made him
like again in nature to God, that is, immortal, and absolutely
blessed. And last of all, he worketh in us a willing endeavour
aptly to resemble the property and conditions of him to whose
likeness we are created, so that we may be holy both body
and soul. They added moreover, that the Word should be incarnate in his due time and appointed age; and also, that
there did remain a great day for judgment, wherein, though
all men were gathered together, yet the righteous only should
receive that reward of heavenly immortality.

So then, this is the brief sum of the holy fathers' tradition,
which it is best to untwist more largely, and to speak of it more
diligently, as it were by parts. First, therefore, the fathers
taught, that the Father, the Son, and the Holy Ghost are one God.
God in the most reverend Trinity, the maker and governor of
heaven and earth and all things which are therein; by whom
man was made, and who for man did make all things, and put Creation of
all things under mankind, to minister unto him things neces- the world.
sary, as a loving Father and most bountiful Lord. Then they
taught, that man consisted of soul and body, and that he indeed was made good according to the image and likeness of
God; but that by his own fault, and egging forward of the Sin and
devil, falling into sin, he brought into the world death and death.
damnation, together with a web of miseries, out of which it
cannot rid itself: so that now all the children of Adam, even
from Adam, are born the sons of wrath and wretchedness;
but that God, whose mercy aboundeth, according to his incomprehensible goodness, taking pity on the misery of man- Grace, life,
kind, did, even of his mere grace, grant[2] pardon for the tion by
offence, and did lay the weight of the punishment upon his Christ.
only Son, to the intent that he, when his heel was crushed
by the serpent, might himself break the serpent's head[3]:
that is to say, God doth make a promise of seed, that is, of
a Son, who, taking flesh of a peerless woman, (I mean, that
virgin most worthy of commendations,) should by his death
vanquish death and Satan, the author of death; and should
bring the faithful sons of Adam out of bondage; yea, and
that more is, should by adoption make them the sons of God,
and heirs of life everlasting. The holy fathers, therefore,

[2 promisisse, Lat.]   [3 Gen. iii. 15.]

Faith.

taught to believe in God, and in his Son, the redeemer of the whole world; when in their very sacrifices they did present his death, as it were an unspotted sacrifice, wherewith he meant to wipe away and cleanse the sins of all the world.

The lineal descent of Messias.

And therefore had they a most diligent eye to the stock and lineal descent of the Messias. For it is brought down, as it were by a line, from Adam to Noe, and from Noe by Sem even to Abraham himself: and to him again it was said, "In thy seed shall all the nations of the earth be blessed[1]:" in which words the promise once made to Adam, as touching Christ the redeemer and changer of God's curse into blessing, is renewed and repeated again. The same line is brought down from Abraham by Isaac unto Jacob[2]; and Jacob, being full of the Spirit of God, pointed out his son Juda to be the root[3] of the blessed Seed, as it is to be seen in the forty-ninth of Genesis. Lastly, in the tribe of Juda the house of David was noted, out of which that seed and branch of life should come.

The league of God.

Moreover, the holy fathers taught, that God by a certain league hath joined himself to mankind, and that he hath most straitly bound himself to the faithful, and the faithful likewise to himself again. Whereupon they did teach to be

The worship of God.

faithful to God-ward, to honour God, to hate false gods, to call upon the only God, and to worship him devoutly. Furthermore, they taught, that the worship of God did consist in things spiritual, as faith, hope, charity, obedience, upright dealing, holiness, innocency, patience, truth, judgment, and godliness. And therefore did they reprehend naughtiness and sin, falsehood, lack of belief, desperation, disobedience, unpatientness, lying, hypocrisy, hatred, despiteful taunts, violence, wrong, unrighteous dealing, uncleanness, riotousness, surfeiting, whoredom, unrighteousness, and ungodliness. They taught, that God was a rewarder of good, but a punisher and

Life eternal and the day of judgment.

revenger of evil. They taught, that the souls of men were immortal, and that the bodies should rise again in the day of judgment: therefore they exhorted us all so to live in this temporal life, that we do not leese[4] the life eternal.

This is the sum of the word of God revealed to the fathers, and by them delivered to their posterity. This is

[1 Gen. xxii. 18.]   [2 per Isaacum *et* Jacobum, Lat. P.]
[3 genearcham, Lat.]   [4 leese: lose.]

the tradition of the holy fathers, which comprehendeth all The true historical narration delivered by the fathers to their children. religion. Finally, this is the true, ancient, undoubted, authentical, and catholic [5] faith of the fathers.

Besides this, the holy fathers taught their children, and children's children, the account of the years from the beginning of the world, and also the true historical course, as well profitable as necessary, of things from the creation of the world even unto their own times; lest peradventure their children should be ignorant of the beginning and succession of worldly things, and also of the judgments of God, and examples of them which lived as well godly as ungodly.

I could declare unto you all this evidently, and in very good order, out of the first book of Moses, called Genesis, if it were not that thereby the sermon should be drawn out somewhat longer than the use is. But I suppose that there are few, or rather none at all, here present, which do not perceive that I have rehearsed this that I have said, touching the tradition of the ancient fathers, as it were word for word, out of the book of Genesis; so that now I may very well go forward in the narration which I have begun.

So then, whatsoever hitherto was of the fathers delivered Moses in an history compileth the traditions of the fathers. to the world by word of mouth, and as it were from hand to hand, that was first of all put into writing by the holy man Moses, together with those things which were done in all the time of Moses' life, by the space of one hundred and twenty years. And that his estimation might be the greater throughout all the world, among all men, and in all ages; and that none should but know, that the writings of Moses were the very word of God itself; Moses was furnished, and as it were consecrated by God, with signs and wonders to be marvelled at indeed, which the almighty by the hand, that is, by the ministry of Moses, did bring to pass: and verily, he wrought them not in any corner of the world, or place unknown, but in Egypt, the most flourishing and renowned kingdom of that age.

Those miracles were greater and far more by many, than that they can be here rehearsed in few words: neither is it needful to repeat them, because you, dearly beloved, are not unskilful or ignorant of them at all. After that also, God by

[5] authentica, orthodoxa, et catholica, Lat. P.]

other means procured authority to Moses. For many and oftentimes God had communication with Moses; and amongst the rest of his talk said he: "Behold, I will come to thee in a thick cloud, that the people may hear me talking with thee, and may believe thee for evermore[1]."

Neither was the Lord therewith content, but commanded Moses to call together all the people, six hundred thousand men, I say, with their wives and children. They are called out to the mount Sina, where God appeareth in a wonderful and terrible fashion; and he himself, preaching to the congregation, doth rehearse unto them the ten commandments. But the people, being terrified with the majesty of God, doth pray and beseech, that God himself would no more afterward preach to the congregation with his own mouth, saying, that it were enough, if he would use Moses as an interpreter to them, and by him speak to the church[2]. The most high God did like the offer; and, after that, he spake to the people by Moses whatsoever he would have done. And for because that the people was a stiff-necked people, and by keeping company with idolaters in Egypt was not a little corrupted, Moses now began to set down in writing those things which the holy fathers by tradition had taught, and the things also which the Lord had revealed unto him. The cause why he wrote them was, lest peradventure by oblivion, by continuance of time, and obstinacy of a people so slow to believe, they might either perish, or else be corrupted. The Lord also set Moses an example to follow. For whatsoever God had spoken to the church in mount Sina, the same did he straightway after write with his own finger in two tables of stone, as he had with his finger from the beginning of the world written the same in the hearts of the fathers[3]. Afterward also, in plain words, he commanded Moses to write whatsoever the Lord had revealed. Moses obeyed the Lord's commandment, and wrote them. The Holy Ghost, which was wholly in the mind of Moses, directed his hand as he writ. There was no ability wanting in Moses, that was necessary for a most absolute writer. He was abundantly instructed by his

[1 Exod. xix. 9.]

[2 Exod. xx. 19.]

[3 See Bullinger's treatise, The Old Faith, in Works of Bp. Coverdale, Parker Soc. Ed. pp. 27, 40.]

ancestors: for he was born of the holiest progeny of those fathers, whom God appointed to be witnesses of his will, commandments, and judgments; suppose[4] Amram, Kahad, Jacob, Sem, Methusalem and Adam. He was able, therefore, to write a true and certain history, from the beginning of the world even until his own time. Whereunto he added those things which were done among the people of God in his own life-time, whereof he was a very true witness, as one that saw and heard them. Yea, and that more is, whatsoever he did set forth in his books, that did he read to his people, and amongst so many thousands was there not one found which gainsayed that which he rehearsed: so that the whole consent and witness-bearing of the great congregation did bring no small authority to the writings of Moses.

Moses therefore contained in the five books, called the five books of Moses, an history from the beginning of the world, even unto his own death, by the space of two thousand four hundred and eighty-eight years: in which he declared most largely the revelation of the word of God made unto men, and whatsoever the word of God doth contain and teach: in which, as we have the manifold oracles of God himself, so we have most lightsome[5] testimonies, sentences, examples, and decrees of the most excellent, ancient, holy, wise, and greatest men of the world, touching all things which seem to appertain to true godliness, and the way how to live well and holily. These books therefore found a ready prepared entrance of belief among all the posterity, as books which are authentical, and which of themselves have authority sufficient, and which, without gainsaying, ought to be believed of all the world. Yea, and that more is, our Lord Jesus Christ, the only-begotten Son of God, doth refer the faithful to the reading of Moses; yea, and that indeed in the chiefest points of our salvation: the places are to be seen, John v. Luke xvi. In the fifth of Matthew he saith: "Do not think that I am come to destroy the law and the prophets; for I am not come to destroy them, but to fulfil them. For, verily, I say unto you, though[6] heaven and earth do pass, one jot or tittle of the law shall not pass, till all be fulfilled. Whosoever, therefore, shall undo one of the least of these commandments, and

The authority of Moses very great.

[4 puto autem, Lat.]
[5 clarissimorum, Lat.]
[6 donec prætereat.—Lat. as in Eng. Ver.]

shall teach men so, he shall be called the least in the kingdom of heaven[1]."

There have verily some been found, that have spoken against Moses, the servant of God. But God hath imputed that gainsaying as done against his divine majesty, and punished it most sharply. The proofs hereof are to be seen in Exod. xvi. and Numeri the xii. And first, of the people murmuring against Moses; then of Mary, Moses's sister, speaking against her brother. But to the people it was said: "Not against the ministers, but against the Lord, are your complaints[2]." As for Mary, she was horribly stricken with a leprosy[3]. Theotectus was stricken blind, and Theopompus fell to be mad, because he had unreverently touched the word of God[4]. For, although the word of God be revealed, spoken, and written by men, yet doth it not therefore cease to be that which indeed it is; neither doth it therefore begin to be the word of men, because it is preached and heard of men: no more than the king's commandment, which is proclaimed by the crier, is said to be the commandment of the crier. He despiseth God, and with God all the holy patriarchs, whosoever doth contemn Moses, by whom God speaketh unto us, and at whose hand we have received those things which the patriarchs from the beginning of the world by tradition delivered to the posterity. There is no difference between the word of God, which is taught by the lively expressed voice of man, and that which is written by the pen of man, but so far forth as the lively voice and writing do differ between themselves: the matter undoubtedly, the sense, and meaning, in the one and the other is all one. By this, dearly beloved, you have perceived the certain history of the beginning of the word of God.

[1 Matth. v. 17-19. Quisquis autem fecerit et docuerit, hic magnus vocabitur in regno cœlorum, Lat.; omitted by the translator.]

[2 Exod. xvi. 8.]

[3 Num. xii. 10. Miriam: Vulg. Maria.]

[4 Theotectus tragœdiarum scriptor, Lat. Theodectes, according to Suidas and Gellius x. 18, was a tragedian, and contemporary with Theopompus, who was an orator and historian, a pupil of Isocrates. Josephus, Lib. xii. cap. 2. Antiq. Jud., and Aristeas de LXX. Interp. relate the story referred to;—namely, that each of these writers was preparing to put forth a part of the scriptures, as their own composition, when they were visited, the former with blindness, the latter with madness, which lasted thirty days.—Ger. Vossius. Lib. i. c. 7. P.]

Now let us go forward to the rest; that is, to add the history of the proceeding of the word of God, and by what means it shined ever and anon very clear and brightly unto the world. By and by, after the departure of the holy man Moses out of this world into heaven, the Lord of his bountifulness gave most excellent prophets unto his church, which he had chosen to the intent that by it he might reveal his word unto the whole world. And the prophets were to them of the old time, as at this day amongst us are prophets, priests, wise men, preachers, pastors, bishops, doctors or divines, most skilful in heavenly things, and given by God to guide the people in the faith. And he, whosoever shall read the holy history, will confess that there flourished[5] of this sort no small number, and those not obscure, even till the captivity of Babylon. Amongst whom are reckoned these singular and excellent men, Phinees, Samuel, Helias, Heliseus, Esaias, and Jeremias. David and Salomon were both kings and prophets. In time of the captivity at Babylon, Daniel and Ezechiel were notably known. After the captivity flourished, among the rest, Zacharias the son of Barachias. Here have I reckoned up a few among many : who, although they flourished at sundry times, and that the one a great while after the other, yet did they all, with one consent, acknowledge that God spake to the world by Moses, who (God so appointed it) left to the church in the world a breviary[6] of true divinity, and a most absolute sum of the word of God contained in writing. All these priests, divines, and prophets, in all that they did, had an especial eye to the doctrine of Moses. They did also refer all men, in cases of faith and religion, to the book[7] of Moses. The law of Moses, which is indeed the law of God, and is most properly called *Thora*[8], as it were the guide and rule of faith and life, they did diligently beat into the minds of all men. This did they, according to the time, persons, and place, expound to all men. For all the priests and pro-

The proceeding of the word of God.

The prophets.

The law.

[5 in populo sive ecclesia Dei, Lat. ; in the people, or church, of God, omitted by the translator.]

[6 compendium, Lat.]   [7 libros, Lat.]

[8 תּוֹרָה, a verbo יָרָה, instituere, docere.—Foster, Lex. Heb. P.— תורה, quam Legem vulgo vertimus, Hebræis ab indicando docendoque dicitur.—Bucer. in Psalm. ii. ed. Steph. 1554. p. 16. See also Hooper's Early Writings, p. 88, Parker Soc. Ed.]

phets, before the incarnation of Christ, did by word of mouth teach the men of their time godliness and true religion. Neither did they teach any other thing than that which the fathers had received of God, and which Moses had received of God and the fathers; and straightways after committing it to writing, did set it out to all us which follow, even unto the end of the world: so that now in the prophets we have the doctrine of Moses and tradition of the fathers, and them in all and every point more fully and plainly expounded and polished, being moreover to the places, times, and persons very fitly applied.

The authority of the holy prophets was very great. Furthermore, the doctrine and writings of the prophets have always been of great authority among all wise men throughout the whole world. For it is well perceived by many arguments, that they took not their beginning of the prophets themselves, as chief authors; but were inspired from God out of heaven by the Holy Spirit of God: for it is God, which, dwelling by his Spirit in the minds of the prophets, speaketh to us by their mouths. And for that cause have they a most large testimony at the hands of Christ[1], and his elect apostles. What say ye to this moreover, that God by their ministry hath wrought miracles and wonders to be marvelled at, and those not a few; that at the least by mighty signs we might learn that it is God, by whose inspiration the prophets do teach and write whatsoever they left for us to remember?

Furthermore, so many commonweals and congregations gathered together, and governed by the prophets according to the word of God, do shew most evident testimonies of God's truth in the prophets. Plato, Zeno, Aristotle, and other philosophers of the gentiles, are praised as excellent men. But which of them could ever yet gather a church to live according to their ordinances? And yet our prophets have had the most excellent and renowned commonweals or congregations, yea, and that more is, the most flourishing kingdoms in all the world under their authority. All the wise men in the whole world (I mean those which lived in his time) did reverence[2] Salomon, a king and so great a prophet, and came unto him from the very outmost ends of the world. Daniel also had the preeminence among the wise men at Babylon,

[1 Dei Filio, Lat.; omitted.]
[2 tantum non adorarunt, Lat.; almost worshipped.]

being then the most renowned monarchy in all the world. He
was moreover in great estimation with Darius Medus, the son
of Astyages[3] or Assuerus, and also with Cyrus that most excellent king.   And here it liketh me well to speak somewhat
of that divine foreknowledge in our prophets, and most assured
foreshewing of things which were to come after many years
passed.   And now, to say nothing of others, did not Esaias
most truly foretell those things, which were afterward fulfilled
by the Jews in our Lord Christ?   Not in vain did he seem
to them of old time to be rather an evangelist than a prophet[4]
foretelling things to come.   He did openly tell the name of
king Cyrus one hundred and threescore years, at the least,
before that Cyrus was born[5]. Daniel also was called[6] of them   _Polyhistor._
in the old time by the name of one which knew much[7].   For
he did foretell those things which are and have been done in
all the kingdoms of the world almost, and among the people
of God, from his own time until the time of Christ, and
further until the last day of judgment, so plainly, that he may
seem to have compiled a history of those things which then
were already gone and past. All these things, I say, do very
evidently prove, that the doctrine and writings of the prophets
are the very word of God: with which name and title they
are set forth in sundry places of the scriptures. Verily, Peter
the apostle saith, " The prophecy came not in old time by
the will of man : but holy men of God spake as they were
moved by the Holy Ghost."

And although God did largely, clearly, plainly, and   _The word of_
God revealed
by the Son
of God.

[3 That Astyages, son of Cyaxares the first, is the Ahasuerus, and
Cyaxares the second, Astyages' son, the Darius the Mede, of scripture,
see Prideaux's Connect. Vol. I. pp. 72, 104, 120, ed. McCaul, Lond.
1845.]

[4 Ita ut a quibusdam evangelista quam propheta potius diceretur
(Esaias).—Augustin. de Civ. Dei. Lib. XVIII. cap. 29. Par. 1531. Tom. V.
Deinde etiam hoc adjiciendum, quod non tam propheta, quam evan-
gelista, dicendus sit (Isaias).—Hieron. Præf. in lib. Isai. Ed. Par.
1693-1706. Tom. I. col. 473.   See also Bullinger's treatise, The Old
Faith, ap. Works of Bp. Coverdale, Parker Soc. ed. p. 66.]

[5 Is. xliv. 28 ; xlv. 1.]

[6 recte appellatus est, Lat.]

[7 Quartus vero (Daniel), qui et extremus inter quatuor prophetas,
temporum conscius, et totius mundi philoïstoros, &c.—Hieron. Ep. L.
Secund. ad Paulinum. Ed. Par. 1706. Tom. IV. par. 2. col. 573.]

simply reveal his word to the world by the patriarchs, by
Moses, by the priests and prophets; yet did he, in the last
times of all, by his Son set it forth most clearly, simply,
and abundantly to all the world. For the very and only-
begotten Son of God the Father, as the prophets had foretold,
descending from heaven, doth fulfil all whatsoever they foretold, and by the space almost of three years doth teach all
points of godliness. For saith John: " No man at any time
hath seen God; the only-begotten Son, which is in the bosom
of the Father, he hath declared him[1]." The Lord himself,
moreover, saith to his disciples: "All things which I have
heard of my Father have I made known to you[2]." And
again he saith: "I am the light of the world: whosoever
doth follow me doth not walk in darkness, but shall have the

The chief contents of Christ's doctrine.

light of life[3]." Our Lord also did teach, that to him, which
would enter into heaven and be saved, the heavenly regeneration was needful[4], because in the first birth man is born to
death, in the second to life; but that that regeneration is
made perfect in us by the Spirit of God, which instructeth our
hearts in faith, I say, in faith in Christ, who died for our sins,
and rose again for our justification[5]. He taught that by that
faith they which believe are justified; and that out of the
same faith do grow sundry fruits of charity and innocency, to
the bringing forth whereof he did most earnestly exhort them.
He taught furthermore, that he was the fulfilling, or fulness,
of the law and the prophets; and did also approve and expound the doctrine of Moses and the prophets. To doctrine
he joined divers miracles and benefits, whereby he declared,
that he himself was that light of the world, and the mighty
and bountiful Redeemer of the world. And, to the intent
that his doctrine and benefits might be known to all the world,

The apostles of Christ.

he chose to himself witnesses, whom he called apostles, because
he purposed to send them to preach throughout the world.
Those witnesses were simple men, innocents, just, tellers of
truth, without deceit or subtilties, and in all points holy and
good; whose names it is very profitable often to repeat in
the congregation. The names of the apostles are these:
Peter and Andrew, James and John, Philip and Bartholomew,

[1 John i. 18.]   [2 John xv. 15.]
[3 John viii. 12.]   [4 John iii. 5.]
[5 Rom. iv. 25.]

Thomas and Matthew, James the son of Alphe, and Judas his brother, whose surname was Thaddæus, Simon and Judas Iscariot, into whose room (because he had betrayed the Lord) came St Matthias[6]. These had he, by the space almost of three years, hearers of his heavenly doctrine, and beholders of his divine works. These, after his ascension into the heavens, did he, by the Holy Ghost sent down from heaven, instruct with all kind of faculties. For, as they were in the scriptures passing skilful, so were they not unskilful, or wanting eloquence, in any tongue. And, being once after this manner instructed, they depart out of the city of Jerusalem, and pass through the compass of the earth, preaching to all people and nations that which they had received to preach of the Saviour of the world and the Lord Jesus Christ. And when for certain years they had preached by word of mouth, then did they also set down in writing that which they had preached. For some, verily, writ an history of the words and deeds of Christ, and some of the words and deeds of the apostles. Other some sent sundry epistles to divers nations. In all which, to confirm the truth, they use the scripture of the law and the prophets, even as we read that the Lord oftentimes did. Moreover, to the twelve apostles are joined two great lights of the world; John Baptist, than whom there was never any more holy born of women[7]; and the chosen vessel[8] Paul, the great teacher of the Gentiles[9].

John Baptist and Paul.

Neither is it to be marvelled at, that the forerunner and apostles of Christ had always very great dignity and authority in the church. For, even as they were the embassadors of the eternal King of all ages and of the whole world; so, being endued with the Spirit of God, they did nothing according to the judgment of their own minds. And the Lord by their ministry wrought great miracles, thereby to garnish the ministry of them, and to commend their doctrine unto us. And what may be thought of that, moreover, that by that word of God they did convert the whole world; gathering together, and laying the foundations of, notable churches throughout the compass of the world? Which verily by man's counsel and words they had never been able to have

The authority of the apostles very great.

[6 Matth. x. 2-4; Acts i. 26.]
[7 Matth. xi. 11.]   [8 Acts ix. 15.]
[9 1 Tim. ii. 7; 2 Tim. i. 11.]

brought to pass. To this is further added, that they which once leaned to this doctrine, as a doctrine giving life, did not refuse to die: besides that, how many soever had their belief in the doctrine of the gospel, they were not afraid, through water, fire, and swords, to cut off this life, and to lay hand on the life to come. The faithful saints could in no wise have done these things, unless the doctrine which they believed had been of God.

Although therefore that the apostles were men, yet their doctrine, first of all taught by a lively expressed voice, and after that set down in writing with pen and ink, is the doctrine of God and the very true word of God. For there-

1 Thess. ii.

fore the apostle left this saying in writing: " When ye did receive the word of God which ye heard of us, ye received it not as the word of men, but, as it is indeed, the word of God, which effectually worketh in you that believe[1]."

The roll of the books of the divine scriptures.

But now the matter itself and place require, that I gather also and plainly reckon up those books, wherein is contained the very word of God, first of all declared of the fathers, of Christ himself, and the apostles by word of mouth; and after that also written into books by the prophets and apostles. And in the first place verily are set the five books of Moses. Then follow the books of Josue, of Judges, of Ruth, two books of Samuel, two of Kings, two of Chronicles; of Esdras, Nehemias, and Hester one a-piece. After these come Job, David or the book of Psalms[2], Proverbs, Ecclesiastes, and Cantica. With them are numbered the four greater prophets, Esaias, Jeremias, Ezechiel, and Daniel: then the twelve lesser prophets, whose names are very well known: with these books the old Testament ended. The new Testament hath in the beginning the evangelical history of Christ the Lord, written by four authors, that is, by two apostles, Matthew and John; and by two disciples, Mark and Luke, who compiled a wonderful goodly and profitable book of the Acts of the Apostles. Paul to sundry churches and persons published fourteen epistles. The other apostles wrote seven which are called both canonical and catholic. And the books of the new Testament are ended with the

[1 1 Thess. ii. 13. Sermonem,—quo Deum discebatis, Lat.; and Erasmus' rendering.]

[2 Solomonis libelli tres, Lat.; omitted by the translator.]

Revelation of Jesus Christ, which he opened to the disciple whom he loved, John the evangelist and apostle; shewing unto him, and so to the whole church, the ordinance of God touching the church[3], even until the day of judgment. Therefore in these few and mean[4], not unmeasurable, in these plain and simple, not dark and unkemmed[5] books, is comprehended the full doctrine of godliness, which is the very word of the true, living, and eternal God[6].

Also the books of Moses and the prophets through so many ages, perils, and captivities, came sound and uncorrupted even until the time of Christ and his apostles. For the Lord Jesus and the apostles used those books as true copies and authentical; which undoubtedly they neither would, nor could, have done, if so be that either they had been corrupted, or altogether perished. The books also, which the apostles of Christ have added[7], were throughout all persecutions kept in the church safe and uncorrupted, and are come sound and uncorrupted into our hands, upon whom the ends of the world are fallen. For by the vigilant care and unspeakable goodness of God, our Father, it is brought to pass, that no age at any time either hath or shall want so great a treasure.

The scripture is sound and uncorrupted.

Thus much hitherto have I declared unto you, dearly beloved, what the word of God is, what the beginning of it in the church was, and what proceeding, dignity, and certainty it had. The word of God is the speech of God, that is to say, the revealing of his good will to mankind, which from the beginning, one while by his own mouth, and another while by the speech of angels, he did open to those first, ancient, and most holy fathers; who again by tradition did faithfully deliver it to their posterity. Here are to be remembered those great lights of the world, Adam, Seth, Methusalem,

---

[3 fata ecclesiæ, Lat.]　　　　　　[4 sobriis, Lat.]

[5 unkemmed or unkempt: uncombed; impexis. —Lat. P.]

[6 The canon of Scripture received by the church of Rome, containing most of those books which we call apocryphal, was first set forth by the council of Trent; and afterwards confirmed by the bull of pope Pius IV. A.D. 1564. On this subject see Burnet on the 6th Article, with the notes in Page's Ed. 1839; and Bishop Cosin's "Scholastical History of the Canon of Scripture." P.]

[7 una cum lege et prophetis, Lat.; omitted.]

Noe, Sem, Abraham, Isaac, Jacob, Amram, and his son Moses, who, at God's commandment, did in writing comprehend the history and traditions of the holy fathers, whereunto he joined the written law, and exposition of the law, together with a large and lightsome[1] history of his own lifetime. After Moses, God gave to his church most excellent men, prophets and priests; who also, by word of mouth and writings, did deliver to their posterity that which they had learned of the Lord. After them came the only-begotten Son of God himself down from heaven into the world, and fulfilled all, whatsoever was found to be written of himself in the law and the prophets. The same also taught a most absolute mean how to live well and holily: he made the apostles his witnesses: which witnesses did afterwards first of all with a lively expressed voice preach all things which the Lord had taught them; and then, to the intent that they should not be corrupted, or clean taken out of man's remembrance, they did commit it to writing: so that now we have from the fathers, the prophets, and apostles, the word of God as it was preached and written.

These things had their beginning of one and the same Spirit of God, and do tend to one end, that is, to teach us men how to live well and holily. He that believeth not these men, and namely[2] the only-begotten Son of God, whom, I pray you, will he believe? We have here the most holy, innocent, upright-living, most praiseworthy, most just, most ancient, most wise, and most divine men of the whole world and compass of the earth, and briefly, such men as are by all means without comparison. All the world cannot shew us the like again, although it should wholly a thousand times be assembled in councils. The holy emperor Constantine gathered a general council out of all the compass of the earth; thither came there together, out of all the world, three hundred and eighteen most excellent fathers[3]: but they that are of the wisest sort will say, that these are not so much as shadows, to be compared to them, of whom we have received the word of God. Let us therefore in all things believe the word of God delivered to us by the scriptures.

[1 luculenta, Lat.]
[2 namely: especially; præsertim. P.]
[3 See before, page 12, where the number is inaccurately stated.]

Let us think that the Lord himself, which is the very living and eternal God, doth speak to us by the scriptures. Let us for evermore praise the name and goodness of him, who hath vouchedsafe so faithfully, fully, and plainly to open to us, miserable mortal men, all the means how to live well and holily.

To him be praise, honour, and glory for evermore. Amen.

OF THE WORD OF GOD; TO WHOM, AND TO WHAT END, IT WAS REVEALED; ALSO IN WHAT MANNER IT IS TO BE HEARD; AND THAT IT DOTH FULLY TEACH THE WHOLE DOCTRINE OF GODLINESS.

THE SECOND SERMON.

DEARLY beloved, in the last sermon you learned what the word of God is; from whence it came; by whom it was chiefly revealed; what proceedings[4] it had; and of what dignity and certainty it is.

Now am I come again, and, by God's favour and the help of your prayers, I will declare unto you, beloved, to whom, and to what end, the word of God is revealed; in what manner it is to be heard; and what the force thereof is, or the effect.

Our God is the God of all men and nations, who, accord-ing to the saying of the apostle, "would have all men to be saved, and to come to the knowledge of the truth[5]:" and there-fore hath he, for the benefit, life, and salvation of all men, revealed his word, that so indeed there might be a rule and certain way to lead men by the path of justice into life ever-lasting. God verily, in the old time, did shew himself to the Israelites, his holy and peculiar people, more familiarly than to other nations, as the prophet saith: "To Jacob hath he declared his statutes, and his judgments to Israel: he hath not dealt so with any nation, neither hath he shewed them his judgments[6]:" and yet he hath not altogether been care-

To whom the word of God is revealed.

[4 progressus, Lat.]　　　[5 1 Tim. ii. 4.]
[6 Psal. cxlvii. 19, 20.]

less of the Gentiles.   For as to the Ninivites he sent Jonas;
so Esaias, Jeremias, Daniel, and the other prophets bestowed
much labour in teaching and admonishing the Gentiles.   And
those most ancient fathers, Noe, Abraham, and the rest, did
not only instruct the Jewish people which descended of
them, but taught their other sons also the judgments of God.
Our Lord Jesus Christ verily, laying open the whole world
before his disciples, said: " Teach all nations: preach the
gospel to all creatures[1]."   And when as St Peter did not yet
fully understand, that the Gentiles also did appertain to the
fellowship of the church of Christ, and that to the Gentiles
also did belong the preaching of the glad tidings of salvation,
purchased by Christ for the faithful; the Lord doth instruct
him by a heavenly vision, by speaking to him out of heaven,
and by the message which came from Cornelius, as you know,
dearly beloved, by the history of the Acts of the Apostles[2].
Let us therefore think, my brethren, that the word of God
and the holy scriptures are revealed to all men, to all ages,
kinds[3], degrees and states, throughout the world.   For the
apostle Paul, also confirming the same, saith: " Whatsoever
things are written, are written for our learning, that through
patience, and comfort of the scriptures, we may have hope[4]."

Let none of us therefore hereafter say, " What need I
to care what is written to the Jews in the old Testament, or
what the apostles have written to the Romans, to the Corinthians, and to other nations?   I am a Christian.   The prophets to the men of their time, and the apostles to those that
lived in the same age with them, did both preach and write."
For if we think uprightly of the matter, we shall see that the
scriptures of the old and new Testaments ought therefore to
be received of us, even because we are Christians.   For Christ,
our Saviour and Master, did refer us to the written books of
Moses and the prophets.   Saint Paul, the very elect instrument of Christ, doth apply to us the sacraments and examples
of the old fathers, that is to say, circumcision in baptism,
Coloss. ii.; and the paschal lamb in the supper or sacrament, 1 Cor. v.   In the tenth chapter of the same epistle
he applieth sundry examples of the fathers to us.   And in

[1 Matt. xxviii. 19.   Mark xvi. 15.]
[2 Acts x.]   [3 Sexubus, Lat.]
[4 Rom. xv. 4.]

the fourth to the Romans, where he reasoneth of faith, which
justifieth without the help of works and the law, he bringeth in the example of Abraham; and therewithal addeth:
"Nevertheless it is not written for Abraham alone, that faith
was reckoned unto him for righteousness, but also for us, to
whom it shall be reckoned if we believe[5]," &c.

"By that means," say some, "we shall again be wrapped
in the law; we shall be enforced to be circumcised, to sacrifice flesh and blood of beasts, to admit again the priesthood
of Aaron, together with the temple and the other ceremonies.
There shall again be allowed the bill of divorcement, or putting
away of a man's wife, together with sufferance to marry many
wives." To these I answer: that in the old Testament we
must consider that some things there are which are for ever
to be observed, and some things which are ceremonial and
suffered only till time of amendment[6]. That time of amendment is the time of Christ, who fulfilled the law, and took
away the curse of the law. The same Christ changed circumcision into baptism. He with his own only sacrifice made
an end of all sacrifices; so that now, instead of all sacrifices,
there is left to us that only sacrifice of Christ, wherein also we
learn to offer our own very bodies and prayers, together with
good deeds, as spiritual sacrifices unto God. Christ changed
the priesthood of Aaron for his own and the priesthood of all
Christians. The temple of God are we, in whom God by his
Spirit doth dwell. All ceremonies did Christ make void, who
also in the nineteenth of Matthew did abrogate the bill of
divorcement, together with the marriage of many wives. But
although these ceremonies and some external actions were abrogated and clean taken away by Christ, that we should not
be bound unto them; yet notwithstanding, the scripture,
which was published touching them, was not taken away, or
else[7] made void, by Christ. For there must for ever be in
the church of Christ a certain[8] testimonial, whereby we may
learn what manner of worshippings and figures of Christ they
of the old time had. Those worshippings and figures of Christ
must we at this day interpret to the church specially[9]; and

The writings of the old Testament are also given to Christians.

[5 Rom. iv. 23, 24.]
[6 Heb. ix. 10. tempus correctionis, Lat.   So Vulgate.]
[7 i. e. or; vel, Lat.]   [8 i. e. a sure; certum, Lat.]
[9 spiritually, ed. 1577; spiritualiter, Lat. P.]

out of them we must, no less than out of the writings of the
new Testament, preach Christ, forgiveness of sins, and repentance.   So then, to all Christians are the writings of the
old Testament given by God; in like manner as the apostle[1]
writ to all churches those things which bore the name or title
of some particular congregations.

To what end the word of God is revealed.   And to this end is the word of God revealed to men,
that it may teach them[2] what, and what manner one God[3]
is towards men; that he would have them to be saved; and
that, by faith in Christ: what Christ is, and by what means
salvation cometh : what becometh the true worshippers of
God, what they ought to fly, and what to ensue.   Neither is
it sufficient to know the will of God, unless we do the same
and be saved[4].   And for that cause said Moses : " Hear,
Israel, the statutes and judgments which I teach you, that ye
may do them and live[5]."   And the Lord in the gospel, confirming the same, crieth : " Blessed are they which hear the
word of God and keep it[6]."

God's good-ness to be praised for teaching us.   And here is to be praised the exceeding great goodness
of God, which would have nothing hid from us which maketh
any whit to live rightly, well, and holily.   The wise and
learned of this world do for the most part bear envy or
grudge, that other should attain unto the true wisdom : but
our Lord doth gently, and of his own accord, offer to us the
whole knowledge of heavenly things, and is desirous that we
go forward therein ; yea, and that more is, he doth further
our labour and bring it to an end.   For "whosoever hath,"
saith the Lord himself in the gospel, "to him shall be given,
that he may have the more abundance[7]."   " And every one
that asketh receiveth, and he that seeketh findeth, and to
him that knocketh it shall be opened[8]."   Whereupon St
James the apostle saith : " If any of you lack wisdom, let
him ask of God, which giveth to all men liberally," that is,
willingly, not with grudging, "neither casteth any man in the

[1 apostles, 1577; apostoli, Lat.]
[2 De Deo et voluntate ejus, Lat.   Omitted by the translator:
concerning God and his will.]
[3 What manner one; qualis, Lat.   P.]
[4 ut salvi fiamus, Lat.]   [5 Deut. v. 1.]
[6 Luke xi. 28.]   [7 Matt. xiii. 12.]
[8 Luke xi. 10.]

teeth, and it shall be given him[9]." Where, by the way, we see our duty ; which is, in reading and hearing the word of God, to pray earnestly and zealously that we may come to that end, for the which the word of God was given and revealed unto us.   But as touching that matter, we will say somewhat more, when we come to declare in what manner of sort the word of God ought to be heard.

Now, because I have said that the word of God is revealed, to the intent that it may fully instruct us in the ways of God and our salvation; I will in few words declare unto you, dearly beloved, that in the word of God, delivered to us by the prophets and apostles, is abundantly contained the whole effect of godliness[10], and what things soever are available to the leading of our lives rightly, well, and holily. For, verily, it must needs be, that that doctrine is full, and in all points perfect, to which nothing ought either to be added, or else to be taken away.   But such a doctrine is the doctrine taught in the word of God, as witnesseth Moses, Deut. iv. and xii. and Salomon, Proverb xxx.[11]   What is he, therefore, that doth not confess that all points of true piety are taught us in the sacred scriptures?   Furthermore, no man can deny that to be a most absolute doctrine, by which a man is so fully made perfect, that in this world he may be taken for a just man, and in the world to come be called for ever to the company of God.   But he that believeth the word of God uttered to the world by the prophets and apostles, and liveth thereafter, is called a just man, and heir of life everlasting.   That doctrine therefore is an absolute doctrine.   For Paul also, declaring more largely and fully the same matter, saith : " All scripture, given by inspiration of God, is profitable to doctrine, to reproof, to correction, to instruction which is in righteousness, that the man of God may be perfect, instructed to all good works[12]."

Ye have, brethren, an evident testimony of the fulness of the word of God.   Ye have a doctrine absolutely perfect in all points[13].   Ye have a most perfect effect of the word of God, because by this doctrine the man of God, that is, the

All points of true godliness are taught us in the holy scriptures.

[9 James i. 5.]   [10 pietatis rationem, Lat.]
[11 Deut. iv. 2; xii. 32.   Prov. xxx. 6.]
[12 2 Tim. iii. 16, 17.]
[13 Habetis omnes partes absolutæ doctrinæ, Lat.]

godly and devout worshipper of God, is perfect, being instructed, not to a certain few good works, but unto all and every good work. Wherein therefore canst thou find any want? I do not think that any one is such a sot, as to interpret these words of Paul to be spoken only touching the old Testament; seeing it is more manifest than the day-light, that Paul applied them to his scholar Timothy, who preached the gospel, and was a minister of the new Testament. If so be then, that the doctrine of the old Testament be of itself full; by how much more shall it be the fuller, if the volume of the new Testament be added thereunto! I am not so igno-

The Lord both spake and did many things which are not written. rant, but that I know that the Lord Jesus both did and spake many things which were not written by the apostles. But it followeth not therefore, that the doctrine of the word of God, taught by the apostles, is not absolutely perfect. For John, the apostle and evangelist, doth freely confess that the Lord did many other things also, "which were not written in his book;" but immediately he addeth this, and saith: "But these are written, that ye might believe that Jesus is Christ the Son of God and that in believing ye might have life through his name[1]." He affirmeth by this doctrine, which he contained in writing, that faith is fully taught, and that through faith there is granted by God everlasting life. But the end of absolute doctrine is to be happy and perfectly blessed. Since then that cometh to man by the written doctrine of the gospel; undoubtedly that doctrine of the gospel is most absolutely perfect.

I know, that the Lord in the gospel said, " I have many things to tell you ; but at this time you cannot bear them :" but therewithal I know too, that he immediately added this saying : " But when the Spirit of truth shall come, he shall lead you into all truth[2]." I know furthermore, that the Spirit of truth did come upon his disciples; and therefore I believe, that they, according to the true promise of Christ, were led into all truth, so that it is most assuredly certain, that nothing was wanting in them.

[1 John xx. 30, 31.]

[2 John xvi. 12, 13. For this and the other texts, by which the Romanists maintain patristical and ecclesiastical tradition, see the treatise "Of Unwritten Verities" in Remains of Abp. Cranmer, Parker Soc. ed. chap. IX.]

But some there are, which, when they cannot deny this, The apostles set down in writing the whole doctrine of godliness. do turn themselves and say, that " the apostles indeed knew all things, but yet taught them not but by word of mouth only, not setting down in writing all those things which do appertain to true godliness[3]." As though it were likely that Christ's most faithful apostles would, upon spite, have kept back any thing from their posterity. As though indeed he had lied which said, " These things are written, that in believing ye might have life everlasting." John therefore did let pass nothing which belongeth to our full instructing in the faith. Luke did omit nothing. Neither did the rest of the apostles and disciples of our Lord Jesus Christ suffer any thing to overslip them. Paul also wrote fourteen sundry epistles : but yet the most of them contained one and the selfsame matter. Whereby we may very well conjecture, that in them is wholly comprehended the absolute doctrine of godliness. For he would not have repeated one and the selfsame thing so often, to so many sundry men, if there had yet been any thing else necessary more fully to be taught for the obtaining of salvation. Those things undoubtedly would he have taught, and not have rehearsed one and the same thing so many times. Verily, in the third chapter of his epistle to the Ephesians he doth affirm, that in the two first chapters of the same his epistle he did declare his knowledge in the gospel of Christ. "God," saith he, "by revelation shewed the mystery unto me, as I wrote before in few words ; whereby when ye read ye may understand my knowledge in the mystery of Christ[4]." And this spake he touching that one and only epistle, yea, and that too touching the two first chapters of that one epistle. Whereunto when the most large and lightsome letters or epistles of St Paul himself, and also of the other apostles, are added, who, I pray you, unless he be altogether without sense, will once think, that the apostles have left in writing to us, their posterity, a doctrine not absolutely perfect ?

[3 Ex quibus omnibus... evidens (est)... quod non omnia, quæ ad religionem nostram pertinent, auctore Christo apostolorum ministerio consignata ecclesiæ, ... in scripturis explicata sint.—Albert. Pigh. Controversiarum præcipuarum, &c. Explicatio. Par. 1549. fol. 95. b. Controv. 3. de Ecclesia.]

[4 Ephes. iii. 3, 4.]

As for those which do earnestly affirm, that all points of godliness were taught by the apostles to the posterity by word of mouth, and not by writing, their purpose is to set to sale their own, that is, men's ordinances instead of the word of God.

But against this poison, my brethren, take this unto you for a medicine to expel it. Confer the things, which these fellows set to sale under the colour of the apostles' traditions, taught by word of mouth and not by writing, with the manifest writings of the apostles; and if in any place you shall perceive those traditions to disagree with the scriptures, then gather by and by, that it is the forged invention of men, and not the apostles' tradition. For they, which had one and the same Spirit of truth, left not unto us one thing in writing, and taught another thing by word of mouth. Furthermore, we must diligently search, whether those traditions do set forward the glory of God, rather than of men; or the safety of the faithful, rather than the private advantage of the priests. And we must take heed of men's traditions, especially since the Lord saith, "In vain do they worship me, teaching doctrines the precepts of men[2]." So that now the surest way is, to cleave to the word of the Lord left to us in the scriptures, which teacheth abundantly all things that belong to true godliness.

It remaineth now for me to tell, in what manner of sort this perfect doctrine of godliness and salvation, I mean, the very word of God, ought to be heard of the faithful, to the intent it may be heard with some fruit to profit them abundantly. I will in few words contain[2] it. Let the word of God be heard with great reverence, which of right is due to God himself and godly things. Let it be heard very attentively; with continual prayers between, and earnest requests. Let it be heard soberly to our profit, that by it we may become the better, that God by us may be glorified, and not that we go curiously about to search out the hidden counsels of God, or desire to be counted skilful and expert in many matters. Let true faith, the glory of God, and our salvation be appointed as the measure and certain end of our hearing and reading. For in Exodus Moses, the holy servant

[1 fained, 1577; confictas, Lat.]
[2 comprehendam, Lat.]

of God, is commanded to sanctify the people, and make them in a readiness to hear the sacred sermon, which God himself did mind to make the next day after.   Moses therefore cometh, and demandeth of the whole people due obedience to be shewed, as well to God, as to his ministers.   Then commandeth he them to wash their garments, to abstain from their wives.   After that he appointeth certain limits, beyond which it was not lawful upon pain of death for them to pass[3]. By this we plainly learn, that the Lord doth require such to be his disciples, to hear him, as do specially shew obedience and reverence to him in all things.   For he, being God, speaketh to us men: all we men owe unto God honour and fear.   A man, unless he become lowly, humble, and obedient to God, is altogether godless.   Then is it required at the hands of those, which are meet hearers of the word of God, that they lay apart worldly affairs, which are signified by the garments; to tread under foot all filthiness and uncleanness of soul and body; to refrain for a season even from those pleasures which are lawful unto us.   The Holy Ghost doth love the minds that are purely cleansed; which yet notwithstanding are not cleansed but by the Spirit of God. Needful it is to have a sincere belief in God, and a ready good-will and desire to live according to that which is commanded in the word of God.   Moreover, we must be wise to sobriety[4].   Over curious questions must be set aside.   Let things profitable to salvation only be learned.   Last of all, let especial heed be taken in hearing and learning.   For saith Salomon: "If thou wilt seek after wisdom as after gold, thou shalt obtain it[5]."   Again he saith: "The searcher out of God's majesty shall be overwhelmed by his wonderful glory[6]."   And again he saith: "Seek not things too high for thee, neither go about to search out things above thy strength; but what God hath commanded thee, that think

[3 Exod. xix. 10—15.]

[4 Rom. xii. 3.   Sapere ad sobrietatem: to think soberly, to sobriety, marg. Author. Ver.]

[5 Prov. ii. 4, 5.]

[6 Prov. xxv. 27, according to the Vulgate version, which is: "Qui scrutator est majestatis, opprimetur a gloria."   "He that is a searcher of majesty (viz. of God), shall be overwhelmed by glory."— Douay Version.   Calvin uses the text in the same sense, Instit. Lib. III. cap. 21. §. 2.]

5

[BULLINGER.]

thou always on: and be not over curious to know his infinite works; for it is not expedient for thee to see his hidden secrets with thine eyes[1]." Whereupon the apostle Paul saith: "Let no man think arrogantly of himself, but so think that he may be modest and sober, according as God to every one hath given the measure of faith[2]." And hereto belongeth that which the same apostle saith: "Knowledge puffeth up, and charity doth edify[3]."

The diseases and plagues of the hearers of God's word.

But chiefly we must beware of those plagues, which choke the seed of the word of God, and quench it without any fruit at all in the hearts of the hearers. Those plagues and diseases hath the Lord rehearsed, or reckoned up, in the parable of the sower[4]. For first of all, wanton and vain cogitations, which always lie wide open to the inspirations of Satan and talk of naughty men, are plagues to the word of God. Also voluptuous and dainty lovers of this world, who cannot abide to suffer any affliction for Christ and his gospel, do without any fruit at all hear God's word, although they seem to give ear unto it very joyfully. Furthermore, "the care of this world, and the deceit of riches," are most pestilent diseases in the hearers of the word of God. For they do not only hinder the seed, that it cannot bring forth fruit in their hearts; but also they do stir up and egg men forward to gainsay the word of God, and to afflict the earnest desirers of God's word. Here therefore we must take heed diligently, lest, being infected with these diseases, we become vain and unthankful hearers of the word of God.

We must pray continually, that the bountiful and liberal Lord will vouchsafe to bestow on us his Spirit, that by it the seed of God's word may be quickened in our hearts, and that we, as holy and right hearers of his word, may bear fruit abundantly to the glory of God, and the everlasting

What the power and effect of God's word is.

salvation of our own souls. For what will it avail to hear the word of God without faith, and without the Holy Spirit of God to work or stir inwardly in our hearts? The apostle Paul saith: "He which watereth is nothing, nor he which planteth; but it is God which giveth increase[5]." We have need therefore of God's watering, that the word of God may

[1 Ecclesiast. iii. 21—23.]   [2 Rom. xii. 3.]
[3 1 Cor. viii. 1.]   [4 Matt. xiii. 1—23.]
[5 1 Cor. iii. 7.]

grow to a perfect age, may receive increase, yea, and may come also to the bringing forth of ripe fruit within our minds. The same apostle Paul saith: "To us also is the word of God declared, even as unto our fathers. But it availed them nothing to hear the word, because it was not joined with faith in them that heard it : for they died in the desert." And immediately after he saith: "Let us therefore do our best to enter into that rest, so that no man die in the same example of unbelief[6]." If therefore that the word of God do sound in our ears, and therewithal the Spirit of God do shew forth his power in our hearts, and that we in faith do truly receive the word of God, then hath the word of God a mighty force and wonderful effect in us. For it driveth away the misty darkness of errors, it openeth our eyes, it converteth and enlighteneth our minds, and instructeth us most fully and absolutely in truth and godliness. For the prophet David in his Psalms beareth witness, and saith: "The law of the Lord is perfect, converting the soul ; the testimony of God is true, and giveth wisdom unto the simple ; the commandment of the Lord is pure, and giveth light unto the eyes[7]." Furthermore, the word of God doth feed, strengthen, confirm, and comfort our souls ; it doth regenerate, cleanse, make joyful, and join us to God ; yea, and obtaineth all things for us at God's hands, setting us in a most happy state : insomuch that no goods or treasure of the whole world are to be compared with the word of God.

And thus much do we attribute to the word of God, not without the testimony of God's word. For the Lord by the prophet Amos doth threaten hunger and thirst, "not to eat bread and to drink water, but to hear the word of God[8]." For in the old and new Testaments it is said, "that man doth not live by bread only, but by every word that proceedeth out of the mouth of God[9]." And the apostle Paul saith, that "all things in the scriptures are written for our learning, that by patience and comfort of the scriptures we might have hope[10]." Also Peter saith : "Ye are born anew, not of corruptible seed, but of incorruptible, by the word of God which liveth and lasteth

[6 Heb. iii. 17, and iv. 2, 11.]
[7 Psal. xix. 7, 8.]
[8 Amos viii. 11.]
[9 Deut. viii. 3 ; Matt. iv. 4.]　　　　[10 Rom. xv. 4.]

for ever. And this is the word which by the gospel was preached unto you[1]." The Lord also in the gospel beareth witness to the same, and saith : "Now are ye clean by the word which I have spoken unto you[2]." Again in the gospel he crieth, saying : "If any man loveth me, he will keep my saying, and my Father will love him, and we will come into him, and make our dwelling-place in him[3]." Jeremy saith also : "Thy word became my comfort[4]." And the prophet David saith : "The statutes of the Lord are right, and rejoice the heart[5]." Whereunto add that saying of the Lord's in the gospel : "If ye remain in me, and my words remain in you, ask what ye will, and it shall be done for you[6]." In another place also the prophet crieth, saying : "If ye be willing and will hearken, ye shall eat the good of the land; but if ye will not hear my word, the sword shall devour you[7]." Moreover Moses doth very often and largely reckon up the good things that shall happen to them which obey the word of God ; Leviticus xxvi., Deut. xxviii. Wherefore David durst boldly prefer the word of God before all the pleasures and treasures of this world. "The fear of the Lord is clean, and endureth for ever ; the judgments of the Lord are true, and righteous altogether : more to be desired are they than gold, yea, than much fine gold ; sweeter also than honey, and the dropping honeycombs. For by them thy servant is plainly taught, and in keeping of them there is a great advantage. Therefore is the law of thy mouth more precious unto me than thousands of silver and gold. Unless my delight had been in thy law, I had perished in my misery[8]." To this now doth appertain that parable in the gospel, of him which bought the precious pearl ; and of him also which sold all that he had, and bought the ground wherein he knew that treasure was hid[9]. For that precious pearl, and that treasure, are the gospel or word of God : which, for the excellency of it, is in the scriptures called a light, a fire, a sword, a maul which breaketh

---

[1 1 Pet. i. 23, 25.]   [2 John xv. 3.]
[3 John xiv. 23.]   [4 Jer. xv. 16.]
[5 Psal. xix. 8.]   [6 John xv. 7.]
[7 Isai. i. 19, 20.]
[8 Psal. xix. 9—11, and cxix. 72, 92.]
[9 Matt. xiii. 44—46.]

stones, a buckler[10], and by many other names like unto these.

Dearly beloved, this hour ye have heard our bountiful Lord and God, "who would have all men saved and to come to the knowledge of the truth," how he hath revealed his word to all men throughout the whole world, to the intent, that all men in all places, of what kind[11], age, or degree soever they be, may know the truth, and be instructed in the true salvation; and may learn a perfect way how to live rightly, well, and holily, so that the man of God may be perfect, instructed to all good works. For the Lord in the word of truth hath delivered to his church all that is requisite to true godliness and salvation. Whatsoever things are necessary to be known touching God, the works, judgments, will and commandments of God, touching Christ, our faith in Christ, and the duties of an holy life; all those things, I say, are fully taught in the word of God. Neither needeth the church to crave of any other, or else with men's supplies to patch up that which seemeth to be wanting in the word of the Lord. For the Lord did not only, by the lively expressed voice of the apostles, teach our fathers the whole sum of godliness and salvation; but did provide also, that it, by the means of the same apostles, should be set down in writing. And that doth manifestly appear, that it was done for the posterity's sake, that is, for us and our successors, to the intent that none of us nor ours should be seduced, nor that false traditions should be popped into any of our mouths instead of the truth. We must all therefore beware, we must all watch, and stick fast unto the word of God, which is left to us in the scriptures by the prophets and apostles.

Finally, let our care be wholly bent, with faith and profit to hear whatsoever the Lord declareth unto us: let us cast out and tread under foot whatsoever, by our flesh, the world, or the devil, is objected to be a let to godliness. We know what the diseases and plagues of the seed of God's word, sowed in the hearts of the faithful, are. We know how great the power of God's word is in them which hear it devoutly. Let us therefore beseech our Lord God to pour into our minds

[10 Psal. cxix. 105; Jer. xxiii. 29; Ephes. vi. 17; Psal. xci. 4.]
[11 sexus, Lat.]

his holy Spirit, by whose virtue the seed of God's word may be quickened in our hearts, to the bringing forth of much fruit to the salvation of our souls, and the glory of God our Father. To whom be glory for ever.

OF THE SENSE AND RIGHT EXPOSITION OF THE WORD OF GOD, AND BY WHAT MANNER OF MEANS IT MAY BE EXPOUNDED.

THE THIRD SERMON.

DEARLY beloved brethren, I do understand that, by means of my doctrine of the word of God, there are risen sundry thoughts in the hearts of many men, yea, and that of some there are sown abroad very ungodly speeches. For some there are which do suppose that the scriptures, that is, the very word of God, is of itself so dark, that it cannot be read with any profit at all[1]. And again some other affirm, that the word plainly delivered by God to mankind doth stand in need of no exposition. And therefore say they, that the scriptures ought indeed to be read of all men, but so that every man may lawfully invent and choose to himself such a sense as every one shall be persuaded in himself to be most convenient[2]. These fellows do altogether condemn the order received of the churches, whereby the minister of the church doth expound the scriptures to the congregation. But I, dearly beloved, if, as ye have begun, so ye will go forward, to pray to the Lord, do trust, by the hope that I have in God's goodness, that I am able plainly to declare, that to the godly the scripture is nothing dark at all, and that the Lord's will is altogether to have us understand it: then, that the scriptures

[1 Scripturæ plurimum frequenter obscuritatis habent, et se trahi accommodarique in diversam sententiam et eludi cauta expositione facile permittunt, etiam quantumvis claræ evidentesque appareant: adeo ut, nisi aptentur ad—ecclesiasticam—traditionis communem sententiam—fiant nobis in laqueum, etc.—Albert. Pigh. Controv. Præcip. Explicatio. Par. 1549. fol. 93. Controv. 3. de Ecclesia.]

[2 Hooker's Preface to Eccles. Pol. Vol. I. p. 180. ed. Oxf. 1820.]

ought always to be expounded. Where also I will teach you the manner, and some ready ways, how to interpret the scriptures. The handling of these points shall take away the impediments which drive men from the reading of the word of God, and shall cause the reading and hearing of the word of God to be both wholesome and fruitful.

And first of all, that God's will is to have his word understood of mankind, we may thereby gather especially, because that in speaking to his servants he used a most common kind of speech, wherewithal even the very idiots[3] were acquainted. Neither do we read that the prophets and apostles, the servants of God and interpreters of his high and everlasting wisdom, did use any strange kind of speech: so that in the whole pack of writers none can be found to excel them in a more plain and easy phrase of writing. Their writings are full of common proverbs, similitudes, parables, comparisons, devised narrations, examples, and such other like manner of speeches, than which there is nothing that doth more move and plainly teach the common sorts of wits among mortal men. There ariseth, I confess, some darkness in the scriptures, by reason of the natural property[4], figurative ornaments, and the unacquainted use of the tongues. But that difficulty may easily be helped by study, diligence, faith, and the means of skilful interpreters. I know that the apostle Peter saith, in the epistles of Paul "many things are hard to be understood[5]:" but immediately he addeth, "which the unlearned, and those that are unperfect, or unstable, pervert, as they do the other scriptures also, unto their own destruction." Whereby we gather, that the scripture is difficult or obscure to the unlearned, unskilful, unexercised, and malicious or corrupted wills, and not to the zealous and godly readers or hearers thereof. Therefore, when St Paul saith, "If as yet our gospel be hid, from them it is hid which perish, in whom the prince of this world hath blinded the understanding of the unbelievers, that to them there should not shine the light of the gospel of the glory of Christ, who is the image of God[6];"

God's will is to have his word understood.

Difficulty in the scriptures.

---

[3] Idiot: an uneducated person, ἰδιώτης. P.]

[4] ex idiomate, Lat.]

[5] 2 Pet. iii. 16.]

[6] 2 Cor. iv. 3, 4. "Lest the light of the gospel of the glory of Christ."—Cranmer's Bible, 1539.]

he doth not lay the blame of this difficulty on the word of God, but upon the unprofitable hearers. Whosoever we are, therefore, that do desire rightly to understand the word of God, our care must be that Satan possess not our minds, and close up our eyes. For our Saviour also in the gospel said : " This is damnation, because the light came into the world, and men loved darkness rather than light[1]." Besides that, the holy prophets of God, and the apostles, did not call the word of God, or the scriptures, darkness, obscureness, or mistiness, but a certain brightness and lightsomeness. David saith : "Thy word is a lantern unto my feet, and a light unto my paths[2]." And what, I pray you, is more evident, than that, in making doubtful and obscure things manifest, no man doth refer to darkness and uncertainties? Things uncertain, doubtful, and obscure, are made manifest by those things that are more certain, sure, and evident. But, as often as any question or controversy doth happen in matters of faith, do not all men agree, that it ought to be ended and determined by the scriptures? It must therefore needs be, that the scriptures are evident, plain, and most assuredly certain.

The word of God requireth an exposition.

But, though the scripture be manifest and the word of God be evident, yet, notwithstanding, it refuseth not a godly or holy exposition; but rather an holy exposition doth give a setting out to the word of God, and bringeth forth much fruit in the godly hearer. And for because many do deny that the scriptures ought to have any exposition, I will shew by examples (which cannot be gainsaid) that they ought altogether to be expounded. For God himself, having often communication with Moses by the space of forty days, and as many years, did by Moses expound to the church the words of the law, which he spake in Mount Sina to the whole congregation of Israel, writing them in two tables : which Moses left to us the Deuteronomy, and certain other books, as commentaries upon God's commandments. After that, immediately followed the prophets, who, interpreting the law of Moses, did apply it to the times, places, and men of their age; and left to us, that follow, their sermons as plain expositions of

A solemn exposition of God's word.

God's law. In the eighth chapter of Nehemias we read these words : " Esdras the priest brought in the law, the book of Moses, and stood upon a turret made of wood, (that is, in the

[1 John iii. 19.]   [2 Ps. cxix. 105.]

holy pulpit.) And Esdras opened the book before the congregation of men and women, and whosoever else had any understanding. And the Levites stood with him, so that he read out of the book, and the Levites instructed the people in the law, and the people stood in their place, and they read in the book of the law distinctly, expounding the sense, and causing them to understand the reading[3]." Thus much in the book of Nehemias. Mark here by the way, my brethren, that the lawful and holy ministers of the church of God did not only read the word of God, but did also expound it.

This manner of reading and expounding the scriptures, or word of God, our Lord Jesus Christ did neither abrogate nor contemn, when, coming in the flesh, he did as a true prophet and heavenly master[4] instruct the people of his church in the doctrine of the new Testament. For entering into the synagogue at Nazareth, he stood up to read; and there was delivered to him the book of the prophet Esay. So he opened the book, and read a certain notable place out of the sixty-first chapter. Then, shutting the book, he gave it to the minister again, and expounded that which he had read, declaring how that in himself now that prophecy was fulfilled[5]. Moreover, after that he was risen from death, he joined himself in company to the two disciples, which went to Emaus; with whom he talked of sundry matters: but at length, "beginning at Moses and all the prophets, he expounded to them whatsoever was written of himself throughout all the scriptures[6]." The apostles, following this example of the Lord, did themselves also expound the word of God. For Peter, in the second chapter of the Acts of the Apostles, doth expound the sixteenth Psalm of Christ's resurrection from the dead[7]. And Philip also doth plainly expound to the nobleman of Ethiope the prophecy of Esay, whereby he bringeth him to the faith of Christ and fellowship of the church[8]. Whosoever doth say, that Paul doth not every where interpret the holy scripture, he hath neither read nor

[3 Nehem. viii. 2—8.]

[4 Adeoque novi Testamenti aut christianæ ecclesiæ doctor:—Lat. omitted by the translator: and so a teacher of the new Testament, or of the christian church.]

[5 Luke iv. 16—21.]   [6 Luke xxiv. 15—27.]

[7 Acts ii. 25—31.]   [8 Acts viii. 30—38.]

seen the deeds nor writings of Paul. Thus have I, I hope, both plainly and substantially shewed, that the word of God ought to be expounded.

What their meaning is that will not have the scriptures expounded. And for those which cry out against the exposition of the scriptures, and would not have the ministers of the word and churches to declare the scriptures in open and solemn audience, neither to apply them to the places, times, states, and persons, their fetch[1] is to seek somewhat else than the honour due unto God. They lead their lives far otherwise than is comely for godly men. Their talk is wicked, unseemly, and dishonest. Their deeds are mischievous and heinous offences. And this would they do without punishment, and therefore desire to have the exposition of the scriptures to be taken clean away. For if a man do read the words of the scripture only, not applying it to the states, places, times, and persons, it seemeth that he hath not greatly touched their ungodly and wicked life. Therefore, when they cry that sermons and expositions of the scriptures ought to be taken away from among men, and that the scriptures ought to be read simply without any addition; they mind nothing else but to cast behind them the law of God, to tread under foot all discipline and rebuking of sin, and so to offend freely without punishment: which sort of men the righteous Lord will in his appointed time punish so much the more grievously, as they do more boldly rebel against their God.

The scriptures are not to be corrupted with foreign expositions. In the mean season, all the ministers of the church must beware, that they follow not herein their own affections any whit at all, or else corrupt the scriptures by their wrong interpretations; and so by that means set forth to the church their own inventions, and not the word of God. Some such like offence it seemeth that the teachers of the ancient people in old time did commit, because the Lord in Ezechiel accuseth them, saying: "Seemeth it a small thing to you to have eaten up the good pasture, but that ye must also tread the residue of your pasture under your feet? and to drink the clearer water, but that ye must trouble the rest with your feet? Thus my sheep must be fain to eat the thing that is trodden down with your feet, and to drink that which ye with your feet have defiled[2]." A sore offence is this, which the Lord according to his justice punisheth most sharply. We

[1 quærunt, Lat.]   [2 Ezek. xxxiv. 18, 19.]

therefore, the interpreters of God's holy word, and faithful ministers of the church of Christ, must have a diligent regard to keep the scriptures sound and perfect, and to teach the people of Christ the word of God sincerely; made plain, I mean, and not corrupted or darkened by foolish and wrong expositions of our own invention.

And now, dearly beloved, the place and time require us to say somewhat unto you touching the interpretation of the holy scriptures, or the exposition of the word of God. Wherein I will not speak any thing particularly of the skilful knowledge of tongues, or the liberal sciences, which are things requisite in a good interpreter; but will briefly touch the generalities alone. And first of all ye must understand, that some things in the scriptures, or word of God, are so plainly set forth, that they have need of no interpretation, neither will admit any exposition: which if any man go about with his own expositions to make more manifest, he may seem to do as wittily as he, which with fagot-light and torches would help the sun at his rising to give more light unto the world. As for those things which are so set down, that they seem to require our help to expound them, they must not be interpreted after our own fantasies, but according to the mind and meaning of him, by whom the scriptures were revealed. For St Peter saith: "The prophecy came not in old time by the will of man; but holy men of God spake as they were moved by the Holy Ghost[3]." Therefore the true and proper sense of God's word must be taken out of the scriptures themselves, and not be forcibly thrust upon the scriptures, as we ourselves lust. And therewithal ye must mark a few certain rules, which I mean briefly to touch and to shew unto you, in those few words which I have yet to speak.

The holy scriptures are not to be expounded according to men's fantasies.

First, since the apostle Paul would have the exposition of the scriptures to agree fitly, and in every point proportionally with our faith; as it is to be seen in the twelfth to the Romans[4]: and because again in the latter epistle to the Corinthians he saith, "Seeing then that we have the same spirit of faith (according as it is written, I believed, and there-

The exposition of the scripture must not be contrary to the articles of our belief.

[3 2 Pet. i. 20, 21. The translator has here omitted, "omnis scriptura prophetica non est privatæ interpretationis." "No prophecy of scripture is of any private interpretation." P.]

[4 Rom. xii. 6. Respondere proportioni fidei, Lat.]

fore have I spoken), we also believe, and therefore do we speak[1]:" let it therefore be taken for a point of catholic religion, not to bring in or admit any thing in our expositions which others have alleged against the received articles of our faith, contained in the Apostles' Creed and other confessions of the ancient fathers.   For saith the apostle: "In defence of the truth we can say somewhat, but against the truth we are able to say nothing[2]."   When therefore in the gospel after St John we read the saying of the Lord, "The Father is greater than I[3]," we must think, that it is against the articles of our faith to make or admit any inequality in the Godhead betwixt the Father and the Son; and therefore, that the Lord's meaning was otherwise than the very words at the first blush do seem to import.   Again, when we read this saying of the apostle, "It cannot be that they which were once illuminated, if they fall away, should be renewed again into repentance[4];" let us not believe that repentance is to be denied to them that fall: for the catholic faith is this, that in every place, at every season, so long as we live on this earth, a full pardon of all sins is promised to all men which turn to the Lord.   In like manner, when we read that the Lord took bread, and said of the bread, "This is my body[5];" let us presently remember, that the articles of our faith do attribute to our Lord the very body of a man, which ascended into heaven, and sitteth at the right hand of the Father, from whence it shall come to judge the quick and the dead; and let us think, that the Lord, speaking of the sacrament, would have us to expound the words of the sacrament sacramentally, and not transubstantially.   Also in reading that saying of the apostle, "Flesh and blood cannot inherit the kingdom of God[6];" let us not by and by upon these words take it simply as the words do seem to signify, but sticking to the article of our faith, "I believe the resurrection of the body[7]," let us understand, that by flesh and blood are meant the affections and infirmities, not the nature and substance, of our bodies.

The exposition must not be repugnant to the love of God and our neighbour.

Furthermore, we read in the gospel, that the Lord doth gather a sum of the law and the prophets, saying: "Thou

[1 2 Cor. iv. 13.]   [2 2 Cor. xiii. 8.]
[3 John xiv. 28.]   [4 Heb. vi. 4—6.]
[5 Matt. xxvi. 26.]   [6 1 Cor. xv. 50.]
[7 hujus carnis, Lat.   Of this body.   See below, page 168.]

shalt love the Lord thy God with all thy heart, with all thy soul, and with all thy mind : this is the chief and great commandment. And the second is like unto it : Thou shalt love thy neighbour as thyself. In these two commandments hangeth the whole law and the prophets[8]." Matt. xxii. Upon these words of the Lord that holy man Aurelius Augustinus, in the thirty-sixth chapter of his first book *De Doctrina Christi*, saith : " Whosoever doth seem to himself to understand the holy scriptures, or any part thereof, so that [with] that understanding he doth not work these two points of charity towards God and his neighbour, he yet doth not understand the scriptures perfectly. But whosoever shall take out of them such an opinion as is profitable to the working of this charity, and yet shall not say the self-same thing which shall be proved that he did mean whom he readeth in that place ; that man doth not err to his own destruction, nor doth altogether by lying deceive other men[9]." Thus much writ Augustine. We must therefore, by all means possible, take heed that our interpretations do not tend to the overthrow of charity, but to the furtherance and commendation of it to all men. The Lord saith : " Strive not with the wicked[10]." But if we affirm that he spake this to the magistrates also, then shall charity towards our neighbours, the safety of them that are in jeopardy, and defence of the oppressed, be broken and clean taken away. For thieves and unruly persons, robbers, and naughty fellows, will oppress the widows, the fatherless, and the poor, so that all iniquity shall reign and have the upper hand. But in a matter so manifestly known I suppose it is not needful to use many examples.

Moreover, it is requisite in expounding the scriptures, and searching out the true sense of God's word, that we mark upon what occasion every thing is spoken, what goeth before, *In expounding the scriptures, we must mark that that*

[8 Matt. xxii. 37—40.]

[9 Quisquis igitur scripturas divinas, vel quamlibet earum partem, intellexisse sibi videtur, ita ut eo intellectu non ædificet istam geminam caritatem Dei et proximi, nondum intellexit. Quisquis vero talem inde sententiam duxerit, ut huic ædificandæ caritati sit utilis, nec tamen hoc dixerit, quod ille, quem legit, eo loco sensisse probatur; non perniciose fallitur, nec omnino mentitur.—Aug. de Doct. Christ. I. 36. Par. 1531. Tom. III. fol. 5. P.]

[10 ne restiteritis malo, Lat. Matt. v. 39.]

goeth before and followeth after, and also the circumstances. what followeth after, at what season, in what order, and of what person any thing is spoken. By the occasion, and the sentences going before and coming after, are examples and parables for the most part expounded. Also, unless a man do always mark the manner of speaking throughout the whole scriptures, and that very diligently too, he cannot choose in his expositions but err very much out of the right way. St Paul, observing the circumstance of the time, did thereby conclude that Abraham was justified, neither by circumcision, nor yet by the law. The places are to be seen in the fourth to the Romans and the third to the Galatians. Again, when it is said to Peter, " Put up thy sword into thy sheath : he that taketh the sword shall perish with the sword[1];" we must consider, that Peter bare the personage of an apostle, and not of a magistrate : for of the magistrate we read, that to him is given the sword to revengement[2].—But it would be over tedious and too troublesome to rehearse more examples of every particular place.

The exposition of God s word must be made by the laying together of divers places. There is also, beside these, another manner of interpreting the word of God; that is, by conferring together the places which are like or unlike, and by expounding the darker by the more evident, and the fewer by the more in number. Whereas therefore the Lord saith, " The Father is greater than I;" we must consider, that the same Lord in another place saith, " My Father and I are all one[3]." And whereas James the apostle saith, that Abraham and we are justified by works[4], there are many places in St Paul to be set against that one. And this manner of interpreting did Peter 2 Pet. i. the apostle allow, where he saith : " We have a right sure word of prophecy, whereunto if ye attend, as unto a light that shineth in a dark place, ye do well, until the day dawn, and the day-star arise in your hearts."

That ancient writer Tertullian affirmeth, that " they are heretics, and not men of the right faith, which draw some odd things out of the scriptures to their own purpose, not having any respect to the rest; but do by that means pick out unto themselves a certain few testimonies, which they would have altogether to be believed, the whole scripture in the mean

---

[1 Matt. xxvi. 52.]   [2 Rom. xiii. 4.]
[3 John xiv. 28, and x. 30.]
[4 James ii. 21, 24.]

season gainsaying it : because indeed the fewer places must be understood according to the meaning of the more in number[5]."

And finally, the most effectual rule of all, whereby to expound the word of God, is an heart that loveth God and his glory, not puffed up with pride, not desirous of vain-glory, not corrupted with heresies and evil affections; but which doth continually pray to God for his holy Spirit, that, as by it the scripture was revealed and inspired, so also by the same Spirit it may be expounded to the glory of God and safeguard of the faithful. Let the mind of the inter-preter be set on fire with zeal to advance virtue, and with hatred of wickedness, even to the suppressing thereof. Let not the heart of such an expositor call to counsel that subtle sophister the devil, lest peradventure now also he do corrupt the sense of God's word, as heretofore he did in paradise. Let him not abide to hear man's wisdom argue directly against the word of God. This if the good and faithful expositor of God's word shall do, then, although in some points he do not (as the proverb saith) hit the very head of the nail[6] in the darker sense of the scripture; yet notwith-standing that error ought not to be condemned for an heresy in the author, nor judged hurtful unto the hearer. And whosoever shall bring the darker and more proper meaning of the scripture to light, he shall not by and by condemn the unperfect exposition of that other : no more than he which is author of the unperfect exposition shall reject the more proper sense of the better expositor, but by acknow-ledging it shall receive it with thanksgiving.

The scriptures must be expounded with a zealous heart after earnest prayer.

Thus much hitherto have I said touching the sense and exposition of God's word : which, as God revealed it to men, so also he would have them in any case to understand it. Wherefore there is no cause for any man, by reason of a few difficulties, to despair to attain to the true understanding of the scriptures. The scripture doth admit a godly and religious interpretation. The word of God is a rule for all

[5 De scripturis ad sententiam suam excerpent, cetera nolentes intueri . . . . cum oporteat secundum plura intelligi pauciora. Sed proprium hoc est omnium hæreticorum. — Tertull. adv. Praxeam, cap. 20. Opp. ed. Semler. Tom. II. p. 183. Hal. Mag. 1828.]

[6 The proverb which Bullinger has adopted is "acu rem tetigisti."]

men and ages to lead their lives by : therefore ought it by interpretation to be applied to all ages and men of all sorts. For even our God himself did by Moses in many words expound and apply to his people the law, which he gave and published in Mount Sina. Furthermore, it was a solemn use among the ancient prophets first to read, and then by expositions to apply, God's law to the people. Our Lord Jesus Christ himself expounded the scriptures. The same did the apostles also. The word of God therefore ought to be expounded. As for those which would not have it expounded, their meaning is, because they would sin freely, without controlling or punishment. But whereas the scripture doth admit an exposition, it doth not yet admit any exposition whatsoever : for that which savoureth of man's imagination it utterly rejecteth. For as by the Spirit of God the scripture was revealed, so by the same Spirit it is requisite to expound it. There are therefore certain rules to expound the word of God religiously by the very word of God itself : that is, so to expound it, that the exposition disagree not with the articles of our faith, nor be contrary to charity towards God and our neighbour ; but that it be thoroughly surveyed, and grounded upon that which went before and followeth after, by diligent weighing of all the circumstances, and laying together of the places. And chiefly it is requisite, that the heart of the interpreter be godly bent, willing to plant virtue and pluck up vice by the roots, and finally, always ready evermore to pray to the Lord, that he will vouchsafe to illuminate our minds, that God's name may in all things be glorified. For his is the glory, honour, and dominion, for ever and ever. Amen.

OF TRUE FAITH; FROM WHENCE IT COMETH; THAT
IT IS AN ASSURED BELIEF OF THE MIND, WHOSE
ONLY STAY IS UPON GOD AND HIS WORD.

THE FOURTH SERMON.

In my last sermon I declared unto you, how that the
perfect exposition of God's word doth differ nothing from the
rule of true faith and the love of God and our neighbour.
For undoubtedly that sense of scripture is corrupted, which
doth square[1] from faith and the two points of charity. I
have now therefore next to treat of true faith and charity
towards God and our neighbour; to the intent, that no man
may find lack of any thing herein. And first, therefore, by
God's help, and the good means of your prayers, I will speak
of true faith.

This word "faith," or "belief," is diversly used in the common talk of men. For it is taken for any kind of religion or
honour done to God: as we say, the Christian faith, the
Jewish faith, and the Turkish faith. Faith, or belief, also is
taken for a conceived opinion of any thing that is told us: as
when we hear any thing rehearsed unto us out of the Indian
or Ethiopian history, we by and by say that we believe it;
and yet notwithstanding we put no confidence in it, nor hope
to have any commodity thereby at all. This is that faith
wherewith St James saith that the devil believeth and trembleth[2]. Last of all, faith is commonly put for an assured
and undoubted confidence in God and his word. Among the
Hebrews faith taketh her name of truth[3], certainty, and assured
constancy. The Latins call that faith, when that is done[4]
which is said. Whereupon one saith, "I demand of thee
whether thou believest or no?" Thou answerest: "I believe." The definitions of
"Do then that which thou sayest, and it is faith." Therefore, faith.

[1 cum fide pugnat.]   [2 James ii. 19.]

[3 אֱמוּנָה faithfulness, from אָמַן to prop, stay, support, to be firm.
אֹמֶן faithfulness, truth. See the Lexicons.]

[4 Fides, quod fiat, quod dicitur, Lat. "Credamus, quia fiat
quod dictum est, appellatam fidem."—Cic. de Off. I. 7.]

in this treatise of ours, Faith is an undoubted belief, most firmly grounded in the mind.

This faith, which is a settled and undoubted persuasion or belief leaning upon God and his word, is diversly defined by the perfecter divines. St Paul saith: "Faith is the substance of things hoped for, the evidence of things not seen[1]." The substance, or *hypostasis*[2], is the foundation, or the unmoveable prop, which upholdeth us, and whereon we lean and lie without peril or danger. The things hoped for are things celestial, eternal, and invisible. And therefore Paul saith: Faith is an unmoveable foundation, and a most assured confidence of God's promises, that is, of life everlasting and all his good benefits. Moreover Paul himself, making an exposition of that which he had spoken, immediately after saith: "Faith is the argument of things not seen." An argument or proof is an evident demonstration, whereby we manifestly prove that which otherwise should be doubtful, so that in him, whom we undertook to instruct, there may remain no doubt at all.

But now, touching the mysteries of God revealed in God's word, in themselves, or in their own nature, they cannot be seen with bodily eyes; and therefore are called things not seen. But this faith, by giving light to the mind, doth in heart perceive them, even as they are set forth in the word of God. Faith, therefore, according to the definition of Paul, is in the mind a most evident seeing[3], and in the heart a most certain perceiving[4] of things invisible, that is, of things eternal; of God, I say, and all those things which he in his word setteth forth unto us concerning spiritual things.

To this definition of Paul's they had an eye which defined faith in this sort: "Faith is a grounded persuasion of heavenly things, in the meditation whereof we ought so to occupy ourselves for the assured truth's sake of God's word, that we may believe, that in mind we do see those things as well, as with our eyes we do behold things sensibly perceived

[1 Heb. xi. 1.]

[2 ὑπόστασις, proprie, *fundamentum, fulcrum,* &c. Schleusner Lex. in voc. In this exposition of Heb. xi. 1, Bullinger and Calvin agree, in several parts, word for word. See Calv. Instit. Lib. III. cap. 2. §. 41.]

[3 saying, ed. 1587, Lat. evidentissima mentis *visio.*]

[4 Comprehensio, Lat.]

and easy to be seen[5]." This description doth not greatly differ from this definition of another godly and learned man, who saith: "Faith is a stedfast persuasion of the mind, whereby we do fully decree with ourselves that God's truth is so sure, that he can neither will, nor choose, but perform that which he in his word hath promised to fulfil[6]." Again: "Faith is a stedfast assuredness of conscience, which doth embrace Christ in the same sort wherein he is offered unto us by the gospel[7]." Another there is which after the same manner almost defineth faith in this sort: "Faith is a gift inspired by God into the mind of man, whereby, without any doubting at all, he doth believe that to be most true whatsoever God hath either taught or promised in the books of both the testaments[8]." The very same author of this definition, therefore, doth extend faith to three terms of time: to the time past, the time present, and the time to come. For he teacheth to believe that the world was made by God, and whatsoever the holy scriptures do declare to have been done in the old world; also that Christ dying for us is the only salvation of them which believe: and that

[5 The editor has not succeeded in tracing this definition to its source. The original Latin gives the definition thus: Fides est rerum divinarum persuasio, quarum cogitationi ita incumbere debemus, propter oraculorum fidem, ut non minus ea cernere animo credamus, quam oculis res sensu perceptas et aspectabiles cernimus.]

[6 This definition is thus given in the original Latin: Fides est firma animi persuasio, qua nobiscum statuimus tam certam esse Dei veritatem, ut non possit non præstare quod se facturum sancto suo verbo recipit.—The editor has not been able to discover these exact words in Calvin's writings; but similar definitions are found in his Institutes, Lib. III. cap. 2. § 42, and Vera Eccles. Reform. Ratio. Tom. VIII. p. 275, ed. Amstel.]

[7 Fides, inquam, firma est conscientiæ certitudo, quæ Christum amplectitur, qualis nobis per evangelium offertur.—Calvin. Vera Eccles. Reform. Ratio. Opp. Tom. VIII. p. 275. a.]

[8 A definition of Faith, almost the same as this, is found in Gropper's Enchiridion, attached to the edition of 1538 of the Canons of a synod of the province of Cologne, and is as follows: Fides est donum menti hominis divinitus infusum, quo citra ullam hæsitantiam credit esse verissima, quæcunque divina eloquia docuerunt.—In Symbol. Apost. fol. 49. Colon. In a later work, also, Gropper says: Fides est præteritorum, præsentium, et futurorum.—Instit. Cathol. p. 232, Colon. 1554.]

by the same God, at this day also, the world and church are governed or preserved, and that in Christ the faithful are saved: last of all, that that shall most assuredly light upon the ungodly and the godly, whatsoever the holy scriptures do either threaten or promise.

The description of true faith.

Out of all these definitions, therefore, being diligently considered, we may, according to the scriptures, make this description of faith: Faith is a gift of God, poured into man from heaven, whereby he is taught with an undoubted persuasion wholly to lean to God and his word; in which word God doth freely promise life and all good things in Christ, and wherein all truth necessary to be believed is plainly declared. Which description of faith I will, by God's help, in this that followeth unfold into parts, and by assertion of places out of the scriptures will both confirm and make manifest unto you. Ye, as hitherto ye have done, so still give diligent ear, and in your hearts pray earnestly to God.

The beginning and cause of faith.

First of all, the cause or beginning of faith cometh not of any man, or any strength of man, but of God himself, who by his Holy Spirit inspireth faith into our hearts. For in the gospel the Lord saith: "No man cometh to me unless my Father draw him[1]." And again: "Flesh and blood," saith the Lord to Peter, confessing Christ in true faith, "hath not revealed this to thee, but my Father which is in heaven[2]." Whereunto the apostle Paul alludeth when he saith: "We are not able of ourselves to think anything as of ourselves, but all our ability is of God[3]." And in another place: "To you it is given for Christ, not only to believe in him, but also to suffer for his sake[4]." Faith therefore is poured into our hearts by God, who is the well-spring and cause of all goodness.

Faith is planted by the word of God.

And yet we have to consider here, that God, in giving and inspiring faith, doth not use his absolute power, or miracles, in working; but a certain ordinary means agreeable to man's capacity: although he can indeed give faith without those means, to whom, when, and how it pleaseth him. But we read, that the Lord hath used this ordinary means even from the first creation of all things. Whom he meaneth to bestow knowledge and faith on, to them he sendeth teachers,

[1 John vi. 44.]   [2 Matt. xvi. 17.]
[3 2 Cor. iii. 5.]   [4 Phil. i. 29.]

by the word of God to preach true faith unto them. Not
because it lieth in man's power, will, or ministry, to give faith;
nor because the outward word spoken by man's mouth is able
of itself to bring faith : but the voice of man, and the preaching of God's word, do teach us what true faith is, or what
God doth will and command us to believe. For God himself
alone, by sending his Holy Spirit into the hearts and minds of
men, doth open our hearts, persuade our minds, and cause us
with all our heart to believe that which we by his word and
teaching have learned to believe. The Lord could by miracle
from heaven, without any preaching at all, have bestowed
faith in Christ upon Cornelius the Centurion at Cesaria[5] : but
yet by an angel he doth send him to the preaching of Peter ;
and while Peter preacheth, God by his Holy Spirit worketh
in the heart of Cornelius, causing him to believe his preaching.   Verily St Paul saith : " How shall they believe in him
of whom they have not heard ?   How shall they hear without a preacher ?   And how shall they preach if they be not
sent ?   So then, faith cometh by hearing, and hearing by
the word of God[6]."   In another place also, " Who is Paul,"
saith he, " or what is Apollos, but ministers, by whom ye
have believed, according as God hath given to every one ?
I have planted, Apollos watered, but God hath given increase.
So then he that planteth is nothing, nor he that watereth,
but God that giveth increase[7]." With this doctrine of St Peter
and St Paul doth that agree which Augustine writeth in the
preface of his book of Christian Doctrine, where he saith :
" That which we have to learn at man's hand, let every one
learn at man's hand without disdain.   And let us not go
about to tempt him in whom we believe ; neither, being deceived, let us think scorn to go to church, to hear or learn
out of books, looking still when we shall be rapt up into the
third heaven.   Let us take heed of such like temptations of
pride, and let us rather have this in our minds, that even the
apostle Paul himself, although he were cast prostrate, and instructed by the calling of God from heaven, was nevertheless
sent to a man to be taught the will of God : and that Corne-

[5 Apud Cæsaream Stratonis, Lat.   Strato's Tower was the
earlier name of Cæsarea Palæstina.—Relandi Palæstin. Illustr. Lib. III.
in voc. Cæsarea.]

[6 Rom. x. 14, 15, 17.]   [7 1 Cor. iii. 5—7.]

lius, although God had heard his prayers, was committed to Peter to be instructed; by whom he should not only receive the sacraments, but should also hear what he ought to believe, what to hope for, and what to love: all which things not-withstanding might have been done by the angel," &c.[1] The same Augustine also, in his Epistle to the Circenses, saith: "Even he worketh conversion and bringeth it to pass, who by his ministers doth warn us outwardly with the signs of things, but inwardly doth by himself teach us with the very things themselves[2]." Also in his treatise, the xxvi. upon John: "What do men" (saith he) "when they preach outwardly? What do I now while I speak? I drive into your ears a noise of words: but unless he which is within do reveal it, what say I, or what speak I? He that is without doth husband the tree, but he within is the creator of it[3]," &c. This said he.

We must pray for true faith.

But, even as the Lord his desire is, to have us believe his

[1 Quod per hominem discendum est, sine superbia discat; et per quem docetur alius, sine invidia tradat quod accepit. Neque tentemus eum cui credidimus, ne talibus inimici versutiis et perversitate decepti, ad ipsum quoque evangelium audiendum atque discendum nolimus ire in ecclesias, aut codicem legere, aut legentem prædicantemque hominem audire, et exspectemus rapi usque in tertium cœlum, sive in corpore, sive extra corpus, sicut dicit Apostolus, et ibi audire ineffabilia verba, quæ non licet homini loqui, aut ibi videre Dominum Jesum Christum, et ab illo potius quam ab hominibus audire evangelium. Caveamus tales tentationes superbissimas et periculosissimas, magisque cogitemus et ipsum Apostolum Paulum, licet divina et cœlesti voce prostratum et instructum, ad hominem tamen missum esse ut sacramenta perciperet atque copularetur ecclesiæ; et centurionem Cornelium, quamvis exauditas orationes ejus eleemosynasque respectas ei angelus nunciaverit, Petro tamen traditum imbuendum, per quem non solum sacramenta perciperet, sed etiam quid credendum, quid sperandum, quid diligendum esse audiret. Et poterant utique omnia per angelum fieri.—August. ex Præf. in Lib. de Doctr. Christiana. Par. 1531. Tom. III. fol. 2.]

[2 Hoc agit ille et efficit, qui per ministros suos rerum signis extrinsecus admonet, rebus autem ipsis per seipsum intrinsecus docet.—Ad Circenses. Ep. cxxx. Tom. II. fol. 124.]

[3 Quid faciunt homines forinsecus annunciantes? Quid facio modo ego, cum loquor? Strepitum verborum ingero auribus vestris. Nisi ergo revelet ille qui intus est, quid dico, aut quid loquor? Exterior cultor arboris: interior est creator.—In Joh. cap. vi. Tract. 26. Tom. IX. fol. 47.]

word, (for the prophet crieth out and saith, "To-day if ye will hear his voice, harden not your hearts;[4]") so in like manner he doth require of us all, which hear his word, that we be not slack in praying. For, in hearing the word of God, we must pray for the gift of faith, that the Lord may open our hearts, convert our souls, break and beat down the hardness of our minds, and increase the measure of faith bestowed upon us. Of this order of prayer there are many examples in the holy scriptures. When the Lord in the gospel said to one, " Canst thou believe ? to him that believeth all things are possible;" he made answer, saying, " I believe, Lord, help thou mine unbelief[5]." The apostles also cry to the Lord, and say: "O Lord, increase our faith[6]." Moreover, this prayer, wherein we desire to have faith poured into us, is of the grace and gift of God, and not of our own righteousness, which before God is none at all. This therefore is left unto us for a thing most certain and undoubtedly true, that true faith is the mere gift of God, which is by the Holy Ghost from heaven bestowed upon our minds, and is declared unto us in the word of truth by teachers sent of God, and is obtained by earnest prayers which cannot be tired. Whereby we learn, that we ought often and attentively to hear the word of God, and never cease to pray to God for the obtaining of true faith.

But that this faith, inspired from heaven, and learned out of the word of truth, doth put into man's mind an undoubted persuasion ; that is, that whatsoever we believe in the word of God, we do believe it most assuredly, without wavering or doubting, being altogether as sure to have the thing, as faith doth believe to have it (for I use this word persuasion, not as it is commonly taken, but for a firm assent of mind, inspired and persuaded by the Holy Ghost;) that this faith, I say, doth put into man's mind this undoubted persuasion, I mean to declare by the example of Abraham's faith, which Paul in the fourth chapter to the Romans describeth in these words: "Abraham, contrary to hope, believed in hope : and he fainted not in faith, neither considered he his own body now dead, when he was almost an hundred years old, nor the deadness of Sarae's womb ; he stackered[7] not at the promise of God

That faith is an undoubted persuasion of the mind.

[4 Psal. xcv. 7, 8.]   [5 Mark ix. 23, 24.]   [6 Luke xvii. 5.]
[7 So in Tyndale's and Cranmer's Versions.]

through unbelief, but became strong in faith, and gave the glory to God, having a sure persuasion, that he, which had promised, was able also to perform[1]."

In these words of the apostle there are certain notes to be observed, which do prove to us that faith doth bring an assured persuasion into the mind and heart of man; and so, that faith is an undoubted confidence of things believed, whereto the heart is made privy; that is, that true faith doth not fly to and fro from place to place in the heart of man, but that, being deeply rooted in Christ, it sticketh in the heart which is enlightened. First, saith the apostle, "Abraham, contrary to hope, believed in hope:" that is to say, there he had a constant hope, where notwithstanding he had nothing to hope after, if all things had been weighed according to the manner of this world. But hope is a most firm and undoubted looking after those things which we believe: so that we see that the apostle did make faith manifest by hope, and by the certainty of hope did declare the assured constancy of faith. After that saith he, "Abraham fainted not in faith, nor stackered at the promise of God through unbelief, but was strong in faith." There are two kinds of stackerings in mankind[2]: the one is that, which, being overcome by evil temptations, doth bend to desperation, and the despising of God's promises. Such was the stackering of those ten spies of the holy land, of whom mention is made in the thirteenth and fourteenth chapters of Numbers. The other stackering is rather to be called a weak infirmity of faith, which also is tempted itself; that now I may not make rehearsal to you, how that in us all, by the spot of original sin, is naturally grafted a certain kind of unbelief, and that man's mind is at no time so enlightened or confirmed, but that cloudy mists of ignorance and doubtings do sometimes arise:

[1 Rom. iv. 18—21.]

[2 Bullinger's words here are very much akin to Calvin's, who writes on Rom. iv. 19, as follows: Duplex enim est fidei debilitas: una, quæ tentationibus adversis succumbendo, excidere nos a Dei virtute facit: altera, quæ ex imperfectione quidem nascitur, non tamen fidem ipsam extinguit. Nam nec mens unquam sic illuminata est, quin maneant multæ ignorantiæ reliquiæ: nunquam sic est animus stabilitus, quin multum hæreat dubitationis.—Comment. in loc. Amstel. Tom. VII. p. 29.]

yet notwithstanding, faith yieldeth not to temptation, neither is drowned nor sticketh in the mire of stackering; but, laying hold upon the promised word of truth, getteth up again by struggling, and is confirmed.   So we read, that, at the promise of God, this came into Abraham's mind: "What, shall there a son be born to thee that art an hundred years old[3]?" This was that infirmity, and stackering, or weakness, of faith. But here the apostle, commending Abraham's faith, which overcame and yielded not, teaching us also of what sort true faith ought to be, that is, a firm and most assured persuasion, saith: "Abraham fainted not in faith, neither considered his own body dead[4], when he was almost an hundred years old, nor the deadness of Sarae's womb."   Lo, this thought came into Abraham's mind: "Shall a son be born to me that am an hundred years old?"   But he fainted not in faith.   The faith of Abraham began not to droop by reason of this temptation.   For he considered not the weakness that was in himself, nothing answerable to the promise of God.   What then? He stackered not at the promise of God through unbelief: that is, he gave no place to unbelief to be tempted of it; he fell not to his own reasons and doubtful inquisitions, as unbelievers are wont to do.   For God's promise being once set before the eyes of his mind, to that, I say, he stuck unmoveably, casting off all doubts and reasons of his own.   For faith hath no respect at all to the weakness, misery, or lack, which is properly in mankind; but setteth her whole stay in the power of God.   So then, I say, Abraham was strong in faith, that is, he prevailed and got the upper hand in his temptation.   For this is an argument, to shew that he had the upper hand[5]: "He fainted not, nor waxed weak in faith."

It followeth in the apostle, "Abraham gave God the glory;" to wit, in believing that God wisheth well to mankind, and that he is a true God and almighty.   For he giveth God his glory, which attributeth to God the properties of God, and doth not gainsay the word and promise of God.   For John the apostle

[3 Gen. xvii. 17.]

[4 Now dead, 1577; jam emortuum, Lat.]

[5 Opponitur enim illi superiori, Lat. For there is opposed to that which went before.   Omitted by the translator.]

saith: "He that believeth not in God, maketh God a liar[1]." Abraham therefore believed in God, and in believing gave God the glory. The apostle Paul goeth forward and saith: " He was throughly persuaded, or certified, that he which had promised was able also to perform." Paul used the Greek word πληροφορηθεὶς, which is all one as if you should say, being certified. For πληροφορέω doth signify, fully to certify: whereupon πληροφορία is an assured faith given unto us, which is made by way of argument, or by the thing itself. And they call that πληροφόρημα, which we call a certification; as when a thing by persuasions is so beaten into our minds, that after that we never doubt any more. Therefore faith did certify Abraham, and with undoubted persuasions did bring him to the point never to doubt, but that God was able to perform what he had promised: in faith therefore he stuck unmoveable to the promise of God, being assuredly certified that he should obtain whatsoever God had promised.

It is certain therefore, and plainly declared by the words of the apostle, that true faith is an undoubted persuasion in the mind of the believer, even so to have the thing as his belief is, and as he is said to have it in the express word of God. Whereby also we learn, that faith is not the unstable and unadvised confidence of him which believeth every great and unpossible thing. For faith is ruled and bound to the word of God; to the word of God, I say, rightly and truly understood. The godly and faithful, therefore, do not by and bye out of the omnipotency of God gather what they list; as though God therefore would do every thing because he can do all things, or that faith should therefore believe every thing, because it is written, "All things are possible to him that believeth." For his faith is therefore a great deal more[2], because that which he doth believe is so set down and declared in the word of God, as he doth believe. Furthermore, where the Lord in the gospel saith, "All things are possible to him that believeth," we must not take that saying to be absolutely spoken, but to be joined to the word, will, and glory of God, and the safety of our souls. For all

Faith believeth not every thing whatsoever.

[1 1 John v. 10.]

[2 Nam *pius* ideo credit, quia, &c., Lat. The translator read *plus*.]

things which God in his word hath promised, all things which God will have, and lastly, all things which make to the glory of God and the safeguard of our souls, " are possible to him that believeth." And for that cause the apostle both openly and plainly said: " Whatsoever God hath promised, that same he is able also to perform." For whatsoever he hath not promised, and whatsoever pleaseth not his divine majesty, or is contrary to the will and express word of God, that cannot God do; not because he cannot, but because he will not[3]. God could make bread of stones; but we must not therefore believe that stones are bread, neither are they bread therefore, because God can do all things. This ye shall understand better and more fully, where as[4] a little hereafter I shall shew unto you, that true faith strayeth not nor wavereth, wandering to and fro, but cleaveth close and sticketh fast to God and his word.

In the mean season, because we have shewed out of Paul's words, by the example of Abraham, that faith is a substance and undoubted persuasion in the heart; and because many do stiffly stand in it, that man is not surely certain of his salvation[5]: I will add a few examples out of the gospel, whereby they may plainly perceive, that faith is a most sure ground and settled opinion touching God and our salvation. And first, verily, the centurion, of whom mention is made in the gospel, had conceived a stedfast hope that his servant should be healed of the Lord. For he understood how great and mighty things he promised to them that believe. He gathered also by the works of Christ, that it was an easy matter for him to restore his servant to health again. Therefore he cometh to the Lord, and among other talk saith: "It is no reason that thou shouldest come under my roof; yea, do but say the word, and my servant shall be made whole." These words do testify, that in the heart and mind of the centurion there was a sure persuasion of most assured health,

Examples of undoubted Faith.

[3 Non quod non possit omnia, sed quod nolit omnia, Lat.]

[4 i. e. where, ubi, Lat.]

[5 Hujus temporis hæreticorum error est, posse fideles eam notitiam habere de sua gratia, ut certa fide statuant sibi remissa esse peccata.—Bellarm. de Justif. Lib. III. cap. 3. p. 949. Colon. Agrip. 1619.]

which by a certain comparison he doth make manifest and more fully express. "For I myself am a man under the authority of another; and under me I have soldiers; and I say to one, Go, and he goeth; and to another, Come, and he cometh; and to my servant, Do this, and he doeth it." When the Lord perceived this certification of his mind by his words most full of faith, he crieth out, "that in all Israel he hath not found so great faith[1]." The same again in the gospel speaketh notably of the woman's faith which was sorely plagued with the bloody flux. And that faith was an undoubted persuasion in her heart once illuminated, we may thereby understand, because she (being first indeed stirred up by the works and words of the Lord) thought thus within herself: "If I do but touch his garment, I shall be whole;" and therefore, pressing through the thickest of the throng, cometh to the Lord[2].

But why heap I together many examples? Doth not the only[3] faith of the Chananitish or Syrophenician woman declare more plainly than that it can be denied, how that faith is a most assured persuasion of things believed? For being over-passed, and, as it were, contemned of the Lord, she wavereth not in faith; but following him, and hearing also that the Lord was sent to the lost sheep of the house of Israel, she goeth on to worship him. Moreover, being put back, and, as it were, touched with the foul reproach of a dog, she goeth forward yet humbly to cast herself prostrate before the Lord, requesting to obtain the thing that she desired. She would not have persevered so stiffly, if faith had not been a certification in her believing mind and heart. Wherefore the Lord, moved with that faith of hers, cried: "Woman, great is thy faith; be it done to thee even as thou wilt[4]."

It is manifest therefore, by all these testimonies of the holy scripture, that faith is a stedfast and undoubted persuasion in the mind and heart of the believer.

Whereunto faith leaneth, and what the object or foundation of faith is. This being now brought to an end, let us see what it is, whereupon man's faith doth lean; and also, how we may clearly perceive, that faith is not a vain and unstable opinion (as a

[1 Matt. viii. 5—10.]   [2 Matt. ix. 20—22.]
[3 una, Lat.]   [4 Matt. xv. 22—28; Mark vii. 26.]

little before we were about to say) of any thing whatsoever, conceived in the mind of man, but that it is tied up and contained within bounds, and, as it were, certain conditions. In the definition therefore of faith we said, that faith bendeth to God-ward, and leaneth on his word. God therefore, and the word of God, is the object or foundation of true faith. The thing whereon a man may lean safely, surely, and without all manner doubting, must needs be stedfast and altogether unmoveable; which doth give health, which doth preserve, and which doth fill up or minister all fulness unto us: for this doth faith seek and request. But this is not elsewhere than in God. On God alone therefore doth true faith bend and lean. God is everlasting, chiefly good, wise, just, mighty, and true of word. And that doth he testify by his works and word. Wherefore in the prophets he is called a strong and unmoveable rock, a castle, a wall, a tower, an invincible fortress, a treasure, and a well that never will be drawn dry[5]. This everlasting God can do all things, knoweth all things, is present in all places, loveth mankind exceedingly, doth provide for all men, and also governeth or disposeth all things. Faith therefore, which is a confidence of God's good-will and of his aid in all necessities, and of the true salvation of mankind, bendeth on God alone, and cannot lean to any other creature, in whom the things are not that faith requireth.

And even as God is true of word, and cannot lie, so is his word true and deceiveth no man. In the word of God is expressed the will and mind of God. To the word of God therefore hath faith an eye, and layeth her ground upon God's word; touching which word the Lord in the gospel said: "Heaven and earth shall pass, but my word shall not pass[6]." The word of God here is compared with the most excellent elements. Air and water are feeble and unstable elements: but heaven, although it turn and move, doth keep yet a wonderful and most stedfast course in moving, and stedfast are all things therein. The earth is most stable and unmoveable. Therefore, if it be easier for these things to be loosed, which cannot be undone, than for the word of God to pass; it followeth, that God's word in all points is most stable, un-

[5 2 Sam. xxii. 2, 3; Psal. xxxi. 2, 3; Prov. xviii. 10; Isai. xxxiii. 6; Jer. xvii. 13.] [6 Mark xiii. 31.]

moveable, and not possible to be loosed. "If" (saith the Lord in Jeremy) "ye can undo the league that I have taken with the day, or the covenant that I have made with the night, so that it neither be day nor night at the appointed time, then may my covenant be of none effect which I have made with David[1]." But not the whole world, laying all their strengths together, is able to make it day when it is once night, nor cause the day to break one hour sooner than the course of heaven doth command. Therefore not all this world, with all the power and pomp thereof, shall be able once to weaken or break, to change or abolish, so much as one tittle in the word of God, and the truth of God's word. Faith therefore, which resteth upon a thing most firm or sure, cannot choose but be an undoubted certification. And since God's word is the foundation of faith, faith cannot wander to and fro, and lean to every word whatsoever: for every opinion conceived without the word of God, or against God's word, cannot be called true faith. And for that cause St Paul, the apostle of Christ, would not ground the true or christian faith upon any carnal props or opinions of men, but upon the truth and power of God. With his words will I conclude this place : "Faith" (saith he) "cometh of hearing, and hearing by the word of God[2]." "By the word of God," he saith, and not by the word of man. Again, to the Corinthians : " My preaching" (saith he) "was not in enticing words of man's wisdom, but in the shewing forth of the Spirit, and of power; that your faith should not be in the wisdom of man, but in the power of God[3]." Whereby also we learn, that some there are, which against all reason require faith at our hands; that is, they would have us to believe that which they are not able to shew out of God's word, or that which is clean contrary to the word of God.

To the better declaring of this that I have said availeth that short abridgement of God's word and of faith, which we in the definition of faith have closely knit up together. There are there rehearsed two chief points of faith and of the word : and first of all, that God in Christ doth freely promise life and every good thing. For God, who is the object or mark

Two chief points of faith.

[1 Jer. xxxiii. 20, 21.]   [2 Rom. x. 17.]
[3 1 Cor. ii. 4, 5.]

and foundation of faith, being of his own proper nature everliving, everlasting[4], and good, doth of himself, from before all
beginning, beget the Son like to himself in all points; who,
because he is of the same substance with the Father, is himself also, by nature, life, and all goodness. And to the end he
might communicate to us, his sons and brethren, both life
and all goodness, he became man; and being conversant, very
God and man, among men, he testified that God the Father, *True faith seeketh all*
through the Son, doth pour himself wholly with all good *good things in God*
things into the faithful, whom he quickeneth and filleth with *through Christ.*
all goodness, and last of all doth take them up to himself
into the blessed place of everlasting life; and that he doth
frankly and freely bestow this benefit, to the end that the
glory of his grace may in all things be praised. This doth
true faith believe; and hereunto belong no small part of the
scriptures, which testify, that God in Christ doth communicate
to the faithful life and godliness. John the apostle crieth out
and saith: " In the beginning was the Word, and the Word
was with God, and God was the Word. And the Word became
flesh, and dwelt among us. And we saw the glory of God,
as the glory of the only-begotten Son of the Father, full of
grace and truth. And of his fulness have all we received[5],"
&c. For the Lord himself, in the Gospel after St John, said:
" Verily I say unto you, whatsoever things the Father doth,
the same also doth the Son. For even as the Father doth
raise the dead to life and quickeneth them, so also doth the
Son quicken whom he will: for neither judgeth the Father
any man, but hath committed all judgment to the Son, that
all men may honour the Son even as they honour the Father.
He that honoureth not the Son, the same honoureth not the
Father which hath sent him. Verily, verily, I say unto you,
he that heareth my word, and believeth on him that sent me,
hath life everlasting, and shall not come into judgment, but is
escaped from death unto life[6]." With these words of the
gospel agreeth that saying of St Paul: " In Christ are laid
up all the treasures of wisdom and knowledge. Because in
him dwelleth all fulness of the Godhead bodily, and ye in
him are fulfilled[7]." But that these great benefits of God are

[4] vivus, æternus, Lat.]
[5] John i. 1, 14, 16.　Conspeximus gloriam *ejus*, Lat.]
[6] John v. 19, 21—24.]　　　　[7] Col. ii. 3, 9.]

freely bestowed upon the faithful, Paul, that vessel of election, declareth in these words: "Blessed be God, who hath chosen us in Christ before the foundations of the world were laid, and hath predestinated us into the adoption of children through Jesus Christ unto himself, according to the good pleasure of his will, to the praise of the glory of his grace, wherein he hath made us accepted in the beloved; through whom we have redemption in his blood[1]," &c. And again: "All have sinned, and have need of God's glory, but are justified freely through his grace, by the redemption which is in Christ[2]:" and so forward. True faith therefore doth believe, that life and every good thing doth freely come to it from God through Christ: which is the chief article of our faith, as in the articles of the belief is more largely laid forth.

True faith believeth the holy scriptures.

The second principal point of God's word and faith is, that in the word of God there is set down all truth necessary to be believed; and that true faith doth believe all that is declared in the scriptures. For it telleth us, that God is; what manner one he is; what God's works are; what his judgments, his will, his commandments, his promises, and what his threatenings are; finally, whatsoever is profitable or necessary to be believed, that doth God's word wholly set down unto us, and that doth true faith receive, believing all things that are written in the law and the prophets, in the gospel and writings of the apostles. But whatsoever cannot be fetched or proved out of those writings, or whatsoever is contrary unto them, that do the faithful not believe at all: for the very nature of true faith is, not to believe that which squareth from the word of God[3]. Whosoever therefore believeth not the fables and opinions of men, he alone believeth as he should: for he dependeth only upon the word of God, and so upon God himself, the only fountain of all truth.

The matter, the argument, and the whole sum of faith is briefly set out unto us in the articles of the christian faith, whereof I will speak at another time. I have this hour declared unto you, dearly beloved and reverend[4] bre-

[1 Ephes. i. 3—7. Qua caros nos reddidit per dilectum, Lat. and Erasmus' rendering.]

[2 Rom. iii. 23, 24.]   [3 Quæ cum verbo Dei pugnant, Lat.]

[4 honorandi, Lat. And there is no *et* (and) in the original.]

thren in the Lord, the definition of faith ; which to the end
that I may surely fasten in every one's mind, and that all
may understand what faith is, I repeat it here again, and
therewithal conclude this sermon.   Faith is a gift of God,
poured into man from heaven, whereby he is taught with an
undoubted persuasion wholly to lean to God and his word;
in which word God in Christ doth freely promise life and
every good thing, and wherein all truth necessary to be believed is plainly declared.   Let us all pray to God our
Father through his only-begotten Son our Lord Jesus Christ,
that he will vouchsafe from heaven to bestow true faith upon
us all, that we, by it knowing him aright, may at the last
obtain life everlasting.   Amen.

THAT THERE IS ONE ONLY TRUE FAITH, AND WHAT THE VIRTUE THEREOF IS.

THE FIFTH SERMON.

BEING cut off with the shortness of time, and detained by
the excellency of the matter, I could not in my last sermon
make an end of all that I had determined to speak touching
faith : now therefore, by the grace of the Holy Spirit, I will
add the rest of the argument which seemeth yet to be behind.   Pray to the Lord that that, which by man's voice is
brought to your ears, may by the finger of God be written
in your hearts.

True faith is ignorant of all division ; for "there is," saith
the apostle, "one Lord, one faith, one baptism, [one] God[5] and
Father of all[6]."   For there remaineth, from the beginning of
the world even unto the end thereof, one and the same faith
in all the elect of God.   God is one and the same for ever,
the only Well of all goodness, that can never be drawn dry.
The truth of God, from the beginning of the world, is one
and the same, set forth to men in the word of God.   Therefore the object and foundation of faith, that is, God and the

Faith is one alone.

[5 unus Deus, Lat.]   [6 Ephes. iv. 5, 6.]

[BULLINGER.]

7

word of God, remain for ever one and the self-same. In one and the self-same faith with us have all the elect ever since the first creation of the world believed, that unto us through Christ all good things are freely given, and that all truth necessary to be believed is declared in the word of the Lord : wherefore the faithful of the old world have always settled their faith on God and his word ; so that now, without all doubt, there cannot be any more than one true faith.

There are many and sundry religions, but no more than one true faith. I know very well, that in the world there are sowed many and sundry faiths, that is to say, religions. For there is the Indian faith[1], the Jewish faith, the faith of the Mahometists, and the faith of the Georgians[2]; and yet notwithstanding there is but one true christian faith, the abridgement whereof is contained in the articles of our belief, and is taught at the full in the sacred scriptures of both the Testaments. I know also that there are sundry beliefs of men, resting upon sundry things, and believing that which is contrary to true faith: but yet, nevertheless, there remaineth but one true belief in God and his word, (which is) an undoubted persuasion and confidence of things most true and assuredly certain.

Faith doth increase and decrease. This confidence doth grow with increase in the minds of the faithful, and, contrarily, decreaseth again and utterly faileth. And for that cause the apostles besought the Lord, saying: " Lord, increase our faith[3]." And Paul the apostle doth in his writings everywhere wish to the faithful the increase of the spirit and faith. David also before him prayed, saying : " O God, create a clean heart within me, and take not thy Holy Spirit from me[4]." For he had seen how that from Saul, whom he succeeded in the kingdom, the good Spirit of God was departed, and that instead thereof the wicked spirit had entered into his mind, which tormented him very pitifully. Hereunto belongeth that saying in the gospel: " To every one that hath shall be given, and from him that hath not

[1 Indiana fides, Lat.]
[2 fides Georgiana, Lat. The Georgians are a branch of the Greek Church.   Mosheim's Eccles. Hist. Book IV. Cent. 16. Sect. 3, Ch. 2. § 10. ed. Soames.   Smith and Dwight's Missionary Researches in Armenia, Letter 8.]
[3 Luke xvii. 5.]
[4 Ps. li. 10, 11.]

shall be taken away that which he hath not," or that he maketh no account of, "and shall be given to him that hath[5]." Neither was it in vain that the Lord said to Peter, " I have prayed for thee, Peter, that thy faith fail not[6]." For Paul speaketh of some in his time, that " made shipwreck of their own faith, and overthrew the faith of other[7]." And to what end, I pray you, do we daily hear the word of God, and make our humble petitions to the Lord, but because we look for increase of godliness, and his aid to keep us that we fall not from true faith ? Verily Paul to the Thessalonians saith : " We pray earnestly day and night to see you personally, and to supply that which is wanting in your faith[8]." And a little before he said : " For this cause I sent Timotheus, that I might be certified of your faith, lest by any means the tempter had tempted you, and so our labour had been of none effect[9]." The same apostle also, in his Epistle to the Ephesians, saith : " Christ gave some apostles, some prophets, some pastors and teachers, to the restoring of the saints, unto the building of the body of Christ, until we all meet together in the unity of faith, and the acknowledging of the Son of God, unto a perfect man, unto the measure of age of the fulness of Christ, so that now we be no longer children[10]." Therefore, so long as we live, we learn, that our faith may be perfect[11]; and if so be at any time it shall be weakened by temptations, that then it may be repaired, and again confirmed. And in this diversity, (I mean) in this increase and weakness of faith, there is no partition or division ; for the self[12] root and substance of faith doth always remain, although it be at some time more, and at some time less. In like manner, faith is not therefore changed or cut in sunder, because one is called general faith, and another particular[13] faith.

General and particular faith.

[5 Luke xix. 26, where the reading of the copies is either *that which he hath*, or, *that which he seemeth to have*.]

[6 Luke xxii. 32.]

[7 1 Tim. i. 19; 2 Tim. ii. 18.]

[8 1 Thess. iii. 10.]

[9 1 Thess. iii. 5.]

[10 Ephes. iv. 11—14.]

[11 may not be perfect, 1587 ; ut perficiatur fides nostra, Lat.]

[12 self-same, 1577.]

[13 specialis, Lat.]

For general faith is no other than that which believeth that all
the words of God are true, and that God hath a good-will to
mankind: particular faith believeth nothing contrary to this;
only that, which is common to all, the faithful applieth particularly to himself, believing that God is not well minded toward others alone, but even unto him also. So then it
bringeth the whole into parts, and that which is general into
particularities. For whereas by general faith he believeth
that all the words of God are true; in the same sort by particular faith he doth believe that the soul is immortal, that
our bodies rise again, that the faithful shall be saved, the
unbelievers destroyed, and whatsoever else is of this sort
taught to be believed in the word of God.

Faith in-
spired and
faith gotten. Moreover, the disputation touching faith poured into us,
and faith that we ourselves get; touching formal faith, and
faith without fashion[1]; I leave to be beaten out of them which
of themselves do bring these new disputations into the church.
True faith is obtained by no strength or merit of man, but is
poured into him of God, as I declared in my last sermon:
and though man obtain it by hearkening unto the word of
God, yet nevertheless it is wholly imputed to the grace of
God; for unless this grace do work inwardly in the heart of
the hearer, the preacher that laboureth outwardly doth bring
no profit at all. We read in the third chapter of St Augustin's book *De Prædestinatione Sanctorum*, that once he
was in an error, because he thought that that faith, wherewith we believe in God, is not the gift of God, but that it
was in us as of ourselves, and that by it we do obtain the
gifts of God, whereby we may in this world live rightly and
holily[2]. But this he confuteth in that book at large, and
that substantially. So then true faith, which bendeth on
Formal faith. God alone[3], and is directed by the word of God, is formal

[1 de fide *infusa* et *acquisita*, de fide *informi* et *formata*, Lat.
The reader who is so disposed may find these points stated in Andr.
Vega. de Justificat. Colon. 1572. Quæst. I. pp. 727, 728.]

[2 Cum similiter errarem, putans fidem, qua in Deum credimus,
non esse donum Dei, sed a nobis esse in nobis, et per illam nos impetrare Dei dona, quibus temperanter et juste et pie vivamus in hoc
seculo.—August. de Præd. Sanct. c. 3. Par. 1531. Tom. VII. fol. 253.]

[3 in unum Deum tendit, Lat.]

enough, or sufficiently in fashion[4]. Verily, the form of faith
is engraven in the heart of the faithful by the Holy Ghost.
And although it be small, and doth not grow up to the highest
degree, yet notwithstanding it is true faith, having force in it
as it were a grain of mustard-seed. The thief, that was
crucified with our Lord, believed in the Lord Jesus, and was
saved, although the force of faith was strong in him but a
very small season, and brought not forth any great store of
fruit of good works: finally, that faith of the thief was not
any whit diverse or contrary from the faith of St Peter and
St Paul, but was altogether the very same with theirs,
although their faith brought forth somewhat more abundantly
the fruit of good works. Peter and Paul were frankly and
freely justified, although they had many good works: freely
was the thief justified, although his good works were very
few or none at all. Let us hold therefore, that true faith is
one alone, which notwithstanding doth increase and is augmented, and, again, may decrease and be extinguished.

There remaineth now for me to declare the virtue and *The power and effect of faith.*
effect of true faith. This hath the holy apostle Paul done[5]
very excellently well, yea, and that most absolutely too. But
although, in the eleventh chapter to the Hebrews, he had said
very much, he is compelled notwithstanding to confess that
he cannot reckon up all: therefore at this time I mean to
rehearse a few virtues of faith, leaving the rest, dearly beloved, to be sought out and considered of yourselves.

True faith before all things bringeth with it true know- *Faith is the true know-ledge that maketh men wise.*
ledge, and maketh us wise indeed. For by faith we know
God, and judge aright of the judgments and works of God, of
virtues and vices. The wisdom that it bringeth with it is
without doubt the true wisdom. Many men hope that they
can attain to true wisdom by the study of philosophy: but
they are deceived as far as heaven is broad[6]. For philosophy
doth falsely judge and faultily teach many things touching
God, the works of God, the chief goodness, the end of good
and evil, and touching things to be desired and eschewed.
But the very same things are rightly and truly taught in the
word of God, and understood and perceived by faith. Faith
therefore is the true wisdom, and maketh us wise indeed. For

[4 Satis est *formalis* aut *formata*, Lat.]
[5 ante me, Lat.; done before me.]   [6 toto cœlo, Lat.]

Jeremy also saith: "Behold, they have cast away the word of the Lord; what wisdom therefore can there be left in them[1]?" The wisdom of Salomon is worshipfully thought of throughout the whole compass of the world; and yet we read that the Lord, in the gospel after St Matthew, uttered this sentence against the Jews: "The queen of the south shall rise in judgment with this generation and shall condemn it; because she came from the ends of the world to hear the wisdom of Salomon: and behold, there is one in this place greater than Salomon[2]." Christ is preferred before Salomon, and the wisdom of Christ before the wisdom of Salomon. But it is well known, that the wisdom of Christ, the Son of God, cannot be attained to without faith. Faith therefore bringeth with it the most excellent wisdom. But herein this wisdom of ours deserveth a singular praise, because they that desire it are not sent to foreign nations, with great cost and labour, to learn it; as to the priests of Egypt, the gymnosophists of India[3], the philosophers of Greece, or to the rabbins of the Jews. God hath dispersed the word of God throughout the whole world, so that now the word of faith is in the hearts of all the faithful. For Paul the apostle saith: "Thus saith the justice that is of faith, Say not in thy heart, Who shall ascend into heaven? that is, to fetch Christ down from above. Or, Who shall descend into the deep? that is, to bring Christ from the dead again. But what saith he? The word is nigh unto thee, even in thy heart: this same is the word of faith, which we preach; for if thou confess with thy mouth the Lord Jesus, and dost believe with thy heart that God hath raised him from the dead, thou shalt be saved[4]."

Faith therefore doth not only make us wise, but happy also; the Lord himself bearing witness thereunto, and saying to his disciples: "Happy are the eyes that see the things that ye see. For I say unto you, that many prophets and kings have desired to see the things that ye see[5], and to hear the

[1 Jer. viii. 9.]   [2 Matt. xii. 42.]
[3 Gymnosophistæ, Lat. A sect of Indian philosophers, who wore no clothing, and practised the severities of standing alternately on one foot, and of fixing their eyes on the sun.—Plin. H. N. vii. 2. med. § 2. Schelleri Lex. totius Latin. sub voc.]
[4 Rom. x. 6—9.]
[5 et non viderunt, Lat. and have not seen them: omitted.]

things that ye hear, and heard them not[6]." We shall there- How man may attain to the chief goodness.
fore find in faith a most certain determination of the most
notable question stirred in, since the beginning of the world,
of learned and most excellent wits; which is, by what means
a man may live, be happy, attain to the chief goodness, be
joined to the chief goodness, and so be justified? There have
been, yea, and yet are, divers opinions touching this matter,
contrary the one to the other. But we do briefly and truly
affirm, that by true faith a man doth live, is happy, attaineth
to the chief goodness, is conjoined to the chief goodness,
and also justified: so that God dwelleth in us, and we in
him; and that by faith we are both happy and blessed.
What, I pray you, could have been spoken more excellently,
worthily, or divinely, touching true faith? For see; faith
quickeneth us, maketh us happy, joineth us to the chief
goodness, so that he[7] in us and we in him may live; and
faith doth also fully justify us.

But now it is best to hear the testimonies out of the
scriptures. Faith maketh us happy. For to St Peter, con- Faith maketh happy.
fessing the Lord Jesus by true faith, it is said: "Happy art
thou, Simon, the son of Jonas. Flesh and blood hath not
revealed this to thee, but my Father which is in heaven[8]."
St Paul, for the proof of faith, bringeth in that sentence of
David: "Happy are they whose iniquities are forgiven, and
whose sins are covered. Blessed is the man to whom the
Lord shall impute no sin[9]." Faith quickeneth or maketh Faith quickeneth.
alive. For "the just liveth by faith[10]." This doth Paul very
often in his writings allege out of the prophets. The same
Paul also saith: "The life which now I live in flesh, I live
by faith in the Son of God, who loved me and gave himself
for me[11]." Faith joineth us to the eternal and chief goodness, Faith joineth to God.
and so maketh us to enjoy the chief goodness, that God may
dwell in us and we in God. For the Lord Jesus himself in
the gospel saith: "He which eateth my flesh, and drinketh
my blood, dwelleth in me, and I in him. As the living Father
sent me, so also I live by the Father, and he that eateth me
shall live by me[12]." But to eat and drink the Lord is to

[6 Luke x. 23, 24.]　　　　　[7 Deus, Lat.]
[8 Matt. xvi. 17.]　　　　　　[9 Rom. iv. 7, 8; Ps. xxxii. 1, 2.]
[10 Gal. iii. 11; Heb. x. 38.]　[11 Gal. ii. 20.]
[12 John vi. 56, 57.]

believe in the Lord, that he hath given himself to death for us. Whereupon John the apostle saith: "We have seen and do witness, that the Father hath sent the Son the Saviour of the world. Whosoever shall confess that Jesus is the Son of God, God dwelleth in him and he in God[1]." Wherefore also Paul said: "I live now; not I, but Christ liveth in me[2]."

Faith justifieth. Moreover faith doth justify. But for because the treatise thereof cannot be fitly and fully made an end of this hour, I mean to defer it till the next sermon that shall be.

At this present, dearly beloved, ye must remember, that there is but one true faith, that is, the christian faith. For although there be said to be many faiths, that is, religions; yet notwithstanding there is only but one true and undoubted faith. And that doth increase, and again decrease, in some men. As for those in whom it is rightly and godly observed, in them it sheweth forth sundry virtues. For it bringeth with it true wisdom; finally, it quickeneth, and maketh us blessed and happy indeed. To God, the Father, the author of all goodness and of our felicity, be all praise and glory, through Jesus Christ our Lord, for ever and ever. Amen.

THAT THE FAITHFUL ARE JUSTIFIED BY FAITH WITHOUT THE LAW AND WORKS.

THE SIXTH SERMON.

BEING ready here, dearly beloved, to speak unto you of faith, which without works doth justify them that believe, I call upon the Father, which is in heaven, through his only-begotten Son Jesus Christ our Lord, beseeching him to open my mouth and lips to the setting forth of his praise, and to illuminate your hearts, that ye, acknowledging the great benefit of God, may become thankful for it, and holy indeed.

Justification. And first of all, I will speak certain things, chiefly necessary to this argument or treatise, touching this term of justification. The term of justifying, very usual and common

[1 1 John iv. 14, 15.]   [2 Gal. ii. 20.]

among the Hebrews, and of a large signification, is not at this day so well understood of all men as it ought to be. To justify is as much to say as to quit from judgment and from the denounced and uttered sentence of condemnation. It signifieth to remit offences, to cleanse, to sanctify, and to give inheritance[3] of life everlasting. For it is a law term belonging to courts where judgment is exercised. Imagine therefore, that man is set before the judgment-seat of God, and that there he is pleaded guilty; to wit, that he is accused and convinced of heinous offences, and therefore sued to punishment or to the sentence of condemnation. Imagine also, that the Son of God maketh intercession, and cometh in as a mean, desiring that upon him may be laid the whole fault and punishment[4] due unto us men, that he by his death may cleanse them and take them away, setting us free from death, and giving us life everlasting. Imagine too, that God, the most high and just judge, receiveth the offer, and translateth the punishment together with the fault from us unto the neck of his Son; making therewithal a statute, that whosoever believeth that the Son of God suffered for the sins of the world, brake the power of death, and delivered us from damnation, should be cleansed from his sins and made heir of life everlasting. Who therefore can be so dull of understanding, but may perceive that mankind is justified by faith?

But that there may be no cause of doubt or darkness left in the mind of any man; that which I have already spoken generally, by the parable and similitude fetched from our common law, I will here particularly bring into certain parts, confirming and manifestly proving every one of them severally out of the holy scriptures, so that even to the slowest[5] wits the power of faith and work of justification may be most evident.

And first, I will shew unto you, that this term of justifi- What it is to justify. cation is taken in this present treatise for the absolution and remission of sins, for sanctification, and adoption into the number of the sons of God. In the thirteenth of the Acts, the apostle Paul saith: "Be it known unto you, men and brethren, that through this Lord Jesus Christ is preached

[3 hæredem constituere, Lat.]
[4 omnis culpa et pœna, Lat.]
[5 vel tardis ingeniis, Lat.]

unto you the forgiveness of sins; and by him all that believe are justified from all things, from which they could not be justified by the law of Moses[1]." See, in Christ is preached unto us the forgiveness of sins; and he that believeth that Christ preached forgiveth sins[2] is also justified. It followeth therefore, that justification is the remission of sins. In the fifth chapter to the Romans saith the same apostle: " Being justified by the blood of Christ, we shall be saved from wrath through him[3]." But the blood of Christ washeth away sins. Justification, therefore, is the washing away or forgiveness of sins. And again, in the same chapter, saith he more plainly: " Judgment entered by one offence unto condemnation, but the gift of many sins unto justification[4]." He maketh justification the contrary to condemnation: therefore, justification is the absolution and delivery from condemnation. What say ye to this moreover, that he doth plainly call justification a gift, that is, the forgiveness of sins? Hereunto also belong those words of his: " Even as by the sin of one condemnation came on all men; so by the righteousness of one good came upon all men to the justification of life[5]." Here again is the justification of life made the contrary of condemnation unto death set as a pain upon our heads because of the transgression: justification of life therefore is an absolution from sins, a delivery from death, a quickening or translating from death to life. For in the fourth to the Romans the same apostle expoundeth justification by sanctification[6], and sanctification by the remission of sins. For in treating of faith, whereby we are justified, or which God imputeth to us for righteousness without works, he saith: " Even as David also doth expound the blessedness of that man, to whom the Lord imputeth righteousness without works, saying: Blessed are they whose iniquities are forgiven, and whose sins are covered[7]." What could be more plainly spoken

[1 Acts xiii. 38, 39.]
[2 qui credit annunciato Christo, remittenti peccata, Lat.]
[3 Rom. v. 9.]   [4 Rom. v. 16.]   [5 v. 18.]
[6 beatificationem, Lat. This is the term which Bullinger employs in this Treatise of Justification, and which the translator, rather unhappily, has rendered *sanctification*. The idea intended by Bullinger is expressed in Rom. iv. 7, which he quotes. — Cf. Calvin, Instit. Lib. iii. cap. 11. § 4. & 22.]
[7 Rom. iv. 7.]

than this? For he doth evidently expound justification by sanctification, and sanctification by remission of sins. Furthermore, what else is sanctification but the adoption whereby we are received into the grace and number of the sons of God? What is he therefore that seeth not, that in this treatise of St Paul justification is taken for adoption? especially, since in the very same fourth chapter to the Romans he goeth about to prove that an inheritance is due to faith, whereunto also he doth attribute justification. By all this it is made manifest, that the question of justification containeth nothing else but the manner and reason of sanctification; that is to say, whereby and how men have their sins forgiven, and are received into the grace and number of the sons of God, and, being justified, are made heirs of the kingdom of God.

And now, let us try whether that which we have said be taught in the scriptures: that Christ before the judgment-seat of God, when sentence of condemnation was to be pronounced against us for our offences, took our sins upon his own neck, and purged them by the sacrifice of his death upon the cross; and that God also laid upon Christ our fault and punishment, so that Christ alone is the only satisfaction and purging of the faithful. This doth the apostle Paul teach most expressly, where he saith: "Who shall lay anything to the charge of God's elect? It is God that justifieth. Who shall condemn? It is Christ that died; yea rather, it is he which is raised up, and is at the right hand of the Father, making intercession for us[8]." And again he saith: "Christ redeemed us from the curse of the law, while he was made the curse for us; (for it is written, Cursed be every one that hangeth on the tree;) that upon the gentiles might come the blessing of Abraham through Jesus Christ[9]," &c. This did the apostle teach out of the writings of Moses. And Moses in his books doth oftentimes make mention, that the sins are laid upon the heads of the beasts which were sacrificed. But those sacrifices bare the type or figure of the death and sacrifice of Christ. Esaias also in his fifty-third chapter saith expressly: "He verily hath taken on him our infirmities, and borne our pains. He was wounded for our iniquities, and smitten for our sins. For the pain of our punishment was laid upon him, and with his stripes are we healed. We all went astray like

Christ hath taken on himself and cleansed our sins.

[8 Rom. viii. 33, 34.]   [9 Gal. iii. 13, 14.]

sheep, every one turned his own way; but the Lord hath thrown upon him all our sins." And immediately after: "He hath taken away the sins of the multitude, and made intercession for the transgressors[1]." Than these words, I think, nothing can be brought more to the matter, or more fit for our present purpose. To this alludeth St Peter when he saith: "The Lord himself bare our sins in his body upon the cross, that we, being dead to sin, may live to righteousness; by the sign of whose stripes we are made whole[2]." Hereunto alluded St John, the forerunner of the Lord, when he said: "Behold the Lamb of God, that taketh away the sins of the world[3]." Moreover, the apostle Paul beareth witness hereto, saying: "Him that knew not sin he made sin for us, that we through him might be made the righteousness of God[4]." Also in his epistle to the Colossians he saith: "It pleased the Father, that in Christ all fulness should dwell; and by him to reconcile all things unto himself, having set peace through the blood of his cross by him, both things in earth and things in heaven[5]." These, I suppose, are testimonies sufficiently evident to prove, that upon Christ are laid our sins, with the curse or condemnation due unto our offences; and that Christ by his blood hath cleansed our sins, and by his death hath vanquished death and the devil, the author of death, and taken away the punishment due unto us.

The pain and offence of sin are taken away by Christ.

Yet because there be some, and those not a few, which deny that Christ by his death hath taken from us sinners both fault and punishment[6], and that he became the only satisfaction of the whole world; I will therefore now allege certain other testimonies, and repeat somewhat of that that I have before recited, thereby to make it manifest, that Christ, the only satisfaction of the world, hath made satisfaction both for our fault and punishment. Esaias verily witnessed, that

[1 Isai. liii. 4—6, 12.]
[2 1 Pet. ii. 24.   Cujus ejusdem vibice, Lat.]
[3 John i. 29.]   [4 2 Cor. v. 21.]   [5 Col. i. 19, 20.]
[6 pœnam et culpam, Lat.   Fingunt sibi (Romanenses theologi) distinctionem pœnæ et culpæ: *culpam* remitti fatentur Dei misericordia; sed culpa remissa *pœnam* restare, quam persolvi Dei justitia postulat.— Calvin, Instit. Lib. III. cap. 4. § 29.   See also Burnet's Expos. of the Thirty-nine Articles, ed. Page. Art. xxii. p. 285, and Palmer's Letters to Dr Wiseman, Let. II.]

both the fault of our offence and the punishment were taken away, when he saith: "He bare our infirmities, and was wounded for our iniquities:" finally, "the discipline of peace" (that is, the discipline, or chastising, or punishment, bringing peace; or the penalty of our correction, that is, the punishment due to us for our offences,) "was laid on his neck." Mark also what followeth: "and with the blueness of his stripes[7] are we healed[8]." This doth evidently teach, that by the pain of Christ our punishment is taken away. For look what pain, penalty, punishment, or correction was due to us, and the same was laid on the Lord himself: and for that cause was the Lord wounded, and received stripes; and with them he healed us. But he had not yet healed us at all, if we should yet look for wounds, stripes, and strokes, that is to say, punishment for our sins. The death of Christ, therefore, is a full satisfaction for our sins. But what, I pray you, should Christ avail us, if yet we should be punished for our offences? Therefore, when we say, that he did bear all our sins in his body upon the cross, what else do we mean, I pray you, but that the Lord by death, that was not due unto him, took from us God's vengeance, that it might not light on us to our punishment? Paul, as often as he maketh mention of our redemption made by Christ, is wont to name it ἀπολύτρωσιν[9]; by which word he understandeth not, as the common sort do, redemption barely and simply, but the very price and satisfaction of redemption. Wherefore also he writeth, that Christ himself did give himself to be the ἀντίλυτρον[10] for us; that is to say, the price wherewith captives are redeemed from their enemies in the war. For that which we do commonly call ransoms, the Greeks do name λύτρα. So then that is ἀντίλυτρον, when man for man, and life for life, is redeemed. But upon them, that are thus ransomed and

[7 livore ejus, Lat. and Vulg.]

[8 Isai. liii. 4, 5.]   [9 Rom. iii. 24; Eph. i. 7.]

[10 1 Tim. ii. 6. This passage is almost word for word Calvin's, as follows: "Ac quoties de redemptione per eum facta meminit Paulus, vocare solet ἀπολύτρωσιν, quo non simpliciter *redemptionem* indicat, qaliter vulgo intelligitur; sed *pretium* ipsum et satisfactionem redemptionis," (the French version adds, que nous appellons Rançon en François). "Qua ratione et Christum ipsum se pro nobis ἀντίλυτρον dedisse scribit."—Calvin. Instit. Lib. III. cap. 4. ed. Amstel. and Vol. II. p. 221. ed. Calvin Translat. Soc. 1845.]

set at liberty, there is no punishment afterward laid, by reason of the translation thereof from one to another. Furthermore, this is the new covenant that God in his Christ hath made with us, " that he will not remember our iniquities[1]." But how could he choose but remember our iniquities, if he ceased not to punish them? So then, this remaineth not to be doubted of, that Christ our Lord is the full propitiation[2], satisfaction, oblation, and sacrifice for the sins, I say, for the punishment and the fault, of all the world: yea, and by himself alone; for in none other is any salvation: "neither is there any other name given unto men whereby they must be saved[3]."

How punishment is laid on us.

I deny not, but that because of discipline, chastisement, and exercise, divers sorts of punishments are laid upon men's necks, and that they are diversely afflicted and vexed because of their offences. But those afflictions, howsoever they be patiently suffered of the faithful, do not yet wash sins away, nor make satisfaction for misdeeds. St Peter saith: "Marvel not that ye are tried by fire, which thing is done for your trial[4], as if any new thing should happen unto you; yea, rather rejoice herein, that ye are partakers of the afflictions of Christ, that in the revelation also of his glory ye may rejoice and be glad[5]." This, I say, is the end and use of afflictions. And by this means the glory of Christ endureth pure and uncorrupted.

God hath appointed that he that believeth should have eternal life and be justified.

It remaineth now for me to prove out of the holy scriptures, that God the Father hath ordained, that he, whosoever doth believe in the only-begotten Son of God, shall be made partaker of Christ his righteousness; that is, shall be justified by him, be absolved from his sins, and be made heir of life everlasting. Esaias therefore saith: " In the acknowledging of him, or in his knowledge, shall my righteous servant justify the multitude, whose sins he himself shall bear[6]." But what

---

[1 Heb. viii. 12.]

[2 propitiationem, Lat. portion, ed. 1587.]

[3 Acts iv. 12.]

[4 This is Erasmus' rendering, which Bullinger adopts: Ne miremini, dum per ignem exploramini, quæ res ad experimentum vestri fit, perinde quasi, &c. The Vulgate is different.]

[5 1 Pet. iv. 12, 13.]

[6 ch. liii. 2. Potest hic tam active quam passive legi dictio דעת, id est, cognitio vel scientia.—Calv. Comment. in loc. Jesai. Accord-

else is the acknowledging or knowledge of Christ, but true faith? Moreover, the Lord Jesus himself in the gospel after St John saith: "And as Moses lift up the serpent in the wilderness, even so must the Son of man be lift up; that whosoever believeth in him should not perish, but have life everlasting[7]." There was none other remedy in the desert against the envenomed bitings of the serpents, but the contemplation or beholding of the serpent lift up and hanged aloft. No plaster did cure them that were poisoned[8], no oblation made to God, not prayer itself offered to God, not any work, nor any way else: the only beholding of the serpent made the poison harmless that then had crept into all their limbs. In like manner, nothing at all doth save us from death but only faith in Christ: for by faith we behold and see Christ lifted up upon the stake of the cross, as it is to be seen in the sixth chapter of John. It followeth in the words of our Saviour: "God so loved the world, that he gave his only-begotten Son; that whosoever believeth should not perish, but have life everlasting. For God sent not his Son into the world to condemn the world, but that the world through him might be saved. He that believeth on him is not condemned: but he that believeth not is condemned already, because he believeth not in the name of the only-begotten Son of God[9]." By these words now the third time is faith beaten into our heads, by which we are made partakers of the Son of God, of his life, salvation, redemption, and all good things beside. In the sixth chapter of the Gospel after John our Lord again saith: "This is the will of the Father which sent me, that every one that seeth the Son, and believeth in him, should have life everlasting, and I will raise him up at the last day[10]." Nothing can be alleged to make more for our present argument than these words of his. For he saith plainly, that the will of God the Father is, that we should believe in the Son, and by this belief have our salvation. Whereupon John, the evangelist and apostle, in his canonical epistle dareth burst forth into these words: "He that believeth not God maketh him a liar, because he believed not the record that

ingly, Bullinger introduces here Calvin's *two* renderings, cognitione sui, vel in scientia sua. The latter is the rendering of the Vulgate.]

[7 ch. iii. 14, 15.]   [8 Wisd. xvi. 12.]
[9 John iii. 16—18.]   [10 John vi. 40.]

God gave of his Son. And this is the record, that God hath given unto us eternal life, and this life is in his Son. He that hath the Son hath life : and he that hath not the Son of God hath not life¹." Dearly beloved, note this. The eternal and unchangeable will of God is, that he will give eternal life unto the world. But he will give the life through Christ, who is naturally life itself, and can give life. The very same God also will that we obtain and have life in us, and that we have it no other ways than by faith. For the apostle Paul taught, that Christ doth dwell in our hearts by faith². Moreover, the Lord himself also witnesseth, and saith, " He that eateth me shall live by me³." But ye know, dearly beloved, that to eat Christ is to believe in him. And therefore we knit up this place with these words of St Peter : " To this Christ do all the prophets bear witness, that whosoever believeth in him shall receive forgiveness of sins through his name⁴."

We have in these a most ample testimony of the whole sacred scriptures. By these I have evidently enough declared, that God hath appointed, that whosoever doth believe in Christ, being cleansed from his sins, shall be made heir of life everlasting.

This will I make more evident yet, by declaring how that

Men are justified by faith alone. faith alone, that is, that faith for itself, and not for any works of ours, doth justify the faithful. For itself I say, not in respect that it is in us a quality of the mind, or our own work in ourselves; but in respect that faith is the gift of God's grace, having in it a promise of righteousness and life ; and in respect that, naturally, of itself, it is a certain and undoubted persuasion resting upon God, and believing that God, being pacified by Christ, hath through Christ bestowed life and all good things on us. Therefore faith for Christ, and by the grace and promise of God, doth justify : and so faith, that is, that which we believe, and wherein our confidence is settled, God, I say, himself by the grace of God⁵ doth justify us through our redemption in Christ : so that now our own works or merits have no place left to them at all, I mean, in justi-

[¹ 1 John v. 10—12.]
[² Ephes. iii. 17.]
[³ John vi. 57.]
[⁴ Acts x. 43.]
[⁵ ipse inquam Deus, ipsa Dei gratia, Lat.]

fication: for otherwise good works have their place in the
faithful, as we in place convenient do mean to shew. For Christ com-
Paul, the teacher of the Gentiles, doth in the way of opposition Adam.
compare Christ with Adam, and sheweth that of Adam, and
so of our own nature and strength, we have nothing but sin,
the wrath of God, and death. And this doth he shew under
the name of Adam, to the intent that no man should seek for
righteousness and life in the flesh. And again, on the other
side, he declareth that we by Christ have righteousness, the
grace of God, life, and the forgiveness of all our sins. In this
opposition, he doth earnestly urge and often repeat this word,
"of one[6]," to no other end verily, but that we should understand, that faith alone doth justify.

To the Galatians he doth very evidently use this kind of God's testa-
argument. "To the last will and testament of a man, if it ment.
once be proved, nobody doth add or take any thing away."
Reason therefore doth rightly require, that no man put to
or take away any thing from the testament of God. But this
is the testament which God confirmed ; that his will is, to bestow the blessing upon Abraham's seed, not in many, or by
many, but through one. "For he saith not, And to the seeds,
as though he spake of many; but as speaking of one he saith,
And to thy seed, that is, Christ[7]." Therefore, it is a detestable
thing to augment or diminish any thing in this testament of
God. Christ alone is the only Saviour still: men can neither
save themselves nor other.

Again, in the same epistle to the Galatians he saith : "We We are not
justified by
know that man is not justified by the works of the law, but the works of
the law, but
by faith in Jesus Christ[8]; insomuch as no flesh shall be jus- by faith.
tified by the works of the law[9]." This is now the third time
that Paul saith, that men are not justified by the works of the
law : in the which clause he comprehendeth all manner of
works of what sort soever. So then, no kind of works do
justify. But what is it then that justifieth ? Faith in Christ,
and that verily alone. For what else can those words import, "We know that man is not justified but by faith in

[6 Rom. v. 12, &c.]
[7 Gal. iii. 16. *in* semine tuo, Lat.]
[8 Et nos in Jesum Christum credidimus, ut justificaremur ex fide
Christi, et non ex operibus legis, Lat. Omitted by the translator.]
[9 Galat. ii. 16.]

[BULLINGER.]

8

Christ?" For the force of these two speeches is all one, "Faith alone doth justify;" and, "It is certain that we are not justified but by faith in Jesus Christ[1]." He addeth the example of the apostles: "And we have believed in Jesus Christ, that we might be justified by faith in Jesus Christ, and not by the works of the law." In like manner also Peter argueth by an example in the Acts of the Apostles, and saith: "We believe that through the grace of our Lord Jesus Christ we shall be saved, even as they." Acts xv.

Moreover, in the very same chapter to the Galatians he saith: "I despise not the grace of God; for if righteousness come of the law, then Christ is dead in vain." For, if we in ourselves had had any thing whereby we might be saved, what needed the Son of God to take our flesh, to suffer, and to die? But for because the Son of God, being incarnate, did suffer and die, and died not in vain; therefore in our flesh there was nothing that could obtain salvation for mankind. Wherefore the only Son of God is our Saviour for ever, and by true faith maketh us partakers of his salvation.

Christ died not in vain.

Paul in the very beginning of his epistle to the Romans doth prove that all men are sinners; that in men there remaineth no strength for them to be saved by; and that the law of God itself doth dig up[2] the knowledge of offences, that is, doth apply them, bring them to light, and make them manifest, but doth not take them away, blot them out, or utterly extinguish them; and that therefore God, for his own goodness' sake, to the end that the work that he hath made should not altogether perish, doth justify the faithful freely by faith in Jesus Christ. I will rehearse a few of the apostle's own words. "The righteousness of God," saith he, "is declared without the law, being witnessed notwithstanding by the law and the prophets; the righteousness of God, I say, cometh by faith in Jesus Christ unto all and upon all them that believe. For there is no difference: for all have sinned, and have need of the glory of God, but are justified freely by his grace through the redemption that

All men are sinners.

[1 Cf. Calvin. Comment. in loc. cit. Maneat igitur illud constitutum: hic propositionem esse exclusivam, Nos non aliter justificari quam fide; aut, Non nisi fide justificari: cui ista æquipollet, Nos sola fide justificari.]

[2 cruore, Lat.]

is in Christ Jesu; whom God hath set forth to be a propitiation through faith in his blood[3]." These words of the apostle, I suppose, are most manifest to them that believe. He plucketh justification from our own merits and strength, and attributeth it to grace, whereby the Son of God is given to the world unto the punishment of the cross, that all they that believe that they are redeemed by the blood of the Son of God may be justified. Again the apostle immediately after addeth: "Therefore we hold, that man is justified by faith without the works of the law." Upon the neck of this again he argueth thus: "Is he the God of the Jews only? Is he not also of the Gentiles? Yes, even of the Gentiles also. For it is one God that shall justify circumcision by faith, and uncircumcision through faith[4]." To be God, is nothing else but to be life and salvation. But God is the God of the Gentiles also, and not of the Jews alone: therefore God is the life and salvation of the Gentiles. This life and salvation he doth communicate to us, not by the law or through circumcision, but by faith in Christ; therefore faith alone doth justify. This may be proved by the example of Cornelius the centurion, who, as soon as St Peter had preached unto him, and he once believed, was by and by justified, when as yet he had not received circumcision, or the law; when as yet he had not sacrificed, nor merited righteousness by any work that he did: for he was freely justified in faith through Jesus Christ. For Peter concluded his sermon to him in these words: "To this Christ do all the prophets give witness, that through his name whosoever believeth in him shall receive remission of sins[5]."

God justifieth as well the Gentiles as the Jews by faith.

After all this, the apostle Paul bringeth forth that notable and singular example of our father Abraham, teaching by what means our father Abraham was justified. For, this being once truly declared, it cannot choose but be plain and manifest to every one, by what means God's will is to justify all men: for the sons cannot be justified any other way than the father before them was justified. Abraham therefore was not justified by circumcision, or receiving of the sacrament; for it is said that he was justified before he was circumcised.

By what means our father Abraham was justified.

[3 Rom. iii. 21—25.]   [4 Ibid. v. 28—30.]
[5 Acts x. 43.]

Afterward was added the sign of circumcision, as "the seal of the righteousness of faith," that is, the sign or sealing that all the seed of Abraham is justified by faith[1]. The same our father Abraham was not justified by the law: for the law was four hundred and thirty years[2] added to the promise, not to take away sin or to work justification, but to make sin appear, and to make us altogether empty; and, when we are once made empty, to send, and as it were compel us to fly, to Christ. Again, Abraham was not justified by his works: and yet, in that most excellent patriarch are found to be good works; yea, and those too good works of true faith, which are both notable and many in number, such and so many as you shall scarcely find in any other. Nevertheless, yet the apostle saith: "What shall we say then that Abraham our father as pertaining to the flesh (who, I say, is our father touching the flesh) did merit or find?"—for both those significations hath the Greek word εὑρηκέναι[3]. For, "if Abraham were justified by works, then hath he to boast; but not before God." For God is only just, and he that only justifieth: all men are corrupt; yea, even Abraham is a sinner, and every man standeth in need of the glory of God. For which cause also the prophet did plainly forbid to boast in any thing, but in the mercy of God. Wherefore Abraham boasted not against God; he acknowledged himself to be a sinner, and that he was to be justified freely, and not for his own merits' sake. The apostle goeth forth and saith: "For what saith the scripture? Abraham believed in God, and it was reckoned unto him for righteousness." Two things are here affirmed: first, that Abraham believed in God; secondly, that that was imputed to him for righteousness. By this it followeth, that Abraham was justified by faith, and not by works. And that doth the apostle prove after this manner: "To him that by works doth merit righteousness righteousness is not imputed. But to Abraham is righteousness imputed: therefore he merited not righteousness by works." Again: "To him verily that worketh not, but believeth, his faith is counted for

---

[1 Rom. iv. 10—12.]

[2 Galat. iii. 17.   post annos, Lat.]

[3 εὑρηκέναι, quod *invenisse* reddunt, significat, teste Budæo, *mereri*.—Bucer. Enarr. Epist. ad Rom. in loc. cit. p. 226, Basil. 1562.]

righteousness. But Abraham believed in God; therefore his faith was reckoned for righteousness[4]."

In the same chapter the same apostle bringeth forth other arguments, altogether as strong as these, to prove that faith justifieth without works. "If they," saith he, "which are of the law be heirs, then is faith but vain, and the promise made of none effect[5]." They are of the law, which seek to be justified by the works of the law. But faith resteth upon the mercy of God. What place then shall grace and the mercy of God have left unto them, if we by works do merit justification? What shall I need to believe, that by the blood of Christ I shall be justified, if God by my works be at one with me again, who for my sins was angry with me? Finally, salvation and righteousness are promised of God. But then the promise endeth, when our own merits begin to come in place. For the apostle to the Galatians saith: "If inheritance be of the law, then is it not now of the promise. But God gave the inheritance to Abraham by promise[6]." Therefore that the promise might remain stable, faith justifieth, and not merits. *Neither is faith nor the promise of none effect.*

Again, in the fourth chapter to the Romans he saith: "Therefore by faith is the inheritance given, that it might be by grace, that the promise might be sure to all the seed; not to that only that is of the law, but to that also that is of the faith of Abraham." He rehearseth here two causes, for which he attributeth justification to faith, and not to works. The first is, that justification may be of free gift, and that the grace of God may be praised. The latter is, that the promise and salvation may remain stedfast, and that it may come upon the Gentiles also: but it should not be given to the Gentiles, if it were due only to the law and circumcision, because the Gentiles lack them both. Finally, the hope of our salvation ought to be stedfastly established: but it should never be surely grounded, or safely preserved, if it were attributed to our own works or merits; for in them is always something wanting. But in God and in the merit of the Son of God can nothing be lacking. Therefore our salvation is surely confirmed, not to be doubted of, and assuredly certain, if that we seek for it by faith in the Son of God, who is our righteousness and salvation. *Justification of free gift.*

[4 Rom. iv. 1—5.]   [5 Ibid. v. 14.]
[6 Gal. iii. 18, 22.]

To all these I will yet add another testimony out of St Paul, which is indeed both most evident and easy to be perceived. In his epistle to the Ephesians he saith: "By grace are ye saved through faith, and that not of yourselves; it is the gift of God: not of works, lest any man should boast himself. For we are the workmanship of God, created in Christ Jesus into good works, which God hath before ordained that we should walk in them[1]."

More than this I will not say, neither will I at large expound the words of Paul. For these testimonies are more clear than the noon-day, and do most evidently testify, that we are justified by faith, and not by any works.

Faith sheweth forth and expresseth itself by good works.

But, reverend[2] brethren in the Lord, good works here come into no jeopardy to be little set by, because of this doctrine, which teacheth that faith alone doth justify. Thus did the apostles of Christ teach; why then should we not teach so too? As for them that think this doctrine, whereby we do constantly affirm that faith alone without works doth justify, to be contrary to religion, let them blame the apostles of Christ, and not find fault with us. Moreover, whereas we

Faith only justifieth.

say, that the faithful are justified by faith alone, or else by faith without works, we do not say, as many think we do, that faith is post alone[3], or utterly destitute of good works: for wheresoever faith is, there also it sheweth itself by good works; because the righteous cannot but work righteousness. But before he doth work righteousness, that is to say, good works, he must of necessity be righteous: therefore the righteous doth not attain to righteousness that goeth before by works that follow after. Wherefore that righteousness is attributed to grace: for the faithful are freely by grace justified in faith, according to that saying, "The just shall live by his faith;" and after that they are justified, they begin to bring forth the works of righteousness. Therefore, in this discourse I mean not to overthrow good works, which have their due place and dignity in the church among the faithful before the face of God: but my mind is, by all the means I may, to prove that the grace of God, and increase[4] of the Son of God, is overthrown and trodden under foot, when we join our merits and works to the merit of Christ,

---

[1 Ephes. ii. 8—10.]   [2 honorandi, Lat.]
[3 fidem esse solam, Lat.]   [4 meritum, Lat.]

and to faith, by which we take hold on Christ. For what can be more manifest than this saying of the blessed apostle? "If we be saved by grace, then not now works[5]; for then grace is no more grace. But if we be saved by works, then is it now no grace[6]; for the work is no more work." Rom. xi. Wherefore these two, grace and merit or work, cannot stand together. Therefore, lest we should overthrow the grace of God, and wickedly deny the fruit of Christ his passion, we do attribute justification unto faith only, because that faith attributeth it to the mere grace of God in the death of the Son of God.

And yet for all this we acknowledge that we are created, according to the doctrine of Paul, unto good works; to those good works, I say, which God hath before ordained[7], which he in his word hath appointed, and doth require us to walk in the same: in which although we walk, and are become rich in good works, yet notwithstanding we do not attribute to them our justification; but, according to the doctrine of the gospel, we humble ourselves under the hand of him that saith: "So ye also, when ye have done all things that are commanded you, yet say, We are unprofitable servants; we have done no more than we ought to do[8]." So then, as often as the godly doth read, that our own works do justify us, that our own works are called righteousness, that unto our own works is given a reward and life everlasting; he doth not by and by swell with pride, nor yet forget the merit of Christ: but, setting a godly and apt interpretation upon such-like places, he doth consider that all things are of the grace of God, and that so great things are attributed to the works of men, because they are received into grace, and are now become the sons of God for Christ his sake; so that at the last, all things may be turned upon Christ himself, for whose sake the godly know that they and all theirs are in favour and accepted of God the Father.

In this that I have said (which is a little indeed in respect of the largeness of the matter, but sufficiently long enough in respect of one hour's space appointed me to speak in,) I have declared unto you, dearly beloved, the great effect of faith; that is to say, that it justifieth the faithful; where, by the way,

Of good works.

[5 ex operibus, Lat.] [6 jam non ex gratia, Lat.]
[7 Ephes. ii. 10.] [8 Luke xvii. 10.]

I have rather briefly touched, than at large discoursed upon, the whole work of justification, both profitable and necessary for all men to know. Now, therefore, I pass over this, and come to the rest.

Faith the root of all good works.

True faith is the well-spring and root of all virtues and good works: and first of all, it satisfieth the mind and desire of man, and maketh it quiet and joyful. For the Lord in the gospel saith: "I am the bread of life: he that cometh to me shall not hunger; and he that believeth in me shall not thirst at any time[1]." For what can he desire more, which doth already feel, that by true faith he possesseth the very Son of God, in whom are all the heavenly treasures, and in whom is all fulness and grace? Our consciences are made clear and quiet, so soon as we perceive that by true faith Christ, the Son of God, is altogether ours; that he hath appeased the Father in our behalf; that he doth now stand in the presence of the Father, and maketh intercession to him for us. And for that cause saith Paul: "Being justified by faith, we have peace with God through our Lord Jesus Christ[2]." Through the same Christ, also, by faith we have a free passage unto the Father[3]. Wherefore we pray to the Father in his Son's name, and at his hand we obtain all things that are available to our behoof. Very well therefore said the apostle John: "And this is the confidence that we have in him, that, if we ask any thing according to his will, he heareth us. And if we know that he heareth us, whatsoever we ask, we know also that we have the petitions that we requested at his hands[4]." They that want faith do neither pray to God, nor yet receive of him the things that are for their welfare. Moreover, faith maketh us acceptable to God, and doth command us to have an eye to the well using of God's good gifts.

Faith the victory of all Christians.

Faith causeth us not to faint in tribulations: yea also, by faith we overcome the world, the flesh, the devil, and all adversities; as the apostle John saith: "For all that is born of God overcometh the world: and this is the victory that vanquisheth the world, even your faith. Who is he that overcometh the world, but he that believeth that Jesus is the Son of God[5]?" Paul saith: "Some were racked, not caring,

[1 John vi. 35.]   [2 Rom. v. 1.]
[3 Ephes. ii. 18.]   [4 1 John v. 14, 15.]
[5 1 John v. 4, 5.]

by faith, to be set at liberty, that they might obtain a better
resurrection. Other some were tried with mocks and stripes,
with fetters and imprisonments; were stoned, were hewed in
pieces, were slain with the edge of the sword: they wandered
in sheep-skins and goat-skins, comfortless, oppressed, afflicted,
(of whom the world was not worthy,) wandering in deserts and
mountains, and in the dens and caves of the earth[6]." For the
Lord himself in the gospel said: "This spake I unto you,
that ye might have peace in me. In the world ye have
affliction; but be of good confidence, I have overcome the
world[7]." Faith therefore both shall be, and is, the force and
strength of patience. Patience is the prop[8], uplifting, and
preservation of hope. Of faith springeth charity. Charity "is
the fulfilling of the law[9]," which containeth in it the sum of all
good works. But unless we have a true faith in God, there
is no charity in us. "Every one that loveth him that begat,"
saith John the apostle, "loveth him also that is born of him[10]."

The hour is past a good while since, and no man is able
in many hours, so substantially as it requireth, to declare
the whole effect of faith.

Ye have heard, dearly beloved, that true faith is the
justification of the church or faithful of God; that it is, I say,
the forgiveness of all sins, a receiving into the grace of God,
a taking by adoption into the number of the sons of God, an
assured and blessed sanctification[11], and finally, the well-spring
of all good works. Let us therefore in true faith pray to
God the Father, in the name of our Lord Jesus Christ, that
he will vouchsafe to fill our hearts with this true faith; that
in this present world, being joined to him in faith, we may
serve him as we ought; and, after our departure out of this
life, we may for ever live with him in whom we believe. To
him be praise and glory for ever. Amen.

[6 Heb. xi. 35—38.]
[7 John xvi. 33.]
[8 *Hæc* fulcit, &c., Lat.   This (faith) is the prop, &c.]
[9 Rom. xiii. 10.]   [10 1 John v. 1.]
[11 beatificationem, Lat.]

OF THE FIRST ARTICLES OF THE CHRISTIAN FAITH CONTAINED IN THE APOSTLES' CREED.

THE SEVENTH SERMON.

In my two last sermons I entreated of true faith and the effects thereof; and among the rest in one place I said, that the articles of the christian faith are, as it were, a brief summary of true faith: now therefore I think it to be not beside the purpose, and part of my duty, to lay before you those twelve articles of our belief. For they are the substance and matter of true faith, wherein faith is exercised: which because it is the ground[1] of things hoped for, here is plainly and briefly declared in these articles what things those are that are to be hoped for. But let no man at this present look for at my hand the busy[2] and full discourse of the articles of our faith: I will but briefly go through them, touching only the most necessary points. They are in another place handled more at large by several parts. Pray ye with me to the Lord, that he will vouchsafe to shew to us his ways, to guide and preserve us in them, to the glory of his own name, and the everlasting salvation of our souls.

The Apostles' Creed.   First, I have to say somewhat touching the common name, whereby the articles of our faith are usually called the Symbol or Creed of the Apostles. A symbol is as much to say as a conferring together, or else a badge[3]. The articles are called a conferring together, because, by the laying together of the apostles' doctrine, they were made and written to be a rule and an abridgement of the faith preached by the apostles, and received of the catholic or universal church. But what he was that first did thus dispose and write these articles, it is not known, nor left in writing of the holy scriptures. Some there are that do attribute it to the apostles themselves, and therefore do call it by the name of the Apostles' Creed. St Cyprian, the martyr, in his exposition of the Apostles' Creed, saith: " Our ancestors have a saying, that after the Lord's ascension, when by the coming of the Holy Ghost the fiery tongues sat upon every one of the apostles, so

[1 substantia, Lat.]   [2 operosam, Lat.]
[3 et collatio, et indicium, Lat.]

that they spake both divers and sundry languages, whereby there was no foreign nation nor barbarous tongue to which they seemed not sufficiently prepared to pass by the way ; they had a commandment from the Lord, to go unto all nations to preach the word of God. When therefore they were in a readiness to depart, they laid down among themselves a platform of preaching for them all to follow, lest peradventure, being severed one from another, they should preach divers things to them that were converted to the faith of Christ. Wherefore being there all together, and replenished with the Holy Ghost, they gathered one every one's several sentence, and made that breviary (as I said) to be a pattern for all their preachings to be framed by, appointing it for a rule to be given to them that should believe[4]." This saith Cyprian. But whether they were of the apostles' own making or no, or else that other, the apostles' disciples, made them, yet this is very well known, that the very doctrine of the apostles is purely contained and taught in them. These twelve articles are called also a badge, because by that sign, as it were by a badge, true Christians are discerned from false.

Now I will declare what order I will use in expounding them unto you. This whole breviary, or abridgement of faith, may be divided into four parts ; so that the three first parts may make manifest the mysteries of the three Persons in one Godhead ; and that the fourth may lay forth the fruits of faith, that is to say, what good things we look for by faith, and what good things God bestoweth on them that put their trust in him. And yet, this notwithstanding, I will proceed

The partition of the Apostles' Creed.

[4 Tradunt majores nostri, quod post ascensionem Domini, cum per adventum sancti Spiritus super singulos quosque apostolos igneæ linguæ sedissent, ut loquelis diversis variisque loquerentur, per quod eis nulla gens extera, nulla linguæ barbaries inaccessa videretur et invia, præceptum eis a Domino datum, ob prædicandum Dei verbum, ad singulas quemque proficisci nationes. Discessuri itaque ab invicem normam prius futuræ sibi prædicationis in commune constituunt, ne forte alius ab alio abducti diversum aliquid his, qui ad fidem Christi invitabantur, exponerent. Omnes ergo in uno positi, et Spiritu sancto repleti, breve istud futuræ sibi (ut diximus) prædicationis indicium, conferendo in unum quod sentiebat unusquisque, componunt, atque hanc credentibus dandam esse regulam statuunt.— Cypr. Expos. in Symb. Apost. in init. ed. Oxon. 1682. This tract is not Cyprian's, but was written by Ruffinus.]

herein even orderly so as the twelve articles are placed or
set down.

The first article of christian faith is this : "I believe in
God, the Father Almighty, maker of heaven and earth."
And this first article of the Creed containeth two especial
points : for first we say generally, I believe in God; then
we descend particularly to the distinction of the Persons, and
add, the Father Almighty. For God is one in substance,
and three in Persons. Wherefore, understanding the unity
of the substance, we say plainly, I believe in God: and
again, keeping and not confounding the Persons, we add, In
the Father Almighty, In Jesus Christ his only Son, and in
the Holy Ghost. Let us therefore believe that God is one,
not many, and pure in substance; but three in Persons, the
Father, the Son, and the Holy Ghost. For in the law it is
written : "Hearken, Israel : The Lord our God is one Lord[1]."
And again, in the gospel we read that the Lord saith :
"Baptize them in the name of the Father, of the Son, and of
the Holy Ghost[2]."

By the way, this is singularly to be marked of us; that,
when we pray, we say, "Our Father which art in heaven,
give us this day our daily bread;" but that, when we make
confession of our belief, we say not, We believe, but, "I believe." For faith is required of every one of us, for every
particular man to have without dissimulation in his heart, and
without double meaning to profess it with his mouth. It was
not enough for Abraham to have faith for all his seed ; neither
will it avail thee any thing for another to believe, if thou thyself art without faith : for the Lord requireth faith of every
particular man for himself. Wherefore, so oft as we confess
our faith, every one of us by himself doth say, "I believe."
But what it is to believe, I have declared already in my fourth
sermon.

It followeth in the confession, "I believe in God." God
is the object and foundation of our faith, as he that is the
everlasting and chief goodness, never weary, but alway ready
at our need. We therefore believe in God; that is to say, we
put our whole hope, all our safety, and ourselves wholly into
his hands, as unto him that is able to preserve and bestow on
us all things that are requisite for our behoof.

God is one
in substance,
and three in
Persons.

I believe in
God.

[1 Deut. vi. 4.]   [2 Matt. xxviii. 19.]

Now it followeth that that God, in whom we rest, and God is called
a Father. unto whose tuition we do all commit ourselves, is "the Father Almighty." Our God is therefore called Father, because from before all beginning he begat the Son like to himself. For the scripture calleth God "the Father of our Lord Jesus Christ." "He," saith the apostle, "is the brightness of the glory of God, and the lively image[3] of the substance of the Father : to whom he said, Thou art my Son, this day have I begotten thee." And again : "I will be his Father, and he shall be my Son[4]." Also God is called Father in respect of the likeness that he hath with our earthly father ; to wit, because of our creation, the favour, love, good-will, and carefulness wherewith he is affected towards us. For God hath created us, God loveth us, God regardeth our affairs, and is careful for us ; yea, and that more exceedingly too than any earthly father is. For saith David : "Even as the father pitieth his children, so doth the Lord pity them that fear him : for he knoweth our estate, remembering that we are but dust[5]." Esaias also in his 49th chapter saith : "Can a woman forget her own infant, and not pity and be fain over[6] the son of her own womb ?   But admit she do forget; yet will not I forget thee." In this is declared God's good-will to us-ward : and we, confessing that God is our Father, do also profess that God to us is both gentle, liberal, and merciful, who wisheth us all things that are available to our health, and purposeth nothing to us-ward but that which is good and wholesome ; and, last of all, that at his hand we receive what good soever we have, either bodily or ghostly.

God is called Almighty, because by his might he can do God is called
Almighty. all things; because he is Lord of all things, and hath all things subject to his commandment. For the same cause also is he called the Lord of hosts. Heaven, earth, and whatsoever is therein, stars, all elements, men, angels, devils, all living creatures, all things created, are in the power of the most high and everlasting God. Whatsoever he commandeth, that they do : nothing is able to withstand his will. What he

[3 expressa imago, Lat. ; Erasmus' rendering. The Vulgate has only *figura.*]
[4 Heb. i. 3, 5.]
[5 Psal. ciii. 13, 14.]
[6 eximie afficiatur erga, Lat.]

will, that must of necessity be done : and also these things he useth even as his own will and pleasure is, and as his justice and man's salvation do require. First we confessed, that God doth will us well; and now we acknowledge, that whatsoever he will, that he is able to bring to pass. For we say that God is Almighty, that is, that there is nothing but he can do it, which is profitable and necessary for us men, as he that is Lord of all, and our strong helper.

God is the maker of heaven and earth. But that God is our good Father, liberal, gentle, merciful, strong, almighty, Lord of all, and our defender and deliverer, it is to be seen by his wonderful works. For he is the "maker of heaven and earth." And in the making of heaven and earth he hath declared the great love that he beareth to mankind. For when as yet they were not, neither were able with deserts and good turns to provoke God to do them any good; then God first of his own mere and natural goodness made heaven and earth, a most excellent and beautiful palace, and gave it them to dwell in, putting under man's dominion all the creatures of this whole world. But how great power he shewed in the making of all these things, it is evident by this, that " he spake the word, and they were made; he commanded, and they were created[1]." Which if thou bring into parts, and severally examine what he made in those six days, in what order, with what beauty, to how great commodity of mankind, and finally how almost with no labour at all he brought them all forth, as it is at large written by Moses in the first of Genesis, thou shalt be compelled to be amazed at the goodwill and power of God. And yet, by the way, we must think the Creator of all things to be such an one, as by his Son, that is, by his eternal Wisdom, hath created all things both visible and invisible; yea, and that of nothing too : and doth moreover at this very present sustain, nourish, rule, and preserve all things by his everlasting Spirit, without which every thing would presently fall to ruin, and come to nought. We do herein therefore confess also the providence of our eternal God, and his exceeding wise government.

And thus in this first part I have declared unto you that which is proper to the Father. For he is a Father; yea, he is the Father of our Lord Jesus Christ, and our Father also,

---

[1 Psal. xxxiii. 9, and cxlviii. 5.]

being Lord of all things, maker of heaven and earth, governor and preserver of all things, by whom all things are,
and in whom all things consist; who from before all beginning begot the eternal Son, equal with the Father, being of
one substance, power, and glory with the Father, by whom
also he made the world. From both them proceedeth the Holy
Ghost, as David witnesseth, and saith: "By the word of the
Lord the heavens were made, and by the breath of his mouth
all the host thereof[2]."

Now followeth the second part, wherein are contained all
the mysteries of Jesus Christ, our Lord, the Son of God.
For the second article of the christian faith is thus word for
word: "And in Jesus Christ, his only Son, our Lord." This
article also comprehendeth two things: the first is, that we
believe in the Son of God; the second, what the Son of God
is. For we confess that we believe, that is, that we put our
whole hope and confidence of life and salvation, as well in the
Son as in the Father. And therefore we say plainly, "I believe
in Jesus Christ," even as before we said, "I believe in God,"
&c. For the Lord Jesus himself, in the fourteenth chapter
of John, saith: "Let not your heart be troubled: ye believe
in God, believe also in me." Again: "This is the work of
God, that ye believe in him whom he hath sent[3]." And
again: "This is eternal life, to know thee, the true God only,
and him whom thou hast sent, Christ Jesus[4]." Moreover, in
the gospel after St John we read, that the Lord, speaking to
the blind whose eyes he opened, said: "Dost thou believe in the
Son of God?" and that the blind, having received his sight,
answered: "Who is he, Lord, that I may believe in him?"
Whereunto the Lord replied: "Thou hast seen him, and he it
is that talketh with thee." And that then again the blind
said, "I believe, Lord;" and therewithal he worshipped him[5].
Therefore let us also believe and worship; let us believe that
Jesus is the very Son of God the Father, being of one power
with the Father, although in Person he differ from the Father:
which David testifying saith, "The LORD said to my Lord,
Sit thou at my right hand," &c.[6]

But if we declare at large, who that Son of God is, in

The second article of our belief.

To believe in the Son of God.

Who the Son of God is.

[2 Psal. xxxiii. 6.]   [3 John vi. 29.]
[4 John xvii. 3.]   [5 John ix. 35—38.]
[6 Psal. cx. 1.]

whom we believe, then must we note three things especially. The first is, that he is called the only Son. If he be the Son, yea, and that too the Son of God, then is his nature and substance a divine nature and substance. For in this signification doth the apostle call him "the brightness of the glory of the Father, and the lively image of his substance." Very well therefore do the holy fathers say, that the Son is of the same

Consubstantial and co-essential. The only Son.

substance and being with[1] the Father. Whereunto belongeth that, that he is called the only Son; and in another place, the only-begotten and first-begotten Son. For we also are called sons, not by participation of nature, or likeness of substance, or naturally, but by adoption. And therefore the Jews were not offended, because he called himself the Son of God, in that sense that all the faithful are called, and are, the sons of God; but because they did perceive, that he did more extol himself in saying that he is the natural Son of God, equal to God, and God himself. For thus we read in the fifth of John: "Therefore the Jews sought the more to kill Jesus; not only because he had broken the sabbath, but said also that God was his Father, and made himself equal with God." Again, where the Lord in the tenth chapter said, "I and my Father are one; then the Jews took up stones to stone him withal: but Jesus answered, Many good works have I done unto you; for which of them do ye stone me?" To which the Jews replied: "For thy good works' sake we stone thee not, but for thy blasphemy, and because thou, being a man, makest thyself God." These are most evident testimonies of the natural Godhead of Christ, which whosoever believeth not, he hath not the Father[2]. For he that honoureth the Son, honoureth the Father; and he that is without the Son hath not the Father: and unless the Son were God by nature, he could not be the Saviour of the world.

Now the second thing that is to be marked is, that the name of the only-begotten Son of God is opened, and he is

Jesus.

called "Jesus Christ." The name is expressly set down, that we may know who it is in whom we believe, lest peradventure we might be deceived in the person. It is Jesus: which name was given unto him by God's appointment from heaven, even

[1 consubstantialis et coessentialis, Lat.]
[2 1 John ii. 23.]

as also it was prefigured in duke Josue and in Jesus the high priest. The angel, in the gospel after St Matthew, instructing Joseph, saith : " Mary shall bring forth a son, and thou shalt call his name Jesus. For he shall save his people from their sins[3]."

So then this Son of God, Jesus, is the Saviour of the world, who forgiveth sins, and setteth us free from all the power of our adversary the devil : which verily he could not do, unless he were very God. He is also called Christ, *Christ.* which is all one as if you say, Anointed. The Jews call him Messias; which word is a title proper to a kingdom or priesthood[4]. For they of old were wont to anoint their kings and priests : they were anointed with external or figurative ointment or oil. But very Christ was anointed with the very true ointment, that is, with the fulness of the Holy Ghost: as is to be seen in the first and third chapters after St John. Most properly therefore is this name Christ attributed to our Lord. For, first, he is both King and Priest of the people of God. Then the Holy Ghost is poured fully by all means and abundantly into Jesus, from whom, as it were by a lively fountain, it floweth into all the members of Christ. For this is that Aaron, upon whose head the oil was poured, " which ran down to his beard, and the nethermost skirts of his garment[5]:" for " of his fulness we have all received[6]."

The last thing that is to be noted now in this second article is, that we call the Son of God "our Lord." The Son *Christ is our* *Lord.* of God verily is for two causes properly called our Lord: first, in respect of the mystery of our redemption. For Christ is the Lord of all the elect, whom he hath delivered from the power and dominion of Satan, sin, and death, and hath made them a people of his own getting for himself[7]. This similitude is taken of lords, which with their money buy slaves for their use, or else which in wars reserve captives, whom they might have slain, or which deliver men condemned from present death. So then by this, lords are, as it were, deliverers, redeemers, or saviours[8]. Hereunto verily alludeth

---

[3 ch. i. 21.]   [4 tam regni, quam sacerdotii, Lat.]
[5 Psal. cxxxiii. 2.]   [6 John i. 16.]
[7 populum acquisitionis, Lat. 1 Pet. ii. 9.]
[8 Dominus redemptoris et assertoris vocabulum est.—Erasm. Colloq. Inquisit. de Fide. Opp. Lugd. Bat. 1703. Tom. I. col. 729.]

[BULLINGER.]   9

Paul, where he saith: "Ye are bought with a price: become not (therefore) the servants of men[1]." And St Peter saith: "Ye are redeemed, not with gold and silver, but with the precious blood of the unspotted Lamb[2]." Moreover, Christ is called Lord in respect of his divine power and nature, by which all things are in subjection to the Son of God. And for because this word "Lord" is of a very ample signification, as that which containeth both the divine nature and majesty, we see that the apostles in their writings use it very willingly. Paul to the Corinthians saith: "Although there be many lords, yet have we but one Lord Jesus Christ, by whom all things are, and we by him[3]."

The third article of our belief.

Now the third article of christian faith is this: "Which was conceived by the Holy Ghost; born of the virgin Mary." In the second article we have confessed, that we believe in Jesus Christ, the Son of God, our Lord: wherein we have, as it were in a shadow, confessed, that we believe assuredly, that God, the Father, hath for us and our salvation given to the world his Son, to be a Saviour and Redeemer; for hitherto belong those names, Jesus, and Lord. Now therefore in this third article I have to declare the manner and order how he came into the world; to wit, by incarnation. This article containeth two things; the conception of Christ, and his nativity: of both which I will orderly speak, after that I have briefly declared unto you the causes of the Lord his incarnation.

The causes of the Lord his incarnation.

Men were in a miserable taking, and all mankind should utterly have perished for sin, which we have all drawn from the first man Adam: for the reward of sin is death. And for that cause we, that were to be cast into hell, could not enter into heaven, unless the Son of God had descended unto

Immanuel.

us, and, becoming God with us[4], had with himself drawn us into heaven. Therefore the chief cause of his incarnation is, to be a Mediator betwixt God and men, and by intercession to join, or bring into one, them that were severed. For

A mediator.

where a mediator is, there also must needs be discord and parties. The parties are God and men: the cause of discord is sin. Now the office of the mediator is to bring to

[1 1 Cor. vii. 23.]   [2 1 Pet. i. 18, 19.]
[3 1 Cor. viii. 5, 6.]
[4 Immanuel, Lat.]

agreement the parties disagreeing : which verily cannot be done, unless that sin, the cause of this variance, be taken clean away. But sin is neither cleansed nor taken away, except that blood be shed, and death do follow. This witnesseth Paul in his ninth chapter to the Hebrews. The mediator ought therefore to take on him our flesh and blood, that he might both die and shed his blood. Furthermore it is needful, that this advocate, or mediator, be indifferently common to both the parties, whom he hath to reconcile : wherefore our Lord Christ ought to be very God and very man. If he had been God alone, then should he have been terrible to men, and have stood them in little stead : if he had been mere man, then could he not have had access to God, which is a consuming fire. Wherefore our Lord Jesus Christ, being both God and man, was a fit Mediator for both the parties. Which thing the apostle witnessing saith : "One God, and one Mediator of God and men, the man Christ Jesus, who gave himself the price of redemption for all[5]." The same apostle, in the second and ninth chapters to the Hebrews, speaketh many things belonging to this place. And in the second chapter, rehearsing another cause of Christ his incarnation, he saith : " It became him in all things to be made like unto his brethren, that he might be merciful and a faithful High Priest in things concerning God, for to purge the people's sins. For in that he himself was tempted, he is able to succour them that are tempted." Another cause, wherefore our Lord was incarnate, was, that he might instruct us men in all godliness and righteousness ; and finally, that he might be the light of the world, and an ensample of holy life. For Paul saith : " The grace of God that bringeth salvation hath appeared unto us, teaching us to renounce ungodliness, and to live holily[6]." To conclude : he therefore became one with us by the participation of nature, that is to say, it pleased him to be incarnate for this cause, that he might join us again to God, who for sin were separated from God ; and receive us into the fellowship of himself, and all other his goodness beside.

The next is for us to declare the manner of his incarnation. The manner of Christ his conception. This article of faith standeth on two members. The first is,

[5 1 Tim. ii. 5, 6.]
[6 Tit. ii. 11, 12.]

9—2

"He was conceived by the Holy Ghost." All we men, Christ excepted, are conceived by the seed of man, which of itself is unclean; and therefore we are born sinners; and Paul saith, "We are born the sons of wrath[1]." But the body of Christ, I say, our Lord, was not conceived in the virgin Mary by Joseph, or by any seed of man, but by the Holy Ghost: not that the Holy Ghost was in place of the seed; for nothing is begotten of the Spirit, but what is spiritual. Neither hath our Lord a phantastical[2], but a very true body, and of the same substance with us. So then our Lord was conceived in the womb of the virgin by the Holy Ghost. For the Holy Ghost by his eternal power did bring to pass, that, the virginity of the mother being uncorrupted, she, I say, being made with child, conceived of her blood, and gave a pure and very human body to the Son of God; as is declared at large by the angel Gabriel in the first chapter of St Luke: of which place I mean to speak elsewhere more largely: I do now pass it over untouched.

God himself straightways after the beginning of the world did foretell, that such should be the manner of that conception. For he said not, The seed of the man shall tread down the serpent's head, but "the seed of the woman[3]." Moreover the Lord by the prophets saith: "I will raise up seed to David." But Moses' law for the raising up of seed to the brother departed is well known: for if the brother died without issue of children, his brother remaining alive was compelled to marry the deceased brother's wife, and of her to beget children, which were called and counted, not by the name of him that was living, but of the dead brother[4]. Wherefore, when there was not to be found a man of David's line, that was sufficiently meet to beget on the virgin the Son of God, the Saviour of the world, God himself raiseth up seed to David, and by his Holy Spirit maketh the virgin with child; who, although she were not with child by a man of

[1 Ephes. ii. 3.]

[2 The Docetæ, an early heretical sect, maintained, that the incarnation and sufferings of our Lord were not real, but phantastical.—See Routh's Reliq. Sacr. Tom. i. p. 461. ed. Oxon. 1846; also Calvin. Instit. Lib. ii. cap. 13.]

[3 Gen. iii. 15.]

[4 Deut. xxv. 5, 6.]

David's line, yet because she was a daughter of David's
stock, and because, God so working, she of her own substance gave substance to the Son of God, this her child
Christ both is, and is called, the Son of David. What doth
that argue moreover, that David in the 110th Psalm saith,
" In the mighty power of holiness the dew of thy birth is to
thee of the womb of the morning;" or, " The dew of thy
birth is to thee of the womb of the morning in the mighty
power of holiness?" That is to say, By a certain mighty
power of holiness, and marvellous means, shalt thou be born.
For thy birth shall be like unto the engendering of the dew,
which cometh of the pure morning, as it were a child born
of the womb. For as in the day-time the sun draweth out
of the earth a vapour, which, by reason of the smallness of
the heat which draweth it upward, is by the coldness of the
temperate night-evenings drawn down again, and resolved
into water; so God, that is the Sun of righteousness, took
blood of the earth, that is, of the body of the untouched
virgin Mary, and by a wonderful means did holily and purely
bring to pass, that of her unspotted womb should be born
and conceived the most holy Son of God.

The causes, why this conception of the Son of God in the _The causes why Christ his conception is pure._
womb of the holy virgin is most pure, are these. He that
is conceived in the womb of a virgin is God; but God is
a consuming fire, which cannot take or suffer any uncleanness in itself. Another cause is this: God came to cleanse
our uncleanness, that is, the uncleanness of us men. He
himself verily ought to be exempt from all original spots, and
in all points most holy, to the end that, being the only unspotted sacrifice offered up for the sins of all the world, he
might clean take away all the sins of the world. For that
which is itself defiled cannot cleanse the thing that is defiled;
but rather the spot or filthiness doth double his uncleanness
by the coming to of that other unclean thing.

The second member of this third article is: He was " born
of the virgin Mary." The Lord was born of Mary his mother, _Of the birth of Christ._
yet she a virgin still. He is therefore very man, which is
born of woman. Moreover his birth is pure : for he was
born of the virgin, so that together she was a mother, and
yet a virgin too. For Esaias saith : " Behold, a virgin shall

conceive, and bring forth a son[1]." A virgin, saith he, shall do both, conceive and bring forth; so that nevertheless she may remain a virgin still. The birth, therefore, of the Son of God is most pure. Also his birth is a true birth, verily and indeed. For he taketh flesh of the substance and womb of the virgin: in which signification also our Lord Jesus Christ is called the Son of David. He could not be called David's son, unless he had taken very human substance of Mary, a maid or daughter of the stock of David. Which that the apostle John might most properly signify and express, he saith: "The Word was made flesh[2]." And the apostle Paul saith: "He doth nowhere take on him the angels, but the seed of Abraham[3]." And in the same place again he affirmeth, that the Lord "was made like to his brethren in all things, sin excepted." To the Philippians he saith: "When he was equal with God, he made himself of no reputation, taking on him the form of a servant, and made in the likeness of men, and found in figure as a man[4]." Again, the apostle John beareth witness, and saith: "Every spirit, that confesseth that Jesus Christ is come in the flesh, is of God; and every spirit, which confesseth not that Jesus Christ is come in the flesh, is not of God[5]." Luke, in his second chapter, hath at large set forth the manner of his nativity; and I do mean elsewhere to speak of it at the full. Let us therefore confess, that Jesus Christ was "conceived by the Holy Ghost, and born of the virgin Mary."

The fourth article of our belief. The fourth article of christian faith is this: "He suffered under Pontius Pilate, was crucified, dead, and buried: he descended into hell." In this fourth article is declared the end, use, and chiefest commodity of the Lord his incarnation. For he became man, that he might suffer and die, and, by dying and suffering, might redeem us from eternal death and the torments of hell, and make us (being once cleansed) heirs of life everlasting. For this is the end of the Lord his death, as I will by and by shew you, and as Paul doth at large declare in the ninth chapter to the Hebrews.

[1 Isai. vii. 14.]   [2 John i. 14.]
[3 Heb. ii. 16, 17. assumit, Lat.; Erasmus' rendering. The Vulgate has *apprehendit*.]
[4 ch. ii. 6—8.]   [5 1 John iv. 2, 3.]

This article also is divided into his parts. First, we confess that our Lord suffered in very deed, and not phantastically Christ did suffer. to the appearance only[6]; and that he suffered verily the calamities and miseries of this world, and after that again the torments of the slaughter-men, and death itself in most bitter pangs. He suffered therefore both in soul and body ; yea, and that too in many fashions. For Esaias saith : "He is a man of sorrows, and hath felt calamities. He beareth our infirmities, and hath carried our sorrows[7]." For the Lord himself also in the gospel said : "My soul is heavy, even unto the death[8]." But verily he suffered all this for us ; for in him was neither sin, nor any cause else why he should suffer.

Secondarily, in this article is noted the time, and Pontius Christ suffered under Pontius Pilate. Pilate the judge under whom the Lord died, and redeemed the world from sin, death, the devil, and hell. He suffered therefore in the monarchy of the Romans, under the emperor Tiberius, when as now, according to the prophecy of Jacob, father of Israel[9], the Jewish people obeyed foreign kings, because there were no more kings or captains of the stock of Judah to have the rule over them : for he foretold, that then the Messias should come[10]. What may be thought of that moreover, that the Lord himself, oftener than once in the gospel, did foreshew that he should be delivered into the hands of the Gentiles, and by them be put to death?

In the third point of this article we do expressly declare the manner of his death; for we add: "He was crucified," and died on the cross. But the death of the cross, as it was most reproachful, so also was it most bitter or sharp to be suffered ; yet took he that kind of death upon him, that he might make satisfaction for the world, and fulfil that which from the beginning was prefigured, that he should be hanged on the tree. Isaac was laid on the pile of wood to be offered up in sacrifice. Moses also stuck the serpent on the stake of wood, and lift it up to be beheld. And the Lord himself said : " I, when I shall be lift up from the earth, will draw all men unto me[11]." Finally, he died on the cross, giving up his ghost to God. For he died verily and indeed, as you shall straightway perceive: where I have briefly to declare unto you,

[6 non putative.]   [7 Isai. liii. 3, 4.]
[8 Mark xiv. 34.]   [9 Jacobi Israelis, Lat.]
[10 Gen. xlix. 10.]   [11 John xii 32]

what the fruit of Christ his death is. First, we were accursed because of sin : he therefore took our curse upon himself, being lift up upon the cross, to the end he might take our curse away, and that we might be blessed in him. Then also, the heritage bequeathed to us by will could not come unto us, unless he which bequeathed it did die. But God bequeathed it : who, that he might die, became man, and died according to his human nature, to the end that we might receive the heritage of life. In another place again Paul saith : " Him that knew not sin did God make sin for us, that we by him might be made the righteousness of God[1]." Our Lord therefore became man, by the sacrifice of himself to make satisfaction for us ; on whom, as it were upon a goat for sin-offering, when all the sins of the whole world were gathered together and laid, he by his death took away and purged them all : so that now the only sacrifice of Christ hath satisfied for the sins of the whole world. And this verily is the greatest commodity of Christ his death taught everywhere by the apostles of Christ. Next after that, also, the death of Christ doth teach us patience and the mortification of our flesh : yea, Christ, by the participation of himself, doth by his Spirit work in us, that sin may not reign in us. Touching which thing the apostle Paul teacheth many things in the sixth chapter to the Romans. The Lord in the gospel saith : " If any man will follow me, let him deny himself, and take up his cross, and follow me[2]." These, and a few more, are the fruits of the Lord his passion, or the death of Christ.

Our Lord was buried.

Fourthly, in this article is added : " He was buried." For our Lord died verily and indeed upon the cross. The very truth of his death was proved by the soldier, which thrust him through the side. After that, he was taken down from the cross, and laid in a sepulchre. In the gospel are expressed the names of them that buried him, Joseph and Nicodemus. There is also shewed the manner how they buried him. The fruit of this his burial the Saviour himself hath taught in these words : " Verily, verily, I say unto you, unless the seed of corn cast into the earth do die, it remaineth alone ; but if it die, it bringeth forth much fruit[3]." Whereupon the apostle exhorteth us to be buried with Christ in his

[1 2 Cor. v. 21.]   [2 Matt. xvi. 24.]
[3 John xii. 24.]

death, that we may rise again in the newness of life[4]; yea, that we may live and reign with him for evermore. If, therefore, our bodies also be buried at any time, let us not therefore be troubled in mind; for the faithful are buried, that they may rise with Christ again.

The fifth part of this fourth article some do put severally by itself, for the fifth article of our faith. I for my part do see no cause why it should be plucked from that that goeth before; nor why it should make by itself a peculiar article of our faith. The words are these: "He descended into hell." Touching this there are sundry opinions among the expositors of the holy scriptures. Augustine, in his book *De Fide et Symbolo*[5], doth neither place these words in the rule of belief, nor yet expound them. Cyprian saith thus: "It is to be known verily, that in the creed of the Latin church this is not added, 'He descended into hell;' nor yet is this clause received in the churches of the east: but yet the sense of that clause seemeth to be all one with that, where it is said, 'He was buried.'[6]" This saith he. So then Cyprian's opinion seemeth to be, that to descend into hell is nothing else but to be laid in the grave, according to that saying of Jacob: "Ye will bring my grey hairs with sorrow to hell, or the grave[7]."

But there are some that think this assertion to be without lawful proof. For it is not likely that they would wrap a thing once already plainly spoken immediately after in a darker kind of speech. Nay rather, so often as two sentences are joined together that signify both one thing, the latter is always an exposition of the first[8]. But in these two

He descended into hell.

[4 Rom. vi. 4.]

[5 August. Opp. Par. 1531. Tom. III. p. 31. "The descent into hell is not in the creed expounded by St Augustine, De Fide et Symbolo."—Pearson on the Creed. Oxf. ed. 1820. Vol. II. p. 278.]

[6 Sciendum sane est, quod in ecclesiæ Romanæ symbolo non habetur additum, *Descendit ad inferna;* sed neque in orientis ecclesiis habetur hic sermo: vis tamen verbi eadem videtur esse in eo quod sepultus dicitur.—Cypr. Expos. in Symb. in loc. p. 22. ed. Oxon. 1682.]

[7 Gen. xlii. 38. ad inferos, Lat. and Vulgate. Ainsworth translates the passage: Ye shall bring down my grey hairs with sorrow unto hell. See also Hutchinson's Works, p. 57. Parker Soc. ed.]

[8 Bullinger here, almost word for word, adopts Calvin's argument,

speeches, "He was buried," and "He descended into hell," the
first is the plainer, and the latter the more intricate. Augustine,
in his ninety-ninth epistle to Evodius, turmoileth himself pitifully in this matter[1]. To Dardanus, *de Dei Præsentia*, he
writeth, that the Lord went into hell, but that he felt no torment[2]. We shall more agreeably to the truth seem to understand this article, if we shall think that the virtue of Christ
his death did flow even to them that were dead, and profited
them too : that is to say, that all the patriarchs and holy
men, that died before the coming of Christ, were for the
death of Christ preserved from death everlasting; as St Peter
also maketh mention, "that the Lord went in the Spirit,
and preached unto the spirits that were in prison[3]." For
verily they by the death of Christ were made to know the
sentence of condemnation justly pronounced against them,
because, when they lived, they believed not with Noe and
them that were with him in the Saviour that was to come.
Or else otherwise, by the lower parts, or by hell, we understand not the place of punishment appointed for the wicked,
but the faithful that are departed, even as also by the higher
parts[4] we understand them that yet are remaining alive.
Wherefore the soul of Christ descended into hell, that is to
say, it was carried into Abraham's bosom, wherein all the

which is: Nam quoties loquutiones duæ rem eandem exprimentes
simul connectuntur, posteriorem esse prioris exegesin convenit.—
Calvin. Instit. Lib. II. cap. 16. § 8.]

[1 Opp. Par. 1531. Tom. II. fol. 86.]

[2 This statement seems to be gathered out of the following passage in the Epistle of Augustine referred to: Non enim facile alicubi
scripturarum inferorum nomen positum invenitur pro bono.   Unde
etiam quæri solet, Si non nisi pœnalia recte intelliguntur inferna, quomodo animam Domini Christi pie credamus fuisse in inferno.   Sed
bene respondetur, ideo descendisse ut quibus oportuit subveniret.
Unde beatus Petrus eum dicit solvisse *dolores inferni, in quibus impossibile erat teneri eum.*   Porro si utraque regis et dolentium et requies-
centium * * * in inferno esse credenda est, quis audeat dicere Dominum Jesum ad pœnales inferni partes venisse tantummodo, nec
fuisse apud eos qui in Abrahæ sinu requiescunt? ubi si fuit, ipse est
intelligendus paradisus, quem lationis animæ illo die dignatus est
polliceri.   Quæ si ita sunt, generale paradisi nomen est, ubi feliciter
vivitur.—August. Epist. 57. Tom. II. ed. Par. 1531.]

[3 1 Pet. iii. 19.   inobedientibus ac in carcere detentis, Lat.]

[4 per superos, Lat.]

faithful already departed were gathered together. Therefore, when he said to the thief that was crucified with him, "This day shalt thou be with me in paradise," he promised him the fellowship of life and of the blessed souls. Touching Abraham's bosom, our Lord spake at large in the sixteenth chapter of the gospel after St Luke. For whereas the Lord is said to have descended, that cometh to pass by the manner of speaking: for otherwise it is evident by Luke, that Abraham's bosom is a place severed a great way from hell, and placed up aloft. But to inquire or reason over curiously of these things is rather the point of a curious fool than of a godly-minded man. We confess in this article, that the souls are immortal, and that they immediately after the bodily death do pass to life, and that all the saints from the beginning of the world, being sanctified by faith through Christ, do in Christ and by Christ receive the inheritance of life everlasting.

I would add to these the fifth article, but that the hour is now already spent. We will therefore defer it unto the next sermon. And now let us all together pray to God, our Father which is in heaven, that he will vouchsafe us his Spirit to inspire us with that true and quickening faith which is in the Father and Son: in the Father, as the maker of all things; in the Son, as the Saviour of the whole world, who therefore came down from heaven, and was incarnate in the womb of the most holy virgin Mary, to the end he might be the Mediator betwixt God and men, and reconcile or make them at one again betwixt themselves; and that he might have wherewithal to make an oblation to appease God's justice, and to purge our sins which he bare on his body, yea, which he took away, and made all the faithful heirs of life everlasting.

Let us now give praise to the grace of God, and thanks to the Son of God: to whom alone all honour and glory is due for ever and ever. Amen.

OF THE LATTER ARTICLES OF CHRISTIAN FAITH CON-
TAINED IN THE APOSTLES' CREED.

THE EIGHTH SERMON.

LET us first of all pray to our God, that he will vouchsafe to grant us an happy, speedy, and very fruitful proceeding in the declaration of the other articles of christian belief.

The fifth article of our belief. The fifth article of our belief is: "The third day he rose
again from the dead." And this article, verily, of our belief is
in a manner the chief of all the rest. Neither are the apostles so busily occupied in declaring and confirming the other,

The glorious resurrection of Christ. as they are in this one. For it had not been enough, if our
Lord had died only, unless he had also risen from the dead
again. For if he had not risen from the dead, but had remained still in death, who should have persuaded us men, that
sin was purged by the death of Christ, that death was vanquished, Satan overcome, and hell broken up for the faithful
by the death of Christ? Yea verily, we have foolish fellows[1]
that would never cease to blaspheme the very God, to make
a mock of our hope, and to say : " Tush, who did ever return
from the dead, to tell us whether there be a life in another
world after this or no, and what kind of life it is? Because
therefore we cannot find, that any man did ever return from
the dead, that is to be doubted of, which these babblers[2] do
tattle touching the life of the world to come." That the
Lord therefore might declare to the whole world, that after
this life there is another, and that the soul dieth not with the
body, but remaineth alive; he[3] returned the third day alive
again to his disciples: and at that instant shewed them, that
sin was purged, death disarmed, the devil vanquished, and
hell destroyed. For the sting of death is sin: or the reward of sin is death : the devil hath the power of death[4],
and shutteth in hell for sins. Now therefore, in that Christ
riseth alive again from the dead, death could have no domi-

[1 absurdi nostri homines, Lat.]
[2 spermologi, Lat. ; Erasmus' rendering, not the Vulgate's, in
Acts xvii. 18.]
[3 Dominus noster, Lat.]
[4 1 Cor. xv. 56; Rom. vi. 23; Heb. ii. 14.]

nion over him : and because death, by suffering the Lord to pass, is broken, it must needs follow, that the devil and hell are vanquished by Christ ; and lastly, that sin, the strength and power of them all, is purely purged. It is evident, therefore, that the resurrection of our Lord Jesus Christ doth, as it were, certify and by seal assure us of our salvation and redemption, so that now we cannot any longer doubt of it.

We confess, therefore, in this article, that our Lord Jesus Christ is risen again, and that he is risen again for our behoof ; that is to say, that he hath wiped away our sins, and that for us he hath conquered death, the devil, and hell, according to the saying of the apostle : " God hath saved us, and hath called us with an holy calling, not according to our works, but according to his own purpose and favour, which was given unto us through Jesus Christ before all beginning, but is declared openly now by the appearing of our Saviour Jesus Christ, who hath verily put out death, and brought forth life, light, and immortality by the gospel[5]." There are many more like this in the fourth of his epistle to the Romans, and in the fifteenth of his first to the Corinthians. For the Lord also in the gospel after St John saith : " I am the resurrection and the life : he that believeth in me, although he be dead, shall live ; and every one that liveth and believeth in me shall not die for ever[6]."

Now also let us throughly consider every word of this article severally by itself. We confess the Lord his resurrection. But a resurrection is to rise again. That riseth which falleth. The body of Christ fell, therefore the body of Christ riseth ; yea, it riseth again, that is to say, the very same body of Christ, which before it fell did both live and stir, doth now rise again ; it doth, I say, both live and stir again. For truly said Tertullian of the resurrection of the flesh, that " this word resurrection is not properly spoken of any thing, save of that which first fell. For nothing can rise again but that that fell. For by rising again, because it fell, we say the resurrection is made ; because this syllable ' re ' is never added but when a thing is done again[7]." Wherefore

What a resurrection is.

[5] 2 Tim. i. 9, 10. ante tempora æterna, Lat. ; Erasmus' rendering ; the Vulgate has, tempora secularia.]

[6] John xi. 25, 26.]

[7] Resurrectionis vocabulum non aliam rem vindicat, quam quæ

the women in the gospel, when they went to anoint the body of the Lord, which hung upon the cross, did hear the angel of the Lord say: " Why seek ye the living among the dead? He is not here, but is risen[1]," &c. This history of the Lord's resurrection is set forth in the twenty-fourth after Luke, and the sixteenth after Mark. Peter the apostle also, in the second of the Acts, affirming the Lord's resurrection by the testimony of David[2], doth expressly shew that the Lord is verily risen again.

Out of or from the dead.

After this we say again, that he is risen out of or from the dead: which member doth express the truth both of his death and resurrection. For the body or flesh dieth, or is destroyed; but, being dead, is raised up again: this body, therefore, or flesh, is raised up again; as though he that maketh confession of his belief should say, Our Lord died even in the very same condition of nature that other mortal men do die in; but he tarried not, nor yet stuck fast among the dead. For the very same mortal flesh, which he had taken unto him, and by dying had laid aside, he now taketh again immortal; as David had foretold before, saying: " Because thou shalt not leave my soul in hell, nor suffer

He was crucified, dead, taken down and laid in his grave upon Good Friday, where his body lay all Saturday, that is, Easter-even, and on Sunday, which is Easter-day, in the morning he rose again from death to life.

thy Holy One to see corruption[3]." For Christ is the first-begotten of them that rise again, in whom, as in the head, there ought to be declared in what sort the resurrection of all Christ his members shall be in the day of judgment.

And we confess that this resurrection was made the third day; I mean the third day after his death. For upon the day of preparation[4] he is taken down from the cross and carried into a sepulchre, where his body resteth the whole sabbath-day; and about the beginning of the first day of sabbaths[5], which, I say, is the first day of the week, and

cecidit. Surgere enim potest dici et quod omnino non cecidit; quod semper retro jacuit: resurgere autem non est nisi ejus quod cecidit. Iterum enim surgendo, quia cecidit, resurgere dicitur: re enim syllaba iterationi semper adhibetur.—Tertul. Adv. Marcion. Lib. v. cap. 9. ed. Semler. Tom. I. p. 347.]

[1 Luke xxiv. 5, 6.]

[2 in prima illa concione sua, Lat. Omitted by the translator: in that his first sermon.]

[3 Psal. xvi. 10.]

[4 in die parasceves, Lat. Mark xv. 42.]

[5 John xx. 1. diei primi sabbatorum, Lat. ; Erasmus' render-

among us at this day is called Sunday[6], in the morning he arose again from the dead. Whereas therefore in the twelfth chapter of the gospel after St Matthew we read that the Lord said, " As Jonas was three days and three nights in the belly of the whale, so shall the Son of man be in the heart of the earth three days and three nights;" yet notwithstanding, in the sixteenth and twentieth chapters, expounding himself as having spoken that by synecdoche, he saith : " I must go to Hierusalem, and suffer many things of the scribes and elders, and be killed, and raised up again the third day[7]."

The sixth article of our faith is: " He ascended into heaven, and sitteth at the right hand of God, the Father Almighty." That body, which is of the same substance with our bodies, taken out of the virgin Mary, and taken verily of the substance of the virgin, which hung upon the cross, and died, and was buried, and rose again; the very same body, I say, ascended into the heavens, and sitteth at the right hand of God the Father. For after that by the space of forty days our Lord had abundantly enough instructed his disciples touching the truth of his resurrection and the kingdom of God, he was taken up into heaven.

The sixth article of our belief.

By that ascension of his he declareth to the whole compass of the earth, that he is Lord of all things, and that to him are subject all things that are in heaven and in earth ; that he is our strength, the power of the faithful, and he of whom they have to boast against the gates of hell. For he, ascending into heaven, hath led captivity captive ; and, by spoiling his enemies, hath enriched his people, on whom he daily heapeth his spiritual gifts. For he sitteth above, that, by pouring his virtue from thence into us, he may quicken us with the spiritual life, and deck us with sundry gifts and graces, and, lastly, defend the church against all evils. For God is our Saviour, King, and Bishop[8]. Whereupon, when as once the Capernaites were offended, because the Lord had called himself the bread of life that came down from heaven to give life unto the world, he saith : " Doth this offend you ?

The glorious ascension of Christ.

ing, not the Vulgate's. The first day of the sabbaths, Cranmer's Bible.]

[6 dominica, Lat.]

[7 ch. xvi. 21, and xx. 18, 19.]

[8 pontifex, Lat.]

What therefore if you shall see the Son of man ascend thither where he was before[1]?" As if he should say : Then verily ye will gather, by my quickening, resurrection, and glorious ascension into the heavens, that I am the bread of life, brought down from heaven, and now again taken up into the heavens, there to remain the Saviour, Life, and Lord of heaven and earth.   Moreover, St Peter the apostle in the Acts saith : " Let all the house of Israel know for a surety, that God hath made the same Jesus, whom ye have crucified, Lord and Christ[2]."

The force of Christ his ascension into heaven.   Furthermore, he did not only rise again from death, and come to his disciples, but also ascended into heaven as they beheld and looked on him, to the end that we thereby might be assuredly certified of eternal salvation.   For by ascending he prepared a place for us, he made ready the way ; that is, he opened the very heavens to the faithful.   God hath placed in heaven the very humanity that he took of us : which is indeed a lively and unreproveable testimony, that all mankind[3] shall at the last be translated into heaven also.   For the members must needs be made conformable to the head. Christ, our Head, is risen again from the dead ; therefore we, his members, shall also rise again.   And even as a cloud took away the Lord from the sight of his disciples; so shall we that believe be carried in the clouds to meet the Lord, and shall wholly in soul and body be, and for ever dwell, in heaven with our Head and Lord, Christ Jesus.   And this doth John evidently teach him that readeth his fourteenth chapter, where the Lord saith : " I go to prepare a place for you, and will come again to you, and take you unto myself, that wheresoever I am, ye may also be."   Paul the apostle also witnesseth, and saith : " We that live, and shall be remaining in the coming of the Lord, shall be carried in the clouds together with them that are raised up from the dead, to meet the Lord in the air[4]."

We confess therefore in this article, that Jesus Christ, being taken up into heaven, is Lord of all things, the King and Bishop, the deliverer and Saviour of all the faithful

[1 John vi. 61, 62.]
[2 ch. ii. 36. hunc Jesum, Lat.]
[3 rather, "our whole manhood." totum hominem, Lat.]
[4 1 Thess. iv. 17.]

in the whole world. We confess, that in Christ, and for
Christ, we believe the life everlasting, which we shall have in
this body at the end of the world, and in soul so soon as we
are once departed out of this world.

But now, by the way, we must weigh the very words of
this article. " He ascended," we say. Who ascended, I pray ^{He ascended into heaven.}
you? He that was born of the virgin Mary, that was cru-
cified, dead, and buried, that rose again from the dead: he (I
say) ascended verily both body and soul. But whither
ascended he? Into heaven. Heaven in the scriptures is not
taken always in one signification. First, it is put for the
firmament, and that large compass[5] that is over our heads,
wherein the birds fly to and fro, and in which the stars are
placed, that are called the furniture and host of heaven. For
saith David: " God is clothed with light, as with a garment:
he spreadeth forth the heaven as it were a curtain." He
saith also: " I shall see thy heavens, the work of thy fingers,
and the moon and stars which thou hast laid." And again:
" Which covereth the heaven with clouds, and prepareth rain
for the earth." And again: " The heavens declare the
glory of God, and the firmament sheweth forth the works of
his hands[6]." Then also, heaven is taken for the throne and
habitation of God: and lastly, for the place, seat, and receptacle of them that are saved, where God giveth himself to
be seen and enjoyed of them that be his. For David, witnessing
again, saith: " The Lord hath prepared his seat in heaven[7]."
Whereupon the Lord in the gospel saith: " Swear not by
heaven; for it is God's seat[8]." And the apostle Paul saith:
" We know, if our earthly mansion of this tabernacle be
destroyed, that we have a dwelling-place for ever in heaven,
builded by God, not made by hands[9]." And therefore, in this
signification, heaven is called the kingdom of God, the kingdom of the Father, joy, happiness, and felicity, eternal life,
peace and quietness. And although God indeed be not shut up
in any place, (for he saith, " Heaven is my seat, and the earth
the footstool of my feet[10];)" yet, because the glory of God
doth most of all shine in the heavens, and because that in
heaven he giveth himself to be seen and enjoyed of them

[5 extentione, Lat.]   [6 Psal. civ. 2. viii. 3. cxlvii. 8. xix. 1.]
[7 Psal. ciii. 19.]   [8 Matt. v. 34.]
[9 2 Cor. v. 1.]   [10 Isai. lxvi. 1.]

[BULLINGER.]   10

that are his, (according to that saying, "We shall see him even as he is[1];" and again, "No man shall see me," saith the Lord, "and live[2];") therefore God is said to dwell in heaven. Moreover Christ our Lord, touching his divinity, is not shut up in any place; but, according to his humanity once taken, which he drew up into heaven, he is in the very local place of heaven; neither is he in the meantime here in earth and every where bodily, but, being severed from us in body, remaineth in heaven. For he ascendeth, which, leaving that which is below, doth go to that above. Christ therefore, leaving the earth, hath placed a seat for his body above all heavens. Not that he is carried up beyond all heavens; but because, ascending up above all the circles[3] into the utmost and highest heaven, he is taken, I say, into the place appointed for those that are saved. For Paul the apostle, speaking plainly enough to be understood, saith: "Our conversation is in heaven, from whence we look for the Saviour to come[4]," &c. In the same manner also Luke the evangelist saith: "And blessing them, he departed from them, and was carried into heaven[5]."

But why do I make so much ado about expounding that which is most evidently declared in the very Creed by that which followeth? For the next is: "He sitteth at the right hand of God, the Father Almighty." For by this we understand what kind of place heaven is, and what our Lord doth in heaven. It is not surely for our frailty over-narrowly to seek out or discuss the secrets of heaven; and yet it is not against religion to inquire after that that is taught us in the scriptures, and so perfectly to remember it as it is taught us. Our Lord is simply said to sit; and that too to sit at the right hand of the Father Almighty. Let us therefore see[6] what the right hand of the Father is, and what it is to sit at the right hand of the Father.

The right hand of the Father in the scripture hath two significations. First, the right hand of God is the place appointed for them that are saved, and the everlasting felicity in

He sitteth at the right hand of God the Father Almighty.

The definition of God's right hand taken here for the place's name.

[1 1 John iii. 2.]
[2 Exod. xxxiii. 20.]
[3 supra omnes orbes, Lat.]
[4 Phil. iii. 20.]
[5 ch. xxiv. 51.]
[6 ex scripturæ testimoniis, Lat. Omitted by the translator: From the testimonies of scripture.]

heaven. This did St Augustine set down to be marked long before us; who, in the twenty and sixth chapter of his book *de Agone Christiano*, writeth, that "the right hand of the Father is the everlasting felicity given to the saints; even as also the left hand is most rightly called the continual misery allotted to the ungodly: not so that by this means, that I have said, the right or left hand is to be understood in respect of God himself, but in respect of his creatures' capacity[7]." And this did St Augustine speak according to the scriptures. For David saith: "The path of life shalt thou make known to me: the fulness of joys is in thy sight; and at thy right hand is gladness for ever[8]." What else is this, than if he had said; Thou shalt bring me into life, I say, into the very heavens, where I shall be filled with joys, both by seeing and beholding thee, and also by enjoying thee: at thy right hand in eternal blessedness are joys everlasting? In the gospel also we read, that the sheep are placed by the Judge at the right hand, and the goats at the left[9]. And when the right hand is taken in this sense, then "to sit" doth signify to rest from all labours, and to live quietly and in happy state. For that saying in the prophet is very well known, "A man shall sit under his vine[10]:" as if he should have said, All things shall be at peace, in safety, and at quiet. So then this that I have said is meant by the right hand of the Father: and where we confess, that the Son doth sit at the right hand of the Father Almighty, we do acknowledge, that our Lord, being delivered from all trouble and mortal infirmities, doth now in his humanity both rest and rejoice in the very local place of heaven, where we believe that both our souls and bodies shall be and live for ever. For the Lord himself in the gospel witnesseth, that in his Father's house there are many mansions, which he goeth to prepare, that they may have a place; and although he did depart, yet that he would return to them again, and take them unto himself, that where

To sit is to be at rest and enjoy felicity.

[7 Dextera Patris est beatitudo perpetua, quæ sanctis datur; sicut sinistra ejus rectissime dicitur miseria perpetua, quæ impiis datur: ut non in ipso Deo, sed in creaturis, hoc modo, quo diximus, intelligatur dextera et sinistra.—August. de Agon. Christ. cap. xxvi. Op. Tom. III. fol. 164. Par. 1531.]

[8 Psal. xvi. 11.]   [9 Matt. xxv. 33.]
[10 Micah iv. 4.]

he is, they also might be in the same place with him[1]. Wherefore we believe, that Christ is at rest in heaven, where he hath
prepared a place of rest for us also, to remain in joys everlasting. And for because our bodies shall not be every where
in felicity, but in the only appointed place; therefore saith
St Augustine truly, that "Christ our Lord, according to the
measure of his very body, is in some one place of heaven[2]."
And St Cyprian saith: "To sit at the right hand of the
Father is the mystery of his flesh taken up into heaven[3]."

God's right
hand the
name of his
power; and
in this signi-
fication to sit
is to reign.

Secondarily, the right hand of God is put for the virtue,
kingdom, protection, deliverance, and power of God. For
David saith: "The Lord's right hand is high: the Lord's
right hand doth mighty things[4]." And Moses said: "Thy
right hand, O Lord, is magnified in power: thy right hand, O
Lord, hath broken the enemy[5]." And when the right hand is
put in this sense, then "to sit" doth signify to reign, to
deliver, to use power, and do the office of a prince. For
saith David: "The Lord said unto my Lord, Sit thou at my
right hand, till I make thine enemies thy footstool[6]." And
the prophet Zachary saith: "Behold the man that is called
the Branch: he shall bud out of his place, and build the temple of the Lord, and sit and rule upon his throne, and be a
priest upon his seat[7]." In this sense the right hand of God
is infinite, and contained in no measure of place. Whereas[8] we
confess, that our Lord doth "sit" at the right hand of the
Father, we do profess, that the Son is exalted above all
things, having all things subject under himself, as Paul,
in his first chapter to the Ephesians, saith; and finally, that
the Son, being so exalted, can do all things, doth reign in
the universal church, doth deliver them that are his, doth
make intercession to the Father in heaven, and in the
power of his Godhead is present in all places. For therefore did the Creed add almightiness to this sitting of his,

[1 John xiv. 2, 3.]

[2 Non dubites (Christum esse) in loco aliquo cœli propter veri
corporis modum.—August. Op. Par. 1679—1700. Lib. ad Dardan.
Tom. ii. col. 692.]

[3 Sedere ad dexteram Patris carnis assumptæ mysterium est.—
Cypr. (Ruffin.) Expos. in Symb. fol. 25. Oxon. 1682.]

[4 Psal. cxviii. 16.]   [5 Exod. xv. 6.]
[6 Psal. cx. 1.]   [7 ch. vi. 12, 13.]
[8 et cum, Lat.   And whereas, 1577.]

where it is said, "He sitteth at the right hand of the Father Almighty." And in St Matthew the Lord saith : " To me is given all might in heaven and in earth : go therefore, and bring all nations unto me[9]."

So then I suppose that briefly thus I have well declared what manner of place heaven is ; to wit, a place of quietness, joy, and everlasting felicity, wherein the Son of God doth sit, doth dwell, and is in his humanity, as we also, that are the members of Christ, shall be in the very same place without all dolour and grief in joy for evermore. And although our Lord be delivered from all grievous business, yet we mean not that he sitteth idly leaning on his elbows[10]. For he is a King, a Priest, and very God in the very temple of God : he cannot choose therefore, of his natural property and office, but work salvation in the elect, and do all things that lie God, a king, and priest, in hand to do. So then now we all know what our Lord doth, as he sitteth in heaven. Neither is it any trouble to him at all to do and work that which he doth ; for he worketh not of compulsion, but naturally, and of his own accord.

Thus, and no otherwise, did the ancient interpreters of the holy scriptures handle this article of our belief; some of whose testimonies I will here allege. St Hierome, in his exposition of Paul's first chapter to the Ephesians, saith : " He hath declared the power of God by the similitude of a man : not because a seat is placed, and God the Father sitteth thereon, having his Son sitting there with him ; but because we cannot otherwise conceive how the Son doth judge and reign, but by such words applied to our capacity. As therefore to be next to God, or to depart far from him, is not to be understood according to the distance of places, but after men's merits, because the saints are heard by him, but the sinners (of whom the prophet saith, ' Behold, they that get themselves from thee shall perish,') are removed far enough from coming near him at all ; even so likewise, to be either at the right or left hand of God is to be taken so, that the saints are at his right hand, and sinners at his left. As our Saviour himself also in the gospel, affirming the same, doth say, that at the right hand are the sheep, and the goats at the left. More-

St Hierome of the right hand of the Father.

[[9] ch. xxviii. 18, 19.]
[[10] non otiosum desidere, Lat.]

over, this very word 'to sit' doth argue the power of a kingdom, by which God is beneficial to them on whom he doth
vouchsafe to sit; insomuch as verily he doth rule them, and
hath them always in his guiding, and doth turn to his own
beck or government the necks of them that before ran out of
way at random and at liberty[1]."

St Augus-
tine of the
right hand
of the Father.
St Augustine, in his book *de Fide et Symbolo*, saith:
"We believe that he sitteth at the right hand of God the
Father. Yet not so therefore, as though we should think
that God the Father is comprehended within the limits of a
man's body; so that they that think of him should imagine,
that he hath both a right and a left side: and whereas it is
said, that the Father sitteth, we must not suppose that he
doth sit with bended hams; lest peradventure we fall into
the same sacrilege, for which the apostle accurseth them that
have changed the glory of the incorruptible God into the
similitude of a corruptible man. For a detestable thing it is
to place God in such a likeness in a christian church: and
much more wicked is it to place it in the heart, where the
temple of God is verily and indeed, if it be cleansed from
earthly desires and error. We must therefore understand,
that 'at the right hand' is as much to say as in greatest happiness, where righteousness and peace and gladness is: even
as also the goats are placed at the left hand, that is, in misery
for their iniquities to their pain and torment. Whereas God
therefore is said to sit, thereby is not meant the placing of
his limbs, but his judicial power, which his majesty never

[1 Per humanam similitudinem Dei potentiam demonstravit: non
quo solium ponatur, et Deus Pater in eo sedeat, secumque Filium habeat
residentem; sed quo nos aliter judicantem atque regnantem nisi per
nostra verba intelligere nequeamus. Sicut ergo proximum esse Deo,
vel ab eo procul recedere, non secundum locorum spatia, sed juxta
merita, sentiendum est; quod sancti juxta eum sint, peccatores vero
(de quibus ait propheta, dicens, Ecce qui elongant se a te peribunt) ab
omni ejus vicinia submoveantur; sic et in dextris vel in sinistris Dei
esse accipiendum est, quod sancti a dextris ejus sint, peccatores vero
a sinistris: Salvatore quoque id ipsum in evangelio comprobante,
quum oves a dextris, hædos esse memoret a sinistris. Sed et ipsum
verbum, *sedere*, regni significat potestatem, per quam beneficium ejus
Deus tribuit, super quibus sedere dignatur; quod scilicet regat eos, et
in curru suo habeat, et ad nutum proprium vaga prius et libera colla
convertat.—Hieron. Comment. in Ep. ad Ephes. cap. I. Par. 1706.
Tom. IV. par. 1, col. 335.]

wanteth in bestowing worthy rewards on those that are worthy of them[2]." And so forth.

The blessed bishop Fulgentius, in his second book to king Trasimundus, saith : " The Lord, to shew that his humanity is local, saith to his disciples, ' I ascend to my Father and to your Father, my God and your God.'" And by and by after : " Declaring the incomprehensibility of his Godhead, he saith to his disciples, ' Behold, I am with you always, even unto the end of the world[3].'"

St Fulgentius. His human-ity is local, that is, con-tained in place ; but his Godhead in-comprehen-sible, as that that is every where, and is not con-tained in any place.

The blessed martyr and bishop of Trent, Vigilius, in his first book against heresies, saith: "This was to go to the Father, and to depart from us; to take away out of this world the nature which he took of us. Thou seest therefore, that it was proper to the same nature to be taken away, and to depart from us; according to the words of the angels which said, 'This Jesus, who is taken up from you, shall come again, even as ye see him go into heaven.' For see the miracle, see the mystery of both his properties: the Son of God in his humanity is departed from us; according to his divinity he saith to us, ' Behold, I am with you always, even unto the end of the world.' If he be with us, how saith he,

St Vigilius.

[2 Credimus etiam quod sedet ad dexteram Dei Patris : nec ideo tamen quasi humana forma circumscriptum esse Deum Patrem arbi-trandum est, ut de illo cogitantibus dextrum aut sinistrum latus animo occurrat: aut id ipsum quod sedere Pater dicitur, flexis poplitibus fieri putandum est; ne illud incidamus sacrilegium quo execratur apostolus eos qui commutaverunt gloriam incorruptibilis Dei in simi-litudinem corruptibilis hominis. Tale enim simulacrum Deo nefas est Christiano in templo collocare; multo magis in corde nefarium est, ubi vere est templum Dei, si a terrena cupiditate atque errore mundetur. ' Ad dexteram' ergo intelligendum est dictum esse in summa beatitudine, ubi justitia et pax et gaudium est: sicut ad sinistram hædi constituun-tur, id est, in miseria propter iniquitates, et labores atque cruciatus. Sedere ergo quod dicitur Deus, non membrorum positionem, sed judi-ciariam significat potestatem, qua illa majestas nunquam caret semper digna dignis tribuendo.—De Fide et Symb. c. 7. Par. 1531. Tom. III. fol. 31.]

[3 (Dominus) ut localem ostenderet humanitatem suam, dicit dis-cipulis suis : Ascendo ad Patrem meum et ad Patrem vestrum, Deum meum et Deum vestrum.—Immensitatem vero suæ divinitatis osten-dens discipulis dicit: Ecce ego vobiscum sum omnibus diebus, usque ad consummationem seculi.—Fulgent. Op. Venet. 1742. ad Trasimund. Lib. II. cap. xvii. p. 50.]

'The time shall come, when ye shall desire to see one of the days of the Son of man, and ye shall not see it?' Both he is with us, and not with us; because them, whom he hath left and departed from in his manhood[1], he hath not left nor forsaken in his Godhead[1]."[2] This saith he.

The seventh article.
Christ a Judge.

The seventh article of our faith is this: "From thence he shall come to judge the quick and the dead." In the former articles there is set forth and confessed the divine goodness, bountifulness, and grace in Christ: now also shall be declared the divine justice, severity, and vengeance that is in him. For there are two comings of our Lord Jesus Christ. First he came basely in the flesh, to be the Redeemer and Saviour of the world: at the second time he shall come gloriously to judgment, to be a judge and revenger that will not be entreated against all unrepentant sinners and wicked doers. And he shall come out of heaven, from the right hand of the Father, in his visible and very human body, to be seen of all flesh, with the incomprehensible power of his Godhead, and being attended on by all the angels. For the Lord himself in the gospel saith: "They shall see the Son man coming in the clouds of heaven with great power and glory, and he shall send his angels with the great sound of a trump[3]," &c.

To judge, what it is.

But now, to "judge" is to sit in the tribunal-seat, to hear and discuss matters, to take up strifes, to determine and give

[1 The words *manhood* and *Godhead* are transposed in ed. 1577.]
[2 Hoc erat ire ad Patrem et recedere a nobis, auferre de hoc mundo naturam, quam susceperat ex nobis. Vides ergo eidem naturæ proprium fuisse ut auferretur et abiret a nobis, quæ in fine temporum reddenda est nobis, secundum attestantium vocem angelorum, Hic Jesus qui receptus est a vobis, sic veniet, quemadmodum vidistis eum euntem in cœlum. Nam vide miraculum, vide utriusque proprietatis mysterium: Dei Filius secundum humanitatem suam recessit a nobis; secundum divinitatem suam ait nobis, Ecce ego vobiscum sum omnibus diebus usque ad consummationem seculi. Si nobiscum est, quomodo ait, Venient dies quando desideretis diem unum Filii hominis, et non videbitis? Sed et nobiscum est, et non est nobiscum; quia quos reliquit et a quibus discessit humanitate sua, non reliquit nec deseruit divinitate sua.—Vigil. adv. Eutych. in Cassandr. Op. Par. 1616. Lib. i. p. 518.]
[3 Matt. xxiv. 30, 31.]

sentence, and lastly, to defend and deliver, and again, to chastise
and punish, and by that means to keep under and suppress
injury and malice. We believe therefore, that our Lord Jesus
Christ in that day shall deliver all the godly, and destroy all
the wicked; according to the words of the apostle, who
saith : " Our Lord shall be revealed from heaven with the
angels of his power, with a burning flame, and shall lay
vengeance on them that have not known God[4];" and again,
" The same just Judge shall give a crown of righteousness to
all them that love his coming[5]."

The manner of this judgment the writings of the evan- The picture
of the last
gelists and apostles do tell us shall be in this sort. When judgment.
once the wickedness of this world shall come to the full, and
that antichrist shall have deceived the world, so that there is
but little faith remaining, and that the wicked shall say, Peace
and quietness; then shall a sudden destruction come. For our
Lord, the Judge, shall send his archangel, to blow the trump,
and to gather together from the four winds all flesh to judgment: by and by after shall the Judge himself, our Lord
Jesus Christ, follow with all the host of heaven: and he shall
descend out of heaven into the clouds: and, sitting aloft in
the clouds as in a judgment-seat, shall be easily seen of all
flesh. For they that shall be then living at the day of
judgment, shall in a very prick[6] of time be changed, and
stand before the Judge; and all the dead shall in a moment
rise up again. Then shall the Judge divide the sheep from
the goats, and, according to justice shall give judgment with
the sheep[7] and against the goats, saying, "Come, ye blessed,"
&c., and, " Go, ye cursed," &c. Presently after shall follow
execution. For the sheep shall by and by be caught up into
the clouds to meet the Lord in the air, and shall ascend with
him joyfully into heaven to the right hand of God the Father,
there to live for ever in glory and gladness. The bottom of
the earth shall gape[8] for the wicked, and shall suck them all
up horribly, and send them down to hell, there to be tormented for ever with Satan and his angels. All this shall be

[4 2 Thess. i. 7, 8.]   [5 2 Tim. iv. 8.]
[6 in puncto, Lat. 1 Cor. xv. 52.   Erasmus, in puncto temporis.
Vulgate, in momento.]
[7 pro ovibus, Lat.]
[8 dehiscet ima tellus, Lat.]

done, not by any long, troublesome, or changeable process, as is used in our courts of law, but even in the twinkling of an eye. For then shall all men's hearts be laid open, and every man's own conscience shall accuse himself. This is more at large set out in Matt. xxiv. and xxv., Wisd. iii. and v., 1 Cor. xv., 2 Cor. v., 1 Thess. iv., v., Rom. ii., 2 Pet. iii. &c.

The quick and dead are judged.

Now we do simply confess, that the quick and the dead shall be judged. This do some expound of the godly and ungodly. But the Symbol or Creed was ordained for the most simple of understanding; and simple things are fittest for to teach simple men. Therefore we say simply, that the dead are all they, that from the beginning of the world even until the last day are departed out of this mortal life: and the living are they, which at that day shall be alive in this world. For the apostle saith: " Behold, I tell you a mystery; we shall not all sleep, but we shall all be changed by the last trump, in a moment of time, and in the twinkling of an eye. For the trump shall sound, and the dead shall rise again incorruptible, and we shall be changed[1]." And again, in another place, the same apostle saith: " This I say unto you in the word of the Lord, that we, which shall live and be remaining at the coming of the Lord, shall not prevent them which are asleep. Because the Lord himself shall come down out of heaven with a great noise, and the voice of an archangel, and the trump of God: and first shall the dead in Christ rise up again; then shall we, which shall be alive and be remaining, be caught up together with them in the clouds into the air to meet the Lord: and so shall we be with the Lord for evermore[2]."

The reward and punishment is most certain.

We confess therefore in this seventh article, that we believe there shall be an end of all things in this world, and that the felicity of the wicked shall not endure for ever. For we believe that God is a just God, who hath given all judgment unto his Son, to repay to every one in that day according to his works, pains to the wicked that never shall be ended, and to the godly joys everlasting. And so in this article we profess, that we look for a deliverance, a ceasing

[1 1 Cor. xv. 51, 52. *per* extremam tubam, Lat. and Erasmus. The Vulgate has, in novissima tuba.]

[2 1 Thess. iv. 15—17.]

from troubles, and the reward of life everlasting. For how should he destroy them that believe in him, his people and his servants, who in the most true gospel saith, " Verily, I say unto you, that ye, which have followed me, in the regeneration, when the Son of man shall sit on the seat of his majesty, ye also shall sit upon twelve seats judging the twelve tribes of Israel[3]?" There are most certain rewards and penalties appointed for the godly and ungodly in the word of truth. He cannot lie that said to Esay: "Say to the righteous, that it shall go well with him; for he shall enjoy the fruit of his study. But woe be to the wicked: it shall be evil with him; for he shall be rewarded according to the works of his own hands[4]." And thus much touching the second part of the Creed. Now are we come to the third part.

The eighth article of our belief is this: "I believe in the Holy Ghost." This third part of the Creed containeth the property of the third Person in the reverend Trinity. And we do rightly believe in the Holy Ghost, as well as in the Father and the Son. For the Holy Ghost is one God with the Father and the Son: and rightly is faith in the Holy Ghost joined to faith in the Father and the Son. For by him the fruit of God's salvation, fulfilled in the Son, is sealed to us, and our sanctification and cleansing is bestowed on us, and derived from him to us, by the Holy Ghost. For the apostle saith: " God, which anointed us, is he also which hath sealed us, and hath given the earnest of the Spirit in our hearts[5]." And again: " Ye were indeed defiled with naughtiness; but now ye are cleansed, and sanctified, and lastly justified, through the name of the Lord Jesus, and by the Spirit of our God[6]." The Father indeed doth sanctify too, but by the blood of Jesus Christ, and poureth the same sanctification out of him into us by the Holy Ghost: so that it is, as it were, the property of the Holy Ghost to sanctify; whereupon he is called Holy or the Sanctifier. Therefore, so often as we hear the Holy Ghost named, we must by and by think of the power in working, which the scripture attributeth

The eighth article of our faith.

[3 Matt. xix. 28.]   [4 ch. iii. 10, 11.]
[5 2 Cor. i. 21, 22.]   [6 1 Cor. vi. 11.]

to him, and we must look after the benefits that from him do flow to us. For the power, operation, or action of the Spirit is that, whatsoever the grace of God doth work in us through the Son: so that of necessity we must believe in the Holy Ghost. And in this eighth article we do profess, that we do verily believe, that all the faithful are cleansed, washed, regenerated, sanctified, enlightened, and enriched of God with divers gifts of grace for Christ his sake, but yet through the Holy Ghost. For without him there is no true sanctification: wherefore we ought not to attribute these gifts of grace to any other means; this glory belongeth to the Holy Ghost only. Of whom I will more largely and fully discourse in my other sermons.

The Father in Christ hath fully given us all heavenly treasures. The hour is spent, which warneth me to wrap up briefly and make an end; therefore I exhort you all to have your faith religiously bent upon the Lord Jesus: for him hath the heavenly Father sent to us, in him hath he wholly expressed and shewed himself to us, and him doth the Holy Ghost print in our hearts and keep in our minds. And in Christ is all man's salvation and every part thereof contained; wherefore we must beware that we derive it not from any thing else. "It pleased the Father," saith the apostle, "that all fulness should dwell in the Son," and in him to recapitulate, and as it were, to bring into a sum, all points of salvation, that in him all the faithful may be fulfilled[1]. For if salvation be sought, then even by his very name are we taught that salvation is in his power: for he is called Jesus, that is, a Saviour. If we desire the Holy Spirit of God and his sundry gifts, we shall find them also in the anointing of Christ: for he is called Christ, the Anointed, I say, the Holy of holies, and the sanctifier, or else the anointer of us with his Spirit. If any man have need of strength and might, of power and deliverance, well, he hath to look for it in Christ his dominion: for Christ is Lord of all. In the same Christ we find redemption: for he hath redeemed us that were sold under Satan's yoke. In his conception we have purity; in his nativity we have sufferance[2]: for he became like to us, that he might suffer grief as well as

[1 Col. i. 19; Ephes. i. 10. ἀνακεφαλαιώσασθαι, id est, recapitulari. —Erasm. Annot. in loc. cit.]
[2 indulgentiam, Lat.]

we[3]. For in his passion we have forgiveness of sins, in his condemnation we have absolution, satisfaction in his offering or cleansing[4] sacrifice, cleansing in his blood, and an universal reconciliation in his descending into hell. In his burial we have the mortification of our flesh, the newness of life; yea rather, the immortality of the soul, and resurrection of our bodies in his glorious resurrection. We have also the inheritance of the heavenly kingdom, with the assured sealing thereof, in his ascension and sitting at the right hand of the Father. And there is he our Mediator, Priest, and King, our safeguard and our head, our defender and most sure rest[5]. From thence he poureth into us his Holy Spirit, the fulness of all good things; and doth communicate himself wholly to us, joining us unto himself with an indissoluble knot. From thence we do with confidence and joy look for him to be our Judge, to be, I say, our patron and deliverer, which shall condemn and send down headlong into hell all our enemies with Satan; but shall take us and all the faithful of every age up into heaven with himself, there to sing a new song, and to rejoice in him for ever. To him be glory for ever. Amen.

OF THE LATTER ARTICLES OF CHRISTIAN FAITH CONTAINED IN THE APOSTLES' CREED.

THE NINTH SERMON.

LET us call to our Father in heaven, through our Lord Jesus Christ, that he will vouchsafe to pour his grace into us, that we may to our no small profit dispatch and expound the last part of the articles of christian belief.

The ninth article of faith is this: "The holy catholic church, the communion of saints." After the confession of our belief in the holy Trinity, and in the mystery of the Son of God, our Lord Jesus Christ, and lastly in the Holy Ghost, the sanctifier and restorer of all; now, in the fourth part, is reckoned up the fruit and power, the effect and end, of faith, and what doth come to, and is bestowed on, the faithful. There cometh to them communion of God and all saints, sanc- *The ninth article of our belief.*

[3 condolere nobis, Lat.]　　　　　　　[4 expiatorio, Lat.]
[5 securitas, Lat.]

tification, remission of sins, the resurrection of the flesh, and life everlasting. Of which I will speak in order as they lie, so far forth as the bountiful Lord shall give me ability.

Now then here we have to rehearse[1] out of the eighth article this word, " I believe :" we must (I mean) say, " I be-lieve the holy catholic church."   Some unlearned there are, which hold opinion, that in this point of our confession we should say, " I believe in the holy church."   The reason that leads them so to think is this; because they find written in the Constantinopolitan Creed, " And in the Holy Ghost, the Lord that giveth life, who proceedeth from the Father and the Son, who together with the Father and the Son is to be worshipped and glorified, who spake by the prophets in one catholic and apostolic church[2]."   For these words they do so distinguish, that, as they do repeat out of the premisses these words, " I believe," and make this the sense, " I believe in the Holy Ghost, the Lord ;" even so here again they do repeat these words, " I believe," making this to be the sense, " I be-lieve in one catholic and apostolic church[3]."   But this is more than needeth, yea, and against all godliness do they wrest these words of the Creed : for this, " In one catholic and apostolic church," is not referred to the verb, " I believe," but to the Holy Ghost, because he spake by the prophets in one catholic and apostolic church.   For our meaning is, and we confess, that one and the same Spirit did all things in both Testaments, contrary to the opinion of them which imagined, that there were two spirits contrary the one to the other.

Moreover St Cyprian, in his exposition of the Apostles' Creed, saith : " He said not, In the holy church, nor, In the remission of sins, nor, In the resurrection of the body.   For if he had added the preposition 'in,' then had the force of those clauses been all one with the force of that that went before. For in those words wherein our belief touching the Godhead is set down, we say, 'In God the Father, in Jesus Christ his Son, and in the Holy Ghost:' but in the rest, where the

Side notes: We must not in our con-fession say, I believe in the church.

Side note: Cyprian.

[1 repetendum est, Lat.]

[2 locutus est per prophetas in unam catholicam, &c., Lat.]

[3 All this is comprised in that principle, I believe the catholic church.   And therefore the council of Nice said, I believe in the church (πιστεύω εἰς τὴν ἐκκλησίαν), that is, I believe and trust the same in all things.—Annot. of Rhiems Test. in 1 Tim. iii. 15.]

speech is not of the Godhead, but touching the creatures or
mysteries, the preposition 'in' is not added, that we may say,
'In the holy church;' but that the holy church is to be believed,
not as we believe in God, but as a congregation gathered
together to God; and that the forgiveness of sins is to be believed, not that we ought to believe in the forgiveness of sins;
and that the resurrection of the flesh is to be believed, not
that we ought to believe in the resurrection of the flesh. So
then, by this syllable 'in' the Creator is discerned from the
creatures, and that that is God's from that that is man's[4]."
This saith Cyprian.

St Augustine, in his book *de Fide et Symbolo*, hath: "I Augustine.
believe the holy church," not, "I believe in the holy church[5]."
There are alleged also his words in his epistle *ad Neophytos*,
touching consecration, Distinct. 4, cap. 1: "We said not,
that ye had to believe in the church, as in God; but understand how we said, that ye, being conversant in the holy
catholic church, should believe in God[6]."

Much more evidently doth Paschasius, in the first chapter Paschasius.
of his first book *de Spiritu Sancto*, say: "We believe the
church, as the mother of regeneration; we do not believe in
the church, as the author of salvation. He that believeth in

[4 Non dixit, in sanctam ecclesiam, nec in remissionem peccatorum, nec in carnis resurrectionem. Si enim addidisset IN præpositionem, una eademque vis fuisset cum superioribus. Nunc autem in
illis quidem vocabulis, ubi de divinitate fides ordinatur, in Deum
Patrem dicitur, et in Jesum Christum Filium ejus, et in Spiritum sanctum: in ceteris vero, ubi non de divinitate, sed de creaturis ac mysteriis sermo est, IN præpositio non additur, ut dicatur, in sanctam
ecclesiam, sed sanctam ecclesiam credendam esse, non ut in Deum, sed
ut ecclesiam Deo congregatam; et remissionem peccatorum credendam
esse, non in remissionem peccatorum; et resurrectionem carnis, non
in resurrectionem carnis. Hac itaque præpositionis syllaba Creator a
creaturis secernitur, et divina separantur ab humanis.—Cypr. (Ruffin.)
Expos. in Symb. Apost. fol. 26. Oxon. 1682.]

[5 Credimus et sanctam ecclesiam, utique catholicam.—August. de
Fid. et Symb. ed. Par. 1531. Tom. III. fol. 32.]

[6 Non ergo diximus, ut in ecclesiam, quasi in Deum crederetis:
sed intelligite nos dicere, et dixisse, ut in ecclesia sancta catholica
conversantes in Deum crederetis. — Gratian. Decret. Par. III. de
Consecr. Distinct. 4. can. 73. The Sermo ad Neophytos, which is
quoted from, is not Augustine's. August. Opp. Tom. VI. Append.
p. 290.]

the church, believeth in man: for man hath not his being of the church, but the church began by man. Leave off therefore this blasphemous persuasion, to think that thou hast to believe in any worldly creature ; since thou mayest not believe neither in angel nor archangel. The unskilfulness of some have drawn and taken the preposition 'in' from the sentence that goeth next before, and put it to that that followeth, adding thereto also too too shamelessly somewhat more than needed[1]." This hath Paschasius in that book of his, which St Gregory the Great, bishop of Rome, liked very well of[2].

What say ye to that moreover, that Thomas of Aquine, reasoning of faith, in the second book, Part. II. Artic. ix. Quæst. 1, saith? "If we say, 'I believe in the holy church,' we must understand, that our faith is referred to the Holy Ghost, which sanctifieth the church ; and so make the sense to be thus: 'I believe in the Holy Spirit, that sanctifieth the church.' But it is better, and according to the common use, not to add at all the syllable 'in,' but simply to say, the holy catholic church: even as also pope Leo saith[3]." This hath Thomas.

St Gregory.

Thomas Aquine.

Pope Leo.

[1 Credimus ecclesiam quasi regenerationis matrem; non in ecclesiam credimus quasi in salutis auctorem. Qui in ecclesiam credit, in hominem credit: nam non homo ex ecclesia, sed ecclesia esse cœpit ex homine. Recede itaque ex hac blasphemiæ persuasione, ut in aliquam humanam te æstimes debere credere creaturam; cum omnino nec in angelum nec in archangelum sit credendum. Nonnullorum imperitia, In, præpositionem hanc, velut de proxima vicinaque sententia, in consequentem traxit ac rapuit, et ex superfluo imprudenter apposuit.—Paschas. de Spiritu Sancto, Lib. I. cap. i. in Biblioth. Patr. Par. 1624. Tom. IX. col. 180.]

[2 Quod Paschasius hujus apostolicæ sedis diaconus, cujus apud nos rectissimi et luculenti de sancto Spiritu libri extant, miræ sanctitatis vir fuerit, eleemosynarum maxime operibus vacans, cultor pauperum et contemptor sui.—S. Gregorii Dialog. IV. 40. Rom. 1613. III. 926. P.]

[3 Si dicatur, In sanctam ecclesiam catholicam, hoc est intelligendum, quod fides nostra refertur ad Spiritum sanctum qui sanctificat ecclesiam, ut sit sensus: Credo in Spiritum sanctum sanctificantem ecclesiam. Sed melius est, et secundum communiorem usum, ut non ponatur ibi, In, sed simpliciter dicatur, sanctam ecclesiam catholicam; sicut etiam Leo Papa dicit.—Aquin. Sum. Tot. Theol. par. II. Quæst. 1. Art. 9, p. 7, Tom. II. Venet. 1594.]

So now ye have heard the opinions of the ancient doctors of the church, Cyprian, Augustine, Gregory, Paschasius, pope Leo; and also of Thomas of Aquine, which taught now in the latter times. And, dearly beloved, ye do understand, by proofs taken out of the canonical scripture, that we must acknowledge and confess the holy catholic church, but not believe in the holy catholic church.

And now we have to see, what that is that is called the church, and what is called the catholic church. *Ecclesia*, which word we use for the church, is properly an assembly; it is, I say, where the people are called out, or gathered together, to hear somewhat touching the affairs of the commonweal. In this present treatise it is the company, communion, congregation, multitude, or fellowship of all that profess the name of Christ. Catholic is as much to say as this fellowship is universal, as that that is extended through all places and ages[4]. For the church of Christ is not restrained into any corner among the Donatists in Africa[5]: it stretcheth out itself through the compass of the world, and unto all ages, and doth contain all the faithful from the first Adam even unto the very last saint that shall be remaining before the end of the world. This universal church hath her particular churches; I mean, the church of Adam and of the patriarchs, the church of Moses and of the prophets before the birth of Christ, the christian church, which is so named of Christ himself, and the apostolical church gathered together by the apostles' doctrine in the name of Christ. And finally, it containeth these particular churches, as the church of Jerusalem, of Antioch, of Alexandria, of Rome, of Asia, of Africa, of Europe, of the east, of the west, &c. And yet all these churches, as it were members of one body under the only head Christ, (for Christ alone is the head of his church,

The catholic church.

[4 Here the translator has omitted: " For all saints are united, just as the members in one body, which depend on one head. Therefore the aggregate and whole multitude of the faithful is called the church." Sancti enim omnes ita uniuntur, ut membra in uno corpore, quæ ab uno dependent capite. Ergo universitas totaque multitudo fidelium dicitur ecclesia.]

[5 For their own body, on account of the sanctity of its bishops, they (the Donatists) claimed exclusively the name of a true, pure, and holy church. This pestilence scarcely extended beyond Africa.— Mosheim, Eccles. Hist. Cent. IV. Book II. part 2, chap. 5.]

not only triumphant, but militant also,) do make one only
catholic church ; in which there are not to be found either
heresies or schisms : and for that cause it is called the true[1]
church, to wit, of the right and true opinion, judgment, faith,
and doctrine. For in the church only is true faith, and
without the church of God is neither any truth, nor yet
salvation.

So then in this article we confess, that all the faithful
dispersed throughout the whole compass of the earth, and
they also that at this time live in heaven, as many, I say, as
are already saved, or shall even until the very end of the
world be born to be saved, are one body, having gotten
fellowship and participation with God and a mutual communion among themselves. And for because no man can be
made one with God, unless he also be holy and pure even as
God is holy and pure; therefore we believe that the church
is holy, that is, that it is sanctified by God the Father in the
blood of the Son and the gift of the Holy Ghost. We have
heard testimonies enough in the former sermons; therefore
this one of Paul shall be sufficient, which he writeth to the
Ephesians : " Christ loved the church, and gave himself for
it, to sanctify and to cleanse it in the fountain of water
through the word, to make it unto himself a glorious church,
not having spot or wrinkle[2]," &c. By which words we understand, that the church is called undefiled and altogether clean,
not in respect of itself, but because of Christ. For the church
of Christ is so far forth holy, as that yet every day it doth
go forward in profiting, and is never perfect so long as it
liveth on the earth. And yet notwithstanding, the holiness
of it is most absolutely perfect in Christ. Whereunto verily
belongeth that notable saying of the Lord : " He that is
washed hath no need but to wash his feet only, for he is
wholly clean[3]." For the faithful are purely cleansed by
Christ, who washeth them with his blood; but yet, because
the flesh doth strive with the spirit so long as life remaineth
on the earth, therefore the godly have need with faith and
the Holy Ghost to wash and wipe their feet, that is, the

Marginal notes: The true church.   We believe the church to be holy.   How the church is holy.

[1 orthodoxa, Lat.]
[2 ch. v. 25—27. mundatam lavacro aquæ, Lat. Erasmus' rendering.]
[3 John xiii. 10.]

reliques and spots wherewith they are distained by their daily conversation in this world.

But now, whereunto belongeth this that is added, "The communion of saints?" These words are neither read in Cyprian, nor Augustine, nor yet by them expounded[4]. Wherefore it is likely, that they were added for the better understanding of that which went before : for, that it might appear that the catholic church is the fellowship or company of the faithful, he added, "The communion of saints;" as if he should have said, which church is a communion of saints. Paul called them saints, which for their faith are sanctified by the blood and Spirit of God. Also this word "communion" is very evident and comfortable. For first, the meaning thereof is, that betwixt God and us there is a communion, that is, a fellowship and participation, and so, consequently, a parting betwixt us of all good and heavenly things. And then also we understand, that we are fellows and partakers with all the saints that are living either in heaven or on earth : for we are members of them under one head, Christ. For the apostle John saith: "That which we have seen and heard we declare unto you, that ye also may have fellowship with us, and that your fellowship may be with the Father, and his Son Jesus Christ[5]." Hereunto appertaineth that trim[6] similitude of the body and members under one head, which the apostle Paul handleth at large in deed. But what is he, that can worthily enough set forth the great goodness of God's gift and benefit, in that we are made fellow-partners of God, with whom we are most nearly conjoined, and have a part in all his good and heavenly things? What can be more delightful to our ears, than to hear, that all the saints, as well in heaven as in earth, are our brethren, and that we again are members, partners, and fellows with them? Blessed be God, which hath so liberally bestowed his blessing on us in Christ his Son.

To this place belongeth the discourse upon the sacraments; of which, and of the church, I mean at another time more fully to entreat. This for the present time is sufficient. For this

[4 See Pearson on the Creed, Oxf. ed. 1820. Vol. II. p. 427.]
[5 1 John i. 3. societas vestra, Lat. But the Vulgate and Erasmus have nostra, as the Greek]
[6 elegans, Lat.]

The communion of saints.

that I have said doth abundantly enough express and set out the fruit of faith in the Father, the Son, and the holy Ghost; to wit, that we have participation with God and all the saints, and that in this fellowship we are sanctified from all filth or uncleanness, being cleansed and holy in Christ our Lord.

The tenth article of our belief.

Now followeth the tenth article of our belief; which is, "The forgiveness of sins." The second fruit or commodity of our belief in God, the Father, the Son, and the Holy Ghost, is here set forth, that is, the remission of sins; which, although it be contained in sanctification spoken of in the last article, is in this place notwithstanding more lively expressed. Without the church, as it were without the ark of Noe, is no salvation: but in the church, I mean, in the fellowship of Christ and the saints, is full[1] forgiveness of all offences. That this may be the better understood, I will divide it into some parts.

The acknowledging and confessing of our sins.

First of all, it is needful to acknowledge and confess, that we are sinners, and that by nature and our own proper merits we are the children of wrath and damnation. For St John doth not in vain nor without a cause call every one a liar, that saith he hath no sin[2]. And God, which knoweth the hearts of men, hath commanded us even till the last gasp to pray, saying: "Forgive us our debts." Moreover, in the gospel we have two excellent examples of men openly confessing their sins to God; the prodigal son, I say, and the publican in St Luke[3]. Let us therefore think, that we are all sinners, as Paul also taught; yea, as he hath evidently proved in the first chapter to the Romans; and let us freely confess to God our sins with David in the 32nd and 51st Psalms, saying: "My sin have I made known to thee, and mine iniquity I have not hid. I have said, I will confess mine unrighteousness against myself; and thou hast forgiven the iniquity of mine offence." "Have mercy on me, O God, according to thy great mercy," &c. The Psalm is known.

Our sins are forgiven of God, not for our merits, but for Christ his sake.

Secondarily, let us believe, that all these sins of ours are pardoned and forgiven of God, not for the acknowledging and confessing of our sins, but for the merit and blood of the Son of God; not for our own works or merits, but for the truth and mercy, or grace, of God. For we do plainly profess,

[1] plenaria, Lat.]
[2] 1 John i. 8.]
[3] ch. xv. 21, and xviii. 13.]

saying: "I believe the forgiveness of sins." We say not, I buy, or by gifts do get, or by works obtain, the forgiveness of sins; but, "I believe the forgiveness of sins." And the word "remission" or "forgiveness" doth signify a free pardoning, by a metaphor taken of creditors and debtors. For the creditor forgiveth the debtor, when he is not able to pay : therefore remission is a forgiving[4], according to the saying of our Saviour in the Gospel : "A certain lender had two debtors; and when they were not able to pay, he forgave them both[5]." Hereunto belongeth that also in the Lord's prayer : "And forgive us our debts ;" for our debts are our sins : them do we request to be remitted, that is, to be forgiven us. In this sense also saith St Paul : "To him that worketh is the reward reckoned not of grace, but of due debt; but to him that worketh not, but believeth on him that justifieth the ungodly, his faith is counted for righteousness : even as David describeth the blessedness of that man, unto whom God imputeth righteousness without works, saying, Blessed are they whose unrighteousnesses are forgiven, and whose sins are covered. Blessed is that man to whom the Lord will not impute sin[6]." Wherefore, in respect of us which have not wherewithal to repay, our sins are freely forgiven ; but in respect of God's justice, they are forgiven for the merit and satisfaction of Christ.

Moreover, it is not the sins of a few men, of one or two ages, or a few and certain number of sins, are forgiven only ; but the sins of all men, of all ages, the whole multitude of sins, whatsoever is and is called sin, whether it be original, or actual, or any other else[7]; to be short, all sins are forgiven us. Which we do hereby learn, because the only sacrifice of Christ is effectual enough to wash away all the offences of all sinners, which by faith come to the mercy-seat of God's grace[8]. And yet by this we do not teach men to sin, because the Lord hath long since made satisfaction for sins : but if any man do sin, we teach him to hope well, and not to despair, but to flee to the throne of grace ; for there we say that Christ, sitting at the right hand of the Father, is "the Lamb of God that taketh away the sins of the world." And in the Creed verily it is

All sins are forgiven.

[4 remissio est donatio, Lat.]
[5 Luke vii. 41, 42.]   [6 Rom. iv. 4—8.]
[7 sive alienum sit, Lat.]
[8 ad thronum gratiæ, Lat.   Heb. iv. 16.]

expressly said, "I believe the forgiveness of sins," and not of sin. For when we say "of sins," we acknowledge that God forgiveth all sins. For to let pass the proofs hereof out of the 3rd and 5th of Paul to the Romans, those out of St John, the apostle and evangelist, shall be sufficient, who in his epistle testifieth, and saith: "The blood of Jesus Christ cleanseth us from every sin[1]." Lo, he saith from every sin. He, I say, that saith from every one, excepteth none, unless it be that which the Lord himself excepted; I mean, the sin against the Holy Ghost; for which the very same St John forbiddeth us to pray[2]. Again also he saith: "If we acknowledge our sins, God is faithful and just to forgive us our sins, and to cleanse us from all our unrighteousness[3]." The apostle thought it not enough to say barely, "To forgive us our sins;" but, that he might declare the thing as it is indeed so plainly that it might easily be understood, he addeth moreover this saying: "And to cleanse us from all our unrighteousness." Lo, here he saith again, "from all unrighteousness." And for because some caviller might peradventure make this objection, and say, This kind of doctrine maketh men sluggish and slow to amendment; for men under the pretence of God's grace will not cease to sin: therefore John in his 2nd chapter answereth their objection, and saith: "Babes, these things write I to you, that ye sin not: and if any man sin, we have an advocate with the Father, Jesus Christ the righteous. And he is the atonement for our sins: and not for our sins only, but also for the sins of all the world[4]." Wherefore it is assuredly true, that by the death of Christ all sins are forgiven them that believe.

God alone, and not man, forgiveth sins.

Moreover, the Lord alone forgiveth sins. For it is the glory of God alone to forgive sins, and of unrighteous to make men righteous. Therefore, whereas men are said to forgive sins, that is to be understood of their ministery, and not of their power. The minister pronounceth to the people, that for Christ his sake their sins are forgiven: and in so saying he deceiveth them not; for God indeed forgiveth the sins of them that believe, according to that saying: "Whose sins ye forgive, they are forgiven them[5]." And this is done so often as the word of the gospel is preached; so that there be no need to feign, that auricular confession and private ab-

[1 1 John i. 7.]   [2 1 John v. 16.]   [3 1 John i. 9.]
[4 1 John ii. 1, 2.]   [5 John xx. 23.]

solution at the priest's hand is necessary for the remission of sins. For as auricular confession was not in use among the saints before the coming of Christ, so we read not that the apostles heard private confession, or used private absolution in the church of Christ. It is enough for us to confess our sins to God, who, because he seeth our hearts, ought therefore most rightly to hear our confessions. It is enough, if we, as St James teacheth us, do one to another betwixt ourselves confess our faults and offences[6]; and so, after pardon asked, return into mutual favour again. It is enough for us to hear the gospel, promising the forgiveness of our sins through Christ, if we believe. Let us therefore believe the forgiveness of sins, and pray to the Lord that he will vouchsafe to give and increase in us this same belief. These things were of old and in the primitive church effectual enough to obtain pardon and full remission of sins: and as they were, so are they undoubtedly at this day sufficient too.

Furthermore, the Lord doth so pardon our sins, not that they should not be any more in us, nor leave their reliques behind them, as a sting in our flesh, but that they should not be imputed to us to our damnation. Concupiscence sticketh fast and sheweth itself in our flesh, striving still with the good Spirit of God, even in the holy ones, so long as life lasteth on this earth. Here therefore we have need of long watching and much fasting, to draw from the flesh the nourishment of evil, and often prayers to call to God for aid, that we be not overcome of the evil. And if any man shall hap to fail for feebleness, and be subdued of temptation, let him not yield himself, by lying still, to be caught in the devil's net: let him rise up again by repentance, and run to Christ, believing that by the death of Christ this fall of his shall be forgiven him. And so often shall he have recourse to him, as he shall be vanquished by concupiscence and sin. For to this end shoot all the exhortations of the prophets and apostles, calling on still to return to the Lord. *How sins are forgiven.*

Finally, the Lord doth so forgive our sins, that he will never once remember them again. For so he foretold us by Jeremiah, in his 31st chapter. He therefore doth not punish us. For he hath not only forgiven the fault, but also the punishment due for the sin. Now then, whereas the Lord *We make not satisfaction for punishment.*

[6 James v. 16.]

sometime doth whip us with his scourges, and whippeth us for our sins indeed (as the holy scripture doth plainly declare), he doth it not to the intent, that with our affliction we should make satisfaction for the sins we have committed; for then should the death of Christ be of none effect: but the Lord with whipping doth chastise us, and by whipping us doth let us understand, that he liketh not of the sins, which we have committed, and he doth freely forgive: by whipping us also he maketh us examples to other, lest they sin too; and cutteth from us all occasion of sinning; and by the cross doth keep our patience in ure[1]. This thus far, touching the forgiveness of sins. Of which I have said somewhat in my sermon of faith that justifieth[2], and elsewhere.

The eleventh article of our faith. The eleventh article is this: "The resurrection of the flesh." These two articles, this and the twelfth, shut up, as briefly as may be, the most excellent fruit of faith, and sum of all perfection; they wrap up, I say, the end of faith, in confessing life everlasting, and the full and perfect salvation of the whole man. For the whole man[3] shall be saved, as well in soul as body. For as man by sin did perish both in body and soul, so ought he to be restored again both bodily and ghostly: and as he ought, so was he by Christ restored again. The soul of man verily is a spirit, and dieth not at all: the body is earthly, and therefore dieth and rotteth. For which cause many hold opinion, that the bodies die, never to be made partakers of joy or pain in the world to come. But we in this article profess the contrary, acknowledging that those our bodies, and so that flesh of ours, shall rise again, and enter into life everlasting.

The resurrection of our flesh. Of this word "resurrection," or rising again, I have spoken in the exposition of that article, "The third day he rose again from the dead." But now this word "flesh" doth a great deal more significantly express the resurrection of this flesh[4] than if we should say the resurrection of the body. Verily Cyprian saith, that in some churches of the east this article was thus pronounced: "I believe the resurrection of this flesh[5]." And Augustine also, in the tenth chapter of his book

[1] i.e. in exercise and practice. exercet, Lat.]
[2] See above, page 109.]   [3 See above, page 144.]
[4] hujus nostræ carnis, Lat.]
[5] Satis cauta et provida adjectione fidem symboli ecclesia nostra

de Fide et Symbolo, saith : " We must without doubting believe, that this visible, which is properly called flesh, shall
rise again. The apostle Paul doth seem, as it were, with
his finger to point at this flesh, when he saith, ' This corruptible must put on incorruption.' When he saith ' this,'
he doth, as it were, put out his finger unto this flesh[6]." This
hath Augustine. Moreover, St Hierome compelleth John,
bishop of Hierusalem, openly to confess the resurrection of the
flesh, not of the body only. " Flesh," saith he, " hath one
definition, and the body another. All flesh is a body ; but
every body is not flesh. That is flesh properly, which is
compact of blood, veins, bones, and sinews. A body, although
it be called flesh, yet sometimes is said to be of like substance
to the firmament, or to the air, which is not subject to touching or seeing ; and oftentimes too may be both touched and
seen. A wall is a body, but it is not flesh[7]." Thus much out
of Hierome. Let us therefore believe, that men's bodies,
which are taken of the earth, and which living men bear
about, wherein they live, and are, which also die and turn
into dust and ashes, that those bodies, I say, are quickened
and live again.

But thou demandest, how this flesh, being once resolved
into dust and ashes, and so into nothing, can rise again in
the former shape and substance : as when it is torn with the
teeth of beasts, or consumed to nothing with the flame of fire,
and when in the grave[8] there is to be found but a small and

Whether the same bodies, that do putrefy, rise again.

docet, quæ in eo quod a ceteris traditur 'carnis resurrectionem,' uno
addito pronomine tradit,'Hujus carnis resurrectionem.'—Cypr. Expos.
in Symb. Apost. fol. 28. Oxon. 1682. See also Becon's Works, Parker
Soc. ed. Vol. II. page 49.]

[6 Hæc ergo visibilis, quæ caro proprie dicitur, sine dubitatione credenda est resurgere. Videtur enim Paulus apostolus eam tanquam
digito suo ostendere, cum dicit, " Oportet corruptibile hoc induere in-
corruptionem." Cum enim dicit Hoc, in eam quasi digitum intendit.—
Opp. Par. 1531. Tom. III. fol. 32.]

[7 Alia enim carnis, alia corporis definitio est. Omnis caro est
corpus ; non omne corpus est caro. Caro est proprie, quæ sanguine,
venis, ossibus, nervisque constringitur : corpus quamquam et caro
dicatur, interdum tamen æthereum vel aërium nominatur, quod tactui
visuique non subjacet ; sed plerunque visibile est atque tangibile.
Paries est corpus, sed non caro, &c.—Hieron. Ep. xxxviii. ad Pam.
adv. Error. Johan. Jerosol. ed. Par. Tom. IV. par. 2. col. 322.]

[8 in monumentis, Lat.]

little quantity of dusty powder ? I refer thee to the omnipotency of God, which the apostle spake of where he saith : " Christ hath transformed this vile body of ours, to make it conformable to his glorious body, by the power wherein he can make all things subject to himself[1]." Wherefore he that in the beginning, when as yet there was not a man in the world, could bring forth man out of the dust of the earth, although the same man be again resolved into that out of which he was taken, I mean, into earth, as the saying is, "Dust thou art, and into dust shalt thou return again[2];" yet notwithstanding, the same God again, at the end of the world, is able to raise man out of the earth. For the Lord in the gospel saith plainly : " The hour shall come, wherein all they that are in the graves shall hear the voice of the Son of God, and shall come forth; they that have done good to the resurrection of life, and they that have done evil to the resurrection of judgment[3]." And now by faith we are throughly persuaded, as the apostle saith, " that he that hath promised is able also to perform[4]." There are moreover lively examples of this matter, and most evident testimonies of the holy scripture. Jonas is swallowed up of the whale in the Syrian[5] sea, but the third day after he is cast up again alive upon the shore out of the beast's entrails; which is a token, that the flesh shall verily rise again. Wherefore, that is not hard to be believed that in the Apocalypse[6] is said, that "the sea casteth up her dead."

[1] Phil. iii. 21. Erasmus, whose rendering Bullinger adopts, has transfiguravit.]

[2] Gen. iii. 19.]

[3] John v. 28, 29.]

[4] Rom. iv. 21.]

[5] The Syrian Sea is that part of the Mediterranean about Cæsarea.—Relandi Palæstina, Lib. III. p. 675, ed. Traject. ad Rhen. 1714. in voc. Cæsarea. Cf. Calvin. Comm. in Jon. i. 3, p. 253, ed. Amstel. 1667.]

[6] in theologia Domini, Lat. The sense, in which Bullinger gives this name to the Apocalypse, is, not only because it is in some copies called the Revelation of John the Divine (see Horne's Introduction, Vol. IV. part 2, chap. 5, §. 1), but because (as he writes in his Comment. in Apocalyps. p. 1. Basil. 1570), est doctrina de rebus ecclesiæ Christi revelata cœlitus a Christo in gloria, et compendium totius pietatis, et prophetarum explicatio et summarium.]

The force of fire had no force to hurt the three companions of Daniel: yea, the rage of wild beasts (contrary to nature) abstained from biting Daniel himself: what marvel is it therefore, if at this day neither the force of fire, nor rage of wild beasts, is able to resist the power of God, being disposed to raise his creatures up again[7]? Did not our Lord Christ raise up Lazarus, when he had lien three days in the grave, yea, and stank too, to life again? Did not he himself, having once broken the tyranny of death, rise up again the third day from the dead? Did he not rise again in the same substance of flesh and form of body, wherein he hanged on the cross, and, being taken down from the cross, was buried? Not without good cause do we look back to Christ, which is called the first-begotten among the dead[8], so often as we think in what manner the resurrection of our flesh shall be. For the members shall rise again in the same order that the Head is risen up before them in: we verily shall not rise again the third day after our death; but in our manner and order shall we rise at the last day; yea, and that too in the very same body wherein now we live.

I will add a few testimonies to prove the resurrection of our flesh. Job, confessing his faith touching the resurrection of the dead, in his great weakness, affliction, and sickness, saith: " I know that my Redeemer liveth, and that in the last day I shall rise out of the earth, and shall be clad again with my skin, and in my flesh I shall see God: whom even I myself shall see, and my eyes shall behold, and none other. This hope is laid up in my bosom[9]." This testimony is so evident as that it needeth no larger an exposition.

Testimonies of the true resurrection.

No less evident are those testimonies out of Esay, chap. xxvi.; Ezech. xxxvii.; Psalm xvi.; Matt. xxii.; John v. vi. xi. Throughout the Acts in every place is often repeated the resurrection of the dead. St Paul, in the fifteenth chapter of his first epistle to the Corinthians, doth make a full discourse of this resurrection. In the fourth chapter of his second epistle he saith: " We which live are always delivered to death for

[7 Cf. Works of Bp. Jewel, Parker Soc. ed. Vol. II. p. 867.]
[8 Coloss. i. 18.   Rev. i. 5.   primogenitus ex mortuis, Lat.]
[9 Job xix. 25—27. The last sentence of v. 27 is in the Vulgate as in Bullinger's Latin, " reposita est hæc spes mea in sinu meo:" and in the Douay Version, " This my hope is laid up in my bosom."]

Jesus' sake, that the life of Jesus also might appear in our mortal flesh[1]." See now, what could be spoken more plainly, than that the life of Christ shall be made to appear in this mortal flesh of ours? For by and by after he saith: "We know that he, that raised up the Lord Jesus, shall raise us up also by the means of Jesus[2]." And in the fifth chapter again: "We must all appear before the judgment-seat of Christ," saith he, "that every man may receive the works of his body, according to that he hath done, whether it be good or evil[3]." Therefore these very bodies of ours shall rise again in the day of judgment.

And now, dearly beloved, I have to declare unto you in what manner our bodies shall rise again, and of what sort *In what sort our bodies shall rise again.* they shall be in the resurrection. In the shutting up and end of all ages, or of this world, our Lord Jesus Christ shall come to judgment with great majesty; and then, whomsoever that day shall find alive, they shall in a moment of time be changed; and first (I say) shall all they that died, from the first Adam to the last that shall die, rise up again, and in their own flesh stand among the living that are changed, before the tribunal-seat of Christ, looking for that last pronounced sentence in judgment. This doth Paul set down in these words: "Lo, I tell you a mystery; We shall not all verily sleep, but we shall all be changed in a moment of time, in the twinkling of an eye, at the sound of the last trump: for it shall sound, and the dead shall rise again incorruptibly, and we shall be changed. For this corruptible must put on incorruption, and this mortal must put on immortality[4]."

Of what fashion our bodies shall be in the resurrection. By this evident testimony of the apostle we may gather in what fashion our bodies shall be in that resurrection. Verily, our bodies shall be none other in the resurrection than now they be; this only excepted, that they shall be clean without all corruption and corruptible affection. For the apostle saith, "The dead shall rise again;" and, "We shall be changed." And again, pointing expressly and precisely to these very bodies which here we bear about, he saith, "This corruptible, this mortal, yea, this body, I say, and no other," as Job also witnessed, shall rise again: and that shall rise again incorruptible, which was corruptible; that shall rise again immortal,

[1 2 Cor. iv. 11.]   [2 ibid. v. 14.]
[3 verse 10.]   [4 1 Cor. xv. 51—53.]

which before the resurrection was mortal. So then this body of ours in the resurrection shall be set free from all evil affections and passions, from all corruption; but the substance thereof shall not be brought to nought, it shall not be changed into a spirit, it shall not lose the own and proper shape. And this body verily because of that purification and cleansing from those dregs, yea, and rather because of these heavenly and divine gifts, is called both a spiritual body, and also a glorious and purified body. A glorious body.

For Paul, in the third to the Philippians, saith: "Our conversation is in heaven, from whence we look for the Saviour, the Lord Jesus Christ, who shall change our vile body, that it may be made like unto his glorious body." See here, the apostle calleth not our resurrection from the dead a transubstantiation, or loss of the substance of our body, but a changing: then also, shewing what kind of body that changed body is, he calleth it a glorious body, not without all shape and void of fashion, but augmented in glory: yea, he setteth before us the very body of our Lord Jesus Christ, wherein he sheweth us what fashion our bodies shall have, being in glory. For in plain words he saith: "He shall make our vile body like to his glorious body." Let us therefore see what kind of body our Lord had after his resurrection. It was neither turned into a ghost, nor brought to nothing, nor yet not able to be known by the shape and figure; for, shewing them his hands and feet, that were easily known by the print of the nails wherewith he was crucified, he said, "See, for I am even he[5]," to wit, clad again with the same body wherein I hung upon the cross. For, speaking yet more plainly, and proving that that body of his was not a spiritual substance, he said: "A spirit hath not flesh and bones, as ye see that I have." He hath therefore a purified body, flesh and bones, and the very same members which he had when as yet his body was not purified. And for this cause did the same Lord offer to Thomas his side[6], and the scars of his five wounds, to be felt and handled; to the end that we should not doubt but that his very body was raised up again. He did both eat and drink with his disciples, as Peter in the Acts[7] witnesseth before Cornelius, that all men might know, that the very self-same body that died rose from death again.

[5 Luke xxiv. 39.]   [6 John xx. 27.]   [7 ch. x. 41.]

Now, although this body be comprehended within a certain limited place, not dispersed all over and every where; although it have a just quantity, figure, or shape, and a just weight, with the own kind and nature[1]; yet notwithstanding it is free from every passion, corruption, and infirmity. For the body of the Lord once raised up was in the garden, and not in the sepulchre, when the women came to anoint it; it meeteth them by the way as they return from the sepulchre, and offereth itself to be seen of Magdalene in the garden; it goeth in company[2] to Emaus with the two disciples that journeyed to Emaus: in the mean time, while he was with them in body, he was not among the other disciples; when they twain are returned to the eleven, the Lord himself at evening is present with them: he goeth before his disciples into Galilee: presently after he cometh into Jury again, where his body was taken up from mount Olivet into heaven. All this doth prove the certain verity of Christ his body. But because this body (although it be a true and very body, of the own proper kind[3], place, disposition, and of the own proper shape and nature) is called a glorified and glorious body, I will say somewhat of that glory, which verily is incident to the true shape and substance of the body once raised up again.

What a glorious body is.

First, glory in this sense is used for a lightsomeness and shining brightness. For Paul saith, that the children of Israel, for the glory of Moses' countenance, could not behold with their eyes the face of Moses[4]: so then a glorious body is a bright and shining body. A very good proof of this did our Lord shew, even a little before his resurrection, when it pleased him to give to his disciples a small taste of the glory to come; and for that cause took aside certain, whom he had chosen, into the top of a certain hill, where he was transfigured before them, so that the fashion of his countenance did shine as the sun, and his clothes were white and glistered as the light[5]. The Lord verily had still the same bodily substance, and the same members of the body, but they were transfigured. But it is manifest, that that transfiguration was in the accidents. For light and brightness was added, so that, the shape and substance of the countenance and body remaining as it was,

[1 sexum et suam naturam, Lat.]
[2 æquis passibus, Lat.]
[3 sui sexus, Lat.]
[4 2 Cor. iii. 7.]
[5 Matt. xvii. 2.]

the countenance and body did glister as the sun and the light. And although we read not that the body of the Lord did within those forty days, wherein he shewed himself alive again to his disciples, make manifest and spread abroad the brightness which it had, and that by reason of the dispensation, whereby also he did eat with his disciples, notwithstanding that clarified bodies need not food or nourishment at all; yet nevertheless his body shineth now in heaven, as John in the first of the Apocalypse witnesseth: and the sacred scriptures lay an assured hope before us, that even our bodies also shall in the resurrection be likewise clarified. For the Lord himself in the gospel, alleging the words of Daniel, saith: "Then shall the righteous shine as the sun in his Father's kingdom[6]." For this cause the glorious bodies are called also clarified, of the clearness of that heavenly brightness wherewith they glister and are adorned.

Secondarily, glory and vileness are made contraries. *Glorious bodies rest free from vileness.* For Paul saith: "He shall change our vile body, to make it in fashion like to his glorious body[7]." In these words vileness and glory are set the one against the other. Vileness comprehendeth the whole pack of miseries and infirmities, passions and affections, which for sin was laid upon the body: from all which our bodies are purged in the resurrection of life; so that then the glorious bodies are bodies drained from the dregs of all corruption, passions, and infirmities, and clad with eternity, heavenly feeling, and glory. For the apostle saith: "It is sown in corruption; it riseth in incorruption: it is sown in dishonour; it riseth in glory: it is sown in infirmity; it riseth in power: it is sown a natural body; it riseth a spiritual body[8]." The gifts therefore of the glorious and clarified bodies are very great and many, as incorruption, glory, power, and the quickening Spirit. For the apostle himself, shewing what he meant by the natural[9] and spiritual body, addeth this immediately, and saith: "There is a natural body, and there is a spiritual body; as it is written, The first man Adam was made a living soul; and the last Adam was made a quickening spirit." And yet again more plainly he saith: "Howbeit, that is not first which is spiritual, but that which is natural, and then that

---

[6 Matt. xiii. 43; Dan. xii. 3.]   [7 Phil. iii. 21.]
[8 1 Cor. xv. 42—44.]
[9 animale, Lat.]

which is spiritual. The first man is of the earth, earthy: the
second man is the Lord from heaven. As is the earthy, such
are they that are earthy: and as is the heavenly, such are
they also that are heavenly. And as we have borne the
image of the earthy, so shall we bear the image of the heavenly." So then Paul calleth that natural body an earthy
body, which we have of our first father Adam, whose quickening is of the soul, and by it doth live. And he calleth the
spiritual body an heavenly body, which we have of Christ,
and made to the likeness of the body of Christ; which
although it be a very body indeed, and the flesh thereof be
very flesh indeed, yet notwithstanding it is quickened and
preserved by the Spirit of Christ, and needeth not any power
vegetative.

The natural and spiritual body.

Although therefore these very bodies and members, which
now we bear, shall after the resurrection be in heaven; yet
nevertheless, because they are clarified and cleansed from all
corruption and feeling of the natural body, there shall not be
verily any natural or corruptible sense or affection, nor use
of the carnal body and members. And this doth the Lord
affirm against the Sadducees (that dreamt of marriages in
heaven, or rather by that absurdity made a mock of the
resurrection), where he saith: "The sons of this world marry
wives, and give in marriage; but they that shall be thought
worthy of that world and of the resurrection from the dead,
do neither marry wives, nor give in marriage; neither can
they die any more. For they are equal to the angels, and
are the sons of God, as soon as they be the sons of resurrection[1]." To which effect also Paul saith: "Flesh and
blood cannot inherit the kingdom of God." And lest peradventure any man should mistake his words, and think that
he spake of the substance of the flesh, he addeth immediately this for interpretation thereof, and saith: "Neither shall
corruption inherit incorruption[2]." Wherefore flesh and blood,
that is to say, the affections and lusts of the flesh, shall not
be in the elect that live in heaven. For the joys of heaven
do differ a great deal from the joys of the earth, and are so
far forth of another condition, that they cannot admit such
corrupt creatures to be inheritors of them; and for that cause

Flesh and blood shall not be in heaven.

Sensu animali.
Animalis.

[1 Luke xx. 34—36. cum sint, Lat.]
[2 1 Cor. xv. 50.]

the corruptible bodies must first be purged from all corruption, and by that means purely clarified.   The Turks therefore are deceived, that look for earthly joys[3].

Moreover, the bodies of the wicked shall also rise again. For Paul, in the Acts, saith : " I believe all that is written in the law and the prophets, hoping in God that the resurrection of the dead, which they themselves look for also, shall be both of the just and unjust[4]."   See here, the apostle saith of the unjust also.   But in this resurrection there shall not be taken out of their bodies the infirmity, corruption, dishonour, and misery ; for even then that very body, rising again in dishonour, shall by the judgment and power of God be surely shut in dishonour and corruption, and so be condemned for ever to bear endless torments, and in death and corruption shall neither die nor yet corrupt : that even as on earth are found certain bodies that do endure even in the fire, so the cursed bodies of the wicked shall not be worn out, nor broken with any torments whatsoever ; for every minute they shall receive new strength to suffer, and so by continual suffering shall abide their deserved punishments for ever and ever and without all end.   For the Lord in the gospel saith, " They that have done evil shall rise again to the resurrection of damnation[5] ;" that is, to an enduring and everlasting damnation.   And Daniel before him said : " And the multitude of them that sleep in the dust of the earth shall awake, some to everlasting life, and some to shame and perpetual contempt[6]."   And in the gospel, again, the Lord saith : "Their worm dieth not, and their fire is not quenched."   And the very same words used Esay before him in his 66th chapter[7].   We must always therefore have that saying of the Lord in our hearts: " Fear him that can destroy both the body and the soul in hell[8]."   Thus much hitherto touching the resurrection of the flesh.

The last article of our belief, which with good luck shutteth up the rest, is this: " And life everlasting."   We have heard and understood, that the souls of men are immortal,

The bodies of the wicked shall also rise again.

The twelfth article of our belief.

[3 See Sale's Prelim. Discourse to his translation of the Koran, Sect. IV.]

[4 ch. xxiv. 15.]

[5 John v. 29.]   [6 Dan. xii. 2.]

[7 Mark ix. 44; Isai. lxvi. 24.]   [8 Matt. x. 28.]

[BULLINGER.]

and that our bodies do rise again in the end of the world. We have confessed that this is our belief. It followeth now, in the latter end of the Creed, whither it is that the immortal soul and body raised up again shall come. Therefore in our confession we say, "And life everlasting;" that is, I believe that I shall have life, and live for ever, both in body and soul. And that everlastingness verily is perpetual and hath no end, as a little before is proved out of the holy scriptures.

Life ever-lasting.

Moreover, the souls are made partakers of this eternal life immediately after they are departed out of the bodies, as the Lord himself witnesseth, saying: "He that believeth in the Son of God shall not come into judgment, but hath escaped from death to life[1]." As for the bodies, they are buried and do putrefy; and yet so, notwithstanding, that they shall not be without life for ever: but they shall then at length be received into eternal life, when, being raised up, they shall after the time of judgment be caught into the air, there to meet Christ, that they may for ever be with the Lord. For then do the souls return out of heaven, every one to his own body, that the whole, perfect, and full man may live for ever both in soul and body. For the soul of Christ dying on the cross did out of hand depart into paradise, and the third day after returned to the body, which rose again and ascended into heaven. Even as, therefore, eternal life came to the Head Christ, so shall it also come to all and every member of Christ.

Now, whereas Paul, citing Esay, saith, "What the eye hath not seen, nor the ear heard, nor hath at any time come into the heart of man, that hath the Lord prepared for them that love him[2];" I suppose verily, if all were said touching eternal life, that might be spoken by all the men of all ages that ever were or shall be, yet that scarcely the very least part thereof hath or shall be throughly touched. For howsoever the scripture doth with eloquent and figurative speeches, with allusions and hard sentences[3], most plainly shew the shadow of that life and those joys; yet, notwithstanding, all that is little or nothing in comparison to speak of, until that day do come wherein we shall with unspeakable joy behold God himself, the Creator of all things, in his glory; Christ our Savi-

[1 John v. 24.]　　　　　　　[2 1 Cor. ii. 9; Is. lxiv. 4.]
[3 ænigmatibus, Lat.]

our in his majesty; and finally, all the blessed souls, angels, patriarchs, prophets, apostles, martyrs, our fathers, all nations[4], all the host of heaven, and lastly, the whole divine and heavenly glory. Most truly therefore said Aurelius Augustine, *Lib. de Civitat. Dei,* xxii. cap. 29: " When it is demanded of me, what the saints shall do in that spiritual body; I answer, not that which I now see, but that that I believe. I say therefore, that they shall see God in that spiritual body." And again: " If I should say the truth, I know not in what sort that action, quietness, and rest shall be. For the peace of God doth pass all understanding[5]." To be short, we shall see God face to face, we shall be filled with the company of God, and yet be never weary of him. And the face of God is not that countenance that appeareth in us; but is a most delectable revealing and enjoying of God, which no mortal tongue can worthily declare. Go to then, dearly beloved brethren; let us believe and live, that when we shall depart from hence we may in very deed have trial[6] of those unspeakable joys of the eternal life to come, which now we do believe.

The face of God.

Hitherto have I, throughout the four last articles, declared unto you the fruit and end of christian faith. Faith leaneth upon one God, the Father, the Son, and the Holy Ghost, which sanctifieth the faithful, and purgeth and halloweth a church to himself: which church hath a communion with God and all saints; all the offences of which church God pardoneth and forgiveth; and doth preserve it both soul and body. For as the saints' souls cannot die, so God raiseth up their bodies again, and maketh them glorious and everlasting, to the end that the whole man may for ever live in heaven with the Lord: to whom be praise and glory world without end. Amen.

[4 et omnem gentem nostram, Lat. And all our race.]

[5 Cum ex me quæritur, quid acturi sint sancti in illo corpore spiritali; non dico quod jam video, sed dico quod credo. Dico itaque, quod visuri sint Deum in ipso corpore...

Illa quidem actio, vel potius quies, atque otium quale futurum sit, si verum velim dicere, nescio.—Ibi est enim pax Dei, quæ, sicut ait apostolus, superat omnem intellectum.—Opp. Par. 1531, Tom. v. fol. 310.]

[6 experiamur, Lat.]

OF THE LOVE OF GOD AND OUR NEIGHBOUR.

THE TENTH SERMON.

IT remaineth, since I have in some sermons discoursed of true faith, that I do now also add one sermon touching love towards God and our neighbour. For in my fourth sermon I promised, so soon as I should have done with the exposition of faith, that then I would speak of love toward God and our neighbour ; because the exposition of the scriptures ought not to go awry out of faith and charity, which are, as it were, the right and holy marks for it to draw unto. Ye, as hitherto ye have done, so cease not yet to pray, that this wholesome doctrine may be by me taught as it should be, and by you received with much increase and profit.

Love and charity. And, first of all, I will not curiously put any difference between charity and love. I will use them both in one and the same sense. St Augustine, *De Doctrina Christiana*, saith: " I call charity a motion of the mind to delight in God for his own sake, and to delight in himself and his neighbour for God's sake[1]." And therefore I call love a gift given to man from heaven, whereby with his heart he loveth God before *Love, from whence it is.* and above all things, and his neighbour as himself. Love therefore springeth from heaven, from whence it is poured into our hearts. But it is enlarged and augmented, partly by the remembrance and consideration of God's benefits, partly by often prayer, and also by the hearing and frequenting of the word of Christ. Which things themselves also are the gifts of the Spirit. For the apostle Paul saith : " The love of God is poured out into our hearts by the Holy Ghost which is given us[2]." For verily the love of God, wherewith he loveth us, is the foundation and cause of our love wherewith we love him ; and of both these jointly consisteth the love of our neighbour. For the apostle saith : " We love him because he first loved us." And again : " Every one that loveth him which begot, loveth him also that is born of him[3]."

[1 Caritatem voco motum animi ad fruendum Deo propter ipsum, et se atque proximo propter Deum.—De Doct. Christ. Lib. III. cap. 10, Vol. III. fol. 11.]

[2 Rom. v. 5.]   [3 1 John iv. 19; v. 1.]

Hereby we gather again, that this gift of love cannot be Double
charity. divided or severed, although it be double. For he that loveth God truly, hateth not his neighbour : and yet, nevertheless, this love, because of the double respect that it hath to God and our neighbour, standeth of two parts. And because of this double charity the tables of God's law are divided into twain : the first whereof containeth four commandments touching the love of God, the second comprehendeth six precepts touching the love of our neighbour. Of which I will speak in their own place. But at this time, because the love of God and of our neighbour are twain, I will first speak of the love of God, and then of the love of our neighbour. " In these two commandments," saith the Lord, " hang the law and the prophets[4]."

With that which we call the love of God, we love God The love of
God. entirely well; we cleave to God as the only, chief, and eternal goodness; in him we do delight ourselves and are well pleased; and frame ourselves to his will and pleasure, having evermore a regard and desire of him that we love[5]. With love we love God most heartily. But we do heartily love the things that are dear unto us, and the things that to us seem worthy to be desired; and we love them entirely indeed, not so much for our commodity, as for because we do desire to join, and, as it were, for ever to give and dedicate ourselves wholly to the thing that we so dearly love. So verily we desire for ever to be joined with God, and are in charity fast linked unto him ; as the apostle saith : " God is charity; and he that dwelleth in charity dwelleth in God, and God in him[6]." And that is the way whereby we cleave to God, as to the only chief and eternal goodness, in whom also we are delighted, and that not a little. On him we rest, thinking assuredly that without him there is no good at all ; and again, that in him there is to be found all manner of goodness. Wherefore our hearty love is set on no good thing but God : and in comparison of him whom we love, we do lightly[7] loathe and tread under foot all things else that

[4 Matt. xxii 40.]

[5 " Here be many propositions together, which we will explain singly and one by one a little more fully :" omitted. P.—Plurima hic simul sunt proposita, quæ sigillatim et per partes copiosius paulo exponemus.]

[6 1 John iv. 16.]   [7 facile, Lat.]

seem to be good in the whole world; yea, verily, the love of

God in us doth overcome all the evils which otherwise seem invincible.　Let us hear Paul with a vehement motion proclaiming this, and saying: "Who shall separate us from the love of God? shall tribulation, or anguish, or persecution, or hunger, or nakedness, or peril, or sword?　(As it is written, For thy sake are we killed all the day long, and are counted as sheep for the slaughter.)　Nevertheless in all these things we overcome through him that loved us.　For I am sure that neither death, nor life, nor angels, nor rule, nor power, nor things present, nor things to come, nor height, nor depth, nor any other creature shall be able to separate us from the love of God which is in Christ Jesu our Lord[1]."　Hitherto have I recited the words of Paul.

The love of God worketh in us a will to frame ourselves wholly to the will and ordinances of him whom we do heartily love.　Yea, it is pleasant and sweet to him that loveth God to do the thing that he perceiveth is acceptable to God, if it be done.　He that loveth doth in mind reverence him whom he loveth.　His eye is never off him whom he loveth.　He doth always, and in all things, wish for his dearling whom he loveth.　His only joy is, as oft as may be, to talk with God, and again to hear the words of God speaking in the scripture.　For the Lord in the gospel saith: "If any man love me, he will keep my word: he that loveth me not doth not keep my words."　Again: "Abide ye in my love.　If ye keep my commandments, ye shall abide in my love, even as I also have kept my Father's commandments, and do abide in his love."　And again: "If any man love me, he will keep my word; and my Father will love him, and we will come to him, and make our dwelling in him[2]."

But now let us hear Moses, the servant of God, declaring and teaching us the way and manner how to love God; to wit, how great love ought to be in the elect.　"Thou shalt," saith he, "love the Lord thy God with all thy heart, with all thy soul, and with all thy strength[3]."　The very same words, in a manner, did our Lord in the gospel repeat, and said: "Thou shalt love the Lord thy God with all thy heart,

---

[1 Rom. viii. 35—39.]　　[2 John xiv. 23, 24; xv. 9, 10.]
[3 Deut. vi. 5.]

with all thy soul, with all thy strength, and with all thy mind[4]." By this we understand, that the greatest love that may be is required at our hands to God-ward ; as that which challengeth man wholly, how big soever he be, and all the parts of man, as peculiar unto itself. In the mind is man's understanding. In the heart is the seat of his affections and will. The strength of man containeth all man's ability, as his very words, deeds, counsel, riches, and his whole substance. Finally, the soul is the life of man. And we verily are commanded to employ all these upon the love of God, when we are bidden to love God with all our soul, with all our strength, with our whole mind, and our whole heart. Nothing is overslipped, but all is contained in this. We are God's wholly and altogether; let us altogether therefore and wholly love God. Let nothing in all the world be dearer to us than God: let us not spare for God's sake any thing of all that which we possess, how dear to us or good soever it be; but let us forsake, spend, and give it for God's sake, and as the Lord by his word appointeth : for in doing so we love God before and above all things.

We are also commanded to stick to God only, and to embrace him alone. For to whom we do wholly owe all that we have, to him is all the whole sincerely, simply, and fully to be given. Here are they condemned, whosoever will at once love God and the world together. The Lord requireth the whole heart, the whole mind, the whole soul, and all the strength ; finally, he requireth all whatsoever we are, or have in possession : he leaveth nothing therefore for thee to bestow on other. By what right then wilt thou give to the flesh, the devil, to other gods, or to the world, the things that properly are God's own ? And God verily alone is the chiefest, eternal, greatest, mightiest creator, deliverer, preserver, most gentle, most just, and best of all. He alone doth give, hath given, and is able to give to man all that is expedient for the safeguard of his body and soul. God alone doth minister to man ability to live well and blessedly : and therefore God deserveth to be loved alone, and that too before and above all other things. This love of God doth bless all the haps and chances of men, and turneth them to their profit, according to that saying : " To them that love God all

God alone to be loved.

[4 Matt. xxii. 37.]

things work for the best[1]." This love of God also containeth this; that it suffereth us not to honour, worship, reverence, fear, or call upon any, neither to trust in, obey, or stick to any other, but to the one and only God, to whom all glory is due.

Who is our neighbour. But now, before we speak of the love of our neighbour, it is requisite that we first shew who it is that is our neighbour; touching which I see some men to doubt and stick uncertainly. For some there are, that take their kinsfolks to be their neighbours: other some there are, that think that their benefactors are their neighbours, and judge them strangers that do them any harm. But our Lord Jesus Christ telleth us, that every one, yea, though he be our enemy, is nevertheless our neighbour, if he stand in need of our aid or counsel. For he imagineth that a Jew, lighting among thieves, and lying on the high-way half dead, and covered with wounds and swelling dry blows[2], was not regarded of his own countrymen, a Levite and a priest, that passed by him; but at last was taken up and healed by a Samaritan. Now there was a deadly enmity between the Jews and the Samaritans; yet notwithstanding, this Samaritan doth good to the Jew, because he saw that the case and necessity of the afflicted man did so require. Now therefore the Lord, applying this to his own purpose, demanded of him that desired to learn who was his neighbour, and saith, "Which of these three seemeth to thee to have been this man's neighbour? He answered, He that shewed mercy. Then said the Lord, Go thou, and do the like[3]." As if he should have said: Like as the Samaritan judged even his enemy to be his neighbour, and dealt friendly with him, when he stood in need of his friendship; so see that thou take every one that needeth thy help to be thy neighbour, and do him good. Aurelius Augustine therefore, according to the right sense of the scripture, said: "We take him to be our neighbour, to whom we shew mercy when need requireth; or to whom we should shew mercy, if at any time he should need[4]." We Switzers do most properly express it, when we call our neighbour *Den nachsten*

[1 Rom. viii. 28.]   [2 tuberibusque, Lat.]   [3 Luke x. 29—37.]
[4 Ut videlicet eum esse proximum intelligamus, cui vel exhibendum est officium misericordiæ si indiget, vel exhibendum esset si indigeret.—August. de Doct. Christ. Lib. I. cap. 30, Par. 1531, Tom. III. col. 4.]

menschen; that is, any man, without difference, whosoever by hap shall light into our company. Moreover, in our country speech we will call our neighbour, *Der abenmensch, namlich ein yeder der so wol ein mensch ist als wir :* meaning thereby any man whatsoever, whether he be our friend or enemy. Hereunto belongeth that saying of Lactantius, in the eleventh chapter of his sixth book : " Why makest thou choice of persons? why lookest thou so narrowly on the limbs ? Thou must take him to be a man, whosoever beseecheth thee therefore, that he may think thee to be a man. Give to the blind, to the impotent, to the lame, to the comfortless ; to whom unless thou be liberal, thou shalt die undoubtedly[5]." Again he saith : " If so be we will rightly be called by the name of men, then must we in any case keep the law of civil humanity. And what else I pray you is it to keep humanity, but therefore to love a man because he is a man, and the very same that we ourselves are[6] ?" The Lord in the gospel verily, speaking of the love of our neighbour, saith : " Love your enemies, bless them that curse you, do good to them that hate you, pray for them that hurt you[7]." And again : " Give to every one that asketh of thee. And if you love them that love you, what thank is that to you? For sinners also love them of whom they are loved[8]." So then every man, whosoever standeth in need of our aid, both is and is to be counted our neighbour.

And yet, all this notwithstanding, there is no cause but that there ought to be an order, a measure, and decent regard in love and well-doing. For rightly said St Augustine, in the twenty-seventh chapter of his book *de Doctrina Christiana :* " No sinner, in that he is a sinner, is to be loved[9]." And in the twenty-eighth chapter : " All men are to be loved alike; but since thou canst not do good to all men, therefore thou

The man next to us.

Any one that is a man as well as we.

An order and measure in loving.

---

[5] Quid personas eligis? quid membra inspicis? Pro homine tibi habendus est, quisquis ideo precatur, quia te hominem putet. . . . Largire cæcis, debilibus, claudis, destitutis : quibus, nisi largiare, moriendum est.—Lactant. Div. Inst. vi. 11, Lugd. Bat. 1660. p. 583. More correctly translated, " to whom unless thou be liberal, *they must die.*" P.]

[6 Conservanda est igitur humanitas, si homines recte dici velimus. Id autem ipsum, conservare humanitatem, quid aliud est, quam diligere hominem, quia homo sit et idem quod nos sumus ?—Ibid. p. 581.]

[7 Matt. v. 44.]　　　　　　　　　　[8 Luke vi. 30, 32.]

[9 Omnis peccator, in quantum peccator est, non est diligendus.—De Doct. Christ. i. 27, Opp. Tom. iii. fol. 4.]

must especially do good to them, to whom thou art, as it were by lot, more nearly joined, by opportunity either of time, of place, or of any other thing whatsoever[1]." And this did Paul, before Augustine, teach, where he saith : " Whosoever worketh not, let him not eat[2]." And again : " While we have time, let us work good to all men ; but specially to them of the household of faith[3]." And in another place he commandeth us not to bestow unto others, and to lack ourselves at home ; but rather he chargeth every one to have a godly care of his own house. The place is known in the fifth chapter of the first epistle to Timothy.

How our neighbour must be loved. Now since I have declared who is our neighbour, let us see also in what sort this neighbour of ours ought to be loved. Our neighbour must be loved simply, without any coloured deceit, with the very self-same love wherewith we love ourselves, or that wherewith Christ hath loved us. For in all things we must stand our neighbour in stead, and do him pleasure, so far as the law of humanity shall be found to require. In this declaration there are four things more fully to be noted.

The love of our neighbour must be sincere. First, that love of our neighbour that is looked for at our hands ought to be so sincere, as that it be without all manner guile, deceit, and coloured craft. For there are many to be found, that have the skill to talk to their neighbours with sugared tongues, and to make a face as though they loved them, when as indeed they do utterly hate them, meaning nothing else but with fawning words to beguile them, that thereby they may work the things that they desire. Paul and John, therefore, the apostles of Christ, go about earnestly to sever hypocrisy from love. For Paul saith : " Let not your love be feigned." Again : " The end of the commandment is love of a pure heart, and a good conscience, and faith not feigned[4]." On the other side, John crieth out, saying : " My babes, let us not love in word, nor in tongue, but in deed and in verity[5]." Moreover, in this sincerity we

[1 Omnes autem homines æque diligendi sunt. Sed cum omnibus prodesse non possis, his potissimum consulendum est, qui pro locorum et temporum vel quarumlibet rerum opportunitatibus constrictius tibi quasi quadam sorte junguntur.—c. 28, ib.]

[2 2 Thess. iii. 10.]   [3 Gal. vi. 10.]

[4 Rom. xii. 9; 1 Tim. i. 5.]   [5 1 John iii. 18.]

contain a free, willing, and merry cheerfulness, that nothing may seem to be done unwillingly or by compulsion. For Paul saith: "Let every man do with a good purpose of mind, not of trouble or necessity; for God requireth a cheerful giver[6]."

Secondarily, it is to be looked for of us, that we should love our neighbour as ourselves. For the Lord hath said, "Love thy neighbour as thyself[7];" that is, most entirely, and as dearly as by any means thou mayest. For there is not any affection that is of more force or vehemency than self-love is. Neither was it the Lord his mind, that the love of our neighbour should be any whit lesser than the love that we bear to ourselves: but rather by this he gave us to understand, that we ought to bestow on others as ardent love as may be, to wit, the very same affection that we bear to ourselves and our own estate; and that we ought to be ready to do good to other, or to keep them from harm, with the same care, faith, and diligence, with the same zeal and good-will, wherewith we provide for ourselves or our own safety. Whereupon the Lord in another place saith: "Whatsoever thou wouldest have done to thyself, that do thou to another. And whatsoever thou wouldest not have done to thyself, do not thou the same to another[8]." And herein doth the Lord require two things at our hands; not to hurt, and to do good. For it is not enough not to hurt a man, but also to do him good, so much as lieth in us to do. For we ourselves desire not only to keep ourselves from hurt, but to do ourselves good also.

We must love our neighbour as ourself.

But if so it be, dearly beloved, that ye do not yet sufficiently understand the manner how we ought to love our neighbour; then mark, I beseech you, the third part of my description of this love, where I said, that we ought to love our neighbour with that same love wherewith the Lord Christ loved us. For in the gospel after St John the Lord saith: "This is my commandment, That ye love one another, as I have loved you[9]." So then, here ye have the manner of our love: we must love our neighbours as Christ hath loved us. But in

We must love our neighbour as Christ hath loved us.

[6 2 Cor. ix. 7.   non ex molestia, Lat. and Erasmus; Vulgate, ex tristitia.]

[7 Matt. xxii. 39.]   [8 Matt. vii. 12.]

[9 ch. xv. 12.]

what sort hath Christ loved us ?   Here again in the gospel he saith : "No man hath greater love than this, that a man bestow his life for his friends[1]."   So then, such must the manner of our love toward our neighbour be, as that we shall not doubt to give our life for our neighbour.   And if so it be then, that for our neighbour's sake we owe the loss of our life, there is nothing verily that we owe him not, considering that to a man nothing is more dear than life : for sooner will he lose all that he hath than once to put his life in jeopardy. Whereupon the apostle John crieth out, and saith : "Hereby perceive we love, because he laid down his life for us : and we ought to lay down our lives for the brethren[2]."   This is easy to be understood by reason of the most evident example. Let us pray earnestly and continually to the Lord, that we may indeed fulfil the thing that we do manifestly understand by the word of God, lest peradventure the same apostle condemn us, who saith : "Whoso hath this world's good, and seeth his brother have need, and shutteth up his compassion from him, how dwelleth the love of God in him[2]?"

How we ought to stand our neighbour in stead.
And now let us also declare the fourth and last manner, how we ought to stand our neighbour in stead, and how to do him good in shewing our dutiful love and civil humanity. That hath the Lord already very finely[3] set out in the very same parable wherein he taught us who is our neighbour : for he hath briefly, and yet very evidently, touched all the points of the love that we owe to our neighbour.   First, the Samaritan, at the sight of the wounded man, was moved with pity.   There is therefore required of us a merciful motion of pity, so to regard other men's calamities as though they were our own : it is looked for at our hands, that we should be as sorrowful-minded for another man's trouble, as he that feeleth the misery, according to that saying of the apostle : "Be mindful of them that are in bonds, as bound with them ; and of them which suffer adversity, as though ye yourselves also, being in the body, suffered adversity[4]."   Secondarily, the Samaritan passeth not by, but cometh unto him ; he doth not

[1 Ibid. v. 13.]   [2 1 John iii. 16, 17.]
[3 eleganter, Lat.]
[4 Heb. xiii. 3.   velut ipsi quoque versantes in corpore, Lat. and Erasmus.   The Genevan Testament renders : As if ye were afflicted in the body.]

with sorrowful words wish health to the wounded, and so, letting him lie, depart to dispatch his own affairs : for James the
apostle saith : " If a brother or sister be naked, and destitute
of daily food, and one of you say unto them, Depart in peace,
be ye warmed and filled ; and yet notwithstanding give them
not those things that are needful to the body, what shall it
profit[5] ?"   The Samaritan therefore cometh unto him, setteth
to his hand, and sheweth the skill that he hath (which was
not much, I wis[6]) to heal the seely[7] mangled man.   He doth
not loathe and turn his face from the ill-favoured colour, bloody
matter, corrupted filth and stench of his wounds; he bindeth
them up himself, not letting them alone for another to do.
He maketh not his excuse, that he is no physician ; but doth
what he can in that necessity, using such medicine as for the
time present he had in a readiness, till more conveniently he
might come by better.   Wine and oil he had taken with him
when he began his journey, which in that necessity he
doth use ; and that not very inconveniently, because wine
purgeth wounds, and oil doth make them supple.   Moreover,
whatsoever he hath, that doth he employ to the seely man's
behoof, and to do him ease doth even disease himself[8] : for
he alighteth from the back of the beast whereon he rode, and
maketh him to serve the maimed man's necessity.   He also
with his own hands lifteth up from the ground the man that
was too weak to stand, and setteth him on the beast.   And
lastly, he himself becometh his guide to lead the way, not
suffering any other to take charge over him.   For when as
he could not readily bring him to his own house, yet did he
convey him into a common inn : where again he spareth not
for any cost or pains-taking ; for he himself taketh charge of
the miserable man, because in common inns sick folks, for the
most part, are slenderly looked unto.   But when his earnest
business calleth on to make haste in his journey, he taketh
out so much money as he doth think to be sufficient till his
return, and giveth it to the inn-keeper[9].   And not being
therewithal content, he giveth to his host an especial charge

[5   James ii. 15, 16.]
[6   quando meliorem (artem) non didicerat, Lat.]
[7   Seely, i. e. weak.]
[8   suum etiam genium defraudans, Lat.]
[9   hospiti meritorio, Lat.]

of the sick man; and also bindeth himself for him, saying: Whatsoever more than this thou shalt lay out about things necessary for his recovery, thou shalt not lose one mite; for at my return I will pay thee all again to the uttermost farthing. So then he promiseth to return, and therewithal declareth that he shall not be quiet until he see him thoroughly healed of all his wounds. Ye have here, dearly beloved, in this the Lord's parable, a most godly and absolute example of love: for the Samaritan doth liberally and willingly employ his whole service upon his needy neighbour's necessity. We therefore owe ourselves wholly and all that we have to our neighbour's behoof; which if we bestow on him, then do we fulfil the duties of love and civil humanity.

The pith of charity. To this we will yet add some testimonies of the scripture, that thereby we may more fully understand the very innermost pith of love; if yet peradventure any thing may seem to be wanting in that which hitherto I have alleged. Paul therefore, writing to the Corinthians, saith: "Love suffereth wrong, and is courteous; love envieth not; love doth not frowardly; love swelleth not, dealeth not dishonestly, seeketh not her own, is not provoked to anger, thinketh not evil, rejoiceth not in iniquity, but rejoiceth in the truth, suffereth all things, believeth all things, hopeth all things, endureth all things [1]." And again, the same apostle in his epistle to the Romans saith: "Love striveth to go before in giving honour to other; love distributeth to the saints' necessity; is given to hospitality, speaketh well of her persecutors, and curseth not them that persecute her; love rejoiceth with them that do rejoice, and weepeth with them that weep, and applieth itself to the weaker sort's infirmity [2]." And again: "Owe nothing to any man, but to love one another. For he that loveth another *Love the fulfilling of the law.* hath fulfilled the law. For this, Thou shalt not commit adultery, Thou shalt not steal, Thou shalt not kill, Thou shalt not bear false witness, Thou shalt not lust, and if there be any other commandment, it is comprehended briefly in this saying, namely, Thou shalt love thy neighbour as thyself. Love worketh no ill to his neighbour; therefore the fulfilling of the law is love or charity [3]."

Works of mercy. Hitherto also pertaineth the works of mercy, which as they

[1] 1 Cor. xiii. 4—7. patiens est, Lat.]
[2] Rom. xii. 10, 13—16.]   [3] Rom xiii. 8—10.]

flow out of love, so are they rehearsed of the Lord in the gospel after Matthew, and are especially these that follow : To feed the hungry, to give drink to the thirsty, to harbour the harbourless[4] and strangers, to cover or clothe the naked, to visit the sick, and to see and comfort imprisoned captives[5]. Hereunto Lactantius, *Lib. Institut.* VI. cap. 12, hath an eye, where he saith : " The chiefest virtue is to keep hospitality, and to feed the poor : to redeem captives also is a great and excellent work of righteousness : and as great a work of justice is it, to save and defend the fatherless and widows, the desolate and helpless, which the law of God doth every where command. It is also a part of the chiefest humanity and a great good deed, to take in hand to heal and cherish the sick, that have nobody to help them. Finally, that last and greatest duty of piety is the burial of strangers and of the poor[6]." Thus much hitherto touching the duty of civil humanity, which true love sheweth to his neighbour in necessity.

But it is not enough, my brethren, to understand how we ought to love our neighbour (though we ought often to repeat it), but rather we must love him exceedingly, and above that that I am able to say. Let us hear the apostle, who with a wonderful goodly grace of speech, with a most excellent, exquisite, and holy example of Christ doth exhort us all to the shewing of charity to our neighbour, and saith : " If therefore there be any consolation in Christ, if any comfort of love, if any fellowship of the Spirit, if any compassion and mercy, fulfil ye my joy, that ye be like-minded, having the same love, being of one accord and mind : let nothing be done through strife or vain-glory, but in meekness let every man esteem one the other better than himself ; look ye not every man on his own things, but every man also on the things of others. For let the same mind be in you that was in Christ

An exhortation to love.

---

[4] colligere vagos, Lat.]　　　[5] Matth. xxv. 35, 36.]

[6] Præcipua virtus est hospitalitas, &c. Captivorum redemptio magnum atque præclarum justitiæ munus est. . . . Non minus magnum justitiæ opus est, pupillos et viduas, destitutos et auxilio indigentes, tueri atque defendere : quod adeo universis divina lex illa præscribit. Ægros quoque, quibus defuerit qui assistat, curandos fovendosque suscipere, summæ humanitatis et magnæ operationis est. . . . Ultimum illud et maximum pietatis officium est peregrinorum et pauperum sepultura.—Lactant. Div. Instit. Lib. VI. cap. 12, Opp. Lugd. Bat. 1660. pp. 585—588.]

Jesus; who, being in the form of God, thought it no robbery to be equal with God, but made himself of no reputation, taking on him the form of a servant; and made in the likeness of men, and found in figure as a man, he humbled himself, made obedient unto death, even the death of the cross. Wherefore God also hath highly exalted him, and given him a name which is above every name, that in the name of Jesus every knee should bow, of things in heaven, and things in earth, and things under the earth, and that every tongue should confess, that the Lord Jesus Christ is the glory of God the [1] Father [2]." To him alone be honour and power for ever and ever. Amen.

[1 quod Dominus sit Jesus Christus ad gloriam Dei Patris, Lat.]
[2 Phil. ii. 1—11.]

THE END OF THE FIRST DECADE OF SERMONS.

THE

SECOND DECADE OF SERMONS,

WRITTEN BY

HENRY BULLINGER.

OF LAWS, AND OF THE LAW OF NATURE, THEN OF
THE LAWS OF MEN.

THE FIRST SERMON.

THE sum of all laws is the love of God and our neighbour; of which and every part whereof because I have already spoken in my last sermon, the next is, that now also I make a particular discourse of laws, and every part and kind thereof. Let us therefore call to God, who is the cause and beginning of laws, that he through our Lord Jesus Christ will vouchsafe with his Spirit always to direct us in the way of truth and righteousness.

A heathen writer, no base[3] author, I wis, made this defi- What law is.
nition of law ; that it is an especial reason, placed in nature, commanding what is to be done, and forbidding the contrary[4]. And verily the law is nothing but a declaration of God's will, appointing what thou hast to do, and what thou oughtest to leave undone. The beginning and cause of laws is God himself, who is the fountain of all goodness, equity, truth, and righteousness. Therefore all good and just laws come from God himself, although they be, for the most part, published and brought to light by men. Touching the laws of men, we must have a peculiar consideration of them by themselves.

For of laws, some are of God, some of nature, and some The division
of men. As concerning God's law, I will speak of it in my of laws.
second sermon : at this present I will touch first the law of nature, and then the law of men.

[3 non obscurus, Lat.]
[4 Lex est ratio summa, insita in natura, quæ jubet ea quæ facienda sunt, prohibetque contraria.—Cicero, de Leg. i. 6.]

[BULLINGER.]

13

The law of natui e. The law of nature is an instruction of the conscience, and, as it were, a certain direction placed by God himself in the minds and hearts of men, to teach them what they have to do Conscience. and what to eschew. And the conscience, verily, is the knowledge, judgment, and reason of a man, whereby every man in himself, and in his own mind, being made privy to every thing that he either hath committed or not committed, doth either condemn or else acquit himself. And this reason proceedeth from God, who both prompteth and writeth his judgments in the hearts and minds of men. Moreover, that Nature. which we call nature is the proper disposition or inclination of every thing. But the disposition of mankind being flatly corrupted by sin, as it is blind, so also is it in all points evil and naughty. It knoweth not God, it worshippeth not God, neither doth it love the neighbour; but rather is affected with self-love toward itself, and seeketh still for its own advantage. For which cause the apostle said, " that we by nature are the children of wrath." Wherefore the law of nature is not called the law of nature, because in the nature and disposition of man there is of or by itself that reason of light exhorting to the best things, and that holy working; but for because God hath imprinted or engraven in our minds some knowledge, and certain general principles of religion, justice, and goodness, which, because they be grafted in us and born together with us, do therefore seem to be naturally in us.

Let us hear the apostle Paul, who beareth witness to this, and saith: " When the Gentiles, which have not the law, do of nature the things contained in the law; they, having not the law, are a law unto themselves; which shew the works of the law[1] written in their hearts, their conscience bearing them witness, and their thoughts accusing one another, or excusing, in that same day, when the Lord shall judge the secrets of men by Jesus Christ according to my gospel[2]." By two arguments here doth the apostle very evidently prove, that the Gentiles are sinners. For first of all (lest peradventure they might make this excuse, and say, that they have no law) he sheweth, that they have a law; and that, because they transgress this law, they are become sinners. For, although they had not the written law

[1 opus legis, Lat.]   [2 Rom. ii. 14—16.]

of Moses, yet notwithstanding they did " by nature the things
contained in the law." The office of the law is to disclose the
will of God, and to teach thee what thou hast to do and
what to leave undone. This have they by nature; that is,
this know they by the law of nature. For that which followeth maketh this more plain: " They, when they have no law,
are to themselves a law :" that is, they have in themselves
that which is written in the law. But in what sort have
they it in themselves ? This again is made manifest by that
which followeth: " For they shew the work of the law
written in their hearts." But who is he that writeth in their
hearts, but God alone, who is the searcher of all hearts ?
And what, I pray you, writeth he there ? The law of nature,
forsooth; the law, I say, itself, commanding good and forbidding evil, so that without the written law, by the instruction
of nature, that is, by the knowledge imprinted of God in
nature, they may understand what is good and what is evil,
what is to be desired and what is to be shunned. By these
words of the apostle we do understand, that the law of nature
is set against the written law of God; and that therefore it is
called the law of nature, because it seemeth to be, as it were,
placed or graffed[3] in nature. We understand, that the law of
nature, not the written law, but that which is graffed[3] in man,
hath the same office that the written law hath; I mean, to
direct men, and to teach them, and also to discern betwixt
good and evil, and to be able to judge of sin. We understand, that the beginning of this law is not of the corrupt
disposition of mankind, but of God himself, who with his
finger writeth in our hearts, fasteneth in our nature, and
planteth in us a rule to know justice, equity, and goodness.

Then also the apostle maketh his second argument, whereby he proveth the Gentiles to be guilty of sin; and this argument he fetcheth from the witness-bearing of their conscience.
For the conscience, being instructed by the law of nature,
doth accuse and condemn the evil committed; because this
conscience only and alone is instead of a thousand witnesses.
And again, it excuseth, that is, it absolveth and acquitteth
them, if nothing be committed contrary to the law. But
although in this present life we do set light by the judgment of our conscience; yet verily we may not then despise

[3 grafted, 1577.]

13—2

or lightly pass over the conscience's accusations, when the Lord shall come with justice and equity to judge the world. So then by all this it followeth, that all nations are sinners; whom unless the Son of God, the common and only Saviour and deliverer of all the world, do cleanse from their offences, it cannot be but that all nations must needs perish in their sins.

Two especial points of the law of nature.   But now we come again to the law of nature, of which there are two points especially for you to be put in mind of. The first is, Acknowledge God, and worship him : the second is, Keep or maintain society and friendship among men. Touching the first, we have these words of Christ his apostle: "Whatsoever may be known of God is manifest among them" (to wit, among the Gentiles) ; "for God hath shewed it to them. For his invisible things, being understood by his works, through the creation of the world are seen; that is, both his eternal power and Godhead : so that they are without excuse; because that, when they knew God, (notwithstanding) they glorified him not as God, neither were thankful[1]," **The Gentiles knew God.** &c. So then, the Gentiles knew God; yea, they knew whatsoever might be known of God. But what teacher had they, or what master? They had God to their master. In what order taught he them, or out of what book? Not out of the written books of Moses, or the prophets; but out of that great and large book of nature. For the things that are not seen of God (in which sort are his everlasting eternity, his virtue, power, majesty, goodness, and Godhead), those he would have to be esteemed of according to the visible things, that is, the things which he hath created. For God's eternal Godhead is known by man's creation, by the continual moving of heaven, and the perpetual course of rivers : for it must needs be, that he is most mighty which sustaineth all these things, which moveth, strengtheneth, and keepeth all things from decay, and which with his beck shakes the whole world. Finally, who doth not see the goodness of him which suffereth the sun to rise upon the good and the evil? But to what intent revealeth he these things to the Gentiles? To the intent, forsooth, that they may acknowledge him to be God, that they may glorify and worship him as God, and be thankful to such a benefactor. When therefore they do not

[1 Rom. i. 19—21.]

this, they are inexcusable, and perish deservedly for their unbelief and unthankfulness' sake. So then it is manifest, that the law of nature doth expressly teach, that there is a God which is to be acknowledged and reverently worshipped.

Touching the latter of these two especial points (that is, for the preserving of friendship and society among men) the Lord in the Gospel saith: "Whatsoever ye would that men should do to you, do ye the same to them[2]." This sentence did Alexander Severus the Emperor turn and express thus: "Whatsoever thou wouldest not have done to thyself, that do not thou to another." Which saying he loved so well, that he commanded it to be written up in his palace and common houses of office[3]. Moreover, to that general law belong these that follow: "Live honestly: hurt not another: give every man his own[4]: provide things necessary for life, and keep it from distress." *Friendship and society of men to be preserved.*

But now, because the law of nature is made opposite to the written law of God, it is requisite that it be answerable also to the law of God: let us therefore see what the wise men and lawgivers of the Gentiles have left in writing to countervail the ten commandments[5], and how far their writings are answerable to the law of God. *The law of nature answerable to the written law.*

Pythagoras, in St Cyril's first book *contra Julianum,* writeth thus of God: "God verily is one; and he too is not, as some do imagine, without the government of the world; but, being wholly in every place of it, doth view all the generations in the whole compass thereof, and is himself the moderation of all ages, the light of his own virtues, the beginning of all works, the light in heaven, the father of all things, the life and quickening of all things, and lastly, the moving of all the circles[6]." See, here Pythagoras confesseth that there is *1. Of God.*

[2 Matt. vii. 12.]

[3 Clamabat (Alexander) sæpius quod a quibusdam sive Judæis sive Christianis audierat, et tenebat; idque per præconem, cum aliquem emendaret, dici jubebat, *Quod tibi fieri non vis, alteri ne feceris.* Quam sententiam usque adeo dilexit, ut et in palatio et in publicis operibus præscribi juberet.—Æl. Lamprid. in Vit. Alexandri Severi apud Hist. August. Scriptores. Hanov. 1611. pp. 352, 3.]

[4 Honeste vivito; Alterum ne lædito; Suum cuique tribuito. Lat. See Early Writings of Hooper, Parker Soc. ed. page 275, note 2.]

[5 quod respondeat Decalogo, Lat.]

[6 Πυθαγόρας γοῦν φησὶν, Ὁ μὲν Θεὸς εἷς· αὐτὸς δὲ οὐχ, ὥς τινες

but one God, who is the maker, preserver, and governor of all things, the father of all, and the light and life of all things. Zaleucus, in the preface of his laws, writeth as followeth : "It is necessary that all men, which inhabit any city or region whatsoever, be throughly persuaded that there are gods; which is evident to be seen by the contemplation of heaven and all the world, and by the goodly disposition and order of that that is therein : for it is not convenient to think that these are the works of fortune or man's ability. Then also the gods must be worshipped and honoured, as they that are the causes of all good things that are done to us by any manner of means. Every one, therefore, must do his best to have his mind purely cleansed from all evil. For God is not honoured of a wicked man; he is not worshipped with sumptuous cost, neither is he delighted with the sight of solemn tragedies, as a wicked man is; but his delight is in virtue, and in a mind that purposeth to do good works and righteousness. Wherefore every one must endeavour himself, as much as he may, both to do well and will well, if he desire to have God to his friend[1]," &c. Cicero, in his second book *de Natura Deorum*, saith : "The best worshipping of the gods, and the most holy and pure religion is, always to honour them with a pure, perfect, and uncorrupted mind and voice[2]."

ὑπονοοῦσιν, ἐκτὸς τᾶς διακοσμήσιος· ἀλλ᾽ ἐν αὐτῷ ὅλος ἐν ὅλῳ, τῷ κύκλῳ ἐπισκοπῶν πάσας γενεάς· ἔστι κρᾶσις ὧν τῶν ὅλων αἰώνων, καὶ φῶς τῶν αὐτοῦ δυνάμεων καὶ ἔργων, ἀρχὰ πάντων, ἐν οὐρανῷ φωστήρ, καὶ πάντων πατήρ, νοῦς καὶ ψύχωσις τῶν ὅλων κύκλων, πάντων κίνασις.—Cyril. Alexandr. Contra Julian. Lib. I. Tom. VI. p. 30, ed. Paris. 1638. See also Early Writings of Bp Hooper, Parker Soc. ed. p. 285.]

[1 Τοὺς κατοικοῦντας τὴν πόλιν καὶ τὴν χώραν πάντας πρῶτον πεπεῖσθαι χρὴ καὶ νομίζειν θεοὺς εἶναι, καὶ ἀναβλέποντας ἐς οὐρανὸν καὶ τὸν κόσμον καὶ τὴν ἐν αὐτοῖς διακόσμησιν καὶ τάξιν· οὐ γὰρ τύχης οὐδ᾽ ἀνθρώπων εἶναι δημιουργήματα· σέβεσθαι δὲ τούτους καὶ τιμᾶν, ὡς αἰτίους ὄντας ἁπάντων ἡμῖν ἀγαθῶν, τῶν κατὰ λόγον γιγνομένων. Ἕκαστον οὖν ἔχειν καὶ παρασκευάζειν δεῖ τὴν αὐτοῦ ψυχὴν πάντων τῶν κακῶν καθαράν· ὡς οὐ τιμᾶται θεὸς ὑπ᾽ ἀνθρώπου φαύλου, οὐδὲ θεραπεύεται δαπάναις οὐδὲ τραγῳδίαις τῶν ἀλισκομένων, καθάπερ μοχθηρὸς ἄνθρωπος· ἀλλ᾽ ἀρετῇ καὶ προαιρέσει τῶν καλῶν ἔργων καὶ δικαίων. Διὸ ἕκαστον δεῖ εἰς δύναμιν ἀγαθὸν εἶναι, καὶ πράξει καὶ προαιρέσει, τὸν μέλλοντα ἔσεσθαι θεοφιλῆ.—Zaleucus ap. Stobæi Florileg. ed. Gaisford. Oxon. 1822. Vol. II. pp. 197, 8.]

[2 Cultus autem Deorum est optimus, idemque castissimus atque sanctissimus, plenissimusque pietatis, ut eos semper pura, integra,

Seneca also, in his fifth book *ad Lucil.* saith: "Our usual custom is to teach men how the gods are to be worshipped. Let us give commandment, that on holy days no man set perchers[3] or taper light before the gods; for they are as much delighted with lights, as men half smouldered have pleasure in smoke. Let us forbid these morning greetings, and solemn kneelings at the temple-doors. This more than needing fiddle-faddle smacks somewhat of ambition. He worshippeth God that knoweth God. Let us forbid to bring napkins and rubbers to Jupiter, and to hold a looking-glass to Juno. God seeketh not such service. Why so? Because he himself, forsooth, doth serve and supply all men's necessities. He is present every where, and at hand with all men. Let every man hear therefore how he ought to worship God as he should. He shall never verily be sufficiently clear from troublesome superstitions, unless he in his mind think of God as he should do; that is, that he hath all things, that he giveth all things, and that he bestoweth benefits freely, not looking for any recompence at all. What is the cause that the gods do good? Their nature, forsooth. He is deceived, whosoever thinketh that they either will or possibly can do harm: they can neither take wrong nor yet do wrong: for to do harm and to suffer harm are coupled together. The chiefest and most excellent nature of all is the nature of them which are themselves exempt from peril, and are not by nature hurtful to others. The first point of worship due to the gods, is to believe that there are gods; then to give them the majesty due unto them, and to ascribe to them their goodness, without the which their majesty is none at all; to confess that they are they that govern the world, that they rule all things as their own, that they do generally look to the safeguards of all mankind, and sometime too are careful for peculiar men. They neither do nor have any evil at all. But some they chastise, keep under, and punish sometime by whipping, in hope to make them good. Wilt thou please the gods, and make them thy friends? Be good thy-

incorrupta et mente et voce veneremur.—Cic. de Nat. Deor. Lib. II. 28.]

[3 The larger sort of wax candles, which were usually set upon the altar.—Bailey apud Johnson in voc. See also Calfhill's Answer to Martiall, Parker Soc. ed. p. 300.]

self then.   He hath sufficiently worshipped them, whosoever hath imitated them in goodness[1]."

The ethnics' sentences are in some places maimed.   In these words of Seneca, although notable indeed, and agreeable to true religion, I find default notwithstanding of two things.   The first is, because not so seldom as once[2] he maketh mention of gods, when as nevertheless in another place he doth frankly confess, that God is one in substance and no more[3].   Neither dare I undertake for him, that he spake after the manner of the scripture, which calleth God *Elohim*, as if you should say "gods," because of the mystery of the most reverend Trinity[4].   And yet I know very well,

---

[1 Quomodo sint Dii colendi solet præcipi. Accendere aliquem lucernam Sabbatis prohibeamus, quoniam nec lumine Dii egent, et ne homines quidem delectantur fuligine. Vetemus salutationibus matutinis fungi, et foribus assidere templorum. Humana ambitio istis officiis capitur: Deum colit qui novit. Vetemus lintea et strigiles Jovi ferre, et speculum tenere Junoni. Non quærit ministros Deus. Quidni? Ipse generi humano ministrat. Ubique et omnibus præsto est. Audiat licet quemadmodum se gerere in sacrificiis debeat, quam procul resilire a molestiis ac superstitionibus, nunquam satis profectum erit, nisi qualem debet Deum mente conceperit, omnia habentem, omnia tribuentem, beneficia gratis dantem. Quæ causa est Diis benefaciendi? Natura. Errat si quis putat illos nocere velle; non possunt: nec accipere injuriam queunt nec facere: lædere enim lædique conjunctum est. Summa illa ac pulcherrima omnium natura, quos periculo exemit, nec periculosos quidem fecit. Primus est Deorum cultus Deos credere: deinde reddere illis majestatem suam, reddere bonitatem, sine qua nulla majestas est; scire illos esse qui præsident mundo; qui universa vi sua temperant, qui humani generis tutelam gerunt, interdum curiosi singulorum. Hi nec dant malum, nec habent. Ceterum castigant quosdam, et coercent, et irrogant pœnas, et aliquando specie [Bulling. text. *spe*] boni puniunt. Vis Deos propitiare? Bonus esto. Satis illos coluit, quisquis imitatus est.—Senec. Opp. Par. 1607. Epist. ad Lucil. 95, p. 427.]

[2 Subinde, Lat.]

[3 Bullinger quotes the passsge (from de Benef. lib. IV. cap. 8) in his treatise *de Origine Erroris*, cap. VIII. p. 36. Tigur. 1539.]

[4 Hoc ipsum nomen (Elohim) non semel in sacris jungitur verbis singularibus, quemadmodum mox ab ipso Genesis initio legis, In principio creavit Dii cœlum et terram. Nam בָּרָא, *Bara*, creavit, singulare est, אֱלֹהִים, *Elohim*, plurale; notaturque Trinitatis mysterium: ut sit sensus, Deus ille trinus in principio creavit cœlum et terram. Verum hac de re docte disputavit Petrus Galatinus.—Bullinger. de Orig. Error. Tigur. 1539, cap. i. p. 5.]

that learned men of our religion have gone about to prove, even by the testimonies of the Gentiles, that the Gentiles also did acknowledge the mystery of the Trinity.   The second is, that (for as much as I can see) Seneca, with the other wise men of the Gentiles, doth not expressly set down and teach the sound trust and confidence that should be had in God.

Moreover, there was not among the Romans any image of God in any temple that they had for the space of one hundred and seventy years after Rome was builded.   For Plutarch, in the life of Numa Pompilius, saith: " As for the decrees that Numa made touching images of the immortal gods, how like are they almost in every point to the doctrine of Pythagoras! Pythagoras thought that that first beginning (he meaneth God) is not subject to sense or any troublesome affection, but is an invisible and uncreated Spirit.   And on the other side, Numa forbade the Romans to think that the shape of God hath the likeness of a man, or else the figure or similitude of any living thing.   Neither was there among them of the old time any painted or fashioned image of God: but in the first hundred and seventy years they builded temples, and set up houses for service to be done in unto the gods, but bodily similitudes they did not make; even as if it were a detestable thing to liken the better unto the worse, and as though God could not otherwise be perceived, but by reason and knowledge only[5]."   The very same doth Marcus Varro testify touching the Romans, in the thirty-first chapter of Augustine's book *de Civitate Dei*.   For he saith, that " the Romans worshipped the gods a hundred and seventy years without any images at all;" and going further he addeth this; " Which if it had endured till now, the gods verily should have been more purely reverenced.   Neither doubteth he to conclude that place with these words, and to say, that

2.
The Gentiles against idols.

[5 Ἔστι δὲ καὶ τὰ περὶ τῶν ἀφιδρυμάτων νομοθετήματα παντάπασιν ἀδελφὰ τῶν Πυθαγόρου δογμάτων.   Οὔτε γὰρ ἐκεῖνος αἰσθητὸν, ἢ παθητὸν, ἀόρατον δὲ καὶ ἀκήρατον καὶ νοητὸν ὑπελάμβανεν εἶναι τὸ πρῶτον· οὗτός τε διεκώλυσεν ἀνθρωποειδῆ καὶ ζωόμορφον εἰκόνα θεοῦ Ῥωμαίους νομίζειν.   Οὐδ' ἦν παρ' αὐτοῖς οὔτε γραπτὸν οὔτε πλαστὸν εἶδος θεοῦ πρότερον· ἀλλ' ἐν ἑκατὸν ἑβδομήκοντα τοῖς πρώτοις ἔτεσι ναοὺς μὲν οἰκοδομούμενοι, καὶ καλιάδας ἱερὰς ἱστῶντες, ἄγαλμα δ' οὐδὲν ἔμμορφον ποιούμενοι διετέλουν· ὡς οὔτε ὅσιον ἀφομοιοῦν τὰ βελτίονα τοῖς χείροσιν, οὔτ' ἐφάπτεσθαι θεοῦ δυνατὸν ἄλλως ἢ νοήσει.—Plutarch. in Vit. Numæ. Lond. 1729. Tom. i. p. 141.]

they which first brought in images among the people, diminished devout fear, and augmented foolish error, in the cities where they governed; wisely judging thereby that the gods may easily be despised under the fondness of imagined likenesses[1]," &c.

3.
The name of God highly esteemed.

Now, as concerning the name of God, how much the Gentiles did set by it, it is evident to be seen by the great religion that they had in taking or giving an oath. There is extant to be seen a notable discourse of this in the eighteenth chapter of the seventh book of Gellius; where among the rest this is to be found written: " An oath among the Romans hath been had and kept holy and uncorrupted: which is declared by many laws and customs[2]." And if so be that among the Gentiles any man should speak opprobriously against God, he was reputed faulty, most sharply to be punished.

4.
The Gentiles keepers of religion.

Furthermore, the Gentiles had their religion[3], their festival-days, ceremonies, and priests of their religion. Melchizedech and Jethro were notable priests of the Gentiles. And although Paul doth flatly say, that "the things which the Gentiles offered were not offered to God, but to devils[4];" yet notwithstanding, because they had in reverence religion and holy ceremonies, they did thereby declare, that God had printed in the minds of men a familiar knowledge of reverence[5] and religion, which afterward is corrupted by false doctrine and wrong opinions touching God and his holy service.

5.
The honouring of parents.

For the honouring of parents and magistrates, for the bringing up of children, and touching the duty of children, there are excellent precepts and sentences of the wiser sort of Gentiles. Hierocles, among his other writings, saith: " If

[1 Dicit (Varro) etiam, antiquos Romanos plusquam annos centum et septuaginta Deos ine simulacro coluisse. Quod si adhuc, inquit, mansisset, castius Dii observarentur.—Nec dubitat eum locum ita concludere, ut dicat, Qui primi simulacra Deorum populis posuerunt, eos civitatibus suis et metum dempsisse et errorem addidisse, prudenter existimans Deos facile posse in simulacrorum stoliditate contemni. —Augustin. Opp. Par. 1531. Tom. v. fol. 57.]

[2 Jusjurandum apud Romanos inviolate sancteque habitum servatumque. Id et moribus legibusque multis ostenditur.—Aul. Gell. Noct. Attic. Lib. vii. cap. 18. init.]

[3 sua sacra, Lat.] [4 1 Cor. x. 20.]
[5 cultus, Lat.]

any man shall call his parents certain second or earthly gods, he shall not do amiss; considering that, for the nigh affinity betwixt us, they ought to be (if it be lawful so to say) more to be honoured of us than the gods themselves. And it is necessary to be persuaded, that we must with a continual readiness of mind do our endeavour to repay the benefits received at their hands with the like again. And although we shall do very much for them, yet notwithstanding all will be too little in comparison of that we ought to do[6]." And so forth as followeth. For sooner will the time fail me, than that I can conveniently rehearse this, and the like belonging hereunto, out of heathen writers: neither did I purpose to reckon up all.

Against murder, wrong, and injury, very severe laws have been made by the Gentiles. From them also came the law called *Lex Julia*, against adultery and detestable lusts[7]. They ordained excellent laws for the contracting and observing of matrimony. And the word of truth doth expressly declare, that the Chananites were wiped away because of their incest in marriage and horrible lusts. Levit. viii. Lycurgus also, Solon, and the Romans, did publish laws for the restraint of outrageous expenses in riotous persons[8]. And here, of purpose, I overpass that which is naturally engraffed in all men, the begetting (I mean) and nourishing of their issue and offspring.

6.
Murder and
adultery.

Against theft, deceit, and usury, for the lawful getting and possessing of goods, for the distributing of riches, and

8.
Theft.

[6 Λεκτέον περὶ τούτων (i. e. γονέων), οὓς δευτέρους καὶ ἐπιγείους τινὰς θεοὺς εἰπὼν οὐχ ἁμάρτοι τὶς ἕνεκά γε τῆς ἐγγύτητος, εἰ θέμις εἰπεῖν, καὶ θεῶν ἡμῖν τιμιωτέρους. Προλαβεῖν δὲ ἀναγκαῖόν ἐστι, ὡς μόνον μέτρον τῆς πρὸς αὐτοὺς εὐχαριστίας ἡ διηνεκὴς καὶ ἀνένδοτος προθυμία πρὸς τὸ ἀμείβεσθαι τὰς εὐεργεσίας αὐτῶν· ἐπείτοι γε πολὺ καταδεέστερα, κἂν πάνυ πολλὰ πράξωμεν ὑπὲρ αὐτῶν.—Hierocl. ap. Stobæi Floril. ed. Gaisford. Oxon. 1822. Vol. III. p. 125.]

[7 This word is substituted for that used by the translator.—In the time of Augustus a lex was enacted (probably about B.C. 17) entitled *Lex Julia de adulteriis coercendis*. The chief provisions of this law may be collected from the Digest (48 tit. 5), and from Paulus (Sentent. Recept. ii. tit. 26. ed. Schultius). Smith's Dict. of Gr. and Rom. Antiq. sub voc. Adulterium.]

[8 See Smith's Dict. of Greek and Rom. Antiq. sub voc. Sumtuariæ leges; and Plutarch's lives of Lycurgus and Solon.]

for bargaining, the Gentiles have very commendable laws. That saying of Ausonius is notably known:

> If greedy gaping after gain
> To get another groat
> Makes usury dispatch apace
> To cut the poor man's throat[1].

9.
Lies.
False witnesses.

All the Gentiles in their writings do worthily commend the truth; and do, by all means they can, cry out on and condemn lying, slandering, and all such kind of knavery. The law of the twelve tables is, that a false witness should be cast headlong down from the top of Tarpey[2]. Charondas Catanæus, among other excellent sayings of his own, hath this also: "Let every one," saith he, "love honesty and truth, and hate dishonesty and lying; for they are the marks whereby virtue is known from vice. We must therefore begin with children, while as yet they are little ones, and inure ourselves to chastise them if they delight to lie, and to make much of them for telling the truth; that thereby the best and fruitfullest branch of virtue may be graffed in every several mind, and so be turned as it were into their nature[3]."

A hill in Rome.
Catana, a town in Sicily.

10.
Concupiscence.

The wiser sort of the Gentiles do utterly condemn concupiscence and evil affections: which the poet in his satires blameth as the root of all mischief, where he saith:

> From thence almost comes every cause
> Of mischief; for no vice,
> That reigns in man, so many times
> Could frantic heads entice
> To mingle poison privily
> To stop another's breath,

[1]   si turpia lucra
Fœnoris, et velox inopes usura trucidat.
          Auson. Idyll. xv. ed. Lond. 1823. Vol. ii. p. 593. P.]
[2 Si falsum testimonium dicassit, saxo dejicitor.—See also A. Gellius, Noct. Attic. Lib. xx. 1, 14; and Works of Becon, Parker Soc. ed. Vol. i. p. 391.]
[3 Τιμάτω δὲ ἕκαστος τὸ καλὸν καὶ τὸ ἀληθές, καὶ μισείτω τὸ αἰσχρὸν καὶ τὸ ψεῦδος· ταῦτα γὰρ ἀρετῆς σημεῖα καὶ κακίας. Διὸ χρὴ συνεθίζειν ἐκ παίδων, κολάζοντας μὲν τοὺς φιλοψευδεῖς, φιλοῦντας δὲ τοὺς φιλαλήθεις, ἵν᾽ ἐμφυσιῶται ἑκάστῳ τὸ κάλλιστον καὶ σπερματωδέστατον τῆς ἀρετῆς.
—Charondas ap. Stobæi Florileg. Vol. ii. p. 220.]

Or else in armour openly
To work his rival's death,
As beastly raging lust hath done[4].

So then by all this we may easily gather, that even in the Gentiles' minds also were graven a certain knowledge of God, and some precepts whereby they knew what to desire, and what to eschew: which notwithstanding they did corrupt, and make somewhat misty, with the evil affections and corrupt judgments of the flesh. For which cause God also, beside the law of nature, did ordain other means to declare his will; I mean, the lively tradition of the fathers, the answers of angels, the voices of prophets[5], wonderful miracles, and written laws which he published by wise and very devout patriarchs[6]. All these did God ordain to be a help to the law of nature. Whatsoever therefore is to be found among the Gentiles agreeable to truth and honesty, that is to be referred to God, the author of all goodness: and on the other side, whatsoever is contrary to the truth, that must be attributed to the corrupt nature and evil affections of mankind.

In all this that I have said ye have to note especially, that here I speak of knowledge, and not of ability. The knowledge of the law is, after a sort, manifest in the Gentiles; but the consent, the will, and ability to fulfil the law is weak, and not easy to be found in them[7]. Wherefore, as we affirm that the understanding of the law must be inspired from heaven; so also we say that ability to fulfil the law must of necessity be given of God above. Nature without grace is *Nature, without grace, of* herein without force and effect. But whereas some of the *none effect.* Gentiles bear the name and praise of righteousness (as Melchizedech, Job, Jethro, and other more), they have that not of their own ability, but of the grace of God: as by the history of Job we may evidently gather by probable arguments. Wherefore, if any of the Gentiles be saved, then are they

[4   Inde fere scelerum causæ, nec plura venena
Miscuit, aut ferro grassatur sæpius ullum
Humanæ mentis vitium, quam sæva cupido
Immodici census.
                        Juvenal. Sat. xiv. 173—6.]
[5 *Oracula* is Bullinger's one word, which the translator has rendered, *the voices of prophets.*]
[6 per homines sapientissimos et religiosissimos, Lat.]
[7 et infirma est et implicatissima, Lat.]

saved, not by the works of nature, or their own deserts, but by the mercy of God in our Lord Jesus Christ.

Moreover, the law of nature is not graffed of God in man to the intent that it, without grace and Christ, should work man's salvation; but rather, to teach us what is good and what is evil, thereby to convince us to be sinners, and without excuse before the Lord. Paul verily, proving that the Gentiles by the law of nature are guilty of sin, as well as the Jews by Moses' law, doth shew that in Christ alone, the Son of God, is justification, life, and all good else. Thus far touching the law of nature.

Laws of men.

The laws of men (for my promise was, that in my second part I would speak of them) are those which are by men ordained and published to the preservation of the common-weal and[1] church of God. Touching these they are of divers kinds. For there are politic laws, there are ecclesiastical laws, and men's traditions. Politic laws are those which the magistrate, according to the state of times, places, and persons, doth ordain for the preserving of public peace and civility. Of this sort there are an innumerable company of examples in the civil law and constitutions of the emperors, especially of Justinian. All which ought to come as near as may be to the laws of God and nature, and not to be contrary to them, or to have any smack of impiety or cruel tyranny. To such laws St Peter willeth us to obey, where he saith: "Submit yourselves unto all manner ordinance of man for the Lord's sake; whether it be to the king, as having the pre-eminence, or unto rulers, as they that are sent by him for the punishment of evil doers, but for the praise of them that do well." For although the apostle by ordinances[2], or men's constitutions, doth inclusively mean the kings and magistrates themselves, as in the second clause of the sentence he doth immediately declare; yet, notwithstanding, he doth bid us therefore obey good laws and just, because by them the magistrates support and rule the commonweal. Moreover, just and honest politic laws are an help to love and tranquillity; do preserve fellowly society among men[3]; do

Laws of policy.

[1 vel, Lat. or.]
[2 See Schleusner, Lex. N. T. in voc. κτίσις. §. 5.]
[3 hominum societatem, Lat.]

defend the good, bring inordinate persons into better order; and lastly, do not make a little only to the setting forward of religion, but do also abrogate evil customs, and utterly banish unlawful mischiefs.   Hereof we have examples in the deeds of Nabuchodonosor, Cyrus, Darius, Artaxerxes, and other princes more.   But touching the magistrate's power, his laws, and office, I will speak of them in another place.

Ecclesiastical laws are those which, being taken out of the word of God, and applied to the state of men, times, and places, are received and have authority in the church among the people of God.   I call these ecclesiastical laws, and not traditions of men, because, being taken out of the holy scriptures, and not invented or brought to light by the wit of man, they are used of that church which heareth the voice of the Shepherd alone, and knoweth not a stranger's tongue.   The congregation cometh together to hear the word of God, and unto common prayers, at morning, at evening, and at such appointed hours as are most convenient for every place and every people; and that the church holdeth as a law.   The church hath solemn prayer times[4], holy days, and fasting days, which it doth keep by certain laws.   The church, at certain times, in a certain place and appointed order, doth celebrate the sacraments according to the laws and received custom of the church.   The church baptizeth infants; it forbiddeth not women to come to the Lord's supper: and that it holdeth as a law.   The church, by judges conveniently appointed, doth judge in causes of matrimony, and hath certain laws to direct them in such cases.   But it deriveth these, and all other like to these, out of the scriptures; and doth for edification apply them to the estate of men, times, and places: so that in divers churches ye may see some diversity indeed, but no discord or repugnancy at all.

Ecclesiastical laws.

Furthermore, ecclesiastical laws have their measure and certain marks, beyond which they may not pass; to wit, that nothing be done or received contrary or differing in any jot from the word of God, sounding against charity and comeliness, either in little or much; that lastly, this rule of the apostle may be effectually observed, " Let all things be done decently, according unto order, and to the edification of the church[5]."   If therefore any man shall go about, under a

Superstitious laws.

[4 supplicationes, Lat.]   [5 1 Cor. xiv. 3, 40.]

coloured pretence of ecclesiastical laws, to bring in, and pop into the mouths of the godly[1], any superstitious, busy[2], and unseemly traditions of men, which withal do differ from the scriptures; their part shall be, first to try that deceit of theirs by the rule of God's word, and then to reject it.

There remain now the traditions of men, which have their beginning, are made and invented, of men, at their own choice; of some foolish intent, or some fond affection of mankind; contrary or without the holy scriptures: of which sort you shall find an infinite number of examples; I mean, the sects, the dominion[3], and single life of spiritual men, the rites and sundry fashioned customs used in their church. Touching all which the Lord in the gospel, citing the prophet Esay, saith: " Why transgress ye the Lord's commandment for your own tradition? Ye hypocrites, rightly did Esaias prophesy of you, where he saith, This people cometh nigh unto me with their mouth, and with their lips they honour me, but their heart is far from me: but they worship me in vain, teaching doctrines the precepts of men[4]." The blessed martyr Cyprian, alluding to these words of Christ, *Epistolarum*, Lib. i. Ep. 8, saith: " It is corrupt, wicked, and robbery to the glory of God, whatsoever is ordained by the giddy madness of men's heads, to the violating of God's disposition. Depart as far as may be from the infective contagiousness of such fellows, and seek by flight to shun their talk, as warily as an eating canker or infecting pestilence; for the Lord forewarneth and telleth you, that they are blind leaders of the blind[5]." Paul also in his epistle to Titus saith: " Rebuke them sharply, that they may be sound in the faith; not taking heed to Jewish fables, and commandments of men turning from the truth." I do of purpose here let pass the words of Paul in his second chapter to the Colossians, because the place is known of all men.

[1 piis obtrudere, Lat.]   [2 operosas, Lat.]
[3 regnum, Lat.]
[4 Matt. xv. 7—9. docentes doctrinas præcepta hominum, Lat. Erasmus', not the Vulgate, rendering.]
[5 Adulterum est, impium est, sacrilegum est, quodcunque humano furore instituitur, ut dispositio divina violetur. Procul ab hujusmodi hominum contagione discedite, et sermones eorum velut cancer et pestem fugiendo vitate, præmonente Domino et dicente: Cæci sunt duces cæcorum.—Cypr. Opp. Ep. 43, pag. 83, Oxon. 1682.]

I will not trouble you, dearly beloved, with too large and busy[6] an exposition hereof. For I suppose that this little that I have said, touching the laws of nature and of men, (I mean laws politic, ecclesiastical, and mere traditions of men,) are sufficient to the attentive and faithful hearers, who at their coming home do more diligently think of every point by themselves, and also read the places of scripture often cited by me, and devoutly expounded[7]. The Lord for his mercy grant, that we do never despise the admonitions of nature's law graffed in our hearts, nor yet be entangled in men's traditions; but that we, in walking lawfully in upright politic laws and holy ecclesiastical ordinances, may serve the Lord: to whom be all glory, honour and dominion, for ever and ever Amen.

OF GOD'S LAW, AND OF THE TWO FIRST COMMAND-MENTS OF THE FIRST TABLE[8].

THE SECOND SERMON.

THE law of God, openly published and proclaimed by the Lord our God himself, setteth down ordinary rules for us to know what we have to do, and what to leave undone, requiring obedience, and threatening utter destruction to disobedient rebels. This law is divided into the moral, ceremonial, and judicial laws: all which parts, and every point whereof, Moses hath very exquisitely written, and diligently expounded. The moral law is that which teacheth men manners, and layeth down before us the shape of virtue[9]; declaring therewithal how great righteousness, godliness, obedience, and perfectness God looketh for at the hands of us mortal men. The ceremonial laws are they which are given concerning the order *What the law of God is.*

The moral law.

The ceremonial law.

[6 operosiore, Lat.]
[7 ac religiose excussis, Lat. This refers to the *hearers,* and not to the *preacher.* The words should be rendered,—and devoutly weigh and test them.]
[8 seu Decalogi, Lat. omitted.]
[9 virtutum formas, Lat.]

[BULLINGER.]

14

of holy and ecclesiastical rites and ceremonies, and also touching the ministers and things assigned to the ministery and other holy uses. Last of all, the judicial laws give rules concerning matters to be judged of between man and man, for the preservation of public peace, equity, and civil honesty. Touching the two latter of these, I will speak of them in place convenient. At this time I mean to discourse upon the moral law.

The judicial law.

First of all, therefore, let no man think, that before Moses' time there was no law, and that the law was by Moses first of all published. For the self-same especial points of the moral law, which Moses setteth down in the ten commandments, were very well known to the patriarchs, even from the beginning of the world. For they worshipped the one true God alone for their God, whom they reverenced, and called upon him. Jacob took away with him the Syrian idols of Laban out of his house[1], and hid them in Bethel under an oak or terebinth tree, which was nigh to Sichem[2]. Abraham, in taking an oath, used always a reverend fear, and a spiced conscience[3]; whereby it followeth, that to him the name of the Lord was holy, and not lightly taken[4]. All the holy fathers did both diligently and devoutly solemnize and observe holy rites and sacrifices. Cham hath his father's curse, because he did unreverently behave himself toward his father. Cain is reproved for murdering his brother. Noe giveth commandment not to shed blood. Joseph is highly commended for refusing to lie with another man's wife; I mean, the wife of his master. Ruben is rebuked, because he did with incest defile his father's bed. Jacob was not angry without a cause with Laban his father-in-law, when he suspected him of theft. All the patriarchs have utterly condemned liars and false witnesses, as well as evil lusts and concupiscence. Wherefore the patriarchs ever, from the beginning of the world even until Moses' time, were not without the precepts of the ten commandments, although they had them not graven in tables or written in parchments. For the

The law was even before Moses' time.

[1 aufert e sua familia, Lat. The translator misrepresents Bullinger's meaning by rendering,—took away *with him*.]

[2 Gen. xxxv. 4.]

[3 sacrosancta erat jurisjurandi religio Abrahamo, Lat.]

[4 celebre, Lat.]

Lord with his finger writ them in their hearts[5], which the lively tradition of the fathers did exquisitely garnish and reverently teach. The law is every where the same, and the will of God is always one, because God is but one and is never changed. Nevertheless, the commandments were first of all set down in tables by God, who was the beginner and writer of them; and after that again were written into books by Moses.

Likewise also the old and holy patriarchs, that were before Moses, did not want the ceremonial and judicial laws. For they had their priests, I say, their fathers of every kindred or household; they had their ceremonies, their altars and sacrifices; they had their solemn assemblies, and purifications. They had their laws for succession in heritage, for the division and possession of goods, for bargaining and contracts, and for the punishing of evil doers. All which Moses gathered together into a certain number of decreed laws; setting down many things more plainly than they were before, and ordaining many things which the patriarchs were either altogether without, or else had used in another order: of which sort were the tabernacle, the holy vessels, the ark of the covenant, the table, the candlestick, the altar for burnt-offerings and for incense, the Levitical priesthood, the holy vestments, with the feasts and holy-days, and whatsoever else is like to this: all which verily are abrogated by Christ, as in place convenient I mean to declare. But for because manners cannot consist, if the ten commandments be broken, therefore the moral law, although it have properly the name of a law, is notwithstanding not abrogated or broken[6]. For the ten commandments are the very absolute and everlasting rule of true righteousness and all virtues, set down for all places, men, and ages, to frame themselves by. For the sum of the ten commandments is this, to shew our love to God, and one love another; and this doth the Lord require at all times, and every where, of all kind of men[7].

The patriarchs before Moses had the ceremonial and judicial laws.

The moral law endureth still.

[5 See above, page 46.]

[6 ut proprie legis nomen obtinuit, ita nunquam abrogatur, Lat.]

[7 Porro Decalogus significat librum seu expositionem et volumen decem capitum præceptorum vel articulorum, Lat. omitted by the translator. Moreover the Decalogue means a book, or exposition and collection, of commandments under ten chief heads.]

14—2

The majesty and dignity of the moral law.

Moreover, this is to be noted touching the dignity of the moral law contained in the ten commandments; that, whereas all the ceremonial and judicial laws were revealed of God to Moses by the angels, and by Moses to the people; and that again by Moses, at God's commandment, they were inserted into written books; yet notwithstanding the moral law of the ten commandments was not revealed by man, or any means of man, but by God himself at the Mount Sina: who there, among other mighty and marvellous wonders, did openly, in a public and innumerable assembly of men and angels, rehearse them word for word, as they are now to be seen. Furthermore, they were written not by the hand of Moses, but with the finger of God, in tables, not made of matter easy to be dissolved[1], but made of stone to endure for ever. Those tables also were kept, as the most precious treasure, in that ark, which of the tables of the covenant (containing in them the chief articles of the eternal league) was named the ark of

Sanctum sanctorum, the most holy place in the temple of God.

the covenant: which ark again was laid up in the holy of holiest. All which circumstances tend to nothing else, but to commend unto us the excellency of the ten commandments, and to warn us to reverence that God which published this moral law, as him that is the Lord of heaven and earth, and which at his own will and pleasure doth order the disposition of all the elements against disobedient rebels. These circumstances also do admonish us, that even now, in our time also, we have to esteem of the ten commandments, as of the dearest jewels to be found in all the world. For the holy reliques, that are remaining in the church of Christ, are the ten commandments, the apostles' creed, the Lord's prayer, and lastly, the whole contents of the sacred bible[2]. Touching the proclamation or first edition of the ten commandments, we have a wonderful large discourse of Moses, Exod. xix. and Deut. iv. and v. chap.

Two tables of God's law.

Now the tables, whereinto the ten commandments of God's law be disposed, are in number two; whereof the first containeth four commandments, and the latter six. For the last commandment, which some divide into twain, is in very deed

[1 non cereas, Lat. not of wax.]
[2 Cf. Bullinger's Comment. in 2 Epist. Petri, cap. i. 12—15. p. 59. (published 1534) and Argument. Epist. ad Galat. ad finem. p. 340. (published 1535).]

II.] 1ST AND 2ND PRECEPTS OF THE TEN COMMANDMENTS. 213

but one alone and undivided[3]. For first the Lord doth
generally command and say, " Thou shalt not covet :" and
then he descendeth particularly, and doth by enumeration
reckon up the things that we must not covet; to wit, our
neighbour's wife, his house, his lands, his cattle, and his substance. Beside that too, this doth argue that it is so, because,
according to the Hebrew disposition, this commandment is
altogether one whole verse, not divided into twain[4]. With
this division of ours agree Joseph. *Antiq.* Lib. III. cap. 5[5];
Origenes *in Exod.* Hom. 8[6]; Ambros. *in* vi. *cap. Epist. ad
Ephes.*[7] But the Master of Sentences, having divided this last
commandment into twain, doth therefore place in the first
table three commandments and no more[8]. He did, perad-

He putteth
three in the
first table, and
seven in the
last, which
added toge-
ther do make
up ten.

[3 Cf. Calvin. Instit. Lib. II. cap. 8, §. 12. Becon's Works, Parker
Soc. ed. Vol. II. pp. 59, 60.]

[4 Exod. xx. 17.]

[5 Μωϋσῆς (τοὺς λόγους τοῦ Θεοῦ) ἐν ταῖς δύο πλαξὶν γεγραμμένους
κατέλιπεν ...... Διδάσκει μὲν οὖν ἡμᾶς ὁ πρῶτος λόγος, ὅτι Θεός ἐστιν εἷς,
καὶ τοῦτον δεῖ σέβεσθαι μόνον· ὁ δὲ δεύτερος κελεύει, μηδενὸς εἰκόνα ζῴου
ποιήσαντας προσκυνεῖν· ὁ τρίτος δὲ, ἐπὶ μηδενὶ φαύλῳ τὸν Θεὸν ὀμνύναι· ὁ δὲ
τέταρτος, παρατηρεῖν τὰς ἑβδομάδας, ἀναπαυομένους ἀπὸ παντὸς ἔργου· ὁ δὲ
πέμπτος, γονεῖς τιμᾶν· ὁ δὲ ἕκτος, ἀποσχέσθαι φόνου· ὁ δὲ ἕβδομος, μὴ
μοιχεύειν· ὁ δὲ ὄγδοος, μὴ κλοπὴν δρᾶν· ὁ δὲ ἔνατος, μὴ ψευδομαρτυρεῖν·
ὁ δὲ δέκατος, μηδενὸς ἀλλοτρίου ἐπιθυμίαν λαμβάνειν.—Joseph. Antiq.
Jud. Lib. III. capp. 4 and 5, Amst. 1726. Tom. I. p. 129.]

[6 Hæc omnia simul nonnulli putant unum esse mandatum. Quod
si ita putetur, non complebitur decem numerus mandatorum ....
Est ergo primum mandatum, Non erunt tibi Dei alii præter me.
Secundum vero, Non facies tibi idolum, &c.—Origen. Opp. ed. Benedict. Par. 1733. Tom. II. p. 157.]

[7 Quia prima quatuor mandata ad Deum pertinent, hæc in prima
tabula contineri subintelliguntur ; cetera ad hominem .... Hæc
sex mandata in secunda tabula videntur scripta, quorum primum est,
Honora patrem et matrem, &c.—Ambros. Opp. ed. Bened. Par. 1690.
Tom. II. Append. p. 249. Comment. in Ep. ad Ephes. cap. vi. verse
3.—But these Commentaries are generally admitted not to be the
work of Ambrose. See James, on the Corruption of Scripture, Councils, and Fathers, Lond. 1843. p. 26.]

[8 Habet decalogus decem præcepta ... quæ sic sunt distributa, ut
tria quæ sunt in prima tabula pertineant ad Deum ...... septem quæ
sunt in secunda tabula ad dilectionem proximi. Primum in prima
tabula est, Non habebis deos alienos. Non facies tibi sculptile, &c.
Hæc Origenes dicit esse duo mandata, sed Augustinus unum.—Pet.
Lombard. Lib. III. Distinct. 37. Par. 1575. fol. 293.—The title of

venture, follow Augustine herein, who, *Quæst. in Exod.* 71, and *Epistola ad Januarium* 119[1], doth also reckon up but three commandments of the first table alone; which he did in respect of the mystical Trinity. And yet, this notwithstanding, he doth not overslip the commandment for abandoning and not worshipping of images; for, undoubtedly, he had always in his mind those words of the Lord in the gospel, where he saith: "Verily I say unto you, though heaven and earth do pass, one jot or tittle of the law shall not pass, till all be fulfilled. Whosoever, therefore, shall break one of the least of these commandments, and shall teach men so, he shall be called the least in the kingdom of heaven." The same Augustine again, in *Quæstionibus Veteris et Novi Testamenti*, Lib. I. cap. 7, maketh four commandments of the first table, and six of the second[2]. And again, he differeth not much from the same order in his third book *ad Bonifacium, &c.*[3]

What the two tables of the law do contain.   Now touching these commandments, the Lord hath divided them into two several orders or tables because of the several difference of matters handled in either of them. For the first of the two appertaineth to God, the second unto man. The first teacheth us what we have to think concerning God, and the

Distinct. 40 is, De sexto et septimo præcepto secundæ tabulæ; and there the *sixth* commandment is, Non desiderabis uxorem proximi tui; and the *seventh*, Non concupisces domum proximi tui, &c. fol. 300.]

[1 Quæritur, decem præcepta legis quemadmodum dividenda sint. ... Mihi tamen videntur congruentius accipi tria illa, et ista septem, quoniam Trinitatem videntur illa, quæ ad Deum pertinent, insinuare diligentius intuentibus.—August. Quæst. super Exod. Opp. ed. Par. 1531. Tom. IV. col. 32.—Hinc est quod etiam in tribus primis præceptis decalogi, quæ ad Deum pertinent (cetera enim septem ad proximum pertinent, id est, ad hominem, quia in duobus præceptis tota lex pendet), tertium ibi de observatione Sabbati positum est: ut in primo præcepto Patrem intelligamus, ubi prohibetur coli aliqua in figmentis hominum Dei similitudo ... ne quisquam Filium Dei verbum ... putaret esse creaturam, sequitur aliud præceptum, Non accipies in vanum nomen Dei tui. Spiritus autem sanctus, in quo nobis illa requies tribuitur, &c.—Id. Ep. Januar. 119. Tom. II. col. 110.]

[2 Hæc quatuor verba sunt de decem; ista ad Deum proprie pertinent. Hæc sunt in prima tabula scripta: deinde in secunda tabula hæc (6) continentur.—Tom. IV. fol. 150.]

[3 Tom. VII. fol. 185. On this subject of the division of the Decalogue, see also Early Writings of Hooper, Parker Soc. ed. pages 349—351; and Calvin. Instit. Lib. II. cap. 8. §. 12.]

worship due unto him; that is, it teacheth us the perfect way to live uprightly and holily in the sight of God. The second is the rule whereby we have to learn our duty toward our neighbour; which also teacheth us humanity, directing us in the way to live peaceably and civilly one with another. And in these two tables are so nearly contained all and every duty looked for at men's hands, that there cannot so much as one jot be added more by all the wise men of the world, concerning a godly life and civil behaviour, which is not contained in these ten commandments.

The first commandment of the ten hath the Lord himself *The first command-* expressly spoken in these very words that follow : " I am the *ment.* Lord thy God, which brought thee out of the land of Egypt, out of the house of bondage : thou shalt have none other gods before me." This commandment standeth of two branches; the very first whereof also containeth divers matters. For first of all, God doth simply offer himself to us, and precisely set down what he will be to us-ward, thereby declaring what he is to all men[4]. Whereupon we again do gather what he, on the other side, doth look for at our hands, and what our duty is to him. Thirdly and last of all, he addeth an evident proof of that, where he said that he is our God.

In the beginning he crieth out and saith : " I am the Lord thy God." Wherein he declareth what he is, and what he will be unto all men. These words are like to the words of the covenant which God made with Abraham, and in Abraham with all faithful believers : " I am," saith the Lord, *The sense is this, I am a* " a strong God, and I am Schaddai;" as who should say, *strong God, and the ful-* *Saturnus a saturando*[5], which is, " to fill." For God is the *ness of all things.* abundant fulness[6] that satisfieth all men and all things : he

[4 exponit nobis qualis sit erga homines, imo qualis erga nos esse velit, Lat. Yea, what he desires to be to us.]

[5 Appellatur (Dominus) etiam Saturnus, quia omnes suas creaturas exsaturat.—Bullinger. de Origine Erroris, cap. VIII. p. 36. Tigur. 1539. Saturnus autem est appellatus, quod saturetur annis.—Cic. de Nat. Deor. Lib. II.]

[6 Copiæ cornu, Lat. On this Divine name שַׁדַּי, Bullinger thus gives his opinion in his book, De Origine Erroris, cap. 1. p. 5 : Magis mihi placet Rabbi Mosis Maimonis filii sententia, quam Petrus Galatinus hisce ferme verbis exponit: Nomen Schaddai compositum est ex verbis דַי Daii, quod est, *sufficit;* et ex litera שׁ, quæ idem pollet quod אֲשֶׁר, qui: ut Schaddai idem sit quod, *qui sufficit,* vel *qui suffi-*

is the everlasting well of all good things, which never is drawn dry. And that doth Jeremy declare at large in the second chapter of his prophecy. All which verily God in effect comprehendeth in these few words: "I am the Lord thy God." 'I, I say, which speak to thee from within the fire, I, and none other.' Here is expressly meant the unity of God. We are here taught to acknowledge one God, and no more; to stick to one, and not to suffer our hearts fantastically to dream of many[1]. "I am thy Lord, I am thy God." He is a Lord, because he alone hath the rule over all creatures; all things are subject to him as to their Lord; all things do bend and obey him, if once he do but beck. He, as Lord alone, doth govern and uphold all things that are[2]. So then in this one word is contained the wisdom of God, his virtue, his power, and infinite majesty. *Deus*, which word we use for "God," is, peradventure, derived of the Hebrew word *Daii*, which signifieth sufficiency or full ability[3]. For God alone, of himself, is unto himself most perfect blessedness and absolute felicity: he is also sufficiently able to minister all things most abundantly to all them that seek after him in truth sincerely, being of himself most liberally wealthy to all that call upon his name. Therefore in this branch the sufficient and full ability, the liberality, the goodness and mercy of God, are to be noted: but most especially in this that he saith, "I am thy God; thy God, I say." For God is not good to himself alone, but even unto us also. He desireth to

ciens aut sufficientia est. Hæc Galat. Poterit itaque Deus appellari Saturnus. Ut enim a die fit diurnus, sic a saturando dicitur Saturnus. . . . . . Itaque licebit nunc summam illam vim ipsum Deum appellare et Schaddai et Saturnum et Copiæ cornu. See also Early Writings of Bp. Hooper, ed. Parker Soc. p. 293.]

[1 non corda pluribus dividere, Lat.]

[2 Est enim cœli et terræ et omnium quæ in eis sunt Conditor, Rector, Conservator, Rex et Princeps summus et maximus, Lat. omitted by the translator. For he is of heaven and earth, and of all things which are therein, the Creator, Ruler, Preserver, and supreme and highest King and Prince.]

[3 A Græco vocabulo deflexa ac transumpta est forte et Latinorum vox *Deus;* nisi cui verisimilius videatur tractam esse ab Hebraica רי, *Daii.*—Bullinger. de Orig. Error. cap. 1. p. 5. From Heb. רי (enough, sufficiency,) the Greeks likewise derived their Δὶς, Gen. Διὸς, &c. (whence Lat. Deus, dius, divus.)—Parkhurst, Heb. Lex. in voc. רי.]

pour and bestow himself wholly, with all his goodness and gifts of grace, upon the faithful and sincere believers. He is no niggard, he is not envious, he rejoiceth and is glad to bestow and divide himself among us abundantly, and to our comfort; to fill us with the enjoying of himself at all times and seasons, but especially in time of our necessity. And God verily saith expressly "thy God," and not your God, that thereby every one of us may understand, that the eternal, most mighty, and holy God both is and will be the God and Lord of every particular man; that is, that he is and will be the keeper, deliverer, redeemer, the unmeasurable mountain and bottomless sea[4] of all good gifts of body and soul, to all them that either are or else ever shall be.

By this now, in the second place, we have to gather what the good and gracious Lord requireth again at our hands, and what our duty to him both is and ought to be. For this, where he saith "thy God," betokeneth an evident relation. For if he will be mine, then I again of duty must be his. He will be my Lord and my God; therefore must I again of duty make account of, and worship him, as my Lord and my God. Wherefore in this commandment there is required at our hands, that we do not only acknowledge the true God to be the true God, and so to stay there; but also, that we do take and account him for our God, our Lord, our King, our Creator, our Preserver, and our Father; and that we do attribute to him his property, to wit, that he is one alone, the only fountain and giver of all good things, that he liveth, and is eternal, righteous, true, holy[5], happy, merciful, mighty, most excellent and chief of all. Let us therefore stick to him alone, let us obey him in all things, let us put our trust in him, let us call on him alone, let us repute him to be the giver of all good things, and crave all good gifts of him; let us thank him for all benefits whatsoever we receive, let us reverence him, and lastly, honour him in fear sincerely, in love most ardently, and in hope as constantly as may be. For hereunto belong those sentences in the books of Moses and the holy gospel: "Thou shalt honour the Lord thy God, and him alone shalt thou serve[6]." And again: "Follow ye the

What this commandment requireth of us.

[4 acervum et mare, Lat.]
[5 beatus, Lat.]
[6 Deut. vi. 13; Matt. iv. 10.]

Lord your God, fear him, keep his commandments, hearken to his voice, serve him, and stick to him[1]." The Lord himself also in the Psalm crieth out and saith : " Offer to the Lord the sacrifice of praise, and pay thy vows unto the Highest. And call upon me in the day of trouble[2]," &c.

The true God is our God.

And now, touching the demonstration, whereby he declareth that he hath been, is, and will be the God and Lord of us all, of our fathers, and of our children that come after us ; the proof thereof is most evident by our[3] delivery out of Egypt. Therein are contained all the virtues of God; his wisdom, his goodness, his righteousness, his truth, his power, and what not? He declareth that he is the Lord in heaven and in earth, in all elements and all creatures. His people the Israelites doth he graciously deliver, defend, with sundry gifts adorn, and mightily preserve, even in despite and maugre all the heads of the whole Egyptian kingdom[4]. And on the other side, he doth by sundry means very terribly, yet notwithstanding justly, punish the Egyptians; and last of all, together with their king, he overwhelmeth them in the Red Sea. By this one miracle of the Lord's the Israelites might have gathered, as God is almighty and the mightiest of all, so also that he would be their God, as heretofore he had been the God of their fathers. For by this wonder he did declare what he was then, and of how great power and goodness he is even at this day among us, and also what he will be in all ages, even unto the end. To us that live in these days the deliverance, which we have obtained by Jesus Christ our Lord, is far more fresh in memory; who hath not delivered us from the bondage of any Egyptian kingdom, nor from the tyrannous hands of any earthly Pharao, but hath set us free from the power of darkness, of sin, death, and the devil. Whereby we gather, that as the eternal, true, excellent, high, and holy God is most mighty, so also he is our God; that he wisheth well to us, and that he careth for and loveth us, according to that saying of the apostle : " Who spared not his own Son, but gave him for us all, how can it be but that

The mystery of our redemption

with him he will give us all things[5]?" Verily, the mystery

[1 Deut. xiii. 4.]   [2 Psal. l. 14, 15.]
[3 *our* is not in the original Latin.]
[4 vel invito et fremente toto regno Ægypti, Lat.]
[5 Rom. viii. 32.]

of our redemption by our Lord Jesus Christ is manifestly contained in the first precept of the ten commandments. For it is evident, that the Israelites' free departure out of Egypt was a type or figure of the delivery of the whole compass of the earth, and of all the kingdoms of the world, which should be wrought by Christ our Lord, who hath now already set all the world free from the bondage of sin and hell. But if any man doubt of this, let him diligently consider with himself the meaning of the ceremony and sacrament of that bodily deliverance, I mean, the very passover. For what is he that knoweth not that the paschal lamb did in a figure represent Christ our Redeemer? Are Paul's words unknown, who saith, " Christ our passover is offered up[6]?" Have not all the apostles and John Baptist called our Lord "the Lamb of God which taketh away the sins of the world[7]?" The words of the prophet Esay also, in his fifty-second chapter, are apparently known; where he compareth the delivery of Israel out of Egypt with the redemption of all the world wrought by Christ from the slavery of sin. Wherefore, in this first precept of the ten commandments is contained the mystery of Christ our Lord, and our salvation: so that, as often as those words of God shall be recited in our ears, we ought not so much to set our eyes and minds upon the ancient delivery of Israel out of Egypt, as upon the new and latter redemption, which we have by Christ Jesus, thereby to quicken our hope, and not to despair, but that the most excellent and mighty God both is and will be our God, as heretofore he hath been theirs.

by Christ contained in the first commandment.

The latter branch of this first commandment flatly forbiddeth us, and every one of us, to have any strange gods; that is, it taketh from us all extraordinary means to seek the safeguard of our lives, where the working finger of God is not, and whatsoever else may be either devilishly devised or unadvisedly chosen beside the very word of God. And therefore the Lord useth a most vehement or earnest kind of speaking: for saith he, " Thou shalt not have any other gods before me[8]." See, he saith, Thou shalt not have, and thou shalt not have before me, or before my face, or with me, or

Strange gods are forbidden.

[6 1 Cor. v. 7.]
[7 John i. 29; Acts viii. 32; 1 Pet. i. 19; Rev. v. 6.]
[8 coram me, Lat.]

by me.   We Germans say, *Zu mir; oder nabend mir; oder
lass michs nit sahen vor meinen augen.*   For so do fathers
speak in their anger, when they do earnestly forbid a wicked
and heinous thing.   See, say they, that thou do it not before
mine eyes for me to see it.   But now God is present every
where; God seeth all things; yea, he beholdeth our hearts,
and hidden secrets of our hearts.   We must not therefore in
any case, either openly or privily, have any strange gods:
that is, none of us must make account of any creature, either
in heaven or earth, as of our God; none of us must attribute
God's properties to his creatures, nor yet the things which
we of duty do owe to God himself.   The properties of God
are these; to be all over[1] and every where, to see all, to
know all, to be able to do all, to give life, to deliver, and
cleanse from sins, to save, preserve, to justify, to sanctify, and
whatsoever else is like to these.   On the other side, our duty
to him is, to reverence God, to call on God, to fear God, to
worship God, to hope in God, to stick to God, to hear God,
to believe God, and to obey God.

Strange gods,
what they
are.

The strange god therefore is that which is not God properly and by nature; yea, it is whatsoever we do make to
ourselves to be our God beside the very living and eternal
God, wherein we trust, wherein we hope, whereon we call,
which we do love and fear, whereon we settle and fasten our
minds, whereupon we do depend, whereof we make account as
of our treasure, help, and safeguard, both in prosperity and
our adversity.   When Rahel asketh children of Jacob, she
hath this answer at his hand: "Am I God, which have made
thee barren[2]?"   And again, when Joram king of Israel had
by Naaman received letters from Benhadad, king of Syria,
requesting to cleanse the leprosy, he rent his clothes for anger,
and cried out, saying: "Am I God, that I can kill, and restore to life again[3]?"   Let God alone, therefore, be our God,
that is, our life and safeguard, our help and refuge, our protection and deliverance, our hope and love, our fear, our
dread, our trembling, and all.   These if we do attribute to
others, and not to God alone, then shall we make other gods
to ourselves.   Moreover, whatsoever is not ordained by God

[1 ubique, Lat.]
[2 Gen. xxx. 2.   Num pro Deo sum, Lat. and Vulgate.]
[3 2 Kings v. 7.]

himself, that is in the scriptures many times called strange, or other. In that sense it is said, that strange fire was carried into the tabernacle[4]; to wit, not that fire which God had commanded for to kindle. In the Proverbs she is called a strange woman[5], whose company the Lord hath not allowed thee to use. They therefore are strange gods, whom we have made to ourselves to hang on, and to seek aid of, when God, notwithstanding, hath not appointed them to have the charge over us. Wherefore the very saints themselves, triumphant now in heaven with Christ our King, shall be reputed for strange gods; the saints themselves, I say, not in respect of themselves, but to us they shall be strange gods in respect of us, which judge very fondly of them, and bestow on them the honour due to God, in worshipping and calling upon them, as we should worship and call upon our tutors and defenders[6]. The very devils and devilish men shall be strange gods, if we for fear shall stand in awe of them more than of God, to whom indeed our fear is due. The stars, the planets, and signs in the firmament shall be strange gods, if we, being deceived with the mathematicals[7], shall wholly hang on them, and in all our doings evermore have regard to the impressions of the sky, directing every minute of our lives to the course of the stars. Likewise, if we shall honour and love money or men with honour or love due unto God, then shall this money and men of ours be imputed to us for strange gods. King Asa is blamed (2 Paral. xvi.[8]) for putting too much confidence in physic and physicians: physic[9] and physicians therefore may be abused, and made strange gods. The Jews are rebuked by the Lord in Esay, chap. xxx. for trusting too much in the Egyptians, their confederates: confederates

(marginal note: Conjurors and witches.)

[4 Levit. x. 1.]
[5 ch. ii. 16.]
[6 pro tutelaribus. See Becon's Works, Parker Soc. ed. Vol. I. pp. 138, 9; Calfhill's Answer to Martiall, pp. 19, 20; and Works of Bp. Jewel, Vol. II. pp. 922, 3.]
[7 i. e. astrologers. Sequitur lauta illa Astrologia seu Mathematica, &c.—Luther. in Decem Præcepta. Opp. Witeb. 1582. Tom. I. p. 3. Olim Genethliaci et similes pro Mathematicis se venditarunt.—Calvin. Opp. Amstel. Tom. I. p. 353. See also Early Writings of Bp. Hooper, Parker Soc. ed. p. 330; Bingham. Orig. Eccles. Book XVI. chap. 5. §. 1.]
[8 2 Chron. xvi. 12.]
[9 Herbæ, Lat.]

therefore may be abused, and made strange gods. But most of all are condemned here the leagues and covenants made with the devil by witchcraft, to have him at commandment. Those blessings also which of right ought rather to be called cursings, I mean, superstitious exorcisms or conjurations, are utterly to be rejected; wherein also this is blameworthy, that the name of the most high God is horribly abused and taken in vain. But what is he, that can exactly reckon up every particular thing wherein this first commandment is transgressed, considering that in it is taught the perfect rule of godliness, which is the inward worship done to God; to wit, to acknowledge God, to believe him, to think rightly of him, to call upon him, to cleave unto him, and in all things to obey him?

The second commandment of God. The second precept of the ten commandments is: "Thou shalt not make to thyself any graven image, nor any likeness of those things which are in heaven above, or in the earth beneath, or in the water under the earth; thou shalt not bow down to them, nor worship them: I am the Lord thy God, strong, and jealous, visiting the fathers' sins in the children unto the third and fourth generation of them that hate me, and shewing mercy unto thousands to them that love me, and keep my commandments." In the first commandment the Lord did teach and draw out before our eyes the pattern of his inward worship and religion: now here, in the second, he amendeth that which might be amiss in the outward rites and ceremonies. If we could have rightly judged of God, and have kept (as devoutly as we should) the first commandment, then should there have been no need of the second: but, because God knew our disposition and nature, he doth therefore expressly forbid the thing that otherwise we would have done. For many there are which think, that God ought to be pourtrayed in some similitude or likeness, and to be worshipped with some bodily or visible reverence, in offering gold, silver, pearls, ivory, and precious things of price. Wherefore the

The end of the commandment is to draw us from strange and foreign worshippings. general end of this commandment is, to draw them from those gross imaginations and carnal worshippings of God, who as he is an incomprehensible power and an eternal spirit, so can he not be resembled to any corruptible similitude: he will be worshipped in spirit and holiness. Under the name of the idol, or imagined likeness, is contained all the outward

reverence done thereunto: when therefore the idols are forbidden, together with them is also forbidden all outward
honour irreligiously exhibited to the true and very God. For
wheresoever an idol is, there must the idolaters set him up a
pillar[1], place him in a seat, erect him an altar, and build him
a temple. And all these again require keepers and overseers,
ministers or priests, sacrifices and offerings, ceremonies, fur-
nitures, holy-days, cost and labour that will never be ended.
In this sense did the prophets say, that idolatrous images were
endless labours and infinite miseries[2]: for after images are
once received, there is no end or measure of expenses and
toil. This doth experience teach to be true.

Now to proceed: this commandment standeth of three *God forbid-*
several parts. For first of all, God flatly forbiddeth to make *deth a graven image.*
a graven image, or other kind of idol; that is, God doth
utterly forbid to set up or hallow to him any image, of
what shape or substance soever it be. For as God will
not, so indeed he cannot, be expressly represented in any
manner of likeness. Now, in this commandment are reckoned
up in a manner all the similitudes of those things, whereunto
we are wont in pourtraying to liken our pictures. Thou
shalt not, saith he, fashion like unto God any shape or figure
of those things which are in heaven; which are, I say, above
us. Above us are the celestial bodies, the sun, the moon, the
planets, the stars, and divers birds of sundry fashions: in all
which figures and shapes almost no small number of the
Gentiles did solemnly honour and reverently worship the
name of God. Thou shalt not liken unto God, saith he, any
shape or fashion of those things that are in the earth. In
the earth are men, beasts, herbs, shrubs, trees, and such-like.
Now it is manifest that the Gentiles worshipped God under
the likeness of men and beasts. Cornelius Tacitus, writing
of the Germans, saith: " But by the greatness of the visible

[1 basim, Lat.]

[2 Bullinger refers to the word עָצָב, which signifies both *trouble* and
an *idol*. And in Psal. xvi. 4, the word עַצְּבוֹתָם is rendered by the
Chaldee Paraphrast and others, *their idols*, and by the English version
and others, *their sorrows*. And Bucer remarks in loc. עַצְּבוֹת *molestias* significat; at עַצַּבִּים pro idolis sæpissime usurpatur.—See also
Calvin. Comment. in loc. cit. ed. Calvin. Translat. Soc. Vol. I. note 1;
and Hooper's Early Writings, p. 43, Parker Soc. ed.]

That is, the sun, moon, and stars.

celestial bodies they do conjecture and verily think, that the gods are neither inclosed in walls, nor yet in favour resembling men's visages; and therefore do they hallow woods and groves, calling that hidden mystery by the name of the gods, which with outward eyes they see not, but with inward reverence alone[1]." Lo, here, our ancestors worshipped God in the likeness of trees and woods : which, nevertheless, men are forbidden here to do, even as also we are prohibited to worship our God in the likeness of any thing that is in or under the water. The Philistines worshipped God in the image of a fish ; for Dagon their God bare the shape of a fish[2]. Egypt honoured God in the similitude of serpents[3]. All which, and many other, Paul knitteth up together in the first to the Romans, where he argueth against the Gentiles, and saith : "Their foolish heart was blinded : when they counted themselves wise, they became fools, and turned the glory of the incorruptible God unto the likeness, not only of a mortal man, but also of birds, and of four-footed beasts, and of creeping beasts." Against this madness is the first part of the law directly given.

The cause why God will not be likened to any thing.

But now, the cause why God will not be represented in any visible or sensible image is this[4]. God is a spirit; God is unmeasurable, incomprehensible[5], unspeakable, all over and every where, filling heaven and earth, eternal, living, giving life unto and preserving all things; and lastly, of a glorious majesty exalted above the heavens. But what is he that can pourtray a spirit in any image or substance ? God is an incomprehensible[6] power, quickening and preserving all and every

[1 De Mor. Germ. c. ix. Ceterum nec cohibere parietibus deos, neque in ullam humanioris speciem adsimulare, ex magnitudine cœlestium arbitrantur : lucos ac nemora consecrant, deorumque nominibus appellant secretum illud, quod sola reverentia vident. They think it not consistent with the greatness of celestial beings, &c.]

[2 Marinum (i. e. piscis) ei (Dagoni) corpus; humana vero facies, manus, item et pedes.—Selden de Dis Syris, Syntag. II. cap. 3. et add.]

[3 The worship of the serpent was in her (Egypt's) early history an important and conspicuous part of her idolatry.—Deane, on the Worship of the Serpent, chap. 2. §. 1.]

[4 in promptu causa est, Lat.]

[5 incircumscriptibilis, Lat.]

[6 immensa potentia, Lat.]

thing.   But David, describing images, saith : " The idols of
the heathen are silver and gold, the works of men's hands.
They have ears, and hear not; noses have they, and smell
not.   They have hands, and handle not; feet have they, and
walk not; neither is there any voice in the throat of them [7]."
Wherefore, if these be compared to God, how like, I beseech
you, are they unto him ?   To go about, therefore, to express
God in any visible likeness is the next way to dishonour God,
and to bring him into contempt.   God's eye beholdeth all
things; idols see nothing.   God's ears hear all things; idols
hear nothing.   By God all things live, move, and are preserved; the idols themselves neither live, nor move, and,
unless they be upheld by the men that make them, they fall
and are dashed in pieces.   An idol breatheth not; God giveth
to other [8] a breathing spirit.   How then, and wherein, are
these twain alike ?   In substance, or in shape ?   If ye say,
in substance ; I answer, Is God then of gold, of silver, or of
wood ?   If in shape ; mine answer is, Hath the invisible power
of God then put on visible and mortal members ?   How
greatly therefore did the Anthropomorphites [9] offend herein ?
If then there be no similitude of God, how cometh it to pass,
I beseech you, that images and idols be called the likeness
and pictures of God ?   Among us he that calleth another an
idol or an image, doth seem to have spoken it too too despitefully [10] in reproach of the other : for we know that idols are
counterfeits of men [11], and not men indeed ; and therefore do
we call him an image, that is a sot, a fool, a dolt, an idiot, and
one that hath no wit, nor knoweth any more than he heareth
of other.   Why then henceforward should we any more call
images the likeness of God ?   God is living : images are
monuments of dead men ; as Salomon [12], the author of the
book of Wisdom, saith : " God is glorious, and heaven and
earth are full of the glory of his majesty ; but idols are with-

They were heretics, affirming, that God hath members like to mortal men.

[7 Ps. cxv. 4—7.]

[8 omnibus, Lat.]

[9 For traces of these heretics, see Mosheim's Eccles. Hist. Cent. 4.
book 2. part 2. ch. 5. §. 23; and Cent. 5. book 2. part 2. ch. 2. §. 10.
note 9; and ch. 5. §. 20. ed. Soames, 1845.]

[10 magna affecisse contumelia, Lat.]

[11 speciem falsam hominis referre, Lat.]

[12 The name, Solomon, is not in the original Latin.]

[BULLINGER.]   15

out all glory, and subject to the scoffs and mocks of men[1]."
Images are tokens of absent friends : but God is present
always and everywhere. And the signs or tokens, which
God did of old ordain and give to his people, were not simply
the signs and images of God, but tokens of God's presence,
signifying that God, who by nature is a spirit, and invisible,
incomprehensible, and unmeasurable, is present still among
them. Such a token was the cloud, the smoke, the fire, and
finally, the very ark of the covenant, which also the cherubin
did cover with their wings, signifying thereby that no mortal
man could look God in the face ; and that therefore the soul,
and the mind, and the spirit, ought by contemplation to be
lifted up into heaven, there to behold him. For to Moses,
who notwithstanding is said to have seen God face to face, it
was said, " No man shall see me and live[2]." When once we
are deceased, then shall we see him as he is, according to the
sayings of the blessed evangelist John[3]. So then these, I
say, are the causes, why the Lord will not have himself represented or pourtrayed in any matter or likeness.

Hereunto now do appertain the places of scripture, and
testimonies of the men that are the chiefest pillars of true
religion and godliness, of Moses, Esay, and Paul. Moses in
Deuteronomy saith: " The Lord spake unto you from the midst
of the fire : and a voice of words ye heard, but likeness saw
ye none, but heard the voice only. Take good heed therefore
unto yourselves, as pertaining unto your souls (for ye saw no
manner of image in that day), lest ye mar yourselves by
making you a graven image, the likeness of any manner of
figure, whether it be the picture of man or woman; the likeness of any manner of beast that is on the earth ; or the
likeness of any manner of feathered fowl that flieth in the air ;
or the likeness of any manner of worm that creepeth on the
earth ; or the likeness of any manner of fish that is in the
waters beneath the earth : yea, and lest thou lift up thine
eyes unto heaven, and when thou seest the sun, the moon,
and the stars, with all the host of heaven, thou shouldest
begin to worship them and reverence them, and shouldest
worship and serve the things which the Lord thy God hath
made to serve all nations under the whole heaven. Take

[1 Wisd. xiv. 15.]
[2 Ex. xxxiii. 20.]   [3 1 John iii. 2.]

heed, therefore, that ye forget not the appointment[4] of the Lord your God, which he hath made with you, and that ye make you no graven image, nor the likeness of any thing that the Lord thy God hath forbidden thee[5]." This hath Moses thus far.

Esaias also, in his fortieth chapter, saith: "Behold, all people" (to wit, compared to God) "are in comparison of him as a drop of a bucketful, and are counted as a little dust sticking on the balance, and weighing nothing at all. Yea, the isles are to him as a very little thing. Libanus is not sufficient to minister fire to his offering, and all the beasts thereof are not enough for one sacrifice. All people in comparison of God are reckoned as nothing; in respect of him they are less than nothing, and as that that is not. To whom then will ye liken God? or what similitude will ye set up to him? Shall the carver make him an image? and shall the goldsmith cover it with gold, or cast it into a form of silver plates? Moreover, shall[6] the poor man, that he may have somewhat to set up, choose a tree that is not rotten, and seek out a cunning workman to carve thereout an image, that moveth[7] not? Know ye not this? heard ye never of it?" And again: "It is he that sitteth upon the circle of the world, whose inhabiters are, in comparison of him, but as grasshoppers. It is he that spreadeth out the heavens like a curtain; he stretcheth them out as a tent to dwell in. It is he that bringeth princes to nothing, and maketh the judges of the earth as though they were not. To whom now will ye liken me, and to whom shall I be like? saith the Holy One. Lift up your eyes on high, and consider who hath made those things, which come out by so great heaps, and he calleth them all by their names." And so forth. Thus much out of Esaias[8].

Moreover, Paul, the apostle of Christ, disputing at Athens of true religion, saith: "God that made the world and all that therein is, seeing that he is Lord of heaven and earth,

[4 fœderis, Lat.]   [5 Deut. iv. 12, 15—19, 23.]
[6 In the original Latin the verbs in these three sentences are *not* in the future tense, nor are the sentences interrogatory. But the two former are interrogatory in the Vulgate.]
[7 ne moveatur loco, Lat.]
[8 Isai. xl. 15—23, 25, 26.]

dwelleth not in temples made with hands, neither is worshipped with men's hands, as though he needed any thing; since he himself giveth life and breath to all and everywhere, and hath made of one blood all nations of men, to dwell on all the face of the earth, and hath determined the times before appointed, and also the limits of their habitation, that they should seek the Lord, if perhaps they might have felt, and found him; though he be not far from every one of us: for by him we live, and move, and have our being; as certain of your own poets have said, For we are also his offspring. Forasmuch then as we are the offspring of God, we ought not to think that the Godhead is like to gold, or silver, or stone, graven by art or man's device[1]."

These testimonies are so evident, and do so plainly declare that which I purposed, that I need not for the further exposition of them to say any more. They were great causes, therefore, that moved St Augustine precisely to pronounce it to be horrible sacrilege for any man to place in the church the image of God the Father, sitting in a throne with bended hams; because it is detestable for a man so much as to conceive such a likeness in his mind. His very words I have rehearsed in the eighth Sermon of my first Decade[2], where I had occasion to speak of the right hand of the Father, and to teach you what it is to sit at the Father's right hand.

All other images are forbidden to be worshipped.

Now, touching other images also, which men erect to creatures or to the heathen gods, they are no less forbidden than the pictures of God himself. For if we may not hallow an image to the true and very God, much less shall it be lawful for us to erect or consecrate an idol to a strange or foreign god. Man in his mind doth choose himself a god, and of his own invention deviseth a shape or figure for it, which lastly he frameth with the workmanship of his hands: so that it may truly be said, that the mind conceiveth an idol, and the hand doth bring it forth. But the Lord, in the first commandment, forbad us to have any strange gods. Now, he that neither hath, nor chooseth to himself, any strange or foreign gods, doth not in his imagination devise any shape for them, and so consequently erecteth no images. For he thinketh it a detestable thing to make an image to the true and very God; he is persuaded that it is a wicked thing to

[1] Acts xvii. 24—29.]   [2] See page 150.]

choose himself a foreign god; and therefore he judgeth it to be most abominable to place the picture of a foreign god in the church or temple of the true and very God. And that is the cause that in the church before Christ his time we do not read, that any images were erected to any saints, whereof at that time there were a great number, (suppose) of patriarchs, judges, kings, priests, prophets, and whole troops of martyrs, matrons, and modest widows. The primitive church also of Christ his apostles had no images, either of Christ himself, or of other saints, set up in their places of public prayer, nor in their churches. The deed of Epiphanius is very well known, which he committed at Anablatha in Syria. It is written in Greek in an epistle to John Bishop of Jerusalem, and translated into Latin by St Hierome. He rent the vail that hung in the temple, bearing in it the image of Christ or some other saint; testifying therewithal, that it is against christian religion, for the picture of a man to hang in the church of God[3]. St Augustine in *Catalogo Hæresewn* maketh mention of one Marcella, a follower of Carpocrates his sect, which worshipped the images of Jesu, Paul, Homer, and Pythagoras, with falling down prostrate before them, and offering incense unto them[4]. Very well and wisely, therefore, did Erasmus of Roterodame, being deeply seen in the works of ecclesiastical writers, when he had wittily spoken many things touching the use of images in churches, at the last - also add this, and say: "There is no decree, no not so much as of men, which commandeth that images should be in churches. For as it is more easy, so is it less perilous, to take all images quite and clean out of the churches, than to be able to bring to pass that, in keeping them still, measure should not be exceeded, nor superstition covertly cloked. For admit that (as some say) the mind be clean from all superstition; yet notwithstanding it is not

[3 Quando—venissem ad villam quæ dicitur Anablatha,—inveni velum pendens in foribus—ecclesiæ, tinctum atque depictum, et habens imaginem, quasi Christi, vel sancti cujusdam.—Cum ergo hoc vidissem, in ecclesia Christi contra auctoritatem scripturarum hominis pendere imaginem, scidi illud.—Epiphan. Opp. Par. 1622. Tom. II. fol. 317.]

[4 Sectæ ipsius (i. e. Carpocratianorum) fuisse traditur socia quædam Marcellina, quæ colebat imagines Jesu et Pauli et Homeri et Pythagoræ, adorando incensumque ponendo.—August. Opp. Par. 1531. Tom. VI. fol. 3.]

without a shew of superstition, for him that prayeth to fall down prostrate before a wooden idol, to have his eyes stedfastly bent upon that alone, to speak to that, to kiss that, and not to pray at all but before an idol. And this I add, that whosoever do imagine God to be any other than indeed he is, they, contrary to this precept, do worship graven images[1]." And again, in the same catechism, he saith: "Even until the time of Hierome there were men of sound religion, which suffered not in the church any image to stand, neither painted, nor graven, nor woven; no, not so much as of Christ, because (as I suppose) of the Anthropomorphites. But afterward the use of images by little and little crept up and came into the churches[2]." This hath Erasmus.

No image must be made for Christ.

Furthermore, for Christ, our Lord and very God, though he have taken on him the nature of us men, yet, that notwithstanding, there ought no image to be erected. For he did not become man to that intent; but he drew up his humanity into heaven, and therewithal gave us a charge, that, so often as we pray, we should lift up the eyes of our minds and bodies into heaven above. Moreover, being once ascended, he sent his Spirit instead of himself unto the church, wherein he hath a spiritual kingdom, and needeth not any bodily or corruptible things. For he commanded that, if we would bestow any thing on him or for his sake, we should bestow it on the poor, and not on his picture or image. And now since, without all controversy, our Christ is the very true God, and that the very true God doth forbid to hallow to him any likeness of man, that is, to represent God in the

[1 Ut imagines sint in templis, nulla præcipit vel humana constitutio. Et ut facilius, ita tutius quoque est, omnes imagines e templis submovere, quam impetrare, ut nec modus prætereatur, nec admisceatur superstitio. Jam ut animus sit ab omni superstitione purus, tamen non caret superstitionis specie, orantem ad ligneum simulacrum procumbere, in hoc intentos habere oculos, ad hoc verba facere, huic oscula figere, nec orare prorsus nisi coram imagine. Illud addam, quicunque sibi aliusmodi fingunt Deum quam est, contra præceptum hoc colunt sculptilia.—Erasm. Symbol. Catec. vi. col. 1188. Opp. Lugd. Bat. Tom. v.]

[2 Usque ad ætatem Hieronymi erant probatæ religionis viri, qui in templis nullam ferebant imaginem, nec pictam, nec sculptam, nec textam; ac ne Christi quidem, ut opinor, propter Anthropomorphitas. Paulatim autem imaginum usus irrepsit in templa.—Ibid. col. 1187.]

shape of a man; it followeth consequently, that to Christ no image is to be dedicated, because he is the true and very God and life everlasting.

In the second part of this commandment we are taught, how far forth it is unlawful for us to make any image of God, or else of feigned gods; and, if so it be that any make or cause them to be made, how and after what sort then we ought to behave ourselves toward them. Images ought not in any case to be made for men to worship, or otherwise to use as means or instruments to worship God in. But if so it happen, that any man make them to the intent to have them worshipped; then must the zealous and godly disposed despise, neglect, not worship nor honour them, nor yet by any means be brought to do them service. For in this precept are two things set down especially to be noted. The first is, " Thou shalt not bow down to them." To bow down is to cap and to knee, to duck with the head and bend the body, to fall down, to honour, to worship, and to reverence. The saints of old did use to bow down (that is, to bend the knee, to uncover the head, and to fall down) to the magistrates, the prophets, the princes, and teachers of the people, and unto all sorts of reverend men. And that they did partly because God had so commanded, who useth their ministery to common men's commodity; and partly again, because men are the lively image of God himself. But deaf, dumb, and blind idols are wood and stone, whereunto we are forbidden to bend or bow down, howsoever we are made to believe that they do bear the likeness of God. The latter is, "Thou shalt not worship them," or else, Thou shalt not do any service unto them. In this clause is forbidden all the outward and unlawful honour done to God, or to the gods, in the way of religion, nay rather, in the way of superstition, and devilish hallowing of churches, reliques, holy-days, and such-like trash and trumpery[3]. For to serve is to worship, to reverence, to attribute some majesty and divine authority to that which we do worship, to have affiance in, to burn incense, to offer gifts, and to shew ourselves dutifully serviceable to that which we worship. There is no man that knoweth not what it is to serve, and what is meant by service, in matters of religion. We are forbidden,

How far forth it is not lawful to make images.

To bow down, what it is.

To serve, what it is.

[3 superstitione et cultu templorum, sacrorum, feriarum, omniumque rerum similium, Lat.]

therefore, to run in pilgrimage to idols, yea, though they be the images of God himself. We are forbidden to do them any service, in offering gifts, or attributing unto them any one jot of God's pre-eminence, thereby to bind ourselves to maintain and uphold their unlawful honour, in mingling such superstitions with better points of true religion. This therefore considered (since we may not attribute to images any serviceable honour[1]), I do not see how we can ascribe to them the office of teaching, admonishing, and exhorting, which are the offices and benefits of God's Holy Spirit and word: for Abacuck the prophet, of whose writings Paul did make no small account, hath left in writing words worth remembering. "What profiteth" (says he) "the image? for the maker of it hath made it: an image and a teacher of lies, though he that made it trusteth therein, when he maketh dumb idols? Woe unto him that saith to the wood, Awake; and to the senseless stone, Arise! Should that teach thee? Behold, it is covered with gold and silver, and there is no breath in it. But the Lord is in his holy temple; let all the earth keep silence before him[2]." What could be said more plainly and agreeable to the truth? Images (saith he) are mere and very lies. But how can that teach the truth, which of itself is nought else but a lie? There is no moving, there is no life, there is no breath in a picture or image. But the Lord sitteth in his holy temple, where he reigneth, and teacheth, by inspiration and the preaching of his word, the sum of godliness, and where he liveth for ever in the hearts of all his saints and servants. Let therefore all the tongues in the whole world be stopped of them that go about to maintain and uphold superstitious idolatry against the true and living God.

Idols teach not.

Now again in the third part of this commandment the Lord doth briefly knit up the pithy handling of sundry things. For, first, he sheweth that men have no just or lawful cause in turning from God, either to make them strange gods, or else to worship God otherwise than they ought to do. "I am" (saith he) "the Lord thy God," a strong God. If I be the Lord, then shouldest thou of duty serve me, honour me, obey me, and worship me, so as thou dost understand that I do desire to be worshipped and honoured. If I be God, then am I of

We have no cause to choose strange gods.

[1 cultum latriæ, Lat.]   [2 Hab. ii. 18—20.]

sufficient ability to minister to all men whatsoever they lack[3]. What canst thou want, therefore, that thou mayest not find in me? why then shouldest thou turn to strange gods? Thou hast no cause at all, undoubtedly, to turn from me. I am, moreover, a strong God, a mighty, yea, an almighty God and Lord. Thou hast no cause to seek a mightier or wealthier prince than me, by him to be delivered out of my hands, and by his liberality to be farther enriched than thou shalt be by my good gifts and blessings. For I am that true and eternal God, the invincible and almighty Prince of the world, the true and only helper and deliverer, the liberal and bountiful giver of all good gifts or benefits. I am also thy Lord and thy God. Those goods of mine are thine. For I am thine: yea, I am thy helper and deliverer out of all adversities and afflictions. Thou art mine: I have created thee: I live in thee, I do preserve thee. Why then shouldest thou turn away from me, and seek after any strange god whatsoever? What needest thou any more hereafter to hunt after senseless idols? Thou art the church and temple of God. Dost thou not feel and perceive within thyself, that I do dwell in thee, and have thine heart in possession? And what, I pray thee, hath the temple of God to do with godless images?

Then also he descendeth, and doth very severely, yet notwithstanding justly, threaten extreme and terrible revengement. "I am" (saith he) "a jealous God." This may be taken two ways very well, and not amiss. For, first, the sense may be thus: I will not have thee to seek any other gods but me, neither will I have thee admit or receive any foreign or unlawful worshipping of me. The cause is, I am a jealous God, envious against my rival, not suffering mine equal, nor by any means abiding to have a mate. I alone will be loved, I alone will be worshipped; and that too, not after any other fashion than I myself have appointed to be observed. For no man is so ignorant but that he knoweth how God in the scripture doth, by the parable of wedlock[4], figuratively set down the assurance and bond wherein by faith we are bound to God[5]. God is our husband and bridegroom: we are his

God suffereth not a mate.

[3 omnisufficientia sum, Lat.]
[4 humani conjugii, Lat.]
[5 religamur Deo (unde et religionis nomen est), Lat. omitted; from which binding the name, religion, is derived. So Augustine: Ad

wife and chosen spouse. A chaste and faithful wife giveth ear alone to her husband's voice; him alone she loveth, him alone she doth obey, and, him excepted, she loveth no man at all. Again, on the other side, a shameless, faithless adulteress and whorish strumpet, not worthy to be called a wife, seemeth outwardly to stick and cleave to her husband; but privily she maketh her body common to many men, and loveth other more than her husband, and for the most part burneth on them, being cold enough to him-ward. But God is a jealous God, and will be loved and worshipped alone, without any partner to rob him thereof. That is spiritual adultery and whore-hunting, when men do partly love and worship God, and yet notwithstanding do therewithal give reverence to strange and other gods. Against this faithless and double dealing all the prophets cry out most vehemently with words that represent a tyrannous and cruel revengement[1]: for of all other sins that is most detestable. I would to God at this day so many were not persuaded, that this kind of honour is the worship that God maketh most account of!

Or else otherwise the sense of those words may be thus: I will not have thee to seek any other gods but me; I will not have thee worship me according to thine own inventions. The cause is, I am a jealous God; that is, I am easy to be provoked, and will not suffer myself and mine honour to be rejected without due punishment for the contempt. And to this sense he seemeth to draw, where he goeth forward, and doth at large expound how he is jealous: for "I visit," saith he, "the fathers' iniquity in the children unto the third and fourth generation of them that hate me." God therefore is a sharp revenger and a just judge against them that follow after strange gods, or serve God unlawfully or irreligiously, and also against all them that swerve from the law of God. For he thundereth out this bitter punishment, especially against idolaters; but therewithal inclusively he threateneth it to them which break the rest of his commandments. For that which the Lord uttereth here is generally spoken, and is of force and effect against all impiety and unrighteousness of all mankind. But for because God's case is far more excellent

unum Deum tendentes, et ei uni religantes animas nostras, unde religio dicta creditur, &c.—De Ver. Relig. cap. 55.]
[1 plane tragicis vocibus, Lat.]

than man's, they therefore do more heinously offend which break the first table, than they that sin against the second; and thereby do deserve a far more grievous pain and heavy punishment.

Now, whereas we see that the Lord saith, that he will visit, and by inquisition punish, the sins of the fathers in the children unto the third and fourth generation; we must not by and by think that God is unjust, and punisheth another man's fault in afflicting the innocent, that is, in whipping him that did not offend: as the Jews in Ezechiel did wickedly taunt and cavil with God, saying, " The fathers have eaten sour grapes, and the children's teeth are set on edge." But it is not so. " For every man shall bear his own offences; neither shall the son bear or abide the father's sin, nor the father the son's iniquity². " This doth the most true God very often and earnestly beat into our heads throughout Ezechiel, and the whole scripture beside. If therefore the children, or childer's children, shall abide in the crooked steps of their fathers, and shall, as their fathers did, do service to idols, and shall think that they shall be safe and remain unpunished because they learned it of their fathers, even as their fathers also were idolaters, and yet flourished in wealth and prosperity; then, I say, I will punish the sin of the fathers in the children: that is, I will sharply revenge the sin that the children have learned of the fathers, and wherein they stiffly stand and abide, being encouraged thereunto by their fathers' example and good fortune; although for the very same sin I did not once touch their fathers before them. And for that cause is this expressly added, " of them that hate me." Hereof have we very many and very evident examples in the books of Kings. The house of Jeroboam is utterly destroyed, because Jeroboam did erect in Israel idolatry and superstition³. Immediately after, the whole stock of king Baasa is clean cut off: and Achab's house is pulled up by the roots. At length, the Israelites are made slaves⁴ to serve the Assyrians. Solomon, the most mighty, wealthy, wise, and happy king of Juda, because of his idolatry and strange superstition, is of a sudden made a wretch of all

How God doth visit the fathers' sins in the children.

[² Ezek. xviii. 2, 20.]
[³ peregrinos cultus, Lat.]
[⁴ captivi abducuntur in Assyriorum regna, Lat.]

other. There is none, unless he never read the holy scriptures, but doth know what happened to his son Roboam, to Joram the son of Josaphat, to Achas, Manasses, Jehoiachim and Zedechias, because of idolatry and foreign worshipping of God.

Let us therefore firmly hold and believe, that the threatenings of God are true in effect, and that God is both a severe and just revenger and punisher of idolaters and wicked superstitious men, and finally, of all and every wicked act done by every man. Although God do sundry times seem to wicked men to slumber, and not to see them, yet notwithstanding he doth awake when he thinks good[1], and payeth home the wicked for all their offences done and past. Although he be long-suffering, yet the righteous Lord doth not always neglect the godly and oppressed, neither doth he always wink at ungodliness, and let the wicked be unpunished for ever : but he giveth them time to repent in, which whosoever do neglect, they do at length feel the greater pains and sharper punishment, according to the saying of the apostle : " What, dost thou despise the riches of God's goodness, suffering[2], and gentleness, not knowing that God's goodness calleth thee to repentance ? But, according to thy hardness and heart that cannot repent, thou heapest up to thyself wrath against the day of wrath, wherein shall be made manifest the just judgment of God, who shall repay to every one according to his deeds[3]," &c.

A most large promise is made to the godly worshippers of the Lord.

Again, the bountiful Lord promiseth great and large rewards to them that worship him, and stedfastly persevere in true godliness and perfect religion. "I am God," saith he, "shewing mercy, or giving bountifully, unto thousands." Here note, that his mercy is greater than his vengeance : for where he is angry, there he punisheth unto the third and fourth generation ; but where he is mercifully liberal, there he is bountiful unto many thousands. For of his goodness and benefits there is no measure or end ; and the mercy of God is far above all his works. Here yet again he addeth two things more : "To them," saith he, "that love me, and keep my commandments." Here, I say, he requireth two things at their hands that are his. The first is, that they love God,

[1 justo tempore, Lat.]   [2 tolerantiæ, Lat.]
[3 Rom. ii. 4—6.   Bullinger has used Erasmus' rendering.]

and make account of and take him to be their God: which if they do, then shall there no room be left in the godly for strange or foreign gods. The second is, that they obey God, and walk in his commandments: which if they do, then are all idols and strange worshippings utterly at an end; then doth the Lord by his word reign in the heart of every godly man, whom the bountiful Lord doth liberally bless with all kind of blessings and good gifts. And this clause verily doth especially belong to this commandment, but inclusively also it is referred to all the rest, as by the very words of God we may easily gather. Let us hold and verily think therefore, that the infinite and unspeakable benefits of God are prepared for them that walk in the law of the Lord.

Thus much had I to speak of these two commandments of the first table, which I cannot now again recapitulate, because an hour and a half is already spent, and for that I hope that I have so orderly proceeded in every point, and taught every thing so evidently and plainly, that there is nothing which ye do not very well perceive and understand. Let us now praise the Lord, and thank him for his goodness, for shewing us his ways; and let us pray that we, walking rightly in them, may at the last come to his eternal[4] joys. Amen.

OF THE THIRD PRECEPT OF THE TEN COMMAND-MENTS[5], AND OF SWEARING.

THE THIRD SERMON.

THE third commandment of the first table[6] is thus word for word: "Thou shalt not take the name of the Lord thy God in vain; because the Lord will not let him go unpunished that taketh the name of the Lord his God in vain." In the second commandment the Lord did set down the worship that he would not have, that he misliked of, and did flatly forbid; to wit, a worldly, earthly, and carnal kind of honour, a base

The third command-ment of God.

[4 cœlestia, Lat.]
[5 primæ tabulæ, seu Decalogi, Lat.]
[6 sive Decalogi, Lat. omitted.]

and vile kind of worship, a service that is directly contrary to the spirit, nature, and majesty of God; that is, to think that God will in shape resemble a man, or any other creature made of earth or corruptible stuff or matter; and then again, to worship him under those shapes and figures with corruptible things, that were first ordained and created for the use and behoof of men, and not of God. For God is an eternal Spirit, which goeth all over[1] and preserveth every thing; whom all the most excellent creatures of the whole world, if they were joined together in one, are not able to resemble, nor yet to represent the least jot of excellency in the living God. God is so far from lacking any corruptible things, that he himself supplieth the want of all our necessities. It is a mere folly therefore to set up a percher[2], a taper, or a smoky torch before the maker and giver of light. It is a very toy to offer flesh of beasts to that eternal Spirit, who in the Psalms saith: "All the beasts of the wood are mine, and the cattle in a thousand hills. I know all birds upon the mountains, and in my power are all the beasts of the field. If I be hungry, I need not to tell thee, since the world is mine, and all that is therein[3]."

Now, therefore, in this third commandment the Lord doth very exquisitely, although very briefly, declare the manner how he will be worshipped, that is, in holy reverencing of his holy name. The names whereby God is called are God, God's majesty, God's truth, God's power, and God's justice. Now the charge of this commandment is, not to abuse the name of God, and not to use it in light and trifling matters; but to speak, to think, and judge honourably, reverently, holily, and purely of God and godly things. But the pith and effect almost of the whole lieth herein, that he saith, " the name of the Lord thy God;" to wit, which is thy chief goodness and felicity, thy Creator, thy Redeemer, and thy tender Father. Now note, that the Lord doth not barely forbid to use his name; but he chargeth not to use it lightly or in vain, that is, beyond necessary use or our behoof, and beside the honour and glory of God. Let us see, therefore, how we ought to sanctify the Lord's name, and how we may devoutly use the name of God, and, last of all, so worship him as he himself hath appointed us to do.

How the Lord's name is sanctified. First of all, we have to think of God as of the chief feli-

[1] omnia permeans, Lat.]
[2] See page 199.]   [3] Ps. l. 10—12.]

city and infinite treasure of all good things, who loveth us exceedingly with a fatherly affection, always wishing and by all means desiring to have us men saved, and to come to the perfect knowledge of the very truth; whose judgments are true and just, whose works for their excellency are wonderful, and whose words are most true, and truth itself. Then ·must this holy name of God continually be called upon in prayers, need, and requests: by that alone we must look to obtain whatsoever is needful for our bodies or souls. We must never cease to give thanks to that for all the good benefits that we do or shall receive; for what good soever men have and enjoy, that have they not from elsewhere than from God, the fountain and giver of all. This glory must ever be given to God. If we be nipped with any adversity, let us not by and by murmur against God's good pleasure and his secret judgments; but rather, suffering and submitting ourselves under his mighty and fatherly hand, let us say with the prophet David: "It is good for me, Lord, that thou hast chastened me[4]." Let not us appoint God what he shall do, but wholly and always submit ourselves to his good will and holy pleasure[5]. Let us in all things give God the glory, in praising openly and plainly professing his name and doctrine before kings and princes, yea, and in sight of all the world, so often as occasion shall be given, and the glory of God shall seem to require. Let us not be ashamed of God our Father, of his truth and true religion. Let us not be ashamed of Christ our Redeemer, nor yet of his cross. But let us be ashamed of errors, idolatry, of the world and vanity, of lies and iniquity. Let us holily, reverently, and devoutly, both speak and think of God, his works, and his word. Let the law of God be holy to us, let his gospel be reverend in our eyes; and let the doctrine of the patriarchs, prophets, and apostles be esteemed of us as that which came from God himself. Let us not take the name of the Lord our God into our mouths, unless it be in a matter of weight. Let us not blaspheme, curse, nor lie in the name of the Lord. Let us not use, nay, rather abuse, the name or word of God in conjuring, juggling, or sorcery[6]: for in these things the name of God is most of all abused. Let us

[4 Ps. cxix. 71, as in Vulgate.]
[5 bonæ, sanctæ et justæ ejus voluntati, Lat.]
[6 ad res magicas, ad circulatoriam, ad incantamenta, Lat.]

precisely and holily keep the oath which we have made by the name of the living and eternal God. Let us in all things tell truth, and lie not; that when this world, that will not see, shall be enforced to see so great a reverence and devotion in us to the name of our God, it may be compelled thereby to glorify our Father which is in heaven. And this verily is the godly using of the Lord's name, and the religion[1] wherein our God is very well pleased.

How the name of God is abused.

Now note by the way, that there are sundry ways whereby we abuse the name of God; and first of all, we abuse it as often as our hearts are without all reverence to God himself; when we do unreverently, filthily[2], wickedly, and blasphemously speak of God, of his judgments, of his word, and of his laws; when we do with scoffing allusions apply God's words to light matters and trifles, by that means turning and drawing the scriptures into a profane and unhonest meaning. Moreover, we do disgrace the name of the Lord our God, when we call not upon his name, but turn ourselves rather to I know not what sort of gods, to man's skill and succour, to things forbidden, to idols, and conjurors[3]; which we fall a-doing then especially, when, being wrapped in misery and calamities, either for our sins, or else because God will try us, we do presently begin to murmur against God, and to accuse his judgments, hardly abstaining from open blasphemy, in grudging to bear the things that for our deserts we do worthily suffer. Hereunto belongeth the abuse of beastly knaves, which do not stick to use the holy name of God in obtaining their filthy lusts, which they call love; and also the naughtiness of them that thereby seek to find and recover the things that are lost, or else are stolen from them. We do unhallow the name of the Lord our God, when we give not to him all honour and glory. We shall, peradventure, do some good deed; there is, perhaps, in us something worthy to be praised : if we, therefore, shall challenge the praise thereof to ourselves, or, at the least, shall pare out a piece of that glory for our own share, and give the rest to God, not referring it all and whole to God the author of all, then do we therein defile the name of God, which ought alone to be praised for ever and ever.

[1 cultus, Lat.]   [2 petulanter, Lat.]
[3 ad magicas artes, Lat.]

Furthermore, if we deny the Lord, or blush at and be ashamed of his holy gospel, because of this wicked world and the naughty men therein; if also we do spot ourselves with a filthy and unclean life, which is to the slander of God's name and the offence of our neighbour; then do we take the Lord's name in vain; yea, we abuse it to his dishonour and reproach. We do abuse the name of the Lord, if we take a solemn oath in a trifle or matter of no effect, or if we do not keep and perform the oath that we have sworn. In our daily talk very often, and almost about godless matters, we are wont to call, and take to witness, the dreadful name of God, having learned it of an ill continuance and custom, or else being stirred up by some evil motion of our naughty mind: we have an innumerable sort of deep and terrible oaths, as wounds, blood, cross, and passion of the Lord, heaven, earth, sacraments, every saint in heaven, and all the devils of hell[4]. Beside all this, we abuse the name of God also sundry and divers ways in telling of lies. The preacher or teacher of the church lieth, when he crieth, "Thus saith the Lord;" whereas the Lord indeed saith nothing so. He maketh the name of God a cloke and a colour to hide his deceit, and doth beguile poor simple souls. The magistrate crieth out, "All power is of God[5];" and so, under pretence of God's name, doth his subjects injury in playing the tyrant and not the magistrate. The common people deceive one another, under the name of the Lord, in contracts and bargaining. And the sturdy rogue, unworthy of alms, will not stickle to stand and make God's name an idle occupation for to get a penny. But who can reckon up all the things, wherein God's name is foully abused? We must all therefore have an eye, that we defile not the name of God, but rather bless it, and holily worship it.

For it followeth in the words of the Lord, what punishment abideth for them that so disgrace his name: "Because," saith he, "the Lord will not let him go unpunished, that taketh his name in vain." And although this commination of the Lord is very horrible indeed, and of itself effectual enough to make the godly sort afraid to pollute the name of God; yet nevertheless I will add one example or twain of

The punishment of them that abuse God's name.

[4 Cf. Becon's Works, Parker Soc. ed. Vol. I. page 359; Latimer, Vol. I. page 231; Hutchinson's Works, page 20.]

[5 Rom. xiii. 1.]

[BULLINGER.]

16

them whom the Lord hath punished for defiling his name. David crieth out, and saith : " The unrighteous shall not stand in thy sight, O Lord : thou hatest them that work iniquity : thou shalt destroy all them that speak lies[1]." But how much more likely is it, that the Lord will destroy all them that speak blasphemy, and abuse his holy name ! Saul, verily, because he called not upon the Lord in his extreme necessity, but asked counsel of the pythonisse[2], was compelled to kill himself with his own hand, after he had seen his people downright slain by the Philistines, his enemies, and his sons lie dead in the midst of the people. Ananias lieth to the Holy Ghost, and defileth the name of the Lord; and, falling down suddenly dead to the ground, down he goeth with shame enough to the devil of hell[3]. Sanherib blasphemeth the name of the eternal God before the walls of Jerusalem ; but anon after he is for his labour bereft of his puissant army, and in his own god's temple is shot through[4] by his own sons. Jehoiachim and Zedechias, both kings of Juda and blasphemers of God's name, are taken captives and slain by Nabuchodonosor, king of Babylon[5]. Achab, Jezebel, and the priests of Baal are utterly wiped out by king Jehu, because they, under the colour of God and godliness, blasphemed the name of God, and persecuted the true religion[6]. In the twenty-fourth of Leviticus, he that blasphemed the name of God was overwhelmed with stones to death.

A pain for blasphemers decreed by an emperor.

And therefore the emperor Justinian, *In Novellis constitu.* 77, writing to the citizens of Constantinople, saith : " Moreover, because, besides unspeakable lusts, some men lash out cursings and oaths of God, thereby provoking him to anger ; we therefore exhort them to abstain from cursings and oaths by his hair and head, and such other words like unto these. For if reproaches done unto men are not left unrevenged,

[1 Psal. v. 5, 6.]

[2 Saul pythonissam consulit; head-note of Vulgate in 1 Reg. xxviii.]

[3 migrat ad inferos, Lat.]

[4 sagittis configitur, Lat. ; with the sword, 2 Kings xix. 37; cum gladio, Vulg.]

[5 2 Chron. xxxvi. 6; 2 Kings xxv. 7. It is not recorded in scripture, although it may be inferred, that these two kings were brought to death by Nebuchadnezzar's treatment of them.]

[6 1 Kings xxii. ; 2 Kings ix. and x.]

much more is he worthy to be punished, that stirreth God to anger with his villany. And for such offences as these do so many dearths, earthquakes, and plagues come unto men. We therefore admonish them to abstain from those crimes : for whosoever, after this admonition of ours, shall be found faulty therein, they shall first shew themselves unworthy to be beloved of men, and, after that too, suffer such punishment as the law shall appoint. For we have given in charge to the right honourable the lieutenant of our royal city to apprehend the guilty, and to punish them extremely : lest peradventure at length for such sinners' contempt, and such heinous offences, not only this city, but also the whole commonweal, be justly destroyed by God's just vengeance[7]." Thus much writeth he. Now by this we may gather, that not the least part of our calamities at these days do happen unto us because of our detestable cursings and horrible blasphemies, which very few magistrates, or none almost at all, do go about to redress, or punish as they should do. The name of the living God is blasphemed with passing deep and horrible oaths, of all sorts, of all kinds[8], and all ages ; so that I think verily, that from the beginning of the world there never was such a blasphemous people as are in this cursed age of ours. And therefore are we vexed with unspeakable and endless calamities. For God is true, and cannot lie,

[7 Ἐπειδὴ δέ τινες—καὶ βλάσφημα ῥήματα καὶ ὅρκους περὶ Θεοῦ ὀμνύουσι, τὸν Θεὸν παροργίζοντες· καὶ τούτοις ὁμοίως παρεγγυῶμεν ἀποσχέσθαι τῶν τοιούτων βλασφήμων ῥημάτων, καὶ τοῦ ὀμνύναι κατὰ τριχός τε καὶ κεφαλῆς καὶ τῶν τούτοις παραπλησίων ῥημάτων· εἰ γὰρ αἱ κατ᾽ ἀνθρώπων γινόμεναι βλασφημίαι ἀνεκδίκητοι οὐ καταλιμπάνονται, πολλῷ μᾶλλον ὁ εἰς αὐτὸ τὸ θεῖον βλασφημῶν ἄξιος ἐστὶ τιμωρίας ὑποστῆναι.— Διὰ γὰρ τὰ τοιαῦτα πλημμελήματα καὶ λιμοὶ καὶ σεισμοὶ καὶ λοιμοὶ γίγνονται. Καὶ διὰ τοῦτο παραινοῦμεν τοῖς τοιούτοις ἀποσχέσθαι τῶν εἰρημένων ἀτοπημάτων—εἰ γὰρ καὶ μετὰ τὴν τοιαύτην ἡμῶν νομοθεσίαν εὑρεθῶσί τινες τοῖς αὐτοῖς ἐπιμένοντες πλημμελήμασι, πρότερον μὲν ἀναξίους ἑαυτοὺς ποιοῦσι τῆς τοῦ Θεοῦ φιλανθρωπίας, ἔπειτα δὲ καὶ τὰς ἐκ τῶν νόμων ὑποστήσονται τιμωρίας. Ἐπετρέψαμεν γὰρ τῷ ἐνδοξοτάτῳ ἐπάρχῳ τῆς βασιλίδος πόλεως τοὺς ἐπιμένοντας ταῖς εἰρημέναις ἀτόποις καὶ ἀσεβέσι πράξεσι— συνέχειν, καὶ ταῖς ἐσχάταις ὑποβάλλειν τιμωρίαις· ἵνα μὴ, ἐκ τοῦ παραβλέπειν τὰς τοιαύτας ἁμαρτίας, εὑρεθῇ καὶ ἡ πόλις καὶ ἡ πολιτεία διὰ τῶν τοιούτων ἀσεβῶν πράξεων ἀδικουμένη.—Justin. Auth. Collat. vi. tit. 6 : Novell. 77. cap. 1, p. 323. Gotting. 1797.]

[8 Sexuum, Lat.]

which saith, that they shall not scape scot free that take his name in vain. The men of our time do not only take it in vain, but do of malice also blasphemously defile it. I would to God the magistrates would more sincerely set forth the worship of God among the people : or else, if this may not be obtained at their hands, yet then at least that they would be no worse nor godless than Caiphas, who, when he heard (as he thought) blasphemy against the name of God, did rent his clothes[1], and cry, that the blasphemer was worthy to die. For surely, unless our christian magistrates do become more sharp and severe against blaspheming villanies, I do not see but that they must needs be a great deal worse than the wicked knave Caiphas. Undoubtedly the Lord is true (as every one of you must severally think within yourselves), and he verily will punish in all men the defiling of his name, but much more the malicious blaspheming of the same.

Of an oath.   This very matter and place do now require, that I also speak somewhat here of taking an oath, or swearing, which is done by calling and taking to witness of God's name. Now, in the handling of this matter, many things are to be thought of and considered. For first of all, I see that some there are, which doubt whether it be lawful to take an oath or no,

Whether it be lawful to swear.   because in Matthew the Lord hath said : " Ye have heard what was said of old, Thou shalt not forswear thyself, but shalt perform thine oaths unto the Lord ; but I say unto you, Swear not at all, &c.[2]" But the Lord's mind in Matthew was not to take clean away the true and ancient law, but to interpret it, and to bring it to a sounder sense, because it was before corrupted and marred by divers forged and counterfeit glosses of the Pharisees. For the people, being taught by them, had evermore an eye to keep their mouths from perjury ; but touching superfluous, unprofitable, and needless oaths, they had no care at all, not thinking that it was amiss to swear by heaven and by earth : wherefore the Lord, expounding his Father's law, saith, that all oaths generally are forbidden, to wit, those wherein the name of the Lord is taken in vain, and whereby we swear when there is no need at all. In the meanwhile, he neither condemned, nor yet took clean

[1 Matt. xxvi. 65, 66.]
[2 Matt. v. 33, 34.]

away, the solemn and lawful oath. Now there is great difference between a solemn oath and our daily oaths, which are nothing else but deep swearings, not only needless, but also hurtful. But a solemn oath is both profitable and needful. The law of God and words of Christ do not forbid things profitable and needful, and therefore they condemn not a solemn and lawful oath. Yea, in the law too is permitted a solemn oath, where there is forbidden alone the unprofitable using of the Lord's name. And Christ, our Lord, came not to break the law, but to fulfil the law. And therefore he, in St Matthew, did not condemn an oath: unless a man should go about to prove that the Son taught a doctrine clean contrary to the doctrine of his heavenly Father; which is a blasphemy against the Father and the Son not to be suffered. Moreover, God himself also sweareth; which undoubtedly he would not do, if an oath could not be taken without any sin. For, after a long exposition of the law, he saith: "Be ye holy, for I am holy; be ye perfect, even as your heavenly Father is perfect[3]." We read also, that the holiest men of both the Testaments, by calling and taking to witness the name of God in matters of weight, did swear, and that they sware without any sin. An oath therefore in the law of Christ is not forbidden; and it is lawful for a christian man both to exact and also to take an oath. I rather, verily, do not see how that man is worthy to be called a Christian, which, being lawfully required to swear, will seem to refuse it. But of this I have more fully disputed in another place against the Anabaptists[4].

Secondarily, we have to consider for what causes we ought to swear. In many commonweals it is an usual and received custom to take an oath upon every light occasion; and for that cause we see that an oath is lightly set by and very little esteemed. For what is this but to take the name of God in vain? Let magistrates therefore learn and know, that an oath ought not to be required but in earnest affairs: as when it standeth for the glory of God, for the safety of our

For what causes we ought to swear.

[3 Levit. xix. 2; Matt. v. 48.]
[4 See H. Bullingeri adversus Anabaptistas Libri VI. nunc primum e Germanico sermone in Latinum conversi per Josiam Simlerum, Tigurinum, Lib. v. cap. 11, pp. 197—202. Tiguri. 1560.]

neighbour, and for the public weal. We must mark therefore, when, and why, the people of God have sworn in the
scriptures. Abraham sware, when he made the league and
confederacy with Abimelech[1]. The people of God doth very
often swear under their kings, in making a covenant with God
for the keeping of true religion[2]. They of old time did clear
themselves of heinous suspicions by taking of an oath. In
Exodus we read: "If any man shall give to his neighbour a
beast to keep, and it shall die, or be stolen away, no man
seeing it, then shall an oath by the Lord go betwixt them
twain, that he hath not laid his hand on his neighbour's thing :
which oath the owner of the thing shall take, and the other
shall not restore it[3]." For Paul, in the sixth to the Hebrews,
saith: "Men verily swear by the greater; and an oath for
confirmation is to them an end of all strife." To this end,
therefore, let magistrates apply the use of an oath; and let
them have an especial regard, in giving an oath, to do it
reverently : let the peers of the people[4] keep inviolably that
which they swear; and let them take heed that they do not
rashly require an oath of light-headed fellows : let them not
compare any thing, or think any thing to be equal, to an oath;
but let them reverently, and last of all, have their recourse to
that, as to the utmost remedy to find out the truth; and
therewithal let them use sharp punishment against perjured
persons[5]. But woe to the people's princes, if through their
wicked negligence an oath be not esteemed! For he, without
doubt, will punish them sharply for it, who saith : " Because
I will not suffer him to go unpunished that taketh the Lord's
name in vain."

What an
oath is.

Thirdly, I will tell you what an oath is, and what it is to
swear. An oath is the calling or taking to witness of God's
name, to confirm the truth of that we say. There is difference betwixt an oath, and that deep kind of swearing, whereby

[1 Gen. xxi. 24.]
[2 2 Kings xxiii. 3 ; 2 Chron. xv. 12—15; Jer. xxxiv. 8—10.]
[3 Exod. xxii. 10, 11.]
[4 proceres populi, Lat.]
[5 Ita minus vilescet in popularium animis juramenti religio, Lat.
omitted by the translator. By these means reverence for an oath will
not be so much weakened in the minds of their people.]

God is blasphemed and torn in pieces. There is difference, too, betwixt an oath and those bitter speeches wherewith we use to curse and ban our neighbours: they are not worthy, doubtless, to be called oaths. But, for because this word *juramentum* is over largely used for any kind of oath, as well in the worse as better part; therefore the godly and lawful oaths are wisely called by the name of *jusjurandum*[6]. For by adding *jus*, which signifieth the law, we are admonished that that kind of oath is lawful and righteous. Now this taking of God's name to witness hath joined to it a calling on, and avowing ourselves to, God's curse and vengeance. For this is the manner of an oath and order of swearing: I will say, or do, it truly indeed and without deceit, so God may help me. Therefore we put ourselves in danger of God's wrath and vengeance, unless we do truly and indeed both speak and do the thing that we promised to do or speak. A very deep and solemn promise-making is this, than the which verily there is not a greater to be found in the world. Here also must be considered the circumstances and ceremonies in swearing. For our ancesters of old were wont to lift their hand up unto heaven, and to swear by the name of the Lord. The Lord our God dwelleth in heaven. We therefore do manifestly declare, that, as in the judges' eyes we lift our hand to heaven, even so in our minds we do ascend, and swear in the presence and sight of God; yea, we give our hand, and plight our faith, to God there, in taking an oath by the name of God. This ceremony used Abraham, the singular friend of God, and father of the faithful[7], when he was wont to swear.

Circumstances and ceremonies in swearing.

I need not therefore to proceed any further, for to declare whether we ought to swear by the name of God alone, or else by the names of saints, or else by laying the hand upon the holy Gospel. For it is manifest, that the faithful must swear by the only eternal and most high God: touching which thing we have most evident precepts, commanding us to swear by the name of the Lord, and again, forbidding us to swear by the names of strange gods. Of the first sort are these: "Thou shalt fear the Lord thy

How we ought to swear.

[6 Jusjurandum est affirmatio religiosa.—Cic. de Offic. Lib. III.]
[7 pater fidei, Lat.—See Gen. xiv. 22.]

God, thou shalt serve him, and swear by his name."
Deut. sixth and tenth chapter. Also the Lord himself in
Esay saith: "To me shall every knee bend, and by me shall
every tongue swear[1]." And again, in the sixty-fifth chapter,
the same prophet saith: "He that will bless himself shall
bless in the Lord, and he that will swear shall swear by the
true and very God." Of the latter sort too are these testimonies of the holy scriptures: Exod. xxiii., "All that I have
said keep ye, and do ye not once so much as think of the
names of strange gods, neither let them be heard out of your
mouth." And Josue, in the twenty-third chapter, saith: "When
ye shall come in among these nations, see that ye swear not by
the name of their gods, and look that ye neither worship nor
yet bow down unto them." In the fifth of Jeremy the Lord
saith : "Thy sons have forsaken me, and sworn by other gods,
which are no gods indeed: I have filled them, and they have
gone a whoring," &c. Moreover, the prophet Sophony
bringeth in the Lord speaking and saying: "I will cut off
those that worship and swear by the Lord, and swear by
Malchom[2]," that is, by their king and defender. And no
marvel though he do threaten destruction to them that swear
by the names of creatures: for an oath is the chief and
especial honour done to God, which therefore cannot be divided
to other. For we swear by the highest, whom we believe
to be the chiefest goodness, the giver of all good things,
and the punishing revenger of every evil deed. But and
if we swear by the names of other gods, then verily shall
we make them equal to God himself, and attribute to them
the honour due to him. And for this cause the blessed
martyr of Christ, Polycarpus, chose rather the flames of fire
than to swear by the power and estate of Cæsar. The
story is to be seen in the fourth book and fifteenth chapter
of Eusebius[3].

An oath is the special honour done to God.

[1 Isai. xlv. 23.]

[2 Zephan. i. 4, 5.—Malkom regem significat. Propheta usurpavit
pro divo aliquo sive patrono deoque tutelari.—Bullinger de Origine
Erroris, cap. xii. p. 54, Tigur. 1539.]

[3 Ἐπιμένοντος δὲ πάλιν αὐτοῦ (τοῦ ἡγουμένου) καὶ λέγοντος, Ὄμοσον
τὴν Καίσαρος τύχην, ὁ Πολύκαρπος, Εἰ κενοδοξεῖς, φησὶν, ἵνα ὀμόσω τὴν
Καίσαρος τύχην, ὡς λέγεις προσποιούμενος ἀγνοεῖν ὅς τις εἰμί, μετὰ παρρησίας
ἄκουε· Χριστιανὸς εἰμί.—Euseb. Hist. Eccles. Lib. IV. cap. 15. See
also Early Writings of Hooper, Parker Soc. ed. page 478.]

Fourthly, we have to consider how we ought to swear, and what the conditions of a just, a lawful, and an honest oath are. Jeremy therefore saith: "Thou shalt swear, The Lord liveth, in truth, in judgment, and righteousness: and the nations shall bless themselves in him, and in him shall they glory[4]." There are therefore four conditions of a just and a lawful oath. The first is, Thou shalt swear, "The Lord liveth." Here now again is repeated that which hath so many times been beaten into our heads, that we ought to swear by the name of the living God. The pattern of our ancestors' oath was this, "The Lord liveth;" as it is evident by the writings of the prophets. Let us not swear therefore by any other but by God. The second condition is: "Thou shalt swear in truth." So then it is required, that not only the tongue, but also the mind, should swear; lest haply we say, The tongue indeed did swear, but the mind sware not at all[5]. Let us be true and faithful therefore, without deceit or guile; let us not lie, nor go about with subtilty to shift off the oath that once we have made. We Germans express this well, when we say, *On alle gfard*[6], or else, *On gfard;* that is, I will not use any double dealing, but will simply and in good faith perform that I promise. There is an excellent pattern of a false and a deceitful oath in *Auli Gellii Noct. Att. Lib.* VII. cap. 18.[7] The third condition is: "Thou shalt swear in," or with, "judgment;" that is, advisedly, with great discretion, not rashly nor lightly, but with consideration of every thing and circumstance, in great necessity, and cases of public commodity. The fourth condition is: "Thou shalt swear in justice," or righteousness; lest peradventure our oath be against right and equity, that is, lest we sin against righteousness or justice, which attributeth that which is theirs both to God and man;

The conditions of an holy oath.

[4 Jer. iv. 2.]

[5 Reference is here made to the well-known line of Euripides, Hippolyt. 608. ἡ γλῶσσ᾽ ὀμώμοχ᾽, ἡ δὲ φρὴν ἀνώμοτος:—and Bullinger uses the words of Cicero's version: Juravi lingua, mentem injuratam gero.—De Offic. Lib. III. cap. 29.]

[6 ohne alle gefáhrde.]

[7 The case referred to by A. Gellius is that of the ten prisoners sent by Hannibal to Rome, after the battle of Cannæ; two of whom evaded their oath, and remained in Rome. P.—See also Cic. de Offic. Lib. I. cap. 13, and Lib. III. cap. 32.]

so that our oath do not directly tend against the love of God and our neighbour.

Here, dearly beloved, ye have heard me express in few words (which God himself hath also taught us), how we must swear, of what sort and fashion our lawful and allowable oaths ought to be, and under what conditions they are contained. But now, if we shall swear against these conditions appointed us by God, then shall our oaths and swearings be altogether unlawful: and furthermore, if we shall go about to perform those unlawful and unallowable oaths, then shall we therewithal purchase and incur the heavy wrath of the revenging Lord.

Whether wicked oaths must be performed.

Now, in these days it is usually of custom demanded, whether we ought to keep or perform wicked or ungodly, unjust or evil vows, or oaths; as if, for example, thy oath or vow should directly tend against God, against true religion, against the word of God, or the health of thy neighbour?

I will here allege and rehearse the usual accustomed answer, which notwithstanding is very true, and grounded upon examples of holy scriptures, as that that squareth not from the truth the narrow breadth of one small hair[1]. The answer therefore is this: If any man shall swear against the faith and charity, so that the keeping of his oath may tend to the worse, then it is better for him to change his oath than to fulfil it.

It is best to break an ill oath.

Whereupon Saint Ambrose saith: "It is sometime contrary to a man's duty to perform the oath that he hath promised, as Herod did[2]." Isidore also saith: "In evil promises break thine oath; in a naughty vow change thy purpose. The thing thou hast unadvisedly vowed, do not perform. The promise is wicked that is finished with mischief[3]." And again, "That oath must not be kept, whereby any evil is unwarily promised. As if, for example, one should give his

[1 veritatique per omnia consentaneam, Lat.]

[2 Est etiam contra officium nonnunquam solvere promissum, sacramentum custodire: ut Herodes, &c.—Ambros. de Offic. apud Gratian. Decret. Par. 1583. Decr. sec. par. caus. xxii. Quæst. 4. can. 2. col. 1574.]

[3 In malis promissis rescinde fidem: in turpi voto muta decretum: quod incaute vovisti, ne facias. Impia enim est promissio, quæ scelere adimpletur.—Isidor. in Synon. Lib. ii. ap. Gratian. Decret. ibid. can. 4. col. 1575. See also Becon's Works, Parker Soc. ed. Vol. i. p. 372.]

faith to an adulteress to abide in naughtiness with her for
ever : undoubtedly it is more tolerable not to keep promise,
than to remain in whoredom still[4]." Beda moreover saith :
"If it shall happen, that we at unawares shall with an oath
promise anything, and that the keeping of that oath shall be
the cause of further evil, then let us think it best upon better
advice to change our oath without hurt to our conscience; and
that it is better, upon such a necessity, for us to be forsworn,
than, for avoiding of perjury, to fall into another sin ten times
worse than that. David sware by God, that he would kill
the foolish fellow Nabal ; but at the first intercession that his
wife Abigal, wiser than himself, did make, he ceased to
threaten him, he sheathed his sword again, and did not find
himself any whit grieved for breaking his hasty oath[5]."
Augustine also saith : "Whereas David did not by shedding of
blood perform his promise bound with an oath, therein his
godliness was the greater[6]." "David sware rashly, but, upon
better and godly advice, he performed not the thing he had
sworn[7]." By this and the like it is declared, that many oaths
are not to be observed. Now he that sweareth so doth
sin : but in changing his oath he doth very well. He that
changeth not such an oath, committeth a double sin; first, for
swearing as he ought not, and then for doing that he should

[4 Non est observandum juramentum, quo malum incaute promit-
titur: veluti si quispiam adulteræ perpetuam cum ea permanendi
fidem polliceatur. Tolerabilius est enim non implere sacramentum,
quam permanere in stupri flagitio.—Isidor. ap. Gratian. Decret. ibid.
can. 13. col. 1576.]

[5 Si aliquid forte nos incautius jurasse contigerit, quod obser-
vatum pejorem vergat in exitum, libere illud consilio salubriore mu-
tandum noverimus, ac magis instante necessitate pejerandum nobis,
quam pro vitando perjurio in aliud crimen gravius esse divertendum.
Denique juravit David per Dominum occidere Nabal, virum stultum et
impium—sed ad primam intercessionem Abigail feminæ prudentis
mox remisit minas ; revocavit ensem in vaginam ; neque aliquid culpæ
se tali perjurio contraxisse doluit.—Beda in Homil. xliv. in natal.
decoll. S. Joan. ap. Gratian. Decret. ibid. can. 6. col. 1575.]

[6 Quod David juramentum per sanguinis effusionem non implevit,
major pietas fuit.—Augustin. ap. Gratian. Decret. ibid. can. 3. col.
1574.   See Becon, Vol. I. p. 374.]

[7 Juravit temere, sed non implevit jurationem majore pietate.—
Gratian. ibid. can. 4. col. 1575, and August. Serm. Opp. Par. 1531.
Tom. x. fol. 304.]

not. Thus much hitherto have I rehearsed of other men's words, which all men verily acknowledge to be true and so indeed. Now by this ye do easily understand, dearly beloved, what ye have to think of those monastical vows and priests' oaths, which promise chastity, (no farther, I wis, by their leave, than man's frail weakness will suffer them.) "For it is better," saith the apostle, "to marry than to burn[1]." And more commendable is it not to perform those foolish, hurtful, and unpure promises, that drive them perforce to filthy uncleanness, than, under the colour of keeping an oath truly, to lie and to live unchastely, God wot[2].

Monastical vows.

Fifthly and lastly, I have briefly to put you in mind, that ye endeavour yourselves, by all the means ye may, devoutly to keep that which ye swear; and therewithal, in few words, to let you understand what reward is prepared for them that do religiously and holily keep and observe the holy oath once solemnly taken. If we love God, if we desire to sanctify his name, if we take the true God for the very true God, and for our God; if we will have him to be gentle and merciful to us-ward, and to be our present deliverer and aider at all assays; then will we have a most diligent care to swear with fear devoutly, and holily to keep and perform the oath that we devoutly make. But unless we do this, then terrible threatenings and sharp revengement of God's just judgment are thundered from heaven against us transgressors. The very heathens shall rise up and condemn us in the day of judgment. For the Saguntines, the Numantines, and they of Petilia, chose rather to die with fire and famine, than to break or violate their promise once bound with an oath[3]. Moreover, the laws of all wise and civil princes and people do adjudge perjured persons to die the death. How great offences, how great corruptions, how great and many mischiefs, I pray you, do rise through perjuries! They entangle, trouble, disgrace, mar, and overthrow the estates, both civil and ecclesiastical. Whosoever, therefore, doth love the commonweal and safeguard of his country; whosoever doth love the church and

How religiously we ought to keep our oaths.

[1 1 Cor. vii. 9.]   [2 parum pudice vivere, Lat.]
[3 Liv. Lib. xxi. cap. 14, and xxiii. capp. 20, 30; Florus, Lib. ii. cap. 18; Valer. Max. Lib. vii. cap. 6. See also early writings of Hooper, Parker Soc. ed. page 336, and Augustin. de Civit. Dei. Lib. iii. cap. 20.]

good estate thereof; he will, above all things, have an especial regard to keep religiously the promise of his oath. Now to those that holily do keep their oaths, the Lord doth promise a large reward. For Jeremy saith: " And the nations shall bless themselves in him, and in him shall they glory[4]." As if he should say: If the people of Juda shall swear holily and keep their oaths, then will the Lord pour out upon them so great felicity and abundant plenty of all good things, that, when as hereafter one shall bless or wish well to another, he shall say, " The Lord shew thee his blessing, as of old he did to the Jews." And whosoever shall praise another, he shall say that " he is like to the Israelites." It is therefore assuredly certain, that they shall be enriched with all good things, and worthy of all manner praise, whosoever shall inviolably keep their oaths and promises.

Let us endeavour ourselves, my brethren, I beseech you, to sanctify the Lord's name, and to add to this third commandment your earnest and continual prayers, saying, as our Lord Jesus hath taught us, O heavenly Father, hallowed be thy name; or, let thy name be holily worshipped. To him be glory for ever and ever. Amen.

A large reward promised to such as keep their oaths.

OF THE FOURTH PRECEPT OF THE FIRST TABLE[5], THAT IS, OF THE ORDER AND KEEPING OF THE SABBATH-DAY.

THE FOURTH SERMON.

THE fourth commandment of the first table is word for word as followeth : " Remember that thou keep holy the sabbath-day. Six days thou shalt labour, and do all thy works ; but on the seventh day is the sabbath of the Lord thy God, in which thou shalt not do any manner of work, neither thou, nor thy son, nor thy daughter, nor thy manservant, nor thy maid-servant, nor thy cattle, nor thy stranger which is within thy gates. Because in six days the Lord

The fourth precept.

[4 Jer. iv. 2.]   [5 seu Decalogi, Lat. omitted.]

made heaven and earth, the sea, and all that is therein; and rested the seventh day : therefore the Lord blessed the sabbath-day, and hallowed it."

The order of the Lord's command-ments. The order, which the Lord useth in giving these commandments, is natural and very excellent. In the first precept the Lord did teach us faith and love to God-ward. In the second he removed from us idols and all foreign kind of worship. In the third he began to instruct us in the true and lawful worship of God: which worship standeth in the sanctifying of his holy name, for us to call thereon, and holily and freely to praise it, and to think and speak of it as religiously as he shall give us grace[1]. The fourth commandment teacheth us also the worship due to God, and the hallowing of his holy name; but yet it bendeth somewhat to the outward honour, although, nevertheless, it frameth to the inward religion. For the sabbath doth belong both to the

The sabbath. inward and outward service of God. Let us see, therefore, what we have to think that the sabbath is, how far forth the use thereof extendeth, and after what sort we have to worship our God in observing the sabbath. Sabbath doth signify rest and ceasing from servile work[2]. And this here I think worthy to be noted, that the Lord saith not simply, " Sanctify the sabbath;" but, " Remember that thou keep holy the sabbath-day;" meaning thereby, that the sabbath was of old ordained, and given first of all to the ancient fathers, and then again renewed by the Lord, and beaten into the memory of the people of Israel. But the sum of the whole commandment is, Keep holy the sabbath-day. This sum doth the Lord by and by more largely amplify, by reckoning up the very days, and particular rehearsing the whole household, to whom the keeping of the sabbath is given in charge[3].

The sabbath is spiritual. The sabbath itself hath sundry significations. For first of all, the scripture maketh mention of a certain spiritual and continual sabbath. In this sabbath we rest from servile work, in abstaining from sin, and doing our best not to have

---

[1] "as he shall give us grace," not in the original.]

[2] שַׁבָּת a cessation, rest.—Lee's Hebr. Lex. in voc.]

[3] Postremo adjicitur exemplum quoque ipsius Dei quiescentis et sanctificantis sabbatum. " Lastly is added also the example of God himself resting on the Sabbath-day and sanctifying it." Omitted by the translator. P.]

our own will found in ourselves, or to work our own works; but, in ceasing from these, to suffer God to work in us, and wholly to submit our bodies to the government of his good Spirit. After this sabbath followeth that eternal sabbath and everlasting rest, of which Esay, in his 58th and 66th chapters, speaketh very much, and Paul also, in the fourth to the Hebrews. But God is truly worshipped, when we, ceasing from evil, and obeying God's holy Spirit, do exercise ourselves in the study of good works. At this time I have no leisure, neither do I think that it is greatly profitable for me, to reason, as largely or as exquisitely as I could, of the allegorical sabbath, or spiritual rest. Let us rather, my brethren, in these our mortal bodies, do our endeavour, with an unwearied good-will of holiness, to sanctify the sabbath, that pleaseth the Lord so well.

Secondly, the sabbath is the outward institution of our religion. For it pleased the Lord, in this commandment, to teach us an outward religion and kind of worship, wherein he would have us all to be exercised. Now, for because the worshipping of God cannot be without a time, therefore hath the Lord appointed a certain time, wherein we should abstain from outward or bodily works; but so yet that we should have leisure to attend unto our spiritual business. For for that cause is the outward rest commanded, that the spiritual work should not be hindered by the bodily business. Moreover, that spiritual labour among our fathers was chiefly spent about four things; to wit, about public reading and expounding of the scriptures, and so consequently, about the hearing of the same; about public prayers and common petitions; about sacrifices, or the administration of the sacraments; and lastly, about the gathering of every man's benevolence. In these consisted the outward religion of the sabbath. For the people kept holy day, and met together in holy assemblies; where the prophets read to them the word of the Lord, expounding it, and instructing the hearers in the true religion. Then did the faithful jointly make their common prayers and supplications for all things necessary for their behoof. They praised the name of the Lord, and gave him thanks for all his good benefits bestowed upon them. Furthermore, they did offer sacrifices, as the Lord commanded them, celebrating the mysteries and sacraments of Christ

The sabbath is the outward institution of religion.

their Redeemer, and keeping their faith exercised and in
ure: they were joined in one with these sacraments, and
also warned of their duty, which is, to offer themselves a
lively sacrifice to the Lord their God. Lastly, they did in
the congregation liberally bestow the gifts of their good-will
to the use of the church: they gathered every man's benevolence, therewith to supply the church's necessity, to maintain the ministers, and to relieve the poor and needy. These
were the holy works of God, which while they, having their
hearts instructed in faith and love, did fulfil, they did therein
rightly sanctify the sabbath and the name of the Lord; that
is, they did on the sabbath those kind [of] works[1], which do
both sanctify the name of God, become his worshippers, and
also are the works indeed that are holy and pleasing in the
sight of God. If any man require a substantial and evident
example of the sabbath or holy day thus holily celebrated,
he shall find it in the eighth chapter of the book of Nehemias: for there the priests do read and expound the word
of God, they praise the name of the Lord, they pray with
the people, they offer sacrifice, they shew their liberality,
and do in all points behave themselves holily and devoutly as
they should.

There is
time enough
allowed to
labour in.

Now, lest any peradventure might make this objection
and say, Ease breedeth vice[2]; or else, I must labour with my
hands to get my living, lest I die with hunger, and my
family perish; he answereth, The Lord alloweth thee time
sufficient for thy labour, for thee to work in to get a living
for thyself and thy household: for six days thou mayest
work, but the seventh day doth the Lord challenge and require to be consecrated to him and his holy rest. Every
week hath seven days: but of those seven the Lord requireth
but one for himself. Who then can rightly complain, I beseech you, or say that he hath injury done unto him?
More time is allowed to work in, than to keep holy the
sabbath: and he that requireth to have this sabbath kept
is God, the maker, the father, and Lord of all mankind.

The master
of the house
must teach
all his family
the keeping
of the sab-
bath-day.

Furthermore, the Lord doth precisely command and give
a charge to plant and bring in this holy rest, this discipline
and outward worship, into the whole family of every several
house. Whereby we gather, what the duty of a good house-

[1 ea operabantur opera, Lat.]   [2 otia dant vitia, Lat.]

holder is; to wit, to have a care to see all his family keep holy the sabbath-day; that is, to do on the sabbath-day those good works which I have before rehearsed. And for because the Lord doth know that man's natural disposition is, where it hath the mastery, there for the most part to rule and reign over-haughtily and too too princelike; therefore, lest peradventure the fathers or masters should deal too hardly or rigorously with their households, or hinder them in observing of the sabbath, he doth in express words and exquisite steps of enumeration command them to allow their family, and every one in their family, a resting time to accomplish his holy service. He doth not exempt or except so much as the stranger. He will not suffer nor allow among them the example of such dullheads[3] as say: "Let faith and religion be free to all; let no man be compelled to any religion." For he commandeth to bind the stranger within the gates of God's people, that is, the stranger that dwelleth in their jurisdiction, to the holy observing of the sabbath-day.

Now, this ease or rest is not commanded in respect of *Ease or rest.* itself, (for idleness always hath been found fault withal,) but it is ordained for the aforesaid especial causes. God's pleasure is, that there should be a place and time reserved for religion: which time and place are not open to them that are busy about bodily and outward works. He is not conversant in the congregation, he heareth not the word of God, he prayeth not with the church, neither is he partaker of the sacraments, which at his master's commandment taketh a journey, or in the market selleth his wares, or in the barn doth thrash or winnow his corn, or in the field doth hedge or ditch, or doth stand at home beating the anvil, or else sitteth still sewing shoes or hosen[4]. Faith, therefore, and religion bid thee to give rest to thy servants and family; yea, they command thee to egg and compel them, if they be slow, to the holy and profitable work of the Lord. Moreover, the Lord's mind is, that they which labour should also refresh and re-create themselves:

> For things that lack a resting time
> Can never long endure[5].

[3 segnium, Lat.]   [4 caligas, Lat.]
[5 Quod caret alterna requie durabile non est, Lat.—Ovid. Ep. IV. 89.]

[BULLINGER.]

17

Wherefore the bountiful Lord, whose mind is to preserve his creatures, doth teach a way to keep them, and doth diligently provide, that his creatures be not too much afflicted by the hard handling or covetousness of their owners. Moses in Deuteronomy addeth the pitiful affection of mercy, saying: "Remember, that once thou thyself wast a servant in the land of Egypt[1]." Charity, therefore, and civil humanity do crave a measure to be kept, so that we do not with endless labours overlade and weary our household servants. Moreover, it is manifest, that the good man of the house[2], by planting godliness in his family, doth not a little advance and set forward his private profit and own commodity: for wicked servants are for the most part pickers[3] and deceitful; whereas, on the other side, the godly are faithful, whom in his absence he may trust to govern his house. In the reckoning up of the household also is mention made of beasts and cattle; which is done, not so much because their owner is a man and ought therefore to use them remissly and moderately, as for because beasts cannot be laboured without the working hand of man to guide them: so then men are drawn from the solemnizing of the sabbath-day by helping their cattle. Wherefore, to the intent that they should not be drawn aside, we are here precisely commanded to allow our cattle that resting time.

The Lord did keep the sabbath-day. Last of all, the Lord doth add his own example, whereby he teacheth us to keep holy the sabbath-day. "Because," saith he, "in six days the Lord made heaven and earth, the sea, and all that in them is, and rested the seventh day: therefore the Lord blessed the seventh day, and hallowed it." The Lord our God wrought six days in creating heaven and earth, the sea, and all that in them is; and the seventh day he rested, and ordained that to be an appointed time for us to rest in. On the seventh day we must think of the works that God did in the six days: the children of God must call to remembrance what and how great benefits they have received the whole week, for which they must thank God, for which they must praise God, and by which they must learn God. We

[1 Deut. v. 15.]
[2 paterfamilias, Lat.; an old term for the master of the house.— Toone's Glossary.   Cf. Matt. xxiv. 43.]
[3 furaces, Lat.]

must then dedicate to him our whole body and soul; we must consecrate to him all our words and our deeds. As that day the Lord did rest from creating, but he ceased not still to preserve; so we upon that day must rest from handy and bodily works, but we must not cease from the works of well doing and worshipping of God. Furthermore, the heavenly[4] rest was no prejudice at all to the things created: neither shall the holy day, or sabbath, spent in God's service, be any let or hinderance to our affairs or business. For the Lord blessed the sabbath-day; and therefore shall he bless thee and thy house, all thy affairs and business, if he shall see thee to have a care to sanctify his sabbath; that is, to do those works which he hath commanded to be done on the sabbath-day. They therefore do err from the truth as far as heaven is wide, whosoever do despise the religion and holy rest of the sabbath-day, calling it an idle ease, and do labour on the sabbath-day, as they do on working days, under the pretence of care for their family and necessity's sake.

The Lord blessed the sabbath-day.

For all these things must we apply to ourselves and our churches. It is most sure, that to Christians the spiritual sabbath is given in charge especially and above all things. Neither is it to be doubted, but that the good Lord's will is, that even in our churches at this day, as well as of the Jews of old, there should be kept and appointed order in all things, but especially in the exercising of outward religion. We know that the sabbath is ceremonial, so far forth as it is joined to sacrifices and other Jewish ceremonies, and so far forth as it is tied to a certain time: but in respect that on the sabbath-day religion and true godliness are exercised and published, that a just and seemly order is kept in the church, and that the love of our neighbour is thereby preserved, therein, I say, it is perpetual, and not ceremonial. Even at this day, verily, we must ease and bear with our family[5]; and even at this day we must instruct our family in the true religion and fear of God. Christ our Lord did no where scatter abroad the holy congregations, but did, as much as he could, gather them together. Now, as there ought to be an appointed place, so likewise must there be a prescribed time, for the outward exercise of religion, and so, consequently, an holy rest. They of the primitive church,

The Christian sabbath.

The Sunday.

[4 quies divina, Lat.]   [5 parci familiæ, Lat.]

17—2

therefore, did change the sabbath-day, lest, peradventure, they should have seemed to have imitated the Jews, and still to have retained their order and ceremonies[1]; and made their assemblies and holy restings to be on the first day of sabbaths[2], which John calleth Sunday[3], or the Lord's day[4], because of the Lord's glorious resurrection upon that day. And although we do not in any part of the apostles' writings find any mention made that this Sunday was commanded us to be kept holy; yet, for because, in this fourth precept of the first table, we are commanded to have a care of religion and the exercising of outward godliness, it would be against all godliness and christian charity, if we should deny to sanctify the Sunday: especially, since the outward worship of God cannot consist without an appointed time and space of holy rest.

I suppose also, that we ought to think the same of those few feasts and holy days, which we keep holy to Christ our

Christmas day, New-year's day, Good-Friday, Easter day, Ascension day, Whit-sunday.

Lord, in memory of his nativity or incarnation, of his circumcision, of his passion, of the resurrection and ascension of Jesus Christ our Lord into heaven, and of his sending of the Holy Ghost upon his disciples[5]. For christian liberty is not a licentious power and dissolving of godly ecclesiastical ordinances, which advance and set forward the glory of God and love of our neighbour. But for because the Lord will have holy days to be solemnized and kept to himself alone, I do not therefore like of the festival days that are held in honour of any creatures. This glory and worship is due to God alone. Paul saith: " I would not that any man should judge you in part of an holy day, or of the sabbaths, which are a shadow of things to come[6]." And again: " Ye observe days, and months, and years, and times; I fear lest I have laboured in you in vain[7]." And therefore we at this day,

[1 See Ignatii, Epist. ad Magnes. cap. 8 and 9.]
[2 prima sabbati, Lat.]　　　　　　　　[3 Rev. i. 10.]
[4 haud dubie, Lat.; omitted.]
[5 Nostra ecclesia ante annos, ni fallor, 12, plura habuit festa: sed abrogatis his solum retinuit diem Dominicam, et festa Christi, Nativitatis videlicet, Circumcisionis et Ascensionis D. Adjecit et missionem Spiritus Sancti superioribus propter celebrationem cœnæ D.—Bullinger. Ep. ad Calvin. in Calv. Opp. Tom. IX. p. 63. Ed. Amstel. dat. Tigur. 29 August. MDLI.]
[6 Coloss. ii. 16, 17. See authorised version, marginal reading.]
[7 Galat. iv. 10, 11.]

that are in the church of Christ, have nothing to do with the Jewish observation; we have only to wish and endeavour to have the christian observation and exercise of christian religion to be freely kept and observed.

And yet, as the hallowing of the Jewish sabbath, so also the sanctifying or exercise of our Sunday, must be spent and occupied about four things, which ought to be found in the holy congregation of Christians, if their Sunday be truly sanctified and kept holy as it should be. First, let all the godly saints assemble themselves together in the congregation. Let there in that congregation so assembled be preached the word of God; let the Gospel there be read, that the hearers may learn thereby what they have to think of God, what the duty and office is of them that worship God, and how they ought to sanctify the name of the Lord. Then let there in that congregation be made prayers and supplications for all the necessities of all people. Let the Lord be praised for his goodness, and thanked for his inestimable benefits which he daily bestoweth. Then, if time, occasion, and custom of the church do so require, let the sacraments of the church be religiously ministered. For nothing is more required in this fourth commandment than that we should holily observe, and devoutly exercise, the sacraments, and holy, lawful, profitable, and necessary rites and ceremonies of the church. Last of all, let entire humanity and liberality have a place in the saints' assembly; let all learn to give alms privately, and relieve the poor daily, and to do it frankly and openly, so often as opportunity of time and causes of need shall so require. And these are the duties, wherein the Lord's sabbath is kept holy even in the church of Christians; and so much the rather, if to these be added an earnest good will to do no evil all the day long.

This discipline now must be brought in and established by every householder in all our several houses, with as great diligence as it was with the Jews. Touching which thing I have nothing to say here, since I have before so plainly handled this point, as that ye perceive that it agreeth even to the church of us that are Christians. This one thing I add more; that it is the duty of a christian magistrate, or at leastwise of a good householder, to compel to amendment the breakers and contemners of God's sabbath and worship. The peers of

The sanctification of the christian sabbath.

The office of every householder.

Numb. xv.

Israel, and all the people of God, did stone to death (as the
Lord commanded them) the man that disobediently did gather
sticks on the sabbath-day[1]. Why then should it not be
lawful for a christian magistrate to punish by bodily imprisonment, by loss of goods, or by death, the despisers of religion,
of the true and lawful worship done to God, and of the
sabbath-day? Verily, though the foolish and indiscreet
magistrate[2] in this corrupted age do slackly look to his office
and duty; yet notwithstanding, let every householder do his
endeavour to keep his several family from that ungodly
naughtiness; let him punish them of his household by such
means as he lawfully may. For if any one householder
dwell among idolaters, which neither have, nor yet desire to
have or frequent, the christian or lawful congregations; then
may he in his own several house gather a peculiar assembly
to praise the Lord, as it is manifest that Lot did among the
Sodomites; Abraham, Isaac, and Jacob, in the land of Canaan,
and in Egypt. But it is a heinous sin and a detestable
schism, if the congregation be assembled, either in cities or
villages, for thee then to seek out byways to hide thyself,
and not to come there, but to contemn the church of God
and assembly of saints: as the Anabaptists have taken an use
to do.

The abuses of the sabbath-day.   Here therefore I have to reckon[3] up the abuses of the
sabbath-day, or the sins committed against this command-
ment. They transgress this commandment, that cease not
from evil works, but[4] abuse the sabbath's rest to the provoking of fleshly pleasures. For they keep the sabbath to
God, but work to the devil, in dicing, in drinking, in dancing,
and feeding their humours with the vanities of this world,
whereby we are not only drawn from the company of the
holy congregation, but do also defile our bodies, which we
ought rather to sanctify and keep holy. They sin against
this precept, which either exercise any handy occupation on
the sabbath-day, or else lie wrapt in bed and fast asleep till
the day be almost spent, not once thinking to make one of
God's congregation. They offend in this precept, that awe
their servants to work, and by appointing them to other

[1 Numb. xv. 32—36.]
[2 si cesset demens et ebrius magistratus, Lat.]
[3 paucis recensendi, Lat.]   [4 imo, Lat.]

business do draw them from the worship of God, preferring other stinking things[5] before the honour due to God. And they, above all other, offend herein, which do not only not keep holy the sabbath-day themselves, but do also, with their ungodly scoffs and evil examples, cause other to despise and set light by religion ; when they do disdain and mock at the holy rites and ceremonies, at the ministery, ministers, sacred churches[6], and godly exercises. And herein, too, do both the good-men and good-wives offend, if they be slack in their own houses to call upon and to see their families keep holy the sabbath-day. Whosoever do contemn the holiness of the sabbath-day, they give a flat and evident testimony of their ungodliness and light regard of God's mighty power.

Furthermore, the keeping or despising of the sabbath doth always carry with it either ample rewards or terrible threats. For the proof whereof, I will recite unto you, dearly beloved, the words of Jeremy, in his seventeenth chapter. "Thus hath the Lord said unto me," saith he; " Go, and stand under the gate of the sons of the people, through which the kings of Juda go in and out, and under all the gates of Jerusalem, and say unto them : Take heed for your lives, that ye carry no burthen upon you on the sabbath-day, to bring it through the gates of Jerusalem, and that ye bear no burthen out of your houses on the sabbath-day : look that ye do no labour therein ; but keep holy the sabbath-day, as I commanded your fathers. Howbeit, they obeyed me not, neither harkened they unto me, but were obstinate and stubborn, and would not receive any correction. Nevertheless, if ye will hear me, saith the Lord, and bear no burthen through this gate upon the sabbath, but hallow the sabbath, so that ye do no work therein ; then shall there go through the gates of this city kings and princes that shall sit upon the throne of David ; they shall be carried upon chariots, and ride upon horses, both they and their princes : there shall come men from the cities of Juda and the land of Benjamin, which shall bring sacrifices, and shall offer incense and thanksgiving in the house of the Lord. But if ye will not be obedient unto me to hallow the sabbath, so that ye will bear your burthens through the gates upon the sabbath-day ; then will I set fire upon the gates of Jerusalem, which shall burn up the great

Promises and threatenings added to the sabbath-day.

[5 res putidas, Lat.]   [6 scholas sacras, Lat.]

The empe-
ror's law for
the keeping
of the sab-
bath.
houses thereof, and shall not be quenched." Very justly,
therefore, did the devout princes, Leo and Anthemius, writing
to Arsemius, their lieutenant, in these words give charge:
"That the holy days, ordained in honour of the high God's
majesty, should not be spent in any voluptuous pleasures,
nor be unhallowed with troublesome exactions. We therefore do decree and ordain, that the Lord's day, or Sunday, as it hath always been accounted well of, so it shall
still be had in estimation; so that upon that day no office of
the law shall be executed, no man shall be summoned, no man
arrested for suretyship, no man attached, no pleading shall be
heard, nor any judgment pronounced," &c. And by and by
after again: " Neither do we, in giving this rest of the holy
day, suffer any man to wallow in any kind of wanton pleasures
at all. For on that day stage-plays are not admitted, nor
fencers' prizes, nor bear-baitings; yea too, and if it happen
that the solemnizing of our birth-day fall upon the Sunday,
then shall it be deferred till the next day after. And we
have determined, that he shall sustain the loss of his dignity,
and have his patrimony confiscate, whosoever shall on the sabbath-day be present at any sight or play, or what summoner
soever of any judge whatsoever shall, under the pretence of
any business, either public or private, do anything to infringe
the statutes in this law enacted[1]."

And yet, nevertheless, they that are Christians do not for-

[1 Impp. Leo et Anthemius. A. A. Armasio. P. P. x.—Dies festos,
majestati altissimæ dedicatos, nullis volumus voluptatibus occupari,
nec ullis exactionum vexationibus profanari.   Dominicum itaque
diem semper honorabilem decernimus venerandum, ut a cunctis exe-
cutionibus excusetur; nulla quenquam urgeat admonitio; nulla fidei-
jussionis flagitetur exactio; taceat apparitio; advocatio delitescat; sit
ille dies a cognitionibus alienus, &c.—Nec hujus tamen religiosi diei
otia relaxantes, obscœnis quibuslibet patimur voluptatibus detineri.
Nihil eodem die vindicet sibi scena theatralis, aut Circense certamen,
aut ferarum lacrymosa spectacula: etiam si in nostro ortu aut natali
celebranda solennitas inciderit, differatur.   Amissionem militiæ pro-
scriptionemque patrimonii sustinebit, si quis unquam hoc die festo
spectaculis interesse, vel cujuscunque judicis apparitor, prætextu ne-
gotii publici seu privati, hæc, quæ lege hac statuta sunt, crediderit
temeranda.——D. Id. Decembr. Constantinop. Zenone et Martiano
Coss.—Justin. Cod. Lib. III. tit. 22. de feriis. p. 411. Tom. I. Lugd.
1551.]

get the words of Christ in the gospel, where he saith : " The The sabbath made for sabbath was made for man, and not man for the sabbath ; and man, and not man for the that[2] the Son of man too is Lord of the sabbath[3]." The sabbath. godly do very well know that God ordained the sabbath for the preservation, and not for the destruction, of mankind ; and that therefore he doth dispense with us for the sabbath, as often as any urgent necessity or saving of a man shall seem to require it. Touching which matter our Saviour Christ himself hath fully satisfied the faithful in the 12th of Matthew, and the 6th and 13th chapters after St Luke. In such things, verily, Christians may use their liberty to occupy themselves in on the sabbath-day[4]. Since the priests and Levites are held excused, which do in the temple openly both kill, slay, burn, and boil beasts, in making their sacrifices, so that they are not thought to break the sabbath-day, because they may without offence to God, even on the sabbaths, dress and make ready the things serving to the outward worship of the Lord ; so likewise may we on the sabbath dress and make ready meat and other necessaries which our bodies cannot lack. We may also minister physic to the sick, visit the weak, and help the needy, that so we may preserve the creature of God. Herein did our Saviour give us an example to follow, who did on the sabbath work the deeds of charity and mercy. We have more than one example of his to be seen in the gospel, but especially in Luke vi. and xiii. and John, the fifth chapter. If then on the sabbath-day it be lawful to draw out of a pit a sheep or an ox in danger of drowning, why should it not be lawful likewise on the sabbath to underset with props a ruinous house that is ready to fall? Why should it not be lawful on the sabbath-day to gather in, and keep from spoiling, the hay or corn, which, by reason of unseasonable weather, hath lain too long abroad, and likely to be worse if it stay any longer? The holy emperor Constantine, writing to Elpidius, saith : " Let all judges in courts of law, and citizens of all occupations, rest upon the Sunday, and keep it holy with reverence and devotion. But they that inhabit the country may freely To plough land on the and at liberty attend on their tillage upon the sabbath-day. sabbath-day. For oftentimes it falleth out, that they cannot upon another day so commodiously sow their seed, or plant their vines ; and

[2 proinde, Lat.]   [3 Mark ii. 27, 28.]
[4 Certe in his versatur libertas Christiana, Lat.]

so, by letting pass the opportunity of a little time, they may hap to lose the profit given of God for our provision[1]." Thus saith the emperor. Now we must consider, that he doth not license husbandmen by all kind of toil continually to defile the sabbath-day. For of the countrymen, as well as of the towns-men, are looked for due honour done to God, and the keeping of the fourth commandment: only this must be remembered, that liberty is granted in causes of necessity. But a godly mind and charity shall be excellent dispensers and mistresses to lead us in such cases as these, lest, under the coloured pre-tence of liberty and necessity, we do deeds not to be borne withal on the sabbath-day, and exercise the works of greedy covetousness, and not of sincere holiness. And thus much had I to say touching the second use of the sabbath-day.

God doth sanctify or make holy.

Thirdly, the sabbath hath a very ample or large significa-tion. For it is a perpetual sign that God alone is he that sanctifieth those that worship his name. For thus saith the Lord to Moses : " Ye shall keep my sabbaths, because it is a sign betwixt me and you to them that come after you, to know that I am the Lord which sanctify you ;" and so forth, as it is to be seen in the 31st of Exodus, and is again repeated in the 20th of Ezechiel[2]. And to this end doth the Lord mutually apply himself[3], as is before said in the declaration of the sabbath's second use and signification. For God doth by his Holy Spirit sanctify his faithful folk and constant believers: which he declareth unto the church by the preaching of the gospel, bearing witness thereunto and sealing it with his sacraments; so that he commandeth us with continual prayers incessantly to crave of him that glorious sanctification. All which things, verily, are practised and put in use upon the sabbath-days especially, to the intent that we may be sancti-fied of God, who is the only sanctifier of us all.

Hitherto have I declared unto you, dearly beloved, as

[1 Imp. Constantinus. A. Elpidio. III.—Omnes judices urbanæque plebes, et cunctarum artium officia, venerabili die solis quiescant. Ruri tamen positi agrorum culturæ libere licenterque inserviant: quo-niam frequenter evenit ut non alio die aptius frumenta sulcis et vineæ scrobibus commendentur; et ne occasione momenti pereat commo-ditas cœlesti provisione concessa.—D. Non. Mart. Crispo II. et Con-stantino II. Coss.—Cod. Just. Lib. III. tit. 12. de feriis. p. 409.]

[2 Exod. xxxi. 13; Ezek. xx. 12.]

[3 mutuam operam confert, Lat.]

briefly as I could, the first table of God's commandments, wherein we have very exquisitely laid down before us the worship due to the name of God. But for because they are not the children of God, which know his mind, but they that do it, let us beseech our heavenly Father so to illuminate our minds, that we may faithfully and indeed worship our Lord and God, who is to be praised world without end. Amen.

OF THE FIRST PRECEPT OF THE SECOND TABLE, WHICH
IS IN ORDER THE FIFTH OF THE TEN COM-
MANDMENTS, TOUCHING THE HONOUR
DUE TO PARENTS.

THE FIFTH SERMON.

Now followeth the second table of God's law, which (by the help of God's Holy Spirit) I will declare as briefly unto you as I have already gone through the first. And as the first contained the love of God, so doth the second teach us the charity due to our neighbour; instructing all men what they owe every one to his neighbour, and how we may in this world live honestly, civilly, and in quiet peace among ourselves. For our good God would have us to live well and quietly. But we that will not know how to live well, nor yet obey his good commandments, do with our sins and iniquities never cease to heap upon our own pates an infinite multitude of miserable calamities.

This table containeth six commandments; the first whereof is, "Honour thy father and thy mother, that thy days may be long in the land which the Lord thy God shall give thee." Very well and rightly doth the Lord begin the second table with the honouring of our parents. For after our duty to God, the next is the reverent love that we owe to our parents, of whom, next after God, we have our life, and by whom we are from our infancy brought up with incredible care and exceeding great labour. Now the very order of nature doth require, that the most excellent and dearest things should always have the first and chiefest place.

And that this commandment may the more easily be un-

The fifth precept.

derstood, I mean to divide my treatise thereof into three parts:
In the first whereof I will declare what degrees and kinds of
men are comprehended under the name of parents: secondarily, I will search out what kind of honour that is, and how
far it extendeth, which the Lord commandeth to give to our
parents: and lastly, I will both touch the promise made to
godly children, and thereupon conjecture and gather the punishment appointed for the ungodly and disobedient offspring.

What is meant by the name of parents. There is none so ignorant but knoweth what parents are.
The Lord our God hath given us them for us to take of them
our beginning of life, that they might nourish and bring us up,
and that of rude and almost brutish things they might make
us very men.   Greater are the good turns that parents do for
their children, greater is the cost and labour that they bestow
on them, and greater is the care, grief, and trouble which
they take for them, than any man, however eloquent soever
he be, is able to express.   And here is not the name of the
father only, but also the name of the mother in express words
set down in the law, lest she peradventure should seem and
be contemptible without any offence to God, because of the
weakness of her frail sex.   The godly and virtuous mothers
do feel and abide more pain and grief in the bearing, bringing
up, and nourishing of their children, than the fathers do.   For
no small cause therefore have we the name of the mother
precisely expressed in this commandment.   We do also comprehend herein the grandfather and grandmother, the great
grandsire and great granddame, and all other like to these.
Our native country. In the second place we do contain every man's country wherein
he was born, which fed, fostered, adorned, and defended him.
Magistrates or rulers. Thirdly, we take princes and magistrates into the name and
title: for the senators and princes are in the holy scriptures
called the fathers and pastors of the people[1]. Xenophon was
persuaded, that a good prince did differ nothing from a good
Guardians or overseers of fatherless children. father[2].   Fourthly, there are to be reckoned under the name
of parents those guardians, which are usually called overseers
of fatherless children or orphans: for they supply the place
of departed parents, taking upon them the charge and defence

[1 2 Kings v. 13; Isai. xxii. 21, and xliv. 28; Jer. xii. 10, and xxv.
34; Micah v. 5.]

[2 Ἀλλὰ πολλάκις μὲν δὴ, ὦ ἄνδρες, καὶ ἄλλοτε κατενόησα, ὅτι ἄρχων
ἀγαθὸς οὐδὲν διαφέρει πατρὸς ἀγαθοῦ.—Xenoph. Cyrop. Lib. VII.]

of their children, whom they must (for that affection ought to be in them) bring up, defend, and advance, even as they would do to their own and those that they themselves did once beget. Among whom also we must make account of such masters and workmen, as teach them an art or occupation: for of them young men and striplings learn some honest science, for every one to get his living honestly; and by them they are taught good manners, being thereby, after a certain sort, out of rude unpolished stuff made perfect seemly men. Fifthly, *Ministers and pastors of the church.* the ministers, doctors, and pastors of the churches, are taken for parents, whom Paul himself did call by the name of fathers, not so much for the care and love wherewith they are affected toward the disciples and sheep of Christ his flock, as for because we are by them through the gospel begotten in Christ. In the sixth place, we must think of our cousins and *Cousins and kinsfolk.* kinsfolks, brother and sister, nephews and nieces, mother-in-law and daughter-in-law, father-in-law and son-in-law, who are by alliance knit together[3], as the members of the body are fastened with sinews. Finally, in the last place, old *Aged persons or old folks.* folks and widows, fatherless children and impotent weak persons, must be reputed among our parents: whose cause and tuition the Lord hath in more places than one commended unto us. So then, my brethren, here ye have heard who they be, that in this first precept of the second table we have to take for our parents, and who and how many are comprehended and commended to us under that name: and now shall ye hear what honour we owe to them, and what the honour is that we should attribute unto them.

To honour, in the scriptures, is diversely taken; but in *To honour, what it is.* this treatise it signifieth to magnify, to worship, to esteem well, and to do reverence as to a thing ordained by God; and also to acknowledge, to love, and to give praise as for a benefit received at God's hand, and as for a thing given from heaven, that is both holy, profitable, and necessary. To honour is to be dutiful and to obey; and so to obey, as if it were to God himself, by whom we know that our obedience is commanded, and to whom we are sure that our service is acceptable. Otherwise we have not in any cause to obey *The honour of God goeth always before.* either our parents or magistrates, if they themselves shall do, or else command us to do, the things that are wicked and

[3 et conservantur, Lat.; omitted.]

unjust. For still the latter commandments have a relation to those that went before. In the second commandment we learned, that God would visit the sins of the fathers in the children; and therefore children ought not to obey their parents, if they command anything contrary to God, or prejudicial to his law. Jonathan obeyed not his father Saul's commandment, who charged him to persecute David: and therefore is he worthily commended in the holy scriptures. The three companions of Daniel obeyed Nabuchodonosor in all that he said, they loved him, and reverenced him as a most mighty, puissant, and bountiful king; but, so soon once as he charged them to fall to idolatry, they set not a button by his commandment[1]. And St Peter, who taught us the honour and obedience that we owe to our parents and magistrates, when he was commanded by the princes and fathers of the people not to preach Christ crucified to the people any more, did answer them, that "we ought to obey God more than men[2]." But what need I thus to stand reckoning up this, when the Lord himself in one short sentence hath knit up this, and all other like to this? "If any man," saith he, "cometh to me, and hateth not his father and mother, his wife, his children, his brethren and sisters, yea, and his own life, he cannot be my disciple[3]." Furthermore, thou dost honour thy parents, when thou dost not contemptuously despise them, unthankfully neglect them, nor shamefully think scorn of them, if peradventure they happen to fall into adversity. Thou honourest thy parents, when with thine help and counsel thou aidest them in their old age and unwieldy crookedness[4]; when thou easest them in time of their need, or succourest them otherwise in any case else. For that indeed is the true and proper honour due to our parents, the Lord himself bearing witness thereunto in the 15th of Matthew, and concluding that we ought to provide and have a care for our parents, to save and defend them, and wholly to give ourselves and hazard our lives in their behalf.

And now, that this that I have said may be more easily and evidently understood, I will confer and apply this honour to those seven several kinds of men which we do comprehend

[1 tantum non contempserunt, Lat. Dan. i. and iii.]
[2 Acts v. 29.]   [3 Luke xiv. 26.]
[4 confectos diuturna ætate, Lat.]

under the name of parents; that thereby every one may see what, and how much, honour he ought to bestow upon his parents, his country, the magistrates therein, and those sorts of people that are afore named.

Whereas of duty we ought to honour our parents, that duty is paid, if we do so worshipfully esteem of them, as to think that they are given to us of God to the end that we should reverence, love, and always have an eye to them, although for nothing else, yet only for the Lord's sake; who is and doth think himself despised, so long as we go on to contemn our parents and to think vilely of them. Neither doth it make any matter to us, whether they be worthy or unworthy, whom the Lord commandeth us to honour. For be they as they may be, yet notwithstanding they did not, without the providence of God, chance to be our parents; in respect of which parentage the lawgiver himself will have them to be honoured. Whatsoever therefore children shall have occasion to speak to their parents, let it always savour of humble reverence and childly affection; and let them with such affection and reverence obey their parents. If they seem to us to be somewhat bitter and ungentle, yet let us wisely wink at, and not seem to know it, by little and little still declining from the evil, which by force they seem to compel us unto; and let us so discreetly handle the matter, that we may give them as small occasion as may be to be offended at us. We have Jonathas, the son of Saul, to be an example to us of a godly and obedient child. He did with great grief and trouble of mind behold his father's madness upon David, and wrongful dealing against himself; yet did he for that present discreetly sustain and wisely dissemble it, finding occasion at another time, and in a place convenient, to tell him of it: he never aided his father in any conceived mischief; he clave alway to the just man and righteous causes; he bewailed his father's stubbornness, and sought not over boldly to resist him and strive against him, when he offered to deal by violent extremity with him, but saved himself by flying away; and yet, for all this, he loved his father never the worse, but prayed still to God for his health and welfare, shewing himself in all things an obedient son to his crabbed father. This verily is the duty of a godly son. This ought every one of us most diligently to follow, in doing our duty and humble obeisance unto our parents, how froward

The honour due to parents.

or crooked soever they be.   Let none give a rough answer
stubbornly ; yea, let none so much as mumble an answer or
mutter against his parents.   Let none curse, or speak evil of,
his father or mother, unless he will perforce seek the way and
means to make the high and mighty[1] God's curse hang over
and light upon his pate.   If haply our parents be poor, if
misshapen in limbs, or otherwise diseased with any infirmity ;
let none of us therefore in mockery flout at or disdainfully
despise them.   Let us not shew ourselves unthankful to them,
to whom, for their good deeds to us-ward, we are of duty
bound for ever.   Let us nourish, cherish, and aid them in all
their necessities : yea, let us wholly bestow ourselves, and all
that we have, to do them good withal.   For all that we
possess undoubtedly is theirs ; and all that we have we enjoy
by them ; for if they were not, then should not we be.

Matt. xv. Let us here call to remembrance the charge that the Lord,
in Matthew, giveth us touching this commandment[2].   Let us
consider what is meant by the Gentiles' ἀντιπελαργεῖν[3], which
is, to requite one good turn with another ; and especially to
nourish and cherish them, by whom thou thyself in thy
youth wast brought up, and tendered[4].   There is, among the
Gentiles, a law extant, worthy to be called the mistress of
piety, whereby it is enacted, that the children should either
nourish their parents, or else lie fast fettered in prison[5].   This
law many men do carelessly neglect, which the stork alone,
among all living creatures, doth keep most precisely.   For
other creatures do hard and scarcely know or look upon
their parents, if peradventure they need their aid to nourish
The stork the
ensign of na-
tural love. them ; whereas the stork doth mutually nourish them, being

[1] justissimi, Lat.]
[2] Inspiciatur cap. 15, Lat. ; omitted.]
[3] ἀντιπελαργέω, to cherish in turn.   Liddell and Scott's Greek
and Eng. Lex. 2nd ed. Oxf. 1845, from πελαργός, a stork.   Metaphora a
ciconiis, quæ parentes senio jam confectos nutrire, et fessos ad terga
recipere, dicuntur ab Aristotl. Scapula. in voc. See also, Calvin. Opp.
ed. Amstel. Tom. I. p. 496, and Tom. II. p. 608.   Early Writings of
Hooper, Parker Soc. ed. page 359, and Erasm. Adag. Chil. p. 282.
Han. 1617.]
[4] ut cum liberi parentes ætate fessos vicissim alunt foventque,
Lat. ; omitted: as when children requite their aged parents by nourishing and cherishing them.]
[5] See Potter's Archæol. Græc. Book I. chap. 26. Vol. I. p. 181.
Lond. 1813.]

stricken in age, and bear them on her shoulders, when for feebleness they cannot fly.

There are to be seen among the Gentiles very religious and excellent sentences touching the honour due unto parents. Isocrates saith : "Shew thyself such an one to thy parents, as thou wouldest wish to have thy children shew themselves to thee[6]." Anaximenes said : "He loveth his father exceedingly well, which doth his endeavour to make him joyful without any trouble at all[7]." Plato also, in his Laws, thinketh, that "he hath a great treasure in his house, whosoever doth nourish at home in his house his father or mother, or any of their parents, in their impotent old age;" and doth suppose that he needeth "no other picture of any of the gods to reverence in his house, because he should turn all his care and diligence to honour his parents[8]." And again, in another place : "Let us pay," saith he, "to our parents, while they are alive, the oldest, first, and greatest debts, that we owe them for our being and bringing up. For every one must think, that all which he hath is theirs, who did beget and bring him up ; so that, according to his ability, he must supply and minister to them all that he doth possess : first of all, the external goods of fortune ; then, of the body ; and lastly, those that do belong unto the mind ; thereby restoring all that he borrowed, and recompensing them in their old age for all their old cares and grief sustained for him. It is seemly also and requisite, that even in words, so long as we live, we should shew reverence unto our parents : for after light and foolish words used to them doth commonly come a terrible plague. For before every man doth Nemesis (the executrice of judgment) stand, and doth throughly think upon all their offences. We must therefore give place to our

The Gentiles' sentences touching honour due to parents.

[6 Τοιοῦτος γίγνου περὶ τοὺς γονεῖς, οἵους ἂν εὔξαιο περὶ σεαυτὸν γενέσθαι τοὺς σεαυτοῦ παῖδας.—Isocrat. Orat. ad Demonicum. ap. Stobæi Floril. ed. Gaisford. Oxon. 1822. Vol. III. p. 113.]

[7 Οὗτος γὰρ μάλιστα πάντων φιλοπάτωρ ἐστὶν, ὅστις ζητεῖ δι' οὗ μηδὲν λυπήσας τὸν πατέρα πλεῖστ' αὐτὸν εὐφράναιτ' ἄν.—Anaximenes, ibid.]

[8 Πατὴρ οὖν ὅτῳ καὶ μήτηρ ἢ τούτων πατέρες ἢ μητέρες ἐν οἰκίᾳ κεῖνται κειμήλιοι ἀπειρηκότες γήρᾳ, μηδεὶς διανοηθήτω ποτὲ ἄγαλμα αὑτῷ, τοιοῦτον ἐφέστιον ἵδρυμα ἐν οἰκίᾳ ἔχων, μᾶλλον κύριον ἔσεσθαι· ἐὰν δὴ κατὰ τρόπον γε ὀρθῶς αὐτὸ θεραπεύῃ ὁ κεκτημένος.—Plato de Legib. Lib. XI. et ap. Stobæi Floril. ubi supra.]

18

parents, when they be angry without a cause, or do what they list, whether it be by word or deed; knowing always, that the father is rightfully angry with his son, though he be angry for nothing else but because he thinks that his son hath done to him the thing that he should not. Let us, therefore, erect to our parents, even when they be dead, monuments seemly for their estate while they were alive: which if we shall do, then shall we undoubtedly be worthily rewarded at the hands of the gods[1]." Thus much hath Plato. St Hierome saith: "Pay to mothers the reverence that ye owe them, who, serving you with the pain of their own wombs, do bear the weight of your bodies; and, carrying about the infant unknown, do, as it were, become servants to them that shall be born. At that time the mother hungereth, not to the filling of her own belly, neither doth she alone digest and feed upon the meat that she eateth: with the mother's meat is the babe nourished that lieth within her; his members are fed with another body's eating; so that the man that shall be is filled with the morsels that the mother swalloweth. What should I rehearse the nourishment that they give to their children, and the sweet injuries of wayward infancy, that they take and put up by means of their little ones? Why should I speak of the meat digested of the mother, which, coming from the other parts of her body into

The pains and travails of mothers in childbirth.

[1] Γονέων δὲ μετὰ ταῦτα τιμαὶ ζώντων, ὡς θέμις ὀφείλοντα ἀποτίνειν τὰ πρῶτά τε καὶ μέγιστα ὀφειλήματα, χρεῶν πάντων πρεσβύτατα· νομίζειν δὲ, ἃ κέκτηται καὶ ἔχει, πάντα εἶναι τῶν γεννησάντων καὶ θρεψαμένων πρὸς τὸ παρέχειν αὐτὰ εἰς ὑπηρεσίαν ἐκείνοις κατὰ δύναμιν πᾶσαν, ἀρχόμενον ἀπὸ τῆς οὐσίας, δεύτερα τὰ τοῦ σώματος, τρίτα τὰ τῆς ψυχῆς, ἀποτίνοντα δανείσματα ἐπιμελείας τε καὶ ὑπερπονούντων ὠδῖνας παλαιὰς ἐπὶ νέοις δανεισθείσας, ἀποδιδόντα δὲ παλαιοῖς ἐν τῷ γήρᾳ σφόδρα κεχρημένοις. Παρὰ δὲ πάντα τὸν βίον ἔχειν τε καὶ ἐσχηκέναι χρὴ πρὸς αὐτοῦ γονέας εὐφημίαν διαφερόντως, διότι κούφων καὶ πτηνῶν λόγων βαρυτάτη ζημία· πᾶσι γὰρ ἐπίσκοπος τοῖς περὶ τὰ τοιαῦτα ἐτάχθη Δίκης Νέμεσις ἄγγελος. Θυμουμένοις τε οὖν ὑπείκειν δεῖ καὶ ἀποπιμπλᾶσι τὸν θυμὸν, ἐάν τ' ἐν λόγοις ἐάν τ' ἐν ἔργοις δρῶσι τὸ τοιοῦτον, ξυγγιγνώσκοντα ὡς εἰκότως μάλιστα πατὴρ υἱεῖ δοξάζων ἀδικεῖσθαι θυμοῖτ' ἂν διαφερόντως. Τελευτησάντων δὲ γονέων ταφὴ μὲν ἡ σωφρονεστάτη καλλίστη, μήθ' ὑπεραίροντα τῶν εἰθισμένων ὄγκων μήτ' ἐλλείποντα ὧν οἱ προπάτορες τοὺς ἑαυτῶν γεννήτας ἐτίθεσαν.... Ταῦτ' ἂν ποιοῦντες καὶ κατὰ ταῦτα ζῶντες ἑκάστοτε ἕκαστοι τὴν ἀξίαν ἂν παρὰ θεῶν καὶ ὅσοι κρείττονες ἡμῶν κομιζοίμεθα.—Plato de Legib. Lib. IV. et ap. Stobæi Floril. Vol. III. p. 116.]

her paps, is turned there into milk and moisture, to fill the
weak and tender jaws with thin and liquid food for nourishment? By nature the infants are compelled to take of their
mothers that which they drink; and when as yet their tooth-
less gums are not able to bite, then do they with the labouring of their lips draw that from their mother's breasts that
they need not to chew. The mother's dug doth serve the
child, and still attendeth upon the swathled babe; her hands
to hold, and her back to bend, are ready still to dandle the
suckling's limbs, that she loves full well, God wot. The
mother desireth often and earnestly to have her youngling
grow, and wisheth full many a time to see him a man. For
these so many and so great good deeds ought the child, once
come to age, to apply himself to do her service with a good
and ready mind and heart. Let nature's debt be paid; let
them that follow have their due. Pay, child, that which
thou owest, and shew thy bounden duty by all manner of
service, whatsoever it be; because no man is able to pay to
his parents so much as he oweth them[2]." Thus far out of
Hierome.

Now touching the country wherein every one is born and brought up; every man doth well esteem of it, love it, and For the ho-
nouring of
our country.

[2 Matribus quoque debitam impendite reverentiam, quæ, vobis
uteri labore servientes, pondus vestri corporis tolerant; atque ignotam
portantes infantiam, famulatum quendam exhibent nascituris. Illo
tempore non sibi tantum mater esurit, nec acceptos sola digerit cibos.
Materno victu alitur et ille qui latet, ejusque membra alterius comes-
tione pascuntur; ut homo futurus alienis morsibus saturetur. Quid
ipsa memorem nutrimenta, et teneræ infantiæ dulces injurias, quas
nutritoris affectus de suis parvulis sumit? Quid cibos in matre confectos, qui fœmineis manantes ex membris lacteum solvuntur in succum,
et fauces invalidas liquido sapore perfundunt? Cogente natura su-
munt infantes de matre quod bibant, et dente non nato hoc sibi curren-
tibus labris eliciunt, quod non sit necesse mordere. Serviunt materna
posteris pectora, serviunt ipsis incunabulis, manus et terga membris
devota lactentium gratos artus accipiunt. Optat mater parvulum
crescere; optat cito videre majorem. . . . . . His tot tantisque præceden-
tibus factis—matri tota debet alacritate serviri. Reddatur naturæ
debitum; reddatur et posteris quod debetur. Exsolve, fili, quod
debes, et officia debita qualicunque exhibe famulatu, quia parentibus
nemo potest reddere quod debetur.—Hieron. Opp. Par. 1706. Tom.
v. p. 97. Epist. de Honorandis Parentibus. The Benedictine editors
consider that this treatise is not Jerome's.]

18—2

Fighting in
defence of
our country.

wish to advance it; every man doth deck it with his virtue and prowess; every one doth help it with all sorts of benefits, stoutly defending it, and valiantly fighting for it, if need be, to save it from violent robbers. What is, I pray you, more to be delighted in, than the good platform of a well ordered city, wherein there is (as one did say) the church well grounded; wherein God is rightly worshipped; and wherein the word of God in faith and charity is duly obeyed, so far forth as it pleaseth God to give the gift of grace; wherein also the magistrate doth defend good discipline and upright laws; wherein the citizens are obedient and at unity among themselves, having their assemblies for true religion and matters of justice; wherein they use to have honest meetings in the church, in the court, and places of common exercise; wherein they apply themselves to virtue and the study of learning, seeking an honest living by such sciences as man's life hath need of, by tillage, by merchandise, and other handy occupations; wherein children are honestly trained up, parents recompensed for their pains, the poor maintained of alms, and strangers harboured in their distress? There are therefore in this commonweal virgins, married women, children, old men, matrons, widows, and fatherless children. If any (by the naughty disposition of nature) transgress the laws, they are worthily punished; the guiltless are defended; peace, justice, and civility doth flourish, and is upheld. Now what is he, that can abide to behold[1] such a commonweal, the country where he is born and bred up, to be troubled, vexed, torn, and pulled in pieces, either by seditious citizens or foreign enemies? In civil seditions and foreign wars all virtue and honesty is utterly overthrown, virgins defiled, matrons uncivilly dealt withal, old men derided, and religion destroyed. Wherefore the valiant captain Joab, being ready to fight against the Syrians in defence of his country, speaketh to his brother Abisai, saying : " If the Syrians be stronger than I, then shalt thou help me; but if the sons of Ammon be too strong for thee, then will I come and aid thee. Be courageous therefore, and let us fight lustily for our people, and for the cities of our God: and let the Lord do the thing that is good in his own eyes[2]." Moreover Judas Machabeus,

[1 æquis et patientibus oculis videat, Lat.]
2 2 Sam. x. 11, 12.]

a man among the Israelites worthily esteemed, and a famous warrior, and singularly affected toward his country, encouraging his soldiers and countrymen against their enemies, said: "They come upon us wrongfully in hope of their force, to spoil and make havoc of us, with our wives and children; but we fight for our lives and liberty of our laws, and the Lord will destroy them before our faces." The people also among themselves, exhorting one another, do cry out and say : " Let us take this affliction from our people, and let us fight for our nation and our religion[3]."

Let not any man make an objection here, and say: "Tush, these are works pertaining to the law, which we, that are of the church of Christ, have nothing to do withal." For the apostle Paul, speaking to the Hebrews, as concerning christian faith, doth say : "These through faith Heb. xi. did subdue kingdoms, wrought righteousness, were valiant in fight, and turned to flight the armies of aliants[4]." Now, since our faith is all one, and the very same with theirs, 2 Cor. iv. it is lawful for us, as well as for them, in a rightful quarrel by war to defend our country and religion, our virgins and old men, our wives and children, our liberty and possessions. They are flatly unnatural to their country and countrymen, and do transgress this fifth commandment, whosoever do (under the pretence of religion) forsake their country afflicted with war, not endeavouring to deliver it from barbarous soldiers and foreign nations, even by offering their lives to the push and prick of present death for the safeguard thereof. St John saith : " By this we know his love, because he gave 1 John iii. his life for us; and we ought to give our lives for the brethren." The hired soldiers[5], who fight unlawful battles for pay of wages, and sell their bodies for greediness of money, shall judge the men that leave their country in peril and danger. For the one put loss of life and limbs in adventure for gain of a few odd crowns; whereas the other dainty fools and effeminate

[3 1 Macc. iii. 20—22, 43.]
[4 Hebr. xi. 33, 34.]
[5 "In 1549, he (Bullinger) by his influence hindered the Swiss from renewing their league with Henry II. of France, representing to them, that it was neither just nor lawful for a man to suffer himself to be hired to shed another man's blood, from whom himself had never received any injury."— Chalmers' Biogr. Dict. Vol. vii. p. 280.]

hearts will not hazard the loss of a limb for their religion, magistrates, wives, children, and all their possessions. What, I beseech you, shall those traitors to their country say in that day, wherein the Lord shall reward the lovers and the unnatural traitors of their country and countrymen; when before their eyes they shall see the Gentiles to excel them in virtue and love to their country-people[1]? Publii Decii, the father and the son, gave their lives freely for the safeguard of the commonweal, and died willingly for the love of their country[2]. Codrus, the natural and loving king of the Athenians, when he understood by the oracle of Apollo that Athens could not be saved but by the king's death, and that therefore the enemies had given commandment that no man should wound the king; this Codrus laid aside his kinglike furniture, and, clothing himself in base apparel, rushed into the thickest of his enemies, and found the means by egging to provoke one of them perforce to kill him[3]. The two brethren, called Phileni, chose rather to lengthen their country with a mile of ground than to prolong their lives with many days; and therefore did they suffer themselves to be buried alive[4]. But what suffer we for the health and safeguard of our country? Hierocles saith: " Our country is as it were a certain other god, and our first and chiefest parent. Wherefore he, that first called our country by the name of *patria*, did not unadvisedly give it that name, but called it so in respect of the thing which it was indeed; for *patria*, 'our country,' is derived of *pater*, 'a father,' and hath his ending or termination in the feminine gender, thereby declaring, that it taketh the name of both the parents. And this reason doth covertly lead us to think that our country, which is but one, ought to be reverenced and loved as well as both our parents, jointly knitting them together, to make them equal in honour[5]."

Lovers of their country.

[1 Curtius Romanus adolescens nobilissimus in hiatum fori ingentem sese præcipitem dedit, ut sua morte spontanea servaret patriam, Lat.; omitted by the translator. Curtius, a most noble Roman youth, cast himself headlong into a vast gulph in the forum, that by his voluntary death he might preserve his country.—Liv. Lib. vii. cap. 6.]

[2 Liv. Lib. viii. cap. 9, and Lib. x. cap. 28.]

[3 Justin. Lib. ii. cap. 6. Vell. Patercul. Hist. Rom. Lib. i. cap. 2. Valer. Max. Lib. v. cap. 6.]

[4 Sallust. de Bell. Jug. p. 333. Lugd. Bat. 1654.]

[5 Ἔστι γὰρ ὡσανεὶ δεύτερός τις θεὸς αὕτη (i. e. ἡ πατρὶς) νὴ Δία,

Furthermore, we must make our earnest prayer for the We must
pray for our
country. safeguard of our country. Babylon was not the country of the Jews; but yet, for because the Jews for their sins were banished by God to Babylon for the space of seventy years, Babylon was counted to them instead of their country. And therefore saith the prophet Jeremy: "Build up houses, and dwell therein; plant gardens, and eat the fruit thereof; marry wives, and beget sons and daughters, and give them in marriage, that they may get children. Seek the peace of that city to which I do carry you, and pray to the Lord for it; because your peace and safeguard is joined to the peace thereof." Chapter twenty and nine. Traitors to their country therefore sin exceedingly, whom the laws of the realm do command for their foul offence to be hanged and quartered.

Touching the magistrate and his office, I mean to speak of For the
honour due
to magis-
trates. them in another place: so much as it is necessarily requisite for this present time St Peter uttereth, where he saith, "Fear God, honour the king[6]." Let us therefore acknowledge and confess, that the magistrate's office is ordained of God for men's commodity, and that God by the magistrate doth frankly bestow on us very many and great commodities. The peers[7] do watch for the common people, if they do rightly discharge their office, not shewing themselves to be detestable tyrants; they judge the people, they take up controversies, they keep justice in punishing the guilty and defending innocents, and, lastly, they fight for the people. And for the excellency of their office, which is both the chiefest and the most necessary, God doth attribute to the magistrate the use of his own name, and calleth the princes and senators of the people gods[8], to the intent that they by the very name should be put in mind of their duty, and that the subjects might thereby learn to have them in reverence. God is just, good, righteous, and one which hath no respect of persons: and such an one

πρῶτος καὶ μείζων γονεύς· παρ' ὃ δὴ καὶ ὁ τοὔνομα τῷ πράγματι τιθέ-
μενος οὐκ ἀνεντρεχὲς ἔθετο, παρασχηματίσας μὲν τῷ πατρὶ, θηλυκῶς δ'
ἐξενεγκὼν, ἵν' οἷον μίγμα τυγχάνοι, τῆς τε τοῦ πατρὸς καὶ τῆς μητρώας.
Καὶ δὴ οὗτος μὲν ὁ λόγος ὑπαγορεύει πατρίδα τιμᾶν, ἐπίσης τοῖς δυσὶ
γονεῦσι τὴν μίαν.—Hierocles ap. Stobæi Floril. ed. Gaisford. Vol. ii.
pp. 75, 76.]

[6 1 Pet. ii. 17.]   [7 principes, Lat.]
[8 Psal. lxxxii. 1, 6; John x. 34, 35.]

ought the good judge or magistrate to be. Monks and heremites[1] do praise their profession or solitary life, extolling it above the skies; but I think verily, that there is more true virtue in one politic man, who governeth the commonweal and doth his duty truly, than in many thousands of monks and here-mites[1], who have not so much as one word expressed in the holy scriptures for the defence of their vocation and vowed order of living: yea, I am ashamed that I have compared the holy office of magistrates with that kind of people, in whom there is nothing found worthy to be compared with them, insomuch as they fly from the labour and ordinance that God hath made profitable for their people and countrymen. Truly, if the prince do faithfully discharge his office in the commonweal, he heapeth up to himself a number of very good works and praise that never shall be ended. Therefore the magistrate must be obeyed, and all his good and upright laws. No sedition or conspiracies ought in any case to be moved against him. We must not curse or speak evil of the magistrate. For God himself in his law doth charge us, saying: "Thou shalt not speak evil of the gods, nor curse the prince of the people[2]." If he chance at any time to sin, let us behave ourselves toward him as to our father; of whom I have spoken a little before.

Against seditious rebels. It happeneth oftentimes, that magistrates have a good mind to promote religion, to advance common justice, to defend the laws, and to favour honesty; and yet notwithstanding, they are troubled with their infirmities, yea, sometime with grievous offences: howbeit, the people ought not therefore to despise them and thrust them beside their dignity. David had his infirmities, albeit otherwise a very good prince. By his adultery he endamaged much his people and kingdom: and, for to make his trouble the more, Absolon sinned grievously[3], and went about to put him beside his crown and kingdom. So likewise in other princes there are no small number of vices, which nevertheless neither move nor ought to move godly people to rebellious sedition, so long as justice is maintained and good laws and public peace defended.

[1 Anachoretæ, Lat.]   [2 Ex. xxii. 28.]
[3 Peccavit tamen graviter Absolon, qui, &c., Lat. Yet Absalom sinned, &c.]

We ought to pray earnestly and continually for the magistrate's welfare. We must aid him with our help and counsel, so oft as need shall serve and occasion be given. We must not deny him our riches or bodies to assist him withal. The saints did gather their substance in common to help the magistrate, so oft as public safeguard did so require. The Israelites of all ages did always fight for their judges, for their kings and other magistrates; and so did all other people upon good advice taken: and likewise, on the other side, did the princes fight for the people. I would therefore that those offices of godly naturalness were of force and did flourish even at this day in all kingdoms, cities, and commonweals. Let every nation give to his magistrate that which by law, or by custom, or by necessity, it oweth him. For Paul the apostle saith: "Give to every one that which ye owe; tribute to whom tribute belongeth, custom to whom custom, fear to whom fear, and honour to whom honour is due." Rom. xiii.

Now, for because the guardians or overseers of orphans do supply the room of parents, and execute the offices of deceased parents to the children that remain, they do worthily deserve to have the reward that is due to parents, whether it be love, reverence, thanks, or obedience. The same also do I judge touching workmen and masters of sciences, who, for the fatherly affection, love, good-will, faith, and diligence shewed to their scholar or apprentice, ought mutually of their scholars to be regarded as a master; to be reverenced, feared, and hearkened unto, as a loving father. But in these unhappy days of ours it is abominable to see the negligence of masters in teaching their scholars, and intolerable to behold the peevish rudeness of untoward scholars. Let masters therefore learn here to shew themselves to be fathers, not being otherwise affected toward their scholars than toward their own children. Let them teach their apprentices their science or occupation, and train them up in manners and all points of civility, with the very same care and diligence that they use in bringing up their own. On the other side, let youths learn to break their natural ingraffed rudeness, and to bridle their youthful lusts; let them learn to be humble and subject, to keep silence, to reverence, to fear, to love, and obey their masters. Let them always remember, that their

The honour due to guardians and masters of occupations.

The office or duty of masters and scholars.

masters are given them of God, and therefore that God is despised in their contemned masters. Let them be diligent, earnest, and trusty in their work. Let them give their masters cause to perceive their earnest desire and ready good-will, that they bear to him, their occupation, and principles of their science. Let every one think upon, and diligently practise indeed, the things that their master teacheth by word of mouth. Let them not grudge to watch and take pains. Let not the masters be grieved, so often as they be asked how to do a thing, to shew it readily in every point as it should be done[1]. Unthankfulness and lack of diligence in the scholar doth many times make the master unwilling and negligent to teach him. Observe this, and, in the rest, fear God, and have an eye to sound religion. When thou art abroad, come not in company of blasphemous and riotous toss-pots[2]; behave thyself honestly, provoke no man to anger, despise no man, speak ill of no man, desire peace and quietness, honour all men, and strive to do good to every one. When thou art at home, help forward thy master's commodity; do not endamage him nor his affairs; if any man either hurt, or doth go about to hinder him, give him warning of it betimes; seek to appease, and hide as much as thou canst, all occasions of falling out and chidings; whatsoever thou hearest at home, do not blab it abroad, and make no tales at home of that that thou hearest abroad. Be silent, quiet[3], chaste, continent, temperant, trusty in deeds, true in words, and willing to do any honest and household business. Beware of them by whom evil suspicions and offences may chance to arise. Do not over-boldly dally with thy master's wife or daughters, nor yet with his maidens; do not stand familiarly talking with them in sight or secretly. Imagine thou (as it is indeed) that thy master's wife is thy mother, his daughters thy sisters; whom to defile, it is a filthy and villanous offence. Let every young man be neat, not nasty; gentle, just, content with a mean diet, not licorice-lipped nor

[1 The translator seems here to have missed Bullinger's meaning. The Latin is: Sit gratus fideliter docenti magistro, ut sæpius roganti de modo agendi dignetur fideliter indicare omnia. Bullinger still declares the duty of the apprentice to his master, and *not* of the masters to their apprentices.]

[2 luxuriosorum, Lat.]   [3 pacificus, justus, Lat.]

dainty-toothed[4]. But why stay I hereabout so long? Let every young man be persuaded and keep in memory, that his duty is to keep himself chaste from filthy defilings, to obey and not to rule, to serve all men, to learn always, to speak very little, not to brag of any thing over arrogantly, not to answer tip for tap[5], but to suffer much and wink thereat.

For the honouring of ministers of the churches, which are the pastors, teachers, and fathers of christian people, many things are wont to be alleged by them who covet rather to reign as lords, than to serve as ministers, in the church of Christ. But we, which are not of that aspiring mind, do acknowledge, that they are given us by the Lord, and that the Lord by them doth speak to us. I speak here of those ministers which tell us not a headless tale of their own dreams[6], but preach to us the word of truth: for of them the Lord in the gospel saith, "He that heareth you heareth me, and he that despiseth you despiseth me[7]." Wherefore the ministery is of the Lord, and through it he worketh our salvation. And therefore must we obey the ministers which do rightly execute their office and ministery; we must think well of them; we must love them and continually pray for them; and since they sow to us their heavenly things, we must not deny them the reaping of our bodily and temporal things. "For the labourer is worthy of his reward." And since the Roman president among the Jews did not deny it, but aided the apostle Paul against the pretended[8] murder and open wrong of the Jewish nation; a christian magistrate, verily, ought not to deny his assistance and defence to the godly ministers of Christ and the churches. Hereunto belong the testimonies of St Paul, that may be alleged. In the last chapter of his first epistle to the Thessalonians he saith: "We beseech you, brethren, to know them which labour among you, and have the oversight of you in the Lord, and admonish you; that ye may have them

The honour due to ministers of the churches.

1 Cor. ix.
Matt. x.

Acts xxiii.
xxiv. xxv.

[4] non palato delicato et moroso, Lat.]
[5] non responsare, Lat. Shakspeare has *tap for tap.* King Henry IV. Part 2. Act II. Scene 1.—Tip, to strike lightly. Wilson's Dict.]
[6] qui non sua nobis adferunt somnia, Lat.]
[7] Luke x. 16.]
[8] conceptum, Lat.]

in reputation through love for their work, and be at peace with them[1]." Again, to the Hebrews he saith : " Obey them that have the rule over you, and give place unto them ; for they watch for your souls, as they that shall give account for them, that they may do it in joy, and not in trembling ; for that is unprofitable for you[2]." For how many and great calamities have fallen upon kingdoms and peoples for the

The contempt of the minis- ters of God's word. contempt of God's word and his ministers, many examples can teach us ; but that especially, which in the last chapter of the second book of Chronicles is set down in these words: " The Lord God of their fathers sent to them by his messengers, rising up betimes, and sending ; for he had compassion on his people, and on his dwelling-place. But they mocked the messengers of God, and despised his words, and jested at his prophets, until the wrath of God arose against his people, and till there was no remedy."

Like unto this are the words of the Lord in the gospel, where he saith : " I send unto you prophets and wise men, some of whom ye shall scourge and kill, that all the righteous blood may light upon you, which hath been shed upon the earth ; from the blood of the righteous Abel, unto the blood of Zacharias, the son of Barachias, whom ye slew between the temple and the altar ;" and so forth : for the place is known to you all, dearly beloved, and is to be seen in the twenty-third chapter after St Matthew. We must beware therefore, in any case, that we do not despise God, who speaketh to us in his word by his servants the prophets.

The honour due to our kinsfolks. We owe, by the force of this commandment, all love, reverence, help, comfort, and humanity to our kinsfolks and alliance. In this commandment[3] are they condemned that shew themselves to be ἄστοργοι[4], that is to say, men without all natural affection and friendly love to their own blood and kinsfolks. There is a certain natural affection, good-will, love, and pitiful mercy (which the scripture calleth the " bowels of

[1] chap. v. 12, 13. pacem habete cum illis, Lat., Erasmus' version. "And be at peace with them," Tyndale's Test. 1525, and Cranmer, 1539.]
[2] Hebr. xiii. 17.]
[3] sicut et Apostolicis scriptis, Lat. ; omitted by the translator. As also in the Apostolical writings.]
[4] Rom. i. 31.]

mercy[5]") in the father and mother toward their children, in brother toward brother, and in cousins toward kinsfolks and friends of their alliance. We have notable examples hereof set down in the scriptures, of Abraham's love toward his son Isaac, and of Joseph's affection toward his father Jacob and his brethren, but especially toward Benjamin his brother by one mother. Mothers and daughters-in-law have a notable example to follow in Noemi and Ruth. Mothers and daughters-in-law (for the most part) do bear a deadly hate the one to the other, which is the cause of much mischief in the houses where they be. Let them learn therefore by this pretty example[6] how to behave themselves on both parts. Let the mother-in-law think the daughter-in-law to be her own daughter; and let the daughter-in-law honour and reverence her mother-in-law, even as if she were her own mother. Many things must be winked at on both sides, many things must be taken in good part, and many things put up with a quiet mind. Many things must be forgiven; and they must both have their ears stopped against tattling tale-bearers and wrongful suspicions. Concord in every house is the greatest treasure that may be, and discord at home is the most perilous and endless mischief that can be invented. Paul his words, touching good turns and honour to be given to our kinsfolks, are very well known, and extant to be seen in the fifth chapter of his first epistle to Timothy.

Last of all also, there is to be found in the word of God a peculiar law for the honouring of old men, which biddeth us to rise before the hoary and grey-haired head[7]. Old men therefore are to be honoured, whom we must worthily magnify, and in whom we must acknowledge the singular grace of God in giving them long life, and that by long and continual experience of all things they have attained to much wit or wisdom, whereby they are able to help us with their counsel. They therefore ought to be praised, that all men may understand[8], that grey hairs are a crown of glory[9]. Moreover, if aged impotent persons are driven into need, then must our abundance supply their necessity. To be short, we must not

For the honour due to old men.

[5] quæ scriptura viscera vocat, Lat. See Gen. xliii. 30; 1 Kings iii. 26; 2 Cor. vii. 15, marg.]
[6] lepido exemplo, Lat.]
[8] et prædicent, Lat.; omitted.]
[7] Levit. xix. 32.]
[9] Prov. xvi. 31.]

deny to old men any duty of humanity wherewith we may pleasure them. In the same sort, also, there are here commended unto us widows, orphans, wards, poor men, strangers, sick and miserable people. And for that cause did the devout and good men of old bestow their goods liberally to the refreshing of old men, widows, fatherless children, and poor

Church goods.

silly [1] creatures. Those goods at this day are called church goods, or ecclesiastical contributions [2]: which, undoubtedly, are very well bestowed, if they be laid out on them for whom they were given. In the emperor's constitutions we may see that there were common houses and substance builded and appointed for all sorts of needy people: for there is mention made of houses for fatherless children, of hospitals for old men, of spittles for beggars, of places for sick men, and nurseries for children [3]. Among us, at these days, there are hospitals and monasteries [4], very many whereof have several places appointed for orphans, old men, poor people, impotent creatures, sick persons, and infants. They therefore do commit an unappeasable offence, whosoever bestow to other uses the substance and places ordained for old and poor people, and lash out (they care not how prodigally) in riot and lustiness the alms bestowed upon poor silly souls.

And now hitherto have I declared how our parents ought to be honoured, and they which are contained under the name of parents.

The promise made to those that worship their parents, and threatenings against such as despise their parents.

There is now remaining the third and last part of our present treatise, wherein we have to see what God promiseth to them that honour their parents religiously; whereby we have to gather, what peril hangs over the heads of them that wickedly neglect and irreligiously despise their parents. The Lord in the law therefore saith: "That thy days may be long in the land which the Lord thy God shall give thee." The meaning of which saying is: Honour thy father and thy mother, that thou mayest for many days enjoy the possession of the land which thou shalt have in testimony of my favour

---

[1 silly, i. e. weak.]   [2 facultates ecclesiasticæ, Lat.]

[3 Orphanotrophiorum, Gerontocomiorum, Ptochotrophiorum, Nosocomiorum, et Brephotrophiorum, Lat. See also Bucer's Script. Anglic. de Regno Christi, p. 82. Basil. 1577. These are often mentioned in Novell. Justinian.]

[4 Cœnobia et Hospitalia, Lat.]

to thee-ward.   These words do properly belong to the Jews. But very well and truly doth a godly minister of Christ, writing upon this place, say : "Because the whole earth is blessed to the faithful, we do nothing amiss, when we reckon this present life among the blessings of God.   Wherefore this promise appertaineth as well to us as to the Jews, because the prolonging of this present life is a testimony of God's especial favour[5]."   He promiseth assuredly to them that do religiously honour their parents, in what land soever they dwell, all kind of blessings, felicity, and store of temporal things, with a sweet prolonging of this present life.   For Paul, interpreting this in the sixth chapter of his epistle to the Ephesians, saith : " That it may go well with thee, and that thou mayest live long upon the earth :" meaning any land whatsoever, and promising a temporal blessing of the Lord.

We therefore gather hereupon, that the contrary is threatened and set as a penalty upon the heads of those that disobediently despise their parents.   By examples, and other places of the scripture, this shall be made more manifest. Cham is cursed of his father Noe for behaving himself unreverently toward him, even in his drunkenness[6].   Joseph is exalted to the chiefest dignity in Egypt, because from his childhood he honoured God and reverenced his father Jacob. Solomon, in the seventeenth chapter of his Proverbs, saith : "Whosoever rewardeth evil for good, evil shall not depart from his house."   Again: " He that despitefully taunteth his father, and despiseth the old age of his mother, shall be confounded and left in reproach."   " The son that leaveth to keep the discipline of his father, shall think of talk of wickedness."   "Whoso curseth his father or mother, his light shall be put out, and the balls of his eyes shall see nought but darkness."   For they are monsters and no men, that are unnatural toward their parents ; and especially they which do not only neglect and despise them, but also beat and uncourteously handle them.   Such fellows doth the Lord command to be slain, as

[5 Quia tota terra fidelibus benedicta est, præsentem vitam inter Dei benedictiones merito reponimus.   Quare ad nos similiter spectat ista promissio, quatenus scilicet divinæ benevolentiæ documentum nobis est præsentis vitæ duratio.—Calvin. Instit. Lib. II. cap. 8. § 37. Tom. IX. p. 101. Amst. 1667.]

[6 Gen. ix. 25.]

people unworthy to see the light, because they forget and will
not acknowledge, that by the means of their parents they
came into the world. " He that curseth father or mother,"
saith the Lord, " let him die the death." And again : " He
that striketh his father or mother, let him die the death[1]."
There is none of you which knoweth not the law, called *Lex
Pompeia*[2], against such as kill their parents. It is not amiss
here to hear what the gentile writers say touching this
matter. Homer saith :

> He did not nourish as he should
> His aged parents dear;
> Therefore the gods did from his youth
> Cut off the jolliest year[3].

And the ancient poet Orpheus saith :

> God sits above, and sees the sons
> That do themselves apply
> To do their fathers' hests, and those
> That shamelessly deny
>
> Them to obey; and as he doth
> Bless th' one with sundry gifts,
> So, for to vex the other, he doth
> Devise a thousand drifts:
>
> For though despised parents die,
> Yet do their ghosts remain,
> And are of force upon the earth,
> To put their sons to pain[4].

[1 Ex. xxi. 15, 17.]

[2 Lex Pompeia de Parricidiis; passed in the time of Cn. Pom-
peius: "He who killed a father or mother, grandfather or grandmother, was whipped till he bled, sewn up in a sack with a dog, cock,
viper, and ape, and thrown into the sea," &c.—See Smith's Dict.
of Gr. and Rom. Antiquities, 286, a. P. ; and Early Writings of
Bp. Hooper, Parker Soc. ed. p. 368.]

[3   οὐδὲ τοκεῦσι

θρέπτρα φίλοις ἀπέδωκε, μινυνθάδιος δέ οἱ αἰὼν
ἔπλεθ'.   Hom. Il. Lib. xvii. 301. P.]

[4   Ζεὺς δ' ἐφορᾷ γονέων ὁπόσοι τίουσι θέμιστας,
ἠδ' ὅσοι οὐκ ἀλέγουσιν ἀναιδέα θυμὸν ἔχοντες.
καὶ τοῖς μὲν πρόφρων τε καὶ ἤπιος ἐσθλὰ δίδωσι,
τοῖς δὲ κακὰ φρονέων νεμεσίζεται ἐμμενὲς αἰεί·
δειναὶ γὰρ κατὰ γαῖαν ἐρινύες εἰσὶ τοκήων.
Orpheus ap. Stobæi Floril. ed. Gaisford. Vol. iii. pp. 111, 112.]

Moreover, the tragical poet, Euripides, hath:

> To him, that while he lives doth love
> His parents to obey,
> Whether he live, or else do die,
> God is a friend alway[5].

And Menander, the comical poet, saith:

> The wretch is worse than mad, that with
> His parents falls at odds[6]:
> For wise men greatly reverence them,
> And honour them as gods[7].

Virgil also, among other horrible vices which are punished in hell with eternal and unspeakable pains, doth say:

> Here they that did their brethren hate,
> While life on earth did last,
> Or beat their parents, &c.

And immediately after:

> He did his country sell for gold,
> And made a tyrant king;
> For bribes he made and marr'd his country's laws and every thing[8].

And Horace in his Odes saith:

> It is a sweet and seemly thing,
> In country's cause to die[9].

And Silius Italicus hath:

> Doubt not of this; forget it not,
> But keep it in thy mind:
> It is a detestable thing
> To shew thyself unkind

[5   Ὅστις δὲ τοὺς τεκόντας ἐν βίῳ σέβει,
ὅδ' ἐστὶ καὶ ζῶν καὶ θανὼν θεοῖς φίλος.
                    Eurip. Heracl. ap. Stobæi Floril. Vol. iii. p. 107.]

[6 Δίκας γραφόμενος πρὸς γονεῖς μαίνῃ, τάλαν.—Menand. ap. Stobæi Floril. Vol. iii. p. 112.]

[7 Θεοὶ μέγιστοι τοῖς φρονοῦσιν οἱ γονεῖς.—Menand. Sentent. Moral. Lugd. 1817.]

[8   Hic, quibus invisi fratres, dum vita manebat,
Pulsatusve parens, &c.
Vendidit hic auro patriam, dominumque potentem
Imposuit, fixit leges pretio atque refixit.
                    Virg. Æn. vi. 608, 9, 21, 22.]

[9   Dulce et decorum est pro patria mori.
                    Hor. Od. Lib. iii. 2, 13.]

[BULLINGER.]

19

Unto thy native country soil;
For no such sin remains
In hell to be tormented there
With utter endless pains,
As that: so doth experience teach [1].

These testimonies have I cited to this end and purpose, that by these, dearly beloved, ye may gather the heinousness of this offence, which the very Gentiles themselves do so grievously cry out against and utterly condemn. Cain slew his brother Abel, but thereby he gat his reward; to be marked with a perpetual blot of ignominy and reproach. Semei did intolerably rail upon David, his ordinary magistrate; and therefore was he punished according to his deserts [2]. Absalom rebelled unnaturally against his father David; but, being wrapped by the hair to a tree, and hanging betwixt heaven and earth, he is horribly thrust through with a javelin [3]. The Lord called them that slew the prophets by the name of adders' brood and sons of the devil [4]. As for them that have reproachfully dealt with old men, or troubled widows, they have not gone unpunished. For the Lord in the law saith: "Thou shalt not afflict the widows nor fatherless children: but if ye do go on to afflict them, they shall undoubtedly cry to me, and I will hear them; and my wrath shall wax hot, and I will slay you with the sword, and your wives shall be widows, and your children fatherless." Thus much hitherto.

St Paul, alleging this law in his epistle to the Ephesians, doth very aptly apply it to our learning and comfort. For he saith: "Children, obey your parents, for this is right; honour thy father and mother, which is the first commandment in promise, that thou mayest prosper and live long on earth. Fathers, provoke not your children to wrath, but

Exod. xxii. (margin)

Eph. vi. (margin)

[1   Jamque hoc (ne dubites) longævi, nate, parentis
       Accipe, et æterno fixum sub pectore serva:
       Succensere nefas patriæ; nec fœdior ulla
       Culpa sub extremas fertur mortalibus umbras.
       Sic docuere senes.

                              Sil. Ital. Punic. Lib. vii. 553.]
[2 2 Sam. xvi. 5—8; 1 Kings ii. 8, 9, 36—46.]
[3 2 Sam. xv. and xviii. 14.]
[4 Matt. xxiii. 33; John viii. 38—44.]

bring them up in instruction and information of the Lord."
In these words he telleth the parents their duty, as well as
the children.   Three things he doth require at the hand of The duty of
parents to
the parents; that is, to bring up their children, to instruct their chil-
dren.
them, and to correct them.   For it is the parents' office to
nourish, to feed, and bring them up, till they be grown
to age, that, being once dispatched from hanging on their
parents any longer, they may get their livings with their
own labour and travail.   It is the parents' office to teach and
instruct their children.   That teaching or instructing consisteth in three things,—in religion, in manners, and skill of an
occupation.

Now touching religion, it hath certain principles, rudi- Children are
to be in-
ments, I say, and catechisms to teach by: secondly, it hath structed in
religion.
the scriptures setting out the word of God, with a full expo-
sition of all things belonging to God: it hath also mysteries,
holy signs and sacraments, to teach and to learn by.   If the
householder be conversant among a people which honoureth
the true religion, and hath received the lawful worship of
God, with true, faithful, and godly ministers and teachers of
Christ his church, let him give charge and see that his children go to the holy congregation, there to be instructed in
religion by the public preacher.   Yet nevertheless, let the
father at home examine his children, and know what they
have learned by hearing the sermon.   Let both the father
and mother also at home privately do their endeavour to
teach their children the ten commandments, the Apostles'
Creed, and the Lord's prayer; and let them teach them a
brief and ready rule out of the scriptures for the understanding of the sacraments.   Let them often and many times
cause them to repeat the catechism, and beat into their heads
such sentences as are most necessary to put them in memory
of their faith and duty of life.   But if so it be, that the Counsel and
advice given
householder have his dwelling with a people that persecuteth to house-
holders in
the christian faith and doctrine, which hateth the true and captivity.
lawful worship of God's name, and cannot abide the congregation and ministers of Christ, (as it happeneth in the Turkish
captivities and troublesome persecutions of our days;) then
shall he take heed and keep himself from idolatry: neither
shall he in his own person go, nor suffer his family to come,

19—2

to those ungodly assemblies, but shall rather in his own house
at home instruct them in true religion, first in the catechism,
and then in deeper divinity. Moreover, so oft as the case
and necessity shall require, he must freely and openly profess
Christ and his gospel. For it is apparently evident by the
epistles of Paul and other histories, that such churches were
in private houses of great cities in the time of the apostles
and thickest of those hot and ancient persecutions[1]. Neither
is it likely that the Jews in their captivity at Babylon, although they lacked the outward use of sacrifices, were altogether without all worship of God. Although Daniel did
not sacrifice, yet did he at certain hours in the day-time
worship God in his own house[2]. The house of Cornelius at
Cesarea was the church, wherein Peter preached in a very
good and ecclesiastical assembly or congregation; and he,
because Joppe had no church for him to pray in, went up to
the higher part of the house to make his prayers there[3].
Neither is it to be doubted, but that the eunuch of queen
Candace's nobility, of whom mention is made in the Acts of
the Apostles, did ordain a church in Æthiopia[4]. And let
them be persuaded, which are without the public and lawful
use of the sacraments, that that shall not be imputed to their
default, which is committed, not by them, but by another's
offence. For even in such a case can the Lord work well
by his Spirit in the minds of his people. But where as[5], by
the grace of God, liberty is given for the congregation to
assemble, and to hear the free, sincere, and true preaching
of the gospel, and lastly, to celebrate the sacraments, there
must those private and domestical churches be broken up and
come to an end : not for because the house of a godly householder is not, nor remaineth still, a church; but for because
the hearing of God's word, prayer, and the celebrating of the
sacraments, ought to be public and common to all the saints.

[1 Rom. xvi. 5; 1 Cor. xvi. 19; Coloss. iv. 15; Philem. 2. Bingham, Orig. Eccles. Book viii. cap. 1. §. 13, and 14; Staveley's Hist. of
Churches, chap. 3. pp. 26—34. Lond. 1712]
   [2 Dan. vi. 10.]   [3 Acts x.]
   [4 Acts viii. 27, &c., and Euseb. Eccles. Hist. Lib. ii. cap. 1. Vol.
i. p. 85. ed. Burton. Oxon. 1838.]
   [5 i. e. where : ubi, Lat.]

For those assemblies by stealth, which the Anabaptists use, and all other sectaries, are both worthily and utterly condemned.

And now let us hear the testimonies of scripture, which command all householders to instruct holily their family in the true religion, and to declare to their children the meaning of the sacraments. Moses in the sixth of Deuteronomy saith: "Hear, Israel, the Lord our God is Lord only[6]: therefore shalt thou love the Lord thy God with all thy heart, with all thy soul, and with all thy might. And these words, which I command thee this day, shall be in thy heart. And thou shalt shew them unto thy children, and shalt talk of them when thou art at home in thine house, and as thou walkest by the way, and when thou liest down, and when thou risest up. And thou shalt bind them for a sign upon thy hand, and they shall be as frontlets between thine eyes[7]." And again: "When thy son asketh thee in time to come, saying, What mean these testimonies, ordinances, and laws, which the Lord our God hath commanded us? Then thou shalt say unto thy son: We were Pharaoh's bondmen in Egypt, and the Lord brought us out with a mighty hand, and shewed signs and mighty wonders before our eyes; and brought us out from thence, and gave us all these precepts and statutes to do and to fear the Lord our God." Hereunto belongeth a great part of the seventy-eighth Psalm. And in the thirteenth of Exodus the Lord doth say again: "Sanctify to me all the first-born. And when thy son shall ask thee in time to come, saying, What is this? Thou shalt say to him, The Lord slew all the first-born of Egypt, and therefore I sacrifice unto the Lord all the males that open the matrix." Also in the twelfth chapter God, or Moses in God's name, expounding the mystery or sacrament of the passover, said[8]: "When your children ask you, saying, What manner of service is this that ye do? ye shall say, It is the sacrifice of the Lord's passover, which passed over the houses

Precepts for the instructing of our children and family.

[6 unus est, Lat.]

[7 Scribes quoque ea super postes domus tuæ et in portis tuis, Lat. omitted by the translator. "And thou shalt write them upon the posts of thy house, and on thy gates."]

[8 inter alia, Lat.]

of the children of Israel," &c. These testimonies are sufficiently evident, and need no further exposition. I will now, therefore, add to these the other things, which parents have to teach their children.

The child must be taught manners.

Let the father instruct his children in manners. We all from our birth are clownish and rude; and all children have unseemly and uncivil manners: which evil is made double as much by evil custom and clownish company. Let the parents, therefore, teach their children manners betimes, which may adorn them at home, and become them abroad. Let him instruct him how to behave himself decently in his going and gesture of his body; how in the church, how in the market, how at the table, how in men's companies, and in all other places of company. There are excellent pretty books set out for that purpose, so that I need not stand to discuss to you the particularities thereof.

Children must learn an occupation.

Lastly, let the father place his children with expert and cunning[1] workmen, to teach them some handycraft whereby to get their living another day. But first, he must make trial of their wits, to see whereunto every one is best apt, and wherein he doth most delight. For " cunning will never be come by, where good will is wanting in him that must learn it[2]." If thou hast any fit for learning, thou shalt do a good and godly deed, to train them up to the ministery of the church, or some other office that standeth by learning. But of all other those parents are to be found fault withal, that bring up their children in lazy idleness. For, although there be left unto them huge heaps of treasure, yet in three or four odd hours all may be wasted and come to nought. Whereunto, then, shall your dainty idle gentleman trust, what shall he do, when there is nothing left but his bare carcass, that is a lump of clay not good for any thing[3]? The inhabiters of Massilia would not admit any into the number of citizens, but such as had learned an occupation to live by[4]. For to a city there is no greater a plague than an unprofitable citizen. But who, I pray you, may be thought to be a worse citizen than

[1 fidis et peritis, Lat.]
[2 Invita Minerva nihil feliciter perfeceris, Lat.—P.]
[3 Quo tunc confugiet miser tellurisque inutile pondus? Lat.]
[4 Valer. Max. Lib. II. cap. 6. § 7.]

he that, being accustomed to ease and delicateness, and of a
sudden by some mishap or else by prodigal riotousness being
deprived of them both, and driven to extreme poverty, is compelled, perforce, to seek out unlawful[5] shifts to get more
wealth again? Furthermore, they of old had a proverb
worthy to be remembered of us[6] at this time: " Every land
maintaineth art[7]." " By this sentence they meant, that learning and science is the surest preparation for every journey.
For they cannot be taken away by thieves, but whithersoever
thou goest, they bear thee company, and are no burden for
thee to bear[8]." If therefore mishap do spoil thy children of
the wealth that thou leavest them; if thou hast taught them
an occupation, it is enough for them to live by. Kings are
deprived of their prince-like dignity, and put beside their
exceeding riches; so that it is no marvel though kings' in-
feriors be spoiled of their wealth, and banished their countries.
Dionysius of Syracuse is reported for his tyranny to have
been thrust beside his seat: but, having lost his kingdom,
he departed to Corinth, where he set up a school, and taught
children their grammar and music, whereby in that necessity
he got his living[9]. He had been hard bested verily, and in
a miserable taking, if he had never learned any thing, but
had settled his hope upon dignity and riches: vain hope had
been his destruction; for he had died in extreme beggary.
Thus much touching the bringing up of children in learning
or knowledge of some occupation.

I have, in that which is behind, to speak somewhat Of correc-
touching the correction of those that are contained under the tion.
name of children. This correction consisteth partly in words,
and partly in stripes. In both there must be had a middle-
mean and measure, that nothing be done outrageously[10]. Let
not the admonition that is given in words be bitterer than the
fault deserves. Let it nip for the time present; but, being

[5 injustissimas planeque seditiosas rationes, Lat.]
[6 omnibus parentibus, Lat.]
[7 Artem quævis alit terra, Lat.—Erasmi. Adag. Hanov. 1617. col.
368, a.]
[8 The quotation is from Erasmus' Adag. in loc. cit.]
[9 Erasmi Adag. in loc. cit.; Justin. Lib. XXI. cap. 5; Cic. Tusc.
Quæst. III. 12.]
[10 ne quid nimis, Lat.]

past, let it be spoken of no more. Continual chiding breeds
contempt. Thou shalt find some children also, with whom
gentle dealing will somewhat prevail[1]. And, unless thou do
sometime praise them and speak well of that which they do,
although peradventure not so well done as thou wouldest
require, thou shalt perceive that utter desperation will take
away hope and courage clean from them. I think it not
good with too heavy a burden to overawe such children as
are willing to bear. Stripes must not be bestowed but for
some great offence, and that too, not in the father's anger,
but moderately ; not to mar, but to amend them. Let the
parents always remember that golden saying of St Paul,
" Fathers, provoke not your children to anger[2]." For the
best wits are hurt by too much rigorousness. Salomon, where
he speaketh of moderate correction, saith : " The rod and
correction giveth wisdom ; but the child that runneth at random bringeth his mother to shame." Again : " Chastise thy
son, and thou shalt be at quiet, and he shall bring pleasure
unto thy soul[3]." These words of his do utterly condemn the
Cockering of father's cockering[4], and the mother's pampering, which is the
children.
marring of very many children. For the parents offend God
as much in too much cockering their children, as they do in
overmuch punishing of them. Heli in the scriptures is ill reported of for doting over his children ; he himself dieth
miserably, and bringeth the shameless wicked knaves, his
sons, to a shameful ending[5]. What is to be thought of that
moreover, that in the twenty-first of Deuteronomy the parents
themselves are commanded to bring their disobedient children
before the judge, and there, by complaint, to sue them to
death ? By this example, which may otherwise seem to be
somewhat too sharp, it pleased God to put other men in
remembrance to keep their children in awe and obedience.
For God is a God of salvation, and not of destruction ; so
that, when disobedient rebels and godless people perish
through their own default, he turneth that destruction of theirs
to the safeguard of his obedient servants. Let parents therefore always remember this saying in the gospel : " It is not

[1 plus efficias, Lat.]   [2 Eph. vi. 4.]
[3 Prov. xxix. 15, 17.]
[4 indulgentiam, Lat.]
[5 1 Sam. ii. 29. & iv.]

the will of your heavenly Father, that one of these little ones should perish. Whosoever offendeth such an one, it were better for him that a millstone were hanged about his neck, and that he were drowned in the depth of the sea[6]."

Now, touching the duty of children, I have spoken of it *The duty of children.* before in the place where I taught, how and after what sort parents ought to be honoured. Paul, as it were in one word, knitteth up much matter, and saith: "Children, obey your parents in the Lord." He telleth the reason why: "For that," saith he, "is righteous." And again he addeth the cause, saying: "For God hath commanded it[7]." Let children therefore consider and think upon the nightly watchings and continual labour that their parents took in bringing them up, and let them learn to be thankful for it, and content with their present estate. When their parents instruct them, let them learn attentively, and shew themselves like to godly Jacob rather than to godless Esau. Let them learn to accustom themselves to good and honest manners. Let them willingly learn the art or occupation whereunto they are set. Let them yield and submit themselves to their parents' correction. Let them not stir up or provoke their parents to anger. Let them choose to learn wit, and obey their parents, of their own mind and accord, rather than to be driven to it by beating and brawling. If parents at their departure leave little behind them for their children to inherit, let not the good children therefore speak ill by the dead. If thy father hath taught thee any art or occupation, he leaveth for thee a sufficient inheritance. Thriftiness, also, and moderate spending, is a very great revenue[8]. If thy father hath well and honestly taught thee good manners, and trained thee up in the true wisdom and perfect religion, then hath he bequeathed thee a patrimony sufficient for to maintain thee. For what else are exceeding great riches, left to a fool or irreligious fellow, but a sword in a madman's hand? Thou art left wealthy enough by thy father's legacy, if that thou art godly, painful, heedful, and honest. For goods gotten by the sweat of our own brows do for the most part continue

[6] Matt. xviii. 14, 6.]
[7] Ephes. vi. 1, 2.]
[8] Frugalitas ac parsimonia magnum est vectigal, Lat. Cf. Erasm. Adag. Chiliad. fol. 269. *a.* Parsimonia summum vectigal.]

longer, and prosper better with us, than those which other leave unto us.

We have again, dearly beloved, spent an hour and a half in handling this matter touching the honour due unto parents. I have stayed you longer than of right I should have done, but ye shall impute it to the love and good will I bear to the matter. I am not ignorant how necessary this argument is, almost to all men: and therefore stick I the longer upon it. For I endeavour myself, not only to teach you things profitable and necessary, but also to beat them into your memories so much as I may, to the end that ye never forget them. God grant you all a fruitful increase of his holy word, which is the seed that is sown in your hearts. Let us pray, &c.

OF THE SECOND PRECEPT OF THE SECOND TABLE, WHICH IS IN ORDER THE SIXTH OF THE TEN COMMANDMENTS, THOU SHALT NOT KILL: AND OF THE MAGISTRATE.

THE SIXTH SERMON.

JUSTICE and innocency are very well joined to[1] the higher power and magistrate's authority; and in this sixth precept both public and private peace and tranquillity are hedged in and inclosed against open tumults and secret discords. And since the life of man is the most excellent thing in the world, whereupon all other things, of how great price soever they be, do wait and attend; and finally, since the body of man is more worth than all other gifts whatsoever; the very natural order doth seem to require, that the sixth commandment should be placed next, which God himself hath plainly expressed in these few words, "Thou shalt not

The sixth precept.

kill[2]." For in this precept justice and innocency are commanded and commended unto us, wherein also it is provided, that no man hurt another's life or body; and so in this pre-

[1 subjungitur, Lat.]
[2 Exod. xx. 13.—duabas duntaxat vocibus proditum, Non occides, Lat.]

cept charge is given to every one to maintain peace and quietness.

Now here are to be observed the steps that lead to murder; wherein we must consider the kinds and causes of hurting and annoying. For the Lord doth not simply forbid murder, but all things else whereon murder doth consist. All egging on, therefore, and provoking to anger is utterly forbidden; slanderous taunts and brawling speeches are flatly prohibited; strife, wrath, and envy, are plainly commanded to be suppressed. And in this sense we have Christ our Lord himself interpreting this law, where in the Gospel after Matthew he saith: "Ye have heard it said of old, Thou shalt not kill; whosoever killeth shall be in danger of judgment. But I say unto you, that whosoever is angry with his brother unadvisedly shall be in danger of judgment. And whosoever shall say unto his brother, Racha, shall be in danger of a council. But whosoever shall say, Thou fool, shall be in danger of hell fire." Thou seest here, therefore, that anger, slander, brawling, and all other tokens of a mind moved to utter ill words, are flatly forbidden. What then must thou do? Thou must, forsooth, come into charity again with him whom thou hast offended; thou must lay aside all wrath and envy, unless thou hadst rather have all the honour that thou dost to God [3] be imputed for sin unto thee, and that, peradventure, thou wouldest choose rather utterly to be condemned. For our Lord goeth on in the gospel, and saith: "If therefore thou bring thy gift unto the altar, and there rememberest that thy brother have any thing against thee, leave there thy gift before the altar," (he speaketh to them, who as then had their temple standing, their altar remaining, and burnt-offerings in use; we, at this day, have another manner of worshipping God,) "and go thy way; first be reconciled to thy brother, and then come and offer thy gift." And again: "Agree with thine adversary quickly, whiles thou art in the way with him; lest at any time the adversary deliver thee to the judge, and the judge deliver thee to the minister, and thou be cast into prison. Verily, I say unto thee, thou shalt not depart from thence until thou hast paid the utmost farthing [4]." But for because

[3 cultum, quem Deo exhibes.]
[4 Matt. v. 23—26.]

so few of us obey this sound and wholesome doctrine of the Lord's, thereby it cometh to pass, that so many great and troublesome tumults happen among men. For small is the substance of them that obey the word of God, but great is the rest and quietness of their consciences. And what pleasure, I pray you, do infinite riches bring to man, since with them a man cannot likely be without troublesome cares of mind, great turmoils and lack of a quiet life? This law therefore, which tends to no other end, but to teach man the way to lead a sweet and pleasant life, doth wholly take from the mind of man such immoderate affections as anger and envy are, two the most pestilent evils that reign among men.

As concerning anger, I mean not at this present to speak over busily, even as also I have determined to be brief touching envy. Of anger many men have uttered many profitable sentences: and yet there is an holy kind of anger, which the scripture disalloweth not; so that, unless a man be angry in that sort, he shall never be a good and godly man. For a good man hath a zeal of God, and in that godly zeal he is angry at the iniquity and naughtiness of mankind; whereof there are many examples to be seen in the scriptures: and this anger doth stomach the sin committed, rather than the person who doth commit the sin. For the good servant of God hateth nothing in the wicked man's person, but his very sin; so that, if the wicked cease once to sin, he will leave to hate or be angry therewithal any longer. This anger is utterly condemned then, when it springs of evil and corrupt affections; when no just cause is given, but that he, which is offended, doth in his anger either fulfil his affection, or else hurt or determine to hurt him with whom he is angry. A great evil it is, and a fruit, which when it is sown doth yield and bring forth one mischief upon another's neck. And therefore doth the apostle of Christ counsel all men not to give any place to anger; and if so be it happen that it enter into our minds, and stick there awhile, yet that we suffer it not to catch fast hold, or take deep root therein. " Be angry," saith he, " and sin not. Let not the sun set upon your anger, and give no place to the devil[1]." For this is the apostle's meaning: if so it happen, that ye be angry, yet sin not; that is, yet bridle your anger. Neither doth the apostle bid

Of anger.

[1 Eph. iv. 26, 27.]

us to be angry, but willeth us not to let our anger to continue long, nor to break out to the working of injury. And παροργισμός (which word Paul useth) signifieth anger indeed, but yet, more rightly, the stirring or provoking to anger; so that thereby we have to understand, that to him, which is by injury provoked to anger, although he be somewhat grieved and touched at the quick, that grief ought to be but of short continuance: neither must we in any case suffer our adversary[2], the devil, to fasten his foot in our hearts, who doth through anger by little and little creep into our minds, and by continual wrath doth work out envy, by which he doth captivate and pervert the whole man, with all his senses, words, and works.

For envy is anger grown into custom by long continu- Of envy. ance, which doth for the most part vex, burn, and (mangle him that doth[3]) envy, more than the party which is envied; although the envious doth never cease to devise mischief against the man whom he doth envy. It is an endless evil, which doth not admit any remedy to take it away. And therefore did the Gentiles bait and canvass it to and fro with wonderful pretty quips and pithy sentences[4]; some of which I will not be ashamed here to rehearse, to the intent that counterfeit Christians, addicted to envy, may be ashamed of it, if peradventure they will learn to blush, when they find themselves touched by heathens and paynims.

Virgil saith:

> In heart, where envy's seed takes root,
>   There grows a poisoned grain,
> Which dries and drinks from every limb
>   The blood of every vein;
> And sucks and soaks the marrow bones,
>   Until they feeble wax;
> (Such is th' envenom'd poison's force,)
>   And yet no bone it cracks[5].

[2 calumniator, Lat.   This exposition of St Paul's words is taken almost verbatim from Erasmus' Annot. in loc.]

[3 invidentem fere torquet, urit, et excarnificat, Lat.   The words between brackets are accidentally omitted in the translation.]

[4 Gentes id exagitarunt miris modis, Lat.]

[5   Livor tabificum malis venenum
Intactis vorat ossibus medullas,
Et totum bibit artubus cruorem.
     Epigr. de Livore. Virgil. Opp. Basil. 1613, p. 1981.]

And therefore saith Horace :

> The Sicil tyrants never found
> A more tormenting hell,
> Than envy was, &c.[1]

Silius Italicus crieth out :

> Ill-favour'd envy, ugly hag,
> And dogged end
> Of mortal men, that never could'st
> Abide to lend
> One word to praise praise-worthy deeds,
> But swell'st to see
> Small things increase, and low things grow
> To high degree[2].

Ovid, speaking of envy, describeth it thus :

> Within did devilish envy sit,
> And eat the flesh of snakes,
> To feed the humour of her vice
> With such kind loathly cates :
> With face of tallow-caked hue,
> And body lean like death,
> With squint eyes turn'd nine sundry ways,
> With rusty stinking teeth.
> Her bitter breast was overspread
> With gaid[3] as green as grass ;
> Her tongue, that ceas'd not to say ill,
> With venom poison'd was.
> She never laugh'd, unless it were
> When grief made others weep ;
> And fretting care within her heart
> Did keep her eyes from sleep.
> She sees, and pines away to see,
> The good success and state
> Of men that prosper on the earth :
> And so her deadly hate
> Is to herself a deadly plague.

[1   Invidia Siculi non invenere tyranni
      Majus tormentum.
                              Hor. Ep. i. 2, 58.]
[2   O dirum exitium mortalibus ! O nihil unquam
      Crescere, nec magnas patiens exsurgere laudes,
      Invidia !
                              Sil. Ital. Punic. Lib. xvii. 188.]
[3 Gaid, withes. Shaw's Gaelic and English Dict. in voc.]

> Where as she goes, she mars the corn
> That grows upon the ground;
> She makes on trees that blossoms bear
> There can no fruit be found;
> And with her breath she doth infect
> Whole houses, realms, and towns[4].

Since, therefore, that envy is so great an evil, and that the Lord commandeth to keep ourselves from it, therein doth appear the Lord's goodness to us-ward; and thereby we may gather how good and profitable his law is, which tendeth, and is given, to none other end, but to set us at liberty from so great a mischief. And here, by the way, we do perceive, that our fault, and not the waywardness of God, is the cause, why many in this world are never at peace and quietness, but are exceedingly vexed with continual torments. For as they cease not to envy the estate of other, so with their anger they disquiet more than themselves, and do at last duly aby[5] and worthily suffer the deserved punishment of their wicked deeds.

And this law doth not only forbid and restrain the mo- *All hurting is forbidden.* tions and evil affections of the mind by wrath, anger, and envy; but doth also give commandment against all manner hurt that riseth by them. Harm and hurt is done by sundry means; by beating, by violent thrusting, by overthrowing, by pulling, and troubling, although in doing so thou dost not wound thy neighbour. But thy sin is the greater, if thou

---

[4]   videt intus edentem
Vipereas carnes, vitiorum alimenta suorum,
Invidiam.—
Pallor in ore sedet, macies in corpore toto:
Nusquam recta acies: livent rubigine dentes;
Pectora felle virent: lingua est suffusa veneno;
Risus abest, nisi quem visi movere dolores.
Nec fruitur somno, vigilacibus excita curis:
Sed videt ingratos, intabescitque videndo,
Successus hominum: carpitque et carpitur una;
Suppliciumque suum est.—
Quacumque ingreditur, florentia proterit arva,
Exuritque herbas, et summa cacumina carpit;
Afflatuque suo populos, urbesque, domosque
Polluit.
                    Ovid. Met. Lib. II. 768, &c.]

[5] luunt pœnas, Lat.]

givest him a wound after what sort soever, either with weapon, or by any means else. And again, thou sinnest yet
more grievously, if thou dost quite cut off, or otherwise break,
any limb of his body; if thou puttest out his eyes, or dashest
a tooth out of his head. So then the better that the limb is
that thou cuttest off, or puttest out of joint, the greater is the
sin, and more grievous thine offence. From whence, without
doubt, the law called *lex talionis*[1] took the beginning, which
commandeth to cut off the hand of him, which did cut off
another's hand; and to pluck out the eye of him, which did
put out another man's eye.

The law of like for like.

Now also, the manner of killing must not be overpassed.
The Lord saith, "Thou shalt not kill." We kill divers
ways: either we ourselves do the deed, or else we use the
help of other to strike the stroke; it is done either privily or
openly. And in this sort again there are very many fashions:
for we commit murder sometime by holding our peace, sometime by dissembling, by giving ill counsel, by consenting, by aid-
ing, or egging forward to evil. Another peradventure would
not do the thing that he doeth, but because he seeth that
thou hastenest him on; but because he knoweth he shall
please thee thereby; and because he perceiveth that thy help
upholdeth him. Although, therefore, that thou with thine
own hand strike not the stroke, yet the murder, that another
committeth by thy setting on, shall be imputed to thee as
well as if thou thyself hadst killed the man. And no marvel,
since John, the apostle and evangelist, calleth hatred manslaughter[2].

The manners of killing.

Moreover, here are to be touched the causes of murder,
or doing of mischief. For hereupon standeth, and from
hence cometh, the mischievous deed and foul offence. Murder is committed, and the neighbour endamaged, either unwittingly, or else upon pretended[3] malice. It is done unwittingly, where as, when a man purposeth another thing, by
ill hap, or, as I should rather say, by the providence of God,
murder doth ensue. As for example; when my mind is to
discharge a gun against a buck, meaning to kill the beast, by

The causes of murder.

[1 See Smith's Dict. of Greek and Rom. Antiq. sub voc. *talio.*
Arnold's Hist. of Rome. Chap. xiv. § 2. Vol. i. p. 286. Lond. 1840.]
[2 1 John iii. 15.]
[3 i. e. designed, premeditated.]

hap I strike a man, who unawares to me was in the same wood, cutting timber: or else where as upon simplicity I give my friend a draught of poison, where mine intent was to have given him a medicine to recover his health. For such chances as these hath the Lord in the law[4], and among all nations, prepared sanctuaries for men to flee to, as places of refuge. Sanctuaries. Murders proceed of pretended malice, when I, being blinded with private greediness, do go about to take from another man that which is his, and for resistance do kill him, if he yield it not to me. Of that sort are many wars and foughten battles now-a-days; and of that sort are robberies and murders committed by the highways' side. That also is pretended murder, when I, for injury that another man doth me, do revenge myself by killing him; or else, when I, being mad with anger, or overcome with wine, do murder the man, whom otherwise, if I were not in that ill-favoured taking, I would make much of and love very heartily.

But now, how foul and detestable an offence murder is, How great an offence murder is. that proceedeth of malice, I think it expedient for me to declare to you, and you to mark in this that followeth. For the consideration thereof, being throughly scanned, must needs undoubtedly work so in the hearts of men, that fewer murders shall be committed, and that every one shall endeavour himself the more, by suppressing anger, to preserve mankind, who is the holy similitude of God himself. The very deed of murder itself fighteth directly and disobediently against the eternal God, who is the life and salvation of the world. For murder destroyeth the very image of God; þecause man is created to the similitude and likeness of God. If a man should of purpose deface[5] the image of the king or prince, set up at their commandment, he should be accused of treason committed: in how great danger is he then, that doth destroy a man, which is the reasonable, lively, and very picture of God himself! We read that Theodosius the emperor did determine to destroy a great number of the citizens of Antioch, for none other cause but for overthrowing of the image that was set up for the honour of Placilla Augusta. But thereunto is added, that one Macedonius, an hermit, came to the emperor's messengers, and said: "O my friends, go say to the emperor, Thou art not an emperor only, but also a man.

[4 Numb. xxxv. 11, &c.]   [5 everteret in foro, Lat.]

[BULLINGER.]

20

Do not thou cruelly destroy the image of God. Thou angerest thy Maker, when thou killest his image. Consider with thyself, that thou art sorry for an image of brass. Now it is evident to all men what difference there is betwixt a thing that is dead, and that which hath life and a reasonable soul. Moreover, it is an easy matter instead of one brasen image to set up more : but it is unpossible to restore one hair to them that once are slain[1]." Finally, murder is clean contrary to the nature of man. For man cherisheth himself, and flesh destroyeth not itself, but preserveth and nourisheth itself so much as it may. But all we men, as many as live, are of one lump, and of the same substantial flesh : and to kill a man therefore is against man's nature. Furthermore, all men are the children of one father, of one stock, and of the same progeny : murder therefore is directly against civil humanity, and is a plague that reigns among men. And doth not the Lord our Redeemer also require charity of all men, which must so abound, that we may not stick to die for our neighbour ? To kill our neighbour, therefore, is flatly repugnant to christian religion. And take this by the way too ; that the blood of man, shed by murder, crieth out of the earth to heaven for revengement : for to Cain, when he had slain his brother, it was said, "The voice of thy brother's blood crieth out of the

[1] Ὁ δῆμος (τῆς Ἀντιόχου πόλεως) τὴν χαλκῆν εἰκόνα τῆς πανευφήμου Πλακίλλης ... κατήνεγκέ τε καὶ ἐπὶ πολὺ τῆς πόλεως κατέσυρε μέρος. Ταῦτα πυθόμενος ὁ βασιλεύς, καὶ χαλεπήνας ... ἐμπρήσειν ἠπείλει καὶ καταλύσειν καὶ εἰς κώμην τὸ ἄστυ μετασκευάσειν. Μακεδόνιος δὲ ὁ θειότατος ... ἐν ταῖς τῶν ὀρῶν κορυφαῖς διαιτώμενος ... τῆς χλανίδος θατέρου (τῶν ἀποστα-λέντων ἀπὸ τοῦ βασιλέως) λαβόμενος, ἀμφοτέρους ἐκ τῶν ἵππων καταβῆναι κελεύει. Ὁ δὲ, της θείας σοφίας ἐμφορηθείς, τοιοῖσδε πρὸς αὐτοὺς ἐχρήσατο λόγοις· Εἴπατε, ὦ φίλοι ἄνδρες, τῷ βασιλεῖ· οὐ βασιλεὺς εἰ μόνον, ἀλλὰ καὶ ἄνθρωπος· μὴ τοίνυν μόνην ὅρα τὴν βασιλείαν, ἀλλὰ καὶ τὴν φύσιν λογίζου· ἄνθρωπος γὰρ ὤν, ὁμοφυῶν βασιλεύεις. Κατ᾽ εἰκόνα δὲ θείαν καὶ ὁμοίωσιν ἡ τῶν ἀνθρώπων δεδημιούργηται φύσις· μὴ τοίνυν ὠμῶς οὕτως καὶ ἀπηνῶς τοῦ Θεοῦ τὴν εἰκόνα κατασφαγῆναι κελεύσῃς· παροξυνεῖς γὰρ τὸν δημιουργόν, τὴν ἐκείνου κολάζων εἰκόνα. Σκόπησον γὰρ, ὡς καὶ σὺ χαλκῆς ἕνεκα δυσχεραίνων εἰκόνος ταῦτα ποιεῖς. Ὅσον δὲ τῆς ἀψύχου διαφέρει ἡ ἔμψυχός τε καὶ ζῶσα καὶ λογική, δῆλον ἅπασι τοῖς γε νοῦν ἔχουσι. Πρὸς δὲ τούτοις λογισάσθω κἀκεῖνα, ὡς ἡμῖν μὲν ῥάδιον ἀντὶ τῆς μιᾶς εἰκόνος πολλὰς δημιουργῆσαι χαλκᾶς· αὐτῷ δὲ πάμπαν ἀδύνατον μίαν γοῦν τῶν ἀναιρεθέντων δημιουργῆσαι τρίχα.—Theodorit. Eccles. Hist. Lib. v. cap. 20. Ed. Reading. Cantab. 1720, pp. 219, 220. See also Calfhill's Answ. to Martiall. Parker Soc. ed. p. 22.]

earth, and is come up to me." For bloodshed verily polluteth and maketh the ground accursed whereon it is shed, and is not cleansed again, nor easily appeased, until it do also drink the guilty blood of them which spilt before the guiltless blood of innocents. Lastly, murders procure and mark the committers thereof with endless spots of reproachful infamy; and, that which is worst of all, it bringeth unto them everlasting damnation. Wherefore Salomon in his proverbs saith : "My son, if sinners entice thee, consent not unto them. If they say, Come with us, we will lay wait for blood, and will lurk privily for the innocent without a cause; We will swallow them up like the grave quick, and whole as those that go down into the pit; We shall find all manner of costly riches, and fill our houses with the prey ; Cast in thy lot among us; we will all have one purse : My son, walk not thou with them, but rather pull back thy foot from their ways. For their feet run to evil, and are hasty to shed blood[2]." Now David saith, that " the blood-thirsty man, and the hypocrite, are abominable to the Lord[3]."

From this law is exempted the magistrate ordained by God, whom God commandeth to use authority and to kill, threatening to punish him most sharply, if he neglect to kill the men whom God commandeth to be killed. This sixth commandment of the law, therefore, doth flatly forbid upon private authority to kill any man : but the magistrate killeth at God's commandment, when he putteth to death those which are by law condemned for their offences, or when in defence of his people he doth justly and necessarily arm himself to the battle. And yet the magistrates may offend in those two points two sundry ways. For either they do by law, that is, under the coloured pretence of law, slay the guiltless, to satisfy their own lust, hatred, or covetousness ; as we read, that Jezebel slew the just man Naboth, with the Lord's prophets[4]: or else by peevish pity and foolish clemency do let them escape scot-free, whom the Lord commanded them to kill; as Saul and Achab are reported to have sinned in letting go the bloody kings whom God commanded to be slain[5]. And Salomon, in the seventeenth of his

The magistrate may kill.

[2 Prov. i. 10—16.]   [3 Psal. v. 6.]
[4 1 Sam. xv; 1 Kings xx. 42.]
[5 1 Kings xxi. & xviii. 13. Hooper's Early Writ. ed. Park. Soc. p. 475.]

20—2

Proverbs, doth testify, that the Lord doth as greatly hate the magistrate that acquitteth a wicked person, as him that condemneth an innocent man[1]. The magistrates also in making or else repelling war do offend two ways in this sort: for either they do unjustly themselves make war upon other men, and entangle their people therein; or else they suffer foreign enemies to rob and spoil the people committed to their charge, and do not with such force as they may keep off and defend[2] that open wrong and manifest injury. Both these offences are of sundry sorts, and therewithal so great that they can hardly be purged. Thou readest therefore, that the holy kings of Israel did never make war upon anybody, unless the Lord commanded them. And they again fought for their people, and suffered them not to be led away captive, as miserable bond-slaves. For so did the blessed patriarch Abraham follow upon and pursue those four kings, nay, rather cutthroat robbers of the east, and recovered by force of arms Lot, Lot's substance, and the people of Sodom that were carried away[3]. And such wars as these are taken in hand, either for the recovery, or else for the confirmation, of peace: so that the magistrates that make war in such a cause are rightly and indeed the children of God, because they are peace-makers; for all peace-makers are the children of God.

What the magistrate is.

And now this place and argument do require, that I speak somewhat touching the office or authority of the magistrate: which (by God's help) I will assay to do, not that I mean or can allege all that may be said thereof, but that which shall seem most properly to declare the meaning of it, and is most necessary for this present treatise[4].

[1 Prov. xvii. 15.]

[2 i. e. repel, keep off.—Johnson. So in Early Writings of Hooper, Parker Soc. ed. p. 107.]

[3 Gen. xiv. 14—16.]

[4 The mischievous tenets of the Anabaptists rendered so necessary in the age of Bullinger the setting forth of the true doctrine concerning civil magistracy. A summary proof of this necessity is thus given by Melancthon: Sæpe et olim et recens fuerunt hypocritæ superstitiosi et fanatici, qui ... magistratuum functiones, judicia, leges forenses, legitimas pœnas, imperia, bella legitima, militiam damnaverunt. Tales furores olim sparserunt Marcion et Manichæi;—circumtulerunt et similes errores ante trecentos annos Flagelliferi, ut vocabantur; et hoc

Magistratus (which word we use for the room wherein Magistratus, what it is.
the magistrate is) doth take the name *a magistris populi designandis,* "of assigning the masters, guiders, and captains of the people." That room and place is called by the name of "power" or "authority," by reason of the power that is given to it of God. It is called by the name of "domination," for the dominion that the Lord doth grant it upon the earth. They are called princes that have that dominion: for they have a pre-eminence above the people. They are called consuls, of counselling; and kings, of commanding, ruling, and governing the people. So, then, the magistracy (that I may henceforward use this word of the magistrate's power and place) is an office, and an action in executing of the same. Aristotle defineth a magistrate to be a keeper of laws[5]. Plutarch, in that book wherein he sheweth that learning is required to be in a king, among other things saith: "Princes are the ministers of God for the oversight and safeguard of mortal men, to the end that they may partly distribute, and partly keep, the good things that he doth liberally give, and frankly bestow upon them[6]." The magistracy, by the scriptures, may be defined to be a divine ordinance or action, whereby the good being defended by the prince's aid, and the evil suppressed by the same authority, godliness, justice, honesty, peace, and tranquillity, both public and private, are safely preserved. Whereby we gather, that to govern a commonweal, and to execute the office of a magistrate, is a worship and service to God himself. God verily is delighted therein. For the office of a magistrate is a thing most excellent, and abounding with all good works, as in my former sermon I have declared.

Now there are three kinds of magistracies or governments Three kinds of magistrates.
of commonweals; the monarchy, the aristocracy, and the Monarchy.

nostro tempore Anabaptistæ passim vagantes adhuc circumferunt hos errores.—Melanc. Loc. Com. Erlang. 1838. Vol. i. pars 2. p. 138.]

[5 Ἔστι δὲ ὁ ἄρχων φύλαξ τοῦ δικαίου.—Aristot. Eth. Lib. v. cap. 6. In Polit. iii. c. 16, Aristotle calls magistrates, νομοφύλακας καὶ ὑπηρέτας τοῖς νόμοις.]

[6 Ἀληθέστερον δ' ἄν τις εἴποι τοὺς ἄρχοντας ὑπηρετεῖν Θεῷ πρὸς ἀνθρώπων ἐπιμέλειαν καὶ σωτηρίαν, ὅπως, ὧν Θεὸς δίδωσιν ἀνθρώποις καλῶν καὶ ἀγαθῶν, τὰ μὲν νέμωσι, τὰ δὲ φυλάττωσιν.—Plutarch ad Princip. Indoct.]

democracy[1]. We may call the monarchy a kingdom, wherein one alone doth by just and upright laws rule all things and causes in the commonweal. For if that justice and equity be once neglected, and that this one doth against all right and reason rule all the roost, then is he a tyrant, and his *Tyranny.* power is tyranny, that is to say, wrong and injury; which is a disease of that troubled kingdom, and a vice that is, as it were, set opposite to be the destruction of that commonweal. *Aristocracy.* The aristocracy is the superior power of a few peers, where a certain number of holy and upright men are chosen to be the guides and rulers of the people. And this did first begin by the fall of tyranny: for when men perceived how dangerous it was to commit the rule of their whole state into one man's hand, they altered the order, and gave the charge thereof to an appointed number of chosen men, who did excel the common sort in power and authority. But if these chief or head men use evil means to come to authority, and, neglecting the commonweal, do hunt after their own advantage; then is their government not to be called an aristocracy, but *Oligarchy.* an oligarchy, that is, the violent lust of a few, and not the good and upright government of chosen peers. So then these few violent rulers are the contrary to the estate, where up- *Democracy.* right headmen have the pre-eminence. The democracy may be called a commonweal, wherein all the people together bear the whole sway and absolute authority. And this democracy began first by the fall of the oligarchy. For when the people saw that their headmen did abuse their power, and waxed violent rulers, they displaced them, and kept the authority to themselves, meaning that every man should freely give his voice in matters touching the commonweal. This kind of government breaketh out commonly into outrageous tumults[2], I mean, into seditions and conspiracies: for no man will suffer himself to be corrected, while every man will challenge to himself full and absolute authority to do what he lusteth, because, forsooth, he is one and a member of the people, in whose hands the whole authority doth consist.

[1 On this subject of the various forms of governments and their abuses, Bullinger seems to have borrowed from Aristot. Ethic. Lib. VIII. cap. 10.]

[2 Systremma, Lat. σύστρεμμα, tumultus e concursu hominum.— Hederic. Lex.]

Now touching the excellency of these forms or kinds of government, it maketh not greatly to my purpose to dispute which ought to be preferred before other. Many have preferred the monarchy before the rest: but therewithal they added, " If he which holdeth the monarchy be a good and upright prince." Which, nevertheless, is rare to be found. They also, which were of that opinion, did themselves live under princes in monarchies. "But it is dangerous to speak against Jupiter." Among many kings of Judah and Israel thou shalt find a very few good, or at least wise tolerable and indifferent, princes; whereby we may perceive that the Lord did not in vain, by the mouth of Samuel, persuade his people to keep their aristocracy, and to be ruled by their priests and elders, as God, by Moses and Jethro, the wisest in the world, had ordained long before. And yet none can deny, but that great perils and infinite discommodities are in the aristocracy, but far more many in the democracy. But such is the condition of mortal men in this corruptible flesh, that nothing among them is absolutely and on every side happy[4]; and therefore that seemeth to them to be most excellent, which, although it be not altogether without inconveniences and some kind of vices, doth nevertheless, in comparison of other, bring fewer perils and lesser annoyance. But howsoever that case doth stand, the apostles of Christ do command us to obey the magistrate, whether he be king, or senate of chosen men. For Paul in his epistle to Titus saith: " Warn them to be subject to rule and power, and to obey magistrates[5]." For to the Romans he saith: " Let every soul be subject to the higher powers: for no power is but of God, and those powers that are are ordained by God[6]." Again, to Timothy he saith: " I exhort you that prayers be made for kings, and for all that are in authority[7]." If therefore any man live in a monarchy, let him obey the king: if in a commonweal of what title soever, let him be ruled by the consuls, tribunes,

A proverb, signifying that it is perilous for a subject to speak against his prince. In English we say, it is ill jesting with saints [3].

The magistrate must be obeyed.

Tit. iii.

[3 The proverb most like this occurs in Ray, as the Italian form of our English one, "No jesting with edge tools, or with bell-ropes:" viz. "Tresca con i fanti, et lascia star i santi; i. e. Play with children, and let the saints alone."—Ray's Proverbs, p. 124.]

[4 Nihil est ab omni parte beatum. Quoted from Hor. Od. Lib. II. 16. 27.]

[5 Titus iii. 1.]   [6 Rom. xiii. 1.]   [7 1 Tim. ii. 1.]

headmen, and elders of the people. For we ought rather to obey the ordinance of God, than over curiously to dispute of the kinds of governments, which is the better or worse than other.

The causes of magistrates, and their beginning.

And in all cases truly, the magistrate is very necessary, and cannot be missing among men; yea, he is so necessary, that without the magistrate's help the state of men can hardly prosper, or easily stand. Neither dost thou read, that the state and commonweal of the Israelites was ever at any time in greater danger and peril of undoing, than it was in the middle time betwixt Sampson and Heli, when they were governed by no magistrates, but did every man what he thought good himself[1]. For all men even from their birth are blindly led with self-love, and therefore they seek their own advantage; nothing pleaseth them but what they do themselves, they utterly mislike the deeds and words of other men: yea, such is our fond affection and opinionative sense, that how evil soever our causes are, yet we will not stick to face them out with a card of ten[2], and to colour them with law and equity. He that will stand in denial hereof, did never consider man's disposition. The people of Israel, at their delivery out of Egypt, saw wonderful signs; they were marvellously fed from heaven in the desert, and did every day behold new miracles. But yet, hearken, my brethren, and consider, what Moses, the meekest and gentlest man that ever was, doth say touching this holy people, this people of God, whom God had chosen to be a peculiar people unto himself: "How shall I alone," saith he to the people, "bear your trouble, your burden, and the strifes that are among you[3]?" What

[1 Judg. xvii. 6.]

[2 Causis nostris licet pessimis jus prætexamus et justitiam, Lat. The proverbial expression used by the translator occurs in Shakspeare's Taming of the Shrew, Act ii. Scene 1. ad fin. and, earlier still, in Skelton:

Fyrste pycke a quarell, and fall out with him then,
And so outface hym with a carde of ten.—
The Bouge of Courte.

The phrase of a card of ten was possibly derived, by a jocular allusion, from that of a hart of ten, in hunting, which meant a full-grown deer; one past six years of age. Nares's Glossary, in voc. Card. I conceive the force of the phrase to have expressed originally the confidence or impudence of one who with a ten, as at brag, faced, or out-faced one who had really a faced card against him.—Ibid. in voc. to face it.]

[3 Deut. i. 12.]

may be thought of that moreover, that in the most sure fellowship of the ancient and apostolic church, yea, in those very vessels which were regenerate, the wrangling disposition of flesh did shew itself? For the Greeks murmured against the Hebrews, because their widows in the daily ministry were little regarded[4]. The Corinthians also go to law before heathen judges; and therefore doth Paul very sharply rebuke them, and chargeth them to appoint honest judges among themselves to take up matters betwixt them that were at variance[5]. Let no man therefore make this objection, and say, that the old people of Israel were a carnal people and not regenerate. For we see, that even in the regenerate the relics of flesh remain, which ever and anon, when occasion is offered, do shew forth themselves, and trouble the quiet state of everything. For I will not now say that the greater sort of men do rather follow the flesh than the spirit. And for that cause God, who loveth man, who keepeth and pre-serveth civility, peace, and human society, hath prepared and applied a medicine against those grievous diseases of men; he hath appointed the magistrate, I say, to step betwixt them that strive with the authority of law and equity, to judge and discuss matters betwixt them that are at variance, to bridle and suppress wrong and affections, and lastly, to save the guiltless and innocents. Whosoever subverteth this or-dinance of God, till such time as men do leave their wayward disposition[6], he bringeth utter confusion to every state, and aideth wrongful dealers and violent robbers to oppress and root out the best sort of people. By this verily, which hitherto we have alleged, it is manifestly apparent, that the magistrate is ordained by God for the safeguard of the good, and punishment of the evil; I mean, for the good and quiet state of mortal men. Wherefore we read, that from the beginning there have been magistrates in the world.

The magistrate ordained by God for the good of men.

Hereunto do appertain these testimonies of the holy scrip-ture. Moses in the law calleth the judges Gods, and this "judg-ment," saith he, "is God's[7]." From whence also Josaphat borrowed that saying, which he spake to the judges, where he saith: "See what ye do: for ye judge not to man, but

[4 Acts vi. 1.]   [5 1 Cor. vi. 1—4.]
[6 priusquam homines angelicum recipiant ingenium, Lat.]
[7 Exod. xxii. 28; Deut. i. 17.]

to the Lord, which is with you in the causes which ye judge: let the fear of God therefore be in your hearts[1]." St Peter saith, that we must "obey the magistrate for the Lord's sake, by whom he is ordained to the praise of the good, and terrifying of the evil[2]." And Paul, the teacher of the Gentiles, saith: "There is no power but of God, and the powers that are are ordained by God: and whosoever resisteth the power, resisteth the ordinance of God; and he that resisteth shall receive to himself damnation. For rulers are not fearful to them that do well, but to the evil. For he is the minister of God, revenger of wrath on him that doth evil[3]." The magistrate therefore is of God; his office is good, holy, pleasing God, just, profitable, and necessary for men: and the rulers, which do rightly execute their office, are the friends and worshippers of God; they are his elect instruments, by whom he worketh man's health and safeguard. We have examples hereof in Adam, all the patriarchs, our father Noe, Joseph, Moses, Josue, Gedeon, Samuel, David, Josaphat, Ezechias, Josias, Daniel, and many other after the time of Christ, who rightly executed the office of magistrates.

Now many there are which will have the magistrate to be of two sorts, to wit, either good or bad. The good magistrate is he who, being lawfully ordained, doth lawfully execute his office and duty. The evil magistrate is he which, when he hath by evil means got the authority, doth turn and dispose it as himself lusteth. And hereupon the question is wont to be demanded: Whether an evil, that is, a tyrannical, magistrate, be of God or no? To this I answer, that God is the author of good, and not of evil. For God by nature is good, and all his purposes are good, being directed to the health and preservation, not to the destruction, of us men. Therefore the good and healthful ordaining of the magistrate, without all doubt, is of God himself, who is the author of all goodness.

But here it is requisite, that we make a difference betwixt the office which is the good ordinance of God, and the evil person that doth not rightly execute that good office. If therefore in the magistrate evil be found, and not the good for which he was ordained, that cometh of other causes, and

A good magistrate and a bad.

Whether an evil magistrate be of God or no.

[1 2 Chron. xix. 6, 7.]   [2 1 Pet. ii. 14.]
[3 Rom. xiii. 1—4.]

the fault thereof is in the men and persons, which neglect God and corrupt the ordinance of God, and not in God, nor in his ordinance: for either the evil prince, seduced by the devil, corrupteth the ways of God, and by his own fault and naughtiness transgresseth God's ordinance, so far, that he doth worthily deserve the name of devilish power, and not divine authority;—(we have an example hereof in the magistrate of Jerusalem: for although he were able to refer the beginning of his power by degrees unto Moses, and so unto God himself who did ordain it; yet, for because he taketh the Saviour in the garden and bindeth him, to his servants it is said, "Ye are come out as it were to a thief with swords and staves; when I was daily with you in the temple, ye stretched not forth your hands against me; but this is even your hour, and the power of darkness[4]." Lo, here he calleth the ordinary magistrate the power of the devil, when he abuseth his power. What could be more evidently spoken? But here ye must mark, that the reproach was in the person, and not in the office. Likewise also the Roman empire was ordained by God, as by the visions of Daniel it is clearly evident: and yet, when Nero, not without God's ordinance, bare the sway in the empire, whatsoever he did as king and emperor, contrary to the office of a good king, that did he not of God, but of the devil: for whereas he hung up and beheaded the apostles of Christ[5], moving a bloody persecution against the church, that sprang not from elsewhere than from the devil, the father of murder. So then, verily, we ought not at any time to defend the tyrannical power, and say that it is of God: for tyranny is not a divine, but a devilish, kind of government; and tyrants themselves are properly the servants of the devil, and not of God:) or else otherwise, some people do deserve by their wicked deeds to have, not a king, but a tyrant. So then the people's sin is another cause that evil magistrates are found in commonweals. In the meanwhile, the king is of the Lord, and sometimes he makes an hypocrite reign. Wherefore the evil magistrate is of God, even as also seditions, wars, plagues, hail, frost, and other miseries of mankind come from the Lord, as punishment of

[4 Luke xxii. 52, 53.]

[5 Paul is said to have been *beheaded*, and Peter *crucified*, at Rome, under Nero.—Euseb. Hist. Eccles. Lib. ii. cap. 25.]

sin and wickedness, which the Lord hath appointed to be executed, as he himself saith: "I will give them children to be their kings, and infants shall rule them; because their tongue and heart hath been against the Lord[1]." Likewise the Lord stirred up the cruel kings of Assyria and Babylon against his city and own peculiar people, whose living was not agreeable to their profession.

How the oppressed must behave themselves under tyrannical princes.

But now, how and after what sort subjects ought to be affected toward such hard, cruel, and tyrannical princes, we learn partly by the example of David, and partly by the doctrine of Jeremy and the apostles. David was not ignorant what kind of man Saul was, a wicked and merciless fellow: yet, notwithstanding, he fled to escape his hands; and when he had occasion given him once or twice to kill him, he slew him not, but spared the tyrant and reverenced him as though he had been his father[2]. Jeremias prayed for Joachim and Zedechias, wicked kings both, and obeyed them until they came to matters flatly contrary to God's religion[3]. For where I spake touching the honour due to parents, there did I by the scriptures prove, that we ought not to obey the wicked commandments of godless magistrates, because it is not permitted to magistrates to ordain or appoint any thing contrary to God's law, or the law of nature. Now the Acts of the Apostles teach us in what sort the apostles did behave themselves in dealing with tyrannical magistrates. Let them, therefore, that are vexed with tyrants, and oppressed with wicked magistrates, take this advice to follow in that perplexity. First, let them call to remembrance, and consider, what and how great their sins of idolatry and uncleanness are, which have already deserved the revenging anger of their jealous God: and then let them think, that God will not withdraw his scourge, unless he see that they redress their corrupt manners and evil religion. So then first, they must go about and bring to pass a full reformation of matters in religion, and perfect amendment of manners amiss: then must they pray continually that God will vouchsafe to pull and draw his oppressed people out of the mire of mischief, wherein they stick fast. For that counsel did the Lord himself, in the eighteenth after

[1 Isai iii. 4, 8.]
[2 1 Sam. xxiv. and xxvi.]
[3 Jer. vii. 16, and xiv.]

Luke, give to those that are oppressed, promising therewithal assured aid and present delivery. But what and how the oppressed must pray, there are examples extant in the ninth of Daniel, and in the fourth chapter of the Acts of the Apostles. Let them also, whose minds are vexed, call to remembrance the sayings of Peter and Paul, the chief of the apostles. "The Lord," saith Peter, "knoweth how to deliver his from temptation, as he delivered Lot." Paul saith: "God is faithful, and will not suffer his to be tempted above their strength; yea, he will turn their temptations unto the best[4]." Let them call to mind the captivity of Israel, wherein God's people were detained at Babylon by the space of seventy years: and therewithal let them think upon the goodly comfort of the captives, which Esay hath expressed from his fortieth chapter unto his forty-ninth. Let us persuade ourselves, that God is good, merciful, and omnipotent, so that he can, when he will, at ease deliver us. He hath many ways and means to set us at liberty. Let us have a regard only, that our impenitent, filthy, and wicked life do not provoke the Lord to augment and prolong the tyrants' cruelty. The Lord is able, upon the sudden, to change the hearts of princes (for "the hearts of kings are in the hands of the Lord, as the rivers of water, to turn them which way he will[5]"), and to make them, which have been hitherto most cruelly set against us, to be our friends and favourable to us; and them which have heretofore most bloodily persecuted the true religion, to embrace the same most ardently, and with a burning zeal to promote it so far as they may. We have evident examples hereof in the books of the Kings, of Esdras, and Nehemias, and in the volume of Daniel's prophecy. Nabuchodonosor, whose purpose was to toast with fire and utterly to destroy the martyrs of God for true religion, was immediately after compelled to praise God, because he saw the martyrs preserved: and he himself doth by edicts given out publicly proclaim and set forth the only true God and his true religion[6]. Darius, the son of Assuerus[7], suffereth Daniel

2 Pet. ii.

1 Cor. x.

[4 imo tentationibus etiam felicem concedet eventum, Lat. 1 Cor. x. 13. So Erasmus expounds; dabit et exitum bonum.—Annotat. in loc. cit.]

[5 Prov. xxi. 1.]   [6 Dan. iii.]

[7 See Prideaux. Connect. Vol. I. pp. 72, 104, 122, ed. Mc Caul. 1845. See also above, page 51, note 3.]

to be cast into the lions' den : but straightway he draweth him out again, and shutteth up Daniel's enemies in the same den, to be torn in pieces by the famishing beasts. Cyrus, the puissant king of Persia, advanceth true religion : Darius, son of Hystaspes, whose surname was Artaxerxes[1], did by all means possible aid and set forward the godly intent of God's people in building up again their city and temple. Let us not doubt therefore of God's aid and helping hand. For God sometime doth utterly destroy, and sometime he chasteneth, untoward tyrants with some horrible and sudden disease : as it is evident that it happened to Antiochus[2], Herod the Great[3], and to his nephew, Herod Agrippa[4], to Maxentius[5] also, and other enemies of God and tyrants over men[6]. Sometime he stirreth up noble captains and valiant men to displace tyrants, and set God's people at liberty ; as we see many examples thereof in the books of Judges and Kings. But lest any man do fall to abuse those examples, let him consider their calling by God : which calling if he have not, or else do prevent, he is so far

Killing of tyrants. from doing good in killing the tyrant, that it is to be feared lest he do make the evil double so much as it was before. Thus much hitherto. Now I return to that which by my digression remaineth yet unspoken of.

The election of magistrates. Here I have to speak somewhat touching the election of magistrates : and first, to whom the choice and ordering of **Who ought to choose them.** the magistrate doth belong ; secondarily, whom and what kind of men it is best to choose to be magistrates ; and lastly, the manner and order of consecrating those which once are chosen.

Touching the election of magistrates, to whom that office should belong, no one and certain rule can be prescribed.

[1 The Artaxerxes, who so much befriended the Jews in the days of Ezra and Nehemiah, and whom, no doubt, Bullinger means, was Artaxerxes Longimanus. Yet the Jewish tradition makes Darius Hystaspis to be Artaxerxes, and Bullinger, perhaps, followed it.— See Prideaux. Con. Vol. I. pp. 201, 244. ed. Mc Caul, 1845.]

[2 Prideaux's Connect. Vol. II. p. 189.]

[3 Ibid. p. 613. Euseb. Eccl. Hist. Lib. I. cap. 8.]

[4 Acts xii. 21—23, *grandson* of Herod the Great ;—nepoti, Lat.— Euseb. Eccles. Hist. Lib. II. cap. 10.]

[5 Gibbon's Decline and Fall, &c. Vol. II. chap. xiv. p. 232. ed. 1820. Euseb. Eccles. Hist. Lib. IX. cap. 9.]

[6 See Jewel's Works.—Parker Soc. ed. pp. 977—8.]

For in some places the whole commonalty doth choose their peers[7]; in other places the peers do choose the magistrates; and in other places princes come to it by succession and birth. In discussing which of these orders should be the best, it were but folly to make much ado. For to every kingdom and every city is worthily left their country fashion, unless it be altogether too too corrupt, and not to be borne withal. But where princes come to it by birth, their earnest prayer must be made to the Lord, that he will grant them to be good.

Now for the good election of magistrates, the Lord him-self declareth whom and what kind of men he will have to be chosen, in these very words: "Look over all the people, consider them diligently, and choose from among them men of courage, such as fear God, speakers of truth, and haters of covetousness, and make them rulers over thousands, rulers of hundreds, rulers of fifties, and rulers of tens, to judge the people at all seasons[8]." Four things the Lord requireth in a good governour. First, that he be a man of courage, of strength or force, that is, which hath ability to do the thing whereunto he is appointed. That ability consisteth in mind rather than in body. For it is required, that he be not a fool, but wise and skilful in that which he hath to do: because the office of a captain is to know how to set his army in order of battle, rather than to fight himself; as also the duty of a surveyor of works is to know how buildings must be erected, rather than to work himself; or as a chariot-man ought rather to know how to guide his cart in driving, than to draw it himself. And therewithal too, there is demanded a boldness of stomach to dare to do the thing that he already knoweth; for constancy and sufferance are very needful in every captain. In the second place that is set down, which indeed is the first; let him fear God, let him be religious, and not superstitious. No idolater preserveth the commonweal, but rather destroyeth it; and a wicked man defendeth not truth and true religion, but persecuteth and driveth them out of his jurisdiction. Let this magistrate of ours therefore be of the right religion, sound in faith, believing the word of God, and knowing that God is present among men and doth repay to whom he list according to their deserts. And for that cause Justinian, the emperor, in *Novellis Constitutionib.* 109, doth freely confess that all

What kind of men ought to be chosen to be magistrates, and the description of a good magistrate.

The magistrate must be sound in religion.

[7 optimates, Lat.]   [8 Exod. xviii. 21.]

his help is of God; and that therefore it is convenient, that
the making of all laws should depend upon him alone. Immediately after he saith: "It is known very well to all men, that
they in whose hands the empire was before it came to us, and
especially that Leo of worthy memory, and the most sacred
prince Justin our father, did in their constitutions flatly forbid
all heretics to be admitted soldiers in any warfare, or dealers
in matters concerning the commonwealth, that the less occasion might be given, by receiving them into the fellowship
of war or handling of public affairs, for any to think that
they corrupt the members of God's holy catholic and apostolic
Church. And this decree do we establish[1]." Thus saith the
emperor. And the godly man verily prayeth to God, and receiveth wisdom at the Lord's hand. And where the princes
are God's friends, and have often conference with God, there
is hope that those commonweals shall prosper and flourish.
But, on the other side, there must needs be feared an unhappy
end of that commonweal, where the enemies of God have the
pre-eminence. Thirdly, there is required of him, which must
be chosen and called to be magistrate, that he be true in word
and deed, so that he be not found to be an hypocrite, a liar, a
deceiver, a turncoat, nor one which out of one mouth doth
blow both hot and cold; but faithful, simple, a plain dealer,
and blameless. He must not be more liberal in promising
than in performing. He must not be one that setteth light by
an oath, not a false swearer, nor a perjured man. Fourthly,
because many that are in office desire riches, and seek to increase their wealth by bribes, the Lord removeth such from
the magistracy, and forbiddeth good magistrates to be covetous: yea, he doth expressly charge them to hate and abhor

[1 Μίαν ἡμῖν εἶναι βοήθειαν ἐπὶ παντὶ τῷ τῆς ἡμετέρας πολιτείας τε καὶ
βασιλείας βίῳ τὴν εἰς Θεὸν ἐλπίδα πιστεύομεν· εἰδότες ὅτι τοῦτο ἡμῖν καὶ
τὴν τῆς ψυχῆς καὶ τὴν τῆς βασιλείας δίδωσι σωτηρίαν· ὥστε καὶ τὰς
νομοθεσίας τὰς ἡμετέρας ἐκεῖθεν ἠρτῆσθαι προσήκει .... Ἴσασι τοίνυν
ἅπαντες, ὡς οἱ πρὸ ἡμῶν βεβασιλευκότες, καὶ μάλιστα Λέων ὁ τῆς εὐσεβοῦς
μνήμης, καὶ Ἰουστῖνος ὁ τῆς θείας λήξεως ἡμῶν πατήρ, ἐν ταῖς ἑαυτῶν
διατάξεσι, τοῖς αἱρετικοῖς ἅπασιν ἀπηγόρευσαν ὥστε μηδεμίαν αὐτοὺς μετ-
ιέναι στρατείαν, μήτε δὲ τὴν οἱανοῦν ἐπὶ δημοσίαις φροντίσι μετουσίαν
ἔχειν· ὅπως ἂν μὴ προφάσει τῶν στρατειῶν τῶν τε δημοσίων ἐπιταγμάτων
τῷ τῆς ἁγίας τοῦ Θεοῦ καθολικῆς καὶ ἀποστολικῆς ἐκκλησίας μέρει φανεῖεν
λυμαινόμενοι· καὶ ἡμεῖς δὲ αὐτὸ τοῦτο πεπράχαμεν.—Justin. Anth. Collat
VIII. tit. 9. Novell. 109. Præfat. p. 431. Gotting. 1797.]

it; as he doth also, in another place, not only forbid them to take bribes, but also command them to shake off and rid their hands of all rewards[2]. Covetousness and greedy desire of bribes are the very plagues that choke good magistrates. By covetous men and takers of bribes law, judgment, liberty, justice, and the country itself, is set to sale and sold to the devil for money. And now, though in this place the Lord hath named only the most pestilent mischief of all other, yet there is no doubt but that he doth inclusively debar all other vices and evils of that sort, commanding them to be strange and far off from the good magistrate and godly governor. Those vices are pride, envy, anger, dicing, surfeiting, drunkenness, whoredom, adultery, and whatsoever else is like to these.

This place is made more manifest by conferring it with other places in the law of God. Moses, in Deuteronomy, saith to the people: " Bring men of wisdom, of understanding, and Deut. i. of an honest life, according to your tribes[3]." Three things here again doth the wise man, Moses, require in them that are to be appointed magistrates in his commonweal. First, saith he, let them be wise. But the beginning of wisdom is the fear of the Lord. Let them therefore be ordained magistrates, that are friends to God and true religion; let them be wise, and not foolish idiots. Secondarily, they must be men of understanding; that is, men of experience, who by long and continual exercise in handling of matters are able at the first brunt to deal in all cases according to the law. Lastly, they must be men of honest report, whose life and sound conversation are by their deeds perfectly tried and sufficiently witnessed of unto the people: and finally, they must be such as bear authority, and not be despised as rascal and vile knaves.

In the book of Numbers also Moses saith: " Let the God Numb. xxvii. of the spirits of all flesh set a man over the congregation, which may go in and out before them, and lead them in and out, that the congregation of the Lord be not as sheep without a shepherd[4]." By these words of the holy prophet we learn who are to be chosen, and how they are to be chosen, into the office of magistrates. Moses prayed to the Lord for a fit and a convenient man: and we therefore must pray to

[2 Isai. xxxiii. 15.]   [3 Deut. i. 13.]
[4 Numb. xxvii. 16, 17.]

[BULLINGER.]

21

God, who searcheth all men's hearts, that he will vouchsafe to send such men to be our magistrates as are meet for that room and calling. The outward shew doth many times deceive us, and we judge him to be a good and godly man who is indeed a notable hypocrite. God alone doth know the mind: we must beseech him, therefore, that he suffer us not in our choice to err or choose amiss. Let him be thought the best and meetest for the purpose, who is instructed with the Holy Spirit of God. Furthermore, he that is appointed to that office must still be the first and the last, and always at one end in all matters of weight and public affairs. Some unprofitable and idle drones there are, that drive other forward, and after the first onset do themselves take their ease. And some wicked fellows there are, which will appoint other what to do, but will themselves do nothing of that which by right belongs unto their office. The guide of the people must be a man of choice elected to be magistrate, whose care is day and night to have an eye that the flock of the Lord be not scattered, endangered, nor utterly destroyed. And thus have I hitherto told you what kind of men they ought to be, to whom the charge is to be committed over the Lord's people.

The manner of consecrating magistrates. Last of all, touching the manner of consecrating magistrates, sundry cities and countries have sundry customs. Let every country freely retain their own usual order. I for my part think best of that manner of consecrating, wherein sumptuous pomp is little or none, but what reason and decency seem to allow. The best and most profitable way is, in consecrating them that are once chosen, to use a certain moderate ceremony, and that too in the face of all the people, that every one may know who they be that are the fathers of the people, to whom they owe honour, whom they ought to obey, and for whose health and welfare they ought to pray. The people of God had a certain prescribed ceremony, which we read that they used in consecrating their kings and magistrates: and it is certain that it was profitably and for good causes first invented, and then commanded by God himself[1].

The rest that is yet behind to be spoken touching the magistrate I mean to defer until to-morrow. And now to end with thanksgiving, let us praise the Lord, &c.

[1 a Deo inventum atque traditum, Lat.]

OF THE OFFICE OF THE MAGISTRATE[2], WHETHER THE
CARE OF RELIGION APPERTAIN TO HIM OR NO,
AND WHETHER HE MAY MAKE LAWS AND
ORDINANCES IN CASES OF RELIGION.

THE SEVENTH SERMON.

THE first and greatest thing, that chiefly ought to be in
a magistrate, is easily perceived by the declaration of his
office and duty. In my yesterday's sermon I shewed you
what the magistrate is, how many kinds of magistrates there
are, of whom the magistrate had his beginning, for what
causes he was ordained, the manner and order how to choose
peers[3], and what kind of men should be called to be magistrates. To this let us now add what the office and duty of a
magistrate properly is.

The whole office of a magistrate seemeth to consist in *The magis-
these three points; to order, to judge, and to punish: of* ^trate's office.^
every one whereof I mean to speak severally in order as
they lie. The ordinance of the magistrate is a decree made
by him for maintaining of religion, honesty, justice, and public
peace: and it consisteth on two points; in ordering rightly
matters of religion, and making good laws for the preservation
of honesty, justice, and common peace. But before I come
to the determining and ordering of religion, I will briefly, and
in few words, handle their question which demand, whether
the care of religion do appertain to the magistrate as part of
his office or no? For I see many that are of opinion, that
the care and ordering of religion doth belong to bishops alone[4],
and that kings, princes, and senators ought not to meddle
therewith.

But the catholic verity teacheth, that the care of religion *Whether the
care of re-
doth especially belong to the magistrate; and that it is not in* *ligion belong
to the magis-
his power only, but his office and duty also, to dispose and* *trate.*

[2 quæ ordinet, Lat.; omitted. What he may regulate.]
[3 proceres, Lat.]
[4 Cf. Becon's Works, Vol. II. p. 303. Parker Soc. ed. The Romish arguments on this topic are alleged and discussed by Melancthon.
—Corp. Reform. Tom. III. No. 1520. pp. 240—58.]

advance religion. For among them of old their kings were priests; I mean, masters and overseers of religion. Melchizedech, that holy and wise prince of the Canaanitish people, who bare the type or figure of Christ our Lord, is wonderfully commended in the holy scriptures: now he was both king and priest together. Moreover, in the book of Numbers, to Josue, newly ordained and lately consecrated, are the laws belonging to religion given up and delivered. The kings of Juda also, and the elect people of God, have for the well ordering of religion (as I will by examples anon declare unto you) obtained very great praise: and again, as many as were slack in looking to religion are noted with the mark of perpetual reproach. Who is ignorant, that the magistrate's especial care ought to be to keep the commonweal in safeguard and prosperity? Which undoubtedly he cannot do, unless he provide to have the word of God preached to his people, and cause them to be taught the true worship of God, by that means making himself, as it were, the minister of true religion. In Leviticus and Deuteronomy the Lord doth largely set down the good prepared for men that are religious and zealous indeed; and reckoneth up, on the other side, the evil appointed for the contemners of true religion. But the good magistrate is commanded to retain and keep prosperity among his people, and to repel all kind of adversity. Let us hear also what the wise man, Salomon, saith in his Proverbs: " Godliness and truth preserve the king, and in godliness his seat is holden up." " When the just are multiplied, the people rejoice; and when the wicked ruleth, the people lamenteth. The king by judgment stablisheth his dominion, but a tyrant overthroweth it. When the wicked increase, iniquity is multiplied, and the just shall see their decay. Where the word of God is not preached[1], the people decay; but happy is he that keepeth the law[2]." Whereby we gather, that they, which would not have the care of religion to appertain to princes, do seek and bring in the confusion of all things, the dissolution of princes and their people, and lastly, the neglecting and oppression of the poor.

Furthermore, the Lord commandeth the magistrate to make trial of doctrines, and to kill those that do stubbornly teach

*Levit. xxvi.
Deut. xxviii.*

[1 quando non est visio, Lat.; cum prophetia defecerit, Vulg.]
[2 Prov. xx. 28; xxix. 2, 4, 16, 18.]

against the scriptures, and draw the people from the true God. The place is to be seen in the thirteenth of Deut. God also forbade the magistrate to plant groves, or erect images : as is to be seen in the seventeenth of Deut. And by those particularities he did insinuate things general; forbidding to ordain, to nourish, and set forth superstition or idolatry ; wherefore he commanded to advance true religion : and so consequently it followeth, that the care of religion belongeth to the magistrate. What may be thought of that moreover, that the most excellent princes and friends of God among God's people did challenge to themselves the care of religion as belonging to themselves ; insomuch that they exercised and took the charge thereof, even as if they had been ministers of the holy things ? Josue in the mount Hebal caused an altar to be builded, and fulfilled all the worship of God, as it was commanded of God by the mouth of Moses[3]. David, in bringing in and bestowing the ark of God in his place, and in ordering the worship of God, was so diligent, that it is wonder to tell. So likewise was Salomon, David's son. Neither do I think that any man knoweth not how much Abia[4], Josaphat, Ezechias, and Josias, laboured in the reformation of religion, which in their times was corrupted and utterly defaced. The very heathen kings and princes are praised, because, when they knew the truth, they gave out edicts for the confirmation of true religion against blasphemous mouths. Nabuchodonozor, the Chaldean, the most mighty monarch of all the world, than who I doubt whether any more great and mighty did reign in the world, publisheth a decree, that he should be torn in pieces, and his house made a jakes, whosoever spake reproachfully against the true God which made both heaven and earth. The place is extant in the third chapter of Daniel's prophecy. Darius Medus, the son of Assuerus, king Cyrus his uncle, saith : " I have decreed that all men in the whole dominion of my kingdom do fear the God of Daniel :" as is to be seen in the sixth of Daniel. Cyrus, king of Persia, looseth the Jews from bondage, and giveth them in charge to repair the temple, and restore their holy rites again[5]. Darius Persa, the son of Hystaspes, saith : " I have decreed for every man which changeth

[3 Josh. viii. 30, &c.]   [4 Asa, in the Latin original.]
[5 Ezra i.]

any thing of my determination touching the reparation of the temple, and the restoring of the worship of God, that a beam be taken out of his house, and set up, and he hanged thereon, and his house to be made a jakes[1]." The very same Darius[2] again, who was also called Artaxerxes, saith: " Whosoever will not do the law of thy God (Esdras), and the law of the king, let judgment straightway pass upon him, either to death, or to utter rooting out, or to confiscation of his goods, or imprisonment[3]." All this we find in the book of Esdras.

An answer to an objection.

The men, which are persuaded that the care and ordering of religion doth belong to bishops alone, do make an objection, and say, that these examples, which I have alleged, do nothing appertain to us which are Christians, because they are examples of the Jewish people. To whom mine answer is: The men of this opinion ought to prove, that the Lord Jesus and his apostles did translate the care of religion from the magistrate unto bishops alone: which they shall never be able to do. But we, on the other side, will briefly shew, that those ancient princes of God's people, Josue, David, and the rest, were Christians verily and indeed; and that therefore the examples which are derived from them and applied to christian princes, both are and ought to be of force and effect among us at this day. I will in the end add also the prophecy of the prophet Esay, whereby it may appear, that even now also kings have in the church at this day the same office that those ancient kings had in that congregation which they call the Jewish church. There is no doubt but that they ought to be accounted true Christians, which, being anointed with the Spirit of Christ, do believe in Christ, and are in the sacraments made partakers of Christ. For Christ (if ye interpret the very word) is as much to say as " anointed." Christians therefore, according to the etymology of their name, are

1 John ii.

anointed. That anointing, according to the apostle's interpretation[4], is the Spirit of God, or the gift of the Holy Ghost. But St Peter testifieth, that the Spirit of Christ was in the

[1 Ezra vi. 11.]

[2 This is not Darius Hystaspis, but Artaxerxes Longimanus.—Prideaux. Connect. Vol. I. p. 249. ed. McCaul. 1845. But, by some writers, Artaxerxes Longimanus is called also Darius.—See Works of Bp. Pilkington, Parker Soc. ed. p. 14.]

[3 Ezra vii. 26.]   [4 1 John ii. 20, 27.]

kings and prophets[5]. And Paul affirmeth flatly, that we have the very same Spirit of faith[6] that they of old had; and doth moreover communicate our sacraments with them, where he saith, that they were baptized under the cloud, and that they all drank of the spiritual rock that followed them, which rock was Christ[7].

Since then the case is so, the examples, truly, which are derived from the words and works of those ancient kings, for the confirmation of faith and charity, both are and ought to be of force with us. And yet I know that every thing doth not consequently follow upon the gathering of examples. But here we have, for the making good of our argument, an evident prophecy of Esay, who foretelleth that kings and princes, after the times of Christ and the revealing of the gospel, should have a diligent care of the church, and should by that means become the feeders and nurses of the faithful. Now it is evident what it is to feed and to nourish; for it is all one as if he should have said, that they should be the fathers and mothers of the church. But he could not have said that rightly, if the care of religion did not belong to princes, but to bishops alone. The words of Esay are these: "Behold, I will stretch out my hand unto the Gentiles, and set up my token to the people; and they shall bring thee thy sons in their laps[8], and thy daughters on their shoulders. And kings shall be thy nursing fathers, and queens thy nursing mothers; they shall fall before thee with their faces flat upon the earth, and lick up the dust of thy feet," &c. Shall not we say, that all this is fully performed in some christian princes? Among whom the first was the holy emperor Constantine, who, by calling a general council, did determine to establish true and sincere doctrine in the church of Christ, with a settled purpose utterly to root out all false and heretical phantasies and opinions. And when the bishops did not go rightly to work by the true rule and touchstone of the gospel and of charity, he blamed them, upbraiding them with tyrannical cruelty, and declaring therewithal what peace the Lord had granted by his means to the churches: adding moreover, that it were a detestable thing, if the bishops, forgetting to thank God for his gifts of peace, should go on among them-

Isai. xlix.

Constantine the great.

[5 1 Pet. i. 11.]
[6 2 Cor. iv. 13.]
[7 1 Cor. x. 2—4.]
[8 in gremio, Lat.]

selves to bait one another with mutual reproaches and taunting libels, thereby giving occasion of delight and laughter to wicked idolaters; when as of duty they ought rather to handle and treat of matters of religion. For (saith he) the books of the evangelists, apostles, and oracles of the ancient prophets, are they which must instruct us in the understanding of God's holy law. Let us expel, therefore, this quarrelling strife, and think upon the questions proposed, to resolve them by the words of scripture inspired from above[1]. After him again, the holy emperors, Gratian, Valentinian, and Theodosius, make a decree, and give out the edict in these very words : " We will and command all people, that are subject to our gracious empire, to be of that religion, which the very religion, taught and conveyed from Peter till now, doth declare that the holy apostle Peter did teach to the Romans[2]." And so forward.

By this, dearly beloved, ye perceive how kings and princes, among the people of the new Testament, have been the foster-fathers and nourishers of the church; being persuaded that the care of religion did first of all and especially belong to themselves.

Osias the leper.

The second objection that they make is the leprosy of Osias king of Juda, which he gat by challenging to himself the office of the priest, while he presumed to burn incense on the incense-altar[3]. They object the Lord's commandment, who bad Josue stand before Eleazar the priest, and gave the king

(margin) Gratian, Valentinian, and Theodosius.

[1] Βασιλεὺς ὁ πανεύφημος τοὺς περὶ τῆς ὁμονοίας τε καὶ συμφωνίας προσενήνοχε λόγους, τῆς τε τῶν τυράννων ἐκείνων ἀναμιμνήσκων ὠμότητος, καὶ τῆς ἐπ' αὐτοῦ θεόθεν παρασχεθείσης ἐντιμοτάτης εἰρήνης· καὶ ὡς δεινὸν εἴη καὶ ἄγαν δεινόν, τῶν πολεμίων καταλυθέντων καὶ μηδενὸς ἀντιτείνειν τολμῶντος, ἀλλήλους βάλλειν, καὶ τοῖς δυσμενέσιν ἡδονὴν καὶ γέλωτα προξενεῖν, ἄλλως τε καὶ περὶ θείων διαλεγομένους πραγμάτων, καὶ τοῦ παναγίου πνεύματος τὴν διδασκαλίαν ἀνάγραπτον ἔχοντας· εὐαγγελικαὶ γάρ, φησι, βίβλοι καὶ ἀποστολικαὶ, καὶ τῶν παλαιῶν προφήτων τὰ θεσπίσματα, σαφῶς ἡμᾶς ἃ χρὴ περὶ τοῦ θείου φρονεῖν ἐκπαιδεύουσι. Τὴν πολεμοποιὸν οὖν ἀπελάσαντες ἔριν, ἐκ τῶν θεοπνεύστων λόγων λάβωμεν τῶν ζητουμένων τὴν λύσιν.—Theodorit. Eccles. Hist. Lib. I. cap. vii. Ed. Reading. Cantab. 1720. pp. 26, 27.]

[2] Cunctos populos, quos clementiæ nostræ regit imperium, in tali volumus religione versari, quam divinum Petrum apostolum tradidisse Romanis religio usque ad hunc ab ipso insinuata declarat, &c.— Grat. Valent. et Theod. Edict. in Corp. Jur. Civil. a Gothof. Amst. 1663. Cod. Lib. I. Tit. i. 1. Tom. II. p. 1. See also, page 34 above.]

[3] 2 Chron. xxvi. 18, 19.]

in charge to receive the book of the law at the Levites' hands[4].
But our disputation tendeth not to the confounding of the
offices and duties of the magistrate and ministers of the church, The several offices of the magistrates and of the ministers must not be confounded.
as that we would have the king to preach, to baptize, and to
minister the Lord's supper ; or the priest, on the other side,
to sit in the judgment-seat, and give judgment against a
murderer, or by pronouncing sentence to take up matters in
strife.   The church of Christ hath, and retaineth, several and
distinguished offices[5]; and God is the God of order, and not
of confusion.   Hereunto tendeth our discourse, by demonstration to prove to all men, that the magistrate of duty
ought to have a care of religion, either in ruin to restore it,
or in soundness to preserve it; and still to see that it proceed
according to the rule of the word of God.   For to that end
was the law of God given into the king's hands by the priests,
that he should not be ignorant of God's will touching matters
ecclesiastical and political, by which law he had to govern the
whole estate of all his realm.   Josue, the captain of God's
people, is set before Eleazar indeed; but yet he hath authority to command the priests, and, being a politic governor, is
joined as it were in one body with the ecclesiastical ministers.
The politic magistrate is commanded to give ear to the ecclesiastical ruler, and the ecclesiastical minister must obey the
politic governor in all things which the law commandeth.
So then the magistrate is not made subject by God to the
priests as to lords, but as to the ministers of the Lord : the
subjection and duty which they owe is to the Lord himself
and to his law, to which the priests themselves also ought to
be obedient, as well as the princes.   If the lips of the priest
err from the truth, and speak not the word of God, there is
no cause why any of the common sort, much less the prince,
should either hearken unto, or in one tittle reverence the
priest.   " The lips of the priest," saith Malachi, " keep knowledge, and they seek the law at his mouth; because he is the
messenger of the Lord of hosts[6]."   To refuse to hear such
priests is to repel God himself.   Such priests as these the
godly princes of Israel did always aid and assist; false priests
they did disgrade; those which neglected their offices they

[4 Numb. xxvii. 22; Deut. xvii. 18.]
[5 officia distincta, Lat.]
[6 Mal. ii. 7.]

rebuked sharply; and made decrees for the executing and right administering of every office.

Of Salomon we read, that he put Abiathar beside the priesthood of the Lord[1] (that he might fulfil the word of the Lord, which he spake to Heli in Silo), and made Zadok priest in Abiathar's stead. In the second book of Chronicles it is said: "And Salomon set the sorts of priests to their offices, as David his father had ordered them, and the Levites in their watches, for to praise and minister before the priests day by day, as their course did require[2]." In the same book again, Joiada[3] the priest doth indeed anoint Joas king; but, nevertheless, the king doth call the priest, and give him a commandment to gather money to repair the temple. Moreover, that religious and excellent prince, Ezechias, called the priests and Levites, and said unto them: "Be. ye sanctified, and sanctify ye the house of the Lord our God, and suffer no uncleanness to remain in the sanctuary. My sons, be not slack now, because the Lord hath chosen you to minister unto himself[4]." [5]He did also appoint singers in the house of the Lord, and those that should play on musical instruments in the Lord's temple. Furthermore, king Ezechias ordained sundry companies of priests and Levites, according to their sundry offices, every one according to his own ministery. What may be said of that too, that even he did divide to the priests their portions and stipends throughout the priesthood? The same king gave charge to all the people to keep holy the feast of passover, writing to them all such letters as priests are wont to write, to put them in mind of religion and hearty repentance. And after all this there is added: "And the king wrought that which was good, right, and just before the Lord his God[6]." When princes therefore do order religion according to the word of God, they do the thing that pleaseth the Lord. This and the like is spoken again by[7] the godly prince Josias. Who therefore will hereafter say, that the care of religion belongeth unto bishops alone?

Princes have done and dealt in religion.

2 Chron. viii.

[1] 1 Kings ii. 27.]   [2] 2 Chron. viii. 14.]
[3] 2 Chron. xxiv.]   [4] 2 Chron. xxix. 5, 11.]
[5] Idem rex mox jubet sacerdotes sacrificare Domino, Lat.; omitted. "The same king presently commandeth the priests to sacrifice to the Lord." P.]
[6] 2 Chron. xxxi. 20.]   [7] by, i. e. concerning; de, Lat.]

The christian emperors, following the example of the an- Princes have
appointed
orders for
religion. cient kings as of their fathers, did with great care provide for the state of true religion in the church of Christ. Arcadius and Honorius did determine that, so often as matters of religion were called in question, the bishops should be summoned to assemble a council[8]. And before them again, the emperors Gratian, Valentinian, and Theodosius, established a law, wherein they declared to the world what faith and religion they would have all men to receive and retain, to wit, the faith and doctrine of St Peter: in which edict, also, they proclaimed all them to be heretics which thought or taught the contrary; allowing them alone to be called catholics, which did persevere in St Peter's faith[9]. By this we gather, that the proper office of the priests is to determine of religion by proofs out of the word of God, and that the prince's duty is to aid the priests in advancement and defence of true religion. But if it happen at any time that the priests be slack in doing their duty, then is it the prince's office by compulsion to enforce the priests to live orderly according to their profession, and to determine in religion according to the word of God. The emperor Justinian, in *Novellis Constitut.* 3, writing to Epiphanius, archbishop of Constantinople[10], saith: "We have, most reverend patriarch, assigned to your holiness the disposition of all things that are honest, seemly, and agreeable to the rule of holy scriptures, touching the appointing and ordering of sacred bishops and reverend clerks[11]." And in the seventeenth constitution he saith: "We give charge and commandment, that no bishop have licence to sell or make away any immovables, whether it be in houses or

[8 Episcopos convenit agitare, Lat.—Impp. Arcad. et Honor. A. A. Apollodoro Proc. Afric.—Quotiens de religione agitur, episcopos convenit judicare, &c.—Dat. 13 Kal. Septemb. Patavi. Theodoro. V. C. Cons.—Cod. Theodos. de religione. Lib. XVI. Tit. 11. p. 527. Par. 1607.]

[9 See above, page 35.]

[10 regiæ urbis archiepiscopum, Lat.]

[11 Ἤδη μὲν κοινῷ τε καὶ ἡγεμονικῷ νόμῳ, πρός τε τὴν μακαριότητα τὴν σὴν πρός τε τοὺς λοιποὺς ἁγιωτάτους πατριάρχας γεγραμμένῳ, τὰ περὶ τῆς χειροτονίας τῶν εὐαγῶν ἐπισκόπων καὶ εὐλαβεστάτων κληρικῶν ... διετυπώσαμεν ἅπερ ἡμῖν ἐδόκει καλῶς τε καὶ προσηκόντως ἔχειν, καὶ τῶν ἱερῶν κανόνων ἀξίως.—Justin. Auth. Collat. I. Tit. 3. Novell. 3. p. 18. Præfat. Gotting. 1797.]

lands, belonging to the churches[1]." Again, in the fifty-seventh constitution, he forbiddeth to celebrate the holy mysteries in private houses[2]. He addeth the penalty, and saith: "For the houses, wherein it is done, shall be confiscate and sold for money, which shall be brought into the emperor's exchequer[3]." In the sixty-seventh constitution, he chargeth all bishops not to be absent from their churches: but if they be absent, he willeth that they should receive no commodity or stipend of the provincial stewards, but that their revenue should be employed on the church's necessities[4]. In the hundred and twenty-third constitution, the lieutenants of every province are commanded to assemble a council for the use and defence of ecclesiastical laws, if the bishops be slack to look thereunto[5]. And immediately after he saith: "We do utterly forbid all bishops, prelates, and clerks, of what degree soever, to play at tables, to keep company with dice-players, to be lookers on upon gamesters, or to run to gaze upon may-games or pageants[6]." I do not allege all this as canonical scriptures, but as proofs to declare, that princes in the primitive church had power, official authority, and a usual custom, granted by God, (as Esay did prophesy,) and derived from the examples

[1] Ἡμεῖς οὖν ... θεσπίζομεν ... μήτε ἄλλον μηδένα πανταχοῦ μήτε πατριάρχην μήτε ἐπίσκοπον ... ἄδειαν ἔχειν ἐκποιεῖν πρᾶγμα ἀκίνητον ἐν οἰκίαις ἢ ἐν ἀγροῖς.—Justin. Auth. Collat. II. Tit. 1. Novell. 7. cap. 1.]

[2] Justin. Auth. Collat. v. Tit. 12. Novell. 58. p. 269.—περὶ τοῦ ἐν ἰδιωτικοῖς οἴκοις ἱερὰν μυσταγωγίαν μὴ γίνεσθαι.]

[3] ... πρὸς τῷ καὶ τὴν οἰκίαν αὐτὴν τὴν ἐν ᾗ τοιοῦτό τι πράττεται γίνεσθαι δημοσίαν, καὶ ὑπὸ τὸ ἱερώτατον ἔρχεσθαι ταμεῖον.—Ibid. p. 270.]

[4] Κἀκεῖνό γε μὴν θεσπίζομεν, ὥστε κατὰ τὸν ἤδη παρ' ἡμῶν φοιτήσαντα νόμον τοὺς θεοφιλεστάτους ἐπισκόπους ταῖς ἑαυτῶν ἐκκλησίαις προσκαρτερεῖν ... εἴπερ ἀπολειφθείη ὁ θεοφιλέστατος ἐπίσκοπος τῆς ἐκκλησίας τῆς αὐτοῦ πλείονα χρόνον, μηδεμίαν αὐτῷ στέλλεσθαι δαπάνην ἐκ τῆς χώρας, ἀλλ' ἐκείνην μὲν περὶ πράξεις εὐσεβεῖς καὶ περὶ τὴν ἁγιωτάτην ἐκκλησίαν δαπανᾶσθαι.—Justin. Auth. Collat. v. Tit. 22. Novell. 67. cap. 3. p. 294.]

[5] ... προνοούντων τοῦ τοιούτου οὐ μόνον τῶν κατὰ τόπον ὁσιωτάτων ἐπισκόπων καὶ τῶν ὑπ' αὐτοὺς κληρικῶν, ἀλλὰ καὶ τῶν πολιτικῶν καὶ τῶν στρατιωτικῶν ἀρχόντων, καὶ τῶν ὑπ' αὐτοὺς τάξεων, καὶ τῶν κατὰ τόπον ἐκδίκων—Justin. Auth. Collat. IX. Tit. 6. Novell. 123. cap. 44. p. 512.]

[6] ... ἀπαγορεύομεν δὲ τοῖς ὁσιωτάτοις ἐπισκόποις καὶ πρεσβυτέροις ... καὶ παντὶ ἄλλῳ οἱουδήποτε εὐαγοῦς τάγματος ἢ σχήματος καθεστῶτι ταβλίζειν, ἢ τῶν τὰ τοιαῦτα παιζόντων κοινωνοὺς ἢ θεωρητὰς γίνεσθαι, ἢ εἰς οἱανδήποτε θέαν τοῦ θεωρῆσαι χάριν παραγίνεσθαι.—Ibid. cap. 10. p. 496.]

of ancient kings, to command bishops, and to determine of religion in the church of Christ.

As for them which object the church's privilege, let them know, that it is not permitted to any prince, nor any mortal man, to grant privileges contrary to the express commandments and very truth of God's word. St Paul affirmed that he had power given him to edify, but not to destroy[7]. I am the briefer, because I will not stand to prove that they are unworthy of indifferent[8] privileges, which are not such as[9] priests and Christ his ministers should be, but are soldiers rather and wicked knaves, full of all kind of mischief. Among other things in the canon law, *Distinct.* 40, we find this written: " See to yourselves, brethren, how ye sit upon the seat: for the seat maketh not the priest, but the priest the seat: the place sanctifieth not the man, but the man the place. Every priest is not a holy man, but every holy man is a priest. He that sitteth well upon the seat, receiveth the honour of the seat: but he that sitteth ill upon the seat, doth injury unto the seat. Therefore an evil priest getteth blame by his priesthood, and not any dignity[10]." And thus much thus far touching this matter.

Ecclesiastical privileges.

Since now that I have declared unto you, dearly beloved, that the care of religion doth belong to the magistrate too, and not to the bishops alone, and that the magistrate may make laws also in cases of religion; it is requisite, that I inquire what kind of laws those are that the magistrates may make in matters of religion. There is no cause why the king or magistrate should suppose, that power is given to him to make new laws touching God, the worship of God, or his holy mysteries; or to appoint a new kind of true justice

What laws the magistrates ought to appoint concerning religion.

[7 2 Cor. xiii. 10.]

[8 Æquis, Lat.]

[9 non sunt hoc quod audiunt, Lat.; are not that which they are called.]

[10 Videte ergo quomodo sedetis super cathedram: quia non cathedra facit sacerdotem, sed sacerdos cathedram; non locus sanctificat hominem, sed homo locum; non omnis sacerdos sanctus, sed omnis sanctus sacerdos. Qui bene sederit super cathedram, honorem accipit ab illa; qui male sederit, injuriam facit cathedræ: ideoque malus sacerdos de sacerdotio suo crimen acquirit, non dignitatem.—Corp. Jur. Can. Decret. I. Pars. Distinct. 40. xii. Joan. Chrysost. id est, Autor. Op. Imperf. in Matt. Hom. 43. ad c. 23. ed. Par. 1687. p. 54.]

and goodness. For as every magistrate is ordained of God, and is God's minister, so must he be ruled by God, and be obedient to God's holy word and commandment, having evermore an eye unto that, and depending still upon that alone. The scripture, which is the word of God, doth abundantly enough set down all that which is proper to true religion: yea, the Lord doth flatly forbid to add to or take anything from his holy word. The magistrate therefore maketh no new laws touching God, and the honour to be given to God; but doth religiously receive and keep, doth put in ure and publish, those ancient laws in that kingdom which God hath allotted him unto. For hereunto appertaineth the giving of the book of God's law unto the kings of Israel[1], that they might learn thereby the way to do the things which they of duty ought to see done. To Josue the Lord doth say : " See that thou dost observe and do according to all the law that Moses my servant commanded thee: thou shalt not turn from it either to the right hand or to the left. Neither shall the book of this law depart out of thy mouth, but occupy thy mind therein day and night, that thou mayest observe and do according to all that is written therein. For then thou shalt make thy way prosperous, and then thou shalt do wisely[2]." Devout and holy princes therefore did do their faithful and diligent endeavour to cause the word of God to be preached to the people, to retain and preserve among the people the laws, ceremonies, and statutes of God; yea, they did their best to spread it to all men as far as they could, and, as time and place required, to apply it holily to the states and persons : on the other side, they were not slack to banish and drive away false doctrine, profane worshippings of God, and blasphemies of his name, but settled themselves utterly to overthrow and root it out for ever. In this sort (I say) godly magistrates did make and ordain devout laws for the maintenance of religion. In this sort they bore a godly and devout care for matters of religion.

Schools.

The cities which the Levites had to possess were of old their schools of Israel. Now Josue did appoint those cities for studies' sake, and the cause of godliness[3]. King Ezechias was no less careful for the sure payment and revenue of the

[1 See Deut. xvii. 18, 19; 2 Kings xi. 12.]
[2 Josh. i. 7, 8.]   [3 Josh. xxi.]

ministers' stipends than he was for the restoring and renewing of every office[4]. For honour and advancement maketh learning to flourish, when need and necessity is driven to seek out sundry shifts: beggary setteth religion to sale, much more the invented lies of men's own mouths. Josaphat sendeth senators and other officers with the priests and teachers through all his kingdom[5]: for his desire was by all means possible to have God's word preached with authority and certain majesty, and, being preached, to have it defended and put in ure to the bringing forth of good works. King Josias doth, together with idolatry and profane worshippings of God, destroy the false priests that were to be found, setting up in their steads the true teachers of God's word, and restoring again sincere religion[6]: even as also king Joas, having rebuked the Levites, did repair the decayed buildings of the holy temple[7]. I am not able to run through all the scriptures, and rehearse all the examples in them expressed: let the godly prince or magistrate learn by these few what and how he ought to determine touching laws for religion.

On the other side, Ahia, the Silonite, saith to Jeroboam: "Thus saith the Lord: Thou shalt reign according to all that thy soul desireth, and shalt be king over Israel. And if thou hearken unto all that I command thee, and wilt walk in my ways, and do that is right in my sight, that thou keep my statutes and my commandments, as David my servant did; then will I be with thee, and build thee a sure house[8]." But the wretch despised those large promises, and rejecting God's word, his temple at Jerusalem, and his lawful worship, refusing also the Levites, he made him priests of the dregs and rascal sort of people; he built himself new temples, which he decked, nay, rather disgraced, with images and idols, ordaining and offering sacrifices not taught in God's word, by that means inventing a certain new kind of worshipping God and a new manner of religion. And although his desire was to seem to be willing to worship God, yet is he by God condemned for a wicked man. Hearken, I pray, the sentence of the Lord, which he denounceth against him: "Thou hast done evil," saith Ahia, as the Lord had taught him, "above all that were

Devisers of new-fangled worships are cursed of God.

[4 2 Chron. xxxi.]   [5 2 Chron. xvii. 7—9.]
[6 2 Kings xxiii.]   [7 2 Kings xii.]
[8 1 Kings xi. 38.]

before thee.   For thou hast gone and made thee other gods and molten images, to provoke me, and hast cast me behind thy back.   Therefore I will bring evil upon the house of Jeroboam, and will root out from Jeroboam even him that pisseth against the wall, and him that is in prison and forsaken in Israel, and will take away the remnant of the house of Jeroboam, as one carrieth away dung till all be gone." And all these things were fulfilled according to the saying of the Lord, as the scripture witnesseth in these words: "When Baasa was king, he smote all the house of Jeroboam, and left nothing that breathed of that that was Jeroboam's." But the very same king, being nothing the better or wiser by another's mishap and miserable example of his predecessor, sticketh not to continue to teach the people, to publish and defend the strange and foreign religion, contrary to the word of God, which Jeroboam had begun.   But what followed thereupon? Forsooth, the Lord by the preaching of Hanani the prophet doth say unto him: "Forasmuch as I exalted thee out of the dust, and made thee prince over my people Israel, and thou hast walked in the way of Jeroboam, and hast made my people Israel to sin, to anger me with their sins; behold, I will root out the posterity of Baasa, and the posterity of his house, and will make thy house like the house of Jeroboam." Which was performed (as the scripture saith) by Simri, captain of the host of Israel: for he destroyed king Hela, the son of Baasa, when he was drunken, and all his posterity[1].   Amri succeeded in the kingdom, who was the father of Achab, that mischievous cut-throat, whom the Syrians slew in fighting a battle[2].   After him reigned his sons Ochosias and Joram. But when they left the religion taught in the word of God to follow the new tradition of king Jeroboam, and had thereunto added the worshipping of the shameful idol Baal, they were utterly (at last) destroyed by the means of Jehu, a very just, although a rigorous prince[3].   The offspring of Amri reigned about the space of forty years, not without the shedding of much innocent blood; but it was at last destroyed, when the measure of iniquity was fulfilled, and was utterly plucked up at the roots by the just judgment of Almighty God[4].

[1 1 Kings xiv. 9, 10; xv. 29; xvi. 2, 3, 9—13.]
[2 1 Kings xxii. 34.]   [3 2 Kings ix. and x.]
[4 The reigns of Ahab, Ahaziah, and Jehoram take up 37 years.]

Let all princes and magistrates therefore learn by these wonderful and terrible examples to take heed to themselves how they devise any new religion, or alter the lawful and ancient manner of worshipping, which God himself hath ordained already.   Our faithful Lord is our good God, who hath fully, simply, and absolutely set down in his word his true religion and lawful kind of worship, which he hath taught all men to keep alone and for evermore : let all men therefore cleave fast unto it, and let them die in defence thereof, that mean to live eternally.   They are punished from above, whosoever do add to, or take away anything from, the religion and kind of worship first ordained and appointed of God. Mark this, ye great men and princes of authority.   For the keeping or not keeping of true religion is the root from whence abundant fruit of felicity, or else utter unhappiness, doth spring and bud out.   He therefore that hath ears to hear, let him hear.   Let no man suffer himself to be seduced and carried away with any coloured intent, how goodly to the eye soever it be, which is indeed a mere vanity and detestable iniquity. To God obedience is much more acceptable than sacrifices are. Neither do the decrees of the Highest need any whit at all our fond additions[5].

Here followeth now the second part of the magistrates' ordinance, which consisteth in making good laws for the preservation of honesty, justice, and public peace ; which is likewise accomplished in good and upright laws.   But some there are who think it mere tyranny to lay laws on free men's backs, as it were a yoke upon necks not used to labour ; supposing that every one ought rather to be left to his own will and discretion.   The apostle indeed did say, " The law is not given for the just, but for the unjust[6] :" but the cause, why the law is not given to the just, is because he is just ; for the just worketh justice, and doth of his own accord the thing which the law exacteth of every mortal man.   Wherefore the law is not troublesome to the just man, because it is agreeable to the mind and thoughts of upright livers, who do embrace it with all their hearts.   But the unjust desireth nothing more than to live as he lusteth : he is not conformable in any point to the law, and therefore must he by the law be kept under,

Laws are necessary for kingdoms, good and requisite for commonwealths.

[5 emblematis,] at.]
[6 1 Tim. i. 9.]

and bridled from marring himself and hurting other. So then, since to good men the laws are no troublesome burden but an acceptable pleasure, which are also necessary for the unjust, as ordained for the bridling of lawless and unruly people; it followeth consequently, that they are good and profitable for all men, and not to be rejected of any man. What may be said of that, moreover, that God himself, who did foresee the disposition of us men, what we would be, and hath still favoured the true liberty which he desired always to have preserved among his people, as one that ever meant them good, and never did ordain the thing that should turn to their hinderance or discommodity; that God himself (I say) was their lawgiver, and hath not suffered any age at any time to live as people without a law? Yea too, those commonweals have been happy always, that have admitted laws, and submitted themselves to be governed by laws; when as, contrarily, those kingdoms have of all other been most miserable, and torn in pieces by civil dissensions and foreign enemies, which, having banished upright laws, did strive to maintain their own kind of freedom, their uncontrolled dealing and licentious liberty, that is, their beastly lust and uncivil rudeness. Good laws therefore are for the health and preservation of the people, and necessary for the peace and safeguard of commonweals and kingdoms.

Wherefore it is a wonder to see the folly of some Christians, since the very heathens have given so honest report of laws and lawgivers. They took their lawgivers for gods, confessing thereby that good laws are the gift of God[1]. But the gift of God cannot be superfluous and unprofitable. Plutarch called laws the life of cities[2]. Demosthenes did expressly confess that laws are the gifts of God[3]. Cicero named laws the bonds of the city (because without laws it is loosed and dispersed), the foundation of liberty, and the well-spring of justice and perfect honesty[4]. For laws undoubtedly are the

---

[1 ΑΘ. Θεὸς ἤ τις ἀνθρώπων ὑμῖν, ὦ ξένοι, εἴληφε τὴν αἰτίαν τῆς τῶν νόμων διαθέσεως; ΚΛ. Θεός, ὦ ξένε, θεός, ὥς γε τὸ δικαιότατον εἰπεῖν.—Plato de Legib. Lib. I. in init.]

[2 Εἴπερ οὖν οἱ νόμους καὶ πολιτείας ἀναιροῦντες τὸν βίον ἀναιροῦσι τὸν ἀνθρώπινον, &c.—Plutarch. adv. Colot. in fin.]

[3 Πᾶς ἐστι νόμος εὕρημα μὲν καὶ δῶρον θεῶν.—Demosth. Orat. adv. Aristog.]

[4 Hoc enim vinculum est hujus dignitatis, qua fruimur in repub-

strongest sinews of the commonweal, and life of the magistrates: so that neither the magistrates can without the laws conveniently live and rule the weal public, nor the laws without the magistrates shew forth their strength and lively force. The magistrate therefore is the living law, and the law is the dumb magistrate[5]. By executing and applying the law, the law is made to live and speak: which those princes do not consider that are wont to say, *Wir sind das recht*, "We are the right, we are the law." For they suppose that they at their pleasure may command what they list, and that all men by and by must take it for law. But that kind of ruling, without all doubt, is extreme tyranny. The saying of the poet is very well known, which representeth the very words of a tyrant:

The magistrate is a law endued with life.

> I say, and it shall be so;
> My lust shall be the law[6].

The prince, indeed, is the living law, if his mind obey the written laws, and square not from the law of nature. Power and authority, therefore, is subject unto laws; for unless the prince in his heart agree with the law, in his breast do write the law, and in his words and deeds express the law, he is not worthy to be called a good man, much less a prince. Again, a good prince and magistrate hath power over the law, and is master of the laws, not that they may turn, put out, undo, make and unmake, them as they list at their pleasure; but because he may put them in practice among the people, apply them to the necessity of the state, and attemper their interpretation to the meaning of the maker.

They therefore are deceived as far as heaven is wide, which think for a few privileges, of emperors and kings granted to the magistrate to add, diminish, or change some point of the law, that therefore they may utterly abolish good laws, and live against all law and seemliness. For, as no

To put to and take from laws.

lica; hoc fundamentum libertatis; hic fons æquitatis: mens, et animus, et consilium, et sententia civitatis posita est in legibus.—Cic. Orat. pro A. Cluent.]

[5 Referring to that saying of Cicero's, (de Legg. Lib. III. cap. 1.) Magistratum legem esse loquentem, legem autem mutum magistratum.]

[6 Hoc volo, sic jubeo; sit pro ratione voluntas.—Juv. Sat. VI. 223.—P.]

22—2

emperors or kings are permitted to grant any privileges contrary to justice, goodness, and honesty; so, if they do grant any such privilege, it ought not to be received or taken of good subjects for a good turn or benefit, but to be counted rather (as it is indeed) their utter destruction and clean overthrow. Among all men, at all times and of all ages, the meaning and substance of the laws touching honesty, justice, and public peace, is kept inviolable: if change be made, it is in circumstances, and the law is interpreted as the case requireth, according to justice and a good end. The law saith, "Let no man kill another: let him that killeth another be killed himself." That law remaineth for ever unchangeable, neither is it lawful for any man at any time to put it out or wipe it away. And yet the rigour of the law may be diminished, and the law itself favourably interpreted: as, for example, if a man kill one whom he loveth entirely well, and kill him by chance, and not of set purpose or pretended malice, so that, when he hath done, he is sorry for it at the very heart, and would (if it were possible) buy his life again with whatsoever he hath to give for it; in such a case the killer ought not to be killed, and therein the magistrate may dispense with the rigour of the law. Another beareth a deadly and continual grudge[1] to one, whom he killeth, and goeth about to colour the matter under the pretence of hap and misfortune: for he sought occasion, that he might for himself have a shew of chance-medley[2]. In such a case as this the magistrate cannot change any jot of the law, but must needs kill him whom the meaning of the law commandeth to kill. I could allege more examples like unto these; but my care is, of purpose, so much as I may, not to be too tedious unto you with too long a discourse. By this that I have spoken it is apparently evident, that laws are good and not to be broken, and how far forth they do admit the prince's $\epsilon\pi\iota\epsilon\iota\kappa\epsilon\iota\alpha\nu$[3], that is, the prince's moderation, interpretation, limitation, or dispensation, lest per-

[1 Vatiniano odio, Lat. Vatinius, in quem acerrime M. Tullius invectus est, in tantum odium populi Romani pervenerat, jam detectis illius flagitiis, ut in proverbium cesserit, Odium Vatinianum.—Erasm. Adag. Chiliad. Hanov. 1617. p. 551. *Odium.*]

[2 casus fortuiti, Lat.]

[3 cf. Aristot. Ethic. Lib. v. cap. 10.]

adventure that old and accustomed proverb be rightly applied unto them, "Law with extremity is extreme injury [4]."

Hitherto I have declared that laws are good, profitable, necessary, and not to be broken: it remaineth now to tell what and what kind of laws the magistrate ought most chiefly to use for the ordering and maintaining of honesty, justice, and public peace, according to his office. Some there are whose opinion is, that the magistrate ought not to use any written laws, but that he should rather give sentence as he thought best according to natural equity, as the circumstances of place, time, persons, and cases do seem to require. Other some there are that do their endeavour to thrust into all kingdoms and commonweals the judicial laws of Moses. And some there are which, having once rejected the law of Moses, will have no judgment given in law, but what is derived out of the laws of heathen princes. But since they that have the pre-eminence and magistrate's authority are men either good or bad; and since that, even in the best men, covetousness, anger, hatred, favour, grief, fear, and other affections, are rife to be found; to whom, I pray you, have they committed the commonweal, which, rejecting all written statutes and certain laws, would have every man that is a magistrate to give judgment as he himself thinketh best? Have they not committed their commonweal to the rule of a beast? But what shall I say then of evil men that are in authority, since in the best men things are so amiss? As good were a kingdom subject to the furies of hell, as bound to the judgments of naughty men. But we will (say they) have them give judgment according to the equity of nature's law, and not after the lust of their corrupt affection. Mine answer is to that; that they will give judgment as affection leadeth them without controlment, and say that they judged by natural equity. They cannot, they will say, judge otherwise, nor otherwise understand the pith of the matter. They think that best which they have determined, and nothing is done contrary to conscience; and thou for thy labour shalt be called *Coram nobis* [5]

What manner of laws the magistrate ought to use.

Written laws are needful.

[4 Summum jus summa injuria, Lat.—Erasm. Adag. Chiliad. p. 619. *Rigor*.]

[5 te in jus vocabunt, Lat. The colloquial phrase of the translator occurs in Latimer's Works, Parker Soc. ed. Vol. II. p. 348, and commonly in Foxe: see Acts and Monuments, Vol. v. pp. 291, 537. ed. 1838.]

for daring find fault with their sentence in judgment. And so shall the just man perish, barbarous affections shall have the upper hand, and naughty men rule all the roost. Yea, and admit we grant all men are good that are called to be magistrates; yet diversity of opinions, that will rise in giving of judgment, will stir up among them endless brawls and continual troubles. If all things therefore be well considered, the best way by a great deal is to put written laws in ure.

Let us learn this by the example of our eternal, wise, excellent, and mighty God, who gave to the Jews, his peculiar people, such laws as at his commandment were set down in writing. The magistrate hath otherwise business enough to judge, that is, to apply and confer the causes with the laws; to see how far and wherein they agree or disagree; and to judge who hath offended against the law, and who have not transgressed the law.

The law of Moses is not to be enforced upon kingdoms and countries. Now it is to be marked, that in Moses' judicial law there are many things proper and peculiar to the Jewish nation, and so ordained, according to the state of the place, time, and persons, that, if we should go about to thrust on and apply them all to other nations, we should seem to shew ourselves more than half mad. And to what end should we bring back and set up again among the people of God[1] the offscourings of the heathen that were cast out a great while ago? The apostles of our Lord Jesus Christ did bind or burden no man with the laws of Moses; they never condemned good laws of the heathens, nor commended to any man naughty laws of the Gentiles; but left the laws, with the use and free choice of them, for the saints to use as they thought good. But therewithal they ceased not most diligently to beat into all men's heads the fear of God, faith, charity, justice, and temperance; because they knew that they, in whose hearts those virtues were settled, can either easily make good laws themselves, or pick and choose out the best of those which other men make. For it maketh no matter whether the magistrate pick out of Moses' Jewish laws, or out of the allowable laws of the heathen, sufficient laws for him and his countrymen, or else do keep still the old and accustomed laws which have before been used in his country, so that he have an eye to cut off such wicked, unjust, and lawless laws, as are found to be thrust in among the better sort. For I suppose that

[1 in forum populi Dei, Lat.]

upright magistrates ought to take off curiosity and new invented novelties. "Seldom," saith the proverb, "is the crow's eye picked out without troublesome stirs[1]:" and curious men's new laws are for the most part worse than the old, that are broken by them and utterly abolished.

Furthermore, all laws are given for ordering of religion or outward worship of God, or else for the outward conversation of life and civil behaviour. Touching the laws of religion, I have spoken of them before. For civil and politic laws, I add thus much, and say, that those seem to be the best laws, which, according to the circumstance of every place, person, state, and time, do come nearest unto the precepts of the ten commandments and the rule of charity, not having in them any spot of iniquity, licentious liberty, or shameless dishonesty. Let them, moreover, be brief and short, not stretched out beyond measure, and wrapped in with many expositions: let them have a full respect to the matter whereto they are directed, and not be frivolous and of no effect.

Now mark, that politic laws do for the most part consist in three especial and principal points—honesty, justice, and peace. Let laws therefore tend to this end, that discipline and honesty may be planted and maintained in the common-weal, and that no unseemly, licentious, and filthy act be therein committed. Let law forbid all uncleanness, wantonness, lightness, sensuality, and riotousness, in apparel, in building, in bibbing and banquetting. Let wedlock be commanded by law to be kept holy. Let stews and brothel-houses be banished the realm. Let adulteries, whoredoms, rapes, and incests, be put to exile. Let moderate feastings be allowed and admitted. Let thriftiness be used, which is the greatest revenue that a man can enjoy[2]. Briefly, whatsoever is contrary to honesty and seemliness, let it by law be driven out and rejected.

Let justice by laws be strongly fortified. Let it by laws be provided, that neither citizen nor foreigner be hurt or hindered in fame, in goods, in body, or life[3]. Let upright laws be made

A proverb used when one will make them blind that were before him, and disannul that which wise men have allowed.

Civil laws; what manner of laws they be.

Laws of honesty.

Laws of justice and equity.

[1] Undecunque fluxerit, perinde valere videtur, *Cornicum oculos configere,* quasi dicas, novo quodam invento veterum eruditionem obscurare.—Erasm. Adag. Chiliad. p. 504. *Mira nova.*]

[2] See above, page 297, note 8.]

[3] Lædens alium violenter vel insidiose puniatur secundum leges, Lat.; omitted by the translator. Whoever injures another by violence or treacherously, let him be punished according to law.]

for the obtaining of legacies and inheritances, for the performing of contracts and bargains, for covenants and agreements, for suretiships, for buying and selling, for weights and measures, for leases and things let to hire, for lending and borrowing, for pawns in mortgage, for use, commodity, and usury of money. Let order be taken for maintenance of peace between the father and his children, betwixt man and wife, betwixt the master and the servant; and, to be short, that every man may have his own. For my meaning is not here to reckon up particularly every several point and tittle of the law.

Laws of peace and unanimity. Lastly, means must be made by giving of laws, that peace may be established, whereby every man may enjoy his own. All violent robberies and injuries must be expelled; privy grudges and close conspiracies must not be thought of. And war must be quieted by wisdom, or else undertaken and finished with manly fortitude.

But, that we may have such a magistrate and such a life, the apostle commanded us earnestly to pray, where he saith: "I exhort you that, first of all, prayers, supplications, intercessions, and giving of thanks, be made for all men; for kings and for all that are in authority, that we may live a quiet and peaceable life in all godliness and honesty [1]."

I am now again compelled to end my Sermon before the matter be finished. That which remaineth I will add to-morrow. Make ye your earnest prayers, with your minds lift up into heaven, &c.

[1] 1 Tim. ii. 1, 2.]

OF JUDGMENT, AND THE OFFICE OF THE JUDGE; THAT
CHRISTIANS ARE NOT FORBIDDEN TO JUDGE: OF
REVENGEMENT AND PUNISHMENT: WHETHER
IT BE LAWFUL FOR A MAGISTRATE TO KILL
THE GUILTY: WHEREFORE, WHEN, HOW,
AND WHAT THE MAGISTRATE MUST
PUNISH: WHETHER HE MAY
PUNISH OFFENDERS IN
RELIGION OR NO.

THE EIGHTH SERMON.

I SPAKE yesterday, dearly beloved, of the magistrate's ordinance : there are yet behind other two parts of his office and duty, that is, judgment and punishment; of both which, by the help of God, I mean to speak as briefly as may be. Give ye attentive ear, and pray ye to the Lord to give me grace to speak the truth.

Judgment is taken in divers significations ; but in this pre- *What judgment is.* sent treatise it importeth the sentence of judges brought in betwixt men at variance ; which sentence is derived out of the laws, according to right and equity, as the case put forth of the parties required, and is pronounced to the intent to take up[2] the strife betwixt them at variance, and to give to every man his own. For at sessions or assizes parties appear and sue one another for some inheritance or possession, which either party affirmeth to be his by law, laying for themselves whatsoever they can to prove and shew what right and title they have to the thing. All which the judges do diligently hear and perfectly note; then they confer the one with the other, and lay them with the law ; lastly, they pronounce sentence, whereby they give the possession to the one party, and take it from the other. The like reason is also in other cases and matters. And this is judgment; yea, this, I say, is the execution of justice. But this kind of quieting and setting parties at one is very mild in comparison of revengement and punishment, which is not executed with words and sentences, but with swords and bitter stripes. And good cause why it

[2 ut dirimat, Lat.]

should be so, since there be divers causes, whereof some cannot be ended but with the sword, and some more gently with judgment in words. But herein consisteth the health and safeguard of the kingdom or commonweal.

Judgment and punishment therefore are in the magistrate the most excellent offices, although peradventure they seem to be somewhat hard and cruel. But unless this which seemeth to be cruelty be put in ure, all ages, states, and sexes shall feel the smart of crueller things, and that which is most cruel indeed. For it is not cruelty, but rather just severity, which (as the Lord commandeth) is put in ure for the safeguard of the guiltless and preservation of peace within the realm and commonweal. Put case there were a commonweal well furnished with most absolute laws for politic manners and matters of religion: suppose also, that in the same commonweal there were no magistrate to execute, and as it were to father[1] those laws, by his authority to bring and reduce all the deeds and sayings of men to the trial of those laws; and that therefore every man breaketh forth to what kind of life he list himself, and doth what he will: tell me, I pray you, what good do those written laws to the men of that country? Believe me, forsooth, not one halfpenny worth of good[2]. The best part therefore of the magistrate's duty consisteth in upright judgment and punishing revengement. And those two points require a man of courage and princely stomach; whom the Lord in his law describeth lively, and telleth what kind of man he would have him to be, and what the office is whereto he is called: which description I will rehearse and expound, because therein the judge's person is chiefly touched.

Moses, at the Lord's commandment, saith to the judges: "Hear the cause of your brethren, and judge righteously betwixt every man and his brother, and the stranger that is with him. Ye shall have no respect of any person in judgment, but ye shall hear the small as well as the great: ye shall not fear the face of any man, for the judgment is the Lord's[3]." The holy prophet in these words toucheth two things chiefly: he declareth what the judge's office is; and what vices or diseases do infect the judge, that he cannot fulfil his office as he ought to do.

Judgment and punishment pertain to the magistrate, as depending upon his office.

The judge's office is described.

[1 qui tueatur, Lat.]　　　[2 nihil prorsus, Lat.]
[3 Deut. i. 16, 17.]

Now touching the office of a good judge, the first point The office of thereof is, that he repel no man, but hear every one, the a good judge is to hear small, the great[4], the citizen, the stranger, the known and and know. unknown. And he must hear the parties willingly, diligently, and attentively. Herein there is admitted no sluggishness of the judge, nor a mind busied about other matters. Judgment before the matter be decided is utterly excluded, because it carrieth away the mind of the judge before the matter is known. The thing itself crieth out, that the matter must first be heard and well understood, before the magistrate proceed to judgment. And the common proverb saith, " Let the other party be heard too[5]." Very wisely said that judge, which told one that made a complaint, " That with the one ear he heard him, and kept the other ear for him upon whom the complaint was made[6]." Herein we contain the perfect knowledge of the judge, and say, that he must not make too much haste in cases unknown, since he must judge them by the thing itself, and not by the parties, secret tales, and privy accusations. Secondarily, let him judge, saith he, The judg yea, let him judge uprightly. To judge is to determine and justly. pronounce truly and justly, according to the laws, what is good, what is evil, what is right, and what is wrong. We Switzers say, *Urteilen, oder erteilen, oder richten;* as if one should say, to distinguish a thing throughly considered, and to plane and make straight a crooked thing. Parties blinded with affections make straight things crooked, which the judge by applying the rule of equity and law doth straighten again; so that to judge is to straighten and to make plain. Moreover, to judge is, by defending and punishing, to keep in liberty. The magistrate doth judge, therefore, when he defendeth the innocent, and bridleth the hurtful person. But he must judge justly, that is, according to justice, and agreeably to the laws, which give to every man that that is his. The judge doth judge unjustly, when of a corrupt mind he pronounceth sentence contrary to all law and equity.

[4 inquilinum, Lat.; omitted.]
[5 Audiatur et altera pars, Lat.]
[6 Λέγεται δὲ καὶ τὰς δίκας διακρίνων ἐν ἀρχῇ τὰς θανατικάς, τὴν χεῖρα τῶν ὤτων τῷ ἑτέρῳ προστιθέναι τοῦ κατηγόρου λέγοντος, ὅπως τῷ κινδυνεύοντι καθαρὸν φυλάττηται καὶ ἀδιάβλητον.—Plutarch. in Vit. Alexandri. Lond. 1723. Tom. IV. p. 60. See also Early Writings of Bp. Hooper, Parker Soc. ed. page 408.]

Now therefore we have to consider the vices which
The faults of judges. usually are wont to reign in judges. The vices that are
in judges be many, and the diseases of their minds are
sundry: but two special diseases there are, and chief of
all the rest. The one of these two vices, which so infecteth the minds of judges that they cannot execute their
Respect of persons. office as they should, is the accepting of faces, or respect of
persons; that is, when the judge in giving judgment hath not
his eye set upon the things themselves, or upon the causes or
the circumstances of the causes as they are indeed; but hath a
regard either of dignity, excellency, humility, poverty, kindred, men of honours, letters[1], or some such like stuff. The
Lord excludeth this evil, and saith : " Ye shall judge justly; ye
shall have no respect of any person in judgment; ye shall hear
Vehement affection. the small as well as the great." The other disease of these
twain is fear; a very vehement affection of the mind, which
disturbeth the very best and most excellent counsels, and
choaketh up virtue before it come to light. Under fear we do
contain hope also, I mean, of commodity; and so by that
means by fear we understand the corruption of bribes. The
judge that stands in fear to lose his life or goods, or is afraid
to displease a nobleman, or is loath to lose the common people's good will; he also that taketh bribes, or is in hope to be
rewarded at one of the parties' hands, doth pervert equity and
advance iniquity. The Lord saith therefore, Ye shall not fear
any mortal man: ye shall not look for any reward at any
man's hand. He addeth the reason why : Because the matter
is not yours, neither were ye called in to do your own business;
but the judgment is the Lord's. The will and law of God
therefore must be respected. For God is able to defend just
judges from the unjust hatred of any, whatsoever they be, and
against all wrong and open violence. Moreover, where it is
said that the judgment is the Lord's, thereby are the judges
warned that they ought to imitate the example of the most
high God. But what, and of what sort, that example of God
The good judge ought to have God before him for a pattern to follow. is, the same Moses, in the first of Deuteronomy[2], expresseth and
saith : " God doth accept neither person nor gift; he doth
justice for the fatherless and widow, and loveth the stranger to

[1 vel clientelam is the Latin, which is here translated, men of
honours, letters.]
[2 It is Deut. x. 17—19.]

give him meat and clothing ; and therefore shall ye love the stranger." And so must godly judges do in the judgment which is God's. Josaphat, without all doubt a very godly prince, speaking to them whom he had made judges, did say : " Take heed what ye do ; for ye execute not the judgments of 2 Chron. xix. man, but of God, which is with you in judgment, Let therefore the fear of the Lord be upon you, and take heed, and be diligent. For there is no unrighteousness with the Lord our God, that he should have any respect of persons, or take any reward."

To these I will yet add a few places of the holy scripture more, which shall partly make manifest those that went before, and partly expound and more plainly express the office of the judge. In Deuteronomy we read : "The judges shall judge the people with equity and justice. Thou shalt not pervert judgment, nor have respect of persons, nor take a reward : for a reward doth blind the eyes of the wise, and perverteth the words of the righteous. Thou shalt do judgment with justice, that thou mayest live and possess the land³." Again, in Exodus we find : "Thou shalt not follow a multitude to do Exod. xxiii. evil, neither shalt thou speak in a matter of justice according to the greater number for to pervert judgment. Neither shalt thou esteem a poor man in his cause. Keep thee far from false matters, and the innocent and righteous see thou slay not; for I will not justify the wicked. Thou shalt take no rewards, for rewards blind the seeing, and pervert the words of the righteous." In Leviticus also we have this : "Ye shall do Levit. xix. no unrighteousness in judgment; thou shalt not favour the person of the poor, nor honour the mighty, but in righteousness shalt thou judge thy neighbour." Again : "Ye shall do no unrighteousness in judgment, in meteyard, in weight, or in measure. True balances, true weights, a true epha, and a true hin, shall ye have. I am the Lord your God," &c. I suppose verily, and am thus persuaded, that in these few words of the Lord our God are comprehended all that which profound philosophers and lawyers of great learning do scarcely absolve in infinite books and volumes of many leaves. Beside all this, the most holy prophet Jeremy crieth to the king, and saith : "Keep equity and righteousness, deliver the oppressed Jer. xxii. from the power of the violent; do not grieve nor oppress the

[³ Deut. xvi. 18—20.]

stranger, the fatherless, or the widow, and shed no innocent blood." Thus much touching the office of judges.

But in the eyes of some men this our discourse may seem vain and fruitless; unless we do also refute their objections, whereby they endeavour to prove, that pleadings and law-matters are at an end, because the Lord in the gospel saith: "To him that will sue thee at the law and take away thy coat, let him have thy cloke also." And again: "While thou art yet with thine adversary upon the way, agree with him quickly, lest he deliver thee to the tormenter[1]." They add, moreover, the strifes in the law, which St. Paul the apostle, in the sixth chapter of his Epistle to the Corinthians, doth flatly condemn. To all which objections mine answer is this: As the doctrine of the evangelists and apostles doth not abrogate the private ordering of particular houses, so doth it not condemn or disannul the public government of common-weals. The Lord, in the gospel after St Luke, chideth with and repelleth the young man who desired him to speak to his brother for an equal division of the inheritance betwixt them. He blamed him, not for because he thinketh ill of him that claimeth an equal division, or that part of the inheritance that is his by right; but because he thought that it was not his duty, but the judges' office, to deal in such cases. The words of our Saviour in that place are these: "Who hath appointed me a judge between you, and a divider of land and inheritance[2]?" And again, as we read in the gospel, "If any man will sue thee at the law, and take away thy coat, give him thy cloke also;" so, on the other side, against this doing of injury there is nothing more busily handled and required in all the evangelical doctrine than charity and well-doing: but a good deed is done in nothing more than in judgment and justice. Since, therefore, that judgment was invented for the practising and preserving of justice and up-right dealing, it is manifest, that to judge in matters of controversy is not forbidden in the gospel. The notable prophets of the Lord, Esay and Zachary, cry out, and say;

"Cease to do evil, learn to do good; seek after judgment, help the oppressed, and plead the cause of the fatherless and

widow." "Execute true judgment, shew mercy and loving-

[1 Matt. v. 40. 25.]
[2 Luke xii. 14.]

kindness every man to his brother. Do the widow, the fatherless, the stranger, and poor, no wrong." They sin, therefore,
that go on to hinder judgment, and to thrust judges beside
their seats; for, as they pull away from the true God no
small part of his worship, so do they open a wide gate to
wrong, robbery, and oppression of the poor.

The Lord, I grant, commanded that which our adversaries
have alleged; meaning thereby to settle quietness among his
people: but because the malice of men is invincible, and the
long-suffering of seely [3] souls makes wicked knaves more mischievous, therefore the Lord hath not forbidden nor condemned
the moderate use of judgments in law. Moreover, we read in
the Acts of the Apostles, that Paul did oftener than once use
the benefit of judgment, not for money or goods, but for his
life, which he endeavoured to save and defend from them that
lay in wait to kill him. Neither consented he to the unjust
judgment of Festus, the president, but appealed to Cæsar [4]:
and yet we know, that Paul did not offend therein against
the doctrine of the gospel of Christ. The same Paul, in
his Epistle to the Corinthians, did not absolutely condemn the
Corinthians for going to law about things belonging to their
living; but because they sued and troubled one another before
heathen judges. It is good and seemly, without doubt, to
suffer wrong with a patient mind; but, because it pleaseth the
Lord to ordain judgment to be a mean of help and succour to
them that are oppressed with injury, he sinneth not at all
that seeks to keep himself from wrong, not by private revengement, but by the upright sentence of judges in law.
And therefore did the apostle command the Corinthians to
choose out to themselves among the faithful such judges as
might take up temporal matters in controversy betwixt them
that fell at variance.

Thus have I declared unto you the second part of the
magistrate's office, which consisteth in judgment. I will now
therefore descend to the exposition of the third and last part,
which comprehendeth revengement and punishment. For the
magistrate, by his office, beareth the sword; and therefore is
he commanded by God to take revengement for the wrong

*Of revenge-
ment taken
by the ma-
gistrate.*

[3 Seely, meek: innocuorum, Lat.]
[4 Acts xxv. 11.]

done to the good, and to punish the evil. For the sword is God's vengeance, or instrument, wherewith he strikes the stroke to revenge himself upon his enemies for the injury done unto him; and is in the scripture generally taken for vengeance and punishment. The Lord in Jeremy crieth out, and saith: "I call a sword upon all the dwellers upon earth[1]." Again, in Ezechiel: "The sword is sharp and ready trimmed to kill the sacrifice." And again: "I will give my sword into the hands of the king of Babel[2]." The kings of Egypt were of their people called Pharaos, as who should say, Revengers[3]. But the sword in the magistrate's hand is to be put unto two uses: for either he punisheth offenders therewith for doing other men injury, and for other ill deeds; or else he doth in war therewith repel the violence of foreign enemies abroad, or repress the rebellions of seditious and contentious citizens at home.

But here again another objection is cast in our way by them which say that, according to the doctrine of the gospel, no man ought either to kill or to be killed, because the Lord hath said, "Resist not the evil[4];" and again to Peter: "Put up thy sword into thy sheath. Every one that taketh the sword doth perish by the sword[5]." My answer to this is: that throughout all the scripture private revengement is utterly forbidden; but that that is done openly by authority of the public magistrate is never found fault withal. But that was private and extraordinary vengeance that the apostle Peter was about to have taken, considering that he was called to be a preacher of the word of God, not to be a judge, a captain, or a man of war. And against private and extraordinary revengement is that sentence rightly pronounced: "Every one that taketh the sword shall perish by the sword."

But that public vengeance and the ordinary use of the sword is not prohibited by God in the church of Christ, I prove by this testimony of the holy apostle. Paul in the twelfth to the Romans hath taught what and how much the perfect-

---

[1 Jer. xxv. 29.]   [2 Ezek. xxi. 9; xxx. 24.]

[3 פָּרַע "apparently, *avenged.* Comp. Syr. ܦܪܥ, retribuit. Judg. v. 2."—Lee's Hebr. Lex. in voc.]

[4 Matt. v. 39.]   [5 Matt. xxvi. 52.]

ness of the gospel requireth of us, and among the rest thus he saith : "Dearly beloved, revenge not yourselves, but rather give place unto wrath : for it is written, Vengeance is mine, and I will repay." But because this might be argued against, and this objection cast in his way, Then, by this means, the long-suffering of Christians shall minister matter enough to murder and manslaughter; he doth therefore immediately after in the next chapter add : "The magistrate is the minister of God to thy wealth, to terrify the evil doers. For he beareth not the sword in vain : for he is God's minister, revenger of wrath to him that doeth evil." We gather therefore by this doctrine of the apostle, that every one of us must let God alone with taking of vengeance, and that no man is allowed to revenge himself by his own private authority. But public revengement, wrought by the ordinary magistrate, is nowhere forbidden. For that God which said to us, "Vengeance is mine, I will repay," doth grant to the magistrate authority to exercise and put that vengeance in ure, which he doth claim as due to himself : so that the magistrate's duty is to punish with the sword the wrongful dealings of wicked men, in the name and at the commandment of God himself. Therefore, when the magistrate punisheth, then doth God himself, to whom all vengeance belongeth, punish by the magistrate, who for that cause is called by the name of God. Moreover, it is written : "Thou shalt not suffer a witch to live[6]." Again : "A wise king will scatter the wicked, and turn the wheel upon them[7]." And again : "He that justifieth the wicked, and he that condemneth the just, they are both abominable in the sight of the Lord[8]."

Neither do we lack examples to prove, that some have incurred the heavy wrath and displeasure of the Lord for their foolish pity in sparing them whom the Lord commanded to strike with the sword. I speak of Saul and Achab[9]. Again, on the other side, there are innumerable examples of most excellent princes, which testify and bear witness of the praise that they deserved for punishing of lewd and wicked offenders. For the prince sinneth not, nor is blame-worthy any whit at all, which killeth or otherwise punisheth the guilty and ungracious man : and for that cause we find in the law so often repeated,

Foolish pity.

[6 Exod. xxii. 18.] [7 Prov. xx. 26.]
[8 Prov. xvii. 15.] [9 1 Sam. xv; 1 Kings xx.]

[BULLINGER.]

23

"His blood be upon himself." But if the blood of the guilty be not shed, then that is imputed as a fault, and laid to the magistrate's charge; because he, neglecting his office, hath pardoned them that were not worthy to be forgiven, and by letting them go hath left the innocent unrevenged. For he is made partaker of the injury done, and shedding of the innocent's blood, which he leaveth unrevenged, by letting the murderer go untouched, on whose neck the Lord gave charge

Severity is
not cruelty.

to let the sword fall. The just severity of the upright magistrate in punishing naughty men is not (as it is falsely judged) extreme cruelty. But overthwart and peevish pity, that spareth offenders which are not worthy to live among men, is utter and mere cruelty indeed. For when the magistrate letteth them go unpunished and at ease, which with their naughty deeds have deserved death, he doth thereby, first of all, give occasion and courage to like offenders to go on and increase in their mischievous wickedness : for they see their own faults borne withal in other men. Secondarily, the men that are not as yet altogether drowned in the mire of wickedness, but are every hour tempted and provoked to naughtiness, will at the last leave to have scruple of conscience, and give their consent to yield to mischief : for they see that mischievous merchants[1] are gently dealt withal. Lastly, offenders set free without any punishment do for the most part become little better : yea, they became twice worse than they were before ; and the increase of his sin shall at length compel thee to kill him for many murders, whom thou wouldest not kill for the murder of one, whereby thou mightest have saved many guiltless men whom that cutthroat, since his first pardon, hath villainously slain. They therefore send wolves and bears among the common people, that let such rakehells[2] escape unpunished.

For what
causes God
commanded
to kill of-
fenders.

Since, now, that I have declared the right use of the sword, and proved that the magistrate hath power to revenge men's injuries, and to kill heinous offenders; let us go on to consider what the causes be for which God commandeth to punish transgressors; let us see, also, when they ought to be punished ; and lastly, what kinds of punishment or penalties the magistrate must use.

[1 facinorosos, Lat.]   [2 nebulones nefarios, Lat.]

The especial causes, for which the Lord doth openly command to punish offenders, are for the most part these that follow. The Lord resisteth force with force, and worketh the safeguard and salvation of men; he revengeth them that suffer wrong, and restoreth again whatsoever may be restored. He declareth his justice also, which rewardeth every one according to his deeds; and therefore he wipeth out reproachful deeds with a reproachful death. He putteth offenders in mind of their crime, and therewithal, for the most part, doth give them sense of repentance unto salvation. For if the wicked do acknowledge his fault, and repent himself of his ill deed, and believe in Christ with all his heart, his sin is forgiven him and he is saved: as we have an evident example Luke xxiii. in the thief that was crucified, whose punishment was an occasion of his salvation; but from the other this salvation was far off, because he did not believe in Christ, and would not be warned by the pain that he felt for his offence to repent for his sins, and to call to God for mercy. Furthermore, by public judgment and open execution all other men may take example to learn to beware of like offences, unless they will suffer like horror of torments.

But let not the magistrate execute any man until he When the magistrate know first perfectly, whether he that is to be punished hath ought to punish of-deserved that punishment that the judges determine; and fenders. whether God hath commanded to punish that offence, that is, whether by God's law that is condemned, which is to be punished. The truth thereof shall be manifestly known, either by the proper and free confession of the man accused, or by the probable testimonies brought in and gathered against the defendant, or by conferring the laws with the offences of him that is to be punished. So then the magistrate may not punish virtue, true religion, nor good, honest, and godly men: for he is ordained of God to terrify, not the good, but offenders.

Now, touching the manner and fashion of punishment, The kinds of punishment. I think it not best over curiously to dispute. Let every nation or city retain still their penalties and order of punishing, unless peradventure their country-custom smack somewhat of rigour and extreme cruelty. For no wise man denieth but that the kind of punishment must be tempered according to the rule of justice and equity. The kinds of punishment are

Diminutio capitis, a kind of judgment whereby one is put out of the king's protection or condemned to bondage. exile or banishment, bondage[1], loss of goods, imprisonment and fetters, scourges, marks with burning irons, loss of limbs, and, lastly, death itself, by killing with the sword, by burning, hanging, drowning, and other such means as every nation useth of custom. Neither is the scripture without a pitiful beadrow[2] of miserable torments. For in the book of Esdras we read: "And whosoever will not do the law of thy God, (Esdras), and the law of the king, let judgment straightways pass upon him, whether it be to death, or banishment, or loss of goods, or imprisonment[3]." This do I add not unadvisedly, because of them that are of opinion that such torments ought not so much as once to be named among christian people.

Discretion and clemency of the judge. But measure and discretion must be used of the judges in punishing offenders, so that heinous faults may be plagued with grievous punishment, lesser crimes may be nipped with smaller penalties, and the smallest and light offences punished more lightly. That sentence in God's law ought to be remembered, "According to the fault, so shall the punishment be[4]:" where also the judge must have a consideration of his clemency and pity. Oftentimes the kind[5] and age excuseth the party accused. The circumstances, being rightly weighed, do sometime excuse the deeds that otherwise are of themselves not all of the best. The judge also must inquire after and diligently consider the former life of the man accused; for which, if it fall out to have been good and honest, then doth he deserve some favour and mercy, unless the offence for which he is troubled be so heinous that it can admit no sparkle of pity. But godliness or the fear of God, with pouring out of prayers unto the Lord and a diligent and lawful examination of the deed or word, that is, of the fault committed, is the best rule for the judge to follow in choosing his time when to use pity,

[1 Diminutio capitis, Lat. "A Roman citizen possessed *libertas, civitas*, and *familia*: the loss of all three, or of libertas and civitas (for civitas included familia) constituted the maxima capitis diminutio."— Smith's Dict. of Gr. and Rom. Antiq. voc. *caput*.]

[2 catalogo, Lat.]　　　　　　　　　[3 Ezra vii. 26.]

[4 Deut. xxv. 2. The last sentence, "according to his fault, by a certain number," is in the Vulgate, "Pro mensura peccati erit et plagarum modus;" which are the words that Bullinger quotes, and which are rendered in the Douay Version, "According to the measure of the sin shall the measure also of the stripes be."]

[5 sexus, Lat.]

and when to deal with extreme rigour. For otherwise decent
clemency is most praiseworthy before God and men.

I have shewed you, dearly beloved, that the magistrate What is to
both may and of duty ought to punish offenders; then, for in offenders.
what causes the Lord will have them to be punished; and,
lastly, how, when, and how much, they are to be punished.
It remaineth now for me to declare wherefore, and for what
offences, they are to be punished: which I mean to lay down
in one word, and briefly too. All words and deeds which are
contrary to the laws of God and the magistrate, that is,
all things that are done mischievously against the laws, are to
be punished: but laws are made either for religion or politic
government; and politic government consisteth in honesty,
justice, and peace. Therefore the magistrate must punish and
keep under all them which do disturb, afflict, trouble, destroy,
or overthrow honesty, justice, public peace, or private tranquillity betwixt man and man. Let him punish dishonesty,
ribaldry, filthy lust, whoredom, fornication, adultery, incest,
sodomy, riotousness, drunkenness, gluttony, covetousness, cozening, cutting usury, treason, murder, slaughter of parents,
sedition, and whatsoever is like to these. The law of the
Lord, published by the ministery of Moses, doth in the eighteenth and twentieth of Leviticus reckon up a beadrow[6] long
enough of such offences as are to be punished. And lest perhaps any man may think, that at this day that which Moses
hath rehearsed is utterly abolished, let him give ear to St Paul,
who saith: "To the just the law is not given, but to the
unjust, and to sinners, to unholy and unclean, to murderers of
fathers and murderers of mothers, to manslayers, to whoremongers, to them that defile themselves with mankind, to man-
stealers, to liars, to perjured men, and if there be any other
thing contrary to sound doctrine[7]." But apostates, idolaters,
blasphemers, heretics, false teachers, and mockers of religion,
do offend against the laws of religion, (and therefore ought
they to be punished by the magistrate's authority[8].)

But the question hath been, and is yet at this day, in con- Whether the
troversy, whether it be lawful for a magistrate to punish any may punish
man in his jurisdiction for the contempt of religion or blas- of religion.
pheming of the same? The Manichees and Donatists were of
opinion that no man ought to be compelled, much less to be

[6 catalogum, Lat.]   [7 1 Tim. i. 9, 10.]
[8 This is added by the Translator. P.]

killed, for any religion; but that every man ought to be left to his own mind and judgment. And yet the scripture doth expressly command the magistrate not to spare false prophets; yea, rebels against God are commanded by holy laws and judges to be killed without mercy. The places are extant to be seen in the holy scriptures; the one in the thirteenth of Deuteronomy, the other in the seventeenth of the same book. In Exodus this same is set down for a rule: "Whosoever sacrificeth to any God, but to the Lord alone, let him be rooted out[1]." In Leviticus, the blasphemer is slain and overwhelmed with stones[2]. In the book of Numbers, the man is slain that did unhallow the sabbath-day[3]. And how many, I pray you, did God's revenging sword destroy of that calvish people that did erect and worship the calf in the wilderness[4]? Helias at mount Carmel killed whole hundreds of false prophets in a solemn set and appointed sacrifice[5]. Eliseus, at the Lord's commandment, anointed Jehu king, to the end that he might root out the house of Achab, and kill at once all Baal's priests[6]. Joiada the priest slew Athalia[7], and good king Josias destroyed together the wicked and stubborn priests of all high places[8]. St Augustine, *Tractatu in Joan.* 11, disputing against the Donatists, doth prove by the example of Nabuchodonozor, that Christian princes do justly punish the Donatists for despising Christ and his evangelical doctrine. Among other things he saith: "If king Nabuchodonosor did glorify God for delivering three children out of the fire; yea, and glorified him so much that he made a decree throughout his kingdom for his honour and worship: why should not the kings of our days be moved so to do, which see not three children saved from the flame alone, but themselves also delivered from the fire of hell, when they behold Christ, by whom they are delivered, burnt up in Christian men, and when to a Christian they hear it said, Say thou that thou art no Christian? This they will do, and yet this they will not suffer. For mark what they do, and see what they suffer. They kill souls; they are afflicted in body. They kill other eternally, and do complain that they themselves do suffer a temporal death[9]."

[1] Exod. xxii. 20.]   [2] Lev. xxiv. 10—16.]
[3] Numb. xv. 32—36.]   [4] Exod. xxxii.]
[5] 1 Kings xviii.]   [6] 2 Kings ix.]
[7] 2 Kings xi.]   [8] 2 Kings xxiii. 20.]
[9] Si Nabuchodonozor rex laudavit et prædicavit et gloriam dedit

Thus much hath Augustine. In the new Testament we have most evident examples of Peter and Paul, Christ's greatest apostles: the one whereof slew Ananias and Sapphira, for their lying hypocrisy and feigned religion[10]; the other struck Elymas the sorcerer blind, and bereft him of his eyes[11]. Neither is there one hair's difference to choose, whether a man be killed with a sword or with a word[12]. For to kill is to kill, by what means or with what instrument soever it be done. God wrought that by his apostles, and doth the like by the magistrate also. For vengeance is God's, who giveth it to the magistrate and chief men to be put in ure and execution upon wicked offenders. There are to be seen many laws made by holy Christian princes for the state of religion, which give an especial charge to kill idolaters, apostates, heretics, and godless people. I will recite unto you, dearly beloved, one law among many, made by the holy emperor, Constantine the Great. For in an epistle, intituled *ad Taurum P. P.*, he saith: " It pleaseth us that in all places, and throughout every city, the temples be out of hand shut up, and liberty denied to wicked men to have access thither to commit idolatry. We will also and command all men to be restrained from making of sacrifice. And if so be it happen that they offend herein, our pleasure is that they be slain with the sword, and the slain man's goods to be confiscate. And we have decreed that the rulers of the provinces shall suffer like punishment, if they neglect to punish the offenders[13]." The very same almost

Deo, quia liberavit de igne tres pueros, et tantam gloriam dedit, ut decretum mitteret per regnum suum, Quicunque dixerint, &c., quomodo isti reges non moveantur, qui non tres pueros attendunt liberatos de flamma, sed seipsos liberatos de Gehenna, quando vident Christum, a quo liberati sunt, exsufflari in Christianis, quando audiunt dici Christiano, Dic te non esse Christianum? Talia facere volunt, et saltem talia pati nolunt. Nam videte qualia faciunt, et qualia patiuntur. Occidunt animas, affliguntur in corpore. Sempiternas mortes faciunt, et temporales se perpeti conqueruntur.—Opp. Par. 1531. Tom. IX. fol. 22. P.]

[10 Acts v.]   [11 Acts xiii. 11.]
[12 gladio, poculis, an verbis, Lat.]
[13 Imp. Constantinus. A. ad Taurum. P. P. I. Placuit omnibus locis atque urbibus universis claudi protinus templa, et accessu vetito omnibus licentiam delinquendi perditis abnegari. Volumus etiam cunctos sacrificiis abstinere. Quod si aliquid forte hujusmodi perpe-

do Theodosius and Valentinianus by proclaimed edicts command *in Codice Theodosiano*, tit. 2. And Valentinianus and Martianus *in Codice Justiniano*, tit. 2. Lib. I.[1] Lastly, without all controversy, adulterers, murderers, rebels, deceivers, and blasphemers, are rightly punished, and not against religion. Wherefore it followeth consequently, that false prophets and heretics are by good right slain: for they are deceivers, blasphemers, and man-quellers[2].

What moderation must be had in punishing.

But in the execution of this punishment there must a great consideration be had and observed; first, of the persons; then, of the errors; and, lastly, of the penalties. For in persons there is great diversity: because there are some standard-bearers, and heady grand captains, which are stout, hypocrites, and full of tongue, and therefore the aptest for to seduce; who, falling headlong without amendment to their own destruction, do with themselves draw other into danger. They must by all means be bridled and kept under, as plagues to the church; lest, like a canker, they spread all over. Again, there are some silly seduced souls, made fools by other men, which err not of malice nor stubborn stomach, but do repent and amend in time. These the magistrate must not straightway condemn, but pray to the Lord, and bear with their error, and teach them in the spirit of gentleness, until they be brought to a better mind.

Moreover, in erroneous doctrines some are more intolerable than other some are. Some there be so wicked and blasphemous, that they are unworthy to be heard, much less to be done[3]. Some there are which do directly and openly tend to the overthrow of the commonweal, unless they be in time appeased and resisted. But those crimes that are brought in and accused, ought first to be by the scripture and manifest truth convinced to be such as they are said to

traverint, gladio ultore sternantur, facultates etiam peremti fisco decernimus vindicari. Et similiter puniri rectores provinciarum, si facinora vindicare neglexerint.—D. Prid. No. Mar. Arbitrione et Lolliano Coss. Justin. Cod. Lib. I. Tit. ii. p. 100. Lugd. 1551. Tom. I.]

[1 Impp. Theod. et Valentin. A. A. Isidoro P. F. P. Cod. Theod. Lib. XVI. Tit. x. p. 526. Par. 1607.—Impp. Valentin. et Mart. A. A. Palladio. P. P. VII. Lib. I. Tit. ii. Cod. Justin. Tom. I. Lugd. 1551. p. 102.]

[2 homicidæ, Lat.]   [3 nedum ferri, Lat.]

be. When the truth is known, and manifest proofs of scripture alleged, then is it lawful most sharply to punish those blasphemers of God and overthrowers of the church and commonweal. But a light and easier penalty must be set on the heads of them whose offence consisteth in light and smaller errors: for some do err so, that by their error God is not blasphemed, the church not subverted, nor the commonweal in any danger at all. Where, by the way, every one must think of that saying of the apostle: " Bear ye one another's burden[4]." And again: " The weak in faith receive ye, not to the doubtfulness of questions [5]."

Furthermore, in punishment and penalties there is great difference. They that err stubbornly, and do their endeavour to draw in and keep other men in their errors, blasphemers, troublers, and subverters of churches, may by law be put to death. But it followeth not thereupon, that every one which erreth must therefore by and by suffer loss of his life. The things, that by threats and fault-finding [6] may be remedied and amended, must not be punished with sharper correction. A mean in every thing is always the best. There is a penalty by payment of money. There are prisons for them to be shut up into, which are corrupted with the poison of false doctrine and lack of belief, lest peradventure they infect others with their contagious disease. There are also other means to punish the body, whereby to keep them under that err from the truth, to keep them from marring those that are sound, and to preserve themselves that they perish not utterly, but that through repentance they may fall to amendment. But the fear of God, justice, and the judge's wisdom shall by the circumstances make him perceive how he ought to punish the naughty doctrine and stubborn rebellion of malicious seducers, and how to bear with the foolish, light belief of silly seduced men, grounded upon simplicity, and not envenomed rancour.

Earnest and diligent admonition is given too late, when the fault is already committed, and is so detestable that it ought straightway to be plagued with the sword: let the

Admonition before punishment.

[4 Gal. vi. 2.]
[5 Rom. xiv. 1.—non ad dijudicationes disceptationum, Lat.; Erasmus' rendering.]
[6 increpationibus, Lat.]

magistrate, therefore, always have an eye to admonish them in time, that are to be warned to take heed of a fault. For earnest admonitions are earnestly commended to men in authority to use to their subjects, when they begin to work any broil. Moreover, godly and wise magistrates have many times pardoned unwitting offenders, whom they saw ready to repent upon giving of warning. The Lord in the gospel biddeth us admonish a sinner; then, if he repent, to pardon his fault; but if he reject a fair warning once given him, then to punish him so much the sharper[1]. And Josue, before he made open war to be proclaimed upon the children of Reuben, did first by embassage command them to dig down the altar, which they seemed to have made contrary to the law of the Lord[2]. The emperor Justinian also granted pardon to them which repented, and turned to a sounder opinion, *Constitut.* 109.[3] Moreover, Josias did not utterly kill all them that were wrapped in error and idolatry, but those especially that were incurable, and would not recant. The magistrate therefore must wisely moderate the matter, and be very circumspect in punishing offenders.

Objections answered.

I cannot here wink and slyly pass over the objections, that some men make against that which hitherto I have said touching punishment; to wit, that the apostle Paul hath not commanded to kill or punish an heretic after the first and second admonition, but to avoid him[4]; again, that faith is the gift of God, which cannot be given or engraffed in any man by rigour of the sword; also, that no man is to be compelled: he that constraineth may make an hypocrite; but a devout and zealous man he cannot make: and lastly, that the apostles required no aid of kings either to maintain or set out the religion of Christ, or else to punish blasphemous railers and enemies of God's word. To all this I answer thus: Paul, when he wrote his epistle to Titus, did write to an apostle: in that epistle, therefore, he instructeth an apostle how to behave himself according to his duty toward an heretic past all reco-

---

[1 Matt. xviii. 15—17.]   [2 Josh. xxii.]

[3 Ἔξεστι δὲ αὐταῖς, τῆς βελτίονος γινομέναις γνώμης, καὶ τὴν ὀρθὴν καὶ ἀληθινὴν ἀσπαζομέναις πίστιν . . . τῶν τοιούτων ἀπολαύειν δωρεῶν τε καὶ προνομίων.—Justin. Auth. Collat. viii. Tit. x. Novell. 109. cap. 2. p. 432. Gotting. 1797.]

[4 Tit. iii. 10.]

very. If he had written to Sergius Paulus, or any lieutenant[5], he would undoubtedly have taught him his office. For the same Paul, standing before Sergius Paulus, then prince of Cyprus, did by his deeds declare unto him the duty of a magistrate: for first, he did not only most sharply rebuke the false prophet Elymas, then forsake his company, eschew and shun him, as the apostle John did Cerinthus[6], but strake him also with bodily blindness.

I grant and confess, that faith is God's gift in the heart of man, which God alone doth search and know. But men are judged by their words and deeds. Admit, therefore, that the erroneous opinion of the mind may not be punished; yet notwithstanding, wicked and infective profession and doctrine must in no wise be suffered. Verily, no man doth in this world punish profane and wicked thoughts of the mind: but if those thoughts break forth into blasphemous words, then are those blaspheming tongues to be punished of good princes. And yet by this I say not, that godliness lieth in the magistrate to give and bestow. Justice is the very gift of God, which none but God doth give to men: but who is so foolish as to gather thereupon, that unjust men, robbers, murderers, and witches are not to be punished, because the magistrate by punishment cannot bestow righteousness upon unrighteous people? We must therefore make a difference betwixt faith, as it is the gift of God in the heart of man, and as it is the outward profession uttered and declared before the face of men. For while false faith doth lurk and lie hid within the heart, and infecteth none but the unbeliever, so long the unbelieving infidel cannot be punished: but if this false and forged faith, that so lay hid, do once break forth to blaspheme, to the open tearing of God and the infecting of his neighbours, then must that blasphemer and seducer be by and by plucked under, and kept from creeping to further annoyance. Not to suppress such a fellow as this, is to put a sword in a madman's hand to kill unwise and weakly men.

Faith is the gift of God; but, where he bestoweth faith, he useth means to give it by: those means he will not have us to neglect. An householder knoweth that faith is the gift

Faith is the gift of God.

[5 præsidem aliquem, Lat.]
[6 Euseb. Eccles. Hist. Lib. IV. cap. 14. Milner's Church History, Cent. i. chap. 13. Vol. I. p. 102, ed. 1834.]

of God; and yet notwithstanding, he instructeth his children in the word of truth, he chargeth them to go to church, to pray for faith, and to learn it at the preacher's mouth. A good father would think much, yea, he would not think well of it, if his son should say : Father, I pray you, teach me not, send me not so much to church, and beat me not if I be not there; for faith is the gift of God, which whipping cannot bring me to. Then what man can quietly abide to hear that faith is the gift of God, and that therefore no man ought for faith, that is, for the corruption of faith and open blasphemy, to suffer any punishment ?

Whether it be lawful to compel one to faith. And yet Petilian, in the eighty-third chapter of St Augustine's second book *contra Petiliani literas*, crieth out, and saith : " God forbid, and far be it from our conscience, to compel any man to our religion[1]." Shall we, therefore, go on to speak the words of heretics, or to say, that the Lord God in the scriptures hath planted hypocrisy, where with threats and punishment he hath driven men to goodness? David saith : " It is good for me, Lord, that thou hast chastised me[2]." And Jeremy saith : " Thou hast chastised me, O Lord, and I am chastised, like an untamed heifer[3]." But if no man ought to be compelled to goodness, to what intent doth Solomon (the wisest of all men) so many times command to chastise children? " He that spareth the rod hateth the child," saith he; " Thou indeed dost strike him, but with the rod thou deliverest his soul from death[4]." Daily experience, and the disposition of men, do plainly teach, that in men there are most vehement affections, which, unless they be remedied and bridled betimes, do both destroy them in whom they be, and other men too, who at the first might easily with light punishment have been preserved. Men in their madness despise compulsion and chastising punishment; but, when they come to themselves again, and see from how great evils they are delivered by those that compelled them, then they rejoice that to their health they were chastised, and praise the compulsion which before they despised.

[1 Augustine says, Noli ergo dicere, Absit, absit a nostra conscientia, ut ad nostram fidem aliquem compellamus. Facitis enim ubi potestis.—Opp. Par. 1531. Tom. VII. fol. 29. P.]

[2 Ps. cxix. 71.]   [3 Jer. xxxi. 18.]

[4 Prov. xiii. 24; xxii. 14.]

Let us hear what Augustine doth think and teach hereof, whose experience in this matter was very much. In his forty-eighth Epist. *ad Vincentium contra Donatist. de vi coercendis hæreticis*, he writeth thus : " My opinion sometime was, that no man ought by force to be compelled to the unity of Christ; that we ought to deal by words, fight in disputations, and overcome with reason, lest peradventure we should have those to counterfeit themselves to be catholics, whom we knew to be open heretics. But this opinion of mine was not confuted with the words of my gainsayers, but with the examples of those which shewed the contrary. For first, mine own city (Hippone) was objected against me ; which, when as sometime it held wholly with Donatus, was by the fear of the imperial laws converted to the catholic unity; and at this day we see it so greatly to detest the naughtiness of your heretical stomachs, that it is thought verily that your heresy was never within it. And many more places by name were reckoned up unto me, that, by the effect of the thing itself, I might confess, that in such a case as this that may be rightly understood where it is written: 'Give a wise man occasion, and he will be the wiser[5].'" And again : " Not every one that spareth is a friend ; nor every one that striketh is an enemy. Better are the stripes of a friend than the voluntary kisses of an enemy. It is better to love with severity, than to deceive with lenity. He that bindeth a frenzy man, and waketh him that is sick of the lethargy, doth trouble them both, and yet he loveth them both. Who can love us more than God himself doth? and yet, as he teacheth us mildly, so he ceaseth not to terrify us to our health. Thinkest thou that no man ought to be compelled to righteousness, when thou readest that the goodman

[5 Nam mea primitus sententia erat, neminem ad unitatem Christi esse cogendum ; verbo esse agendum, disputatione pugnandum, ratione vincendum, ne fictos catholicos haberemus, quos apertos hæreticos noveramus. Sed hæc opinio mea non contradicentium verbis, sed demonstrantium superabatur exemplis : nam primo mihi opponebatur civitas mea, quæ cum tota esset in parte Donati, ad unitatem catholicam timore legum imperialium conversa est; quam nunc videmus ita hujus vestræ animositatis perniciem detestari, ut in ea nunquam fuisse credatur : ita aliæ multæ, quæ mihi nominatim commemorabantur; ut ipsis rebus agnoscerem etiam in hac causa recte intelligi posse, quod scriptum est, Da sapienti occasionem, et sapientior erit.—Opp. Tom. II. fol. 34. P.]

of the house said to his servants, ' Whomsoever ye find, compel them to come in;' when thou readest that he, that was first called Saul and afterward Paul, was constrained by the violent force of Christ, which compelled him to know and keep fast the truth of the gospel[1]?" And the same Augustine again, in Epist. *ad Bonifacium comitem* 59, saith: " Where is that now that they were wont to cry and say, that it is at every one's free choice to believe, or not to believe? Whom did Christ constrain? whom did he compel? Lo, here they have the apostle Paul for an example : let them confess in him, that Christ first compelled him, then taught him; first struck him, and afterward comforted him. And it is wonderful how he, which by the punishment of his body was compelled to the gospel, did after his entering in labour more in the gospel than all they that were called by word alone : and whom the greater fear compelled to charity, his charity, once perfect, did cast out all fear. Why then should not the church therefore compel her lost children to return, since the lost children have compelled other to their destruction[2]?"

Again, in the same epistle, the same Augustine saith : " Whereas some, which would not have upright laws ordained

[1 Non omnis qui parcit amicus est, nec omnis qui verberat inimicus. Meliora sunt vulnera amici, quam voluntaria oscula inimici. Melius est cum severitate diligere, quam cum lenitate decipere... Qui phreneticum ligat, et qui lethargicum excitat, ambobus molestus, ambos amat. Quis nos potest amplius amare quam Deus? Et tamen nos non solum docere suaviter, verum etiam salubriter terrere non cessat ... Putas neminem debere cogi ad justitiam, cum legas patrem familias dixisse servis, Quoscunque inveneritis cogite intrare; cum legas etiam ipsum primo Saulum, postea Paulum, ad cognoscendam et tenendam veritatem magna violentia Christi cogentis esse compulsum?—Aug. Ep. 48. ad Vincentium Opp. Par. 1531. Tom. II. fol. 33. P.]

[2 Ubi est quod isti clamare consueverunt, Liberum est credere vel non credere? Cui vim Christus intulit? Quem coegit? Ecce habent Paulum apostolum: agnoscant in eo prius cogentem Christum et postea docentem, prius ferientem et postea consolantem. Mirum est autem quomodo ille, qui pœna corporis ad evangelium coactus intravit, plus illis omnibus qui solo verbo vocati sunt in evangelio laboravit; et quem major timor compulit ad caritatem, ejus perfecta caritas foras misit timorem. Cur ergo non cogeret ecclesia perditos filios ut redirent, si perditi filii coegerunt alios ut perirent?—Opp. Tom. II. fol. 42. P.]

against their ungodliness, do say, that the apostles did never The apostles required no aid of the magistrate for the maintenance of religion against the adversaries of the same. require any such things of the kings of the earth; they do not consider, that that was another time (not like to this), and that all things are done in their due time and season. For what emperor did at that time believe in Christ, to serve him by making laws in defence of religion against ungodliness? when as yet that prophecy was in fulfilling, 'Why did the heathen rage, and the people imagine a vain thing? The kings of the earth stood up, and the rulers took counsel against God and against his Christ.' For as yet that was not begun which followeth in the Psalm, where it is said: 'And now understand, ye kings, and be ye learned, ye that judge the earth; serve him in fear and rejoice in trembling.' But how do kings serve God in fear, but by forbidding and punishing with devout severity those things which are done against God's commandments? For in that he is a man, he serveth him one way; but in that he is a king, he serveth him another way: because in that he is a man, he serveth him by living faithfully; but in that he is a king, he serveth him by establishing convenient laws to command that which is just, and to forbid the contrary:—as Ezechias served him, by destroying the groves and temples of idols, and those high places that were erected against the Lord's commandment: as Josias served him, by doing the like: as the king of Ninivie served him, by compelling the whole city to please and appease the anger of the Lord: as Darius served him, by giving the idol into Daniel's power to be broken in pieces, and by casting his enemies in among the lions: as Nabuchodonosor served him, by a terrible proclamation, which forbade all men within his dominion to blaspheme the true and very God. In this therefore should kings serve God, in that that they are kings, by doing those things which none can do but kings. Wherefore, when as in the apostles' times the kings did not as yet serve the Lord, but imagined a vain thing against the Lord and against his Christ, that the prophet's sayings might be fulfilled, there could not as then, I say, any laws be made to forbid ungodliness, but counsel be rather taken to put ungodliness in practice. For so the course of times did turn, that both the Jews should kill the preachers of Christ, thinking that thereby they did God good service; and that the Gentiles also should fret and rage

against the Christians, and make the martyrs' constancy overcome the flames of fire. But afterward, when that began to be
fulfilled which is written, 'And all the kings of the earth shall
worship him, all nations shall serve him;' what man that were
well in his wits would say to kings, 'Tush, take ye no care
how, or by whom, the church of your Lord is defended or
defaced within your kingdom; let it not trouble you to mark
who will be honest, and who dishonest within your dominion?'
For since God hath given man free will, why should adultery
be punished, and sacrilege left untouched? Is it a lighter
matter for the soul to break promise with God, than a woman
with a man? Or, for because those things which are not
committed by contempt, but by ignorance of religion, are to be
more mildly punished, are they therefore to be utterly neglected? It is better (who doubteth?) for men to be brought
to the worshipping of God by teaching, rather than for to be
compelled to it by fear or grief of punishment: but because
these are the better, they, which are not such, are not therefore to be neglected. For it hath profited many men (as we
see by experience) first to have been compelled with fear and
grief, that afterward they might either be taught, or follow
that in deed which they had learned in words[1]."

[1 Quod enim dicunt qui contra suas impietates leges justas con-
stitui nolunt, non petisse a regibus terræ apostolos talia, non considerant
aliud fuisse tunc tempus, et omnia suis temporibus agi. Quis enim
tunc in Christum crediderat imperator, qui ei pro pietate contra impietatem leges ferendo serviret, quando adhuc illud propheticum com-
plebatur, Quare fremuerunt gentes et populi meditati sunt inania;
astiterunt reges terræ et principes convenerunt in unum adversus
Dominum et adversus Christum ejus? Nondum autem agebatur, quod
paulo post in eodem Psalmo dicitur, Et nunc, reges, intelligite, erudimini
qui judicatis terram: servite Domino in timore, et exultate ei cum
tremore. Quomodo ergo reges Domino serviunt in timore, nisi ea,
quæ contra jussa Domini fiunt, religiosa severitate prohibendo atque
plectendo? Aliter enim servit quia homo est, aliter quia etiam et rex
est. Quia homo est, ei servit vivendo fideliter: quia vero etiam rex
est, servit leges justa præcipientes et contraria prohibentes convenienti
vigore sanciendo: sicut servivit Ezechias, lucos et templa idolorum,
et illa excelsa quæ contra præcepta Dei fuerant constructa, destruendo:
sicut servivit Josias, talia et ipse faciendo: sicut servivit rex Ninivi-
tarum, universam civitatem ad placandum Dominum compellendo:
sicut servivit Darius, idolum frangendum in potestatem Danieli dando,
et inimicos ejus leonibus ingerendo: sicut servivit Nabuchodonosor,

Hitherto I have rehearsed the words of St Augustine's answer to the objections of them which are of opinion, that by no law disobedient rebels, seduced people, and deceivers, ought to be punished in cases of religion.

I see my hope doth fail me, wherein I thought that I could have been able in this sermon to have made an end of all that I had to say touching the magistrate. But I perceive that here I must stay, unless I should go on, dearly beloved, and be too tedious unto you all. I mean to-morrow, therefore, to add the rest that is yet behind. Make ye your humble prayers unto the Lord upon your knees, and then depart in peace.

de quo jam diximus, omnes in regno suo positos a blasphemando Deo lege terribili prohibendo. In hoc ergo serviunt Domino reges, in quantum sunt reges, cum ea faciunt ad serviendum illi, quæ non possunt facere nisi reges. Cum itaque nondum reges Domino servirent temporibus apostolorum, sed adhuc meditarentur inania adversus eum et adversus Christum ejus, ut prophetarum prædicta omnia complerentur, non utique tunc possent impietates legibus prohiberi, sed potius exerceri. Sic enim ordo temporum volvebatur, ut et Judæi occiderent prædicatores Christi, putantes se officium Deo facere, sicut prædixerat Christus ; et gentes fremerent adversus Christianos, et omnes potentia (patientia) martyrum vinceret. Postea vero quam cœpit impleri quod scriptum est, Et adorabunt eum omnes reges terræ, omnes gentes servient illi; quis mente sobrius regibus dicat, 'Nolite curare in regno vestro a quo tueatur (teneatur) vel oppugnetur ecclesia Domini vestri: non ad vos pertineat in regno vestro, quis velit esse sive religiosus sive sacrilegus. ... Cur enim, cum datum sit divinitus homini liberum arbitrium, adulteria legibus puniantur, et sacrilegia permittantur ? An fidem non servare levius est animam Deo, quam fœminam viro ? Aut si ea, quæ non contemptu sed ignorantia religionis committuntur, mitius vindicanda, numquid ideo negligenda sunt ? Melius est quidem (quis dubitaverit?) ad Deum colendum doctrina homines duci, quam pœnæ timore vel dolore compelli. Sed non quia isti meliores sunt, ideo illi, qui tales non sunt, negligendi sunt. Multis enim profuit, quod experimentis probavimus, prius timore vel dolore cogi, ut postea possint doceri, aut quod jam verbis didicerant opere sectari.—Opp. Tom. II. fol. 42. P.]

24

OF WAR; WHETHER IT BE LAWFUL FOR A MAGISTRATE
TO MAKE WAR. WHAT THE SCRIPTURE TEACHETH
TOUCHING WAR. WHETHER A CHRISTIAN MAN
MAY BEAR THE OFFICE OF A MAGISTRATE.
AND OF THE DUTY OF SUBJECTS.

THE NINTH SERMON.

To the right of the sword, which God hath given to the
magistrate, doth war belong: for in my last sermon I taught
you, that the use of the sword in the magistrate's hand is
twofold, or of two sorts. For either he punisheth offenders
therewith; or else repelleth the enemy that spoileth or would
spoil his people, or cutteth off the rebellious purposes of his
own seditious citizens.

Whether it be lawful for a magistrate to make war. But many make a doubt whether it be lawful for a magistrate to make war or no [1]. And it is marvel to see them as
blind as beetles in a matter of itself as plain as may be. For
if the magistrate doth by God's law punish offenders, thieves,
and harmful persons; and that it maketh no matter whether
they be few or many in number, as I declared in my yesterday's sermon; even by the same law may he persecute,
repel, and kill rebellious people, seditious citizens, and barbarous soldiers, who, under the pretence of war, do attempt
that openly which thieves and robbers are wont to do privily.
The prophet, I confess, did among other things prophesy of
us Christians, and say: "They shall turn their swords into
spades, and their javelins into scythes [2]:" for Christians have
peace with all men, and do altogether abstain from armour;
for every one doth that to another which he would wish to
have done to himself. But, for because all are not so minded,
but that many unruly persons, wicked thieves, and oppressors
of the poor, do live and dwell among honest and good-mean-
ing men, as wild beasts among harmless creatures; therefore
God from heaven hath given the sword into the magistrate's
hand, to be a defence for harmless people against unruly

[1 Of these doctrines of the Anabaptists, Latimer also makes mention, Parker Soc. ed. Vol. I. pp. 495, 6. See also Bullinger. adv. Anabaptist. Lib. v. cap. 10.]

[2 Isai. ii. 4.]

cut-throats. But we read not in any place that we are for-bidden to suppress and kill wolves, wild boars, bears, and such other beasts that do annoy and prey upon men or cattle. What let then should there be why we should not, by lawful war begun in a good quarrel, repel the unjust injury of violent robbers, since thieves, robbers, barbarous soldiers, and sedi-tious citizens, do differ little or nothing from wild beasts? The scripture, verily, doth not vouchsafe to call them by any other names than by the names of beasts. Hereunto consenteth the common sense of nature; and herewithal agreeth the doctrine of faith and religion. " If it be possible," saith the apostle, " as much as lieth in you, live quietly with all men; not revenging yourselves." See here, " as much as lieth in you," saith he, and, " if it be possible :" otherwise, he addeth immediately after : " The magistrate beareth not the sword in vain [3]." He meaneth, for them that trouble all things, and do annoy the men which do desire to live at peace. And this is confirmed by the examples of the most holy and excellent men that have been in the world, which have taken war in hand for the defence of their country and harmless country-men; as I have already declared out of St Paul's Epistle to the Hebrews, when as in the exposition of the fifth precept I shewed what honour every man doth owe to his country [4].

I will add to these some reasons of St Augustine, uttered *contra Faustum Manichæum,* Lib. XXII. cap. 74. " Neither let him," saith he, " marvel or be astonied at the wars made by Moses; for because even in them too he followed God's commandment, not like a tyrant, but like an obedient servant. Neither did God rage with cruelty, when he commanded those wars; but justly paid home them that deserved it, and terrified those that were worthy of it. For what is blame-worthy in war? Is it to be blamed that they do die which once must die, that they which live may rule in peace ? To find fault with that is rather a cowardly touch, than the part of a religious Christian. Desire to hurt, cruelty in revenging, an unappeased stomach, bruteness in rebelling, greediness to rule, and whatsoever else is like to these, are the things that in war are worthy to be blamed, and by right of law to be sharply punished. Against the violence of injurious enemies, at the commandment either of God himself or any other lawful

[3 Rom. xii. 18; xiii. 4.]   [4 See before, p. 277.]

power, even good men are wont to take war in hand; since
their state in the world is such, that politic order doth justly
bind the magistrate in such a case to command it, and the
subjects to obey it. Otherwise John, when the soldiers came to
him to be baptized, saying, 'And what shall we do?' would have
answered them, and said: Cast off your armour, forsake your
soldier's life, strike, wound, or kill nobody. But, because
he knew that while they did so, as soldiers in the war, they
were not man-quellers, but ministers of the law, not revengers
of their own injuries, but defenders of the commonweal, he
said unto them, 'Strike no man, do no man injury; be content with your wages.' But because the Manichees have of
use blasphemed or spoken against John, let them hear the
Lord Jesus Christ himself commanding to give to Cæsar that
stipend which John did say the soldier should be content
withal. 'Give,' saith he, 'to Cæsar that which is Cæsar's, and
to God the things that do belong to God.' For to this end
is tribute paid, that the soldier in the war may have his pay
out of hand for his pain. Very well, therefore, when the
centurion said, 'And I am a man set under power, having
soldiers under me; and I say to one, Go, and he goeth, and to
another, Come, and he cometh, and to my servant, Do this, and
he doeth it,'—did the Lord commend his faith, and not command him to forsake his soldiership[1]." Hitherto also apper-

[1 Nec bella per Moysen gesta miretur aut horreat, quia et in illis
divina secutus imperia, non sæviens, sed obediens fuit: nec Deus, cum
jubebat ista, sæviebat, sed digna dignis retribuebat, dignosque terrebat.
Quid enim culpatur in bello? An quia moriuntur quandoque morituri,
ut dominentur in pace victuri? Hoc reprehendere timidorum est, non
religiosorum. Nocendi cupiditas, ulciscendi crudelitas, impacatus atque
implacabilis animus, feritas rebellandi, libido dominandi, et si qua
similia, hæc sunt quæ in bellis jure culpantur, quæ plerumque ita culpantur ut etiam jure puniantur. Adversus violentiam resistentium,
sive Deo sive aliquo legitimo imperio jubente, gerenda ipsa bella
suscipiuntur a bonis, cum in eo rerum humanarum ordine inveniuntur,
ubi eos vel jubere tale aliquid, vel in talibus obedire juste ordo ipse
constringit. Alioquin Joannes, cum ad eum baptizandi milites venirent,
dicentes, Et nos quid faciemus? responderet eis, Arma abjicite, militiam istam deserite, neminem percutite, vulnerate, prosternite neminem.
Sed quia sciebat eos, cum hæc militando facerent, non esse homicidas
sed ministros legis, et non ultores injuriarum suarum sed salutis pub-
licæ defensores, respondit eis, Neminem concusseritis, nulli calumniam
feceritis, sufficiat vobis stipendium vestrum. Sed quia Manichæi

taineth that which followeth in the same 75th chapter and 76th next after. But I do of purpose willingly bear somewhat with you, not meaning by overlong rehearsing of too many sentences to be tedious unto you.

Thus hitherto I have shewed you that it is lawful for the magistrate for to make war. Where, by the way, also we gather, that the subjects do lawfully, without any offence to God, take armour to battle, when they take it in hand at the magistrate's bidding. But if the magistrate's purpose be to kill the guiltless, I declared in my former sermons that then his people ought not to obey his wicked commandments. *Let the people obey the magistrate when he commandeth them to war.*

Let the magistrate therefore have an eye to himself, that he abuse not his lawful authority. And although the magistrate be licensed to make war for just and necessary causes; yet, notwithstanding, war is a thing most full of peril, and draweth with itself an endless troop of mischievous evils. By war the just judgment of God doth plague the men whom his fatherly warning could never move; but among them many times, too, the guiltless feel the whip. In war, for the most part, soldiers misuse themselves, and thereby incur God's heavy displeasure: there is no evil in all the world that war upholdeth not. By war both scarcity of every thing and dearth do arise: for highways are stopped, corn upon the ground is trodden down and marred, whole villages burnt, provision goeth to wrack, handicrafts are unoccupied, merchandise do cease, and all do perish, both rich and poor. The valiant strong men are slain in the battle; the cowardly sort run away for their lives to hide their heads, reserving themselves to be tormented with more exquisite and terrible kinds of cruel punishments: for wicked knaves are promoted to dignity, and bear the sway, which abuse mankind like savage beasts. Hands are wrung on every side; widows and children *War, a thing full of peril and danger.*

Joannem aperte blasphemare consueverunt, ipsum Dominum Jesum Christum audiant, hoc stipendium jubentem reddi Cæsari, quod Joannes dicit debere sufficere militi. Reddite, inquit, Cæsari quæ Cæsaris sunt, et Deo quæ Dei sunt. Ad hoc enim tributa præstantur, ut propter bella necessario militi stipendium præbeatur. Merito et illius centurionis dicentis, Et ego homo sum sub potestate constitutus, habens sub me milites, et dico huic, Vade, et vadit; et alii, Veni, et venit; et servo meo, Fac hoc, et facit; fidem laudavit, non illius militiæ desertionem imperavit.—Opp. Par. 1531, Tom. VI. fol. 89. P.]

cry out and lament; the wealth, that hath been carefully gathered to help in want to come, is spoiled and stolen away; cities are rased, virgins and unmarriageable maidens are shamefully deflowered, all honesty is utterly violated, old men are handled unreverently, laws are not exercised, religion and learning are nothing set by, godless knaves and cut-throats have the dominion: and therefore in the scriptures war is called the scourge of God. For with war he plagueth incurable idolaters, and those which stubbornly contemn his word; for that was the cause why the city of Jerusalem with the whole nation of the Jews was utterly destroyed; "because they knew not the day of their visitation" (as the Lord in the gospel saith), but went on to kill the Lord's apostles, bringing on upon their own necks " the shedding of all the blood, from the righteous Abel unto Zacharias[1]." For murder, idolatry, incest, and detestable riot, we read that the Canaanites were rased out and cut off[2]. The Moabites, as Esay witnesseth, were quite overthrown for cruelty, inhumanity, and contempt of the poor[3]. The men of Ninivy did by war unjustly vex other nations, making havoc of all, to fill their greedy desire: and therefore, saith the prophet Nahum, other men measured to them with the same measure that they had measured to other before[4]. Micheas, in his sixth chapter, affirmeth flatly that God sendeth war upon unjust men for their covetousness and false deceit. In Jeremy arrogancy and pride, in Esay riot and drunkenness, are said to be the causes of war[5].

But the evil and misery that war bringeth with it sticketh so fast to commonweals and kingdoms, where it once hath hold, that it cannot be removed, taken away, or shaken off, at our will and pleasure, by any worldly wisdom, by any leaguemakings, with any wealth, by any fortifications, by any power or manhood; as it is to be seen in the prophet Abdias[6]. Our sincere turning to God alone is the only way to remedy it, as Jeremy testifieth in his fifth chapter. Now this turning to the Lord consisteth in free acknowledging and frank confession of our sins, in true faith for remission of sins through the grace of God and merit of Christ Jesus: secondarily, it consisteth in hatred and renouncing of all unrighteousness, in love of

War is the scourge of God.

[1 Luke xix. 44; Matt. xxiii. 34—38.]   [2 Lev. xviii. 27, 28.]
[3 Isai. xvi.]   [4 Nahum iii. 19.]
[5 Jer. xiii. 9; Isai. v.]   [6 Obad. 3, 4, 8, 9.]

justice, innocency, charity, and all other virtues; and, last of all, in earnest prayers and continual supplications.

Again, thou mayest see perhaps, that some by war have *War for profit.* no small commodity, profit, and inestimable riches, with very little loss or no damage at all. Such was the war which the Israelites had with the Canaanites under their captain Josue. But I would not that gaping after gain should draw any man *They that have the* from right and equity. And many times the magistrates sup- *juster quarrel are overcome* pose that their quarrel is good, and that of right they ought *of the unjust.* to make war on others and punish offenders; when as notwithstanding the righteous God by that occasion draweth them on into peril, that their sins may be punished by the men in whom they did purpose to have punished some grievous crime. We have evident examples hereof in the scriptures. The eleven tribes of Israel in a good quarrel made war on the Benjamites, purposing to revenge the detestable crime that a few wicked knaves had horribly committed, wherein the whole tribe bare them out and upheld them, being partners thereby of their heinous offence: but twice the Israelites were put to the worse, and the wicked Benjamites had the upper hand in the battle[7]. In the time of Heli the Israelites minded to drive the tyrannous rule of the idolatrous Philistines out of their country; but they are slain, the ark of God is taken, and carried into the cities of their idolatrous enemies[8]. Likewise that excellent prince Josias is overthrown and slain by the Chaldees, because the Lord had purposed to punish and bring evil upon the whole people of Israel, which he would not have so holy a prince his servant to see with his eyes, to his sorrow and grief[9]. Whereby we have to gather, that the truth of religion is not to be esteemed by the victory or overthrow of any people, so that that religion should be true and right whose favourers have the upper hand, and that again be false and untrue whose professors and maintainers are put to the worse: for we must distinguish betwixt religion and the men or persons that keep that religion, which do for other causes suffer the Lord's visitation.

But all this admonisheth us, that the magistrate hath need of the great fear of God before his eyes, both in making and

[7 Judg. xx.]   [8 1 Sam. iv.]
[9 2 Kings xxii. 20, and xxiii. 29.—"In his days Pharaoh Necho, king of *Egypt*," &c. P.]

repelling wars, lest while he goeth about to avoid the smould-
ering coalpit, he hap to fall into the scalding limekiln[1]; or lest,
while he supposeth to ease his shoulders of one evil, he doth,
by the way whereby he sought ease, heap up either more
or far greater evils.   Princes therefore must precisely look
into, and throughly examine, the cause of wars, before they
The causes
of war.   begin or take them in hand.   The causes are many, and of
many sorts; but the chief are these that follow.   For either
the magistrate is compelled to send aid and raise the siege of
his enemy, which doth environ the garrisons that he hath
appointed for the defence of some of his cities; because it
were an offence, and part of parricide, to forsake and give
over, against oath and honesty, his cities and garrisons that
are in extremity : or else the magistrate of duty is compelled
to make war upon men which are incurable, whom the very
judgment of the Lord condemneth and biddeth to kill without
pity or mercy.   Such were the wars as Moses had with the
Madianites, and Josue[2] with the Amalechites.   Of that sort
are the wars wherein such men are oppressed, as of invincible
malice will both perish themselves and draw other to destruction as well as themselves, with those also which, rejecting all
justice and equity, do stubbornly go on to persist in their
naughtiness.   Such were the Benjamites, which were destroyed
by sword and fire of the other eleven tribes.   Such are at this
day those arrogant and seditious rebels as trouble commonweals
and kingdoms, as of old Absalom was in Israel, and Seba the
son of Bochri; of whom mention is made in the second book
of Samuel[3].

Wars taken
in hand for
the defence
of religion.   Hereunto appertain the wars that are taken in hand for the
defence of true religion against idolaters and enemies of the
true and catholic faith.   They err, that are of opinion that no
wars may be made in defence of religion.   The Lord, indeed,
blamed Peter for striking with the sword, because he was
an apostle; but thereby, notwithstanding, he bade not the
magistrate to be negligent in looking to religion, neither forbad he him to defend and maintain the pureness of faith.
For if it be lawful for the magistrate to defend with the sword
the things of account, of which sort are liberty, wealth, chas-

[1 ne dum vitant carbonariam, incidant in calcariam, Lat.—Cf.
Erasm. Adag. Chiliad. pp. 493, 4. Hanov. 1617.]
[2 a Saule, Lat.—not Joshua.]   [3 2 Sam. xx.]

tity, and his subjects' bodies ; why should he not defend and
revenge the things of greater account, and those which are of
greatest weight? But there is nothing of more and greater
weight than sincere and true religion is. There is, moreover,
a manifest and flat commandment of God touching this matter
to be seen in Deuteronomium. For the Lord commandeth
that every city, within the jurisdiction of every magistrate,
which departeth from God and the worship of God, should be
set on with warriors, and utterly rased, if it revolted not from
idolatry betimes. The place is extant in the thirteenth of
Deut. But if the magistrate be commanded to punish apostates by war, then is it lawful for him by war to defend the
Church in danger to be drawn by any barbarous prince from
true religion unto false idolatry. Josue would by war have
suppressed the Reubenites with their confederates for building
an altar against God's commandment. Judas Machabeus fought
for the people of God against the people and soldiers of king
Antiochus, who purposed to tread down the Jewish religion,
which at that time was the true worship of God, and perforce
to make all men receive and profess his heathenish superstition. Likewise also Paul commended greatly those Jewish
captains or judges, which by faith withstood and turned away
foreign enemies' invasions. And Paul himself did war in
Cyprus against Elymas the false prophet, and struck him with
blindness: he addeth the reason why he struck him blind, which
he fetcheth from the keeping of religion, and saith : " Ceasest
thou not to pervert the right ways of the Lord? &c." Act. xiii.
For the same Paul again forty men do lie in wait, supposing, if
he were once made away, that a good part of the preaching
of the gospel would then come to an end, and that thereby
the Jewish religion (which, notwithstanding, was utterly false)
should have been set up and maintained for truth. But Paul *Since he
was not negligent to remedy this case, neither turned he the *asked aid of*
other cheek to have that stricken too ; but earnestly and hum- *great deal*
bly requireth delivery and defence, which he requested not of *required it*
a christian magistrate (when as yet there was none), but of *of christian*
a Roman centurion : neither did he once gainsay him, when he *there had*
saw that he chose out four hundred footmen and seventy *been any.*
horsemen, whom he placed in order of battle array, to conduct
him safely from Hierusalem to Antipatridis : and by that
means was Paul, the vessel of election, preserved by an armed

band of Italian soldiers[1]. Of the Armenians, whom Maximinus the emperor did tyrannously oppress, Eusebius in the ninth book and eighth chapter of his Ecclesiastical History saith: " The people of Armenia, having been long time both profitable and friends to the people of Rome, being at length compelled by Maximinus Cæsar to change the use of Christian religion (whereunto the whole nation was most holily bent) into the worship of idols, and to honour devils instead of God, of friends became enemies, and of fellows adversaries; and preparing by force of arms to defend themselves against his wicked edicts, do of their own accord make war upon him, and put him often to much trouble and business[2]." Thus saith he. It is lawful, therefore, for the magistrate to defend his people and subjects against idolaters, and by war to maintain and uphold true religion.

Like to this there is another cause why the magistrate may take war in hand. For either some barbarous enemy invadeth the people committed to thy charge, tearing and spoiling them most cruelly, like a wolf in a flock of sheep; when as notwithstanding thou didst not first provoke him thereunto by injury, but also after his causeless beginning thou hast offered equal conditions of peace to be made: in such a case as this the magistrate is commanded to stand forth like a lion, and to defend his subjects against the open wrong of merciless cut-throats: (so did Moses, when he fought against Arad, Sehon, and Og, kings of the Amorites[3]: so did Josaphat, when he fought against the Ammonites and inhabitants of mount Seir[4]: so did David, when he understood[5] the war made on him by the Syrians:) or else the magistrate doth aid his confederates (for the magistrate may make league with the nations about him, so that thereby nothing be done against the word of God), when by tyrants they be wrongfully oppressed. For so did Josue deliver the Gabionites from the

[1 Acts xxiii.—Romanorum militum, Lat.]

[2 Τούτοις προσεπανίσταται τῷ τυράννῳ ὁ πρὸς Ἀρμενίους πόλεμος, ἄνδρας ἐξ ἀρχαίου φίλους τε καὶ συμμάχους Ῥωμαίων· οὓς καὶ αὐτοὺς Χριστιανοὺς ὄντας, καὶ τὴν εἰς τὸ θεῖον εὐσέβειαν διὰ σπουδῆς ποιουμένους, ὁ θεομισὴς εἰδώλοις θύειν καὶ δαίμοσιν ἐπαναγκάσαι πεπειραμένος, ἐχθροὺς ἀντὶ φίλων καὶ πολεμίους ἀντὶ συμμάχων κατεστήσατο.—Euseb. Hist. Eccles. Lib. IX. cap. 8.]

[3 Numb. xxi.]   [4 2 Chron. xx.]
[5 propellens, Lat.—2 Sam. viii.]

siege of their enemies, and Saul the men of Jabes Galaad, fighting for them against Nahas, a prince full of tyranny[6]. In such cases as these magistrates and princes do lawfully make war, and their soldiers and subjects do rightly obey them; yea, they do with great glory die a happy death, that die in so just a quarrel, as for the defence of religion, of the laws of God, of his country, wife, and children. They therefore that enter into warfare to sustain the troublesome toil of battle, must not set their minds upon gain or pleasure, wherein they look, when peril is past, to lie still and wallow: but justice, public peace, defence of truth and innocency, must be the mark for them all to shoot at: to the intent, when the wicked are vanquished, the victory obtained, and the enemies put to flight, slain out of hand, or brought to better order, that then religion may flourish, judgment and justice may be exercised, the Church upheld, the ceremonies, rites, ordinances, and discipline thereof maintained, study and learning cherished, the poor provided for, widows and children defended and cared for; that all sorts may live in quiet peace, that old men in reverence, maidens in chastity, and matrons in honesty, may serve God, praise God, and worship God, without fear or danger. This was the mark whereto our fathers Abraham, Moses, Josue, David, and other valiant men of famous memory[7], did direct the eyes of their bodies and minds: upon this only their hearts were settled, so often as they warred and went to battle against ungodly tyrants in defence of the church and commonweal: to whom, and to all other valiant and godly soldiers, eternal praise is duly given of all the church and faithful saints. But to fearful and cowardly soldiers, to wicked, covetous, and blaspheming warriors, to riotous knaves, and unconstant traitors, by whose cowardice, gluttony, lust, and unnatural treason, excellent kingdoms do come to nought[8], and flourishing commonweals are quite overthrown, is reproach and infamy worthily due: for God himself hath cursed such knaves for evermore.

Therefore it is not lawful to make any war, unless it be against open enemies, and wicked men that are incurable. The wars are unjust, that men do make upon their own fellows,

The commendation of war and warriors.

Unjust wars.

[6 Josh. x.; 1 Sam. xi.]

[7 denique beatæ recordationis patres nostros, Lat. P.]

[8 hodie, Lat., omitted; at this day.]

against innocent persons, or people in whom there is hope of amendment. Those wars also are unjust, that are not begun by lawful means for matters of weight. All things must first be assayed, before it come to be tried out by battle. Other men's territories must not be desired : the liberty of other people or thine own subjects must not be repressed: thou must not follow any affection, which may withdraw or seduce thy mind ; of which sort are desire of rule, covetousness, greediness of gifts, envy, and other affections like unto these. War is to commonweals a remedy indeed, but perilous and dangerous, even as lancing or cutting is to the members. The hand is poisoned, and the arm in danger to be envenomed too, whereby the whole man perhaps may be cast away : but yet thou cuttest not off thy hand until, when thou hast tried all other medicines, thou dost plainly perceive that no other means can remedy the sore but cutting off alone. Likewise, when all helps fail, then at the last let war begin; so yet, nevertheless, that the prince do remember to begin with war before all help and hope of recovery be utterly past[1].

The word of God hath made laws of war. For the word of God is so far off from finding fault with war begun upon a just quarrel, that it doth both make laws of war, and sheweth a number of examples of upright wars, of wise and worthy warriors. The laws of war are recited in the 20th chapter of Deuteronomy, both profitable and necessary, and therewithal so evident, that they need no words of mine to expound them. Moreover, in every place of the scripture these laws of war are still bidden to be kept. First of all, the chief and uppermost place must be given to religion in every camp and garrison : for the Lord himself hath appointed priests and ministers of true religion to attend and serve in wars. Secondarily, let upright laws be of force in camps abroad, as well as in cities at home : let soldiers live honestly, justly, and rightly, as order and discipline are wont to require when as they are in the city at home. For that saying cometh not of God, but of the devil, which is commonly spread abroad, Let laws in war be hushed and still[2]. Thirdly, let him that is chosen to be guide and general of the war be godly, just, holy, valiant, wise, and fortunate; as, among them of old, were Josue, David, Judas Machabeus, Constantine,

[1 ut meminerint tamen principes, Ne quid sero nimis, Lat.]
[2 Sileant inter arma leges, Lat.—See Cic. pro Mil.]

Theodosius[3], and many more. To all this there must be added a chosen band of tried men: for choice of soldiers must be made, unless perhaps the army do consist in a troop of bastards and unskilful men, of perjured and blaspheming knaves, of cut-throats and rakehells, of drunkards and gluttons, and a beastly drove of filthy swine. Victory consisteth not in the multitude of men, but in the grace of God and a chosen band. The proverb is common which saith, "Where a multitude is, there is confusion." Great and innumerable armies are a let to themselves very greatly; as we do learn by daily experience, and as examples of every age do testify to us. Moreover, loiterers in camps are always reproved. Let the christian soldier, therefore, be idle at no time; let him ever be busy, and still doing something: let him be courageous, faithful to his country, ready to take pains, obedient to his captains, fit to take time when occasion is offered, and evermore occupied in warlike discipline; no effeminate milksop, but of manly stomach; not cruel and merciless, but severe and pitiful, as time requireth. What he may preserve, that let him not destroy. But, above all things, let him not forget or think scorn, both in peril and out of peril, evermore to make his prayers and supplications to God his Saviour. In God's name let him begin all things; without God let him attempt nothing: in adversity, and when he hath the overthrow, let not his courage quail, nor his heart and hope forsake him; in prosperity let him not be puffed up with pride and arrogancy, but let him give thanks to God, and use the conquest like a merciful victor: let him wholly depend upon God's helping hand, and desire nothing rather than the defence of the commonweal, laws, religion, justice, and guiltless people.

The description of a christian soldier.

Many, I know, will marvel to see me require at the hands of a soldier the things that seem to be enough, as the common saying is, to be looked for of a right good and godly man; as though, indeed, that none could be soldiers but irreligious and naughty men. Soldiers, I confess, are for the most part such kind of fellows: but what fruit, I pray you, reap we at this day of so evil seed? The Turks overrun and spoil us; we are to all the heathen a jesting-stock to

[3 Mascelzer, Lat.; omitted by the translator.—See Gibbon, Decl. and Fall. chap. xxix.; and Universal Hist. Ancient Hist. Vol. xvi. p. 473. Lond. 1748. Book iv. chap. 5.]

laugh at; kingdoms decay and are made subject to devilish Mahometism, and every day we are wrapped in more mise-

What manner of soldiers the ancient Christians were in times past.

ries than other[1]. But what kind of soldiers they of old were, which went to the war from out of the church or congregation of the Christians, we may easily gather even by that one history, worthy the remembrance, which Tertullian to Scapula setteth down thus: "Marcus Aurelius also in his wars with the Germans, by the prayers which christian soldiers made unto God, obtained showers of rain in that great drought. At what time have not droughts been turned away by our prayers and fastings? Then the people crying out

The Latin copy hath, *E. qui solus potens*, by which I think I e meant the emperor.

for joy to the God of gods, and the emperor himself, under the name of Jupiter, confessed the wonderful working of our God[2]." Thus much Tertullian. But Eusebius, in his Ecclesiastical History, hath more largely and fully set down the same history, and saith: "Histories report that Marcus Aurelius, brother to Antoninus Cæsar, making war upon the Germans and Sarmatians, when his army was in danger to be lost with drought, being at his wits' end because he knew not what way to seek for remedy in that distress, did at the last light upon a certain legion wherein christian soldiers were, whose prayers God heard, when they, as the manner of our men is, had upon their knees cried out unto him; so that on a sudden, when no man looked for it, with the pouring down of sufficient showers, the thirst of the army that then was in danger, for which the Christians had made supplications, was presently quenched; but their enemies, that hovered there to have been their destruction, were stricken and scattered with thunder and fire in lightning from heaven : which deed is reported by heathen historiographers; but that it was obtained at the prayers of our men, they do not report : for with them the other miracles, which are done by our men, have no place of credit. But among our men Tertullian

[1] See Works of Becon, Parker Soc. ed. Vol. I. p. 239.]

[2] Marcus quoque Aurelius in Germanica expeditione christianorum militum orationibus ad Deum factis imbres in siti illa impetravit. Quando non geniculationibus et jejunationibus nostris etiam siccitates sunt depulsæ? Tunc et populus adclamans Deo deorum, qui solus potens, in Jovis nomine Deo nostro testimonium reddidit.—Tertul. ad Scapulam. cap. 4. pag. 162. Tom. III. ed. Semler. 1829. Bullinger's quotation reads : et qui solus potens.]

maketh mention hereof; and among the Greeks Apollinaris, Legio ful-
who also affirmeth, that for the miracle of that notable deed minea.
that legion's name was changed by the emperor, and called
The Legion of Thunder. Tertullian addeth, that the letters of
Marcus the emperor are yet to be had, wherein the full and
manifest truth of this matter is plainly declared[3]."

Hitherto Eusebius. Whereby we gather that christian
soldiers of old were not only given to prayer, but to justice
also, and holiness of living. For who knoweth not that James
the apostle said, "The earnest prayer of a righteous man availeth much : Elias was a man under infirmities even as we are,
and he prayed in his prayer, and the heavens gave rain, and
the earth brought forth her fruit[4]?" It is most evident,
therefore, that soldiers of old were very godly and religious
men. Our soldiers at these days, because they are far from
religion, yea, because they are enemies to true religion, do,
instead of victory, suffer overthrows abroad, and loss and
destruction of their cities at home. And worthily do commonweals suffer such plagues for trusting so much in such wicked
soldiers. For to trust them is all one as if they should put

[3 Τούτου δὴ ἀδελφὸν Μάρκον Αὐρήλιον Καίσαρα λόγος ἔχει, Γερμανοῖς
καὶ Σαρμάταις ἀντιπαρατατόμενον μάχῃ, δίψει πιεζομένης αὐτοῦ τῆς στρατιᾶς,
ἐν ἀμηχανίᾳ γενέσθαι, τοὺς δὲ ἐπὶ τῆς Μελιτινῆς οὕτω καλουμένης λεγεῶνος
στρατιώτας, διὰ πίστεως ἐξ ἐκείνου καὶ εἰς δεῦρο συνεστώσης, ἐν τῇ πρὸς
τοὺς πολεμίους παρατάξει γόνυ θέντας ἐπὶ γῆν, κατὰ τὸ οἰκεῖον ἡμῖν τῶν
εὐχῶν ἔθος, ἐπὶ τὰς πρὸς τὸν Θεὸν ἱκεσίας τραπέσθαι. Παραδόξου δὲ τοῖς
πολεμίοις τοῦ τοιούτου δὴ θεάματος φανέντος, ἄλλό τι λόγος ἔχει παραδοξό-
τερον ἐπικαταλαβεῖν αὐτίκα· σκηπτὸν μὲν εἰς φυγὴν καὶ ἀπώλειαν συνελαύ-
νοντα τοὺς πολεμίους, ὄμβρον δὲ ἐπὶ τὴν τῶν τὸ θεῖον παρακεκληκότων
στρατιὰν, πᾶσαν αὐτὴν ἐκ τοῦ δίψους μέλλουσαν ὅσον οὔπω διαφθαρή-
σεσθαι, ἀνακτώμενον. Ἡ δὲ ἱστορία φέρεται μὲν καὶ παρὰ τοῖς πόρρω τοῦ
καθ᾽ ἡμᾶς λόγου συγγραφεῦσιν .... Τοῖς μὲν ἔξωθεν ἱστορικοῖς, ἅτε τῆς
πίστεως ἀνοικείοις, τέθειται μὲν τὸ παράδοξον, οὐ μὴν καὶ ταῖς τῶν ἡμετέρων
εὐχαῖς τοῦτο ὡμολογήθη γεγονέναι· τοῖς δέ γε ἡμετέροις, ἅτε ἀληθείας φίλοις, ἁπλῷ καὶ ἀκακοήθει τρόπῳ τὸ πραχθὲν παραδέδοται. Τούτων δ᾽ ἂν
εἴη καὶ Ἀπολινάριος, ἐξ ἐκείνου φήσας τὴν δι᾽ εὐχῆς τὸ παράδοξον πεποιη-
κυῖαν λεγεῶνα οἰκείαν τῷ γεγονότι πρὸς τοῦ βασιλέως εἰληφέναι προσηγορίαν,
Κεραυνοβόλον τῇ Ῥωμαίων ἐπικληθεῖσαν φωνῇ. Μάρτυς δὲ τούτων γένοιτ᾽
ἂν ἀξιόχρεως ὁ Τερτυλλιανός .... Γράφει δ᾽ οὖν καὶ αὐτὸς λέγων, Μάρκου
τοῦ συνετωτάτου βασιλέως ἐπιστολὰς εἰσέτι νῦν φέρεσθαι, ἐν αἷς αὐτὸς
μαρτυρεῖ ἐν Γερμανίᾳ ὕδατος ἀπορίᾳ μέλλοντα αὐτοῦ τὸν στρατὸν διαφθεί-
ρεσθαι ταῖς τῶν Χριστιανῶν εὐχαῖς σεσῶσθαι.—Euseb. Hist. Eccles. Lib.
v. cap. 5.]

[4 James v. 16—18.]

confidence in the very devils, whom these soldiers do, for the most part, exceed in all kind of filthiness, uncleanness, cruelty, and villainy.

Examples of war and captains out of the scripture. But now the word of God doth set before our eyes an innumerable sort of examples almost of holy and upright wars, and of excellent kings and captains. Abraham, our father, setting forward with a very small army, pursueth the four most puissant kings or robbers of the world; he overthroweth and putteth them to flight; and, having recovered his people, and restored to them their substance again, he giveth the thanks to God, as to the author of that unlikely victory [1]. Moses and Josue destroyed about thirty-nine kings; they punished severely the unspeakable wickedness of all those nations; and planted the people committed to their charge in the land which God had promised to give them. The Judges of the people of Israel had notable wars against the heathens and infidels, whereby they brake the tyranny of those wicked men, unlawfully usurped among God's people, restoring them again to their liberty and religion. The prophet Samuel is here to be numbered among the notable captains of God's people. Jonathas, Saul's son, was a worthy captain, and a singular example of a godly man. Than David none was more excellent or worthy to be praised. In war he vanquished the Philistines, the Idumites, the Syrians, and a good part of the East beside; by war he revenged injuries; by war he maintained his liberty, and kept God's people from a number of mischiefs: and yet, notwithstanding, he that warred thus is said to be a man according to God's heart's desire, and the father of our Lord Jesus Christ touching his flesh or his humanity [2]. In David's posterity thou mayest find many excellent warriors and valiant captains, Abia, Asa, Josaphat, Amasia, Osia, Ezechias, and other more. Among these Judas Machabeus hath not the last nor least place of all, who fought very stoutly for the law, religion, and people of God, and died at the last in the midst of the battle, in defence of religion and his country quarrel. I will not add to these the examples of Constantine, Gratian, Theodosius, and other more that were excellent in feats of war. Of these and other writeth St Augustine in the end of his fifth book *de*

[1 Gen. xiv.]
[2 1 Sam. xiii. 14; Rom. i. 3.]

Civitate Dei[3], and Orosius very largely in the seventh book of his history unto the end of the 28th chapter [4]. This is sufficient for godly magistrates. Hitherto have I discoursed of war to be made by the magistrate, and the use of the sword in the magistrate's hand; touching which I gave some notes by the way in that sermon wherein I expounded the Fifth Commandment.

This being thus ended, I have now to prove that christian men may bear the office of a magistrate; which treatise I mean therefore to take in hand, because our mad-headed Anabaptists, and some other builders of a devised commonweal [5], by gainsaying that which hitherto we have alleged, do go about to prove that a Christian may not bear the office of a magistrate: their reason is, because Christians, as they say, may not strive in law, nor kill any man, nor recover by war things violently taken away, nor revenge any injury that is done unto them. And although these causes of theirs be answered every one in his fit and several place; yet will I briefly gather here together a few substantial arguments, by which a politic and christian man may understand, contrary to the madness and dreams of the Anabaptists, if he be called to bear rule and authority, that then he both may, and of duty ought, to serve the Lord his God in taking upon him and executing the office of a magistrate. For, whereas they feign that the doctrine of the gospel doth utterly cut off all kind of defence, and whatsoever else belongeth to the defence of christian men's goods and bodies, that is nothing so, and they are deceived as far as heaven is wide: for the truth doth teach us clean contrary.

For whatsoever things are ordained by God for a means of men's safeguard and good estate, they are so far from misbecoming and being unseemly for a christian man, if he

A christian man may be a magistrate.

Respublica Utopiana.

[3 Chap. xxv. "De prosperitatibus, quas Constantino Imp. Christiano Deus contulit," and xxvi. "de fide et pietate Theodosii Augusti."—Opp. Par. 1531. Tom. v. fol. 69. P.]

[4 a 28 cap. ad finem usque, Lat.—Pauli Orosii adv. Paganos Histor. Libri Septem. Mogunt. 1615. In the chapters of the 7th Book from the 28th are related the successes of Constantine, Gratian, Theodosius, &c.]

[5 Utopianæ reipublicæ extructores, Lat.—See Preface of Hooker's Eccles. Pol. Vol. i. p. 183. Oxf. 1820.]

use them and apply himself unto them, that, if he refuse and neglect, he cannot rightly be called a true Christian. For the first and greatest care of every Christian is, by all means that he may, to set forward and maintain the health and safeguard of all sorts of men. But the magistrate is not ordained by any man, but by God himself, for the health and wealth of all mankind; as it is expressly witnessed by the prophets and apostles, but by Paul especially in the 13th to the Romans. Who then cannot thereby perceive that a Christian may praiseworthily execute a magistrate's office?

Furthermore, no man will deny, I know, that a christian man's faith is, not in words only, but in deeds also, to give a proof of justice and mercy, by all means to care for public peace and tranquillity, to do judgment with justice, to defend the fatherless, widows, and children, and to deliver poor oppressed people. Neither doth he contemn, flee from, nor reject, occasion, places, and means, by which he may put those good works in ure. And therefore a Christian refuseth not the place or office of a magistrate: for the magistrate's office is to do judgment with justice, and to provide for public peace.

Moreover, it is undoubtedly true, as before we have declared, that Moses, Samuel, Josue, and David, are not excluded from the name of Christianity: but since they were in authority and bare the names of magistrates, what let is there, I pray you, why a true christian man may not[1] bear the office of a magistrate in his commonweal? What may be thought of this, moreover, that in the new Testament certain notable men are well reported of, who, when they were in authority, were not put beside their offices because they were Christians and of a sound religion? Touching Joseph of Arimathea, thus we read in Luke: " And, behold, there was a man named Joseph, a counsellor," (Mark saith, " a noble senator[2]), who was a good man and a just; the same had not consented to the counsel and deed of them; which was of Arimathea, a city of the Jews, which waited also for the kingdom of God[3]." Mark here, I beseech you, how notable a testimony this man hath here. Joseph is a counsellor or

Honestus
senator.

[1 vel hodie, Lat., omitted; at this day too.]

[2 The Vulgate has, "nobilis decurio;" but "honestus senator," which Bullinger adopts, is the rendering of Erasmus in Mark xv. 43.]

[3 Luke xxiii. 50, 51 ; Mark xv. 43.]

senator; yea, and that more is, a noble senator too: he sat in the senate, and among those judges which did condemn our Saviour Christ; but, because he consented not to their deed and judgment, he is acquited as guiltless of that horrible murder. The same is said to have been a good man and a just, and of the number of them that look for the kingdom of God; that is, of the number of those which of Christ are called Christians: and yet, nevertheless, he was a counsellor or senator, and that too[4] in the city of Jerusalem. A Christian therefore may lawfully bear the office of a magistrate. Hereunto belong the examples of the Æthiopian treasurer, Acts viii.; of Cornelius the centurion, Acts x.; and of Erastus the chamberlain[5] of Corinth, Rom. xvi. 2 Tim. iv. But our desire is to have the Anabaptists prove and declare out of the scriptures that which they object here, in saying that these men, being once converted to the faith, did straightway put off their robes of estate, and lay aside their magistrate's sword[6]. For we have a little before, by the words of St Augustine upon John Baptist's answer[7], (who did himself also preach the gospel,) already proved, that the soldiers that were baptized were not put beside their office, nor commanded by John to give over armour and cease to be soldiers.

They object, again, that the Lord conveyed himself privily away, when the people were minded to have made him a king[8]: which, say they, he would not have done, but because by his example he would commend humility to all Christian people; and, as it were, thereby to command them, not to suffer the charge to rule any commonweal to be laid on their necks. They add, moreover, these sayings of the Lord: " My kingdom is not of this world." Again: " Kings of nations have dominion over them; but ye shall not be so[9]." But they understand not that the cause, why the Lord conveyed himself away, was for the fond purpose of the foolish people, which went about, by making him a king, not to do

The Lord conveyeth himself away, while the people would have made him a king.

[4 et manet, Lat.]
[5 quæstor ærarius, Lat.—Erasmus' rendering.]
[6 deposuisse trabeam et gladium, Lat.]
[7 See page 372.]
[8 John vi. 15.—creare et salutare regem, Lat.]
[9 John xviii. 36; Luke xxii. 25.]

the will of God, but, being blinded with affections, to seek to bring those things to pass that were for the ease and filling of their bellies. For insomuch as he had fed them miraculously a little before, therefore they thought that he would be a king for their purpose, who was able to give his subjects meat without any cost or labour at all. Furthermore, our Lord came not to reign on the earth after the manner of this world, as the Jews imagined, and as Pilate feared, who dreamed the Messias should reign as Salomon did: and for that cause the Lord doth rightly say, "My kingdom is not of this world." For he is ascended into heaven, and sitteth at the right hand of his Father, having subdued all kings to himself, and all the world beside, wherein he reigneth by his word and his Spirit, and which he shall come to judge in the end of the world. And although Christ denieth that his kingdom is of this world, yet, notwithstanding, he never denied that kings and princes should come out of the world into the church, to serve the Lord therein, not as men alone, but as kings and men of authority. But kings cannot otherwise serve the Lord as kings, but by doing the things for which they are called kings [1]. And unless that Christians, when they are once made kings, should continue in their office and govern kingdoms according to the rule and laws of Christ, how, I beseech you, should Christ be called "King of kings, and Lord of Lords [2]?" Therefore, when he said, "Kings of nations have dominion over them, but so shall not ye be;" he spake to his apostles, who strove among themselves for the chief and highest dignity: as if he should have said, Princes, which have dominion in the world, are not by my doctrine displaced of their seats, nor put beside their thrones; for the magistrate's authority is of force still in the world, and in the church also. The king or magistrate shall reign; but so shall not ye: ye shall not reign, ye shall not be princes, but teachers of the world and ministers of the churches. Thus briefly I have answered to the Anabaptists' objections, which in other places also I have many times confuted somewhat more largely. By this that here I have said, I think I have sufficiently proved, that a christian man can not only, but ought of duty also, to take upon him the office of a magistrate, if it be lawfully offered unto him.

My kingdom is not of this world.

But so shall not ye.

[1 See page 367.]   [2 Rev. xix. 16.]

Now, before I make an end of the discourse of this place, Of the duty of subjects. I will briefly add what the duty of subjects is, and what every man doth owe to his magistrate. First of all, the subjects' duty is, to esteem honestly, reverently, and honourably, not vilely nor disdainfully, of their magistrates or princes. Let them reverence and honour them as the deputies and ministers of the eternal God. Let them abroad also give them the honour that is usually accustomed in every kingdom and country. It is a foul thing for subjects to behave themselves undecently towards their lords and men of authority. But a false, a light, or ill opinion, once conceived, breedeth a contempt of the things and persons, touching whom, that opinion is once taken up. Some evident testimonies of scripture, therefore, must be gathered and graffed in every man's heart, that thereby a just estimation and worthy authority of magistrates and officers may be bred and brought up in all people's minds. Here, by the way, let princes and magistrates take heed to themselves, that by a spotted and unseemly life they make not themselves contemptible and laughing-stocks, and so by their own default lose all their authority among the common people. The Lord our God, verily, vouchethsafe to attribute his own name to the princes and magistrates of the people, and to call them gods. Exod. xxii.; Psalm lxxxii. The apostles called them the deputies and ministers of God. 1 Peter ii.; Rom. xiii. But who will not think well of gods, and them which are the deputies and ministers of God, by whom God worketh the wealth of the people? He that despiseth him that is sent, despiseth him that sendeth[3]. He that honoureth the deputy seemeth to give more honour to him that appointed the deputy than to him that is the deputy. Moreover, Salomon in the sixteenth of his Proverbs saith : " Prophecy is in the lips of the king; therefore his heart shall not go wrong in judgment[4]." And in the eighth of the Preacher : " I must keep the king's commandment because of the oath that I have made to God for the same[5]." Again, Proverbs xxiv. : " My son, fear thou the Lord and the king, and keep no company with them that

[3 Luke x. 16.]
[4 Prov. xvi. 10.—divinatio, Lat.]
[5 Eccles. viii. 2.—et rationem habere juramenti Dei, Lat.]

slide back from the fear of them[1]: for their destruction shall rise suddenly." And Paul said: "Whosoever resisteth the power, resisteth the ordinance of God; but they that resist shall receive judgment to themselves[2]." Of this sort I have rehearsed certain testimonies in the exposition of the fifth precept.

Secondarily, let subjects pray for their princes and magistrates, that the Lord may give them wisdom, knowledge, fortitude, temperance, justice, upright severity, clemency, and all other requisite virtues, and that he will vouchsafe to lead them in his ways, and to preserve them from all evil; that we may live under them in this world in peace and honesty. This doth Paul require at the hands of subjects, in the second chapter of his first epistle to Timothy, and Jeremy, in the twenty and ninth of his prophecy. I have in another place recited their very words; therefore at this time I let them pass. The minds of many men are herein very slow and careless, and that is the cause many times why they feel the things that willingly they would not, and bear the burdens, with grief enough, that otherwise they should not; and worthily too: for if they would but do their duty willingly, in praying for their magistrate earnestly, their case undoubtedly would be far better than it is. But how fervent a desire they in the primitive church had to pray for their magistrate, we may gather even by these words of Tertullian, in the thirtieth chapter of his Apology: "We pray always," saith he, "for all emperors, desiring God to give them long life, a sure reign, a safe house, valiant armies, faithful counsellors, honest subjects, a quiet world, and whatsoever else a man or emperor may desire[3]."

Obedience to magistrates' laws.   Let the people also obey the good and upright laws of their princes or magistrates; yea, let subjects obey them holily, reverently, and with a devout mind; not obeying their laws as the laws of men, but as the laws of the ministers and

[1 Qui defectores sunt, Lat.]   [2 Rom. xiii. 2.]
[3 Precantes sumus omnes semper pro omnibus imperatoribus, vitam illis prolixam, imperium securum, domum tutam, exercitus fortes, senatum fidelem, populum probum, orbem quietum, et quæcunque hominis et Cæsaris vota sunt.—Tertul. Apol. cap. xxx. Tom. v. p. 62. ed. Semler.]

deputies of God himself: for Peter biddeth us obey them for the Lord; and Paul saith, "We must not obey them for anger only, but for conscience sake also[4];" that is, we must not obey the magistrate only for fear, lest our contempt and disobedience do breed our punishment; but we must obey him, lest we sin against God himself, and so our own conscience do argue our wickedness. But in the fifth commandment I proved by testimonies and examples out of the scriptures, that we ought not to obey godless magistrates, so oft as they command any wicked thing, which is flatly contrary to the word of God. The apostles and faithful men of the primitive church did choose rather to be shut up in prison, to be sent in exile, to be spoiled of their substance, to be cast to wild beasts, to be killed with the sword, to be burnt with fire, and to be strangled, than to obey any wicked commandments. That blessed martyr, bishop Polycarpus, answered the Roman proconsul, and said: "We are taught to give to princes, and to the powers that are of God, such honour as is not contrary to true religion[5]." And St John Chrysostom said to Gaina: "It is not lawful for a godly emperor to assay any thing contrary to God's commandments[6]."

Lastly, let subjects pay tribute to their magistrates; yea, let them, if necessity so require, not stick to bestow their bodies and lives for the preservation of their magistrate and country, as I have already taught you in the fifth commandment. The Lord in the gospel doth simply say, "Give to God that which belongeth to God, and to Cæsar that which belongeth to Cæsar[7]." They therefore are worthily blamed, that pinch, grudge at, or defraud the magistrate of any part of his tribute. Taxes and tributes are due to the magistrate, as the hire of his labour, and as it were the sinews of public tranquillity and commonweal. For "who goeth to warfare

[4 1 Pet. ii. 13; Rom. xiii. 5.]

[5 Πολύκαρπος ἔφη ... δεδιδάγμεθα ... ἀρχαῖς καὶ ἐξουσίαις ὑπὸ Θεοῦ τεταγμέναις τιμὴν κατὰ τὸ προσῆκον τὴν μὴ βλάπτουσαν ἡμᾶς ἀπονέμειν.— Euseb. Hist. Eccles. Lib. iv. cap. 15.]

[6 Ὁ δὲ μέγας Ἰωάννης ἀντέλεγε φάσκων, οὐκ ἐξεῖναι βασιλεῖ τῶν θείων κατατολμᾶν, εὐσεβεῖν γε προαιρουμένῳ.—Theodorit. Eccles. Hist. Lib. v. cap. 32. ed. Reading. Cantab. 1720, p. 232. Bullinger gives the history more at length in his treatise de Script. Sac. Author. &c. fol. 123. Tigur. 1538.]

[7 Luke xx. 25.]

of his own proper cost[1]?" Every man liveth by that labour wherein he is occupied. The prince taketh pains in governing the commonweal, and preserving it in peace; he neglecteth his own private and household business, whereby he should live, and provide things necessary for himself and his family, by looking and attending on his country's affairs: it were against reason, therefore, but that he should be fed and maintained upon the public treasure and cost of his country. It is requisite, also, that kingdoms and commonweals be sufficiently furnished with money and substance to help in distress, either of war, famine, fire, and other miseries[2]; or else to the setting up again of men fallen into poverty, or putting away of greater calamities. I say nothing now touching the keeping in reparation of common buildings, as the city-walls, bulwarks, trenches, ditches, gates, bridges, highways, wells, conduits, judgment-halls, and market-places, with many more of the same sort. There are also certain common persons, as serjeants, watchmen, and such like, which are to be nourished and maintained of the common cost and treasury; and, unless that money be still at hand and in readiness, there can no kingdom nor any commonweal stand long in assurance. They, therefore, that grudge to pay tribute deny the hire of the magistrate's labour, and go the next way to work to subvert the commonweal, and to bring it to nought. The men that in the commonweal's affairs (as some of custom be) are negligent and careless, sin not against any one lord, but against the whole commonweal: and therefore thou mayest see that such slothful workmen are seldom times enriched with the good blessings of God.

But now here, by the way, all magistrates and princes must be admonished to love the people subject to their charge and government, to bear with them bountifully, and not to nip them with immoderate exactions: which is easily done, if they themselves will be thrifty, and keep themselves moderately from riotous gluttony and over sumptuous pride. Let a good prince consider what a sin it is to have his palace abound in riotousness and surfeiting, while his cities and towns are tormented and pined with famine and hunger. Let magistrates consider that tributes and subsidies are not the private goods of them in authority, but the public sub-

Common cost or treasures.

[1 1 Cor. ix. 7.]   [2 calamitatibus publicis, Lat.]

stance of the whole commonweal. God hateth pillers and robbers. God abhorreth immoderate exactions. God curseth polling tyrants; but blesseth profitable and moderate magistrates. But, in peace and war, agreement and concord are much more available than money unjustly gotten; and stronger is that kingdom, and firmer that commonweal, which is upheld by the love and agreement of the prince and commonalty, although the common treasure there be very small, than that country or city which hath innumerable riches heaped up together and wrung out of the citizens' entrails, when as continual grudge and ill-will makes the prince and people at continual variance. I say no more here than the very truth is; experience of all ages is a witness that it is so.

Thus much hitherto have I laid down before your eyes, dearly beloved, as briefly as I could, touching the magistrate; taking occasion upon the sixth commandment, "Thou shalt not kill," and declaring to what end and purpose God did ordain him, what his duty is toward his subjects, and what his subjects' duty is toward him. Now let us pray, and beseech the Lord that he will grant both to magistrates and subjects to walk worthily in their vocations.

OF THE THIRD PRECEPT OF THE SECOND TABLE, WHICH IS IN ORDER THE SEVENTH OF THE TEN COMMANDMENTS: THOU SHALT NOT COMMIT ADULTERY OF WEDLOCK; AGAINST ALL INTEMPERANCE; OF CONTINENCY.

THE TENTH SERMON.

THE nearest to our life and body is every one's several mate in wedlock; for by wedlock two bodies are joined together[3], and are made one: for the Lord said, "And two shall be one flesh[4]." In this third precept, therefore, which is next after the forbidding of murder, commandment is given for the holy keeping of honourable wedlock, and for the true

[3 conjugio enim conjunguntur, Lat. P.]
[4 Gen. ii. 24; 1 Cor. vi. 16.]

sanctifying of the body against adulteries, wandering lusts, and all incontinency. Wedlock is prepared to this end and purpose, that honesty and chastity may flourish among good men, and children may be brought up in the fear of the Lord. This commandment again is briefly expressed in as few words as may be : "Thou shalt not commit adultery[1]." In the exposition of this commandment, by the help of God's good Spirit, I will first speak of holy matrimony; then, of adultery; thirdly, I will shew you what is contained under the name of adultery ; and lastly, I will make an end with a treatise of continency.

The seventh precept.

Wedlock, which is also called matrimony, is an alliance or holy joining together of man and woman, coupled and brought into one by mutual consent of them both, to the intent that they, using all things in common betwixt themselves, may live in chastity, and train up their children in the fear of the Lord. The gospel verily calleth wedlock a joining together which God hath made: for Christ said, "What God hath joined together, let no man separate[2]." Neither is it lawful to make any other the author of matrimony than God himself. God did, by the mean and ministery of his angels and chosen men, appoint other good and necessary ordinances for mankind's commodity ; but he himself did immediately, without the ministery of any person, ordain matrimony ; he himself did establish and ratify it with laws for the purpose; he himself did couple the first married folks; and he, being the true high priest indeed, did himself bless the couple then whom he did join together.

What wedlock is.

By this we may easily gather the excellent dignity of marriage or matrimony. For God did ordain it; yea, he ordained it in paradise, when man as yet was free from all kind of calamities. Adam, when he was in the great felicity of paradise, seemed not yet to live commodiously nor sweetly enough, except a wife were given to be joined unto him. "It is not good," saith God, "for man to be alone ; I will make him a helper to tarry or dwell with him[3]." For God brought to Adam all living creatures, which he had created, for him to name them : but among them all there was no-

The excellency or dignity of marriage.

[1 Exod. xx. 14.—duobus exprimitur verbis, Non mœchaberis, Lat.]
[2 Matt. xix. 6.]
[3 Gen. ii. 18.—adjutorium, quod ei cohabitet, Lat.]

thing that Adam had lust unto; his mind and nature did utterly abhor to be coupled with any of them. God therefore, casting Adam into a dead sleep, doth out of his side, as he slept, frame up a woman; which so soon as Adam set his eye upon, when she was brought unto him by God who had made her, he straightway crieth, that this was such a one as he desired, that this was such a one as he' could love, and wherewith his nature could very well agree. "This now," saith he, "is bone of my bones, and flesh of my flesh." I have found, saith he, I have found an help fit for me, which hath part of my flesh, of my blood, and my very substance. From hence riseth and yet remaineth that natural proneness of men toward women: when, on the other side, overthwart mingling and meddling of cursed men with beasts, contrary to man's nature, was long ago destroyed by fire; which shewed that God did abhor it. The Lord moreover said: "A man shall forsake his father and his mother, and cleave to his wife, and two shall be one flesh[4]." But in the exposition of the fifth commandment we perceived, how much God doth set by the love and good-will of children to their parents, and what a charge he giveth to children to honour them. It must needs be, therefore, that wedlock is a most heavenly ordinance, since it is preferred before the honouring of parents: and yet, nevertheless, it is so preferred, as that, by the law of matrimony, the precept for the honour due to parents may not be abolished; but that thereby married folks may know to behave themselves so, if their parents go about to breed discord betwixt them and their spouses, that then they suffer not themselves for their parents' words to be severed, but in all things else to honour them as they should.

The holy patriarchs kept the law of matrimony, and reverenced wedlock very devoutly[5]. For no small parcel of the first and most excellent book of the bible, called Genesis, is spent in rehearsing the marriages of holy men. Neither is Moses, the peerless servant of God ashamed to make mention of the business and works of wedlock as pure and excel-

[4 Gen. ii. 24; Mark x. 7, 8.]
[5 Nec puduit sanctum dei Spiritum multis recensere et describere matrimonia ipsorum, Lat. Nor was the Holy Spirit of God ashamed to recount and describe their marriages in many words.—Omitted by the translator.]

lent, which seem to many at this day to be foul and filthy. Christ himself (who, being the very natural Son of God, was himself born in wedlock, although of a pure and uncorrupted virgin) did honour and commend the knot of matrimony, while he did vouchsafe to shew his first miracle at a wedding; which was such a miracle, as did declare that the Lord is able to make the bitterness of marriage sweet, and the scarcity thereof abound with plenty. As the apostles were married men, according to the examples of the patriarchs, kings, princes, priests, and prophets[1]; so Paul, the chief of all the apostles, crieth out and saith : " Wedlock is honourable among all and the bed undefiled: but whoremongers and adulterers God will judge[2]." He saith, that wedlock is honourable among all men: he meaneth, all nations ; for very few people shall you find that do not greatly commend the state of marriage. Xenophon thinketh, that among all God's ordinances scant any one can be found that is more commendable or profitable than wedlock is[3]. Musonius, Hierocles[4], and other ancient sages think marriage to be so necessary to live well and conveniently, that the life of man without marriage seemeth to be maimed. Even they (the heathens I mean) do make the evils and discommodities of marriage to consist in the married folks, and not in marriage. For marriage of itself is good ; but many use not well the thing that is good, and therefore they feel the smart of their foul abuse worthily. For who knoweth not, that the fault of drunkenness is not to be referred to wine, which is the good and wholesome creature

---

[1 Bullinger, in his treatise de Scriptur. Authorit. et de Episcop. Instit. et Funct. establishes this statement by Euseb. Eccles. Hist. Lib. III. cap. 30, and Lib. v. cap. 24, and Lib. VIII. cap. 10; and Tripart. Hist. Lib. I. cap. 10, and Lib. IX. cap. 38. See also Jewel's Works, pp. 882, 3, and Original Letters, Vol. I. pp. 116, 146, and Becon's Works, Vol. III. p. 235. Parker Soc. ed.]

[2 Hebr. xiii. 4.]

[3 Ἐμοὶ γάρ τοι, ἔφη φάναι, καὶ οἱ θεοὶ, ὦ γύναι, δοκοῦσι πολὺ διεσκεμμένως μάλιστα τὸ ζεῦγος τοῦτο συντεθεικέναι, ὃ καλεῖται θῆλυ καὶ ἄρρεν, ὅπως ἔτι ὠφελιμώτατον ᾖ αὐτῷ εἰς τὴν κοινωνίαν.—Xenoph. Œcon. cap. vii. p. 39. Tom. v. ed. Schneider. Oxon. 1813.]

[4 Ὥστε ὁ ἀναιρῶν ἐξ ἀνθρώπων γάμον ἀναιρεῖ μὲν οἶκον, ἀναιρεῖ δὲ πόλιν, ἀναιρεῖ δὲ σύμπαν τὸ ἀνθρώπειον γένος. Musonius.—οἶκός τε ἡμιτελὴς μὲν τῷ ὄντι ὁ τοῦ ἀγάμου, &c.—Hierocles ap. Stobæi Floril. ed. Gaisford. Oxon. 1822. Vol. III. pp. 8, 10.]

of God, but to the excessive bibbing and over-great greediness of
man, which abuseth God's good creature? "That which cometh
out of the heart of man," saith the Lord in the gospel, " and
not that which goeth in by the mouth, defileth the man[5]."
Hereunto belongeth that saying of Paul, the apostle of Christ,
where he attributeth sanctification to wedlock ; "for the bed,"
saith he, " is undefiled :" and in another place he testifieth,
that "the unbelieving husband is sanctified by the believing
wife[6] :" he affirmeth also, that children born in wedlock are
holy or clean. Moreover, the same Paul maketh Christ an
example of love betwixt man and wife, and shadoweth the
mysteries of Christ and the church by the colour of wedlock :
he figureth, I say, a heavenly thing by an holy type that
God doth allow[7]. Whereupon in another place the same
apostle doth say, that their doctrine is a very " doctrine of
devils," which forbid men to marry[8]. And so, consequently,
it followeth, that that is an heavenly doctrine, proceeding
from God, which permitteth marriage freely to all men, and
doth commend and reverence it.

The excellency and dignity of matrimony being thus The causes
of marriage.
understood, let us now seek out and look on the causes for
which God hath ordained marriage for men to embrace. God,
according to his natural goodness, directeth all his ordinances
to the great good and abundant commodity of mortal men :
and therefore it followeth, that he ordained matrimony for
the preservation of mankind, to the end that man's life might
be pleasant, sweet, and thoroughly furnished with joys sufficient. But all these causes may be reduced into the number
of three. First, God himself doth say, " It is not good for
man to be alone; let us make him an help therefore to be
before him," or to dwell with him[9]. So, then, the first cause
why wedlock was instituted is man's commodity, that thereby
the life of man might be the pleasanter and more commodious;
for Adam seemed not to live half happily nor sweetly enough,
unless he had a wife to join himself unto : which wife is not
in the scriptures called an impediment or necessary evil, as
certain poets and beastly men who hated women have fool-

[5 Matt. xv. 11, 17, 18.]
[6 1 Cor. vii. 14.—intercedente matrimonio, Lat. ; omitted.]
[7 Eph. v. 22, &c.]   [8 1 Tim. iv. 1, 3.]
[9 Gen. ii. 18.]

The wife is
the arm of
her husband. ishly jangled; but she is the help or arm of the man. Antipater, an heathen writer, *in Sermone de Nuptiis,* doth
wonderfully agree with this saying of the scripture, and
expresseth plainly what kind of help and what manner of arm
the wife is to her husband. " Whosoever," saith he, " hath
not had trial of wife and children, he is utterly ignorant of
true mutual good-will. Love in wedlock is mutually shewed,
when man and wife do not communicate wealth, children, and
hearts alone, as friends are wont to do; but have their bodies
in common also, which friends cannot do. And therefore
Euripides, laying aside the deadly hate that he bare to
women, writ these verses in commendation of marriage:

> The wife that gads not, gigglot[1] wise,
> ⠀⠀With every flirting gill[2],
> But honestly doth keep at home,
> ⠀⠀Not set to gossip still,
> Is to her husband in his cares
> ⠀⠀A passing sweet delight;
> She heals his sickness all, and calls
> ⠀⠀Again his dying sprite.
> By fawning on his angry looks
> ⠀⠀She turns them into smiles;
> And keeps her husband's secrets close,
> ⠀⠀When friends work wily guiles.

"For like as a man, having one hand or one foot, if by any
means he get himself another, may thereby the more easily
lay hold on what he listeth, or go whither he will; even so
he that hath married a wife shall more easily enjoy the
healthful pleasures and profitable commodities of this present
life: for married folks for two eyes have four, and for two
hands as many more, which being joined together, they may
the more easily dispatch their handy business. Again, when
the one's two hands are wearied, the hands of the other supply
their room, and keep their work in a forwardness still.
Marriage therefore, which, instead of one member, is by
increase compact of twain, is better able to pass through the
course of this world than the single and unwedded life[3]."

[1 gigglot: a wanton; a lascivious girl.—Johnson's Dict.; Shakspeare, Measure for Measure, Act v. Sc. 1.]
[2 gill, (from *gillian,* the old English way of writing Julian, or Ju-
liana): the appellation of a woman in ludicrous language.—Ibid.]
[3 Συμβέβηκε δὲ καὶ τὸν μὴ πεῖραν ἐσχηκότα γαμετῆς γυναικὸς καὶ

Thus much out of Antipater. Hierocles also in his book *De Nuptiis* saith: " To live with a woman is very profitable, even beside the begetting of children: for, first, she doth welcome us home, that are tired abroad with labour and travail; she entertaineth us serviceably, and doeth all she may to recreate our weary minds; she maketh us forget all sorrow and sadness: for the troublesome cases of our life, and generally of care and business, while we are occupied in matters abroad, in bargaining in the country, or among our friends, are not easily suffered to be troubled with our domestical and household affairs; but when we have dispatched them, and are once returned to our wives at home, so that our minds are at quiet, and we restored to our ease and liberty, then are our cumbersome businesses well lightened and eased, whereby they cease to trouble us any longer. Neither is a wife troublesome undoubtedly, but lighteneth things that are troublesome to us; for there is nothing so heavy that a man and wife, living in concord, are not able to bear, especially if they be both willing to do their endeavour[4]." And so forth.

τέκνων ἄγευστον εἶναι τῆς ἀληθινωτάτης καὶ γνησίου εὐνοίας.... Οὐ γὰρ μόνον τῆς οὐσίας καὶ τῶν φιλτάτων πᾶσιν ἀνθρώποις τέκνων καὶ τῆς ψυχῆς, ἀλλὰ καὶ τῶν σωμάτων οὗτοι μόνοι κοινωνοῦσι.... καὶ ὁ Εὐριπίδης εἰς ταῦτα ἀποβλέψας, καὶ ἀποθέμενος τὴν ἐν τῷ γράφειν μισογυνίαν, ταῦτ' εἴρηκεν·

Γυνὴ γὰρ ἐν νόσοισι καὶ κακοῖς πόσει
ἥδιστόν ἐστι, δῶματ' ἢν οἰκῇ καλῶς,
ὀργήν τε πραΰνουσα καὶ δυσθυμίας
ψυχὴν μεθιστᾶσ'· ἡδὺ καὶ ἀπάται φίλων....

'Ομοιότατον γάρ ἐστιν, ὡς εἴ τις μίαν ἔχων χεῖρα ἑτέραν ποθὲν προσλάβοι, ἢ ἕνα πόδα ἔχων ἕτερον ἀλλαχόθεν ἐκτήσατο. 'Ως γὰρ οὗτος πολὺ ἂν ῥᾷον καὶ βαδίσαι οὗ θέλοι, καὶ προσαγάγοιτο· οὕτως ὁ γυναῖκα εἰσαγόμενος ῥᾷον ἀπολήψεται τὰς κατὰ τὸν βίον σωτηρίους καὶ συμφερούσας χρείας. 'Αντὶ γοῦν δύο ὀφθαλμῶν χρῶνται τέσσαρσι· καὶ ἀντὶ δύο χειρῶν ἑτέραις τοσαύταις, αἷς καὶ ἀθρόως πράττοι ἂν ῥᾷον τὸ τῶν χειρῶν ἔργον. Διὸ καὶ ἐὰν αἱ ἕτεραι κάμνοιεν, ταῖς ἑτέραις ἂν θεραπεύοιτο· καὶ τὸ σύνολον δύο γεγονὼς ἀνθ' ἑνός, μᾶλλον ἂν ἐν τῷ βίῳ κατορθώῃ.—Antipater ap. Stobæi Floril. Vol. III. pp. 17—19.]

[4 "Επειτα καὶ πρὸ γενέσεως τέκνων λυσιτελὴς ἡ μετὰ γυναικὸς συμβίωσις. Πρῶτον μὲν γὰρ ἀποτετριμμένους τοῖς θυραίοις καμάτοις ὑποδέχεται θεραπευτικῶς ἀναλαμβάνουσα, καὶ μετ' ἐπιμελείας ἀνακτωμένη πάσης· ἔπειτα τῶν ὄντων δυσχερῶν ἐν τῇ διανοίᾳ λήθην ἐντίθησι. Τὰ γὰρ σκυθρωπὰ τοῦ βίου, περὶ μὲν τὴν ἀγοράν, ἢ τὸ γυμνάσιον, ἢ τὸ χωρίον, ἢ καθόλου πάσης μερίμνης ἀσχολίας, καὶ περὶ τοὺς φίλους τε καὶ συνήθεις διατρίβουσιν ἡμῖν, οὐκ ἔστι πρόχειρα τοῖς ἀναγκαίοις ἐπιπροσθούμενα περισπασμοῖς· ἀνεθεῖσι

The begetting and bringing up of children.

The second cause why matrimony was ordained is the begetting of children for the preservation of mankind by increase, and the bringing of them up in the fear of the Lord: for the Lord blessed Adam and Eva, saying, "Increase and multiply, and replenish the earth." Paul the Apostle in his Epistle to Titus saith: "Speak to the elder women, that they may teach honest things, that they may make the younger women to be sober-minded, to love their husbands, to love their children, to be discreet housekeepers, good, obedient to their husbands." And again, to Timothy: "Adam was not deceived, but the woman was seduced; notwithstanding, through bearing of children she shall be saved, if they continue in faith, and charity, and holiness with modesty[1]." But the begetting of children were altogether unprofitable, if they were not well brought up; for she that loveth her children indeed doth bring them up in the fear of the Lord: which bringing up is no small commodity to the commonweal and church of God. The glory also and worship of God is greatly augmented, when as by wedlock there doth spring up a great number of men that acknowledge, call upon, and worship God as they ought to do.

The bed in wedlock undefiled.

The third cause why matrimony was ordained the Apostle Paul expresseth in these words: "To avoid whoredom, let every man have his own wife, and every woman her own husband. It were good and expedient for a man not to touch a woman," and to live single[2]; but because this is "not given to all men[3]," as the Lord in the gospel testifieth, and that concupiscence of the flesh doth, for the most part, burn the greatest sort of men, the Lord hath appointed marriage to be, as it were, a remedy against that heat; as the Apostle in another place witnesseth, saying, "Let them marry which

δ' ἐκ τούτων, εἴς τε τὴν οἰκίαν ἐπανελθοῦσι, καὶ οἶον εὐσχόλοις τὴν ψυχὴν γενομένοις, ἐμπελάζει καιρῷ χρώμενα τούτῳ τοῦ ἀνιᾶν ἡμᾶς, ὅτ' ἄν γε ἔρημος εὐνοίας καὶ μονήρης ὁ βίος. . . . Οὐ γὰρ ἡ γυνὴ, μὰ Δία, βάρος ἢ φορτίον ἐστί . . . ἀλλ' ἥδε μὲν κἀκ τῶν ἐναντίων κοῦφόν τι καὶ ῥᾶστα φέρεσθαι δυνάμενον, μᾶλλον δὲ καὶ τῶν ὄντως ἐπαχθῶν καὶ βαρέων κουφιστικόν. Οὐδὲν γὰρ οὕτω φορτικόν ἐστι τῶν ὄντων, ὥστε μὴ ῥᾷστον εἶναι συμφρονοῦσί γε ἀνδρὶ καὶ γυναικὶ, καὶ κοινῇ φέρειν αὐτὸ βουλομένοις.—Hierocles ap. Stobæi Floril. Vol. III. pp. 12—14.]

[1 Titus ii. 3—5; 1 Tim. ii. 14, 15.]

[2 1 Cor. vii. 2, 1.]

[3 Matth. xix. 11.]

cannot abstain; for it is better to marry than to burn[4]." By this we learn, that the natural company of a man with his own wife is not reputed for a fault or uncleanness in the sight of God. Whoredom is uncleanness in the eyes of the Lord, because it is directly contrary to the law of God: but God hath allowed wedlock and blessed it; therefore married folks are sanctified by the blessing of God through faith and obedience. Neither lack we here any evident arguments and testimonies of Paul to prove it by; for to the Hebrews he said, "Wedlock is honourable among all men, and the bed undefiled; but whoremongers and adulterers God will judge[5]." The Apostle here spake very reverently; and by "the bed" he understood the natural company of a man with his wife, which he saith plainly is undefiled. What God hath made Acts x. clean who shall call unclean? Who can deny that to the Tit. i. clean all things are clean? Paphnutius, therefore, both bishop and confessor, judging rightly of this, did in the Nicene council say openly, that "the lying of a man with his own wife is chastity[6]." Neither was the most modest apostle ashamed to make laws betwixt a man and his wife; for to the Corinthians he saith, "Let the husband give to the wife due 1 Cor. vii. benevolence; likewise also the wife to the husband. The wife hath not the power of her own body, but the husband; likewise also the husband hath not the power of his own body, but the wife. Defraud ye not the one the other, except it be with both your consents for a time, that ye may give yourselves to fasting and to prayer; and afterward come together again, that Satan tempt you not for your incontinency." These words of the Apostle are so evident, that they need no exposition at all. In the same Epistle again he saith, "If thou marriest a wife, thou sinnest not." And again, "If a virgin marry, she hath not sinned[7]." Now what is more excellent, pure, and holy, than virginity is? But a virgin sinneth not, if she change virginity for holy matrimony. Very well therefore doth Chrysostom in a certain homily say,

[4 1 Cor. vii. 9.]   [5 Hebr. xiii. 4.]

[6 Ἀναστὰς δὲ Παφνούτιος ὁ ὁμολογητὴς ἀντεῖπε· τίμιον δὲ τὸν γάμον ἀποκαλῶν, σωφροσύνην δὲ τὴν πρὸς τὰς ἰδίας γυναῖκας συνουσίαν.—Sozomen. Eccles. Hist. Lib. i. cap. 23. See also Early Writings of Hooper, Parker Soc. ed. page 376.]

[7 1 Cor. vii. 28.]

[BULLINGER.]

26

"The first degree of chastity is unspotted virginity; the second is faithful wedlock[1]." St Augustine also calleth marriage chastity or continency: the place is to be seen in the 19th and 20th chapters, *de bono conjugali*[2], and in the 199th epistle[3]. This is the head from whence doth spring the greatest part of public honesty; for God alloweth wedlock,

Honesty. but disalloweth fornication and all kind of uncleanness. It pleased him by his ordinance to exclude all uncleanness from his believing servants. Let the saints therefore, but magistrates especially, have an especial eye not to be slack in promoting holy wedlock, but diligent to punish severely all filthy fornication and other uncleanness.

This have I hitherto rehearsed somewhat largely out of the holy scripture, to the intent I might prove to all men, that wedlock is holy, and that therefore no man can be

No man forbidden to marry. defiled with the moderate, holy, and lawful use thereof; and so, consequently, that marriage is permitted to all sorts of men. For the apostle saith: "Let a bishop be the husband of one wife; let him rule his own house well, and have faithful children[4]." For it is manifest, by the testimonies of scripture and ecclesiastical writers, that the apostles of Christ and other apostolical teachers of the primitive church were married men, and had wives and children[5]. Neither is there anything, next after corrupt doctrine, which doth more infect the church of Christ, and subvert all ecclesiastical discipline, than if the ministers of the churches, which should be lights of the whole congregation, be fornicators or adulterous persons. That offence especially, above all other, is an hinderance and blot to all kind of honesty. But touching this I purpose not at this time to discourse so largely and fully as I might.

[1 Nam primus est gradus castitatis sincera virginitas: secundus autem fidele conjugium.—Chrysost. Opus Imperf. in Matt. Hom. xxxii. p. 133. Tom. vi. Par. 1724. But this work is not Chrysostom's.]

[2 Restat ut videamus, utrum saltem continentes nostri conjugatis illis patribus comparandi sint, &c. And, Nuptiis sanctorum patrum, non quas nuptias, sed quam continentiam comparem quæro," &c.—De Bon. Conj. capp. 19, 20. Opp. Par. 1531. Tom. vi. fol. 165. col. 1.]

[3 Tom. ii. fol. 156. col. 3. P.]

[4 1 Tim. iii. 2, 4; Titus i. 6.]

[5 See Bullinger. de Episcop. Instit. et Funct. fol. 96—8. Tigur. 1538; and Jewel's Works, Park. Soc. ed. pp. 882, 3.]

To this I add, that the band of wedlock is indissoluble and *The knot of wedlock is indissoluble.* everlasting, that is to say, such a knot as never can be undone. For of two is made one flesh and one body, which if you sever, you do utterly mar it. " What God hath joined together, therefore, let not man separate⁶." They therefore do make a slaughter of this body, that do commit adultery. For the laws of God and men admit a divorcement betwixt a man and his adulterous wife. And yet, let not any less or lighter cause dissolve this knot betwixt man and wife, than fornication is. Otherwise God, which in the gospel hath permitted the less, doth not forbid the greater, to be causes of divorcement. And in the primitive church, the epistles and constitutions of christian princes do testify, that once committing of fornication was no cause of divorcement. Of which I have spoken in another place.

But that this holy knot may be the surer, it is available, *How matrimony must be contracted.* that marriages be made holily, lawfully, and with discretion, in the fear of the Lord. Let them not be unwillingly agreed unto and made up by compulsion. First, let the good liking of their consenting minds be joined in one, whom the open profession of mutual consent and outward hand-fasting must afterward couple together. Let them be matched together, that are not severed by alliance of blood and nighness of affinity. Let them be coupled in one, that may marry together by the laws of God and their country, with the consent and counsel of their friends and parents. Let them, which mind marriage, have a sincere heart purposely bent to seek their own safeguard and continual felicity; that is, to respect only the will and pleasure of God, and not admit any evil affections as counsellors to make up the marriage betwixt them. Hierocles, in his book *De nuptiis*, saith: " It is mere folly and lack of wit which make those things, that of themselves are easy to be borne, troublesome, and make a wife a grievous clog to her husband. For marriage to many men hath been intolerable, not because the wedded state is, by default of itself or own proper nature, so troublesome or cumbrous; but for our matching as we should not, it falleth out as we would not, and causeth our marriages to be grievous and noisome. To this end, verily, our daily marriages do commonly come. For they marry wives usually, not for the

[⁶ Matth. xix. 6.]

begetting of children or society of life : but some for a great
dowry, some for a beautiful body ; and some, being seduced
by such kind of causes, as it were men abused by unfaithful
counsellors, have no regard to the disposition and manners of
their spouse, but marry at adventures, to their own decay
and utter destruction[1]." Hereunto belongeth Plutarch's admonition to parents, in his treatise of bringing up of children,
where he counselleth men to bestow such wives on their sons
as are not much wealthier nor mightier than their children.
For a very pithy saying is that usual proverb, " Marry a
wife of thine own degree[2]." To be short, let the fear of
God, the word of God, and earnest prayer poured out to God,
be always annexed to the beginning of marriages.

Against poly-
gamy, or
the having of
many wives. But it is not convenient, that in lawful matrimony any
more should be than two alone, to be joined together under
one yoke of wedlock. For the use of many wives, which
our fathers usurped without any blame, may not stablish
polygamy for a law among us at these days. The time of
correction[3] is now come to light, and Messias now is come into
the world, who teacheth all rightly, and reformeth things
amiss. He therefore hath reduced wedlock to the first prescribed rule and law of matrimony. " Two," saith the Lord,
" shall be one flesh." And the apostle saith: " Let every
man have his own wife, and every woman her own husband[4]."
The multitude of Salomon's concubines therefore appertain

[1 Βαρὺ δέ ἐστιν ὡς ἀληθῶς ἀφροσύνη καὶ δύσοιστον τοῖς αὐτὴν κεκτη-
μένοις, ὑφ' ἧς δὴ καὶ τὰ φύσει κοῦφα γίνεται βαρέα, τά τε ἄλλα καὶ γυνή.
Τῷ ὄντι γὰρ καὶ συχνοῖς δή τισιν ἀφόρητος ἐγένετο ὁ γάμος, ἀλλ' οὐχὶ παρ'
ἑαυτῷ, οὐδὲ τῷ φύσει τοιάνδε τὴν μετὰ γυναικὸς εἶναι κοινωνίαν· ἀλλ' ὅτ'
ἂν γαμῶμεν ἃς μὴ δεῖ, μετὰ τοῦ καὶ αὐτοὶ παντάπασιν ἀπειροβίως διακεῖσθαι
καὶ ἀπαρασκεύως ἔχειν πρὸς τὸ ἀγαγεῖν ὡς χρὴ τὴν ἐλευθέραν ἄγεσθαι, τὸ
τηνικαῦτα συμβαίνει χαλεπὴν καὶ ἀφόρητον γίνεσθαι τὴν κοινωνίαν. Ἀμέλει
καὶ ταύτῃ χωρεῖ τοῖς πολλοῖς ὁ γάμος. Οὐ γὰρ ἐπὶ παίδων γένεσιν καὶ
βίου κοινωνίαν ἄγονται γυναῖκας· ἀλλ' οἱ μὲν διὰ προικὸς ὄγκον, οἱ δὲ δι'
ἐξοχὴν μορφῆς, οἱ δὲ δι' ἄλλας τινὰς τοιουτοτρόπους αἰτίας, αἷς χρώμενοι
κακοῖς συμβούλοις, οὐδὲν περὶ τῆς διαθέσεως καὶ τοῦ ἤθους τῆς νύμφης
πολυπραγμονήσαντες, ὄλεθρον αὐτῶν θύουσι τὸν γάμον.—Hierocles ap.
Stobæi Floril. Vol. III. p. 15.]

[2 Ἐγγυᾶσθαι δεῖ τοῖς υἱοῖς γυναῖκας μήτε εὐγενεστέρας πολλῷ μήτε
πλουσιωτέρας· τὸ γὰρ, τὴν κατὰ σαυτὸν ἔλα, σοφόν.—Plutarch. de Liberis
Educand. See also Erasm. Adag. Chiliad. Hanov. 1617. p. 124. col. 2.]

[3 correctionis tempora, Lat.—Heb. ix. 10.]

[4 1 Cor. vi. 16, and vii. 2.]

not to us. We have not to follow the example of Jacob, who married two sisters. And yet, notwithstanding, the word of truth condemneth not the second, third, or many marriages which a man maketh, when his wife is deceased. For that saying of the apostle is general to all men, and endureth in all ages: "Let them marry, that cannot abstain; for it is better to marry than to burn[5]." Which sentence is taken out of these words in the gospel: "All men cannot receive this saying, save they to whom it is given. For there are some chaste, which were so born out of their mother's womb; and there are some chaste, which were made chaste of men; and there are some chaste, which have made themselves chaste for the kingdom of heaven's sake. He that is able to receive it, let him receive it[6]." Let him therefore, that cannot receive it, marry a wife, so often as necessity compelleth him thereunto.

The second and third marriages after the first wife.

But now, especially, it standeth us in hand to know, how married folks must behave themselves, what they must do in wedlock, to what end they must direct their deeds and thoughts, and how they ought to be affected toward that holy ordinance of God Almighty. Touching which thing I will not speak much, but briefly note out the most necessary points, to give all men occasion to think with themselves, and call to mind both more and greater matters which I leave untouched.

The reverend behaviour which is required in the estate of marriage.

First of all, let married folks be throughly persuaded and assuredly certain, while they live in matrimony, that they are in the work of God, that they please God, and do an acceptable thing in the sight of the Lord, because of God's word wherein he blessed that kind of life, and sanctified all wedded people, which by faith do live in that work and ordinance of the living God. Therefore, when married couples do patiently suffer the troubles that follow the married life, while they labour faithfully, while they do those things decently which belong to the charge and office of married people; as, while the wife doth love her husband, while she doth dutifully obey him, while she doth bring forth her children with grief and pain, and, when they are brought forth, doth diligently nourish them, and labour to bring them up; while the husband doth love his wife, while he doth mutually help

[5 1 Cor. vii. 9.]   [6 Matth. xix. 11, 12.]

her, and faithfully in all things shew himself a careful father
for his family and household; in doing these things they
please God no less than they do when they go to church to
hear the word of God and to worship the Lord. For these
works of wedlock are reputed for good works, as well as
giving of alms, justice, and making of peace. Married folks
therefore have need especially of true faith in God, the author
of wedlock: for by wedlock in faith they shall please the
Lord. This our monks[1] could not abide to hear of, although
the word of God doth urge it upon them; they ceased not
to magnify their counterfeit holiness and hypocritical vows.

Married
folks must
be faithful.

Secondarily, it is required at the hands of wedded couples
to be mindful of the faith which they give and take, that they
do not falsely deceive one another, but holily keep the promise
that they make and troth that they plight, and to keep it
sincerely both in body and mind. Let neither of them lust
after the body of a stranger, nor conceive an hatred or loathsomeness of their wedded spouse. And thy body, thou that
art a married man, is not thy body, but thy wife's; as also
thy wife's body is not thy wife's, but thine. Thou stealest
and dost commit a robbery, if thou take away another body's
goods; and, when thou hast conveyed it from the proper
owner, dost give it to another. Let the mind of wedded
mates be unspotted, and the body untouched. Every one,
when he first cometh to solemnize wedlock by the holy ceremony ordained for that purpose, doth promise with an oath in
the name of the Lord before God and the church, that he will
use the company of no woman but her, that he will cleave to,
love, and cherish her alone without any other. This faith
once given whosoever doth violate, he is falsely forsworn, and
is a breaker of a godly promise and God's holy truth.

They must
dwell toge-
ther with
knowledge.

Neither is it sufficient for thee to be faithful, unless thou
be courteous or tractable toward thy wife, and dwell with her
" according to knowledge," as St. Peter saith[2]. Let the husband be the head of the wife, to wit, her adviser and counsellor,
her ruler and guide, her sweet yokefellow and admonisher in
all her affairs, her assured aid and faithful defender. Let the
wife be obedient unto her husband, even as we see the members
obey the head: let her yield herself to her husband to be

[1 Hæc non urserunt monachi, quæ tamen jubentur urgere, Lat. P.]
[2 1 Pet. iii. 7.]

ruled and governed; let her not despise his honest counsels and indifferent commandments[3]. Let them think that they twain are one body, or the members of one body. And therefore let them learn by the government of this mortal body, how to behave themselves in the guiding of wedlock. The worthier members do not despise the more unworthy limbs, but do rather honour them, lighten their labour, and aid and help them. Again, the more unworthy limbs are in love with the worthier, not envying their pre-eminence any whit at all. One member breaketh not or hurteth another; but all do mutually cherish themselves, and defend one another from harm and injury. Such a mutual knitting together, and working, and love, and charity, and good-will, and fellowship, let there be betwixt man and wife. For to that end the woman was taken out of the man's body, that the husband should cherish (his wife) his own body. And for that cause the apostle saith: Ephes. v. " So must husbands love their wives, even as their own bodies. He that loveth his wife doth love himself; for no man at any time hath hated his own flesh, but loveth and cherisheth it, as the Lord doth the church." What may be said to that, moreover, that the apostle, in the very same place, hath made the Son of God and the holy Church an example for married folks to follow in keeping of wedlock; requiring at the husband's hand to love his wife, even as Christ hath loved the church; and of the wife to reverence her husband and to love him again, as the church doth Christ? Than which example there is none in the world more holy and effectual. For there is no love greater than the love of Christ toward his church, neither is there any love more chaste than that which the church doth bear to Christ. It is therefore required at the hands of wedded mates mutually to bear most ardent and holy love the one to the other. Let them use all things in common : let them be partakers both of the same prosperity and the same adversity. Let them both draw under one yoke, and bear betwixt them one another's burden. Briefly, let them twain be the members of one and the very same body. I have more at large set down these offices of man and wife in my treatise which is called " The Institution of Christian Matrimony[4]."

[3 æqua dogmata, Lat.]
[4 See Becon's Works, Parker Soc. ed. Vol. I. p. 29, n. 2.]

Let them beget and bring up children.

Lastly, let them bring up their children in holy discipline and the fear of God, to the health of their own house and the whole commonweal. Paul saith: "I would have the younger women marry, to get children, and to govern the house; for that is honest and acceptable before God[1]." But touching the bringing up of children, I have already spoken in the fifth Sermon of this Decade. Now, the very begetting of children alone is very profitable both to every private or particular house, and also to the commonweal: for here I will not stand to shew, that the honour and glory of God is very greatly augmented, if children be not only begotten, but also brought up in the fear of God and knowledge of his word. Hierocles saith: "I confess that marriage is profitable, especially because it bringeth children forth, which is indeed a goodly fruit: for they, being of our very blood, do while we are in health aid us in all our affairs; and in old age, when years come upon us, they succour us well with all that they may: they are familiar companions of our joy in prosperity, and in adversity are our partners in sorrowing with us for our heavy mishaps[2]." And so forth. Antipater also saith: "Man, which is endued with a civil disposition to maintain society, must augment his country and commonwealth with increase of children: for cities could not have been preserved by any means at all, unless the head men of every city, and the sons of noble gentlemen, seeing their ancestors wither and fall away like goodly leaves of a fair tree, had married in time convenient, and left behind them children as worthy plants, to succeed in their country, thereby to make it flourish for ever; doing their best, so far as they could, to keep it from the assaults and conquests of enemies and strangers. They therefore, shooting at nothing more than to defend and assist their country, both in their lifetime and when they were dead, did think it most necessary and especially convenient to marry and be married, desiring thereby both to do all things that nature

[1 1 Tim. v. 14.]

[2 *Φημὶ τοίνυν καὶ σύμφορον εἶναι τὸν γάμον, πρῶτον μὲν ὅτι θεῖον ὡς ἀληθῶς φέρει καρπὸν τὴν παίδων γένεσιν, οἳ παραστάται μὲν ἡμῖν οἷον συμφυεῖς ἔτι καὶ αὐτοῖς ἐῤῥωμένοις ἐν ἁπάσαις γίγνονται πράξεσιν· ἀγαθοὶ δὲ ἐπίκουροι κάμνουσιν ὑφ' ἡλικίας καὶ γήρᾳ πιεζομένοις, οἰκεῖοι μὲν ἐν εὐπραγίαις εὐφροσύνης κοινωνοὶ, συμπαθεῖς δὲ ἐν τοῖς ἐναντίοις καιροῖς διάδοχοι τῶν ἀνιαρῶν.*—Hierocles ap. Stobæi Floril. Vol. III. p. 12.]

requireth, and also those that touch the health and increase of their country, and most of all the worship of God, &c.[3]"

Since therefore that lawful matrimony is of so great effect, and so available to live well and happily, the faithful do not without cause begin their marriages with religion and religious rites. The Lord, verily, did presently in the beginning[4] bless the first marriage of our parents, Adam and Eve, and did himself couple them in wedlock. Whereupon the church of God hath received a custom, that they which join in marriage, before they dwell together, go into the temple of the Lord, where, after prayer made in the midst of the congregation, they are joined together, and blessed by the minister of God in the name of God himself. Wherefore in wedlock the first and chiefest things that be required, are the earnest and continual prayers of the married folks to God, that he will vouchsafe to make the husbands wise, religious, modest, gentle, honest, painful sufferers[5], and lovers of their wives; and that it will please him to make the wives obedient, meek, chaste, faithful lovers of their husbands and children, housewives, and fruitful[6]. For no one man is able to declare all the evils that come even of one corrupt and naughty marriage. Through it whole houses are wonderfully disquieted, all wealth and honesty do utterly decay, the children are bastards, God is offended and provoked to anger, and an endless mischief brought to the whole commonweal. God, therefore, must be earnestly beseeched to bless all married people, that both the glory of his holy name, and the

Marriages must be begun with religion.

[3 ... Ταῦτα δὲ δὴ κατανενοηκὼς ὁ εὐγενής, καὶ ὡς φύσει πολιτικὸν γενόμενον, συναύξειν τὴν πατρίδα δεῖ. Καὶ γὰρ οὐκ ἂν ἄλλως δύναιντο αἱ πόλεις σώζεσθαι, εἰ μὴ οἱ βέλτιστοι ταῖς φύσεσι τῶν πολιτῶν, ἢ τῶν γενναίων παῖδες, τῶν προτέρων καθαπερεὶ φύλλων καλοῦ δένδρου ἀπομαραινομένων καὶ ἀπορρεόντων, οὗτοι καθ' ὥραν γαμοῖεν, καθαπερεί τινας γενναίους βλαστοὺς διαδόχους τῇ πατρίδι καταλιπόντες, οἳ θάλλειν αὐτὴν ἀεὶ ποιοῖεν, καὶ τὴν ἀκμὴν ἀΐδιον φυλάττοιεν, καὶ ὅσον ἐφ' ἑαυτοῖς μηδέποτ' εὐεπίθετον τοῖς ἐχθροῖς, στοχαζόμενοι τοῦ καὶ ζῶντες καὶ μεταλλάξαντες ἀμύνειν τῇ πατρίδι καὶ βοηθεῖν, τῶν ἀναγκαιοτάτων καὶ πρὸ τῶν καθηκόντων νομίζουσι τὸ συγκραθῆναι εἰς γάμον, πᾶν μὲν τὸ τῇ φύσει ἐπιβάλλον σπεύδοντες ἐπιτελεῖν, πολὺ δὲ μάλιστα τὸ εἰς τὴν τῆς πατρίδος σωτηρίαν καὶ αὔξησιν ἀνῆκον, καὶ ἔτι μᾶλλον εἰς τὴν τῶν θεῶν τιμήν.—Antipater ap. Stobæi Floril. Vol. iii. p. 16.]

[4 protinus ab initio, Lat.]   [5 patientes, Lat.]
[6 œconomicas, Lat.]

commonweal's prosperity, may thereby daily increase more and more.

Against adultery.

I am now come to speak of adultery, which is a sin whereby the husband goeth to another woman, or the wife turneth aside after another man, to whom they make common the use of their bodies, which are not their own bodies now, but their mates' in wedlock. Some there are that flatter themselves, and are of opinion, that they are not culpable of adultery, if they have the company of any unbetrothed maiden, or one that is unmarried; or if a woman play the harlot with an unwedded man: they will have it (in God's name[1]) to be fornication, and not adultery. But the scripture teacheth the contrary. Thou goest to another woman, thou art an adulterer: thou breakest thy faith, thou art forsworn: thy body is not thine, but thy wife's; when therefore thou bestowest thy body on another, thou committest adultery. If thou, being wedded, dost lie with a married wife, thou doublest the sin of thine adultery. This offence was plagued with most sharp punishment even in the beginning almost, and as soon as the world was created. Pharao, the king of Egypt, commanded Sara, Abraham's wife, to be taken away and carried to his palace, that he might use her as his wife; thinking verily that she had been Abraham's sister. But

Gen. xii.

the scripture saith, "The Lord vexed Pharaoh and all his house with great plagues, because of Sara, Abraham's wife." Lo, here the king of Egypt is punished with grievous plagues for his adultery; and yet he knew not that Sara was Abraham's wife: how great plagues therefore are prepared for the men that wittingly and willingly, without all shame, commit adultery! To Abimelech, king of the Philistines, the Lord

Gen. xx.

doth say, "Lo, thou shalt die, because of the woman which thou hast taken away from her husband." And yet this king also had taken away Sara, not knowing that she was Abraham's wife. Joseph, being provoked to adultery by his

Gen. xxxix.

master's wife, doth simply say, "How should I do this great wickedness, and sin against God?" Every word doth bear some weight: for adultery is an heinous sin. Whereupon in

Job xxxi.

the book of Job we find these words of Job himself: "If mine heart have been deceived by a woman, or if I have laid

[1 Not in the original Latin.]

wait at my neighbour's door[2]; then let my wife be another
man's harlot, and let other men have to do with her. For
this is a wickedness and sin that is worthy to be judged to
death : yea, it is a fire that utterly should consume and root
out all mine increase." Job saith that he hath not only not
committed adultery, but that he hath not so much at any time
as once given the attempt to defile another man's wife. He
confesseth that adultery is a sin, and so grievous an offence,
that it doth deserve to have the adulterer's wife to be defiled
with adultery. He addeth, that adultery is a fire that utterly
consumeth and devoureth all things ; and, lastly, that it is a
sin to be judged, and punished by death.

Moreover, Salomon, the wisest of all men, saith : " May
a man take fire in his bosom, and his clothes not be brent[3]? Prov. vi.
Or can one go upon hot coals, and his feet not be brent?
Even so he that goeth in to his neighbour's wife, and toucheth her, cannot be unguilty. Men do not utterly despise a
thief that stealeth to satisfy his soul, when he is hungry ;
but if he may be gotten, he restoreth again seven times as
much, or else he maketh recompence with all the substance
of his house: but whoso committeth adultery with a woman, he
lacketh understanding; and he that doeth it, destroyeth his
own soul. He getteth himself a plague and dishonour, and
his reproach shall never be put out. For the jealousy and
wrath of the man will not be entreated ; neither accepteth
he the person of any mediator, nor receiveth any gifts, how
great soever they be." In these words of Salomon many
things are to be noted. First, as it cannot otherwise be, but
that fire must burn the garment wherein it is carried; so
no man can commit adultery without damage and danger of
further punishment. Secondarily, comparison is made betwixt
a thief and an adulterer : not that theft is thereby defended;
but because thieves, although they be infamous, do seem yet
to sin a great deal less than adulterers do. For a thief may
make satisfaction by restoring the worth of the thing that he
stole to him from whom he stole it away ; but for adultery
no amends can be made. And what is he that would not

[2 nimirum ut corrumperem uxorem ejus, Lat.; omitted by the
translator: namely, with the intent of corrupting his wife.]
[3 brent, i. e. burnt.]

rather wish to have thieves ransack his chest, and take away his substance, than to have his wife, his darling, defiled with adultery? Moreover, Salomon calleth the adulterer mad, and without understanding. Adultery is judged to be a sin worthy of death and endless infamy. For the Lord in the law doth not say only, " Thou shalt not commit adultery;" but in another place also goeth on, and addeth, "And he that committeth adultery with another man's wife, even he that committeth adultery with his neighbour's wife, let both the adulterer and the adulteress be slain." Levit. xx. And this punishment of adultery by death was not abrogated or changed by the very Gentiles; for the Roman law *Lex Julia* is very well known, how it commanded adulterers to be put to death[1]: which law was of force in the time of St Hierome, as we may gather by the history which he wrote of an adulteress, at the chopping off of whose head seven strokes were given[2].

Neither is it marvel, undoubtedly, that adultery was among them of old, and is yet at this day, according to the laws[3], to be punished by death; for upon that one many sins do depend. First of all, the adulterer is a perjured man; for he hath broken and violated the faith, which he gave openly, before God and the face of the congregation, by calling to witness the most holy and reverend Trinity, when the minister of Christ did solemnise the marriage, and couple him to his wife, by giving hand in hand. Secondarily, the adulterer hath committed theft and robbery; for when the adulteress doth make her body common to another man, then doth she set to sale, defile, and mar, not her own, but her husband's body. Thirdly, bastards born in adultery do oftentimes

[1 " The Lex Julia, passed about B. C. 17, did not inflict the punishment of death on either party; and in those instances under the emperors, in which death was inflicted, it must be considered an extraordinary punishment, and beyond the provisions of the Julian Law. By a constitution of Constantine, confirmed by Justinian, the offence in the adulterer was made capital. The Julian Law, however, *permitted the father in certain cases* to kill the adulterer and adulteress."—Dict. of Gr. and Lat. Antiq. s. v. *Adulterium*. P.]

[2 Hieron. Epist. xvii. ad Innocentium de muliere septies percussa. Par. 1706. Tom. IV. col. 23—26.]

[3 See Becon's Works, Parker Soc. ed. Vol. II. p. 649; and Early Writings of Bp. Hooper, p. 376.]

enjoy an equal part of inheritance with the right-begotten children; which cannot be without great wrong done to the lawful heirs and legitimate offspring: for they are against all right robbed of their due inheritance, whereof an equal portion is given to him to whom by law no parcel is due. Lastly, beside all these, innumerable mischiefs do spring of adultery. Since therefore that it is a serpent with so many heads, both the laws of God and men do rightly punish adulterers with loss of life.

But some jolly fellows there are, forsooth[4], that of adultery do make but a sport. They are persuaded that David's adultery doth make on their side; and that place of scripture where we read, that the Lord was favourable to the adulteress that was taken even as the deed was in doing. Why do not these merry conceited men consider how severely the Lord did punish David for that offence? The bloody house[5] of David was immediately after defiled with filthy incest. For Amnon doth perforce deflour his sister Thamar. And straightway, upon the neck of that again, his house is defamed by most cruel parricide, while Absalom in a banquet murdered his brother Amnon. The very same Absalom also, David's son, defileth or defloureth his father's wives, and that openly too, laying all fear of God and shame aside. He driveth his father out of his kingdom, and hasteneth on to shorten his days. All which calamities David confesseth that he doth worthily sustain, for the adultery and murder by him committed. Lastly, many thousands of his people were slain in the battle; David himself is hardly and with much ado restored to his kingdom; and afterward, being restored, he repented his sin all the days of his life[6]. Now it is marvel if adulterers, considering these punishments, will go on yet to allege the example of David in defence of their naughtiness. Our Saviour did not come into the world to be a judge, but a saviour; neither did he in any place usurp the right of the sword. Who, therefore, will make any marvel at it, to see the adulteress not condemned by him to be stoned to death? Yet he said: "Hath no man condemned thee[7]?" as if he minded not to have resisted the law, if

David's adultery.

The Lord absolveth adultery.

[4 Si diis placet, Lat.]   [5 funesta domus, Lat.]
[6 2 Sam. xi—xix.]   [7 John viii. 10.]

judgment had once passed upon her. For he came not to be a patron to adulterers, nor to break the law, but to fulfil it. But if it like adulterers well, that the adulteress was not condemned of the Lord, then let them also like that sentence, wherewith the history is ended, when the Lord saith : " Go thy ways, and sin no more." Let them, therefore, leave off to defile and destroy themselves with filthy adultery.

What other things are forbid under the title of adultery.

The Lord in his law hath expressly named adultery alone ; but therewithal he doth inclusively understand all kinds of lust and luxury, and all things else which do edge forward and stir up fire in men to wantonness, which he forbiddeth as severely as adultery itself. The Lord in the gospel doth not only forbid the outward work of adultery, but the very affection also and wanton lust of the heart and mind. " Ye have heard," saith he, " that it was said to them of old, Thou shalt not commit adultery. But I say unto you, That whosoever looketh on a woman to lust after her, hath committed adultery already with her in his heart[1]." In the same place he teacheth us to pluck out our eyes, and cut off our hands, that is, to extinguish unclean affections that rise in our minds, while yet they be young and begin to bud, lest peradventure they break out from thoughts to deeds. So then in this precept every unclean thought, all ribald talk, and filthiness of bodily deeds, are utterly forbidden.

Fornication.

In this precept is forbidden fornication, or that kind of whorehunting, which is said to be the meddling of a single man with an unmarried woman. This kind of whoredom is thought of many either to be a very small offence, or none at all. But such kind of men doth the devil hearten on, bewitch, and by all those ill thoughts drive on to commit that sin ; when as the doctrine of the evangelists and apostles

Acts xv.

doth teach us the contrary. For the apostles, in that synodal epistle, which they sent from Hierusalem to all nations,

1 Pet. iv.

do expressly name and forbid fornication. St Peter reckoneth fornication among those filthy sins, from which he would

1 Cor. x.

have Christians to be most clear. St Paul saith, " Flee fornication." Again, " Let us not be defiled with fornication, as some of them committed fornication, and fell in one day three and twenty thousand[2]." Fornication doth directly

[1 Matt. v. 27, 28.]   [2 1 Cor. vi. 18 and x. 8.]

fight with the covenant of God, whereby he is joined to us, and we to him : and whoredom also spoileth God of his glory, and doth most filthily pollute the temple of the Lord. Let us hear what the apostle Paul saith touching this matter: 1 Cor. vi. " Know ye not that your bodies are the members of Christ ? shall I therefore take the members of Christ, and make them the members of an harlot ? God forbid. What, know ye not that he that is coupled to an harlot is one body ? For two, saith he, shall be one flesh. But he that is coupled to the Lord, is one spirit. Flee fornication. Every sin that a man doeth is without the body ; but he that committeth fornication sinneth against his own body. What, know ye not that your body is the temple of the Holy Ghost which is in you, whom ye have of God, and ye are not your own? for ye are bought with a price." Therefore fornication shutteth fornicators out of the kingdom of God. For the same apostle saith : " Neither whoremongers nor adulterers Ephes. v. shall inherit the kingdom of God." And therefore in another place he suffereth not fornication to be so much as once named among Christians[3]; so far was he[4] from admitting stews and brothel-houses among God's people. Moreover, whoredom doth fill the whole body with sundry diseases : it depriveth whore-haunters of all their goods and substance ; it bringeth them to poverty and extreme misery, and driveth them at last to utter desperation. It overthroweth their fame and good name with shame and ignominy : the view whereof is lively expressed in the holy scriptures by the example of Samson, the strongest man among all the Israelites. Salomon, therefore, the most wise of all other, doth very fitly, in time and place convenient, admonish all men to fly the enticing baits and flattering allurements of whorish strumpets. For the end of them is deadly poison, and they throw a man down headlong into a bottomless pit of endless miseries[5].

By this law also that kind of whoredom is prohibited, Rapes forbidden. which consisteth in defloration of virgins, and violent rapes, by which children are perforce defiled and carried from their

[3 Eph. v. 5, 3.]
[4 servus Jesu Christi. Lat. So far was the servant of Jesus Christ, &c.]
[5 Prov. vii. 23, &c.]

parents. There is difference betwixt a rape perforce, and the deflouring of a maid done without violence. Sichem defiled Dina, the daughter of Jacob; and although he desired to have the defloured maid to his wife, and to change his religion, yet notwithstanding he himself is slain by Levi and Simeon, the brethren of Dina; his city is rased and filled with the blood of murdered men, whose goods were ransacked and laid open to spoil. The history is extant in the thirty-fourth chapter of Genesis. For the rape which Roderichus, king of the Goths in Spain, committed upon the daughter of Julianus, a lieutenant, all Spain in a manner was mingled with fire and blood. For Volaterranus, in his second book of his Geography, saith: "Roderichus reigned three years, whose filthy lust brought an end, as well to the name, as to the quiet kingdom, of the Goths in Spain, by means of the Saracens that invaded their land. For when it fell out, that he had defloured the daughter of one Julianus, a lieutenant of that part of Mauritania that is called Tingitana, private grief did prick her father to seek revengement, whereto he used the commodity of the place. Wherefore Julianus doth privately call the Saracens out of Africa; who, in the year of grace 714, under the conduct of their captain Muzta, being sent by Mirmemolinus their king at that time, entering in through the straits of Morocco, did in two years' space subdue all Spain almost, except Asturia: in the space of which time it is reported that seven hundred thousand men on both sides were destroyed by that war; wherein also the king, which had defloured the virgin, with all his nobility, was utterly slain[1]."

Asturia, a country in Spain, between Galatia and Portugal.

[1 Roderychus tres annos regnavit; cujus fœda libido finem attulit Gothorum non tam generi quam pacifico imperio, Saracenis supervenientibus. Nam cum filiam cujusdam Juliani præfecti, qui Tingitanam administrabat provinciam, vitiasset, dolor domesticus patrem ad ultionem sollicitavit, loci fretum commoditate. Quare Julianus clam ex Aphrica Saracenas evocat: qui anno salutis 714 duce Muza, misso a Mirammelino eorum tunc rege, per angustias Herculei freti ingresso, biennii spatio omnem fere Hispaniam occupant præter Astures. In quo temporis spacio dicuntur ad septies centena hominum millia in eo bello utrinque absumpta.—Volaterrani Commentar. Urban. Geograph. Lib. II. p. 17, Basil. 1559. The author of the modern part of the Universal History, (Vol. XVI. p. 87, Lond. 1782) observes on this account, in a note: "The reign of Roderic was so short and so full of troubles, and his own personal character in other respects so fair,

In Israel, for the Levite's concubine, whom the citizens of Gibea of the tribe of Benjamin had violently ravished, were twenty-five thousand Benjamites slain, beside them which perished from among the other eleven tribes, whose number amounted to forty thousand men[2]. Neither is it unknown to any, that the kings were expelled out of the city of Rome, and Troy, being wearied with ten years' war, (which troubled both the east and west,) was at the last utterly sacked and clean overthrown, because Tarquinius had perforce ravished Lucretia, and Alexander Paris had stolen out of Greece Menelaus his Helena, another man's wife[3]. Every age almost doth minister an innumerable sort of such like examples. For the most just God hath always by evident examples declared, how greatly he is offended with deflourers of virgins and ravishers of women. And for that cause are laws and very sharp punishments ordained and appointed for such lascivious knaves. Rapes and such villainies committed perforce the laws do punish with loss of life; but to him that doth deflour a maid not violently the Lord doth say, "Marry and endow her[4]." Other laws appoint other penalties: touching which more is spoken in the civil law.

Moreover, incest is especially prohibited. They call in- Incest. cest an unlawful meddling of a man with a woman against the honour of blood and affinity. For "cestus" signifieth the marriage-girdle, which the bride did wear, to shew that the marriage was just and lawful[5]. We Germans call this sin by the name of "Bloutschand;" whereby we signify the sin committed in corrupting or defiling our own blood or kindred. In Leviticus, after the degrees of blood, in which we are forbidden to marry, the Lord doth presently add : "In all these be not ye defiled: for in all these things are the nations defiled, which I cast out before you. And hereby the land is defiled, and I have visited the iniquity thereof upon it, and the

that nothing can be more improbable with respect to him than this imputation."]

[2 Judges xx.]

[3 See also Early Writings of Hooper, Parker Soc. ed. p. 354.]

[4 Deut. xxii. 28, 29.]

[5 ab *in* priv. et *castus*. Facciol. Alii ducunt ab *in*, et *cesto*, Veneris cingulo, quo amor maritalis in legitimis nuptiis conciliari putabatur.— Holyoke's Dict. in voc. 1677.]

[BULLINGER.]   27

land hath spewed out the inhabitants thereof. Ye shall therefore keep my statutes and mine ordinances, and shall not do any of all these abominations. For whosoever shall do so, he shall be cut off from among his people[1]." And in the twentieth chapter of Leviticus he hath appointed death to be the punishment of incest; which is not changed by the civil laws or imperial constitutions.

Sodomy. The abominable sin of sodomy, and meddling with beasts, also is plainly forbidden : against which we have most evident and express laws set down in the eighteenth and twentieth chapters of Leviticus. We have also a very severe, but yet a most just, punishment laid by God himself upon the pates of the detestable Sodomites : for with fire and stinking brimstone sent down from heaven he consumed those filthy men to dust and ashes; which ashes he washed away with the waves of the Dead Sea, because he would not have so much as the very cinders to remain of so wicked men. Moreover, their whole cities and fruitful fields were burnt with fire. For it was not requisite[2] that any one jot of the substance of those most wicked men should remain undestroyed. The place where those cities sometime were situated is at this day overflown with water, and called the Dead Sea. Whereby we do consequently gather, that the most just God will not spare the Gentiles, entangled in the very same sin, although for a time he wink at and dissemble it. Fire shall destroy both them and theirs; and they themselves shall for ever burn in hell, where nothing shall remain of them but a reproachful memory. For in the Revelation[3] of our Lord Jesus Christ to his apostle John we read: "And fire came down from God out of heaven, and devoured them; and the devil, which deceived them, was cast into a lake of fire and brimstone, where the beast and the false prophet shall be tormented day and night for evermore." Apoc. xx.

Allurements forbidden. Furthermore, all things else are forbidden, that do incite or allure us to unlawful lusts; which baits are the over-nice pranking and decking the body, evil and wanton company, gluttony, surfeiting, and drunkenness. For Ezechiel, among the rest of his prophecies, saith : " This was the iniquity of

[1 Lev. xviii. 24—29.]
[2 oportebat, Lat.]
[3 in Theologia Domini nostri Jesu Christi, Lat. See p. 170, n. 6.]

Sodom, pride, gluttony, abundance of all things, and idleness[4]." Men are provoked to lust either by hearing or reading of dishonest ditties and bawdy ballads; or by looking on and beholding wanton dances, unseemly sights, ribald talk, and filthy examples. They therefore are by this law reproved, which wink at or cherish, which are the bawds or bringers together of adulterous persons. Unto the wicked the Lord in the Psalms doth say: "Why dost thou take my covenant in thy mouth, whereas thou hatest to be reformed, and dost cast my words behind thee? When thou sawest a thief, thou consentedst unto him; and hast been partaker with the adulterers," &c. The just Lord therefore doth punish all these offences in wicked men, every one according to the greatness of the sin. For some sins are far more heinous than other some are. He is an adulterer, that in his mind doth lust after another man's wife: but he sinneth more grievously, if he endeavour to finish in deed his wicked thought; he offendeth yet more deeply, if he do the deed; and sinneth most of all, if, after once, he fall unto it again. Likewise the adulterer sinneth; so doth the bawd, and he also that upholdeth his adultery. The whoremonger sinneth deeply; but he that defileth himself with incest sinneth more grievously; and he most heinously of all, that in meddling with beasts committeth filthy sodomy. So then in this seventh precept charge is given for the maintenance of shamefacedness, modesty, sobriety, temperancy, chastity, public honesty, and true holiness of soul and body.

The next is for me to say somewhat now touching continency. By abstinence we refrain from other men's goods, and take from no man the thing that is his. Some there are that will have temperancy to extend farther than continency; for they will make the one to be but a part of the other[5]. I, in this treatise, do simply make continency the contrary to intemperancy or incontinency. For continency is a virtue or power of the mind received from the Spirit of God, which suppresseth affections, and doth not in any wise permit unlawful pleasures. This is conversant and doth shew itself in

Psal. 1

Of continency.

[4 Ezek. xvi. 49.]
[5 Temperantia est rationis in libidinem atque in alios non rectos animi impetus firma et moderata dominatio. Ejus partes sunt continentia, clementia, modestia.—Cic. de Orat. Lib. ii. cap. 60.]

27—2

the common and usual talk of men, in pleasures that are allowed, in apparel, in buildings and dwelling-houses, in meat and drink, and in other things also. I at this present will only examine those points of continency which are already rehearsed.

The continency or the bridling of the tongue.

First of all, it is required of us to keep in our tongue, and not to let it loose at random to the blaspheming of God's glory or hurt of our neighbour. Let the talk of a christian man be honest, profitable, and seasoned with salt; let it be unacquainted with scoffing, lightness, lying, ribaldry, and filthiness. St James in the third chapter of his epistle hath spoken sufficiently of the tongue's properties. In his first chapter also he saith: "Let every man be swift to hear, slow to speak, and slow to anger." And Paul saith: "Let no filthy communication proceed out of your mouth, but that which is good to edify withal, as oft as need is, that it may minister grace unto the hearers; and grieve not the Holy Spirit of God, by whom ye are sealed unto the day of redemption[1]." And again: "Let not fornication, or any uncleanness, or covetousness, be once named among you, as it becometh saints; neither filthiness, nor foolish talking, neither jesting, which are not seemly; but rather giving of thanks. Let no man deceive you with vain words; for for such things cometh the wrath of God upon the children of disobedience[2]." For in another place he citeth this sentence out of Menander, and saith: "Ill words corrupt good manners[3]." Moreover, a man's mind is bewrayed by his talk; for "of the heart's abundance the mouth doth speak[4]." If therefore in any thing, then in tongue especially, it behoveth Christians to be sober and continent.

Granted pleasures.

The Lord, I confess, hath granted man the use of certain pleasures. For he may lawfully, without offence to God, clothe his body with garments soberly, thereby to keep his limbs from cold. God hath and doth allow the embracings of man and wife in holy wedlock. He granteth choice of a dwelling-place conveniently situated against the untemperateness of the air, and biddeth us not to wander, like beasts and

[1 Eph. iv. 29, 30.   quoties opus est, Lat.   Erasmus' rendering.]
[2 Eph. v. 3, 4, 6.]
[3 1 Cor. xv. 33.]
[4 Matt. xii. 34.]

cattle, through fields and desolate woods. He hath, for our necessity and pleasant feeding, allowed us the use of meat and drink. He granteth us quietness, ease, and sleep, which doth wonderfully refresh the strength, that is decayed and tired with pains. Therefore, so often as a godly man doth enjoy them, doth use them, and is delighted with the honest pleasure of them, let him give thanks to God, and use them moderately in the fear of the Lord. For in so doing he sinneth not against the Lord : but by the abuse of those things, by unthankfulness for them, and by immoderate using of them, he doth offend his God and maker.

For what is allowed or permitted to married folks I have already declared in this very sermon : so that I need not here again to repeat it unto you. Solomon saith : " Be glad with the wife of thy youth ; let her be as the beloved hind and pleasant roe; let her love always refresh thee, and be thou still delighted therein[5]," &c. In the meantime, let every one refrain from all abuse and intemperancy : and, if necessity at any time require it, let man and wife lie asunder, as Paul doth counsel them[6]; or else let them give ear to the prophet Joel, who saith : " Proclaim an holy fast, gather the people together ; let the bridegroom come forth of his chamber, and the bride out of her closet[7]."

Our garments must be cleanly and honest, according to our country fashion, to cover and become us, unless our country fashion be too far out of order : there must be in them no hypocritical sluttishness, beyond-sea gauds, new-fangled toys, nor unseemly sights[8]. The chief apostles of Christ, Peter and Paul, were not ashamed in their epistles to write somewhat largely touching the manner and ordering of women's apparel; because that kind of people do most of all bend to that foolish bravery. Let every faithful body think what is seemly for them to wear, not so much by their degree in dignity or condition of riches, as by their religion. Excess in every thing is discommended in Christians. And to what end do we jag and gash[9] the garments that are sewed

Continency in apparel.

1 Pet. iii.
1 Tim. ii.
Tit. ii.

[5] Prov. v. 18, 19.]
[6] 1 Cor. vii. 5.]
[7] Joel ii. 16. de velo suo, Lat.   But edit. 1587 reads, *his* closet.]
[8] nihil peregrinum, leve et indecorum, Lat.]
[9] discindere, Lat.]

together to cover our bodies, but that thereby we may, as it were, by a most fond and ridiculous anatomy, open and lay forth to the eyes of all men what kind of people we are in our inward hearts, jagged (God wot) and ragged[1], vain, light, and nothing sound? And a linen or woollen garment doth as well cover and become the body, as damasks and velvets[2], the cost whereof doth overlade thy purse with expenses to buy them, and mis-shape thee like an ill-favoured picture, when thou wearest them upon thee[3].

Continency in buildings.

In buildings God forbiddeth not cleanliness and necessary cost, but sumptuous expense and gorgeous excess. For these over-brave buildings are seldomtimes finished without extorting wrong and over-great injury done to the poor. Jeremy bringeth in the Lord speaking against the king of Judah, and saying: "Woe to him that buildeth his house with unrighteousness, and his parlour with the goods that are wrongfully gotten; which never recompenseth his neighbour's labour, nor payeth him his hire; who saith to himself, I will build me a wide house and gorgeous parlours; who causeth windows to be hewn therein, and the ceilings and joists maketh he of cedar and painteth them with sinoper[4]. Thinkest thou to reign now that thou hast inclosed theeself with cedar? Did not thy father eat and drink and prosper well, as long as he executed justice and equity[5]?" Let none of us, therefore, build sumptuous houses by robbing the poor of their hire for their labour. Let every one dwell in a house agreeable to his profession, degree, and condition. St Hierome condemneth sumptuous cost even in churches and temples[6]. Neither do I see what gorgeous buildings bring to a man, but mischief and misery. Lord[7], how unwillingly do we die and depart

[1 discissi videlicet, laceri, Lat.]
[2 holoserica, Lat.]
[3 quæ te non decent, et luxuriosa sunt, Lat.]
[4 Vulg. *sinopide;* a red stone found in Sinopis in Pontus.—Plin. Hist. Nat. Lib. xxxv. cap. 5. § 13. Usus, si lignum colorare libeat.]
[5 Jer. xxii. 13—16.]
[6 Hieron. Ep. xxxiv. ad Nep. de Vit. Cler. Par. 1706. Tom. iv. col. 263. See Bullinger de Scriptur. Sanct. Authoritate, &c. Lib. ii. fol. 115. Tigur. 1538. and de Orig. Error. cap. 21. fol. 102. Tigur. 1539.]
[7 This expression is not in the original Latin.]

from goodly dwellings, whereby we double the fear of death and terror of sickness! The patriarchs, verily, did dwell in tents, whereby they witnessed that they were pilgrims, and sought another country, the heavenly Hierusalem[8].

Continency in meat and drink is not the loathing of wine and victuals, but the moderate using of them to supply our necessity, and not to cloy us with gluttony. God in the scripture doth condemn gluttony, surfeitings, riotous after-banquets, and drunkenness, which he forbiddeth most of all: for of drunkenness do spring endless miseries and innumerable mischiefs, grievous diseases, poverty, and pinching beggary. Solomon saith: "Who hath woe? who hath sorrow? who hath strife? who hath brawling? who hath wounds without a cause? who hath red eyes? even they that follow the wine, and seek excess thereof[9]. Look not thou upon the wine, how red it is, and what a colour it giveth in the glass. It goeth down sweetly, but at the last it biteth like a serpent, and poisoneth like an adder[10]." I will not rehearse all which I could allege out of heathen writers against surfeiting and drunkenness. Solomon alone in that one sentence containeth a great deal of matter. Moreover, he that heareth not Christ, whom is it likely that he will give ear unto in all the world? Now Christ, in the gospel, by the parable of the rich glutton[11] doth marvellous evidently set forth the woeful end of insatiable paunches[12]. In the same gospel also he taketh occasion to touch the surfeitings and drunkenness of our age, (I mean the age which is immediately before the judgment-day,) where he saith: "As it happened in the days of Noe and Lot; they did eat and drink, even until the day that Noe entered into the ark, and that Lot departed from among the Sodomites; and then incontinently the deluge came, and fire and brimstone poured down from heaven, and destroyed them all[13]." Again, he addeth: "Take heed to yourselves, lest at any time your hearts be overcome with surfeiting and drunkenness and cares of this life; and so that day come upon you at unawares. For

Continency in meat and drink.

Christ against drunkenness.

[8 Heb. xi. 9, 10, 13—16.]
[9 qui veniunt inquisitum ubi misccatur, Lat.]
[10 Prov. xxiii. 29—32.]
[11 Luke xvi. 19, &c.]
[12 epulones, Lat.]
[13 Luke xvii. 26—29.]

as a snare shall it come upon all them that dwell upon the face of the whole earth. Watch ye therefore, at all times praying, that ye may escape all these things, and stand before the Son of man[1]." And I would to God that all men would not write this golden, heavenly, and divine admonition of our Saviour in their halls and dining-parlours only, but in their several hearts also. For since drunkenness hath in these our days so good entertainment with all degrees, estates, kinds[2], and ages, we do daily feel the woeful miseries that God doth threaten to drunkards in the fifth and twenty-eighth chapters of Esay's prophecy. And it is to be feared greatly, that the day of the Lord shall suddenly light upon an innumerable sort of drunkards, to their endless pain and utter destruction. Let him hear, therefore, which hath ears to hear.

SaintMartin's doctrine of continency.

Some say that this Martin was abbot of the monastery of Dumia.

Neither can I here refrain, but needs must recite unto you, dearly beloved, that which St Martine, the bishop, not of Tours in France, but of Dumia [in Germany,] who flourished in the days of Justinian the emperor, did write to Miro, king of Gallicia, touching the ordering and leading a continent life: " If (saith he) thou dost love continency, cut off superfluity, and keep under thine appetite. Consider with thyself, how much nature requireth, and not how much lust desireth. Bridle thy concupiscence, and cast off the alluring baits that serve to draw on hidden pleasures. Eat without undigested surfeiting, and drink without drunkenness. Neither glut thyself with present delicates, nor long after deintrels[3] hard to be come by. Let thy diet be of cates good-cheap, and sit not down for pleasure, but for meat. Let hunger, not sauces, provoke thee to eat. Pay but little for pastimes to delight thee, because thy only care should be to leave such pleasures, that thereby thou, in fashioning thyself to the example of God, mayest, as much as thou canst, make haste to reduce thyself from the body to the spirit. If thou lovest continency, then choose not a pleasant but a wholesome dwellingplace; and make not the lord to be known by the gorgeous house, but the house by the honest landlord. Boast not thyself of that which thou hast not, nor that which thou hast, neither covet to seem more than thou art. But rather take heed that thy poverty be not uncleanly, nor thy niggishness filthy, nor thy

[1 Luke xxi. 34—36.]   [2 sexus, Lat.]
[3 daintrel, a delicacy.—Webster's Dict. 1831.]

simplicity contemptible, nor thy lenity fearful; and though thy estate be poor, yet let it not be in extreme misery. Neither be out of love with thine own degree, nor wish after the estate of another man's life. If thou lovest continency, avoid dishonest things before they happen, and fear no man above thine own conscience. Think that all things are tolerable, dishonesty excepted. Abstain from filthy talk, the liberty whereof doth nourish unshamefacedness. Love rather profitable communication than merry conceits and pleasant talk, and set more by the blunt-spoken truth than by fair soothing speeches. Thou mayest sometime mingle mirth with matters of weight ; but it must be done moderately, without the hurt or detriment of thine estate and gravity : for laughter is blameworthy, if it be immoderately used, childishly squeaked, or taken up by fits, as women are wont to do. Esteem not saucy scoffing, but civil mirth with courteous humanity. Let thy conceits of mirth be without biting, thy sports not without profit, thy laughter without unseemly writhing of thy mouth and visage, thy voice without shrieking, and thy pace in going without hasty shuffling. Let not thy rest be idleness; and when other play, take thou some holy and honest thing in hand. If thou art continent, take heed of flattery, and let it grieve thee as much to be praised of naughty men, as if thou were praised for thine own naughty deeds. Be the gladder for it, if thou displeasest evil men, and impute the evil opinions which naughty men have of thee for the best praise that can be given thee. The hardest work of continency is to put away the soothing courtesies of dissembling flatterers, whose fawning words undo the mind with pleasant sensuality. Presume not too much upon thyself, neither be thou arrogant. Submit thyself so far as thou mayest keep thy gravity ; and yet make not thyself a footstool or cushion for every man to lean on. Be told of thy faults willingly, and suffer thyself gladly to be reprehended. If any man for a cause be angry with and chide thee, acknowledge thy fault, and let his chiding profit thee : but if he chide thee without any cause, think that thereby he would have profited thee. Fear not sharp, but sugared, words. Do thou thyself eschew all sorts of vices, and be not an over-busy searcher-out of other men's faults : be thou no sharp fault-finder, but an admonisher without upbraiding, so that still thy warning may bear the shew of cheerful mirth : and condescend easily to pardon the error. Neither praise nor dispraise any man overmuch. Be still, and give ear to them that speak, and be ready to instruct them that do hearken : to him that asketh give a ready answer, to him that despiseth thee give place easily, and fall not out to chiding and cursing. If thou art continent, have an eye to the motions of thy body and mind, that they be not unseemly : and set not light by them because nobody seeth them; for it maketh no matter if no body see them, so thou thyself dost spy and perceive them. Be moveable, not light; constant, not stubborn. Be liberal to all men, fawning on no man : familiar with few, and upright to every one. Believe not lightly every rumour, accusation, or conceived suspicion. Despise vainglory, and be no sharp exactor of the goods that thou hast. Use few words thyself, but suffer them that speak. Be grave, not rough, nor contemning the merry nature. Be desirous and applicable to be taught wisdom : impart what thou knowest to him that demandeth without any arrogancy, and desire to learn the things that thou knowest not without hiding thine ignorance. A wise man will not change his common country fashion, nor make the people gaze on him with new-found devices[1]."

[1] Continentiam si diligis, circumcide superflua, et in arctum desideria tua constringe. Considera tecum quantum natura poscat, et non quantum cupiditas expetat. Impone concupiscentiæ tuæ frœnum et modum, omniaque blandimenta, quæ occultam voluptatem trahunt, rejice. Ede citra cruditatem, bibe citra ebrietatem. Nec præsentibus deliciis inhærebis, nec desiderabis absentes. Victus tibi ex facili sit; nec ad voluptatem, sed ad cibum accede. Palatum tuum fames excitet, non sapores. Desideria tua parvo redime, quia hoc tantum curare debes, ut desinant; atque, quasi ad exemplar compositus divinum, a corpore ad spiritum, quantum potes, te festina reducere. Si continentiæ studes, habita non amœne, sed salubriter : nec dominum esse velis notum a domo, sed domum a domino. Non tibi ascribas quod non eris, nec quod es, nec major quam es videri velis. Hoc magis observa, ne paupertas tibi immunda sit, nec parsimonia sordida, nec simplicitas neglecta, nec lenitas languida : et si tibi res exiguæ sunt, non tamen sint angustæ. Nec tua defleas, nec mireris aliena. Si continentiam diligis, turpia fugito antequam accidant; nec quenquam alium vereberis plusquam te. Omnia tolerabilia præter turpitudinem crede. A verbis quoque turpibus abstineto, quia eorum licentia impudentiam nutrit. Sermones utiles magis quam facetos et amabiles ama, rectos potius quam obsecundantes. Miscebis interdum seriis jocos, sed tem-

Thus much have I hitherto recited touching continency out of the writings of the blessed bishop, Martine of Dumia. We, for our parts, must pray to the Lord, that he will vouchsafe to bestow on us his holy Spirit, by which the force of continency in all things may take root in our hearts, to the bringing forth of fruit in our deeds, agreeable to the prescript rule of this commanded continency. For, unless the Holy

peratos et sine detrimento dignitatis ac verecundiæ. Nam reprehensibilis risus est, si immodicus, si pueriliter effusus, si muliebriter fractus. Non erit tibi scurrilitas, sed grata urbanitas. Sales tui sint sine dente, joci non sine utilitate, risus sine cachinno, vox sine clamore, incessus sine tumultu. Quies tibi non desidia erit; et cum ab aliis luditur, tu sancti aliquid honestique tractabis. Si continens es, adulationes evita, sitque tibi tam triste laudari a turpibus, quam si laudaris ob turpia. Lætior esto quoties displices malis, et malorum de te existimationes malas veram tui laudationem ascribe. Difficillimum continentiæ opus est assentationes adulatorum repellere, quorum sermones animum voluptate resolvunt. Non eris audax, nec arrogans. Submittes te, non projicies, gravitate servata. Admoneberis libenter, et reprehenderis patienter. Si merito objurgabit aliquis, scito quia profuit: si immerito, scito quia prodesse voluit. Non acerba, sed blanda, timebis verba. Esto vitiorum fugax ipse, aliorum vero neque curiosus scrutator, neque acerbus reprehensor; sed sine exprobratione correptor, ita ut admonitionem hilaritate prævenias; et errori facile veniam dato. Nec extollas quenquam, neque dejicias. Dicentium esto tacitus auditor, audientium promptus receptor: requirenti facile responde, contemnenti facile cede, ne in jurgia execrationesque discedas. Si continens es, animi tui motus corporisque observa, ne indecori sint; nec illos ideo contemnas, quia latent: nam nihil differt, si nemo videat, cum tu ipse illos videas. Mobilis esto, non levis; constans, non pertinax. Cunctis esto benignus, nemini blandus, paucis familiaris, omnibus æquus; rumoribus, criminibus, suspicionibus minime credulus vel malignus. Vanæ gloriæ contemptor, et bonorum, quibus præditus es, non acerbus exactor. Rari sermonis ipse, sed loquentium patiens. Severus, non sævus, sed hilarem non aspernans. Sapientiæ cupidus et docilis, quæ nosti sine arrogantia postulanti imparties; quæ nescis, sine occultatione ignorantiæ tibi postula impartiri. Non conturbabit sapiens mores publicos, nec populum in se vitæ novitate convertet.— D. Martini Episcopi Dumiensis formula honestæ vitæ, sive de quatuor virtutibus cardinalibus liber unus, ap. Max. Biblioth. Vet. Patr. Lugd. 1677. Tom. x. fol. 383.—This Martin, a monk born in Pannonia, became abbot and bishop of Dumium, (*not in Germany*, the translator's mistake,) and finally bishop of Braga in Portugal, A. D. 563—583. —Mosheim's Eccles. Hist. ed. Soames. Cent. VI. Book 2. part 2. chap. 2. p. 37, note 4. Bingham's Antiq. B. IX. chap. 6. § 16.]

Ghost do quicken and inspire us, we do in vain give ear to so
many and so good commandments; and, unless we live and
lead a temperate and a sober life, we are utterly unworthy to
bear the name of Christians.

Of fasting. To this place also doth the treatise of fasting belong;
which I mean to handle in as few words as conveniently can
be. Christian fasting is a discipline, ordering, and chastening
of the body for the present necessity, which we begin and
keep of our own accord, without compulsion, and wherewith
we humble ourselves in the sight of God, by drawing from
the body the matter that setteth the flesh on fire, thereby to
make it obey the spirit. For so long as we mortal men do
live in this body, the flesh doth still resist the spirit; and
most of all rebelleth then, when we with delicates do pamper
the body. Wherefore fasting doth draw from the body every
evil which stirreth up and strengtheneth it against the good
commandments of God's holy Spirit.

Two kinds of fastings. Now the necessity for which we keep this fasting is of
two sorts, public and private. We fast for the public or
common necessity, when some calamity doth either oppress,
or else hang over the head of the church. Of such a manner
of fasting we see examples in the second chapter of Joel, and
in the third of Jonas his prophecy: which very same order
in fasting was used in the time of our Lord's apostles, as it
is evidently extant in the Acts of the Apostles[1]. And this kind
of fasting doth seem to have differed very little, among them
of old, from a general mourning; yea, it seemeth altogether
to have been nothing else but a kind of lamenting. In the
scriptures every book is full of examples, which teach and
instruct us how the holy saints did humble themselves in the
sight of God with true repentance for their sins and offences.
Private necessity is that for which every particular man doth
fast, when he feeleth himself to be vexed with bodily concupiscence, that thereby he may take from the flesh the flame
and fuel, lest the body at last be fired and burned. For the
Lord in the gospel said, that the children of the bride-chamber
do fast when the bridegroom is taken from them[2], that is, in
a hard and dangerous time. The marriage doth signify the
bond whereby we are knit to Christ in faith and the Holy

[1 Acts xiii. 3. and xiv. 23.]
[2 Mark ii. 19, 20.]

Ghost. This yet notwithstanding, the godly man doth still rejoice[3]. He doth with giving of thanks and temperance both eat and drink so much as is sufficient, and is delighted also in these external gifts of God: but when he feeleth that the bridegroom is ready for to depart, or that he is now already almost departed out of his heart; that is, when he feeleth that the spirit is extinguished by the flesh's wantonness, and that faith doth once begin to be cold; then doth he settle himself to prayer, and doth appoint a solemn fasting, thereby either to keep the bridegroom still, or else to pull him back being ready to depart.

But neither public nor private fastings can abide to be enforced: for they will not be compelled, but desire to proceed of a free, cheerful, and voluntary mind. Unwilling men do nothing well. God requireth a cheerful giver. Moreover, let fastings be moderated according to the quality of places, persons, perils, and temptations: if they be not continual, yet let them be often, till such time as we be delivered and rid utterly of them. Let them be without superstition and feigned hypocrisy, as our Lord in the sixth of St Matthew's gospel hath taught us. Herewithal do the words of St Hierome agree very well, which he wrote to Nepotianus, touching fasting, as followeth: "Prescribe to thyself so long a time to fast in as thine ability will suffer thee to bear. Let thy fastings be pure, uncorrupt, simple, moderated, and not superstitious. What availeth it to eat no oil, and to seek out such seldom fond cates as are hard to be come by, as figs, pepper, nuts, dates, pure flour for overfine bread, and honey? The gardens, with digging for novelties, are turned over and over, because we will not eat common cribble[4] bread; and so, while our dainty mouths seek after delicates, our souls are pulled from the kingdom of heaven. I hear, moreover, that some men there are, which (contrary to nature) refuse to drink water and feed upon bread; but suck up and swallow very costly suppings, dainty herbbroths, and the juice of beets, not out of a cup, but out of a shell. O shame! blush we not at such fond toys, and are

Of what quality and kind our fastings must be.

[3 Hoc integro, perpetuo gaudet pius, Lat. This remaining unbroken, the godly man continually rejoices.]

[4 cribble, coarse flour, or meal.—Webster's Dict.]

we not ashamed of such superstition[1]?" Thus much saith
Hierome. And it is evident, that even at this day this vice
is especially received among our wealthy and religious men.

The end of
fastings.

But the end of christian fastings are, that the church, or
sinner, should submit and humble themselves before the Lord,
that the flesh should be obedient and subject to the spirit,
that the flesh should not hinder the sinner to work righteousness, and that the intent and mind of him that prayeth
should be the more earnestly bent toward God. For fasting
is of the number of those works which of themselves are not
absolute and perfect, but have another meaning, for which
they are ordained to another end and purpose: therefore
fasting is a certain help to the prayers and virtues of godly
men. Whereupon in the prophets we find, that the fastings
of the Jews displeased the Lord: for they did nought else
but fast alone; that is, they did at a certain and appointed
time abstain from their usual manner of eating, but they
restrained not themselves from sin and wickedness, but let
their flesh have the bridle at will, when as indeed they
should have ceased to have pampered it, that thereby it being
the weaker, the spirit might be the stronger to do and fulfil
all sort of good works. And therefore saith the Lord: " I
have not chosen such a manner of fasting ;" and the rest, as
it followeth in the fifty-eighth chapter of Esay, and in the
seventh and eighth chapters of Zachary's prophecy.

The true
fast.

The apostle Paul, verily, doth expressly say, that " meat
commendeth us not to God: for neither if we eat, have we
anything the more; neither if we eat not, have we anything
the less[2]." He therefore doth not fast truly, which doth

[1 Tantum tibi jejuniorum modum impone, quantum ferre potes.
Sint tibi pura, casta, simplicia, moderata, et non superstitiosa jejunia.
Quid prodest oleo non vesci, et molestias quasdam difficultatesque
ciborum quærere, carycas, piper, nuces, palmarum fructus, similam,
mel, pistacia? Tota hortorum cultura vexatur, ut cibario non ves-
camur pane; et dum delicias sectamur, a regno cœlorum retrahimur.
Audio præterea quosdam, contra rerum hominumque naturam, aquam
non bibere, nec vesci pane; sed sorbitiunculas delicatas et contrita
olera, betarumque succum, non calice sorbere, sed concha. Proh pu-
dor! non erubescimus istiusmodi ineptiis, nec tædet superstitionis?—
Hieron. Opp. Par. 1706. Epist. xxxiv. ad Nepot. de Vit. Cler. Tom. iv.
pars 2. col. 264.]
[2 1 Cor. viii. 8. Erasmus' rendering.]

abstain only, at a certain appointed time, from certain manner of meats; but he, which doth therefore refrain from the pleasures of the flesh, that thereby he may make it subject to the spirit, and do the works of faith and charity, which are acceptable in the sight of the Lord. If therefore thou dost desire to fast a true fast, eat, drink, and sleep, and take heed to thy body, that it wax not insolent; fast from all sin, eat not the meat of malice, taste not the juncats[3] of lust and pleasure, and be not set on fire with the wine of wantonness. Fast from evil deeds, abstain from evil words, and refrain thyself from naughty thoughts. For Basil also saith: "True fasting consisteth in freeness from vices, in continency of tongue, in suppressing of anger, in cutting off concupiscence, backbiting, lying, and perjury[4]," &c. But even as the good works themselves, which are done by faith, do not merit the kingdom of heaven (for that glory is due to the merit of Christ alone); even so fasting, which is an aid and help to good works, doth not meritoriously deserve the kingdom of God.

But now I see a doubtful disputation arise among the most divines of this our age, touching the time and manner of fastings, and also of the choice of meats. Some there are which affirm and uphold the fasts of Lent[5], and embering days, and such other, to be the fasts which God hath appointed. There are that say, thou hast not fasted, if by any means thou taste any flesh: and there are which prescribe and appoint some certain hours to fast in. But I, for my part, see not any such doctrines to be taught us in the scriptures. For the Lord in the gospel kept not any of their devised fasts, when he fasted forty days; but did altogether abstain from all kinds of meat, even as Moses and Helias had also done: wherefore he by that deed of his did not give us any law to fast so. Moreover, the Lord in the gospel doth evidently teach, that the thing, which entereth in by the mouth, doth not defile the man, but that which issueth out from his heart[6].

Of the manner and time of fasting, and of the choice of meats.

[3 epulas, Lat.]

[4 ἀληθὴς νηστεία ἡ τοῦ κακοῦ ἀλλοτρίωσις, ἐγκράτεια γλώσσης, θυμοῦ ἐποχή, ἐπιθυμιῶν χωρισμός, καταλαλιᾶς, ψεύδους, ἐπιορκίας.—Basil. Hom. II. de Jejunio, T. II. p. 15. Paris. 1722.]

[5 stata jejunia quadragesimæ, quatuor temporum, Lat. See Bingham's Orig. Eccles. Lib. XXI. cap. 1. and cap. 2. § 1.]

[6 Matt. xv. 11, 18.]

" To the pure are all things pure[1]." And Paul saith : " I know, and am persuaded through the Lord Jesus Christ, that nothing is common of itself; but to him that thinketh that any thing is common, to him is it common." Again : " Let not him which eateth despise him which eateth not ; nor let him which eateth not judge him which eateth : for him that eateth the Lord hath taken[2]." Moreover, the place is evident, which the same Paul writeth in the fourth chapter of his first epistle to Timothy, where he affirmeth, that the forbidding of meats is a "doctrine of devils." Neither needeth any man here to tell us any whit of the Tatians and Encratites[3] ; for they did slander the good creatures of God. Paul speaketh of them who, although they do not utterly condemn meat and marriage, do yet notwithstanding forbid the use of meat.

Difference in fastings.

Furthermore, we do not read that any laws were ordained in that age which followed next after the preaching of the apostles, which did command and prescribe any time and order of fasting, or choice of meats. I will rehearse unto you, dearly beloved, the words of Irenæus the martyr, which in the Ecclesiastical History of Eusebius are to be found word for word, as they are here set down: " The controversy is not only touching Easter-day, but also touching the manner of fasting. For some do think that the fast ought to be kept but one day only, other two, other more, and some whole forty days ; so that, counting the hours of the night and day, they make a day. Which difference of observing the times is not now first of all in our age begun, but was brought in a great while ago (as I suppose) of them, which did not simply keep that which was taught from the beginning, but, either by negligence or unskilfulness, fell afterward into a worse use and custom. And yet notwithstanding, all these, though they jarred in the observation of times, were nevertheless and are

[1 Titus i. 15.]
[2 Rom. xiv. 14, 3.]
[3 The Tatiani or Tatianists, who were also called Encratitæ, or *abstainers*, were the followers of Tatian in the second century of the Christian era. They held *matter* to be the source of all evil, and therefore discarded all the external comforts and conveniences of life, and fasted rigorously.—Mosheim. Eccles. Hist. Book i. Cent. ii. part 2. chap. 5. § 9. Vol. i. p. 195. ed. Soames. See also Early Writings of Hooper, Parker Soc. ed. p. 375.]

agreeable with us; neither hath the discord about fasting broke our concord in faith⁴." Thus much Irenæus. Moreover, Socrates Constantinopolitanus in the ninth book and thirty-eighth chapter of his⁵ Tripartite History witnesseth, that about the year of our Lord 453, in the reign of Theodosius the younger, the same diversity was in the church, and setteth it down in these words following: "Furthermore, they have not the same kind of abstinence from meat. For some do altogether abstain from living creatures; some among living creatures do eat fish only; some with fish do feed on fowls also, saying, that they (as Moses saith) have their substance of water; some are known to abstain from herbs and eggs; some do feed of dry bread only; some not so much as that: some, fasting nine hours, do then without difference use any kind of meat: and innumerable customs are found among sundry men." Now the very same Socrates, shewing his opinion upon that diversity, doth say: "And for because no ancient writing is found touching this thing, I think that the apostles left it free to every man's judgment, that every one may work, not by fear or necessity, the thing that is good⁶." Thus far Socrates. The fasts of Christians, therefore, ought

The Latin copy hath caulis, which I turn herbs: it may also be taken for roots.

Fastings must be

[⁴ Οὐδὲ γὰρ μόνον περὶ τῆς ἡμέρας ἐστὶν ἡ ἀμφισβήτησις, ἀλλὰ καὶ περὶ τοῦ εἴδους αὐτοῦ τῆς νηστείας. Οἱ μὲν γὰρ οἴονται μίαν ἡμέραν δεῖν αὐτοὺς νηστεύειν, οἱ δὲ δύο, οἱ δὲ καὶ πλείονας· οἱ δὲ τεσσαράκοντα ὥρας ἡμερινάς τε καὶ νυκτερινὰς συμμετροῦσι τὴν ἡμέραν αὐτῶν. Καὶ τοιαύτη μὲν ποικιλία τῶν ἐπιτηρούντων οὐ νῦν ἐφ᾽ ἡμῶν γεγονυῖα, ἀλλὰ καὶ πολὺ πρότερον ἐπὶ τῶν πρὸ ἡμῶν, τῶν παρὰ τὸ ἀκριβές, ὡς εἰκὸς, κρατούντων, τὴν καθ᾽ ἁπλότητα καὶ ἰδιωτισμὸν συνήθειαν εἰς τὸ ᾽μετέπειτα πεποιηκότων. Καὶ οὐδὲν ἔλαττον πάντες οὗτοι εἰρήνευσάν τε, καὶ εἰρηνεύομεν πρὸς ἀλλήλους, καὶ ἡ διαφωνία τῆς νηστείας τὴν ὁμόνοιαν τῆς πίστεως συνίστησι.—Euseb. Histor. Eccles. Lib. v. cap. 24. ed. Burton.]

[⁵ Not *his*, but the history compiled from him and others.]

[⁶ Sed etiam ciborum abstinentiam non similem habent. Nam alii omnino ab animatis abstinent: alii ex animantibus pisces solummodo comedunt: quidam cum piscibus vescuntur et volatilibus, dicentes hæc secundum Mosen ex aqua habere substantiam: alii vero etiam caulibus et ovis abstinere noscuntur: quidam sicco tantummodo pane vescuntur: alii neque hoc. Alii, usque ad nonam jejunantes horam, sine discretione ciborum reficiuntur. Et innumeræ consuetudines apud diversos reperiuntur. Et quia nulla lectio de hoc invenitur antiqua, puto apostolos singulorum hoc reliquisse sententiæ, ut unusquisque operetur non timore, non necessitate, quod bonum est.—Hist. Tripart. ap. Cassiodori Opp. Lib. ix. cap 38. Tom. v. p. 348. Rotomag. 1679.]

[BULLINGER.]

28

free, and not
bound to
laws. to be free, and not bound to laws. Apollinus, a certain ancient and ecclesiastical writer, disputing against Montanus, the heretic, saith : " This is he which taught that marriages are undone, and which first of all hath appointed laws for men to fast by [1]."

And verily, to go about to set down to all men and nations one manner of fasting in one appointed time, one prescribed order and choice of meat, is a mere folly, and a brain-sick kind of madness. For, according to the choice of air, so are men's bodies of sundry temperatures, and one kind of meat doth not stir men of sundry complexions to one kind of affection. The most godly way, therefore, and profitable order for the church is, that all pastors in every congregation should teach sobriety, temperancy, and the true fast indeed: not presuming to prescribe any laws for the choice of meats or times, but leaving that free to every man and nation, who undoubtedly will have an especial eye to temper themselves from the things by which they perceive that their health [2] will be endangered ; but most of all in the time when the flesh beginneth to wax over wanton, or when some great peril hangeth over their head. For the time of fasting is not prorogued till an appointed number of years or days be expired, but till the looseness or wantonness of the flesh, temptations, or motions, be utterly bridled. Fastings being so ordered, as they be the exercises of godliness, obtain great praise indeed in the church of the Lord.

The sum of
the seventh
precept or
command-
ment. Thus much hitherto touching fasting. Now, to shut up this seventh precept, I say it forbiddeth all intemperance, it commandeth holiness, and the clean and lawful use of all the members of the whole body. And therefore in this short precept there is contained a good part of the doctrine of Christ and his apostles. For Paul to the Thessalonians saith : " We beseech you, brethren, and exhort you by the Lord Jesus, that ye increase more and more, as ye have received of us how ye ought to walk, and to please God. For ye know

[1 Auctor Euseb. Ecclesiast. Hist. Lib. v. cap. 18, Lat. Οὖτός ἐστιν ὁ διδάξας λύσεις γάμων, ὁ νηστείας νομοθετήσας.—Euseb. Hist. Eccles. Lib. v. cap. 18. ed. Burton. The writer is *Apollonius.*—Routh, Reliq. Sacr. Tom. I. p. 466. Oxon. 1846. See also Calvin. Comment. in I. Ep. ad Tim. cap. IV. v. 3. Tom. VII. p. 455. ed. Amst.]

[2 Suæ integritati, Lat.]

what commandments we gave you by the Lord[3] Jesus. For this is the will of God, even your holiness; that ye should abstain from fornication; that every one of you should know how to possess his vessel[4] in holiness and honour; not in the lust of concupiscence, as the Gentiles, which knew not God. God is a revenger of all such, as we have forewarned you and testified. For God hath not called us unto uncleanness, but unto holiness[5]." And straightway after again: "The God of peace sanctify you throughout, that your whole spirit, and soul, and body, may be preserved blameless in the coming of our Lord Jesus Christ[6]."

I have again, my brethren, passed beyond the appointed time of an ordinary sermon, staying you longer than I am wont to do. Pardon this fault; for, I hope, I have not troubled you, almost two whole hours, without profiting you any whit at all. Make your prayers now, and depart in peace. By the help and will of God I will, within these few days, add the rest of the ten commandments. The grace of our Lord and Saviour Jesus Christ be with you all. Amen.

[3 Dominum nostrum, Lat. our Lord.]

[4 suum inquam corpus, Lat. omitted by the translator:—I mean, his body.]

[5 1 Thess. iv. 1—7. immunditiæ causa, Lat. Erasmus' rendering.]

[6 1 Thess. v. 23. The rendering in Cranmer's Bible is more agreeable with Bullinger's text: viz. "So that in nothing ye may be blamed in the coming of our Lord Jesus Christ."]

ERRATA.

PAGE	NOTE	LINE	FOR	READ
10	2	1	*hæc*	*hanc*
138	2	8	*regis*	*regio*
—	—	12	*lationis*	*latronis*
202	1	2	*ine*	*sine*

ADDENDA.

15 note 7 line 8 παθόντα,

—   —   12 ἢ τρεπτόν,

29 line 9 " sat at the right hand of God," should have been noted as an interpolation of the Translator's.

53   13 of the Saviour : ab ipso Salvatore, Lat.

54   33 Mark,

64   21 dele², and insert [Matt. xv. 9.]

83 note 5 The definition is taken from Budæi Comment. Ling. Græc. p. 103.

91   3 cf. Tertull. adv. Praxean. cap. 10. Tom. II. p. 161. ed. Semler. Hal. Mag. 1828, which passage, no doubt, Bullinger had here in his mind, as he has referred to it also in his Exposit. Epist. ad Roman. iv. 20, 21. p. 47. Tigur. 1537.

112 line 32 So in his Expos. Epist. ad Rom. iii. 26. p. 35, Bullinger writes : Hactenus exposuit (Paulus) fidem, videlicet in Christum, id est, ipsum Christum Jesum, Dei filium, cui fidimus, veram esse pii hominis justitiam.

123 note 4 line 13. Of this treatise Bullinger himself says in his Comment. in Lucam. Lib. i. p. 17. Tigur. 1546.—quæ S. Cyprianus, *sive is Ruffinus est,* scripsit.

129 line 22 cf. Augustine's Enarrat. in Psalm. cit.

154   9 See Pearson on the Creed. Art. 7. p. 455. Vol. i. and Vol. ii. p. 365. Oxf. 1820.

158   23 Symbolum secundo conditum disertis verbis in hunc modum confitendum docet : πιστεύω εἰς τὸ Πνεῦμα τὸ ἅγιον τὸ Κύριον, τὸ λαλῆσαν διὰ τῶν προφητῶν εἰς μίαν καθολικὴν καὶ ἀποστολικὴν ἐκκλησίαν, hoc est, Credo in Spiritum sanctum Dominum, qui loquutus est per prophetas in unam catholicam et apostolicam ecclesiam. Audis unum atque eundem esse Spiritum, qui per prophetas loquator in unam generalem ecclesiam, olim quidem a prophetis, nunc ab apostolis, verbo veritatis, qui Sancti Spiritus instinctus est, collectam. Bullingeri Comment. in 1 Epist. Petri. cap. i. p. 11.

195   36 See Erasmi Adag. Chili. p. 500, conscientia mille testes.

212 note 2 See an anecdote of Celio Secundo Curio in M'Crie's Hist. of Reform. in Italy, p. 102. Lond. 1827.

320 line 1 cf. Bp. Hooper's Early Writ. ed. Park. Soc. p. 78.

350   5 These were the Anabaptists' objections. See Bullinger. adv. Anabapt. Lib. v. cap. 4.

CONTENTS.

ERRATA AND ADDENDA.

IN VOLUME I.

Advertisement, p. viii. line 27, for *Œcolampadius* read *Zuingle*.

Page 2. In the Fac-Simile Title-page the N. B. should have been rather: "This triple table is in the editions of 1577 and 1584 *prefixed*, but in that of 1587 *affixed*, to the Decades."

 60, note 1, substitute: "Apostles, edd. 1577 and 1587. The reading *Apostle* is in ed. 1584. Apostoli, Lat."

 83, note 8. Bullinger's quotation here seems to have been from Erasmus, Opp. Tom. v. coll. 1078, 9. Lugd. Bat. 1704.

 82, note 3,⎫
 99, — 11,⎬ for "1587" read "edd. 1584 and 1587."
 110, —   2,⎪
 421, —   7,⎭

 152, —   1, for "in ed. 1577" read "in edd. 1577, 1584, and 1587."

IN VOLUME II.

Page 30, note 2, after "wanting in"⎫
 80, — 2, — "but in"⎬ add "1584 and."
 142, — 1, — "ed."⎪
 199, — 5, —   —⎭

 41, — 3, read "page 33."

 53, — 4, — "page 30."

 59, line 18, for *faint* read *feint*.

 69, — 7, dele comma at "what"

 73, — 17, —— at "it"

 76, — 22, —— at "enough"

 95, — 18, dele 4 at "Christ," and add it at "present," l. 20.

 ib. note 4, for *præsentissimum* read *præsentissimam*.

 96, line 18, dele comma at "Jesus"

 110, note 3, read "page 79"

 116, — 1, for xi. read xix. and after "fol. 8, 9" add "14, &c."

 135, line 33, for "be" read "he"

 145, — 1,⎱ at "temple" add a colon.
 150, — 32,⎰

 153, note 8, add "See above page 45, note 7."

 163, line 3, for "holy" read "only."

 ib. dele note 6.

 164, note 2, read "page 179."

 173, — 5, — "page 141."

 179, — 6, — "page 172."

 197, — 5, — "page 165, note 9."

 234, line 21, dele comma at "done"

 248, — 19, for "after flesh" read "after the flesh."

 ib. — 20, after "called" add a comma.

 ib. note 4, read "page 256, note 5."

Page 257, line 36, read "page 248."
    265, note 11, — "page 165."
    281, — 8, add "See Vol. i. page 286, note 3."
    290, line 6, for "death ?" read "death."
    294, — 5, for "worshsip" read "worship."
    304, — 5, at "afflictions" add a comma.
    312, — 8, at "such" add note : "great, ed. 1577."
    313, note 9, read "page 304, note 5."
    341, — 2, — "page 333, note 7."

FIFTY SERMONS

DIVIDED INTO

FIVE DECADES.

THE THIRDE AND

fourth decade of sermons,

WRITTEN TO THE

MOST RENOVMED KING

of England, Edward the sixt, by

Henrie Bullinger.

The second Tome.

IESVS.

This is my beloued sonne, in whom I am
well pleased. Heare him. *Matth.* 17.

TO THE MOST RENOWNED

PRINCE EDWARD THE SIXTH,

KING OF ENGLAND AND FRANCE, LORD OF IRELAND,
PRINCE OF WALES AND CORNWALL, DEFENDER
OF THE CHRISTIAN FAITH[1].

GRACE AND PEACE FROM GOD THE FATHER THROUGH
OUR LORD JESUS CHRIST.

YOUR Majesty would, I know right well, most royal king,
admit a stranger to talk with your grace, if any new guest
should come and promise, that he would briefly out of the
sentences and judgments of the wisest men declare the very
truest causes of the felicity and unhappy state of every king
and kingdom : and therefore I hope that I shall not be excluded from the speech of your Majesty, because I do assuredly promise briefly to lay down the very causes of the
felicity and lamentable calamities of kings and their kingdoms
so clearly and evidently, that the hearer shall not need to
trouble himself with over-busy diligence to seek out my
meaning, but only to give attentive ear to that which is
spoken.   For, by the help of God, I will make this treatise
not to be perceived only by the wit and true judgment of
learned heads, but also to be seen as it were with the eyes,
and handled as it were with the hands, of very idiots[2] and
unlearned hearers ; and that too, not out of the doubtful
decrees and devices of men, but out of the assured word of
the most true God.   Even the wisest men do very often
deceive us with their counsels, and greatly endamage the followers thereof: but God, which is the Light and eternal
Wisdom, cannot any time either err, or conceive any false
opinions or repugning counsels ; much less teach others any-

[1 Bishop Hooper urged Bullinger to dedicate one of his writings
to King Edward at this time.   Original Letters, Parker Soc. pp.
73, 78.   Interesting particulars concerning the conveyance, presentation, and reception in England of this Volume occur, in chronological
order, in the same Original Letters, as follows: pp. 662, 560, 665, 269,
88.   See also Strype, Eccles. Mem. Book I. chap. 30, Vol. II. part 1,
p. 390, Oxf. 1822.]

[2 Idiots: uneducated persons.   See Vol. I. p. 71, n. 3.]

thing but truth, or seduce any man out of the right way. The Wisdom of the Father doth in the holy gospel cry out and say: "I am the light of the world: he that followeth me shall not walk in darkness, but shall have the light of life." This eternal wisdom of God, as it doth not disorderly wrap things up together and make them intricate, but layeth down in order and teacheth them plainly; so it doth not only minister wholesome counsels, but bringeth them to the effect which they wish that obey her. Oftentimes, verily, men do give good counsels, that are not unwholesome; but yet in their counsels that is altogether omitted, which should have been first and especially mentioned.

All the wise men almost of the world have been of opinion, that kings and kingdoms should be most happy, if the king of the country be a wise man; if he have many wise, aged, faithful, and skilful counsellors; if his captains be valiant, warlike, and fortunate in battle; if he abound with substance; if his kingdom be on every side surely fortified; and lastly, if his people be of one mind and obedient. All this I confess is truly, rightly, and very wisely spoken: but yet there is another singular and most excellent thing, which is not here reckoned among these necessaries, without which no true felicity can be attained, nor, being once gotten, can safely be kept; when as contrarily, where that one thing is present, all those other necessaries do of their own[1] accord fall unto men, as they themselves can best wish or devise. The Lord our God therefore, who is the only giver of wise and perfect counsels, doth far more briefly and better shut up all shortly, and say in the gospel: "But seek ye first rather the kingdom of God, and the righteousness thereof, and all these things shall easily be given[2] unto you." Again, "Blessed are the eyes which see that ye see: for I say unto you, that many kings and prophets have wished to see the things that ye see, and to hear the things that ye hear, and have neither heard nor seen them." And again, "Nay rather, blessed are they that hear the word of God, and keep it." And this thing[3] above all other is very necessary: "Mary hath chosen the good part, which shall not be taken from her." Having my warrant therefore out of the word of God, I

[John viii. 12.]

Matt. vi.

Luke x.

Luke xi.

[Luke x. 42.]

From whence issueth the

[1 *own* wanting in 1587.]   [2 adjicientur, Lat.]
[3 this one thing, 1577.]

dare boldly avow, that those kings shall flourish and be in ^{felicity or calamity of} happy case, which wholly give and submit themselves and their ^{kings and kingdoms.} kingdoms to Jesus Christ, the only-begotten Son of God, being King of kings, and Lord of lords; acknowledging him to be the mightiest prince and monarch of all, and themselves his vassals, subjects, and servants: which, finally, do not follow in all their affairs their own mind and judgment, the laws of men that are contrary to God's commandments, or the good intents of mortal men; but do both themselves follow the very laws of the mightiest king and monarch[4], and also cause them to be followed throughout all their kingdom, reforming both themselves and all theirs at and by the rule of God's holy word. For in so doing the kingdom shall flourish in peace and tranquillity, and the kings thereof shall be most wealthy, victorious, long-lived, and happy. For thus speaketh the mouth of the Lord, which cannot possibly lie: "When the king sitteth upon the seat of his kingdom, ^{Deut. xvii.} he shall take the book of the law of God, that he may read in it all the days of his life, that he may do it, and not decline from it either to the right hand or to the left; but that he may prolong the days in his kingdom both of his own life and of his children." And again, "Let not the ^{Josh. i.} book of this law depart out of thy mouth," (Josue, or thou, whatsoever thou art that hast a kingdom), "but occupy thy mind therein day and night, that thou mayest observe and do according to all that is written therein: for then shalt thou make thy way prosperous, and then shalt thou be happy." It is assuredly true, therefore, confirmed by the testimony of the most true God, and in express words pronounced, that the prosperity of kings and kingdoms consisteth in true faith, diligent hearing, and faithful obeying the word or law of God: whereas their calamity and utter overthrow doth follow the contrary.

This will I make, as my promise is, in this annexed demonstration, both evident to the eyes, and as it were palpable to the very hands, by the examples of most mighty kings, not taken out of Herodotus or any profane author, but out of the infallible history of the most sacred scriptures. Saul, the first ^{Saul.} king of Israel, was both most fortunate and victorious, so long as he did in all things follow the word of God: but when he

[4 æterni, Lat. *eternal* monarch, ed. 1577.]

once gave place to his own good intents and meaning, being utterly forsaken of the Lord, he heareth Samuel say to his face : "Thou hast refused and cast off the word of the Lord ; therefore hath God also cast thee away, that thou shalt not be king of Israel." I will not here stand over largely to declare the miseries and calamities, wherein he was wrapped from that time forward. For as he himself was horribly haunted and vexed with the evil spirit, so did he not cease to vex and torment his people and kingdom, until he had brought them all into extreme danger, where he and some of his were slain and put to the worst by the heathen, their enemies, leaving nothing behind him but a perpetual shame and endless ignominy. Next after Saul doth David succeed in the seat and kingdom, who without all controversy was the most happiest of all other kings and princes. But what store he did set by the word of the Lord, it is evident to be seen by many notable acts of his, and especially in that alphabetical psalm, which in order and number is the hundredth and nineteenth[1] : for therein he setteth forth the praise of God's word, the wholesome virtue whereof he doth at large wonderfully expound, in teaching what great desire and zeal we ought to have thereto. For he was schooled and had learned before, by private mishaps and shameful deeds, and lastly, by the unhappy sedition of his graceless son Absolon, what an evil it is to decline from the word of the Lord. Salomon, the son of David, the wisest and most commended king of all the world, did so long enjoy prosperity and praise at the mouth of the Lord, as he did not neglect with reverence to obey his word. But when once he had transgressed the Lord's commandment, straightway the Lord did say unto him : " Forasmuch as this is done of thee, and that thou hast not kept mine ordinances and my statutes, which I commanded thee, I will rend thy kingdom from thee, and will give it to thy servant." And now mark, that, according to that saying, immediately after Salomon's death the kingdom was rent into two parts, and

1 Sam. xiii. xiv. xv. &c.

Solomon. 1 Kings iv. & xi.

[1 This Psalm is divided (probably for the advantage of memory), according to the number of letters which compose the Hebrew Alphabet, into twenty-two portions, of eight verses each ; and not only every portion, but every verse of that portion, begins with the letter appropriated to it. See Bp Horne, Comment. on Psalms, Argum. to Psalm cxix.]

that ten tribes followed Jeroboam, the servant of Salomon; two tribes clave still to Roboam, Salomon's son. He, for neglecting the word of the Lord, and following after strange gods, is overwhelmed with an infinite number of woful miseries: for the scripture testifieth, that the Egyptians came up against Hierusalem, and did destroy the city, palace, and temple of the Lord.

Roboam.
2 Chron. xii.

Abia, the son of Roboam, overcame the host of Israel, and bare away a triumphant victory, when he had wounded and slain five hundred thousand men of the ten tribes of Israel: and of this so great a victory no other cause is mentioned, but because he believed the word of the Lord. Next after Abia did his son Asa, a renowned and most puissant king, reign in his stead; of whom the holy scripture testifieth, that he abolished all superstition, and did restore sincere religion according to the word of God: whereby he obtained a most flourishing kingdom in peace and quietness by the space of forty years. Again, of Josaphat, Asa his son, we read: "The Lord was with Josaphat, because he walked in the former ways of his father David, and sought not Baalim, but sought the God of his father, and walked in his commandment." And therefore for his prince-like wealth and famous victories he was renowned through all the world. But to his son Joram, who forsook the word of God, Helias the prophet said: " Because thou hast not walked in the ways of Josaphat thy father, and in the ways of king Asa, but hast walked the ways of the kings of Israel; behold, with a great plague will the Lord smite thy folk, thy children, thy wives, and all thy goods; and thou shalt suffer great pain, even a disease of the bowels, until thy bowels[2] fall out." And whatsoever the Lord threatened to bring upon him by the mouth of the prophet, that did the unhappy king feel with unspeakable torments to his great reproaches: being made an example of wretchedness and misery, which doth light on all the pates of them that do forsake the word of God. Neither was the hap of Ochosias[3], son to king Joram and Athalia, in any point better: for at the commandment of Jehu he was stabbed in, and slain wretchedly; because he chose rather to follow the laws and rites of the kings of Israel than the very

Abia.
2 Chron. xiii.

Asa.
2 Chron. xiv.

Josaphat.
2 Chron. xvii.

Joram.
2 Chron. xxi.

Ochosias.
2 Kings ix.

[2 Substituted for another word used by the translator.]
[3 Ahaziah.]

Joas.
2 Chron.
xxiii. xxiv.

true laws of the Lord his God. Moreover Joas, a child yet but seven years old, being by the labour, faith, and diligence of the faithful priest Joiada restored to and settled in the place of his father, who was slain before him, reigned, after the wicked Athalia was put to death, most happily and in a prosperous state, so long as Joiada the priest did live[1]. But when the high priest was once departed out of this world unto the Lord, the king, being immediately seduced by the malice and wiliness of his wicked counsellors, left off to follow the word of the Lord : and as he ceased to follow the Lord, so did felicity and glory forsake to follow him. For the Syrians, coming on with a very small power of armed men, do destroy and put to flight an infinite host of Jewish people ; they put to the sword all Joas his counsellors, and make a spoil of all his kingdom. And Joas, for rejecting the Lord, deserved with excessive grief first to behold this misery, then to pine away with a long consuming sickness, and lastly, upon his bed, to have his throat cruelly cut of his own household servants.

Amasias.
2 Chron. xxv.

Amasias[2], the son of Joas, is renowned for a famous victory which he obtained upon the Idumites, for no other cause but for obeying the word of the Lord. But afterward, when he began to rebel against God and his prophets, he is in battle vanquished by Joas, king of Israel; by whom when he was spoiled, and compelled to see the overthrow of a great part of the walls of Hierusalem, he was himself at the last by conspirators entrapped, and miserably murdered. Next after him suc-

Osias.
2 Chron. xxvi.

ceeded his son Osias[3], who also, as well as the father, enjoyed a singular felicity and most happy life, so long as he gainsaid not the mouth of God : but when he would usurp and take upon him that office, which God had properly appointed to the Levites alone, directly opposing himself against the word of the Lord, he was stricken with a leprosy, and for his uncleanness was compelled severally[4] to dwell aloof in banishment from the company of men, even until his last and dying day.

Jotham.
2 Chron
xxvii.

Jotham also, the son of Osias, is reported to have been wealthy and victorious in his wars : the cause of this felicity

[1] Hujus enim suggestione et vigilantia ad normam verbi Domini in omnibus respexit rex, Lat. omitted by the translator. For by his instructions and watchful superintendence the king had regard in all things to the rule of the Lord's word.]

[2] Amaziah.]   [3] Uzziah.]   [4] severally, apart.]

the scripture doth briefly add, and say : " Jotham became mighty, because he directed his ways before the Lord his God." But contrarily, Achaz, the son of Jotham, as he was of all Achaz. 2 Chron. the Jewish kings almost the wickedest, so was he in his life xxviii. the most unfortunate. For insomuch as he forsook the law of the Lord his God, the Lord delivered both him and his people first into the hands of the king of Syrians, and after-ward into the hands of the Israelites, who in one day slew one hundred and twenty thousand Jews, and took captive away with them two hundred thousand women and children. So Achaz himself, and all that were his, by feeling had proof of all kind of calamities, being made an example to terrify all other that do gainsay the word of God.

The good and godly king Ezechias succeeded his ungodly Hezechiah. 2 Kings xviii. father in the seat and kingdom. Of him we have this testimony in the scripture : " He did that which was right in the sight of the Lord, according to all that his father David did. He put away the high places, and brake the images, and cut down the groves, and all-to[5] brake the brasen serpent which Moses had made : for unto those days the children of Israel burnt sacrifice to it. He trusted in the Lord God of Israel. For he clave to the Lord, and departed not from him, but kept his commandments, which the Lord commanded Moses." And now, let us hear what followed upon this obedience and faith of his. The scripture goeth forward, and saith : " And the Lord was with him, so that he prospered in all things that he took in hand." While he did reign, the most ancient and puissant monarchy of the Assyrians was broken and dimin-ished : for when Senacherib, king of Assyria, besieged the city of Jerusalem, the angel of the Lord in one night slew in the Assyrian camp one hundred fourscore and five thousand soldiers. And the king of Babylon also did very honourably by his ambassadors send prince-like gifts unto Ezechias, desiring earnestly his amity and friendship : for the glory of that most godly king was blown abroad, and known in all the world. Again, when his son Manasses, a very wicked man, did not Manasses. 2 Kings xxi. tread the path and express the deeds of his most holy father, but, being made king in the twelfth year of his age, did of purpose cross the word of God, and brought in again all the superstition which his father had abolished, he was taken

[5 all-to : entirely.]

captive and carried away to Babylon: and although, by the
goodness and mercy of God, he was restored to his seat again,
yet, when he died, he left a maimed and a troublesome kingdom
unto his son Ammon; who also, for his rebelling against the
word of God, as a most unfortunate man reigned but two years
only, and was at the last wretchedly slain by his own household servants.

Ammon.
2 Kings xxi.

In place of his murdered father was his son Josias settled
in the kingdom, being, when he was crowned, a child but
eight years old. Of all the kings of Juda he was the flower
and especial crown. He reigned quietly and in all points
most happily by the space of one and thirty years. Now
the scripture, which cannot lie, doth paint out to our eyes the
faith and obedience which he did devoutly shew to the word
of God, for which that felicity did accompany his kingdom.
He was nothing moved with the admonitions of his father
Ammon's counsellors; but so soon as he had heard the words
of the law read out of the book, which Helkia the high priest
found in the temple at Hierusalem, he straightway committed
himself wholly to God and his word. Neither stayed he to
look for the minds and reformations of other kings and kingdoms; but, quickly forecasting the best for his people, he began
to reform the corrupted religion, which he did especially in
the eighteenth year of his age. And in that reformation he
had a regard always to follow the meaning of the holy scripture alone, and not to give ear to the deeds of his predecessors,
to the prescribed order of long continuance, nor to the common
voices of the greatest multitude. For he assembled his people
together, before whom he laid open the book of God's law,
and appointed all things to be ordained according to the rule
of his written word. And thereupon it cometh which we find
written, that he spared not the ancient temples and long accustomed rites, which Solomon and Jeroboam had erected and
ordained against the word of God. To be short, this king
Josias pulled down, and overthrew, whatsoever was set up in
the church or kingdom of Juda against the word of God. And
lest, peradventure, any one should cavil and say, that he was
over hardy and too rough in his dealings, the scripture giveth
this testimony of him, and saith: "Like unto him was there
no king before him, which turned to the Lord with all his
heart, with all his soul, and all his might, according to all the

Josias.
2 Kings xxii.

law of Moses: neither after him arose there any such as he." Whereas we read therefore, that this so commended and most fortunate king was overcome and slain in a foughten battle, that death of his is to be counted a part of his felicity, and not of his misery. For the Lord himself said to Josias: "I will gather thee unto thy fathers, and in peace shalt thou be buried, that thine eyes may not see all the evil which I will bring upon this place." For there is no greater argument, that the people and very princes of the kingdom under that most holy king were mere hypocrites and idolaters, than for because, next and immediately after his death, both his sons and peers, rejecting the word of God, did bring in again all superstition and blasphemous wickedness. Whereupon we read that for the whole twenty-two years, wherein the kings of Juda did reign after the death of Josias, there was no peace or quietness in Hierusalem, but perpetual seditions and most bloody murders. Next after Josias reigned his son Joachas: but within three months after he was taken, bound, and led captive away into the land of Egypt. After the leading away of Joachas, his brother Joachim ware the crown: who in the eleventh year of his reign, being bound in chains, was slain by Nabuchodonoser, and lastly (as Jeremy saith) was buried in the sepulchre of an ass[1]. In Joachim's stead was his son Jechonias set up; but, about three months after, he with his princes and substance was taken captive and led away to Babylon. After him the kingdom was given to Zedechias, the son of Josias: but, because he would not obey the word of God preached by the prophet Jeremy, he loseth both his life and kingdom in the eleventh year of his reign: in whose time also the temple is set of fire, Hierusalem[2] is sacked, and the people slain for the most part, or led away captive. Thus much hitherto touching the kings of Juda. For in Zedechias both the kingdom and majesty or dignity thereof did fail and make an end.

To these if we add the ends and destinies of the kings of Israel, we shall again be compelled to confess, that all felicity of kings and kingdoms do consist in hearing and following the word of God; and that contrarily, calamities and miseries do rise by the contempt and neglecting of the same. For Jero-

[2 Kings xxii. 18—20.]

Joachas. Joachim. Jechonias & Zedechias. 2 Kings xxiii. xxiv. xxv.

[Jer. xxii. 18, 19.]

The kings of Israel.

[1 sepultura asini, Lat.]

[2 sedes regni vetustissima, Lat. omitted: the most ancient seat of the kingdom.]

boam, the first king of the separated Israelites, letting pass the word of God, did ordain new rites to worship the Lord by, and erected new temples; but by so doing he overthrew [1 Kings xii. himself, his house, and all his kingdom. After him doth —xv.] Baasa succeed both in the kingdom and idolatrous religion, [1 Kings xv. which was the cause why he and his were utterly destroyed. 33, 34, and xvi. 1—14.] Then followeth Amri, the father of Achab; who, for augment-[1Kings xvi. 25—28.] ing idolatrous impiety, is horribly slain with all his family, so that not one of his escaped the revenging sword of God's anger and jealousy.   And for because Jehu was faithful and valiant in killing those tyrants, in dispatching Baal's priests, and rooting out of idolatrous superstition, the Lord doth promise, [2 Kings x. and say unto him : "Because thou hast zealously done that 30] which thou hast done, according to all that is right in my sight[1], therefore shall thy children, unto the fourth generation, sit on the seat of Israel."   And we read verily, that his sons and nephews were notable princes, which succeeded in the kingdom, even Joachas, Joas, Jeroboam the second of that [2 Kings xii name, and Zacharias.   The other kings, as Sellum, Manahe[2], —xiv.] Pekaiah, Peka, and Osee, had their kingdom altogether like to the kingdom of the son of Josias, to wit, in a seditious, trou-blesome, and a most miserable taking.   For they despised the [2 Kings xv. mouth of the Lord : therefore were they utterly cut off, and and xvii.] for the most part either slain, or carried away captive, by their enemies the Assyrians.   From the division of the people into two several kingdoms after the death of Solomon, there were in number nineteen kings of Israel, and eighteen of Juda. The kings of Israel altogether reigned about two hundred and seventy-two years, and they of Juda about three hundred and ninety-three[3].   Now by the space of so many years, in the most renowned and peculiar people of God, which was as it were a glass set before the eyes of all nations to view and behold themselves in, there might the truest causes of felicity and calamities of all kings and kingdoms in the whole world be so lively represented and perfectly painted, that there

[1 juxta omnia quæ fuerunt in corde meo, Lat.]
[2 Manahem, Lat.]
[3 Strictly speaking, the number of the kings of Judah was 19,—not including Athaliah's usurpation. According to Usher, the kingdom of Judah lasted 388 years; and the kingdom of Israel 254 years. Annal. Vet. Test.]

should be no need to fetch from elsewhere a more plain and evident demonstration of the same.

And yet for all that, we are not without other foreign Foreign kings. examples, whereby to prove it. For the Pharaos of Egypt were the destruction both to themselves and also to their[4] kingdom, by[5] their stubborn rebellion against God's word. Again, Darius Priscus[6] and the great Nabuchodonosor enjoyed no small felicity, because they despised not the counsels of Daniel. Balthasar, king of Babylon, a despiteful contemner of God and his word, is in one night destroyed with all his power : Babylon, the most ancient and famous city of the world, is taken, set on fire, sacked, and overthrown, and the kingdom translated to the Medes and Persians. [Dan. iv—vi.] Neither were the kings of Persia unfortunate at all, I mean, Cyrus, and Darius, otherwise called Artaxerxes[7]; because Kings which they favoured the word of God, and did promote his people favoured God's word, and true religion. But on the other side we read that An- and kings tiochus, surnamed[8] Epiphanes, was most unfortunate; who, secuted the as it were, making war with God himself, did most wickedly burn and make away the books of holy scripture[9]. Furthermore, we have as great store of examples, also, even out of those histories which followed immediately the time of Christ his ascension. For so many Roman emperors, kings, and princes as persecuted the preaching of the Gospel and Church of our Lord Jesus Christ, and advanced idolatry and superstitious blasphemy, so many, I say, did die a foul and shameful death. Of this are Eusebius and Orosius, renowned historiographers, assured witnesses[10]. Again, St Augustine, Lib. v. *de Civit. Dei*, affirmeth, that incredible victories, very great glory, and most absolute felicity hath been given by God unto those kings, which have in faith sincerely embraced

[4 vetustissimum, Lat.; omitted by the translator :—most ancient.]

[5 sola, Lat.; omitted by the translator: by nothing but by their rebellion.]

[6 i. e., Darius the Mede, or Cyaxares the second, uncle of Cyrus. Bulling. in Apocalyps. Serm. LXXI. See also Vol. I. p. 51. n. 3.]

[7 See Vol. I. p. 318, note 1.]

[8 licet cognominatus, Lat; although surnamed.]

[9 1 Maccab. i. 20—57. Prideaux's Connection, Vol. II. pp. 172—188, ed. Mc Caul. Lond. 1845.]

[10 Euseb. Hist. Eccles. Lib. VIII. cap. 16. Oros. adv. Pagan. Hist. Lib. VII. capp. 7, 22, &c.]

Christ their Lord, and utterly subverted idolatry and superstitious blasphemy[1]. It is evident therefore, that felicity
cometh by good-will and obedience to the word of God, and
that all kings and kingdoms shall be unhappy, which forsake
the word of God, and turn themselves to men's inventions.
And this I have, I trust, declared hitherto so plainly, that
the hearers may seem not only to understand, but also to
see before their eyes, and as it were to feel with their hands,
the pith and material substance of this whole treatise.

But whereunto doth all this tend? That your royal Majesty, forsooth, may undoubtingly know, and be assuredly
persuaded, that true felicity is gotten and retained by faithful
study in the word of God: to wit, if you submit yourself
altogether and your whole kingdom to Christ, the chief and
highest prince; if, throughout your whole realm, you dispose
and order religion, and all matters of justice, according to
the rule of God's holy word; if you decline not one hair's
breadth from that rule, but study to advance the kingdom
of Christ, and go on (as hitherto you have happily begun)
to subvert and tread under foot the usurped power of that
tyrannical antichrist. Not that your Majesty needeth any
whit at all mine admonitions or instructions: for you have
undoubtedly that heavenly teacher in your mind (I mean,
the Holy Ghost[2]), which inspireth you with the very true
doctrine of sincere and true religion. Your Majesty hath the
sacred Bible, the holiest book of all books, wherein, as in a
perfect rule, the whole matter of piety and our true salvation
is absolutely contained and plainly set down[3]. Your Majesty
hath noble men, and many counsellors, belonging to your kingdom, faithful, valiant, and skilful heads both in the law of God
and men, who for their wisdom and love that they bear to the
sincere truth are greatly commended among foreign nations.
And for that cause all the faithful do think and call your
Majesty most happy. But that happy king Ezechias, although

[1 Aug. de Civit. Dei, Lib. v. cap. 24. Quæ sit Christianorum im-
peratorum, et quam vera felicitas. See also Vol. I. p. 385, n. 3.]

[2 Not in the original Lat.]

[3 Habet doctos, sapientes, pios, fideles in regno doctores et pastores multos, Lat. omitted by the translator: (your majesty) hath in
your kingdom many learned, wise, pious, and faithful teachers and
pastors.]

he did especially use the help of those excellent men Esay and Micheas, did not despise faithful admonishers, even among the meanest sort of Levites: neither thought they, that in admonishing the king they lost and spent their labour in vain[4]. [2 Chron. xxx. 22.] I therefore, having good affiance in your Majesty's good and godly disposition, do verily hope, that this short discourse of mine, touching the true causes of the felicity and calamities of kings and kingdoms, shall have a profiting place[5] with you. Even I, which twelve years since did dedicate unto your father of famous memory, Henry the Eighth, a book touching the authority of the holy scripture, and the institution and function of bishops[6], against the pontifical chuffs[7] of the Romish superstition and tyranny ; and now by experience know, that that labour of mine brought forth no small fruit within the realm of England ; am now so bold again as to dedicate these my sermons unto your royal Majesty.

In these sermons I handle not the least and lowest points or places of Christian religion, the law, sin, grace, the Gospel, and repentance. Neither do I, as I think, handle them irreligiously. For I use to confer one scripture with another; than which there is no way better and safer to follow in the handling of matters touching our religion. And for because you are the true defender of the Christian faith, it cannot be but well[8] undoubtedly, to have Christian sermons come abroad under the defence of your Majesty's name. My mind was, according to mine ability and the measure of faith which is in me, to further the cause of true religion, which now beginneth to bud in England, to the great rejoicing of all good people. I have therefore written these sermons at large, and handled the matter so, that of one many more may be gotten : wherein the pastor's discretion shall easily

[4 oleum et operam perdere, Lat.]

[5 et locum et fructum habituram, Lat.]

[6 Interesting particulars of the reception of this book in England in 1538 occur in Original Letters, Parker Soc. pp. 611, 618. See also p. 313 for a testimony to the usefulness of Bullinger's writings in England.]

[7 antistites, Lat.; *chuff*, a word of no certain etymology, but signifying a rough uneducated clown of portly appearance. Toone's Glossary, in voc. Lond. 1834. See Shakspeare's Henr. IV. Part I. Sc. 2, Act 2, —" ye fat chuffs."]

[8 minime erit ingratum, Lat.]

discern what is most available and profitable for every several church. And the pastor's duty verily is rightly to mow[1] the word of truth, and aptly to give the fodder of life unto the Lord's flock. They will not think much[2], I hope, because in these sermons I do use the same matter, the same arguments, and the very same words, that other before me, both ancient and late writers, (whom I have judged to follow the scriptures), have used yer[3] now, or which I myself have elsewhere alleged in other books of mine own heretofore published. For as this doctrine, at all times, and in all points agreeable to itself, is safest to be followed, so hath it always been worthily praised of all good and godly people. If the Lord grant me life, leisure, and strength, I will shortly add the other eight sermons of the fourth decade, which are behind[4]. And all that I say here, I speak it still without all prejudice to the judgment of the right and true Church.

Our Lord Jesus, the King of kings, and Lord of lords,
lead you with the Spirit[5], and defend you to
the glory of his name, and safety of all
your realm. At Tigure, in the
month of March, the year
of our Lord,
1550.

Your Majesty's dutifully bounden
and daily Orator[6],

HENRY BULLINGER,

Minister of the Church at Tigure in Swicerland.

[1 secare, Lat. 2 Tim. ii. 15, Erasmus' version:—recta sectio (verbi veritatis) est, explicandi ratio ad ædificationem formata. Calv. Comment. in loc.]

[2 His non ingratum fuerit, Lat.]

[3 yer: ere, before. See Tyndale's Doctrinal Treat. Park. Soc. p. 51, note 1, and 455, note 1.]

[4 Bullinger fulfilled this promise in the following August. See Dedication prefixed to the Third Sermon of the fourth Decade.]

[5 Spiritu suo, Lat. ; his Spirit.]

[6 Orator: bead-man, or prayer-man. See note 3, Tyndale's Doctrinal Treatises. Parker Soc. ed. p. 331.]

THE

THIRD DECADE OF SERMONS,

WRITTEN BY

HENRY BULLINGER.

OF THE FOURTH PRECEPT OF THE SECOND TABLE,
WHICH IS IN ORDER THE EIGHTH OF THE TEN COM-
MANDMENTS, THOU SHALT NOT STEAL.
OF THE OWNING AND POSSESSING OF PROPER
GOODS, AND OF THE RIGHT AND LAW-
FUL GETTING OF THE SAME;
AGAINST SUNDRY KINDS
OF THEFT.

THE FIRST SERMON.

For the sustaining and nourishing of our lives and families, we men have need of earthly riches. Next therefore
after the commandments touching the preservation of man's
life, and the holy keeping of wedlock's knot, in this fourth
commandment a law is given for the true getting, possessing,
using and bestowing of wealth and worldly substance; to the
end that we should not get them by theft or evil means, that
we should not possess them unjustly, nor use or spend them
unlawfully. Justice requireth to use riches well, and to give to
every man that which is his: now, since the laws of God be the
laws of justice, they do very necessarily by way of commandment say, "Thou shalt not steal." These words, again, in The eighth
number are few; but in sense, of ample signification. For in ment.
this precept theft itself is utterly forbidden; all shifting
subtilties are flatly prohibited; deceit and guile is banished;
all cozening fetches are clean cut off; covetousness, idleness,
prodigality, or lavish spending, and all unjust dealing, is
herein debarred: moreover, charge is here given for maintaining of justice, and that especially in contracts and bargains.
Wonderful turmoils, verily, are raised up and begun among
men of this world about the getting, possessing, and spending
of temporal riches: it was expedient therefore, that God in

2

his law, which he ordaineth for the health, commodity, and peace of us men, should appoint a state, and prescribe an order, for earthly goods: as in this law he hath most excellently done. And that ye may the better understand it, I will at this present, by the help of God's Holy Spirit, discourse upon the proper owning and upright getting of worldly riches: in which treatise the whole consideration of theft in all his kinds shall be plainly declared.

Of the proper owning of substance.

For the proper owning and possessing of goods is not by this precept prohibited; but we are forbidden to get them unjustly, to possess them unlawfully, and to spend them wickedly: yea, by this commandment the proper owning of peculiar substance is lawfully ordained and firmly established. The Lord forbiddeth theft; therefore he ordaineth and confirmeth the proper owning of worldly riches. For what canst thou steal, if all things be common to all men? For thou hast stolen thine own, and not another man's, if thou takest from another that which he hath. But God forbiddeth theft; and therefore, by the making of this law, he confirmeth the proper possession of peculiar goods. But because there is no small number of that furious sect of Anabaptists, which deny this propriety of several[1] possessions[2], I will by some evident testimonies of scripture declare that it is both allowed and ratified of old. Of Abraham, who in the scripture is called the father of faith, Eliazer, his servant, saith: "God hath blessed my master marvellously, that he is become great; and hath given him sheep and oxen, silver and gold, menservants and maidservants, camels and asses[3]; and to his son hath he given all that he hath." Lo then, Abraham was wealthy, and did possess by the right of propriety all those things which God had given him; and he left them all, by the title of inheritance, as peculiar and proper goods unto his son Isaac. Isaac therefore and Jacob possessed their own and proper goods. Moreover God, by the hand of Moses, brought the Israelites, his people, into the land of promise, the grounds whereof he did by lot divide unto the tribes of

[Gen. xxiv. 35, 36.]

[1 several: separate, particular.]

[2 See Articles of Religion, Art. xxxviii. and Bullinger adversus Anabaptistas. Lib. i. cap. 9, p. 22, and Lib. iv. cap. 9, p. 143, Tigur. 1560.]

[3 camels and asses, not in original Lat. of Bullinger.]

Josue[4] his servant, appointing to every one a particular portion to possess; and did by laws provide that those in- [Levit. xxv. Numb. xxvii.] heritances should not be mingled and confounded together. In Salomon and the prophets there are very many precepts and sentences tending to this purpose.

But I know very well that these troublesome wranglers do make this objection, and say : That christian men are not bound to these proofs, that are fetched out of the old Testament[5]. And although I could confute that objection, and prove that those places out of the old Testament do in this case bind us to mark and follow them; yet will I rather, for shortness' sake, allege some proofs out of the scriptures of the new Testament, to stop their mouths withal. Our Lord Jesus Christ doth greatly commend in his disciples the works of mercy, which do consist in feeding the hungry, in giving drink to the thirsty, in clothing the naked, in visiting prisoners and those that be sick, and in harbouring strangers and banished men. He therefore granteth to his disciples a propriety and possession of peculiar goods, wherewith they may frankly do good unto other, and help the needy and the man in misery. But, the proper owning of several goods being once taken away, good deeds and alms must of necessity be utterly lacking : for if all things be common, then dost thou give nothing of that which is thine, but all that thou spendest is of the common riches. Yet Paul the apostle, in his epistle [1 Cor. xvi. 1—4.] to the Corinthians, biddeth every one to lay up alms by himself, which he might receive when he came to Corinth. He hath also commanded every one to bestow so much as he can [2 Cor. viii. 11—15, & ix. 6, 7.] find in his heart willingly to give, and according to the quantity that every one possesseth, not according to that which he possesseth not; and yet not to bestow it so, that they to whom it is given should have more than enough, and they which give should be pinched with penury and lack of things necessary. The same apostle saith : " We beseech you, brethren, that you study to be quiet, and to do your

---

[4 per Josue, Lat; by Joshua.]

[5 ... inter abominandos Anabaptistas eos statuimus, qui vetus testamentum rejiciunt, qui testimonia quæ ex illo adducuntur ad declaranda et confirmanda dogmata Christianæ fidei, aut ad errores et falsa dogmata refutanda, non recipiunt, &c.—Bullinger adv. Anabap. Lib. II. cap. 15, p. 74.]

own business, and to work with your own hands, as we commanded you: that you may walk honestly to them that be without, and that ye may have lack of nothing." I could, out of other his[1] epistles, allege many more proofs of this same sort: but these are enough to declare sufficiently, that propriety of goods is in both the Testaments permitted to christian men.

In the Acts of the Apostles we read[2], that among them of the primitive and apostolic church all things were common; but that which followeth in the same book doth declare what kind of communion that was which they had: for Luke saith, "None of them said that any thing was his of that which he possessed." Lo here, the first Christians possessed houses, grounds, and other riches, by the right of propriety; and yet they possessed them not as their own goods, but as the goods of other men, and as it were in common, so notwithstanding that the right of propriety did still remain in possessors' own hands: and if so be at any time necessity so required, they sold their lands and houses, and helped the need of them that lacked. If they sold, then that which they sold was undoubtedly their own: for no good man doth sell another man's substance, but that which is his own, or that which he hath taken in hand to husband as his own. Moreover, St Peter, compounding all this controversy, saith to Ananias, "Whiles the land remained, was it not thine own? and when it was sold, was it not in thy power? How is it then, that thou liest to the Holy Ghost, and keepest back part of the price of the land, and makest, notwithstanding, as though thou hadst brought the whole price unto us?" It was in Ananias his power not to have sold the land; and, when it was sold, to have kept to himself the whole sum of money: and yet for that deed he should not have been excluded from the church of the faithful. It was free therefore at that time, even as at this day also it is, either to sell, or not to sell, their[3] lands and possessions, and to bestow it commonly for the relieving of the poor. Therefore that place in the Acts of the Apostles doth not take away the right of propriety, nor command such a communion of every man's goods as our mad-headed Anabaptists go about to ordain.

Marginal notes:
[1 Thess. iv. 11, 12.]
How in the apostles' age all things were common.
[Acts iv. 32.]
[Acts v. 3, 4.]

[1 his, not in original Lat.]
[2 sane, Lat. omitted: indeed.]
[3 their, not in original Lat.]

And for because I perceive that some do very stiffly stick to the letter, and urge that communion of substance, it shall not be tedious to recite unto you, dearly beloved, other men's judgments touching this point; I mean, the opinions of them which by conference of scriptures have made this matter most plain and manifest[4].

Whereas we read in the second chapter of the Acts, that all which believed were joined in one[5], it must not so be understood as though they, like monks, forsaking every one his proper house, did dwell together in common, all in one house; but that they, as it is immediately after added, continued daily in the temple with one accord: not that they left off every man to eat in his own house and to provide things necessarily required of nature, or that every one sold the house that he had; since there is afterward added, "breaking bread from house to house." If they brake bread from house to house, let these Anabaptists answer, in what houses the Christians at Jerusalem did break their bread. In the houses of unbelievers? I think, nay. Therefore they brake bread and ate meat in the houses of the faithful. How therefore did they all sell or forsake their lands and houses? How did they live together like cloisterers? Whereas Luke saith therefore, that "so many as believed were joined in one," that is to be understood, that they did oftentimes assemble in the temple: so then that communicating of goods among the Christians was nothing else but a sale, which the wealthier sort made of their lands and houses, to the end that by bestowing that money the poor might be relieved, lest they, being compelled by penury and famine, should turn from Christianity to Judaism again. Moreover, we read in many places of the Acts, that Christians kept to themselves the use of their houses and ordering of their substance; as in the ninth of the Acts we find of Tabitha, who was full of good works, making coats and clothing for widows and poor people. In the twelfth of the Acts we read that Peter the apostle, being brought out of prison, "came to the house of Mary, the

[4 Most of the ensuing arguments from scripture occur in Melancthon's Epist. adv. Anabap. Corp. Ref. Tom. I. col. 970—3, and Calvin's Instruct. adv. Libertinos, cap. 21, p. 393, Tom. VIII. Amstel. 1667. See also Bullinger, adv. Anabapt. Lib. IV. cap. 9.]

[5 Acts ii. 44, erant conjuncti, Erasmus' rendering.]

mother of John, whose surname was Mark, where many were gathered together to pray:" he saith not, to dwell, but to pray; whereby thou mayest understand that the congregation was assembled in that house to pray. Again, in the ninth chapter, Peter stayeth many days in the house of Simon the tanner, which was a christian man, and dwelt in his own house. And in the eleventh chapter, "the disciples, according to every one's ability, sent help to the brethren which dwelt in Jury." Lo here, "as every one," saith he, "was of ability." But what ability could any of them have had, unless they had somewhat of their own in possession? In the sixteenth chapter, Lydia, the woman that sold purple, when she was baptized, did say, "If ye have judged me to be faithful to the Lord, come into my house, and abide there." Why said she not, sell my house; but, "come into my house:" but for because she did so possess her house after she believed, as that she made it common to the apostles? In the twentieth chapter, Paul doth glory that he hath not desired any man's gold, silver, or precious clothes. But what sense or reason could be in these words, unless it were lawful for christian men to keep the possession of that which is theirs? And in the twenty-first chapter, Philip had at Cæsarea a house and four daughters: why sold he not his house? Philemon [Philem. 16, 22.] also, Paul's host, had both a house and a servant too. It is therefore most plain and evident, that the Holy Ghost's meaning is not to have such an order of life observed, as these people do devise; but that every man should govern well his own house and family, and relieve the brethren's necessity, according as his ability will suffer and bear. To this end also do other places belong; 1 Timothy v., Titus ii., 1 Thess. iv., 2 Thess. iii. And when in all his Epistles almost he prescribeth to parents and children, to husbands and wives, to masters and servants, their office and duties; what doth he else, but teach how to order our houses and families? Thus much thus far.

What may be said of that, moreover, that many wealthy men in the gospel are reported to have been worshippers of God? Joseph of Arimathea, which buried the Lord after he was crucified, is said to have been a wealthy man, and a disciple of Christ also. The women were wealthy, which followed the Lord from Galilee, and ministered to him and his disciples of their goods and substance. The eunuch[1] treasurer of Queen Candace was a wealthy man. Tabitha of Joppa, whom Peter raised from death to life, was rich, and spent her substance freely upon poor and needy people. Lydia, the seller of purple, was wealthy too; and innumerable more, who were both godly and faithful people. Whereas the Lord therefore did say to the young man, "If thou [Matt. xix. 21.] wilt be perfect, go, and sell that which thou hast, and give to the poor, and thou shalt have treasure in heaven; and come and follow me;" that is no general law, or simple doctrine belonging to all men; but is a demonstration only, to shew that the young man to whom he spake had not yet so perfectly fulfilled the law, as he thought verily that he had done: for he thought he had done all, and that nothing was wanting. For the young man set more by his goods than he did by God and the voice of God's commandment: for he departed sadly, and did not as the Lord had bidden him; and thereby declared that he had not yet fulfilled the law. Moreover, we may out of other places gather that the Lord did not cast down his disciples to misery and beggary. Neither was Paul the apostle ashamed to make laws for rich men, and to prescribe an order how they ought to behave themselves. "To them that be rich," saith he, "in this [1 Tim. vi. 17—19.] world, give charge that they be not high-minded, nor trust in uncertain riches, but in the living God, which giveth us abundantly all things to enjoy; that they do good, that they be rich in good works, that they be ready to give, glad to distribute, laying up in store for themselves a good foundation against the time to come, that they may lay hold upon eternal life." Hereunto belong the admonitions of our Sa- [Matt. vi. 24, & xiii. 22, & xix 23, 24.] viour, who saith: "Ye cannot serve God and mammon at once." Again, "Riches are thorns that choke the seed of the word of God." And again, "Verily, I say unto you, a rich man shall hardly enter into the kingdom of heaven. It is easier for a camel to go through the eye of a needle, than for a rich man to enter into the kingdom of God." And as the minds of wealthy men are not utterly to be discouraged and driven to desperation, as though it were impossible for them to be saved; so are they to be admonished of the imminent perils, lest peradventure they sleep securely

[1 Substituted for another word used by the translator.]

over their riches, being seduced by Satan to abuse their wealth, when as indeed they ought rather to use it after the rule of the Apostle, which I did even now recite. The Gangresian synod[1], a very ancient council, verily condemned them which taught, "that faithful rich men could have no hope to be saved by the Lord, unless they did renounce and forsake all the good that they did possess[2]." St Augustine enrolleth and reckoneth the Apostolics in his catalogue, or bead-row, of heretics: "They, taking arrogantly this name to themselves, did not admit into their company any of them which used the fellowship of their own wives, or had in possession any proper substance." After that he addeth: "They therefore are heretics, because, separating themselves from the church, they think that they have no hope to be saved which use and enjoy the things that they themselves lack. They are like unto the Encratites, and are called also by the name of Apotactites[3]." Touching riches, they of themselves verily are not evil, but the good gifts of God; it is the abuse that makes them evil. But for the use of them, I will speak hereafter.

Here followeth now the treatise of the getting of wealth and riches, which be necessary for the maintenance of our lives and families. Touching the getting whereof there is a large discourse among our lawyers: for they say, that goods are gotten by the law of nations, and by the peculiar law of every particular country: by the law of nations; as by prevention in possession, by captivity, by finding, by birth, by casting up of water, by changing the kind, by increase in bondage, by mixture, by building, planting, sowing, tilling in

Gangresis Synodus.

False doctrine concerning riches and rich men condemned.

Of the lawful getting of riches.

[1 The Synod of Gangra in Paphlagonia was held after that of Nice, but before that of Antioch, i. e. between A.D. 325 and 341; but the exact year is not known.]

[2 — τῶν χρημάτα ἐχόντων, καὶ μὴ ἀναχωρούντων αὐτῶν, κατεγίνωσκον (οἱ περὶ τὸν Εὐστάθιον)—κατὰ τούτων οὖν ἱεροὶ ἀθροισθέντες πατέρες κανόνας ἐξέθεντο. Zonaras in Can. Apost. &c. Lutet. Paris. 1618. p. 310.]

[3 Apostolici, qui se isto nomine arrogantissime vocaverunt, eo quod in suam communionem non reciperent utentes conjugibus et res proprias possidentes ... Ideo isti hæretici sunt, quoniam se ab ecclesia separantes nullam spem putant eos habere, qui utuntur his rebus quibus ipsi carent. Encratitis isti similes sunt; nam et Apotactitæ appellantur.—August. Opp. Par. 1531, Tom. VI. p. 4, col. 3.—Ἐγκρατῖται, *continents;* ἀποτακτικοὶ, *separatists.* See Vol. I. p. 432, n. 3.]

a ground free from possession, and by delivery: by the peculiar law of every particular country; as by continuance of possession, by prescription, by giving, by will, by legacy, by fiefment, by succession, by challenge, by purchase[4]. Of all which particularly to speak, it would be a labour too tedious, and for you to hear, dearly beloved, little profitable.

That therefore which we are to say we will frame to the manners and customs of our age; and we will utter that which shall tend to our avail. Principally, and before all things, we must close and shut up an evil eye, lest we be carried away with too much concupiscence and desire. "The [Matt. vi. 22, 23.] light of the body," saith our Saviour Christ in the Gospel, "is the eye: if therefore thine eye be single, thine whole body shall be lightened: but if thine eye be evil, thy body shall be all dark." The mind of man, being endued with faith and not infected with concupiscences and naughty lusts, doth give light to all things that he shall take in hand, go about, and do: but if his mind be corrupt and unclean, then shall his deeds savour also of corruption and uncleanness. Wherefore faith and upright conscience must subdue and beat down too much concupiscence and covetousness, which take their original and roots from distrust, making unholy and unclean all the counsels of man, all his thoughts, all his words and deeds. And that we may be able and of force sufficient to captivate and bring them into subjection, necessary it is, that the grace of Christ assist us; which every godly-minded man and woman doth ask of God with godly and faithful prayers.

Behoveful it is that we always set before our eyes, and have deeply graven in our hearts, the doctrine of our Saviour Christ touching these, and the instruction also of his holy apostles; which is not so much but it may be well borne away. We will, therefore, rehearse unto you, dearly beloved, three several places, two of them out of the Gospel,

---

[4 Jure gentium, et jure civili. . . . Occupatione, captivitate, inventione, nativitate, alluvione, specificatione, accessione, confusione, ædificatione, plantatione, satione, cultura, traditione. . . Usucapione, præscriptione, donatione, testamento, legato, fidei commisso, successione, arrogatione, adjectione.—Corp. Jur. Civil. Digest. Lib. XLI. Tit. i. col. 1447, &c. Tom. I. Par. 1628.—All these terms of the civil law are very fairly explained in the translation.]

and the third out of Saint Paul: in which places, as it were in a perfect abridgement, you may have comprised what things soever can be required of such as worship God in truth. In the Gospel according to St Matthew thus saith our Lord and Saviour: " Hoard not up for yourselves treasures in earth, where the rust and moth doth corrupt, and where thieves break through and steal: but lay up treasure for you in heaven, where neither moth nor rust doth corrupt, and where thieves do not break through and steal. For where your treasure is, there will your hearts also be. No man can serve two masters: for either he shall hate the one, and love the other; or else he shall lean to the one, and despise the other: ye cannot serve God and mammon. Therefore I say unto you, be not careful for your life, what ye shall eat or drink; nor yet for your body, what ye shall put on: is not the life more worthy than meat, and the body more worth than raiment? Behold the fowls of the air, for they sow not, neither do they reap, nor carry into barns; yet your heavenly Father feedeth them: are not ye much better than they? Which of you, by taking careful thought, can add one cubit to his stature? And why care ye for raiment? Consider the lilies of the field, how they grow: they labour not, neither do they spin; and yet I say unto you, that even Salomon in all his royalty was not arrayed like one of these. Wherefore, if God so clothe the grass of the field, which, though it stand to day, is to-morrow cast into the furnace; shall he not much more do the same for you, O ye of little faith? Therefore take no thought, saying, What shall we eat, or, What shall we drink, or, Wherewith shall we be clothed? For after all these things do the Gentiles seek: for your heavenly Father knoweth that ye have need of all these things. But seek ye first the kingdom of God[1], and all these things shall be added unto you. Care not then for to-morrow; for the morrow shall care for itself. Sufficient unto the day is the evil thereof." Thus saith the Lord in the sixth of Matthew's Gospel.

Again, in the twelfth chapter of St Luke's gospel he[2] saith: "Take heed, and beware of covetousness: for no man's

[1 et justitiam ejus, Lat.; omitted by the translator: and his righteousness.]

[2 idem Dominus noster, Lat.; the same our Lord.]

life standeth in the abundance of things which he possesseth :" that is, the life hath no need of superfluity, or, no man's life hath need of more than enough. "And he put forth a similitude, saying, The ground of a certain rich man brought forth fruits plentifully ; and he thought within himself, saying, What shall I do, because I have no room where to bestow my fruits ? And he said, This will I do ; I will pull down my barns, and build greater, and therein will I gather all my fruits and my goods; and I will say to my soul, Soul, thou hast much goods laid up in store for many years; take thine ease, eat, drink, and be merry. But God said unto him, Thou fool, this night do they require thy soul again from thee[3] : then whose shall these things be which thou hast provided ? So is he that gathereth riches to himself, and is not rich to God-wards." Paul, the vessel of election, following in all things his teacher and master, crieth out, and saith : "Godliness is a great lucre, if a man be content [1 Tim. vi. 6—11.] with that he hath : for we brought nothing into the world, and it is certain that we may carry nought away ; but, having food and raiment, we must therewith be content. For they that will be rich fall into temptations and snares, and into many foolish and noisome lusts, which drown men in perdition and destruction. For covetousness, and the love of money, is the root of all evil; which while some have lusted after, they erred from the faith, and wrapped themselves in many sorrows. But thou, O man of God, flee these things ; and follow after righteousness, godliness, faith, love, patience, meekness, &c."

Whosoever, therefore, meaneth by bodily labour or any kind of traffic to get a living and things necessary for himself and his family, let him take these godly precepts instead of treacle[4] and other wholesome medicines, to strengthen his mind against the envenomed force of poisoned greediness, and the infecting plague of covetousness. And when he hath with this medicine against poison, compounded of the doctrine of the evangelists and apostles, fortified his mind against the Labour is commended and idleness condemned.

[3 animam tuam repetunt abs te, Lat. So the Vulgate and Erasmus. The original is, τὴν ψυχήν σου ἀπαιτοῦσιν ἀπὸ σοῦ. See the marginal reading of our authorised version.]

[4 theriaca, Lat. ; a compound medicine against the bites of poisonous animals; treacle. Facciolati Tot. Lat. Lex. in voc.]

plague, then let him immediately bend himself to some labour
and kind of occupation. But let every one pick out and
choose an honest and profitable occupation, not a needless
art, or a science hurtful to any other man. And finally, let
all men fly idleness, as a plague or contagious disease. And
now again let us in this case hear the heavenly words of that
holy apostle Paul, who saith: "We charge you, brethren, in the
name of our Lord Jesus Christ, that ye withdraw yourselves
from every brother that liveth inordinately, and not after the
institution[1] which he received of us. For when we were with
you, this we warned you of, that if any would not work, the
same should not eat. For we hear say, that there are some
which walk among you inordinately, working not at all, but
be busy-bodies. Them that are such we command and
exhort, by our Lord Jesus Christ, that they, working in
quietness, eat their own bread."

[2 Thess. iii. 6, 10—12.]

In all ages, and among all honest men, both idleness and
needless occupations have been always condemned. Hesiodus
said :

> Both gods and men abhor
> The lazy hand-inbosom'd lout[2],
> That works not in a common weal,
> But lurks, and lives without
> Pains-taking; like the idle drone,
> That lives upon the spoil
> Of that, for which the busy bees
> Do tire themselves with toil.

And Sophocles said :

> Where idleness doth sit a-brood,
> There's never good egg hatch'd[3].

For God doth not assist slothful persons and idle slow-
backs. Now I call those needless occupations, which idle
and ill-disposed people do use, thereby to be troublesome
to their neighbours, and to deceive other men; exercising,

Needless oc-
cupations.

[1 institutionem, Lat.; Erasmus' rendering. See Fulke's Defence
of Translations of the Bible, Parker Soc. ed. pp. 151, 166.]

[2 to bosom, to conceal in privacy. Johnson's Dict.; lout, to bow,
bend, or do obeisance; and hence a clown or rustic was so called.
Toone's Glossary. Lond. 1834.]

[3 Hesiodi Ἔργ. καὶ Ἡμ. 301. Sophocl. Iphig. apud Stobæi Floril.
Tit. xxx. ed. Gaisford, Vol. ii. p. 30.]

I confess, an occupation, but such an one as is utterly unlawful and unprofitable to all men, themselves only excepted, to whom it brings in excessive gains: of which sort are usurers, engrossers, hucksters[4], and other moe, that have many arts to frank themselves with an idle shew of business, like a swine shut up to be fatted in a sty[5]. As for them whose wealth is come to them, not by their own labour, or their own industry[6], but by inheritance of their ancestors' leaving, let them consider with themselves by what means the riches were gotten, which now by inheritance are fallen to their lot: and, if they perceive that they be heirs of unjust-gotten goods, let them be liberal, and make amends for them[7], not doubling the evil in possessing unjustly, and more wickedly digesting the thing that before was naughtily come by. Let them put no trust or confidence in their ill-gotten riches, neither let them give themselves to idleness, but still be busy in some honest thing. But yet most commonly it cometh to pass, that ill-gotten goods are spent very lewdly[8]. The best way therefore is, either to be heir to a good, just, and liberal man; or else to seek means, by their own toil and travail[9], to have of thine own wherewithal to sustain both thine own life and the lives of thy family.

Wealth by inheritance.

But many men make a doubt here, and call it into question: first, whether bargaining, and buying and selling, be lawful or no; and then, what one occupation it is, among all other, that doth best beseem a godly man. Them which stick upon these doubts I wish to consider these reasons that follow. First, it is manifest, that contracts are for the most part voluntary, and that bargains are made with the mutual consent of the buyer and seller; so that each one may take deliberation, and make choice of that which he would have, to see whether it be best for his purpose or no. Of this sort are the exchange of things, suretyship, letting, hiring, mortgaging, borrowing, lending, covenanting, buying, selling, and

Whether bargaining and buying and selling be lawful or no.

[4 monopolæ et propolæ, Lat.]
[5 negotioso otio se saginantes, Lat.]
[6 negotiatione æqua, Lat.; by fair trading.]
[7 and make amends for them; not in the original Latin.]
[8 male partum male dilabatur, Lat. See Erasmi Adag. Chiliad. p. 727, Hanov. 1617.]
[9 negotiatione justa, Lat.]

other moe like unto these. These things, as experience doth prove, even the holiest men cannot be without, so long as they live in this frail world. Neither doth the Lord of the law in any place forbid these kind of contracts, but planteth them rather in his commonweal of Israel, that the people might know and acknowledge them to be the ordinances of God : the abuse, deceit, guile, and confidence in them is flatly forbidden by the word of the Lord. If, therefore, any man do use them moderately, not staying himself upon them, nor reposing his trust in them, in so using them he sinneth not. And here again let us hear the words of the apostle, who saith:

[1 Cor. vii. 29—31.] "Let them which have wives be as though they had none ; and them which weep, as though they wept not; and them which rejoice, as though they rejoiced not; and them which buy, as though they possessed not; and them which use this world, as though they used it not[1]: for the fashion of this world doth pass away." In like manner, we do in no place read that just and lawful gains have been at any time forbidden : yea, the Lord doth bless the labour and travail of his servants, which love him, that even as in virtue, so also they may increase in riches and substance. This do the examples of Abraham, Isaac, and Jacob evidently tes-

[1 Tim. iii. 3, 8; Titus i. 7, 11.] tify. And the very apostles bid us not[2] to look after no gain, but charge us only to keep ourselves from gaping after filthy gain.

Sundry kinds of occupations. There are among men many and divers occupations ; and the state and conditions, wherein men are, do stand in need of many and sundry things. There is an occupation or grosser kind of labour, which is put in practice by force of hand and strength of body rather than by art, although it wanteth not altogether wit and discretion. There is also a more fine and subtile labour of the wit, which, although it be not done without the body and strength of man, is yet, notwithstanding, accomplished by the wit rather than by the bodily force of him which laboureth. Of the first sort are all those occupations or sciences which are commonly called handicrafts; and in that number we reckon also merchandising, husbandry, and

[1 So Tyndale, 1534, and Cranmer, 1539; and the Vulgate and Erasmus agree with Bullinger's text, tanquam non utantur.]

[2 non jubent nos nullum sperare lucrum, Lat. So 1577; not, is wanting in 1587.]

grazing of cattle. Of the latter sort are the study of tongues, of physic, of law, of divinity especially, and of philosophy, and lastly, the governing of a commonweal. The patriarchs, verily, who were most innocent and excellent men, did, for the most part, either exercise husbandry, or else breed and feed up cattle to increase. There are many examples, of Abel, Noe, Abraham, Isaac, Jacob, Job, and other more. The Levites and prophets lived by their study and ecclesiastical ministry. The feat[3] of merchandising is nowhere condemned throughout the holy scriptures; but those merchants are condemned, which neither fear nor seek after God, but use odd shifts and subtile sleights to deceive and cozen their brethren and neighbours. For James, the apostle of Christ our Lord, saith: "Go to now, ye that say, To-day, and to-morrow, let us go into such a city, and continue there a year, and buy, and sell, and win: and yet cannot tell what shall happen on the morrow; for what is your life? it is even a vapour, that continueth for a little time, and then vanisheth away. For that ye ought to say, If the Lord will, and if we live[4], let us do this or that." Neither is Lydia, the seller of purple, found fault withal, in the Acts of the Apostles, for that she did sell purple: for Salomon, where he setteth forth the praise of a good house-wife, doth commend her greatly for exercising merchandise. All notable kings have lived by governing of their common-wealths; even as Joseph, the preserver of Egypt, and Daniel, the chief next to the king in Babylon and Media, did in like sort. For as in man's body there are many members, and sundry uses whereunto they are applied, when as notwith-standing they do all agree in one, and tend together to the preservation and safeguard of the body; even so God hath ordained divers arts and occupations for men to labour in, so yet nevertheless, that he would have them all to serve to the commonweal's commodity.

    But now it is not for me definitively to pronounce which of all these occupations a godly man ought chiefly first to choose, and then to put in practice. Let every man weigh with himself the things that hitherto I have alleged; then let him search and make trial of himself, to what kind of life and

[James iv. 13—15.]

Prov. xxxi.

1 Cor. xii.

What occupation a godly man ought chiefly to use.

[3 feat: employment.]
[4 So Tyndale, 1534, and Cranmer, 1539; and the Vulgate and Erasmus, as Bullinger, et si vixerimus.]

occupation his mind is most willing, and whereunto he himself is most fit and profitable: let him also have a diligent regard to consider, what arts they are that be most simple and agreeable to nature; and what occupations have least need of craft and deceit; and lastly, what sciences do least of all draw us from God and just dealing. And when this is scanned, then let every man choose to himself that which he taketh to be best convenient, and most wholesome both for his soul and also his body. We cannot all of us manure the ground, neither are all heads apt to take learning; a few among many do govern the common-weal; and all are not fit to be handicrafts-men. Every one hath his sundry disposition; every one is inspired by God; every one hath the aid and counsel of his friends and well-willers; every one hath sundry occasions; and every one hath the rule of God's word: let him be content with and stay himself upon them, so yet that God's commandments may still have the pre-eminence.

Beware of prodigality. But for him that laboureth and taketh pains in his occupation, these rules of admonition which follow are as necessary as those which are already rehearsed. For first of all, every one must take heed of prodigality or riot, in meat, drink, apparel, nice pranking of the body, and gorgeous buildings; needless expenses must always be spared. For the Lord's will is, that every man should keep, and not lash out, the wealth that he hath, where no need requireth it: for the Lord doth hate and detest riot and needless cost to maintain pride withal. Moreover the man, that is prodigal of that which is his own, is for the most part desirous of other men's goods; from whence arise innumerable mischiefs, threats, conspiracies, downright deceit, shameless shifts, murders, and seditions. Secondarily, let him which laboureth in his vocation be prompt and active; let him be watchful and able to abide labour; he must be no lither-back[1], unapt, or slothful fellow. Whatsoever he doth, that let him do with faith[2] and diligence. Sloth and sluggishness do displease God utterly. The Lord mislikes the yawning mouth and folded arms, the signs of sleep, which commonly follow the careless man, who doth neglect the state and condition of

[1 lither, lazy, idle, slothful. (North-country word.) Grose's Provincial Glossary. Lond. 1787.]
[2 fideliter, Lat.]

his house and family³.   But on the other side, the scripture commendeth highly faithful labourers, and good and painful people in work.   Let us hear, I beseech you, the golden words of Solomon, the wisest among all men; who, where he blameth sluggards, saith: " Go to the emmet, thou sluggard; [Prov. vi. 6 consider her ways, and learn to be wise.   She hath no guide, —11.] nor overseer, nor ruler; and yet in the summer she provideth her meat, and gathereth her food in the harvest.   How long wilt thou sleep, thou sluggard? when wilt thou arise out of thy sleep?   Yea, sleep on still a little, slumber a little, fold thine hands together yet a little, and take thine ease: and in the meanwhile shall poverty come upon thee like a traveller, and necessity like a weaponed man."   Again, David in the psalms crieth, saying⁴: " The labours of thine hands shalt thou eat: O well is thee, and happy shalt thou be."   What may be thought of that moreover, that the Lord God would not have Adam to live idly in paradise, that happy place for his state and condition? for he enjoined him the tending and dressing of that goodly garden.   Idle people, therefore, are the most unhappy of all mortal men; and slothful drowsy-heads are nothing else but an unprofitable lump of unoccupied earth⁵.   Lastly, let the artificer have a regard, that he hurt no man by his art or occupation.   And let this be the rule for him to keep his eye upon in all business and affairs of his science: " Whatsoever thou wouldest have done to thyself, the same do thou to another; and whatsoever thou wouldest not have done to thyself, that do not thou to another⁶."   Moreover, thou doest hurt to another man two sundry ways; that is, by keeping back, and taking away: as for example, if thou withholdest that which thou owest and is not thine own; or if thou takest away that which is another man's, and that which he doth not owe unto thee.   But of the hurt done in withholding and taking away, I will at this present speak somewhat

[³ This whole sentence is a paraphrase of the Latin; displicet (Deo) supina rei familiaris negligentia.]

[⁴ Beati omnes qui timent Dominum, qui ambulant in viis ejus, Lat. omitted by the translator; Blessed are all they that fear the Lord, and walk in his ways. Psal. cxxviii. Prayer Book Version.]

[⁵ telluris inutile pondus, Lat. See Erasmi Adag. Chiliad. p. 138, Hanov. 1617.]

[⁶ See Vol. I. p. 197.]

largely, that thereby ye may the better understand the Lord's commandment, " Thou shalt not steal," and more perfectly perceive what kinds and sorts of theft there be.

Theft.   Theft, they say, is a deceitful fingering of another man's goods, moveable and bodily, which is done against the owner's will, to the intent to make gain either of the thing itself, or of the use of the thing, or of the possession of the same. Therefore they say, that a mad man doth not commit theft ; because in him there can no endeavour of craft or deceit be possibly found. Neither can, say they, that man be argued of[1] theft, which by mistaking, and not of set malice, did take away another man's good instead of his own. But he alone is not called a deceitful fingerer, which layeth hand upon the thing; but he who by any manner of means conveyeth it from the possession of the true owner. Now they say, that it is done against the owner's will, not only if it be perforce and violently taken from him : but also if he know not of the taking it away ; or if he do know, yet if he cannot forbid them ; or, if he can forbid them, yet if for some certain causes he will not. Neither is it added without a cause, that theft is committed for gain and profit's sake. For if one in jest, or for some other honest cause, take any thing away, he doth not thereby deserve to be called a thief. But of theft they make two sorts : the manifest theft, as that wherewith the thief is taken ; and the theft not manifest, as when, after the deed, one is convinced of theft. Of these there is a large discourse, *Digestorum* Lib. xlvii. tit. 2[2]. Let us return to the further opening of our present proposition.

Sundry sorts of damage done by withholding.   Thy withholding doth hurt another man, when thou in buying and selling dost use false measure or false weights. To this rule is referred unjust and false exchange[3] ; I mean, exchange of money in bank[4]. Touching these points we will recite the commandments and sentences only of the Lord our God, who in Leviticus setteth this for a law : " Ye shall do no unrighteousness in judgment, in meteyard, in weight,

[Lev. xix. 35, 36.]

[1 be argued of : be convicted of, found fault with for.]
[2 The foregoing definitions of the Civil Law are collected in Jul. Pacii Isagog. in Instit. &c. p. 395, Traject. ad Rhen. 1680.]
[3 Collybus, Lat.]
[4 Collybus autem, ait Pollux, est permutatio pecuniæ, Lat. omitted by the translator. Cf. Schleusneri Lex. N. T. sub voc. κολλυβιστής.]

or in measure: true balances, true weights, a true ephah,"
(that is, a bushel, or a peck⁵ in measure, of dry things,)
" and a true hin," (that is, in measure of liquid things a pint
and an half, or the twelfth part of a pint and an half,⁶) " shall
ye have.   I am the Lord your God, which brought you out
of the land of Egypt." In Deuteronomy we read : " Thou [Deut. xxv. 13—16.]
shalt not have in thy bag two manner of weights, a great and
small.   Neither shalt thou have in thy house divers measures,
a great and a small," (to the end, that in receiving or buying
thou mayest use the greater, and in laying out or selling thou
mayest use the lesser,) " but thou shalt have a just and a right
weight, and a just and right measure shalt thou have ; that
thy days may be prolonged upon the land, which the Lord
thy God giveth 'thee.   For all that do such things, and all
that do unrightly, are abominable unto the Lord thy God."
Hereunto appertaineth that sentence of Salomon's in the
Proverbs, where he saith: "Two manner of weights, and two [Prov. xx. 10.]
manner of measures, both these are abominable unto the
Lord."   But what can be heard, or thought of, more grievous
and horrible, than a man to be abominable in the sight of his
God?   In the sixth chapter of Micheas also the Lord doth
threaten divers and grievous punishments, which he mindeth
to lay upon the necks of them that use not justice in weights
and measures.   Why therefore do we not rather fly from
doing wrong and unrighteousness, choosing sooner to be
happy than unhappy ;   and hearken unto the Lord, who
saith, " Good measure, and pressed down, and shaken to- [Luke vi. 38.]
gether, and running over, shall they give into your bosom ;
for with the same measure that ye mete to other, shall other
mete to you again ?"   Let us be throughly persuaded therefore, that riches gotten by craft and theft can neither
flourish long, nor yet be for our health to enjoy.

Again, other men are endamaged by the withholding of
them which possess inheritances due unto other : which break
promise, and deceive men in contracts, bargains, and covenants : which make a face, as though they gave the thing,

[⁵ modium vel quartale, Lat. The ephah is generally reckoned to
have been nearly equal to 6½ gallons of our dry measure.   Horne's
Introd. Vol. III. p. 534, Lond. 1828.]

[⁶ sextarium vel cyathus, Lat. The hin was 1 gallon, 2 pints, English.   Ibid.]

which they do either change, or retain to themselves by some coloured shift, or else do give it, when they themselves have marred, or utterly destroyed it. Both the one and the other, verily, is fraud and guile and flat deceit. But now, by the way, mark this manifest and usual point of God's just judgment; that wrongful possessors of other men's heritages are both short-lived, and the unfortunatest men of all other people.

[Prov. x 2, & xxviii. 8.] Touching these wrongful withholders Salomon pronounceth, that they shall find no gain. For gain unjustly gotten, how great soever it be, deserveth rather to be called a loss more truly than a gain.

Things found. To this precept do things that are found belong, which thou deniest to the demander, as though thou either hast not found them, or else dost challenge them to be thine own Pledges and pawns. by law. Hereunto appertaineth the pledge, or pawn, which thou withholdest. A man that taketh a journey into a far country hath put thee in trust with certain silver plate, and a pound weight of gold, to keep for him against his return, because he had hope that thou wouldest keep them safely; but at his coming back, when he demandeth them, thou deniest the thing: in so doing thou hast stolen it from him, and cracked the credit that thy friend had in thee, and, last of all, thou hast doubled the sin. A poor man hath guaged[1] to thee some precious thing, that he setteth much by; which when he claimeth again, with ready money in hand to pay the sum which he borrowed upon it, thou deniest him the pledge, thou quarrellest with him, and usest subtilty to defraud him of his pawn: in so doing thou stealest it from him. Moreover, the Lord gave to his people other laws to this end and effect, touching the taking of pledges or guages. [Deut. xxiv. 6, 10—13.] For in Deuteronomy he saith, "No man shall take the nether or the upper millstone to pledge: for he hath laid his life to pledge to thee." For it is all one, as if he had said: Thou shalt not take that at thy neighbour's hand instead of a pledge, wherewith he getteth his living and doth maintain his family: for thereby thou shouldest take from him both life and living. And immediately after he saith: "When thou lendest thy brother any thing, thou shalt not go into his house to fetch a pledge from thence; but thou shalt stand without, that he which borrowed it of thee may bring it out

[1 gaged: impawned, Johnson.]

of doors to thee." The Lord forbiddeth cruelty, and would
not have rich men to be too sharp in ransacking poor men's
houses, nor over curious in taking of pledges at poor men's
hands. For he addeth afterward: "And if it be a poor
body, thou shalt not sleep with his pledge; but deliver him
the pledge when as the sun goeth down, that he may sleep
in his own raiment, and bless thee; and that shall be imputed
for righteousness unto thee before the Lord thy God.

Lastly, they do most of all endamage their neighbours, *The withholding of
labourers
hire.* which do withhold the labourer's wages. The labourer's hire
is withheld two sundry ways: for thou dost either never
pay it; or else thou payest it with grudging and grunting,
thou dost delay the payment too long, or otherwise dimi-
nishest some part of his hire. But mark now, that the name
of hirelings is of ample signification, and is extended to all
kinds of artificers. The common sort of wealthy men have
a cast now-a-days to use the help of handicrafts-men, and
bid them keep a reckoning of their hire and wages in books
of accounts: in the mean while, though they perceive that
these poor men lack money, yet will they not pay so much
as one penny; yea, when they require the debt that is due,
they take them up with bitter words, and send them empty
away, till they themselves be disposed to pay. And so these
foolish and wicked wealthy men do not cease to lash out in
riot prodigally the things that are not clearly their own, but
which they withhold from other poor men. Let us hear
therefore the laws and judgments of the Lord our God
touching this horrible abuse and detestable fault. In Deuteronomy we read: "Thou shalt not deny, nor withhold, the [Deut. xxiv.
14, 15.] wages of an hired servant, that is needy and poor, whether
he be of thy brethren, or of the strangers that are in thy
land and within thy gates; but shalt give him his hire the
same day, and let not the sun go down thereon, for he is
needy, and by the hire he˙holdeth his life[2]," (that is, he layeth
the hope of his life therein, as he that looks to live thereby,)
"lest he cry unto the Lord, and it be turned unto sin to thee."
With this law of the Lord do the words of James the
apostle most fitly agree, where he saith: "Behold, the hire
of labourers, which have reaped down your fields, which hire
is of you kept back by fraud, crieth; and the cries of them

[2 et ad mercedem tollit animum suum, Lat.]

which have reaped are entered into the ears of the Lord of Sabboth[1]." What can be more terrible to the hearer's ears? The labourer's hire, which is withheld, doth cry, and crieth even up into heaven; and, that which is most of all, doth enter into the ears of the most just, severe, and mighty God. What now may these defrauders look for at God's hand, but heavy punishment to light upon their cursed heads? Tobie therefore most rightly and briefly concludeth this matter, and giveth excellent counsel to all sorts of peo-[Tobit iv. 14.] ple, saying: "Whosoever worketh any thing for thee, give him his hire immediately, and let not thy hired servant's wages remain with thee at all. For in so doing, and fearing God, thou shalt have thanks."

Damage that is done by taking away. Now followeth the second member or part of detriment, which doth consist in taking away another man's goods. And this taking away also is of sundry sorts. Now, the first place of these sorts is attributed to theft itself (of which we have spoken somewhat before); which theft is committed, not in taking away of money only, but in wares also, and wrongful dealing in other men's grounds, in removing land-marks or mere-stones[2]; and whatsoever is translated, denied, or clean taken away, against all right; or is maliciously, against all conscience and consent of the other party, that is, of the true owner, delayed, or foaded off[3], till a longer time than it ought to be. For in the nineteenth of Leviticus the Lord setteth this down for a law, and saith: "Ye shall not steal, ye shall not lie; no man shall deal with his neighbour [Eph. iv. 25, 28.] deceitfully." And Paul to the Ephesians saith: "Laying lies aside, speak ye every one the truth to his brother; for we are members one of another. Let him which stole steal no more; but rather labour with his hands in working the thing that is good, that he may give to him that hath need." This may we extend almost to all the offices and duties of men. For whosoever denieth the debt and duty which of right he oweth, the same doth sin against this commandment:

[1 James v. 4, Sabaoth, Lat. In Cranmer's Bible, 1539, it is Sabbaoth; and in the Geneva New Testament, 1557, "the Lord of Armies."]

[2 mere: a boundary, Johnson.]

[3 To fode out, or fode forth, with words: to keep in attention and expectation, to feed with words. Nares' Glossary in voc.]

as for example, if the householder deny the duty that he oweth to his family; again, if the family consume the householder's substance, and do deceive the good man, whose care is bent to maintain his charge, and are set to undo him by prodigal spending his money and goods, which they filch from him privily.   Again, if the lord, or master, (although this point may well be referred to the title of damage that is done by withholding) be too rough to his hinds, or husbandmen[4]: or if the ploughfolks do idly waste their master's substance, or slackly look to their tillage and business, or spend in riot his wealth and riches.   So then, the servant offendeth against this commandment, if he doth not seek all the means that he may to have a diligent care for his master's affairs, and faithfully augment his wealth and possessions. And in like manner do maidservants, in the duties which they owe, offend against their mistresses.   And therefore Paul, having an eye to this precept, giveth Titus in charge, and saith: "Exhort servants to be obedient unto their own mas- [Titus ii. 9, 10.] ters, and to please them in all things; not answering again, nor pickers, but shewing all good faithfulness, that they may adorn the doctrine of God our Saviour in all things."   And like unto this is that which the same apostle repeateth in the sixth chapter to the Ephesians, the third to the Colossians, and the first to Timothy, the sixth chapter: for in this commandment his doctrine of the duties of masters and servants hath a fit place (so far as concerneth the householder's riches), and whatsoever else is like unto this.

To this precept also robbery and deceit do fully belong, Robbery and deceit. both which extend far, and contain many kinds.   Fraud is infinite: for the iniquity of men is bottomless, their crafts are diverse, and of so many sorts that no one man can number them all.   And robbery is not always armed with force and weapons, but is sometimes furnished with sleights and coloured words: neither do robbers lurk and lay wait in woods and wide open fields alone, but are conversant also in the thickest throngs of every good city.   Thou takest away thy neighbour's goods under the false title and pretence of law; thou robbest him, I say, while by thy suit, thy gifts, or other fetches, thou dost extort from the judges corrupted

[4 hinds or husbandmen, colonis suis, Lat.; hind, a servant, Johnson; a peasant or rustic. Toone's Glossary.]

sentence, to maintain thy wrongful claim. Some there are which, under the title of a deed of gift, stick not to wrest whole heritages from legitimate heirs. These and other shifts, or cozenings like unto these, are contained partly under robbery, partly under deceit, but altogether and flatly under plain thievery.

Dicing and carding.

Although at dice players do give their mutual consent to fall to gaming: yet, for because each one's desire is greedily set to get the other's money, and that they make blind fortune (I mean, the dice or cards) to be the divider of their goods betwixt them ; therefore are the dice and cards worthily condemned of all good divines. And Justinian the emperor, as it is extant, *Cod.* Lib. III. tit. ultimo, having a regard to his subjects' commodity, decreed, that it should be lawful for no man, either in public or in private houses, to play at dice. For although dice-play hath been used of great antiquity, yet hath it ended and burst out into tears. For many, having lost all the substance that they have, do at the last in play break forth to the cursing and blaspheming of God[1]. Otherwise there is none so ignorant but knoweth well enough, that such exercises of the wit or body as are free from the poisoned desire of the filthy gain, whereon neither the hurt of our neighbour nor ourself doth depend, are lawful enough to be used of Christians.

Usury.

Usury[2] is, when thou grantest to another the use of thy goods, as of land, houses, money, or any thing else, whereof thou receivest some yearly commodity. For thou hast a manor, a farm, lands, meadows, pastures, vineyards, houses, and money, which thou dost let out to hire unto another man upon a certain covenant of gain to return to

[1 Imp. Justinianus A. Joanni P. P. xv. Alearum usus antiqua res est, et extra opera pugnatoria concessa: verum pro tempore prodiit in lacrymas, extranearum multa nationum suscipiens. Quidam enim ludentes, nec ludum scientes, sed numeratione tantum, proprias substantias perdiderunt, die noctuque ludendo argento, apparatu, lapidibus, et auro: consequenter autem ex hac inordinatione blasphemare Deum conantur, et instrumenta conficiunt. Commodis igitur subjectorum prospicientes, hac generali lege decernimus, ut nulli liceat in publicis vel privatis domibus ludere, neque inspicere, &c.—Codex Justin. Lugd. 1551, Tom. I. p. 515, Lib. III. tit. 43.]

[2 See Jul. Pacii Isagog. in Digest. Lib. XXII. tit. 1. pp. 189—200, Traject. ad Rhen. 1680.]

thee for the use thereof. This bargain, this covenant, is not of itself unlawful, nor yet condemned in the holy scriptures. And the very name of usury is not unhonest of itself: the abuse thereof hath made it unhonest, so that not without a cause it is at this day detested of all men. For usury is in the scripture condemned, so far as it is joined with iniquity and the destruction of our brother or neighbour. For who will forbid to let out the use of our lands, houses, or money to hire, that thereby we may receive some just and lawful commodity ? For buying, setting to hire, and such like contracts are lawfully allowed us. And as the part of him that giveth is to do good; so is it the duty of him that taketh not to use a good turn without all manner of recompence, to the hurt and hinderance of him that giveth it. In bestowing of mere benefits there is another consideration, whereof we read in the sixth of Luke : "If ye lend to them, of whom ye hope to receive again," &c. And the lawyers did discuss this matter thus : that it is no usury, when the debtor giveth a pension, and some yearly fee, in recompence of the money which he hath borrowed, saving the principal sum which he hath borrowed whole, by a covenant that was made before of selling it back again ; because the thing doth cease to be lent, which is so granted to another man's use, that, unless the debtor will, the creditor cannot claim the thing so long as the debtor payeth his pension ; for the assured payment whereof he hath put himself in bond : for such a crediting is a flat contract of buying. They say therefore, that usury is committed in lending alone (which ought to be without hire), and not in other contracts or bargains. Let them therefore, which deal in these kind of trades, have this always before their eyes, as a rule to be led by : "Whatsoever thou wouldest have done to thyself, that do thou to another : and whatsoever thou wouldest not have done to thyself, that do not thou to another[3]." And let them think of those words of the apostle : "Let no man [1 Thess. iv. 6.] beguile his brother in bargaining." I know very well, that touching money they are wont to allege, that it endureth not as lands and vineyards, but is consumed and made less with use and tossing from man to man ; and that therefore

[3 See page 34.]

no commodity ought to be taken for the use thereof[1]. But if a man put money into another man's hand, wherewith he buyeth himself a farm, a manor, lands, or vineyards, or otherwise occupieth it to his gain and profit, I see no cause why a good Christian and an honest man may not reap some lawful commodity of the hire of his money, as well as of the letting or leasing of his land. It is in the power of him which so letteth out his money, with that money to buy a farm, and so to take the whole gain to himself; but now we see that, in letting the other have it, he granteth him the use of his money, whereby he is a very great gainer. This fellow, to whom this sum is lent, or otherwise given upon covenants of contract, doth with the money get some stay of living, with the revenue whereof he nourisheth all his family, paying to his creditor the portion agreed on; of which when he hath once made a full restitution, he maketh the living his own for ever, and acquitteth himself from the yearly pension. In this kind of covenanting no man, I think, will say, that the poor is oppressed, when the thing itself doth rather cry, that by such usury the poor is greatly helped. Usury therefore is forbidden in the word of God, so far forth as it biteth (for here I use the very term of the scriptures[2]) his neighbour, while it hindereth him, or otherwise undoeth him. For thus saith the Lord in Leviticus: " If thy brother be waxen poor, and fallen in decay[3], whether he be a stranger or indweller, relieve him, that he may live with thee. Thou shalt take no usury of him, or more than right; but fear the Lord, that thy brother may live with thee. Thou shalt not give him thy money upon usury, nor lend him thy victuals for increase[4]. I am the Lord your

[Lev. xxv. 35—38.]

[1 Nec vero arguta illa ratio Aristotelis consistit, fœnus esse præter naturam, quia pecunia sterilis est, nec pecuniam parit, &c.—Calvin. Comment. in quat. libr. Mosis. ed. Amstel. 1671, Tom. I. p. 528.]

[2 נֶשֶׁךְ interest (from נָשַׁךְ momordit) from its involving an injurious, biting, system. Lee's Lexicon in voc. and Calvin. Comment. Tom. I. p. 527, col. 2.]

[3 nutaveritque manus ejus tecum, Lat. (and his hand faileth with thee. Auth. Vers. Marg. reading;) id est, si facultas ejus apud te deficere inceperit, Lat., omitted by the translator: that is, if his means with thee begin to fail.]

[4 ad nimium, sive excessum, sive superabundantiam, Lat.; for too large, or for excess and superabundance of, increase.]

God." Therefore the Lord misliketh all arts of covetous and deceitful men, wherewith they do not only exceed measure in exacting usury, but do of purpose let out their money and substance to hire, that by that occasion they may wipe their debtors of all that they have.

No man, I think, can in few words express all the wicked fetches of subtile usurers; they invent such new ones every day. I will therefore recite here the judgment of the Lord against a few wicked arts and detestable deeds of usurers, in lending, letting, and selling; to the end that, these being once considered, all men may judge and take heed of the like. The prophet Amos in the eighth chapter saith: "Hear this, O ye that swallow up the poor, and make the needy of the land to fail, saying: After a month[5] we will sell corn, and at the week's end we will set forth wheat, we will make the ephah small, and the sicle[6] great, and falsify the weights by deceit; that we may buy the poor for silver, and the needy for shoes, and sell the refuse of the wheat. The Lord hath sworn by the excellency of Jacob, Surely I will never forget any of their works. Shall not the land tremble for this? shall not every one mourn that dwelleth therein? and it shall rise up wholly as a flood," &c. *That is, the measure small and the price great.*

Wherefore, that the wrath of God may be turned away from falling upon commonweals and kingdoms for unjust extortion in usury and detestable usurers, it is the part of a holy magistrate to bridle usurers with upright laws; and, according to the quality of times, places, states, and persons, to appoint a lawful, just, and honest lucre, that usurers may not, in lending, letting, buying, and selling, oppress the poor people, but that equity and justice may be kept in all things. Of this duty of his the magistrate hath a notable example in Nehemias, suppressing the covetousness, cruelty, and extreme injury of usurers, and other oppressors of his Jewish commonalty. It is at large set down in the fifth chapter of the history of Nehemias. In this therefore, which I have hitherto alleged, I mean not to father or defend unjust occupiers, usurers, or their insatiable covetousness; but I affirm *Against usurers.*

[5 The authorised Version has "the new moon;" but in the margin "month."]

[6 So Coverdale's Bible, 1535, has "sycle," from the Latin, *siclum*, shekel. See Becon's Works, Parker Soc. ed. Vol. II. p. 109.]

flatly, that they live of the blood and bowels of their brethren and countrymen, and that they shall be undoubtedly
damned, unless they repent them of their sin and extortion.
The very law of nature doth make greatly against them,
which I object here, and say unto them: "Whatsoever thou
wouldest not have done to thyself, that do not thou to ano-
[Luke iii. 12, 13.] ther." "The publicans also came to John, that they might
be baptized of him, and said, Master, what shall we do?
To whom he said: Exact no more than is appointed for you."
These publicans were such as lived upon the public toll and
customs, which they had farmed at the Romans' hands for a
certain sum of ready money. Now, he bade not these publicans to leave off their toll-gathering, but willed them to be
content with their appointed duty. In like manner I urge
the same sentence, and say to all usurers and occupiers:
"Exact no more than is appointed for you." But if ye want
a certain constitution and ordinance, set down by the magistrate, for the gain of your money in every several trade;
then let equity, humanity, and charity prevail in your minds,
and let the common law sink into your hearts, which saith:
"Whatsoever ye would that men should do to you, the
same do ye to them." "If thine eye," saith the Lord, "be
single, all thy body is lightsome; but if the light that is in
thee be darkness, how great then is that darkness!"

Sacrilege.   Sacrilege is the spoiling of holy things which are consecrated to God and the use of the church. For the church
of God hath hallowed goods and riches, wherewith it doth
partly maintain sincere doctrine and the holy ministry of
the church; and partly relieve the needy saints and impotent
brethren. The church also hath goods and possessions, to
keep the places of prayer, spiritual houses[1], and hospitals[2]
in due reparations; and lastly, for the public help of all
people in common calamities and grievous afflictions. They
therefore are church-robbers, which do convert the church-
goods from the lawful and holy purpose, for which they
were ordained, into a profane and godless use; spending them
prodigally in hunting, gay clothing, superstition, whore-
hunting, dicing, drinking, and excessive banqueting: in
which things bishops and magistrates of these days do greatly

[1 ædium sacerdotalium, Lat.]
[2 xenodochiorum aut hospitalium, Lat.]

offend[3]. And it cannot otherwise be, but that some great misfortune, and more calamities than one, must needs follow that foul abuse of ecclesiastical riches and spiritual goods. For as Christ our Lord, the very Son of God, is spoiled and defrauded in the poor and needy ; so doctrine and godliness come to an end, honest studies do utterly decay, the sheep of Christ are altogether destitute of good and faithful shepherds, and are left for a prey to ravening wolves and merciless robbers. But yet we must have a regard not to account in the number of church-robbers such heads and overseers of holy religion, as some kings of Juda were, but Ezechias especially, and many other bishops and pastors of the primitive church, who, in many troublesome broils, when either wars did waste their countries and commonweals, or else when hunger or some other public calamity did oppress and pinch their silly[4] countrymen, did not stick to bestow the church-goods liberally, and to empty the treasure of the hallowed money, that thereby they might do the poor oppressed some good : but they had undoubtedly been wrongful church-robbers, if they, to spare money and other vessels which are without life, would not have redeemed living creatures, their countrymen, from death and penury. There is an excellent place of this matter in St Ambrose, *Officiorum*, Lib. ii. cap. 28[5]. There are also notable examples hereof in the ecclesiastical history[6].

Moreover, in the number of church-robbers divines account Simoniacs, that is, merchants[7], I mean, buyers and Simoniacs.

[3 See Seckendorf. Comm. de Luth. Lib. iii. Sect. 21. § lxxviii. Add. 1.]

[4 silly, see Vol. i. pp. 189, 351.]

[5 The title of this chapter, in the treatise *de Officiis Ministrorum*, is : Misericordiam etiam cum invidia propria largius exercendam : ad quod refertur memorabilis vasorum sacrorum in captivorum redemtionem ab Ambrosio fractorum historia, et pulcherrima de auri et argenti quæ ecclesia possidet legitimo usu præcipiuntur, &c.—Ambrosii Opp. Tom. ii. col. 102, Par. 1690.]

[6 In his treatise, *De Episcoporum Instit. et Funct.* Bullinger instances such an example of Achatius, Tripart. Hist. Lib. ii. cap. 16, and of Cyril, ibid. Lib. v. cap. 37. He alleges also the examples and words of Ambrose, Laurentius, Exuperius, Jerome, and Augustine: cap. 9. fol. 117, Tigur. 1538.]

[7 Chananæi, Lat. See Hos. xii. 7.]

sellers of spiritual and ecclesiastical dignities. For such an one is Simon Magus, their grand patriarch, reported to have been in the Acts of the Apostles. In the civil law, whosoever went about with privy gifts to buy the voice of any man to speak on his side, when public offices were for to be bestowed, he was guilty of ambition; and, beside the shame and open infamy, was compelled to pay an hundred crowns for his offence[1]. But, because this belongs not to sacrilege, we let it pass, and return to our matter.

They are church-robbers, whosoever either do not pay at all, or else do pay unwillingly, the goods that are due to the church; I mean, their tithes and yearly revenues. It is to be seen in the scriptures, how terribly the prophets do threaten church-robbers. Haggeus testified, that the ground brought forth so ill and little fruit for nothing else, but for because the people did not truly pay that which of duty they ought to the temple. In Malachy, God promiseth the people to make their ground fruitful, if they will pay liberally the stipends and tributes due to the temple. Now the ministers of the churches may use those revenues, or stipends, by as good law and right as they that use the profit of the ground, which they themselves have husbanded. For so doth the Lord expressly teach them in the eighteenth of the Book of Numbers; wherewithal Paul's saying agreeth in the ninth chapter of his First Epistle to the Corinthians. And the Lord Jesus himself also gave alms to the poor of the stipend which he had, as it is to be seen in the thirteenth chapter of St John's Gospel.

Moreover, beggars commit sacrilege, who abuse the name of Christ, and make their poverty a cloak to keep them idle still. The apostle commandeth Timothy not to cherish such idle hypocrites and wandering vagabonds with the alms and expenses of the church goods.

But now the greatest sacrilege of all is, if a man translate the glory of God, the Creator, unto a creature.

There is a kind of theft called Peculatus, which is committed in filching the common treasure, or purloining away the prince's substance[2]. This kind of robbery breedeth every

Marginal notes: [Acts viii. 18, &c.] Ambition.   [Hag. i.]   [Mal. iii. 10 —12.]   [1 Tim. v. 5, &c.]   Peculatus.

[1 See Jul. Pacii Isagog. in Digest. Lib. XLVIII. tit. 14. p. 422, and Smith's Dictionary of Greek and Roman Antiquities, sub voc. *Ambitus*.]

[2 See Jul. Pacii Isagog. in Digest. Lib. XLVIII. tit. 13. p. 421.]

hour new exactions, and giveth wicked magistrates good cause and fit opportunity to poll[3] the poor commonalty. Of this sort of robbers did Cato happily[4] speak, when he said: "Private thieves do lead their lives in chains and fetters, but public thieves in gold and purple[5]." Under this title of robbery are all those contained, that either do not pay at all, or else pay with ill-will, the tributes and taxes that are due to their magistrates. Lastly, all they are counted faulty in this kind of thievery, whosoever do abuse the public wealth or treasure of the commonweal.

Other some there are, that take up children, whom they *Plagium* know very well, and sell them to other, thereby to get advantage; or else do steal away other men's servants. This kind of theft the lawyers call Plagium[6]. And of this offence are those people guilty, which, by evil whispering, persuasion, and seditious doctrine, do draw servants and handmaids from obedience to their masters, and children from doing reverence and duty to their parents. And when captains, that are hired of strange princes to serve for money in foreign wars, do, against the parents' will and knowledge, carry away whole *This is used in no place* bands of silly young men, whom they entice with many fair *so much as in Bullinger's* promises, and entrap with sundry sleights, leading them to *own country, where the* wars wherein they perish and never return to their friends *Swicers, who serve all men* again; such captains, I say, are to be reckoned in the number *for money, do practise* of men-stealers[7]. This offence of old was punished by death, *it daily.*

[3 poll: plunder.]   [4 happily, or *haply;* Lat. forte.]

[5 Sed enim M. Cato in oratione, quam de præda militibus dividenda scripsit, vehementibus et illustribus verbis de impunitate peculatus atque licentia conqueritur. Ea verba, quoniam nobis impense placuerunt, adscripsimus: Fures, inquit, privatorum furtorum in nervo atque in compedibus ætatem agunt; fures publici in auro atque in purpura.—A. Gell. Noct. Attic. Lib. XI. cap. 18. See also Becon's Works, Parker Soc. ed. Vol. II. p. 600; and Calvin. Comment. Tom. I. p. 531. col. ii. Amstel. 1671.]

[6 See Jul. Pacii Isagog. in Digest. Lib. XLVIII. tit. 15. p. 422, and Smith's Dict. sub voc. *plagium.*]

[7 "By a law no less politic than humane, established among the cantons (of Switzerland), their troops were not hired out by public authority to both the contending parties in any war. This law the love of gain had sometimes eluded, and private persons had been allowed to enlist in what service they pleased, though not under the public banners, but under those of their officers."—Robertson's Hist. of Charles V. book II. Vol. II. p. 189, Lond. 1782.]

as it is evident in the twenty-first of Exodus, and in the law of Constantine, which is to be seen *Cod.* Lib. IX. tit. 20[1].

Another sort of thieves there is, which we call felons; and those be they which steal and drive away other men's cattle. In this order of thieves are those people placed, which do misuse the cattle that is lent them; and they also, which, when they may, will not help another man's cattle that is in jeopardy: for the Lord in the law commanded to bring back that which goeth astray, and to restore it to the right owner.

Thus much hitherto have I spoken, my brethren, touching the sundry kinds of theft, of the just and lawful getting of goods, and also of the proper owning of peculiar riches.

OF THE LAWFUL USE OF EARTHLY GOODS; THAT IS, HOW WE MAY RIGHTLY POSSESS, AND LAWFULLY SPEND, THE WEALTH THAT IS RIGHTLY AND JUSTLY GOTTEN: OF RESTITUTION, AND ALMS-DEEDS.

THE SECOND SERMON.

I DID in my last Sermon, dearly beloved, declare unto you, by what means goods are rightly gotten, and how many kinds of theft there be, and sundry sorts of getting wealth unlawfully. There is yet behind another treatise for me to add, and therein to teach you what is the true use of goods rightly gotten, and how we may lawfully possess them, and justly spend and dispose them in this transitory life.

[1 Imp. Constantinus A. ad Celerem vicarium Africæ XVI. Plagiarii, qui viventium filiorum miserandas infligunt parentibus orbitates, metalli pœna cum ceteris ante cognitis suppliciis teneantur. Si quis tamen ejusmodi reus fuerit oblatus, posteaquam super crimine claruerit; servus quidem, vel libertate donatus, bestiis subjiciatur; ingenuus autem gladio consumatur. D. Kal. Augu. Constantino A. IIII. et Licinio. Coss.—Codex Justin. Lugd. 1551, Tom. II. p. 701, Lib. IX, tit. 20.]

[2 Abigei dicuntur, qui gregem ovium aut pecorum—vel equum de grege, vel bovem de armento abducunt.—Jul. Pacii Isagog. in Instit. Lib. XLVII. tit. 14. p. 406, Traject. ad Rhen. 1680.]

For justice doth not only not defraud any man, but doth, so much as it may, endeavour itself to do good to all men; neither is it enough for a godly man not to hurt any body, unless also he do good to all that he can. And in this point do many men sin, while they are persuaded that they have done all the duty that they owe, if they hurt no man, and if they possess that which they have without trouble to any man; although in the meanwhile they have no regard, whether they help or do good to any man, or no. And he sinneth as greatly in the sight of the Lord, which doth not use rightly goods justly gotten, as he that hath heaped up wealth in wickedness and naughty means. I will tell you therefore, so far as God shall give me grace, how, and in what sort, godly men may holily possess and dispose these earthly goods.

First of all, that the use of worldly wealth may be healthful to the owner, holy men have a diligent care, that nothing of another man's remain in their possession: that is, they do carefully separate wealth rightly come by from unjust-gotten goods, and do faithfully restore whatsoever they find, in that which they have, to belong of right unto other men. For they are throughly persuaded, and do verily believe, that by this means the wealth that is left them, although by restitution it be somewhat diminished, will yet notwithstanding prosper the better, endure the longer, and be far more fruitful unto them. *Nothing of another man's must be possessed.*

Now this restitution is flatly commanded, and also very necessary to be put in practice: for the Lord in the law doth by sundry means, and that very carefully, give charge of it too, as is to be seen in the twenty-second of Exodus. Moreover, so often as the just and holy commandment of God was, through the covetousness and wickedness of mankind, cast off and neglected, the Lord raised up grievous and almost unspeakable evils against the contemners thereof, and scattered abroad the unjust-gotten goods by wars, mishaps, and divers calamities. For the prophet Esay crieth, saying: "The Lord shall enter into judgment with the elders and princes of his people, and shall say unto them, It is ye that have burnt up my vineyard, the spoil of the poor is in your houses." And Amos in the third chapter of his prophecy crieth: "They store up treasures in their palaces by violence *Restitution is necessary.* *Exod. xxii.* *Isai. iii.*

and robbery. Therefore thus saith the Lord God: Miseries shall invade thee on every side of the land, and thy enemies shall bring down thy strength, or riches, from thee, and thy Luke xix. palaces shall be spoiled." We read therefore in the gospel, that Zacheus, of his own accord, promised restitution four-fold double, that is, a full and absolute recompence of whatsoever he had taken wrongfully away; and it is assuredly certain, that he performed that promise: for he understood by the inspiration of the Holy Ghost, that a restitution of his ill-gotten goods was especially necessary, and that he should never be happy until he had made a full amends for all his wrongful dealings. Very rightly therefore said St Augustine in his fifty-fourth epistle to Macedonius, where he writeth : " If, when thou mayest, thou dost not restore that which thou hast of another man's goods, then is not repentance truly performed, but falsely feigned: but if repentance be truly taken, then is not sin forgiven, unless restitution be made of that which was taken away; but, as I said, when it may be restored[1]."

When restitution is to be made..   But touching the time, when restitution ought to be made, the example of Zacheus teacheth us; who, so soon as he was received unto the favour of Christ, and did understand the works of truth and equity, did immediately promise restitution, and out of hand perform the same. Wherefore we must not foad off from day to day to make restitution. No man hath need to double his offence. For thou needest not by thy morrow and over-morrow delays to augment his discommodity and hinderance any longer, from whom thou hast, by thy subtil means and wicked violence, wrested the goods that he hath; considering, that he to his loss hath lacked them long enough, and been without them too long, God wot[2].

To whom restitution is to be made.   If thou demandest, to whom thou oughtest to make restitution? I answer, to him from whom thou tookest it, if thou knowest from whom thou hast had it, and who it is whom thou hast defrauded. But by that means, sayest thou, I shall bring myself into obloquy and infamy. I bid thee not

[1] Si enim res aliena, propter quam peccatum est, quum reddi possit, non redditur, non agitur pœnitentia, sed fingitur: si autem veraciter agitur, non remittetur peccatum, nisi restituatur ablatum; sed, ut dixi, cum restitui potest.—Aug. Opp. Par. 1531, Tom. ii. fol. 48, col. 4.]

[2] This expression is the translator's.]

do so : but, if thou didst invent a means to take it, then find out some handsome way to restore it again, whereby thou mayest escape and not incur the note of infamy.   And pray to the Lord, that he will vouchsafe to shew thee a ready way and apt for to accomplish the thing that thou mindest.   If thou meanest in good sadness[3] to make true restitution, thou shalt undoubtedly find a way to do it without reproach and obloquy.   But if thou dost but dally and jest with the Lord, thou wilt not be without a thousand excuses, the best and the soundest whereof will never set thy conscience at quiet liberty. Neither is God mocked.   I cannot tell, sayest thou, from whom I have taken it, and therefore I know not to whom I should restore it.   If in very deed thou knowest not from whom thou hast taken it; then hast thou the poor and needy, on whom to bestow it : to those thou oughtest to deal thy unjust-gotten goods, and not to superstition, or the ministers thereof.

Now, let every one make restitution of so much as he hath taken away ; or at the least, of so much as he is able to restore.   For many have spent, and so prodigally wasted other men's goods, that they are not able to make restitution of any thing again.   Let such fellows acknowledge their fault, and repent their folly, from the bottom of their hearts. And if it happen at any time afterward that they come by goods, then let them be so much more liberal of their own, as before they were prodigal in spending other men's.   But if all the riches which thou possessest be other men's goods, and gotten of thee by theft and robbery, so that, if thou madest a full restitution, there should no penny be left for thee, but that thou must needs go beg ; then art thou verily hard bestead, and in too woeful a taking ; yea, thou art mad and far beside thyself, if thou wilt not stick, but still go on to paint thy pride, and maintain a port with other men's pence, and satisfy thy lust in the bowels, blood, and sweat of poor men's brows.   Why dost thou not rather abase thy self to poverty, and use thy unjust-gotten goods, as needy people use their alms ?   For thou livest of that that should be the poor's. Therefore lay down thy pride, and forsake thy ruffling[4]

[marginal note: How much every one ought to restore.]

[marginal note: Good counsel or advice.]

[3 sadness: seriousness, earnestness.]
[4 ruffling: to ruffle, to put out of form or discompose; but used by old writers to signify the acting in a rough, turbulent, or disorderly manner.—Toone's Glossary.]

4—2

riot. Consider with thyself, who thou art, and whereupon thou livest: and still do thy endeavour to make restitution, so far as thou canst; and let it grieve thee to see thyself not able to restore the whole again. If it be not a grief to thee for a time to suffer poverty, to labour and faithfully to exercise some honest occupation, and to train up thy children, leading them as it were by the hand, to work ; then thou shalt not want whereon to live, although thou restorest all, whatsoever thou hast, of other men's goods. But there is very small and almost no faith at all in many men ; whereby it cometh to pass, that very few, or none, can be persuaded to make true restitution. To this I add (before I go any further) that they ought especially to think of a restitution, which have with evil words corrupted the minds of simple souls; with privy backbiting raised slanders on other men ; or with perverse counsel stirred up the mightier men against the weaker sort: for these things do pass and are far above all earthly riches.

Ample or large discourses have been made touching restitution.

Thus much have I said hitherto touching restitution, of which other men have left very ample discourses. I for my part do see, that to a godly mind this work of restitution is short and plain enough ; and therefore have I spoken of it so shortly as I have. For a godly and well disposed man doth with all his heart desire and seek to obey the law of God ; and therefore, by calling to God for aid, he shall easily find a way to work justice and equity. As for those whose desire is rather to seem just men than to be just indeed, and do love this world more than it becometh them to do; they, with their over many questions and innumerable perchances and putcases[1], do make the treatise of restitution so tedious and intricate, that no man shall ever be able to make it so plain that they will understand it. I will not therefore answer them any more, but only warn them to examine their own conscience, and see what that doth bid them do. Now I would have that conscience of theirs to be settled in, and be mindful of, the general law, which saith : " Whatsoever thou wouldest have done to thyself, that do thou to another; and whatsoever thou wouldest not have done to thyself, that do not thou to another."

[1 *put case*, an elliptical expression for *suppose that it may be so.* Johnson.]

After this now I will somewhat freely discourse upon *We must not set our minds* the just possessing, using, or disposing of well-gotten earthly *on riches.* substance. First of all, no man must put any confidence in riches, which are indeed things transitory and do quickly decay: we must not settle our minds upon nor be in love with them; but by all means take heed that they drive us not to idolatry, nor hinder the course that we have to pass. Heaven is the goal whereat we run[2]. Here again we must all give ear to the divine and heavenly words uttered by the prophet David, who said: "Put your trust in God *Psal. lxii.* always, pour out your hearts before him; for God is our refuge. As for the children of men, they be but vain: the children of men are deceitful upon the weights, they are altogether lighter than vanity itself. Trust not in wrong and robbery, give not yourselves to vanity: if riches increase, set not your hearts upon them[3]." The apostle Paul, being endued with the same spirit, biddeth us to use the world and worldly things, as though we used them not[4]. Again, he calleth covetousness the worshipping of idols; and chargeth *[Coloss. iii.* rich men not to put their trust in uncertain riches, but in *5.] [1 Tim. vi.* the living God, who ministereth to all creatures living suffi-*17.]* ciently enough. And therefore the Lord in the gospel forbiddeth to heap up treasures upon earth.

Now, on the other side, we are not bidden by the apostles *Prodigality forbidden.* to spend our goods prodigally, in riot and wantonness. For we may not abuse the wealth, that the Lord hath lent us, in pride and luxury, as many do, who lash out all in dicing, sumptuous building, strange clothing, excessive drinking, and over-dainty banqueting. The end and destruction of such kind of people the Lord doth very finely[5], though not without terror to them that hear it, set down in the parable of the rich glutton, who, after his delicate fare and costly apparel, was after this life tormented in hell with unspeakable thirst, and toasted there with unquenchable fire. Therefore these temporal goods must be rightly, holily, and moderately used, without excess.

Every man must acknowledge these terrestrial goods to be *Riches are the gift of* the mere and free gifts of our bountiful and heavenly Father, *God for*

[2 Ad cœlos tendimus, Lat.]
[3 See Prayer-book Version.]
[4 1 Cor. vii. 31. See page 31.]   [5 venuste, Lat.]

which he
must be
thanked. and not to be given for our deserts, or gotten by our might. For we have of God's liberality all things necessary to maintain our lives. It is the Lord which blesseth and doth prosper our labour. Finally, they are not evil, but the good gifts of God, which he giveth to the maintenance of our lives, and not to our destruction: the fault is in ourselves, that riches are a snare to bring many men to evil ends. Moreover, the Lord himself requireth, and in his word commandeth us, to be thankful unto him for his good benefits bestowed on us; to use them with thanksgiving; to praise his name for all things; and to rejoice in his fatherly goodness shewed unto us. For thus doth Moses, the servant of God, in Deutero-

[Deut. viii.] nomy, charge the Israelites[1]: "When thou hast eaten therefore, and filled thyself, then thank the Lord thy God in that good land which he hath given thee. Beware that thou forget not the Lord thy God, that thou wouldest not keep his commandments, his laws and ordinances, which I command thee this day: yea, and when thou hast eaten, and filled thyself, and hast built goodly houses, and dwellest therein; and when thy beasts and thy sheep are waxen many, and thy silver and thy gold is multiplied, and all that thou hast is increased; then beware, lest thine heart rise, and thou forget the Lord thy God, which brought thee out of the land of Egypt, and from the house of bondage. Say not then in thine heart, My power and the might of mine own hand hath prepared me this abundance. Remember the Lord thy God: for it is he that giveth thee power to get substance, &c."

[1 Tim. iv. 4.] Moreover Paul the apostle saith, that all the creatures of God are good, created to the good and preservation of us men; and biddeth us use them with the fear of God and

[1 Cor. x. 31.] giving of thanks. And again: "Whether ye eat or drink, or whatsoever ye do, do all to the glory of God." And in

[Heb. xiii. 5, 6.] another place: "Let your manners be far from covetousness; and be content with the things that ye have: for he hath said, I do not forsake, nor leave thee. So that we may boldly say, The Lord is my helper, I will not fear what man can do unto me."

[1 Dominus Deus tuus dabit tibi terram præstantissimam, in qua nulla re indigebis, Lat. omitted by the translator; The Lord thy God shall give thee a most excellent land, wherein thou shalt not lack any thing.]

Let earthly goods also serve our necessity. Now necessity Goods serve to supply our necessity. requireth a commodious dwelling-place, so much victuals as are sufficient, comely apparel, and honest company-keeping with our neighbours and equals. Let every man measure and esteem these circumstances, first by his own person, then by his family or household. For an householder must warily provide and foresee, that no necessary thing be wanting in his family. Of this care of the householder there are sundry testimonies of scripture extant; but specially that of St Paul, in the fifth chapter of his first epistle to Timothy. And here note, that by necessity all things are meant, which the body or life of man doth necessarily require and stand in need of; and finally, whatsoever the honesty and beseeming of every man doth crave or demand. And thus far verily, and to this end or purpose, it is lawful for any man to lay somewhat up in store against years to come. The man, whose charge is much in keeping a great house, hath need of the more to maintain it withal: and he, whose family is not so big, needeth so much the less as his house is the smaller. And one state of life, and a greater port, becometh a magistrate; when another countenance, and a lower sail, beseemeth a private person. But in these cases let every man consider what necessity requireth, not what lust and rioting will egg him unto. Let him think with himself, what is seemly and unseemly for one of his degree.

And yet we do not in this treatise make so strict a Necessity excludeth not allowed pleasure. definition of necessity, as that thereby we do utterly condemn all pleasure and moderate liberty for sensuality and luxury. For I know that God hath granted and given to man, not only the use of necessity,—I mean, the use of those things which we as men cannot be without,—but also doth allow him all moderate pleasures wherewithal to delight him. Let no man therefore make scruple of conscience in the sweet and pleasant use of earthly goods, as though with that sweet pleasure which he enjoyeth he sinned against God; but let him which maketh conscience, make it rather in the just and lawful use of those terrestrial riches. For the Lord hath in no place forbidden mirth, joy, and the sweet use of wealth, so far forth that nothing be done undecently, unthankfully, or unrighteously. For the prophet Jeremy, alluding to the promises of God's law contained in the twenty-sixth of Leviticus and the twenty-eighth of Deuteronomy, saith: "They shall come and rejoice in Sion, and shall have plenteousness of goods which the Lord shall give them, namely, in wheat, wine, oil, young sheep and calves; and their soul shall be as a well watered garden; for they shall no more be sorrowful. Then shall the maid rejoice in the dance, yea, both young and old folks : for I will turn their sorrow into gladness, and will comfort them, and make them merry. I will make drunken the hearts of the priests with fat, and my people shall be filled with my goodness, saith the Lord." Jeremy thirty-first. Moreover[1] in the fourth chapter of the third book of Kings we read: "And under Solomon they increased, and were many in number, as the sand of the sea, eating and drinking, and making merry[2]." Again, in the eighth chapter of the same book we find: "And Solomon made a solemn feast, and all Israel with him, a very great congregation, which came together out from among all the people, even from the entering in of Hemath unto the river of Egypt, before the Lord seven days and seven days, that is, fourteen days in all. Afterward he sent away the people, and they thanked the king, and went unto their tents very joyfully, and with glad hearts, because of all the goodness that the Lord had done for David his servant, and for Israel his people[3]." Like unto this is that which we read in the eighth chapter of Nehemias, in these words: "And Esdras, with the Levites, said to all the people which was sad and sorrowful, This day is holy unto the Lord your God : be not ye sorry, and weep ye not; but go your way to eat the fat, and drink the sweet, and send part unto them that have not, &c." And the Lord, verily, doth not require us men to be without all sense and feeling of those pleasures which he of his grace hath given us to enjoy ; neither would he have us to be altogether benumbed, like blocks and stocks and senseless stones: for he himself hath graffed in us all the sense and feeling of good and evil, of sweet and sour. And the same our God and Maker hath, of his eternal goodness and wisdom, ordained a certain natural excellency in his creatures, and

[1 in sacra historia, Lat. omitted ; in the sacred history.]

[2 1 Kings (commonly called, The Third Book of the Kings, Auth. Ver.) iv. 20.—In Juda et Israela, Lat. omitted by the translator.]

[3 universo populo, Lat.]

hath adorned them, and made them so delectable, that we may delight in and desire them ; yea, and that more is, our God hath planted in them a nourishing force and virtue to cherish us men, and to keep our bodies in fair and good liking. For David saith : " And (he maketh grow out of the [Psal. civ. 15, &c.] earth) wine that maketh glad the heart of man, and oil to make him have a cheerful countenance, and bread to strengthen man's heart. The trees of the Lord are full of sap, wherein the birds make their nests, and sing, &c." Moreover, it is reported that Jacob, the patriarch, did drink to drunkenness; and of Joseph and his brethren the scripture saith : "And in drinking with him they were made drunken with wine[4]." Now no man will take this drunkenness of theirs for that excessive bibbing, which the holy scripture doth every where The common English translation hath, condemn; but for a certain sweet and pleasant measure in they were drinking, wherewith being once satisfied they were made the made merry. merrier. For that mad kind of drunkenness bereaves the senses, and is so far from causing men to be jocund and merry, that, clean contrariwise, it maketh them wayward, uncivil, out of order, beastly, swinelike, and filthy. A like phrase of speech useth Haggeus the prophet, where he saith : [Hag. i. 6.] " Consider your own ways in your hearts ; ye sow much, but ye bring little in ; ye eat, but ye have not enough ; ye drink, but not unto drunkenness:" that is, not unto sweet and pleasant sufficiency, that, being filled and jocund therewith, ye need desire no more, but for that plenty give thanks to the Lord, your good benefactor, for bestowing it on you. This do I somewhat more largely declare, because of the Anabaptists[5], and certain senseless Stoics, and other new sprung up hypocrites, the Carthusian monks[6], who, as they go about to make men mere blocks, so do they, with most tragical outcries, condemn utterly all allowable pleasure and

[4 There seems to be some oversight in the mention of Jacob. Concerning Gen. xliii. 34, Ainsworth, in loc. remarks : "largely drank, or drunk themselves merry: were drunken, which word is used for large drinking unto mirth, but with sobriety, Hag. i. 6 ; John ii. 10".]

[5 Bullinger, adv. Anabap. Lib. I. cap. 10, Tigur. 1560.]

[6 The Carthusian order of Monks, so called from their first settlement at Chartreuse, near Grenoble in France, arose in the year 1084 or 1086. They were a branch of the Benedictines, and were the most austere of all the religious sects.—Mosheim, Cent. xi. Part 2. Book 3. chap. 2. § 27.]

lawful delights. They, to colour and commend their odd opinion to the ears of men, abuse many places of the sacred [Luke vi. 25.] scriptures: "Woe (say they) to you which now are full, and do laugh now; for the time will come, when ye shall hunger and weep:" when as indeed this and such like sayings were uttered of God against the wicked, and such as do unthankfully abuse the benefits and creatures of their good God. And therefore, for a conclusion of that which I have hitherto said, I add this; that godly men must still take careful heed, that they let not loose the reins to lust, and so exceed the golden mean[1]. For mean and measure in these allowed pleasures also is liked and looked for, as well as in other things.

Riches must serve to do honour, and shew courteous behaviour between man and man. Furthermore, let goods and earthly substance serve to do honour, and shew curteise[2] humanity in one man to another. For we do of duty owe honour and humanity to our kinsfolks and alliance, our friends and acquaintance, our countrymen and strangers. For we must not only do good to them that are familiar with us, but to them also whom we did never see before, in keeping hospitality for wayfaring strangers, so far as our substance will stretch to maintain it. For if otherwise thy wealth be slender, as that it will do no more but maintain thine own house and family, no parcel of God's law[3] doth bind or bid thee to distribute to other men the wealth which thou thyself dost need as much or more than they. It is sufficient for thee to provide that they of thine own household be not a burden to other men's backs. So then the man, whose wealth is small, is not compelled to spend that little which he hath[4] in doing honour or shewing courtesy to other men: it is enough for him to bear with a valiant heart his own hard hap, and to take heed that his poverty procure him not to offend against right and honesty. Let those who are indifferently stored[5], and richer men who have wealth at will, be courteous and liberal to entertain strangers with frank hospitality. Let their minds be set to use liberality to their own praise and honesty, and not given to filthy greediness and unhonest sparing of every odd halfpenny. For some thou shalt find, who, though they be indifferent well stored with

[1 ne quid nimis, Lat.]   [2 i. e. courteous.]
[3 nulla Dei vel æqua lex, Lat.; no law of God or equity.]
[4 quod non habet, Lat.; that which he hath not.]
[5 mediocres, Lat.]

wealth and possessions, are yet notwithstanding so wholly
given over to the gathering of more, that neither for their
own honesty's sake, nor for any shew of courtesy, they will
once bestow a dodkin[6] upon any man whatsoever, be he their
own countryman, or a stranger unknown. These kind of fellows are always chambered, and keep themselves close in secret
counting-houses; their bags are their pillows whereon they
sleep and dream of their ruddocks[7]; they are not seen to stir
abroad, lest peradventure occasion should be offered them to
give entertainment, or to shew some civility to aliens and
strangers. The scripture doth give a far better report of the
most holy and famous patriarchs, our grand predecessors.

Lot sat in the gates of Sodom to wait for strangers and
wayfaring men, to the end he might take them home to his
house, and give them entertainment so well as he could. And
if it fell out that he met with a stranger, he did not desire
him home to his house for fashion's sake only, that is, with
faint or feigned words; but he used in earnest all the means
he could to compel him perforce to take up his inn, and lodge
with him that night. Of our father Abraham ye read
in Genesis, that in the very heat of the day, as he sat
in the door of his tent, he espied three men that were travellers, whom at the first sight, although he knew them
not, he entertained very lovingly, and bade them welcome
heartily. For he stayeth not to look when they should
come and request to refresh themselves with him; but start-
eth up, and meeteth them before they come to the door of his
tent, where he himself preventeth them in speaking first unto
them; and, when he had courteously after his country-manner
with obeisance saluted them, he biddeth them very lovingly
home to his house, and saith: " I beseech thee, my Lord, if
I may find favour in thy sight, pass not away, I pray thee,
from thy servant." Lo, here he calleth a traveller, and a
stranger too, by the name of Lord (even as we Germans,
in the entertaining of strangers, are wont to say: *Sind mir*

[marginal note: The patriarchs' hospitality. [Gen. xix.]]

[marginal note: [Gen. xviii.]]

[marginal note: We say in English, Sir.]

[6 teruncium, Lat. Dodkin, a small coin, the eighth part of a
stiver, a little doit: used as a contemptuous term for things of the
smallest value.—Toone's Glossary.]

[7 This is a free translation of the original Latin,—saccis in-
dormiunt. Ruddock, the bird called the robin red-breast: it is also
metaphorically used to signify gold coin.—Toone's Glossary.]

Gott wol kommen, lieben herren und guten freunde.) And
although he were in the land, where he dwelt, a man of high
authority and very great name, yet notwithstanding he did,
as it were, forget himself and say : " Pass not, I pray thee,
away from thy servant." He calleth himself a servant of
strangers. He goeth on moreover, and saith : " Let a little
water be fet[1], and wash your feet, and refresh yourselves
under the tree. And I will fet a morsel of bread to comfort
your hearts ; and then shall ye go on your way." In these
few words he containeth, in a manner, all the points of civil
courtesy. Neither did Abraham use these words to make a
shew only of bounteous liberality : but when he had by en-
treaty requested them to stay, and by their grant obtained
his desire, he bestirreth his stumps to accomplish in deeds
the thing that he had promised ; he maketh haste to Sara,
which was in the tent, and saith : " Make ready at once

Or pecks. three measures of fine meal, knead it, and make cakes." The
scripture yet addeth further this clause : " And Abraham,
running unto his beasts, caught a calf tender and good, and
gave it to a young man, which hasted, and made it ready at
once. And he took butter and milk, and the calf which he
had prepared, and set it before them, and stood himself with
them ;" that is, did himself serve them, as they ate under
the tree. This is wonderful verily, and to be thought on
deeply. Those goods were well and worthily bestowed upon
so bountiful, liberal, and courteous a man as Abraham was,
which knew how to use his wealth so honestly and with so
commendable courtesy. Neither was he alone in all his house
so frank and liberal ; as his wife and family were readily
given and very willing to put that holy exercise in ure and
practice. All things therefore were ready with a trice. In
making preparation, also, no diligence was wanting ; choice
was made of all things ; for riffraffe and refuse-gear was
not served to these strangers, but the best and likeliest of
all that was found. The good man himself taketh pains like
a servant. He himself bringeth in his country fare, which
far doth excel all costly cates and princelike dishes ; and setteth his guests to meat with butter and milk, and serveth
the last course with veal, well fed, and housewife-like dressed.
Neither was he content with this courtesy and entertainment,

[1 fet : fetched.]

but humbled himself further yet, and waited at the table, while his guests were at meat. The table, lo, was served by him, which had those great and ample promises made him by God; which is the father of all the faithful, which is the root and grandsire of Christ our Lord, which was the friend of God and confederate to puissant kings, being himself the most honourable prince in all the land, as he that had in war overcome and vanquished four of the mightiest kings of all the East, and brought them back again to slavery and bondage, delivering his people whom they had taken captive.

This excellent and worthy man, I say, may well be a pattern for all wealthy men to follow, in bestowing honour, courtesy, and hospitality upon strangers and men unknown. For, lastly, beside his rare and seldom seen hospitality, he shewed moreover this point of courtesy, that, when they rose from meat, he bare them company some part of the way. Let our wealthy pinchpence, therefore, at the last be ashamed of, and leave their niggish lives and insatiable covetousness. What pleasure, I pray you, have they of their riches? to whom do they good? whom do they honour with their close-kept coin? Or what honour or honesty doth their money procure or get them, while they live among men? Why do not the wiser sort of wealthy men rather leave this crew of miserable wretches, and hearken to the apostle's words, who saith, "Remember to keep hospitality; for by that means [Heb. xiii. 2.] many have lodged angels unwittingly and unawares?" And verily, he speaketh there of Lot and Abraham. Neither is it to be doubted, but that we entertain the very angels of God, and Christ himself, as often as we shew courtesy and hospitality to good and godly mortal men.

Lastly, let the goods of wealthy men serve, not to the entertainment of men of credit only, but to the relief also of poor and needy creatures. For that wholesome saying of Paul must be beaten into their heads: "Charge them that [1 Tim. vi. 17 —19.] are rich that they do good, that they be rich in good works, that they be ready to give, glad to distribute, laying up in store for themselves a good foundation against the time to come, that they may lay hold upon eternal life." With this doctrine of the apostle[2] doth the prophet Esay very well

Goods must serve to relieve the poor.

[2 congruit prophetica per omnia. Isaias enim &c., Lat. ; the doctrine of the prophets agrees in all points. For Isaiah &c.]

[Isai. xxiii. 18.] agree, where he saith touching Tyre: "Their occupying also and their wares shall be holy unto the Lord: their gains shall not be laid up nor kept in store; but it shall be theirs that dwell before the Lord, that they may eat enough, and have clothing sufficient." Lo, here Esaias teacheth us the means to lay up treasure that ever shall endure. Moreover, in the sixth chapter of Matthew the very same is repeated that was spoken of before. Let every one also call to his memory the other wholesome sentences of the Lord his God, to stir him up to the giving of alms. In [Deut. xv.] Deuteronomy Moses saith: "Beware that thou harden not thine heart, nor shut to thine hand from thy needy brother: but open thine hand liberally unto him. Thou shalt give him, and let it not grieve thine heart to give unto him: because that for this thing the Lord thy God shall enrich and bless thee in all thy works, and in all thou puttest thine hand unto. The Lord[1] shall never be without poor; and therefore I command thee, saying, Open thine hand liberally unto thy brother that is poor and needy in the land." In the [Psal. cxii. 5, 9.] Psalms we find: "A good man is merciful, and lendeth; and guideth his words with discretion. He disperseth abroad, and giveth to the poor: his righteousness remaineth for ever; his horn shall be exalted with honour." Solomon also saith: [Prov. iii.] "Let mercy, or well-doing, or faithfulness never part from thee: bind them about thy neck, and write them in the tables of thine heart; so shalt thou find favour and good estimation in the sight of God and men." Again, "Honour the Lord with thy substance, and of the firstlings of all thine increase give to the poor: so shall thy barns be filled with plenteousness, and thy presses shall flow over with sweet wine." And [Prov. xxi. 13.] again, "Whosoever stoppeth his ear at the cry of the poor, he shall cry himself, and not be heard." With these in all points do the sayings of the apostles and evangelists plainly [Matt. v. 42.] agree. "Give to every one that asketh of thee." Again: [Matt. xxv. 40.] "Verily, I say unto you, inasmuch as ye have shewed mercy to the least of these my brethren, ye have shewed it to me." Which sentence surely is worthy to be noted, and deeply printed in the hearts of all Christians. For if the Lord Jesus reputeth that to be bestowed on himself, which thou bestowest on the poor; then undoubtedly he thinketh himself

[1 A misprint in all the editions for "the land."]

neglected and despised of thee, so often as thou neglectest
or despisest the needy. This is undoubtedly true and most
surely certain: for the Lord and Judge of all people as-
sureth us by promise, that at the end of the world, in that
last judgment, he will give sentence in this manner and order:
"Come, ye blessed of my Father, possess the kingdom, &c.
For I was hungry, and ye gave me meat; I was thirsty, and
ye gave me drink :" and so forward, as is to be seen in the
twenty-fifth chapter of St Matthew's Gospel. Hereunto also
belongeth the words of St John the apostle, where he saith:
"Whoso hath this world's good, and seeth his brother have [1 John iii.
need, and shutteth up his compassion from him, how dwelleth 17.]
the love of God in him?" And from hence, undoubtedly,
did first arise the common voice of them of old, which were
wont to say : "If thou seest a needy body die with hunger,
and dost not help him, while thou mayest, thou hast killed
him, and given consent unto his death[2]." Let him therefore, which hath store of earthly goods, know for a surety,
and in his heart be throughly persuaded, that he is bound
especially to do good to the needy.

Moreover let him that is wealthy do good to all men, so To whom we
near as he can. For the Lord saith: "Give to every one that good.
asketh of thee." And Tobias giveth his son this lesson, saying:
"Turn not thy face from any poor man[3]." But if thou canst
not, through lack of ability, do good to all men, then succour
them chiefly whom thou perceivest to be godly-disposed, and
yet pinched with penury : for St Paul saith, "Let us do good [Gal. vi. 10.]
to all men, but to them especially that are of the household
of faith." Let us therefore aid, succour, and relieve fatherless children and poor widows, old men and impotent people,
those that are afflicted and persecuted for the profession of the
truth, and such as are oppressed with any misery and calamity.
Let us further and help forward good and holy learning, and
all the worshippers and true ministers of God that live in
want and scarcity. Finally, let us relieve strangers, and
whomsoever else we may.

[2 See Bingham, Antiq. of Christ. Church, Book xvi. chap. 10.
sect. 15.]

[3 Tobit iv. 7. This lesson is given by Tobit to his son, Tobias,
according to the authorised Version ; but in the Vulgate the names
of the father and son are alike Tobias; as also in the earlier English
translation of the Bible.]

How we
ought to do
good.

[2 Cor. ix. 7.]

How far we
must do
good.

Now our duty is to aid, and stand them in stead, with counsel, comfort, help, money, meat, drink, lodging, raiment, commendations, and with all things else wherein we perceive that they lack our helping hand: touching which I spake somewhat in the tenth sermon of the first Decade[1]. We must also succour them readily, with a willing heart and a cheerful mind: "for God requireth a cheerful giver." And in helping them let us do liberally: for Tobias saith, "Be merciful after thy power[2]: If thou have much, give plenteously; if thou have little, do thy diligence gladly to give of that little. For in so doing the Lord shall bless both thee and thine."

Thus much, my brethren, have I hitherto said touching the lawful use of earthly goods. God grant that every one of you may print these sayings in his heart, and put in practice this holy work. Let us pray to the Lord that he will vouchsafe so to direct us in his ways, that for the getting of those transitory goods we lose not the everlasting treasure of his heavenly kingdom.

OF THE PATIENT BEARING AND ABIDING OF SUNDRY CALAMITIES AND MISERIES: AND ALSO OF THE HOPE AND MANIFOLD CONSOLATION OF THE FAITHFUL.

THE THIRD SERMON.

I SHALL not do amiss, I think, my reverend[3] brethren, if to the treatise which I have already made of earthly riches, and of the use and abuse of the same, I do here also add a discourse of the divers calamities, wherewith man, so long as he liveth in this frail flesh, is continually vexed and daily afflicted. For since that many men do either lose their temporal goods, or else can by no means get them, which are the causes why they be oppressed with penury and neediness; it cannot be but profitable and very necessary too for every good man to know out of the word of God the very reason

[1 Vol. i. p. 188.]

[2 quomodo potueris, ita esto misericors, Lat. and Vulgate. This sentence, however, is omitted in the authorised Version, though retained in the service of the Offertory in the Book of Common Prayer, and given in Coverdale's Bible, 1535.]

[3 fratres honorandi, Lat.]

and ground of his consolation in his miseries; lest, being swallowed up of too great sorrow, and entangled in utter desperation, he give himself over to be Satan's bond-slave. Now this treatise serveth for the whole life of man. For I mean not to speak of any one calamity alone, as of poverty, or penury, but generally of all the miseries that happen to man. Verily, since man is born to grief and misery, as birds to flying[4] and fishes to swimming; his life can never possibly be either sweet or quiet, unless he know the manner and reason of his calamity. And if so be he know the reason thereof, religiously taken and derived out of the word of God; then his life cannot choose but be sweet' and quiet, howsoever otherwise it seem to be most bitter and intolerable. The mind of man, verily, is sorely afflicted and grievously tormented with lamentable miseries; but the same, on the other side, is sweetly eased and mightily upholden by the true knowledge of those miseries, and holy consolations, derived and taken out of the word of God.

First of all, it is requisite to lay before our eyes and reckon up the several kinds and especial sorts of mortal men's calamities. The evils verily are innumerable, which daily fall upon our necks; but those which do most usually happen are the plague or pestilence, sundry and infinite diseases, death itself, and the fear of death, whose terror to some is far more grievous than death can be. To these be added the death and destruction of most notable men, or such of whom we make most account; robberies, oppressions, endless ill chances, poverty, beggary, lack of friends, infamy, banishment, persecution, imprisonment, enforced torments, and exquisite punishments of sundry sorts and terrible to think on, unseasonable and tempestuous weather, barrenness, dearth, frost, hail, deluges, earthquakes, the sinking of cities, the spoiling of fields, the burning of houses, the ruin of buildings, hatred, factions, privy grudges, treasons, rebellions, wars, slaughters, captivity, cruelty of enemies, and tyranny; also the lack of children; or troubles, cares, and hellish lives[5] by the matching of unmeet mates in wedlock, by children naugh-

The kinds of calamities.

[4 Job v. 7: homo nascitur ad laborem, et avis ad volatum.— Vulgate. "Man is borne unto mysery, like as the byrde for to fle."— Coverdale's Bible, 1535.]

[5 miseriæ, Lat. without any epithet.]

5

tily disposed, maliciously bent, disobedient and unthankful to
father and mother; and lastly, care and continual grief in
sundry sorts for sundry things, which never cease to vex our
minds. For no man can in never so long a bead-row[1] reckon
up all the evils whereunto miserable mankind is woefully endangered, and every moment tormented. New miseries rise
up every day, of which our elders did never hear; and they
are appointed to be felt and suffered of us, who with our new
and never heard of sins do daily deserve new and never seen
punishments, when as otherwise the miseries, which our forefathers felt, had been enough and sufficient to have plagued
us all.

The good
and evil are
afflicted with
calamities.
But now with these evils, as well the good and godly
worshippers of God, as the wicked contemners of his name,
are troubled and put in ure: yea, the saints are through all[2]
their life time afflicted and vexed, when as contrarily the
wicked abound with all kinds of joy and delightful pleasures:
whereupon it cometh, that great temptations and complaints
arise in the minds of the godly. The wicked do gather by
their happy state and pleasant life, that God doth like their
religion, and accept their manner of dealing, whereby they
are confirmed and grounded in their errors. And on the
other side the godly, by reason of the miseries which they
have long suffered, do revolt from godliness, and turn to the
ungodly, because they think that the state of the wicked is
far better than theirs. Now it is good to know, and severally
to learn, all this out of the scriptures. That the godly are
and have been afflicted, as well as the wicked, since the beginning of the world, it is manifest to be seen in the example
of Abel and Cain: for, as the one was pitifully slain of the
other for his sincere worshipping of God, so was the other for
the murder made a vagabond, not daring for fear to abide in
any place to take his rest in. Jacob, surnamed Israel, is read
to have been vexed with many calamities. The same is
reported also of the Egyptians, while they persecuted the
Israelites. Saul was vexed, and David afflicted. The Lord
our Saviour, with his disciples, bare the cross of grief and
trouble: again, on the other side, the Jews, who cruelly
persecuted Christ and his disciples, were horribly destroyed,

[1 catalogo, Lat.]
[2 omnem prope, Lat.; almost all.]

and that worthily too, for their villainous injury. Unspeakable are the evils which the church of Christ did suffer in those ten most bloody persecutions[3] before the reign of Constantine the great: but Orosius, the notable, diligent, and faithful historiographer, maketh mention, that due and deserved punishments were out of hand laid upon the necks of those persecuting tyrants; of whom I will speak somewhat in place convenient[4]. And by the testimonies both of God and man, and also by manifold experience, we see it proved, that as well the godly as ungodly are touched with miseries. Yea truly, the best and holiest men for the most part are troubled and afflicted, when the wicked and worser sort are free from calamities, leading their lives in ease and pleasures. And while the good do suffer persecution and injuries, the wicked rejoice thereat. For the Lord in the gospel saith to his disciples: "Verily, verily, I say unto you, ye shall weep and lament, the world shall be glad; but ye shall be sorrowful." *The godly are afflicted when the wicked live in pleasures.* *[John xvi. 20.]*

But now, what kind of temptations those be, which arise in the hearts of the godly through their tribulations; and what those men, which are not altogether godless nor the enemies of God, do gather of the felicity wherein the wicked are, the scripture in many places teacheth us, and especially in that wonderful discourse of Job and his friends. The prophet Abacuch complaineth, and saith: "O Lord, how long shall I cry, and thou not hear? how long shall I cry out to thee for the violence that I suffer, and thou not help? why am I compelled to see iniquity, spoiling, and unrighteousness against me? why dost thou regard them that despise thee, and holdest *Habak. i.*

[3 The persecutions of the Christians by the Romans have, for many ages, been accounted *ten* in number. But the ancient history of the Church does not support precisely this number.—Some Christians of the fifth century were led into a belief by certain passages of scripture, especially by one in the Apocalypse, that the Christian body was fated to undergo *ten* calamities of the heavier kind; to which opinion they then accommodated history, though against her will, not, however, all in the same way.—Mosheim Eccles. Hist. cent I. Book 1. part i. chap. 5. § 4. ed. Soames, and note in loc.]

[4 See p. 109, &c. Orosius frequently notices these punishments in the 7th book of his Histor. adv. paganos; and the title of the 27th chapter of the same book is, "Collatio populi Israelitici et Christiani, Ægyptiaci item et Romani, quomodo illi pro Deo in adflictionibus, hi a Deo in plagis, similia fere passi sunt."]

thy tongue while the wicked treadeth down the man that is more righteous than himself? The wicked doth circumvent the righteous; and therefore wrong judgment proceedeth." In

Mal. iii. Malachi the hypocrites do cry: "It is but vain to serve God: and what profit is it that we have kept his commandments, and that we have walked humbly before the face of the Lord[1]? Now therefore we call the proud and arrogant blessed and happy: for the workers of wickedness live happily and are set up; and they tempt God, go on in their wickedness, and are delivered[2]." The holy prophet Asaph containeth all this most

Psal. lxxiii. fully and significantly in the Psalm, where he saith: "My feet were almost gone, my treadings had well nigh slipped: for I was grieved at the wicked, when I did see the ungodly in such prosperity. For they are in no peril of death[3]; they are, I say, troubled with no diseases, whereby they are drawn, as it were, to death, but are lusty and strong. They come into no misfortune like other men; but are free from the evils wherewith other folk are plagued: and this is the cause that they are so holden with pride, and wrapped in violence as in a garment. Their eyes swell with fatness, and they do even what they lust[4]. They stretch forth their mouth unto heaven, and their tongue goeth through the world: yea, and they dare to say, Tush, how should God perceive it[5]? Lo, these are the ungodly, these prosper in the world, and these have riches in possession. Then, said I, have I cleansed my heart in vain, and washed mine hands in innocency: and I bear punishment every day. And while I thought thus to myself, I had almost departed from the generation of God's children."

The causes of calamities. Now since this is so, it followeth consequently to beat out[6] the causes of these calamities: for in so doing we shall

[1 coram Deo exercituum, Lat.; God of hosts.]

[2 qui Deum tentant, Lat.; "for they tempte God, and yet escape." Coverdale's Bible, 1535.]

[3 neque enim sunt illis nexus ad mortem, Lat.; (eo quod non trahantur ad mortem quasi captivi.—Calvin, Comment. in loc.); for there are no bands in their death.—Auth. Vers.]

[4 dum eis videlicet pro voto omnia succedunt, Lat.; omitted,— while, that is, all things go according to their desire.]

[5 quomodo cognosceret omnia Deus? estne cognitio apud Altissimum? Lat.; How should God know all things? is there knowledge in the most High?]

[6 ut diligentissime excutiamus, Lat.]

be the better able to judge rightly of the miseries both of the godly and wicked sort of people. The causes of calamities are many, and of many sorts: but the general and especial cause is known to be sin. For by disobedience sin entered into the world, and death by sin; and so, consequently, diseases, and all evils in the world. They are very light-headed and vain fellows, that refer these causes to I cannot tell what, blind constellations, and movings of planets. For[7] we by our evil lusts and corrupt affections do heap up day by day one evil on another's neck. And at our elbows standeth the devil, who roundeth[8] us in the ears, and eggeth us forwards; and, as helps to spur us on, there are a crew of naughty packs[9], that never cease to train us in. And daily there do rise up divers instruments of tribulation, wherewith the most wise and just God doth suffer us men to be exercised and tormented.

But the same causes of affliction are not always found to be in the holy worshippers of God, as are in the wicked despisers of his name. The saints are often afflicted, that by their trouble the glory of God may be known to the world. For when the disciples of Christ did see the blind man in the gospel, which was blind from his mother's womb, they said to the Lord: "Master, who sinned, this man, or his parents, that he was born blind? Jesus answered, Neither did this man sin, nor his parents; but that the works of God might be made manifest in him." Likewise, when the Lord heard say that Lazarus was sick, "This disease (saith he) is not to death, but to the glory of God, that by it the Son of God may be glorified." And yet, if we touch this matter to the quick, there can none in the world be found without sin; so that, if the Lord will mark our iniquities, he shall always find somewhat to be punished in us: as it is at large declared in the book of Job.

The cause why the saints are afflicted.

[John ix. 2, 3.]

John xi.

Furthermore, the Lord doth suffer his spouse, the church, which he loveth full dearly, to be troubled and afflicted to this end and purpose; that he may openly declare, that the elect are defended, preserved, and delivered by the power and aid of God, and not by the policy or help of man. For Paul

We are delivered by the goodness of the Lord, not by our own means or ability.

[7 ceterum, Lat.; but.]

[8 to round, Johnson; to roun, Toone: to whisper or speak in secrecy.]

[9 pack, a loose or lewd person.—Johnson's Dict.]

saith : " We have this treasure in earthen vessels, that the excellency of the power may be God's, and not of us : while we are troubled on every side, but not made sorrowful; we are in poverty, but not in extreme poverty ; we suffer persecution, but are not forsaken therein ; we are cast down, but we perish not; we always bear about in the body the dying of the Lord Jesus, that the life of Jesus might also be made manifest in our body. For we which live are always delivered unto death for Jesus' sake, that the life also of Jesus might be made manifest in our mortal flesh[1]." Also the same apostle saith : " Virtue is made perfect in infirmity[2]."

Again, as the afflictions of the holy martyrs and faithful saints of Christ are testimonies of the doctrine of faith, as our Saviour in the gospel saith, " They shall deliver you up to councils, and in their synagogues they shall scourge you; yea, ye shall be brought before kings and rulers for my sake, that this might be for a witness to them and the people:" even so, in like manner, are the saints, overladen with miseries, made examples for us to learn by how to overcome and despise[3] the world, and to aspire to heavenly things.

Afflictions are testimonies of the doctrine of faith. [Matt. x. 17, 18.]

Finally, the Lord doth try those that be his by laying the cross upon their necks, and purgeth them like gold in the fire : he cutteth from us many occasions of evil, that he may bring us to the bearing of greater and more plentiful fruit. The wisdom of the Lord doth therein follow the manner of goldsmiths, who put their gold into the fire to purge, and not to mar it : and he imitateth also good husbandmen, who, when their corn is somewhat too rank, do mow it down ; and prune their trees, not to destroy, but to make them bear more abundant fruit. And this flesh of ours, verily, in peace and quietness is luskish[4], lazy, drowsy, and slow to good and honest exercises ; it is content, and seeketh no further than earthly things; it is wholly given to pleasures ; it doth utterly forget God and godly things : now therefore it is not expedient only, but also very necessary, to have this dull and sluggish lump stirred up and exercised with troubles, afflictions, and sharp persecutions. The saints herein are like

We are tried by afflictions.

[1 2 Cor. iv. 7—11. Bullinger has adopted the translation of Erasmus.]
[2 2 Cor. xii. 9. This is the Vulgate, and not Erasmus', version.]
[3 calcare, Lat. ; to tread under foot.]
[4 luskish, somewhat inclinable to laziness or indolence.—Johnson.]

to iron, which by use is somewhat worn and diminished, but by lying still unoccupied is eaten more with rust and canker. Most truly therefore said St Peter: "Dearly beloved, think 1 Pet. iv. it not strange, that ye are tried with fire, which thing is to try you, as though some strange thing happened unto you: but rejoice rather, in that ye are partakers of the afflictions of Christ; that, when his glory is revealed, ye may be merry and glad[5]." For Paul to Timothy saith: "Remember that 2 Tim. ii. Jesus Christ of the seed of David was raised from the dead according to my gospel; for which I am afflicted, as an evil doer, even unto bonds: and yet I suffer all things for the elect's sakes, that they might also obtain the salvation which is in Christ Jesus with eternal glory. It is a faithful saying: For if we be dead with him, we shall also live with him: if we be patient[6], we shall reign with him: if we deny him, he shall also deny us[7]." For in his epistle to the Romans he saith: "Those which he knew before he did Rom. viii. also predestinate, that they should be like-fashioned unto the shape of[8] his Son, that he might be the first-begotten among many brethren. Moreover, whom he did predestinate, them also he called; and whom he called, them also he justified; and whom he justified, them also shall he glorify[9]." Again, in the same epistle he saith: "We rejoice Rom. v. also in tribulations; knowing that tribulation worketh patience; patience proof; proof hope: and hope maketh not ashamed[10], &c." This do the private examples of the saints, and public examples of the whole church, very plainly declare. Abraham, Isaac, and Jacob, had never known that God's helping hand had been so faithful and always present with them; they had never been grounded in so sure hope, nor shewed such especial fruit of their excellent patience; if they had not been exercised with many perils, and, as it were, oppressed with infinite calamities. Whereupon it cometh, that David cried: "It is good for me, Lord, that thou hast troubled me." The church Psal. cxix. of Israel was oppressed in Egypt; but to the end that it [71.]

[5 1 Pet. iv. 12, 13; Erasmus' translation.]
[6 So Tyndale's and Cranmer's translations.]
[7 Erasmus' translation chiefly.]
[8 So Tyndale's and Cranmer's translations.]
[9 glorificabit, Lat.; the Versions have glorificavit.]
[10 Erasmus' translation.]

might with the more glory be delivered, and pass into the land of promise. The Jewish church was afflicted by them of Babylon and the Assyrians, so that their temple was overthrown, and the saints carried captive with the worst of the people. But the godly sort in their very captivity do feel the wonderful help of God, and by that means are made the better[1] by their afflictions; so that the name of the Lord was known[2] among the Assyrians, the Chaldees, the Medes and Persians, to his great glory and renown, as it is at large declared in the histories of Daniel, Hester, and Esdras[3].

Certain punishments appointed as plagues to certain sins. Here also is to be noted, that certain punishments are appointed of the Lord as plagues for certain sins; so that most commonly a man is plagued by the very same things wherein he sinned against the Lord. David offended God with murder and adultery; and therefore is he punished with the shame of his own house, with whoredom, incest, and detestable murder of his own children; and lastly, driven out and banished his kingdom. It was pride and arrogance, wherein Nabuchodonosor sinned; and therefore, being distract of his wits and turned into a beastly madness, he led his life for a certain time[4] with beasts of the field. But as Nabuchodonosor was, when God thought good, restored to his kingdom; so David did in time convenient feel the mercy of the Lord in settling him in his seat again. For this saying of the Lord is firmly ratified for ever, not only to David, but to every one that believeth, which is in these words set down in the scriptures: *[Psal. lxxxix. 30—34.]* "If his children forsake my law, and keep not my commandments, I will visit their sins with rods, and their iniquities with scourges: yet will I not utterly take my goodness from him; I will not break my covenant, neither will I change the thing that is once gone out of my mouth." Therefore it is to our profit that the Lord afflicteth us; as he himself testifieth in the revelation of Christ[5], uttered[6] by John the *Rev. iii.* apostle and evangelist, saying: "Them which I love I rebuke

[1 puriores fiunt, Lat.]
[2 quam latissime, Lat.; to the widest extent.]
[3 Ezra and Nehemiah. See Sixth Art. of Religion; "First Book of Esdras, Second Book of Esdras." So also Vulgate.]
[4 destinato tempore, Lat.]
[5 in theologia sua, Lat. See Vol. I. p. 170. n. 6.]
[6 edita, Lat.; put forth, published.]

and chasten." And Salomon, long before that, did say : "My Prov. iii.
son, refuse not the chastening of the Lord, neither faint when
thou art corrected of him. For whom the Lord loveth, him he
chasteneth ; and yet delighteth in him, as a father in his son[7]."

Now, touching the persecutions and terrible plagues laid Sin is the cause of the church's persecutions.
upon the neck of the whole church of God, or several martyrs
of the same; as they were, for the most part, breathed out of
worldly tyrants against the saints for their open confession
and testimonies of their faith, and truth of the gospel, so most
commonly the causes of those broils were the sins and offences
of the saints, which the justice of God did visit in his holy
ones, no doubt to the good and salvation of the faithful.
For of that bloody persecution under the emperors Diocletian
and Maximinian, which caused many thousands, yea, many
millions, of martyrs to come to their endings, we read this
following in the history of Eusebius of Cesaria, who learned
it, not by hear-say, but was himself an eye-witness of the
same : "When as by too much liberty and wantonness the
manners of the church were utterly marred, and the discipline
thereof corrupted ; while among ourselves we envy one
another, and diminish one another's estimation ; while among
ourselves we snatch at and accuse ourselves, moving deadly
war among ourselves; while dissimulation sitteth in the face,
deceit lurketh in the heart, and falsehood is uttered in words,
so that one evil is heaped still on another's neck ; the Lord
beginneth by little and little, and with the bridle to check the
mouth of his tripping church, and, reserving the congregations
untouched, he beginneth first to suffer them to feel persecution which served as soldiers in the camps of the Gentiles.
But when as by that means the people could not be made to
remember themselves, insomuch that they ceased not to
persist in their wickedness, and that the very guides of the
people and chief of the church, unmindful of God's commandment, were set on fire among themselves with strife, envy,
hatred, and pride, so that they might think they rather exercised tyranny than the office of ministers, because they had
forgotten christian sincerity and pureness of living ; then at
length the houses of prayer and churches of the living God

[7 Prov. iii. 11, 12 ; et tanquam pater in filio delectatur, Lat. ; "and
yet delyteth in him even as a father in his owne sonne."—Coverdale's
translation, 1535.]

were thrown to the ground, and the holy scriptures set on fire in the broad and open streets[1]." Thus much, word for word, out of the eighth book of his ecclesiastical history.

What kind
of sins the
saints' sins
are.
And yet here I make difference betwixt sin and sin. For the saints sin, but yet they abstain commonly from heinous crimes; although now and then too they fall into them, as it is evident by the example of David : but yet, for the most part, they fly from theft, murder, whoredom, and other grievous[2] sins like unto these. And while the saints are afflicted by tyrants, it is not for the neglecting of justice and true religion; but for the contemning of superstition, and stedfast sticking to Christ and his gospel. The Lord therefore doth forgive, and in the blood of Christ wash away, the sins of the holy martyrs, reputing them to suffer death not for the sins which they have committed, but for the zeal and love of true religion. He also punisheth the tyrants for the death of his martyrs; because, in putting them to death, they follow their own tyrannous affection, and not the just judgment of the living God. The Lord's mind, verily, was by tyrants to chasten his people Israel : but the tyrants (as Esay in his tenth chapter witnesseth) did not take it to be so; but rather, following their own affections, they passed all measure in afflicting them, and never sought after justice and equity : they therefore are punished of the Lord for killing his

[1 Bullinger has followed the Latin translation of Eusebius : Ubi ex multa libertate multaque indulgentia vitiati sunt mores, et disciplina corrupta est, dum alter alteri invidemus, et alter alteri derogamus; dumque nos invicem mordemus et incusamus, et adversum nosmetipsos intestina prœlia commovemus; dum simulatio in vultu, dolus in corde, fallacia profertur in verbis, et malorum per singula cumulus intumescit; aggreditur (Dominus) primo sensim refrœnare lapsantes, congregationibusque manentibus, indulget interim eos, qui erant in militia tantum gentilium, persecutione pulsari. Sed cum nullus ex hoc clementiœ ejus intellectus populis redderetur, et persisterent in malis suis, atque ipsi qui duces populi videbantur et principes, divini mandati immemores effecti, adversum se invicem contentionibus, zelo, livore, superbia, inimicitiis atque odiis inflammarentur, ita ut tyrannidem potius quam sacerdotium tenere se crederent, christianœ humilitatis et sinceritatis obliti; tunc demum...domus orationis et ecclesiœ Dei vivi ad solum deductœ sunt; divinœ vero scripturœ in medio platearum igni crematœ sunt.—Euseb. Eccles. Hist. Ruffino Aquil. interprete, lib. VIII. cap. 1. p. 183. Basil. 1539.]

[2 morte expianda, Lat.]

innocent and guiltless servants. For the thing which the Lord did persecute in his people, (their sins, I mean, and offences,) that do the tyrants neither punish nor persecute: but the thing that pleased God, (the love, I mean, of true religion, and the utter detesting of idolatry,) that they are mad upon, and persecute it with sword and fire and unspeakable torments. To this therefore doth that saying of St [1 Pet. iv. 15, 16.] Peter belong: "See that none of you be punished as a murderer, or as a thief, or as an evil-doer, or as a busy-body in other men's matters: but if any man suffer as a christian man, let him not be ashamed, but rather glorify God on this behalf."

Yet, for all this, I would not that heinous offenders should any whit despair. They have the example of the thief that was crucified with Christ; that let them follow: let them, I say, confess their faults, believe in Christ, commit themselves wholly to his grace and mercy, and lastly, suffer patiently the pain of their punishment; and, in so doing, there is no doubt but they shall be received of Christ into Paradise, and live there for ever, as the thief doth with Christ.

And although the godly be slain among transgressors, yet *Why God doth punish the good with the evil.* is he no more defiled by suffering with them than Christ our Lord was, being hanged among thieves. For though the godly and ungodly be wrapped and coupled together in one kind of punishment, yet are they severed by their unlike ending; while the wicked, after this bodily death, is carried to hell, there to burn without intermission; and the godly taken immediately into heaven, to live with Christ his Lord, to whom he committed and commended[3] himself. Touching this matter, and the causes of the afflictions of the holy men of God, I will not be aggrieved to recite unto you, dearly beloved, a notable place of St Augustine out of his first book *De civitate Dei*. "Wheresoever (saith he) good men do suffer the same and like punishment that the evil sort do, it is to be marked, that there is not therefore no difference betwixt them, because there is no diversity in the thing that they suffer. For as in one and the same fire gold doth shine, and chaff doth smoke; and under one flail the husk is broken, and the corn purged; and as the scummy froth is not mixed with the oil, although one weight of the same press doth crush both out at once: even

[3 obtulit, Lat.; offered.]

so one and the self-same misery, falling upon the good and the bad, doth try, fine, and melt the good; and on the other side condemn, waste, and consume the evil sort. Whereupon it cometh to pass, that in one and the same affliction the evil do detest and blaspheme the Lord, when contrarily the good do pray unto and praise his name for that he layeth upon them. So much matter maketh it in afflictions to mark not what, but with what mind, every man doth suffer. For stir up dirt and sweet ointments alike, and you shall have the one stink filthily, and the other cast forth a sweet-smelling savour. Therefore in that hurly-burly, and irruption made by the barbarous people, what did the Christians suffer which was not rather to their profit, while they did faithfully consider those troubles? especially because they, humbly considering the sins for which God, being wroth, did fill the world with so many and great calamities, although they be far from committing heinous, grievous, and outrageous offences, do yet nevertheless not repute themselves so clear of all faults, as that they judge not themselves worthy to suffer temporal calamity for the crimes they commit every hour and moment. For over and besides that every man which liveth peradventure laudably enough, doth in some points yield a little to carnal concupiscence, although not to the outrageousness of horrible sins, to the gulf of heinous offences and abominable iniquities, yet notwithstanding he yieldeth to some sins, which either he haunteth very seldomly, or else committeth so much the oftener as they are the lesser; over and besides this therefore I say, what man is there which, when he seeth and knoweth very well the men for whose pride, lascivious lives, covetousness, and damnable iniquity, God (as he hath threatened) doth plague the earth, doth so esteem them as they are to be thought of, and live so with them as he ought to live with such kind of people? For oftentimes many things are wickedly dissembled, while wicked doers are not taught, corrected, chidden, and admonished of their evil behaviours, either because we think the pain too much to tell them their faults; or while we are afraid to have the heavy looks of them with whom we live; or else avoid their displeasure, lest peradventure they should hinder or hurt us in temporal matters, when as either our greediness desireth to have somewhat more, or our infirmity feareth to lose the things which it hath already in hold and possession: so that, although the life of the wicked displease the good, for which cause they fall not into the same damnation, which is after this life prepared for the evil; yet, since they do therefore bear with, and forbear, their damnable sins, because they fear them in lighter and smaller trifles, they are justly scourged with them in this temporal life, albeit they be not punished with them eternally. While they be punished by God with the wicked, they do justly feel the bitterness of this life, for the love of whose sweetness they would not be bitter in telling the wicked of their offences. This therefore seemeth to me to be no small cause why the good are whipped with the evil, when it pleaseth God to punish the naughty manners of men with the affliction of temporal pains. For they are scourged together, not for because they lead an evil life together, but because they love this temporal life together. I do not say alike, but together; when the better sort ought to despise it, that the evil, being rebuked and corrected, might obtain the eternal life; to the getting whereof if they would not be our fellows and partners, they should be carried and lovingly drawn, even while they be our enemies; because, so long as they live, it is always uncertain whether their minds shall be changed to be better or no. Wherefore they have not the like but a far greater cause to admonish men of their faults, to whom the Lord saith by the mouth of the prophet: ' He verily shall die in his sin, but his blood will I require at the hand of the watchman.' For to this end are the watchmen, that is, the guides of the people, ordained in the churches, that they should not forbear to rebuke sin and wickedness. And yet, for all this, that man is not altogether excusable of this fault, which, although he be no guide or overseer of the people, doth, notwithstanding, know many things worthy controlment, and yet wink at them in those with whom he liveth and is conversant, because he will give them none offence, for fear lest he lose those things, which in this world he useth as he ought not, or is delighted in so as he should not[1]." And so forth. For all this have I hitherto rehearsed out of St Augustine.

[1 Hæc cum ita sint, quicunque boni malique pariter afflicti sunt, non ideo ipsi distincti non sunt, quia distinctum non est quod utrique perpessi sunt.—Nam sicut sub uno igne aurum rutilat, palea fumat, et sub eadem tribula stipulæ comminuuntur, frumenta purgantur; nec

The last and hindermost cause of the calamities which
oppress the holy saints of God is, because the Lord, in afflict-

ideo cum oleo amurca confunditur, quia eodem preli pondere exprimitur: ita una eademque vis irruens bonos probat, purificat, eliquat;
malos damnat, vastat, exterminat. Unde in eadem afflictione mali
Deum detestantur atque blasphemant, boni autem precantur et lau-
dant. Tantum interest, non qualia, sed qualis quisque patiatur. Nam
pari motu exagitatum et exhalat horribiliter coenum, et suaviter fragrat
unguentum. . . . Quid igitur in illa rerum vastitate Christiani passi sunt,
quod eis non magis fideliter ista considerantibus ad profectum valeret?
Primo, quod ipsa peccata, quibus Deus indignatus implevit tantis
calamitatibus mundum, humiliter cogitantes, quamvis longe absint a
facinorosis, flagitiosis, atque impiis, tamen non usque adeo se a delictis
deputant alienos, ut nec temporalia pro eis mala perpeti se judicent
indignos. (Bullinger's text has *dignos*.) Excepto enim quod unusquisque, quamlibet laudabiliter vivens, cedit in quibusdam carnali concupiscentiæ, etsi non ad facinorum immanitatem et gurgitem flagitiorum
atque impietatis abominationem, ad aliqua tamen peccata vel rara vel
tanto crebriora quanto minora:—hoc ergo excepto, quis tandem facile
reperitur, qui eosdem ipsos, propter quorum horrendam superbiam,
luxuriam, et avaritiam, atque execrabiles iniquitates et impietates Deus,
sicut minando prædixit, conterit terras, sic habeat ut habendi sunt;
sic cum eis vivat, ut cum talibus vivendum est? Plerumque enim ab
eis docendis, admonendis, aliquando etiam objurgandis et corripiendis
male dissimulatur; vel cum laboris piget, vel cum os eorum (coram)
verecundamur offendere; vel cum eorum inimicitias devitamus, ne
impediant et noceant in istis temporalibus rebus, sive quas adipisci
adhuc appetit nostra cupiditas, sive quas amittere formidat infirmitas:
ita ut quamvis bonis vita malorum displiceat, et ideo cum eis non incidant in illam damnationem, quæ post hanc vitam talibus præparatur;
tamen quia propterea peccatis eorum damnabilibus parcunt, dum eos in
suis licet levibus et venialibus metuunt, jure cum eis temporaliter flagellantur, quamvis in æternum minime puniantur. Jure istam vitam,
quando divinitus affliguntur cum eis, amaram sentiunt, cujus amando
dulcedinem peccantibus eis amari esse noluerunt. . . . Non mihi itaque
videtur hæc parva esse causa, quare cum malis flagellentur et boni,
quando Deo placet perditos mores etiam temporalium poenarum afflictione punire. Flagellantur enim simul, non quia simul agunt malam
vitam, sed quia simul amant temporalem vitam : non quidem æqualiter,
sed tamen simul; quam boni contemnere deberent, ut illi correpti atque
correcti consequerentur æternam: ad quam consequendam, si nollent
esse socii, ferrentur et diligerentur inimici; quia donec vivunt, semper
incertum est, utrum voluntatem sint in melius mutaturi. Qua in re
non utique parem, sed longe graviorem habent causam, quibus per
Prophetam dicitur, 'Ille quidem in suo peccato morietur, sanguinem
autem ejus de manu speculatoris requiram.' Ad hoc enim speculatores,

ing his friends, doth thereby give a most evident testimony of his just judgment, which shall fall upon his enemies for their contemning of his name and majesty. For St Peter saith: "The time is that judgment[1] must begin at the house of God: if it first begin at us, what shall the end be of those which believe not the gospel of God? And if the righteous scarcely be saved, where shall the ungodly and sinner appear?" And like to this is that notable sentence of the Lord's, which he spake, when he went to the place of execution, saying: "If they do this in a moist tree, what shall be done in the dry?" If the saints, by whom are meant the fruitful[2] trees bringing forth most precious fruits of good works, are, by the sufferance of God, in this world so miserably tormented and wrongfully vexed; what shall we say, I pray you, of the wicked, which are so far from virtue and good works? They shall, undoubtedly, be plagued with unspeakable pains and punishments.

For touching the causes of those calamities wherewith the wicked are tormented; they can be none other than the heinous crimes which they commit from day to day; and are therefore punished by God's just judgment, to the end that all men may perceive, that God hateth wicked men and wickedness alike. So we read that Pharao was afflicted. Saul fell upon his own sword, and was slain in the mount Gilboe, with many thousand Israelites, because he had sinned against the Lord, which purposed to destroy him for an example of his judgment, and a terror to them that should follow after. Antiochus Epiphanes, Herod the Great, Herod Agrippa, and Galerius Maximianus, the emperor, were taken horribly with grievous diseases, and died of the same[3]. The

The affliction of the godly is an argument of God's just judgment against the wicked. [1 Pet. iv. 17, 18.]

Luke xxiii.

The causes of afflictions in the wicked sort.

hoc est, populorum præpositi, constituti sunt in ecclesiis, ut non parcant objurgando peccata. Nec ideo tamen ab hujuscemodi culpa penitus alienus est, qui, licet præpositus non sit, in eis tamen, quibus vitæ hujus necessitate conjungitur, multa monenda vel arguenda novit, et negligit, devitans eorum offensiones propter illa quibus in hac vita non indebitis utitur, sed plusquam debuit delectatur.—August. Opp. de Civit. Dei. Lib. I. capp. 8, 9. Tom. v. p. 4, col. 4. p. 5, col. 1, 2, 3. Par. 1531.]

[1 Afflictio inquam et tribulatio, Lat.; omitted by the translator; I mean, affliction and tribulation.]

[2 Si sanctæ arbores frugiferæ, Lat.; if the holy fruitful trees.]

[3 See Vol. I. p. 318. For the miserable end of Maximian see

reason was, because they sinned against God and his servants; on whom he determined to take a vengeance, and to make them proofs of his just judgment; so to be examples for tyrants to perceive what plagues remain for those which seek the blood of the godly and faithful. And although our good God doth ordain all things for the best to his creatures, and sendeth in a manner all calamities and miseries to draw us from wickedness; yet because hypocrites and wicked people despise the counsels and admonitions of God, and neither will acknowledge God when he striketh, nor turn to him when he calleth them, all things do turn to their destruction (even as to them which love the Lord all things work to the best), and therefore do they perish in their calamities: for in this world they feel[1] the wrath of the almighty God in most horrible punishments; and in the world to come, when once they are parted out of this life, do for ever[2] bear far greater[3] and bitterer pains than any tongue can tell.

The infelicity of the ungodly. But if it happen that the wicked and ungodly sort do not in this life feel any plague or grievous affliction, then shall they be punished so much the sorer in the world to come. There is no man that knoweth not the evangelical parable of the rich unmerciful glutton, who, when as in this life he lived as he lusted, in passing delights, was notwithstanding in hell tormented with unquenchable thirst, and parched with fire[4] which never ceased burning. The felicity therefore of the wicked in this life is nothing else but extreme misery. *James v.* For St James the Apostle saith: "Ye have lived in pleasure upon earth, and been wanton; ye have nourished your hearts, as in a day of slaughter[5];" which, I say, will turn to you, as to well-fed beasts, that are fatted *Jer. xii.* up to be slain to make meat of[6]. For Jeremy goeth a little

Euseb. Hist. Eccles. Lib. VIII. cap. 16, and Lactantius de Mor. Persecut. cap. 33, and Gibbon, chap. XIV. p. 213. Vol. II. ed. Lond. 1820.]

[1 persentiscere incipiunt, Lat.; they begin to feel.]

[2 So 1577, but in 1587, *therefore bear.* æternum perferunt, Lat.]

[3 eadem, imo longe majora, Lat.; the same, nay far greater.]

[4 ignibus infernalibus, Lat.; fire of hell.]

[5 James v. 5. Bullinger has adopted Erasmus' renderings.]

[6 In his Commentary Bullinger prefers the other explanation of this comparison: in deliciis lascive pascitis cuticulam vestram, quotidiana agitantes convivia, non minus splendida quam alii solent festo die mactata victima.]

more plainly to work, and saith: "O Lord, thou art more righteous than that I should dispute with thee: yet notwithstanding I will talk with thee. How happeneth it that the way of the ungodly doth prosper so well, and that it goeth so well with them which without shame offend in wickedness? Thou hast planted them, they take root, they grow, and bring forth fruit." And immediately after: "But draw thou them out, O Lord, like a sheep[7] to be slain, and ordain or appoint them[8] against the day of slaughter." With this also doth that agree, which the prophet Asaph, after he had roundly and largely reckoned up the felicity of the wicked, addeth, saying: "Thou, verily, hast set them in slippery places; thou shalt cast them down headlong, and utterly destroy them[9]. O with how sudden calamities are they oppressed; they are perished and swallowed up of terrors! Even as a dream that vanisheth so soon as one awaketh; thou, Lord, shalt make their image contemptible in the city." For David also before him did cry, saying: "Yet a little, and the ungodly shall be nowhere; and when thou lookest in his place, he shall not[10] appear. I have seen the ungodly in great power, and flourishing[11] like a green bay-tree: and I went by, and, lo, he was gone; I sought him, but he could not be found." In like manner also doth Malachi the prophet witness, that there is great difference, in the day of judgment, betwixt the worshipper and despiser of God, and betwixt the just and unjust dealer: "For the day of the Lord shall come, in which the proud, and those that work wickedness, shall be burnt as stubble with fire from heaven, so that there shall remain unto them neither root nor branch." They that are wise, therefore, will never hereafter be offended at the felicity of the wicked: they will never desire and long to be made partakers of their unhappy prosperity: they will not grudge at all to bear the misery of the cross, which they do daily hear to be laid by God[12]

Psal. lxxiii. [18—20.]

Psal. xxxvii.

[Mal. iii. 18, and iv. 1.]

[7 sicut pecudem e grege, Lat.]

[8 consecra sive destina, Lat.; sanctify or set apart; הִקְדִּשׁ, Heb. sanctifica, Vulg.]

[9 ut prorsus dissiliant, Lat.; that they may burst altogether.]

[10 nuspiam, Lat.; nowhere.]

[11 et virentem ac sese diffundentem, Lat.]

[12 a clementissimo Deo, Lat]

upon his saints, to the end they may be tried and fined from the dross of the flesh and this unclean world. Thus far have I sufficiently reasoned of the causes of calamities.

How the godly behave themselves in their calamities. Let us now see, my reverend brethren[1], how, and in what order, the godly and sincere worshipper of God doth behave himself in all calamities and worldly afflictions. His courage quaileth not, but kicketh rather all desperation aside[2], because he understandeth, that he must manfully in faith bear all sorts of evils. Therefore doth he arm himself with hope, patience, and prayer. There are, verily, among men some which, so soon as they feel any affliction, do presently cry, as the common voice is, That it had been best if they never had been born, or else destroyed as soon as they were born. A very wicked saying is this, and not worthy to be heard in a christian man's mouth. But far more wicked are they which stick not to destroy themselves[3], rather than by living they would be compelled to suffer any longer some small calamity, or abide the taunts of the open world. And

The Stoics were of opinion, that a valiant man ought not to be grieved for any misery or calamity. yet on the other side again men must reject the unsavoury opinion of the Stoics, touching their *indolentia*, or lack of grief: touching which I will recite unto you, dearly beloved, a most excellent discourse of a notable doctor in the church of Christ, set down in these words following:

Against the Stoics' indolentia. " We are too unthankful towards our God, unless we do willingly and cheerfully suffer calamities at his hand. And yet such cheerfulness is not required of us, as should take away all sense and feeling of grief and bitterness : otherwise there should be no patience in the saints' suffering of the cross of Christ, unless they were both pinched by the heart with grief, and vexed in body with outward troubles. If in poverty there were no sharpness, if in diseases no pain, if in infamy no sting, and in death no horror, what fortitude or temperancy were it to make small account of and set little by them ? But since every one of them doth naturally nip the minds of us all with a certain bitterness engraffed in them, the valiant stomach of a faithful man doth therein shew itself, if he, being pricked with the feeling of this bitterness, howsoever he is grievously pained therewith, doth notwithstanding

[1 honorandi fratres, Lat.]
[2 calcat, Lat.]
[3 sibi ipsis violentam et armatam manum inferunt, Lat.]

by valiant resisting and continual struggling worthily vanquish and quite overcome it. Therein doth patience make
proof of itself, if, when a man is sharply pricked, it doth
notwithstanding so bridle itself with the fear of God, that it
never breaketh forth to immoderate unruliness. Therein doth
cheerfulness clearly appear, if a man, once wounded with
sorrow and sadness, doth quietly stay himself upon the
spiritual consolation of his God and creator. This conflict,
which the faithful sustain against the natural feeling of sorrow
and grief, while they study to exercise patience and temperance, the apostle Paul hath finely described in words as
followeth: 'We are troubled on every side, but not made [2 Cor. iv.
sorrowful: we are in poverty, but not in extreme poverty: 8, 9.]
we suffer persecution, but are not forsaken therein: we are
cast down, but we perish not.' Thou seest here, that to
bear the cross patiently is not to be altogether senseless and
utterly bereft of all kind of feeling: as the Stoics of old did
foolishly describe the valiant man to be such an one, as,
laying aside the nature of man, should be affected alike in
adversity and prosperity, in sorrowful matters and joyful
things; yea, and such an one as should be moved with nothing
whatsoever[4]. And what did they, I pray you, with this
exceeding great patience[5]? Forsooth, they painted the image
of patience, which neither ever was, nor possibly can be, found
among men. Yea, while they went about to have patience
over exquisite and too precise, they took away the force
thereof out of the life of man. At this day also there are
among us Christians certain new upstart Stoics, which think it
a fault not only to sigh and weep, but also to be sad and
sorrowful for any matter. And these paradoxes, verily, do
for the most part proceed from idle fellows, which, exercising
themselves rather in contemplation[6] than in working, can do
nothing else but daily breed such novelties and paradoxes.
But we Christians have nothing to do with this iron-like Ferrea philo-
philosophy, since our Lord and master hath not in words sophia.
only, but with his own example also, utterly condemned
it. For he groaned at and wept over both his own and other
men's calamities, and taught his disciples to do the like.

[4 instar lapidis, Lat.; like a stone.]
[5 Calvin's word is *sapientia*; but Bullinger reads *patientia*.]
[6 speculando, Lat.]

[John xvi. 20.] 'The world (saith he) shall rejoice, but ye shall be sorrowful, ye shall weep.' And lest any man should make that weeping to be their fault, he pronounceth openly, that they are [Matt. v. 4.] happy which do mourn. And no marvel: for if all tears be misliked of, what should we judge of the Lord himself, out of whose body bloody tears did trill[1]? If all fear be noted to proceed of unbelief, what shall we think of that horror, wherewith we read that the Lord himself was stricken[2]? If we mislike all sorrow and sadness, how shall we like of that where the Lord confesseth that his soul is heavy unto the death?

"Thus much did I mind to say, to the intent that I might revoke godly minds from desperation; lest peradventure they do therefore out of hand forsake to seek after patience, because they cannot utterly shake off the natural motions of grief and heaviness: which can not choose but happen to them which of patience do make a kind of senselessness, and of a valiant and constant man a senseless block, or a stone without passions[3]. For the scripture doth praise the saints for their patience, while they are so afflicted with the sharpness of calamities as that thereby their stomachs are not broken, nor their courage is utterly quailed; while they are so stung with the prick of bitterness as that they are filled with spiritual joy; while they are so oppressed with heaviness of mind as that yet they be cheerful[4] in God's consolation. And yet is that repugnancy still in their hearts, because the natural sense doth fly from and abhor the thing that it feeleth contrary to itself; when as, on the other side, the motions of godliness doth even through these difficulties, by striving, seek a way to the obedience of God. This repugnancy did the Lord exJohn xxi. press when he said to Peter: 'When thou wast younger, thou girdedst thyself, and wentest whither thou wouldest: but when thou shalt be old, another shall gird thee, and lead thee whither thou wouldest not.' It is not unlike verily[5], that Peter, when it was need to glorify God by his death, was

[1 trill: trickle, fall in drops. Johnson.]
[2 non leviter consternatum, Lat.]
[3 or a stone, &c. not in Lat.]
[4 exhilarati respirent, Lat.]
[5 This translation is wrong. The Latin is, Non est sane verisimile; *It is not indeed likely.*]

with much ado against his will drawn unto it: for if it had been so, his martyrdom had deserved little praise or none. But howsoever he did with great cheerfulness of heart obey the ordinance of God; yet because he had not laid aside the affections of his flesh[6], his mind was drawn two sundry ways. For while he saw before his eyes the bloody death which he had to suffer, he was undoubtedly struck through with the fear thereof, and would with all his heart have escaped it: and on the other side, when he remembered that he was by God's commandment called thereunto, overcoming and treading down all fear, he did willingly and cheerfully yield himself unto it. If therefore we mean to be Christ his disciples, our chief and especial study must be, to have our minds endued with so great obedience and love[7] of God as is able to tame and bring under all the ill[8] motions of our minds to the ordinance of his holy will. And so it will come to pass, that, with what kind of cross soever we be vexed, we may, even in the greatest troubles of our minds, constantly retain quiet sufferance and patience. For adversity will have a sharpness to nip us withal; likewise, being afflicted with sickness and diseases, we shall groan and be disquieted and wish for health: being oppressed with poverty, we shall be pricked with the sting of care and heaviness: in like manner, we shall be stricken with the grief of infamy, contempt, and injury done unto us; also at the death of our friends nature will move us to shed tears for their sakes. But this must still be the end of our thoughts, Why, the Lord would have it so[9]; let us therefore follow his will." Thus much hath he[10].

Wherefore the faithful, being once over-taken and entangled with calamities, do chiefly remedy their miseries with patience: which (as Lactantius saith) " is the quiet bearing, with an indifferent mind, of those evils which are either laid or do fall on our pates[11]." For the faithful man by patience, having his eyes throughly fastened upon the word of God, doth in faith

<small>Of the saints'
patience.</small>

[6 humanitatem non exuerat, Lat.]

[7 observantia, Lat.]   [8 contrarias, Lat.]

[9 Atqui Dominus ita voluit; Well, but so is the will of the Lord!]

[10 Calvini Instit. Lib. III. cap. 8. § 8, 9, 10. ed. Amstel. Tom. IX. p. 185.]

[11 Patientia est malorum, quæ aut inferuntur, aut accidunt, cum æquanimitate perlatio.—Lactant. Divin. Instit. Lib. v. cap. 22, p. 530. Lugd. Bat. 1660.]

and hope stick fast to God and cleave to his word; he suffereth all adversities whatsoever bechance him, moderating always
the grief of his mind and pains of his body with wonderful[1]
wisdom, so that at no time, being overcome with the greatness
of grief or sorrow, he doth revolt from God and his word, to
do the things that the Lord hath forbidden. By patience
therefore he vanquisheth himself and his affections, he overcometh all calamities, and standeth still stedfast with a quiet
mind and well-disposed heart to God-ward. And although
the faithful do with patience suffer all things, yet doth he find
fault with the things that are wicked, and hardly bear with
aught that is against the truth. For our Saviour, Christ Jesus,
the only perfect example of patience, did most patiently yield
his hands and his whole body to be bound of the wicked; and
yet nevertheless he reproveth their iniquity, saying: "Ye are
come forth as to a thief with swords and staves, although I
was daily with you in the temple: but this is your hour and
power of darkness[2]."

The image of patience. To this now belongeth that excellent description, or lively
image[3], of patience laid down by Tertullian in words as follow-
eth: "Go to now, let us see the image and habit of patience.
Her countenance is calm and quiet; her forehead smooth,
without furrowed wrinkles, which are the signs of sorrow or
anger; her brows are never knit, but slack in cheerful wise,
with her eyes cast comely down to the ground, not for the
sorrow of any calamities, but only for humility's sake. Upon
her mouth she beareth the mark of honour, which silence
bringeth to them that use it. Her colour is like to theirs that
are nigh no danger, and are guiltless of evil. Her head is
often shaken at of the devil[4], and therewithal she hath a
threatening laughter. Moreover, the clothes about her breasts
are white, and close to her body, as that which waggeth not
with every wind, nor tosseth up with every blast. For she
sitteth in the throne of that most meek and quiet spirit, which
is not troubled with any tempest, nor overcast with any clouds;

[1 cœlesti, Lat.]
[2 Luke xxii. 52, 53. Bullinger has adopted Erasmus' translation.
The Vulgate reads the former sentence interrogatively, as our English
authorised version.]
[3 prosopopœia, Lat.]
[4 Her head is often shaked at the devil, ed. 1577.]

but is plain, open, and of a goodly clearness, as Helias saw
it the third time. For where God is, there also is Patience, [1 Kings xix.
his darling, which he nourisheth[5]." 12.]

Moreover, the blessed martyr Cyprian, in his sermon *De* The force
bono patientiæ, reckoneth up the force or works of patience, and effects of
patience.
and saith: "Patience is that which commendeth us to God, and
preserveth us. Patience is that which mitigateth anger,
which bridleth the tongue, governeth the mind, keepeth peace,
ruleth discipline, breaketh the assaults of lust, keepeth under
the force of pride, quencheth the fire of hatred, restraineth
the power of the rich, relieveth the need of the poor, maintaineth in maidens unspotted virginity, in widows chastity,
in married people unseparable charity; which maketh humble
in prosperity, constant in adversity, meek in taking injury;
which teacheth thee to forgive quickly those that offend thee,
and never cease to crave pardon when thou offendest others;
which vanquisheth temptations, which suffereth persecutions,
and finisheth with martyrdom[6]. This is that which groundeth
surely the foundations of our faith: this is that which doth
augment the increase of our hope: this is that which guideth
us, so that we may keep the way to Christ, while we do go
by the suffering thereof: this is that which maketh us continue the sons of God, while we do imitate the patience of our
Father[7]." Thus much Cyprian.

[5 Age jam, si et effigiem habitumque ejus (patientiæ) compre-
hendamus: vultus illi tranquillus et placidus, frons pura, nulla mœroris
aut iræ rugositate contracta: remissa æque in lætum modum super-
cilia, oculi humilitate, non infelicitate, dejectis. Os taciturnitatis honore
signatum. Color, qualis securis et innoxiis. Motus frequens capitis
in diabolum, et minax risus. Ceterum amictus circum pectora can-
didus et corpori impressus; ut qui nec inflatur nec inquinatur (Bullinger's text is the *various reading,* inquietatur). Sedet enim in throno
spiritus ejus mitissimi et mansuetissimi, qui non turbine glomeratur,
non nubilo livet, sed est teneræ serenitatis, apertus, et simplex, quem
tertio vidit Helias. Nam ubi Deus, ibidem et alumna ejus, patientia
scilicet.—Tertull. de Patientia. ed. Semler. Tom. iv. p. 87. Hal.
Mag. 1824.]

[6 Bullinger has, persecutiones et martyria.]

[7 Patientia est, quæ nos Deo commendat, et servat. Ipsa est quæ
iram temperat; quæ linguam frænat; quæ mentem gubernat, pacem
custodit, disciplinam regit, libidinis impetum frangit, tumoris violentiam comprimit, incendium simultatis extinguit; coercet potentiam
divitum, inopiam pauperum refovet; tuetur in virginibus beatam inte-

To this, if it please you, you may add, for a conclusion, that short but very evident sentence of the Lord in the gospel, "Through your patience possess your souls;" and these words of the apostle, "Cast not away your confidence, which hath great recompence of reward. For ye have need of patience, that after ye have done the will of God ye might receive the promises. For yet a very little while, and he that shall come will come, and will not tarry. And the just shall live by faith: and if he withdraw himself, my soul shall have no pleasure in him. We are not of them which withdraw ourselves unto perdition: but we pertain to faith unto the winning of the soul[1]."

But since patience is not born in and together with us, but is bestowed of God from above, we must beseech our heavenly Father that he will vouchsafe to bestow it upon us, according to the doctrine of James the apostle, who saith[2]: "If any of you lack wisdom, let him ask of God, which giveth to all men indifferently, and casteth no man in the teeth: and it shall be given him. But let him ask in faith, nothing wavering."

Now the sound hope of the faithful upholdeth christian patience. Hope, as it is now-a-days used, is an opinion of things to come, referred commonly as well to good as evil things: but in very deed hope is an assured expectation or looking for of those things which are truly and expressly promised of God, and believed of us by faith. So then there is a certain relation of hope to faith, and a mutual knot betwixt them both. Faith believeth that God said nothing but truth,

Side notes: Luke xxi. Heb. x. James i. The hope of the faithful.

gritatem, in viduis laboriosam castitatem, in conjunctis et maritatis individuam caritatem: facit humiles in prosperis, in adversis fortes, contra injurias et contumelias mites; docet delinquentibus cito ignoscere; si ipse delinquas, diu et multum rogare; tentationes expugnat, persecutiones tolerat, passiones et martyria consummat. Ipsa est quæ fidei nostræ fundamenta firmiter munit (Bullinger's text has, ponit). Ipsa est quæ incrementa spei sublimiter provehit. Ipsa actum dirigit, ut tenere possimus viam Christi, dum per ejus tolerantiam gradimur. Ipsa efficit ut perseveremus filii Dei, dum patientiam Patris imitamur. —Cypr. Opp. p. 219. Oxon. 1682.]

[1 Heb. x. 35—39. Erasmus' version. So also Tyndale's and Cranmer's translations.]

[2 Patientia perficit, Lat.; omitted by the translator: Patience makes perfect; opus perfectum habet. Vulg.]

and lifteth up our eyes to God; and hope looketh for those things which faith hath believed. But how shouldest thou look for aught, unless thou knowest that the thing that thou lookest for is promised of God, and that thou shalt have it in time convenient? Faith believeth that our sins are forgiven us, and that eternal life is through Christ our Redeemer prepared for us: now hope looketh, and patiently waiteth, to receive in due time the things that God hath promised us, howsoever in the mean time it be tossed with adversities. For hope doth not languish nor vanish away, although it seeth not that which it hopeth: yea, it quaileth not, although that things fall out clean cross and contrary, as if the things, which it doth hope, were nothing so. And therefore Paul said: "We are saved by hope: but hope, that is seen, is no hope. For how can a man hope for that which he seeth? But and if we hope for that we see not, then do we with patience abide for it." Abraham hoped that he should receive the promised land, when as yet he possessed not one foot of ground in it, but saw it inhabited of most puissant nations. Moses hoped that he should deliver the people of Israel out of Egypt, and place them in the land of promise, when as yet he saw not the manner and means how he should do it. David hoped that he should reign over Israel, and yet he felt the peril of Saul and his servants hanging over his head[3], so that oftener than once he was in danger of his life. The apostles and holy martyrs of Christ did hope that they should have eternal life, and that God would never forsake them; and yet nevertheless they felt the hatred of all sorts of people, they were banished their countries, and lastly were slain by sundry torments. So (I say) hope is the hope and looking for of things not present, and things not seen; yea, it is a sure and most assured looking for of things to come[4]: and that, not of things whatsoever, but of those which we believe in faith[5], and[6] of those which are promised to us by the very true, living, and eternal God. For St Peter saith: "Hope perfectly in the grace which is brought unto you[7]." Now they hope

Hope is of things absent.

[Rom. viii. 24, 25.]

Hope is of things absent and not seen.

Hope is of things that are most certain.

[3 Saulinos potentissimos, Lat.; the partisans of Saul, who were most powerful.]

[4 Et expectatio quidem, sed expectatio certa, imo longe certissima, Lat.]

[5 vera fide, Lat.]   [6 adeoque, Lat.; and so.]

[7 1 Pet. i. 13, our Translation, hope "to the end:" in the margin,

perfectly, which do without doubting commit themselves wholly to the grace of God, and do assuredly look for to inherit life everlasting.

Furthermore, the apostle Paul calleth hope, as it were, [Heb. vi. 19.] the safe and sure anchor of the soul. And by how much the promise of God is the surer, by so much is hope the more firm and secure. For hope is not the looking for of anything whatsoever, but of faith; that is, of the thing that faith hath believed, and which we know to be promised to us in the word of God. And therefore doth Paul expound [Heb. xi. 1.] faith by hope, where he saith: "Faith is the ground of things hoped for, the evidence of things not seen." Faith therefore is, as it were, the foundation whereupon hope doth rest; and so God himself, and his infallible word, is the object to our [1 Tim. i. 1.] hope. And for that cause Paul calleth God our hope, and so do the prophets also. To this belongeth the ninety-first Psalm, where the faithful crieth: "Thou art my hope, O Lord; thou hast set thine house very high[1]." Like to this thou shalt find an innumerable sort of places in the book of the Psalms. But hope cannot be sure, where there is no sound faith and express promise of God. Now, since God's promises are as well of things temporal as eternal, hope also is as well of things transitory as everlasting.

Hope, the gift of God.

And as faith is the gift of God's grace, and not the power or effect of our own nature; so hope is given us from above, and confirmed in us by the Spirit of God. For in our looking after things, there are both groanings and longings for them. Temptations assail and urge us sorely, as though the thing were utterly denied, which is for a season deferred; or as though God knew not our state and condition, because he seemeth somewhiles, and as it were for ever, to neglect and not set by our earnest expectation: wherefore our hope hath need of much consolation and confirmation of the Spirit of God; which, if it be sound, sustaineth and upholdeth the mind of man[2] overladen howsoever with very weak infirmities. And when the Lord deferreth his promises,

perfectly : the original is τελείως. Tyndale's, Cranmer's, and the Geneva Versions all render it, "trust perfectly on the grace that is brought unto you." Bullinger has adopted Erasmus' translation.]

[[1] Psal. xci. 9, Prayer-book Version.]

[[2] animum cupidum quidem boni, sed interim tamen, Lat.; the mind of man, eagerly longing after good, howsoever in the mean time, &c.]

and seemeth somewhat too long either to neglect our cala- Though the Lord put off the perform-ance of his promises unto us for a season; yet he doth not deceive us, because he is faithful and just.
mities, or else to lay more troubles on the backs of us that
are otherwise sufficiently afflicted; then cometh hope, which,
doing her duty, biddeth us pluck up our hearts, and stay
the Lord's leisure, who, as he cannot possibly hate them
that worship him, so he never faileth nor in the least point
deceiveth them; for he himself is the eternal truth and everlasting goodness.

Here now the places of scripture, touching the certainty
of hope, are very profitable to teach that the people that
hoped in God were never confounded, although he did delay
very long to aid them with his helping hand.   The Lord promiseth the land of Canaan to the seed of Abraham; but four
hundred and thirty years do first come about, before he settleth them in possession of it; yea, before he brought them to
it, he led them whole forty years about in the wilderness[3].
He delivereth the Israelites from the captivity of Babylon;
but not till seventy years were spent[4]. What may be thought
of this also, that God, having immediately after the beginning
promised his only Son, did notwithstanding not send him till
and toward the latter end of the world?   The saints must
therefore still endure, and always wait the Lord's good leisure[5], because truth cannot possibly fail them, and all that
hope in it are surely saved.   David crieth: "Our fathers Psal. xxii.
hoped in thee; they hoped in thee, and thou didst deliver
them.   They called upon thee, and were saved: they hoped
in thee, and were not confounded."   And again: "The Lord [Psal. xxxiv. 8.]
is good; happy is the man that hopeth in him."   And again:
"They that hope in the Lord shall be like mount Sion; they Psal. cxxv.
shall not be moved, but shall stand fast for ever."   And
Paul, in his temptations, crieth out in his Epistle to the
Philippians, saying: "I know that my affliction shall turn [Phil. i. 19, 20.]
to my salvation, according to my earnest expectation and my
hope, that in nothing I shall be ashamed."

Thus much have I said hitherto, to teach you how the General consolations.
faithful do behave themselves in sundry calamities: for they

[3 per desertum vastissimum, Lat.]

[4 Exempla hujus rei in scripturis innumera sunt, Lat.; omitted by
the translator.   There are in the scriptures examples to this effect
without number.]

[5 hoc potissimum nomine, Lat.; on this consideration above all.]

despair not, but confirm their hearts with assured hope, and suffer all evils with a patient mind, quietly waiting for the Lord in their troubles, who is the only hope of all the faithful. Now to the end of this I mean to add a few general consolations, which may the more confirm the hope of the faithful, induce them to patience in suffering calamities, and cheer up their heavy spirits to all manner afflictions.

From whence affliction cometh.

First of all, let the afflicted weigh with himself from whence affliction cometh. Evil men, the devil, sickness, and the world, are they that afflict us; but not without God, who suffereth them to do it. Satan could not trouble Job, neither in goods or body, but by God's sufferance. And the prophet David crieth: "Thou art he that took me out of my mother's womb; thou wast my hope, when I hanged yet upon my mother's breasts. I was left to thee as soon as I was born: thou art my God; my time is in thy hand[1]." And the

[Matt. x. 29, 30.]

Lord in the gospel saith: "Are not two sparrows sold for one farthing? and one of them lighteth not upon the ground without your Father: yea, even all the hairs of your head are numbered." Now God, by whose government all things are ruled, is not a God and a Lord only, but also a Father to mortal men. And his will is good and wholesome to us-ward, besides that, whatsoever he doth, he doth it all in order and justly. But if the will of God be good toward us, the thing cannot choose but be good to us, which happeneth by the sufferance and will of him that loveth us so dearly. And herein do the children of the world differ much from the sons of God. For these (I mean the sons of God)[2], in comforting one another in their calamities, do say: Suffer, and grudge not at the thing that thou canst not alter: it is God's will that it shall be so, and no man can resist it: suffer therefore the power of the Lord, unless thou wouldest rather double the evil that thou canst not escape. But the worldlings, on the other side[3], being demanded, Do they suffer the hand of the Lord; and, Whether they submit themselves to

[1 Psal. xxii. 9, 10 (Prayer-book version), and xxxi. 15.]
[2 The translator has made here a great mistake; for Bullinger now proceeds to describe the conduct and language of the children of this world, *not* of the sons of God, under afflictions.]
[3 For all this read, These (children of this world). On the other side, is not in Lat.]

God or no? do make this answer: "I must whether I will or no[4], since I cannot withstand it." If therefore they could withstand it, by this we may gather that they assuredly would[5]. But the children of God do patiently bear the hand of God, not because they cannot withstand it, nor because they must by compulsion suffer it; but for because they believe that God is a just and merciful Father[6]. For therefore they acknowledge and confess, that God of his just judgment doth persecute the sins of them, that have deserved far more grievous and sharp punishment than he layeth upon them: they do acknowledge also that God doth, as a merciful father, chasten them to the amendment of their lives and safeguard of their souls; and therefore do they, for his chastening of them, yield him hearty thanks; and, forsaking utterly themselves and their opinions, do wholly commit themselves, whether they live or die, into the Lord's hands. The Apostle, going about to settle this in the hearts of the faithful, saith: "God speaketh to you as to his sons; My son, despise not thou the chastening of the Lord, neither faint when thou art rebuked of him: for whom the Lord loveth he chasteneth, and scourgeth every son that he receiveth. If you endure chastening, God tendereth you as his sons; for what son is he whom the father chasteneth not? But if ye be without chastisement, whereof all are partakers, then are ye bastards, and not sons. Since therefore, when we had fathers of our flesh, they corrected us, and we reverenced them; shall we not much more rather be in subjection to the Father of spirits, and live?" [Heb. xii. 5 —9.]

Secondarily, let the faithful believer, which is oppressed with calamities, consider and weigh the causes for which he is afflicted. For either he is troubled and persecuted of worldlings for the desire that he hath to righteousness and true religion: or else he suffereth due punishment for his sins and offences. Let them which suffer persecution for righteousness' sake rejoice and give God thanks, as the apostles did, for that he thinketh them worthy to suffer for the name of [Acts v. 41.]

The causes of our afflictions.

[4 Bullinger here also gives the German phrase,—Ich musz wohl.]

[5 The Latin is more lively: Si ergo possis, audio quid facturus sis. Had you then but the power, your words tell me what you would do.]

[6 justum et patrem benignissimum, Lat. ; is just, and a most merciful Father.]

Matt. v.

Christ. For the Lord in the gospel said: "Blessed are they that suffer persecution for righteousness' sake; for theirs is the kingdom of heaven. Blessed are ye, when men shall revile and persecute you, and shall say all manner evil saying against you[1], for my sake: rejoice ye, and be glad; for great is your reward in heaven: for so persecuted they the prophets that were before you." But if any man for his sins doth feel the scourge of God, let him acknowledge that God's just judgment is fallen upon him; let him humble himself under the mighty hand of the Lord; let him confess his sins to God; let him meekly require pardon for them, and patiently suffer the plague which he with his sins hath worthily deserved. Let him follow the examples of Daniel and David. Daniel confesseth his sins unto the Lord, and saith: "We have

Dan. ix.

sinned, we have committed iniquity, and have done wickedly; we have not obeyed thy servants the prophets, which spake to us in thy name. O Lord, unto thee doth righteousness belong, and unto us open shame. Thou hast visited and afflicted us,

2 Sam. xv.

as thou didst foretell by Moses thy servant." And David, when through Absalom's treason he was compelled to forsake Hierusalem and go in exile, said to the priests which bare the ark after him: "Carry back the ark of God into the city again. If I shall find favour in the eyes of the Lord, he will bring me back again, and will shew me both himself and his tabernacle. But if he thus say, I am not delighted in thee[2]; then, here am I; let him do with me what seemeth good in his eyes." And verily, it is much more better and expedient to be punished in this world, and after this life to live for ever, than to live here without afflictions, and in another

1 Cor. xi.

world to suffer everlasting pains. Paul, verily, doth plainly say: "When we are judged, we are chastened of the Lord, that we should not be damned with the world." And the very end of all chastenings and calamities, wherewith the saints are exercised, tendeth to nothing else, but that, by despising and treading down the world, they may amend their lives, return to the Lord, and so be saved. But touching the end of afflictions, we have spoken of it before.

Furthermore the men, that bear the yoke of afflictions,

[1 mentientes, Lat.; speaking falsely.]

[2 neque mihi gratus es, Lat. omitted; neither art thou pleasing to me.]

do lay before themselves the plain and ample promises of God, The promises made to the afflicted. from which, and from the examples of the saints, they never turn their eyes. There are innumerable examples of them which have felt God's helping hand ready in all needs to aid and deliver them. Now our good God doth promise to help and deliver, not them only which are afflicted for righteousness' sake, but them also whom he doth visit for their faults and offences. For David saith : "The Lord doth heal the contrite [Psal. cxlvii. 3, and cxlvi. of heart[3] : The Lord doth loose them that are bound in chains : 7, 8, and ciii. 9, 10, 12.] The Lord giveth sight unto the blind : The Lord setteth up again them that do fall. He is not angry for ever ; neither doth he always chide. He dealeth not with us after our sins, nor rewardeth us after our iniquities. And how wide the east is from the west, so far hath he set our sins from us." To this belongeth the whole thirtieth chapter of Jeremy's prophecy. And Paul doth bear witness to this, and saith : "As the afflictions of Christ are many in us, so is our comfort [2 Cor. i. 5.] great through Christ[4]."

Neither are we without examples enough to prove this same by, and to lay before our eyes the present delivery of the saints, and the repentance of sinners in extreme calamities. Our ancestors, the patriarchs, Noe and Lot, with their families, were by the mighty hand of God delivered from the deluge, that drowned all creatures under the heavens, and the horrible fire that fell upon Sodom. Jacob and Joseph, being wrapped in sundry tribulations, were by their merciful God wound out[5] and rid from all : even as also the children of Israel were brought forth and delivered from the servile bondage of Pharao in Egypt[6]. The people of Israel did in the wilderness under their guides and judges[7] sin often and grievously against the Lord, for which they were punished roundly, and sharply scourged ; but they were quickly delivered again by the Lord, so oft as they did acknowledge their sins, and turn themselves to him again. There are also notable peculiar[8] examples of God's deliverance of his people in David, Josaphat, Ezechias, Manasses, and many

[3] et obligat contritiones eorum, Lat. omitted ; and bindeth up their wounds.]

[4] præsentissimum, Lat. ; most ready.]   [5] explicantur, Lat.]

[6] plane ferrea, Lat. omitted ; which was truly iron.]

[7] sub Judicibus et Regibus, Lat.]

[8] peculiaria sed egregia, Lat.]

Examples of God's deliverance. other. There are to be seen in the gospel innumerable places, where Christ delivered his professors[1] from sin, from diseases, from perils, and from the devil.   In the Acts of the apostles there are found most excellent patterns of present delivery by the mighty hand of God.   The apostles are imprisoned, and fast bound in fetters; but they are loosed and brought forth by the angel of God, and placed in the temple to preach the [Acts v. 18—20.] gospel openly.   Peter likewise is delivered out of prison, when Agrippa had determined the next day following to make [Acts xii. 6—10.] an end of and dispatch him.   The apostle Paul, being oppressed with an infinite sort of calamities, did always feel the present hand of God at all times ready to rid him out of misery: and setting this tribulation and delivery of his for [2 Tim. iii. 10—12.] an example to all the faithful, he saith to Timothy: "Thou knowest my persecution and afflictions[2], which came to me at Antioch, at Iconium, at Lystra; which persecutions I suffered patiently: but from them all the Lord delivered me.   Yea, and all that will live godly in Christ Jesus, shall suffer persecution."   Many more examples doth the same apostle reckon up together in the eleventh chapter to the Hebrews.   All this, I say, do the saints consider, and in time of temptation and affliction do comfort and strengthen themselves therewith. [Rom. xv. 4.] For so doth Paul teach us, where he saith: "Whatsoever is written, for our learning is it written, that through patience and comfort of the scriptures we might have hope.

The Lord's commandments of bearing the cross. Beside this also, the faithful sort call to their minds the commandments of Christ our Lord, wherewith he, commending patience unto us, hath laid the cross upon us all.   For [Matt. xvi. 24—27.] in the gospel he saith: "If any man will go after me, let him forsake himself, and take up his cross, and follow me. For whosoever will save his life shall lose it; and whosoever shall lose his life for my sake shall save it.   For what doth it advantage a man, to win the whole world, and lose his own soul?   Or what shall a man give for a ransom of his soul?   For the Son of man shall come in the glory of his Father with his angels: and then shall he reward every man according to his work."   And again, in another place he saith: "If any man come to me, and hate not his father, and mother, and wife, and children, and brethren, and sisters,

[1 his professors, not in the Latin.]
[2 patientiam afflictionesque, Lat.; my patience and afflictions.]

yea, and his own life also, he cannot be my disciple. And [Luke xi. 26, whosoever doth not bear his cross, and come after me, he 27.] cannot be my disciple." After which words the Lord bringeth in certain parables, by which he teacheth us to make trial of our ability before we receive the profession of the gospel. To the precepts[3] of their master Christ the faithful apostles, Peter and Paul, had an especial eye, exhorting us to the patient bearing of the cross of Christ. " For Christ," saith Peter, "was afflicted for us, leaving to us 1 Pet. ii. 21.] an example, that we should follow[4] his steps." And Paul said : " Through many tribulations we must enter into the [Acts xiv. 22.] kingdom of God."

Another comfort that the faithful have in their afflictions The time of is this, that the time of affliction is short; that the joy and affliction is short, but the reward in the world to come is unspeakably far more large ample and and excellent than the tribulation of this life is troublesome, eternal. so that there can be no comparison betwixt the joy of the one and grief of the other : and lastly, that our good God doth not lay such burdens on us as we are not able possibly to bear. Touching all which points, I think it convenient here to rehearse proofs out of the scriptures, to prove them true. St Peter calleth the time of affliction short, or momentary[5]. And the prophet Esay, or the Lord rather in Esay's prophecy, long before Peter's time, did say : " Go, my people, [Isai. xxvi. enter into thy chambers, and shut the doors after thee; hide 20.] thyself a little while[6], until mine indignation be overpast." Paul also saith : " The fathers of your flesh did for a few [Heb. xii. days chasten you after their own pleasure ; but the Father 9—11.] of Spirits doth (for a short time) correct you to your profit, that ye might be partakers of his holiness. But no chastising for the present seemeth to be joyous, but grievous : nevertheless afterward it bringeth the quiet fruit of righteousness to them that are exercised thereby." Again he saith : " We suffer with Christ, that with him we may be glorified. For I am certainly persuaded that the afflictions of this time are not comparable to the glory that shall be shewed upon us. For the momentany lightness of our affliction doth wonderfully, above all measure, bring forth to us an everlasting

---

[3 Ad præcepta certa, Lat.]   [4 insequeremini, Lat.]
[5 1 Pet. i. 6. ad breve tempus, Erasmus' translation, which Bullinger adopts.]   [6 paululum vel ad momentum, Lat.]

weight of glory; while we look not for the things that are seen, but the things that are not seen: for the things that are seen are temporal; but the things that are not seen are eternal[1]." Again, in his first Epistle to the Corinthians the [1 Cor. x. 13.] same Apostle saith: "God is faithful, which shall not suffer you to be tempted above that you are able; but shall with the temptation make a way to escape, that ye may be able to bear it." But if it so happen, that the Lord doth seem to us to extend our tribulation longer than justice would seem to require, then must we by and by remember, that we may not prescribe to God any end of his will, but must permit him freely to afflict us[2] without all controlment, so much, so long, and by such means, as shall seem to be best to his godly wisdom. He who is himself the eternal wisdom, and loveth us men entirely well, doth know well enough his time and season, when to make an end of our miseries, and rid us from afflictions. There are in the scriptures sundry examples to comfort the men whose afflictions endure for any [Mark v. 25, 26.] long time. The woman in the gospel was troubled with an issue of blood by the space of twelve years, which had almost driven her to utter desperation of her health's recovery. Another lay beddred[3] whole eighteen years. By the pool [John v. 2—9.] Bethesda[4] lay the silly[5] creature, who had been diseased eight and thirty years. This space, surely, was very troublesome. But yet at last they[6] were restored to health again by God, who knoweth best at what time and season his help is most expedient and profitable for mankind. Let us therefore wholly submit ourselves to his good, just, and most wise will, to be delivered when and how he shall think best.

No afflictions do separate the godly from their Lord and God. But the chiefest comfort and greatest hope in tribulation is, that not any force or misery can possibly separate the faithful and elect servants of God from God himself. For [John x. 27—30.] the Lord in the gospel crieth out, and saith: " My sheep hear

[1 Rom. viii. 17, 18. 2 Cor. iv. 17, 18. Erasmus' translation.]
[2 Suæ manui subditos, Lat. omitted; who are subject to his hand.]
[3 Luke xiii. 11. Decubuit contracta, Lat.]
[4 Ad probaticam piscinam, Lat.; so the Vulgate, est autem Jerosolymis probatica piscina: and the Douay Version; Now there is at Jerusalem a pond, called Probatica. Bethesda is not in Bullinger's original.]
[5 silly, weak, poor, Lat. miser.]
[6 omnibus, Lat.; all these were.]

my voice, and I know them, and they follow me; and I give them eternal life, and they shall never perish, neither shall any man pluck them out of my hand. My Father, which gave them me, is greater than all; and no man is able to take them out of my Father's hand. I and my Father am[7] one." Hereunto belongeth that outcry[8] of St Paul, which he useth to the encouragement of us Christians, where he saith: "Who shall separate us from the love of Christ[9]? Shall tribulation, or anguish, or persecution, or hunger, or nakedness, or peril, or sword? As it is written, For thy sake are we killed all day long, and are counted as sheep for the slaughter. Nevertheless, we overcome in all these things through him that loved us. For I am sure, that neither death, nor life, nor angels, nor rule, nor power, nor things present, nor things to come, nor height, nor depth, nor any other creature, shall be able to separate us from the love of God, which is in Christ Jesu our Lord."

Rom. viii.

The saints, I confess, in their calamities do feel grief and many discommodities; but so yet that even in their discommodities they have far many more commodities: they are therefore diminished one way, but augmented another way, so that the cross of theirs is not their destruction, but an exercise for them and a wholesome medicine. And therefore I think that that same worthy and golden sentence of St Paul can never be too often beaten into our minds, where he saith: "We are troubled on every side, yet are we not without shift; we are in poverty, but not in extreme poverty; we suffer persecution, but are not forsaken therein; we are cast down, but we perish not." The faithful therefore do in this world lose these their earthly riches; but do they thereby lose their faith? Lose they their upright and holy life? Or lose they their riches[10] of the inner man, which are the true riches in the sight of God? The apostle crieth: "Godliness is a great lucre with a mind content with that that it hath. For we brought nothing into the world, and it is certain that we may carry nought away: but having food and raiment we must therewith be content." And the Lord,

Discommodities that the saints suffer are recompensed with other commodities.

[2 Cor. iv. 8, 9.]

[1 Tim. vi. 6 —8.]

[7 sumus, Lat.; are.]
[8 tripudium ac celeusma, Lat.; triumph and encouragement.]
[9 a dilectione Dei, Lat. and Erasmus, from the love of God: but the Vulgate has, a charitate Christi.]
[10 bona, Lat.; good things.]

verily, who of his goodness hath created heaven and earth and all that is therein for the use of men, which even feedeth the ravens' young ones, will not cause the just man to die with hunger and penury. Moreover, that man doth not lose his treasure in this world, which gathereth treasure as the Lord hath commanded him; with whom the faithful know that a most wealthy treasure is laid up in heaven for them, which are in this world spoiled of their terrestrial goods for their Lord and master's sake. That worthy and notable servant [Job i. 21.] of God, Job, doth cry: "Naked I came out of my mother's womb, and naked shall I turn to the earth again[1]: the Lord gave, and the Lord hath taken away; as the Lord pleased, so is it happened[2]. Blessed be the name of the Lord."

To deny the truth is not the way to keep our goods.

Last of all, it is manifest, that to deny the truth, thereby to escape persecution, is not the way to keep our wealth and quiet state, but rather the means to lose them; yea, by so doing we are made infamous to all good men of every age and nation. For we see that they which would not for Christ and the cause of his truth hazard their riches, but chose rather by dissimulation and renouncing of the truth to keep their worldly wealth[3], did retain for ever infamous reproach, and daily augment most terrible torments, which vexed horribly their guilty conscience, losing nevertheless in the devil's name the wealth which they would not once hazard in the cause of their Saviour[4]. But they, on the other side, which jeoparded themselves and all their substance in the quarrel of Christ, despising manfully all dangers that could happen, did always find a sweet and pleasant comfort, which strengthened the minds of their afflicted bodies. For they cry with the [Phil. iv. 11—13.] apostle: "We have learned, in whatsoever state we are, therewith to be content. We know how to be low, we know also how to exceed: every where and in all things we are instructed both to be full and to be hungry, both to have plenty and to suffer need. We can do all things through Christ who strengtheneth us." They know that the same

[1 Heb. שָׁמָּה, thither, Auth. Ver. Cyprian quotes it,—naked also shall I go under the earth. Adv. Jud. Lib. III. cap. 6.]

[2 So the Vulgate and Coverdale, The Lord hath done his pleasure: and Cyprian.]

[3 vel retinere vel augere, Lat.; either to keep, or to increase.]

[4 non jam in nomine Christi, sed in nomine diaboli, Lat.]

apostle hath said : " Ye have suffered with joy the spoiling of [Heb. x. 34.] your goods, knowing that ye have in heaven a far more excellent substance, which will endure." For the Lord in the gospel also said: " Verily I say unto you, There is no man that hath forsaken house, or brethren, or sisters, or father, or mother, or wife, or children, or lands, for my sake, and the gospel's, but he shall receive an hundred fold now at this present, with persecutions; and in the world to come eternal life." Mark x. So then the saints and faithful servants of God are oppressed with servitude in this present world: but therewithal they know and consider that the Lord himself became a servant for us men[5]; whereby[6] they, that are servants in this world, are made free through Christ, and by terrestrial servitude a way is made to celestial liberty.

The faithful are exiled, or banished their country : but Affliction in exile. the heathen poet saith, " A valiant-hearted man takes every country for his own[7]." Verily, in what place of the world soever we are, we are in exile as banished men. Our Father is in heaven, and therefore heaven is our country. Wherefore, when we die, we are delivered from exile, and placed in the heavenly country and true felicity. In like manner, whom the tyrant killeth with hunger and famine, those doth Affliction in he[8] rid of innumerable evils. And again, whomsoever famine famine. doth not utterly kill but only torment, them doth it teach to live more sparingly, and afterward to fast the longer and devoutly. Now in this case the faithful, which suffer famine, do call to remembrance the examples of the ancient saints, of whom when Paul speaketh, he saith: " They wandered about [Heb. xi. 37, 38.] in sheep skins and goat skins; being destitute, afflicted, and tormented; of whom the world was not worthy: they wandered in wilderness, and in mountains, and in dens, and caves of the earth." Christians also consider, that the state of famished Lazarus, who died among the tongues of the dogs that licked his blains, was far better than the surfeiting of the strut-bellied glutton, who being once dead was buried

[5 prius, Lat.; before us.]
[6 adeoque, Lat. ; and that so.]
[7 Omne solum forti patria est. Ovid. Fast. Lib. i. 493.]
[8 ceu morbus aliquis, Lat. omitted; like some disease.]

Affliction in wars by deflouring of women.

in hell[1]. Moreover, it is to be abhorred, detested, and (yet) lamented of all men, to see a crew of barbarous villains and unruly soldiers abuse perforce, not honest matrons only, but tender virgins also, that are not fit yet nor ripe for a man. But the greatest comfort that we have in so great a mischief and intolerable ignominy is, that chastity is a virtue of the mind. For if it be a treasure of the mind, then is it not lost though the body be abused : even as in like sort the faith of a man is not thought to be overcome, although the whole body be consumed with fire. And chastity is not lost, verily, where the body is defloured ; because the will of the abused body persevereth still to use that chastity, and doth what it may to keep it undefiled. For the body is not holy therefore, because the members thereof are undefiled, or because the secret parts thereof are not undecently touched : considering that the body, being wounded by many casualties, may suffer filthy violence ; and since physicians for health's sake may do to the members the thing that otherwise is unseemly to the eyes. Wherefore so long as the purpose of the mind (by which the body must be sanctified) remaineth, the violent deed of another's filthy lust taketh not from the body that chastity, which the persevering continency of the defloured body doth seek to preserve. And in the meanwhile there is no doubt but the most just Lord will sharply punish those shameless beasts and monsters of nature, which dare undertake to commit such wickedness.

The saints in suffering the cross do feel no new or unwonted miseries.

The saints are confirmed in their tribulation by the innumerable examples of their fore-fathers ; whereby they gather, that it is no new thing that happeneth unto them, since God from the beginning hath with many afflictions and tribulations exercised his servants and the church, his spouse, whom he loveth so dearly. And here I think it to be very expedient, and available to the comforting of afflicted minds, to reckon up the best and choicest examples that are in scriptures : of which there are many both private and public. The chances and pilgrimages of the latter patriarchs (because I mean not to speak of them before the deluge[2]) are those, which I call

[1 sepulti et demersi in inferos, Lat. ; who was buried, and plunged into hell.]

[2 veterum, Lat.]

private examples. For our father Abraham is by the mouth of God called from out of Ur of the Chaldeans to go into Palestine, from whence he is driven by a dearth into Egypt, where again he is put to his shifts, and feeleth many pinches. After that, when he came again into Palestine, even till the last hour of his life, he was never without some one mishap or other, to trouble and vex his mind. His son Isaac felt famine also, and had one misfortune[3] upon another's neck to plague him withal. He sinneth not that calleth Jacob[4] the wretchedest man that lived in that age, considering the infinite miseries wherewith he was vexed. While he was yet in his mother's womb and saw no light, he began to strive with his brother Esau: afterwards, in his stripling's age, he had much ado to escape his murdering hands by exiling himself from his father's house into the land of Syria; where again he was kept in ure and exercised sharply in the school of afflictions[5]. At his back-return into his country he was wrapped in and beset with perils enough, and endless evils. The detestable wickedness of his untoward children had been enough to have killed him in his age[6]. In his latter days, for lack of food, he goeth down as a stranger into the land of Egypt, where in true faith and patience he gave up the ghost[7]. Of Moses, the great and faithful servant of God, the scripture testifieth, that in his youth he was brought up in the Egyptian court; but, when he came to age, he refused to be called the son of Pharao's daughter, choosing rather to be afflicted with the people of God, than to enjoy the temporal commodities of this sinful world[8], because he counted the rebuke of Christ greater riches than all the treasures of the Egyptians. The same Moses was grievously afflicted, first by Pharao and his princes, and after that again by them of his own household, and his own country people whom he had brought out of the land of Egypt. David also, the anointed of the Lord, was troubled a great while with his master Saul, that was mad upon him to have

Examples of afflictions in the patriarchs.

[Heb. xi. 24—26.]

[3 domestica infortunia, Lat. ; in his family.]
[4 a Domino Israelem cognominatum, Lat. omitted; whom God surnamed Israel.]
[5 in exquisitissima afflictionum palæstra seu officina, Lat.]
[6 optimum senem tantum non enecant, Lat.]
[7 sanctum Deo tradit spiritum, Lat.]
[8 peccati, Lat. ; of sin.]

brought him to his end: but having at the last (for all that Saul could do) obtained the kingdom, afflictions ceased not to follow him still; for, after many troublesome broils, he was by Absalom thrust beside his kingdom, and very straitly dealt withal: and yet in the end God of his goodness did set him up again.

Christ and Paul examples unto us.

In the new Testament, Christ himself, our Lord and Saviour, and that elect vessel, his apostle Paul, are excellent examples for us to take comfort by. The Lord in his infancy was compelled to fly the treason and murdering hands of cruel tyrants; in all his lifetime he was not free from calamities; and at his death he was hanged among thieves. And Paul,

[2 Cor. xi. 23—28.]

speaking of himself, doth say: "If any other be the ministers of Christ, I am more; in labours more abundantly, in stripes above measure, in imprisonments more plenteously, in death[1] often. Of the Jews five times received I forty stripes save one; thrice was I beaten with rods, once stoned; thrice I suffered shipwreck; a day and a night have I been in the depth; in journeying often; in perils of waters, in perils of robbers, in perils of mine own nation, in perils among the heathen, in perils in the city, in perils in the wilderness, in perils in the sea, in perils among false brethren; in labour and travail, in watchings often, in hunger and thirst, in fastings often, in cold and nakedness. Beside those things that outwardly come unto me, the trouble, which daily lieth upon me, is the care of all the churches." These, I say, are private examples.

Examples of afflictions of the old church.

We have a public example in the church of Israel afflicted in Egypt, many times troubled under their kings and judges, and lastly led captive by the Assyrians and men of Babylon. Afterward, being brought home again by the goodness of God, they pass many brunts, and are sharply afflicted under the monarchies of the Persians, Greeks, and Romans. What shall

The ten horrible persecutions of the church of Christ.

I say of the apostolic church of Christ, which, even when it first began, like an infant, to creep by the ground[2], did presently feel the cross, and yet flourished still in those afflictions, which even to this day it doth patiently suffer? Histories make mention of ten persecutions, wherewith the church of Christ (from the eighth year of Nero, till the reign of Constantine the great, by the space of three hundred and eighteen

[1] in mortibus, Lat.]
[2] ab ipsis incunabulis, is Bullinger's phrase.]

years[3]) was terribly shaken and sharply afflicted, without intermission or respite of time for it to breathe in, and rest itself
from troublesome broils and merciless slaughters[4].

The first persecution of those ten[5] did Nero, that beast
and lecherous monster, raise against the Christians, wherein,
it is said, that Peter and Paul, the Apostles of Christ, were
brought to their endings. The second was moved by Fla-
vius Domitianus, which banished the Apostle John into the
Isle of Patmos. The third persecutor after Nero was
Trajan the emperor, who published most terrible edicts
against the Christians: under him was the notable martyr
and preacher Ignatius, with many other excellent servants of
Christ, cast to wild beasts, and cruelly torn in pieces. The
fourth persecution did the Emperor Verus most bloodily stir
up through all France and Asia; wherein the blessed Polycarpus was burnt in fire alive, and Irenæus, the bishop of
Lyons, was headed with the sword[6]. In the fifth persecution
of the church of Christ, Septimius Severus through many
provinces did bloodily crown many a saint with the garland
of martyrdom: among whom is reckoned Leonidas the father
of Origenes. Julius Maximinus was the sixth after Nero that
played the tyrant against the church. In that persecution
the preachers and ministers of the churches were especially
murdered: among whom, beside an innumerable sort of other
excellent men, Pamphilus and Maximus, two notable lights,

[3 The persecution in Nero's reign began A.D. 64, (he became
emperor A.D. 54), and Constantine succeeded Maxentius, A.D. 312; so
that the interval is 248 years. See Burton's Hist. of Christ. Church,
Chap. V. p. 128, and Chap. XVII. p. 392. Lond. 1845.]

[4 Bullinger's words are: Concessis tamen nonnunquam intervallis
quibusdam, satis quidem accisis, quibus respiraret ecclesia: although
indeed occasionally some intervals were granted, short enough in good
sooth, wherein the church might take breath.]

[5 Primam (persecutionem) quippe computant (nonnulli) a Nerone
quæ facta est, secundam a Domitiano, a Trajano tertiam, quartam ab
Antonino, a Severo quintam, sextam a Maximino, a Decio septimam,
octavam a Valeriano, ab Aureliano nonam, decimam a Diocletiano et
Maximiano.—Aug. de Civ. Dei, Lib. XVIII. cap. 52. Par. 1531. Tom. v.
fol. 251. See Euseb. Eccl. Hist. III. 18, 36; IV. 15; VI. 1, 41; VII. 11,
30, &c.]

[6 We have no account of the death of Irenæus upon which we can
absolutely depend; and there is a doubt whether he was martyred or
not.]

were especially slaughtered.   The seventh blood-sucker after
beastly Nero was Decius the Emperor, who proclaimed most
horrible edicts against the faithful.   In his time was St
Laurence, a deacon of the church, broiled upon a grate-iron;
and the renowned Virgin Apollonia, for her profession, did
leap into the fire alive.   Licinius Valerianus was as cruel
as the rest in executing the eighth persecution against the
faithful professors of Christ and his gospel.   In that broil
were slain many millions of Christians, and especially St
Cornelius and Cyprian, the most excellent doctors in all the
world.   Valerius Aurelianus did rather purpose, than put
in execution, the ninth persecution : for a thunder rushed
before him to the great terror of them that were about him;
and, shortly after, he was slain as he journeyed, and so his
tyranny by his death was ended.   But Caius Aurelius Valerius Diocletianus, Maximinianus Maxentius, and Marcus
Julius Licinius, being nothing terrified with this horrible
example, did raise the tenth persecution against the church
of Christ, which, enduring by the space of ten whole years,
brought to destruction an infinite number of Christians in
every province and quarter of the world.   This broil doth
Eusebius Cæsariensis passingly[1] paint to the eyes of the
reader : for he himself was an eye-witness and looker-on of
many a bloody pageant and triumphant victory of the martyrs, which he rehearseth in the eighth book of his ecclesiastical history.   In that slaughter were killed the first apostles
of our Tigurine church, both martyrs of Christ and professors
of his gospel, S. Fœlix and his sister Regula[2].

A. D. 306.

After those ten persecutions there followed many more
and more terrible butcheries, stirred up by many kings and
barbarous men, in sundry quarters of the earth ; upon the
neck whereof did follow the merciless blood-sheddings committed by the Saracens, Turks, and Tartars[3]: moreover, the

[1 graphice, Lat.]
[2 These martyrs (ex Thebœa legione) are thus mentioned in the
Ephemeris, Bed. Opp. Tom. I. p. 206. Col. Agrip. 1612.   Septemb. 3 Id.]
    Has simul et Felix felici morte dicavit,
    Martyrio Regulæ juncto, pariterque beavit.
They suffered September 11, A. D. 281.   See Hospinian. de festis Christian. p. 143. Genev. 1674.]
[3 Tartarorum, Turcarum denique, Lat. ; and lastly of the Turks.]

butcherly bishops[4] of Rome did annoy extremely the church of God, by shedding in civil and foreign wars more christian blood than any tongue can possibly tell. No new thing therefore doth at this day happen to us that in the church of Christ do suffer divers persecutions and afflictions; for we have examples of great efficacy, both new and old, to confirm our hearts, that they faint not in calamities.

And therefore did the prophets and apostles, and their Lord and master, Jesus Christ, foretel these perils, calamities, and all persecutions; because they would have us to fortify our minds against these miseries at all times and seasons, lest, by being shaken with them at unawares, we should revolt from our faith, and forsake our profession. "Because I have chosen you out of the world," saith the Lord to his disciples, "therefore the world doth hate you. Remember the words which I spake unto you, saying, The servant is not greater than his master. If they have persecuted me, they will also persecute you; if they have kept my words, they will also keep yours. But all these things shall they do to you for my name's sake, because they know not him that sent me. This have I said to you, that ye should not be offended. They shall drive you from their synagogues: and the time shall come, that whosoever killeth you shall think he doth God good service."

Their afflictions were foretold.

[John xv. 19—21; xvi. 1, 2.]

The rest that is like to this I mean not at this time to recite out of the prophets and apostles, because it cannot be briefly rehearsed[5]: let every one pick out, and apply to his own comfort, the plainest and most evident testimonies, that by reading he shall light upon.

And although the saints do not rejoice at the destruction of their persecuting enemies, whom they could wish rather to be converted, and so saved, than in this present world to be punished, and in the world to come to be damned for ever; yet they are glad, when they see the Lord punish their afflicters[6], because thereby they perceive that God hath

Persecutors are recompensed for their persecuting tyranny.

[4 pseudo-pontifices, Lat.; the false bishops: *butcherly* is not in the original.]

[5 The following texts are put in the margin of the Latin original of Bullinger; Psal. xxii. lxix. Isai. xlix. li. Dan. vii. viii. xi. Zech. xiii.]

[6 hoc potissimum nomine, Lat.; for this reason specially.]

a care over those that be his servants. They do gather also by the present vengeance of God upon the wicked, that as afflictions are for the health and amendment of the faithful, so they are to the hurt and destruction of the unbelievers: for, while they persecute other, they themselves are destroyed; and while they trouble the church of the living God, they kindle a fire of the wrath of God against themselves, that will never be quenched. For in the prophecy of Zacharias thus we read that the Lord speaketh touching his church: "Behold, I make Jerusalem a cup[1] of poison unto all the people that are round about her: yea, Juda himself shall be in the siege against Jerusalem[2]. And in that day I will make Jerusalem a heavy stone for all people; so that all such as lift it up shall be torn and rent, and all the people of the earth shall be gathered together against it." A like saying to this hath the Lord in Jeremy, where he speaketh against the persecutors of his church, and saith: "Take this wine-cup of indignation from my hand, and make all the people, to whom I send thee, to drink of it; that when they have drunken thereof, they may be mad, and out of their wits, for fear of the sword which I will send among them. For I begin to plague the city that is called after my name; and think ye then that ye shall escape unpunished? Ye shall not go unpunished." And this is that whereto St Peter alluding saith: "The time is that the judgment of God beginneth at the house of God: if it first begin with us, what shall the end of them be, that believe not the gospel?"

I have a little above rehearsed in order the ten persecutions, which the Roman emperors stirred up against the church of Christ: now histories make mention, that there was not one of them but was requited with some notable calamity. And, beside the peculiar revengements that followed every several persecution, it is to be noted, that the most just Lord, after the space of three hundred and forty-two years (for so many years are reckoned from the last of Nero unto the second

Marginal notes:
[Zech. xii. 2, 3.]
[Jer. xxv. 15, 16, 29.]
[1 Pet. iv. 17.]
Vengeance taken of blood.

[1 calix soporis, Lat.; a cup of trembling, Auth. Ver.; slumber, marg. reading.]

[2 So also Coverdale, 1535. Calvin in loc. remarks: Miror cur omittant quidam interpretes particulam בְּ, et ita vertant, Erit etiam Jehudah in obsidione contra Jerusalem.]

year of the emperors Honorius and Theodosius[3]), did begin more abundantly to requite the death of his saints upon the necks of the blood-thirsty Rome. For within the space of one hundred and nine and thirty years Rome was six times taken and brought into subjection to the barbarous nations[4]. For in the four hundredth[5] year of grace, which was the second of Honorius and Theodosius his reign, the Wisigothes, under their captain Alaricus, both took and sacked the city, using notwithstanding great mercy in their victory. After that again, the Vandals, under their guide Genserichus, brake into the city cruelly, and spoiled it very greedily[6]. After them came the Herules, and the remnant of Atthilas his army, with their captain Odacer, who took the city, and got the kingdom to themselves, extinguishing utterly the rule of the Romans in the west part of the world[7]. Then again, when about fourteen years were come and gone, in cometh Theodoricus Veronensis with his Ostrogothes, who slew the Herules, and obtained the city[8]. But, it, being recovered by the faith and industry of the valiant captain Belisarius, and restored to Justinian the emperor of the east, was immediately again taken by Totylas[9], a prince of the Goths; who with fire and sword did sack it, pull down houses, and overthrew a great part of the walls thereof, whereby Rome was so defaced, that for the space of certain days there was no man that dwelt within it. That spoil of the city happened about the five hundred and forty-eighth year after Christ his incarnation[10]. And thus did Christ, in revenging his church, lay deserved plagues upon the neck of bloody Rome; beside other miseries (I pass that over)

[3 Nero destroyed himself A.D. 68, and the second year of Honorius and Theodosius was A.D. 410. Usher's Annals, Vol. II. p. 694. Lond. 1654. Gibbon's Dec. and Fall, ch. 32, Vol. V. p. 411. Lond. 1820.]

[4 Bullinger details more fully these invasions of Rome in his treatise on the Revelation. Sermons LVII. & LXXVI.]

[5 412, Lat. and ed. 1577. The date in Gibbon is Aug. 24, 410. Vol. V. p. 310, ch. 31.]

[6 A.D. 455, June 15—29. Gibbon, ch. 36, Vol. VI. p. 151.]

[7 A.D. 476, or 479. Gibbon, Vol. VI. p. 226, &c.]

[8 A.D. 493. Gibbon, ch. 39, Vol. VII. p. 15.]

[9 A.D. 536. Gibbon, ch. 41, Vol. VII. p. 224.]

[10 A.D. 546. Gibbon, chap. 43, Vol. VII. p. 366; and again, after a repulse, finally taken A.D. 549. ibid. p. 375.]

which it did suffer by the Huns and Lombards[1]. For this is enough to shew how miserably Rome was plagued for afflicting the church of Christ; which nevertheless, maugre the tyrants' heads, remained safe, and overcame those brunts, and shall reign with Christ for evermore. In like manner were the Saracens extinguished and utterly destroyed, when first they had suffered many a great overthrow, and had been plagued throughout the world with sundry mishaps and overthwart calamities. The Turks also do daily feel their woes and miseries, and are likely hereafter to feel sharper punishments. Moreover, the popes[2] with poison are one slain by another, and are strangely vexed with wonderful terrors. They are in no place sure of their lives, but even in the midst of all their friends are beset with miseries; they live in fear continually, all the whole pack of them. Furthermore, even they among them, that live most happily, do rot away with the disease that followeth filthy pleasures; than which there is no kind of death either sharper to the patient, or more detested among all men. And their adherents, which by their setting on do persecute the church of Christ, do either

They were eaten of worms alive, and stank so horribly, that no man could abide them. drop away with the like disease that waiteth upon filthy lust, or do by little and little consume away, as Herod and Antiochus[3] did; which death is long before it dispatch them, but doth torment them beyond all measure: yea, and besides these bitter plagues, they destroy one another with endless civil wars. The Lord therefore is righteous, and his judgments are just and equal, who never forgetteth to revenge his friends by finding out his own and his servants' enemies, to punish them for their deserts.

The conclusion. Since then, my brethren, that the case so standeth, let us, I beseech you, patiently suffer the hand of the Lord our God, as often as we are touched with any calamity, or tempted of the Lord our God; knowing this, that the Lord doth strike us that he may heal us, and trouble us that he may comfort us and receive us to himself into joys everlasting. And that we may so do, since we are otherwise too weak of ourselves, let us pray to our Father which is in heaven, through Jesus Christ our Lord, that he will vouchsafe to be present with us in our

[1 A.D. 568—570. Gibbon, chap. 45, Vol. VIII. p. 126, &c.]
[2 pseudo-pontifices, Lat.]   [3 See above, p. 80.]

temptations, and guide us in the way of constancy, peace, and righteousness. And for an example, let every one set before his eyes the order that Christ our Saviour and master did use; who, a little before the cross of his passion, betook himself to prayer. For going up into the mount of Olives, he beseecheth his Father humbly, and prayeth to him ardently. He is instant in prayer[4], and lieth upon him earnestly[5]; and yet so, that he submitteth all to his will and pleasure. Let us also do the like, that we may have trial of our Father's present aid with the effectual comfort of our minds, and that we for his goodness may give him praise for evermore. Amen.

OF THE FIFTH AND SIXTH PRECEPTS OF THE SECOND TABLE, WHICH ARE IN ORDER THE NINTH AND TENTH OF THE TEN COMMANDMENTS, THAT IS, THOU SHALT NOT SPEAK FALSE WITNESS AGAINST THY NEIGHBOUR: AND, THOU SHALT NOT COVET THY NEIGHBOUR'S HOUSE, &c.

THE FOURTH SERMON.

WE are now come to the exposition of the two last precepts of the ten commandments. The ninth commandment is: "Do not speak false witness against thy neighbour." By this precept is confirmed faith in covenants and contracts: it ruleth the tongue, and commendeth unto us verity, the fairest virtue of all other, and teacheth us to use modesty and sincerity both in word and deed. Hitherto yet have we heard nothing in all God's commandments touching the tongue, but a little only in the third commandment. But of the tongue do arise the greatest commodities and discommodities of our life. "For the tongue" (saith James) "is a little member, and boasteth great things. Behold, how great a matter a little fire kindleth. And the tongue is fire, even a world of wickedness. So is the tongue set among our members, that it defileth the whole body, and setteth on fire the course of nature, and it is set on fire of hell. All the nature of beasts, and of birds, and of serpents, and things of the sea, is meeked and

The ninth commandment.

The tongue.

[James iii. 5 —10.]

[4 preces suas iterat, Lat.]   [5 patrem urget, Lat.]

tamed of the nature of men[1]: but the tongue can no man tame, it is an unruly evil, full of deadly poison. Therewith we bless our God and Father; and therewith curse we men that are made after the similitude of God. Out of one mouth proceed both blessing and cursing." Therefore very well and necessarily is the way set down in this ninth precept, how men should frame and order their tongues.

Now summarily this precept doth command us to use our tongues well, that neither privately or publicly we do our neighbour harm, either in his life, good name, or riches, by word or writing, or otherwise by painting, neither by simulation nor dissimulation, nor yet so much as by a beck or a nod. All things are forbidden that are against truth and sincerity. There is required at all our hands simplicity, plain speaking, and telling of the truth. Briefly, we are commanded every man to do his endeavour mutually to maintain plain dealing and verity. For in the twenty-third of Exodus we read that the Lord did charge us, saying: "Thou shalt not have to do with a false report." And in the nineteenth of Leviticus, "Ye shall not steal, saith the Lord, nor lie, nor deal falsely one with another." And the apostle James, after he had touched the evils of the tongue (especially because out of one mouth proceeded good and bad) doth add: "These things, my brethren, ought not to be so. Doth a fountain at one hole send forth sweet water and bitter also? Can the fig tree, my brethren, bear olive berries? either a vine, figs? So can no fountain give both salt water and fresh also." Verily, since God hath given to man a tongue, that by the means of it one man may know another's meaning, that it may bless or praise God, and do good to all men[2]; it is altogether requisite that it should be applied to the use that it was made for[3], that thereby a man out of a good heart might utter good talk, clear from deceit and hurt, from blasphemy and railings, and from filthy speaking.

Of bearing witness.

But it is best for us by parts more nearly to sift the special points of this precept or argument. First of all, in this commandment it is forbidden every man in the court before a judge to bear false witness. Therefore all witness-

Marginal notes: Exod. xxiii. / Levit. xix. / [James iii. 10—12.]

[1 domatur et domita est, Lat.]
[2 etiam sibi ipsi. Lat. omitted: and to one's self also.]
[3 ut imago respondeat archetypo, is Bullinger's Latin.]

bearing simply is not forbidden us, but false witnessing only. "Do not speak (saith he) false witness." It is lawful, therefore, to bear true witness, especially if a magistrate demand it of thee. And therefore the Hebrew phrase is very significant, and saith, "Answer not false witness against thy neighbour[4]." Now he answereth, that is asked a question. And in bearing of witness, he that speaketh must have a regard of God alone and simple truth; he must lay aside all evil affections, hatred, fear, or all part-taking; he must hide nothing, nor dissemble in his speech: he must not devise any thing of his own making, nor corrupt the meaning of his words that spake; as those false witnesses did in the Gospel, when before the judges they said, "I will destroy this temple, and in three [Matt. xxvi. 61.] days build it again;" for they corrupted the meaning of Christ. And the Lord in the law doth say, "Thou shalt not [Exod. xxiii. 1, 2.] take up a false report, neither shalt thou put thine hand with the wicked to be an unrighteous witness. Thou shalt not follow a multitude to do evil, neither shalt thou speak in a matter of justice according to the greater number, for to pervert judgment." He therefore, that beareth false witness, committeth sin against God and his neighbour. For first of all, he staineth himself with sacrilege and perjury, and so by telling a lie in the name of God he doth despite to God himself. Moreover, he doth to his neighbour so much hurt, as he taketh damage by the judge's sentence either in body, goods, or loss of life. For it is manifest that the judge, being moved with thy false witness, did punish the accused party in body, goods, or life itself: which he would not have done, had he not been drawn thereunto by thy false witnessing. And therefore a very good and just law is that, which Moses hath uttered in these words: "If a false witness be [Deut. xix. 18—21.] found among you, then shall ye do unto him as he had thought wickedly to have done to his brother: and thou shalt put evil away from the midst of thee: that the rest may hear and fear, and dare after that do no more such wickedness among you. Thou shalt have no compassion on him; but life for life, eye for eye, tooth for tooth, hand for hand, and foot for foot." To this belongeth the saying of Salomon in the Pro- [Prov. vi. 16, 19, & xix. 5, verbs, where he crieth, "God hateth a false witness." And 9.]

[4 לֹא־תַעֲנֶה. Ainsworth translates, Thou shalt not answer.]

[Hist. Sus. 61—2.] again, "A false witness shall not scape unpunished." We have an example in the two false witnesses that rose against the chaste[1] and honest Susanna.

False and wrongful accusations. In this law are condemned also all false and wrongful accusations, and unjust judgments bought for money at the mouth of unrighteous judges. And as those deeds are worthily forbidden, so likewise are they misliked that set their tongue to sale; I mean, such merchants as for a morsel of bread will easily be hired either to bless or curse the innocent. Of which sort of cursing, spiteful, and soothing tongues thou mayest find a great number in every degree and state, both of rich and poor, of spiritual and of lay people.

Furthermore, we have here commended unto us the inviolable keeping of bargains, covenants, and contracts; and, on the other side, are we especially charged not to use either guile, or deceit, or craft, or any kind of cozening. Of which I have spoken where I treated of theft.

A lie, and the kinds of lies. But now the especial thing that is forbidden the faithful herein is to tell a lie, that is, to speak an untruth, either upon purpose therewith to hurt his neighbour, or upon any vain and light occasion, or otherwise upon some evil affection. For among men many kinds and sundry sorts of lies are reckoned up. St Augustine, in his fourteenth chapter *ad Consentium de Mendacio*, maketh mention of eight kinds of lies[2]. I among many will name a few only. There is a jesting lie; as when I say that I lie, or other men know that I do lie, by which lie of mine they take some profit, or (as I should rather say) some pastime or pleasure. To lie in that sort, although it be no great and heinous sin, is yet a sign of very great lightness; which the apostle misliketh in the faithful, as it Ephes. v. may appear in the fifth chapter of his epistle to the Ephesians. And yet I think not that devised fables, parables, and feigned narrations are hereby forbidden: which, as they are in the scripture everywhere used in matters of most importance, so have they also a very good grace, being of themselves very necessary, and profitable for the readers. Notwithstanding St Augustine will not have jesting mirth[3] in the number of lies.

[1 pudicissimam fœminarum, Lat.]
[2 August. Opp. Par. 1531. Tom. iv. fol. 5. col. 1.]
[3 Exceptis jocis, quæ nunquam sunt putata mendacia.—August. Tom. iv. fol. 2.]

There is, moreover, an officious lie; that is, when I fitten[4] or tell an untruth, for duty's sake, to the end that by my lie I may keep my neighbour harmless from the evil or mischief that hangeth over his head. Of this sort there are many examples in the holy scriptures. The midwives of Egypt did save the Hebrews' children alive, whom Pharao [Exod. i. 17—19.] commanded to be slain at their birth; and, being accused before the king for breaking the law, they did by an officious and a very witty lie excuse themselves, and pretend a certain speediness of travail in the Hebrews' wives, more than the Egyptian women had. Rahab doth with a very strange tale [Josh. ii. 4—6.] deceive the citizens[5] of Jericho, and by her lie preserve the spies of the people of God. And Michol, David's wife, with [1 Sam. xix. 13, 14.] a lie did save her husband's life, and sent away her father Saul's servants without their purpose, for which the king had sent them. And Jonathan feigneth many a thing at his father's [1 Sam. xx. 28, 29.] table, for the good-will that he bare to David, whom by honest shifts and godly deceits he did rid from the bloody hand of his cruel father Saul. The holy widow Judith also [Judith x. &c.] by lying and dissembling doth enter the tent of captain Holophernes; and by cutting off his head doth set her afflicted country-folks at liberty again.

Now it hath been a question among the divines of the primitive church, whether they, whose examples I have here alleged, did sin in lying or no. Origen, and they that followed him, did permit a wise and godly man to lie, if so be it were for the welfare of them for whom the lie was made[6]. Neither was St Hierome without suspicion of Origen's opinion: for upon the epistle of Paul to the Galatians he writ, that Peter and Paul, to serve the time, did use a kind of simulation[7]. But St Augustine, admonishing Hierome of that

[4 fingo, Lat.—to fitton, to form lies or fictions.—Nares.]

[5 civibus suis, Lat. her citizens.]

[6 Ex quo perspicuum est, quod nisi ita mentiti fuerimus, ut magnum nobis ex hoc aliquod quæratur bonum, judicandi simus quasi inimici ejus, qui ait: Ego sum veritas.—Hæc Origenes scripsit, negare non possumus....docetque magistris mentiendum. Hieron. Apol. adv. Rufin. Lib. i. Tom iv. col. 369. Par. 1706.]

[7 Restitit (Paulus) secundum faciem publicam Petro et ceteris; ut hypocrisis observandæ legis ... correptionis hypocrisi emendaretur. —Utilem vero simulationem, et assumendam in tempore, Jehu regis Israel nos doceat exemplum, &c.—Hieron. Comment. in. Ep. ad Gal. cap. ii. Opp. Tom. iv. col. 243.]

matter, denieth flatly that we ought once to suspect that a lie is allowed in the sacred scriptures. On the other side again, St Hierome telleth Augustine, that the best interpreters of the ancient church are full and wholly of his mind. There are, to and fro, very learned and large epistles written on both sides, which are extant now, and to be seen amongst us; and therefore I need not stick hereupon any longer[1]. The same Augustine, in the fifteenth chapter of his book that he wrote *ad Consentium contra Mendacium,* saith: "He which saith that some lies are righteous, is to be thought to say nothing else but that some sins are righteous, and so, consequently, that some unrighteousness is righteous: than which what can be spoken more absurd? For whereupon is sin, but because it is contrary to righteousness? But those things that are done against the law of God cannot be righteous. Now it is said to God, Thy law is truth; and therefore that which is against the truth cannot be righteous. But who doubteth but that every lie is against the truth? Therefore no lie can possibly be righteous[2]." And so forth as followeth. Now on the other side, very notable learned men have thought, that Augustine was somewhat too stubbornly set against lying. And therefore some there are, which, going as it were betwixt both, do say, that they (whose examples I alleged even now) were not altogether without all sin; and yet they suppose, that their fault in those lies was a very small sin. I would wish those, which will allow themselves to lie officiously, to take heed to themselves, lest, by following their own affections more than enough, they do at last take that for an officious lie which is indeed a pernicious lie.

[1 Jerome's Epistle on this subject is Ep. 74. Opp. Tom. IV. col. 618-626. Augustine's letters are given in the same place, and in August. Opp. Ep. VIII. IX. XI. Tom. II. fol. 8, 9. Par. 1531.]

[2 Nihil autem judicandus est dicere, qui dicit aliqua justa esse mendacia, nisi aliqua justa esse peccata, ac per hoc aliqua justa esse quæ injusta sunt. Quo quid absurdius dici potest? Unde enim est peccatum nisi quia justitiæ contrarium est?... Ea vero quæ contra legem Dei fiunt, justa esse non possunt. Dictum est autem Deo, Lex tua veritas: ac per hoc, quod est contra veritatem justum esse non potest. Quis autem dubitet contra veritatem esse mendacium omne? Nullum ergo justum esse potest mendacium.—August. Opp. ad Consent. Tom. IV. fol. II. col. 2. Par. 1531.]

For the last and worst kind of lie is a pernicious lie: and that proceedeth of a corrupt mind, and tendeth to the damage of thy neighbour, which hath deserved no hurt at thy hand. This kind of lie is everywhere cried out upon throughout the scriptures: and the fault thereof increaseth according to the quantity of the mischief that it doth. For divines and ecclesiastical preachers do lie of all other most perniciously, while with lies and corrupt doctrine they kill the souls of men, and make the bodies and goods of silly seduced people both subject to the curse of God and in danger of a thousand perils more. And hereunto belongeth hypocrisy also, which the Lord Jesus doth in the gospel wonderfully taunt and bait exceedingly. Now hypocrisy doth shew itself, not only and so much in crafty and deceitful words, as also, and far more, in the whole conversation of our lives; as when we make semblance, or else dissemble such things as are not, by that means lying to God and beguiling our neighbour.

Furthermore, in this law are forbidden tale-bearings, privy slanders, backbitings, close whisperings, and all suspicions which rise by such occasions. Despiteful quips therefore, and heads that are ready to speak evil of all men, are plainly condemned. For some there are which are without honesty, not sticking to slander all estates and conditions, both high and low, private and public, and people of all ages: and for that purpose do they cast abroad infamous libels, they stick up written pasquils, and set out pictures to defame men withal. And to themselves they seem very eloquent, while with bitter words they check, and find fault with, all sorts of men: yea, they account the malapert prattling of their unbridled tongues to be a commendation of uncontrolled liberty and free licence of speaking. But they sin very grievously, which take delight in cursed speaking; that is, which carry about a tongue full of bitterness, curses, and deceit: even as they also are not without sin, that love a-life [3] to hear envenomed speech and hurtful talking.

But we make a difference, and do except from wrongful quarrels such accusations as are justly made and openly shewed, either by writing or word of mouth; and such kind

Carrying of tales, and a tongue disposed to speak lewdly and slanderously.

Pasquil is, as I think, an image in Rome, whereupon the people are wont to stick up writings to the defamation of them whom they hate; therefore Bullinger calleth such writings by the name of that image.

Just accusations.

[3 a-life, as my life, exceedingly. Nares' Glossary in voc.]

of chidings and chastenings also as preachers use in sacred
sermons: for they, which do in that sort chastise and pursue
wicked vices and errors, do purpose nothing else but the
glory of God and safeguard of men's souls, which they desire
to advance by all the means they can, not seeking to utter
their spite or wreak the malice of their naughty affections.

But we may gather by many arguments, that it is a
heinous crime falsely to slander and wickedly to backbite our
brethren and neighbours. For there is scarcely any thing
that doth so much disgrace us as backbiting doth. We are
made to the similitude and likeness of God, that we may be the
sons of God; but false accusations do make us, of the sons of
God, to be the sons of the devil. Now we all abhor and utterly
detest the name of the devil: but if thou art a wrongful slanderer, then art thou the very same that thou dost so detest:
for the devil taketh his name of wrongful accusing, and is
called a slanderer[1]. Moreover, in the book of Proverbs, God
is said to hate backbiters and wrongful slanderers. And in
the twenty-fourth chapter we read: "The thought of a fool
is sin, and a slanderer is hated of men." For a good name (as
the same Salomon witnesseth) is a precious treasure. When
as therefore the fame and good name of a man is put in
hazard by the false reports and slanders of a wicked tongue,
the chiefest jewel that a man hath is put in jeopardy; so that
in very deed a slanderer doth seem to sin more deeply than
a thief, unless a man make more account of his transitory
riches than of his name and good report: and therefore it
is strange at this day, that a thief for stealing is never pardoned, and backbiters for slanders are never once touched[2].
I would to God that magistrates would once rightly weigh
the sundry circumstances of sundry matters, and punish every
fault with penalties agreeable to the offence, and revenge the
greater crimes with great and sharper punishments. For
God truly doth require of and charge every one of us, to do
our best in maintaining truth, for the defence of our neighbour's good name, and preservation of his earthly substance.

Backbiting is pernicious.

[Prov. xxii. 1.]

[1] Διάβολος,—speciatim ita dicitur qui est ad calumniandum pro-
clivis, calumniator. 1 Tim. iii. 11; Tit. ii. 3; 2 Tim. iii. 3. Schleusneri
Lex. in voc.]

[2] aut minimum. Lat. omitted: or as gently as possibly may be.]

In this law also it seemeth that flattery is forbidden, Flattery. which, as the proverb doth truly say, maketh a fool mad, and causeth him that is mad to be incurably mad. And therefore Salomon saith, that a flatterer is worthy to be cursed of all men. "They (saith he) which say to the wicked, thou art just, [Prov. xxiv. shall be cursed of the people, and hated of the tribes." And 24.] in another place: "The words of a tale-bearer be as though [Prov. xxvi. they were simple[3], and yet they pierce to the inward parts of 22, 25.] the heart. When he speaketh softly, believe him not: for there are seven mischiefs in his heart." And therefore in Ecclesiastes it is very well said: "It is better to hear the rebuke [Eccles. vii. of a wise man than the song of a fool," that is, of a flatterer. 5.] And yet, although flattery be so great an evil, it is notwithstanding favoured of all men; so that as an infecting plague it is crept into[4] the church[5], into princes' palaces, into judges' courts, and every private house. For, like an alluring mermaid, it hath a song that doth delight our flesh. For we, like fools, are blinded with self-love, and do not mark that flatteries and allurements do breed our destruction. Ezechiel blameth greatly all flattering preachers, and saith: "Woe unto them [Ezek. xiii. that say unto the people, Peace, peace, when there is no 10, 11, 18.] peace; which daub with untempered morter, which sew enticing pillows under every elbow, and put alluring kerchiefs upon every head[6], to hunt after and catch souls." Of such kind of teachers, that delight more in lies and flattery than in sincere verity, the apostle Paul saith: "The time shall come [2 Tim. iv. that they shall not abide to hear sound doctrine; but they, 3, 4.] whose ears do itch, shall get them teachers according to their lusts, and shall turn their ears from the truth, and shall be turned into fables[7]." And David, praying against this plague, as the thing that is most pernicious to all kings and princes in authority, doth say: "The righteous shall smite me friendly[8]: but the precious balms of the wicked shall not anoint my head[9]." And again, "Lord, deliver me from lying lips and [Ps. cxx. 2.]

[3 Bullinger follows the Vulgate.]

[4 adde et occuparit, Lat. nay, has gained possession of, omitted.]

[5 Sacram in templo cathedram, Lat.]

[6 qui consuunt blandos pulvillos sub omni axilla aut cubito, et cervicalia blanda sub omni capite, Lat.]

[7 unto, 1577, ad fabulas, Lat.]

[8 et increpabit me, Lat. omitted : and shall reprove me.]

[9 oleum autem peccatoris non impinguabit caput meum, Lat. after the Vulgate, Psal. cxli, 5.]

The tenth commandment of God. [Exod. xx. 17.] a deceitful tongue." Thus much have I hitherto said for the exposition of the ninth commandment.

Now followeth the tenth and last commandment, which, word for word, is expressed thus: "Thou shalt not covet thy neighbour's house, thou shalt not covet thy neighbour's wife, Deut. v. nor his man-servant, nor his maid-servant, nor his ox, nor his ass, nor any thing that is thy neighbour's." Which words the Lord in the fifth of Deuteronomy doth lay down in this manner and order: "Thou shalt not covet thy neighbour's wife, thou shalt not covet thy neighbour's house, nor his field, nor his man-servant, nor his maid-servant, nor his ox, nor his ass, nor any thing that is thy neighbour's." Neither is there any difference or contrariety in the thing itself, although in Exodus, "Thy neighbour's house," and in Deuteronomy, "Thy neighbour's wife," be set first in order. Now this maketh[1] somewhat against them that divide this last precept into two commandments, which is indeed but one, as it may be partly gathered by this order thus inverted in the setting of it down in two sundry places.

Coveting. In this precept coveting is especially forbidden; I mean, evil longing and corrupt desiring. For coveting is a word indifferently used, as well in the better as the worse signification. For David affirmeth that he did long after God and Ps. cxix. his law: "I have wished for (saith he), O Lord, thy salvation." And, "I have longed after thy commandments." Psal. cxix. We must here, therefore, be able with discretion to judge betwixt that good affection, which God did first create in man; and that other motion, the root of evil, that groweth in our nature by the descent of corruption from our first father Adam. There was in Adam before his fall a certain good appetite with pleasure and delight. He was not so hungry, that hunger did pain his empty bowels (which is indeed a plague for sin), but he did eat with a certain sweet and delectable appetite. He was delighted with the pleasures of Paradise. He did with a certain holy desire both love and long after the woman, which God had brought and placed before him. And this good appetite or desire proceeded from God himself, who made both Adam and all his affections good at the first. Yea, and at this day also there are in men certain natural affections and desires, as, to eat, to drink, to sleep, and such like, belonging to the preserva-

[1 Facit autem. Lat. But this maketh. See Vol. I. p. 213.]

tion[2] of man's life, which of themselves are not to be accounted among the number of sins, unless by corruption of original vice they pass the bounds for which they are ordained. But in this treatise upon the tenth commandment desire is used in the worser part, and is taken for the concupiscence or coveting of evil things. This concupiscence, being translated from Adam into us all, is the fruit of our corrupt nature, or offspring of original sin, whose seat is in the heart of man; and is the fountain and head-spring of all sin and wickedness that is to be found in mortal men. For the Lord in the gospel doth expressly say: "Whatsoever entereth in by the mouth [Matth. xv. 17—20.] goeth into the belly, and is cast out into the draught: but the things that come out of the mouth proceed from the heart; and those defile the man. For out of the heart do come evil thoughts, murders, adulteries, whoredoms, theft, false witness-bearings, despiteful speaking: these be they that do defile the man." And the apostle James, speaking altogether as plainly in [James i. 13 —15.] another place, doth say: "Let no man, when he is tempted, say that he is tempted of God: for every one is tempted while he is drawn away, and enticed with the bait of his own concupiscence. Then when lust hath conceived, it bringeth forth sin; and sin, when it is finished, bringeth forth death."

Concupiscence, therefore, is a motion or affection of the *Concupiscence.* mind, which of our corrupt nature doth lust against God and his law, and stirreth us up to wickedness, although the consent, or deed itself, doth not presently follow upon our conceit. For if the deed do follow the lust, then doth the sin increase by steps and degrees. For[3] first we must consider the very blotting out, or corrupting, of the image of God in us, original sin, and that disease that lieth hid in our members, which is by us called evil affections. Secondarily, we must consider that it increaseth by our delight and pleasure therein. Thirdly, it is augmented, if we consent[4] and seek after counsel to commit the crime. And, lastly, if the consent break forth to the deed-doing, then is it greater and greater, according to the qualities of accidents or circumstances. Now all these are reckoned in the number of sins,

[2] ad conservationem ac propagationem, Lat., to the preservation and propagation.]

[3] In peccato enim, Lat. omitted: for in the case of sin.]

[4] Inde sequitur fere consensus, Lat. Thence follows usually consent.]

though by degrees the one of them is greater than the other: touching which I will, by God's sufferance, speak somewhat more largely, when I come to the treatise of sin. Wherefore that evil and unlawful affection, which is of our natural corruption, and lieth hid in our nature, but bewrayeth itself in our hearts against the pureness of God's law and majesty, is that very sin, which is in this law condemned. For, although there be some which think that such motions, diseases, blemishes, and affections of the mind are no sins, yet God, by forbidding them in this law, doth flatly condemn them. But if any man doubt of this exposition, let him hear the words of the apostle, who saith: " I knew not sin, but by the law: for I had not known lust, except the law had said, Thou shalt not lust. Without the law sin was dead: I once lived without law ; but when the commandment came, sin revived, and I was dead." And again, " The affection of the flesh is death, but the affection of the Spirit is life and peace : because the affection of the flesh is enmity against God; for it is not obedient to the law of God, neither can be. So then they that are in the flesh cannot please God." The affection of concupiscence therefore doth condemn us; or, as I should rather say, we are worthily condemned by the just judgment of God for our concupiscence[1], which doth every hour and moment bewray itself in the thoughts of our hearts. There are (I confess) sundry fantasies and many thoughts in the minds of men, which, while they tend not to the offence of God or our neighbour, nor do contain any uncleanness or self-love, are not to be counted in the number of sins: as I did immediately after the beginning declare unto you.

So hitherto, verily, God hath forbidden the grosser sins which man doth daily commit against him ; and now at last he cometh to the concupiscence and corrupt nature of man, the well-spring of all evil, which in this precept he goeth about to stop up and cause to sleep: or, as I should rather say, to detect to the eyes of all men the infirmity and weakness of mankind. For what is he that hath not some whiles felt concupiscence ? yea, what is he, that is not every hour and moment pricked with the sting of fleshly concupiscence ? What man is there, I pray you, that is not diseased with the

[Rom. vii. 7—9.]

[Rom. viii. 6—8.]

Man is convinced of sin.

[1 in nobis latentem atque, Lat., omitted : which lurketh in us, and.]

natural sickness common to us all, and spotted with the blemish of original guiltiness? Being therefore convinced of sin before the Lord, we are not able to excuse our fault, nor escape the sentence of the judge that doth condemn all flesh. For the just Lord doth expressly condemn our natural corruption and wicked inclination, which is a continual turning from God, and rebellion against the sincerity which he requireth at our hands. For they are called happy that are clean in heart, because they shall see God. They therefore, whose hearts are wrapped in lusts, diseased with concupiscence, and spotted with the poison of original guilt, shall not see God. But such are all we that are the sons of Adam. And therefore this law doth convince us all of sin, infirmity, natural corruption, and of damnation which followeth upon the neck of our corruption.

Moreover, God in his law doth not only require the outward cleanness of the body, but the inward pureness also of the mind, the soul, and all our affections; and giveth charge that all, whatsoever we think, determine, go about, or do, should tend to the health and profit of our neighbour. This commandment therefore may be referred to all the other that went before. For the Lord himself expounding this commandment, " Thou shalt not commit murder," addeth : " Whosoever is angry with his brother shall be in danger of judgment," &c. Matt. v ; and again, in expounding this precept, " Thou shalt not commit adultery," he addeth ; " Whosoever looketh on another man's wife to lust after her, he hath committed adultery already with her in his heart."

What pureness God requireth of man.

Matth. v.

And here he doth exactly rehearse the things which we do covet, and, in longing after which, we are wont to sin. Now our covetousness consisteth in the desire either of things or persons. The things that we covet are either immoveable or moveable : as we Germans do usually say, *Die guteren sind etliche ligende, etliche farende*[2]. The immoveable things are houses, farms, lands, vineyards, woods, meadows, pastures, fishpools, and such like. Things moveable are money, cattle, honour[3], office, and dignities. The persons are wife, children, man-servants and maid-servants. These and such like, which our neighbour hath in possession, none of us ought to covet

What it is that we must not covet.

[2 Helvetice, Lat., in our Swiss phrase.]
[3 honores, Lat. honours.]

to his hurt or hinderance : or if any man happen to covet them, yet let him not consent to the concupiscence, nor take delight therein; let him not seek to obtain the thing that he so desireth, nor suffer his ill-conceived purpose to break out to the deed-doing, in taking from his neighbour his things or persons: for God requireth at the hands of those that worship him such kind of righteousness as is altogether sound and absolutely perfect, not in the outward deed alone, but also in the inward mind and settled purpose of the heart. [Matt. v. 20.] Whereupon the Lord in the gospel saith: "Unless your righteousness exceed the righteousness of the scribes and Pharisees, ye shall not enter into the kingdom of God." But touching the manner how God's commandments are fulfilled, and that faith is the absolute righteousness, I will hereafter in another sermon tell you, as I have already said somewhat in the sermon that I made upon true faith.

Hitherto in twelve sermons I have run through and declared the ten precepts of the moral law, in which I told you that the form of virtue is laid before our eyes, thereby to frame our manners according to the will of God. God himself hath divided all the branches of his moral law into two tables. The first doth shew the duty of us men to our Creator, and teacheth how to worship aright our God and governor. The second table, in six whole precepts, doth declare what, and how much, every man is bound to owe to his neighbour, and how we may all live both quietly, well, and civilly one with another. It commandeth us to honour our parents, and all those which God hath ordained instead of our parents. It forbiddeth murder, or doing injury to any man in his life and body. It forbiddeth whoredom, adultery, and wicked lusts, commending wedlock, cleanness, and a continent life[1]. It forbiddeth lies, false witness-bearings, and evil[2] desires; and biddeth us to love our neighbours with all our hearts, being ready at all times with all our power to do them good.

To God, our Lord and most prudent lawgiver, be all praise and thanks for ever and ever. Amen.

[1 Prohibet furta, dolos, imposturas, Lat. omitted: it forbiddeth thefts, cheatings, and impositions.]
[2 et noxias, Lat. omitted: and hurtful.]

OF THE CEREMONIAL LAW OF GOD, BUT ESPECIALLY
OF THE PRIESTHOOD, TIME, AND PLACE, AP-
POINTED FOR THE CEREMONIES.

THE FIFTH SERMON.

In the partition of God's laws, next after the moral law
we placed the ceremonial law[3]: and therefore, since the moral
law is already expounded, I have now next, by the help of
God, to treat of the law of ceremonies. And, that I may not
hide any thing from you, note this by the way: that some
write *Ceremoniæ*, and some *Cerimoniæ*; which two words are
used for ceremonies; considering that sundry men have sundry
opinions touching the word, from whence it should come.
For some (after the opinion of Servius Sulpitius) do think
that they are called *Ceremoniæ a carendo*[4]. But Festus
affirmeth, that[5] ceremonies did first take their name of the
town Cæres, or Cærete[6]. For Livy in his fifth book saith,
that the relics[7] of the Romans were kept by the towns-men of
Cæres in the French wars, at what time the Frenchmen invaded Rome[8]. By which occasion it is likely that, for remembrance of the benefit, all the worship due to God, and all the
holy rites or customs, were, according to the name of the
town, usually called ceremonies. But from whencesoever
the word is derived, we in this treatise use it for the holy
deed of worshipping God, and the ecclesiastical rites of sacred
religion.

Now ceremonies are holy rites belonging to the ministers Ceremonies generally,
of religion, and also to the place, time, and holy worship ex- what they are.
hibited to God; all which, how they ought to be kept and

[3 Vol. I. p. 209.]

[4 Servius Sulpicius religionem esse dictam tradidit, quæ propter
sanctitatem aliquam remota ac seposita a nobis sit, quasi a relinquendo
dicta, ut a carendo ceremonia. Macrob. Saturn. Lib. III. cap. 3. See
also Aul. Gell. Noct. Attic. Lib. IV. cap. 9. Augustine adopted this
derivation. Retract. cap. 37.]

[5 alii existimant, Lat. omitted: some persons think that.]

[6 Cærimoniarum causam alii ab oppido Cære dictam existimant;
alii a caritate dictam judicant. Festus, Lutet, 1576.]

[7 Sacra Romanorum, Lat.]

[8 —Sacra in plaustrum imposuit (L. Albinius), et Cære, quo iter
sacerdotibus erat, pervexit. Liv. Lib. V. cap. 40.]

observed according as they should be, the laws called ceremonial do exactly teach and precisely describe. Ceremonies therefore are the actions and rites, which the laws or rules, called ceremonial, do frame or appoint.

Now ceremonies are ordained either by God or men. As touching those which God hath instituted, they are of two sorts: the one sort whereof he did ordain in the old Testament to the ancient Israelites; and the other, at the coming of Christ, to us that are the people of the new Testament or covenant. Of the ceremonies of the new Testament I mean to speak, when I come to treat of the church and the sacraments thereof. At this time I will discourse of the ceremonies of the old Testament, which were holy rites and actions ordained and delivered by God himself to the people of Israel until the time of amendment, partly to represent, and in a shadow to shew[1], the mysteries of God; and partly to worship God by them, and also with them to keep the people of God in a lawful religion, and in the society of one ecclesiastical body.

Human ceremonies.

But men also have brought in very many and sundry sorts of ceremonies: as among the heathen the arch-flamines did, who were the priests and ministers of idols; which offices and rooms both their kings and princes did some times supply. [1 Kings xii. 26—33.] Among the Hebrews, Jeroboam, king of Israel, to the destruction of him and his, did change the ceremonies which God had ordained into his own, that is, into men's inventions and detestable blasphemies.

In this latter age of the world, wherein we live, there is no ho[2] of ceremonies that are instituted daily by brain-sick[3] people: the misery whereof many learned men both have and do yet at this day lament and bewail. Augustine complaineth that in his time ceremonies did increase too fast in the church of God: what would he say (think you), if he were alive to see them now-a-days[4]? But of this I will speak at another time.

[1 velandaque, Lat. and to veil.]
[2 ho, i.e. stop, bound, limit. Johnson. See Tyndale's Doctr. Treat. Park. Soc. ed. p. 25.]
[3 This epithet is not in the Lat.]
[4 ... ipsam religionem, quam paucissimis et manifestissimis celebrationum sacramentis misericordia Dei esse liberam voluit, servilibus

Now, for because the word ceremonies is attributed as a name to any heathenish rites whatsoever, I in this treatise would have you to know, that I speak not of every ceremony, but of those only which were delivered of God by Moses to the people of Israel; not at the will of Moses, but at the will of God, by the means or ministery of Moses, according as it was said unto him: "See, that thou doest all things according to the pattern that was shewed thee in the mountain." The original therefore or beginning of these ceremonies, which we treat of, are referred to God himself, the most true and assured author thereof; and they did therefore please God, because they were godly, and might be exhibited in faith. Contrarily, the ceremonies in religion that are devised and ordained of men are utterly condemned, as is to be seen in the twelfth of Deuteronomy[5]. In the seventeenth chapter of the fourth of Kings also we find: "Israel walked in the ordinances, or ceremonies, which they themselves had made to themselves." It is known to all men, what happened to Jeroboam and his household, and all the kings of Israel, that walked in the ways of Jeroboam[6]. So then these ceremonies of ours, I mean, the ceremonies whereof I speak, are actions and rites not in profane but holy matters, which God himself did first ordain, and which God's people doth use and exercise.

[Exod. xxv. 40. Acts vii. 44. Heb. viii. 5.]

[2 Kings xvii. 8.]

These ceremonies were not delivered to all people or nations, but to the people of Israel only, and that too, as the apostle saith, "until the time of amendment," as that which should lie upon the shoulders of the Jews till the coming of Messiah; at what time they should be taken away, and after that appear no more. And in this sense, verily, the apostle Paul calleth the law the schoolmistress[7] until Christ.

Divine ceremonies.

[Heb. ix. 10.]

We have, moreover, to note the end whereunto ceremonies were ordained. Ceremonies do especially belong to the doctrine of piety and faith. For they were added to the first table, as a shore, or prop, to uphold or stay it. For they

The end whereto ceremonies were ordained.

---

oneribus premunt (ceremoniæ), ut tolerabilior sit conditio Judæorum. —August. Januario Ep. cxix. Par. 1531. Tom. ii. fol. 112. col. 1.— A very similar passage, with the same quotation from Augustine, occurs in Wicliffe's Apology for the Lollards, Camden Soc. ed. p. 75. Lond. 1842.]

  [5 locus illustris est Deuteronomii xii. Lat.]

  [6 See Vol. i. pp. 335, 6.]　　　　[7 Gal. iii. 24; pædagogia, Lat.]

teach the outward worship of the true God, which godly
men do give unto him; and by them were the Israelites
drawn not only from strange gods, but from strange worships
also, wherewith they were too much and too long inured and
trained up in the land of Egypt; to the end they should
not have any occasion to receive or admit any strange kinds
of worships, when they were furnished, and as it were wrapped
in so exquisite sorts of curious ceremonies.   This doth Moses
in the twelfth of Deuteronomy make to be the cause why
God appointed such busy ceremonies.   Therefore ceremonies,
and the use of ceremonies, are in the scripture expressly called

The worship of God. the worship of God.   For with them it pleaseth God to be
worshipped; and with them he did retain his people in the
true worshipping of him, and in the true religion and communion of one ecclesiastical body.   For the church is severed
and divided by the admitting or bringing in of new or strange
ceremonies; as it is evident in the states and dealings of Salomon and Jeroboam.   Moreover the apostle Paul said;

1 Cor. x. "Are not they which eat of the sacrifice partakers of the
altar," and so consequently of the whole religion?   Furthermore, the chief or especial mysteries of Christ and his church
were shadowed in ceremonies[1], and were the sacraments of the
Jewish people, wherewith the Lord would bind them unto
him, put them in mind of his benefits, and lastly, keep the
piety, obedience, and faith of his people in ure and exercise.
And because the Lord did especially require faith and faithful
obedience at the hands of his servants in the observing of
ceremonies, therefore those ceremonies did not please but
utterly displease his majesty, so oft as the people were ignorant of the meaning of the secret mysteries contained in
those figurative shews; so oft, I say, as they were without
faith, and observed only the outward actions or ceremonies,
without inward zeal and touch of conscience.   For the Lord

When God liketh, and when he mis-liketh, cere-monies. [Jer. vii. 21 —23.] in Jeremy crieth out and saith: "Heap up your burnt-
offerings with your sacrifices, and eat the flesh: for when I
brought your fathers out of Egypt, I spoke no word unto
them of burnt-offerings or sacrifices; but this I commanded
them, saying, Hearken unto and obey my voice, and I will

[Exod. xxix. 18, 25, 41— 46. Numb. xv. &c.] be your God, and ye shall be my people."   And yet, in another place, we read that the offering of sacrifices, and that

[1 velata abscondebantur, Lat.; being veiled, were hidden.]

external action of the people in worshipping God, was acceptable and of a sweet-smelling savour in the nose of the Lord. Now, whereupon riseth this diversity, I pray you, but upon the difference of the minds of them that worship the Lord? For sacrifices pleased him, and the honour that was done unto him in simple obedience and faith alone did please him too: but that religion he did utterly mislike of, wherein he was worshipped with outward shews, and not with the faith and sincere obedience of the inward heart: in which sort we read that Cain did sin; for God commanded not to sacrifice in that manner that Cain did.

Again, he commanded to sacrifice and to worship him with external ceremonies[2] in faith that Christ should come to be the Saviour of the world[3]: not that they should hope to be justified by the external action, but by him that was prefigured in all their ceremonies, Christ Jesus, the sacrifice once to be offered to save them all[4]; who was the life and meaning whereunto all those ceremonies did lead, that are expressed in the law.

But it is not amiss here particularly to examine and look into not all and every one, but the chiefest ceremonies, and those which are more significant than the rest. Let this labour of mine not seem to any man to be more curious than needeth, or less profitable than it sheweth for. For it is undoubtedly very available to the sound understanding of the abrogation of the law[5]. All things, whatsoever God hath laid down in the holy scriptures, are altogether profitable to our edification, and do carry with them a divine authority, whereby we may confirm our minds: they therefore are very fools and godless people, or, to use a more gentle term, they are shuttle-witted[6], and ignorant of all good things, whose stomachs do rise at the ceremonies that God hath taught, and whose ears are offended to hear a sober and godly treatise upon the exposition of those divine ceremonies. Some there are, and that no small number, who think it very profitable

The knowledge of the ceremonies is not unprofitable.

[2 legitime et, Lat. omitted: lawfully, and.]
[3 in fide Christi venturi Messiæ, Lat.]
[4 the sacrifice—all; not in the original.]
[5 rather, of the law that has been abrogated: legis abrogatæ, Lat.]
[6 temerarii, Lat. Shittle or shuttle; light, volatile, giddy. Richardson's Dict. in voc.]

and an excellent thing to construe Homer and Virgil allegorically; in divine ceremonies only foolish heads are persuaded that no profit or wisdom lieth secretly hidden: when indeed, in all the world again, there is nothing more profitable, more pleasant, more fine, more excellent, or more full of wisdom in allegorical types, than the ceremonies are that God hath ordained. For in them are the mysteries of Christ and his catholic church very finely, plainly, and notably described.

The sum of the ceremonies.

Now, in reckoning up and touching these several ceremonies, I will chiefly follow the very natural order. Ceremonies do appertain to the ecclesiastical worship of God. Therefore it is necessary that there should be persons appointed in the church to be the masters, or rather public ministers, of those ceremonies, to exercise and put them in practice, as the Lord ordained them. It is necessary also, that there be a certain place and time appointed, wherein and when God should be especially worshipped rather than at another place or season. Moreover, the holy rites, that is, the very ceremonies, must be appointed and certainly numbered, that the worshippers of God may know what and how great the honour

The priesthood.

is that they are bound to give unto him. And first of all, I mean to say somewhat of the persons, that is, the priests or Levites; referring still the hearers to the reading of the holy Bible, wherein the whole is fully contained and largely described.

The beginning of priesthood.

The beginning of priesthood among the old people is derived or brought from the creation almost[1]: for they say, that in every family the first-begotten were always the priests.

[Exod. xiii. 2, 15.]

It is certain, that, when the firstborn of Egypt were slain, the Lord did by a law consecrate to himself the first-begotten of the Israelites. And the preeminence, or dignity, of the first-begotten hath always been very great by the civil law[2]. The first-begotten did always rule and bear the sway in his father's house, and was, as it were, a king among his brethren: to the first-begotten the inheritance was due, to the other brethren were portions given: the first-begotten did

I think his meaning was to have said

excel the rest in the dignity of the priesthood. Therefore when Cain and Abel did strive about their birthright, they

[1] In his treatise de Episcop. instit. et funct. cap. i. Bullinger shews that he here follows the *vetus Judæorum traditio.*]

[2] vel in legibus civilibus, Lat.: even in civil laws.]

contended not about a trifle, but about a matter of very great weight. Whereupon, when the mother-virgin is said in Luke to have borne the first-begotten son, let no man think that she was the mother of the second-begotten, or many sons more. For in that Luke calleth Christ her first-begotten son, therein is noted his dignity and excellency. For to Christ our Lord doth belong the kingdom, priesthood, and inheritance: by whose bountiful liberality we are adopted to be his partners both in the kingdom, priesthood, and inheritance of life everlasting and all heavenly things. *Esau and Jacob, instead of Cain and Abel[3]. Christ the first-begotten. [Luke ii. 7.]*

But to return to our purpose again. The dignity of priesthood, among the people of Israel, did of right belong to Reuben, because he was the first-begotten; but he, by committing detestable incest, did lose his right. Next to him, therefore, was Levi[4], who also lost that dignity for the sin which he committed in killing the men of Sychem traiterously, and profaning the sacrament of circumcision. But because the tribe of Levi did behave itself manfully, not only in the bringing of the children of Israel out of Egypt, but also in punishing idolaters, I mean, the men that worshipped the golden calf; therefore did they receive the office or dignity of priesthood in reward of their virtue, and at that time were the Levites chosen to the place of the first-begotten of all the seed of Israel. For thus we read: "And Moses said unto the Levites, Consecrate your hands unto the Lord this day, every man upon his son, and upon his brother; that there may a blessing be given you this day." And again: "And the Lord spake unto Moses, saying, Behold, I have taken the Levites from among the children of Israel for all that first openeth the matrice among the children of Israel; and the Levites shall be mine; because all the firstborn are mine: for the same day that I smote all the firstborn in the land of Egypt, I hallowed to myself all the firstborn in Israel." And so forth. By this it appeareth that the tribe of Levi was appointed to the priesthood in the church of Israel. Moreover this dignity, or ministry, was singularly confirmed to this tribe immediately upon the insurrection of Korah, Dathan, and Abiron, by the wonderful miracle that the Lord *[Gen. xlix. 3, 4. 1 Chron. v. 1.] [Gen. xxxiv. xlix. 5—7.] The Levites chosen to be priests. Exod. xxxii. [29.] Numb. iii. [12, 13.]*

[3 This correction of the translator is perhaps not necessary. Bullinger probably took Calvin's view.—Conf. Calv. Comment. in loc.]

[4 successit ergo Levi, Lat.]

wrought upon Aaron's rod, which budded alone among the other eleven twigs, for a witness that God had appointed the tribe of Levi alone to the office and function of holy priesthood. And for that cause was the same rod put into the ark, and kept in the tabernacle, to the end that none other tribe should affect the priesthood at any time thereafter. All which is largely declared in the sixteenth and seventeenth chapters of the Book of Numbers.

Certain degrees among the priests. Now there was among the Levites a certain order; there were degrees, and, as it were, appointments unto sundry offices. For the Levites were divided into three families, that is, into Cahatites[1], Gersonites, and Merarites : and they again were parted into four orders. For first of all, out of the family of Cahat were chosen princes, to bear the sway and rule the rest : to them the remnant of the Cahatites, and the other two orders, the Gersonites and Merarites, were subject, and did obey the first sort of Cahatites that were their governors. For Aaron, the chief priest, with Ithamar and Eleazar his sons, had the preeminence among the rest. For thus we read in the third of Numbers : " And thou shalt give the Levites unto Aaron and to his sons ; for they are given unto him of the children of Israel. And thou shalt appoint Aaron and his sons to wait on their priests' office ; and the stranger that cometh nigh shall be slain." Therein did Aaron, the chief priest, bear the type or figure of Christ, the true, the best, and greatest king and bishop, to whom all Christians are subject, as to their chief bishop and head, whose dwelling is in heaven[2].

Among the Levites such were chosen to the ministry as were most fit for it. And here observe, that all the Levites did not serve in the tabernacle, nor that they all did everywhere through the land of Israel instruct and teach. There were certain ordinances touching the choice and refusal of those among the Levites that were to be called to the ministry or priesthood. Time will not serve me to reckon all the laws appointed for that purpose ; the chief whereof are to be seen in the twenty-first and twenty-second chapters of Leviticus. In the eighth chapter of the book of Numbers the age is appointed of them that should be thought fit for the ministry ; that is, from the twenty-fifth to the fiftieth year of their age. The priests, that were called

[1 Cahatites : Kohathites.]
[2 quorum ipse summus pontifex et caput in cœlis est, Lat.]

and chosen to the ministry, were also consecrated. The manner of consecrating them is far more large and busy than that I can in few words declare it. By their consecration was meant, that they ought to be adorned with sundry gifts, and endued with holy conversation, that serve the church in the office of priesthood. For to this doth especially belong the anointing of the priests, which is a type of the Holy Ghost, wherewithal unless an ecclesiastical minister be endued, he exerciseth the office to his own destruction. This ceremonial anointing of priests is set down by Moses in the twenty-ninth of Exodus, the eighth of Leviticus, and the eighth chapter of the book of Numbers. To this we must add also the habit or apparel that the priests did use. The priests ware, when they did not minister in their charge or office, such kind of garments as laymen did, as we may gather out of Ezechiel[3]; but when they did serve in the ministry, then did they wear ceremonial raiment according to God's commandment. A very large description whereof Moses doth very well set down in the twenty-eighth and thirty-ninth chapters of Exodus. *1 John ii.*

There are in number nine sorts of ceremonial garments[4]; yet some do reckon up but eight; Josephus maketh ten[5]. First of all, the priests, before they went about their offices, did wash themselves in water[6], and then put on their holy garments. Among those garments, some there were indifferently used both of the inferior and chief priests. And first, their privities are hidden with linen breeches coming down to their knees and hams; the upper part whereof was tied above their hips with a gathering band, like the upper part of our common slops[7], to the end that, if they should chance to *The priests' raiment.* *Breeches.*

[3 Ezek. xlii. 14.—alienis, id est, vulgaribus vestimentis amicti (sacerdotes) multitudini admiscebantur. Œcolampadius, Comment. in loc. cit. fol. 264. Argent, 1534.]

[4 In the following account of the garments of the Jewish priests Bullinger has largely borrowed from Jerome's Epist. ad Fabiolam, de veste sacerdotali. Hieron. Opp. Par. 1693—1706. Tom. ii. col. 574, &c.]

[5 Joseph. Antiq. Lib. iii. cap. 7.]

[6 aqua munda, Lat. pure water.]

[7 caligarum nostrarum, Lat. Slops: trowsers, Johnson. Homily (Oxf. ed. 1832, p. 285) Against excess of Apparel. But the corresponding word in the auth. ver. of Isai. iii. 20, there quoted, is "the ornaments of the legs."]

fall, while they were busy in killing their sacrifices, or in bearing of burdens to and fro, the parts should not appear which shame doth bid to cover.

The close frock or cassock. Upon their linen breeches they had a close coat, made of double linen, which (as Josephus saith) was made of silk[1]. That was plain, or close to the body, without plait or gathering[2], and came down just to the calf of the leg. Such[3] were soldiers wont to wear, and called them cassocks[4]; so fit for their limbs and close to their bodies, that they were light, and without let either to run or fight. And therefore the priests, making themselves ready to the ministery of God, put on such a cassock, that, being comely clad, they might, notwithstanding, with much expedition discharge their office, and exercise their ministery.

The girdle The third kind of raiment, that was a belt or girdle, did gird that cassock about the priest. This girdle was woven of purple, scarlet, and blue silk[5], like to an adder's skin, hanging down beneath the knee, but in the holy ministery tucked up again upon the left shoulder[6].

The cap or mitre. The fourth kind of ornament was a mitre, or a round little cap, which covered his head almost to the ears, in fashion like as if a man should cut a bowl even in the midst, and set the upper part upon his head[7].

The Ephod. Then was the ephod, (whereof mention is made, not in Exodus, where the ceremonial garments are reckoned up as it were of purpose, but in other places of holy scripture,) [Judg. xvii. 5; xviii. 14. 1 Sam. ii. 18.] which garment was indifferently common to all the priests. This ephod is thought to have been a linen cloak; such an [2 Sam. vi. 14.] one as David ware when he danced before the ark. Of the priests which Saul slew by the hands of Doeg the Edomite, [1 Sam. xxii. 18.] thus we read: "And he killed that same day eighty-five men that ware linen ephods." His meaning is, not that they were slain while the ephods were on their backs; but that they were killed, when they were of that age and order, that

[1 —διπλῆς σινδόνος βυσσίνης. Joseph. ibid. § 2. Exod. xxviii. 40.]
[2 Adhæret corpori plana, Lat.]   [3 lineas, Lat.]
[4 camisia, Lat. a linen coat, which soldiers wore close to their body. Ainsworth.]
[5 bysso hyacinthoque. Lat. and Joseph. ibid. μετὰ ὑακίνθου καὶ βύσσου.]
[6 Joseph. ibid. § 2.]
[7 Joseph. ibid. § 3. Exod. xxviii. 40.]

they might wear an ephod; that is, that they might minister
in the priesthood of the Lord.   Therefore in Osee we read, [Hos. iii. 4.]
"Thou shalt be without ephod, and teraphim;" that is, without priesthood and religion.   For the ephod began to be used
for the very priesthood; the garment, or the sign, for the
thing signified.   But if any man will take these words of Osee
to be spoken of the more notable ephod (of which I shall
have cause to speak anon), I will not greatly gainsay him.
Now this linen ephod seemeth not to differ much from that
which the Papists do[8] call a surplice[9].   These five garments
the chief priest and under priests did use alike.   The other
four do properly belong to the high priest alone.

   The first of the four was called megil, and was a coat *The megil.*
down to the ancles[10]; a garment of all blue silk, from the neck
down to the sole of the foot, being close on every side, unless
it were the places to put his head and arms out at: at the
hems beneath did hang seventy-two bells, and as many pomegranates, so placed that still between two bells there hung
one pomegranate, and betwixt two pomegranates one bell:
the cause thereof is made to be this, that, when the high
priest went into the holy of holies, the sound might be heard;
because he should by and by die the death unless he did so[11].

   Now followeth the ephod of the high priest, which differ- *The breast-
eth much from that whereof I spake before.   For it was not lap or high
of linen, but woven with weaver's work of divers colours of priest's
gold, purple, and silk; being unlike to the other in shape and ephod.*
making.   For it belonged to the high priests alone, and was
a breast-lap, coming over the bulk from the neck to the hips:
for, like a curet[12], it covered the breast; it came over the
hinder part of the shoulders, and about both the sides under
the arm-holes: bearing the same fashion that at this day
women's stomachers do, which we Switzers call *libli*[13].   This
ephod be ware upon the top of his megil, that came down to

[8 hodie, Lat. omitted: at this day.]
[9 pallium, camisiam, vel vestem chori, Lat.]
[10 vestis inquam sinuosa, Lat. omitted: a plaited garment.]
[11 Exod. xxviii. 31-35. Joseph. ibid. § 4.]
[12 curet, or curiet, a breastplate or corslet, from *cuir*, leather;
breastplates being at first made of that material.   Toone's Glossary
in voc.]
[13 The word which Luther's version has is *leibrock*.]

[Exod. xxviii. 6—14.]

The breast-lap of judgment.

[Exod. xxviii. 30.] Urim and Thummim.

the ancles[1]. Upon each shoulder he bare an onyx-stone, called schoham[2]; wherein were graven the names of the children of Israel: against the breast there was nothing woven in it, but a place was left void for the breast-lap of judgment. For the breast-lap of judgment, which is called hosen, was the eighth ornament of their attire; and it was a woven cloth made of gold, purple, and silk, about an handbreadth square, and double, and hemmed about on every side, because it should not ravel out. In that there was woven precious stones of a wonderful greatness (for the kind) and of a marvellous price; which were placed so in four sundry rows, that every rank contained three stones; in which, as in the onyx-stones, were graven the names of the children of Israel[3]. They glistered with a wonderful brightness; for no stones were set in the breast-lap but such as shone exceedingly. Whereby it seemeth that Urim and Thummim was nothing else but these rows of precious stones: for Urim and Thummim signify light and perfectness; for, as these stones did give great light, so were they pure without all manner of spots. And they thought that the high priest did never say right in a matter of weight, nor, when he was asked, did utter truly the answers and oracles of God, but when the breast-lap of judgment did hang on his breast. Now this breast-lap of judgment was tied to the ephod, or the other breast-lap, by golden rings beneath; and above, it hung down the shoulders by golden chains, that were fastened under the onyx-stones. This was the most precious and excellent part of the high priest's apparel. For it was the coffer of wisdom, and treasure of all law and knowledge, of equity and justice, from whence the Israelites did fetch, as it were, the determinate answers to such doubts as at any time they stuck upon: which is the cause (as it seemeth) that some have translated Urim and Thummim into the Greek δήλωσις καὶ ἀλήθεια[4];

[1 Joseph. ibid. § 5. and de Bell. Jud. Lib. v. cap. 5. § 7.]

[2 gemmæ pretiosæ, Lat. omitted: precious stones.]

[3 Exod. xxviii. 15-29. Josephus, ib. § 5.]

[4 Levit. viii. 8. LXX. ἐπέθηκεν ἐπὶ τὸ λογεῖον τὴν δήλωσιν καὶ τὴν ἀλήθειαν. Hoc vero quid significabatur aliud, quam quod in pectore sacerdotis debet esse verum judicium de rebus divinis, quod deinde non sibi retineat, sed coram ecclesia proferat cum veritate?—Bullinger. de Epic. instit. et funct. Lib. ii. fol. 70.]

that is (say they) doctrine and truth is in the priest's breast.

The last of all is the golden plate. For upon the high priest's head there was a blue silk lace, whereupon this plate was put, which was broad beneath and sharp above; in fashion somewhat like to the label of a bishop's mitre; wherein was written, "Holy to the Lord," or, "The holiness of the Lord." For Christ, our Lord, alone is holiest of all, and he that sanctifieth us all. He is an antichrist that doth usurp that name or title. Some think, that in that plate was written that name of God that was not lawful for any man to utter[5]. This plate was tied to the cap[6], full upon the forehead, with a blue silk lace, and was as it were a crown upon his head[7]. Thus, I say, were the high priest and under priests arrayed at the first.

These sundry ceremonies have sundry and godly significations. The use and end of these ordinances the Lord declared by Moses to be for glory and comeliness' sake: for they were invented, partly for the winning of credit and authority to the ministers of religion, and partly for the commendation or advancement of religion itself; because the things are most regarded, that are set forth with so great solemnity. Moreover, it was profitable and especially necessary with these busy ceremonies to set awork the people, which, if they had been without such ceremonies of their own, was very profane, and ready to have embraced the idolatrous rites of heathen nations.

Furthermore, those ceremonial clothes, used by the priests, Aaron's successors, do offer to us the beholding[8] of Christ, the true and highest priest. He was apparelled with the garment of righteousness, temperance, and virtue; which garment is common unto us also. For all Christians must put on and be clad with Christ. And yet Christ hath the pre-eminence, as the high and chiefest priest among us all; not only because he

The golden plate.

That name was Jehovah, which wheresoever the Israelites did find it written, they did not call Jehovah, but expressed it by the word Adonai, which signifieth Lord: so greatly did they reverence the majestical name of God.

The meaning of the priests' apparel.

[5 In qua (i. e. lamina aurea) scriptum est nomen Dei Hebraicis quattuor litteris, jod, he, vav, he, quod apud illos ineffabile nuncupatur. Hieron. Ep. ad Fabiol. Tom. II. col. 581. Par. 1693—1706.]

[6 commune omnium sacerdotum. Lat. omitted: which was common to all the priests.]

[7 Exod. xxviii. 36-38. Joseph. ibid. § 6.]

[8 exhibent spectandum, Lat.]

doth sanctify us, and endue us with virtue; but also because he hath certain properties peculiar to himself, as he that is both very God and the Saviour of the world. He beareth us upon his breast and shoulders, as Aaron did the precious stones[1]: for we are not vile, but very dear, in the sight of God. Out of the breast of our high priest, Christ, doth glister and shine the light of eternal wisdom : for in him, as it were in the treasury of God's eternal wisdom, are all the riches of knowledge and wisdom laid up and locked. He is the light of the world; he is both truth and perfectness; so that all the world should of right require and seek at Christ alone for laws, ordinances, answers, and whatsoever else is needful to perfectness and true happiness. He is the Holy of holies, the very majesty and holiness of God: upon his head is the crown of glory very rightly placed, as he that sanctifieth only, reigneth in glory, and liveth for evermore.

Besides all this, the priests were by these ceremonies taught to understand, by their very apparel, what was required at their hands, and what kind of men they ought to be. Let the priests be always ready to the executing of their office; let them walk honestly before God and men ; let them be temperate and far from lust and sensuality; let their loins be girded with the belt of justice and verity; let their breast, their sides, and back be furnished with the word of God; let their head be covered with the helmet of salvation; upon that let Christ Jesus, the Saviour, be placed; and let him be the chief of the ministers and of the ministry: but chiefly let the priest be heard in the church : for if he be dumb, he shall die the death; but if he ring out the name of the Lord, and preach his law, then doth he stir up in the church a savour, far passing the smell of sweet pomegranates, in the nose of God. Therefore under these clothes is hidden the signification of the priests' manners, of their virtues and vices. Next after a man's talk, there is nothing that doth commend him sooner than his apparel. For as the man is, such is his talk, such is his clothing: therefore the raiment doth note of what conversation the priest ought to be. Whereupon it cometh that in the scriptures we are bidden to put on other clothing; when the meaning of the Holy Ghost is,

[1 Gestat nos in humeris suis et in pectore suo, veluti gemmas pretiosas, Lat.]

that we should change our wicked conversation: so that the very garments do partly instruct the priests what they have to do, and what is seemly for them.

But now the time and course of this treatise inviteth me to speak somewhat of the priests' office. Their office did consist in many things, but especially in teaching and instructing. For the chief cause why the priests were ordained of God was to instruct the church in true piety, and to teach the people the law of God.   For thus we read that the Lord did say unto Aaron: "Thou and thy sons that are with thee, shall drink neither wine nor strong drink, when ye enter into the tabernacle of witness, lest haply ye die.   Let it be an everlasting ordinance among your posterities, that ye may put difference both betwixt holy and unholy, and betwixt clean and unclean; and that ye may teach the sons of Israel all the statutes which the Lord hath spoken unto them by the ministery of Moses." Levit. x.   The same law doth Ezechiel in as many words almost rehearse in the forty-fourth chapter of his prophecy.   And Malachi declareth it also, as it is to be seen in the second of his prophecy. They therefore are utterly deceived, which think that the Levitical priests were appointed only for to kill the sacrifices.   Moreover, the Lord doth every where in his laws minister matter for the Levitical priests to instruct the people in; and that matter was not the heathenish philosophy, the edicts of kings, or decrees of senators, but the very word of God, delivered to them by God himself.   And that this doctrine might be the more commodiously uttered to the people, the priests appointed certain holy days[2], wherein the people should assemble together, to hear them preach the word of God.

The next point of their duty[3], after teaching, was to bless the people.   That blessing was not free for every priest to use as he listed, but was bound to a certain form of words, very solemnly uttered, which is thus expressed in the sixth of Numbers: "And the Lord spake unto Moses, saying, Speak unto Aaron and his sons, saying, On this wise ye shall bless the children of Israel, and say unto them: The Lord bless thee and keep thee: the Lord shew his face unto thee, and be

The priests' office.

Let priests teach.

Let them bless.

Numb. vi.

[2 indicebant fastos, Lat.]
[3 non minimum officiorum, Lat. : and that, not the least of their duties.]

merciful unto thee; the Lord lift up his countenance upon thee, and give thee peace." This manner of blessing did they use undoubtedly in their holy assemblies, especially at the breaking up of the congregation, when the people did depart. In another place it is said, that God did bless; but here, that Aaron and his sons did bless the people: whereupon we have to note, that God doth work inwardly, and perform in the faithful, whatsoever the priests in that form of blessing did wish unto the people[1]; so that still to bless is the only and proper work of God alone. And therefore, very significantly, after that solemn blessing uttered by the mouth of the priest, God doth add: "And they shall call, or put, my name over, or upon the children of Israel; and I will bless them." The priests, therefore, do lay before the people the name of the Lord; they commend unto them the mighty power of his Godhead; and shew them that all goodness doth flow from God, teach[2] them how they may obtain[3] it through faith in Christ, who is the blessed Seed that blesseth all them that call upon his name.

Now in this solemn blessing six principal points are chiefly contained. First the priest saith, "The Lord bless thee:" that is, the Lord bestow upon thee whatsoever belongeth to the safety of thy body and soul. Secondarily he saith, "The Lord keep thee;" for it is not sufficient to receive good things[4] at the hand of the Lord, unless they be preserved by his power, and not taken from us by his wrathful indignation, nor lost again by our own negligence. Thirdly he saith, "The Lord shew thee his face," or, "the Lord make his face shine upon thee." The Lord doth then shew us his loving face, when after his anger he sheweth us his favour, and doth become good and gracious to us. And therefore in the fourth clause doth follow a more plain exposition, where the priest saith, "The Lord be merciful unto thee:" as if he should have said, The Lord be always gentle and favourable unto thee in all that thou goest about, either in words or deeds. The fifth blessing is, "The Lord lift up his countenance upon thee." Now the Lord lifteth up his countenance, when he looketh upon us, when he watcheth over us, and doth direct and guide our ways. The last desire is, "Peace;" which is taken for the salvation and chief goodness

[1 externis sensibus ingerunt sacerdotes, Lat.]
[2 teaching, ed. 1577.]   [3 possimus, Lat.]
[4 corporis et animæ, Lat. omitted: of the body and soul.]

that happeneth unto mankind, although in another sense it is put for the contrary to war or battle: and the peace of the conscience is no small felicity to mortal men[5]. These were the good things that the priests did wish to light upon the people, teaching them withal to beseech the Lord for those blessings with ardent prayers and earnest supplications. Even till this day there do remain the psalms that the priests did make for the people's sake to sing. For after that David had brought music into the temple, then did the playing upon musical instruments, with sweet melody and singing of psalms, begin to be taken for an office amongst the priests. Touching this music used in the temple the first book of Chronicles speaketh very much, where it treateth of David and his dealings, how he distributed the singers into twenty-four orders, and that by course.

Moreover, the priests were commanded[6] to minister the sacraments, and to sacrifice. For they did circumcise the infants[7]; their office was to see the passover eaten, and to offer sacrifices of sundry sorts unto the Lord: of which I will speak hereafter in place convenient. And that they might more commodiously offer their sacrifices, David, by the inspiration of the Holy Ghost, divided the two families of Eleazar and Ithamar into twenty-four orders: for they did minister by course, as is to be seen in the twenty-fourth chapter of the first of Chronicles. All the while that their turn to minister did last the priests remained still within, and never did set a foot out of the temple. For there were houses builded within the temple for the priests to dwell in, when their lot did come to serve the Lord; they never went unto their own houses until their course were expired, and their time to minister were fully finished. The priests also did keep the holy vessels and make them clean; they kept the candles burning, and the holy fire, that it should not go out: to be short, they had the charge of all things which seemed to belong to the service of God, as oil, frankincense, and such like things.

Sacrifices and ministering of the sacraments was commanded to the priests.

Now before the temple was erected, and that the Israelites had obtained a place where to settle themselves in the land of promise, the priests' office was to see the tabernacle pitched

The priests carried the tabernacle and vessels of the Lord.

[5 juge convivium, Lat.: a continual feast. Prov. xv. 15.]
[6 rem facere divinam, administrare inquam, Lat.: to perform the service of God, I mean &c.]
[7 The Mosaic Law did not require the priests to be the operators.]

down, and taken up again, and carried to and fro. For in the third of Numbers thus we read: "The Levites shall keep all the instruments of the tabernacle of the congregation, and have the charge of the children of Israel, to do the service of the tabernacle." For the tabernacle was so appointed, that when they journeyed it might be taken into many pieces[1]. Therefore, when the Israelites were ready to remove their camp, Aaron and his sons came with the coverings appointed for the purpose, to wrap up and carry the holy vessels in. The Cahatites bare the ark, the table, the altar[2], and instruments belonging thereunto. The Gersonites had charge over the cords, the coverings, the hangings, the curtains, the veils, and ropes, belonging to the tabernacle. The Merarites did bear the harder stuff that was made of wood and brass, as the pillars, bars, stakes, and planks. All which whosoever desireth to understand more nearly, let him read the third and fourth chapters of the book of Numbers. When the temple was builded, there

[1 Chron. xxvi. 1, &c.] Doorkeepers. Trumpeters. were porters and warders of the temple appointed among the Levites. The trumpets also, wherewith the congregation was called together, were in the Levites' hands[3]; as we read

The priests were appointed to serve in war. in the tenth of Numbers. The priests also were appointed to be ready and serve in the wars, as is to be seen in the twentieth of Deuteronomy. For the Lord would not have the laws to be hushed where armour did clatter; for victories do avail greatly to godliness and the study of religion.

The priests did judge betwixt cause and cause. Beside this also the priests had yet another office; that was, to judge betwixt cause and cause, between clean and unclean: both which are more largely declared in the seventeenth of Deuteronomy, and in the thirteenth and fourteenth chapters of Leviticus. For as often as any difficult matter happened to rise among them, the hearing of it was brought to the mother city Hierusalem[4]: and if any man were suspected to be a leper, the Levitical priests did judge of his disease according to the laws that were prescribed them. So hitherto I have summarily laid down the offices of priesthood among the old people, reckoning up only the especial parts belonging to their service.

[1 So ed. 1577: places, ed. 1587; partes, Lat.]
[2 aras, Lat. altars.]
[3 sacerdotum, Lat.: in the priests' hands.]
[4 Hierusalem is not in the Latin.]

Now as those priests did serve the Israelitish church, so did they live of the revenues of the church. For the Lord appointed them certain stipends and dwelling-places in the land of promise. For he assigned forty-eight cities for them to inhabit in the land of Israel, six whereof were cities of refuge for men to fly unto, as unto sanctuaries. Moreover he commanded to lay out and appoint, for the sustenance of the priests' cattle and families, the suburbs and ferms without the walls of the cities, within a thousand cubits' compass on every side. In those cities were schools, so conveniently placed throughout all the land, that all men might easily go with very small pain from the places thereabout unto the synagogues, to hear the word of God. In those cities there was no sacrifice made: for they were commanded to sacrifice in one place alone; and thrice a year they went up to the temple to sacrifice unto the Lord: but every sabbath-day the law was taught in every town where the synagogues were. Moreover the rents belonging to the priests were great and ample; as is to be seen in the eighteenth of the book of Numbers, and in the last of Leviticus. The wealth of the priests was enough and sufficient to maintain their families, and to live themselves honestly. And they with that stipend did not give themselves to riot and idleness; but, living moderately, did apply themselves to learning, and teaching of the people. Thus much hitherto touching the persons belonging to the ministry of holy religion.

And for because by law they could not sacrifice but in one place alone, there was a certain place appointed to the people, wherein, as in an holy shop, the priests should exercise their holy ministry in sacrificing to the Lord; and therefore now the very order and course of this argument doth require, that I say somewhat touching that holy place. That place in the beginning was the tabernacle built by Moses, and afterward the temple which Salomon did make. The law, which forbad them to sacrifice any where but in that one place alone, unless it were by dispensation, is extant in the twelfth of Deuteronomy, and in the seventeenth chapter of Leviticus; and doth contain the mystery of Christ, who was offered up but once, and in one place, to cleanse the sins of the world. Of whom I will speak somewhat more hereafter.

Now that tabernacle, or tent, (being called the tabernacle

Side notes:

The stipends and dwelling-places assigned to the priests.

A thousand cubits geometrical make one mile, three quarters of a mile, and 500 paces, reckoning five feet to every pace.

A synagogue was a place for people to assemble themselves together in to hear the word or law of the Lord. [Deut. xvi. 16.]

The holy place.

of appointment[1], because the Lord appointed it both to give answers in, and to have his lawful worship duly accomplished in) was to the people instead of a temple, so long as they wandered and dwelt in the wilderness. For insomuch as they strayed forty years in the desert, it was not convenient for them to have a settled temple, but such an one as in their journeys they might carry to and fro, so oft as they removed. That tabernacle was erected in this order, and was in a manner of this form and fashion. First of all there were stuck into the earth, close by the ground, silver sockets to fasten in and set boards upon, to make a wall withal: under every plank, or board, were two sockets. For every board had two tenons, like pikes, whereby they were stuck into the sockets.

The fashion of the tabernacle.

The boards on either side of the tabernacle, north and south, were twenty in number: at the upper end, which was toward the west, were ten boards, or planks, all laid over with gold, and ten cubits high apiece. These, when they were set up, were stuck or fastened into the sockets: upon the back sides those boards had golden rings, through which were bars of sittim wood (which is thought to be white-thorn) thrust; partly, to join the boards close together, that they might be like a wall without chink or crevice; and partly, to make them stand stedfast without wagging to and fro. The *sanctum* on the east side was shut up with a veil. Moreover, there were made ten curtains, or hangings, of broidered work[2], which were coupled together with loops or taches. These curtains were laid upon the tops of the boards that were set upright, as it had been the rafter or roof of an house: over which curtains were three coverings more, the uppermost whereof was of taxus leather[3], well able in rain to keep water out.

[Exod. xxvi. 15—29.]

[Exod. xxvi. 31—33.]

Now the tabernacle was in length thirty cubits, and in breadth ten cubits; as may be gathered by the measure of the boards. It was divided also into three parts: the first was called *sanctum sanctorum*, holy of holies, and *adytum ædis* (the house[4] into which no man came but the high priest alone),

[Exod. xxvi. 1—14.]

[1 אֹהֶל מוֹעֵד. The tabernacle of the congregation. Auth. ver.]

[2 opere Phrygio, Lat. Pictas vestes…acu facere Phryges invenerunt, ideoque Phrygioniæ appellatæ sunt.—Plin. Hist. Nat. VIII. 74.]

[3 תְּחָשִׁים, badgers' skins. Auth. ver.]

[4 the house—alone, not in the Lat.]

or the chancel of the temple[5] the second was the *sanc-tum*, whose length was twenty cubits, as the length of the first was ten: the third part was called *atrium*, the court, which had in length an hundred cubits, and in breadth fifty. This *atrium* was compassed about with fifty-three pillars, that were fastened down into brasen sockets, and were in height five cubits; upon which there hung hangings of network, through which a man might easily see: at the very entry was hanged a veil twenty cubits long upon four pillars. The *sanctum sanctorum* was divided from the *sanctum* by the most precious veil, hanged upon four pillars of silver: and the *sanctum* was severed from the *atrium* with the second veil, that was very precious, and hung upon five pillars laid over with gold. In the midst of the *atrium* did stand the inner house, I mean, the tabernacle, that is divided (as I said even now) into the *sanctum* and the *sanctum sanctorum*.

Into the *sanctum sanctorum* no man did enter but the high priest only once in a year. Therein was laid the ark of the covenant of our Lord betwixt the cherubin; whereunto some (upon the apostle's words) do add the golden censer. But other there be which think that by θυμιατήριον is meant the incense altar, and not the censer. It should seem thereby (if these fellows be not deceived), that at the time when the apostle writ, the golden altar did stand within the veil in the *sanctum sanctorum*. But it is manifest by the fortieth chapter of Exodus, (as I mean to shew you anon,) that the golden altar from the beginning was placed in the *sanctum* before the veil. And thereunto agreeth that which may be gathered out of the first chapter after St Luke. But howsoever it was, this is sure, that the ark of the covenant was not seen of any mortal man, but of the high priest alone, when he offered incense in the *sanctum sanctorum*, once in a year. For it was hid with the first veil, the staves wherewith it was borne appearing a little within the *Sanctum*, by the bearing up of the veil which was somewhat thrust out with the ends of the staves; so that he which stood any thing nigh in the *sanctum* might easily discern it, but of him that stood farther off it could hardly be perceived. For in the eighth chapter of the third book of Kings thou readest: "And they drew out the staves, that the ends of

What things were laid in the tabernacle. [Heb. ix. 4.]

[Exod. xl. 26, 27. Luke i. 9.]

[1 Kings viii. 8.]

[5 *oraculum templi*, Lat.]

them might appear out of the *sanctum sanctorum* into the *sanctum*, but they were not seen without." The *sanctum* was open daily for the priests, that did by course supply the place of ministry before the Lord. In the *sanctum*, before the veil, was placed the golden table furnished with shew-bread, upon the north side[1]: right over against it, upon the south side[2], was set the golden candlestick. Now in the midst, betwixt[3] those twain, before the veil and the ark, did stand the golden altar, called the altar of incense, which was consecrated to the burning of sweet perfumes. And in the *atrium*, not very far from the second veil of the *sanctum*, did appear the altar of burnt-offerings; and betwixt the altar and the veil was put the laver, out of which the priests did wash themselves, when they began to go about their ministry. All the people, which came to the sacrifice, might easily on every side see to the altar. And of this sort was the holy tabernacle, which was to the Israelites instead of a temple: touching which he shall read more largely and fully, whosoever will look in the twenty-sixth, twenty-seventh, thirty-sixth, thirty-eighth, and fortieth chapters of Exodus.

Now so much as I have hitherto spoken touching the building of the tabernacle hath a very good end to be applied unto, and containeth and comprehendeth no obscure signification. For first of all, it was profitable to nourish and maintain the unity of the catholic faith. For with that one tabernacle, as with a sure bond, they[4] were tied, first to God and his religion, and then among themselves one to another, as it were, sundry members compact and knit into one body. For to that tabernacle the whole people was gathered, as to one parish-church, to worship and pray unto one God and Lord. And for because the children of Israel did dwell in tabernacles, it pleased the Lord also to have a tabernacle builded for himself, and placed in the midst of them, that thereby he might testify that he himself doth dwell in the midst of his people. The tabernacle therefore being as it were the palace of God, the most high and mighty king, did stand in the midst of the people, as a testimony of his divine presence, to strike the fear and reverence of God into the

Marginal notes: The Latin copy here doth square from the words of the twenty-sixth of Exodus, where we find (as I have turned it) that the table stood on the north side, whereas the Latin copy saith, on the south side, and calleth it *pars australis*.

The meaning of the tabernacle.

[1 in parte australi, Lat.]   [2 in latere meridionali, Lat.]
[3 Joseph. Antiq. Lib. III. cap. VI. § 8.]
[4 Israelitæ, Lat.; the Israelites.]

hearts of all his subjects.   We men lay up in our tabernacles, or houses, the things that we have; and will be sought for and asked after at our houses.   And therefore the Lord did place in the tabernacle the holy things, as it were his treasure; and would be inquired after in the tabernacle, promising that there he would hear the prayers and requests of all the faithful that called upon his name.

Moreover in those ceremonies are contained the secret mysteries of Christ and his church.   For Paul calleth us the temple of God, and our bodies the tabernacle of the Lord: for in us the Lord doth[5] dwell.   The boards of the tabernacle are, as it were, the rafters, beams, and pillars of the church. And the church hath her pillars, which are doctors and other excellent men inspired with the Holy Ghost[6]: and every several faithful man is a board laid over with gold, if he keep sincerity, and remain in the unity of the faith.   The boards of the tabernacle were joined together with bars: and so must sound doctrine keep all the faithful (which are the boards of the mystical tabernacle) in their duty and quiet concord, without crack or crevice.   The curtains, though they were many, yet were they knit together with golden loops, as if they had been but all one piece: and therefore the sundry members of the church must be gathered together, and by charity be knit together in one, that they may be one among themselves, and, as it were, a roof of righteousness in the church of God.   The coverings of the church, to keep out storms, are faith, repentance, and[7] desire to do good.   Christ [1 Cor. iii. 11.] himself is the socket thereof; "for none other foundation can be laid than that is already laid, even Christ Jesus." Moreover, the veil that was spread before the *sanctum sanc-* Heb. ix. *torum* doth signify, as the apostle[8] saith, that the way of the saints, which they had to go in, was not as then made manifest, so long as the first tabernacle did stand.   Therefore, when Christ was come, and with his death had finished all, then the veil that hung in the temple was rent from the top to the very ground: whereby all men might understand, that

[5 vult, Lat.; will, ed. 1577.]
[6 heroico vel principali spiritu præditos, Lat.; referring to Psalm li. 14, which the Vulgate renders, spiritu principali confirma me.]
[7 vel, Lat.; or.]
[8 did signify, as the holy apostle, ed. 1577.]

the way was opened into the *sanctum sanctorum*, that is, into the very heavens; and that satisfaction was made for all men in respect of the law[1]. In the tabernacle also did hang other veils, which were as shadows of the flesh[2] of Christ. Those veils did hang at the very entry into the *sanctum* and the *atrium*. Now Christ, our Lord, is the way and the door, by whose incarnation and death we have an entry made into the kingdom of God. Yea, Christ himself is our tabernacle, in whom we dwell and live, and in whom we worship and please our God: he is the curtain and ceiling, the rafter and ornament of his church: he is the trusty and most assured covering, that doth defend us from the injuries of man and the devil: he is the bar of the church, which joineth the members thereof together, and keepeth them in the unity of faith[3]: he is the pillar and socket of his church; he is the head[4], and only all-in-all both of our life and true salvation. In those figures, therefore, they of old had the chief mysteries hidden of Christ and the church; in which Christ is now no otherwise to be beheld, than he was in the beginning of the world beheld of the ancient patriarchs, to wit, very God and very man, the only and highest king and priest, the true Saviour of the world, in whom and by whom alone the faithful have their whole salvation.

The history of the ark of God.

To proceed now: this tabernacle, by the Lord's appointment, was erected in Silo, as soon as they came into the land of promise, and did continue there until the time of Heli; as is evident in the eighteenth of Josue, and first of Samuel, first and third chapters. Under Heli the ark was taken by the Philistines, and carried into Palestine[5]; from whence it was restored again, and placed in Bethsemes; from thence again

[1 Sam. vii. 1.]

it was carried to Kirjath-jearim, into the house of Abinadab in Gibea, that is, on the hill; for his house was set upon a high place. For in the sixth of the second book of Samuel we read: "David went with all the people to Baala Juda (which

Josh. xv.

in the fifteenth of Josue is called Kirjath-jearim), to fetch from

[1 et omnibus in lege satisfactum, Lat.]
[2 purissimæ carnis, Lat.; of the most holy flesh.]
[3 ac omnis boni, Lat.; omitted: and of every good thing.]
[4 et virtus, Lat.; omitted: and strength.]
[5 in urbes Palæstinorum, Lat.; among the cities of the Philistines.
1 Sam. v.]

thence the ark of God." And presently after; "And they fetched it out of the house of Abinadab that was in Gibea," that is, on the hill. For there was an high place in Kirjath-jearim, wherein Abinadab dwelt. Some other, which take Gabaa for the proper name of the town[6], do say, that the ark was translated from Palestine into Gabaa. But this is sure, the ark was conveyed from the house of Abinadab into the house of Obed-edom, and from thence into the city of David, that is, into Sion. For so is the city [of] David expounded in the eighth chapter of the third book of Kings. [2 Sam. vi. 10, 12. 1 Kings viii. 1.]

In Sion did David pitch a new tabernacle for the ark of God, wherein he did place it, and appointed priests to minister there before the Lord : as it is at large described in the sixteenth chapter of the first book of Chronicles. And yet, by building that new tabernacle, David neglected not the old tabernacle of appointment. For after the time of Heli, and the taking of the ark by the Philistines, it seemeth that it was translated diversely from place to place. Silo verily, wherein it was first placed, was desolate, as is to be seen in the seventy-eighth Psalm and the seventh chapter of Jeremy. Therefore, when Saul did reign, it appeareth to have been pitched in Gilgal, where he offered peace-offerings in sign of thanksgiving unto the Lord for victory against the Ammonites, as is to be seen in the eleventh chapter of the first book of Samuel. In the twenty-first chapter of the same book it is apparent, that the tabernacle was for a time in Nob (a town not very far from Hierusalem, Isaiah x.), where Ahimelech, the priest, gave to David the fresh shew-bread that was taken from the golden table. In the time when David reigned it was erected in Gabaon, a city of the Benjamites : for in the twenty-first of the first of Chronicles thus we read : "The tabernacle of the Lord, which Moses made in the wilderness, and the altar of burnt-offerings, was at that time (when the angel appeared to David with a sword ready drawn) in the hill of Gabaon[7]." In that place was it also in the reign of Salomon, and to that hill did Salomon go to pray to the Lord before the temple was builded. For in the first chapter of the second

The history of the Lord's tabernacle.

Isai. x.

[6 Accordingly, the one and self-same Hebrew word is rendered in our authorised version, in 1 Sam. vii. 1, *in the hill*, and in 2 Sam. vi. 3, *in Gibeah*.]

[7 vel excelso, Lat. ; or high place.]

book of Chronicles we find : " And Salomon, with all the congregation, went to the high place that was at Gabaon; for
there was the tabernacle of God's appointment, which Moses
the servant of the Lord made in the wilderness. But the ark
of God had David brought from Kirjath-jearim into the place
which David had prepared for it : for he had pitched a tent
for it at Hierusalem. Moreover the brasen altar, that Beza-
leel the son of Uri had made, was there before the tabernacle
of the Lord : and Salomon and the congregation went to visit
it." Therefore, whereas we read in the third chapter of the
[1 Kings iii. third book of Kings, " Salomon loved the Lord, and walked
3.] in the ways of his father David; only he sacrificed and burnt
incense in the high places :" that is not spoken in the dispraise, but in the praise, of Salomon, as he that did not at
adventures sacrifice in every place, but in the high places, to
wit, upon that consecrated altar which was appointed of the
Lord, whereof I spake even now before. Other there are
which think that Salomon was not simply blamed in these
words for offering upon the altar of burnt-offerings (for that
was altogether lawful), but because he had till then deferred
the building of the temple. But that which goeth before and
followeth after do make greatly that those words were spoken
in that sense and signification which I did first allege. The
same Salomon, when the temple was builded, did command
and see that the old ark, with all the instruments belonging
thereunto, should be brought by the priests as a precious
treasure from Gabaon, and placed in the temple which he had
caused to be built for that purpose : the holy scripture bearing witness thereunto and saying; " And they brought the
ark of the Lord, and the tabernacle of appointment, and all
the holy vessels that were in the tabernacle : the priests and
Levites, I say, brought them into the temple"—the third
[1 Kings viii. of Kings, eighth chapter, and the second of Chronicles, fifth
4. 2 Chron. v.
5.] chapter. And so was the tabernacle of the Lord, which stood
four hundred and seventy eight[1] years, abrogated at the last,
and instead thereof the temple was erected.

Of Solomon's   Touching the temple of the Lord, which was prepared by
temple.
David, but builded and made an end of by Salomon, I need
not make many words in the description thereof, because it is
[1 Kings vi. in the third of Kings and second of the Chronicles very busily
& 2 Chron.
iii. and iv.]   [1 According to Usher, 486 years, viz. from A. C. 1490 to A. C. 1004.]

set down, and painted out at the full. The place, where the temple was afterward builded, is reported to have been shewed to David by the angel of the Lord; and that David did first of all make sacrifice there unto the Lord; and addeth these words: "This is the house of the Lord God, and this altar is for the sacrifice of Israel." As if he should have said: This plat of ground is appointed for the temple; in this piece shall be built the house of the Lord; yea, here shall be offered that only and effectual[2] sacrifice for all men, the very Son of God, Christ Jesus incarnate. For all the interpreters of the holy scriptures agree that the place was at Jerusalem, upon the mountain Moria, where Abraham once would have offered his son Isaac; and that in that appointed or fatal place the temple was erected; and that the hill Golgotha, or Calvary, was not far off, but in the very top of the mountain Moria, which was the place and the holy hill, wherein the holy gospel doth testify that Christ was offered for the sins of all the world; which was prefigured in a type of the ancient sacrifices and other ceremonies belonging to the temple[3]. The use and end of the temple was none other than the use and end of the tabernacle was before.

Jeroboam therefore and the kings of Israel did sin most grievously, when they forsook the temple to make sacrifices in the high places, in their cathedral churches at Bethel and at Dan, and in other high and pleasant places. The people of Juda with their kings did sin most grievously, either for sacrificing to God in the high places, or else because they did not utterly cut down those high places. For the Lord would, and his will was to be worshipped in one place, which he had chosen unto himself. The plain law touching that matter is extant in the twelfth of Deuteronomy, and is very expressly set down in the seventeenth of Leviticus, in these words following: "Whosoever of the house of Israel shall kill an ox, or a sheep, or a goat, within the host or without the host, (to wit, for a sacrifice unto the Lord; for otherwise they might lawfully kill a beast for their sustenance in any place wheresoever,) and shall not bring it to the door of the tabernacle of

Marginal notes: [1 Chron. xxii. 1.]   The sin of them that sacrifice in the high places.

[2 aternum efficax, Lat.; everlastingly effectual.]
[3 quem sacrificia et templi et veterum omnia præfigurarunt, Lat.: of whom all the sacrifices both of the temple and of the ancients were a type.]

the congregation, to offer his sacrifice before the dwelling-place of the Lord; blood shall be imputed to that man, as if he had shed blood. Wherefore when the children of Israel bring their offerings, let them bring them to the Lord before the door of the tabernacle of appointment, unto the priest, that he may offer them. And let them no more offer their offerings to devils[1], after whom they have gone a whoring. This shall be an ordinance to them for ever in their generations. And he that doth not this shall be rooted out from among his people." There are in these words three things to be noted: first, that it was not lawful to sacrifice but in that one place only, that was, before the altar of burnt-offerings: secondarily we have to mark, that that commandment was given, to the end that all men should understand that the sacrifice was made to God, to whom the tabernacle did belong: thirdly, that to offer sacrifice out of the place, against God's commandment, was to make sacrifice unto the devil; that the offerer was to be judged as a murderer; and that he was excommunicated by the Lord God, as he that was excluded from the company of God and his holy saints[2]. But whereas Samuel, Helias, and certain other patriarchs, did, by God's sufferance, make sacrifices upon some especial causes in other places, and not before the altar in the tabernacle, they did it by dispensation. They therefore that sacrifice in high places, not to strange gods only, but even to the very true God, did sin first of all by disobedience: for God doth mislike, yea, he curseth, all the worship done unto him, which we ourselves do first invent without the warrantise of his word; it is faithful obedience that pleaseth him best. Secondarily, they sinned by making a schism in the unity of the ecclesiastical body. Thirdly, for despising the mystery of Christ, that was to be offered in the mount of Golgotha; and for not referring the meaning of their sacrifices to Christ, the only truth of all their typical ceremonies. Lastly, they sinned by trusting in their sacrifices, as in well-wrought works, to justification, and by neglecting the worship of God, and changing it into trifles of their own inventions[3].

The temple stood, from the time that Salomon did first build it until the first destruction of it under king Zedekias,

[1 satyris vel dæmonibus, Lat.]   [2 Isai. lxvi. Lat.]
[3 cultum peculiarem finxerunt, Lat.]

four hundred and forty years[4]. And from the reparation of it unto the utter overthrow[5] under Vespasian, it stood five hundred and eighty two years[6]. Other there be that do account it otherwise. Thus have I hitherto spoken a little of a great deal concerning the temple.

Now it remaineth for me to touch and lightly to pass over[7] the holy instruments belonging to the tabernacle and temple of the Lord: among which the ark of the covenant was the chief; which ark was so called, because of the tables of the covenant that were put within it. It was also called the ark of the Lord God of hosts, which dwelleth upon it betwixt the cherubim; and by that means the Lord himself was called by the name "of him that sitteth betwixt the cherubim," because he did from thence give answers unto his servants, and had placed it in the midst of his people to be a sign that his presence was always among them. Touching the stuff whereof, and the form how, the ark was made, I will say nothing here. For the matter and fashion are in their colours very lively painted out in the twenty-fifth chapter of Exodus. Of the meaning, mystery, and use of the ark, I will speak somewhat now. We men lay up in our coffers and chests the treasures that we most set by. And therefore we understand, that in the ark was laid the treasure of the church, and all the substance of which the faithful made most account. We must not therefore seek for them in men, in Noah, Abraham, Isaac, Jacob, Moses, David, St Mary, John, Peter, or Paul; much less in the Romish indulgentiary[8]; but in him in whom all fulness dwelleth, and in whom all the treasures of God's wisdom and knowledge are heaped up in store; who is not seen here on the earth, but in the *sanctum sanctorum*, in heaven, I say, above, and is called Jesus Christ; whose divinity is figured by the most pure gold, and his humanity by the sittim-wood, that is, of

The signification and ministry of the ark.
[*Deut.* xxxi. 26.]

Arca is an ark or a coffer, and what was laid therein.

[4] According to Usher, 416 years; viz. from A.C. 1004 to A.C. 588.]
[5] ad secundum excidium, Lat.; until the second destruction.]
[6] According to Usher, 585 years; viz. from A.C. 515 to A.D. 70.]
[7] per transennam inspiciamus, Lat.—proverbialis locutio, qua significatur, non propius, neque sigillatim, sed procul, obiter, et summatim inspicere. Facciolati Tot. Lat. Lex. in voc. Erasmi Adag. Chil. p. 364. Hanov. 1617.]
[8] in cista Chananaica ac Romanensi indulgentiaria, Lat.; in the Canaanitish and Romish indulgence-chest.]

cedar, or rather white-thorn: for he took upon him flesh like to our sinful flesh; even the very flesh that we have in all points, saving that it was not sinful[1]. Out of this ark do the faithful fetch all good and necessary things for the use of their life and eternal salvation. For in the ark we read that there was laid the tables of the covenant, the pot of manna, and Aaron's rod that budded. For we heard that in Christ were hidden the jewels of the church. Christ is our wisdom, the word[2] of the Father, the fulfilling of the law; he is just himself, and our righteousness also. In Christ is the heavenly food: for he is the bread of life that came down from heaven, to the end that every one that eateth of it may live eternally. In Christ did the priesthood bud again: it seemed verily, at the death of Christ upon the cross, to have been cut down for growing any more; but at his resurrection it budded again, and he took the everlasting priesthood, that never shall be ended: for even now, as he standeth at the right hand of the Father in heaven, he maketh intercession to him for us. Moreover the ark was compassed with a crown, because Christ our Lord is a king, which delivereth us his faithful servants from all evil, and maketh us the sons of God. Upon the ark we read that there was placed the mercy-seat, which was either the cover of the ark, or else a seat set upon the ark. By it was figured, as the apostles John and Paul interpret it, Christ our Lord, who is the throne of grace, and the propitiation for our sins; not only for ours, but also for the sins of all the world. Out of the propitiatory, or mercy-seat, also were uttered the oracles and answers of God. For the use of the mercy-seat is read in the holy scripture to have been this, that Moses, entering into the tabernacle, did at the mercy-seat receive the answers and commandments of God, which he declared unto the people. And Christ is he by whom our heavenly Father declareth his will to us, and whom alone he hath given us to hear, saying, "This is my beloved Son, in whom I am well pleased; hear him." Two cherubim have their faces turned toward the mercy-seat, and do as it were look one to another:

Christ his priesthood compared to Aaron's rod.

The mercy-seat.

[Rom. iii. 25. 1 John ii. 2.]

[Exod. xxv. 21, 22.]

[1 nulla in eo peccati spina existente, Lat. omitted: there being in him no thorn of sin. The allusion in this phrase is, of course, to the *white-thorn*, or sittim-wood, mentioned above.]

[2 lex et verbum, Lat.; the law and word.]

whereupon St Peter saith, that "the angels do desire to [1 Pet. i. 12.] behold" the Saviour of the world, which is declared in the gospel. The same angels do always serve our Lord and Master, and are ready at his beck, as to him that is Lord over all. Now none did carry the ark of the Lord but the priests alone[3]. For they only which are anointed by the Holy Ghost, and endued with true faith, do receive Christ, and are made partakers of his heavenly gifts. Neither must we wink at and let pass the note that is given in the fourth and fifth chapters of the first book of Samuel, where it is said, that the Israelites, for abusing the ark and turning *The use and abuse of the* it to another use than that for which it was given, and for *ark.* attributing unto it more than the scripture willed, were slain by the Philistines, and that the ark was carried into captivity; to the end that all men might learn thereby not to attribute more to the sacraments and mysteries of God than is convenient, and not to apply them to any other use than that for which the Lord hath ordained them. For the ark was not ordained to the end it should be taken for God, although it bare the name of God[4]; neither was it made to the end that they should look for grace and help to proceed from it, as we read that they did: but it was given them as a token, that God, their confederate[5], was in the midst of his people, so long as they did keep the tables of the covenant that were closed within the ark, and did cleave to God alone, at whose hands they should look for all good things through Christ, his Son, which was prefigured by the ark.

Next to the *adytum*, or *sanctum sanctorum*, in the *sanc-* *The golden* *tum*, did stand the golden table, the matter and fashion whereof *table.* is declared in the twenty-fifth chapter of Exodus. Upon the *Exod. xxv.* table we men do set our meat and sustenance; by the table we are refreshed; and at the table we forget our cares, and

[3 sacerdotes Domini, Lat.; the priests of the Lord.]

[4 ... disertis verbis appellatur (Arca) Dominus exercituum. Nam 2 Samuelis, 6 cap. scriptura testatur, et ait: Et surgens David abiit una cum toto populo, ut transferret arcam Dei, super quam invocatum est nomen, nomen Domini exercituum insidentis cherubim super eam. Hoc enim Hebraico idiomate tantundem valet, ac si tu dicas: cui nomen inditum est ut appelletur, Jehovah, sive Deus exercituum, habitans super cherubim.—Bulling. de Episcop. Instit. et funct. cap. 6. fol. 88. Tig. 1538.]

[5 utpote confœderatum, Lat.]

are merry and jocund. Therefore the table can be none other but Christ our Lord, and christian doctrine : for Christ is the sustenance of our life; he is the joy and mirth of the faithful. The table was of gold without, and all wood within, because Christ, our table[1], is both God and man. The table (which is the type of christian doctrine[2]) is set forth in the church : it is not therefore to be sought at Athens, among[3] the sophisters, nor among the Gymnosophists of India[4], nor in the Jewish synagogues. Upon the table are set twelve new loaves, divided into two parts. For the bread of life, which is new and sweet[5], doth feed and fill both the Jews and the Gentiles. Moreover, that bread was holy and not profane, and none might eat it but the priests alone. In like manner the faithful only are worthy of Christ, the bread of life, and they that believe receive it only. The loaves were called by the name of shew-bread, or the bread of sight[6]; whereby is meant, that the bread of life (which is christian doctrine[7]) should always be in sight before our eyes. And as those loaves were to be set always before the Lord in the sight of all men; so must not the doctrine of Christ be privily hidden, but openly shewed unto all people. A vessel with frankincense was set upon the shew-bread, because they that eat the heavenly bread do offer to God prayers and thanksgivings without intermission, which is to God as sweet as frankincense[8]. In the twenty-fourth of Leviticus it is at large declared in what sort the shew-bread is prepared.

The golden candlestick is in the *sanctum*, and standeth before the veil on the one side, or over against the table. We have the description of it in the twenty-fifth chapter of Exodus. Candles are set up in our common houses to give light to all them that are in the house. And Christ our Lord is come[9] a light into the world, that whosoever follow-

Marginal notes:
[Lev. xxiv. 9. Matt. xii. 4.]

The shew-bread.

The golden candlestick.

Exod. xxv.

[1 cibus noster, Lat. ; our food.]
[2 which—doctrine, not in the original.]
[3 aut apud, Lat.; or among.]
[4 See Vol. i. p. 102. note 3.]
[5 et exsaturans, Lat. omitted ; and satisfying.]
[6 panes propositionis, sive facierum, Lat. In Hebr. called *bread of faces*, or *of presence.* Ainsworth on Exod. xxv. 30.]
[7 which—doctrine, not in the original.]
[8 which—frankincense, not in the original.]
[9 datus est, Lat. ; has been given. John viii. 12.]

eth him should get the light of life.   Out of Christ do proceed, and upon Christ do stick, other noses of candlesticks[10],
which have their light from Christ, the chief candlestick.
For the Lord did say unto the apostles, "Ye are the light
of the world." So then Christ is the shank, or shaft, of the
candlestick, upon which shank many snuffs or noses do stick,
which hold the light up to the church[11]: for what light
soever is in the ministers of the church, they have it all of
Christ, who is the head of light, and very light itself.   The
candlestick is wholly all of gold.   And Christ is very God
indeed, the light and wisdom of the Father: and the ministers of Christ must be sincere and throughly snuffed[12] from
all affections of the flesh: and to that end belongeth the use
of the snuffers that did pertain unto the candlestick.

In the midst, betwixt the table and the candlestick, before
the veil, in the *sanctum*, did stand the golden altar of incense, The incense
which is exactly painted out in the thirtieth chapter of Exodus. Exod. xxx.
That altar was ordained for two uses.   For first, there was
offered upon it every day incense or perfume, which it was
not lawful to offer or prepare to any other God or creature.
That was done twice every day, at morning and at evening.
Zacharias, the father of John Baptist[13], was in that ministery,
when he saw the angel, and for his unbelief's sake was made [Luke i. 9—
20.]
dumb for a season.   Secondarily, incense was offered upon
that altar after a certain solemn manner once in a year, that
was, at the feast of cleansing, as is declared in the sixteenth Lev. xvi.
chapter of Leviticus.

Now by incense, or perfume, is to be understood the
prayers of the faithful; as David witnesseth where he saith:
" Let my prayer be set forth in thy sight as the incense; [Psal. cxli.
2.]
and let the lifting up of my hands be an evening sacrifice."
Now there was but one incense altar alone.   Whosoever
builded any more, he was condemned of blasphemous wickedness.   By that only altar is figured Christ our Lord, both
God and man, the mediator and intercessor betwixt God and
man; by whom all the saints do offer all their prayers to

[10 cannæ et luminaria, Lat.]
[11 cannæ in suprema parte habentes lumina, Lat.; reed-like
branches having lights at their extremities.]
[12 repurgatos, Lat.]
[13 divi Baptistæ, Lat.]

God, their Lord and heavenly Father. They therefore build many altars, which choose to themselves creatures to be their intercessors, by whose mediation they desire to obtain that which they lack at the hands of God. In the end of the thirtieth chapter it is expressly said: " Whosoever shall make like incense to that, to smell thereto, shall perish from among his people." Therefore through Christ alone the faithful church of Christ doth offer her prayers to God the Father. This altar, whereof we speak, was bound about with a crown of gold: for Christ, our Lord and altar, is a very king and priest, and weareth the crown of glory[1]. Now we must pray at morning and evening, that is, continually and very earnestly[2]. And we must always pray in and through the name of Christ. And Christ is he alone, through whom God hath been pleased with the prayers of them that have prayed in the morning, that is, at the beginning of the world; and is at this day pleased with them that pray to him at evening, that is, in the end and these last days of the world. They therefore sinned most grievously against the Lord, that offered incense in the high places everywhere: for as they were rebellious and disobedient to God, preferring their own inventions before the laws of God, which they neglected; so did they despise the mystery of Christ, the only mediator, in departing from that only altar.

The altar of burnt-offerings.

In the court, or *atrium*, did stand another altar, which was called the brasen altar, or the altar of burnt-offerings, which is finely described in the twenty-seventh of Exodus. Of this sort also there was but this one. For it was not lawful for any religious man to sacrifice in any other place, saving in the holy place where this altar was, unless it were by some singular dispensation. Therefore, when the Reubenites with their confederates had built an altar by the banks of Jordan, and the fame thereof was brought to the ears of the other tribes of Israel, they did all agree with one consent, [Josh. xxii. 10, &c.] that the crime was to be punished with open war. Whereby we may again gather the greatness of their fault, which, neglecting that altar, did offer sacrifice in the high places: of which I also spake before. Now that only and catholic

[1 Nam Christus Dominus noster verus est rex et pontifex, Lat.; and—glory, not in the original.]
[2 perpetuo et jugiter, Lat.]

altar of ours is Jesus Christ, who offered himself a living sacrifice for us to God. Neither is there any sacrifice in all the world that can cleanse sin, but that alone. Neither do any sacrifices of the faithful please the Father, but those that are by faith offered upon the altar, Jesus Christ. For Christ doth sanctify us; and, being sanctified, we do by him offer the sacrifice that he doth well accept of. This have I taken out of the apostle's doctrine in the thirteenth to the Hebrews, and the twelfth to the Romans.

The last of the holy vessels was the brasen laver, which was placed in the *atrium*, betwixt the veil of the *sanctum* and the altar of burnt-offerings. It is described in the thirtieth chapter of Exodus. In it was contained the water wherewith the priests, that ministered before the Lord, did wash themselves. By that laver was Christ signified, which is the washing of the faithful. And by it was meant, that holy things were not to be handled with unwashed hands and feet. They wash themselves, that by the Holy Ghost are purified, and by the grace of God are made fit to the ministry of religion: but he is in danger of death, that is not a partaker of the grace of life.

The brasen laver.

[Exod. xl. 30.]

Beside these, there are also reckoned other instruments belonging to the tabernacle: but these in a manner are the chief. I thought not good, by beating out busily every particularity, to rehearse unto you every small thing, lest peradventure by too long a treatise I should be too tedious unto your patience.

Now the same holy vessels, that were in the tabernacle, were in the temple also; saving that in Salomon's temple there was a far more goodly shew and pomp than in the tabernacle: for none other cause, undoubtedly, but that the mysteries of Christ and of the church should increase every day more and more to the sight of the world. Christ, the true Salomon, and king of peace and tranquillity, the very eternal felicity itself, hath raised up in this world to himself a church, which stretcheth to the ends of the world; of which the prophets have spoken very largely, Zachary especially, and the famous prophet Nathan, second of Samuel, chapter seven. Thus much hitherto of the holy place.

After the holy place in the sacred ceremonies, the next to be handled is the holy time. For as to the outward reli-

The holy time.

gion a certain place was given, so to the same also an appointed time was assigned. And holy days are to be employed upon holy actions. For actions are either those which we call handy works[1], invented for to get victuals, clothing, and other things necessary for the use of our bodies; or else they are holy or religious, which are done for the exercise of outward religion. We must not consume all our time in handy works and profane business; neither can we bestow all times upon outward religion. But those actions are not without time: for every action is contained in time. Therefore God hath divided the time into sundry parts for sundry actions: so that he will have some working days, to serve for handy actions; and other holy days, for the exercise of outward religion. Not that the working days are not holy and dedicated to the Lord, (for he doth challenge all days and times to himself, and will at all seasons be worshipped in heart;) but for because the holy days are singularly, and, as it were, more precisely, consecrated to the outward worship of God, than the working days are.

What an holy day is.   Therefore the festival or holy day, which by God's appointment is holy to the Lord, was kept for the devout exercising of God's outward worship. Therefore those days are not holy, nor those feasts lawful, which are not held to the one and only God, Jehovah: neither are those holy days lawful, in which the lawful service of God is not lawfully exercised. And for those causes the sabbaths and festival-days of the Israelites are in the prophets many times rejected, because they were unlawfully solemnized, without pure faith and sincere affections.

To what end the holy days were ordained.   Now all holy days had one common name, and were called sabbaths, feasts[2], holy days[3], meetings and assemblies. All holy days, what name soever they were called by, were ordained to God alone, not to creatures, not for surfeiting and wanton chambering. All holy days were invented for the health, profit, and recreation of mankind: for holy days are no burden, but the easing of our burdens. Profane works, I confess, are profitable, but ease is also necessary: for without rest labour cannot continue. The Lord's will

[1 et quasi prophanæ, Lat. omitted: and, as it were, profane.]
[2 item festa, Lat.; also feasts.]
[3 dies stati et sancti, Lat.; omitted.]

therefore is, to give man a time of recreation, and biddeth his servants to be merry on the holy days in holiness and modesty; so that their ease may be an honest recreation, and not reproachful sensuality. Again, ease of itself is not good, but in respect of another thing it is good. God biddeth to cease from work, but yet he setteth us on work another way; he willeth us to cease from bodily labour, and begin to work in heart and mind, and wholly apply ourselves to his holy service. And therefore it is needful to have holy assemblies, the reading of the holy scriptures, public prayers, sacrifices (for it is prescribed in the twenty-eighth and twenty-ninth chapters of the book of Numbers what they ought to offer at every feast and holy day), the celebration of the sacraments, and whatsoever else the Lord hath commanded to be done at festival-days and solemn seasons. For that one thing is here required especially, which Mary found, as she sat at the feet of Jesus, and heard his word. Moreover, all feasts [Luke x. 39, 42.] generally do contain the memory, and put us in the remembrance, of notable things; every feast according to the name. The sabbath did put them in mind of God's good benefit in The Sabbath. creating the world for the behoof and profit of us men. It was also, as Moses witnesseth, Exodus thirty-first, a sign of the true sanctification, which God alone bestoweth upon the people that call upon his name. The other holy days did beat into them the memory of the other benefits that God had shewed them, and had (as I will anon declare) their several significations.

Now there was a measure and certain number of holy days, which were distinguished, and very wisely ordered: A measure and certain number in holy days. first into seven-nights[4], whereof every one had in it one sabbath, that was the seventh day: then into months; for the first day of every month was holy to the Lord, and was called the feast of the new moon[5]: and lastly, they were divided into yearly feasts, which returned once every year at an appointed season: of that sort of feasts there were three in number, the passover, pentecost, and the feast of tabernacles[6]. Besides these, there were also other made holy days, which God had not commanded, but were received by the church

[4 septimanas, Lat.]   [5 vel calendas, Lat.]
[6 The Latin is, et septimi mensis; and (the feast) of the seventh month.]

to the glory of God and remembrance of his great benefits. For the feast of lots, which they called Purim, and was brought in by Mardocheus, was received of all the church, as is to be seen in the ninth of Esther. The feast of dedication was ordained by Judas Maccabeus, with the consent of all the church, in memory that the temple was restored and the people delivered from the tyranny of king Antiochus, as is to be read in the fourth chapter of the first book of Mac-

[John x. 22, &c.]
Solemn fast-
ings.

cabees: and Christ our Lord did honour that feast of dedication with an holy sermon. Moreover, there were solemn fastings appointed to be kept among the people of God : as in the fifth month, wherein the city was set on fire ; in the seventh month, wherein Godolias was slain ; and in the tenth month, wherein Hierusalem was besieged : of which fastings the prophet Zachary speaketh in his seventh and eighth

[Esth. ix. 20
—32.]

chapters : and in the time of Esther a fast was ordained in the month Adar, for a remembrance of the calamity which was wrought, or rather purposed, against the Jews by the wicked Aman.

The Sabbath.

Of the sabbath, and the signification thereof, I spake a little above, and in another place also, where I expounded the ten commandments[1]. The sabbath was observed by a natural[2] and divine law ever from the first creation of the world, and is the chief of all other holy days. For it was not then first ordained by Moses, when the ten commandments were given by God from heaven: for the keeping of the sabbath was received of the saints[3] immediately from the beginning of the world. And therefore we read that the Lord in the commandments did say : " Remember that thou keep holy the sabbath-day." And before the law was given, there is evident mention made of the sabbath in the sixteenth of Exodus, and the second of Genesis.

The new
moon.

The second kind of holy days was the new moons[4], which were solemnized in the beginning of every month. Mention is made of them in the x. and xxviii. chapters of the book of Numbers, 1 Samuel xx., Psalm lxxxi., Ezekiel xlvi., and 2 Chronicles ii. That solemnization is reported to have been

[1 See Vol. i. Dec. 2. Serm. iv.]   [2 quasi naturali, Lat.]
[3 a sanctis, Lat.]
[4 Secundum genus Sabbati sive feriarum sunt calendæ vel neo-
meniæ, id est novilunia. Lat.]

ordained in remembrance of the light created; to admonish
the people not to ascribe the months to Janus or Mars, or
any other[5] planet, but to the one and holy[6] God, the maker,
governor, and ruler of all things and seasons. Moreover, it
was a sign of the reparation or renewing of faithful minds
by the heavenly illumination: that we Christians may truly
and in deed solemnize the new moon, when, being brought
forth of darkness into light by the Son of God, we walk as
becometh the children of light, and reject the works of the
devil and darkness.

The third kind of holy days doth contain the feasts that
return once every year; of which I find to be three: the
passover, the pentecost, and the feast of tabernacles[7]. Now
the Lord's will was, that in these three feasts there should
be general assemblies and solemn meetings in the holy place,
to wit, at the tabernacle, and, after the tabernacle, at Salomon's
temple. For thus saith Moses in Deuteronomy: " Thrice in
the year shall every male appear before the Lord thy God
in the place which he hath chosen; that is, in the feast of
sweet bread, in the feast of weeks, and in the feast of tabernacles: neither shall he appear empty in the sight of the
Lord; every one according to the gift of his hand[8], and
according to the blessing of the Lord thy God, which he
hath given thee:" that is to say, every man shall offer to
the Lord according as he can, and according to the measure
of riches which the Lord hath given him. Now those three
solemn feasts were divided into three several months, most
apt to journey and to travel in. In the spring time was the
passover holden, when first the corn began to spindle[9], or
turn into ears. About harvest, when the first work belonging to husbandry was done and finished, they kept the feast
of pentecost. And lastly, when all their fruits were in, they
went up to the feast of tabernacles. And so many went to
it as possibly could go. Some are of opinion, that they, which
had once in the year appeared before the Lord, were dispensed withal, and might lawfully tarry at home at the other
two feast-times. But I think verily that religious men did

The three year's meetings or assemblies of the Jews.

[Deut. xvi. 16, 17.]

[5 divo vel, Lat.; god or.]   [6 soli, Lat.; only, ed. 1577.]
[7 festum mensis septimi, Lat.; the feast of the seventh month.]
[8 So the marg. of Auth. Ver.]
[9 to shoot into a long small stalk. Johnson's Dict.]

[Exod.xxxiv. 24.] seldom times use such dispensations. The Lord in one place promiseth that he will defend and keep the bounds and substance of them that travel to seek his name. Howsoever those dispensations were admitted, yet this is most sure, as appeareth by all histories, that at those feasts were very great assemblies[1].

Passover. Now the feast of passover was called by many names[2], but especially it was termed the feast of sweet, or unleavened, bread: for by the space of seven whole days they fed upon unleavened bread. The ceremonies of that feast, with the sacrifices that were to be offered thereat, are at large described in the twelfth of Exodus, and twenty-third of Leviticus. In that feast was eaten the paschal lamb, in no other place but at the tabernacle, or afterward at the temple, Deut. xvi., for a remembrance of that notable deliverance of Israel and all the faithful out of the Egyptian servitude and slavery. In that feast God would have the first-fruits of their land offered unto him, in token of the manna wherewith he fed their fathers. Moreover, that feast did signify that passing over and delivering of the faithful, which in the shedding of of blood was accomplished by Christ. Whereupon the apostle said, "Christ our passover is offered up." 1 Cor. v. But of the passover I will speak more in my next sermon.

Pentecost. [Exod.xxxiv. 22.] The pentecost was also called the feast of weeks, and new corn; for at that feast was set forth shew-bread made of the new year's corn[3]. They reckoned from the next day after the passover seven weeks, that is, fifty days; and upon the fiftieth day they did celebrate the memory of the law of God, revealed and given by God himself from heaven unto his people Israel. For the fiftieth day of their departure out of Egypt we read that the Lord himself spake to them at the mount Sinai, and gave to them the law of the ten commandments: so that the pentecost was a memorial, that, as then, the church was illuminated with the very word of God. And that old pentecost was a figure of the day wherein Christ the Lord, being the end of the law, did send the Holy Ghost upon his disciples, and did illuminate his spouse the church[4].

[1 conciones fuisse longe frequentissimas, Lat.]
[2 See below, page 182.]
[3 two loaves, Levit. xxiii. 16, 17.]
[4 universam ecclesiam, Lat.—his spouse, not in Lat.]

The ceremonies belonging to this feast are expressed by Moses in the twenty-third chapter of Leviticus.

They kept the feast of tabernacles in the seventh month, as Moses commanded in Deuteronomy, saying: "When thou hast gathered in the crop of thy land and vineyards[5], then shalt thou keep the feast of tabernacles by the space of seven days: and thou shalt be merry in thy holy day, thou, and thy son, and thy daughter, thy manservant, and thy maidservant, the Levite, the stranger, the fatherless, and the widow, that are within thy gates. Seven days shalt thou keep holy unto the Lord thy God, in the place which the Lord hath chosen to himself; because the Lord thy God hath given thee happy success in all thy fruits, and in all the work of thy hands. See therefore that thou rejoice." Moreover, the manner of this feast, solemnly celebrated, is to be read in the eighth chapter of Nehemias, where, whosoever looketh, he shall find it described at the full.

The feast of the seventh month, or of the tabernacles. [Deut. xvi. 13—15.]

Now this feast of tabernacles of the seventh month was divided into four solemnities[6]. For the first day of the month was the feast of trumpets, or sounding of trumpets; which was a memorial of those troublesome wars, which the people did happily achieve, by the help and aid of God, against the Amalekites[7], and[8] all other their heathen enemies. And by that feast was signified, that the whole life of man upon the earth is a continual warfare.

The feast of trumpets.

Upon the tenth day of the same month was held the feast of cleansing. In that feast the priest, in a solemn form of words, began to confess aloud the people's sins; and every man, quietly following in the same words, did recite them privately to himself, and in his mind did quietly speak unto the Lord[9]. To those confessions was added the ceremony used with the scape-goat, and the sacrifice, which is at large set down in the sixteenth chapter of Leviticus. And so were

The feast of cleansing.

[5 de area tua et de torculari tuo, Lat. and Marg. of Auth. Ver.; thy floor and thy winepress.]

[6 Bullinger here recounts the chief religious anniversaries of the seventh month, Tisri, in which also the feast of tabernacles occurred: cohærent enim inter se festa quatuor, as he says in his Comment. in Joan. Lib. iv. fol. 78. Tigur. 1556.]

[7 primo quidem, Lat.; in the first instance.]

[8 deinde vero, Lat.; and afterwards.]

[9 Levit. xvi. 21. See Lightfoot's Temple Service, chap. xv.]

the sins of the people cleansed: which was a type of the cleansing that should be through Christ; who, being once offered, did with the only sacrifice of his body take away the sins of all the world. It did also contain the doctrine of true repentance.

The feast of tabernacles.   Upon the fifteenth day began the feast of tabernacles. For by the space of seven whole days, that is, from the fifteenth to the twenty-second, the people dwelt in tabernacles. The end of this ceremony the scripture doth declare to be, that the posterity should know that the Lord did place their forefathers in tabernacles: whereby they were put in mind of the good that he did to them while they were in the wil- *[Lev. xxiii. 42, 43.]* derness. For they were kept forty years in the wilderness, so that they lacked neither victuals nor clothing. And by that feast we are warned that the life of this world is but as a stage, and that we have no abiding place to stay for ever, but are still looking for the world to come; as the apostle Paul taught us, 2 Cor. v., Heb. xiii.

The congregation.   The fourth feast of this month was held upon the twenty-second day, and was called the congregation, or assembly. Upon that day was gathered the offering and stipend given to the ministry, for reparations of the temple, for the cost of sacrifices, and maintenance of the ministry[1]. It is thought that in that feast was sung the eighty-fourth Psalm: "How pleasant are thy tabernacles," &c., and certain other Psalms called *Torculares Psalmi*[2], which they did use. Thus much hitherto concerning the feasts that fall out once in every year.

The year of jubilee.   Here also I think it necessary to make mention of the year of jubilee. Now this year of jubilee was every fiftieth as it fell by course, which is at large described, with all the ceremonies belonging thereunto, in the twenty-fifth of Leviticus. It was declared to all the people in the land of promise by the sound of a trumpet made of a ram's horn, with a proclamation of freedom to all them that were wrapped in servitude or bondage.

In that jubilee was contained very evidently the mystery

[1 For this statement Bullinger refers, in his Comment. in Joan. Lib. iv. fol. 78, to Lev. xxiii. and Numb. xxix.]

[2 Psal. viii., lxxx., and lxxxiii., as they are numbered in the Vulgate, bear the title, Pro torcularibus, *for the presses* (Douay Bible): the title in our Auth. Ver. is *upon Gittith.*]

of Christ our Lord, who declared to us the meaning of that ceremony out of the sixty-first chapter of the prophecy of Esay, in St Luke's Gospel, chap. iv., where he saith, that he is he that doth indeed proclaim the jubilee, the true freedom and acceptable year of the Lord. Now he hath pronounced remission and freedom to all the faithful, not with a trumpet made of a ram's horn, but with the gospel. For by the mercy of God in the merit of Jesus Christ, the Son of God, all debts or sins are forgiven to all the faithful that live upon the face of all the earth, upon condition that we, whose sins are forgiven, should likewise forgive the trespasses of them that offend us. And in Christ, verily, we have[3] the true and everlasting rest, that shall never fail us. By Christ we have return granted us to our possession or country[4], from whence we were fallen, that is, to heaven, the place of the faithful.

Thus much have I said of the holy time or holy days, as briefly as possibly I could. The rest is at the full to be seen in the twenty-third of Exodus, Levit. xxiii., Numb. xxviii. and xxix., Deut. xvi. That which is behind touching this argument (I mean, touching the Jewish ceremonies) I will by God's leave make an end of in the next sermon. Now let us make our humble prayers and supplications unto God, &c.

OF THE SACRAMENTS OF THE JEWS; OF THEIR SUNDRY
SORTS OF SACRIFICES, AND CERTAIN OTHER
THINGS PERTAINING TO THEIR
CEREMONIAL LAW.

THE SIXTH SERMON.

In my last sermon I spake of the holy persons, I mean, the ministers of God's religion, the Levitical priests; and the place and time assigned to God's service. There remaineth now for us to consider the holy thing which those holy persons did exercise in the holy time and place; I mean, the very worship and holy rites so ordained, taught, and prescribed by God himself, that all men might easily understand

[3] vocationem et, Lat., omitted; our calling and.]
[4] veterem nimirum, ad terram viventium, Lat.; that is, the ancient country, to the land of the living:—'that is—faithful,' is the translator's addition.]

how to do service, and what honour to give unto the Lord. In this treatise we have first to consider the Jewish sacraments, and then their sacrifices.

Two sacraments of the synagogue. The ancient church of the saints had two especial sacraments; circumcision, and the paschal lamb. Of both which I will speak severally, and agreeably to the word of God, according to the grace which the Lord shall vouchsafe to give unto me.

Circumcision, what it is. Now circumcision was the holy action, whereby the flesh of the foreskin was cut away for a sign of the covenant that God made with men. Or, to describe it more largely, circumcision was a mark in the privy members of men, betokening the eternal covenant of God; and was ordained by God himself, to testify his good-will toward them that were circumcised, to warn them of regeneration and cleanness, and to make a difference betwixt the confederates of God and other people or nations.

The original or beginning of circumcision.

[John vii. 22.]

The author, therefore, of circumcision is God himself: the beginning of it is of great antiquity. For the Lord himself in the gospel saith: "Circumcision began not at Moses, but at the patriarchs." Moses verily did renew, or repair, the law or custom of circumcision; but Abraham, the renowned friend of God, was the first that was circumcised, in the ninetieth year[1] of his age, and in the very same day that God, making a covenant with him, did first ordain·the use of circumcision. For he added circumcision as a seal to the league which he made with Abraham and with his seed for ever. The place is extant in the seventeenth chapter of Genesis. It was first ordained in the 2046 year after the creation of the world, 390 years after the deluge, when Sem, the son of Noah, was 487 years old. So that Moses is found to have been born 320 years after the first institution of circumcision: whereby it appeareth, that circumcision was in use among the patriarchs 400 years before the law was given to the Israelites by the hand of Moses[2].

[1 Nonagesimum nonum, Lat.; ninety years old and nine. Gen. xvii. 24.]

[2 According to Abp. Usher, these dates are as follows: Circumcision was instituted A.M. 2107, after the deluge 450 years, when Shem was 549 years old, before Moses' birth 326 years, and before the giving of the law 406 years. But see Vol. I. page 42, note; and The Old Faith, in works of Coverdale, Parker Soc. ed. p. 36.]

Now for because circumcision is added as a sign or seal Of the league of God and man. to the league that was made betwixt God and Abraham, I must briefly, and by a short digression, touch the manner or order of that covenant. God, in making of leagues, as he doth in all things else, applieth himself to our capacities, and imitateth the order which men use in making confederacies. Men do by leagues, as by most sure and stedfast bonds, bind themselves to the society and fellowship of one body or people; in which society, to the end they may be the safer, and live more quietly from the wrongs and injuries of all other nations, they do mutually hazard both lives and livings, the one in defence of the other's liberty. In these leagues they do precisely express what they be that make the confederacy, upon what conditions, and how far the covenant shall extend. And therefore, when God's mind was to declare the favour and good-will that he bare to mankind, and to make us men partakers wholly of himself and his goodness, by pouring himself out upon us, to our great good and profit, it pleased him to make a league or covenant with mankind. Now he did not first begin the league with Abraham, but did renew to him the covenant that he had made a great while before. For he did first of all make it with Adam, the first father of us all, immediately upon his transgression, when he received him, silly wretch[3], into his favour again, and promised his only-begotten Son, in whom he would be reconciled to the world, and through whom he would wholly bestow himself upon us, by making us partakers of all his good and heavenly blessings, and by binding us unto himself in faith and due obedience. This ancient league, made first with Adam, he did afterward renew to Noah, and after that again with the blessed patriarch Abraham. And again, after the space of four hundred years, it was renewed under Moses at the mount Sinai, where the conditions of the league were at large written in the two tables, and many ceremonies added thereunto. But most excellently of all, most clearly and evidently, did our Lord and Saviour Jesus Christ himself[4] shew forth that league; who, wiping away all the ceremonies, types, figures, and shadows, brought in instead of them the very truth, and did most absolutely fulfil and finish the old league,

[3 jam profugum, Lat. ; now become an outcast.]
[4 tandem, Lat. ; at length.]

bringing all the principles of our salvation and true godliness into a brief summary, which, for the renewing and fulfilling of all things, and for the abrogation of the old ceremonies, he called the new league, or new testament. In that testament Christ alone is preached, the perfectness and fulness of all things; in it there is nothing more desired than faith and charity; and in it is granted holy and wonderful liberty unto the godly: of which I will speak at another time. But now I return to the league which was renewed with Abraham.

Between whom the league was made.

We are expressly taught in Genesis, who they were that made the league; that is, the living, eternal, and omnipotent God, who is the chief maker, preserver, and governor of all things; and Abraham with all his seed, that is, with all the faithful, of what nation or country soever they be. For so doth the Apostle expound the seed of Abraham, especially in his epistle to the Galatians, where he saith, "If ye be Christ's, then are ye the seed of Abraham, and heirs by promise."

[Gal. iii. 29.]

The time, how long this league should last.

The time, how long this league should endure, is eternal, and without end or term of time. For although, in the renewings or declarations of the league, many things were added which afterward did vanish away, especially when Christ was come in the flesh; yet notwithstanding, in the substantial and chiefest points, ye can find nothing altered or changed. For God is always the God of his people: he doth always demand and require of them faithful obedience; as may most evidently be perceived in the new Testament.

The conditions of the league or covenant.

For there are two points, or especial conditions, contained in this league: the first whereof declareth what God doth promise, and what he will do for his confederates; I mean, what we may look for at his hands: the second comprehendeth the duty of man, which he doth owe to God, his confederate and sovereign prince. Therefore God for his part saith, "I will be thy God, and Saddai[1], that is, thy fulness and sufficiency; I will, I say, be thy God, and the God of thy seed after thee." God of himself is wholly sufficient to most absolute perfectness and blessedness; neither needeth he the help of any other, since whatsoever is in any place

God is all in all to his confederates.

wheresoever, it is both of him, and hath abiding by him; God alone sufficeth man, and he alone is the giver of all that men desire, or doth belong to perfect felicity. And therefore

[1 See Vol. I. p. 215, note 6.]

Saturnus (peradventure by occasion of the word Saddai) took his name among the heathen, and signifieth to suffice, or satisfy. For he alone is able to satisfy or suffice all, who is himself very fulness and sufficiency itself. But now God sheweth, by two arguments, that he will be the sufficiency, or all in all, to the seed of Abraham. For first he saith : " To [Gen. xv. 18, & xvii. 8.] thy seed will I give the land of Canaan." In which promise he comprehendeth all earthly and bodily benefits; to wit, great wealth, felicity, tranquillity, abundance of all things, health, glory, notable victories, and whatsoever else pertaineth to the preservation and temporal happiness of mankind. Now how he did perform this promise to the seed of Abraham, the holy scripture doth declare; by that means teaching, that the very true God was the God of Abraham's seed, as he had promised to their father Abraham. Secondarily, he promiseth that Seed wherein all the nations of the [Gen. xii 18.] earth were to be blessed; to wit, Christ the Saviour, whom he had promised to Adam many years before. To bless is to enrich with all spiritual benediction : wherein he comprehendeth all the spiritual gifts of God ; the forgiveness of sins, the reviving of life, and glory everlasting. To bless also is to take away a curse; so that this promise of God's to Abraham is all one with that which he made to Adam, saying ; " The seed of the woman shall tread down the serpent's head." [Gen. iii. 15.] For the head of the old dragon is nothing else but the power and kingdom of Satan. His power is the curse, sin, and death. Therefore, when his head is crushed or trodden down, the curse is taken away ; and instead of the curse succeedeth a blessing. By this, I say, he doth declare that he will be the God of Abraham and of his seed.

The second condition of the league betwixt God and man What is required of prescribeth to man what he must do, and how he must behave men in the league. himself toward God, his confederate and sovereign prince. " Walk before me," saith God to man, " and be upright." [Gen. xvii. 1.] Now they walk before God, which do direct all their life, words, and works, according to the will of God. His will is that we should be upright. That uprightness is gotten by faith, hope, and charity ; in which three are contained all the offices of saints, which are the friends and confederates of the Lord. Therefore this latter condition of the league doth teach the confederates what to do, and how to behave themselves before the Lord; to wit, to take him for their God, to stick to him alone, who is their only all in all, to call upon him alone, to worship him alone, and, through the Messiah, to look for sanctification and life everlasting. These were the conditions of the covenant; to which the number of ceremonies were not added in Abraham's time, which afterward were given to the Israelites under the leading of their captain Moses.

Circumcision was the sign or seal annexed to the league.

To this confederacy the Lord did add circumcision as a sign or seal, to confirm it withal. Seals are put to writings for an effectual force and confirmation's sake. The tables, or writings, do contain and give evidence of all the points of the whole league. Circumcision, therefore, is added to the league instead of the writing[1], and also of the seal; and for that cause circumcision is called the league itself[2]: even as the writings or letters of covenants among us are commonly called the very covenant[3], when as in deed they are nothing else but the evidences of the league, which contain in writing all the order of the confederacy, and confirm it with a seal. It is very usual that the signs do take the names of the things which they do signify; so that it is no marvel though circumcision be called the league, when as in deed the league is not the cutting of the skin, but the communion of fellowship which we have with God. In the seventeenth of Genesis thus saith the Lord touching this sign of outward circumcision: " This is my covenant, which ye shall keep betwixt me and you, and thy seed after thee; every male shall be circumcised among you. Ye shall circumcise the flesh of your foreskin, and it shall be for a sign of the covenant betwixt me and you," &c. Lo here circumcision, in these words of the Lord's, is first named the covenant; and afterwards, for exposition's sake, it is called the sign of the covenant. In the same sense doth St Stephen call it a testament, in the seventh chapter of the Acts, when he meant that it was the sign or seal of the testament.

Gen. xvii.

Acts vii.

Moreover, the manner of circumcision is declared: " Ye

[1 tabularum, Lat.]
[2 See Gen. xvii. 9, 13. *My covenant*, that is, *the sign* of my covenant, or testament, as is explained in verse 11. Ainsworth on Gen. xvii. 10.]
[3 der bund, ipsum inquam fœdus, Lat.]

shall," saith God, "circumcise the flesh of your foreskin[4]." The manner and order of circumcision. [Gen. xvii. 11.
The cutting or taking away of this flesh was called circum-
cision. But now, whose office it was to cut that skin away,
we find not expressed. It appeareth that the most honourable in every house or family, I mean, the first-begotten, or
ancient of every household, did circumcise, before the law;
which office was turned to the priests, when once the law was
given[5]. It is a singular example, and no more to be found
like unto it, that Zipporah, the wife of Moses, did circumcise
her son. Exodus, chap. iv.

Now also the time of circumcision is set down, to wit, the
eighth day, when the new-born child began to be of a little
more strength. And we gather out of the fifth chapter of the
book of Josue, that they did circumcise them not with knives
of iron, but of stone: for in that chapter the Lord doth in
express words command to circumcise the sons of Israel with
knives of stone[6]. But it is manifest by the rites of the sacraments, that God doth alter nothing in the ceremonies of the
sacraments: and therefore we conjecture and gather, that
Abraham used none other but knives of stone, especially
since we read that Zippora, Moses his wife, did circumcise
her son with a stone.

The rest of the Jewish trifles, which they sow abroad
touching the ceremonies of circumcision, I do of purpose here
let pass: for they are utterly unworthy to be heard, and
have no mystery contained in them. But the knife of stone
is of force in the exposition of the mystery of circumcision:
for circumcision had a mystery and a most certain meaning
hidden within it.

For, first, circumcision did signify that the whole nature The mystery and meaning of circumci- sion.
of man is unclean and corrupt; and therefore that all men
have need of cutting and regeneration. And for that cause
that cutting was made in the member wherewith man is
begotten[7]. For we are all begotten and born the sons of
wrath in original sin. Neither doth any man deliver us from
that damnation, but he alone that is without sin, to wit, the
blessed Seed, Jesus Christ our Lord, who was conceived by

[4 A sentence of the original and of the translation is here omitted.]
[5 See above, p. 143.]
[6 verse 2, sharp knives, Auth. Ver.; marg. knives of flints.]
[7 Cf. Augustin. Expos. in Evang. Joan. Tract. xxx.]

the Holy Ghost, and born of the virgin Mary; who with the shedding of his blood (which was prefigured in the blood shed in circumcision) doth cleanse us from sin, and make us heirs of everlasting life. And now this circumcision maketh sorely against them that deny original sin; and putteth them to their shifts, that attribute justification and salvation to our own strength and virtue. For if we were clean, if we by our own power could get salvation, what needed our fathers to be cut in that sort? The things that are cut off are either unpure, or else superfluous. But God made nothing unpure or superfluous. Now he made the flesh of the foreskin. If the flesh of the foreskin had been evil, God had not made man with the flesh of the foreskin. The skin, therefore, is not evil of itself, nor yet superfluous: but the cutting of the foreskin doth rather serve to teach us to understand, that by our birth and nature we are corrupt, and that we cannot be cleansed of that corruption but by the knife of stone. And for that cause, verily, was circumcision given in that member, and in none other. I will anon add another cause out of Lactantius, why it was given in none other part of all the body.

Moreover, circumcision did signify and testify that God Almighty, of his mere grace and goodness, is joined with an indissoluble bond of covenant unto us men, whom his will is first to sanctify, then to justify[1], and lastly to enrich with all heavenly treasures through Christ, our Lord and reconciler. For that was the meaning of the stony knife; because Christ, the blessed Seed, is the rock of stone out of which do flow most pure and cleansing waters; and he by his Spirit doth cut from us whatsoever things do hinder the mutual league and amity betwixt God and us: he also doth give and increase in us both hope and charity in faith, so that we may be knit and joined to God in life everlasting, which is the blessed and happy life indeed.

Deut. xxx.   Now here it is expedient to hear the testimonies of the law and the apostles. In the thirtieth of Deuteronomy Moses saith: "The Lord thy God shall circumcise thy heart, and the heart of thy seed, that thou mayest love the Lord thy God." Now the outward and visible cutting was a sign of this inward circumcision. And Paul also, speaking of

[1 quos velit sanctificatos justificare, Lat.]

Abraham, saith: "And he received the sign of circumcision, [Rom. iv. 11.] as the seal of the righteousness of faith which he had being yet uncircumcised; that he should be the father of all them that believe, though they were not circumcised; that righteousness might be imputed to them also," &c. Lo here, Abraham's circumcision was a sign that God by his grace had justified Abraham; which justification he received by faith before his circumcision: which is an argument, that they which believe, though they be not circumcised, are nevertheless justified with faithful Abraham; and again, that the Jews, which are circumcised, are[2] justified of God by faith. And for that cause was circumcision given in the very body of man, that he might bear in his body the league of God, and be thereby admonished that he is justified by grace through faith.

Whereby we gather also, that the grace of God, and the The grace of God is not tied to circumcision. justification of the godly, is not tied to the sign: for if it had, then had not Abraham been justified before his circumcision, but even in his circumcision. Furthermore, if it had been so, then the Lord, whose will is to have mankind saved, would not have given commandment to have them circumcised upon the eighth day: for many children died before the eighth day, and never came to circumcision; and yet they were not damned. To which we may add that Sara, Rebecca, Rahel, Jochabeth, and Mary, Moses' sister, with innumerable more matrons and holy virgins, could not be circumcised; and yet they were saved by the grace of God through faith in the Messiah that was to come. The grace of God, therefore, was not tied to the sacrament of circumcision: but yet it was not despised and neglected of the holy saints of the old church, but used to the end for which it was ordained, that is, to be a testimony and a seal of free justification in Christ[3], who Coloss. ii. circumciseth us spiritually without hands by the working of the Holy Ghost.

Furthermore, God by the outward and visible sign did By circumcision the circumcised are gathered into one body. gather into one church them which were circumcised; in which number those which he had chosen before[4] he did join to himself with the bond of his Spirit. For St Paul, for the

[2 sciant se, Lat.; may know that they are.]
[3 venturo, Lat.; who was to come.]
[4 ex quibus electos, Lat.]

very same cause, did call the people of one religion the circumcision, as is evident by the fifteenth chapter to the Romans, and the third to the Philippians. Therefore by circumcision God did separate his people from the unbelieving nations. Whereupon it came, that to be called uncircumcised was as great reproach among them, as to be called dog is now-a-days among us: for an uncircumcised person was reputed for an unclean and profane man, and for such an one as had no part in God nor his covenants.

1 Sam. xvii.
Acts xi.

Finally, circumcision did put the circumcised in mind of their duty all their life long; to wit, that every man should think that he had taken upon him to profess God, and to bear in his body the sacrament of the Lord. For that is the cause why the Israelites were named, or had their names given them, in their circumcision: for it is evident in Luke, that John Baptist and Jesus our Saviour had their names given them at their circumcision; even as also the first circumcised at his circumcision was called Abraham, whose name before was said to be Abram.

Circumcision
putteth a
man in mind
of his duty.

[Luke i. 59.
& ii. 21.]

[Gen. xvii.
5.]

It did admonish the circumcised of his duty, forsomuch as he had given his name unto the Lord, his confederate, to be enrolled in the register of God among the names of them that give themselves unto the Lord: wherefore he ought, by covenant and duty, to frame his life, not after his own lust and pleasure[1], but according to the will of God, to whom he did betake himself. For the condition of the covenant was, that the circumcised should not defile themselves with idolatry and strange religions; that they should not pollute with unclean living the bodies and minds that were hallowed to the Lord; but that they, persevering in true faith, should ensue godliness, shew the works of repentance, and be obedient to God in all things. For thus saith Moses in the tenth of Deuteronomy: "Circumcise the foreskin of your hearts, and harden not your necks any longer." To which words the prophet Jeremy alludeth in his fourth chapter, saying: "Be ye circumcised to the Lord, and cut away the foreskin of your heart." And the martyr St Stephen, rebuking the unbelieving Jews, saith: "Ye stiff-necked, and of uncircumcised heart and ears, ye always resist the Holy Ghost." Very rightly, therefore, doth the holy apostle Paul, in his Epistle to the Romans, the second chapter,

Jer. iv.

[Acts vii. 51.]

[1 aut aliorum voluntate, Lat., omitted; or the will of others.]

declare that there are two sorts of circumcision: the one of the letter, in the flesh, the outward circumcision, that is made with hands; the other in the heart, of the Spirit, the inward circumcision, which is made by the means of the Holy Ghost. The circumcision of the heart God doth well like of in those that be his; but that in the flesh he doth utterly mislike of, if, as the flesh is, the heart be not circumcised. The liking and misliking of these two circumcisions is in that which went before so plainly already declared, that I need not to stick any longer upon it.

Two circumcisions, one of the spirit, the other of the letter.

And here I think it not amiss, before I make an end of circumcision, to rehearse unto you, dearly beloved, the words of the ancient writer Lactantius, Lib. Instit. IV. chap. 17. where he speaketh of circumcision in this manner: "The meaning of circumcision was, that we should make bare our breasts; to wit, that we should live with a simple and plain dealing heart; because that part of the body, which is circumcised, is partly like to a heart, and an object of shame[2]: and the cause why God commanded to make it bare was, that by that sign he might admonish us not to have a covered heart, that is, that we should not cover within the secrets of our conscience any crime whereof we ought to be ashamed. And this is the circumcision of the heart, whereof the prophets speak, which God hath translated from the mortal flesh to the immortal soul. For the Lord being wholly set and fully minded, according to his eternal goodness, to have a care for our life and safeguard, did set repentance before our eyes for us to follow, as a way to bring us thereunto: so that, if we make bare our hearts, that is, if by confession of our sins we satisfy the Lord, we should obtain pardon, which is denied to the proud and those that conceal their faults by God, who beholdeth not the face as man doth, but searcheth the secrets of the breast[3]." Thus much hitherto hath that ancient writer

Lactantius touching circumcision.

[2 substituted for another term; et pudenda, Lat.]

[3 Hujus secundæ circumcisionis figura erat, (illa carnis circumcisio) significans, nudandum esse pectus, id est, aperto et simplici corde oportere nos vivere; quoniam pars illa corporis, quæ circumciditur, habet quandam similitudinem cordis, et est pudenda. Ob hanc causam Deus nudari eam jussit; ut hoc argumento nos admoneret, ne involutum pectus haberemus, id est, ne quod pudendum facinus intra conscientiæ secreta velemus. Hæc est cordis circumcisio, de qua prophetæ loquuntur; quam Deus a carne mortali ad animam transtulit,

12

of the church, Lactantius Firmianus, declared unto us touching the mystery of circumcision.

The sum of circumcision. Now all this, which hitherto I have said touching the meaning and mystery of circumcision, was set forth, as in a picture, to be seen of all men's eyes, so often as circumcision was solemnized in the church. There was the league, as it were, renewed, which God did make with men. There was the grace of God, his sanctification, and our corruption, declared: therein did Christ, the rock of stone, appear, who with his Spirit doth cut and wash away all spots of the church. Moreover, the worshippers of God did learn by that sign, and so by all the holy ceremony, that they, being in one celestial[1] body, ought to do their endeavour by pureness of living to win the favour of God, their confederate; because by the visible circumcision there was, after a sort, an open confession made of the true religion, of free consent to the true religion, and of a binding by promise unto the same. He therefore that did despise or unadvisedly neglect that holy ceremony was sharply punished, as may be gathered by the seventeenth of Genesis, and the fourth chapter of Exodus. And so much hitherto concerning circumcision.

Of the paschal lamb. There followeth now the second sacrament of the ancient church, I mean, the paschal[2] lamb. It is an Hebrew word, not signifying a passion, as it should seem if it were derived according to the Greek etymology[3]; but it signifieth a skipping, a leaping, or a passing over: for the Hebrew signifieth [Exod. xii. 23.] to leap or pass over[4]. The cause of this word Moses sheweth in the law, where he saith : "The Lord shall go over to strike the Egyptians; and when he shall see the blood upon the upper post, and the two side posts of the door, the Lord will

quæ sola mansura est. Volens enim vitæ ac saluti nostræ pro æterna sua pietate consulere, pœnitentiam nobis in illa circumcisione proposuit, ut si cor nudaverimus, id est, si peccata nostra confessi satis Deo fecerimus, veniam consequamur; quæ contumacibus et admissa sua celantibus denegatur ab eo, qui non faciem, sicut homo, sed intima et arcana pectoris intuetur.—Lactant. Instit. Lib. iv. cap. 17. Lugd. Bat. 1660, p. 406.]

[1 ecclesiastico, Lat.; ecclesiastical, ed. 1577.]

[2 Pascha, Lat.]

[3 Eam (i. e. vocem πάσχα) quidam patrum a voce πάσχειν pati derivarunt. Schleusner. Lex. in voc.]

[4 פָּסַח Passed, stood, over for defence. Lee's Hebr. Lex. in voc.]

pass over that door, and will not suffer the destroyer to come within your houses." This sacrament is known also and called by other names. For it is called a sign, a remembrance, a solemnity, an holy assembly[5], the feast of the Lord, a worship, an observation, an oblation, and a sacrifice. But whereas that ceremony is called a passing over, that is not done without a trope. For the passing over was the very benefit, wherein the angel of the Lord did pass over the Jews, leave their houses untouched, and save their lives; but for because the paschal lamb was a memorial and a renewing of that benefit, therefore it took the name of the benefit: even as I admonished you before[6], that it is usual in sacraments for the signs to be called by the names of the things that they signify, because of the likeness and mutual proportion that is betwixt them.

Let us see now what the passover was, and what kind of ceremony did belong unto it. The passover was an holy action, ordained by God, in the killing and eating of a lamb; partly to the end that the church might keep in memory the benefit which God did for them in the land of Egypt, [7]to be a testimony of God's good will toward the faithful, to be a type[8] of Christ, and partly[9] also to gather all the partakers thereof into the fellowship of one body, and to put them in mind to be thankful and innocent. *What the passover was.*

This sacrament was first ordained by God himself, and not by man. For Moses delivered to the children of Israel whatsoever he received at the Lord's hand: as it is to be seen at large in the twelfth chapter of Exodus. And he instituted that ceremony even at that very time when he brought the Israelites from out of Egypt. Now since this ceremony came first from God, it followeth consequently, that all the passovers which followed, even until that passover which the Lord did hold with his disciples a little before his death, were holy and divine actions. To flesh and worldly wisdom many points, I may say, all the parts, of this sacrament do seem to be merely absurd and altogether needless; but faith, which looketh up to God, the author of this sacrament, hath a great respect unto, and reverenceth greatly, all the mysteries contained *The first author of the passover, and the time when it first began.*

[5 πανήγυρις, in Lat.]   [6 p. 176.]
[7 deinde, Lat.; next.]
[8 typum quoque, Lat.; to be also a type.]   [9 denique, Lat.]

12—2

therein[1]. For even as God is the chief and most absolute wisdom, so are all[2] his ordinances most absolute and passing profitable.

Here now is noted the time when this sacrament was first delivered to the church of Israel; to wit, in the four hundreth and thirtieth year (counting from the promise made to Abraham, or from the time that he departed from his country first), which was the 2447th year from the beginning of the world, 791 years after the general flood[3]. The time is also appointed when the passover should be holden, to wit, every year, in the month Nisan, which taketh part of our March and part of April. Moreover, the very day is named, that is, the fourteenth of the month, beginning their account at spring time's equinoctial. For on the tenth day they chose the lamb that should be eaten, and on the fourteenth day they killed it. There is also set down the hour of the day when it should be slaughtered: that was, about eventide[4], to wit, betwixt three and five of the clock in the afternoon, according to the course of our dials; and, as the Jews were wont to reckon the hours of the day, it was to be killed betwixt nine and eleven o'clock. And in that killing of the lamb at eventide did this meaning lie hid, that Christ should be slain in the latter days of the world; yea, the very hour and moment, wherein Christ should die, was therein foretold: for he gave up the ghost about the ninth hour. Whereupon St Peter saith, that the prophets did search at what moment, or minute of time, the Spirit of Christ, which was in them, did signify that Christ should come and suffer[5].

The Equinoctial is, when the day and night is both of one length, and cometh twice in a year, to wit, the 8th of April, and the 8th of October. The Jews began to reckon from one to twelve, as we begin to reckon from seven in the morning till six at night; and so it was, that our three o'clock was nine o'clock to them, and our five, eleven to them. The ninth hour of the Jews is three o'clock in the afternoon to us.

[1 omnia, Lat.; all things in it.]

[2 omnia et singula, Lat; all and every one of.]

[3 According to Abp. Usher the Passover was instituted, as Bullinger also says, 430 years after Abraham's call, Gen. xii., but A.M. 2513, and 857 years after the deluge. But see Bullinger's Treatise, The Old Faith, in Coverdale's Fruitful Lessons, &c. p. 36.]

[4 inter vesperas, Lat.; between the two evenings. Marg. Auth. Ver. Exod. xii. 6.]

[5 1 Pet. i. 11. Bullinger has adopted the translation, not of the Vulgate, but of Erasmus:—scrutantes ad quem aut cujusmodi temporis articulum significaret qui in illis erat Spiritus Christi: where also Erasmus notes; Nec est tempus, quod Græci vocant χρόνον, sed καιρὸν, quod articulum vertimus: est enim certius quiddam quam tempus. Calvin similarly understands the apostle's phrase: prophetas scrutatos

Furthermore, there was a certain appointed place assigned The place appointed to this sacrament[6]. In Egypt, verily, they did eat it by for the eating of the companies here and there in several houses. But when they passover. were once come into the land of promise, it was not lawful to hold passover in any place but at the tabernacle of appointment; and after that, at the the temple in Hierusalem. Being divided therefore into several houses at Hierusalem, they did eat it by companies, as is to be seen in the twenty-second chapter of St Luke's gospel. And that was a type, that Luke xxii. Christ, which was to be offered but once upon the mount of Calvary, should be effectual for ever to cleanse the sins of all his people.

There was also appointed, who they should be that should Who were the guests at hold the passover; to wit, the whole circumcised congrega- the eating of the lamb. tion of Israel, being assembled by houses and families in so great companies as were sufficient to eat a lamb[7]. For as Christ is the Saviour of us all, so all sinners (for we all are sinners) are the cause why Christ our Lord was offered upon the altar of the cross.

Moreover, there is great diligence[8] used in describing the The manner or rite of manner of killing and eating the lamb. First, they chose to eating the passover. themselves this lamb from among other lambs and kids : the fifth day after they cut the throat thereof, and saved[9] the blood in a platter, which with a bush of hyssop, made like a holy-water stick[10], they sprinkled upon the two sides and upper posts of the door. The lamb itself they did eat publicly, not boiled with water, but roasted with fire; and that whole also, I mean, both head and feet, and purtenance too; and with it they did eat lettuce or sour herbs, and unleavened bread. And while they were at it, they stood about it with their loins girded, with shoes on their feet, and staves in their hands. They did eat it in haste : they neither brake nor cast a bone

esse quo temporis articulo advenerit Christi regnum. Comment. in loc. cit.]

[6 huic sacro, Lat.]

[7 Exod. xii. 43—49.—φρατρία περὶ ἑκάστην γίνεται θυσίαν, (τοῦ Πάσχα) οὐκ ἔλασσον ἀνδρῶν δέκα—πολλοὶ δὲ καὶ σὺν εἴκοσιν ἀθροίζονται. Joseph. de Bell. Jud. Lib. VI. cap. 9. § 3.]

[8 multa fide et diligentia, Lat. ; great faithfulness and diligence.]

[9 excipiebant, Lat. ; received.]

[10 aspergillo hysopi, Lat.]

of it unto the dogs, but burnt the bones with fire. From evening until morning no man did set one foot out of doors.

The end whereto this ceremony tended.

All these ceremonies had their ends whereunto they tended, contained great mystéries, and bare a very evident signification of things past, things present, and things to come. They did also join the whole congregation, or Jewish church, into one body and profession of one religion; and did also warn all those that did eat of the lamb to be thankful to God, and zealous in religion: as I will by parts touch, and teach you as briefly as I can.

The Lord's benefit was kept in memory by the eating of the passover.

For, first of all, the Lord's will was to keep in memory, and as it were for ever to prolong the remembrance of that great benefit, which he did once for his people of Israel[1], in preserving marvellously his chosen flock, when he slew in one night all the first-born of the Egyptians, and the next day after led his elect from out of Egypt, where they had a long time sustained great misery in bondage. This benefit he would not have only to be preached by word of mouth (for it is certainly sure, that in that feast were made most effectual sermons touching God's benefits and grace shewed to their fathers); but would have them also laid before their eyes by an holy action and ceremony, as it were by a looking-glass and lively picture, even as though their deed were newly in doing again before their faces. For the visible action did, after a sort, make a sermon to their eyes and other senses. Wherefore Moses, when he did interpret the ceremony and holy

[Exod. xii. 26, 27.]

action, did say : " When your children shall say unto you, What meaneth this worship of yours ? ye shall say unto them, This sacrifice is the passing over of the Lord, who passed over the houses of the children of Israel in Egypt, when he slew the Egyptians, and delivered our houses."

The testimony of God's good will towards his people.

But this ceremony was the signification of a thing already past: and therefore it should have little availed that age of man which followed, to celebrate a benefit which did nothing at all belong unto them, unless the Lord had applied it to every age and season. God therefore would have this to be a testimony to the posterity of his favour, goodness, and perpetual assistance[2]; to put them in mind, that he was not only the God of their fathers and ancestors, but that he would be

[1 in Ægypto, Lat. ; in Egypt.]
[2 liberationis perpetuæ, Lat.]

the God of all the posterity of the Israelites; that he would bear with and spare them for the blood of Christ; and finally, that he both would and could defend them from all evil, and bestow upon them all good and fatherly blessings. For in the 136th Psalm we read: "O praise the Lord, for he is good, because his mercy endureth for ever: which struck the first-born of the Egyptians; for his mercy endureth for ever: with a strong hand and a stretched out arm; for his mercy endureth for ever[3]." Besides the remembrance, therefore, of the benefit which God did for their fathers, the posterity did by the use of that ceremony stir up their faith, to believe that God would have mercy on and do good for them according to his natural goodness, even as he did to their fathers before them. And by that means this ceremony was no small exercise of faith in the children of Israel.

Furthermore, those ceremonies did contain the mysteries, that were to come, of Christ, the Saviour of us all. For in them was prefigured what Christ should be, what he should do for the world, by what means the faithful should be partakers with him, and how they should behave themselves before him. For among many other beasts there was none thought to be more fit for this sacrament than a lamb; not so much for the signification of simplicity and patience that was in Christ, like to the quietness of a lamb, as for because a lamb was the daily sacrifice that was offered to the Lord[4]. For Paul saith: "Christ our paschal Lamb is offered up." And a lamb by the law was every morning and evening offered up in sacrifice. For Christ is the Lamb that was killed since the beginning of the world; of whom John Baptist testified, saying, "Behold the Lamb of God, that taketh away the sins of the world[5]." And for because we all did go astray like sheep, every one after his own way, the Son of God came down unto us, and became a sheep, of our very substance and nature. But yet he[6] was sound and without spot, without sin and wickedness; conceived by the Holy Ghost, and born of the virgin Mary. He was a male,

The lamb was a type of Christ, of his passion and redemption.

[1 Cor. v. 7.]

[Exod. xxix. 38, 39.]

[Rev. xiii. 8.]

[3 verses 1, 10, 12. The eleventh verse is also quoted in the Latin.]
[4 quam quod victima est, Lat.]
[5 John i. 29. peccatum mundi, Lat.]
[6 hic noster, Lat.]

and of a year old; that is to say, strong, and all one, the same to-day that he was yesterday, and the same for ever, to wit, the Saviour of all the world[1]. The ceremonial lamb was chosen and taken from among other lambs and goats: for Christ descended lineally of righteous men and sinners ; as is to be seen in the first chapter of Matthew's Gospel. Likewise, for the shedding of the lamb's blood God did bear with the whole church of the Israelites : for the blood of Christ (whereof[2] the lamb's blood was a type) was to be shed, that by it[3] all the faithful might be cleansed, and that by the shedding of that the anger of God the Father might be appeased, and he reconciled again unto the church[4]. The blood was sprinkled upon the upper and two side-posts of the house with a bunch of hyssop. Hyssop, verily, is a base herb and of small account ; and the preaching of the Gospel seemeth to be foolish, vile, and of no value : and yet by the preaching of the gospel the blood of Christ unto the remission of sins must be sprinkled[5] on us which are the house of God. Now we receive the Lamb to life, when we do eat, that is, when we believe that Christ did suffer for us: for Christ is eaten by faith, as it is at large declared[6] in the sixth chapter of St John. The lamb is dressed with fire, and not with water: it is not eaten raw, but roasted. For Christ was not man alone, but very God also, the true burnt-offering. He is able fully to absolve us, so that there needs no addition of ours : all our additions are mere water, and altogether cold. Moreover, the whole Lamb was to be eaten ; the head, the feet, and purtenance : for unless we believe that Christ is very God and very man, and that he is our wisdom and righteousness, we do not eat him wholly. They eat not the head, which deny that Christ is God : they eat not the feet, which do deny that Christ is man: they eat not the purtenance, which do not acknowledge the gifts that are in Christ, which he doth communicate unto the faithful, to wit, righteousness, wisdom, sanctification, redemption, and life. The bones of the Lamb were neither broken nor thrown to the dogs, but burnt with fire : for in Christ there

[1 universi orbis, Lat.]   [2 whereof—a type, not in Lat.]
[3 ejus sanguine, Lat. ; by his blood.]
[4 toti ecclesiæ, Lat.]   [5 aspergi sive prædicari, Lat.]
[6 ipse fuse exponit, Lat. ; he himself at large declares.]

was not one bone broken; as the apostle John beareth witness in the nineteenth chapter of his gospel.   Herein also lieth John xix. hid another[7] mystery.   For although the Son of God did suffer[8] in his humanity, yet in his divinity he remained still without any passion.   Now the things in Christ, which we cannot attain unto by reason of the excellency of his Godhead, we do[9] earnestly wish for and greatly desire.   Moreover, Christ is the meat of the reasonable and faithful soul, and is not to be cast to dogs and unbelieving miscreants[10]. The Lamb was to be eaten in haste, without delay : for Christ must be eaten by faith, out of hand, without foading off[11], and that too with a sharp desire and eager appetite. With the lamb they were commanded to eat sour herbs and unleavened bread : for the faithful must repent them of their life[12] ill-spent, and wholly betake themselves to a purer trade of living.   For here followeth[13] the manner how they ought to behave themselves toward their Redeemer. They stood to eat the lamb, having their[14] loins girded, with shoes on their feet, and staves in their hands.   Such was the habit of wayfaring men, or pilgrims.   We therefore must so behave ourselves in this present world, as doth become pilgrims and strangers, which do contemn this world, and look for another country.   In their journey, therefore, let them give themselves to temperate modesty ; let their feet be shod with the preaching of[15] the gospel of peace ; let them wholly lean upon the staff of God's aid and succour ; and let them depart with as much haste as may be from the bondage and corruption of this naughty world[16].

This very same ceremony was, as it were, a confession of The badge the true religion, and as a cognisance, whereby the people sion of faith. of God were known from other people and nations.   Therefore all the Israelites were gathered together into one church and society : wherein, by celebrating of the passover, they

[7 præterea, Lat.]
[8 in eo quod pati potuit, Lat. omitted; in that which could suffer.]
[9 merito, Lat. omitted; we do justly.]
[10 impiis, Lat.]   [11 See p. 38, note 3.]
[12 præteritæ, Lat. ; past.]
[13 copiosius, Lat. omitted ; more at length.]
[14 renibus vel, Lat. ; their reins or.]
[15 Eph. vi. 15.—the preaching of, not in the original.]
[16 hujus seculi, Lat.]

did profess that they were the redeemed, the libertines[1], and the people of the living God. For thereunto belongeth the commandment which charged them that no stranger should eat of the lamb, but that the circumcised alone should be partakers of it; that it should not be divided into many parts; that it should be eaten nowhere but in one place alone, and that too by companies of all the Israelites[2]; and lastly, that no man should once set a foot out of doors until the next morning. By which thing it is given us to understand, that neither Christ, nor our salvation, is to be found without the church, in the sects or schisms of wicked heretics. Christ, the Lamb of God, doth gather all the faithful into one church, wherein he keepeth them, and lastly doth save them.

At the tabernacle first, and afterward at the temple.

Last of all, this ceremony did put God's people in mind of their duty, of thankfulness especially[3], of the study of godliness and harmless innocence. They therefore did give thanks to God for these and all other his benefits; they praised his name; and did utterly abstain from all leavened bread. For ye shall find nothing so severely forbidden in this ceremony as the eating of leavened bread. "Whosoever eateth leavened bread," saith the Lord, "his soul shall perish from among the congregation of Israel, whether he be a stranger, or an Israelite born." The same saying is afterward oftentimes repeated, and throughly beaten into their brains. Now the apostle Paul, whose cunning and learning was much in the law of Moses, expounding what was meant by the leavened bread, doth say : "Therefore let us keep the feast, not in the old leaven, nor in the leaven of malice and unrighteousness[4], but in unleavened bread, that is, in sincerity and truth[5]." Thus much hitherto touching the eating of the paschal lamb.

The paschal lamb did warn the communicants of their duties.

[Exod. xii. 19.]

To these sacraments were also added sacrifices of sundry sorts and many kinds: which were not first invented and taught by Moses, but were taken up and used immediately after the world was created. For Cain and Abel offered burnt sacrifices to God the maker of the world: the one, of

Of sacrifices, and their first beginnings.

[1 libertos, Lat. ; freed men.]   [2 ab universo Israele, Lat.]
[3 gratitudinis præsertim et, Lat.; especially of thankfulness, and, &c.]
[4 versutiæ, Lat.]
[5 1 Cor. v. 8, Erasmus' rendering.]

the fruits of the earth; and the other, of the cattle that was in his flock. Likewise Seth, Noah, Sem, Abraham, Isaac, and Jacob, with all the other patriarchs, are known[6] to have sacrificed unto the Lord. Now since the heathenish sacrifices of the Gentiles, as the very heathen writers themselves did testify, were partly like unto, and in many points all one with, the Jewish sacrifices; it is not unlikely but that the grand patriarchs[7] of the Gentiles did teach every one his own nation the manner of sacrificing, which they had learned of their forefathers, Sem, Cham, Japhet, and of the holy patriarch Noah himself. But it is undoubtedly certain, that the holy fathers did bring in nothing of their own invention, nor add any thing to the sacrifices more than they had received and learned of God, who is the author of all goodness; although Moses did more precisely distinguish and certainly order the sorts, the kinds, and differences betwixt sacrifice and sacrifice: and yet whatsoever he did, that did he at the Lord's appointment. God instructed Moses in all that he did. For the book of Leviticus, wherein are specially described all the kinds of sacrifices, doth immediately after the very beginning testify, that Moses was called by God, and that he learned of the Lord all the ceremonies of the sacrifices which he commanded the Israelites to keep. And in the seventh chapter of the book of Numbers we read: "And when Moses Num. vii. came into the tabernacle of appointment, he heard the voice of God speaking unto him out of the mercy-seat."

Now, as I was about to say, there were divers sacrifices sun- Sacrifices have some things com-mon, and some things peculiar. drily differing in many points among themselves, and yet having many things common and general one with another. It was general to all sacrifices, not to be offered in any other but one appointed place alone. It was general to all sacrifices, that they ought of duty to be offered by faith, according as they were taught by the word of God. It was general to all sacrifices, to be made according to the Lord's commandment, with holy fire, and not with strange fire, or fire profanely kindled. Nadab and Abihu, the sons of Aaron, were slain for nothing else but for because they used profane or strange fire in sacrificing to the Lord. For when the Israelites, or Levites, did first of all sacri- [Lev. ix. 24.] fice, as the Lord had commanded them, in the tabernacle of

[6 creduntur, Lat.]   [7 genearchas, Lat.]

appointment, then did God, by sending fire from heaven, give a token that he did like of that manner of sacrifice. Whereupon in the sixth of Leviticus the priests are charged to maintain or keep the holy fire always burning, first in the tabernacle, and then in the temple: which thing it is manifest The vestal virgins were nuns consecrated to the goddess Vesta. that the heathen did imitate, in commanding the vestal virgins at Rome always to keep the holy fire burning. By this perpetual fire is meant the perpetual working of the Holy Ghost in the church of Christ; which must be kept quick and stirred up in the hearts of the faithful with fervent prayers, with the sincere doctrine of the Lord, and with the right use of the holy sacraments. It was also general to all sacrifices, that in them neither wild nor unclean beasts were offered to the Lord. Moreover, this general rule of sacrifices is given by Moses in the twenty-second chapter of Leviticus, saying: "Let no deformity be in the thing that thou shalt offer: if it be blind, or lame, or maimed; if it have pushes[1], or scabs, or tetter[2], ye shall not offer it unto the Lord, neither shall ye put ought of it upon his altar." Verily, if any man had brought a deformed oblation unto the Lord, he shewed himself plainly to be a contemner, and utterly unthankful toward his maker. And therefore the Lord in Malachi crieth [Mal. i. 8.] out, and saith : "When ye bring the blind for sacrifice, do ye not sin? and when ye bring the lame and sick, do ye not sin? Offer it now, I pray thee, to thy prince or captain; will he be content with it? or will he accept thy person? saith the Lord of hosts. And so I say, My name is in contempt and of no estimation among you." The just and true God, therefore, doth at all times require truth, liberality, sincerity, and integrity in them that worship him; and on the other side, he abhorreth and utterly detesteth uncleanliness, lying, and hypocrisy.

There are certain other things also, which be generally common to all sorts of sacrifices: but I will not at this time make particular rehearsal of every several jot or minute. But what peculiarities every sundry sacrifice hath, it will evidently appear in the exposition of their sundry sorts: which I will now speak of in order as they lie.

[1 push, a pimple, an eruption. Johnson's Dict.]
[2 tetter, a scab; a scurf; a ringworm. Ibid.]

First of all, I will expound to you that kind of sacrifice Holocaustum, the which in the scripture is called Holocaustum[3].   That sacrifice burnt-offering. was wholly consumed with fire, so that nothing but the skin or hide of the beast was left for the priest.   The word is derived of the Greek : for it is called *holocaustum*, as one should say ὅλον καυστόν, that is, wholly burnt or consumed with fire[4].   This sacrifice was of three kinds : I mean, it was made after three sorts, to wit, with greater, with little, and with less, living creatures ; namely, with an ox, a bullock, or a calf ; or, if any man's ability were not sufficient to stretch to that expense, then did he offer a lamb, or a kid : and yet again, if he could not offer that by reason of his poverty, it was lawful for him to sacrifice birds, not geese, or cocks, or other unclean fowls, but turtles, and doves, and such kind of [Lev. i.] clean birds.

Now the manner of making this burnt sacrifice was in this order.   The beast, that was to be offered, was placed at the one side of the altar ; upon which the priest did presently lay his hands, and cut the throat of it.   The blood was saved, to be sprinkled round about the altar ; the skin was flayed from the slaughtered beast, and that alone was all the fees that fell to the portion or share of the priest : the legs were chopped off, and washed together with the purtenance.   Immediately after, a fire was made upon the altar, whereupon was laid the whole sacrifice, to wit, the head, the body, the legs, and the purtenance, and were altogether burnt upon the altar before the Lord.   But if so be it happened that a turtle or a dove were offered for a sacrifice, then did the priest with his finger wreath about and break the neck thereof, and the blood was let drop about the sides of the altar.   The feathers also were cast at the one side of the altar into a place where ashes lay ; the wings were jointed ; and last of all, the whole body was burnt upon the altar. This was the manner of the sacrifice, or oblation, which they did commonly call a burnt-offering : the signification whereof was most cheerful and pleasant to them which were persuaded, that by burnt-offering was prefigured the very Son of God, to be incarnate of the unspotted virgin, and to be

[3 עוֹלָה.]

[4 The corresponding Hebrew name is כָּלִיל.   Deut. xxxiii. 10. Ps. li. 19.]

sacrificed once for the cleasning of all the sins of the whole world. For they in the glass of that sacrifice did behold the cross and passion of the Lord, which took our sins upon himself[1], and, being slain, did shed his blood for the remission of sins, offering himself wholly to God the Father in the fire of charity and heavenly zeal. The very same Christ is the turtle or pigeon.

Moreover, beside these ceremonies in the burnt sacrifice, it was required that no burnt sacrifice of beasts should at any time be made without that kind of offering which they called *minha*[2]. That oblation was an handful of corn, or of meal, or else of crusty bread sodden in a caldron, or a bowed[3] piece of bread (which we call a cracknel) baked in an oven or in a frying-pan, which was burnt with oil and frankincense upon the altar of burnt sacrifices. And Christ, verily, is the bread [Heb. ix. 14.] of life, who by the eternal Spirit, as saith the apostle, did offer himself to God the Father for us, to be the meat and preservation of our life.

The daily sacrifice. In the number of burnt sacrifices are reckoned the daily sacrifices that were offered every morning and every evening, and the sacrifices of the anointing or consecrating of priests. Of the daily sacrifice a large exposition is made in the twenty-ninth of Exodus and the sixth chapter of Leviticus. It was called the daily offering, because every morning and evening two lambs were offered, to wit, one in the morning, and another at the evening. In these lambs was Christ most manifestly prefigured; who is that Lamb of God that taketh away the sins of the world; whose virtue is always effectual and of power to take away the sins of the faithful. For the Lamb[4] was killed from the beginning of the world; he was once slain upon the cross: but yet his merit and effectual power endureth still, and doth absolve all them that are delivered from their sins.

[1 Omitted: "for to this pertaineth the laying on of hands, which was a sign of communion." Huc enim pertinet maxime manuum impositio, quæ communionis erat symbolum." P.]

[2 מִנְחָה, a gift to God in sacrifice,—generally unbloody, and consisting of various fruits, flour, oil, &c. opp. τῷ זֶבַח. Lee's Heb. Lex. in voc.]

[3 bowed: bent.]

[4 that Lamb, ed. 1577; agnus ille, Lat.]

Now the sacrifices of consecrating, I mean, of the priests, of the tabernacle, and of all the vessels or instruments belonging to the holy ministery, are in many points all one with the burnt-offerings, and in some things differing from them: as is fully to be seen in the twenty-ninth of Exodus and the eighth of Leviticus. And Christ our Lord did first begin the priesthood by his passion, and after that hallowed all the faithful to be priests unto himself.

The second kind of sacrifices was the oblation, which they called *minha;* a gift, reward, or sacrifice of a wheaten cake; and by another name was called a meat-offering[5]. This sacrifice was of the fruits of the earth, and was not offered always after one sort: for there are reckoned three kinds of this sacrifice. For there was offered either parched wheat, sticking in the ears; or wheat out of the ears, or else clean meal, unbaked; or, at leastwise, meal made up into bread; which bread again was made three sundry ways, and in three sundry fashions. For either it was baked in an oven, or furnace; or else sod in a pot, or a caldron; or else fried in a frying-pan, like unto cakes. To these there was added, as sauce to the sacrifice, salt, oil, and frankincense. Honey and leaven were by a general rule utterly barred from all sorts of sacrifices. For cakes made with honey were never allowed of, nor admitted in their offerings: yet in the feast of thanksgiving they did eat leavened bread. Therefore, when any man did offer wheat, it was first anointed by the priest with oil, then seasoned with salt, and last of all had frankincense put upon it: after that the priest took one handful from out of all (but in the sacrifice for the priest all was burnt), and burnt it upon the altar; the rest he did reserve, as a share to himself. [Lev. vi. 23.] And in all meat-offerings frankincense was always used, except in the sacrifice for sin and in the sacrifice of jealousy; as is to be seen in the fifth of Leviticus and the fifth of the book of Numbers. The rest that belongeth to the full rites and ceremonies of the meat-offerings whosoever is desirous to know, he shall find them in the second chapter of Leviticus. For I mean not here particularly to repeat every jot and tittle of their accustomed ceremonies.

Now even as Christ was before prefigured in beasts and birds, so also is he represented in this bread or cakes. For

The meat-offering.

[5 cibarium, Lat.]

he is the bread of life, and hath sundry fashions of infirmity and glory. In Christ thou shalt not find any leaven, that is, sin, uncharitableness, hypocrisy, or pride. There is in Christ no sweetness, nor honey-like taste, of worldly or wicked pleasures. But salt thou mayest find in him, a well seasoned temperature altogether heavenly, and most absolute wisdom. Because of Christ, and for his sake, all things of ours are acceptable unto God; for Christ his sake our prayers are heard of God the Father: upon Christ, therefore, there is a sweet-smelling frankincense in the nose of God the Father[1]. And in these ceremonies are also shadowed the manner and matter of our sacrifices; to wit, that they should be without hypocrisy, bitterness, hatred, envy, and fleshly pleasure, and should be seasoned with godly and continual prayers.

The drink-offerings. With the meat-offerings we may place the drink-offerings also[2]. For in those sacrifices wine was poured out unto the Lord, as is evident in the twenty-ninth of Exodus, the twenty-third of Leviticus, and the twenty-eighth chapter of the book of Numbers. Now Christ is our wine, our drink, and joy unto eternal life. He poureth himself into the minds of the godly, that he may fill them with joy, and live in them and they in him. And therefore did he consecrate in wine the memory of his blood that was shed for us to the remission of our sins.

With these meat-offerings may be joined the sacrifices of the first-fruits, of the first-begotten, and of the tenths: touching all which there is much to be read in divers places of the law; as in the thirteenth and twenty-third of Exodus, in the eighteenth of Deuteronomy, and the eighteenth of the book of Numbers. Now Christ is the first-begotten and the first-fruits of all the faithful, for whose worthiness and merit we are all spared, and by whom we, being sanctified, are made the sons and[3] heirs of God. To him, as to our Maker and Redeemer, we owe, as tenths, our very souls, and whatsoever else is dear unto (and good in) us. Moreover, it is a point of thankfulness frankly to bestow upon God part of our earthly riches, which we have at his hands, to the main-

[1 The Latin is only, Est ergo thus super Christo.]
[2 נֶסֶךְ.]
[3 adeoque et, Lat.; and so also.]

tenance of his true worship, and the relief of all that be in poverty.

The third kind of sacrifice is that which is offered for sin, and is therefore called *Hattah*[4], a cleansing[5], or *Ascham*[6], a sacrifice for sin. We in one word may call it a cleansing sacrifice[7]. For it was offered for sin committed unwittingly or by ignorance; (which by the degrees of the sinners were divided into four sorts ; as, if the chief priest did sin, if the whole church did sin, if the prince did sin, or if some man of the meaner sort did sin :) or else they did offer it for sin committed willingly, or of a set purpose, being yet a mean or excusable[8] sin; or else for a great and heinous crime, which ignorance could by no means excuse. The ceremony used in this sacrifice is very ample and large, so that I mean not presently once to touch it[9]. It is most exquisitely set down in the fourth, fifth, sixth, and seventh chapters of Leviticus. Neither is it to be doubted but that Christ was laid before their eyes, as well in that sacrifice, as in all their other oblations. For Christ is the end of the law, (and the mark whereto the ceremonial laws did tend[10].) And Esay in the fifty-third chapter of his prophecy saith: "Whereas he never did unrighteousness, nor any deceitfulness was found in his mouth ; yet hath it pleased the Lord to smite him with infirmity ; that when he had made his soul an offering for sin[11]," (for here is put אָשָׁם *Ascham*,) "he might see seed, and might prolong his days, and that the advice of the Lord might prosper in his hand." To this belongeth that whole disputation of the apostle Paul in his Epistle to the Hebrews, wherein he sheweth that Christ is the true sacrifice for sin, that cleanseth all the church and the sins thereof[12]. In this ceremony were shadowed[13] the disposition[14] of sins[13], the passions of Christ, and the power and strength of death[15].

The sin-offering.

Isai. liii.

[4 חַטָּאת.]   [5 piaculare, Lat.]

[6 אָשָׁם.]   [7 sacrificium expiatorium, Lat.]

[8 *mediocri* is Bullinger's one word here.]

[9 adeo ut in præsenti per compendium commemorare non placeat, Lat.]

[10 This sentence between brackets is an addition of the translator's.]

[11 hostiam delicti, vel victimam pro culpa, Lat.]

[12 et peccata omnia, Lat.]   [13 partim, Lat. omitted; partly.]

[14 ingenia, Lat.]   [15 passionis Christi et mortis virtus, Lat.]

13

The yearly sacrifice.

Now these many and sundry sacrifices, appointed for sins, were kept uncertainly[1], because they were wont to be offered of them that sinned at that very time when they did commit the sin : but the certain, the yearly, and universal sacrifice was that which is at large described in the sixteenth of Leviticus, and may be referred in this place to the number of cleansing sacrifices. For in the feast of atonement, upon the tenth day of the seventh month every year, was solemnized the sacrifice of cleansing, or atonement, for all the sins universally of all the people. The manner of this general sacrifice I will not over-busily at this time describe, since it is as clearly as the light set down in that place of Leviticus which even now I cited; and since I, in expounding the mystery thereof, do mean to shew, and make plain, so many shadows in it as are needful to be marked. For I will say somewhat touching the meaning and mystery thereof.

In that most pleasant glass was figured the whole passion, and effect of the passion, of Jesus Christ, our Lord and Saviour ; which by that sacrifice was every year laid before the eyes and renewed to the minds of all the faithful church of God. For this manner of representing our redemption and salvation did please God, by sacraments, rather than by pictures, colours, or by stage-plays; which are at this day greatly set by, although scarce godly, by no small number of trifling and fantastical heads[2].

Now mark, that the high priest only did all that was to be done in this solemn sacrifice; save only that two ministers were joined unto him, the one to lead away the scape-goat, and the other to carry out of the host the bullock and he-goat that was to be offered. Yea, charge is very precisely given, that no man should join himself to the high priest, when he entereth into the tabernacle, and maketh an atonement for the sins of the people. " Let no man," saith the Lord, " be in the tabernacle of appointment, when he goeth in to make sacrifice in the sanctuary, until he do come out again." For no man must be joined to Christ in finishing the work of our salvation and redemption. For he alone is

[Lev. xvi. 17.]

[1 conceptiva erant, Lat.]
[2 Viz. the Miracle Plays, or Mysteries—the Easter representations of our Lord's crucifixion and resurrection, &c. Brand's Pop. Antiq. Vol. I.]

the Saviour; he alone hath trode the press, and he alone was crucified for us.   The patriarchs, prophets, apostles, martyrs, and all other creatures, are utterly excluded from having any thanks for our redemption and salvation.   Christ alone remaineth the Saviour and Redeemer of the world.   To attribute our salvation to creatures, to our own works and our own merits, is to admit creatures with the high priest into the tabernacle, and to incur the indignation, that is, the terrible curse, of the almighty, true, and everliving God. For by the Jewish high priest is prefigured to us Christ our Saviour, who, as the apostle Paul saith, hath a priesthood, which by succession cannot go from him to any other[3].

Now Aaron did take a bullock for a sin-offering, and a ram for a burnt-offering, of his own; and of the people he took two he-goats.   Therefore Christ our Lord, the true and only priest of his church, did offer for us the thing that he took of us, to wit, the substance of our flesh.   There is added also, that Aaron, (by which name we understand every one that was the high priest among the people of God), when he went about to sacrifice, did clothe himself with the usual and common garments of the other priests (I mean, such as the other priests were wont to wear), saving only that they were holy and without spot.   For, although Christ the Son of God did take our nature upon him, and did become like unto us, being clad, as it were, in the usual garment of us men; yet, notwithstanding, his fleshly garment (I mean, his body that was like to ours) was altogether free from corruption[4], and clean without all spots of sin.

Aaron did first of all kill a steer for himself and his family: whereby he declared that he was not the very and true high priest, but the type of him that was the true priest. For Paul saith: "Our high priest had no need, as those high [Heb. vii. 26, 27.] priests had, first to offer sacrifices for their own sins, and then for the sins of the people.   For he did that once, when he offered up himself."   Afterwards Aaron drew lots at the door of the tabernacle, to try betwixt the two goats, which should be slain for the sacrifice, and which should be sent away as

[3 Heb. viii. 24, "hath an unchangeable priesthood;" ἀπαράβατον ἔχει τὴν ἱερωσύνην, one that cannot pass on to a successor. See Schleusner. P.]

[4 his fleshly—to ours, not in Lat.; he is altogether, &c.]

the scape-goat into the desert. The two goats do signify Christ our Lord, very God and very man, in two natures unseparated. He is slain, and dieth[1] in his humanity; but is not slain nor dieth in his divinity. Yet he, being one and the same Christ, unseparated, is the Saviour of the world, and doth work the redemption of us mortal men. So in the two goats was a mystery hidden. And for because, as Solomon saith, the lots are guided by the Lord's will, it was not without the especial will of the Father that the Son was sacrificed, and killed on the cross.

[Prov. xvi. 33.]

Moreover, the high priest did take the blood, first of the bullock, then of the slain goat, and a censer in his hand, and went within the veil, where with the incense he did make a cloud of smoke before the mercy-seat, and with his finger did sprinkle the blood seven times toward the mercy-seat. All which the apostle Paul expounding in the ninth to the Hebrews saith, that "Christ entered not into the tabernacle made with hands, but into the very heavens; not with the blood of a bullock, or a goat, but with his own blood, and found for us a perpetual cleansing and remission of our sins." For "he is our propitiation; not for our sins only, but also for the sins of all the world." And hereunto did the apostles allude, as often as they called Christ our propitiation; as St Paul in the third to the Romans, and St John in the second and fourth chapter of his first epistle. Now the seven times sprinkling of the blood betokened the full perfection, or perfect fulness, of the cleansing. We have need also to be sprinkled with the finger, not of man, but of Christ[2] Jesus, our Lord and Saviour, whose finger is the Holy Ghost, by whom our cleansing doth come upon us. To the sprinkling of the blood is also added sweet-smelling incense[3]: for, as the apostle testifieth, Christ, our high priest, did offer prayers for us with tears, and was heard in that which he feared[4]. Whereupon, by the cloud of smoke, that is, by the great quantity of smoke, was noted the great efficacy of earnest prayers.

[1 John ii. 2.]

When that was done, the high priest went again into the

[1 secundum id quod mori potuit, Lat.]
[2 summi nostri Pontificis, Lat.; our High-priest.]
[3 incensum aromaticum contusum, Lat.; of beaten, pounded, aromatics.]
[4 Heb. v. 7, pro reverentia, Lat.; for his piety. Auth. Ver. marg.]

sanctum, and set the blood upon the golden altar of incense. For in the work of our redemption both innocent blood and earnest prayer for us must be joined together. Out of the *sanctum* again he came to the altar of burnt-offerings, which stood in the court (which was called *atrium*), and there he gave the other goat to a convenient man to be carried away into the wilderness: but in the delivering of the goat he used a precise manner and singular ceremony. For the high priest laid both his hands upon the goat, and over his head did confess the sins of the people, who also did themselves confess their sins, following the priest, clause by clause, in all the confession[5] which he rehearsed: and then, so soon as all the sins were laid upon the head of the goat, he was sent away, that by that means he might carry the sins of all the people[6] into the desert. From this ceremony did the Gentiles undoubtedly borrow their kind of cleansings or purgings of the people, called in Greek καθάρματα[7], and in Latin *piamina*. For their manner was, in extreme perils, that one should give himself for all the rest, whom they took, and did either kill and burn upon the altar, or cast into the water; praying therewithal, that all their evil luck might go with him, and that the gods being pacified with the death of him[8] might again be favourable to all the rest. But the wretches erred as far as heaven is wide: for Christ the Son of God was made sin for us, that is, he was made a sacrifice for sin, yea, he became a curse for us, that we by him might receive a blessing. For to this had the prophet Esay an eye, when he said: "We all went astray like sheep; every one turned after his own way: but the Lord hath thrown down upon him[9] all our sins." Again: "He was wounded for our offences, and smitten for our wickedness." And again: "The pains of our punishment were laid upon him, and he bare our griefs[10]."

[5 See Lightfoot's Temple Service, chap. 15. Works, Vol. i. p. 963. Lond. 1684. See above, p. 169, note 8.]

[6 totius ecclesiæ, Lat.]

[7 καθάρματα—homines ignobiles et scelerati, qui publice alebantur et grassante peste aliove malo graviore immolabantur ad expiandum urbem aut civitatem Deorumque iram avertendam. Schleusner, in voc.]

[8 unius, Lat.]

[9 effecit in illum incurrere, Lat.]

[10 Isai. liii. 6, 8, 5. For the payne of oure punyshmēt shal be layde upō him. Coverdale, 1535. But this last quotation in the Latin

Now the goat did carry the sins into the desert, not that the sins should not be, but that they should not be any more imputed unto them. For in the church verily there is sin in the saints, but it is not imputed unto them. Sin is imputed to all them that are without the church, in the desolate wilderness. The convenient man, that should carry away the scape-goat, can be none other than Christ himself, who in the days of his flesh did observe the convenient time and fit occasion, repeating oftentimes that his hour was not yet come; but at the last, when time convenient was come for him to die, he said that then his hour was come. And by dying he carried away conveniently the scape-goat, I mean[1], the sin of all the world.

When this also was thus accomplished, the high priest did again wash himself; and, putting off the common garments of the inferior priests, did again put on his high priest's attire. Now this often and manifold washing in the holy ceremony is a shadow, or type, of the most absolute remission of sins; even as also the changing of a garment is a sign or figure of glorification; as is at the full to be seen in the third chapter of Zachary's prophecy. And Christ, being glorified, did enter into heaven, there to appear in the sight of God, the only and effectual sacrifice for us mortal men. Therefore did Aaron sacrifice a ram for a burnt-offering : for Christ is the sacrifice which endureth always, and purgeth all the faithful.

Moreover, Aaron sent the bullock and the other goat unto the holy place without the host, that there they might be burned. Which thing Paul expoundeth thus, and saith : "The bodies of those beasts, whose blood is brought into the holy place by the high priest for sin, was burnt without the tents : therefore Jesus also, that he might sanctify the people with his blood, did suffer without the gate." Heb. xiii.

And although in this which I have hitherto alleged I have by fits[2] declared the end and fruit of this ceremony, yet will I not think it much here again particularly to repeat the same again ; since I see that the Holy Ghost in the scripture doth, as it were, take pains very busily to beat the same into our heads.

is of verse 4 : Vere languores nostros ipse tulit, et dolores nostros ipse portavit.]

[1 adeoque, Lat.]   [2 sparsim, Lat.]

The end of all this stir and solemnity is[3], that all the sins, I say, all the sins of God's universal church, are by the one and only sacrifice, once only offered, most perfectly blotted out[4] and absolutely purged. Let us, therefore, hear the very words of the Holy Ghost, which speaketh in the scripture most plainly and evidently, saying: First, "And the high [Lev. xvi. 21 priest shall confess over the goat all the iniquities of the ^{22, 30, 34.]} children of Israel, and all their trespasses and all their sins." Secondly, "And the goat shall bear upon him all their misdeeds into the desert." Thirdly, "The same day shall the priest make an atonement for you, to cleanse you, that you may be clean from all your sins before the Lord." Fourthly, "And let this be an everlasting ordinance unto you, to cleanse the children of Israel from all their sins once every year." But who is so very a sot or dull head as to think, that all the sins of the people are washed away with the blood of beasts? "If," saith the apostle, "they had once fully cleansed sins, then [Heb. x. would they have ceased to offer any more." By this cere- ^{1, 2.]} mony, therefore, the mystery of Christ to come was beaten into all men's brains, and once every year laid forth to the eyes of all men to behold. For of this ceremony did Zachary borrow his prophecy of Christ, in his third chapter, where Zech. iii. he saith: "Behold, I bring forth the Branch, my servant. For, lo, the stone that I lay before Josua, upon one stone shall be seven eyes: behold, I will cut the graving thereof, saith the Lord of hosts, and I will take away the sin of this land in one day." The Lord doth promise the Messiah, which was prefigured by the priests, and especially by[5] the high priest Josua. Christ is the stone, upon which the eyes of all men are stedfastly fixed, as upon their only Saviour. He is digged in, and cut, in his passion; and by suffering and dying once he purgeth the sins of all the earth.

Of this ceremony, and of this place of scripture, did Paul, the holy apostle of Christ, borrow his whole discourse almost in his epistle to the Hebrews, touching the sacrifice of Christ once offered for all the sins of the whole world: in which discourse he doth very often repeat out of the law the word "once," and that with a certain emphatical vehemency.

[3 omnium, Lat.; stir and solemnity, not in Lat.]
[4 e medio sublata, Lat.]
[5 of, ed. 1587.]

The only sacrifice of Christ is sufficient for all the world.

Now, to appoint other priests, to institute another time, and to ordain another manner of sacrifice, is utterly to kick at, and tread under foot, this heavenly and most evident truth. But this doctrine of the only sacrifice of Christ is the true, ancient, sound, unreproveable, and everlasting doctrine: by which all they are saved that are saved, and by which all they have been saved, that have been saved since the beginning of the world. The enemies or adversaries of this doctrine Paul, the apostle of Christ and the Gentiles, (whose skill in the law was inferior to no man's,) doth call

[1 Cor. xvi. 22; 2 Cor. xi. 3, 13; Gal. i. 8, 9; iii. 1, 3; v. 4; Eph. iv. 14; Phil. iii. 2.]

fools, mad, unconstant, light-headed, carried with every puff of wind, wicked, apostates, which have revolted from Christ, liars, false prophets, false apostles, deceivers, schismatics, dogs, enchanters, witches, detestable, and cursed. Therefore, if an angel from heaven teach us any otherwise, let him be to us accursed.

Yet by the way this must not be concealed, that in that yearly sacrifice it was required and looked for at men's hands, first, that they should confess their sins; then, that they should be sorry in their minds, in good earnest and indeed, for their sins committed; and lastly, that they should keep sabbath,—I do not mean an idle resting from honest business, but a quietness in the faith of Christ and a ceasing from ill deeds. Whosoever doth so prepare himself in the feast of atonement, that is, in the time of the preaching of the grace of God through Christ, he is without doubt throughly cleansed by that only sacrifice of Christ Jesus: of which I have hitherto not without good cause spoken so largely as you perceive that I have. For this one place doth give a wonderful light both to the understanding of many places in the scriptures, and also of the mystery of our redemption, and of Christ our Redeemer, so plainly, that no other place[1] doth so clearly expound, set forth, and lay them open before our eyes to be seen and looked on: it doth also teach us to understand the words of Christ our Lord in the

[John v. 45, 46.]

gospel of St John, where he saith, "There is one which accuseth you, even Moses, in whom ye hope: for had ye believed Moses, ye would then have believed me; for he wrote of me."

This water was also called the water of

Now with the sacrifice of atonement and the other cleansing sacrifices we do advisedly number the sacrifice of the red

[1 vix alius, Lat.; scarce any other.]

cow; I mean, of the cleansing, or of the cleansing or holy *separation, and the water* water, that was ordained against all sorts of defilings and *of expiation; because they,* uncleannesses. For there were sundry kinds of uncleannesses; *upon whom it was sprin-* of which there is a large discourse to be seen in Moses his law: *kled, were separated for* and by them is laid before us the type of our corrupt nature *a time from the rest of* and continual sins. There is fully described, in the nineteenth *the people, till by it* chapter of the book of Numbers, first the very ceremony and *they were cleansed.* sacred rite; then is declared the manner how to make the holy cleansing water against all defilings; lastly is added the use and effect of that holy water.

　　There was brought to Eleazar the priest a red cow with- *The sacrifice of the red* out spot, which never felt the yoke, and that was out of *cow.* hand carried out and slain without the host. Part of the blood was saved by the priest, and with his finger he sprinkled it seven times towards the tabernacle of appointment: but the whole cow he burnt with fire, so that no part of it was left; and into the fire he cast cedar-wood, hyssop, and a scarlet lace. This being once done, the priest did wash himself in water, and in his stead came another that was clean[2], who, gathering the ashes, did lay them up in a clean place. Therefore, so often as need required, they did put off those ashes into an earthen vessel, into which they poured running water[3]; and in that sort was the holy cleansing water always prepared, which they did sprinkle with a sprinkler made of hyssop upon all such as were defiled. This was the manner and ceremony of the cleansing, the use and end whereof doth immediately follow.

　　The apostle Paul doth testify, that the circumstances of this ceremony did lay before us a most evident type of Jesus Christ: for in the ninth chapter to the Hebrews he saith: "If the ashes of a young cow, sprinkled, doth sanctify them *Heb. ix.* that are partakers of it to the purifying of the flesh, how much more the blood of Christ!" Therefore both the priest and the cow did bear the type of Christ. The female kind in the cow doth note the infirmity of man's nature; the red colour doth admonish us of the Lord his blood, by which we are washed from our uncleanness. There was no spot to be found in Christ; for he was the Holy of holies, and altogether free from and without all sin. He was not brought to death by the yoke of necessity ; for he offered himself unto it of

[2 vir mundus, Lat.]　　　　　　[3 aqua viva, Lat.]

his own free will: yea, he offered himself willingly to go to
his death, and that too without the host or walls of the
city, in the mount of Calvary: which thing the apostle Paul
doth touch in the thirteenth to the Hebrews. Christ, both
God and man, was wholly offered in body and soul: whose
blood is wholesome[1] for us, if by the Holy Ghost it be
sprinkled in our hearts. The faithful also must die with
Christ; they must be humbled, and burn in love to God-ward
as red as scarlet[2]: and that was the meaning of the cedar-
wood, the hyssop, and the scarlet lace, which were cast into
the fire.

Moreover, the ashes which came of the sacrifice were
gathered up and preserved to purify and cleanse withal.
Those ashes were nothing else but the type or figure of the
effect of Christ his death or sacrifice; I mean, the very cleansing and remission of our sins. For therefore did blood and
water gush abundantly out of the pierced side of Christ[3], that
we might learn that out of the death of Christ doth flow our
cleansing and our life: for in blood life doth consist, and
water purgeth and is a sign of cleansing. The ashes were
gathered by a man that was clean, who nevertheless was
made, and did remain, unclean until the evening. Finally,
the water was sprinkled with a sprinkler made of hyssop upon
the defiled, to the end that thereby he might be sanctified or
purged. The water was kept in an holy place: for marga-
rites[4], and that which is holy, ought not to be cast to dogs
and filthy swine. The Lord also doth require preachers to
teach the effect of Christ his passion, and in the contemptible
and lowly[5] preaching of the gospel to lay before the world
our redemption and sanctification in the death and blood of
Christ: he doth require, I say, such holy teachers as are
themselves faithful and cleansed in the blood of Christ. And
yet those teachers, with the whole church beside, do even till

[1 salutaris, Lat.]

[2 ardere amore divino et extolli, Lat. 'As red as scarlet,' is the
translator's addition.]

[3 morientis et jam extincti Christi, Lat.; of Christ, when dying,
and now already dead.]

[4 margaritæ, Lat.; pearls, Matth. vii. 6.]

[5 coram mundo, Lat.; as the world esteems it. The translator
missed the meaning of these words, when he rendered them, "to lay
before the world." Bullinger had in his mind 1 Cor. i. 20—29.]

the evening, I mean, the ending of their lives, pray still, "Forgive us our trespasses." For the Lord himself said; "He that is washed is clean, and hath no need but to wash his feet only." To this do appertain the often washings used in this ceremony, which signify that by the grace of God all sins are purged; that the saints have always an holy care to watch against the assaults of sin; and that those sins are cleansed none other ways but by the water of Christ his grace. Lastly, it is most often and earnestly repeated in the law, that they all remain unclean, how many soever, being once defiled, are not again cleansed with the holy water of separation. For the Lord said to Peter, "Unless I wash thee, thou shalt have no part with me." [John xiii. 10.] [John xiii. 8.]

My meaning is not to run through every particular point of this ceremony, but to touch the especial matters only. Therefore now I proceed to that which remaineth.

To these cleansing sacrifices may also be added the sacrifices whereby the bodily defilings, which were figures of the defilings of sin, were purified and cleansed: of which sort were the defilings of the seed, the eating and touching of unclean creatures, the leprosy, and of the woman in child-bed: all which Moses doth largely handle from the twelfth of Leviticus unto the fifteenth of the same. And in all this there is nothing else prefigured to the church of God but our natural corruption and original wickedness, with the free cleansing of the same by the grace of God in the blood of Christ our Saviour. *Sacrifices for the defilings of the body.*

With these we may also number the sacrifice of jealousy; which is thoroughly treated of in the fifth chapter of Numbers: although the manner and order thereof seemeth rather to belong unto the judicial laws of God. *The sacrifice of jealousy.*

The fourth kind of sacrifices was the sacrifice of thanksgiving[6], which they called *schelamim*, or *scholomim*[7], the sacrifice of health, or the peace-offering: for it was offered to give thanks withal, to wit, either for the recovery of health, or for felicity and prosperity; I mean, when they had received some good turn at the hands of God, or else by his aid had escaped the brunt of some mishap or evil fortune. In this sacrifice they used a beast either of the herd or of the *The sacrifice of thanksgiving.*

[6 sacrificium eucharistiæ, gratiarum actionis, vel gratulatorium, Lat.]

[7 שְׁלָמִים.]

fold: it was not lawful to offer birds; for it was done either
with a bullock or an heifer, with a male or a female lamb, or
with an he or she-goat. It was slain before the *atrium:* the
hide or skin thereof was the priest's fee. The blood was
sprinkled about the altar. The kidneys, the caul of the liver,
the rump of the lamb, and all the fat, was burnt upon the
altar of burnt-offerings. The right shoulder was heaved, the
breast was waved toward the ends of the world[1]. (For

Thruma and
thnupha. *thruma* and *thnupha*[2], that is, the heaving and waving, were
not kinds of sacrifices, but ceremonies only, which the priests
did use in making their sacrifices and oblations. By the
heaving was signified, that Christ should be heaved or lifted
up, and that he, being once lifted up, should draw all men
unto him. The waving of the breast toward every part of the
world was a token, that the preaching of Christ should be
spread in every corner of the world.) The breast and the
shoulder were both the priest's portion, together with the jaw-
bone and the paunch or belly. The rest of the flesh returned
to him that made the oblation, and was eaten by him in an
holy banquet. The remnant of ceremonies belonging to this

[Lev. vii.
11—13.] sacrifice are to be found in the third chapter of Leviticus.
For if it were *thoda*[3], a confession, a praise, or a protestation,
then was added to the sacrifice a cake of pure wheat flour and
salt steeped in oil, or sodden cracknels, or bread baken in
pans: part whereof was heaved, and fell to the priest's share;
the rest returned to the offerer, even as also leavened bread
was allowed to be eaten in the banquet.

Now in this kind of sacrifice also Christ was preached,
with the effect and power of his death and passion; and in it
was shewed the whole manner and order of giving thanks to
God for his good benefits. There are sundry sorts of benefits.
If a man received a good turn, if an ill turn had not befallen
him, if he had recovered his health or had escaped some
misfortune, he offered a sacrifice to the Lord. There are
also other ancient benefits common to all men[4]; as, that God

[1 in cardines mundi, Lat.]

[2 תְּרוּמָה, a *heave-offering.* תְּנוּפָה, *waving, shaking* of sacrifices
before Jehovah, a particular rite in offering. Gesenius, Heb. and Eng.
Lex. in voc.]

[3 תּוֹדָה, Heb. confession, praise.]

[4 common to all men, not in Lat.]

hath made the world and all that is therein; and that through Christ he hath redeemed all the faithful: there are daily benefits; yea finally, all things are full of God's good benefits. For all which benefits we must offer our sacrifice to God alone, and not to any creatures which he hath made: yea, we must offer to him with all our hearts; all our affections must be hallowed to the Lord. For out of the beasts which were sacrificed to the Lord for thanksgiving, those parts were chosen and given to the Lord in which the especial power of life consisteth. For in the kidneys is the power of generation; in the blood the vital spirit; in the liver the spring of all the blood, &c. Now we must give thanks by a sacrifice, that is, by Christ, for[5] we are saved for Christ his sake; and all good things are bestowed on us by God, not for our own sakes, nor for any creatures' sakes, but for Christ his sake, our only Saviour and Redeemer. To them which offered was allowed a sober and merry banquet, because the felicity of those that are not unthankful is for the most part augmented two-fold double. And the knowledge of Christ is a delicate banquet and a continual feast.

With the sacrifices of thanksgiving those offerings do much agree which are called vows and free-will-offerings[6]. The free-will-offering was that which proceeded of mere good will and devotion of the mind, without necessity or compulsion of any law or ordinance; as when a servant giveth to his master the thing that he oweth him not, for a declaration only of the good will that he beareth unto him. But herein the free-will-offerings do differ from the sacrifice of thanksgiving; because in the sacrifice of thanksgiving charge was given, that whatsoever was left, which was not spent the first day, should not be eaten on the morrow, but be burnt with fire: on the other side, in the free-will-offerings it was lawful for them to eat the remnant upon the second day, and[7] to burn their leavings upon the third day. Now the vowed sacrifices were those which were offered by covenant to the Lord; as for example, a man, being in peril, doth vow to make a sacrifice to God, if he be delivered out of that imminent danger: it falleth out that he is delivered, and he

The free-will-offering.

[5 porro, Lat.; further.]

[6 נֶדֶר, a vow, נְדָבָה, a voluntary offering.]

[7 jubebantur, Lat.; they were commanded.]

for his delivery doth offer up the sacrifice : the thing that
is so offered is called a vowed sacrifice. The ceremonies of
the twain[1] did wholly agree with the sacrifice of thanksgiving.
More of them is to be seen in the seventh chapter of Leviticus.

The meaning of these sacrifices was, that all good benefits
are bestowed upon us for Christ his sake; and[2] with those
benefits we receive the very good will which we have to
serve the Lord.

Thus much have I hitherto said touching the sacrifices
of the people of God : not that I have touched every point,
but so many only as are of most importance. In these
sacrifices, as in a lively action, were set forth Christ our
Lord, his passion, and the effectual merit of his death : so
that we may call the holy actions of the sacrifices sermons
upon the passion of Christ, and instructions[3] of our redemption
by our Lord and Saviour.

Of vows. Now, for because we have already spoken hitherto of
vowed sacrifices, we must here consequently borrow leave,
for a digression, to say somewhat of their usual vows. For
vows belong to the Jewish ceremonies. Of the making, performing, and redeeming of vows there is a large discourse
in the law of God, but especially in the twenty-seventh of
Leviticus. To vow is to promise any thing[4] with an oath
solemnly, either for our own or another's welfare. And
therefore a vow was an action referred to God alone, and
that too in an holy and lawful thing. But in vows there
was a difference; because vowed things were divided into
four kinds : for sometimes they vowed men, sometimes
they vowed other living things, sometimes houses, and sometimes lands or other immoveable substance[5]. Again, there
was a difference in men according to their ages, and after[6]
their ages they might be redeemed. For clean living creatures there was no redemption permitted at all. It was
free either to leave their houses to the use of the ministery,
or else to redeem them with such a sum as the priest should

[1 of the twain, not in Lat.]
[2 atque adeo, Lat.; and so too.]
[3 catecheses, Lat.]   [4 Deo, Lat.; unto God.]
[5 res inanimes, Lat.; lifeless things.]
[6 juxta, Lat.; according to.]

value them at[7]. In lands, redemption was sometimes admitted, and sometimes not admitted. And in the thirtieth chapter of the book of Numbers there is a precise commandment given touching the votaries, when their vows are of force, and when of small effect; where it is diligently beaten into their heads, that vows lawfully made to God are not to be called back again, but straitly kept and throughly performed. Rash or unlawful vows the Lord did never like of nor receive.

Of the lawful vows, and such as are made to the true and only God, the prophet speaketh, where he saith, "Make vows, and pay them." We read not that any of the godly [Ps. lxxvi. 11.] sort did make any vows to any saints or any other creatures; neither that they vowed any thing that was not in their power to vow, nor that which was contrary to the will of God to whom they vowed it, nor that which was to their neighbour's hinderance, nor the thing that had not in it some evident commodity. And verily, these kinds of vows were for none other cause permitted to the Israelites till the time of amendment, but that they should remain in the worship of one true God, and not make their vows to any other strange God.

To the treatise of vows belongeth the discipline and order of the Nazarites; of which there is a large discourse in the sixth chapter of the book of Numbers. The Nazarites were those who, because they would the more freely, without let, attend upon God's service, or else because they had heretofore lived too licentiously, did of their own accord and will take upon them a more strict and severe trade of life than the common people used, and kept it for a discipline, to make other men to follow their example of virtue and honest living. Whereupon it cometh to pass, that some do take the Nazarites to have their name of separation, because *Nazir* among the Hebrews signifieth a separation; and that the Nazarites, separating themselves from the common trade of life that other men did lead, did give themselves to a peculiar form of living for God and godliness' sake. That severe and strict discipline did continue in some by the length of all their lifetime, as in Samson and Samuel. [Jud. xiii. 7; I Sam. i. 11.]

Moreover, such as did wholly give themselves to the

The discipline of the Nazarites.

[7 æstimatione æqua, Lat.; fair valuation.]

[Amos ii. 11;
Lam. iv. 7.] study of the scriptures were, by the prophets Amos and Jeremy, because of their most temperate life (which is required of students), and because they were wholly dedicated to the ministry of God, called Nazarites. Sometimes also it did endure but for the space of certain days or months. These Nazarites did abstain, according to the commandment of the law, from certain things, from which they were not barred by any other law, and which were not unlawful for other men to use which were without the necessity of that vow. First of all they abstained from wine, from all things that the vine brought forth, and whatsoever else did make men drunken. But it is manifest, that as wine is the good creature of God, so no drink is forbidden by the law. Yet for because the Nazarites were consecrated to the Lord, and sanctified by a certain peculiar kind of living; and for because wine is the means that leadeth to drunkenness, which is the gulf of all sin and filthiness; therefore did the Nazarites not without a cause abstain from wine. They did also take heed of idleness, the mother of mischief, and utterly despised all worldly pleasures. Furthermore, so long as the time of their vow endured, they did not clip their hair, but let their locks grow out a length. And thereupon, as some do think, they took their names, and were called Nazarites: for insomuch as *Nazer* signifieth hair, they suppose that they were called Nazarites, as who should say, long-locked or shaggy-haired people[1]. But the apostle Paul biddeth the woman to pray, or to come into the congregation to hear a sermon, with her head covered, for none other cause, but for that she is not in her own power, but subject to another, that is, to her husband. And therefore the Nazarites did let their hair grow, because by the vow which they had made to God they were no longer in their own power, but were wholly yielded into the power of God. And the head, which is the tower of the body and the most excellent part thereof, being covered[2] with a bush of hair, was a token that the whole man was by vow given to the Lord, to whom alone he ought to have an eye, and upon whom alone he ought wholly to depend. Moreover it

[1] נֶזֶר, *consecration.* Hence meton. *the consecrated head* (of a Nazarite);—and even (the primary idea being neglected), *the long, unshorn hair* (of a woman). Genesius, Heb. and Eng. Lex. in voc.]

[2] veluti obvelata, Lat. ; covered as with a veil.]

was required at the hands of the Nazarite, that he should not defile himself with the contagious company of wicked and naughty persons. Whereunto also belongeth the commandment, which charged the Nazarite not to be present at the death or burial of his parents, or children, or wife, or brethren, or sisters. For he ought to settle the eyes of his mind upon God alone, and in comparison of him to set light by and loathe the things which were most dear and precious unto him. But if it so fell out, that[3] at unawares he were defiled by seeing of a dead body[4], he was not therefore acquitted of his vow, as one whose former life had been sufficient for the performance of the same : for he was commanded to sanctify himself the seventh day, and then to undertake the keeping of his vow again.

By all this we may plainly perceive what and how great the sin of Samson was, who was a Nazarite to the Lord. For because he did not only lurk in the brothel-house with the harlot, but did also bewray the secret of God unto her, and cast behind him the covenant made with God, whereof his hair was a sure testimony ; therefore did the Lord forsake him, and that wonderful strength which he had from heaven was clean taken from him. For the strength of Samson lay not in his hair, so that by the cutting off his hair his strength was cut away also ; but it lay in the Spirit of the Lord, which was given him from God above. And therefore do we find this sentence so often in the scripture, "And the Spirit of the Lord came upon Samson." Therefore when the Spirit of God departed, his strength departed also : but it departed from him, when he, being wholly joined unto the harlot, was made one soul with her, and did prefer her before God and his commandment, so that he suffered his hair to be polled, and utterly revolted from the ordinance of the Lord : for by that means did the Spirit of God forsake him. Whereupon immediately after he was brought into the hands of his enemies the Philistines ; where when he was miserably vexed, and when he heard the name of God evil spoken of[5] and blasphemed because of his captivity, he repented heartily, and

[marginal notes:] Samson a Nazarite to the Lord ; how greatly he sinned.

[Judg. xiii. 25 ; xiv. 6, 19; xv. 14.]

[3 vel, Lat. ; even at.]
[4 super mortuo, Lat. ; by a dead body. *Seeing of,* not in Lat.]
[5 Rather, and when on his account the name of God (male audiret, Lat.) was evil spoken of.]

called upon the name of the Lord: whereby it came to pass, that, when his hair grew forth again, his strength returned ; that is, the Spirit of the Lord came upon him again, being brought unto him, not by the growing of his hairs, but by his repentance and earnest calling upon the Lord. Neither did Samson desire to revenge his own private injury so much as to suppress the blasphemous mouths, and to deliver the people of God[1] from fear and slavery. The strength of God, therefore, returned again, wherewith he bending the pillars of the theatre was himself slain with the fall of the palace, and at his death slew many mo than he had killed in all his life time before.

But now we return again to the purpose, to add the other ceremonies that do belong to the exposition of the vow of the Nazarites.

When the time was expired, therefore, which the Nazarite had taken upon him for to observe, he came to the tabernacle of the Lord, and offered the sacrifices that are prescribed in the law: whereby he testified that he was a sinner, and plainly confessed that all goodness and virtue[2], that was to be found in him, was given and bestowed from God above. And therefore he polled his head, and cast his hair into the fire[3], wherein the peace-offering was a burning. At last, when all this was in this manner accomplished, it was lawful for the Nazarite, as one loosed of his bonds, to return unto his old life again. Thus much hitherto touching the discipline of the Nazarites.

Of the clean and unclean creatures. Now touching the clean and unclean, there is a long discourse in the law of Moses. I in my former treatise did lightly touch and pass over some certain things; but now at the last (for here I mean to make an end to speak of ceremonial laws) I will add somewhat touching the choice of meats, I mean, of clean and unclean meats.

God, verily, in the beginning created all things; and he so created them, that, as the Creator is good, even so all his creatures even at this day are good also: neither doth he gainsay himself now, when he forbiddeth certain meats, as

[1 ad quos vocatus fuerat, Lat. omitted; unto whom he had been called.]

[2 id est, si quid virtutis, Lat.; that is, whatever virtue.]

[3 craticulam, Lat.; gridiron.]

though somewhat of itself were unclean. There are other mysteries, that lie hidden under this doctrine of the choice of meats.

The laws, which are given touching meats and victuals, seem to be small and of little value; but it pleased the Lord in a small thing to admonish us what we have to do in a greater, and that even in the smallest things the authority of his Godhead ought to be regarded. For the authority of the law dependeth upon God: God is the lawgiver, and the law is his invention. This suppresseth the malapertness of mortal men, which maketh, undoeth, and every day deviseth new laws and ordinances. Therefore God in these kind of laws doth commend to his people faithful obedience to be shewed unto him: even as, in the beginning, he commanded Adam not to taste of the tree of knowledge of good and evil, requiring thereby faithful obedience to be shewed unto him. Verily, the obedience and faith, which was in the Maccabees, in old Eleazar, and in certain other godly men, that stood against king Antiochus, even to the shedding of their blood and suffering of most bitter death, did please the Lord exceedingly. Other more abstained from swine's flesh, whereby they obtained neither praise nor glory among wicked men[4]. When the word of God saith that a thing is holy, it is holy indeed; and that, because he is holy that commandeth it. When God saith that any thing is unclean, it is unclean indeed, so that to eat any thing against the word of God is to defile the eater. " Ye now," saith the Lord in the Gospel, " are clean because of the word which I said unto you." It is needful, therefore, that we believe the word of God, and that obedience go before faith[5]; and then it cannot be but that the deed or work that is of faith, as Eleazar's was, who would not taste the swine's flesh, must needs be acceptable unto God, with whom whatsoever is not of faith is sin and wickedness.

Moreover, the Lord in[6] these laws of his touching the abstaining from the flesh of certain living creatures had a great respect unto the health and soundness of mortal men's

Margin notes:
Why God forbad the eating of certain meats.

The constant obedience of certain holy men, who abstained from things unclean. [1 Mac. ii. 2; 2 Mac. vi. 18, &c.; vii.]

[John xv. 3.]

[Rom. xiv. 23.]

[4 among wicked men, not in Lat.]

[5 et præcedat obedientia fidei, Lat.; the obedience of faith go before.]

[6 in quibusdam, Lat.; in some of.]

14—2

bodies. For some of those which he forbiddeth to be eaten are by physicians[1] scarcely thought to be wholesome for our bodies. And thereupon the saints do gather this syllogism: If God hath care for the health of our bodies, he is far more careful verily for the preservation of our souls. What may be thought of this, that many nations have tempered[2] themselves from the eating and touching of some living creatures? Therefore, that the people of Israel, who of themselves were sufficiently superstitious and curious enough, should not be their own carvers, and invent such toys as they thought best, God gave them such laws for choice of their meat as did contain hidden mysteries in them, thereby to draw them from their own devices, and to sever them from all other nations; as Moses testifieth in the fourteenth chapter of Deuteronomy, saying: "Thou art an holy people unto the Lord thy God, and the Lord thy God hath chosen thee from among all the nations upon the face of the whole earth, to be a peculiar people unto himself." To St Peter[3], in the Acts of the Apostles, a vision is shewed, wherein by the unclean beasts are meant the Gentiles. Lastly, God would have the nature and disposition of the beasts, that he forbad to be eaten, to be throughly scanned. For in their diet at the table he did by figures lay before their eyes the heavenly philosophy, giving them occasion, even in their meat, to think and speak of the true holiness of the mind, to the end that men should not be filthy, impudent, foul, and unclean. And therefore is this clause so many times repeated, "I the Lord your God am holy;" as if he should say: All these ceremonies tend to this end, that ye may give yourselves to holiness. Wherefore in those figures he taught the godly what to follow, and what to fly from.

[Lev. xix. 2; xx. 7, 8; xxi. 8, &c.]

Now in the law of the clean and unclean he doth first of all put certain generalities; then he descendeth by specialities, and doth in a beadrow[4] reckon up certain particular things in a very natural course and order. The place is at the full set out in the eleventh chapter of Leviticus and the fourteenth of Deuteronomy. Those beasts were allowed

[1 et a medicis, Lat.]
[2 sibi temperarunt, Lat.; have abstained.]
[3 certe, Lat.; without a doubt.]
[4 per catalogum, Lat.]

to be eaten, which cleave the hoof, and chaw the cud. Here are two things set down, in which the duty of a good man is notably contained : for if we will be clean, we must divide the hoof, and also chaw the cud. Our affection is the foot of our minds, which affection must not be followed. We must have discretion in all things to judge betwixt affections. And as in a cleft there be two parts or sides, the right and the left ; so a good man chooseth the good, and flieth from the evil. Chawing of the cud is our judgment. For we must not admit everything which we hear and see, but those things only which we have examined exactly, and found to be contrary neither to God nor to his law.

There are then repeated many living things particularly, which were not lawful to be eaten among the people of the Lord. Those were either four-footed beasts upon the earth, or fishes, or birds, or such as creep upon the ground. Of four-footed beasts four by name we are especially forbidden : the camel, whose long and lofty neck doth teach us, that pride and arrogancy must be eschewed[5]; the coney, or the mountain mouse[6]; for God doth utterly mislike the men that are altogether overwhelmed, like coneys, in the earth, and never lift up their minds unto heaven[7]; the hare, a fearful beast, which doth warn us to shake off all cowardly fearfulness ; even as also the hog doth put us in mind to avoid all uncleanness ; for a hog is the very type and picture of nasty filthiness, and of it doth the byword rise, to call an uncleanly person a beastly swine[8]. And of Circe the fable goeth, that she with her enchantments did turn Ulysses his men into a sort of loathly hogs[9]. Furthermore of fishes, so much was allowed for meat, as was found to have fins and scales upon them : if they lacked either of them, they were forbidden ; as the eel, which though it hath fins yet lacketh it scales, and therefore was not to be eaten. For as the bodies of fishes are ruled with the fins, so must the whole man be governed by hope[10]. The scales are hard and cover the body :

[5 modis omnibus, Lat. ; by all means.]

[6 שָׁפָן, the jerboa. The name is probably derived from the animal's *burrowing*. Lee's Lex. in voc.]

[7 and never—heaven, not in Lat.]

[8 qui et proverbiis locum dedit, is the Lat. of this sentence.]

[9 Hom. Od. Lib. x.]   [10 spe firma, Lat.]

and we, unless we be constant and patient in the Lord's work, are worthy to be abhorred of the Lord our Maker. Of birds those are forbidden, which are the greatest raveners, devourers; which love and live by unclean meats; which fly abroad at owl-light, at midnight, and in the dark; and such as are crafty, unstable, and nothing cheerful[1]. Herein therefore is commended unto us well-doing, abstinence, temperance, simplicity, light, constancy, cheerfulness, soundness and pureness of living. Lastly, of such as creep by the ground no small number are noted: for men altogether wrapped in worldly muck do utterly displease the Lord.

I have of purpose not reckoned up all the names of the forbidden creatures, partly because it would have been too tedious unto you, and partly because the interpreters of the Bible do wonderfully stick[2] in the interpretation of their names: so that I can never marvel enough at the extreme blind stubbornness of the Jewish people, in keeping so strictly the choice of their meats, when their own rabbins do stick, and cannot tell certainly what creatures they be that the Lord did forbid them.

To this belongeth, that even before the law, in the time of Noah, God did forbid to eat the blood and the flesh with the blood of any thing torn by wild beasts, or strangled. Before the deluge the fathers did eat the herbs and fruits of the earth. After the flood they had leave given to eat the flesh of living creatures; but so yet, that they should cut the throat off, and drain the blood out of the body. The place is extant in the ninth chapter of Genesis. Moreover, in the law the Lord with great severity saith: "Whatsoever man it be of the house of Israel, or of the strangers that sojourn among you, that eateth any manner of blood, I will set my face against that soul, and will cut him off from among his people." Leviticus xvii. And the same law is repeated in the nineteenth chapter of the same book, and in the twelfth and fifteenth chapter of Deuteronomy. It is again rehearsed in the third and seventh chapter of Leviticus. Neither is it without very just and great causes, that he did so severely forbid the eating of blood. For first of all, after the words above rehearsed, he addeth immediately: "For the life of the flesh is in the blood; and I have given it unto you upon the altar, to

The eating of blood and strangled is forbidden.

Lev. xvii.

[1 alacres, Lat.]　　　　　　[2 laborant ac variant, Lat.]

make an atonement for your souls: for blood shall make an atonement for the soul. Therefore I said unto the children of Israel, Let no soul among you eat blood, &c." Lo, in these words a most evident reason is given why it was not lawful to eat blood; because blood was the most excellent and precious thing, as that which was ordained for the sanctification of mankind. For God gave blood to be as the price, wherewith sins should be cleansed; to be, I say, the price of redemption, whereby men should be absolved of their sins. Blood also is the life, that is, the nourishment of life.

The blood, therefore, was a sign of the blood of Christ, that was to be shed upon the cross: by which, as by a most full and absolute atonement, the faithful are cleansed and thoroughly sanctified; and in which is the nourishment of the soul to life everlasting: and as it was not lawful to eat the flesh of the sacrifices, whose blood was carried into the *sanctum*[3] for sin, but to burn it without the host; so it was unlawful to eat the[4] blood, which[5] was the cleansing for their sins. He therefore did eat blood, which attributed to his own strength or works the atonement which was made by the blood of Christ, esteeming his blood to be profane, and not attributing unto it the full satisfaction for all sins. Again, he did not eat, but pour the blood down at the altar, who did ascribe the benefit of our redemption to the only merit of Christ, and did esteem it of so great value as it ought by right to be esteemed.

Lastly, God would have it deeply printed in the minds of men, that no man should shed another's blood, nor live of the blood and bowels of other men: as mercenary soldiers, covetous persons, usurers, and cozeners do, in sucking out and shedding the blood of silly people with subtle sleights and open injury. And God, talking with Noah, did with terrible threats[6] beat into all murderers an horrible fear, saying: "If [Gen. ix. 5, 6.] men be slack, I will take vengeance upon the shedding of blood." For man was made to the image and likeness of God: how can God choose then but take the reproach as done to himself, which is done unto his image? For whosoever

[3 in sancta, Lat.; into the holy places.]
[4 blood, not *the* blood.]
[5 utpote, Lat.; inasmuch as it was.]
[6 et rationibus, Lat.; and reasons.]

casteth down the image of the king, he offendeth against the king, and is accused of treason.

But now touching strangled, this law was given: "Eat not with blood." And again, "Eat not of that which dieth of itself, nor of that which is torn with wild beasts, &c." But by strangled and carrion that dieth of itself are signified the dead works, from which he is bidden to purge himself[1], whosoever desireth to get God's favour. He therefore did eat strangled, whosoever did live in wickedness, without repentance, not regarding[2] the blood of Christ his Saviour.

The touching of unclean things. Now also the touching of unclean things is set down in the law by these three notes; as if thou touchest an unclean thing, or if thou bear it, or if it fall by chance into some vessel or garment of thine. He verily is defiled by the falling of a thing, whosoever sinneth unwittingly. But he sinneth more heinously, whosoever sinneth[3] willingly and of a set and pretended purpose[4]. But he sinneth most grievously of all, that upholdeth[5] wickedness, and compelleth other to commit the same.

But whereas in touching, and in other places, it is said that the uncleanness shall abide till evening; that is an evident prophecy of Christ, to wit, that the Messiah should come at evening, that is, in the end of the world, to purge the sins of all the earth.

I have enough, and long enough, thus far by two whole sermons (I pray God it may be to your profit, dearly beloved) stayed in and stuck upon the ceremonial laws: therefore, that I may now come to an end, I will bring the chief points whereof I have spoken into a brief sum. I did divide the whole treatise of the ceremonial laws into three especial branches: for I spake of the holy persons, of the holy time and place, and of the holy things which the holy persons did exercise in the sacred place; I mean, the sacraments, the sacrifices, and other holy ceremonies. The holy persons are the priests: I shewed you their first beginning, their ordering, their mystical apparel, and their sundry offices. When I spake of the holy time and place, I did describe unto you the taber-

[Exod. xxii. 31; Lev. vii. 24; xix. 26.]

[1 per divinam gratiam, Lat.; by the grace of God.]
[2 neque magnopere curabat, Lat.]
[3 sciens, Lat. omitted; with knowledge.]
[4 dedita opera, Lat.]   [5 defendit, Lat.]

nacle, and noted unto you what was within the tabernacle; to wit, the ark of the covenant, the golden table, the golden candlestick, the altar of incense, the altar of burnt-sacrifices, and the brasen laver: the mysteries of all which I declared unto you. In the treatise of the holy time I touched all the kinds of holy-days and solemn feast-days, with all their certain and uncertain holy-days. Last of all, in our discourse upon the holy things[6], I told you of the two sacraments of the old church, circumcision and the passover; and also of the sacrifices, whereof some were burnt-offerings, some meat-offerings, some peculiar, and some of thanksgiving[7]: wherein we spake somewhat also touching free-will-offerings and vowed sacrifices: finally of vows, of the discipline[8] of the Nazarites, of clean and unclean creatures, of the choice of meats, of blood and strangled, and of the touching of unclean things.

The Lord Jesus enlighten your hearts, that all this may tend to the glory of his name, and the health of your souls! Amen.

OF THE JUDICIAL LAWS OF GOD.

THE SEVENTH SERMON.

In prosecuting the treatise of God's laws, I have now lastly to speak of that sort which are called the judicial laws: of which I will entreat, dearly beloved, as briefly as I can, so far forth as I shall be persuaded to be expedient for your edification. This treatise will not be unpleasant nor unprofitable to every zealous hearer, although it doth specially belong to courts of law, where judgment is exercised: for the judicial laws were with wonderful faith and diligence set out of God[9] by the ministry of his servant Moses; and God is not wont to reveal any thing to mankind with so precise and exquisite diligence, unless it do directly tend to mankind's great commodity.

The judicial laws are profitable.

[6 et cultum sacrum, Lat.; and upon the holy worship.]
[7 gratulatoria seu eucharistica, Lat.]
[8 vel instituto, Lat.; or institution.]
[9 ab optimo et sapientissimo Deo, Lat.; of the most excellent and most wise God.]

Now although these judicial laws are very few in number, and not to be compared in multitude with the huge volumes of the laws and decrees of emperors, kings, and wisest sages; yet do they in their short breviary contain the chief points of judgment and justice, and, in effect, as much almost as is contained in the books of the laws and constitutions of the emperors and civil lawyers. The good Lord would not by too long and burdensome a pack of laws be too burdenous and troublesome unto his people; neither was it needful over curiously to stick upon every several thought of ill-disposed persons : it is sufficient for all wise men, people, and nations, if every one have so much law as is sufficient for the conservation of peace, civil honesty, and public tranquillity ; as all the holy scripture[1] witnesseth that the people of Israel had.

Most ancient laws.   Now these judicial laws are the most ancient, and very fountains of all other good laws which are to be found almost in all the world. Moses was before all other lawgivers that were of name and authority : among whom Mercurius[2] Trismegistus and Rhadamanthus the Lycian[3] are thought to be the eldest. The Egyptians called their Mercurius by the name of Thoth, who, as Lactantius affirmeth, slew Argus that had so many eyes, and upon the murder fled into Egypt[4].

He was called Diphyes, that is, Geminus, or duplicis naturæ, because he first ordained matrimony among the Grecians.   Now Argus and Atlas lived about the time of Cecrops Diphyes ; and Cecrops is reported to have been in the same time that Moses was[5]. Rhadamanthus also is supposed to have lived after the days of Joshue, Moses his servant and successor.

[1 universa historia sacra, Lat.; all the sacred history.]

[2 He is by Augustine (de Civit. Dei, Lib. xviii. cap. 8 and 39) made a late contemporary of Moses.]

[3 In Euseb. Chron. a.m. 3765 are placed "Rhadamanthus et Sarpedon reges Lyciorum." Moses is there placed from a.m. 3608 to 3728. Augustine (de Civit. Dei, Lib. xviii. cap. 12.) places Rhadamanthus in the interval between the Exodus and the death of Joshua.]

[4 legislatorem suum, Lat.; their lawgiver. Lactantius, on the authority of Cicero (de Nat. Deor. Lib. iii.) having stated that there were five Mercuries, says:—quintum fuisse eum, a quo occisus sit Argus: ob eamque causam in Ægyptum profugisse; atque Ægyptiis leges ac literas tradidisse. Hunc Ægyptii Thoth appellant.—Lactant. Div. Instit. Lib. i. cap. 6. pp. 29, 30. Lugd. Bat. 1660.]

[5 Cecrops is placed by Abp. Usher, b.c. 1556, a little after the birth of Moses. In Euseb. Chron. under date a.m. 3615, it is said: Quidam scribunt Athlantem fratrem Promethei, et Argum cuncta cernentem his fuisse temporibus ; alii vero ætate Cecropis (i. c. a.m. 3640.)]

But the most famous lawgivers of the greatest and most His image was with two faces, or two heads. ancient nations did follow long after the death of Moses; Draco and Solon among the Athenians, Minos with the Cretians, Charondas of the Tyrians [Thurians], Phoronæus to the Argives, Lycurgus to the Lacedæmonians, Pythagoras to the Italians, Romulus and Numa unto the Romans. Plato writ of laws a little before the reign of Philip, king of Macedon and father to Alexander the Great[6]. And Cicero, Lib. II. *de Legibus*, saith: " I see therefore that the opinion of the wisest sort was, that law was neither invented by men's wits, nor yet was the decree or ordinance of people; but a certain eternal thing, ruling the whole world with discretion to command or forbid, to do or leave undone. So they said that the chief and highest law is the wisdom of God, which commandeth or The Latin copy hath mentem Dei, for the which I call the wisdom of God. forbiddeth all things by reason. Whereupon that law, which the gods have given to mankind, is rightly commended: for it is the reason and discretion of the wise which is able either to command or else forbid;" and so forth[7]. Therefore the judicial laws of God are commended unto us, not so much for their antiquity, as for the authority which they have of God.

Now that we may plainly and distinctly discourse upon To judge, a Judge, judgment, and the judicial laws, what they be. this matter, ye have to mark, that to judge is an action; and in this treatise is taken for an action done in the courts of judgment: for it signifieth to take up and determine of matters betwixt such as be at variance, or else upon the hearing of a cause to give sentence or judgment. Finally, to judge doth signify, to deliver them that be in danger, to relieve the oppressed, to defend the afflicted, and with punishment to keep under mischievous offenders. Judgment, therefore, is not the sitting or meeting of judges in assizes or sessions; but is rather the very diligent discussing of causes, the giving of sentence according to right and equity by the laws of God, and also the assertion and defence whereby the good are delivered, and the punishment that is executed upon the ill-

[6 Draco, B.C. 624. Solon, 594. Minos is placed by Euseb. Chron. thirty years later than Rhadamanthus. Charondas at Thurium, 446. Phoroneus is placed in Euseb. Chron. about the 110th year of Isaac's age. Lycurgus, 884. Pythagoras, 547. Romulus, 753. Numa, 715. Plato de Legibus, cir. 367. See also Polydor. Vergil. de rer. invent. Lib. II. cap. 1; and Augustin. de Civit. Dei. Lib. XVIII. cap. 3, 8, 25.]

[7 Cic. de Legib. Lib. II. cap. 4.]

disposed and wicked offenders. The judges are the overseers of judgment and justice; I mean, such as do justly
according to the laws give sentence betwixt them that are at
discord, which do defend and deliver the good, and punish
and bridle the wicked. And so the judicial laws are those
which inform the judges how to determine of controversies and
questions, how to judge justly, how to punish the wicked, and
how to defend the good, that peace, honesty, justice, and
public tranquillity may be among all men; which is the end
and mark alone whereto both the judge and all the judicial
laws do tend and are directed. For God, our good Lord and
lawgiver, would have it to go well with man, that we may live
happily, civilly, and in tranquillity. And therefore we do not
in this treatise exclude the care and defence of pure religion,
but do make it one of the especial points which the judicial
laws do look unto.

The judicial laws belong to the ten commandments. And now even as the ceremonial laws, so also are the
judicial laws added by God unto the ten commandments, to
expound and confirm them therewithal. For the precepts
of the ten commandments are the chief and principal precepts,
whereunto we must refer all laws, as to the eternal mind or
will of God. I think I need not to stand and shew you,
dearly beloved, to what precepts of the ten commandments
every several judicial law is to be referred: for that is
very plain and evident to every one that will take but small
pains to confer and lay them together. For the judicial
laws that are set out against murder and injury are appertaining to this precept: "Thou shalt do no murder." And
whatsoever is spoken against adultery, fornication, and filthy
lusts, are added to the commandment: "Thou shalt not
commit adultery." Likewise, whatsoever is said in the judicial laws against deceits, shifts, cozenings, and usury, do
belong to the commandment: "Thou shalt not steal." Lastly,
all the laws touching the bridling of heretics and suppressing
of apostates by force are set down to make plain the first,
second, third, and fourth commandments of the first table:
for some laws may be applied to more precepts than one of
the ten commandments. But this is easy and plain to be
perceived of every man: therefore I will not stand any
longer about it.

The laws of judges. Now for because the judicial laws do first of all require judges, such, I mean, as should maintain and put the laws in execution (for the laws without executors seem to be dead, and on the other side are alive under a just magistrate, who is for that cause called the living law[1]); therefore before all other laws are placed those judicial laws which were given by God touching the magistrate or judges, with their office and election. Of their election thus we read: "Bring ye," [Deut. i. 13.] saith Moses to the people, "men of wisdom and of understanding, and expert[2], according to your tribes, and I will make them rulers over you." Again: "I will make thee[3] [Deut. xvi. 18.] rulers and judges to judge the people, according to thy tribes, in all thy cities which the Lord thy God giveth thee." And yet again more plainly: "Seek" (saith Jethro, being [Exod. xviii. 21—23.] inspired from above, unto Moses) "out of all the people men of courage, and such as fear God, true men, hating covetousness," (to wit, such as hate to take money and bribes), "and make of them over the people rulers of thousands, rulers of hundreds, rulers of fifties, and rulers of tens: and let them judge the people at all seasons. Which if thou dost, thou shalt both keep the ordinances of God[4], and the people in peace and safety." To this doth belong that which we read in the book of Numbers, where Moses prayed, saying: "Let [Num. xxvii. 16—23.] the God of the spirits of all flesh set a man over this congregation, which may go out and in before them; that the congregation of the Lord be not as sheep without a shepherd." Herein Moses hath left an example for us to imitate, in making our prayers to God for the election of our judges. For oftentimes our opinions or judgments of men do utterly deceive us; but the God of spirits doth behold the minds and hearts, and knoweth what every one is in thoughts and inward meaning[5]. He therefore must be besought to give and shew to us not hypocrites to be our judges, but men of truth and virtue. In the same place doth Moses leave to us the description of consecrating new chosen judges: for they were set before the Lord, and hands were laid upon them

[1 See Vol. i. p. 339.]

[2 spectatæ probitatis viros, Lat.; men of tried probity. Heb. and Auth. Ver. *known*. Vulg. quorum conversatio sit probata.]

[3 Constitues tibi, Lat.; thou shalt make thee.]

[4 servabis instituta Dei, Lat.; implebis imperium Dei, et præcepta ejus poteris sustentare, Vulg.]

[5 intus et in cute, Lat.]

with making of prayers and supplications. Moreover the office of judge is very briefly, but yet in most effectual and absolute sentences, described of the Lord, by the mouth of Moses, in these words: "Hear the causes of your brethren, and judge righteously betwixt every man and his brother, and the stranger that is with him. Ye shall have no respect of any person[1] in judgment : but hear the small and the great alike ; and fear not the face of any man : for the judgment is God's." Again : "Judge the people with just judgment. Decline not in judgment[2] : have no respect of persons, neither take thou any bribes ; for rewards do blind the eyes of the wise, and doth pervert just causes. Do judgment with justice, that thou mayest live, and possess the land which the Lord thy God shall give thee." And again : "Do no unjust thing in judgment ; accept not the face of the poor, neither fear thou the face of the mighty, but judge thou justly unto thy neighbour." Again : "Thou shalt not have to do with a false report ; thou shalt not follow a multitude to do evil ; neither shalt thou speak in a matter of justice according to the greater number for to pervert judgment :" that is, if thou seest an innocent to be condemned of the multitude, do not thou therefore condemn him because the multitude hath condemned him ; but judge thou justly, and commit not evil because of the many voices of the multitude. "Thou shalt not esteem a poor man in his cause : neither shalt thou hinder the poor of his right in his suit. Keep thee far from a false matter ; and the innocent and righteous see that thou slay not[3]. Thou shalt not oppress the stranger ; seeing ye yourselves were strangers in the land of Egypt."

And God verily, when he had delivered the people from the tyranny of the kings of Egypt, did not put them in subjection to kings again, nor burden them with the tributes which kings are wont to exact of their subjects : for he made them a commonweal, or an aristocracy, which was the most excellent kind of regiment, wherein the choicest men in all

Marginal notes:
[Deut. i. 16, 17.]
[Deut. xvi. 18—20.]
[Lev. xix. 15.]
[Exod. xxiii. 1—3, 6, 7, 9.]
The institution of a king and of princes.

[1 non agnoscetis facies, Lat. ; ye shall not acknowledge faces. Auth. Ver. Marg.]

[2 ne flectas judicium, Lat. ; thou shalt not wrest judgment. Auth. Ver.]

[3 Non enim justificabo impium, Lat. omitted by the translator ; for I will not justify the wicked.]

the multitude were picked out to bear the sway and to rule
the rest: but yet because he was not ignorant of his people's
foolishness, and that they, being weary of their liberty, would
crave a king (which thing he did afterward also dissuade
them from [4] by his servant Samuel), he made laws for a king 1 Sam. viii.
also, that he might understand that he was to live under the
laws, and to give judgment according to the laws.   The discipline or institution of a king is thus expressed in the seventeenth chapter of Deuteronomy: "When thou art come into
the land which the Lord thy God giveth thee, and shalt say,
I will set a king over me, like as all the nations that are
about me; then thou shalt make him king over thee, whom
the Lord thy God shall choose.   One from among the midst
of thy brethren shalt thou make king over thee; and thou
mayest not set a stranger over thee, which is not of thy
brethren.   But he shall not gather many horses unto himself,
nor bring the people back again into Egypt, to increase the
number of horses;" that is, to get himself a strong troop of
horsemen: "forasmuch as the Lord hath said, Ye shall henceforth go no more again that way.   Also let him not take
many wives to himself, lest his heart turn away: neither let
him gather too much silver and gold.   And when he is set
upon the seat of his kingdom, he shall write him out a copy
of this law in a book, according to the copy of the book
which the priests the Levites do use: and it shall be with
him, and he ought to read therein all the days of his life;
that he may learn to fear the Lord his God, and to keep all
the words of this law, and these ordinances, for to do them.
And let not his heart arise above his brethren, neither let
him turn from the commandment, either to the right hand or
to the left; that he may prolong his days in his kingdom,
both he, and his sons, in the midst of Israel."

Thus much hitherto of the magistrates, of judges, and of
kings.

Now I suppose that in this institution of a king all things
are contained, which are most largely set out by other authors
touching the discipline and education of a prince.   And by
the way this is especially to be noted; that kings are not set
as lords and rulers over the word and laws of God; but are,

[4 multis et validis rationibus, Lat. omitted; with many and powerful reasons.]

as subjects, to be judged of God by the word, as they that
ought to rule and govern all things according to the rule of
his word and commandment.

And here I have to rehearse unto you some of the judicial
laws; I mean, not all and every several one, but those alone
which are the chief and choicest to be noted: by which ye
may consider of the rest, and plainly perceive, that the people
of Israel were not destitute of any law which was necessary
and profitable for their good state and welfare. I will recite
them unto you as briefly as may be, and in as natural and
plain an order as possibly can be.

Holy things. Of the holy buildings, of the not making away of such
things as were consecrated to the Lord, and finally, of the
maintaining and publishing of true religion, there is large
speech everywhere throughout the whole scripture. Neither
do I think it to be greatly to the purpose word by word to
recite all the laws, nor particularly to make mention of all
the commandments touching those matters. Verily, of the
heathen, and of the overthrowing of their temples and superstitious holy toys, this commandment is briefly given by the
[Deut. vii. 1—6.] Lord himself: "When the Lord thy God hath cast out many
nations before thee, thou shalt root them out; neither shalt
thou make league with them, nor pity them, nor join affinity
with them: because they will seduce thy sons to serve strange
gods; and so my fury wax hot against thee, and I destroy
thee. But this shalt thou do to them: ye shall dig down
their altars, ye shall break their idols[1], ye shall cut down
their groves, and burn their images with fire. For an holy
people art thou unto the Lord thy God; and the Lord thy
God hath chosen thee to be a peculiar people unto himself."
The same law is set down in the twenty-third of Exodus, and
is again repeated in the twelfth of Deuteronomy. Hereunto
Idolatry. belong the laws that were published against idols and images.
In the nineteenth of Leviticus the Lord saith: "Look not back
to idols, neither make you molten gods: I am the Lord your
God." Also in the twenty-sixth chapter: "Ye shall make you
no idols nor graven image, neither rear you up any pillar,
neither shall ye set you up any image of stone[2] in your land,

[1 statuas, Lat.; statues, or pillars. Auth. Ver. Marg.]
[2 lapidem figuratum, Lat.; a stone of picture, or figured stone.
Auth. Ver. Marg.]

to bow down unto it: for I am the Lord your God." Again in the sixteenth of Deuteronomy: "Thou shalt plant no grove of any trees nigh unto the altar of the Lord thy God: neither shalt thou set thee up any image, which the Lord thy God hateth." There are, beside these, also many other laws to this end and purpose in every place through all the volume of the scriptures.

Of the well handling and entreating of the poor, of widows³, *The poor.* of orphans, and strangers, the Lord giveth this commandment: "Ye shall not afflict the widow, nor the fatherless. But if ye [Exod. xxii. 22—24.] go on to afflict them, without doubt they shall cry to me, and I will assuredly hear them, and will be angry with you, and will slay you with the sword, and your wives shall be widows, and your children fatherless." To this belongeth a good part of the fifteenth chapter of Deuteronomy. In the twenty-fourth chapter the Lord saith: "Do not pervert the judgment of the stranger, of the fatherless, and of the widow. Remember that thou wast a stranger in the land of Egypt."

Of the receiving and refusing of witnesses and their wit- *Witness and witness-bearings.* ness-bearings in judgment these few notes are given in the law: "One witness shall not be of force against a man, [Deut. xix. 15, 16, 18, 19.] whatsoever his sin or offence shall be: but in the mouth of two or three witnesses shall every word be established. If a false witness rise up against a man, to accuse him of trespass, the judges shall make diligent inquisition; and if they find that the witness hath borne false witness against his brother, then shall they do to him as he had thought to have done to his brother; and thou shalt put evil away from out of the midst of thee."

Now, for the oath which the judges have to exact, or they that are at variance, or else the witnesses, have to take, that doth the Lord command to be done by the calling to record of his holy Name, and that too of none other but his name alone. Deuteron. x. &c.

Moreover, that in effect is a kind of appeal, where Moses *An appeal.* doth so often bid the judges in an hard and doubtful matter to have recourse unto the high priest, and so, as it were, to God himself, or the oracle of God, for the declaration of the same; as is to be seen in the eighteenth chapter of Exodus, and in the first and seventeenth chapter of Deuteronomy.

[³ pupillis, Lat. omitted; fatherless.]

Marriage.   Of lawful wedlock, against incestuous and unprofitable marriages, and also of the degrees of consanguinity and affinity, there are exquisite precepts as well in the eighteenth chapter of Leviticus, as also in other places of the books of Moses. Verily, where lawful marriages are not, there is no matrimony : therefore the children that are so born are counted bastards; neither is there for them any dowries or inheritance.

Parents and children.

[Deut. vi. 6—9.]

The Lord in many places of his law doth charge parents to bring up their children honestly, and to instruct them in the fear of God. Among the rest he saith : "The words which I command thee this day thou shalt shew unto thy children, and shalt talk of them when thou art at home in thine house, and as thou walkest by the way, and when thou liest down, and when thou risest up. And thou shalt bind them for a sign upon thine hand, and they shall be as frontlets betwixt thine eyes; and thou shalt write them upon the posts of thine house, and upon thy gates, &c."

Again, for the honouring, reverencing, and nourishing of parents, there are not in the moral law only, but also in the judicial laws, some things set down wherein the honour and duty to be given to parents is diligently commended to all sorts of people : of which I will speak when I come to treat of parricide, under which title I do comprehend the evil handling and naughty demeanour of men to their parents.

Of the power and authority of fathers.

[Exod. xxii. 16, 17.]

Now, how great the authority of fathers over their children was, we may conjecture by that especially, where, in the twenty-first of Exodus, it is permitted to the father, that is in poverty, to sell his daughter. Again, in another place, leave is given to the father either to deny, or else to give, his deflowered daughter in marriage to him that did defile her. And again, it was in the father's power to break the vow[1] which the child had made without his knowledge or consent, Numbers xxx.

Disinheriting. But that to disinherit the children (if the children had not deserved it, but that some corrupt affection had blinded the parents) lay not in the power or will of the parents, that law doth shew, which is published in the twenty-first chapter of Deuteronomy; and doth forbid the father to place the second in the right of his eldest or first-begotten son.

Inheritance.   Concerning the coming to inheritance, and the succession

[1 Deo nuncupatum, Lat. ; made to God.]

of goods, or the lawful succession by kindred, there is a precise law in the twenty-seventh chapter of the book of Numbers. There is set down the case of the daughters of Zelphad, who did request that their father's name should not be wiped out, but that their father's inheritance and name might be given unto and still remain with them. Upon that occasion was the law made, that if the sons did die, the heritage should be conveyed over and given to the daughters, or, at leastwise, to those that were nearest of affinity. And thereunto belongeth the law of raising seed unto the deceased brother, and the whole thirty-sixth chapter almost of the book of Numbers. Upon this law also doth hang the right which cometh by adoption.

Furthermore, of whoredoms, adulteries, and the ravishing of virgins, there are many profitable, honest, and wholesome laws. In the twenty-third of Deuteronomy it is said, "There shall be no whore of the daughters of Israel, nor whoremonger of the sons of Israel." And in the same place he forbiddeth to bring oblations which are the price of an harlot's hire. In Leviticus charge is given, saying: "Set not out thy daughter for hire, to make her play the harlot; lest the land be defiled, and filled with sin." Therefore, in the twenty-second of Deuteronomy, the maid that was deflowered, and yet feigned herself to be a virgin still, when she was given to an husband, was commanded to be stoned to death before the doors of her father's house; to the end that parents, being terrified with so grievous a thing, might be stirred up to look more warily unto their children. In the twenty-second of Exodus this law is given: "If a man entice a maid that is not betrothed, and lie with her, he shall endow her and take her to wife." There are most sharp laws against whoredoms and adulteries, Deuteronomy xxii.; for there adulterers are punished with death. The same punishment was appointed for him that did by violence ravish a virgin.

For suspicions and jealousy there are rules given in the fifth chapter of Numbers. Against detestable, unlawful, and altogether devilish lusts, there are most severe and yet most just laws expressed; as against most filthy incest, abominable sodomy, horrible and unnatural bestiality, and such sins as God hath cursed, and are not once worthy to be named among men. Levit. eighteenth and twentieth chapters.

Whoredom and adultery.

[Lev. xix. 29.]

15—2

Divorce-
ments.
Divorcements and separations were permitted by the law in the twenty-fourth of Deuteronomy, for nothing else but [Matt. xix. 8.] for the hardness of the Jewish people's hearts, and for the avoiding of some greater inconvenience; to wit, lest peradventure any man should poison, strangle, or otherwise kill the woman, his wife, which he hated, when he could by none other means rid his hands of her. And they that were in that manner divorced might at their pleasures be married to others.

The division
of goods.
Moreover, that justice might be maintained, and that every man might enjoy his own, in the law there was charge very diligently given for the division of things, for the partition of the land of promise by equal portions, and for the peculiar possession of proper goods; that to every tribe possessions might be given by lot, and that no man should by any means make away the possessions which were given him. For hereunto belongeth that which is spoken by Moses in the thirty-second, thirty-third, thirty-fourth chapters of the book of Numbers, and oftentimes in other places also.

Buying and
selling, &c.
And yet notwithstanding, this law was nothing prejudicial to traffic by exchange. For there were many and very upright laws published for buying and selling, for letting and hiring, for borrowing and lending, for usury and things left in custody. Whosoever desireth to see the places in the law, he shall have them in the twenty-fifth of Leviticus, in the twenty-second of Exodus, in the fifteenth and twenty-third chapters of Deuteronomy. And I suppose that to this is to be referred the Pawns and
pledges.
[Exod. xxii.
26, 27.] law which is given concerning pawns or pledges: "If thou hast taken thy neighbour's garment to pledge, thou shalt restore it him again before the sun be set. For that is his only covering:" that is, it is the garment wherewith he covereth his flesh, and wherein he sleepeth. "For it shall come to pass, that if he cry to me, I will hear him; because I [Deut. xxiv.
6.] am merciful." Again; "Thou shalt not take the nether or upper mill-stone to pledge: for he hath laid that whereon he liveth to pledge to thee."

Things left
in custody.
The laws for things left in custody, or committed to the credit of another man, and for taking of oaths, commandeth every man to make true restitution of the thing which was given unto him to keep. But if it were stolen away from him to whom the custody of it was committed, then he that

kept it ought to purge himself by an oath before a magistrate, to shew that he consented not to the conveying of the thing away. The same order is commanded to be observed in things borrowed, that are lost, or otherwise broken : as is to be seen in the twenty-second chapter of Exodus.

And for because it is manifest that no small part of the *Bondage.* goods of the ancient Israelites did consist in the multitude of bondmen, therefore the law of God doth stick long upon the discourse of bondage and bondmen, and of the binding and manumission of them. And yet it doth diligently command to handle bondmen mercifully like men, and every sixth year[1] to set them free from slavery. But if it so fell out, that at *Mancipation.* the sixth year's end any bondman were desirous to stay still in his master's house, he was permitted so to do, upon condition that his voluntary bondage should be confirmed by the ceremony of mancipation; to wit, that the bondman, being *[Exod. xxi. 1—6.]* brought before the judges, should there testify that he would serve in bondage voluntarily ; and thereupon the nether lap of his ear should be bored with an awl, and fastened to the door. And that was the sign or token of faith and obedience. For David, alluding thereunto, did say, that the Lord had bored through his ear, that is, that by faith he had bound him to obedience.

Moreover, the Lord did in these laws limit out the time *Manumission.* of bondmen's manumission, because the lords of bondmen should not use them over-cruelly for their gain and commodity's sake : all which are at full set down in the twenty-first chapter of Exodus. We must also refer that to the clemency that ought to be shewed to servants, where as in the twenty-third chapter of Deuteronomy it is said : " Thou shalt not deliver unto his master the servant which is escaped from his master unto thee ; but let him dwell in any place whereunto he is fled." And yet manstealing is most sharply forbidden. Now they commit the offence called Plagium[2], that is to say, *Plagium.* manstealing, whosoever do entice other men's bondmen to run from their masters, or which do, by theft or robbery, steal other men's servants, whom they do either keep to themselves, or else sell to others. Against such this law is given : " Whosoever stealeth a man, and selleth him, if he be *[Exod. xxi. 16.]*

[1 sexennio finito, Lat.]
[2 See above, page 47.]

convinced of the crime, let him die the death." And the same law is again repeated in the twenty-fourth of Deuteronomy.

Bastards. Of free men little is said in the law; but they were exempted from bearing office in the commonwealth, which were known to be harlots' children, whose fathers[1] no man knew. Strangers also, as the Ammonites and Moabites, were utterly barred from rule and authority in the Israelitish weal public. Deuteronomy xxiii.

All deceit, cozening, robbery, shiftings, and subtil crafts, are flatly forbidden in the law under the title of theft. For in the nineteenth of Leviticus we read : " Ye shall not steal, nor deal falsely, nor lie one to another." And in the nineteenth of Deuteronomy : " Thou shalt not remove thy neigh-

Theft and deceit.

Restitution. bour's meerstone[2]." In the twenty-second of Exodus the Lord doth punish theft with four or five-fold double restitution : which whosoever did not perform, he was sold, and brought into extreme bondage. But if the stolen thing were found with the thief, and recovered again, then did the stealer restore to the owner double the value of that which was stolen. To this law belonged whatsoever was spoken con-

Sacrilege. cerning sacrilege, stealing of cattle, robbing of the common treasury, and carrying away of other men's bond-slaves; of which I spake somewhat a little before[3]. And to this doth

The hireling's wages. appertain that excellent law which saith : " Thou shalt not

[Deut xxiv. 14, 15.] deny, nor keep back, the wages of an hired servant that is poor and needy, whether he be of thy brethren, or of the strangers that are within thy land; thou shalt give him his hire the same day[4], and that before the sun go down; because he is needy, and doth therewith sustain his life[5]: lest he cry against thee unto the Lord, and it be sin unto thee."

The doing and receiving of damage. Concerning doing and receiving damage, and the making of full restitution for the harm that is done, there are many

[Exod. xxi. 33, 34.] constitutions in the law of the Lord. " If any man," saith

---

[1 and whose, Lat.]   [2 mere: a boundary. Johnson.]
[3 sacrilegium, abigeatum, et peculatum, Lat. See above, p. 44-48.]
[4 die suo, Lat.; at his day. Auth. Ver.]
[5 Sustentat ex eo vitam suam, Lat. So Vulg. and Coverdale, 1535, "and his life (is) susteyned therwith." Ainsworth in loc.: "And unto it he lifteth up his soul; that is, hopeth for and desireth it for the maintenance of his life."]

the law, "doth dig a well, and do not cause it to be covered, so that an ox or a sheep of another man's do fall into it; then let him that owneth the well take to himself the beast that perished, and pay the worth of the beast to him that is the owner thereof." The like law is made in the twenty-first of Exodus touching an ox that pusheth with his horns. In the twenty-second chapter is given the law of restitution in giving like for like; if either one man's pasture be eaten up by another man's cattle, or if one man hurt another's corn or vineyard. For the law commandeth to restore other pasturings, other corn-ground, and other vineyards, not of the worst, but of the best, to him that had the damage done him. Likewise if any man had set thorns on fire, and by [Exod. xxii. 5, 6. Lev. xxiv. 18—21.] his negligence had suffered it to catch hold upon corn, either standing in the field upright, or stacked up in mows[6] at home; then he, by whose negligence the fire began, did make amends for the loss that the other received. The same law is again repeated in the twenty-fourth of Leviticus. In the twenty-second of Deuteronomy there are many things expressed that must be referred unto this title: of which sort is the law that biddeth us to bring back the ox that goeth astray, and to restore the things that are found to him that lost them; to keep our buildings in good reparations, that by misfortune in the fall of them our brethren be not mischieved. And like to these is the law also which saith: "Thou shalt have [Deut. xxiii. 12, 13.] a place without the host to go forth unto; and shalt bear a paddle-stick at thy girdle, wherewith as thou sittest thou shalt dig a hole to hide thy ordure, or cover thine excrements in." And in the civil law the like matter in effect is handled[7]: for very necessity doth require, that in commonweals there should be laws concerning draughts, and order of buildings, so that no man by his excrements or building of new houses should trouble or annoy his neighbours about him. To this place, also, we may add the laws that were made concerning the separating of lepers from them that were clean, lest peradventure the contagious disease should by little and little infect the healthful. The laws of lepers and the leprosy are

[6 mow, a heap of corn or hay; when laid up in a house, said to be in *mow*; when heaped together in a field, in *rick*. Johnson's Dict.]
[7 Codex Justin. Lib. viii. tit. 10, de ædificiis privatis. Tom. ii. Lugd. 1551.]

at large set down in the thirteenth and fourteenth chapters of Leviticus.

Weight and measure. Just weights and just measures the Lord commanded to be kept in the law, where he saith : " Thou shalt not have in thy bag two manner of weights, a great and a small : neither shalt thou have in thine house divers measures, a great and a small. But thou shalt have a right and a just weight, and a perfect and a just measure shalt thou have : that thy days may be lengthened in the land which the Lord thy God giveth thee. For all that do such things, and all that deal unrightly, are abomination unto the Lord thy God." This law is given in the twenty-fifth of Deuteronomy, and is again repeated in the nineteenth chapter of Leviticus.

The punishment of the guilty.

[Exod. xxii. 18 ; Deut. xxiv. 16.]

Of public judgments, of witchcrafts, and the punishment of offenders, there are many laws set down in the book of the Lord. " Thou shalt not," saith the Lord, " suffer witches to live." Again : " The fathers shall not be killed for the sons, nor the sons for the fathers : but every one shall be slain for his own offence." Neither doth the law conceal the manner of killing : for it giveth the use of the sword, of stones, and of fire, into the magistrate's hands. And sometime it is left to the judge's discretion to punish the offender according to the circumstance of the crime committed, either in body or goods, in loss of limbs or life, in scourging with rods, or selling into bondage. In the twentieth chapter of Leviticus all the offences are almost reckoned up that are to be punished with present death. And in like manner the like are repeated in the eighteenth and twenty-first chapter of the same book.

Witches and soothsayers. Against witches and soothsayers[1] there is precise charge given in the eighteenth of Deuteronomy. In the nineteenth of Leviticus this short precept is given : " Ye shall not seek after witches, nor observe your dreams : ye shall not decline to sorcerers, nor inquire of soothsayers to be defiled by them." Against such the law doth expressly give judgment of death and extreme punishment, Leviticus xx. In the twenty-second of Exodus this strait sentence is sharply pronounced : " Let not a woman live that is a witch."

Heretics and false prophets. Against heretics, schismatics, apostates, and false prophets, the law giveth judgment in the thirteenth and eighteenth

[1 Mathematicis, Lat. See Vol. I. p. 221, note 7.]

chapters of Deuteronomy; where it doth most plainly teach how such kind of people are to be handled. And like to this is the law for the stoning of blasphemers, which is contained in the twenty-fourth of Leviticus; and also the law for contemners and breakers of the Lord's sabbath, Numbers xv.

Against seditious rebels and secret slanderers there is much to be found in many places of the law. Chore, Dathan, and Abirom were rebels, of whose ends ye may read in the sixteenth of the book of Numbers. If any man did maliciously bring up a slander upon his wife's chastity, and was not able to prove it true, he was merced at a sum of money, or punished with stripes, as is to be seen in the twenty-second of Deuteronomy. In the nineteenth of Leviticus this precept is given: "Thou shalt not go up and down with tales among thy people: neither shalt thou hate thy brother in thine heart; but shalt rebuke him and tell him thy mind plainly." Also in the twenty-second of Exodus it is said, "Thou shalt not rail upon the gods (or judges[1]), nor blaspheme the ruler of thy people." *[Rebels and slanderers.]*

Moreover there are sundry kinds of murder, whereof some are greater or smaller than other. The most detestable murder of all is parricide, (when one killeth his father or his kinsman[2]), under which we do comprehend the evil-entreating or currish handling of parents by their children. "Whosoever striketh father or mother, or curseth them," saith the law, "let him die the death." Again, they are bidden to kill the rebel that dareth stand up to resist the upright decrees and holy ordinances of the elders, Deuteronomy xvii. And also in the twenty-first of Deuteronomy we find: "If any man have a stubborn, a froward, and rebellious son, that will not hearken to the voice of his father, and the voice of his mother, and they have chastened him, and he would not hearken unto them: then shall his father and his mother take him, and bring him out unto the elders of that city, and to the gate of that place; and say unto the elders of the city, This our son is stubborn and disobedient, and will not hearken to our voice; he is a rioter and a drunkard: and straightway all the men of that city shall stone him with stones until he die: and thou shalt put evil from thee: and all Israel shall hear and fear." *[Murder.]* *[Exod. xxi. 15, 17.]*

[2 The translator's addition.]

Furthermore, murder is either committed willingly or else unwillingly. Of murder unwillingly committed there is an example in the nineteenth chapter of Deuteronomy, where the case is put as followeth : Two friends go to the wood to hew wood together ; and as the one fetcheth his stroke, the head of the axe falleth from the helve, and striketh the other so that he dieth upon it. This deed the Lord doth neither impute, nor would have it to be imputed to the man, but to himself; and therefore he giveth licence to the man to fly unto the sanctuary. For his mind was that the sanctuaries should be a safeguard to such kind of people as killed men unwillingly, and not to bladers[1] and cutters, not to them that poison, or otherwise kill their neighbours of a set pretence or purpose[2] : of which there is much to be seen in the thirty-fifth of Numbers, the fourth and the nineteenth chapters of Deuteronomy. To the law for murder unwillingly committed doth the case belong[3] that is thus put forth : Two men fight together, and in their fight they strike a woman with child, so that either she falleth in travail before her time, or else doth presently die out of hand. In such a case what is to be done, the Lord did teach in the twenty-first of Exodus, where the law of like for like is also set down: "An eye for an eye, a tooth for a tooth, a hand for a hand," &c. In the same place, also, is put another kind of murder, which is committed either by thy beast, as by thine ox that pusheth with his horns, or by thy wolf, or by thy dog that thou keepest in thine house; or else by some instrument, or building, that is in thy possession. Now thou didst either know, or not know, the fierceness of thy beast, the peril in thine instrument, or the rottenness of thy building. If thou knewest it not, thou wast then excused : but if thou knewest it, and didst not seek a way to prevent the mischief, the Lord gave charge that thou shouldest die for it. But if of clemency it were granted thee to redeem thy life, thou shouldest not refuse to pay any sum of money, how great soever it were.

Now wilful murder, committed upon pretended malice[4],

The sanctuary.

[1 bladers, latronibus, Lat.]
[2 non veneficis aut parricidis, Lat.]   [3 etiam, Lat.; also.]
[4 quæ fit voluntate destinata per insidias aut malevolentiam, Lat.; which is perpetrated of set purpose by lying in wait or malice.]

is utterly unpardonable in the law of God.   "Such an one," [Exod. xxi. 14.]
saith the law, "thou shalt pull from mine altar, that he may
be killed."   In this case redemption of life is not permitted,
but the blood of the murderer is straitly required.   Many
cases of this severity, and many other things tending to
this end, are to be read in the thirty-fifth chapter of Numbers
and the twenty-first of Exodus.   In the twenty-first of Deuteronomy is described the action, partly ceremonial, and
partly judicial, which was solemnized when any man was
found to be slain, and no man knew who was the murderer;
where also the manner is prescribed, how to make an atonement for the murder : whereby we may gather how horrible
a sin murder is in the sight of God and the catholic church.

Lastly, the law doth not leave the order of war untouched: War.
for it giveth precepts concerning the beginning, the making,
and the ending of war; which are to be read in the twentieth
chapter of Deuteronomy.   Moreover in the law there are set
out the examples of terrible wars; as that with the Amalachites
in the seventeenth of Exodus, and that with the Madianites
in the thirty-first of the book of Numbers : where somewhat
also is said touching the division of spoils gotten in the wars.

I know, my brethren, that I have been somewhat tedious Conclusion.
unto you in making this rehearsal of the laws unto you : but
for because the most wise and mighty God doth nothing without especial causes and the evident profit of mankind, I could
not therefore suffer this part of the law to pass me untouched;
considering that I see it so diligently taught by God himself,
and that it maketh much to the opening and maintaining of
the moral law.   Our good God, who knoweth all things, doth
also know the dulness and overthwart slackness of man's wit,
and how it requireth to be driven perforce many times to do
good and eschew evil.   And therefore the holy Lord hath
in these judicial laws added an holy kind of compulsion to
drive men on withal.

In the morals he frameth our manners, and teacheth us
what to do, and what to leave undone.   With the ceremonials
he helpeth forward the morals; and doth under types and
figures lay before the eyes of our body and mind the mysteries of God[5] and his heavenly kingdom.   And lastly, by

[5 mysteria regni Dei, Lat.]

the judicials he compelleth us to the keeping of the laws, and doth preserve the integrity of the same. Now all these together do tend to this end only, that man may be saved, that he worship God aright, and live according to the will of the Lord.

Thus much have I spoken hitherto, by the help of God, concerning his holy laws. Now let us praise the goodness of the Lord, who doth not suffer his people to lack any thing that is necessary for their commodity; and doth even at this day instruct us with these laws to the glory of his name and health of our souls.

OF THE USE OR EFFECT OF THE LAW OF GOD, AND
OF THE FULFILLING AND ABROGATING OF THE
SAME: OF THE LIKENESS AND DIFFERENCE
OF BOTH THE TESTAMENTS AND
PEOPLE, THE OLD AND
THE NEW.

THE EIGHTH SERMON.

ALTHOUGH I have hitherto in large sermons laid forth[1] the law of God by several parts, yet methinketh I have not said all that should be said, nor made an end as I should do, unless I add now a treatise of the use, effect, fulfilling, and abrogating of the law of God; albeit I have here and there in my sermons[2] touched the same argument. Now by this discourse or treatise, dearly beloved, ye shall understand, that the Testament of the old and new church of God is all one; and that there is but one means of true salvation for all them that either have or else at this present are saved in the world: ye shall also perceive wherein the old Testament[3] doth differ from the new. Moreover this treatise will be necessary and very profitable both to the understanding of many places in the holy scripture, and also to the easy perceiving and most wholesome use of those things which I have said hitherto touching the law. God, who is the author, the

[1 qua potui diligentia, Lat.; with my best diligence.]
[2 in hisce nostris sermonibus, Lat.]
[3 quid novum testamentum differat a veteri, Lat.]

wisdom, and the perfect fulness of the law, give me grace to speak those things that are to the setting forth of his glory, and profitable for the health of your[4] souls.

The use of God's law is manifold and of sundry sorts; *Of the use and effect of God's law.* and yet it may be called back to three especial points, and we may say that the use thereof is threefold or of three sorts.

For first of all, the chief and proper office of the law is, to convince all men to be guilty of sin, and by their own fault to be the children of death. For the law of God setteth forth to us the holy will of God; and, in the setting forth thereof, requireth of us a most perfect and absolute kind of righteousness. And for that cause the law is wont to be called the testimony of God's will, and the most perfect exemplar of his divine pureness. And hereunto belong those words of the Lord in the gospel, where he, reciting shortly the sum of God's commandments, doth say: "The first of all the com- *Absolute perfectness is required of us in the law.* mandments is: Hear, O Israel, the Lord our God is one Lord: *[Mark xii. 29 —31.],* and thou shalt love the Lord thy God with all thy heart, and with all thy soul, and with all thy mind, and with all thy strength. This is the first commandment. And the second is like to this, Thou shalt love thy neighbour as thyself. There is none other commandment greater than these." Therefore to this doth also appertain that saying of the apostle Paul: "The end of the commandment is charity out of a pure heart, *[1 Tim. i. 5.]* and a good conscience, and faith unfeigned." But since the law doth require at all our hands most absolute righteousness, charity, and[5] a pure heart, it doth[6] condemn all men of sin, unrighteousness, and death. For in the law of God it is expressly said: "Cursed is every one which abideth not in all *[Deut. xxvii. 26; Gal. iii. 10.]* that is written in the book of the law to do it." But what *No man living is perfect and unspotted.* one of us fulfilleth all the points of the law? What man, I pray, either heretofore hath had, or at this day[7] hath, a pure heart within him? What man hath ever loved, or doth now love, God with all his heart, with all his soul, and with all his mind? What man is he that did never lust after evil? Or who is it now that lusteth not every day? Therefore imperfection and sin is by the law, or by the bewraying of the

[4 nostrarum, Lat.; our.]
[5 adeoque, Lat.; and so a.]
[6 certe, Lat. undoubtedly.]
[7 etiam hodie, Lat.]

law[1], revealed in mankind[2]. What shall we say to this? Where, I pray you, doth there appear in any man that divine and most absolute righteousness, which the law requireth? Job crieth, "I know verily that a man, compared to God, cannot be justified[3]." Or, "How shall a man be found right-

[Job ix. 2, 3, 15.]
eous, if he be compared to God? If he will argue with him, he shall not be able to answer one for a thousand. [4]If I have any righteousness in me, I will not answer him, but I will beseech my judge." Likewise, these[5] are the words of the apostle John, who saith: "If we say we have no sin, we

[1 John i. 8, 10.]
deceive ourselves, and the truth is not in us." Again, "If we say we have not sinned, we make him a liar, and his word is not in us." Therefore by this means the law is a certain

The law doth make our sins manifest, and bring our misery to light.
looking-glass, wherein we behold our own corruption, frailness, imbecility, imperfection, and our judgment, that is, our just and deserved damnation. For the apostle doth expressly say, that the law was given to the end that it might make manifest men's transgressions, and by that means drive them to the acknowledging of their imperfection and guilt in sinning. For none of us doth look into his own bosom, nor into the secrets of his own breast, but we do all flatter ourselves, and will not be persuaded that our thoughts and deeds[6] are so corrupt as they be in very deed; and therefore doth the law creep in, and lay open the secrets of our hearts, and bringeth to light our sin and corruption. "Before the law," saith the apostle, "although sin were in the world, yet was it not imputed[7]."

[Rom. iv. 15; iii. 20.]
The same apostle also saith : "The law worketh wrath; for where there is no law, there is no transgression." And again, "By the law cometh the knowledge of sin." For in the seventh to the Romans the same apostle doth say more fully : "I knew not sin, but by the law: for I had not known lust, except the law had said, Thou shalt not lust. But sin, taking

---

[1] indicio legis, Lat.]

[2] ut non dicam hic aliud gravius, Lat. omitted; not to allege here any severer charge.]

[3] So the Vulgate; and Coverdale, 1535.]

[4] item, Lat.; again.]

[5] succinit huic, Lat. ; like to these, ed. 1577.]

[6] res nostras, Lat.]

[7] non imputabatur, vel reputabatur, Lat.; or not considered, Rom. v. 13.]

occasion[8] by the commandment, wrought in me all manner of concupiscence. For without the law sin was dead. I once lived without law; but when the commandment came, sin revived, and I was dead[9]. And it was found, that the same commandment, which was ordained unto life, was unto me an occasion of death, &c." For a good part of that chapter is spent in that matter. Therefore the proper office of Moses, and the principal use and effect of the law, is to shew to man his sin and imperfection[10].

As for those which stay here, and go no further to make any other use and effect of the law, but as though Moses did nothing but kill, and the law nothing but slay; they are diversly, and that not lightly, deceived. I do here again repeat it, and tell them, that the very proper office of the law is, to make sin manifest; and also that Moses his chief office is, to teach us what we have to do, and with threatenings and cursings to urge it, especially when the law is compared with the gospel. For in the third chapter of the second epistle to the Corinthians Paul calleth the law the letter; and immediately after, the ministration of death; then again, he calleth it a doctrine written in letters and ink, and[11] figured in tables of stone, which should not endure, but perish and decay. The same apostle, on the other side again[12], doth call the gospel the ministration or doctrine of the Spirit, which endureth and decayeth not, which is written in men's hearts, and giveth life to the believers[13]. Whereupon we do freely confess, that the law doth properly make manifest our infirmity[14]; but the gospel giveth a medicine, and a remedy to that which was almost past hope.

And now here we must think that our holy ancestors had not the law, alone to convince them of sin; nor Moses, to do nothing else but kill and slay; nor that Moses was given to wound them, but to heal them[15]: and that, not by his own power or virtue, but by the guiding of them to him that cherisheth the contrite in heart, and healeth all their sor-

Moses doth not only slay, nor the law only kill.

[8 occasione accepta, peccatum per præceptum genuit, Lat.; and Erasmus.]

[9 mortuus sum, Lat.]   [10 morbum, sive peccatum, Lat.]
[11 rursus, Lat.]   [12 protinus, Lat.; and immediately.]
[13 to the believers, not in Lat.]   [14 morbum, Lat.]
[15 ut mederetur etiam, Lat.; but to heal also.]

rows: that is Christ Jesus, who also wrought by the min-istery of Moses. For we must not think, from the beginning of the world, nor from Moses his time till the coming of Christ[1], that the bare letter was preached only, and that the grace and Spirit of God was idle and wrought not in the minds of the faithful: for in that the law doth shew us, and invincibly prove to us, that in us, I mean, in our flesh, that perfection is not, which the most holy and perfect God doth in his law require of us, it doth therein revoke and pull back mankind (not by the virtue of itself, but by the power of the quickening Spirit of Christ) from confidence of the flesh[2], as that wherein there is no health nor jot of perfection; and so consequently doth give us occasion to turn ourselves to Christ our mediator, who is alone our sanctification and perfection. And so, for this occasion[3], the law is a path and ready way, and, as it were, a schoolmaster[4] given by God to us men, to draw us from all confidence in our own strengths, from all hope of our own merits[5], and from the trust in any kind of creatures, and to lead us directly by faith to Christ, who was made by God (as I said even now) our "righteousness, sancti-fication, and redemption," without whom there is no salvation under the sun. Therefore Moses did not only urge the law, but did also preach Christ and life in Christ. For the Lord in the gospel saith to the Jews: "Think not that I will accuse you to my Father[6]; there is one that accuseth you, even Moses, in whom ye trust. For if ye had believed Moses, ye would undoubtedly have believed me: for he wrote of me." And Paul to the Galatians saith: "If there had been a law given which could have given life, then no doubt right-eousness should have been by the law. But the scripture hath concluded all under sin, that the promise by the faith of Jesus Christ should be given unto them that believe. But before faith came, we were kept under the law, and were shut up into the faith which should afterward be revealed. Wherefore the law was our schoolmaster unto Christ, that we should be jus-

[1 Cor. i. 30.]

Moses doth also lead to Christ. [John v. 45, 46.]

[Gal. iii. 21—24.]

[1 ad Christum usque, Lat.]   [2 ab omni carne, Lat.]

[3 juxta hanc concomitantiam vel occasionem, Lat.]

[4 adeoque et pædagogus, Lat.]

[5 ab omni operum nostrorum respectu, Lat.; from all regard of our own works.]

[6 apud Patrem, Lat.]

tified by faith." Lo, what could be said more plainly, than that the law hath concluded all under sin? But to what end? " That the promise by the faith of Christ Jesus should be given unto them that do believe." And again: "Before faith came," that is, before he came to whom our faith is directed, and upon whom it is grounded[7], " we were kept under the law." How? Forsooth, being shut up unto the faith that was to be revealed. Therefore our fathers were shut up in the law, that they should not break out at any time, and seek for life and salvation any where else but in Christ alone. Wherefore the law did lead us[8] by faith directly unto Christ. And yet more plainly he saith: " The law was our schoolmaster unto Christ." Lo, here again the law doth bring us to Christ[9]. And again he addeth; "That we should be justified by faith." Therefore the law setteth forward the true doctrine of justification, teaching plainly that we are justified by faith in Christ, and not by the merits of our own works. In which point it is openly like unto the gospel[10], and taketh to itself the office of the gospel: and no marvel, since to many men, through their own fault, the gospel[11] doth become and is made the letter. Furthermore, the same apostle doth in another place say, that " in sacrifices they called their sins [Heb. x. 2, to remembrance," and we know that in them was prefigured[12] 3.] the purging of sins. Therefore even the ceremonial laws also led them to Christ, testifying and teaching them that he alone doth cleanse us from all our sins. Whereupon I conclude that the office of Moses and of the law both was and is, to open to us our sin and judgment; and yet not to condemn us only, but also by occasion to lead us to Christ.

By which we learn also, that the law doth not only The law teach us the first principles and rudiments of righteousness, perfect righteousness. but the very true and absolute righteousness. For Moses doth expressly say, that he taught a most perfect and absolute [Deut. xxx. kind of doctrine, as that wherein both life and death doth 15.] wholly consist. And the apostle saith, that the law leadeth

[7 See Vol. i. Addend. in pag. 112, line 32.]
[8 us, not in Lat.]   [9 En, ducit lex ad Christum etiam, Lat.]
[10 miscetur evangelio, Lat.]
[11 ipsum evangelium, Lat.; the gospel itself.]
[12 also prefigured, Lat.]

us by the hand to Christ, that we should be justified by faith. Now the righteousness of faith is the most perfect right-eousness. Therefore, whereas the precepts of the law are in some places called the rudiments of the world[1], that is for two especial causes: the first whereof is, because the law is, as it were, the first instructions or elements, which, when the doctrine of the gospel cometh, is finished, and giveth place to it as to more absolute principles; the latter cause is, because ceremonies are taught under outward things or signs, when as in those outward things they do prefigure, and set forth to be seen, the inward things, even Christ him-self and his holy mysteries.

The precepts of the law are the rudiments of the world.

And out of that which I have hitherto said we may also learn, that the ancient saints, which lived under the old testament, did not seek for righteousness and salvation in the works of the law, but in him which is the perfectness and end of the law, even Christ Jesus; and therefore that they used the law and the ceremonies as a guide and school-mistress to lead them by the hand to Christ their Saviour. For so often as they heard that the law required perfect righteousness at their hands, they did by faith through grace[2] understand, that in the law Christ was set forth to be the most absolute righteousness, to whom all men ought to fly for the obtaining of righteousness. So often as they met together in the holy congregation[3], to behold the holy cere-monies which God hath ordained, they did not look upon the bare figures only, nor think that they did please God, and were purged from their sins, by that external kind of worship[4]; but they did cast the eyes of their minds and of faith upon the Messiah to come, who was prefigured in all the ceremonies and ordinances of the law. They therefore did abuse the law, who thought that they were acceptable to God, and that they served him as they should, because they were busy in those ceremonial works. For those thoughts and persuasions the prophets in their sermons did sharply accuse, and evermore cry out upon. And in that sense, and for that cause, the people of Israel is many times called a carnal people: not that all the patriarchs and fathers before the coming of Christ were carnal or fleshly; but for

The kind of righteousness which was in the people of the old ancient world.

A carnal or fleshly people.

[1 Gal. iv. 3. Marg. Coloss. ii. 8, 20.]   [2 donata ex gratia, Lat.]
[3 in loco sacro, Lat.]   [4 propter cultum illum, Lat.]

because they did as yet live then under those external shadows and outward figures[5]; and for because there were
peradventure among the people some that did not perceive
the spiritual things shadowed under those external figures,
and did think perhaps that they were acceptable to God for
the working and doing of that external work[6].

The second use and another office of the law is, to teach *The law frameth the life of man.*
them that are justified in faith by Christ what to follow and
what to eschew, and how the godly and faithful sort should
worship[7] God. For the law of God doth comprehend a
most absolute doctrine both of faith in God, and also of all
good works. For in the first use of the law I declared how
the moral and ceremonial law doth teach us faith in God
and Christ his Son, and how it bringeth man to the knowledge of himself, that he may understand how that in himself,
that is, in the nature of man, there is no good thing nor any
life ; but that all the gifts of life, of virtues, and salvation, are
of God the Father, the only well-spring of all goodness,
through Christ his Son our Saviour[8]. In this second argument of the end[9], the use, or office of the law of God, we
must acknowledge all the forms of virtues, and the treasure
of all goodness[10], to be set forth unto us in the law of the
Lord; and that the apostle applieth the precepts of the law
to exhortation and consolation. The first of the two tables
of the moral law doth teach us what we owe to God, and
how he will be worshipped of us : the second table frameth
the offices of life, and teacheth us how to behave ourselves
toward our neighbour. The ceremonies also do belong to
religion[11] ; and the judicials teach the government of an
house or a commonweal, so that by them we may live honestly among ourselves and holily to God-wards. Therefore
the law doth teach all justice, temperance, fortitude, and
wisdom, and instructeth a godly man in every good work

[5] elementis et figuris, Lat.]
[6] propter opus externum operatum aut perfectum, Lat. See also
Bullinger, adv. Anabapt. Lib. iv. cap. 3.]
[7] rite colant, Lat.]
[8] per Christum, sive Messiam, Lat.]
[9] In præsenti, id est, in consideratione secundi finis, &c. Lat.]
[10] omnium bonorum operum, Lat.]
[11] ad cultum, Lat. ; to the worship (of God).]

16—2

wherein it is necessary that an holy worshipper of God should be instructed. Wherefore so often as the holy prophets of God would set up again and restore the worship of God and true religion that was decayed; so often as they would cry out upon and rebuke[1] the faults and errors of men; and lastly, when they would teach them to do those good works, which are good works indeed, they led them always[2] unto the law, and cited all their testimonies out of the law. Whereof we have evident examples in the fifteenth Psalm of David, and in the first and thirty-third chapter of Esay's Prophecy, and in the eighteenth of Ezekiel also. Paul in the thirteenth to the Romans referreth all the offices of our life to the law of charity; for the Lord himself, before Paul, had done the same in the gospel. Moreover the prophet David in the ninety-fourth Psalm crieth, " Blessed is the man, O Lord, whom thou instructest in thy law;" and in the seventy-eighth Psalm, " He made a covenant to Jacob, and gave a law in Israel, that the posterity might know it, and put their trust in the Lord, and not forget the works of God, but keep his commandments." Again, in the nineteenth Psalm he saith: " The law of the Lord is an undefiled law, converting the soul: the testimony of the Lord is sure, and giveth wisdom unto the simple: the statutes of the Lord are right, and rejoice the heart: the commandment of the Lord is pure, and giveth light unto the eyes. The fear of the Lord is holy, and endureth for ever: the judgments of the Lord are true and righteous altogether[3]: more to be desired are they than gold and precious stone[4]; and sweeter than honey and the honeycomb." And to this end tendeth the sense of all the alphabetical psalm, which is in order of number the 119th.

The law bridleth the unruly.   The third use or office of the law[5] is to repress the unruly; and those whom no reason can move to orderliness the law commandeth to constrain with punishment, that honesty, peace, and public tranquillity, may be maintained in christian

[1 corrigere, Lat.]
[2 semper ac unice, Lat.; always and alone.]
[3 justificata in semetipsa, Lat. and Vulg.; justified in themselves, Douay.]
[4 lapidem pretiosum, Lat. and Vulg.]
[5 divinæ legis, Lat.]

commonweals[6].   For some there are, and that no small
number of people, which do refrain from doing evil, and live
somewhat tolerably, not so much for the love of virtue, as for
the fear of punishment that will ensue their inordinate living.
Therefore it pleased the goodness of God, by giving the law,
to put in a caveat, and to make a proviso for the tranquillity
of mankind.   And to this it seemeth that the apostle had
an eye when he said: "We know, that the law was not given ⎡1 Tim. i. 9,
to the just, but to the unjust, to the lawless and disobedient, ⎣10.]
to the ungodly and to sinners, to unholy[7] and unclean, to
murderers of fathers and murderers of mothers, to manslayers, to whoremongers, to them that defile themselves
with mankind, to man-stealers, to liars, to perjured; and if
there be any other thing that is contrary to wholesome doctrine," &c.

After the declaration of the use, the end, and the office ⎡It is unpossi-
of the law, I have next to teach you how, and by what ⎢our own
means, the law of God is fulfilled.   It is unpossible for any ⎣fulfil the law.
⎢ble for us of
⎢strength to
man, of his own strength, to fulfil the law, and fully to satisfy
the will of God in all points.   For it is manifest that in the
law there is not required the outward work only, but also the
pureness of the inward affections, and, as it were, as I said
even now, a certain heavenly[8] and absolute perfectness.   For
the Lord himself in one place crieth, "Be ye perfect, even as [Matt. v. 48.]
your Father which is in heaven is perfect."   But so absolute
a perfectness is not found in us so long as we live in this flesh:
for the flesh, even to the very last end of our life, doth keep
still her corrupt disposition; and although it doth many times
receive an overthrow by the spirit, that striveth against it,
yet doth it still renew the fight[9]; so that in us there is not
found, nor in our strength there doth remain[10], that heavenly
and most absolute perfectness[8].   But let us hear the testimony
of the holy apostle Paul touching this matter, who saith:
"We know that the law is spiritual: but I am carnal, sold ⎡Rom. vii.
under sin.   For that which I do I allow not: for what I ⎣14, 15.]
would, that do I not; but what I hate, that do I."   And

[6 in christian commonweals, not in the original.]

[7 irreverentibus, Lat.]   [8 divinam perfectionem, Lat.]

[9 usque tamen recurrit, Lat. Cf. Horat. Ep. Lib. I. 10, 24.]

[10 ex nostris viribus derivetur, Lat.]

again: "I know that in me, that is, in my flesh, dwelleth no good thing: for to will is present with me; but I find no means to perform that which is good." Again: "I delight in the law of God after the inward man: but I see another law in my members, rebelling against the law of my mind, and subduing me unto the law of sin which is in my members." And at the last he concludeth, and saith: "So then with the mind I myself[1] serve the law of God; but with the flesh the law of sin." Now some there are which think that Paul spake these words not of himself, but of the persons of others which were carnal men and not as yet regenerate. But the very words of the apostle do enforce the reader, whether he will or no, to confess, that the words recited may be applied even to the man that is most spiritual[2]. Augustine, 1. Lib. *Retractat.* cap. 23, saith, that he himself was sometime of opinion, that those words of the apostle ought to be expounded of the man which was under the law, and not under grace; but he confesseth, that he was compelled by the authority of others' writings and treatises to think that the apostle spake them of such men as were most spiritual, and of his own person: as he doth at large declare in his book[3] against the Pelagians[4]. Even St Hierome also, who is said to have thundered out a most horrible curse against them that taught that the law did command things unpossible[5], doth expressly write to Rusticus, that Paul in this place speaketh of

Rom. vii. Paul spake in the 7th chapter to the Romans of his own person.

[1 idem ego, Lat., and Erasmus.]

[2 maxime spiritualibus competere, Lat.]

[3 libris, Lat.; books, ed. 1577.]

[4 In (eo) libro, " *Quod autem ait,*" inquam, " *Scimus quia lex spiritalis est, ego autem carnalis sum, venundatus sub peccato,* satis ostendit, non posse impleri legem, nisi a spiritalibus, quales facit gratia Dei." Quod utique non ex persona Apostoli accipi volui, qui jam spiritalis erat; sed hominis sub lege positi, nondum sub gratia. Sic enim prius hæc verba sapiebam, quæ postea lectis quibusdam divinorum tractatoribus eloquiorum, quorum me moveret auctoritas, consideravi diligentius et vidi etiam de ipso apostolo posse intelligi, quod ait, Scimus quoniam lex spiritalis est, ego autem carnalis sum. Quod in eis libris quos contra Pelagianos nuper scripsi, quantum potui diligenter ostendi." —Retract. 1. 23. Aug. Opp. Par. 1531. Tom. 1. fol. 7. col. 3.]

[5 Execramur etiam eorum blasphemiam, qui dicunt impossibile aliquid homini a Deo præceptum esse. Symboli Explan. ad Damasum. Hieron. Opp. Tom. v. col. 124. Par. 1706. But this treatise is not Jerome's.]

his own person[6]. But if the flesh and the corrupt disposition thereof remain, whereby it doth uncessantly strive with the spirit, then, verily, that heavenly perfectness is never perfit in us so long as we live; and so, consequently, so long as we live, none of us fulfilleth the law.

Here also is to be inserted that disputation of Paul, where he proveth that no mortal man is justified by the works of the law: his meaning is, not that no man is justified by the very works of the law, but that no man is justified by the works of our corrupt nature[7], which doth not perform that which the law of God requireth; for, as the same apostle saith, it is not able to perform it. And very well truly[8] saith he; "We know that a man is not justified by the deeds of the law, but by the faith of Jesus Christ: and we have believed in Jesus Christ, that we might be justified by the faith of Christ, and not by the deeds of the law; because by the deeds of the law no flesh shall be justified." Neither must we by the deeds of the law understand the ceremonies only: for even as the ceremonies do not, so likewise do not the morals, justify us men. The apostle speaketh of the morals, when he speaketh of the deeds of the law. For in the third chapter to the Romans the same apostle saith: "By the deeds of the law there shall no flesh be justified in his sight." And immediately after he addeth the reason why, saying; "for by the law cometh the knowledge of sin." But in the seventh chapter he sheweth by what law, to wit, the moral law. For the moral law saith, "Thou shalt not lust." But the apostle saith, "I knew not sin but by the law; for I had not known concupiscence, if the law had not said, Thou shalt not lust." In his epistle to the Ephesians he speaketh to the Gentiles, and saith simply that works do not justify: but, speaking to the Gentiles, he could not mean it of ceremonial laws, but of the very moral virtues, that is, all kinds of works that seemed to be good. To the Galatians he saith: "As many as are of the deeds of the law are under the curse."

No man is justified by the works of the law.

The works of the law.

[Gal. ii. 16.]

[Ephes. ii. 9.]

[Gal. iii. 10.]

[6 Hieron. Opp. Tom. IV. par. sec. col. 772. Ep. 95. Bullinger, Expos. in Ep. ad. Rom. Cap. VII. p. 66. Tigur. 1537.]

[7 The translator has here (from, 'his meaning is,' &c.) entirely mistaken Bullinger's words, which are; non legis quidem, sed corruptæ naturæ nostræ vitio: not indeed through any fault of the law, but through the fault of our corrupt nature.]

[8 diserte quidem, Lat.]

And to prove that, he addeth; "For it is written, Cursed is
every one that continueth not in all things which are written
in the book of the law to do them." Now unless we do by
the deeds of the law understand the morals, as well as the
ceremonials, I do not see how his proof can hang to that
which went before. For he saith expressly, "In all things
which are written in the book of the law[1] to do them." Now
who knoweth not that the ceremonials were not written alone,
but that the morals were written also? And St Augustine in
his book, *De Spiritu et litera*, cap. VIII.[2] doth by many
arguments prove, that Paul by the deeds of the law did understand the morals also[3].

Now that we may conclude this place, I will here recite
the words of the apostle in the eighth chapter to the Romans[4],
saying: "What the law could not do, inasmuch as it was
weak through the flesh, that God performed by sending his
own Son in the similitude of sinful flesh, and by sin condemned
sin in the flesh; that the righteousness of the law might be
fulfilled in us, which walk not after flesh, but after the spirit."
The apostle in these words teacheth us two things: first,
that the law neither can now, nor never could, justify us men.
The fault of this weakness or lack of ability he casteth not
upon the law, which is of itself good and effectual, and is the
doctrine of most absolute righteousness; but he layeth the
fault thereof upon our corrupt flesh. Our flesh neither could,
nor can, perform that which is required of us by the law[5] of
God. Whereupon St Peter, in the council held at Hierusalem,
[Acts xv. 10.] is read to have said: "Now therefore why tempt ye God, to
put on the disciples' necks the yoke, which neither our fathers
nor we were able to bear?" The latter is inferred upon the

[1 legis hujus, Lat.; of this law.]

[2 præsertim cap. 8, Lat.; and more especially in chap. 8.]

[3 Ac ne quisquam putaret hic Apostolum ea lege dixisse neminem
justificari, quæ in sacramentis veteribus multa continet figurata præcepta, unde etiam ipsa est circumcisio carnis, quam die octavo accipere
parvuli jussi sunt; continuo subjunxit quam legem dixerit, et ait, *Per
legem enim cognitio peccati*, &c.—Lib. de Spiritu et Litera. ch. VIII. Aug.
Op. Par. 1531, Tom. III. fol. 172. col. 2. Several similar passages are
contained in the same treatise.]

[4 verses 3. 4. Bullinger has adopted Erasmus' rendering. But
see below, p. 258, note 1.]

[5 bona lege, Lat.; by the good law.]

first, to wit, when the law could not give us life, nor we were able to do that which the law required at our hands, then God, who is rich in mercy and goodness, sent his Son into the world, that he, being incarnate, should die for us, and so take away the sin of our imperfection, and bestow on us his perfectness and fulness of the law[6]. By this therefore it is manifest that Christ hath fulfilled the law, and that he is the perfectness of all the faithful in the world.

But here this place requireth a more full exposition, how Christ hath fulfilled the law, and how he is made our perfectness. First of all, whatsoever things are promised and prefigured in the law and the prophets, all those hath Christ our Lord fulfilled. For those promises; "The seed of the woman shall crush the serpent's head: In thee shall all the kindreds of the earth be blessed;" and other more innumerable like to these did our Lord fulfil, when he, being born into this world, made an atonement for us, and brought back life to us again. In like manner he fulfilled all the ceremonials, while he himself, being both priest and sacrifice, did offer up himself, and is now and ever an effectual and everlasting sacrifice, and an eternal high priest, making intercession always at the right hand of the Father for all faithful believers. He also doth spiritually circumcise the faithful, and hath given them instead of circumcision the sacrament of[7] baptism. He is our passover, who instead of the paschal lamb hath ordained the Eucharist, or supper of the Lord. Finally, he is the fulfilling[8] and perfectness of the law and the prophets. Moreover our Lord fulfilled the law, in that he did most absolutely in all points satisfy the will of God, being himself the holiest of all[9], in whom there is no spot, no evil concupiscence, nor any sin: in him is the love of God most perfect, and righteousness altogether absolute; which righteousness he doth freely communicate to us that are most unperfect, if we believe and have our hope fast settled in him[10]. For he forgiveth us our sins, being made a cleansing sacrifice for us,

Christ hath fulfilled the law, and is the perfectness of the faithful.

[Gen. iii. 15; xii. 3.]

[6 perfectionem suam nobis conferret in fide, qui est perfectio et plenitudo legis, Lat.; and bestow on us his perfectness in faith, being himself the perfectness and fulness of the law. Ed. 1577.]

[7 the sacrament of, not in Lat.]

[8 et mens, Lat. ; omitted.]   [9 sanctus sanctorum, Lat.]

[10 and have—him, not in Lat.]

and maketh us partakers of his own righteousness; which is for that cause called imputed righteousness[1]. Whereunto the testimonies of the apostle do appertain. "God," saith Paul, "was in Christ reconciling the world unto himself, not imputing their sins unto them. For him, which knew no sin, he made sin for us, that we might be made the righteousness of God by him[2]." Again: "Abraham believed God, and it was imputed to him for righteousness, without works[3]. So also, if we believe in God through Christ, our faith shall be imputed to us for righteousness." For by faith we lay hold on Christ, whom we believe to have made most absolute satisfaction to God for us, and so consequently that God for Christ his sake is pleased with us, and that his righteousness is imputed to us as our own[4] (and is indeed by gift our own), because we are now the sons of God.

[Rom. iv. 3, 24.]

These things being diligently weighed, it shall be easy for us to answer them which make this question, and do demand: Since no mortal man doth of himself exactly satisfy the law, how then is righteousness, life, and salvation, promised to them that do observe the law? Our answer is forsooth, that that promise hath a respect to the perfect righteousness of Christ, which is imputed unto us. Otherwise it is assuredly certain, that the holy scripture doth not so much as in one jot disagree or square[5] in any point from itself. The apostle doth plainly say: "If there had a law been given which could have given life, then had righteousness been of the law: but now the scripture hath shut up all under sin, that the promise might be given by faith to them that do believe." Wherefore he keepeth or doth fulfil the law, even of the ten commandments, who doth the thing for which the law was chiefly ordained. But the law was chiefly ordained (as I did declare a little before) to the end, that it might convince us all of sin and damnation, and so by that means send us from ourselves, and lead us by the hand to Christ, who is the fulfilling of the law

Life is promised to them that keep the law.

[Gal. iii. 21, 22.]

[1 imputativa, Lat.]

[2 2 Cor. v. 19, 21, per illum, Lat.; Erasmus' rendering. Calvin retains the "in ipso" of the Vulgate; melius enim quadrat menti Paulinæ illa significatio. Com. in loc. cit.]

[3 certe absque operibus, Lat.]

[4 Christi justitiam gratis imputari, Lat.]

[5 discrepare, Lat.]

unto justification to every one that doth believe. And therefore How we may keep the law. he doth fulfil and keep the law, who hath no confidence in himself and his own works, but, committing himself to the very[6] grace of God, doth seek all righteousness in the faith of Christ. Whereupon now it is evident, that these two sentences of Christ our Lord are of one sense and meaning; "Whoso- [John vi. 47; Matt. xix. 17.] ever believeth in me, he hath life everlasting:" and, "If thou wilt enter into life, keep the commandments." For Paul also in the thirteenth chapter of the Acts saith: "Be it Acts xiii. known unto you, brethren, that through Christ is preached to you the forgiveness of sins; and by him all that believe are justified from all the things, from which he could not be justified by the law of Moses." And to this place now belongeth all the work[7] of justification, of which I have at large disputed in another place[8].

Now that faith, wherewith we believe that Christ hath How we may keep the law. satisfied the law, and that he is our righteousness and our perfection, is neither of our own nature, nor of our own merits, but is by the grace of God poured into us through the Holy Spirit which is given into our hearts. This Spirit abiding in our hearts doth inflame our breasts with the love and desire of God's law, to do our endeavour to the expressing[9] and shewing of the law in all our works and conversation: which desire and endeavour, although they be never fully accomplished by reason of the flesh's frailty[10], or weakness of man's nature, which remaineth in us even till the last gasp and end of our life, is notwithstanding acceptable to God by grace[11] for Christ his sake alone; neither doth any godly man put any confidence in this other, but in the first fulfilling of the law[12], as that which is only absolute and perfect. For Paul in his epistle to the Romans crieth out: "O wretched man that I am! who shall deliver me from the body of this death[13]?" And yet immediately after he answereth; "I thank God," to [Rom. vii. 24, 25; viii. 1.] wit, because he hath redeemed me from death, "through Jesus Christ our Lord. So then I myself with the mind serve the

---

[6 veræ gratiæ, Lat.; true grace.]
[7 negotium, Lat.]   [8 See Decade I. Serm. 6.]
[9 legitime, Lat.; omitted.]   [10 carnis ingenium, Lat.]
[11 sed duntaxat, Lat.]   [12 tantum, Lat.; omitted, alone.]
[13 ex hoc corpore morti obnoxio, Lat.; Erasmus' rendering.]

law of God, but with the flesh the law of sin. There is then[1] no condemnation to them which are graffed[2] in Christ Jesu, which walk not after the flesh but after the spirit," &c. Wherefore, since we are in Christ, we are in grace, and therefore is God pleased with our works, which, being given to us by faith[3] and by the liberal Spirit[4], do proceed from an heart that loveth God, the giver of them all[5]. For John said: "This is the love of God, that we keep his commandments; and his commandments are not grievous." He addeth also the reason thereof, and saith; "For all that is born of God overcometh the world:" now every one is born of God that doth believe; as is declared in the first of St John.

[1 John v. 3, 4, 12, 13.]

God's commandments are not heavy to be borne.

By which it is easy to reconcile these two places, which seem at a blush to jar one with another: The laws of God are heavy, which neither we nor our fathers were able to bear: and, The laws of God are not grievous, or heavy to be borne. For they are not heavy to the faithful which are in Christ[6], and to those which have the gift of God's Spirit, that is, to those that are reconciled to God by Christ their Lord and Saviour. Without Christ and faith in Christ they are most grievous and heavy to be borne of every unbeliever[7]. So the faithful, being stirred up by the Spirit of God, doth voluntarily and of his own accord do good to all men, so far as his ability doth suffer him, and will not in any case do hurt to any man: not for because he feareth the punishment that in the law is appointed for the disobedient, unjust, and wrongful dealers; but for because he loveth God. And so also he fulfilleth the judicial law.

[Acts xv. 10; 1 John v. 3.]

Of the abrogation of the law.

Here I know full well that thou wilt make this objection and say: If the law be fulfilled, and that the fulfilling[8] thereof hath a place in the saints and faithful ones, what needed then, I pray you, the abrogating of the law? What

[1 nunc, Lat.; omitted: now.]

[2 qui insiti sunt, Lat., and Erasmus.]   [3 ex fide, Lat.]

[4 ex liberali spiritu, Lat.; referring to Psalm li. 12, where Calvin and Bucer read, spiritu liberali. See also p. 147, note 6.]

[5 the giver of them all, not in Lat.]

[6 insitis in Christo, Lat.]

[7 and heavy—unbeliever, not in Lat.]

[8 that the fulfilling thereof, not in Lat.]

needed Paul, and all the best divines, to dispute so largely of the abrogation of the same? I will therefore say somewhat of the abrogation of the law, first generally, and then by parts peculiarly. But first of all, these words of the Lord in the gospel must be beaten into the head of every godly hearer[9] : " Think not," saith he, " that I am come to destroy [Matt. v. 17—19.] the law or the prophets: yea, I came not to destroy, but to fulfil them. Verily, I say unto you, heaven and earth shall pass[10], but one jot or tittle of the law shall not pass, till all be fulfilled. Whosoever therefore shall loose one of the smallest of these commandments, and shall teach men so, he shall be called the least in the kingdom of heaven: but whosoever shall do and teach them, he shall be called great in the kingdom of heaven." Let every one therefore be assuredly persuaded that the law of God, which is the most excellent and perfect will of God, is for ever eternal, and cannot be at any time dissolved, either by men, or angels, or any other creatures. Let every man think that the law, so far as it is the rule how to live well and happily, so far as it is the bridle wherewith we are kept in the fear of the Lord, so far as it is a prick to awake the dulness of our flesh, and so far as it is given to instruct, correct, and rebuke us men, that so far, I say, it doth remain unabrogated[11], and hath even at this day her commodity in the church of God: and therefore the abrogating of the law consisteth in this that followeth.

I told you that God's commandments require the whole man, and a very heavenly[12] kind of perfectness; which whosoever performeth not, he is accursed and condemned by the law. Now no man doth fulfil that righteousness: therefore are we all accursed by the law. But this curse is taken away, and most absolute righteousness is freely bestowed on us, through Christ Jesus. For Christ redeemed us from the curse of the law, being made the curse, righteousness, and sanctification for us men. And so in this sense the law is abrogated; that is, the curse of the law is through Christ taken from the faithful, and true righteousness is bestowed upon us through grace by faith in the same Christ Jesus[13].

[9 insculpenda erunt animo pio, Lat.]
[10 donec prætereat, Lat.; as in Auth. Ver.]
[11 intactam, Lat.]   [12 plane divinam, Lat.]
[13 through grace—Jesus, not in Lat.]

For he is that blessed Seed in whom all the kindreds of the earth are blessed. He is our righteousness. For Paul saith, " By him every one that believeth is justified from all things, from which ye could not be justified by the law of Moses." Therefore the law is put for the curse of the law: or else the law of God is taken for that which is bewrayed or made manifest by the law, that is to say, it is taken for sin; for by the law cometh the knowledge of sin. Therefore the law is abrogated, that is, sin is taken away, not that it should not be, or not shew itself[1] in us, but that it should not be imputed unto us and condemn us; "for there is no damnation to them that are in Christ Jesu[2]." Moreover the law is taken for the vengeance or punishment which is by the law appointed for transgressors. Therefore the law is abrogated, because the punishment appointed by the law is taken from the necks of the faithful believers; "for the law is not given to the righteous man." For Christ delivered the faithful from eternal punishments, whiles he being guiltless did suffer afflictions for wicked sinners. Furthermore, the apostle saith: " The fleshly mind is enmity against God: for it is not obedient to the law of God, neither can be." But now this hatred or enmity of God's law is by faith pulled out of the hearts of the faithful; and instead of it is graffed in the love of God's most holy will: so that, in this sense also, the law is said to be abrogated, because the hatred of the law is taken away. And therefore the apostle compareth them that are under the law to bond-slaves, and them that are free from the law to sons and children[3]: to whom also he attributeth the spirit, not of bondage, but of adoption. " For because ye are sons[4]," saith he, " God hath sent the Spirit of his Son into your hearts, which crieth, Abba, Father, &c." To these may be added, that the law of God hath types and shadows, and that the ceremonies are very[5] burdensome, even as also the whole law is called a yoke. But now the Son of God came into this world, who, fulfilling the figures, shewed to us the very truth, and did abolish those types and shadows; so that now no man can

Side notes:

[Acts xiii. 39.]

2

3

[1 Tim. i. 9.]

[Rom. viii. 7.]
4

Gal. iv.

5

[1 exserat suas vires, Lat.]   [2 Rom. viii. 1, qui insiti sunt in.]
[3 liberis sive filiis, Lat.]   [4 ejus filii, Lat.; his sons.]
[5 satis alioqui, Lat.; are otherwise sufficiently.]

condemn us[6] for neglecting or passing over those ceremonies or figures: and so again in that sense the law of God is abrogated, that is to say, that kind of government which Moses ordained did come to nought, when Christ did come and his apostles began to teach. For they, without regard of the ecclesiastical regiment appointed by Moses, did congregate churches, to which they taught not that kind of regiment which Moses had ordained. For they did constantly reject the priesthood of Aaron, the sacraments, the sacrifices, and choice of days, of meats, and of apparel, which Moses had taught their elders; and instead of all those rites they preached Christ alone, and his two sacraments, &c.[7]

This have I said hitherto generally[8] touching the abro- *The moral law is not* gation of the law; and now again I will more largely expound *abrogated.* the same by several parts.

The whole law[9] is divided into the moral, the ceremonial, and the judicial laws. The moral law now is contained in the ten commandments, the first precept whereof doth teach us to honour and worship one God alone, and not to match 1 any strange gods with him. This commandment did our Lord Jesus in the gospel so earnestly urge and diligently teach, that we may perceive very well that in it nothing is altered. The second precept forbiddeth idolatry, that is, the worshipping and honouring of all manner images, whether they be 2 the images of God himself, or of any of his creatures. But it is known that the apostles, in the doctrine of the gospel, did use all means that they could to banish and drive away all kind of idolatry. Paul and John cry, "Flee from idolatry." [1 Cor. x. 14. 1 John v. 21.] And whereas Christ and his apostles do most diligently teach 3 us to sanctify and glorify God's holy name, they do thereby give their consent to the establishing of the third[10] commandment, which doth forbid to defile God's name by taking it in vain. The fourth alone of all the commandments[11], concerning the sanctifying of the sabbath-day, is of St Augustine called 4 ceremonial[12]. But it must not be simply understood to be

[6 nos judicare, Lat.]
[7 et paucula sacramenta, &c., Lat. ; and very few sacraments.]
[8 et breviter, Lat.; omitted, and in few words.]
[9 lex Dei, Lat.]   [10 the third, not in Lat.]
[11 in universo decalogo, Lat.; omitted, of all the ten.]
[12 Inter omnia illa decem præcepta, solum ibi quod de Sabbato

ceremonial: for so far forth as the outward worship of God requireth a certain appointed time to be exercised in, and carrieth with it the[1] sacrifices of the law, so far, I say, it is ceremonial; but in respect that it teacheth to meet in holy assemblies to worship God, to pray, to preach, to be partakers of the sacraments, and to offer spiritual sacrifices, therein it is eternal and not ceremonial: as I have before declared in

5 the exposition of the sabbath[2]. The fifth precept, touching the honour due to parents, the Lord himself doth ratify in the fifteenth chapter of Matthew's gospel; even as he doth also

6 very diligently teach the sixth against murder, and the

7 seventh against adultery, in the fifth chapter of the same gos-

8 pel. The eighth, which is against theft, is renewed by the

[1 Thess. iv. 6; Eph. iv. 28.] apostle, who giveth charge, that no man deceive[3] his brother, and that no man steal any more; but that every one should labour with his hands, that he may have things necessary for

9 himself, and be able to give to him that wanteth. The ninth precept, which is for the bridling of the tongue, so that no lie be made nor false witness borne against our neighbour, is by Christ himself and his apostles confirmed so often as they give rules for the ordering of the tongue, and charge every

10 man to speak the truth to his neighbour. And they also do condemn evil lusts and affections, whereby they do not abrogate but repair the tenth[4] commandment, which doth forbid all manner of concupiscence. Therefore the whole abrogation of the ten commandments, so far forth as they are abrogated, doth consist in those points whereof I spake even now: to wit, that Christ in faith is our perfect and absolute righteousness, &c. the apostle bearing witness thereunto, and saying: "What the law could not do, inasmuch as it was weak through the flesh, God, having sent his own Son in the similitude of sinful flesh, even by sin condemned sin in the flesh; that the righteousness of the law might be fulfilled in us, which walk not after the flesh, but after the spirit:" as is to be seen in the eighth to the Romans[5]. I have therefore discussed the

positum est, figuratè observandum præcipitur.—Aug. Januario. Ep. 119. c. 12. Op. Par. 1531. Tom. II. fol. 110. col. 4. In the Bened. ed. it stands ad Inquis. Jan. II. 55. c. 12. P.]

[1 externa, Lat.; omitted.]   [2 See Decade II. Serm. 4.]

[3 fraudet in negotio, Lat.]   [4 tenth, not in Lat.]

[5 verses 3, 4. Bullinger varies in this quotation from himself at

brieflier of this matter, in this place, because I have at the full spoken of it in the treatise of the ten commandments.

I am now come to speak of the ceremonials. These ceremonials were given and granted until the time of amendment, to wit, until Messiah should come. Messiah is already come; therefore all the ceremonies, even to the coming, death, resurrection, and ascension of Christ our Lord into the heavens, are come to an end, and have no place any longer in the church of the Christians. And yet here we must and do make a difference[6] betwixt the writings concerning the ceremonies, and the very things of the ceremonies that are set down in writing; I mean, the very ceremonies themselves, or actions that were used. For the writings concerning the ceremonies, which were set forth by the Spirit of God, are not taken away from Christians[7], nor abrogated, so that they may not be read, retained, or used in the church: as I declared in the second sermon of the first decade[8]. For they are effectual to instruct us in Christ Jesu, while in them we do behold the manner how Christ was preached and prefigured to the ancient church of the holy fathers. Paul, verily, did most significantly preach Christ out of the ceremonies; which no man will deny that readeth diligently his epistle to the Hebrews: for he doth wonderfully in that epistle lay Christ and all his gifts before the eyes of all the church. Therefore the ceremonials both may and ought to be read in the church; so yet that in them Christ be sought, and, when he is found, be aptly preached. And for that cause, in the fifth and sixth sermons of this decade, where I handled the ceremonials, I annexed unto them certain notes of their significations, that I might open a way for the students of the scriptures and lovers of Christ to go forward and proceed in that kind of argument.

Now the ceremonial[9] things, or stuff of the ceremonies, of which sort are the priesthood, the place, the time, the sacrifice, and whatsoever else is like to these, are utterly.

How far forth the ceremonials are abrogated.

page 253, and from Erasmus' rendering, in these points: he reads *eo quod* (which Calvin also prefers), instead of ea parte qua imbecillis erat;—and sub specie carnis *peccatricis*, instead of carnis peccato obnoxiæ;—and instead of de peccato, *per peccatum* condemnavit peccatum.]

[6 necessario, Lat. omitted.]   [7 from Christians, not in Lat.]
[8 Vol. I. p. 59.]   [9 res ceremoniales, is Bullinger's own term.]

17

[BULLINGER, II.]

abrogated, so that henceforth they are neither used, nor have any place in the church of Christ. This did Jeremy foretell in the third chapter of his prophecy, saying: "In those days[1] they shall make no more boast of the ark of the Lord's covenant[2]: no man shall think upon it, neither shall any man make mention of it; for from thenceforth it shall neither be visited, neither shall such things be done any more[3]." By the ark the prophet meaneth those points of the law[4] which are abolished by the coming of Christ. St Paul, in his epistle to the Hebrews, by the promise that God made to Jeremy[5], saying, "that he would make a new covenant," doth gather

Heb. viii. this observation: "In that he saith, A new covenant, he hath worn out the first; for[6] that which is worn out, and waxed old, is ready to vanish away." The same apostle to the Ephesians saith: "Christ is our peace, which hath made both one, and broken down the middle wall, that was a stop between us; taking away in his flesh[7] the hatred, even the law of commandments contained in ordinances, for to make of twain one new man in himself, so making peace." Ephes. ii. God verily severed the Jews from the Gentiles, while he chose and consecrated them to be a peculiar people unto himself, not by the calling of the word only, but also by the sacraments. For there were ceremonies prescribed and given, which, as a middle wall betwixt the Jews and the Gentiles, should compass in and contain[8] the heritage of the Lord: so that in the ceremonies the note of difference[9] did consist, whereby the Jews were known to be the lawful heirs[10] of God's good promises, whereof the Gentiles had no part or portion. But Christ came into the world, to the intent that of two people, the Jews and the Gentiles, he might make one church; and

Ceremonies the middle wall or partition. therefore did he break down the middle wall that parted them, that is, he did clean take away the ceremonial ordi-

---

[1 dicit Dominus, Lat. omitted; saith the Lord.]

[2 non dicant amplius, arca fœderis Domini, Lat.]

[3 neque fiet ultra, Lat.; neither shall that be done any more. Auth. Ver.]

[4 etiam alia legalia, Lat.]   [5 apud Jeremiam, Lat.]

[6 porro, Lat.]   [7 per carnem suam, Lat.]

[8 includerent, Lat.; inclose.]

[9 discriminis professio, Lat.]

[10 ac (adeo ut) Judæis, ceu justis hæredibus addiceretur hæreditas, Lat.]

nances which were a stop betwixt them[11]. For Christ in that case did the same that princes are wont to do, who, when they go about to bring two nations, that are at variance, into one kingdom and under one authority, do first take away the diversity of arms[12], which are the cognisances of their ancient hatred, that when the cause of the remembrance of the grudge is taken from their eyes, they may the better agree betwixt themselves in mind and behaviour. For even so did Christ take away circumcision, the sacrifices, and all the ceremonies[13], to the end that of the Jews and Gentiles he might make one church and fellowship[14]. Paul, to the Colossians, compareth the ceremonies to an obligation, or hand-writing[15], whereby God hath us bound, as it were, so that we cannot deny the guilt. But he saith that we were so delivered by Christ from the guilt, that the obligation or hand-writing was cancelled or torn in pieces. But by the cancelling of the hand-writing the debtor is acquitted and set at liberty. And therefore we read, that at the death of our Lord the veil of the temple was torn in pieces from the bottom up to the very top; that thereby all people might understand, both that sins were then forgiven them, and that the people of God was set at liberty from all the burden and yoke of the law. Verily, when the wicked, stiff-necked, and disloyal[16] people of the Jews did, after the death of Christ, go on to exercise, prorogue[17], and to obtrude[18] to all men the ceremonies, which were finished and abrogated at the coming of Messiah[19]; then Christ, sitting at the right hand of the Father, did by the means of the Roman princes utterly deface their city, and overthrow[20] the temple, wherein they boasted[21]: which thing the prophet Daniel, and Balaam many

Ceremonies hand-writing

The city and temple of Jerusalem destroyed.

Dan. ix. Num. xxiv.

[11] which—them, not in Lat.]
[12] diversas tesseras, Lat.; the variety of badges.]
[13] legalibus, Lat.]   [14] and fellowship, not in Lat.]
[15] Coloss. ii. 14. Calvin's words, in his Commentary on this passage, are here again largely adopted by Bullinger. See also Calfhill's Answer, p. 123.]
[16] perfidus, Lat.]
[17] prorogare, Lat.; to continue or prolong.]
[18] pietatis ergo in templo, Lat. omitted; as a matter of religion in the temple.]
[19] at the coming of Messiah, not in Lat.]
[20] funditus, Lat. omitted; to its foundations.]
[21] wherein they boasted, not in Lat.]

17—2

hundred years before Daniel's time, foretold and said should come to pass. Neither hitherto yet, by the space of 1500 years and more, have they had any place to restore and set up again their city and temple.

In Theodoretus and Ruffinus we read that in the reign of Julian the emperor the Jews, with very great hope and presumption, went about to build a new temple; and that they sought the foundation thereof in the place where that temple stood which was burnt by Titus, son and general[1] to the emperor Vespasian: but Christ our Lord (who in the gospel foretold out of Daniel's prophecy the desolation thereof, and did among other speeches say, "And Hierusalem shall be trodden under foot of the Gentiles, till the time of the Gentiles be fulfilled,") did mightily repress their wicked endeavours, and hinder their labour for going forward. For when they had gathered and brought together many thousand bushels of lime and chalk, then suddenly came a whirlwind with a wonderful storm and blustering, which scattered abroad and carried away the store of stuff by them provided. There happened also a terrible earthquake, by which all the buildings almost of the whole place were swept away, and made even with the ground. Finally, when a great company, which were busy in the work, did the same night remain, or take their rest, in a certain porch or gallery near to the new begun city and temple, the whole building and roof thereof, falling down on a sudden, slew all the number that were within the reach thereof. In the morning they which remained alive ran together to seek every man for his friend among them that were slain by the ruinous building. And when those terrors could do no good, nor turn them from their purpose, then suddenly out of the trenches, foundations, and storehouses hard by, where their tools and other necessaries lay, there sprang forth a fearful fire, which burnt many that urged the work, and compelled the rest to take their heels. For in that one day it brake forth sundry times, and so at last repressed the stubborn rashness of that stiff-necked people. And for because these things should not be thought to have happened casually or at adventures, the night before and the night following there appeared in the sky a bright or glistering sign of the cross, and the garments of the Jews were filled over

[1 and general, not in Lat.]

with crosses, not bright but black, which could not be rid
away or wiped out by any pains-taking or manner of means.
They therefore, in spite of their teeth and full sore against
their wills, being compelled with those horrible terrors, fearful
judgments, and bitter plagues of Christ our Lord, forsook the
place, and fled every man to his house, leaving the work undone, and openly confessing, that Jesus Christ, whom their
forefathers had crucified, is a most mighty God, howsoever
Julian, with Pharao[2], and the chief of the Jews, did persevere
still in their disloyalty and despiteful blasphemy against him[3]
and his holy church[4].

But howsoever the Jews do even at this day abide in
their wilful stubbornness, the Lord did from heaven declare
openly enough, that he is no longer delighted with the[5]
ceremonial rites, because he destroyed all the instruments
belonging to that ancient kind of worship; and made the
very shop of that old religion, I mean the temple and city
of Hierusalem, level with the ground. Touching the temple,
the Lord in the gospel spake to his disciples, when they
with wondering did behold it[6], and said: "Do ye not see [Matt. xxiv.
all these things? Verily I say unto you, there shall not be 44.] 2; Luke xix.
left here one stone standing upon another." And again, weeping over the unthankful city, he said: "They shall not leave
in thee one stone standing upon another, because thou
knewest not the time of thy visitation." And now, that all
this was word for word accomplished and fully finished,
Josephus, an eye-witness of the same, doth largely testify in
the eighteenth chapter of his seventh book *De Bello Judaico*[7].
Even very now I told you, that from one thousand and five
hundred years ago unto this present time the Jews never
had any place given them to build their temple up in again:
whereby, if they were not beside themselves, they might

[2 licet cum Pharaone, et Julianus et potior Judæorum turba, Lat.]

[3 contra Christum, Lat.; and his holy church, not in Lat.]

[4 Vide Theodoret. Eccl. Hist. III. 20. et Ruffin. Aquil. Hist. Eccles.
Lib. I. cap. 37. 38. 39.]

[5 legalibus vel, Lat.]

[6 commonstrantibus, Lat.; point it out.]

[7 This reference is according to the Latin edition of Josephus,
Basil, 1540. In the more modern editions the account is contained in
the chapters of the sixth, and the first chapter of the seventh book, de
Bell. Jud.]

easily gather, that the Messiah is already come into the world, and that he hath abrogated all the ceremonial rites.

Rites or ceremonies, how they are perpetual or everlasting. It is a very slender, or rather no defence at all for the Jews to allege the words in the law, which are many times rehearsed, where the ceremonies are described : " Ye shall keep it for an everlasting ordinance." For in this sense everlasting is taken for long lasting and unchangeable, so far forth as it hath respect unto the will or authority of mankind[1]. For the Lord did with threatening of grievous punishments forbid that mankind's unadvisedness should change or abrogate the holy ceremonies. And yet, since he did ordain those ceremonies until the time of amendment, he[2] doth neither sin, nor yet incur the crime of unconstancy, when he doth change or take away the ceremonies according to the determinate purpose which he intended from the beginning. Moreover, so long as the thing signified[3] doth not decay, and that the shadow only, or momentany figure[4], doth vanish away, it is assuredly certain that the ceremony doth yet remain in full effect and substance[5]. The whole man doth live for ever ; and yet the things that are temporal or corruptible in him do perish in death, and are abolished in his clarification[6].

The priesthood abrogated. But that all these things may appear as clear as the daylight, I will particularly run through and touch the more notable sort of ceremonies. That the priesthood of Aaron is utterly abrogated, it is evident by the words which[7] the [Psalm cx. 4; Heb. v. 6.] apostle citeth out of David, saying : " The Lord hath sworn, and will not repent, Thou art a priest for ever after the order of Melchisedech." Christ, therefore, is the one and only high priest, and that too an everlasting priest, having an immutable priesthood, which cannot by succession pass from him to any other man or angel. For he now, standing at the right hand of the Father in heaven, the very true temple which was prefigured by the tabernacle and temple at Jerusalem, doth make intercession for us, and doth all the offices of an high priest : of whom the apostle of Christ, St Paul, doth speak very largely in his epistle unto the Hebrews.

[1 quantum attinet homines, Lat.] [2 Deus, Lat.]
[3 per ritum, Lat.; by the ceremony.]
[4 cadit et, Lat. ; falls, and.] [5 in substantia sua, Lat.]
[6 i. e. glorification.] [7 id maxime arguit quod, Lat.]

This Christ Jesus, our high priest, hath consecrated all the faithful to be kings and priests unto himself. And yet notwithstanding he doth ordain ministers of the church, by doctrine and examples to instruct the church, and to minister the sacraments; I mean, not those old and ancient ones, but those which the Lord hath substituted instead of the old ones. What doctrine they must teach, he doth expressly declare. The mystical attire and garments of the priesthood he neither did commend to his apostles, nor leave to his church, but took them away with all the ceremonies[8] that are called the middle wall betwixt the Jews and Gentiles. The Lord himself and his apostle Paul will have the pastors of the people clad with righteousness and honesty; and do precisely remove the ministers of the church from superiority and secular affairs. They do also appoint stipends for the ministers to live upon; yet not those which the law allowed them, but such as were most tolerable and convenient for the state and condition of every church. *Matt. x. 1 Cor. ix.*

The Lord left the place to serve and worship God in free, without exception or binding to any one prescribed or peculiar place, when in the gospel after John he said: "The hour shall come, and is already, when the true worshippers shall worship the Father neither in this mountain, nor at Jerusalem, but in the spirit and in truth: for such the Father requireth to worship him. God is a Spirit; and they that worship him must worship him in spirit and in truth." The apostle followed the Lord in this doctrine, and said; "I will that men pray in every place, lifting up pure hands, without anger." Neither did the Lord in vain, as I shewed you even now, suffer the temple to be utterly overthrown, considering that at his death he had rent the veil thereof. And yet, for all that, the ecclesiastical assemblies are not thereby condemned: of which I spake in the exposition of the fourth precept[9], "Remember that thou keep holy the sabbath-day." Verily, the tabernacle and the temple bare the type of the catholic church of God, out of which there are no prayers nor oblations acceptable to the Lord. But the church is extended to the very ends of the world. And yet it followeth not thereupon, that all are in the church which are in the world: they alone are in the church, which through the

The place for to worship God in is free for every man to choose where he listeth, and the congregation liketh. [John iv. 21, 23, 24.]

[1 Tim. ii. 8.]

[8 decretis, Lat.]   [9 See Vol. I. page 255.]

catholic faith are in the fellowship of Christ Jesus, and by the agreement of doctrine, by charity, and by the participation of the sacraments (unless some great necessity hinder them), are *To sacrifice in high places.* in the communion of the holy saints. But they burn incense and sacrifice in high places, whosoever seek after any other sacrifice than the one and only oblation of Christ Jesus; or look for any other to offer their prayers to God the Father than Christ alone[1], as they are taught by the mouth of the pastor sincerely preaching the word of God. Moreover the church of God hath no need now of any ark, any table, any shewbread, any golden candlestick, any altar either of incense or burnt-offerings, nor yet of any brasen laver: for Christ alone is all in all[2] to the catholic church; which church hath all these things spiritually and effectually in Christ Jesus, and can seek for nothing in any other creatures; insomuch that, if it perceive any man to bring in again either these or such like ceremonial instruments, it doth sharply rebuke and bitterly curse[3] him for his unwarrantable rashness and blasphemous presumption in the church of Christ. For what need hath the church of shadows and figures, when it doth now enjoy[4] the thing itself, even Christ Jesus, whose shadow and figure the ceremonies bare? Moreover the church hath signs enough, in that it hath received of Christ two sacramental signs, wherein are contained all the things which the old church did comprehend[5] in sundry and very many figures.

The holy time is free.
[Mark ii. 27, 28.]
Furthermore, he hath left the holy time, to worship God in, free to our choice, who in the gospel saith: "The sabbath was made for man, not man for the sabbath: therefore the Son of Man is Lord also of the sabbath." And the apostle [Coloss. ii. 16, 17.] Paul saith: "Let no man therefore judge you in meat, or drink, or in part of an holy day[6], or of the new moon, or of the sabbaths: which are the shadows of things to come; but the body is of Christ." Of the christian sabbath I spake in

[1 et alium in orando et sacrificando modum tenent, quam verbo pastoris in ecclesia est traditum, Lat.; and practise another method of prayer and sacrifice than, &c.]

[2 hæc omnia, Lat.; is all these things.]

[3 execretur, Lat.; for his—Christ, not in Lat.]

[4 per fidem, Lat. omitted; by faith: whose—bare, not in Lat.]

[5 habuit, Lat.]   [6 So Auth. Ver. marg.]

the exposition of the fourth commandment[7]. As for the new moons, they are not solemnized by the church of Christ, insomuch as it is taught by Christ to attribute to God[8], not the beginning of months only, but the whole year also, and the commodity[9] thereof, with the light of the sun, the moon, and all the stars in heaven.

Moreover the Christians do celebrate their passover more spiritually than bodily; even as also they do solemnize their Pentecost, or Whitsuntide[10]. For as he sent his Spirit upon his disciples, so doth he daily send it upon all the faithful. And that is the cause that in the faithful the alarm is stricken up to encourage them as soldiers to skirmish with their enemies[11]. For the flesh lusteth against the spirit, and the faithful are daily assaulted, and provoked to battle, by the world, and by the devil the prince of the world[12]. Furthermore, the feast of propitiation, being once finished upon the cross, endureth for ever: neither do the saints any more send out a scapegoat, to bear their sins into the desert[13]; for Christ our Lord came once, and was offered up, and by his sacrifice took away the sins of all the world. Finally, since the faithful do daily consider and bear in their minds, that they have no abiding place in this transitory world, but that they look after a place to come; they need not, as the Jews did, once a year to celebrate the feast of tabernacles. In like manner, the faithful do no more acknowledge any year of jubilee: for Christ came once, and preached unto us that acceptable year, even the gospel, whereby it is proclaimed that all our sins and iniquities are clearly forgiven us. For so doth Christ himself interpret it[14] in the fourth of St Luke's gospel, taking occasion to speak of it out of the sixty-first chapter of Esay's prophecy. And thus the holy time and festival days are abrogated by Christ in his holy church; which notwithstanding is not left destitute of any holy thing or necessary matter.

[7 Decade II. Serm. 4.]
[8 creatori, Lat. omitted; the maker of them.]
[9 proventum, Lat.]
[10 or Whitsuntide, added by the translator.]
[11 Semper autem hic classicum canunt ad pugnam, Lat. See above, page 169.]
[12 hujus seculi, Lat.]
[13 to bear—desert, not in Lat.]   [14 hæc declarat, Lat.]

But now because this present year, wherein this book is first of all printed, is the year of grace 1550, and according to the Romish tradition is called the year of jubilee; I am therefore compelled, as it were of necessity, to make a little digression, and speak somewhat of the Romish jubilee.

I do therefore call it the Romish, and not the christian, jubilee, because, as I shewed you even now, the church of Christ, after our redemption wrought by Christ and preached by the gospel, doth neither acknowledge nor receive any other year of jubilee. In the ancient Jewish year of jubilee there is to be considered the meaning of the letter, and of the spirit[1]. According to the letter, bondmen were set at liberty, and lawful heirs did receive again their patrimony and possessions, which either was changed away or otherwise gone from them. The meaning[2] of that order, as it could not be brought again into all kingdoms in these latter days[3] without the trouble of all estates, so it is little set by and the care of the oppressed utterly neglected by the holy popes[4], who now of late[5] brought in the year of jubilee, and preached it unto the foolish world, not for any zeal they had to help the oppressed, but for the desire they had, by robbing the world, to augment their own treasures[6]. The spiritual and hidden mystery of the jubilee did commend[7] unto them of old the free remission of all sins through Christ by faith in Christ: which free grace cannot, without reproach to Christ, be otherwise preached than it hath been already taught by the holy gospel. Therefore the church was without the observation of any year of jubilee by the space of 1300 years after Christ his incarnation. At last, up start Bonifacius, the eighth of that name, bishop of Rome[8], who first of all invented that wicked ordinance. For Platina, in the life of that Bonifacius, saith: "This is he that first brought in the jubilee, in the year of Christ 1300, wherein he granted full remission of all

[1] consideratur litera et spiritus, Lat.]
[2] Is ritus, Lat.]   [3] hodie, Lat.]
[4] non admodum curant beatissimi patres, Lat.]
[5] now of late, not in Lat.]
[6] ut opibus suis plurimum accedat, is the Lat., rendered by, not for any—own treasures.]
[7] Christum et gratuitam ejus, Lat.; Christ, and his free, &c.]
[8] cujus nomine et Sextus Decret. prodiit, Lat. omitted; under whose name the sixth book of Decretals also was put forth.]

their sins to as many as visited the see apostolical. And the same did he ordain to be observed every hundredth year." So then the church of Christ was without this jubilee, without peril of salvation, by the space of 1300 years. And therefore may we also be without it without all peril and damage, yea, to our great profit and commodity. For if our Romanists go on to obtrude it to the world as a thing necessary to salvation, then shall they condemn the universal church which was before pope Boniface his time, who first brought in this unacquainted jubilee. Thus we are so far from not[9] being able to be without it, that we ought by all means possible to detest and abhor it as a very wicked and blasphemous ordinance; considering that we have to believe that the jubilee is utterly abrogated by Christ, and also that all sins are freely through Christ forgiven to all that believe, in what place of the world soever they live and are conversant in.

This pope Boniface doth to his false promise and unpure place annex the remission of sins. Now I doubt whether this blasphemous antichrist[10] could do any thing more horrible, and more against the honour of the Saviour[11]. For therein is defiled the glory of the only-begotten Son of God, who is the only health[12] of all the world. Therein is defiled the salvation of many thousands, for which Christ died upon the cross. And therein also is defiled the glory of christian faith, by which alone we are made partakers of eternal salvation. This ungracious and wicked pope was he of whom that common proverb runneth: "He entered like a wolf, he reigned like a lion, and died like a dog[13]." For verily so blasphemous an ordinance was worthy of such an author; so foolish a people was worthy of such a pastor; and so devilish a pope was worthy of such an end[14]. Platina writeth, that in that

[9 non tantum illo carere possumus, Lat.]
[10 "blasphemous antichrist" is not in the original.]
[11 et execrandum, Lat.; and to be abhorred.]
[12 Salvatoris, Lat.; Saviour.]
[13 See Homily for Whit-sunday, Part II. page 425. Oxford, 1832. "It is reported, that Celestine" (his predecessor) "prophesied of him, Ascendisti ut vulpes, Regnabis ut leo, Morieris ut canis.—Of this Pope (Boniface) a certain versifier wrote thus:

Ingreditur vulpes, regnat leo, sed canis exit;
Re tandem vera, si sic fuit, ecce chimera."]
[14 and so—end, not in the original.]

year of jubilee there came so great heaps of people to Rome, that although the city were indifferently large enough, yet one man could not for throng pass by another[1]. For the world will needs be deceived: if it were not so, they would give ear unto the Lord which crieth, "O all ye that thirst, come to the waters, and ye that have no money, draw nigh. Why spend ye your money upon a thing of nought, &c." Esay lv., and John iv. vii. Now all the while that the world was set thus on madding, the righteous Lord was not asleep, nor yet did dissemble how much they displeased him with that devilish[2] invention. For the very same year he stirred up Ottoman[3], the patriarch and first founder of the Turkish empire, by whose means he did notably scourge the church of Rome and the corrupt manners that were crept into Christendom. A few years after succeeded Clement the sixth[4], Paul the second, and Sixtus the fourth[5], as wicked men as he, as is to be found in the histories of their lives; who changed the year of jubilee from every hundreth to every fiftieth year, and so at last to every five and twentieth year, that so they might suck the more advantage out of men's foolishness. But now to the matter again.

[1 Jubileum idem (Bonifacius VIII.) retulit anno millesimo trecentesimo, quo plenam delictorum omnium remissionem his præstabat, qui limina apostolorum visitassent.—Idem etiam centesimo quoque anno observari mandavit.—Ob hanc rem eo anno tanta undique hominum multitudo Romam venit, ut vix incedere per urbem, amplam quidem et vastam, liceret.—Platin. de Vit. Pontif. Rom. p. 245. Colon. 1568.]

[2 devilish, not in Lat.]

[3 From that very year (viz. of the institution of the jubilee), as most stories do record, the Turks do begin the first count of their Turkish emperors, whereof the first was Ottoman. Foxe's Acts and Monum. Vol. ii. p. 586. ed. Lond. 1837. See also Bullinger in Apocalyps. Conc. xxx. on Rev. vi. 1—4, and xli. on ix. 12-19.]

[4 Petentibus Romanis, ut quemadmodum Bonifacius octavus olim concesserat, ut centesimo quoque anno plenam peccatorum omnium remissionem visitantibus limina apostolorum Petri et Pauli, quinquagesimo quoque anno id facere libenter annuat (Clemens VI.) cum dicerent ætatem hominum jubileum illum centum annorum attingere non posse. Platin. de Vit. Pontif. Rom. p. 258.]

[5 Quum vero annus Jubileus instaret, quem ex quinquagesimo ad xxv contraxit (Xystus IV.) primusque anno salutis mccccLxxv. celebravit, &c. Platin. p. 350.—This was in confirmation of the bull of his predecessor, Paul the Second.]

The sacraments also of the ancient Jews are flatly abro- The Jewish sacraments and sacrifices are utterly abrogated.
gated, and in their places are substituted new sacraments,
which are given to the people of the new covenant.

Instead of circumcision is baptism appointed[6]. The apos- 1
tles, in the synod held at Hierusalem, did oppose themselves
against those which were of opinion that circumcision was
necessary unto salvation; and in that council they allowed of
Paul's doctrine, who both thought and taught the contrary.
For Paul in one place saith; "Lo, I Paul say unto you, that [Gal. v. 2—4.]
if you be circumcised, Christ shall profit you nothing. For
I testify to every man which is circumcised, that he is a
debtor to the whole law to do it. Christ is made of none
effect to you: as many of you as are justified by the law, are
fallen from grace." Neither is it right or convenient that
in the church of Christ there should remain so bloody a sacrament[7] as circumcision was, when once that blood was shed
upon the cross which stancheth and taketh away the blood[8]
of the old Testament.

Instead of the paschal Lamb is the Lord's supper or- 2
dained[6], which by another name is called the eucharist, or a
thanksgiving. For so the Lord himself in Luke expoundeth
it, saying, that he did then eat the last passover with his
disciples; at the end whereof he did immediately ordain the
sacrament of his body and blood, which he biddeth them to
celebrate in remembrance of him[9], until he return to judgment again. Therefore the Lord left[10] the supper to be an
unchangeable sacrament until the end of the world.

Moreover, that all sorts of sacrifices contained in the law
are utterly abrogated, no man, I suppose, will once deny,
which doth but consider, that both the temple and the two
altars, with all the holy instruments, are utterly overthrown
and come to nothing. I told you that those sacrifices were
remembrances of sins, and types or figures of the cleansing
and atonement that was to be made by Christ Jesus[11]. Therefore when Christ was come and offered up for the sins of all
the world, then verily did all the sacrifices of the ancient Jews[12]
come to their ending. For where there is a full and absolute

[6 subiit, Lat.]   [7 signum, Lat.]   [8 omnem sanguinem, Lat.]
[9 in remembrance of him, not in Lat.]
[10 ecclesiæ, Lat.; to the church.]   [11 expiationis futuræ, Lat.]
[12 veterum, Lat.; Jews, not in Lat.]

remission of sins, there is no longer any sacrifice for sin. But in the new Testament there is a full remission of sins: therefore in the new Testament there is no longer any sacrifice offered for sins. For Christ is only and alone instead of all the sacrifices. For he was once offered up, and after that is offered no more: who by the once offering up of himself hath found eternal redemption; so that all, which be sanctified, are sanctified by none other oblation but that of Christ upon the cross made once for all. Wherefore Christ, being once offered upon the cross for the sins of all the world, is the burnt-offering of the catholic church: he is also the meat-offering, which feedeth us with his flesh offered upon the cross unto eternal life, if we receive and feed on him[1] by faith. Moreover he is the drink-offering of the church, which with his blood doth quench the thirst of the faithful unto life everlasting. He is the purging and daily sacrifice of the church; because he is "the Lamb of God that taketh away the sins of the world[2]." His death and passion cleanseth all men from their sins, their errors, and iniquities[3]. Finally, he is the church's sacrifice of thanksgiving; because by Christ we offer praise to God, and by Christ we render thanks unto the Lord[4].

The eucharist, or supper of the Lord, is to Christians instead of all sacrifices. To conclude: the only supper of the Lord, which we call the eucharist, containeth in it all the kinds of ancient sacrifices: which are in effect but of two sorts; to wit, of purging and of atonement, as those which were offered for sin; or else of thanksgiving, as those which rendered thanks and offered praise unto the Lord. Now the supper is a testimony, a sacrament, and[5] a remembrance of the body of Christ which was given for us, and of his blood that was shed for the remission of our sins. For the body and blood of our Lord, which were but once offered upon the cross[6], and neither can nor ought to be offered any more of men, are not sacrificed afresh in the celebration of the supper: but in the celebrating of it there is reiterated a remembrance of the thing, I mean, of the oblation, which was but once made, and in once offering

[1 si percipiatur, Lat.; if it (his flesh) be received.]
[2 John i. 29, peccatum, Lat.]
[3 omnia vitia mortalium, omnes errores, omnia scelera, Lat.]
[4 Deo Patri, Lat.; to God the Father.]
[5 adeoque, Lat.; and so.]
[6 pro peccatis, Lat.; for sins.]

was sufficient. Again, in the supper we render thanks to God for our redemption, for which also the universal church doth offer praise unto his name. Wherefore the supper of the Lord doth comprehend the whole substance and matter, which was prefigured in those ancient sacrifices: so that, in that point, the church is not destitute of any good or necessary thing, although it doth no longer retain those sacrifices of the elder church. Yea, they ought not any longer to be solemnized in the church, because they were nothing else but the figures, types, and sacraments of Christ to come. But the church doth now believe, and that rightly too, that Christ is already come, and that he hath fulfilled and accomplished all things; as we read that he himself did testify, when on the cross he cried, saying, " It is finished."

Moreover all vows are come to an end, because all sacri- *Vows abrogated.* fices, wherein[7] the vows consisted, are vanished and gone. Likewise the discipline of the Nazarites is now decayed, because the temple with all the ceremonies belonging thereunto is vaded away. There remaineth still in the church a christian and moderate discipline, but not that which is described in the law: and the saints do perform to God the vows which they have made in the church, not contrary to faith and godliness; but they are sparing, wary, and very religious in making vows. For what have we to give to God, which we have not first received at his hands; and to the performing of which we were not bound before in baptism ?

Christ doth not so distinguish between clean and unclean *The choice of meats abrogated.* in the gospel, as Moses doth in the law. " That," saith he, *[Matt. xv. 11.]* " which entereth into the mouth defileth not the man; but that which cometh out of the mouth." And the apostle Paul doth flatly say, that "to the clean all things are clean." And *[Tit. i. 15.]* like to this he speaketh much in the fourteenth to the Romans, and in other places moe. In his epistle to the Colossians he saith : " If ye be dead with Christ from the rudiments of the world, why, as living in the world, are ye led with traditions, (touch not, taste not, handle not;) all which do perish in abusing[8] ?" And so forth. To Peter also it is said : " What

[7 wherein—consisted, not in Lat.]
[8 Coloss. ii. 20-22, ipso pereant abusu, Lat. ; and Erasmus : whych all peryshe thorow the very abuse. Cranmer, 1539.]

Blood and strangled forbidden of the apostles.

God hath sanctified, that call not thou unclean." Therefore whereas, in the synodal epistle set forth by the apostles in the fifteenth of the Acts, both blood and strangled is forbidden and exempted from the meat of men, that commandment was not perpetual, but momentany, for a time only. For it pleased the apostles, for charity's sake, to bear therein with the Jewish nation, who otherwise would have been too stubborn and self-willed. The Jews at that time did every day so rifely hear the reading of the law, which did expressly forbid to eat blood and strangled, as if the preaching of the gospel had not begun to be sowed among them; and therefore they could not but be greatly offended to see the Gentiles so lavishly to use the things prohibited. Wherefore the apostles would have the Gentiles for a time to abstain from the things that otherwise were lawful enough, to see if peradventure by that means they might win the Jews to the faith of Christ. For the epistles, which Paul wrote a few years after the council at Hierusalem, do sufficiently argue that the decree of the apostles against blood and strangled was not perpetual. But the commandments given against things offered to idols, and against fornication, (in using whereof the Gentiles thought that they did not greatly offend,) are perpetual, because they be morals, and of the number[1] of the ten commandments. But of that matter I have spoken in another place.

And now, because I am come to make mention of the synodal decree ordained by the apostles and elders of the council at Hierusalem, I think it not amiss to recite unto you, dearly beloved, as a conclusion to this place, the whole epistle

The decree of the synod held at Hierusalem.

sent by the synod, because it doth bear an evident, full, and brief testimony, that the law is abrogated after that manner which I have declared. Now this is their epistle, or constitu-

[Acts xv. 23—29.]

tion : " The apostles, and elders, and brethren, send greetings unto the brethren which are of the Gentiles, that are in Antiochia, Syria, and Cilicia. Forasmuch as we have heard, that certain which departed from us have troubled you with words, and cumbered[2] your minds, saying, Ye must be circumcised, and keep the law ; to whom we gave no such commandment : it seemed good therefore to us, when we were come together with one accord, to send chosen men unto you,

[1 legum primarum atque, Lat.; of the first laws and, &c.]
[2 labefactantes, Lat.]

with our beloved Paul and Barnabas, men that have jeoparded their lives for the name of our Lord Jesus Christ. We have sent therefore Judas and Silas, which shall also tell you the same things by mouth. For it seemed good to the Holy Ghost and to us, to charge you with no more than these necessary things; (that is to say) that ye abstain from things offered to idols, and from blood, and from strangled, and from fornication: from which if ye keep yourselves, ye shall do well. So fare ye well." This is word for word the catholic, the synodal, apostolic, and ecclesiastical epistle of the council held at Hierusalem, both brief and easy : for as the speech of truth is simple, so also may true religion and christian faith be easily laid down in very few and evident words.

Immediately, in the beginning, after their accustomed manner of subscribing and inscribing their epistle, they do out of hand fall to, and touch the false apostles with whom Paul and Barnabas were in controversy, and do declare what kind of doctrine that of the false prophets was, which they had till then preached unto the churches as the catholic, true, and apostolic doctrine ; to wit, that they which will be saved must be circumcised and keep the law of Moses. For they thought not that faith in Christ, without the help of the law, was sufficient enough to full and absolute justification. They made their boasts, that they were sent from Hierusalem[3] by the apostles and disciples of the Lord, who did all with one consent teach the same doctrine that they did preach; and they said that Paul with his companion Barnabas alone did, schismatic-like, sow in the churches a certain doctrine, peculiar to himself, touching faith which justified without the works of the law. Wherefore the apostles straightways, after the beginning of their epistle, do declare what they think of such false teachers and their unwarranted doctrine : " We confess," say they, "that those false teachers went from hence out of Hierusalem, but we deny that they were either sent or instructed by us. For we gave no commandment to any such." And so they do testify that it is utterly false, which those fellows taught, to wit, that the apostles and disciples of the Lord did preach that the law is requisite to full justification. Yea, they do yet go on more plainly to declare

The false apostles' doctrine. They subscribe their own names, and inscribe the names of them to whom the epistle is sent.

[3 ex urbe sancta, Lat.]

18

what the doctrine of those false apostles was : "They trouble you," say they, "with words, and cumber your minds, commanding you to be circumcised and to keep the law." The sum therefore of their doctrine was, that, unless a man were circumcised and did keep the law, he could not be saved : whereby they did ascribe salvation to the keeping of the law, or to the merit of their works. Unto this doctrine the apostles

1 do attribute two perilous effects. The first is, "They trouble you with words." They be words, say they, which do rather amaze, than appease, comfort, or pacify your minds; yea, they do trouble you so, that ye cannot tell what to believe, or whereto to trust : and do moreover stir up strifes, discords, and jarrings among you. To these words of the apostles doth Paul seem to have alluded in his epistle to the Galatians,

[Gal. i. 6, 7.] saying : "I marvel that ye are so soon turned from Christ[1], which called you by grace, unto another gospel; which is not another gospel indeed, but that there be some which trouble you, and intend to pervert the gospel of Christ." The latter effect is,

2 "They cumber or weaken your minds." For they, which lean to the law and to works, have nothing stable or stedfast in their minds : for since the law requireth a most exact and absolute righteousness, and doth thereby kill, because such righteousness is not found in us; therefore those minds are weakened and subverted that are taught to lean to the works of the law, which law no man doth keep as of right he ought to do.

[Rom. iv. 14—16.] Therefore Paul to the Romans saith: "If they that do belong unto the law are heirs, then is faith vain, and the promise made of none effect[2]." And immediately after again : "Therefore the heritage is given by faith, as according to grace; that the promise may be sure to all the seed," &c. The false apostles therefore did subvert and weaken minds, by teaching that salvation is gotten by the law : which, verily, is a grievous judgment against those which with them do teach the like.

Paul his doctrine is allowed and commended to the churches. Then also they do with like liberty go on to the other side, to shew their opinion of Paul and Barnabas; yea, they do adorn them, as their messengers, with a most holy tes-

[1 a Christo qui vocavit vos per gratiam, Lat.; and Erasmus : from Christ which called you by grace. Cranmer, 1539.]

[2 Nam lex iram operatur, Lat. omitted; for the law worketh wrath.]

timonial[3], to the end that they may among all men have the more authority, and that all men may understand that betwixt them twain and the other apostles there was a full agreement and consent of doctrine and religion. "We being gathered together with one accord," say they, "have sent messengers unto you." Lo here, of the false apostles they testified that they sent them not, nor gave them any commandment: but these men they send, and do with one accord give them a commandment. But who be they whom they send? "Our beloved Paul and Barnabas, which have jeoparded their lives for the name of Christ Jesus." These twain are most choice apostles, and holy, glorious martyrs, our dearly-beloved brethren, being of the same religion and doctrine with us, who have declared what their lives and doctrine is by their manifold virtues[4] and manful suffering of peril and dangers.

But for because Paul and Barnabas were themselves no small doers in that controversy and disputation, there were joined to them two other chosen men, Judas and Silas, to the end that they might indifferently, without suspicion, declare the things which in the council were alleged for both sides; as I mean to shew you in the exposition of the general decree.

For now they do in few words comprehend the very decree of the whole and universal synod; in the laying down whereof they do first of all name the author of the decree, saying: "It seemed good to the Holy Ghost and to us." They first set down the Holy Ghost, and then themselves; making him to be the author of truth, and themselves to be the instruments by which he worketh: for he worketh in the church by the ministry of men. But men's authority without the inspiration of the Holy Ghost is none at all. Therefore do the apostles very significantly say: "It seemed good to the Holy Ghost and to us:" that is, after that we were assembled in that synod to treat of the matter of justification and of the law, (about which things Paul and his adversaries did stand in controversy,) we followed not our own judgments, neither did we use proofs of our own inventions; but, searching out and hearing the doctrine of the Holy Ghost, we do upon his warrant write this unto you.

The exposition of the general decree of the synod held at Hierusalem.

[3 et elogio, Lat, omitted; and encomium.]
[4 editis, Lat.; displayed.]

In the second place, they do set down the sum of the decree, saying: "That we might not charge you with greater burdens than these necessary things, (that is to say) that ye abstain from things offered to idols, and from blood, and from strangled, and from fornication." Therefore, say they, the doctrine of the gospel which Paul hath hitherto preached with us, is sufficient to the obtaining of life and salvation. We intend not to lay any greater burden upon you than the doctrine of the gospel and abstinence from those few things. In which sentence they seem to have had an eye to the opinion of St Peter, who in the council said: "Ye

Acts x. know that I, being called by God, did go to the Gentiles, and did preach to them salvation through the gospel. Ye know, that to the Gentiles, being neither circumcised, nor keeping the law, while I preached to them faith in Christ Jesus, the Holy Ghost was given from above, so that their hearts were purified of God himself by faith, not by the law, and that they were made heirs of eternal life." And upon

[Acts xv. 7—11.] this he inferreth: "Now therefore why tempt ye God, to lay upon the disciples' necks a yoke, which neither we nor our fathers were able to bear? But we believe that through the grace of the Lord Jesus Christ we shall be saved, even as they." See here, St Peter called the law a burden and a yoke: and therefore, where the apostles say that they will not lay upon the church any greater burden, they do thereby signify that the law is flatly abrogated. They do therefore set the church free from the burden of the law, and do acquit it from all burdens like to the law.

Men have unjustly thrust upon the church of God many ceremonies. We now do gather by those words of the apostles, that those burdensome and innumerable ceremonies, which the church hath received by councils and synods since the time of the apostles, were unjustly and against the apostolic spirit then laid upon the church, and at this day wickedly retained and defended in the church. For they in express words said: "It seemed good to the Holy Ghost and to us to burden you with no more than these things necessary."

But if any man object and say, that those ceremonies were for the rudeness of the people laid upon the churches' necks, as a rule or instruction[1] to guide or teach them by; mine answer is, that that kind of instruction is clean

[1 pædagogiam, Lat.]

taken away, which whosoever goeth about to reduce, he desireth nothing else but to bring in Judaism again. God knew very well what kind of church that would be, which he purposed to gather together of Jews and Gentiles; and yet he abolished those external ceremonies. Now who doth better know than God what is expedient, or not expedient, for his church? Therefore the things that be abolished were not expedient for the faithful: whereupon the apostles did rightly and very well pronounce; "It seemed good to the Holy Ghost and us not to lay upon you any greater burden." Let them therefore be ashamed of their doings, which lay so great a burden upon the shoulders of the church, that otherwise ought to be most free.

Now also here is added the conclusion of the sentence: "Than these necessary things, (that is to say) that ye abstain from things offered to idols," &c. In these words they had an eye unto the sentence of St James, the apostle and brother of the Lord: for he, confirming and allowing of St Peter's opinion touching justification by faith and the not laying of the law upon the Gentiles' necks, doth allege a testimony of scripture out of Amos; who did foretell that the Jews should be cut off because of their sins, and that in their steads the Gentiles should be taken, among whom the true church of God should be; which was prefigured by the ruin and reparation of David's tabernacle. The same prophet did also foretell a reason how, and a cause why, the Gentiles should be received into the church; not for circumcision's sake, nor yet by the help of the law, but by grace through faith. For he saith: "The remnant of the men shall seek after the Lord, and all the heathen upon whom my name is called, saith the Lord, which doth all this: all these works of God are known to him from before the world began." Lo here, they shall seek the Lord, and shall be received into his fellowship, upon whom his name shall be called. This phrase of speech doth signify, that they which are elect shall be the sons of God; for upon them the name of the Lord is called, which are named the sons of God, and are his elect. Now the whole scripture attributeth that to faith. By faith, therefore, we are made the members of the church, and sons and[2] heirs to God our maker. But if any man do murmur against the counsel of

St James alloweth of St Peter's opinions.

[Amos ix. 11, 12.]

[Acts xv. 17 —18.]

[2 adeoque, Lat.; and so.]

God, and say, Why doth God so? let him think, that this deed is the deed and work of God, whom it is not lawful for man to gainsay, and all whose works are known from the beginning of the world to have been done in judgment and righteousness: whereupon it doth consequently follow, that this counsel of his is good and righteous, whereby he doth through faith in Christ join to himself and sanctify[1] the heathen nations[2].

Now upon these words of the prophet St James (subscribing as it were to St Peter's opinion) doth gather and infer : " Wherefore my sentence is, that we trouble not them which from among the Gentiles are turned to God :" that is to say, I think that they are not to be molested, or charged with the observation of the law. But lest the Gentiles, once hearing that the law was abolished, should thereby think that they might freely do whatsoever they would, and so by that means abuse their liberty ; and also, against all charity, despise and give offence unto the Jewish brethren ; therefore James addeth : " But I think it best for us to write unto them, that they abstain from filthiness of idols." For there were at that time certain converts of the Gentiles, who thought it lawful for them to enter into idol-temples, and be partakers of things offered to idols ; because an idol is nothing, since there is but one only God alone : whereupon they gathered that those sacrifices were nothing, that they did neither good nor harm ; and therefore that Christians might with a safe conscience be partakers of them. But St James and Paul also, 1 Cor. viii. ix. and x., will have the heathen converts to abstain utterly from the worship of idols, that is, from the idols themselves, and from those things which are in the idol-temples offered to false and feigned gods.

From some certain things must the saints abstain.

Moreover he addeth : " Let them beware of fornication." The Gentiles, verily, did by good laws forbid the adulteries and defilings of virgins and matrons, with very sharp punishments suppressing the violent deflowerers of honest women : but they thought it a very light and in a manner no fault at all for such to commit whoredom as did of their own accords set their chastity to sale ; or if an unwedded man

[1] beatificat, Lat. See Vol. I. page 106, note 6.]
[2] citra legis observationem, Lat. omitted ; without keeping of the law.]

should have to do with a single woman : and therefore the apostle James, even as Paul also, 1 Cor. vi. and 1 Thess. iv. doth very severely require the holy and pure use of the body, without all filthy and unclean beastliness.

Last of all[3], he willeth the Gentiles to be restrained of eating blood and strangled. He addeth the cause why, and saith : " For Moses of old time hath in every city them that preach him in the synagogues, where he is read every sabbath-day." Of which constitution (touching blood and strangled) I spake somewhat, before that I made this same digression.

Now therefore, since the matter is at that point, it is evident that they are without a cause offended with St James, which think that he did without all right and reason make and publish[4] this decree; and that the fruit of that synod was very perilous, nothing wholesome, and flatly contrary to christian liberty. For it is assuredly certain, that the meaning of James did in no point differ from the mind of St Paul, who nevertheless did very well and praiseworthily[5] say: " Let us follow the things that make for peace, and things wherewith we may one edify another. Destroy not the work of God for meat's sake. All things are pure ; but it is evil for that man that eateth with offence. It is good neither to eat flesh, nor to drink wine, nor any thing whereby thy brother stumbleth, or falleth, or is made weak," &c. Romans xiv. It is also most certain, that St Paul, who was so sharply set to defend the christian liberty that he withstood Peter openly[6] at Antioch, would not have been behindhand to resist St James, if he had thought that this constitution either had been, or should be, prejudicial to christian liberty. Verily, he would neither have preached, nor yet commended, this tradition of the apostles to the churches of the Gentiles, if he had not thought that it had been both wholesome and profitable for them all to embrace. But he did preach and commend it unto the churches, as is to be seen in the sixteenth of the Acts : and therefore is St James without a cause murmured against of some, because he forbad to eat blood and strangled.

Finally, the conclusion of their epistle is : " From which

St James defended.

[3 in tertio loco, Lat. ; in the third place.]
[4 aut proposuisse, Lat.]   [5 cum laude omnium, Lat.]
[6 et in faciem, Lat. ; and to the face.]

if ye keep your selves, ye do well; so fare ye well." They praise that abstinence, and teach it as a good work, because it is also commended to us in all the scriptures.

Thus have I digressed, not far, I trust, from our purpose, to speak of the decree of the apostolic synod held at Hierusalem: and thus much at this time touching the abrogation of the ceremonial laws.

The abrogation of the judicial laws.

It remaineth here for me to say somewhat concerning the abrogation of the judicial laws. Now therefore the judicial laws do seem to be abrogated in this sense, because no christian commonweal, no city or kingdom, is compelled to be bound and to receive those very same laws, which were by Moses in that nation, according to the time, place, and state, published and set out of old. Therefore every country hath free liberty to use such laws as are best and most requisite for the estate and necessity of every place, and of every time and persons: so yet that the substance of God's laws be not rejected, trodden down, and utterly neglected. For the things which are agreeable to the law of nature and the ten commandments, and whatsoever else God hath commanded to be punished[1], must not in any case be either clean forgotten, or lightly regarded. Now the end whereunto all these laws do tend is, that honesty may flourish, peace and public tranquillity be firmly maintained, and judgment and justice be rightly executed. Of which because I have at large disputed in the exposition of the precept[2], "Thou shalt do no murder," I will here be content to be so much the briefer.

The holy apostle Paul commandeth to obey the magistrate: he alloweth of the authority of the sword, which he confesseth that the magistrate hath not in vain received at the hand of God. And therefore he did not disallow or find fault with the election of the magistrate, the use of the sword, the execution of the judgment and justice, nor with upright and civil laws.

Now whosoever doth confer the laws and constitutions of princes, kings, emperors, or christian magistrates, which are to be found either in the Code, in the book of Digests or Pandects, in the volume of New Constitutions[3], or else in any

---

[1 quæ Deus semper et apud omnes gentes punire jussit, Lat.]
[2 Decade II. Sermons 6, 7, 8.]
[3 The Code is the Codex Justinianeus, or collection of imperial

other books of good laws of sundry nations, with these judicial laws of God; he must needs confess, that they draw very near in likeness, and do very well agree one with another[4]. Justinian, the emperor, forbad by law either to sell or otherwise to make away the possessions of the church[5] and things consecrated unto God. For the sincere confessing and pure maintaining of the catholic faith the emperors, Gratian, Valentinian, and Theodosius, did make a most excellent and holy law[6]. Constantine the great gave charge to Taurus, one of his lieutenants, to shut the idol temples, and with the sword to destroy such rebels as went about to set them open, and to sacrifice in them[7]. That laws were made for the relief of the poor, and that kings and emperors had a care over them, it is to be seen in more places than one of the emperor's laws and constitutions. It is very certain, that whosoever readeth the Code, Lib. I. tit. 2, he shall find much matter belonging to this argument[8]. For the honest training up of children, and the liberal sustaining of aged parents, there are very commendable laws in the books of the heathens[9]. Concerning the authority that parents have over their children, there is much and many things to be found in writing : likewise of wedlock, of incest, and unmeet marriages, Honorius, Arcadius, and many other princes, have made very tolerable and laudable decrees : where they speak also very well and wisely of

constitutions in twelve books, each of which is divided into titles, which was promulgated at Constantinople, under Justinian, Nov. 16, A.D. 534.—The Pandects, so called because of the *comprehensiveness* of the work, or Digests, so called because of the *arrangement* of its materials, was a compilation out of ancient juristical writings, which was ordered by Justinian, and finished in the close of A.D. 532. It contained fifty books, which were divided into seven parts, and subdivided into titles. After the code was completed, Justinian supplied what was deficient in that work by a collection which he called Novellæ Constitutiones. Theodosius II. had published his code of laws, A.D. 438; and his Novellæ, or additions, about nine years later.—See Smith's Dict. of Greek and Roman Antiq., and Duck's Jur. Civil. Lib. I. cap. 3. § 8. and cap. 4.]

[4 Vol. I. pages 197—205.]   [5 Vol. I. page 331.]
    [6 Vol. I. pages 34, 35, 328, 331.]   [7 Vol. I. page 359.]
    [8 De—orphanotrophis, et xenotrophis, et brephotrophis, et ptochotrophis, &c. In his omnibus locis piis aluntur seu recipiuntur pauperes, &c., &c. Pacii Isagog. in Cod. Lib. I. 3. p. 460.]
    [9 Vol. I. pages 202, 273, 288—290.]

the law of divorcement[1]. But if I go on to add or oppose to every several title of the judicial laws contained in this sermon sundry and peculiar laws out of the decrees of christian princes, I shall, I know, be too tedious unto your patience; for then would this treatise pass the time of an ordinary sermon. Let it therefore suffice us at this time, by the declaration of these notes[2] to have opened and made a way to the diligent lovers of the truth to come to the understanding of other things, which we have here omitted; and that they may believe[3] that the substance of God's judicial laws is not taken away or abolished, but that the ordering and limitation of them is placed in the will and arbitrement of good christian princes; so yet that they ordain and appoint that which is just and equal, as the estate of time, place, and persons shall best require, that honesty and public peace may be thereby preserved[4], and God the Father duly honoured through his only-begotten Son Christ Jesus, to whom all praise is due for ever. For we do see that the apostles of Christ did neither require nor command any nation, in the administration of politic affairs, to bind themselves to the strict keeping of Moses' law. This rule must always be kept and observed.

[1 Pet. ii. 13, 14.] St Peter doth simply command, and say: "Submit yourselves to all manner ordinance of man[5] for the Lord's sake; whether it be unto the king, as having the preeminence, or unto rulers, as unto them that are sent of him for the punishment of evil-doers, but for the laud of them that do well." And [Acts v. 29.] yet the same apostle affirmeth that "we ought rather to obey God than men," so often as men do publish laws against true religion, justice and equity; concerning which I spake in the exposition of the common place of the magistrate[6]. And so, thus much I thought good to say touching the abrogation of the judicial laws.

The likeness and difference of the old and new testament and people.   Now if every one of you do throughly ponder with himself the things that I have hitherto said touching the law of

[1 Bingham, Orig. Eccles. Book xvi. chap. 11.; and Book xxii. chap. 5.]

[2 et vestigiis, Lat.; and traces.]

[3 tenereque in præsentiarum, Lat.]

[4 in gente quavis, Lat. omitted; in every nation.]

[5 cuivis humanæ creaturæ, Lat.]

[6 Vol. i. pages 269, 316.]

God, the parts of the law, the use or effect, the fulfilling and abrogating of the same; it will be a thing of no difficulty to determine what every one ought to think concerning that point or title of this treatise, whereof I promised, in the beginning of this sermon, that I would speak somewhat toward the end; to wit, that the testament of the old and new church[7] is all one, and that there is but one way of true salvation to all that either are, or have been, saved in this world: and also, wherein the new testament doth differ from the old. For since I have already shewed[8] that all the points of the law have a respect and a kind of relation unto Christ, and that he was in the law preached[9] to the fathers to be the only Saviour, in whom alone they were to be saved; who is it which cannot perceive, that they had none other but the very same manner and way to be saved which we at this day do enjoy by Christ Jesus[10]? And yet, that this may appear more evident, I will not stick to bestow some pains to make this matter more manifest unto you with as plain a demonstration as possible may be, although a plainer cannot likely be than that which I have already shewed you.

Verily, there is no difference of the people, of the testament, of the church, or of the manner of salvation betwixt them, among whom there is found to be one and the same doctrine, the same faith, the same Spirit, the same hope, the same inheritance, the same expectation, the same invocation, and the same sacraments. If therefore I shall be able to prove that all these things were indifferently common to them of the old church as well as to us, then have I obtained that which I shot at; to wit, that in respect of the substance there neither was, nor is, any more than one testament; that the old fathers are one and the same people that we are, living in the same church and communion, and saved not in any other but in Christ alone, the Son of God, in whom also we look for salvation.

The fathers and we are all one church, and people of one and the same testament.

That they and we have all one and the same doctrine, I prove thus. Our doctrine is the doctrine of the gospel. But that the fathers were not without the same doctrine, it is evident by St Paul, who testifieth, saying: "God verily promised the gospel of God afore by his prophets in the holy

That the fathers and we have all one doctrine.

[Rom. i. 1—4.]

[7 ecclesiæ Dei, Lat.]
[9 propositum esse, Lat.]

[8 apertissime, Lat.; most clearly.]
[10 by Christ Jesus, not in Lat.]

scriptures, of his Son, which was made of the seed of David after the flesh, and hath been declared to be the Son of God with power by the Spirit," &c. What could be said more plainly? The gospel, which is at this day preached[1], was of old promised by the prophets in the holy scriptures; to wit, that the Son of God should come into the world to save all faithful believers. This gospel also teacheth, that the faithful are not justified by the works of the law, but freely by grace through faith in Christ[2]. St Paul saith: [Rom. iii. 20—22.] " By the deeds of the law there shall no flesh be justified in his sight: for by the law cometh the knowledge of sin. But now is the righteousness of God declared without the law, being witnessed by the testimony of the law and the prophets: the righteousness of God cometh[3] by the faith of Christ Jesus unto all and upon all them that believe." With Paul St Peter also doth fully agree, where, in the synod held [Acts xv. 10, 11.] at Hierusalem, he saith: " Neither we nor our fathers were able to bear the yoke of the law, but do believe, even as they, to be saved through the grace of our Lord Christ Jesus." And so, consequently[4], in all other substantial and material points there is no difference in doctrine betwixt us and them.

The fathers and we have all one faith. [Rom. x. 17.] To proceed now: they, whose doctrine is all one, must of necessity have all one faith; " for faith cometh by hearing, and hearing by the word of God." What doth that argue, that Abraham and the rest of the[5] holy fathers are set before our eyes as examples of faith for us to follow? We see that it is so in the holy gospel of the Lord, and the sacred writings[6] of the apostles. But who would give us such foreign examples to imitate, as do not concern the thing for which they are given? Paul in many places, but especially in the fourth chapter to the Romans, sheweth that faith must be imputed to us for righteousness; as we read that it was imputed unto Abraham. Now that faith of his was not another, but the very same faith with ours, which resteth upon the promise of God and the blessed Seed: for he calleth Abraham the father, not of those only which are born of the circumcision, but of those also which walk in the steps

[1 ecclesiæ, Lat.; to the church.]   [2 in Christ, not in Lat.]
[3 cometh, not in Lat.]   [4 and so consequently, not in Lat.]
[5 patres nostri, Lat.; *our* fathers.]
[6 literis, Lat.; epistles.]

of the faith which was in Abraham before he was circum- [Rom. iv. 12.]
cised. Besides that also, the confirmation of the christian
rule, I mean[7] the apostles' creed, or articles of our belief, is
fetched out of the scriptures of the fathers of the old Testament; which is undoubtedly a most manifest argument that
their faith and ours is the very same faith. They did believe in the Messiah that was then to come; and we believe
that he is already come, and do more fully perceive and
merely[8] see all that which was spoken of before in the prophets: as I will anon declare, when I come to shew the
difference betwixt the two Testaments.

That all one and the same Spirit did govern our fore- The fathers
fathers and the people of the new covenant, who can doubt, all one Spirit.
considering that the Spirit of God is one alone; and that St
Peter doth in express words testify, that the Spirit of Christ [1 Pet. i. 11.]
was in the prophets? And St Paul also saith: "Since we [2 Cor. iv.
have the same spirit of faith, according to that which is 13.]
written, I believed, and therefore I spake; and we believe,
and therefore do we speak." Therefore, although the same
apostle doth in another place say, that the faithful "have [Rom. viii.
not received again the spirit of bondage unto fear, but the 15.]
spirit of adoption, whereby they cry, Abba, Father;" yet
doth he not deny but that the faithful fathers had the same
spirit that we have. For even they also cried to God as to
their father, although they obtained it not by the law (which
terrifieth), but by the grace of Messiah. Again, the same
apostle saith: "Whosoever are led by the Spirit of God, [Rom. viii.
they are the sons of God:" which sentence we may thus 14.]
convert, and say, that the sons of God are led by the Spirit
of God. But there is none, unless it be such an one as
never read the scriptures, which will deny that the ancient
fathers were the sons of God, and were so called both by Exod. iv.
the Lord himself, and also by his servant Moses. Deut. xiv.

What may be thought of that moreover, that our forefathers were called kings and priests, and so, consequently,
a royal priesthood and a priestly kingdom? which names
St Peter applied to the faithful believers in Christ Jesus. [Exod. xix.
Now such a kingdom and priesthood cannot be, or consist, 6; 1 Pet. ii.
without the unction of the Spirit. 9.]

[7 quam alias appellamus, Lat.]
[8 merely, absolutely, Johnson; exactius, Lat. but ed. 1577, nearly.]

[John vii.
39.]
The holy apostle John, I confess, in his gospel said: "The Holy Ghost was not yet, because Jesus was not yet glorified." But as he spake not of the substance of the Holy Ghost, which is coeternal with the substance[1] of the Father and of the Son; so he doth not altogether deny that the fathers had the Holy Ghost. For in that place he speaketh of the excellent gift, which after the ascension of the Lord was poured out upon the people that did believe. For John himself, interpreting himself, doth immediately before say: "These words, 'Whosoever believeth on me, out of his belly shall flow rivers of water of life,' spake he of the Holy Ghost[2], which they that believe on him should receive." The gift therefore of the Holy Ghost was not at that time, when the Lord spake those words, so commonly and plentifully poured upon all men, as it was upon the faithful after the glorification of the Lord Jesus.

And verily our forefathers and the holy prophets could not have so precisely and expressly foretold all the mysteries of Christ and the church, which the evangelists and apostles do testify to be now accomplished and fulfilled[3], unless in their prophecies they had been governed by the very same Spirit wherewith the apostles were afterward instructed. For it is a wicked thing for us to think that the prophets and patriarchs[4] did, like madmen, babble they knew not what, and speak such words as they themselves understood not. Abraham saw the day of Christ, and was glad of it: for by that spiritual sight of his, he had[5] and felt within himself a certain kind of spiritual joy. How many times doth David in the Psalms testify, that the service of God and the holy congregation did delight him at the very heart! Which words he uttered not so much for the joy that he had in the external ceremonies, but for that he did, by the Spirit and by faith, behold in these ceremonies[6] the true Messiah and Saviour of the world[7]. And since it is evident that our forefathers were justified by the grace of God, it is manifest that that justification was not wrought without the Spirit of

[1] essentiæ, Lat.]   [2] de Spiritu, Lat.]
[3] ad verbum, Lat.; to the letter.]   [4] patres nostros, Lat.]
[5] capiens, Lat.]
[6] sive ritibus sacris, Lat. omitted; or holy rites.]
[7] Christum, Lat.; the true—world, not in Lat.]

God; through which Spirit even our justification at this day is wrought and finished. Therefore the fathers were governed by the very same Spirit that we of this age are directed by.

Of this opinion was St Augustine, whose words, dearly beloved, I mean to recite unto you word for word out of his second book, *de Peccato Orig. contra Pelag., et Celest.* Cap. 25. "Things to come," saith he, "were foreseen of the prophets by the same spirit of faith, by which they are of us believed to be already finished. For they, which of very faithful love could prophesy these things unto us, could not choose but be themselves partakers of the same. And whereupon is it that the apostle Peter saith, 'Why tempt ye God, to lay upon the disciples' necks the yoke that neither our fathers nor we were able to bear; but we believe that through the grace of the Lord Jesus Christ we shall be saved even as they:' whereupon is it, I say, that Peter saith this, but for because they are saved by the grace of the Lord Jesus Christ, and not by Moses' law, by which doth come, not the salving, but the knowledge of sin? But now the righteousness of God is without the law made manifest, witnessed by the law and prophets. Therefore if it be now at this time made manifest, then must it needs be that it was before, although as then it were hidden: the hiding whereof was prefigured by the veil of the temple, which, when Christ died, was rent in pieces, for a signification that it was then revealed. And therefore this grace of the only Mediator of God and man, the man Christ Jesus, was then in the people of God, but it was hidden in them, as it were rain in a fleece, which God doth separate unto his inheritance, not of duty, but of his own voluntary will: but now, that fleece being as it were wrung out, that is, the Jewish people being reprobated, it is openly seen in all nations, as it were upon the bare ground in an open place[8]." This much out of Augustine.

[8 Eodem Spiritu fidei ab illis hæc futura videbantur, quo a nobis facta creduntur. Neque enim, qui nobis ista fideli dilectione prophetare potuerunt, eorum ipsi participes non fuerunt. Et unde est quod dicit Apostolus Petrus, Quid tentatis Deum imponere jugum supra collum discipulorum quod neque patres nostri neque nos potuimus portare; sed per gratiam Domini Jesu credimus salvi fieri, quemadmodum et illi; nisi quia et illi per gratiam Domini Jesu Christi salvi

The fathers
had the same
hope and
inheritance
that we have. Now also there was set before the eyes of Israel a carnal and temporal felicity, which yet was not all that they
hoped upon; for in that external and transitory felicity was
shadowed the heavenly and eternal happiness. For the
apostle, in the fourth and eleventh chapter to the Hebrews,
saith that the fathers out of that visible and temporal inheritance did hope for another invisible and everlasting
heritage. Neither was Christ to any other end so expressly
promised them, nor the blessing and life in Christ for any
other purpose so plainly laid before them, nor Christ himself
almost in all their ceremonies so often prefigured, for any
other intent, but that they thereby might be put in hope of
the very same life into which we are received through Christ
our Redeemer. For the Lord in the gospel saith, that we
shall be gathered into the kingdom of heaven, into the same
glory with Abraham, Isaac, and Jacob.

That salva-
tion was not
promised
only, but also
performed
unto the
fathers. But here is an objection made, that life and salvation was
promised only, and not performed, unto the fathers; but that
they, being shut up in prison, did look for the coming of
Messiah. I, for my part, do not find any thing in the scriptures to be written of such a prison, whereinto the holy
patriarchs were fast locked up. Peter, verily, maketh mention
of a prison; but in that prison he will have the disobedient,
Ad inferos. and not the obedient, spirits to be. But if any man object,
that Christ descended to them below, we verily do not deny
it: but yet we say withal, that he descended to the departed
saints; that is, that he was gathered to the company of the
blessed spirits, which were not in the place of punishment,
Ad inferos. that is, in torments, but in the joys of heaven; as the Lord
himself confirmeth the same, when, being ready to descend to

facti sunt, non per legem Moysi, per quam non sanatio, sed cognitio
est facta peccati? Nunc autem sine lege justitia Dei manifestata est,
testificata per legem et prophetas. Si ergo nunc manifestata est,
etiam tunc erat, sed occulta. Cujus occultationem significabat templi
velum, quod est ad ejus significandam revelationem Christo moriente
conscissum. Et tunc ergo ista gratia unius mediatoris Dei et hominum,
hominis Christi Jesu, erat in populo Dei, sed tanquam in vellere
pluvia, quam non debitam sed voluntariam segregat Deus hæreditati
suæ, inerat latens: nunc autem, velut siccato illo vellere, hoc est, Judaico populo reprobato, in omnibus gentibus, tanquam in area, cernitur
patens.—Aug. Opp. Par. 1531. De Peccat. Orig. cap. 25. Tom. VII.
fol. 164. col. 3.]

them below, he did say unto the thief, "This day shalt thou be with me in Paradise." It may also by many places of scripture be proved, that the ancient holy fathers, from Adam's time until the death of Christ, at their departure out of this life did presently for Christ his sake enter not into prison, but into eternal life. For our Lord in the gospel after St Mark doth say : "God is not the God of the dead, [Mark xii. but of the living." But he is the God of Abraham, of Isaac, and of Jacob : therefore, consequently, Abraham, Isaac, and Jacob, do live, or are now alive ; and yet not in body, corporally : for their bodies, being buried, were rotten long since ; therefore their souls do live in joy ; and their very bodies shall rise to judgment again. In the gospel after St Luke the Lord maketh mention of Abraham's bosom, into [Luke xvi. which are gathered all the blessed spirits ; and of it he testi-fieth, that it is placed aloft, and that it is not a place of pain and punishment, but of joy and refreshing. And therefore we do often read in the scriptures of the holy fathers, that they were gathered unto their people ; that is to say, that they were received into the fellowship of those fathers, with whom they had in this world remained in the same faith and same kind of religion. For the sequences and circumstances of those places do manifestly declare, that those words cannot be expounded corporally of the burial of the body. Again, in the gospel after St Matthew the Lord saith : "I say unto you, [Matt. viii. that many shall come out of the east and out of the west, and shall rest themselves with Abraham, Isaac, and Jacob, in the kingdom of heaven : but the children of the kingdom shall be cast out into utter darkness ; there shall be weeping and gnashing of teeth." Now if the Gentiles must be gathered into the kingdom of heaven, and that they must be placed in the fellowship of the fathers ; then must it needs be that the fathers were already in heaven, and felt the joys thereof at that very time when the Lord spake these words : who also in the gospel after St John doth plainly say : "Abraham [John viii. was glad to see my day ; and he saw it, and rejoiced :" which saying although we understand to be spoken of the justification and joy of the conscience, yet do we not separate from it the joy of eternal life ; because the one doth of necessity depend upon and follow the other.

Moreover we must here consider the occasion upon which

19

these words of the Lord do seem to have been spoken[1]. The
Lord had said : " Verily, verily, I say unto you, if a man keep
my saying, he shall never taste of death :" which words the
Jews took hold on, and said, " Abraham is dead, and the prophets are dead ; and yet sayest thou, If a man will keep my
saying, he shall never see death ? What, art thou greater than
our father Abraham, which is dead ? and the prophets are dead
also. Whom makest thou thyself?" To this the Lord made
answer, and shewed that Abraham is quickened, or else preserved in life and heavenly joy, through faith in the sayings
of Christ Jesus ; and that, howsoever he is dead in body, yet
notwithstanding his soul doth live in joy for ever with God, in
whom he did put his trust. To this may be added, that David
in the sixteenth psalm, calling God his hope, his expectation,
and his inheritance, doth among other things say : " The
Lord is always at my right hand. Therefore my heart is
glad, my glory rejoiceth, and my flesh shall rest in hope.
For thou wilt not leave my soul in hell, neither wilt thou
suffer thine Holy One to see corruption. Thou wilt make me
to know the path of life : in thy presence is the fulness of
joy, and at thy right hand there be pleasures for evermore."
And although St Peter and St Paul do in the Acts of the
Apostles apply this testimony of David, as a thing spoken
prophetically, unto Christ Jesus ; yet notwithstanding, no man
can deny but that the same may, after a certain manner, be
referred unto David, who in that psalm maketh a profession
of his faith, declareth his hope, and expresseth his *Michtam*,
that is, his delight, or the arms or cognisance whereby
he would be known[2]. Those words therefore do first appertain to Christ, and then to David and all the faithful : for
the life and resurrection of Christ is the life and resurrection
of the faithful. Again, in another place the same prophet
[Psal. xxvii.
13]. saith : " I believe verily to see the goodness of the Lord in
the land of the living." Now in the land of the living there
is neither death nor dolour, but fulness of joy and everlasting
pleasures : these joys and delights David by faith did look to
obtain at the hand of God through Christ his Saviour, and
did indeed, according to his hope, possess the same im-

[1 petitum ac pronunciatum, Lat.]
[2 insignia, aureolum, aut cleynodium, Lat. מִכְתָּם.]

mediately after he did depart out of this life, although it were many years after his death or ever Christ did come in the flesh; even as we also at this day are saved by him, although it be now one thousand five hundred and odd years ago since he in his flesh did depart from the earth[3].

But whereas Paul in the eleventh to the Hebrews saith; "And all these holy fathers, having through faith obtained good report, received not the promise, because God had provided a better thing for us, that they without us should not be made perfect;" I think simply, that it must be understood of the perfect[4] or full felicity, in which the holy fathers without us are not consummated, or made perfect; because there is yet behind the general resurrection of all flesh, which must first come : and when that is once finished, then is the felicity of all the saints consummated or made perfect; which felicity shall then not be given to the soul alone, but to the body also. St Peter also doth constantly affirm, that salvation is first of all by Christ purchased for the souls of the holy saints; then that they by the same Christ[5] are immediately upon their bodily death received to be partakers of the same salvation; and lastly, that in the end of the world the bodies of the saints being raised from death, as the bodies of all men be, shall appear before Christ to be judged by him. "The Lord," 1 Pet. iv. saith he, "shall judge both the quick and the dead.   For to this end was the gospel preached to the dead, that in the flesh they should be judged like men[6], but in the spirit they should live with God[7]:" that is to say, the death of Christ is[8] effectual to the fathers that died in the faith : so that now in soul they live with God, and that they again are to be judged in their flesh[9] like to all other men, at what time the Lord shall come to judge the quick and the dead.   Therefore our salvation is not as yet perfect nor consummated, but shall be made perfect in the end of the world.

Moreover, our forefathers did not pray to any other but

[3 licet venerit ante annos mille quingentos quadraginta novem, Lat. ; one thousand five hundred and forty-nine.]

[4 ut ipse Paulus dicit, Lat. omitted ; as Paul himself speaks.]

[5 by the same Christ, not in Lat.]

[6 secundum homines, Lat.]

[7 juxta Deum, Lat.]   [8 fuit, Lat.; was.]

[9 carne sive in corporibus suis, Lat.]

The fathers and we have all one manner of invocation. God alone, the only Creator of all things; and did believe verily that he would be merciful unto mankind for the blessed Seed's sake. And although they did not so usually call upon God, as we at this day do, through the Mediator and intercessor Christ Jesus; even as the Lord in the gospel [John xvi. 24.] did himself testify, and say, "Hitherto have ye not asked any thing in my name: ask, and ye shall receive;" yet were they not utterly ignorant of the Mediator, for whose sake they were heard of the Lord. Daniel in the ninth chapter of his prophecy maketh his prayer, and desireth to be heard of God for the Lord's sake, that is, for the promised Christ his sake. Finally, so often as the holy saints did in their prayers say, "Remember, Lord, thy servants, Abraham, Isaac, and Jacob," they did not look back to the persons or souls of the deceased patriarchs, but to the promise that was made to the patriarchs. Now since that promise is, "In thy seed shall all the kindreds of the earth be blessed;" and since Paul doth testify, that Christ is that blessed Seed; it followeth consequently, that the holy fathers in their prayers had an eye to the blessed Seed, and that they did desire God to hear them for Christ his sake. For in one place also the Lord [2 Kings xix. 34.] promiseth deliverance to king Ezechias, saying: "I will defend this city for mine own sake, and for my servant David's sake." But in the seventh and twenty-eighth chapter of Esay's prophecy it is manifest that the city was spared for Christ his sake, the son of the virgin, which is the foundation placed in Sion; whom Ezechiel in the thirty-fourth [Matth. xxii. 42, 45.] chapter calleth by the name of David, and the gospel calleth David's son.

The fathers and we have the very same sacraments. Last of all, the apostle Paul doth shew that the ancient fathers had amongst them the very same sacraments which we now have; as he doth in other places also make us partakers and apply to us both circumcision and the passover, the sacraments which were given to them of old; as doth appear in the second to the Colossians, and 1 Corinthians, the fifth chapter. In the tenth chapter he threateneth grievous punishment to the Corinthians at the hands of God, unless they abstain from things offered to idols, and from all heathenish sensuality. And thereupon he bringeth in the example of the Israelites, which he doth after this manner apply to his purpose: "I would not, brethren, that ye should be ignorant, that our fathers were the church of God, and that they had the same sacraments which we at this day have. For they were all baptized unto Moses (that is, by Moses, or by the ministery of Moses) in the cloud and in the sea. (For the cloud and the sea were figures of baptism.) And they did also[1] eat of the same spiritual meat, and did drink of the same spiritual drink." And immediately after he interpreteth his own meaning, and saith : "For they drank of the spiritual rock that followed them ; which rock was Christ." Manna verily, and the rock, did typically represent the spiritual food wherewith Christ refresheth both us and them, who is himself the bread and drink of eternal life. But although they did bodily, outwardly, and visibly receive their sacraments; yet for because they were destitute of faith and the Holy Ghost, because they were de-filed with the worshipping of idols, with surfeiting and fornica-tion, they displeased God, and were by him destroyed in the desert. And therefore, unless ye also abstain from those filthy vices, neither shall baptism nor the sacrament of the Lord's supper[2] avail you, but ye shall undoubtedly be destroyed of the Lord.

Since therefore it is by[3] most evident proofs of scripture declared, that the old fathers had the same sacraments, the same invocation of God, the same hope, expectation, and inhe-ritance, the same Spirit, the same faith, and the same doctrine, which we at this day have ; the mark, I hope, whereat I shot is fully hit ; and I have, I trust, sufficiently proved, that the faithful fathers of the old testament, and we the believers of the new covenant, are one church and one people, which are all saved under one congregation, under one only testament, and by one and the same manner of means, to wit, by faith in Christ Jesu.

Thus much have I hitherto said touching the likeness, the agreement, and the unity betwixt the old and new testament, or people of God. I will now add somewhat touching the diversity betwixt them, and the things wherein they differ.

Of the dif-ference of the old and new testament and people.

In the very substance, truly, thou canst find no diversity: the difference which is betwixt them doth consist in the manner of administration, in a few accidents, and certain circumstances.

[1 omnes, Lat. omitted; all.]
[2 aut spirituale epulum, Lat. ; or the spiritual banquet.]
[3 his testimoniis, Lat. ; these proofs.]

For to the promise or doctrine of faith, and to the chief and principal laws, there were annexed certain external things, which were added until the time of amendment; so that the whole ecclesiastical regiment, the manner of teaching the doctrine of godliness, and the outward worshsip of God, was among the old fathers of one sort, and is among us of another. But the especial things wherein they differ may be rehearsed and set down in these few principal points.

All things more evident in the new people or covenant than were in the old. First and foremost, all things of the new covenant are more clear and manifest than those of the old testament. The preaching[1] of the old covenant had always in it, for the most part, some misty or cloudy thing, and was still covered and wrapped up in shadows and dim shews: but the publishing of the new testament is clear and manifest, so that it is called the light which is without all mists and darkness. Moses did with a vail cover his face, neither could the children of Israel behold his countenance: but we, beholding not only the countenance of Moses which is now uncovered, but the pleasant and amiable[2] face of Christ himself, do greatly rejoice to see our salvation openly revealed before our eyes. In that sense did the Lord say that his disciples were happy, where he brake out into these words: "Happy are the eyes which see the things that ye see. For I say unto you, that many prophets and kings desired to see the things that ye see, and saw them not; and to hear the things that ye hear, and heard them not." The just man Simeon did in this sense call himself as happy a man as lived, and did thereupon promise that [Luke ii. 29– 32.] he was willing to die, saying: "Lord, now lettest thou thy servant depart in peace, according to thy word. For mine eyes have seen thy salvation; which thou hast prepared before the face of all people; to be a light to lighten the Gentiles, and to be the glory of thy people Israel."

But although our forefathers had not so much light as doth shine to us in Christ since his coming in the flesh, yet was that little light which they had sufficient to the getting of salvation by faith in Christ. Even we ourselves, although we see him[3] far more clearly than our forefathers did, do notwithstanding behold him but in a mist[4], in comparison of the bright-

[1 revelatio, Lat.]
[2 clarissimam et amœnissimam, Lat.]   [3 him, not in Lat.]
[4 in ænigmate, Lat.; 1 Cor. xiii. 12.]

ness wherein he shall appear⁵. For we shall hereafter see him³ face to face in the glory of his majesty⁶: and yet notwithstanding even this sight of him⁷, which now we have, is sufficient to salvation. Therefore it is a very fine similitude, and prettily said of them which say, "Although at day-break the brightness of the sun is not so great as it is at noon-day, yet wayfarers or travellers do not stay till the sun be at the highest, but take the morning before them to go their journey in, and have light enough to see the way." For in like manner they think, that to our forefathers even that little portion of light, which was in the morning, was sufficient by the leading of faith to bring them through all impediments to eternal felicity. In the mean time, we have great cause to rejoice⁸, that Christ, the very sun and light of righteousness⁹, doth, after the misty light of the day-star of the law¹⁰, shine forth to us in the new testament.

Moreover the forefathers in the old testament had types, shadows, and figures of things to come, but we have now received the very thing itself which was to them prefigured. Therefore the thing which God did promise to them he hath performed and given to us. They verily did believe that Christ should come and deliver all the faithful from their sins; and we believe that he is already come, that he hath redeemed us, and hath fulfilled all that the prophets foretold of him. Therefore the Lord in the gospel said: "The prophets and the law prophesied unto John; since that time the kingof God is preached, and suffereth violence of every man." Whereupon it is gathered, when the thing prefigured is come and present, that then the figures and shadows, which did foreshew the things to come, do come to an end and vanish away. Therefore the yoke and burden, which our fathers did bear, is thereby taken from our necks. The worshipping of God, which they did use externally, was very busy¹¹ and

The new testament hath no figures or types, but is the fulfilling of all figures.

[Luke xvi. 16.]

Christ hath taken all burdens from our shoulders.

[⁵ in comparison—appear, not in Lat.]
[⁶ The Latin is only, in gloria, in glory.]
[⁷ of him, not in Lat.]
[⁸ et propter quod æternas Deo nostro agamus gratias, Lat. omitted; and we should render to our God everlasting thanks for it.]
[⁹ clarissimus Sol, Lat.]
[¹⁰ post luciferum istum et stellas lucidissimas, Lat. ; after that day-star and the very bright stars.—of the law, not in Lat.]
[¹¹ operosus, Lat.]

burdensome; as the Aaronical priesthood, the tabernacle or temple that was to be throughly furnished with most exquisite things and instruments, their sundry sorts of sacrifices, and many moe ceremonies like unto these. Now from all this cost and business we, which be the people of the new covenant, are freely disburdened and set at liberty. And he by whom we are disburdened is Jesus Christ, in whom alone we have all things necessary to life and salvation. For it pleased God the Father to recapitulate in him, and, as St Paul saith, to bring into a sum[1], all things requisite to life and salvation; that the things which seemed before to be dispersed here and there should in Christ alone be fully exhibited and brought unto us. For Christ is the fulfilling of all the types and ceremonies; by whose Spirit since we do now possess the thing prefigured, we have no longer need of the representing types and shadows. The external things that Christ hath ordained are very few, and of very small cost. Therefore the people of the new testament doth enjoy a passing great and ample liberty.

To this, I suppose, doth belong that excellent place of St Paul, which is to be seen in the fourth to the Galatians, where, in handling this matter diligently, he feigneth that there are two mothers, the one whereof doth gender to bondage, and the other unto liberty; and that he doth under the type of Agar and Sara: by which he noteth the two doctrines; that of the law, and that of the gospel. That of the law gendereth to bondage, but that of the gospel doth gender unto liberty. Therefore the law did gender the holy fathers and the prophets unto bondage, not that they should abide bond-slaves for ever, but that it might keep them under discipline; yea, that it might lead them unto Christ, the full perfection of the law. The liberty of the fathers was by the weight and heap of ceremonies so oppressed and covered, that although they were free in spirit before the Lord, yet notwithstanding they did in outward shew differ little or nothing from very bond-slaves, by reason of the burden of the law that lay upon their shoulders. For insomuch as the law was not as yet abrogated, they were compelled precisely to observe it. But when Christ was come and had fulfilled all things, then did the shadows vanish away, and that

Gal. iv.

The bondage of the law in the old testament.

[1 Eph. i. 10. See Vol. I. page 156.]

heavy yoke was taken from the neck of us Christians. So by this means our mother Sara gendereth us unto liberty. She is the mother of us all. Of that mother (which is also called the holy mother church) we have the seed of life: she hath fashioned us, and brought us forth into the light; she colleth[2] us in her bosom, wherein she carrieth both milk and meat, (I mean the word of God,) to nourish, save, and bring us up.

Now the bonds being cancelled, and the middle wall, which was a stop, being broken down, God doth more liberally rule his church, and not retain it any longer under so strait a custody. For neither is the people of God contained within the bounds of the land of promise; for they are dispersed to the ends of the world: neither are the circumcised, and those that keep the law, his people now, (although it is not to be doubted but that even then, when circumcision was of force[3], he had some that were his people among the Gentiles, as Job, and other moe which he himself did know;) but those are his people, which do acknowledge Christ, although they be neither circumcised nor busied with the law. This is a new people, gathered together out of all the world by faith and the Holy Ghost. To this new testament hath Christ given his own name: wherein the Jews have none inheritance, unless they forsake their stubborn opinion of the law, and cleave to Christ alone without affiance in the law. All the books of the prophets are fully fraughted with testimonies touching the calling of the Gentiles unto the communion and fellowship of God, and also touching the reprobation of the Jews, who for their unreclaimable affiance in the law are utterly rejected.

Furthermore, the apostle Paul putteth another difference betwixt the two testaments, alluding to the prophecy of Jeremy, as it is to be seen in the eighth chapter of his Epistle to the Hebrews. For he attributeth to the people of the new testament certain excellent gifts, to wit, absolute and full remission of their sins: for he saith, "Because I will be merciful to their unrighteousnesses, and I will no more remember their sins and iniquities." He doth also attribute to the people of the new testament a most exquisite refor-

Margin notes:
The people of the new testament are new and without all number.

So that the people of this testament are after the name of Christ called Christians.

The gifts of the new testament are most ample and manifold.

[2 fovet, Lat. To coll: to embrace.]
[3 when—of force, not in Lat.]

mation and absolute illumination of their minds: for he saith, "I will plant my laws in their minds, and write them in their hearts; and then shall no man teach his neighbour, or his brother, saying, Know the Lord; for they shall all know me, from the little unto the great." But of the law it is written, that it was graven in tables of stone. Yet for all this let no man think that the fathers obtained no remission of their sins. For as they by faith had free forgiveness of their sins, so did God[1] both write his law and pour his Spirit into their hearts. For which of us at this day can say, that we excel in knowledge and in faith[2] either Abraham, Moses, Samuel, David, Esay, Daniel, or Zacharias? So then the difference is not, in that the fathers of the old testament were without the remission of sins and the illumination of the Holy Ghost, and that we alone, which are the people of the new testament, have obtained them: but the difference doth consist in the greatness, ampleness, largeness, and plentifulness of the gifts, to wit, because they are more liberally bestowed and more plentifully poured out upon more now than they were of old. For all nations, being called do not by dropmeal, but by whole handfuls, draw the water of life. The Lord doth pour out his Spirit upon all flesh. Of old God was known in Jury only; but now, since Christ is come into the world, his disciples are gone through all the corners of the earth, and teach all kingdoms to know the Lord. Of old the worthy men[3] and prophets were not so many but that they might be numbered; because the land of promise in a manner alone did breed such good and holy men; but who is at this day able to reckon all the kings, princes, noblemen, prophets, bishops, doctors, martyrs, and excellent persons of every sex, estate, and age, which have been and are at this day bred, not only in Jurie, but also in Arabia, Idumea, Phœnicia, Mesopotamia, Persia, Asia, Egypt, Africa, Greece, Italy, the east, the south, the west, and the north? Free remission of sins is preached to all countries and kingdoms. All the faithful in every nation under heaven are through Christ received into the grace and favour of God the Father. All have received in great abundance the gift

[1 olim quoque, Lat.; of old also.]
[2 illuminatione, Lat. omitted; and in illumination.]
[3 heroes, Lat. omitted.]

of the Holy Ghost. All have prophesied. All have known the Lord.

Finally, the law maketh no man perfect[4]. The gospel simply maketh perfect, and doth directly, without any stop, lead us to Christ, and causeth us to rest and to content ourselves in him alone.

Last of all, I will not slip over this difference, although it be of little weight, and such an one as other like unto it may be easily observed; that the law, appointing out a certain land, peculiarly separated from other nations, did promise to the old fathers the possession of the same, so long as they did keep the law; but if they did transgress the law, then did it threaten that they should be rooted up and utterly cast out of that good land. But to us no one limited land is expressly promised: "for the earth is the Lord's, and the fulness thereof; the round world, and all that therein is." But although he doth not here assign to us, as he did to our forefathers of old, any certain or peculiar thing, yet doth he not at any time neglect us: for he feedeth, blesseth, and preserveth us in every land and nation. Therefore the promises which were of old made to our forefathers concerning the land of promise, being come to an end, are utterly vanished away; so that they, which for an age or two ago did incite many nations to arm themselves for the recovery of the holy land, do seem to have been besides their wits. Christ by his coming into the world hath sanctified all the earth: for there are in every nation of the world some sons and heirs of God and his kingdom.

The new testament hath no promise of any certain earthly country.

[Psal. xxiv. 1.]

Touching the likeness and agreement, the unlikeness and difference of both, I mean, the old and new testaments or people, I have therefore spoken the more briefly, because I have in the first sermon of the first decade, and in the sixth sermon of the third decade, already handled the selfsame matter. Finally, I have but shortly touched the abrogation of the law, because I did a good while ago set forth two treatises; the one Of the ancient faith[5], the other Of the only and eternal covenant of God[6]; which treatises I know to be familiar among you.

[4 Sed ducebat ad spem potiorem, Lat. omitted; but led to a better hope.]

[5 See the Old Faith, in Bp. Coverdale's Works, Fruitful Lessons, Parker Soc. ed. The Latin translation was published at Zurich, 1544.]

[6 This latter treatise,—De Testamento seu Fœdere Dei unico et

I will not here, in the conclusion, recapitulate unto you the special points of this sermon; partly because I have already been somewhat too long; and partly because I have, as I hope, used so plain an order, that every point is indifferently well settled in every man's memory. Thus have I, by God's grace and sufferance, made an end to treat of God's holy law, wherein I have been occupied a good sort of days by several sermons. Blessed be God and our heavenly Father world without end; whom I beseech to bless us all through Jesus Christ our Lord and Saviour. Amen.

OF CHRISTIAN LIBERTY, AND OF OFFENCES. OF GOOD WORKS, AND THE REWARD THEREOF.

THE NINTH SERMON.

I HAVE already through many sermons discoursed long upon God's laws. Now therefore, because upon the consideration and handling of the law there do arise certain points not[1] to be omitted, which do depend upon, and are annexed hand in hand unto, the law; of which sort are christian liberty, good works, the reward[2] of good works; [3]sin, and the reward or punishment of sin; I will speak of them in order, as God shall put into my mouth: whom I shall desire you to pray unto with me, beseeching him not to suffer me to speak, in these or other points of holy doctrine, the thing that shall sound against his holy will.

Of christian liberty. Upon the abrogation of the law doth christian liberty depend and follow, as the effect of the abrogating of the law; which liberty doth minister us occasion to speak of offences.

Now concerning christian liberty the most holy apostle of Christ, St Paul, hath reasoned very diligently and largely; whereby we may gather that the consideration of christian liberty is neither of no weight, nor yet of little profit. But the treatise thereof is especially necessary to us of this age,

æterno,—Bullinger published at Zurich, A.D. 1534, and afterwards appended to his Commentaries in Epistolas Apostolorum canonicas septem.]
[1 non contemnenda, Lat. omitted; not to be thought lightly of.]
[2 merces sive proemium, Lat.]
[3 denique, Lat. omitted; lastly.]

among whom there are no small number of men, which do either not understand what christian liberty is; or else, if they know it, do foully abuse it, thereby to fulfil the lusts of the flesh. I will therefore tell you who is the deliverer that setteth us at liberty; who they are that he setteth at liberty; and wherein[4] and how far forth he setteth them at liberty: which things being once known, it will be an easy matter to perceive what christian liberty is, what the property or disposition of those is which are so set at liberty, and how far forth they must beware from giving offence to any man, and from abusing their granted liberty.

There is none other deliverer promised, given[5], and preached unto us, than Christ Jesus, the Son of God. For he which doth deliver other men, must be himself free from the bands wherewith they are tied, that wish and look to be set at liberty. But throughout all ages there is none such to be found in all the world, nor yet in heaven, but Jesus Christ[6] alone, the Son of God; who for that cause did in the gospel say, "If the Son set you at liberty, then are ye free indeed." *Who is our deliverer.* *[John viii. 36.]*

Now they, whom the Lord delivereth, are bond-slaves; wherefore he doth deliver them from bondage, and doth incorporate them in the liberty of the sons of God. He doth set all bond-servants at liberty, excluding none but such as do by their own default, their own unbelief and disobedience, exclude themselves. For the coming of the Son of God was to set all such at liberty as were entangled in bondage. Therefore he doth so far forth deliver us, as we are bond-servants. For bondage and liberty are one opposed and contrary to the other, so that without the consideration of the one we cannot conceive the meaning of the other. Wherefore I think it best here to speak so much of bondage as this present argument shall seem to require. *Who they be that Christ doth set at liberty.*

First, bondage is nothing else but the state or condition wherein bond-servants be. Now those that are in bondage are either bondmen born, or else made bond-servants. The children that issue of bond-servants are bond-slaves born. The other, that are made bond-servants, are so made either by captivity, whereupon they take their names, and are called captives; for Pomponius saith, Slaves were thereupon so *What bondage is.*

[4 a qua re, Lat.]   [5 exhibetur, Lat.]
[6 Jesus Christ, not in Lat.]

called, because the captains commanded to sell them for money, when they were in wars taken captives by their soldiers; and so by that means to spare their life and save them: these bondmen are in Latin also called *Mancipia, eo quod ab hostibus manu caperentur,* because they were taken prisoners by the hand of their enemies: or else they are made bondslaves by the civil law; as when a freeman, above twenty years of age, doth for lucre sake suffer himself to be sold for money[1]. Bondmen therefore have lost all liberty, and do wholly hang upon their masters' government, in whose power it lieth to kill them if they list.

Now of bondage there are two sorts; the politic[2], and the spiritual. The politic bondage is not by grace and the preaching of the gospel taken out of the church of the faithful, so that there should be no bondmen at all, or that they should not do their duty, or not do the service that of right they do owe. For the apostle Paul saith: "Let every man walk according as he is called[3]. And so ordain I in all churches. Art thou called being a servant? care not for it: but yet if thou mayest be free, use it rather." And again: "Servants, obey them that are your bodily masters with fear and trembling and singleness of heart, as unto Christ; not with eye-service, as men-pleasers; but as the servants of Christ, doing the will of God from the heart; with good will serving the Lord, and not men; knowing that whatsoever good thing any man doth, that shall he receive again of the Lord, whether he be bond or free." And in his epistle to Timothy he saith: "Let as many servants as are under the yoke count their masters worthy of all honour, that the name of God and his doctrine be not blasphemed. And they which have believing masters, despise them not, because they are brethren; but rather do service, forasmuch as they are believ-

Marginal notes:
Two sorts of bondage.
Bodily bondage.

[1 Cor. vii. 17, 21.]

[Eph. vi. 5—8.]

[1 Servi autem ex eo appellati sunt, quod Imperatores captivos vendere, ac per hoc servare nec occidere solent: qui etiam *mancipia* dicti sunt, eo quod ab hostibus manu capiuntur. Servi autem aut nascuntur, aut fiunt: nascuntur ex ancillis nostris; fiunt autem jure gentium, i. e. ex captivitate; aut jure civili, cum liber homo major 20 annis ad pretium participandum sese venundari passus est.—Corp. Jur. Civil. Par. 1628, Tom. I. p. 9, Instit. Lib. I. tit. 3, de jure personarum.]

[2 sive civilis, Lat.]

[3 ut vocavit eum Dominus, Lat.]

ing and beloved, and such as are partakers of the benefit[4]."
And yet in this bondage the faithful have this comfort by the
preaching of the gospel, that howsoever they be bond in body,
yet they are free in mind and soul. For the apostle again A paradox
doth say : "He that is called a bondman in the Lord is the [1 Cor. vii.
Lord's freeman ; likewise he that is called free is bond to 22.]
Christ."

This is a comfort to the faithful in all their afflictions, which
know that their spirit is safe and free, howsoever their body
is straitly imprisoned or sharply tormented. Therefore the
saints are at their liberty, although they be never so narrowly
looked to and shut up in custody ; they are victorers and van-
quishers, howsoever they are bound and oppressed ; finally,
they enjoy most exquisite pleasures even then when they are
vexed[5] with most infinite evils. I know that the children of
this world do mock and scoff at these pleasures and liberty of
the faithful believers, as though they were mere dreams and
fantasies of very fools and asses : but God[6] doth soundly pay
them home for their scoffs and mockery, not in the world to
come only, but also in this present life; while they themselves,
like miserable caitiffs, being in extreme captivity, do notwithstanding even in that slavery[7] think themselves at liberty and
in most absolute felicity. For they serve a filthy service in
detestable slavery, making themselves bondmen to abominable
whoredom, to beastly mad drunkenness, to the wicked mammon[8], and to other most vile pleasures, wherein they die and
rot with endless shame and infamy. But of the service and
afflictions of the saints, who do even in their afflictions enjoy
their liberty and rejoice in the Lord, the apostle Paul speaketh
where he saith : "We are troubled on every side, yet are we
not made pensive ; we are in poverty[9], but not in extreme
poverty ; we suffer persecution, but are not utterly forsaken
therein ; we are cast down, but we perish not; bearing about

[4 1 Tim. vi. 1, 2, et qui beneficia rependere possunt, Lat.]

[5 acerbissime, Lat.]

[6 justo judici, Lat. omitted ; the righteous judge.]

[7 Rather, inasmuch as they are in most extreme captivity and
thrice miserable, even then when they think themselves most at liberty,
&c.]

[8 Luke xvi. 9 ; mammonæ iniquitatis, Lat. and Vulg.]

[9 laboramus, Lat.]

always in the body the dying of the Lord Jesus, that the life
of Jesus might also appear in our body[1]." And again: "In
all things we do our endeavour to shew ourselves as doth
become the ministers of Christ; in much suffering, in afflictions in necessities, in sorrows, in stripes, in imprisonments, in
seditions, in labours, in watchings, in fastings; in glory and
ignominy, in reproaches[2] and praises; as deceivers, and yet
speakers of truth; as unknown, and yet known; as dying,
and lo, we live; as chastened, and not killed; as sorrowful,
and yet always rejoicing; as poor, and yet making many rich;
as having nothing, and yet possessing all things." Lo, here
ye see how the saints in extreme servitude have a cheerful
consolation and are always at their liberty : as is to be seen
by infinite examples in the Acts of the Apostles, and other
ecclesiastical histories.

[2 Cor. vi. 4, 5, 8—10.]

Spiritual bondage.

Now we come to the second part of bondage. The
spiritual bondage hath a certain likeness to the bodily servitude. For Adam by his own fault became a bondman; and
we of him are all born bondmen[3]. He was once at liberty,
and .had the Lord to be his friend and favourer[4]; but he
did disloyally revolt from God, and got himself another
master, the devil, a tyrant as cruel as may be, who for his
sin having gotten power over him did, like a merciless lord,
miserably handle him like a bond-servant. Now we of our
corrupt grandsire are born corrupt and sinners, and for our
sin are also under the devil's dominion ; we are in danger of[5]
the law, and of the curse thereof: for we are the bond-slaves
of sin ; we are made subject to sundry calamities by reason
of our sin. This therefore is called the spiritual bondage, not
because it is only in the mind of man, but because of the opposition whereby it is opposed to the bodily bondage[6]. For
otherwise sin hath made our body also subject to the curse :
neither do we sin in mind alone, but in the body also ; for
every part and all the members of our bodies are subject unto

[1 2 Cor. iv. 8—10, in nostra mortali carne, Lat. ; in our mortal
flesh : as in verse 11.]

[2 per gloriam—per convicia, Lat.]

[3 nascimur ex servo servi, Lat.]

[4 habuerat Dominum optimum et clementissimum, Lat.]

[5 subjicimur, Lat. Tyndale's Doct. Treat. ed. P. S. p. 9, n. 6.]

[6 civili vel corporali, Lat. ; to civil or bodily.]

sin, and infected with iniquity.   Therefore we serve in most Abortion is made when a woman is before her time delivered of her child. miserable bondage, while, being under the devil's dominion, we do the things that please the flesh, by the egging on of evil affections, to the bringing forth of fruit, or rather to the making of abortion with peril of our lives, to the devil, our cruel and our rigorous master; for this verily is our hardest and most lamentable servitude and bondage.

Now on the other side, let us see what christian liberty The spiritual liberty, and how far forth we are made free by Christ. is; that is to say, from what, and how far forth, the Lord hath made us free.   In one word we do briefly say, that Christ our Lord hath delivered us from a grievous bondage[7]; to wit, that he hath so far forth made us free, as we by sin[8] were slaves and bond-servants.   This we may more largely expound and say: The Son of God came into this world; and, having first oppressed the tyranny of Satan and crushed his head by his death and passion, he hath translated us into his own kingdom, and hath made himself our Lord and king. Secondarily, he hath adopted us to be the sons of God, and with his blessing took away the bitter curse of the law; for he took away all sins, and purged all the faithful from their iniquities.   Thirdly, he did most liberally bestow the free gift of the Holy Ghost, to the end that the sons of God should willingly and of their own accord submit themselves to the will of God, and to do the things that the Lord would have them: for the hatred of the law doth not remain, although the weakness of the flesh abideth still.   Lastly, the same our Lord and King hath taken from the shoulders of his elect the burden of the law, the types and figures, with all the costs belonging to the same; and hath forbidden us, being once set at liberty, to entangle ourselves again with any laws and traditions of men.   Of all this being laid together we make this definition: To deliver is to make free, Christian liberty. and to set at liberty from bondage.   He is free, or manumissed, that, being delivered from bondage, doth enjoy his liberty: therefore manumission, or liberty, is nothing else but the state of him that is made free; the commodity, I say, which a free-made man hath received and doth enjoy by reason of his deliverance; to wit, in that he, being delivered from the tyranny of Satan, from sin, from the curse of the

[7 a gravi illa servitute, Lat.; from that grievous bondage.]
[8 by sin, not in Lat.]

law, and from death, is made the son of God and heir of
everlasting life; and also that he hath received the Spirit of
liberty, by which he doth wholly give himself to be the servant of God, to do him service all his life long; and lastly,
that, being delivered from the law of Moses and from all
mortal men[1], he doth altogether depend upon the gospel
only, having at liberty free use of external things, as of
meat, of drink, of clothing, and of such like indifferent
things: and in these three last rehearsed points doth christian liberty chiefly consist.

Testimonies
to prove
christian
liberty by.
Now to this I will add such testimonies of scripture as
shall both better confirm and more plainly declare my exposition. And, first of all, I will allege those testimonies
which are to be found in the books of the holy evangelists;
and then those that are extant in the writings of the apostles.

Luke i.
Zacharias the priest, and father of John Baptist, in his
hymn of thanksgiving, Luke i. doth declare the truth and
goodness of God in performing that to us which he promised
to our forefathers; to wit, "That we, being delivered out of
the hands of our enemies, might serve him without fear in
holiness and righteousness before him all the days of our
life." In this testimony of his we have the true liberty; that
freedom, I mean, wherein we, being by the Lord delivered
from all our enemies, both visible and invisible, should no
longer serve them with fear, but[2] serve our God[3] in joy and
gladness. There is added also the manner and order how
to serve him; "in holiness and righteousness." Holiness
doth cut off and cast away all uncleanness and inconveniency[4]:
righteousness giveth to every man that which is due, to wit,
the things which we of duty do owe to every man, and doth
contain in it both freedom and benevolence. And in this
kind of service do they, which are made free, serve the Lord
their God, not for a day or two, or a certain few years, but
all the days of their life. Therefore true christian liberty
is the perpetual service which we owe and do to God.

In the eighth chapter of St John's gospel, to the Jews

[1 ab omnibus hominum legibus, Lat.; from all laws of mortal men,
ed. 1577.]
[2 citra timorem, Lat.; without fear.]
[3 ipsi Deo, Lat.; God himself.]
[4 intemperantiam, Lat.; incontinency, ed. 1577.]

which made great brags of the vain and silly liberty which they received of their ancestors, Christ our Lord maketh this objection : " Verily, verily, I say unto you, that whosoever John viii. committeth sin, he is the servant of sin. And the servant abideth not in the house for ever; but the Son abideth for ever : if the Son therefore shall make you free, then are ye free indeed." In these words he[5] maketh mention both of bondage and of liberty. He is a bondman to sin, as to a cruel master or a never-contented tyrant, whosoever doth commit any sin; for he doth obey, as one that is bound to sin. Such bondmen are all the sons of men; whose punishment is[6] to have none inheritance in their Father's house, which is the heavenly Hierusalem[7]. As for those which the Son of God restoreth to freedom, they are partakers of the heavenly kingdom and fellow-heirs with the Son of God. But Christ maketh none free but them that are faithful[8] : therefore the sons of God and fellow-heirs of Christ are for Christ his sake their only deliverer made free and set at liberty. Neither is there any other in heaven or in earth, beside Christ Jesu, which is able to set us at freedom and at liberty.

Paul in the sixth chapter to the Romans saith : " Let Rom. vi. not sin reign in your mortal bodies, that ye should thereunto obey by the lusts of it[9]; neither give ye your members as instruments[10] of unrighteousness unto sin ; but give yourselves unto God, as they that are alive from the dead, and your members as instruments[10] of righteousness unto God. For sin shall not have power over you; because ye are not under the law, but under grace." In these words he exhorteth them that are purged and made free by Christ to live holily in their spiritual bondage. Now he saith not, Let not sin be in you, or in your mortal body : but he saith, "Let not sin reign in you, or in your mortal body." But when reigneth sin ? Forsooth sin reigneth then, when we obey

[5 Dominus, Lat.]

[6 id supplicii conjunctum, imo irrogatum habentes, Lat.; whose punishment is adjoined, nay imposed.]

[7 in cœlesti utique patria, Lat. ; which is the heavenly country.]

[8 credentes, Lat. ; believers.]

[9 ut obediatis ei per cupiditates ejus, Lat. and Erasmus. That ye shulde ther unto obey by the lustes of it. Cranmer, 1539.]

[10 arma, Lat.]

20—2

it through the lusts thereof; that is, when we resist not, but do fulfil the lusts of the flesh. Sin therefore doth not reign in our mortal body, so long as it is but felt in the body and not obeyed or permitted to rule, but rather resisted and trod under foot[1]. The same sentence doth he expound by another somewhat more easy to be understood: I would not have you to permit your members to sin, as to a tyrant, to use them as instruments to work all unrighteousness: I rather require you to give yourselves to be ruled and governed by God. For since he hath set you free from death and brought you to life again, it is requisite[2] that ye should give your members to God, as lively instruments, to work all righteousness. And that shall ye be easily able to do, because "ye are not under the law, but under grace."

Upon this doth all the rest of that chapter depend[3] unto the end. "What then?" saith he; "shall we sin, because we are not under the law, but under grace? God forbid. Know ye not, how that to whomsoever ye commit yourselves as servants to obey, his servants ye are to whom ye obey; whether it be of sin unto death, or of obedience unto righteousness? But God be thanked, that ye were the servants of sin, but ye have obeyed with heart the form of doctrine into the which ye are brought unto[4]. Being then made free from sin, ye are become the servants of righteousness." And yet he sheweth, that the freemen of Christ do not abuse their liberty, and give themselves again to be governed by their old and tyrannous master sin: for he maketh sin and righteousness to be, as it were, two masters; and addeth to each of them the hire, or reward, that they give to their servants; the one life, the other death. Lastly, he saith generally, that we are his servants to whom we give ourselves to obey. Upon which he inferreth: "Being redeemed by the grace of God from the bondage of sin, and from death which is the reward of sin, we are translated into the bondage of righteousness, (whose reward is life[5],) that thereby we may live."

[1 quin calcantur magis cupiditates, Lat.]
[2 æquum est, Lat.; it is just.]   [3 huc pertinent, Lat.]
[4 in eam in quam traducti estis formam doctrinæ, Lat. and Erasmus: unto the rule of the doctrine that ye be brought unto, Cranmer, 1539; whereto ye were delivered, Marg. Auth. Ver.]
[5 whose—life, not in Lat.]

For he doth more significantly express his meaning in that which followeth, saying : "I speak after the manner of men, because of the infirmity of your flesh. As ye have given your members servants to uncleanness and iniquity unto iniquity ; even so now give your members servants to righteousness unto holiness. For when ye were the servants of sin, ye were free from righteousness. What fruit had ye then in those things, whereof ye are now ashamed ? for the end of those things is death. But now ye, being made free from sin and made the servants of God, have your fruit unto holiness, and the end everlasting life. For the reward of sin is death; but the gift of God is eternal life through Jesus Christ our Lord." All this is so plain and evident, that it needeth no larger exposition of mine.

And yet in the seventh chapter next following he doth by comparison in a parable more fully expound all that he said before. "The woman," saith he, "which is in subjection to the man, is by the law bound to the man as long as he liveth. If, while the man liveth, she go aside to another, she is counted an adulteress; but if the man be dead, she may couple herself with another man. Even so, I say, we are dead to the law." For Christ died for us, and was in his body offered up to be a sacrifice, or oblation, to cleanse and purge our sins, that we might thenceforth be united and coupled to him ; and that we, being conceived and made with child[6] with the Holy Spirit, may travail, bring forth, and be delivered of an excellent issue and holy fruit of good works : even as, while we served sin, and were subject unto it as to our master, we brought forth an ill-favoured babe of death ; I mean, iniquity and wickedness, for the punishing whereof death is appointed and ordained. But let us now hear the very words of the holy and blessed apostle, saying : "Even so, my brethren, we also[7] are dead concerning the law[8] by the body of Christ, that we should be coupled to another[9], who is raised from the dead, that we should bring forth fruit unto God. For when we were in the flesh, the lusts of sin[10], which were by the law, wrought in our members to bring forth fruit unto death. But now are we delivered from the

[6 impraegnati, Lat.]   [7 vos quoque, Lat.; ye also.]
[8 legi, Lat.; to the law]   [9 nimirum ei, Lat.; even to him.]
[10 effectus peccatorum, Lat.]

law, and dead unto it, whereunto we were in bondage[1]; that
we may serve in newness of spirit, and not in the oldness of
the letter."

That place in the eighth chapter to the Romans is un-
Rom. viii. known to no man, where he saith : " The law of the spirit of
life through Christ Jesus hath made me free from the law of
sin and death." The manner of this deliverance he doth immediately after add, saying : " For what the law could not do,
that God did by sending his own Son:" and so forth as
followeth : for the words are sufficiently plain, and understood of all men[2].

1 Cor. vii. In the seventh chapter of the first epistle to the Corinthians he saith: " Ye are bought with a price; do not ye
become the servants of men." In these words the holy apostle
exhorteth servants under the colour or pretence of worldly[3]
bondage not to commit anything for their earthly masters'
pleasure, which soundeth against sincerity and is repugnant
to pure religion : to wit, although[4] they be called by the
name of servants, yet they should not obey the wicked laws
and ungodly ordinances of mortal men. The cause that
ought to pull and draw us from it is, because we are redeemed and set at liberty by the price of Christ his blood.
It would therefore be too too bad and unworthy a thing, if we,
contrary to the effect of our liberty, should obey the naughty
laws and ordinances of man.

Free from
the laws and
ordinances
of men.
This also is extended and stretcheth out to the laws of
men which are made in matters of religion. For in the
fifteenth chapter of the holy gospel written by the evangelist
Matt. xv. St Matthew the Lord and Saviour saith, " In vain do they
worship me, teaching doctrines the precepts of men ;" and,
" Let them alone : they are blind leaders of the blind." And
[Col. ii. 20—
23.]
the apostle St Paul saith: " If ye be dead with Christ from
the rudiments of the world, why, as yet living in the world,
are ye led[5] with traditions, (Touch not; taste not; handle
not ; which all do perish in abusing[6],) after the commandments

[1 So Cranmer, 1539; and marginal reading of Auth. Ver., being
dead to that wherein we were held.　Bullinger adopts Erasmus' rendering; mortui ei in quo detinebamur.]
[2 notissima sunt omnibus, Lat.]　　[3 vel civilis, Lat.; or civil.]
[4 quia, Lat. ; because.]　　　[5 tenemini, Lat. ; are ye bound.]
[6 quæ sunt omnia in corruptionem ipso abusu, Lat., after Erasmus :
whych all peryshe thorow the very abuse, Cranmer, 1539.]

and doctrines of men? Which things have a shew of wisdom in superstition and humbleness of mind, and in neglecting of the body; not in any honour to the satisfying of the flesh." First of all he sheweth, that the faithful ones of Christ Jesu have nothing to do with the decrees of man's inventions, and that they are not bound to observe men's traditions, because they are dead to traditions with Christ; that is to say, they are by Christ Jesu[7] redeemed and set free from traditions; which traditions did in Christ his death finish and come to an end, while he did make us his own, and set us at liberty. Then also he doth by imitation counterfeit the words of them which make those decrees[8], and say, " Oh, touch not, taste not, handle not."

These three precepts stretch very far, and comprehend many petit decrees; all which he doth immediately confute with these probable arguments. First, because they appoint the worship of God to be in things that perish in the use thereof; but the kingdom of God is neither meat nor drink, but doth consist in spiritual things; and that which entereth in by the mouth doth not defile the man. Secondarily, because they are not made of God, the author of all goodness; but have their beginning of man's inventions: " But in vain do they worship me," saith the Lord in [Matt. xv. 9.] the gospel, " teaching doctrines the precepts of men." Neither doth the holy apostle St Paul wink at and slily pass over, because he will not answer to[9], the things which do most commend these traditions. First of all, they are commended For what it is that men's for the shew and appearance of wisdom that is in them; for traditions are wont to be they seem to have been not without great wisdom ordained of commended. wise men, in that they do so fitly serve to every person, time, and place. The earnest defenders of men's traditions cry out, and say: Our ancestors were no fools, their laws are full of wisdom. But Jeremy crieth out on the other side, saying: " They have rejected the word of God; therefore what wisdom [Jer. viii. 9.] can be in them?" Another cause why traditions are commended is the Greeks' ἐθελοθρησκεία; that is to say, a chosen

[7 per mortem Christi, Lat.]

[8 qualia sint illa decreta commemorat per Mimesim, Lat.: μιμη-τικῶς subjungit; Bulling. Comment. in loc.]

[9 because—answer to, not in Lat.]

kind of worship[1], which we of our own brains have chosen, and taken ourselves to serve and do God worship withal; for men do gladly and willingly receive the traditions of men, because they are agreeable to their inclination[2]. Yea, Christ

[John xv. 19.]

in the holy gospel saith; "If ye had been of the world, the world would have loved her own: now for because I have chosen you out of the world, the world doth hate you." And again he saith: "That which men set such store by, is abominable unto God[3]." Moreover men's traditions are commended for humility: which is understood in two manners or respects. For first, that is said to be humility, if any man do readily obey and easily yield to that which is urged, obtruded, and thrust upon him by men of countenance and authority: secondarily, the laws of men do seem to exercise humbleness, and keep men in humility. But such obedience and humility may rather be called sacrilege, because it is not ruled and directed by the word of God, as the thing whereby alone it should be tempered and squared, but doth transfer and convey over the honour of God from God to men. Last of all, men's traditions are commended for the neglecting of the flesh: for, Oh, that discipline and chastisement of the flesh seemeth to them a goodly thing, by which the wantonness of the flesh is somewhat bridled and tamed. Finally the apostle addeth,

The care of the body.

" Not in any honour to the satisfying of the flesh:" that is to say, Which things, although they have a shew of religion and holiness, have notwithstanding in very deed no honour at all, considering that those external things are ordained of God for the ease and relief of men's necessities. Yea, Paul doth flatly find fault with those decrees, because they give the body no honour for the satisfying of the same, that is, according to the measure of the body's necessity. For a moderate care and looking to the body is not only permitted, but also commanded, lest we perhaps by too much lack and nearness[4] do mar the body, and make it unapt to do good works. Neither is the care of the flesh in any place forbidden[5], unless it tend to

[Rom. xiii. 14.]

lusts and sensuality. Wherefore the apostle saith, " Cherish not the flesh unto concupiscence." Therefore God hath granted to man for his necessity the use of meat, drink,

[1 Cultus electitius, Lat.]　　　　[2 ingenio humano, Lat.]
[3 Luke xvi. 15; coram Deo, Lat.]
[4 inedia, Lat.]　　　　[5 simpliciter, Lat. omitted; in itself.]

sleep, clothing, rest, allowable pleasures, and other things necessary[6].

In the fourth chapter to the Galatians St Paul saith: "When the fulness of the time was come, God sent his Son, *Gal. iv.* born of a woman, and made under the law, to redeem them that were under the law, that we might receive by adoption the right (or inheritance)[7] of children. Now because ye are sons, God hath sent the Spirit of his Son into your hearts, crying, Abba, Father. Wherefore thou art no more a servant, but a son: if thou be a son, thou art also an heir of God through Christ." And immediately after again: "Stand fast in the liberty wherewith Christ hath delivered us, and be not again wrapped in the yoke of bondage."

In the second to the Hebrews he saith: "Christ was *Heb. ii.* made partaker of flesh and blood with us, to the end that through death he might expel[8] him that had lordship over death, that is, the devil; and that he might deliver them which through fear of death were all their life time in danger of[9] bondage." Thus I hope these testimonies of scripture suffice for our purpose.

These things being well weighed and throughly consi- *The estate, property.* dered will plainly teach, what kind of liberty they have *or duty of them that are free by Christ.* which are made free by Christ, and what their property and inclination is; to wit, most religious, and altogether given to holy things; that is to say, in all points addicted to the Spirit, without which there is no liberty, and by which all the sons of God are always governed. The Lord's freemen do most diligently beware that they do unadvisedly offend no man by their liberty, nor vainly abuse their purchased freedom; for they have continually before their minds and eyes the weighty sayings of the holy apostles of their Lord Christ Jesu. St Peter in the second chapter of his first Epistle saith[10]: "As free, and not having the liberty for a cloak of maliciousness, but even as the servants of God." And Paul

---

[6 In this exposition Bullinger has borrowed *literally* from Calvin's Comment.; and both from Erasmus' Annotations, in loc. cit.]

[7 ut adoptione jus filiorum acciperemus, Lat. and Erasmus: that we thorow eleccion myght receave the inheritaunce that belongeth unto the naturall sonnos. Cranmer, 1539.]

[8 aboleret, Lat.]   [9 See page 307, note 10.]

[10 verse 16, prætextum vel velamen habentes malitiæ, Lat.]

saith : " Brethren, ye have been called unto liberty; only let not liberty be an occasion to the flesh, but by love serve one another. For I, when I am free, have made myself servant to all, that I may win the more[1]."

The abuses of christian liberty.

They therefore do specially[2] abuse christian liberty, who, seeking after carnal things under the colour and pretence of the Spirit and of liberty, do make their brags, that they by the preaching of the gospel are set free from all bodily debts and duties : and therefore they do deny to their masters, creditors, magistrates, and princes, the duty that they owe them; by that means revolting and rebelling against them[3]. These fellows are seditious stirrers, and not the reverencers of the evangelical doctrine. Paul crieth : " Give to every one that which is due: tribute to whom tribute belongeth; custom to whom custom is due; fear to whom fear; and honour to whom honour doth appertain. Owe nothing to any man, but this, that ye love one another."

[Rom. xlii. 7, 8.]

Moreover they also do abuse christian liberty, who, when they have not[4] received the Spirit of liberty and of the sons of God, when they are not as yet delivered from Satan nor justified by Christ, do notwithstanding promise liberty to all men ; and think that, for the opinion which they have conceived of their liberty, they may do whatsoever it pleaseth them; by that means gainsaying good laws and severe discipline with exclamations and outcries that liberty by laws is entrapped, betrayed, and trod under foot. Against such, and especially against the teachers of that vain and pernicious liberty, St Peter taketh stomach, and saith : " These are wells without water, clouds that are carried with a tempest; to whom the mist of darkness is reserved for ever. For when they have spoken the great swelling words of vanity, they entice through lusts in the voluptuousness of the flesh[5] such as were clean escaped from them which are

[2 Pet. ii. 17—19.]

[1 Gal. v. 13; 1 Cor. ix. 19; liber sim ab omnibus, Lat.; when I am free from all.]

[2 primum, Lat.; in the first place.]

[3 See Bullinger, adv. Anabapt. Lib. II. cap. 2, and Hooker, Eccles. Pol. Pref. Vol. I. p. 183, Oxf. 1820.]

[4 nondum, Lat.; not as yet.]

[5 inescant homines per concupiscentias carnis voluptatibus, Lat. and Erasmus: they entyse thorow lustes in the volupteousnes of the flessh. Cranmer, 1539.]

wrapped in error, while they promise them liberty; whereas they themselves are the bond-servants of corruption: for of whom a man is overcome, into the same is he brought in bondage:" and so forth as followeth.   Now when men do after that manner abuse liberty, that licentious lust is not worthy to be called by the name[6] of liberty. *Licentious-ness.*

Last of all, they do abuse christian liberty, whosoever do abuse things indifferent, and have no regard of their weak brethren, but do offend them unadvisedly.   We must therefore in this case always have in mind this notable saying of St Paul: "All things are lawful for me, but all things are not expedient: all things are lawful for me, but all things do not edify."   Touching this matter there is more to be seen in the fourteenth chapter of St Paul's Epistle written to the Romans. *[1 Cor. vi. 12; x. 23.]*

And here by occasion, yea, rather being compelled by necessity, I will speak a little, and so much as shall be requisite for the godly-disposed to know, touching offences. *Scandalum*, which word the Latins borrow of the Greeks, doth signify a falling, a tripping, a stumbling-block, an offence, a let or hinderance: such as are stones in a street that stick up higher than the rest, or gins that are of purpose subtilly set or hid to snare the feet of them that pass over them: for they which do either light on or stumble at them, do fall, or else are turned out of the straight path. *Of offences.*

Now this kind of snare or stumbling-block is by a metaphor transferred to the estate of religion and manners of men.   For he giveth an offence, whosoever doth with overthwart, foolish, or unseasonable words or deeds either do or say to another man anything whereby he taketh an occasion to sin.   Therefore *scandalum* is an occasion given to sin and do wickedly, and the very impulsion or driving to a fall or to wickedness.   Other there are that do define *scandalum* to be an offence joined with a contempt[7]: for an offence doth usually draw a contempt with it; or, as we may say also, an offence doth rise upon a contempt.   To conclude therefore, it is put for an injury offered by one man to another.

[6 sancto vocabulo, Lat.; the sacred name.]
[7 So Zuingle defines it, De vera et falsa religione, Comment. p. 412, Tigur. 1525.]

Now we offend other men either by our words, or else by our deeds. The offence that is given by words is partly in evil, foolish, and unseasonable doctrine, and partly our daily talk or communication. The greatest offence is that which doth arise of wicked doctrine, directly contrary to the true doctrine of the holy gospel. The next to this is that offence which doth arise of foolish and unseasonable doctrine; which, though it be derived out of the word of God, is notwithstanding either unaptly uttered, or unwisely applied. For the preacher may sin either by too much suffering[1] or lenity; or else by too much sharpness and overthwart waywardness[2], so that the hearers being offended do wholly draw back from all hearing of the gospel. And yet, for all this, the light of the gospel must not be hidden, nor the truth slily winked at[3], because men will be offended; but preachers must with all their diligence take heed that the word of God be wisely set forth and aptly dispensed[4]. Whatsoever things are against the laws of God, those must most constantly be accused, and without fear most diligently confuted, howsoever the world and worldlings do storm against the same.

Now they do by their daily talk cause their brethren to stumble, whosoever let their tongues run loose to talk they care not what; and at their pleasure, without advice, to babble they care not how: of which sort are filthy speech and ribaldry, but especially such blasphemous words as are unreverently uttered against God, the holy scriptures, and articles of our faith; for evil words corrupt good manners. I do not here exclude the letters or writings of men which do unadvisedly offend their brethren.

Lastly, stumbling-blocks of offence are laid before many men either by promises or else by threatenings: so often, I mean, as by alluring enticements of many fair promises, or else by terrible threats and torments, they are turned from the right path of truth into byways and errors; for
so did Pharao lay a stone of offence before king Zedechias, by causing him to make a league with him, and by that

[1 licentia, Lat.]
[2 nimia mordacitate et morositate, Lat.]
[3 dissimulanda, Lat.]
[4 recte secetur, Lat.; 2 Tim. ii. 15.]

means to trust more in the power of Egypt than in the mighty hand of God[5]. Tyrants do oftentimes give weak Christians causes of offence, while they by torments drive them to deny the name of their master Christ.

Now the deeds, whereby men are offended, be of two sorts; that is to say, they be either lawful and at our free choice, or else unlawful and utterly forbidden us. But even lawful deeds are by abuse made unlawful. For it is lawful for the faithful to eat what they lust: for to the clean all things are clean. But thy eating is made unlawful, if thou dost eat with the offence of thy weak brother: for he doth not understand that it is lawful to eat indifferently every kind of thing; and thou knowest very well that, if thou eatest, he will be offended; and yet notwithstanding thou dost eat and despise him : assure thyself in so doing thou givest cause of offence, and sinnest not a little against thy weak brother. To this we add all unseasonable using of free things and indifferent.

But here we must note, that the doctors of the church do Weaklings and stubborn persons. diligently distinguish and make a difference betwixt weak brethren and stubborn persons. The weaklings are such as be utterly ignorant in some points of religion; and yet notwithstanding are tractable enough, and fear the Lord; not erring of purpose with malicious overthwartness, but touched with a certain weakness of faith and religion, suffering themselves nevertheless willingly to be instructed. Of such the [Rom. xiv. 1.] apostle saith : "Him that is weak in faith receive ye, not to strifes of disputations." But the stubborn and obstinate people are they which, when they know the truth and liberty of the saints, do notwithstanding harden their minds, and set themselves against the truth of liberty[6] which they know; desiring to have much granted them, and every man to bear with them, not so much for that they do ever mean to give place to the truth, as to the end that by this occasion once granted them they may at last subvert the truth and christian liberty, and in stead thereof set up their trifles and superstitious vanities. Of such men the Lord speaketh in [Matt. xv. 14.] the gospel, saying: "Let them alone; they be blind leaders of the blind." And Paul in the second chapter to the Ga- Gal. ii.

[5 potentiæ et liberationi divinæ, Lat.]
[6 veritati et libertati, Lat.; the truth and liberty, ed. 1577.]

latians saith: "Titus, being a Greek, was not circumcised, because of incomers, being false brethren, which came in privily to spy out our liberty which we have in Christ Jesus, that they might bring us into bondage. To whom not so much as for an hour we gave any place by subjection; that the truth of the gospel might continue with you."

An offence given and an offence taken. Moreover to this place is to be referred the difference that some men do very wisely make betwixt the giving and the taking of an offence.

An offence is given then, when by thy fault, by thy importunity, I say, and thy lightness, thou either doest or sayest a thing for which thy brother hath a cause to be offended[1]. The other kind of offence is not given, but taken or picked out, not by thy fault, but by the malice or wickedness of another man: as for example, when thou dost sin neither in word nor deed, when thy deeds are nothing insolent, nor thy words unseasonable, when thou either sayest or doest the thing that is both free and lawful for thee to say and do; and yet another taketh pepper in nose[2] and is offended with that liberty of thine: which is all one, as if a man that walketh in a plain path[3] should hap to trip or stumble, and presently quarrel with his companion[4], as though he had laid a block in his way.

Now the unlawful and forbidden deeds wherewith men are offended do tend against God and his laws, are done contrary to all seemliness, equity, right, and reason, and stir up others to imitate the like revels and desire of ill rule[5]: for such are idolatry, murder, whoredom, covetousness, pride, and luxury. So did the wicked king Jeroboam set up the golden calves to be a stumbling-block unto all the people of Israel. And in like manner do many, with their drunken tippling and overnice bravery in gaudy apparel, not only offend others, but also make them worse, and by their ill example draw them into like and more foolish vanities.

[1 merito, Lat.]
[2 This proverbial term for an angry person (see Ray's Proverbs, pp. 140, 197. Lond. 1817) is added by the Translator.]
[3 in quo nulla posita est offensio, Lat. omitted; where no stumbling-block has been laid.]
[4 The mention of a *companion* is an addition of the Translator's.]
[5 ad paria studia et scelera, Lat.]

Finally, to give an offence is a very great sin; as the saying[6] of the Lord in the gospel affirmeth. For in Matthew he saith: "Woe unto the world because of offences. It must needs be that offences come; but woe to the man by whom the offence cometh! Whosoever offendeth one of these little ones that believe in me, it were better for him that a millstone were hanged about his neck, and that he were drowned in the depth of the sea." And Paul the apostle, speaking to the brethren that give offence, doth say : "Through thy giving of offence perisheth thy brother for whom Christ died." And again: "And so ye sinning against your brethren, and wound-ing their weak consciences, do sin against Christ himself." But what can be devised more heinous than to sin against Christ? Let us all therefore take heed, that by abusing christian liberty we give no occasion of offence to the weak, but always do the things that do belong to charity.

Last of all, we must especially confirm our minds against the enemies of the gospel, who cease not daily to lay innu-merable heaps of offences upon the preachers and zealous followers of the evangelical doctrine. "Ye," say they, "are the causes of all the broils, seditions, wars, and hurly-burlies, wherewith the world is at this day disquieted." Against these offensive outcries, I say, we must confirm our minds with that notable saying of Christ in the gospel: "I came not to send peace, but a sword. For I am come to set a man at variance with his father, and the daughter against her mother, and the daughter-in-law against her mother-in-law: and a man's foes shall be they of his own household." Here we must call to remembrance, and lay before our eyes, the nota-ble examples of the prophets and apostles. King Achab said to Helias the prophet, that he was the disturber and plague of the kingdom; but the prophet replieth, that not he, but the king, was the troubler of the country. The rebellious Jews objected against Jeremy, that, since the time they began to leave the worship of their (idol) gods, and to hearken to the preaching of the word of God, they never had one jot of felicity, but that mishaps by troops fell one upon another's neck. To which objection they were answered, that those misfortunes did light upon them because of their sins, and especially for their rebellion and unthankfulness' sake. The

To give offence is a great sin.

[Matt. [xviii. 6, 7.]

[1 Cor. viii. 11, 12.]

Offences rise not of the gospel, but of the enemies of the gospel.

[Matt. x. 34—36.]

[1 Kings xviii. 17, 18.]

[Jer. xliv. 15—23.]

[6 unica sententia, Lat.]

unbelieving Jews at Thessalonica cried out against Paul and
[Acts xvii. 6.] Silas, saying: "These fellows, that have troubled the whole
world, are come hither also." But Paul, speaking against
[1 Thess. ii. 15, 16.] the Jews his enemies and persecutors, said: "They, as they
have killed the Lord Jesus and their own prophets, so do
they persecute us: they please not God, and are adversaries
to all men; resisting us that we should not preach the gospel
unto the Gentiles to their salvation, that they may still fulfil
their sins; and so at last the endless[1] anger of God may fall
upon them." These sayings and such like let the faithful
think upon and have in their minds, and let them persevere
still with constancy and patience to spread abroad the doctrine
of the gospel, howsoever the world doth fret and cast offences
in the way. And thus much hitherto touching offences[2].

Of good works. It remaineth now, as my promise in the beginning was,
to say somewhat in the end of this sermon concerning good
works. For we have learned that christian liberty is not
licentiousness, but an adoption into the number of the sons
of God, which do bestow all their life upon the study of
godliness and virtues: we have learned that the law of God
is the rule and doctrine of good works: the course of order,
therefore, doth now require to have somewhat said touching
good works.

What works do signify in the scripture. First of all, let us determine of the very true and certain signification of works, because the word is used diversly,
and is of ample signification. For works are the labours
and busy exercises of men, by the which they get their
livings: for Paul commandeth every man to work with his
own hands; the law forbiddeth us to do any work on the
sabbath-day; and the Israelites were oppressed in Egypt
with hard and wearisome work and toil. There are also
workmen, to whom the Lord in the gospel commandeth to
pay the hire that is their due. A work also is the thing
which is made or expressed by the artificer or workman;
[Jer. xviii. 3.] for the prophet Jeremy, speaking of a potter, saith: "He
made a work upon a wheel." Moreover a work doth sig-
[2 Tim. iv. 5.] nify an office or duty; for Paul saith, "Do the work"

[1 in finem, Lat.]
[2 This treatise of "offences" is transferred by Bullinger from his
Comment. in Matt. cap. xviii. Lib. VIII. fol. 172, Tiguri. 1542. Cf.
Calvin. Instit. Lib. III. cap. 19, § 11, 12.]

(meaning the office) "of an evangelist:" and the Holy Ghost, speaking in the church at Antioch, saith, " Separate [Acts xiii. 2.] me Paul and Barnabas for the work whereunto I have chosen them." Furthermore, the works of the Lord are[3] the mighty deeds of God, whereby he doth declare his power and goodness unto men: and in that signification heaven, earth, and man himself, are said to be the works of God's hands. Works also are the benefits of God bestowed upon us men; for in the gospel he saith: "I have shewed you many good works:" (as if he should have said, I have done [John x. 32.] you many good turns[4].) There are also evil works, I mean works of iniquity: whereupon some men are called workers [Job xxxiv. 22. Psal. v. 5, &c.] of iniquity, whose deeds are[5] the works of the flesh and of darkness. Again, there are good works, I mean sundry virtues, the fruits of faith; of which sort are justice, temperance, charity, patience, hope, &c. For the Lord in the gospel said: "Let your light so shine before men, that [Matt. v. 16. they may see your good works, and glorify the Father which is in heaven." The apostle saith that we are made for [Eph. ii. 10.] good works, to walk in them. Those same are called the [Matt. iii. 8. Acts xxvi. fruits of repentance, and works worthy of repentance. They 20.] are called the works of light[6], and the fruits of the Spirit. [Gal. v. 22.] The same are the works of humanity, benevolence, and charity: such are commended in Tabitha, which is read to [Acts ix. 36.] have been full of good works. Paul saith: " Let us work [Gal. vi. 10.] good, while we have time, to all; but especially to them of the household of faith." Such a like work of humanity and charity did Mary bestow upon Christ our Saviour, who said: [Matt. xxvi. 10.] " She hath wrought a good work on me." This being thus declared, we will now describe good works in their colours and qualities.

Good works are deeds, or actions, wrought of those Good works, what they which are regenerate by the Spirit[7] of God, through faith, are. and according to the word of God, to the glory of God, the

[3 vocantur, Lat.; are called.]
[4 This parenthesis is the Translator's.]
[5 illis respondent, Lat.]
[6 The express phrase, *works of light*, does not occur in Scripture; but Bullinger seems to refer to Rom. xiii. 12; for, in his exposition of that passage, he says: Hic palam audimus—quæ (sint) opera tenebrarum, quæ lucis, p. 106, Tigur. 1537.]
[7 spiritu bono, Lat.; by the good Spirit.]

honesty[1] of life, and the profit of our neighbour. This brief description I will prosecute by parts, and expound so well as the Lord shall give me grace.

The original cause of good works.

First, I will by proof shew that there is none other well-spring, from whence good works do flow, than God himself, which is the author of all good things. For the prophet saith: "All men are liars; God alone doth speak the truth[2]."

[Matt. xix. 17.]

And the Lord in the gospel saith: "None is good but God alone." Good works therefore must have their beginning, not of man, who is a liar and corrupt, but of God himself, the well-spring of all goodness. And God doth by his Spirit and by faith in Christ Jesus renew all men, so that they, being once regenerate, do no longer their own, that is, the works of the flesh, but the works of the Spirit, of grace, and[3] of God himself. For the works of them that are regenerate do grow up by the good Spirit of God that is within them; which Spirit, even as the sap giveth strength to trees to bring forth fruit, doth in like manner cause sundry virtues to bud and branch out of us men, as the Lord himself

[John xv. 4, 5.]

doth in the gospel testify, and say: "I am the vine, ye are the branches. As the branch cannot bear fruit of itself, unless it abide in the vine; so cannot ye also, unless ye abide in me. Whosoever abideth in me, and I in him, he bringeth forth much fruit: for without me ye can do nothing." To the same cause is that to be referred, where as[4] we say that a good work is done by faith. For faith is the gift of God, whereby we lay hold on Christ, through which we are both justified and quickened; as the scripture saith,

[Hab. ii. 4.]

"The just shall live by his faith." And in another place saith Paul: "By faith Christ dwelleth in our hearts[5]." And

[Gal. ii. 20.]

again: "I live; yet now not I, but Christ liveth in me: and the life which now I live in the flesh, I live by the faith of the Son of God, who loved me, and gave himself for me." Now he that liveth doth the works of life through him, no doubt, by whom he is quickened; and he that is justified doth the works of righteousness through him that justified

[1 ornamentum et honestatem, Lat.]
[2 Ps. cxvi. 11; Rom. iii. 4: where the Vulgate has, *est* Deus verax; Erasmus renders, *sit*.]
[3 adeoque, Lat.; and so.]   [4 cum dicimus, Lat.]
[5 Eph. iii. 17; in cordibus vestris, Lat.]

him: that is, the righteous do through Christ work righteousness, and righteousness containeth the whole company of virtues. So then God alone remaineth still the only well-spring and author of good works.

But let us now see the testimonies of scripture, by which we may evidently learn, that the works of them that be regenerate are attributed to God himself, who by his Spirit and by faith doth work in the hearts of the regenerate. Moses testifieth, saying: "The Lord shall bless thee, and the Lord thy God shall circumcise thy heart, and the heart [Deut. xxx. 5, 6.] of thy seed, that thou mayest love the Lord thy God with all thy heart, and with all thy soul, that thou mayest live." Lo, here the cause that godly men do rightly love the Lord doth proceed of the circumcision of the heart. Now who, I pray you, doth circumcise the heart beside the Lord? The prophet Esay doth more plainly say: "Thou, Lord, shalt ordain peace: for even thou hast wrought all our works [Isai. xxvi. 12.] in us." In the gospel after St John our Saviour saith: "He that worketh verity cometh to the light, that his works [John iii. 21; xv. 5.] may be seen, because they are wrought by God." And again: "Whosoever abideth in me, and I in him, he bringeth forth much fruit; for without me ye can do nothing." Paul also to the Philippians saith: "To you it is given for Christ, [Phil. i. 29.] not only to believe in him, but also to suffer for him." And yet again more plainly: "It is God that worketh in you both to will and to do according to the good purpose of the mind[6]." Likewise also St James saith: "Every good giving [James i. 17.] and every perfect gift is from above, and cometh from the Father of lights." Moreover St Peter, ascribing all the parts of good works to God, doth say: "The God of all [1 Pet. v. 10.] grace, who hath called you to his eternal glory through Christ Jesus, restore, uphold, strengthen, and stablish you." For "we are not able," as Paul in another place saith, "of [2 Cor. iii. 5.] ourselves to think any thing as of ourselves; but all our ability is of God." Therefore God alone remaineth still the only well-spring of all good works, from whom, as from

[6 Phil. ii. 13; pro bono animi proposito, Lat. and Erasmus. Sensus est, Deus operatur in nobis velle et perficere, idque facit quod propenso in nos animo sit, quod nos amat, et familiariter admodum complectitur. Bullinger, Comment. in loc.]

a spring-head, good works[1] do flow into the saints, as into sundry streams and channels[2].

Good works are imputed to men.

  Yet here by the way this must be added, that good works, although they do in deed proceed from God, and are in very true and proper phrase of speech the fruits of the Spirit and of faith, both are notwithstanding, and are also said to be, ours; that is to say, the works of faithful men: partly because God worketh them by us, and useth our ministery in the doing of the same; and partly because we are by faith the sons of God, and are therefore made the brethren and joint-heirs with Jesus Christ. For by this right of inheritance all the works of God, which are in us God's gifts, do begin to be not another's, but our own and proper works. Yea, the very scripture doth attribute them to us, as unto sons and freeborn children; for the Lord in the gospel saith: "The servant abideth not in the house for ever; the son abideth for ever." Therefore, as all things in the father's house do, by right of inheritance and title of propriety, come to the son, although the son hath not gotten them by his own industry, nor gathered them by his own labour, but hath received them by the liberality of his parents; even so the works of God, which he doth work in us and by us, which are God's gifts bestowed upon us, both are, and are said to be, our own, because we are the sons of the household, as it were, by adoption, and therefore are the lawful heirs. Wherefore it were the sign of a very unthankful mind for an adopted son, being forgetful of his father's beneficence and liberality, to make his brags, that all those goods, which he enjoyeth by right of inheritance, were gotten and come by through his own labour and travail. Whereupon Paul said very religiously: "What hast thou that thou hast not received? If thou hast then received it, why dost thou yet boast as though thou receivedst it not?" Very well thought the holy martyr of Christ, St Cyprian, who was wont to say: "We should boast of nothing, because we have nothing of our own[3]." And to this

[John viii. 35.]

[1 Cor. iv. 7.]

[1 opera vere bona, Lat.]
[2 as—channels, is the Translator's addition.]
[3 In nullo gloriandum, quando nostrum nihil sit.—Cypr. Testim. III. ad Quirinum 4. Op. Par. 1633, p. 373.]

place belongeth[4] that saying of the prophet Esay: "Shall the axe boast against him that heweth with it; or shall the saw brag against him that draweth it[5]?" We, verily, are the instruments or tools of God, by which he worketh; for the apostle saith: "We are joint-workers with God; ye are God's husbandry, ye are God's building. According to the grace which God hath given me." Therefore, according to the meaning of the apostle's writing, St Augustine, *Lib. de Gratia et libero arb.*, in the sixth chapter, doth say: "When grace is given, then do our merits begin to be good, and that through grace. For if grace be taken away, then man doth fall, not being set up, but cast down headlong, by free-will. Wherefore, when man beginneth to have good works, he must not attribute them to himself, but unto God, to whom it is said in the Psalm, Be thou my helper: O forsake me not. In saying, Forsake me not, he sheweth, that if he be forsaken, he is able to do no good of himself[6]." So then in these words St Augustine doth plainly enough declare, that good works are ours after that sort, that yet notwithstanding they cease not to be the works of God; yea, that they ought nevertheless to be ascribed to the grace of God that worketh in us[7].

[margin: 1 Cor. iii. 9, 10.]

Now by this which we have hitherto alleged out of the scriptures touching the true original cause of good works, we may easily understand how and after what manner the scripture doth attribute righteousness unto our merits. For I have in another place[8] sufficiently declared (and will again say somewhat, when I come to the treatise of the gospel) that faith, not works, doth justify us in the sight of God: which is the especial point and chief foundation of the evangelical and apostolical doctrine.

[margin: No works do justify. 1]

[4 pertinere videtur, Lat.]
[5 Is. x. 15; qui ipsam agitat, Lat. and Calvin.]
[6 Sed plane cum data fuerit (gratia), incipiunt esse etiam merita nostra bona, per illam tamen. Nam si illam subtraxerit, cadit homo, non erectus, sed præcipitatus libero arbitrio. Quapropter quando cœperit homo habere merita bona, non debet sibi tribuere illa, sed Deo, cui dicitur in Psalmo, Adjutor meus esto, ne derelinquas me. Dicendo, ne derelinquas me, ostendit quia si derelictus fuerit, nihil boni valet ipse per se.—Aug. Opp. Par. 1531, Tom. vii. fol. 268, col. 1.]
[7 Cf. Calvin. Instit. Lib. ii. cap. 5, § 14.]
[8 Decad. i. Serm. 6, Vol. i. p. 104.]

All our works generally are either the works of nature or the flesh, or else the works of the law, or else the works of faith or grace. Now the works of nature or the flesh do not justify, but condemn us; because " that which is born of flesh is flesh." But "the lust of the flesh is death, and enmity against God." What the apostle thought and said touching the works of the law, I did declare[1] to you in my former sermon: " By the works of the law," saith he, "shall no flesh be justified." But if we beat out and examine the works of grace and of faith, we shall find that they both are, and have been, done by faithful and just men.

Whereupon it is manifest, that justification did always go before the works of righteousness: for the just man doth work righteousness; so that righteousness is the fruit that the just do bring forth. Man, verily, is justified freely by grace, and not by works, which follow after justification. What may be said to that, where the scripture saith[2], that even Abraham, the father of all that believe, was not justified by the works of grace and of faith? He lived 430 years before[3] the law; he believed in God, and by true faith did most excellent works: and yet by those his works of faith he was not justified. For Paul doth plainly argue thus: " If Abraham were justified by works, then hath he wherein to boast; but not before God. For what saith the scripture? Abraham believed God, and it was counted unto him for righteousness. To him[4] that worketh is the reward not reckoned of grace, but of duty[5]: but to him that worketh not, but believeth on him that justifieth the ungodly, his faith is counted for righteousness." Now whereas we conclude, that we also shall be justified according to the example of Abraham by faith, and not by works, we ground that conclusion, not upon our own minds, but upon the apostle's doctrine, who saith: " Nevertheless it was not written for him[6] only, that faith was imputed to him for righteousness;

Marginal notes:

2
[Rom. viii. 6, 7.]

[Rom. iii. 20.]

[Rom. iv. 2—5.]

[Rom. iv. 23.]

[1 copiose exposui, Lat.]
[2 aperte testatur, Lat.]
[3 Gal. iii. 17. Hoc loco Apostolus 430 annos a promissione facta Abrahæ ad legem usque numerat. Bullinger, Comment. in loc.]
[4 Ei vero, Lat.; now to him.]
[5 See Tyndale's Doctrinal Treatises, Park. Soc. ed. p. 103.]
[6 propter Abraham, Lat.]

but it was written for us also, to whom it shall be reckoned, if we believe in Christ." Touching this matter I have already disputed in the sixth sermon of the first Decade. I verily am persuaded that this doctrine of the apostles and evangelists ought to be laid up in the bottom of every faithful heart : that we are justified by the grace of God, not by merits[7]; through faith[8], and not through works.

But while we urge and repeat this doctrine unto the people, we are said of many to be the patrons of all naughtiness, and utter enemies to all good works and virtues. But we, by this our preaching and doctrine of faith which doth only justify, do not contemn good works, nor think them to be superfluous. We do not say that they are not good; but do cry out upon the abuse of good works, and the corrupt doctrine of good works, which is defiled with the leaven of the Pharisees. For we teach to do good works, but we will not have them to be set to sale, and to be bought I cannot tell in what order of bargaining. We will not have any man to put confidence in them ; we will not have any man to boast of the gifts of God ; we will not have the power to justify, or to merit life everlasting, to be simply attributed unto them. For by that means Christ should wax vile and contemptible[9], who hath with his death alone merited for us the heavenly kingdom of God Almighty. Neither do we by this, as many think we do, separate good works from faith. Our doctrine is, that works and faith are not severed, but cleave together as closely as may be : so yet notwithstanding, that justification is properly ascribed to faith, and not to works. For works do consist in our worthiness, but faith doth cleave to the promise of God, which setteth before us both righteousness and life in the only-begotten Son of God, Christ Jesus our Saviour. And Christ is sufficiently able of himself, and by his own power and virtue, to justify them that believe in his name, without any aid or help of ours at all.

I will not wink at some men's objection, but freely confess, that the scriptures here and there do after a sort attribute both life and justification unto good works. But the scripture is not contrary to itself : therefore we must search

Good works are not rejected, but their abuse is by this doctrine condemned.

In what sense the scripture doth attribute justification unto good works.

[7 non meritis nostris, Lat.]
[8 per fidem in Christum, Lat.]
[9 et oppugnaretur, Lat. ; and be fought against.]

and examine, in what sense, and how, life and justification are ascribed to our works. St Augustine doth so answer this objection, that he referreth our works[1] unto the grace of God; for in his book *De gratia et libero arbitrio*, the eighth chapter, he writeth : "If eternal life be of duty given to good works, as the scripture doth most plainly testify, saying, 'Because God will reward every man according to his works;' then how is eternal life of grace, considering that grace is not given as due to works, but freely and without deserts? as the apostle Paul doth say, 'To him that worketh the reward is not reckoned of grace, but of duty ;' and again, ' The remnant,' saith he, ' are saved by the election of grace :' and immediately after he addeth, 'If it be of grace, then it is not now of works; for then grace is no more grace.' How then is eternal life, which is gotten by works, a gift? Or else did not the apostle say, that everlasting life is a gift? Yes, verily; he said it so plainly that we cannot deny it. Neither are his words so obscure that they require a sharp understander, but an attentive hearer. For when he had said, 'The reward of sin is death;' he addeth straightways : 'But the gift of God is life everlasting in Jesu Christ our Lord.' Methinketh therefore, that this question can be none otherwise resolved, unless we understand, that even our good works, to which eternal life is given, must be referred to the grace and gift of God ; because the Lord Jesus saith, 'Without me ye can do nothing:' and the apostle, when he had said, 'Ye are saved by grace through faith,' doth presently add, ' and that not of yourselves; it is the gift of God : not of works, lest any man should boast[2].'" Thus much hitherto out of St Augustine.

[1 bona opera, Lat.]

[2 Si enim vita æterna bonis operibus redditur, sicut apertissime dicit scriptura, Quoniam Deus reddet unicuique secundum opera ejus; quomodo gratia est vita æterna, cum gratia non operibus reddatur, sed gratis detur? ipso apostolo dicente, Ei qui operatur merces non imputatur secundum gratiam, sed secundum meritum; et iterum, Reliquiæ, inquit, per electionem gratiæ salvæ factæ sunt; et mox addidit, Si autem gratia, jam non ex operibus, alioquin gratia jam non est gratia. Quomodo est ergo gratia vita æterna, quæ ex operibus sumitur? An forte vitam æternam non dixit apostolus gratiam? Imo vero sic dixit, ut negari omnino non possit; nec intellectorem acutum, sed tantummodo intentum desiderat auditorem. Cum enim dixisset, Stipendium peccati mors; continuo subdidit, Gratia autem Dei vita

Now although this answer of St Augustine be godly and plain enough to him that simply searcheth for the truth, yet I am sure that some there are which never will be answered with it. They will, I know, go about upon St Augustine's words to infer that works, and not faith alone, do justify us men. For thus they argue: We are justified, and do obtain eternal life, by grace: good works do belong to the grace of God: therefore good works do justify us. *The cavils of them which attribute justification unto works.*

Now it is not amiss to close and buckle hand to hand with these disputers, that in this little ye may perceive that they be mere shifts of sophistry, which they set to sale under the name and colour of very sound arguments. And first of all, there is no man so foolish, if he hath read the doctrine of St Paul, but knoweth very well that those two propositions cannot hang together: we are justified by grace; and, we are justified by works. For that sentence of St Paul is as clear as the sun, where he saith, "If of grace, then now not of works: for then grace were no grace." We do freely grant both their propositions; to wit, that we are justified by grace, and that works belong to the grace of God, or be the gift of God: but we deny their consequence, and say that it is false; to wit, that works do justify. For if that be true, then may we in like manner truly say, A man doth see; an hand doth belong unto a man: and thereupon infer, therefore a hand doth see. But who would gather so vain a consequent? For all do understand, that a man doth consist of sundry members, and that every member hath his effects[3] and offices. Again, what is he which knoweth not, that the grace of God, which is otherwise undivided, is divided and distinguished according to the diverse operations which it worketh? For there is in God a certain (as it were) general grace, whereby he created all mortal men, and by which he sendeth rain upon the just and unjust: but this grace doth not [Rom. xi. 6.]

æterna in Christo Jesu Domino nostro. Ista ergo quæstio nullo modo mihi videtur posse dissolvi, nisi intelligamus et ipsa bona opera nostra, quibus æterna redditur vita, ad Dei gratiam pertinere, propter illud quod ait Dominus Jesus, Sine me nihil potestis facere. Et ipse apostolus cum dixisset, Gratia salvi facti estis per fidem; et hoc non ex vobis, sed Dei donum est, non ex operibus ne forte quis extollatur; vidit utique, &c.—Aug. Opp. Par. 1531, Tom. vii. fol. 268, col. 3.]

[3 suas vires, Lat.]

justify; for if it did, then should the wicked and unjust[1] be justified. Again, there is that singular grace, whereby he doth, for his only-begotten Christ his sake, adopt us to be his sons: he doth not, I mean, adopt all, but the believers only, whose sins he reckoneth not, but doth impute to them the righteousness of his only-begotten Son our Saviour. This is that grace which doth alone justify us in very deed. Moreover there is a grace, which, being poured into our minds, doth bring forth good works in them that are justified. This grace doth not justify, but doth engender the fruits of righteousness in them that are justified. Therefore we confess and grant, that good works belong to grace, but after a certain manner, order, and fashion[2].

Again, they object and say: But grace or faith and works, justification also and sanctification, are so joined together, that they cannot be severed one from another: therefore the thing that agreeth to one is also appliable unto the other.

I verily neither dare nor do in any case gainsay, that faith and works do cleave together; but I do utterly deny that they twain are all one, so that the thing which is attributed to the one may also be applied unto the other. For faith, although it be weak and unperfect in us, doth notwithstanding lean and stay upon Christ his perfection alone, and so far forth it doth justify us. But our works have in them (for I use the mildest phrase of speech) some sprinkling of vice and sparkle of error, because of the original disease that is natural in us all: but it followeth not therefore, that the grace of God is polluted by any vice or fault of ours; which should of necessity follow consequently, if, by reason of the strait knot betwixt them, the properties of the one were common to the other. Although the light of the sun be not separate from the heat thereof, yet is not the light the same that the heat is. Neither is it a good consequence to say, The sun giveth light to the world; therefore the heat of the sun giveth light to the world, because in the sun the heat and light cannot be separated. Yea rather, the sun in respect of his light doth lighten the world, not in respect of the heat that it hath. And yet the sun doth both warm and

[1 omnes impii, Lat.]
[2 sed sua ratione, suo modo, Lat.]

lighten the earth at once.   In like manner we are freely justified by the merciful grace of God, for Christ his sake, our Lord and Saviour, not in respect and consideration of the works of grace, that are found in us; although these works are engendered and brought forth by that free grace.   And so we must attribute all glory wholly to the grace of God, and not part stakes with him, and take to our own share any part of his glory.

These wranglers have yet another shift, and say: Although we say that eternal life is given by God to all faithful believers, not for faith only in Christ Jesus, but also for the works of faith; all the glory nevertheless shall redound to God; namely since we acknowledge and confess that those works are wrought in us by the power and grace of God.

To this our answer is; that glory must so be given to God as he doth please to have it given him.   If the will, purpose, and counsel of God were to receive us into his friendship for the works' sake, which his Spirit and grace doth bring forth in us; then should he unadvisedly, without discretion, have sent his only-begotten Son into the world, and rashly have appointed him to the terrible pangs of bitter death.   But God, in all that he hath created either in heaven or earth, much less in this case, which is the greatest that belongeth to man, the chief and most excellent creature that he hath made[3], did never at any time do any thing rashly, without great advisement.   Wherefore it is assuredly certain, that it was never the counsel and purpose of God for our own good works[4] and virtues to redeem us from the tyranny of Satan, and to accept us for his sons; but for the only sacrifice and satisfaction of his only-begotten Son Christ Jesus, our Lord and Saviour.   For the judgment of Paul in this matter remaineth firm and invincible, where he saith: "If righteousness [Gal. ii. 21.] come of the works of the law, then did Christ die in vain." And that divine saying of St Peter remaineth for ever uncontrollable : " There is salvation in none other."   [Acts iv. 12.]

Again, they do lay certain places of scripture together, and thereupon do argue thus: Although Paul in one place doth say, " Ye are saved by grace through faith;" yet in [Eph. ii. 8; Rom. viii. another place the same Paul doth say, " We are saved by 24.]

[3 that belongeth—hath made, not in Lat.]
[4 opera fidei, Lat. ; the works of faith.]

hope." Now who knoweth not that hope is, as it were, upheld and strengthened by patience?—Christ himself in the gospel agreeing thereunto, and saying, "In your patience ye shall possess your souls." Therefore not faith only, but hope and patience do bring us to salvation.

[Luke xxi. 19.]

To this we answer thus; That the holy apostle doth sufficiently expound himself, if a man will take the pains to read him throughout, and weigh with himself the end and cause for which he spake every several sentence. "Ye are," saith he, "saved by grace through faith; and that not of yourselves, it is the gift of God; not of works, lest any man should boast," &c. Hath he not in these few words most evidently declared what his belief is touching grace or faith, and works? Who would desire a plainer speech? There is none so very a dorhead[1] as that he understandeth not, that the benefit[2] of salvation is wholly and merely ascribed to grace. For he doth not divide salvation or justification partly to faith or grace, and partly to works; neither doth he attribute the first place to faith, and the second place to works: he doth utterly exclude all boasting. "Ye are," saith he, "saved by grace through faith." And immediately after he addeth, "and that not of yourselves." He annexeth the cause: "it is the gift of God." And again: "not of works." He sheweth why: "Lest any man should boast." He that understandeth not this doth undoubtedly understand nothing at all.

Loqui contra solem : a proverb applied to them that speak against the truth. He that wresteth or otherwise cavilleth at this doth speak against the sun, and saith that the light is darkness. Now whereas the same apostle doth in another place say, "We are saved by hope;" it is by the marking of the whole place to be gathered, that his meaning is as if he had said: "I told you, that they which believe in Christ are the sons and heirs of God, and have thereby their salvation and felicity; but I would have every one to understand it in hope and expectation, not in enjoying the very thing itself, and present fruition." Now who can hereupon infer, Therefore hope doth justify? But we do rather make this argument: Patience is no patience at all, unless the patient man be first justified by true faith: therefore the commendation of patience[3]

[1 bardus, Lat. Dor: a drone.]
[2 totum beneficium, Lat.]
[3 patientiæ laus et virtus, Lat.]

doth wholly depend upon faith, and not the praise of faith upon patience; although faith be declared and shewed forth by patience.

For it is a sentence utterly unworthy to come out of a christian man's mouth, to say, that faith is made perfect by good works; that is to say, where faith doth want a piece, that there good works do patch it up. For when we name faith, we do not name simply the quality of believing which is in our minds, but we have an eye to Christ himself[4], our Lord and Saviour, together with his righteousness and heavenly gifts; upon whom alone, as upon a base and sure foundation, our faith doth rest and firmly stand. But to go about to supply the want of any thing in Christ Jesus, is nothing else but with devilish blasphemy to disgrace the Son of God. The faith of saints, I confess, doth declare and shew itself by works; but it followeth not thereupon, that works do therefore make perfect that which seemeth to be wanting in Christ his perfection. For there is nothing lacking in our deliverance, redemption, and justification wrought by Christ. The apostle James did say indeed, "Seest thou how faith was made perfect by works?" But [James i. 22.] his meaning was none other but to say, Seest thou how faith, by the works which followed it, did declare itself to be a true and righteous faith, and not an hypocritical faith? For before these words he said: "Seest thou how his faith was effectual through works?" Again, the apostle Paul said: "I fulfil[5] that which is lacking to the afflictions of Christ in my flesh for his body's sake, which is the church." But you may better translate the Greek τὰ ὑστερήματα to be that rather which is behind, than that which is lacking to[6] the afflictions of Christ: for the Greeks call τὰ ὑστερήματα not only those things that are wanting, but also the remnant (which word St Ambrose also used)[7], I mean the remnant

[4 See Vol. I. addend. p. 112, line 32.]

[5 Col. i. 24. Suppleo vel adimpleo, Lat. The former is the rendering of Erasmus, the latter of the Vulgate.]

[6 quæ supersunt, quam quæ desunt, Lat.]

[7 —qui nunc gaudeo in passionibus pro vobis, et suppleo relliquias pressurarum Christi, &c. Ambros. Comment. in Ep. ad Coloss. cap. 1, v. 24, Tom. II. Append. pág. 266, Par. 1690. But these commentaries are not genuine. See James' Corruption of Scripture, Councils, and Fathers, ed. Cox, Lond. 1843, p. 26.]

and those things that are remaining behind. And St Peter saith, that "Christ suffered for us, leaving behind him an example for us, that we might follow his trace and footsteps." Therefore the apostle affirmeth, that he by suffering fulfilled the remnant which was behind[1].

[1 Pet. ii. 21.]

Another objection. [1 Cor. xiii. 2.]

After this again they allege the words of the apostle Paul, where he saith: "If I have all faith, so that I can remove mountains out of their place, and yet have not charity, I am nothing." For upon this they infer, "Therefore not faith only, but also charity, yea, rather charity than faith, doth justify."

But we say that Paul in this sentence doth neither deny that faith alone doth justify, nor yet doth attribute the justification of the saints to charity. For when we affirm that we are justified by faith, or when we make faith the cause of justification, (which thing must be by often repetition beaten into our memories,) we do not understand that faith, as it is a virtue in us, doth work, and by the quality[2] that sticketh to us doth merit, righteousness in the sight of God; but so often as we make mention of faith, we understand the grace of God exhibited in Christ, which is through faith freely applied to us, and received[3] as the free gift of God bestowed upon us. And in that sense doth Paul[4] use the name of faith, when he affirmeth that faith doth justify. But in this place of the thirteenth chapter to the Corinthians he doth not so take the name of faith, but putteth it for the power of working miracles; as is manifest by that which followeth, where he saith, "so that I can remove mountains." That faith doth not comprehend Christ wholly, but only the power in shewing of miracles: and therefore it may be sometime in an unjust man and an hypocrite; as it was in Judas Iscariot, to whom the faith of miracles profited nothing, because he was without the justifying faith; which faith is never without, but of itself engendereth, charity.

Again, whereas they object that saying out of the gospel of St John, "Whosoever knoweth[5] my commandments and keepeth them, he it is that loveth me; and my Father will

John [xiv. 21, 23.]

[1 hasce relliquias, Lat.]
[2 qualitate sua, Lat.; its quality.]
[3 apprehenditur recipiturque, Lat.]
[4 et Paulus, Lat.; doth Paul also.]   [5 habet, Lat.]

love him, and we will come to him, and make our abiding in him ;" therefore for the observation of the commandments, that is, for our works' sake, God is joined to us : we again allege this saying of the same evangelist and apostle John : " By [1 John iv. this we know that we abide in him, and he in us, because he 13.] hath given us of his Spirit." But that Spirit of God is a free gift : therefore we are joined to God by mere and free grace.

It followeth in John : " And we have seen and do testify, that the Father hath sent the Son to be the Saviour of the world." Thou hearest, I hope, by what it is that the world is saved, and what Christ the Saviour of the world is [6]. Now who knoweth not that he was sent unto us of the Father by the mere and only grace of God? It followeth now, how that grace is received : " Whosoever confesseth that Jesus is the Son of God, God abideth in him, and he in God." But in the sixth of John, instead of ' confesseth,' is put ' be- John vi. lieveth :' and no marvel, since out of a true faith a true confession doth arise. By faith therefore are we saved [7], and by faith are we joined unto God. But letting pass these wranglers, who will never be without store of such sophistical shifts, we do again return to our purposed argument, to shew you how, and in what sense, life and justification are attributed to works.

They that are well exercised in the reading of the holy The places of faith and scriptures, that they may reconcile the places of scripture works, that seem at a that seem at a blush to be at discord, do teach that faith and blush to disagree, works in very deed are not separated one from another. For are here reconciled. the same Holy Spirit which giveth faith doth therewithal also regenerate the understanding and will, so that the faithful doth ardently desire, and do his endeavour in all things, to do service to God his maker. Therefore, for the unseparable knot betwixt faith and good works, which always keep company and attend upon [8] faith, we say, that justification is sometimes [9] somewhat unproperly attributed to works, which is somewhat more properly to be attributed to faith, but most properly of all to be ascribed to Christ apprehended by faith, who is in very deed the foundation and subject of our faith.

[6 rather, and who the Saviour of the world is, namely Christ.]
[7 recipimus salutem, Lat.]   [8 sequuntur, Lat.]
[9 rather, that there is attributed to works that which, &c. ; ' justification' is not in Lat.]

I will yet essay to make this more manifest.   In true faith there are two things to be considered, reconciliation and obedience : reconciliation, because by faith we understand and verily believe, that God is reconciled to us for Christ his sake, by whom we are adopted into the number of the sons of God; and obedience, because they that are reconciled do wholly yield themselves to him to whom they be reconciled, with earnest desire and zeal to do his will and pleasure.   So then we say that faith[1] is of two sorts, the justifying and the obeying faith[2].   Of the justifying faith[2] St Paul maketh mention, [Rom. v. 1, 2.] where he saith : "Being justified by faith, we have peace toward God through the Lord Jesus Christ, by whom we are reconciled."   Again he maketh mention of the obeying faith[2], [Rom. vi. 16.] where he saith : "Know ye not, that to whom ye give yourselves as servants to obey, his servants ye are to whom ye do obey ; whether it be of sin unto death, or of obedience unto righteousness?"—that is to say, which obedience maketh you to do the things that are righteous, and to be the servants of righteousness, which shall turn to you to eternal life ; and not the servants of sin, which turneth unto death.   Now therefore justification is properly attributed to the reconciling righteousness through Christ Jesus, and is improperly ascribed to the obeying righteousness, or righteousness of obedience. For the obeying righteousness is of the reconciling, and without the reconciling righteousness obedience should not be called righteousness.   To which this is also to be added, that they which are justified do not put any confidence in this obedience, as that which is always spotted in this world by reason of our flesh.

To this also agreeth this other explication which I will here annex.   The most proper work of faith is purification [Acts xv. 9.] and sanctification; for St Peter doth expressly say, that by faith our hearts are purified.   But in sanctification the holy scriptures do shew to be two especial things: first, that all the faithful are freely purified by the blood of Christ Jesus; [1 Pet. i. 18, 19.] for again the same St Peter saith : "Ye know that you are redeemed not with transitory things, as gold and silver; but with the precious blood of Christ, as of an unspotted Lamb." St Paul saith: "Ye are sanctified[3] by the will of God through

---

[1 justitiam, Lat. ; righteousness.]   [2 faith, not in Lat.]
[3 Heb. x. 10, 14, sanctificati sumus, Lat.]

the oblation of the body of Jesus Christ once made. For
with that one oblation he made them perfect for ever which
are sanctified." St John also saith : "The blood of Jesus [1 John i. 7.]
Christ the Son of God doth cleanse us from all sin." Therefore the most proper phrase of speech is to say, that we are
sanctified through faith by the blood of Christ, who said : "I [John xvii. 19.]
sanctify myself for them, that they also may be sanctified
through the truth." The latter is, that they which are sanctified by the blood of Christ through faith, do day by day
sanctify themselves, and give their minds to holiness ; to the
doing and study whereof the apostles do most earnestly exhort
the saints. For Peter saith: "As he which called you is holy,
so be ye also holy in your conversation⁴; because it is written,
Be ye holy, for I am holy." St Paul saith : "This is the will of
God, even your holiness," &c. 1 Thessal. iv.   St John saith:
"Now are we the sons of God; and yet it doth not appear [1 John iii. 2, 3.]
what we shall be : but we know that, when he shall appear,
we shall be like him ; for we shall see him as he is. And every
one that hath this hope in him purifieth himself, even as he
also is pure." Now this purging or purification, which is
made by our care and industry, is called by the name of
sanctification, not because it is made by us as of ourselves, but
because it is made of them that are sanctified by the blood of
Christ, in respect of Christ his blood⁵. For unless that sanctification, which is the very true and only sanctification in
deed, do go before, our sanctification (I mean, that which we
work) is none at all. But if that go before, then is this of
ours imputed for sanctification, although in the meanwhile the
spots of sin remaining in us do defile it, and that we do put
no confidence in it. Therefore, so often as thou shalt read in
the holy scriptures that righteousness is attributed to our good
works, thou shalt think straightways, that it is done for none
other causes than those which I have hitherto already declared unto thee. For the apostolical Spirit cannot be repugnant or contrary to itself.

This will yet be made a great deal more manifest, if we [The apostles against the righteousness of works.]
call to remembrance and do consider, that the apostles had to
deal with two kinds of men : the one sort whereof did affirm,

[⁴ 1 Pet. i. 15, 16, in omni conversatione, Lat.]
[⁵ in respect of Christ his blood, is an addition of the translator's.]

that they were sufficiently able of their own strength to satisfy or fulfil the law, and that they could by their deserts and good works merit eternal life; yea, they affirmed that the merit of Christ was not sufficient enough[1] to the getting of salvation, unless the righteousness of men were added thereunto. Against these Paul disputed very constantly and pithily in all his epistles; for they made Christ and the grace of God of none effect. The other sort of men were such as, abusing the doctrine of grace and faith, did wallow like swine in all filthy sins, because they thought that it was sufficient unto salvation if they did say that they believed; but they never declared their faith or belief by any good works, although occasion thereunto were given them. Against these did St Peter very well and wisely[2] dispute in the first chapter of his second epistle, and St James in the second chapter of his epistle. For he affirmeth, that Abraham was not justified by faith only, but by works: that is to say, that he was not justified by a vain opinion, but by faith which bare and was full of good works. For James doth use the names of faith and justification in one sense, and Paul in another. Paul putteth faith for an assured confidence in the merit of Christ; and he useth justification for absolution and remission of sins, for adoption into the number of the sons of God, and lastly[3] for the imputing of Christ his righteousness unto us. But in James faith doth signify a vain opinion: and justification doth import, not the imputing of righteousness, but the declaring of righteousness and adoption. For it is undoubtedly true, that the holy[4] apostles of Christ, St Peter and St James, would not by their writings make void the grace and merit of Christ, to advance the merits of mortal men; but rather to withstand the unpureness of them which put the faith of Christ in peril of disgracing[5], to the offence of all good men, living in the mean while most wickedly in detestable sins without repentance. Therefore the apostles of Christ, requiring good works at the hands of the faithful, do first of

The apostles against the abusers of grace and faith.

[1 per se, Lat. omitted; of itself.]
[2 constanter et acriter, Lat.]
[3 adeoque et, Lat.; and thus also.]
[4 fidelissimos, Lat.; the most faithful.]
[5 rather, which made a boast of faith in Christ to the offence, &c.]

all require a true and lively faith, and do refer them both[6] unto the grace of God.

Let us therefore most firmly hold, that the apostles do attribute justification, life, and salvation, to good works improperly; to true faith properly; but most properly to Christ, who is the subject and foundation of true faith. For although true faith[7] is not without good works, yet doth it justify without good works, by itself alone. For it is most certain, that life and salvation are bestowed on us after the same manner that health and life was given to the children of Israel, which in the wilderness were poisoned of the serpents. They had their health restored them not by any works, but by the only beholding and looking upon the brasen serpent: therefore we also are made partakers of eternal life by faith alone, which is the true beholding and looking up to Christ. "As Moses," saith our Saviour, "did lift up the serpent in the wilderness, so must the Son of man be lifted up; that every one which believeth in him should not perish, but have eternal life." And the apostle Paul saith: "Ye are saved by grace through faith; not of yourselves; it is the gift of God: not of works, lest any man should boast," &c. [John iii. 14, 15.] [Eph. ii. 8, 9.]

Faith justifieth without works.

With this doctrine of the evangelists and apostles do the testimonies of certain doctors of the church agree: some of which I will recite unto you, dearly beloved, not because these testimonies of the scripture are not sufficient, but because we will not seem to be the beginners and bringers in of new doctrines: although in very deed that can not be new, which is derived out of the evangelical and apostolic doctrine, albeit that all the doctors of the church should gainsay or deny it. Now therefore give ear how some, even of the best of them, do not in words only say and write, but also by proofs shew, that faith alone doth justify.

Origen, a very ancient writer, upon the third chapter of the epistle of St Paul to the Romans, doth say: "Paul saith that the justification of faith alone is sufficient for a man; so that every one that doth believe only is justified, although no works are once wrought by him. Now if we require an example, where any was ever justified by faith alone without good works; that thief, I suppose, is example good enough, *Origen in iii. ca. ad Roma.*

[6 omnia, Lat.; all.]
[7 communi lege, Lat. omitted; by a general law.]

who, being crucified with Christ, did cry from the cross, 'Lord Jesu, remember me when thou comest into thy kingdom.' In the writings of the evangelists there is mention made of no good work which he in his life time did; and yet, [Luke xxiii. 42, 43.] because of this his faith only, Jesus said unto him: 'Verily I say unto thee, this day thou shalt be with me in paradise.' Therefore this thief was through faith justified without the works of the law. For after this request and prayer of his the Lord made no inquisition what his works were all his life long; neither did he look what works he would do after this faith and believing; but did immediately, upon his confession, both justify, and take him as a companion to go with him to paradise. Moreover to the woman, of whom mention is made in the gospel after St Luke, not for any work of the law, but for [Luke vii. 48, 50.] faith only he said, 'Thy sins are forgiven thee.' And again, 'Go in peace, thy faith hath made thee safe.' Furthermore, in many places of the gospel we find that our Saviour used the like kind of speech, making faith always to be the cause of men's salvation. And a little while after the same [Gal. vi. 14.] apostle saith: 'God forbid that I should glory in any thing but in the cross of our Lord Jesus Christ, by whom the world is crucified to me, and I to the world.' Thou seest here that the apostle glorieth not of his own righteousness, or chastity, or wisdom, or other works or virtues of his own, but doth most plainly pronounce and say: 'Let him that glorieth glory in the Lord;' and so by that means all boasting is excluded[1]." And so forth, with many other sayings tending to this purpose.

[1] Dicit (Paulus) sufficere solius fidei justificationem, ita ut credens quis tantummodo justificetur, etiamsi nihil ab eo operis fuerit expletum. Imminet igitur nobis, qui integram esse scripturam apostoli conamur asserere, et ordine suo cuncta constare, ut requiramus, quis sine operibus sola fide justificatus sit. Quantum igitur ad exemplum pertinet, sufficere arbitror illum latronem, qui, cum Christo crucifixus, clamavit ei de cruce, Domine Jesu, memento mei cum veneris in regnum tuum. Nec aliud quicquam describitur boni operis ejus in evangeliis, sed pro hac sola fide ait ei Jesus, Amen dico tibi, hodie mecum eris in paradiso...Per fidem enim justificatus est hic latro, sine operibus legis. Quia super hoc Dominus non requisivit quid prius operatus esset, nec exspectavit quid operis cum credidisset expleret, sed sola confessione justificatum comitem sibi eum paradisum ingressurus assumpsit. Sed et mulier illa, de qua in evangelio secundum Lucam refertur...ex

St Ambrose in his exposition of Paul his epistle unto the Ambrose.
Romans, upon the third and fourth chapters, doth say : "They
are freely justified, saith St Paul, because, when they work
nothing, nor do any thing for God again, they are yet through
faith only justified by the gift of God[2].

"'According to the purpose of God's grace,' saith Paul :
it. was so ordained of God, that, laying the law aside, the
grace of God should require faith only unto salvation[3]."

" This doth by the example of the prophet confirm the
blessedness of the man to whom the Lord imputeth righteousness without works : he calleth them blessed, with whom
the Lord hath covenanted, that without labour and keeping
of the law they should be justified before their Maker[4]."

St John Chrysostom, treating of faith, of the law of Chrysost.
nature, and of the Holy Ghost, doth expressly say : " I cannot
prove that he which worketh the works of righteousness
without faith doth enjoy eternal life : but I can by good
proof shew that he which believed, without works, did both
live and obtain the kingdom of heaven.   No man without
faith hath obtained life ; but the thief believed only, and for
his faith was justified by the most merciful God.   And whereas

nullo legis opere, sed pro sola fide, ad eam (ait), Remittuntur tibi
peccata tua: et iterum, Fides tua te salvam fecit, vade in pace.   Sed
et in multis evangelii locis hoc sermone usum legimus Salvatorem, ut
credentis fidem causam dicat esse salutis ejus... Audi quid dicit (apostolus): Mihi autem absit gloriari, nisi in cruce Domini mei Jesu Christi,
per quem mihi mundus crucifixus est, et ego mundo.   Vides apostolum
non gloriantem super justitia sua, neque super castitate, neque super
sapientia, neque super ceteris virtutibus vel actibus suis, sed apertissime
pronunciantem et dicentem, Qui gloriatur, in Domino glorietur; et
sic exclusa est Judaica gloriatio, &c.—Orig. Comment. in ep. ad
Roman. Lib. III. Tom. IV. Par. 1733—59, pp. 516, 17.]

[2 Justificati sunt gratis, quia nihil operantes, neque vicem red-
dentes, sola fide justificati sunt dono Dei.—Ambros. Comment. in ep.
ad Rom. cap. III. v. 24, Tom. II. Append. Par. 1690, col. 46.   But see
above, page 336, note 3.]

[3 Secundum propositum gratiæ Dei] Sic decretum dicit Paulus a
Deo, ut cessante lege solam fidem gratia Dei posceret ad salutem.—Ib.
cap. iv. v. 5, col. 48.]

[4 Sicut et David dicit.]   Hoc ipsum munit exemplo prophetæ
beatitudinem hominis cui Deus accepto fert justitiam sine operibus.
Beatos dicit, de quibus hoc sanxit Deus, ut sine labore et aliqua observatione sola fide justificentur apud Deum.—Ib. cap. IV. v. 6, col. 48.]

here, peradventure, thou wilt object, that he wanted time to
live justly, and to do good works: I answer, that I do not
greatly strive about that; but this only I stick to, that faith
alone did justify and save him. For if he had lived any
longer, and had neglected faith and works, he had undoubtedly
fallen from salvation. But the only end and argument
whereat I now shoot is, that faith of itself doth bring salvation, and that works of themselves did never save any
workers that wrought them:" as Chrysostom doth at large
declare by the example of the captain[1] Cornelius[2].

These testimonies, I suppose, are sufficient to wits that
will be answered and do not stand obstinately in quarrellings
and janglings; otherwise I could allege a great number
more. But I will not be over-tedious unto you, dearly beloved, nor seem to be endless[3] in an evident matter.

Of merits or
of the reward
of good
works.

But now because to this treatise of the righteousness of
works there is a question annexed touching the merits of
good works; I will therefore summarily say somewhat of
merits, or rather, of the hire and reward of good works: to
this end specially, lest any man, thinking irreligiously of the
merits of good works, do thereby win to himself not good
but evil works.

No good
merits in
man.

The name of merits is an unacquainted term, not used in
the scriptures. For in that signification wherein our merit-
workers use it, to wit, for meritorious works; for that, I
mean, whereunto both life and the grace of God is of duty
given as debt that is due; in that signification, I say, it doth
obscure the grace of God, and maketh man too proud and
arrogant. What, I pray you, can our works deserve, since

[1 centurionis, Lat.]

[2 Ἄνευ πίστεως τὸν ἐργαζόμενον ἔργα δικαιοσύνης οὐ δύνῃ παραστῆσαι
ζήσαντα, ἄνευ δὲ ἔργων τὸν πιστὸν δύναμαι δεῖξαι καὶ ζήσαντα καὶ βασιλείας
ἀξιωθέντα. Οὐδεὶς ἄνευ πίστεως ἔζησεν· ὁ δὲ λῃστὴς πιστεύσας μόνον
ἐδικαιώθη. Καὶ μή μοι λέγε, οὐκ ἔσχε καιρὸν πολιτεύεσθαι· οὐδὲ γὰρ ἐγὼ
τοῦτο φιλονεικῶ, ἀλλ' ἐκεῖνο παρέστησα, ὅτι ἡ πίστις καθ' ἑαυτὴν ἔσωσεν.
Εἰ γὰρ ἐπέζησε τῇ πίστει, καὶ ἔργων ἠμέλησεν, ἐξέπιπτε τῆς σωτηρίας. Τὸ
δὲ σκοπούμενον νῦν καὶ ζητούμενον, ὅτι καὶ ἡ πίστις καθ' ἑαυτὴν ἔσωσεν, ἔργα
δὲ καθ' ἑαυτὰ οὐδαμοῦ τοὺς ἐργάτας ἐδικαίωσε. Καὶ θέλεις ἰδεῖν ἀκριβῶς,
ὅτι ἔργα ἄνευ πίστεως οὐ ζωοποιεῖ; Μεμαρτύρητο Κορνήλιος, &c.—Chrysost.
Serm. de Fide et Lege Naturæ et Sancto Spir.   Opp. Tom. I. Par.
1718, p. 826. But this treatise is not Chrysostom's.]

[3 spinosus, Lat.]

none of the saints durst be so bold as to plead their merits before the Lord? Job crieth: "If I will justify myself, [Job ix. 20, 30.] mine own mouth shall condemn me. If I will go about to shew myself to be an innocent, he[4] shall prove me a wicked doer. If I wash myself with snow-water[5], and make my hands never so clean at the well[6], yet shalt thou dip me in the mire, and mine own garments shall defile[7] me." David crieth: "Enter not into judgment with thy servant; for in [Psal. cxliii. 2.] thy sight shall no man living be justified." Christ our Lord in the gospel saith: "When ye have done all things that are commanded you, then say, We are unprofitable servants; we have done that we ought to do." But a little before our Lord said: "Doth the master thank the servant which doth [Luke xvii. 9, 10.] the things that are commanded him to do?" The holy apostle St Paul also crieth: "I do not despise the grace of [Gal. ii. 21.] God: for if righteousness be of the law, then did Christ die in vain." Again, in the gospel after St Luke, the Pharisee [Luke xviii. 9—14.] is greatly blamed, which could not be content to put confidence in his own righteousness, but would needs boast of his merits also. And Nabuchodonosor felt no little plague for saying [Dan. iv. 28—33.] that the kingdom of Babylon did come unto him by his own art, industry, power, and virtue. By how much a greater punishment, therefore, shall we think them to be worthy of which are persuaded, and make their brags, that they by their merits have deserved or earned the kingdom of heaven?

And yet all this doth not tend to the making void of [A reward is given to good works.] the stipend of good works, or to the denying of the reward that is prepared for virtues: for he is true which promised, and what he promised he will perform. Now he promised rewards to them that work righteousness: even as also according to his justice and truth he hath threatened terrible punishments to wicked and impenitent sinners. But the promises of God are of two sorts; to wit, they lay before our eyes the gifts and rewards of this present life, and of the life to come. For the Lord in the gospel after St Mark doth say: "Verily I say unto you, there is no man that [Mark x. 29, 30.] hath forsaken house, or brethren, or lands, for my sake

[4 So Coverdale, 1535.]
[5 quasi aquis nivis, Lat.; as it were with.]
[6 at the well, not in Lat.]
[7 abominabuntur me, Lat.]

and the gospel's, but he shall receive an hundreth-fold now at this present with persecutions; and in the world to come life everlasting." And Paul saith: "Godliness is profitable to all things, having promise of the life that is now, and of that which is to come. This is a sure saying, and by all means worthy to be received. For therefore we both labour and suffer rebuke, because we have our hope settled in the living God, &c." And here it will do well to reckon up and cite the testimonies of scripture, which do concern the reward of good works. I will therefore recite a few, but such as shall be evident and pertaining to the matter. The Lord in Esay crieth: "Say to the just, that it shall go well with him; for he shall eat the fruit of his study, or travail. And woe to the wicked sinner; for he shall be rewarded according to the works of his hands." In Jeremy we read: "Leave off from weeping; for thy labour shall be rewarded thee." And in the gospel the Lord saith: "Blessed are ye, when men speak all evil sayings against you, lying, for my sake. Rejoice ye, and be glad; for great is your reward in heaven." The apostle Paul also saith: "Glory, honour, and peace, to every one that worketh good, to the Jew first, and also to the Gentile." Again: "We must all appear before the judgment-seat of Christ, that every one may bear the deeds of his body, according to that which he hath done, whether it be good or bad." And again: "Every one shall receive a reward according to his labour[1]."

Now let us remember, that the reward is promised and great gifts are prepared for them that labour manfully. To sluggards and slow-backs are imminent the evils of this present life, and also of the life to come. To them that strive lawfully the garland is due. But if it happen that the reward be deferred, and that they which strive receive not the promises by and by out of hand; yet let the afflicted think that their afflictions tend to their commodity, and that they are laid upon them by their heavenly Father. Let not their courage therefore fail them, but let them shew themselves men in the fight, and call to God for aid; for "whosoever persevereth unto the end, he shall be saved." Let every one call to his remembrance the old examples of the holy fathers, to whom many promises were made, the

Marginal notes:
[2 Tim. iv. 8—10.]
[Isai. iii. 10, 11.]
[Jer. xxxi. 16.]
[Matt. v. 11.]
[Rom. ii. 10.]
[2 Cor. v. 10.]
To whom the rewards are promised.
[Matt. xxiv. 13.]

[1 1 Cor. iii. 8; suam mercedem, Lat.]

fruit whereof they did not reap till many a day were come and gone, wherein they strove against and did overcome full many a sharp temptation. The apostle Paul crieth : " I [2 Tim. iv. 7, 8.] have fought a good fight, I have fulfilled my course, I have kept the faith. Henceforth there is laid up for me a crown of righteousness, which the Lord, the righteous judge, shall give me in that day : not to me only, but to them also that have loved his appearing." They must lay before their eyes the truth of God, who saith : " Heaven and earth shall [Matt. xxiv. 35.] pass, but my word shall not pass." The Israelites, verily, were a long time holden captive in Egypt : but the Lord did not forget his promise ; for in a fit and convenient time he set them out at liberty with abundant joy and glory for the triumph gotten over their oppressors. The Amalechites and Chanaanites did a great while, I confess, exalt themselves in sin and wickedness ; but when the measure of their iniquity was fully filled, then were they throughly recompensed for their pains by him that is the severe revenger of unrepented wickedness. The scripture therefore exhorteth all men to have sure hope, persevering patience, and constancy invincible : of which I spake in the third sermon of this third Decade. To this place do belong, as I suppose, those excellent words of St Paul, where he saith : " It is a faithful saying : for if we be dead with him, we [2 Tim. ii. 11—13.] shall also live with him : if we be patient, we shall also reign with him : if we deny him, he also shall deny us : if we be unfaithful, he abideth faithful ; he cannot deny himself." And again : " Cast not away your confidence, which hath great recompence of reward. For ye have need of patience, that, after ye have done the will of God, ye may receive the promise. For yet a very little while, and he that shall come will come, and will not tarry. And the just shall live by faith : and if he withdraw himself, my soul shall have no pleasure in him. But we are not of them that withdraw ourselves unto perdition ; but we pertain to faith, to the winning of the soul[2]."

Yet for all this we must not abuse these and such like testimonies touching the reward of works, nor the very name of merits, where it is found to be used of the fathers ; neither must we wrest it against the doctrine of mere grace and *We must not abuse these places, which confirm the reward of good works.*

[2 Heb. x. 35—39. So Cranmer, 1539.]

Hire is due, but heritage proceedeth of the parents' good-will.

the merits of Christ our Saviour. We must think that the kingdom of heaven and the other special gifts of God are not as the hire that is due to servants, but as the inheritance of the sons of God. For although in the last day of judgment the judge shall reckon up many works, for which he shall seem as it were to recompense the elect with eternal life; yet, before that recital of good works, he shall say:

[Matt. xxv. 34.]

" Come, ye blessed of my Father, possess the kingdom prepared for you since the beginning of the world." Now if thou demandest, why he shall in the day of judgment make mention rather of works than of faith; mine answer is, that it is a point or usual custom in the law for judgment not only to be just, but also by the judge's pronunciation to have the cause made manifest to all men wherefore it is just. And God doth deal with us after the order of men: wherefore he doth not only give just judgment, but will also be known of all men to be a just and upright judge. But we are not able to look into the faith of other men, which doth consist in the mind; and therefore we judge by their words and deeds. Honest words and works bear witness of a faithful heart; whereas unhonest pranks and speeches do bewray a kind of unbelief. The works of charity and humanity do declare that we have faith in deed: whereas the lack of them do argue the contrary. And therefore the scripture admonisheth us, that the judgment shall be according to our works. To this sense agreeth that in the twelfth of Matthew, where it is said, " By thy deeds[1] thou shalt be justified, and by the same thou shalt be condemned." To Abraham, after

[Gen. xxii. 16, 17.]

he had determined to offer his son Isaac, it was said: "Because thou hast done this thing, and hast not spared thine only-begotten son, I will bless thee, and multiply thee exceedingly, &c." But it is manifest that God made that promise to Abraham before Isaac was born; yea, he made it as soon as Abraham was brought out of his country: therefore the promise was not now first of all annexed as a reward unto the works of Abraham, &c.

How or in what sense God is said to give a reward unto our good works.

Therefore God examineth our works according to his own favourable mercy, and not with the extremity and rigour of law; and doth reward them with infinite benefits, because they proceed from faith in Christ, albeit that, for the sin

[1 verse 37; but Bullinger's Latin is ex dictis tuis, by thy words.]

which abideth in us, they be unpure and nothing meritorious. Now he doth hereby give us a proof that he hath a regard of us and our works; because, in testifying the greatness of his love toward us, he doth vouchsafe so to honour not only us, but also his own gifts in us, which he of his great goodness hath graciously bestowed upon us. Our bountiful God doth herein imitate the manner of dealing which fleshly fathers use in this world toward their children: for they bestow gifts upon their children as rewards of their well-doing, thereby provoking them to greater virtues, when as in very deed all things belong to the children by right of inheritance; and the true and proper cause of this reward, which the father giveth to the child, is not the obedience of the son, but the mere good-will and favour of the father. Moreover herein are two things to be observed. First, although God doth after the manner of men allure us with rewards, draw us on with gifts, and keep us in good works with manifold recompences; yet must not the reward or recompence be the mark whereat the worker ought to look, respecting rather his own glory and commodity than the love and honour that he oweth to God.   God will be worshipped for love's sake only; and he will be loved of mere good-will, and not for the hope of any reward.   For as he requireth a cheerful giver, so doth he look for such an uncoacted[2] affection, voluntary love, and free good-will, as children do naturally bear to their parents.   The last is, that our works, which some call merits, are nothing else but the mere gifts of God.   Now he were a very unthankful person, which, when of another man's liberality he hath licence given to occupy his land to his best commodity, will at length go about to translate the right thereof from the true owner, which lent it him, unto himself.   But because I would be loath, by drawing out this treatise too far, to detain you longer than reason would, I will recite unto you, dearly beloved, a notable conference of places in the scripture made by St Augustine, whereby ye may evidently understand and infer a conclusion, that the rewards of good works, or merits of the saints, are the very free and mere grace of God.

Therefore in the seventh chapter of his book, *De Gratia* et *Libero Arbitrio*, thus he saith: "John the forerunner of

St Augustine
his sentence
touching the

[2 uncoacted: uncompelled.]

merits of the our Lord doth say, 'A man can receive nothing, unless it
saints.
[John iii. 27.] be given him from heaven.' If therefore thy good works be
the gifts of God, then God crowneth thy merits, not as thy
merits, but as his own gifts. Let us therefore consider the
merits of the apostle Paul, (that is to say, the merits which
he saith are in himself,) whether they be the gifts of God or
[2 Tim. iv. no. 'I have,' saith he, 'fought a good fight, I have ful-
7.] filled my course, I have kept the faith.' First of all, these
good works had been no good works, unless good thoughts
had gone before them. Give ear, therefore, what he sayeth
[2 Cor. iii. 5.] of those good thoughts: 'not because we can think anything
of ourselves, as of ourselves, but our ability is of God.'
Then also let us consider every several particularity. 'I have
fought,' saith he, 'a good fight.' I demand, by what power
he fought? whether by that which he had of himself, or
by that which was given him from above? It is unlikely
that so great a teacher of the Gentiles as the holy apostle
St Paul was should be ignorant of the law, which in Deu-
[Deut viii. teronomy is heard to say: 'Say not thou in thy heart,
17, 18.] Mine own strength and the power of mine own hand hath
done this wonderful thing: but thou shalt remember the Lord
thy God, because he giveth thee strength and power to do
it.' But what doth it avail to fight well, unless the victory
do ensue? And who, I pray you, giveth the victory, but
[1 Cor. xv. he of whom St Paul himself doth say, 'Thanks be to God,
57.] which giveth us the victory through our Lord Jesus Christ?'
And in another place, when he had cited the place out of
the Psalms, where it is said, 'Because for thy sake we are
killed all day, and are counted as sheep appointed to the
[Rom viii. slaughter,' he did immediately add, and say: 'But in all
36, 37.] these things we overcome, or have the victory, through him
which loved us.' We have the victory, therefore, not
through ourselves, but through him that loved us. After
that again he said: 'I have fulfilled my course.' But as
[Rom. ix. he said this, so in another place also he saith: 'It is not
16.] of the willer, nor of the runner, but of God which taketh
mercy.' Which sentence cannot be by any means so
inverted, that we may say, It is not of God which taketh
mercy, but of the willer, and of the runner. For whosoever
dare take upon him so to invert that sentence of the holy
apostle, he doth openly shew that he flatly gainsayeth the

words of St Paul.   Last of all he said ; ' I have kept the
faith :' but in another place again he confesseth, saying,
' I have obtained mercy that I might be faithful.'   He said [1 Cor. vii.
not, I have obtained mercy because I am faithful; but, 'that
I might be faithful :' declaring thereby that faith itself cannot be obtained without the mercy of God; and that faith is
the gift of God, as he doth most evidently teach where he
saith, ' Ye are saved by grace through faith; and that not of [Eph. ii. 8.]
yourselves, it is the gift of God.'   For they might say, We
have therefore received grace, because we have believed;
by that means attributing, as it were, faith to themselves,
and grace to God : but, to prevent that insinuation, the holy
apostle St Paul, when he had said, ' By faith,' doth straightways add, 'And that not of yourselves, it is the gift of God.'
Again, lest they should say that they by their works did
meritoriously deserve such a gift, he doth presently annex,
' Not of works, lest any man should boast.'   Not because
he did deny or make void good works, considering that he
saith, that God doth reward every man according to his
works; but for because works are of faith, and not faith of
works.   And so by this means our works of righteousness
proceed from him, from whom that faith doth also come,
touching which it is said, ' The just doth live by faith[1].' ''

[1 Dicit et Joannes, præcursor Domini nostri, Non potest homo
accipere quicquam, nisi fuerit ei datum de cœlo . . . Si ergo Dei dona sunt
bona merita tua, non Deus coronat merita tua tanquam merita tua, sed
tanquam dona sua.   Proinde consideremus ipsa merita apostoli Pauli,
—et videamus, utrum merita ipsius, tanquam ipsius, id est, ex ipso ei
comparata, an dona sint Dei.   Bonum, inquit, certamen certavi, cursum
consummavi, fidem servavi.   Primo, ista bona opera, si non ea præ-
cessissent cogitationes bonæ, nulla essent.   Attendite itaque quid de
ipsis cogitationibus dicat; ait enim scribens ad Corinthios, Non quia
idonei sumus cogitare aliquid a nobis, tanquam a nobismetipsis, sed
sufficientia nostra ex Deo est.   Deinde singula inspiciamus: Bonum,
inquit, certamen certavi.   Quæro qua virtute certaverit, utrum quæ illi
ex semetipso fuerit, an quæ desuper data sit ?   Sed absit ut tantus
doctor gentium ignoraverit legem Dei, cujus vox est in Deuteronomio:
Ne dicas in corde tuo, Fortitudo mea et potentia manus meæ fecit
mihi virtutem magnam hanc; sed memoraberis Domini Dei tui : quia
ipse tibi dat fortitudinem facere virtutem.   Quid autem prodest bonum
certamen, nisi sequatur victoria ?   Et quis dat victoriam, nisi ille de
quo dicit ipse, Gratias Deo qui dat nobis victoriam per Dominum
nostrum Jesum Christum ?   Et alio loco, cum commemorasset testi-

All this have I hitherto word for word recited out of St Augustine: wherein all that may be said concerning the merits of good works are sufficiently well contained, and so soundly confirmed by proofs of scripture, that I mean not to add any thing unto them: for I see it sufficiently manifest for all to understand what and how the ancient fathers thought and taught of the merits of sinful men. For what can be said more briefly, sincerely, and fully, than that a reward is prepared for the good works of men? but yet that that reward is nothing else but the grace, and that the merits or good works of the saints are the gift[1], of God; which merits while he crowneth, he crowneth his own gifts. In all this therefore the ecclesiastical and apostolic doctrine remaineth still immutable and unreprovable; that we are justified and saved by the grace of God[2] through faith, and not through our own good works or merits.

Good works must be done according to the rule of the word of God.

We do now again return to good works, and are come to expound the description or definition of good works which we did set down in the beginning of this treatise. Now therefore,

monium de psalmo, Quoniam propter te mortificamur tota die, deputati sumus ut oves occisionis; subjecit atque ait, Sed in his omnibus supervincimus per eum qui dilexit nos. Non ergo per nos, sed per eum qui dilexit nos. Deinde dixit, Cursum consummavi. Sed ille hoc dixit, qui alio loco dicit, Non volentis, neque currentis, sed miserentis est Dei. Quæ sententia nullo modo potest etiam sic converti ut dicatur, Non miserentis Dei, sed volentis atque currentis est hominis. Quisquis enim hoc ausus fuerit dicere, aperte se ostendit Apostolo contradicere. Postremo dixit, Fidem servavi. Sed ille hoc dixit qui alibi ait, Misericordiam consecutus sum ut fidelis essem. Non enim dixit, Misericordiam consecutus sum, quia fidelis eram; sed, ut fidelis essem: hinc ostendens etiam ipsam fidem haberi nisi Deo miserante non posse, et esse donum Dei: quod apertissime docet dicens, Gratia salvi facti estis per fidem; et hoc non ex vobis, sed Dei donum est. Possent enim dicere, Ideo accepimus gratiam quia credidimus, tanquam sibi fidem tribuentes, gratiam Deo: propter hoc Apostolus cum dixisset, per fidem, et hoc, inquit, non ex vobis, sed Dei donum est. Rursus, ne dicerent se suis operibus donum tale meruisse, continuo subjecit, Non ex operibus, ne forte quis extollatur: non quia negavit aut evacuavit opera bona, cum dicat Deum unicuique reddere secundum opera ejus; sed quia opera sunt ex fide, non ex operibus fides; ac per hoc ab illo sunt nobis opera justitiæ, a quo est ipsa fides de qua dictum est, Justus ex fide vivit.—Augustin. de Grat. et Lib. Arb. ad Valentin. Opp. Par. 1531, Tom. VII. p. 268, coll. 2, 3, capp. 6, 7.]

[1 gratiam, Lat.]　　　　　　[2 sola gratia Dei, Lat.]

unless our works do spring in us from God through faith, they cannot have the name of good works: but contrarily, if they do proceed from God through faith, then are they also framed according to the rule of the word of God. And for that cause did I in the definition of good works significantly say, that they are done of them which are regenerate by the good Spirit of God, through faith, according to the word of God. For God is not pleased with the works which we of ourselves do of our own brains and authority[3], without warrantise of his word, imagine and devise. For the thing that he doth most of all like and look for in us is faith and obedience, which is most evident to be seen in the very example of our grandfather Adam; and contrarily, he doth mislike and utterly reject the works of our own choice and our good intents, which spring in and rise upon our own minds and judgments; as I will by these testimonies of scripture declare unto you.

In the twelfth of Deuteronomy we read: " Every man Deut. xii. shall not do that which is righteous in his own eyes. Whatsoever I command you, that shall ye observe to do it: neither shalt thou add anything to it, nor take anything from it." Moreover in the history of Samuel there is a notable example of this matter to be seen. For Saul, the king of Israel, received a commandment to kill all the Amalekites, with all their beasts and cattle: but he, contrary to the precept, through a good intent (as he thought) of his own, and for a religious zeal's sake of his own choosing, reserved the fattest oxen for to be sacrificed: and for that cause the prophet came and said unto him, " Is a sacrifice so pleasant and acceptable to the [1 Sam. xv. Lord as obedience is? Behold, to obey is better than sacrifice; 22, 23.] and to hearken is better than the fat of rams. For rebellion[4] is as the sin of witchcraft, and stubbornness[5] is as the vanity of idolatry." Lo, here in these few words thou hast the goodly praise and commendation of the religion of our own inventing, and of our own good works which do arise of our own good intents and purposes. They which do neglect the precepts of the Lord to follow their own good intents and forecasts are flatly called[6] witches, apostates, and wicked idolaters. They

[3 et intentione bona, Lat. omitted; and good intention.]
[4 apostasia sive rebellio, Lat.]
[5 vel nolle obsequi, Lat. omitted; or unwillingness to be obedient.]
[6 a veritate divina, Lat. omitted; by the truth of God.]

seem in their own eyes verily to be jolly fellows, and true worshippers of God, and zealous followers of the traditions of the holy fathers, bishops, kings, and princes : but God, which cannot lie, doth flatly pronounce that their works do differ nothing from witchcraft, apostasy, and blasphemous idolatry, than which there can be nothing more heinous by any means devised. Therefore the Lord in the gospel, citing that place out of Esay's prophecy, doth plainly condemn, reject, and tread under foot all those works which we choose to ourselves, having their beginning of our own good intents and purposes, where he saith : "In vain do they worship me, teaching doctrines the precepts of men. Every planting, which my Father hath not planted, shall be plucked up by the roots. Let them alone; they be blind leaders of the blind." And thereupon it is that St Paul did so boldly affirm, that the precepts of men are contrary to the truth, and are mere lies. The same Paul in one place saith, "Whatsoever is not of faith is sin :" and in another place, "Faith cometh by hearing, and hearing by the word of God."

[Matt. xv. 9, 13, 14.]

[Tit. i. 14.]

[Rom. xiv. 23; x. 17.]

Whereupon we may gather, that the works which are not framed by the express word of God, or by a sure consequence derived from it, are so far from being good works, that they are plainly called sins. Enforce thou, I pray thee, never so great a good turn upon a man against his will, and see what favour thou shalt win at his hand, and how thou shalt please him with that enforced benefit. Therefore good works do first of all require the precise and express observing of God's will, to which alone they ought to tend[1]. In his epistle to the Colossians the same apostle doth openly condemn the Greek ἐθελοθρησκείαν, that is, the voluntary religion which they of their own choice and mind brought in to be observed. And what need have we, I pray you, to invent to ourselves other new kinds of good works, considering that we have not yet done those works which God himself[2] prescribeth, and doth in express words require at our hands? By this now our adversaries may perceive, that we do not altogether simply condemn good works, but those alone which we, by rejecting the word of God, do first set abroad by our own imaginations and fantastical inventions: of which sort are many

[1 to which—tend, not in Lat.]
[2 jure, Lat. omitted; of good right.]

upstart works of our holy monks and sacrificing shavelings[3]. But to conclude: the works that are repugnant to the word of God are by no means worthy of any place or honour.

And that we may more rightly perceive the sense or meaning of good works, we must in mine opinion diligently observe these words of the apostle: "We are created in Christ Jesus unto good works, which God hath before ordained that we should walk in them." He maketh here two notes concerning those that are good works indeed. The first is, "We are," saith he, "created in Christ Jesus unto good works." It doth therefore necessarily follow, that good works are wrought of him which is by true faith graffed in Christ Jesu: for unless the branch abide in the vine, it cannot bring forth fruit. All the works therefore of the unfaithful, howsoever they shine with the title of righteousness, are notwithstanding not good works in very deed. The latter is, "Which God hath before ordained, that we should walk in them." We must not therefore make account, that all the works which men may do are to be counted good works indeed; but those only which God hath ordained of old that we should walk in them. Now what works those be, the Lord in his law (which is the eternal will of God) hath very plainly expressed. And thereupon it is that the Lord in the gospel, being demanded questions concerning eternal life and the very true virtues, sendeth the demander unto the law, and saith: "What is written in the law?" And again; "If thou wilt enter into life, keep the commandments." Therefore the ten commandments are a most sure and absolute platform of good works: which that ye may the better understand, I will briefly recapitulate, and as it were in a picture lay it before your eyes.

Good works indeed.

[Eph. ii. 10.]

[Luke x. 26.]

[Matt. xix. 17.]

The ten commandments are a platform of good works.

To the first precept thou shalt refer the fear, the faith, and love of God, with assured hope, persevering patience, and constancy invincible in trouble and afflictions. To the second belongeth the true and sincere worship wherewith God is pleased, with the utter refusal of all superstition and perverse religion. Upon the third doth depend the reverence of God's majesty, the free confession of his might, the holy[4] invocation of his name, and the sanctification of the same. In the fourth

[3 monachorum et sacrificorum, Lat.]
[4 et perseverantem, Lat. omitted; and enduring.]

is comprehended the moderate conservation of the ecclesiastical ceremonies, the preaching of God's word, public prayers, and whatsoever else doth belong to the outward service or external worship due to God. To the fifth thou mayest annex the natural love of children toward their parents, of men toward their country and kinsfolks, the due obedience that we owe to the magistrates and all in authority, and lastly, the offices of civil humanity. To the sixth thou shalt join justice and judgment, the protection of widows and orphans, the delivering of the oppressed and afflicted, well-doing to all men, and doing hurt to no man. To the seventh thou shalt add the faith of wedded couples, the offices of marriage, the honest and godly bringing up of children, with the study of chastity, temperance, and sobriety. To the eighth is to be reckoned upright dealing in contracts, liberality, bountifulness, and hospitality. Under the ninth is couched the study of truth through all our life-time, faith in words and deeds, with decent, honest, and profitable speech. In the tenth and last thou mayest remember good affections, holy wishes, with all holy and honest thoughts. And so this is the compendious platform of good works. Now if thou desire to have it more briefly expressed than this that thou seest, then turn thyself, and hearken to the words of Christ our Lord, who gathereth these ten into two [Matt. xxii. 37, 39; and vii. 12.] principal points, and saith: "Thou shalt love the Lord thy God with all thy heart, with all thy soul, and with all thy mind; and thy neighbour as thyself. Whatsoever therefore ye would that men should do to you, even so do ye to them."

What be good works in very deed, according to the testimonies of the ancient prophets. Upon these precepts of the Lord all the faithful, which desire to do good works, must surely fix their eyes and minds, and that too so much the more diligently and constantly as they do more surely and evidently perceive and see, that God in the law and the prophets doth require nothing else nor any other works at the hand of his elect and chosen servants. Go to now therefore, let us hear out of the holy prophets some such evident testimonies touching good works as do consent and wholly agree with the law of the Lord. [Deut. x. 12, 13.] Moses in Deuteronomy crieth: "And now, Israel, what doth the Lord thy God require of thee, but to fear the Lord thy God, and to walk in all his ways, to love him, and to serve the Lord thy God with all thy heart and with all thy soul; that thou keep the commandments of the Lord, and his ordi-

nances, which I command thee this day?" And the kingly
prophet David in the fifteenth Psalm asketh this question:
"Lord, who shall dwell in thy tabernacle?" and presently
answereth it himself, saying: "Even he that walketh uprightly, and doth the thing that is just and right;" and so
forth, as it is contained in the ten commandments. Esay
also, in his thirty-third chapter, moveth the same question,
and answereth it even so as David had done before him.
Jeremy, in the twenty-second chapter, doth urge and reiterate
these words to the Jews: "Thus the Lord commandeth:
keep equity and righteousness, deliver the oppressed from the
power of the violent, do not grieve nor oppress the stranger,
the fatherless, nor the widow, and shed no innocent blood in
this place." And Ezechiel, in his eighteenth chapter, knitteth
up a beadrow[1] of good works, in no point unlike to these,
saving only that it is somewhat more largely amplified. In
Osee the Lord saith: "I desire mercy[2] more than sacrifice, [Hosea vi. 6.]
and the knowledge of God more than whole burnt-offerings."
Micheas doth diligently inquire what the worshipper of God [Mic. vi. 8.]
should do to please him withal, and what works he should do
to delight the Lord; and immediately, by the inspiration of
the Holy Ghost, he maketh answer, saying: "I will shew
thee[3], O man, what is good; and what the Lord requireth of
thee: namely, to do justly, to love mercy, and with reverence
to walk before thy God." In like manner the prophet
Zachary, to them that demanded of him certain questions
touching virtues and such good works as please the Lord,
gave this answer, saying: "Thus saith the Lord of hosts; [Zech. vii. 9,
Execute true judgment, shew mercy and loving-kindness every 10; and viii. 17.]
man to his brother: do the widow, the fatherless, the stranger
and the poor, no wrong: let no man imagine evil in his heart
against his brother: neither be ye lovers of false oaths: for
these are the things which I do hate, saith the Lord."
      With this doctrine of the prophets doth the preaching of
the evangelists and apostles fully agree, teaching in every
place that charity, righteousness, and innocency are the
scope and sum of all good works. The apostle James saith:
"Pure religion and undefiled before God and the Father is [James i. 27.]

[1 catalogum, Lat.]
[2 beneficentiam, pietatem seu misericordiam, Lat.]
[3 So Coverdale's Bible, 1535, and the Vulgate.]

this, To visit the fatherless and widows in their adversity, and to keep himself unspotted of the world."

To what end good works must be done.It remaineth now for me to draw to an end, and in the rest that is yet behind to be spoken touching the description of good works to confer places of the scripture for the confirmation and plain exposition of the same. Now therefore we said, that good works indeed are wrought by them that are regenerate, to the glory of God, the ornament of our life, and the profit of our neighbour. For the Lord in the gospel [Matt. v. 16.] prescribeth this end to good works, where he saith: "Let your light so shine before men, that they may see your good works, and glorify your Father which is in heaven." The apostle Paul also oftener than once, exhorting us to good works, doth, as a most effectual cause to set them forward, [Tit. ii. 10.] add: "That by those works of ours we may adorn the doctrine of our Lord and Saviour Christ Jesus." And even as a comely and cleanly garment adorneth a man, so do good works indeed set forth the life of christian people. For hereupon it riseth, that the apostles of Christ did so often [Eph. iv. 22 —24; Col. iii. 9, 10.] persuade us to put off the old man, and put on the new which is created in the similitude and likeness of God. For thereby we obtain both honour and glory; we both are, and are called, the servants, yea, and the sons of our Lord God, whose property and virtue shineth in us, to the glory and praise of his holy name. And as he doth require good works at our hands, so, if we do them, we on the one side do please and delight him, and he on the other doth honour us again: as may be proved by many testimonies of the holy scripture. But the thing itself is so plain and without all controversy, that it needeth no business to prove it at all. He, verily, doth every minute augment in us his gifts, while we are intentive to do [2 Matt. xxv. [8, 29.] good works; for in the gospel he saith: "To every one that hath shall be given, and he shall abound; and from him that hath not shall be taken even that which he hath, and shall be given to him that hath." To this also may be added, that God is favourable to them that work righteousness, and doth enrich them even with many temporal gifts, and at the last bring them to life everlasting. For the apostle Paul doth [Rom. ii.] expressly say: "God shall reward every man according to his deeds; to them which, by continuing in well-doing, seek for glory, and honour, and immortality, eternal life;" and

again, " Glory, and honour, and peace, to every one that
worketh well:" although the godly in all their good works
do not (as I told you before) respect so much the recompence
and reward at God's hand, as the advancement of God's glory,
the fulfilling of his will, and the profit of our neighbour. For
Paul saith : " Do all things to the glory of God :" and again,
" Let no man seek his own, but every one another's profit : [1 Cor. x. 31,
even as I do in all things please all men, not seeking mine   24, 33.]
own commodity, but the profit of many, that they may be
saved." Therefore all the godly do so direct and temper
their works, that they may please, delight, and honour God,
and profit many men; for in so doing they express, or represent, the nature of God, whose sons they both are, and are
also called ; for he doth liberally pour out his benefits upon
all creatures ; and therefore his sons are beneficial and bent to
do good to all men.

Thus much had I hitherto to say touching the nature or
property, cause, end, and effect, that is, the very true and
right meaning[1], of good works : by which I hope it[2] is evident
to be perceived, how and in what sense the Lord in the
scriptures is said to attribute the name of righteousness and
justification[3] unto the good works of the saints his servants :
and that true principle[4] of our religion remaineth[5] firm
and unreproveable, wherein we confess and hold that " we
are justified by the grace of God for Christ his sake through
faith, and not for works." Now therefore there is nothing
more behind but this only ; for us to make our humble petition
to God for true faith in Christ our Lord, and that by his
grace he will so guide us, that we may now in works put that
in practice which hitherto we have been taught in the words of
this treatise[6] ; that is to say, that we may in good works
indeed express the faith which we in words profess that we
have in Jesus Christ our Lord.   Amen[7].

[1 ratione, Lat.]   [2 etiam illud, Lat.]
[3 mercedemque reddere, Lat. omitted; and to render a reward.]
[4 orthodoxum et primarium dogma, Lat.]
[5 nihilominus, Lat. omitted; notwithstanding.]
[6 de bonis operibus, Lat. omitted; concerning good works.]
[7 The greater part of this ninth Sermon is extracted from Bullinger's treatise, De vera hominis Christiani justificatione, which, dated
at Zurich, August 1543, forms the preface to his Commentary on the
Gospel of St John.]

OF SIN, AND OF THE KINDS THEREOF; TO WIT, OF
ORIGINAL AND ACTUAL SIN, AND OF SIN AGAINST
THE HOLY GHOST: AND LASTLY, OF THE
MOST SURE AND JUST PUNISH-
MENT OF SINS.

THE TENTH SERMON.

WE have lastly now to discourse of sin, which, as I told
you, is to be referred to the treatise of the law. Of which
that I may lawfully, religiously, rightly, and profitably speak
to the edifying of you all, I shall desire you to make your
humble prayers with me to God the Father, in the name of
Christ his Son, our gracious Lord and Mediator[1].

The name of sin, whereupon it riseth.

Sin is of most men taken for error; for that, I mean,
whereby we do not only err from the thing which is true,
right, just and good, but do also follow and decline to that
which is naught. The Latins derive their word *peccatum*,
sin, of *pellicatus*, whore-hunting; which is a fault of wedded
people that are corrupted with the spirit of fornication, as
when men prefer harlots before their lawful wives. And
this definition, verily, doth wonderfully agree to this present
treatise. For all we that do believe are by faith hand-fasted
to our God, as to our spouse and husband: if therefore we
prefer other gods before him, or choose rather to serve
them; if, I say, we let pass the true goods in deed, to
follow the shadow of goods, vain hopes, and the pernicious
pleasures of this world; then do we sin indeed, and commit
fornication against our spouse and husband[2]. But the
learned sort do for the most part put a difference betwixt
peccatum and *delictum*, which both, in effect, do signify
sins[3]: but they call that *delictum*, when the thing is not
done that should be done; and that they call *peccatum*,
when that is done that should be left undone. St Hierome
seemeth to have taken *delictum* for the first fall to sin[4].

[1 The Father—Mediator, added by the translator.]
[2 and—husband, an addition of the translator's.]
[3 which—sins, the translator's.]
[4 —quærimus quid significent (delicta), quove distent a peccatis...
Aiunt enim quod παραπτώματα (delicta) quasi initia peccatorum sint:
cum cogitatio tacita subrepit, et ex aliqua parte conniventibus nobis,
necdum tamen nos impulit ad ruinam... Peccatum vero esse, quum

St Augustine sayeth that *peccatum* is committed of him that sinneth wittingly, and *delictum* of him that sinnneth of ignorance[5]. I see that those words are in some places confounded, and that the one is used for the other. In some places the error, or *delictum*, is used as the milder term; *peccatum*, in a more grievous sense; and an heinous crime, a mischief, a revolting or wickedness, for the greatest of all[6]. For St Augustine saith : " Neither is every *peccatum crimen*[7], because every *crimen* is *peccatum*." Therefore we say, that the life of a man[8] living in this transitory world may be found to be without that heinous offence, *crimen*, for which all the world doth cry out upon and accuse him[9]: but "if we say we have *nullum peccatum*, no sin," (as the apostle saith,) [1 John i. 8.] " we deceive ourselves, and the truth is not in us." Among the Hebrews sin is called by sundry names, which do import and signify overthwartness, perverseness, a fault, an error, a revolting, infirmity, vice, ignorance, and transgression. For to transgress doth signify to depart from the truth[10], from our duty or office, not to keep the right path, but to turn away from the prescript rule of the law of God. Now that rule, or law of God, is of the Hebrews called *Thora*, that is to say, a direction, or a leading by the hand[11]; for it doth direct a man in the ways that are acceptable to the Lord : and therefore the Greeks call sin by the names of ἀνομία καὶ παρανομία. Again, in the Hebrew tongue, sin is as much to say as a turning away from good to evil; also a revolting, as when thou drawest thy neck from out of the yoke of his power to whom thou art a servant : finally, it signifieth the crime or guilt whereby we endanger ourselves to the rod of punishment.

quid opere consummatum pervenit ad finem.—Hieron. Comment. in Ep. ad Ephes. cap. 2, Tom. IV. col. 338, Par. 1706.]

    [5 Potest etiam videri illud esse delictum quod imprudenter, id est, ignoranter; illud peccatum quod ab sciente committitur.—Aug. Quæst. sup. Levit. cap. 20, Opp. Tom. IV. fol. 43, col. 2, Par. 1531.]

    [6 Crimen vero, scelus, defectionem et impietatem multo gravissimam, Lat.; but *crimen* for heinous wickedness, &c.]

    [7 Neque enim quia peccatum est omne crimen, ideo crimen est etiam omne peccatum.—Aug. Enchir. ad Laurent. cap. 64, Opp. Tom. III. fol. 37, col. 4.]

    [8 sanctorum hominum, Lat.; of saints.]

    [9 for which—accuse him, added by the translator.]

    [10 a recto, Lat.]   [11 See Decade I. Serm. I. p. 49.]

The defini-
tion of sin.
Verily St Augustine taketh much pains to find out a
proper definition of sin. In his second book *De Consensu
Evangelistarum* he saith : " Sin is the transgression of the
law[1]." *Ad Simplicianum*, Lib. I. : "Sin is an inordinateness
or perverseness of man; that is, a turning from the more
excellent Creator, and a turning to the inferior creatures[2]."
De Fide contra Manichæos, cap. 8, he saith : " What is
it else to sin, but to err in the precepts of truth, or in the
truth itself[3]?" Again, *Contra Faustum Manichæum*, Lib.
XXII. cap. 27 : " Sin is a deed, a word, or a wish, against
the law of God[4]." The same Augustine, *De duabus ani-
mabus contra Manichæos*, cap. 11, saith : " Sin is a will to
retain or obtain that which justice forbiddeth, and is not free
to abstain[5]." And *In Retract.* Lib. I. cap. 15, he saith :
" That will is a motion of the mind, without compulsion,
either not to lose or else to obtain some one thing or
other[6]."

All which definitions as I do not utterly reject, so do I
wish this to be considered and thought of with the rest:
Sin is the natural corruption of mankind, and the action
which ariseth of it contrary to the law of God, whose
wrath, that is, both death and sundry punishments, it bringeth
upon us. Thou hearest how well this definition doth consist
upon his parts. Thou hearest in it of our natural corruption ; in the naming whereof appeareth, how this definition

[1 Porro peccatum est legis transgressio.—Aug. de Consens. Evang.
Lib. II. cap. 4, Tom. IV. fol. 85, col. 4.]

[2 Est autem peccatum hominis inordinatio atque perversitas ; id
est, a præstantiore conditore aversio, et ad condita inferiora conversio.
—Id. ad Simplic. Lib. I. Tom. IV. fol. 135, col. 3.]

[3 Peccare enim quid aliud est, nisi in veritatis præceptis, vel in
ipsa errare veritate?—Id. de Fide con. Manich. cap. 8, Tom. VI. fol.
117, col. 4.]

[4 Ergo peccatum est factum, vel dictum, vel concupitum aliquid
contra æternam legem.—Id. cont. Faust. Manich. Lib. XXII. cap. 27,
Tom. VI. fol. 84. col. 1.]

[5 Ergo peccatum est voluntas retinendi vel consequendi quod justitia vetat, et unde (Bullinger reads, *et non*, probably by mistaking the
abbreviation in old copies *et un.*) liberum est abstinere —Id. de duab.
anim. cont. Manich. cap. 11, Tom. VI. fol. 32, col. 2.]

[6 Ipsam voluntatem definivi dicens: Voluntas est animi motus,
cogente nullo, ad aliquid vel non amittendum vel adipiscendum.—Id.
Retract. Lib. I. cap. 15, Tom. I. fol. 5, col. 3.]

doth not agree to the sin of our first parents, in whom there
was no natural corruption : of which I mean to speak in
place convenient. Thou hearest the action named, which
ariseth of the natural corruption, and is repugnant to the
law of God. Thou hearest that sin doth bring upon us the
wrath of God, that is, death and sundry sorts of punishments appointed by the mouth of God to plague us for our
sins. Of which I will speak in order as they lie, so far
forth as the Lord shall give me grace and ability.

Now therefore it seemeth that this treatise may most
aptly be begun at the discussing of the original cause and
beginning[7] of sin. Some there be that do derive the original
cause of evil or sin from the influence of the planets, saying, " I sinned, because I was born under an unlucky
planet." Other there are, which, when they sin and are
rebuked for it, do make this answer : " Not I, but the devil
is in fault, that I have committed this grievous crime." And
sometime, laying aside all excuses, they[8] do directly cast
the blame upon God, and say : " Why, God would that it
should be so ; for if he would not have had it so, I had
not sinned." Another saith : " Since God could have letted
it, and would not, he is the cause and author of my sin."
But it is no new thing now that men do whet their blasphemous tongues against God, the maker and ruler of all
things ; for our first parents, when they had sinned and
were accused of it by God himself, found a shift for to
translate the sin, which they committed, from themselves to
other, and would not confess the truth as it was in very
deed. Such is the abominable wickedness of man. For
Adam, as it were, answering God overthwartly, casteth the
fault of his offence, not only[9] upon his wife which God had
coupled unto him, but also upon God himself. " The woman," [Gen. iii. 12]
saith he, " whom thou gavest to be with me, gave me of
the tree[10], and I did eat." As if he should have said : If
thou hadst not given me the woman, I had not sinned. But
the Lord coupled him to a wife, not to the end that she
should be an occasion of evil, but that the man might be in

The cause or beginning of sin.

[7 et auctore, Lat. omitted ; and author.]
[8 homines, Lat. ; men.]
[9 non tam—quam, Lat.; not so much upon his wife, as upon God.]
[10 dedit mihi pomum, Lat. ; gave me the apple.]

the better case and condition. Again, the woman doth simply impute the cause of that evil unto the devil, saying: "The serpent beguiled me, and I did eat." Lo, these are most corrupt, false, wicked, and detestable opinions touching the original cause of sin, wherewith the justice and truth of God is mightily offended. Neither is the nature of man the cause of sin. For God, which created all things, did also create the nature of man, and made it good, even as all things else which he created were also good[1]. Therefore the nature of man was good. For it is an accidental quality that happened to man either in, or immediately after, his fall, and not a substantial property, to have his nature so spotted with corruption as now it is[2]. Now we, being born in sin of sinful progenitors, have sin by descent as our natural property; for St Augustine, writing, *De Fide contra Manichæos*, cap. 9, saith: "And if we say that any men are evil by nature, we mean, that they are so because of the original descent of our first parents' sin, wherein we mortal men are wholly born[3]." But this now requireth a more exact and ample declaration.

That the devil alone is not the author of sin, so that, when we sin, the blame thereof should redound to him, and we that sinned escape without fault, this doth greatly argue; because it is in his power to egg and persuade, but not to enforce a man to do evil. For God by his power restraineth the devil from being able to do the thing that he would do: he can do no more than God permitteth him to do. For if he had no power over an herd of filthy swine, how much less authority hath he over the excellent souls of God's most excellent creatures! He hath, I confess, great subtilties, and more than rhetorical force, wherewith to persuade us: but God is stronger, and never ceaseth to prompt good and wholesome counsels unto the souls of his faithful servants. Neither doth he permit more to Satan than is for our commodity: as is to be seen in the example of that holy man, the patient Job; and

The nature of man is not the cause of sin.

The devil alone is not the cause of sin.

[1 valde bona, Lat.; very good.]

[2 mox ab initio talis qualis nunc est indita, Lat.; which is even from the first imparted so as it now is.]

[3 Sed et si aliquos naturaliter dicimus malos, propter originem veteris peccati dicimus, in quo jam nostra mortalitas nascitur.—August. de Fide cont. Manich. cap. 9, Opp. Tom. vi. fol. 117, col. 4.]

also in the example of Paul, 2 Cor. xii., and in his words, saying, " God is faithful, which will not suffer us to be tempted
above that we are able to bear⁴." They therefore are vainly
seduced, which cast the fault of their sin upon the devil's
shoulders.

To proceed: if thou demandest of them which lay the That destiny
blame of their sin upon their evil destiny, what destiny is? cause of sin.
they will answer, either that it is a course knit together by
eternity and linked to itself, as it were a certain chain and
continual row of counsels and works necessarily following one
upon another's neck according to the disposition and ordinance of God; or else that it is the evil stars or planets.
Now, if thou demandest again, who made the stars? they have
none other answer but God: it followeth therefore, consequently, that they enforce the cause of their sin upon God
himself. But all the ancient and best philosophers did never
pretend or allege destiny, much less such Christians as did
freely confess the mighty power of their God and Maker⁵.
And even among our men, I mean, among them that would
seem to be Christians, they which stood in the opinion of destiny
and constellations, were such kind of fellows as wise men
would be ashamed to follow them as authors. Bardesanes⁶
imputed to destiny the conversations of mortal men. And
the Priscillianists, who were condemned in the first council
held at Toledo, thought and taught that man is tied to fatal
stars, and hath his body compact according to the twelve
signs in heaven, placing Aries in the head, Taurus in the
neck, and so consequently to every sign his several limbs⁷. St

[⁴ 1 Cor. x. 13, vos—potestis, Lat.]
[⁵ as did—maker, not in Lat.]
[⁶ Bardesanes was a Syrian, of Edessa, and lived in the second
century of the Christian era.   Euseb. Hist. Eccles. Lib. iv. cap. 30.
Mosheim, Eccles. Hist. Book i. cent. 2, part 2, chap. 5, § 8.]
[⁷ Astruunt etiam (Priscillianistæ) fatalibus stellis homines colli-
gatos, ipsumque corpus nostrum secundum duodecim signa cœli esse
compositum, sicut hi qui mathematici vulgo appellantur: constituentes
in capite arietem, taurum in cervice, geminos in humeris, cancrum in
pectore; et cetera nominatim signa percurrentes, ad plantas usque
perveniunt, &c.—August. de Hæres. cap. 70, Opp. Tom. vi. fol. 6, col.
4.   Priscillian lived in the middle of the fourth century, in Spain.
Mosheim, Eccles. Hist. Book ii. Cent. 4, part 2, chap. 5, §§ 21, 22.—
The first council of Toledo was held A.D. 405.]

Augustine, *In opusculo* LXXXIII. *quæstionum, Quæst.* 45, confuting soundly the destinies of planets, among other his reasons
saith : " The conceiving of twins in the mother's womb, because
it is made in one and the same act, as the physicians testify
(whose discipline is far more certain and manifest than that of
the astrologers), doth happen in so small a moment of time,
that there is not so much time as two minutes of a minute
betwixt the conceiving of the one and the other. How therefore cometh it, that in twins of one burden there is so great a
diversity of deeds, wills, and chances, considering that they of
necessity must needs have one and the same planet in their
conception, aud that the mathematicals do give the constellation of them both as if it were but of one man[1] ? " To these
words of St Augustine great light may be added, if you annex
to them and examine narrowly the example of Esau and
Jacob's birth and sundry dispositions.   The same Augustine,
writing to Boniface against two epistles of the Pelagians, Lib.
II. cap. 6, saith : " They which affirm that destiny doth rule,
will have not only our deeds and events, but also our very
wills, to depend upon the placing of the stars at the time
wherein every man is either conceived or born, which placing
they are wont to call constellations.   But the grace of God
doth not only go above all stars and heavens, but also above
the very angels themselves.   Moreover these disputers for
destiny do attribute to destiny both the good and evil that
happen to men.   But God, in the evils that fall upon men,
doth duly and worthily recompense them for their ill deserts :
but the good, which they have, he doth bestow upon them not
for their merits, but of his own favour and merciful goodness
through grace, that cannot be looked for of duty ; laying both
good and evil upon us men not through the temporal course
of planets, but by the deed and eternal counsel of his severity
and goodness.   So then we see that neither the falling out of

[1 Conceptus autem geminorum, quoniam uno concubitu efficitur
attestantibus medicis, quorum disciplina multo est certior atque mani-
festior, tam parvo puncto temporis contingit, ut in duas minutas mi-
nutarum non tendatur.   Unde ergo in geminis tanta diversitas actionum
et eventuum et voluntatum, quos necesse est eandem constellationem
conceptionalem habere, et amborum unam constellationem dare mathe-
maticos, tanquam unius hominis?—Lib. de divers. quæst. 83. quæst.
45, Tom. IV. fol. 116, col. 4.]

good or evil hath any relation unto the planets[2]." Therefore this place may be concluded with the words of the Lord in the prophet Jeremy, saying: "Thus saith the Lord, Ye shall [Je not learn after the manner of the heathen, and ye shall not be afraid for the tokens of heaven; for the heathen are afraid of such. Yea, all the observations of the Gentiles are vanity[3]." For the planets have no force to do either good or evil. And therefore the blame of sins is not to be imputed thereunto.

I have now to prove unto you, that God is not the cause of sin, or the author of evil. "God," say they, "would have it Goc so. For if he would not have had it so, I had not sinned; for of who may resist his power?" Again, "Since he could have letted it, and would not, he is the author of my sin and wickedness." As though we knew not the crafty quarrels and subtle shifts of mortal men. Who, I pray you, knoweth not, that God doth not deal with us by his absolute power, but by an appointed law and ordinance; I mean, by commodious means and a probable order[4]? God could, I know, by his absolute power keep off all evil; but yet he neither can nor will either corrupt or mar his creature and excellent order. He dealeth with us men therefore after the manner of men: he appointeth us laws, and layeth before us rewards and punishments: he commandeth to embrace the good and eschew the evil; to the performing whereof he doth neither deny us his grace, without which we can do nothing; neither

[2 Fatum quippe qui affirmant, de siderum positione ad tempus quo concipitur quisque vel nascitur, quas constellationes vocant, non solum actus et eventa, verum etiam ipsas nostras voluntates, pendere contendunt. Dei vero gratia non solum omnia sidera et omnes cœlos, verum etiam omnes angelos supergreditur. Deinde fati assertores et bona et mala hominum fato tribuunt: Deus autem in malis hominum merita eorum debita retributione persequitur, bona vero per indebitam gratiam misericordi voluntate largitur; utrumque faciens non per stellarum temporale consortium, sed per suæ severitatis et bonitatis æternum altumque consilium. Neutrum ergo pertinere videmus ad fatum.—Id. cont. duas epist. Pelag. ad Bonifac. Lib. ii. cap. 6, Tom. vii. fol. 182, col. 2.]

[3 Ergo quod sidus Saturni inclemens et asperum vel crudele, Veneris benignum et mite ab astrologis appellatur, vanitas est vanitatum, omitted; therefore, that the star of Saturn is called by astrologers unkind and harsh or cruel, and the star of Venus kindly and mild, is vanity of vanities.]

[4 legitimo, Lat.]

doth he despise our diligent good-will and earnest travail. Herein if man be slack, the negligence and fault is imputed to man himself, and not to God, although he could have kept off the sin[1], and did not; for it was not his duty to keep it off, lest peradventure he should disturb the order and destroy the work which he himself had made and ordained. Therefore God is not the author of sin or naughtiness. Touching which matter I will first add some[2] testimonies of the holy scripture; then answer to sundry objections of the adversaries of this doctrine; and lastly declare the original cause or head-spring of sin and wickedness.

God being good himself created all things good which he created.

The testimonies which teach that God is not the author of sin or naughtiness are many in number: but among the rest this is an argument of greatest force and probability, because God is said to be good naturally; and that all which he created were made good[3] in their creation. Whereupon it

[Wisd. i. 13 —16.]

is that Solomon[4] saith: " God hath not made death; neither hath he delight in the destruction of the living: for he created all things, that they might have their being; and the beginnings of the world were healthful; and there is no poison of destruction in them, nor the kingdom of hell upon the earth: for righteousness is immortal, (but unrighteousness bringeth death[5]:) and the ungodly call it to them both with words and works, and thereby come to nought:" and so forth, as is to be seen in the first chapter of the book of Wisdom; which words do passingly agree with the first chapter[6] of that most excellent prophet Moses.

In the fifth psalm David saith: " Thou art the God that hast no pleasure in wickedness: neither shall any evil dwell with thee. The unjust shall not stand in thy sight: for thou hatest all them that work iniquity. Thou shalt destroy them that speak leasing: the Lord doth abhor both the bloodthirsty and deceitful man." Lo, thou canst devise nothing more contrary to the nature of God than sin and naughtiness: as

[1 potentia sua, Lat. omitted; by his power.]
[2 clara, Lat. omitted; clear.]   [3 valde bona, Lat.]
[4 sapiens ille, Lat.; the wise man. Bullinger says *not* Solomon. Cf. Vol. i. p. 225, note 12.]
[5 This parenthesis is not in Bullinger's Latin, nor in the Septuagint, nor Vulgate, nor Auth. Ver.; but it is in Coverdale's Bible, 1535.]
[6 cum primis capitibus, Lat.]

thou mayest more at large perceive in the thirty-fourth chapter of the book of Job.

The wise man saith: "God created man good; but they sought out many inventions of their own." And therefore the apostle Paul[7] deriveth sin, damnation, and death, not from God, but from Adam; and from God he fetcheth grace, forgiveness, and life, through the mediator Jesus Christ. That place of Paul is far more manifest than that it needeth any large exposition: let it not only be considered and[8] diligently weighed of the readers and hearers; whom I would wish always to bear in mouth and mind the very words and meaning of this notable sentence[9]: "Even as by one man sin entered into the world, and death by sin:" and so forth as followeth. [Eccles. vii. 29.]

The same apostle in the seventh to the Romans doth evidently declare that the law is holy, the commandment good and just; and thereby he doth insinuate, that in God or in his will there is not, and in his law, which is the will of God, there springeth not, any spot or blur of sin or naughtiness. In our flesh, saith he, the evil lurketh, and out of us iniquity ariseth. "I know," saith he, "that in me, that is in my flesh, there is no good." In that chapter there are many sentences to be found which do wonderfully confirm this argument.

Again, in the third to the Romans the same apostle saith: "If our unrighteousness setteth forth the righteousness of God, what shall we say? Is God unrighteous which taketh vengeance? (I speak after the manner of men;)" that is, I use the words of wicked people;) "God forbid: for how then shall God judge the world? For if the truth of God hath more abounded through my lie unto his glory; why am I as yet judged as a sinner?" &c. Verily, if God were the author of sin and all evil, and that he would have the wicked to be such as in very deed they are, then why, I pray you, should he judge or punish them as transgressors, since they by sinning fulfilled his will? Rom. lii.

[7 ad Roma. 5 cap., Lat.]

[8 rather, but:—But ed. 1577 has, let it only be considered and diligently, &c.]

[9 The translator has here paraphrased Bullinger's one word, *Recita.*]

To this place also doth belong that testimony of the blessed evangelist and apostle John, in his canonical epistle, where he saith : "If any man love the world, the love of the Father is not in him. For all that is in the world, as the lust of the flesh, and the lust of the eyes, and the pride of life, is not of the Father, but of the world. And the world passeth away, and the lust thereof: but he that fulfilleth the will of the Father[1] abideth for ever." Lo here, God is utterly free from all evil: evil, saith he, is not of the Father, but of the world. And he which doeth the will of the Father[1] doeth not what the world will, but what God will. Therefore these two, good and evil, sin and the will of God, are directly opposed and repugnant the one against the other. These testimonies, though few in number, are notwithstanding, in my judgment, sufficiently significant and able to persuade a godly-disposed hearer.

[1 John ii. 15—17.]

Now upon this we do first infer a conclusion, and boldly warrant that point of Catholic doctrine, which hath ever since the apostles' time always been defended with much diligence against the unpure philosophy of some, (although yet I do not utterly condemn all the parts of philosophy, knowing very well that some points thereof are very necessary and profitable to the zealous lovers of God and godliness,) that God is not the author of evil, or cause of sin. Then out of the same testimonies we gather, that the original cause of sin or evil is derived of man himself, and his suggester and provoker, the devil : so yet that we say, that the devil, being first himself corrupted, did corrupt man, being nevertheless not able of himself to have done anything, had not man of his own accord consented unto evil.

The true cause of sin or evil.

And here we must set before our eyes the fall of our first father Adam, that by the consideration thereof we may be the better able to judge of the original cause of sin and iniquity.

God created Adam, the first father of us all, according to his own similitude and likeness ; that is to say, he made him good, most pure, most holy, most just, and immortal, and adorned him with every excellent gift and faculty, so that there was nothing wanting to him in God, which was available to perfect felicity. Touching this similitude or

[1 Dei, Lat.]

likeness to God I shall take occasion upon the words of Paul to speak hereafter. So then he was endued with a very divine, pure, and sharp understanding. His will was free, without constraint, and absolutely holy: he had power to do either good or evil. Moreover God gave him a law, which might instruct him what to do and what to leave undone. For God in saying, "Thou shalt not eat of the [Gen. iii. 3.] fruit of the tree of knowledge of good and evil," did simply require at his hands faith and obedience, and that he should wholly depend upon God: all which he had to do, not by compulsion or necessity, but of his own accord and free good-will. For very truly and holily writ the wise man in the fifteenth of Ecclesiasticus[2], saying: "God made man in the beginning, and left him in the hand of his counsel. He gave him his commandments and precepts: if thou wilt, thou shalt keep my commandments, and they shall preserve thee."

Therefore, when the serpent tempted the mind of man, and did persuade him to taste of the forbidden tree, man knew well enough what peril was laid before him, and how the serpent's counsel was flatly repugnant to the Lord's commandment. In the mean time neither did God compel him, nor Satan in the serpent enforce him to sin, while he resisted and did withstand him. For God had said: "Ye shall not eat of that tree, nor touch it: if ye do, ye shall die for it." Therefore he was at his own free choice, and in the hand of his own counsel, either to eat or not to eat: yea, God declared his mind unto him in giving precise commandment, that he should not eat; and to the commandment he annexed the danger of the breach thereof, withdrawing him thereby from the eating of the fruit, and saying, "Lest perhaps thou die." And as Satan could not, so also he did not, shew any violence, but used such probable words to counsel him as he could, and did indeed at length persuade him. For when the woman's will gave ear to the word of the devil, her mind departed from the word of God; whereby she rejected the good law of God, did of her own perverse will commit that sin, and drew her husband that yielded of his own accord into the fellowship of the same offence: as the scripture doth most significantly express in these words:

[2 verses 14—16, according to the Vulgate. Our Authorised Version is a little different, following the Greek LXX.]

"And the woman, seeing that the tree was good to eat of, and pleasant to the eyes, and a tree to be desired to make one wise[1], took of the fruit thereof, and did eat, and gave to her husband with her, and he did eat also." Lo, here thou hast the beginning of evil, the devil: thou hast heard what it was that moved the mind or will of man unto that evil, to wit, the false persuasion of the devil, or his subtle praise of the fruit of the tree, and so consequently a mere lie; and the pleasant shew of the delicate tree. But that which our first parents did, they did of their own accord and free good will, being led by hope to obtain a more excellent life and profounder wisdom, which the seducer had falsely promised them. We do therefore conclude, that sin doth spring not of God, which hateth and doth prohibit all evil, but of the devil; the[2] free election of our grand-parents and their corrupted will, which was depraved by the devil's lie, and the false shew of feigned good. So then the devil and the yielding or corrupted mind[3] of man are the very causes of sin and naughtiness.

Sin springeth of the devil's suggestion and our corrupt will. To proceed now : this evil doth by descent flow from our first parents into all their posterity, so that at this day sin doth not spring from elsewhere but of ourselves, that is to say, of our corrupt judgment, depraved will, and the suggestion of the devil. For the root of evil is yet remaining in our flesh by reason of that first corruption: which root bringeth forth a corrupt branch in nature like unto itself: which branch Satan even now, as he hath done always, doth by his sleights, subtilties, and lies, cherish, tend, and tender, as an imp of his own planting; and yet notwithstanding he laboureth in vain, unless we yield ourselves to his hands to be framed as he listeth.

Now therefore, that there may herein appear less doubt or darkness, I will, for confirmation's[4] sake, add two most evident testimonies; the one out of the writings of the evangelists, the other out of the doctrine of the apostles.

John viii. [44.] The Lord in the gospel saith: "The devil was a murderer from the beginning, and stood not in the truth, because the truth is not in him. When he speaketh a lie, he speaketh of his own; because he is a liar, and the father

[1 concupiscibile ad contemplandum, Lat.]   [2 and the, Lat.]
[3 voluntas, Lat.]   [4 et declarandi, Lat.]

of lies." By these[5] words of the Lord we gather, that
evil is to be referred to the devil, who, being created in
truth and goodness, did not stand fast in truth and goodness,
but degenerated from his nature wherein he was made
good, and fell[6] into another nature corrupt and wicked,
and hath out of himself dispersed all evil (as it appeared
by the history of our first parents) into the world; to wit,
murder and lies (under which two are comprehended all
other evils), of which he is expressly said to be the father,
that is, the cause, the author, the well-spring, and beginning:
not because he was made such an one of God, but because
he stood not fast in the truth. To them therefore that do
demand[7], of what beginning Satan came, and whether God
made him or no? our answer is, That God indeed made all
the angels, and those also which afterward did become reprobates and wicked devils: but we do not therefore say
that the cause of evil doth redound to God. For we know
that God in the beginning made all the angels good; for
all things which he made were good. Furthermore it is
said that the devil stood not in the truth; that is, that he
revolted from the truth: from which he could not have revolted, if he had never stood in it. Therefore God in the
beginning did place all his angels in the truth. He required
of them truth, faith or fidelity, and the duty that they
ought[8] him: which they were able to have done, if they
themselves would. But they did disloyally fall from their
allegiance, and sinned, as the apostle Peter testifieth, against [2 Pet. ii. 4.]
the Lord; and therefore the fault of their falsehood and
of all their naughtiness was not in God, but in the rebellious
and revolting angel. For since the time of his fall there
is no truth, no fidelity, no integrity, no fear of God, no
light or goodness to be found in him. Therefore truly
said St John in the canonical epistle: "He that committeth [1 John iii.
sin is of the devil; for the devil sinneth from the beginning." 8.]
For he is the first sinner, and the beginning of sin. To
this also may this note be added[9], that of Peter and John
the devil is said to sin. For sin is repugnant to the will of

[5 disertissimis, Lat.; most express.]
[6 sua culpa, Lat. omitted; by his own fault.]
[7 objicientibus, Lat.]   [8 i. e. owed.]
[9 in his omnibus illud observabile, Lat.]

God: therefore God would not have had him perish: whereupon, since he perished, it followeth that he perished, not
by the fault of God, but by his own fault.

Let us now hear the other testimony concerning the corrupt will of man, which is in very deed the cause of sin.
St James the apostle saith: "Let no man say when he is
tempted, I am tempted of God: for God cannot be tempted
with evil, neither tempteth he any man. But every man is
tempted, when he is drawn away and enticed of his own
concupiscence. Then when lust hath conceived, it bringeth
forth sin; and sin, when it is finished, bringeth forth death."
In these words St James, I hope, doth evidently enough
make God to be free from all fault of sin, and doth derive
it of us ourselves, shewing by the way the beginning and
proceeding of sin. Neither doth James in this place gainsay
the place in Genesis, where Moses said, "God tempted
Abraham." For in Moses to tempt doth signify to make
a trial or a proof: but in this argument of ours it signifieth
to stir or draw to evil, and so to corrupt us. Therefore
God, as he cannot, saith he, be tempted of evil; that is to
say, as God is by nature good and uncorrupt; so doth he
not corrupt, deprave, or defile[1] any man with evil; for that is
contrary to the nature of God. From whence then hath
sin his beginning? The holy apostle answereth, saying:
"Yea, every one is tempted, corrupted, and drawn into evil,
while he is withdrawn and enticed with his own concupiscence." Lo here, sin taketh beginning of our concupiscence,
and is accomplished and finished by our own work and labour.

Note here, by the way, what a weight and emphasis
every one of the apostle's words doth carry with it. For
first, he maketh concupiscence our own, or proper to us all,
even as the Lord before did say of Satan, "When he
speaketh a lie, he speaketh of his own." Now because
concupiscence is our own, therefore sin is our own also. For
concupiscence doth withdraw us from that that is true, just,
and good, to that which is false, unjust, and evil. The same
concupiscence enticeth us, that is, by making a shew of false
hope it doth deceive us: as fowlers are wont with meat to
entice birds into their nets, which, when they have deceived
them, they catch up and kill. What, I pray you, could be

[James i.
13—15.]

[Gen. xxii.
1.]

[1 immergit, Lat.]

spoken more plainly? We are by our own concupiscence cast into evil: this concupiscence draweth us from God; it doth entice, and utterly deceive us. And then, having laid the foundation of sin and opened the well-spring from whence it floweth, he doth very properly allude and by an allegory shew us the genealogy, that is, the beginning and proceeding of sin. That concupiscence, saith he, which is proper unto us all, doth, as it were a matrix, conceive sin in us; and immediately after doth bring it forth; to wit, when our lust bursteth out into the act, when we do greedily prosecute that which we lusted after, and, being once obtained, we do enjoy it against the law of God: upon the neck whereof death doth follow without intermission; "for the reward of sin is death."

I have, I trust, by these evident proofs of scripture plainly declared that God is not the cause of evil; but our corruptible[2] will or concupiscence, and the devil, which stirreth, provoketh, and inflameth our depraved nature to sin and wickedness, as he which is the tempter and utter enemy to mankind and his salvation[3].

It will not be amiss here to hear the objections of certain cavillers against this doctrine, and to learn how to answer them according to the truth. Some there are which, when they see that we derive sin not of the nature of God but of the corruptible will of man and false suggestion of the devil, do presently object, that God created Adam, and so consequently created sin in Adam[4]. To this we answer; that sin is the corruption of the good nature made by God, and not a creature created by God either in or with man. God created man good: but man, being left to his own counsel, did through the persuasion of Satan, by his own action and depraved will, corrupt the goodness that God created in him: so now that sin is proper to man[5], I mean, man's corrupt action against the law of God, and not a creature created in him of God. To this they reply: But the will and ability that was in Adam, was it from elsewhere than from God himself? Undoubtedly, no: it was from God. Therefore, say they, sin is of God. I deny it; for God gave not to Adam will and power of working, to the end that he

Objections are answered.

[2 corruptam, Lat.]

[4 in Adam, not in Lat.]

[3 omnis boni, Lat.]

[5 proprium hominis, Lat.]

should work evil; for by express commandment he forbad him to do wickedness. Therefore Adam himself did naughtily apply the will and power, which he received of God, by using them untowardly. The prodigal son received money at his father's hand; whose meaning was, not that he should waste it prodigally with riotous living, but that he might have whereupon to live and supply the want of his necessities. Wherefore when he had lavishly lasht it out, and utterly undone himself, the fault was in himself for abusing it, and not in his father for giving it unto him[1]. Furthermore, to have the power to do good and evil, as Adam had of God, is of itself a thing without fault: even as also to have poison, to bear a weapon, or wear a sword, is a thing that no man can worthily blame. They have in them a force to do good or harm; they are not naught unless they be abused: and he that giveth thee them doth leave to thee the use thereof. If he be a just man, he putteth them into thy hand not to abuse, but to use as equity and right requireth. Wherefore, if thou abusest them, the fault is imputed to thyself, and not to him that gave thee them. Now since God, which gave Adam that will and power, is of himself most absolutely just, it followeth consequently, that he gave them to Adam not to do evil but good: why then is the most just God blamed in such a case as sinful man is without all blame in? We do therefore conclude: because affection in Adam, being moved by sense and egged on by the serpent, did persuade him to eat of the forbidden fruit, when nevertheless his understanding did yet hold the word of God which forbad him to eat; and that his will was at free choice and liberty to incline to whether part it pleased him; he did notwithstanding[2] will and choose that which God had forbidden him; we do therefore, I say, conclude, that sin is properly to be imputed to man which willingly transgressed, and not to God[3] which charged him that he should not sin.

Here again the adversaries ask this question, Why God

[1 sua, non patris, culpa perit, tametsi pecuniam acceperit a patre, Lat.]

[2 in pejorem inclinavit, Lat. omitted; incline to the worse part, and.]

[3 legislatoris, Lat.; not to the lawgiver.]

did create man so frail, that he of his own will might incline to Why God created man so fickle that he should fall. evil: why did he not rather confirm in him the goodness and perfect soundness of nature, that he could not have fallen or sinned? To this the scripture answereth, saying: "What art thou that disputest with God? Woe to him that striveth with his Maker! Woe to him that saith to the father, Why begottest thou? and to the mother, Why broughtest thou forth⁴?" Unless God had made man fallable⁵, there had been no praise of his works or virtue; for he could neither have willed nor choosed but of necessity have been good. Yea, what if man ought altogether to be made fallable? For so did the counsel of God require him to be. God giveth not his own glory to any creature. Adam was a man, and not a God. But to be good of necessity is the proper glory of God, and of none but God⁶. And as God is bountiful and liberal, so also is he just: he doth good to men; but will therewithal that men acknowledge him and his benefits, and that they obey him, and be thankful for the same. He had bestowed innumerable benefits upon Adam: there lacked nothing therefore but to give him an occasion to declare and shew his thankfulness and obedience to his good God and benefactor; which occasion he offered him by the making of that law, or giving his commandment. We see therefore that God ordained not that law to be a stumbling-block in Adam's way, but rather to be a staff to stay him from falling: for in the law he declareth what he would have him to do. He sheweth, that he wisheth not the death or destruction of Adam: he teacheth him what to do, that he may escape death and live in felicity and perfect happiness. For which cause also he To what end God gave the law to Adam. provided that the law should be a plain and easy commandment: "Of the tree of knowledge of good and evil thou shalt not eat," saith the Lord; "for if thou doest, thou shalt die the death: but of any other tree in the garden thou shalt eat." What else was this, than as if he should have said, Thou shalt in all things have an eye to me; thou shalt stick to me, obey me, be subject unto me, and serve me: neither shalt thou from elsewhere fetch the forms of good and evil than of me; and

[⁴ Rom. ix. 20. Isai. xlv. 9, 10. Coverdale's Bible, 1535, also has *Why*. Bullinger's Latin is *Quid*.]

[⁵ i. e. liable to fall; labilis, Lat.]

[⁶ But to be—but God, the translator's addition.]

in so doing thou shalt shew thyself obedient and thankful
unto me thy Maker? Did God in this desire any unjust
thing, or more than he should, at the hands of Adam? He
shewed him the tree as a sacrament or[1] sign of that which he
enjoined him by the giving of the law; to wit, that the tree
might be a token to put him in memory that he ought to
obey the Lord alone, as a wise, bountiful, excellent, and
greatest God and Maker. And what difficulty, I pray you,
or darkness was there herein? St Augustine is of the same
opinion with us, who in his book *De Natura Boni adversus
Manichæos,* cap. 35, saith: " He did therefore forbid it, that
he might shew that the nature of the reasonable soul ought
to be, not in man's own power, but in subjection unto God;
and that by obedience it keepeth the order of her salvation,
which by disobedience it doth corrupt and mar. And hereupon it cometh, that he called the tree, which he forbad, by
the name of the tree of knowledge of good and evil; because
Adam, if he touched it against the Lord's commandment,
should by trial feel the punishment of his sin, and by that
means know what difference there was betwixt the good that
followeth obedience and the evil which ensueth the sin of
disobedience[2]." Now therefore, when the serpent was crept
in and began to tell man of other forms of good and evil
directly contrary to the law of God, and that man had once
received them as things both true and credible[3], he did disloyally revolt from God, and by his own fault through disobedience he wrought his own destruction. Therefore God did
always deal justly with him; and man contrarily dealt too too
unjustly, and was utterly unthankful, howsoever men will go
about to cloak or not to hear of his unthankful stubbornness[4].

[1 a sacrament or, not in Lat.]
[2 Ad hoc enim prohibuerat, ut ostenderet naturam animæ ratio-
nalis, non in sua potestate, sed Deo subditam esse debere, et ordinem
suæ salutis per obedientiam custodire, per inobedientiam corrumpere.
Hinc et arborem quam tangi vetuit sic appellavit, dignoscentiæ boni et
mali: qui, cum eam contra vetitum tetigisset, experiretur pœnam peccati, et eo modo dignosceret, quid interesset inter obedientiæ bonum et
inter inobedientiæ malum.—August. de Nat. Boni adv. Manich. Opp.
Tom. vi. fol. 115, col. 4, Par. 1531.]
[3 as—credible, not in Lat.]
[4 howsoever—stubbornness: utcunque rem æstimes, Lat.]

But whereas we say that man was made fallable, we will not have it to be so understood, that any man should think that there was in Adam any one jot or prick of infirmity before his fall; for as he was in all points most absolutely perfect, so was he in no point created so frail that he should sin or perish by death. For God, which is one in substance and three in persons, said: "Let us make man in our image, after our own likeness." Note here, that *Zælœm* doth signify the picture or counterfeit of another thing, and that *Demuth* importeth the very pattern whereby any picture is drawn or image portrayed[5]. Therefore in God is the example or pattern, to the resemblance whereof there was a picture or similitude framed : but that representing likeness cannot be this body of ours; for God is a Spirit, in no point like to the nature of dust and ashes[6] : we must of necessity therefore resemble the image of God to spiritual things, as to immortality, truth, justice, and holiness. For so hath the apostle Paul taught us, where he saith, "Be ye renewed in the spirit of your mind; and put on that new man, which after God is shapen in righteousness and holiness of truth[7]." Wherefore there was no want in our grandfather Adam of any thing that was available to absolute perfectness : so that even a blind man may perceive, that man was not created to death and destruction, but unto life, felicity, and absolute blessedness.

There was no corruption or infirmity in Adam before his fall.

The image of God.

But, say they, God did foreknow the fall of man, which, if he would, he could have withstood : now, since he could and would not, God is to be blamed because Adam sinned. It is a goodly matter indeed[8], when, all fear of God being laid aside, men will at their pleasure fall flatly on railing against the majesty of God almighty. I answered in the beginning of this discourse to this objection; and yet this I add here moreover, that upon God's foreknowledge there followeth no necessity, so that Adam did of necessity sin because God did foreknow that he would sin. A prudent father doth foresee, by some untoward tokens, that his son will one day

God did foreknow the fall of man.

---

[5] דְמוּת is more than צֶלֶם : this expresses the *general form or delineation;* that, the *conformity* or *resemblance of the parts.* Parkhurst, Heb. Lex. in voc. דְמָה.]

[6] luti, is Bullinger's *one* word.]

[7] Eph. iv. 23, 24. Marg. Auth. Ver.]

[8] egregia censebitur disputatio, Lat.]

come to an ill ending[1]: neither is he deceived in his foresight; for he is slain, being taken in adultery. But he is not therefore slain, because his father foresaw that he would be slain; but because he was an adulterer. And therefore St Ambrose, or whosoever it is that was author of the second book *De Gentium Vocatione*, cap. 4, speaking of the murder which Cain committed, saith: "God verily did foreknow to what end the fury of the mad man would come. And yet, because God's foreknowledge could not be deceived, it doth not thereupon follow, that necessity of sinning did urge the crime upon him[2]," &c. And St Augustine, *De Libero Arbitrio*, Lib. XIII. cap. 4, saith: "As thou by thy memory dost not compel those things to be done that are gone and past, so God by his foreknowledge doth not compel those things to be done which are to come. And as thou rememberest some things that thou hast done, and yet hast not done all things which thou rememberest; so God foreknoweth all things which he doth, and yet doth not all which he foreknoweth. But God is a just revenger of that whereof he is no evil author[3]." And so forth.

An objection. Like unto this is another objection, which they make that say: God did before all beginnings determine with himself to deliver mankind from bondage: therefore it could not otherwise be, but that we should first be tangled in bondage: therefore it behoved us to be drowned in sin, that by that means the glory of God might shine more clearly; as the [Rom. v. 20.] apostle said, "Where sin was plenteous, there was grace more plenteous." But it is marvel that these cavillers do not better consider, that God of himself, without us, is sufficient to himself unto absolute blessedness and most perfect felicity; and that his glory could (as it doth) of itself reach above all

[1 perimendum gladio, Lat.]

[2 Et utique præsciebat Deus ad quem finem insanientis esset progressura conceptio. Neque ex eo, quod falli scientia divina non poterat, necessitate peccandi urgebatur facinus voluntatis.—De Vocat. Gent. Lib. II. cap. 4, col. 540, Ambros. Opp. Tom. IV. Par. 1614.]

[3 Sicut enim tu in memoria tua non cogis facta esse, quæ præterierunt; sic Deus præscientia sua non cogit facienda quæ futura sunt. Et sicut tu quædam quæ fecisti meministi, nec tamen quæ meministi omnia fecisti; ita Deus omnia quorum ipse auctor est præscit, nec tamen omnium quæ præscit ipse auctor est. Quorum autem non est malus auctor, justus est ultor.—August. de Lib. Arbit. Lib. III. cap. 4, Tom. I. fol. 141, col. 3, Par. 1531.]

heavens, although there had never been any creature brought into light. Is not God without beginning? But we his creatures had a beginning. God is glorious from before all beginnings: therefore he is glorious without us: and his glory would be as great as it is, though we were not[4]. But what dullard is so foolish as to think, that that eternal light of God doth draw any brightness of glory at our darkness, or out of the stinking dungeon[5] of our sin and wickedness? Should God's glory be no glory, if it were not for our sins? The wise man in Ecclesiasticus saith: "Say not thou, It is the Lord's fault that I have sinned: for thou shalt not do the thing that God hateth. Say not thou, He hath caused me to do wrong; for he hath no need of the sinner:" or, for the wicked are not needful unto him. " God hateth all abomination of error; and they that worship God will love none such." Why therefore do we not change our manner of reasoning, and so consider of the matter as it is in very deed? God, of his eternal goodness and liberality, whereby he wisheth himself to be parted[6] among us all to our felicity, did from everlasting determine to create man to his own similitude and likeness: but for because he did foresee that he would fall headlong into a filthy and miserable bondage, he did therefore by the same his grace and goodness ordain a deliverer to bring us out of thraldom; to the end that so he might communicate himself unto us, that we might praise his gracious favour, and render thanks to his fatherly[7] goodness. And so, whatsoever we men have sinned and turned to our own destruction, that same doth God convert again to our commodity and salvation: even as he is read to have done in the case of Joseph and his brethren; which is, as it were, a certain type of spiritual things[8] and cases of salvation. And we must wholly endeavour ourselves to do what we may in reasoning of this argument so to turn it, that all glory may be given to God alone, and to us nothing else but silence in the sight of God[9].

[Ecclus. xv. 11—13.]

[4 and his glory—were not, the translator's addition.]
[5 a putore illo, Lat.]
[6 distrahi quasi, Lat.; as it were parted.]
[7 fatherly, not in Lat.]
[8 harum rerum, Lat.; of these things. The rest is the translator's paraphrase.]
[9 confusio faciei, Lat. Dan. ix. 8. in—God, not in Lat.]

Now last of all, there are yet behind some places of scripture, which must by the way be run through and ex-

[Rom. i. 28.] How God giveth men over to a reprobate sense. pounded. The apostle[1], verily, saith: " God gave them up to a reprobate sense." But this kind of giving over is, as Augustine also saith[2], a work of judgment and justice ; for they were worthy to be given up unto a reprobate sense. The cause is prefixed in the words of the apostle : for God had made himself manifest unto them ; but they were not only unthankful towards him, but waxed wise also in their own conceits, and went about to obtrude unto him I wot not what manner of religion and worship. Therefore, that they might by proof see that they were fools and ungodly, God gave them up unto filthy lusts. In like manner king Amazias would not give ear and hearken to the Lord, because God had determined to punish his iniquities ; as is to be read in the fourth book of Kings, the fourteenth chapter, and second Paralipom. twenty-fifth chapter. Likewise did the Lord put the spirit of error into the mouths of the false prophets, and they seduced Egypt : Esay nineteen. So also did a seducing spirit[3] go out from the Lord of judgment, and was a lying spirit in the mouth of all the prophets : as is to be seen in the last chapter of the third book of Kings. Now the Lord doth all these things with just and holy judgment.

God is said to make men blind. Again, God is said to blind men's eyes, so often as he doth revoke, or take away, the contemned light of his truth and sincerity, leaving them that delight in darkness to walk and stick in their darkness still. For then the Lord permitteth his words to be preached to the unthankful and ungodly receivers unto their judgment or condemnation ; for so, verily, doth the evangelical and apostolical doctrine teach us [John iii. 19.] to think. " This," saith the Lord, " is condemnation," or, this is judgment, " that" the Son of God, the very true " light, came into the world, and the world loved darkness more [2 Cor. iv. 3, 4.] than light." And Paul said : " If yet the gospel[4] be hid, it is hid in them that perish : in whom the God of this world hath blinded the senses of the unbelievers," &c.

[1 Paulus, Lat. omitted.]

[2 Augustine treats of these words of St Paul in Psalm lvii. enarr. Opp. Tom. viii. fol. 121, col. 2, and argues that these sins of the heathen are just punishments from God.]

[3 vel cacodœmon, Lat.]

[4 evangelium nostrum, Lat.]

In the same sense God is said to harden man. For when To harden.
the Lord calleth man and he resisteth, making himself unworthy of the kingdom of heaven, he doth then permit him
unto himself: that is, he leaveth man unto his own corrupt
nature, according unto which the heart of man is stony, which
is mollified and made tractable by the only grace of God:
therefore the withdrawing of God's grace is the hardening of
man's heart; and when we are left unto ourselves, then are
we hardened. Pharao, king of Egypt, did by his murdering
of the Israelitish infants, by his tyranny, and many other
vices horribly committed against the law of nature, offend
the eyes of God's most just and heavenly majesty : therefore
it is no marvel that he hardened his heart. But if any man
will not admit or receive this exposition, yet can he not deny
that God in the scriptures doth use our kinds of phrases and
manner of speeches. Now we are wont to say, This father
doth by too much cockering or over gentle dealing mar or
harden his son[5], he maketh him stubborn and stiff-necked;
and yet the father doth not tender[6] him to destroy, but to save
him : the son indeed by the abuse of his father's clemency
doth both destroy and harden himself. Therefore whereas
the son is hardened, that cometh by his own and not his
father's fault, although the father bear the name to have
hardened him, or made him past grace[7]. And verily, if thou
dost diligently consider the history of Pharao[8], thou shalt
oftener than once find this sentence repeated there : " And God harden-
ed Pharao's
God hardened Pharao's heart," namely, when some benefit or heart.
delivery from evil was wrought before : as though the scripture should have said, By this benefit of delivering him from
evil did God harden the heart of Pharao, while he abused the
goodness of God, and supposed that all things would be afterwards out of peril and danger, because God had taken away
this present punishment and did begin to do him good. And
yet I confess, that God, before he had benefited, or laid any
punishments upon, Egypt, did immediately upon the calling of
Moses say : " I know that the king of Egypt will not let you [Exod. iii.
depart;" and again : " See that thou do all these signs and 19; iv. 21.]

[5 Macht in halsztarck, omitted, but interpreted, by the translator.]
[6 non ideo indulget, Lat.]
[7 or—grace, the translator's addition.]
[8 in Exodo, Lat. omitted.]

wonders, which I have put in thy hand, before Pharao: but I will harden Pharao's heart, that he shall not let the people go." But these sayings do not tend hereunto, that we should make God the author of all Pharao's falsehood, rebellion, and stubborn dealing against the Lord; but rather they were spoken to the comfort and confirmation of Moses, who is therefore so premonished, that, when he dealeth earnestly with the king and yet cannot obtain his suit, he should notwithstanding know that he had God's business in hand, and that God by his long sufferance is the cause of that delay[1], when as notwithstanding at the last he would temper all things to his own honour and glory. The case, by a similitude, is all one as if an householder should send his servant to his debtors, saying: Go thy way, and demand my debts; but yet I know that thou shalt receive none of them; for I by my sufferance and gentle dealing will cause them to be the slacker to pay it: but yet do thou thy duty; and I in the meanwhile will see what is needful to be done.

To this may be added, that even in those very chapters where it is so often said, "God hardened Pharao's heart," this also is afterward annexed, which layeth the hardening of Pharao's heart upon Pharao's own head, saying, "He hardened his heart, and hearkened not unto them." In the ninth of Exodus, when Pharao was well whipped, he crieth: " I have now sinned; the Lord is just, but I and my people are unjust or wicked:" and immediately after again: "But when Pharao saw that it ceased raining, he sinned yet more, and hardened his heart, and it was hardened." So then these and such like places must be conferred with these words, " I have hardened Pharao's heart;" and out of them must be gathered a godly sense; such a sense, I mean, as maketh not God[2] the author of evil.

Amos iii.

Now also the prophet Amos doth very plainly say : "There is no evil in a city, but the Lord doth it." But Augustine, *contra Adimantum*, cap. 26, did very religiously[3] write : " Evil in this place is not to be taken for sin, but for punishment ; for the word (evil) is used in two significations : the one is the evil which a man doeth ; the other evil is the pain which he suffereth. Now the prophet in this place speaketh

How God is said to do evil.

[1 pertinaciæ illius, Lat. ; of that stubborn dealing.]
[2 Deum justissimum, Lat.]   [3 orthodoxe, Lat.]

of that evil which is the punishment that men do suffer. For Note here, the first evil is the deed; the second, the punishment of the evil deed. by the providence of God, which ruleth and governeth all things, man doth so commit the evil which he will, that he may suffer the evil which he would not. Therefore the evil that God doth is not evil in respect of God, but is evil to them upon whom his vengeance lighteth. So then he, in respect of himself, doth good ; because every just thing is good : that vengeance of his is just, and so consequently it is good[4]." The place of Esay also must be none otherwise understood in his forty-fifth chapter, saying : " I am the Lord, and there is else none. It is I that created light and darkness : I make peace and evil : yea, I, even I the Lord, do all these things." For here he taketh evil for war, and maketh it the contrary to peace.

Again St Augustine, *De Natura Boni contra Manichæos* chap. 28, saith : "When we hear that all things are of him, All things are of God, by God, and in God. and by him, and in him, we must understand it to be spoken of all the natures that are naturally. For sins are not of him, because they do not keep, but defile, nature ; which sins the holy scriptures do diversly testify to be of the will of them which commit them[5]." Thus much St Augustine.

Neither is it a matter of any great difficulty to answer to that sentence of Salomon's, where he saith, " God created all things for his own sake; yea, the ungodly against the evil day." Proverbs xvi. For we believe that the most just God hath appointed a day[6] of affliction, judgment, or punishment[7], which shall come upon them in due time and season.

[4 Malum hoc loco non peccatum, sed pœna intelligenda est. Dupliciter enim appellatur malum ; unum quod homo facit, alterum quod patitur pœna. De pœnis ergo loquebatur Propheta, cum hoc diceret. Divina enim providentia cuncta moderante et gubernante, ita homo male fecit quod vult, ut male patiatur quod non vult.—Ita ergo Deus malum facit, quod non ipsi Deo malum est, sed eis in quos vindicat. Itaque ipse, quantum ad se pertinet, bonum facit ; quia omne justum bonum est, et justa est illa vindicta.—August. Opp. Tom. vi. fol. 43, col. 3. Par. 1531.]

[5 Cum autem audimus, Omnia ex ipso, et per ipsum, et in ipso ; omnes utique naturas intelligere debemus quæ naturaliter sunt. Neque enim ex ipso sunt peccata, quæ naturam non servant sed vitiant ; quæ peccata ex voluntate esse peccantium multis modis sancta scriptura testatur.—Id. Tom. vi. fol. 115, col. 2.]

[6 certum diem, Lat.]

[7 impiis, Lat. omitted ; for the ungodly.]

[Rom. ix. 18.]

But whereas the apostle saith, "He hath mercy on whom he will, and whom he will he hardeneth;" we must not so wrest it to say, that God doth of necessity drive any man to sin, and that therefore he is the cause of sin. For the will of God is good and just, and willeth nothing but what is expedient, and not repugnant to nature and the word of God. And therefore it is that the prophet crieth: "The Lord is just in all his ways, and holy in all his works." Psal. cxlv.

Thus have I out of much that may be said picked out a little, and laid it before your eyes, dearly beloved, for you to consider, of the cause of sin.

The differences of sin. We are now come to demonstrate the first parts which were set down in the description of sin immediately upon the beginning of this sermon. They are in number two: the first is, "Sin is the natural corruption of mankind;" the latter is, "And the action that riseth of it contrary to the law of God." Some verily, in setting down the kinds or differences of sins, do very well and advisedly say, "Of sins, one is original, and another actual." I mean in order to speak of both, so far as God shall give me grace: and first, of the same natural corruption in mankind; that is, of original sin.

Original sin. Now therefore it is called original sin, because it cometh from the first beginning, being derived from our first parents into us all by lineal descent and continual course from one to another; for we bring it with us in our nature from our mother's womb into this life.

Of this sin there are many definitions made, which as they do not disagree among themselves, so yet is one of them more full and evident than another of them is. Some say, Original sin is the corruption of nature from the first perfectness. Other some say, It is the corruption of man's nature, which maketh that we do not truly obey the law of God, and are not without sin. Again; some call it a want, or defect; other call it concupiscence; which might better seem to be the fruit of original sin, that is, of our corruption. Other call it an inordinateness of appetites, which is left in nature[1]. Anselmus, a late writer, saith: "Original sin is the want of

[1 The various definitions of original sin from the fathers and schoolmen, &c., are collected in Jod. Coccii Thesaur. Cathol. p. 100, &c. Colon. 1620.]

original righteousness[2]." But this is thought to have been spoken somewhat too briefly; for the force of sin seemeth to be not sufficiently expressed: for our nature is not only void and barren of goodness, but also most abundant and fruitful of all evils and naughtiness. Therefore the definition of Hugo is taken for the better, who saith: "Original sin is ignorance in the mind, and concupiscence in the flesh[3]." But yet this seemeth to be a far fuller and better definition: "Original sin is the vice or depravation of the whole man, whereby he cannot understand[4] God and his will; but of a perverse judgment of things doth overthwartly, and perverteth all things[5]."

And now among all these definitions I wish you, dearly beloved, to consider of this also: Original sin is the inheritably descending naughtiness or corruption of our nature, which doth first make us endangered to the wrath of God, and then bringeth forth in us those works which the scripture calleth the works of the flesh. Therefore this original sin is neither a deed, nor a word, nor a thought; but a disease, a vice[6], a depravation, I say, of judgment and concupiscence; or a corruption of the whole man[7], that is, of the understanding, will, and all the power of man; out of which at last do flow all evil thoughts, naughty words, and wicked deeds.

This sin taketh beginning at and of Adam; and for that cause it is called the inheritably descending naughtiness and corruption of our nature. Concerning the corruption and sin of Adam, out of whom we are all born sinners, I have already sufficiently spoken, where I treated of the cause of sin[8]; and by and by hereafter shall follow somewhat more of the same

The beginning of original sin.

[2 Hoc peccatum, quod originale dico, aliud intelligere nequeo in eisdem (al. ipsis) infantibus, nisi ipsam, quam supra posui, factam per inobedientiam Adæ justitiæ nuditatem.—Anselmi Opp. de Concept. Virg. et Orig. Pec. cap. 27. p. 106. Lutet. Par. 1675.]

[3 Hoc autem vitium originis humanæ duplici corruptione naturam inficit: ignorantia scilicet mentem, et concupiscentia carnem.—Hugo de S. Victore de Sacr. Fid. Lib. I. par. 7. Tom. III. p. 397. col. 2. Mogunt. 1617.]

[4 nec animo persequi, Lat. omitted; nor follow after with his mind.]

[5 Vid. Bucer. de Vera Eccles. &c. compos. p. 105. ed. 1543.]

[6 morbus sive vitium, Lat.]

[7 totius humanæ naturæ, Lat.]　　　[8 See above, page 371.]

argument; so that I have no need to repeat anything here : I will therefore now pass forth to the rest.

The Pela-
gians. The Pelagians denied that this evil of original sin was hereditary ; for these are the very words of Pelagius himself : " As without virtue, so are we also born without vice ; and before the action of our own will, that alone is in man which God created[1]." These words of his are somewhat obscure ; but Cœlestius, the partner of Pelagius, did more openly spue out this poison, and say : "We did not therefore say that infants are to be baptized into the remission of sins, to the end that we should seem thereby to affirm that sin is *ex traduce,* or hereditary ; which is utterly contrary to the catholic sense : because sin is not born with man, but is afterward put in ure by man ; because it is declared to be, not the fault of the nature, but of the will[2]." Again Pelagius said, "That that first sin did not hurt the first man only, but all mankind also, his issue and offspring :" but he doth immediately add, "not by propagation, but by example ;" that is to say, not that "they which came of him drew any vice of him, but because they that sinned afterward did in sinning imitate him that sinned first and before them[3]." This is to be seen in Aurelius Augustinus *De peccato originali contra Pelagium et Cœlestium,* Lib. II. cap. 6, 13, and 15.

That heredi-
tary evil is
in, and is
born together
with man. We therefore must prove by the testimonies of holy scripture, that the evil is hereditary in man ; and that original sin is born together with us, that is, that all men are born sinners into the world. The prophet therefore doth plainly cry, Psalm li., " Behold, I was born in wickedness,

[1 Ut sine virtute, ita et sine vitio procreamur : atque ante actionem propriæ voluntatis id solum in homine est, quod Deus condidit.— August. de Pec. Orig. contra Pelag. et Celest. Lib. II. cap. 13. Opp. Tom. VII. fol. 163. col. 2.]

[2 In remissionem autem peccatorum baptizandos infantes, non idcirco diximus, ut peccatum ex traduce firmare videamur : quod longe a catholico sensu alienum est; quia peccatum non cum homine nascitur, quod postmodum exercetur ab homine; quia non naturæ delictum, sed voluntatis esse demonstratur.—Ibid. Tom. VII. fol. 162. col. 3.]

[3 Dicit (Pelagius) non tantum primo homini, sed etiam humano generi primum illud obfuisse peccatum, non propagine sed exemplo : id est, non quod ex illo traxerint aliquod vitium, qui ex illo propagati sunt; sed quod eum primum peccantem imitati sunt omnes, qui postea peccaverunt.—Ibid. fol. 163. col. 2.]

and in sin hath my mother conceived me[4];" or, as another
translation out of the Hebrew saith: " Behold, I was shapen
in iniquity, and in sin my mother cherished or warmed me[5]:"
that is to say, sin did then immediately cleave unto me,
when I was once conceived and nourished in my mother's
womb.   Now that happened, undoubtedly, not by any vice
of matrimony, (for the wedlock-bed is holy and undefiled;)
but *ex traduce*, and by propagation.   For Job in his fourteenth chapter saith manifestly: "Who can make or bring
forth a pure or clean thing of that which is unclean[6]? no
body undoubtedly is able to do it."   Of that sort also there
are many other sayings in the fifteenth and five and twentieth chapters of the same book.   And Paul, the holy apostle
of Christ, in the fifth to the Romans, doth most evidently
say : " As by one man sin entered into the world, and death
by sin ; even so death entered into all men, insomuch as all
have sinned.   For unto the law was sin in the world : but
sin is not imputed when there is no law.   Nevertheless
death reigned from Adam unto Moses, over them also that
had not sinned with like transgression as did Adam," &c.
Doth not the apostle in these words manifestly shew the
propagation of sin, saying, " Sin entered by one man into
the world; death entered into all men, insomuch as they
have all sinned;" to wit, insomuch as they are all subject to
corruption ?   And, that no men either before or after Moses
might be excepted, he addeth : " Death reigned from Adam
unto Moses over them also which had not sinned with the
like transgression as did Adam ;" that is to say, over them
which had not[7] sinned of their own will, as Adam had, but
drew from him original sin by propagation.   St Augustine
doth more fully excuss and handle this argument in his first
book *De peccatorum meritis et remissione*, in the ninth,
tenth, and eleventh chapter, and the rest as they follow in
order[8].   Again, Paul in the seventh to the Romans calleth
this evil the sin that dwelleth in us, that is to say, the sin

[4 Vulg. Vers. Ps. l. 7.]   [5 Calvin. in loc. cit.]
[6 ex immunda (nimirum massa) Lat.; out of an unclean (he
means) lump.]
[7 nondum, Lat. ; not yet.]
[8 Hoc autem apostolicum testimonium in quo ait, Per unum hominem, &c.—Aug. Opp. Tom. vii. fol. 135. col. 1.]

that is begotten and born with us: for he addeth, "I am carnal, sold under sin;" and, "I know that in me (that is, my flesh) there dwelleth no good." And therefore the [1 John i. 8.] blessed apostle and evangelist John telleth us, that "if we say we have no sin, we deceive ourselves, and the truth is not in us." He saith very significantly, 'we have,' and not, 'we have had,' or, 'we shall have;' for by our corrupt nature we have that proper unto us. Therefore it is manifest that the fiction of the Pelagians is false, whereby they affirm that we are born without vice: it is false, that the voluntary action only, and not the corruption or depravation which is not yet burst forth to the deed[1], is sin.

Voluntary sin.

And Augustine doth in one place call even that voluntary sin original sin; and that two sundry ways: first, not simply of itself, but in respect of Adam; because it, being committed by the naughty will of Adam, is drawn and made hereditary in us: secondly, because a naughty lust may be named a will[2]. For *Lib. Retract.* i. cap. 15, he saith: "If any man doth say, that even the very lust is nothing else but will, such a will yet as is vicious and subject to sin, he needeth not to be gainsaid: for where the thing is manifest, we must not strive about terms and words. For so it is proved, that without will there is no sin either in deed or in propagation[3];" that is, either actual or original[4]. Thus much Augustine, who doth also allege other sayings like to this in his third book *Contra Julianum Pelagianum*, chap. 5.[5] It shall be sufficient to us even without them to learn by the testimonies of the holy scriptures, that sin is not only

[1 in opus pravum, Lat.; to the evil deed.]

[2 Et illud quod in parvulis dicitur originale peccatum ... non absurde vocatur etiam voluntarium, quia ex primi hominis mala voluntate contractum, factum est quodammodo hæreditarium.—Aug. Retract. Lib. i. cap. 13. Opp. Tom. i. fol. 4. col. 3.]

[3 Quod si quisquam dicit etiam ipsam cupiditatem nihil esse aliud quam voluntatem, sed vitiosam peccatoque servientem, non resistendum est, nec de verbis, cum res constat, controversia facienda est. Sic enim ostenditur sine voluntate nullum esse peccatum, sive in opere sive in origine.—Id. ibid. cap. 15. Tom. i. fol. 5. col. 4.]

[4 that is—original; the translator's addition.]

[5 Frustra itaque putas ideo in parvulis non esse delictum, quia sine voluntate, quæ in eis nulla est, esse non potest, &c.—Id. contr. Jul. Pelag. Lib. iii. cap. 5. Tom. vii. fol. 204. col. 4.]

a voluntary action, but also an hereditary corruption or depravation that cometh by inheritance.

Not unlike to all this[6] is that sentence in Ezechiel, where
the Lord saith : "The son shall not bear the iniquity of the
father, but every man shall die in his own sin." For
Adam's fall should do us no harm, if it were not so that
even from him there is sprung up in us such a perverseness
as is worthy of God's just judgment. But now, since all the
inclination, disposition, and desire of our nature, even in a
child but one day old, is repugnant to the pureness and will
of God, which is only good; no man therefore is punished
for his father, but every one for his own iniquity : and calamities fall even on the youngest babes, whom we see to be
touched with many afflictions by the holy and just judgment
of the most just God.

Neither is their objection any whit stronger which say,
that the children of holy parents cannot draw or take any
spot of their parents; for they have their lineal descent
of the fleshly generation, and not of the spiritual regeneration. And whereas the apostle said, "The unbelieving
husband is sanctified by the wife, and the unbelieving wife
is sanctified by the husband : else were your children unclean; but now are they clean :" it is not repugnant to our
former allegations. For they are called holy, not by the
prerogative of their birth or generation, as though children
were born[7] holy without any spot or vice at all; but for
because they, being born by nature corrupt, are by the
virtue of the covenant and grace made pure, and uncleanness
is not imputed to them, for Christ his sake, or the remission
of sins which is pronounced in these words : "I will be thy
God, and the God of thy seed after thee." For of old,
even those children which of the seed of Abraham were
holy and blessed received notwithstanding the sign of circumcision. Now what need, I pray you, had they had of
circumcision, or purging, if by their birth they had had no
uncleanness in them ?

That therefore is utterly false which ye heard even now
that Cœlestius, the Pelagian, did utter in these words : "We
did not therefore say that infants are to be baptized into

Marginal notes:
The son shall not bear the iniquity of the father. [Ezek. xviii. 20.]

To be born of holy parents.

[1 Cor. vii. 14.]

The catholic doctrine of original sin.

[6 His omnibus nihil repugnat, Lat.]
[7 sic, Lat. omitted; under these circumstances.]

the remission of sins, to the end that we should thereby seem to affirm that sin is *ex traduce*, or hereditary; which is utterly contrary to the catholic sense." For it is catholic and true doctrine, that the children of the Jews were circumcised, not so much only because they were partakers of the divine covenant, as for because that all the antiquity of holy fathers did so confess, that in infants there was somewhat which had need of cutting, that is, which had need to be remitted by the grace of God, and not be imputed to them unto death. It is catholic and true doctrine, that the infants of Christians are baptized, not so much because they are the children of God and freely received into the covenant; as for because there is in them, even from their birth, somewhat which the Lord by his grace doth wash away, lest it should bring upon them death and damnation. Yea, that cannot be catholic, which doth so manifestly repugn so many evident places of scripture, which prove that in infants there is sin by propagation. To confirm this we may add, that St Augustine in his first book *Contra Julianum Pelagianum*, cap. 2, gathereth together the testimonies of the most excellent learned bishops and doctors in the primitive[1] church, by which he proveth that all the ministers of the churches, even from the apostles' time, did both acknowledge and openly teach original sin. In that place he citeth the testimonies of Irenæus, Cyprian, Reticius, Olympius, Hilary, and Ambrose, his father and master in christian doctrine[2], Innocent, Gregory, Basil, and John Chrysostom; and at length he inferreth : "Wilt thou now call so great a consent of catholic priests a conspiracy of naughty men? Neither think thou that St Hierome is to be contemned, because he was but a priest only, and no bishop; who, being skilful in the Greek, Latin, and Hebrew tongues, and passing from the west unto the east church, lived in holy places and the study of the sacred scripture, even to his crone[3] and crooked age. He read all, or in a manner all, the works of them which in both parts of the world did write of ecclesiastical doctrine; and yet he neither held nor taught any otherwise of this point of doctrine[4]." And again the same Augustine,

All the ancient doctors or fathers of the church confess (with one assent) original sin.

The east and west churches.

[1 primitive, not in Lat.]   [2 in Christo, Lat.]
[3 crones: old ewes who have lost their teeth. Grose's Provincial Glossary, in voc.]
[4 An tantam consensionem sacerdotum catholicorum conspira-

in his third book *De Peccatorum Meritis et Remissione,* cap. 6, saith : " Hierome, expounding the prophecy of Jonas, when he came to that place where mention is made that even the little children were chastened with fasting, saith : 'It began with the eldest, and came even to the youngest. For there is none without sin; no, not he which is but one day old, nor he whose grey head hath seen many years. For if the stars are not clean in the sight of God, how much more unclean are dust[5] and putrefying earth, and those which are in subjection to the sin of Adam's transgression !'" To these words of Hierome doth Augustine himself annex this that followeth : "If it were so that we might easily ask it of this most learned man, how many teachers of the holy scriptures in both the tongues, and how many writers of christian treatises would he reckon up, which, since the time that Christ his church was first planted, have themselves neither thought, of their predecessors learned, nor taught their successors, any other than this doctrine touching original sin! I verily, though I have read nothing so much as he, do not remember that I have read any other doctrine of Christians which admit or receive both the testaments, whether they were in the unity of the catholic church, or otherwise in schisms and heresies : I do not remember that I have read any other thing in them, whose writings touching this matter I could come by to read them, if either they did follow, or thought that they did follow, or would have men believe that they did follow, the canonical scriptures[6]." Thus far hath Augustine ; teaching, in

tionem dicturus es perditorum? Nec sanctum Hieronymum, quia presbyter fuit, contemnendum arbitreris ; qui Græco et Latino, insuper et Hebræo eruditus eloquio, ex occidentali ad orientalem transiens ecclesiam, in locis sanctis atque in literis sacris usque ad decrepitam vixit ætatem. Hic omnes vel pene omnes, qui ante illum ex utraque parte orbis de doctrina ecclesiastica scripserant, legit, nec aliam de hac re tenuit prompsitque sententiam.—Aug. Opp. Tom. VII. fol. 197. col. 1.]

[5 vermis, Lat. ; a worm.]

[6 Nam in eo quod in Jonam prophetam scripsit (Hieronymus), cum ad eum venisset locum, ubi commemorantur etiam parvuli jejunio castigati : Major, inquit, ætas incipit, et usque ad minorem pervenit. Nullus enim absque peccato, nec si unius quidem diei fuerit vita ejus, et innumerabiles anni vitæ illius. Si enim stellæ mundæ non sunt in conspectu Dei, quanto magis vermis et putredo, et ii qui peccato offendentis Adam tenentur obnoxii ! Hunc doctissimum virum si facile

the very beginning, that all the saints did by a full consent
and agreement in doctrine most expressly grant and confess,
that original sin is even in new-born infants. Methinketh
that St Hierome did not only in Jonas, but also much more
evidently in Ezechiel, confess and affirm original sin. His words
are to be seen, *Comment. lib.* xiv. in cap. 47, *ad Ezechielem*,
and are verbatim as followeth: "What man can make his
boast that he hath a chaste heart, or to whose mind by the
windows of the eyes the death of concupiscence, or (to use a
milder term) the tickling of the mind, doth not enter in? For
the world is set in wickedness; and even from his childhood
the heart of man is set to naughtiness; so that not the very
first day of a man's nativity his nature is free from sin and
naughtiness. Whereupon David in the Psalm saith: 'For
behold I was conceived in iniquity, and in sin my mother conceived me.' Not in the iniquities of my mother, or in mine
own sins; but in the iniquities of our mortal state. And
therefore the apostle saith, 'Death reigned from Adam to
Moses, over them also which had not sinned with the like
transgression as did Adam[1].'" Thus much hath Hierome.
And we have hitherto alleged all these sayings, to the end

interrogare possemus, quam multas utriusque linguæ divinarum scripturarum tractatores et Christianarum disputationum scriptores com-
memoraret, qui non aliud ex quo Christi ecclesia est constituta
senserunt, non aliud a majoribus acceperunt, non aliud posteris tradiderunt! Ego quidem, quamvis longe pauciora legerim, non memini
me aliud audisse a Christianis, qui utrumque accipiunt testamentum,
non solum in catholica ecclesia, verum etiam in qualibet hæresi vel
schismate constitutis; non memini me aliud legisse apud eos, quos de
his rebus aliquid scribentes legere potui, qui scripturas canonicas
sequerentur, vel sequi se crederent credive voluissent.—August. Opp.
Tom. vii. fol. 148. col. 4.]

[1 Quis enim hominum gloriari potest castum se habere cor? vel
ad cujus mentem per oculorum fenestras mors concupiscentiæ non
introivit, et, ut parum dicam, animi titillatio? Mundus enim in ma-
ligno positus est; et a pueritia appositum est cor hominis ad malum: ut ne unius quidem diei a nativitatis suæ exordio sine peccato sit
humana conditio. Unde et David confitetur in Psalmo, Ecce enim in
iniquitatibus conceptus sum, et in peccatis concepit me mater mea.
Non in iniquitatibus matris meæ, vel certe meis; sed in iniquitatibus
humanæ conditionis. Unde et apostolus dicit, Regnavit mors ab Adam
usque ad Moysen, etiam super eos qui non peccaverunt in similitudinem
prævaricationis Adæ.—Hieron. Opp. Tom. iii. col. 1055. Par. 1704.]

we might prove that original sin is the natural or hereditary corruption of man's nature.

Let us now see what and how great the hereditary naughtiness or corruption of our nature is, and what power it hath to work[2] in man. Our nature verily, as I shewed you above, was before the fall most excellent and pure in our father Adam : but after the fall it did by God's just judgment become corrupt and utterly naught, which is in that naughtiness by propagation, or *ex traduce*, derived into all us which are the posterity and offspring of Adam; as both experience and the thing itself do evidently declare, as well in sucklings or infants as those of riper years. For even very babes give manifest tokens of evident depravation so soon as they once begin to be able to do anything; yea, before they can perfectly sound any one syllable of a whole word. All our understanding is dull, blunt, gross, and altogether blind in heavenly things. Our judgment in divine matters is perverse and frivolous. For there arise in us most horrible and absurd thoughts and opinions touching God, his judgments, and wonderful works. Yea, our whole mind is apt and ready to errors, to fables, and our own destruction : and when as our judgments are nothing but mere folly, yet do we prefer them far above God's wisdom, which we esteem but foolishness in comparison of our own conceits and corrupt imaginations ; for he lied not which said : " The natural man perceiveth not the things of the Spirit of God ; for they are foolishness unto him ; neither can he know them, because they are spiritually discerned." Now Paul calleth him the natural man[3], which liveth naturally by the vital spirit, and is not regenerate by the Holy Ghost : and since we all are such, we are therefore wholly overcome and governed of *philautia*, that is, too great a self-love and delight in ourselves, whereby all things that we ourselves do work do highly please us ; looking still very busily to our own selves and our commodity, when in the meantime we neglect all others, yea, rather do afflict them. Neither did Plato unadvisedly esteem that vice of self-love to be the very root of every evil[4]. Furthermore, our whole will is

Marginal notes: What and how great the corruption of our nature is.

[1 Cor. ii. 14.]

[2 quid efficiat, Lat.]
[3 animalem hominem, Lat.]
[4 Stobæi Floril. Tit. xxiii. Tom. i. p. 427. ed. Gaisford. Oxon. 1822.]

led captive by concupiscence, which, as a root envenomed with poison, infecteth all that is in man, and doth incline, draw on, and drive men to things carnal, forbidden, and contrary to God, to the end that he may greedily pursue them, put all his delight in them, and content himself with them. Moreover there is in us no power or ability to do any good: for we are slow, sluggish, and heavy to goodness; but lively, quick, and ready enough to any evil or naughtiness. And, that I may at last conclude, and briefly express the whole force and signification of our hereditary depravation and corruption; I say, that this depravation of our nature is nothing else but the blotting of God's image in us. There was in our father Adam before his fall the very image and likeness of God; which image, as the apostle expoundeth it, was a conformity and participation of God's wisdom, justice, holiness, truth, integrity, innocency, immortality, and eternal felicity. Therefore what else can the blotting or wiping out of this image be but original sin; that is, the hatred of God, the ignorance of God, foolishness, distrustfulness, desperation, self-love, unrighteousness, uncleanness, lying, hypocrisy, vanity, corruption, violent injury, wickedness, mortality, and eternal infelicity? This corrupt image and likeness is by propagation derived into us all, according to that saying in the fifth of Genesis: "Adam begat a son in his own similitude and likeness." Therefore as our father Adam was himself corrupted, depraved, and full of calamities, so hath he begotten us his sons corrupt, depraved, and full of miseries[1]: so that all we which do descend of his unpure seed are born infected with the contagious poison of sin. For of a rotten root do spring as rotten branches, which in like manner put over their rottenness into the little twigs that shoot out and grow upon them.

Our deprava-tion is the blotting out of the image of God in us.

Original sin condemneth.

And this evil verily, this corruption and this sin, although it lie hid in infants, and by reason of their tender age doth not break forth into any deed-doing, yet notwithstanding it is a sin; and such a sin verily as maketh them endangered unto God's wrath, and separateth them from the fellowship of God. For with the most holy God, who " is a consuming fire," no man can abide but he that is unspotted and clean from the filthiness of sins. And Paul saith : " All have sinned,

[Rom. iii. 23.]

[1 corrupt—miseries, the translator's addition.]

and are destitute, or have need, of the glory of God." This glory of God is the very image of God: whereof because they are destitute, they being corrupted with original sin are worthily excluded from the fellowship of God.   To this place doth belong the whole treatise of concupiscence in the fourth sermon of this third Decade: where I taught you, that bare concupiscence, which is not yet burst forth to the deed-doing, is a sin; and that too such a sin as maketh all men subject to the curse of God. For it is written: "Cursed [Deut. xxvii. 26; Gal. iii. 10.] be every one which abideth not in all things that are written in the book of this law."   Therefore the first effect of original sin is this, that it bringeth wrath, death, and damnation upon very infants, and so consequently upon all mankind: whereof, that it may the more firmly be settled in every man's mind without all scruple of doubting, I will by some store of testimonies out of the scripture make manifest proof unto you, not by repeating those places again which I have already cited in this sermon, and in the fourth sermon of this third Decade.

The Lord in the gospel saith to Nicodemus: "Verily, I say unto thee, unless a man be born from above[2], he cannot see the kingdom of God."   And again[3]: "Unless a man be [John iii. 3, 5, 6.] born of water and of the Holy Ghost[4], he cannot enter into the kingdom of God.   That which is born of the flesh is flesh; and that which is born of the Spirit is spirit."   In these words are comprehended two things worthy to be remembered, and very consonant to our present argument. First, none enter into the kingdom of heaven but those that be regenerate from above[5] by the Holy Ghost: therefore our first birth tendeth to death, and not to life; for in our first nativity we are born to death.   The latter is, "That which is born of flesh is flesh:" therefore in our first nativity we are all born flesh.   But touching the disposition of the flesh and the force thereof, the apostle saith: "The fleshly mind is [Rom. viii. 7.] enmity against God: for it is not obedient to the law of God, neither can be."   Therefore that fleshly birth engendereth us, not the friends and sons, but the enemies, of God; and so consequently doth make us endangered to the wrath of God.

[2 So margin of Auth. Ver.]
[3 Amen dico tibi, Lat. omitted; Verily, I say unto thee.]
[4 et spiritu, Lat.]   [5 e cœlo, Lat.]

Paul in his second chapter to the Ephesians saith: "We were by nature the sons of wrath, even as other." In which words he pronounceth that all men are damned. For all those that are damned, or are worthy of eternal death, and all such with whom God hath good cause to be offended, he calleth the sons of wrath, after the proper phrase of the Hebrew speech. For the wrath of God doth signify the punishment which is by the just judgment of God laid upon us men. And he is called the child of death, which is adjudged or appointed to be killed. So is also the son of perdition, &c. Now mark, that he calleth us all the sons of wrath, that is, the subjects of pain and damnation, even by nature, in birth, from our mother's womb. But whatsoever is naturally in all men, that is original: therefore original sin maketh us the sons of wrath; that is, we are all for our original corruption made subject to death and utter damnation. This place of Paul for the proof of this argument is worthy to be remembered[1].

The same apostle in the first to the Colossians saith: "God hath delivered us from the power of darkness, and hath translated us into the kingdom of his dear Son." Now if we be translated into the kingdom of the Son of God, then were we once in the kingdom of the devil. And to this place belong very many testimonies of the same apostle in the fifth chapter of his Epistle to the Romans: "By one man's sin many are dead." Again; "By one that sinned came death; for judgment came by one unto condemnation." Again; "For the sin of one death reigned by the means of one." And again; "By the sin of one sin came upon all men[2] unto condemnation." Finally, original sin is by David and Paul expressly called sin: therefore death is due to original sin; for "the reward of sin is death."

Original sin is proper to all.

We do therefore conclude, that infants do bring damnation with them into this world even from their mothers' wombs; because they bring with them a corrupt nature: and therefore they perish not by any others', but by their own, fault and naughtiness. For although St Augustine doth in one place seem to call this sin *Peccatum alienum*, that is, another's sin, (that thereby he may shew how it is by

[1 valde est insignis, Lat.]
[2 propagatum est malum, Lat. and Erasmus.]

propagation derived from other into us,) yet doth he confess that it is in very deed and truly proper to all and every several one of us[3]. And although it be so, that for lack of age in a new-born babe this disease hath not already brought forth the fruit of his iniquity ; yet notwithstanding the very whole nature of the babe is nothing but filthy corruption, and a certain seed of sin and wickedness, which cannot choose but be abominable unto the Lord : for God doth hate all manner of uncleanness[4].

With this agreeth[5] that sentence of Paul, where he saith : "Where no law is, there is no transgression." For the apostle doth not absolutely say that the sin or transgression (which is sin in very deed in the sight of God) is no sin; but he respecteth the estimation of men, how they do repute it. For men, before sin doth appear and is opened unto them by the law, do not so repute or think of sin as it ought in very deed to be esteemed. The same Paul in another place saith : " Sin without the law was once dead:" and, " I once lived without law ; but when the law came, sin revived." If so be now that sin revived, then did it live before the law, afore it was stirred up by the law, although it did not so rifely then, as now, shew forth the strength and force of itself. To this also is to be added that saying of Paul : " Sin was in the world even to the law ; but sin is not imputed when there is no law." Lo here, sin was in the world before the law, but it was not imputed; not because God did not impute it, but because men do not impute it to themselves. Under cinders doth fire lie hid; which is very fire indeed, but, because it casteth out no flame or light of itself, it is not thought to be fire. And for that cause the learned and godly man of famous memory, Ulderick Zuinglius[6],

Where there is no law there is no transgression. [Rom. iv. 15.]

Rom. vii.

[Rom. v. 13]

Ulderick Zuinglius of original sin.

[3 Nec sic dicuntur ista *aliena peccata*, tanquam omnino ad parvulos non pertineant... Sed dicuntur *aliena*, quia nondum ipsi agebant vitas proprias, sed quicquid erat in futura propagine vita unius hominis continebat.—August. Marcellino de Baptism. Parv. Epist. 16. Opp. Tom. ii. fol. 180. col. 3. Par. 1531.]

[4 This paragraph is borrowed almost literally from Calvin, Instit. Lib. ii. cap. 1. § 8.]

[5 His nihil repugnat, Lat.]

[6 Peccatum bifariam in evangelica doctrina accipitur: primum, pro morbo isto, quem ex generis auctore contrahimus, quo amori nostri addictis suum... Eum morbum intelligit Paulus Rom. vii. quum dicit,

did diligently distinguish betwixt sin and disease or infirmity, when once he had occasion to dispute of original sin, which he chose rather to call a disease than sin: because by the name of sin all men do understand the naughty act committed by our own consent and will against the law of God; but by the name of disease or sickness they understand a certain corruption and depravation of the nature that was created good, and the miserable condition of bondage whereinto it is brought: even as also we read[1] before, that Augustine did call this original sin *peccatum alienum*, another's sin, that thereby he might give us to understand that it is hereditary, and doth descend from others into us; and yet he denied not but it is proper to every several one of us. In like manner Zuinglius denied not original sin, as some did falsely slander him: he thought not that by itself it is unhurtful to infants, but so far forth as it is by the grace of God, through the blood of Jesus Christ, in the virtue of God's promise and covenant, made harmless unto them[2]. His mind was to make an exquisite difference betwixt the actual and original sins[3]. For in rendering an account of his faith in the council held at

Jam non ego operor illud, sed inhabitans in me peccatum . . . Secundo loco accipitur peccatum pro eo quod contra legem fit; ut, per legem cognitio peccati. Rom. vii. Actio ergo quæcunque tandem, quæ contra legem fit, peccatum appellatur.—Zuingl. de Vera et Falsa Relig. Comment. p. 116. Tiguri. 1525.]

[1 audivimus, Lat.; heard, ed. 1577.]

[2 Vitium hoc et morbus homini, quoad bonum et malum non discernit, pro peccato et culpa imputari nequit, utcunque gravis sit et pestifer. Unde colligimus peccatum originale morbum quidem esse, qui tamen per se culpabilis non est, nec damnationis pœnam inferre potest, . . . donec homo contagione hac corruptus legem Domini transgreditur; quod tum demum fieri consuevit, cum legem sibi positam videt et intelligit . . . Peccatum ergo originale damnationem non meretur, si modo quis parentes fideles nactus fuerit. Quæcunque enim hoc loco de originali infantium vel parvulorum peccato loquimur, ad fidelium duntaxat infantes referri debent, et de solis illis intelligi.— Id. De Baptismo. Tom. II. pp. 90, 89.]

[3 Diximus originalem contagionem morbum esse, non peccatum, quod peccatum cum culpa conjunctum est; culpa vero ex commisso vel admisso ejus nascitur qui facinus designavit . . . Morbus ergo iste ac vitium, primi parentis culpa inflictus, infecit sobolem, non soboles seipsam. Cum ergo peccatum appellatur in scripturis, per denominationem hoc fieri constare jam satis arbitror.—Id. De Pecc. Orig. ad Urban. Rheg. Tom. II. p. 116.]

Augusta[4], the year of our Lord 1530, he said : "I acknowledge
that original sin is by condition and contagion born in and with
all them that are begotten by the act of a man and a woman :
and I know that we are the sons of wrath. Neither am I anything against it, that this disease and condition should, as Paul
termeth it, be called sin : yea, it is such a sin, as that they,
whosoever are born in it, are the enemies and adversaries of
God Almighty. For hither doth the condition of their birth
draw them, and not the committing of wickedness, except it
be so far forth as our first parent committed it. The very
true cause therefore of our disloyalty and death is the crime
and wickedness which Adam committed ; and that in very
deed is sin : and this sin which cleaveth to us is in very deed
a disease and condition, yea, it is a necessity of dying[5]." And
so forth as followeth ; for hitherto I have rehearsed his
very words.

There is now remaining the other effect of original sin for
me to expound.   It breaketh out and bringeth forth in us
those works that the scriptures call the works of the flesh ;
even like as when an oven set on fire doth cast out flames
and sparkles ; or as a fountain that ever springeth doth
pour out water in great abundance[6].   There is no quietness
in the nature of man : for covetousness with filthy lust ariseth
in it, ambition cleaveth to it, anger invadeth it, pride puffeth
it up and causeth it to swell, drunkenness delighteth it, and
envy torments both thyself and others.   Therefore the Lord
in the gospel saith : " Out of the heart proceed evil thoughts, [Matt. xv. 19.]
murders, adulteries, whoredoms, thefts, false-witness-bearings,
and evil speakings."   Again, Paul in the fifth chapter to the

Original sin bringeth forth the works of the flesh.

[4 Augsburg.   See Sleidan. Comment. de Statu Relig. Lib. VII.]

[5 Originale peccatum per conditionem et contagionem agnasci
omnibus, qui ex adfectu maris et fœminæ gignuntur, agnosco, et nos
esse natura filios iræ scio . . . . Quanquam nihil moror hunc morbum et
conditionem, juxta Pauli morem, appellari peccatum.   Imo tale est
peccatum, ut quicunque in eo nascuntur hostes et adversarii Dei sunt.
Huc enim trahit illos nativitatis conditio, non sceleris perpetratio, nisi
quantum hoc semel perpetravit primus parens.   Vera igitur perdu-
ellionis et mortis causa est perpetratum ab Adam crimen ac nefas ;
atque hoc vere est peccatum : at peccatum istud, quod nobis adhærescit,
et vere morbus et conditio, imo necessitas est moriendi.—Id. ad Carol.
Rom. Imp. Fidei ratio. Tom. II. p. 539.]

[6 aut scaturigo aquam perenniter profundit, Lat.]

Galatians doth reckon up no small number of the works of the flesh; even as he doth the like also in the first and third chapters of his epistle to the Romans. In the fourth to the Ephesians he doth very properly[1] describe those works of the flesh, which spring out of the natural corruption of all them[2] which are not regenerate by the Holy Ghost. "This I say," saith he, "and testify unto you[3], that ye henceforth walk not as other Gentiles walk, in vanity of their mind; darkened in cogitation, being alienated from the life of God by the ignorance that is in them, by the blindness of their hearts: which being past feeling have given themselves over unto wantonness, to work all uncleanness with greediness." This, though it be but little, shall suffice for this place; for I will more largely prosecute it in the treatise of actual sin: to the handling whereof I will presently pass, so soon as I have by the way admonished you, that I have not without good cause thus far in many words spoken of the cause of original sin, that is, of man's depravation and the corruption of all his strength.

On these points the foundations of our faith are laid.

For as in these are opened the veins of pure doctrine, so in them are placed the foundations of our faith and whole belief. For if there be no original sin, then is there no grace: or if there be any, yet shall it have nothing to work in us. If our own strength is whole and sound, then have we no need of any physician. In vain therefore came the Son of God into the world[4]; for then shall men be saved by their own strength and ability: and so shall the foundation of our faith be quite turned upside down. Therefore St Augustine is very vehement in this cause; whose golden words I will recite unto you, dearly beloved, out of his second book *De Originali Peccato contra Pelagium et Coelestium.* In the twenty-third and twenty-fourth chapters I find written as followeth: "There is great diversity in these questions, which are thought to be beside the articles of faith, and those wherein (keeping sound the faith whereby we are Christians) it is either not known what is true, and so the sentence definitive is suspended; or else it is otherwise guessed at by human and unassured suspicion than the thing itself in very deed is: as for example, when it is demanded of what sort and where

[1 graphice, Lat.]   [2 in omnibus, Lat.]
[3 per Dominum, Lat. omitted; by the Lord.]
[4 missus, Lat. omitted; being sent.]

paradise is, where God placed man whom he had made of the dust of the earth, when as notwithstanding christian faith doubteth not but that there is a paradise." And after the recital of a few more such questions, at last he saith : "Who may not perceive in these and such like sundry and innumerable questions, appertaining either to the most secret works of God, or the most dark and intricate places of the holy scriptures, which it is hard to comprehend or define in any certain order, both that many things are unknown without the peril of christian faith, and also that in some points men do err without any crime of heretical doctrine ? But concerning the two men; by the one of whom we are sold under sin, by the other redeemed from sin ; by one we are cast headlong into death, by the other we are made free unto life; because that man did in himself destroy us by doing his own will and not the will of him that made him, but this man hath in himself saved us by doing not his own will but the will of him that sent him ; therefore, in the consideration of these two men christian faith doth properly consist. For there is one God and one Mediator of God and man, the man Christ Jesus ; because there is none other name under heaven given unto men in which they must be saved ; and in him hath God appointed all men to trust, raising him up from death to life. Therefore christian verity doubteth not but that without this faith, that is, without the faith of the only Mediator of God and man, the man Christ Jesus ; without the belief, I say, of his resurrection, which God hath prescribed to men, which cannot be truly believed without the belief of his incarnation and death ; without the faith therefore of the incarnation, death, and resurrection of Christ, none of the ancient just men could be cleansed and justified of God from their sins : whether they were in the number of those just men whom the holy scripture mentioneth ; or in the number of those just men whom the scripture nameth [not], and yet are to be believed to have been either before the deluge, or betwixt the deluge and the law, or in the very time of the law ; not only among the children of Israel, as the prophets were, but also without that people, as Job was. For even their hearts were cleansed by the same faith of the Mediator, and charity was poured into them by the same Holy Spirit, which breatheth where he listeth, not following after merits, but even working the very merits

Christian faith consisteth in the consideration of two men.

Some were saved beside Israel, but not without Christ.

themselves. For God's grace will not be by any means, unless it be free by all means. Although therefore death reigned from Adam unto Moses, because the law given by Moses could not overcome it; for there was no such law given as could quicken, but such a law as whose office was to shew, that the dead, to the quickening of whom grace was necessary, were not only overthrown by the propagation and dominion of sin, but were also condemned by the hidden[1] transgression of the very law itself; not that every one should perish that did then understand it in the mercy of God, but that every one, being through the dominion of death appointed unto punishment and detected to himself by the transgression of the law, should seek for the help of God; that where sin abounded, grace might more abound, which alone doth deliver from the body of this death. Although therefore the law given by Moses could not rid any man from the kingdom of death, yet in the very time of the law were the men of God not under the terrifying, convincing, and punishing law, but under the delectable, saving, and delivering grace. There were among them some which said, 'In iniquity was I conceived, and in sin hath my mother fed me in her womb[2].' " And so forth; for hitherto I have cited the very words of St Augustine.

[1] The translator read *abdita* for *addita*.]

[2] Longe aliter se habent quæstiones istæ, quas esse præter fidem arbitratur, quam sunt illæ, in quibus, salva fide qua Christiani sumus, aut ignoratur quid verum sit et sententia definitiva suspenditur, aut aliter quam est humana et infirma suspicione conjicitur: veluti cum quæritur qualis vel ubi sit paradisus, ubi constituit Deus hominem quem formavit ex pulvere, cum tamen esse illum paradisum fides christiana non dubitet..... Quis enim non sentiat in his atque hujusmodi variis et innumerabilibus quæstionibus, sive ad obscurissima opera Dei sive ad scripturarum abditissimas latebras pertinentibus, quas certo aliquo genere complecti ac definire difficile est, et multa ignorari salva christiana fide, et alicubi errari sine aliquo hæretici dogmatis crimine? Sed in causa duorum hominum, quorum per unum venundati sumus sub peccato, per alterum redimimur a peccatis; per unum præcipitati sumus in mortem, per alterum liberamur ad vitam; quoniam ille nos in se perdidit faciendo voluntatem suam, non ejus a quo factus est, iste nos in se salvos fecit non faciendo voluntatem suam, sed ejus a quo missus est; in horum ergo duorum hominum causa proprie fides christiana consistit. Unus est enim Deus, et unus mediator Dei et hominum, homo Christus Jesus: quoniam non est aliud nomen sub cœlo datum hominibus, in quo oporteat

I have thus far spoken of original sin, of the native and hereditary corruption of our nature, which is the first part in the definition of sin. Here followeth now the latter part; to wit, the very action which ariseth of that corruption, the actual sin, I say, which is so called *ab actu*, that is, an act or a deed-doing. For insomuch as that corruption which is born together with and is hereditary in us doth not always lie hid, but worketh outwardly and sheweth forth itself, and doth at last bring forth an imp of her own kind and nature, which imp is actual sin; therefore we define actual sin to be an action, or work, or fruit, of our corrupt and naughty nature, expressing itself in thoughts, words, and works against the law of God, and thereby deserving the wrath of God.

nos salvos fieri, et in illo definivit Deus fidem omnibus, suscitans illum a mortuis. Itaque sine ista fide, hoc est, sine fide unius mediatoris Dei et hominum, hominis Christi Jesu; sine fide, inquam, resurrectionis ejus, quam Deus hominibus definivit, quæ utique sine incarnatione ejus ac morte non potest veraciter credi; sine fide ergo incarnationis et mortis et resurrectionis Christi, nec antiquos justos, ut justi essent a peccatis, potuisse mundari et Dei gratia justificari, veritas christiana non dubitat; sive in eis justis quos sancta scriptura commemorat, sive in eis justis quos quidem illa non commemorat, sed tamen fuisse credendi sunt vel ante diluvium, vel inde usque ad datam legem, vel ipsius legis tempore, non solum in filiis Israel, sicut fuerunt prophetæ, sed etiam extra eundem populum, sicut fuit Job. Et ipsorum enim corda eadem mundabantur mediatoris fide, et diffundebatur in eis caritas per Spiritum sanctum, qui ubi vult spirat, non merita sequens, sed etiam ipsa merita faciens. Non enim Dei gratia gratia erit ullo modo, nisi gratuita fuerit omni modo. Quamvis ergo mors regnaverit ab Adam usque ad Moysen, quia non eam potuit vincere nec lex data per Moysen, non enim data est quæ posset vivificare, sed quæ mortuos, quibus vivificandis esset gratia necessaria, non solum peccati propagatione et dominatione prostratos, verum etiam ipsius legis addita prævaricatione convictos, deberet ostendere, non ut periret quisquis hoc in Dei misericordia etiam tunc intelligeret, sed ut per regnum mortis ad supplicium destinatus etiam sibi ipsi per prævaricationem legis manifestatus Dei quæreret adjutorium, ut ubi abundavit peccatum superabundaret gratia, quæ sola liberat a corpore mortis hujus. Quamvis ergo nec lex per Moysen data potuerit a quoquam homine regnum mortis auferre, erant tamen et legis tempore homines Dei, non sub lege terrente, convincente, puniente, sed sub gratia delectante, sanante, liberante: erant qui dicerent, Ego in iniquitatibus conceptus sum, et in peccatis mater mea in utero me aluit.—August. Opp. Par. 1531. Tom. VII. fol. 164. col. 2. 3. de Pecc. Orig. contra Pelag. et Celest. Lib. II. capp. 23, 24, 25.]

So then by this the cause of actual sin is known to be the very corruption of mankind, which sheweth forth itself through concupiscence and evil affections : affections entice the will; and will, being helped with the other faculties in man that work together with it, doth finish actual sin. And that ye may more clearly perceive that which I say, I wish you to note, that our mind hath two parts : the understanding, or reason, or judgment; and the will or appetite. In the reason are the laws of nature, whereunto must be added the preaching, or reading, or knowledge of God's word. And now, as of good works in man there are two especial causes, to wit, sound judgment well framed by the word of God, and a will consenting and obeying thereunto, (and yet notwithstanding there is principally to be required the coming to of the Holy Ghost from heaven[1], to illuminate the mind and move forward the will;) even so we may most properly say that actual sin is finished, when any thing is of set purpose, with advised judgment and the consent of our will, committed against the law of God. And yet to these there do many times happen other outward causes both visible and invisible ; for evil spirits move men, and evil men[2] move men, and other infinite examples of corruption that are in the world. Hope, fear, and weakness, do also move men. Augustine, *Quæst. in Exodum* xxix. saith: "The beginning of vice is in the will of man : but the hearts of men are moved by sundry accidental causes, now this, now that ; sometimes the causes are all one ; the difference is in the manner and order, according to every one's proper qualities, which do arise of every several will[3]." Again in the seventy-ninth psalm he saith : "Two things there are that work all sins in mortal men, desire and fear. Consider, examine, and ask your hearts, search your consciences, and see, if any sins can be but by desiring, or else by fearing. Thou art promised, if thou wilt sin, to have such a reward given thee as thou dost delight in ; and for desire of the gift thou crackest thy conscience, and dost commit sin. And again on

[1 extrinsecus aut cœlitus accedens, Lat.]

[2 homines, Lat. ; *not* evil men.]

[3 In voluntate quippe hominis est origo vitiorum; moventur autem causis corda hominum, alia sic, alia vero sic ; etiam non diversis causis, sæpe diverso modo secundum proprias qualitates quæ ex voluntatibus veniunt.—August. Opp. Tom. IV. fol. 29. col. 2.]

the other side, though peradventure thou wilt not be seduced
with gifts, yet being terrified with threatenings thou dost, for
dread of that which thou fearest, commit the iniquity that
otherwise thou wouldest not. As for example, some one man
or other would with gifts corrupt thee to bear false witness.
Thou presently hast turned thyself to God, and hast said in
thy heart, 'What doth it advantage a man, if he gain the
whole world, and suffer the loss of his own soul?' I will not
be hired with gifts to lose my soul for the gain of money.
Thereupon he, which before enticed thee, doth now turn himself to terrify thee; and for because his gifts did fail to hire
thee, he beginneth to threaten unto thee damage, banishment,
wounds, and death.   In such a case now if greediness could
not, yet fear perhaps might cause thee to sin⁴." The same
Augustine again, in his book *De Sermone Domini in Monte*,
saith : "Three things there be by which sin is accomplished,
suggestion, delectation, and consent. Suggestion, whether it
be wrought by the memory, or senses of the body ; as when
we see, hear, smell, taste, or touch any thing. Now if we be
delighted to have it, that unlawful delight must be restrained:
as for example, when we fast, if at the sight of meat our
appetite do arise, it is not done without delectation : but we
must not give our consent to that delectation, but suppress it
with the power of reason ; for if the consent be given, then is
the sin accomplished. These three things are correspondent
to the circumstances of the history that is written in Genesis :
so that of the serpent was made that suggestion ; in the
carnal appetite, as in Eva, was the delectation ; and in reason,
as in Adam, did the full consent appear : which being finished,

[⁴ Omnia peccata duæ res faciunt in homine, cupiditas et timor.
Cogitate, discutite, interrogate corda vestra, perscrutamini conscientias ;
videte utrum possint esse peccata, nisi aut cupiendo aut timendo.
Proponitur tibi præmium, ut pecces; id est, quod te delectet: facis
propter quod cupis. Sed forte non induceris donis, terreris minis :
facis propter quod times. Corrumpere te vult aliquis ut dicas, verbi
gratia, falsum testimonium... Attendisti tu Deum, et dixisti in animo
tuo, Quid prodest homini, si totum mundum lucretur, animæ autem
suæ detrimentum patiatur? Non adducor præmio ut perdam animam
meam pro lucro pecuniæ. Convertit ille se ad incutiendum metum,
qui præmio corrumpere non valuit; incipit minari damnum, et expul-
sionem, cædes, fortassis mortem. Ibi jam si cupiditas non valuit,
forte timor valebit ut pecces.—Id. Tom. viii. fol. 185. col. 4.]

man is expelled as it were out of paradise, that is, out of the blessed light of righteousness into death and damnation[1]." Thus much saith Augustine touching the cause of sin.

But here we must especially note in the definition of actual sin the very property or difference, whereby this action is discerned from all other actions, and whereby the most proper note of sin is made manifest. This action therefore, even as all sins else do, doth directly tend against God's law. But what the law of God is, I have in my former sermons at large declared. Verily, it is none other but the very will of God. Now the will of God is, that man should be like unto his[2] image, that is, that he should be holy, innocent, and so consequently saved.

This will of his did God express, first by the law of nature, then by the law which he writ in two tables of stone, and lastly by the preaching of the holy gospel. Now those three tend all to one end, to wit, that man should be holy, innocent, and so consequently saved. And whatsoever things are done of men, either in thought, word, or deed, against that holy law of God, they both are, and are called, actual sins. Therefore in the judging or esteeming of men's sins, the law of God must be only looked unto; for the things that are not contrary to God's law are not sins: neither hath any man authority to make new[3] laws, for the transgressing whereof men should be counted sinners. That glory belong-
[Psal. li. 4.] eth to God alone, to whom David crieth: "To thee alone have I sinned, and against thee have I wrought wickedness." Neither is it any part of our office to take upon us by our own

[1 Nam tria sunt quibus impletur peccatum; suggestione, delectatione, et consensione. Suggestio, sive per memoriam fit, sive per corporis sensus, cum aliquid videmus aut audimus, vel olfacimus, vel gustamus, vel tangimus. Quo si frui delectaverit, delectatio illicita refrænanda est: velut cum jejunamus, et, visis cibis, palati appetitus assurgit, non fit nisi delectatione; sed huic tamen non consentimus, si eam dominantis rationis jure cohibemus. Si autem consensio facta fuerit, plenum peccatum erit... Tria ergo hæc, ut dicere cœperam, similia sunt illi gestæ rei, quæ in Genesi scripta est, ut quasi a serpente fiat suggestio et quædam suasio; in appetitu autem carnali, tanquam in Eva, delectatio; in ratione vero, tanquam in viro, consensio: quibus peractis, tanquam de paradiso, hoc est, de beatissima luce justitiæ in mortem homo expellitur.—Id. Tom. iv. fol. 248. col. 3, 4.]

[2 id est divinæ, Lat. omitted; that is, to the divine.]

[3 new, not in Lat.]

judgments to determine which be the smallest and which the greatest sins. For which of us would think, that it were sin to say to his brother, "Thou fool?" And yet the Lord in the gospel pronounceth it to be sin: who in the same gospel also affirmeth, that we "shall give account for every idle word at [Matt. v. 22; and xii. 36.] the latter day of judgment." Very rightly therefore saith St Augustine in his second book *De Bapt. contra Donatistas*, capit. 6 : "In esteeming of sins let us not bring in deceitful balances, wherein to weigh both what we list and as we list, after our own mind and phantasy, saying, This is heavy, and that is light: but let us bring in the weights of God's holy scriptures, as out of the secret treasuries of the Lord, and thereby let us weigh what is heavy, and what is light; nay rather, let not us weigh them, but acknowledge and so accept them as they are weighed by the Lord[4]."

And although this might seem to be sufficient, as that which hath sufficiently declared the nature of actual sin; yet will we more at large consider the sundry sorts or kinds and differences of sins. The Stoics were of opinion that all sins were equal: whom perhaps Jovinian following (as the patriarchs of heresies are by Tertullian said to be philosophers[5]) is written to have affirmed the very same with them, as is extant in St Augustine's catalogue of heretics[6]. The holy scripture teacheth us that God is just: whereupon we do conclude, that all sins therefore are not equal; for we see that God, as he is a just judge, doth punish some sins more sharply than other some. For in his gospel the Lord saith : *The kinds and sorts of sins.*

That all sins are not equal.

[4 Non afferamus stateras dolosas, ubi appendamus quod volumus et quomodo volumus, pro arbitrio nostro dicentes, Hoc grave, hoc leve est: sed afferamus stateram divinam de scripturis sanctis, tanquam de thesauris Dominicis, et in illa quid sit gravius appendamus; imo non appendamus, sed a Domino appensa recognoscamus.—August. Opp. Tom. VII. fol. 80. col. 3. Par. 1531.]

[5 Sane et sibi præstitit aliquid Materia, ut et ipsa cum Deo possit agnosci, coæqualis Deo, imo et adjutrix: nisi quod solus eam Hermogenes cognovit, et hæreticorum patriarchæ philosophi.—Tertull. adv. Hermog. cap. 8. Tom. II. p. 68. ed. Semler. Hal. Mag. 1828. Also de Anim. cap. 3. Tom. IV. p. 185.]

[6 A Joviniano quodam monacho ista hæresis orta est ætate nostra, cum adhuc juvenes essemus. Hic omnia peccata, sicut Stoici philosophi, paria esse dicebat, &c.—Aug. de Hæres. No. 82. Tom. VI. fol. 7. col. 1.]

[Matt. xxiii. 14.] " Woe to you, scribes and Pharisees, hypocrites ! which devour widows' houses under the pretence of long prayer: therefore shall you receive the greater damnation." And [Matt. x. 15.] again; " It shall be easier," saith the Lord, " for the land of Sodom in the day of judgment, than for the city" that rejecteth the preaching of the gospel. Likewise in the eleventh of Matthew he saith : " It shall be easier for Tyre and Sidon in the day of judgment, than for you." To Pilate also he [John xix. 11.] said : " The man that delivered me to thee hath the more [Luke xii. 47, 48.] sin." Again : " The servant that knew his master's will, and prepared not himself, neither did according to his will, shall be beaten with many stripes. But he that knew not, and did commit things worthy of stripes, shall be beaten with few stripes."

Sins increase by degrees and circumstances. To proceed now, sins do arise by steps, and increase by circumstances. For first, there is a hidden sin, contained in the very affection or desire of man. But I have already told you, that affections and desires are of two sorts; to wit, natural affections, which are not repugnant to the law of God; of which sort are the love of children, parents, and wife, and the desire of meat, drink, and sleep : although I know and do not deny but that sometimes those affections are defiled with the original spot. Again, there are carnal desires or affections in men, directly contrary to the will of God. Those affections are nourished and do increase by vain thoughts and carnal delights increasing in thy bosom; and at last they break out into the sin of the mouth, yea, after that, to the deed-doing, or actual sin itself. As for example : Thou lustest after another man's wife, and settlest the lust in the bottom of thy heart, still delighting thyself with vain cogitations, while thou callest to mind her passing beauty and lineaments of body, and dost by thy often and vehement imagination both delight and set thyself on fire ; and not being content herewithal alone, thou ceasest not to lie at[1] her, whom thou lovest, with words and writings to spot her chastity ; and, if occasion serve thee, thou dost by thy deed-doing defile her, and also dost reiterate the sin which thou hast once committed ; and lastly, laying aside the fear of God's plague and the shame of the world, thou dost daily frequent it, and openly use it. Seest thou here, by this example, how one and the same sin

[1 solicitas, Lat.]

doth increase by degrees, and doth still require a sharper punishment, according to the greatness and enormity of the crime?
Verily, the Lord in the gospel after St Matthew confirmeth this,
and saith: "Ye have heard how it was said to them of old, [Matt. v. 21,
Thou shalt not kill: Whosoever killeth shall be in danger of 22.]
judgment. But I say unto you, That whoso is angry with
his brother unadvisedly[2] shall be in danger of judgment: and
whosoever shall say unto his brother, Racha, shall be in
danger of a council: but whosoever shall say, Thou fool,
shall be in danger of hell-fire." In these words of the Lord's
thou hearest first the differences of sins, as anger, the tokens of
angry minds, and open scoldings, which do for the most part
end in open fightings; and then thou hearest that, as the
sin increaseth, so the greatness and sharpness of the punishment is still augmented. It was therefore no unapt or silly distinction that they made in actual sin which said, that there is
one sin of the thought, another of the mouth, and another of
the deed; which they did again divide into certain kinds and
sorts: reducing them again partly into *Scelera*, and partly Scelera and
into *Delicta*. delicta.

    Scelera are those heinous crimes which are conceived
and committed of set purpose and pretended malice: of which
sort are those especially which are called the crying sins, as Peccata
murder, usury, oppression of the fatherless and widows, clamantia.
sodomy, and the withheld hire of the needy labourer. For
touching murder, the voice of the Lord in Genesis saith:
"The voice of thy brother's blood crieth unto me." And in [Gen. iv. 10.]
the twenty-second of Exodus he saith: "If ye vex the fatherless and widows, and they cry to me, I will hear them and
slay you." The word of God doth with bitter quips bate
usury and utterly condemn it. The sin of the Sodomites
ascended up to heaven, requiring vengeance to light upon the
villanous beasts[3]. And James the apostle saith: "Behold, [James v. 4.]
the hire of the labourers which have reaped down your fields,
which hire of you is kept back by fraud, crieth; and the cries
of them which have reaped are entered into the ears of the
Lord of sabaoth." To these sins other men do also annex The seven
those seven principal vices, pride or vain-glory, anger, envy, principal
sloth, covetousness, gluttony, and lechery. Yea, they make the seven
these the seeds and first beginnings of all sins and wickedness, deadly sins.

[2 unadvisedly, not in Lat.]   [3 to light—beasts, not in Lat.]

and therefore do they call them the principal sins; as is to be seen in the Sentences of Peter Lombard[1].

Moreover they call those sins *delicta*, which are committed of infirmity or unwittingly; to wit, when the good is forsaken, and duty to God or man neglected, by a certain kind of idle sluggishness; where peradventure are to be numbered the sin of ignorance, the sin called *alienum*, and the sin of unwillingness: although even they also are oftentimes made both heinous crimes and detestable offences.

Peccatum alienum, another's sin, is when another is made to sin by our means, as ye shall hereafter perceive.

Ignorance is said to be of two sorts: the one is natural and very ignorance, which springeth of original sin; the other is affected or counterfeit, which riseth of a set purpose and pretended malice. The natural ignorance is a disease, a fault, and a sin; because it springeth of a poisoned original, and is a work of darkness, as it appeared above by the testimony of the apostle St Paul[2]. Verily St Augustine in his third book *De Libero Arbitrio*, cap. 19, saith: "That which every one by ignorance doth not rightly, and that which he cannot do though he willeth rightly, are therefore called sins, because they have their beginning of the sin of free-will. For that precedent did deserve to have such consequents. For as we give the name of tongue, not to that member only which moveth in the mouth while we speak; but even to that also which followeth upon the moving of that member, to wit, the form and tenour of words which the tongue doth utter; according to which phrase of speech we say, that in one man there are divers tongues, meaning the Greek and the Latin tongues; even so we do not only call that sin which is properly called sin (for it is committed of a free will wittingly), but that also which followeth upon the punishment of the same[3];" of which I have said somewhat before.

The sin of ignorance.

[1 Præterea sciendum est septem esse vitia capitalia vel principalia, ut Greg. super Exod. ait: scilicet, Inanem gloriam, Iram, Invidiam, Acidiam vel Tristitiam, Avaritiam, Gastrimargiam, Luxuriam.—Lombard. lib. Sent. Lib. II. distinct. 42. fol. 221. Par. 1575.]

[2 See page 394.]

[3 Nam illud quod ignorans quisque non recte facit, et quod recte volens facere non potest, ideo dicuntur peccata, quia de peccato illo liberæ voluntatis originem ducunt. Illud enim præcedens meruit ista sequentia. Nam sicut linguam dicimus non solum membrum, quod movemus in ore dum loquimur, sed etiam illud quod hujus membri motum consequitur, id est, formam tenoremque verborum, secundum

Other do cloak their ignorance with that saying of the Lord in the gospel: "If I had not come and spoken unto them, they had wherewithal to cloak their sin," or they should have had no sin. For hereupon they infer: Therefore they to whom nothing hath been preached are free from blame and accusation of sin. But the Lord said not so. For first, he spake of their pretended colour[4], and not of their innocency; and every pretence is not just and lawful. He said, I confess, "they should have had no sin:" but he addeth presently, "Now have they nothing to cloak their sin withal." Secondarily, he doth not universally acquit the ignorant from all kind of sin, but from the sin of rebellion only: for St Augustine upon John saith: "They have an excuse not for every sin; but for this only, that they believed not in Christ, because he came not unto them. For all, which neither have heard nor do hear, may have this excuse, but they cannot escape condemnation. For they that have sinned without law, shall perish without law[5]." And Paul also, in the first to Timothy, the first chapter, saith: "I thank him because he hath counted me faithful, putting me into the ministery; who was before a blasphemer, and a persecutor, and an oppressor: but yet I obtained mercy, because I did it ignorantly, in unbelief." Lo, here the apostle saith that he obtained mercy because he sinned through ignorance: this ignorance he deriveth of unbelief, and attributeth to it most filthy fruits.

Furthermore we call that false and counterfeit ignorance, which is of very malice feigned by obstinate and stubborn

[John xv. 22.]

quem modum dicitur alia lingua Græca, alia Latina; sic non solum peccatum illud dicimus, quod proprie vocatur peccatum, libera enim voluntate et ab sciente committitur; sed etiam illud quod jam de hujus supplicio consequatur necesse est.—August. Opp. Tom. I. fol. 145. col. 3. Par. 1531.]

[4 prætextu, Lat.]

[5 Domino donante respondeo, Habere illos excusationem, non de omni peccato suo, sed de hoc peccato, quo in Christum non crediderunt, ad quos non venit, et quibus non est locutus . . . Restat inquirere, utrum hi qui priusquam Christus veniret in ecclesiam ad gentes, et priusquam evangelium ejus audirent, vitæ hujus fine præventi sunt seu præveniuntur, possunt habere hanc excusationem? Possunt plane, sed non ideo possunt effugere damnationem. Quicunque enim sine lege peccaverunt, sine lege peribunt.—Id. Expos. in Evang. Joan. Tract. LXXXIX. Tom. IX. fol. 94. col. 3, 4.]

people: as if thou, when a thing displeaseth thee[1], shouldest say, that thou dost not understand it; or if, when thou mayest, thou wilt not understand it.   Such is the ignorance that was in the Jews, the professed enemies of God's grace in Christ[2].

[Rom. x. 2, 3.] For Paul saith: "I bear them witness that they have a zeal of God, but not according to knowledge.   For being ignorant of God's righteousness, and seeking to set up their own, they were not subject to the righteousness of God."   For the Lord in the gospel said to the Pharisees, when they demanded if *[John ix. 40, 41.]* they were blinded also; "If ye were blind, ye should have no sin: but now ye say, We see; therefore your sin abideth."

Peccata aliena, others' sins. The sins called *aliena* are not those which we ourselves commit, but those which other men do, yet not without us; to wit, while we allow, help forward, persuade, command, wink at, give occasion, or do not resist or gainsay them, when we *[1 Tim. v. 22.]* may.   The apostle Paul forbiddeth Timothy to lay hands on any man hastily, nor to communicate with other men's sins. Therefore to give an unfit man orders, and to place him in the ecclesiastical ministery, is that kind of sin which we do call another's sin: for to thee is worthily imputed what unseemliness soever is committed against God and his church by the ignorance of the man whom thou hast so ordained.   They *Both these sins are referred to the compeller, the one in respect of the man compelled, the other in respect of the compeller himself.* sin another's sin, which offer violence, and do by torments and threatenings compel men to deny the truth, or to commit some heinous offence.   For the denial of the truth is *peccatum alienum*, another's sin, to him which compelleth the denier to renounce it; and therewithal to the same man his own sin, in respect of himself, is impiety, tyranny, sacrilege, and murder, for causing the other to renounce the truth.

Where, by the way, we are well admonished, that of sins some are wilful, and some unwilful or enforced.

Peccatum voluntarium et involuntarium. They call that the unwilful sin, which is committed either by another man's enforcing, or else by our own ignorance. Therefore that which is done neither by compulsion, nor by ignorance, is concluded to be the voluntary or wilful sin.

Again, of enforced sin they make two sorts; whereof they call one absolute, the other conditional.   Now they think that the absolute violent sin is, when it lieth not in us either to do or not to do, but when it cometh from some other man,

[1 thee, not in Lat.]   [2 in Christ, not in Lat.]

without the consent of him to whom the violence is offered :
even as if the wind should drive us to any place unlooked for ;
or if the king's officers do perforce compel thy hands to offer
incense to idols, while thou to thy power resistest, and dost
deny it so far as thou canst.   In such a case they acquit the
man, so compelled, from all blame, punishment, and reproach[3].

Now touching the second kind of violent sin, which they
call conditional, they think that it riseth upon sundry causes.
But that we may not stick too long upon this point, we do
simply say : the unwilful or violent sin either hath, or hath not,
the consent of him which is compelled.   If he give his consent,
as for example, either to the renouncing of the evangelical truth
which he hath hitherto professed, or to the committing of other
grievous and horrible crimes, then is not the man compelled
void of blame.   For neither can the fear of death, nor
torments, be an excuse for him.   Choose death rather than to
deny the truth, to commit any heinous crime, or to be compelled to consent to a wicked and horrible sin[4].   If thou shalt
rather choose to die than to do a filthy deed, the tyrant shall
not enforce or compel thee against thy will.   He may indeed
kill thee : but to compel thee to do evil against thy will he is
not able ; for by dying thou confessest the truth, and by
dying thou declarest that thou wilt not do that which, while
thou livest, they do exact of thee.   And by that means they
neither overcome nor compel thee ; but are themselves overcome and compelled to see and have trial of that which
grieveth them full sore.   Antiochus Epiphanes did what he
might to have polluted the holy bodies of the Maccabees with
the use of unclean and forbidden meat : but they, choosing
rather to die than by living to be defiled, did by dying overcome the tyrant, and could not be compelled.   And verily it
is a thing received and approved among all professors of sound
religion, that death and all extremities whatsoever must sooner
be tasted than any thing committed which is by nature filthy
and repugnant to religion.

To proceed now ; if consent be not given, but mere and
unavoidable violence is offered to a godly man, (for here we
make a difference betwixt him that upon compulsion doth

*See Augus-
tine, de
Mendacio ad
Consentium,
cap. 9 and 10,
&c.*

[2 Mac. vii.]

[3 laude et vituperatione, Lat. ; praise and blame.]
[4 Aug. de Mend. ad Consentium, 9. and 10.   Tom. IV. fol. 3.
col. 4. and fol. 4. col. 1, 2.]

yield to do wickedness, and him which by compulsion cannot be brought unto it[1];) that violence spotteth not his uncorrupt and holy mind.   As for example; if a godly man, having his feet bound and arms fast pinioned, be perforce brought into an idol temple, and there compelled to be present at their detestable sacrifice; or if an unspotted virgin or honest matron be in the wars or barbarous broils villanously abused, without their consent to the deed-doing, and cannot have leave rather to die untouched than so to be undecently handled, she is, assure yourselves, unspotted before the face of God. For very wisely said St Augustine: "Not to suffer unjustly, but to do unjustly, is sin before God[2]." *Lib. de Libero Arbitrio*, III. cap. 16.   Again, *De Mendacio ad Consentium*, cap. 7, he saith: "That which the body, where lust went not before, doth violently suffer ought rather to be called vexation than corruption.   Or if all vexation be corruption, yet all corruption is not filthy; but that corruption only which lust hath procured, or whereunto lust hath consented[3]." Again, in his first book *De Civitate Dei*, capit. 18, he saith: "Where the purpose of the mind remaineth constant, by which the body is sanctified, there the offered violence of another's lust taketh not from the body the purposed holiness, which the constant perseverance of the party's own chastity doth still retain[4]." Much more like to this hath he in the same place, and also in the sixteenth, nineteenth, and twenty-eighth chapters of the same book, &c.

Mad men's death is unwilful, and therefore to be construed to the best.

No man must hasten his own death.

So also we must think the best of the unwilful death of men beside their wits, that in their madness kill themselves. For otherwise it cannot be found in the canonical books of holy scripture, that God did either give leave or commandment to us mortal men to kill ourselves, thereby the sooner

[1 discernimus hic inter eum qui coactus malum facit, et qui patitur, Lat.]

[2 Non enim injuste aliquid pati, sed injuste aliquid facere, peccatum est.—August. Opp. Tom. I. fol. 144. col. 4. Par. 1531.]

[3 Quod enim violenter non præcedente libidine patitur corpus, vexatio potius quam corruptio nominanda est. Aut si omnis vexatio corruptio est, non omnis corruptio turpis est, sed quam libido procuraverit, aut cui libido consenserit.—Id. Tom. IV. fol. 3. col. 3.]

[4 Proposito animi permanente, per quod etiam corpus sanctificari meruit, nec ipsi corpori aufert sanctitatem violentia libidinis alienæ, quam servat perseverantia continentiæ suæ.—Id. Tom. V. fol. 8. col. 4.]

to obtain immortality, or to avoid imminent evil. For it must be understood that we are forbidden so to do by the law which saith, " Thou shalt not kill:" namely since he addeth not, "thy neighbour;" as he did in another precept, where he forbiddeth to bear false witness. (For because he nameth not thy neighbour, he doth in that precept include thyself also[5].) Therefore is the doctrine of Seneca to be utterly condemned, which counselleth men in misery to despatch themselves, that by death their misery may be ended[6]. And St Augustine, disputing against them that do therefore murder themselves because they will not be subject to other men's filthy lusts[7], doth say : " If it be a detestable crime and a damnable sin for a man to murder himself, as the truth doth manifestly cry that it is; who is so mad to say, Let us sin now, lest peradventure hereafter we happen to sin ; let us now commit murder, lest hereafter perhaps we fall into adultery ? If iniquity have so far the upper hand, that not innocency but mischief is most set by, is it not better by living to hazard the chance of an uncertain defloweration in time to come, than by dying to commit a certain murder in the time present ? Is it not far better in such extreme times of calamity to commit such a fault as by repentance may be forgiven, than to do such a sin whereby no time is left to repent in ? This have I said because of those wilful men and women, which, to avoid not others' but their own sin, lest perhaps under another's lust they should consent to their own being stirred up, do think that they ought to rid themselves from it by shortening their lives. But far be it from a christian mind, which trusteth in our God and with a settled hope doth stay on him as on his surest aid ; far be it, I say, from such a mind to yield to any pleasures of the flesh unto the consenting to filthiness. But if the concupiscential disobedience, which dwelleth yet in our mortal members, is against the law of our will stirred up or moved by a law of her own ; how much rather is it without blame in the body of him that consenteth not, if it be without blame in the body of him that

[5 This explanation is the translator's.]

[6 Si pugnare non vultis, licet fugere.—Senec. de Provident. cap. 6. In his Comment. in Matth. chap. xvi. 25. Lib. VII. p. 613, Bullinger's reference on this topic is to Senec. ad Lucil. Ep. 71.]

[7 et peccent, Lat. omitted ; and commit sin.]

sleepeth[1]!" Thus much out of Augustine: now do we return to our purpose again.

Sins hidden and manifest.

To proceed therefore: they divide actual sins into hidden or private, and into manifest or public sins. Those hidden sins are not such as are hidden from men, being known to none but God alone; of which sort is hypocrisy and the depravation of man's disposition; but such as are not utterly without witnesses, although they be not openly known and made manifest to all men. For on the other side the manifest and public sins are committed with the knowledge and offence of the whole church. And these verily are of both the greater, and those the lighter, because they touch the church and procure the offence of many men[2]: touching which the apostle speaketh in the fifth chapter of the first epistle to Timothy.

Sins mortal and venial.

But the most vulgar and apt distinction of actual sin, which doth in a manner contain in itself all the other kinds and parts thereof, is that wherein it is called either mortal or venial sin[3]. They think that mortal sin is every sin which is committed of an unfaithful person; and that venial sin is

[1 Veruntamen si detestabile facinus et damnabile scelus est etiam seipsum hominem occidere, sicut veritas manifesta proclamat; quis ita desipiat, ut dicat, Jam nunc peccemus ne postea forte peccemus; jam nunc perpetremus homicidium, ne forte postea incidamus in adulterium? Nonne, si tantum dominatur iniquitas, ut non innocentia sed potius peccata eligantur, satius est incertum de futuro adulterium quam certum de præsenti homicidium? Nonne satius est flagitium committere, quod pœnitendo sanetur, quam tale facinus ubi locus salubris pœnitentiæ non relinquitur? Hæc dixi propter eos vel eas, quæ non alieni sed proprii peccati devitandi causa, ne sub alterius libidine etiam excitatæ suæ forte consentiant, vim sibi qua moriantur inferendam putant. Ceterum absit a mente christiana, quæ in Deo suo fidit, in eoque spe posita ejus adjutorio nititur; absit, inquam, ut mens talis quibuslibet carnis voluptatibus ad consensum turpitudinis cedat. Quod si illa concupiscentialis inobedientia, quæ adhuc in membris moribundis habitat, præter nostræ voluntatis legem, quasi lege sua, movetur; quanto magis absque culpa est in corpore non consentientis, si absque culpa est in corpore dormientis!—August. de Civ. Dei, Lib. I. cap. 25. Opp. Tom. v. fol.11. col. 2, 3.]

[2 Et hæc (i. e. publica) quidem sunt graviora, illa autem (i. e. privata) leviora, quod videlicet attinet homines et multorum offensionem, Lat.]

[3 Aquinat. prim. sec. par. Summæ. quæst. 88. fol. 148, &c. Par. 1615.]

every sin that is done of a faithful man. I do simply and according to the scriptures suppose, that all the sins of men are mortal; for they are done against the law or will of God. But death is due to sins; for the prophet crieth: "The soul that [Ezek. xviii. 20.] sinneth shall die itself;" and the apostle saith: " The reward [Rom. vi. 23.] of sin is death." Yea, and deadly sins do take the name of death. To this now do belong these testimonies of the apostle: " This ye know, that every fornicator, or unclean person, or [Eph. v. 5; Gal. v. 19— covetous person, which is a worshipper of idols, hath none 21; 1 Cor. v. 11; vi. 9, 10.] inheritance in the kingdom of Christ and God." The same sentence, being again rehearsed[4] in the fifth to the Ephesians, is again to be found in the fifth to the Galatians, and the fifth and sixth chapters of the first to the Corinthians.

But the sins which are of their own nature mortal are through grace in the faith of Jesus Christ made venial; because they are through Christ forgiven by God's great favour and mercy. And therefore the apostle in the sixth chapter to the Romans did not say, " Let not sin be in your mortal body;" [Rom. vi. 12; viii. 1, 12, 13.] but, " Let not sin reign in your mortal body, that ye should obey to it through the lusts thereof." And again; " There is therefore no condemnation to them that are in Christ Jesus, which walk not after the flesh, but after the spirit." And again; " Brethren, we are debtors, not to the flesh, to walk after the flesh. For if ye live after the flesh, ye shall die: but if by the spirit ye shall mortify the deeds of the flesh, ye shall live." Therefore there is sin in our body always so long as we live; but by grace it is not imputed unto death: and they to whom it is not imputed, do by all means endeavour to walk after the spirit, and not after the flesh: and yet they do very oftentimes slip and fall; which falls and slippings nevertheless, together with that infirmity[5] of mortal men, are counted sins,—I mean sins pardonable and not to be punished eternally.

Now to mortal sins is that sin especially to be referred, which is called the sin against the Holy Ghost; which some do not without a cause suppose to be most properly called mortal sin: of which I will speak, when first I have somewhat briefly answered to certain questions that do depend upon this argument.

First of all here is demanded, Whether that sin or dis- Whether that the sin ease, which after baptism remaineth in infants, be sin in very remaining in

[4 edita, Lat.; being rehearsed.]   [5 cum morbo illo sontico, Lat.]

27

infants after
baptism is a
sin or no. deed? Now it is manifest, that concupiscence remaineth in
them that are baptized; and that concupiscence is sin; and
therefore that sin remaineth in them that are baptized : which
sin, notwithstanding, is through the grace of God in the
merit of Jesus Christ not imputed unto them.   So did St
Augustine resolve this knot in the first book *De Peccatorum
Meritis et Remissione,* cap. 39, where he saith : " In infants
verily it is so wrought by the grace of God, through the
baptism of him that came in the likeness of sinful flesh, that
the flesh of sin should be made void.   And yet it is made
void so, not that the concupiscence which is spread and bred
in the flesh, while it liveth, should of a sudden be consumed,
vanish away, and not be; but that it should not hurt him
now being dead, in whom it was even at his birth.   For it is
not given in baptism to them of more years, that the law of
sin which is in their members contrary to the law of their
mind should utterly be extinguished and not be at all; but
that all the evil, whatsoever is said, done, or thought of man,
when with his captive mind he served that concupiscence,
should be utterly wiped out, and so reputed as though it never
had been done[1]."   Thus much hath Augustine.

Whether
the virtuous
works of the
heathen are
sins, or no?   Another question is, Whether those works, that the Gentiles do, which have a shew of virtue and goodness, are sins,
or else good works?   It is assuredly true, that God even
among the Gentiles also had his elect.   Now so many such
as were among them were not without the Holy Ghost and
faith.   Therefore their works which were wrought by faith
were good works, and not sins.   For in the Acts of the Apos-
[Acts x. 2, 4.] tles mention is made, that the prayers and alms-deeds of
Cornelius the centurion were had in remembrance before God ;
and the same Cornelius is said to have been a devout man
and fearing God: whereupon I infer that he was faithful;
whose faith afterward is made fully perfect, and upon whom

[1 In parvulis certe, gratia Dei, per baptismum ejus qui venit in
similitudine carnis peccati, id agitur, ut evacuetur caro peccati. Eva-
cuatur autem, non ut in ipsa vivente carne concupiscentia conspersa
et innata repente absumatur et non sit; sed ne obsit mortuo quæ inerat nato... Nam nec grandibus hoc præstatur in baptismo... ut lex
peccati quæ inest in membris, repugnans legi mentis, penitus extinguatur et non sit; sed ut quicquid mali ab homine factum, dictum,
cogitatum est, cum eidem concupiscentiæ subjecta mente serviret,
totum aboleatur, ac velut factum non fuerit habeatur.—August. Opp.
Tom. VII. fol. 141. col. 3.]

the gift of the Holy Ghost is more plenteously bestowed. Moreover the worthy deeds of the heathens are not to be despised nor utterly contemned; for as they were not altogether done without God, so did they much avail to the preserving and restoring of the tranquillity of kingdoms and commonweals. And therefore did the most just Lord enrich certain excellent men and commonweals with many and ample temporal gifts; for upon the Greeks and many Roman princes he bestowed riches, victories, and abundant glory: and verily, civil justice and public tranquillity was in great estimation among many of them. Other received infinite rewards, because they did constantly and manfully execute the just judgments of God upon the wicked rebels and enemies to God. Neither is it to be doubted but that the Lord granted that invincible power to the Roman empire under Octavius Augustus and other Roman princes, to the end that by their strength he might break and bring down the invincible malice of the Jewish people, and so by the Romans revenge the blood of his Son, his holy prophets, and blessed apostles, which had been shed by those furious and blasphemous beasts. Note here, that[2] immediately after the subversion of Hierusalem the Roman empire began to decline. Now let us return to the matter again.

Lastly they do demand, Whether the good works of the saints and faithful ones be sins or no? Verily, if thou respectest our corruption and infirmity, then all our works are sins, because they be the works of us which are ourselves not without filthy spots; and therefore the works which be wrought by us cannot be so perfect as otherwise they ought to be in the sight of God. And yet the very same works, for the faith's sake in us and because we are received into the grace of God, and that therefore they are wrought of us which are now by grace the sons of God, both are indeed and also called good[3]. For to this end tendeth that saying of the apostle: "With the mind the same I, or even I, do serve the law of God; but with the flesh the law of sin." Lo here, one and the same apostle, even being regenerate, doth retain in himself two sundry dispositions; so that his very work, working in divers respects, is both sin and a good work also. For inasmuch as in mind he serveth God, so far forth he doth a good work; but insomuch as he again did serve the law of

Whether the good works of the saints are sins or no?

[Rom. vii. 25.]

[2 Certe, Lat.; unquestionably.]   [3 and also called, not in Lat.]

the flesh, therein his work is not without a spot. For he himself a little before in the same seventh chapter said: "I find, when I would do good, that evil (παράκειται, that is to say) is present with, by, and in me[1]:" which evil undoubtedly, making always a shew of itself in all our words, works, and thoughts, doth cause that the work which is done of us, when we are regenerate, cannot be so pure as God's justice doth look that it should be. By the grace therefore and the mercy of God it is reputed and esteemed as pure.

Hereunto now doth that sentence of our Lord in the gospel after St John belong, where he saith : " He that is washed hath no need save to wash his feet, but he is clean every whit." For if he be clean every whit, what need hath the clean to wash his feet? But if his feet must be washed, how then is he clean every whit? And yet these sayings are not repugnant betwixt themselves; even as also that saying is not, where we say that good works[2] are sins. For according to the plentifulness and imputation of God's grace and mercy we are clean every whit, being throughly purged from all our sins, so that they shall not condemn us; and yet, for because there is always in us the law of sin which sheweth itself in us[3] so long as we live, therefore our feet, that is, those evil motions and naughty lusts of ours, must be resisted and to our power repressed. Finally, we must acknowledge that we ourselves[4] and our very works are never without an imperfection ; and therefore consequently, that all our works and we do stand in need of the grace of God. These questions being thus resolved, we are now come to expound the sin against the Holy Ghost.

[John xiii. 10.]

The sin against the Holy Ghost is a perpetual blaspheming of the revealed and known[5] truth; to wit, when we against our conscience falsely revolting from the known truth do without intermission both inveigh and rail against it. For blasphemy is the evil speech or despiteful taunts wherewith we inveigh against or slander any man, by casting forth wicked and detestable speeches against him, whereby his credit and estimation is either cracked or utterly disgraced. We do therefore blaspheme the magistrates, our elders[6], and other good men, when we do not only withdraw our obedience

Of the sin against the Holy Ghost.

[1 insideat, vel adjaceat, aut inhæreat ac insitum sit, Lat.]
[2 opera fidelium bona, Lat.] [3 in membris nostris, Lat.]
[4 ex nobis ipsis, Lat.] [5 agnitæ, Lat.] [6 parentes, Lat.]

and the honour due unto them, but do also with reproachful words bait them, not ceasing to call them tyrants, bloodsuckers, wicked heads, and odible guides [7]: but we do especially blaspheme God, when we detract his glory, gainsay his grace, and of set purpose do stubbornly contemn and dispraise his truth revealed unto us and his evident works declared to all the world.

Every sin verily is not blasphemy, but all blasphemy is sin; for because it tendeth against God and his will, it is sin: but therewithal this property more and singularity it hath, that it doth also despise God and speak reproachfully against his works. Many do sin against the doctrine of the truth, because they do either neglect and not receive the truth; or else because, when they have received it, they do not reverence and set it forth [8]: but these kind of men, though they be sinners, do yet not deserve to be called blasphemers. But if they begin once with taunts and quips to mock the doctrine which they neglect, calling it heretical, schismatical, seditious, and devilish, then may they rightly be termed blasphemers. *What blasphemy is properly.*

Wherefore the property of the sin against the Holy Ghost is, not only to revolt from the truth, but also against all conscience to speak against the truth, and with flouts incessantly to overwhelm both the very work and most evident revelation of the Lord. For the conscience, being by the evidence of the revelation or work of the Holy Ghost convinced, suggesteth or telleth them that they ought not only to temper themselves from reproachful speeches, but that they ought to do another thing too, that is, that they ought to yield to the truth and give to God his due honour and glory. But now, to exclude this inspiration of the Holy Spirit, to reject and overwhelm it with stubborn falsehood, flat apostasy, wicked contradiction, and perpetual contempt, is flatly to commit sin against the Holy Ghost. And this verily taketh beginning of original sin, and is nourished and set forward by devilish suggestions, our perverse affections, by indignations, envy, hope or fear, by stubborn and self-wilful malice, and lastly by contumacy and rebellion. *The beginning of this sin against the Holy Ghost.*

But now the course of the matter requireth to hear what the Lord said in the gospel concerning this sin. In the twelfth

[7 execrandos, Lat. ; *guides* is the translator's addition.]
[8 ornant, Lat.]

of Matthew he saith: "Every sin and blasphemy shall be forgiven unto men; but the blasphemy against the Holy Ghost shall not be forgiven unto men. And whosoever speaketh a word against the Son of man, it shall be forgiven him; but whosoever speaketh against the Holy Ghost, it shall not be forgiven him, neither in this world, nor in the world to come." The same sentence of our Saviour is thus expressed in the third chapter of St Mark's gospel:[1] "All sins shall be forgiven unto the children of men, and blasphemies wherewith soever they shall blaspheme: but he that speaketh blasphemy against the Holy Ghost hath never forgiveness, but is in danger of eternal damnation." In the twelfth chapter after St Luke these words in a manner are uttered thus: "Whosoever speaketh a word against the Son of man, it shall be forgiven him; but unto him that blasphemeth the Holy Ghost it shall not be forgiven." In these words of the Lord we have here mention made of blasphemy against the Son of man, and of blasphemy against the Holy Ghost: of which that against the Holy Ghost is utterly unpardonable, but that against the Son

Blasphemy against the Son of man. of man is altogether venial. Blasphemy against the Son of man is committed of the ignorant, which are not yet enlightened; and doth tend against Christ, whom the blasphemer doth think to be a seducer, because he knoweth him not. Such blasphemers the word of the Lord doth manifestly testify that Paul himself before his conversion and a great part of the Jews were; for upon the cross the Lord prayed,

[Luke xxiii. 34.]
[1 Cor. ii. 8.] crying: "Father, forgive them; for they wot not what they do;" and the apostle Paul saith: "If they had known the Lord of glory, they would not have crucified him." Whereupon St Peter in the Acts, speaking to the Jews, saith: "I know that ye did it through ignorance; now therefore turn you, and repent, that your sins may be wiped out." Acts iii.

The blasphemy against the Holy Ghost. But the blasphemy against the Holy Ghost is said to be a continual fault-finding or reproach against the Holy Spirit of God; that is, against the inspiration, illumination, and works of the Spirit. For when he doth so evidently work in the minds of men that they can neither gainsay it nor yet pretend ignorance, and that for all this they do resist, mock, despise, and continually snap at the truth[2], which they in their

[1 Amen, dico vobis, Lat. omitted. Verily, I say unto you.]
[2 revelationem aut operationem illam Spiritus, Lat.; that revelation or working of the Spirit.]

consciences do know to be[3] most wholesome and true[4]; in so doing they do blaspheme the Holy Spirit and power[5] of God. As for example: the Pharisees, being by most evident reasons and unreprovable miracles convinced in their own minds, could not deny but that the doctrine and works of our Lord Jesus Christ were the truth and miracles of the very God[6]; and yet, against the testimony of their own consciences, they did of mere envy, rebellious doggedness, and false apostasy, continually cavil that Christ did all by the means and inspiration of Beelzebub[7], the devil.   And little or nothing better than the Pharisees are those which, when they have in these days once understood[8] that the very truth and assured salvation are most simply and purely set forth in Christ, do notwithstanding forsake it, and allow of the contrary doctrine, condemning and with mocks[9] railing upon the sound and manifest truth; yea, and that more is, they cease not to clap their hands and hiss at it, as a damnable heresy.

As this sin is of all other the filthiest, so is it not venial, but utterly unpardonable; for in the gospel the Lord hath expressly said: "It shall not be forgiven him, neither in this world, nor in the world to come." Which sentence in St Mark is thus pronounced: "He hath never forgiveness, but is in danger of eternal damnation." The cause is manifest. For it is unpossible without faith to please God; without faith there is no remission of sins; without faith there is no entrance into the kingdom of God.   But the sin against the Holy Ghost is mere apostasy and flat[10] rebellion against the true faith which the Holy Ghost by his illumination doth pour into our hearts: which illumination these untoward apostates do incessantly call darkness; they name it a mere seduction, and do with taunts blaspheme it openly.   Therefore this sin is never forgiven them; for they tread under foot the grace of God, and do despise and make a mock of the way which leadeth to

Sin against the Holy Ghost is no remitted.

[3 optimam, Lat. omitted; the best.]

[4 contra conscientiam propriam, Lat. omitted; against their own conscience.]

[5 and power, not in Latin.]

[6 divina esse, Lat.; were divine.]   [7 Beelzebub, not in Latin.]

[8 evangelica doctrina, Lat. omitted; by the preaching of the gospel.]

[9 contra animi sui sententiam, Lat. omitted; against the judgment of their mind.]

[10 perstans, Lat.; obstinate.]

salvation[1]. Wherefore St Paul in the tenth to the Hebrews saith: "If we sin willingly after we have received the knowledge of the truth, there remaineth no more sacrifice for sins, but a fearful looking for of judgment and violent fire, which shall devour the adversaries." Now, I pray you, what is it to sin willingly? Forsooth, to sin willingly is not to sin through infirmity, or oftentimes to fall into one and the same sin: but to sin willingly is with a most stubborn contempt to sin; as they are wont to do, which wittingly and willingly do reject and spurn at the grace of God, not ceasing to make a mock of the cross and death of Christ, as though it were foolish and not sufficiently effectual to the purging of all our sins: for to such there is prepared none other sacrifice for sins. And such the apostle calleth the adversaries, that is, the contemners and enemies of God. And therefore the same apostle in the sixth chapter of the same epistle saith: "It cannot be that they which were once lighted, and have tasted of the heavenly gift, and were become partakers of the Holy Ghost, and have tasted of the good word of God, and the powers of the world to come, and they fall away, should be renewed again into repentance; crucifying to themselves the Son of God afresh, and making a mock of him." He speaketh not here of every fall of the faithful; but of wilful and stubborn apostasy. For Peter fell and was restored again through repentance: which happeneth to more than Peter alone; for all sinners are through repentance daily restored. But unrepentant Judas is not restored, because he was a wilful[2] apostate. Mockers and blaspemers are not restored through repentance, because they do obstinately stand against the known verity, and cease not to blaspheme the way by which alone they are to be led unto eternal life. Therefore those places of St Paul do make never a whit for the Novatians[3], but do expound to us the nature and envenomed force of the sin against the Holy Ghost.

St John the apostle and evangelist, disputing of this sin in his canonical epistle, saith: "If any man see his brother sin a sin which is not unto death, he shall ask, and he shall give him life for them that sin not unto death. There is a sin

[1 John v. 16—18]

[1 ad gratiam, Lat.]   [2 pertinax, Lat.]
[3 Their peculiarity was, that they would not receive into the church persons who after being baptized fell into the greater sins. They did not, however, exclude them from all hopes of eternal salvation.—Mosheim, Eccles. Hist. Book I. Cent. 3. Part 2. ch. 5. § 18.]

unto death; I say not that thou shouldest pray for it[4]. All unrighteousness is sin: and there is a sin not unto death. We know that whosoever is born of God sinneth not; but he that is begotten of God keepeth himself, and that evil toucheth him not." St John here maketh mention of two sorts of sins: the one unto death, that is, mortal and unpardonable, for which we must not pray, that is to say, prayers cannot obtain pardon for it. That sin is contumelious reproach against the Holy Ghost, revolting apostasy, and incessant mocking of the gospel of Christ; for in the gospel after St John we read: "Verily, verily, I say unto you, if a man [John viii. keep my sayings, he shall not see death for ever;" and again: 52, 24.] "If ye believe not that I am, ye shall die in your sins." And apostasy in very deed is iniquity, and a purposed and perpetual sin; for what is more sinful or unjust than to strive against[5], and make a mock of[6] the known verity? The other sin is venial, not unto death; the which, of what sort it is, St John declareth when he addeth: "We know that every one which is born of God sinneth not." Now that saying must not be so absolutely taken, as though he sinned not at all: but we must understand, that he sinned not to death; for otherwise the very saints are sinners, as it is evident by the first chapter of this epistle. Furthermore, that which doth immediately follow in John maketh manifest that which went before: "He that is begotten of God," saith he, "keepeth himself;" that is, he standeth stedfastly in the known truth, and taketh heed to himself, that that evil[7] touch him not; that is, that he entrap him not, stir him up against God, nor retain him in rebellion. Thus much have I hitherto said touching the sin against the Holy Ghost[8], which Augustine did in one place call final impenitency, which doth follow Or endless upon apostasy, blasphemy, and contempt of the Holy Ghost, unrepent-ance. or of the word of truth revealed by the Holy Ghost.

[4 ut roges, Lat.; and Erasmus.]
[5 indesinenter, Lat. omitted: without ceasing.]
[6 medium ostendere digitum, is the proverb which Bullinger uses.]
[7 malus ille, Lat.]
[8 Peccatum in Spiritum Sanctum est finalis impœnitentia: de qua dicit Aug.—Gratian. Decret. Par. II. caus. 1. quæst. 1. cap. 81. p. 673. Par. 1583. The treatise De Ver. et Fals. Pœnitent. in which occur the words,—Soli peccant in Spiritum Sanctum, qui impœnitentes existunt usque ad mortem,—is considered to be spurious.]

Of the just and certain punishment of sinners. And although I have already, in the handling of original sin and sin against the Holy Ghost, partly touched the effects of sin; yet to conclude this treatise withal, I will briefly shew you somewhat touching the just and assured punishment that shall be laid upon sinners. For in the definition of sin I said, that sin brought upon us the wrath of God with death and sundry punishments: of which in this place I mean to speak. It is as manifest, as what is most manifest, by the scriptures, that God doth punish the sins of men, yea, that he punisheth sinners for their sins. For many places in the scriptures declare, that God is angry and grievously offended at the sins of mortal men. David crieth: "The Lord loveth the just; as for the wicked and violent, his soul doth hate them. Upon the ungodly he shall rain snares, fire and brimstone, storm and tempest; this shall be their portion to drink. For the righteous Lord loveth righteousness: with his countenance he doth behold the thing that is just." In like mannner Paul saith: "The wrath of God is revealed from heaven against all ungodliness and uncleanness of men, which withhold[1] the truth in unrighteousness." And what may be thought of that moreover, that the wrath of God for the sins of us men would be by no means appeased[2] but by the death of the Son of God? Wherein verily the excellency of the great price of our redemption doth argue the greatness and filthiness of our sin. To all which we may add, that the good Lord, who loveth mankind so well, would not have overwhelmed us[3] with so many pains and exceeding calamities, had not our sin been passing horrible in the sight of his eyes. For who[4] can make a full beadrow of all the calamities of miserable sinners[5]? The Lord for our sins absenteth himself from us[6]. But if the sun be out of the earth, how great are the mists and cloudy darkness in it? If God be away from us, how great is the horror in minds of men? Here therefore, as punishments due to sinners, are reckoned the tyranny of Satan, a thousand torments of conscience, the death of the soul, dreadful fear, utter desperation[7], innumerable calamities of body and of our

[Psalm xi. 5—7.]

[Rom. i. 18.]

The plague of sins.

[1 detinent, Lat.; withhold, Tyndale 1525, and Cranmer 1539.]
[2 peccata mortalium non potuerunt expiari, Lat.]
[3 genus humanum, Lat.]
[4 paucis et in transcursu, Lat. omitted; in few words and by the way.]
[5 peccatorum pœnas, Lat.]   [6 alienatur, Lat.]
[7 et infandi dolores, Lat. omitted; and griefs not to be described.]

other faculties, which Moses the servant of God doth at large rehearse in the twenty-sixth of Leviticus and the twenty-eighth chapter of Deuteronomy. And now, since new sins are daily scourged with new kinds of punishments, what end, I pray, is any man able to make, if he should go about to reckon them all[8] ?

It is not to be doubted, verily, but that the Lord doth punish sinners justly; for he is himself a most just Judge. And for because it is a mad man's part to doubt of the justice, omnipotency, and wisdom of God; it followeth therefore consequently, that all religious and godly men do hold for a certainty[9] that the punishments, which God doth lay upon men, are laid upon them by most just judgment.

But how great and what kind of punishment is due to every fault and several transgression, belongeth rather to God's judgment to determine, than for mortal men too curiously to inquire. Whereupon St Augustine, *Tracta. in Joan.* 89, saith: "There is a great diversity of punishments, as of sins; which how it is ordained, the wisdom of God doth more deeply declare, than man's conjectures can possibly seek out, or utter in words[10]." He verily which in his law given to men gave this for a rule, "According to the measure of the sin, so shall the measure of the punishment be[11];" being himself most equal and just, doth not in judgment exceed measure. Abraham, in the notable communication had with God which is reported in the eighteenth of Genesis, doth among other things say: "Wilt thou destroy the just with the wicked? That be far from thee, that thou shouldest do such a thing, and slay the righteous with the wicked, and that the righteous should be as the wicked. That is not thy part, that judgest all the earth: thou shalt not make such judgment[12]." Hereunto also belongeth that notable demonstration, which the Lord useth toward[13] Jonas being angry

The Lord doth pu:... sinners justly.

[8 quis, oro, pœnarum finis, aut quis genera omnia commemoret? Lat.]

[9 imo compertissimo, Lat. omitted; yea, for a most assured certainty.]

[10 Tanta est autem suppliciorum, quanta diversitas peccatorum; quæ quomodo sese habeat, altius indicat sapientia divina quam conjectura scrutatur aut effatur humana.—August. Opp. Tom. IX. fol. 94. col. 4. Par. 1531.]

[11 Deut. xxv. 2. cf. Vol. I. page 356, note 4.]

[12 Gen. xviii. 23, 25. Vulgat.]

[13 prophetam, Lat. omitted; the prophet.]

with the Lord because of his judgments: for he sheweth that he hath justly a care of the infants, yea, and of the cattle in Ninive. The place is extant[1] in the fourth chapter of the prophecy of Jonas. Let us therefore stedfastly hold, that the Lord, when he punisheth, doth injury to no creature which he hath made. Here therefore the disputations and questions come to an end, wherein men are wont to demand, Why the Lord doth sometimes use so sharp torments towards infants or sucklings? or why he rewardeth temporal offences with eternal punishments? "For the Lord is righteous in all his ways, and holy in all his works." As David did most truly witness, where as in another place he saith: "Thou art just, O Lord, and thy judgment is right." Blessed is he that stumbleth not here, and doth not murmur against the Lord.

[Psalm cxlv. 17.]

[Psalm cxix. 137.]

God punisheth most sharply.

But if it so happen that the Lord at any time do somewhat long defer the judgment and punishment, we must not therefore think that he is unjust, because he spareth the wicked, and sharply correcteth[2] his friends and their vices. Let us rather lay before our eyes the evangelical parable of the rich glutton and poor silly Lazarus: for Lazarus, though he was the friend of God, did notwithstanding die for want of food: the other, though he was God's enemy, did spend his life in dainty fare and pleasures, and felt none ill. But hearken after this life what their judgment was. Abraham saith to the rich glutton: "My son, remember that thou in thy lifetime receivedst thy good, and Lazarus likewise received evil: but now he rejoiceth, and thou art tormented." Therefore if the godly be at any time afflicted in this present life, they shall be abundantly rewarded for it in the life to come: but if the wicked be spared in this world, they are more grievously punished in the world to come: for God is just, and[3] rewardeth every man according to his merit.

[Luke xvi. 25.]

If hereafter therefore thou shalt chance to see the wicked live in prosperity, think not thou by and by that God is unjust: suppose not that his power is abated[4]; and say not that he sleepeth, and seeth them not. For that saying of the prophet, which is also used by the apostle Peter,

[1 notus est, Lat.; is well known.]
[2 interim, Lat. omitted; in the mean season.]
[3 ergo, Lat.; and therefore.]
[4 Noli putare Deum esse ficulneum, Lat. See Erasmi Adag. Chiliad. p. 95. col. 2. *auxilium infirmum.*]

is assuredly true : "The eyes of the Lord are upon the just, [Psal. xxxiv.
and his ears open unto their prayers;" again : "The eyes ^{15, 16; 1 Pet.} iii. 12.]
of the Lord are upon them that do wickedness." We must
in such a case fortify our minds with the just examples of
God's judgments, gathered together out of the holy scriptures.
Let us consider that the world was destroyed with the ge- Examples of
neral deluge, when God had in vain a long time looked after God justly
punishing.
repentance. Let us remember that Sodom, Gomorrha, and
the cities adjacent thereabout, were burnt with fire sent down
from heaven. Let us think upon Egypt, how it was stricken
with divers plagues[5], and the inhabitants drowned in the Red
sea. Let us call to mind the things that happened by the
holy and just judgment of God to the Amorhites, the Chanaanites, the Amalechites, and the very Israelites, first under
their judges, then under their kings. Their measure at last
was fully filled. Neither did they at any time despise God and
his word, but were at the last paid home for their labour.
They never sinned and went scot-free long[6]. The history of
Paulus Orosius, yea, the universal history of all the world,
do minister unto us innumerable examples like unto these,
declaring the certainty of God's judgment[7]. Let us think[8]
that God doth not therefore allow of sins, because he is
slack in punishing them ; but let us persuade ourselves, that God's long
forbearing.
he by the prolonging of punishment doth of his unmeasurable
goodness both look and stay for the repentance and conversion of miserable sinners. For in the gospel the Lord biddeth [Luke xiii.
6—9.]
not to cut down the barren fig-tree, because he looked to see
if it would bring any fruit the next year following. The
apostle Paul saith : "Despisest thou the riches of his good- [Rom. ii. 4—
9.]
ness and patience and long-sufferance ; not knowing that the
goodness of God leadeth thee to repentance ? But thou,
after thy stubbornness and heart that cannot repent, heapest
unto thyself wrath against the day of wrath and declaration
of the righteous judgment of God, which will reward every
man according to his deeds: to them which by continuing
in well-doing seek for glory, and honour, and immortality,
eternal life ; but unto them that are contentious, and do not
obey the truth but obey unrighteousness, shall come indig-

[5 primum—deinde, Lat. omitted; first, and then.]
[6 Cf. above, pages 6—13.]
[7 justi judicii, Lat. ; the justice of God's judgment.]
[8 præterea, Lat. omitted; besides.]

nation and wrath, tribulation and anguish, upon every soul of man that doth evil." This, I say, let us firmly hold, and with this let us content ourselves, not grudging to see[1] the wicked live long in prosperity without pain or punishment. The holy, just, wise, and mighty God knoweth best what to do, how to do, why and when to do everything conveniently. To him be glory for ever and ever. Amen.

Why sins are plagued with temporal punishments, considering that they are forgiven by the grace of God. To this belongeth also, that God doth as well afflict the good as the bad; touching which I spake at large in the third sermon of this third Decade[2]. Now here therefore some there are which demand, why God doth with divers punishments persecute those sins which he hath already forgiven to men? For he forgave Adam his sin, and yet he laid on him both death and innumerable calamities of this life beside.

[2 Sam. xii. 13, 10.] To David we read that the prophet Nathan said, "The Lord hath taken thy sin away:" and yet immediately after the same prophet addeth: "The sword shall not depart from thy house." To this we answer simply, that these plagues, which are laid on us before the remission of our sins, are the punishments due to our sins; but that after the remission of our sins they are conflicts and exercises, wherewith the faithful do not make satisfaction for their sins, which are already remitted by grace in the death of the Son of God; but wherewith they are humbled and kept in their duty, having an occasion given of the greater glory.

And here I will not stick to recite unto you, dearly beloved, St Augustine's judgment touching this matter in his second book *De Peccatorum Meritis et Remissione*, chap. 33, and 34, where he saith: "Things, the guilt whereof God absolveth or remitteth, to the end that after this life they should do no harm, and yet he suffereth them to abide unto the conflict of faith, that by them men may be instructed and exercised, profiting in the conflict of righteousness," &c. And presently after: "Before forgiveness, they are the punishments of sinners; but after remission, they are the conflicts and exercises of just men." And again, after a few words more he saith: "The flesh which was first made was not the flesh of sin, wherein man would not keep righteousness among the pleasures of paradise. Wherefore God ordained that, after his sin, the flesh of sin being increased should endeavour with pains and labours

[1 Rather, however the wicked may, &c. utcunque, Lat.]
[2 See above, page 75.]

to recover righteousness again. And for that cause Adam being cast out of paradise dwelt over against Eden, that is, against the place of pleasures; which was a sign that with labours, which are contrary to pleasure, the flesh of sin was then to be inured, which, being in pleasures, kept not obedience before it was the flesh of sin. Therefore even as those our first parents, by living justly afterward, whereby they are rightly thought to be by the blood of Christ delivered from utter punishment, deserved not yet in that life to be called back again into paradise; so also the flesh of sin, although when sins are forgiven a man live righteously in it, doth not presently deserve not to suffer that death which it drew from the propagation of sin. Such a like thing is insinuated to us in the book of the Kings concerning the patriarch David; to whom when the prophet was sent, and had threatened unto him the evils that should come upon him through the anger of God because of the sin which he had committed, by the confession of the sin he deserved forgiveness, according to the answer of the prophet who told him that that sin and crime was forgiven unto him; and yet those things betided him which God had threatened unto him, to wit, that he should so be humbled by the incest of his son, &c. And what is the cause that they demand not, If God for sin did threaten that scourge, why then, when he had pardoned the sin, did he fulfil that which he threatened? but for because they know (if they demand that question) that they shall rightly be answered, That the remission of the sin was granted to the end the man should not be by his sin hindered to obtain eternal life: but the effect of God's threatening did follow after the remission of the sin, to the end that the godliness of the man might be tried and exercised in that humility. In like manner God hath for sins laid bodily death as a punishment upon the body of man; and after the forgiveness of sins hath not taken it away, but left it in the body to be a mean to the exercise of righteousness[3]." Thus far hath Augustine.

Absolon defiled his father's bed, whereby he saith that David was humbled.

[3 —res, quarum reatum, ne post hanc vitam obsint, Deus solvit, tamen eas ad certamen fidei sinit manere, ut per illas erudiantur et exerceantur proficientes in agone justitiæ ... respondemus dicentes, ante remissionem esse illa supplicia peccatorum; post remissionem autem certamina exercitationesque justorum ... Caro enim, quæ primo facta est, non erat caro peccati, etc.—August. Opp. Tom. VII. fol. 147. col. 1. 2. 3.]

How the wicked are punished.

Now as concerning the punishments of the wicked, (if the most just God do in this world touch them with any,) let us know that they be the arguments[1] of God's just judgment, who in this world beginneth to punish them temporally, and in the world to come doth not cease to plague them everlastingly. The wicked, verily, perish through their own default; for God beginneth to whip them in this life, to the end that they, being chastened, may begin to be wise, and turn to the Lord: but they[2], by his chastisement, are the more indurate, and murmur at the judgments of God, converting that to their own destruction which was ordained to have been to their health. For as to them that love God all things work to the best, so to them that hate the Lord all things do work to their utter destruction. This argument might be extended further yet; but for because I have already spoken a great deal to this effect in the third sermon of this third Decade, that which is here left out may there be found; and therefore I refer you to the looking upon that[3]. And so now hitherto touching sin.

I have with somewhat too long a sermon, dearly beloved, by more than the space of two whole hours detained you here. That therefore I may now make an end, let us humbly acknowledge our sins, and meekly cry with prayers unto the Lord, which sitteth in the throne of grace, saying: Have mercy upon us, O Lord, for against thee have we sinned, and do confess our offences. Thy debtors are we; forgive thou us our debts, as we forgive our debtors: and lead us not into temptation: but deliver us from evil. Amen.

The End of the Third Decade of Sermons.

[1 i. e. proofs, evidences.]
[2 non convertuntur ad se percutientem, sed, Lat. omitted; are not turned to him that smiteth them, but, &c.]
[3 See above, page 79.]

The Decades of Henry Bullinger

The Decades of Henry Bullinger

Volume 2

Edited by Thomas Harding

With new introductions by
George Ella and Joel R. Beeke

Reformation Heritage Books
Grand Rapids, Michigan

Reformation Heritage Books
3070 29th St. SE
Grand Rapids, MI 49512
616-977-0889
orders@heritagebooks.org
www.heritagebooks.org

Printed in the United States of America
23 24 25 26 27/11 10 9 8 7 6 5 4 3

ISBNs
978-1-892777-38-6 (vol. 1)
978-1-892777-39-3 (vol. 2)
978-1-60178-827-6 (2 vol. set)

This reprint is photolithographed from the 4-volume Parker Society edition (1849–1852), edited by Thomas Harding, and published by the University Press at Cambridge. Volumes 1 (the first and second Decades) and 2 (the third Decade) of the Parker Society edition are printed as volume 1 of this edition. Volumes 3 (the fourth Decade) and 4 (the fifth Decade) of the Parker Society edition are printed as volume 2 of this edition.

For additional Reformed literature, request a free book list from Reformation Heritage Books at the above regular or email address.

CONTENTS.

ADDENDA.

Page 229, line 23. See Bullinger de Orig. Error. Lib. i. cap. 5. fol. 22. Tigur.
1539.
245, — 37. Owe: own, possess. Shakspeare. Twelfth Night. A. i. Sc. 5.
Ourselves we do not *owe*.

ERRATA.

Page 73, note 9, } for "above" read *Vol. II.*
102, — 2, }
185, — 5, for " spinosa" read *spinose.*
196, line 33, read, representation *or* likeness.
209, note 1, for "133" read "132."
223, line 5, place a comma at *obedient.*
229, — 24, } for " animœ " read *animœ.*
231, — 20, }
304, — 9, place a comma after *curiously.*
318, note 1, for " note 2 " read *note* 1.
348, dele " note 4 " and substitute [⁴ See above, page 329, and Hutchinson's
Works, ed. Parker Soc. p. 134.]
353, — " note 3."

THE
FOURTH DECADE OF SERMONS,

HENRY BULLINGER.

OF THE GOSPEL OF THE GRACE OF GOD, WHO HATH
GIVEN HIS SON UNTO THE WORLD, AND IN
HIM ALL THINGS NECESSARY TO SAL-
VATION[1], THAT WE, BELIEVING
IN HIM, MIGHT OBTAIN
ETERNAL LIFE.

THE FIRST SERMON.

AFTER the exposition of the law, and those points of
doctrine that depend upon the law[2], I think it best now to
come to the handling of the gospel, which in the exposition
of the law and other places else hath been mentioned oftentimes. Now therefore, dearly beloved, as I have been hitherto helped with your prayers to God, so here again I
request your earnest supplications[3] with me to the Father,
that I by his holy Spirit may speak the truth to your edification[4] in this present argument.

Evangelium is a Greek word; but is received of the *Evangelium,*
Latins and Germans, and at this day used as a word of their the gospel.
own. It is compounded of εὖ, which signifieth good, and
ἀγγέλλω, to tell tidings. For *Evangelium* signifieth the
telling of good tidings, or happy news: as is wont to be
blown abroad, when, the enemies being put to foil, we raise
the siege of any city, or obtain some notable victory over
our foes. The word is attributed to any joyful and lucky
news concerning any matter luckily accomplished.

[1 veræ salutis omnia, Lat.; all things pertaining to true salvation.]
[2 aut legi utcunque adhærent, Lat. omitted; or are in some way
connected with the law.]
[3 Rather, your supplications, and those most earnest.]
[4 with me—edification, the translator's addition.]

1

The apostles did willingly use that term; not so much because the prophets had used it before them[1], as for that it doth wonderfully contain, and doth as it were lay before our eyes, the manner and work of our salvation accomplished by Christ, whereunto they have applied the word *Evangelium*[2]. The prophet Esay, as Luke interpreteth it, bringeth in Christ our Lord speaking in this manner: "The Spirit of the Lord upon me, because he hath anointed me εὐαγ-γελίσασθαι; that is, to preach the gospel hath he sent me, to heal the broken-hearted, to preach deliverance unto the captive, and recovering of sight unto the blind, freely to set at liberty them that are bruised, and to preach the acceptable year of the Lord." Lo here, the Saviour of the world doth in the prophet and the evangelist expound to us what *Evangelium* is, and whereunto it tendeth. "The Father," saith he, "hath sent me to preach *Evangelium*, the gospel, to the poor." And immediately after, to shew who those poor should be, he addeth: "which are broken-hearted, or broken-minded;" to wit, such as find in themselves no soundness or health; but, utterly despairing of their own strength, do wholly depend upon the help of Christ their cunning and willing physician[3]. Now the gospel, or good tidings, which is shewed to the[4] afflicted, is this; that the Son of God is descended from heaven to heal the sick and diseased souls. To which also, to make it more evident, he addeth another cause[5], saying, that the Son of God is come "to preach deliverance unto captives, and the recovering of sight to the blind," &c. For all men are held captive in the bonds of damnation: they do all serve a sorrowful slavery under their cruel enemy Satan: they are all kept blind in the darkness of errors; and to them it is that redemption, deliverance, and the acceptable year[6] of the Lord, is preached. Now this joyful tidings is called *Evangelium*, the gospel.

Isai. lxi.
Luke iv.

[1 Bullinger refers to the Hebrew word בִּשֵׂר, which the LXX. often render by εὐαγγελίζω. See his Comment. in Matth. fol. 1. Tigur. 1542. whence much also of this definition of the gospel is extracted.]

[2 whereunto—Evangelium, the translator's addition.]

[3 cunning (skilful) and willing, not in Lat.]

[4 his, Lat.; to these.]   [5 alia, Lat.; other benefits.]

[6 verus utique annus jubileus, Lat.]

Therefore the gospel is of all men in a manner after The gospel, what it is. this sort defined: The gospel is a good and a sweet word, and an assured testimony of God's grace to us-ward, exhibited in Christ unto all believers. Or else: The gospel is the most evident sentence of the eternal God, brought down from heaven, absolving all believers from all their sins, and that too freely, for Christ his sake, with a promise of eternal life. These definitions are gathered out of the testimonies of the evangelists and apostles; for St Luke bringeth in the angel of the Lord speaking to the amazed shepherds, and saying: "Fear not; for, behold, I bring you good tidings of great joy, that shall be to all people: for unto you is born this day in the city of David a Saviour, which is Christ the Lord." Lo here, he taketh from the shepherds all manner of fear with the bringing of good tidings; that is, with the preaching of health, which is a thing that is full of joy and always bringeth gladness with it. The tidings are, that there is born the Saviour of the world, even the Lord Jesus Christ: he is born; and that too unto and for us; that is, to the health and salvation of us mortal men. St Paul saith, that "the gospel was promised afore of God by the [Rom. i. 1—4.] prophets in the holy scripture of his Son, which was made of the seed of David after the flesh; who hath been declared to be the Son of God with power, after the Spirit that sanctifieth, by his resurrection from the dead." And again: "The gospel is the preaching of Jesus Christ, according to [Rom. xvi. 25, 26.] the revelation[7], which hath been kept close from before beginnings, but is now made manifest, and by the writings of the prophets opened to all nations unto the obedience of faith, according to the appointment of the eternal God." And yet again more briefly he saith: "The gospel is the power [Rom i. 16.] of God unto salvation to all that do believe;" that is to say, the gospel is the preaching of God's power, by which all they are saved that do believe. But Christ is the power of God: for he is said to be the arm, the glory, the virtue, and brightness of the Father. Now Christ bringeth salvation to every one that doth believe: for he is the Saviour of all.

Of all this we do now gather this definition of the holy The definition of the gospel. gospel: The gospel is the heavenly preaching of God's grace

[7 revelationem mysterii, Lat.]

1—2

to us-ward, wherein it is declared to all the world, being set
in the wrath and indignation of God, that God the Father
of heaven is pleased in his only-begotten Son, our Lord Christ
Jesus, whom, as he promised of old to the holy fathers, he
hath now in these latter times[1] exhibited to us, and in him
hath[2] given us all things belonging to a blessed life and
eternal salvation, as he that for us men was incarnate, dead,
and raised from the dead again, was taken up into heaven,
and is made our only Lord and Saviour, upon condition
that we, acknowledging our sins, do soundly and surely[3] believe in him.

This definition, I confess, is somewhat with the longest:
but yet withal I would have you think, that the matter,
which is in this definition described, is itself very large and
ample; which I have therefore in this long definition or
description, with as great light as I could, endeavoured myself to make manifest to all men. Wherefore I neither
could nor should have expressed it more briefly. This definition consisteth of just parts, which being once severally
expounded and throughly opened, every man, I hope, shall
evidently perceive the nature, causes, effects, and whatsoever
else is good to be known, concerning the gospel.

That the
gospel is
tidings from
heaven.

First of all; that the gospel is tidings come from heaven,
and not begun on earth, that doth most of all argue, because
God our heavenly Father did himself first preach that tidings
to our miserable parents after their fall in paradise, promising his Son, who, being incarnate[4], should crush the serpent's head. Then again, the apostle Paul doth in express

[Heb. i. 1,
2.]

words say: "God in time past, at sundry times, and in
divers manners, spake unto the fathers by the prophets, and
hath in these last days spoken to us by his Son." And

[John i. 18;
iii. 31, 32.]

John before him is read to have testified, saying: "No man
hath seen God at any time; the only-begotten Son, which
is in the bosom of the Father, he hath declared him." And
again: "He that cometh from on high is above all: he that
is of the earth is earthly, and speaketh of the earth: he that
cometh from heaven is above all. And what he hath seen

[1 now—times, not in Lat.]
[2 plene, Lat. omitted; fully.]
[3 modo credamus, Lat.—soundly and surely, not in Lat.]
[4 incarnandus, Lat.; being to be incarnate.]

and heard, that he testifieth." To this belongeth, that the prophets were believed to have prophesied by the inspiration of the Holy Spirit. Now they did in the holy scriptures foreshew the gospel: the especial or chief points whereof were by angels descending from heaven declared unto men. For the incarnation of the Son of God is by the archangel Gabriel told first to the holy virgin, and after that again to Joseph, the supposed Father of Christ, and tutor[5] of the unspotted virgin. The same angel did preach to the shepherds the birth of the Son of God. Moreover, to the women that came to the grave, minding after their country-manner to anoint the body of the Lord, the angels declared that he was risen from the dead again. The same angels at the Lord's ascension did testify to the apostles, whose eyes were turned and surely fixed into the clouds, that he was taken up into heaven, and that from thence he should come again to judge the quick and the dead. And to all these testimonies may be added the voice of the eternal Father himself uttered from heaven upon our Lord and Saviour, saying, "This is my beloved Son, in whom I am pleased; hear him:" which [Matt. iii. 17; Luke ix. 35.] testimony of the Father the blessed apostle Peter doth in the zeal of the Spirit repeat in the first chapter of his second epistle. Therefore the preaching of the gospel is a divine speech, unreprovable, and brought down from heaven: which whosoever believe, they do believe the word of the eternal God; and they that believe it not, do despise and reject the word of God. For it ceaseth not to be the word of God because it is preached by the ministery of men. For of the apostles we do read that the Lord did say: "It is not ye that speak, but the Spirit of my Father which is within you." [Matt. x. 20.] And therefore we read, that they departed not from Hierusalem, until they were first instructed from above, and had received the Holy Ghost. Neither is there any cause why the word of God should be tied to the apostles only, as though after the apostles no man did preach the word of God. For our Lord in St John's gospel doth plainly say: "Verily I say unto you, He that receiveth whomsoever I send receiveth me; and he that receiveth me receiveth him [John xiii. 20.] that sent me." Now our Lord, the high priest and chief bishop of his catholic church, doth send, not apostles only,

The gospel is the word of God, although it be uttered by the ministry of men.

[5 i.e. guardian.]

but all them also that are lawfully called and do bring the word of Christ. Therefore we understand it to be spoken concerning all the lawful ministers of the church, where the Lord doth say, " Whose sins soever ye forgive, they are forgiven them; and whose sins soever ye retain, they are retained :" and again, " Whatsoever thou loosest on earth, shall be loosed in heaven ; and whatsoever thou bindest on earth, shall be bound in heaven." For in another place the Lord saith : " Verily I say unto you, It shall be easier for the land of Sodom and Gomorrha in the day of judgment, than for that city that receiveth you not, and heareth not your sayings." Now who knoweth not with how filthy and horrible sin the men of Sodom did defile themselves; and that the Lord rained fire, brimstone, and pitch from heaven, wherewith he burnt up both the city and her inhabitants ? Who therefore cannot gather thereupon, that rebels and blasphemers of the gospel of Christ do sin more grievously than the Sodomites did; and that God, which is a sure revenger, will surely plague them for it, either in this life, or in the world to come, or else in both, with unspeakable miseries and endless torments ? Let us therefore believe the gospel of the Son of God, first preached to the world by God the Father, then by the patriarchs, after that of the prophets, and lastly of the only-begotten Son of God Christ Jesus, and his apostles ; whose heavenly voice doth even at this day sound to us in the mouths of the ministers, sincerely preaching the gospel unto us.

The gospel preacheth grace.

Secondarily, we have to consider what it is that the heavenly preaching of the gospel doth shew unto the world ; to wit, the grace of God our heavenly Father. For the apostle Paul in the twentieth chapter of the Acts saith, "that he received the ministry of the Lord Jesus, to testify the gospel of the grace of God." Now therefore I will at this present say so much of the grace of God as is sufficient for this place.

The word, grace.

The word "grace" is diversly used in the holy scriptures, even as it is in profane writings also. For in the Bible it signifieth thanksgiving, and also a benefit, and alms; as 2 Cor. viii. Moreover, it signifieth praise and recompence, as in that place where the apostle saith : "If, when ye do well, ye are afflicted, and yet do bear it; that is praiseworthy

Marginal notes:
[John xx. 23.]
[Matt. xviii. 18.]
[Matt. x. 15.]

before God[1]." It doth also signify faculty or licence; as when we say, that one hath gotten grace to teach and execute an office. For the apostle saith that he received grace; and im- [Rom. i. 5.] mediately, to expound his own meaning, he addeth, to execute the office of an apostle. Moreover the gifts of God are called grace, because they are given gratis, and freely bestowed without looking for of any recompence. And yet Paul, in the fifth to the Romans, distinguisheth a gift from grace: for grace doth signify the favour and good-will of God toward us; but a gift is a thing which God doth give us of that good-will, such as are faith, constancy, and integrity. They are said to have found grace with God, whom God doth dearly love and favour more than other. In that sense Noah found grace in the eyes of the Lord: Joseph found grace in the eyes of the lord of the prison: and the holy virgin is read to have found grace with the Lord, because she was beloved of God, and very dear unto the Lord, as she whom he had singularly chosen from among all other women. But in this *The grace of God, what it is.* place and present argument "grace" is the favour and goodness of the eternal Godhead, wherewith he, according to his incomprehensible goodness, doth gratis, freely, for Christ his sake embrace, call, justify, and save us mortal men.

Now here methinketh, before we go any further, it is not amiss to examine and search out the cause of this God's love to us exhibited. For we see that there is a certain relation[2] betwixt the favour of God and us men to whom his favour is so bent. It is a matter neither hard nor tedious to be found out. For in us there is nothing wherewith God can *The cause of God's grace.* be in love, or wherewithal he may be moved or stirred up to embrace us: yea, insomuch as we are all unpure[3] sinners, and that God is holy, just, and a revenger of iniquities, he hath matter enough to find in us, for which he may be angry at and with just revengement plague us. So then the cause of God's love to us-wards must of necessity be not in us, nor in any other thing beside God (considering that nothing is more excellent than man), but even in God himself[4]. Moreover the most true scripture doth teach us, that God is of his own inclination naturally good, gentle, and, as Paul calleth him, *phil-* [Titus iii. 4.]

[1 gratia apud Deum, Lat.; 1 Pet. ii. 20. Auth. Marg. *thank.*]
[2 correlationem, Lat.]   [3 impurissimi, Lat.]
[4 ejusque natura, Lat. omitted; and in his nature.]

anthropon, a lover of us men, who hath sent his own[1] Son, of his own nature, into the world for our redemption: whereupon it doth consequently follow, that God doth freely, of himself and for his Son's sake, love man, and not for any other cause. Whereby immediately all the preparaments, incitaments, and merits of men, being dissolved by the fire of God's great love, do vade and pass away like smoke. For the grace of God is altogether free; and unless it be so, I cannot see how it can be called grace. But it behoveth us in a thing so weighty to cite some evident testimonies of the holy scripture, to confirm our minds withal against all sophistical trifles and temptations of the devil. Our Lord in the gospel said: "So God loved the world, that he gave his only-begotten Son for the world, that every one which believe in him should not perish, but have life everlasting." Lo here, this good-will of God, which is the favour and love wherewith God embraceth us, is the cause of our salvation. For Christ, having suffered for us, is our salvation. Now God[2] of very love hath given Christ both to us, and for us[3]. Neither may we think, that God was first moved by our love to him-ward to shew like mutual love to us again, and to give his Son for us; for he had determined, before the beginning of the world, to work our redemption through Christ his Son. And John the Evangelist in his canonical epistle saith: "Herein is love, not that we loved God, but that he loved us, and sent his Son to be an atonement for our sins."

To these testimonies, although sufficiently plain and strong enough, I will yet add some proofs out of the apostle Paul; that so this argument may be more evident, and that the great agreement may appear which is betwixt evangelists and apostles in this doctrine of grace[4]. Paul therefore saith[5]: "All have sinned, and stand in need of[6] the glory of God; but are justified freely by his grace, through the redemption that is in Christ Jesu." Again to the Ephesians he saith: "Ye are saved through grace by faith, and that not of yourselves, it is the gift of God: not of works, lest any man

Marginal notes:

[John iii. 16.]

[1 John iv. 10.]

[Rom. iii. 23, 24.]

[1 unicum, Lat.; only.]
[2 Pater Deus, Lat.; God the Father.]
[3 and for us, not in Lat.]   [4 totius doctrinæ, Lat.]
[5 ad Romanos, Lat. omitted.]
[6 destituuntur, Lat. and Erasmus.]

should boast[7]." Again to Titus: "The grace and love of God our Saviour towards all men hath appeared, not of the works of our own righteousness which we did, but according to his mercy hath he saved us[8]." Likewise, in the second Epistle to Timothy, the first chapter, he saith: "God hath saved us, and hath called us with an holy calling, not according to our works, but according to his own purpose and grace, which was given us in Christ Jesus[9]." I think, verily, that if a man had been set of purpose to have feigned anything for the defence of this matter, he could not have framed any sentence so fit and evident as these words are. So now it is manifest, that the grace of God is altogether free, as that which excludeth all our works and merits; and this free love of God is the only cause and true beginning of the gospel: for which cause Paul calleth the gospel the preaching of grace.

The cause of the gospel.

But now, although the grace of God doth not depend upon us or our works[10], yet doth it not idly abide in God, as if it were utterly without us and altogether far from us, as the thing that is neither felt nor yet worketh in us. For we understood by the cited testimonies, that grace is the favour of God wherewith he loveth us men; we understood that men are saved by grace: for since God loveth men, he would not have them perish; and therefore he hath through grace sent his Son to deliver them from destruction, and that in him the justice and mercy of God might be known to all the world. But none are delivered save those that believe; therefore grace hath somewhat whereby to work in man[11]: for by the pouring of the Holy Ghost into our hearts, the understanding and will are instructed in the faith. To be short, grace (as I have already[12] told you) doth call, justify, save, or glorify the faithful: so that we must make our account, that the whole work of our salvation and all the virtues of the godly do proceed of the only grace of God alone, whose working we do at all times acknowledge

The working of God's grace.

[7 Eph. ii. 8. 9, gratia per fidem, Lat.]
[8 Titus iii. 4. 5, erga homines, Lat.]
[9 per Christum, Lat. and Erasmus.]
[10 or our works, not in Lat.]
[11 Rather, therefore again grace hath something to work in man.]
[12 in finitione, Lat. omitted; in the definition.]

and confess[1]. And that is again proved both by divine and human testimonies. Paul to the Romans saith: "Those which he knew before, he also did predestinate: and those which he did predestinate, he also called: and those whom he called, he also justified: and those whom he justified, he also glorified. What shall we then say to these things? If God be on our side, who can be against us? Which spared not his own Son, but gave him for us[2], how shall he not with him also give us all things?" Again, in the first chapter of his Epistle to the Ephesians, he hath referred the whole work of election and salvation, with all the parts thereof, unto the grace of God. Moreover, the holy fathers in the council *Mileventanum*, among whom also St Augustine was present, made this decree touching the grace of God: "If any man say, that mercy is without the grace of God bestowed from above upon us, believing, willing, desiring, endeavouring, studying, asking, seeking, and striving, (as of ourselves;) doth not confess, that even to believe, to will, and to be able to do all these things as we should do, is wrought by the pouring in and inspiration of the Holy Ghost; if he join the humility or obedience of man as an help unto grace[3]; and if he doth not consent that it is the very gift of grace, even that we are humble and obedient; he is directly contrary to the apostle, who saith, 'For what hast thou that thou hast not received?' and, 'By the grace of God I am that I am[4].'" Thus much say they. Now these divine and human testimonies being throughly

[1 ubique, Lat.; throughout.]   [2 pro nobis omnibus, Lat.]

[3 More correctly, and maketh the help of grace to follow after either man's humility or obedience.—Beveridge on the Thirty-Nine Articles, Vol. I. p. 383. Oxf. 1840.]

[4 There is a mistake in the reference: the following is the canon meant: Si quis sine gratia Dei credentibus, volentibus, conantibus, laborantibus, vigilantibus, studentibus, petentibus, quærentibus, pulsantibus nobis misericordiam dicit conferri divinitus; non autem ut credamus, velimus, vel hæc omnia sicut oportet agere valeamus per infusionem Spiritus Sancti in nobis fieri confitetur; et aut humilitati aut obedientiæ humanæ subjungit gratiæ adjutorium, nec ut obedientes et humiles simus ipsius gratiæ donum esse consentit; resistit apostolo dicenti, *Quid habes quod non accepisti?* et, *Gratia Dei sum id quod sum.* —Concil. Arausic. II. can. 6. Concil. Labb. et Cossart. Tom. IV. col. 1668. Par. 1671. This second council of Orange was held A.D. 529. Augustine was dead long before.]

considered, there is none, I hope, which may not understand
that the grace of God is the same that I told you; to wit,
the favour and good-will of the eternal Godhead, wherewith
he according to his incomprehensible goodness doth embrace,
call, justify, and save men freely for Christ his sake, our
Lord and Saviour.

The blessed man Aurelius Augustine had a sharp conflict
with Pelagius the Briton concerning the grace of God. For
the heretic did by grace understand nothing but the benefit
of the creation; which as Augustine denied not to be grace,
so did he vehemently urge that the apostle[5] did especially
speak of that free grace, whereby, without any merit of ours,
we are freely saved for Christ his sake. This did he urge therefore the more earnestly, because he saw that[6] the heretic
affirmed that his own human nature was sufficient unto him[7],
not to do only, but also to do perfectly, the commandments
of God by free-will. But of these matters St Augustine
doth very largely and religiously dispute in his ninety-fifth
Epistle, *Ad Innocentium*[8].

Many of the late writers, for teaching's sake, have divided grace into grace that doth things acceptable, and grace
that is gratis or freely given: again, they have divided it into
working grace, and joint-working grace: finally, they part
it into grace that goeth before, and grace that followeth after.
And the very same writers also reckon up the operations
or effects of grace after this manner almost: grace healeth

Marginal notes: The contro-versy betwixt Augustine and Pelagius touching the grace of God.

1. Gratia gratum faciens. 2. Gratia gratis data. 3. Gratia operans, et gratia co-operans. 4. Gratia præveniens, et gratia subsequens.

[5 Apostolos, Lat.; the apostles.]
[6 Pelagium, Lat. omitted.]
[7 Rather, that human nature was sufficient unto itself.]
[8 Aurelius aliique episcopi, inter quos Augustinus, Innocentio
Papæ, de Pelagio quem audierant jam ad presbyterii gradum evec-
tum.—Aug. Ep. 95. (in the Benedictine Edition, 177.) Op. Par. 1531.
Vol. II. fol. 83. col. 2. In the course of this epistle it is charged
against Pelagius,—illum dicere gratiam, quam etiam cum impiis habemus, cum quibus homines sumus; negare vero eam qua Christiani
et filii Dei sumus:—and it is replied,—Etsi enim quadam non im-
probanda ratione dicitur gratia Dei, qua creati sumus.... quia non
præcedentium aliquorum operum meritis, sed gratuita Dei bonitate
donata est; alia est tamen qua prædestinati vocamur, justificamur,
glorificamur. It is also stated that Pelagius affirmed,—non solum
ad facienda, verum etiam ad perficienda mandata divina per liberum
arbitrium humanam sibi sufficere naturam,—as here alleged by Bullinger.]

the soul, and maketh it first to will well, and then to work effectually the thing that it willeth : so it causeth it to persevere in goodness, and at length to come to eternal glory. But I am not so careful to reckon up the sentences of writers, to shew you every one's several opinion, (which both were an excessive labour, and also more than my ability is to do) ; as I am willing to cite the places of scripture (which is the one and only rule how to think, and how to judge rightly), to shew you thereby what the scripture would have you think : as I have in my former treatise, Of the grace of God, both briefly and evidently enough, I hope, declared unto you. And also the discourse of Christ[1], which followeth hereafter, (through whom the Father hath poured the most excellent and heavenly grace into us,) shall help to make up that which seemeth to be wanting here.

We are justified by grace.

But now, before I depart from this argument, I thought good to admonish you, that the sentences of God's word do not jar among themselves, when we do in sundry places read and hear, first, that we are saved freely or by the grace of God ; then, that we are saved by the love of God ; thirdly, that we are saved through the mercy of God ; fourthly, that we are saved through Christ ; fifthly, that we are saved through the blood, or death, or incarnation of Christ ; and lastly, that we are saved through faith in Christ, or in the mercy or grace of God. For all these speeches tend to one and the same end, and do ascribe the whole glory and cause of man's salvation unto the very mercy or grace of God. The pledge of grace, yea, and our only Saviour, is the only-begotten Son of God betrayed unto death. Sincere faith layeth hold on mere grace in Christ, and nothing else.

God exhibiteth his grace to us in Christ.

Now therefore, having thus expounded according to my small ability that which I had to speak in general of the grace of God, I do here descend to handle that singular or particular work of God's grace, which is nothing else but that the merciful Father hath exhibited to us his Son in that manner and order as he promised him to us in the old prophets, and that in him he hath fully given us all things requisite to eternal life[2] and absolute felicity ; because he is the Lord and Messiah, or only and true Saviour, which was

[1 disputatio de Christo, Lat.]
[2 salutis, Lat.]

incarnate, dead, raised to life, and taken up into heaven
for us and our salvation. For Christ is both king and high
priest, that is, our Saviour; he is the mark, the star, and
very sun-light of the preaching of the gospel. Now in expounding these things particularly I will use this course and
order. First of all, I will out of the law and the prophets
recite unto you some evident promises of Christ[3] made by God
unto the church; which shall be those especially that the
apostles themselves have already touched and expounded.
Secondly, I will prove unto you that God hath now performed that which he promised so long ago; to wit, that he
hath already exhibited to us his only-begotten Son; and that
he is that true and so long-looked-for Lord and Messiah, which
should come to save the world. Lastly, I will shew you how that
in this Son the Father is pleased and reconciled to the world
again: in whom also he hath fully given us all things requisite
to eternal life and absolute felicity. For he for us and for
our salvation was incarnate, dead, raised to life again, and
taken up into heaven, there to be a Mediator for ever and
advocate unto his Father[4]. And in these points do lie
the lively veins of the gospel, which flow with wholesome
waters unto eternal life; for in them doth consist the sound
consolation of the faithful, and the enduring tranquillity of a
quiet conscience: without them there is no life or quiet rest.

The promises made by God concerning Christ, which are
uttered in the holy scriptures, are threefold, or of three sorts:
I therefore, to make them the plainer unto you, do divide the
promises of one and the same sort according to the times.
The first promises were made to the patriarchs or ancient
fathers before the giving of the law: and these again consist
of two sorts; for one sort of them are plain, uttered evidently in simple words, without all types and figurative
shadows; the other sort are figurative and couched under
types.

The first and most evident promise of all was made by the
very mouth of God unto our first parents, Adam and Evah,
being oppressed with death, calamities, and the horrible fear
of God's revenging hand for their transgression[5]; which pro-

The promises touching Christ our Saviour.

The first evangelie, gospel, or preaching of glad tidings. Gen. iii.

[3 eximias promissiones de Christo, Lat.]
[4 there to be—Father, not in the original.]
[5 of God's—transgression, not in Lat.]

mise is, as it were, the pillar and base of all christian religion, whereupon the preaching of the gospel is altogether founded, and out of which all the other promises in a manner are derived. That promise is contained in these words of the Lord : " I will put enmity betwixt thee" (meaning the serpent, the devil, I say, in the serpent)[1] "and the woman[2], and betwixt thy seed and her seed ; and it shall tread down thy head, and thou shalt tread upon his heel." God in these words promiseth seed ; the seed, I say, not of man, but of woman ; and that too, of the most excellent woman, to wit, that most holy virgin Mary, the woman that was blessed among all other women. For she conceived, not by any man, but by the Holy Ghost ; and, being a virgin still, was delivered of Christ our Lord : who by dying and rising again did not only vex or wound, but also crush and tread down, the head, that is, the kingdom of Satan, to wit, sin, death, and damnation ; taking away and making utterly void all the power and tyranny of that our enemy and deceiver. In the meanwhile Satan trod on Christ his heel ; that is to say, he, by his members Caiphas, Pontius Pilate, the Jews and Gentiles, did with exquisite torments and death vex and kill the flesh, which was in Christ the lowest part, even as the heel is to the body[3]. For the Lord in the Psalms saith : "I am a worm, and no man. They have brought my life into the dust." But he rose again from the dead. For had he not risen again, he had not trodden down the serpent's head. But now, by his rising, he is become the Saviour of all that do believe in him. Out of this promise is derived that singular and notorious one, which the angel of the Lord reciteth unto our father Abraham in these words following : " In thy seed shall all the nations of the world be blessed." But Paul, in his epistle to the Galatians, doth in express words declare, that that blessed seed is ours[4], which was promised to Abraham. Now our Lord is called by the name of seed because of the first promise made to Adam and Evah, and because he was for us incarnate and made very man. Neither is this promise re-

[Psal. xxii. 6, 15.]

[Gen. xxii. 18.]

[Gal. iii. 16.]

[1 in the serpent, not in Lat.]
[2 et inter illam mulierem, Lat.]
[3 even as—body, not in Lat.]
[4 Christum illud esse semen benedictum, Lat. ; that that blessed seed is Christ.]

pugnant to the first: for although Christ our Lord be here called the seed, or son, of Abraham; yet is he no other way referred unto Abraham than by the virgin, which was the daughter of Abraham and mother of Christ. Now what good doth the son of Abraham to us by his incarnation? Forsooth, he blesseth us. But a blessing is the contrary unto a curse. Therefore what cause[5] soever we drew from the sin of Adam, that doth Christ heal in us, and bless us with all spiritual blessing. Neither doth he bestow this benefit upon a few alone, but upon all the nations of the world that do believe in him.

The patriarch Jacob, being inspired with the Holy Ghost, foretold the chances that should betide his children[6]; and at length when he came to Juda among the rest, he saith: "The sceptre shall not depart from Juda, and a law-giver[7] [Gen. xlix. 10.] from between his feet, till `Schilo come; and unto him shall the gathering of the people be." Lo here, in these words the Messiah is not only promised, but the very time also is prescribed, when he should be incarnate, with a declaration both what and how far forth he should be. The kingdom, saith he, shall remain under Juda until the coming of the Saviour[8]: and albeit that the tribe of Juda shall not always have kings to govern them, yet shall it not lack nobles, captains, lawgivers, learned men and sages, to rule the people. And therefore the evangelical history doth faithfully witness, that Christ came at that time when all power, authority, and rule was translated to the Romans, unto whose emperor, Octavius Augustus, the Jews were enforced to pay taxes and tribute. Now *Schilo* signifieth felicity, or the author of felicity; it signifieth plenty, store, and abundance of all excellent things. For Christ is the treasury of all good things. And the Chaldee interpreter, where he findeth *Schilo*, translateth it Christ. Finally, to him, as to their Saviour, shall all people be gathered: as the prophets did afterward most plainly declare, Esay in the second, and Micheas in the fourth chapters of their books or prophecies.

Furthermore, the types and figures of Christ are Noah

[5 A misprint in all the editions for *curse:* quicquid maledictionis, Lat.]

[6 et res futuras, Lat. omitted; and things to come.]

[7 vel scriba, Lat. omitted; or a scribe.]　　　[8 Christi, Lat.]

preserved in the ark; for in Christ are the faithful saved; as St Peter testifieth, 1 Pet. iii. Abraham offereth up Isaac, his only-begotten son, upon the top of the same mountain where many years after the only-begotten Son of God was offered upon the cross[1]. Joseph is by his brethren sold to the heathen, he is cast in prison; but being delivered he doth become their Saviour, and is of all the people called the preserver of the Egyptian kingdom. In all these things was Christ our Lord prefigured.

The later promises also are of two sorts; either openly uncovered, or hidden as it were under a veil or figure. They are contained in the law and the prophets even till the time of the captivity of Babylon. The blessed apostle Peter doth in the third chapter of the Acts cite the prophecy of Moses touching the coming of the greatest of all prophets. The prefigured promises[2] of Christ are the sacrifices, which Paul in his epistle to the Hebrews doth in a wonderful summary shortly declare. The same Paul, in the fifth of the first to the Corinthians, applieth the paschal lamb to Jesus Christ. The like doth Peter in his first epistle[3]. Again, the stony rock that was struck, and gushed out with water[4], St Paul calleth Christ. And Christ himself in the gospel after St John doth say, that he was prefigured in the brasen serpent, which was lift up in the desert: the mystery whereof I have in another place more fully declared[5]. Many more there are like unto these; a good part whereof I have already touched, when I had occasion to treat of the ceremonies and their signification[6]; where he that listeth may read of it at large.

The unfigured and uncovered promises are almost without number in the Psalms and the prophets. Yea, the Lord himself in the gospel after St Luke doth testify, that the description of all his office and business is at large contained in the law, the prophets, and the Psalms. And when St Peter had preached the gospel, wherein he promised both Christ and the full remission of sins to all that believed, he did immediately

Margin notes:
1 Pet. i.
[1 Cor. x. 4.]
John [iii. 14, 15.]
Luke [xxiv. 44.]

[1 See Vol. II. page 151.]

[2 Rather, the promises in a figure.]   [3 in I. capite, Lat.]

[4 Rather, and the water that flowed out. Cf. Bullinger, Comment. in loc. cit.]

[5 See Vol. II. p. 339; also, The Old Faith, p. 44.]

[6 See Decade III. Serm. 6.]

add: "All the prophets also from Samuel and these that [Acts iii. 24.] followed in order, as many as have spoken, have likewise told you of these days." David verily, in the second, twenty-second, and hundred and tenth Psalms, hath notably set down the two natures of Christ, his Godhead and his manhood. Again, he hath laid before all men's eyes[7] his wholesome[8] preaching, his eternal priesthood, his everlasting redemption, and most bitter[9] death and passion[10]. What shall I say of the prophet Esay? who was, by no small doctor of the church of Christ, very worthily called an evangelist[11] rather than a prophet: as if he had written a story of things already past and done by Christ, and not of things that should be done: so truly did he foretell the state of Christ[12]. Now he maketh[13] Christ to be very God and very man, born after the flesh of the unspotted virgin; who had to preach the word of life, like a good shepherd to feed his fearful sheep, to be the light of the Gentiles unto the utmost parts of the earth, to give sight to the blind, to heal the lame and diseased; to be betrayed by his own, to be spit upon, to be smitten, to be hanged betwixt thieves, to be offered up a sacrifice for sin, and finally to make intercession for transgressors, that he himself being just might justify all that believe in his name. Read Esay, seventh, eighth, ninth, eleventh, twenty-eighth, fortieth, forty-ninth, fiftieth, and fifty-third chapters; and also all the last chapters of all his prophecy, wherein he doth most fully describe the church or congregation of Christ Immanuel[14]. Jonas bare the most manifest type of the Lord's sharp death and joyful resurrection[15]. Micheas also doth name Bethlehem [Mic. v. 2.] to be the place wherein Messiah should be born, whose beginning, to wit, of his divine nature, he doth refer to be before all beginnings[16]. He doth also foretell that the preaching of [Mic. iv. 2.] the gospel should from out of Hierusalem be sown abroad

[7 tantum non inspectanda, Lat.; almost so as to be seen.]
[8 salutarem, Lat.]
[9 per mortem, Lat.; through a most bitter death.]
[10 See The Old Faith, p. 53, &c.]
[11 Augustine. See Vol. I. p. 51.]
[12 so—of Christ, not in Lat.]
[13 proponit, Lat.]
[14 Immanuel, an addition of the translator's.]
[15 The epithets are the translator's.]
[16 refert ad æternitatem, Lat.]

[Jer. xxiii. 5.] through all the compass of the world. Jeremy saith, that God would raise up to David a true seed or branch, that is, the looked-for Messiah; and in that prophecy he alluded to the law concerning the raising up of seed to the deceased brother. For the virgin, conceiving by the Holy Ghost, Deus verus brought forth a Son, whose name is Jehovah, being very et essentialis. [Isai. vii. 14.] God in very deed, whom Esay calleth Immanuel, and is the true righteousness of all that do believe in him; for by Christ [Isai. xxxi. 33, 34.] are the faithful justified. For the same prophet[1] in the thirty-first chapter doth promise in Christ full or absolute remission of sins and abundant grace of the Holy Ghost: Joel [ii. 28–32.] which thing Joel also did not conceal. Thus out of many testimonies I have picked out only these few in number; for the whole books of the prophets are occupied in the description of Christ and his offices.

The last promises concerning Christ were by God revealed to the prophets, and by them declared to the church of God, even in the very time of the captivity at Babylon, or else immediately upon their return to Hierusalem[2]. Ezechiel prophesieth of the shepherd David, and of the sheep receiving John [x.] that shepherd: which prophecies the Lord doth in St John's gospel expound of himself. The same prophet treateth very much of grace and frank and full remission of sins through the Saviour Christ, especially in the thirty-fourth, thirty-sixth and thirty-seventh chapters of his prophecy. Daniel, verily, hath visions and many dreams; but in them he doth so set Christ out unto us, that it is unpossible to have him more better, more evidently and excellently described. In his second chapter he teacheth us of his eternal kingdom, and telleth us that Christ should come under the Roman monarchy, at what time the Roman princes, being by affinity allied together, should mutually in battle destroy one another: which was fulfilled when Pompey and Julius Cæsar, Antony and Octavius Dan. ix. Augustus, maintained civil war[3]. Moreover, Daniel's weeks[4] are unknown to no man, wherein he doth as it were with his finger point[5] at Christ, the coming[6] of Christ, and the reprobation of the Jews because of their disloyalty and unbelief.

[1 iterum, Lat.; again.]
[2 mox post captivitatem, is Bullinger's Lat.]
[3 imperitantibus, Lat.]   [4 in 9 cap. Lat.]
[5 toti mundo, Lat.; to all the world.]   [6 tempora, Lat.]

Haggee[7] the prophet foretold the manner how the temple should be builded, I mean, the true temple indeed; to wit, the church of Christ. Zachary doth excellently paint[8] to us many mysteries of Christ: he layeth before us the kingdom and priesthood of our Lord and Saviour: he commendeth to us that one and only eternal sacrifice, which is effectual enough to cleanse the sins of all the world: Zach. third, ninth, and fourteenth chapters. Yea, he prophesieth of nothing else but of Christ and his kingdom. Malachias foresheweth[9] the forerunner of the Lord, and handleth no small number of mysteries concerning Christ. Whereby we do perceive that Paul writ most truly in the first to the Romans, saying, that God did afore promise the gospel by his prophets in the holy scriptures. Rom. i.

Now by these holy promises we do gather this also, that there are not many or divers gospels, (although we deny not, but that the same gospel[10] was penned by divers evangelists;) but that there is one alone, and that too, as it were, eternal. For the very same gospel which is at this day preached to us was at the beginning of the world preached to our first parents[11]. For it is assuredly certain, that by the gospel were saved Adam, Evah, Abel, all the patriarchs, prophets, and faithful people of the old Testament: which thing we have in another place at large declared[12]. The gospel is not divers.

We are now come to the second part, where we have to shew you that God the Father hath faithfully performed to us that which he promised to our forefathers in giving to us his only-begotten Son, who is that true and looked-for Messiah, that is to be blessed[13] world without end. In making this matter manifest the evangelists and apostles of our Lord have taken great pains, and set it forth so well and faithfully that it cannot be bettered. God the Father hath through Christ performed to us that which he promised to our forefathers.

They shew that Christ doth come of the stock of David, descending lineally of the seed of Abraham: they tell that

[7 chap. ii. 7—9. Haggæus templum extruit, is Bullinger's phrase.]
[8 tradit, Lat.]   [9 præmittit, Lat.]
[10 eandem historiam evangelicam, Lat.]
[11 Rather, was from the beginning of the world preached to the fathers.]
[12 This is the topic of Bullinger's treatise, The Old Faith. See also Vol. II. page 283.]
[13 benedictus, Lat.; who is blessed.]

his mother was the virgin, which did conceive by the Holy
Ghost, and, being a virgin still, brought him into the world.
They note the time wherein Christ was revealed, in all points
correspondent to the prophets' prophecies. They add, that
the place of his nativity was answerable to that which Micheas foretold. In the East there appeareth a star, which
moveth the princes[1], or wise men, to go and salute the new-
born King. They come therefore, and even in Hierusalem[2]
do openly profess that the Messiah is born, and that they
are come out of the East to worship and honour him. According to their words so were their deeds: for when by
the leading of the star they had once found him, they fall
down before him, and do, by offering to Christ the gifts
that they brought, not obscurely declare how joyful they
were, and how much they set by their Lord and Saviour[3].
In the very city of Hierusalem[4] the most just man Simeon
with great joy of heart and godly gratulation doth in the
temple openly testify, that God according to his eternal
goodness[5] and constancy had given to the world his only-
begotten Son, whom he had promised unto the fathers;
therewithal protesting that he was willing to die[6]. He addeth
the cause; "For that," saith he, "mine eyes have seen thy
salvation," to wit, that *Schilo*, the Saviour[7], whom thou, O
God, hast determined to "set before all people, a light to
lighten the Gentiles, and to be the glory of thy people Israel:"
that is, that he, shaking off all darkness, should bring the
light of truth and life unto the Gentiles, to lighten them
withal; and that he should be the glory and life of the people
of Israel. Hereunto also belongeth the testimony of that
notable man Zachary, the holy priest of God, saying:
"Blessed be the Lord God of Israel; for he hath visited
and redeemed his people, and hath raised up a horn of salvation for us in the house of his servant David; as he spake
by the mouth of his holy prophets, which have been since

[Luke ii. 30—
32.]

[1 magos viros primarios et sapientissimos, Lat.]
[2 in urbe Hierosolymorum regia, Lat.; in the royal city.]
[3 quanti Christum faciant, Lat.; how joyful they were, the translator's addition.]
[4 urbe regia, Lat.]   [5 veritate, Lat.; truth.]
[6 tranquillissimo animo, Lat.; with most peaceful mind.]
[7 felicitatorem salvatoremque, Lat.]

the world began:" and so forth, as is to be seen in the
first of Luke's gospel. Moreover John the son[8] of this Zachary, surnamed the Baptist, than who we read not that
any one more holy was ever born of women, did with his
finger point at Christ Jesus, and openly declare that he is
that looked-for Messiah, whom all the prophets promised; Jesus is
Christ, that
and that God, by giving him unto the world, hath done that is that
looked-for
he promised, and wholly poured himself with all his benefits Messias.
into and upon all faithful believers. "And as the people
waited" (saith Luke), "and thought in their hearts of John, [Luke iii. 15, 16.]
whether he were very Christ; John answered, saying to them
all, Indeed I baptize you with water; but one stronger than
I cometh after me, whose shoe-latchet I am not worthy to
unloose; he shall baptize you with the Holy Ghost and with
fire." And in the Gospel after St John we read: "The [John i. 29–34.]
next day John seeth Jesus coming unto him, and saith, Behold the Lamb of God, which taketh away the sin of the
world. This is he of whom I said, After me cometh a man
which is preferred before me[9], because he was before me;
and I knew him not: but that he should be declared unto
Israel, therefore am I come baptizing with water." And
immediately after he saith: "I saw the Spirit descending
from heaven like unto a dove, and it abode upon him. And
I knew him not: but he that sent me to baptize with water,
the same said unto me, Upon whom thou shalt see the Spirit
descending, and tarrying still on him, the same is he which
baptizeth with the Holy Ghost. And I saw, and bare record
that this is the Son of God." Again, when the disciples of
John did envy the happy success of Christ, and that it
grieved them to see their master John as it were neglected
in comparison of Christ, John said to his disciples: "Ye your- [John iii. 28
–30, 35, 36.]
selves are witnesses, that I said, I am not Christ, but I am sent
before him. He that hath the bride is the bridegroom; but
the friend of the bridegroom, which standeth and heareth
him, rejoiceth because of the bridegroom[10] : therefore this
my joy is fulfilled. He must increase, but I must decrease.
The Father loveth the Son, and hath given all things into

[8 filius beatissimus, Lat.; the most blessed son.]
[9 qui me antecessit, Lat. and Erasmus; qui ante me factus est,
Vulg.]
[10 gaudio gaudet propter vocem sponsi, Lat.]

his hand. He that believeth in the Son hath life everlasting: he that believeth not in the Son shall not see life, but the wrath of God abideth upon him."

These testimonies are firm, clear, and evident enough, and might suffice for the confirmation of this cause. But let us yet of a many moe pick out and add a few, which may declare that Christ is already exhibited unto us. Therefore our Lord himself, whom we believe to be Messiah, when he had a great while been very greatly commended by the testimony of John, doth at length come abroad and preach the word of life. But it is not read, that in any age, before or since, there was ever any that taught with so great grace. And therewithal he shewed almost incredible and wonderful miracles, which do easily argue who he was, and were sufficient to win such a man with whom no words might possibly prevail. He was loving and gentle to sinners, repeating still and beating into their heads that he was come to save them, and call them to repentance. Therefore, when the disciples of John did once [Matt. xi. 3—5.] come unto him, saying, "Art thou he that should come, or shall we look for another?" he answered, "Go ye and tell those things to John which ye see and hear : the blind receive their sight, and the lame walk, the lepers are cleansed, and the deaf hear, the dead are raised to life, and to the poor is preached the glad tidings of the gospel." Now by these, his doctrine I mean, and his works or miracles, his mind was to shew, that he was exhibited the true Messiah unto the world, and that none other is to be looked for. Moreover in the synagogue at Nazareth, where he read and expounded Esay's prophecy of the coming of Messiah, he declared there that that scripture was in himself[1] fulfilled. And to the history is [Luke iv. 16—22.] immediately annexed : "And all bare record unto him, and wondered at the gracious sayings that proceeded from his mouth." Again, in the tenth chapter of St John his gospel : "The Jews came round about the Lord, and said, How long dost thou make us to doubt? If thou be Christ, tell us plainly. Jesus answered them, I told you, and ye believe not : the works that I do in my Father's name, these bear witness of me. But ye believe not, because ye are not of my sheep." And presently after he addeth : "Ye say that I blaspheme, because I said, I am the Son of God. If I do not

[1 in himself, not in Lat.]

the works of my Father, believe me not: but if I do, and if
ye believe not me, believe my works; that ye may know and
believe that the Father is in me, and I in him." In the
seventh of John we read : " They that believed in him said,
Will Christ, when he cometh, shew more signs than this man
hath shewed ? " that is to say : Admit we grant that there is
another Christ to be looked for; yet this is most sure, that the
other Messiah cannot do more and greater miracles than this
man doth. Let us therefore believe that this is the true
Messiah. Before Caiaphas, the high priest, and the whole
council of the peers of Israel, also before Pontius Pilate in the
judgment-hall of the Roman empire, our Lord Christ did
openly in express words confess that he is that true and looked-
for Messiah.

He verily, as the prophets foretold of him, did of his
own accord die for sinners ; the third day after that he rose
again from the dead; he ascended into heaven, and sitteth on
the right hand of God the Father. And the evangelists,
reciting faithfully the words and deeds of Christ, do to the
most notable ones always add : " All this was done or said,
that it might be fulfilled which was spoken by the prophet."
Wherefore it were not worth the labour here to gather
together the prophecies of the prophets, by them to examine
the words and deeds of Christ, and by the manifest agreement
betwixt them for to conclude, That God hath performed to
us that which he promised unto our fathers in giving to us his
only-begotten Son Christ Jesus, which is the true and looked-
for Messiah. For this have the evangelists already done,
and that too with so great faith and diligence, that for the
plainness of the thing it cannot be bettered. To this place
now ye may refer all that I have in my former sermons said
touching the signification, or mysteries, fulfilling and abrogating,
of the law.

And, to content ourselves with a smaller number of testimonies, might not this one, which is read in the fourth of St
John, be instead of many thousand confirmations? The
woman of Samaria saith to the Lord : " I know that the
Messiah shall come, which is called Christ: therefore when
he cometh, he shall tell us all things. Jesus answered her,
I am he that speak to thee." Lo, what could be had[2] more

[2 said, edd. 1577 and 1587. dici, Lat.]

plainly? "I," saith he, "am the Messiah; even I, I say, that do even now speak to thee, and did at the first say, If thou knewest the gift of God, and who it is that saith to thee, Give me to drink, thou wouldst have asked of him, and he would have given thee water of life. For whosoever shall drink of the water that I shall give him, he shall never be more athirst: but the water that I shall give him shall be in him a well of water springing up into eternal life." They therefore are the most thirsty and unfortunate[1] of all men, which long for and look after another Messiah beside our Lord and Saviour Christ Jesus. The apostle St Peter in a meetly long oration, well grounded and confirmed with scripture and strong reasons, in the second of the Acts, doth shew that our Lord Jesus is that true Messiah: for with this sentence he shutteth up his sermon: "Therefore let all the house of Israel surely know, that God hath made both Lord and Christ this Jesus, whom ye have crucified." To the same mark tendeth that large and learned oration of the first martyr St Stephen, which is extant to be seen in the seventh chapter of the Acts[2]. Philip doth out of Esay's prophecy declare to the eunuch of Æthiope that Jesus is Christ. St Paul in all the Jewish synagogues putteth forth none other proposition to preach on but this; Jesus is Christ, that is, Jesus is the king, the bishop, and the Saviour of the faithful. And in the thirteenth chapter he doth at large declare and prove that proposition true.

So now these most evident and clear testimonies of holy scripture cannot choose but suffice such heads as are not of purpose set to cavil and wrangle. I will not at this present too busily and curiously dispute against the overthwart Jews, who look for another Messiah, and do deny that our Lord Jesus, the Son of God and the virgin Mary, is the true Messiah. The wretches feel that to be true, which the Lord in his gospel did foretell them, saying: "When ye shall see the abomination of desolation, spoken of by Daniel the prophet, standing in the holy place, let him that readeth understand. Then let them that are in Jurie flee to the mountains. But woe to them that are with child and give suck in those days; for great shall the affliction be." And again, speaking of the city of Hierusalem, he saith: "The days shall come

The Jews deny that Christ is come, or that Jesus is Christ.

[Matt. xxiv. 15, 16, 19, 21.]

[Luke xix. 43, 44.]

[1 aridissimi, Lat.]   [2 in 8 cap. Lat.]

upon thee, that thine enemies shall compass thee with a
trench, and hem thee in, and lay seige to thee on every side,
and shall make thee even with the ground, and thy sons that
are within thee ; and they shall not leave in thee one stone
standing upon another ; because thou knowest not the time of
thy visitation." And again ; " There shall be wrath upon this [Luke xxi.
people ; and they shall fall with the edge of the sword, and $^{23, 24.]}$
shall be led captive into all nations ; and Hierusalem shall be
trod under foot of the Gentiles, until the times of the Gentiles
be fulfilled." Now since they feel these things to be so finished[3]
as they were by Christ foretold in the gospel ; why do not
the wretches give God the glory, and in other things believe
the gospel, acknowledging Jesus Christ, the Son of God and the
virgin Mary, our Lord and Saviour, to be[4] the true and looked-
for Messiah ? What have they wherewith to cloak their stubborn incredulity ? They have now by the space of more than
a thousand and five hundred years been without their[5] country;
I mean, the land of promise that flowed with milk and honey;
they have wanted their prophets ; and lacked their solemn
service and ceremonial rites.   For where is their temple ?
where is the high priest ? where is the altar ? where are the
holy instruments ? where be the sacrifices that ought to be
offered according to the law ? All the glory of God's people is
now translated unto the Christians. They joy to be called the
sons of the faithful Abraham ; they enjoy the promises made
unto the fathers ; they talk and make mention of the fathers;
they judge rightly of the law and covenant of the Lord;
they have the holy scriptures, and in expounding them they
have great dexterity ; they have the true temple, the true
high priest, the true altar of incense and burnt-offerings, even
Christ Jesus, the Lord and Saviour ; they have the true
worship, which was of old prefigured only in those external
ceremonies : as I have already declared unto you in that
place where I handled the Jewish ceremonies.   The Gentiles
are out of every quarter of the world called unto Christ Jesu.
All the promises touching the calling of the Gentiles have
been hitherto most abundantly fulfilled, and are even at this
day. Now are we the chosen flock[6], according to the doctrine

[3] ad verbum, Lat. ; to the letter.]
[4] venisse, Lat. ; to have come.]
[5] the, ed. 1577. patria sua, Lat.]   [6] genus, Lat. ; nation.]

[1 Pet. ii. 9.] of St Peter: "We are the royal priesthood, an holy nation, a peculiar people; being called hereunto, that we should preach the power of him[1] which hath called us out of darkness into his marvellous light." Therefore let the unhappy Jews (unless perhaps they had rather to be entangled in greater errors, to be vexed daily with endless calamities, and so at last perish eternally[2]) turn unto Christ by faith, and together with us begin to worship him in whom their fathers hoped, and in whom alone is life and salvation. For, that I may with the

[1 Tim. iii. 16; Rom. ix. 33.] apostle's words conclude this place: "God is made manifest in the flesh, justified in the spirit, seen to the angels, preached to the Gentiles, believed in the world, and received in glory[3]. And every one that believeth in him shall live eternally, and never be confounded."

God the Father being angry with the world, is pleased with it in the Son. We have now behind the last part to expound; the contents whereof are, that God the Father, who before was angry with the world, is pleased now in his only-begotten Son Jesus Christ our Lord.

First of all therefore I have to shew you that God was angry with the world: which is no hard matter to prove. For God is angry at sins. But the whole world is subject to sin; therefore it must of necessity be, that the most just God

[Rom. i. 18.] is mightily angry with all the world. And Paul saith: "The wrath of God is revealed from heaven against all ungodliness and unrighteousness of men." Again, the same apostle saith, that "all men are subject unto sin." For confirmation whereof he citeth these sentences of the holy scriptures, saying: "There is none righteous, no, not one: there is none that understandeth, or seeketh after God: they are all gone out of the way: they are all become unprofitable: there is none that doth good, no, not one. Their throat is an open sepulchre; they have used their tongues for to deceive; the poison of asps is under their lips: whose mouth is full of cursing and bitterness: their feet are swift to shed blood. Heart's grief and misery are in their ways: and the way of peace have they not known. There is no fear of God before their eyes."

[1 ut prædicemus vires illius, Lat.]

[2 juxta Christi Domini comminationem, Lat. omitted; according to the threatenings of Christ the Lord.]

[3 in gloria, Lat.; received up in glory. Tyndale 1525, and Cranmer 1539.]

Now lest the Israelites should answer, that these things do not pertain to the people of God, but to the heathen and ungodly alone, he addeth: "We know that whatsoever the law [Rom. iii. 9 —19.] saith, it saith it to them which are under the law; that every mouth may be stopped, and that all the world may be endangered[4] to God." No man is here excepted. For to the Galatians the same apostle saith: "He hath shut up all under sin, [Gal. iii. 22.] that he may have mercy on all." It followeth therefore, that all the world was subject to the wrath or indignation of the most just and righteous God: as is at large proved in the second, fourth, and fifth chapters to the Ephesians.

But the heavenly Father is appeased, or reconciled to this wicked world, through the only-begotten Son our Lord Jesus Christ. And this I hope I shall abundantly prove by the only testimony of God himself. For the Father, by sending down a voice from heaven unto the earth upon Christ, first ascending newly out of the water after his baptism, and then again at his transfiguration in the sight of his disciples, did significantly say: "This is my beloved Son, in whom I [Matt. iii. 17; xvii. 5.] am delighted, pleased, or reconciled[5]; hear him." This testimony is read to have been foreshewed in the forty-second chapter of Esay's prophecy. And Peter the apostle repeateth the same in the first chapter of his second epistle. Paul also did as it were expound this, and say: "It pleased the [Col. i. 19, 20.] Father that in the Son should dwell all fulness; and by him to reconcile all things unto himself, since he hath set at peace through the blood of the cross by him both the things in earth and the things in heaven." In heaven is God, and we men here upon earth. Now Christ is the Mediator, which goeth betwixt us, and reconcileth us unto his Father, so that now we are the beloved of the Father in his beloved Son. For in the epistle to the Ephesians the same apostle saith: "He hath made us accepted in the beloved; in whom we have [Eph. i. 6, 7.] redemption through his blood, the forgiveness of sins, according to the riches of his grace." All this shall be more fully understood by that which followeth.

For now I must prove that God the Father hath in his All things requisite to Son given us all things that are necessary to a happy life and life and salvation are eternal salvation. I name here two things; a happy life, fully given us in Christ Jesus.

[4 See Tyndale's Doct. Treat. ed. Parker Soc. p. 502, n. 1.]
[5 placata, reconciliata vel propitiata est anima mea, Lat.]

and everlasting salvation. By a happy life I understand a holy and godly life, which we live and lead quietly and honestly in this present world. Eternal salvation is that felicity of the life to come, which we with assured hope do verily look for.

Now we have in Christ a most absolute doctrine of a happy life taught us by the gospel; wherein also we do comprehend the example of Christ, his own trade of life. Verily, our heavenly Father hath made him our teacher, in saying, "Hear him." And he himself in the gospel after St Matthew sayeth: "Be ye not called masters; for ye have one master, even Christ;" who in the gospel after St John is called "The light of the world." In another place also he testifieth that his doctrine is contained in the holy scriptures; whereupon it cometh that he referreth his disciples to the diligent reading of the holy scriptures: touching which scriptures Paul, the teacher of the Gentiles and[1] the universal church of Christ, doth say: "All scripture is given by inspiration[2] of God, and is profitable to doctrine, to reproof, to correction, to instruction which is in righteousness; that the man of God may be perfect, instructed in all good works." Wherefore, although the whole world be mad, and that the obstinate defenders of the traditions[3] rather than the scriptures do whet their teeth for anger; yet, maugre their heads, the word of the apostle shall abide most firm[4], wherein he testifieth that the doctrine of the scriptures, otherwise called the christian doctrine, is in all points most absolute and thoroughly perfect. Touching which matter, because I have already spoken in the first sermons of the first Decade, I am therefore here a great deal the briefer.

Now concerning the eternal salvation fully purchased[5] for us by Christ, thus ye must think. Eternal salvation is the seeing and enjoying of the eternal God, and so, consequently, an unseparable joining or knitting unto him. For David saith, "There is fulness of joys in thy sight; and at thy right hand are pleasures for evermore:" and St John saith, "Now are

[Matt. xxiii. 8; John viii. 12.]

[2 Tim. iii. 16, 17.]

[Psal. xvi. 11.]
[1 John iii. 2.]

[1 adeoque, Lat.; and so.]
[2 Omnis scriptura, divinitus inspirata, est utilis, &c. Lat. So Tyndale and Cranmer.]
[3 traditionum vivarum, Lat.; of the lively traditions.]
[4 stat stabitque, Lat.; abides and shall abide.]
[5 paratam sive partam, Lat.]

we the sons of God, and yet it appeareth not what we shall
be; but we know that, when he shall appear, we shall be like
him; for we shall see him as he is." Moreover the Lord in
the gospel saith, "Blessed are the pure in heart: for they [Matt. v. 8.]
shall see God." But all men are endued with unpure hearts:
therefore no man shall see God; because no uncleanness
abideth in consuming fire; (and God is a consuming fire[6];)
therefore we cannot be partakers of salvation unless we be
purely cleansed. But without the shedding of blood there is
no cleansing or remission of sins : I do not mean the blood of
rams or goats, but of the only-begotten Son of God, our Lord
Christ Jesus. He[7] therefore took our flesh and blood; he came
into the world, died willingly for us, and shed his blood for
the remission of our sins; and so by that means purged the
faithful, so that now, being clean, they may be able to stand
before[8] the most holy God, who is a consuming fire. To this
may be annexed the consideration of the incarnation of our
Lord Jesu Christ, his death, resurrection, and ascension into
heaven, whereof I did above make mention in the definition of
the gospel; for in those points doth consist the whole mystery of our reconciliation: touching which I do in this
place speak so much the more briefly, because in the exposition
of the apostles' creed I have handled so much as seemeth to
concern these points of doctrine; which whosoever will know,
may look and find them there.

　　Now that Christ alone is our most absolute life and sal- Christ alone
vation, it may be gathered by that which is already spoken; and salva-
and yet notwithstanding I will here allege some testimonies tion.
more, to the end that the verity and sincerity of the evangelical truth may be the more firm and evident to all men.
That in Christ alone our life and salvation doth consist, so
that without Christ there is no life and salvation in any other
creature, the Lord himself doth testify[9], saying: "Verily, [John x. 1,
verily, I say unto you, He that entereth not by the door into 7, 8.]
the sheepfold, but goeth in some other way, he is a thief and
a robber. Verily, verily, I say unto you, I am the door of
the sheep : as many as came before me are thieves and robbers." Lo here, there is but one door only, through which

[6 The translator's addition.]
[7 Dei filius, Lat.; the Son of God.]
[8 habitare cum, Lat.]　　　　[9 in evangelio, Lat.; in the gospel.]

the way doth lie unto eternal life : and Christ is that door. They therefore, which do by other means than through Christ strive to come to life and salvation, are thieves and robbers; for they steal from Christ his honour and glory, considering that he both is and abideth the only Saviour: and in so doing they kill their own souls. The same Saviour in the gospel [John xiv. 6.] saith : "I am the way, the truth, and the life. No man cometh to the Father but by me." Hath he not in these few words rejected and utterly excluded all other means of salvation, making himself alone our life and salvation ? [1]This phrase of speech, "No man cometh to the Father but by me," is the same that this is, "Through Christ alone we come unto the Father." Moreover the Lord's apostles have so laid Christ alone before our eyes, that no man can choose but understand, that without Christ Jesus there is no life to be found in any other creature. The holy apostle St Peter in the Acts saith: [Acts iv. 12.] "There is in none other any salvation : for there is none other name under heaven given among men wherein we must be saved." And St Paul, in the fifth chapter to the Romans, doth oftentimes repeat, that "by the righteousness of one man, Jesus Christ, all the faithful are justified." Again, the same [Acts xiii. 38, 39.] Paul saith : "Through him is preached to you the remission of sins; and through him is every one that believeth justified from all the things, from which ye could not be justified by Moses' law." Like to this also he hath other testimonies in the second chapter of his epistle written to the Galatians. It is manifest therefore, that through Christ alone the forgiveness of sins and life everlasting are freely bestowed upon all the faithful; which gifts, as they are not without Christ at all, so are they not bestowed by any other means than through Christ alone. Concerning the remission of sins, which is the chief tidings of the gospel, I have at large already discoursed in the ninth sermon of the first Decade and other places more.

Christ doth fully work our salvation.   Now for the proof that our Lord doth fully absolve from sins, fully remit sins, and fully save repentant sinners[2], so that nothing more can be desired or wished for, and consequently, that the Lord himself is the most absolute fulness of all the faithful, without whom they that believe neither

[1 Certe, Lat. ; Without doubt.]
[2 repentant sinners, not in Lat.]

do nor can wish for anything else to life, salvation, and absolute felicity, he doth himself in the gospel say[3] : " Every one that drinketh of this water shall thirst again ; but whosoever shall drink of the water which I shall give him, he shall live eternally." And again : " I am the bread of life ; he that cometh to me shall not hunger, and he that believeth in me shall never thirst." The apostles therefore, after they had eaten this celestial bread, that is, after they had once believed in Christ[4], when many departed and did forsake Christ, being demanded whether they also would leave him, did answer, " Lord, to whom shall we go ? Thou hast the words of eternal life. And we believe and know that thou art Christ, the Son of the living God." Lo here, they neither will nor can forsake Christ ; because there is none other to whom they may join themselves : for he alone is the life and salvation of them that believe ; and that too, so absolute and perfect, that in him alone they may content and stay themselves. With the writings of the evangelists doth the doctrine of the apostles fully agree. For Paul to the Colossians saith : " It pleased the Father that in the Son should dwell all fulness." And again : " In the Son doth dwell all the fulness of the Godhead bodily ; and ye are fulfilled in him." And in the Epistle to the Hebrews he affirmeth, that the faithful have full remission of sins, because sacrifices for sin do cease to be offered ; and that God doth by the prophet Jeremy promise so absolute remission of sins, that he will not so much as once remember or think on them hereafter[5]. To this place belongeth the whole epistle written to the Hebrews ; and the conclusion of the eighth sermon in the first Decade, wherein I reckoned unto you the treasures that God the Father doth give to us in Christ his Son our Lord and Saviour.

Upon this now doth follow consequently, that they have not yet rightly understood the gospel of Christ, nor sincerely preached it, whosoever do attribute to Christ Jesu our Lord,

[John iv. 13, 14; vi. 35.]

[John vi. 68, 69.]

[Coloss. [i. 19; ii. 9, 10.]

[Heb. x. 2; Jer. xxxi. 33.]

The unsincere preaching of the gospel.

[3 rursus, Lat. ; again.]

[4 Dei filium, Lat. omitted ; the Son of God.]

[5 Proinde quicunque Christum fide possident, plenissime omnia vitæ et salutis possident, Lat. omitted ; And therefore, whosoever has Christ by faith, has most abundantly all things belonging to life and salvation.]

the true Messiah, either not only, or else not fully, all things requisite to life and salvation. It is a wicked and blasphemous thing to ascribe either to men, or to things inferior and worse than men, the glory and honour due unto Christ. The principal exercises of christian religion cannot, by derogating from the glory of Christ[1], challenge anything[2] unto themselves. For sincere doctrine doth directly lead us unto Christ. Prayer doth invocate, praise, and give thanks in the name of Christ. The sacraments do serve to seal and represent to us the mysteries of Christ. And the works of faith are done of duty, although also of free accord; because we are created unto good works. Yea, through Christ alone they do please and are acceptable to God the Father; for he is the vine, we are the branches. So all glory is reserved untouched to Christ alone: which is the surest note to know the true gospel by.

The sum of the gospel.

Thus hitherto we have heard that God, the Father of mercies, according to his free mercy taking pity upon mankind when it stuck fast and was drowned in the mire of hell, did, as he promised by the prophets, send his only-begotten Son into the world, that he might draw us out of the mud, and fully give us all things requisite to life and salvation. For God the Father was in Christ reconciled unto us, who for us and our salvation was incarnate, dead, raised from death to life, and taken up into heaven again.

And although it may by all this be indifferently well gathered, to whom that salvation doth belong, and to whom

Salvation preached in the gospel doth belong to all.

that grace is rightly preached; yet the matter itself doth seem to require in flat words expressly to shew, that Christ and the preaching of Christ his grace declared[3] in the gospel doth belong unto all. For we must not imagine that in heaven there are laid two books, in the one whereof the names of them are written that are to be saved, and so to be saved, as it were of necessity, that, do what they will against the word of Christ and commit they never so heinous offences, they cannot possibly choose but be saved; and that in the other are contained the names of them which, do what they can and live they never so holily, yet cannot avoid

[1 by derogating—Christ, not in Lat.]
[2 hujus, Lat. omitted; of this (glory).]
[3 allatam vel annunciatam, Lat.]

everlasting damnation. Let us rather hold, that the holy gospel of Christ doth generally preach to the whole world the grace of God, the remission of sins, and life everlasting. And in this belief we must confirm our minds with the word of God, by gathering together some evident places of the holy scriptures, which do manifestly prove that it is even so. Of which sort are these sayings following: "In thy Seed shall all the nations of the earth be blessed," Genesis xxii. "Every one that calleth upon the name of the Lord shall be saved," Joel ii. "We have all gone astray like sheep; and God hath laid upon him the iniquity of us all," Esay liii. "Come to the waters, all ye that thirst," Esay lv. There are of this sort innumerable places in the old Testament. Now in the gospel the Lord saith: "Every one that asketh receiveth; and he that seeketh findeth," &c. Matt. vii. "Come to me, all ye that labour and are heavy loaden, and I will ease you of your burden," Matt. xi. "Teach all nations, baptizing them in the name of the Father," &c. Matt. xxviii. "Go ye into the whole world, and preach the gospel unto all creatures: whosoever believeth and is baptized, he shall be saved," Mark xvi. "So God loved the world, that he gave his only-begotten Son, that every one which believeth in him should not perish, but have eternal life," John iii. In the Acts of the Apostles St Peter saith: "Of a truth I perceive that there is no respect of persons with God; but in every nation he that feareth him, and worketh righteousness, is acceptable unto him," Acts x. Paul in the third to the Romans saith: "The righteousness of God by faith in Jesus Christ cometh unto all and upon all them that believe." And in the tenth chapter he saith: "The same Lord over all is rich to all them that call upon him." In his Epistle to Titus he saith: "There hath appeared the grace of God that is healthful to all men[4]." And in the first to Timothy, the second chapter, he saith: "God will have all men to be saved, and to come to the knowledge of the truth." These and such like are the manifest testimonies, whereupon all the faithful do firmly stay themselves.

But now if thou demandest, how it happeneth that all men are not saved, since the Lord would that all should be saved and come to the knowledge of the truth; the Lord

Wherefore all men are not saved.

[4 chap. ii. 11, marg.]

[Matth. xx. 16.] in the gospel doth himself answer thee, saying: "Many indeed are called, but few are chosen." Which sentence he doth in the fourteenth of St Luke's gospel more plainly expound, where he doth in a parable shew the causes why a great part of mortal men doth not obtain eternal salvation, while they prefer earthly things and transitory before celestial or heavenly matters. For every one had a several excuse to cloke his disobedience withal: one had bought a farm; another had five yokes of oxen to try; the third had newly married a wife. And in the gospel after St John [John iii. 19.] the Lord saith: "This is condemnation, because the light came into the world, and men loved darkness more than the light." With this doctrine of the evangelists doth that saying of the apostle agree, 2 Cor. iv. And in the first to Timothy, the fourth chapter, he saith: "God is the Sa- The faithful are saved. viour of all men, especially of those that believe." Where-upon we gather, that God, in the preaching of the gospel, requireth faith in every one of us: and by faith it is manifest that we are made partakers of all the goodness and gifts of Christ. And verily there is a relation[1] betwixt faith and [Mark xvi. 16.] the gospel; for in the gospel after St Mark the Lord an-nexed faith to the preaching of the gospel. And Paul [Rom. i. 5, 16.] saith, that "to him was committed the preaching of the gospel, unto the obedience of faith." Again he saith: "The gospel is the power of God unto salvation to all them that do believe." And in the tenth chapter to the Romans he doth by gradation shew that the gospel is received by faith. But that faith may be rightly planted in the hearts of men, it is needful that the preaching of repentance do first go before: for which cause I, in the latter end of the definition of the gospel, added, "So that we, acknowledging our sins, may believe in Christ:" that is to say, the Lord will be our Saviour and give us life everlasting, if we acknowledge our sins, and do believe in him. And therefore here now may be annexed the treatises of faith and repentance. Touching faith, I have already largely spoken in the fourth, fifth, and sixth sermons of the first Decade. Concerning repentance I will hereafter speak in a several sermon by itself. In this place I will only touch summarily such points of repentance[2] as seem to make for the demonstration of the gospel.

[1 correlatio, Lat.]   [2 of repentance, not in Lat.]

Our Lord Christ Jesus doth in the preaching of the gospel require faith and repentance: neither did he himself, when he preached the gospel, proceed any other way. For Mark hath: "Jesus came into Galilee, preaching the gospel of the kingdom of God, and saying, The time is fulfilled, and the kingdom of God is at hand; repent, and believe the gospel." Neither did he otherwise instruct his disciples, when he sent them to preach the gospel unto all nations; for St Luke saith: "Christ said to his disciples, So it is written, and so it behoved Christ to suffer, and to rise again the third day from the dead; and that in his name should be preached repentance and the forgiveness of sins unto all nations." St Paul, like a good scholar following his master, in the Acts of the Apostles saith: "Ye know that I have held back nothing that was profitable unto you, but have shewed you, and have taught you openly and throughout every house, witnessing both to the Jews, and also to the Greeks, the repentance that is toward God, and the faith that is toward our Lord Jesus Christ." [3]In his Epistle to the Romans, where he doth compendiously[4] handle the gospel, he taketh occasion to begin the preaching thereof at sin, convincing both Jews and Gentiles to be subject thereunto. Now he beginneth at sin to this end and purpose, that every one, descending into himself, may see and acknowledge that in himself he hath no righteousness, but that by nature[5] he is the son of wrath, death, and damnation: not that such acknowledging of sins doth of itself make us acceptable unto God, or else deserve remission of sins and life everlasting; but that after a sort[6] it doth prepare a way in the minds of men to receive faith in Christ Jesus, and so by that means to embrace Christ Jesus himself, who is our only and absolute righteousness; for "the whole need not the physician, but such as are sick and diseased." They therefore, which think themselves to be clear without sins and righteous of themselves, do utterly reject Christ, and make his death of none effect[7]: but on the other side, they that feel the diseases of the mind, and do from the bottom

Side notes: The gospel teacheth faith and repentance. [Mark i. 14, 15.] [Luke xxiv. 46, 47.] [Acts xx. 20, 21.]

[3 Certe, Lat.; Without doubt.]　　　　[4 methodice, Lat.]
[5 sua natura, Lat.; by his own nature.]
[6 suo modo, Lat.]
[7 and make—effect; an addition of the translator's.]

of their hearts confess that they are sinners and unrighteous,
not putting any trust in their own strength and merits, do
How Christ is received. even pant for the haste that they make to Christ; which
when they do, then Christ doth offer himself in the gospel,
promising unto them remission of sins and life everlasting,
as he that came to heal the sick and to save repentant
sinners. But the promise is received by faith, and not by
works: therefore the gospel, and Christ in the gospel, are
received by faith. For we must diligently distinguish betwixt the precepts and the promises. The promises are received by faith: the precepts are accomplished by works.
[Gal. iii. 18.] Whereupon Paul is read to have said: "If the inheritance
be of the law, then is it not now of promise: but God gave
Abraham the inheritance by promise." The same apostle
to the Romans, conferring the law and the gospel together,
[Rom. x. 5— 9.] doth say: "The righteousness which is of the law doth say,
Whosoever doth these things shall live by them; but the
righteousness of faith doth say, If thou believest, thou shalt
be saved." The law therefore is grounded upon works,
whereunto it seemeth to attribute righteousness: but because
no man doth in works fulfil the law, therefore is no man
justified by works, or by the law. The gospel is not grounded
upon works: for sinners acknowledge nothing in themselves
but sin and wickedness; for they feel in themselves that
they are wholly corrupted: and therefore they fly to the
mercy of God, in whose promises they put their trust, hoping
verily that they shall freely obtain remission of their sins,
and that for Christ his sake they are received into the number
of the sons of God.

I would speak more in this place concerning faith in Jesus
Christ, the remission of sins, and the inheritance of life everlasting, if I had not already in the first Decade declared
them at large. Here by the way ye have to remember,
that the gospel is not sincerely preached, when ye are taught
that we are made partakers of the life of Christ for our
own deserts and meritorious works. For we are freely
saved[1], without respect of any works of ours, either first or
last[2].

And although I have oftener than once handled this

[1 per fidem, Lat. omitted; through faith.]
[2 operum nostrorum, sive præcedentium, sive sequentium, Lat.]

argument in these sermons of mine; yet because it is the hook whereupon the hinge of the evangelical doctrine (which is the door to Christ[3]) doth hang; and that this doctrine (to wit, that Christ is received by faith, and not by works) is of many men very greatly resisted; I will, for the declaration and confirmation sake thereof, produce here two places only, but such as be apparent enough and evident to prove and confirm it by: the one out of the gospel of Christ our Lord, the other out of Paul's Epistles.

Christ is received by faith, and not by works.

Our Lord Jesus Christ, being about to teach briefly the way to true salvation, that is, to preach the glad tidings of life unto Nicodemus, in the gospel after St John, doth first of all begin at repentance, and doth wholly take Nicodemus from himself, leaving him no merits of his own wherein to put his trust. For while he doth utterly condemn the first birth of man, as that which is nothing available to obtain eternal life, what doth he, I beseech you, leave to Nicodemus, wherein he may brag or make his boast? For he doth expressly say: "Verily, verily, I say unto thee, Unless a man be born from above[4], he cannot see the kingdom of God." If the first birth and the gifts[5] thereof were able to promote a man to the kingdom of God, what need then should he have to be born the second time? The second birth is wrought by the means of the Holy Ghost, which, being from heaven poured into our hearts, doth bring us to the knowledge of ourselves, so that we may easily perceive, assuredly know, and sensibly feel, that in our flesh there is no life, no integrity, or righteousness at all; and so consequently, that no man is saved by his own strength or merits. What then? The Spirit forsooth doth inwardly teach[6] us that which the sound of the gospel doth outwardly tell us, that we are saved by the merit of the Son of God[7]. For the Lord in the gospel saith: "No man ascendeth into heaven, but he that descended from heaven, the Son of man that is in heaven." For in another place he doth more plainly say: "No man cometh to the Father but by me." And again, to Nicodemus he saith: "As Moses did lift up the serpent in the wilderness, so must the Son of man be

How Christ did preach the gospel.

Of regeneration more largely is spoken in the sermon of repentance.

[John iii. 13; xiv. 6; iii. 14, 15.]

[3 which—to Christ, not in Lat.]
[4 So Marg. Auth. Ver. John iii. 3.]   [5 facultates, Lat.]
[6 pergit et docet, Lat.]   [7 fide, Lat. omitted; by faith.]

lift up; that every one which believeth in him should not perish, but have eternal life." Now Moses did hang up the brasen serpent for the health and recovery of them that were poisoned[1] by the bitings of the serpents. For they died presently that were stung with the serpents[2], unless they did immediately look up to the brasen serpent; for at the very sight thereof the poisoned sting did lose all force, and the person envenomed was out of hand restored and cured again. Neither was there in the host of the Israelites any other medicine but that alone, which whosoever despised he died without remedy. For the force of the poison was not expelled, and the life of the infected was not preserved, either by the power of prayers, or the multitude of sacrifices, or medicinable herbs, or any kind of physic, or other means of man's invention[3]: if any would escape the peril of death, it behoved him to behold the brasen serpent aloft. Now that brasen serpent was a type or figure of Christ our Lord; who, being lift up upon the cross, is ordained of God to be the only salvation. But now to whom doth that saving health befall? To them, forsooth, that do behold him being so lift up. The Lord himself telleth us what "to behold" doth signify, and instead thereof doth put "to believe." Therefore no works, none other means, nor merits of ours do save us from eternal death and from the force of sin, that is, the poison wherewith we are all infected by the old serpent, our adversary Satan. Faith alone, whereby we believe in Christ, who was lift up for the remission of our sins, and in whom alone our life and sure salvation doth assuredly consist, is the only thing that quickeneth us which are already dying by the envenomed sting of Satan, which is sin[4].

Hear, moreover, what the Lord doth add, instructing Nicodemus yet more fully in the true faith, and making the only cause of our salvation to be the mere and only grace of God, which is received by faith in Christ. "For so" (saith he) "God loved the world, that he gave his only-begotten Son, that every one which believeth in him should not perish, but have eternal life. For God sent not his Son[5]

[1 morientum e veneno, Lat.; that were dying of the poison.]
[2 dipsades, Lat.]   [3 See The Old Faith, p. 44.]
[4 which are—sin; an addition of the translator's.]
[5 in mundum, Lat.; into the world.]

to condemn the world ; but that the world might be saved
by him. He that believeth in him is not condemned : but
he that believeth not in him is already condemned, because
he believeth not in the name of the only-begotten Son of
God." Lo, what could be spoken more plainly ? By faith
we are made partakers of Christ. By repeating faith so
often his meaning was so to beat it into our heads, that no
man should hereafter do once so much as doubt of so manifest
and evident a piece of doctrine. But if here now thou dost
little set by the authority of Christ, then whose authority
wilt thou esteem ? But thou wilt not, I know, reject his
testimony. Yet albeit that his warrant is sufficient, give ear
notwithstanding to that disciple whom the Lord loved, who
in his epistle expounding as it were the words of the Lord,
and by the way of exposition repeating and beating them
into all men's minds, doth strongly cry out : " If we receive 1 John v.
the witness of men, the witness of God is greater : for this
is the witness of God which he testified of his Son. He that
believeth in the Son hath the testimony in himself : he that
believeth not God doth make him a liar, because he believed
not the record that he[6] gave of his Son. And this is the
record, that God hath given us eternal life, and this life is
in his Son. He that hath the Son hath life ; and he that
hath not the Son of God hath not life." But what else is
it to have the Son of God than to believe in him ? For
this sense is gathered by that which went before, being of
itself so evident, that for me to add anything unto it, is to
do nothing else but as it were to go about with a tallow-
candle to help or adlight the sun at his rising.

Now are we come to the place of St Paul, which is to be How Paul
seen in the third and fourth chapters of his epistle to the the gospel.
Romans. " The righteousness of God," saith he, " without
the law is made manifest, being witnessed by the testimony
of the law and the prophets." Paul in this place doth
preach the gospel most evidently ; for I know not any other
place wherein he doth it more plainly. He teacheth herein
how we are justified before God, what is the true righteousness and salvation of mankind, and by what means it cometh
unto us. He saith, that the righteousness of God, that is to
say, the righteousness which God bestoweth, or which doth

[6 Deus, Lat. ; God.]

prevail[1] before God, is revealed without the law; that is to
say, doth come unto us without the help of the law, to wit,
without the aid and merits of the works of the law. For
touching the testimony of the law and the prophets, they
witness both together, that they which believe are justified by
the righteousness of God. Now what that righteousness is,
he doth immediately declare, saying : " The righteousness of
God cometh by the faith of Jesus Christ unto all and upon all
them that believe." The righteousness, saith he, whereof we
speak[2], is not human or of mortal man, but altogether divine,
or of God himself. For as God alone is only just, so the
righteousness of God is the true and only righteousness of
God[3] that saveth us : which righteousness God maketh us to
be partakers of by that faith of Jesus Christ, to wit, if we
believe in Christ, and hope in him for to be saved[4]. Neither
is there here any man excluded from righteousness and salvation; for Paul doth plainly say, "Unto all and upon all
that do believe." Wherefore God doth repute and esteem all
them to be righteous, which do believe in Jesus Christ, his
only Son, our Lord and Saviour. Now he doth presently
annex the cause why he attributeth salvation unto the righteousness of God, and not of man, or why the gospel commendeth to us the righteousness of God, saying : " For there
is no difference; all have sinned and have need of the
glory of God." For because all men of their own nature are
destitute of the glory of God, that is, since they are without
the true image of God, to the likeness whereof they were
created in the beginning; therefore all men, verily, are unrighteous and sinners : whereupon it followeth, that in them
there is no righteousness, and that they have nothing wherein
to boast before the righteous God. For what else, I beseech
you, do sinners carry from the judgment-seat of God, but
confusion and ignominy ? And for because all men are such
and in that case, therefore the apostle doth very wisely add :
" But they are justified freely by his grace through the redemption in Christ Jesus ; whom God hath set forth to be a
propitiation, or reconciliation, through faith in his blood."

[1 consistit et valet, Lat.]
[2 quæ justificat et salvat, Lat. omitted; which justifies and saves.]
[3 of God, not in the original.]
[4 and hope—saved, not in Lat.]

Which is all one as if he had said : Men are justified for Christ
his sake by the mere grace or mercy of God, without any
help or merit of their own, if so be they do but believe that
God hath given his Son to the world, to shed his blood, and
to reconcile the purified sinners unto his Father in heaven.
In which words there are most fully and plainly declared the
whole manner and order of sanctifying, purifying, and justifying
of sinners.

The manner and order of our sanctification, purification, and justification.

But it is good here to repeat the apostle's words, and
more nearly to examine and deeply to consider them. "They
are," saith he, "freely justified." But wherefore freely?
Because, forsooth, they are justified by the mere grace of God,
without the help of their own works or merits. For all men are
sinners, and therefore they have nothing of themselves to allege for their justification: whereupon it followeth, that, since
some are justified, they are justified freely by the grace of God.
For the same apostle in the eleventh to the Romans saith: "If
we be saved by grace, then now not of works; for then grace
is no more grace: but if by works, then is it now no grace."

But there followeth in Paul immediately that which doth
yet make that argument more manifest, which is notwithstanding very manifest already; "through the redemption,"
saith he, "that is in Christ." Our righteousness and salvation
is the work of mere grace, because we are redeemed. For
in respect of ourselves, our works, and merits, we were the
servants of death and the devil, insomuch as we were sinners
and subject to sin. But God, by sending his Son, redeemed
us, when as yet, being his enemies, we were bound to the
devil, his open adversary[5]. Therefore he did freely redeem
us; as Esay the prophet did in his fifty-second chapter
plainly foretell that it should come to pass. But true salvation is not in any other, whatsoever he be, save in Christ
alone, our true Lord and Saviour. For the heavenly Father
did by his eternal counsel set forth his Son, our Lord
Jesus Christ, to be our propitiation, to wit, that he might be
our reconciliation, for whose sake only the Father being
pacified adopteth us into the number of the sons of God:
which is accomplished by none other way but through faith
in his blood; that is, if we believe that the Son, being sent
of the Father, did shed his blood, thereby to set us, cleansed,

[5 to the devil, his open adversary; an addition of the translator's.]

justified, and sanctified, before his heavenly Father. Wherein
we see again that our salvation doth freely consist in faith in
Jesus Christ.

These points being thus unfolded, the apostle, proceeding
to shew how far the benefit of redemption and justification
doth stretch, doth immediately add : "To declare his right-
ousness by[1] the forgiveness of the sins that are past, which
God did suffer, to shew at this time his righteousness." God,
saith he, hath set forth Christ to be the only propitiation,
that he might shew that there is but one and the same righteousness of all ages; Christ, I say, himself, who is the righteousness of all that believe. Now here he maketh mention of
two several times; that ancient age of the fathers, and this
present time wherein we now live. The ancient age is that
which went before the coming of Christ: this latter age of
ours is that which beginneth at Christ, is now at this present,
and shall be extended to the end of the world. And God
verily did of his long sufferance bear with and suffer the sins
of that old age for Christ his sake, by whom, and for whom,
he hath forgiven them : neither doth he set before us at this
day any other righteousness, save Christ alone, to be received
and embraced by faith.

For the apostle doth not obscurely afterward add: "That
he might be just, and the justifier of them that believe on
Jesus." As if he should have said : Now the meaning of all
this is, that we should understand that all men are unrighteous and altogether sinners; but that God alone is righteous,
without whom there is no righteousness at all: and that he
doth communicate his righteousness to all them that do believe
in Christ, to wit, which do believe that for Christ his sake
the Father is pleased and reconciled unto us, and that for him
we are reputed both just and holy.

By these words of the apostle there are two very wicked
and blasphemous errors of certain fellows notably refuted.
The one of the twain is the error of them which say, that our
fathers were justified, not by faith in Christ, but by the law
and their own merits; affirming that Christ suffered not for
the fathers, but for them alone that lived when he was upon
the earth, and for them that followed after his death. The
other error is theirs which say, that Christ offered up his

Marginal notes:
Who they be
that Christ
hath re-
deemed.

Errors
refuted.

[1 propter, Lat. ; for.]

body for the fathers, for original sin only, not for us and all
our sins; and therefore that we must make satisfaction for
our own sins. But the apostle Paul doth in this place condemn both these opinions. And the holy evangelist John,
agreeing with Paul, doth say : " The blood of the Son of God [1 John 1. 7;
doth cleanse us from all sin. For he is the propitiation for   ii. 2.]
our sins; not for our sins only, but for the sins of all the
world." Therefore the merit of Christ his redemption doth
extend itself to all the faithful of both the testaments.

The apostle Paul proceedeth, and upon that which he had
said he inferreth : " Where is the boasting ? It is excluded.
By what law ? Of works ? Nay, but by the law of faith."
He gathereth by the evangelical doctrine[2] hitherto taught,
that all the boasting of every man's own righteousness, and all
the bragging of every one's merits, is utterly taken away,
altogether exempted, and vanished : not by the law of works;
that is, not by the doctrine concerning works, which is wont
for the most part to puff men up and make them swell; but
by the law of faith; that is, by the doctrine concerning faith,
which doth empty and leave in us nothing but an humble
confession and acknowledging of our own lack of merits, attributing all our help to grace in Christ Jesus. And at the
last, gathering the chief proposition, he saith : " We do therefore hold that a man is justified[3] without the works of the law."

This is the sum and breviary of the whole gospel, that
we are justified, that is to say, absolved from sins, from
the definitive sentence of death and damnation, and sanctified
and adopted into the number of the sons of God, by faith,
that is, by an assured confidence in the name of Christ,
which is given by the Father to be our only Saviour.
And here are works by name excluded, to the end there
should be given to us no occasion to entangle faith with
works, or to attribute to works the glory and title due to faith
alone, or rather to Christ, upon whom our faith is grounded
and upheld.

This proposition being once put forth he doth presently
after confirm with arguments, shewing withal that this salvation is common both to the Jews and Gentiles, saying : " Is he

[2 de fide justificante, Lat. omitted; concerning the faith that
justifieth.]
[3 fide, Lat. ; by faith.]

the God of the Jews only? Is he not also of the Gentiles? Yes, even also of the Gentiles : for it is one God that shall justify the circumcision by faith, and the uncircumcision through faith." He fetcheth the confirmation of that which he said from the nature of God. There is but one God, who is of his own nature both life and righteousness; and he is the God both of the Jews and the Gentiles : therefore he is the life and righteousness of both the people : which righteousness he bestoweth on them by faith : therefore faith doth justify, or make them both righteous.

This is declared by the example of Cornelius the centurion. For he is justified, or, as I should rather say, being once justified he is declared to be acceptable to God, by the sending down of the Holy Ghost in a visible form upon him, when as he neither was circumcised, nor yet had kept the law, but had only heard the preaching of the gospel, and had believed in Jesus Christ. Now God did not justify Cornelius so alone, but will also justify all other nations by faith; even as he will not by any other means than by faith alone justify the Jews.

It followeth in Paul: "Do we then destroy the law through faith? God forbid : but we rather maintain the law." For the defenders or the disputers in the defence of works, or rather of justification by works, are wont to object : If faith alone in Christ doth justify, then is the law, or doctrine of the law, altogether unprofitable. For to what end are we commanded to do good works, if good works do not justify? The apostle answereth, That the law is not abolished by faith, but rather maintained : for since faith doth directly tend to Christ, in whom alone it doth seek and find all fulness; and that the law itself is the school-mistress unto Christ, and doth shut up all under sin, so that justification is by faith given to the faithful; it is most evident, that the law is not destroyed or darkened, but confirmed and made light, by the doctrine of faith.

How Abraham the father of the faithful is justified.

The apostle goeth on in his confirmation, and saith: "What shall we say then that Abraham our father as pertaining to the flesh did find? For if Abraham were justified by works, then hath he wherein to boast; but not before God. For what saith the scripture? Abraham believed God, and it was counted unto him for righteousness." There

are verily many examples of the holy fathers: but among
all the rest, the apostle chose out this of Abraham[1] to handle
it at large. For he in the scriptures is called the father of
them that do believe. Whereupon it is assuredly certain,
that the children shall be justified after the same sort that
their father was; as the apostle hath in express words taught
in the latter end of the fourth chapter. Moreover, Abraham was famous for[2] good works above all the rest of the
holy fathers: therefore if any other could have been justified
by his good works or merits, much more might Abraham
before all the rest. But for because he was justified by
faith and not by works, it is manifest therefore that all the
saints also both have been, and are, justified by faith and
not by works. Furthermore, Abraham lived 430 years before the law was revealed by Moyses[3]: whereupon it followeth,
that his works cannot be called the works of the law by
them that are the deniers of the justification by faith without
the law. Therefore the works that he did, he did them of
faith, and his works were the works of faith; and yet was
he not justified by them, but by faith. Therefore the glory
of the justification of faith remaineth sound, unspotted, and
unmingled with anything else. "What," saith he, "shall
we say that our father Abraham found concerning the flesh;"
to wit, so far forth as he is a man, and we also men of him?
What, I say, shall we say that he deserved[4]? To this demand this answer must be added: He found nothing, and
by his works he deserved nothing. For the proof followeth:
If by his works he deserved anything, or was by his merits
justified, then hath he wherein to boast. But he hath nothing
wherein to boast: therefore is he not justified by his works.
For God alone is righteous, and keepeth this his glory unto
himself alone without any partner or joint-possessor with
him, freely justifying them that are of the faith of Jesus
Christ, to the end that his grace may be always praised.

But Paul himself, by bringing in a place of scripture,
doth shew that Abraham had nothing wherein to make his
boast. "For what," saith he, "doth the scripture say?
Abraham believed God, and it was counted unto him for

[1 solius, Lat.; alone.]　　　　　[2 multis, Lat.; for many.]
[3 Gal. iii. 17. See Vol. II. page 180.]
[4 See Vol. I. p. 116, and note 3.]

righteousness." Lo here, the scripture doth most plainly
say, that Abraham was justified by faith; or rather, that
faith was imputed to him for righteousness; and therefore
that Abraham was for his faith counted righteous before the
most just and righteous God.

But let us hear Paul, how he applieth this place of
scripture unto his purpose. It followeth then: "To him
that worketh is the reward not reckoned of grace, but of
duty. But to him that worketh not, but believeth in him
that justifieth the ungodly, his faith is counted for righteousness." Which words, verily, may be briefly reduced into
this kind of argument. Whosoever doth with his works
deserve anything, to him the reward is given as a thing of
duty due unto him, and not imputed freely as though it
were no debt. But faith is imputed to Abraham unto righteousness; therefore he received righteousness, not as a reward
of duty ought[1] unto him, but as a gift not due but freely
given him. And again: "To him that worketh not, but
believeth in him that justifieth the ungodly, his faith is
reckoned for righteousness." But to Abraham faith was
imputed unto righteousness: therefore he obtained righteousness by faith, and not by works.

Now there is an emphasis in that he saith, "But believeth in him that justifieth the ungodly." For thereby is
signified, that he which is to be justified doth bring nothing
with him but the only acknowledging of his own misery and
ungodliness, to seek for mercy at the hand of the Lord. For
he understandeth, that he is destitute of good[2] works, and
such as may abide the trial of God's just judgment. He
doth therefore fly to the mercy of God, presuming for a
certainty that the righteousness of faith is the aid or help of
the sinner, that must be freely saved by the grace of God.

The right-
eousness of
Christians is
imputative.

Here, by the way, ye must note, that Christians' righteousness both is, and is said to be, imputative righteousness:
which thing alone is able to break the neck of all our
boasting; for imputation is the contrary unto debt. God
is not of duty bound to us, either for our own sakes, or for
our works' sakes; but so far forth as he hath bound himself
to us of his free grace and goodness: and in us there are
many things that hinder the perfection of righteousness in

[1 i. e. owed.]   [2 perfectis, Lat.]

us. Whereupon David cried: "Enter not into judgment [Psal. cxliii.
with thy servant: for in thy sight shall no man living be ^2.]
justified." Therefore God doth freely impute to us the
righteousness of faith; that is, he reputeth us for righteous
because we believe him through his Son. So we read that
in the evangelical parable the Lord did say: "But when [Luke vii.
the debtors were not able to pay, he forgave them both the ^42.]
debt." For God also forgiveth us our debts or sins, not
reputing them unto us, but counting us for righteous for
Christ his sake. For the same apostle, most evidently testifying the same thing, in the second Epistle to the Corinthians,
saith: "God was in Christ reconciling the world unto himself, by not imputing sins to men." And after that again:
"Him, which knew no sin, he made sin for us, that we might [2 Cor. v. 19,
be the righteousness of God in him." What canst thou ^21.]
require more evident, than that we are counted righteous
before God, because by Christ his sacrifice our sins are so
purged, that we should hereafter be no longer held with the
guilt of the same?

We proceed now to reckon up the other arguments of
St Paul, as firm and manifest as these that are already rehearsed.

In the same chapter therefore it followeth: "Even as What David
David describeth the blessedness of the man, to whom the justification.
Lord imputeth righteousness without works, saying, Blessed
are they whose unrighteousnesses are forgiven, and whose
sins are covered. Blessed is that man, to whom the Lord
will not impute sin." In the beginning he doth with clear
and evident words express the thing that he intendeth to
prove or confirm; to wit, that God imputeth righteousness
to the saints without works. What could be said more
plainly? And, to prove it to be so, here he inferreth the
testimony of David, which doth in a manner contain three
sundry members or clauses: first, "Blessed," saith he,
"are they whose unrighteousnesses are forgiven;" then,
"Blessed are they whose sins are covered;" and lastly,
"Blessed is that man to whom the Lord will impute no
sin."

Now the force of the argument or demonstration doth
consist in the words, Forgive, Cover, and Not impute. The
creditor forgiveth the debtor that which he hath not paid

him, whether he be able or not able to pay it him. We in respect of our sins, which are our debts, are able to pay nothing to God. Forgiveness therefore of those debts or sins of ours is the gift of God's mere grace and liberality. For the creditor cannot forgive the thing that is already paid unto him; for when he giveth back the thing that he hath received, in so doing he doth not forgive, but give; and that deed in the scriptures is called *Donum*, a gift, not *Remissio*, a forgiving. Whereupon St Paul saith, "God gave to Abraham the inheritance:" therefore Abraham with his works did not merit the same. Secondarily, some filthy thing that offendeth the eyes of men is usually wont to be covered; and yet notwithstanding the filthy thing abideth filthy still[1], although it doth not appear outwardly unto the eyes of men. And our merciful God hath covered our sins, not that they should not be, but that they should not appear or come to judgment; which thing is the gift of grace, and not of merits. For the covering is nothing else than the blood of the Son of God; for for his blood's sake we sinners are not damned. Lastly, God might by right and justice impute sin unto us; but of his grace he imputeth it not. And all these laid together do confirm and prove, that righteousness is freely, by faith, without works, imputed unto us.

This very same place of St Paul taken out of David doth discuss and make plain unto us other points of doctrine also, whereof there is some controversy. For we learn that justification is nothing else but sanctification[2], forgiveness of sins, and adoption into the number of the children of God. We learn that St Paul speaketh not only of the ceremonial works of the law, but also of the saints' good works of every sort. Furthermore we learn, that both sins and iniquities, that is, all manner sins of the faithful, are freely pardoned and utterly forgiven. Moreover we learn that sins are fully remitted, not the fault only, but the punishment also: which punishment, some say, is retained; but God doth not impute sins. In another place he saith, "that he will not have any remembrance of our sin at all." Lastly, we learn that the satisfactions for sin of man's invention is a most vain lie, and flatly opposite to the apostle's doctrine.

[Jer. xxxi. 34; Heb. x. 17.]

[1 latet adhuc sub tectorio, Lat.; lurketh still under the covering.]
[2 beatificatio, Lat. See Vol. I. page 106, note 6.]

I have hitherto alleged two most evident places; the one out of the gospel of Christ, the other out of St Paul his epistle written to the Romans: by which I meant to prove, that Christ, being preached to us by the gospel, is received not by works but by faith; and I hope I have by divine testimonies so declared this matter of importance, that no man shall need hereafter either to doubt or waver in the same. To all this now I add this note, still most necessary to be observed; that all good and holy men in the church of Christ must with all their power do their endeavour that this doctrine of the gospel may abide sincere and utterly uncorrupted. For they must in no case admit that justification is partly attributed to faith and the mercy of God, and partly to the works of faith and our own merits : for if that be admitted, then doth the gospel lose all force and virtue. I think therefore, that all men must only and incessantly urge this, That the faithful are justified, saved, or sanctified[3] by faith, without works, by the grace and mercy, I say, of God through Christ alone. And I suppose, verily, that this doctrine of the gospel must be kept sincere and uncorrupt in the church for very many causes, but among all other for these especially which follow hereafter.

First of all, it is manifest, that the often-repeated doctrine of the grace of God, which in his only Son doth through faith alone work justification, is by so many divine testimonies, even from the beginning of the world, by so many demonstrations, and so many determinations of unreproveable councils, both so plainly declared and throughly inculcated, that the very consent of all ages in the truth revealed from heaven, and the authority of the most holy men in all the world, do sufficiently invite us to retain, maintain, and keep that doctrine uncorrupted. We have the justification of our blessed father Abraham a little[4] above expounded by no obscure author, but even by Paul, the teacher of the Gentiles and elected vessel of God himself. We have the doctrine of justification taught by the most glorious king and prophet[5] David, a man even after God's heart's desire, the great grandsire of Christ our Lord, declared and expounded by the same apostle Paul. Now Abraham and David were always

Why the doctrine of faith that justifieth without works is to be kept uncorrupted in the church of Christ.

[3 beati, Lat.; blessed.]
[4 paucis, Lat.; in few words.]   [5 and prophet, not in Lat.]

men of chief account in the church of God. With which twain the whole company of the prophets do wholly agree; for [Acts x. 43.] the apostle Peter saith: "All the prophets bare witness to Christ, that by his name every one which doth believe in him should receive remission of his sins." And even now by the mouth of Paul we heard say, that by the testimonies of the law and the prophets it is proved, That the righteousness of God is freely bestowed by faith, without the law.

We have also the very Son of God, Jesus Christ, our Lord, whose authority, excelling far all the world's beside[1], may confirm us well enough in this piece of doctrine[2]. For he, as it were in certain assembled councils, did determine and decree that which we in this place do counsel all men to retain. For having gathered together his disciples at Cæsarea Philippi, he demanded of them, what men did think of him. Now when they answered diversely, according to the diversity of opinions that the common people had of him, he inquired of them what they themselves thought of him[3]. Then Peter in the name of all the rest said, "Thou art that Christ, the Son of the living [Matt. xvi. 16, 17.] God." To whom the Lord replied: "Happy art thou, Simon Bar-jona; for flesh and blood hath not revealed this to thee, but my Father which is in heaven." In these words he concludeth two several things: first, that true faith doth make us happy; neither is it to be doubted but that "to make happy" is used here in that signification, which ye heard out of Paul even now that David used it in: lastly, that that sanctifying[4] faith is not the work of our own nature, but the heavenly gift of God. And then also he taketh occasion, upon that notable confession of true faith, to give a new name to Simon Peter, for the eternal memory of the thing[5], and for the imprinting of the signification of that mystery in all men's minds. Peter confessed that Christ was a stone, or rock; therefore Christ surnameth Peter a *Petra*, that is, a stone: as if one should call him a living stone laid upon a living stone, or of Christ a Christian. Yea, and lest peradventure any man should tie the thing, universally belonging to the whole

[1 omnes in mundo præstantissimos, Lat.]
[2 may—doctrine, not in Lat.]
[3 certam confessionem, Lat.]   [4 beatificantem, Lat.]
[5 ad æternam rei memoriam,—alluding to the opening phrase of the decrees and bulls of the popes, &c.]

church, unto Peter alone, the Lord himself doth apply it unto all the church, and saith : "And upon this stone will I build my church ; and the gates of hell shall not prevail against it." As if he should have said : That which now is done in thee, Peter, shall hereafter be done in all the faithful. Thou by faith art laid upon me which am the stone, and art made a member of the church : I therefore do ordain, that whosoever confesseth me to be the stone shall be a member of the church, sanctified[6], justified, and delivered from the devil and the power of death. Thy confession (that is, I, Christ the Son of God, whom thou confessest,) shall be the foundation of the church ; upon which foundation whosoever are laid[7], they shall be justified[8] and freely saved. For Paul also said : "Another [2 Cor. iii. foundation cannot be laid than that that is already laid, which 11.] is Christ Jesus." And the apostle John saith : "This is the [1 John v. 4.] victory that hath overcome the world, even your faith." Now lest Peter and his other fellow-disciples should not know the way how other men should be admitted into the fellowship of the church and received into the communion of Christ, he addeth immediately : "And I will give thee the keys of the kingdom of heaven ; and whatsoever thou loosest in earth, shall be loosed in heaven," &c. He gave the keys when he sent the apostles to preach the gospel. Therefore by the preaching of the gospel (which is the key of the kingdom of heaven) is heaven opened, and the way pointed out how we, being graffed in Christ and the church, may be made the heirs of eternal life ; to wit, through faith in Christ, which we are taught by the gospel of Christ. Thus much touching the council whereof Christ himself was president, held at Cæsarea Philippi[9].

There is extant in John another council, held at Caper-naum[10], both famous and full of people. For in a great multitude of his disciples and other men he doth determine, that eternal life is gotten by faith in Christ ; and that there is none other way for us to come to life than this, "to eat his flesh, and to drink his blood ;" that is, to believe in him. And when among the audience there was a schism by reason that many revolted from Christ, he demanded of them that were

[6 beatus, Lat.]   [7 fide, Lat. ; by faith.]   [8 beati, Lat.]
[9 Hæc de Cæsarien. concilio hactenus,—is all that Bullinger says.]
[10 Capernaiticum, Lat. John vi.]

his nearest disciples, whether they also would forsake him? Then Peter in the name of all the rest did answer : Since in thee, O Christ, there is life and salvation, if we depart from thee we cannot be partakers of life; and therefore by faith we will firmly stick and cleave close to thee for ever.

Moreover here are to be reckoned two councils also that were held by the apostles; the one of which no man can deny to be very general or universal[1]; for in it there were devout men of every nation under heaven. In that council did Peter the apostle in express words teach, That Christ is the Saviour of the world; whom whosoever believeth, he shall have life everlasting. The place is known in the Acts of the Apostles, the second chapter. Before the chief of the Jews the same apostle declareth, that there is salvation in none other than in Christ alone. The place is [Acts iv.] extant in the Acts of the Apostles, the third chapter. The like he doth to the first-fruits of the Gentiles, Cornelius and his household, in the tenth chapter. The second council, which was famous also and passingly adorned with all good gifts, is described in the fifteenth chapter of the Acts : in which council this proposition was allowed, That faith See the order without works doth justify freely. Touching which matter of the Acts[2] of the Apos- I have spoken at large in another place.

tles, and
the eighth Now by all this I would have it proved, that the doc-
sermon of
the third trine of Faith that justifieth without works ought to be
decade. retained unmingled and uncorrupt in the church, because, as I may so say, it is most catholic and altogether unreproveable : to the breach whereof this curse or *anathematism* [Gal. i. 8.] of the apostle is added, saying : " If we, or an angel from heaven, shall preach to you any other gospel than that which we have preached, let him be accursed."

The second cause, why it is expedient that this doctrine be kept sincere in the church, is ; because if it be once put out of joint, the glory of Christ shall be in danger of wrack and in jeopardy. For the glory of Christ is darkened and corrupted in the minds of men (although of itself it remaineth always sound and clear), if we begin to divide the righteousness whereby we stand and appear before God, attributing it to our own merits and good works of our own. For this is the glory of the Son of God, that " under heaven

[1 vero œcumenicum, Lat.]   [2 scriem in Act. Lat.]

there is none other name given unto men in which they
must be saved." Hereupon it is that Paul said : "Christi is [Gal. v. 4;
ii. 21.]
made of none effect to you, whosoever are justified by the
law; ye are fallen from grace." And again : "I do not
despise the grace of God; for if righteousness be of the law,
then did Christ die in vain." If he died in vain, then is
the glory of Christ his cross perished.

The third cause is, the certain and assured reason of
our salvation. Our salvation should be utterly uncertain,
if it did depend upon our works and merits; who, because
of our natural corruption, unless we be beside ourselves, do
say or ought to say with Job: "If I have any righteous- [Job ix. 15.]
ness, I will not answer, but humbly beseech my judge."
Therefore did Paul very rightly say: "If the inheritance [Rom. iv. 14,
16.]
be of the law, then is faith void, and the promise made of
none effect. Therefore is it of faith, as according to grace[3];
that the promise may be firm to all the seed."

The fourth cause is; because by this doctrine especially
there is repaired in us the image of God, to the likeness
whereof we were at the first created. For by faith Christ
dwelleth and liveth in us, who is also delighted in our humility. But then is the image of the devil stirred up in
us, when we begin once to be proud in ourselves, and to
usurp the glory of God; which is done undoubtedly so often
as we do attribute our righteousness and salvation unto ourselves, as though by our own works or merits we had deserved the kingdom of God. The devil swelleth with pride,
and doth his endeavour to rob[4] God of his glory. The
saints do know and acknowledge that they are saved by the
true grace and mercy of God; and do therefore attribute to
him all honour and glory, and to themselves confusion and
ignominy. Whereunto undoubtedly belongeth the parable
in the gospel of the Pharisee boasting in his good works,
and of the publican praying and saying, "God be merciful [Luke xviii.
9—14.]
to me a sinner:" of which twain the publican is read to have
gone heavy[5] to his house rather justified than the other.

[3 ut secundum gratiam, Lat.]
[4 ad se rapere, Lat.; to take to himself.]
[5 descendisse, Lat.; to have gone down. *Heavy* is doubtless in all
the editions a misprint for *home*, which Tyndale's and Cranmer's
versions have.]

The fifth cause is, the value or estimation of the sin. For that seemeth to be no great fault, which may by men's works be blotted out before God. But the holy scripture teacheth, that sins could be by none other means cleansed, but by the death and innocent blood of the[1] Son of God. Now by that every man that hath any understanding may easily gather, that sin in the sight of God is a most abominable and detestable thing : whereupon there doth arise in the faithful saints a careful and diligent watching against sin, and a continual bewailing of our miserable condition, with a passing humility and exquisite modesty.

I could yet add to these some causes more, why all men ought to strive and endeavour to keep this doctrine (that the catholic church is justified by the grace of God in his only-begotten Son, through faith, and not through works) sincere and uncorrupt in the church of Christ : but these I hope are sufficient for them that are not of purpose set to quarrel against us. And yet, notwithstanding, there is no peril why by this doctrine good works should be neglected : of which I have spoken in place convenient[2]. But if there be any that cease not of purpose to cavil against the manifest truth of the gospel, I object against them that saying of Paul : that neither we, nor the churches of God, do stand to wrangle in so manifest a light.

[1 Cor. xi. 16.]

The conclusion and sum of all. To conclude ; the sum of all that which hitherto I have said touching the gospel is this : That all men that be in the world are of their own nature the servants of sin, the devil, and eternal death, and cannot be loosed or set at liberty by any other means but by the free grace of God, and the redemption which is in the only-begotten Son of God our Lord Christ Jesus ; of which redemption they only are made partakers that do believe and trust in him. For whosoever do by true faith receive Christ Jesus through the preaching of the gospel, they are therewithal justified ; that is, acquitted from their sins, sanctified, and made heirs of eternal life : but they that by their unbelief and hardness of heart do not receive Christ, are given over to the eternal John iii. 36.] pains and bonds of hell ; for "the wrath of God abideth upon them."

Let us therefore give hearty thanks to God our Re-

[1 ipsius, Lat. ; of the very.]   [2 Vol. I. p. 118.]

deemer, and humbly beseech him to keep and increase us in the true faith, and lastly to bring us to life everlasting. Amen.

OF REPENTANCE, AND THE CAUSES THEREOF; OF CONFESSION, AND REMISSION OF SINS; OF SATISFACTION AND INDULGENCES; OF THE OLD AND NEW MAN; OF THE POWER OR STRENGTH OF MEN, AND THE OTHER THINGS PERTAINING TO REPENTANCE.

THE SECOND SERMON.

I PROMISED in my last sermon, that I made of the gospel of Jesus Christ, to add a discourse of repentance; which by the help of God and your good prayers I purpose in this sermon for to perform.

They among the Latins are said to repent, which are aggrieved at or ashamed of the thing that they have done. Thou hast done a good turn, and thinkest him unworthy of it for whom thou hast done it, and for that cause art sorry to thyself: that sorrow of thine is repentance. We Germans call it *Den reuen*. The Greeks do name it *Metanœam*. Now they which are skilful of that tongue say, that μετα-νοεῖν signifieth to bethink afterward : so that *Metanœa* is there properly used, where a man, having once slipped by doing something foolishly, doth notwithstanding at length come to himself again, and verily purpose to correct his own error[3]. It is therefore referred, not to the thought of the mind only, but also to the deed done. For he that perceiveth that he hath offended, doth devise with himself how to amend it. So now the thing beginneth to displease thee, which before did please thee : so now thou eschewest the thing that before thou ensuedst[4]. Moreover the Hebrews call repentance *Theschubah*[5], that is, a conversion, or returning to the right way or mind again. The metaphor seemeth to

To repent.

[3 Bullinger here refers to Erasmus' annotation on Matth. iii. 2: μετάνοια dicta est a μετανοεῖν, hoc est, a posterius intelligendo, ubi quis lapsus, re peracta, tum demum animadvertit erratum suum.]

[4 cupidissime, Lat. omitted; most eagerly.]

[5 תְּשׁוּבָה.]

be taken of them which once did stray from the right path, but do again at length return into the way : which word is translated to the mind, to the manners, and deeds of men.

The diverse use of this word repentance.

But now this word is diversely used; for repentance signifieth the changing of the purpose once conceived, or of

[Jer. xviii. 8.]

any other thing. For by Jeremy the Lord saith : " If they turn from evil, I will also repent me of the evil which I meant to lay upon them." Therefore God doth then repent, when he changeth his purpose : he repenteth not, when he

[Rom. xi. 29.]

doth not alter it. Paul saith : " The gifts and calling of God

[Psal. cx. 4.]

are without repentance." And David said : " The Lord hath

Repentance in God, how and what it is.

sworn, and will not repent." Elsewhere repentance is figuratively attributed to God, like to the affection of mortal

[Gen. vi. 7.]

men : as when he saith, " I repent[1] me that I have made man." For God of his own nature doth not repent as men do, so that he should be touched with grief, and that the thing should now mislike him which he before did like of; but he doth barely alter that which he hath done. Among ecclesiastical writers they are said to repent, which after a prescribed manner of punishment do penance for their sins which they have committed. The scripture in another place doth use it for the whole effect and matter of the gospel :

[Acts xi. 18.]

for in the Acts we read, that God gave to the Gentiles repentance unto life. But we, in this disputation of ours, will use repentance for a converting or turning to the Lord, for the acknowledging of sins, for the grief conceived for sins committed, for mortification, and the beginning to lead a new life ; and finally[2] for the change, correction, and amendment of the life from evil to better : that which we Germans call *Bekeerung, Enderung oder Besserung*[3].

What repentance is.

And as diversely too is repentance defined of the ecclesiastical writers : howbeit all agree that it is a conversion or turning to the Lord, and an alteration of the former life and opinion. We therefore do say, that repentance is an unfeigned turning to God, whereby we, being of a sincere fear of God once humbled, do acknowledge our sins, and so, by mortifying our old man, are afresh renewed by the

[1 It repenteth, ed. 1577.]
[2 breviter, Lat.; shortly.]
[3 bekehrung, conversion; aenderung, changing; besserung, correction.]

Spirit of God[4]. This definition doth consist upon her parts, which, being somewhat more largely opened and diligently expounded, will declare unto us and lay before our eyes the whole nature of repentance.

First we say, that repentance is an unfeigned turning *Conversion to God.* unto God. For I will hereafter shew you, that there are two sorts of repentance; to wit, feigned and unfeigned. And the apostle Peter saith: "Repent, and turn, that your sins [Acts iii. 19.] may be blotted out;" expounding, as it were, the first by the last, to wit, repentance by returning; (he meaneth) to him from whom they had turned themselves away. For there is a certain relation betwixt turning to and turning fro. If thou hadst never turned away, then hadst thou had no need to have turned to again. But we have all turned away from the true, just, and good God, and from his holy will, unto the devil and our own corrupt affections. And therefore must we again turn us from the devil, and from our old naughty life and will, unto the living God and his most holy will and pleasure. We do here significantly say, to God, and not to creatures or any help of man. For the Lord in Jeremy doth say: "If, Israel, thou wilt return, [Jer. iv. 1.] return to me." Whosoever therefore do not turn to God, nor make themselves conformable to his holy will, howsoever they do turn to creatures and other means of man's invention, yet are they not[5] to be esteemed or counted penitents.

Now there is none so blind but seeth, that for the stir- *The doctrine of verity is needful to repentance.* ring of us up to repentance the preaching or doctrine of the truth is needful and requisite, to teach us what God is to whom we must be turned; what the goodness and holiness is, to which we must be turned: who the devil is, and what the evil and wickedness[6] is, from which we must be turned; and lastly, what the thing is that must be amended in our mind and life, and also how it must be altered and amended. Truly the prophets and apostles of the Lord, in exhorting men unto repentance, do travail much and stick very long in describing of God's nature, goodness, righteousness, truth and mercy; in painting out the laws and offices of the life of man; and in accusing and heaping up[7] the sins of men;

[4 spiritualiter.]
[5 revera, Lat. omitted; in truth.]   [6 falsum, Lat.]
[7 exaggerandis, Lat.]

whereunto they add the grievous and horrible tokens[1] of God's just judgments : as is in every place of the prophets' writings to be found very rifely. And therefore some there are which bid us even now to preach the law to those men whom we would draw unto repentance : which thing as I do not gainsay, but very well like it, so do I withal admonish them, that the preaching of the gospel also doth object to men their sins, and grievously accuse them. For the Lord [John xvi. 8, 9.] in the gospel saith : " When the Holy Ghost cometh, it shall argue the world of sin, because they believed not in me." Whereupon St Peter, in the Acts of the Apostles, upbraiding to the Jews their sins committed, and preaching unto them Christ and faith in Christ, exhorteth them unto repentance. The places are very well known. Acts ii. and iii. St Paul, going about to draw the Athenians unto repentance, doth [Acts xvii. 30, 31.] say : " God, who hath hitherto winked at the times of this ignorance, doth now preach to all men everywhere that they should repent; because he hath appointed a day, in which he will judge the world with righteousness through Christ." Let them therefore, to whom charge is given to draw men[2] unto repentance, learn here to use much liberty and wisdom, that all men may acknowledge their sin and the greatness of their iniquity. Moreover God doth stir up men to repentance, not by his word only, but also by divers afflictions and sundry sorts of punishments : yea, all the calamities that happen in the world are certain sermons, as it were, persuading and drawing us unto repentance. For, that I may in silence overpass that which is written in the prophets ; did not our Lord himself in the gospel, when he heard tidings of the slaughter which Pontius Pilate had made upon the Galileans, and the death of the eighteen men upon [Luke xiii. 1—5.] whom the tower in Siloe fell, presently say, " Think ye that they were greater sinners than the rest? No, verily ; but unless ye repent, ye shall all likewise perish." It is assuredly certain therefore, that war, famine, and plagues[3] do always invite us unto repentance ; that is, they premonish us, by laying sin aside, to be converted unto God, and wholly to give ourselves to sincere integrity.

[1 minas graves et horrendas hypotyposes, Lat.]
[2 doctrina, Lat. omitted; by doctrine.]
[3 pestes omnes, Lat. ; all plagues.]

But in vain is repentance preached unto us, unless by The fear of fear and trembling conceived in our minds we do reverently God in all penitents. dread the wrath and judgment of Almighty God conceived against us because of our sins and wickednesses. Now this fear is outwardly stirred in us by the external preaching or discipline of the minister[4], as I told you before; but that external doctrine availeth nothing alone, unless inwardly, that is, in our hearts, we be moved by the Holy Spirit of our heavenly Father. And therefore Jeremy in his Lamentations crieth: "Turn us, O Lord, and we shall be turned." And [Lam. v. 21.] in the thirty-first chapter: "Turn thou me, O Lord, and I [Jer. xxxi. 18, 19.] shall be turned; because thou art the Lord my God. And after I was turned, it repented me of evil." We read that St Peter, being provoked by the words of the damsel that kept the door, and of the soldiers, did foully deny his master Christ; but, being revoked at the cock's crowing, he repented his fault or folly from the bottom of his heart. And yet it was not the crowing of the cock of itself alone, that stirred that motion in him; but that and the word of Christ together, who had said unto him: "Verily I say unto thee, the cock shall not crow till thou hast denied me thrice." Whereupon St Matthew saith; "And Peter remembered the words of the [Matt. xxvi. 34, 75.] Lord, which had said unto him, Before the cock crow, thou shalt deny me thrice," &c. With these also is joined a more secret touching of Peter's mind; for the good Lord touched the heart of Peter, as the evangelist testifieth, saying: "And [Luke xxii. 61.] the Lord, turning himself about, looked upon Peter." That looking back of the Lord made Peter's heart to melt, and drew it from the destruction whereinto it was about to fall. Therefore if our ears be pierced with the word of God, and our hearts touched with his Holy Spirit, then shall we, like true penitents, unfeignedly reverence and dread the Lord.

And therewithal, being humbled before the most just and Our humbling and acknowledging of our sins. holy God, whom we with our sins do so much offend and provoke to wrath and indignation, we confess his judgment to be just against us, and freely acknowledge all the sins and iniquities that in the word of God are objected against us, crying out and saying with the prophets: "Thou, verily, [Jer. xii. 1; Psal. cxix. O Lord, art righteous, thou art true, and thy judgments just; 75; Isai. lxiv. 6; Dan. ix. 5, but we are most unrighteous, liars, wicked, and wholly over- 6, 8, 9.]

[4 of the minister, not in Lat.]

whelmed with detestable iniquities. There is nothing sound or sincere within us. All that we have is corrupt and miserable. We have sinned, we have been wicked, we have done unjustly, we have forsaken thee. We have gainsaid thy servants the prophets, we have not obeyed the words of thy mouth. To thee therefore, O God, doth righteousness belong, and to us wretches shame and confusion." This humiliation and free confession of sins doth God require of penitent sinners: touching which I will hereafter speak somewhat more; for now I return more fully to expound the fear of the Lord.

The fear of God is of two sorts.

At this present I speak of the sincere fear of God: for we confess that the fear of God is of two sorts, sincere and unsincere. The sincere fear of God is perceived in the faithful, and is a godly reverence consisting in the love and honour of God. For the prophet bringeth in God saying: "The son honoureth the father, and the servant the master: therefore if I be a father, where is my honour? if a lord, where is my fear?" And Paul saith: "Ye have not received the spirit of bondage again unto fear; but ye have received the spirit of adoption, by which we cry, Abba, Father." Therefore the sincere fear of God in them that do repent is not the servile dread of punishment, but a careful study mixt with the love and honour of God. An honest wife feareth her husband, and a gracious daughter feareth her father[1]; and yet each of them doth therewithal love, the one her father, the other her husband, and doth with an holy love endeavour herself to keep his favour, and fear lest at any time she should do anything to lose it. And therefore penitents do not only fear[2], because they know, being taught by the Spirit of God, that they have committed sins, for which they have deserved to be forsaken of the Lord; but do also love him as their merciful Father, and are therefore sorry with all their hearts for their sins committed; and do above all things most ardently require to be reconciled again to their merciful God and loving Father.

[Mal. i. 6.]

[Rom. viii. 15.]

Sorrow to God-ward.

For with this sincere fear of God is joined the grief or sorrow, which is conceived by the Spirit of God for our sins that we commit. St Paul maketh mention of two sorts of sorrows. "The sorrow that is to God-ward," saith he, "doth bring forth repentance[3] not to be repented of; but, contrarily, the

[2 Cor. vii. 10.]

[1 parentem, Lat.]   [2 Deum, Lat. omitted; God.]
[3 ad salutem, Lat. omitted; to salvation.]

sorrow of the world bringeth death." The king and prophet David sorrowed to God-ward, when he cried: " Thine arrows stick fast in me, and thy hand doth press me sore. There is no whole part in my flesh, because of thy displeasure : there is no rest in my bones by reason of my sin : " and so forward, as is to be seen in the thirty-eighth Psalm ; which, although it were written of his grievous disease or sickness, doth yet notwithstanding, as it were in a shadow, shew us the great grief that is in the saints for offending their good and gracious Father with their continual[4] sins. To God-ward was the sinful woman sorry in St Luke, who, falling prostrate at [Luke vii. 38.] the Lord's heels, did wash his feet with tears, and wiped them with her hair. To God-ward was St Peter sorry, and wept [Luke xxii. 62.] (as we read) full bitterly for his offence. The godly are greatly grieved because they do so oftentimes offend so foully so good a God and gracious Father. No words, I think, can possibly express the grief and sorrow that they conceive. But the prophet Jeremy, describing the contrary affection of impenitent sinners, doth say : "Do men fall, so that they may Jer. [viii. 4– 6.] not rise again ? Doth any man go so astray, that he may not turn again ? How doth it happen then that this people of Hierusalem is turned away so stubbornly ? I gave ear and hearkened, they spake not rightly : there was none that did repent him of his wickedness, to say, What have I done ? Every one of them turned to his own course, like a fierce horse headlong to the battle."

The worldly grief is the sorrow of such men as know not God, and are without faith and the true love of God; yea, of such as yield under the burden of sorrow, adversities, and[5] very sins. Like to this also, in a manner, is the consideration of the unsincere fear of God. For the wicked, with their head the devil, do fear God, not as a father, whom they are sorry to offend, and to whom they desire to be reconciled as to a father; but as a tormentor, because they know that he will revenge their evil deeds; and therefore with Judas[6] they run[7] to the rope. There is in them no love of God, no honour, no good-will, no reverence, but mere hatred[8], horror,

[4 continual, not in Lat.]
[5 adeoque et, Lat.; and so of their sins also.]
[6 Iscariotha, Lat. omitted.]   [7 tandem, Lat.; at last.]
[8 odium Dei, Lat.]

and utter desperation. But such fear the apostle and evangelist John denied to be in charity, saying that "perfect charity casteth out all fear:" I mean not that fear of the Lord that is the beginning of wisdom; but that of which I have spoken all this while; the fear, I mean, that is in the devil and wicked men his members[1].

[1 John iv. 18.]

Faith is needful in them that repent.

And now by this we gather, that unto penitents faith in God and the merit of Christ is most of all and especially needful. In which sense it is, I think, that many have made faith a part of repentance: which as I do not greatly deny, so yet do I see that St Paul made as it were a difference betwixt faith and repentance, when in the twentieth of the Acts he saith, that "he witnessed both to the Jews and Gentiles the repentance that is toward God, and the faith in Jesus Christ." Therefore repentance and faith seem to be diverse: not that true repentance can be without faith; but because they must be distinguished, and not confounded. We do all know that true faith is not without works, as that which of necessity sheweth forth good works[2]; and yet we make a difference betwixt faith and works, so yet that we do not separate them or rend the one from the other: and in like manner we acknowledge that true faith and true repentance are undividedly knit together, and closely fastened the one to the other. I will not stand in argument, whether faith be a part of repentance, or doth by any other means depend upon it. It seemeth to me a notable point of folly to go about to tie matters of divinity[3] to precepts of logic: for we learn not that of the Lord's apostles. I admonished you before in a sermon of the gospel[4] (which thing I do here repeat again), that the acknowledging of sins doth not of itself obtain grace or forgiveness of sins; even as the bare acknowledging of a disease is not the remedy for the same: for even damned men also do acknowledge their sins, and yet are not therefore healed. The acknowledging of sin is a certain preparative unto faith; as the acknowledging of a disease doth minister occasion to think upon a remedy. To this at this present we add, that not the very fear of God, how sincere soever it be; not the very sorrow conceived for our

[1 the fear—members, not in Lat.]
[2 lege utique communi, is Bullinger's parenthesis.]
[3 ubique, Lat. omitted; in all cases.]   [4 See above, p. 35.]

sins, how great soever it be; nor the very humiliation, how submiss soever it be, do of themselves make us[5] acceptable to God: but rather that they prepare an entrance and make a way for us unto the knowledge of Christ, and so consequently do lead us to Christ himself being incarnate and crucified for us and our redemption, and lay us upon Christ alone, by him to be quickened and purely cleansed. For he that is truly converted to God is utterly turned from himself and all hope of worldly aid. Whoso doth truly fear God and is sorry in very deed from the bottom of his heart, he doth fear and is sorry for his sins committed; and not for that alone, but because he findeth himself to be corrupted wholly, and to have in himself no soundness or integrity: yea, because he reverenceth God as his Father, he doth disclose to him his wounds as to a chirurgeon, desiring instantly to be reconciled to him as to his loving Father. And whereas here true godliness doth cry, that no man can be reconciled to God the Father but by the only-begotten Son; the penitent doth by faith lay hold on the Son, and so seek the means of his reconciliation[6]. Faith is grounded upon the only grace or mercy of God exhibited to us in Christ Jesus, and the penitent believeth that he is accepted of God for Christ his sake alone: and therefore he maketh his supplications to God, committing himself wholly unto his mercy; as we read that David, and the prodigal son in the fifteenth chapter of St Luke's gospel, did. To this place might be annexed the doctrine of[7] the gospel, of faith in Jesus Christ, and of the remission of sins; touching which I have already spoken.

And here I think it not amiss, that the minds of penitents must by all means be confirmed with many and evident places of scripture plainly uttered concerning the full remission of sins, to the end that hereafter we have no scruple of conscience to cause us to despair or doubt in our temptations: wherein notwithstanding I repeat again and again this note to be throughly marked, for the confirmation of the glory of the only-begotten Son of God, our Lord Christ Jesus, that penitent sinners have their sins remitted, not for their repentance, in respect that it is our work or action; but in respect

Sins are fully and surely forgiven unto penitents.

[5] pœnitentes, Lat.]
[6] and so—reconciliation; an addition of the translator's.]
[7] de, Lat.; concerning.]

that it comprehendeth the renewing of man by the Holy
Ghost, and true faith, which delivereth us to Christ our physician, that he may heal all our diseases and bind up all our
griefs[1]. And although this treatise doth properly belong to
the common place of faith and the gospel, of which I have so
briefly as I could already discoursed; yet notwithstanding I
will here recite some evident sentences touching the grace of
God and free remission of our sins.

David in the hundreth and third psalm saith: "Praise
the Lord, O my soul, and forget not the things that he hath
done for thee: which forgiveth all thy sins, and healeth all
thine infirmities: which saveth thy life from destruction, and
crowneth thee with mercy and loving-kindness. He hath not
dealt with us after our sins, nor rewarded us according to our
wickedness. For look how high the heaven is in comparison
of the earth; so great is his mercy toward them that fear
him. And look how far the east is from the west; so far hath
he set our sins from us. Yea, like as a father pitieth his own
children, so is the Lord merciful to them that fear him. For
he knoweth that we are frail (prone to sin), and doth remember
that we are but dust."

Esay in the first chapter of his prophecy saith: "Thus
saith the Lord, Though your sins be as red as scarlet, they
shall be made whiter than snow; and though they be red as
purple, they shall be made like undyed[2] wool." Again, in the
forty and third chapter, he bringeth in the Lord saying:
"I am he that blot out the[3] transgressions, and that for mine
own sake, and I will not remember thy sins."

In the thirty-first chapter of Jeremy, which saying is
also alleged by Paul in the eighth and tenth chapters to the
Hebrews, the Lord saith: "This is my covenant that I will
make with them after these days; I will be merciful unto
their iniquities, and not remember their sins any more."

In the thirty-sixth chapter of Ezechiel the Lord saith:
"I will sprinkle clean water upon you, and ye shall be
cleansed from all your uncleanness. A new heart also will
I give you, and a new spirit will I put within you: as for
that stony heart, I will take it out of your flesh, and give
you a fleshy heart. I will deliver you from all your un-

[1 contritiones, Lat.]   [2 nativa lana, Lat.]
[3 tuas, Lat.; thy.]

cleannesses. But I will not do this for your sakes, saith the Lord, be ye sure of it, &c."

Daniel in his ninth chapter leaveth to us a manifest example of confession of sins, and doth in express words say that by the Messiah sins are forgiven, iniquity purged, and everlasting righteousness brought in instead of it[4]. So doth the prophet Zachary in his third chapter affirm, that the iniquity of the earth is purged by the only sacrifice of Christ Jesus.

The Lord, in the gospel after St Matthew, doth say: "They that are whole need not the physician, but they that [Matt. ix. 12, 13.] are sick. Neither did I come to call the righteous, but sinners to repentance." And therefore is he called Jesus, that is, a Saviour: for the angel said, "He shall save his people [Matt. i. 21.] from their sins." And St Paul to Timothy saith: "It is a [1 Tim. i. 15.] sure saying, and worthy by all means to be received, that Jesus Christ came into the world to save sinners."

In the same gospel the Lord saith: "Every sin and [Matt. xii. 31, 32.] blasphemy shall be forgiven men; but blasphemy against the Holy Ghost shall not be forgiven men. And whosoever shall say a word against the Son of man, it shall be forgiven him: but whosoever speaketh a word against the Holy Ghost, it shall not be forgiven him, neither in this world, nor in the world to come." Concerning sin against the Holy Ghost I have already spoken in another place[5]. Now to this place do belong all the examples of that most liberal kind of forgiveness, which is expressed in the gospel: as for example, of the sinful woman, Luke vii.; also John iv. and Matthew viii.; of Zachee, St Peter, and the thief upon the cross. But who is able briefly to reckon them all? To this also do appertain the three parables in the gospel[6] after the evangelist St Luke.

In the gospel after St John the forerunner of the Lord [John i. 29; xx. 23.] doth cry out, saying: "Behold the Lamb of God, that taketh away the sins of the world." And the Lord himself did say to his disciples: "Whose sins soever ye forgive, they are forgiven."

Peter the apostle in the Acts doth cry and say: "All [Acts x. 43.] the prophets bear witness to Christ, that whosoever believeth

[4 instead of it, not in Lat.]

[5 See Vol. II. p. 420.]   [6 ex 15 cap. Lat. omitted.]

in him should by his name receive remission of his sins."
[1 Pet. ii. 24.] The same apostle again in his Epistle saith : " Christ his own self bare our sins in his body upon the cross[1], that we, being dead to sin, might live to righteousness : by whose stripes ye are healed."

The apostle Paul in the fifth chapter of his second Epistle to the Corinthians saith : " God was in Christ reconciling the world unto himself, not imputing their sins unto them. For him, that knew not sin, he made sin for us ; that we through him might be made the righteousness of God." And in the tenth to the Hebrews he hath : " Christ, having offered one sacrifice for sin, is set down at the right hand of God for ever ; from henceforth tarrying till his foes be made his footstool. For with one offering hath he made perfect for ever them that are sanctified."

Moreover the blessed apostle and evangelist John doth
[1 John i. 7.; ii. 2.] no less truly than evidently testify, saying : " The blood of Jesus Christ the Son of God doth cleanse us from all sin." And again : " And he is the propitiation for our sins ; not for ours only, but for the sins also of the whole world."

Against the Novatians and Anabaptists.   But now most vain and the very messengers of Satan himself are the Novatians and Anabaptists, which feign that we are by baptism purged into an angelical life, which is not polluted with any spots at all : but if it be polluted, then can he that is so defiled look for no pardon at all[2]. For, to pass over many other places of holy scripture, was not St Peter consecrated to God in baptism ? Had he not tasted of God's good grace ? [3]After that notable confession which
[Matt. xvi. 17.] he made, the Lord said unto him : " Happy art thou, Simon Bar-Jona ; flesh and blood hath not revealed this unto thee, but my Father which is in heaven." Again, when the Lord
[John vi. 67 —69.] demanded of his disciples, saying, " Will ye depart also ?" then Peter in the name of them all answered ; " Lord, to whom shall we go ? Thou hast the words of eternal life ; and we believe and know that thou art Christ, the Son of the living God." And yet this very same Peter, after his baptism and tasting of the grace of God, sinned notwith-

[1 super lignum, Lat.]
[2 See Vol. ii. p. 424. n. 3. and Bullinger, adv. Anabapt. Lib. i. cap. 11.]
[3 Certe, Lat. omitted ; unquestionably.]

standing, and that too not lightly[4], in denying and for-
swearing his Lord and Master.   Now was he, for this sin of
his, altogether unpardonable?   Was his return to God again
stopped up by his stumbling?   No, verily.   For when he
heard the cock crow, he remembered presently the words of
the Lord, he descended into himself, he considered what he
had done, he wept bitterly and mourned lamentably.   And
yet he was not long tormented in that grief without consolation.   For the third day after, to the women which came
to the Lord's sepulchre it was said by the angels: "Tell
his disciples, and Peter, that he is risen, and goeth before
you into Galilee."   Lo here, the Lord will have it known
to Peter by name, that he was risen.   And why to Peter
by name?   Because, forsooth, he had sinned more grievously
than the other: not that the Lord did like of Peter's sin;
but because he would thereby declare to us that penitents
do obtain forgiveness of their sins, so often as they do turn
to the heavenly grace of God again.   And not many days
after he restored Peter to the ministry again, commending
to him the charge of his sheep.

Moreover the Lord in Jeremy speaketh to the people
of Israel, saying: "If any man put away his wife, and she[5] [Jer. iii. 1.]
marry to another man, will her first husband turn to her
again?   But is not this land defiled?   Hast thou not committed fornication with many?   Yet turn thee to me again,
saith the Lord."   And the Galatians, being once rightly instructed by the apostle Paul, but after that seduced by the
false apostles, revolted from the truth and preaching of the
gospel: yet notwithstanding they obtained pardon.   The
Corinthians also, after they had received grace, did wittingly
and willingly sin in many things: but yet upon repentance
the apostle Paul promised them forgiveness of their sins at
the hands of the Lord.

And what is more manifest than this, that all the saints
do daily in earnest and truly, not hypocritically or falsely,
pray saying, "Forgive us our trespasses?"   They which pray
thus do plainly confess that they are sinners; and the Lord
promiseth to hear those that pray with faith.   Therefore even
those sins are forgiven at the prayers of penitents, which

[4 sed gravissime, Lat. omitted; but most heinously.]
[5 ab ipso divertens, Lat. omitted; turning aside from him.]

are committed after the grace of God is once known and obtained.

Now the places in the epistle to the Hebrews, which the Novatians allege for the confirmation of their opinion, I have in another place so thoroughly discussed[1], that I need not here busily to stand long upon them.

The sum of the true doctrine of repentance.

But now to gather a sum of those things which I have hitherto said concerning repentance; let us hold, that repentance is a turning to God, which, although he doth by his word and other means stir it up in us, is notwithstanding especially by the Holy Ghost so wrought in us, that with fear we love and with love we fear our just God and merciful Lord[2], from whom we were turned back, being sorry now with all our hearts that we with our sins did ever offend so gracious a Father. For being humbled before his eternal and most sacred majesty, we acknowledge the sins that are objected against us by the word of God : yea, we acknowledge that in us there is no integrity or soundness ; but do heartily desire to be reconciled with God again : and since that reconciliation cannot be otherwise made than by the only Mediator the Lord Christ Jesus, we do by faith lay hold on him, by whom we, being acquitted from all our sins, are reputed of God for righteous and holy. This benefit whosoever do sincerely acknowledge, they cannot choose but hate sin and mortify the old man.

I would therefore now add other members belonging to this treatise of repentance, to wit, the mortification of the old man, and the renewing of the spirit, were it not that the very matter itself doth require to have somewhat said touching the confession[3] of sins and satisfaction for the same. For some there are that, when they speak of repentance, do speak some things contrary to the truth[4]. To the end therefore, dearly beloved, that ye be not ignorant what to think of these points according to the truth, I will not stick to stay somewhile in the exposition of the same. And I hope ye shall out of my words gather such fruit as ye shall not hereafter repent yourselves of.

[1 See Vol. II. p. 424.]

[2 ut revertamur ad ipsum, Deum, inquam, justum, a quo &c. Lat.]

[3 de confessione, Lat. But ed. 1587 has *forgiveness*.]

[4 de his, Lat. omitted ; touching these points.]

To confess, or a confession, is in the holy scriptures *Of the confession of* diversely used. For it signifieth to praise the Lord, and to *sins.* give him thanks for the benefits that we receive at his hands; and therefore confession is put for praise and thanksgiving. For the prophet saith: "O praise the Lord; for he is good, and his mercy endureth for ever[5]." Paul in his epistle to Titus, speaking of hypocrites, saith: "In words they confess[6] that they know God, but in their deeds they deny him." Here to confess doth signify to say, to profess, or to boast. In another place it is taken for to trust, to stay upon God's goodness, and to testify that confidence as well by words as deeds: and in that sense did St John use it in the fourth chapter of his epistle, and Paul in the tenth to the Romans. Moreover, to confess is to give glory to God, and freely to acknowledge thy sin and the judgment which is objected to thee for thy sin. Salomon in the twenty-eighth chapter of his Proverbs saith: "Whosoever hideth his iniquities" (or[7] doth as it were defend them), "nothing shall go well with him: but whoso confesseth and forsaketh them, to him shall be shewed mercy." The Hebrew tongue useth[8] the word *Jadah* for that which we call, to confess. Now *Jadah* signifieth to let slack, or loose[9], as when a bow once bended is unbended again. And *Modeh*[10], which cometh of *Jadah*, is as if one should say, confessing, yielding, or granting to be vanquished[11]. For God accuseth us, and pleadeth us guilty of sin and endangered[12] to punishment: which our flesh doth presently[13] acknowledge, but yet standeth stiff like a bended bow, until at length, when that stiffness is unbended, it doth acknowledge every thing that God objecteth against us. This acknowledging is called *Modeh*, that is, a confession. And we Germans say, *Es hat*

[5 Psal. cxxxvi. 1. Confitemini Domino.]
[6 Chap. i. 16. they confesse, Tyndale, 1534. Cranmer, 1539.]
[7 imo et, Lat.; nay also.]
[8 in hac sententia, Lat. omitted; in this sentence.]
[9 projicere vel dimittere, Lat.]
[10 ידה *to cast, cast forth, cast out.* מודה *confessing.* Parkhurst, Heb. Lex. in voc.]
[11 herbam præbens, Lat. For this proverbial phrase see Erasm. Adag. Chil. p. 707. col. 1. Hanov. 1617.]
[12 endangered to. See Tyndale's Doctr. Treatises, ed. Park. Soc. pp. 236, 502.]
[13 non protinus, Lat.; doth *not* presently.]

gelassen, Er hat geschnellt, when we mean that anything hath yielded, or that a man hath at last confessed that which he did afore either flatly deny or else dissemble.

Confession of sins ordained of God.

But now confession of sins is of more sorts than one ; for the one is divine, the other human. I will first speak of the divine confession, then of the human.

We call that divine, whereof there be evident testimonies or examples in the holy scriptures, and which is instituted by God himself. That is a free acknowledging and flat confession of the sin which God[1] objecteth against us, whereby we do attribute all glory to God, and to ourselves shame and confusion ; and therewithal do crave pardon of God, and of our neighbour, against whom we have sinned. Now sin is objected to us by God himself, who outwardly by the word, or the ministry of men, and sometimes by signs and wonders, and inwardly by the secret operation of his Holy Spirit, doth plead us guilty of sin and endangered to punishment, requiring of us a free and voluntary confession of our sins. For he liketh of a free and voluntary, not a feigned or extorted, confession. Truly, the citizens of Hierusalem and people of the Jewish religion did of their own accord come to the baptism of John, confessing their sins which John[2] in his preaching had objected against them. And after the ascension of Christ into heaven St Peter accused the sins[3] of the Jews; and immediately upon the accusation it followeth in the history : "When they heard this, they were pricked in their hearts, and said to Peter and the other apostles, Men and brethren, what shall we do ?"— and so forth, as followeth in the second of the Acts. Likewise also the keeper of the prison at Philippos[4], feeling the earthquake, sprang out, and being instructed with the apostles' words confessed his sins and was baptized[5]. And the men of Ephesus which were given to magical arts, when they heard the

[Acts xix. 13—19.] calamity which the devil brought upon the sons of Sceva, their fellows and practisers in magic and sorcery, did fear exceedingly, and came and did confess their sins. Upon these causes for the most part doth the confession of sins especially arise.

[1 God, not in the original: quæ objicitur nobis, Lat.]
[2 beatus Joannes, Lat.]
[3 peccatum, Lat.]
[4 magister carceris Philippici, Lat. Acts xvi. 26—33.]
[5 and was baptized, not in Lat.]

Again, of the confession instituted by God there are two *The confession which* sorts, whereof the one is made to God, the other to our *is privately made to* neighbour. That which is made to God is either private or *God.* public. We do then make our confession to God privately, when we disburden our hearts before God, open the secrets of our hearts to him alone, and, in acknowledging the sins that are in us, do earnestly beseech him to have mercy upon us. This confession is necessary to the obtaining of pardon for our sins: for unless we do acknowledge our own corruption and unrighteousness, we shall never by true faith lay hold on Christ, by whom alone we are to be justified. But here we think not that penitents must hasten to any other confessor to confess their sins unto, but unto God alone; for he alone doth forgive and blot out the offences of penitents[6]. He is the physician, to whom alone we must discover and open our wounds. He it is that is offended with us, and therefore of him we must desire forgiveness[7] and reconciliation. He alone doth look into our hearts and search our reins; to him alone therefore we must disclose our hearts. He alone calleth sinners unto him: let us therefore make haste unto him, prostrate ourselves before him, confess our faults unto him, and crave pardon for them of him. This confession, if it be made of a zealous mind to God-ward, although it cannot be made by word of mouth by reason of some impediment or want of the tongue[8], is notwithstanding acceptable to God[9], who doth not so much respect the mouth as the mind of man. On the other side, if we make confession with the mouth, and in heart are not thoroughly bent to the same[10], although we make that confession to God or the high-priest, yet doth not the Lord regard so vain a confession.

Concerning that true confession to God I have already spoken, where as[11] in the definition of repentance I said that penitents do acknowledge their sins: of which the scripture doth in many places substantially speak. David in the Psalms

[6 of penitents, not in Lat.]

[7 pax, Lat.   Bullinger here borrows largely from Calvin. Instit. Lib. III. cap. 4. § 9.]

[8 by reason—tongue, the translator's addition.]

[9 cordium inspectore, Lat. ; who looketh at the heart.—who—man, is the translator's paraphrase.]

[10 in Deum intenti non simus, Lat.]   [11 cum, Lat.]

[Psal. li. 1, &c.] doth pray[1] saying: "Have mercy upon me, O God, according to the greatness of thy mercy. For I acknowledge my sins, and my sin is ever before me. To thee alone have I sinned, and done evil in thy sight." And so forth. And in another [Psal. xxxii. 5.] Psalm: "I have made my fault known unto thee, and mine unrighteousness have I not hid. I said, I will confess mine unrighteousness unto thee[2] against myself[3], and thou hast forgiven the wickedness of my sin." In the gospel the Lord teacheth to pray, and in prayer to confess and say: "Forgive us our debts, as we forgive our debtors." And, when we pray so[4], he biddeth us to go aside into our chamber, that our heart and the devotion of our hearts may there appear unto our heavenly Father alone. The prodigal son doth in the field, where none but swine alone were to be seen, privately both make and offer the confession of his sin unto his father[5]. And that publican in the gospel, which is compared with the Pharisee, knocketh his breast, and with a lamentable [Luke xviii. 13.] voice doth to himself confess and say, "Lord, be merciful to me a sinner." Let us now also hear John, the holy apostle and evangelist, comprehending all that may be truly spoken [1 John i. 8, 9.] touching this confession in this one saying: "If we say that we have no sin, we deceive ourselves, and the truth is not in us. If we confess our sins, God is faithful and just to forgive us our sins, and to cleanse us from all iniquity." With this private confession, which is made to God, is that voluntary confession always joined that is made before men. For penitents are humbled so often as the matter, the glory of God, and safeguard of our neighbour requireth, and do before men openly testify[6] that they have sinned unto God. For so David, when Nathan the prophet told him of his sin, cried [2 Sam. xii. 13.] out, saying: "I have sinned to the Lord." So also Zacheus, [Luke xix.] understanding that the Lord was upbraided for receiving him[7], doth openly confess his sin, and promise amendment.

[1 et confitetur, Lat.; and confess.]

[2 Domino, Lat.; unto the Lord.]

[3 confitebor adversus me, Lat.; accuse myself. Coverdale, 1535; and see Ainsworth in loc.]

[4 confitentesque, Lat.; and confess.]

[5 Rather, Among the swine frames the confession of his sin, and offers it to his father alone. Luke xv.]

[6 etiam testantur, Lat.; also testify.]

[7 for receiving him, added by the translator.]

We verily do publicly make our confession to God so as Public or open confession. I told you a little above; but so much the rather yet, when after the hearing of the word of truth we do after that public or solemn manner, either in the church, or otherwise in some congregation or holy assembly[8], recite our sins committed, and cry to God for mercy and pardon of the same. Truly, of old the Lord appointed in our forefathers' days, that, the priest Levit. xvi. going before in words premeditated for the purpose, the whole people should follow him word for word, and openly confess their sins in the temple[9]. Whereupon undoubtedly it is at this day received in the church of the Christians, that, the pastor or doctor of the church going before in words conceived, at the end of the exposition of the scriptures[10], before the assembly is dismissed, all the people should openly in the temple confess all their sins against God, and heartily desire him of his mercy to forgive them the same[11]. The public confessions of sins are notably known, which were made by Daniel, Esdras, and Nehemias. And I say plainly[12] that that was a public confession of sins, which St Matthew in his third chapter saith that the Jews did make: for all Jewry came out to John the forerunner of the Lord, "and were baptized of him in Jordan, confessing their sins." For when they did publicly receive baptism, then did they thereby declare and openly confess their sins. For baptism is the sign of the cleansing of sins: therefore they that are baptized confess that they are sinners. They that were not baptized thought

[8 or holy assembly, not in Lat.—coram hominibus, Lat. omitted; before men.]

[9 See above, pages 165, 197.]

[10 et paulo antequam, Lat.; and a little before.]

[11 The divines of Cologne, in the Enchiridion appended to the canons of their provincial Council, 1538, having referred, as Bullinger here, to Nehemiah iv. and ix., also observe: Hinc finita concione, generalem et publicam confessionem ad populum pronuntiat (sacerdos) ac monet, ut se pronuntiantem populus eisdem verbis prosequatur. fol. 140.—In the reformed churches the general confession of the minister and people was ordinarily placed at the opening of public worship. Durel's View of the Government, &c. in Reformed Churches beyond the seas, p. 35. Lond. 1662. Sect. I. § 38. But see The Order of the Church in Denmark, &c. Works of Bp. Coverdale, ed. Park. Soc. p. 472.]

[12 interpretor, Lat.]

themselves to be otherwise purged, and that they need[1] not any sanctification. The Ephesians did publicly confess their sins, when, gathering their books of witchcraft together, they burned them in the fire: for by the burning of those books they did confess, that they had committed wickedness that was to be purged with fire.

Confession that is made to our neighbour. Now the confession that is made to our neighbour is of this sort: Thou hast offended thy brother[2], or else he perhaps hath done thee injury, for which ye are at discord, and do hate one another: in this case verily ye must think of reconciliation. Let the one therefore go to the other, and confess, and ask pardon for the fault committed; and let him that is innocent in the matter[3] freely forgive him that confesseth his fault, and so become his friend again. Of this confession the apostle James spake, saying: "Confess your faults one to another, and pray one for another, that ye may be healed." [James v. 16.] And[4] our Lord and Saviour did before James teach us, saying: "If thou offerest thy gift at the altar" (for he speaketh to those among whom at that time the sacrifices of the law were yet in use), "and dost remember there that thy brother hath any thing against thee, leave there thy gift before the altar, and go thy ways; first be reconciled to thy brother, and then thou mayest come and offer thy gift." [Matt. v. 23, 24.] To this also doth belong that parable, which the Lord putteth forth and expoundeth in the eighteenth chapter after St Matthew, of him that was cast into perpetual prison, because, when he had found favour at his Lord's hand, he was over cruel upon his fellow-servant, to whom he would not forgive so much as a farthing. For in the sixth chapter after St Matthew the Lord saith: "If ye forgive men their trespasses, your heavenly Father will also forgive you. But if ye forgive not men their trespasses, no more will your Father[5] forgive you your trespasses." Not that for our forgiving of others our sins are forgiven us; for so the forgiveness of our sins should not be free, but should come by our merits and as a recompence of our deserts: but now when our sins are freely forgiven through faith, verily that unreconcileable and

[1 needed, ed. 1577.]　　　[2 proximum, Lat.; neighbour.]
[3 that is innocent in the matter, not in Lat.]
[4 Quia, Lat.; Because.]
[5 pater cœlestis, Lat. Matth. vi. 14, 15.]

hard heart is an assured argument that there is no faith
in a hard, stubborn, and unappeasable man.   But where
there is no faith, there is no remission.   Therefore voluntary forgiveness in a man towards his neighbour is not that[6]
for which we are forgiven of God our Father, but is an
evident sign and natural fruit of true faith and the grace of
God in us[7].

To these two kinds of confession some men add that Consultation.
whereby they, that are oppressed in conscience with any
grievous sin, doth[8] consult or ask counsel either of the pastor
of the Lord's flock, or else of some other that is expert and
skilful in the laws[9] of God.   But that is rather to be termed
a consultation than a confession; and it is in no place either
commanded or forbidden, and therefore left free at every
man's choice.   Wherefore no man ought to be compelled to
this consultation.   But if any brother do demand counsel either
of the minister of the church, or of any other private brother,
then charity commandeth thee to satisfy him, if so be that
thou canst.   Yea, if he demandeth not, and thou dost see thy
brother to be in danger, charity again commandeth thee to
admonish him that is so in danger, and to handle him as
a brother.   For Paul to the Galatians saith : " Brethren, if a [Gal. vi. 1,
man be prevented in any fault, ye which are spiritual restore ²·]
such an one in the spirit of meekness, considering theeself
lest thou also be tempted.   Bear ye one another's burden,
and so fulfil the law of Christ."   But this belongeth nothing
to confession; therefore we return to our purpose again.

Thus much have we hitherto said touching the confession Confessions
of sins which God hath instituted.   Now we will annex some- dained of
what touching the confession of sins that men have ordained. men.
That confession also is of two sorts: the one is public, ritual or
ceremonial, which for the most part they call Ἐξομολόγησις ; Exhomolo-
the other is private or secret, and is called auricular.   gesis.

I call the public confession ritual, not so much because it
is the acknowledging or confession of sin, as for that it is the
penitential action for the sin committed.   For Isidore the bishop,
Libro Etymol.[10] vi. cap. 18, saith : *Exhomologesis* " is the

[6 is not that—but, the translator's addition.]
[7 within us, ed. 1577.]   [8 do, ed. 1577.]
[9 law, ed. 1577. legis, Lat.]
[10 Hispalen. Episcopus, Lat. : Bishop of Seville, A.D. 595.]

discipline of prostrating and humbling men in habit, in living, to lie in sack and ashes, to deface the body with filth, to mourn and lament with a sorrowful mind, and through sorrow to amend that wherein they sinned before[1]." These words of bishop Isidore I would not have recited unto you, dearly beloved, who is an author not very famous, unless I had seen the same words in a manner to be read in the book which Tertullian wrote of repentance[2]; and unless I had found an example thereof in Eusebius, who in the fifth book and last chapter of his Ecclesiastical History saith: "Natalis the martyr, being seduced by heretics, and at length understanding his error, riseth up in the morning, and putting on a sackcloth, sprinkling himself with ashes, and with many tears bewailing his error, casting himself prostrate at the feet of Zephyrinus the bishop and all other, not clerks only, but laymen also, with great lamentation and exceeding sorrow provoked all the congregation with earnest and continual prayers to request of Christ Jesus to pardon his offence[3]."

Touching the rites of repentance I will hereafter speak. Now this ritual or ceremonial repentance, as it was used among them of old, appeareth not to have been commanded of God, that whosoever at this day committeth any sin should be compelled presently to confess[4] it openly in such

I find him otherwise called Natalius.

[1 Exomologesis prosternendi et humiliandi hominis disciplina est habitu, atque victu; sacco et cineri incubare; corpus sordibus obscurare; animum mœroribus dejicere; illa, quæ peccavit, tristi tractatione mutare.—Isidor. Opp. Etymolog. Lib. vi. cap. 19. § 79. Tom. iii. p. 292. Rom. 1798.]

[2 Tertulliani Opp. de Pœnit. cap. 9. Tom. iv. p. 52. ed. Semler. Hal. Mag. 1824.]

[3 Confessor quidam erat apud nos, Natalis (Ναΰάλιος Gr. ed. Burton) nomine. . . . Hic, deceptus aliquando ab Asclepiodoto quodam et Theodoto collectariis, ... adquievit ut . . . . episcopus illius hæresis nominaretur. . . . Ad ultimum a sanctis angelis per totam noctem verberatus, ... mane consurgens, cilicio se induit, et cinere conspergit, ac multis lacrymis errorem suum deflens, ante pedes se Zephyrini episcopi prosternit, et vestigiis omnium, non modo clericorum, sed etiam laicorum, multa cum lamentatione provolutus, in lacrymas et miserationes omnem provocavit ecclesiam, ut indulgentiam sibi a Christo continuis et jugibus pro ipso precibus implorarent.—Euseb. Eccles. Hist. Lib. v. cap. 28. Ruffinus' translation, which Bullinger adopts. Basil. 1539. p. 126.]

[4 pœnitere, Lat.]

sort as they were wont to do it.   For where is it read that
such penance was enjoined to the sinful or adulterous woman   Luke vii.
that is mentioned in the gospel?   Many other sinners are   John viii.
received by Christ into the grace of God without such outward penance.   For it is very well known how Christ dealt
with Matthew, with Zacheus, with Peter that denied him, and
with many other.   Therefore we do not amiss[5] believe that
the old bishops and priests did invent that public kind of
penance for discipline's sake, and that they of their times
might have less liberty to sin.   Truly Hermius[6] Sozomenus
Salaminius, that notable writer of the Ecclesiastical History, in
his seventh book and sixteenth chapter saith : " In the beginning it pleased the priests, that as it were in a theatre, where
all the congregation might bear record of the same, the sins
of offenders should be openly punished."   Lo here, he saith,
" It pleased the priests."   He addeth also, that there was
a priest appointed, to whom they that sinned should come and   An elder.
confess their sins, and should hear of him the penance, to wit,
what they should do, or how they should aby[7] for their transgression.   Immediately after he describeth the manner of
penance in the Romish church used.   And to that again he
addeth, that " in the church at Constantinople there was a
priest appointed to hear penitents ; which office remained still,
till at the length a certain gentlewoman, which for the sins
that she had confessed was enjoined by such a penitentiary to
fast, and to pray to God, and thereby having occasion to be
long in the church, was at last bewrayed to have played the
whore with a deacon : for which cause the priests were evil
spoken of.   But Nectareus the bishop, devising how it were
best to deal with such a grievous crime, deprived the deacon,
that had done the sin, of his deaconship.   And for because
some persuaded them[8] to leave it free to every one, according
to his own conscience and confidence, to come to the communion of the mysteries, he did quite take away the office of that
penitentiary priesthood : and ever since that time hath that
counsel given to Nectareus prevailed, and doth even to this
day endure."   And so forth.   The same in the beginning of
the chapter saith : " Nectareus, the bishop of Constantinople,
did first take out of the church the priest that was appointed

[5 non temere, Lat.]   [6 Hermias.]
[7 quid luendum, Lat.]   [8 him, ed. 1577.]

78 THE FOURTH DECADE. [SERM.

to hear the confession of penitents, whom all the other bishops did in a manner follow¹." Thus far he.

But the bishop Nectareus would not have abrogated that *Exhomologesis*, (being so holy a man as indeed he was,) if he had understood that it had been instituted by God himself: neither had it been lawful for him to have abrogated it. Therefore he knew, even as Sozomen doth also confess, that by the counsel of the bishops that order of penance was usurped in the church. Neither do we read that John Chrysostom, who succeeded Nectareus², and was a very diligent and severe bishop, did ever restore that ritual penance which his predecessor had abrogated before him. For in the thirty-first homily upon St Paul's Epistle to the Hebrews he writeth: "I bid thee not to bewray theeself openly, nor yet to accuse thyself to others; but I will have thee to obey the holy prophet, who saith, Open thy way unto the Lord. Therefore confess thy sins before God, the true and upright Judge, with prayers for the injury committed³: not with thy tongue, but with the memory of thy conscience. And then at length believe that thou mayest obtain mercy, if thou hast it⁴ in thy mind continually⁵." And so forth. Again

John Chrysostom's doctrine concerning confession.

[¹ Ἐν τούτῳ δὲ τὸν ἐπὶ τῶν μετανοούντων τεταγμένον πρεσβύτερον οὐκέτι συνεχώρησεν εἶναι πρῶτος Νεκτάριος, ὁ τὴν ἐκκλησίαν Κωνσταντινουπόλεως ἐπιτροπεύων· ἐπηκολούθησαν δὲ σχεδὸν οἱ πανταχοῦ ἐπίσκοποι... φορτικόν, ὡς εἰκὸς, ἐξ ἀρχῆς τοῖς ἱερεῦσιν ἔδοξεν, ὡς ἐν θεάτρῳ ὑπὸ μάρτυρι τῷ πλήθει τῆς ἐκκλησίας τὰς ἁμαρτίας ἐξαγγέλλειν· (The Tripartite History gives these words of Sozomen, as Bullinger also,—but *incorrectly*—propterea visum est antiquis pontificibus, ut velut in theatro sub testimonio ecclesiastici populi delicta pandantur.) πρεσβύτερον δὲ τῶν ἄριστα πολιτευομένων ἐχέμυθόν τε καὶ ἔμφρονα, ἐπὶ τοῦτο τετάχασιν, ᾧ δὴ προσιόντες οἱ ἡμαρτηκότες τὰ βεβιωμένα ὡμολόγουν· ὁ δὲ, πρὸς τὴν ἑκάστου ἁμαρτίαν, ὅ τι χρὴ ποιῆσαι ἢ ἐκτίσαι ἐπιτίμιον θεὶς, ἀπέλυε..... Τάδε μὲν ἀρχῆθεν οἱ Ῥωμαίων ἱερεῖς ἄχρι καὶ εἰς ἡμᾶς φυλάττουσιν. Ἐν δὲ τῇ Κωνσταντινουπόλει ἐκκλησίᾳ, &c.—Sozomen. Hist. Eccles. Lib. VII. cap. 16, pp. 299, 300. ed. Reading. Cantab. 1720. Tom. II. See also Works of Bp. Pilkington. ed. Parker Soc. p. 553.]

[² Socratis Hist. Eccles. Lib. VI. cap. 2. Sozomen. Hist. Eccles. Lib. VIII. cap. 2.]

[³ Bullinger has here read, delicta *pro injuria*, for delicta *pronuncia*, as this passage is quoted, Lombard. Sentent. Lib. IV. distinct. 17. c.]

[⁴ it, wanting in ed. 1587.]

[⁵ Οὐ λέγω σοι, ἐκπόμπευσον σαυτὸν, οὐδὲ παρὰ τοῖς ἄλλοις κατηγόρησον, ἀλλὰ πείθεσθαι συμβουλεύω τῷ προφήτῃ λέγοντι, Ἀποκάλυψον πρὸς

upon the fiftieth Psalm: "If thou art ashamed to tell thy sins to any man because thou hast sinned, yet say them daily in thine own heart; I bid thee not confess them to thy fellow, that he should upbraid thee: tell them to thy God who doth regard them. If thou tellest them not, God is not ignorant of them; for he was at hand when thou didst them[6]." And again in another place he saith: "I bring thee not forth into the theatre of thy companions: I compel thee not to discover thy sins unto mortal men. Rehearse thy conscience before God, and declare it unto him. Shew thy wounds unto the Lord, thy best physician, and ask of him a salve for the same[7]." Again: "Take heed that thou tell not a man of thy sins, lest he bewray thee and upbraid thee for them. For thou needest not to confess them to thy companion, that he should bring them abroad, but to the Lord which hath the care of thee, who also is a gentle physician: to him therefore thou shalt shew thy wounds[8]." Moreover he bringeth in the Lord speaking and saying: "I compel thee not to come into the open theatre, and to make many privy to thy sins: tell thy sin privately to me alone, that I may heal thy sore[9]." Thus much out of Chrysostom. Now all this doth manifestly argue, that that ceremonial penance (as it was once used in the church), not instituted by God,

Κύριον τὴν ὁδόν σου. Ἐπὶ τοῦ Θεοῦ ταῦτα ὁμολόγησον, ἐπὶ τοῦ δικαστοῦ ὁμολόγει τὰ ἁμαρτήματα, εὐχόμενος, εἰ καὶ μὴ τῇ γλώττῃ, ἀλλὰ τῇ μνήμῃ, καὶ οὕτως ἀξίου ἐλεηθῆναι. Ἄν ἔχῃς τὰ ἁμαρτήματα διηνεκῶς ἐν τῇ μνήμῃ, &c.—Chrysost. Hom. xxxi. in Ep. ad Hebr. cap. 12. Tom. xii. pp. 289, 290. Par. 1718—38.]

[6 Ἀλλ' αἰσχύνῃ εἰπεῖν διότι ἥμαρτες; λέγε αὐτὰ καθ' ἡμέραν ἐν τῇ εὐχῇ σου. Καὶ τί; μὴ γὰρ λέγω εἰπὲ τῷ συνδούλῳ τῷ ὀνειδίζοντί σε· εἰπὲ τῷ Θεῷ τῷ θεραπεύοντι αὐτά· οὐ γάρ, ἐὰν μὴ εἴπῃς, ἀγνοεῖ αὐτὰ ὁ Θεός. Μὴ γὰρ παρὰ σοῦ βούλεται αὐτὰ μαθεῖν; ὅτε ἔπραττες αὐτά, παρῆν.—Id. Hom. in Psal. L. Tom. v. p. 589. But this treatise is spurious.]

[7 Οὐδὲ γὰρ εἰς θέατρόν σε ἄγω τῶν συνδούλων τῶν σῶν· οὐδὲ ἐκκαλύψαι τοῖς ἀνθρώποις ἀναγκάζω τὰ ἁμαρτήματα. Τὸ συνειδὸς ἀνάπτυξον ἔμπροσθεν τοῦ Θεοῦ, καὶ αὐτῷ δεῖξον τὰ τραύματα, καὶ παρ' αὐτοῦ τὰ φάρμακα αἴτησον.—Id. de Incomprehens. Dei Nat. Hom. v. Tom. i. p. 490.]

[8 Μὴ γὰρ ἀνθρώπῳ λέγεις, ἵνα ὀνειδίσῃ σε; μὴ γὰρ συνδούλῳ ὁμολογεῖς, ἵνα ἐκπομπεύσῃ; τῷ δεσπότῃ, τῷ κηδεμόνι, τῷ φιλανθρώπῳ, τῷ ἰατρῷ τὸ τραῦμα ἐπιδεικνύεις.—Chrysost. Conc. de Lazaro. iv. Tom. i. p. 757.]

[9 Οὐκ ἀναγκάζω, φησίν, εἰς μέσον ἐλθεῖν σε θέατρον, καὶ μάρτυρας περιστῆσαι πολλούς· ἐμοὶ τὸ ἁμάρτημα εἰπὲ μόνῳ κατ' ἰδίαν, ἵνα θεραπεύσω τὸ ἕλκος.—Ibid. p. 758. See also Calvin. Instit. Lib. iii. cap. 4. § 8.]

was without any injury taken out of the church, and not[1] restored again by the bishops that succeeded. They do not altogether in vain tell us that some relics of that ritual repentance abided still in the Roman church[2]. But what have we to do what every church hath taken to itself, either to keep or else to lay away? We rather ought to inquire, what Christ hath delivered unto us, and what his apostles have taught us ; of whose doctrine I have, I think, spoken enough already.

Of auricular confession.

The private or secret confession of sins was wont to be made when none were by but the priests alone. For one goeth secretly, and whispereth his sins in the ear of the priest that was appointed to hear those secret confessions ; and, being by him absolved, doth think that by the recital of a few ordinary words he is purged from all his sins: and therefore I call it auricular confession. This was unknown in the apostles' times ; and although it be now a good sort of years ago since it first took root, yet notwithstanding it was free from the beginning. At last we read that it was commanded and roughly extorted by the bishop of Rome, when the state of the church was most corrupted, about the year of grace 1215. And yet it was about eighty years or more in controversy, before it was by decree laid upon all men's necks, " whether it were enough for a man to confess himself to God alone, or else to a priest also, for the purging of his sins?" Hugo in his book of the church's power to bind and loose doth say : " I dare boldly say, if before the priest's absolution any man do come to the communion of the body and blood of the Lord, that he doth assuredly eat and drink his own damnation, although he repent him never so much, and doth never so greatly lament his offences[3]." This did Hugo say boldly without his warrant,

[1 neque mox, Lat.]

[2 Credimus hanc confessionem—nunquam penitus abolitam fuisse, non solum in Romana, sed ne in Græca quidam ecclesia.—Enchirid. Colon. fol. 145.]

[3 Audacter dico, si ante sacerdotis absolutionem ad communionem corporis et sanguinis Christi accesserit, judicium sibi pro certo manducat et bibit, etsi eum peccasse jam multum pœniteat, et vehementer doleat et ingemiscat.—Ricardi Sancti Victor. Scoti Opp. Colon. Agrip. 1621. Tract. de Potest. Ligandi et Solvendi. cap. XXI. p. 519. par. I.— He died abbot of St Victor, A.D. 1173. Gall. Christ. Tom. VII. p. 669.

unless the word of God doth instruct us falsely. He lived about the year of our Lord 1130. Within a little while after him upstarted Peter Lombard, commonly called the Master of Sentences, because he gathered together the sentences of the fathers, and laid forth their doctrine as it were in a summary: of whose work I mean not here to tell my judgment what I think. It is thought that he flourished about the year of Christ 1150[4]. He, *Sententiarum*, Lib. IV. *Dist.* 17, and 18, doth by the authority of the fathers shew, first, that it sufficeth to make the confession of sins to God alone: then he annexeth other sentences which teach the contrary; and lastly concludeth of himself and saith: "By these it is undoubtedly proved, that we must offer our confession first to God, then to the priest, and that otherwise we cannot enter into paradise, if we may (have a priest)." Again: "It is certified that it is not sufficient to confess to God without a priest; neither is he truly humble and penitent, that doth not desire the judgment of a priest[5]." Gratian, that gathered the decretals together[6], was somewhat honester than Peter Lombard, who lived and flourished at the same time with Lombard. He determineth nothing definitively; but shewing sentences for either side, both that we must confess our sins to the priest and not confess them, doth leave it indifferently unto the reader's judgment. For thus he concludeth: "Upon

Watt's Biblioth. Brit. Mosheim, Eccles. Hist. Vol. II. p. 439. ed. Soames, note 7.—Hugo of St Victor, whom Bullinger names by mistake, was born A.D. 1096, and died 1140. Mosheim, ibid. note 6.]

[4 He died bishop of Paris, A.D. 1164. Mosheim, Eccles. Hist. Book III. cent. 12. part II. chap. 2. § 23. ed. Soames. Vol. II. p. 440, note 2.]

[5 The title of Sentent. Lib. IV. distinct. 17 c. is, Si sufficit soli Deo confiteri; and there Lombard says, Quibusdam visum est sufficere, si soli Deo fiat confessio sine judicio sacerdotali et confessione ecclesiæ: p. 340. But the title of the following section is, Quod non sufficit soli Deo confiteri, si tempus adsit, si tamen homini possit; and then Lombard concludes in the words quoted by Bullinger: Ex his aliisque pluribus indubitanter ostenditur, oportere Deo primum, et deinde sacerdoti offerri confessionem, nec aliter posse perveniri ad ingressum paradisi, si adsit facultas; p. 341: and in the next section, E. p. 342, Certificatum est, quod non sufficit confiteri Deo sine sacerdote: nec est vere humilis et poenitens, si non desiderat et requirit sacerdotis judicium.]

[6 He completed his Decretum about A.D. 1151. Mosheim, Eccles. Hist. Vol. II. p. 411, note 2.]

what authority and reasons both the opinions of confession and satisfaction are grounded, we have briefly here declared. But to which of these we ought rather to stick, that is reserved for the reader to choose; for both parts have wise and religious men to their fautors and defenders[1]." Thus saith Gratian about the end of the first distinction of penance.

A law made, wherein auricular confession was first commanded.

About fifty years after followed Lotharius Levita[2], a doctor of Paris, the scholar[3] and earnest follower of Peter Lombard. He, being once made bishop of Rome and named Innocent the Third, called together at Rome a general council called *Lateranense*[4], in which he made a law, which Gregory the Ninth reciteth in his decretal of penance and remission, Lib v. chap. 12, almost in these very words: "Let every person of either sex, after they are come to the years of discretion, faithfully confess alone, at least once in a year, their sins unto their own proper priest, and do their endeavour with their own strength to do the penance that is enjoined them; receiving reverently at Easter at the least the sacrament of the Eucharist, unless peradventure by the counsel of their own priest, for some reasonable cause, they think it good for a time to abstain from receiving it. Otherwise in this life let them be prohibited to enter into the church; and when they are dead, to be buried in christian burial[6]."

The Latin copy hath, *semel in animo*: falsely I think for *semel in anno*[5].

This is that new law which containeth many absurd and

[1 Quibus auctoritatibus vel quibus rationum firmamentis utraque sententia confessionis et satisfactionis innitatur, in medium breviter exposuimus. Cui autem harum potius adhærendum sit, lectoris judicio reservatur. Utraque enim fautores habet sapientes et religiosos viros. —Gratian. Decret. pars II. caus. 33. quæst. 3. de Pœnitent. dist. 1. cap. 89. ad fin.]

[2 Lothaire Conti, born in A.D. 1160 or 1161, studied in the university of Paris, and was elected pope A.D. 1198. Mosheim, Vol. II. p. 508, note 7. Lotharius Levita, or the Deacon, was the name under which he wrote before he became pope. Centur. Magd. cent. XII. Watt's Biblioth. Brit.]

[3 the scholar, not in Lat.]

[4 The Fourth Lateran, called by the Romanists the Twelfth General Council, was held A.D. 1215. Mosheim, Eccles. Hist. Book III. cent. 13. part 2. chap. 3. § 2. Vol. II. p. 559. n. 2.]

[5 This error is corrected in the London reprint by H. Midleton. P.]

[6 Omnis utriusque sexus fidelis, postquam ad annos discretionis pervenerit, omnia sua solus peccata confiteatur fideliter saltem semel

wicked blasphemies. And, to let pass very many of their absurdities, I will recite unto you not past one or twain of the foulest of them. Is it not a wicked thing, to send a sinner to I wot not what kind of priest of his own, when Christ hath given but ministers and preachers to his church only, being still himself the universal priest, and proper priest to every one in the church, even until the end of the world; to whom alone all the faithful ministers do send sinners from themselves for to confess their sins to him? For John said: "I am not Christ, [John iii. but am sent before him to bear record of him." What may be said to this moreover, that it is a detestable blasphemy to attribute the remission of sins to our own confession and the priest's absolution, as to the works of mortal men? And who, I pray you, is able to reckon up all his sins unto the priest? Doth not Jeremy cry, "The heart of man is evil and un- [Jer. xvii. 9.] searchable?" Doth not David say, "Who knoweth his [Psal. xix. sins? Cleanse me from my hidden faults." It is unpossible for a man to confess all his sins. While therefore a man, compelled by the law, doth consider these reasons and ponder them in himself, he cannot choose but must needs be drowned in the bottomless depth of desperation: so great a burden is laid upon the free necks of Christ his faithful people, as a thing so necessary that without it they cannot obtain eternal salvation, directly contrary to the apostles' decree that is to be seen in the fifteenth of the Acts. And lastly, what, I pray you, is a sinner able to do of his own strength? What power, I pray you, have we silly wretches[7] of ourselves to do good?

But it grieveth me, and I am ashamed of these men's impudency, to see that they will have this their auricular confession to be instituted of God, and that they go about to uphold and confirm it by the scriptures; guilefully[8] wresting

Auricular confession can be proved by no place in all the scripture.

in anno proprio sacerdoti; et injunctam sibi pœnitentiam studeat pro viribus adimplere: suscipiens reverenter ad minus in Pascha eucharistiæ sacramentum; nisi forte de consilio proprii sacerdotis, ob aliquam rationabilem causam, ad tempus ab ejus perceptione duxerit abstinendum: alioquin, et vivens ab ingressu ecclesiæ arceatur, et moriens christiana careat sepultura.—Concil. Lateran. IV. in Concil. stud. Labb. et Coss. Tom. XI. par. 1. coll. 172, 3. Lutet. Par. 1671. See also Decret. Gregor. IX. Lib. V. tit. 38. fol. 314. col. 4. Lugd. 1510.]

[7 silly (weak) wretches, not in Lat.]

[8 proferunt, Lat.; guilefully wresting, the translator's paraphrase.]

that place in the gospel where the Lord saith to the leper, "Go thy way, shew thyself to the priest." Now they do not impudently wrest this place alone, contrary to the true sense; but do also corrupt all the other testimonies of holy scriptures which they are wont to cite. Among all the rest I will tell you of this one. Bonaventura, in his Commentaries, *Ad Sententias Magistri*, Lib. iv. Dist. xvii. Quæst. 3, imagineth two things to be in confession: the one formal, to wit, absolution, or the power to heal; and this he saith was instituted by the Lord at the giving of the keys: the other is material, to wit, the disclosing of the sin; and this he saith that the Lord himself did not institute, but only insinuate. For immediately after he addeth these words: "And therefore confession was insinuated by the Lord, instituted by the apostles, and openly proclaimed by James the bishop of Hierusalem. For as he proclaimed the decree of not keeping the ceremonial laws, Acts xv.; so also he published and laid upon all them that sin the necessity of confession, saying, Confess your sins one to another." Thus much hath Bonaventura[1]. But who will not wonder at the blindness of that age? This writer acknowledgeth that auricular confession was not instituted by the Lord, but obscurely[2], and as it were by conjectures of the consequents[3]; that the apostles expounded the mind of Christ and instituted it; and that St James in the name of all the apostles did by a decree openly proclaim it. He addeth, that the words of the proclamation were, "Confess your sins one to another." Now what is it else to wrest the scriptures, if this be not to wrest them? Even he that is the blindest doth easily see, that these cham-

[1 Dicendum quod duo sunt in confessione: unum formale et completivum; et hoc est absolutio, sive potestas absolvendi vel medicandi; et hanc Dominus instituit, qui potestatem clavium concessit; et penes hos residet virtus. Aliud autem est materiale; et hoc est detectio peccati sive morbi: et hoc Dominus non instituit in se, sed insinuavit. ... Et ideo confessio fuit a Domino insinuata, ab apostolis instituta, ab episcopo Hierosolymitano, scilicet Jacobo, promulgata: sicut enim sententia de non servandis legalibus promulgata (Actor. xv.) fuit, sic et confessio omnibus peccantibus indicta et imposita fuit, Confitemini alterutrum peccata vestra.—Bonavent. Opp. Sent. Lib. iv. dist. 17. quæst. 1. par. 2. art. 1. quæst. 3. Tom. v. p. 224. Mogunt. 1609.]

[2 implicite, Lat.]

[3 ex quadam consequentia, Lat.]

pions are unweaponed in this same combat[4], bringing forth a
spear made of a wrapt-up wisp of hay[5], which they shake and
keep a coil with[6], as if it were the lance-staff of Hector or
Achilles. It is most evident that the apostle speaketh not of
secret and auricular confession, but of that confession which
by a certain reciprocation is made of them that have mutually
offended one another; and now again, freely confessing their-
selves one to another, are mutually reconciled, and pray one
for another again: of which I have said somewhat already
a little before. They do not see that in the apostle's words
there are two things, which being diligently considered do make
them mere mocking-stocks to them that perceive them. For
first the apostle in that place useth this word ἀλλήλους, which
signifieth mutually, one another, one for one, and as it were
reciprocally. Thereupon we infer thus: If according to the
apostle's precept we must confess ourselves one to another, and
that ἀλλήλους doth signify mutually or reciprocally, that is,
that we must confess ourselves by turns, as it were first I to him
and then he to me, as it signifieth so in very deed; then must it
needs be, that after the laymen have confessed themselves to the
priests, the priests should again confess themselves unto the
laymen; for that is to make confession one to another: for
we say, φιλοῦσιν ἀλλήλους, that is, they love one another
mutually, he him and he him again. But if this trouble the
priests[7], to have their confessions heard of laymen[8]; let them
then acknowledge that this place of the apostle doth make
nothing for their secret and auricular confession, which they
have devised for their own commodity. Then the apostle
addeth: "And pray ye one for another, that ye may be
healed." He doth therefore associate, and as it were join
under one yoke, both confession and prayer. And upon that
we do again gather, If we must confess to none but priests,
then must we pray for none but priests[9]. But we must not
pray for priests alone; ergo, we must not confess to priests

[4 inermes in hac palæstra, Lat.]
[5 telum hujusmodi, non fraxineum, sed prorsus betaceum: made
of beet.]
[6 coil: noise, tumult, difficulty. Nares' Gloss.]
[7 presbyteris, Lat.]
[8 to have—laymen, the translator's addition.]
[9 This argument is also Calvin's, Instit. Lib. III. cap. 4. § 6.]

alone, but every one one to another. The same place of St James must not be understood of secret and auricular confession, but of that open or public confession by which they return into charity again by the mutual confession of their faults, which had before offended each other with mutual injuries; and, being now again reconciled, do pray one for another that they may be saved. We do therefore leave this for an undoubted truth, that the disputers for auricular confession neither have proved, nor can prove, that it was instituted and ordained of God.

Whether auricular confession ought to be received in the church for discipline's sake

But when they see that this their confession will to wrack[1], they go about with weak props, God wot[2], to stay it up, and say that that confession is to be retained still in the church, if it were for nothing else but for discipline's sake, to make men blush when their sins come to light; which is a cause many times that men do sin the seldomer. And also they say, that it is to be retained for private absolution and peculiar or singular consolation of the godly. But if auricular confession be so needful and profitable for the church as they will seem to have it, how chanced it that the church for the space of a thousand years[3] after the apostles' times was utterly without it? It is marvel then that the apostles did in no place either use it or command it. And again, it is manifest that the times which were before the coming of Christ did not once so much as dream of this confession: neither did the apostles leave the church of God destitute of anything necessary unto salvation. Now what discipline this auricular confession, planted in the church of God, is, the abominable deeds and wicked acts that ensued it do plainly declare. For both he that doth confess, and he that heard the confession, learned horrible wickedness even by the examination and beating out the circumstances of sins committed. By that means there were given and taken causes and occasions of whoredoms and adulteries. Under the pretence of those confessions the chastity of matrons and virgins hath been assaulted, and also corrupted, oftener times and more sundry ways than[4] is decent to be named. Those confessors fished

[1 wrack: ruin, destruction. Johnson.]
[2 quibusdam, Lat.; God wot, the translator's phrase.]
[3 amplius mille, Lat.; more than a thousand.]
[4 quam prosit aut, Lat.; than it is expedient or.]

out the secrets of every man's conscience: which thing availed greatly to the establishing of their tyranny.   By those confessions the confessors could cunningly spoil and rob their shrift-children, as they called them, of their goods and substance; because they knew what riches every one had, and how he came by them.   And when the peers of every common-wealth knew that the priests were privy to their faults, they could not choose but fear the priests: and so it came to pass, that they did not so strongly as they might set themselves against the extreme corruption and lust of the priests, that was otherwise not to be suffered[5].   They have been heard to say: "I have learned by confessions, and know at my fingers' ends, what kind of men, of women, and of maidens are in this city.   I know how to handle every one according to his disposition.   They do all fear and stand in awe of me, because they know that I am privy to their most secret deeds and thoughts of their minds."   The secrets told in confession are many times foolishly babbled abroad with the peril of the silly soul that first confessed them.   By the means of confessions no small and many treasons are hatched up and put in practice.   And surely it is a goodly matter, when we for the fear or carnal blushing that we have by the means of one man (I mean, as some term him, of our ghostly father[6]) we shall cease to sin, rather than for the sincere fear that we have of God; when as in deed we do not blush at all to think that he[7] shall be a witness against our conscience, nor yet do fear the severity of his judgment that shall lighten upon us.   What may be said to this moreover, that by this auricular confession, once established in the church, nothing else is wrought, but that the word of God should be the less regarded through our traditions, and we made the slacker to confess our sins to him, to whom of right we ought for to confess them[8]?   For so often as we remember our sins, we do earnestly[9] put them off again until the time of confession come: and when it is come, then who, I pray you, goeth to it with a cheerful mind?   Let wise men therefore judge what kind of discipline this is, and how well it pleaseth God[10].

[[5] in populo Dei, Lat. omitted; in the people of God.]
[[6] confessoris inquam, Lat.]   [[7] Deum, Lat.]
[[8] to whom—them, the translator's addition.]
[[9] securi, Lat.; carelessly, 1577.]
[[10] Cf. Works of Bp. Pilkington, Parker Soc. ed. p. 554. Remains

Whether
auricular
confession is
to be kept in
the church
for private
absolution's
sake, or not.
That which they allege of private absolution is a mere device of man's invention, which hath not in the sacred scriptures any precept or example to back itself withal. For in very deed none doth absolve us men from sin, blame, and punishment[1], but God alone, to whom alone that glory doth belong. The minister, by the preaching and consolation of the gospel, doth pronounce and testify that to the faithful their sins are forgiven. Therefore this preaching of forgiveness, being fetched from out of the mouth or word of God, is the absolution wherewith the minister absolveth. Neither is that absolution made any whit the more effectual, if the minister do privately whisper it into the sinner's ear. The public preaching of the gospel, as it is instituted by Christ our Lord, doth satisfy a faithful mind, which doth not so much respect the demeanour of the minister, as he regardeth the truth of him in whose name the minister doth it. But if a sinner, say they, do hear privately said unto him, "I absolve thee from thy sins," and that by the virtue of the keys; he doth far better understand that his sins are remitted than when forgiveness of sins is generally preached and publicly pronounced. But we do in this case set against them the apostle's example; whom when the men of Jerusalem had heard to preach, they were pricked in heart, and said: "Men and brethren, what shall we do? To whom Peter answered, Repent, and be baptized every one of you in the name of Christ Jesus unto the remission of your sins, &c. And there were added to the church that same day about three thousand souls." Now who understandeth not, that[2] upon so great a multitude baptism was at once bestowed, and the remission of sins universally preached unto them all; and not that every one had this saying or the like whispered severally into his ear, 'Brother, thy sins are forgiven thee?' And verily a godly-minded man may learn true faith in Jesus Christ (through which his sins are forgiven him) as well by the public preaching of the gospel, as by the private whisperings of privy penitentiaries and absolving confessors: namely[3] since that

[Acts ii. 37—41.]

of Bp. Latimer, Vol. II. p. 179. Foxe, Monuments, Vol. III. p. 205; v. p. 191. Lond. 1838.]

[1 a pœna et culpa, Lat.]

[2 simul, Lat. omitted; at one and the same time.]

[3 præsertim, Lat.]

public preaching doth contain the commandments of God[4], when as those whisperings do nothing so; and finally, since that the public preaching of the gospel doth apply to every one the grace of God, and that the sacraments do testify the remission of sins and the heavenly gifts prepared for all them that do[5] believe in Jesus Christ. And yet I say not this because I think it amiss, when occasion serveth so to do, if the minister do preach privately to one or two the gospel of our Lord, or else in the words of Christ do promise remission of sins to him that believeth: but I do here dispute against them which do suppose that public and general preaching, as it was used of the apostles, declaring to all and every man[6] the remission of sins, is not sufficient, except the sinner, going to the priest, do confess his sins, and privately ask and receive private or peculiar absolution of him for the same. For they think that, for that private absolution's sake, this private or auricular confession must be retained in the church.

But we will not, say they, that all and every peculiar sin with the circumstances thereof should be reckoned up or rehearsed. What of that then? Who, I pray you, commanded us to whisper any sins at all into the priest's ear? The primitive church was wont to confess to the priests, neither few nor many, nor any sins at all. Bonaventura recorded that before pope Innocent the Third they were not counted heretics which affirmed, that confession made to God alone, without any priest, is sufficient to them that do faithfully believe; but after the decree which he published, touching confession to be made of every man unto his own priest, they were judged heretics that taught men to be confessed to God only[7]: as though it lay in pope Innocent to make a new article of faith, which the church was without by more than the space of twelve hundred years after Christ. Therefore if all they that lived before Innocent were without

[4 habeat præceptum, Lat.]

[5 Rather, testify that remission of sins and heavenly gifts are theirs who do, &c.]

[6 fidelibus, Lat. omitted; that believe. every several man, ed. 1577.]

[7 Dicendum quod si quis esset modo hujus opinionis (i. e. quod sufficiat si soli Deo fiat confessio), esset hæreticus judicandus, quoniam in concilio generali hoc determinatum est sub Innocentio III. Sed ante hanc determinationem hoc non erat hæresis.—Bonavent. Opp. Sentent. Lib. IV. par. 2. dub. 1. Tom. v. p. 220. Mogunt. 1609.]

suspicion of heresy in that point; and since we read that Nectarius and the church of Constantinople was not condemned of heresy for abrogating and casting out of the church their *exhomologesis*, which seemeth to be far better than this auricular confession; no godly man undoubtedly shall condemn us, which maintain the confession instituted by God, that is wont to be made to God and our neighbour, but do only reject and hiss at that secret and auricular confession, as that which bringeth more discommodity than honest profit to the church of God.

Of the satis-
faction of
works.

And for because I have hitherto said thus much of secret or auricular confession, upon which the treatise of satisfaction doth depend, I should here even of necessity say somewhat of satisfaction, had I not sufficiently spoken of it in mine other sermons of this work; as in the sixth and ninth sermons of the first Decade, and in the third Decade, where I entreat of the saints' affliction; in the tenth sermon of the same Decade, and also in the fourth Decade, where I spake of the gospel. The priests and monks do teach that repentance of the sin committed, and faith in Christ, are not sufficient for the purging of sins without the satisfaction of our own works and merits[1]; which they make to be, wearing of sackcloth, fasting, tears, prayers, alms-deeds, offerings, sundry afflictions of the body, pilgrimages, and many other odd knacks[2] like unto

Note here the
difference
that they
make betwixt
pœna and
*culpa pec-
cati.*

these. For they affirm, that by these means penalty due to sins (the guilt whereof, they say, is only pardoned) is washed away, as with a shower of water poured down upon it[3]. But we already have taught out of the canonical scriptures, that God doth not only forgive freely the guilt, but also the penalty of our sins. We have already taught, that men are not justified by their own works and merits, but by the mere grace of God through the faith of Christ Jesus: for otherwise he should in vain have taken our flesh upon him, and in vain should Christ have given himself unto the most bitter and reproachful death of the cross. Now we add, If we are not justified by works, then do we not with our works make satisfaction for our sins. For in effect (although I acknow-

[1 and merits, not in Lat.]

[2 odd knacks, translator's phrase.]

[3 See Vol. I. p. 108, note 6. Lombard. Sent. Lib. IV. distinct. 10. cap. 10.]

ledge that there is a difference, and do not confound them)
justification and satisfaction come both to one end.   By the
justification of Christ we are absolved: by the satisfaction
of Christ, or rather for his satisfaction's sake, we are also
absolved.   Christ is our righteousness, and therefore also our
satisfaction.   The price of our redemption is in Christ, not in
ourselves.   If we make satisfaction for ourselves, then is the
price of our redemption in ourselves.   And therefore are we
both Christs and Saviours unto ourselves: which thing doth
flatly make Christ of none effect, and therefore is it extreme
blasphemy.   Moses in his law doth with little business or
none dissolve all the arguments for satisfaction wrought by
our works.   For where he describeth the manner of cleansing
sins, he placeth no jot thereof in the works of men, but sheweth that it all consisteth in the ceremonial sacrifices.   Now
we do all agree and jointly confess, that in those sacrifices the
only sacrifice of Christ was plainly prefigured.   And to that
is added, that that only preaching and promise of the new
testament is this: "I will be appeased upon their unright- [Jer. xxxi.
eousness and sins, and will no more remember their iniquities." 34.]
Now where such a remission is, there is no oblation or satisfaction for sin.   And we in the creed verily do believe the
forgiveness of sins.   But if the debtor make satisfaction to the
creditor, then what, I pray you, doth the creditor forgive him?
Therefore this article of our faith, the principal promise
and preaching of the new testament, is utterly subverted, if
we admit the doctrine of the satisfaction of our works for sin.

  We do acknowledge that tears, fastings, wearing of sack- God afflict-
cloth, alms-deeds, and the other works of piety, humiliation, whose sins
and charity, have a place[4] in repentance; of which I will forgiven.
speak in place convenient: but we deny[5] that with them we
make satisfaction for our sins, lest we should make the price
of Christ his redemption of none effect.   We acknowledge that
at some times the Lord hath whipped[6] them whose sins he hath
forgiven, as he did to our parents Adam and Evah, and to king
David after his adultery and murder of Urias.   But I have
already shewed[7] you that those afflictions were not satisfactions

[4 suum locum, Lat.; their own place.]
[5 modis omnibus, Lat. omitted; by all means.]
[6 sumpsisse supplicium vel pœnam, Lat.]
[7 See Vol. II. p. 430.]

for the sins which God had pardoned, but exercises of God's discipline and humiliation; which doth by those means keep his servants in their dutiful obedience, and doth declare to all men how heartily he hateth sins, although he doth freely forgive and pardon them. Therefore lest we, because of that free forgiveness, should be the more inclined and prone to sin, he punisheth them whom he maketh to be examples for us to take heed by.

Neither do we read that the saints did simply attribute the benefit of justification or satisfaction unto their afflictions. I confess that Daniel the prophet gave counsel to the most mighty king Nabuchodonosor, and said: "Let thy sins be redeemed in righteousness, and thine iniquities in shewing pity to the poor[1]:" but in these words the king was taught how to lead the rest of his life that was yet behind, and how to rule the state of his kingdom. The king had till then oppressed many nations, and sinned in merciless cruelty: whereupon he persuadeth him to change his old kind of life, to embrace justice, and deal well with all men. Therefore he speaketh not of the satisfaction of his sins before God, but before men. For there is salvation in none other than in Christ alone. But if any man do stubbornly stick upon the letter, we say, that the righteousness of Christians is faith, by which their sins are properly cleansed: and that faith is not without good works and charity[2], to which justification is unproperly ascribed. Of which matter I spake in the treatise that I made of good works[3].

[1 Pet. iv. 8; Prov. x. 12.] Therefore, when St Peter doth cite that place in Salomon, "Charity covereth the multitude of sins;" the word 'covereth' is not there used for purging; for by the only blood of Christ all sins are purged and wiped away: but it is taken for turning away. For as self-love in a manner is the root of all sins, so charity is thought to be the driver away of all mischiefs; for "love doth none ill to his neighbour[4]."

Many sins be forgiven her because she loved much. Now whereas they object that sentence of the gospel, where the Lord saith, "Many sins[5] be forgiven her, because

[1 justitia redimantur, Lat. Dan. iv. 27.]
[2 beneficentia vel caritate, Lat.]   [3 See Vol. ii. p. 327.]
[4 Rom. xiii. 10. Bullinger has here borrowed from his Commentary on St Peter, loc. cit.]
[5 Luke vii. 47. peccata ejus, Lat.]

she loved much:" they do miss herein, because they understand not that the word ὅτι, which is commonly Englished[6],
because, or, *for that*, is here a note of inferring somewhat,
and that no other sense is gathered than this: "Many sins
be forgiven her, therefore she loved much; or, whereby it
cometh, that she loveth much." Neither do we here wrest
the words of the gospel to maintain a wrong opinion; for in
the history there goeth before, first, "When they were not
able to pay, he forgave them both." If he forgave them,
and if they were not able to pay, he did not then forgive
them for their love; for if they had been able to pay, he
would not have forgiven them. Secondarily, there goeth
before, "Whether of these will love him more?" Simon
saith, "He to whom he forgave the more." Therefore the
Lord's answer could in effect be nothing else but this: "I
have forgiven her[7] very much, therefore hath she loved
much." So then, I say, love is of forgiveness, and not forgiveness of love. And then it followeth immediately: "And
he said to the woman, Thy faith hath saved thee, go in peace."
We do therefore conclude, that there is but one only satisfaction for the sins of all the world, to wit, Christ once[8] offered
up for us which are by faith made partakers of him.

But now, as we do not acknowledge or admit the satis- *Of indul-*
factions that are obtruded unto us in the doctrine of the *gences.*
priests and monks, so do we by all means detest the indulgences of the bishops of Rome. They called these indulgences a beneficial pardoning of crimes, or remission of the
punishment, or of the guilt, or both; to wit, by the power of
the keys bestowed by the Lord; and for the merit of the
martyrs' blood (for so they say) granted or given to them
that are rightly contrite in heart, and do confess their sins.
For these fathers of indulgences[9] are wont with their indulgences to remit·again the rigour and severity of the satisfaction, which lieth in them to order at their discretion[10]. Truly,
as one said, "The fathers' gentle indulgence doth make the
children naught[11];" so have their indulgences utterly corrupted true repentance. But thou canst read in no place that

[6 redditur, Lat.; rendered.]   [7 huic mulieri, Lat.; this woman.]
[8 once, not in Lat.]   [9 indulgentes patres, Lat.]
[10 suo impositam arbitrio, Lat.]
[11 Blanda patrum segnes facit indulgentia natos.—Joan. Baptist.
Mantuan. Parthen. Lib. I. 164. Tom. I. Par. 1531.]

such power[1] was given to the popes as they did feign. We read that to the apostles the keys were given by the Lord: but those keys were nothing else but the ministry of preaching the gospel; as I in place convenient will shew unto you. Now the gospel promiseth to us remission both of the guilt and penalty for Christ his sake and faith in Christ, and doth admonish us that in the latter times there shall come men that shall say, We are Christs; that is, which shall attribute to themselves the things that do properly belong to Christ alone, such as is especially the forgiveness of sins. But it commandeth us to fly from them, and by all means to take heed of them, as of wicked seducers.

The same evangelical truth doth teach, that the faithful are cleansed by the only blood of the Son of God. Their indulgences do promise men the cleansing of their sins through the blood of St Peter, St Paul, and other holy martyrs. And for that cause are they the profanation of the blood of the Son of God. The saints do wash their garments in the blood of the Lamb, not in the pardoning bull, or box of indulgences, nor in the martyrs' blood. Yea, Paul himself denieth that either he, or Peter, or any other of the saints was crucified for the church of God. And yet their indulgences were so set forth, as though God were pleased with us for the blood of the martyrs. Therefore their indulgences are flatly contrary to the apostles' doctrine. And I admonished you in my sermon of good works[2] in these words of Paul, "I fulfil that which is behind of the afflictions of Christ in my flesh for his body's sake, which is the church;" that that fulfilling is not referred to the work of the purging or propitiation of Christ, which is consummate, unless Christ at his death did testify falsely, saying, "It is consummate;" but to those afflictions wherewith the members of Christ, that is, the faithful, are exercised by the cross so long as they live in this frail flesh. Verily the Lord maketh account of the afflictions laid upon the faithful, as of his own: for to Paul he said, "Saul, Saul, why persecutest thou me?" Moreover, when he saith, "For the church," he meaneth not, for the expiation of the church, but for the edification and profit of the same[3]. And Paul sustained

[Acts ix. 4.]

[1 clavium potestatem, Lat.; power of the keys.]

[2 See Vol. II. page 333.]

[3 Calvin's words, Instit. Lib. III. cap. 5. § 4. Foxe, Acts and Mon. Vol. v. p. 611. Lond. 1838.]

grievous afflictions at the hands of the Jews because he preached the gospel to the Gentiles: and it was expedient that in him there should be shewed to the church an example of patience so rare as could not lightly be found again. Yea, other have oftentimes objected against these indulgence-defenders this godly saying of the holy man, pope Leo, in his eighty-first epistle: "Although the death of many saints is precious in the sight of the Lord, yet the slaughter of no man subject to sin is the propitiation for the sins of the world." Again, "The righteous have received, not given, crowns of glory: and of the manful constancy of the martyrs are sprung examples of patience, not the gifts of righteousness: for their deaths were singular; neither did any one by his ending pay the debt of another, since there is one Lord Jesus Christ, in whom they are all crucified, dead, buried and raised up again[4]." Thus much out of pope Leo. We have therefore by divine and human testimonies evidently proved, that the indulgences given to sinners by the merit or treasure of the martyrs' blood are mere blasphemies against God, and open injuries against his holy martyrs.

The holy saints' suffering is not our redemption.

I have hitherto spoken of those indulgences which were of old freely bestowed by the popes of Rome[5], although at this day they be few in number and curtailed too: now therefore I will say somewhat of their indulgences, which they for the most part do sell and make traffic of. To sell indulgences in the church of God is a sin so detestable, as that it is hard to name any one more horrible. And yet it is and hath been a common practice and merchandise[6] these many years with the bishops of Rome and their factors, whom they call apostolics, not having any word in the scripture wherewith to cloak that

The filthy mart of indulgences.

[4 Quamvis enim multorum sanctorum in conspectu Domini pretiosa mors fuerit, nullius tamen insontis (Bullinger has *sontis*) occisio propitiatio fuit mundi. Acceperunt justi, non dederunt, coronas: et de fortitudine fidelium exempla nata sunt patientiæ, non dona justitiæ. Singulares quippe in singulis mortes fuerunt; nec alterius quispiam debitum suo fine persolvit, cum inter filios hominum unus solus Dominus noster Jesus Christus extiterit, in quo omnes crucifixi, omnes mortui, omnes sepulti, omnes etiam sunt suscitati.—Leon. Opp. Ep. LXXXIII. ad Palæst. Episc. p. 152. The same is repeated in Ep. XCVII. ad Leon. Aug. cap. 2. pp. 171, 172, and Serm. XII. p. 59. Par. 1662.]

[5 of Rome, not in Lat.]   [6 and merchandise, not in Lat.]

wicked invention. And now, though I slip over and do not
shew how indulgences are nothing but a bare name without
any stuff or matter, and that under that vain name miserable
men and silly souls are foully deceived; yet note, that Christ,
the chief and only high priest of his catholic and holy church,
in the days of his flesh did with a whip drive the buyers and
sellers (as impudent dogs) out of the church[1] of God: which

[John ii. 13—
16; Matt.
xxi. 12, 13.]
thing he did twice; once at the beginning of his preaching,
and another time a little before his passion[2]. At the first
time he added: "Away with these things from hence, and
make not my Father's house an house of merchandise." At
the latter time he said: "It is written, My house shall be
called the house of prayer; but ye have made it a den of
thieves." And Simon Magus also, in the Acts of the Apostles,
seeing that by the laying on of the apostles' hands the Holy
Ghost was given, did offer them money, saying: "Give me
this power also, that on whomsoever I lay my hands, he
may receive the Holy Ghost." But hearken how Peter

[Acts viii.
18—21.]
accepteth his petition. "Thy money (said he) perish with
thee; because thou hast thought that the gift of God may be
obtained with money. Thou hast neither part nor fellowship
in this business; for thy heart is not right in the sight of
God." Lo, the gifts of God are not gotten with money.
Lo, their heart is not right that make merchandise of religion[3].
Lo, they have no part or fellowship in the inheritance of the
kingdom of heaven, or in the preaching of the glad tidings[4].
Therefore what shall we say now of the indulgences which
the pope's apostolics do set to sale for money? What shall
we say of the very indulgenciaries, and the pope himself,
whose hirelings they be? We must confess, verily, that they
are the fellows of Simon (not Peter, but) Magus: for Peter
did by the just sentence of God curse such kind of merchants:
"Your money (saith he) perish together with you." This is
a heavy and terrible, but yet a most just judgment of the
most just God. The same apostle Peter, foreseeing that in
the church there would be many such merchants, doth in his

[2 Pet. ii. 1—
3.]
last epistle say: "There were false prophets among the people,

[1 e templo, Lat.]
[2 Rather, nearly at the end, i. e. of his ministry.]
[3 in rebus religionis, Lat.]
[4 vel in evangelica ratione, Lat.]

even as there shall be false teachers among you, which privily bring in damnable heresies, even denying the Lord that hath bought them, and bring upon themselves swift damnation. And many shall follow their damnable ways, by whom the way of truth shall be evil spoken of. And with covetousness through feigned words shall they make merchandise of you." For what is it with feigned words through covetousness to make merchandise[5] of the miserable idiots[6], if this is not, when they say that they do give full remission of sins unto all them that are contrite, and do confess their sins? For if any man do acknowledge his sins, and with a true faith convert[7] himself to God through Christ, even without their indulgences he doth obtain plenary remission of all his sins. Those foxes therefore make money of smoke, deceiving simple souls[8], and selling for coin the thing which they never had, neither possibly can be purchased with money.

And thus much hitherto of bought and sold indulgences; of which other writers have made very long discourses. I suppose that by this little any man may easily understand how to judge of them aright.

We are now at length come past those rocks and shelves to which we did of purpose sail, that, when we had viewed the most perilous places, we might admonish the unskilful passengers to take heed how they strike upon them for making shipwreck of their souls, by thinking that in these indulgences doth lie the true force of sufficient repentance; wherein there is nothing but the utter displeasing of God's most holy majesty. Therefore letting that alone as it is, we do now return to declare the last members of repentance, whereby we said that penitents do mortify the old man, and are renewed spiritually.

First of all therefore, it seemeth good to tell, What the old man is, What the new or regenerated man is, and What the power or strength of man is: for by the demonstration thereof we shall the better understand what it is to mortify the old man, and to be renewed in the spirit.

[5 lucrumque facere, Lat. omitted; and to make gain.]
[6 ex misera plebecula, Lat. Cf. Vol. I. p. 71, note 3.]
[7 convertatur, Lat.]
[8 fucum faciunt simplicibus versutissimi, Lat. Cf. Erasm. Chiliad. Adag. p. 305, *imposturæ.*]

The old and new man.

We say that the old man is all that which we have of nature, or of our first parents, to wit, not the body only or the flesh, I mean the grosser and substantial part of the body; but even the very soul, with the strength, the power and faculties of the same. Therefore, whereas in some places of the holy scriptures the flesh is put for man, we must not only understand the massy substance and grosser part of the body; but the very flesh together with the soul and all the faculties thereof, that is, the whole man not yet regenerate. For the [John iii. 6.] Lord in the gospel saith: "That which is born of the flesh is flesh, and that which is born of the spirit is spirit." And this he speaketh concerning regeneration, which is not according to the flesh (as Nicodemus did falsely imagine), but according to the spirit. The word "flesh" therefore doth import[1] the natural power and faculties[2] of man; even all that, I mean, which we have or take of our first grandsire Adam. The new man is said to be he that is regenerate by the Spirit of God in Christ, or is renewed according to the image of Christ, with all the gifts and virtues of the Holy Ghost. And as the flesh is usually put for the old man, so[3] is the spirit by an antithesis commonly used and taken for the new man.

The flesh taken in scripture for the old man.

Now here the very place requireth to discourse somewhat of the power and virtues of man: of which although I have elsewhere disputed already, as in the sermon of freedom and bondage, and of sin[4], yet again I will touch such points as I think to suffice for this present argument.

Of the power of man.

There are two parts or faculties of our soul, understanding and will. Understanding doth discern in things object, what to receive or what to refuse; and is as it were the light and guide of the soul. Will chooseth, for in it doth lie both to will and to nill: which are again impelled by other Understanding. powers and faculties. Now the understanding is of two sorts; for we understand either earthly or heavenly things. I call those earthly things, which do appertain not to the life to come, but to the life present: whereunto we refer all liberal arts and handicrafts, the governing of public weals,

[1 comprehendit, Lat.]
[2 naturalis animæ, Lat.; the powers and faculties of the natural soul.]
[3 and as—so, not in Lat.]
[4 See Sermons 9, 10. of the Third Decade.]

and the ruling of private houses. By heavenly things I understand God himself, eternal felicity, and life everlasting, the knowledge of God and all kinds of virtues, faith, hope, charity, righteousness, holiness, and innocency of life.

Now let us see what this understanding of man is able to do, and what power it hath. The judgment and understanding of man in earthly things is not altogether none at all: but yet it is weak and very small, God wot. The understanding therefore that is in man doth come of God: but in that it is small and weak, that cometh of man's own fault and corruption. But the bountiful Lord doth augment in men those gifts of his; whereby it cometh that man's wit bringeth wonderful things to pass. For which cause we read in the holy scriptures, that the arts and wits of men are in the hands of God. But in the knowledge or understanding of heavenly matters there is not one small spark of light in man: his wit of itself is nothing but darkness, which at the beginning was created by God most sharp and lightsome, but was afterwards by man's[5] corruption utterly rebated[6] and darkened again. For therefore it is that Christ in the gospel said: "No man cometh to me, unless my Father draw him." And [John vi. 44, 45.] in the Prophets it is written: "All shall be taught by God." And Paul saith: "The natural man perceiveth not the things [1 Cor. ii. 14.] that are of the Spirit of God; for they are foolishness unto him; neither can know, because they are spiritually discerned." The natural man (that is, that old man which is not yet regenerate by the Holy Ghost) is not a block altogether without all sense or feeling: for if he were utterly without all the discourses of reason, then how should the preaching of the gospel seem foolishness unto him? He doth therefore by the gift of God hear and understand the words and sense of the holy scripture; but by reason of his natural corruption he is not touched with them, he doth not rightly judge of them: they seem mere folly unto him: neither doth he perceive that they must be discerned spiritually, because he is not regenerate, and is yet without the true light of God's most holy Spirit. For in another place the apostle saith: "We are not able to think any good[7] as of ourselves, but all our ability is of God." And therefore it is that we

[5 parentis nostri, Lat.]   [6 rebated: blunted. Johnson.]
[7 2 Cor. iii. 5; good, not in Lat.]

do so often in the scriptures find mention of enlightening or illumination: which should without cause be expressed or named, if so be man's understanding were clear, and of itself not dark and misty. There is therefore born together with all men a blindness of heart and mind, a doubting in the promises of God, and an unbelief and perverse[1] judgment in all heavenly things. For albeit that man hath at God's hand received understanding, yet by reason of his own corruption ignorance is a peculiar and proper heritage belonging unto him. For he is then in his[2] kingdom, when he is blind, when he doth err, when he doth doubt, when he doth not believe, nor use the gifts that God hath given him rightly, as he should, that is, to his own salvation and the glory of his Maker[3].

Let us now see what the will of the old man is able to do. Therefore, since this will doth follow a blind guide, God wot, that is to say, corrupt[4] affection, it is unknown to no man what foolish[5] choice it maketh, and whereunto it tendeth. And although the understanding be never so true and good, yet is the will like to a ship tossed to and fro with stormy tempests, that is, of affections. For it walloweth[6] up and down with hope, fear, lust, sorrow, and anger, so that it chooseth and followeth nothing but evil. For the holy apostle speaking of himself doth say: " I know that in me, that is, in my flesh, there dwelleth no good thing. For to will is present with me, but I find no means to perform that which is good. For the good that I would, do I not: but the evil which I would not, that do I." But now, since the apostle spake this of himself when he was regenerate, what, I pray you, shall we say of the will of the old man? The old man willeth all things which God willeth not, and, breaking into all kind of wickedness, doth foully fulfil his filthy lusts: that is to say, he giveth his members servants unto uncleanness and wickedness, from one iniquity unto another. We have of this very many examples exhibited unto us, both by the holy scriptures and daily experience.

[Rom. vii. 18, 19.]

Of the new man, and of regeneration.   Let us now against this oppose or set the new man, that is, the man which is regenerate by the Spirit of God through

[1 perversissimum, Lat.]   [2 suo, Lat.; his own.]
[3 Dei, Lat.]   [4 corruptissimum, Lat.]
[5 foolish, not in Lat.]   [6 raptatur, Lat.]

the faith of Jesus Christ. Now regeneration is the renewing of the man, by which through the faith of[7] Jesus Christ, we, which were the sons of Adam and of wrath, are born again the sons of God, and do therefore put off[8] the old man, and put on the new, which both in understanding and will doth freely serve the Lord. This regeneration is the renewing of the mind, not of the body : as we heard in another place, out of the third chapter of St John's gospel[9]. The author of this regeneration is the Holy Ghost, which is from heaven given unto man, I mean, to a faithful man. For the gift of the Holy Ghost is given for Christ his sake, and that too unto none but those that do believe in Christ. This Spirit of God doth testify with our spirit that we are the sons of God, and therefore the heirs of his kingdom. We are therefore a new creature, repaired now according to the image of God, and endued with a new nature or disposition : whereby it cometh to pass, that we do daily put off that old man, and put on the new : which thing is done when we walk[10], not in concupiscence, after the carnal inclination[11] of the flesh, but in newness of sense, according to the working of the Holy Ghost by whom we are regenerate. The same substance and form of the body abideth still ; the mind is changed, the understanding and will renewed. For by the Spirit of God the understanding is illuminated, faith and the understanding of God and heavenly things is plenteously bestowed, and by it unbelief and ignorance, that is, the darkness of the old man, are utterly expelled, according to that saying of the apostle, "Through Christ ye are made rich in all things, in all speech and knowledge :" again, "We have not received the spirit of the world, but the spirit which is of God, to know what things are given of Christ to us." And again, "We have (or know the spirit or)[12] mind of Christ." And again, "Ye have no need that any man teach you : but as the very anointing doth instruct you of all things, and is true, abide ye in it[13]."

[Rom. vii. 16, 17.]

[1 Cor. i. 5; ii. 12, 16.]

And in this regeneration of man the will also doth receive

[7 per Spiritum sanctum in fide J. C., Lat. ; through the Holy Spirit in the faith of.]

[8 in diem, Lat. omitted ; day by day.]

[9 See above, p. 37.]   [10 dum ambulamus, Lat.]

[11 pro ingenio, Lat.]

[12 The parenthesis is the translator's.]

[13 1 John ii. 27, in ea, Lat. and Erasmus ; in it, Marg. Auth. Ver.]

an heavenly virtue, to do the good which the understanding perceived by the Holy Ghost: so that it willeth, chooseth, and worketh the good that the Lord hath shewed it; and on the other side nilleth, hateth, and repelleth the evil that the Lord hath forbidden it. For Paul saith: "I know to be humble, and I know to exceed. I can do all things through Christ who strengtheneth me[1]." And again to the Philippians he saith: "To you it is given for Christ, not only to believe in him, but also to suffer for him." And again yet he doth more plainly say: "It is God that worketh in you both to will and to perform, according to the good purpose of the mind[2]." But now note this, that whatsoever they do which are regenerate by the Spirit of God, they do it freely, not by compulsion, nor against their wills. For like as God requireth a cheerful giver; so "where the Spirit of the Lord is, there is free liberty and hearty good-will[3]." And Zachary, the father of

[Luke i. 74, 75.]

John Baptist, said: "That we, being delivered from the hands of our enemies, might serve him without fear, in holiness and righteousness before him all the days of our life." Yea, and our Lord himself in the gospel saith: "If ye abide in my sayings, ye shall be my disciples indeed, and ye shall know the truth, and the truth shall make you free." And again:

[John viii. 31, 32, 36.]

"If the Son set you at liberty, or make you free, then shall ye be free indeed." Touching this liberty of the sons of God I have already discoursed in the ninth sermon of my third Decade.

What, and of what kind, the liberty is that is in man.

This liberty of the sons of God we do willingly acknowledge and freely confess: but the arrogant disputations of some blasphemous praters[4] concerning free-will, as though it were in our power of ourselves to do any heavenly thing, we do utterly reject and flatly deny. And yet we do not make man subject to fatal necessity, nor turn upon God the blame of iniquity, as we have elsewhere more at large declared[5]. And St Augustine in his controversy with the Pelagians did so attemper his disputation, that he attributed the good to the grace of God, and the evil unto our nature: so that, the sense being sound, uncorrupted, and well weighed, he attributeth

[1] Phil. iv. 12. excellere, Lat. and Erasmus; excede, Tyndale, 1534.]
[2] Phil. i. 29; ii. 13. See above, p. 323, note 6.]
[3] 2 Cor. iii. 17, and hearty good-will, not in Lat.]
[4] blasphemous praters, not in Lat.]　　[5] See Decade III. Serm. 10.]

free-will, which he granteth to be in us, unto the grace that worketh in us, yea, to the regeneration of the Spirit, rather than to ourselves or our own power.

I will here cite and rehearse unto you, dearly beloved, this one testimony only out of all his writings, as it is to be found in the first chapter of his book *De Correptione et Gratia*, where he saith: "We must confess that we have free-will to do both evil and good: but in the doing of evil every one is free from righteousness, and bound to sin; but in good no man can be free, unless he be made free by him which said, 'If the Son make you free, then shall ye be free indeed.' And yet not so that, when every one is set free from the condemnation of sin, he should then no more stand in need of his deliverer's aid: but so rather, that, where he heareth his deliverer say, 'Without me ye can do nothing,' he should presently say to him again, 'Be thou my helper; O forsake me not.' And verily, I am glad that in our brother Florus I found this faith, which, without doubt, is the true, prophetical, and apostolical faith. For here must the grace of God through Jesus Christ our Lord be needs understood; by which alone we men are delivered from evil, and without which we do no good, either in thought, will, love, or deed: not only that by the shewing, or teaching of grace, men should no more but know what is to be done; but also, that by the very working and performing of grace they should with love do the thing that they know[6]." And so forth. For I have hitherto rehearsed unto you St Augustine's opinion

[6 Liberum itaque arbitrium et ad malum et ad bonum faciendum confitendum est nos habere: sed in malo faciendo liber est quisque justitiæ, servusque peccati; in bono autem liber esse nullus potest, nisi fuerit liberatus ab eo qui dixit, Si vos Filius liberaverit, tunc vere liberi eritis. Nec ita ut cum quisque fuerit a peccati damnatione liberatus, jam non indigeat sui liberatoris auxilio; sed ita potius ut ab illo audiens, Sine me nihil potestis facere, dicat ei et ipse, Adjutor meus esto, ne derelinquas me. Hanc fidem, quæ sine dubio vera et prophetica et apostolica fides est, etiam in fratre nostro Floro invenisse me gaudeo. Intelligenda est enim gratia Dei per Jesum Christum Dominum nostrum, qua sola homines liberantur a malo, et sine qua nullum prorsus sive cogitando, sive volendo et amando, sive agendo faciunt bonum: non solum ut monstrante ipsa quid faciendum sit sciant, verum etiam ut præstante ipsa faciant cum dilectione quod sciunt.—August. Opp. Tom. VII. fol. 272. col. 2. Par. 1531.]

touching free-will, of which this is sufficient for a note by the way : now I return to my purpose again.

We have heard what the old man is, what the new man is, and how we are renewed by the Holy Spirit : now therefore, when we say that penitents do mortify the old man, and are renewed by the Spirit, or spiritually, we say nothing else but that to all penitents the affections, senses or lusts, of the flesh (I mean, even the very understanding which we have of the old Adam, together with the will,) are not only suspected, but also convicted of impiety ; and that therefore[1] in all their thoughts, words, and deeds, they do never admit their affections into their counsel, but do by all means resist them, and continually study to break the neck of them : and on the other side, in all our counsels, words, and deeds to admit and receive, yea, and with prayers to call unto us, that heavenly guide, the Spirit of Christ, by whose conduct and leading we may perceive, judge, speak, and work, that is to say, either omit or do, that which we have learned in our grand pattern Christ, according to whose likeness we must be reformed, that henceforth we may apply ourselves to holiness, righteousness, and good works to God-ward[2].

But now all this we shall understand more rightly and plainly by the words of the apostle, where he saith : "This I say, and testify in the Lord[3], that ye henceforth walk not as other Gentiles walk, in vanity of their mind, darkened in cogitation, being alienated from the life of God by the ignorance that is in them, by the blindness of their hearts; which being past feeling have given themselves over unto wantonness, to work all uncleanness with greediness. But ye have not so learned Christ, if so be ye have heard him, and have been taught in him, as the truth is in Jesus; to lay down, according to the former conversation, the old man, which is corrupt according to the lusts of error, but to be renewed in the spirit of your mind; and to put on that new man, which after God is shapen in righteousness and holiness of truth :" and so forth, as followeth in the fourth chapter to the Ephesians[4]. The same apostle in the third to the Colossians saith : "Mortify your members which

[1 in gerendis rebus, Lat. omitted; in all their transactions.]
[2 beneficentiæque, Lat. ; to God-ward, not in Lat.]
[3 per Dominum, Lat. and Erasmus.]
[4 verses 17—24, holiness of truth, Marg. Auth. Ver.]

are upon the earth; fornication, uncleanness, inordinate affection[5], evil concupiscence, and covetousness, which is idolatry; for which things' sake the wrath of God cometh upon the children of disobedience: among whom ye also walked sometime, when ye lived in them. But now put ye off also all these things, wrath, fierceness, maliciousness, blasphemy, filthy communication out of your mouth : lie not one to another, seeing that ye have put off the old man with his works; and have put on the new man, which is renewed into the knowledge and image of him that made him. Put on therefore, as the elect of God, holy and beloved, bowels of mercy, kindness, modesty, meekness, long-suffering ; forbearing one another, and forgiving one another, if any man have a quarrel against any :" and so forth. To which if thou addest that which the apostle hath of the same matter in the sixth chapter to the Romans, every point will be more express and plain unto the hearer.

Now these words of the apostle do not only teach us Of the worthy fruits, or of the fruits worthy of repentance. what the old man is, what the new man is, what it is to mortify the old man, and how penitents are renewed in the newness of the spirit, or of the mind ; but do also shew what the fruits be that are worthy of repentance, to wit, those rehearsed virtues, or those offices of life toward God and our neighbour. We owe to God fear and[6] reverence, humbleness of mind, the knowledge[7] of ourselves, faith, hope, the hatred of sin, the love of righteousness; charity towards our neighbour[8], welldoing towards all men[9], and innocency in all things. These kind of fruits did the holy man John Baptist require of the Jewish nation, when he said : "Bring forth fruits that become [Luke iii. 10, &c.] repentance." For in St Luke, being demanded of the people, of the publicans, and of the mercenary or garrison soldiers[10], what thing they should do worthy of repentance, he prescribeth none other than that which we even now recited. For the Lord himself by Esay, in the fifth chapter of his prophecy, rehearsed up none other fruits than those. And in the reve-

[5 mollitiem, Lat. and Erasmus ; unnatural lust, Tyndale 1534, and Cranmer 1539.]

[6 sive, Lat. ; or.]   [7 agnitionem, Lat.]

[8 Rather, to our neighbour (we owe), &c.]

[9 towards all men, not in Lat.]

[10 a satellitibus vel stipendiariis, Lat. In his Comment. in loc. cit. Bullinger explains at length what soldiers these were.]

lation[1] made to St John, speaking to the minister of the church of Ephesus, he saith: "Remember from whence thou art fallen, and repent, and do the first works." Whereunto agree the words of St Paul, speaking to Agrippa, and saying:

[Acts xxvi. 20.]

"I have preached to the Jews and Gentiles, exhorting them to repent, and to turn to God, and to do such works as become them that repent." And again, in the seventh chap-

2 Cor. [10, 11.]

ter of the second epistle to the Corinthians, he saith: "Sorrow which is to God-ward causeth repentance unto salvation not to be repented of. For, behold, this self-same thing that ye were made sorry to God-ward, how much carefulness it hath wrought in you; yea, what clearing of yourselves; yea, what indignation; yea, what fear; yea, what vehement desire; yea, what zeal; yea, what punishment[2]!" Now this carefulness is an intentive diligence to correct that which is amiss. Verily, out of careless looseness doth arise inured custom to commit sin, and negligent security. Penitents do not stand in defence of their sins, but make their supplicant apology to God, to have them remitted. Hypocrites excuse themselves, and seek out shifts and starting holes, not confessing freely their sins and offences, nor praying to God to have them forgiven. He which repenteth truly and in very deed is angry with himself because of his wicked manners and life already lewdly spent. The punishment which he doth exercise upon himself[3] preventeth and turneth away the revenging and imminent wrath of God. Moreover with fear he doth take heed how he sinneth any more: for the contempt of God is the original of mischiefs, and bond of an impenitent life. Furthermore, he which doth truly repent is ravished with the passing vehement desire or love of God and heavenly things: he burneth with zeal, whereby it cometh to pass that he neither foadeth[4] off from day to day, nor yet doth coldly nor slackly go about, that which he hath learned by the word of God to be required at his hand to be done and performed. Briefly, whatsoever he doth he doth it with all his mind, even from the very bottom and root of his heart. For so saith the great

[Deut. xxx. 2, 3.]

prophet of God, the holy man Moses: "If thou wilt turn to

[1 revelatione sua, Lat.; his revelation. chap. ii. 5.]
[2 So Tyndale 1534, and Cranmer 1539.]
[3 affligendo semetipsum, Lat. omitted; by afflicting himself.]
[4 foadeth off. See Vol. II. page 38, note 3.]

the Lord thy God, and hearken unto his voice, with all thy heart, and with all thy soul; the Lord thy God also shall turn thy captivity, and shew pity upon thee in the bowels of mercy." Thus much touching the fruits of repentance.

Now upon all the premises we infer this consequent, that repentance (whose only scope, whereto it tendeth[5], is the renovation by the Spirit of Christ of the image of God, which was by Adam's fall of old defiled) is not a work of a day or twain, or of a prescribed number of years, but a continual observance of our whole life, and so consequently a daily putting off and renewing of the old man for ever[6]. For they that are regenerate by the Holy Spirit of God are never so purged that they feel no motions of the flesh, of sin, and of carnal affections. There is always object to the eyes of the faithful this sentence of St Paul, that cannot by any means be plucked out of their minds : " I know that in me, that is, in my flesh, there dwelleth no good thing. For to will is present with me, but I find no means to perform that which is good. For the good, that I would, I do not; but the evil, that I would not, that do I." For we bear about the relics of the flesh through all our life. Whereupon it cometh that in the saints there is a perpetual and very sharp battle. For they do partly obey the spirit, and are partly weakened of the flesh : by the spirit they are lifted up to the contemplation and desire of heavenly things; but by the flesh they are thrust down to earthly things, and troubled with the allurements of this naughty world. For even the apostle, feeling that combat in himself, said : " The flesh lusteth contrary to the spirit, and the spirit contrary to the flesh. For they are so at enemity betwixt themselves, that what ye would ye cannot do." And in another place he saith : " Even I, the same, do in the mind serve the law of God, but in the flesh the law of sin." And, to help the matter forward withal, there lacks no deceit, no craft, and a thousand[7] temptations of the subtle crafts-master, our enemy the devil. Therefore the labour and peril of the true penitent, that is, of a christian man, is far greater than that our prayers are comparable unto it.

But now who doth not here perceive how great watching,

Marginal notes:

Repentance is a work not of a day or twain, but of all our life.

[Rom. vii. 18, 19.]

[Gal. v. 17.]

[Rom. vii. 25.]

[5 in nobis, Lat. omitted; in us.]

[6 adeoque innovationem quotidianam, is all Bullinger says.]

[7 incessabiles, Lat. omitted; endless.]

What things are necessary in penitents. abstinence, constancy [1], fortitude, and patience, are needful for those that do repent? what great need they have of earnest and continual prayers? Let us in this sharp conflict lay before our eyes the instruction of that valiant champion the apostle Paul; for that which he saith may be to us instead of a large and ample commentary. For he will in few words passingly instruct us how to behave ourselves in this troublesome combat, how to vanquish, and how to triumph when the victory is gotten. In his epistle to the Ephesians thus he saith: "Brethren, be strong in the Lord, and in the power of his might. Put on all the armour of God, that ye may stand against the assaults of the devil. For we wrestle not against flesh and blood only, but against rules, against powers, against worldly governors [2] of the darkness of this world, against spiritual subtilties in heavenly things. Wherefore take unto you the whole armour of God, that ye may be able to resist in the evil day, and, having finished all things, to stand fast. Stand therefore, having your loins girt about with the truth, and having on the breast-plate of righteousness, and your feet shod in the preparation of the gospel of peace: above all, taking the shield of faith, wherewith you may quench all the fiery darts of the wicked: and take the helmet of salvation, and the sword of the Spirit, which is the word of God; praying always in all prayer and supplication in the Spirit, and watching for the same with all instance." And so as followeth in the sixth to the Ephesians.

The outward exercises of repentance. Here therefore are also to be rehearsed the outward exercises of repentance or rites of penance, wherewith the saints do exercise themselves, partly to tame and keep under the motions of flesh, and partly to testify their repentance unto the congregation. Those exercises are, carelessness of the flesh, tears, sighs, sackcloth, fastings, weeping, lamenting, neglecting and hatred of dainty diet, trimming of the body, and also of allowable pleasures: which, although they be done, and yet do not proceed from the very heart and from true faith, are notwithstanding nothing available to him that useth them. But it is best here to learn, and as it were in a painted table to behold them pictured in the word [3] of God. Joel [ii. 12—17.] The prophet Joel saith: "Turn ye to me, saith the Lord,

[1 assiduitate, Lat.]   [2 rectores, Lat. omitted; rulers of.]
[3 in verbo sincero, Lat.]

with all your hearts, with fasting, with weeping, and with mourning: and rent your hearts, and not your garments, and turn to the Lord your God; for he is gracious and merciful, slow to anger, and of great goodness, and he will repent him of the evil. Who knoweth whether the Lord[4] will return and take compassion, and will leave behind him a blessing? Blow up a trumpet in Sion, proclaim fast, call an assembly, sanctify the congregation, gather the people, gather the elders, assemble the children and sucking babes. Let the bridegroom come forth of his chamber, and the bride out of her closet. Let the priests, the Lord's ministers, weep betwixt the porch and the altar, and let them say: Spare thy people, O Lord, and give not over thine heritage unto reproach, that the heathen should rule over them. Wherefore should they among the heathen say, Where is their God?" To these divine and evident precepts let us annex that notable example of the truly repentant Ninivites out of the holy scriptures; of whom the holy prophet Jonas hath left this in writing: "The men of Ninive believed God, and proclaimed a fast, and put on sackcloth from the greatest of them unto the least of them. And word come to the king of Ninive, which arose from his throne, and put off his robe, and covered himself in sackcloth, and sat down in the ashes." Moreover by the king's commandment proclamation was made throughout the whole city, saying: "Let neither man nor beast[5] taste anything, neither feed, nor yet drink water: but let both man and beast put on sackcloth, and cry mightily unto God; yea, let every man turn from his evil way[6], and from the wickedness that is in his hands. Who can tell whether God will turn, and be moved with repentance, and turn from his fierce wrath, that we perish not?" And now it is good to hear how effectual true repentance is in the sight of the Lord. Therefore it followeth in the same chapter: "And God saw their works, that they turned from their evil ways, and he repented of the evil which he said he would do to them, and did it not."

And here also, dearly beloved, ye must note, that repentance is of two sorts, to wit, private or secret, and public or manifest. Every one doth secretly to himself repent

Jonah [iii. 5—10.]

Private and public repentance.

[4 the Lord, not in Lat.]
[5 neque greges, Lat. omitted; nor flocks.]
[6 et a violentia et injuria, Lat.]

privately, so often as, when he hath sinned against God, he doth descend into himself, and with the candle of God's word doth search all the corners of his heart, and confess to God all his offences; being grieved that he hath offended him, and yet doth turn unto him, believing verily that he will be reconciled unto him in Christ his Saviour; and for his sake doth utterly hate sin, and entirely love righteousness and innocency, in following them so near as he can[1]. The public or solemn repentance is used in great calamities, in dearth, in pestilence and war: and of that repentance it is that the prophet Joel speaketh, whose words ye heard a little afore. And yet private repentance is in many points all one with the public. For Peter weepeth bitterly; and private penitents do fast privately, and abstain severely even from all allowed pleasures, much more then from the allurements and baits of the world[2]. But they that do truly repent either publicly or privately, both do and must specially hate

Repentance must be voluntary, not coacted.
coloured hypocrisy and vain ostentation. Moreover, both kinds of repentance are free and voluntary, not extorted or coacted, but proceeding of a willing mind. The pastor of the church and teacher of the truth, I confess, doth severely call upon all sinners without delay to repent themselves truly for their sins committed: but yet he doth by express law lay upon no man's neck any precise order, prescribing the time, manner, place, or number; but leaveth it free to every one's choice, so that they do the thing that is decent, according to the prescript rule in the word of God. But public repentance is for the most part wont to be proclaimed, and openly received of the whole congregation, so often as piety requireth it, and necessity compelleth it; and doth out of the word of God therewithal declare what and how all things must be done and decently ordered.

False and true repentance.
Again, it is manifest that there are two sorts of repentance more: for there is true repentance and false repentance. The true repentance is that which he doth exercise that is regenerate by the Spirit of God[3]; and is without all colour and craft, containing in it all those things that I have hitherto told you of. The scriptures contained in the old

[1 in following—he can, not in Lat.]
[2 carnis ac mundi, Lat.; of the flesh and of the world.]
[3 in fide Jesu Christi, Lat. omitted; in the faith of Jesus Christ.]

and new Testament do minister to us many examples of true
repentance, which I have at large laid forth unto you in that
that I have already spoken.   Those examples are excellent,
which we find of our parents Adam and Evah, of the people
of Israel's often repenting[4] in the thirty-third of Exodus, in
the book of Judges, and the books of Kings.   Yet more
excellent than the rest is that of David in the twelfth chapter
of the second of Samuel, and i. Par. 21; and that of Manasses [1 Chron.
and Josias, ii. Reg. xxxiii. and xxxiv.   In the gospel also ^{xxi.]}
we have to see the examples of Matthew, Zacheus, the sinful
woman, and Peter; beside other more that here for shortness'
sake I do wittingly pass over.

But false or counterfeit repentance proceedeth of a feigned
heart: and though at a blush it seem to have the circumstances of true repentance, yet for because it wanteth a
turning to God and a sound confidence in him, it is unsincere
and utterly false.   For of all other it is most certain, that
the repentance of Judas Iscariot was false and counterfeit:
and yet he confessed his sin, he bare record to the truth,
and did with much anger and sorrow restore to the priests
the price which he took for the innocent blood; but because
he did not wholly turn to Christ and put his whole confidence in his mercy and goodness, all his repentance was
without all fruit.   And without all profit do hypocrites, and
those that are without the faith of the gospel, torment themselves, and make a shew of outward repentance.

But they are most happy and in an heavenly case[5], that True peni-
do with all their hearts truly repent with faith unfeigned: an happy
for they receive infinite goodness of their most bountiful and case.
liberal God, who is at one again with penitents, and doth
now love them that before he did for their sins most heartily,
and yet most justly, hate and abhor.   The punishments also,
which he determined to lay upon them, he turneth into
benefits: for he doth fill, and as it were load[6] penitents
with all manner of good things, both temporal and eternal.
Now ye understand, dearly beloved, by my former sermons,
that God bestoweth so great benefits upon us, not for our
works of repentance, but for Christ his sake, in whom alone
the saints do trust, not putting any confidence in their works

[4 often repenting, not in Lat.]
[5 and in—case, not in Lat.]   [6 and—load, not in Lat.]

of repentance, how holy and commendable soever they be. For insomuch as the Father loveth Christ, and that we by faith are graffed in him, God doth therefore love us, and our works do please him; which works of ours when he doth recompense, he crowneth not our works, as our own works, but crowneth in us the grace which he himself hath given us[1].

Unrepentants are unhappy.
Again, it must needs be that unrepentants are most unhappy. They hear with what sins and transgressions they have offended God, and provoked his just vengeance against themselves; but therewithal they think not how to prevent the wrath of God being readily imminent to take vengeance of them[2], nor how to obtain his favour again. What else therefore doth remain behind for them, but a most certain and just destruction both of body and soul, of all their goods, and whatsoever things else they do most esteem in this transitory life? It is good here to call to mind that notable sentence of the Lord Jesus in the gospel, saying: [Matt. xi. 21, &c.] "Woe be to thee, Chorazin; woe be to thee, Bethsaida: for if the wonders had been done in the city of Tyre and Sidon, that have been done in you, they would have repented long ere this in sackcloth and ashes. But I say unto you, it shall be easier for Tyre, Sidon, and Sodoma in the day of [Matt. xxi. 19, &c.] judgment, than for you." The parable[3] of the unfruitful fig-tree is known to all men, whereof mention is made in the gospel, which withered up by the judgment of God, to be an example to teach and terrify all impenitent sinners. What shall fall, may we think, upon the men of these days, that do so boldly despise repentance now so many years so plainly preached unto them, and beaten into their heads[4]? Some there are, a God's name[5], that will outwardly for a shew's sake only seem to be desirous of the evangelical truth: other are utter enemies, contemners, and persecutors of the gospel: and an infinite rabble thou shalt find of Lucianists, Epicures, Nullifidians[6], and Atheists. Now since all

[1] gratiam suam in nobis coronat, is all Bullinger says.]
[2] sontibus, Lat. omitted; that are guilty.]
[3] The parable, not in Lat. Bullinger says, Notissima est omnibus arbor ficus infrugifera.]
[4] and—heads, not in Lat.]   [5 a God's name, not in Lat.]
[6] Nullifidians, not in Lat. Cf. Becon, ed. Park. Soc. Vol. III. pp. 401, 503: and for Lucian, see Abp. Grindal's Works, ed. Parker Soc. p. 8.]

these do equally in a manner sweetly deride, or rather scoff-ingly mock at, this hearty repentance, we cannot do other-wise but still expect and look when the terrible judgment of God's mighty arm should fall upon such unrepentant sinners. Let them that wish well to themselves speedily turn to the Lord, and consider with themselves continually and earnestly how great the damage is, to keep the transitory joys of this present life, and so to lose the eternal joys of the kingdom of heaven.   Let every one make haste to do that which he perceiveth to be done the better by so much, by how much the sooner it is taken in hand.

Let not repentance be deferred.

And yet I would not that any man should despair in his sins, if so be that he doth not stubbornly despise the remedy of repentance; nor because of the facility and gentleness of his heavenly Father doth not maliciously, by the way of contempt, defer repentance even till the very end.   And if any man be hindered by the flesh, the world, and the devil, so that it be late or ere he apply his mind to repentance, neither would I have him to fall to desperation.

But now, because I have somewhat more long drawn out this discourse of repentance than I had thought to have done, that I may here at last make an end of my sermon, I will instead of a conclusion recite unto you these golden words of the holy martyr St Cyprian, bishop of Carthage, where he writeth against Demetrian to this effect following: " Believe and live; and ye, that now for a time do persecute us, rejoice with us for ever.   When ye are once out of this life, then is there no place for repentance, nor any effect of satisfaction.   In this world the life is either won or lost.   In this world eternal salvation is provided for by the unfeigned worshipping of God and the fruits of true faith.   Let not any man, either by his sins or years, be held back from coming to lay hold upon salvation.   So long yet as a man is in this world, no late repentance doth come out of season.   The entry is open unto God's indulgence; and to them that seek and understand the truth, the path to pardon is passing plain. Thou, even at the very end and last gasp of this temporal life, ask pardon for thy sins at the hands of him which is the true and only God; call to him for the confession and faith of his knowledge: to him that confesseth pardon is granted, and to him that believeth salvation is given, and he even pre-

No repentance cometh too late.

sently upon his departure doth pass to immortality. This grace doth Christ communicate : this gift he doth attribute unto his own mercy, by making death subject unto the triumph of the cross, by redeeming him that believeth with the price of his blood, by reconciling man to God the Father, by quickening the mortal by the heavenly regeneration. Let us all, if it be possible, follow him. Let us all profess his sign and sacrament. He openeth to us the way of life. He bringeth us to paradise again. He leadeth us to the kingdom of heaven. With him we shall always live; and being by him made the sons of God, we shall with him always rejoice, being restored by the shedding of his blood. We shall be Christians glorified together with Christ, blessed in God, rejoicing with perpetual pleasure always in the sight of God, and evermore giving thanks to God. For he cannot choose but be merry always and thankful, who, being once in danger and fear of death, is now made secure in immortality[1]."

[1 Credite et vivite : et qui nos ad tempus persequimini, in æternum gaudete nobiscum. Quando istinc excessum fuerit, nullus jam pœnitentiæ locus est, nullus satisfactionis effectus : hic vita aut amittitur, aut tenetur; hic saluti æternæ cultu Dei et fructu fidei providetur. Nec quisquam aut peccatis retardetur, aut annis, quo minus veniat ad consequendam salutem. In isto adhuc mundo manenti pœnitentia nulla sera est. Patet ad indulgentiam Dei aditus, et quærentibus atque intelligentibus veritatem facilis accessus est. Tu sub ipso licet exitu et vitæ temporalis occasu pro delictis roges; et Deum, qui unus et verus est, confessione et fide agnitionis ejus implores. Venia confitenti datur, et credenti indulgentia salutaris de divina pietate conceditur; et ad immortalitatem sub ipsa morte transitur. Hanc gratiam Christus impertit, et hoc munus misericordiæ suæ tribuit, subigendo mortem trophæo crucis, redimendo credentem pretio sanguinis sui, reconciliando hominem Deo Patri, vivificando mortalem regeneratione cœlesti. Hunc, si fieri potest, sequamur omnes; hujus sacramento et signo censeamur : hic nobis viam vitæ aperit, hic ad paradisum reduces facit, hic ad cœlorum regna perducet. Cum ipso semper vivemus, facti per ipsum filii Dei : cum ipso exultabimus semper, ipsius cruore reparati. Erimus Christiani cum Christo simul gloriosi, de Deo Patre beati, de perpetua voluptate lætantes semper in conspectu Dei, et agentes Deo gratias semper. Neque enim poterit nisi et lætus esse semper et gratus, qui cum morti fuisset obnoxius, factus est de immortalitate securus.— Cyprian. Tract. ad Demetrian. fin. p. 196. Oxon. 1682.]

TO[2] THE MOST RENOWNED[3] PRINCE

EDWARD THE SIXTH,

KING OF ENGLAND AND FRANCE, LORD OF IRELAND, PRINCE OF WALES AND CORNWALL, DEFENDER OF THE CHRISTIAN FAITH,

GRACE AND PEACE FROM GOD THE FATHER, THROUGH OUR LORD JESUS CHRIST.

THE promise, that not long ago[4] I made to your most royal majesty, I do now perform, offering here the other eight sermons of the fourth Decade, which I dedicate unto your royal majesty, that of me you may have two decades of sermons full and wholly finished. In March I sent twelve sermons unto you, which were favourably accepted of your royal majesty, as I understand by the letters of that godly and worthy learned man, Master J. Hooper[5], the most vigilant bishop of Glocester, my brother and reverend fellow-father in Jesus Christ: who also by the commendation of your royal majesty's good will to me-ward hath heartened me on, so that now, with far more confidence and liberty than before, I send unto your majesty this other part of my work, entreating of most weighty and holy matters. In this my dedication I respect nothing else but that which I declared in my former epistle; to wit, that I, according to the gift that the Lord hath endued me withal, may help forward and advance the state of christian religion, now again happily springing up in the famous realm of England by your royal majesty's good beginnings and counsels of your worthy nobles. All they of every nation that is in Christendom, which do truly believe in Christ Jesus, do heartily rejoice, on your majesty's behalf and the behalf of your most flourishing kingdom, for this renovation of true religion; and do earnestly pray to Christ the Lord, that he will happily bring to a good end the thing that you in the fear of him have happily begun.

Your royal majesty verily hath adventured upon a work ^{Whether they that}

[2 See Orig. Lett. ed. Park. Soc. pp. 671, 673.]
[3 Serenissimo, Lat.]   [4 See Vol. II. p. 16, note 4.]
[5 Orig. Lett. ed. Parker Soc. Vol. I. p. 88.]

mind to
reform the
churches
must stay to
look for the
determi-
nation of a
council.
Matt. xxviii.
both very great and full of troubles: but he will never fail
your godly endeavours, that said, "Behold, I am with you
for ever unto the end of the world." And now also, even
as it hath been always from the first beginning of the church,
there are many lets and great impediments, that are object
against most holy and wholesome intents, doing what they
can to hinder and trouble the reformation of religion[1]: and
among other stops this is one of the greatest, that no small
number even of the wisest sort do say, that there ought no
such haste to be made upon private authority, but that the
determination of the general council in controversies of religion must needs be stayed for, and altogether looked after;
without the judgment whereof, say they, it is not lawful for
a kingdom[2], much less for any other commonweal, to alter
any one point in religion once received and hitherto used.

Jer. viii.
But the prophets and apostles do not send us to the councils
of priests or elders, but to the word of God: yea, in Jeremy
we read, "How say ye, We are wise, we have the law of the
Lord among us? Truly, the lying pen of the scribes have
wrote a lie[3]. The wise have been ashamed, they were afraid
and were taken: for lo, they have cast out the word of the
Lord; what wisdom then can there be among them?" Again,
Luke ix.
in the Gospel we read, "No man, that layeth his hand to the
plough, and looketh back, is fit for the kingdom of God."
Therefore the authority of the prophets and evangelists giveth
counsel, fully to absolve and perfectly to end the reformation
of religion once begun with the fear of God, out of or by
the word of God; and not to look for or stay upon councils,
which are directed, not by the word of God, but by the
affections and motions of men.

What coun-
cils have been
in these later
ages cele-
brated.
For the late examples of some ages within the space of
these 400 last years or thereabout do sufficiently teach us
what we may look for by the determination of general councils. The causes of councils of old were the corruption
either of doctrine or else of the teachers, or else the ruin of
ecclesiastical discipline. And good and zealous men have
strongly cried now by the space of 500 years and more, that

[1 cœptam, Lat. omitted; which is begun.]
[2 ne regno quidem, Lat.; not even for a kingdom.]
[3 the false pen of the scribes worketh for falsehood. Marg. Auth.
Ver.]

there are crept into the church superstitions, errors, and abuses; that the salt of the earth is unsavoury, that is, that the ministers of the churches are by sloth, ignorance, and wickedness become unseasonable; and that all discipline in the church is fallen to ruin.   Bernard Clarevallensis[4], being one among many, is a notable witness of the thing[5] and condition.   And for that cause there have been many councils of priests celebrated, at the calling together of the bishop of Rome, together with the mutual aid of many kings and princes.   But what became of them, what was done in them, and what small amendment or correction of doctrine, teachers, and discipline there was by them obtained, the thing itself (the more it is to be lamented) doth plainly declare.   For the more that councils were assembled, the more did superstition and error prevail in doctrine, abuse in ceremonial rites, pride, riot, covetousness, and all kind of corruption in the teachers or priests, and a foul blurring out of all honest discipline.   For such men were made presidents of the councils, as had need first of all themselves either to be brought into a better order, or else to be utterly excommunicate out of the congregation of the saints; and they being presidents did in the councils handle causes neither lawful nor lawfully. For the word of God had among them neither due authority nor dignity; neither did they admit to the examination and discussing of causes those men whom it was decent to have chiefly admitted, but them whom they themselves did think good to like of; and in them they sought not the glory of God and the safeguard of the church, but sought themselves, that is, the glory and pleasures of this transitory world. Therefore in the holding of so many general councils we see no amendment or reformation in the church obtained, but rather errors, abuses, and the kingdom and tyranny of the priests confirmed and augmented[6].

And even at this day, although we would wink and not see it, yet we cannot choose but even with our hands feel what we may look and hope for in a general council. There shall at this day no council have any authority, unless it be

What Christians at this day may look for by general councils.

[4 Bernard largely complains of the pride and corruption of the clergy, De Offic. Episc. capp. VII. IX; in Cantic. Serm. x. § 3, LXXVII. § 1.]

[5 hujus rei, Lat.; and condition, not in Lat.]

[6 See Bullinger Von den Conciliis, Par. II. cap. 11. Zurich, 1561.]

lawfully (as they expound lawfully) called together. None seemeth to be lawfully called together but that which the bishop of Rome doth call together, and that which is holden according to the ancient[1] custom and laws received; namely, that wherein they alone do sit, and have, as they call it, deciding voices, to whom power is permitted to determine[2] and give sentence in the council; and to them who shall think it an heinous crime, and directly contrary to the oath that is given them, to do once so much as think, much more to speak, anything against the bishop and see of Rome, against the decrees of the fathers, and constitutions of the councils.

What therefore may you look for in such a council ? That forsooth which I told you that now by the space of 400 years and more the afflicted church of God, to the detriment of godliness, hath seen and felt; namely, that the sincere doctrine of Christ being trode under foot, and holy discipline utterly oppressed, we see that every day more and more, with the great and intolerable[3] tyranny of the see and church of Rome, there do increase and are confirmed unsound and faulty doctrine, most filthy abuses, and too too great licentiousness and wicked living of the priests. They forsooth do cry, that it is an heresy to accuse the pope of error, in the chest of whose breast all heavenly doctrine is laid up and contained. They cry that all the decrees of the apostolical see must be received even so as if they were confirmed by the very voice of Peter himself. They cry that it is a wicked thing to move any controversy, or to call into doubt the doctrine and ceremonies received and used in the church of Rome; especially touching their sacraments, whereof they to their advantage do make filthy merchandise. They cry that the church of Rome hath power to judge all men, but that no man hath any authority to judge of her judgment. There are in the decretals most evident canons that do set out and urge these things, as I have told them[4]. Now what manner reformation shall we think that they are likely to admit, which stand so stiffly to the defence of these things? Truly, they would rather that Christ with his gospel, and the true church his spouse, should wholly perish, than they would depart one inch from their decrees, rites, authorities, dignities, wealth, and

[1 hucusque consueto, Lat.]   [2 residendi, Lat.]
[3 imo intoleranda, Lat.]   [4 as I have told them, not in Lat.]

pleasures. They verily come into the council, not to be judged of others, that they may amend those things which even their own consciences and[5] all the world do say would be amended; but they come[6] to judge and yoke all other men, to keep still their power and authority, and to overthrow and take away whatsoever withstandeth their lust and tyranny. For afore, there were sent out horrible thunders against the accusers or adversaries of the see apostolic; that is, of the papistical corruption: after, followed the hot bolts of that thunder, even sentences definitive of excommunication. The secular power hath now by the space of thirty years and more been called on, and persecution hath been everywhere raised up against guiltless Christians[7], not for committing heinous crimes and defending naughtiness, but for inveighing against mischiefs and mischievous men, and for requiring the reformation of the church: and yet even at this day most cruel edicts are out, and cruelty is exercised every day more and more, against them that confess the name of Christ: yea, such is their impudency and brasen-faced boldness, they dissemble not that the council, if any must be celebrated, shall be called for the rooting out of heresies; yea, they do openly profess, that the council, once held at Trent, was to this end assembled.   Now since these things more clearly than the sun are perceived to be most true, thou shalt, most holy king, do wisely and religiously, if, without looking for the determination of a general council, thou shalt proceed to reform the churches in thy kingdom according to the rule of the books of both Testaments, which we do rightly believe, being written by the inspiration of the Holy Ghost, to be the very word of God.

But now, that it is lawful for every christian church, much more for every notable christian kingdom, without the advice of the church of Rome and the members thereof, in matters of religion depraved by them, wholly to make a reformation according to the rule of God's most holy word, it is thereby manifest, because Christians are the congregation, the church, or subjects of their king, Christ, to whom they owe by all means most absolute and perfect obedience.   Now the Lord

It is lawful for every christian church to reform things out of order.

[5] adeoque, Lat.; and so.]

[6] conabuntur, Lat.; they will use every effort.]

[7] homines, Lat.; men. The bull of Leo X. against Luther was issued June 15. 1520.]

gave his church a charge of reformation: he commended unto it the sound doctrine of the gospel, together with the lawful use of his holy sacraments: he also condemned all false doctrine, that I mean that is contrary to the gospel: he damned the abuse and profanation of the sacraments; and delivered to us the true worship of God, and proscribed the false. Therefore Christians, obeying the laws and commandments of their prince, do utterly remove or take away all superstition, and do restore, establish, and preserve the true religion, according to the manner that Christ their prince appointed them. He verily is a fool or a madman, which saith that the church of Christ hath none authority to correct such errors, vices, and abuses as do daily creep into it[1]. And yet the Romish tyranny hath so bewitched the eyes of many men, that they think that they cannot lawfully do any thing[2] but what it pleaseth Rome to give them leave to do. The ecclesiastical histories make mention of provincial synods, held in sundry provinces, wherein there were handled matters of faith and the reformation of the churches, and yet no mention once made of the bishop of Rome. What may be thought of that moreover, that in certain synods, not heretical but orthodoxastical and catholic, thou mayest find some that were excommunicated for appealing from their own churches unto the church of Rome[3]? St Cyprian, writing to Cornelius[4] the bishop of Rome, doth say: "Since that it is ordained by us all, and that it is just and right, that every man's cause should be heard there where the crime is committed; and that to every several pastor is appointed a portion of the flock, which every one must govern, and make account of his doings before the Lord: it is expedient, verily, that those, over whom we have the charge, should not gad to and fro, by that means with their subtle and deceitful petulancy to make the concord of bishops to be at jar; but to plead their causes there where they may have their accusers present, and witnesses of their crime committed[5]."

[1 as—into it, not in Lat.]   [2 hic, Lat. omitted; in this matter.]
[3 Bingham, Book IX. chap. 1. § 11; and XVII. chap. 5. § 14.]
[4 beato Cornelio, Lat.]
[5 Nam cum statutum sit omnibus nobis, et æquum sit pariter ac justum, ut uniuscujusque causa illic audiatur, ubi est crimen admissum; et singulis pastoribus portio gregis sit adscripta, quam regat unusquisque et gubernet, rationem sui actus Domino redditurus: oportet utique eos quibus præsumus non circumcursare, nec episcoporum concordiam

But letting pass the testimonies of men, we do now come to the testimonies in the book of God. The most holy *Holy king Josias.* king Josias, most godly prince, may alone in this case teach you what to do and how to do, with the warrant and authority of God himself. He by the diligent reading of the holy book of God, and by the contemplation of things present, and the manner of worshipping God that then was used, did understand, that his ancestors did greatly and very far err from the plain and simple truth; for which cause he calleth together the princes and other estates of his kingdom, together with all the priests, to hold and celebrate a council with them. In that council he standeth not long disputing whether the examples of the elders ought rather to be followed, or God's commandment simply received: whether he ought rather to believe the church, or the scripture: and whether all the judgment of religion ought to be referred to the high priest. For laying abroad the book of the law, he submitteth both himself and all his unto the sacred scripture. Out of the book of the law both he himself doth learn, and biddeth all his to learn, what thing it is that pleaseth God, namely, that which was commanded and learned in the reading of the law of God. And presently he gave charge, that all men should do and execute that, not having any regard to the ancient custom, or to the church[6] that was at that time: he made all subject to the word of God. Which deed of his is so commended, that, next after David, he is preferred before all the kings of Judah and Israel.

Now your royal majesty cannot follow any better or safer *Faith cannot be reformed but by the word of God.* counsel than this, considering that it proceedeth from God, and that it is most fit for the cause which is even now in hand. The disputation is of the reformation of religion, and the true faith of Christ. You know that that doth spring from heaven, namely, that it is taught by the word of God, and poured into our hearts by the Holy Ghost; for Paul saith: "Faith cometh by hearing, and hearing by the word of *Rom. x.* Christ." Therefore as true faith is not grounded upon the word of man, so is it not taught or planted by the same. For in another place the same apostle saith: "My preaching was *1 Cor. ii.*

cohærentem sua subdola et fallaci temeritate collidere; sed agere illic causam suam, ubi et accusatores habere et testes sui criminis possint. —Cyprian. Opp. Epist. LIX. p. 136. Oxon. 1682.]

[6 ipsius etiam ecclesiæ, Lat.]

not in the enticing words of man's wisdom, but in the shewing of the Spirit and of power; that your faith might not be in the wisdom of man, but in the power of God." Not without good cause, therefore, do we refuse the traditions of men, and turn only to the doctrine of the word of the Lord, without which it is assuredly certain that there is no doctrine nor any foundation of true faith.

The scriptures do sufficiently minister a full platform how to reform the church.

Neither are they worthy to be heard, who think that the canonical scriptures are not plain enough, full enough, or sufficient enough, to minister a perfect platform of reformation. They blaspheme the Spirit of God, imputing unto it obscureness and imperfection, which faults no profane writer can well abide to hear of. St Paul in defence of the truth saith:

2 Tim. iii. 16, 17.

"All scripture given by inspiration of God is profitable to doctrine, to reprove, to correction, to instruction which is in righteousness; that the man of God may be perfect, instructed unto all good works." What now, I pray you, is omitted in these words, that may seem to appertain to a most absolute reformation? What, I beseech you, have those impudent fellows to say against this? Proceed, therefore, proceed, most holy king, to imitate the most godly princes, and the infallible rule of the holy scripture: proceed, I say, without staying for man's authority, by the most true and absolute instrument of truth, the book of God's most holy word, to reform the church of Christ in thy most happy England[1].

The Lord Jesus, the head and mighty prince of this
church[2], preserve and lead thee his most faithful
worshipper in the way of his truth until
the end, to the glory of his name, and
the good estate and welfare of
the whole christian church.
At Tigure, in the month
of August, the year
of our Lord,
1550.

Your royal majesty's most dutifully bounden,
HENRY BULLINGER,
Minister of the church at
Tigure in Switzerland.

[1 ecclesias Christi Anglicanas, Lat.; most happy, not in Lat.]
[2 his church, ed. 1577; ecclesiæ suæ, Lat.]

OTHER EIGHT SERMONS

FOURTH DECADE,

WRITTEN BY

HENRY BULLINGER.

OF GOD; OF THE TRUE KNOWLEDGE OF GOD, AND OF THE DIVERSE WAYS HOW TO KNOW HIM; THAT GOD IS ONE IN SUBSTANCE, AND THREE IN PERSONS.

THE THIRD SERMON.

I HAVE hitherto in thirty-two sermons discoursed upon the word of God, and the lawful exposition of the same; upon christian faith, the love of God and our neighbour. I have also spoken of the law of nature, of man's law, and God's law, and of the parts of God's law, namely, the moral, the ceremonial, and the judicial laws; of the use of the law, and of the fulfilling and abrogation of the same; of the likeness and difference betwixt the two testaments and people, the old and the new; of christian liberty; of offences; of the effect[3] and merits of good works; of sin, and the sundry sorts thereof: and also of the grace of God, or the gospel of Jesu Christ, in whom our heavenly Father hath given us all things belonging to life and eternal salvation: finally, I have treated of repentance, and of the things that do especially seem to belong thereunto. And for because our purpose is to dispute discreetly upon the principal points of christian religion[4], and that[5] in the premises we have heard often mention made of God, of the knowledge and worship of God, of Jesus Christ, of the Holy Ghost, of good and evil spirits, of the church, of prayer, of the sacraments, and such like holy things; since we are now come to an end of those former points, necessity itself doth here require, that we should speak somewhat now of all and every one of these latter

---

[3 ratione, Lat.]   [4 religionis nostræ, Lat.]
[5 præterea, Lat.; and more especially.]

principles according to the holy scripture, so far forth as the Lord shall give me grace and ability to do the same.

Sundry opinions concerning God. Concerning God there were of old many erroneous opinions, not among the ruder sort of people only, but even in the whole pack of philosophers, and conventicles of false Christians. As touching the philosophers, that ancient and learned writer, Tertullian, was wont to say, that 'philosophers are the patriarchs of heretics[1]:' and touching false Christians the apostle John said, "They went out from us, but they were not of us; for if they had been of us, they would have remained with us." Neither do I see what gain you should get by it, if I should proceed to reckon up unto you all their opinions. It is good perhaps to know wherein they[2] erred, lest we also do strike upon the same rock that they did. Therefore if any that have a desire unto it do wish to see the opinions of the heathen sort and of heretics[3] concerning God, let them search Plutarch in his *Placitis Philoso. lib.* I. cap. 7. or in other heathen writers; or[4] in Cyril's first book *Contra Julianum;* and[5] in the 4. cap. *Dogmatum vel definitionum Ecclesiast.*[6] I will[7] at this time trouble the attentive

1 John ii. 19.

Whereupon the diversity of opinions concerning God do rise, and from whence the true knowledge of him must be fetched. ears and minds of the godly hearers with that burden. That diversity of opinions is derived from none other fountain than from the boldness and unskilfulness of men, which are not ashamed of their own device and brain to add and apply[8] to God the things from which he is most far and free. And now, that here I may not stick long in declaring the narrow straitness and misty darkness of man's wit; who, I pray you, is able with his understanding to conceive the being[9] of God, when as indeed no man did ever fully understand of what fashion the soul of man is, of what sort many other things are that be in man's body, and of what manner substance[10] the sun and moon are made? There are given many reasons of natural philosophy; but the work of God doth still abide more great and wonderful than that the wit or speech of man

---

[1 See Vol. II. p. 407, note 5.]   [2 alii, Lat.; others.]
[3 exercitationes exterorum, et hæreticorum sententias, Lat.]
[4 aut etiam, Lat.; or even.]   [5 denique, Lat.; lastly.]
[6 A treatise among the works of Augustine.]
[7 nolo, Lat.; I will *not.*]
[8 affingere, Bullinger's one word.]   [9 essentiam, Lat.]
[10 So ed. 1577; what manner of substance, 1587.]

is able to comprehend or express it. Let no man therefore,
that goeth about to know any certainty of God, descend into
himself to search him out with thoughts of his own[11]; neither
let him ground his opinion upon men's determinations and
weak definitions[12] : for otherwise he shall always worship the
invention of his own heart, mere folly, trifles and foolish
phantasies. But on the other side again, the man cannot
choose but think rightly, judge truly, and speak well of God,
that attributeth nothing to himself, deviseth nothing of his
own brain, nor followeth the toys of other men's inventing;
but in all things giveth ear to the word of God, and followeth always his holy revelation[13]. Therefore let this stand as
it were for a continual rule, that God cannot be rightly
known but by his word; and that God is to be received and
believed to be such an one as he revealeth himself unto us
in his holy word. For no creature verily can better tell what,
and what kind of one God is, than God himself.

Now since this God doth in his word, by the workman- *That there is a God.*
ship of the world, by the holy scriptures, and by his oracles
uttered by the mouth of the patriarchs, prophets, and apostles,
yea, and the very minds[14] and consciences of men, testify
that he is, therefore did the kingly prophet David[15] say: "The *Psal. xiv.*
fool hath said in his heart, There is no God." For he must needs
be an ass or a fool, which denieth the thing that is evident to
all men in the world which are not beside their wits, namely,
that there is a God: considering that even Cicero, an heathen
author, in his book *de Natura Deorum*, doth say[16], "It is
bred and born together with men, and graffed in their hearts,
to think that there is a God[17]." Truly, they that deny God
do deny him whom nevertheless they fear; and therefore by
that fear they confess that he is, by that means convincing
themselves of lying and falsehood.

Again, this is to be noted; that in demanding who and *A measure is to be kept in*
what God is, although that question is made and doth arise *demanding and inquiring what God is.*

[11 to search—his own, the translator's addition.]
[12 aut humano innitatur judicio, Lat.]
[13 revelationem Dei, Lat.]
[14 in the very minds, ed. 1577 ; in animis denique, Lat.]
[15 merito, Lat.; with good reason, omitted.]
[16 inter alia, Lat.; among other things, omitted.]
[17 Cic. de Nat. Deor. Lib. I. cap. 17.]

even by the beating out and discussing of the scriptures, yet a measure is to be kept and in any case observed. For to go about over curiously to inquire after, search out, and seek[1] the very eternal being of God, is both perilous and also flatly

Prov. xxv. forbidden. Salomon crieth, "As it is not good to eat much honey; so he, that is an over curious searcher out of God's majesty, shall be confounded of his glory[2]." Before that sin-

Exod. xix. gular and notable communication, wherein our God in the mount Sinai talked[3] with the whole people of Israel, it is said to Moses: "Set bounds unto the people round about the mountain, and say unto them, Take heed to yourselves that ye go not up into the mount, or touch the border of it. Whosoever toucheth the mount, let him die the death," &c. Lo here, it was present death to pass the limits or bounds prescribed. Therefore our studies are and ought to be defi- nite, not infinite[4]. Truly we read in many places of the holy scriptures, that the most entire and excellent friends of God stood amazed trembling, so often as God in any outward shew did of his own accord offer himself unto their eyes. I need not to busy myself too much in reckoning up examples. Ye know how Abraham behaved himself in the talk which he had with God, Gen. xviii. Ye know what the parents of Gedeon said in the book of the Judges[5]; and what Helias spake, 3 Reg. xix. Peter, after that he by the miraculous taking of the great draught of fishes did understand that Christ

Luke v. was more than a man, cried out, saying: "Go out from me, O Lord, for I am a sinful man." Therefore the saints, if in any other matters belonging to God, then in this especially, are humble, modest, and religious; understanding that his eternal and incomprehensible power and unspeakable majesty are altogether uncircumscriptible[6], and cannot be compre- hended in any name whatsoever.

The name of God is un- speakable and passeth man's utter- ance. Very eloquently, truly, and godly doth Tertullian in his book *De Trinitate* say: 'The proper name of God cannot be uttered, because it cannot be conceived. For that is called by a name, that is conceived by the condition of its own

---

[1 inspicere, Lat.] [2 See Vol. I. p. 65, note 6.]

[3 congreditur, Lat.] [4 not infinite, not in Lat.]

[5 So Latin also, *Gedeonis*, for Samson. Both Gideon and Manoah expressed the same apprehension. Judg. vi. 22, and xiii. 22.]

[6 nulla definitione, Lat.; by any definition.]

nature: for a name is the significant notifying of that thing which may be conceived by the name. But when the thing, which is handled, is of such sort that it cannot be rightly conceived by our very senses and understanding, how shall it be rightly named by an apt term and fit nomination? which, while it is beyond understanding, must needs also be above the significancy of the term whereby it is named: so that when God upon certain causes or occasions doth annex or declare to us his name in words, we may think and know that the very property of the name is not expressed so much in words, as a certain significancy is set down, to which while men in prayers do run, they may seem to be able by it to call upon and obtain the mercy of God[7].' And again he saith: 'Concerning God and those things that are of him and in him, neither is the mind of man able to conceive what they be, how great they be, and of what fashion they be; neither doth the eloquence of man's mouth utter in speech words in any point answerable unto this majesty[8]. For to the thinking upon and uttering out of his majesty all eloquence is mute and dumb, and the whole mind is too too little. For it is greater than the mind; neither can it be conceived how great it is: because, if it can be conceived, then must it needs be less than man's mind, wherein it may be comprehended. It is also greater than all speech, and cannot be spoken; because if it may be spoken, then is it lesser than man's speech, by which, if it be spoken, it may be compassed and made to be understanded. But whatsoever may be thought of him shall still be less than he: and whatsoever in speech is shewed of him, being compared with him,

[7 Ex quo effectum est, ut nec nomen Dei proprium possit edici, quoniam non possit nec concipi. Id enim nomine continetur, quidquid etiam ex naturæ suæ conditione comprehenditur. Nomen enim significantia est ejus rei quæ comprehendi potuit ex nomine. At quando id, de quo agitur, tale est, ut condigne nec ipsis intellectibus colligatur; quomodo appellationis digne vocabulo pronuntiabitur? Quod dum extra intellectum est, etiam supra appellationis significantiam sit necesse est: ut merito quando nomen suum Deus ex quibusdam rationibus et occasionibus adjicit et præfert, non tam legitimam proprietatem appellationis sciamus esse depromptam, quam significantiam quandam constitutam, ad quam dum homines decurrunt, Dei misericordiam per ipsam impetrare posse videantur.—Lib. de Trinitate. cap. IV. Tertull. Opp. Par. 1664, p. 709.]

[8 his, ed. 1577.]

shall be much less than he. For in silence to ourselves we may partly perceive him : but as he is, in words to express him, it is altogether impossible. For if you call him Light, then do you rather name a creature of his than him, but him you express not: or if you call him Virtue, then do you rather name his power than him, but him you declare not: or if you call him Majesty, then do you rather name his honour than him, but him you describe not. And why should I, in running through every several title, prolong the time? I will at once declare it all. Say all of him whatsoever thou canst, and yet thou shalt still rather name something of his than himself. For what canst thou fitly speak or think of him, that is greater than all thy words and senses? Unless it be, that after one manner, and that too as we can, as our capacity will serve, and as our understanding will let us, we shall in mind conceive what God is, if we shall think that he is that which cannot be understood, nor can possibly come into our thought what kind of thing, and how great it is. For as at the seeing of the brightness of the sun the sight of our eyes doth so dazzle and wax dim, that our sight cannot behold the very circle of the same by reason that it is overcome of the brightness of the beams that are object against it; even so fareth it with the sight of our mind in all our thoughts of God; and by how much more she settleth herself to consider of God, by so much more is she blinded in the light of her cogitation. For (to repeat the same thing again) what canst thou fitly think of him that is above all loftiness, higher than all height, deeper than all depth, lighter than all light, clearer than all clearness, brighter than all brightness, stronger than all strength, more virtuous than all virtue, fairer than all fairness, truer than all truth, greater than all greatness, mightier than all might, richer than all riches, wiser than all wisdom, more liberal than all liberality, better than all goodness, juster than all justice, and gentler than all gentleness? For all kinds of virtues must needs be less than he that is the Father and God of all virtues : so that God may truly be said to be such a certain being as to which nothing may be compared. For he is above all that may be spoken[1]." Hitherto have I cited the words of Tertullian.

[1 De hoc ergo ac de eis quæ sunt ipsius et in eo sunt, nec mens hominis quæ sint, quanta sint, et qualia sint, digne concipere potest,

Although now these things are so, and that no tongue either of angels or of men can fully express what, who, and of what manner God is, seeing that his majesty is incomprehensible and unspeakable; yet the scripture, which is the word of God, attempering itself to our imbecility, doth minister

The forms and manners of knowing God.

nec eloquentia sermonis humani æquabilem majestatis ejus virtutem sermonis expromit. Ad cogitandam enim et ad eloquendam illius majestatem, et eloquentia omnis merito muta est, et mens omnis exigua est. Major est enim mente ipsa, nec cogitari possit quantus sit; ne, si potuerit cogitari, mente humana minor sit, qua concipi possit. Major est quoque omni sermone, nec edici possit; ne, si potuerit edici, humano sermone minor sit, quo quum edicitur, et circumiri et colligi possit. Quidquid enim de illo cogitatum fuerit, minus ipso erit; et quidquid enuntiatum fuerit, minus illo comparatum circum ipsum erit. Sentire enim illum taciti aliquatenus possumus; ut autem ipse est, sermone explicare non possumus. Sive enim illum dixeris lucem, creaturam ipsius magis quam ipsum dixeris; ipsum non expresseris: sive illum dixeris virtutem, potentiam ipsius magis quam ipsum dixeris, et deprompseris: sive dixeris majestatem, honorem ipsius magis quam illum ipsum descripseris. Et quid per singula quæque percurrens longum facio? semel totum explicabo. Quidquid omnino de illo retuleris, rem aliquam ipsius magis et virtutem quam ipsum explicaveris. Quid enim de eo condigne aut dicas aut sentias, qui omnibus et sermonibus et sensibus major est? Nisi quod uno modo, et hoc ipsum quomodo possumus, quomodo capimus, quomodo intelligere licet, quid sit Deus, mente capiemus; si cogitaverimus id illum esse, quod quale, et quantum sit non possit intelligi, ne in ipsam quidem cogitationem possit venire. Nam si ad solis aspectum oculorum nostrorum acies hebescit, ne orbem ipsum obtusus inspiciat obviorum sibi superatus fulgore radiorum; hoc idem mentis acies patitur in cogitatione omni de Deo, et quanto ad considerandum Deum plus intenditur, tanto magis ipsa cogitationis suæ luce cæcatur. Quid enim de eo (ut iterum repetam) condigne dicas, qui est sublimitate omni sublimior, et altitudine omni altior, et profundo omni profundior, et omni luce lucidior, et omni claritate clarior, omni splendore splendidior, omni robore robustior, omni virtute viritior, omni pulchritudine pulchrior, veritate omni verior, et fortitudine omni fortior, et majestate omni major, et omni potentia potentior, et omnibus divitiis ditior, omni prudentia prudentior, et omni benignitate benignior, omni bonitate melior, omni justitia justior, omni clementia clementior? Minora enim sint necesse est omnium genera virtutum eo ipso qui virtutum omnium et Deus et parens est: ut vere dici possit, id Deus esse, quod ejusmodi est cui comparari nihil potest. Super omne est enim quod dici potest.—Ibid. cap. II. pp. 707, 708. This treatise, de Trinitate, is found among the works of Tertullian, but is an abridgment of a book of Tertullian's by Novatian.]

unto us some means, forms, and phrases of speech, by them to bring us to some such knowledge of God as may at least-wise suffice us while we live in this world: so yet notwith-standing that still we should think that the thing that is incomprehensible cannot be defined, but that by those phrases an occasion is only given, by which we are to be brought to greater things through the illumination of the Spirit; and that we should in this disputation have still before the eyes of our mind that true and assured sentence of the eternal God unto his servant Moses, saying: "Thou canst not see my face; for no man shall see me and live." For when we are once departed out of this life, and are unburdened of this mortality and mortal frailty, then shall we see the majesty of God; for the apostle St John said: "We know that when he appeareth, we shall be like unto him; for we shall see him as he is." And to these let us annex the words of the apostle Paul, where he saith: "Now we see in a glass, even in a dark speaking[1]; but then we shall see face to face." Therefore let no man go beyond the limited bounds, or prevent the time appointed, nor yet presume by wicked boldness and curiosity[2] in this life to behold the face, that is, the very essence or being, of God. Let that revelation of God suffice every one which God himself voucheth safe in his word to open unto us, namely, so much as he of his goodness thinketh necessary and profitable for us to know. And I do here with warrant say, that that wisdom is the true wisdom, which will not in this matter go about to know or savour more than the eternal wisdom doth teach to know.

Exod. xxxiii.

1 John iii.

J Cor. xiii. 12.

The names of God.

The first and chiefest way to know God is derived out of the very names of God attributed unto him in the holy scripture. Those names are many and of sundry sorts, because his virtue, his wisdom, I mean, his goodness, justice, and power are altogether infinite. I will reckon up and expound unto you, according to my skill the most excellent and usual among the rest.

Jehovah.

Among all the names of God that is the most excellent which they call *Tetragrammaton*, that is (if we may so say), the four-lettered name: for it is compounded of the four

[1 in a riddle. Marg. auth. ver.]
[2 in hac carne et, Lat. omitted; in this flesh and.]

spiritual[3] letters, and is called JEHOVAH.   It is derived of
the verb-substantive, *Hovah*, before which they put *Jod* and
make it Jehovah, that is to say, Being, or, I am; as he that
is αὐτουσία, a being of himself, having his life and being not
of any other but of himself; lacking nobody's aid to make
him to be, but giving to be unto all manner of things; to
wit, eternal God, without beginning and ending, in whom we
live, we move, and have our being.   To this do those words
especially belong, which we find to have passed betwixt God
and Moses in the third chapter of Exodus: "And Moses said
to God, Behold, when I come unto the children of Israel,
to whom thou dost now send me, and shall say unto them,
The God of your fathers hath sent me unto you; and they
shall ask me, saying, What is his name? what answer shall
I make them?   And God said to Moses, I am that I am; or,
I will be that I will be: and he said, Thus shalt thou say
to the children of Israel, I am, or Being, or I will be, hath
sent me unto you."   That is, I am God that will be, and
he hath sent me who is himself Being, or Essence, and God
everlasting.   For their future tense containeth three sundry
times, He that is, He that was, and, He that will be, hath
sent me.   Truly the evangelist and apostle John seemeth in
his Revelation to have had an eye to these words of the Lord,
which also he went about to interpret, saying in the person
of God: "I am Alpha and Omega, the beginning and the end, Rev. i.
or the first and the last, saith the almighty Lord, which is,
and which was, and which shall be."

Some there are which observe this for a note, that in all
tongues almost, even of the barbarous sort, the name of God
is written with four letters.   Concerning his name in Hebrew
it is assuredly so; and in the Greek, Latin, and German Cabala is a
tongues it is so also.   For God in Greek is called Θεὸς, in the Jews, left
Latin *Deus*, and with us Germans he is called *Gott*.   They Moses, not in
add moreover, that the Persians call him Σύρη, and the Egyp- from the
tians Θωὺθ, or Θεὺθ, and by contraction, Θωθ.   And in the son, wherein
four letters the Cabalists say that there are wonderful mys- as well the
teries contained: of which as other have written very di- mystical
ligently, so I have liefer[4] here not to stand upon them[5], or to included in
trouble your patience with them. the holy
scripture.

tradition of
to them by
writing, but
father to the
is contained
secrets of
nature, as the
sense
the words of

[3 spiritalibus literis.]
[4 liefer, rather.]   [5 his subtilitatibus, Lat.]

Jah and Hu. Like to this also are these names of God, *Jah*, and *Hu*. Whereof the first is oftener found in the Psalms than once: Psal. cxi. for David saith, "*Hallelu-Jah*," that is, "Praise ye the Lord." The latter is also mentioned by David, saying, *Hu*, that is, "he," I say, God, the Being and creator of all things, [Isai. xlii. 8.]
Hu signifieth
he or this. "spake the word and it was done; *Hu*, he commanded and it was." In Esay the Lord saith: "I am the Lord, *Hu* is my name[1], and my glory will I give unto none other." Now those words also are derived of being, and do teach us that God is always like himself, an essence which is of itself eternally, and which giveth to be unto all things that are: as he by whom, in whom, and to whom all things are, being himself a perpetual and most absolute ἐντελέχεια, or perfit havingness[2].

But the Hebrews do not read or express the four-lettered name of God by calling it Jehovah, but instead of it they Adonai. use the word *Adonai*. For they say that Jehovah must not be uttered. Now all interpreters in their translations, where they turn it into Latin, do call it *Dominus*, that is, Lord: for God is the Lord of all things, both visible and invisible. Neither is there in all the world any other Lord but this one, and he alone, to whom all things in the world are subject and do obey: for he hath a most mere dominion and absolute monarchy over all his creatures. And therefore for plainness sake sometime the word *Sabbaoth* is annexed to the The Lord of
Sabbaoth or
of hosts. name of God[3]; which some translate "the Lord of powers," and some "the Lord of hosts." For God, being almighty, doth by his power or strength shew forth and in his host declare, what mighty things he is able to do, and of how great power and might he is. For since that he is the God of all creatures, and that he doth dispose and use them as a captain doth his soldiers, to work mighty and marvellous things, he doth even by small things[4] declare how great he himself is, and how great his power is. In the host of God are all the Dan. vii. angels, of whom Daniel said, "Thousand thousands and hundred thousands did minister unto him:" one of which angels did in one night kill in the Assyrians' camp, under the banner

[1 Hu est nomen meum. Bibl. Tigur. Lat. 1544.]

[2 perfectihabia, Lat.]

[3 Dicitur enim Dominus Sabaoth, Lat. omitted; for he is called the Lord of Sabaoth.]

[4 minima, Lat.; the smallest.]

of the most puissant king Senacherib, one hundred four-score and five thousand soldiers.   In the host of God are all the winds, all the stars, and all the fiery, airy, and watery impressions.   In the host of God are all evil spirits, all men, kings and princes, all the warlike furniture of every nation, and finally, all creatures, both visible and invisible : and all these he useth according to his own pleasure, yea, according to his own good and just will, when, how much, and how long he listeth, to finish and bring to pass his own will and judgments.   In punishing the first world at the deluge he used water : in destroying of Sodoma and the cities there-about he used fire : and in rooting out the Canaanites and Jews he used the means of mortal men, or soldiers.

Sometimes there is ascribed to the Lord[5] the word *Æleon*, and the Lord is called *Æleon*[6], that is to say, high.   For in the one hundred and thirteenth psalm we read : "The Lord is higher than all nations, and his glory is above the heavens. Who is like the Lord our God, which setteth himself so high in his habitation?"   And in the ninety-seventh psalm he saith : "Thou, Lord, art higher than all that are in the earth ; thou art exalted far above all gods." *The high Lord.* *Psal. cxiii.* *Psal. xcvii.*

Again, God is called *El*, because of his strength.   For what he will, that can he do, and therefore is he called a strong God, or a giant[7].   For Jeremy saith : "The Lord is with me as a strong giant."   Esay saith : "The Lord shall come forth like a giant, he shall take stomach unto him[8] like a man of war, he shall roar and overcome his enemies." And like to this is the word Eloah, whose plural number is Elohim: That name betokeneth the presence of God, which never faileth his workmanship and worshippers[9].   Jeremy bringeth in God speaking, and saith : "Am I God, that seeth but the thing that is nigh at hand only, and not the thing that is far off[10]? may any man hide himself, so that I shall not *El.* *Jer. xx.* *Isai. xlii.* *Eloah.* *Jer. xxiii.*

[5 additur vocabulo Domini, Lat. ; there is added to the name of Lord.]

[6 עֶלְיוֹן *high* in situation or power, *the most High*. Lee's Lex.]

[7 heros vel gigas, Lat.]   [8 So Coverdale, 1535.]

[9 Nam אֵל significat *ad*, cui additur הּ relativa particula, quod Deus se referat ad omnia.—Bulling. de Orig. Error. fol. 4.]

[10 Annon Deus de propinquo ego, et non Deus de longinquo? Lat.; Coverdale, 1535, renders the sentence as the translator here.]

see him, saith the Lord? do not I fill heaven and earth?"

Psal. cxxxix. For before him also David said: "Whither shall I go from the breath of thy mouth[1]? And whither shall I flee from thy countenance? If I ascend into heaven, thou art there: and if I descend into hell, thou art there also. If I take the wings of the morning, and dwell in the uttermost parts of the sea, even there thy hand shall rule me, and thy right hand Acts xvii. shall hold me fast." Therefore the apostle Paul saith: "God is not far from every one of us. For by him we live, we move, and have our being." And for that cause peradventure God was of the Greeks called Θεὸς, to wit, ἀπὸ θέειν, because of his readiness and present succour; because he never faileth mortal men, but always and in all places doth aid and relieve them. Likewise Plato in Cratylo, and his interpreter Proclus, do think that Θεὸς (God) is derived ἀπὸ τοῦ θέειν, that is, of running: but that course or running is not referred to the presence or help of God, but to another thing[2]. For when men saw the sun, the moon, the stars, and heaven itself by running still to be turned about, they thought that they were gods. Some there are that will derive it ἀπὸ τοῦ δέους, that is to say, of fear or dread: for fear of religion[3] believeth and persuadeth men that there is a God. The Latins perad- Deus. venture framed their *Deus* (God) of the Greeks' Θεὸς. But some do think rather that *Deus* is derived *a dando*, of giving, because he giveth all things unto all men. For so among the Hebrews he is called Θεὸς[4] (as I will anon declare), or *Schaddai*, because he is sufficient to himself, he lacketh nothing, but giveth to all men all good things and necessary[5]. Some other will have God in Latin to be called *Deus, quod ipsi nihil deest*, that is, because there is nothing wanting in him.

Elohim. But now the scripture doth attribute the plural number, *Elohim*, not to God alone, but also to angels, to judges, and to men in authority: because God is always present with them, while they labour in that office which he hath appointed them unto; and doth by the ministry of them work the things which he himself will, and which are expedient for the welfare of mortal men. And although the word *Elohim* be of the

[1 a Spiritu tuo, Lat.]
[2 Platon. Cratyl. ed. Bekker. Tom. IV. p. 224. Lond. 1826.]
[3 vel religio, Lat.; *or* religion. So ed. 1577.]
[4 Hebræis Dai nuncupatur, Lat.]   [5 See Vol. I. p. 216, note 3.]

plural number, yet is it set before verbs in the singular number; as in the first of Genesis we find, " In the beginning," *Bara Elohim, Creavit Dii,* " God created" (for *Bara, created,* is the singular number) heaven and earth. In that phrase of speech is shewed unto us the mystery of the reverend Trinity : for Moses seemeth to have said in effect, In the beginning that God in the Trinity created heaven and earth. In the seventh chapter of the second book of Samuel, *Elohim* in the plural number is joined with verbs of the plural number[6], to declare that there is a difference of persons in the blessed Trinity.

This Dii importeth as much as if one should say, Gods.

Moreover, in the league which God maketh with our father Abraham God giveth himself another name. For he saith : "I God am *Schaddai,*" that is, sufficient, or sufficiency. Therefore God is called *Schaddai.* Some in their translations turn it *Vastator,* a destroyer, as if God should name himself a just revenger. But Moses Ægyptius[7] saith : " The noun *Schaddai* is compounded of the verb *Daii* (which signifieth, *he sufficeth*) and the letter *Schin,* which hath the same meaning that *Ascher* hath, and signifieth, *he that.* So that *Schaddai* is as much to say as, " he that sufficeth to himself, and is the sufficiency or fulness of all things." Peradventure the heathen have upon this occasion derived their *Saturnus,* which name they gave to them whom they did wickedly take to be gods: for as *Diurnus* cometh of *Dies,* a day; so is *Saturnus* derived a *saturando,* of satisfying or filling[8]. Therefore God is that He, to whom nothing is lacking, which in all things and unto all things is sufficient to himself; who needeth no man's aid, yea, who alone hath all things which do appertain to the perfect felicity both of this life and of the world to come; and which only and alone can fill and suffice all his people and other creatures. For this cause the Germans call him *Gott,* as who should say *Guot,* good, or best[9]; because, as he is full of all goodness, so he doth most liberally bestow upon men all manner of good things. The German word is

Schaddai.

Gen. xvii.

Saturn.

It seemeth that we Englishmen do borrow of the Germans their word Gott, and turn their double T into D, which we sound God, as if we should say, good.

<hr>

[6 Verse 23, הָלְכוּ־אֱלֹהִים.]

[7 Moses Maimonides, a celebrated Jewish rabbi, born at Cordova, in Spain, lived long, and died in Egypt, A.D. 1204.]

[8 See Vol. I. p. 215, notes 5, 6.]

[9 das höchste oberist güt, German, omitted; the highest good over all.]

not much unlike to the ancient name whereby the Egyptians called God; for they called God *Theuth*, or *Thoth*: now if we for *Th* put *G*, then is it *Goth*, and we say, *Gott*.

The Lord himself, in the sixth chapter of Exodus, putteth these two names[1] together, *Schaddai* and *Jehovah*, as two of the most excellent names that he hath, and saith: "I am Jehovah. And I appeared to Abraham, Isaac, and Jacob, as God Schaddai: but in my name Jehovah I was not known unto them." Not that the patriarchs had not heard or known the name[2] Jehovah: for that name began to be called upon in the time of Seth, immediately after the beginning of the world. Therefore it seemeth that the Lord meant thus in effect: "I opened myself unto the patriarchs as God Schaddai, who am able in all things sufficiently to fill them with all goodness; and therefore I promised them a land that floweth with milk and honey: but in my name Jehovah I was not yet known unto them, that is, I did not perform unto them that which I promised." For we have heard already, that he is called Jehovah of that which he maketh to be; and therefore he bringeth his promise to performance. "Now therefore" (saith he) "I will indeed fulfil my promise, and shew myself to be, not only *Deum Schaddai*, an all-sufficient or almighty God[3], but also to be Jehovah, an essence or being eternal, immutable, true, and in all things like myself, or standing to my promise[4]."

Last of all we read in the third of Exodus that God said to Moses: "Thus shalt thou say to the children of Israel, The Lord God of our[5] fathers, the God of Abraham, the God of Isaac, and the God of Jacob, hath sent me unto you. This is my name for ever, and this is my memorial from one generation unto another." So then here now we have another name of God; for he will be called the God of Abraham, of Isaac, and of Jacob. "This," saith he, "shall be my memorial from one generation unto another; to wit, wherein I will keep in memory my benefits bestowed upon those patriarchs, that by them the posterity may know me and remember me." For when we hear the names of those patriarchs, they do put us in mind of all the excellent and

Gen. iv.

The God of Abraham, Isaac, and Jacob.

[1 vocabula sua, Lat.; his names.]
[2 nomen Dei, Lat.]
[3 an all—God, not in Lat.]
[4 or—promise, not in Lat.]
[5 vestrorum, Lat.]

innumerable benefits which God bestowed on our forefathers[6]: which are not in vain with so great diligence peculiarly reckoned up of Moses in[7] his first book called Genesis. For he will be our God, even as he was theirs, if so be we do believe in him as they did believe. For to us that believe he will be both Schaddai and Jehovah, eternal and immutable truth, being, life, and heaped-up store of all manner good things.

And now by the way, it is not without a mystery that, when he is the God also of other patriarchs, as of Adam, Seth, Enos, and especially of Enoch and Noah, yet out of all the number of them he picked those three, Abraham, Isaac, and Jacob, and to every one of their names prefixed severally his own name[8], saying: "I am the God of Abra- Trinity. ham, the God of Isaac, and the God of Jacob." For so he did evidently teach the mystery of the Trinity in the unity of the divine substance, and that every one of the persons is of the same divinity, majesty and glory; that is, that the Father is very God, the Son very God, and the Holy Ghost very God; and that these three are one God; for he saith, "I am God, &c." Of which I will speak in place convenient.

Thus much hitherto concerning the names of God, out of which an indifferent knowledge of God may easily be gathered. I know that one Dionysius[9] hath made a busy Dionysius, of the names of commentary upon the names of God: but I know too, that God. the godly sort, and those that are studious of the apostles' doctrine do understand, that the disciples of the apostles did far more simply handle matters belonging unto religion. I know that other do make account of seventy-two names of God out of the scriptures and books of the Cabalists, which as I have in another place rehearsed[10], so will I hereafter out of Exodus[11] repeat to you the chiefest of them.

Secondarily, God is in the word of God exhibited to be Visions and prosopo- seen, to be beheld, and to be known by visions and divine graphy of God.

[6 ipsis, Lat.; on them.]   [7 per, Lat.; throughout.]
[8 id est, Dei nomen, Lat. omitted; that is, the name of God.]
[9 Dionys. Areop. ad Timoth. episc. Ephes. lib. de div. nom. This work is spurious: it is supposed to have been written in the fourth or fifth century.]
[10 Bulling. de Orig. Error. cap. i. fol. 6.]
[11 ex Exodi 34. cap. Lat.]

Prosopography is a picturing or representing of bodily lineaments.

mirrors, as it were in a certain parable, while by *Prosopography, Prosopopœia,* or mortal shapes[1] he is set[2] before our eyes. And yet we are warned not to stick upon those

Prosopopœia is where those are brought in to speak that do not speak.

visible things, but to lift up our minds from visible things to things invisible and spiritual. For neither is God bodily in his own substance, because he is in visions exhibited to us in a bodily shape like a man; neither did any of the old saints before the birth of Christ express God in the shape and picture of a mortal man, because God had in that shape exhibited himself to be seen of the patriarchs and prophets.

Anthropomorphites.

It is the doating error of the Anthropomorphites[3] to say, that God is bodily, and that he hath members like to a mortal man. And that no man do in this case deceive himself, by attributing falsely to God the thing that is against his honour, I will here, instead of a remedy against that poison, recite unto you, dearly beloved, the words of St Augustine, which he out of the pure understanding of the holy scriptures and assured testimonies of[4] catholic true doctors writ to Fortunatus, *De Videndo Deo,* against the Anthropomor-

How members are attributed to God who is bodiless.

phites. "Concerning the members of God (saith he), which the scripture doth in every place make mention of, know this; that, lest any man should believe that, according to the fashion and figure of this flesh we are like to God, the same scripture did also say that God hath wings, which it is manifest that we men have not. Therefore even as, when we hear wings named, we understand God's protection and defence; so when we hear of hands, we must understand his operation; when we hear mention made of feet, we must understand his present readiness; when we hear the name of eyes, we must understand his sight, whereby he seeth and knoweth all things: and when we hear of his face, we must understand his justice, whereby he is known to all the world: and whatsoever else like unto this the same scripture doth make mention of, I believe verily that it must be understood spiritually. Neither do I alone, or am I the first, that think thus; but even all they also which even with a mean understanding of the scriptures do withstand the opinion of them that are, for that cause, called Anthropo-

[1 aut icones, Lat.]   [2 quasi, Lat. omitted; as it were.]

[3 See Vol. I. p. 225, note 9.]

[4 aliorum, Lat. omitted; of other.]

morphites.   Out of whose writing because I will not cite over
much, to cause too long a stay, I do here mean to allege
one testimony out of St Hierome.   For when that man,
most excellently learned in the holy scriptures, expounded the
Psalm, where it is said, ' Understand, ye unwise among the Psal. xciv.
people; ye fools, at length be wise: he that planted the ear,
shall he not hear; or he that made the eye, shall he not see?'
[he] did among other things say: ' This place doth most of all These words
make against the Anthropomorphites, which say that God of Hierome
are taken out
hath members even as we have.   As for example, he is said of Tertullian.
to have eyes: The eyes of the Lord behold all things; the
hand of the Lord maketh all things.   And Adam heard
(saith he) the sound of the feet of the Lord walking in
paradise.   They do understand these places simply as the
letter lieth, and do refer mortal weakness to the magnificent
mightiness of the immortal God.   But I say that God is all
eye, all hand, and all foot.   He is all eye, because he seeth
all things; all hand, because he worketh all things; all
foot, because he is present everywhere.   Therefore mark ye
what he saith: ' He that planted the ear, shall he not hear?
or he that made the eye, shall he not see?'   He said not,
therefore hath he no eyes?   But he said, ' He that planted the
ear, shall he not hear; or he that made the eye, shall he not
see?'   He made the members, and gave them the efficient
powers.'"   And a little afterwards the same St Augustine saith:
"In all this which I have cited out of the saints and doctors,
Ambrose, Hierome, Athanasius, Gregory (Nazianzene), and
whatsoever else like these of other men's doings I could
ever read or come by (which I think to be too long here
severally to rehearse), I find that God is not a body, or that
he hath members like to a man; neither that he is divided
by the distance of places, but by nature unchangeably invisible.   And I do in the help of God without wavering believe,
and so far as he giveth me grace I do understand, that not
by the same invisible nature and substance, but by a visible
shape taken unto him, he appeared, as it pleased him to
them to whom he did appear, when in the holy scriptures
he is reported to have been seen with corporal eyes."   Thus
much out of Augustine [5].

[5 Nam de membris Dei quæ assidue scriptura commemorat, ne
quisquam secundum carnis hujus formam et figuram nos esse crederet

To these now I will also add the words of Tertullian, a very ancient ecclesiastical writer, in his excellent book *De Trinitate.* "By members (saith he), are shewed the efficient powers of God, not the bodily fashion of God, or corporal lineaments. For when the eyes are described, it is set down because he seeth all things; and when the ear is named, it is therefore named because he heareth all things; and when the finger is mentioned, then is there a certain signification

similes Deo, propterea et eadem scriptura et alas habere Deum dixit, quas nos utique non habemus. Sicut ergo alas cum audimus, protectionem intelligimus; sic et cum audimus manus, operationem intelligere debemus; et cum audimus pedes, præsentationem; et cum audimus oculos, visionem qua cognoscitur (Bullinger read, *cognoscit*); et cum audimus faciem, justitiam qua innotescit: et si quid aliud eadem scriptura tale commemorat, puto spiritaliter intelligendum. Neque hoc ego tantum, aut ego prior; sed omnes qui qualicunque spiritali intelligentia resistunt eis qui ob hoc anthropomorphitæ nominantur. Ex quorum literis ne multa commemorando majores moras faciam, hoc unum sancti Hieronymi interpono . . . Cum ergo ille vir, in scripturis doctissimus, psalmum exponeret ubi dictum est, Intelligite ergo, qui insipientes estis in populo, et stulti aliquando sapite; Qui plantavit aurem non audiet? aut qui finxit oculum non considerat?— inter cetera, Iste locus, inquit, adversus eos maxime facit qui anthropomorphitæ sunt, qui dicunt Deum habere membra quæ etiam nos habemus. Verbi causa, dicitur Deus habere oculos: Oculi Domini aspiciunt omnia; manus Domini facit omnia: et, Audivit, inquit, Adam sonum pedum Domini deambulantis in paradiso. Hæc simpliciter audiunt, et humanas imbecillitates ad Dei magnificentiam referunt. Ego autem dico, quod Deus totus oculus est, totus manus est, totus pes est: totus oculus est, quia omnia videt; totus manus est, quia omnia operatur; totus pes est, quia ubique est. Ergo videte quid dicat: Qui plantavit aurem non audiet? aut qui finxit oculos non considerat? Et non dixit, Qui plantavit aurem, ergo ipse aurem non habet? non dixit, Ergo ipse oculos non habet? Sed quid dixit? Qui plantavit aurem non audiet? qui finxit oculos non considerat? Membra tulit, efficientias dedit . . . Denique in iis omnibus quæ de opusculis sanctorum atque doctorum commemoravi, Ambrosii, Hieronymi, Athanasii, Gregorii, et si qua aliorum talia legere potui, quæ commemorare longum putavi, Deum non esse corpus, nec formæ humanæ habere membra, nec eum esse per locorum spatia divisibilem, et esse natura incommutabiliter invisibilem; nec per eandem naturam atque substantiam, sed assumpta visibili specie, sicut voluit, apparuisse iis quibus apparuit, quando per corporis oculos in scripturis sanctis visus esse narratur, in adjutorio Domini inconcusse credo, et quantum ipse donat intelligo.—August. ad Fortunat. Ep. cxi. Opp. Tom. ii. fol. 101. col. 4. Par. 1531.]

of his mind declared; and when the nose-thrills are spoken
of, the receiving of prayers, as of sweet smells is thereby
notified; and when the hand is talked of, it argueth that
he is the author of all creatures; and when the arm is specified, thereby is declared that no nature can withstand the
power of God; and when the feet are named, that putteth
us in mind, that God filleth all things, and that there is nothing where he is not present. For neither members nor
the offices of members are necessary to him, to whose will
only, without any words, all things obey and are ready at
hand. For why should he require eyes, which is himself
the light? Or why should he seek for feet, which is himself present everywhere? Or how should he go in, since
that there is nowhere for him to go out from himself? Or
why should he wish for a hand, whose will without words
doth work all things? Neither doth he need ears, that
knoweth the very secret thoughts. Or wherefore should
he lack a tongue, whose only thinking is a commanding?
For these members were necessary to men, and not to God;
because the counsel of men should be of none effect, unless
the body did fulfil the thoughts: but to God they are not
needful, whose will the very works do not only follow without
all stirring business, but do even immediately with his will
proceed and go forward. But he is all eye, because he
wholly seeth: he is all ear, because he wholly heareth: he
is all hand, because he wholly worketh; and all foot, because
he is wholly everywhere. For whatsoever is simple, that
hath not in itself any diversity of itself. For those things
fall into a diversity of members, whatsoever are born unto
dissolution; but the things that are not compact together cannot feel [1]diversity[2]." And so as followeth: for all these
hitherto are the words of Tertullian.

[1 In ed. 1577 diversity is placed within brackets.]

[2 Efficaciæ igitur ibi divinæ per membra monstrantur: non habitus
Dei, nec corporalia lineamenta ponuntur. Nam et cum oculi descri-
buntur, quod omnia videat exprimitur; et quando auris, quod omnia
audiat proponitur; et cum digitus, significantia quædam voluntatis
aperitur; et cum nares, precum quasi odorum perceptio ostenditur;
et cum manus, quod creaturæ sit omnis auctor probatur; et quando
brachium, quod nulla natura contra robur ipsius repugnare possit edicitur; et quando pedes, quod impleat omnia, nec sit quicquam ubi
non sit Deus, explicatur. Neque enim sunt ei aut membra aut mem-

How the
patriarchs
did see God.   Therefore when we read that Moses did see God face
to face, and that Jacob, Israel, and the prophets saw God
plainly and not obscurely ; thereby is meant, that to them
was exhibited a vision most manifest, effectual, and very
familiar. For truly said Theodoretus, the bishop of Cyrus:
"We say that the fathers did not see the divine nature or
substance, which cannot be circumscribed, comprehended, or
perceived in the mind of man, but doth itself comprehend
all things : but we say that they saw a certain glory and
certain visions, which were answerable to their capacity, and
did not pass the measure of the same[1]." For these assured
sentences of the holy scripture do always remain most true :

John i.
1 Tim. vi.   "No man did ever see God at any time." "God dwelleth in
the light that no man can attain unto, whom no man hath

Exod. xxxiii. seen nor can see;" and again, "No man shall see my face,
and live;" that is, so long as he liveth upon this earth in the
corruption and imperfection of this our flesh no man shall
behold the essence of God, which is eternal and light that
cannot be looked upon. For when we are once delivered
from this corruption and are clarified, then shall we see

brorum officia necessaria, ad cujus solum etiam tacitum arbitrium et
serviunt et adsunt omnia. Cur enim requirat oculos, qui lux est?
Aut cur quærat pedes, qui ubique est? cur ingredi velit, cum non sit
quo extra se progredi possit? aut cur manus expetat, cujus mens ad
omnia instituenda artifex est, et silens voluntas? Nec auribus eget,
qui etiam tacitas novit voluntates. Aut propter quam causam linguam
quærat, cui cogitare jussisse est? Necessaria enim hæc membra hominibus fuerunt, non Deo; quia inefficax hominis consilium fuisset, nisi
cogitamen corpus implesset : Deo autem non necessaria, cujus voluntatem non tantum sine aliqua molitione opera subsequuntur, sed ipsa
statim opera cum voluntate procedunt. Ceterum ipse totus oculus,
quia totus videt : et totus auris, quia totus audit : et totus manus, quia
totus operatur : et totus pes, quia totus ubique est. Non enim habet
in se diversitatem sui, quicquid est simplex. Ea enim demum in diversitatem membrorum recidunt, quæ veniunt ex nativitate in dissolu-
tionem. Sed hæc, quæ concreta non sunt, sentire non possunt.—Novat.
de Trin. Lib. apud Tertull. Opp. Par. 1664, p. 710.]

[1 Ἡμεῖς δὲ καὶ λογισμοῖς εὐσεβέσι χρησάμενοι, καὶ ταῖς ἀποφάσεσι ταῖς
θείαις πιστεύοντες, αἳ βοῶσι διαρρήδην, Θεὸν οὐδεὶς ἑώρακε πώποτε, φαμὲν
αὐτοὺς οὐ τὴν θείαν φύσιν ἑωρακέναι, ἀλλ' ὄψεις τινὰς τῇ σφῶν δυνάμει
συμμέτρους ... οὕτω τοίνυν καὶ περὶ τῶν ἀγγέλων νοήσομεν ... οὐ γὰρ τὴν
θείαν οὐσίαν ὁρῶσι τὴν ἀπερίγραπτον, τὴν ἀκατάληπτον, τὴν ἀπερινόητον,
τὴν περιληπτικὴν τῶν ὅλων, ἀλλὰ δόξαν τινὰ τῇ αὐτῶν φύσει συμμετρου-
μένην.—Theodoret. Opp. Dial. I. p. 15. Tom. IV. Lut. Par. 1642.]

him as he is. Therefore God is said to have been seen of the fathers, not according to the fulness of his divinity, but according to the capacity of men.

Tertullian thinketh that all things in the old Testament were done of God the Father by the Son, who, taking upon him a competent shape, appeared to men and spake unto the fathers. Paul in the beginning of his Epistle to the Hebrews doth significantly speak of the Son of God incarnate, not denying absolutely that the Father did ever any thing by the Son. Tertullian saith: "To the Son was given all power in heaven and in earth. But that power could not be of all things, unless it were of every time. Therefore it is the Son that always descended to talk with men, from Adam unto the patriarchs and prophets, in vision, in dream, in a mirror, and in oracle. So always it pleased God to be conversant in the earth with men, being none other than the Word which afterward was to be made flesh. And it pleased him so to make a way for us to faith, that we might the more easily perceive that the Son of God descended into the world, and that we might know that such a thing was done[2]." And so as followeth; for all these are the words of Tertullian. After this premonition we will now add the visions of God's majesty exhibited to holy men.

God did do all things with the fathers by his Son.

God exhibited to his servants many and sundry visions, wherein he after a manner did shadow forth his majesty unto them: all which visions it would be too long a labour for me to rehearse and expound unto you. Ye shall find the most notable ones, Exodus xix, Esay vi, Ezechiel i, Daniel vii, and in the Apocalypse of the blessed evangelist and apostle John: it is sufficient to have put you in mind of them. But now the most renowned and excellent one of

God shadowed in visions.

[2 Omnem dicens potestatem, et omne judicium, et omnia per eum facta, et omnia tradita in manu ejus, nullam exceptionem temporis permittit, quia omnia non erunt, si non omnis temporis fuerint. Filius itaque ... ad humana semper colloquia descendit, ab Adam usque ad patriarchas et prophetas, in visione, in somno, in speculo, in ænigmate: ordinem suum præstruens ab initio semper quæ erat persecuturus infinita, semper ediscebat, et Deus in terris cum hominibus conversari, non alius quam Sermo qui caro erat futurus. Ediscebat autem, ut nobis fidem sterneret, ut facilius crederemus Filium Dei descendisse in seculum, et retro tale quid gestum cognosceremus.—Tertull. Adv. Prax. cap. 16. Tom. II. pp. 176, 177. ed. Semler.]

them all I will here recite and handle at large. It is to be seen in the thirty-third and thirty-fourth chapters of Exodus.

Moses had trial of the facility and goodness of God, and that there was nothing which he obtained not at God's hand : therefore he taketh upon him boldly to ask this also *Moses desireth to see God in his majesty and glory.* of the Lord, to see God in his substance, glory, and majesty ; which thing all the true wise men of every age did only wish and long for. For Moses saith : " Because I understand that thou, O God, wishest well[1] unto me, and that thou canst deny nothing ; go to, I beseech thee, shew me thy glory :" that is, suffer me, I pray thee, to see thee so as thou art in thy glorious substance and majesty. Now God answering to this request, which is the greatest of all other, doth say unto him : " I will make all my good to pass by before thee, and I will cry the name of the Lord, or in the name of the Lord[2], before thee." In which words he promiseth two things to Moses. The one is, "All my good shall pass by before thee." But this chief good of God can be nothing else than the good and mighty God himself, or rather, the Word of God, I say, the very beloved Son of God, in whom we believe that all the treasures of wisdom, divinity, goodness, and perfectness are placed and laid up. For he set before Moses' eyes the shew of him in a human and visible shape, such in sight as he in the end of the world should be incarnate in. The other thing that he promised is, "I will cry the name of the Lord, or, in the name of the Lord, before thee;" that is, I will proclaim the names of my glory, by which thou mayest understand who I am, and see me in thy mind.

God giveth his gifts freely without respect of man's merits. But now, that no man should attribute so excellent a vision to the merit of Moses, the Lord doth add this sentence following : ' This vision doth not happen to thee because of thine own merit. For without man's merits I reveal myself to whom I will, and without respect of persons will have compassion on whom it pleaseth me ;' which consideration of the free grace and liberal goodness of God doth greatly belong to the true knowledge of God. Then the Lord goeth to again, and doth more significantly declare to Moses

---

[1 peroptime, Lat.]

[2 בְּשֵׁם יְהֹוָה, Exod. xxxiii. 19. in nomine Domini, Vulgate.]

in what manner and order he will exhibit or shew himself unto him. " Thou mayest not (saith he) in this life see my face;" that is, thou mayest not fully see me in my substance; for that is reserved for the blessed spirits and clarified bodies in the world to come. I will therefore in this fashion shew myself unto thee. Thou shalt go up into the mountain; there in a rock I will shew thee a clift, wherein thou shalt place thyself: and I will lay mine hand upon thee, that is, a cloud, or some such thing, that, as I come toward thee, thou mayest not look directly in my face. In that phrase of speech the Lord doth imitate the fashion of men, whose order is to spread their hands over the eyes of him whom they would not have narrowly to behold any thing. The Lord then addeth: And in the mean while I will pass by; that is, the image which I take, to wit, the shape of a man, wherein I will exhibit myself to be seen, shall pass by before thee. And when I am once past, so that thou canst not see my face, I will take away the hand wherewith I hid thine eyes, and then thou shalt behold the back of the figure, or my hinder parts. Now the hinder parts of God are the words and deeds of God, which he leaveth behind him that we by them may learn to know him. Again, the beholding of God's face is taken for the most exact and exquisite knowledge of God; but they that see but the back only do not know so well as they that see the face. And in the hinder or latter times of the world God sent his Son into the world, born of a woman[3]; whom whosoever do in faith behold, they do not see the Godhead in his humanity, but do by his words and deeds know who God is, and so they see the Father in the Son. For they learn that God is the chief good, and that the Son of God is God, being co-equal and of the same substance with the Father.

Now let us see how God (according to his promise made) did exhibit himself to be seen of Moses. Moses, rising up betimes, ascendeth up into the mountain cheerfully unto the rock which the Lord had shewed him, placing himself in the clift, and looketh greedily for the vision or revelation of God. At length the Lord descended in a cloud, and came upon the mountain unto the clift of the rock wherein Moses stayed for him. And presently, when Moses' face was

How God did shew himself to Moses.

[3 Cf. August. de Trinitate. Lib. II. cap. 16.]

10

hidden, the figure of God, that is, the shape of a man which God took upon him, did pass by before him: and when as now the back of the figure was toward Moses, so that he could no more see the face thereof, the Lord took his hand away, and Moses beheld the hinder parts of the same[1]. Whereby he gathered that God should once, that is to say, in the hinder times of the world, be incarnate and[2] revealed to the world. Of which revelation we will hereafter speak somewhat more. And when the Lord was once gone past, he cried, and as his promise was, so in a certain catalogue he reckoned up his names, whereby, as in a shadow, he did declare his nature. For he said, "Jehovah, Jehovah, God, merciful and gracious, long-suffering, and abounding in goodness and truth; keeping mercy in store for thousands, forgiving wickedness, transgression, and sin: and yet not suffering the wicked to escape unpunished, visiting the wickedness of the fathers upon the children and children's children, unto the third and fourth generation." What else is this than if he

What God is. had said 'I am the uncreated essence, being of myself from before all beginning, which giveth being to all things, and keepeth all things in being; I am a strong and almighty God; I do not abuse my might, for I am gentle and merciful; I love my creatures, and man especially, on whom I do wholly yearn in the bowels of love and mercy; I am rich and bountiful, and ready at all times to help my creatures; I do freely, without recompence, give all that I bestow; I am long-suffering, and not irritable to anger, and hasty to revenge, as mankind is; I am no niggard or envious, as wealthy men in the world are wont to be; I am most liberal and bountiful, rejoicing to be divided among my people, and to heap up benefits upon the faithful: Moreover, I am true and faithful; I deceive no man, I lie in nothing; what I promise, that I stand to, and faithfully perform it: Neither do I nor can I so waste my riches[3], that all at length is spent, and I myself drawn dry; for I keep good turns in store for a thousand generations, so that although the former age did live never so wealthily with my riches, yet they that come and are born even until the very end of the world shall nevertheless find in me so much as shall suffice

[1 Domini, Lat.; of the Lord.]   [2 atque ita, Lat.; and so.]
[3 spargens in homines, Lat. omitted; scattering them upon men.]

and satisfy their desire; for I am the well-spring of good
that cannot be drawn dry; and if any man sin against me
and afterward repent him of the same, I am not unappeasable; for even of mine own free-will I do forgive errors,
sins, and heinous crimes: and yet let no man therefore
think that I am delighted with sins, or that I am a patron
of wicked doers; for even I, the same, do punish wicked
and impenitent men; and chasten even those that are mine
own, that thereby I may keep them in order and office: but
let no man think that he shall sin and escape unpunished,
because he seeth that his ancestors did sin and were not
punished; that is, did sin and were not utterly cut off and
wiped out[4]; for I reserve revengement till just and full
time, and do so behave myself[5], that all are compelled to
confess me to be a God of judgment?' Now when Moses
the servant of God had heard and seen these things, he made
haste, and fell down prostrate to the earth, and worshipped.
Let us also do the same, being surely certified that the Lord
will not vouchsafe, so long as we live in this transitory God doth
world, to reveal himself and his glory any whit more fully most evi-
dently open
and brimly[6], than in Christ his Son exhibited unto us. Let himself
through
therefore the things that sufficed Moses suffice us also: let Christ.
the knowledge of Christ suffice and content us.

For the most evident and excellent way and mean to
know God is laid forth before us in Jesu Christ, the Son of
God incarnate and made man. For therefore we did even
now hear, that before Moses was set the shadow of Christ,
when it pleased God most familiarly to reveal himself unto
him. And the apostle Paul placeth the illumination or ap- 2 Cor. iv.
pearing of "the knowledge of the glory of God to be in the
face of Jesus Christ." And in another place the same Paul
calleth Christ "the brightness of his Father's glory, and the Heb. i.
lively image of his substance." Truly he himself in the gospel
doth most plainly say, "No man knoweth the Father but Matth. xi.
the Son, and he to whom the Son will reveal him." For John xiv.
he is the way unto the Father, and the Father is seen and
beheld in him. For we do again in the gospel read, "No John i.
man hath ever seen God at any time; the only-begotten Son,

[4 protinus, Lat. omitted; immediately.]
[5 modis omnibus, Lat. omitted; in all respects.]
[6 brim: public.]

which is in the bosom of the Father, he hath revealed him
1 Cor. i. unto us." But again the apostle saith, "After that in the
wisdom of God the world through their wisdom knew not
God, it pleased God through foolishness of preaching to save
them that believe." That which he in this place calleth the
wisdom of God is the very creation and workmanship of
the world, and the wonderful works of God, in which God
would be known to the world; and in the beating out and
considering whereof all the wisdom of all the wise men till
then did altogether lie. But for because the consideration
of those things did no good, by reason of man's wisdom for
the most part referring the causes of things to somewhat
else than to God, the true and only mark whereto they
should be referred; and while men thought themselves wise,
Rom. i. as the same apostle[1] teacheth us, even in their own reason-
ings they became fools; it pleased God by another way to be
known to the world, to wit, by the foolish preaching of the
gospel, which is in very deed most absolute and perfect wisdom, but to the worldly wisdom of mortal men it seemeth
foolishness. For it seemeth a foolish thing to the men of
this world, that the true and very God, being incarnate or
made man, was conversant with us men here in the earth,
was in poverty, was hungry, did suffer and die. And yet
even this is the way whereby God is most evidently known
to the world, together with his wisdom, goodness, truth,
God's wisdom appeareth. righteousness, and power. For the wisdom of God, which
no tongue can utter, doth in the whole ministry and won-
derful dispensation of Christ shine out very brightly; but
far more brimly if we discuss and beat out the causes (of
which I spake elsewhere), and throughly weigh the doctrine
God's goodness appeareth. of Christ. In the incarnation of the Son of God it appeareth,
how well God wisheth to the world being sunk and drowned
in sin, as that to which he is bound by an indissoluble league;
and doth through Christ adopt the sons of death and of the
devil into the sons and heirs of life everlasting. Now
God's truth appeareth. whereas Christ doth most exactly fulfil all those things which
the prophets by the revelation of God did foretell of him,
and whereas he doth most liberally perform the things which
God the Father did promise of him[2]; that doth declare how

[1 idem doctor gentium, Lat.; the same teacher of the Gentiles.]
[2 in ipso, Lat.; in him.]

unchangeable and true the eternal God is. In the deeds or ^{God's power and long-suffering appeareth to the world.} miracles of Christ our Lord, in his resurrection, in his glo- rious ascension into heaven, and most plentiful pouring out of his holy Spirit upon his disciples, but especially in con- verting the whole world from paganism and judaism to the evangelical truth, do appear the power, long-suffering, ma- jesty, and unspeakable goodness of God the Father. In the ^{God's justice appeareth.} death of Christ the Son of God doth shine[3] the great justice of God the Father, as that which, being once offended with our sins, could not be pacified but with such and so great a sacrifice. Finally, because he spared not his only-begotten ^{God's mercy appeareth.} Son, but gave him for us that are his enemies and wicked rebels, even therein is that mercy of his made known to the world, which is very rightly commended above all the works of God. Therefore in the Son, and by the Son, God doth most manifestly make himself manifest to the world; so that whatsoever is needful to be known of God or of his will, and whatsoever is belonging to heavenly and healthful wis- dom, that is wholly opened and throughly perceived and seen in the Son. Therefore, when Philip said[4] to Christ, "Lord, shew us the Father, and it sufficeth us;" we read ^{John xiv.} that the Lord answered, "Have I been so long with you, and do ye not yet know[5] me? Philip, he that hath seen me hath seen the Father; and how sayest thou, Shew us the Father? Dost not thou believe, that I am in the Father, and the Father in me?" Now herein he calleth back all the faithful from over-curious searching after God, laying before them the mystery of the dispensation wherein he would have us to rest and to content ourselves, namely in that that God was made man. Therefore whosoever desire to see and know God truly, let them cast the eyes of their mind upon Christ, and believe the mystery of him contained in words and deeds, learning by them what and who God is. For God is such an one as he exhibiteth himself[6] to be known in Christ, and in that very knowledge he doth appoint eternal life to be, where he saith: "And this is eternal life, that they might ^{John xvii.} know thee, the only true God, and Jesus Christ whom thou hast sent." Let him that wisheth well to himself take heed

[3 maxime, Lat. omitted; most especially.]
[4 roganti, Lat.; asked.]   [5 cognovistis, Lat. and Vulgate.]
[6 nobis, Lat. omitted; to us.]

that he go not about to know any more than God himself doth teach us in Christ. But whosoever, neglecting Christ, doth follow the rule and subtilties of man's wit, he verily doth come to nought and perish in his thoughts.

God is known by his works. Psal. xix. The fourth mean to know God by is fetched out of the contemplation of his works. David saith, "The heavens declare the glory of God, and the firmament sheweth forth the Rom. i. works of his hands." And the apostle Paul saith, "His invisible things, being understanded by his works through the creation of the world, are seen, that is, both his eternal power and Godhead." Lo, the power and Godhead of God are these invisible things of God; and yet they are understood by the consideration of God's works: therefore even The works of God are two ways considered. God himself is known by the works of God. But now the works of God are doubly considered, or be of two sorts. For either they are laid before us to be beheld in things created for the behoof of men, as in heaven and in earth, and in those things that are in heaven and in earth, and are governed and preserved by the providence of God; of which sort are the stars and the motions or courses of the stars, the influence of heaven, the course[1] of time, living creatures of all kinds, trees, plants, fruits of the earth, the sea and whatsoever is therein, stones, and whatsoever things are hid within and digged out of the earth for the use of men. Of these St Basil and St Ambrose have written very learnedly and godly in their books intituled, "The work of six days," the which they called *Hexaëmeron*[2]. Here may be inserted that history of nature, which the glorious and worthy king Psal. civ. David doth in the Psalms, especially after the hundredth psalm, most fitly apply to our purpose. But lest we should entangle and make intricate the course of this present treatise, I will hereafter speak of the creation of the world, and of God's government and providence in the same. At this present it shall suffice to know[3], that heaven and earth and all that is therein do declare to us, and set as it were before our eyes, an evident argument that God, as he is most wise, is also most mighty, wonderful, of an infinite majesty, of an incom-

[1 vicissitudo, Lat.]
[2 Basil. Opp. Tom. i. pp. 1—87. Par. 1721. Ambros. Opp. Tom. i. pp. 2—142. Par. 1686.]
[3 agnoscere, Lat.; to acknowledge.]

prehensible glory, most just, most gracious, and most excellent[4]. Esay therefore, a faithful teacher of the church,
giving good counsel for the state of mortal men, doth say
unto them[5]: "Lift up your eyes on high, and consider who Isai. xl.
hath made these things that come forth by heaps[6], calling
them all by their names; whose strength is so great, that
none of them doth fail." For although that even from the
beginning the stars have shined to the world, and have in
their course performed that for which they were created;
yet are they not worn by use, nor by continuance[7] consumed away or darkened ought at all; for by the power
of their maker they are preserved whole. Jeremy also
crieth: "O Lord, there is none like unto thee. Thou art Jer. x.
great, and great is thy name with power. Who would not
fear thee, O king of the Gentiles? For thine is the glory:
for among all the wise men of the heathen, and in all their
kingdoms, there is none that may be likened unto thee." And
immediately after again: "The Lord God is a true and living
God and king[8]: if he be wroth, the earth shaketh, neither
can the Gentiles abide his indignation. He made the earth
with his power; with his wisdom doth he order the whole
compass of the world; and with his discretion hath he spread
the heavens out. At his voice the waters gathered together
in the air[9]; he draweth up the clouds from the uttermost
parts of the earth; he turneth lightning to rain, and bringeth
the winds out of their treasures[10]."

Or else the works of God are set forth for us to behold in
man, the very lord and prince of all creatures: not so much in
the workmanship or making of man, which Lactantius and
Andreas Wesalius[11] have passingly painted out for all men to
see; as in the works which toward man, or in man, or by man,

[4 maximum, Lat. omitted; most great.]

[5 optime, Lat. omitted; exceeding well.]

[6 producens in numero exercitum eorum, Lat.; Coverdale's rendering, 1535, is like the translator's.]

[7 vetustate, Lat.]

[8 Deus et rex sempiternus, Lat.; God and an everlasting king.]

[9 ingens aquarum vis in aëre erit, Lat.]

[10 their treasuries, Coverdale, 1535. his treasures, Auth. Ver.]

[11 Lactantii de Opificio Dei, capp. 8—19.—Andrew Vesalius, a
celebrated anatomist and physician, born at Brussels about A.D. 1514,
wrote a work, De humani corporis fabrica.]

the Lord himself doth finish and bring to pass. For God doth justly punish some men; and by punishing them he doth declare that he knoweth the dealings of mortal men, and hateth all wrong and injury. Upon other he heapeth up very large and ample benefits; and in being bountiful unto them he declareth that he is rich, yea, that he is the fountain of goodness that cannot be drawn dry, that he is bountiful, good, merciful, gentle, and long-suffering. Hereof there are innumerable examples in the history of the Bible. Cain, for the murder committed upon his brother, lived here in earth a miserable and wretched life: for the just Lord doth revenge the blood-shed of the innocent. The first world was drowned in the deluge[1]; a plague was laid on it for the contempt of God; but Noah and his were saved in the ark by the mercy of God. God bringeth Abraham from Ur of the Chaldees, and placeth him in the land of Canaan, blessing and loading him with all manner of goods. He doth wonderfully keep Jacob in all his troubles and infinite calamities. Through great afflictions he lifteth up Joseph from the prison[2] unto the throne of Egypt: he doth grievously plague the Egyptians for the tyranny shewed in oppressing Israel, and for the contempt of his commandment. But it would be too long and tedious to make a beadrow of all the examples. Now by these and such like works of God we learn who, and how great, our God is, how wise he is, how good, how mighty, how liberal, how just and rightful; and withal we learn that we must believe and in all things obey him. For Asaph

Psal. lxxviii. saith: "The things that we have heard and known, and such as our fathers have told us, those we will not hide from our sons; but will shew to the generations to come the praise of the Lord, his mighty and wonderful works which he hath done: that the children which are born, when they come to age, may shew their children the same; that they may put their trust in God, and not forget the works of God, but keep his commandments." And so as followeth in the seventy-eighth Psalm.

God is shadowed to us by comparisons. Another way to know God by, next to this, is that which is gathered upon comparisons: for the scripture doth compare all the most excellent things in the world with God,

[1 immisso cœlitus, Lat. omitted; which was sent from heaven.]
[2 from the prison, not in Lat.]

whom it preferreth before them all; so that we may thereby gather, that God is the chief good, and that his majesty is incomprehensible. This one place of Esay may stand instead of many, where in the fortieth chapter he saith: " Who hath Isai. xl. measured the waters with his fist ? Who hath measured heaven with his span ? Who hath held the dust of the earth betwixt three fingers[3], and weighed the mountains[4] and hills in a balance ? Who hath directed the Spirit of the Lord ? Who gave him counsel ? Who taught him ? Who is of his counsel, to instruct him ? Behold, all people are in comparison of him as a drop of a bucket-full, and counted as the least thing that the balance weigheth. Yea, he shall cast out the isles as the smallest crumb of dust. Libanus were not sufficient to minister him wood to burn, nor the beasts thereof were enough for one sacrifice unto him. All people in comparison of him are reckoned as nothing; and if they be compared with him, they are counted as less than nothing. Isai. xl. Understand ye not this ? hath it not been preached unto you since the beginning ? have ye not been taught this by[5] the foundation of the earth ? It is he that sitteth upon the circle of the world, whose inhabiters are (in comparison of him) but as grasshoppers. He spreadeth out the heavens as a covering, and stretcheth them out as a tent to dwell in. He bringeth princes to nothing, and maketh the judges of the earth as though they were not[6]." And so forth. To this place now do belong the *Prosopopeial* speeches of God, of which thou shalt find sundry and many, beside the visions which we placed in the second way or mean to know God. But the most excellent are extant in the eighteenth Psalm, and in the fifth chapter of Salomon's Ballad[7]: both which I pass over untouched, because I mean not to stay you too long; for we must descend to the other points.

Last of all, God is known by the sayings or sentences God is learned by uttered by the mouths of the prophets and apostles; of the sayings and sentences which sort is that notable speech of Jeremy[8], where he saith: of the pro-

[3 So Vulgate and Coverdale, 1535.]
[4 in statera, Lat. omitted; in scales.]
[5 a, Lat.; from; since, Coverdale, 1535.]
[6 ut sint inanes, Lat.]
[7 Salomon's Balettes, called Cantica Canticorum; Coverdale, 1535.
See Fulke's Defence, &c. ed. Parker Soc. pp. 571, 572.]
[8 beati Jeremiæ, Lat.]

phets and
apostles.
Jer. ix.

"Let not the wise man glory in his wisdom, nor the strong man in his strength, nor the rich man in his riches[1]: but let him that glorieth glory in this, that he understandeth and knoweth me, that I am the Lord, and do mercy, judgment, and righteousness upon earth: therefore am I delighted in such things alone, saith the Lord." Now by the mercy of God we are saved, and adorned with sundry great benefits; by his judgment he punisheth the wicked and disobedient according to their deserts, and therewithal he keepeth equity: even as also his righteousness doth truly perform that which he promiseth. Therefore we say that God is a Saviour, a liberal giver of all good things, an upright Judge, and assured truth in performing his promises.

And hither now is to be referred the doctrine of the prophets and apostles, which teacheth that to be the true God is one in essence, or being. knowledge of God, that acknowledgeth God to be one in essence, and three in persons. Concerning the unity of the divine essence (by the allegation whereof the plurality of the heathen gods are utterly rejected and flatly condemned), I will cite those testimonies out of the holy scripture that seem to be more evident and excellent than all the other, which are in number so many that a man can hardly reckon them all. The notablest is that which is grounded upon the prophetical and evangelical authority, and, being cited out of the Deut. vi. Mark xii. sixth chapter of Deuteronomy, is in the twelfth of Mark set down in these words: "Jesus said, The first of all the commandments is, Hearken, Israel, the Lord our God is one Lord. And thou shalt love the Lord thy God with all thy heart, with all thy soul, with all thy mind, and with all thy strength. This is the first commandment. And the second like this is, Thou shalt love thy neighbour as thyself. There is none other commandment greater than these." It followeth now in the gospel: "And the Scribe said, Well, Master, thou hast said the truth; that there is one God, and that there is none other but he; and that to love him with all the heart, with all the mind, with all the soul, and with all the strength, and to love a man's neighbour as himself, is greater than all the burnt-offerings and sacrifices." With this testimony also do all the other notable ones agree, that

[1 neque glorietur, Lat.; repeated in these two sentences, but omitted by the translator.]

are in the law. For in the twentieth of Exodus we read, Exod. xx. that the Lord himself with his own mouth did in mount Sina say: "I am the Lord thy God, which brought thee out of the land of Egypt, out of the house of bondage; have thou none other gods but me[2]." Again, Moses in the end of his song bringeth in God saying: "See now how that I, I Deut. xxxii. am God, and there is none other God but I. I kill, and make alive again: I wound, and I heal, neither is there any that can deliver out of my hand." With the testimonies in the law do those of the prophets also agree. For David in the eighteenth Psalm saith: "The way of God is an undefiled Psal. xviii. way, the word of the Lord also is tried in the fire. He is the defender of all them that put their trust in him. For who is God but the Lord? or who hath any strength[3] except our God?" There are of this sort many other places in the volume of the Psalms. The Lord in Esay and by Esay Isai. xlii. crieth and saith: "I am the Lord, Hu[4] is my name, and Or, this is my my glory will I not give unto any other, nor mine honour name. to graven images." "I am the first and the last, and beside Isai. xliv. me there is no God. And who is like to me? (If any be), let him call forth and openly shew the thing that is past, and lay before me what hath chanced since I appointed the people of the world[5]; and let him tell what shall happen hereafter, and come to pass." "I the Lord do all things, I spread out the heavens alone, and I only have laid forth the earth by myself. I make the tokens of witches of none effect, and make the soothsayers fools. As for the wise, I turn them backward, and make their wisdom foolishness. I set up the word of my servant, and do fulfil the counsels of my messengers." "I am the Lord, and there is else none; Isai. xlv. which createth[6] light and darkness, and maketh peace and trouble: yea, even I the Lord do all these things." To these testimonies of the prophets we will now add one or two out of Saint Paul, the great instructor and apostle of the Gentiles. He in his Epistle to Timothy saith: "There 1 Tim. ii. is one God, and one mediator of God and men, the man Christ Jesus." And again he saith: "One Lord, one faith, Ephes. iv.

[2 coram me, Lat.; before me.]

[3 quis est petra, Lat.; who is a rock, Auth. Ver.]

[4 See above, page 132.]   [5 populum seculi, Lat.]

[6 created, ed. 1577.]

one baptism, one God and Father of all, which is above all, and through all, and in you all." Again, the same apostle to the Corinthians saith : "There is none other God but one. And though there be that are called gods, whether in heaven or in earth, (as there be gods many, and lords many ;) yet unto us there is but one God, even the Father, of whom are all things, and we in him ; and one Lord Jesus Christ, by whom are all things, and we by him." Now I suppose these divine testimonies are evident enough, and do sufficiently prove that God in substance is one, of essence incomprehensible, eternal, and spiritual.

But under the one essence of the Godhead the holy scripture doth shew us a distinction of the Father, of the Son, and of the Holy Ghost. Now note here, that I call it a distinction, not a division or a separation. For we adore and worship no more Gods but one : so yet that we do neither confound, nor yet deny to take away [1], the three subsistences or persons of the divine essence, nor the properties of the same. Noetus (Anoetus in very deed,) and Sabellius the Libyan, a godless, bold, and very rude ass, of whom sprang up the gross heresy of the Patripassians, taught that the Father, the Son, and the Holy Ghost did import no distinction in God, but that they were diverse attributes of God. For they said that God is none otherwise called the Father, the Son, and the Holy Ghost, than when he is named good, just, gentle, omnipotent, wise, &c. They said, the Father created the world ; the same in the name of the Son took flesh and suffered ; and again, in changing his name, he was the Holy Ghost that came upon the disciples. But the true, prophetical, and apostolical faith doth expressly teach, that the names of the Father, the Son, and the Holy Ghost do shew to us what God is in his own proper nature. For naturally and eternally God is the Father, because he did from before beginnings unspeakably beget the Son. The same God is naturally the Son, because he was from before beginnings begotten of the Father. The same God is naturally the Holy Ghost, because he is the eternal Spirit of them both, proceeding from both [2], being one and the same God both with them [3].

Marginal notes:

1 Cor. viii.

In the one essence of God there is a distinction of persons.

Noetus is as much to say, as a man of understanding, which term was the proper name of a man. *Anoetus* signifieth a fool, or one without understanding.

The gross error of the Patrispassians.

[1 negantes auferamus, Lat. ; deny or take away, ed. 1577.]
[2 from them both, ed. 1577.]
[3 An error in all the editions for, with them both.]

And when in the scriptures he is called a gentle, good, wise, merciful, and just God, it is not thereby so much expressed what he is in himself, as what a one he doth exhibit himself to us. The same scripture doth openly say, that the Father created all things by the Son : and that the Father descended not into the earth, nor took our flesh upon him, nor suffered for us ; for the Son saith, "I went out from the Father, John xvi. and came into the world ; again, I leave the world, and go unto the Father." The same Son falling prostrate in the mount of Olives prayeth, saying, "Father, if it be possible, let Matth. xxvi. this cup pass from me." Again, in the gospel he saith, "I John xiv. will pray to the Father, and he shall give you another Comforter[4]." Lo, here he saith, the Father shall give you another Comforter. And yet again, lest by reason of those persons and properties of those persons we should separate or divide the divine nature, the Son in the gospel saith, "I and the Fa- John x. ther are one." For when he saith "one," he overthroweth them that separate or rent the divine substance or nature : and when *He speaketh* he saith, "We are," and not "I am," therein he refuteth them *plurally.* that do confound the subsistences or persons in the Trinity. Therefore the apostolic and catholic doctrine teacheth and doth confess, that they are three, distinguished in properties ; and that of those three there is but one and the same nature, or essence, the same omnipotency, majesty, goodness, and wisdom. For although there be an order in the Trinity, yet can there be no inequality in it at all. None of them is in time before other, or in dignity worthier than other : but of the three there is one Godhead, and they three are one and eternal God.

And the primitive church verily under the apostles, and the times that came next after them, did believe so simply, despising and rejecting curious questions and needless disputa- *A disputation* tions. And even then too did arise pestilent men in the church *of God* *sprung up.* of God, speaking perverse things, whom the apostle doth Acts xx. upon good cause call "grievous wolves, not sparing the flock." They first brought in[5] very strange and dangerous questions, and sharpened their blasphemous tongues against heaven itself. For they stood in it, that three persons could not be one nature or essence ; and therefore that, by naming the Trinity, the Christians worshipped many Gods, even as the heathen do.

[4 alium paracletum vel consolatorem, Lat.]
[5 contexuerunt, Lat.]

And again, since there can be but one God, they infer consequently, that the same God is Father, Son, and Holy Ghost unto himself. For so it was agreeable that they should doat in folly, whom the word of God did not lead, but the gross imagination of mortal flesh: and God did by these means punish the giant-like boldness of those men, whose minds, being without all reverence and fear of God, did wickedly strive to fasten the sight of the eyes of the flesh upon the very face of God. But the faithful and vigilant overseers and pastors of the churches were compelled to drive such wolves from the folds of Christ's sheep, and valiantly to fight for the sincere and catholic truth, that is, for the Unity and Trinity, for the monarchy and mystery of the dispensation. That strife bred forth divers words, with which it was necessary to hold and bind those slippery merchants[1]. Therefore immediately after the beginning there sprang up the terms of Unity, Trinity, essence, substance, and person. The Greeks for the most part used *ousia, hypostasis,* and *prosopon*[2] : which we call essence, subsistence, and person.

What terms were usurped in this disputation.

Of these again there did in the churches spring up new and fresh contentions[3]. They disputed sharply of the essence and subsistence, whether they are the same or sundry things. For Ruffinus Aquileiensis, in the twenty-ninth chapter and first book of his ecclesiastical history, saith: "There was moved a controversy about the difference of substances and subsistences, which the Greeks call οὐσίας and ὑποστάσεις. For some said that substance and subsistence seem to be all one; and because we say not that there are three substances in God, therefore that we ought not to say, that there are three subsistences in him. But on the other side again, they that took substance for one thing and subsistence for another did say, that substance noteth the nature of a thing and the reason whereupon it standeth; but that the subsistence of every person doth shew that very thing which doth subsist[4]."

Essence and substance or subsistence.

[1 homines, Lat.]　　　　[2 οὐσία, ὑπόστασις, πρόσωπον, Lat.]
[3 posterioribus annis, Lat. omitted; in after years.]
[4 Sed et de differentia substantiarum et subsistentiarum sermo eis per scripturam motus est. Græci οὐσίας et ὑποστάσεις vocant. Quidam etenim dicebant substantiam et subsistentiam unum videri; et quia tres substantias non dicimus in Deo, nec tres subsistentias dicere debeamus. Alii vero, quibus longe aliud substantia quam subsistentia

Basilius Magnus wrote[5] a learned epistle to his brother Gregory about the difference of essence and subsistence[6]. And Hermius Sozomenus, in the twelfth chapter of his fifth book of Histories, saith: "The bishops of many cities, meeting together at Alexandria do, together with Athanasius and Eusebius Vercellensis, confirm the decrees of Nice, and confess that the Holy Ghost is co-essential with the Father and the Son, and name them the Trinity; and teach that the man, which God the Word took upon him, is to be accounted perfect man, not in body only, but in soul also; even as the ancient doctors of the church did also think. But for because the question about *Ousia* and *Hypostasis* did trouble the churches, and that there were sundry contentions and disputations concerning the difference betwixt them; they seem to me to have determined very wisely, that those names should not at the first presently be used in questions of God; unless it were that, when a man went about to beat down the opinion of Sabellius, he were compelled to use them, lest by lack of words he should seem to call one and the same by three names, when he should understand every one peculiarly in that three-fold distinction[7]." Socrates in the seventh chapter and third book of his History addeth: "But they did not bring into the church a certain new religion devised of them-

significare videbatur, dicebant, quia substantia ipsa rei alicujus naturam rationemque qua constat designet; subsistentia autem uniuscujusque personæ hoc ipsum quod exstat et subsistit, ostendat.—Eccles. Hist. Ruffino autore. Lib. x. cap. 29. ed. Basil. 1539.]

[5 scripsit et, Lat.; also wrote.]

[6 Basil. Opp. Ep. 43. ad Gregorium fratrem de οὐσίας et ὑποστάσεως differentia. Tom. II. p. 28. Basil. 1540. Or Tom. III. p. 115. Ep. 38. Paris, 1721.]

[7 Ἐν τούτῳ δὲ πολλῶν πόλεων ἐπίσκοποι συνελθόντες εἰς Ἀλεξάνδρειαν ἅμα Ἀθανασίῳ καὶ Εὐσεβίῳ τὰ δεδογμένα ἐν Νικαίᾳ κρατύνουσιν· ὁμοούσιόν τε τῷ Πατρὶ καὶ τῷ Υἱῷ τὸ ἅγιον Πνεῦμα ὡμολόγησαν, καὶ τριάδα ὠνόμασαν· οὐ μόνῳ τε σώματι, ἀλλὰ καὶ ψυχῇ, τέλειον χρῆναι δοξάζειν ἄνθρωπον, ὃν ὁ Θεὸς Λόγος ἀνέλαβεν, εἰσηγήσαντο, καθὰ καὶ τοῖς πάλαι ἐκκλησιαστικοῖς φιλοσόφοις ἐδόκει. ἐπεὶ δὲ ἡ περὶ τῆς οὐσίας καὶ ὑποστάσεως ζήτησις τὰς ἐκκλησίας ἐτάραττε, καὶ συχναὶ περὶ τούτων ἔριδες καὶ διαλέξεις ἦσαν, εὖ μάλα σοφῶς μοι δοκοῦσιν ὁρίσαι, μὴ ἐξ ἀρχῆς εὐθὺς ἐπὶ Θεοῦ τούτοις χρῆσθαι τοῖς ὀνόμασι, πλὴν ἡνίκα τις τὴν Σαβελλίου δόξαν ἐκβάλλειν πειρῷτο· ἵνα μὴ ἀπορίᾳ ὀνομάτων ταὐτὸν δόξῃ τὶς τρισὶ προσηγορίαις καλεῖν, ἀλλ᾽ ἕκαστον ἰδίᾳ νοοῖτο τριχῇ.—Sozomen, H. E. Lib. v. cap. 12. p. 198. ed. Reading. Cantab. 1720.]

selves, but that which from the beginning even till then the ecclesiastical tradition taught, and prudent Christians did evidently set forth[1]." And so forth.

All things that are to be believed of God are fully contained in the canonical scriptures. Therefore away with the pope's champions to the place whereof they are worthy, which, when we teach that all points of true godliness and salvation are fully contained and taught in the canonical scriptures, by the way of objection do demand; in what place of the scripture we find the names of Trinity, person, essence, and substance; and finally, where we find that Christ hath a reasonable soul? For although those very words consisting in those syllables are not to be found in the canonical books (which were by the prophets and apostles written in another and not in the Latin tongue), yet the things, the matter, or substance, which those words do signify, are most manifestly contained and taught in those books: which things likewise all and every nation may in their language express, and for their commodity and necessity speak and pronounce them. Away also with all sophisters, which think it a great point of learning to make the reverend mystery of the sacred Trinity dark and intricate with their strange, their curious, and pernicious questions. It is sufficient for the godly, simply, according to the scriptures and the apostles' creed to believe and confess, that there is one divine nature or essence, wherein are the Father, the Son, and the Holy Ghost. Neither is it greatly material whether ye call them substances, or subsistences, or persons, so that ye do plainly express the distinction betwixt them, and each one's several properties; confessing so the unity, that yet ye confound not the Trinity, nor spoil the persons of their properties.

Testimonies out of the Gospel to prove the Trinity. And here now it will do very well[2] out of the scriptures to cite such evident testimonies as may evidently prove the mystery of the Trinity with the distinction and several properties of the three persons. The Lord in the Gospel after **[Matt. xxviii. 19, 20.]** St Matthew saith: "All power is given to me in heaven and in earth: go ye therefore and teach all nations, baptizing

[1] Οὐ γὰρ νεαράν τινα θρησκείαν ἐπινοήσαντες εἰς τὴν ἐκκλησίαν εἰσήγαγον, ἀλλὰ ἅπερ ἐξ ἀρχῆς καὶ ἡ ἐκκλησιαστικὴ παράδοσις ἔλεγε, καὶ ἀποδεικτικῶς παρὰ τοῖς Χριστιανῶν σοφοῖς ἐφιλοσοφεῖτο.—Socrates, H. E. Lib. III. cap. 7. p. 178. ed. Reading.]

[2] præstat, Lat.; it is better.]

them in the name of the Father, and of the Son, and of the Holy Ghost; teaching them to observe all things whatsoever I have commanded you." Tertullian, alleging those words against Praxea, saith: "He did last of all command his disciples to baptize into the Father, and the Son, and the Holy Ghost. We are baptized not into one, nor once, but thrice at every name, into every several person[3]." Thus much Tertullian. Now as every several person is severally expressed, so the divinity of them all is therein singularly taught to be one and common to them all, because he biddeth to baptize, not only into the name of the Father, but also of the Son, and[4] the Holy Ghost. The apostle and elected vessel, Paul, doth flatly deny that any man either ought to be, or ever was, baptized[5] into the name of any man which is nothing else but mere man. "Were ye," saith he, "baptized in the name of Paul?" So then the Father is God, the Son is God, and the Holy Ghost is God, into whose name we are baptized.

Tertullian contra Praxeam.

1 Cor. i.

The same Lord in the Gospel after St John saith: "When the Comforter cometh, whom I will send unto you from the Father, that is, the Spirit of truth, he will lead you into all truth. He shall not speak of himself: but whatsoever he shall hear, that shall he speak. He shall glorify me, for he shall receive of mine, and shall shew unto you. All things that the Father hath are mine: therefore said I unto you, that he shall take of mine, and shew unto you." In these words of the Lord's thou hearest mention made of the person of the Father from whom the Spirit is sent, of the person of the Son which sendeth him, and of the person of the Holy Spirit which cometh unto us. Thou hearest also of the mutual and equal communion of the divinity and all good things betwixt the three persons. For the Holy Ghost speaketh not of himself, but that which he heareth. "He shall," saith the Son, "take of mine." And again: "All things that the Father hath are mine." And therefore what

John xiv. & xvi.

[3 Novissime mandans (Christus) ut tinguerent (discipuli) in Patrem et Filium et Spiritum Sanctum, non in unum: nam nec semel, sed ter, ad singula nomina in personas singulas tinguimur.—Tertull. adv. Prax. cap. XXVI. Tom. II. p. 199. ed. Semler.]

[4 and of, ed. 1577.]

[5 ab Apostolis, Lat. omitted; by the Apostles.]

things the Son hath, those are the Father's: and the divinity, glory, and majesty of them all is co-equal.

With these most evident speeches do these two manifest testimonies of John[1] Baptist agree. First he saith: "He whom God hath sent doth speak the words of God; for God giveth not the Spirit by measure unto him. The Father loveth the Son, and hath given all things into his hand. He that believeth on the Son hath everlasting life, &c." Lo, here again, in the one Godhead thou hearest the three persons distinguished by their properties: for the Father loveth and sendeth the Son, and giveth all things into his hand; the Son is sent, and receiveth all things; but the Holy Ghost is given of the Father, and received of the Son according to fulness. Then again the same Baptist crieth the second time, and saith: "I saw the Spirit descending from heaven like unto a dove, and it abode upon him. And I knew him not: but he that sent me to baptize with water, the same said unto me, Upon whomsoever thou shalt see the Spirit descending, and tarrying still upon him, the same is he which baptizeth with the Holy Ghost. And I saw, and bare record that this is the Son of God." Here again are shewed unto us, as clearly as the day-light, the three persons distinguished and not confounded. For he that sendeth John is the Father: the Holy Ghost is neither the Father, nor the Son, but appeareth upon the head of Christ in the likeness of a dove: and the Son is the Son, not the Father, and that too the Son of the Father, upon whose head the Holy Ghost did abide. And now to this place doth belong the testimony of the Father, uttered from heaven upon his Son Christ. For he saith: "This is my beloved Son, in whom I am well pleased." But one and the same cannot be both father and son unto himself. The Father is one, and the Son is one: and yet not divers things, but one and the same God, of one and the same nature. For the Son in one place doth most plainly say: "I and the Father are one, &c."

Moreover, what could be more clearly spoken for the proof of the express distinction and properties of the three persons in the reverend Trinity, than that where the archangel Gabriel in St Luke, declaring the sacrament[2] of the

Marginal notes: John iii.   [John i. 32—34.]   Matth. iii. & xvii.   John x.

[1 beatissimi Joannis.]
[2 sacrament : mystery.]

Lord's incarnation, doth evidently say unto the virgin, the
mother of God[3]: "The Holy Ghost shall come upon thee, Luke i.
and the power of the Highest shall overshadow thee; therefore also that holy thing that shall be born shall be called
the Son of God?" What, I pray you, could have possibly
been invented of purpose to be more manifestly spoken for
the proof of this matter, than these words of the angel?
Thou hast here the person of the Highest, that is, of the
Father. For in the words of the angel, a little afore, it is
said: "He shall be great, and shall be called the Son of
the Highest." Now the Son is the Son of the Father. We
have also the persons of the Son and of the Holy Ghost
expressed, with their properties, neither mingled nor confounded. The Father is not incarnate, nor yet the Holy
Ghost, but the Son. To the Father is born of the virgin a
Son, even he that was the Son by the eternal and unspeakable manner of begetting. But the Holy Ghost, which is
the power of the Most Highest, did overshadow the virgin,
and made her with child. And so by this means thou mayest
see here the persons distinguished, not divided; and how they
differ in properties, not in essence of deity, or in nature.

Here now (although these places might seem to suffice The apostles'
testimonies
any reasonable man[4]) I will yet add other testimonies of the concerning
the Trinity
holy apostles, and that too of three the most excellent among
all the apostles. St Peter, preaching the word of the Gospel
before the church of Israel, as Luke testifieth in the Acts of
the Apostles, doth among other things say: "This Jesus Acts ii.
hath God raised up, and exalted him to his right hand; and
he, having received of the Father the promise of the Holy
Ghost, hath shed forth this which ye now see and hear."
Lo, God the Father raiseth up and doth exalt the Son: the
Son is raised up, exalted, and sitteth at the right hand of
the Father: and the Son, receiving of the Father the Holy
Ghost, doth bestow it upon the apostles. Therefore the
Spirit proceedeth from the Father and the Son, subsisting in
his own person, but being one and the same Spirit of them
both. Moreover, in the sermon made at Cæsarea in the con- Acts x.
gregation of the Gentiles, that is, in the house and family of
Cornelius the centurion, the same apostle doth as plainly

[3 Deiparæ, Lat.]
[4 any reasonable man, not in Lat.]

express the person of the Father, of the Son, and of the
Holy Ghost; and knitteth the Trinity together into one essence of the divine nature.

Rom. i.
St Paul[1] in the beginning of his Epistle to the Romans
saith, that he was "appointed to preach the gospel of God,
which he had promised afore by his prophets in the holy
scriptures, of his Son; which was made of the seed of David
after the flesh, and hath been declared to be the Son of
God with power after the Spirit that sanctifieth[2]." Again,

Gal. iv.
to the Galatians he saith: "God sent his Son, made of a
woman, that we by adoption might receive the right of sons.
And because ye are sons, God hath sent forth the Spirit of
his Son into your hearts, crying, Abba, Father." And again,

Tit. iii.
to Titus he saith: "God according to his mercy hath saved
us by the fountain of regeneration and renewing of the
Holy Ghost[3], which he shed on us richly through Jesus Christ
our Saviour." Therefore St Cyril, speaking very truly of
the apostle Paul, *Libro in Joan.* ix. cap. 45, doth say:
"That holy man did rightly know the enumeration of the
sacred Trinity: and therefore he teacheth, that every person
doth properly and distinctly subsist; and yet he preacheth

Identitas.
openly the immutable selfsameness of the Trinity[4]." Concerning which matter, if any man would gather together
and reckon up all the testimonies that Paul hath for the
proof of it, he must of necessity recite all his epistles.

1 John ii.
The blessed apostle and evangelist John doth more strongly
and evidently than the other[5] affirm and set forth the mystery
of the Trinity, and distinction of the persons, as well in his
evangelical history as in his epistle. Among many this one
at this time shall be sufficient. In his canonical epistle he
saith: "Who is a liar but he that denieth that Jesus is Christ?
The same is antichrist, that denieth the Father and the Son.
Whosoever denieth the Son, the same hath not the Father.

[1 Apostolus, Lat. omitted.]

[2 per potentiam et Spiritum sanctificantem, Lat.]

[3 Per lavacrum regenerationis ac renovationis, &c.]

[4 οἶδε γὰρ τῆς ἁγίας καὶ ὁμοουσίου τριάδος τὴν ἀπαρίθμησιν, καὶ ἰδίᾳ
μὲν ἕκαστον τῶν σημαινομένων ὑφεστάναι διδάσκει, τό γε μὴν ἐν ἀπαραλλάκτῳ
κεῖσθαι ταυτότητι τὴν ἁγίαν τριάδα διακηρύττει σαφῶς.—Cyril. Opp. Lib.
ix. in Joann. Tom. iv. p. 812. Lutet. 1638.]

[5 ceteris, Lat.; the others.]

Therefore let that abide in you which you have heard from
the beginning." And presently after he saith again : "Ye
need not that any man teach you, but as the same anointing
teacheth you of all things, and it is true, and not lying." In
these words ye hear the Father, ye hear the Son, ye hear the
anointing, that is, the Holy Ghost. The Father is not the
Son; the Son is not the Father; neither is the Holy Ghost the
Father, or the Son : but the Father is the Father of the Son,
the Son is the Son of the Father, and the Holy Ghost[6] proceedeth from them both ; and yet those persons are so joined
and united, that he which denieth one of them hath in him
none of them. Yea, whosoever denieth this Trinity is pronounced to be antichrist : for he denieth God, which is one
in Trinity and three in Unity ; and so consequently confounding or taking away the properties of God, he denieth God to
be such a one as he is in very deed.

Now I suppose that these so many and so manifest testimonies do suffice the godly ; for they believe the scriptures,
and do not over-curiously pry into the majesty of God, being
content with those things alone wherein it hath pleased God
of his goodness to appear and shine to us mortal men. Some
there are which do their endeavour by certain parables or
similitudes to shadow this matter ; that is to say, to shew how
the three persons are said to be distinguished, and yet notwithstanding to be one God. But in all the things that God hath
made (as I did admonish you in the beginning of this treatise)
there is nothing which can properly be likened to the nature
of God : neither are there any words in the mouth of men
that can properly be spoken of it : neither are there any
similitudes of man's invention that can rightly and squarely
agree with the divine Essence. And St Basil, disputing
de Ousia et Hypostasi, saith : "It cannot be that the comparisons of examples should in all points be like to those
things, to the use whereof the examples do serve[7]." Thou
mayest say that injury is done to the majesty of God, if it be
compared with mortal things. But for because the holy scripture doth not a little condescend and attemper itself to our

The mystery of the Trinity is shadowed by simili- tudes.

[6 unctio autem, Lat. ; and the anointing.]

[7 Οὐ γὰρ δυνατόν ἐστι διὰ πάντων ἐφαρμοσθῆναι τὸ ἐν τοῖς ὑποδείγμασι
θεωρούμενον τοῖς πρὸς ἃ ἡ τῶν ὑποδειγμάτων χρεία παραλαμβάνεται.—Basil.
Opp. Epist. 38. Tom. III. p. 169. Paris. 1839.]

infirmity, I will put a similitude, although in very deed much
unlike, which is usually taken and commonly used. Behold
the sun and the beams that come from it, and then the heat
that proceedeth from them both. As the sun is the head-
spring of the light and the heat, so is the Father the head-
spring of the Son, who is light of light: and as of the sun
and the beams together the heat doth come, so of the Father
and the Son together the Holy Ghost proceedeth. But now
put case or imagine that the sun were such as never had
beginning, nor ever shall have ending; and should not then, I
pray you, the beams of this everlasting sun be everlasting
too? And should not the heat, which proceedeth of them
both, be everlasting, as well as they? Finally, should not the
sun be one still in essence or substance, and three by reason

*Tertullian
contra
Praxeam.*

of the three subsistences or persons? This parable of the sun
did Tertullian use, whose words, which do also contain other

*I would wish
the skilful in
the Latin
tongue to
read this
similitude in
the Latin
copy; for
though it be
here trans-
lated ad
verbum, yet
our English
tongue will
not bear it so
lively as the
Latin doth.*

similitudes, I will not be grieved to recite unto you. "I will not
doubt (saith he) to call both the stalk of a root, the brook of a
spring-head, and a beam of the sun, by the name of a son;
for every original is a parent, and everything that issueth of
that original is a son: much more then the Word of God
(may be called a Son), which even properly hath the name of
Son: and yet neither is the stalk separated from the root, nor
the brook from the spring-head, nor the beam from the sun;
no more is the Word separated from God. Therefore according to the fashion of these examples I profess that I say there
are two, God and his Word, the Father and his Son. For the
root and the stalk are two things, but joined in one; and
the spring-head and the brook are two kinds, but undivided;
and the sun and the beams are two forms, but both cleaving
the one to the other. Everything that cometh of anything
must needs be second to that out of which it cometh, and
yet it is not separated from that from which it proceedeth.
But where a second is, there are two; and where a third is,
there are three. For the third is the Spirit of God and the
Son; even as the third from the root is the fruit of the stalk,
the third from the spring-head is the river of the brook, and
the third from the sun is the heat of the beam: yet none of
these is alienated from the matrix, of which they take the
properties that they have. So the Trinity, descending by
annexed and linked degrees from the Father, doth not make

against the monarchy*, and doth defend the œconomical state,
that is, the mystery of the dispensation. Understand everywhere that I profess this rule, wherein I testify that the
Father, the Son, and the Holy Ghost, are unseparated one
from another; and so thou shalt know how everything is
spoken[1]." And so forth; for all these are the words of
Tertullian, who flourished in Africa, not long after the age of
the apostles.

But letting pass the parables, similitudes, or comparisons The certainty
of the doc-
of man's invention, let us stedfastly believe the evident word trine touch-
ing the
of God. What man's capacity cannot attain unto, that let Trinity.
faith hold fast. What the sacred scriptures declare unto us,
what Christ in his flesh did teach us, what was by so many
miracles confirmed for our sakes[2], what the Spirit of God in
the true church doth tell us, that must be thought more true
and certain than that which is proved by a thousand demonstrations, or that which all thy senses are able to conceive.
Paul denieth that he would hear an angel, if he should speak
anything contrary to the gospel of Christ. Yea surely, it is
a prank of arrogant foolishness, to doubt of the things that
are in the scriptures with so great authority laid forth and
taught us: but it is a greater madness, if a man will not

[1 Nec dubitaverim filium dicere et radicis fruticem, et fontis
fluvium, et solis radium; quia omnis origo parens est, et omne quod
ex origine profertur progenies est: multo magis Sermo Dei, qui etiam
proprie nomen filii accepit: nec frutex tamen a radice, nec fluvius a
fonte, nec radius a sole discernitur, sicut nec a Deo Sermo. Igitur,
secundum horum exemplorum formam, profiteor me duos dicere, Deum
et Sermonem ejus, Patrem et Filium ipsius. Nam et radix et frutex
duæ res sunt, sed conjunctæ; et fons et flumen duæ species sunt, sed
indivisæ; et sol et radius duæ formæ sunt, sed cohærentes. Omne
quod prodit ex aliquo, secundum sit ejus necesse est de quo prodit;
non ideo tamen est separatum. Secundus autem ubi est, duo sunt:
et tertius ubi est, tres sunt. Tertius enim est Spiritus a Deo et Filio,
sicut tertius a radice, fructus ex frutice; et tertius a fonte, rivus ex
flumine; et tertius a sole, apex ex radio; nihil tamen a matrice alienatur, a qua proprietates suas ducit. Ita trinitas, per consertos et con-
nexos gradus a Patre decurrens, et monarchiæ nihil obstrepit, et οἰκονομίας statum protegit. Hanc me regulam professum, qua inseparatos
ab alterutro Patrem et Filium et Spiritum testor, tene ubique: et ita,
quid quomodo dicatur, agnosces.—Tertull. adv. Prax. capp. 8 and 9,
pp. 157, 158.]

[2 for our sakes, not in Lat.]

believe the oracles of God for none other cause but for that
our understanding cannot attain to the knowledge of all
things, when as nevertheless we know that our understanding
is naturally blind and hateth God. Among philosophers he
is counted an impudent fellow which rejecteth the authority
of any notable and approved writer. It was enough to persuade the scholars of Pythagoras for a man to say to them,
αὐτὸς ἔφη, "he said it." And then dareth a Christian seek
starting-holes, and jangle about asking of curious questions,
when it is said unto him, 'God said it, and taught thee to
believe it?' No man doubteth of the king's letters patents,
if so be the seal be acknowledged: therefore what a folly is
it to doubt of the divine testimonies, which are so evident, and
firmly sealed with the Spirit of God!

The sum of things to be believed concerning the Trinity.

Wherefore, that I may here recapitulate and briefly express
the principal sum of this our exposition, I will recite unto you,
dearly beloved, the words of the holy father Cyril, which are
to be found *Libro in Joan.* IX. cap. 30, in the sense following: "True faith is in God the Father, and in the Son, not
simply, but incarnate, and in the Holy Ghost. For the holy
and consubstantial Trinity is distinguished by the differences
of names, that is, by the properties of the persons. For the
Father is the Father, and not the Son: and the Son is the
Son, and not the Father: and the Holy Ghost is the Holy
Spirit proper to the Father and the Son. For the substance
of the Deity is all one, or the same: wherefore we preach
not three, but one God. Therefore we must believe in
God; but, distinctly and more fully expounding our faith, we
must so believe, that we may refer the same glorification to
every person. For there is no difference of faith. For we
ought not to have a greater faith in the Father than in the
Son, and in the Holy Ghost; but the measure and manner of
it must be one and the same, equally consisting in each of the
three persons: so that by this means we may confess the
unity of nature in the trinity of persons. This faith must
firmly be grounded in our minds, which is in the Father, and in
the Son, (and the Son, I say, even after that he was made
man,) and in the Holy Ghost[1]." Thus much out of Cyril.

[1 Δεῖ γὰρ πιστεύειν τοὺς οἵγε φρονοῦσιν ὀρθῶς, εἴς γε Θεὸν πατέρα,
καὶ οὐχ ἁπλῶς εἰς υἱόν, ἀλλὰ καὶ ἐνανθρωπήσαντα, καὶ εἰς τὸ πνεῦμα τὸ
ἅγιον. ἡ μὲν γὰρ ἁγία τε καὶ ὁμοούσιος τριὰς καὶ ταῖς τῶν ὀνομάτων δια-

Now all these points shall be thoroughly confirmed with more full testimonies, when we come once to prove the divinity of the Son of God, and of the Holy Ghost; which I mean to reserve till time convenient.

But let no[2] man think that this belief of the unity and trinity of the Godhead was either invented by the fathers or bishops of the churches, or first of all preached by the apostles immediately upon Christ his death and ascension[3]. For after the same manner that I have hitherto declared unto you, even from the beginning of the world did all the holy patriarchs, prophets, and elect people of God believe and ground their faith. Although I deny not but that the mystery of the Trinity was more clearly expounded to the world by Christ, yet is it evident by some undoubted testimonies, which I will add anon, that the mystery of the Trinity was very well known unto the patriarchs and the prophets. But first by the way I will admonish you, that the holy patriarchs and prophets of God did hold themselves content with the bare revelation and word of God, not raising curious questions about the unity and trinity of God. They did clearly understand that there is one God, the Father of all, the only Saviour and author of all goodness; and that without or beside him there is none other God at all. And they again did evidently see, that the Son of God, that promised Seed, hath all things common with the Father: for they did most plainly hear that he is called the Saviour, and is the Redeemer,

The mystery of the Trinity was very well known to the patriarchs and prophets.

φοραῖς καὶ τῶν προσώπων ποιότησί τε καὶ ἰδιότησι διαστέλλεται· πατὴρ γάρ ἐστιν ὁ πατήρ, καὶ οὐχ υἱός, καὶ υἱὸς πάλιν ὁ υἱός, καὶ οὐ πατήρ, καὶ πνεῦμα τὸ πνεῦμα τὸ ἅγιον ἴδιον τῆς θεότητος· καὶ εἰς τὸν αὐτὸν τῆς οὐσίας ἀνακεφαλαιοῦται λόγον, οὐ τρεῖς ἡμῖν, ἀλλ᾽ ἕνα Θεὸν ἐπιγράφουσα. πλὴν εὐδιαστόλως φημὶ δεῖν ἡμᾶς ποιεῖσθαι τὴν πίστιν, οὐχ ἁπλῶς λέγοντας, πιστεύομεν εἰς Θεόν, ἀλλ᾽ ἐξαπλοῦντας τὴν ὁμολογίαν, καὶ ἑκάστῳ προσώπῳ τὸν αὐτὸν τῆς δόξης ἀνατιθέντας λόγον. διαφορὰ γὰρ πίστεως οὐδεμία μὲν ἐν ἡμῖν· οὐ γὰρ μείζων μὲν ἐν ἡμῖν ἡ πίστις ἐν πατρὶ, ἐλάττων δὲ ἐν υἱῷ, ἢ καὶ ἐν τῷ ἁγίῳ πνεύματι· ἀλλ᾽ εἷς τε καὶ αὐτὸς τῆς ὁμολογίας ὅρος τε καὶ τρόπος διὰ τριῶν ἐρχόμενος ὀνομάτων ἐν ἴσῳ τῷ μέτρῳ, ἵνα πρὸς ἑνότητα φύσεως καὶ διὰ τούτων ἰοῦσα φαίνηται πάλιν ἡ ἁγία τριὰς, ἀκατηγόρητός τε παντελῶς ἡ περὶ αὐτὴν διαλάμπουσα δόξα, καὶ ἐν ταῖς ἡμετέραις ὁρᾶτο ψυχαῖς εἰς πατέρα καὶ εἰς υἱὸν ἡ πίστις, καὶ ὅτε γέγονεν ἄνθρωπος, καὶ εἰς τὸ πνεῦμα τὸ ἅγιον.—Cyril. Opp. Lib. IX. in Joann. Tom. IV. p. 762. Lutet. 1638.]

[2 let a man, an error in all the editions.]

[3 Christi seculo, Lat.]

from whom all good things do proceed and are bestowed upon the faithful; whereby now it was easy for them to gather that the Father and the Son are one God, although they differ in properties. For insomuch as they were assuredly certain that the damnable doctrine of the plurality of gods did spring from the devil, they did not worship many but one God, whom notwithstanding they did believe to consist of a trinity of persons. For Moses, the undoubted[1] servant of God, in the very first verse of his first book saith: "In the beginning (*creavit Dii*) God created heaven and earth." He joineth here a verb of the singular number to a noun of the plural number, not to make incongruity of speech, but to note the mystery of the Trinity. For the sense is as if he should have said, That God[2] which doth consist of three persons created heaven and earth. For a little after God, consulting with himself about the making[3] of man, doth say, "Let us make in our image." Lo, here he saith, "Let us make," and not, "Let me make," or, "I will make." And again he saith, "In our image," and not, "In my image." But lest any man should think that this consultation was had with the angels, let him hear what God himself doth say in Esay: "I the Lord," saith he, "make all things, and stretch out the heavens alone of myself," (that is, of mine own power, without any help or fellow with me,) "and set the earth fast." Therefore the Father consulted with the Son, by whom also he created the world. And again, lest any man should think, as the Jews object, that these things were after the order and custom of men spoken of God in the plural number for honour's sake and worship, thou mayest hear what followeth in the end of the third chapter: "Behold, this man is become as one of us, in knowing good and evil." Now here, by *enallage* he putteth these words, "is become," for "shall become," or, "shall happen:" so that his meaning is as if he should have said, "Behold, the same shall happen to Adam that shall come to one of us," that is, to the Son; to wit, that he should have trial of good and evil, that is, that he should feel sundry fortunes, namely sickness, calamities, and death, and (as the proverb is) should feel both sweet and sour; for that is the lot or condition

Gen. i.

As who should say, Gods created, respecting the trinity of the Godhead.

[Isai. xliv. 24.]

[1 eximius, Lat.]   [2 Deus ille trinus, Lat.—P.]
[3 de producendo vel condendo, Lat.]

of man.   But the Son being incarnate for us, not the Father
nor the Holy Ghost, was found in shape as a man, and had
trial of sundry fortunes and of death: which was foretold to
Adam, as it is manifest, for consolation's sake, and not in the
way of mockage.   For as the good Lord did with a garment
strengthen the body of our first parent[4] against the unsea-
sonableness of the air, when for his sin he purposed to banish
him out of paradise; so did he comfort and cheer up his
sorrowful mind with a full example of the Son's incarnation
and suffering.   And when he had so armed him in body and
soul, he casteth him out of the garden of felicity into a
careful and miserable exile.

There are in every place many examples of this matter
like unto this.   For Abraham saw three; but with them three   Gen. xviii.
he talked as with one, and worshipped one.   And, "The Lord
rained upon Sodom and Gomorrha brimstone and fire from   Gen. xix.
the Lord out of heaven, and overthrew those cities."   But
lest any man should interpret it and say, The Lord rained
from the Lord, that is, from heaven; he himself doth presently add, "From heaven."   For as the Father created all
things by the Son, so doth he by him preserve all things,
and doth even still by him work all things.

Next after Moses, the notablest prophet, David, in his
Psalm[5] doth say: "By the word of the Lord were the hea-   Psal. xxxiii.
vens made, and all the hosts of them by the breath of his
mouth."   So here thou hearest that there is one Lord, in
whom is the Word and the Spirit, both distinguished but not
separated.   For the Lord made the heavens, but by the
Word: and the whole furniture of heaven doth stand by the
breath of the mouth of the Lord.   The same David saith:
"The Lord said to my Lord, Sit thou on my right hand,   Psal. cx.
until I make thine enemies thy footstool."   Note, that in another place the same David doth flatly say, that beside the
Lord there is none other: and yet here again he doth as
plainly say, "The Lord said to my Lord;" meaning the
Father, who had placed the Son, which was David's Lord,
at his right hand in heaven.

Out of Esay may be gathered very many testimonies;
but the notablest of all the rest is that which Matthew the

[4 protoplastorum, Lat.; parents.]
[5 Psalmis, Lat.; Psalms, ed. 1577.]

Isai. xlii.
Matth. xii.
apostle citeth in these words : " Behold, my Son whom I have chosen; my beloved, in whom my soul is pleased : I will put my Spirit upon him, &c." With this agreeth that which
Isai. lxi.
Luke iv.
Luke citeth, saying : " The Spirit of the Lord upon me, because he hath anointed me, to preach the gospel to the poor hath he sent me, &c." In these testimonies here thou hast the Father, the Son, and the Holy Ghost. A few out of many ; for I do not covet[1] to turn over the whole scriptures of the old Testament.

The mystery of the Trinity must not be joined with curious disputations. So then this faith, wherewith we do believe in God, the Father, the Son, and the Holy Ghost, we have received of God himself, being delivered unto us by the prophets and patriarchs, but most evidently of all declared by the Son of God himself, our Lord Jesus Christ, and his holy apostles : whereupon now we do easily gather, wherefore it is that all the sincere bishops or ministers of the churches, together with the whole church of Christ, have ever since the apostles' time with so firm a consent maintained and had this faith in honour. It were verily a detestable impiety to leave this catholic and true rule of faith, and to choose and follow one newly invented. There are even at this day extant most godly and learned books of[2] ecclesiastical writers, wherein they have declared and defended this catholic faith by the holy scriptures against all wicked and blasphemous heretics. There are extant sundry symbols of faith, but all tending to one end, set forth and published in many synodal assemblies of bishops and fathers. There is at this day extant, learned and rehearsed of the universal Church and all the members thereof, both learned and unlearned, and of every sex and age, that creed commonly called the Apostles' Creed ; wherein we profess nothing else than that which we have hitherto declared, namely, that we believe in one God, to wit, the Father, the Son, and the Holy Ghost. And for because this consent of all the saints concerning this true faith hath been ever since the beginning of the world so sure and firm, it was very well and godly provided of ancient kings and princes, that no man should once dare be so bold either to call into doubt, or with curious questions and disputations to deface or make intricate, this belief concerning the unity and

[1 affectamus, Lat.]
[2 multorum, Lat.; of many.]

trinity of the almighty God[3].   He of old among the Israel- Exod. xix.
ites was stricken through and slain, which passed beyond the
bounds that the Lord had limited out: and we also have
certain appointed bounds about the knowledge of God, which
to pass is hurtful unto us; yea, it is punished with assured
death.

God grant that we may truly know, and religiously wor- The con-
clusion.
ship, the high, excellent, and mighty God, even so, and such,
as himself[4] is. For hitherto I have, as simply, sincerely, and
briefly as I could, discoursed of the ways and means how to
know God, which is in substance one, and three in persons:
and yet we acknowledge and do freely confess, that in all
this treatise hitherto there is nothing spoken worthy of or
comparable to his unspeakable majesty. For the eternal,
excellent, and mighty God is greater than all majesty, and
than all the eloquence of all men; so far am I from thinking
that I by my words[5] do in one jot come near unto his excellency. But I do humbly beseech the most merciful Lord,
that he will vouchsafe of his inestimable goodness and liberality to enlighten in us all the understanding of our minds
with sufficient knowledge of his name, through Jesus Christ
our Lord and Saviour. Amen.

THAT GOD IS THE CREATOR OF ALL THINGS, AND GOVERNETH ALL THINGS BY HIS PROVIDENCE: WHERE MENTION IS ALSO MADE OF THE GOODWILL OF GOD TO USWARD, AND OF PREDESTINATION.

THE FOURTH SERMON.

DEARLY beloved, it remaineth now for me in this day's
sermon, for a conclusion to that which I have hitherto spoken
concerning God, briefly to add somewhat of that creation or
work of God, whereby he, being the maker of all things,
hath to mankind's commodity wholesomely created all things,
both visible and invisible, and doth now as always most

[3 See Vol. I. p. 34.]   [4 he himself, ed. 1577.]
[5 mea infantia, Lat.]

wisely govern and order the same. For by so doing we shall obtain no small knowledge of God; and many things shall be more openly laid forth unto us, which we in our last treatise did but touch and away[1]. In the searching out, considering, and setting forth of the creation of the whole and the parts thereof, all the diligence of all wise men[2] hath been set on work, doth labour, and shall be troubled so long as this world endureth. For what is he, though he were the wisest, the cunningest, and diligentest writer of the natural history, that leaveth not many things untouched for the posterity to labour in, and beat their brains about? Or what is he at this day, which, although he use the aid and industry of most learned writers, is not compelled to wonder at more and greater things than either they ever did, or he ever shall, attain unto you[3]? The most wise Lord will always have witty men, that are enriched with heavenly gifts, to be always occupied and evermore exercised in the searching out and setting forth the secrets of nature and of the creation. But we do simply by faith conceive, that the worlds were made of nothing, and of no heap of matter[4], of God through the Word of God; and that it doth consist by the power of the Holy Ghost, or

Psal. xxxiii
Heb. xi. Spirit of God. For so did king David, and Paul the teacher of the Gentiles, both believe and teach. But although the order of the whole, and the manner of the creation, cannot be knit up or declared in few words, yet will I do my endeavour to utter somewhat, by which the sum of things may partly appear to the diligent considerer.

And here I choose rather to use another man's words than mine own; especially because I suppose this matter cannot be more lively expressed than Tertullian, in his book *De Trinitate*,

The history of the creation contained in few words. setteth it forth as followeth: "God hath hung up heaven in a lofty height; he hath made the earth massive with a low and pressed down weight; he hath poured out the seas with a loose and thin liquor; and hath planted all these, being decked

The sky and stars. and full with their proper and fit instruments. For in the firmament of heaven he hath stirred up the dawning risings

[1 parcius delibavimus, Lat.]

[2 externorum domesticorumque sapientum, Lat.; of wise men both without and within the church.]

[3 So in all the editions; assequatur, Lat.]

[4 præjacente materia, Lat.]

of the sun; he hath filled the circle of the glittering moon for
the comfort of the night with monthly increasings of the world;
and he lighteneth the beams of the stars with sundry gleams
of the twinkling light" (the night, he meaneth); "and he would
that all these should by appointed courses go about the compass
of the world, to make to mankind days, months, years, signs,
times, and commodities. In the earth also he hath lift up *The earth.*
high hills aloft, depressed down the valleys below, laid the
fields out evenly, and profitably ordained flocks of beasts for
sundry services and uses of men. He hath made the massive
oaks of the woods for the behoof of man; he hath brought
forth fruits to feed them[5] withal; he hath unlocked the mouths
of springs, and poured them into running rivers. After all
which necessary commodities, because he would also procure
somewhat for the delight of the eyes, he clad them all with
sundry colours of goodly flowers, to the pleasure and delight
of those that beheld him[6]. In the sea also, although for the *The sea.*
greatness and profit thereof it were very wonderful, he framed
many sorts of living creatures; some of a mean, and some
of a monstrous bigness; which do by the variety of the
workmanship give special notes of the workman's wit. And
yet not being therewithal content, lest peradventure the rage
and course of the waters should with the damage of the
earth's inhabitants break out and occupy another element,
he closed up the water's limits within the shores; that thereby,
when the raging waves and foaming water did rise up from
the depth and channel, it might turn into itself again, and
not pass beyond the bounds appointed, keeping still the prescribed course; to the end also that man might be so much
the more ready to keep God's laws, when he perceived that
even the very elements did observe and keep them. Last of *Man.*
all he setteth man to be lord over the world; whom he made
to the likeness and image of God: to whom he gave reason,
wit, and wisdom, that he might imitate God; whose body,
although it were made of earth, was yet notwithstanding inspired with the substance of the heavenly breath and Spirit
of God: to whom when he had put all things in subjection,
he would have him alone to be free without subjection. And
lest that liberty, being let loose at random, might come into

[5 So ed. 1584 also: but ed. 1577 has, fruit to feed him.]
[6 them, ed. 1577.]

peril again, he gave a commandment; by the means of which commandment it could not be said that evil was out of hand or by and by present in the fruit, but should then be in it, when once he perceived in the will of man the contempt of that commandment.   For both he ought to be free, lest the image of God should seem to be bound undecently; and also a law was to be given, lest at any time the unbridled liberty should break out to the contempt of him that gave the liberty: that he might consequently receive either due rewards of obedience, or merits of punishment for disobedience, having that given him to whether part he was willing by the motion of the mind for to incline; whereby the envy of mortality doth return to him who, when by obedience he might have escaped it, did yet run headlong into it, while he made too much haste to become a God," &c.   The same addeth: " In the parts above the firmament which are not now to be beheld of our mortal eyes, that first there were ordained angels; then there were ordained spiritual virtues; then there were placed thrones and powers, and many other unmeasurable spaces of the heavens; and that many works of holy things were there created[1]," &c.   Thus far Tertullian.

[1 Regula exigit veritatis, ut primo omnium credamus in Deum Patrem et Dominum omnipotentem, id est, rerum omnium per-fectissimum conditorem, qui cœlum alta sublimitate suspenderit, terram dejecta mole solidaverit, maria soluto liquore diffuderit, et hæc omnia propriis et condignis instrumentis et ornata et plena diges-serit.   Nam et in solidamento (firmamento) cœli luciferos solis ortus excitavit, lunæ candentem globum ad solatium noctis mensuris (Bul-linger read, menstruis) incrementis orbis implevit, astrorum etiam radios variis fulgoribus micantis lucis (noctem) accendit: et hæc omnia legitimis meatibus circumire totum mundi ambitum voluit, humano generi dies, menses, annos, signa, tempora, utilitatesque fac-tura.   In terris quoque altissimos montes in verticem sustulit, valles in ima dejecit, campos æqualiter stravit, animalium greges ad varias hominum servitutes utiliter instituit.   Sylvarum quoque robora humanis usibus profutura solidavit, fruges in cibum elicuit, fontium ora resera-vit et lapsuris fluminibus infudit.   Post quæ ne non etiam ipsis quoque deliciis procurasset oculorum, variis florum coloribus ad voluptatem spectantium cuncta vestivit.   In ipso quoque mari, quamvis esset et magnitudine et utilitate mirabile, multimoda animalia, nunc mediocris nunc vasti corporis, finxit, ingenium artificis de institutionis varietate testantia.   Quibus non contentus, ne forte fremitus et cursus aquarum cum dispendio possessoris humani alienum occuparet elementum, fines

Now the sum of all this is : God did by his power create of nothing heaven, earth, and the sea; which he did immediately adorn and enrich with all kinds of good things. And into this world, which taketh the name of furniture that is in it, as in a most sumptuous palace well furnished with all sort of excellent necessaries, it pleased him to bring man, to whom he did put all things in subjection : as David doth with David celebrateth the wondering and marvelling set it forth, where he saith : " O creation of the world. Lord, our governor, how excellent is thy name in all the world ! For thy glory is lift up above the heavens. Out of the mouths of very babes and sucklings hast thou ordained strength, because of thine enemies ; that thou mayest destroy the enemy and the avenger. For I will consider the heavens, even the works of thy fingers ; the moon and the stars, which thou hast ordained. What is man, that thou art so mindful of him; or the son of man, that thou hast care over him ? Thou madest him somewhat lower than the angels (or, than God); thou crownest him with glory and honour, thou madest him to have dominion over the works of thy hands. Thou hast put all things in subjection under his feet; sheep and oxen, and the beasts of the field, the fowls of the air, and the

litoribus inclusit; quo cum fremens fluctus et ex alto sinu spumans unda venisset, rursum in se rediret, nec terminos concessos excederet, servans jura præscripta : ut divinas leges tanto magis homo custodiret, quanto illas etiam elementa servassent. Post quæ hominem quoque mundo præposuit, et quidem ad imaginem Dei factum : cui mentem et rationem indidit et prudentiam, ut Deum posset imitari : cujus etsi corporis terrena primordia, cœlestis tamen et divini halitus inspirata substantia. Quæ cum omnia in servitutem illi dedisset, solum liberum esse voluit. Et ne in periculum cederet rursum soluta libertas, mandatum posuit, quo tamen non inesse malum in fructu arboris diceretur, sed futurum si forte in voluntate hominis de contemptu datæ legis præmoneretur. Nam et liber esse debuerat, ne incongruenter Dei imago serviret; et lex addenda, ne usque ad contemptum dantis libertas effrænata prorumperet : ut et præmia condigna et merita pœnarum consequenter exciperet, suum jam habens illud, quod motu mentis in alterutram partem agitare voluisset : ex quo mortalitas, invidia utique in ipsum redit, qui cum illam de obedientia posset evadere, in eandem incurrit, dum ex consilio perverso deus esse festinat... Quanquam etiam superioribus, id est, super ipsum quoque solidamentum, partibus, quæ non sunt hodie nostris contemplabiles oculis, angelos prius instituerit, spirituales virtutes digesserit, thronos potestatesque præfecerit, et alia multa cœlorum immensa spatia et sacramentorum infinita opera condiderit.—Novatian. de Trin. cap. 1. Tertul. Opp. Par. 1664.p. 707.]

fishes of the sea, which walk through the paths of the sea. O Lord, our governor, how excellent is thy name in all the world!" Psalm viii. The same again in another place doth Psal. lxxix. say: "The heavens are thine, O God, and the earth is thine; thou hast laid the foundation of the round world, and all [Psal. lxxiv. 16, 17.] that therein is." "The day is thine, and the night is thine; thou hast ordained the light[1] and the sun: thou layedst all the borders of the earth; thou hast made both summer and winter." Now who is so very a sot as that he doth not by these proofs easily gather, how great our God is; how great the power of God is; how good, rich, and liberal to man, who never deserved any such thing at his hand, our God is, which hath created so great riches, so exquisite delights, and such furniture as cannot be sufficiently praised, for man alone, and hath made them all subject, and will have them all to obey man as their lord and master?

God governeth all things. But here by the way, in the creation of the world, we have to consider the preservation and government of the whole by the same God. For neither doth the world stand and endure by any power of its own; neither do those things move and stir of their own accord, or (as we say) at all adventures, which are stirred or moved howsoever. For the Lord John v. in the gospel saith: "My Father worketh hitherto, and I Heb. i. work." And Paul saith: "God by his Son hath made the worlds, and doth rule and uphold them with the word of his Acts xvii. power." And again: "By God we live, and move, and have our Acts xiv. being." And again: "God left not himself without witness, in that he shewed his benefits from heaven, giving us rain and fruitful seasons, filling our hearts with food and gladness." And Of God's providence. Theodoret, *De Providentia*, saith: "It is a most absurd thing to say, that God hath created all things, but that he hath no care of the things which he hath made; and that his creature, as a boat destitute of a steersman, is with contrary winds tossed to and fro, and knocked and cracked upon shelves and rocks[2]." Therefore in this place we have to say some-

---

[1 lights, ed. 1577; luminaria, Lat.]

[2 Τῶν γὰρ ἄγαν ἀτοπωτάτων πεποιηκέναι μὲν αὐτὸν τὰ σύμπαντα λέγειν, ... ἀμελεῖν δὲ ὧν ἐποίησε, καὶ περιορᾶν τὴν κτίσιν, οἷόν τι σκάφος ἀνερμάτιστόν τε καὶ ἀκυβέρνητον ὑπὸ τῶν ἐναντίων ἀνέμων τῇδε κἀκεῖσε πεμπόμενον, καὶ σκοπέλοις καὶ βράχεσι προσρηγνύμενον.—Theodoret. Hæret. Fab. Lib. v. cap. 10. p. 275. Tom. iv. Lut. Par. 1642.]

what of God's providence and government: which all the
wicked, together with the epicures, do at this day[3] deny,
saying in their hearts: " Is it likely, that he that dwelleth in
heaven should regard the things on earth? And doth the
Almighty observe and mark the very smallest of words[4] and
works? He hath given to all creatures a certain inclination
and nature, which he hath made their own; and so leaveth
them now in the hand of their own counsel, that they of their
own nature may move, increase, perish, and do even what
they lust. Tush, God neither knoweth, nor doth greatly
trouble himself about these toys." Thus do the wicked reason
very wickedly: but the scripture doth expressly in many
places pronounce and prove[5], that God by his providence doth
care for and regard the state of mortal men and of all the
things that he hath made for the use of mortal men. And
therefore here it is profitable and necessary to cite some testimonies out of the holy scriptures for the proof of this argument.

David in his Psalms saith: " The Lord shall reign for Psal. cxlv.
ever, and his kingdom is a kingdom of all ages, and his
dominion from generation to generation." Lo, the kingdom
of God (saith he) is a kingdom of all ages, and his dominion
throughout all generations. Therefore God hath not only
created the world and all things that are in the world; but
doth also govern and preserve them at this day, and shall
govern and preserve them even till the end. For the same
kingly prophet, celebrating the providence of God about man
and his estate, doth say: " Thou, O Lord, knowest my down- Psal. cxxxix.
sitting and mine uprising; thou spiest out all my ways. For
there is not a word in my tongue, but thou, O Lord, dost
know it altogether. Thou hast fashioned me behind and
before, and laid thine hand upon me;" and so forth, as followeth in the hundred and thirty-ninth psalm, which psalm
doth wholly make to this purpose. With this doctrine of
David doth the testimony of Salomon agree, where he saith:
"The king's heart is in the hand of the Lord; like as the Prov. xxi.
rivers of water, he may turn it whithersoever he will. Every
man's way seemeth right in his own eyes; but the Lord
driveth[6], or ruleth, the heart." And in the gospel the Lord

[3 etiam hodie, Lat.]
[4 our words, ed. 1577; dicta et facta nostra, Lat.]
[5 imo demonstrat, Lat.]   [6 impellit, Lat.]

Matth. x.   said: "Are not two little sparrows sold for a farthing? And one of them shall not light on the ground without your Father. Yea, even all the hairs of your head are numbered."

There are besides these other evident testimonies also of the providence of God. Daniel, the wisest man of all the east, and

Dan. ii.   the most excellent prophet of God, doth say: "Wisdom and strength are the Lord's: it is he that changeth the times and seasons[1]: he taketh away kings, and setteth up kings: he giveth wisdom unto the wise, and understanding to those that understand: he revealeth the deep and secret things: he knoweth the thing that lieth in darkness; for the light dwelleth

Psal. lxxxix.   in him." Moreover, Ethan the Ezrachite saith: "Thou, Lord, rulest the raging of the sea; thou stillest the waves thereof, when they arise. Thou hast an almighty arm; thou strengthenest thy hand, and settest up thy right hand. In justice and equity is thy royal throne stablished; goodness and

Psal. civ.   faith do go before thy face." And David saith: "Of the fruit of thy works, O God, shall the earth be filled. And he bringeth forth grass for cattle, and herb for the use of man; and bread to strengthen the heart of man, and wine to make him merry." And immediately after in the same psalm: "All things do wait upon thee, that thou mayest give them their meat in due season. When thou givest it, they gather it; and when thou openest thine hand, they are filled with good. If thou hidest thy face, they are troubled; and if thou takest away their breath, they die, and are turned into their

Psal. cxlv.   dust." Again: "The Lord upholdeth all such as fall, and lifteth up all those that be down. The Lord looseth men from their fetters: the Lord giveth sight unto the blind. The

[Psal. cxlvi.]   Lord keepeth the stranger; he defendeth the fatherless and widow; and the way of the wicked he turneth upside down."

Psal. cxlvii.   "Great is our Lord, and great is his power; and of his wisdom there is none end. He telleth the number of the stars, and calleth them all by their names. He covereth the heavens with clouds, and prepareth rain for the earth. He giveth fodder unto the cattle, and meat to the young ravens that call upon him[2]. He giveth snow as wool, and scattereth the hoar frost like ashes. He casteth forth his ice like morsels: who shall abide before the face of his cold? He shall send out his word, and melt them; he shall blow with his wind, and the waters

[1 et quæ fiunt in tempore, Lat.]   [2 upon him, not in Lat.]

shall flow." And again: "I know that the Lord is great; and Psal. cxxxv.
that he is above all gods. What pleased him, that hath he
done in heaven and earth, and in the sea, and in all deep
places. He lifteth up the clouds from the ends of the world,
and turneth lightning unto rain, and bringeth the winds out
of their treasuries[3]." There are many testimonies like to
these to be seen in the thirty-eighth and thirty-ninth chapters of
the book of Job; and rifely[4] in the Psalms, and books of the
holy prophets: but these that hitherto I have recited are
sufficient enough, testifying abundantly that God by his providence doth govern this world and all things that are
therein, and especially man himself the possessor of the world,
for whom all things were made.

We do here attribute nothing to destiny, either stoical or Against Gentilism.
astrological; neither have we anything to do with that eth-
nick fortune, either good or ill. We do utterly detest philosophical disputations in this case, which are contrary to the
truth of the prophets' writings and doctrine of the apostles.
We content ourselves in the only word of God; and do therefore simply believe and teach, that God by his providence doth
govern all things, and that too according to his own good will,
just judgment, and comely order, by means most just and
equal: which means whosoever despiseth, and maketh his
boast only on[5] the bare name of God's providence, it cannot
be that he should rightly understand the effect of God's providence. They make this objection: "Because all things in
the world are done by God's providence, therefore we need
not to put in our oar[6]: we may snort idly and take our ease:
it is sufficient for us to expect the working or impelling of
God; for if he need our aid, he will, whether we will or no,
even impel us to the work which he will have to be wrought
by us." But the saints in the scripture are laid before us The saints do not
and shewed to have thought, spoken, and judged more sin- neglect good means.
cerely of God's providence. The angel doth in express words
say to Lot: "Haste thee to Zoar, and save thyself there: Gen. xix.
for I can do nothing until thou art come thither." Lo, here
by God's providence Lot with his are saved; the citizens of

[3] his treasuries, Auth. Ver.]
[4] rifely; passim, Lat.]
[5] So also ed. 1584: but ed. 1577 has *of*.]
[6] nostram industriam, Lat.]

Sodom are destroyed, and of all the cities thereabout: and yet even in the very work of his preservation Lot's labour is required, and he bidden to do his good-will to save himself. Yea, "I cannot," saith the Lord, "do anything till thou art come into Zoar." The king and prophet David doth plainly

Psal. xxxi. say, "I have hoped in thee, O Lord; I have said, Thou art my God: my days are in thy hand." And yet even he, which did wholly betake himself to the providence of God, did earnestly consider with himself, how with his diligence and industry he might deceive and escape from the layings in

1 Sam. xix. wait of Saul his father-in-law. Neither doth he despise the aid and shifts of his wife[1] Michol: he doth not reply to her again and say, "All things are done by the providence of God; therefore there needs no wiles to be wrought. The Almighty is able to take me out of the hands of our father's soldiers, or otherwise to save me by some miraculous means: let us content ourselves, and suffer God to work his will in us." He did not argue thus; but did understand that, as God's providence doth proceed in a certain order by middle means, so that it is his part to apply himself to means in the fear of God, and by all assays to do his best for his own defence[2]. St Paul doth

Acts xxiii. hear the Lord flatly saying: "As thou hast borne witness of me at Hierusalem, so must thou bear record of me at Rome." And although he did nothing doubt of the truth of God's promises, and was not ignorant of the power of God's providence; yet notwithstanding he did privily send his sister's son, which told him that the Jews had conspired to kill him, unto the tribune, to desire of him that Paul might not be brought forth at the Jews' request. Neither did he shew himself uncourteous or unthankful to the soldiers that carried him to Antipatridis, nor to the horsemen that went with him[3] to Cæsarea. Again, as he sailed in the Adriatic sea, when he was in peril of dangerous shipwreck, and that all his company

Acts xxvii. were stricken with fear, he said: "Sirs, I exhort you to be of good cheer; for there shall be no loss of any man's life among you, but[4] of the ship. For there stood by me this night the

[1] dilectæ conjugis, Lat.]

[2] omnemque movere lapidem, Lat. Erasmi Adag. Chiliad. p. 228, *experientiæ.*]

[3] inde, Lat. omitted; thence.]

[4] sed tantum, Lat.; but only.]

angel of God, whose I am and whom I serve, saying, Fear
not, Paul: thou must be brought before Cæsar; and lo, God
hath given thee all them that sail with thee. Wherefore,
sirs, be of good cheer; for I believe God, that it shall be
even as it was told me." But a while after, when the mariners
went about to leave the ship, the same Paul said to the centurion and to the soldiers: "Unless these abide in the ship, ye
cannot be saved."

Therefore means do belong to the providence of God,
by which he worketh; and therefore are they not to be
neglected. Truly, it is by God's government or providence,
that we have all these impressions* of what sort soever, *Meteors, im-
either fiery, or airy, or watery. For by the power of God, pressions or
and not by any power of their own[5], doth the air make times for
the earth fruitful, the water[6] flow and ebb again, and the earth and strange-
doth bring forth her increase. And although the saints think men to
verily, that none of all this is done for any sake of theirs[7], marvel.
because the Saviour himself in the gospel saith, "The Father Matth. v.
sendeth rain upon the just and unjust;" yet for all that they
do never forget the words of the prophet, where he saith,
"If ye will be willing and obedient, ye shall eat the good of Isai. i.
the land: but if ye be obstinate and rebellious, ye shall be
devoured with the sword: for the mouth of the Lord hath
spoken it." For the great prophet Moses, long before Esay,
had said: "If thou shalt hearken diligently unto the voice of Deut. xxviii.
the Lord thy God, to observe and do all his commandments,
all these blessings shall come upon thee. Thou shalt be
blessed in the city, and blessed in the field. Blessed shall the
fruit of thy body be, and blessed shall the fruit of the ground[8]
be. The Lord shall open heaven unto thee, and give rain to
thy land in due season. But if thou wilt not hearken unto
the voice of the Lord thy God, to observe and do his commandments, then all these curses shall come upon thee.
Cursed shalt thou be in the city, and cursed in the field. The
heaven above thy head shall be brass; and the Lord shall
smite thee with many plagues," &c. And histories bear
record, that all these things happened to the people of God

[5 neque temere, Lat. omitted; nor of chance.]
[6 So also 1584: but ed. 1577, *waters*, and Lat. aquæ.]
[7 propter sua merita, Lat.; for any merits' sake of theirs, ed. 1577.]
[8 So also ed. 1584: but ed. 1577, thy ground.]

even as they are here foretold; and that too, not without the providence of the Lord their God. All good successes and prosperity are the good blessings of God; and on the other side, all calamities and adversities are the curses of God. Therefore hereupon the saints do gather, that men's affairs and state are wholly governed by God's providence, so yet that they must not therefore sit (as we say) with their hands in their bosoms idly, and neglect good means; but rather watchfully and diligently walk by the grace of God in the ways and means, or precepts and ordinances, of the Lord. For the providence of God doth not disturb the order of things; it doth not abrogate the offices of life, nor labour and industry; it doth not take [away] a just dispensation[1] and obedience: but by these things it worketh the health of those men which do through the help of God religiously apply themselves to the decrees, purpose, or working of the Lord; to whom they do rightly ascribe what good soever doth chance or betide them; imputing to man's corruption, to our own unskilfulness, and to our sins, what evil soever doth happen unto us. Therefore the saints acknowledge, that although wars, plagues, and divers other calamities do by God's providence afflict mortal men, yet notwithstanding that the causes thereof do arise of nothing else than the sins of man. For God is good, which wisheth us rather well than evil: yea, oftentimes he of his goodness turneth our evil purposes unto good ends; as is to be seen by the history of Joseph in the book of Genesis.

God's good-will is learned by his providence.

Truly, upon the earnest consideration of God's providence all the godly sort do gather, that their good God wisheth all well[2] unto man. For he hath a great care over us, not in great things only, but also in the smallest. He knoweth the number of the days of our life. In his sight are all our members, as well within as without. For the Lord in the gospel saith, that "all the hairs of our head are numbered." He by his providence defendeth us from all manner diseases and imminent perils. He feedeth, refresheth, and preserveth us: for as he made all creatures for man's health and behoof, so doth he preserve and apply them to man's good and commodity.

[1 œconomiam, Lat.]
[2 So also ed. 1584: but ed. 1577, wisheth well.]

The doctrine of the foreknowledge and predestination of God, which hath a certain likeness[3] with his providence, doth no less comfort the godly worshippers of God. They call foreknowledge that knowledge in God, whereby he knoweth all things before they come to pass, and seeth even present all things that are, have been, and shall be. For to the knowledge of God all things are present; nothing is past, nothing is to come. And the predestination of God is the eternal decree of God, whereby he hath ordained either to save or destroy men; a most certain end of life and death being appointed unto them. Whereupon also it is elsewhere called a fore-appointment[4]. Touching these points some have diversely disputed; and many verily, curiously and contentiously[5] enough; and in such sort surely, that not only the salvation of souls, but the glory of God also, with the simple sort is endangered. The religious searchers or interpreters of the scriptures confess, that here nothing is to be permitted to man's wit; but that we must simply and wholly hang upon whatsoever the scripture hath pronounced[6]. And therefore these words of St Paul are continually before their eyes and in their minds: "O the depth of the riches of the wisdom and knowledge of God! how unsearchable (or incomprehensible) are his judgments, and his ways past finding out! For who hath known the mind of the Lord? or who was his counsellor? or who hath given unto him first, and he shall be recompensed?" They never forget the admonition of the most wise man, Jesus Syrach, saying: "Seek not out the things that are too hard for thee; neither search after things which are too mighty for thee: but what God hath commanded thee, think thou always thereupon, and be not too curious in many of his works; for it is not needful for thee to see with thine eyes the things that be secret." In the mean time truly, they do not contemn neither yet neglect those things which it hath pleased God by the open scriptures to reveal to his servants touching this matter.

Of God's foreknowledge there are many testimonies, especially in the prophecy of Esay, chap. xli. and in the

Of God's predestination, or fore-appointment.

Rom. xi.

Ecclus. iii.

[3 cognationem, Lat.]   [4 præfinitio, Lat.]   [5 spinosa, Lat.]

[6 agnoscunt modum, ut in rebus omnibus, ita in his imprimis, servandum; Lat. omitted; they acknowledge that, as in all things, so in these matters especially, moderation is to be kept.]

chapters following; whereby also the Lord doth declare that he is the true God. Furthermore, God by his eternal and unchangeable counsel hath fore-appointed who are[1] to be saved, and who are to be condemned. Now the end or the decree of life and death is short and manifest to all the godly. The end of predestination, or fore-appointment, is Christ, the Son of God the Father. For God hath ordained and decreed to save all, how many soever have communion and fellowship with Christ, his only-begotten Son; and to destroy or condemn all, how many soever have no part in the communion or fellowship of Christ, his only Son. Now the faithful verily have fellowship with Christ, and the unfaithful are strangers from Christ. For Paul in his Epistle to the Ephesians saith: "God hath chosen us in Christ, before the foundations of the world were laid, that we should be holy and without blame before him through love: who hath predestinate us into his sons[2] through Jesus Christ into himself, according to the good pleasure of his will; that the glory of his grace may be praised, wherewith he is pleased with us[3] in his beloved." Lo, God hath chosen us; and he hath chosen us before the foundations of the world were laid; yea, he hath chosen us, that we should be without blame, that is, to be heirs of eternal life: howbeit, in Christ, by and through[4] Christ hath he chosen us. And yet again more plainer: he hath "predestinate us," saith he, "to adopt us into his sons," but by Christ; and that too hath he done freely, to the intent that to his divine grace glory might be given. Therefore whosoever are in Christ are chosen and elected: for John the apostle saith: "Whoso hath the Son hath life; whoso hath not the Son of God, hath not life." With the doctrine of the apostles agreeth that also of the gospel. For in the gospel the Lord saith: "This is the will of him that sent me, the Father; that every one which seeth the Son, and believeth in him, should have everlasting life: and I will raise him up in the last day." Lo, this is the

Ephes. i.

1 John v.

John vi.

[1 debeant, Lat.; who ought.]

[2 ut adoptaret in filios, Lat.]

[3 placatus est nobis, Lat. ἐχαρίτωσεν significat, gratificavit, sibi caros, gratos, ac dilectos reddidit, adeoque et placatus est. Bulling. Comment. in Eph. i. 6. See Vol. I. p. 96, note 1.]

[4 per vel propter Christum, Lat.; through or for the sake of Christ.]

will or eternal decree of God, saith he, that in the Son by faith
we should be saved.   Again, on the contrary part, touching
those that are predestinate to death, the Lord saith: "He John iii.
that believeth not is condemned already, because he hath
not believed in the name of the only-begotten Son of God.
And this is the condemnation, that light is come into the
world, and men have loved darkness more than light." There- Who is
                                                            elected and
fore, if thou ask me whether thou art elected to life, or pre- predestinate
                                                            to life.
destinate to death; that is, whether thou art of the number
of them that are to be damned, or that are to be saved;
I answer simply out of the scripture, both of the evangelists
and the apostles: If thou hast communion or fellowship with
Christ, thou art predestinate to life, and thou art of the
number of the elect and chosen: but if thou be a stranger
from Christ, howsoever otherwise thou seem to flourish in
virtues, thou art predestinate to death, and foreknowledged,
as they say, to damnation.   Higher and deeper I will not
creep into the seat of God's counsel.   And here I rehearse
again the former testimonies of scripture: "God hath predestinate us, to adopt us into his sons through Jesus Christ.
This is the will of God, that whoso believeth in the Son
should live; and whoso believeth not should die."   Faith
therefore is a most assured sign that thou art elected; and
whiles thou art called to the communion of Christ, and art
taught faith, the most loving God declareth towards thee his
election and good-will.

    The simpler sort, verily, are greatly tempted and exceed- A sore
                                                            temptation in
ingly troubled with the question of election.   For the devil this case.
goeth about to throw into their minds the hate of God, as
though he envied us our salvation, and had appointed and
ordained us to death.   That he may the more easily persuade this unto us, he laboureth tooth and nail wickedly to
enfeeble and overthrow our faith; as though our salvation
were doubtful, which leaneth and is stayed upon the uncertain[5]
election of God.   Against these fiery weapons the servants
of God do arm their hearts with cogitations and[6] comforts
of this sort fetched out of the scripture:

    God's predestination is not stayed or stirred with any

[5 So ed. 1577, rightly; incertæ Dei electioni, Lat.; but ed. 1584
and 1587, certain.]

[6 adeoque, Lat.; and so with.]

worthiness or unworthiness of ours; but of the mere grace and mercy of God the Father, it respecteth Christ alone. And because our salvation doth stay only upon him, it cannot but be most certain. For they are wrong, that think those that are to be saved to life are predestinate of God for the merit's sake, or good works, which God did foresee in them. For notably saith the apostle Paul: "He hath chosen us in Christ into himself, according to the good pleasure of his will, that the glory of his grace might be praised." And again: "It is not in him that willeth, nor in him that runneth, but in God that sheweth mercy." Again: "God hath saved us, and called us with an holy calling, not according to our works, but according to his own purpose and grace, which was given unto us through Christ Jesus before the world was, but is now made manifest by the appearing of our Lord Jesus Christ." Freely therefore, of his mere mercy, not for our deserts, but for Christ's sake, and not but in Christ, hath he chosen us, and for Christ's sake doth embrace us, because he is our Father and a lover of men. Of whom also speaketh the prophet David: "The Lord is full of compassion and mercy, slow to anger, and of great kindness. And as a father hath compassion on his children, so hath the Lord compassion on them that fear him: for he knoweth whereof we be made, and remembereth that we are but dust." Moreover, in the prophet Esay we read: "Can a woman forget her child, and not have compassion on the son of her womb? Though she should forget, yet will I not forget thee." Truly, in Christ, the only-begotten Son of God exhibited unto us, God the Father hath declared what great store he setteth by us. Thereupon doth the apostle gather: "Who spared not his Son, but gave him for us all, how can it be that he should not also with him give us all things?" What thing therefore should we not reckon upon and promise ourselves from so beneficial a Father? For thou canst not complain that he will not give unto thee his Son, or that he is not thine, who, as the apostle saith, was given for us all. Moreover, the Lord himself, crying out in the gospel, saith: "Come unto me, all ye that labour and are heavy laden, and I will refresh you." And again to his disciples: "Go ye into all the world, and preach the gospel to every creature. He that shall believe, and be baptized, shall be saved." Where-

[Ephes. i. 4—6.]

[Rom. ix. 16.]

[2 Tim. i. 9, 10.]

Psal. ciii.

Isai. xlix.

Rom. viii.

Matth. xi.

Mark xvi.

upon also Paul saith: "God our Saviour will that all men 1 Tim. ii. shall be saved, and come unto the knowledge of the truth." In old times long ago it was said to Abraham: "In thy Gen. xxii. Seed shall all the tribes (or nations) of the earth be blessed." And Joel saith: "And it shall be, that whosoever shall call Joel ii. upon the name of the Lord shall be saved." The which Peter also hath repeated in the Acts, chapter ii.; and Paul to the Romans, chapter x. Esay also saith: "We have all Isai. liii. gone astray like sheep; we have turned every one to his own way: and the Lord hath laid upon him the iniquities of us all." And therefore durst St Paul say: "As by the offence Rom. v. of one the fault came on all men to condemnation; even so also by the justification of one the benefit abounded[1] towards all men, to the justification of life." Therefore the Lord is read in the gospel to have received sinners and publicans with outstretched arms and embracings, adding moreover these words: "I came to seek that which was lost. Neither Matth. ix. came I to call the righteous, but sinners to repentance." All Luke xix. which sayings do hitherto belong, that, being more narrowly weighed, they might confirm and establish us of God's good-will towards us, who in Christ hath chosen us to salvation: which salvation, truly, cannot but be most certain, and by all means undoubted; especially for that the Lord himself in the gospel saith: "My sheep hear my voice, and I know them, and they John x. follow me: and I give unto them eternal life; and they shall never perish, neither shall any pluck them out of my hand," &c.

I know what here again doth sting and grieve[2] the minds Of the drawing of of many. "The chosen sheep," say they, "of Christ, do know those that are Christ's voice; and, being endued with a stedfast faith, stick predestinate to life. in Christ inseparably, since they have felt that drawing, whereof the Lord speaketh in the gospel: 'No man cometh John vi. to me, unless my Father draw him:' as for me, as I feel no such manner of drawing, so do I not with a full and perfect faith stick in the Son of God." First of all, verily, true faith is required of the elect: for the elect are called; and being called, they receive their calling by faith, and frame themselves like him that called them[3]. "He that believeth not is already

---

[1 propagatur bonum, Lat.; and Bibl. Lat. Tigur. 1544, and Erasmus' version.]

[2 angat, Lat.; Bullinger's one word.]

[3 se accommodant vocanti, Lat.]

condemned." Whereupon also Paul saith: "God is the Saviour of all men, specially of the faithful." Furthermore, unless we be drawn of the heavenly Father, we cannot believe. And we must be very careful, lest we, conceiving vain opinions of that divine drawing, neglect the drawing itself. God verily drew Paul violently, but he doth not draw all unto him by the hair. There are also other ways of drawing, by which God draweth man unto him; but he doth not draw him like a stock or a block. The apostle Paul saith: "Faith cometh by hearing, and hearing by the word of God." God therefore doth then draw thee, when he preacheth unto thee the gospel by his servants; when he toucheth thy heart; when he stirreth thee to prayer, whereby thou mayest call and cry for his grace and assistance, his enlightening and drawing. When thou feelest these things in thy mind, I would not wish thee to look for another drawing: despise not thou grace offered, but use it whiles time present serveth, and pray for the increase of grace. For to greater and perfecter things thou aspirest godlily afterwards; in the mean space, there is no cause why thou shouldest despise the lesser. In the gospel after St Matthew they receive large[1] riches, who, having received but a few talents, occupied the same faithfully: but he that despised the talent wherewith he was put in credit, and cloaked his slothfulness with I wot not what care, is greatly accused; yea, he is spoiled of the money which was once given him, and is thrown into everlasting torments, being bound with bonds of condemnation. For the Lord pronounceth generally: "Whosoever hath, to him shall be given, and he shall have abundance; but whosoever hath not, from him shall be taken away even that which he hath." He hath, who acknowledgeth, magnifieth, and reverenceth[2] the grace of God: to this[3] heap of graces more is added, so that it is made more abundant. He hath not, which doth not acknowledge the gifts of God, and imagineth other, I cannot tell of what kind; in the mean time he doth not put in ure the grace received, and which is present. And these are wont to use excuses, that that drawing came not to them as yet; and that it is a matter very dangerous to use occupying, or to make merchandise, of the

[1] ampliores, Lat.; larger.]
[2] excolit, Lat.]
[3] So also ed. 1584: but ed. 1577, to *his* heap.]

gifts of God. But St Paul, judging far otherwise, saith : "So 2 Cor. vi.
we as workers together beseech you, that ye receive not the
grace of God in vain." And to Timothy: " I put thee in re- 2 Tim. i.
membrance, that thou stir up the gift of God which is in thee."
Not that without God we are able to do any thing of ourselves,
but that the Lord requireth our endeavour, which notwithstanding is not without his assistance and grace. For truly
saith the selfsame apostle : "God worketh in us both to will Phil. ii.
and to do even of his good pleasure." Again: "Not that we 2 Cor. iii.
are sufficient of ourselves, to think any thing of [4] ourselves:
but all our sufficiency is of God."

Furthermore, I wish not any man to despair, if by and Faith hath
by he feel and try [5] not in his mind a most ripe and perfect her increasings.
faith. The gospel saith : "Of her own accord doth the earth Mark iv.
bring forth fruit; first the blade, then the ear, and afterwards
full corn in the ear." For so likewise hath faith her increasings ; and therefore did the very apostles of the Lord pray :
" Lord, increase our faith." Furthermore, in Mark truly a [Mark ix. 22,
&c.]
woeful man crieth unto our Saviour : " If thou canst do anything, Lord, have compassion upon us, and help us." But he
heard the Lord straightways saying unto him : " If thou
canst believe it, all things are possible to him that believeth."
And this silly [6] soul cried out: " I believe, Lord; help mine
unbelief." Lo, this woeful wretch believed, feeling in his mind
faith given him of God, which notwithstanding he perceived to
be so weak, that he stood in need of God's help and aid. He
prayeth therefore, " help mine unbelief," that is, my faith,
which, if it be compared with an absolute and perfect faith,
may seem but unbelief. But hear, I beseech you, what this
faith, how little soever it was, wrought and brought to pass ;
what an humble mind and hanging upon the only mercy of
God was able to do. For straightways he healed the child of
the woeful father ; and, being restored unto health, and as it
were raised up from the dead, giveth him again to his faithful father. If any therefore doth feel faith in his mind,
let him not despair, although he know that it is weak enough,
God wot [7], and feeble : let him cast himself wholly upon God's
mercy ; let him presume very little, or nothing at all, of his

[4 So also ed. 1584: but ed. 1577, as of.]
[5 experiatur, is Bullinger's one word.]   [6 miser, Lat.]
[7 This expression is the translator's.]

own merits[1]; let him pray incessantly for the increase of faith. In which purpose verily the[2] words of our Saviour, very full of comfort, out of the gospel, may confirm and strengthen any man most wholesomely : " Ask, and it shall be given you : seek, and ye shall find : knock, and it shall be opened unto you. For whosoever asketh, receiveth : and whosoever seeketh, findeth : and to him that knocketh, it shall be opened. Is there any man among you, who, if his son ask him bread, will give him a stone? or, if he ask fish, will give him a serpent? If you therefore, which are evil, can give good gifts unto your children ; how much more shall your heavenly Father give good things, even the Holy Ghost itself, if you shall ask of him?" These and such like sayings, set forth unto us in the holy gospel for our consolation, ought more to move and establish our minds of the good, yea, the right good-will of God towards us than the eggings of the devil, wherewith he goeth about not only to overwhelm the hope of our election, but to make us suspect and doubt of God, as though he had his creature in hatred, whom he had rather have destroyed than saved. But he is well enough known to the saints by his subtilties and trains ; for so he deceived our first parents. Let us keep it deeply printed in our breasts, that God hath chosen us in Christ, and for Christ his sake predestinate us to life ; and that therefore he giveth and increaseth faith to Christ-ward in them that ask it ; and that it is he that puts it in our hearts[3]. For all things that tend to our salvation come from the grace of God; nothing is ours but reproach and shame.

These things, brethren, thus far have I laid before you concerning the marvellous and wonderful work of the creation wrought by the eternal, true, and living God, without any trouble (doubtless) or pains-taking. " For he spake the word, and they were made. He commanded, and they were created." A little we have added touching the most wise and excellent governing of all things by God's divine providence, which is always just and most righteous : likewise of God's good-will towards us ; of predestination[4]; and certain other

Marginal notes:

Matth. vii.
Luke xi.

Gen. iii.

[1] viribus, Lat. ; strength.]

[2] So also ed. 1584: but ed. 1577, *these ;* hæc verba, Lat.]

[3] eundemque ut petamus inspirare, Lat.; and that it is even he that puts it into our hearts to ask.]

[4] Cf. Orig. Lett. ed. Parker Soc. CLIV, CLV.]

points unto these belonging. All these things truly have we rehearsed, to beautify the glory and knowledge of God our creator; to whom both the perpetual and universal course of nature, as well of things invisible as also visible, beareth witness; whom the angels worship, the stars wonder at, the seas bless, the earth reverenceth, and all infernal things behold[5]; whom the mind of every man feeleth, albeit it doth not[6] express him; at whose beck all things are moved, the springs cast forth their streams, rivers decrease[7], the waves arise aloft, all things bring forth their increase, the winds are forced to blow, showers to fall, seas to rage, all things in all places to deliver abroad their fruitfulness; who planted a peculiar garden of felicity for our first parents, gave them a commandment, and pronounced sentence against their sin; delivered righteous Noe from the dangers of the deluge; translated Enoch into the fellowship of his friendship; did choose Abraham to himself; defended Isaac; increased Jacob; appointed Moses the captain over his people; set free from the yoke of bondage the groaning children of Israel; wrote a law; brought the offspring of the fathers into the land of promise; instructed his prophets with his Spirit, and by all these promised his only-begotten Son again; and at the same instant that he had promised to give him hath sent him; through whom also he would be acquainted and come in knowledge with us; and hath poured forth upon us all his heavenly graces. And because of himself he is liberal and bountiful, lest this whole world, being turned away from the rivers of his grace, should wax dry, he would have apostles to be sent by his Son as teachers throughout the whole world, that the state of mankind might acknowledge their Maker[8]; and, if they followed him, might have instead of a God one whom in their petitions and prayers they might call Father; whose providence hath not only extended itself, and is now extended, not only severally unto men, but also unto very towns and cities, the ends of which he foretold by the voices of his prophets, yea, throughout the whole world; whose ends, plagues, decays, and punishments for their unbelief he hath described. And lest any should think, that this in-

[5] suspiciunt, Lat.; look up to.]
[6] So also ed. 1584: but 1577, do not.]   [7] labuntur, Lat.]
[8] institutorem, Lat.]

[BULLINGER, III.]

fatigable providence of God extended not to everything, though never so small, the Lord saith: "Of two sparrows, the one of them falleth not to the ground without the will of the Father;" and, "the hairs of your head are all numbered:" whose care also and providence suffered not the garments of the Israelites to wax old, nor their simple[1] shoes on their feet to be worn and torn. And not without good reason: for if this God comprehendeth that which containeth all things, and all things and the whole doth consist of parts and particulars; then shall his care reach consequently even to every part and particular, whose providence hath reached already to the very whole, whatsoever it is. To this God be all glory.

OF ADORING OR WORSHIPPING, OF INVOCATING OR CALLING UPON, AND OF SERVING THE ONLY, LIVING, TRUE, AND EVERLASTING GOD: ALSO OF TRUE AND FALSE RELIGION.

THE FIFTH SERMON.

Touching God, what he is in person, what in quality, and what in substance[2], I have told you already; not as I ought, but as I was able. I have likewise shadowed out how good and ready his will is towards man, whom he hath ordained to life everlasting in his only-begotten Son; whom also he hath made Lord of all things in this present world, all things being brought in subjection unto him.

Now, that man should not be ignorant what he oweth to so mighty a God, and to a Father so loving and liberal, I will anon join a disputation touching this living, true, and everlasting God, of man to be adored, called upon, and worshipped. For man is neither created nor born to behold and gaze upon the stars, as the philosopher doted[3]; but that he should be the image and temple of God, in whom God might dwell and reign; and that he should therefore acknowledge God, reverence, adore, call upon, and worship, and also[4] be

[1 vilissima, Lat.]   [2 quantus sit, Lat.]
[3 Seneca, de otio Sapientis, cap. 32.]
[4 adeoque, Lat.; and so.]

joined unto God, and live with him eternally. And first of all I will speak of adoring God; next of calling upon God; and lastly, of serving God: whereupon we shall perceive without any trouble at all which is the true religion, or which is the false. The places truly expounded[5] are very plentiful; but in few words I will comprehend what the scripture doth teach us concerning them; howbeit not every one particularly, but the chiefest, and so much as seemeth sufficient for our salvation and sound knowledge.

To adore or worship, in the holy scriptures, doth signify, for honour's sake to uncover the head, to bend the body, to incline or bow the knee, or with the whole body to lie prostrate upon the ground, to fall flat on the face at one's feet, after the fashion of suppliants or petitioners, in token of humility, submission and obedience[6]; and it is referred chiefly to the gesture or habit of the body. The Hebricians use one only word *Schahah*[7], which all interpreters have expounded by this word *adorare*, to adore, bend, bow, and lie along with the face downward. The Grecians have expounded it by the word προσκυνέω, that is, I bow the knees, I uncover or make bare the head, I humbly beseech or adore. And προσκύνησις, adoration, is so called either of kissing, or of moving the hat; for κυνέω signifieth, I kiss. And that a kiss was sometimes a sign of worshipping, reverencing, or adoring, it is to be gathered out of the thirty-first of Job. What, and is it not a fashion very much used even at this day, for honour and reverence' sake to kiss the hand? Again, κυνῆ signifieth a hat, a bonnet, or a cap; so that, to adore, is to make bare and uncover the head for reverence' sake. The Latinists also, peradventure, had an eye to the habit of the body; for *orare*, to pray, signifieth both as well to crave as to speak a thing. He therefore doth adore, that, casting his countenance upon a man, doth crave something suppliantly. Likely it is that the Germans also had a respect hereunto: for they turn *adorare*, to adore, by this word *anbatten;* which might moreover have been turned *Zu fussen fallen*[8].

To adore and worship, what it is.

[5 So also ed. 1584: but ed. 1577 propounded; propositi, Lat.]

[6 deditionisque, Lat.]

[7 More correctly, the Hithpahel form of this verb, viz. הִשְׁתַּחֲוָה signifies, *to worship*.]

[8 to fall at the feet.]

In the ninth of Matthew thou dost read: "Behold, a certain ruler came to Jesus, and worshipped (or adored) him." But Mark, writing the same history, "And behold," saith he, "there came one of the princes of the synagogue, whose name was Jairus; and when he saw him, he fell down at his feet, and besought him instantly (or much;)" thus expounding to us what to adore is, to wit, to fall down at one's feet, and to submit and beseech like a suppliant. For so we read in the old Testament of Jacob Israel, our father: "And he, going before them, bowed himself to the ground seven times, until his brother Esau approached and drew near." Of David and Abigael thus we read in Samuel: "When Abigael saw David, she hasted, and lighted off her ass, and fell before David on her face, and worshipped on the ground, and she fell at his feet, saying: Let that iniquity be counted mine, my lord, &c." Likewise of Nathan the prophet, it is read thus written: "And when he was come in to the king he worshipped" (or made obeisance) "upon his face on the ground." For God, communicating this honour, doth allow the same unto men, either for their old age, their authority, or worthiness' sake: for man is the lively image of God. And it pleaseth God himself to call men that excel other in authority, gods. Whereupon the apostles of Christ, Peter and Paul, instructing the people of God, taught them, he verily, "Fear God, honour the king;" and this, "The magistrate is God's minister: give therefore to all men, honour to whom honour belongeth; fear to whom fear is due." In the law the Lord saith: "In the presence of a hoar head rise up;" and, "Honour thy parents." In consideration of this commandment of God the godly do reverence the aged, their parents, and magistrates; and please God also with faithful obedience.

But to adore, worship, or honour images, what representation likeness soever they bear, the Lord doth nowhere like or allow; for he saith in the law: "Thou shalt not bow down nor worship them[1]." And by his prophet Isaie, "None (saith he) considereth within himself of this matter, and saith: One piece of the wood I have burnt in the fire, I have baked bread with the coals thereof, I have roasted flesh therewithal, and eaten it; and should I now of the residue make an abominable idol, and fall down and worship a rotten piece

[1 Vol. I. p. 231.]

Marginal notes:
Mark v.
Gen. xxxiii.
1 Sam. xxv.
1 Kings i.
To adore or worship men.
Psal. lxxxii.
1 Pet. ii.
Rom. xiii.
[Levit. xix. 32.]
[Exod. xx. 12.]
Exod. xx.
Isai. xliv.

of wood²?" In the same prophet thou readest with much indignation pronounced: "Their land is full of vain gods (or   Isai. ii.
idols;) before the works of their hands have they bowed
themselves and adored it; yea, even before the thing that their
own fingers have made. There kneeleth the man, there
falleth the man down (before them³): therefore forgive them
not." Therefore that ancient writer, Lactantius, inspired   In his second
book and
with a prophetical spirit, disputing against the Gentiles, hath   eighteenth
chapter.
thus left it written: "The images themselves which are wor-
shipped are representations or counterfeits of dead men. And
it is a perverse and an absurd thing, that the image of a man
should be worshipped of the image of God, to wit, man; for
he worshippeth the thing that is worser and weaker. Besides
that, the very images of saints, which most vain men do serve,
are void of all sense and feeling, because they be⁴ earth. And
where is he that understandeth not, that it is a wicked and
sinful act for an upright and straight creature to be bowed
down, and to adore and worship earth; which to that end is
under our feet, that it should be trodden upon, and not adored
of us; who therefore are made to go upright and look upward,
that we should not lie grovelling downward, that we should
not cast this heavenly countenance to the earth, but thither
look and direct our eyes, whither the condition of their nature
hath guided them? Whosoever therefore endeavoureth to   ch. xix.
maintain the mystery of man's creation, and to hold the reason
of his nature; let him raise up himself from the ground, and
with a raised mind bend his eyes unto heaven: let him not
seek a god under his feet, nor dig from under his footsteps that
which he may adore or worship; because whatsoever lieth
under or is subject to man, the same must needs be inferior unto
man. But let him seek aloft, let him seek in the highest place;
because nothing can be greater than man, but that which is
above man. But God is greater than man: he is therefore
above, not beneath; neither is he rather to be sought in the
lowest, but in the highest region or room. Wherefore there
is no doubt, but that wheresoever an image is, there is no
religion. For if religion consist in divine things, and that
nothing is divine unless it be among heavenly things, then do

[² truncum ligneum, Lat.]
[³ incurvavit se homo, et humiliatus est vir, Lat. and Vulgate.]
[⁴ So also ed. 1584: but ed. 1577, they are.]

images lack religion ; because in that which is made of earth
there can be no heavenly thing. Which matter even by the
very name itself may appear and be manifest to a wise man :
for whatsoever is counterfeit, that must needs be false;
neither can that which hath a representation or gloss of truth
at any time take unto it the name of truth. If then not
every representation or counterfeit be, not a thing in earnest,
but as it were a toy and a sport, religion is not in images, but
there is less religion where they be. That which is true
therefore is to be preferred before all things that are false.
Earthly things must be trodden under foot, that we may get
or obtain heavenly things[1]." These words not unadvisedly
have we cited hitherto out of Lactantius. We return now to
our purpose.

Spiritual ado-
ration or
worshipping.

But because the outward gesture or habit of the body is

[1 Simulacra ipsa, quæ coluntur, effigies (sunt) hominum mortuorum:
est autem perversum et incongruens, ut simulacrum hominis a simulacro Dei colatur; colit enim quod est deterius et imbecillius ... Ipsæ
imagines sacræ, quibus inanissimi homines serviunt, omni sensu carent,
quoniam terra sint. Quis autem non intelligat, nefas esse rectum
animal curvari, ut adoret terram; quæ idcirco pedibus nostris subjecta
est, ut calcanda nobis, non adoranda, sit; qui sumus ideo excitati ...
ut non revolvamur deorsum, ne hunc cœlestem vultum projiciamus ad
terram, sed oculos eo dirigamus, quo illos naturæ suæ conditio direxit?
... Quicunque igitur sacramentum hominis tueri, rationemque naturæ
suæ nititur obtinere, ipse se ab humo suscitet, et erecta mente oculos
suos tendat in cœlum, non sub pedibus quærat Deum; nec a vestigiis
suis eruat quod adoret, (quia quicquid homini subjacet, infra hominem
sit necesse est,) sed quærat in sublimi, quærat in summo; quia nihil
potest homine majus esse, nisi quod fuerit supra hominem. Deus
autem major est homine : supra ergo, non infra est; nec in ima potius
sed in summa religione (Bullinger read, regione) quærendus est.
Quare non est dubium, quin religio nulla sit, ubicunque simulacrum
est. Nam si religio ex divinis rebus est, divini autem nihil est nisi in
cœlestibus rebus, carent ergo religione simulacra; quia nihil potest esse
cœlestis in ea re quæ sit ex terra. Quod quidem de nomine ipso appa-
rere sapienti potest: quicquid enim simulatur, id falsum sit necesse
est; nec potest unquam veri nomen accipere, quod veritatem fuco et
imitatione mentitur. Si autem (non, Bullinger's text) omnis imitatio
non res potissimum seria, sed quasi ludus ac jocus est; non religio in
simulacris, sed mimus (Bullinger read, minus) religionis est. Præ-
ferendum est igitur verum omnibus falsis; calcanda terrena, ut cœlestia consequamur.—Lactant. de Orig. Error. Lib. II. capp. 17, 18. pp.
227—230. Lugd. Bat. 1660.]

commonly framed according to the inward quality of the mind, and the outward habit of his body which adoreth submitteth, yieldeth, and maketh subject him that worshippeth to him which is worshipped; therefore adoration is translated likewise to the inner man: so that to adore is to reverence and respect God, to bequeath ourselves wholly unto him, and to cleave inseparably unto him, upon him only and alone to hang in all things, and to have recourse unto him in all our necessities whatsoever. Furthermore, the outward adoration doth immediately, when it is needful and ability granted, follow a mind rightly endued with true faith and holy fear of God. For adoration is two-fold, or of two sorts: one of the mind or spirit, which is inward, sound, sincere and true; another of the body, which is outward, unsound, counterfeit, and false, which may proceed from him in whom there is no sparkle of religion. True adoration is the fruit of true faith and holy fear of God; namely, a lowly or suppliant yielding and humble consecrating, whereby we bequeath ourselves, yield and submit ourselves, unto our God, whom as we understand to be our best and most merciful Father, so to be our most high and almighty God: upon him therefore alone we do wholly depend, and to him only we have respect: which also forthwith, so soon as occasion is ministered unto us, we express and testify by outward adoration. All this we shall the better understand by these testimonies of scripture following. David saith: " O come, let us sing unto the Lord; let us heartily rejoice in God our salvation. Let us come before his presence with thanksgiving, and shew ourselves joyful in him with psalms. For the Lord is a great God, and a great king above all gods: because in his hand are the corners of the earth, and the height of the hills are his. For the sea is his and he made it, and his hands fastened the dry land. O come let us adore (or worship) and fall down, and kneel[2] before the Lord that hath made us: because he is the Lord our God ; and we are the people of his pasture, and the sheep of his hands." Thou perceivest therefore that we must adore or worship God, and that we must cleave unto him, and sing praises to his name, because he is the most mighty God, Creator of all things, yea, our Creator, our Father, and our Shepherd. Likewise, in the gospel according

Adoration or worshipping is of two sorts.

Psal. xcv.

[2 ploremus, Lat.]

to Matthew, adoration doth follow faith, and doth as it were grow out of it, and by it is nourished. For after that the disciples, being taught by miracles, believed that Jesus was Christ, they came (saith Matthew) and adored (or worshipped)

Matt. xiv. him, saying: "Thou art truly the Son of God." Again, thou readest in John that the Lord asked the blind man that was excommunicate or cast out of the synagogue, whom he re-

John ix. stored to his sight, saying, "Dost thou believe in the Son of God?" and that the blind man answered, "Who is he, Lord, that I might believe in him?" and that Jesus answered, and said: "Thou hast both seen him, and he it is that talketh with thee." Moreover upon this by and by followeth in the history: "But he said, I believe, Lord; and he worshipped him." Hitherto now belongeth that which the Lord

[John iv.] said to the Samaritan in the gospel: "The true worshippers shall worship the Father in spirit and in truth." For the Lord doth allow spiritual and inward adoration or worshipping; not that outward, counterfeit, or hypocritical worshipping, but that which proceedeth from a mind regenerated by faith through the Holy Ghost, and that tendeth sincerely towards

In the history of the Kings. one God. For we read in the history of the old Testament, that those princes worshipped in truth, which consecrated and made holy themselves unto one God with their whole heart, and on him only depended: again, that they worshipped not the Lord with their whole heart, which, being destitute and void of sincere faith, depended also upon creatures. Now a reason of this adoration or worshipping the Lord adjoineth in the gospel. Worship (saith he) ought in all points to agree with him that is worshipped. But God that is worshipped is spirit and truth, and is delighted with spiritual worship and unfeigned faith. In spirit and truth therefore he must be worshipped.

Truly to adore and worship God, what it is. Wherefore the saints have a special care and regard that the inward worship of the mind be sound, and that first of all they worship in heart, and truly, with a sincere faith and a reverence of God's majesty: and whiles they are inwardly so occupied, they do no less outwardly, falling on their faces with humility, and do worship in God's presence. For the outward worship is a companion of the inward, and followeth it. Hypocrites also worship God in body, suppliantly and lowly enough; but because their minds go a wool-gathering, and neither with

faith nor reverence cleave unto the Lord, they hear this
spoken of the Lord by the prophet: "This people honoureth Isai. xxix.
me with their lips, but their heart is far from me : but in vain Matt. xv.
do they worship me, teaching doctrines precepts of men."
And this verily is the counterfeit and false worshipping. And
that worshipping also is false, nay, it is most wicked and
abominable, wherewith the creatures are worshipped, either
with God, or for God, or without God. And, to say sooth, they
do not worship God at all, which neither fear God, neither
believe in God, nor yet depend or hang only upon God.

All men truly confess that God must be worshipped, but That God
every one doth not surely[1] acknowledge and confess that God only and
only and alone is to be worshipped. It remaineth therefore worshipped.
to be declared, that God only and alone is to be worshipped
of men.   Adoration or worshipping is joined with true faith
and perfect or sincere reverence of God's majesty ; which
seeing they are due to God alone, it followeth that God alone
is to be worshipped : and therefore is this saying so often cited
and beaten upon in the law and the prophets : "Thou shalt
worship the Lord thy God, and a strange god thou shalt not
worship."   Now a strange god is whatsoever without and
beside the only, living, true, and everlasting God thou
choosest unto thyself to be worshipped[2]. The only and alone
true, living, and everlasting God therefore is to be worshipped.   In the history of the gospel we read, that the devil Matt. iv.
tempted our Lord Christ; and, having led him up into an high
mountain, shewed him from thence all the kingdoms of the
world and the glory of them, and said : "All these will I
give thee, if thou, falling down, wilt worship me :" and that
the Lord made answer : "Avoid, Satan; for it is written, Thou
shalt worship the Lord thy God, and him only shalt thou
serve."   And surely worshipping and serving are linked
mutually the one with the other, that they cannot be severed
or put asunder.   Whereupon it followeth, that, seeing the
Lord requireth only and alone to be served, he will doubtless
in like manner only and alone be worshipped.   And Heli, the
great prophet of God, teaching that God can in no case abide to
have one joined unto him in worship, crieth out unto the people
worshipping God and with him their god Baal : "How long 1 Kings
(saith he) do you halt on both parts ?   If the Lord be God, xviii.

[1 sincere, Lat.]   [2 Vol. I. p. 220.]

follow him: if Baal be god, go after him." As if he should have
said, You cannot worship God and Baal at once. "No man
can serve two masters." For the Lord our God requireth, not a
piece, but our whole heart, our whole mind and soul: he leaveth
nothing therefore for us to bestow upon any other. In the epistle
to the Hebrews Paul sheweth, that Christ is more excellent
than angels, because that angels adore or worship Christ, but
they again are not worshipped. If then the angels are not
worshipped, whom shall we grant, beside the living, true, and
everlasting God, that deserveth to be worshipped? God
therefore only and alone is to be worshipped. For in the
revelation of Jesus Christ, made unto the blessed apostle and
evangelist John, thus we read written: "And I saw another
angel flying through the midst of heaven, having the everlasting gospel to preach unto them that dwell upon the earth,
and to all nations, and kindreds, and tongues, and people,
saying with a loud voice: Fear God and give him honour,
because the hour of his judgment is come; and worship him
that hath made heaven and earth, the sea, and fountains of
waters." And again in the same book we read: "And I fell
down before the feet of the angel, to worship him. And he
said unto me: See thou doest it not; I am thy fellow-servant
and of thy brethren having the testimony of Jesu; worship
God." Again, in the end of the same book thou dost read:
"And after I had heard and seen, I fell down to worship
before the feet of the angel, which shewed me these things.
And he said unto me, See thou dost it not; for I am thy
fellow-servant, and of thy brethren the prophets, and of them
that keep the words of this book." With this thing the
saying and doing of St Peter doth not greatly disagree, at
whose feet when Cornelius the centurion fell down and worshipped, Peter said, "Arise, I also myself am a man;" and
therewithal laying his hand on him, which lay along, did lift
him up, and set him on his feet. Right religiously therefore
wrote Augustine touching true religion, saying: "Let not
religion be unto us the worshipping of man's handy work. For
better are the workmen themselves, which make such; whom
notwithstanding we ought not to worship. Let not religion
be to us the worshipping of mortal men: because, if they have
lived godlily, they are not to be esteemed as those that
would seek such honours; but their will it is, that he should

Matt. vi.

Heb. i.

[Rev. xiv.
6, 7.]

Rev. xix.

Rev. xxii.

Acts x.

In his book
intituled De
Vera Re-
ligione, c. 55.

be worshipped of us, who enlightening them, they rejoice that
we are made fellow-partakers of his merit.　They are to be
honoured therefore for imitation or following sake, not to be
worshipped for religion's sake.　And if they have lived ill,
they are not to be worshipped, wheresoever they be[1]." The
same Augustine in his first book *De consensu Evangelista-*
rum, of the consent of the evangelists, and eighteenth chapter,
reasoning why the Romans never received both the God
and the worship of the God of the Hebrews, considering that
they received the gods almost of all the Gentiles to be worshipped; and he answereth, that that came to pass by none
other occasion, than because the God of the Hebrews would
only and alone be worshipped without a mate or partner.
If any require his words, they are these: "There resteth
nothing for them to say, why they have not received the holy
rites and worship of this God, save only because he would be
worshipped alone; and hath forbidden them to worship the
gods of the Gentiles, whom nevertheless these people did
worship.　For the sentence or opinion of Socrates (who, as by
oracle it was ratified, was the wisest of all men) is, that every
god ought in such sort to be worshipped, as he himself hath
given commandment he would be worshipped.　Therefore
were the Romans of very necessity forced not to worship the
God of the Hebrews; because, if they would worship him
after another fashion than he himself said he would be worshipped, they should not then worship him, but that which
they themselves had devised and made: and if they would
in that manner worship him as he himself prescribed, then
they saw that they were debarred from worshipping other
gods, whom he forbad to be worshipped.　And upon this they
refused the worship of the only true God, to the intent they
might not offend many counterfeit and false gods; thinking
that the anger of them would rather be more to their dis-

Why the Romans never received the God of the Hebrews to be worshipped.

[1 Non sit nobis religio humanorum operum cultus. Meliores
enim sunt ipsi artifices, qui talia fabricantur, quos tamen colere non
debemus.... Non sit nobis religio cultus hominum mortalium: quia si
pie vixerint, non sic habentur, ut tales quærant honores; sed illum a
nobis coli volunt, quo illuminante lætantur meriti sui nos esse con-
servos. Honorandi ergo sunt propter imitationem; non adorandi
propter religionem. Si autem male vixerint, ubicunque sint, non sunt
colendi.—August. de Vera Relig. cap. 55. Opp. Tom. I. fol. 155. col. 4.
fol. 156. col. 1. Par. 1532.]

profit than the good-will of him to their benefit[1]." Thus saith Augustine. And although these things are written concerning the worship and service of God, and that we dispute of adoring God's majesty; yet notwithstanding they are not impertinent or beside our purpose; for the worshipping and serving of God are inseparably linked and knit together. Of this serving of God we will speak more heareafter. But by the words cited before we do gather, that only and alone the true, living, and everlasting God is to be worshipped, according Deut. x. ing to that commonly known sentence of the law : " Thou shalt worship the Lord thy God ; him shalt thou fear, and him only shalt thou serve: to him shalt thou cleave, and in his name shalt thou swear."

Rewards and punishments for them that do and do not worship God. Furthermore, God from the beginning hath promised and performed, yea, and will perform whiles this world standeth, great rewards to his true worshippers. Contrariwise, we believe that great mischiefs or punishments are prepared for those which either do not at all worship God, or else instead of the true God do worship strange gods. The Lord in his Revelation, shewed to John the apostle, saith : Rev. xxi. " The fearful, and unbelieving, and the abominable, and murderers, and whoremongers, and sorcerers, and idolaters, and all liars, shall have their part in the lake that burneth with fire and brimstone, which is the second death."

To invocate or call upon, what it is. These things have we hitherto spoken of worshipping God : we will now speak, in the second place, of invocating

[1 Veruntamen diligentius ab istis quærendum est, quemnam putent esse Deum Israel, cur eum colendum non receperint, sicut aliarum gentium deos quas Romanum subegit imperium, &c. . . . Nihil ergo restat ut dicant cur hujus Dei sacra noluerint recipere, nisi quia solum se coli voluerit; illos autem deos gentium, quos isti jam colebant, coli prohibuerit. . . . Certe sententia illius eorum philosophi proditur, quem sapientissimum omnium hominum etiam oraculo fuisse firmarunt. Socratis enim sententia est, unumquemque deum sic coli oportere, quomodo se ipse colendum præceperit. Proinde istis summa necessitas facta est non colendi Deum Hebræorum, quia si alio modo eum colere vellent quam se colendum ipse dixisset, non utique illum colerent, sed quod ipsi finxissent. Si autem illo modo vellent quo ipse diceret, alios sibi colendos non esse cernebant, quos ille coli prohibebat: ac per hoc respuerunt unius veri Dei cultum, ne multos falsos offenderent; magis arbitrantes sibi obfuturam fuisse istorum iracundiam, quam illius benevolentiam profuturam.—August. de Consensu Evangelist. Lib. I. capp. 17, 18. Opp. Tom. IV. fol. 81. col. 3.]

or calling upon God, of which point we promised to speak.
To call upon, and calling upon, is diversely taken in the
scriptures. For it signifieth to bring forth as a witness,
or a calling to witness. So Moses calleth heaven and earth Deut. xxxii.
to witness against the children of Israel, by the figure *Pros-*
opopœia. Again, the name of any one to be called upon
over another, is to be called by, or after, his name. "Let Gen. xlviii.
my name" (saith Jacob) "be called upon them," that is,
upon Ephraim and Manasseh; that is, let them be named by
my name, as if they were my children; and let them be
called, not the sons of Joseph, but the sons of Jacob Israel.
So say the wives to their husbands[2], "Let thy name be Isai. iv.
called upon us;" that is, suffer, or give leave, that we may
be named by thy name, and that we may be made thy
wives: for those women, through the knot of wedlock, take
unto them their husbands' names. After the same manner
do we oftentimes read in the prophets and holy history of
the Bible, "The house upon which thy name is called;"
that is, the house which is called after thy name, and is
named the Lord's house. Likewise Joab, general of the
king's army, saith unto David: "Take thou the city" (Rab- 2 Sam. xii.
bah, the chief city or seat royal of the Ammonites), "lest I
take it, and my name be called upon it;" that is, lest I be
called the conqueror of Rabbah. Most ignorant therefore
and unskilful are they of the scriptures and the phrases of
speech used in the scripture, which cite that saying of Jacob,
which even now we declared, in defence and maintenance of
the invocation of saints; as though Jacob would have his
name to be called upon of his posterity and offspring. In
Daniel thou dost read, "A people upon whom the name of Dan. ix.
God is called:" which signifieth nothing else than, a people
that is called God's people. Here is no mention of invocating, whereby we ask or desire any thing. Furthermore,
invocation, or calling upon, is taken for religion. For Luke
saith in the Acts: "Saul had power (or authority) to bind Acts ix.
all those that called upon the name of the Lord." And Paul
saith: "Let every one that calleth upon the name of the 2 Tim. ii.
Lord depart from iniquity." Also, "Seek after peace with
all them that call upon the name of the Lord," that is, which

[2 So also ed. 1584: but ed. 1577 has rightly, *husband;* maritum,
Lat.]

are of the true christian religion. Lastly, to invocate or call upon signifieth, to cry or call for help, and with continual outcries to crave somewhat.

Invocation or calling upon God, what it is.That invocation therefore or calling upon God, whereof at this time we entreat, is a lifting up of man's mind to God in great necessity or in some desire, and a most ardent craving of counsel and assistance by faith; and also a bequeathing or committing of ourselves into the protection of God, and as it were a betaking of ourselves to his sanctuary and only safeguard. In invocation therefore (true invocation, I mean) a faithful mind is first of all required, which doth acknowledge God to be the author and only giver of all good gifts; who is willing to hear them that call upon him, and is able to grant us all our requests and desires whatsoever. An uncessant and ardent petition or beseeching is also required. But of these points more shall be said, when God shall give us leave, in our sermon of the prayer of the faithful; for invocation is a kind of prayer.

That God is to be called upon.Now verily I will shew, that in all our desires God is to be called upon, yea, only and alone to be called upon. Surely there are express commandments of God, charging us to call upon the name of the Lord, who promiseth, that for the goodwill and love which he beareth us he will hear our requests and suits, and largely give unto us things tending to our health and benefit. Of many I will cite one or two testimonies. 1 Kings viii.Salomon, the wisest of all men, doth teach us to call upon God in all and every one of our necessities, making a particular rehearsal of men's special desires. The same argument doth Salomon's father, that most holy king David, handle throughout the whole hundred and seventh Psalm. He reckoneth up therefore the divers casualties, chances, and miseries of men, their affliction or oppression, their wanderings and dangers in their journey, their bonds and imprisonments, their diseases, and the fear of death, which sometimes is more terrible and hideous than death itself, their jeopardies on the sea and rough waters[1], barrenness, scarcity, calamities, contempt, shame, and ignominy. 'Those crosses,' saith he, 'if they light on any man, let him not ascribe them either to his god to whose defence he hath committed himself[2], or to fortune, or to his constellation and

[1 fluminibus, Lat.]   [2 deo tutelari, Lat.]

destiny; but to that God that knoweth all things, and can
do all things, and upon that God let him call earnestly by
faith.' For often doth the prophet repeat these words:
"And when they cried unto the Lord in their tribulation,
he delivered them out of their distress." And for that cause
doth he so often reiterate those words, to the end that we,
having conceived a perfect trust in our hearts and sure
belief, might learn in all chances to call upon the name of
the Lord. For Salomon in his Proverbs yet again saith: Prov. xviii.
"The name of the Lord is a most strong tower: unto it
doth the righteous man run, and he shall be advanced[3]," or,
he shall be set free from danger. Asaph also in his holy
songs saith: "Sacrifice unto the Lord a sacrifice of praise, Psal. l.
and pay thy vows unto the Most Highest." And, "Call upon
me in the day of trouble, and I will deliver thee, and thou
shalt glorify me." And he bringeth in the Lord himself
speaking, and requiring sacrifices, not of beasts, not of gold
or silver, but of praise and invocation. Therewithal he promiseth help; and witnesseth, that by invocating and praising
he is honoured (or glorified); whereupon David said: " In Psal. xviii.
my trouble I will call upon the Lord, and I will cry unto
my God; and he shall hear my voice out of his holy temple,
and my cry shall enter into his ears." Joel also said:
"Every one that calleth upon the name of the Lord shall Joel ii.
be safe." And the Lord by the prophet Jeremy saith: " Ye Jer. xxix.
shall call upon me, and ye shall live[4]: ye shall pray unto
me, and I will hear you; ye shall seek me, and ye shall
find me, if with your whole heart ye seek me." Furthermore, we do not read that our holy and blessed fathers in
their petitions and requests[5], were they small or were they
great, called upon any other than that God who liveth
everlastingly world without end. For the Lord himself by
Asaph saith: "In thine extremities and troubles, O Israel, [Psal. lxxxi.
thou calledst upon me, and I delivered thee." Also David 7.]
saith: "Our fathers hoped in thee, [6]and thou deliveredst Psal. xxii.

[3 exaltabitur, Lat.; is set aloft. Marg. Auth. Ver.]

[4 Bullinger appears to have read *vivetis* for *ibitis* (which also Bibl.
Lat. Tigur. 1544 has), ye shall go.]

[5 So also ed. 1584: but ed. 1577, *or* requests.]

[6 speraverunt, Lat. omitted; but found in ed. 1577, they hoped in
thee.]

them. Unto thee they cried, and were delivered; in thee they trusted, and were not confounded." Now add unto all these the commandment of Christ our Lord: "When you pray, say, Our Father," &c. Add also the words which follow in Luke xi. and Matthew vii. "Ask, and it shall be given you;" and so forth. We conclude, therefore, that the true, living, and everlasting God ought of all men in all their necessities to be called upon.

That God only and alone is to be called upon.

But to no purpose, peradventure, I take pains in this point, seeing that there are but a few, or none at all, which deny that God is to be called upon. This seemeth to require a more diligent declaration, that God only and alone is to be called upon. For many doubtless do call upon God, but together with God, or for God, certain chosen patrons; whereupon ensueth that they call not upon God only and alone. Now that he alone is to be called upon, in this sort we declare. By invocation or calling upon we require help or succour, either that good things may be given to us, or that evil things may be turned away from us: which needeth no further proof, seeing it cannot be denied of any that is ruled by his right wits. Now God only and alone is our helper, who only giveth good things, and taketh away evil things. For the Lord saith in the gospel: "There is none good but one," to wit, God; where one is taken for one only and alone. Again in the law, by the mouth of Moses, the Lord saith: "Behold, that I am God alone, and that there is none other God beside me." And again by Isaie: "Am not I the Lord? and there is none other God beside me: a just God and a Saviour; there is none other beside me." And David: "Who," saith he, "is God, besides the Lord? and who is mighty (or a rock), save our God?" In very evil part therefore did the worshippers of God take it, so often as men asked of them those things which are in the Lord's hands only to give. Rahel said to Jacob: "Give me children, or else I die." But the scripture by and by addeth: "And Jacob being angry said, Am I in God's stead, which hath denied thee" (or withholden from thee) "the fruit of the womb?" So when the king of Syria desired and besought Joram, the king of Israel (a king, I wis, not so godly), that he would heal Naaman, who was infected with the leprosy, Joram saith: "Am I a God, that I should be

Marginal notes:
Matt. xix.
Deut. xxxii.
Isai. xlv.
Psal. xviii.
Gen. xxx.
2 Kings v.

able to kill and to give life? For he sendeth to me, that I should heal a man from his leprosy." Wherefore most certain it is, that to God only it belongeth to give good things, and to turn away evil things. Whereupon it doth consequently follow, that God only and alone must be called upon. For if those patrons, whom they call upon as their helpers and succourers that do not call upon the only God, be able either to give those things that are good, or to turn away those things that are evil, then certainly there is not one only God; for those should likewise be gods. But gods they are not, because there is but one God, who only and alone giveth (or bestoweth) good things, and taketh away (or removeth) evil things. God only and alone therefore is to be called upon: patrons are not to be called upon, insomuch as they are able to do us neither good nor harm. As touching that which of their own heads some do here object, that patrons do us good and harm, not of themselves, but of God; it is doubtful, yea, it is most false. For the Lord himself by the prophet saith: " I am the Lord: Hu Isai. xlii. (this or being)¹ is my name; and my glory I will not give to another, neither my praise to a graven image²." So that all glory belongeth to God, because he is only³ and alone, not only the well-spring of all good graces, which is never drawn dry, but also a most just and equal distributer of the same; and for that cause he is called upon, worshipped, and served of men. Psalm l.

Furthermore, insomuch as we ought to sacrifice unto none but to one God, certain it is that we must worship but one only God. The Lord crieth in the law: " He that offereth Exod. xxii. unto other gods than to the only God, let him be rooted out." And therefore Paul and Barnabas, when the people of Lystra Acts xiv. were preparing sacrifices to offer unto the apostles, they rent their clothes thereat, as at intolerable blasphemy. For in the law of the Lord we read again: "Whosoever shall make Exod. xxx. for himself a composition (or perfume) of incense, to smell thereto, he shall be cut off from among his people." But the sacrifices of the godly are prayers, thanksgivings, and invocations on God's name. For David saith: "Unto thee will I Psal. cxvi.

[¹ See above, page 133.]
[² So also ed. 1584: but ed. 1577, to graven images; sculptilibus, Lat.]
[³ Rather, But the glory of God is this, that he is only, &c.]

sacrifice a sacrifice of praise, and I will call upon the name of the Lord." And again: "Let my prayer be directed in thy sight as incense; and the lifting up of my hands as an evening sacrifice." Paul likewise saith: "By Christ we offer the sacrifice of praise always unto God, that is, the fruit of lips which confess his name." For the prophet[1] Osee biddeth us "offer the calves of our lips." Forsomuch therefore as one only God is to be sacrificed unto, therefore one only God is to be called upon. Neither is it possible, that they, whom such as call not upon the only God name heavenly patrons, would, if they be saints, require of men such manner of invocations: nay rather, both against God and against the saints do these offend, ascribing that to such which no blessed spirits do acknowledge. St Augustine saith, that they are not the angels of the good God, but wicked devils, which will have not the only and most high God, but themselves, to be worshipped and served with sacrifices[2]. Besides that, the blessed spirits (or saints) during the time that they lived in their mortal bodies prayed, "Thy will be done, as in heaven so in earth:" therefore, being now delivered and set free from all corruption, they do much more fully, yea, most perfectly agree unto the will of God, which commandeth all men to worship and call upon the only God.

Again, he that looketh into and seeth the hearts of them that call upon him, heareth their petitions or requests, and is able to fulfil the desires of all men living, he (I say) is lawfully and fruitfully called upon. And surely it is requisite and necessary that he know all things, that he be almighty, and the searcher of hearts. Wherefore, seeing the only God is he, the only God without further question ought to be called upon. For that God only is the searcher of hearts, comprehended in no place, but present everywhere, and omnipotent, Salomon in these words doth testify: "Behold, the heavens and the heaven of heavens are not able to contain

Psal. cxli.

[Heb. xiii. 15.]

Hos. xiv.

1 Kings viii.

[1 et propheta, Lat.; also the prophet.]

[2 Dic mihi, dæmonia colis, an spiritus bonos, quales sunt angeli? Sunt enim angeli sancti, et sunt spiritus maligni. Ego dico quia in templis tuis non coluntur nisi spiritus maligni, qui sibi exigunt superbi sacrificium, et volunt se coli tanquam Deos. Maligni sunt, superbi sunt.—Aug. Enarr. in Ps. xcvi. Opp. Par. 1531. Vol. viii. fol. 226. col. 2.]

thee: how much more unable then is this house that I have built! Thou therefore shalt hear in heaven, in the place of thy habitation (or, in thy dwelling-place), and shalt have mercy. For thou only knowest the hearts of the sons of men. Thou shalt do (and give) to every one according to all his ways, which knowest his very heart." As for the heavenly patrons, as these men call them, they do neither know the thoughts of men; neither is their power spread throughout the heaven, the earth, and the seas; neither do they know all things, or yet are everywhere present, or be omnipotent. For if it were so with them, they should be transformed and changed into a divine nature, and should cease any more to be creatures: but although by Christ they enjoy everlasting blessedness, yet notwithstanding they remain creatures still, neither do they know all things, neither are almighty; therefore are they at no hand to be called upon. In one prick and moment of time truly innumerable thousands of mortal men offer up their vows, and make their petitions: so that he verily which heareth must at a pinch, and in a very moment, and not at sundry seasons or degrees of time, know and be able to do all things; yea, and in a moment also reach out his helping hand unto all: which as no creature, though never so excellent, can do; so the only God, that knoweth all, and is omnipotent, can do all things, and therefore only and alone is to be called upon.

I wot well what the defenders of heavenly patrons (or saints) object against that which I have spoken; to wit, that they of their own nature do neither see nor yet hear what is done of us upon the earth; but in the face of God, as in a most lightsome looking-glass, do see all things, whatsoever God vouchsafeth to reveal to them, and that so they have an under-knowledge of all our affairs, and also help us[3]. But this imagination or forgery, in all points doubtful, can be proved by no authority out of the holy scriptures. But touching the celestial saints the scripture doth rather affirm the flat contrary. For in Isaie the people of God cry out: "Thou, O God, art our Father: though Abraham be ignorant Isai. lxiii. of us, and Israel know us not; yet thou, O Lord, art our Father, and our Redeemer." If then the patriarchs, so studious

[3 Sentiments like the above are frequently met with in Romish writers: ex. gr. in Pighius, Controv. præcip. &c. fol. 194. Par. 1549.]

and careful for their people, knew not what they did; which of the saints (I pray you) shall we grant or point out, that knoweth what we do, and that intermeddleth with the affairs of the living? True doubtless is that that the holy psalm soundeth:

Psal. xxvii. "Because my father and my mother have left (or forsaken) me, the Lord hath taken me up." If our parents forsake and leave us, how (I pray you) can they tell, or do they care, how it fareth with us? Let that suffice us wherewith David held himself throughly content, saying: "The Lord hath taken

2 Kings xxii. charge over me." We read that Josias was translated out of this life into another, to the end he should not see the mischiefs, (or plagues and punishments,) which the Lord determined to bring upon the Israelitish people for their most wicked and naughty life. The blessed souls therefore enjoy the sight of God, and thereby participate light and endless joy or gladness; they know none of our affairs, neither is it needful they should know them, considering that the Lord alone hath all things in his government.

Now is that also most certain, that invocation springeth from faith, as the fruit from the root. For Paul, using that saying

Rom. x. of the prophet, "Whosoever calleth upon the name of the Lord shall be safe," doth by and by add: "But how shall they call upon him, in whom they have not believed?" See how the apostle bringeth in one upon another: he is not called upon, who is not believed. Wherefore, in whom we believe, upon him we do also call. But in God only and alone do we believe; therefore on him only do we call. For wheresoever true faith is, there likewise is the gift of the Holy Ghost.

Rom. viii. For the apostle saith: "If any have not the Spirit of Christ, this man is none of his." And again: "You have not received again the spirit of bondage unto fear; but you have received the spirit of adoption, by which we cry, Abba, Father." They therefore, that are endued with a true belief in God, call upon God, whom they do acknowledge and confess to be the only

Matt. vi. Father of all. Neither might so much as the least part in that solemn form and order of invocation, delivered unto us by the Son of God, be attributed by any means unto patrons, or saints. The only God therefore is to be called upon.

The heart of sinful man trembleth and quaketh to ap-

Of the inter-cessor with God. proach near unto so great a majesty. For who may seem worthy in himself to appear and come before the presence of

the most holy, the most just, and the most terrible God?
Here therefore some supply and make up the matter with the
patronship or intercession of celestial saints, by whose mediation, and making way before us, passage lieth open for us
unto God. But this they bring forth without the warrant
of the scripture. The scripture hath laid before us a law, as
it were, of calling upon God, and thereunto hath annexed
most ample or large promises: so the commandment doth set
forth unto us by and through whom we should call upon
God, adding thereunto a most excellent promise, and opening
unto us through Christ Jesus only a ready way to the
Father. For in the gospel the Lord saith: "Verily, verily, John xvi.
I say unto you, Whatsoever ye shall ask the Father in my
name, he shall give it to you. Hitherto you have not asked
anything in my name. Ask, and ye shall receive, that your
joy may be perfect," (or full). And, "Whatsoever ye shall John xiv.
ask in my name, I will do it; that the Father may be glorified
by the Son. If you shall ask anything in my name, I will
do it." What could be spoken more fully and clearly than
these words? Christ biddeth us by (or in) his name to call
upon God the Father, and promiseth that he will give the
faithful whatsoever they ask in Christ his name. Who doubteth now any whit at all of the truth and constancy of him
which promiseth? What need we therefore henceforth the
intercession of saints? Of calling upon them, or of coming
to God by their mediation, we have no testimony of scripture, we have no promise. Whereunto I add, that he con-
temneth the commandment and precept of God, whosoever
seeketh by any other than by Christ and his intercession to
come to the Father. He that obeyeth the commandment of
Christ, and in his name maketh invocation, the same needeth
not at all the mediation of saints. Hath not he all things
plentifully in Christ? We say therefore, and affirm, that Christ alone
only Christ is the mediator, intercessor, and advocate with is the intercessor and ad-
the Father in heaven of all men which are in earth; and in vocate with
the Father.
such sort the only mediator, &c. that after him it is needless to have other advocates.

Many do grant that Christ is given unto us an intercessor with God; but because they join with him many other, A mediator
of redemp-
they do not surely send all unto him alone, neither yet do tion and
intercession.
they preach one only mediator. They imagine that Christ is

the mediator of redemption, yea, and the only mediator ; howbeit not the only mediator of intercession, but together with him many more.   But the scripture setteth forth unto us Christ, as the only mediator of redemption, so also of intercession.   The office of a mediator touching redemption and intercession is one and the selfsame.   A mediator putteth himself in the midst between them that are at variance or disagreement; and he is joined to each in disposition and nature. An intercessor putteth himself in the midst between them that are at strife and dissension ; and unless he be indifferent for either side, he cannot be an intercessor.   On both parts reconciliation[1] (or atonement) is required and looked for.   There must needs therefore be a certain cause of discord ; which being taken away, the discord or debate doth also cease.   The cause of discord is sin.   It is the duty therefore of a mediator or intercessor quite to rase out sin, that disagreement may no longer remain.   For this there is no amends or satisfaction made with words or with prayers, but with blood and death. Hebrews ix.   Whereupon we do necessarily gather, that only Christ is the mediator or intercessor with the Father.   For principally Christ[2] may set himself in the midst between God and men, because he only is partaker of both natures.   The saints participate but only one ; for they are men ; but Christ is both God and man.   Furthermore, he that is an intercessor must also be a reconciliator, or an atonementmaker.   For the end, whereat he that maketh intercession doth shoot, is reconciliation.   But Christ is the only reconciliator of men, therefore also the only intercessor.   For it belongeth to an intercessor to dissolve the cause of contention and discord, that is to say, to abolish and take away sin. But Christ alone, and no creature, taketh away sin.   It remaineth therefore that Christ is the only intercessor.   Hitherto do now

1 Tim. ii. pertain the testimonies of scripture.   Paul saith : " There is one God, and one reconciler (or mediator) of God and men, the man Christ Jesus, who gave himself the price (or ransom) for the redemption of all."   And although the apostle speak expressly of redemption, yet notwithstanding these words

[1 reconciliatio dissidentium, Lat. ; reconciliation of parties at variance.]

[2 Principio enim solus Christus, Lat. ; For, in the first place, only Christ, &c.]

are placed in the midst between the disputation of the invocation upon God, which is done by Christ, who is the only
mediator of redemption and intercession. For as he alone
redeemed us, so doth he alone even now commend us, being
redeemed, unto the Father. Touching this let the apostle be
heard once again, saying to the Romans: "Christ, when as Rom. v.
yet we were sinners, died for us: much more therefore now
being justified (or made righteous) by his blood, we shall be
saved from wrath through him." And yet again somewhat
plainer: "For if, when we were enemies, we were reconciled
to God by the death of his Son; much more, being reconciled,
we shall be saved by his life." For in another place the
same apostle saith: "Christ ever liveth" for this end, " to Heb. vii.
make intercession for us." And again: "It is God that Rom. viii.
justifieth: who is he that can condemn? Christ is he that
died; yea, that is raised up; who also is at the right hand of
God, and maketh intercession for us." The same Christ openeth the way, or maketh access, for us unto the Father[3].
Hebrews, chapter iv. and Ephesians, chapter ii. For the Lord
Jesus himself in the gospel doth not shew unto us many
doors, but one only door. "I am (saith he) the door." And John x.
again: "I am (saith he) the way, the truth, and the life. John xiv.
None cometh to the Father but by me." Doth not he which
saith, "I am the way, the truth, and the life," yea, and
such a way, that there is access to the Father by none other
than by me, that is, by me only and alone, exclude all other
means, all other ways, and all other patrons or advocates
whatsoever? Also in another place of the gospel, lest any
through shamefacedness, knowledge of their own unworthiness,
and guiltiness of sins, or the majesty and glory of Christ the
Son of God, should be hindered from calling upon God in the
name of Christ, and committing themselves to Christ his
defence; he in his own person, plainly and lovingly calling all
unto him and to the benefit of his defence, crieth: "Come Matth. xi.
unto me, all you that labour and are heavy loaden, and I will
give you rest."

Out of the epistle to the Hebrews no less evident testimonies than these, and that good store, may be gathered.

[3 Idem rursus aditum nobis ad Patrem aperit per Christum in
epistola, &c.; the same (apostle) again opens for us access to the
Father through Christ in his epistle, &c.]

Amongst other this one is excellent : " Christ, for that he endureth for ever," saith the apostle, "hath an everlasting priesthood. Wherefore he is able perfectly to save them that come unto God by him, seeing he ever liveth (for this end) to make intercession for them. For such an high priest it became us to have, (which is) holy, harmless, undefiled, separated from sinners, and made higher than the heavens, &c." Mark, I pray you, how many arguments in this testimony of Paul we have, to prove that Christ is the only intercessor of the faithful in heaven with the Father. The proper or peculiar office of the priest is, to make intercession : but only Christ is priest in the presence of God : he therefore is the only intercessor. Now also the priesthood of Christ is ever-lasting, or unchangeable. Therefore, not by once offering up hath he redeemed us, being made the alone and only Mediator of redemption; but the everlasting and perpetual Mediator also of intercession, making intercession for us even till the end of the world. For albeit our Lord be a judge[1], yet notwithstand-ing he is a judge of the unfaithful, a defender and upholder of the faithful, and at the length, when the world is at an end, a judge of all. And if so be he have an everlasting priesthood, and (ἀπαράβατον) not conveyable, I say, or removeable, which cannot, either by succession, resignation[2], or part-taking, pass over to any other; then certainly Christ only and alone remaineth intercessor of the faithful. Moreover, there is no cause why we should choose and take to ourselves, either after Christ, or with Christ, other intercessors. For he is able himself alone to work our salvation at the full; leav-ing unto others nothing at all whereabout to busy themselves. Let us also first of all[3] note that which expressly he doth add, "That come unto God by him :" by him, I say, that is, our mediator, priest, and intercessor, Christ : for by him only and alone the way lieth open for us to go to the Father. Unto which also is annexed, "That he liveth; and (for this end) he liveth to make intercession for us." The heavenly saints also do live in the kingdom of God with Christ : but they live for themselves (or for their own benefit), not for us (or our advantage). Christ liveth for us, and maketh inter-cession for us : therefore he alone maketh intercession. Saints

[1 et judex, Lat.; a judge too.]
[2 resignation, not in Lat.]   [3 imprimis, Lat.; especially.]

do not make intercession.   These reasons do prove unto us
most manifestly, I think, that the apostle speaketh of the
mediation of intercession, not of redemption.   Last of all, he
requireth in an intercessor such manner of marks (or properties) as a man cannot find in any save in Christ the Lord
only and alone.   For although the angels be innocent and
harmless, yet notwithstanding they are not higher than the
heavens.   The heavenly saints, although they be now purged
and made clean from sins, yet for all that by nature they are
not separated from sinners, neither are they made higher
than the heavens, as being lords over angels and over every
creature.   Only the Son is such a one, and for him this glory
is reserved and kept: he alone therefore is the intercessor of
the faithful with the Father.

Unto these testimonies of Paul we will yet join one of
St Peter, and another of the most blessed apostle and evan- 1 Pet. ii.
gelist John.   St Peter doth teach that the saints, that is, we
which are faithful in this world, are laid, as lively stones, by
faith upon Christ the lively stone; and that we are made a
spiritual building (or house), and an holy priesthood, to offer
spiritual sacrifices, acceptable to God by Jesus Christ.   Lo,
we are laid, not upon saints, but upon Christ, the lively stone;
by whom we are both quickened and preserved in the building.
We are made a spiritual house, and an holy priesthood, for
this end; that we should offer, not sacrifices of beasts, but
spiritual sacrifices, to wit, our own selves and our prayers,
unto God by Jesus Christ, not by saints.   For they also are
the spiritual house with us, the lively stones, laid upon Christ,
and living through Christ.

Furthermore, John writeth: "My babes, these things 1 John ii.
write I unto you, that ye sin not: and if any man sin, we
have an advocate with the Father, Jesus Christ, the just
(or the righteous).   And he is the propitiation (or reconciliation) for our sins; and not for ours only, but also (for
the sins) of the whole world."   I do not think that any
thing could be devised or spoken[4] more agreeable to our purpose, more evident, more strong or better than this.   We
hear that Christ is appointed and made unto us of God not
only a mediator of redemption, once to redeem, but to be

[4 vel confingi posse, Lat.; could even be devised :—or spoken, the
translator's addition.]

an everlasting mediator, yea, of intercession; who so often standeth an advocate before God the Father, how often sinful man offendeth and hath need of his help and defence; unto whom also the guilty may boldly have access, and commit unto him their cause to be pleaded before God. "If any man sin," saith John, "we have an advocate with the Father." Lo, John calleth him an advocate, whom the defenders (or maintainers) of the patronship of saints do call a mediator of intercession. For *advocatus*, παράκλητος, and advocate, signifieth a tutor, a defender, a favourer, a comforter, a patron, or a proctor, which pleadeth, or hath a cause[1] in handling. But mark whom he defineth and setteth forth to be our advocate: not the holy virgin, not Peter or Paul, not himself or Stephen, but Jesus Christ. If he had thought or believed that the patronship of heavenly saints had been over and besides necessary and wholesome for men, then would he have joined them with Christ the Lord: now he setteth forth unto us Christ alone. He addeth, "the just" (or the righteous); as if he had said, there is no cause why any should distrust or stand in doubt of his patronship, or think him a patron not in his Father's favour and love. He is the Son, he is Christ, he is the just or righteous: therefore he is highly in his Father's favour, and most acceptable; who in the presence of the most just God may appear for us that are unjust. Such righteousness is not found in any one of Adam's children. But it is required in an intercessor. Indeed, he doth communicate his righteousness to the saints by faith; but that righteousness is imputed to the saints, and it is imputative. In Christ righteousness is natural, and as it were born in him; yea, it is properly his own. For Christ Jesus, he is the only righteous in heaven and in earth; who needeth not first for his own sins, and then for the offences of the people, either to pray or to offer sacrifice; for he only hath no sin, and he is the righteousness of all: he[2] therefore maketh intercession with the Father, because none naturally and properly is righteous but Christ alone. And it is not amiss in this place first of all[3] to mark, that Christ is called a propitiation, or satisfaction, not for sinners or people of one

[1] So also ed. 1584: but ed. 1577, *our* cause; causam nostram, Lat.]
[2] solus, Lat.; he only.]
[3] in primis, Lat.; most especially.]

or two ages, but for all sinners and all faithful people throughout the whole world. One Christ therefore is sufficient for all: one intercessor with the Father is set forth unto all. For how often thou sinnest, so often thou hast ready a righteous intercessor with the Father. Not that we should imagine in heaven, as in a court, the Father upon his throne to sit as a judge, and the Son our patron so often to fall down on his knees, and to plead or entreat for us, as we sin and offend: but we understand with the apostle, that Christ is the advocate and the universal priest of the church, and that he only appeareth in the presence of the Father: because as the power and force of his death, (albeit he die not daily,) so the virtue of his intercession, is always effectual. Let us therefore draw near and come to God by Christ, the only mediator of our redemption and intercession, our only intercessor and advocate. We cannot but be acceptable unto God the Father, if we be commended unto him by his only-begotten Son. *What manner of intercession Christ's is.*

Furthermore, weak are the arguments wherewith the maintainers of the heavenly patrons go about to establish their patronship or intercession. The Spirit, say they, maketh intercession for us according to the doctrine of the apostle; therefore Christ alone doth not make intercession. I answer, that Paul speaketh not of another intercessor in heaven, but of the spirit of man praying in this world; which, being enlightened and kindled with the Spirit of God, groaneth and maketh intercession for the saints. The words of the apostle are plain. *An answer to certain arguments or reasons of the adversaries. Rom. viii.*

These men do yet add: We read in scripture of the prayers of angels, and that they offer the prayers of the faithful in God's presence: therefore not Christ alone prayeth or maketh intercession for us in heaven, but also the saints. We deny that this followeth; because the scripture teacheth that angels are ministering spirits; and, according to their office, offer prayers only as ministers in the presence of God, but not to make intercession, or that men are heard for angels' sakes, but for Christ's sake, who maketh intercession, and for whose sake the prayer which is brought and offered unto God is acceptable unto him. Now if so be they will bring forth the like also touching the blessed souls of the saints, and reason, *a simili*, from that that is like; let them *Prayer of angels.* *Heb. i.*

first teach that souls are appointed and made ministering spirits. But they cannot: and if they could, yet had they not proved that the heavenly saints are intercessors. For not the angels themselves, doubtless, are therefore intercessors, because they offer the prayers of men unto God.

They agree, say they, and are knit unto us in the same knot of charity and love; and for because the spirits of the blessed which live in heaven do love us here in earth, therefore, according to the nature and disposition of this love, they also pray for us. We answer, that they gather this without warrant of scripture. For, that we may without wrangling grant them this, that the saints in heaven are not without the love of their neighbour; yet notwithstanding we add, that this love in the heavenly saints hath not now that nature or disposition, and those offices, which in times past it had in earth. Otherwise, we should attribute many more absurdities to the saints; as though they either did or suffered those things, which they neither do nor yet suffer. Whilst they lived in earth, according to the disposition and nature of love, they were sorry, and they were glad, and they prayed with us, yea, they also made intercession for us: but now that they have put off this corruption and have left us, leading their lives in heaven with the Lord, they neither know our affairs, neither are moved with any earthly affections. They understand that it is passing well with us[1] without their help. They understand likewise that the work of our salvation is already wrought and accomplished[2], so that they may acquiet themselves, and rest from their labours, and rejoice in Christ; who is doubtless the only intercessor with the Father of all men living in their misery, because he knoweth all, and can do all, neither is he moved at, neither wearied or tired with, or yet is ignorant of any thing; but taketh upon him most absolutely and dispatcheth all things, whatsoever are incident or belong to an intercessor. They understand that this glory agreeth unto the only Son of God; and therefore they go not busily about it, that they in Christ's stead might appoint or make themselves in-

[1 nobis abunde consultum esse, Lat.; that we are full well cared for.]

[2 constitutum esse salutis negotium, Lat.; that the work of salvation is ordered.]

tercessors: for here the love that they bear to God surpasseth the love of their neighbour.

But these men object, that the saints pray not in heaven
after the rite and fashion of that only intercessor, but after
the same manner that they prayed for their fellow-brethren in
earth.   Even now we said that it did not follow, This they did
in earth, therefore they do the same in heaven.   Neither can
it be proved by manifest scriptures that the saints in heaven
pray for us.   Why then do they set forth unto us doubtful
opinions for certain?   For, that we may grant them that the
saints pray in heaven, (which thing not a few of the fathers
have written[3];) it doth not therefore follow that the saints are
to be called upon.   For that sentence of St Augustine is very
well known, which is read written in his book *De civitate
Dei*, xxii. chap. 10: "The Gentiles did both build temples,
made altars, ordained priests, and offered sacrifices unto their
gods.   But we do not erect temples to our martyrs, as unto
gods; but remembrances as unto dead men, whose spirits live
with God.   Neither do we there set up altars, upon which we
might sacrifice unto martyrs; but we sacrifice to one God,
who is the sacrifice both of the martyrs, and also our sacrifice:
according to which sacrifice, as men of God, that have overcome the world in the confession of him, they are named in
their place and order.   Howbeit, they are not called upon of
the priest that sacrificeth, because he is God's priest, and not
theirs.   Now the sacrifice itself is the body of Christ, which is
not offered unto them; because they also themselves are
the same[4]."   Thus saith he: testifying plainly enough, that
the saints are not called upon, or to be called upon, because
sacrifice belongeth unto God, and not to the saints.

[3 Bullinger quotes some passages from Cyprian, Augustine, and
Jerome, in his treatise, De Orig. Error. capp. 14, 15, 16, 17.]

[4 Denique illi talibus diis suis et templa ædificaverunt, et statue-
runt aras, et sacerdotes instituerunt, et sacrificia fecerunt.   Nos autem
martyribus nostris non templa sicut diis, sed memorias sicut hominibus
mortuis, quorum apud Deum vivunt spiritus, fabricamus.   Nec ibi
erigimus altaria, in quibus sacrificemus martyribus, sed uni Deo et martyrum et nostro sacrificium immolamus; ad quod sacrificium, sicut
homines Dei, qui mundum in ejus confessione vicerunt, suo loco et
ordine nominantur; non tamen a sacerdote, qui sacrificat, invocantur;
quia Dei sacerdos est, non illorum.   Ipsum vero sacrificium corpus est
Christi, quod non offertur ipsis, quia hoc sunt et ipsi.—Augustin. de
Civit. Dei, Lib. xxii. cap. 10. Opp. Tom. v. fol. 302. col. 4. Par. 1531.]

Wherefore, when the adversaries add, that the church many years called upon the saints, that the church erred not, and therefore they that call upon the saints do not err ; we answer, that the church doth not err, when she heareth the voice of her bridegroom and shepherd : but that she doth err, when, neglecting the voice of her shepherd, she followeth her own decrees.   The whole church of Israel erred, together with their high priest Aaron and the elders of the people, when, transgressing the law of God, they worshipped God represented by an image with singings and dancings, otherwise than he himself had appointed.   Neither are the Israelites absolved from error and sin, for that many years they put not down their high places.

They add again, the saints have helped when they have been called upon ; therefore they are to be called upon. Oftentimes that falleth out well which is instituted against the word of God.   But who can thereupon gather that that is good which is instituted against the word of God ? As though the innocent and harmless were therefore to be spoiled with war, because we see that by war merciless soldiers wax rich.   The gods of the Gentiles likewise seemed to hear the petitions of their suppliants; but are the gods of the Gentiles therefore to be called upon ?

But we mean not to answer to every one of their arguments, because we have done that already elsewhere, according to our talent[1].   We conclude, therefore, that the word of truth, uttered out of the mouth of God, doth teach us invocation of God's name by the mediation of Jesus Christ : neither do we read that any holy man, either in the old or the new Testament (of whom the scripture undoubtedly hath made mention), called upon any, though never so excellent a patriarch or prophet, departed this life, or upon any apostle, or apostle's disciple, otherwise than by the name of Jesus Christ.   Let us therefore hold fast, that that doctrine is most perfect and most safe, which biddeth us all to call upon God alone by his only Son, and that God himself requireth this of every one of us ; and that when we obey, we please God.

The last place, touching the serving of God, doth remain behind.   This word *colere* is in Latin of large signification.

[1 Bulling. de Orig. Erroris, Lib. i. capp. 18, 19. Tigur. 1539.]

For we say, *colere amicitiam*, to maintain friendship, *colere
literarum studia*, to love learning, *colere arva*, to till or husband our lands, and *colere senes*, to reverence old men. We
in this place use *colere* for *servire*, that is, in all points like a To serve,
what it is.
servant to be dutiful, and to shew himself obedient to rever-
ence, or have in veneration, and to do worship. The Hebricians
use their word *abad*, which the Latin interpreter translateth
servivit, coluit, or *sacrificavit*[2]; that is, he served, worshipped,
or sacrificed. In the book of Kings thou dost read: "And 1 Kings xvi.
Achab served Baal, and worshipped him." The Grecians call
this service either λατρεία or δουλεία. The one is taken
for the other: though indeed *servire*, to serve, be more than
colere, to worship: for thou canst abide without any ado to
worship some man; but to serve the same, thou canst not so
well away withal. We say therefore that the service[3] of The service
of God.
God is a service whereby men submit themselves reverently
unto God, and obey him, and according to his will worship
him. They therefore serve[4] God, which serve[5] him earnestly,
behave themselves dutifully in obeying him, serving[6] him
inwardly and outwardly, as he hath appointed.

For the service[7] of God is twofold, or of two sorts; the The service
of God is
twofold, or
of two sorts.
true and the false. The true is called true religion, true
faith, and godliness. The false is called superstition, idolatry,
and ungodliness. For that is the true service[7] of God, which
springeth from the true fear of God, from a sincere faith, which
submitteth itself in all things to the will of God[8]. The false
service consisteth in the contrary: touching the which we
will say more, when we come to speak of superstition.

The true service of God is divided again, for perspicuity
or plainness' sake, into the inward service of God, and the
outward. The inward service is known to God alone, who is
the searcher of hearts. For it is occupied in the fear of God,
and perfect obedience, in faith, hope, and charity, from whence
do spring the worshipping of God, the calling upon him,
thanksgiving, patience, perseverance, chastity, innocency, well-

[2 Exod. xx. 5; vii. 16. Vulgate.]

[3 cultum, Lat.] 　　　　　　　　　[4 colunt, Lat.]

[5 timent, Lat.; fear him.] 　　　　[6 colentes, Lat.]

[7 cultus, Lat.]

[8 So also ed. 1584: but ed. 1577, which submitteth itself to God
alone, and applieth itself in all things, &c. So Lat.]

The inward
service of
God. doing, and the rest of the fruits of the Spirit.   For with these
gifts of God and spiritual things God, who is a Spirit, is
truly served : without these no service is allowed of God,
howsoever in the sight of men it seem gay, glorious and pure.
This service of God hath testimonies both divine and human ;
but first of all of the law, the prophets, and the apostles.   For
Deut. x.   in the law Moses saith : "And now, Israel, what doth the
Lord thy God require of thee, but that thou shouldest fear
the Lord thy God, and walk in all his ways, that thou
shouldest love him, and that thou shouldest serve the Lord thy
God with all thy heart, and with all thy soul, that thou
shouldest keep the commandments of the Lord, and his ordinances, which I command thee this day for thy wealth ?"
Micheas the prophet bringeth in one asking questions concerning the true service of God, in what things the same consisteth,
Mic. vi.   and he maketh answer : "I will shew thee[1], O man, what is
good, and what the Lord doth require of thee : surely to do
justly (or judgment), to love mercy, and to humble thyself to
Rom. xii.   walk with thy God[2]."   St Paul the apostle saith : "I beseech
you, brethren, by the mercies of God, that ye give up your
bodies a living sacrifice, holy, acceptable unto God, (which is)
your reasonable serving of God.   And fashion not yourselves
like unto this world, but be ye changed by the renewing of
your mind, that ye may prove what is the will of God, and
what is good and acceptable and perfect[3]."   The same apostle,
comprehending in few words the true service of God to be a
turning from idols unto God and the faith of Jesus Christ,
1 Thess. i.   saith : "They of Macedonia, and other nations (or quarters),
shew of you, how you are turned to God from idols, that ye
might serve the living and true God, and look for his Son
from heaven, whom he raised from the dead, even Jesus, who
delivereth us from the wrath to come."   Moreover, St James
James i.   the apostle saith : "Pure religion and undefiled before God the
Father is this, to visit the fatherless (or orphans) and widows
in their adversity, and to keep himself unspotted of the

[1 So Coverdale, 1535, and Vulgate.]

[2 to be lowly, and to walk with thy God, Coverdale, 1535. et soli-
citum (Bullinger adds, vel submissum, which word is used in Bibl. Lat.
Tigur. 1544) ambulare cum Deo tuo. Vulgate.]

[3 —ut quotidiano docti exercitio tandem discernere possimus, quid
Deus velit, quodnam illud bonum et rectum sit, quid illi placeat, et
quæ sit illa absoluta felicitas.—Bulling. expos. in loc.]

world⁴." These divine and evident testimonies of holy scripture declare plentifully enough, dearly beloved, which is the
true inward service of God.   Human testimonies nevertheless,
nothing disagreeing from divine, there are many and everywhere found in ecclesiastical writers.   Lactantius, lib. *Institut.* vi. cap. 9, saith: "Therefore the knowledge of God and
his service is all in all: in this consisteth all the hope and
salvation of man: this is the first step (or degree) of wisdom,
that we should know who is our true Father, that we should
reverence him alone with due godliness, that we should obey
him, and most devoutly serve him: and to obtain his favour,
let all labour, care, and industry be bestowed⁵." Of this kind
the same author citeth⁶ other testimonies also largely in the
tenth chapter of the same book; and in the first chapter of
his book, *de vero Dei Cultu,* he giveth us manifest⁷. But
instead of many we like well the citing of that one testimony,
touching the true service of God, freely uttered by the mouth
of a Roman martyr⁸ before judge Asclepiades at the Roman
consistory. For after he had both courageously and religiously
told what God was in person, and what in substance, he
addeth:

The testimony of a Roman martyr concerning the true service of God

> Thou knowest God: now understand as well
> The form and manner how he served is;
> What kind of church it is where he doth dwell;
> What gifts to give he thought it not amiss;
> What vows he asks: whom he (beside all this)
>   Will have his priests, and in his church likewise
>   What he commands to bring for sacrifice.
>
> Unto himself, even in the mind of man,
> A church he hath vouchsafed up to rear;

God's temple or church.

[⁴ So ed. 1577: but 1584, 1587, in the world; a mundo, Lat.]

[⁵ In Dei agnitione et cultu rerum summa versatur; in hoc est spes
omnis ac salus hominis: hic est sapientiæ gradus primus, ut sciamus
quis sit nobis verus pater, eumque solum pietate debita prosequamur,
huic pareamus, huic devotissime serviamus; in eo promerendo actus
omnis et cura et opera collocetur.—Lactant. Instit. Lib. vi. cap. 9.
p. 576. Lugd. Bat. 1660.]

[⁶ recitat, Lat.]

[⁷ et luculentissima de vero Dei Cultu, cap. 1. Lat.; and (the same
author) gives the most clear description of the true worship of God in
the first chapter (of the same book).—The sixth book of Lactantius'
Institutes is entitled, *De Vero Cultu.*]

[⁸ Rather, of the martyr Romanus.]

A lively, feeling, breathing church, which can
Not sundred be, fair, beautiful, and clear,
And never like destruction's dint to fear,
　　With lofty top, and painted pleasantly
　　With colours fresh of great diversity.

God's priest.

At th' holy porch a priest is standing there,
And keeps the doors before the church which been.
Faith is her name, a virgin chaste and clear,
Her hair tied up with fillets like a queen.
For sacrifices simple, pure, and clean,
　　And which she knows are pleasing, bids this priest
　　Offer to God, and to his dear Son Christ;

God's sacri-
fices.

A shamefac'd look, a meek and harmless heart,
The rest of peace, a body pure and chaste,
The fear of God, which sinners doth convert:
The rule likewise of knowledge truly plac'd,
A sober fast from all excessive waste
　　Of gluttony, an hope which doth not faint,
　　A liberal hand which gives without restraint.

From these oblations a vapour doth arise,
Which savours sweet by virtue's force compels:
It doth ascend and pierce the azure skies;
The scent of balm and saffron it excels,
Yea frankincense, and Persian spices' smells:
　　From earth to heaven it mounteth up aloft,
　　And pleaseth God therewith delighted oft[1].

[1 Cognostis ipsum? nunc colendi agnoscite
　　Ritum modumque; quale sit templi genus;
　　Quæ dedicari sanxerit donaria;
　　Quæ vota poscat; quos sacerdotes velit;
　　Quod mandet illic nectar immolarier.

Ædem sibi ipse mente in hominis condidit,
　　Vivam, serenam, sensualem, flabilem,
　　Solvi incapacem posse, nec destructilem,
　　Pulchram, venustam, præminentem culmine,
　　Discriminatis inlitam coloribus.

Illic sacerdos stat sacrato in lumine,
　　Foresque primas virgo custodit Fides,
　　Innexa crines vinculis regalibus.
　　Poscit litari victimas Christo et Patri,
　　Quas scit placere, candidatas, simplices;

Frontis pudorem, cordis innocentiam,
　　Pacis quietem, castitatem corporis,
　　Dei timorem, regulam scientiæ,
　　Jejuniorum parcitatem sobriam,
　　Spem non jacentem, semper et largam manum.

And so forth as followeth to this purpose.   These things I think sufficient, concerning the inward service of God : wherein I confess in the meanwhile to be somewhat which may be referred also to the outward service of God.

The outward service of God springeth from the inward : The outward neither is it known to God alone, as this other, but is open service of to the judgment of man ; and it is a keeping or executing of God. the rites instituted of God himself, whereby we do both testify unto men the inward service, and practise them to the glory of God and our profit.   Of this kind were among the ancient people the temple, the priesthood, and all the ceremonies instituted of God, which are very often called the service of God.   And this service had his appointed limits ; for it was not lawful for every one to feign a service of God after their own pleasure, as is shewed at large in the law and in the holy history.

Now that outward service served to the glory of God and the profit of the faithful : which thing I have declared when I was in hand with the Jewish[2] ceremonies.   Furthermore, as Christ abrogated those old rites, so in their stead he placed again a very few.   For he instituted an holy assembly, wherein his will is that his word should be preached and expounded out of the holy scripture to his own glory and to our profit ; common prayer to be made ; and the sacraments to be ministered and received.   To which things a convenient place is necessary, fit time, due order, and holy instruments.   Where again the godly do in nothing follow their own wills ; for from the word of that God, whom they serve, they fetch the whole manner and order of serving him.   Whereof somewhat is spoken in the fourth commandment of the first table, and shall be spoken more at large in due place and order.

> Ex his amœnus hostiis surgit vapor,
>   Vincens odorem balsami, turis, croci,
>   Auras madentes Persicorum aromatum ;
>   Sublatus inde cœlum adusque tollitur,
>   Et prosperatum dulce delectat Deum.
>   Prudentii Peristeph. Hymn. xiv. 341—365.
> Romanus, whose address to Asclepiades, prefect of the city, is thus
> versified, was a martyr at Antioch in the fourth century.   Magdeb.
> Centur. Cent. iv. cap. 12.]
>   [2 Israeliticis, Lat.]

To be short, they serve God with outward service, who by faith and obedience gather themselves into the holy assembly at limited times; who keep the ecclesiastical discipline derived out of the word of God; who hear the word of God, or the holy exposition of the sacred scriptures; who pray publicly with the church; who religiously participate the sacraments; and observe other lawful and wholesome rites or ceremonies. By this their service they glorify God among men, and receive of God no small reward[1], namely, his blessing, and increase of heavenly gifts.

There is no need, I think, in this place, of testimonies of the scriptures, to confirm these things that we have hitherto spoken touching the outward service of God. For everywhere in the history of the Gospel, in the Acts and Epistles of the Apostles, very many are to be found. For the Lord Jesus doth everywhere gather together holy assemblies, to whom he preacheth the gospel, and commendeth prayer. Of Mary sitting at his feet and hearing his preaching he

Luke x.

saith: "This one thing is necessary; Mary hath chosen the good part, which shall not be taken from her." And in

Luke xi.

another place: "Blessed are they," saith he, "which hear the word of God, and keep it." Surely the Lord himself instituted and put in use the sacraments. For to John, not consenting to baptize him at his asking, and saying, "I have need to be baptized of thee, and comest thou to me?" he answered, "Let it be so now: for so it becometh us to fulfil all righteousness." Whereupon the apostle Paul likewise, diligently commending ecclesiastical discipline to the churches, ordained most decently holy assemblies. The places are very well known unto all; 1 Cor. xi. 14, 16; likewise 1 Tim. ii. and elsewhere.

That only God is to be served.

But before I conclude this place, I will shew that only God is to be served[2]. And surely the service itself, whereof we have hitherto entreated, cannot be bestowed upon any creature, neither angels nor celestial saints; to God alone it agreeth. Wherefore there is none so blind but may see that God alone must be served with these. And when God requireth of us his service or duty, he requireth our whole heart: nothing therefore is left us to bestow upon other.

Deut. xiii.

Moses, full of the Spirit of God, saith in his law: "Ye shall

[1 utilitatem, Lat.]   [2 colendum, Lat.]

walk after the Lord your God, and fear him; his commandments shall ye keep; and ye shall hearken unto his voice,
and ye shall serve him, and cleave unto him." Neither
makes it any matter that here the word "alone" is not
added, seeing that the words are uttered with an emphasis
or force. For when he saith, "Him shall ye serve, and
to him ye shall cleave," what other thing do we understand,
than to him and not to any other, therefore to him alone?
Furthermore, in the sixth chapter of Deuteronomy, thou
dost not read, "Thou shalt fear the Lord thy God, and him
alone shalt thou serve, and thou shalt swear by his name;"
but, "Thou shalt fear the Lord thy God, and him" (em-
phatically) "shalt thou serve, and thou shalt swear by his
name." Furthermore, the Lord in the gospel, bringing these
words of the law against the tempter, and making the emphasis plain, "It is written," (saith he), "Thou shalt worship Matt. iv.
the Lord thy God, and him only shalt thou serve." Which
testimony doubtless, being most effectual and pithy, is only
sufficient for our demonstration, that God alone is to be
served.

I will moreover add hereunto the testimony of a man,
howbeit established by divine authority, which we also elsewhere set down in our books. St Augustine, *de Quantitate
Animæ*, doth shew that God alone is to be served in this
sort: "Whatsoever the soul doth serve as God, needful it
is that she think the same better than herself. But we must
believe that neither the earth, nor the sea, nor the stars,
nor the moon, nor the sun, nor anything at all that may be
felt, or seen with these eyes; to be short, not heaven itself,
which cannot be seen of us, is better than the nature of the
soul: yea rather, that all these are far worse than is any
soul, assured reason doth convince[3]." And anon; "If therefore there be any other thing of those that God hath created, something is worse, something is as good: worse, as

[3 Quicquid enim anima colit ut Deum, necesse est ut melius esse
quam seipsam putet. Animæ autem natura nec terra, nec maria, nec
sidera, nec luna, nec sol, nec quicquam omnino quod tangi aut his
oculis videri potest, non denique ipsum, quod videri a nobis non potest,
cœlum, melius esse credendum est. Imo hæc omnia longe deteriora
esse, quam est quælibet anima, ratio certa convincit.—August. de Quant.
Animæ. cap. 34. Opp. Tom. i. fol. 130. col. 4. Par. 1532.]

the soul of a beast; equal, as the angels: but nothing is better: and if happily something of these better, this cometh to pass by sin and not by nature; by which sin notwithstanding it becometh not so ill, that the soul of a beast is either to be preferred before it, or to be compared with it. God therefore alone is to be worshipped of it, who alone is the author of it. And as for any other man, though he be most wise and most perfect, or any soul endued with reason, and most blessed, they are only to be loved and followed; and according to desert and order, that is to be exhibited unto them, which agreeth and is fit for them. For it is written, 'Thou shalt worship the Lord thy God, and him only shalt thou serve[1].'" These be St Augustine's words. And thus far have we entreated of one only, living, true, and everlasting God to be served.

How saints are to be worshipped.

Of true religion.

Moreover, whosoever cleave unto God with a sincere faith, and worship, call upon, and serve one God lawfully, they are rightly named religious: their study and action is true religion. Some will have religion to be derived *a relinquendo*[2], because thereby we leave or forsake false gods, all errors, and earthly desires, and seek after the true God, after truth, and heavenly things. Massurius Sabinus saith: "That is religious, which for some holiness' sake we put by and severally set aside. The word 'religion' hath his name *a relinquendo*, as *Ceremoniæ a carendo*[3]." But M. Cicero supposeth that *Religio* is so called *a relegendo* (of selecting or putting apart), because they that be religious do carefully choose all

[1 Si quid ergo aliud est eorum quæ Deus creavit, quiddam est deterius, quiddam par: deterius, ut anima pecoris; par, ut angeli: melius autem nihil. Et si quando est aliquid horum melius, hoc peccato ejus fit, non natura; quo tamen non usque adeo fit deterior, ut ei pecoris anima præferenda aut conferenda sit. Deus igitur solus ei colendus est, qui solus ejus est auctor. Homo autem quilibet alius, quanquam sapientissimus et perfectissimus, vel prorsus quælibet anima rationis compos atque beatissima, amanda tantummodo et imitanda est, eique pro merito atque ordine, quod ei congruit, deferendum. Nam Dominum Deum tuum adorabis, et illi soli servies.—August. ibid.]

[2 Vol. II. p. 125, note 4.]

[3 Massurius Sabinus, in commentariis quos de indigenis composuit, Religiosum, inquit, est quod propter sanctitatem aliquam remotum ac sepositum a nobis est; verbum a relinquendo dictum, tanquam cærimoniæ a carendo.—Aul. Gell. Noct. Att. Lib. IV. cap. 9. p. 280. Lugd. Bat. 1700.]

things which seem to belong to the service of the gods. But he is confuted, in many words, of Lactantius Firmianus, an ancient writer of the church, Lib. *Instit.* iv. cap. 28, where among other things he saith: " On this condition we are born, that being born we might do to God just and due service, that we should know him alone, and that him we should follow. With this bond of godliness we are straitly bound and tied unto God ; whereupon religion itself took her name." And anon after: " We said that the name of religion was derived from the bond of godliness, because God hath tied and bound man unto himself in godliness : for that it is needful that we serve him as a lord, and obey him as a father [4]." Other ecclesiastical writers also following him, as Hierome and Augustine, derived religion *a religando*, of tying or binding. For Hierome in his commentary upon the ninth chapter of Amos saith: "This bundle tied up with the religion of the Lord, which is one. Religion therefore took her name *a religando*, of tying together, and binding into the Lord's bundle [5]." And Augustine in his book *de Quantitate Animæ*, chapter 36, saith : "True religion is, whereby the soul tieth herself through reconciliation to one God, from whom through sin she had as it were broken away [6]." The same Augustine, in his book *de Vera Religione*, and last chapter, saith : "Let religion tie us unto one God Almighty, whereof it is believed to be named religion [7]."

[4] Hac conditione gignimur, ut generanti (Bullinger read, generati) nos Deo justa et debita obsequia præbeamus; hunc solum noverimus; hunc sequamur. Hoc vinculo pietatis obstricti Deo religati sumus; unde ipsa religio nomen accepit: non, ut Cicero interpretatus est, a relegendo; qui in libro de natura deorum secundo (cap. 28) dicit ita, &c. &c. .... Diximus nomen religionis a vinculo pietatis esse deductum; quod hominem sibi Deus religaverit, et pietate constrinxerit: quia servire nos ei, ut domino, et obsequi, ut patri, necesse est.—Lactant. Instit. Lib. iv. cap. 28.]

[5] Iste fasciculus una Domini religione constrictus est. Unde et ipsa religio a religando, et in fascem Domini vinciendo, nomen accepit. —Hieron. Comment. in Amos. cap. 8. Opp. Tom. iii. col. 1448. Par. 1693—1706.]

[6] Est enim religio vera, qua se uni Deo anima, unde se peccato velut abruperat, reconciliatione religat.—Aug. Opp. Par. 1532. Tom. i. fol. 131. col. 1.]

[7] See the quotation, Vol. i. p. 233, note 5. Aug. Opp. Tom. i. fol. 156, col. 3.]

We say, therefore, that true religion is none other thing
than a friendship, a knitting, and an unity (or league) with the
true, living, and everlasting God; unto whom we being linked
by a true faith do worship, call upon, and serve him alone;
upon whom we do wholly depend, living in all things according
to his will, or according to the prescript rule and law of his
word. Therefore most rightly is the whole matter of salvation
and faith comprised in this one word, religion: which elsewhere
is called in scripture a league or covenant, and elsewhere again,
marriage or wedlock. For as they which be confederate are
united and made one by a league; so God and man are knit
together by religion: and as by marriage the husband and
the wife are made one body, so by religion we are knit into
a spiritual body with God, as with our husband, and with the
very Son of God, as with our bridegroom and our head.
Hitherto therefore doth belong whatsoever things are uttered
in the scriptures touching the keeping of the league or covenant, and the faith of marriage. Truce-breakers are they,
disloyal, and infamous through their adultery, whosoever,
being not knit to one God by faith, worship him alone, call
upon him through Christ, and serve him also as he himself
hath said in his word he would be served.

The very same are also called superstitious. For superstition is false religion, which doth not serve God but somewhat
else for God, or not God alone, or not rightly or lawfully.
This word superstition stretcheth itself even to old wives'
tales and doting errors: for in Dutch we call superstition,
aberglauben, mis-glauben, und mis-bruch. But Lactantius,
reasoning most exactly of this word, in his fourth book of
Institutions, and twenty-eighth chapter, writeth in this
sort: " Religion is the service of the true God; superstition,
of the false. They are said to be superstitious, not that
wish their children to outlive them, for that we do all wish;
but either they that reverence the memory remaining of
the dead; or else they that, while their parents were alive,
worshipped their images within their houses, like household
gods. For those which did take unto themselves new rites,
to the intent they might instead of gods honour the dead,
whom they thought were taken from among men and received
into heaven; those (I say) they called superstitious: but those

that worshipped and served public and ancient gods they named religious. Whereupon saith Virgil:

> Vain superstition, ignorant
> Of th' old and ancient gods.

But seeing we do find that our ancients have been in semblable manner consecrated gods after their death, they therefore which serve many and false gods are superstitious. But we are religious, which pray and make our supplications to one God, being the true God, &c.[1]"

Superstition consisteth chiefly in these points; either when the Lord is not served, but other gods in his stead, the only one, true, and living God being left and forsaken; or else when the Lord is served, but not alone, but other together with him; or else when he is served, but not with his lawful service. *To leave, or forsake the true God, and to serve strange gods.*

In the first kind of superstition did the Gentiles in a manner[2] offend, who knew not the true God; insomuch that they, instead of the true God, worshipped false, feigned, or strange gods. And that the Israelites also, God's people, were sick of the same madness, the holy prophet Jeremy is a witness; who, expostulating and reasoning the matter with the people, saith: "Hear ye the word of the Lord, O house of Jacob, and all the families of the house of Israel. Thus saith the Lord, What iniquity have your fathers found in me, that they are gone far from me, and have walked after vanity, and are become vain? For they said not, Where is the Lord that brought us[3] out of the land of Egypt; that led us through the wilderness, through a desert and waste land, through a dry *Jer. ii.*

[1 Superstitiosi vocantur, non qui filios suos superstites optant (omnes enim optamus), sed aut ii, qui superstitem memoriam defunctorum colunt; aut qui parentibus suis superstites colebant imagines eorum domi tanquam deos penates. Nam qui novos sibi ritus assumebant, ut deorum vice mortuos honorarent, quos ex hominibus in cœlum receptos putabant, hos superstitiosos vocabant; eos vero, qui publicos et antiquos deos colerent, religiosos nominabant. Unde Virgilius:
> Vana superstitio, veterumque ignara deorum.

Sed cum veteres quoque deos inveniamus eodem modo consecratos esse post obitum, superstitiosi ergo qui multos ac falsos deos colunt: nos autem religiosi, qui uni et vero Deo supplicamus.—Lactant. Instit. Lib. iv. cap. 28. p. 445. Lugd. Bat. 1660.]

[2 fere, Lat.; generally.]

[3 brought us up out, ed. 1577.]

land, and by the shadow of death, by a land that no man passed through, and where no man dwelt? And I brought you into a plentiful country, to eat the fruit thereof and the commodities of the same : but when ye entered, ye defiled my land, and made mine heritage an abomination. The priests said not, Where is the Lord? and they that should minister the law, knew me not: the pastors also offended against me; and the prophets prophesied in Baal, and went after things that did not profit (or followed idols). Wherefore I will yet plead with you, saith the Lord; and I will plead with your children's children. For go ye to the isles of Chittim, and behold; and send unto Kedar, and take diligent heed; and see whether there be such things. Hath any nation changed their gods, which yet are no gods? But my people have changed their glory for that which doth not profit (or for an idol). O ye heavens, be astonied at this; be afraid, and utterly confounded, saith the Lord. For my people have committed two evils: they have forsaken me, the fountain of living waters, to dig them pits, even broken pits, that can hold no water." Thou dost hear that the people of Israel by an heinous offence, and for the which no amends might be made, forsook God, the lively spring, and digged unto themselves broken pits. The waters do signify the perfit good, wherewith the desire both of the soul and the body may be satisfied. Such a plentiful spring is God alone, the highest, excellentest, and perfittest good. This being forsaken, they digged, that is, with very great pains and costs they provided for themselves, pits; that is, they turned themselves to creatures, to them that are no gods, neither yet are able to satisfy their desires. This mischief even at this day also is common; whiles many, having forsaken God, are turned unto celestial saints, of whom they desire that which was to be desired of God, neither can be given but of God alone.

Here hath idolatry a place, that is, the worshipping of images. For they not only[1] are superstitious, which feign unto themselves false gods, having forsaken the true God; or that put their trust in things of nothing: but they also which worship and reverence the images either of God, or of gods, are also superstitious. For images or counterfeits[2] are set up either to the true God himself, or else to false gods, to

[1 not they only, ed. 1577.]   [2 simulacra, Lat.]

creatures (I say) themselves. But it is not lawful by any image or counterfeit to represent the exceeding great, everlasting, and living God world without end. Neither is it lawful to worship or serve him being expressed by an image or likeness: much less therefore is it lawful to consecrate unto creatures images or counterfeits, to worship and serve them. There are very many testimonies of scripture extant against idolatry; as in Exodus xx. Esay xl. xliv. Psalm cxv. 1 Corinthians vi. x. Romans i. Galatians v. 1 Thessalonians i. 1 Peter iv. 1 John v. Jeremy x. &c. Furthermore, I do here diligently admonish the simpler sort, that they suffer not themselves to be deceived. For none can avoid the name of an idolater, that doth worship, reverence, and fear images ; that putteth some part of his confidence in them ; that lieth along before them ; that offereth them gifts ; that keepeth them in a place of solemnity and honour ; that sticketh up tapers and burneth incense unto them ; that loveth, beautifieth, maintaineth, enricheth, and serveth them with any kind of sacrifice or holy service whatsoever. But concerning idolatry we have spoken very largely elsewhere[3].

Furthermore, they served (who doubts it ?) the God of Israel ; howbeit not alone, but with the true God other gods also, of whom we read in the history of the kings : " And yet they served," (or feared) "the Lord : and they appointed out priests (even of the basest) unto themselves for the high places, who prepared for them sacrifices in the houses of the high places. And when they served the Lord, they served their own gods also, after the manner of the nations from whence they were brought into Samaria." And again : " So these nations feared the Lord, and served their images also; so did their children, and their children's children : as did their fathers, so do they unto this day." This mischief, in like manner, is altogether common at this day. For a man may find worshippers and servers of God who will at no hand be persuaded that God alone is to be served, yea, boldly affirming that it is flat and damnable heresy to deny that together with God saints are both to be worshipped, called upon, and served. Against whom we have elsewhere[4], and in this our present sermon also, sufficiently disputed.

Here likewise cometh next to hand to be marked the

Not to worship God alone, but to worship other gods also together with the true God.

2 Kings xvii.

[3 Decade II. Serm. 2.]   [4 Bulling. de Orig. Error. Lib. I.]

diverse manner and sundry fashion of serving God super-stitiously. For neither doth he only and alone serve God superstitiously, who indeed first feigneth or imagineth in his mind a God, and then afterwards expresseth the same God by an image or counterfeit, whereunto by and by upon that he offereth sacrifices and incense, and, lying prostrate upon the ground, worshippeth in presence of the same, and suppli-antly serveth it with all reverence : but he principally serveth God superstitiously, who doth communicate the incommuni-cable properties of God to creatures, albeit he express God by no representation, likeness, or counterfeit; or he which thinketh that the gifts, which he hath received from heaven at the hands of God, are given and bestowed upon him of celestial saints. Furthermore, the incommunicable properties of God are, able to do all things, to know all things, to be present in every place, to hear all things, to help, succour, or assist, to be loving, bountiful, just, righteous, and merciful. Verily, Esay, the best learned of the prophets and of singular authority, proveth and convinceth by these most strong and substantial arguments or reasons, that the gods of the Baby-lonians and Gentiles are no gods : " Because they cannot foretel or know things that are to come hereafter, neither yet can do good or evil." Wherefore, able to enrich and store with all manner of benefits, and to chastise with due deserved punishments ; so also to know all things, and to be of power to compass and do all things ; they are the pro-perties of God alone, communicable to no creature. He there-fore is superstitious, which attributeth these properties to celestial saints, and for that cause doth serve and call upon them. Osee the prophet doth very sore inveigh against the Jews, who gave and attributed to strange gods the gifts of God, insomuch that he nameth the synagogue of such a strumpet or harlot. " I will have no pity" (saith he) " upon her children : for they be the children of fornications. For their mother hath played the harlot : she that conceived them hath done shamefully. For she said, I will go after my lovers, that give me my bread and my water, my wool and my flax, mine oil and my drink." And anon after : " Now she did not know that I gave her corn, and wine, and oil ; and multiplied" (or gave her much) " her silver and gold, which they bestowed even upon Baal." And it is a

Marginal notes:

The pro-perties of God are in no case to be attributed unto strange gods.

Isai. xli. xlii. &c.

God's gifts are not to be attributed to strange gods. Hosea ii.

thing much used at this day, to ascribe unto celestial saints, and not to the only God, the increase of the earth, and the temperate or sharp seasons of the year, as though they came from them.   But that is superstition, not godliness or religion.

Furthermore, God is superstitiously served, when indeed he is served alone, howbeit not after a lawful manner.   Unlawful service proceedeth from the will and imagination of men ; and it is contrary to the word and ordinance of God. For God is then lawfully served, when he is served according to his own will and word.   In the law thus hath the Lord commanded : "Beware that thou seek not after the gods of the Gentiles, saying, How did these nations serve their gods, that I may do so likewise ?   Thou shalt not do so unto the Lord thy God, &c.   (Therefore) whatsoever I command you, take heed you do it : thou shalt put nothing thereto, nor take ought therefrom."   Nadab and Abihu offer strange fire unto the Lord : therefore are they burned up in the presence of the Lord with fire from heaven.   Oza also perished, because he handled the ark of God otherwise than the Lord had commanded in his law.   Micha, in the book of Judges, instituted unto the true God, whose name is Jehovah, an image, an altar, a chapel, and a service : but it is reproved in the sacred scripture, because it was not only not fetched out of the holy scripture, but was in all respects quite contrary and utterly against the law of God.   Jeroboam also ordained passing sumptuous service ; he instituted cathedral churches, and set up golden images, all to the God of Israel : but for that they were not agreeable to the word of the Lord, they are all, one with another, utterly condemned for execrable and accursed sacrileges.   Yea, what we may think in general of all the services which are neither instituted of God, nor agreeing with the word of God, but feigned upon a good intent and meaning of our own, that only testimony of the most excellent prophet Samuel doth declare to us, which he pronounced against Saul and his sacrifices in these words : " Hath the Lord as great pleasure in burnt-offerings and sacrifices, as when the voice of the Lord is obeyed ?   Behold, to obey is better than sacrifice, and to hearken (is better) than the fat of rams.   For rebellion is as the sin of witchcraft, and transgression is wickedness and idolatry."   Here-

To serve God, but not lawfully.

Deut. xii.

Levit. x.

[2 Sam. vi.]

Judges xvii.

1 Kings xii. xiii.

1 Sam. xv.

Isai. lxvi. unto maketh that which we read in Esay : " He that killeth a bullock is as if he slew a man ; he that sacrificeth a sheep, as if he cut off a dog's neck; he that offereth an oblation, as if he offered swine's blood ; he that remembereth incense, as if he blessed an idol. All these things have they chosen in their own ways, and their soul is delighted in their own abominations." Vain therefore and abominable are those services which are not reduced and framed to the pure word Isai. xxix. Matt. xv. of God : for the same prophet saith, " In vain do they serve me, teaching doctrines of men."

The living, true, and everlasting God, who will and ought only and alone to be worshipped, to be called upon, and to be served, give unto all men true religion, and deliver them from all vain superstition, through Jesus Christ our Lord. Amen. A. F.

THAT THE SON OF GOD IS UNSPEAKABLY BEGOTTEN OF THE FATHER ; THAT HE IS CONSUBSTANTIAL WITH THE FATHER, AND THEREFORE TRUE GOD. THAT THE SELFSAME SON IS TRUE MAN ; CONSUB-STANTIAL WITH US : AND THEREFORE TRUE GOD AND MAN, ABIDING IN TWO UNCONFOUNDED NATURES, AND IN ONE UNDIVIDED PERSON.

THE SIXTH SERMON.

THE things themselves and their order do require, that after I have spoken generally of God, of his unity, and of his trinity, I further entreat particularly of the persons of the reverend Trinity ; and first of all, of our Lord Jesus Christ, true God and man ; then of the Holy Ghost : where-with if our minds be endued, all things whatsoever we speak and hear shall tend to the glory of God's name, and to the salvation of our souls. Let us therefore pray, &c.

The Son is begotten of the Father, un-speakably, from ever-lasting. The everlasting Father, the original and author of all things, begot the Son by an everlasting and unspeakable begetting. For the whole scripture with one agreement doth call God a Father, yea truly, an eternal or everlasting Fa-ther. But none is a father of his own self, but a father

of his son : and for because he is the everlasting Father, he
must therefore necessarily have an everlasting Son, equal
unto himself in all respects, co-eternal, and consubstantial
with him. St Paul undoubtedly for the confirmation of
this catholic verity allegeth out of the old Testament two
testimonies. "Unto which," saith he, "of his angels said [Heb. i. 5.]
God at any time, Thou art my Son, this day have I begotten
thee ?" and again, "I will be his Father, and he shall be
my Son:" all which words he applieth unto Christ Jesus,
the Son of God. Of whom also Micheas beareth witness,
saying : "And thou, Bethlehem Ephrata, art little to be Micah v.
among the thousands of Judah; yet out of thee shall he
come forth unto me, that shall be the ruler in Israel : whose
goings forth" (or spreadings abroad)[1] "have been from the
beginning and from everlasting." Whereupon the Son of
God himself, in the Gospel after John, saith : "Verily I say John viii.
unto you, Before Abraham was, I am." And John saith :
"In the beginning was the Word, and the Word was with John i.
God, and God was the Word." But he doth understand by
"The Word," not the word which is spoken and so vanisheth,
not the counsel of God, but the person of the Son. For by
and by he addeth, "And the Word became" (or was made)
"flesh." And we do know that the Son of God, not the
determination[2] or purpose of God (as heretics do vainly imagine), was incarnate. But he which in time was incarnate was
with the Father from everlasting and before all beginnings, and
therefore also true God with the true God. For, "The Word,"
saith he, "was with God, and God was the Word:" because
in the beginning, namely, from everlasting, he was with God.

These simple and plain testimonies, delivered unto us
out of the scriptures, and therefore most true, concerning
the everlasting begetting of the Son by the Father, are sufficient, I think, for them that are not curious. For the scripture doth not here fulfil[3] the vain desires of curious men,
neither yet reasoneth of these points subtilly; but rather
delivereth and setteth down but a few things, in which it is
our parts to believe. But that which the scripture either
doth not set down, or else in few words shadoweth out,
either we are ignorant of to our health, or else, sticking

[1 emanationes, Lat.]   [2 cogitationem, Lat.]
[3 non explet, Lat.]

to that that is set down, we seek not further for more. The holy father Cyril, expounding that saying of the evangelist John, "In the beginning was the Word," saith: "Let us not, seeking things infinite and which cannot be contained within bounds, busy our brains about a consideration that cannot be expressed, and never can have an end. For neither will we grant a beginning of beginning, neither yet will we yield that the Son was begotten of the Father in time: but we will confess that he is with the Father from everlasting. For if he was in the beginning, what mind may be able at any time to climb beyond that WAS? Or when shall we so comprehend in our mind that WAS, that it go not before or outreach our thoughts? Upon good reasons therefore and worthily the prophet Esay, being astonished, crieth out, 'And who shall declare his generation*?' For he, passing all capacity of minds, and being far above and beyond all reason of man, is unspeakable." And anon after he saith: "Because the Son is before all worlds, he cannot be begotten in time: but he is evermore in the Father as in a fountain; as he saith of himself, 'I went out and came from the Father.' For we do understand the Father as a fountain, in whom the Word is his wisdom, his power, the engraven form of his person, his brightness, and his image. Wherefore, if there never were any time wherein the Father was without his wisdom, his power, the engraven form of his person, his brightness, and finally his image; we must of necessity and force confess, that the Son also is co-eternal and everlasting with him, since he is the wisdom, power, &c. of the Father everlasting. For how is he the engraven form of his Father's person, or how is he the most perfect image of his Father, unless he have perfectly obtained and possess the beauty of him, whose image he is? And it is not absurd that we said, the Son is to be understood in the Father as in a fountain. For the name of fountain doth signify nothing else than as from whom: and the Son is in the Father and from the Father; not flowing abroad, but either as brightness from the sun, or as heat from the fire wherewith it is endued. For in these examples we see one from one to be brought forth, and both to be so co-everlasting, that the one can neither be without the other, nor yet keep and retain the quality of their nature. For how shall it be the

* Or age, as other translate it.

sun, if it be deprived of his brightness; or how shall brightness be, unless there be a sun from whence it doth come? And how shall that be fire that wanteth heat? or from whence should heat come but from the fire, or else from somewhat else peradventure not far distant from the substantial quality of fire? As therefore the qualities which proceed from these bodies are together with them from whence they do proceed, and evermore declare from whence they do come; so is it to be understood in the only-begotten. For he is understood to be of the Father, but he is believed to be likewise in the Father: not differing from the nature of his Father, neither yet next his Father second in nature: but always in the Father himself, and with him, and from him, according to the manner of his unspeakable begetting[1]."

[1 Οὐκοῦν ἀρχὴ μὲν ἀρχῆς οὐκ ἔσται, κατὰ τὸν ἀκριβῆ τε καὶ ἀληθῆ λογισμόν, ἀλλ' εἰς ἀμήρυτον μέντοι καὶ ἀκατάληπτον ὁ περὶ αὐτῆς ἀποδημήσει λόγος. τέλος δὲ οὐκ ἐχούσης τῆς ἀεὶ πρὸς τὸ ἀνόπιν φυγῆς, καὶ τὸ τῶν αἰώνων ἀναφοιτώσης μέτρον, οὐκ ἐν χρόνῳ γεγονὸς ἀϊδίως δὲ μᾶλλον ὑπάρχων μετὰ πατρὸς εὑρεθήσεται· ἦν γὰρ ἐν ἀρχῇ. εἰ δὲ ἦν ἐν ἀρχῇ, ποῖος, εἰπέ μοι, δυνήσεται νοῦς τὴν τοῦ ῏ΗΝ ὑπερανίστασθαι δύναμιν; πότε δὲ ὅλως τὸ ῏ΗΝ ὡς ἐν τέλει στήσεται, προανατρέχοντος ἀεὶ τοῦ διώκοντος λογισμοῦ καὶ τῆς ἑπομένης αὐτῷ προαναπηδῶν ἐννοίας; ἐπὶ τούτῳ δὴ ἄρα καταπεπληγμένος ὁ προφήτης φησὶν Ἡσαίας, Τὴν γενεὰν αὐτοῦ τίς διηγήσεται; ὅτι αἴρεται ἀπὸ τῆς γῆς ἡ ζωὴ αὐτοῦ. αἴρεται γὰρ ὄντως ἀπὸ τῆς γῆς ὁ περὶ τῆς γεννήσεως λόγος τοῦ μονογενοῦς· τοῦτ' ἔστιν, ὑπὲρ πᾶσάν ἐστι διάνοιαν τῶν ὄντων ἐπὶ τῆς γῆς, καὶ ὑπὲρ πάντα λόγον, ὡς εἶναι λοιπὸν ἀνεξήγητον...... ἐπειδήπερ καὶ αὐτῶν ἐστι τῶν αἰώνων πρεσβύτερος ὁ υἱός, τὸ μὲν ἐν χρόνῳ γεγενῆσθαι διαφεύξεται· ἦν δὲ καὶ διὰ παντὸς ὡς ἐν πηγῇ τῷ πατρί, κατὰ τὸ παρ' αὐτοῦ λελεγμένον, Ἐγὼ ἐκ τοῦ πατρὸς ἐξῆλθον καὶ ἥκω. πηγῆς τοιγαροῦν νοουμένου τοῦ πατρός, ἦν ὁ λόγος ἐν αὐτῷ σοφία, καὶ δύναμις, καὶ χαρακτήρ, καὶ ἀπαύγασμα, καὶ εἰκὼν ὑπάρχων αὐτοῦ. καὶ εἰ χρόνος ἦν οὐδείς, ὅτε λόγου χωρὶς καὶ σοφίας καὶ χαρακτῆρος καὶ ἀπαυγάσματος ἦν ὁ πατήρ, ἀνάγκη συνομολογεῖν ἀίδιον ὑπάρχειν τὸν υἱόν, ὃς ταῦτά ἐστι τῷ ἀιδίῳ πατρί. πῶς γὰρ ὅλως ἐστὶ χαρακτήρ, πῶς δὲ εἰκὼν ἀκριβής, εἰ μὴ πρὸς ἐκεῖνο μεμορφωμένος ὁρᾶται τὸ κάλλος, οὗ καὶ ἔστιν εἰκών; ἀδικήσει δὲ ὅλως οὐδὲν τὸ ὡς ἐν πηγῇ τῷ πατρὶ τὸν υἱὸν ὑπάρχειν ἐννοεῖν· μόνον γὰρ τὸ ἐξ οὗ τὸ τῆς πηγῆς ἐν τούτοις ὄνομα σημαίνει. ἔστι δὲ ὁ υἱὸς ἐν πατρὶ καὶ ἐκ πατρός, οὐκ ἔξωθεν, ἢ ἐν χρόνῳ γεγονώς, ἀλλ' ἐν τῇ τοῦ πατρὸς ὑπάρχων οὐσίᾳ, καὶ ἐξ αὐτῆς ἀναλάμψας, ὥσπερ ἐξ ἡλίου τυχὸν τὸ ἀπαύγασμα αὐτοῦ, ἢ καθάπερ ἐκ πυρὸς ἢ ἔμφυτος αὐτοῦ θερμότης. ἐν γὰρ τοῖς τοιούτοις παραδείγμασιν ἐν μὲν ἐξ ἑνὸς γεννώμενον ἔνεστιν ἰδεῖν, ἀεὶ δ' οὖν ὅμως συνυπάρχον καὶ ἀχωρίστως προσόν, ὡς δίχα τοῦ ἑτέρου μὴ εἶναι δύνασθαι καθ' ἑαυτὸ τὸ ἕτερον, καὶ διασώζειν ἀληθῆ τὸν τῆς οἰκείας φύσεως λόγον. πῶς γὰρ ὅλως ἥλιος οὐκ ἔχων ἀπαύγασμα, ἢ πῶς ἀπαύγασμα μὴ

Thus far Cyril. And these points surely concerning the Father, and the unspeakable begetting of the Son of God, are stedfastly to be believed according to the scriptures.

Furthermore, touching the Son of God, let us firmly hold and undoubtedly believe, that he is consubstantial (or, of the same substance) with his Father, and therefore true God: that the selfsame Son, being incarnate for us and made man, subsisteth in either nature, as well of God, as also of man; howbeit so that these natures are neither confounded between themselves, nor yet divided: for we do believe one and the selfsame our Lord Jesus Christ to be true God and true man. All and every one of which points throughout their parts we will plainly, and according to the measure of grace that God shall give us, declare unto you.

About the word *homoousius*, which the Latinists agreeably[1] have translated *consubstantiale*, consubstantial, the ecclesiastical history doth testify that there hath been long and much altercation among the ancient writers. What it signifieth, and how it was taken of that most famous and solemn synod of Nice, the most learned and godly Eusebius Pamphili, bishop of Cæsarea, briefly and pithily expounded in this sort: "In that the Son is said to be consubstantial with the Father, it hath an express signification, for because the Son of God hath no similitude or likeness with creatures that were made, but is resembled and likened to the Father alone who begat him; neither is he of any other substance, essence, or being, than of the Father." And the same Eusebius anon after saith: "Unto which sentence and opinion, in this manner expounded, it appeareth we may well subscribe: seeing we do know that the best learned and famous bishops and interpreters among those that were ancient, reasoning of the Godhead

ὄντος ἡλίου τοῦ ἀπαυγάζοντος αὐτό; πῶς δὲ καὶ πῦρ, εἰ τὸ θερμαίνειν οὐκ ἔχει; πόθεν δὲ τὸ θερμὸν, εἰ μὴ ἐκ πυρὸς, ἢ παρά τινος ἑτέρου τῆς τοῦ πυρὸς οὐσιώδους ποιότητος οὐ μακράν που κειμένου; ὥσπερ οὖν ἐν τούτοις τὸ ἐνυπάρχειν τὰ ἐξ αὐτῶν οὐκ ἀναιρεῖ τὴν συνύπαρξιν, ἀεὶ δὲ συντρέχοντα τοῖς γεννῶσι δεικνύει τὰ γεννώμενα, καὶ μίαν ὡς πρὸς αὐτὰ τὴν φύσιν κληρωσάμενα· οὕτω καὶ ἐφ' υἱοῦ. κἂν γὰρ ἐν πατρὶ καὶ ἐκ πατρὸς νοῆται καὶ λέγηται, οὐκ ἔκφυλος ἡμῖν καὶ ξένος ἢ ὡς μετ' αὐτὸν δεύτερος εἰσβήσεται, ἀλλ' ὢν ἐν αὐτῷ, καὶ συνυπάρχων ἀεὶ, καὶ ἐξ αὐτοῦ πεφηνὼς, κατὰ τὸν ἄῤῥητον τῆς θείας γεννήσεως τρόπον.—Cyril. Opp. Lib. I. in Joann. Tom. IV. pp. 11, 2. Lutet. 1638.]

[1 concorditer, Lat.]

of the Father and the Son, used this word *homoousius*." These
be Socrates his words in the first book of histories and the
eighth chapter [2].   Surely the godly governors of churches,
being constrained by the hypocrisy, craftiness, and malice of
heretics, did themselves use, and caused others also to use,
words most pithy and as little doubtful as might be, whereby
partly they might manifestly express the sound truth, and
partly discover and reprove, yea, and also thrust out, the
deceits and malicious practices of heretics.   Arius confessed
that the Son of God was God ; but in the meanwhile he
denied that the Son was consubstantial with his Father :
wherefore he declared that he did not sincerely confess the
true Godhead of the Son.   Neither makes it any great matter,
though there be not expressed in the holy scripture some apt
and fit word to set out and declare the thing in so many
letters as it is written in another tongue, so that that be read
to be manifestly expressed in the scriptures, which by the word
is signified. Wherefore, if we shew that the Son is of the same
substance or nature with the Father, and so equal with and
like unto God, and one with him; we have then made sufficient
and plentiful demonstration, that the Son is *homoousius,* or
consubstantial with the Father.   The prophet Zachary, bringing in the person of God speaking, sayeth : " Arise, O thou [Zech. xiii.
sword, upon my shepherd, and upon the man that is my 7.]
fellow (or my co-equal): smite the shepherd, and the sheep (of
the flock) shall be scattered abroad."   Lo, God calleth the
shepherd, that is smitten, his fellow or co-equal.   And who is
that shepherd that was smitten, the history of the gospel doth
declare ; pointing out unto us the very Son of God himself, our
Lord Jesus Christ.   Neither doth it hinder but further our
cause, that Hierome readeth not, " The man that is co-equal
with me ;" but, " The man cleaving unto me."   For as he
denieth not that *Amith* doth signify co-equal, so he setteth
down another word no less effectual.   For when he translat-

[2 Παραστατικὸν δὲ εἶναι τῷ πατρὶ τὸ ὁμοούσιον, τὸ μηδεμίαν ἐμφέρειαν
πρὸς τὰ γεννητὰ κτίσματα τὸν υἱὸν τοῦ Θεοῦ ἐμφαίνειν· μόνῳ δὲ τῷ πατρὶ
τῷ γεγεννηκότι κατὰ πάντα τρόπον ἀφωμοιῶσθαι, καὶ μὴ εἶναι ἐξ ἑτέρας τε
ὑποστάσεως καὶ οὐσίας, ἀλλ' ἐκ τοῦ πατρός. Ὡι καὶ αὐτῷ τοῦτον ἑρμηνευ-
θέντι τὸν τρόπον, καλῶς ἔχειν ἐφάνη συγκαταθέσθαι· ἐπεὶ καὶ τῶν παλαιῶν
τινὰς λογίους καὶ ἐπιφανεῖς ἐπισκόπους καὶ συγγραφέας ἔγνωμεν ἐπὶ τῆς τοῦ
πατρὸς καὶ υἱοῦ θεολογίας τῷ τοῦ ὁμοουσίου συγχρησαμένους ὀνόματι.
—Socrates, Hist. Eccles. Lib. I. cap. 8. p. 25. ed. Reading.]

eth it, " The man cleaving unto me," he would express the inward and very substantial (that I may so term it) inherence or co-equality of the Father and the Son. For he addeth in his commentaries : " And the man which cleaveth unto God, who is it but even he that saith, ' I am in the Father, and the Father in me[1]?'"

[John v. 18.] Again we read in the gospel of John : " The Jews therefore sought to kill Jesus, not only because he had broken the sabbath-day, (ἀλλὰ καὶ πατέρα ἴδιον ἔλεγε τὸν Θεόν,) but said also that God was his Father, (even his proper, or very own :) making himself (ἴσον) equal to God." Furthermore[2] the Grecians expound ἴσος, that is to say, equal, by this word, ὅμοιος, that is to say, like. Neither can that equality anywhere else have place than in the substance. For the Jews understand that whereof the Arians will be ignorant, that the Lord after a certain peculiar and special manner calleth[3] God his Father ; to wit, ἴδιον, his proper or very own Father, by nature or by birth, of whom the Son being naturally begotten is natural and consubstantial with his Father. For it followeth : " Making himself equal to (or with) God," namely in virtue or power, in everlastingness, and essence. For the same Lord sayeth in the same evan-[John viii. 42.] gelist : " I proceeded and came from God." He did not say only, " I came," but, " I proceeded." He proceeded from the Father such a one in substance as the Father is, surely "Light of light, very God of very God." For he sayeth again to the Jews : " Verily I say unto you, Before Abraham was, I am." He doth not say, " I have been," or, " I will be;" but, " I am ;" alluding to the name of the Lord Jehovah, and declaring that the substance of his Godhead is the very same with the substance of the Father, and that he is therefore consubstantial with the Father. For yet again he sayeth [John x. 30.] more plainly : " I and the Father are one :" one, I say, not *Identitate et essentia. in concord or agreement, but in *selfsameness and being ; for

[1 Super virum cohærentem mihi. . . . Pro eo quod nos vertimus, super virum cohærentem mihi, id est, προσκεκολλημένον μοι, Aquila interpretatus est, super virum contribulem meum, id est, σύμφυλόν μου : Symmachus, super virum populi mei, quod Hebraice dicitur *Amithi.* Jerome proceeds to explain " vir cohærens Deo," by John xiv. 10, and Luke xxiii. 46.—Hieron. Opp. Tom. III. p. 1789. Par. 1704.]

[2 cæterum, Lat.; now.]

[3 So also ed. 1584: but ed. 1577 *called;* appellasse, Lat.]

in that place the power and majesty of God are handled. And when the Jews would without further stay stone the Lord to death, having spoken these words, they declared plainly enough after what sort they understood his words: for they stoned blasphemers to death, who with revilings either impaired God's glory, or else usurped and took the same unto themselves.

Hitherto belongeth that which Paul speaketh concerning the Son of God, saying: "Who is the image of the invisible [Col. i. 15.] God, the first-born of all creatures, because all things were created by him." For if he be the image of the invisible God, he must needs be fellow (or co-equal) with God. For in another place Paul calleth the same Christ, "the engraven [Heb. i. 3.] form of God, and his express image," and answerable in all respects most truly to his pattern or first figure. An image verily and likeness is of things that are not unequal or unlike, but of things equal and like. And he is called "the first-born," because he is Prince and Lord[4], not that he is reckoned among creatures. For all things that were made, by him they were made: therefore he is no creature, but true God, to wit, of the nature and substance of God, one with the Father.

The same apostle saith to the Philippians, that the Son is "in the form (or shape) of God." But to be in the form (or shape) of God is nothing else than in all respects to be fellow (or equal) with God, to be consubstantial with him, and so indeed God himself. For what it is to be in the form or shape of God, is by the contrary clause very manifestly declared. For it followeth: "He took upon him the form of a [Phil. ii. 6—8.] servant." Which is again expounded by that which followeth: "Being made in the likeness of men;" that is to say, being made very man, unlike in nothing to all other men, sin excepted; which in another place is plainly expressed. [Heb. iv. 15.] And here he addeth again; "And found in figure as a man." Therefore, to be in the form of God is to be co-equal and consubstantial with God: for he addeth, "He thought it no robbery to be equal with God." For robbery is the taking away of that which another doth owe; for it is possessed by injury. The Son therefore is co-equal with the Father, and true God by nature and after the most proper manner. And this is the meaning of St Paul his words: Albeit the Son were

[4 See Vol. II. p. 130.]

of the same glory and majesty with the Father, and could have remained in his glory without humiliation or debasement; yet had he rather abase himself, that is to say, take unto him the nature of a man, and cast himself into dangers, yea, even into death itself. For otherwise according to his Godhead he suffered no change; for God is unchangeable, and without variableness.

Since the case so standeth, godly is the saying of St Ambrose in his book *de Fide* against the Arians, and fifth chapter : "Seeing therefore thou dost know this unity of substance in the Father and the Son, not only by the authority of the prophets, but also of the gospel; how sayest thou that *Homoousius*, consubstantial, is not found in the sacred scriptures? as though *Homoousius* were somewhat else than that he saith, 'I went out from God the Father ;' and, 'I and the Father are one[1]?'" &c. The scholar, St Augustine, following his master, Ambrose, in his controversy had with Pascentius confirmeth *Homoousius* by places of scripture, and declareth that this is holily used in our faith and religion[2]. The same doth he also in his third book against Maximinus, bishop of the Arians, and fourteenth chapter[3]. But what needeth heaping up of more words? For I trust it is plainly enough declared by evident places of holy scripture, that the Son is consubstantial with the Father, and that so it must be believed. We hope also that in the treatise following this selfsame point shall not a little be made manifest by testimonies of scriptures.

[1 Cum ergo hanc unitatem substantiæ in Patre et Filio non solum prophetica sed et evangelica auctoritate cognoscas; quomodo dicis in scripturis divinis ὁμοούσιον non inveniri, quasi aliud sit ὁμοούσιον quam quod dicit, Ego de Patre exivi; et, Ego et Pater unum sumus?—De Fide Orthodoxa cont. Arrian. cap. 5. Ambros. Opp. Tom. II. Append. col. 352. Par. 1686—90. The Benedictines consider this not to be a work of Ambrose. See also James on Corrupt. of Script. &c. p. 31. ed. 1843.]

[2 Homoousion, quod in auctoritate divinorum librorum cogebamur ostendere, etiam si vocabulum ipsum ibi non inveniamus, fieri posse ut illud inveniamus, cui hoc vocabulum recte adhibitum judicetur.—Aug. Pascent. Ep. 173. Opp. Par. 1532. Vol. II. fol. 150. col. 3.]

[3 Hoc et illud homoousion, quod in concilio Niceno adversus hæreticos Arianos a catholicis Patribus veritatis auctoritate et auctoritatis veritate formatum est. ... Quid est, inquam, homoousion nisi, Ego et Pater unum sumus?—Id. Vol. VI. fol. 151. col. 1.]

Arius with his complices denied that the Son of God, our That the Son of God is true and very God. Lord Jesus Christ, is true God. But the most true scripture doth so evidently prove and confirm it, that none which loveth the truth from his heart can doubt anything at all thereof. We will presently[4] cite some testimonies and arguments that are most plain and apparent, whereby, through the assistance of the Holy Ghost, our faith may be established, and the catholic and sound truth itself made manifest.

In the third chapter of Matthew, the heavens are opened to our Lord as he was baptized by John Baptist, and the Holy Ghost came down in the likeness of a dove, and alighted upon the head of our Lord Jesus Christ; and forthwith was a voice heard out of the clouds, pronounced by the glorious God in this sort: "This is my beloved Son, in whom my soul is well pleased." And John saith in his gospel[5]: "I [John i. 32—34.] saw the Spirit descending from heaven in the likeness of a dove, and it abode upon him; and I knew him not, but he that sent me to baptize with water, he said unto me, Upon whom thou shalt see the Spirit descending and abiding upon him, this is he which doth baptize with the Holy Ghost. And I saw and bare witness that this is the Son of God." Hereunto belongeth that which Peter, being asked of the Lord, "But whom do ye say that I am?" answered in the Matt. xvi. name of all the disciples; "Thou art that Christ, the Son of the living God." And again, the Lord objecting this, "Will you also be gone?" Peter again made answer in the name of them all; "Lord, unto whom shall we go? Thou John vi. hast the words of everlasting life. And we believe and have known, that thou art Christ, the Son of the living God." We also verily are called the sons of God, howbeit by adop- Christ is the natural son of God. tion: but Christ not by adoption, neither by imputation, but by nature. For in the fourteenth chapter of Mark the high priest saith unto our Lord: "Art thou Christ, the Son of the blessed?" In Matthew also the same high priest saith: "I [Matt. xxvi. 63, 64.] adjure" (or charge) "thee by the living God, that thou tell us whether thou be[6] the Son of the living God. Jesus answered, I am. For ye shall see the Son of man sitting at the right hand of power, and coming in the clouds of hea-

[4 in præsenti, Lat.]
[5 Et Joannes Baptista apud Joannem Evangelistam, Lat.]
[6 Christus, Lat. omitted.]

ven." Which appeareth to be repeated out of the seventh chapter of Daniel. Furthermore, they bring this confession of the Lord before Pilate as blasphemous, and not to be satisfied but with death, crying: "We have a law, and according to our law he ought to die; because he made himself the Son of God." But they themselves in the history of the gospel thunder out these words against the Lord: "We are not born of fornication; we have one Father, even God." It is certain therefore, that the Jews accused our Saviour for none other cause of high treason committed against God's majesty, than for that he named himself the natural, not the adopted, Son of God; for the first did not deserve death, but the last was worthy of death[1]. For we read also in the fifth of John: "Therefore the Jews sought the more to kill him[2], not only because he had broken the sabbath-day, but also for that he said that God was his Father, making himself equal with God," (or God's fellow.)

Lo, thou hast the manner how he called himself the Son of God, not by adoption, or reputation, but by nature and substance. For yet again the Lord himself objecteth this to them that would have stoned him: "Many good works have I shewed you from my Father: for which of these good works do ye stone me? The Jews answered again, saying, For thy good works" (or well-doing) "we do not stone thee, but for blasphemy; namely, because thou, being a man, makest thyself God." Lo, what could be spoken more plainly? "Thou makest thyself God." And what, I pray you, had he spoken, whereof they gathered these things? "I give unto my sheep everlasting life, neither shall they perish for ever, neither shall any pluck them out of my hand. My Father which gave them me is greater than all: and none can pull them out of my Father's hand. I and the Father are one." To give life everlasting doth belong to the power of God: to preserve, and so to preserve that none may be able to pluck them out of his hands, belongeth to the same power. Now the Lord proveth this[3] saying with this argument or

[1 Rather, For the last did not deserve death, but the first was worthy of death. Hoc enim non erat capitale, illud erat capitale, Lat.]

[2 Jesum, Lat.]

[3 So also ed. 1584: but ed. 1577 *his* saying; suam assertionem, Lat.]

reason : None is able to pull the sheep out of my Father's hands : therefore none can pull them out of my hands.   The proof of his antecedent, Because the Father is greater than all ; that is to say, is the greatest of all, whose divine power is above all.   The proof of his consequent, Because I and my Father are one ; to wit, not in will and agreement only, but in majesty also and power, whereof we do at this present entreat ; not of concord or agreement, but of power to make alive and to preserve.   Touching which the Lord himself most plentifully discourseth throughout the whole fifth chapter of St John's gospel, shewing that he forgiveth sins, that by his power he maketh alive and raiseth up from the dead, even as his Father doth ; therefore that he is of one and the same divine power and majesty with God the Father. These things are so evident, plain, and manifest, that albeit we had none other testimony [4], yet these may abundantly suffice to prove the assertion of the true divinity or very Godhead of the Son of God, that the Son indeed is true and very God.

Again the selfsame our Lord and Saviour with great liberty of speech and plainness of words, without any manner [5] of riddle, dark sentence, and obscurity of words, openly and expressly saith to his disciples : " Let not your heart be troubled (or vexed).   You believe in God, believe also in me. I am the way, the truth, and the life.   He that hath seen me hath seen the Father.   Do ye not believe that I am in the Father, and the Father in me ? "   And certain it is that Christ our Lord is the heavenly doctor or teacher, the most constant defender of the truth, who neither hath seduced neither yet could seduce and lead out of the way, no, not so much as one.   But [he] biddeth us believe in him as true and very God.   Therefore our Lord and Saviour is true and very God.   For in another place he saith most plainly : " I am the lively bread (or the bread of life) that came down from heaven : he that believeth in me hath life everlasting." *John xiv.*

John vi.

He again in the gospel plainly pronounceth, and saith : " Father, the hour is come ; glorify thy Son, that thy Son may also glorify thee : as thou hast given him power of all flesh, that so many as thou hast given him, he might give them life *John xvii.*

[4 So also ed. 1584 : but ed. 1577 testimonies ; testimonia, Lat.]
[5 So also ed. 1584 : but ed. 1577 *all* manner.]

everlasting. And this is everlasting life, that they should know thee only true God, and whom thou hast sent, Jesus Christ." By which words he hath expressly proved both the unity of God (that is to say, that there is but one God), against the Ethnicks who worshipped many gods; and notably touched the distinction of the persons, in the meanwhile likewise declaring himself to be very God with the Father. For by and by he addeth: "Glorify thou me, O Father, with thine own self, with the glory which I had with thee before this world was."

Here I think must not be over-slipped of me the argument of Tertullian, which I will recite unto you, dearly beloved, out of his book, *De Trinitate*, wherein he doth gather together very many most sound and strong reasons of Christ his divinity or Godhead. "If (saith he) Christ be only man, why hath he appointed and set us down such a rule to believe, wherein he should say, 'And this is life everlasting, that they might know thee the only true (or very) God, and whom thou hast sent, Jesus Christ?' If also he would not be known to be God, why doth he add, 'And whom thou hast sent, Jesus Christ,' but for that he would be taken also for God? Because, if he would not be known to be God, he would have added, 'And whom thou hast sent, the man Jesus Christ:' but now Christ neither hath added, neither yet hath delivered unto us in doctrine, that he is man only, but hath joined himself to God; to the end he would be known by this conjunction or joining together, that he also is God, as indeed he is. We must therefore believe, according to the prescript rule, in one Lord true and very God; and consequently in him whom he hath sent, Jesus Christ: who had at no hand (as we have said) joined himself to the Father, unless he would be known to be God also. For he would have separated himself from the Father, if he would not have been known to be God. For he would have placed himself among men only, if he had known that he was man only : neither would he have joined himself with God, if he had not also known himself to be God. Now also touching as he is man, he saith nothing; because no man doubteth that he is man: and he joineth himself to God not without good cause, that he might set down a form of his divinity or Godhead to them that should believe. If Christ be only man, how is it that he saith, 'And now

glorify me with the glory which I had with thee before the world was?' If before the world was he had glory with God, and possessed glory with the Father, then was he before the world. Neither had he had glory, if he had not been afore, that he might possess glory : for none can have a thing, unless he which possesseth the thing be afore. But Christ had glory before the creation of the world ; therefore he was before the creation of the world. For if he had not been before the creation of the world, he could not have had glory before the creation of the world, when he himself was not. But he could not as a man[1] have glory before the creation of the world, who then was[2], when the world was made. But Christ had glory; he was therefore before the world was made: he was not therefore man only, who was before the world was made. Therefore he is God, because he was before the world was made, and possessed glory before the world was made[3]." After these words Tertullian doth

[1 So also ed. 1584: but ed. 1577 as man.]

[2 Rather, who then was *not*. See Latin original.]

[3 Si homo tantummodo Christus, quare credendi nobis talem regulam posuit, quo diceret, Hæc est autem vita æterna, ut sciant te unum et verum Deum, et quem misisti Jesum Christum? Si noluisset se etiam intelligi, cur addidit, Et quem misisti Jesum Christum; nisi quoniam et Deum accipi voluit? Quoniam si Deum nollet intelligi, addidisset, Et quem misisti hominem Jesum Christum. Nunc autem neque addidit, nec se hominem nobis tantummodo Christus tradidit, sed Deo junxit, ut et Deum per hanc conjunctionem, sicut est, intelligi vellet. Est ergo credendum secundum præscriptam in Dominum unum verum Deum, et in eum quem misit Jesum Christum conse-quenter; qui se nequaquam Patri, ut diximus, junxisset, nisi Deum quoque intelligi vellet: separasset enim ab eo, si Deum intelligi se noluisset. Inter homines enim tantummodo se collocasset, si hominem se esse tantummodo sciret; nec cum Deo junxisset, si se non et Deum nosset. Nunc et de homine tacet, quoniam hominem illum nemo dubitat; et Deo se jungit merito, ut credituris divinitatis suæ formu-lam poneret. Si homo tantummodo Christus, quomodo dicit, Et nunc honorifica me gloria quam habebam apud te priusquam mundus esset? Si antequam mundus esset gloriam habuit apud Deum, et claritatem tenuit apud Patrem, ante mundum fuit; nec enim habuisset gloriam, nisi ipse prius fuisset, qui gloriam posset tenere: nemo enim habere aliquid poterit, nisi ante ipse fuerit qui aliquid tenet. Sed enim Christus habet gloriam ante mundi institutionem: ergo ante insti-tutionem mundi fuit. Nisi enim ante institutionem mundi esset, ante mundi institutionem gloriam habere non posset, quum ipse non esset. Sed enim homo gloriam ante mundi institutionem habere non potuit,

shew, that these things are not meant of the predestination, but of the substance, of Christ. But thus far of this.

St Paul the apostle in his epistle to the Romans declareth in plain words not once or twice, that our Lord Jesus Christ is true and very God. For he speaking of Christ in his ninth chapter saith: "Which is God in all things to be praised for ever." The words are very well known which the same apostle writeth in his first epistle to the Corinthians, and eighth chapter. St John the apostle and evangelist doth so manifestly declare the divinity or Godhead of the Son in his canonical epistle, that he which seeth and perceiveth it not is blind both of body and mind. In the end of the epistle he saith: "We know that the Son of God is come, and hath given us a mind, that we should know him who is true: and we are in him that is true, in his Son Jesus Christ. This same is true (or very) God, and eternal (or everlasting) life."

Now it is God by "whom we live, move, and have our being," as Paul witnesseth: but by Christ our Lord we live, move, and have our being, as he himself hath expressly taught in the gospel after John: Christ therefore is true and very God.

In the forty-third and forty-fifth chapters of Esay the Lord saith: "I am, I am the Lord; and there is no Saviour without me. A just God and a Saviour, there is none beside me." But Jeremy in his twenty-third chapter calleth Christ the son of David, Jehovah, and our Righteousness. Likewise in Esay the Father speaking of his Son saith: "I have given (or made) thee the light of the Gentiles, that thou mayest be my health unto the end of the world." Moreover, seeing there is no other God but one, none other salvation and righteousness save that divine righteousness only, it followeth consequently, doubtless, that Christ is true and very God, in all respects co-equal with his Father.

In the same Esay the Lord saith: "I have sworn by mine ownself, the word of righteousness shall go out of my mouth, and it shall not be drawn back again: because every knee

Marginal references: Rom. ix. | 1 John ix. | Acts xvii. | Jer. xxiii. | Isai. xlix. | Isai. xlv.

qui post mundum fuit: Christus autem habuit; ante mundum igitur fuit. Non igitur homo tantummodo fuit, qui ante mundum fuit. Deus est igitur, quoniam ante mundum fuit, et gloriam ante mundum tenuit.—Tertull. Opp. Novatian. de Trinitate. cap. 24. p. 723. Par. 1664. See above, p. 129, note.]

shall bow unto me, and all tongues shall swear (by my name)[1]."
And Paul saith: "There is a name given unto Christ which is Phil. ii.
above all names, that in the name of Jesus everything[2] should
bow, of things in heaven, of things in earth, and of things
under the earth; and that every tongue should confess that the
Lord is Jesus Christ, to the glory of God the Father." It
must needs be therefore that Christ is true and very God.
For seeing he is worshipped and also served, seeing we confess him to be Lord; that surely turneth not to the reproach
and ignominy, but to the honour and glory, of God the Father.
For in the gospel after John thus saith the Lord: "The John v.
Father hath given all judgment (to wit, all jurisdiction, and
all government, all glory, power, and authority) to the Son;
that all might honour the Son as they honour the Father.
He that honoureth not the Son, honoureth not the Father
that sent him." Hereunto therefore belongeth that[3] which
we read in the prophet Esay: "I the Lord, *Hu* (or, myself[4]) Isai. xlii.
is my name[5], and my glory I will not give to another," (or to
a stranger, &c.) But he giveth his glory to the Son: he
therefore in his substance, according to his divinity or Godhead, is not a stranger or severed from the Father, albeit he
be acknowledged to be another several person. What doth
the Lord in the gospel after John say? "And now, O Father, John xvii.
glorify thou me with thine ownself with the glory which thou
gavest me with thee before this world was?" No, but, "which
I had with thee ere the world[6] was." "I had," saith he, not,
"I received;" albeit the scripture doth oftentimes use this
word for the mystery of dispensation.

    In Micheas the Christians say: "All people (one with Mic. iv.
another) walk in the name of their God: as for us, we will
walk in the name of our God." Furthermore, they walk in
the name and the way of Jesus Christ, saying in the gospel,
"I am the way," and "the door:" "I am the light of the world; John x. xiv.
viii.
he that followeth me doth not walk in darkness." That
Christ therefore is God, who is he that can be ignorant? For
the Lord saith in Ezechiel, "I will feed my flock myself Ezek.
xxxiv.
alone:" and anon he addeth, "My servant David shall feed
it;" meaning Christ, the son of David, that only universal

[1 The translator's addition.]   [2 genu, Lat.; knee.]
[3 iterum, Lat. omitted; again.]   [4 I myself, ed. 1577.]
[5 See above, page 132.]   [6 hic mundus, Lat.; this world.]

pastor or shepherd of the church, and therefore true God. For the universal pastor or shepherd must be a king and a priest[1], must be everlasting, must know all things, must be omnipotent, must be present with all men in all places. The Son of God therefore is true and very God, because he is the Messias.

Furthermore, what is more manifest and less called in controversy, than that God only forgiveth sins? It must needs be therefore, that nothing is more evident and less doubtful, than that we believe Christ to be true and very God, because "He is the Lamb of God that taketh away the sins of the world."

Again, whereas Paul truly calleth Christ "our hope;" (for Esay foretold, "In him shall the Gentiles trust;") and whereas Jeremy crieth, "Cursed be the man that putteth his trust in man, but blessed is the man that putteth his trust in God;" we must necessarily confess that Christ is God. For in John he oftentimes repeateth: "Verily I say unto you, he that believeth in me hath everlasting life."

I could bring innumerable examples of this kind out of the scriptures, which witness that the Son of God, our Lord Jesus Christ, is of one and the selfsame nature with the Father, and therefore is very God of very God: but I trust that to holy hearers and not given to contention those which I have already cited will suffice.

It remaineth that we declare unto you, that the Son of God was incarnate for us, and was born very man of the virgin Mary, consubstantial, or of the selfsame substance, with us in all points, sin excepted. The law, the prophets, and the apostles, shew unto us most manifest arguments of the true flesh or humanity of the Son of God.

For in the law the Lord saith: "The Seed of the woman shall crush the serpent's head." But who knoweth not that the head of the serpent is the kingdom, force, or power of the devil? And that Jesus Christ brake this power, the whole scripture doth witness. And here he is called the Seed of the woman. And truly he is called seed, to verify his true human nature: and he is termed the seed of the woman, not of the man, because of his conception by the

Marginal notes: Mark ii. | John i. | 1 Tim. i. | Isai. xi. | Jer. xvii. | Of the incarnation or true humanity of Christ. | Gen. iii.

[1 Rather, For the universal Shepherd, King and Priest, must be, &c.]

Holy Ghost, and his birth of the virgin Mary. And because she was the daughter of David, of Abraham, and Adam, it followeth that the son of Mary was very man. For as we have heard it said to Adam, "The Seed of the woman shall bruise the serpent's head;" so also we read that the same promise was renewed and repeated to Abraham in these words: "In thy seed shall all the nations of the world be Gen. xxii. blessed." And Paul to the Galatians manifestly saith, that Gal. iii. this Seed of Abraham, wherein we have obtained blessing, is Christ Jesus. The same apostle saith, "For in no sort took Heb. ii. he the angels, but he took the seed of Abraham:"—by angels doubtless excluding all manner of spiritual substances: by the seed of Abraham understanding the very substance itself of the flesh of man. For he addeth: "Wherefore in all things Heb. ii. it became him to be made like unto his brethren. And because they be partakers of flesh and blood, he also himself likewise took part with them (of the same)." Verily, the scripture draweth the lineal descent of Christ most diligently from the loins of Abraham unto Jacob, and from him again to Judas, and from him in like sort to David. To him again the promises of the incarnation of the Son of God are renewed. For Nathan saith to David: "Thus saith the Lord, When 2 Sam. vii. thy days be fulfilled, thou shalt sleep with thy fathers, and I will set up thy seed after thee, which shall proceed out of thy body, and will stablish his kingdom: he shall build a house for my name, and I will stablish the throne of his kingdom for ever." Neither is there any cause why any man should interpret this of Salomon. For he was born while his father David lived, and his kingdom quickly decayed. But Nathan speaketh of a son which should be born to David after his death: "When thou shalt sleep with thy fathers," saith he, "I will set up thy seed after thee." And what manner of seed this should be, he most evidently declareth, and saith, "which shall proceed out of thy body." For in the 132nd Psalm we read; "Of the fruit of thy body will I set upon thy seat."

Furthermore, Mary the virgin descended lineally from the seed[2] of David, of whom Christ our Lord was begotten and born, of whom the angel speaking, and expounding those old and ancient prophecies, saith unto the virgin: "And the Luke i.

[2 So also ed. 1584: but ed. 1577 *of* the seed.]

Lord God shall give unto him the seat of his father David, and he shall reign over the house of Jacob for ever, and of his kingdom there shall be none end." Hereunto also belongeth that which Elisabeth saith to the virgin which came out of Galilee into the hill-country of Juda: "And whence cometh this to me, that the mother of my Lord should come to me? Blessed art thou among women, and blessed is the fruit of thy womb." Truly Matthew and Luke draw the lineal descent of Christ from the loins as it were[1] of David even unto the virgin Mary, which conceiveth by the Holy Ghost, that is, the Holy Ghost making her fruitful. She, when the months were fulfilled that she should be delivered, brought forth a son: and he which is born in all respects appeareth to be true and very man: he is laid in a manger, wrapped in swathling clouts; he grew in stature, and increased in years, according to the manner of man's body; he is wearied, he is refreshed, he is glad, he is sad, he is hungry, he is thirsty, he eateth, he drinketh, he feareth, and, to be short, he dieth: which the truth of the history of the gospel in many words declareth.

Neither is the scripture itself ashamed to call Mary the mother of our Lord, not the putative or supposed, but the true and natural mother, which of the substance of her own body gave true flesh and substance of man to the Son of God; the angel of God so witnessing with Esay, and saying, "A virgin shall conceive in her womb, and shall bring forth a son." Lo, he saith, "in her womb." And again, in Matthew the selfsame angel saith, "That which is conceived in her is of the Holy Ghost." Whereupon the apostle unto the Galatians saith, that "the Son of God is made of a woman," to wit, according to man's nature. For Christ is the fruit of the body of David, and of the virgin Mary, begotten and born of the loins of David: and John also, the apostle and evangelist, saith, "The word was made flesh, and dwelt among us." In calling God flesh, doubtless he calleth him very man. For the same apostle in another place saith: "Every spirit that confesseth that Jesus Christ is come in the flesh, is of God; and every spirit which confesseth not that Jesus Christ is come in the flesh, is not of God." Therefore we freely pronounce that Valentinus, Marcion, Apelles,

Matt. i.
Luke iii.

Matt. i.
John ii.

Isai. vii.
Luke i.

Matt. i.

Gal. iv.

John i.

1 John iv.

[1 ex prosopia et veluti lumbis, Lat.]

and Manichæus, denying the true and very flesh of Christ, are
of the devil; and therefore that they by all means, together
with all their disciples and sectaries, are to be avoided.   This
treatise of the true flesh of Christ we knit up with these
most plain words of Paul: "When Christ was in the form of Phil. ii.
God, he made himself of no reputation, taking on him the
form of a servant, and made in the likeness of men, and found
in figure as a man. He humbled himself, being made obedient
unto death, even the death of the cross." Wherefore it is
without doubt, that the Son of God took true and human flesh,
and in the same is consubstantial or of the selfsame substance
with us in all points, sin excepted.

Neither did our Lord, after he was risen again from the The Lord,
dead, though he were glorified, put off or lay aside his true after he was
risen, laid
body which he had once taken and put on; and his glo- not aside his
true and very
rification doth not take away the truth of his nature.   For body.
he saith unto his disciples, "A spirit hath not flesh and bones [Luke xxiv.
39.]
as ye see me have."   Wherefore he carried that his true and
very flesh into heaven with him; in his true flesh he appeareth always for us in the sight of God the Father; in his
true flesh he will come to judge the quick and the dead; in
his true flesh they shall see him which crucified[2] him.   Christ
according to this nature (who in respect of his Godhead is
no creature, but a Creator) is a creature; for the flesh of
Christ hath beginning, and lineally descended from Adam,
who is the creature of the living God.   And albeit these
things be sufficiently fenced with the force of the scriptures,
yet it shall not seem irksome unto you, dearly beloved, to
rehearse the opinion of the blessed father Cyril, which concerning the same matter he hath left written in his epistle
unto Successus, bishop of Isauria diocese[3], in these words:
"Because I found in your advertisement such a kind of
thing, as though the holy flesh of Christ, the Saviour of us
all, were turned into the nature of his deity after his resurrection, so that now he should seem to be wholly and solely
God, we thought good also to make answer unto this."   And
a few words after: "After the resurrection certainly it was the

[2 confixerunt, Lat.; which pierced.]

[3 Isauriæ Diocæsariensis, Lat. Diocæsarea was one of the dioceses
in the province of Isauria, and under the patriarchate of Antioch.—
Bingham, Antiq. of Christ. Ch. Book IX. chap. 3. § 16.]

selfsame body which suffered, but yet not having now in itself man's infirmities. For we affirm not that it abideth hunger, labour, or any such like thing, but we confess that now it is incorruptible : and not this only, but also that quickeneth and giveth life. For it is a body that both hath and giveth life, that is to say, of the only-begotten Son of God; and it is glorified with the most worthy brightness of God; and it is known and taken to be the body of God. Therefore if any man say that that is God's body, as the body of a man is man's body, he swerveth not from allowable reason.

2 Cor. v.

Whereupon I think that most blessed Paul also said, 'Though we have known Christ after the flesh, now yet henceforth know we him no more.' For being, as I said, the proper body of God, it far passeth all human bodies. But a body made of earth could not abide to be turned into the nature of the deity or Godhead. For this is impossible : otherwise we abase the Godhead, as if it were made, and as if it had taken somewhat into itself which according to nature doth not properly belong to it. Hereby it is proved to be as much folly to say that the body is turned into the nature of the Godhead, as that which is the Word to be changed into the substance of flesh. For as this is impossible, because it is proved to be a body not able to be turned and changed ; so also it is not possible that any creature can be turned into the essence or nature of the Godhead : but flesh is also created ; and therefore we say that the body of Christ is divine, because it is the body of God, and beautified with unspeakable glory. And now let us confess that it is uncorruptible, holy, and giving life : but that it is changed into the nature of the Godhead, neither have any of the holy fathers so thought or taught, neither do we so think[1]." Thus

[1 Ἐπειδὴ δὲ εὖρον ἐν τῷ ὑπομνηστικῷ ἔμφασίν τινα λόγου τοιαύτην, ὅτι μετὰ τὴν ἀνάστασιν τὸ ἅγιον σῶμα τοῦ πάντων ἡμῶν σωτῆρος Χριστοῦ εἰς θεότητα, φησὶ, μετακεχώρηκεν, ὡς εἶναι τὸ ὅλον θεότητα μόνην, δεῖν ᾠήθην καὶ πρός γε τοῦτο εἰπεῖν. . . . Μετά γε τὴν ἀνάστασιν ἦν μὲν αὐτὸ τὸ σῶμα τὸ πεπονθὸς, πλὴν οὐκέτι τὰς ἀνθρωπίνας ἀσθενείας ἔχον ἐν ἑαυτῷ· οὐ γὰρ ἔτι πείνης, ἢ κόπου, ἢ ἑτέρου τῶν τοιούτων τινὸς δεκτικὸν εἶναι φαμὲν αὐτό· ἀλλὰ λοιπὸν ἄφθαρτον· καὶ οὐχὶ τοῦτο μόνον, ἀλλὰ καὶ ζωοποιόν· ζωῆς γὰρ ἔστι σῶμα, τοῦτ' ἐστι, τοῦ μονογενοῦς· κατελαμπρύνθη δὲ καὶ δόξῃ τῇ θεοπρεπεστάτῃ, καὶ νοεῖται Θεοῦ σῶμα. Τοιγάρτοι, κἂν εἴ τις αὐτὸ λέγοι θεῖον, ὥσπερ ἀμέλει τοῦ ἀνθρώπου τὸ ἀνθρώπινον, οὐκ ἂν ἁμάρτοι τοῦ πρέποντος λογισμοῦ. Ὅθεν οἶμαι καὶ τὸν σοφώτατον Παῦλον

far Cyril. And Theodoretus, bishop of Cyrus, *Dialog.* II.
Eranist. saith: "I will shew that the body of the Lord,
yea, after the ascension, was called a body.   Hear Paul
therefore saying, 'Our conversation is in heaven, from   Phil. iii.
whence we look for a Saviour, the Lord Jesus Christ: who
shall change our vile body, that it may be fashioned like
unto his glorious body.' Therefore it is not changed into
another nature, but remaineth indeed a true and very body,
replenished with divine glory, and casting forth beams of
light.   But if it be changed into another nature, their bodies
also shall likewise be changed ; for they shall be fashioned
like unto him. But if the bodies of saints keep the substance of their nature, the body of the Lord likewise hath
his substance unchangeable[2]."   Thus far Theodoret.

Furthermore, when we profess that Christ hath true and   Christ hath a
very flesh, we do not mean flesh without soul.   For we must   reasonable
soul.
confess, that Christ hath a reasonable or human soul, not

εἰπεῖν· Εἰ γὰρ ἐγνώκαμεν κατὰ σάρκα Χριστόν, ἀλλὰ νῦν οὐκέτι γινώσκομεν.
Θεοῦ γὰρ, ὡς ἔφην, ἴδιον σῶμα ὑπάρχον ὑπερέβη πάντα τὰ ἀνθρώπινα.
Μεταβολὴν δὲ τὴν εἰς τὴν τῆς θεότητος φύσιν οὐκ ἐνδέχεται παθεῖν σῶμα τὸ
ἀπὸ γῆς· ἀμήχανον γάρ· ἐπεὶ καταγορεύομεν τῆς θεότητος, ὡς γενητῆς, καὶ
ὡς προσλαβούσης τὶ ἐν ἑαυτῇ, ὃ μή ἐστι κατὰ φύσιν ἴδιον αὐτῆς. Ἴσον γάρ
ἐστιν εἰς ἀτοπίας λόγον τὸ εἰπεῖν, ὅτι μετεβλήθη τὸ σῶμα εἰς θεότητος φύσιν,
καὶ μὴν κἀκεῖνο, ὅτι μετεβλήθη ὁ λόγος εἰς φύσιν σαρκὸς, τῷ λέγειν μετα-
κεχωρηκέναι τὴν θεότητα εἰς φύσιν σαρκός. Ὥσπερ δὲ τοῦτο ἀμήχανον,
ἄτρεπτος γὰρ καὶ ἀναλλοίωτός ἐστιν, οὕτω καὶ τὸ ἕτερον· οὐ γάρ ἐστι τῶν
ἐφικτῶν εἰς θεότητος οὐσίαν ἤτοι φύσιν μεταχωρῆσαί τι δυνάσθαι τῶν κτι-
σμάτων· κτίσμα δὲ καὶ ἡ σάρξ. οὐκοῦν θεῖον μὲν εἶναι φαμὲν τὸ σῶμα
τοῦ Χριστοῦ, ἐπειδὴ τοῦ Θεοῦ σῶμά ἐστι, καὶ ἀρρήτῳ δόξῃ κατηγλαϊσμένον,
ἄφθαρτον, ἅγιον, ζωοποιόν· ὅτι δὲ εἰς θεότητος φύσιν μετεβλήθη, οὔτε τὶς
τῶν ἁγίων πατέρων ἢ πεφρόνηκεν ἢ εἴρηκεν, οὔτε ἡμεῖς οὕτω διακείμεθα.—
Cyrill. Epist. I. ad Successum. Opp. Tom. v. Part. II. pp. 139, 140.
Lutet. 1638.]

[2 Δείξω δὲ ὅμως, καὶ μετὰ τὴν ἀνάληψιν σῶμα καλούμενον τοῦ Δεσ-
πότου τὸ σῶμα. Ἄκουσον τοίνυν τοῦ ἀποστόλου διδάσκοντος· Ἡμῶν γὰρ
τὸ πολίτευμα ἐν οὐρανοῖς ὑπάρχει, ἐξ οὗ καὶ σωτῆρα ἀπεκδεχόμεθα Κύριον
Ἰησοῦν· ὃς μετασχηματίσει τὸ σῶμα τῆς ταπεινώσεως ἡμῶν, εἰς τὸ γενέσθαι
αὐτὸ σύμμορφον τοῦ σώματος τῆς δόξης αὐτοῦ. Οὐ τοίνυν εἰς ἑτέραν μετα-
βέβληται φύσιν, ἀλλὰ μεμένηκε σῶμα, θείας μέντοι δόξης πεπληρωμένον, καὶ
φωτὸς πέμπον ἀκτῖνας ... Εἰ δὲ εἰς ἑτέραν ἐκεῖνο μετεβλήθη φύσιν, καὶ
τὰ τούτων (i. e. τῶν ἁγίων) ὡσαύτως μεταβληθήσεται· σύμμορφα γὰρ ἐκείνῳ
γενήσεται· εἰ δὲ τὰ τῶν ἁγίων φυλάττει τὴν χαρακτῆρα τῆς φύσεως, καὶ τὸ
δεσποτικὸν ἄρα ὡσαύτως τὴν οἰκείαν οὐσίαν ἀμετάβλητον ἔχει.—Theodoret.
Dial. II. pp. 83, 84. Opp. Tom. IV. Lutet. 1642.]

void of a mind. Arius taught that the Son of God took flesh only without soul[1], and that the Word was in place of the soul. And Apollinarius did attribute unto Christ a soul, but he took away the mind, denying that it was reasonable[2]. The scripture doth both attribute unto Christ a soul, and taketh not away the mind from the soul. The Lord himself sayeth in the gospel: "The Son of Man came not to be ministered unto, but to minister, and to give his soul a redemption for many." The same Matthew hath left written of him: "He began to be sorrowful and heavy. And Jesus said, My soul is heavy, even unto the death." And in another place the Lord himself saith: "Now my soul is troubled." And if so be that this soul of Christ lack the mind, which is the chiefest part of the soul, how hath he a soul? how could he be sorrowful, and understand, desire, and remember? "With hearty desire (saith the Lord) have I desired to eat this passover with you before I suffer." But this desire came not from his Godhead, neither from his flesh only, nor from his soul wanting a mind, but from his perfect manhood of body and mind. Moreover we read in the gospel that the Lord said: "The Son of Man came not to destroy men's souls, but to save them." Therefore he took not flesh only, but a reasonable soul also. For man had perished both soul and body: therefore that he might be saved both body and soul, our Saviour Christ took a very man's body and a reasonable soul, that is to say, a most perfect man. Therefore blessed Athanasius, teaching us according to the scriptures the confession of true faith, said: "Christ is God of the substance of his Father, begotten before all worlds; and man of the substance of his mother, born in the world: perfect God, and perfect man, of a reasonable soul and human flesh subsisting."

Matt. xx.

Matt. xxvi.

John xii.

Luke xxii.

Luke ix.

The heretical error and the sound truth touching the mystery of Christ's incarnation. Thus far in these words have we shewed that Jesus Christ our Lord is very God and very man; consubstantial or of the same substance with the Father according to his Godhead, and consubstantial or of the same substance with us according to his manhood. For he hath a reasonable soul and human flesh in very deed. We will speak furthermore of the conjunction or uniting of these natures into one person; in which matter histories declare, that certain ancient writers in old

[1 without a soul, ed. 1577.]
[2 Augustin. de Hæres. cap. 55.]

time foully erred.　For Eutyches admitted one nature only in Christ, and the same made, that is, meddled or confounded together of a divine and human nature: from whom the Monothelites were not far beyond, acknowledging only one will in Christ.　Nestorius, willing to avoid a coal-pit, fell into a lime-kiln[3].　For he, confessing two natures, seemeth to affirm that there are so many persons, teaching that the Word is not united to the flesh into the selfsame person, but that it only dwelleth therein: whereupon also he forbad the holy virgin to be called God's mother.　Against whom the common assertion of the whole church, holding opinion according to the scripture, hath taught that two natures in Christ and the properties of those natures are to be confessed; which are so coupled together into one undivided person, that neither the divine nature is changed into the human, nor the human into the divine, but either of them retain or keep their own nature, and both of them subsist in the unity of person.　For Christ[4] according to the disposition of his divine nature is one and the selfsame, immortal: according to the disposition of his human nature, mortal: and the selfsame immortal God and mortal man is the only Saviour of the world.　Of which thing we will speak anon, by God's grace, somewhat more largely and plainly.

A proverbial kind of speech, whereby is meant, that in avoiding a less error he fell into a greater.

Touching the very conjunction or uniting of the true Godhead and manhood in Christ, the prophets and apostles have not crabbedly[5] nor craftily disputed.　For they speaking simply said, "God was made man;" or, God took on him man.　For John the apostle and evangelist saith: "The Word was made flesh," that is, God was made man, or the Word of God became flesh.　St Paul saith: "God was made manifest in the flesh."　And again: "The Son of God in no sort took the angels, but he took the seed of Abraham."　Therefore we, according to the doctrine of the apostles, expounding the mystery of the conjunction of the divine and human nature in Christ, say: God was incarnate or made man; God took on him man; God appeared or was made manifest in human flesh.　He that will sift out deeper matters than these, it is to cast himself into great dangers.

Of the uniting of Christ his Godhead and manhood.

John i.

1 Tim. iii.

Heb. ii.

[3] illam carbonariam, Lat.　See Vol. I. p. 376. n. 1.]

[4] Rather, For one and the same Christ is according to, &c.]

[5] spinose, Lat.]

Some there are who, in expounding these points more fully, use the words of society or fellowship, participation, and communion, or part-taking; and that, not without authority of the scriptures; Paul saying, "Forasmuch then as the children are partakers of flesh and blood, he also himself like-wise took part with them."

Christ re-
taineth both
natures
unmeddled,
or uncon-
founded
together.

Nevertheless we must here first of all take heed, that we do not meddle or confound the two natures joined together in one person, nor that we rob them of their properties. For God of his own nature is everlasting and unchangeable. God therefore, remaining always one and the selfsame, is not changed into an human or into any other nature, but joineth, coupleth, taketh, yea, and uniteth unto himself the human nature. Again, unless in his human nature he remain a creature, and be the selfsame which he is said to be, it is not an human nature: this therefore remaining in its own sub-stance is taken to the divine nature. Therefore two natures remain in the one person of Christ, the divine and the human; and either of them doth retain their own disposition and their own property: which we will now declare by some places of scripture.

Esay in his seventh chapter saith: "A virgin shall con-ceive, and bring forth a Son; and his name shall be called Immanuel." He acknowledgeth both natures in Christ: for according to his divine nature he is called "Immanuel," that is to say, "God with us;" according to his human nature he is conceived and born. The same prophet saith: "A child is born unto us, and a son is given unto us," &c. For he is given who is from everlasting; and he is born whose beginning and being is in the world[1]. Wherefore one and the selfsame retaineth both the divine and the human nature.

For Micheas also saith: "And thou, Beth-lehem Ephrata, art little indeed among the thousands of Judah. Out of thee shall he come forth unto me, which shall be the governor in Israel, whose outgoings have been from the beginning, and from everlasting." Lo, what could be spoken more plain? One and the selfsame hath two offsprings: for insomuch as he is God, his generation is from everlasting; and as he is man, he is born in Beth-lehem. Wherefore one and the self-same Christ is very God and very man. Again in the gospel

[1 qui in seculo esse incipit, Lat.]

according to St Matthew, the Lord asketh the Pharisees, saying: "What think you of Christ? whose Son is he? *Matt. xxii.* They said unto him, The Son of David. He saith unto them, How then doth David in spirit call him Lord, saying, The *Psal. cx.* Lord said unto my Lord, Sit thou on my right hand until I make thine enemies thy footstool? If David call him Lord, how is he then his Son?" As if he said: Since Christ without doubt is the Son of David, and he calleth him Lord (not by human affection, but by the Holy Ghost), that is to say, very God of the selfsame power with the Father, the sequel[2] is that Christ is very man and very God. The angel Gabriel, noting no less plainly both these natures, saith to the virgin Mary: "That holy thing which shall be born shall be called *Luke i.* the Son of God." For of the virgin he is born, very man of very man: and this is the Son of God. For Elisabeth also calleth the virgin the mother of the Lord; to wit, of God. Moreover, in the gospel of John thou mayest read very many sayings of this sort, which point out, as it were with the finger, both natures in the selfsame Christ. "Ye *John xiv.* believe," saith the Lord, "in God, believe also in me." And again, "The Father is greater than I." Also, "I went out *[John xvi. 28.]* from the Father, and came into the world: again I leave the world, and go to the Father." And again in another place: "The poor shall ye have always with you, but me *Mark xiv.* always ye shall not have." And again: "Behold, I am *Matt. xxviii.* always with you, even unto the end of the world." Which sentences truly, as it were contrary, cannot be all true at once, unless we acknowledge that Christ retaineth the properties of (both) natures unconfounded or unmingled. Paul unto the Romans manifestly saith, that "he was called to *Rom. i.* be an apostle to preach the gospel of God, which he had promised afore by his prophets in the holy scriptures, concerning his Son; which was made of the seed of David according to the flesh; and declared mightily to be the Son of God, touching the Spirit of sanctification, by the resurrection from the dead." The apostle therefore acknowledgeth both natures in Christ: for according to the flesh (saith he) Christ is the Son of David; but if we behold the power of his miracles, his resurrection from the dead which giveth life, and that Christ sendeth the Holy Ghost and

[2 *consequens est*, Lat.; it follows.]

sanctifieth all the faithful, it appeareth that he which is the
Son of David after the flesh is also the Son of God according
to his divine power.   The same apostle, in the second chapter to the Philippians, doth no less plainly and evidently
affirm both natures in Christ.   But because that place
hath been already oftentimes alleged, I pass over to the citing
of other.

The natures in Christ are not mingled or confounded.
St Augustine, expounding not only the confession of
his own faith, but of the whole church in all the world which
flourished in his time, in his epistle to *Dardanus*, LVII. hath
thus left written: "Doubt not that the man Christ Jesus is
there now, from whence he shall come; and have in ready
remembrance and faithfully hold the christian confession:
because he rose from the dead, ascended into heaven, sitteth
at the right hand of the Father, neither shall come from
elsewhere than from thence, to judge the quick and the dead:
and in such sort shall he come, that voice of the angel so
witnessing, as he was seen to go into heaven; that is to say,
in the selfsame shape and substance of flesh, to which indeed
he gave immortality, (but) took not the nature away.   According to this shape he is not to be thought everywhere
present.   For we must beware lest we so fortify the divinity of man, that we take clean away the truth of his body.
For it doth not consequently follow, that that which is in
God should be so[1] everywhere as God.   For the scripture
which cannot lie saith even of us, that 'in him we live, move,
and have our being,' howbeit we are not everywhere as he
is: but he is after another sort man in God, because he is
also otherwise God in man, after a certain proper and singular manner.   For one person is God and man, and both
of them is one Jesus Christ; everywhere in that he is God,
but in heaven in that he is man."   And the same author saith
a little after: "Take away space of places from bodies, and
they shall be nowhere: and because they shall be nowhere,
they shall be no bodies.   Take the very bodies from the
qualities of the bodies, and there shall be no place for them
to be, and therefore it must needs be that they have no
being."   And in the end of the Epistle the same Augustine
saith: "Doubt not that Christ our Lord, the only-begotten
Son of God, co-equal with the Father, being also the Son

[1 So also ed. 1584: but ed. 1577, should so be.]

of man, whom the Father exceedeth in greatness, both to
be present everywhere as he is God, and also to be in the
same temple of God as God dwelling there; and yet to be
in some certain place of heaven according to the manner of
his true body[2]." The selfsame thing the same author as yet
expoundeth more at large in his fiftieth treatise upon John[3];
and *Contra Felicianum Arianum,* cap. 9, 10, and 11[4]; also
in his treatise *De Agone Christi,* cap. 24 unto cap. 27[5]. To

[2 Noli itaque dubitare, ibi nunc esse hominem Christum Jesum
unde venturus est, memoriterque recole et fideliter tene Christianam
confessionem : quoniam resurrexit a mortuis, ascendit in cœlum, sedet
ad dexteram Patris, nec aliunde quam inde venturus est ad vivos
mortuosque judicandos; et sic venturus est, illa angelica voce testante,
quemadmodum ire visus est in cœlum, id est, in eadem carnis forma
atque substantia, cui profecto immortalitatem dedit, naturam non
abstulit. Secundum hanc formam non est putandus ubique diffusus.
Cavendum est enim ne ita divinitatem astruamus hominis, ut veritatem
corporis auferamus. Non est autem consequens, ut quod in Deo est
ita sit ubique ut Deus. Nam et de nobis verissima scriptura dicit,
quod in illo vivimus, movemur, et sumus; nec tamen sicut ille ubique
sumus: sed aliter homo ille in Deo, quoniam aliter et Deus ille in
homine, proprio quodam et singulari modo. Una enim persona Deus
et homo est, et utrumque est unus Christus Jesus : ubique, per id quod
Deus est; in cœlo autem per id quod homo... Nam spatia locorum
tolle corporibus, nusquam erunt; et quia nusquam erunt, nec erunt.
Tolle ipsa corpora qualitatibus corporum, non erit ubi sint, et ideo
necesse est ut non sint... Christum autem Dominum nostrum, unigenitum Dei Filium, æqualem Patri, eundemque hominis filium, quo major
est Pater, et ubique totum præsentem esse non dubites tanquam Deum,
et in eodem templo Dei esse tanquam inhabitantem Deum, et in loco
aliquo cœli propter veri corporis modum.—Augustin. ad Dardan. Ep.
LVII. Opp. Tom. II. fol. 53. col. 3. fol. 54. col. 2. fol. 56. col. 1. Par.
1531.]

[3 Secundum præsentiam majestatis semper habemus Christum; secundum præsentiam carnis, recte dictum est discipulis, Me autem non
semper habebitis.—Id. Tom. IX. fol. 76. col. 3.]

[4 Fel. Scire cupio quo pacto ad filium transeat dignitas patris, et
ad patrem non recurrat humilitas prolis? Aug. Non secundum naturam ista nunc dici, quotidianarum rerum exempla nos docent, &c.—
Id. Tom. VI. fol. 160. col. 3.—This treatise is not genuine.]

[5 Nec eos audiamus qui negant tale corpus Domini resurrexisse,
quale positum est in monumento, &c. c. 24. Nec eos audiamus qui
negant ipsum corpus secum levasse in cœlum Dominum nostrum, &c.
c. 25. Nec eos audiamus qui negant ad dextram Patris sedere Filium,
&c. c. 26.—Id. Tom. III. fol. 164. col. 2. P.]

which we will also join the testimony of the holy martyr
Vigilius, bishop of Trident. For he, disputing against Eutyches in the defence of both natures in Christ, saith: "If
the nature of the Word and flesh be one, how is it that since
the Word is everywhere, the flesh also is not found everywhere? For when the flesh was in earth, surely it was
not in heaven; and because it is now in heaven, surely it is
not in earth: and so far is it from being in the earth, that
according to flesh we do look for Christ to come from heaven,
whom according to the Word we believe to be with us on
earth. Therefore, according to your opinion, either the Word
is contained with his flesh in place, or else the flesh with the
Word is in every place: whereas one nature receiveth not
into itself anything contrary and unlike. But it is contrary
and far unlike to be limited within a place, and to be everywhere: and because the Word is in every place, but his
flesh is not in every place, it is evident that one and the selfsame Christ is of both natures; and that he is everywhere
according to the nature of his Godhead, and is contained in
place according to the nature of his manhood; that he is
both created, and also without beginning; that he is subject
to death, and also cannot die; one of which is agreeable to
him by the nature of the Word, whereby he is God; the
other by the nature of the flesh, whereby the selfsame God
is man. Therefore one and the selfsame Son of God, being
also made the Son of man, hath a beginning by the nature
of the flesh, and hath no beginning by the nature of his
divinity: by the nature of his flesh he is created, and by
the nature of his divinity he is not created: by the nature
of his flesh he is limited in place, and by the nature of his
divinity he is not contained in place: by the nature of his
flesh he is inferior also to angels, and according to his divinity he is equal to the Father: by the nature of his flesh
he died, but by the nature of his divinity he died not. This
is the catholic faith and christian confession, which the apostles
delivered, the martyrs confirmed, and the faithful even unto
this day do observe and keep[1]." Hitherto we have rehearsed

[1] Si Verbi et carnis una natura est, quomodo cum Verbum ubique
sit, non ubique inveniatur et caro? Nam quando in terra fuit, non
erat utique in cœlo: et nunc quia in cœlo est, non est utique in terra;
et in tantum non est, ut secundum ipsum Christum spectemus ven-

the words of Vigilius, martyr and bishop, to this end, that
the most notable agreement of the holy scripture, of the universal church, and of the most godly and learned fathers in
this principle might be understood, wherein we confess that   Christ in
the properties of both natures in Christ remain unconfounded.   one person
remaineth
undivided.

Again, we must by all means take heed, lest through defending and retaining the properties of the two natures we
divide and pull asunder the unity of the person; as though
there were two Christs, whereof the one should be subject to
suffering and mortal, the other not subject to suffering and
immortal.   For there is but one and the same Christ, who
according to his Godhead is acknowledged immortal, and
mortal according to his manhood.   Nestorius denied that the
blessed virgin Mary was the mother of God; for he said
God was unchangeable, and therefore that he could not be
born, and that he had no mother.   Whereupon sprang a suspicion, that he should say the Lord was bare man, and that
he should maintain the heretical opinion of Paulus Samosa-
tenus and Photinus: which thing Socrates handleth at
large, *Historiarum* Lib. vii. cap. 32[2].   But Nestorius was

turum de cœlo, quem secundum Verbum nobiscum esse credimus in
terra.   Igitur secundum vos aut Verbum cum carne sua loco continetur, aut caro cum Verbo ubique est, quando una natura contrarium
quid et diversum non recipit in seipsa.   Diversum est autem et longe
dissimile circumscribi loco et ubique esse; et quia Verbum ubique est,
caro autem ejus ubique non est, apparet unum eundemque Christum
utriusque esse naturæ; et esse quidem ubique secundum naturam divinitatis suæ, et loco contineri secundum naturam humanitatis suæ;
creatum esse, et initium non habere; morti subjacere, et mori non
posse: quod unum illi est ex natura Verbi, qua Deus est; aliud ex
natura carnis, qua idem Deus homo est. Igitur unus Dei Filius idemque
hominis factus filius habet initium ex natura carnis suæ, et non habet
initium ex natura divinitatis suæ; creatus est per naturam carnis suæ,
et non est creatus per naturam divinitatis suæ; circumscribitur loco
per naturam carnis suæ, et loco non capitur per naturam divinitatis
suæ; minor est etiam angelis per naturam carnis suæ, et æqualis est
Patri secundum naturam divinitatis suæ; mortuus est natura carnis
suæ, et non est mortuus natura divinitatis suæ.   Hæc est fides et confessio catholica, quam apostoli tradiderunt, martyres roboraverunt, et
fideles nunc usque custodiunt.—Vigilii contra Eutychen. Lib. iv. fol.
73. Tigur. 1539.]

[2 Socratis Hist. Eccles. Lib. vii. cap. 32.   De Anastasio presbytero, a quo Nestorius ad impietatem perductus est.   ed. Cantab. pp.
380, 381.]

injurious to the scripture and to true faith. For Elisabeth, the wife of Zachary and the mother of St John Baptist, being full of the Holy Ghost, in express words saluteth the holy virgin Mary, and calleth her the mother of the Lord, that is, the mother of God. And albeit his heavenly nature be without generation and corruption, yet notwithstanding it is most certain that he whom Mary brought forth was God in very deed. For " that which is born of her," saith the angel, " is the Son of God :" therefore she brought forth God, and she worthily is called the mother of God. For if she bare not God, she brought forth bare man, neither hath the Son of God coupled man unseparably to himself. In like manner, since God of his own nature is immortal, truly he cannot die : but if any man for that cause should absolutely deny that God was crucified and offered, yea, and died for us, he should gainsay Paul saying, " Had they known it[1], they would not have crucified the Lord of glory." But who is ignorant that the God of glory, or glorious God, cannot be crucified ? In the meanwhile, since he which according to the flesh suffered and was nailed on the cross was God, not bare man only, we rightly say that God suffered and was nailed on the cross for us ; though he which suffered suffered according to that only which could suffer. For Peter the apostle saith, " Christ hath suffered for us in the flesh." The first Toletan council following him decreed in these words : " If any shall say or believe that the Godhead may be born, let him be accursed. If any shall say or believe that the deity of Christ may be turned, changed, or subject to suffering, let him be accursed. If any shall say or believe that the nature of the Godhead and the manhood is one in Christ, let him be accursed[2]." And Damasus bishop of Rome saith : " If any shall say, that in suffering on the cross the Son of God and God suffered pain, and not the flesh with the soul which he put on in the form

Cor. ii.

[1 Pet. iv. 1.]

[1 ipsum, Lat. ; him.]

[2 Si quis dixerit vel crediderit Deitatem nascibilem esse: anathema sit. Si quis dixerit vel crediderit Deitatem Christi convertibilem fuisse, vel passibilem: anathema sit. Si quis dixerit vel crediderit Deitatis et carnis unam in Christo esse naturam: anathema sit.—Assertio Fidei Concil. Toletan. I. Magd. Centur. Cent. v. cap. 9. foll. 467, 468. Basil. 1624. The first of these three determinations is not found, and the second is given somewhat differently, in Concil. Labb. et Coss. Tom. II. col. 1228.]

of a servant, which he took on him as the scripture saith, let
him be accursed³." Therefore, whereas Paul saith, that
"God hath purchased to himself a church with his own ^{Acts xx.}
blood," who is so mad to believe that the divine nature hath
or ever had blood? In the meanwhile who is such a dor-
head⁴ that he understandeth not, that the flesh which God
took hath blood? And since that God accounteth not that as
another's, but his own, which he took unto himself; we most
truly say, that God with his own blood redeemed the world.
Whereupon Theodoretus also, bishop of Cyrus, *Dialog. Eran.* 3,
a little before the end, saith: "If Christ be both God and
man, as both the holy scripture teacheth, and as the most
blessed fathers have always preached, then as man he suffered,
but as God he was not subject to suffering. But when we
say the body, or flesh, or humanity suffered, we do not
separate the divine nature: for as it was united to his human
nature, which was hungry and thirsty, and weary, yea, and
slept also, yea, and was vexed with sorrow and heaviness for
the passion which he should suffer, abiding indeed none of
those, but suffering that to abide the affections and passions
of nature; even so it was joined unto him when he was
crucified, and permitted that his passion should be throughly
ended, that by his passion he might suffer death, not feeling
grief truly by his passion, but making his passion agreeable
and convenient for himself as the passion of his temple or
dwelling-place and of his flesh joined unto him; by the which
also they that believe are called the members of Christ:
he himself is called the head of those that believe⁵." Thus
far he.

[³ Εἴ τις εἴπῃ, ὅτι ἐν τῷ πάθει τοῦ σταυροῦ τὴν ὀδύνην ὑπέμεινεν ὁ Υἱὸς
τοῦ Θεοῦ θεότητι, καὶ οὐχὶ σαρκὶ καὶ ψυχῇ λογικῇ, ἥνπερ ἀνέλαβεν ἐν τῇ
τοῦ δούλου μορφῇ, ὡς εἴρηκεν ἡ ἁγία γραφὴ, ἀνάθεμα ἔστω.—Damasi Opp.
Epist. ad Paulin. Thessalon. Episc. p. 116. Romæ, 1638.]

[⁴ tam stupidus, Lat.; dor, a drone. Johnson.]

[⁵ Εἰ ὁ Χριστὸς καὶ Θεὸς καὶ ἄνθρωπος, ὡς καὶ ἡ θεία διδάσκει γραφὴ,
καὶ οἱ πανεύφημοι πατέρες κηρύττοντες διετέλεσαν, ὡς ἄνθρωπος ἄρα πέπον-
θεν, ὡς δὲ Θεὸς διέμενεν ἀπαθής. . . . Ὅταν τὸ σῶμα, ἢ τὴν σάρκα, ἢ τὴν
ἀνθρωπότητα πεπονθέναι λέγωμεν, τὴν θείαν οὐ χωρίζομεν φύσιν· ὥσπερ
γὰρ ἥνωτο πεινώσῃ καὶ διψώσῃ καὶ κοπιώσῃ, καὶ μέντοι καὶ καθευδούσῃ, καὶ
ἀγωνιώσῃ τὸ πάθος, οὐδὲν μὲν τούτων ὑφισταμένη, συγχωροῦσα δὲ ταύτῃ
δέχεσθαι τὰ τῆς φύσεως πάθη· οὕτω συνῆπτο καὶ σταυρουμένῃ, καὶ συνε-

This figure of speech is called of some ἀλλοίωσις, alteration or changing; of John[1] Damascenus ἀντίδοσις, mutual giving or an interchanging of properties. That is wont to be called a communicating of properties[2], to wit, when that property is given to one nature which is proper to another: as for example; "No man hath ascended up into heaven (saith the Lord) but he that came down from heaven, even the Son of man which is in heaven." Truly, his human nature was not then in heaven, when the Lord spake this, but in earth: yet notwithstanding, because flesh is taken into the fellowship of his Godhead, that which is proper to this is attributed to his manhood. And bishop Fulgentius, making mention of[3] this interpretation, in his second book to king Thrasimundus hath thus left written: "He said this, not that the human substance of Christ is present in every place; but because one and the selfsame Son of God and Son of man, very God of the Father as he is very man of man, though according to his true humanity he was then locally in earth, yet according to his divinity (which by no means can be contained in place) he did wholly fill heaven and earth[4]." Thus saith he. Wherefore the sentences, bearing witness of Christ in the writings of the evangelists and apostles, are diligently to be marked. For some are peculiarly referred to his divine nature, as are these: "I and the Father are one." "Before Abraham was, I am." "In the beginning was the Word, and the Word was with God, and God was that Word." "He is before all things, the image of the invisible God, by whom all things are

χώρει τελεσιουργηθῆναι τὸ πάθος, ἵνα λύσῃ τῷ πάθει τὸν θάνατον, ὀδύνην μὲν ἐκ τοῦ πάθους οὐ δεχομένη, τὸ δὲ πάθος οἰκειωσαμένη, ὡς ναοῦ γε ἰδίου, καὶ σαρκὸς ἡνωμένης, δι᾽ ἣν καὶ μέλη Χριστοῦ χρηματίζουσιν οἱ πιστεύσαντες, καὶ τῶν πεπιστευκότων αὐτὸς ὠνόμασται κεφαλή.—Theodoret. Demonstrat. per Syllog. Opp. Tom. IV. p. 186. Lutet. Par. 1642—84.]

[1 Joan. Damascen. Orthodoxæ Fid. Lib. III. cap. 3. p. 174. Bas. 1575.]

[2 idiomatum communicatio, Lat.]

[3 agnoscens, Lat.; recognising.]

[4 —Non quia humana Christi substantia fuisset ubique diffusa, sed quoniam unus idemque Dei filius atque hominis filius, verus Deus ex Patre sicut homo verus ex homine, licet secundum veram humanitatem suam localiter tunc esset in terra, secundum divinitatem tamen, quæ loco nullatenus continetur, cœlum totus impleret et terram.—Fulgent. ad Trasimund. Lib. II. cap. 17. p. 50. Venet. 1742.]

made." And some are particularly referred to his human nature, or to the mystery of his embassage or ministration[5]: of which sort are these: "The Father is greater than I." "Thou madest him a little inferior to the angels." "My soul is heavy even to the death." Again, there are testimonies which have respect to both natures, but to neither of them severally do they sufficiently agree. Such are these: "My flesh is meat indeed, and my blood is drink indeed." "I have power to forgive sins, to raise to life whom I will, and to give righteousness and holiness. I am the shepherd, the door, the light, the way, the truth, and the life." "No man cometh to the Father but by me." For these do set forth and commend unto us the very substance of Christ, the person I mean of our true Saviour and Mediator, God and man. For no man forgiveth sins but God only. Again, they are not forgiven without death and shedding of blood, as the apostle witnesseth in the ninth chapter to the Hebrews. Again, there are testimonies, which cannot aptly be declared but by communicating of words[6]. Touching which I hope this is sufficient.

Again, he doth not divide the person of our Mediator, God and man, whosoever for the unity's sake of natures doth not so far extend his humanity as his divinity is[7] extended. For in the gospel after St Matthew, the Lord goeth not with his body into the house of the centurion; whereas yet notwithstanding there is no doubt that, his Godhead being present and not absent, the servant of the centurion was cured of this disease. And who will say that therefore the person is divided by St Matthew, for that he hath not extended the humanity of Christ even unto his divinity? The angels, speaking to the women concerning the body of Christ risen from the dead and now glorified, say: "He is not here, he is risen." But we are not ignorant that his divinity is in every place. And yet the angels divided not his inseparable person, in that they did not make equal in all respects the human body of Christ with his Godhead. The angels themselves[8] do not divide the person of Christ, when, his body being taken up from the mount Olivet into heaven, they standing on the earth testify that he shall come again after the same manner as they saw

The person of Christ is not divided.

Matt. viii.

Mark xvi.

[Acts i. 11.]

[5 sive ad missionem, dispensationisque mysterium, Lat.]
[6 idiomatum, Lat.]   [7 ut sic dicam, Lat. omitted; so to say.]
[8 Illi ipsi angeli, Lat.]

him depart from them. But who dare deny that the Lord was then also present with them? Therefore our Lord after the manner of his very body is in heaven not in earth: but according to his infinite Godhead he is everywhere, in heaven and in earth. Man consisteth of soul and body; and these most contrary in natures between themselves make one person, not two; and whosoever attributeth and defendeth that which is proper to either of them, doth not divide the person. The body sleepeth, the soul sleepeth not: these properties of parts make not two persons. Hereunto seemeth to belong that which Theodoret hath left written in his third Dialogue, saying: "We do not divide the natural unity of the soul and the body, neither separate we the souls from their own proper bodies: but consider those things which properly belong to their natures. Therefore when the scripture saith, 'And devout men carried Stephen to his burial, and made great lamentation over him;' wilt thou say that his soul was buried with his body? I think not. And when thou shalt hear Jacob the patriarch saying, 'Bury ye me with my fathers,' thou dost understand that to be spoken of his body, not of his soul. Again thou dost read, 'There they buried Abraham and Sara his wife,' &c. In which speech the scripture doth not make mention of the body, but in all points signifieth the soul and body together. But we rightly divide and say, that the souls are immortal, and that the bodies only of the patriarchs are buried in the double cave. Even so we also are wont to say, In this or that place this or that man was buried. We do not say, this man's body, or that man's body, but this man or that man; for whosoever is well in his wits knoweth we speak of the body. So whereas the evangelists so oftentimes make mention of Christ's body buried, at the length they set down the name of the person and say, that Jesus was buried and laid in the grave[1]," &c. Thus far Theodoret.

Acts viii.

[1 Ὀρθ. Οὐδὲ ἡμεῖς, ὦ ἀγαθὲ, διαιροῦμεν τὴν ἕνωσιν, ἀλλὰ θεωροῦμεν τὰ τῶν φύσεων ἴδια....Ὅταν οὖν ἡ θεία λέγῃ γραφὴ, Συνεκόμισαν δὲ τὸν Στέφανον ἄνδρες εὐλαβεῖς, καὶ ἐποίησαν κοπετὸν μέγαν ἐπ᾽ αὐτῷ, καὶ τὴν ψυχὴν εἴποι ἄν τις μετὰ τοῦ σώματος παραδεδόσθαι ταφῇ; Ἐραν. Οὐ δῆτα. Ὀρθ. Καὶ ὅταν ἀκούσῃς Ἰακὼβ τοῦ πατριάρχου λέγοντος, Θάψατέ με μετὰ τῶν πατέρων μου, περὶ σώματος ἢ περὶ ψυχῆς ταῦτα εἰρῆσθαι τοπάζεις; Ἐραν. Δῆλον ὡς περὶ σώματος. Ὀρθ. Ἀνάγνωθι δὲ καὶ τὰ ἑξῆς. Ἐραν. Ἐκεῖ ἔθαψαν Ἀβραὰμ, καὶ Σάῤῥαν τὴν γυναῖκα αὐτοῦ....Ὀρθ. Οὐδ᾽ ἐν τούτοις...

And since it is without controversy, that this faith and
doctrine from Christ's time even unto our age hath flourished in the holy church of God, and against innumerable
assaults of Satan and heretics hath remained most stedfast;
and the selfsame is delivered and confirmed by testimonies of
scripture and consents[2] of holy councils; I exhort you, dearly
beloved, that, calling on the name of Christ, you may persevere and continue in the same doctrine, and being joined by
true faith and obedience to Christ, very God and man, you
may give continual thanks, worshipping him that reigneth for
ever.

OF CHRIST, KING AND PRIEST; OF HIS ONLY AND EVERLASTING KINGDOM AND PRIESTHOOD; AND OF THE NAME OF A CHRISTIAN.

THE SEVENTH SERMON.

I HAVE declared unto you, dearly beloved, that Christ
Jesus our Lord is very God and man: which will bring more
plentiful profit, if we understand what the fruit of that thing
is; which is chiefly known by the offices of Christ our Lord.
He is king and priest of the people of God; therefore he
hath a kingdom and a priesthood: which things if we shall
somewhat more diligently consider, they shall declare unto
us the exceeding great benefit of the divinity and humanity
of Christ.

Christ Jesus is a king; therefore he is Lord of all, ruler Christ
and governor of all things which are in heaven and in earth, of all.
and specially of the catholic church itself, which is the communion of saints. And forsomuch as he is King and Lord,
truly by his royal or kingly office he is the deliverer or
preserver, the revenger and defender, and, finally, the lawgiver of his elect. For he crushed the serpent's head, the Gen. iii.
Luke xi.

σώματος ἐμνημόνευσεν ἡ θεία γραφή· ἀλλὰ διὰ τῶν ὀνομάτων τὴν ψυχὴν
ὅμου καὶ τὸ σῶμα ἐδήλου. Ἡμεῖς μέντοι διαιροῦμεν ὀρθῶς, καὶ φαμὲν τὰς
ψυχὰς ἀθανάτους εἶναι, μόνα δὲ τῶν πατριαρχῶν τὰ σώματα ἐν τῷ διπλῷ
κατατεθῆναι σπηλαίῳ.—Theodoret. Dial. III. Opp. Tom. IV. pp. 129, 130.
Lutet. Par. 1642.]

[2 symbolis, Lat.]

strong and most cruel enemy of God's people; whom when he had conquered he bound and spoiled. He delivered the elect out of the power of darkness, and set them into the

1 Pet. ii.

liberty of the sons of God; that we might be his peculiar people, sanctified through the blood of our king, a purchased people, to serve him in righteousness and holiness. He is humble, loving, and gentle; which the history of the gospel also out of Zachary rehearseth of him, Matth. xxi. He watcheth for us, he defendeth and guardeth us, he enricheth us with all manner of good things, and furnisheth us against our enemies with spiritual armour, and giveth us abundantly power to resist and to overcome. He hath purged the temple of God, casting out the Canaanites[1]; he hath cancelled unrighteous laws, he hath delivered us from them; and now he ruleth and governeth us with the sceptre of his mouth, exceeding good and most just laws being proclaimed. For he is God and man; therefore he is the only monarch, the

Christ is a monarch.

King of kings, and the Lord of lords: for he hath all the kings and rulers in the world subject unto him; some verily of their own accord, through faith, being obedient; and other, though striving and rebelling against him, made subject by

Psal. ii.

his power. And therefore saith the prophet David: "Be wise, O ye kings, be learned, ye that are judges of the earth; serve the Lord with fear, and rejoice unto him with reverence. Kiss the Son, lest he be angry, and so ye perish from the right way[2]." For in another place the same prophet saith:

Psal. cx.

"The Lord said to my Lord, Sit thou on my right hand, until I make thine enemies thy footstool. The Lord will send forth the rod of his power out of Sion; be thou ruler even in the midst among thine enemies." Esay also, bringing

Isai. xlix.

in the Lord speaking, saith: "I will lift up my hands unto the Gentiles, and set up my standard to the people[3]; and they shall bring thee their sons upon their shoulders: for kings shall be thy nursing fathers, and queens shall be thy nursing mothers." Which thing ecclesiastical histories declare more largely. Of this king Christ the prophets prophesying

Isai. xvi.

said: "And in mercy shall the seat be prepared; and he

[1 Cf. Vol. II. p. 45, n. 7, and p. 153, n. 8; and see Bullinger. in Apocalyps. Conc. XXI. p. 58, and Conc. XXVIII. p. 76, and Conc. LXXVIII. p. 245. Basil, 1557.]

[2 in via, Lat.]

[3 inter populos, Lat.]

shall sit upon it in truth in the tabernacle of David, judging and seeking judgment, and making haste unto righteousness." And again : " Behold, the time cometh, saith the Lord, that I Jer. xxiii. will raise up the righteous Branch of David, which king shall bear rule; and he shall prosper with wisdom, and shall set up equity and righteousness again in the earth. In this time⁴ shall Juda be saved, and Israel shall dwell without fear : and this is the name that they shall call him, The Lord our Righteousness."

And because our Lord is a king, therefore he must needs Of the kingdom of God. have a kingdom. As well the realm and dominion subject to a king is called a kingdom, as principality, empire, power, and manner of government itself. Therefore the church, the communion or fellowship of saints, being obedient and subject to their king Christ, is called the kingdom of God. For Micheas saith, " And the Lord shall reign over them in mount Sion :" Mic. iv. therefore Sion (which signifieth the church) is the kingdom of God. And God is said to reign, when in the church he ruleth, governeth, keepeth, and defendeth those that be his, and endueth and maketh them fruitful with divers graces. For Paul saith, " The kingdom of God is not meat and drink, but righteousness, and peace, and joy in the Holy Ghost." Moreover the kingdom of God is that eternal glory and felicity which God doth communicate to his elect. For the Lord saith in the gospel, " Come, ye blessed of my Father, Matt. xxv. inherit the kingdom which is prepared for you from the beginning of the world." And the thief even at point of death making his prayer to the Lord, who was ready to die on the cross, and desiring to be partaker of this kingdom, saith, " Lord, remember me when thou comest into Luke xxiii. thy kingdom." Again, since the gospel teacheth us how God reigneth in us in this world, in time to translate us unto himself into that other ; that is, since the gospel is that thing by which the Lord reareth up his dominion; it is not unadvisedly called of Matthew, in his thirteenth chapter, the kingdom of God⁵. In another place, for the same cause it is called " the word of the kingdom." To be short, we at this present by the kingdom of God understand the congregation

[⁴ So also ed. 1584 : but ed. 1577, in *his* time.]
[⁵ Our Lord's phrase in Matthew is, The kingdom of *heaven :* in the other Evangelists, of *God.*]

of saints itself, the catholic church, I mean, and the power
or administration of God reigning therein, that is, preserving,
governing, and glorifying the same.

The kingdom of God, which is one, is two ways considered.
And this kingdom of God is verily but only one; for
there is but one God only, one king Christ only, one church,
and life everlasting. But this one kingdom of God according to the dispensation of the same is considered two ways:
first, according to the omnipotency of God; for he, since
he is the highest and omnipotent, hath and executeth over
all creatures, visible and invisible, most just rule and equal
power, nill they or will they be obedient: secondly, according to his Spirit, whereby he reigneth in his elect. And
so the kingdom of God is again two ways considered: for
either it is earthly, and is called the kingdom of grace; or
else it is heavenly, and is called the kingdom of glory.

God's king-dom of grace in earth.
The earthly kingdom of grace is not therefore called
earthly, as though it were carnal and earthly, like the kingdom of Babylon, Persia, Alexandria, or Rome; but because it
is on earth. For a good part of the holy church of God is
conversant on this earth, being partaker of flesh and blood
while it liveth on the earth, though it live not an earthly
life according to the flesh; for according to the Spirit,
whereby it is ruled, it liveth a heavenly life. Not that the
Prov. xxiv. 2 Sam. vii.
partakers of the kingdom of God sin not: for "the just
man falleth and riseth seven times in a day." Whereupon
it is also called the kingdom of grace: for as long as
we live in this world, our king and Lord never denieth his
How Christ reigneth on earth in his kingdom.
grace and mercy to us that crave pardon. And the faithful
do wholly hang upon the grace of their king: they embrace[1]
continual repentance, and endeavour themselves to things
of more perfectness; for they frame all that they do according to the laws of their king and prince. For he reigneth in his elect by the word of truth, and by the Holy
Ghost. By the word of truth he teacheth what the saints
should do, and what they should avoid: by his Holy Spirit
he moveth their hearts, and giveth strength to fly evil and
follow that is good. For truly our king reigneth not so much
Rev. i.
for himself as for us: for he maketh us also kings, that we,
being delivered from the devil, damnation, sin, and the curse,
may be lords over the devil, damnation, sin, and the curse,

[¹ agunt, Lat.]

yea, and over all things; and joint-heirs with the Son of God
himself.

For these causes the kingdom of God is called a spi- The spiritual
ritual kingdom. For the partakers of the kingdom of God, kingdom of God.
endued with the Spirit of God, do bring forth the fruits of
the Spirit, not the works of the flesh; and, to be short, are
governed with the Spirit of God. Neither truly doth our
Lord reign after the manner of the kings of this world, saying to Pilate, "My kingdom is not of this world." Which
sentence some abuse, gathering that there is no outward
government in the church of God: under which name they
also take away the office of a magistrate; and speak so subtilly
of the kingdom of God, that a man cannot tell where the
kingdom of God is, or who be partakers of this kingdom.
They understand not that the meaning must be gathered upon
the occasion of that saying. The Jews, accusing the Lord
before Pilate, laid to his charge that he ambitiously sought
after a kingdom. The Lord, clearing himself of this crime,
sheweth Pilate that his kingdom shall not be such a one
which, after he had cast out Tiberius Cæsar, should be gotten
and kept with arms, and be governed after the manner of
this world. Declaring that, he addeth: "If my kingdom were John xviii.
of this world, then would my servants surely fight, that I
should not be delivered to the Jews." Therefore he inferreth,
"But now is my kingdom not from hence:" and therefore
they fight not for me, to place me in the throne of the kingdom, Tiberius being cast out. And anon he saith: "For this
cause was I born, and for this cause came I into the world,
that I should bear witness unto the truth: and all that are of
the truth hear my voice." As therefore Christ by truth
(not by lying, deceits, and crafty practices, like the princes of
this world) prepareth himself a kingdom; so by truth he doth
both retain and govern his kingdom: and whosoever embrace
truth are partakers of Christ's kingdom, whether they be
princes or of the commonalty: all these obey the voice of
their King, and serve their highest Prince.

Here nevertheless we expressly add, that kings can no
otherwise serve their Lord and King than kings, that is, in
doing those things which kings ought to do, namely, to execute
judgment and justice. For albeit these be in the world, yet
rule they not after the world, because they are now governed

by the Spirit of their King Christ, and direct all their doings
to the prescript rules of God's word, and in all things yield
themselves to be guided by the Spirit of God: and so far
surely their kingdom is not of this world. Of these things I
have elsewhere cited much out of St Augustine according to
the scripture[1]. And our King Christ defendeth his church
and his ministers sometime by the aid of princes; sometimes
he preserveth and spreadeth abroad the same lying open
to persecutions through infirmity and weakness: for it is
pressed down, but not oppressed, or kept under still; Christ
the mightiest prince always reigning and overcoming in those
that be his.

The bounds
of Christ's
kingdom in
earth.

Now the bounds of this earthly kingdom of Christ reach
unto the uttermost parts of the earth; for all the kingdoms
of the world and all nations pertain unto the kingdom of
Christ. Hereunto belong all the testimonies of the prophets
touching the calling of the Gentiles[2], whereof thou mayest find
very many in Esay and Zachary, who excellently describe
the kingdom of Christ in earth. Whereupon the Jews took
occasion to feign I wot not how great and glorious things of
the majesty and victories of the Messias, which nevertheless
long since were abundantly fulfilled in Christ, but more spiritually than carnally. But they, while they dream of and look
for carnal things, loathe spiritual, and lose both. But the
faithful, through the bountifulness and liberality of Christ
their King, most abundantly obtain those good things which
the prophets promised, namely, plentiful peace both with God
and men, and all kind of felicity; always to be blessed,
always to be safe (though they fight continually) from all
enemies, as well visible as also invisible, and to enjoy everlasting salvation. Which things the prophets in their writings
have set forth in a most large kind of style, yet understanding
nothing else than as even now we said; that the faithful shall
be most happy, and shall possess in Christ all good gifts both
of soul and body, as much indeed as is necessary and healthful for the saints. And this is that kingdom (now we understand both, as well that of grace as this of glory) which that
Joseph of Aramathia, just Simeon, and Anna the prophetess,
with other saints, awaited and looked for. This same kingdom
Philip the deacon preached to them of Samaria, and St Paul

[1 Vol. I. pp. 365-369.]   [2 omnium gentium, Lat.]

the apostle to them of Rome: which thing Luke doth testify
in the Acts of the Apostles, chapter viii. and xxviii.

But the seat or throne and[3] palace of our king is heaven. *The seat of our king, Christ.*
For he ascended a conqueror into heaven, and sitteth at the
right hand of God the Father almighty: from thence as the
sun of righteousness he shineth to all which live in his church,
or in his kingdom; yea, and he chooseth the hearts of the
faithful to himself wherein he may dwell[4]. Furthermore,
that we may understand our king, though not corporally
present in earth but ascended into heaven, not therefore to
be absent from his kingdom; he verily in his word compareth
himself to the head and us to the body or the members.
Now therefore as the body is never without the head, so
the kingdom of God is not without Christ the prince. And
as the vital spirit from the heart, and the power or virtue
of feeling and moving from the head, is poured into the body:
so are we quickened or made alive by our prince Christ; he
justifying, preserving, comforting, confirming, and defending
us from all evil. As all the members are ruled by the head,
so all the faithful in the kingdom of Christ are governed
by their king Christ. Paul therefore saith: "God raised *Ephes. i.*
Christ from the dead, and set him on his right hand in heavenly places, far above all rule, and power, and might[5], and
every name that is named, not only in this world, but also
in the world to come; and hath put all things under his
feet, and gave him to be the head over all things to the
church, which is his body, the fulness of him that filleth all
in all." Of which kind there are very many other to be
found in the writings of the apostles: first of all[6] that
"Christ is the head of the church, and he it is which *Ephes. v.*
giveth salvation to the body; for he gave himself for the
church, to sanctify it when he had cleansed it in the fountain
of water in the word, that he might present it unto himself a
glorious church," &c.

And thus much hitherto of the kingdom of Christ in

[3 adeoque, Lat.; and so.]

[4 Alioqui nullam in terris sedem vel palatium regni habet, Lat.
omitted; Otherwise, he has no seat or palace of his kingdom upon
earth.]

[5 et dominium, Lat. omitted; and dominion.]

[6 in primis, Lat.; especially.]

earth, which is both called the kingdom of grace and the church militant.

God's king-dom of glory in heaven. Moreover the kingdom of God is called the kingdom of heaven and of glory for that occasion, because those whom our Lord and king hath sanctified on earth, and guided with his Spirit, yea, and also justified, being delivered from the flesh and taken out of this world he glorifieth in heaven, and receiveth them into joy and into the fellowship both of himself and of all the saints. For the souls of the faithful, even as soon as they depart out of their bodies, are forthwith received into heaven, to reign with Christ the everlasting King, and for ever to rejoice with all the saints. But in the last judgment, wherewith we believe that the quick and dead shall be judged of Christ our king, the bodies of the saints shall be raised up, clarified[1], coupled again to their souls; and how many soever have cleaved unto Christ their king from the beginning of the world shall live for ever and reign in glory together with Christ their king and prince. Of this kingdom of the saints the prophets and apostles have

Rev. xxi. & xxii. spoken much, and chiefly the apostle St John in his Revelation. Some have called this kingdom the church triumphant.

The kingdom of Christ is an everlasting kingdom. This kingdom of God, or of Christ, is an everlasting kingdom : for as even to the world's end the church shall be on earth, howsoever this world and the prince of the world do rage ; so the faithful after judgment shall live and reign with Christ, happy for ever both in body and soul.

Matt. xvi. Matt. xxiv. For the Lord saith in the gospel : "The gates of hell shall not prevail against the church." Also the last times shall be as the days of Noe were, wherein, though the wicked did far in number exceed the church of the faithful, yet Noe and his were saved in the ark, but the wicked were destroyed with the flood: in such sort surely shall iniquity by all means prevail in the end of the world ; but in the meanwhile those that are elected into the kingdom of Christ shall be saved by Christ, whom they shall look for to be their judge, and shall see their Redeemer coming in the clouds of heaven.

Dan. vii. Daniel also in his prophecy describeth the rising and falling of all kingdoms and of antichrist also, but attributeth no end to the kingdom of the saints or holy people, but wit-

[1 See Vol. I. pp. 172-176.]

nesseth that it shall be everlasting. The same doth the prophet Zachary also in his twelfth chapter. For the saints reign on the earth by Christ; and, being translated from the earth into heaven, they shall reign together with their king Christ for ever. And the scripture is wont oftentimes to speak of one of these kingdoms only. Of both these kingdoms we understand many places of scripture: first of all, that which is spoken by our Saviour: "When ye pray, say, Our Father, which art in heaven, hallowed be thy name, thy kingdom come." For we pray that he would reign in us while we live on earth, that we also may reign over the world and the prince of the world; and that we be not ruled by Satan, neither that sin reign in us; but rather that we, here being governed by himself, may in time to come reign with Christ in heaven.

Matt. vi.

Contrariwise, what manner of kingdom the kingdom of the world is, it appeareth by considering the head or the king and prince thereof, which is the devil, the author of sin, of uncleanness, and of death. He reigneth in the world, the prince doubtless of the kingdom of darkness. Not that God and his Christ is not king of all things; but because unfaithful apostates, through their own proper malice, revolting from God to the devil, do appoint him for the prince[2]; to whom even of their own accord they submit and yield themselves to be governed, living in all ungodliness, wickedness, and uncleanness; framing themselves like to their head the devil; with whom they shall be punished everlastingly in the world to come, as in this world they have suffered themselves to be governed of him, doing his will.

The kingdom of the world, what manner of one it is.

This "prince of this world," elsewhere also called "The god of this world," hath Christ the true king and monarch of the world overcome, and hath destroyed his kingdom: not that he should not be as long as this world endureth, but that he should not hurt the elect. Satan doth live and shall live for ever, howbeit in misery, (which life in very deed is death), but he hath no power against them that be redeemed by Christ the prince. He hath and shall have a kingdom even unto the end of the world, but in the children of unbelief. This kingdom also in this world is in decaying, and as

John xii.
2 Cor. iv.
1 John iii.

[2 So also ed. 1584: but ed. 1577, *their* prince. Sibi principem, Lat.]

it were momentany and for a short time; for the world
passeth away, and all worldly things perish. But all the elect
of God are very strangers from this kingdom; yea, they are
as it were sworn enemies of this kingdom. Neither can the
prince of darkness by his power put away the partakers of
the kingdom of Christ into his kingdom of iniquity. Truly,
he goeth about this diligently, and with divers temptations
vexeth the elect: but those overcome through him which
in time past vanquished that false king and prince of thieves,
and taught us that, despising this filthy prince and the world
and the lusts of the world, giving our minds to innocency,
we should yield ourselves to that good Spirit to be governed.

These things have I thus far declared, as briefly as I
could, touching the king Christ and his only and everlasting
kingdom.

Christ Jesus the High Priest. And now Christ our Lord is a priest, yea, that chiefest,
only, and everlasting priest, whom the high priests of the old
people did prefigure and shadow out. For David in his song
Psal. cx. altogether divine saith: "The Lord sware, and will not repent
him, Thou art a priest for ever after the order of Melchizedek." Which words the blessed apostle alleging and expounding in his epistle to the Hebrews, hath left these words
Heb. vii. written: "The forerunner (saith he) is for us entered into
heaven, after the order of Melchizedek made a priest for
Gen. xiv. ever. For this Melchizedek, king of Salem, priest of the
most high God, who met Abraham coming from the slaughter
of kings, and blessed him, to whom also Abraham gave the
tenths of all things; who first indeed is called by interpretation
the king of righteousness, then also king of Salem, which is,
king of peace; of an unknown father, of an unknown mother,
of an unknown kin, neither having beginning of days, nor end
of life, but likened to the Son of God, remaineth a priest for
ever[1]." Surely our Lord Jesus Christ is both a righteous
and peaceable king, and the righteousness and peace of the
faithful: and he is that everlasting priest, who according
to his humanity is believed to be born of the virgin without
seed of man, and therefore of an unknown father; and according to his divinity begotten of the Father, and therefore of an
unknown mother; and unspeakably begotten from everlasting, and therefore of unknown kin, having neither beginning

[1 Erasmus' version.]

nor end of life.   For albeit according to his humanity he was
dead and buried, yet according to his divinity he remaineth
God immortal and everlasting.   The selfsame which is a king
is also acknowledged a priest, not according to the order of
Aaron, but according to the order of Melchizedek.   For as
the scripture remembereth this one a priest; so one Christ
remaineth priest for ever, having an everlasting priesthood.
But high priests in time past were called and anointed; they
did not thrust themselves into such an office by force or
deceit.   Whereupon the apostle said: "No man taketh the Heb. v.
honour to himself, but he that is called of God, as was Aaron.
So also Christ took not glory to himself to be made high
priest, but is made and confirmed of him who said unto him,
Thou art my Son, this day have I begotten thee.   As he saith Psal. ii.
also in another place: Thou art a priest for ever after the
order of Melchizedek."   But thou dost nowhere read that our
priest was anointed with visible oil: for he was anointed with Christ is
invisible oil, namely, with the fulness of the Holy Ghost; as the anointed.
prophet witnesseth: "Thy God[2] hath anointed thee with the Psal. xlv.
oil of gladness above thy fellows."   And again: "The Spirit Isai. lxi.
of the Lord upon me: for the Lord hath anointed me, and
sent me to preach good tidings unto the poor."

Furthermore, when we read that the office of priests in
times past was to serve in the tabernacle, to teach the people,
to make intercession between God and men, to pray for the
people and to bless them, to sacrifice also, and to consecrate or
sanctify; and that now it is manifest that Jesus Christ is the
lawful priest; it is certain that he is tied to the selfsame offices,
but indeed to so much more excellent than these by how
much he hath obtained a more excellent priesthood.   Those How Christ
priests after the order of Aaron served in the corruptible and doth the
figurative tabernacle: but our Lord, being taken up into the a priest.
true tabernacle, heaven itself, ministereth to all the saints of
God.   For heaven and the church of saints is the true tabernacle and temple of our high priest.   Christ our priest is the Christ the
only and everlasting teacher and master of his universal the church.
church.   For not only that age hath he so taught, which lived
in the days of his flesh; but the Spirit of Christ was in the
prophets, by whom now also he ruleth all the seats[3] of his
catholic church.   Christ himself as yet speaketh unto us, and

[2 Deus, Deus tuus, Lat.]   [3 cathedras, Lat.]

will speak even unto the end of the world, by the mouth or writings of the holy apostles and all teachers preaching the doctrine of the apostles. And this doctrine is sufficient for the catholic church; for it comprehendeth all those things fully which pertain to the holy[1] and happy life. Christ our high priest maketh intercession for all the saints in his own temple. For he, being the only advocate and patron of all the faithful, prayeth to the Father for us on the right hand of God; for he ascended unto the right hand of God the Father, that he should always appear there in the presence of God, to follow all our suits[2] faithfully: of which thing I have spoken more at large in my last sermon[3], where I entreated of invocation and intercession. The same our Lord only blesseth us. For he was made a malediction and curse for us, that we might be blessed in him, according to that notable and ancient prophecy: "In thy seed shall all the nations of the world be blessed." Moreover Christ our Lord sacrificeth for us: for he offereth incense when he maketh supplication for us, and appeareth on the right hand of God. And he offereth a sacrifice for sins unto the living God, not a sacrifice of a beast, but himself, always an effectual sacrifice, to make satisfaction for all the sins of the people. Whereof since I have entreated abundantly in the treatise of ceremonies[4], here of purpose I am the briefer. Again, since our Lord Jesus Christ is the holy of holiest, doubtless he sanctifieth and consecrateth his catholic church, anointing it with the oil of the Holy Ghost, that we may be made both holy and priests to offer spiritual sacrifices to God. For we read that that holy ointment, poured on Aaron's head, ran down to his beard, and even to the skirts of his clothing. For Christ, the high priest of his universal church, poureth his Spirit as well upon them that are very far off as upon them that are near at hand; for he crieth in the gospel: "If any man thirsteth, let him come unto me and drink. He that believeth on me, as the scripture hath said, out of his belly shall flow rivers of water of life." And again: "For their sakes sanctify I myself, that they also might be sanctified in the truth."

Marginalia:
Christ maketh intercession.
Christ blesseth.
[Gen. xxii.]
Christ sacrificeth.
Christ sanctifieth.
John vii.
John xvii.

[1 So also ed. 1584: but ed. 1577, *a* holy.]
[2 negotia exequatur, Lat.]
[3 Sermon (not the last, but) v. pp. 212—219.]
[4 Vol. II. Decade III. Sermon v.]

To be short, when we say and confess that Jesus
Christ is the priest or bishop[5] of the faithful people, we say
this; that Christ is our chosen and appointed teacher and master, to govern and teach his universal church, to make intercession for us, and to plead all our suits[6] faithfully before the
Father in heaven; which is the only patron, mediator, and
advocate of the faithful with God; who by the sacrifice of his
body is the perpetual and only satisfaction, absolution, and
justification of all sinners throughout the whole world[7]; who
consecrateth into priests those that believe, that they also
might offer to God the Father through Jesus Christ acceptable
sacrifices, and might be the house and tabernacle of God.

Out of this it shall be easy to judge what manner of *Of Christ's priesthood.*
priesthood Christ's is, who is our high priest and bishop.
His priesthood is the very office or very function and working of the priest, whereby Christ the priest himself executeth
all things in heaven and in the catholic church, which belong to his priestly office.   Wherefore it must needs be,
that this priesthood of Christ our high bishop is not visible
and corporal, but altogether spiritual.   For very well saith
Paul, " Christ were no priest, if he were on the earth :" where *Heb. viii.*
they that are of the tribe of Levi do minister in the tabernacle or temple; where there is a temple or tabernacle with
manifold holy garments and vessels.   But Christ our Lord
is of the tribe of Juda; born, I say, of a royal tribe: albeit
we are not ignorant in the meanwhile, that the royal tribe,
that is, the tribe of Juda, and the priestly tribe, that is,
the tribe of Levi, were mingled together; for we read *[Luke i. 36.]*
that Elizabeth, which was of the daughters of Aaron, was
cousin to the Virgin, the mother of God, she being of the
line of David.   Neither is our Lord read at any time to
have used the temple or the holy vessels in his ministery.
For although sometime he taught in the temple, yet he
taught not only in the same.   He never sacrificed in the
temple at the holy altars either of incense or of burnt-offerings.   He never used priestly garments, which were figurative;
whereof I spake when I expounded the ceremonial laws[8].

[5 summum pontificem, Lat.]   [6 negotia agat, Lat.]
[7 omnium peccatorum totius mundi, Lat.; of all the sins of the
whole world.]
[8 Vol. II. Decade III. Serm. v.]

Heb. xiii. Therefore, when he would sacrifice for the satisfaction of the sins of the whole world, he suffered without the gate, and offered himself a lively and most holy sacrifice, according as the shadows or types, prophecies and figures foreshewed in the law of Moses: whereof in like manner I have entreated in the discourse of the ceremonial laws. And when he had offered the sacrifice of his body, he ascended into heaven, and sitteth at the right hand of the Father, that from thence he may give light unto his church, and there appear always for us in the presence of God the Father. And therefore he doth not now corporally execute his priestly office on earth, in like sort teaching us now as in the days of his flesh he taught the men of his age. For now he doth illuminate with his Spirit the minds of his, and daily repaireth or reneweth the evangelical doctrine of the apostles; and yet, for all that, he himself speaketh by the mouth of them that teach and preach the gospel. He blesseth us from heaven, that is to say, he enricheth us with all heavenly blessings.
1 John ii. Of him the apostle speaking saith: "And the anointing, which ye have received of him, dwelleth in you: and ye need not that any man teach you; but as the same anointing teacheth you of all things, and it is true and not lying, and as it hath taught you, ye shall abide in it[1]." Of him the
Isai. xliv. divine prophet speaking saith: "I will pour water upon the thirsty, and floods upon the dry ground: I will pour my Spirit upon thy seed, and my blessing upon thy stock[2]," (or buds:) "they shall grow together like as the grass, and as the willows by the water's side." By which words we learn that Christ our high priest hath no need of a bishop, suffragan, or vicar in his church; for he himself is present with his church, and governeth it by his Spirit. The selfsame Christ, at the right hand of the Father in heaven, doth not so oftentimes humbly fall down on his knees and make
Heb. v. intercession for us as we do sin. "In the days of his flesh, when he did offer up prayers and supplications[3], with strong crying and tears, he was once heard in that which he feared[4]."

[1 manete in ea, Lat.; and Erasmus, and Bibl. Lat. Tigur. 1544. Marg. Auth. Ver.]

[2 So Coverdale, 1535; stirpem tuam, Lat. and Vulg.]

[3 pro nobis, Lat. omitted; for us.]

[4 exauditus est a Patre pro reverentia, Lat.; Erasmus' Version.]

For now he always appeareth for us in the presence of God. All our matters are manifest in his sight; and the Father beholdeth the face of his Christ, for whose sake he is pleased with all his members, hearing them and giving them whatsoever healthful things they require, according to that saying of our Saviour: "Verily, verily, I say unto you, Whatsoever ye shall ask the Father in my name, he shall give it you." Therefore here we must imagine no turmoils, no molestation, no labour wherewith he should be wearied which is the intercessor, advocate, and priest of all before God the Father in heaven: whereof also I put you in mind in my last sermon, where I entreated of invocation and intercession[5]. Wherefore our priest, executing his office before God in heaven, hath need of no altar of incense, no censer, no holy vessels or garments: much less hath he need of the altar of burnt-offerings; for on the cross, which was his altar, he offered up himself but once for all. Neither was there any mortal man worthy to offer to the living God the living Son of God. And that only sacrifice is always effectual to make satisfaction for all the sins of all men in the whole world.

And though in the discourse of the ceremonial laws I have alleged many testimonies touching these things, yet I cannot stay myself here, but must cite unto you some that be notable. For this matter, wherein the fruit of Christ's divinity and humanity, to be short, all our salvation consisteth, cannot worthily and diligently enough be printed in men's hearts. Paul unto the Hebrews, speaking of the priests of the old Testament, and comparing Christ our high priest with them, yea, by all means preferring him, saith: "And [Heb. vii. 23—27.] among them many were made priests, because they were not suffered to endure by reason of death. But Christ, because he endureth for ever, hath an everlasting," or unchangeable[6], "priesthood, for that it doth not pass over to another by succession. Wherefore he is able also perfectly to save them that come unto God by him, seeing he ever liveth to make intercession for them. For such an high priest it became us to have, (which is) holy, harmless, undefiled, separate from sins[7], and made higher than the heavens: which needed not

[John xvi.]

[5 See above, p. 219.]
[6 immigrabile, Lat. See Vol. II. p. 195, n. 3.]
[7 a peccatoribus, Lat.]

daily, as those high priests, to offer up sacrifice, first for his own sins, and then for the people's; for that did he once, Heb. ix. when he offered up himself." And again he saith: " Christ is not entered into the holy places made with hands, which are the similitudes of the true sanctuary, but into heaven itself, to appear now in the sight of God for us: not that he should offer himself often, as the high priests[1] entered into the holy places every year in strange" (or with other) " blood; for then must he have often suffered since the foundation of the world: but now in the end of the world hath he appeared once, to put away sin by the sacrifice of himself. And as it is appointed unto men that they shall once die, and after that cometh the judgment; even so Christ, once offered to take away the sins of many, the second time shall be seen without sin of them which wait for him unto Heb. x. salvation." And again the same Paul saith: " Every priest appeareth daily ministering, and oftentimes offereth one manner of offering, which can never take away sins: but this man, after he had offered one sacrifice for sins, sitteth for ever at the right hand of God, and from henceforth tarrieth till his enemies be made his footstool. For with one offering hath he made perfect," or consecrated, " for ever them that are sanctified." All these sayings hitherto are the apostle Paul's. And I think that these testimonies are not to be made manifest and agreeable to our purpose by a larger interpretation; for they are all even without any exposition of ours most evident, and very aptly[2] agree to the matter which we have in hand. For they do plainly set forth and lay before our eyes to behold the whole priesthood of Christ, specially that which belongeth to the intercession and the only and everlasting sacrifice or satisfaction for sins. It belongeth also to the same priesthood to consecrate priests unto God all the faithful: not that we should offer for the satisfaction of sins, but that we should offer our prayers, thanksgivings, and ourselves, and the duties of godliness as it were every moment. For St John the apostle and evan-Rev. i. gelist saith: " Jesus Christ, prince of the kings of the earth, loved us, and washed us from our sins in his own blood, and made us kings and priests unto God and his Father." We 1 Pet. ii. may find the same sentence also in the epistle of St Peter.

[1 pontifex, Lat.]   [2 quam apertissime, Lat.]

So that in these[3] we may see what fruit riseth and floweth unto us from the divinity and humanity of Christ our king and high priest. For he could not be prince of kings and high priest, unless he were God and man.

Here this place requireth to speak somewhat of the name of a Christian, and of the duties of a christian man. *Of the name of a Christian.*

We have the name of Christians of Christ, to whom being unseparably knit we are the members of that body whereof he is head. And Christ is not his proper name (for he is called Jesus), but a name of office, derived from the Greek word χρίσμα, which signifieth anointing[4]; so Christ signifieth as much as *anointed*. Therefore Tertullian saith, it is not a proper name, but a name attributed. And he addeth, "Anointed is no more a name than clothed or apparelled, a thing accident to the name[5]." But the kings and high-priests were anointed with oil; therefore Christ signifieth unto us him that is king, high-priest, or bishop. And because we are named Christians of Christ, who hath anointed us with the Holy Ghost, truly we also are kings and priests. Where you may see how great a benefit we have received of Christ, God and Man; for he hath made us kings and priests. *Christians are kings and priests.*

We see what the duty of Christians is; namely, to maintain this dignity even to the last gasp, lest it be taken from us again by Satan. Furthermore if we be kings, we are lords over things, and are free, ruling, not ruled or in subjection: free, I say, from sin and everlasting death, and from all uncleanness; lords over Satan, prince of this world, and over the world itself. For we rule the world and the flesh: we are not ruled by them. Hereunto belong those words of the apostle: "Let not sin reign in your mortal body, that ye should thereunto obey by the lusts of it. Neither give ye your members as instruments (or weapons) of unrighteousness unto sin: but give yourselves unto God, as they that are alive from the dead, and your members as instruments (or weapons) of righteousness unto God. For sin shall not have power (or *Christians are kings.* *Rom. vi.*

[3 in omnibus his, Lat.; in all these.]

[4 a chrismate, Lat. Cf. Tertul. de Baptismo, cap. 7. Tom. iv. p. 164. ed. Semler. Hal. Magd. 1824.]

[5 Si tamen nomen est Christus, et non appellatio potius. Unctus enim significatur: unctus autem non magis nomen est, quam vestitus ... accidens nomini res.—Tertull. Adv. Prax. Op. Par. 1634, p. 660.]

dominion) over you." And therefore when the prince of this world, yea, and the world itself, and the flesh, and sin, the wicked affection thereof, do what they can to draw us again out of freedom into bondage, we must (because we are kings) valiantly resist them, and, continuing in conflict, vanquish and overcome them by the virtue of Christ reigning in us. For

1 John v. St John the apostle saith: "All that is born of God overcometh the world; and this is the victory which hath overcome the world, even your faith." Hitherto belongeth the doctrine of freedom and bondage, whereof I entreated in the former Decade[1]. By all these we gather, that the principal duty of Christians is always to stand in battle array, and to keep their place, to watch and endeavour by all force and means, lest at any time being overcome of their enemy Satan they be spoiled of their royal or kingly dignity, and be haled down into the bondage of hell. Truly, if we overcome in Christ and with Christ, we shall reign together with him; that is, we shall live with him and all the saints in glory for ever and ever. And thus are we kings in Christ; thus are we Christians.

Christians
are priests. Again, because we are Christians, that is to say, anointed, surely we are priests also; and therefore, according to our priestly office, we teach, we admonish, we exhort, and comfort all our brethren, and all men that are committed to our charge. Where notwithstanding we do necessarily make a difference between the christian priesthood and the ecclesiastical ministery. All Christians truly, as well men as women, are priests, but we are not all ministers of the church: for we cannot all one with another preach publicly, administer the sacraments, and execute other duties of pastors, unless we be lawfully called and ordained thereunto. This our priesthood common to all is spiritual, and is occupied in common duties of godliness, not in public and lawful ministeries of the church. Whereupon one may and ought to instruct and admonish another privately, and while he so doth, he executeth a priestly office; as when the good-man of the house[2] instructeth his children at home in godliness; when the good-wife of the house teacheth and correcteth her daughters; to be short, when every one of us exhort every neighbour of ours to the desire and study of godliness. For the apostle

[1 Decade III. Serm. IX.]   [2 Vol. I. page 258, note 2.]

Paul saith: "Exhort ye one another daily, while it is called Heb. iii. to-day; lest any of you be hardened through the deceitfulness of sin." Moreover, since we be priests, we must offer sacrifices worthy of our God. And we have sufficiently testified, that, after Christ our high and only priest or bishop in all ages and in all the whole world, none doth offer a satisfactory sacrifice to take away sin: for when he offered up himself, he offered a sacrifice but once, howbeit always effectual to cleanse the sins of all. Therefore we offer unto him thanksgiving and praise, celebrating the memory of that one only sacrifice: we offer prayers: we offer ourselves, that is to say, our bodies, a lively and a reasonable sacrifice to God, together with all kind of godliness and well-doing. For Paul saith: "By Christ we offer the sacrifice of praise always unto God, Heb. xiii. that is, the fruit of lips confessing his name. To do good and to distribute forget not; for with such sacrifice God is well pleased." But touching these sacrifices I have spoken more in my former sermon[3], wherein I entreated what the true service of God is. But since all sanctification is and riseth from one high priest, Christ Jesus, we can sanctify ourselves no otherwise than with honest and pure conversation of life, which thing is required at our hands; namely, that we be holy, and that we sanctify the name of our God with an innocent life, that it be not evil spoken of through us by men, but that they may see the good works of the faithful, and glorify the Father which is in heaven. There is none but may see that all the duties of a christian man are comprehended in these points; wherein unless we exercise ourselves earnestly, I do not see that we are worthy of so excellent a name.

That this most holy name was first given to the faithful at Antioch in Syria, Luke is witness: which yet let no man so understand, as if that name afore had been altogether unknown to all men. For now it is become most common; in time past it was the name only of most excellent and holy men, and of such as rather were so indeed than so accounted, though also by name they were in some manner so acknowledged. For Eusebius in his ecclesiastical history maketh mention, that the ancient fathers Adam, Seth, Noe, Abraham, and other like unto these, were all Christians; and therefore christian religion to be the very purest, perfectest, and the

The name of a Christian, most ancient. [Acts xi. 26.]

[3 See above, p. 224.]

19—2

ancientest. The words of Eusebius, if any require, are these : " The nation of the Hebrews is not new, but unto all men in antiquity famous, and known to all. Their books and writings do contain ancient fathers, of whom they make report before the flood, rare indeed and few in number, howbeit in godliness and righteousness and in all kind of virtues most excellent ; and after the flood, of other of the sons and nephews of Noe, as of Tharam and Abraham, of whom as their captain and progenitor the posterity of the Hebrews do boast. So that if any man shall say that all these from Abraham himself even to the first man, being beautified with the testimony of righteousness, through their works, though not in name, were Christians, truly he should not stray from the truth. For a Christian signifieth a man which excelleth other in knowledge and doctrine of Christ, with moderation of mind, and righteousness and continency of life, and through fortitude of virtue and confession of godliness toward the one and only God of all creatures. And this name those ancient fathers did no less esteem than we do. Neither had they care of the corporal circumcision, as we also have not ; neither of keeping the Sabbath-day, as we also have not ; nor of abstaining from meats, nor other differences : which things afterwards Moses first of all ordained, and figuratively delivered them to be performed : as such things also even at this day pertain not to Christians. But they saw plainly the Christ or anointed of God : as also it is declared already before, that he both appeared unto Abraham, and gave answer unto Isaac and Israel, and spake to Moses, and after him to the prophets. Whereby thou shalt find that these godly men also obtained the name of Christ, according to that saying spoken of them, to wit, Touch not my Christs (or mine anointed), and do my prophets no harm. Therefore it is manifest that this godly invention of those men who lived holily in the time of Abraham, which of late by the doctrine of Christ is preached to all nations, is the first, most ancient, and eldest of all[1]." Thus much Eusebius.

[1 Οὐ νέον, ἀλλὰ καὶ παρὰ πᾶσιν ἀνθρώποις ἀρχαιότητι τετιμημένον ἔθνος, τοῖς πᾶσι καὶ αὐτὸ γνώριμον, τὸ Ἑβραίων τυγχάνει. Λόγοι δὴ παρὰ τούτῳ καὶ γράμματα παλαίους ἄνδρας περιέχουσι, σπανίους μὲν καὶ ἀριθμῷ βραχεῖς, ἀλλ᾽ ὅμως εὐσεβείᾳ καὶ δικαιοσύνῃ καὶ πάσῃ τῇ λοιπῇ διενεγκόντας ἀρετῇ· πρὸ μέν γε τοῦ κατακλυσμοῦ, διαφόρους· μετὰ δὲ καὶ τοῦτον, ἑτέρους τῶν

Furthermore, if we behold ourselves in this looking-glass There are but few Christians. of a christian name, we shall see that very few at this day are worthy of this name[2]. Truly all of us are commonly so called, and we will be[3] named Christians; but few of us live a life worthy of our profession. We are named Christians of holy anointing. The holy anointing is the Holy Ghost himself. "Upon whom shall my Spirit rest?" saith the Lord; Isai. lxvi. "even upon him that is poor, and of a lowly troubled spirit, and standeth in awe of my words." But we set light by the word of God, we have very troublesome heads, we are corrupt with evil affections and lewd lusts, we swell with pride; and therefore we want the ointment of holy oil, or are void of the Holy Ghost[4]. Who therefore can say that we be Christians? We are all of us in manner ruled by wicked desires, by the flesh, the world, and the prince of this world; few of us rule the world, and the flesh, and those things which are in them. Therefore not the Spirit of God, but the spirit of the world

τε τοῦ Νῶε παίδων καὶ ἀπογόνων, ἀτὰρ καὶ (τὸν Θάραν, alii) τὸν Ἀβραὰμ, ὃν ἀρχηγὸν καὶ προπάτορα σφῶν αὐτῶν παῖδες Ἑβραίων αὐχοῦσι. Πάντας δὴ ἐκείνους δικαιοσύνῃ μεμαρτυρημένους, ἐξ αὐτοῦ Ἀβραὰμ ἐπὶ τὸν πρῶτον ἀνιοῦσιν ἄνθρωπον, ἔργῳ Χριστιανούς, εἰ καὶ μὴ ὀνόματι, προσειπών τις οὐκ ἂν ἐκτὸς βάλοι τῆς ἀληθείας. Ὁ γάρ τοι δηλοῦν ἐθέλοι τοὔνομα, τὸν Χριστιανὸν ἄνδρα διὰ τῆς τοῦ Χριστοῦ γνώσεως καὶ διδασκαλίας, σωφροσύνῃ καὶ δικαιοσύνῃ καρτερίᾳ τε βίου καὶ ἀρετῆς ἀνδρίᾳ, εὐσεβείας τε ὁμολογίᾳ ἑνὸς καὶ μόνου τοῦ ἐπὶ πάντων Θεοῦ διαπρέπειν, τοῦτο πᾶν ἐκείνοις οὐ χεῖρον ἡμῶν ἐσπουδάζετο. Οὔτ᾽ οὖν σώματος αὐτοῖς περιτομῆς ἔμελεν, ὅτι μὴ δὲ ἡμῖν· οὐ σαββάτων ἐπιτηρήσεως, ὅτι μὴ δὲ ἡμῖν· ἀλλ᾽ οὐδὲ τῶν τοιῶνδε τροφῶν παραφυλακῆς, οὐδὲ τῶν ἄλλων διαστολῆς, ὅσα τοῖς μετέπειτα πρῶτος ἁπάντων Μωϋσῆς ἀρξάμενος ἐν συμβόλοις τελεῖσθαι παραδέδωκεν, ὅτι μὴ δὲ νῦν Χριστιανῶν τὰ τοιαῦτα· ἀλλὰ καὶ σαφῶς αὐτὸν ᾔδεσαν τὸν Χριστὸν τοῦ Θεοῦ, εἴγε ὦφθαι μὲν τῷ Ἀβραὰμ, χρηματίσαι δὲ τῷ Ἰσαὰκ, λελαληκέναι δὲ τῷ Ἰακὼβ, (Ἰσραὴλ, alii) Μωϋσεῖ τε καὶ τοῖς μετὰ ταῦτα προφήταις ὡμιληκέναι προδέδεικται. Ἔνθεν αὐτοὺς δὴ τοὺς θεοφιλεῖς ἐκείνους εὕροις ἂν καὶ τῆς τοῦ Χριστοῦ κατηξιωμένους προσωνυμίας, κατὰ τὴν φάσκουσαν περὶ αὐτῶν φωνήν· Μὴ ἅψησθε τῶν χριστῶν μου, καὶ ἐν τοῖς προφήταις μου μὴ πονηρεύησθε. Ὥστε σαφῶς πρώτην ἡγεῖσθαι δεῖν καὶ πάντων παλαιοτάτην τε καὶ ἀρχαιοτάτην θεοσεβείας εὕρεσιν, αὐτῶν ἐκείνων δὴ τῶν ἀμφὶ τὸν Ἀβραὰμ θεοφιλῶν ἀνδρῶν, τὴν ἀρτίως διὰ τῆς τοῦ Χριστοῦ διδασκαλίας πᾶσιν ἔθνεσι κατηγγελμένην.—Euseb. Hist. Eccles. Lib. I. cap. 4. Tom. I. pp. 31, 32. ed. Burton. Oxon. 1838.]

[2 sacro nomine, Lat.]

[3 So also ed. 1584: but ed. 1577, we will be *all*; omnes volumus, Lat.]

[4 or—Ghost, the translator's addition.]

and the flesh beareth rule in us. The devil, the world, and the flesh have dominion over us; for in them we live, and them we do obey: whereupon, being estranged and let loose from all righteousness and holiness, we are become slaves, serving a most vile and filthy slavery. For we, not desiring to be delivered, do neither seek a redeemer; nor, being impatient of their tyranny, rise and rebel against them: but like faint-hearted cowards, we yield ourselves to be brought in subjection, and to be kept under their tyranny: nay, it repenteth and irketh us of our labours, watchings, prayers, and of all duties of godliness; and, being careless, we lie lurking as in a place of voluptuousness. But who would vouchsafe such swine the most holy name of a Christian, but he that is both exceeding foolish and wicked? No marvel then if such be thrust down into hell, there eternally to burn, and there eternally to be yoked unto him whom[1] they have most wickedly chosen to themselves to follow. And now what one of us is there that doth teach, admonish, and exhort those that boast and brag of this christian name? I speak nothing here concerning the doctors or teachers of the church; but my talk doth touch the office and duty of a christian man. Truly, the most part of us are slow in instructing our families and fellow-brethren: for either it grieveth us to take the pain, or else we fear danger. Therefore we turn the office of admonishing and instructing upon the public ministers of the church, as though nothing at all of this matter were required of us. For this cause speeches in a manner unseemly to be spoke are heard uttered of men: "I have not the office of a minister, I am no (*pfaff*) priest; why therefore should I instruct? why should I admonish?" And these care not how blasphemous and filthy things be spoken either at home or abroad; for they live to themselves, and think that the glory of God and the soul's health of their neighbour belongeth nothing unto them. But what sacrifices offer we worthy of God and our name? where are prayers and thanksgivings? where is the mortification of our flesh, and the denying of this world? where is compassion, or well-doing? where is an holy and harmless life? The contrary (if need so required) I could reckon up in a long bead-row: but to what end were it to make a large discourse of those things that are manifest unto all men? For who,

[1 hic, Lat. omitted; here.]

I pray you, doth deny, that the life of this present age (of men, I mean, which brag and boast of their christian name) is filthy, stinking, and pestilent? Which things since they be too too true and evident, I have nothing done amiss in saying a little before, that at this day there are few Christians. They that are wise and desire to be according to their name, let them hear our Saviour speaking in the gospel of Matthew : "Strive to enter in at the strait gate; for wide is the gate, Matt. vii. and broad is the way, that leadeth to destruction, and many there be which go in thereat : because strait is the gate, and narrow is the way, which leadeth unto life, and few there be that find it."

Furthermore they (which thing ought first of all to have Against false been spoken) do very greatly offend against religion and christian Christians. profession, which as they do not sincerely acknowledge the priesthood and kingdom of Christ, so they boast themselves to be chiefly praise-worthy, commendable, and catholic, because they commit those things which by all means obscure and darken the kingdom and priesthood of Christ. Christians, being content with this only title and name, do not ambitiously seek after or admit another name : but these men, as though the name of a Christian were but a light and trifling name, never rest until they be also called by other names; as though they were baptized into the name of Brion[2], Benet[3], Robert[4], or Francis[5]. Christians, cleaving only to their law-giver, master, and teacher Christ, do not acknowledge the voice of strangers, neither go a straw's breadth from the divine scriptures : but these men charge thee with heresy, unless thou receive and worship for heavenly oracles all kind of constitutions of the Romish church, though they be flat contrary to the words and teaching of Christ. Christians acknowledge themselves to have one king, one deliverer, one Saviour, and one head in heaven : these men worship his vicar in earth, and attribute salvation not only to trifling

[2 Brunonis, Lat.; Bruno, founder of the Order of Carthusians.]

[3 Benedicti, Lat.; Benedict of Nursia (or Norcia), in Italy, established the Benedictine order about A.D. 529.]

[4 Robert or Rodbert, born at Arbrissel, near Rennes in France, founded the order of Fontevraud, a new sect of Benedictines, A.D. 1100.]

[5 St Francis of Assisi, in Italy, established his order of Fratres Minores, or Minorites, about A.D. 1208.]

things, but to very stinking and loathsome things. Christians put all their trust in God, to whom they offer all their vows and prayers by Jesus Christ, whom they believe to be the only high priest and most faithful patron and advocate of all that believe: they[1] make their prayers to creatures and men's imaginations, and choose to themselves so many patrons and intercessors as there do live saints in heaven. Christians know that the sacrifice of Christ once offered is always effectual to make satisfaction for all the sins of all men in the whole world, and of all men of all ages: but these men with often outcries say, that it is flat heresy not to confess that Christ is daily offered of sacrificing priests, consecrated to that purpose. Therefore the name of a Christian is common to all, but the thing signified and meant by the name is common to the faithful only who cleave unto one Christ.

The conclusion.

Now I conclude my whole discourse of Christ, a king and a priest, with these words of St Augustine : " The Son of God, which made us, is made among us; and being our king ruleth us: and therefore we are Christians, because he is Christ. He is called Christ a *Chrismate*, that is to say, of anointing. Kings also and priests were anointed, and he was anointed king and priest. Being a king, he fought for us: being a priest, he offered himself for us. When he fought for us, he was as it were overcome, yet by right he hath overcome in very deed : for he was crucified, and on his cross whereon he was nailed he slew the devil, and then he was our king. But wherefore is he a priest? Because he hath offered himself for us. Let a priest have somewhat to offer. What could man find to give? A clean sacrifice? what sacrifice? what clean thing can a sinner offer ? O wicked sinner! O ungodly wretch! whatsoever thou shalt bring, it is unclean. Seek within thyself what to offer, thou shalt find nothing. Seek out of thyself what to offer, he is not delighted in rams or goats or bullocks; they are all his, though thou offer them not. He found nothing clean among men, which he might offer for men; therefore he offered himself a clean offering, an undefiled sacrifice. Therefore he did not offer that which we gave unto him, but that which he took of us; and that he offered pure and clean. He took flesh in the womb of the virgin, that he might offer pure and clean flesh for us that were unclean. He

[1 Isti, Lat.; these.]

is a king, he is a priest.   In him let us rejoice[2]."   To him be glory for ever and ever.   Amen.

OF THE HOLY GHOST, THE THIRD PERSON IN TRINITY TO BE WORSHIPPED, AND OF HIS DIVINE POWER.

THE EIGHTH SERMON.

IT remaineth that, after we have expounded the mysteries of the Son of God our Lord Jesus Christ, we consequently[3] speak of the Holy Ghost and of his divine power and operation.   For unless he inspire our minds and rule our tongue, we shall never be able worthily or profitably either to speak or hear anything concerning him.   For as no man knoweth those things which are of God, but the Spirit of God; so men fetch the understanding of heavenly things and the knowledge of the Holy Ghost from nowhere else than from the same Spirit of God.   Let us therefore pray and beseech God the Father, that by his Son[4] Jesus Christ he would vouchsafe to enlighten our dark and misty

[2 Filius Dei, qui fecit nos, factus est inter nos, et rex noster regit nos...et ideo Christiani (sumus) quia ille Christus.   Christus a chrismate dictus est, id est, ab unctione.   Reges autem ungebantur et sacerdotes; ille vero unctus est et rex et sacerdos.   Rex pugnavit pro nobis; sacerdos obtulit se pro nobis.   Quando pugnavit pro nobis, quasi victus est, jure autem vere vicit.   Crucifixus est enim, et de cruce sua, in qua erat fixus, diabolum occidit, et deinde rex noster. Unde autem sacerdos?   Quia se pro nobis obtulit.   Date sacerdoti quod offerat.   Quid inveniret homo quod daret?   Mundam victimam?   Quam victimam?   Quid mundum potest offerre peccator?   O inique, O impie, quicquid attuleris immundum est... Quære apud te quid offeras, non invenies: quære ex te quid offeras; non delectatur nec arietibus, nec hircis, nec tauris: omnia ipsius sunt, etsi non offeras...Nihil mundum invenit in hominibus quod offerret pro hominibus: seipsum ergo obtulit mundam victimam, hostiam immaculatam....Non ergo hoc obtulit quod nos illi dedimus; imo hoc obtulit quod a nobis accepit, et mundum obtulit.   Carnem enim...de utero virginis (accepit), ut mundam offerret pro immundis.   Ipse rex, ipse sacerdos: in eo lætemur.—August. Enarrat. in Psal. 149. Opp. Tom. VIII. fol. 361. col. 1. Par. 1532.]

[3 consequenter, Lat.; next.]

[4 Dominum nostrum, Lat. omitted; our Lord.]

minds, by sending this his holy Spirit into our hearts, and to direct us in the sincere way of truth according to the holy scriptures.

And first of all it seemeth not unprofitable to expound the word, spirit, because in the scripture it is diversly taken and very often used; so that not seldom times he shall greatly err, which is ignorant of the force of that word. Spirit properly is the signification[1] of an element, signifying air, wind, breath. In that signification we read this spoken of our Saviour: "The wind bloweth where it lusteth, and thou hearest the sound thereof, but canst not tell whence it cometh, and whither it goeth." And Paul saith: "If I pray with an unknown tongue, my spirit prayeth, but my understanding is made unfruitful." Lo, the apostle useth spirit for the breath or voice; for he joineth it to the tongue, and setteth it against the mind. By a metaphor it is translated to every bodiless substance, and is set against the body. Spirit therefore signifieth an angel, either good or bad. For the prophet (whose words Paul ·hath also rehearsed) saith: "Which maketh his angels spirits, and his ministers a flaming fire." And again: "Are they not all ministering spirits?" These testimonies are understood of good angels. When the scripture speaketh of evil angels, commonly it addeth somewhat, as an evil spirit, or an unclean spirit. We call also spirits or ghosts, which have taken some shape that cannot well be discerned, spirits. So the apostles not believing that the Lord was risen again with his true body, when they saw him they thought they had seen a spirit: to whom, shewing his feet and his hands, he saith, "A spirit hath not flesh and bones as ye see me have." Again, spirit is taken for the breath of life; as with the Latins, to breathe[2] is to live, to leave breathing[3] is to die. David saith: "When thou givest it them, they gather it; when thou openest thy hand, they are filled with good. When thou hidest thy face, they are troubled; when thou takest away their breath, they die, and are turned again to their dust." And the Lord in Moses saith: "I will destroy all flesh, wherein there is breath of life." The reasonable soul also of man is peculiarly called spirit, insomuch that spirit is very often taken in the

The word *Spirit* is expounded.

Spirit is air or wind. John iii.

1 Cor. xiv.

Spirit signifieth an angel.

Psal. clv.

Heb. i.

[Luke xxiv. 39.]

Spirit signifieth life. Psal. cxlv. civ.

Gen. vi.

Spirit signifieth the soul of man.

[1 nota, Lat.]
[2 spirare, Lat.]
[3 expirare, Lat.]

holy scripture for the reasonable soul of man. For in the gospel thou dost read, "Jesus, when he had bowed down his head, gave up the ghost," (or the spirit). And thou dost read of the holy martyr Stephen, "They stoned Stephen calling on and saying, Lord Jesu, receive my spirit." For Solomon said before : " The dust shall be turned again unto earth from whence it came⁴, and the spirit shall return unto God who gave it."   And sometimes spirit signifieth the affection and motion, readiness and provocation of the mind. For Solomon saith : "A man that refraineth not his appetite," or spirit, "is like a city which is broken down." Thou mayest oftentimes find in the scriptures the spirit of pride, anger, lust, or envy, taken for a proud, angry, lustful, or envious affection.   Also in Luke xiii. the very sore disease, or source of sickness, is called the spirit of infirmity. The spirit also signifieth those spiritual motions which the Holy Ghost stirreth up in the hearts of the saints, yea, and the very gifts poured into the hearts of men by the Spirit; which in every place in Paul is to be seen. Elsewhere spirit is opposed against the letter, the body, the figure, the type or shadow; and is used for a more high or mystical meaning, and for the very pith of the thing; as when Paul saith : "The circumcision of the heart is the circumcision which consisteth in the spirit, not in the letter." And again: "The Lord hath made us able ministers of the new Testament, not of the letter, but of the spirit. For the letter killeth, but the spirit giveth life." Therefore thou mayest find spirit to be taken for inspiration, revelation, and doctrine. For John saith : "Believe not every spirit, but prove the spirits, whether they be of God or not." And again : "Quench not the Spirit, despise not prophecies." Last of all, God is called that unmeasurable and unspeakable power of the Spirit. "God," saith our Lord, "is a Spirit, and they that worship him must worship him in spirit and in truth." By this means the word spirit is common to all the persons of the reverend Trinity : howbeit it is peculiarly applied to the third person in Trinity, of whom we make this sermon.

And albeit the Holy Ghost, forsomuch as he is God, can be compassed within no limits, (for by his own nature he is

[⁴ sicut fuit, Lat. ; as it was, Auth. ver.]

Luke xxiii.
John xix.

Acts vii.

Eccles. xii.

Spirit signifieth affection of mind.

[Prov. xxv. 28.]

Spirit signifieth spiritual motions.

Rom. ii.

2 Cor. iii.

Spirit signifieth revelation.

1 John iv.

1 Thess. v.

John iv.

What the Holy Ghost is.

unspeakable, unmeasurable, incomprehensible, everlasting ;) yet notwithstanding, that I may say somewhat in a certain order concerning him, if it will be no otherwise, I will at the least[1] shadow out that which the scripture, the inspiration of the Holy Ghost himself, very largely declareth of him. The Holy Ghost is the third person in Trinity to be worshipped, very God, proceeding from the Father and the Son, which enlighteneth, regenerateth, sanctifieth, and fulfilleth the faithful with all good graces. But that the Holy Ghost is the third person in the holy Trinity, I think it is sufficiently at large declared in the third sermon of this Decade. Surely this only sentence of our Saviour, "Baptize them in the name of the Father, and of the Son, and of the Holy Ghost," doth abundantly confirm to godly minds that the Holy Ghost is the third person in Trinity.

[Matt. xxviii. 19.]

That the Holy Ghost is very God.

Moreover that he is very God, of the same power, glory, majesty, and being with the Father and the Son, that especially proveth, because he is the third person in the holy Trinity Neither must we think that he is lesser than they, because he is reckoned in the third place. For though the blessed Trinity be remembered of us in order, yet notwithstanding there is no degree, no time, no place, or number in the blessed Trinity. For blessed Athanasius made his confession according to the scripture, and said : "The catholic faith is this, that we worship one God in Trinity, and Trinity in Unity ; neither confounding the persons, nor dividing the substance. For there is one person of the Father, another of the Son, and another of the Holy Ghost : but the Godhead of the Father, of the Son, and of the Holy Ghost is one ; the glory equal, the majesty co-eternal. Such as the Father is, such is the Son, and such is the Holy Ghost. The Father uncreate, the Son uncreate, and the Holy Ghost uncreate. The Father incomprehensible[2], the Son incomprehensible, and the Holy Ghost incomprehensible. The Father eternal, the Son eternal, and the Holy Ghost eternal : and yet are they not three eternals, but one eternal," &c. And Augustine also, in his fifteenth book *de Trinitate*, cap. 26, saith : "In that high Trinity, which is God, there are no distances of times, whereby it may be shewed or at least de-

<hr>

[1 at the last, ed. 1577, 1587 : saltem, Lat.]
[2 immensus, Lat.]

manded, whether the Son were first born of the Father, and
afterward the Holy Ghost to proceed from them both [3]," &c.

Truly, we confess that the Father, the Son, and the Holy
Ghost is one God, and that the same is eternal.　Therefore
let it trouble no man, that the Spirit is put in the last place.
For when the apostle in his epistle to the Corinthians framed
his blessing, he said : "The grace of our Lord Jesus Christ, 2 Cor. xiii.
and the love of God, and the fellowship of the Holy Ghost,
be with you all." He maketh mention of the Holy Ghost in
the last place.　But the same Paul saith, " There are diversities of gifts, but it is the selfsame Spirit : and there are 1 Cor. xii.
differences of administrations, but it is the selfsame Lord :
and there are divers manners of operations, but it is the
selfsame God, which worketh all in all:" setting the Spirit in
the first place, teaching that the order of names doth not
make difference of dignities.　After this manner also in the
former testimony, he placed the Son before the Father ; not
overthrowing the order which the Lord hath set down in
Matthew, but shewing the equality of the Trinity in honour [4]. [Matt. xxviii.
For what canst thou more plainly say than that which the 19.]
scripture saith, that the Holy Ghost doth sanctify, renew,
regenerate, give life, and save ? and these are operations
agreeable to God only.　By operations therefore we manifestly acknowledge, that the Holy Ghost is God, of the same
essence and power with the Father and the Son.　For the
Holy Ghost from the beginning before all creatures, visible
and invisible, is a Creator, not a creature, as Job witnesseth :
"His Spirit hath garnished the heavens." Again : "The Job xxvi.
Spirit of God hath made me, and the breath of the Almighty [Job xxxiii.
hath given me life." Zacharias the priest and father of St 4.]
John Baptist saith : "Blessed be the Lord God of Israel, for Luke i.
he hath redeemed his people : as he spake by the mouth of

[3 In illa summa Trinitate, quæ Deus est, intervalla temporum
nulla sunt, per quæ possit ostendi aut saltem requiri, utrum prius de
Patre natus sit Filius, et postea de ambobus processerit Spiritus Sanctus.—Augustin. de Trinitate. Opp. Tom. III. fol. 101. col. 1. Par. 1531.]

[4 Ἐν μὲν τῇ προτέρᾳ ἐπιστολῇ (1 Cor. xii. 4—6) πρῶτον ἔταξε (ὁ
ἀπόστολος) τὸ Πνεῦμα, ἐνθαῦτα δὲ (2 Cor. xiii. 14) τελευταῖον· διδάσκων
ὡς οὐ ποιεῖ τῶν ὀνομάτων ἡ τάξις ἀξιωμάτων διαφοράν.　Ταύτῃ τοι τὸν
Υἱὸν προέταξε τοῦ Πατρὸς, οὐ τὴν τάξιν ἀνατρέπων ἣν ὁ Κύριος τέθεικεν,
ἀλλὰ τὸ ὁμότιμον τῆς Τριάδος ἐπιδεικνύς.—Theodoret. Hæret. Fab. Lib. v.
cap. 3. p. 258. Tom. IV. Lut. Par. 1642.]

his holy prophets, which have been since the world began."
And[1] St Peter saith : " For the prophecy came not in old time
by the will of man, but holy men of God spake as they were
moved by the Holy Ghost."   By this, I pray you, who cannot gather that the Holy Ghost is God? For God spake
by the mouth of the prophets; and the Holy Ghost spake by
the mouth of the prophets : therefore the Holy Ghost is
God.   The same Peter also in express words hath called the
Holy Ghost God, when he accused Ananias of theft, yea, and
also of sacrilege : for when he had said, " How is it that
Satan hath filled[2] thy heart to lie unto the Holy Ghost ? "
by and by he addeth, "Thou hast not lied unto men, but
unto God."   To the doctrine of St Peter agree those things
in all points, which St Paul the doctor of the Gentiles hath
taught.   For he called the believers the temples of God.
"Know ye not (saith he) that ye are the temple of God, and
that the Spirit of God dwelleth in you ?"   And again :
"Know ye not that your bodies are the temple of the Holy
Ghost which is in you, whom ye have of God, and ye are not
your own?"   To be the temple of God, and to be the temple of the Holy Ghost, Paul taketh to be one and the selfsame
thing : it followeth therefore that the Holy Ghost is God.
For in his Epistle to the Corinthians he expressly nameth
the Holy Ghost God : for after he had said, " There are
diversities of gifts, but it is the selfsame Spirit ;" and had
reckoned up the kinds of gifts; by and by he addeth, "And
all these things worketh even one and the selfsame Spirit,
distributing to every man severally even as he will."   And
he himself had said a little afore, " There are divers manners of operations; but it is the selfsame God, which worketh
all in all."

But Didymus Alexandrinus, a man of excellent learning,
doth knit up a most evident argument of the Godhead of
the Holy Ghost, declaring also that his nature doth altogether differ from the nature of angels.   For in his *Lib.* i.
de Spiritu Sancto, he hath left this written, St Hierome so
interpreting it : "If the Holy Ghost were a creature, he
should have at the least a limitable substance, as have all
things which are made.   For although invisible creatures are
not limited within place and bounds; yet in property of

Margin notes:
2 Pet. i.
Acts v.
1 Cor. iii.
1 Cor. vi.
1 Cor. xii.

[¹ At, Lat. ; But.]   [² seduxit, Lat.]

substance they are limited : but the Holy Ghost, since he is in many places, hath not a limitable substance. For Jesus sending forth the preachers of his gospel, he filled them with the Holy Ghost. But neither did all the apostles go to all nations together, but some into Asia, some into Scythia, and other dispersed into other nations, according to the dispensation of the Holy Ghost which they had with them, even as they also heard the Lord saying, 'I am with you always, even unto the end of the world.' Hereunto doth that also agree : ' Ye shall be witnesses unto me, even unto the uttermost parts of the world.' If therefore they, being sent into the furthest parts of the earth to bear witness of the Lord, were severed one from another with a very great distance of place, and yet had present with them the Holy Ghost dwelling within them, whose substance is not limitable ; it is manifest that the power of angels doth far differ from this power of the Spirit. For, to use an example : the angel which was present with the apostle when he prayed in Asia could not together at the selfsame time be present with other, which were abiding in other parts of the world. But the Holy Ghost is not only present with men being severed one from another, but is also a continual dweller in every angel, principality, throne, and dominion[3]," &c. Now who cannot here-

[3 Spiritus Sanctus, si unus de creaturis esset, saltem circumscriptam haberet substantiam, sicut universa quæ facta sunt. Nam etsi non circumscribantur loco et finibus invisibiles creaturæ, tamen proprietate substantiæ finiuntur: Spiritus autem Sanctus, cum in pluribus sit, non habet substantiam circumscriptam. Mittens quippe Jesus prædicatores doctrinæ suæ replevit eos Spiritu . . . Neque enim omnes apostoli ad omnes gentes pariter sunt profecti ; sed quidam in Asiam, quidam in Scythiam, et alii in alias dispersi nationes, secundum dispensationem illius quem secum habebant Spiritus Sancti, quomodo et Dominum dicentem: Vobiscum sum omnibus diebus usque ad consummationem seculi. His et illud congruit . . . Eritis testes mihi . . . usque ad extremum terræ. Si ergo hi in extremis finibus terræ, ob testimonium Domini constituti, distabant inter se longissimis spatiis, aderat autem eis inhabitator Spiritus Sanctus, incircumscriptam habens substantiam, demonstratur angelica virtus ab hoc prorsus aliena. Angelus quippe qui aderat, verbi gratia, apostolo in Asia oranti, non poterat simul eodem tempore adesse aliis in ceteris partibus mundi constitutis. Spiritus autem Sanctus non solum sejunctis a se hominibus præsto est, sed et singulis quibusque angelis, principatibus, thronis, dominationibus inhabitator adsistit, &c.—Didymi Alexandrini de Spiritu Sancto liber

by gather, that the Holy Ghost is true and very God ? The selfsame author hath gathered very many[1] arguments of the true Godhead of the Holy Ghost; and next him the holy father Cyril[2]; and holy Athanasius hath absolutely discoursed upon that matter, *Lib. de Trinitate* ii., to Theophilus[3]. These few testimonies, thus far rehearsed, we think shall suffice those that obey and love the truth.

They that stedfastly believe these things are not moved with any strange opinions and questions, curiously yea, wickedly brought in about this matter by ill-occupied persons. For some are reported to have denied the Holy Ghost to be Lord; for they have taught that he is a minister, and as it were a certain instrument of the Father and the Son[4]. But Christ our Lord joined the Holy Ghost to himself and to the Father, when he delivered the form of baptism; for he saith, "Baptizing them in the name of the Father, and of the Son, and of the Holy Ghost."   And yet it is manifest that a creature is not joined to the Creator in baptism, neither that there is any servile condition in the Godhead. Therefore the council of Constantinople in their creed[5] give to the Holy Ghost certain terms, whereby they might destroy certain errors, calling him "Lord, and Giver of life:" for when he maketh him Lord[6], he maketh him equal to the Son, and excludeth the condition of a servant or minister. Beside that, he denieth that he is their instrument; for there is one Lord: there are not many lords; and the Son is not lord of the Holy Ghost; but the lordship is common to the three persons, which are only one Lord. And seeing the Holy Ghost is the Lord, surely he is not appointed to a servile ministery, but endued with lordly authority; neither is he an under-servant to do the work, but is a joint worker with the

The Holy Ghost is neither minister nor instrument.

unus, S. Hieronymo interprete. cap. 6. p. 265. Biblioth. Vet. Pat. Tom. vi. Venet. 1770, or Hieron. Opp. Tom. iv. Par. i. col. 497. Par. 1706. In the works of Jerome the treatise is divided into three books.]

[1 alia, Lat. omitted; other.]

[2 Cyril. Dial. ad Hermiam presb. de Sancta Trin. cap. 7. De Sancto Spiritu, quod Deus sit, et ex Deo secundum naturam. Opp. Tom. v. Par. i. pp. 631, &c. Lut. 1638.]

[3 Athanasii Opp. de Trin. et Spir. S. pp. 587, &c. Par. 1627.]

[4 The Macedonians.]   [5 See Vol. i. pp. 13, 16, 17.]

[6 So also ed. 1584: but ed. 1577, when he *calleth* him Lord: cum Dominum vocat, Lat.]

Father and the Son; yea, and he himself doth work as Lord.

Again, certain other are reported to have taught that the Holy Ghost is not a substance or a person, but as it were an accident, that is to say, a stirring up, a provocation, or a motion of a godly and renewed mind. And in very deed our mind being illuminated with the Holy Ghost is oftentimes called spirit; but we must wisely distinguish the creature from the Creator, and the accident from the substance. The blessed apostle distinguished our spirit from the holy Spirit of God, when he said; "As many as are led by the Spirit of God, they are the sons of God. The Spirit itself beareth witness to our spirit, that we are the sons of God." And the same apostle saith: "The flesh lusteth contrary to the spirit, and the spirit contrary to the flesh." And who understandeth not, that the mind of man instructed of the Holy Ghost is here called the spirit; not the third person himself in the reverend Trinity? And that mind, as touching illumination, is not of itself, but proceedeth from the Holy Ghost illuminating it; neither cometh it from any other than from him which is the third person in Trinity: but that mind is not the very person of the Holy Ghost: as imagination proceedeth from the soul, and yet it is not the soul itself. That stirring of the spirit in us is an accident; but God is not an accident, neither is mingled with the accident. We must therefore confess, according to the scriptures, that the Holy Ghost is a⋅ person subsisting, co-equal in nature or essence with the Father and the Son, and therefore to be worshipped and glorified of us, as very God and Creator: again, that a godly and holy motion stirred up in the minds of holy men by the Spirit is the effect and working[7] of this Holy Spirit, and is called a holy spirit, but after a certain manner proper to it. Otherwise we deny not that the Holy Ghost himself, being promised, is communicated unto us, but after our capacity and as he will. For what is he amongst men that is able to comprehend the fulness of the everlasting and incomprehensible God?

Furthermore, touching the proceeding of the Holy Ghost from the Father and the Son, the divines have curiously, subtilly, and busily disputed. For the question is asked, Whether he proceed from the Father alone, or from the Son

The Holy Ghost is a substance, not an accident.

Rom. viii.

Gal. v.

Of the proceeding of the Holy Ghost.

[7 creaturam, Lat.]

also?   In which question the Latinists seem to disagree very much from the Grecians.   The question is also asked, What manner of proceeding this is?   We, omitting many curious questions, will briefly declare those things unto you which are wholesome and agreeable with the holy scriptures.   For who shall be able to canvass out all the questions of curious men, and all the bold and unclean thoughts of idle heads, without offence to good men, and especially of the simple hearers?

The Holy Ghost proceedeth from the Father and the Son. That the Holy Ghost proceedeth from the Father and the Son, the scripture manifestly teacheth, which most plainly sheweth that he is the Spirit of either or both of them.   For

Gal. iv. he it is of whom the apostle saith: "Because ye are sons, God hath sent the Spirit of his Son into your hearts."   And

Matt. x. the Son speaking of the same Spirit saith: "For it is not you that speak, but the Spirit of your Father, he it is which speaketh in you."   Again, the same Son saith of the Holy

John xv. Ghost, "Whom I will send unto you from the Father."   And

John xiv. again he saith elsewhere, "Whom the Father will send in my name."   Therefore he proceedeth from both, as well from the Father as from the Son.   For although this be read else-

John xv. where to be spoken of the Holy Ghost, "Which proceeded from the Father;" yet it is not denied that he proceedeth from the substance of the Son also.   But that more is, Cyril, a Greek writer, expounding the gospel of St John, and interpreting this selfsame place, lib. x. cap. 33, saith: "When he had called the Comforter the Spirit of truth, that is to say, his Spirit (for he is the truth), he addeth, that he proceedeth from the Father.   For as he is the Spirit of the Son naturally in his abiding, and through him proceeding, so also surely is he the Spirit of the Father.   But unto whom the Spirit is common, surely they cannot by any means be dissevered in substance[1]."   Again, St Augustine in his fifteenth book

John v. *De Trinitate*, cap. 26, saith: "Who may understand by this that the Son saith, as the Father hath life in himself, that he gave life unto the Son as being then without life; but that he

---

[1 Ἰδοὺ γὰρ, ἰδοὺ πνεῦμα τῆς ἀληθείας, τοῦτ᾽ ἔστιν ἑαυτοῦ, τὸν παράκλητον εἰπὼν, παρὰ τοῦ πατρὸς αὐτὸν ἐκπορεύεσθαι φησίν. ὥσπερ γὰρ ἐστιν ἴδιον πνεῦμα τοῦ υἱοῦ φυσικῶς, ἐν αὐτῷ τε ὑπάρχον, καὶ δι᾽ αὐτοῦ προϊὸν, οὕτω καὶ τοῦ πατρός. οἷς δὲ τὸ πνεῦμα κοινὸν, τούτοις εἴη δήπου πάντως ἂν καὶ τὰ τῆς οὐσίας οὐ διωρισμένα.—Cyril. in Joann. Lib. x. Opp. Lutet. 1638. Tom. iv. p. 910.]

so begat him without time, that the life, which the Father
gave to the Son in begetting him, is co-eternal with the life
of the Father which gave it him : let him understand, as
the Father hath power in himself that the Holy Ghost
might proceed from him, so hath he given to the Son that the
same Holy Ghost may proceed from him, and both without
beginning; and so it is said that the Holy Ghost proceedeth
from the Father, that that which proceedeth from the Son
might be understood to be of the Father and the Son. For if
the Son have ought, he hath it of the Father : surely he hath
it of the Father, that the Holy Ghost proceedeth from him[2]."
Thus far he. By all this we gather that the Holy Ghost
proceedeth as well from the Father as from the Son.

Now as concerning the manner of proceeding we say[3], The pro-
that the proceeding of the Holy Ghost is two-fold or of two   *ceeding of*
sorts, temporal and eternal. Temporal proceeding is that   *the Holy*
whereby the Holy Ghost proceedeth to sanctify men; the   *Ghost is*
eternal proceeding is that whereby from everlasting he pro-   *twofold, or*
ceedeth from God. The Spirit proceedeth from both parts[4]   *of two sorts.*
from both of them, as well from the Father as the Son.
Neither doth he proceed from the Father into the Son
severally[5], and from the Son into creatures : for I say the
nature and substance of the Father and the Son is one and
the selfsame, inseparable, and co-everlasting too.

Temporal proceeding commonly is called a sending and *Temporal*
gift. For the Holy Ghost is sent two manner of ways unto men : *proceeding.*
visibly, that is to say, under some visible form, as of a dove,
and of fiery tongues ; as he is read in the gospel, and in the

[2 Qui potest intelligere in eo quod ait Filius, Sicut habet Pater
vitam in semetipso, sic dedit Filio vitam habere in semetipso, non sine
vita existenti jam Filio vitam (Patrem) dedisse, sed ita eum sine tempore genuisse, ut vita, quam Pater Filio gignendo dedit, coæterna sit
vitæ Patris qui dedit; intelligat, sicut habet Pater in semetipso, ut de
illo procedat Spiritus Sanctus, sic dedisse Filio, ut de illo procedat
idem Spiritus Sanctus, et utrumque sine tempore; atque ita dictum
Spiritum Sanctum de Patre procedere, ut intelligatur, quod etiam pro-
cedit de Filio, de Patre esse et Filio. Si enim quicquid habet, de Patre
habet Filius ; de Patre habet utique, ut de illo procedat Spiritus Sanctus.
—August. de Trin. Lib. xv. cap. 26. Opp. Tom. iii. fol. 101. col. 2. Par.
1532.]

[3 videmus, Lat. ; we see.]　　　[4 utrobique, Lat. ; both ways.]
[5 divisim, Lat.]

Acts of the Apostles, to have been given to Christ and the apostles : invisibly, he is daily and as it were every moment given to the faithful, the Spirit of Christ watering us with his grace, and giving faith, hope, and charity unto us.

Eternal proceeding.

Moreover, the eternal proceeding of the Holy Ghost, whereby he proceedeth out of the substance of the Father and the Son, is unspeakable, as the begetting of the Son by the Father. Whereupon it is not said in the gospel, hath proceeded, or, shall proceed, but, "proceedeth:" for so the Lord declareth his eternity of proceeding, and that the substance of the Father and of the Son and of the Holy Ghost is co-eternal, and unseparable, and nothing at all differing. St Augustine in his fifteenth book *De Trinitate* and twenty-sixth chapter saith : " He that is able to understand the begetting of the Son by the Father without time, let him also understand the proceeding of the Holy Ghost from them both without time[1]." And if any ask this question, Since the Holy Ghost proceedeth from the substance of the Father and the Son, how cometh it to pass that he is not called the Son? I answer, that the scripture calleth the second person the Son, and testifieth that he is the only-begotten of the Father; and that the same nowhere maketh any mention that the Holy Ghost is begotten, or that he is called the Son. Neither have the ancient fathers made any other answer to this question. And I like the similitude which is here expressed : if one stream should flow from two springs, it might well be said to flow from them both, yet it could be said to be the son of neither of them. Hereunto I shall not seem unfruitfully nor beside the purpose to add the disputations of Didymus concerning sending; lest any should understand that perversely, and according to the flesh, which is spiritually to be interpreted by faith. " The Holy Ghost the Comforter is sent of the Son (saith he), not according to the ministry of angels, or prophets, or apostles, but as it becometh the Spirit of God to be sent of the wisdom and truth of God, having an unseparable nature with the selfsame wisdom and truth. For the Son, being sent of the Father, abiding in the Father, and having the Father in himself, is not separated nor sundered

[1] Qui potest intelligere sine tempore generationem Filii de Patre, intelligat sine tempore processionem Spiritus Sancti de utroque.—August. Opp. Tom. III. fol. 101. col. 2.]

from the Father. And the Spirit of truth also, being sent of the Son, after the manner aforesaid, proceedeth from the Father, not from elsewhere removing unto other things; for this is impossible and blasphemous likewise. For if this Spirit of truth be limited within a certain space, according to the natures of bodies, leaving one place he goeth to another: but even as the Father, not consisting in place, is far above and beyond the nature of all bodies; so also the Spirit of truth is not limited within space of place, seeing he is bodiless, and, as I may more truly say, excelling all and every reasonable creature. Because therefore it is impossible and wicked to believe these things which I have said in bodily creatures[3]; we must understand that so the Holy Ghost went out and came from the Father, as our Saviour doth bear witness that he himself went out and came from the Father, saying, 'I went out and came from God.' And as we separate places and changings of places from bodiless things, so also we do separate these speeches, inwardly (I mean) and outwardly, from the nature of things intellectual: for these two words pertain to bodies that may be touched and have bigness. Therefore we must believe the unspeakable word, which faith only and alone maketh known unto us; that our Saviour is said to come out from God, and the Spirit of truth to proceed from the Father[4]," &c. Other questions both scrupulous

Look in the third Sermon of this Decade, about the beginning[2].

[2 See above, page 157.]

[3 ista quæ diximus in corporalibus credere, Lat. Bullinger's reading: but see the quotation in the next note.]

[4 Spiritus Sanctus Consolator a Filio mittitur, non secundum angelorum aut prophetarum aut apostolorum ministerium, sed ut mitti decet a sapientia et veritate Spiritum Dei, indivisam habentem cum eadem sapientia et veritate naturam. Etenim Filius missus a Patre non separatur nec disjungitur ab eo, manens et habens illum in semetipso. Quin Spiritus veritatis supradicto modo missus a Filio de Patre egreditur, non aliunde ad alia transmigrans. Impossibile quippe hoc pariter et blasphemum est. Si enim... Spiritus veritatis juxta naturam corporum certo spatio circumscriptus, alium deserens locum ad alium commigrabit: sed quomodo Pater non consistens in loco, ultra omnem corporum est naturam; ita et Spiritus veritatis nequaquam locorum fine clauditur, cum sit incorporalis, et, ut verius dicam, excellens universam rationalem creaturam. Quia ergo impossibile est et impium ista quæ diximus de incorporalibus credere; exire de Patre Spiritum Sanctum sic intelligendum, ut se Salvator de Deo exisse testatur, dicens, Ego ex Deo exivi et veni. Et sicut loca et commuta-

and very many I pass over untouched : in these things
I require a mind religious, and not a curious ; a faithful mind,
and not a subtil.

Now there is but one Holy Ghost, because he is always
one and the selfsame God.　It is the same Spirit therefore,
which spake unto the patriarchs, prophets, and apostles, and
which at this day speaketh to us in the church.　For therefore the council of Constantinople is thus read to have confessed their faith : " I believe in the Holy Ghost, the Lord ;"
and anon after : " Who spake by the prophets.　And I
believe one catholic and apostolic church[1]."　These sayings
are taken out of the holy scripture.　For St Peter testifieth
in express words, that the Spirit of Christ was in the prophets, and there was none other spirit in the apostles than
the Spirit of Christ.　And Paul the apostle saith : " Seeing
then we have the same Spirit, as it is written, I believed,
and therefore have I spoken, we also believe, and therefore
speak."　Upon which testimony Tertullian inferreth, and (no
doubt) soundly : " It is one and the selfsame Spirit therefore,
which was in the prophets and the apostles[2]."　He promiseth
that the selfsame Spirit shall be always in the church. They
erred therefore, yea, foully they erred, whosoever among
them of old feigned one God and Spirit of the old Testament, and another of the new Testament[3].　Didymus Alexandrinus, the bright light in his age of all the Grecian
churches, in his first book entitled *De Spiritu Sancto*, saith :
" Neither ought we to think that the Holy Ghost is divided
according to substances, because he is called the multitude

1 Pet. 1.

2 Cor. iv.

tiones locorum ab incorporalibus separamus; sic et probationes, intus
dico et foris, ab intellectualium natura discernimus; quia istæ corporum sunt recipientium tactum et habentium vastitates.　Ineffabili
itaque et sola fide noto sermone credendum est, Salvatorem dictum
esse exisse a Deo, et Spiritum veritatis a Patre egredi.—Didymi Alex.
de Spir. Sanct. capp. 25, 26, p. 273. Biblioth. Vet. Patr.　Tom. VI.
Venet. 1770. or Hieron. Opp. Lib. II. coll. 509, 510.　Tom. IV. Pars I.
Paris. 1706.]

[1 Qui loquutus est per prophetas in unam catholicam et apostolicam ecclesiam, Lat.　See Vol. I. p. 158, and Addenda, p. 436.]

[2 Unus ergo et idem Spiritus, qui in prophetis et apostolis, nisi
quoniam ibi ad momentum, hic semper.—Novatian. de Trin. cap. 29.
Tertull. Opp. Col. Agrip. 1617. p. 741.]

[3 So Manes and his followers.]

of good graces.   For he cannot suffer, he cannot be divided,
neither yet be changed; but, according to his divers manners
of workings and understandings, he is called by many names
of good graces, because he doth not endue his partakers
with his communion after one and the selfsame power[4]," &c.
Furthermore, the Holy Ghost hath increasing or fulness, *Increasings of the Spirit.*
and diminishing and want in man: not that in God (who,
as it is commonly and truly said, neither receiveth more or
less) there is any change to be found; but because man,
according to his capacity, receiveth the Spirit plentifully and
liberally, or measurably and sparingly, even as it pleaseth
the Holy Ghost.   The portion of the Spirit of Helias was *2 Kings ii.*
given double from heaven to Heliseus.   And it is said of
our Saviour, that "the Father gave him the Spirit not by *John iii.*
measure."   For the Lord himself elsewhere saith: "Whoso- *Matt. xiii.*
ever hath, to him shall be given, and he shall have more
abundance; but whosoever hath not, from him shall be taken
away even that he hath."   Saul had received excellent *1 Sam. xvi.*
graces; but because he did not use and exercise them, the
good Spirit of God departed from him, and the evil spirit
succeeded and tormented him.   And the Spirit of God departeth, even as it cometh also, at one instant: for when
we are forsaken of the Lord, the Spirit of God departeth
from us.   Whereupon we read that David prayed: "Cast *Psal. li.*
me not away from thy presence, and take not thy holy
Spirit from me."   And again: "Stablish me with thy principal Spirit[5]."

Next after these things it seemeth that we must dili- *Of the effect and power of*
gently search out, what the effect and what the power of *the Holy Ghost.*
the Holy Ghost is.   The power of the almighty and everlasting God is unspeakable; therefore no man can fully declare what the power of the Holy Ghost is: yet somewhat
I will say, making those things manifest which he worketh
chiefly in men.   For otherwise the Father by the Spirit

[4 Nec existimare debemus Spiritum Sanctum secundum substantias esse divisum, quia multitudo bonorum dicatur.   Impassibilis enim
et indivisibilis atque immutabilis est; sed juxta differentes et efficientias et intellectus multis bonorum vocabulis nuncupatur: quia participes suos non juxta unam eandemque virtutem communione sui donet
&c.—Didymi Alex. ibid. cap. 9. p. 266. Hieron. ibid. col. 499.]

[5 See Vol. II. p. 147, note 6.]

worketh all things: by him he createth, sustaineth, moveth, giveth life, strengtheneth, and preserveth all things : by the selfsame he regenerateth his faithful people, sanctifieth, and endueth them with divers kinds of graces.   Whereupon in the description above mentioned of him, comprising in four members his principal powers and effects which shew themselves by their working in men, I said, that he doth illuminate, regenerate, sanctify, and fulfil the faithful with all good graces : which things that they may the better be understood, it shall be good first of all to declare (as well as we can) the appellations or names of the Holy Ghost, which the holy scripture giveth him ; and then to recite one or two places of the old and new Testament, to set forth and declare the power of the Holy Ghost.

The Holy Ghost.

First, he is called the Holy Spirit of God, because all creatures as many as are sanctified are sanctified by him. The heavenly Father sanctifieth with his grace, but through the blood of his beloved Son ; and sanctification is derived unto us[1] and sealed by the Spirit.   Therefore the holy Trinity, being one God, doth sanctify us.   It is a wicked thing therefore to attribute sanctification to strange and foreign things : it is a wicked thing to translate purification and justification from the Creator unto the creature.   Moreover he is called holy, to make a difference of him from other spirits.   For we read in the scriptures, that there was and is a spirit of the world, a spirit of infirmity[2], a spirit of fornication and uncleanness, and a spirit of pride.   From all these the Holy Ghost is separated, which inspireth into us the contempt of this world; which openeth unto us the scriptures, and confirmeth us in truth; which purifieth our hearts, and maketh our minds chaste, and so preserveth them: finally, which maketh us lowly and gentle, and driveth away from us all maliciousness.

The Holy Ghost is the Spirit of God and of the Son.

The same Holy Ghost is called the Spirit of God and of the Son: of God, to make a difference between it and the spirit of Satan ; and it is called the Spirit of the Son, because it is the proper and natural Spirit of the Son, which he also communicateth unto us that we also might be the

[1 So also ed. 1584: but ed. 1577, *into* us.]
[2 vertiginis, Lat. and Vulgate; of giddiness, Douay Bible, Isai. xix. 14.]

sons of God. For Paul saith: "Ye are the temple of God, 1 Cor. iii. and the Spirit of God dwelleth in you." Again: "If any Rom. viii. man have not the Spirit of Christ, the same is none of his." And again: "Because ye are sons, God hath sent the Spirit of his Son into your hearts, crying, Abba, Father."

Moreover our Lord himself, in the history of the gospel, The Holy Ghost is the calleth the Holy Ghost a Comforter, saying: "I will pray Comforter. John xiv. the Father, and he shall give you another Comforter, that he may abide with you for ever; even the Spirit of truth, whom the world cannot receive, because the world seeth him not, neither knoweth him: but ye know him; for he dwelleth with you, and shall be in you." For παράκλητος signifieth a comforter, a stirrer up or a provoker, an exhorter, an advocate or patron which pleadeth the cause of his client. For the Holy Ghost is the mouth, the eye, the heart, the counsel, the hand, and the foot of all the faithful. Didymus, in his The Holy Ghost is a work entitled *De Spiritu Sancto*, saith: (Christ), "giving comforter, and giveth the Holy Ghost a name answerable to his working, calleth joy and gladness. him the Comforter; because he doth not only comfort those whom he findeth worthy of him, and setteth them free from all heaviness and trouble of mind; but giveth unto them a certain incredible joy and gladness, insomuch that a man, giving God thanks because he is counted worthy of such a guest, may say, Thou hast given me gladness in my heart: for everlasting joy and gladness is in the heart of them in whom the Holy Ghost dwelleth[3]." The Holy Ghost, verily, alone maketh the consciences of men void of care, quiet, and at peace before God in the matter of justification and in all temptations of the world. Paul saith: "This only I desire [Gal. iii. 2.] to learn of you, whether ye have received the Spirit by the works of the law, or by the preaching of faith." The apostles being beaten with rods, when they were endued with the Holy Ghost and had that Comforter present in their

[3 Consolatorem autem venientem Spiritum Sanctum dicit (Salvator), ab operatione ei nomen imponens: quia non solum consolatur eos quos se dignos repererit, et ab omni tristitia et perturbatione reddit alienos; verum incredibile quoddam gaudium et hilaritatem eis tribuit, in tantum ut possit quis Deo gratias referens, quod tali hospite dignus habeatur, dicere, Dedisti lætitiam in corde meo. Sempiterna quippe lætitia in eorum corde versatur, quorum Spiritus Sanctus habitator est.—Didym. Alexandr. de Spir. Sanct. cap. xxv. Biblioth. Vet. Patr. Tom. vi. fol. 272. col. 2. Hieron. Opp. Tom. iv. Pars 1. col. 509.]

[Acts v. 41.] minds, went rejoicing from the presence of the council, because they were counted worthy to suffer reproach for the name of Christ. So we read in the ecclesiastical history that the martyrs of Christ, being full of the Holy Ghost, even in extreme torments and most bitter deaths were most patient, and sang praises and gave thanks unto God.

The Holy Ghost is the Spirit of truth. John xv.

Furthermore, we have heard that the Holy Ghost is called of the Lord the Spirit of truth. For in another place also he beautifieth him with that name; for he saith, "When the Comforter shall come, whom I will send unto you from the Father, even the Spirit of truth, which proceedeth from the Father, he shall bear witness of me." And he is called the Spirit of truth, because there is another hypocritical spirit[1], an erroneous and lying spirit in the mouth of all false prophets. This our Spirit worketh in his worshippers sincerity, gentleness of mind[2], and integrity. Those he teacheth all truth. For our Lord elsewhere in the gospel

John xiv.

saith: "That Comforter, which is the Holy Ghost, whom the Father will send in my name, he shall teach you all things, and bring all things to your remembrance, whatsoever I have said unto you." Therefore the Spirit of truth hath taught the apostles all truth that is to be believed and all godliness; and they have delivered the same fully to the church. For the Holy Ghost driveth away all errors, destroyeth all heresies, confoundeth[3] all idolatry and ungodliness, and poureth true faith into our hearts, and establisheth true religion in the church. The Acts of the Apostles afford us very many of examples. By this Spirit of God the apostles foretold things to come, shadowing out among other things antichrist and the corruption of this our last age, and admonishing the church lest the elect should be entangled in errors and blasphemous wickedness.

The Spirit of promise.

Now he is called the Spirit of promise, for that he was promised of God by the prophets through Christ to the fathers, to the apostles, and to all that believe the apostles' doctrine[4], and was at length also through the same Christ fully given and performed. This word putteth the godly

[1 Spiritus impostor, Lat. omitted; a spirit which is a deceiver.]
[2 candorem, Lat.]
[3 profligat, Lat.]
[4 Rather, Because he was promised from God to the fathers by

in mind, that they should not ascribe the having of this so great and healthful a gift to their merits, but to the mere grace of God.   And the Holy Ghost is granted, yea, given Gal. iii. unto us, by the promise of God.   Whereupon it followeth that all the gifts of God are freely given: which thing the apostle Paul principally proveth, and earnestly beateth into our heads, in his epistles, specially to the Romans and the Galatians.

In Luke the Lord saith : " If I with the finger of God The Holy
Ghost the cast out devils, no doubt the kingdom of God is come upon finger of God.
[Luke xi. 20. you."   St Matthew, rehearsing the same words, saith : " If Matt. xii. 28.] I by the Spirit of God cast out devils, then is the kingdom of God come upon you."   Therefore the Holy Ghost is called the finger of God, to wit, the might and power of God. Men of occupations[5] work with their fingers : God work- eth his works by his divine power, I mean, by his Spirit ; whose power is so great, that even his little finger (give me leave so to speak) surpasseth all the power and strength in the world.   That appeared in those sorcerers of Egypt. Exod. viii. Didymus rehearseth a parable touching the unity of the divine substance, and admonisheth diligently and conveniently, Look in the
third Sermon that we should not for corporal things forge and feign unto of this De-
cade, what ourselves a corporal meaning of spiritual things.   For he things are
spoken saith : " But beware lest thou, being cast down unto base against the
heretics things, dost imagine in thy mind diversities of corporal ac- called the
Anthropo- tions, and begin to forge to thyself magnitudes, and inequa- morphites[6]. lities, and other members of the body greater and lesser, saying, that the finger from the hand, and the hand from him whose hand it is, doth differ by many inequalities; because the scripture doth now speak of bodiless things, purposing to shew the unity only, and not the measure of substance also.   For as the hand is not divided from the body by the which it worketh and bringeth all things to an end, and is in him whose hand it is ; so also the finger is not separated from the hand whose finger it is.   Therefore away with inequalities and measurings when thou thinkest of God ; and understand the unity of the finger, of the hand, and of the

the prophets, and to the apostles and all who believe the doctrine of the apostles by Christ.]

[5 opifices, Lat.]

[6 See above, page 138.]

whole substance, by which finger the law was written in tables of stone[1]." Thus far he.

The Spirit is called water, and a lively fountain. Now the Holy Ghost is read, as well in the writings of the prophets as also of the apostles, to be shadowed out by water, and a lively or continual running fountain. "I will pour out," saith the Lord by Esay, "waters upon the thirsty, and rivers upon the dry ground." And anon by interpreta- Isai. xliv. tion he addeth: "I will pour my Spirit upon thy seed, and my blessing upon thy stock." And in the gospel the Lord John vii. saith: "If any man thirst, let him come unto me and drink. He that believeth in me, as saith the scripture, out of his belly shall flow rivers of water of life." To which in way of exposition the holy evangelist[2] addeth: "But this he spake of the Spirit, which they that believe in him should receive." Surely water maketh barren grounds fruitful, cleanseth things defiled, giveth drink to them that be thirsty, and cooleth them that are in a heat: so the grace of the Holy Spirit maketh barren minds fruitful, to bring forth fruit to the living God; by the selfsame grace our hearts are cleansed from all uncleanness; the same quencheth the thirst of the soul, and comforteth it when it is afflicted, and fulfilleth all the desires thereof.

The Holy Ghost is fire. Fire is simple and pure; and some bodies it consumeth, and other some it purgeth, making them more fine and clean: it warmeth also, and hath many profitable and necessary operations in man. Therefore the Holy Ghost is rightly shadowed out unto us by fire. For he is pure and simple, he consumeth the ungodly, cleanseth the faithful from the

[1 Verum cave ne ad humilia dejectus... depingas in animo tuo corporalium artuum (Bullinger read *actuum*) diversitates, et incipias tibi magnitudines et inæqualitates et cetera corporum majora vel minora membra confingere; dicens digitum a manu, et manum ab eo cujus est manus, multis inæqualitatibus discrepare; quia de incorporalibus nunc scriptura loquitur, unitatem tantum volens, non etiam mensuram substantiæ demonstrare. Sicut enim manus non dividitur a corpore, per quem cuncta perficit et operatur, et in eo est cujus est manus; sic et digitus non separatur a manu cujus est digitus. Itaque rejice inæqualitates et mensuras cum de Deo cogitas, et intellige digiti et manus et totius substantiæ unitatem; quo digito lex in tabulis lapideis scripta est.—Didym. Alex. de Spir. Sanct. capp. 20, 21. Biblioth. Vet. Patr. Tom. vi. pp. 270, 271. Hieron. Opp. Tom. iv. Par. i. col. 506.]

[2 historicus sacer, Lat.]

filthiness of sins, and maketh them to burn with the love of God and their neighbour, setting them on fire doubtless with the fire of his love.

When he was given to the apostles in the day of Pentecost, there was heard a sound as it had been with the force of a mighty wind coming: by which thing was signified, that the doctrine of godliness should be spread throughout the whole world by the power of God and wonderful success, maugre the might of the whole world setting shoulder against the same all in vain.   For the wind (no man staying it) bloweth through the whole world, pierceth all places, and no man can keep it out; it hath also wonderful effects in bodies to change them. And the Holy Ghost pierceth all things; softeneth men's hearts; and of froward, stubborn, and rebellious, he maketh most lowly, modest, and obedient men. *The Holy Ghost a mighty wind.*

Fiery tongues appear upon the heads of the apostles and disciples endued with the Holy Ghost; signifying doubtless the operation or working of the Holy Ghost, of which they were signs and assurances. For he instructeth, exhorteth, and comforteth the faithful: neither doth he arm his faithful apostles with cold tongues, but fiery tongues.   The apostles, when they preached the gospel, seemed not to speak, but to lighten and to thunder: whereupon also certain of them were called of our Saviour "The sons of thunder." *The Holy Ghost a fiery tongue.*

Furthermore, the Holy Ghost appeareth in the likeness of a dove upon the Son of God, even then when he was baptized of John Baptist.   For a dove is mild and gentle, without malice or harm[3]: whereof sprung the proverb, "manners like a dove, dove-like simplicity;" and, "more gentle than a dove."   For a dove is among birds as a sheep among four-footed beasts, which thinketh no hurt to any living creature: whereupon Christ is also called a sheep or a lamb.   Of the Spirit of God therefore the wise man saith very well: "The spirit of wisdom is holy, one only, manifold, subtle, quick, moving[4], clear[5], undefiled, plain[6], sweet, loving the thing that is good, sharp, which cannot be letted, doing good, kind to man, stedfast, sure, free from care, having all power, circumspect in all things, and passing through all understanding and clean, yea, most subtle spirits." *The Holy Ghost a dove. Isai. liii. John i. Acts viii. Wisd. vii.*

[3 felle carens, Lat.]   [4 disertus, Lat. ; lively, A. V.]
[5 illustris, Lat.]   [6 certus, Lat.]

The Holy
Ghost oil and
anointing. Again, they that are endued with the Holy Ghost are called the anointed of the Lord. For the Holy Ghost is called both oil and anointing: for unless we be watered of the Holy Ghost, we wax barren and waste away; for we are void of lively and heavenly moisture, and of our own nature always wither and wax dry. And of this anointing there went a notable figure before, in the ceremonial anointing of 1 John ii. kings and priests. St John saith: "And the anointing which ye have received of him dwelleth in you, and ye need not that any man teach you; but as the same anointing teacheth you of all things, and it is true, and not lying, and as it taught you, abide in it[1]." For the Lord also saith in Jer. xxxi.
Heb. viii. Jeremy: "This shall be the covenant that I will make with the house of Israel after those days; I will plant my law in the inward parts[2] of them, and write it in their hearts; and will be their God, and they shall be my people. And from henceforth shall no man teach his neighbour or his brother, saying, Know the Lord; for they shall all know me, from the lowest unto the highest, saith the Lord. For I will forgive their misdeeds, and will never remember their sins any more."

But we shewed a little before that the Holy Ghost is the universal teacher of all truth. Hitherto that seemeth to belong 2 Cor. i. which St Paul saith: "It is God which hath anointed us, which hath also sealed us, and hath given the earnest of the Spirit in our hearts." For now the Holy Ghost is not only called anointing, but also the sealing up or earnest of our salvation: The Holy
Ghost is the
earnest of
our inherit-
ance. for ἄῤῥα, or ἀῤῥαβών, is a part of payment, which maketh assurance of the whole sum to be paid, to wit, a pledge. And surely the Holy Ghost doth now testify, yea, it doth seal and assure us, that we are the sons of God, and that, when time is, we shall be received into the everlasting inheritance. Paul Ephes. i. again saith: "Ye are sealed with the holy Spirit of promise, which is the earnest of our inheritance, unto the redemption of the purchased possession, unto the praise of his glory." Ephes.i. That assurance doth marvellously confirm and comfort the minds of the faithful in temptations; encourageth them besides that to patience in adversity, and to holiness of life. For here- 1 John iv. upon said St John: "Little children, ye are of God, and have overcome them; for greater is he that is in you, than he that

[1 See above, p 286, and note 2.]   [2 in mentem, Lat.]

is in the world." And again: "Now are we the sons of God, 1 John iii. and yet it doth not appear what we shall be: but we know that, when he shall appear, we shall be like unto him, for we shall see him as he is. And every man that hath this hope in him purgeth himself, even as he also is pure."

And as the Holy Ghost is an unspeakable knitting to- The Holy Ghost love gether, whereby the three persons are inseparably coupled or charity. one with another in everlasting love and concord; even so the same coupleth the spouse of Christ with her spouse with a knot that cannot be loosed, and joineth together between themselves all the members of his mystical body in an ever-lasting covenant. For as the members of our body are joined together whole and sound by the benefit and enjoying of life[3], so the mystical body of Christ is united together by the Holy Ghost. Therefore it is no marvel that he is called Rom. v. or noted with the name of love, which poureth love into our hearts.

And albeit by these names of the Holy Ghost his opera- The opera-tions of the tion may be understood, yet will I add certain testimonies of Holy Ghost. scripture, out of which his power or effect, especially in us, may be more fully understood. Esay almost in the beginning Isai. xi. of his prophecy, describing the person of the King our Messias, among other things saith: "The Spirit of the Lord shall rest upon him; the spirit of wisdom and understanding, the spirit of counsel and strength, the spirit of knowledge and of the fear of the Lord; and shall make him of deep judgment in the fear of God[4]." Though he declared many, yet hath he not reckoned up all the powers of the Spirit. Therefore it is not for us to bring into a strait, and with the common sort to comprise in a narrow number of seven, the powers of the Spirit. For we have heard hitherto that there is the spirit of promise, of doctrine, of humility, and gentleness, &c. To which beside these there are reckoned up very many to-gether; for he is the spirit of wisdom: but how great this is, and how far it reacheth, it is manifest even in the words[5] of Solomon. To wisdom is joined understanding, which is Wisdom. said to be the action and applying of wisdom ordered or Under-standing. framed to things, places, times, and persons. Counsel is re- Counsel.

[3 beneficio spiritus, Lat.]
[4 faciet cum spirare timorem Domini, Lat.]
[5 in rebus, Lat.; in the affairs.]

quired and given in doubtful matters, and sheweth what we
Strength.   may most conveniently do.   Strength ministereth sufficient
force and constancy to execute and perform, yea, and patiently
bear, whatsoever by counsel we have learned either to be
Knowledge.   done or to be suffered.   And now knowledge is an experience
Fear.   obtained and gotten by long time and use.   Unto these is
fear added, that is to say, godliness and true religion; whereunto unless we refer all our sayings and doings, wisdom,
understanding, counsel, strength and knowledge, shall nothing
profit us.   To be short, whosoever is endued with the Spirit
of God, whatsoever he shall either do or say will savour of
the fear[1] of God; finally, he shall say and do all things unto
the glory of God : and all these things truly are freely and
fully drawn out of the only fountain of the Holy Ghost.

Paul the apostle, in his epistle to the Romans, describing
the wonderful force of the Holy Ghost working in us being
new-born, saith : " They that are in the flesh cannot please
Rom. viii.   God.   But ye are not in the flesh, but in the Spirit, if so be
The Spirit
doth mortify
and quicken.   the Spirit of God dwell in you.   If any man have not the
Spirit of Christ, the same is none of his.   And if Christ be in
you, the body is dead because of sin ; but the spirit is life for
righteousness' sake.   But if the Spirit of him that raised up
Jesus from the dead dwell in you, even he that raised up Christ
from the dead shall also quicken your mortal bodies, because
that his Spirit dwelleth in you."

The Spirit
or Holy
Ghost re-
vealeth the
mysteries of
the kingdom
of God.
1 Cor. ii.   The same apostle in his epistle to the Corinthians teacheth, that by the revelation of the Holy Ghost the mystery of
the kingdom of God is very manifestly opened unto us.
" God," saith he, " hath revealed them unto us by his Spirit ;
for the Spirit searcheth all things, yea, the deep things of God.
For what man knoweth the things of man, save the spirit of
man which is in him ?   Even so the things of God knoweth no
man, but the Spirit of God.   And we have not received the
spirit of the world, but the Spirit which is of God, that we might
know the things which are given to us of Christ[2]."   Hitherto
pertain these words of our Lord and Saviour out of the holy
John xvi.   gospel : " I tell you the truth, it is expedient for you that I go
away ; for if I go not away, that Comforter will not come
unto you ; but if I depart, I will send him unto you.   And when

[1 spirabit timorem, Lat.]
[2 a Christo, Lat. So Erasmus and Calvin.]

he is come, he will rebuke the world of sin, and of righteousness, and of judgment : of sin, because they believe not on him[3] :
of righteousness, because I go to the Father, and ye see me
no more : of judgment, because the prince of this world is
judged already."   And it is evident, that in all these clauses
the whole sum of religion is contained which the Holy Ghost
most plentifully hath delivered unto the church : which we also
touched in the exposition of the names of the Holy Ghost.
It followeth in the gospel : " I have yet many things to say
unto you, but ye cannot bear them away[4] now.   Howbeit,
when he is come, which is the Spirit of truth, he will lead
you into all truth.   He shall not speak of himself ; but whatsoever he shall hear, that shall he speak, and he will shew
you things to come[5]."   And since it is certain that the Holy
Ghost is come, it is evident that he led the apostles into all
truth : insomuch that whatsoever agreeth not with their
writings is worthily suspected of a lie.   Otherwise I doubt
not but he at this day speaketh in the church by those
which are his : but it is without controversy, that the Holy
Ghost doth not gainsay himself.   And that things to come
were revealed to the apostles by the Spirit, we have touched
in the exposition of the names of the Holy Ghost.   Neither
is it doubtful but at this day he revealeth many things to the
saints in the church, even those things which pertain to the
preservation of the gospel of Christ[6] and the saints.

The Spirit foresheweth things to come.

   Again, we read in the epistle of Paul to the Corinthians :
" The manifestation," saith he, " of the Spirit is given to
every man to profit withal : for to one is given by the Spirit
the word of wisdom, to another the word of knowledge by
the same Spirit ; to another is given faith by the same Spirit ;
to another the gifts of healing by the same Spirit ; to another
power to do miracles ; to another prophecy ; to another discerning of spirits ; to another divers kinds of tongues ; to
another the interpretation of tongues.   But all these worketh that one and the selfsame Spirit, dividing to every man
severally even as he will."   All these things are manifest,
neither need they any further exposition.   These are great

[1 Cor. xii. 7—11.] The divers gifts of the Holy Ghost.

[3 in me, Lat.]   [4 So Tyndale and Cranmer; portare, Lat.]
[5 Ille me glorificabit : quia de meo accipiet, et annunciabit vobis,
Lat. omitted.]
[6 veritatis Christianæ, Lat.]

and evident gifts of the Holy Spirit. Unto which also if we add
those words which the same apostle hath set down concerning
Gal. v. the same Spirit of God, we will make an end[1] : " The fruit
of the Spirit," saith he, " is love, joy, peace, long-suffering,
gentleness, goodness, faith, meekness, temperance."   These I
say and all other virtues the Holy Ghost, which worketh all
good things in all men, graffeth, planteth, preserveth, defendeth,
and bringeth unto full ripeness in the minds of the faithful.

Tertullian's
notable trea-
tise of the
Holy Ghost.   To all these we will now add, instead of a conclusion, the
most notable[2] treatise of Tertullian touching the Holy Ghost.
The same is this : " Because the Lord was departing into
heaven, he did necessarily give to his disciples a comforter,
lest he should leave them in a manner orphans, which was not
convenient, and forsake them without a certain advocate and
tutor.   For it is he that strengthened their minds and understandings, which distinguished the sacraments of the gospel,
which was in them the giver of light in heavenly things, by
whom being strengthened and established they neither feared
imprisonments nor chains for the name of the Lord ; but
rather set at nought the very powers and torments of this
world, being now armed and emboldened through him, having
in them the gifts which this selfsame Spirit doth distribute
and direct, as it were certain ornaments to the church, which
is the spouse of Christ.   For it is he that appointeth prophets
in the church, instructeth the teachers, guideth tongues,
worketh miracles, and giveth health, bringeth to pass wonderful works, sheweth the discerning of spirits, establisheth
governments, endueth with counsel, ministereth and ordereth
and disposeth all other spiritual gifts ; and therefore maketh
the church of God on all sides and in all things perfect and
absolute.   It is he which in the likeness of a dove, after the
Lord was baptized, descended and remained upon him, dwelling only in Christ fully and wholly, not maimed or minished
in any measure or portion, but plentifully received into him
with his whole abundance, that others might obtain from him
a certain distribution of gifts; the fountain of the fulness of the
Holy Ghost wholly remaining in Christ, that from him might
be derived veins of gifts and miracles, the Holy Ghost most
Isai. xi. abundantly dwelling in Christ. For Esay prophesying the same
said : ' And the spirit of wisdom and understanding, the spirit

[1 vela colligemus, Lat.]   [2 elegantissimam, Lat.]

of counsel and strength, the spirit of knowledge and godliness, resteth upon him. And the spirit of the fear of the Lord filled him.' The like and selfsame saying he hath also in another place in the person of the Lord himself: 'The Spirit of the Lord Isai. lxi. upon me, because he hath anointed me; to preach the gospel to the poor hath he sent me.' Likewise David: 'Wherefore Psal. xlv. thy God hath anointed thee with the oil of gladness above thy fellows.' Of this Spirit the apostle Paul speaketh: for 'he that hath not the Spirit of Christ, the same is none of his.' Rom. viii. 'And where the Spirit of the Lord is, there is liberty.' This 2 Cor. iii. is he which by water worketh the second birth of regeneration[3], being a certain seed of heavenly generation; and he that consecrateth the heavenly nativity, being a pledge of the promised inheritance, and as it were a certain handwriting of everlasting salvation; who maketh us the temple of God, and bringeth to pass that we be his dwelling-house; who performeth the office of an advocate, maketh intercession for us in the hearing of God with sighs that cannot be uttered; and pouring forth his gifts of defence, is given to be a dweller in our hearts and a worker of holiness; who exercising that in us, bringeth our bodies into everlastingness and unto the resurrection of immortality, while he accustometh them to be partakers in him of his heavenly power, and to be coupled with the heavenly eternity of the Holy Ghost. For our bodies are trained up in him and by him to proceed to immortality, whilst they learned to behave themselves moderately according to his ordinances. For it is he that lusteth contrary to the flesh, because the flesh fighteth against him. It is he which bridleth insatiable lusts, which tameth immoderate concupiscences, which quencheth unlawful desires, which vanquisheth flaming affections, which abhorreth drunkenness, which banisheth covetousness, which abandoneth riotous banquetings, which knitteth the knot of love and charity, which subdueth the affections, driveth away sects, sheweth the rule of truth, convinceth heretics, casteth out the wicked, and is a defence to the gospel. Of him the apostle also saith: ' For [1 Cor. ii. 12.] we have not received the spirit of the world, but the Spirit which is of God.' Of this Spirit he triumpheth and saith: 'And I think verily that I have the Spirit of God.' Of him 1 Cor. vii. he saith: 'And the Spirit of the prophets is subject to the 1 Cor. xiv.

[3 So also cd. 1584: but ed. 1577, or regeneration.]

21—2

1 Tim. iv. prophets.' Of him he saith again: 'Now the Spirit speaketh evidently, that in the latter times some shall depart from the faith, giving heed unto spirits of error and doctrines of devils, which speak false in hypocrisy, having their conscience 1 Cor. xii. seared with an hot iron.' 'No man being guided by this Spirit calleth Jesus execrable;' no man denieth that Christ is the Son of God, or forsaketh God the Creator; no man uttereth any of his own words against the scriptures, neither doth any man establish other wicked decrees; no man commandeth contrary [Mark iii. 29.]
[Matt. xii. 32.] laws. 'Whosoever blasphemeth against this Spirit shall never have forgiveness, neither in this world, nor in the world to come.' It is he that in the apostles beareth witness to Christ, that sheweth constant faith of religion in martyrs, that planteth marvellous continency of assured love in virgins, that keepeth the laws of the Lord's doctrine uncorrupted and undefiled in others, that confoundeth heretics, reformeth the froward, reproveth the unfaithful, revealeth dissemblers, and punisheth the wicked, and preserveth the church chaste and unstained in pureness of perpetual virginity and holiness of truth[1]." Thus far Tertullian.

[1 Quoniam Dominus in cœlos esset abiturus, paracletum discipulis necessario dabat, ne illos quodammodo pupillos (quod minime decebat) relinqueret, et sine advocato et quodam tutore desereret. Hic est enim qui ipsorum animos mentesque firmavit, qui evangelica sacramenta distinxit, qui in ipsis illuminator rerum divinarum fuit, quo confirmati pro nomine Domini nec carceres nec vincula timuerunt, quinimo ipsas seculi potestates et tormenta calcaverunt, armati jam scilicet per ipsum atque firmati, habentes in se dona quæ hic idem Spiritus ecclesiæ Christi sponsæ quasi quædam ornamenta distribuit et dirigit. Hic est enim qui prophetas in ecclesia constituit, magistros erudit, linguas dirigit, virtutes et sanitates facit, opera mirabilia gerit, discretiones spirituum porrigit, gubernationes contribuit, consilia suggerit, quæque alia sunt charismatum dona componit et dirigit; et ideo ecclesiam Domini undique et in omnibus perfectam et consummatam facit. Hic est qui in modum columbæ, posteaquam Dominus baptizatus est, super eum venit et mansit, habitans in solo Christo plenus et totus, nec in aliqua mensura aut portione mutilatus, sed cum tota sua redundantia cumulate distributus et missus, ut ex illo delibationem quandam gratiarum ceteri consequi possint, totius Sancti Spiritus in Christo fonte remanente, ut ex illo donorum atque operum venæ ducerentur, Spiritu Sancto in Christo affluenter habitante. Hoc etenim prophetans Esaias aiebat: Et requiescit, inquit, super eum Spiritus sapientiæ et intellectus, Spiritus consilii et virtutis, Spiritus scientiæ et pietatis, et implevit eum Spiritus timoris Dei. Hoc idem

Thus far, not without trembling, we have entreated of A sum of the most holy mystery of the reverend Trinity, the Father, the Son, and the Holy Ghost, which we have learned out of the scriptures: and here now we will stay, humbly worship-

atque ipsum et alio in loco ex persona ipsius Domini : Spiritus Domini super me, propter quod unxit me, evangelizare pauperibus misit me. Similiter David : Propterea unxit te Deus, Deus tuus, oleo lætitiæ a consortibus tuis. De hoc Apostolus Paulus : Qui enim Spiritum Christi non habet, hic non est ejus : Et, Ubi Spiritus Domini, ibi libertas. Hic est qui operatur ex aquis secundam nativitatem, semen quoddam divini generis, et consecrator cœlestis nativitatis, pignus promissæ hæreditatis, et quasi chirographum quoddam æternæ salutis ; qui nos Dei faciat templum, et nos ejus efficiat domum ; qui interpellat divinas aures pro nobis gemitibus ineloquacibus, advocationis implens officia et defensionis exhibens munera, inhabitator corporibus nostris datus, et sanctitatis effector ; qui id agens in nobis, ut ad æternitatem et ad resurrectionem immortalitatis corpora nostra perducat, dum illa in se assuefacit cum cœlesti virtute misceri, et cum Spiritus Sancti divina æternitate sociari.   Erudiuntur enim in illo et per ipsum corpora nostra ad immortalitatem proficere, dum ad decreta ipsius discunt se moderanter temperare.   Hic est enim qui contra carnem desiderat, quia caro contra ipsum repugnat.   Hic est qui inexplebiles cupiditates coercet, immoderatas libidines frangit, illicitos ardores extinguit, flagrantes impetus vincit, ebrietates rejicit, avaritias repellit, luxuriosas comessationes fugit, caritates nectit, affectiones constringit, sectas repellit, regulam veritatis expedit, hæreticos revincit, improbos foras exspuit, evangelia custodit.   De hoc item Apostolus : Non enim spiritum mundi accepimus, sed Spiritum qui ex Deo est.   De hoc exultat et dicit : Puto autem quia et ego Spiritum Dei habeo.   De hoc dicit : Et Spiritus prophetarum prophetis subjectus est.   De hoc refert : Spiritus autem manifeste dicit quia in novissimis temporibus recedent quidam a fide, attendentes spiritibus seductoribus, doctrinis dæmoniorum in hypocrisi mendacia loquentium, cauteriatam habentium conscientiam suam.   In hoc Spiritu positus nemo unquam dicit anathema Jesum, nemo negavit Christum Dei Filium, aut repudiavit creatorem Deum ; nemo contra scripturas ulla sua verba depromit, nemo alia et sacrilega decreta constituit, nemo diversa jura conscribit.   In hunc quisquis blasphemaverit, remissionem non habet, non tantum in isto seculo, verum etiam nec in futuro.   Hic in apostolis Christo testimonium reddit, in martyribus constantem fidem religionis ostendit, in virginibus admirabilem continentiam signatæ caritatis includit, in ceteris incorrupta et incontaminata doctrinæ dominicæ jura custodit ; hæreticos destruit, perversos corrigit, infideles arguit, simulatores ostendit, improbos quoque corrigit, ecclesiam incorruptam et inviolatam perpetuæ virginitatis et veritatis sanctitate custodit.—Novatian. de Trin. cap. 29. Tertull. Opp. pp. 741, 742. Col. Agrip.]

ping this Unity in trinity and Trinity in unity. And let us keep in mind and acknowledge this distinction or division most manifestly declared in the scriptures, and the unity also commended unto us with exceeding great diligence. For in the scripture the beginning of doing and the flowing fountain and well-spring of all things is attributed to the Father; wisdom, counsel, and the very dispensation in doing things is ascribed to the Son; and the force and effectual power of working is assigned to the Holy Ghost. Howbeit, let us take heed lest through the distinction we separate the unity of the substance of God; for there is but one God in whom those properties are. It is but one fire, though there be three things seen in it, light, brightness, and heat. For these rise together, and cease all at once. The light goeth not before the brightness, neither the brightness before the heat. And though one thing be attributed to the light, another thing to the brightness, and a third thing to the heat; yet they work unseparably. Therefore when we read that God created the world, we understand that the Father from whom are all things, by the Son by whom are all things, in the Holy Ghost in whom are all things, created the world. And when we read that the Son became flesh, suffered, died, and rose again for our salvation, we believe that the Father and the Holy Ghost, though they were not partakers of his incarnation and passion, yet notwithstanding that they wrought that our salvation by the Son, whom we believe never to have been separated from them. And when sins are said to be forgiven in the Holy Ghost, we believe that this benefit and all other benefits of our blessedness are unseparably given and bestowed upon us from one, only, true, living, and everlasting God, who is the Father, the Son, and the Holy Ghost. To whom be praise and thanksgiving for ever and ever. Amen.

OF GOOD AND EVIL SPIRITS; THAT IS, OF THE HOLY
ANGELS OF GOD, AND OF DEVILS OR EVIL
SPIRITS; AND OF THEIR OPERATIONS.

THE NINTH SERMON.

NEXT unto this sermon of the Holy Ghost I will add
a treatise of good and evil spirits, that is, of the holy angels
of God, and of devils or wicked spirits, and of their operations: of whom since the holy scripture delivereth us an
assured doctrine and in all points profitable, it seemeth that
we ought not lightly to regard it, but with as much faith
and diligence as we can to bring it unto light. It were a
foul fault in him that studieth after godliness, to be ignorant
of the dispositions of good and evil angels, of whom so
often mention is made in the holy scriptures; yea, it were
a thing most dangerous, not to know what manner of creatures the devils are, which under that name might easily
deceive and spoil us. But first we will speak of holy angels,
and then of devils or spirits[1].

The word *angel* some say to be a name of office[2], not An angel.
of nature, and is common to the Latins and Greeks, of whom
it is borrowed, and it signifieth an ambassador or legate, and
therefore it hath a larger signification. For the preachers of
the truth are called angels, as in Malachy, and in the apostle Mal. ii. & iii.
Paul[3]; for they are the ambassadors or "messengers of the 1 Cor. xi.
Lord of hosts." St Peter also calleth evil spirits angels: as Paul [2 Pet. ii. 4.]
also doth saying, that the faithful shall one day judge the [1 Cor. vi. 3.]
angels[4]; and that the angel or messenger of Satan was sent 2 Cor. xii.
unto him. Howbeit the scripture peculiarly calleth angels the
blessed spirits of God, ministers, and messengers, and heavenly
armies[5].

[1 or spirits, not in Lat.]

[2 Angelus enim officii nomen est, non naturæ.—August. Tract. de
eo quod dictum est a Deo ad Moysen, Ego sum qui sum. (Incerti auctoris.) Opp. Tom. vi. fol. 179. col. 4. Par. 1532.]

[3 In his Commentary on 1 Cor. xi. 10, Bullinger first explains
"the angels" of the heavenly beings, and then says: Alii per angelos
verbi ministros intelligunt.]

[4 Hunc locum exponens (Theophylactus) angelos, ait, dæmones
ipsos appellat. Sunt enim et hi per nos condemnandi. Bulling. Comment. in 1 Cor. vi. 3.]

[5 satellites, Lat.; heavenly, the translator's addition.]

That there
are angels.
[Acts xxiii.
8.]
But the Sadducees denied that there be angels; for
Luke in the Acts of the Apostles saith: "The Sadducees say
that there is no resurrection, neither angel nor spirit; but the
Pharisees confess both." And indeed the whole scripture
doth testify that there are angels, making mention in many
places that they have appeared unto men, and have revealed
unto them the will of God, or otherwise accomplished his
work. Truly the Lord Jesus reasoning against the Sadducees
Matt. xxii.
in the gospel saith: "Ye err, not knowing the scriptures, nor
the power of God. For in the resurrection they neither marry,
nor are given in marriage, but are as the angels of God in
heaven." Let us therefore believe that there are angels. For
the authority of the Son of God, and the irrevocable truth of
the holy scriptures, ought worthily to win more credit with
us than the toys of all Sadducees and wicked men. What,
A. Steuchus
in his 6th
and 6th book
de Perenni
Philosophia[1].
have not the heathenish poets and philosophers confessed
that there are angels, whom they call gods? For they,
feigning that gods in the likeness of men were lodged and
entertained of righteous men, seemed to all learned men to
have meant nothing else than that which the holy scriptures
make mention of, how Abraham and Lot received angels into
their houses resembling strangers. But howsoever the case
standeth, most certain it is, both by the holy scripture and
by manifold experience, that there are blessed spirits of God,
that is to say, good angels.

What angels
are.
Now what the nature of angels is, it cannot throughly be
declared of any man. For there are many things in the
order of creatures, whose nature cannot directly and perfitly
be expounded: they may nevertheless after a sort, according
to our capacity, be shadowed out. Some therefore there are
which say that angels are good spirits, ministers, of a fiery
nature, created for the ministery or service of God and good
men. Other some say angels are heavenly spirits, whose
ministery and service God useth to execute all things which
he hath determined. Wherefore we shall not seem to miss
much of the mark, if we say that angels are good spirits,
heavenly substances (I mean uncorruptible), created for the
ministery or service of God and men.

[1 Augustini Steuchi Eugubini de perenni philosophia. Lib. viii.
cap. 6, 8. in which he quotes Callimachus, Homer, Catullus, and Virgil.
Opp. Tom. ii. foll. 140, 142. Venet. 1591.]

That angels are created of God, the writings of the That angels
are created. prophets and apostles do witness. For Paul citeth that saying of David, "Which maketh his angels spirits, and his Heb. i. ministers a flame of fire." The same apostle saith : "By Col. i. Christ all things are created, that are in heaven and that are in earth, visible and invisible, whether they be majesties[2] or lordships, either rules or powers." Wherefore heretics have set forth toys, saying that angels are workers in the creation of all things and co-eternal with God : for God in time by the Son as well created angels as all other creatures.

Now touching the time when angels were created, When angels
were created. whether with the light before man, or after man, and all the works of God, let him tell that can; the holy scripture passing it over with silence, and pronouncing no certainty thereof. Epiphanius[3] and Augustinus[4], ancient interpreters of the scriptures, learnedly and truly confess that there is nothing delivered in the scriptures of that matter : and that which is not delivered in the scriptures cannot without danger be inquired after, but without danger we may be ignorant thereof. It is sufficient to acknowledge that angels were created, at what time soever it seemeth they were created. Let us rather give God thanks that he hath created for mankind so excellent ministers. Let us live an holy and angel-like life in the sight of God's holy angels. Let us watch lest he, which transfigureth and turneth himself into an angel of light, under a good shew and likeness deceive us.

Now we must further see what manner of creatures Angels are
substances. angels are : they are heavenly spirits, and incorruptible and most swift substances. We say expressly that angels are substances, that is to say, creatures having essence or being. For some deny that they are substances, subsisting in their proper essence or being; for they imagine that angels are nothing else than qualities, motions, or inspirations of good minds. But the canonical scripture calleth them ministers. Heb. i.
[Matt. xxii. Our Saviour saith, that they which rise again shall be like 30.]

[2 throni, Lat.]

[3 Οὐδαμοῦ γὰρ τηλαυγῶς σημαίνει τὸν χρόνον τῆς τῶν ἀγγελων ποιήσεως.—Epiphan. adv. Hær. Lib. II. Tom. II. p. 611. Opp. Tom. I. Par. 1622.]

[4 Augustin. de Genesi ad lit. Opp. Tom. III. fol. 102. col. 4. De Incarnat. Verbi. Tom. IV. fol. 209. col. 3.]

[Heb. i. 6.] unto the angels of God. St Paul declareth that the Son of God is more excellent than the angels, for that they worship Heb. ii. him as God their creator. The selfsame apostle saith : "For ye shall read in no place that the Son taketh on him the angels, but the seed of Abraham taketh he on him." Which testimonies most manifestly teach that angels are substances, not qualities or motions in men's minds ; that I say nothing now, how they have oftentimes appeared unto men in likeness or shape of men. Let us therefore hold and confess that angels are substances.

What manner of substances angels are. Furthermore, what substances angels are, other peradventure have better declared : for the which I bear no man grudge. I confess that there are good spirits, to make difference of them that are evil : whereof shall be spoken hereafter. I confess that they are good, not so much for the goodness of their nature in which they continued, as for their operation or working ; for they always stir up and further us to that which is good. I confess also that angels are spirits, that is to say, spiritual, heavenly, incorruptible, and exceeding swift substances : for the scripture witnesseth Psal. civ. and saith, "Which maketh his angels spirits, and his ministers a flame of fire." The scripture, I say, nameth angels spirits and a flame of fire, not that angels of their own nature and substance are corporal fire, but because fire after a sort resembleth them which in clearness, beauty, and incorruptibleness, and also in swiftness, quickness, and brightness, are the Bodily substances. most beautiful and exellent creatures. The schoolmen's definitions [1] grossly enough say, that the angels are bodily substances, but of their own kind ; for God only is without body. In these words therefore thus they have set down : "Every creature is bodily ; angels and all heavenly powers are bodily, though they consist not of flesh. Now hereby we believe that they are bodily, because they are limited in place, as the soul also is clothed [2] with flesh. (Angels peradventure at this day are more aptly said to be local or in place, not circumscriptively, but definitively [3].) We must believe that nothing by nature is bodiless and invisible but God only, that is to say, the Father, the Son, and the Holy Ghost : who

[1 *Definitiones ecclesiasticæ*, Lat.]
[2 So also ed. 1584 : but ed. 1577, *inclosed*.]
[3 G. Majoris Opp. Tom. II. fol. 522. Witeb. 1569.]

therefore is rightly believed to be bodiless, because he is in every place, and fulfilleth and conserveth all things; and therefore he is invisible to all creatures, because he is without body[4]." Thus much from them.

But those bodies either of young men or old men, in which angels oftentimes appeared unto the fathers, were not their proper or natural bodies, but taken upon them and as it were borrowed from elsewhere for a time and for the weakness of our capacity. And what manner of bodies those same very bodies were which they took, or from whence they were taken, or where they were bestowed when they had ended their business[5], it is very hard to declare. St Augustine, in his *Enchiridion ad Laurent.* cap. 59, saith: "Who can declare with what manner bodies they have appeared unto men, that they might not only be seen but be touched, and again convey not with sound substance of flesh but by spiritual power certain visions, not to the bodily eyes, but to the eyes of the spirit or mind, or tell something not in the ear outwardly but inwardly in the mind of man, even they themselves being therein; as it is written in the book of the prophets, 'And the angel said unto me, which spake in me?' (for he saith not which spake unto me, but in me;) or that appear even in one's sleep, and talk together after the manner of dreams? for we have in the gospel, 'Behold the angel of the Lord appeared unto him in his sleep, saying,' &c. for by these means angels do as it were declare that they have not bodies which can be handled. And they make a very hard question, how the fathers did wash their feet; how Jacob by taking so fast hold wrestled with the angel. When these things come in question, and every one giveth his conjecture as he is able, their heads are not unfruitfully occupied, if a moderate dis-

(margin: What bodies are taken of angels.)

(margin: [Matt. i.])

[4 Nihil incorporeum et invisibile natura credendum, nisi solum Deum, id est, Patrem et Filium et Spiritum sanctum. Qui ideo recte incorporeus creditur, quia ubique est et omnia implet atque constringit; ideo et invisibilis omnibus creaturis, quia incorporeus est. Creatura omnis corporea est: angeli, et omnes coelestes virtutes corporeæ; licet non carneæ subsistant. Ex eo autem corporeas esse credimus, quod localiter circumscribuntur, sicut et anima humana, quæ carne clauditur.—August. de Eccles. Dogm. capp. 11, 12. Opp. Tom. iii. fol. 42. col. 3. Par. 1532.]

[5 post dispensationem, Lat.]

putation be taken in hand, and the error of them which think they know that which indeed they know not be removed. For what needs it that these and such like things be affirmed or denied, or defined with danger, since we may be ignorant of them without blame[1]?" Thus far he. In these and such like causes let us acknowledge his omnipotency and wonderful dispensation, who doth what he will: to whom truly it is not hard to create substances fit and agreeable for his purpose and appointment, since of nothing he made all visible and invisible creatures.

Angels are incorruptible. Moreover we affirm that angels through the grace and power of God are incorruptible substances, yea, and unchangeable in their felicity, without burden and hinderances. For St Augustine also, *ad Pet. Diac. de Fide,* cap. 23, saith, " that unchangeableness was not by nature graffed in angels, but freely given by the grace of God[2]." The same Augustine, *De Vera Religione,* cap. 13, saith: " We must confess that angels by nature are changeable, if God only be unchangeable; but in that will, wherewith they love God rather than themselves, they remain stedfast and stable in him, and enjoy his majesty, being subject most willingly to

[1 Itemque angeli quis explicet cum qualibus corporibus apparuerint hominibus, ut non solum cernerentur, verum etiam tangerentur; et rursus non solida corpulentia sed spiritali potentia quasdam visiones non oculis corporeis, sed spiritalibus vel mentibus ingerant; vel dicant aliquid non ad aurem forinsecus, sed intus in animo hominis, etiam ibidem ipsi constituti; sicut scriptum est in prophetarum libro, Et dixit mihi angelus, qui loquebatur in me? (non enim ait, Qui loquebatur ad me, sed, in me :) vel appareant et in somnis, et colloquantur more somniorum? Habemus quippe in evangelio: Ecce angelus Domini apparuit illi in somnis, dicens. His enim modis velut indicant se angeli contrectabilia corpora non habere. Faciuntque difficillimam quæstionem, quomodo patres eis pedes laverint? quomodo Jacob cum angelo tam solida contrectatione luctatus sit? Cum ista quæruntur, et ea sicut potest quisque conjectat, non inutiliter exercentur ingenia, si adhibeatur disceptatio moderata, et absit error opinantium se scire quod nesciunt. Quid enim opus est ut hæc atque hujusmodi affirmentur, vel negentur, vel definiantur cum discrimine, quando sine crimine nesciuntur?—August. Enchirid. ad Laurent. cap. 59. Opp. Tom. III. fol. 37. col. 1.]

[2 Sed hoc ipsum, quod ab illo statu beatitudinis, in quo sunt, mutari in deterius nullatenus possunt (angeli), non est eis naturaliter insitum, sed postquam creati sunt gratiæ divinæ largitate collatum. —Id. de Fide ad Petrum Diac. Opp. Tom. III. fol. 49. col. 4.]

him alone[3]." With these words agree those which are read in *Definit. Eccles.*, cap. 61, in this wise: "The angelical powers, which continued stedfast in the love of God when the proud angels fell, received this in way of recompence, that henceforth they should never feel the fretting bite of the tooth of sin to seize upon them, and that they should continually enjoy the sight of their Creator without end of felicity; and in him so created should continue in everlasting stedfastness[4]." Thus far he. Truly the scripture, shewing the incorruptibleness of angels, affirmeth that we in the resurrection shall be like the angels; for we shall rise incorruptible: therefore angels are incorruptible. For thus saith our Saviour: " The children of this world marry wives, and are married: but they that shall be counted worthy to enjoy that world, and the resurrection from the dead, do not marry wives, neither are married, neither can they die any more; for they are equal with the angels, and are the sons of God, insomuch as they are the children of the resurrection." Whereupon Theodoretus, *In Divinis Decretis*, hath thus inferred: " We do not therefore reckon the angels in the number of gods, as the poets and philosophers of the Grecians do; neither do we divide natures that are without bodies into the male and female kind. For to a nature immortal, or that cannot die, division of kind is superfluous: for they have no need of increasing, since they feel no diminishing[5]," &c.

1 Cor. xv.

Luke xx.

But that the angels are most free and swift, and without

Angels are

[3 Fatendum est enim et angelos natura esse mutabiles, si solus Deus est incommutabilis; sed ea voluntate, qua magis Deum quam se diligunt, firmi et stabiles manent in illo, et fruuntur majestate ipsius, ei uni libentissime subditi.—Id. de Vera Relig. cap. 13. Opp. Tom. I. fol. 149. col. 3.]

[4 Virtutes angelicæ, quæ in divino amore fixæ perstiterunt, lapsis superbientibus angelis, hoc munere retributionis acceperunt, ut nulla jam rubigine surripientis culpæ mordeantur, ut et in contemplatione conditoris sine felicitatis fine permaneant, et in hoc sic conditæ æterna stabilitate subsistant.—Id. de Eccles. dogmat. cap. 61. Opp. Tom. III. fol. 42. col. 4.]

[5 Τοὺς δὲ ἀγγέλους οὔτε κατὰ τοὺς τῶν Ἑλλήνων ποιητὰς καὶ φιλοσόφους θεοποιοῦμεν, καὶ εἰς θῆλυ καὶ ἄρρεν τὴν ἀσώματον διακρίνομεν φύσιν .... τῇ δὲ ἀθανάτῳ φύσει περιττὴ τοῦ γένους ἡ διαίρεσις, οὔτε γὰρ αὐξήσεως δέονται μὴ μειούμενοι.—Theodoret. Hæret. Fab. Lib. v. cap. 7. p. 265. Tom. IV. Lut. Par. 1642.]

most free, swift, and speedy. Acts v.

impediment, burden, and let, the scripture in many places declareth. In the Acts of the Apostles thus we read : " The priests put the apostles in the common prison; but the angel of the Lord by night opened the prison-doors, and brought them forth, and said, Go and stand and speak in the temple unto the people all the words of this life. But when the officers came, and found them not in the prison, they returned and told, saying, The prison truly found we shut with all diligence, and the keepers standing without before the doors."

Acts xii.

In the same book thus again we read written : " Herod put Peter in prison ; and Peter slept between two soldiers, bound with two chains, and the keepers before the door kept the prison. And behold the angel of the Lord was there present," or stood by him, "and a light shined in the prison : and he smote Peter on the side, and stirred him up, saying, Arise up quickly; and his chains fell off from his hands. And anon, when they were past the first and second watch, they came unto the iron gate that leadeth unto the city, which opened unto them by the own accord." Behold, no impediments or lets, how strong and mighty soever they were, hindered or stayed the angel of the Lord, that he might not execute most speedily the commission which he had from God. All things give place and make way to the Lord's ambassador. The iron chains fell from Peter's hands of their own accord : he walketh safe through the thick troops of soldiers, the angel going before him : the lock of the prison-door, no man opening it, is unlocked ; and when the servants of God were gone out, it is shut again. These angels, that is to say, these heavenly ambassadors, being of their own nature most swift and speedy spirits, are now conversant in heaven, the power of God so willing and working : but so soon as it shall please the Lord of all, by and by they are present with men in earth, unto whom they are sent of God from heaven. And they are present in earth, sometime with one, and sometime with another. Not that they are not contained in their proper place : for when the angel told the women of Christ's resurrection, he was not at the same instant in heaven and by the grave or sepulchre at once. For God only is not contained in place ; for he is present in every place. But angels go not forward fair and softly, neither are they moved with labour or toiling, after the manner of

corruptible bodies.　Yet in the scriptures they are expressly
said to ascend into heaven, and from thence to descend unto
us.　We very rightly believe that our souls, as soon as they
depart out of the bodies, do forthwith enter into the kingdom[1] of heaven : for the Lord hath said in the gospel,
" But hath escaped from death unto life ; " and, " To-day John v.
shalt thou be with me in paradise."　And thou dost read of Luke xxiii.
Lazarus the beggar : " And it came to pass that the beggar Luke xvi.
died, and was carried by the angels into Abraham's bosom."
To this also now seemeth that saying of Daniel to belong :
" As I was yet a speaking, making supplication, and con- Dan. ix.
fessing mine own sin and the sin of my people Israel, and
pouring forth my prayers before the Lord my God for the
holy hill of my God ; yea, while I was yet speaking in my
prayer, the man Gabriel, whom I had seen before in the
vision, came flying hastily unto me."　Lo, our souls are
carried up into heaven by the angels, which notwithstanding
are elsewhere said at an instant to be taken up into heaven.
Afterward, as soon as Daniel had prayed unto the Lord, the
angel, without any longer delay, flying speedily, (for so the
scripture speaketh for our capacity,) is present with him that
prayeth, and sheweth him that he is heard of God.　Angels
therefore are swift and passing speedy, being kept down
with no weight, neither hindered nor stayed from performing those things for which they are sent from heaven ; albeit
they are contained in place as creatures (though not limited),
and are moved with a certain order and manner agreeable
to that spiritual nature.

　　This treatise requireth peradventure that something also The strength
be spoken of the might, power, and strength of the angels. of angels.
But what need many words in a manifest matter ?　For
since the Lord, who sendeth forth his angels, is almighty,
there is nothing but that angels can do it in those their
ambassages and ministeries.　There is nothing in the whole
course of nature, that is able to withstand the ministers of
the almighty God.　For angels are not called powers and
virtues for nought.　I will shew one example among many,
and yet not the chiefest.　One angel in one night, without [2 Kings xix.
any furniture or much ado, slew in the tents of the Assy- 35.]
rians, at the walls of Hierusalem, a hundred fourscore and

[1 regiam, Lat.; the palace.]

five thousand of the valiantest soldiers. In Daniel we have such a description of an angel, whereby both the power and excellency of angels may be gathered. "His body," saith he, "was like the Turkish or jasper stone, his face to look upon was like lightning, his eyes as lamps of fire, his arm and feet were like in colour to polished brass[1], and the voice of his words was like to the voice of a multitude." So that it is not needful to make a long discourse of the knowledge and wisdom of angels; for this is not a thing that passeth capacity, seeing angels are creatures. But insomuch as pertaineth to their ambassages and ministeries, surely they are most wise, in all points furnished, and in no part diminished. For he that sendeth them is everlasting wisdom itself, and he furnisheth his ambassadors most perfitly.

Furthermore, touching the multitude and order of angels certain divines have wittily and wisely enough disputed. The scripture simply affirmeth that angels are innumerable. For Daniel saith: "A thousand thousands ministered unto him, and ten thousand thousands stood before him." It is also read that Christ said to Peter: "Thinkest thou that I cannot pray unto my Father, and he shall send unto me more than twelve legions of angels?" Paul also saith: "Ye are come into the city of the living God, the heavenly Jerusalem, and to an innumerable company of angels." Many distinguish that innumerable multitude into nine companies; and these again they bring into three hierarchies or holy principalities, of which they affirm that each of them have three orders: the first, seraphim, cherubim, thrones; the second, lordships, virtues, powers; the third, principalities, archangels, and angels. They add in what they differ between themselves, and what is proper to every one of them. But St Augustine, in his *Enchir.* cap. 58, saith: "Wherein lordships, principalities, and powers do differ between themselves, let them tell that can: if yet they are able to prove that they say. I confess myself to be ignorant of these matters[2]." And the same Augustine, *Ad Orosium contra*

Dan. x.

The knowledge of angels.

Of the multitude and order of angels.

Dan. vii. [10.]

Matt. xxvi. [53.]

Heb. xii. [22.]

[1 æris candentis, Lat.]
[2 Et quid inter se distent quatuor illa vocabula, quibus universam ipsam cœlestem societatem videtur apostolus esse complexus, dicendo, Sive sedes, sive dominationes, sive principatus, sive potestates, dicant qui possunt; si tamen possunt probare quod dicunt. Ego me ista

Luscillianistas, saith: "Truly the apostle saith, Whether seats (thrones), whether lordships, whether principalities, whether powers. And therefore that there are seats, lordships, principalities, and powers in the hosts of heaven, I stedfastly believe; and that they differ somewhat between themselves, I hold it for an undoubted truth: but what they are, and what they differ between themselves, I know not. Neither truly do I think myself for the ignorance thereof to be endangered, as I am for disobedience if I neglect the Lord's commandments[3]." And anon in 'the same place he sheweth that we must not busily and curiously search after these things: whose counsel we do willingly obey, perceiving that the scriptures, which minister unto us all things necessary and healthful, have set down nothing concerning them.

Yet this we cannot deny, that those names (or if you will so call them, orders of angels) are expressed in the holy scriptures: whereupon for our weakness it is meet after a sort to expound them as we may. These blessed spirits of heaven seem generally and simply to be called angels, because they be the messengers and ambassadors of the most high God: who it appeareth are called archangels, when they be sent in message in God's greatest matters, to shew or do things altogether hard and heavenly. For so we read in Paul, that "the Lord himself shall descend from heaven in a shout, and in the voice of an archangel, and in the trump of God." For, that we may compare small things with great, we see that kings and princes in weighty affairs appoint none to be their ambassadors but noblemen. It appeareth that they are called thrones, because they stand always in the throne[4] of God; or else because God is read

The exposition of names given to angels.

Archangels.

1 Thess. iv.

Thrones and seats.

ignorare confiteor.—August. Enchirid. ad Laurent. cap. 58. Opp. Tom. III. fol. 37. col. 3. Par. 1532.]

[3 Certe ait apostolus, Sive sedes, sive dominationes, sive principatus, sive potestates. Et esse itaque sedes, dominationes, principatus, et potestates in cœlestibus apparatibus firmissime credo, et differre inter se aliquid indubitata fide teneo: sed ... quænam ista sint, et quid inter se differant, nescio. Nec ea sane ignorantia periclitari me puto, sicuti inobedientia, si Domini præcepta neglexero.—Id. lib. ad Orosium contra Priscillianistas et Origenistas. Opp. Tom. VI. fol. 134. col. 1.]

[4 So also ed. 1584: but ed. 1577, *at* the throne.]

in the prophets to have made and placed his own seat in angels, and to be carried of them as it were in the coach of a king; as David saith: "He bowed the heavens and came down, and there was darkness under his feet. He rode upon the cherubims," or was carried upon the cherubims[1], "and did fly: he came flying upon the wings of the wind." Furthermore, the description of the chariot and throne of God in Ezechiel is known. They seem to be called lordships, principalities, and powers, because God executeth his government, and exerciseth his own power in the world, by the ministry of angels. For so also they are called powers and armies, or the host of heaven: for they encompass the Lord round as his guard; and he who is called the God of Sabaoth, or of hosts, the Lord, I say, of all angels, spirits, and creatures, whose ministry he useth, when, where, how, and as much as it pleaseth him, useth them also as his soldiers. St Hierome thinketh they are called cherubims, of their exceeding knowledge[2]. Other expound them swift. Seraphims have their name of ferventness; or else because they are compared to most pure and clear fire; or for that they are burning in the love of God[3].

By these names in the meanwhile are shadowed out the manifold offices and divers operations of angels; which we being desirous to comprehend in few words, have said that angels are created of God for the ministry of God himself and men. For David said: "Which maketh his angels spirits, and his ministers a flame of fire." And again in another place: "O praise the Lord, all ye angels of his; ye that excel in strength, ye that fulfil his commandments, and hearken unto the voice of his words. O praise ye the Lord, all ye hosts[4]; ye servants of his that do his pleasure." And of angels Paul also saith: "Are not all ministering spirits, which are sent out into the ministry for their sakes which shall be heirs of salvation?" But God useth the ministry of angels upon no necessity, but of his own good-will. For he might be without

Marginal notes:
Psal. xviii.
Lordships. Principalities.
Powers.
Cherubim.
Seraphim.
God useth the ministry of angels.
[Psal. civ. 4.]
Psal. ciii.
[Heb. i. 14.]

[1 ascendit super, Lat. and Vulgate.]

[2 Cherubim, quod interpretatur *scientiæ multitudo*.—Hieron. Epist. 50. Opp. Tom. IV. Par. II. col. 574. Par. 1693-1706.]

[3 of God, not in Lat.]

[4 So also ed. 1584: but ed. 1577, all *his* hosts; virtutes ejus, Lat.]

them, since by his own word[5] he bringeth to pass what he
will: " For he spake, and they were made; he commanded, [Psal. xxxiii.
and they were created;" not one of all the angels jointly 9.]
working with him. So at this day also he is able, without the
help of angels, to bring to pass what he will. But because
of his special goodness he created them to the partaking
of everlasting life and salvation, he useth their ministry to
us-ward, as he also doth the service of other creatures, to
whom they declare their faith and obedience to God-ward;
and God exerciseth his unspeakable good-will both toward
them, whom by grace he hath made partakers of everlasting
joy, and also toward us, whom he hath vouchsafed to honour
with the service of so excellent a company. For among
other innumerable and the greatest benefits of God, whereat
not without cause we are astonished, this is not to be accounted the least, that he hath given us angels to be our
servants. Truly this is an exceeding great token of his
fatherly care and regard to us-ward, first of all[6] because he
frameth himself so sweetly to our capacities and dispositions.
In time past the Lord himself spake with his own mouth in
mount Sina with the church or congregation of the Israelites;
but when he understood that they had rather he should speak
by their interpreter Moses, he took their wish and offer, and
afterward he spake by Moses, using his ministry toward them. Exod. xix.
Truly God is able to pour most perfite faith into our minds Deut. v.
by his Holy Spirit without any joint working of men; but
because he knew it was profitable for us that it should so be,
he instituted the ministry of his word, and planteth the faith
of the apostles by the preaching of the gospel. And that
ordinance once made he doth so precisely observe, that when he
might have done the same by angels, yet by the angels themselves he sendeth them that are to be instructed in the faith
to the apostles. For it is manifest what the angel of the Lord
in the Acts of the Apostles did with Cornelius, whom he sendeth unto the preaching of Peter[7]. Therefore, when God seeth Acts x.
the ministry of angels convenient for us, then of good-will,
upon no necessity, he useth their ministry toward men. And
doubtless angels love men exceedingly; and that which they

[5 nutu suo, Lat.; by his nod.]
[6 imprimis, Lat.]
[7 See Vol. I. pp. 84-86.]

do, they do of their own accord, not of constraint or unwillingly. For they cannot but exceedingly love them whom they see to be so dear to their Creator, that for their sakes he spared not his only-begotten Son, but for them[1] delivered him up into most bitter death: that I make no mention here of the most ready obedience which they perform to their God, who willeth and commandeth them to serve him and

Luke xv. men. The Lord in the gospel witnesseth, "that the angels in heaven rejoice at the conversion and turning of men that be Zech. i. sinners." In Zachary the angel of the Lord is brought in very sorrowful for the misery of the captives in Babylon, and careful for their deliverance from their captivity[2]. All which things commend unto us the love and affection of angels toward mankind. For otherwise those blessed spirits are not moved with affections, carefulness or sorrow, as we are in the flesh; but they be glad, and rejoice, as blessed spirits can rejoice, in whom there is no human affection: which affections nevertheless are not only attributed to them, but to God himself tropically or by a figure, and as they say $\dot{a}\nu\theta\rho\omega\pi\text{o}\pi\alpha\theta\tilde{\omega}s$, that is, after the affection of man, to the end our minds may the better understand and more easily conceive spiritual and heavenly things, as it were by parables. Howbeit let us think that parables do not always contain all things: therefore our minds must be lifted up to higher things, and spiritual things must spiritually be judged.

What the ministries of angels are. The ministry of angels extendeth very far; which I will declare by rehearsing certain kinds of them as briefly and as plainly as I can.

First, they do service unto God himself in all things; which I think is sufficiently declared in that which went afore. The same God they all magnify together with everlasting praises, worshipping, glorifying, and rejoicing in him. For Theodoret, reciting certain testimonies of scriptures concerning this matter, saith: "The ministry or service of angels is the praising of God, and singing of hymns or songs. For the holy prophet Esay saith of the seraphim, that they cried and Isai. vi. said, 'Holy, holy, holy is the Lord God of Sabaoth; heaven and earth are full of his glory.' And of the cherubim the

[1 pro omnibus, Lat.]
[2 So also ed. 1584: but ed. 1577, from captivity; ex captivitate, Lat.]

heavenly prophet Ezechiel saith, that he heard them saying, 'Blessed be the glory of the Lord out of his place[3].'" The whole host of heaven also singeth a birth-song to Christ their prince, when he was born, as is to be seen in St Luke, saying: "Glory be to God on high, and in earth peace, and among men good-will." So they go before with an example for men to follow, teaching what they also should do, that is, offer praise and thanksgiving to God on high, whom the angels also reverence and worship with us.

Moreover the angels love the truth, and are desirous to have the same spread abroad and the glory of God by all means furthered; and therefore they lay blocks in the way of false prophets, hating them with their accursed doctrine and antichrist. For St Peter testifieth that the angels desire to behold the gospel of the Son of God[4]. In the Revelation of Jesus Christ made to John the apostle the angel of the Lord bindeth Satan; and the angels, furthering the gospel of Christ[5], set themselves everywhere against false Christians and false teachers. For even in the end of the world, " the Son of Man shall send forth his angels, and they shall gather out of his kingdom all things that offend, and them which do iniquity, and shall cast them into a furnace of fire." They themselves stand in the presence of the Almighty God, waiting his commandment; who, so soon as he shall command them to go forth and to execute his commandments, by and by they make speed. They come therefore unto men to declare the will and commandments of God. So the angel Gabriel came first to Zachary, the father of John Baptist; afterward he came to the blessed virgin, to shew unto her the incarnation of the Son of God. Innumerable examples of this kind are everywhere found in the holy scriptures.

Margin notes: Ezek. iii. / Luke ii. / 1 Pet. i. / [Matt. xiii. 41, 42.] / Luke i.

[3 Λειτουργία δὲ τῶν ἀγγέλων ἡ ὑμνῳδία· περὶ μὲν γὰρ τῶν Σεραφὶμ ὁ μακάριός φησιν Ἡσαΐας, ὅτι ἐκέκραγον καὶ ἔλεγον, Ἅγιος, ἅγιος, ἅγιος, Κύριος Σαβαώθ· πλήρης ὁ οὐρανὸς καὶ ἡ γῆ τῆς δόξης αὐτοῦ. Περὶ δὲ τῶν Χερουβὶμ ὁ θεῖος εἶπεν Ἐζεκιὴλ, ὡς ἤκουσε λεγόντων, Εὐλογημένη ἡ δόξα Κυρίου ἐκ τοῦ τόπου αὐτῆς.—Theodoret. Hæret. Fab. Lib. v. cap. 7. p. 267. Tom. v. Lut. Par. 1642-84.]

[4 Nam S. Petrus commemorat evangelium Filii Dei admodum jucundum gratumque spectaculum esse angelis, Lat. For St Peter testifies that the gospel of the Son of God is a most pleasant and grateful spectacle to angels.]

[5 veritatem Christianam, Lat.]

They watch for our safety, being careful for us, yet without molestation; whereof I told you before. They advertise the faithful in time convenient, foreshewing dangers to come; and they also do comfort the afflicted. For the wise men, being warned by the angel that they should not return unto Hierusalem to Herod, avoid great peril. Joseph also being commanded by the angel flieth into Egypt, delivering the Christ or anointed of the Lord[1] out of the bloody hands of Herod. Christ also at the mount of Olivet, being in a bloody sweat, is comforted by the angel. And Hagar, the handmaid of Sara, being in extreme danger, is recreated by the consolation of an angel. As also the apostle St Paul, being very near shipwreck, heareth this voice of the angel of the Lord: "Fear not, Paul; thou must be brought before Cæsar: and, lo, God hath given thee all them that sail with thee."

Again, angels are sent for revengement of mischievous persons; to take punishment, I mean, of those that be wicked and impenitent. For the first-born of the Egyptians are smitten of the angel. In the Acts of the Apostles the angel of the Lord smiteth Herod Agrippa. It is said that in the camp of the Assyrians many were smitten and slain of one angel. And David saw an angel with a sword drawn hovering between heaven and earth, afflicting the people with a most grievous plague. So we believe that the holy angels shall come with the Son of man unto judgment, as Paul witnesseth, and saith: "Our Lord Jesus Christ shall be revealed from heaven, with the angels of his power, in flaming fire, rendering vengeance unto them that know not God, and that obey not the gospel of our Lord Jesus Christ." For in the Revelation of Jesus Christ also the angels pour out vials full of the wrath of God upon the heads of false Christians[2].

Moreover, they take upon them the charge and defence of us, God so commanding: they are our keepers, ready at hand watching over us that no adversity happen unto us, and do guide our ways: for hitherto belong the testimonies of the Psalms, and very many examples of the scripture. David saith: "This poor (or afflicted) man cried, and the Lord heard him, and saved him out of all his troubles. The angel of the Lord pitcheth his tents round about them that fear him, and delivereth them." And in another psalm he saith:

Matt. ii.

[Luke xxii. 43, 44.]
Gen. xvi.

Acts xxvii.

Exod. xii.
Acts xii.
2 Kings xix.

[2 Sam. xxiv. 16, 17.]

2 Thess. i.

Rev. xvi.

Psal. xxxiv.

[1 Christum Dominum, Lat.]   [2 antichristianorum, Lat.]

"There shall no evil come unto thee, neither shall any plague _{Psal. xci.} come near thy tabernacle (or dwelling). For he shall give his angels charge over thee, to keep thee in all thy ways. They shall bear thee in their hands, that thou hurt not thy foot against a stone. Thou shalt go (or walk) upon the lion and adder (or asp); the young lion and the dragon shalt thou tread under thy feet." And the Lord in the gospel plainly saith, that little children have angels without doubt to be their _{Matt. xviii.} keepers. Jacob the patriarch, greatly fearing his brother _{Gen. xxxii.} Esau, seeth angels coming to meet him; and understandeth that angels were given unto him as guides and keepers of him in his way against the fierceness of his brother. In the _{2 Kings vi.} affairs of Heliseus we read, that the king of Syria besieged the city Dothan with a great host, wherein Heliseus at that time led his life, whom he had purposed to take. When the servant of Heliseus perceived that, and was troubled in mind, and lamented his master's case, Heliseus said, "Fear not; for they that be with us are more than they that be with them." The prophet also prayed and said, "Lord, I beseech thee, open his* eyes[3], that he may see. And the Lord opened the eyes of _{*Servant's.} the servant, and he looked, and behold, the mountain was full of horses and fiery chariots;" that is to say, he was armed and defended with the guard of an host of angels. Abraham also saith to his servant: "The Lord God of heaven, which _{[Gen. xxiv.} said unto me, Unto thy seed will I give this land, he shall _{7.]} send his angel before thee," namely, to direct thy way, to defend thee, and bring to pass that thou mayest obtain thy desire. For the Lord himself said to Moses in Exodus: "Behold, I will send my angel before thee, to keep thee in _{[Exod. xxiii.} the way, and to lead thee to the place that I have prepared." _{20.]} In the Acts of the Apostles thou dost often read that angels served the apostles, furthered their purpose, and defended them against their adversaries.

In Daniel angels are brought in for princes, and presi- _{Dan. x.} dents or governors, of kingdoms: as Michael with Gabriel, princes of the Israelitish kingdom; another of the Persian kingdom; another of the Grecian kingdom; and each of them debate the matter touching his own kingdom, and fight for the same. Not that there is any variance or disagreement in heaven, where doubtless there is plentiful peace, everlast-

[3 oculos pueri, Lat.]

ing concord and quietness; neither that there are conflicts or battles fought between the angels, as between those gods whom the poet Homer describeth; but by a parable and allusion heaven is compared to the court of some puissant and renowned prince, where ambassadors of sundry countries debate their divers causes: which is done in consideration of our weak wit and slender capacity. For thus we ought to conceive in our mind; that God, who is the only Lord of all kingdoms, heareth all men's suits, and taketh in hand all men's matters; and that angels, at the word[1] and will of God, minister and do service unto God, when it pleaseth him to use their ministry and service. For so Nabuchodonosor also saw in a vision a watchman coming down from heaven, and fore-telling the destiny of the tree that was to be hewn down.

Dan. iv.

We must not attribute too much unto angels.

Nevertheless we must here take heed lest, contrary to the nature of true religion, we attribute too much to angels; that we worship them not; that we call not upon them, nor serve them. Indeed, when men hear that angels are given unto them of God for ministers, and that God by them doth good unto us, by and by they think that some honour[2] is to be ascribed and given unto them. But sincere religion doth teach us to acknowledge God the author of all good things; that the angels are the ministers of God, and as it were instruments by whom he worketh, as we see the sun, the moon, and the stars, the patriarchs, the prophets, and the apostles, to be and to have been. But who being well in his wits hath wor-shipped, called upon, or served, the sun or the stars, though they be creatures very excellent and beneficial unto men? And what partaker, I pray you, of true faith and belief hath worshipped, called upon, or served the patriarchs, the pro-phets, and the apostles, though they were endued with most precious gifts, and wonderful in working of miracles? We do all worship, call upon, and serve God; and we confess that

Saints will not be wor-shipped of us.

God worketh by his saints; who together with the holy angels of God require nothing less than to be worshipped, called upon, and served of us. For truly said Lactantius, *lib. Institut.* II. cap. 16: "Angels, since they be immortal, neither suffer nor yet are willing to be called gods: whose only office it is alone to attend upon God with their service, to be at his beck, and to do nothing at all but at his commandment.

[1 pro nutu, Lat.]   [2 nihil non honoris, Lat.]

For we say that God so governeth the world, as a king
ruleth his kingdom; whose officers no man will say are fellows
with him in ruling his kingdom, albeit affairs be dispatched
by their ministry and service[3]." And therefore we read that
St Augustine also said: "When the angels of God hear, he
himself heareth in them, as in his true temple, not made with
hands[4]." Verily, if we look more narrowly into and weigh
the holy scripture, we shall find not in one or two places
that the name of God and angels are set down without difference. For angels are causes further off, and instrumental,
as they term them; but God is the nearest and most principal cause. For in the Acts of the Apostles we read that Acts vii.
Stephen said, "And when forty years were expired, there
appeared unto him in the wilderness of mount Sinai an angel:"
and by and by he addeth, "And the voice of the Lord came
unto him saying, I am the God of thy father," &c. He calleth
the selfsame Lord, whom a little before he had called an
angel: to wit, because he believed that an angel both saith
and doth all things at God's commandment; that the word
and the work is proper to God, and the angels are as instruments. Likewise in the book of Judges, cap. vi. he is called
Lord, which even now was called an angel. Hagar, the hand- Gen. xvi.
maid of Sara, received a great benefit in the desert by the
angel of the Lord; yet she accounteth not the same received
of the angel, but of the Lord: she giveth not thanks to the
angel, neither doth she consecrate the memory thereof to the
angel; much less doth she worship and call upon the angel;
nay rather she referreth her speech also unto God. For so
the holy scripture witnesseth: "And she called the name of
the Lord which spake unto her, Thou God lookest on me,"
&c. The children of Israel, before whom the angel of the
Lord went in the wilderness, never offered sacrifice to their
guide or captain, never worshipped or served him. Even so

[3 Neque angeli, cum sint immortales, dici se deos aut patiuntur
aut volunt: quorum unum solumque officium est servire nutibus Dei;
nec omnino quicquam nisi jussu facere. Sic enim mundum regi a
Deo dicimus, ut a rectore provinciam: cujus apparitores nemo socios
esse in regenda provincia dixerit, quamvis illorum ministerio res ge-
ratur.—Lactant. Instit. Lib. ii. cap. 16.]

[4 Nam et cum exaudiunt angeli ejus, ipse (Deus) in eis exaudit,
tamquam in vero nec manufacto templo suo.—Augustin. de Civit. Dei.
Lib. x. cap. 12. Opp. Tom. v. Par. 1532.]

the servant of Abraham, being committed to the angel, doth not make supplication unto him, desiring him well to prosper his purpose; but he prayeth unto God, and requireth of him to shew and give trial of his mercy toward his master Abraham. In Daniel the angel of the Lord appeareth [Dan. iii.] walking among Daniel's fellows which were cast into the burning oven; but when they were delivered from the violence of the flame, they do not praise the angel, neither account the benefit of their delivery received of him, but of God only: for they sing, "Blessed art thou, O Lord God of our fathers; right worthy to be praised and honoured in that name of thine for evermore[1]." So in like manner Paul in express words confesseth that it is God whose he is, and whom he worshippeth; though in the meanwhile he had made mention also of an angel: for so he saith in the Acts, Acts xxvii. "There stood by me this night the angel of God, whose I am, and whom I serve," that is to say, God. For in another place John being willing to worship at the angel's feet, the Rev. xxii. angel crieth, "See thou do it not; for I am thy fellow-servant, and of thy brethren the prophets, and of them which keep the words of this book." These plain and manifest testimonies of holy scripture evidently teach us, that although God use the ministry of angels toward us, yet that they are to be acknowledged and confessed of us to be ministers of God and fellow-servants, and therefore not to be worshipped or called upon; but that God only must be worshipped, called upon, and served.

From this holy doctrine of scripture certain ministers and ecclesiastical writers of the ancient church have nothing swerved. For Lactantius in that book which we cited a little before saith: "Angels will have no honour given unto them, whose honour is in God. But they which revolted and fell from the ministry of God, because they are enemies of the truth and offenders, they go about to challenge to themselves the name of God and the worship of gods[2]." And now St

[1 Song of the three holy children, 3 Dan. iii. 26, (Apocryphal,) Vulgate.]

[2 Nullum sibi honorem tribui volunt (angeli), quorum omnis honor in Deo est. Illi autem, qui desciverunt a Dei ministerio, quia sunt veritatis inimici et prævaricatores Dei, nomen sibi et cultum deorum vendicare conantur.—Lactant. Instit. Lib. II. cap. 16.]

Augustine, being of the same judgment in this matter, hath thus left written : "Whom might I find" (now he speaketh unto God) "to reconcile me unto thee? What, should I go unto angels? With what prayer, with what vows? Many endeavouring to return unto thee, and not being able of themselves, have assayed (as I hear) these ways, and have fallen into a desire and longing after curious visions, and are counted worthy to be deceived[3]." These things are extant, Lib. x. *Confess.* cap. 42. After which he sheweth at large, that Jesus Christ is the only Mediator and Intercessor for all the faithful. The same Augustine, in his tenth book *de Civitate Dei*, cap. 16, declareth in many words, that the good angels of God require sacrifices not for themselves but for God[4]. In his last chapter of his book *de Vera Religione*, he saith: "Let us believe that the best angels will that God be served with the best and most excellent ministry ; that together with them we should worship one God, in the contemplation and beholding of whom they are blessed. For we are not blessed by seeing the angels, but by seeing the truth ; whereby we also love the very angels, and rejoice together with them. Wherefore we honour them for love, not of duty. Neither do we build temples unto them; for they are unwilling in such sort to be honoured of us; because they know that we ourselves, if we be good, are the temples of the most high God. It is well written therefore that an angel forbad a man to worship him, but willed him to worship one only God, under whom he also was a fellow-servant with him[5]." The

The worshipping of angels greatly condemned.

[3 Quem invenirem qui me reconciliaret tibi? Ambiendum (Bullinger read, An eundum) mihi fuit ad angelos? Qua prece? quibus sacramentis? Multi conantes ad te redire, neque per seipsos valentes, sicut audio, tentaverunt hæc, et inciderunt in desiderium curiosarum visionum, et digni habiti sunt illusionibus.—August. Confess. Lib. x. cap. 67. (alii 42).]

[4 ... per sacrificium non sibi, sed ei (Deo) nos subdere volunt (angeli boni).—Id. Opp. Tom. v. fol. 123. col. 3, 4.]

[5 Hoc etiam ipsos optimos angelos et excellentissima Dei ministeria velle credamus, ut unum cum ipsis colamus Deum, cujus contemplatione beati sunt. Neque enim et nos videndo angelos beati sumus, sed videndo veritatem, qua etiam ipsos diligimus angelos, et his congratulamur ... Quare honoramus eos caritate, non servitute; nec eis templa construimus; nolunt enim se sic honorari a nobis, quia nos ipsos, cum boni sumus, templa summi Dei esse noverunt. Recte

same Augustine therefore in his catalogue of heretics reckoneth worshippers of angels among heretics, naming them *angelici*, angel-worshippers[1]. For in his disputation against Maximinus, bishop of the Arians, Lib. I. proving the Holy Ghost to be God, he manifestly calleth worshippers of angels sacrilegious persons, and cursed of Christ and his church. The words of the author, if any require, are these: "If we should make a temple (saith he) of wood and stone to the holy angel, that is most excellent, should we not be cursed of the truth of Christ, and of the church of God? because we do that service to a creature, which only is due to one God. If therefore by building a temple to any kind of creature we should rob God of his honour, how is not he the true God to whom we build not a temple, but we ourselves are his temple[3]?" Thus saith he.

Mark what he thinketh of the temple built to St Michael in Mount Garganus[2].

Of evil spirits. These things have I hitherto spoken in brevity of the holy or good angels of God: now I pass over to discourse of evil spirits, of wicked angels I mean and revolting, that is to say, of evil spirits, or devils. Hereof I will briefly and plainly speak that which the holy scriptures minister unto me.

That there are devils. That there are devils the Sadducees in times past denied, and at this day also some scarce religious, nay rather epicures, deny the same[4]: who, unless they repent, shall one day feel, to their exceeding great pain and smart, both that there are devils, and that they are tormentors and executioners of all wicked men and epicures. For the whole scripture and all

itaque scribitur hominem ab angelo prohibitum, ne se adoraret, sed unum Deum, sub quo ei esset et ille conservus.—Id. de Vera Relig. cap. 55. Tom. I. fol. 156. col. 2.]

[1 Angelici, in angelorum cultu inclinati, quos Epiphanius jam omnino defecisse testatur.—Id. de Hæres. cap. 39. Opp. Tom. VI. fol. 4. col. 3.]

[2 This highly-venerated church, dug out of the solid rock, is in a cave of Mount St Angelo, the ancient Mons Garganus. Cramer's Italy, Vol. II. p. 277.]

[3 Nonne, si templum alicui sancto angelo excellentissimo de lignis et lapidibus faceremus, anathematizaremur a veritate Christi et ab ecclesia Dei? quoniam creaturæ exhiberemus eam servitutem quæ uni tantum debetur Deo. Si ergo sacrilegi essemus faciendo templum cuicunque creaturæ; quomodo non est Deus verus, cui non templum facimus, sed nos ipsi templum sumus?—August. contra Maxim. Lib. I. Opp. Tom. VI. fol. 142. col. 1.]

[4 See above, p. 330, note 3.]

godly and wise men, as many as have lived from the beginning of the world even unto this day, have confessed that
there are evil spirits or devils.

Now what thing devils are, it is no less hard and doubt- What the
devil is.
ful exactly to define by reason, than I said it was difficult to
describe fully the nature of angels : howbeit I will shadow
them out by one or other kind of description, to the end
I may entreat of them in a certain order. Evil angels are
corrupt and wicked spirits, and, for their revolting or falling
away, everlastingly condemned : subject indeed they are to
God, but yet nevertheless adversaries to God and men, for
that they turn all their travails and studies to the contempt
and despising of God, and to the deceiving and destruction
of men.

First, that the devil is a creature, hereby it is manifest ; That the
devil is a
because there is but one creator only, to wit, that God in creature.
Trinity and Unity. He created all spirits : but the devil
also falleth in the reckoning of spirits. We said before[5] that
the time of their creation is not set down in the scripture,
when as we shewed that it was nowhere expressed at what
time, whether before man or after man, angels were created.
Hereunto we do now add, that evil angels became evil, not by The devil was
not created
creation, but by their own revolting and falling away. For evil.
all things which God created were and are exceeding good :
all angels therefore, as men in like manner, were naturally
created good. But they continued not stedfast in this good- Of the fall
of angels
ness granted, given, and graffed in them of God ; but they from heaven.
being corrupt with their own malice, as men also are, fell, and
were by the most just God thrown out of heaven, as out of
the felicity or happiness which was given them. Now when
or at what time this was done, the scripture doth not again
express : howbeit it seemeth to have been done before the
fall of man ; for the devil by the serpent egged our parents
to sin, and drew them into misery and death. Neither doth
the same scripture peculiarly define what manner of sin the
devil's was : neither doth it expressly and particularly shew
the manner how they were cast out of heaven. It saith generally, that there was folly or wickedness found in the angels,
and that therefore they were thrown down headlong into hell.
For we read in the book of Job : "Behold, he found no truth [Job iv. 18.]

[5 See above, page 329.]

in his servants[1], and in his angels there was folly" (or wickedness). St Peter, nothing disagreeing from this, said, that
" God spared not the angels which sinned, but cast them down
into hell, and delivered them into chains of darkness, to be
kept unto judgment." But Judas also, the brother of James,
the apostle of the Lord, surnamed Thaddeus, rehearsing the
same sentence in a manner, said : " The angels which kept not
their first estate (to wit, the nature wherein they were
created), but left their own habitation, (to wit, their road[2],
their office, and their faith,) the Lord hath reserved in everlasting chains unto darkness[3] unto the judgment of the great
day." What, doth not our Lord and Saviour Christ speaking of the devil say thus, "He was a murderer from the
beginning, and abode not in the truth?" For hereupon we
may gather, that the devil sometime abode or was in the
truth, but shrunk and forsook it by faithless falling away.

Those testimonies, which witness that an angel sinned by
revolting, and was thrown down headlong into hell, are sufficient for godly minds and such as are not curious. Furthermore, out of Esay[4] and Ezechiel[5] there are recited of others
testimonies making for the same matter : which as we reject
not, so we doubt not but that by an allegory they are applied
unto these of ours. That which is alleged out of Luke, " I
saw Satan as it had been lightning falling down from heaven,"
is not so properly expounded of the first fall of angels : for
there is another fall of the devil, to wit, whereby he fell from
his own tyranny (whereby he had possessed the minds of
men, and ensnared them with wickedness and sin) through
the coming of Christ into the world, and through the sincer
preaching of the gospel. Now there is no doubt that all
angels were created good, and that the evil fell through their

Marginal notes:
2 Pet. ii.

[John viii.]

Isai. xiv.
Ezek.
xxviii.

[1 Ecce qui serviunt ei non sunt stabiles, Lat. and Vulgate. He
hath found unfaithfulness among his own servants, Coverdale, 1535.]

[2 stationem, Lat.]

[3 So all the editions ; but the Lat. sub caligine.]

[4 Quod de Satana exposuerunt hunc locum, id ignorantia factum
est. Calv.—Scimus Satanam cecidisse : verum Luciferum in scripturis
alicubi vocatum non reperimus. Musculus, apud Maldonat. Expos.
Eccles. in Isai. xiv. 12.]

[5 Qui allegorias sectantur, per Principem Tyri Luciferum intelligunt ... freti dicto Domini, Videbam Satanam de cœlo cadentem sicut
fulgur.—Œcolampad. Comment. in Ezech. fol. 173. Argentor. 1534.]

own, and not through God's fault and folly ; whereof I spake
somewhat also in the tenth sermon of the third decade, where
I entreated of the beginning of sin[6]. To which I will now add
the most notable and evident declaration of Theodoret, bishop
of Cyrus, taken out of the secrets of the scriptures; who in his
Epitome Divin. Decret. saith : " Let us consider whether the
devils justly suffer punishment, since they received of him
that made them a nature like his. And how can he which is
good be called the creator of wickedness ? And how is he
righteous and just, that punisheth the nature which can do
nothing that good is, but is tied and bound with fetters of
wickedness and vice ? But we know that the God of all
things, and the fountain of justice and righteousness, is righteous and just. Therefore he will not punish the devils unjustly. And we know that God was their guide and captain,
and that the good angels are his workmanship, and that he
is called good of all such as are rightly minded. He therefore made not the nature which could do nothing that is good,
travailing and bringing forth wickedness only, and doing
things contrary to his will and mind. If God therefore did
neither make the evil nature, (for he is the maker and worker
of all good things, as he himself is good,) then doth he not so
much as once think to punish unjustly : for he is just and the
lawgiver of justice or righteousness, and he will punish the
devil and such also as serve and are under him. Therefore
the devil of his own will and accord is evil, and they that take
his part. For as God made man good in the beginning, and
with free will of mind, these doubtless, to wit, good angels,
kept their nature which they received pure and uncorrupt :
but those (to wit, men) declined and fell into the worse, and
corrupted their heavenly shapes, and they that were like unto
God made themselves brutish: so also the devil and rout of
devils, which were with other bodiless creatures, did not follow
the good will of them toward the Lord God ; but being puffed
up with the disease of haughtiness and pride, betook themselves unto that which was the worse, and fell from their
former state and condition[7]." Thus far he. With Theodoret

[6 See Vol. II. p. 366.]

[7 Ὅτι μὲν οὖν κολασθήσονται (οἱ δαίμονες), σαφῶς ἐδιδάχθημεν. Σκο-
πήσωμεν δὲ λοιπόν, εἰ δικαίως τοῦτο πείσονται, φύσιν τοιαύτην παρὰ τοῦ
πεποιηκότος δεξάμενοι. Πῶς δ᾽ ἂν ἀγαθὸς εἰκότως κληθείη τῆς κακίας ὁ

doth St Augustine agree in his book entitled *de Vera Rel.*
cap. xiii. saying: " The devil, inasmuch as he is an angel, is
not evil; but inasmuch as he is perverse and wicked of his
will: for, setting more by himself than by God, he would not
be in subjection unto him, but, swelling through pride, he fell
from his chief essence and excellent being[1]." And again, in
his treatise upon Job, xlii.: " Dost thou demand from whence
the devil is? From whence also the other angels are: but the
other angels constantly continued in their obedience; he by
disobedience and pride fell from an angel and became a devil[2]."

The devil is
everlastingly
condemned.

Now that which I affirmed touching those wicked spirits,
who for their revolting and falling away are adjudged to
damnation, I see it denied of some, who promise to condemned spirits redemption from their punishments a little
before the judgment-day. But against these very many
doctors of the church have disputed, all and every one of
them condemning with one voice an opinion which the scrip-

ποιητής; πῶς δὲ δίκαιος ὁ φύσιν κολάζων ἀγαθόν τι δρᾶσαι μὴ δυναμένην,
ἀλλὰ τοῖς τῆς κακίας πεπεδημένην δεσμοῖς; Ἀλλὰ δίκαιον ἴσμεν τὸν τῶν
ὅλων Θεὸν, καὶ δικαιοσύνης πηγήν· οὔκουν ἀδίκως κολάσει τοὺς δαίμονας καὶ
τὸν ἐκείνων ἡγούμενον. Καὶ ἀγαθῶν ἐπιστάμεθα δημιουργὸν τὸν ἀγαθὸν
Θεὸν παρὰ τῶν εὖ φρονούντων ἁπάντων ὀνομαζόμενον. Οὔκουν ἐδημιούρ-
γησε φύσιν δρᾶσαι μὲν οὐδὲν ἀγαθὸν δυναμένην, κακίαν δὲ μόνην παρὰ γνώμην
ὠδίνουσαν. Εἰ δὲ μήτε φύσιν πονηρὰν ἐδημιούργησεν ὁ Θεὸς, (ἀγαθῶν γάρ
ἐστιν ὡς ἀγαθὸς ποιητής,) μήτε ἀδίκως κολάζειν ἀνέχεται, (δίκαιος γάρ ἐστι
καὶ δικαιοσύνης νομοθέτης,) κολάζει δὲ τὸν διάβολον καὶ τοὺς ὑπ' ἐκείνῳ
τελοῦντας· γνώμῃ ἄρα πονηρὸς ὁ διάβολος καὶ οἱ τῆς ἐκείνου συμμορίας.
ὥσπερ γὰρ τὸν ἄνθρωπον ἀγαθὸν ἐξ ἀρχῆς ἀγαθὸς ἐδημιούργησεν ὁ Θεὸς,
αὐθαιρέτῳ δὲ γνώμῃ οἱ μὲν ἐφύλαξαν ἀκήρατον ἣν ἔλαβον φύσιν, οἱ δὲ ἐπὶ
τὸ χεῖρον ἀπέκλιναν, καὶ τοὺς θείους χαρακτῆρας διέφθειρον, καὶ τοὺς θεοειδεῖς
θηριώδεις ἀπέφηναν· οὕτως ὁ διάβολος καὶ τῶν δαιμόνων τὸ στῖφος, σὺν
τοῖς ἄλλοις ἀσωμάτοις γενόμενοι, τὴν μὲν ἐκείνων περὶ τὸν δεσπότην Θεὸν
οὐκ ἐζήλωσαν εὔνοιαν, τὸ δὲ τοῦ τύφου καὶ τῆς ἀλαζονείας εἰσδεξάμενοι
πάθος, ἐπὶ τὸ χεῖρον ἐτράπησαν, καὶ τῆς προτέρας ἐξέπεσον λήξεως.—Theodoret. Hæret. Fab. Lib. v. cap. 8. p. 269. Tom. iv. Lut. Par. 1642.]

[1 Ipse (diabolus) in quantum angelus est, non est malus, sed in
quantum perversus propria voluntate... Ille autem angelus magis seipsum quam Deum diligendo subditus ei esse noluit, et intumuit per
superbiam, et a summa essentia defecit et lapsus est.—August. de Vera
Relig. cap. 13. Opp. Tom. i. fol. 149. col. 3. Par. 1532.]

[2 Quæritis autem fortasse, unde ipse diabolus? Inde utique unde
et ceteri angeli: sed et ceteri angeli in sua obedientia perstiterunt;
ille inobediendo et superbiendo lapsus est angelus, et factus est diabolus.—Id. Expos. in Evang. Joan. Tract. 42. Opp. Tom. ix.]

tures long ago condemned. For the judge in the end of the
world, pronouncing definitive sentence against Satan and all
the wicked, shall say : " Depart from me, ye cursed, into ever- Matt. xxv.
lasting fire, which is prepared for the devil and his angels."
And by and by the apostle and holy evangelist, a witness of
the truth, doth add: "And these shall go into everlasting
punishment, but the righteous into life everlasting." For in
Mark the Lord also said: " In hell their worm dieth not, Mark ix.
and the fire is not quenched." And in John in more plain
and pithy words he saith: " They that have done good shall John v.
come forth unto the resurrection of life, and they that have
done evil unto the resurrection of condemnation." He doth not
say, they shall go either into life or into condemnation, but
into the resurrection either of life or condemnation, that is,
to remain everlastingly in life or death. For Daniel, of whom
the Lord borrowed these words, hath said: "And many of Dan. xii.
them that sleep in the dust of the earth shall awake; some to
everlasting life, and some to shame and perpetual contempt."
For John the apostle saith, that the smoke of those that are Rev. xiv.
condemned and thrown headlong into hell for evermore shall
ascend up. It is certain therefore, that the condemnation of
the wicked shall be altogether without end and everlasting.

Furthermore, in calling the revolting angels spirits, we Devils are
do not understand by spirit the wicked affection of the heart, substances.
or the quality or passion of the mind, or corruption and sin.
For the world is not without some which think the devil is
nothing else but a mischievous man, or a mischievous and sinful
commotion or outrage of the mind[3]. By spirits therefore we
understand spiritual substances, endued with feeling and understanding. For in the first chapter of Job Satan came and Job i.
shewed himself among the children (or servants) of God, speaking with the Lord. The gospel also reporteth unto us, that devils,
being cast out of a man, entered into the herd of swine, and Matt. viii.
drowned them in the depth of the sea or lake of Gaderen[4].
Moreover the gospel recordeth, that the devil sinned from John viii.
the beginning, that he continued not in the truth, that he is a
liar and a murderer. Judas maketh mention that the angel [Jude, 9.]
fought with the devil. In Mark the devils cry out, and say :
" What have we to do with thee, thou Jesus of Nazareth? art Mark i.

[3 See above, p. 330, note 3.]
[4 See Bulling. Comment. in Matth. Lib. iv. fol. 88. Tigur. 1542.]

thou come to destroy us?" But yet for all that our Saviour,

Matt. xxv. being already appointed and made judge, shall say to the devils: "Go into the everlasting fire." All which testimonies agree to substances by themselves subsisting, and not to qualities. Devils therefore are spiritual substances. But what

What manner of bodies they be which the devils take. bodies they be which they oftentimes take, and in which they appear unto men, no man I think can perfectly tell: which also we told you a little before, when we entreated of the bodies which good angels took. For truly that devils put on bodies and shapes differing from their own, the history of Samuel raised

1 Sam. xxviii. up by a witch manifestly proveth. It was not Samuel that was raised from the dead, but the captain-coiner of lies, counterfeiting Samuel, deceived king Saul[1]. And Paul witnesseth that

2 Cor. xi. Satan doth transform himself into an angel of light. Histories also declare, that the devil is a marvellous juggling deceiver, in taking on him divers forms and shapes.

The devil is quick, crafty, and mighty. And as I said of good angels, that they are speedy in their ministery, without burden or lets; so there is no doubt that devils in their kind and work are well prepared. For the scriptures declare, that they have a thousand shifts, wonderful craftiness and subtilty, and that their knowledge is passing quick and reacheth very far; finally, that they are very ready and never weary to attempt and perform all things. They pass through the whole world with exceeding swiftness, they handle all their matters very craftily; and therefore are marvellous names shadowing out their force and

[Rev. xii. 9. John xiv. 30. Eph. ii. 2. 1 Pet. v. 8.] power allotted unto them. For he is called "Satan the old serpent, a deceiver, the prince of this world, the prince of darkness, which hath power over the air, a roaring lion." Of which and of other not unlike I will speak anon more at

An infinite rout of devils.
Mark xvi. large, when I have first told you this, that there are an infinite rout of devils. For seven devils are cast out of Mary

Matt. xii. Magdalen. That devil of whom Matthew speaketh, being no sooner cast out, museth and consulteth how he may be wholly restored again, taking to him seven other spirits worse than

Mark v. himself. Moreover, in Mark's gospel there is mention made of a legion: for the unclean spirit, being asked of the Lord what his name was, answered, "My name is legion, because we are many." Therefore, when there is mention made of Satan elsewhere in holy scripture, it is not so to be taken, as

[1 Fulke's Defence of Translat. &c. ed. Parker Soc. p. 313.]

though there were either but one substance or person of the
devil; for they are comprehended as the members under the
head, and as particularities under generalities. The scripture
truly elsewhere maketh mention of the prince of the devils;
for the enemies of Christ do often cry out: "He casteth out Mark iii.
devils by the prince of devils." But yet that saying doth not
express what manner of principality that is, and whether
orderly among themselves those evil spirits be distinguished.
And it is certain that all the ungodly are under one head, as
all the godly are under one Christ the Lord. It is certain
that all the devils are of the selfsame corrupt will, bending
all their force only to this end, to be adversaries to God
and hurtful enemies to men. But of the operations, works,
or effects of devils I will speak where I shall by the way
expound[2] their names or attributes.

Corrupt and wicked spirits generally are called devils,
which is as much as if you should say slanderers or false accusers. For διαβολή with the Greeks signifieth slander, &c.;
and the word *devil* is fetched from the Grecians[3]. For he Devil.
soweth slanders in accusing men unto God, and in setting men
at variance between themselves: that now I say nothing how
he goeth about to bring God and his works into suspicion
among men. Therefore he is elsewhere called a liar, and A liar.
the author of lies, and the father of all hypocrites; and
therefore the spring of all errors, heresies, and wickednesses.
And because Judas was an hypocrite, a liar, a false accuser,
and traitor, the Lord rightly gave him the name of a devil. John vi.

The apostle Peter called the devil an adversary. For Satan or an
the Lord also himself called him, "The envious man[4]," which 1 Pet. v.
sowed tares in the Lord's field. For he is the enemy of Matt. xiii.
God and men, setting himself against the will of God, whose
glory also he laboureth to take away, and hindereth the salvation of men, and soweth infinite offences in the Church of
God. And truly the Hebrews call him Satan, whom we call Matt. iv.
an adversary. That word is translated unto men. For in
that Peter set himself against the counsel and purpose of
God, he heareth this voice of the Lord: "Get thee behind [Matt. xvi.
23.]
me, Satan." And David also said to his nephew[5] Abisai, [2 Sam. xix.
22.]

[2 Rather, when I shall have expounded.]
[3 See Vol. II. p. 118, note 1.]　　　[4 inimicum hominem, Lat.]
[5 ad nepotem ex sorore, Lat.: 1 Chron. ii. 16.]

the son of Zeruia: "What have I to do with you, ye sons of Zeruia, that this day ye should be adversaries unto me?" For Abisai gainsayed the counsel and decree of David.

The devil is called *dæmon*, to wit, knowing, crafty, and cunning in many things, ἀπὸ τοῦ δαίω, which signifies, I know. For Plato truly in *Cratylo*, according to the opinion of Hesiodus, doth think that devils, whom we commonly call by this word dæmons, are called and as it were named δαήμονας, that is, wise, prudent, and knowing[1]. Hereunto the word

Gen. iii. serpent must be referred. "The serpent," saith the scripture, "was subtiler than all the beasts of the field." Therefore did the devil choose the serpent to be his dwelling-place, by whom he might put his guileful devises in practice and

A serpent and dragon. deceive our first parents. For he is called the deceiver, the beguiler, and seducer of the world, the old serpent and dragon. For what seducing soever there is in the world, what wicked devices and deceitful practices, they flow from this one fountain of all his mischief. In profane writers this word is used in a far contrary signification. For Socrates in Plato saith: "I affirm that every man is dæmon, that is to say, wise, whosoever is good, and that he is *dæmoniacus*, that is to say, wise and happy, both alive and dead[2]." Wherefore it is a thing very much and often used of Homer to adorn noble personages with this name[3]. But in the history of the gospel *dæmoniaci* are such as are possessed with a devil.

1 Tim. iv. Paul, in his first Epistle to Timothy, reduceth and draweth the whole body of deceits and doctrines coloured with a shew of false wisdom unto this head.

1 Pet. v. A roaring lion. St Peter saith: "Be sober and watch, for your adversary the devil, as a roaring lion, walketh about, seeking whom he may devour; whom resist stedfastly in faith." By the lion he shadoweth out unto us the nature or disposition of the devil; for the devil hath exceeding great strength, he is full of greedy raveny and most cruel fierceness: whereupon

A murderer. [John viii. 44.] he is also called of some a cruel beast. The Lord calleth him a murderer: for he inspired into Cain and all manslayers horrible murders; and at this day also he soundeth the alarum to all wars, to all broiling battles, to all slaughters and se-

---

[1 Plat. Cratyl. p. 226. Vol. iv. ed. Bekker. Lond. 1826.]
[2 Plat. Cratyl. ubi supr.]
[3 Hom. Il. a'. 222. 561. λ'. 480, &c.]

ditions; to be short, he kindleth wrath, he soweth hatred, and nourisheth envy. He is named "a tempter;" for he is A tempter. always egging men to mischief, sparing nothing whatsoever he thinketh can entice and draw us to things most wicked.

In the history of the gospel, and in the writings of the An evil and unclean spirit. apostles, the devil hath well-nigh[4] the name of an unclean, of a mischievous or malignant, of a filthy and wicked spirit. For he fell not from his pureness only through his own fault, in which he was first created of the most pure God; but even now also he is delighted with unpureness, and allureth all men to uncleanness. From this master of mischief proceed all filthy lusts, all whoredoms, adulteries, all excess, drunkenness and surfeiting, all beastliness and vanity, pride and arrogancy, &c.

Now the devil also in the gospel is called Beelzebub, because that sometime they of Accaron in Palestine, thinking they worshipped God, worshipped in very deed the devil. St Paul saith: "What agreement hath Christ with Belial?" [2 Cor. vi. 15.] He setteth Belial against Christ, to wit, the devil against God. But Moses put the cogitation of Belial for a wicked and evil thought[5]. Therefore the devil is wicked and ungodly, rebellious and obstinate against God. For they say that Belial signifieth altogether as much as if a man would say, lawless, without yoke and without discipline[6]. There are some also which think that in the Book of Job the devil is figured or signified by Behemoth and Leviathan. Job xl. and xli. chapter.

St Paul giveth the devils divers names, saying, that the godly hath battle "against principalities and powers, against worldly governors of the darkness of this world[7], against [Eph. ii. 2; vi. 12.] spiritual wickedness in heavenly (places), against the governor that ruleth in the air, against the spirit that now worketh in the children of disobedience:" whom also in another place he calleth "the god of this world." And as God exerciseth his power in the world and in the good for

---

[4 fere, Lat.; generally.]

[5 Deut. xv. 9. "Beware that there be not a thought in thy wicked (marg. Belial) heart,—that there be not a poynte of Belial." Coverdale. 1535.]

[6 Hebræis componitur vox (Belial) a בְלִי et יַעַל, significans vel absque jugo vel absque utilitate.—Bulling. Comment. in loc. cit.]

[7 adversus principes mundi et tenebrarum seculi hujus, Lat.]

the most part by good angels, who for that cause, I said, are called principalities and powers; so because the same God of his just judgment doth suffer the devil to have rule over the wicked, they are rightly called principalities and powers: not that God delivereth unto him the mere and chiefest rule, (for all power belongeth to God only;) but because he suffereth him to execute his tyranny. For he plainly saith that he is the " prince of the world," to wit, of the wicked ; for by interpretation it followeth, " He is the prince of the darkness of this world :" and who knoweth not that in the scriptures darkness doth signify ignorance, blindness, unbelief, ungodliness, and wickedness ; and, to be short, ungodly men which are drowned in these vices ? And again, there is added that which declareth the true meaning : " Which worketh in the children of disobedience." Therefore the faithful and obedient, who are in the kingdom of Christ and not in the kingdom of the devil, are exempted from this rule and government.

The god of this world.

Neither is Satan called god upon any other consideration ; for there is added, " of this world." For in very deed the devil is not a god; but because there are found in the world certain madmen who take him for god, he hath the name of God. The blessed father Augustine expounded this no otherwise ; for in his treatise upon John xxv. he saith : " God forbid we should think the devil were so called the prince of the world, that we should believe that he is able to rule over heaven and earth: but the world (for he is called the prince of this world) is said to be in wicked men, which are dispersed throughout the whole compass of the earth[1]." And again the same Augustine in his first chapter

The prince of this world cast out.

de Agone Christiano saith: " The prince of this world is cast out; not that he is cast out of the world, but out of their minds which cleave to the word of God and love not the world whereof he is prince, because he hath dominion over them which love temporal goods, which are contained in this visible world : not for that he is lord of this world, but prince of those concupiscences whereby everything is co-

[1 Absit autem ut diabolum mundi principem ita dictum existimemus, ut eum cœlo et terræ dominari posse credamus: sed mundus appellatur in malis hominibus, qui toto orbe terrarum diffusi sunt.— August. Tract. in Joan. 25. Opp. Tom. IX. fol. 78. col. 2. Par. 1532.]

veted that is transitory. By this concupiscence the devil reigneth in man, and holdeth his heart in possession[2]." The same doctor in his treatise upon John lii. asketh the question, " Whether Satan were not cast out of the minds of the prophets and patriarchs, since it is reported in the gospel that he is cast out by Christ?" And he maketh answer: "Verily, he is cast out quite. How therefore is it said, 'He shall now be cast out?' How think we, but because that which came to pass in very few men is even now foretold that it shall come to pass shortly in many and mighty people; as that saying, 'But the Holy Ghost was not yet given, because Jesus was not yet glorified,' may have the like question and the like answer? For the abundance of spiritual grace was not given as yet, which afterward was given[3]." Thus far he.

Furthermore, when the apostle saith, that " we fight against spiritual wickednesses in heavenly places:" by heavenly he meaneth not heavenly joys, placing the devils in heaven again; but the air, that is, the lower part of the world, yea, and the world itself. For he saith elsewhere: "According to the spirit that ruleth in the air." And truly the princes of this world are in the air, above, beneath, and about us, assaulting us on every side. Otherwise, neither heaven nor the lower region of the air is subject to the rule

Prince of the world.

[2 Princeps hujus mundi missus est foras; non quia extra mundum missus est, ... sed foras ab animis eorum qui cohærent verbo Dei, et non diligunt mundum cujus ille princeps est; quia dominatur eis qui diligunt temporalia bona, quæ hoc visibili mundo continentur. Non quia ipse dominus est hujus mundi, sed princeps cupiditatum earum, quibus concupiscitur omne quod transit. .. Per hanc cupiditatem regnat in homine diabolus, et cor ejus tenet.—Id. de Agon. Christ. cap. 1. Opp. Tom. III. fol. 162. col. 1.]

[3 Sed dicit aliquis, Nunquid de cordibus patriarcharum et prophetarum veterumque justorum non ejectus est (diabolus) foras? Ejectus est plane. Quomodo ergo dictum est, Nunc ejicietur foras? Quomodo putamus, nisi quia tunc quod in hominibus paucissimis factum est, nunc in multis magnisque populis jam mox futurum esse prædictum est? Sic et illud quod dictum est, Spiritus autem nondum erat datus, quia Jesus nondum fuerat glorificatus, potest similem habere quæstionem et similem solutionem ... Spiritus nondum erat datus, id est, illa abundantia gratiæ spiritalis, qua congregati linguis omnium loquerentur, &c.—Id. Tract. in Joan. 52. Opp. Tom. IX. fol. 78. coll. 1, 2.]

of devils, that therein they may do what they will, or abuse it as they list; but so far forth as God of his just judgment shall permit. For in this disputation we must always hold for a confessed and undoubted truth, that our Lord God is king and governor of all creatures, and that he keepeth still his dominion over all creatures, and exerciseth the same after a most just and equal manner.

The opera-
tions of the
devil. And although out of all these things might be gathered how great and what manner of operation the devil's is, yet thereunto will I add somewhat more, lest anything should seem to be wanting in this matter. In the description of the devil I drew into two heads all his effects, works, or operations. For devils are adversaries to God and enemies to men, whose whole endeavours and drifts tend to the despising of God, and to the deceiving and destruction of men. The sum therefore is this: They bend all their force to the contempt of God and destruction of men. And that their power to hurt is not small, and their understanding also quick to bring all their purposes to effect, we have heard once or twice already. That they have a will to do hurt, there is no cause why any man should doubt. For the Lord said to

Luke xxii. his disciples in the gospel: "Behold, Satan hath earnestly
Matt. xxvi. desired to sift you as it were wheat." And again: "Watch and pray, lest ye enter into temptation." And St Peter saith:
1 Pet. v. "Your adversary, as a roaring lion, rangeth up and down, seeking whom he may devour." And that he withstandeth God, and with continual labour gainsayeth God, and stirreth up all creatures to the hating and despising of God, the scripture doth everywhere testify. He did wickedly instil into the minds of our first parents an opinion altogether unworthy of God, as though maliciously he did envy at their
Gen. iii. blessed state. For he said by the serpent: "Hath God said ye shall not eat of that tree?" And anon: "Ye shall not die the death. For God doth know, that the same day that ye eat thereof your eyes shall be opened, and ye shall be as gods, knowing good and evil." Unto which deceitful words when they gave credit, they themselves perished, and drew with them the whole world into ruin and destruction. Neither at this day verily ceaseth he to slander and speak evil as well of God himself as also of his works, to the intent that he might draw us together with him into the hating

of God, into distrust and desperation, and to everlasting destruction; for he envieth us our salvation whereunto we are
ordained by Christ. But it is better to speak somewhat more
distinctly of this thing.

Satan hurts men in their minds, in their bodies, and in
their goods. For he enticeth and provoketh our minds to
sin. Furthermore he also troubleth the minds of men, and
driveth them into an outrage; and being out of quiet in this
their outrage, he miserably vexeth, tormenteth, and dispatcheth[1] them. Hereupon thou mayest read that some
physicians call this madness or outrage an evil spirit or
wicked devil. But he diversely plagueth their bodies, chiefly
with diseases. We have the most holy man Job for an example. In the gospel after St Luke it is said, that that Luke xiii.
woman, which was bowed together, was bound by Satan
eighteen years. Again, in the gospel according to St Mark
we read of a child which had a dumb spirit: "And whenso- Mark ix.
ever he taketh him, he teareth him, and he foameth, and
gnasheth with his teeth, and pineth away;" and casting himself on the ground, lieth grovelling. This selfsame evil spirit
taketh away from men their goods, wasteth and diminisheth
their substance and worldly wealth. Which thing again is
manifest in the history of Job and of the gospel: for Job
is spoiled of all his substance, Satan so ordering the matter,
by soldiers and robbers. The herd of swine also, being
drowned and strangled in the sea, wrought great loss to the
Gergesites; and, being violently carried away of the devils,
were tumbled headlong into the sea. Furthermore, this
mischievous miscreant in accomplishing these things doth
somewhat by himself and by wicked angels his fellows, and
somewhat by other creatures. By himself he worketh outwardly and inwardly, by tempting and provoking men. For
he casteth before our eyes counterfeit and deceitful shapes;
changing himself into an angel of light, he windeth himself
into the minds of men. He speaketh unto us, setting before
us gay promises and most grievous threatenings, howbeit all
of them coloured with deceits and lies. For oftentimes he
bringeth reasons, probable indeed and apparent, yea, and
places of scripture at a blush very agreeable, but yet maliciously wrested to his own purpose. And by this means he

[1 conficit, Lat.]

either hindereth and maimeth true faith in the minds of men; or else he taketh it away and utterly overthroweth it, and by and by possesseth them wholly, and driveth them into most certain perdition. So it is said that when he had entered into Judas' heart, he cast him wholly headlong into everlasting destruction. The heart of man is open unto God only, for he only is the searcher of the heart and reins. But the devil, by circumventing men with his guileful practices; and by putting wicked persuasions into their hearts, is said to enter into men's hearts. And he worketh against man by other creatures also, as by elements, when he raiseth fire, winds, waters, hail, and such like calamities against us. Furthermore, he stirreth up men against us, our friends to vex and betray us, and our enemies to consume and bring us to our end with persecutions, battles, and bloodsheds. The history of Job yet again beareth witness of these things. Whereunto thou mayest reckon persecutions laid upon the worshippers of God. Now also he eggeth false prophets and enchanters against us. Whereunto belong deceitful jugglings and all kinds of sorcery and witchcraft; which the works of the sorcerers of Egypt, and of Simon, and the place of Moses in Deut. xiii. testify to be most effectual. Hereunto chiefly belong false miracles and corrupt answers or oracles. By these truly in times past he did very much hurt to the church of God, as histories testify, neither ceaseth he at this day to do hurt: which thing experience itself doth teach and verify.

For though it be certain that Satan is not cast out by the power of Satan; yet one giveth place to another for a time, to this end, that they may the more easily deceive men, and obtain a kingdom. Christ truly and the apostle Paul foretold, that even the last times should be wonderfully bewitched with deceitful signs and powers. Most evident places touching that thing are extant in Matthew xxiv. 2 Thessalonians ii. chapter. More might be spoken, dearly beloved, and that at large, concerning the operations or workings of the devil; but I trust these things being gathered together in brevity are sufficient, and give occasion to muse of higher things.

But let no man so understand these things, as if the devil were able to do all things, and that what he will he can also

John xiii.

Matt. xii.

do by and by. For his power is definite, or limited and restrained, so that he cannot do so much as he would: otherwise all things had been overthrown and perished long ago. Therefore not without consideration I added in the describing of the devil, that he is subject to God; for he can do nothing without God's permission. Now God permitteth him, either to exercise and try the patience of those that are his, and to hasten their salvation; as it is manifest in the history of Job, and in the words of Paul to the Corinthians, saying, " Lest I should be exalted out of measure through the abundance of the revelations, there was given unto me a prick to the flesh, the messenger of Satan to buffet me." Neither is it doubtful, that in most grievous torments of persecutions he exalteth many notable martyrs, yea, and at this day doth and in times past hath exalted such, unto glory and everlasting rest. Or else he giveth the devil leave to execute violence and cruelty upon men, by that means to chastise their wickedness or to punish their unbelief. For verily the devils are the instruments of God's wrath, to execute his vengeance. For Paul saith: " The coming of antichrist is after the working of Satan, in all power, and signs, and wonders of lying, and in all deceiveableness of unrighteousness in them that perish; because they received not the love of truth, that they might be saved. And therefore God shall send them strong delusion, that they should believe lies; that all they might be damned which believed not the truth, but had pleasure in unrighteousness." And this in a manner is the strength and power of sorcery and enchanting, which is feeble in the faithful.

Wherefore there is no cause why any man should miserably fear the devil: " But rather sanctify ye (saith Esay) the Lord of hosts[1]; let him be your fear and your reverence." Some say that certain nations of the East worshipped the devil for this cause, that he should not hurt them[2]. But these are stark staring mad. For if it be not God's will, which even now I began to tell you, or if he give no leave, Satan cannot touch so much as a hair of thine. For he could not enter into the herd of swine, which were feeding nigh the lake

The power of the devil is definite or limited.

2 Cor. xii.

2 Thess. ii.

We must fight manfully against the devil, but we must not fear him.

[1 ipsum, Lat. omitted; himself.]
[2 Selden de Diis Syris. Syntag. ii. cap. 6. et Add. Beyeri. p. 134. Amstel. 1680.]

Genezaret at Gadara[1], and destroy them, but by the Lord's permission. St Augustine also, expounding the thirty-second Psalm, allegeth in these words the history of Job: "What could the devil himself do? durst he take away one silly sheep from the holy man Job, before he said, Lay thy hand on him, that is to say, give me power? He was willing, but God did not suffer him. When God gave him leave, then he was able: therefore the devil was not able, but God which gave him leave. Therefore Job being well instructed did not say, as we now are wont to say, The Lord gave, and the devil hath taken away; but, The Lord gave, and the Lord hath taken away[2]." And these things do exceedingly comfort the godly in temptations; who understand that nothing can happen to them without God's permission, and that he permitteth nothing but that which maketh for our amendment and salvation, and therefore that we are always preserved by the providence and bountifulness of God. For whatsoever hath hitherto been spoken concerning the power and workings of the devils pertained not hitherto, to dash us out of courage and cast us down; but to make us more vigilant or watchful. The Lord, that overcame the devil and sheweth us the way to overcome him, commandeth us to watch. For therefore he encountered with Satan the first, second, and third time, to instruct us how we should fight against the enemy of mankind. He overcame him for us, that we should not despair of ability and power easily to overcome him, since he is already weakened and wounded. By faith, doubtless, we shall overcome him: for by faith we are knit unto Christ, and by faith we draw the Spirit of Christ, by the force and virtue whereof we shall triumph. Truly for that cause St Peter willeth us "to resist by faith." St Paul, exhorting us unto this conflict, and furnishing us with excellent complete

Matt. iv.

1 John v.

1 Pet. v.

[1 prope paludem Gadarenam apud Gadaram, Lat. See above, p. 353, note 4.]

[2 Quid ipse diabolus? Ausus est vel unam oviculam tollere viro sancto Job, nisi prius diceret, Mitte manum tuam, hoc est, da potestatem? Ille volebat, sed ille non sinebat. Quando ille permisit, ille potuit: non ergo ille potuit, sed qui permisit. Ideo bene eruditus ipse Job non ait, sicut jam commemorare vobis solemus, Dominus dedit, et diabolus abstulit; sed, Dominus dedit, et Dominus abstulit.—August. Enarrat. pars 2. in Psal. xxxii. Opp. Tom. vii. fol. 46. col. 1.]

armour, saith: "Take unto you the whole armour of God, Ephes. vi. that ye may be able to resist in the evil day, and, having finished all things, to stand fast. Stand therefore, having your loins girt about with the truth, and having on the breast-plate of righteousness, and your feet shod that you may be prepared to the gospel of peace; above all things taking the shield of faith, wherewith you may quench all the fiery darts of that wicked. And take the helmet of salvation, and the sword of the Spirit, which is the word of God, praying always in all prayers and supplication in the spirit[3]," &c. Whereunto that also belongeth, which the same apostle witnesseth: "God doth not suffer us to be tempted above that we 1 Cor. x. are able to bear, but shall with the temptation make a way to escape." Let us therefore reverence this God; let us beseech him, that through his power and might we may overcome. Amen.

OF THE REASONABLE SOUL OF MAN; AND OF HIS MOST CERTAIN SALVATION AFTER THE DEATH OF HIS BODY.

THE TENTH SERMON.

ALL men do confess that the reasonable soul of man hath affinity or likeness with spirits; neither is there any wise man, as I think, which doth deny that the knowledge of the reasonable soul of man, whereof the scripture teacheth so many things, and that too so diligently, is most wholesome and necessary to all the godly. The order therefore, the profit, and the very necessity also of things[4] do require, that I speak somewhat likewise of the reasonable soul of man: wherein I will follow the plainness of the scripture and of the interpreters thereof, leaving physical or natural points unto them to be expounded unto whom it belongeth by duty and profession; saving that we will so far deal in them as we cannot want them in this discourse of ours. The holy scripture and the interpreters thereof neither move curious questions of the soul of man; neither do they satisfy curious heads, when they desire to know those things which cannot be declared,

[3 Erasmus' translation.]
[4 Rather, The order of things therefore, profit, and very necessity.]

or, if they could, yet it would always seem unto them that nothing were unto them more aptly spoken; for they always stagger, they are always learning and yet doubt, they never come to the knowledge of the truth with a quiet mind, they never abide in the plain truth when it is found, they search after other and many more and subtiler matters than they understand. But we know that all things which are necessary and for our salvation are simply and plainly delivered in the holy scriptures, and that we must simply, godlily, and religiously rest in them : therefore those things that are not delivered in them touching the matter of our salvation, we know that they are not to be sought after of us, and that they hinder not our salvation if we be ignorant of them.

The word anima (which we call soul) is diversely taken.

Gen. i.

The word *anima*, which we call soul, is diversely taken in the holy scripture. First of all *anima*, the soul, is taken for every living thing; for Moses bringeth in the Lord speaking, "Let the earth bring forth living creature[1] after his kind, cattle, worm, and beast of the earth after his kind." For who knoweth not that there are reckoned three kinds or parts (give me leave so to speak for instruction's sake) or three principal powers of the soul? For there is the soul vegetative which worketh in plants; there is the soul sensitive, which is not without the soul vegetative, and it giveth life to brute beasts and other creatures endued with life and feeling[2]; there is also the reasonable soul wherewith men are endued, which is furnished with many powers or abilities, and comprehendeth both the other. Hereof *anima*, the soul, is taken in the scripture for breath which men draw in and let go again, and also for the life of man, or of a living creature. Thus we read, *Anima ejus* &c., "His life is in him :" and, "I will do thee no more harm (saith Saul to David), because (*anima mea*) my life was precious in thine eyes this day." The Grecians call *anima*, the soul, ψυχὴν, as it were ἀναψυχήν, because by drawing breath it refresheth. The Hebricians call it *Næphæsch*, of comforting[3]. Again, *anima*, the soul, is taken in the scriptures for the thing itself that hath life, yea, even for any, or rather for the whole man. For it is said in the law : "The soul that worketh with a

The soul is breath and life.

[Acts xx. 10.]
[1 Sam. xxvi. 21.]

Soul is taken for man.

Levit. xx.

[1 animam viventem, Lat.]
[2 and other—feeling, not in Lat.]
[3 a refocillando, Lat.]

spirit, or that is a soothsayer, shall die." Likewise in Paul we read : "Let every soul be subject to the higher power." Rom. xiii. And again, in Genesis, the king of Sodom saith to Abraham : "Give me the souls, and take the substance or goods to thy- Gen. xiv. self." For the scripture is wont to name the whole by a part : for as by the soul he means the whole man, rehearsing the nobler part, so by flesh also he signifies the whole baser part. Moreover since man and also other living creatures Soul a desire. have an appetitive or desiring soul, soul is used in the scripture for affection, will, desire, or lust. For Ezekiel saith, "They Ezek. vii. shall not satisfy their souls" (in Dutch, *Sy werden iren glust nit bussen*), "neither shall their bellies be filled." Lastly, *anima*, Soul is the spirit of man. the soul, signifieth the reasonable soul of man : whereof we will entreat (God assisting) at this present. Yet here I cannot dissemble, that among very famous writers there is controversy *de anima, et animo*, about the soul and the mind, whether they are one and the selfsame, or diverse ; and that there are reasons on both sides. They that make a difference between The soul and mind. them say, that by the soul we live, and that with the mind we understand : which thing Lactantius saith in his 18th chapter *de Opificio Dei*[4]. I know that all the best and most approved writers use them both indifferently, and take the one for the other.

For we must not think that there are two souls in man. That there is but one soul. For very well have the school definitions[5] defined, uttering these words in the fifteenth chapter : "We do not say that there are two souls in one man, as Jacobus and certain of the Syrians write; one natural, whereby the body hath life, and is mingled with blood; the other spiritual, which ministereth reason : but we say there is one and the selfsame soul in man, which both quickeneth the body with his fellowship, and ordereth himself by his own reason[6]." Therefore we do not That there is a soul.

[4 Sequitur alia et ipsa inextricabilis quæstio : Idemne sit anima et animus; an vero aliud sit illud quo vivimus, aliud autem quo sentimus et sapimus.—Lactant. de Opif. Dei. cap. 18.]

[5 definitiones ecclesiasticæ, Lat.]

[6 Neque duas animas esse dicimus in uno homine, sicut Jacobus et alii Syrorum scribunt; unam animalem, qua animetur corpus et immixta sit sanguini, et alteram spiritalem, quæ rationem ministret: sed dicimus unam esse eandemque animam in homine, quæ et corpus sua societate vivificet, et semetipsam sua ratione disponat.—August. de Eccles. dogm. cap. 15. Opp. Tom. III. fol. 42. col. 4.]

think that there is any consideration to be had of them which altogether deny that there is a soul; for these are as mad as they which deny that the sun shineth. For all of us do see and feel the sun: as also we live by the benefit of the soul.

What the soul is.

Furthermore, what the reasonable soul of man is, the wise heads of this world could not as yet with one agreement define. For they so differ that a man shall hardly find two which say one thing; and there are opinions not a few contrary between themselves. What, do not the old interpreters of the scriptures doubtingly proceed in defining the soul? Lactantius, in his book *de Opificio Dei*, denieth that man can attain to the reason and nature of the soul[1]. Therefore nothing at all did they err from the truth, which thought the soul could be comprehended in no absolute definition, wherein his nature might be expressed throughly and at the full; yet that the nature or disposition of the same might after a sort be shadowed out, and that by the works or actions thereof, and by such qualities as the scripture doth attribute. There are some therefore which have said, that the soul is the spirit of life, created after the image of God, and breathed into the body of man. One there is which describes it thus: The soul is a spirit, whereby the body to which it is coupled doth live, made apt to the knowledge of God through love, and hereby meet to be joined with him unto everlasting blessedness. Another defineth it after this sort: A reasonable soul is an understanding spirit, one part of the substance of man; neither dieth it when it is departed from the body, but is immortal. Cassiodore defineth it: The soul of man is created of God, a spiritual and peculiar substance, which quickeneth the body whose own it is, reasonable indeed and immortal[2]. We will set down a description fetched from the scripture, to be weighed and considered upon of the godly, and to direct and rule this our whole discourse. The soul is a spiritual substance, poured of God into man's body, that, being joined thereunto,

[1 Quid autem sit anima, nondum inter philosophos convenit, nec unquam fortasse conveniet. Etenim alii sanguinem esse dixerunt, alii ignem, alii ventum, &c.—Lactant. de Opif. Dei. cap. 17.]

[2 Anima hominis est a Deo creata, spiritalis propriaque substantia, sui corporis vivificatrix, rationabilis quidem et immortalis.—Cassiodor. Opp. de Anima. p. 286. Par. 1579.]

it might quicken and direct the same; but being dissevered
from the body, it should not die but live immortal for ever.

Some deny that the soul is a substance; for they contend that it is nothing else than the power of life in man, and
indeed[3] a certain quality.   But the holy scripture acknowledgeth that the soul is a subtance subsisting; for the Lord
in the gospel witnesseth, that a soul may be tormented in
hell: which forthwith by the selfsame authority of the
gospel is shewed as it were to be viewed with our eyes, in
the soul of the rich glutton.   The same Lord which cannot
lie said to the thief, "To day shalt thou be with me in
Paradise:" which words cannot be expounded of any other
part in the thief than of the soul; for his body was nailed,
and did hang on the cross.   Whereupon also the apostle and
evangelist saw "under the altar the souls of them that were
slain for the word of God."   He heard them "crying with
a loud voice, and saying: How long tarriest thou, Lord,
which art holy and true, to judge, and to avenge our blood
on them that dwell on the earth?"   The same John saw
long white garments given to every one of the souls, these
words being therewithal spoken of the Lord: "Rest yet for
a little season, until your fellow-servants, and your brethren
that shall be killed as ye are, shall be fulfilled."   All which
verily agree not to qualities, but to substances which have
their being: therefore the souls of men are substances.   Which
thing that they might most plainly and pithily express,
certain ecclesiastical writers, I think, have set down that the
souls of men are bodily, that is, substances of their kind,
having their proper being.   Neither do I think, dearly
beloved, I shall be tedious unto you, if I recite word for
word that which St Augustine hath reasoned of this matter
on both parts in his epistle to St Hierome, which is in order
the twenty-eighth, saying: "That the soul is bodiless, though
it be hard to persuade it to the duller sort, yet I confess that
I am so persuaded.   But that I may not move controversy
about a word to no purpose, I will willingly be silent; because
where there is no doubt of the thing, there is no need to
strive about the name.   If every substance or essence be a
body, or if that which after some sort is in itself is more
aptly called something, then the soul is a body.   But if you

Marginal notes: That souls are substances. / Luke xxiii. / Rev. vi.

[3 adeoque, Lat.; and so.]

will call that only a bodiless nature, which is altogether unchangeable and is wholly everywhere, then the soul is a body, because the soul is no some such thing. Furthermore, if nothing be a body but that which with some length, breadth, and height resteth, or is moved in space of place, that the greater part thereof taketh the greater room and the lesser part the lesser room, and be less in part than in the whole, then the soul is not a body. For that which giveth the power of life unto the body is stretched through the whole body, not by local spreading of itself, but by a certain lively extending of itself. For the whole soul is present in all and every part of the body at once, and not lesser in the lesser parts nor greater in the greater parts; but in some places more vehement and quick, in some more remiss and faint, and in all it is the whole and in every part the whole. For that whole soul which in some parts of the body feeleth not, in some other parts where it feeleth it doth wholly feel in itself, and not only in some part of itself. For where any part of the quick flesh is pricked with a sharp thing, although that place be not only not of the whole body, no, not so much almost as seen in the body, yet the whole soul feeleth that pricking; and yet is not that pain that is felt dispersed over all the parts of the body, but 'is only felt where it is. How then cometh that by and by to the whole soul, which is not felt but in one place of the body, but because that the whole soul is there where the smart is felt, and yet leaveth not the other parts of the body that it might be there wholly and all in all? For those parts of the body live also by the presence of the soul, where no such thing is done. If it were so that the grief were in more places than one at once, it should be felt by the whole soul in each place. Therefore the whole soul could not be both in all and in every part of the body, whose own it is, all at once, if it were so spread through those parts as we see bodies are by spaces of places, their lesser parts taking the lesser room and their greater parts the greater room. Wherefore if the soul be to be termed a body, surely it is not such a body as is in substance like the ·earth, or like the water, or the air, or the celestial bodies. For all such bodies are greater in greater places and lesser in lesser places, and nothing of them is wholly in any some part of theirs; but as the parts of the places be, so are they filled with the parts of the bodies. Whereupon the soul is perceived, whether it be a body or whether it is to be called bodiless, to have a certain proper nature, created of a more excellent substance than all the elements of the earthly mould: which cannot be conceived by any phantasy or imagination of bodily shapes which we attain unto by the senses of our flesh, but is understood in the mind and felt in the life[1]." Thus far have I rehearsed Augustine's words.

[1 Incorpoream quoque esse animam, etsi difficile tardioribus persuaderi potest, mihi tamen fateor esse persuasum. Sed ne verbi controversiam vel superfluo faciam, vel merito patiar; quoniam cum de re constat, non est opus certare de nomine: si corpus est omnis substantia vel essentia, vel si quid aptius nuncupatur id quod aliquo modo est in seipso, corpus est anima. Item si eam solam incorpoream placet appellare naturam, quæ summe incommutabilis et ubique tota est, corpus est anima, quoniam tale aliquid ipsa non est. Porro si corpus non est, nisi quod per loci spatium aliqua longitudine, latitudine, altitudine ita sistitur vel movetur, ut majori sui parte majorem locum occupet et breviore breviorem, minusque sit in parte quam in toto, non est corpus anima: per totum quippe corpus quod animat, non locali diffusione, sed quadam vitali intentione porrigitur. Nam per omnes ejus particulas tota simul adest, nec minor in minoribus et in majoribus major, sed alicubi intensius, alicubi remissius, et in omnibus tota et in singulis tota est. Neque enim aliter quod in corpore etiam non toto sentit, tamen tota sentit. Nam cum exiguo puncto in carne viva aliquid tangitur, quamvis locus ille non solum totius corporis non sit, sed vix in corpore videatur, animam tamen totam non latet; neque id quod sentitur per corporis cuncta discurrit, sed ibi tamen sentitur ubi fit. Unde ergo ad totam mox pervenit, quod non in toto fit, nisi quia et ibi tota est ubi fit, nec ut tota ibi sit cetera deserit? Vivunt enim et illa ea præsente ubi nihil tale factum est. Quod si fieret, et utrumque simul fieret, simul utrumque totam pariter non lateret. Proinde et in omnibus simul et in singulis particulis corporis sui tota simul esse non posset, si per illas ita diffunderetur, ut videmus corpora diffusa per spatia locorum minoribus suis partibus minora occupare et amplioribus ampliora. Quapropter si anima corpus esse dicenda est, non est certe corpus, quale terrenum est, nec quale humidum aut aëreum aut æthereum. Omnia quippe talia majora sunt in majoribus locis et minora in minoribus locis, et nihil eorum in aliqua sui parte totum adest, sed ut sunt partes locorum, ita occupantur partibus corporum. Unde intelligitur anima, sive corpus sive incorporea dicenda est, propriam quandam habere naturam, omnibus his mundanæ molis elementis excellentiore substantia creatam; quæ veraciter non possit in aliqua fantasia corporalium imaginum, quas per carnis sensus per-

24—2

The soul is bodiless, or a spirit.

The scripture also aimeth chiefly at this mark[1], to teach that the soul is bodiless; for advisedly and expressly it calleth the same a spirit. For the Lord in the gospel after John saith: "I will put my life from me, and I will take it again. No man taketh it from me, but I put it away of myself." And in the same evangelist you read: "And Jesus said, It is finished: and when he had bowed his head, he gave up the ghost." For he crieth out in another evangelist: "Father, into thy hands I commend my spirit." And Matthew saith: "And Jesus, when he had cried again with a loud voice, yielded up the ghost." Whereunto doubtless may be referred that which we read in the Acts of the Apostles of the first martyr, Stephen: "And they stoned Stephen, calling on and saying, Lord Jesu, receive my spirit." But by these things I cannot more plainly and pithily express[2] what manner of substance the soul of man is, which I believe to be a spirit, having indeed a substance created of God proper and peculiar to itself. For Augustine, whose words I alleged a little before, saith yet again, 1 cap. *de Quantitate Animæ:* "I cannot name the substance of the soul, for I do not think the same to be of these usual and known natures which we touch with the senses of our body. For I think that the soul consisteth not of earth, nor of water, nor of air, nor of fire, neither yet of all these joined together, nor of any one of them. The nature of the soul may be called simple, because it consisteth not of other natures[3]." Which words of Augustine Cassiodore willing to rehearse and express by imitation saith: "The soul of man created of God is a spiritual and peculiar substance[4]." Therefore I simply affirm

John x.

John xix.

Luke xxiii.

Matt. xxvii.

Acts vii.

What manner of substance the soul of man is.

cipimus, cogitari, sed mente intelligi vitaque sentiri.—August. Ep. 28. Hieronymo de Natura et Origine Animarum. Opp. Tom. ii. fol. 19. col. 4. Par. 1532.]

[1 huc maxime inclinat, Lat.]

[2 His vero significantius, Lat.; more expressively than these texts.]

[3 Substantiam vero ejus (animæ) nominaro non possum: non enim eam puto esse ex iis usitatis notisque naturis quas istis corporis sensibus tangimus. Nam neque ex terra, neque ex aqua, neque ex aëre, neque ex igni, neque ex his omnibus, neque ex aliquibus horum conjunctis constare animam puto .... Simplex animæ natura dici potest, quia ex aliis naturis non est.—August. de Quant. Animæ. Opp. Tom. i. fol. 122. col. 4.]

[4 See above, p. 368, n. 2.]

that the soul hath a singular, yea, a certain more excellent substance, and differing from other spirits, having his true being and working always from his Creator[5]; but such as we in our speech cannot compass, neither are able to utter.

In the meanwhile we do not allow of them who, minding to express what manner of substance the soul is, say that the soul is God, or else surely a part or portion of God[6]. For the scripture reproveth them both. For truly the soul is a creature, and is drowned in variableness and sins : but a creator, and clean of itself, it is not. And because God the Creator is immutable and indivisible, the soul cannot be a portion of God. Therefore elegantly and truly Aurelius Prudentius in his *Apotheosis*, after he had in many words confuted these filthy errors, gathering at length all the meaning of the truth, saith :

> To say the soul is GOD, or part of him,
> 'Tis folly great, and too absurd a thing:
> Since chief and heavenly joys it tastes, which swim
> From always fresh and everlasting spring.
> Now it obeys, anon it falls to sin ;
> One while in joy, another while in pain:
> For due desert such guerdon it doth win :
> Now punish'd 'tis, anon 'tis free again[7].

The soul is neither God nor part of God.

To the end that we might overthrow this error, and discern the soul from other spirits and spiritual substances, we added in our description ; "That the soul of man is poured into the body of man by God :" whereby every man understandeth without any ado, that it is created, and also is a spirit, not angelical, but human, that is, breathed into man's body by God, of his own essence and nature.

Where again a new question touching the original of souls doth offer itself to us to be expounded. For it is wont to be asked, from whence souls come ? When or how they enter into their bodies ? St Hierome is the author, that in

Of the original of the soul.

[5 a creatione sua, Lat.; from its creation.]

[6 Manichæorum, delirio—quod rursus hac ætate invehere tentavit Servetus.—Calv. Instit. Lib. I. cap. 15. § 5.]

[7 Absurde fertur Deus aut pars esse Dei ; quæ
    Divinum summumque bonum de fonte perenni
    Nunc bibit obsequio, nunc culpa aut crimine perdit;
    Et modo supplicium recipit, modo libera calcat.
                    Prudent. Apoth. 952—955.]

time past there were many opinions, and those same most
contrary between themselves, touching the original of souls.
For he, writing to Marcellinus and Anapsychias, saith: "I
remember your question, nay rather forsooth, the question
of the church, touching the state of the soul: whether it
fell from heaven, as Pythagoras the philosopher, and all Pla-
tonists and Origen do think: or whether it be of the proper
substance of God, as the Stoics, Manicheus, and the heresies
of Priscillianus of Spain do suppose: whether they be counted
in God's treasury, long since laid up there, as certain churchmen foolishly persuaded think: whether they be daily made
of God and sent into bodies, according to that which is
written in the gospel, "My Father worketh hitherto, and I
work:" or whether, *ex traduce*, that is, by the generation
of the parents, as Tertullian, Apollinarius, and the greatest
part of the west churches conjecture; that as a body is
born of a body, so a soul is born of a soul, and hath his
being after the like state as brute beasts have[1]." But all
those opinions are confuted of ecclesiastical writers with sound
arguments.   That opinion is received and avouched for the
truest which holdeth, That the soul is created of nothing,
and poured of God into the body, when the child is made
perfect in shape and in every part of his body in the womb
of his mother.   For thus the ecclesiastical definitions do declare: "We say that the Creator of all things doth only
know the creation of the soul; and that the body only is
sowed by (carnal) copulation in marriage; that by the true
appointment of God it thickeneth in the matrice, becometh a
substance and receiveth shape; and that when the body is

[1 Super animæ statu memini vestræ quæstiunculæ; imo maxime
ecclesiasticæ quæstionis: Utrum lapsa de cœlo sit, ut Pythagoras phi-
losophus, omnesque Platonici et Origines putant; an a propria Dei
substantia, ut Stoici, Manichæus, et Hispana Priscilliani hæresis sus-
picantur; an in thesauro habeantur Dei, olim conditæ, ut quidem ecclesiastici stulta persuasione confidunt; an quotidie a Deo fiant, et
mittantur in corpora, secundum illud quod evangelio scriptum est,
Pater meus usque modo operatur, et ego operor; an certe ex traduce,
ut Tertullianus, Apollinaris, et maxima pars Occidentalium autumant;
ut quomodo corpus ex corpore, sic anima nascatur ex anima, et simili
cum brutis animantibus conditione subsistat.—Hieron. Epist. 78. (al.
82.) ad Marcellin. et Anapsych. Opp. Tom. IV. Pars 2. col. 642. Par.
1706.]

fashioned, the soul is created and poured into it[2]."   Whereupon St Hierome also to Pammachius, disputing against the
errors of John, bishop of Hierusalem, after he had rehearsed
divers opinions touching the original of the soul, he saith :
" Whether truly God createth souls daily, in whom his will
is his work, and never ceaseth to be a creator of them ?
Which is an ecclesiastical opinion, according to the opinion of
our Saviour, The Father worketh hitherto, and I work ;
and according to that of Esay, Which formeth the spirit of
man in him; and in the Psalms, Which fashioneth their
hearts in every one of them[3]."   Thus far he.

The scripture truly in express words doth teach, that the
soul hath not original out of earth, neither that it is created
before the body ; but it proceedeth out of the mouth of the
Creator, to wit, from the secret power of God, and that it is
poured into the body when it is fashioned.   For Moses, describing the creation of God our Father[4], doth first make mention,
that the body of Adam was fashioned and made, and that
afterwards the spirit of life was breathed into his body being
perfectly made and fashioned.   " The Lord God," saith he, [Gen. ii. 7.]
" made man of the clay of the earth, and breathed upon his
face or into his nostrils the breath of life, and man was made
a living soul."   For the breath of life doth signify the living
and reasonable soul, that is to say, the soul of man, which
thou seest breathed or poured into the body when it is fashioned.   And when the same Lord created the woman of
Adam's rib, he took not life from Adam, or out of his soul,
and put it into Eve, but of his goodness and power he poured
the same into her body when it was perfectly made.   And

[2 Sed dicimus creationem animæ solum creatorem omnium nosse,
et corpus tantum per conjugii copulam seminari, Dei vero judicio coa-
gulari in vulva et compingi atque formari, ac formato jam corpore animam creari et infundi.—August. de Eccles. Dogm. Opp. Tom. III. fol.
42. coll. 3. 4. Par. 1532.]

[3 An certe (quod ecclesiasticum est secundum eloquia Salvatoris,
Pater usque modo operatur, et ego operor; et illud Isaiæ, Qui format
spiritum hominis in ipso; et in Psalmis, Qui fingit per singulos corda
eorum;) quotidie Deus fabricatur animas : cujus velle fecisse est, et
conditor esse non cessat?—Hieron. ad Pammach. adv. error. Johan.
Jeros. Ep. 38. Opp. Tom. IV. Pars 2. fol. 318.]

[4 Formationem patris nostri, Lat.; rather, the creation of our
father, i. e. Adam.—God, is the translator's addition.]

that we are no otherwise created of the Lord at this day, than that the soul may be poured into the body when it is fashioned, Job is a witness sufficient, saying: "Thy hands, O God, have made me and fashioned me round about. Hast thou not poured me as it were milk, and turned me to curds like cheese? Thou hast covered me with skin and flesh, and joined me together with bones and sinews." Lo, thou hast here in these words both the conception and also the fashioning of man's body in his mother's womb most excellently described. And touching the soul, it followeth in Job immediately: "Thou hast given me life and grace, and thy visitation hath preserved my spirit." Behold, "life," that is, the soul, is by God poured into the body after it is shapen. "Thou hast given me life," saith he, "and grace." He addeth grace or mercy to life: for it is a marvel the child should live in the mother's womb, seeing it is wrapped within so many coverings; therefore a singular benefit of the mercy of God sheweth itself in this. But it followeth by way of interpretation: "And thy visitation," that is, thy providence and preservation, "hath kept or preserved my spirit." For now he calleth that "spirit," which first he had called "life;" that is to say, the soul. Wherefore we rightly hold and according to the scriptures, that the souls of men are created of God, and poured into the bodies when they be already fashioned in the womb; though we touch not every point and particular matter of this cause, and (as the saying is) hit the nail on the head.

Now it resteth to see what the soul worketh in the body of man. We comprehended that briefly in the description, saying that, being joined to the body, it giveth life to man and directeth him. For the reasonable soul comprehendeth the powers vegetative and sensitive, and thereby it giveth life to the body. Moreover the soul hath two parts, distinguished in offices, not in substance; namely, Understanding and Will; and thereby it directeth man. For by the understanding, which is called both the mind and reason, it conceiveth, judgeth, and knoweth things that are to be understood, and discerneth what to follow and what to avoid. But by will or appetite he chooseth that which he knoweth, following one thing and refusing another. Which things again stretch very far. Therefore I will handle every part more largely.

First of all " the soul by his presence giveth life to this Out of the 13 cap. of August. de Quantitate Animæ. mortal and earthly body ; it knitteth it together, and with a wonderful embracing keepeth it, and suffereth it not to grow out of order or pine away ; it equally distributeth the food throughout the members, giving to every one sufficient ; it preserveth a comely form and measure therein not only in beauty, but also in making and growth.   But all these things may seem also common to plants, as well as to man : for we see and confess, that they also live ; and that every one of them is preserved in his kind, nourished, increased, and engendered.   Therefore let us see what the soul is able to do, and what it worketh in the senses, where a more perfect view of life is perceived.   The soul sheweth itself in the sense of feeling, and thereby knoweth and discerneth the things that are hot, cold, rough, smooth, hard, soft, light, and heavy.   Moreover, the soul determineth the innumerable differences of tastes, savours, sounds, and shapes, by the senses of tasting, smelling, hearing, and seeing.   And among all these things it chooseth and coveteth those things which are according to the nature of the body whereunto it is joined, and refuseth and shunneth the contrary ; and also consenteth not only to the procreation of children, but to the cherishing, defending, nourishing, and preserving of them.   But all these things again no man denieth but the life which is in beasts may do also.   Let us therefore consider what is the proper force of the soul of man.   And here weigh with me the wonderful power of understanding and reasoning, and not a common memory as is in brute beasts, but a remembrance of innumerable things commended unto us, and kept in mind by signs and deep consideration : consider with me so many devices of craftsmen, tilling of lands, building of cities, manifold wonderfulness of sundry buildings and devices ; the inventions of so many forms in letters, in words, in gesture, in sound, in pictures, and feigned shews ; so many tongues of nations, so many things ordained, so many new things, so many things reformed ; such a number of books, and of such like monuments for the maintenance of memory, as having a care of them which come after ; the orders of offices, powers, honours and dignities, either in families, or in the common weal in peace or in war, either in profane or in holy matters. Weigh with me the marvellous force and virtue of devising the rivers of eloquence, the variety of verses in poetry, a thousand-fold devices and merriments to move pleasure and pastime, skilfulness in playing on instruments and in singing, cunning in measuring, readiness in numbering, conjecturing of things past and things to come by things present[1]."

These verily are great powers or operations in the soul of man, but they are common to the good and bad. Therefore the true goodness and praise, which riseth from the powers of the soul unto man, aud which are found in the godly only, do follow. The soul is bold to prefer itself before the whole body, and to think that the goods of the body are not his, but rather to despise them; and thereby how much the more he delighteth himself, so much the more he withdraweth himself from filthiness, and cleanseth himself

[1 Corpus hoc terrenum atque mortale præsentia sua vivificat (anima), colligit in unum atque in uno tenet; diffluere atque contabescere non sinit; alimenta per membra æqualiter, suis quibusque redditis, distribui facit; congruentiam ejus modumque conservat, non tantum in pulchritudine, sed etiam in crescendo atque gignendo. Sed hæc omnia homini etiam cum arbustis communia vīderi queunt: hæc enim etiam dicimus vivere, in suo vero quidque illorum genere custodiri, ali, crescere, gignere videmus atque fatemur... Intendit se anima in tactum, et eo calida, frigida, aspera, lenia, dura, mollia, levia, gravia, sentit atque discernit. Deinde innumerabiles differentias saporum, odorum, sonorum, formarum, gustando, olfaciendo, audiendo, videndoque dijudicat. Atque in his omnibus ea quæ secundum naturam sui corporis sunt asciscit atque appetit, rejicit fugitque contraria:... fœtibus quoque non jam gignendis tantummodo, sed etiam fovendis, alendis, atque conservandis conspirat... Sed hæc rursus omnia posse animam etiam in bestiis nemo negat... Cogita memoriam non consuetudine inolitarum, sed animadversione atque signis commendatarum ac retentarum rerum innumerabilium; tot artes opificum, agrorum cultus, extructiones urbium, variorum ædificiorum ac moliminum multimoda miracula; inventiones tot signorum in literis, in verbis, in gestu, in hujuscemodi sono, in picturis atque figmentis; tot gentium linguas, tot instituta, tot nova, tot instaurata, tantum librorum numerum et hujusmodi monumentorum ad custodiendam memoriam, tanquam curam posteritatis; officiorum, potestatum, honorum, dignitatumque ordines, sive in familiis, sive domi militiæque in republica, sive in prophanis, sive in sacris apparatibus; vim ratiocinandi et excogitandi fluvios eloquentiæ, carminum varietates, ludendi ac jocandi causa milleformes simulationes, modulandi peritiam, dimetiendi subtilitatem, numerandi disciplinam, præteritorum ac futurorum ex præsentibus conjecturam.—August. de Quant. Animæ. cap. 33. Opp. Tom. I. fol. 130. coll. 1, 2. Par. 1532.]

wholly by faith and the Holy Ghost, and strengtheneth himself against all things which go about to put him by from his good intent, and maketh great account of fellowship or society, loveth men tenderly, and willeth nothing to another which he would not have happen to himself. For he followeth the word or doctrine of God, and believeth that by this God speaketh unto him: he is joined by the Holy Ghost and faith with God himself, in whom he delighteth and liveth in true felicity, bringing forth all kind of virtues. In this so excellent a study of the soul there is yet great labour. For the soul fighteth fiercely with the world and the flesh, and is never safe and at rest from the assaults or invasions of Satan: but being strengthened by the Lord, he goeth away with notable victories and triumphs. The souls therefore (I mean, of saints and holy men) work all manner of holy works; for the souls of the wicked commit heinous sins of all sorts. There are many other operations of souls, which I cease to rehearse, lest I should be longer than were meet.

Hitherto I have entreated of the soul of man as yet joined to the body: in which discourse the wonderful goodness of God appeareth, the most bountiful Creator of the soul, yea, of the whole man; from whose grace we worthily account it received, whatsoever praise is given to the soul. Now I will speak of the soul separated from the body.

The soul, being separated from the body, ceaseth not to be that which it was; but, the body being dead, the soul abideth alive in his own essence, altogether immortal, and void of all corruption. For the death of man is not the extinguishing or destruction of the soul, but only a separation or departure from the body. Thou takest a candle out of a lantern; thou hast taken the light from the lantern, but thou hast not put out the candle. The lantern truly, because the candle is taken away, remaineth full of darkness; but the candle feeleth so little hurt by removing of it, that, being taken away from the lantern, it then shineth more clearly, and casteth forth the beams of his light more at large. So truly the soul, being separated from his earthly or slimy body, doth so little feel any discommodity, that, being delivered from the trouble and burden of the body, it liveth more at liberty, and worketh more effectually. But the common sort understand not this. They see the body only

Of the soul separated from the body.

The soul is immortal.

among the dead, spoiled of the soul; and because this wanteth all feeling and moving, yea, and rotteth away, they think that the whole man perisheth.   Neither is the world without some shameless and ungodly wretches who have in their mouth, that no man ever returned from death or from below, who by his return proved that the souls remain alive when the body is dead.   But maliciously they lie, dissembling that they know not that which certainly they know.   For who knoweth not that Christ the Son of God died, and was buried, and the third day was raised again from the dead, the very self-same soul returning into his body, which before death gave his body life and ruled it?   Who knoweth not that Christ with his true body and with his reasonable and natural[1] soul ascended into heaven, and sitteth at the right hand of the Father, that he, laying down there as it were a most assured pledge, might testify unto the whole world that both our own proper souls and our own proper bodies shall one day be translated thither?   Who knoweth not that so many which were dead, being raised from death to life, received not new souls, but those their old souls?   Which should not have come to pass, if by the death of the body the souls of men were extinguished.

Of the death of souls.   They object, that the scripture itself maketh mention of the death of the soul.   I confess no less indeed.   For the soul of man is both mortal and immortal, after a certain manner of his own.   For the soul is not all manner of ways immortal *1 Tim.i. & vi.* as God is, of whom it is said that he only hath immortality. And truly the death of the soul in the holy scripture is to be remembered; but the same is referred to the state and condition, not to the substance, of the soul.   For if God be the life of the soul, surely to be forsaken of God, and to be left unto thyself, is the death of the soul.   But nevertheless the reasonable soul liveth in his proper essence or being, so that, when it liveth miserably, a miserable life is in very deed called death.   But desperation also is the very death of the *Gal. ii.* soul; for by hope we live: and Paul saith, "I live, yet not I, but Christ liveth in me; and the life which I now live in the flesh, I live by the faith of the Son of God." Therefore they that are destitute of faith are dead, and they that have faith live.   St Augustine, cap. 10, *De Fide et Symbolo*, saith:

[1 genuina, Lat.]

" The soul, as it may be called corruptible by reason of sin
and wickedness, so it may be called mortal.   For the death
of the soul is the revolting or falling from God; which first
sin of the soul was committed in paradise, as is declared in
the holy scriptures[2]."   And the same Augustine again, Lib.
de Trinitate, 14, cap. 4, saith : " The soul also hath his death,
when it lacketh a blessed life, which is to be named the true
life of the soul.   But for this cause it is called immortal, for
that, whatsoever life it liveth, yea, though it be most miserable,
yet it never ceaseth to live[3]."   We therefore freely confess,
that the souls of men, separated or taken out of their bodies, do
not die, but live immortal for ever ; the faithful in everlasting
joy and felicity, but the unbelievers in eternal damnation.

Which thing I will now go on to confirm by some sub- Testimonies
stantial testimonies of scripture.   But first take this with tality of
you, that testimonies of scripture in this case are far more souls.
lively than man's reasons framed out of philosophy.   For
these testimonies are fetched from the very mouth of the
living God himself, which preserveth us in life ; who, since he
is true, cannot lie, and who, since he giveth life and is life
itself, is able to witness most certainly above all other touching
life.   Neither is it doubtful that the Spirit of God worketh
jointly with the word of God ; of whom unless the hearts of
men be touched, the reasons of philosophy, how manifest soever
they be, shall prevail nothing, especially in the danger of
death and in other temptations.   They are fleshly therefore
and brutish altogether, which are not ashamed to say, That
they cannot be persuaded or brought to believe the immortality of souls by the scriptures only.   Nay, which is more ;
that shall never be stedfast and stable in temptations, which
shall proceed from flesh and blood.   We will therefore add
some certain testimonies, and those too most manifest.

David, the most puissant and happiest king in the world,

[2 Potest enim et anima, sicut corruptibilis propter morum vitia,
ita etiam mortalis dici.   Mors quippe animæ est apostatare a Deo,
quod primum ejus peccatum in paradiso sacris literis continetur.—
August. de Fide et Symb. cap. 10. Opp. Tom. III. fol. 32. col. 3. Par.
1532.—Works of Coverdale, ed. P. S. Remains, p. 201.]

[3 Habet quippe et anima mortem suam, cum vita beata caret,
quæ vera animæ vita dicenda est.   Sed immortalis ideo nuncupatur,
quoniam qualicunque vita, etiam si miserrima est, nunquam desinit
vivere.—Id. de Trin. Lib. XIV. cap. 4. Opp. Tom. III. fol. 91. col. 2.]

comprising in one verse both the immortality of souls and the resurrection of bodies, saith: "Thou, O Lord, shalt not leave my soul in hell: neither shalt thou suffer thine Holy one to see corruption." Man consisteth of body and soul. The body rotteth away when it is dead, and is turned into dust; but it shall not therefore perish: for as the body of Christ which was buried did not rot, but rose again the third day; so in the day of judgment shall our bodies be raised up, and by Christ be delivered from corruption. And our soul goeth not into hell there to remain[1]: but as the soul of Christ returned from the nether parts unto his body, and ascended into heaven in his body which he had taken again; even so shall our souls also live by Christ, they shall not die.

Salomon, the son of David, excelling all kings and mortal men in wisdom, in one verse likewise expounding the providence of God touching the soul and the body, saith: "The dust shall be turned again unto earth, from whence it came; and the spirit shall return unto God, who gave it." Salomon calleth man's body dust, because it is said in Moses that God made it of the dust of the earth. Therefore the body turneth again unto dust; for it putrefieth and is resolved into that which first it was, even until the judgment-day, as the Lord saith: "For dust thou art, and into dust shalt thou be turned again." But the spirit, that is to say, the reasonable soul, dieth not with the body: it is not resolved into dust, because it is not taken out of the dust; neither is it scattered into the air, because it doth not consist of air; but returneth alive from death unto God. And therefore it returneth unto God, because God gave the soul, and after a singular manner made man after his own likeness and image, breathing into his face the spirit of life,—of life I say, that is, of lively power, not the spirit of death. Therefore the soul cannot perish, because it receiveth immortality from God; who, since he is life, is able to preserve that breath of life which he hath made.

The Lord Jesus, the true and very Son of God, the life and resurrection of the faithful, saith plainly in the gospel: "Fear (ye) not them which kill the body, but are not able to kill the soul; but rather fear him which is able to destroy

Psal. xvi.

Eccles. xii.

Gen. iii.

Matt. x.

[1 there to remain; not in Lat.]

both body and soul in hell." If when the body being slain
by tyrants the soul is not killed, then it remaineth alive after
the body is destroyed; and so assuredly it remaineth, that,
having put off the body, it should be cast of the most just
God into hell, there everlastingly to burn for his unfaithfulness. For in the same gospel the Lord saith again, " Who- Matt. xv.
soever will save his life shall lose it:" again, "whosoever
will lose his life for my sake, shall find it." For not he only
loseth his life or soul, which bridleth it from the pleasures
of the world and liveth most temperately; but he also who
offereth himself into the bloody hands of tyrants to be slain
for the confession of christian faith. And he findeth his life
or soul which he lost. Therefore the souls of men, even
after the death of the body, remain alive and immortal.

In the gospel according to St John the Lord saith:
"Verily, verily, I say unto you, He that heareth my word, John v.
and believeth on him that sent me, hath everlasting life, and
shall not come into judgment; but is escaped from death
unto life." Thou hast in these words of the Lord the death
of the body. But forthwith afterward he witnesseth, that we
"escape unto life:" therefore men's souls remain alive after
death. For now he speaketh nothing of the raising again
or of the salvation of the body, but of the life of the soul
after death. In the same gospel the Lord saith again:
"Verily, verily, I say unto you, If a man keep my saying, John viii.
he shall never see death." But it is evident that all men Heb. ix.
are ordained once to die, namely, with bodily death: therefore the soul liveth after the death of the body. For it
must needs be that a faithful man shall never see or feel
death, unless he told a lie who affirmeth with an oath that
which he spake. For in every other place[2] he addeth an
oath, saying, " Verily, I say unto you;" that we should not
doubt of the immortality of souls. There are very many
testimonies, and those most evident, of Christ the Son of God
in the same gospel, as in the sixth and eleventh chapters: to
which we will join one or two out of the writings of the
blessed apostles of Christ.

St Peter, speaking of the souls of the fathers which were 1 Pet. iv.
dead a great while ago, saith, that " the gospel was preached
also to the dead, that they should be judged like other men

[2 utrobique; Lat. in both places.]

in the flesh, but should live before God[1] in the spirit."
Spirits are souls of the blessed fathers, whose bodies being
buried a great while ago do wait for the universal sentence
of that general and last judgment: that is, that their flesh
may be raised up again and be judged with other men in
the last day; but in the meanwhile their souls live with God.
So that men's souls are alive, though their bodies were rotten
a great while ago.

2 Tim. i.St Paul in his epistle to Timothy saith, that life and
immortality is made manifest and brought by Christ[2]. The
same Paul everywhere doth so plainly avouch the immortality
of souls, that he must needs be blind which seeth it not.

Rev. vi.St John, the apostle and evangelist, saw under the altar in
heaven (that is, under the protection of Christ who is the
sacrifice and propitiation for the sins of the world) living souls
lying and crying: "How long tarriest thou, Lord, to revenge
our blood?" He saw them clothed with white garments, and
enjoying everlasting rest. But these souls were the souls of
the martyrs of Christ, whose bodies died, being murdered on
the earth under tyrants and persecutors of the christian faith.
Therefore the souls of men are immortal.

Most true therefore, yea, and undoubted, are those words
Wisd. ii.which are read in the book of Wisdom, uttered in this manner:
"The souls of the righteous are in the hand of God, and there
shall no torment touch them. In the sight of the unwise they
appeared to die, and their end is taken for a misery, and their
departing from us to be utter destruction; but they are in rest.
For though they suffer pain before men, yet is their hope
full of immortality. They are punished but in few things;
nevertheless in many things shall they be well rewarded. For
God proveth them, and findeth them meet for himself. As
gold in the furnace doth he try them, and receiveth them as
a burnt-offering: and when the time cometh, they shall be
looked upon. They shall shine and run through, as the
sparkles among the stubble. They shall judge the nations,
and have dominion over the people, and their Lord shall reign
for ever."

Wherefore most truly and according to the canonical

[1 juxta Deum; Lat. and Erasmus.]
[2 manifeste vitam et immortalitatem per Christum esse repa-
ratam; Lat.]

scripture do the ecclesiastical definitions pronounce, cap. 16 : " We believe that man only hath a substantial soul, which, having put off the body, liveth and keepeth his senses and disposition lively. It doth not die with the body, as Aratus affirmeth; nor a little while after, as Zenon saith; because it liveth substantially. But the souls of beasts and other mortal creatures are not substantial, but are born with their flesh through the life of their flesh, and with the death of their flesh are at an end and do die[3]."

Furthermore, that truth touching the immortality of souls, as it were by the law of nature, is written and imprinted in the minds of all men. Whereupon it is no marvel that all the wise men among the Gentiles could never abide that the soul should be called mortal. For the consent of all, which is thought the voice of nature, specially of the chiefest, declareth that souls are immortal. And M. Tully also affirmeth that, saying: "As by nature we think there are Gods, and by reason we know what they be, so we hold opinion with the consent of all nations, that souls do still continue[4]." All the ancient writers therefore, and all that followed them, have said that souls are everlasting or immortal; as Trismegistus, Museus, Orpheus, Homerus, Pindarus, and Pherecydes the Syrian, the master of Pythagoras[5], and his scholar Socrates. Plato himself, who to learn the opinions of Pythagoras sailed into Italy[6], was not only of the same opinion that Pythagoras was of, touching the immortality of souls, but brought reasons also to confirm the same. These reasons, as Tully witnesseth, are many, that he which readeth his book cannot seem to desire any thing further[7]. Seneca so plainly affirmeth and proveth the immortality of souls, that nothing can be more plain[8]. And Epicte-

All wise men have thought that souls are immortal.

[3] Solum hominem credimus habere animam substantivam, quæ exuta corpore vivit, et sensus suos atque ingenia vivaciter tenet. Non cum corpore moritur, sicut Aratus asserit; neque post modicum intervallum, sicut Zenon dicit; quia substantialiter vivit. Animalium vero animæ non sunt substantivæ, sed cum carne ipsa carnis vivacitate nascuntur, et cum carnis morte finiuntur et moriuntur.—August. de Eccles. Dogm. 16. Opp. Tom. III. fol. 42. col. 4. Par. 1532.]

[4] Cic. Tusc. Quæst. Lib. I. cap. 16.]

[5] Id. ibid.]   [6] Id. ibid. cap. 17.]

[7] Tot autem rationes attulit (Plato), ut velle ceteris, sibi certe persuasisse videatur.—Cic. ibid. cap. 21.]

[8] Senec. Epist. 117.]

tus, a famous philosopher, who lived in the time of Seneca, hath done no less[1]. If as yet there be any light-headed men to whom the immortality of the soul seemeth doubtful, or which utterly deny the same, these truly are unworthy to have the name of men; for they are plagues of the commonwealth, and very beasts, worthy to be hissed and driven out of the company of men. For he lacketh a bridle to restrain him, and hath cast away all honesty and shame, and is prepared in all points to commit any mischief, whosoever believeth that the soul of man is mortal.

In what place souls live when they are separated from their bodies.

I shewed that souls[2] by death being separated from their bodies do not die, but remain alive: it resteth now behind that I teach you, where the souls, when they are destitute of the dwelling-place, their bodies, lead their life and are conversant.

While they were coupled to the bodies, they used them as their dwelling-houses; so that, though they be said not to be limited in place, yet they do not wander out of their bodies, but they are as it were shut up in them as in prisons[3], until the time they be dissolved and set at liberty. Those same souls therefore being now dissevered from their bodies, since they retain their sound senses, their nature or disposition, and their whole substance in lively manner, albeit they are said, no, not even now to be limited in place, yet are they not let loose and run astray, having their abiding in no place; but being compact and set fast in their own essence or being are in some place again, having no new bodies, (for the souls are free even till the judgment-day, when they shall be joined again to their bodies;) howbeit certain abiding-places are prepared for them of God, wherein they may live. Although other, by my lieve, very subtilly and wittily do reason, how spirits are contained in place or not contained: I simply affirm with the scripture, that souls separated from bodies are taken up either into heaven itself, or else are drowned in the depth of hell; and that their being and abiding is even so there, that when they are here they are not elsewhere. For the Lord most plainly and pithily saith in the gospel, that the soul of beggarly Lazarus was carried into Abraham's bosom, and the soul of the rich glutton was cast down into hell. But

Luke xvi.

[1 Simplicii Comment. in Epicteti Enchirid. cap. 39.]
[2 hominum, Lat. omitted; of men.]
[3 ergastulis, Lat.]

that more is, it forthwith followeth in the history: "Between
us and you" (for the blessed and cursed souls talk together)
"there is a great gulf stedfastly set; so that they which would
go from hence to you cannot, neither can they that would
come from thence to us." And Paul also desireth "to be dis- Phil. i.
solved, and to be with Christ." We are dissolved by death:
for when the soul departeth, the body is dissolved and dieth;
the soul flieth unto Christ. But the scripture sheweth us
that Christ is in heaven at the right hand of the Father.
Now where heaven is, there is none but can tell; and we
elsewhere have largely entreated of that matter[4].

In the gospel after St John the Lord himself calleth the
conversation[5] of souls, which is prepared for the souls after
they are separated from the bodies, both a place and mansion,
and habitation or dwelling; adding these words thereupon,
"I will receive you (even) unto myself, that where I am, John xiv.
there may ye be also." And therefore St John saw souls Rev. vi.
in heaven, abiding and taking their rest under the altar or
protection of Christ: for thither, when they departed from
their bodies, he had gathered them unto himself. Hereunto
belongeth that notable place of the apostle Paul, marvellous
fit for this purpose, written in the second to the Corinthians [v. 1.]
in these words: "We know that if our earthly house of this
tabernacle were destroyed, we have a building of God, even
an habitation not made with hands, but eternal in heaven," &c.
Lo, while our souls were joined to our bodies, they inhabited
and dwelt in them as in their houses; but after our corruptible
house is destroyed, God hath builded another better and of
longer continuance, heaven I mean itself, into the which he
lovingly receiveth our souls departing out of our bodies. For
that manner body which we now have he calleth the house
of this tent or tabernacle. For as tents for a time are made
of light stuff, and pitched without any strong foundation,
and a while after are pulled down, or do fall of their own
accord; so a mortal body is given to men as a ruinous
cottage, wherein they inhabit a few days, and immediately
pack away again. St Peter used the like allegory. Against 2 Pet. i.
this (tent) he opposeth a building of everlasting continuance,
heaven I mean itself: for when he had said that we have

[4 See Vol. I. page 145.]
[5 contubernium, Lat.]

"a building of God," he addeth by interpretation, (even) an "habitation not made with hands;" and yet more plainly, "eternal in heaven." Neither doth that which by and by followeth hinder this, or import another meaning: "for therefore sigh we, desiring (upon our clothing) to be further clothed with our house which is from heaven." For "from heaven" signifieth as much as if thou wouldest say, heavenly. Therefore the house of the soul is heavenly or heaven itself, a

The soul returneth to the body, but not before judgment. place, I say, appointed for blessed spirits. For verily the faithful soul shall dwell in heaven even unto that day, wherein the Lord shall judge the world with that his general judgment: then at the length the soul shall return to the body again being raised up, that after judgment the whole man, both soul and body, may live for ever with God. For

1 Thess. iv. thus witnesseth the apostle St Paul: "The Lord himself shall descend from heaven in a shout, and in the voice of the archangel, and in the trumpet of God, and the dead in Christ shall rise first: then we which live, which remain, shall be caught up together with them in the clouds, to meet the Lord in the air; and so shall we ever be with the Lord," namely, in the heavens which are above us where the clouds are seen. Therefore, omitting vain speculations and curious disputations, let us believe that there is a house prepared by the Lord in heaven for souls being separated from their bodies, into the which the faithful may be received; and again, that there is everlasting fire prepared, whereunto all the souls of all infidels or unbelievers may be cast.

How souls should be translated to their appointed place. We have taught, that heaven is the seat or habitation prepared of God to receive souls being separated from their bodies. It remaineth behind, that we shew after what manner and what time they should be translated thither after death. Touching the manner, I can say nothing else but that it is fully known unto God; and that, so far forth as seemeth sufficient for us, it is shadowed out in the scriptures; namely, that it is brought to pass by angels carrying up our souls with a most swift flight or moving. For the Lord saith in the gospel, that the soul of Lazarus was carried by angels into Abraham's bosom: of which thing also we spake before when we preached of God's angels[1]. But what man-

[1 de angelis bonis, Lat.; of good angels, ed. 1577. See above, p. 335.]

ner of moving this is, whether natural or supernatural, I mean not to make search. I believe that what God promiseth, the same he performeth and accomplisheth; and he promising saith, "He is passed from death to life." Again, he said to John v. the thief, "To-day shalt thou be with me in paradise," com- Luke xxiii. prehending that his passage as it were in a moment. Hereunto we also necessarily add this, that it must be attributed to the merits of Christ that we are taken up into heaven; for he is the door and the way.

But at what time souls should be carried up into heaven, At what or cast down into hell, seemeth to be a question at this time souls be carried up present not only profitable, but by all means necessary to be into heaven. discussed; for in this our age there are evil-disposed persons who have corrupted the pure simplicity of this matter. For you shall find some will say, that the souls departing from the bodies go not by and by the right and ready way to heaven, but that, being as it were taken with a slumbering lethargy, they sleep until the last day of judgment[2]. You shall find other some contending, that souls cannot come into heaven unless they be perfectly purified with cleansing fire, which they call purgatory; as though they were intercepted by pirates and robbers in the midst of their journey, and cast into torments, until either they themselves make satisfaction, or other for them have paid as it were the debt which they had elsewhere borrowed[3]. But both of these things do I deny, and utterly deny: and I affirm that souls do not sleep, neither are they purged by any torments after the death of their body; but are waking and alive, and are forthwith after the death of the body, and even in a moment, either carried into heaven, being freed from all kind of torments, or otherwise cast down into hell.

These sleepy-heads[4] have nothing to allege for this their Souls sepa- lethargy or imagination of the sleep of the soul, but that the rated from their bodies scripture oftentimes, describing the death of the saints, maketh do not sleep. mention of sleeping and laying to sleep; as, "he fell asleep, and was gathered unto (or laid by) his fathers;" and Paul

[2 Bullinger. adv. Anabapt. Lib. IV. cap. 10.]
[3 Canones Concil. Trident. Sess. xxv. decret. de Purgatorio.]
[4 Dormitantii, Lat. See Jerome's *play* on Vigilantius' name.—Hieron. Opp. Tom. IV. Par. II. pp. 280, &c. Par. 1706. and Gilly's Vigilantius and his times, pp. 349, 392. Lond. 1844.]

saith, speaking of those that die, "I would not have you
ignorant concerning them which are asleep." But even as
souls, when they were joined to these frail bodies, never slept,
neither could sleep: so being delivered from the burden of the
body, they are much less to be thought to sleep. To the
body therefore is sleep to be referred. For whosoever dieth
in a true faith, he sleepeth in the Lord. And as they that
sleep, when their limbs are therewith refreshed, do immediately awake, rise, and labour; even so the body is not
altogether extinguished by death, that it should not live
again any more, but now verily it is received into rest, and
at the day of judgment it riseth again and liveth. And for
this cause holy men are said in the scriptures to sleep, not
to die, that thereby the mystery of the resurrection of our
flesh may be signified. Which thing these gross-headed men
understand not: whereupon they attribute that to the soul
which is proper to the body. Other arguments which they
bring to confirm their madness are unworthy to be rehearsed:
for either they violently wrest the scripture from the natural
sense; or else by their corrupt reasoning they gather falsehood out of those things that are false.

Souls separat-
ed from the
bodies are
not carried
into purga-
tory.

But they do err and are no less deceived than these
sleeping doctors, which think that souls departing from their
bodies go not by and by the right and ready way into
heaven, but are caught in the midst of their journey, and
carried into that purgatory fire, wherein they may be purged
from the filthy spots of sins which they have gotten in the
flesh; and that after they be purged, they are carried by
angels into the presence of the most holy God. For either
the souls are purged with that purgatory fire from the filth
of their sins, or else they are washed and cleansed through
the pain and grief of torments which there they do suffer.
If sins be purged by virtue of that fire, then it followeth, that
sinners are not sanctified by the only blood of the Son of God.
But by what scriptures have they proved unto us that this
power of purging is given to the fire? Hath God altered his
mind and purpose, and set this fire instead of Christ to work
our sanctification? Fie for shame! But if for our sufferings
and torments' sake sins are forgiven, then it followeth that we
are not purged by the cross and passion of Christ only.
Let them teach us out of the scripture, that such worthiness is

attributed by God to our sufferings. But by the only blood and
passion of Christ all those are sanctified that be sanctified, whosoever they be. Therefore purgatory is a wicked device of the
devil, which darkeneth, yea, and maketh void the cross and merits
of Christ. For what other thing do they account purgatory
but a satisfaction for sins made by the souls separated from
their bodies? In the gospel of John there is a question moved Souls are
by the disciples of John the Baptist, touching the purifying purged by the
of souls; and John Baptist declareth that the faithful are of Christ.
through Christ purified by faith; which thing he is believed to
have testified also by the holy baptism. Moreover, the most
excellent apostles do expressly witness, that all the faithful
are cleansed by the only blood of Christ, and by his only
passion and most sufficient merits. For Peter, who saith in
the Acts, "Neither is there salvation in any other: for Acts iv.
among men there is given no other name under heaven
whereby we must be saved;" he, I say, hath written in his
first canonical epistle: "Ye know that you were not redeemed 1 Pet.
with corruptible things, as with silver and gold, but with the
precious blood of the immaculate Lamb." John the apostle
also saith: "The blood of Christ Jesus, the Son of God, 1 John i.
cleanseth us from all sin." And he again: "Christ loved us, Rev. i.
and washed us from our sins by his own blood." And Paul, Ephes. v.
both to the Ephesians and to Titus, sheweth that we are Tit. iii.
purified by the only blood of the Son of God. Unto the
Hebrews he saith: "By himself hath he purged our sins, and Heb. i.
sitteth on the right hand of God in the highest places." It
was not without signification that he said, "By himself,"
that he might thereby exclude all other means. For elsewhere he saith thus: "If righteousness come by the law, Gal. ii.
then Christ died in vain." For after the same manner we
also do reason: If we be cleansed by purgatory fire, then
in vain did Christ shed his blood to purge us; for what
needed he to have suffered most grievous punishment, if we
could have been cleansed by purgatory fire? Moreover, the
whole scripture teacheth us, that Christ is our only satisfaction and propitiation: which thing we have at large shewed
in other places[1]. And therefore souls make no satisfaction in
purgatory, unless we will confess that men have no need
of Christ.

[1 See Vol. i. pages 136, 167, Vol. ii. page 200.]

These men do further feign, that the power to purge is given to the fire of purgatory by grace, or by the blood and merits of Christ, and that this fire purgeth not by his own virtue, but by the power of the Son of God[1]. But they have also forged this most wickedly. For the scripture in every place (as we also said even now) sendeth us back to the Son of God and the price of his blood and cleansing, whereof it teacheth that we are made partakers, while we live in this world, by faith and the Holy Ghost: but of purgatory it speaketh not a word in any place; neither saith it in any place that we by the grace of God are purged in another world. Therefore they steal away the glory which is proper unto the Son of God, and give it to a fire which is altogether forged and blasphemous. Furthermore, they appoint another time of grace out of this world, which is altogether strange unto the scriptures. For our Lord crieth in the gospel:

[John ix. 4.] "I must work the works of him that sent me, while it is day; the night cometh, when no man can work." And St Paul

Gal. vi. saith: "Let us do good," that is to say, let us be bountiful and liberal towards the poor, "while we have time." Which saying he seemeth to have taken out of Solomon's book of

Eccles. xi. the Preacher, saying: "When the clouds are full, they pour out rain upon the earth: and when the tree falleth, whether it be toward the south or north, in what place soever it fall, there it remaineth." He useth two allegories or dark speeches, by the which he teacheth the rich to be liberal. The first is taken from the clouds. The clouds from the earth do gather up vapours, which being thickened are immediately, as out of a sponge, pressed out and poured upon the earth to water it. Let rich men do the like, distributing again among men such riches as they have gotten among men. The second is taken of trees, which being felled lie in the same places in which they fall. The wise man therefore warneth us to do that in due season which we ought to do; for when we are departed from hence, there is no place of repentance. And in the gospel a tree is oftentimes put for a man; where also the right hand is put for heaven or the place of blessedness, as the left hand for hell or the place of damnation. Therefore this is his meaning: When thou art dead, thou shalt remain for ever either in damnation or blessedness. Men's testimonies are

[1 Alexander de Hales. Sum. Theol. Par. IV. quæst. 8.]

agreeable to the heavenly.   For St Cyprian against Deme-
trianus saith: "When we shall be departed hence, there
is then no place of repentance, satisfaction is of no value.
Here life is either lost or gotten.   Here is provision made for
eternal salvation, by the serving of God and the fruit of
faith[2]."

They object again, that souls when they depart from the
body are purged indeed by the blood of the Son of God, but
not fully; for there remains some filth to be washed away in
purgatory[3].   For they depart out of this world not having a
full and perfect faith, and therefore they be not altogether
good: and again, since they have some faith, they be not altogether evil: and because they are not perfectly good, they
cannot enter into heaven; again, since they are not altogether
evil, they cannot be damned: and therefore there remaineth a
middle place, wherein they may be fully tried[4], and at the
length being purified may be presented into the sight of God.
But these men after their manner feign what they list.   But
we have shewed by the holy scriptures, that the souls of the
faithful are purged by the only blood of the Son of God
through faith, and not by purgatory.   Now will I also shew
in that which followeth, that the sins of all men are purified
fully, that is to say, most absolutely, by the only sacrifice of
Christ; and further, that by the grace of God in the blood of
Christ is forgiven in the very instant of death whatsoever
infirmity and remnants of sin are behind in the souls of the
faithful departing from the body.   For the Lord saith in the
gospel, "He that is washed, needeth not save to wash his
feet, but is clean every whit."   Behold he saith, "He is clean
every whit;" that is, washed by the grace of Christ, so that
the foulness of the feet, that is to say, the infirmity and imperfection which remaineth after regeneration, cannot bring
him again into the number of those that are unclean.   For
the Lord saith again in the gospel, "And for their sakes
sanctify I myself, that they also might be sanctified through
the truth."   The Lord gave up himself to be a sacrifice for
our sins, to the end that we might be sanctified, that is,

Marginal notes: That souls are fully purged by the blood of Christ.

John xiii.

John xvii.

[2 See above, p. 114.]

[3 Bellarmin. Controv. vi. Lib. i. cap. vii. col. 1358.   Cranmer's
Remains, ed. Parker Soc. p. 181.]

[4 excoquantur, Lat.]

purged from our sins truly, that is to say, fully and most perfectly. For Paul saith, "For with one offering hath he made perfect for ever them that are sanctified." Mark, I pray you, the apostle's words: "Christ with one oblation" (lo, he saith, with one) "hath perfectly sanctified all that are sanctified," and are made heirs of eternal life. Hereupon we gather: If by the one sacrifice of Christ once offered for us all souls are purified, and that indeed perfectly purified, so that there is nothing wanting to their purifying; what, I pray you, findeth purgatory to purify? Therefore it is a shameless forgery and horrible blasphemy against the merit of the purifying of Jesus Christ the Son of God. If there seem any thing to be diminished or wanting unto the soul now departing, Christ by his grace performeth and maketh it up whilst it is yet in the world. It is a wicked speech and unworthy to be heard among christian people, that by our sufferings in purgatory that is fulfilled which was not as yet fully satisfied[1] with the blood and passion of Christ: as if our sufferings were better and more effectual than the passion of the Son of God.

These men object unto us the weakness of faith in them that die: and we on the other side object unto them the mercy of God, fully pardoning his faithful people. The father of the lunatic mentioned in the gospel, requiring help of the Lord, heareth: "If thou canst believe" (to wit, that I am able to heal thy son), "all things are possible to him that believeth." And albeit he felt his faith not altogether perfect, but that therein remained much weakness, yet the help of God was not hindered by the weakness thereof: for because he humbly submitted himself unto the mercy of the Lord, beseeching and saying, "Lord, I believe, help my unbelief;" the Lord by and by succoured him, and without delay healed his son. So there is no doubt that the most merciful Lord will fail his faithful people, to whom he hath promised most full forgiveness, acknowledging their weakness in the hour of death, and therefore also calling for the mercy of God; but that upon the instant of the going out of the soul he forthwith perfectly sanctifieth it with his Spirit for Christ's sake, and beautifieth it with all kind of graces, that, being truly purged from all the filth of sins, it may flee up, and deserve to appear in the presence of God. And this should

[1 expiatum, Lat.]

be beaten into the heads of them that are a dying. For there are extant most large promises of God; there are extant examples of many holy men dying and calling upon God.

Furthermore it is certain by those things which we have already alleged, that the death of Christ hath made full satisfaction for sins ; so that now there remaineth nothing further to be cleansed with the fire of purgatory. Souls, after the death of the body, do flee the right and ready way into heaven, taking nothing away with them which needeth purging. Therefore that fire of purgatory is nothing else in very deed than a traffic or merchandise of most covetous men, whereby craftily and cunningly they purge the purses, not the souls, both of rich and poor[2].

These men by and by under-prop their purgatory building, which is a falling, with two posts. The first is this : They *Of prayer for the dead.* of old (say they) prayed for the salvation of souls separated from the body ; therefore there is a purgatory. For since in heaven they have no need of prayers; surely in hell[3] prayers do no good, since in hell is no redemption ; truly there is a middle place left wherein souls are kept, unto whom the prayers of the living do good : that place is purgatory[4]. Thus indeed they reason, howbeit imagining all things of their own heads, without the authority of the scriptures. But this is that they have to say, that they of old prayed for the dead. I know what Augustine, that famous doctor of the church, what Chrysostom, that golden-mouthed man, and other ancient and notable men have left written touching this matter. But I ask the question, Whether that which they did were well done ? For not all things which the holy fathers said and did (who oftentimes have suffered something of man's invention) are absolutely to be allowed or followed. Those things are not to be allowed and followed, which are set down by them against the decrees of the scripture, (which thing they themselves unfeignedly confess[5];) but those things only which

[2 Tyndale's Exposit. ed. Parker Soc. pp. 161-163. Answer to More, p. 146. Doctr. Treat. pp. 244, 303, 318. Sermons of Latimer, p. 50.]

[3 ex inferis, Lat.]

[4 Thomas Aquinas contra Gentiles. Lib. IV. cap. 91. Bellarmin. disput. de Controversiis, Lib. I. cap. 5. Controv. VI.]

[5 See Confutation of Unwritten Verities. Cranmer's Remains, &c. ed. Parker Soc. chap. II. pp. 22-36.]

are uttered and confirmed by the authority of holy scriptures, which largely and plainly contain whatsoever is necessary to be known in the doctrine of godliness. But thou canst find nothing in them of prayer for the dead. For that which some allege out of the second book of Maccabees proveth nothing; for that book is not canonical: which thing it behoved them to have learned long since even out of Hierome [1].

They add, That prayer for the dead is an unwritten tradition of the apostles [2]. I hear them; but I know well enough that the unwritten traditions of the apostles are not contrary to their written doctrines. I know well enough that the written doctrines of the apostles no where command prayers for the dead, and in no place allow them. When Paul the apostle exhorted the Thessalonians to moderation in lamenting for the dead [3], the time being then very fit and most convenient to give commandment concerning offering of prayers for the souls of the dead, if he had thought them any whit profitable and necessary; yet notwithstanding he maketh no manner mention of them, yea rather, he simply teacheth what they ought to believe touching the souls of the faithful being separated from their bodies, namely, that they live in everlasting blessedness with Christ, waiting and looking for the resurrection of their bodies [4]. But who cannot see that this certainty and plainness of the apostle's doctrine is entangled and perilously shaken with this feigned apostolic tradition? For if we believe in Christ, let us believe his words and promises. He himself said that he is the resurrection and life of the faithful, and that the souls of the believing even immediately upon the death of the body do escape and pass into life. If (I say) we believe these most true words of the Lord, why then do we, as yet being careful for the salvation of the souls of the dead, pray and make

1 Thess. iv.

[1 Machabæorum libros legit quidem ecclesia, sed inter canonicas scripturas non recipit.—Hieron. Præf. in Prov. Solom. Opp. Tom. I. fol. 939. Par. 1693. See also Bp. Cosin's Scholast. Hist. of Canon of Script. Chap. VI. § 71. p. 72. Lond. 1683. Fulke's Defence, &c. ed. Parker Soc. p. 24. Remains of Abp. Grindal, p. 23.]

[2 Bellarmin. Controv. I. Lib. IV. cap. 7. col. 164. Controv. VI. Lib. II. cap. 16. col. 1404. Jewel's Defence of Apology, ed. Parker Soc. p. 559.]

[3 mortem suorum, Lat.; the death of their brethren.]

[4 Cf. Sermons of Abp. Sandys, ed. Parker Soc. p. 163.]

supplication for them, as though they had not yet obtained salvation? By these our prayers truly ye give a manifest proof that we doubt of our faith, and hope not after that, as concerning the salvation of our souls, which we do both profess with tongue, and which also the words of Christ and the apostles command us to hope after. The stedfast faith truly and assured hope of those that believe and stay themselves upon the promises of Christ do forbid us here to take and wear black mourning-garments in offerings for the dead, whose souls we believe to have already put on white garments: they forbid us to give occasion either to unbelievers, or to weaklings in faith, of reprehending us worthily, because we mourn and lament for them who we say do live with God, as if they were cast into hell-fire[5], and busily set ourselves awork with making humble prayers unto God to deliver the miserable souls out of torments; that is to say, because the faith, which we profess with tongue and voice, we condemn by the testimony of our heart and mind, yea, and of our outward works. If we go on after this sort, truly we are double-dealers in our hope and in our faith. The things which we speak seem to be dissembled, false, and feigned. For it availeth nothing in words to vaunt of virtue, and with deeds to destroy truth. Therefore let him that will receive this tradition (as they call it) of the apostles, touching the offering of prayers for the faithful departed: as for me, I mean to receive nothing repugnant to true faith and disagreeing from the apostles' doctrine, neither do I persuade any man to receive such vanity.

This also I cannot choose but tell you, that that which they call the tradition of the apostles St Augustine calleth the tradition of the fathers received of the church. For in his sermon, *de verbis Apostoli*, 32, he saith: "This which the fathers delivered the whole church observeth; to wit, that prayers should be made for them in the communion of the body and blood of Christ, when they in their own place are rehearsed at the very sacrifice, and the same is mentioned to be offered for them also[6]." And again, *de Cura pro Mortuis gerenda*, cap. 4,

[5 in ignes, Lat.; hell, not in Lat.]
[6 Hoc enim a patribus traditum universa observat ecclesia, ut pro eis qui in corporis et sanguinis Christi communione defuncti sunt, cum ad ipsum sacrificium loco suo commemorantur, oretur, ac pro illis

he saith: "Supplications or prayers for the souls of the dead are not to be neglected, which the church hath received to be made for all that be departed in the christian brotherhood; not rehearsing them by name, but in a general remembrance of them altogether[1]." Thus far he: who though in some place he stretch the traditions of the apostles very far, yet by these words this seemeth more expressly to be his meaning; that this rite or order of praying for the dead was delivered to the church by the fathers, and doubtless many years after the apostles' time was received of the church. The same Augustine defendeth in more places than one, that the receiving of the eucharist, or sacrament of the Lord's supper, is as necessary for infants being new come forth of their mother's womb to the attaining of salvation, as the sacrament of baptism. The chief and notable places, wherein he handleth that matter, are in his first book against Julianus Pelagianus, &c., and in his first book *de Peccatorum Meritis et Remissione*, against the Pelagians[2]. Neither doth he urge that opinion with less earnestness than the tradition, because that was received and very usual in the church in that age. But who at this day receiveth that ceremony as apostolical? Who seeth not that those good fathers, otherwise most faithful pastors, in that thing suffered some invention of man? The written doctrine of St Paul deserveth at this day more to be esteemed than that ancient tradition of the church. Paul writeth: "Let every man examine himself, and so let him eat of this bread and drink of this cup." Whereby all men understand that the eucharist, or sacrament of the Lord's supper, is for them to receive that are of perfect age, and not for infants. For that cause it was lawful for our elders to forsake that tradition, and to draw more near to the scripture. Let them therefore in this matter give us leave also to depart from the uncertain tradition of the fathers, and to cleave to the most assured faith and doctrine of the apostles.

1 Cor. xi.

quoque id offerri commemoretur.—August. de Verbis Apost. Serm. xxxii. Opp. Tom. x. fol. 84. col. 1. Par. 1532.]

[1 Non sunt prætermittendæ supplicationes pro spiritibus mortuorum, quas faciendas pro omnibus in Christiana et catholica societate defunctis, etiam tacitis nominibus quorumque sub generali commemoratione, suscepit ecclesia.—Id. Tom. iv. fol. 200, col. 2.]

[2 Id. Tom. vii. fol. 192, &c., and fol. 134, &c. Par. 1532.]

But Ærius (say they) was condemned for this cause, for *Æriani con-* that he believed prayers were unprofitable for the dead[3]. I *demned.* know indeed that Ærius was condemned, neither do I take upon me to defend him, whom Phylastrius, Epiphanius, and Augustine do make mention to have been an Arian, and a man polluted with other foul errors[4]. But touching prayers for the dead, whether they be profitable or unprofitable, there is no doubt that they are catholics and not heretics, who believe that which is delivered and set down in the Apostles' creed: for according to the tradition of this creed we believe the forgiveness of sins, the resurrection of this flesh, and life everlasting. They which believe these things obtain undoubtedly whatsoever they believe. For the Lord said to the Centurion: "Go thy way, and as thou hast be- *Matt. viii.* lieved, so be it done unto thee." Therefore whosoever believeth forgiveness of sins and life everlasting hath obtained forgiveness of sins, and surely he shall live in everlasting life. Which thing, if that be true, as it cannot be false, which is delivered unto us in the Apostles' creed, what place, I pray you, shall prayers have for the dead? For the dead have their sins forgiven them: therefore all lets and delays unto life are taken away, and so they live with God. But they which have not believed have retained and kept their sins still, and, being cast down into the bottomless lake, stick fast in the mire of hell. Which things since they are so of a certainty, truly there is no use of praying for the dead, neither before God, nor among the faithful. Hereunto are annexed so many examples of the saints in both the Testaments, which are to be preferred both before traditions and condemnations of men. Which, I pray you, of the holy fathers ever prayed for their dead? Did Adam pray for his Abel? Did the sons pray for their father Adam? What prayers did Abraham offer to God for the soul of his father Thare, or for the soul of his most dear wife Sara? What prayers poured Esau and Jacob forth for their father Isaac when he died? the twelve sons of Israel for Jacob? Salo-

[3 Bellarmin. Controv. vi. Lib. i. cap. 2. col. 1325.]
[4 S. Philastrii Lib. de Hæres. p. 491. § 44. Vet. Pat. Biblioth. Tom. vii. Ven. 1670. Epiphan. adv. Hæres. Lib. iii. Tom. i. § 1. p. 905. Opp. Tom. i. Par. 1622. August. Opp. Tom. vi. fol. 6. col. 1. Par. 1532.]

mon for David? In the new Testament John Baptist is beheaded of Herod, Stephen stoned of the Jews, James his head is cut off by the shoulders at the commandment of Agrippa; their disciples bury their bodies, and do all things religiously belonging to their burials: but in so many funerals there is no mention made of prayer for the souls of the dead; for they believed that they forthwith after death were carried into everlasting life. Who then after so many notable examples, and after so clear profession of the catholic and sincere faith, can tie us to the necessity of praying for the souls of the dead? Who can say hereafter that we are heretics, who fulfil that in work which we profess in profession of faith or confession of the mouth; yea, which do no other thing than the most excellent worshippers of God of both Testaments have done before us?

Appearing of spirits. The last post, wherewith they underprop their purgatory, lest it should fall, is the appearing of spirits[1]. For Rabanus, a bishop, sheweth out of the testimonies of pope Gregory and reverend Beda, that the souls of dead men have very often appeared, and taught that oblations and prayers do profit them very much[2]. But I wonder that men of learning would ground their work upon so rotten and ruinous foundations; *Deut. xviii.* for the Lord in the law forbiddeth to ask the truth of the spirits or souls of the dead. In the Prophets we are sent *Isai. viii.* from such oracles to the law and the testimony. In Luke *Luke xvi.* the rich glutton crieth in torments, and saith: "I pray thee, father Abraham, that thou wouldest send Lazarus to my father's house, for I have five brethren, that he may witness unto them, lest they also come into this place of torment." But he heareth: "They have Moses and the prophets; let them hear them." But when the rich glutton had answered, "No, father Abraham; but if one come unto them from the dead, they will believe and[3] repent;" he heareth again, "If they hear not Moses and the prophets, neither will they believe,

[1 Bellarmin. disput. de Controversiis. Controv. vi. Lib. i. cap. 7. coll. 1361, 2, 1375, 1384, 1390. Magdeb. Centur. Cent. viii. cap. 13. col. 498. Vol. ii. Cent. x. cap. 14. col. 385. Cent. xii. cap. 13. col. 886. Vol. iii. Basil. 1624.]

[2 Rabani Mauri de Instit. Cleric. Lib. ii. cap. 44. Tom. vi. fol. 27. col. 1. Col. Agrip. 1626.]

[3 believe and, not in Lat.]

if one rise from death." Therefore it is most certain, and confirmed by the authority of the gospel, that blessed souls[4] are not sent of God unto us to teach us any thing. Who, I pray you, would give ear to wicked and condemned souls? The gospel of Christ sendeth us all to the canonical scripture. Whereupon it followeth, that the testimonies which are fetched from oracles or appearings of the spirits of the dead are of no weight, but most deceivable and full of lying.

Man's testimonies are agreeable with God's; which also teach us, that souls being separated from their bodies cannot wander or stray in these regions. The words are too long to rehearse, which Tertullian learnedly disputeth of this matter in the end almost of his book *De Anima;* yet they are all levelled to this mark, to shew that souls separated from their bodies, and appointed to their places, do not return again into this world. To the objection of some that boast of art magic, and also that by the power of God many have returned from the dead into this life, he answereth: "But although the power of God hath called back again some souls into their bodies, to give us instruction of his might and right; yet therefore that shall not be communicated with the credit and boldness of magicians, and the deceitfulness of dreams, and licentiousness of poets: but in the examples of the resurrection, when God's power, either by prophets, or by Christ, or by apostles, bringeth souls into bodies, it is manifestly declared by sound, evident, and full truth, that it is the shape of a true body: that thou mightest judge all appearings of dead men without bodies to be delusions[5]." Therefore Chrysostom in his twenty-ninth Homily upon Matthew demanding: "What then shall we answer to those speeches; I am such a soul?" he answereth; "It is not the soul of that dead body which speaketh these things, but the devil, who de-

That souls separated from their bodies do not wander in these regions.

[4 ne beatas quidem animas, Lat. ; that not even blessed souls.]

[5 Sed etsi quasdam revocavit in corpora Dei virtus, in documenta juris sui, non idcirco communicabitur fidei et audaciæ Magorum, et fallaciæ somniorum, et licentiæ poëtarum. Atquin in resurrectionis exemplis, cum Dei virtus, sive per prophetas, sive per Christum, sive per apostolos in corpora animas repræsentat, solida et contrectabili et satiata veritate, præjudicatum est hanc esse formam veritatis, ut omnem mortuorum exhibitionem incorporalem præstigias judices.—Tertull. de Anim. cap. 57. Opp. ed. Semler. Tom. IV. p. 287. Hal. Magd. 1824.]

viseth these things to deceive them that hear him." And
anon he saith : " Wherefore these are to be counted the words
of old wives and of dotards, and children's toys and phantasies." And again: "A soul separated from the body
cannot wander in these regions. For the souls of the righteous are in the hands of God, and the souls of infants likewise : for they have not sinned. And the souls of the wicked
after this life are by and by carried away : which is made
apparent by Lazarus and the rich glutton. But in another
Luke xii. place the Lord also saith : 'This night they shall require thy
soul again from thee.' Therefore the soul, when it departeth
from the body, cannot wander here with us : and that not
without cause. For if they which go a journey, chancing
into unknown countries, know not whither they are like to
go, except they have a guide ; how much more shall the soul
be ignorant whither it shall go, after it hath left the body
and entereth altogether into a new life and strange way,
unless it have a guide ! Out of many places of the scripture
it may be proved, that the souls of just and righteous men
Acts vii. do not go astray[1] after death. For Stephen saith, 'Lord
Phil. i. Jesu, receive my spirit.' And Paul desired to be loosed and
Gen. xxv. to be with Christ. Of the patriarch the scripture also saith,
'He died in a quiet (or good) age, and was gathered unto (or
Luke xvi. laid by) his fathers.' And that the souls of the wicked cannot
tarry or have their abiding here, give ear what the rich
glutton saith, and consider what he craveth, and obtaineth not.
For if the souls of men might be conversant here, he had come
himself as he desired, and had certified his brethren of the
torments of hell. Out of which place of scripture this also
plainly appeareth ; that souls after their going out of the body
are carried into some certain appointed place, from whence
they cannot return of their own accord when they will
return, but wait and look for that terrible day of judgment[2]."
Thus much hitherto out of Chrysostom.

[1 non errare hic, Lat.; do not wander up and down here.]

[2 Αὐτοὶ, φησὶν, οἱ δαιμονῶντες βοῶσιν, ὅτι ψυχὴ τοῦ δεῖνος ἐγώ.
Ἀλλὰ καὶ τοῦτο σκηνή τις καὶ ἀπάτη διαβολική. Οὐ γὰρ ἡ ψυχὴ τοῦ τελευ-
τηκότος ἐστὶν ἡ βοῶσα, ἀλλ' ὁ δαίμων ὑποκρινόμενος ταῦτα ὥστε ἀπατῆσαι
τοὺς ἀκούοντας.... Ὥστε γραϊδίων μεθυόντων ταῦτα τὰ ῥήματα, καὶ παίδων
μορμολύκεια. Οὐδὲ γὰρ ἔνι ψυχὴν ἀπορραγεῖσαν τοῦ σώματος ἐνταῦθα
πλανᾶσθαι λοιπόν· ψυχαὶ γὰρ δικαίων ἐν χειρὶ Θεοῦ· εἰ δὲ αἱ τῶν δικαίων,

Against these things they oppose the appearing of Samuel _{Samuel} *(margin: Samuel after his death appeared not to Saul.)*
fetched from the holy scriptures; whereby they go about to
prove that souls return again after death, and instruct men
touching things which they shall demand. We answer in
few words, that that disguised masker, which seemed to be
Samuel, was called Samuel by a trope or figure, but in very
deed he was not Samuel: for of a certainty it was a spirit, *1 Sam. xxviii.*
a juggling and delusion of Satan. For sorcery is straitly
forbidden in the law of the Lord: therefore blessed spirits
obey not forbidden ways and unlawful practices, which, when
they were as yet joined with their fleshly bodies, by all means
abhorred and resisted them in their assaults: as for damned
spirits, they exercise themselves therein. But who would
believe their oracles? Samuel[3] (say they) foretold what
happened the morrow after. And what of that? That was
no hard matter for the devil, since that the true and living
Samuel foretold many things a little while before: but this
crafty fox might foreknow the judgment of God which was
to come, even by things present, and by the fear and quaking
of the hosts. Tertullian in his book *De Anima* saith:
" God forbid we should believe that the soul of any saint,
much less the soul of a prophet, can be fetched up by the devil;
since we have learned that Satan is transformed into an

καὶ αἱ τῶν παίδων· οὐδὲ γὰρ ἐκεῖναι πονηραί· καὶ αἱ τῶν ἁμαρτωλῶν δὲ
εὐθέως ἐντεῦθεν ἀπάγονται. Καὶ δῆλον ἀπὸ τοῦ Λαζάρου καὶ τοῦ πλουσίου.
Καὶ ἀλλαχοῦ δέ φησιν ὁ Χριστός· Σήμερον τὴν ψυχήν σου ἀπαιτοῦσιν ἀπὸ
σοῦ. Καὶ οὐχ οἷόν τε ψυχὴν ἐξελθοῦσαν τοῦ σώματος ἐνταῦθα πλανᾶσθαι·
καὶ μάλιστα εἰκότως· εἰ γὰρ ἐν γῇ βαδίζοντες τῇ συνήθει καὶ γνωρίμῳ, καὶ
σῶμα περικείμενοι, ὅταν ξένην ὁδὸν ὁδεύωμεν, ποίαν ἐλθεῖν δεῖ οὐκ ἴσμεν
ἂν μὴ τὸν χειραγωγοῦντα ἔχωμεν, πῶς ἡ τοῦ σώματος ἀπορραγεῖσα ψυχή,
καὶ τῆς συνηθείας ἐξελθοῦσα πάσης, εἴσεται ποῦ δεῖ βαδίζειν ἄνευ τοῦ
καθοδηγοῦντος αὐτήν· καὶ πολλαχόθεν δὲ ἑτέρωθεν ἄν τις κατίδοι, ὅτι οὐκ
ἔνι ψυχὴν ἐξελθοῦσαν ἐνταῦθα μεῖναι· καὶ γὰρ ὁ Στέφανός φησι· Δέξαι τὸ
πνεῦμά μου· καὶ ὁ Παῦλος, Τὸ ἀναλῦσαι καὶ σὺν Χριστῷ εἶναι πολλῷ
μᾶλλον κρεῖττον· καὶ περὶ τοῦ πατριάρχου δέ φησιν ἡ γραφή· Καὶ προσε-
τέθη πρὸς τοὺς πατέρας αὐτοῦ, τραφεὶς ἐν γήρει καλῷ. Ὅτι δὲ οὐδὲ αἱ τῶν
ἁμαρτωλῶν ψυχαὶ διατρίβειν ἐνταῦθα δύνανται, ἄκουσον τοῦ πλουσίου πολλὰ
ὑπὲρ τούτου παρακαλοῦντος, καὶ οὐκ ἐπιτυγχάνοντος. Ὡς εἴγε ἦν δυνατόν,
αὐτὸς ἂν ἦλθε καὶ ἀνήγγειλε τὰ ἐκεῖ γεγενημένα. Ὅθεν δῆλον ὅτι μετὰ τὴν
ἐντεῦθεν ἀποδημίαν εἰς χώραν τινὰ ἀπάγονται αἱ ψυχαί, οὐκ ἔτι κύριαι οὖσαι
ἐπανελθεῖν, ἀλλὰ τὴν φοβερὰν ἐκείνην ἡμέραν ἀναμένουσαι.—Chrysostom.
Hom. in Matth. xxviii. (al. xxix.) foll. 336, 7. Tom. vii. Par. 1727.]

[3 Sed prædixit, Lat.; But Samuel, &c.]

angel of light, much more into a man of light; yea, that he will pretend that he is God, and will shew wonderful signs, to overthrow, if it were possible, even the elect[1]," &c. St Augustine is of the same judgment concerning that appearing. Lib. *ad Simplicianum* II. quæst. 3; and *ad Dulcitii* quæst.[2] &c.

By these testimonies it is abundantly declared, I trust, that souls of men separated from bodies do not wander or appear after death in these regions; for they remain until judgment in the places appointed for them by the determination and providence[3] of God. Wherefore they are neither sent by God, neither can they enter in unto men to instruct and warn them either of things present or of things to come. Whereupon it followeth, that appearing of souls, that revelations and oracles, are mere delusions of Satan, ordained contrary to the sincerity and pureness of true religion. And because they which do what they can to prove unto us that there is purgatory use the defence and safeguard of these vanities; it is undoubtedly true that they prove a falsehood by deceit, and an uncertain thing by a thing of much more uncertainty. Furthermore, it remaineth undoubtedly true, that purgatory, wherein souls having put off their bodies should be purged unto life everlasting, cannot be shewed out of the scriptures.

Souls certainly and immediately after the death of the body are blessed.

And because we have removed and put by the lets which were cast in the way to hinder the most speedy journey, we return to our purpose; wherein we intended to declare that the souls of the faithful, separated by death from the body, do immediately after the death of the body pass the right and ready way into heaven, and so most certainly and upon the sudden be saved. Likewise we understand, that the souls of the unfaithful are thrust down the right and ready way into hell, and that by and by after the death of the body they perish with most certain and sudden damnation. For the

[1 Absit alioquin ut animam cujuslibet sancti, nedum prophetæ, a dæmonio credamus extractam, edocti quod ipse Satanas transfiguretur in angelum lucis, etiam Deum se adseveraturus, signaque portentosiora editurus, ad evertendos, si fieri possit, electos.—Tertull. de Anim. cap. 57. ed. Semler. Tom. IV. p. 286.]

[2 August. Opp. Tom. IV. fol. 139. col. 1. and fol. 142. coll. 3, 4. Par. 1532.]

[3 and providence, not in Lat.]

Lord expressly saith in the gospel: " He that believeth in the John iii.
Son of God is not condemned (or judged); but he that believeth not is condemned (or judged) already, because he hath
not believed in the name of the only begotten Son of God."
Again : " He that believeth in the Son of God hath eternal [v. 36.]
life; but he that believeth not the Son shall not see life, but
the wrath of God abideth on him." And yet again : " This [vi. 40.]
is the will of him that sent me, that every one which seeth the
Son, and believeth on him, hath everlasting life; and I will raise
him up at the last day." Now the last day of man is the The last day
point of death: in it Christ saveth us by his power, lest our of man.
soul should either perish or feel any torments, but that it
might live and enjoy everlasting blessedness. Moreover[4],
the last day is that last day of judgment, wherein Christ shall
raise again and judge all flesh, glorifying the bodies of his
faithful people unto life everlasting.

Again the Lord saith in the gospel: "Verily, verily, I John v.
say unto you, He that heareth my word, and believeth on him
that sent me, hath everlasting life, and shall not come into
judgment (or damnation); but is escaped from death unto
life." These only words of our Lord are able enough (without any gain-saying) to set forth, declare, prove, and confirm
sufficiently our opinion concerning the most certain and sudden
salvation of souls. For first of all, lest any man should doubt
of the most assured truth touching the matter which he was
setting forth, immediately upon the beginning most holily he
sweareth, that is to say, he confirmeth the truth by giving
witness thereunto with an oath. Afterwards he annexeth
the whole manner of our salvation; which consisteth in hearing
the word of God, and in true faith which receiveth the truth of
God's word: for it is not enough to have heard the word of
the gospel, unless we cleave unto the same by true faith.
But now mark with what assurance Christ promiseth life and
salvation to them that believe in him : " He hath life everlasting," saith he: he said, "he hath," not, he shall have. Therefore he left no space either to doubting, or to space of time.
Yea, yet more plainly, by interpretation expounding when and
how the faithful have or obtain life, he saith : " He shall not

[4 Est præterea, &c. Lat. Again the last day is. In these two
senses Bullinger also explains "the last day" in Comment. in Joan. in
loc. cit.]

come into judgment (or damnation), but is escaped from death unto life." They come into judgment, which have their cause to be examined and discussed before the judge. They come also into judgment, which by the sentence of the judge are punished for their evil cause. But the faithful have no cause to be tried and discussed before the judge; for their sins are fully forgiven them. "It is God which justifieth and forgiveth. Who is he that condemneth?" Therefore they are not subject to any punishments; for Christ bare the punishment of the cross, that his faithful people might be delivered and saved harmless from all torments. But rather, lest any man should think there were a stay or space of time between the death of the body and the life of the world to come, he saith: "But is escaped from death unto life." Lo, he saith, "He is escaped," not, He shall escape; that by the verb of the preter tense he might signify the certainty of the time past[1], and might shew that the souls of them that believe are by and by after the death of the body caught up into life everlasting. And I know well enough that the adversaries here have no sound argument to set against so manifest and invincible a truth. Indeed, with their wrangling words and their sophistry they may wrestle with the truth; but to overthrow the truth they are never able. For the souls of the faithful even out of the very mouth (as is commonly said, " *Von mund auf zu himmel faren*[2]") upon a sudden enter into their blessed seats, and by faith enjoy everlasting felicity.

Rev. xiv. Again, we read in the revelation of our Lord Jesus Christ made to John the apostle, that it was said: "And I heard a voice from heaven, saying unto me, Write, Blessed are the dead which hereafter die in the Lord[3]: even so saith the Spirit, that they may rest from their labours, and their works follow them." In these words an heavenly and undoubted oracle touching the blessednesses of all such as die in faith is knit up: and St John is commanded to write the oracle from

[1 of the time past, not in Lat.]

[2 Ascend to heaven from the very mouth.]

[3 So Tyndale, 1525; Coverdale, 1535; Cranmer, 1539; and the Geneva version, 1557. The Vulgate reads, Amodo jam dicit Spiritus, (From henceforth now, saith the Spirit, Douay); but Erasmus notes: Græci sic distinguunt, ut amodo sit finis sententiæ, ut sit sensus, *Posthac* fore beatos, qui in Domino fuerint mortui. Annot. in loc.]

heaven, that it may remain to all times, and be read of all people. The sum of the oracle is this, " Blessed are the dead, which hereafter die in the Lord." But they die in the Lord, whosoever depart out of this life in the faith of Jesus Christ; for so the apostle useth this kind of speech in the 1 Cor. xv. and 1 Thess. iv. Furthermore, they which depart out of this life in the faith of Jesus Christ are simply and truly pronounced blessed, to wit, happy and free from all misery. Yea, a note of the time when they shall obtain this blessedness is added, namely, Hereafter ($\dot{a}\pi\dot{a}\rho\tau\iota$), that is to say, presently, at an instant[4], by and by, out of hand, to wit, as the Lord saith in the gospel, forthwith after the death of the body. There is added also another testimony, whereby again the certainty of felicity is expressed, and perfection too not delayed till the morrow : " Even so, saith the Spirit, that they may rest from their labours." The Spirit, I mean, of truth, which cannot lie, saith, $\nu a\acute{\iota}$, that is to say, Amen, so it is: truly the faithful are blessed indeed; and even at an instant they are blessed; and so blessed, that " they rest from their labours." The labours of the faithful are miseries, calamities, afflictions, sorrow, fear or dread, and other evils of this sort, wherewith in this world they are vexed, yea, rather exercised in faith. From these things the souls of the faithful departing from their bodies are delivered: therefore they are not purged by torments and vexations, they are not scorched in the midst of their journey ; but, being happy and blessed, are forthwith delivered from all anguish and trouble. And if so be that they suffered anything whiles they were yet living in the body, if they did any good works in faith, they "do follow them." Let no man think that those works, because they now cease, were and are vain ; for they receive their reward in that blessed life. For that it is, that " their works do follow them." And let us mark, that he saith not, the works of other follow them, to deliver them forsooth out of purgatory; but, their own works follow them. For in the gospel also, the wise virgins, which had oil ready in their lamps, went in with the bridegroom to the marriage: the foolish virgins,

[4 $\dot{a}\pi\dot{a}\rho\tau\iota$ significat, ab instanti, ab illa hora, protinus et continuo, einswegs, von stund an. Bulling. in Apoc. Conc. 65. p. 205. Basil. 1570.]

which had[1] prepared themselves no oil, but did hope to have from elsewhere to serve their turn, are excluded and shut out from joy.

To the omnipotent God therefore, our most merciful Father, and continual running fountain of all good graces and which is never drawn dry, who fashioned our body in our mother's womb, and breathed or poured into it a reasonable soul, which might whilst it is joined to the body quicken and direct us, and when it is separated from the body might forthwith after the death of the body be translated into heaven, there to live in joy and happiness until it return again unto the body being raised from the dead in the last judgment, with the which it may rejoice and be glad for ever and without end; to that God, I say, through Jesus Christ, for whose sake we are made partakers of so great a benefit, be glory, praise, and thanksgiving for evermore. Amen.

[[1] in vita, Lat. omitted; in their lifetime.]

CONTENTS.

BIOGRAPHICAL NOTICE

OF

HENRY BULLINGER.

[To avoid multiplying references it is here generally stated, that the following abstract of Bullinger's life has been compiled from a Diary of Bullinger's, in the Library of Zurich (Acta Eccles. Mscr. F. 106); from a memoir of Bullinger, in the 1st volume of Miscell. Tigur. part 2; from the biographies of Simler, Melchior Adam, and Pastor Hess; and from D'Aubigne's History of the Reformation, (Books VIII. XI. XV. XVI.), where much use has been made of Bullinger's own "Chronick."]

HENRY BULLINGER, the fifth child of Henry Bullinger and Anna Widerkehr[1], was born on the 18th of July, 1504, at Bremgarten, a small town, of which his father was parish-priest and dean, about ten miles west of Zurich. In his childhood he was preserved several times from imminent perils: once from the plague, and risk of premature interment; again, when by a fall in the street a whistle which was in his hand was driven into his neck; and again, when the enticement of a beggar would have stolen him from his home and friends.

His earliest education was commenced in his fifth year in the school of his native place: but such was his fondness for learning, application, and forwardness, that in his twelfth year, June 11, 1516, his father sent him to a grammar-school at Emmerich on the Rhine. There he continued three years, and made rapid advances, especially in his Latin studies. Meanwhile his pecuniary resources were kept so straitened, that he was obliged to beg for a livelihood from one neighbour's door to another with singing. This severe discipline his father exercised, not out of necessity, nor from covetousness, but (as he thought) to train his son to moderation in his own habits, and to sympathy with the sufferings of the poor[2].

[1] They were not *formally* married until December 31, 1529, at the cathedral in Zurich.—Bullinger's Diary. Miscell. Tig. Tom. I. par. 2. p. 4.

[2] Bullinger drily observes in his diary: "Intra hoc triennium secundo me vestivit parens; dedit præterea aureos 33."

Nor was this hardship, connected as it was with the superstitious notions of his day, uncongenial with young Bullinger's
own temperament: rather he has left it on record, that he
already purposed with himself to become after a few years a
Carthusian monk, because it was the most strict of all the
orders.

From Emmerich Bullinger was removed to the university
of Cologne; and entered July 8, 1519,[1] at the college *Bursæ-
Montis*. There the works of the school-divines, and chiefly of
Peter Lombard and Gratian, soon engrossed his attention;
and, in the providence of God, were converted into instruments
for detaching him from the religion of Rome. For in this
course of reading meeting with frequent extracts from the
fathers, he felt an earnest desire quickened within him to
peruse their entire writings. Accordingly, he solicited and
obtained admission to a well-stored library of the Dominicans;
and there studied with intense ardour several treatises of
Chrysostom, Ambrose, Origen, and Augustine. Simultaneously
the earlier tracts of Luther, especially his " Babylonish Captivity" and treatise " On Christian Liberty," with the " Loci
Communes" of Melancthon, came into his hands. He procured
for himself also a copy of the New Testament[2], and devoted
days and nights to the perusal of it, with the aid of the Commentaries of Jerome. The result of these pursuits was, that
Bullinger's mind and heart opened gradually to the knowledge and reception of the gospel in its purity[3].

In this transition state, and having taken his bachelor's
degree in October 1520, and his master's in February 1522,[4]
Bullinger returned in April of the last-mentioned year to his
father's roof at Bremgarten. There he devoted himself to
the study of the Bible with still greater eagerness; and joined
to it the writings of Athanasius, Cyprian, and Lactantius, and

[1] In this same year Bullinger's father set himself to oppose Samson, the preacher of indulgences, at Bremgarten.—D'Aubigne, Hist.
of Ref. Book VIII. chap. 7.

[2] Of the ignorance of scripture among the priests of this time
Bullinger affirms in his preface to the Epistles :—inter trecentos non
reperti sunt triginta qui ordinarie Biblia legerint.

[3] — totus a papistica doctrina abhorrere incipio.—Bullinger's
Diary.

[4] — In recipiendis titulis una cum aliis insaniebam, ut tum erat
moris.—Bullinger's Diary.

several of Luther's treatises, especially " On the Abrogation of the Mass," and " On Vows." These occupations powerfully promoted, under God, his improved views of christian truth[5].

But his profiting was not to be for himself only. The Cistercian abbot of Cappel, Wolfgang Joner, since his elevation in 1519, had laboured much to improve the moral and intellectual condition of his convent. Having heard therefore of Bullinger's excellent character, studiousness, and abilities, he sent an invitation to him early in 1523, to become lecturer and teacher of the monks and other students in his monastery; and as the offer was disconnected with any constraint of vows, profession, or observances, that could interfere with his enlightened conscience[6], Bullinger consented to enter (17th January) upon the proposed duties. The engagement, however, was a further development of God's gracious providence toward him[7]; and as it allowed him to discourse on the holy scriptures, with the writings of the fathers and Erasmus and Melancthon, it was a signal means to himself and his hearers of advancement in sound christian doctrine[8], notwithstanding severe oppositions even to the risk of life. Six years were passed by Bullinger in this useful retirement; where also he composed, principally for his own practice and improvement, more than fifty treatises, mostly on religious topics: of which the larger part remained in manuscript[9]; but some were either published afterwards, or incorporated in his later writings, or distributed among his friends[10].

During the same interval Bullinger formed an intimate

[5] See Bp Cox's testimony; Zurich Letters, A. p. 244.

[6] Bullinger testifies in his Diary: "Abbas quidem non dominus mihi erat, sed præstabat mihi patrem."

[7] Ego vero indies magis atque magis abstrahebam a superstitione ad veram religionem.—Bulling. Diar.

[8] In the course of the years 1525 and 1526 images were removed from the church, and the mass was superseded by the Lord's supper, at Cappel. The abbot also married in 1527.—Bulling. Diar.

[9] In his "Ratio Studiorum," p. 45, Bullinger gives a detail of some of these compositions, and says concerning them: " ne literam quidem inter tot chiliades eo animo scripsi ut ederetur." Several of these treatises, in Bullinger's hand-writing, are yet extant in the library at Zurich; and a few were in the possession of Hottinger, when he wrote his " Schola Tigurinorum Carolina," A.D. 1664, where also the titles of most of them are to be found.—Append. I. p. 88.

[10] Biblioth. Tigur. Mscr. F. 106.

acquaintance with Zwingle and Leo Judæ, and was much influenced by the religious sentiments of the former, especially on the subject of the eucharist[1]. Indeed, in the end of June 1527, he obtained from his abbot leave of absence for five months, to attend Zwingle's lectures at Zurich; where also he availed himself of the opportunity to perfect his acquaintance with Hebrew and Greek literature.

In December of the same year, the senate of Zurich deputed Bullinger to accompany Zwingle to the important disputation at Berne[2]. On his return he was prevailed on to undertake the pastoral office[3]; and preached his first sermon on Sunday, June 21, 1528, at the village of Husen, near Cappel.

A new sphere of usefulness now opened on Bullinger; and, yielding to the advice of his relatives and patron[4], and to the solicitations of the inhabitants, he went back to Bremgarten, June 1, 1529, and by incessant preachings and expositions there and in neighbouring places greatly furthered the spreading cause of the Reformation[5]. On the 17th of August he was

---

[1] In a letter to Crodelius, March 12, 1545, Bullinger writes of himself: "Circa finem anni 1523 primum vidi Zwinglium, nihildum de eucharistia disputantem: ubi vero inceperat corpoream Christi præsentiam et manducationem oppugnare, expendi hominis argumenta, ac veritatem apertam, firmius assertam scripturis, et jam ante imbibitam priusquam novissem Zwinglium, non illibenter recepi, et me partibus ejus junxi, scribendo, docendo, disputando, prædicando, veritatis causam juvans."—Hess, p. 28.

[2] See Orig. Lett. p. 718, note 1.

[3] Bullinger's own account of this *ordination* is: "In Junio convocata est Tiguri synodus, in quam ipseque vocabar; ubi ex pastoribus præsidebat Huldr. Zuinglius, Leo Judæ, Heinrich Engelhard; et e senatoribus Diethelmus Roestius, consul, Rodolph Binderus, plebis tribunus, et alii. His rogatus solenne illud juramentum præstiti, atque ita ad prædicandum evangelium Christi vocatus, recusare amplius, quemadmodum feceram hactenus, non potui.—Bulling. Diar.

[4] Bullinger was greatly attached to his abbot, Wolfgang Joner, and constantly in his writings refers to him as "Mæcenas ille noster, omniumque studiosorum patronus." He was slain with Zwingle at the battle of Cappel.

[5] In February of this year Bullinger's father had publicly proclaimed at Bremgarten his conviction, that he had hitherto, in the time of darkness, misled his parishioners; but that now he would endeavour to guide them in the right way of life, out of holy scripture alone, and through Jesus Christ, our only Saviour.—Hess, Le-

united in marriage in the church of Birmenstorf, a small village near Bremgarten, by his brother John, the curè, to Anne Adlischweiler, to whom he had been pledged during his visit to Zurich two years previously, and who had formerly been a nun in the convent of Œtenbach, where daughters of the first families in Zurich were received[6]. During the two years of this residence at Bremgarten, Bullinger composed some of his Commentaries on parts of holy Scripture; and disputed in public often, and largely wrote against the prevailing errors of the anabaptists.

In consequence of the disastrous defeat of the protestant confederates at Cappel, October 11, 1531,[7] Bullinger was compelled to remove with his family and parents into Zurich for safety[8]. There he settled on the 21st of November; and on the 9th of December following (at the same time that the senate of Bale applied for him as successor to Œcolampadius, and the senate of Berne solicited him for a pastor[9]) he was appointed by the authorities of Zurich[10] to supply the vacancy in the preachership of their cathedral, which had been created by the melancholy death of Zwingle[11]. In this important post Bullinger continued for the remainder of his long life, labouring with most assiduous diligence and wide-spread influence. For several years, from 1531 to 1538, his preachings

bensgeschichte Bullingers, Vol. I. p. 9. Zurich. 1828. He died at Zurich, April 8, 1533, aged 64 years.

[6] Six sons and five daughters were the fruit of this marriage.— See Zurich Letters, A. p. 30, note 2.

[7] Sleidan. Comment. de Stat. Relig. Lib. VIII. p. 204. Francof. 1610. Orig. Letters, ed. Park. Soc. p. 552, note 1.

[8] In this unhappy crisis Bullinger had always recommended less warlike measures, and most publicly in a sermon preached at Bremgarten, before a general diet in the summer of 1531.—D'Aubigne's Hist. of Reform. Book XVI. chap. 5.

[9] See letters of application in Biblioth. Tig. Mscr. F. 106. No. A. fol. 32, dated Nov. 27 and 28, 1531, from Basle; and fol. 33, dated Dec. 6 and 11, from Berne.

[10] — piissimus Tigurinorum senatus . . . mandabant ne vel Basileam vel Bernam proficisceret.—Bulling. Diar.

[11] Of Bullinger's first sermon at the cathedral of Zurich, preached three days after his arrival, Myconius wrote to a friend: "Talem concionem detonavit, ut multi putarent Zuinglium non defunctum, sed ad phœnicis modum renatum esse."—Hotting. Helvet. Hist. Eccl. Tom. III. p. 602.

were daily, sometimes twice in the day; his publications, of which many were suggested by passing events, were voluminous[1] and frequent; his pastoral and synodical, civil and ecclesiastical, engagements were unceasing and very various; his correspondence was exceedingly extensive and critical: and his house was always open, and his interpositions ready to shelter and befriend especially refugees from every country where religious persecution raged[2]. And during the protracted efforts to effect a reconciliation between the Lutherans and the church of Zurich on the sacramentarian question, his moderation and sincerity were eminently conspicuous[3].

In the middle of January 1536 Bullinger was deputed with Leo Judæ to attend the conference of deputies from all the Swiss reformed churches at Basle[4]. There he assisted in drawing up the first Helvetic Confession of Faith, and commenced a personal acquaintance with Calvin. His hospitalities also were liberally experienced at Zurich by Englishmen, John Butler[5], Nicolas Partridge[6], and William Woodroofe, in the month of August of the same year. Bartholomew Traheron[7] joined them in September of the year following[8].

A fatal plague in 1541 deprived Bullinger of his aged mother (August 16) and one of his sons (September 30); and in the next year, of his beloved colleague Leo Judæ (June 19), in the midst of his invaluable labours on the Biblia Tigurina[9].

[1] It is stated sometimes, that Bullinger's writings are published in ten volumes. But this is a mistake. For his own convenience Bullinger collected the principal of them into ten volumes (Biblioth. Tigur. Mscr. F. 98. no. 6); but they have never been published in any complete form. See also Hottinger, Schola Tigur. Tig. 1664 Append. I. p. 75; and Gesneri Biblioth. Tigur. 1583.

[2] "That common father of the afflicted," is Pilkington's feeling description of Bullinger.—Orig. Lett. ed. Park. Soc. p. 135.

[3] Melch. Adam. in Vit. Bullingeri. p. 483. Francof. 1653. Hess, Lebensgeschichte H. Bullingers, Vol. I. p. 360. This moderation sometimes exposed Bullinger to unkindly suspicions.—See Orig. Lett. p. 611.

[4] Orig. Lett. p. 611, note 3.

[5] Ibid. p. 311, note 2; and p. 621, note 2.

[6] Ibid. pp. 608, 124.   [7] Ibid. pp. 316, 623, 624.

[8] Mentioning in his diary Traheron, and Partridge, and Eliot, Bullinger observes, " exposui illis multa Isaiæ capita."—Cf. Orig. Lett. pp. 623, 619.

[9] Orig. Lett. p. 235, note 7. Hess, L. H. B. Vol. I. p. 382.

The preface to this translation, which Bibliander had principally completed, was written by Bullinger in February 1543.

In his extant diary Bullinger has marked March 29, 1547, as the day when Hooper and his wife, in their exile[10], accomplished their long-cherished desire of visiting him[11]; and March 24, 1549, when they left him for England with their daughter Rachel, his god-child[12]. In the end of May of the last-mentioned year also Calvin and Farell came to Bullinger, and a " consensus " or agreement was completed on the subject of the Lord's supper, between the churches of Geneva and Zurich[13]. At the same instant, as appeared by various decrees in the year following[14], the whole weight of the papal party, imperial and ecclesiastical, was combining to condemn Bullinger and all his writings. But nothing turned him aside from his steady course of usefulness; and early in 1554 the largest influx of English refugees enjoyed his sympathy and interest. Among them were Parkhurst, Jewel, Horn, Pilkington, Lever, Humphrey, and Cole[15]. Italian exiles from Locarno also sought and obtained like shelter in Zurich, through his interventions, in the spring of the year following[16].

From 1556 to 1564 Bullinger's time and exertions were largely and painfully consumed in combating the errors of Joachim Westphalus[17], Stancari[18], George Blandrata[19], Bren-

---

[10] Orig. Lett. p. 35, note 2.   [11] Ibid. pp. 34, 42, 254.

[12] Ibid. pp. 48, 50, note 1.

[13] Ibid. pp. 88, 121, note 2. 267, 479, 493.

[14] Hoc anno (1550) missa sunt ad me edicta: primum ex Italia, ubi apud Venetos legatus S. Pontificis me et libros meos damnavit... secundum, ex inferiori Germania, ubi damnavit libros meos Theologus Lovaniensis : Ipse Cæsar Carolus V. me una cum multis aliis decreto vulgato et ipse damnavit. Tertium, ex Gallia, ubi Theologi Parisienses me et libros meos condemnarunt.—Bulling. Diar. A testimony to the value of Bullinger's Commentaries in Italy is found in Orig. Lett. p. 358.

[15] Orig. Lett. pp. 126-131, 136-7, 751. Zurich Lett. A. p. 87.

[16] Orig. Lett. p. 148. M'Crie's History of Reform. in Italy, p. 283. Lond. 1833.

[17] A minister of Hamburg, who revived the sacramentarian controversy.

[18] An Italian, who, besides approving Lutheran sentiments offensively to the Swiss, advocated dangerous opinions concerning the two natures of Christ.

[19] A physician of Savoy, and a partizan of Socinus.

tius[1], and Ochin[2]: while in the last-mentioned year a pestilence deprived him of his wife[3], and his second daughter, married to Lavater; and in the year following, of two other daughters,— his eldest, the wife of Zwingle jun.; and his third, who had married Josiah Simler[4]. By the same plague he had himself also been brought to the brink of the grave[5]; and not long after his sufferings from the stone commenced, which embittered the remainder of his days[6]. Notwithstanding declining health, family bereavements, and public trials, however, Bullinger's manifold labours continued unabated; and in the year 1571 he exerted himself most indefatigably in relieving his destitute country people during a very grievous famine.

Early in October 1574, his last and fatal disorder attacked him[7]. In the first instance, indeed, the severity of the seizure yielded so far to the remedies that were applied, that he was able to resume his public duties. But the disease returned on the 24th of May in the year following with excruciating violence, and lasted until the 17th of September: when, after exhibiting a bright example of christian patience, and having taken a touching personal farewell of all his colleagues, and written a letter to the senate of Zurich, to be delivered after his decease—(one object of which was to commend to them Rodolph Gualter as his successor),—he expired, in the exercise of much prayer and in the peace of the gospel, in the 71st year of his age[8].

His remains were deposited in the cathedral of Zurich, amid the sincere and lively regrets of all classes of his townspeople.

[1] A chief advocate of the Ubiquitarian doctrine.—Zurich Lett. A. p. 108, note 8.

[2] Bernard Ochin, an Italian, of Siena, dangerously advocated polygamy, and is said to have impugned the doctrine of the Trinity.

[3] Zurich Lett. A. pp. 144, 171.

[4] Ibid. pp. 142, note 1; and 171, note 3.

[5] Ibid. pp. 142, 3. 151.

[6] Ibid. pp. 212, 216, 314. Cœpi hoc anno (1569) ex ischia ægrotare, cui calculus accessit.—Bulling. Diar.

[7] See Zurich Lett. A. p. 317.

[8] See Bp Cox's beautiful letter on Bullinger's death, Zurich Lett. A. p. 318. See also B. p. 268.

His principal works, in the chronological order in which they were written or published, are the following:

1. Vergleichung der uralten und unser zeiten Ketzereyen, zu warnen die einfältigen Christen. ["A comparison of the heresies of ancient and of our times, a caution to plain Christians." This was Bullinger's first printed treatise. It was published, 1526, under the name of Octavius Florence.]

2. Ratio Studiorum, sive De institutione eorum, qui studia literarum sequuntur, &c. 12mo. Tigur. [This treatise was one of those which Bullinger composed at Cappel, in 1527. The MS. was given in 1532, by the author, to his great friend Berthold Haller of Berne, and preserved among his connections until published in 1594, by Ulrich Zwingle, jun.]

3. De Origine Erroris in negotio Eucharistiæ ac Missæ. 4to. Basileæ, &c. 1528. [There is added, "Appendix de Romani Pontificis authoritate, quando, a quibus, quave arte, in tantam imperii gloriam subvectus sit." This treatise also was composed at Cappel by Bullinger, after the model of Lactantius, and is dedicated to Wolfgang Joner, Peter Simler, and Andrew Curian. Œcolampadius saw the treatise on Bullinger's visit to Basle in 1527, and was so pleased with it that he prevailed to have it published. It was printed also in German at Heidelberg. Zanchi (Epist. lib. II. p. 278. Opp. Tom. VIII. Heidelb. 1613) gives a pleasing testimony to the usefulness of this book. The anecdote is quoted by M'Crie, Hist. of Reform. in Italy, p. 320, note, 2 ed. See below, No. 23.]

4. De hebdomadis quæ apud Danielem sunt, opusculum. 8vo. Tigur. 1530. [This treatise Bullinger composed at Bremgarten; but afterwards retracted it in his Homilies on Daniel. This book was forbidden in England in 1531. Foxe, Vol. IV. p. 669. Lond. 1837.]

5. Von dem unverschampten &c. leeren der selbsgesandten Widertöuffern, 12mo. &c. [This treatise against the Anabaptists was also composed by Bullinger at Bremgarten, in the end of 1530, and published at Zurich 1531. It is written in the form of a dialogue, between Simon, an anabaptist, and Joiada, his opponent. Two tracts follow; the former on the lawfulness of interest; the latter, dedicated to his brother John, on tithes. This treatise, enlarged with additions from Zwingle's "in Catabaptistarum Strophas Elenchus," was translated into Latin by Leo Judæ, and published in four books, in the year 1535.[9] Of these treatises, Zwingle says in his

[9] Ames mentions (Vol. III. p. 1461,) "Three Dialogues between the seditious libertine or rebell Anabaptist, and the true obedient Christian: wherein obedience to magistrates is handled. By Hen. Bul-

Annotations on Jeremiah, published March 11, 1531 : " Scripsit nunc de ea (re, i. e. usura, &c.) germanice Heinrychus Bullingerus, frater ac conterraneus noster, juvenis acris ac solertis ingenii, qui contra Catabaptistas disputationem, velut δᾷδα, ex nostris sumpsit mani- bus. Deo gratia." p. 149. Tig. 1531.]

6. De prophetæ officio, et quomodo digne administrari possit, oratio. 8vo. Tigur. 1532. [This sermon, which was circulated among the clergy of the canton of Zurich, because the troubled state of the time prevented their assembling to hear it, contains an encomium on Zwingle, and a defence of his death on the field of battle.]

7. Auff Johansen Wyenischen Bischoffs trostbüchlin, &c. Tig. 1532. [An answer to Faber bishop of Vienna, who boasted that the Zurichers had been defeated at Cappel because they had forsaken the true church.]

8. In Epistolam Joannis Apostoli et Evangelistæ Canonicam Commentariolus. 8vo. Tig. 1532.

9. Commentarius in Ep. Pauli ad Hebræos. 8vo. Tig.⸱1532. [The dedication to Philip, landgrave of Hesse, contains a defence of Zwingle's death and of the reformed religion. In the course of the commentary on chapter x. Bullinger also gives an account of the mode of celebrating the Lord's supper at Zurich.]

10. Expositio in sanctissimam Pauli ad Romanos epistolam. 8vo. Tig. 1533. [In his dedication to Berthold Haller Bullinger addresses him as " hujus mei operis maxima causa."]

11. In Acta Apostolorum Commentariorum libri vi. 8vo. Tig. 1533. [This work is dedicated to the senate of Frankfort-on- the-Maine, " qui mox " (Bullinger notes in his diary) "honorificas misere literas ac aureos numeros 12, quos ego senatui obtuli, qui pauperibus in xenodochio legavit." It was republished in fol. with corrections and additions in 1540.]

12. In D. Petri Apostoli Epistolam utranque commentarius. 8vo. Tig. 1534. [Dedicated " omnibus per Germaniam fratribus nomine Christi evangeliique afflictis et exulibus."]

13. In priorem D. Pauli ad Corinthios epistolam commentarius. 8vo. Tig. 1534. [In his notes on chap. xiv. Bullinger describes the public lectures in the church at Zurich since the Reformation.]

14. De Testamento seu fœdere Dei unico et æterno brevis

lynger, and translated out of Latin by John Veron, printed at Wor- cester, &c. 1551." But Lowndes also notices; " An holsome Antidotus agaynst Anabaptistes, newly translated by John Veron," and published in 1548; and " A Dialogue between the seditious Anabaptist and the true Christian, about obedience to Magistrates," printed at Worcester, in 1549.

expositio. 8vo. Tig. 1534. [This treatise was appended to the edition of Bullinger's Commentaries on the Epistles, 1537, and translated into German in 1539. (Von dem einigen und ewigen Testament oder Pundt Gottes...kurtzer bericht, &c.) It was composed against those who rejected the authority of the Old Testament among Christians. See Vol. II. p. 299, note 6.]

15. Utriusque in Christo naturæ tam divinæ quam humanæ, contra varias hæreses, pro confessione Christi catholica, assertio orthodoxa. 8vo. Tig. 1534. [Also added in 1537 to the Commentaries on the Epistles. This discourse was delivered in the convocation of the clergy of the canton of Zurich, on the festival of the martyrs, Felix and Regula, (see Decade III. p. 106,) chiefly in consequence of the Socinian doctrines of Claude of Savoy, who was in Zurich at that time. Mosheim, Vol. III. p. 555, note 6, ed. Soames.]

16. In posteriorem D. Pauli ad Corinthios Epistolam Commentarius. 8vo. Tig. 1535.

17. In D. Apostoli Pauli ad Galatas, Ephesios, Philippenses et Colossenses epist. Commentarii. 8vo. Tig. 1535.

18. In D. Apostoli Pauli ad Thessalonicenses[1], Timotheum, Titum, et Philemonem epistolas Commentarii. 8vo. Tig. 1536. [The Commentary on the epistles to Timothy is dedicated to Werner Steiner, to whom Bullinger had promised such a work (he says) ten years before, and who lodged him and his family for some weeks in 1531, when Bullinger came from Cappel to settle in Zurich.—" The Sum or Substance of the Second Epistle of St Paul to the Thessalonians, by H. Bullinger, translated by R. H," was printed in 8vo, in 1538, by James Nicholson. Ames, Vol. III. p. 1450.]

19. In Epistolas Divi Jacobi Apostoli, et in secundam et tertiam Joannis Apostoli, et unam Judæ, Commentarii. 8vo. Tig. 1537. [In this same year, 1537, Bullinger published all his Commentaries on the Epistles together in one volume, fol. with a general preface.]

20. Das der Christen gloub von anfang der wält gewart habe, &c. 4to. Basil, 1537.—[This treatise was afterwards published at Zurich in 1539, under the title, "Der alt gloub."—It was composed by Bullinger against the boast of the papists, that the defeat at Cappel had proved theirs to be the true and ancient religion.— Cellarius translated it into Latin, and published it in 1544, with the title "Antiquissima Fides," &c.—Coverdale translated it (as it should seem, from the German original) into English. See Coverdale's

---

[1] The greater part of the Commentary on the second chapter of the Second Epistle to the Thessalonians was published separately, in German, by Melchior Ambach, at Frankfort, in 1541, with the title, Vom Antichrist und seinem reich,—Of Antichrist and his kingdom.

Works, ed. P. S. "The Old Faith." See also Decade III. Serm. VIII. Vol. II. p. 299, note 5.]

21. De Scripturæ Sanctæ authoritate, certitudine, firmitate, et absoluta perfectione; deque Episcoporum, qui verbi Dei ministri sunt, institutione et functione, contra superstitionis tyrannidisque Romanæ antistites; ad sereniss. Angliæ regem Heinrychum VIII. Heinrychi Bullingeri libri duo. 4to. Tig. 1538. [These treatises were composed, and dedicated, at the suggestion of some of the Englishmen who were then sojourning in Zurich.—An English translation of the former of these treatises, made by William Gybson, and dedicated to the duke of Somerset, exists in MS. in the British Museum. (Biblioth. Reg. 18. B. XXVII. p. 101.)—See also Orig. Lett. ed. P. S. pp. 611, 618; and Decades, Vol. II. p. 15, note 6.]

22. Bericht der krancken. 12mo. Tig. 1538. [Translated into Latin "per studiosum quendam" in 1540, with the title, " Quo modo cum ægrotantibus ac morientibus agendum sit." Bullinger composed this treatise during the prevalence of a plague in Zurich. Hottinger. Schol. Tigur. Append. I. p. 77.]

23. De Origine Erroris, libri duo. 4to. Tig. 1539. [An enlarged edition of the treatise, No. 3. It was translated into French, 1560; and into German, 1574. It was also published in folio, at Zurich, 1568. Of the usefulness of this treatise to Bp Grindal, see Zurich Letters, A. p. 182, also pp. 207-8.]

24. Orthodoxa et erudita D. Joachimi Vadiani, &c. epistola, &c. Accesserunt huic D. Vigilii Martyris et Episcopi Tridentini libri v. 12mo. Tig. 1539. [Bullinger published these treatises on the two natures in Christ, with a preface, life of Vigilius, and summaries of each of his books.]

25. Expositio de omnibus sanctæ Scripturæ libris, eorumque præstantia et dignitate. 8vo. Tig. 1539. [This treatise Bullinger enlarged, and published in fol. 1543: and prefixed in 1544 to the Biblia Tigurina.]

26. Der Christlich Eestand. 12mo. Tig. 1540. [This treatise was translated into English by Coverdale, under the title, " The Christian state of Matrimony; when, where, how, and of whom it was instituted and ordained; what it is; how it ought to proceed; what be the occasions, fruit, and commodities thereof. Contrariwise, how shameful and horrible a thing whoredom and advoutry is. How one ought also to choose him a meet and convenient spouse, to keep and increase the mutual love, truth, and duty of wedlock; and how married folks should bring up their children in the fear of God." It was printed by John Goughe, 1543, (see Works of Becon, ed. P. S. Vol. I. p. 29, note 2,) and was among the forbidden books in Eng-

land in the reign of Henry VIII. Foxe, Vol. iv. p. 679. It was
also translated into Latin by John ab Ulmis, and presented to lady
Jane Grey; (Orig. Lett. ed. P. S. pp. 406, 422,) and parts of it were
by her translated into Greek, (ibid. p. 427.)]

27. In Sacrosanctum Jesu Christi Domini nostri Evangelium
secundum Matthæum Commentariorum libri xii. fol. Tig. 1542.
[The treatise on the Resurrection at the end of these Commentaries,
(Lib. xii. foll. 267—279,) was translated by Frisius into German, with
the title, " The Hope of the Faithful," and published August 18,
1544. It is this treatise, and not Wermuller's, which is placed under
the same title in Coverdale's Remains, ed. P. S. p. 135, &c.[1] Hence
the reference in p. 181, note 1, of that volume, should be to the Commentaries of Bullinger on the Epistles of St Paul. See also Orig. Lett.
ed. P. S. p. 224. The Commentaries were published in August.]

28. In divinum Jesu Christi Domini nostri Evangelium secundum Joannem Commentariorum libri x. fol. Tig. 1543. [The preface to this Commentary, " De vera hominis Christiani Justificatione,"
is dated in August. This Commentary was especially commended by
Melancthon. Corp. Reform. Tom. v. col. 342.]

29. Ad Joannis Cochlei de canonicæ Scripturæ et catholicæ
Ecclesiæ authoritate libellum pro solida Scripturæ canonicæ authori-
tate tum et absoluta ejus perfectione veraque catholicæ Ecclesiæ
dignitate Heinrychi Bullingeri orthodoxa Responsio. 4to. Tig. 1544.
[This was a reply to Cochlæus' attack on Bullinger's treatise, No. 21.
See Orig. Lett. ed. P. S. p. 244.]

30. Brevis Antiβολή, sive Responsio secunda Heinrychi Bullingeri ad maledicam implicatamque Joannis Cochlei de Scripturæ et
Ecclesiæ authoritate Replicam, una cum expositione de sancti Christi
catholica Ecclesia, ad illustrissimum Principem et Dominum D.
Ottonem Heinrychum Palatinum Rheni et utriusque Bavariæ Ducem,
&c. 4to. Tig. Nov. 1544.

31. In sacrosanctum Evangelium Domini nostri Jesu Christi
secundum Marcum Commentariorum lib. vi. fol. Tig. 1545. [The
preface, " De Jesu Christo pontifice maximo, et rege fidelium summo
regnante in ecclesia sanctorum," is dated in August.]

32. Absoluta de Christi Domini et catholicæ ejus ecclesiæ Sacramentis tractatio. [This treatise was *composed* in the year 1546; and
sent first to Calvin, who approved of it; and then to John-a-Lasco,
and by him published at London, " An. 1551. Men. Apri." with
a dedication to the princess Elizabeth. This English edition is
extremely rare. The Rev. W. Goode has a copy of it, which he

---

[1] Qu. Is this the book referred to in Orig. Lett. p. 245?

obligingly lent to the editor, and which seems to have been a presentation copy from John-a-Lasco to the bishop of Ely. The substance of this treatise was embodied by Bullinger in his Decad. v.
Serm. vi. vii. See also Orig. Lett. ed. Park. Soc. pp. 497, 681. The
printing of this treatise Abp Cranmer encouraged, although he had
not read it, saying, that Bullinger's writings needed no examination.
Gerdesii Scrin. Tom. iv. par. 1. pp. 470-2.]

33. In luculentum et sacrosanctum Evangelium Domini nostri
Jesu Christi secundum Lucam Commentariorum lib. ix. | fol. Tig.
1546. [The preface, "qua demonstratur, Deum Patrem in Filio
suo unigenito—omnia dedisse ecclesiæ suæ, quæ ad vitam et salutem hominis pertinent," &c., is dated in August. See Orig. Lett.
ed. Park. Soc. p. 255.]

34. Series et digestio temporum et rerum descriptarum a beato
Luca in Actis Apostolorum. 4to. Tig. 1548.

35. Sermonum Decas prima et secunda. 4to. Tig. 1549. [Pub-
lished in the beginning of March. See Orig. Lett. p. 266. The ninth
sermon of the 2nd Decade was published in English with a dedication to Edward VI. by Walter Lynne, with the title, "A
Treatise or Sermon of Henry Bullinger, much fruitful and necessary
for this time, concerning magistrates and obedience of subjects, &c.
Made in the year of our Lord 1549." A copy of this book is in
the British Museum. See Orig. Lett. p. 396, note 1.]

36. Sermonum Decas tertia et quarta. 4to. Tig. 1550. [The
second *volume* of the Decades, of which the former part was dedicated in March, and the latter in August, to Edward VI. See
Orig. Lett. pp. 269, 560, 141, 483, 665, 673. The former part was
translated into English immediately, by Thomas Caius; Orig. Lett.
p. 415.]

37. Sermonum Decas quinta. 4to. Tig. 1551. [This decade
was dedicated in March to lord Grey. Orig. Lett. pp. 3, 121, 436,
493, 498, 574. Extracts from this decade, and the dedication, with
a few passages from the second Decade, were published in English
with the title, "The Judgment of the Reverend Father, Master
Henry Bullinger, &c. in certain matters of religion being in controversy in many countries, even where as (where) the gospel is
taught." 1566.]

The Decades were published together, in folio, in 1552; and have
been translated into German and Dutch, under the name of Hausbuch, (Zurich Lett. Second Series, p. 118), French, and English.

38. Die rechten opffer der Christenheit. 12mo. Tig. 1551.
[The true Christian Sacrifice. A sermon from Hebr. xiii. preached
by Bullinger, 14 August, at Zurich, and dedicated to Conrad Pellican.

Of this sermon Bullinger has noted : " Hunc sermonem Latinum fecit D. Johannes Parkhurstus, Nordovicensis in Anglia episcopus: sed non est, quod *ego* sciam, excusus." Hottinger. Schola Tigur. Append. I. p. 79.]

39. Brevis ac pia institutio Christianæ religionis ad dispersos in Hungaria ecclesiarum Christi ministros et alios Dei servos scripta. [This treatise was written in 1551, but *printed*, " Ovarini," in 1559, 8vo.]

40. Antithesis et compendium evangelicæ et papisticæ doctrinæ, &c. 8vo. Tig. 1551. [Composed at the desire of George, count of Wirtemberg; and written also in German.]

41. Perfectio Christianorum, sive de Jesu Christo, Christianorum perfectione unica, demonstratio. 8vo. Tig. 1551. [Written in German also, (Der Christenheit rechte volkommenheit, &c.) and dedicated in the month of September to Henry II. king of France, when with several of the princes of Germany he sought the liberation of the duke of Saxony and the Landgrave of Hesse.—Sleidan, Comment. Libb. xxiii. xxiv. See also Orig. Lett. p. 6.]

42. Ecclesias Evangelicas neque hæreticas neque schismaticas, sed plane orthodoxas et catholicas esse Jesu Christi ecclesias, Apodixis ad illustrissimum principem et dominum D. Georgium comitem Wirtenbergen. et Montis Bellgardi, &c. 8vo. Tig. 1552. [The preface is dated in February. The treatise was also published in German, Das die Evangelischen Kilchen, &c.]

43. Von der verklärung Jesu Christo: et vom waaren Messia. 12mo. Tig. 1552. [Two sermons from Matth. xvii. 1—8, preached at Zurich by Bullinger, in October 1552; but *not published* till 1556.]

44. Von dem heiligen Nachtmal, &c. Zwo predginen. 12mo. Tig. 1553. [These two sermons were preached by Bullinger at Zurich; and afterwards translated into Latin, and published " a studioso quodam," with the title, " De Sacrosancta Cœna Domini nostri Jesu Christi, qua forma, quo ritu, et in quem finem eam instituerit; quomodo item ad ipsam nos præparari oportet." A translation of this book was made out of a French version in English "by J. T.," and dedicated to " Thomas [Bentham], bishop of Coventry and Lichfield." It was "imprinted at London, nigh unto the Three Cranes in the Vintry, for William Ponsonby." A copy is in the library of Lambeth Palace : no date.—Qu. Is this treatise the book which Lever mentions, Orig. Lett. Let. lxxix. p. 156 ?]

45. Dispositio et Perioche historiæ Evangelicæ per iiii. Evangelistas contextæ, necnon Actorum Apostolorum, Epistolarum quoque Pauli xiiii. et Canonicarum vii. ex commentariis H. Bullingeri petita et in formam Enchiridii redacta. 8vo. Tig. 1553.

46. De gratia Dei justificante nos propter Christum per solam fidem absque operibus bonis, fide interim exuberante in opera bona, libri IIII. ad sereniss. Daniæ regem Christianum, &c. large 8vo. Tig. 1554. [This treatise was composed by Bullinger with the object of conciliating in Denmark a greater confidence in the Swiss Reformation. Melancthon was much delighted with this work.—Corp. Reform. Tom. VIII. col. 523. See also Orig. Lett. p. 744.]

47. Von dem zytlichen Gut, &c. zwo predigten. 12mo. Tig. 1554. [These two sermons of Bullinger's, on the right use of worldly possessions, were composed by him in Latin, and published in this German translation by John Haller.]

48. "A treatise of the cohabitation of the faithful with the unfaithful. Whereunto is added a Sermon made Of the confessing of Christ and his Gospel, and of the denying of the same. Anno 1555. Apocal. xviii. 'Come away from her, my people, that ye be not partakers of her sins, that ye receive not of her plagues.'

A Sermon of the true confessing of Christ and the truth of the Gospel; and of the foul denying of the same: made in the convocation of the clergy at Zurich, the 28. day of January, in the year of the Lord 1555, by H. B."

[This book has neither place, nor printer's name, nor date. The type is foreign, and the spelling bad. A copy of it is in the British Museum. Ames, Vol. II. p. 1581.]

49. Das jungste Gericht, &c. 12mo. Tig. [These two sermons on the last Judgment, from Matt. xxiv. 31—46, are dedicated by Bullinger to Wolfgang Waydner of Worms, in February 1555, but appear not to have been published at Zurich until 1559.]

50. Von dem heil der gloübigen &c. 12mo. Tig. 1555. [A sermon preached by Bullinger, at Zurich, May 26, 1555, On the setting forth of man's salvation always by the word of God and the sacraments.]

51. Summa Christlicher Religion, &c. 8vo. Tig. 1556. [This treatise was published also in the same year in Latin, with the title, "Compendium Christianæ Religionis x. libris comprehensum." It is a kind of epitome of the Decades. It was published in English[1], January 1572, by George Byshop, under the title of "Commonplaces of Christian Religion compendiously written," &c. The translator, John Stockwood, "Minister of Battel," dedicated the work to Henry, earl of Huntingdon. A copy of the book is in the British Museum. Bullinger's original treatise is dedicated to William, landgrave of Hesse.]

52. Apologetica Expositio, qua ostenditur Tigurinæ Ecclesi

---

[1] Ames, Vol. II. pp. 1007, 1147.

ministros nullum sequi dogma hæreticum in Cœna Domini, &c. 12mo. Tig. 1556. [This treatise was also published in German in 1557. It was written in consequence of the revival of the sacramentarian controversy, and the bitter denunciations of several of the Lutheran party and of Westphalus.]

53. In Apocalypsim Jesu Christi, &c. conciones centum. fol. Basil. 1557. [These sermons are dedicated "Ad omnes per Germaniam et Helvetiam, Galliæ, Angliæ, Italiæ, aliorumque regnorum, vel nationum Christi nomine exules," &c.; and the dedication is acknowledged on the part of some English refugees at Arau and Frankfort, in Orig. Lett. pp. 169, 763. The sermons were delivered by Bullinger in lectures at Zurich during the years 1555 and 6. See Orig. Lett. p. 158. The work has been translated into German, French, and Polish. In England a translation was made and published by John Daus of Ipswich, in 1561 (Zurich Lett. p. 99); and another revision, "faithfully corrected and amended," in 1573. Both editions were printed by John Daye[2]. Bp Parkhurst ordered his clergy to procure copies of this translation, or of the original Latin sermons. Zurich Letters, p. 99.]

54. Conciones XXVI. in cap. vi. Jeremiæ. 8vo. Tig. 1557.

55. De fine sæculi et judicio venturo Domini nostri Jesu Christi, deque periculis nostri hujus seculi corruptissimi gravissimis, et qua ratione fiant innoxia piis; orationes duæ, habitæ in cœtu cleri per Heinrychum Bullingerum. Basil. 1557. [These sermons on Matt. xxiv., Dan. vii., and 2 Tim. iii., were preached, the former 12 Sept. 1555, and the latter 28 January, 1557. They were "englished by Thomas Potter;" and "imprinted at London, at the long shop in the Pultrie, by John Allde." A copy of this book is in the Library of Lambeth Palace: no date. But Ames gives the date 1596. Vol. II. p. 892.]

56. Sermones in vii—xiv. capp. Jeremiæ. 8vo. Tig. 1558.

57. De Cœna Domini Sermo. 8vo. Tig. 1558.

58. Festorum dierum Domini et Servatoris, &c. sermones ecclesiastici.—Accessit illis præterea præfatio de Sabbato et Feriis Christianorum. fol. Tig. 1558. [These discourses, dedicated to the palatine of Wilna, were composed and published by Bullinger at the request of his colleagues, to promote an improved style of preaching. See Orig. Lett. p. 700.]

59. Sermones XXXII. in capp. xiv—xxx. Jeremiæ. 8vo. Tig. 1559.

60. Bericht wie die so von wägen unsers herren Jesu Christi, &c. ires gloubens ersücht, &c. antworten und sich halten mögind, &c. 12mo. Zurich, 1559. [This treatise was composed by Bul-

[2] Herbert's Ames, Vol. I. p. 634.

linger for the benefit of persecuted protestants in Bavaria. It was published in a Latin translation in 1560, by Josiah Simler, with the title, "Institutio eorum qui propter Dominum nostrum Jesum Christum de fide examinantur et variis quæstionibus tentantur[1]." It was also translated into English. Zurich Letters, A. p. 278. See also p. 110.]

61. Catechesis pro adultioribus scripta. 8vo. Tig. 1559. [This Catechism was composed by Bullinger at the request of the ministers of Zurich; and about the year 1578 was recommended by statute to be used in the University of Oxford, "for the benefit of youth, and the informing them in true religion." Wood's Hist. and Antiq. of Univ. of Oxford. Vol. ii. part i. p. 193. ed. Gutch. Oxf. 1796. Cardwell's Document. Ann. Vol. i. p. 300. Oxf. 1844.]

62. Der Widertoufferen ursprung, &c. in vi. bucher. 8vo. Tig. 1560. [This improved treatise of Bullinger's on the Anabaptists (see above, No. 5) was immediately translated into Latin and published by Josiah Simler, with the title, "H. Bullingeri adversus Anabaptistas libri vi." &c. See Zurich Letters, A. pp. 87, 95, 96, 110.]

63. Von den Conciliis. 12mo. Tig. [This treatise was composed in November 1560, and published early in 1561. It was also published in 1561 in Latin with the title, "De Conciliis &c. brevis ex historiis commemoratio." See Zurich Letters, A. pp. 97, 208.]

64. Tractatio verborum Domini, In domo patris mei mansiones multæ sunt, &c. 12mo. Tig. [This tract was written by Bullinger in December 1560, and published in 1561, at Zurich. It was also translated by Lavater into German.—It was composed against the Ubiquitarian doctrine. See Zurich Letters, A. p. 92, note 1, and p. 98.]

65. Sermones lxxiv. in caput xxx. Jeremiæ ad finem. 8vo. Tig. 1561.

66. Threnorum seu Lamentationum Jeremiæ explicatio. 8vo. Tig. 1561.

67. Gegenbericht Heinrychen Bullingers uff den bericht herren Johansen Brentzen von dem himmel und der gerachten Gottes, &c. [This treatise against Brentius was composed by Bullinger in December 1561. It was published also in Latin in 1562; Responsio, qua ostenditur sententiam de cœlo et dextera Dei, &c. Bullingeri &c. non esse eversam, &c. See Zurich Letters, A. pp. 108, 110, 121.]

68. Vester grund, &c. 8vo. Zurich, 1563. [Another treatise of Bullinger's against the errors of Brentius. It was published also

[1] See Gerdesii Scrin. Tom. iv. par. 2. p. 440.

at the same time in Latin with the title, "Fundamentum firmum, cui tuto fidelis quivis inniti potest," &c. See Zurich Letters, A. p. 131.]

69. Repetitio et dilucidior explicatio consensus veteris orthodoxæ catholicæque Christi Ecclesiæ, &c. de inconfusis proprietatibus naturarum Christi Domini in una indivisa persona permanentibus, &c. 8vo. Tig. 1564. [Another treatise against the errors of Brentius.]

70. Von rächter hilff und errettung in noten. 12mo. Zurich, 1564. [This sermon, on deliverance in affliction, from Matth. xiv. 22—33, was preached by Bullinger at Zurich, 12 July, 1564.]

71. Daniel sapientissimus Dei propheta, qui a vetustis Polyhistor, id est, multiscius est dictus, expositus Homiliis LXVI. &c.— Accessit huic operi Epitome temporum et rerum ab orbe condito ad excidium usque ultimum urbis Hierosolymarum sub Imperatore Vespasiano. fol. Tig. 1565. [See Zurich Letters, A. pp. 145, 150, 151, 220. B. p. 164.]

72. Isaias excellentissimus Dei propheta, &c. expositus Homiliis cxc. &c. fol. Tig. 1567. [Zurich Letters, A. pp. 172, 191, 194, 220; B. p. 164.]

73. Reformationsgeschichte. [This history of the Reformation in Switzerland, extending from 1519 to 1532, was finished by Bullinger, 10th Nov. 1567: but was never published until 1838 and 1840.]

74. Von der bekerung dess menschen zu Gott und dem waaren glouben; VI. predigen, &c. [These six sermons on Conversion, from Acts viii. 27, &c. were published by Bullinger in October 1569. See Zurich Letters, A. pp. 220, 224.]

75. Ad Testamentum D. Joannis Brentii nuper contra Zuinglianos publicatum Responsio brevis necessaria et modesta a ministris Ecclesiæ Tigurinæ universis fidelibus ad judicandum proposita. 8vo. Tig. 1571. [This reply was written by Bullinger in the name of all the pastors of Zurich. It was published also at the same time in German. See Zurich Letters, A. pp. 241, 243, 258, 266; B. p. 245.]

76. De Scripturæ Sanctæ præstantia et dignitate. 8vo. Tig. 1571.

77. Bullæ papisticæ ante biennium contra sereniss. Angliæ, Franciæ, et Hyberniæ reginam Elizabetham, et contra inclytum Angliæ regnum promulgatæ, refutatio, orthodoxæque reginæ et universi regni Angliæ defensio, Henrychi Bullingeri. S.—Londini, apud Johañem Dayum, Typographum. Small 4to. 1571. [This treatise was composed by Bullinger at the suggestion of some of

his friends among the English bishops. (See Zurich Lett. A. pp. 221, 244; B. p. 179). It was also published in English, (Zurich Lett. A. pp. 242, 3, 258, 266, 269; B. pp. 183, 192,) and in 1578 was translated into German, and published by John Conrad Ulmer, preacher at Schaffhausen.]

78. Vermanung an alle diener des Worts Gottes &c. 12mo. Zurich, 1572. [An exhortation of Bullinger's to Christian concord and agreement. It was translated by Josiah Simler into Latin, with the title, "Adhortatio ad omnes in Ecclesia Domini nostri Jesu Christi verbi Dei ministros, ut contentiones mutuas deponant, &c. (Zurich Letters, A. p. 270) and was also translated into English by John Cox, and published 1575. Ames, Vol. II. p. 890.]

79. Von der schweren langwirigen verfolgung der heiligen christlichen Kirchen, &c. 12mo. Zurich, 1573. [This treatise was composed by Bullinger on occasion of the St Bartholomew massacre in France. It was translated into Latin and published the same year by Josiah Simler, with the title, "De Persecutionibus Ecclesiæ Christianæ." It appeared in English, in 16mo. under the title of, "The Tragedies of Tyrants[1], exercised upon the Church of God from the birth of Christ unto this present year 1572." &c. London, 1575. The translator was Thomas Twynn: and his translation is dedicated to Parker, archbishop of Canterbury. A copy of the book is in the British Museum.—See Zurich Letters, A. pp. 300, 303, 308.]

80. Zwo predigen über den cxxx. owch cxxxiii. psalmen Davids durch Heinrychen Bullinger, &c. 12mo. Zurich, 1574. [See Zurich Letters, A. pp. 303, 308.]

81. Antwort Heinrych Bullingers &c. uff D. Jacoben Andresen über die siben klagartickel erinnerung. 12mo. Zurich, 1574. [This answer to James Andreæ[2], who took up the defence of Brentius, was translated into Latin by Josiah Simler, with the title, "Ad septem accusationis capita, quæ hodie maxima importunitate per calumnias summaque cum injuria quidam inquieti, scriptis illis suis, in capita coacervant ministrorum Tigurinæ Ecclesiæ, quos per contumeliam Zuinglianos nuncupant, Heinrici Bullingeri &c. Responsio."—See Zurich Letters, B. p. 245.]

Besides the above works, Bullinger drew up the Confession of the Church of Zurich on the Lord's Supper[3] against the misrepresentations of Luther in 1545. (Warhaffte Bekantnuss, &c. Rodolph

---

[1] Ames, Vol. II. p. 775.

[2] See Zurich Lett. A. p. 302, note 1. B. pp. 98, 100, 274.

[3] Orig. Lett. p. 681. See John-a-Lasco's opinion of it, Gerdesii Scrin. Tom. IV. par. 2. p. 460.

Gualter translated it into Latin ; "Orthodoxa Tigurinæ Ecclesiæ ministrorum confessio," &c. See Orig. Lett. P. S. p. 681.) Several of his letters also and admonitions to his son Henry, and grandson Felix Lavater, have been published in Miscell. Tig. Vol. I. par. 3, and in Merkwürdige Züge. H. Bulling. Bern. 1828.[4] In a letter of Martin Micronius (Orig. Lett. p. 560) Bullinger's *Decades on the Kings* are mentioned : but no such Decades were published. The Latin must have been "decades ad *regem ;*" and the reference is to the second volume of the Decades, which Bullinger dedicated, and a copy of which he specially sent, to Edward VI. (See Orig. Lett. pp. 662 and 88).

Besides English translations of some of Bullinger's writings mentioned in the foregoing list, there was printed in 1548, in 12mo. "at London, by Robert Stoughton," "Two Epistles: one of H. Bullinger, with the consent of all the learned men of the church of Tigury; another of John Calvin, chief preacher of the church of Geneva: whether it be lawful for a christian man to communicate or be partaker of the mass of the papists, without offending God and his neighbour or not:" (dated "Tiguri, Feb. 18, 1541,") which probably was among the books alluded to in Orig. Lett. p. 396. Another edition came out in 1549. (Lowndes; and Ames, Vol. II. p. 750.)

N. B. The Editor cannot close this list of Bullinger's publications without acknowledging his great obligations to M. Horner, the librarian of the Zurich Library, for the great facilities which he afforded him in making needful researches in that invaluable collection of books and documents.

THE ENGLISH TRANSLATION OF BULLINGER'S DECADES.

THERE were *three* editions of the English translation[5] of Bullinger's Decades ; viz. in the years 1577, 1584, and 1587. The Parker Society has reprinted the latest edition.

Copies of any of the editions are seldom perfect. In most cases the title-pages are *fac-similes,* extremely well executed,

---

[4] Hottinger also mentions a tragedy of Bullinger's, "Brutus sive Lucretia," which was published (but without his name) and acted at Basle, A.D. 1533.—Schola Tigur. Append. I. p. 88. Tig. 1664.

[5] Made, says Strype (Ann. II. ii. p. 144. Oxf. ed.) by a "person of eminency in the church."

but bearing another date than that of the edition to which they are prefixed; and leaves of different editions are found supplied in one copy. On page 1085 of the old editions also (Vol. IV. page 437 of this reprint) variations in the text of all the copies (whatever the edition) occur, which can be accounted for only on the supposition, that, for some unexplained reason, the publisher cancelled former or printed new leaves.

In a copy of the ed. 1587 (as the editor has been informed by the Rev. G. C. Gorham), which is in the possession of Dr Bayford, there is a remarkable addition in the last lines of the title-page, as follows: "Imprinted at London by Raph Newberie, dwelling in Flete-Street, a little above the Conduit, *who hath store of these bookes for those that want them, both in Latine*[1] *and English.* Cum gratia et privilegio Regiæ Majestatis, 1587." The added words are here given in italics, and are not found in other copies of the same year.

On the debated question of the degree of authority which was given to these Decades of Bullinger in the reign of queen Elizabeth in the English church, the Editor deems it most consistent with the principles and practice of the Parker Society, that he should confine himself to *facts*, and leave *conclusions* to be drawn from them by others. These facts may most conveniently be presented under the following heads:

1. The earlier registers of the Convocation of the province of Canterbury were destroyed in the great fire of 1666.[2]

2. But in archbishop Whitgift's Register, at the archiepiscopal palace of Lambeth[3], there are found, "Orders for the better increase of learning in the inferior ministers, and for more diligent preaching and catechising:" which had been introduced, it appears, into the upper house of Convocation on the second day of December, 1586, by the archbishop, and which contain the following directions:

"I. Every minister having cure, and being under the

---

[1] In 1586 Newbery had a licence to print Bullinger's Decades in Latin.—Ames, Vol. II. pp. 918, 1134.

[2] Cardwell's Synodalia, Preface, page i.

[3] Tom. I. fol. 131. a. Cardwell's Synodalia, Vol. II. page 562.

degrees of master of arts, and batchelors of law, and not licensed
to be a public preacher, shall before the second day of February next provide a Bible, and Bullinger's Decads in Latin
or English, and a paper book, and shall every day read over
one chapter of the holy scriptures, and note the principal contentes thereof briefly in his paper booke, and shall every
week read over one sermon in the said Decads, and note
likewise the chief matters therein contained in the said paper;
and shall once in every quarter (viz. within a fortnight before
or after the end of the quarter) shewe his said note to some
preacher nere adjoyninge to be assigned for that purpose.

"II.   Item, The bishop, archdeacons, or other ordinary,
being a publick preacher, shall appoint certaine grave and
learned preachers, who shall privately examine the diligence,
and view the notes of the said ministers, assigninge sixe or
seaven ministers, as occasion shall require, to every such
preacher, that shall be next adjoyning to him, so as the
ministers be not driven to travell for the exhibitinge of their
notes above sixe or seaven miles (if it may be), and the said
preacher shall by lettres or otherwise, trulie certifie to the
archdeacons, or other ordinarye of the place, themselves being
publick preachers, and resiant within, or nere to their jurisdiction, and for want thereof, to the busshop himself, who do
performe the said exercises, and how they have profited
therein, and who do refuse or neglecte to perform the same;
the archdeacons and others receiving the said certificates,
shall signifye the same, once in the yere, to the busshope, and
that about Michalmas.

"III.   Item, Such as shall refuse to perform the exercises, or shall be negligent therein, and shall not after admonition by the bishop, archdeacon, or other ordinary aforesaid,
reform himself, if he be beneficed, shall be compelled thereunto by ecclesiasticall censures; if he be a curate, shall be
inhibited to serve within the jurisdiction."

"VIII.   It is concluded that the exercises above written,
and no other, shall be henceforth publicly or privately used
within any parts of this province."

Afterwards, in the seventh session of the same Convocation by prorogation, on March 10th, "the prolocutor" of
the lower house "prayed that the articles agreed on by the
bishops for the increase of learning in inferior ministers might

be read; which was done.   And then the archbishop exhorted
all the clergy to do their duty[1]."   And in archbishop Whitgift's register a letter to the archdeacon of Canterbury[2] (William Redman) is inserted, in which the archbishop, under
date March 29, 1587, transmits to him the Orders above
mentioned to be observed throughout the whole diocese; and
Strype records, in his Life of Bishop Aylmer[3], that "the
bishop's pious and painful son, Dr Theophilus Aylmer, now
archdeacon of London, the 6th of January ensuing, called for
the clergy (as he frequently used to do) intending this meeting chiefly for such ministers as were not preachers, but of
the inferior sort: for the bringing forward of which were
these particulars enjoined.... 2. Every person to have Bullinger's Decads. 3. Each to have his paper book, and therein
to write the quantity of one sermon every week," &c.

    Yet in archbishop Whitgift's Register[4] again, a copy of
a letter is extant, apparently designed as a circular to the
bishops[5] of his province, dated Nov. 1, 1588, in which the
archbishop writes: "After my right hearty commendations to
your lordship.   Where secundo Decembris, when we were
assembled in the synod kept in the year 1586, it was thought
fit and necessary to me and to the rest of my brethren then
present in that synod, although not as a judicial act or conclusion by the authority of the convocation, that the articles of
the tenor of the copy herein enclosed should be put in execution by your lordship and all the rest of my said brethren
the bishops of this province; forasmuch as it is like it will be
looked for at this next parliament, how the same articles have
been accordingly used, and likewise how the canons agreed
upon by all our consent in the convocation holden the xxiiii of
November, in the year of our Lord 1584, and allowed by the
queen's majesty, have been observed; &c." and in the margin
of the register this letter is described, "A copy of my lord
grace his letters for the exercises:"—so that *the " Articles,"*

---

[1] Strype, Whitgift, Vol. I. page 499.

[2] Tom. I. fol. 132.

[3] Strype's Life of Bp Aylmer, p. 83. Oxf. 1824.

[4] Tom. I. fol. 151. a.

[5] Strype gives this letter as addressed *to the bishops,*—Whitgift,
Vol. I. page 531.   It appears in Wilkins' Concil. as directed to the
bishop of London.—Vol. IV. p. 338. Lond. 1737.

which the archbishop here mentions, are *the "Orders"* quoted above.

3. In her majesty's State Paper Office, also, a contemporary copy of archbishop Whitgift's " Orders " is preserved; and a duplicate copy of them, made, for greater security, by Sir Joseph Williamson in the reign of Charles II.: but these papers are only endorsed, " Orders for the discipline of the Church ;" no signature of a Secretary of state, nor any memorandum whatsoever, is to be traced upon them ; and the Editor is informed at the Office, that the preservation of these documents among the State papers is no proof, of itself, that they had received any state or royal sanction.

4. The edition of the Decades of 1587 had on its title-page, " Cum gratia et privilegio Regiæ Majestatis ;" an inscription, which neither of the former editions presented. But these words only declared a licence to publish ; and did not intimate that the book had received any regal sanction and authority.

The " Epistles " of Bullinger " concerning the Apparell of Ministers and other indifferent things[6]," which were added to the English edition of the Decades, 1587, and which are mentioned in the title-page, are not inserted in this reprint, as they are found among the Zurich Letters, A. Append. Let. III. and IV. ed. Park. Soc.

[6] Ames, Vol. II. p. 697.

FIFTY SERMONS

DIVIDED INTO

FIVE DECADES.

THE FIFT AND LAST

decade of sermons,

WRITTEN BY

Henrie Bullinger.

The third Tome.

IESVS.

This is my beloued Sonne, in whom I am
well pleased. Heare him. *Matth.* 17.

FIFTH DECADE OF SERMONS,

WRITTEN BY

HENRY BULLINGER.

¶ OF THE HOLY CATHOLIC CHURCH; WHAT IT IS,
HOW FAR IT EXTENDETH, BY WHAT MARKS IT IS
KNOWN, FROM WHENCE IT SPRINGETH, HOW
IT IS MAINTAINED AND PRESERVED, WHE-
THER IT MAY ERR. ALSO OF THE
POWER AND STUDIES OF THE
CHURCH.

THE FIRST SERMON.

THE order and course of things[1] so leading us, next after
God, the workman and author of all things, we come to speak
of his most excellent work, to wit, the church.   For so great
is the goodness of our good God and most loving Father,
that not he himself is desirous to live happily and blessedly
alone, but moreover to bestow and pour upon us men, his
beloved creatures, all kind of blessedness[2]; and that we
should enjoy his goods by all means possible.   And for that
intent he chooseth men to himself who live in this world, that
he may once[3] translate unto himself: in whom also (even
while they live here) he may dwell, whom he may enrich
with all his goods, in whom he may reign; and that they
should be called by his name, to wit, a people, a house, a
kingdom, an inheritance, a flock, a congregation or church,
of the living God.   Of which church I will speak (being
aided with your prayers) such things as the Lord of the
church shall grant unto me to utter.

This word *Ecclesia*, which signifieth a church or con- Ecclesia, a
gregation[4], is a Greek word, used and received among the congregation.

[1 rerum cohærentium, Lat.: of things mutually related to each
other.]

[2 et bona sua omnia, Lat. omitted: and all his good things.]

[3 aliquando, Lat.]   [4 which—congregation: not in Lat.]

Latins, signifying, as I said, a congregation, communion, or assembly (in the Dutch tongue, *Ein Gemeind*), or a people called together to hear of matters of the commonwealth: for so it is found that St Luke used this word in the nineteenth chapter of the Acts of the Apostles. But it was translated to an holy use, and began to be called a congregation, assembly, or company of the faithful, calling upon the name of the Lord. St Paul saith that he persecuted the congregation or church of God: who in another place saith, "I received authority from the high priests to bind all those that call upon the name of Christ[1];" for now doth he term them such as call upon the name of Christ, or Christians, whom before he named the church. Or else this word *Ecclesia*, the church or congregation, is so called of calling forth together: for in the Greek tongue ἐκκαλέω signifieth to call forth. For God calleth forth from all parts of the wide world, and from the whole congregation of men, all believers together with their seed[2], that they may be his peculiar people, and he again may be their God; that is to say, that they may be the church of the living God. In times past the congregation or assembly of the Jewish people, being God his flock, was called a synagogue; for this word synagogue signifieth as much as *Ecclesia*, the congregation. But because of the stubbornness of the Jews, and the unappeasable hatred which they bear towards christian religion, this word synagogue is not esteemed, but is almost quite grown out of use. But we will not dispute by due and right order of the churches either of the Jews or the Turks, or of other strange churches of the Gentiles[3], whereof we know there are many sorts and kinds. We will speak of the christian church and congregation of the faithful: which the Germans do call *Die kirch*, alluding peradventure to the Greek word κυριακή. For they call κυριακήν anything belonging to the Lord, to wit, a house or a people; as the Germans do call *Die kirchen* both the people of God themselves, and also the place wherein they assemble together to worship

Margin: 1 Cor. xv.
Margin: Acts xxii.
Margin: Synagogue.

[1 Ananias says this of Saul. Acts ix. 14.]
[2 ex hoc mundo, Lat. omitted: out of this world.]
[3 vel aliarum exterarum gentium, Lat.: or (of the churches) of other nations that are without.]

God. But first of all we will describe a little plainlier[4] what the church or congregation is.

The church is the whole company and multitude of the faithful, partly being now in heaven, and partly remaining yet here upon earth: where it doth agree plainly in unity of faith or true doctrine, and in the lawful partaking of the sacraments: neither is it divided, but joined and united together as it were in one house and fellowship. *What the church is.*

This church was usually[5] called catholic, that is to say, universal. For she bringeth forth[6] her branches in all places of the wide world, in all times of all ages; and generally doth comprehend all the faithful of the whole world. For the church of God is not tied to any one region, nation, or kindred; to condition, age, sex or kind: all the faithful generally and each one specially, wherever they or he be, are citizens and members of this church. St Paul the Apostle saith: "There is neither Jew nor Greek, neither bondman nor free, neither man or woman; for ye be all one in Christ Jesu." *The catholic church.* *Gal. iii.*

The church is distinguished into the triumphant and the militant. The triumphant is that great company of holy spirits in heaven, triumphing[7] for the victory gotten against the world, sin, and the devil, still[8] enjoying the sight of God, wherein consisteth all fulness of all kind of joy and pleasure: whereupon they set forth God's glory, and praise his goodness for ever. This church doth St John the Apostle set forth very notably[9] in his Revelation[10], saying: "After this I saw, and, behold, a great company which no man was able to number, of all nations, peoples, and tongues, standing before the throne, and in the sight of the Lamb, clothed in white raiments[11], and palms in their hands: and they cried out with a loud voice, saying: Salvation belongeth to him that sitteth on the throne of our God[12], and to the Lamb." And a little after he saith: "And one of the elders answered *The distinction of the church. The triumphant church.* *Rev. vii.*

[4 paulo rudius, Lat.]   [5 solet, Lat.: is usually.]
[6 profert, Lat.: sendeth forth into.]
[7 modo, Lat. omitted: now.]   [8 still, not in Lat.]
[9 graphice, Lat.]   [10 Revelations, ed. 1577.]
[11 So also ed. 1584: but ed. 1577, white *garments*.]
[12 So Erasmus: and Bibl. Lat.: Tigur. 1544; and Tyndale, 1534; and Cranmer, 1539.]

and said unto me : These which are clothed in white garments, who are they ? or from whence come they ? And I said unto him, Thou knowest, Lord. And he said unto me, These are they that have come out of great affliction, and have spread abroad[1] their garments, and have made them white in the blood of the Lamb : therefore are they before the throne of God, and serve[2] day and night in his holy[3] temple. And he that sitteth on the throne shall dwell over them[4]. They shall neither hunger nor thirst henceforth any more : neither shall the sun shine[5] on them, or any heat : because the Lamb, who sitteth[6] in the midst of the throne, shall govern them, and bring them to the springs of the water of life[7]. And the Lord shall wipe away all tears from their eyes." Brethren, ye have heard a notable[8] description of the triumphant church in heaven, and that too triumphing truly through the blood of Jesus Christ, by whom they conquered and do now reign. For Christ is that " Lamb of God, that taketh away the sins of the world ;" by whom all which be sanctified are sanctified, and shall be sanctified, and do live, from the first creation of the world unto the end

of all times. St Paul, in a certain place giving unto us also a notable description of this church, telleth that we which as yet are busied[9] in the militant church shall sometime be translated to the same, and be made fellows with the[10] angels of God, received among the orders of the patriarchs, and placed in the company of the blessed spirits, with the most high God himself and the mediator our Lord Jesus Christ. For he, preaching the greatness of God's grace brought unto us by the gospel, and exhorting us to receive the same with a true faith, " Ye came not (saith he) unto mount Sina, to a fire, to a whirlwind, a stormy tempest, and

---

[1 So Bibl. Lat. Tigur. and Tyndale and Cranmer, "and made their garments large." Mea autem sententia rectius et simplicius legere videtur codex Compluten. et Aretas, Et ἔπλυναν, quod et vetus Interpres vertit, Abluerunt.—Bullinger. in Apoc. Conc. 36. p. 103. Basil. 1570.]

[2 serviunt ei, Lat.: serve him.]   [3 holy, not in Lat.]

[4 Super eos, Lat.: super illos, Bibl. Lat. Tigur. 1544. and Vulgate, and Erasmus.]

[5 cadet, Lat.]   [6 est, Lat.]

[7 ad vivos fontes aquarum, Lat.]   [8 elegantissimam, Lat.]

[9 qui versamur, Lat.]   [10 sanctis, Lat. omitted: holy.]

darkness; but unto mount Sion, to the city of the living God, to heavenly Hierusalem, and to the innumerable company of angels, and to the church or congregation of the first-begotten which are written in heaven, and to God the judge of all, and to the spirits of the perfect just, and to the mediator of the new Testament, Jesus Christ[11], speaking better things than the blood of Abel spake[12]." And therefore all the saints in heaven do belong unto our company, or rather, we belong unto their fellowship; for we are companions and fellow-heirs with the saints from Adam unto the end of all worlds, and God's household. Which containeth the greatest comfort of all man's life, and moveth most of all to the study of virtue: for what more worthy thing is there, than to be of God's household? Or what may be thought more sweet to us, than to think ourselves fellows with the patriarchs, prophets, apostles, martyrs, of all angels and blessed spirits? This benefit, I say, Christ hath bestowed on us. To him therefore be praise, glory, and thanks for ever and ever. Amen.

The militant church is a congregation of men upon earth, professing the name and religion of Christ, continually[13] fighting in the world against the devil, sin, flesh, and the world, in the camp and tents and under the banner of our Lord Christ. This church is to be considered[14] two ways. For either it is to be taken strictly, comprehending them only which be not only called but are in very deed the church, the faithful and elect of God, lively members, knit unto Christ, not[15] with bands and other outward marks and signs[16], but in spirit and faith: and oftentimes by these means[17] without the other: of which matter we will speak hereafter. This inward and invisible church of God may be well named the elect spouse of Christ, only known unto God, who alone knoweth who are his. When we be first taught to know this church, we confess her with the Apostles' creed,

The militant church.

The holy church.

[11 and to the blood of sprinkling, omitted by Bullinger.]
[12 loquebatur, Lat. and Bibl. Lat. Tigur. 1544. and Erasmus.]
[13 et adhuc, Lat.: and still.]
[14 rursus, Lat. omitted: again.]
[15 non modo, Lat.: not only.]
[16 rather, with outward bands or marks.]
[17 duntaxat, Lat. omitted: only.]

I believe
the holy
catholic
church.

saying[1]: " I believe the holy catholic church, the communion of saints." And in these few words we comprehend that there is a church, also what is the church, and what manner one it is. For first we confess that there hath been, and is, a church of God, and that it shall continue for ever. Then, professing what it is, we add this, " The communion of saints." That is to say : We believe the church to be nothing else but the company of all those saints that are, have been, and shall be, as well in this present age, as in the world to come, who enjoy all good things in common granted unto them by God. Also we express what manner of thing the church is, to wit, holy, even the spouse of Christ, cleansed and blessed.

1 Cor. vi.

For St Paul calleth them holy, which are cleansed with the Spirit and blood of our God, of which a great part have received crowns of glory[2]: the residue labour here upon earth, hoping to receive them in heaven. And truly, in consideration of the church, the chiefest matter is that through the grace of God we be made the members of Christ's body, and partakers of all heavenly gifts with the angels[3]; for we confess none to be more holy than our own selves[4].

The church
doth compre-
hend the
wicked.

Or the church more largely considered comprehendeth not only those that are the very faithful and holy indeed, but also them who although they believe not truly or unfeignedly, neither be clean or holy in the conversation of their life, yet do they acknowledge and profess true religion with the true believers and the holy men of God : yea, they speak well and allow of virtues and reprove evil, neither do sever themselves[5] from the unity of this holy church militant. In which consideration, not so much as the wicked and hypocrites (such as we read to have been in the church in the time of Christ and the apostles, as Judas, Ananias and Sapphira, Simon Magus, also Demas, Hymenæus, Alexander, and many other) are excluded and put from the church; which church may well be called the outward and visible church.

[1 Hanc in primis confitentes symbolo edocti apostolico dicimus, Lat. Confessing this church especially we say, as we are taught by the Apostles' Creed.]

 [2 of glory, not in Lat.]

 [3 cum sanctis omnibus, Lat. : with all the saints.]

 [4 Rather, for we confess none more than ourselves to be holy.]

 [5 adhuc, Lat. omitted : as yet.]

But this church, whereof we speak, is to be accounted of[6] either by reason of some part thereof, or else of the whole; for it is to be considered generally and particularly. And the particular church is that which is comprised in a certain number, and is known by some sure and certain place: for of the place it taketh the name, being called after the names of cities, as the churches of Zurick and Bernes, &c. The Greeks called those particular churches παροικίας[7], which we commonly call parishes[8]. And we call[9] that a parish, which hath dwelling-houses and streets joined together in neighbourhood. But in cities and towns[10] unto certain portions are usually ascribed both churches and parish priests to serve them, and all that whole circuit is called a parish[11]; in the Dutch tongue, *Ein barchi*[12], 'oder pfarkirch, oder ein kirchhory.* And in the old time the parish priest was a provider; for he provided and gave necessaries to strangers, and chiefly salt and wood[13]. Some called him the maker of the feast, other call him a preparer of virgins[14]. Therefore because the pastors of churches be as it were preparers of virgins for the Redeemer and head of the church, which is Christ, bringing unto him a chaste and undefiled virgin; and to be short, because they themselves provided things most necessary for the people of God, and also prepared heavenly meats and banquets, the pastors of the Lord's flock are very well called parish priests, or the curates of souls[15]. Of the particular church the Lord speaking in the gospel saith: "If he that offendeth the church will not regard when he is warned, complain unto the church."

The particular church.

Parish and parish-priest.

Matt. xviii.

[6 rursus, Lat. omitted: again.]

[7 Bingham's Antiq. Book IX. chap. II. § 1.]

[8 Vulgus dicit parochias, alii et rectius dixere parœcias, Lat.]

[9 vocant, Lat.]　　[10 et in agro, Lat.: and in the country.]

[11 Pacii Isagog. in Decretal. Lib. III. tit. 29. de parœciis.]

[12 parochie, Dutch translation, 1567.]

[13 Parochus (πάροχος), qui legatis et aliis iter facientibus necessaria (nominatim salem, lignum, fœnum) publico sumtu *prœbenda* suscepit vel redemit. Idem Latine a *prœbere* (παρέχειν) apud Ciceronem Offic. I. 15. dicitur *prœbitor.*—Doering. in Hor. Sat. I. 5. 46.]

[14 paranymphum, Lat. The bride-man, as he rode in the carriage with the bride and bridegroom, was sometimes called the πάροχος. —Smith, Dict. of Antiq. p. 599. Lond. 1842.]

[15 Bullinger seems here to have borrowed from Polydor. Vergil. De Rerum Inv. Lib. IV. cap. 9.]

But it is not possible that the universal church through the whole world should assemble and come together, that the rebellious and obstinate should be brought before it: wherefore judgment is referred to be given on the stubborn by the particular churches. To conclude, the universal church consisteth of all the particular churches throughout the whole world, and of all the visible parts and members thereof. This is the same which we shadowed out of late, when we spake more at large thereof.

The church of God hath been, and shall be, for ever.

But the catholic church of God doth abide with us[1] (as we began to tell a little before) continually from age to age from the beginning, and is at this time dispersed throughout the whole world, both visibly and invisibly; and the Lord's people and God his house shall continue upon earth unto the world's end. For there was never yet any world[2], neither shall be any age, wherein God hath not sanctified or will not sanctify some unto himself, in whom he will dwell, and that they shall be his flock and holy house: for the testimonies[3] of ancient prophets do record that the church is perpetual. For thus we find it written in the 132nd psalm: "The Lord hath chosen Sion, he hath chosen her for an habitation for himself. This is my resting-place for ever and ever; here *[Ps. lxxxix. 35, 36.]* will I dwell, because I have chosen her." And again: "I have sworn unto David in my holiness, his seed shall remain for ever, and his seat shall continue before me as the sun." But who knoweth not that all this is to be understood of Christ, the Son of David, and of his throne and spiritual Sion, which is the church? He also, signifying the continuance of the *Matt. xxviii.* church, saith in the gospel: "I will remain with you continu- *John xiv.* ally unto the end of the world." And again: "I will ask of my Father, and he shall give you another Comforter, the Spirit of truth, that he may abide with you for ever." To *Matt. xvi.* this belongeth also that saying in the gospel: "And the gates of hell shall not prevail against the church." Which saying truly is a great comfort to the faithful in so many and so great persecutions intended to the utter destruction and overthrow of the church.

The church of the devil and antichrist.

But as Christ had always his church here upon earth, hath now, and for ever shall have; so likewise the devil, as

[1 *ad nos usque decurrit*, Lat.]   [2 *seculum*, Lat.]
[3 *etiam*, Lat. omitted: also.]

long as the world shall continue, shall never want his people in whom he may reign.   This church of the devil took her first beginning of Cain, and shall continue to the last wicked person, comprehending also all those evil peoples that have been in the meantime and shall be betwixt the beginning and the ending.   But they, living here on earth, have society and common with them that are tormented in hell.   For as all that be godly, being under one head Christ, do make one body; so all the wicked, under one head Satan, are one incorporate body.   This may right worthily be called the wicked church[4], Sodom and Gomor, Babylon, the congregation of Chora, Dathan, and Abirom, a synagogue, a school, and a stews of the devil, the kingdom of antichrist, or any other of like sort. In this church are reckoned up all such as are wicked and infidels, separating themselves from the society of our holy mother the church, or forsaking the communion thereof : and specially such as are mockers of God and his holy word, blasphemers and persecutors of Christ and his church.   Such in these days are the heathen, Turks, Jews, heretics, schismatics, and generally all such as are professed enemies to christian religion.   And to these also we may add hypocrites; for it is no small offence that the Lord himself in every part of the gospel[5] doth so earnestly persecute and blame.   Among other things he saith : "The Lord of that servant shall come in the day wherein he looketh not for him, and in an hour that he shall not know of, and shall divide him, and shall give him his portion with hypocrites, where shall be weeping and gnashing of teeth."   Out of all doubt he signified the greatness of the offence by the sharpness of the punishment.   This church doth follow the motions of the devil, and the devices or imaginations of her own heart, and is busied and exercised in all kind of blasphemy and wickedness, wherein she excelleth herself; and at last sinketh down to hell, that she be not in any place separated from that head whereunto she hath so diligently or rather obstinately joined herself.

  I know right well that ye will object against me, for that I have reckoned the hypocrites to be in the outward communion and fellowship of the militant church, and now again to account them of the company of the devil's church.   Moreover

Matt. v. vi. xxiii.

Matt. xxiv.

How hypocrites are, or may be accounted in the church of God.

[4 ecclesia malignantium, Lat. : Psalm xxv. 5. Vulgate.]
[5 in sancto evangelio, Lat.]

you will say, That it is impossible that the same hypocrites may take part of both churches differing betwixt themselves[1]; for that the Lord saith : " Either make the tree good and the fruit good, or else the tree naught and the fruit naught." And St Paul also saith, that there is no " fellowship betwixt Christ and Belial, twixt light and darkness, twixt truth and lying ;" and that hypocrisy is lying and darkness.

Here therefore I perceive a fit place to shew, by what means and how far I may account hypocrites to be of the congregation of the church. First we make a distinction or difference of hypocrites. For there are certain hypocrites that put their confidence in their human justice and equity, doing all their works openly that they may be seen of men, firmly trusting and stiffly standing to men's traditions. To these it is a custom and property not only to fly from the church which teacheth the righteousness of Christ, but also to curse, detest, and to persecute it with all cruelty. Such kind of people were the Jews and Jewish Pharisees, with whom our Lord Jesus Christ had much contention, and with whom even at this day the church contendeth and maketh wars. These be the plain and visible members of the devil's church, and they are not to be counted of the outward[2] church, yea, they are not once worthy to be named in the church of Christ. Again, there are some kind of hypocrites that are dissemblers, which neither give any confidence to their own righteousness and justice, neither yet do greatly regard the traditions of men. These kinds of people neither hate the church, nor fly from it, nor persecute it; but outwardly they agree with it, professing the same faith, and participating the selfsame sacraments : but inwardly and in mind they neither believe unfeignedly and sincerely, neither do they live holily. Of this sort, some of them for a season will cleave to the fellowship and company of the church ; and having any occasion given they will fall from it, as heretics and schismatics are wont to do, and such as of friends are become enemies. Other there be again that never fall from the church, but keep themselves in the fellowship of the church all their lifetime, outwardly pretending and feigning religion ; but inwardly giving themselves up to their own errors, faults, and wickedness : unto whom without doubt the

Marginal notes:
Matt. xii.
2 Cor. vi.
Hypocrites.

[1 diversissimis inter se, Lat.]
[2 vel exterioris, Lat.: even of the outward.]

outward behaviour and fellowship profiteth nothing at all.　For we ought to live for ever and to participate all heavenly gifts with them that desire them, to join in fellowship[3] with the church of God not only by outward and visible society, but by inward communion and fellowship, wherein consisteth life and salvation : of which matter we will speak in convenient place.　Such hypocrites or dissemblers, hanging[4] on the ecclesiastical body, are called members of the body, and are said to be of the church. Which matter that it may the better be understood of you all, we will set it forth by certain parables.

We say that the wicked or hypocrites be in like sort in the church, as chaff is in the corn ; which indeed is of another nature, and is no corn.　Like as therefore ofttimes there hang members unto men's bodies, either dry, or rotten, or feeble, which members although they have no society nor take part with the lively members in the vital spirit, yet by coupling together and certain strings they cleave fast unto the lively members, by means whereof they are also called by men members and parts of the body ; who, lest they should infect the other, they cut them off ; ofttimes[5] they let them alone, lest by cutting them off the whole body should be in danger of life : even so in like sort[6], we say that hypocrites are in the church of Christ, though they be not united to the church either by the bond of the Spirit, or of faith and love ; neither are they to be taken for lively members ; yet are they suffered, lest some worse mischief happen to the whole body of the church ; and ofttimes they are cut off, whereby the better health may come to the ecclesiastical body.

But let us hear what the evangelical and apostolical testimony saith. The Lord saith plainly in the gospel, that in the Lord's field cockle groweth up, being sown by a wicked man ; which he forbiddeth to be plucked up, lest that therewith the corn be plucked up also.　Behold, cockle sown by an evil man (I say) by the devil himself, which is no corn, yet doth it increase, and is in the Lord's field.　Again, the Lord saith in the gospel : " The kingdom of heaven is like unto a net, which, being cast into the sea, draweth all manner of things up with

Matt. xiii.

[3 Rather ; For they that desire to live for ever, and to participate in all heavenly good things, must join in fellowship, &c.]

[4 adhuc, Lat. omitted : still.]　　　　　　[5 nonnunquam, Lat.]

[6 ratione certa et suo quodam modo, Lat.]

it; and when it is filled, it is brought to the shore; and there men sitting reserve that which is good in a vessel, and that which is evil they cast away." Again behold, how ye may see both good and bad to be drawn in the selfsame net; and therefore in the selfsame kingdom both good and evil to be

Matt. xxii. reckoned. Also in another parable, there entereth one in among the guests which hath not on his wedding-garment; who is suffered for a season, but yet at last is cast out of

Matt. iii. doors by the lord of the feast. In another place it is said that he hath a fan[1] in his hand, and cleanseth the floor, and

1 Cor. v. burneth the chaff with unquenchable fire. [2]St Paul in his epistle to the Corinthians putteth a difference betwixt the professed and open enemies of Christ's church, and the impure sort of men who as yet are not quite repugnant and adversaries of the church and the name of Christ[3]. " If any man (saith he) that is called a brother be a thief, or a whoremonger, or a covetous person, &c. with such an one see that ye eat no meat. For what doth it belong unto me to judge of them that be without? For God judgeth them that are without." Without, that is to say, without the bounds of the church, he placeth them that are not called brethren, to wit, such as do not acknowledge the name of Christ or of the church: within, that is to say, in the society of the church (I mean of the outward church), he reckoneth up them that as yet do acknowledge the name of Christians, neither yet do withstand ecclesiastical discipline, though themselves[4] in meantime be defiled and spotted with much mischief[5]. Of all

1 John ii. men St John the apostle spake plainly[6], saying : " They went out from us, but they were none of us ; for if they had been of us, they had tarried still with us." This seemeth to be a new kind of speech. For if they which go out of the church had not been in the society of the church, how could they go out of the church? Can a man come forth of a place, in the which he never came, or in which he never was? Therefore if hypocrites and evil men are gone out of the church, surely

---

[1 vannum aut ventilabrum, Lat.]
[2 Proinde, Lat. omitted. For this reason.]
[3 to the name of the church and of Christ, Lat.]
[4 they themselves, ed. 1577.]   [5 sceleribus, Lat.]
[6 So also ed. 1584: but ed. 1577, spake *plainliest*: significantissime, Lat.]

they were sometime in the church; then, to wit, when they had not as yet gone out of it and did plainly shew what manner ones they were indeed.   Again, for that they went out of the church, they manifestly shew that they were never indeed the true and lively members of Christ and the church, yet for a while they were numbered among the members of the church.   The apostle giveth the reason: it is the disposition of Christ's true members never to forsake Christ and his church, but to continue and also to prosper and increase daily more and more.   The saints and holy men truly do offend or fall, but yet they do not forsake Christ utterly. David, having committed adultery and manslaughter, crieth out, saying: "Make me a clean heart, O Lord, and renew a Psal. li. right spirit within me.   Cast me not away from thy presence, and take not thy Holy Spirit from me.   O give me the comfort of thy help[7] again, and stablish me with thy free Spirit[8]."   St Peter denieth the Lord, and the weak flesh Luke xxii. overcame a good spirit: but immediately (the Lord stirring up his heart) he repented, and, departing from evil company, he adjoineth himself to the good fellowship of the Lord, who foretold him of this great fall, and thereto added these words: "I prayed for thee that thy faith should not fail; and thou, when thou art converted, confirm thy brethren."   The same Peter also in another place, what time many fell from Christ, John vi. being demanded whether he also provided[9] to depart, answered: "Lord, to whom shall we go?   Thou hast the word[10] of eternal life.   And we believe and know, that thou art Christ, the Son of the living God."   Wherefore St John said very truly: "They went out from us, but they were none of us."   He addeth the reason: "If they had been of us, they had still tarried with us."   Therefore because they continued not still with us in the society of Christ and the church, they shewed by their defection and falling away[11] what manner ones hitherto they have been: we accounted them to be members of the church, but they by their falling away did declare that they were chaff in the Lord's corn.   For as

---

[[7] salutaris tui, Lat.]

[[8] spiritu principali, Lat.   See Vol. II. p. 147, note 6; and p. 252, note 4.]

[[9] paret, Lat.]   [[10] verba, Lat.]

[[11] a nobis, Lat. omitted: from us.]

chaff, being not[1] stirred nor fanned, doth seem to be heavy with a grain of wheat in it, but being once fanned it appeareth empty and light, and is put apart from the corn; so hypocrites, being light by reason of their defection[2], do manifestly prove that they were never heavy with the seed of God's word, and that they were never of the true corn[3] of Christ.

All that be in the church be not the church.From hence a general and ancient[4] opinion is gathered, that all that are said to be the church, and beautify themselves with the title of the church, are not by and by the church. For St John plainly addeth : "But that it may be evident, that all be not of us." [5]We read how that St Paul to

Rom. ix.the Romans saith : "They are not all Israelites which came of Israel; neither are they all children straightway, because they are the seed of Abraham : but in Isaac shall thy seed be called." Therefore the faithful are the true and lively members of Christ and of the saints. In mean season truly, so long as hypocrites or wicked persons not yet putting off their visors[6] shall by their sayings and doings declare what they are, that they may lawfully be cut from the church, who not yet breaking away by their own accord do forsake Christ in the open field and fly to the tents of antichrist or the devil, are known and taken to be the true[7] inhabitants of the church, and are called the church and the members of the church, although God, who beholdeth the hearts of all men, do well enough discern them[8]. I will again make

John xiii.this matter plain by an example. As long as Judas, the betrayer of Christ and manslayer, did not utter his crafty or rather most wicked device either by open deed or word, neither forsook the company of Christ and the apostles, but did preach and provide necessary things of household for Christ, he was accounted for an apostle and the steward of Christ, yea, and for a member of the apostolic church. Yet

John vi.the selfsame Judas was called by the Lord a devil, and when he spake of the elect and of his true and lively mem-

[1 nondum, Lat. : not yet.]
[2 rather, by their light defection: levi sua defectione, Lat.]
[3 So also ed. 1584: but ed. 1577, never the true corn.]
[4 orthodoxa, Lat.]   [5 unde, Lat. : whence.]
[6 necdum deterso fuco, Lat.]   [7 true, not in Lat.]
[8 rather, judges otherwise of them.]

bers, he was most plainly shut out; so that there is no occasion
of doubt to think that Judas was no member of the inward John xiii.
and holy church of God, though he were a member of the
outward church, being reckoned in the number of the holy
men. And therefore they speak not without great advice, The visible and invisible,
that said, that of God's church there was one visible and the outward and inward
outward, another invisible and inward. The visible and out- church.
ward church is that which is outwardly known by men for a
church, by hearing God's word and partaking of his sacraments, and by public confession of their faith. The invisible
and inward is so called, not that men are invisible, but because
it is not to be seen with man's eye, and yet doth appear
before God's eyes, who believe truly and who feignedly. For
the true believers are the true and lively members of this
inward church; which before I called the militant church
more strictly considered: but the other visible church, comprehending both good and bad, is more largely considered.

Now forasmuch as we have said that the church militant Of the out-
upon earth is marked by God with certain tokens and marks ward marks of the church
whereby it may be known in this world; it followeth next of God.
that we should speak of those outward marks of the church
of God. And there are two special and principal marks,
the sincere preaching of the word of God, and the lawful
partaking of the sacraments of Christ: where as some add
unto these the study of godliness and unity, patience in
affliction, and the calling on the name of God by Christ; but
we include them in these twain that we have set down. St
Paul writing to the Ephesians saith: "Christ gave himself
for the congregation, that he might sanctify it, and cleanse it
in the fountain of water through the word." Ye have in this
testimony of the apostle the marks of the church, to wit, the
word and the sacrament, by the which Christ maketh to
himself a church. For with his grace he calleth, with the
blood of Christ he purifieth; that which he sheweth[9] by his
word to be received by faith, and sealeth with sacraments,
that the faithful should doubt of nothing touching their salvation obtained through Christ. And these things truly do
properly belong unto the faithful and the holy members.
Whereas hypocrites are not purified, the fault lieth in themselves, and not in God or his holy ministry: they are surely

[9 id quod annunciat, Lat.: which thing he proclaims.]

sanctified visibly, whereupon they are counted holy amongst men; and these things do improperly belong unto them. St Peter in this point differeth not a whit from St Paul, who when he preached the word of God to the people of Jerusalem, and they demanding what they should do, Peter answer-

Acts ii. eth: "Repent, and be ye every one baptized in the name of Jesus Christ for the remission of sins." St Peter therefore joined baptism with doctrine, the sacrament with the word. Which thing he had learned of our Saviour himself in the

Matt. xxviii. gospel written by St Matthew, saying: "Teach ye all nations, baptizing them in the name of the Father, and of the Son, and of the Holy Ghost." So that ye read in the Acts no other mysteries of the word and sacraments of the church

Acts ii. than are recited[1] in these words, "They continued in the doctrine of the apostles, and in doing almsdeeds[2], and in breaking of bread, and prayer:" where ye may see the supper of the Lord, another sacrament, adjoined to the sacrament of baptism, also the desire and study of unity and love, and the calling upon the name of God.

These things being thus sufficiently plain and firm enough, yet notwithstanding I will add other testimonies out of the holy scriptures. Concerning the token of God's word, or the preaching of his gospel, the Lord himself speaketh by Esay

Isai. lix. the prophet, saying: "I will make this covenant with them, My Spirit that is come upon thee (the church), and my words which I have put in thy mouth, shall never go out of thy mouth[3], nor out of the mouth of thy childer's children, saith the Lord, from this time forth for evermore." For in the

John viii. gospel also the Lord Jesus saith: "He that is of God doth
John x. hear the word of God:" again, "My sheep hear my voice, and I know them[4], and I give to them everlasting life; and
John xiv. they shall not perish for ever:" and again, "He that loveth me will keep my commandments; he that loveth me not will

[1 Rather, So that you read recounted in the Acts no other tokens of the church than these of the word and sacraments.]

[2 beneficentia. Communicatio.....e caritate Christiana est, et officia Christiana instituit, et opera misericordiæ habet.—Bulling. Comment. in Act. loc. cit. Tigur. 1540.]

[3 neque de ore seminis tui, Lat. omitted: nor out of the mouth of thy seed.]

[4 So also ed. 1584: but ed. 1577, and they follow me.]

not keep my commandments:" again, "Whoso is of the John xviii.
truth will hear my voice." Now as touching the marks and
tokens of the sacraments, St Paul, speaking of holy baptism,
saith: "Through one Spirit we are all baptized in one body[5]." 1 Cor. xii.
And he also speaking of the Lord's supper saith: "Though 1 Cor. x.
we be many, yet are we one bread and one body; for we are
all partakers of the same bread. Is not the cup of blessing
which we bless partaking of the blood of Christ?" It is most
certain therefore, for that it is approved[6] by testimonies of holy
scriptures, that the outward marks and tokens of the church
are the word and the sacrament. For these bring us into the
society of one ecclesiastical body, and keep us in the same.

All these testimonies properly (as I said a little before) do How these
belong unto the elect members of God, being endued with the church.
faith and true obedience: but unto the hypocrites, which are
void of faith and due obedience, they nothing at all[7] belong:
notwithstanding, because these also do hear the voice of the
shepherd outwardly, and ensue virtue, and openly or outwardly are annexed to the elect and true believers in the partaking
of the sacraments, yea, unto the true body of Christ, for those
outward signs' sake they are accounted to be in the church so
long as they depart not from it. In which point, for perspicuity sake, having treated of the marks of the church, we must
add this thereunto, that by common order[8] these marks do declare and note the members of the church. For there are
certain special members, who although they want these marks,
yet are they not excluded from the society and communion of
the true church of Christ. For it is most evident[9] that there
are many in the world which do not hear the ordinary preaching of God's word, neither do come into the congregation and
company of them that call upon God or that receive[10] the sacraments: not for that they despise them, or that it is a delight
unto them to be from sermons and the preaching of God's
word[11]; but because through necessity, as imprisonment, sickness, or being let by some other urgent cause[12], they cannot

[5 in unum corpus, Lat.]   [6 traditum, Lat.]
[7 improprie, Lat.]
[8 lege communi, Lat.]   [9 certissimum, Lat.]
[10 rather, or receive, i. e. they do not receive.]
[11 and—word, not in Lat.]
[12 aliorum malorum vi, Lat.: by the constraint of other evils.]

2—2

attain unto that which they earnestly desire; and yet for all that
they are the true and lively members of Christ and of the
catholic church.   In times past the Lord instituted or appointed to the people[1] of Israel a visible church, which he established by a certain law, and set it forth by visible signs.   If
any man had despised this church, or refused, when he might,
to hear the doctrine of the church, and to enter in among the
holy company, and to do sacrifice ; or else had railed at it ; or
instead of the order of worshipping God that was appointed
had embraced any other kind ; truly he was not accounted at
all to be of the order and number of the people of God.   And
yet it is certain, that there were an innumerable company of
men dispersed throughout the whole world among the gentiles,
who never did, nor could, communicate with this visible company and congregation of God's people ; and yet notwithstanding they were holy members of this society and communion[2],
and the friends of almighty God.   There were a great many
of the children of God with Joachim[3] and Jechonias[4] taken
prisoners by Nabucodonosor and brought captive into Babylon,
to whom it was no prejudice, neither did they[5] hurt them, that
they were separated from the people of God, the church, and
worshipping of God, being then visibly upholden by Zedechias
at Jerusalem[6] : even as in very deed it did little avail a great
many, to be in the visible assemblies and congregations with
the people of God in God's temple, when their minds and hearts
were not sound and perfit.   We may in these days find out
a great many of the faithful dispersed on the seas, condemned
to the galleys for the confession of the true faith : we may
find many that be holden in captivity under antichrist, of the
which we will speak in the next sermon following : we may
find also a wonderful many in Græcia, Natolia, Persia, Arabia,
or in Africa, being the servants of Jesus Christ and worthy
members of the catholic church of Christ, being shut out and
debarred from the holy mysteries[7] of the Christians through

[¹ in populo, Lat. : among the people.]
[² cœtus sancti membra, Lat.]   [³ cum rege Joachim, Lat.]
[⁴ Or Jehoiachin. See Vol. II. p. 11.]
[⁵ So also ed. 1584 : but ed. 1577, did *it*.]
[⁶ rather, that they were separated from the people of God, who
still had the temple and visible worship at Jerusalem under Zedekiah.]
[⁷ a sacris, Lat.]

impiety and cruelty of Mahomet: nevertheless we shall find them almost[8] nearly joined together in one spirit and one faith with all the true[9] members of the church, and marked[10] also with the visible signs. Therefore the word and the sacraments by common decree are the marks of the church, not putting apart or differing the faithful from the communion and society of other faithful being by some necessity shut out from the visible company of those that are faithful[11].

But to the perfect understanding of the marks of the church this belongeth also, and that most principally; that it is not enough to brag of the word of God, or of the scripture, unless also we embrace, retain, and determine[12] the true sense and that which is agreeing with the articles of faith. For if we corrupt[13] the sense of the scripture, and urge the same in the church, then dost thou not bring forth the sincere scripture itself, but thine own opinion and thy fancies which thou hast devised of thine own mind. The church of the Arians did not refuse the word of the Lord, but rather laboured both to beautify and defend their own blasphemous errors by the testimonies of holy scripture. That church denied our Lord Jesus Christ to be of one substance with God the Father: which thing, sith that the sense of the scriptures and of the ancient[14] faith among the chiefest points of our faith doth both affirm and urge, truly it alleged not the sincere and pure word of God, howsoever it boasted of it, but an adulterate word; yea, and thrust in and defended her heretical opinion for the true and perfect meaning of the holy scripture: and therefore it had not the true mark of the church, neither was it the true church of God. By this one unhappy example we may judge of all other churches of heretics: who though they seem not to be void of the testimony of God's word, yet for all that in very deed they have no purity of God's word in them.

That which we have said concerning the word of God is also necessarily to be understood of the use of the sacraments: for except they be orderly and lawfully used, I say, in that

What manner of God's word it ought to be that is the mark of the church.

After what sort the sacraments ought to be used.

[8 rather, most.]
[9 true, not in Lat.]   [10 rather, who are also marked.]
[11 rather, which yet do not put aside from the communion of the faithful those believers, who by some necessity are shut out of the visible company of the faithful.]   [12 tueamur, Lat.]
[13 corrumpas, Lat.: if ye corrupt, ed. 1577.]   [14 orthodoxæ, Lat.]

order in the which the Lord himself instituted them, they
are no marks or signs of the church of God. Jeroboam
truly sacrificed, yea, he sacrificed unto God; but because he
sacrificed not lawfully, he was accounted a stranger, and a
faller off from the true church of God. Yea, David himself
brought with great devotion and much joy and melody the
ark of the Lord of hosts; but because he carried it not lawfully upon the shoulders of the priests, by and by, instead of
great joy, the exceeding sorrow which followed declared that
it is not enough to use the sacraments and ordinances of God,
unless ye use them lawfully; which if you do, God will acknowledge you for his. Moreover, those which of old were
baptized of heretics were not for that cause baptized again
by the ancient catholics: because the heretics baptized not
into the name of any man, or into the society of their errors[1]
or heresies, but baptized " in the name of the Father, and of
the Son, and of the holy Ghost;" neither did they invocate
their own name, or the name of arch-heretics, but of Jesus
Christ. Wherefore not the baptism of heretics, but the
baptism of the church, yet ministered by heretics, they not
refusing, they allowed not the churches of heretics as known
to be true by true signs: but they acknowledged that heretics
use things properly[2] belonging unto the true church; neither
that it doth anything at all derogate or take from a good
thing, if any wicked or evil man do administer it. We do not
acknowledge at this day the upstart Romish church of the
pope (we speak not now of that old apostolic church) to be
the true church of Christ; yet we do not rebaptize those
which were baptized of the priests embrued with popish corruption: for we know that they are baptized with the
baptism of Christ's church, and not of the pope, in the name
of the holy Trinity, to the articles of the catholic faith, not to
errors, not to superstitions and papistical impieties. Finally,
we confess that not at this day[3] the unworthiness of the
minister can derogate anything from the service of God[4].
In like sort also we refuse not the Lord's prayer, or the
Apostles' Creed, or finally the canonical scriptures themselves,
because the Romish church doth also use them: for she hath
them not of herself, but received them from the true church

1 Kings xii.

2 Sam. vi.

*Baptized of
heretics are
not rebap-
tized.*

[1 ignorantiæ, Lat.]　　　　　[2 peculiariter, Lat.]
[3 ne hodie quidem, Lat.]　　　[4 rei divinæ, Lat.]

of God. Wherefore we use them in common with her, not for the Romish church's sake; but because they came from the true church of Christ do we use them.

Beside those outward marks of the church which the true believers have common with hypocrites, there are certain inward marks specially belonging only to the godly; or else, if you will, rather call them bonds or proper[5] gifts. These do make the outward marks to be fruitful, and, without the outward marks being by some necessity absent, do make men worthy or acceptable in the sight of God[6]. For without these no man can please God: in these therefore is the true mark[7] of God's children. And those be the fellowship of God's Spirit, a sincere faith, and double charity: for by these the faithful, being the true and lively members of Christ, are united and knit together, first unto their head Christ, then to all the members of the ecclesiastical body. And the consideration hereof doth chiefly belong to the knowledge of the true church of God; which though she should suffer rotten members, yet is she not defiled of them through their outward conjunction; for with continual study she laboureth by all means to keep herself undefiled to God. And first of all the evangelical and apostolical doctrine doth teach us, that Christ is joined to us by his Spirit, and that we are tied to him in mind or spirit by faith, that he may live in us and we in him. For the Lord crieth out in the gospel, saying: "If any man thirst, let him come to me and drink. *John vii.* He that believeth in me (as the scripture saith) shall have streams of living water flowing out of his belly." To which saying by and by the evangelist addeth this: "But this he spake concerning the Spirit, which they should receive that believed in him." Again he, promising in his gospel his Spirit unto his disciples, yea, even unto all his faithful, which should abide with them for ever, saith: "In that day ye *John xiv.* shall know that I am in my Father, and you in me, and I in you;" to wit, by the Holy Ghost: John the apostle expounding it, and saying, "By this we know that he dwelleth *1 John iii.* in us, by the Spirit that he gave unto us;" and again: "By *1 John iv.* this we know that we dwell in him, and he in us, because he hath given of his Spirit unto us." St Paul, the vessel of

Of the inward marks of the church of God.

[5] peculiaria, Lat.]
[6] acceptos vel gratos Deo, Lat.]   [7] typus, Lat.]

election, differeth not from St John, writing and saying to
the Romans: "If any man hath not the Spirit of Christ,
the same is none of his. And whosoever are led by the
Spirit of God, they are the children of God." Now as
touching true faith, which tieth us unto the Lord, St Paul
saith: "I live now; yet not I, but Christ liveth in me. But
the life which I now live in the flesh, I live yet through the
faith of the Son of God, who loved me, and gave up himself
for me." And again he saith: "Christ dwelleth in our hearts
through faith." With which sayings St John the apostle
agreeing again saith: "Whosoever confesseth that Jesus
Christ[1] is the Son of God, God dwelleth in him, and he in
God." For the Lord himself before that said in the gospel: "He that eateth my flesh, and drinketh my blood,
dwelleth in me, and I in him:" and he eateth Christ's flesh
and drinketh Christ's blood that believeth. Therefore Christ
our Lord is joined unto us in spirit, and we are tied to him
in mind and faith, as the body unto the head: they therefore that lack this knot and bond, that is, that have not the
Spirit of Christ, nor true faith in Christ, are not the true
and lively members of Christ; the Lord himself in the gospel
witnessing[2] and saying: "If a man abide not in me, he is
cast forth as a branch and withereth; and men gather them,
and cast them into the fire, and they burn." Which words
of our Saviour the apostle imitating (as we said even now)
said: "He that hath not the Spirit of Christ is none of
his." But they that are not destitute of the Spirit of Christ
are inflamed with the love of God. Neither do we separate
love from faith, the same St John so teaching us[3] and saying:
"God is love; and he that dwelleth in love dwelleth in God,
and God in him." For the Lord saith in the gospel: "If a
man love me, he will keep my word; and my Father will love
him, and we will come unto him, and will dwell with him."

But although properly faith join us to our head Christ,
yet the same also doth knit us to all Christ's members upon
earth. For whereas there is but one faith of them all, and
therefore the same Spirit; there cannot but be the same mouth,
the same mind, and the same sentence amongst them all:
although faith be not now taken only for a confidence in the

Side notes:
Rom. viii.
Gal. ii.
Eph. iii.
1 John iv.
John vi.
John xv.
1 John iv.
[John xiv. 23.]

[1 Christ, not in Lat.]   [2 rursus, Lat. omitted: again.]
[3 iterum, Lat. omitted: a second time.]

mercy of God through Jesus Christ, but also for an outward
confession of faith.   For we all confessing one faith and one
and the selfsame head, with one spirit and mouth we also together profess that we all are members of one and the selfsame
body.   Neither is there anything else in the world that more
unappeasably dissevereth the minds of men than the diversity
of faith or religion; and therefore there is nothing that may
more nearly join us together than unity of faith.

We come now to speak of love, which, I said, joineth
together the members of the ecclesiastical body mutually
amongst themselves.   The Lord saith in the gospel: "A new John xiii.
commandment give I unto you, that ye love one another; as
I have loved you, that ye also love one another.   By this
shall all men know that ye are my disciples, if ye have love
one to another."   It is therefore out of doubt, that the only
mark of the church next after faith is love, a bond most
firmly knitting together all the members.   This groweth
from the communion of Christ and unity of the Spirit.   For
insomuch as Christ, the king, the head and high bishop, of the
catholic church, enduing us all with one and the same Spirit,
hath made us all his members, the sons of God, brethren and
fellow-heirs, whom undoubtedly he loveth tenderly; every
faithful man cannot choose but with fervent love embrace
the members and fellow-heirs of their king, their head, and
their high bishop.   For John the apostle saith: "Every one [1 John v. 1.]
that loveth him that begat, doth love him also that is born of
him."   "If any man say, I love God, and hateth his brother, he 1 John iv.
is a liar: for how can he that loveth not his brother whom
he hath seen, love God whom he hath not seen?"   Paul, to
the end that he might most properly express before our eyes,
and as it were set to view and behold, this unity and agreement
of the members, useth a parable taken from the members of
a man's body, and saith: "For as we have many members in Rom. xii.
one body, and all members have not one office; so we being
many are one body in Christ, and every one one another's
members."   The same in the twelfth chapter of the first epistle
to the Corinthians, more largely and plainly expounding joining
together of the heads and the members, and that chiefly by
the said parable of the members of a man's body, and publishing it very eloquently[4], witnesseth, that between the highest

[4 elegantissime expoliens, Lat.]

members of the church and the lowest members of the same there is a very great and apt consent, and moreover a diligent care, and a help both continual and most faithful. Of all which it appeareth, that the marks of the true and lively church of Christ are the communion of the Spirit of Christ, sincere faith, and christian charity; without the which things no man is partaker of this spiritual body. By these things also it shall be easy to judge whether thou art in the fellowship of the church, or thou art not.

Of the original of the church. Moreover, we gather out of those things which we have hitherto disputed touching the marks of Christ's church, from whence is her original, and also how the church is planted, spread abroad, and preserved. Her original is heavenly; for St *Gal. iv.* Paul, speaking of the church, saith: "Jerusalem which is above is free, which is the mother of us all." Therefore he calleth the church heavenly, not that it dwelleth altogether in heaven, but that she, being here on earth, hath a heavenly beginning. For the children of God are not born of flesh and blood, but from heaven, by the renewing of the Holy Spirit, who through the preaching of God's word planteth faith in our hearts, by which faith we are made the true members of Christ and his *1 Pet. i.* church. For Peter saith: "Ye are born anew, not of mortal seed, but of immortal, by the word of God, which liveth and *1 Cor. iv.* lasteth for ever." And Paul saith: "I begat you in Christ Jesu through the gospel." And the same apostle saith in another place: "Faith cometh by hearing, and hearing cometh by the word of God."

Rom. x. Since therefore faith cometh by hearing, and hearing by the word of God, and that specially[1] by the word of God, the church truly can by no means spring or be builded by the *The church is not built by the doctrine of men.* decrees and doctrines of men. Therefore we affirm, that only the word of God is apt for the building up of the church of God. Men's doctrines set up men's churches, but Christ's word buildeth the christian church. For the doctrines of men proceed of flesh and blood. But Peter, confessing Christ with a pure[2] faith, and therefore grounded upon Christ who is the foundation of the church, heard these words of Christ himself: *Matt. xvi.* "Flesh and blood hath not revealed these things unto thee, but my Father which is in heaven." And therefore Paul *Gal. i.* saith: "When it pleased God that I should preach his Son

[1 Significanter, Lat.]   [2 vera, Lat.]

among the gentiles, I conferred not of the matter with flesh and blood, &c." He also, most manifestly abolishing all doctrines of men from the setting up and building of faith and the church, and only commending the word of God, saith to the Corinthians: "My word and preaching stood not in the enticing speech of man's wisdom, but in plain evidence of the Spirit, and of power[3]; that your faith should not be in the wisdom of men, but in the power of God." To this now pertaineth these testimonies of Christ. "He that is of God heareth God's word." Again, "He that is of the truth will hear my voice." And again, more plainly he saith, "The sheep will follow the shepherd, because they know his voice. They will not follow a stranger, but will run away from him, because they know not the voice of strangers." But under the voice of strangers we include all traditions and[4] decrees of men differing from the doctrine of Christ: to which traditions the apostle St Paul doth attribute the shape of wisdom, but the truth he denieth them, and calleth them superstitious. For our Lord himself in the gospel bringeth forth of the prophet Esay that immutable[5] saying: "They worship me in vain, teaching for doctrines men's precepts." Let us therefore hold that the true church is not built by man's decrees, but that she is founded, planted, gathered together, and builded only by the word of Christ. *1 Cor. ii.* *John viii.* *John xviii.* *John x.* *Colos. ii.* *Tit. i.* *Matt. xv.*

We do add that it is out of doubt that the church of God is preserved by the same word of God, lest at any time it should be seduced, or lest it should slip and perish; and that neither can it at any time be preserved by any other means: Paul again witnessing, and saying: "Christ hath given some to be apostles, and some prophets, and some evangelists, some pastors and teachers, for the gathering[6] together of the saints, for the work of the ministry (that is to say, to teach and preach the word), and for the edification of the body of Christ; till we all meet together in the unity of faith, and knowledge of the Son of God, unto a perfect man, and unto the measure of the age of the fulness of Christ; that we henceforth be no more children, wavering and carried about with every wind *The church is preserved by the word of God.* *Ephes. iv.*

[3 but in plain—power, the Translator's addition.]
[4 traditions and, not in Lat.]   [5 irrefragabile, Lat.]
[6 ad administrationem, Lat.: that the saints might be gathered together, Geneva, 1557.]

of doctrine, by the deceit of men, (mark, I pray, how men's doctrines are condemned again with great and inviolable authority,) and with craftiness, whereby they lay in wait to deceive. But let us follow the truth in love, and in all things grow up into him which is the head, that is, Christ; by whom all the body being coupled and knit together by every joint, for the furniture thereof, (according to the effectual power which is in the measure of every part,) receiveth increase of the body unto the edifying of itself in love, (increaseth the body unto the edifying of itself through love.)" These words of the apostle are so plain, that they need no better exposition than they have of themselves.

In this place also the order and manner of the church[1] by the preaching of God's word should of right be set down, which many do term and call the ministry of the word, or of the church : but we will speak of that (God willing) in the third sermon. It shall be sufficient in this place to defend, that our Lord God, having given doctors unto the church, doth found, build, maintain, and enlarge the church by his word, yea, by his word only.

The prophetical, apostolical, and orthodoxical church. There come two things now to be considered. First, that the church of God, for the continual and constant study of the word of God, is called prophetical and apostolical, yea, and also orthodoxical. For it is called prophetical or apostolical, because by the travail of the prophets and apostles it was first builded, and by their doctrine is preserved even at this time, and shall by it be spread abroad even unto the end of the world. It is called orthodoxical, because it is sound of judgment, opinion, and faith : for without the church there is no true faith, neither any perfect doctrine touching true virtue and felicity. The faith and doctrine of the church was revealed from God himself[2] by Adam and the patriarchs, by Moses and the prophets, by Christ and the apostles : whereby she elsewhere is named a mother; whereof we will speak in the next sermon.

Of the continual succession of bishops. Secondarily, that the succession of doctors or pastors of the church doth prove nothing of itself without the word of God. The champions and defenders of the papistical church do boast, that they have a most certain mark of the apostolic

[1 ordo gubernandi ecclesiam, Lat.]
[2 cœlitus ab ipso Deo, Lat.: from heaven by God himself.]

church, to wit, in the continual succession of bishops coming from St Peter by Clement the first, and so to Clement the seventh, and to Paul the third who died of late, and so continuing to Julius the third not long ago created[3]. Moreover they add, that all such members are cut off as do separate themselves from that church in the which only that apostolical succession is found. And we do not deny but that the right succession of pastors in the primitive church was of great weight. For they which then were called pastors were pastors indeed, and executed the office of pastors. But what manner of pastors they have been a great many years, which of the rout of cardinals, mitred bishops, and sophisters have been called pastors[4], none is ignorant but he which is altogether without any understanding. The prophet Zachary heard these words spoken to him from the Lord: "Take to thee yet the instruments of a foolish shepherd; for Zech. xi. lo, I will raise up a shepherd in the land, which shall not look for the thing that is lost, nor seek the tender lambs[5], nor heal that that is hurt, nor feed that that standeth up: but he shall eat the flesh of the fat, and tear their hoofs in pieces[6]. Wo be to the idle[7] shepherd, that forsaketh the flock, &c." Therefore never a whit more do these men prove by their continual succession of bishops, who teach not the word of God sincerely nor execute the office and duty of pastors, than if they should set before the eyes of the world a company of idols. For who dare deny but that a great part, yea, the most part of the bishops of Rome since Gregory the Great, were such manner of idols, such kind of wolves and devourers, as are described by the prophet Zachary? What then, I pray you, can the continual succession of such false pastors prove? Yea, and they which were of the latter time, did they not fill almost the universal church with the traditions of men, and partly oppressed the word of God, and partly persecuted it? In the ancient church of the Israelites there was a continual order of

[3 Paul III. died Nov. 10, 1549; and on Feb. 7, 1550, John Maria de Monte, who took the name of Julius III., was chosen to succeed him.—Sleidan. Comment. Lib. xxi. ad fin.]

[4 Romanæ ecclesiæ pastores, Lat.: pastors of the church of Rome.]

[5 derelicta non visitabit, dispersum non quæret, Lat]

[6 ungulas eorum dissolvet, Lat.]

[7 væ pastori idolo, Lat. *Idle* appears to be a mere mistake.]

succession of bishops, without any interruption thereof, even from Aaron to Urias[1] who lived under Achas, and to other wicked bishops[2] also falling from the word of God to the traditions of men, yea, and also idolatry.   But for all that, that succession did not prove the idolatrous bishops[2], with the church that clave unto them, to be the true bishops[2] of God, and the true church of God.   Truly the true prophets of God, the sound and catholic fathers[3], preaching only the word of God without men's[4] traditions, yea, clean against all traditions, were not able to reckon up any continual succession of priests their predecessors to whom they themselves should succeed; and yet notwithstanding, they were most excellent lights, and worthy members of the church of God; and they which believed their doctrine were neither schismatics nor heretics, but even to this day are acknowledged to be the true church of Christ.   When Christ our Lord, the blessed Son of God, did teach here on earth, and gathered together his church, the succession of bishops[2] was on his adversaries' part : but they for that cause were not rulers of the true church of God, and Christ of the heretical church.   The apostles of our Lord could not allege for themselves and their doctrine a succession of bishops[2] not interrupted : for they were ordained of the Lord, who was also himself created of God the High Priest for ever after the new order of Melchisedech, without the succession[5] of the order of Levi; and yet the church that was gathered by them is acknowledged of all men to be the true and holy church.   The apostles themselves would have none other to be accounted for their true fellows[6] and successors but those who walked upright in the doctrine and way of Christ ; for notable and manifest is the saying of

1 Cor. xi.

Paul : " Be ye the followers of me, even as I am of Christ." And though he speaketh these words to all the faithful, and not only to the ministers of God's word; yet those would he chiefly have such followers of him, as the residue of common Christians, that is to say, every man in his vocation and calling.   The same apostle, speaking at Miletum with the

Acts xx.

bishops of Asia, among other things saith : " I know this,

[1 2 Kings xvi. 10.   His name is omitted in 1 Chron. vi.]
[2 pontifices, Lat.: high-priests.]
[3 viri, Lat.]   [4 men's, not in Lat.]
[5 extra successionem, Lat.]   [6 imitatoribus, Lat.]

that after my departing shall grievous wolves enter in among
you, not sparing the flock. Moreover, of your own selves
shall men arise speaking perverse things, to draw disciples
after them." Paul the apostle not from any other place than
out of the apostolic church itself, yea, out of the company or
assembly of apostolic bishops and pastors, fetcheth out the
wolves and devourers of the church. But could not these
(think you) allege the apostolic succession for themselves and
their most corrupt cause, that is to say, that they be descended from apostolic pastors? But forsomuch as, forsaking the truth, they be fallen from the faith and doctrine
of the apostles, the offspring and apostolical succession doth
nothing at all make for them. Therefore we conclude, that
the continual succession of bishops by itself proveth nothing;
yea, rather that that is no lawful succession which wanteth
the purity of the doctrine of the scriptures and apostles[7].

And therefore Tertullian, greatly esteeming (and that worthily) the continual succession of pastors in the church, yet requireth the same to be approved by the sincerity of apostolic doctrine; yea, he acknowledgeth those churches which are instructed with pure doctrine, and yet not able to make any reckoning of succession of bishops, to be apostolic churches. If any man require the words of the author, they be these: "But if there be any churches that dare presume to plant themselves in the very age of the apostles, that therefore they may seem to have been planted by the apostles, because they were under the apostles, we may say thus: Let them bring forth the first beginning of their churches, let them turn over the order of succession of their bishops, so by successions going from the first beginning that that first bishop of theirs may be found to have for his author and predecessor some one of the apostles and aposto-lical sort of men, and yet such an one as continued with the apostles. For by this means the apostolic churches give their judgment: as the church of Smyrna testifieth that they had Polycarpus placed there by St John; and as the church of Rome sheweth that Clemens was appointed by St Peter; and as in like sort also other do shew for themselves, who have their offspring of apostolic seed, placed in their bishop-ricks by the apostles. Let heretics feign some such matter; (for after their blasphemies, what is unlawful for them?) but

Tertullian of the continual succession of pastors.

[7 doctrinæ evangelicæ et apostolicæ, Lat.]

albeit they do feign, they shall not prevail. For their own
doctrine being compared with the doctrine of the apostles, by
the diversity and contrariety thereof shall shew that it had
neither apostle nor apostolical man for the author; because,
as the apostles taught nothing that was contrary among
themselves, even so apostolical men set forth nothing contrary
to the apostles; but only such as fell away from the apostles,
and taught other doctrine[1]."   In this manner therefore may
those churches appeal, who albeit they can bring for their
author none of the apostles or apostolic men, as those that
are of far later time and are but now daily erected, yet they,
agreeing in one faith, are nevertheless counted apostolical, for
the likeness of the doctrine.

The doctrine of the ancient church of Rome.

The selfsame author, speaking of the ancient church of
Rome, and gathering the sum of that it either taught or
learned, said[2]: "Happy is that church to which the apostles
have uttered all their doctrine with their blood: where
Peter in suffering is made like to the Lord: where Paul is
crowned with the like end that John had: where the apostle
John, after that he was plunged in hot scalding oil, felt no
pain, and was banished into the isle. Let us see what it
learned, and what it taught, and how it doth agree with the
churches of Africa. It acknowledgeth one God the maker of
all things, and Jesus Christ the Son of God, the creator,

[1 Ceterum, si quæ audent interserere se ætati apostolicæ, ut ideo
videantur ab apostolis traditæ, quia sub apostolis fuerunt; possumus
dicere: Edant ergo origines ecclesiarum suarum: evolvant ordinem
episcoporum suorum, ita per successiones ab initio decurrentem, ut
primus ille episcopus aliquem ex apostolis vel apostolicis viris, qui
tamen cum apostolis perseveraverit, habuerit auctorem et anteces-
sorem. Hoc enim modo ecclesiæ apostolicæ census suos deferunt:
sicut Smyrnæorum ecclesia Polycarpum ab Joanne conlocatum refert:
sicut Romanorum, Clementem a Petro ordinatum itidem: perinde
utique et ceteræ exhibent, quos ab apostolis in episcopatum constitutos apostolici seminis traduces habeant. Confingant tale aliquid
hæretici. Quid enim illis post blasphemiam inlicitum est? Sed, etsi
confinxerint, nihil promovebunt. Ipsa enim doctrina eorum, cum apostolica comparata, ex diversitate et contrarietate sua pronuntiabit,
neque apostoli alicujus auctoris esse, neque apostolici: quia sicut
apostoli non diversa inter se docuissent; ita et apostolici non contraria
apostolis edidissent, nisi illi qui ab apostolis desciverunt, et aliter præ-
dicaverunt.—Tertul. de Præscript. Hæret. cap. 32. apud Script. Eccles.
Opusc. ed. Routh. Vol. I. p. 147. Oxon. 1840.]

[2 So also ed. 1584: but ed. 1577, *saith*; dicit, Lat.]

born of the virgin Mary ; and the resurrection of the flesh :
it joineth the law and the prophets with the doctrine of the
evangelists and apostles, and from them drinketh that faith ;
baptizeth with water, clotheth with the Holy Ghost, feedeth with
the Lord's supper, exhorteth with martyrdom ; and contrary
to this institution receiveth no man. This is the institution[3]."
Thus far Tertullian in his book which he entitled, *Of the
Prescription of Heretics.*

The last thing that is to be noted is this ; that the Lord
God not only of old and unto this time, but in these days
also, giveth doctors and pastors to the church: doctors, I
say, and not leaders[4] and captains of hosts and armies of
men[5], not princes, not soldiers, not crafty men, using deceitful means which in these days they call practices.   For by
no other means or manner, nor by no other instrument, than
by the doctrine of truth and sound and simple godliness[6], is
that holy and catholic church of God built up, fenced, and
preserved, whereof at the beginning simple men and Christ's
apostles by the preaching of the gospel laid the foundation.
Paul therefore removeth all worldly wisdom, and saith : " I
was among you, Corinths, in weakness, and in fear, and in
much trembling ; neither stood my word and my preaching in
the enticing speech of man's wisdom, but in plain evidence of
the Spirit and of power ; that your faith should not be in the
wisdom of men, but in the power of God."   The same apostle
also banisheth all crafty counsel with all sorts of deceit,

The church is not built by war or deceit.

[1 Cor. ii. 3—5.]

[3 Si autem Italiæ adjaces, habes Romam, unde nobis quoque
auctoritas præsto est. Ista quam felix ecclesia! cui totam doctrinam
apostoli cum sanguine suo profuderunt: ubi Petrus passioni dominicæ adæquatur: ubi Paulus Joannis exitu coronatur: ubi Apostolus
Joannes, postea quam in oleum igneum demersus nihil passus est, in
insulam relegatur; videamus quid didicerit, quid docuerit, quid cum
Africanis quoque ecclesiis contesserarit. Unum Deum novit creatorem
universitatis, et Christum Jesum ex virgine Maria Filium Dei creatoris,
et carnis resurrectionem: legem et prophetas cum evangelicis et apostolicis literis miscet, et inde portat [al. *potat*] fidem : eam aqua signat,
sancto Spiritu vestit, eucharistia pascit, martyrium exhortatur, et ita
adversus hanc institutionem neminem recipit. Hæc est institutio,
&c.—Id. ibid. cap. 36. p. 151.]

[4 doctores quidem, non ductores, Lat.]

[5 and armies of men, not in Lat.]

[6 quam doctrina veritatis et pietatis sincera et simplici, Lat.]

when writing to the Thessalonians he saith: "Our exhortation was not by deceit, nor by uncleanness, nor by guile. But as we were allowed of God that the gospel should be committed unto us, even so we speak; not as they that please men, but God, which trieth our hearts. Neither yet did we ever use flattering words, as ye know; nor coloured covetousness, God is record; neither sought we praise of men," &c. Wherefore he is greatly deceived and mad, that thinketh the church can either be gathered together, or being gathered can be maintained and preserved, with practices, that is to say, with crafty counsels and subtle deceits of men. It is truly said of the common people, that "the same is overthrown again by man's wisdom, which was first built by man's wisdom." Besides this, the Lord himself doth remove force and arms from the building of the church, since he forbids his disciples the use of sword; and unto Peter, ready prest[1] to fight, saith, "Put up thy sword into the scabbard." Neither do we ever read that any were sent of the Lord as soldiers, which with armed force should bring the world in subjection; but rather the scripture witnesseth the great enemy of God, Antichrist, shall be destroyed with the breath of God's mouth. Wherefore there is no doubt that all those things which are read in divers places of the prophets, and chiefly in the twelfth of Zachary, concerning wars to be made against all nations by the apostles and apostolical men, ought to be figuratively expounded. For the apostles, according to their manner, fight as apostles; not with spear, sword, and bow of carnal warfare, but of spiritual. The apostolical sword is the word of God. Yet in the mean time no man denieth but that the weapons of carnal or corporal warfare have been profitable sometime to apostolical men and to the church, and do good even at this day. No man denieth that God doth oftentimes use the help of soldiers and magistrates in defending the church against the wicked and tyrants: yea, rather all men will confess, that a good and godly magistrate oweth a duty[2] toward the church of God. For not without great cause the worthy[3] prophet of God, Isay, calleth "kings nursing fathers, and queens nursing mothers." Paul, being oppressed of the Jews in the temple of Jerusalem for preaching of the gospel

Margin notes:
1 Thess. ii.
Matt. xxvi.
Luke xxii.
2 Thess. ii.
Isai. xlix.
Acts xxi.

[1 prest, prepared.]
[2 operam suam, Lat.]   [3 clarissimus, Lat.]

amongst the gentiles, by the army of Claudius Lysias, the Acts xxiii.
Roman tribune, is taken away and rescued. And not long
after there was sent with the apostle by the same tribune no
small company of soldiers, to wit, a troop of horsemen and
certain companies of footmen, by whom he was brought safely
to Antipatris and Cæsarea before Felix the proconsul of
Judea: which thing is not rashly with so great diligence
and at large remembered by Luke in the Acts of the Apostles.
The ecclesiastical history reciteth many examples of holy
princes which have defended and succoured the church[4].
But these things in another place in some manner I have
entreated of in the seventh and eighth sermons (as I remember) of the Second Decade. And thus far of the original of
the church of God, and of the increase and preservation of
the same, have we spoken.

In this place it seemeth unto me not unfitly may the Whether the church of God may err.
famous question be handled or briefly expounded, Whether the
church of God may err? which that it may more plainly be
understood, I will briefly discuss the parts of this question.
I have taught that the catholic church of God doth comprehend, first the blessed spirits in heaven, then all faithful
Christians here on earth; unto whom I said did cleave the
wicked, or hypocrites, feigning faith for a season. Now
therefore, if we understand by the church the blessed spirits
in heaven, the church can never err. But if we understand
the wicked or hypocrites joined and mingled with the good,
and the wicked alone by themselves, they do nothing else but
err; but as they are joined unto the good and faithful,
and follow them, they either err, or they err not. For the
church of the good and faithful here upon earth doth err, and
doth not err. Which thing we will declare, when we have
weighed the diversities of errors, and gathered the number of
them together wholly in a bundle. Errors some be of doctrine and faith, and some be of life and manners: and what
manner of ones either of them be, I think there is no man
but knoweth. Let us see then, whether the church of the
faithful upon earth do err or no; and if it err, in what point
or how far it erreth. As concerning the manners and life
of the church, it cannot wholly and clearly acquit itself of
errors; that is to say, from sin. For always, so long as it is

[4 ecclesiam Dei, Lat.]

living here on earth, it prayeth heartily: "And forgive us our trespasses, as we do forgive them that trespass against us." And God for his mercy's sake doth always purge in his saints all dregs and infirmities, as long as they live in this world, continually renewing and fining the elect[1]. I am not ignorant what may hinder thee, faithful hearer. If the church (sayest thou) be not holy and pure, how is it called of the apostle holy, without spot and wrinkle? I answer, If thou wilt acknowledge no church upon earth but that which is altogether without blemish, thou shalt be forced to acknowledge none at all. For there shall never be any such kind of church remaining on earth, where the most righteous God, as the scripture witnesseth, "hath shut up all things under sin, that he might take mercy on all men." St Paul therefore doth call the church pure, without spot or wrinkle, through the benefit of Christ's sanctification[2]: not that by herself, while she is in the flesh, she is without spot; but for that those spots, indeed otherwise cleaving unto her, through the innocency of Christ, to those that embrace Christ by faith are not imputed: finally, for that the selfsame church in the world to come shall be without spot or wrinkle. For having put off the flesh and cast off all miseries, it shall at length be brought to pass that she shall want nothing. Besides this it is said that the church is without spot, because of the continual study of the church, whereby she laboureth and travaileth by all means, that as far as it is possible she may have as few spots as may be. And by that means, and chiefly by the benefit of imputation, the church erreth not, but is most pure and without sin[3].

Moreover, as touching doctrine and faith the church of Christ doth not err. For it heareth the voice of the shepherd only, but the voice of strangers she knoweth not: for she followeth her only shepherd Christ, saying: "I am the light of the world: he that followeth me shall not walk in darkness, but shall have the light of life." Paul also to Timothy saith: "These things hitherto have I written unto thee, that thou mayest know how thou oughtest to behave thyself in the house

Marginal notes:
John xiii. xv.
Rom. vii.
How the holy church is without spot and wrinkle. [Eph. v. 27.]
John viii.
1 Tim. iii.

[1 So also ed. 1584: but ed. 1577, and defiling the elect.—Subinde recurrentes et polluentes electos, Lat.]

[2 propter Christi beneficium et sanctificationem, Lat.]

[3 velut impeccabilis, &c. Lat.: as it were without sin.]

of God, which is the church of the living God, the pillar and The church is the pillar
ground of truth." But the church is the pillar and ground of and the ground of
truth, for that, being stablished upon the foundation of the pro- the truth.
phets and apostles, Christ himself, which is the everlasting truth
of God and the only strength of the church, [she] receiveth
this by fellowship which it hath with him, that she also might
be the pillar and foundation of the truth. For the truth of
God is in the church; and the same through the ministry of
the church is spread abroad; and, being assaulted and warred
against by the enemies, abiding sure, is not overcome: so far
forth as being made one body with Christ she doth persevere
in the fellowship of Christ, without whom she can do nothing.
Again, the same church doth err in doctrine and faith, as
often as she, turning from Christ and his word, goeth after
men and the councils and decrees of the flesh; for she forsaketh that thing that hath hitherto stayed[4] that she erred
not, which is the word of God and Christ. I think no man
will deny that the great congregation of the people of Israel Exod. xxxii.
in the desert was an excellent church of God; with the which
the Lord made a covenant, and bound himself unto it by sacraments and ordinances. And yet how shamefully she erred
whilst neglecting God's word, and, Aaron the high priest of
religion not constantly and earnestly resisting, she both made
a molten calf, and worshipped it as a god, no man is ignorant.
Where also surely it shall be necessary[5] more diligently to
look into and mark the whole number of the church; for
many in the church erring, it followeth not that none at all
is free from error. For as in the church of Israel the Lord
reserved a remnant to himself, I mean Moses, Joshua, and
undoubtedly many more, as well in that congregation as elsewhere without[6], which did never worship the calf; so there is
no doubt, although there do many err in the church, but that
the Lord through his mercy doth preserve to himself a certain
number who both understand aright, and by whose faithful
diligence[7] errors are destroyed, and the wandering flock of
the Lord brought back again into the holy fold.

The church therefore is said to err, when a part of it,
having lost God's word, doth err: and the same erreth not
wholly and altogether; forasmuch as certain remnants (through

---

[4 obstitit, Lat.]   [5 opportunum erit, Lat.]
[6 extra, Lat.]   [7 quorum fide et diligentia, Lat.]

the grace of God) are reserved, by whom the truth may flourish again, and may again be spread abroad in every place. St Paul called the churches of the Corinthians and Galatians "the holy churches of God;" yet these erred greatly, in doctrine, in faith, and in manners: and yet who doubteth that there were many among them who were most sincere followers of the pure doctrine preached by St Paul? That holy church therefore erred, so far forth as it continued not stedfastly in true doctrine: and it erred not, so far forth as it departed not from the truth delivered by the apostles[1]. From hence it plainly appeareth to the whole world, that those are most vain liars which commend unto us churches not builded upon the foundation of the prophets and apostles, but upon the decrees of men, which they shame not to commend unto us for most true churches and such as cannot err.

[Psal. cxvi. 11.]
Jer. viii.

David crieth out: "Only God is true, and every man a liar." Jeremy also crieth: "They have rejected the word of the Lord, and what wisdom is in them?" Therefore those churches do err, neither be they the true churches of God. The true church groundeth upon Christ Jesus, and is governed by his word only.

Of the power of the church.

Unto this treatise of the word of God, which is the only rule whereby all things are done in the church, the disputation of the power of the church of God in earth, and of the studies thereof which also are directed according to the word of God, is very like[2]. But before I will bring forth my judgment, that is to say, the judgment delivered by the scriptures, I will briefly rehearse the sum of those things, which the papists have left in writing concerning this matter, and do undoubtedly maintain for sound doctrine. John Gerson (not much amiss, unless he have an evil interpreter[3]) hath defined ecclesiastical authority to be "a power supernaturally and spiritually given of the Lord to his disciples and to their lawful successors unto the end of the world, for the edification of the church militant according to the laws of the gospel for the obtaining of eternal felicity[4]." But

---

[1 apostolum, Lat.]   [2 affinis est, Lat.]

[3 So also ed. 1584: but ed. 1577, an *ill* interpreter.]

[4 Potestas ecclesiastica est potestas, quæ a Christo supernaturaliter et specialiter collata est suis apostolis et discipulis ac eorum successoribus legitimis usque in finem seculi ad ædificationem eccle-

Peter de Aliaco, the cardinal, saith, that this authority is six-fold; to wit, of consecration; of administering the sacraments; of appointing ministers of the church; of preaching; of judicial correction; and receiving things necessary unto this life[5].

They call that the power of consecration, whereby a priest being rightly ordered may consecrate[6] the body and blood of Christ on the altar. This power they say was given to the disciples of the Lord by these words: "Do this in re-membrance of me." But unto the priests in these days they think it to be given of the bishop giving with the bread the chalice, and saying: "Receive ye power to offer up and to consecrate[7] Christ's body both for the quick and the dead." This moreover they call the power of orders, and a mark or character that cannot be wiped out. The power of adminis-tering the sacraments, and chiefly of the sacrament of penance, they call the power of the keys. The keys they make of two sorts: the keys of knowledge, that is to say, the authority of knowledge in the cause of a sinner making his confession; and the keys of giving of sentence and judgment, or of opening and shutting up of heaven, of forgiving or retaining of sins. They say that this power was promised to Peter in Matthew, the Lord saying, "Unto thee will I give the keys of the kingdom of heaven:" but that it was given to all the disciples in John, Christ saying, "Whose sins soever ye for-give, they are forgiven to them:" and in these days is given to the priests by the bishops[8], in their consecration laying their hands on the priests at the giving of them their holy orders[9], saying, "Receive ye the Holy Ghost; whose sins soever ye forgive, they are forgiven them." They call the power of placing ministers of the church ecclesiastical jurisdiction, and to consist in a certain prelacy; and[10] the fulness of it to rest

Power of consecration.

The power of the keys.

Power of jurisdiction.

siæ militantis, secundum leges evangelicas pro consecutione felicitatis æternæ.—Gerson. de Potest. eccles. Opp. Tom. I. col. 3. Par. 1606.]

[5 Petri de Alliaco Tract. de ecclesiæ auctoritate ap. Gerson. Opp. Tom. I. col. 898. Par. 1606.]

[6 conficere potest, Lat.]

[7 conficiendi, Lat.]

[8 So also ed. 1584: but ed. 1577, by the bishop: ab episcopo, Lat.]

[9 in sacerdotum ordinandorum capita, Lat.: on the heads of the priests who are to be ordained.]

[10 adeoque, Lat.: and so.]

only in the pope, having respect to the whole universal church. For it belongeth only to the pope to appoint rulers and prelates in the ecclesiastical hierarchy, because it was said to him, "Feed my sheep." Moreover they say, that all jurisdiction ecclesiastical doth come from the pope to the inferior rulers either mediately or immediately : in which things authority is limited at his pleasure that hath the fulness of power ; for a bishop hath authority only in his diocese, and a curate in his parish, &c. Power of apostleship or preaching the word of God they call the authority of preaching, which the Lord had given to his disciples, saying : "Go ye into all the world, preaching the gospel to all creatures." But doctors in these days affirm, that none ought to be sent[1] to preach but only by Peter, that is, his successor, mediately or immediately, &c. They say that the power of judicial correction was given to Peter by God, to whom he said, "If thy brother shall offend or trespass against thee, &c :" for the words of the Lord are known well enough in St Matthew, cap. xviii. They say therefore that God gave authority unto priests not only of excommunicating, but also of determining, judging, and establishing commandments, laws, and canons ; because in that place it is said, "Whatsoever ye bind upon earth, it shall be bound in heaven." To conclude ; they say that the power and authority to receive things necessary for this life, in reward of their spiritual labours, was given by these words of the Lord : "Eating and drinking such as they have."

Power of preaching.

Power of judgment or judicial correction.

Power to receive.

These things do these men teach concerning ecclesiastical power, not only foolishly, but also falsely. Of the power of consecration and sacrificing, how vain and foolish it is, we have oftentimes said in other places[2]; and perhaps will say more (if God grant life) in convenient place and time. Of the power of the keys we will dispute (God willing) about the end of the next sermon ; and something we brought, when we disputed of penance and auricular confession[3]. But they are foolish and shameless trifles which they babble of ecclesiastical jurisdiction, of the fulness of the high power (that is to say)

[1 So also ed. 1584: but ed. 1577, sent out.]
[2 See Vol. I. pp. 157, 165. Vol. II. p. 270. Bullinger. de Episc. Instit. &c. fol. 78. Tigur. 1538.]
[3 See Vol. III. pp. 75, &c.]

of the bishop of Rome; which I doubt not are known well
enough to the whole world long ago: and of that matter there
shall follow hereafter some arguments for the confutation
thereof in these our sermons.   Whereas they usurp unto
themselves the office of teaching, and cry out that no man
can lawfully preach but such as are ordained by them; they
thereby seek the overthrow of God's word and the defence
and assertion of their own errors: which shall also be entreated
of in his due place.   The power of excommunicating they have
so filthily and shamefully abused, that the church (through
their negligence and wicked presumption) hath not only lost
true discipline, but also excommunication itself hath been a
great many years nought else with the bishops of Rome but
fire and sword, wherewith they first[4] raged against the true
professors of God's word, and persecuted the innocent worshippers of Christ.   Moreover, that there is no power given
of God to the ministers of the church to make new laws, we
will shew in place convenient.   The authority and power to
receive wherewith to live have they put in execution to the
uttermost: but in recompence of their temporal harvest they
have not sown spiritual things, but rather, being asleep, they
have suffered him that is our enemy to sow cockle in the
Lord's field, and that not by any other but by their own
means.   For have not they, not being contented with things
necessary for this life, under that colour subtilly invaded kingdoms, and most shamefully and cruelly possessed them?
Wherefore he that seeth not that ecclesiastical authority, as
it is by these men affirmed and also by them put in practice,
is but a mere tyranny over simple souls, it is plain he seeth
nothing at all.

We will now hereunto join a true, simple, plain, and mani-
fest doctrine concerning ecclesiastical jurisdiction.   Power is _{What power}
defined to be a right which men have to do some thing by.   _{is.}
It is called in Greek Ἐξουσία, and Δύναμις: whereof the first
word signifieth right and power; the second, ability to execute power or authority; for oftentimes it cometh to pass that
a man shall have authority to do a thing, but is destitute of
ability to perform it.   But God can do both; and hath given
them both unto the apostles against those that were possessed _{Luke ix.}
with devils, as Luke witnesseth, saying: ἔδωκεν αὐτοῖς δύναμιν

[4 fere, Lat.: generally.]

καὶ ἐξουσίαν: "He gave them power and authority over all
Two kinds of devils," &c.   And there is also one sort of power, which is free
power. and absolute; and another sort of power which is limited, which
is also called ministerial. Absolute power is that which is altogether free, and is neither governed or restrained by the law or
will of any other : of which sort is the power of Christ which
Matt. xxviii. he speaketh of in the gospel, saying : " All power is given unto
me in heaven and in earth : go therefore, and teach all nations,
baptizing them," &c.   He, speaking again of this power in the
Rev. i. Revelation shewed unto St John the apostle, saith : " Fear
not; I am the first and the last; and I am alive, but was dead;
and behold, I am alive for evermore.   And I have the keys
Rev. iii. of hell and of death."   And again : " These things saith he
that is holy and true; which hath the key of David, which
openeth and no man shutteth, and shutteth and no man openeth."   The power which is limited is not free, but subject to
an absolute or greater power of another; which cannot of
itself do everything, but that only that the absolute power
or greater authority doth suffer to be done, and suffereth it
under certain conditions : of which sort surely is the ecclesiastical jurisdiction, and which may rightly be called the
ministerial power ; for the church of God useth her authority committed unto her for this purpose by her ministers.
St Augustine, acknowledging this distinction, and speaking of
baptism in his fifth treatise upon John, saith : " Paul baptized as a minister, and not as one that had power of himself;
but the Lord baptized as he that had power of himself.   Behold, if it had pleased him, he could have given this power to
his servants, but he would not : for if he should have given
this power unto his servants, that it should also have been
theirs which was the Lord's, then there should have been as
many sundry baptisms as servants[1]," &c.   In the church
Christ reserveth that absolute power to himself ; for he
continueth the head, king, and bishop of the church for ever :
neither is that head, which giveth life, separated from his body

---

[1 Baptizavit ergo Paulus tanquam minister, non tanquam ipsa
potestas ; baptizavit autem Dominus tanquam potestas. Intendite, et
potuit hanc potestatem servis dare, sed noluit: si enim daret hanc
potestatem servis, id est, ut et ipsorum esset quod Domini erat, tot
essent baptismata quot servi.—August. Tract. 5. in Joan. Opp. Tom.
ix. fol. 9. col. 2. Par. 1531.]

at any time: but that limited power he hath given unto the church. Which thing it ought to acknowledge; to wit, an ecclesiastical jurisdiction, hemmed in with certain laws, which proceedeth from God; and for that cause it is effectual, and therefore in all things ought to have chief regard unto God; and that ecclesiastical jurisdiction is for that purpose given unto the church, that it might be put in practice for the profit of the church. For St Paul saith: "The Lord hath given us power, to the intent we should edify, and not for the destruction of the church." And therefore that power, which tendeth to the hinderance and destruction of the church, is a devilish tyranny, and not an ecclesiastical power proceeding from God. And it behoveth us diligently to mark and retain this end of ecclesiastical power. *2 Cor. xii.* *[2 Cor. xiii.]*

But the limited power of the church consisteth very near in these points; to wit, in ordaining of the ministers of the church, in doctrine, and in the discerning between doctrines, and finally, in the ordering of ecclesiastical matters. Of every one of which points in their order we will speak a little; declaring what manner of authority the church hath, and how far it is limited in every part thereof. *In what points ecclesiastical power consisteth.*

The Lord himself appointed the chief[2] doctors of the church, which were the apostles, that all men might understand that the ecclesiastical ministry is the divine institution of God himself, and not a tradition devised by men. And therefore after that the Lord was ascended into heaven, St Peter, calling the church together, speaketh out of the scriptures of placing another apostle in the stead of the traitor Judas; by that very fact shewing that power was given unto the church by God to elect ministers or teachers. The same church also not long after, by the persuasion of Peter and the apostles, so persuading undoubtedly by the inspiration of the Holy Ghost, chose seven deacons. The church of Antioch, being manifestly instructed by the Holy Ghost, doth ordain and send Paul and Barnabas, although they were long before that time assigned to the ministry. It is read also in the Acts of the Apostles that the churches, by the commandment of the apostles, did ordain doctors for the holy ministry, as often as need required: and yet notwithstanding they did not ordain every one without choice, but such only as *To ordain ministers of the church.* *Acts i.* *Acts vi.* *Acts xiii*

[2 primos, Lat.: the first.]

were fit for that office; that is to say, such as afterward by
express laws they themselves did describe; to wit, " If any man
were faultless, the husband of one wife, watchful, sober," &c.
The rule set down by the apostle is sufficiently known, as appeareth in the 1 to Tim. iii. cap. But as touching the ordaining
of ministers (God willing) we will speak in the third sermon
of this decade. But if the church have received power to
appoint fit ministers for the church, I think no man will deny
that the church hath authority to depose the unworthy and
wicked deceivers; and also to correct and amend those
things which, being lacking, may seem necessary for this
order.

And forasmuch as ministers are chosen chiefly to teach,
it must follow that the church hath power to teach, to
exhort, to comfort, and such like, by her lawful ministers:
and yet no power to teach every thing, but that only which
she received, being delivered unto her from the Lord by the
doctrine of the prophets and apostles. " Teach them (saith
the Lord) that which I commanded you." " Go ye, and preach
the gospel to all creatures." And St Paul saith : " I am put
apart to preach the gospel of God, which he promised before
by his prophets in the holy scriptures." But this ministry
and office of preaching is nothing else but the power of the
keys which the church hath received; the office (I say) of binding and loosing, of opening and shutting heaven. In another
place also the apostles received power from the Lord over all;
over all, I say, not absolutely, but over all devils, and not
over all angels and men: and yet that authority and power
they received over devils, they received it not absolutely; for
it is added unto it, that they should expel and cast them out.
And therefore they could not deal with devils after their own
fancy; but that only, and so far forth as he would have them
to do who hath absolute power over all devils: and that
they might cast devils out of men, but not to send them into
men, though they would have desired it never so much. And
so also as touching diseases, they could not do what they
would : else would not St Paul have left Trophimos sick at
Miletum, who might so greatly have been profitable unto him
in the holy ministry. The two disciples, if they had been
able to have done what they would, would have commanded
fire from heaven to have fallen down upon Samaria, and so

1 Tim. iii.

Power to teach.

Matt. xxviii.
Mark xvi.
Rom. i.

The power of the keys.

Matt. x.

2 Tim. iv.

Luke ix.

would have taken vengeance of the uncourteous and barbarous people of Samaria, for that they denied to harbour the Lord Christ. In like manner the same apostles received keys, that is to say, power to bind and to loose, to open and shut heaven, to forgive and to retain sins; but perfitly limited: for they could not loose that which was bound in hell, neither bind them that were living in heaven. For he said not, Whatsoever ye bind in heaven, but, "Whatsoever ye bind upon earth;" neither said he, Whatsoever ye loose in hell, but, "Whatsoever ye loose upon earth." Again, they were not able either to bind or loose whom they would, not so much as upon earth. For they were not able to loose, that is to say, to pronounce a man free from sin, that was without faith: again, they could not bind, that is to say, pronounce condemned, him that was lightened with faith, and was truly penitent. And surely such as teach other doctrine than this touching the power of the keys deceive the whole world: of which we will more largely entreat in place convenient. Likewise the church hath received power from Christ to administer the sacraments by ministers, but not according to her own will and pleasure, but according to God's will and the form and manner set down by the Lord himself. The church cannot institute sacraments, neither yet alter the ends and use of the sacraments. *Power to, administer the sacraments.*

Finally[1], that the church hath power to give judgment of doctrines, even by this one sentence of the apostle Paul appeareth: "Let the prophets (saith he) speak two or three at once[2], and let the other judge." And in another place he saith: "Prove all things, and keep that which is good." And St John saith: "Dearly beloved, believe not every spirit; but try the spirits, whether they are of God." But of this kind of power to judge there is also a certain order. For the church doth not judge at her own pleasure, but after the sentence of the Holy Ghost, and according to the order and rule of the holy scriptures. And here also order, moderation, and charity, is observed. Therefore if at any time the church of God, according to that authority which she hath received from the Lord, do call a council together for some weighty matter, as we read that the apostles of the Lord did in the Acts of the Apostles; it leaneth not here *Power to judge of doctrines.* *1 Cor. xiv.* *1 Thess. v.* *1 John iv.* *To call a council.* *Acts xv.*

[1 Porro, Lat.]   [2 at once, not in Lat.]

to her own fleshly judgment, but giveth over herself to be guided by the Spirit, and examineth all her doings by the rule of the word of God and of the twofold charity. Wherefore the church maketh no new laws; as the church of Jerusalem, or rather the apostolic church, saith, that "it seemeth good both to the Holy Ghost and to the church, that no other burden should be laid upon" the faithful Christians, but only a few and those very necessary things, and neither

Power to dispose the affairs of the church.

beside nor contrary to the holy scriptures. Now ecclesiastical matters are of divers sorts, the good ordering and well-disposing whereof for the commodity of men is in the power of the church: of which sort those things are which concern outward worship in place and in time, as is prophesying, or interpretation of tongues, and schools. Also the church hath to judge in causes of matrimony; and chiefly it hath correction of manners, admonitions, punishments, and also excommuni-

2 Cor. xiii.

cating or cutting off from the body of the church: for the apostle also saith, that this power is given him, and yet to the intent he should therewith edify, and not destroy. For all these things which we have remembered, and such like, are limited with the rule of the word and of love, also with holy examples and reasons deduced out of the holy scriptures: of all which we will perchance more largely speak in their place.

Thus much have I hitherto said concerning ecclesiastical power; the contrary whereof I have declared with how open a mouth our adversaries do publish: but yet they handle these matters so grossly, that it may appear even unto children what they seek or what they would defend; to wit, not the ecclesiastical power, but their own covetousness, lust, and tyranny. The canonical truth teacheth us that Christ himself doth hold and exercise absolute or full power in the church; and that he hath given the ministerial power to the church, who executeth it for the most part by ministers, and religiously executeth it according to the rule of God's word.

These things being in this sort considered, it shall not be greatly laboursome to know the studies of the holy church of God. For it executeth (as I said even now) that power which it hath received of God most carefully and faithfully, to the end that it may serve God, that it may be holy, and that it may please him. And that I may reckon up some of her studies specially : first of all it worshippeth, calleth upon, loveth and serveth[1] one God in Trinity ; and taketh nothing in hand, not having first consulted with the word of this true God.   For she ordereth all her doings according to the rule of God's word : she judgeth by the word of God ; and by the same she frameth all her buildings, and being built maintaineth them, and being fallen down she repaireth or restoreth them again.   The assemblies and congregations of saints upon earth she fervently furthereth and loveth.   In these things[2] it hearkeneth diligently to the preaching of the word of God : she is partaker of the sacraments devoutly, and with great joy and desire of heavenly things.   It prayeth to God by the intercession of our only mediator Christ with a strong faith, fervently, continually, and most attentively.   It praiseth the[3] majesty of God for ever, and with great joy giveth thanks for all his heavenly benefits.   It highly esteemeth all and every the institutions of Christ, neither doth it neglect any of them.   But chiefly it acknowledgeth that it receiveth all things belonging either to life[4], salvation, righteousness, or felicity, of the only Son of God, our Lord Jesus Christ; as he who only chose her, and then by his Spirit and blood sanctified her, and made her a church, that is, a chosen people, whose only king, redeemer, high priest, and defender, he is, and without whom there is no salvation.   Therefore in God alone by our Lord Jesus Christ she only resteth; him she only desireth and loveth; and for his sake she rejoiceth to lose all things that appertain to this world, yea, and to spend her blood and her life.   And therefore it cleaveth unto Christ by faith inseparably ; neither doth it hate any thing more bitterly than falling away from Christ and desperation: for without Christ there seemeth nothing in all this whole life to be pleasant.   With Satan, as with a deadly enemy, she hath unappeasable enmity.   Against heresies and errors it striveth both constantly and wisely.   The simplicity of the christian faith, and the sincerity of the doctrine of the apostles, it most diligently keepeth.   She keepeth herself as much as lieth in her unspotted of the world and of the flesh, and from all carnal and spiritual infection.   And therefore she fleeth

[1 colit, Lat.]   [2 In his, Lat.: i. e. in these assemblies.]
[3 bonitatem et, Lat. omitted : goodness and.]
[4 suæ, Lat. : its life, &c.]

from and by all means detesteth all unlawful congregations
and profane religions, with all wicked men; and willingly and
openly confesseth Christ both by word and deed, even with
the damage of her life.   It is exercised with afflictions, but
yet never overcome.   It keepeth unity and concord carefully.
All and every the members of her body she most tenderly
loveth.   It doth good unto all men, as much as power and
ability will suffer.   It hurteth no man.   It forgiveth willingly.
It beareth with the weak brotherly, till they be brought
forth forward to perfection.   She is not puffed up with pride,
but through humility is kept in obedience, in modesty[1], and in
all the duties of godliness.   But who (I pray you) is able to
recite all and every one of the studies of the church[2] in a
very large discourse, much less in this short recital?   And
who would not desire to be a member of so divine and heavenly
a congregation ?

I would by and by join hereunto that which remaineth
touching the unity of the catholic church, of the division
thereof, and of other things belonging to the consideration
hereof, but that I do perceive you, being already weary of
hearing, do earnestly look for an end of this sermon.   Therefore we will put off the residue till to-morrow.   And
now, lifting up our minds into heaven, let us give thanks
to the Lord our God, who through his beloved
Son hath purified us and gathered us
together, to be a chosen people to
himself, and to be heirs of all his
heavenly treasures. To him
therefore be all praise
and glory, world
without end,
Amen.

[1 moderatione, Lat.]   [2 sanctæ ecclesiæ, Lat.]

⁋ THAT THERE IS ONE CATHOLIC CHURCH: THAT
WITHOUT THE CHURCH THERE IS NO LIGHT OR SAL-
VATION.　AGAINST SCHISMATICS.　WHEREFORE
WE DEPART FROM THE UPSTART CHURCH OF
ROME.　THAT THE CHURCH OF GOD IS
THE HOUSE, VINEYARD, AND KINGDOM
OF GOD; AND THE BODY, SHEEP-
FOLD, AND SPOUSE OF CHRIST;
A MOTHER AND A VIRGIN.

THE SECOND SERMON.

I SEE you are assembled, brethren, with attentive minds
to the exposition of those things which rest to be spoken of the
catholic church of God; which we affirm to be one and unseparable, according to the holy oracles of the sacred scripture.
Solomon in his Canticles saith: "One is my dove and my
beloved." Whereunto doubtless the doctor of the Gentiles
had respect, when he said: "There is one body, and one
spirit; even as ye are called in one hope of your vocation.
There is one Lord, one faith, one baptism; one God and Father
of all, which is above all, and through all, and in you all."
To these heavenly testimonies agree the testimonies of men.
For Cyprian, the bishop and martyr, in his book *De Simplicitate Clericorum*, saith: "The church is one, which is spread
further and further abroad by fertile increase: even as there
are many beams of the sun and but one light, and many
boughs of a tree, yet but one oak grounded upon a stedfast root; and whereas many brooks issue out of one spring,
though the number seem to be increased by the abundance
of store, yet is it but one at the head. Pluck a beam of
the sun from the globe; that one once separated is void of
light. Break a bough from the tree, it can bring forth no
fruit. Cut a brook from the spring, and being cut off it
drieth up. Even so the church, lightened with God's light,
spreadeth abroad the beams of her light through all the
world; yet it is but one light, which is spread everywhere,
neither is the unity of the body separated: she extendeth
her branches with plenteous increase throughout all the earth,
she sendeth out her plentiful rivers all abroad; yet is there

There is one holy church of God.

Cant. vi.

Ephes. iv.

but one head, and one spring, and one mother plentiful with fertile succession[1]." And so forth.

Moreover, where we read that divers names are given to the church, we must not imagine that there are many churches in the world, neither is that body to be separated which can bear or suffer no kind of division. Writers call the church catholic, which undoubtedly signifieth universal, because it is but one, neither can there be any more. For albeit this be distinguished into the church triumphant and militant; into the church of the old fathers, and the congregation of people of latter time; yet do all these members remain perpetually knit together in one body under one head, Christ. And even as the several conditions of bond and freemen separateth not a kingdom or commonwealth into parts; so neither doth the quiet rest or felicity of the blessed spirits triumphing in heaven, and the labours and sorrows wherewith we warring as yet in this world under Christ's ensigns are exercised, make two churches. The holy angel saith to St John in the Apocalypse: "I am thy fellow-servant, and of thy brethren the prophets." He therefore acknowledgeth both the prophets and apostles to be the sons and servants of one God. Whereof we read in the gospel, that one only vineyard, not two or divers, was let out to husbandmen, though they were divers. For even so there is but one church of the old fathers which were before the coming of Christ, and ours or the new people since Christ's coming taken out of the Gentiles. But what

Rev. xxii.

Matt. xxii.

[1 Ecclesia quoque una est, quæ in multitudinem (Bullinger read latitudinem) latius incremento fœcunditatis extenditur. Quomodo solis multi radii, sed lumen unum; et rami arboris multi, sed robur unum tenaci radice fundatum; et cum de fonte uno rivi plurimi defluunt, numerositas licet diffusa videatur exundantis copiæ largitate, unitas tamen servatur in origine. Avelle radium solis a corpore, divisionem lucis unitas non capit; ab arbore frange ramum, fractus germinare non poterit; a fonte præcide rivum, præcisus arescet: sic ecclesia Domini luce perfusa per orbem totum radios suos porrigit, unum tamen lumen est quod ubique diffunditur, nec unitas corporis separatur; ramos suos in universam terram copia ubertatis extendit, profluentes largiter rivos latius expandit; unum tamen caput est, et origo una, et una mater fœcunditatis successibus copiosa.—Cyprian. Lib. de Unit. Eccles. (al. de Simplicitate Prælatorum.) Opp. p. 108. Oxon. 1682.]

they differ from us, or we from them, hath been said in the eighth Sermon of our third Decade. Again, there are mingled with the holy church evil men and hypocrites; but the church is not separated· for evil men: for even as traitors mingled with citizens and not yet discovered make not two commonwealths; so although evil men cleave to good, yet are they both gathered into one church. And when hypocrites depart from the unity of the church, the church is not rent in pieces, but becometh purer. For excellently[2] saith St Augustine, that evil men or hypocrites are that in the church that chaff is amongst wheat, cockle in standing corn, traitors in a city, and runagates amongst soldiers. But it is plain, that wheat is the cleaner, standing corn the lustier, citizens safer, and soldiers the stronger, when runagates, traitors, cockle and chaff, are separated from them: yea, and except sometimes rotten members of the church be cut off from the ecclesiastical body, the church cannot be in safety. And particular or several churches are as towns or cities in a kingdom: the multitude of cities divideth not a kingdom. Of particular churches dispersed throughout all the world, as a body of many members, is gathered and compacted together the catholic and universal church, which is the fellowship of all the saints. Therefore most certain it is that there is but one only church of God, not many, whereof the only monarch is Jesus Christ; to whom be glory.

The unity and united society of this church of God is so great, that out of her fellowship is there no people found acceptable unto God, any true salvation or safety, any light or truth; for without the pale of God's church are no wholesome pastures found, all are infected with poison. No religion pleaseth God out of the church of God. If of old time any man had sacrificed to God himself without the tabernacle or temple, in the high places, he was accounted to have sacrificed to devils, and esteemed to have shed innocent blood. Rightly therefore the blessed martyr and bishop of Carthage, Cyprian, hath left in writing: " Whosoever separated from the church is joined to an adulterous church, the same man is separated from the promises of the church: neither pertaineth he to Christ's merits, which hath left the church of Christ. He is a stranger, he is unclean, he is an

Without the church is no light or salvation.

De Simplicitate Prælatorum.

[2 eleganter, Lat.]

4—2

enemy. He cannot now have God his father, who hath not the church his mother. If he might scape that was out of the ark of Noah, he may also escape that is abroad out of the church. He must needs be a most wicked man, whosoever he be, that leaveth his own country and the fellowship of very good men, and falleth away to the enemies[1]." Lactantius therefore most truly says: "It is only the catholic church, which retaineth true religion. Here is the fountain of truth: this is the household of faith: this is the temple of God; into which if one enter not, or out of which if any depart, he is excluded from the hope of salvation and life everlasting[2]." For our Saviour first said, that out of the sheepfold life is not found.

Institut. Lib. v. cap. 30.

Against certain schismatics.

Wherefore I cannot marvel enough at the corrupt and schismatical manners of certain men, who separate themselves for every light cause from the most wholesome and pleasant company or society of the church. For you shall find in these days captious and fantastical men not a few, which of many years have had fellowship with no church, nor as yet have fellowship with any; for in every man that is they find some kind of fault, in themselves only they find nothing worthy reprehension. Therefore they conceive with themselves a wonderful fashion of the church, which except they see somewhere established after that fashion which they themselves have devised, they contend (with shame enough) that there is as yet no true church of Christ in the world. They are worthy surely to be master-builders in Utopia or Cyribiria, where they might set up a building fit for themselves.

[1 Quisquis ab ecclesia segregatus adulteræ jungitur, a promissis ecclesiæ separatur; nec pervenit (Bullinger read pertinet) ad Christi præmia, qui relinquit ecclesiam Christi. Alienus est, profanus est, hostis est. Habere jam non potest Deum patrem, qui ecclesiam non habet matrem. Si potuit evadere quisquam, qui extra arcam Noe fuit, et qui extra ecclesiam foris fuerit evadet. Sceleratissimus sit oportet, quisquis patriam suam optimorumque virorum consortium deserit, ac ad hostes deficit.—Cyprian. Lib. de Unit. Eccles. Opp. p. 109.]

[2 Sola igitur catholica ecclesia est, quæ verum cultum retinet. Hic est fons veritatis; hoc est domicilium fidei; hoc templum Dei; quo si quis non intraverit, vel a quo si quis exiverit, a spe vitæ ac salutis æternæ alienus est.—Lactant. Instit. Lib. IV. cap. 30. p. 450. Lugd. Bat. 1660.]

But it seemeth unto them they have just cause of schism. For they will not communicate with our church, for that it seemeth the doctrine of the ministers in the church is not yet sufficiently cleansed and polished, neither yet lofty (as they themselves term it, *Hoch gnug gericht*), subtle, and spiritual enough. Elsewhere they complain that in our churches are divers customs used. Furthermore, they desire the rigour and severity of discipline, and finally an exact pureness of life; for they fear they shall be defiled with the unclean company of certain men. Many for the faults and vices of certain ministers either forsake or fly the congregation of the church: of which sort at this day are the anabaptists[3]. But there is as yet no sufficient cause alleged by these men, for which of right they ought not either to be joined unto us, or for the which they may be separated from us. We acknowledge that there be just causes for the which the godly both may and ought to separate themselves from wicked congregations, in which not only the lawful use of the sacraments is altogether corrupted and turned into idolatry, but also the sound doctrine is altogether adulterated, the preachers or pastors are not now prophets, but false prophets which persecute God's truth, and finally to them that sit to receive the food of life they minister poison. But none of these things (God be thanked!) can they object against us.

For as concerning doctrine, it consisteth partly in sure opinions, and those as it were numbered, firm, and immutable: of which kind are the articles of faith, and those without addition and corruption, lawfully and sincerely understood; and of that sort are also those principles: That all men are sinners, conceived and born in sin; That none but those that are regenerate can enter into the kingdom of God; That men, not by their own deserts, but through the grace of God, by the only merits of Christ, are justified by faith; That Christ once sacrificed for sin is no more sacrificed, that he is the only and perpetual priest; That good works are done of those that are justified; and those are indeed good works which the Lord hath prepared for us to walk in; That the sacraments of the Lord and of the church are to be received, and not to be despised; That we must pray continually, and

For the diversity of doctrine schism must not be made.

[3 Bullinger. adv. Anabapt. Lib. III. capp. 2. 3. Hooker, Eccles. Pol. Preface. Vol. I. p. 179. Oxf. 1820.]

that in that manner which the Lord hath appointed us; and
if there be any more of the same sort. But it sufficeth if
these and other like grounds be uniformly, purely, and simply
taught in the church according to the scriptures, though
there be added no rhetorical figures, nor no painted eloquence be heard. For aptly the blessed martyr Irenæus,
after the rule of faith set out in his first book against heresies: "Since there is but one only faith, (saith he,) neither
he which can say much of it saith more than he ought;
nor he which saith little thereby diminisheth it[1]." Therefore
when the doctrine of ministers expoundeth those things in
the church which are agreeable to the true and sincere faith,
which it also corrupteth not, what have these captious smat-
terers of rhetoric and self-learned[2] to require, though eloquence and plentiful learning be wanting in the teachers?
Was not the doctrine of the apostles and prophets most
simple and most free from all subtilty, that rightly it might
be said, how much more simple it seemed to be, so much
the safer it was? But in the mean season I despise not
true eloquence, (as that which is a singular gift of God), [as]
I have elsewhere often witnessed.

And partly doctrine consisteth in the daily expounding of
the scriptures, and in the applying of them to our time, place,
and affairs. In that kind was ever great variety and diversity, for which notwithstanding no wise man ever yet, separated himself from the fellowship of the church. For it cometh
to pass very often, that two or three or else more may
expound one place not after one manner, but after most
divers sorts. There may be one that expoundeth very darkly,
and another expoundeth more plainly: this man hitteth the
mark, he comes not near it: and this man applieth the place
which he handleth very fitly, some other useth not like simplicity of application: in the mean season, notwithstanding, he
saith nothing contrary to the soundness of faith and the love
of God and our neighbour, and useth[3] all things to edification.
I say, that of this diversity no man taketh just occasion to
depart from the church. For all godly men prove all things,
and keep that which is good; and in all sermons and holy
exercises[4] refer their whole study only unto edifying. And

[1 See Vol. i. p. 27.]   [2 erudituli, Lat.]
[3 profert, Lat.]   [4 auscultationibus, Lat.]

moreover the preachers agree well among themselves, and hereunto direct all things, that both themselves and their hearers may become better; not that they may seem better learned, or to have uttered that which no man saw heretofore. And the best learned loathe not their sermons which are not so learned: for albeit they may seem not altogether to have hit the mark, yet forasmuch as they have taught wholesome things, they are praised and not condemned; albeit in fit time and place they be somewhiles admonished[5]. Again, they that are unskilful do not envy the gifts of the learned, nor refuse to labour for more perfection, neither loathe they or condemn they learned sermons of those that be better learned; but they praise God, and being warned strive to more perfection. For wisely said St Aurelius Augustine, in his first book of christian doctrine, the six and thirtieth chapter: "Whosoever (saith he) seemeth to himself to have understood the holy scriptures or any part of them, so as of that understanding he gather not the twofold charity of God and his neighbour, he yet understandeth nothing. But whosoever gathereth such a sense thereof as may be profitable to him for the increase of charity, and yet gathereth not that sense that it may probably seem he whom he readeth meant in that place, he is not perniciously deceived, neither lieth he at all[6]." The same anon after: "He is notwithstanding to be corrected, and must have it shewed him, how much more profitable it were for him not to leave the high way, lest by accustomable straying he be forced either to go cross or crooked[7]." Thus far he. Therefore where an ecclesiastical interpreter doth err grossly, it is lawful to a better learned brotherly to admonish him; but to make a schism it is not lawful. The authors of schism lightly are somewhat proud and arrogant, and swell[8] with envy, and therefore are void of all charity and modesty[9]: they allow nothing but what they themselves bring forth, neither will

---

[5] amice, Lat. omitted: in a friendly manner.]

[6] See Vol. I. p. 77, note 9.]

[7] Corrigendus est tamen, et quam sit utilius viam non deserere demonstrandum est, ne consuetudine deviandi etiam in transversum aut perversum ire cogatur.—August. de Doct. Christ. I. cap. 36. Opp. Tom. III. fol. 5. col. 1. Par. 1531.]

[8] tabescunt, Lat.]   [9] moderatione, Lat.]

they have anything common with others; they are always musing some high matter, and nothing that is common or simple. Unto these men very well agreeth the saying of the apostle Paul: "Knowledge puffeth up, but love edifieth." Therefore godly teachers in the church, and also godly hearers, for doctrine which is not altogether foolish and though it be somewhat gross, yet being godly and tending to edification, they neither leave or forsake the fellowship of the church, neither strive they or contend, but rather use charity in all things.

And if the ministers' lives be attached with grievous vices, and yet in the mean season they be faithful in teaching, admonishing, exhorting, rebuking and comforting; if they lawfully distribute the lawful sacraments; no man hath just occasion to forsake the church. The Lord expressly saith in the gospel: "The scribes and the Pharisees sit in Moses' seat. All therefore whatsoever they bid you observe, that observe and do; but after their works do not; for they say, and do not." Behold the Lord saith, They say, and do not; therefore the teachers' lives were not agreeable to their doctrine: yet for that they stood in Moses' seat, that is to say, because they taught the word of God lawfully and sincerely, he biddeth to receive their sincere doctrine; but their life not being agreeable to their doctrine, that he biddeth to refuse: and therefore to make a schism for the preachers' evil lives' sake, the Lord doth forbid. Surely he commands to flee from false prophets; but not an evil life, but false doctrine, maketh a false prophet. A great conflict about this matter had the holy father St Augustine with the Donatists, who contended that the ministry was of smaller power through the imperfection of the ministers: which case is to be considered in another sort.

But now what cause have they to leave[1] and forsake our churches for the unlikeness or variety of ceremonies? In the baptism of children, say they, you observe not one order: and so also in the celebration of the supper. Some take the bread of the Lord in their hands sitting, some do come and take it at the hands of the ministers[2], who also put it in the mouths of the receivers. Some celebrate the communion[3]

Marginal notes:

1 Cor. viii.

For the vices of the ministers schism must not be made.

Matt. xxiii.

For the diversity of ceremonies schism must not be made.

[1 adversari, Lat.: to oppose.]   [2 præsidentium, Lat.]
[3 cœnam Domini, Lat.]

often; some seldom, and that but upon set days. And you use not one form of prayer. Neither have all your assemblies one manner, neither meet they at one time. But how shall we believe that the spirit of unity and peace is in you, in whom is found so great diversity? For just causes therefore we do not communicate with you. But of these customs we shall speak more fitly in their proper place. But it is marvel that men not altogether rude and ignorant of ecclesiastical matters bring no other arguments for defence of their wicked schism. Are the poor wretches ignorant how great diversity there hath been always in ceremonies, unity notwithstanding always remaining undivided in the catholic church[4]? Socrates, the famous writer of the ecclesiastical history, in the fifth book of his history, the twenty-second chapter, setteth out at large the diversity of ceremonies in the church of God. Amongst other things he saith: "No religion," saith he, "keepeth all one kind of ceremonies, albeit it agree in doctrine about them. For they which agree in faith differ in ceremonies." And again: "It shall be both laboursome and troublesome, yea, and impossible, to describe all the ceremonies of all the churches in each city and region[5]." The blessed martyr Irenæus, writing to Victor, bishop of Rome, rehearseth a great diversity of the churches in their fastings and[6] keeping the feast of Easter; and then addeth: "And yet notwithstanding all these, even when they varied in their observations, were both peaceable among themselves and with us, and yet are; neither doth the disagreement about fasting break the agreement of faith[7]." And again: "Blessed Polycarpus," saith he, "when he came to Rome under Anicete, and having some small controversy about certain other matters were by and by reconciled; but of this kind of matter they contended not a whit. For neither could Anicetus persuade Polycarpus, that he should not observe those things which with John the disciple

---

[4 Christi, Lat. omitted: of Christ.]

[5 Οὐδεμία τῶν θρησκείων τὰ αὐτὰ ἔθη φυλάττει, κἂν τὴν αὐτοῦ περὶ τούτων δόξαν ἀσπάζηται. Καὶ γὰρ οἱ τῆς αὐτῆς πίστεως ὄντες διαφωνοῦσι περὶ τὰ ἔθη πρὸς ἑαυτούς.... Πάντα δὲ τὰ ἐν ταῖς ἐκκλησίαις ἔθη κατὰ πόλεις καὶ χώρας γενόμενα ἐγγράφειν ἐργῶδες, μᾶλλον δὲ ἀδύνατον.—Socrat. Hist. Eccles. Lib. v. cap. 22. Cantab. 1720. pp. 294. 298.]

[6 denique, Lat.]   [7 See Vol. I. p. 433, note 4.]

of our Lord and the rest of the apostles, with whom he had
been conversant, he had always observed; neither did Polycarpus persuade Anicetus not to keep that custom, which by
the tradition of those elders to whom he succeeded he said
he was to keep. And, these matters thus standing, they had
fellowship one with another[1]." Thus far he. Moreover, the
ancient church used great liberty in observation of ceremonies, yet so always as it brake not the bond of unity. Yea,
and St Austin, prescribing unto Januarius what in this diversity of ceremonies he should either do or follow, biddeth not
him to make a schism, but judging moderately and wisely,
"No rule," saith he, "in these things is better than a grave
and wise christian, who will do in such sort as he shall see
every church do unto which by chance he cometh. For
that which neither contrary to faith nor good manners is
commanded is to be counted indifferent, and according to
their society amongst whom we live to be observed." Again,
lest under pretence of this rule and counsel any might force
upon every man what ceremonies they would, he addeth:
"The church of God, placed amidst much chaff and cockle,
suffereth many things; and yet whatsoever is either contrary
to faith or good life she alloweth not, neither holds she her
peace, neither doth she it[2]."

For the im-
pure life of
men conver-
sant in the

Last of all, whereas these men think that there is no
true church where as yet faulty manners are to be seen in

[1 Καὶ τοῦ μακαρίου Πολυκάρπου ἐπιδημήσαντος ἐν τῇ Ῥώμῃ ἐπὶ Ἀνι-
κήτου, καὶ περὶ ἄλλων τινῶν μικρὰ σχόντες πρὸς ἀλλήλους εὐθὺς εἰρήνευσαν,
περὶ τούτου τοῦ κεφαλαίου μὴ φιλεριστήσαντες εἰς ἑαυτούς. Οὔτε γὰρ ὁ
Ἀνίκητος τὸν Πολύκαρπον πεῖσαι ἐδύνατο μὴ τηρεῖν ἅτε μετὰ Ἰωάννου τοῦ
μαθητοῦ τοῦ Κυρίου ἡμῶν, καὶ τῶν λοιπῶν ἀποστόλων οἷς συνδιέτριψεν, ἀεὶ
τετηρηκότα, οὔτε μὴν ὁ Πολύκαρπος τὸν Ἀνίκητον ἔπεισε τηρεῖν, λέγοντα
τὴν συνήθειαν τῶν πρὸ αὐτοῦ πρεσβυτέρων ὀφείλειν κατέχειν. Καὶ τούτων
οὕτως ἐχόντων, ἐκοινώνησαν ἑαυτοῖς.—Euseb. Hist. Eccles. Lib. v. cap.
24. ed. Burton. Tom. I. p. 371. Oxon. 1838.]

[2 Nec disciplina ulla est in his melior gravi prudentique Christiano, quam ut eo modo agat quo agere viderit ecclesiam ad quam-
cunque forte devenerit. Quod enim neque contra fidem neque contra
bonos mores injungitur, indifferenter est habendum, et pro eorum
inter quos vivitur societate servandum. . . . . Sed ecclesia Dei, inter
multam paleam multaque zizania constituta, multa tolerat; et tamen
quæ sunt contra fidem vel bonam vitam, non approbat, nec tacet,
nec facit.—Ep. p. 118, 9. August. Opp. Tom. II. fol. 108. and 112.]

men conversant in the church, by whose conversation they church schism must not be made. fear to be polluted, unless either they come not at the church or else quickly forsake it, they fall into the madness of the heretics called *Catharoi*[3], who[4], deceived with the false imagination of exact holiness and using sharp cruelty[5], fled from those churches in which the fruits of the doctrine of the gospel plainly appeared not. Against these we set both the prophetical and apostolical, to wit, the most holy churches. For Esay and Jeremy rebuking the manners of their time do greatly inveigh against corruption of doctrine and manners; neither charge they them with light and common faults, but heinous. Esay crieth that " from the crown of the head to the sole of the foot there is no whole place;" and yet he departed not from the church, nor planted himself a new[6], albeit from all ungodliness and corruption he kept himself very diligently. How many faults, nay, how many errors, I pray you, were there amongst the apostles of Christ themselves! What, did our Lord depart from them? The church of Corinth was corrupted, not only in manners but also in doctrine. There was in it contentions, factions, and brawlings; whoredom and breaking of wedlock undoubtedly was common among them. What think you of that, that many of them were present at profane sacrifices? Surely it was no small error that they esteemed baptism according to the worthiness of the minister[7]. They had defiled the Lord's supper with their private and[8] prodigal banquets; yea, and of the resurrection of the dead they thought not aright. But did the apostle for that cause either depart from them himself, or command others to depart? yea, rather he calleth them[9] a holy church; and, greatly rebuking their contentions, he exhorteth all men to observe[10] the unity of the church in the sincerity of truth. It is not to be doubted, therefore, that they greatly sin which abstain from the fellowship of our or rather the catholic church, in which albeit there be

[3 An appellation of the *Novatians*. Vol. II. p. 424, note 3.]
[4 qui et ipsi, Lat.: who likewise.]   [5 rigiditatem, Lat.]
[6 Novam sibi constituebat, Lat.: formed for himself a new church.]
[7 baptismum referebant ad homines, Lat.]
[8 adeoque, Lat.]   [9 talem, Lat. : such a church.]
[10 colendam, Lat.: to cultivate.]

great corruption of life, yet the doctrine is sincere and the sacraments are purely ministered.

For the unworthy partakers of the Lord's supper schism must not be made.

But these men object: Ye admit all men without exception to the receiving of the Lord's supper, wicked men, drunkards, covetous men, soldiers, and such like kinds of men, with whom the holy apostle forbids us to eat common bread: so far off is it that he granteth us to be partakers at the Lord's table[1] with such. Except therefore we like to be defiled with the fellowship of the wicked, it is needful either not to join with this society, or else altogether to flee from it. But of the Lord's supper and the receiving thereof, if I live, I will speak in another place apt for it. At this time this only we bring against them; that Paul, the most faithful servant of Jesu Christ, was not sharper than his master. But it is manifest that he admitted Judas to the holy table, whom he knew, as it is wont to be said, *intus et in cute*, that is to say, thoroughly within and without[2], and yet he did not put him by. But he would have rejected him, if he had known the rest of his disciples would have been polluted with his company. Judas himself was polluted, for his mind and conscience were corrupt: but the rest of the apostles, whose minds were pure through perfect[3] faith, could not be defiled by another man's treachery. Therefore

1 Cor. xi.

saith Paul the apostle: "Let a man prove himself, and so let him eat of that bread, and drink of that cup." He biddeth every man to prove himself, not to judge another man's servant, who standeth to his Lord or falleth. If thou beest endued with faith, and dost lawfully participate at the Lord's table, thou art not defiled with another man's wickedness. Therefore, to avoid pollution, there is no cause why thou shouldest be separated from the church, in which thou seest the bad mingled with the good to be partakers of the Lord's supper. But if so be thou beest separated, thou plainly declarest thyself, being hardened with arrogancy, to be partaker with these whom St Augustine in his third book against *Parmenian*, the first chapter, painteth forth with these proper and lively colours: "They are evil children, who, not for the hatred of other men's iniquities but through the study

[1 dominicum frangere panem, Lat.]
[2 that—without, the Translator's explanation of the proverb.]
[3 veram, Lat.]

of their own contentions, go about either wholly to allure
or at least to divide the simple people provoked with the
bragging titles of their names, puft up with pride, foolish
with frowardness, subtile with slanders, troublesome with
seditions: who, lest they should be detected to want the light
of truth, pretend the shadow of sharp severity: and those
things which in the holy scriptures, the sincerity of love
being saved and the unity of peace being kept, are commanded for the correction of the faults of their brethren,
wherein moderation also should be used, they usurp to the
sacrilege of schism and occasion of cutting off." The same
author, amongst other things godlily and wisely disputed in
the two chapters following, gives this counsel to modest wits:
" That quietly they should correct what they may, and what
they cannot mend they should patiently suffer and lovingly
mourn, till God himself either amend it, or in the day of
judgment fan away the chaff[4]."

Furthermore, concluding this place, I will recite unto *Unity must*
you the words of the blessed martyr Cyprian. He in his *be kept, and schism*
third book, and third epistle, hath thus left it written: " If *eschewed.*
cockle appear to be in the church, yet ought neither our
faith nor our charity be letted, that, because we see cockle
in the church, we ourselves depart from the church: we must
rather labour to be good corn, that when the corn shall be
laid up in the Lord's barn, we may receive the fruit of our
labour and travail. The apostle saith in his epistle: ' But in
a great house are not only vessels of gold and silver, but also
of wood and of earth; and some vessels of honour, some of
dishonour.' Let us endeavour and labour what we may, that

[4 Illi filii mali, qui non odio iniquitatum alienarum, sed studio
contentionum suarum, infirmas plebes jactantia sui nominis irretitas,
vel totas trahere vel certe dividere affectant, superbia tumidi, pervi-
cacia vesani, calumniis insidiosi, seditionibus turbulenti; ne luce veritatis carere ostendantur, umbram rigidæ severitatis obtendunt; et quæ
in scripturis sanctis salva dilectionis sinceritate, et custodita pacis
unitate, ad corrigenda fraterna vitia moderatiori curatione fieri præcepta sunt, ad sacrilegium schismatis et occasionem præcisionis usur-
pant... Misericorditer igitur corripiat homo quod potest; quod autem
non potest, patienter ferat, et cum dilectione gemat atque lugeat,
donec aut ille desuper emendet et corrigat, aut usque ad messem differat eradicare zizania.—August. contra Epist. Parmen. capp. 1. and
2. Opp. Tom. VII. fol. 11. col. 3. and fol. 13. col. 3. Par. 1531.]

we may be a vessel either of gold or of silver : but the Lord only hath liberty to break in pieces the earthen vessels, to whom also is given an iron rod. The servant cannot be greater than the Lord[1]. Neither let any man think it lawful for him to challenge that to himself which the Father hath given only to his Son, that he might now be able to purge the floor, or fan the chaff, or by all the wit man hath to separate all the chaff from the corn. This is a proud obstinacy and wicked presumption, which lewd fury taketh to himself. And while some men always take to themselves a further dominion than peaceable justice requireth, they perish from the church : and whiles they proudly lift up themselves, blinded with their own presumption, they are bereft of the light of the truth[2]." The Lord Jesus reduce the wandering sheep into the unity of the catholic church, and living in unity keep and uphold them. Amen.

Of the departing from the church of Rome.

These adversaries of ours being overcome, there arise up new and cruel enemies, that is to say, the defenders of the Roman monarchy and of the apostolic see, as they call it, and the most ancient church : for they cry even while they be hoarse, that we are guilty of the same crime whereof we condemned the anabaptists and certain other fantastical fellows. For they say, that we with wicked schism and

---

[1 So also ed. 1584: but ed. 1577, *his* Lord.]

[2 Etsi videntur in ecclesia esse zizania, non tamen impediri debet aut fides aut caritas nostra, ut quoniam zizania esse in ecclesia cernimus, ipsi de ecclesia recedamus : nobis tantummodo laborandum est, ut frumentum esse possimus, ut cum cœperit frumentum dominicis horreis condi, fructum pro opere nostro et labore capiamus. Apostolus in epistola sua dicit, In domo autem magna non solum vasa sunt aurea et argentea, sed et lignea et fictilia; et quædam quidem honorata, quædam vero inhonorata. Nos operam demus et quantum possumus laboremus, ut vas aureum vel argenteum simus : ceterum fictilia vasa confringere Domino soli concessum est, cui et virga ferrea data est. Esse non potest major domino suo servus; nec quisquam sibi, quod soli filio pater tribuit, vindicare potest, ut aream ventilandam et purgandam palam ferre se jam posse, aut a frumento universa zizania humano judicio segregare. Superba est ista obstinatio, et sacrilega præsumptio, quam sibi furor pravus assumit. Et dum dominium sibi semper quidam plus quam mitis justitia deposcit assumunt, de ecclesia pereunt; et dum se insolenter extollunt, ipso suo tumore cæcati veritatis lumen amittunt.—Cyprian. Ep. LIV. Opp. p. 100. Oxon. 1682.]

forced by no necessity have forsaken the old Romish church, and have set up for ourselves new and heretical synagogues. And they allege that the holy scripture hath as yet her authority in the church of Rome, that it is read as yet in all the churches[3], that they fetch their disputations out of it in all their schools, yea, and also that the sacraments have their right place and use; and therefore that we are wicked schismatics, who without any necessary cause to go away are departed from the catholic church, most of all for the faults of some of the clergy and of the bishops. I must needs therefore digress a little, and contend with these defenders of the popish church, and shew that we never departed from the catholic church of Christ.

And because in this matter it chiefly behoveth us to know who is truly said to be an heretic or who is a schismatic, of these matters I will first of all speak these few words. St Augustine thinketh that this difference there is between an heretic and a schismatic, that an heretic doth corrupt the sincerity of faith and doctrine of the apostles with his wicked doctrine; and a schismatic, although he sin not at all against the pure doctrine and sincere faith, yet he rashly separates himself from the church, breaking the bond of unity[4]. And surely he properly is an heretic, whosoever he be, that contrary to the scripture which is the word of God, against the articles of faith, or against the sound opinions of the church grounded on the word of God, through hope of any temporal commodity, of his own brain and fleshly choice, chooseth, receiveth, teacheth, followeth strange things, and stiffly retaining doth both defend them and spread them abroad. By the imperial edict of Augustus Cæsar Gratian, Valentinian, and Theodosius, they are defined to be catholics or Christians, who continue in that religion which St Peter taught the church of Rome, and which blessed Damasus and St Peter bishop of Alexandria did teach, that is to say, confessing,

Who is an heretic, and who a schismatic.

[3 So also ed. 1584: but ed. 1577, *their* churches. The Latin is, in omnibus templis.]

[4 Hæretici...ex...evangelii semine et Christi nomine procreati, pravis opinionibus ad falsa dogmata convertuntur...Solet autem etiam quæri, schismatici quid ab hæreticis distent, et hoc inveniri; quod schismaticos non fides diversa faciat, sed communionis disrupta societas.—August. Quæst. ex Matth. Opp. Tom. IV. fol. 78. col. 1. Par. 1531.]

according to the teaching[1] of the apostles and doctrine of the gospel, the only Godhead of the Father and of the Son and of the Holy Ghost in equal majesty and in an holy Trinity. And again they are by them declared to be heretics, who follow contrary opinions, whom they account both mad and infamous and worthy of punishment[2]. And he is a schismatic, whosoever he be, that separateth himself from the unity of the true church of God, and either himself gathereth together new assemblies, or joineth himself to congregations gathered by others, albeit in doctrine he err little or nothing. And I think no man can either desire or gainsay anything in these descriptions.

And therefore the defenders of the Romish monarchy do greatly offend against us, evermore having in their mouths against us the most heinous crimes of heresy and schism. For we teach nothing against the sincerity and truth of the holy scriptures, or against the articles of faith, or against the opinions of the catholic church which be sound and established by the canonical scriptures. If it had liked us to have sought earthly commodity, we would surely have continued in the popish doctrine, in which all things are gainful; but because we have received the doctrine of Christ, we are open to every man's reproach: whereof we were not ignorant when we departed from the doctrine of the pope. For no hope therefore of temporal commodity do we embrace the doctrine of Christ, neither do we presumptuously[3] affirm anything; for if any man can teach us any better out of God's word, we will not refuse to embrace that which is better. And moreover, with open voice and with all our hearts[4] we condemn all heresies and heretics, whosoever they be, which the ancient church either in general councils or without councils hath killed with the sword of God's word. But we strive against the false doctrine of the pope, his new decrees which fight against the word of God, and most filthy abuses and corruptions in the church. The bishops of Rome have taken to themselves with their conspirators a tyranny over the church, playing the part of very antichrists in the temple of God: their tyranny therefore and antichristianism we flee

[1 disciplinam, Lat.]   [2 See Vol. I. p. 34.]
[3 pertinaciter, Lat.: obstinately.]
[4 sincero corde, Lat.]

and refuse, Christ and his yoke we refuse not, the fellowship of saints we flee not : yea, rather to that end we may
remain in that society and become[5] the true members of
Christ and of his saints, flying out of the popish church, we
are gathered together again into one holy catholic and apostolic church.   And this church we do acknowledge to be the
very house of God, and the proper sheepfold of Christ our
Lord, whereof he is the shepherd.

For freely we confess, and with great joy giving thanks *A free con-*
to God that hath delivered us we publish abroad, that we *fession of departing*
are departed from the Romish church, and that we do at *from the Romish*
this day also abhor the same.   But first of all we distinguish *church.*
and put a diversity between the old church of Rome and
the late upstart church.   For there was sometime at Rome
a holy and faithful church, which apostolic men and the
apostles of Christ themselves did establish and preserve by
the word of God : which ancient church was not only without
the ceremonies there used and received at this day, but if
she had but seen them, she would surely have accursed them.
That ancient church wanted the decrees whereupon the church
of Rome at this day altogether stayeth herself.   She was
ignorant of that monarchy and all that stately court.   Therefore from that ancient and apostolic church of Rome we
never departed, neither will we ever depart.   We acknowledge, moreover, all that are at Rome, who at this day do
worship Christ and keep themselves from all popish pollution,
to be our beloved brethren; of which sort we doubt not but
Rome hath a great many.   Finally, we do not acknowledge
that upstart church of Rome to be the true church of Christ,
which doth acknowledge and worship the pope as Christ his
vicar in earth, and is obedient to his laws.   Wherefore we
cannot be schismatics, who, leaving the church of Rome, have
not departed from the true church of God.

For the holy catholic church cleaveth unto her only *The upstart*
shepherd Christ, believeth his word, and liveth holily ; but *church of Rome is not*
you shall find all things quite contrary in the church of *the church.*
Rome, so as it cannot come within the compass[6] neither of
the outward and visible, neither of the inward and invisible,
church of God.   The godly bear with many things in the
church, that is to say, in the members of the church and in

[5 esse, Lat. : be.]   [6 censum, Lat.]

the ministers (as I shewed of late when I entreated against schismatics); but in that upstart church of Rome thou shalt not find small and tolerable faults either of doctrine or of life or of errors: all these faults in her are heinous, desperate, and abominable. What manner of charity should it be therefore that could hope for better of the[1] most untoward and lamentable things[2]? Hypocrites and evil men are accounted to be parcel of the outward and visible church of God, and are suffered in the same: but these Romanists are neither evil men or hypocrites, but the very worst and the most cruel enemies of Christ his truth, openly blaspheming the gospel and persecuting those that believe in Christ; and therefore they neither have the outward nor yet the inward marks of the church[3]. The Spirit of the Lord resteth upon those that tremble at the word of God: these men fret and fume if any man unfeignedly reverence the word of God. True faith attributeth only unto Christ all the means whereby it cometh unto everlasting life[4]: these men do persecute the faithful, because they attribute unto Christ Jesus alone all the means whereby they attain unto everlasting life[4], and will not part stakes in the means of salvation with popish fancies. Instead of charity they exercise cruelty against their brethren and against their neighbours. What shall a man say of them who abuse the public goods of the church, and spend them according to their own private lusts? For that which of old time the faithful have of charity given to the use of the church and for the sustentation of the poor, that do these men waste, living most lecherously and filthily. Which thing the elect apostles of the Lord, Peter and Thaddeus, did foretel the church of God of concerning them.

The church of Rome hath not the outward marks of the church, what shall I say? These men say that the canonical scripture hath authority in the church of Rome, and that the same word is read both in their churches and in their schools, and that the sacraments have their force and are effectual amongst them. But I can shew the contrary. First of all, they will make subject the interpretation of the holy and sacred scriptures unto their see, and the right of judgment in all cases

Marginal notes: The church of Rome hath not the inward marks of the church of God. — 2 Pet. ii. and in the epistle of Jude. — The church of Rome hath not the outward marks of the church of God.

[1 So also ed. 1584: but ed. 1577, these.]
[2 de pertinacissimis deploratissimisque rebus, Lat.]
[3 ecclesiæ Dei, Lat.]   [4 omnia vitæ, Lat.]

they give unto their idol the pope of Rome. For that canon
every man knoweth: "Whatsoever he decreeth, whatsoever
he establisheth, is of all men to be observed for ever inviolably[5]." And again: "The whole church throughout the
universal world knoweth, that the holy church of Rome hath
authority to give judgment of all things, neither is it lawful
for any to give judgment of her judgments[6]." Therefore she
also judgeth the scriptures and expoundeth them, and turneth
and windeth them which way she listeth. I will not now
remember how by manifest words the standard-bearers of that
see do write, that the canonical scripture taketh her authority of the church[7], abusing this sentence of the ancient father
St Augustine, "I would not have believed the gospel, if the
authority of the holy church had not moved me[8]," &c. This
will I affirm, which cannot but be manifest unto all men, that
the Romish church, or the rulers of the same church, do take
away the natural sense and true meaning of the holy scriptures, and have set down a strange sense instead of it; which
sense, to the end it may the better be liked of men, they call
the sense of the holy mother the church; which sense also
they urge with so great wickedness, as if you oppose against
it the native sense, you shall receive for your labour the reproachful name of an heretic. In few words, except you
bring out the whole scripture wrested after their mind and
gain, that is to say, tempered with their devilish decrees as
with poison, it will be said that you have not brought out the
holy scriptures, but that you have taught heresy. By examples the matter will be made the plainer. The scripture
teacheth that Jesus Christ is the only head of the church:
but unless you also join the pope to be the head of the church
militant in earth, you will be called an heretic. The scrip-

[5 —ab omnibus quidquid statuit, quidquid ordinat (Romana ecclesia), perpetuo et irrefragabiliter observandum est.—Corp. Jur. Can.
Decret. I. par. distinct. 19. cap. 5. Tom. I. p. 24. Par. 1687.]

[6 Cuncta per mundum novit ecclesia, quod sacrosancta Romana
ecclesia fas de omnibus habeat judicandi, neque cuiquam de ejus
liceat judicare judicio.—Ibid. Decret. II. par. caus. 9. quæst. 3. cap.
17. p. 211.]

[7 See Jewel's Def. of Apol. Park. Soc. ed. pp. 218, 247. part I.]

[8 Ego vero evangelio non crederem, nisi me catholicæ ecclesiæ
commoveret auctoritas.—August. contra epist. Manichæi. Opp. Tom.
VI. fol. 24. col. 3. Par. 1531.]

ture teacheth that Jesus Christ is the only intercessor or mediator, priest, and only sacrifice propitiatory of the faithful :
but unless you join hereunto, that Christ is indeed the mediator of redemption, but that the saints together with Christ
are the mediators of intercession, and that the priests do daily
offer an unbloody sacrifice, so as the saints may be acknowledged to be intercessors together with Christ in heaven, and
that the priests in earth do daily offer in their mass a sacrifice for the quick and for the dead, you will else be called an
heretic.   The scripture teacheth that Jesus Christ is the
righteousness of the faithful, which righteousness we receive
by faith : but unless you will part stakes between this righteousness of Christ and works or men's merits, you will be
called an heretic.   The scripture teacheth that Christ ascended into heaven, and hath established[1] a vicegerent power, to
wit, the Holy Ghost; and that also he will not come again
into the world bodily but only at the day of judgment : but
unless you do acknowledge the same Christ to be also corporally present in the bread of the sacrament, and dost also
worship him there, thou wilt else be called an heretic.   Christ
our Lord said at his last supper, reaching the cup to his disciples, " Drink you all of this :" but and if thou wilt contend
that both the kinds of the sacrament ought to be given to all
the faithful, thou wilt be called an heretic.   God said in his
law, Thou shalt not make an image, thou shalt not worship it,
thou shalt not serve it: but unless thou understand by an
image the idols of the gentiles, as of Saturn or Mercury,
but not of the true God or any saint, thou wilt be called an
heretic.

Many more things of this sort I could bring forth, if I
spake to them that were ignorant.   What authority therefore,
or what place, shall we say the word of God had in that see ?
Who seeth not that these filthy beasts do tread under foot as
a captive the most holy word of God; that they establish
and re-establish laws of God according to their own giant-like
boldness? It is therefore as clear as anything may be clear,
that the Romish church is destitute of the holy word of God.
I have shewed plainly in the first sermon of this decade[2], that
it is not enough to boast out the words of the holy scripture,
unless therewithal the natural sense be retained uncorrupted.

[1 misisse, Lat. : hath sent.]   [2 See above, p. 21.]

The church of Rome hath corrupted the sense and meaning of the holy scriptures, and thrust upon the simple people opinions contrary to the scriptures : and therefore the church of Rome is not the true church of Christ.

The sacrament of baptism ministered by popish priests albeit we do not reiterate, for that they baptized in the name of the Father and of the Son and of the Holy Ghost (as in the first sermon of this decade I have shewed[3]); yet the breaking of bread or distribution of the Lord's supper they so defiled, and also corrupted the same with doctrines contrary to the sound faith, and turned the same into such a filthy merchandise, as no man that is of a sound judgment can with a safe conscience and without corruption of his religion communicate with them. Of the most filthy life and wicked manners of the priests of the Romish church I will at this time say nothing. For already it appeareth, I doubt not, to them that are not wilfully blind[4], that the see of Rome hath not the outward marks of the true church of God, joined with the pure word of God[5], and sound preaching of the gospel. It wanteth (I say) a heavenly ministry, and lawful ministers of the church, and also the wholesome use of the Lord's supper : and therefore it is not the true church of God from which no man may depart without being guilty of schism.

By this means, some man will say, Christ shall have no church left him in the earth ; for they that be the governors of the church, if they err, and corrupt and forsake the word of God, what hope (I pray you) remaineth of the church ? Or where the marks of the church appear not, where (I pray you) is the church ? I answer, that Almighty God in such calamities of the church, in the which the governors fall away from the word and true worship of God, and do embrace and bring in new laws and new ordinances into the church, the true outward marks of the church being for a time either darkened or worn out of use, doth yet notwithstanding reserve unto himself a church in the earth ; which church also he furnisheth[6] and repaireth with true teachers whom he sendeth into the same, albeit they be not acknow-

The Lord reserveth to himself a church, though the governors of it err.

[3 See above, p. 22.]
[4 vel cæcis, Lat.: even to the blind.]
[5 Rather, seeing it wanteth the pure word of God, &c.]
[6 fulcit, Lat.]

ledged for true ministers and teachers of God's church by those who will seem to be the true and the ordinary governors of the church, but are rather condemned as seditious disturbers of the church and execrable heretics. By examples taken out of the scriptures the matter will be made more manifest. In the time of Achas king of Juda, (Urias the high priest winking at it, and the princes of the land and priests not resisting,) the king shut up the temple of the Lord, and took away the holy altar[1]: which thing the scripture expressly witnesseth; and therefore both the ministry of the word and the lawful or ordinary ministration of the sacraments[2] ceased: but yet notwithstanding there was a holy church in the kingdom of Juda, in the which (as I may say) extraordinarily no man doubteth the prophet Esay with certain other did preach. Under Manasses, the nephew[3] of king Achas, true doctrine and administration of the sacraments was banished, except only circumcision; and that falling away continued until the church was reformed by that most godly king Josias: and yet in the mean season prophets were sent, and God had his church in Juda, albeit the most part of the people with their governors did both follow and defend the wickedness and defection of Manasses. In the kingdom of Israel king Jeroboam thrust out of their offices[4] the teachers and preachers of the law of the Lord and of the sound truth[5], and instead of them gave unto the people profane and unlearned priests and rulers; and moreover built new temples, yea, and those were cathedral churches, and set up new idols or calves, a new religion, new altars, and new feasts; and by this means abrogated the true religion of God to that end that there might no outward marks at all of the church of God appear in Israel: and yet there is no doubt but God had a notable church in Israel, for the preservation and repairing whereof from time to time God sent his prophets, albeit they were not acknowledged to be the true prophets of God at the hands of the false church and of the false prophets. Under Jeroboam, the second of that name, Amos the prophet, a shepherd or neat-herd of Tecoa, taught and preached the true word of God: but he

Marginal references:
2 Kings xvi. 2 Chron. xxviii.
2 Kings xxi. xxii. 2 Chron. xxxiii. xxxiv.
1 Kings xii. 2 Chron. xi.
Amos ii.

[1 cathedram, Lat.]   [2 sacrificiorum, Lat.]
[3 nepote, Lat.: grandson.]
[4 Levitas, Lat. omitted: the Levites.]
[5 doctores legis Domini et prædicatores veritatis sinceræ, Lat.]

heard at the hands of Amasias the high priest of the kingdom, " Get thee quickly hence, and go into the land of Juda, Amos vii.
and prophesy or preach there ; but prophesy no more at
Bethel, for it is the king's chapel, and it is the king's court."
Furthermore, when Achab passed all the kings before him in
wickedness, and added moreover to the ungodliness and falling away of Jeroboam the abominable religion of Baal, and
had filled all the kingdom of Israel with superstitions, idol-
atries, enchantments, and sacrileges, yea, and moreover persecuted the pure word[6] of God in his prophets most cruelly,
there was yet found in Israel a most famous church of God.
Elias, that great and most excellent prophet of God, because
of that horrible falling away from God and loathsomeness of
that most miserable people, in whom there appeared no one
token of the true church of God, flying into the wilderness,
hid himself in corners; and being asked of the Lord what he
did there, he answered : " I have been very jealous for the 1 Kings xix.
God[7] of hosts; for that the children of Israel have forsaken
thy covenant, cast down thine altars, and slain thy prophets
with the sword; and I only am left, and they seek my life
to take it away." But straightways he is sent back into the
land of Israel from whence he was fled, and heard moreover
these words : " I have left unto myself seven thousand men in Rom. xi.
Israel, who have neither bowed their knees to Baal, neither
kissed him." Behold, this mighty prophet thought that only
he himself had been left of all the number of the faithful
in Israel : but he heard that God had reserved seven thousand holy men who had not bowed their knees, that is to say,
had never served Baal so much as with outward reverence.
But who knoweth not that the prophet understood by the
number of seven an exceeding great number of the true servants of God, who undoubtedly were circumcised not into the
covenant of Baal, but into the covenant of the eternal God?
The same men lacked not faith, and therefore they were not
without doctrine, though the same were not so common, neither
seemed to the Baalites to be either ordinary or catholic : but
undoubtedly they wanted the use of the sacrifices; for seeing
they were not lawfully offered, they would not be partakers of

[6 doctrinam, Lat.]
[7 So also ed. 1584: but ed. 1577, the *Lord* God; pro Domino
Deo, Lat.]

those that were unlawful; but in the mean season they were not destitute of the things which were signified by the outward[1] signs or sacraments, being partakers through faith of all the gifts of God.

Though the Romish church be not the church, yet God hath a church in earth.

After the self-same sort, since the bishop of Rome after the manner of king Jeroboam, having forsaken the sound preaching of the gospel, and having corrupted the first and simple institution of the Lord's supper, and depraved and wrested to his own profit other commandments[2] of God, and placed himself[3] in the throne or temple of God, or in the church of God[4], bragging that he is a God in earth; surely the church of God, oppressed with grievous tyranny, could very hardly hitherto be discerned by outward marks. For instead of the sincere preaching of the gospel a certain kind of doctrine mixed and corrupted with men's decrees was set forth; and instead of the Lord's supper popish mass was celebrated; and instead of other ordinances of God came in a high heap of foolish and superstitious ceremonies, whereunto a great number of men yielding made themselves subject to the see of Rome. In the mean space notwithstanding, the church of God was not utterly extinguished throughout all the world, neither the holy ministry of the word of God and the true worship of God utterly decayed amongst all men. For there were found spread abroad in every place not a few men, who neither allowed the pope and his conspirators, neither his corruption in matters of the church; but they worshipped the Lord Christ, whom they acknowledged to be the only author of salvation, and therefore they kept themselves free from popish filthiness. And God also sent almost in every age since the beginning of popedom men that were grave, godly, and learned, who grievously accused the pope's kingdom and tyranny (even as the prophets did of old time in the days of Jeroboam the idolatrous corruption), constantly requiring the reformation of the church from popish corruptions, and also teaching the true doctrine of salvation and the true use of the sacraments. And whereas a pure reformation by reason of antichrist's tyranny could not be obtained, there was notwithstanding found a continual study of purity and a godly desire of the

Dan. ix.
2 Thess. ii.

[1 outward, not in Lat.]   [2 institutis, Lat.]
[3 Rather, hath placed himself.]
[4 imo in ipsum Dei templum vel ecclesiam, Lat.]

lawful use of the sacraments : even as I said there was in the elect members of the true church of God in the days of Jeroboam, Achab[5], Manasses, and in the time of the captivity of Babylon.   But even as in those times the true prophets of God were not acknowledged for true prophets of the priests of Baal, but were condemned for schismatics and heretics ; even so in certain ages past the bishops of Rome with their conspirators did excommunicate and persecute godly and learned men, who preached the word of God and called for the reformation of the church, and many of them did they put to death with fire and sword : which thing our Lord and Master himself with the prophets and apostles did foreshew should come to pass.

Moreover, God could undoubtedly reserve to himself a mighty church even under the papism ; even as we doubt not but he hath done a very great under Mahometanism : for who will think that no members of the church of God are remaining in all Asia and Africa ?   Could not our merciful God with his mighty power, in that last calamity and ruin of God's church, reserve again (as sometime he did) seven thousand men, of whom never a one had worshipped the beast or received his mark ?   What hath been done in Turkey or what at this day is done, let them declare that can do it best and most rightly.   What hath been done amongst us in these last ages no man can deny.   Through the great goodness of God we see it is come to pass, that even as circumcision, the sign of God's covenant of old, was given unto the people of God even in the midst of the falling from God ; so also at this day, in the greatest darkness of antichrist, most holy baptism was given to the Christians to be as a seal[6] of the forgiveness of sins and inheritance of the children of God.   Surely the pureness of doctrine was profaned with infinite most gross traditions by the pope's sworn friends ; yet in the mean time it was not altogether abolished.   For, that I repeat not again any thing of the which I have said of godly and learned men, sent of God, crying for reformation of the church, and greatly profiting withal the children of God ; was it not with a certain universal consent received for most certain and undoubted, that in the decalogue, or ten commandments, there was set down a short and most absolute sum of all the commandments

[5 Achas, Lat. omitted.]   [6 in obsignationem, Lat.]

of God; and that in the Lord's prayer was taught us a most ample form of prayer unto God; and that in the apostles' creed was contained a most perfect rule of faith, or of that which was to be believed? Surely the custom was to recite the creed almost unto every one that was departing out of this world, and to those that lay even at the last gasp, as a most perfect rule of that faith which bringeth salvation[1]. Neither do we doubt that the merciful God and Father of mercies (who vouchsafed to save the thief upon the cross even at the giving up of his life) had mercy upon those that were oppressed with the tyranny of antichrist; and through his unmeasurable grace touched the hearts of men, both living and ready to die, and taught them by his Holy Spirit; and that they, confessing[2] one God the Father and Maker of all things, and one Jesus Christ the Son of God, redeemer of the world, to have suffered and risen again, and one Holy Ghost, and finally the holy catholic church, that he hath sanctified them[3], forgiving them all their sins, and hath translated the souls of such faithful men into life everlasting (according as they believed); into which place also we believe our flesh (being raised again) shall be carried in the end of the world. They have here therefore their answer also, who ask, Whether all our elders who died before these last times wherein the gospel is revealed be damned? Let therefore those that be alive rather look, lest for their contempt of the word of God and contentions raised against the word of God they come to worse end than their fore-fathers came. Therefore though we acknowledge not the popish church to be the true church, yet it followeth not thereof that there neither is or was any church of God in the earth. For we say that is the true church of God, which believeth in Christ and forsaketh not his word, which church also we have plentifully enough described. We know more-over that we ourselves, which at this day believe in Christ, are the true church of Christ our Lord: for[4] we cleave by faith to our only head Christ and to all the members of the catholic church; so we are not destitute of the true marks of the true church of God.

[1 Palmer's Antiq. of English Ritual, chap. viii. Vol. II. p. 224. Oxf. 1832.]

[2 Rather, and that he hath sanctified them, confessing, &c.]

[3 that he—them, should be omitted.]

[4 ut cohæremus, Lat.: as we cleave.]

But we read not, say they, that under the bishops, priests, and kings of the church of the Jews, either the prophets, that is to say, the guides of the faithful, or else the faithful themselves, did depart away from the high priest, from the king, and from[5] their universal church, and ordained unto themselves new particular sacrifices, as you at this day do: for you, departing from the bishop of Rome, from kings and governors, and from the universal church, do congregate unto yourselves a church far unlike the universal church both in preaching and ministering of the sacraments.   Whereunto I answer, that the old fathers before the coming of our master Christ for a certain prescribed cause did not seek places to offer new sacrifices in, the temple being abused[6] and defiled with idolatry; for it was unlawful to offer sacrifice without the bounds of the temple; as is to be seen in the seventeen of Leviticus and the twelfth of Deuteronomy.   Neither was there any other cause why that the people, being kept in bondage by the space of seventy years in the captivity of Babylon, offered no sacrifices; yet most certain it is notwithstanding, that both the prophets of God and the holy and true worshippers of God separated themselves both from the worship and sacrifices which were used, being contrary to the word of God.   Surely we read in all the sermons of the prophets, that both those sacrifices and also that church are condemned. For which cause they themselves[7] also were condemned of the high priest[8] and other priests of Baal as most abominable heretics and schismatics; even as now-a-days also we are thrust through with the darts of your curses, for that we will not communicate with the popish church and her holy service, and do reject their holy service itself. To this may be added, that, the sacrifices of the law being now fulfilled and abrogated by the Lord[9], the apostles with manifest defection departed not only from the high priests and church of Hierusalem, but moreover gathered unto Christ a new church by the preaching of the gospel and badge of the sacraments; which church in the Acts of the Apostles we have described: and according to whose pattern all churches ought of right to be reformed, even

[5 So also ed. 1584: but ed. 1577, *or* from, vel ab, Lat.]
[6 occupato, Lat.]   [7 vicissim, Lat. omitted: in return.]
[8 a pontificibus, Lat.]
[9 Rather, fulfilled by the Lord, and abrogated.]

as many as would be called apostolic churches. What have we therefore offended now-a-days, reforming churches after the likeness of the apostolic church; which churches were of old profaned by that see of Rome and the members thereof? We read that the church of God before the coming of Christ in the flesh was oftentimes defiled with filthy pollutions of corrupt men, and that the same was purged again and renewed after the likeness of the old church, according to the word of God. And why should not we take the same course in our age in the very same cause?

There remain moreover prophecies of our Saviour Christ and of the holy apostles and prophets, lively painting out this grievous oppression of the church of Christ under the fury of antichrist's tyranny in this our last age : there remain most weighty commandments, commanding to fly from antichrist, from idolatry and false prophets. For the Lord saith in St Matthew's gospel : "There shall arise false Christs, and false prophets, and shall shew great signs and wonders ; so that, if it were possible, they should deceive the very elect. Behold, I have told you before. Wherefore, if they shall say unto you, Behold, he is in the desert, go not forth ; behold, he is in the secret places, believe it not." And again : " Beware of false prophets, which come to you in sheep's clothing, but inwardly they are ravening wolves." Also : " Can the blind lead the blind? shall they not both fall into the ditch ?" St Peter also saith very gravely : "Save yourselves from this froward generation." And also in his second and third chapters of his second Epistle he entreats very largely of this matter. And also St Paul, agreeing in all things with the holy gospel and with St Peter, and painting forth antichrist and those last times of antichrist and corrupt men, not lights but firebrands of the church, commandeth the saints to depart from them, and to gather themselves together unto Christ and his sincere truth. If any man ask for the places, he shall find them, 2 Thess. ii.; 1 Tim. iv.; 2 Tim. iii. and iv. The same apostle in another place, even as the apostle John, doth also say : " Fly from idolatry." And in the sixth chapter of the second Epistle to the Corinthians by express words and most manifest opposition he sheweth, that there can be no agreement between Christ and Belial, light and darkness, and between idols and the temple of

(margin notes)
Apostolic churches.

Departure from the Romish church is commanded.

Matt. xxiv.

Matt. vii.

Luke vi.
Acts ii.

1 Cor. x.
1 John v.
2 Cor. vi.

God.   And therefore he addeth by and bye after: "Wherefore come out from among them, and separate yourselves, (saith the Lord,) and touch none unclean thing, and I will receive you."   To this appertaineth that which the blessed apostle John in his Revelation shewed him by the Lord Christ, seeing the works[1] of Babylon, heareth also therewith a voice coming from heaven, and commanding after this manner: "Go out of her, my people, that ye be not partakers of her sins, and that ye receive not of her plagues."   The same apostle very often threateneth everlasting destruction to those that worship the beast, but life and glory to those that forsake and flee from the beast, so as they cleave only to the only Saviour of the world, Jesus Christ.   Therefore that departure of ours from the see or church of Rome is not only lawful, but also necessary, as that which is commanded us of the Lord himself and by his holy apostles[2], unto whom unless we obey, we cannot be saved.

Otherwise we are not ignorant that fallings away are *The kinds of falling away.* altogether abominable and to be blamed; amongst the which notwithstanding except we distinguish, it will not plainly appear what we either allow or disprove, either else what we follow or flee from.   There is a defection of apostasy: in the which, through hatred of faith or religion, atheists or godless men, of mere ungodliness and contempt of God, with their wicked ringleaders Lucian and Julian the apostata[3], fall away from the sound and catholic faith, and finally from the fellowship of the faithful; and moreover do blaspheme and rail upon the christian verity, and either laugh to scorn or persecute the very church of God.   There is also an heretical defection: that is to say, wherein with Valentine, Marcion, Arius, Manicheus, Artemones[4], and other such monsters, certain proud, arrogant, and malapert wicked persons, either refusing the very scripture or wresting[5] the same, despise

[1 fata, Lat.]   [2 per sanctos apostolos, Lat.: not, *and* by.]

[3 Lucian, of Samosata, died A.D. 180: and Julian the Roman emperor declared his apostasy A.D. 361.—Mosheim, E. H. ed. Soames. Vol. I. p. 296.]

[4 Valentine an Egyptian, and Marcion, a native of Pontus, were of the Gnostic heresy in the second century; and Artemon in the same century denied the divinity of Christ: Manichæus, or Manes, arose in the third, and Arius in the fourth century.—Mosheim, E. H. Vol. I. pp. 199, 193, 205, 262, 381.]   [5 interpolantes, Lat.]

and tread it under their feet; or else do deny, overthrow, and resist certain articles of faith and the sound and ancient[1] opinions of the church of God, and affirm the contrary, and so frame to themselves heretical churches, and depart from the true, ancient[1], and catholic church. There is, moreover, a schismatical defection: such as was the Donatists', who separated themselves from the true church of God under the pretence of obtaining a more absolute kind of holiness[2]; whereof I have spoken very largely but a little before. And the above remembered two kinds of defection are altogether abominable and wicked, even as also the third kind can by no means be defended. But none of all these kinds can be imputed unto us now-a-days, departing from the church of Rome. For the departure is void of all crime, which is made not from the true, but from the false church; not from the people of God, but from the persecutors of God's people; not from the articles of faith and sound opinions of the church, but from errors which obscure the articles of faith and from the wicked traditions and corruptions of men; which, moreover, is made not through any lightness, but of necessity; not for innovation[3], but for true religion's sake[4], that leaving the fellowship of darkness we may be gathered together again with Christ, the true light, and all his members. And in this sort now-a-days have we forsaken that see of Rome, flowing with false doctrine, idolatry, and the blood of innocent martyrs; and have embraced the doctrine of the gospel and of the apostles, and therefore Christ himself the head of the church, which is the fellowship of all saints believing in Christ. And this hitherto have I spoken by digression. I now return to the treatise of the catholic church, that I may make an end of those things which remain to be spoken.

And to that end, that greater light and force may be added to those things which I have hitherto spoken of the church, I will now bring out certain parables out of the holy scriptures, whereby those things are[5] as it were painted out

[1 ancient, not in Lat.]   [2 See Vol. I. p. 161, note 5.]

[3 non novandi, Lat. All the editions read *invocation* for *innovation.*]

[4 propter veram fidem recuperandam, secundum testimonia æternæ veritatis, Lat. omitted: that we may recover the true faith, according to the testimonies of eternal truth.]

[5 quibus illa statuitur, Lat.: whereby it (i. e. the church) is, &c.]

before our eyes.   And so shall it be easy for every man to put a difference between the inward and the outward church; and to know what either appertaineth properly to every one, or else what is not proper.

First of all, the church is set forth unto us under the shape and fashion of a house.   A house is builded to this end, that men may dwell in it; and it is builded by workmen of matter of all sorts, of wood, of stones, and mortar, the foundation being first laid, upon which are set walls, which are joined together with a corner-stone: last of all is added or placed aloft the roof, without which the whole building, by little and little rotting, would fall down and decay.   I said that the church is the house of God, the chief master-builder whereof is God himself; who in the figure thereof, that is to say, in the tabernacle made by Moses and temple builded by Salomon, did deliver both unto Moses and David the fashion of the temple, according to which pattern they should build it.   For God from the beginning kept the angels that they should not fall; but repaired man, being fallen into sin and death, even straightways after the beginning of the world sanctifying a church unto himself, which he also severed out, compassing it about with his word.   And this fashion of the church it is altogether needful that we keep, and that we receive not any other fashion, either of emperor or pope, or delivered by any other man. The true master-builder of this house of God[6] saith in the gospel: "Upon this rock I will build my church."   For the same Son of God is he that maketh us worthy of his kingdom; he giveth us faith, by which we are made true members of the church of God.   But albeit the Lord himself be the only and principal builder of his church, yet he refuseth not the labours of men in the building; yea, rather he joineth men with him in building of the church, whom also he vouchsafeth to call master-builders[7].   For Paul saith: "As a skilful master-builder I have laid the foundation."   And again: "Who is Paul, and who is Apollos, but the ministers by whom ye believed, and as the Lord gave to every man?   I have planted, Apollos watered, but God gave the increase. So then neither is he that planteth anything, neither he that watereth, but God that giveth the increase."   Again: "We

The church is the house of God.

Matt. xvi.

1 Cor. iii.

[6 veri Dei domus, Lat.]   [7 architectos, Lat.]

together are God's labourers[1]: ye are God's husbandry and God's building." We will make the matter plain by an example.

What time God would raise up a house unto himself among the Gentiles, first of all he endued with his grace Cornelius, the governor of the Italian band placed by Cæsar[2], or the captain and centurion: by and bye after, sending the apostle Peter, he prepared and made ready that house for himself. For Peter teacheth and baptizeth; Cornelius with his household hearkeneth, believeth, is baptized, and becometh the house of God, the true church; which church the Lord dwells in by his Spirit. For even as a house is dwelt in by men, so God dwelleth in the church: as Paul witnesseth, saying, "The temple of God is holy, which ye are." Again: "Know you not that your body is[3] the temple of the Holy Ghost, which is in you?" &c. The foundation of this house is Christ; for Christ saith by Esay: "Behold, I put or lay in Sion (that is to say, in the church) a stone, a tried stone, a precious corner-stone, a sure foundation. He that believeth shall not make haste." Which prophecy the Lord expounding in St Matthew's Gospel, and applying it to himself as the foundation of the church, saith unto Peter confessing Jesus to be the true Son of the living God[4], the Messias that was looked for: "And upon this rock I will build my church, and the gates of hell shall not overcome it." There is moreover to be added hereunto the exposition of St Peter the apostle, who, reciting the very same words of the prophet Esay, and alluding to that saying of David, "The stone which the builders refused is[5] the head of the corner," saith expressly, that Christ is that "living stone, refused of men, but chosen of God, a sure foundation, upon whom whosoever stayeth shall not be confounded." And also Paul the apostle agreeth with Peter, for he saith: "And the rock was Christ." And again: "Another foundation can no man lay than that which is laid, which is Jesus Christ." Therefore, whereas he in another place nameth the self-same foundation the foundation of the prophets and apostles, it is not so to be

Margin notes:
Acts x.
1 Cor. iii.
1 Cor. vi.
Isai. xxviii.
Matt. xvi.
Psal. cxviii.
1 Pet. ii.
Acts iv.
1 Cor. x.
1 Cor. iii.
Ephes. ii.

[1 Dei sumus cooperarii, Lat.]
[2 apud Cæsaream, Lat.: at Cesarea.]
[3 corpora vestra sint, Lat.]
[4 veri Dei, Lat.]　　　　　　　　[5 factus est, Lat.]

taken, as if the apostles and prophets were the foundation of the church; but that they laid Jesus Christ for the foundation of the church, and builded the whole building upon this foundation, yea, even themselves also. For mortal men cannot be the object of faith, and foundation of the church, whereupon the faithful may stay. David crieth: "The way *Psal. xviii.* of God is uncorrupt: the word of the Lord is tried in the fire: he is a shield to all that trust in him. For who is God, besides the Lord? And who is mighty (or a rock)[6], save our God?" And Jeremy saith: "Thus saith the Lord, *Jer. xvii.* Cursed be the man that trusteth in man, and maketh flesh his arm, and withdraweth his heart from the Lord. Blessed be the man that trusteth in the Lord, and whose hope the Lord is." So the writings of the prophets and apostles with one consent shew us the rock, that is to say, the foundation of the church, to be Christ, and that it is he only and alone.

Greatly do they err therefore, whosoever they be, that *Peter or the bishop of Rome is not the foundation of the church.* do attribute to the bishop of Rome this divine praise, power, and prerogative, which is due only to the Son of God. And if so be it that they object, that many interpreters, both Greek and Latin[7], have understood by the rock Peter himself; we refuse man's authority, and do affirm and bring forth heavenly authority. Christ said not, I will build my church *Matt. xvi.* upon thee, but upon a rock; and that self-same rock that thou hast confessed. Yea, and Peter taketh his name of Petra, which signifieth a rock[8], even as a Christian of Christ. And Peter also himself by the rock understood Christ. Hereunto maketh the authority of Paul, saying: "The rock was Christ." *1 Cor. x.* And, "Other foundation can no man lay, than that which is *1 Cor. iii.* laid, which is Jesus Christ." For David before said: "Who is God, besides the Lord; or who is a rock, save our God?" These testimonies I repeat not unadvisedly: for all those that are not beside their wits will confess there is more credit to be given to these most manifest testimonies, witnessing Christ only to be the rock and placing him for the foundation of the

[6 who hath any strength, Prayer-Book Ver.: who is a rock, Auth. Ver.]

[7 Tertullian. de Pudic. cap. 21. Cyprian. Epist. ad Jubaian. and Cornel. and De Unit. Eccles. § 3. Chrysost. Homil. 69. in Petr. Apost.]

[8 which—rock, the translator's explanation.]

church, than unto those that teach both Peter and the bishop of Rome, together with Christ, to be rocks and foundations of the church. I will use no sharper speech at this time against them, forasmuch as it is most manifest unto all men what manner of men they be, most unworthy to be reckoned with Peter, but most worthy to be counted amongst Simoniacs. Peter foresaw what manner of men they would be; and therefore, lest any man should be deceived by them, he painted them out in their colours in the second chapter of his second epistle. But leaving them, we will return to the exposition of the parable we had in hand.

Who be God's house.

The matter of the house, as the walls and other parts, are faithful men, builded upon the foundation Christ. Which thing those famous and principal workmen of this building, Peter and Paul, witness and explain in these words. Peter saith:

1 Pet. ii.

"To Christ ye come as unto a living stone, disallowed of men, but chosen of God, and precious. And ye, as lively stones, be made a spiritual house, and holy priesthood, to offer up spiritual sacrifices, acceptable to God by Jesus Christ." And

Ephes. ii.

Paul saith: "Now therefore ye are no more strangers and foreigners, but citizens with the saints, and of the household of God; and are built upon the foundation of the apostles and prophets, Jesus Christ himself being the chief cornerstone; in whom all the building coupled together groweth unto an holy temple in the Lord: in whom ye are also built together to be the habitation of God by the Spirit." By the

Christ the corner-stone.

authority therefore of the apostles we learn, that Christ is the corner-stone in the house of God, who, lest the walls should fall down, coupleth them together, and upholdeth the whole building. He is also the roof of the church, that is to say, the defender and ruler, under whose defence the church liveth safe, happy, and blessed. Hereunto appertaineth the

The tabernacle and temple figures of the church.

consideration of the tabernacle of Moses, and of the temple of Salomon: for either of them is called the house of God. The tabernacle was distinguished into the holiest of all, the holy place, and the court: and albeit these several parts be named, yet is it called one house of the Lord, because there is but only one universal church, which nevertheless hath, as it were, her parts. "The holiest of all" is a figure of the triumphant church in heaven, where are our fellow-servants and brethren, the patriarchs, prophets, apostles, martyrs, and all the blessed spirits. There doth Christ our Lord appear always in the sight of God; who is our ark, wherein is contained the treasures of the church, which is the fulfilling of the law, the certainty of the covenant, and our propitiation; thence have we[1] our oracles. In this part of the temple all things are sumptuous, gold and precious stones; for in heaven perfect joy is attained. In the temple are forms of angels, palms and flowers, for because in the life to come the elect shall be as the angels of God. Here they that do overcome are green for evermore. "To him that overcometh," saith the Lord, "will I give to eat of the tree of life, which is in the midst of the paradise of God." Here all things shine: for in Christ and in the life to come we shall be made bright. "The holy place" representeth unto us the militant and inward church, sanctified with the blood of Christ; which hath not a shew of godliness only, but godliness itself: for by faith they cleave fast unto God, and with mutual charity they are knit together amongst themselves. They serve God in spirit, hearing God's word, and being partakers of the sacraments. In the holy place therefore Salomon placed ten candlesticks, ten tables, and ten caldrons; for in the church the saints are daily lightened, nourished, and purged through repentance. Finally, "the court" received the whole assembly of the people; for the church is the assembly of all those that profess faith, having also hypocrites mingled with them. Between the holy place and the court or porch are two pillars in Salomon's temple, dedicated[2] to the posterity of David; for it is Christ that beareth up the church, by whom the way is open into the church. Through the benefit and power of Christ the church hath obtained, that, if she continue in Christ, she should also be "the pillar and ground of the truth." But besides[3] the tabernacle and temple of God there is no place, but in the church, wherein God receiveth the service done unto him; God is only favourable in the church of his saints[4]. Let the Jews, Turks, and Saracens, therefore, do works which in outward shew are never so excellent, yet without Christ and his fellowship no man pleaseth God.

Rev. ii.

Again, the church of God is compared by Esay to a most excellent vine, who saith by plain words: "The vineyard of

The church is God's vine. Isai. v.

[1 redduntur nobis, Lat.]
[2 inscriptæ, Lat.]   [3 extra, Lat.]
[4 Cf. Vol. II. pp. 147, 153.]

the Lord of hosts is the house of Israel, and the men of Juda
are his pleasant plant." And also in the gospel our Lord in
the parable of the vine plainly expoundeth, that men are the
branches of this vine. Yea, and in John he saith : "I am that
true vine, and my Father is an husbandman. Every branch
that beareth not fruit in me he taketh away; and every one
that beareth fruit, he purgeth it, that it may bring forth more
fruit. As the branch cannot bear fruit of itself, except it abide
in the vine ; no more can ye, except ye abide in me. I am the
vine, you are the branches : he that abideth in me, and I in
him, the same bringeth forth much fruit : for without me ye
can do nothing. If a man bide not in me, he is cast forth as
a branch, and withereth; and men gather them, and cast them
into the fire, and they burn." There is one church therefore ;
for it is one vine. Out of her come branches, partly fruitful,
and partly unfruitful : for both the good or godly and true
worshippers of God, and evil men or hypocrites, are counted
to be in the church ; but hypocrites in their time are cut off,
and thrown into everlasting fire. That the good remain in
the vine, and are not cut off but bring forth fruit, that are
they indebted for to Christ, the foundation of the church, and
also the head and preserver of the same ; who by his spiritual
and lively juice makes them fruitful in good works. Herein
most evidently appeareth the knitting together of the head
and the members, Christ and the faithful ; whereof we spake
at first, and of which the Lord addeth in the gospel : "If ye
abide in me, and my words abide in you, ask what you will,
and it shall be done to you."

The church is the kingdom of God. Moreover, this church of the faithful is called the kingdom
of God : for the Son of God himself, Christ Jesus, is the king
of the church, that is to say, of all the faithful ; who by his
Spirit and word governeth the church ; and she again willingly
submitteth herself to his government. Neither are there
found many kingdoms in the world, because there is one only
King of glory, Christ. Of this king and kingdom I have
entreated in the seventh sermon of my fourth decade.

The church is shadowed out by man's body. Now we have also said oftentimes, that the church is
likened to man's body. In the body the head is the chief,
which is never absent from the body ; and being stricken
off, leaveth a dead body void of sense. And albeit this have
very many members, yet is there a most pleasant agreement

of them all amongst themselves; every one agreeth and consenteth together amongst themselves: they are sorry one with another, and help each one another. The same thing likewise do all faithful people perform one towards another, that one member doth to another member. They are united to their head Christ by faith; the head itself is joined to the members through grace and the Spirit. Christ is never separated from the church: neither hath she life elsewhere but from Christ; who although he be absent in body from the militant church, yet is he continually present in spirit, in operation, and in government: so as he needeth no vicar in earth, since he governeth alone, and continueth for ever the only head, the only king, the only priest and saviour of his church. For the Lord saith in Ezechiel: "I will raise up over my sheep Ezek. xxxiv. a shepherd, who shall feed them, to wit, my servant David: he shall feed them, and he shall be their shepherd. And I the Lord will be their God, and my servant David shall be their prince among them. I the Lord have spoken it." This last thing he added, lest any should doubt of the faith and certainty of those things which are spoken. God is the eternal truth, and he hath spoken it: therefore that which he hath spoken cannot but be most true. But what hath he spoken? That there shall be and is one pastor and prince of the church. Behold, that he said one, is not without signification. But who is that one? He expoundeth that, and saith, "My servant David," to wit, Christ Jesus, that branch of David's posterity, whom the authority of the gospel calleth everywhere the Son of David. He shall be a shepherd, not in name and title only, but in deed; for he shall feed his sheep, and therefore shall be in the midst of them. For in the gospel he saith expressly: "Wheresoever two or three are gathered Matt. xviii. together in my name, there am I in the midst of them." And again: "Behold, I am with you always, even to the end of the Matt. xxviii. world." Now, if he be present with his church, she hath no The church need of a vicar; for a vicar supplieth the place of him that of God hath is absent. Wheresoever therefore Christ his vicar is acknowledged, there is no Christ, and therefore there reigneth antichrist. This will be made as yet much more clear and sure, if we weigh what it meaneth, that Christ is said to be the head of the church. The head is the life, salvation, and light, or that The head of which giveth light to the church, the supreme governor of the the church.

faithful, who both can and will always be present to the whole congregation of saints, of all ages, and dispersed throughout the whole world; hear her prayers and requests, and moreover send her succour in all things: and briefly, who is able perfectly to govern the whole church, and both provide for[1] and bring to pass all her matters, and that in all things. But this privilege, as I think, thou canst give to no creature without blasphemy and sacrilege: only therefore Christ, perfect God and man, is and remaineth the only head of the church.

The pope is not the head of the church. Those that acknowledge the pope of Rome to be the head of the church militant either know not what they do and say, or willingly and wittingly do blaspheme the Son of God, whom they will not have to reign over his church alone.

But let us now hear the testimonies of St Paul the apostle of this matter. "God," saith he, "hath raised up Christ from the dead, and set him at his right hand in the heavenly places, far above all principalities and powers, and might and domination, and every name that is named, not in this world only, but also in that that is to come: and hath made all things subject under his feet, and hath appointed him over all things, to be head to the church; which is his body, even the fulness of him that filleth all in all things." Behold, Christ is the head, for he ruleth all things in heaven and in earth; he governeth all things; he hath all things subject unto himself; and maketh the church his body, ministering unto her those things whereof she hath need, and fulfilling all her desires.

Ephes. v. Again, the same apostle saith: "Christ is the head of the church, and the same is the saviour of the body." It is the part of the head to preserve and govern the body: but that no man performs, but only Christ. He remaineth therefore the only head of his church; specially since the church is the spiritual body of Christ, and therefore cannot have a carnal head, without you will make of the church a poetical monster: for Christ is the head of the church, not because he is man, but because he is God and man.

But and if the defenders of the Romish idol and champions of the monarchy of Rome by the head do understand the prince or governor in earth, as Saul in the scripture is called the head over Israel, and so do understand the chief bishop ruling in the chief see; let them again hear the scrip-

Ephes. i. (margin)

[1 sarcire, Lat.]

ture itself confuting their filthy error, and saying : " And there _{Luke xxii.} arose also a strife among the apostles, which of them should seem to be the greatest.   But Jesus said unto them : The kings of the Gentiles reign over them, and they that bear rule over them are called gracious lords[2].   But ye shall not be so : but let the greatest among you be as the least ; and the chiefest, as he that serveth.   For who is greater, he that sitteth at table, or he that serveth ? is not he that sitteth at table ? and I am among you as he that ministereth." That primacy therefore of the church of Rome is of men ; it is not of the doctrine or institution[3] of Christ : yea rather, quite contrary it is and repugnant unto the institution, doctrine, and example of Christ ; who will not have the apostles or apostolic men to reign like unto the princes of this world.   He instituted ministers of the church, who should serve the church.   She sitteth at the table ; the ministers set that food before her which they receive of the Lord, and rightly divide the word of the Lord.   Did not Christ himself refuse a crown upon earth, and did not he that is Lord of all minister ?   Doth not he himself disallow that any minister should seek any prerogative, no, not in respect of eldership ?   "He that is greatest among you (saith he) let him be as the younger."   He therefore commandeth an equality amongst them all.   And therefore St Jerome judgeth rightly, saying, that by the custom of man, and not by the authority of God, some one of the elders should be placed over the rest, and called a bishop ; whereas of old time an elder or minister[4] and a bishop were of equal honour, power, and dignity[5].   And it is to be observed, that St Jerome speaketh not of the Romish monarchy, but of every bishop placed in every city above the rest of the

<small>Hierome in his commentaries upon Titus, and in his epistle to Evagrius.</small>

[2 benefici, Lat.]   [3 traditione, Lat.]
[4 or minister, not in Lat.]

[5 Hæc propterea, ut ostenderemus apud veteres eosdem fuisse presbyteros quos et episcopos: paulatim vero, ut dissensionum plantaria evellerentur, ad unum omnem sollicitudinem esse delatam. Sicut ergo presbyteri sciunt se ex ecclesiæ consuetudine ei qui sibi præpositus fuerit esse subjectos ; ita episcopi noverint se magis consuetudine, quam dispositionis dominicæ veritate, presbyteris esse majores.—Hieron. Comment. in Ep. ad Tit. cap. 1. Opp. Tom. IV. par. 1. col. 413.   Audi et aliud testimonium, in quo manifestissime comprobatur eundem esse episcopum atque presbyterum, &c.—Hieron. ad Evangelum. Ep. 101. Opp. Tom. IV. par. 2. col. 803. Par. 1706.]

ministers. Which thing I bring not out, to that end we should stay upon the authority of man; but to that end I might shew, that even by the witness of man it may be proved, that that majority, as they call it, hath not the original from the Son of God and from God's word, but out of man's brain[1]; and that therefore both Christ remaineth the only head of his church, and the bishop of Rome is nothing less than the head of the church militant. And therewithal we cleave most stedfastly to the sacred and holy gospel, and to the undoubted doctrine of the apostles; which doctrine taketh away all pride of supremacy, and commendeth unto us a faithful ministry and the equal authority and humbleness of the ministers; the apostles again witnessing and saying: "Let a man so think of us, as of the ministers of Christ, and disposers of the secrets of God."

The church is the sheep-fold of Christ.

Hereunto belongeth almost the whole tenth chapter of John, wherein the Lord named himself the true and also the only shepherd of the universal church. The only sheepfold of this shepherd is the catholic church, gathered together by the word out of the Jews and Gentiles. And[2] sheep of this fold are all the faithful people in the world, hearing and giving themselves over wholly to be governed by this chief shepherd Christ: who albeit he also communicate this name of pastor, or shepherd, unto the ministers appointed to the ministry of the church, yet notwithstanding, he retaineth unto himself the charge of the chief shepherd, and also the chief power and dignity. Men that are pastors of churches are all ministers, and are all equal: Christ our Lord is the universal pastor, and chief and Lord of pastors. The more worthy diligence and trust is in the pastors, the more worthy it maketh them. Therefore, when the Lord

John xxi.

said unto Peter, "Feed my sheep," he committed not unto Peter any empire either over the world or over the church, but a ministry to the behalf of his redeemed. "Teach," saith he, "and govern with my word, my sheep; my sheep, I say, whom I have redeemed with my blood;" for Paul

Acts xx.

saith: "Take heed unto yourselves, and to the whole flock, whereof the Holy Ghost hath made you overseers, to feed the church of God, which he hath purchased with his own blood." The bishop of Rome therefore is deceived, who by

[1 ex arbitrio hominum, Lat.]   [2 Proinde, Lat.: Therefore.]

the Lord's word spoken unto Peter thinketh that full power is given unto him over all in the church[3].   Let the apostle Peter himself be heard, talking with his fellow-elders, and as it were opening those words of the Lord spoken unto him: "The elders that are among you," saith he, "I beseech, which am also an elder, and a witness of the sufferings of Christ, and also a partaker of the glory that shall be revealed. Feed the flock of God, which dependeth upon you[4], caring for it not by constraint, but willingly; not for filthy lucre, but of a ready mind.   Not as though ye were lords over God's heritage[5], but that ye may be ensamples to the flock." Peter speaketh not of any empire and lordship, yea, by express words he forbids lordly dignity.   For even as he is appointed of the Lord a minister and an elder, not a prince and a pope[6]; so also he appointed no princes in the church, but ministers and elders, who with the word of Christ should feed Christ's flock, and that willingly and lawfully, all wicked devices at once set apart.   Hereto belongeth the whole thirty-fourth chapter of Ezechiel, which a little before we alleged. But had not the heart been hardened and the eyes blinded of the bishop of Rome and his, they should long ago have seen, that they could in no part nor by no means have been numbered amongst the shepherds of the church and disciples of Peter.   They would at least have marked that sentence of their own Gregory, which sentence he reciteth unto Maurice the emperor, almost in these words: "I affirm boldly, that whosoever he be that calleth himself the universal priest, is a forerunner of antichrist."   And anon after: "But forasmuch as the truth itself saith, Every one that exalteth himself shall be brought low, thereby I know that every puffing up is so much the sooner broken, how much the greater it is swollen[7]."   These are his sayings.

1 Pet. v.

The office of a pastor is not a lordly dignity.

[3 Cf. Jewel's Apology, &c. ed. P. S. p. 289.]

[4 quantum in vobis est, Lat. and Erasmus.]

[5 neque ceu dominium exercentes adversus cleros, Lat. and Erasmus.]

[6 summus pontifex, Lat.]

[7 Ego autem fidenter dico, Quia quisquis se universalem sacerdotem vocat...antichristum præcurrit...Sed quoniam veritas dicit, Omnis qui se exaltat humiliabitur, scio quia quælibet elatio tanto citius rumpitur, quo amplius inflatur.—Gregor. Mauricio Augusto. Opp. Tom. IV. Epist. 30. p. 203. Rom. 1591.]

The church is
the spouse of
Christ.
John iii.
Last of all, the estate[1] of Christ and the church is shadowed out by the similitude of marriage between the husband and the wife; for Christ is called the husband of the church, and the church is called the spouse of Christ.

John iii.
St John saith to his disciples: "Ye yourselves are my witnesses, that I said, I am not the Christ, but that I am sent before him. He that hath the bride is the bridegroom; but the friend of the bridegroom, which standeth and heareth him, rejoiceth greatly because of the bridegroom's voice. This my joy therefore is fulfilled. He must increase, but I must decrease." And in the prophets this allegory is very

Ezek. xvi.
common. In a certain place is feigned a damsel, despised and polluted, to lie in her filthiness; and a certain nobleman cometh by, who, plucking her out of the mire, and making her clean from her filthiness, and also sumptuously apparelling her, chose her unto his wife. And albeit this allegory declareth that heavenly benefit which God shewed unto his people, being in bondage in Egypt, by the wonderful deliverance and adopting them into his peculiar people; who, notwithstanding, seeth not, that all mankind from his first original is defiled with sin and wickedness, and sticketh fast in the mire of hell? Who knoweth not, that the Son of God came down from heaven, and washed all mankind in his blood; and having purged her, hath joined to himself a glorious church, having neither spot nor wrinkle, nor any such thing? Surely, by marriage is made a mutual participation in common between those that are contracted of all their goods, and as it were a certain knitting together into one body, not to be dissolved. Therefore when Christ took upon him our flesh, both he became ours in all things, and we also

Ephes. v.
are members of the same body, of his flesh, and of his bones. In us there is infirmity, sin, and death: the same things hath our husband also taken unto himself, that he might make them hurtless unto us. In Christ our husband is justification, sanctification, and life; the same things doth he communicate unto us his spouse, that in him we might be just and holy, and might live through him.

The church
or mother
begetteth
children.
Of that lawful joining together of the Lord and the church are born lawful children unto God; whereupon the church is called a mother, and a freewoman, that is to say,

[1 negotium, Lat.]

a matron and mistress. For the apostle Paul saith : " Jeru- Gal. iv.
salem which is above is free; which is the mother of us
all." For even as through the joining of man and woman
together, by propagation of seed, are born children: so Christ
hath coupled the church unto himself, wherein he hath left
the seed of his word. By the word our mother, the church,
begetteth children (whereof before I admonished you, when
I spake of the original of the church[2]) ; that is to say, whiles
she, retaining the seed of the word, by the preaching of the
word doth fashion and nourish us in her womb, and after
bringeth us forth into light; whom afterwards she nourisheth 1 Cor. iii.
Ephes. iv.
with milk, and bringeth up with stronger meat, until we grow
up into a perfect man. But even as without a husband,
without true faith plighted, and without seed, there is no
mother; even so the church without Christ, without true
faith and the seed of God's word, is not that our mother, that
is a free woman, and our mistress. We have by these things
by the way learned, why the church of God is called a
mother. The same notwithstanding is also called a virgin; The church
a virgin.
for of this holy mother, the church, the Lord before all things
requireth faith and integrity. For the apostle Paul saith : 2 Cor. xi.
" I have coupled you to one man, to present you a chaste
virgin unto Christ." Therefore it is the part of the spouse,
to bring unto her husband for her dowry her virginity, and
to keep the same undefiled. But what manner of virginity
is that ? Sincere faith in Christ, which wholly, or with all
her mind, cleaveth for ever unto one : which cometh to pass,
when we give ear only to our spouse, and love none but
him alone; to be short, when we persevere in the simplicity
of the gospel. For it followeth in the words of the apostle:
" But I fear, lest it come to pass that, even as the serpent
deceived Eve with his subtilty, so your minds should be corrupt from the simplicity that is in Christ." That simplicity
acknowledgeth Christ to be the means[3] of salvation, the recovery[4] of life and all heavenly treasures; without whom
there is no salvation, nor no good thing. But who will call
her a chaste matron, who giveth ear to bawds, and setteth
her heart also upon the love of others, neither contenteth
herself with her husband only ? Will not all men cry out
that she is a naughty pack, and an adulteress, lying with others, Adultery and
fornication.

[2 See above, p. 26.]   [3 compendium, Lat.]
[4 recapitulationem, Lat. cf. Vol. i. p. 156, note 1.]

and bringing forth children of strange seed? And in the holy scriptures spiritual adultery and fornication is much spoken of: all the sermons of the prophets are full of such allegories. They call those men or churches adulterers, whoremongers, and fornicators, which receive strange seed, that is to say, doctrine differing from the word of God: for such as they, going a whoring from God, cleave not unto God only; they love not alone him with all their heart; they do not worship, serve, and call upon him only; yea rather, they choose unto themselves others, whom they may worship and call upon either instead of God, or together with God. Hereunto pertaineth a good part of the fifth chapter of Jeremy, and all the second chapter of Osee. Amongst other things the Lord saith: "I will not have compassion upon her children, because they are children of fornications: for their mother hath played the harlot; for she hath said, I will go after my lovers," &c.

The church of Rome is not the holy mother church.

Since these things are thus, brethren, there is no cause why any man should[1] reverence the church of Rome, decking herself with the title and beauty of the holy mother, the church; for she is not the holy mother church, she is not an uncorrupted matron and virgin. For where is the husband, who is the only husband of this chaste matron? where is the faith and integrity kept with her husband? hath she not defiled herself with strange seed? hath not she received and taught a new and strange doctrine from the word of God, and by that means begetteth many children, not to Christ, but to antichrist? St John, beautifying this church

Rev. xvii.

with her apt title, calleth her, " Great Babylon, the mother of whoredoms and abominations of the earth; and a woman drunken with the blood of the saints, and with the blood of the martyrs of Jesu Christ." Our holy mother, the church, is an undefiled virgin, hearing only the voice or doctrine of her only well-beloved husband, placing all the means of life and salvation in him alone, and depending only upon him in all things.

With many other allegories doth the scripture paint out the mystery of Christ and the church: but thereof it sufficeth to have spoken thus much. The Lord Jesu, the true and only Shepherd of his church, bring home again lovingly the wandering sheep into his fold; and being gathered together in his church, preserve them for ever. Amen.

[1 hodie, Lat. omitted: at this day.]

OF THE MINISTRY, AND THE MINISTERS OF GOD'S WORD;
WHEREFORE AND FOR WHAT END THEY ARE INSTITUTED
OF GOD.   THAT THE ORDERS GIVEN BY CHRIST
UNTO THE CHURCH IN TIMES PAST WERE
EQUAL.   WHENCE AND HOW THE PRE-
ROGATIVE OF MINISTERS SPRANG.
AND OF THE SUPREMACY OF
THE BISHOP OF ROME.

THE THIRD SERMON.

THE exposition touching the church of God shall be trulier
understood, brethren, by those things which remain to be
spoken out of the word of the Lord concerning the ministry
and ministers of the church. For I said, the church of God is
builded and preserved by the word of God; and that, through
ministers appointed for that purpose by the Lord: so that now
it followeth to speak of the ministers of the church, and of
their ministry, that is, of that order wherewith God governeth
his church.

And truly, the ecclesiastical ministry is extended both to
stir up, and also to maintain, public prayers and the administration of the sacraments, and especially it is occupied in
preaching of the word of God. Of the two former I will
speak in place and time convenient: of the ministry of the
word I will entreat at this present.

In consideration whereof, first it is expedient to view,
wherefore God in instructing men useth the aid or ministry
of men; and what men perfect[2] or work in the ministry itself,
and what God. He verily, for his exceeding goodness and *Wherefore God useth the ministry of men in building his church.*
mercy toward us, coveteth to pour himself wholly into us,
(which I think good to repeat often, that it may be the
deeper rooted in our hearts, and that we also may bethink
ourselves what we owe unto God,) that we may both be
strengthened and blessed in him; and may perfectly understand
his will to us-ward, and finally our duty whereby we be
bound unto him. As he therefore furthereth our salvation
very diligently in all things, so, lest there should be anything
wanting to true doctrine, he himself cometh forth to instruct

[2 præstent, Lat. : supply.]

men. But such is our weakness and corruption through sin, we cannot abide the meeting of his eternal and wonderful[1] majesty: which is apparent by much communication[2] of God had with our fathers, but especially at his meeting with the whole church of Israel in mount Sina. For when he came down on the mount, not without glory and heavenly[3] majesty, and uttered with his own mouth a brief sum of his whole religion and of all the laws, (which sum we call the decalogue, or ten commandments,) the people, being astonied with his divine majesty, said unto Moses: "Talk thou with us, and we will hear: but let not God talk with us, lest we die." And God, receiving this offer, said: "I have heard the voice of the words of this people, which they have spoken unto thee: they have well said all that they have spoken. Oh that there were such a heart in them, that they would fear me, &c." Insomuch that this manner of teaching by men, which men themselves have chosen for themselves, God[4] will have to be perpetual, and never to be broken: so as when he sent his Son into the world, he clothed him with flesh, that he might after that manner speak[5] unto us by him.

Exod. xix. xx.

Deut. v.

God indeed might by the secret illumination of his Spirit, without man's ministry (as his power is tied to no creature), regenerate the whole world, and govern the church itself: but as he despiseth not his creatures, nor destroyeth the work of his own hands, and doeth all things in order; even so from the first beginning he forthwith spake to the world by patriarchs, then by prophets, afterward by apostles; neither at this day ceaseth he to give unto the world doctors and pastors: so that it becometh us not to tempt God, that is, not to look for a secret inspiration with the heretics Enthusiastæ[6]; but to acknowledge a just order, and that God himself speaketh unto us by men, of whom he would have us to learn religion. The eunuch of Candace, queen of Ethiopia, did read the holy scriptures, and the Lord could have taught him by secret

By the ministry of the word God worketh salvation in his church.

Acts viii.

[1 immensæ, Lat.] [2 ex multis colloquiis, Lat.]
[3 divina, Lat.] [4 Deus quoque, Lat.]
[5 Rather, and after that manner spake, &c.]
[6 So the Messalians or Euchites were called.—Mosheim, Eccles. Hist. Book II. Cent. 4. Part 2. chap. v. § 24. ed. Soames. note 5. Vol. I. p. 409. But Bullinger probably referred to a sect of the Anabaptists, called Enthusiasts. See Bulling. adv. Anabapt. Lib. II. cap. 1.]

inspiration the mystery[7] of faith; but he giveth him Philip to
be a teacher and an interpreter. Likewise Paul, the doctor of Gal. i.
the Gentiles, taken up into the third heaven, and instructed by
Christ himself, not by men, of all the principles of our religion,
is nevertheless referred over unto a man called Ananias. The Acts ix.
angel of God is sent to Cornelius, captain of the Italian band, Acts x.
being at Cæsarea, which might have instructed him in all
points of true religion; but he willeth[8] him to call for Peter
the apostle: "He (saith the angel) will tell thee what thou
must do." For this cause ministers are called saviours: they
are said to convert men : their word is called, not the word of
man, but the word of God; he which despiseth them, seemeth
to despise God himself. It is also said, that they themselves
do bind and loose, and retain and forgive sins. For Abdias
the prophet saith, that saviours shall ascend into the mount
Sion; which many[9] interpret of the apostles. Paul, pleading
before king Agrippa, and rehearsing the words of God which
came unto him in a vision, saith : "I send thee unto the Gen- Acts xxvi.
tiles, to open their eyes, that they may be turned from darkness to light, &c." And[10] Gabriel the archangel said before
that, speaking of John, "He shall go before the Lord with Luke i.
the spirit and power of Elias[11], to turn the hearts of the fathers
to the children, and the disobedient to the wisdom of the just
men." Moreover, the apostle to the Thessalonians, "We thank 1 Thess. ii.
God (saith he), because when ye had received of us the word of
the preaching of God[12], ye received it not as the word of men,
but as it is indeed, the word of God, which worketh also in you
that believe." Again: "He therefore that despiseth these 1 Thess. iv.
things[13], despiseth not man, but God, who hath even given
you[14] his Holy Spirit." For the Lord saith in the gospel : Luke x.
"He that heareth you, heareth me; and he that despiseth you,
despiseth me." And again : "Whatsoever ye shall loose on Matt. xviii.
earth, shall be loosed in heaven; and whatsoever ye shall bind
on earth, shall be bound in heaven." And again : "Whose John xx.

[7 negotium, Lat.]   [8 jubet, Lat. : cf. Vol. I. p. 86.]
[9 nemo non, Lat.]
[10 Etenim, Lat. : For.]
[11 in spiritu Heliæ, Lat. : and power, not in Lat.]
[12 quo Deum discebatis, Lat., and Erasmus.]
[13 rejicit nos, Lat. The Vulgate reads, hæc spernit.]
[14 in nos, Lat., but Erasmus, in vos.]

sins soever ye remit, they are remitted unto them; and whose sins soever you do retain, they are retained."

Let every thing be given to him that it be-longeth: I mean, both to God and the minister.

But some, wresting these places of the holy scripture against the natural sense, do give the ministers an equal power in a manner with Christ; and that which only pertaineth unto him, they communicate also unto them. But they say, that by such means the ministry must be set out, lest it wax vile and of no estimation among profane men. Other some again so speak of the inward drawing of the Spirit, that they seem as it were to make superfluous, or to take clean away, the out-ward ministry, and to attribute nothing at all unto it. There-fore the ministry must be limited with his bounds, lest it be drawn hither and thither with the affections and lusts of men, and either too much or too little be attributed unto it. Let the ministry indeed be beautified and kept in authority, but let it be done without the dishonouring of God. Neither indeed becometh it us, under the pretence of the ministry, to attribute that to man's labour which is only God's office, on whom all men ought to depend, and unto whom, as the only well-spring and giver of all godliness[1], they ought to have respect. Therefore the faithful ministers of the Lord Jesus ought only to have regard hereunto, that they may keep the glory and authority of Christ unblemished, and his priest-hood sound unto himself in every point. For the Lord Jesus himself, sitting at the right hand of the Father in the true tabernacle, which God pight[2] and not man, remaineth a priest, yea, the only high priest of his church for ever, executing as yet all the duties of a priest in the church. For he, as the only teacher and master in the church, teacheth his disciples, that is, the church or congregation of the faithful; enduing them with the Holy Ghost, regenerating and drawing them, sanctifying and making them free from their sins: which

Unto the office of the ministry belongeth the place of the 2 Cor. v.

thing the scripture in every place plainly teacheth. This glory, this power, he hath given unto none, neither doth any minister, unless he be blinded with devilish pride, take that unto him-self, as though he did work these works that are proper unto Christ, either for Christ, or in Christ's stead, or together with Christ. The apostles, being Christ his most faithful ministers and most chosen instruments of God, did not give the Holy

[1 So also ed. 1584: but ed. 1577, *goodness.* Omnis boni, Lat.]
[2 pight: pitched.]

Ghost, did not draw men's hearts, did not inwardly anoint men's minds, did not regenerate souls ; they themselves did not deliver from sin, death, the devil, and hell : for all these things be the works of God, which he hath not communicated to any. Wherefore the most holy Baptist in plain words denied that he was Christ ; he denied that he himself baptized with the Holy Ghost. "I (saith he) baptize with water : but he John i. baptizeth with the Holy Ghost. I am the voice of a crier in the wilderness, Prepare the way of the Lord." And Paul, pleading his cause before Agrippa, wisheth of God that king Acts xxvi. Agrippa were such a one as Paul himself was, except his bonds : but such a wish had not needed, if he himself could draw, sanctify, and absolve. There are infinite other of this kind to be seen in the scriptures.

Yet nevertheless the ministry of the church is not The ministry is not ap- needless. The king's counsellors and officers have not equal pointed in vain. power with the king, neither are they kings with the king or for the king ; but for all that, their service is not in vain. Therefore that thing which Christ, the Son of God, who is the greatest, the best, and the chief high priest of his church, worketh in his catholic church inwardly and in their minds, as the only searcher of the hearts ; the very same outwardly he declareth and testifieth by his ministers, whom the scripture for that cause calleth witnesses, ambassadors, or messengers. "You (saith the Lord to his apostles) shall bear John xv. Acts i. witness, because ye have been with me from the beginning." And Paul saith : "I am ordained a preacher[3], and an apos- 1 Tim. ii. tle, and a teacher of the Gentiles." Therefore the same apostle, in another place, calleth the same gospel both a testimony, and preaching, of our Lord Jesus Christ[4]. And John the apostle affirmeth, that he was banished into the isle of Pathmos "for the word of God, and for the witnessing of Rev. i. Jesus Christ." And therefore when ministers bear witness of the Son of God, and out of his word promise life everlasting, their word is not called man's word, but the word of God ; and they are said to save, and to release from sin ; for they are the true messengers and heralds of the King, who is the deliverer, who hath sent them to publish remis-

[3 præco evangelii, Lat.]

[4 1 Cor. i. 6 ; 2 Tim. i. 8, *testimonium* ; 2 Tim. iv. 17, *præconium* ; Erasmus, and Bibl. Lat. Tigur. 1544.]

sion of sins[1]: whereupon also they attribute all the means of life, salvation, and delivery, to the only deliverer Christ.

1 Cor. iii. iv. Paul in another place calleth ministers, "fellow-labourers with God;" and afterward again, "disposers of the secrets of God." For the salvation which the Son of God hath only wrought, and which he also only giveth, the ministers preach or dispose[2], and so they are "fellow-labourers." The same apostle out of the doctrine of the gospel, which resem-

Matt. xiii. bleth the teacher in the church to one that soweth seed, compareth the ministers to gardeners and planters of trees; to whom he committeth the outward manuring, reserving

1 Cor. iii. the inward working to Christ our Lord, saying: "Who is Paul then, and who is Apollos, but ministers by whom ye believed; and as the Lord gave to every man? I have planted, Apollos watered; but God gave the increase. So then neither is he that planteth anything, neither he that watereth; but God that giveth the increase."

With which testimony of the scripture Augustine being instructed, learned so to speak and write of the ministry of the church, as nothing should be diminished from the glory of God, which inwardly moveth and teacheth us; and yet in the mean time the office of the ministry should not be taken away, or despised as unprofitable. For in his epistle *ad Circenses*, which in order is accounted the 130, speaking of the secret drawing of God and the outward ministry of men: "These are not (saith he) our works, but God's; I would not at all attribute these things unto man's working: no, not if, when we were with you, so great a conversion of the multitude through our speaking and exhortations should happen. That thing he worketh and bringeth to pass, who by his ministers outwardly warneth by tokens or signs of things; but by the things themselves he inwardly teacheth by himself." Thus far he. But lest it might seem to any man, that he spake too briefly and sparingly, and not worthily enough, of the ministry of the church, even he himself immediately addeth, and saith: "Neither therefore ought we to be more slow to come unto you, because whatsoever is done praiseworthy among you cometh not of us, but of him which alone doth wonderful things; for we ought more carefully to run to behold the works of God than our own works; because

[1 of sins, not in Lat.]　　　　　　[2 dispensant, Lat.]

even we ourselves, if we have any goodness in us, we are
his work, and not man's.   Therefore the apostle said:
'Neither is he that planteth anything, nor he that watereth;
but God that giveth the increase[3].'"   The same writer, speaking of the very same thing in his twenty-sixth treatise upon
John : " All the men of that kingdom (saith he) shall be
such as are taught of God; they shall not hear by men : and
though they hear by men, yet that which they understand
is inwardly given; it shineth inwardly; it is inwardly revealed.
What do men in preaching outwardly?   What do I now
when I speak?   Make you to hear a noise of words with
your ears.   But unless he reveal it, which is within, what say
I ? or what speak I ?   The outward workman is the planter
of the tree, and the inward is the creator.   He that planteth,
and he that watereth, worketh outwardly ; that do we :
but neither is he that planteth anything, nor he that watereth; but God that giveth the increase.   This is the meaning of,
' They shall be all taught of God[4].'"   Thus far Augustine.

Wherefore, when in another place St Paul saith, " Ye 2 Cor. iii.
are the epistle of Christ, ministered by us, written not with

[3 Non sunt hæc opera nostra, sed Dei; non hæc humanis operibus
omnino tribuerem; nec si cum apud vos essemus tanta conversio multitudinis nobis loquentibus et hortantibus proveniret.   Hoc agit ille
et efficit, qui per ministros suos rerum signis extrinsecus admonet,
rebus autem ipsis per seipsum intrinsecus docet...Nec ideo pigrius
moveri nos oportet ad visendos vos, quoniam quicquid in vobis lauda-
bile est factum, non a nobis, sed ab illo factum est, qui facit mirabilia
solus.   Multo enim alacrius debemus accurrere ad spectanda opera
divina quam nostra, quia et nos, si quid boni sumus, opus illius, non
hominum sumus.   Unde apostolus dixit, Neque qui plantat est aliquid,
neque qui rigat; sed qui incrementum dat, Deus.—August. Ep. 130.
Opp. Tom. II. fol. 124. col. 4. Par. 1531.]

[4 Omnes regni illius homines docibiles Dei erunt, non ab hominibus audient.   Etsi ab hominibus audiunt, tamen quod intelligunt
intus datur, intus coruscat, intus revelatur.   Quid faciunt homines
forinsecus annunciantes?   Quid facio ego modo cum loquor?   Strepitum verborum ingero auribus vestris: nisi vero revelet ille qui
intus est, quid dico, quid loquor?   Exterior cultor arboris, interior
est creator.   Qui plantat et qui rigat, extrinsecus operatur; hoc facimus nos: sed neque qui plantat est aliquid, neque qui rigat; sed qui
incrementum dat, Deus.   Hoc est, Erunt omnes docibiles Dei.—
Id. Tract. in Joan. 26. Tom. IX. fol. 47. col. 1. See also Vol. I.
p. 86.]

ink, but with the Spirit of the living God; not in stony tables, but in fleshy tables of the heart;" we must diligently put a difference between the work of the Spirit, and the work of man or of the minister. The minister doth not take on him the honour of God and the work of the Spirit, but his own work, that is to say, the ministry. Paul preacheth, and writeth with ink; but the Spirit of God moveth the heart; and with his grace, or anointing, he writeth in the very heart: so he worketh together with God, Paul working his proper work, and the Spirit working his work. The apostles are preachers and ministers of the gospel, not of the letter, but of the Spirit: not that they give the Holy Ghost, but because they are preachers of the gospel, that is, of that which giveth the Spirit of Christ[1], yea, which poureth it into the believers: but they are not preachers of the letter of the law, which doth not give grace and remission of sins, but worketh wrath and bringeth sin to light. Touching the keys and the power of the keys, there will be elsewhere a more fit place to speak. And moreover it seemeth that here is a meet place for those things, which I have disputed of in the first sermon of this decade, touching the power and ministry of the church.

Again; whereas the Lord useth in teaching his church man's help, and us as labourers together in finishing the salvation of mankind[2], he sheweth most evidently how greatly he loveth us, and how much he esteemeth of us; who hath laid up so great a treasure in earthen vessels, and even in us ourselves worketh whatsoever is most excellent, and overcometh all the high excellency of the world. Whereby we learn again to attribute all the glory unto Christ, Paul again teaching us, and saying: "We preach not ourselves, but Jesus Christ the Lord; and ourselves your servants for Jesus' sake. For it is God, that commanded the light to shine out of darkness, who hath shined in our hearts, for to give the light of knowledge of the glory of God in the face of Jesus Christ. But we have this treasure in earthen vessels, that the excellency of the power may be of God, and not of us. We are afflicted on every side, yet are we not in distress, &c."

Moreover, all the members of the ecclesiastical body are

2 Cor. iv.

[1 prædicatores evangelii, id est, Christi spiritum conferentis.]
[2 of mankind, not in Lat.]

wonderfully glued together by the ecclesiastical ministry: for this chiefly helpeth to make concord and continue unity, because we want mutual instruction; and unto every church is one peculiar pastor appointed as a governor, as it were some faithful householder, governing and keeping in order his whole family. Truly it cannot be denied, that in time past that[3] most exquisite order[4] of the tabernacle, and temple, and the tribe of Levi consecrated to the priesthood, were to this end ordained of God: which as soon as that ungodly king Jeroboam through wicked presumption forsook, he rent the kingdom in pieces, and at the length utterly overthrew both his own house and the whole kingdom[5]. St Paul also, speaking of the ends of the holy ministry instituted of God, doth not forget the unity of the ecclesiastical body; whereunto also he joineth other notable good things. If any man desire his words, they are these: "He instituted ministers, for the gathering together[6] of the saints, for the work of the ministry, and for the edification of the body of Christ: till we all meet together in the unity of faith, and knowledge of the Son of God, unto a perfect man, and unto the measure of the age of the fulness of Christ: that we henceforth be no more children, wavering, and carried about with every wind of doctrine, by the deceit of men, and with craftiness, whereby they lie in wait to deceive; but let us follow the truth in love, and in all things grow up into him, which is the head, that is, Christ," &c. These ends of the ecclesiastical ministry are manifest in the preaching of the word of God. God hath instituted a ministry in the church, that all the members may be brought into the unity of the body, and that they may be subject and cleave to Christ their head, that thereby we may grow to be of full age, and become perfect men; that we be not always children, and that we lie not open to the deceits and bewitchings of all heretics; but, being joined together in true faith and charity, let us hold fast the pure and simple truth of Christ; and serving Christ unfeignedly in this world, we may after death reign with him in heaven.

Out of these things let us also derive this; that the eccle-

The end of the ministry.

Ephes. iv.

[3 totum, Lat.: all that.]   [4 cultum, Lat.]
[5 See Vol. II. p. 128.]
[6 instaurationem, Lat. and Erasmus.]

siastical ministry, though it be executed by men, yet is it

The begin-
ning of the
ministry, and
the worthi-
ness thereof.

not of man, that is to say, invented by man. For the beginning thereof is from heaven, and the author or institutor thereof is God himself; and therefore the worthiness of it doth greatly excel.

The first preacher in paradise was God himself, yea, the Son of God himself: who by the ministry of the Holy Ghost always spake to the fathers; even as afterwards, being incarnate, he was given of the Father to be a master and teacher to the whole world. He preached unto our parents, Adam and Eve, remission of sins and repentance. He ordained and revealed a sacrifice, instead of a sacrament; wherein might be represented and ratified[1] unto them the price of the redemption, promised by the seed in time convenient to be paid, &c. There succeeded in the ministry Adam with his sons and nephews, Seth, Enos, Enoch, Noe, Sem, Abraham, with their sons and nephews, even unto Moses; in whose time, while he governed the church, and after him, there are given prophets and priests, even unto the time of John Baptist and Jesus, the promised seed, I mean Christ, our king and high priest. He in like wise[2] sent into the world his disciples, that is to say, the apostles, who ordained for their successors bishops and doctors: of which thing I have spoken more largely in another place[3]. God himself therefore is heard in the voice or doctrine of his ministers; so that we are commanded to give ear to the ministers, preaching the gospel, as to the very angels of God, yea, as to the Lord himself. For this cause Paul praiseth the Galatians, saying: "Ye despised not neither abhorred my trial which was in the flesh; but received me as an angel of God, yea, as Christ Jesus." Whereupon St Augustine also in his thirtieth treatise upon John: "Let us hear (saith he) the gospel, as if the Lord were present; and let us not say, Oh, happy are they who could hear him: because there were many of them which saw him, and yet consented to kill him, and many among us who have not seen, and yet believed. For that also which sounded precious out of the mouth of the Lord, is both written for our sakes, and kept for us, and is also read for our sakes, and for our posterity's sake shall

Gal. iv.

How minis-
ters are to
be heard.

[1 obsignaretur, Lat.]   [2 rursus, Lat.]
[3 De Episcoporum Instit. et Funct. cap. 5.]

be read unto the end of the world.   The Lord is above; yea,
and the Lord, which is the truth, is here also.   For the
body of the Lord wherewith he rose may be in one place,
but his truth is spread abroad everywhere.   Let us therefore hear the Lord, and that also which he shall give us of
his words[4]."   Thus much he.   The Lord, our high priest,
speaketh unto us even at this day by the ministers preaching his word.   And[5] we have all things, whatsoever the Lord
spake by the patriarchs, prophets, and apostles, set out in
the scriptures, which the ministers of the church do read
and declare before us.   Who therefore hereafter can despise
the ministry and the faithful ministers of Christ, especially
since our Lord and Saviour took upon him the ministry, and Rom. xv.
Heb. iii.
was made the apostle and minister of the church of the Jews?
What and if those first ministers were such, as no age, in
any doctrine of religion, in holiness and excellency, had their
fellows, much less their betters?   At this day, insomuch as
they are the last times, wherein scoffers and epicures have
their full range, the ministry of God's word is of no value.
But if you run over and weigh all the ages, even unto the
beginning of the world, you shall find that the wisest, justest,
and best men in the whole world had nothing in more reverence than the word of God, and the prophets, and the
holy apostles of God.

But before we proceed any further in other things That the
ministry
of the word
of God re-
maineth in
the church.
belonging to this matter, we will make answer to some, which,
even under the pretence of the holy scriptures, endeavour to
pervert the ministry of the word.   For they allege this text
of Jeremy : "No man shall teach his neighbour, for all shall Jer. xxxi.
know me[6]."   As we deny not that Jeremy hath so written;

[4 Nos itaque sic audiamus evangelium tanquam præsentem Dominum, nec dicamus, O illi felices, qui eum videre (Bullinger read
audire) potuerunt : quia multi in eis qui viderunt, et occiderunt;
multi autem in nobis qui non viderunt, et crediderunt.   Quod enim
pretiosum sonabat de ore Domini, et propter nos scriptum est, et nobis
servatum est, et propter nos recitatur, et propter posteros recitabitur,
et donec seculum finiatur.   Sursum est Dominus, sed etiam hic est
veritas Dominus.   Corpus enim Domini, in quo resurrexit, uno loco
esse potest : veritas ejus ubique diffusa est.   Dominum ergo audiamus,
et quod ipse donaverit de verbis ejus.—August. Tract. in Joan. xxx.
Opp. Tom. ix.]

[5 Imo, Lat. : Nay.]   [6 Bullinger. adv. Anabapt. Lib. ii. cap. 4.]

so we say, by that kind of speech and figurative saying that he meant nothing else, than that the knowledge of God and heavenly things should be very common in the whole world; which Joel also foretold would come to pass, and which Peter allegeth in the Acts, second chapter. In the meanwhile these two prophets, as also all other very often, do make mention of the teachers of the church, whom the Lord should send unto his people: which they would not have done, if they had understood that all preachers should be taken clean away. Whereas other object, that all have the office of teaching committed alike unto them, to wit, parents to teach their children, and every one to admonish his neighbour; therefore that there is no need of the ministry of the word of God in the church: it is sophistical. For all of us can and ought privately to teach and admonish our children and our neighbours; but therefore the public ministry of the word of God is not superfluous. For the same God, which commanded parents and us all that they should instruct their children in godliness, and that every one of us also should teach and admonish our neighbours, hath given public ministers unto the church. It is their office to teach openly or publicly in the church; neither is this permitted to whomsoever will, but only to them that be lawfully ordained; lest happily, if other teach, they should not go forward in the right path; for then it were lawful for every one, being inspired with the Spirit of God, at what time and place soever, both soberly to gainsay and to affirm the truth. Therefore the public ministry of the word remaineth nevertheless, and that perpetually, in the church.

Thus much have we spoken in general of the ministry and the ministers of the word of God. Now that which remaineth of this matter we will discuss by their kinds and parts. And first we will shew what orders, or what offices, the Lord hath instituted from the beginning, or whom he hath put in authority in the holy ministry of the church; then, what manner men, and after what sort, it is meet for us to ordain ministers; last of all, what manner of office it is that they have, that are ordained in the church. And that we be not troublesome unto you, beginning a long discourse from the patriarchs, we will begin at our Lord Christ himself; of whom Paul the apostle speaking: "He that descended," saith he, "is even the same which ascended up far above all heavens, to fulfil all things.

How all may teach.

Deut. vi.

What orders the Lord hath instituted in the church.

And he gave some apostles, and some prophets, and some
evangelists, and some pastors and doctors, to the gathering
together of the saints, into the work of ministration, into the
edifying of the body of Christ :" and so forth, as is read in the
fourth chapter to the Ephesians. Therefore our Lord ordained
apostles, prophets, evangelists, pastors, and doctors, by whose
labour he meant to build, preserve, and govern the church.

Let us now see what the scripture teacheth us of them. Apostles.
Apostle is a new name, given of the Lord himself to those
twelve, which he chose peculiarly, and ordained teachers and
masters to (all) nations. For thus we read in the sixth of
Luke : "The Lord called his disciples : and of them he chose Luke vi.
twelve, whom also he called apostles." For apostle signifieth,
one that is sent, a messenger, ambassador, or orator ; for in
the gospel after St John we read : "The apostle (or messenger) John xiii.
is not greater than he that sent him." And truly, there is
very often mention made of sending, in the prophets and in
the old Testament[1]; from whence it seemeth the Lord borrowed
that name. We read of no certain bounds appointed to the
apostles ; for the Lord saith in the gospel : "Go ye into the Mark xvi.
whole world, and preach the gospel to all creatures." These
are the master-builders of the first church of God, from whom
among ancient writers they took the name of apostolic
churches ; those, I mean, which the apostles first founded : as
was the church at Antioch, Ephesus, Corinth, and many other
mentioned in the Acts of the Apostles.

The name of a minister and[2] prophet is exceeding large :
whereof is spoken in another place[3]. Prophets in this place Prophets.
are they which excel in singular revelation, and by whom the
Lord foretelleth things that shall come to the church : such a
one as we read Agabus was, which both foretold to St Paul Acts xi. xxi.
the famine which was to come, and his bonds[4]. Wise and
godly men, endued with a singular gift of interpreting the
scripture, in times past were called prophets : as it may appear
by the words of the apostle, 1 Corinth. xiv. chapter.

An evangelist is a preacher of the gospel of Jesus Christ, Evangelists.
sent with apostolic authority. Such we read were Philip and
Timothy, &c.

[1 in antiqua historia, Lat.]
[2 minister and, not in Lat.]   [3 See Vol. I. p. 49.]
[4 rather, which both foretold the famine, &c. and to St Paul, his
bonds.]

Pastors.

Pastors watch over the Lord's flock, having care of the Lord's people, feeding the church with the word of truth, and keeping the wolves from the sheepfolds. The chief of these John x. xxi. is that good Shepherd, Christ, which saith unto Peter, "Feed my sheep;" whereby he also joineth himself to shepherds.

Doctors or teachers.

Doctors or teachers have their names of teaching. Neither do I see what they differ from shepherds, but that they did only teach, and in the meanwhile were not burthened with the care that belongeth to the pastor: of which sort in a manner are the interpreters of scriptures, and governors of christian schools.

There are also found other names of the overseers of the church in the scriptures. The apostle Paul saith unto the Bishops. shepherds, gathered together in the council at Miletum: "Take Acts xx. heed therefore unto yourselves, and to all the flock, over the which the Holy Ghost hath made you overseers, to feed the church of God." But bishops are called superintendents, seers, keepers, watchmen, and rulers. The people of Athens called them, whom they sent to their tributary cities subject unto them, diligently to see and mark what they did in every city, $\epsilon\pi\iota\sigma\kappa\acute{o}\pi o\nu\varsigma$[1] and $\phi\acute{u}\lambda\alpha\kappa\alpha\varsigma$, that is to say, spies and watchmen[2]. The apostles called bishops watchmen, and keepers of the Lord's flock, and the stewards of Christ, or disposers of Elders. the secrets[3] of God in the church. And presbyter, an elder, hath his name of age and ancient years. In times past the care of the commonwealth was committed unto the elders, as to those that were exercised with manifold experience and long use of things; for governors of cities are both called seniors and senators. And as commonweals have their senators, so hath the church her elders; as it appeareth in the Acts xiv., xv., xx., and xxi. chap. It seemeth that the ordaining[4] of elders came into the church out of the synagogue; for thus Numb. xi. we read in the book of Numbers: "Gather unto me (saith he) threescore and ten men of the elders of Israel, whom thou knowest to be the elders of the people, and officers over them; and I will take of the spirit which is upon thee, and put upon them, and they shall bear the burden of the people with thee,

[1 Budæi Comment. Ling. Græc. (p. 290. 1529.) apud Bullinger. Expos. in Heb. v. 5. 6. p. 673. Tig. 1537.]

[2 The interpretation is the translator's.]

[3 mysteriorum, Lat.]   [4 constitutio, Lat.]

lest thou be constrained to bear it alone." Wherefore the
elders in the church of Christ are either bishops, or otherwise
prudent and learned men added to bishops, that they[5] may
the more easily bear the burden laid upon them, and that the
church of God may the better and more conveniently be
governed.   For Paul saith: "The elders that rule well, let 1 Tim. v.
them be counted worthy of double honour; most specially
they which labour in the word and doctrine." There were
therefore certain other in the ecclesiastical function, who albeit
they did not teach by and bye[6], as did the bishops, yet were
they present with them that taught in all businesses. Perhaps
they are called of the same apostle elsewhere governors, that 1 Cor. xii.
is to say, which are set in authority concerning discipline and
other affairs of the church.

And because we are come thus far in this present treatise,
we will also declare other names of offices in the church. There
is much speech in the scriptures of deacons, and, among eccle- Deacons.
siastical writers, of priests.   In the primitive church the care
of the poor was committed to deacons; as it is plainly gathered
out of the sixth chapter of the Acts of the Apostles.   There
are also laws to be seen, which are prescribed unto them by
the apostle in the first to Timothy, the third chapter.   The
office of deacons was separated from the function of pastors;
and therefore we do not reckon them in the order of pastors.
The ancient fathers referred them to the ministry, but not to
the priesthood.   We read also, that women, not wedded, but Women
widows, ministered in the primitive church; and among other deacons.
Phebe, of the church of Cencrea, highly praised of the apostle, Rom. xvi.
is very famous.   But he forbiddeth women to teach in the 1 Cor. xiv.
church, and to take upon them public offices.   How therefore,
or in what thing, did women minister in the church? Undoubtedly, they ministered unto the poor in duties appertaining 1 Tim. ii.
to women.   They ministered unto the sick; and with Martha,
Christ's hostess, they did with great care and diligence cherish
the members of Christ: for what other offices could they
have?

Moreover, the name of priest seemeth to be brought into Priests.
the church out of the synagogue; for otherwise ye shall not
find in the new Testament the ministers of the word of God
and of churches to be called priests, but after that sort that

[5 episcopi, Lat.: the bishops.]   [6 continue, Lat.]

1 Pet. ii.

all Christians are called priests by the apostle Peter. But it appeareth that the ministers of the new Testament, for a certain likeness which they have with the ministers of the old Testament, of ecclesiastical writers are called priests; for as they did their service in their tabernacle, so these also, after their manner and their fashion, minister to the church of God. For otherwise the Latin word is derived of holy things, and signifieth a minister of holy things: a man, I say, dedicated and consecrated unto God to do holy things. And holy things are not only sacrifices, but what things soever come under the name of religion; from which we do not exclude the laws themselves, and holy doctrine. In the old Testament we read that David's sons were called priests[1]: not that they were ministers of holy things, (for it was not lawful for them, which came of the tribe of Juda, to serve in the tabernacle, but only to the Levites); but because they, living under the government and discipline of priests, did learn good sciences and holy divinity.

2 Sam. viii.

There is an interchanging between those names.

Here it seemeth it must not be dissembled, that those names, which we have entreated of, are in the scriptures one[2] used for another. For Peter, the apostle of Christ our Lord, calleth himself an elder; and in the Acts of the Apostles he calleth the apostleship a bishoprick. For St Paul also calling the elders together at Miletum, and talking with them, he calleth them bishops; and in his epistle unto Titus he commandeth to ordain elders town by town, whom immediately after he calleth bishops[3]. And that they also are called both doctors and pastors, there are none so gross-headed to deny.

What manner of order remaineth in the church.

Now by all these things we think it is manifest to all men, what orders the Lord himself ordained from the beginning, and whom he hath consecrated to the holy ministry of the church, to govern his own church. He laid the foundation of the church, at the beginning, by apostles, evangelists, and prophets; he enlarged and maintained[4] the same by pastors and doctors. To these elders and deacons were helpers: the deacons in seeing to the poor; and the elders in doctrine, in discipline, and in governing and sustaining other weightier

[1 chief rulers, Auth. Ver.: princes, marg.: Heb. כֹּהֲנִים *priests.*]

[2 frequens, Lat. omitted: often.]

[3 1 Pet. v. 1; Acts i. 20, xx. 28; Tit. i. 5.]

[4 consecravit, Lat.]

affairs of the church. Nevertheless, it appeareth that the order of the apostles, evangelists, and prophets, was ordained at the beginning by the Lord unto his church for a time, according to the matter, persons, and places. For many ages since, and immediately after the foundation of Christ's kingdom in earth, the apostles, evangelists, and prophets ceased; and there came in their place bishops, pastors, doctors and elders; which order hath continued most stedfastly in the church: that now we cannot doubt, that the order of the church is perfect and the government absolute, if at this day also there remain in the church of God bishops or pastors, doctors also or elders. Yet we deny not, that after the death of the apostles there were oftentimes apostles raised up of God, which might preach the gospel to barbarous and ungodly nations. We confess also, that God even at this day is able to raise up apostles, evangelists, and prophets, whose labour he may use to work the salvation of mankind. For we acknowledge, that holy and faithful men, which first preach the truth of the gospel to any unbelieving people, may be called apostles and evangelists. We acknowledge that men inspired with singular grace of the Spirit, which foresee and foreshew things to come, and be excellent interpreters of the scriptures, or divines illuminated, may be called prophets; as we have shewed[5] elsewhere more at large.

But in the order of bishops and elders from the begin- Equality between bishops and elders. ning there was singular humility, charity, and concord; no contention or strife for prerogative, or titles, or dignity ; for all acknowledged themselves to be the ministers of one master, co-equal in all things touching office or charge. He made them unequal, not in office, but in gifts, by the excellency of gifts. Yet they, that had obtained the excellenter gifts, did not despise the greater[6] sort, neither did they envy them for their gifts. St Paul saith: " Let a man so esteem of us, as 1 Cor. iv. the ministers of Christ, and disposers of the secrets of God." The same Paul in more than one place calleth the preaching of the gospel the ministry ; for that took deep root in the ancient bishops' hearts, which the Lord, when his disciples strived for dignity, and (as they say) for the majority, that is,

[5 ostendi, Lat.: Bullinger. de Episc. Instit. et Funct. capp. 1. and 5.]

[6 So also ed. 1584: but ed. 1577, meaner: mediocres, Lat.]

which of them should be the greatest[1], setting a child in the
Matth. xviii. midst of them, said : " Verily, verily[2], I say unto you, Except
ye turn, and become as little children, ye shall not enter into
the kingdom of heaven." Truly the martyr of God, St Cyprian, standing in the council of the bishops at Carthage, wisely
said[3]: " Neither hath any of us appointed himself to be a
bishop of bishops, or by tyrannous fear compelled his fellows in
office to necessity of obeying : since every bishop hath, according to the licence and liberty of his power, his own free choice ;
as if he might not be judged of another, since neither he himself can judge another. But let us all look for the judgment
of our Lord Jesus Christ, who only and alone hath power
both to prefer us in the government of his church, and to give
sentence of our doing[4]." Thus far he. At that time, therefore, bishops contended not for I know not what primacy or
patrimony of Peter ; but that one might excel the other in
pureness of doctrine and holiness of life, and mutually to help
one another. And then undoubtedly the affairs of the church
went forward prosperously ; insomuch that, though the most
puissant princes of the world should have persecuted the
church of Christ with fire and sword, yet nevertheless against
all the assaults of the devil and the world she had stood unmoveable, having won the victory, and had daily been more
enlarged and also renowned. Oh happy had we been, if this
order of pastors had not been changed ; but that that ancient
simplicity of ministers, that faith, humility, and diligence, had
remained uncorrupted!

When the
prerogative
of bishops
began, and in
what sort.

But in process of time all things of ancient soundness,
humility, and simplicity, vanished away ; whiles some things are

[1 The translator's explanation.]
[2 Amen, Lat.: not repeated.]
[3 disertis verbis, Lat.: in express words.]
[4 Neque enim quisquam nostrum episcopum se episcoporum constituit, aut tyrannico terrore ad obsequendi necessitatem collegas suos
adigit; quando habeat omnis episcopus, pro licentia libertatis et potestatis suæ, arbitrium proprium, tamque judicari ab alio non possit,
quam nec ipse potest judicare : (Bullinger read, tanquam judicari ab
alio non possit, cum nec ipse possit alterum judicare :) sed exspectemus
universi judicium Domini nostri Jesu Christi, qui unus et solus habet
potestatem, et præponendi nos in ecclesiæ suæ gubernatione, et de
actu nostro judicandi.—Cyprian. ap. Concil. Carthag. Opp. p. 229.
Oxon. 1682.]

turned upside down ; some things either of their own accord were out of use, or else are taken away by deceit; some things are added to. Verily, not many ages after the death of the apostles there was seen a far other hierarchy (or government) of the church[5] than was from the beginning ; although those beginnings seem to be more tolerable, than at this day all of this same order are. St Hierome saith :

You shall find more upon this place of St Hierome elsewhere, in these words: "Let no man think that the holy man speaketh of the primacy and monarchy of the bishop of Rome : for he speaketh of the bishops of every several province. For in St Hierome's time the liberty of the church as yet remained safe: therefore every several province chose unto themselves him that was best, whom they called both bishop, superintendent, and metropolitan[8]."

" In times past churches were governed with the common counsel and advice of the elders : afterward it was decreed, that one of the elders, being chosen, should be set over the other; unto whom the whole care of the church should pertain, and that the seeds of schisms should be taken away[6]." Thus much he. In every city and country, therefore, he that was most excellent was placed above the rest. His office was to be superintendent, and to have the oversight of the ministers[7] and the whole flock

He had not (as we understood even now out of Cyprian's words) dominion over his fellows in office or other elders: but, as the consul in the senate-house was placed to demand and gather together the voices of the senators, and to defend the laws and privileges, and to be careful lest there should arise factions among the senators; even so no other was the office of a bishop in the church : in all other things he was but equal with the other ministers. But had not the arrogancy of the ministers and ambition of bishops in the times that followed further increased, we would not speak a word against them. And St Hierome affirmeth, that "That

[5 in ecclesia, Lat.]

[6 — Communi presbyterorum consilio ecclesiæ gubernabantur. Postquam vero . . . decretum est, ut unus de presbyteris electus superponeretur ceteris, ad quem omnis ecclesiæ cura pertineret, et schismatum semina tollerentur.—Hieron. Comment. in Ep. ad Tit. cap. 1. Tom. IV. par. 1. col. 413. Par. 1706.]

[7 presbyteris, Lat.]

[8 This extract from Bullinger's treatise De Episcop. Instit. et Funct. cap. 16, fol. 143, is not given in edd. 1577 and 1584; nor in the folio Latin ed. of the Decades, Tiguri, 1552. It appears however in the octavo edition of the Latin Decades, "Londini excudebat Henricus Midletonus;" no date.]

preferment of bishops sprang not by God's ordinance, but by the ordinance of man. These things have we remembered," saith he, "to the end we might shew, that, among the old fathers, bishops and ministers were all one; but by little and little, that the plants of dissensions might be plucked up, all the care was committed unto one. Therefore, as ministers know, that they by the custom of the church are subject to him which is set over them; so let bishops know, that, rather by custom than by the truth of the Lord's disposition, they are greater than the other ministers; and that they ought to govern the churches together in common, following the example of Moses, who, when it was in his power alone to govern the people of Israel, chose out threescore and ten other, with whom he might judge the people[1]." Thus he writeth in his commentary upon the third chapter of the epistle of Paul unto Titus.

The dignity and prerogative of bishops increased.

But the ancient fathers kept not themselves within these bounds. There were also ordained patriarchs at Antioch, Alexandria, Constantinople, and Rome. There are appointed archbishops, or metropolitans; that is to say, such as have government over the bishops throughout provinces. And to bishops of cities, or inferior bishops, there are added such as were called chorepiscopi (or bishops of the multitude)[2]; that is to say, at such time as the country or region was larger than that the care and oversight of the bishop placed over the city would suffice: for these were added as vicars and suffragans, who might execute the office of the bishop throughout that part of the country. But we know that the functions of suffragans, or vicars general, in these last times, are of a far other manner in bishops' courts and dioceses. And also under deacons were placed subdeacons. And when wealth increased, there were archdeacons also created; that is to say, overseers of all the goods of the church. They as yet were not mingled with the order of ministers[3] or bishops, and of those that

[1 The former part of this quotation is given above, p. 87, n. 5. Jerome then proceeds: Et in commune (noverint episcopi) debere ecclesiam regere, imitantes Moysen, qui, quum haberet in potestate solus præesse populo Israel, septuaginta elegit, cum quibus populum judicaret.—Hieron. Comment. in Ep. ad Tit. cap. 1. Opp. Tom. IV. par. 1. col. 413.]

[2 The translator's explanation.]   [3 sacerdotum, Lat.]

taught; but they remained as stewards, or factors, of the goods of the church: as neither the monks at the beginning executed the office of a priest or minister in the church; for they were counted as laymen, not as clerks, and were under the charge of the pastors. But these unfortunate[4] birds never left soaring, until in these last times they have climbed into the top of the temple, and have set themselves upon bishops' and pastors' heads: for monks have been and are both popes, archbishops, and bishops; and what are they not? It is rehearsed out of the register of Gregory, that he (who nevertheless was very favourable to the monks) himself would put him out of the clergy, who being a monk would take the degree of an abbot; forasmuch as the one dignity would hinder the other[5].

Clerks (who are the Lord's inheritance, or whose lot the Clerks. Lord is) in times past such were called as were students, or professors of divinity[6]; that is to say, the very seed of pastors of the church, and such as were even as it were consecrated to succeed in the ministry of the church: that is, such as lived under government, and were trained up by the doctors and elders in the study of the liberal sciences and holy scriptures[7]. This institution is ancient, not new, neither invented by man; for in time past, among the old people of the Jews, they were called Nazarites[8]. And that the most excellent churches have continually had famous schools, even from the time of the apostles, Eusebius doth often witness[9]. But unto those students, the affairs of the church somewhat increasing, it seemeth that the charge of opening and shutting the temple or church was committed; and to prepare all things in the church; and further, to read openly before the people such places of scripture as the bishop appointed them. Whereupon, perhaps, the names of door-keepers and readers sprang, which are at

[4 inauspicatæ, Lat.]

[5 Presbyteros, diaconos, ceterosque cujuslibet ordinis clericos ... abbates per monasteria esse non permittas.—Greg. Maximiniano Episc. Syracus. Regist. Lib. III. indict. 12. Epist. XI. p. 98. Opp. Tom. IV. Rom. 1591.]

[6 candidati theologiæ, Lat.]

[7 See Bingham, Antiq. Book I. chap. 5. § 7—9.]

[8 See Vol. II. p. 208.]

[9 See Bullinger, de Episc. Instit. et Funct. cap. 8. De scholis Christianorum priscis, &c.]

8

this day reckoned amongst ecclesiastical orders[1]. But they which were more familiarly present with the bishops and accompanied them, and were esteemed as those who after the decease of the bishops might succeed in their places, were called *Acoluthi,* as if you would say, "followers;" for it is a Greek word. And as in time, for the most part, all things become worse, even so these things, the further off from their first institution, the more filthily were they wrested. In some things you shall see nothing left but the bare name; some things utterly lost; some things are turned altogether to another use. And here for witness I allege Isidorus, Rabanus, Innocentius, Durandus, and other writers of this kind[2]. They make two sorts of ecclesiastical persons; one of dignity, another of order: of dignity; as pope, patriarch, primate, archbishop, archpriest, archdeacon, and provost: of order; as the minister[3] or priest, the deacon, &c. But some account six orders, other some eight. All with one accord do reckon doorkeepers or porters, readers or singers, exorcists, acoluthes, subdeacons, deacons, elders or priests. Those again they divide into greater and lesser orders. Among the greater orders are the priest or elder, the deacon, and the subdeacon. The rest are called the lesser orders; of which orders there remaineth nothing in a manner beside the bare name. The office of doorkeepers is turned over to the sextons, which they call holy-water clerks[4]. There are no readers; for that ancient reading is worn out of use. The psalmists, or singers, do understand nothing less than that they rehearse or sing. Touching the exorcists this they say: Josephus writeth, that king Solomon found out the manner of exorcism, that is, of conjuring, whereby unclean spirits were driven out of a man that was possessed by Eleazar the exorcist, so that they durst no more come again[5]. To this office they that are

[1 Horum mentio fit in Carthaginen. Concilio IV. Lat. marg. These are mentioned in the fourth Council of Carthage. Labb. et Coss. Tom. II. col. 1200. capp. 8, 9. Par. 1671.]

[2 Isidorus, Etymol. Lib. VII. cap. 12. Tom. III. p. 339. Rom. 1798. Rabanus, de Instit. Cleric. Lib. I. cap. 9. Opp. Tom. VI. Col. Agrip. 1626. Innocent. III. Epist. Lib. I. p. 44. Lib. II. p. 452. Opp. Tom. I. Par. 1682. Durand. Rational. Divin. Lib. II.]

[3 presbyter, Lat.]   [4 ædituos, quos vocant sacristas, Lat.]

[5 Refert Josephus, regem Salomonem excogitasse modos exorcismi, id est, adjurationis, quibus immundi spiritus, expulsi ab homine,

named exorcists are called; of whom it is read in the gospel: "If I through Beelzebub cast out devils, by whom do your *Matth. xii.* children (to wit, your exorcists or conjurers) cast them out?" Thus much they say; which I rehearse to this end, that it may appear to all men, that these men are the very same of whom the apostle foretold that it should come to pass, that they "shall not suffer wholesome doctrine, but shall be turned unto *2 Tim. iv.* fables." For who knoweth not, that it is most fabulous which is reported of Solomon? Who knoweth not, that the apostles of the Lord were not exorcists, neither used at any time any manner of enchantments or conjurations? For with a word they cast out unclean spirits, that is, by calling upon and by the power of the name of Christ. Those gifts[6] ceased long ago in the church of God. Those sons of Scæva the priest, *Acts xix.* in the Acts of the Apostles, were said to be exorcists; whom the evil spirit, though they called on the names of Jesus and Paul, ran upon, and tare the clothes from their backs, and so, by God's appointment, made known unto all men how much the eternal God is delighted with exorcists: and yet these fellows thrust them upon us as yet. Touching the acoluthes, or followers, thus they write: hear, I pray you, how trimly they reason. "The acoluthes," say they, "are wax-bearers, because they carry wax-candles. For when the gospel must be read, or mass is to be said, wax-candles are lighted, to signify the joy of the mind[7]." Who hearing these things will say, that these men do unlearnedly handle no mysteries? Subdeacons and deacons are no longer providers for the poor; but, being made ministers of superstition, they attend on the popish mass. The deacon's office is to sing the gospel; the subdeacon's, to sing the epistle. In few words I cannot express what foolish men do fondly chatter concerning these matters. Over these they have set an archdeacon, which is a name of dignity and preeminence[8].

ulterius reverti non sunt ausi.—Rabani Mauri de Instit. Cleric. cap. 10. Opp. Tom. vi. p. 6. Col. Agripp. 1626.]

[6 ea gratia, Lat.]

[7 Acolythi Græce, Latine Ceroferarii dicuntur a deportandis cereis, quando legendum est evangelium, aut sacrificium offerendum: tunc enim accenduntur luminaria ab eis... ad signum lætitiæ demonstrandum.—Isidor. Etymol. Lib. vii. cap. 12.]

[8 See on the above mentioned orders of ecclesiastical persons, Bingham, Antiq. Book ii. chap. 21; and Book iii. chap. 1—7.]

Sacrificers, who are also called priests[1], are diversely distinguished; for there are regular priests, and secular priests.
By regular priests they understand monks: whereas they are
nothing less than those they are said to be. Truly, they
resemble those that of old were called monks in no point of
their doings: a great part of them are a rule and law unto
themselves. Of these men some are doctors appointed to
the office of preaching, but yet rather occupied in saying of
their hours, and in singing and saying of masses: and these
men sow superstition, and most obstinately defend it, and
most bitterly do persecute true religion. Another sort, and
the greatest part, of these monkish priests do nothing else
but sing in the church, and mumble mass, and that for a
very slender price. But you may sooner number the sands
of the coast of Libya than the whole rabble of these. But
they are unprofitable both unto God, and to the church, and
also even to themselves; men utterly unlearned, and " slow
bellies," and yet in the mean season sworn enemies to the
truth of the gospel.

Among the secular priests, the chief are canons; which for
the most part are idle persons, given over to voluptuousness,
gluttons, and in very deed secular, that is to say, worldly[2].
They think they have gaily discharged their duty, if they
make an end of the hours which they call canonical, and be
present gazers on at the mass; and if they honour and
beautify with their presence God's service, as they call it.
They seem to be more strait, and not to be secular priests, who
say mass both for the quick and for the dead. There are
reckoned also in the number of secular priests parish priests,
whom they call *Plebani*; that is, priests appointed for the
people, who only represent some shadow of the old institution
in this, that they preach and administer the sacraments;
which nevertheless you cannot allow, because they minister
them after popish traditions, and not after the doctrine of the
apostles. And many other things they do by reason of their
office, which godliness by all means doth disallow. There
are added unto these hirelings, helpers or vicars. There are
also joined unto these *Sacellani*, whom they call chaplains, of
whom there is an exceeding number. These, even as the

*Popish regu-
lar priests.*

*Popish secu-
lar priests.*

[1 Sacerdotes qui et presbyteri, Lat.]
[2 The translator's explanation.]

monkish priests, do account the chief parts of their duty to be saying over their hours, but especially in massing : as for doctrine, they attribute nothing to it; for of this company you shall find some who never in all their life made one sermon. For the charge of preaching they commit only to their parish priests, and their vicars; they serve those gods, to whom their altar or their chapel is consecrated, &c. By all which things even unto blind men it plainly appeareth, how shamefully the first institution of ministers[3] or pastors is corrupted and turned upside down. They set over the priests archpriests. I have used that word in my preface or epistle in the beginning of the first decade[4]: and I hear that some brethren are offended at it, as though there stuck some piece of popish leaven still about us; or as though we thought to bring in again some unworthy dignity into the church. But I would not have those brethren to fear. With us there are no popish archpriests : neither understood I any popish dignity by that word, but the office of overseeing, which others call visiting. For they have the charge of all degrees in our country, in admonishing and correcting : they have no prelacy or superiority; they reap no rewards thereby, &c.

Archpriests.

But we return to our purpose. They derive priests, or sacrificers, from the seventy disciples, whom it is read in the gospel that the Lord did choose ; the order of bishops, from Peter himself, and the residue of the apostles. And immediately they divide the order of bishops into three parts; namely, patriarchs, archbishops, and bishops[5]. They account the patriarchs the fathers of princes, or highest fathers ; and them also they call primates. And primates, say they, have authority over three archbishops, as a king also hath authority over three dukes. Here I think cardinals have their place, in whom the church of Rome is turned as a gate upon the hinges ; for in the Decretals of Gregory, *De Officio Archip.*, it is thus read : " Cardinals have their name *a cardine*," that

Kinds of bishops.

[3 presbyterorum, Lat.]

[4 The dedicatory preface of the Latin original of the Decades is directed, " Clarissimis viris, Rodolpho Gualthero, Petro Symlero, &c. Decanis, seu *archipresbyteris*, &c. See Appendix.]

[5 Gratian. ap. Corp. Jur. Can. Decret. I. par. distinct. XXI. Tom. I. p. 26. Par. 1687.]

is, of the hinge of a gate; "for as by the hinge the gate is ruled, so by cardinals the universal church is governed[1]." Archbishops are, as it were, the princes of bishops: they are also surnamed metropolitans, because they have their government in the chiefest cities. In very deed metropolis with the Greeks is as it were a mother-city, from whence colonies are deducted, that is, people are sent to inhabit some new place[2]. Whereupon he is called the metropolitan bishop, who governeth some one province, and hath other bishops under him. And these are called both bishops[3], chief priests[4], and presuls. But if you compare all these things with that which I said before of the bishops and governors of the primitive church, you will say there is very great difference between them.

The pope or chief bishop.

But that which they write touching the pope, or chief bishop, is far[5] from the writings of the apostles and evangelists, and from the first ordaining of ministers made by our Saviour Christ. All those bishops, say they, our most holy lord, the pope, doth excel in dignity and power: who is called pope, that is, the father of fathers: he is also called universal, because he is chief of the universal church: and he is also called apostolical, and the chief bishop, because he supplieth the room of the chief of the apostles[6]. For he is Melchizedech, whose priesthood other are not to be compared unto, because he is the head of all bishops[7], from whom they descend as members from the head; and of whose power they all do receive, whom he calleth to be partakers of his care and burden, but not to be partakers of the fulness of power[8]. They therefore define the pope to be the

[1 Dicuntur cardinales a cardine: quia sicut in cardine regitur ostium, ita per istos debet in ecclesia regi officium: unde etiam dicti sunt cardinales, quia per eos regitur universalis ecclesia.—Gregor. Decretal. Lib. i. tit. 24. cap. 2. col. 319. Par. 1585.]

[2 This explanation is the translator's.]

[3 pontifices, Lat.]   [4 antistites, Lat.]

[5 quam alienissimum, Lat.: as alien as possible.]

[6 Rather, and he is also called apostolical, because he supplieth the room of the chief of the apostles; and chief bishop (et summus pontifex, Lat.) for he is &c.—See Epist. Decretal. Tom. i. pp. 342, 448, 498, 553. Tom. ii. p. 644, Rom. 1591.]

[7 pontificum, Lat.]

[8 Illius autem prælatus papa i. pater patrum vocatur; et univer-

supreme head of the church in earth, and the only universal
shepherd of the whole world, who cannot err, neither ought
to be judged of any man: for, they say, he is the judge of
all men, having absolute power. For thus saith Innocent, the
ninth, pope, in his third quest.: "Neither of the emperor,
neither of all the clergy, neither of kings, nor of the people,
ought the judge to be judged." Upon which place he that
wrote the gloss writeth thus: "A general council cannot
judge the pope; as appeareth in the Extravagants, in the title
of election, cap. *Significasti*. Therefore, if the whole world
should pronounce sentence in any matter against the pope, it
seemeth that we must stand to the pope's judgment[9]." Hereunto pertain those common grounds of the clawback, flattering lawyers of the pope's court, very plausible and authentical: "That all the laws of the pope are to be received of
all men, as if they proceeded from the very mouth of Peter[10]:
That the authority of the pope is greater than the authority
of the saints[11]: That the pope is all, and above all[12]: That God
and the pope have one consistory;" which thing also Hostien.
affirmeth, *In C. Quanto de Transl. prœl.*[13]: "That the pope
cannot be brought into order by any man, though he be
accounted an heretic[14]: That he hath supreme power, neither

salis, quia universæ ecclesiæ principatur; et apostolicus, quia principis
apostolorum vice fungitur; et summus pontifex, quia caput est omnium pontificum, a quo illi tanquam a capite membra descendunt, et
de cujus plenitudine omnes accipiunt, quos ipse vocat in partem sol-
licitudinis, non in plenitudinem potestatis . . . . Hic est Melchisedec,
cujus sacerdotium non est ceteris comparatum.—Durand. Rat. Div.
Offic. Lib. II. cap. I. 17. fol. 46. Lugd. 1565.]

[9] Neque ab Augusto, neque ab omni clero, neque a regibus, neque
a populo, judex judicabitur.—Corp. Jur. Can. Decret. Gratian. Decr.
Sec. Par. Caus. IX. Quæst. iii. can. 13, col. 877. Concilium non
potest papam judicare, ut Extravag. de Elect. Significasti. Unde si
totus mundus sententiaret in aliquo negotio contra papam, videtur
quod sententiæ papæ standum esset.—Gloss. ibid. Papam nullus
mortalium judicare potest.—Ibid. Caus. XII. quæst. II. col. 1238.]

[10] Sic omnes apostolicæ sedis sanctiones accipiendæ sunt, tanquam
ipsius divini Petri voce firmatæ sint.—Agatho ap. Corp. Jur. Can.
Decret. I. pár. distinct. 19. Tom. I. p. 24.]

[11] The editor has not been able to verify this reference.]

[12] See Jewel's Works, ed. Parker Soc. Vol. I. pp. 69, 93, 443.]

[13] Consistorium Dei et papæ unum et idem est censendum.
—Hostiens. de Transl. Episc. Opp. fol. 75. Par. 1512.]

[14] The editor has not been able to verify this reference.]

hath he any fellow[1]: That he hath all laws within his breast:
That there is a general council where the pope is[2]: That
he hath all laws in his breast[3]: That he hath both swords,
whereby he may rightly be called an emperor; yea, that he
is above the emperor: That he only can depose the emperor,
and pronounce the sentence of the emperor to be of no effect:

Read Anton.
de Rosellis in
his treatise of
the power of
the pope and
the emperor. That he only may spare whom he will; and may also take
away the right of one man, and give it to another; and
finally, may take away privileges." To be short, they say,
" he is lord of lords, and hath the right of the king of kings
over his subjects; yea, and also hath fulness of power over the
temporal things in earth[4]. Yea, and also the whole world is
the pope's diocese, wherein he is the ordinary of all men[5]:
and it standeth upon the necessity of salvation, that every
man be subject to the bishop of Rome[6]." Hereunto, for

[1 — eam potestatem (papæ) cui nulla par in terris esse potest.
—Jo. Hieron. Albani. de Potest. Pap. par. II. num. 300. apud Tract.
tract. tom. XIII. fol. 82. Venet. 1584.]

[2 The editor has not been able to verify this reference.]

[3 Romanus pontifex ... jura omnia in scrinio pectoris sui censetur
habere.—Bonifac. VIII. Corp. Jur. Can. Sexti Decretal. tit. II. de Constit. cap. I. Tom. II. p. 285.]

[4 — est hodie apud pontificem gladius uterque et utraque
jurisdictio. Par. I. cap. 11. Papa.... eum (imperatorem) deponit
.... sic ipse solus dici debet monarcha. cap. 5. — nullas sententias
principis esse declarat (pontifex). cap. 9. — fateri oportet pontificem
Cæsare superiorem. cap. 44. Papa... debet juste dici princeps regum
terræ. cap. 12. — quoniam Christus fuit Dominus terrenorum et judex
.... ergo et papa, vicarius ejus. cap. 17. Pontifex.... habet plenitudinem potestatis, et.... ei est commissa.... administratio temporalium. Par. II. cap. 7. — cui (pontifici) cuncta temporalia et spi-
ritualia subsunt. cap. 3. Papa solus omnibus et in omnibus præest.
cap. 4. — in terris dicitur habere cœleste arbitrium.—Anton. de
Rosellis de Monarchia, apud Goldast. Hanov. 1611. The treatise
abounds with similar statements.]

[5 ... cum dominus Papa sit judex ordinarius omnium hominum.
Decret. Gregor. IX. Lib. II. tit. XXVIII. Gloss. in cap. 59. col. 962. Par.
1585. Universa Christianitas provincia sua (i.e. papæ) intelligitur.
Hostiens. Aur. Sum. Lib. I. cap. 6. fol. 36. Colon. 1612.]

[6 Igitur ecclesiæ unius et unicæ unum corpus, unum caput....
Christus videlicet, et Christi vicarius, Petrus, Petrique successor;
dicente Domino ipsi Petro, Pasce oves meas.... per quod commisisse
sibi intelligitur universas.... In hac ejusque potestate duos esse
gladios, spiritualem videlicet et temporalem, evangelicis dictis instrui-
mur ...Si suprema (potestas, i.e. ecclesiastica, deviat) a solo Deo,

conclusion, I will add the words of the glosser, who saith, *In Ca. Quinto de Transl. Episcopi.* Tit. vii. " The pope," saith he, "is said to have a heavenly power; and therefore he altereth the very nature of things, by applying the things that are of the substance of one thing unto another: and of nothing he can make something; and that sentence which is of no force he can make to be of force; because in those things with him, what he willeth, his will is instead of reason. Neither is there any may say unto him, Why dost thou so? for he can dispense above the law, and of unrighteousness make righteousness, correcting and changing laws; for he hath the fulness of power[7]." Thus far he.

But who heareth these things without horror both of body and mind? Who understandeth not, that the saying of Daniel is fulfilled, "He shall think that he may change times and laws?" Who understandeth not, that the saying of Paul[8] is fulfilled, who saith, "I know this, that after my departing shall grievous wolves enter in among you, not sparing the flock; also of your own selves shall men arise, speaking perverse things, to draw away disciples after them?" For from bishops, and from them that advance bishops, came forth this man of sin; who placeth himself in the throne of the Lamb, and challengeth those things to himself which are proper only to the Lamb: of which sort are the supreme government, priesthood, lordship, and full power in the church; whereof I have spoken enough in the former sermons. Whom doth it now not move to think, that that saying of Paul is fulfilled, " The adversary, or enemy[9] of Christ shall be revealed, and

(margin) Dan. vii. viii.

(margin) Acts xx.

(margin) 2 Thess. ii.

non ab homine, poterit judicari .... Porro subesse Romano pontifici omni humanæ creaturæ declaramus, dicimus, definimus, et pronunciamus omnino esse de necessitate salutis.—Bonifac. VIII. de Majorit. et Obed. Extrav. Comm. Lib. I. tit. 8. cap. I. Corp. Jur. Can. tom. II. p. 394. Par. 1687.]

[7 Papa dicitur habere cœleste arbitrium: et ideo etiam naturam rerum immutat, substantialia unius rei applicando alii; et de nullo (nihilo) potest aliquid facere: et sententiam quæ nulla est aliquam facere (facit aliquam): quia in his quæ vult ei est pro ratione voluntas; nec est qui ei dicat, Cur ita facis? Ipse enim potest supra jus dispensare, et de injustitia facere justitiam, corrigendo jura et mutando: nam plenitudinem obtinet potestatis.—Corp. Jur. Can. Decretal. Greg. IX. Lib. I. De Transl. Episc. Tit. 7. Gloss. in cap. 3. col. 217. Lugd. 1624.]

[8 Pauli quoque, Lat.]   [9 æmulus, Lat.]

shall be exalted above all that is called God, or that is worshipped[1]; so that he, as God, sitteth in the temple of God,
shewing himself that he is God?"

But the pope's champions dispute, that it is for the profit
and salvation, yea, necessary for the church, to have some one
bishop to have preeminence over the other, both in dignity
and power. But let them dispute and set forth this their idol
as they please: they which will simply confess the truth must
needs freely acknowledge, that the pope is antichrist; for that
which these men babble of the supremacy of the pope is flatly
repugnant to the doctrine of the gospel and of the apostles.
For what more evident thing can be alleged against their disputations, than that which the Lord said to his disciples, when
they strived for sovereignty? "The kings of the Gentiles reign
over them, and they that bear rule over them are called gracious lords. But ye shall not be so; but let the greatest among
you be as the least; and the chiefest, as he that serveth. For
who is greater; he that sitteth at table, or he that serveth? is
not he that sitteth at table? And I am among you as he that
serveth." This place I alleged and discussed briefly also in
my former sermon[2]. This simple and plain truth shall continue invincible against all the disputations of these harpies*.
The most holy apostles of our Lord Christ will not be lords
over any man under pretence of religion[3]; yea, St Peter in
plain words forbiddeth lordship over God's heritage, and commandeth bishops to be examples to the flock.

Whereas they object, that Christ said to Peter, "Thou art
Peter, and upon this rock I will build my church; and I will
give unto thee the keys of the kingdom of heaven," &c.
and, "Feed my sheep;" and thereupon that St Peter was
appointed over all the apostles, and in them over all priests,
ministers[4] and bishops, the chief and prince, yea, and the
monarch of the whole world; it maketh nothing at all to
establish their dominion or lordship. We willingly grant, that
St Peter is the chief of the apostles; and we also ourselves do
willingly call St Peter the prince of the apostles; but in that
sense that we call Moses, David, Helias, or Esay, the chief or
prince of the prophets; that is to say, such as have obtained
far more excellent gifts than the rest. But that Peter was the

[1 numen, Lat. and Erasmus.]   [2 See above, page 87.]
[3 fidei, Lat.]   [4 presbyterorum, Lat.]

chief or prince, after that sort that these men will have him, we deny, and deny again most constantly. And therewithal we defend St Peter, and clear him from those spots, wherewithal these men strive to defile him even being dead. He had not remained faithful towards his master, if he had taken to himself rule or dominion. In all places we read that Peter was equal with the other disciples; but in no place in the scripture that he was their master. And St Paul, in the beginning of his epistle to the Galatians, sheweth in many words, that he in apostleship is nothing inferior to Peter : neither, when he came to Jerusalem, came he to that end he might kiss his feet, or to profess subjection; but that by their meeting and friendly conference together every one throughout all churches might understand there was perfect consent in opinions between Peter and Paul, and that, as touching apostleship, their authority was equal. In the same place Paul calleth James, Peter, and John, pillars : he doth not attribute that prerogative to Peter alone; which notwithstanding he had rightly done, if he had received supremacy at the hands of the Lord, as these men do affirm. How cometh it, that Peter doth nothing of his own head, but referreth ecclesiastical matters to the rest of the disciples, as to his fellows in authority? which thing we may see in the Acts. In another place he calleth himself a fellow-elder, not the prince of priests. When he was sent by the apostles with John into Samaria, he requireth not another to be sent, lest his supremacy should seem to be diminished, but willingly obeyeth. But if we should grant, that Peter was chief of the apostles after that sort as these men do affirm; would it thereupon follow, that the pope is the prince of the whole church, yea, of the whole world? For as the pope is not Peter; so the twelve or eleven apostles are not the whole world. Moreover, Peter could not give that he had not: he had not an empire over the whole world; therefore he gave it not.

But Constantine gave it to Sylvester, say they. But if we never so perfectly agreed, that the donation of Constantine were true, and not feigned or forged (which yet the best learned men do affirm); yet would not Sylvester himself have received an imperie, or dominion, though it had been offered

Of the donation of Constantine[5].

[5 On the Donation of Constantine, see Fulke's Answers, ed. Parker Soc. page 360, note 4.]

him.   For the voice of the high and heavenly prince, Christ,
had been of more authority with him, ("The kings of the
nations bear rule over them, but it shall not be so with you,")
than the foolish affection of an earthly emperor.   Shall we
believe that Peter[1] would have received secular power with
imperial government, if the emperor Nero had proffered it
him? No, in no wise. For this word of the Lord took deep
root in his inward bowels: "But it shall not be so with you."
Before he had received the Holy Ghost, wandering in blindness with the rest of the multitude of Jews, he imagined that
the kingdom of Christ in earth should be an earthly kingdom:
but after he received the Holy Ghost, he understood that the
throne of Christ, the chief king and emperor, was not on the
earth, but situated in heaven[2].   He knew that Christ our
Lord fled into the wilderness, when the people thought to
2 Kings v. make him a king.   He knew that Helisæus by most wholesome counsel refused the reward of Naaman, the prince; and
that Giesi his servant, to his everlasting reproach and overthrow of his own health, required it afterward at his hand.
St Peter would not take upon him the charge of the poor,
lest he should thereby with less diligence attend upon prayer
and preaching of the word of God; which thing the Acts of
the Apostles do witness.   Who therefore thinketh it likely
that he, casting aside the office of apostleship, would have
received the empire even of the whole world?   He denieth
that one man can both happily execute the charge of the ministry of the word, and also minister unto the necessity of the
poor[3].   But what pope will they give unto us, that hath the
Spirit more fully than Peter had? which can perform that
which Peter could not? which can not only now both serve
at tables, but also can govern the whole world?   Therefore
they are trifles which they rehearse to us touching the donation
of Constantine.   Constantine was more sound than that he
would frame such a donation, which he knew was repugnant
to the doctrine of Christ.   Sylvester was more upright than
to receive that which he knew could not be received without
the utter overthrow of the ministry of the word.   But if

[1] Petrum apostolum, Lat.]
[2] Ac regnum ejus non esse ex hoc mundo, Lat. omitted; and
that his kingdom is not of this world.]
[3] mensis ministrare, Lat.]

Constantine gave that altogether, which he is said to have given; and that Sylvester did not refuse his donation; both of them offended, because both dealt against the word of God.

I saw what of late years Augustine Steuchus, a man other- Augustine Steuchus of the donation of Constantine.
wise well learned and of much reading, hath written touching
Constantine's donation against Laurentius Valla[4] : but he
bringeth no sound arguments, though he wonderfully rage[5],
and put all the force of his eloquence in ure, and finally, do
busily heap together from all places whatsoever by any manner means may seem to further this cause. And truly, that
book seemeth better worthy to be trodden under foot, than to
be occupied[6] in good men's hands. For, that I make no
words, that he calleth that ecclesiastical kingdom of Rome
oftentimes eternal[7], whereas the kingdom of Christ and the
saints is only eternal; doth he not most manifestly place the
pope in the seat of Christ our Lord? For, after he had recited the testimony of one pope Nicolas, he forthwith addeth: "Thou hearest that the high bishop of Constantine is
called God, and counted for God. This verily was done, when
he adorned him with that famous edict; he worshipped him as
God, as the successor of Christ and Peter. As much as he
could, he gave divine honours unto him, he worshipped him
as the lively image of Christ[8]." Thus far he in the sixty-
seventh section of his book. Neither hath he written that
which is unlike unto this, twenty-eighth section. For he,
remembering certain imaginations of his own conceived of the
pope, he feigneth I cannot tell what fruit would come thereof,
if it were made known among the furthest Indians, that all

[4 Augustini Steuchi Eugubini Bibliothecarii contra Laurentium Vallam, De falsa Donatione Constantini. Libri duo. Opp. Tom. III. fol. 253, &c. Paris. 1577.]

[5 ringatur, Lat.]   [6 teratur, Lat.]

[7 Vere profertur a nonnullis de ecclesia carmen Virgilianum oraculum summi Jovis, *Imperium sine fine dedi.* Hoc inquam de eccle-sia, de Romanæ sedis majestate vere profertur, quæ fecit ut imperium Romanorum esset sine fine renatum in ipsa ecclesia.—Steuchi de falsa Don. Con. fol. 258.]

[8 Audis summum pontificem a Constantino Deum appellatum, habitum pro Deo. Hoc videlicet factum est, cum eum præclaro illo edicto decoravit, adoravit uti Deum, uti Christi et Petri succes-sorem: divinos honores ei quoad ejus potuit contulit; velut vivam Christi imaginem veneratus est.—Ibid. fol. 277.]

the kingdoms of the world are governed by the pope's beck; that kings worship him, as being a thing very well known to them, that he is the successor of Christ; and therefore that they receive him not so much a mortal man, as God himself in him, who hath substituted him in his room on earth; and therefore we ought to abstain from reproachful words, if he sin in anything as a man, because in him they worship the Son of God[1]. These wicked rejoicings, and these flattering or rather sacrilegious voices, would Peter have suffered, think you; who lifted up Cornelius, when he fell down before him, and would have worshipped him, and said, "Arise; I myself also am a man?" We read also, that the angel himself said unto John, which fell down and would have worshipped at the angel's feet: "See thou do it not; for I am thy fellow-servant, and of thy brethren the prophets." It is also written of Herod Agrippa, because he repressed not the flattering voices of the people, which cried when he had ended his oration, "It is the voice of a God, and not of a man," that therefore he was stricken of the angel of God, and he rotted away, being eaten of worms. Therefore we, since we know that Christ himself, the Son of God, doth reign as yet in the church, as to whom only all glory and power is given; and hath not substituted any man on the earth, in whom he will be worshipped and served; we worship and serve Christ Jesus, the Son of God, only; and utterly abhor the pope as antichrist, and a dunghill-god, or, if you will, a god of the jakeshouse, together with the sacrilegious[2] clawbacks and blasphemous flatterers.

The Lord in very deed said to St Peter: "Thou art Peter; and upon this rock I will build my church: and I will give thee the keys of the kingdom of heaven," &c. But what make these sayings to establish the monarchy, prerogative,

Marginal notes: Acts x. Rev. xxii. Acts xii. Thou art Peter, &c.

[1 Cur non potius inducat (Laurentius) Sylvestrum nescio quam cogitationem concipientem quæ mihi interdum occurrit: Si quis apud remotissimos Indos degens.... prædicaret esse....religionem; cujus caput.... tantæ potestatis.... habeatur, ut omnia regna nutibus ejus regnantur;.... quem reges adorent, quibus perspectissimum sit.... successorem esse Christi.... Ob hanc causam solitum esse apud eos, ut non tam mortalem illum hominem, quam in eo Deum ipsum, qui eum sibi in terris suffecisset, suspicientes.... abstinentesque maledictis, si quid is ut homo peccet, propterea quod in eo venerentur filium Dei.—Ibid. fol. 258.]

[2 ed. 1577, *his* sacrilegious. Sacrilegis suis, Lat.]

and dignity of the pope? Peter is commended of the Lord for the constancy of his faith: whereupon also he received his name, being called Peter *a petra*, that is, of the rock, wherein he settled himself by a true faith. Christ is that rock whereunto Peter stayed. He heareth, that this shall be the perpetual foundation of the church; that all shall be received into the fellowship of the church, who with a true faith confess with Peter, that Jesus Christ is the very Son of God, and rest upon him as the only rock and salvation. Moreover, the keys of the kingdom of God are promised unto Peter: but when they are delivered, they are not given to Peter alone, but to all the apostles. For " the keys" are not (as these men imagine) a certain dominion and jurisdiction; but the ministry of opening and shutting the kingdom of heaven; to let into the church, and to shut out; which is wrought by the preaching of the gospel, as it shall anon be said more abundantly. After the same manner, when Christ said to Peter, " Feed my sheep," he did not give unto Peter the monarchy of the whole world and dominion over all creatures, but committed unto him a pastoral cure; of which thing I have spoken in my last sermon; as also elsewhere both often and largely against the supremacy of the bishop of Rome[3]. Unto the ancient writers of the church which they object unto us, testifying I know not what of the supremacy of Peter, we will answer in one word; that we care not so much what the old writers thought herein, as what Christ the Son of God instituted; and what the apostles (whose authority doth far excel the judgment[4] of the old writers) practised, and what they have left both in their writing and examples for us to judge and follow: whereof I have also spoken in the second sermon of this decade.

We have almost gone further than we determined: therefore, that we may draw to an end, we have spoken of the order or office, which the Lord instituted in his church; and whom he hath placed over it, by whose labour he will establish[5], govern, further, and preserve his church. These things which remain to be spoken we will put off until to-morrow: for they are longer than at this time can be finished; but more worthy and more excellent than that they ought to be restrained into few words, &c.

[3 See above, page 88, and Bullinger de Episc. Instit. et Funct. cap. 13, fol. 137. Tigur. 1538.]

[4 auctoritatem, Lat.]   [5 fundare, Lat.]

OF CALLING UNTO THE MINISTRY OF THE WORD OF
GOD. WHAT MANNER OF MEN, AND AFTER WHAT
FASHION, MINISTERS OF THE WORD MUST BE
ORDAINED IN THE CHURCH. OF THE KEYS
OF THE CHURCH. WHAT THE OFFICE OF
THEM IS THAT BE ORDAINED. OF
THE MANNER OF TEACHING THE
CHURCH; AND OF THE HOLY
LIFE OF THE PASTORS.

THE FOURTH SERMON.

In this present sermon, by God's assistance, we will, as
briefly and plainly as we can, set forth unto you, dearly beloved, what manner of men ministers should be; and after what
sort at this day it behoveth us[1] to ordain ministers; not
speaking again of the office, but of persons meet for the office.
For neither do I think it necessary or profitable to shew at
large, that that order or function instituted by Christ in the
church sufficeth even at this day to gather[2], govern, and
preserve the church of God on earth; yea, without these orders,
which in these last ages new invention hath instituted: for
that doth the thing itself witness, and the absolute perfection
of the primitive church avoucheth it.   But that it may be
plainly understood of all men, whom it behoves the church at
this day to ordain ministers, we will speak a little more amply
of the calling of the ministers of the church.

Of the calling unto the ministry, and the kinds of calling.   Calling is no other thing than a lawful appointing of a
meet minister.   The same also may be called both ordination
and election, though one word be more large in signification
than the other.   Election goeth before by nature; for whom
we choose, those we call.   Ordination comprehendeth either of
them.   But there are numbered almost of all men four kinds
of calling.   The two former are lawful, the two latter are unlawful.   And the first kind is, whereby ministers are called,
neither of men, nor by man, but by God; as it is read, that
Esay the prophet and the apostle Paul were called.   This
kind for the most part is confirmed with signs or miracles, and
is called a heavenly[3] and secret calling.   The second kind of

[1 nobis conveniat, Lat.]   [2 ad excitandam, Lat.]
[3 divina, Lat.]

calling is made of God indeed, but by the ordination of men: after which sort it is read that St Matthew, Luke, and Timothy, were created ministers of the church. This kind is ordinary, public, used of men, and at this day common: wherein indeed God calleth, bestowing necessary gifts upon his ministers, and appointing laws to those that do elect; and they, following those laws, do ordinarily elect him whom they by signs conjecture to be first called of God: I mean by signs, gifts necessary for ministers.

Now the third kind of calling, which of the unlawful callings is the first, cometh indeed from men, but not from God; when as for favour and rewards some unworthy person is ordained. And here is sin committed, as well of those that are ordained, as of those that bear rule in the ordination. Of those that are ordained; when they desire to be placed in the ministry, for which either they do not understand, or they will not understand, that they be very unfit, being destitute of necessary gifts: or else, when they are sufficiently furnished with knowledge of the scriptures and other things, yet they take not the right path to this function, that is to say, when they respect not the glory of God but their own gain. For there is required of them that are to be ordained a testimony of their own conscience, and a secret calling, to wit, whereby we are well known to ourselves to be moved to take upon us this office, not through ambition, not for covetousness, not for desire to feed the belly, nor of any other lewd[4] affection; but through the sincere fear and love of God, and of a desire to edify the church of God: of which thing very eloquently[5] and holily hath St Paul written in 1 Thess. ii. Besides this, the testimony of other of sound learning and skilfulness in things is also required: for all of us please ourselves, and esteem ourselves to be worthy, to whom the government of the church may be committed; whereas we foully deceive ourselves. And they that have the authority of ordination do offend, when as in ordaining of ministers they regard not what God by laws set down hath willed herein to be done, and what the state and safety of the church requireth; but what is for the commodity of him that is to be ordained. Oftentimes, therefore, unworthy persons are ordained; or such as are unlearned, and not very sound[6]; or else such as are

Calling by favour and gifts.

[4 pravo, Lat.]   [5 elegantissime, Lat.]   [6 parum sinceri, Lat.]

sufficiently learned, but not of good conversation; or such
as are simple and are good Christians, but unfit and unskilful
pastors: and unto this they are allured through favour or
bribes. Wherefore they provoke the most heavy wrath of
almighty God upon themselves, and make themselves partakers
of all those sins, whereof they are the authors, in that they do
not uprightly execute the charge which is committed unto them.

Simony.

Our elders[1] called this sin simony, an offence punishable with
no less punishment than shameful reproach[2] and death everlasting. Anthemius, the emperor, writing to Armasius, among
other things saith: "Let no man make merchandise of the
degree of priesthood by the greatness of price; but let every
man be esteemed after his deserts, not according to that he is
able to give. Let that profane thirst of covetousness cease to
bear rule in the church, and let that horrible fault be banished
far off from holy congregations. After this manner in our
time let the bishop be chosen; being chaste and lowly, so as in
what place soever he come he may purge all things with the
uprightness of his own life: let a bishop be ordained not with
price, but with prayers. He ought to be so far from desire
of promotion, that he must be sought for by compulsion: and
being desired, he ought to shun it; and if he be entreated, he
ought to fly away: let this only be his furtherance, that he is
importune by excuses to avoid from it. For truly he is unworthy of the ministry, that is not ordained against his will[3]."
Thus much he; who, if he should at this day come to Rome,
he would think without doubt he were come into a strange
world; yea, into the mart of Simon, not of Peter, but both of
Magus the Samaritan, and Giesi the Israelite.

[1 vetustas, Lat.]

[2 nunquam delendo probro, Lat. See Bingham, Orig. Eccles.
Book IV. chap. iii. § 14; and Book XVI. Chap. vi. § 28.]

[3 Nemo gradum sacerdotii venalitate pretii mercetur; quantum
quisque meretur, non quantum dare sufficit, æstimetur... Cesset alta-
ribus imminere profanus ardor avaritiæ, et a sacris adytis repellatur
piaculare flagitium. Itaque castus et humilis nostris temporibus
eligatur episcopus, ut quocumque locorum pervenerit, omnia vitæ
propriæ integritate purificet. Non pretio, sed precibus, ordinetur
antistes. Tantum ab ambitu debet esse sepositus, ut quæratur cogen-
dus, rogatus recedat, invitatus effugiat, sola illi suffragetur necessitas
excusandi. Profecto enim indignus est sacerdotio, nisi fuerit ordinatus invitus.—Justin. Cod. Lib. I. tit. 4. cap. 29. Tom. I. p. 43. Lugd.
1551.]

The fourth kind of calling is that, whereby any man thrusteth himself into the ministry of his own private affection[4], being neither ordained of God, neither yet by man. Of these kind of men the Lord saith in Jeremy: "I have not sent them, and yet they ran." Cyprian, writing unto Antonianus, calleth such schismatics, who usurp unto them the office of a bishop, no man giving it them[5]. And this kind of calling is unproperly called a calling.

Jer. xxiii.

Wherefore it is evident, that in the church there must needs be a calling, and that public and lawful; as well for many other causes, as especially for these : that the ordinance of God be not neglected, and that the discipline of the church be retained, and that all men in the church may know who are preferred to the ecclesiastical ministry. Albeit therefore Paul, the apostle and doctor of the Gentiles, in the beginning were not sent of men, neither by men, but of God only; yet the same Paul, at the commandment of the Holy Ghost, is separated by the church of Antioch, together with Barnabas, to the ministry of the Gentiles. After the same manner many other were sent or called of God; whom nevertheless it behoved to be ordained also by men. For Paul in another place saith : " And no man taketh this honour unto himself, but he that is called of God, as was Aaron." And again : " How shall they hear without a preacher, and how shall they preach except they be sent ?" &c.

A calling necessary in the church.

Acts xiii.

Heb. v.

Rom. x.

As concerning that second kind of calling, which is common, and at this day received in the church, and yet appointed[6] by the Lord, there are three things to be considered : first, who they be that call; that is, who have right and authority to call, or to ordain ministers : secondly, who, or what manner of men, are to be ordained : lastly, after what manner they that be called are to be ordained.

And first of all ; that the Lord hath given to his church power and authority to elect and ordain fit ministers, we have declared before, in the second sermon of this decade, by the example of the ancient[7] churches in the world, Jerusalem and Antioch : of which two, the church of Hierusalem did not only ordain seven deacons, but also Matthias the apostle ; and the

Who may choose ministers in the church.

[4 arbitrio, Lat.]

[5 Quisquis ille fuerit ... profanus est, alienus est, foris est.—— Cyprian. Ep. LV. Opp. p. 104. Oxon. 1682.]

[6 traditam, Lat.]   [7 vetustissimarum, Lat.]

church of Antioch separated into the ministry the famous apo-
Acts xiv. stles of Christ, Paul and Barnabas[1]. Whereunto appertaineth[2],
that the churches of the Gentiles, being instructed of Paul and
Barnabas, ordained[3] them elders or governors of their churches
by election had by voices[4]. The chiefest in this election were
the pastors themselves; for Peter governing the action, Matthias was created apostle by the church. This form or order
the ancient church diligently observed many years. For Cyprian, *Epist.* Lib. I. Epist. 4 : " The common people," saith he,
" hath especially power either to choose worthy priests, or to
refuse them that be unworthy. Which thing also we see to
descend from the authority of God; that the priest be chosen in
the presence of the common people, before all men's eyes, and
be allowed worthy and meet by public judgment and witness:
Numb. xx. as in Numbers the Lord commanded Moses, and said : ' Take
Aaron thy brother, and Eleazar his son, and bring them up
into the mount, before all the congregation.' God commandeth
the priest to be ordained before the whole congregation : that
is, he teacheth and sheweth that the ordaining of priests ought
not to be done without the knowledge of the people being
present; that in their presence either the vices of the evil
might be discovered, or the deserts of the good commended;
and that that is a just and lawful ordaining, which shall be examined by the election and judgment of all[5]." Thus far he.
This custom and manner endured to the time of St Augustine;

[1 See above, page 43.]   [2 Quibus accedit, Lat.]
[3 delegerunt, Lat.]

[4 collatis suffragiis, Lat.   Illud χειροτονήσαντες ita ponitur, ut
presbyteros vel populi delectos esse suffragiis, vel manuum impositione
inauguratos fuisse, possimus intelligere.—Bullinger. de Episc. Instit.
&c. fol. 98. Tig. 1538.]

[5 Quando ipsa (plebs) maxime habeat potestatem vel eligendi
dignos sacerdotes, vel indignos recusandi. Quod et ipsum videmus
de divina auctoritate descendere, ut sacerdos, plebe praesente, sub
omnium oculis deligatur, et dignus atque idoneus publico judicio ac
testimonio comprobetur; sicut in Numeris Dominus Moysi praecepit,
dicens, Apprehende Aaron fratrem tuum, et Eleazarum filium ejus,
et imponas eos in montem coram omni synagoga...Id est, instruit
et ostendit (Deus) ordinationes sacerdotales non nisi sub populi assis-
tentis conscientia fieri oportere, ut plebe praesente vel detegantur
malorum crimina, vel bonorum merita praedicentur; et sit ordinatio
justa et legitima, quae omnium suffragio et judicio fuerit examinata.—
Cypr. Opp. Epist. 67. pp. 171, 2.   Oxon. 1682.]

for it is to be seen in his hundred and tenth epistle, which witnesseth that, the people giving a shout, Augustine ordained Eradius for his successor[6]. In these latter times, because the people made often tumults in the elections of pastors, the ordination was committed to chosen men of the pastors, magistrates, and people. These three kinds of men propounded or named notable men, out of whom he which was thought the best was chosen. There is somewhat of this *In Justiniani Imperat. Novel. Constitut.* 123.[7]

They which think that all power of ordaining ministers is in the bishops', diocesans', or archbishops' hands, do use these places of the scripture: "For this cause I left thee in Creta" (saith Paul to Titus), "that thou shouldest ordain elders in every city." And again: "Lay hands suddenly on no man." But we say, that the apostles did not exercise tyranny in the churches; and that they themselves alone did not execute all things about election or ordination, other men in the church being excluded: for the apostles of Christ ordained bishops or elders in the church, but not without communicating their counsel with the churches; yea, and not without having[8] the consent and approbation of the people; which may appear by the election or ordination of Matthias, which we have now once or twice recited. Truly, the Lord in the law saith to Moses: "Thou shalt appoint thee judges." But in another place he saith[9]: "Thou shalt seek out among all the people whom thou mayest make rulers." And again, Moses unto the same people[10]: "Bring you men of wisdom and understanding, and I will make them rulers over you," &c. Therefore, as Moses doth nothing of his own will in the election of the magistrate, though it were said to him, "Thou shalt appoint thee judges," but doth all things communicating his counsel with the people; so undoubtedly Titus[11], though it were said unto him, "Ordain elders in every city," yet he understood, that hereby nothing was permitted to him which

Marginal notes:
That bishops alone have not power to make ministers. Tit. i.
1 Tim. v.
Deut. xvi.
Exod. xviii.
Deut. i.

[6 — in omnium vestrum notitiam profero, presbyterum Eradium mihi successorem volo. A populo acclamatum est, Deo gratias, &c.—August. Ep. cx. Opp. Tom. ii. fol. 100. col. 2. Par. 1531.]

[7 — ex tribus illis personis...maxime idoneus ordinetur.—Justin. Novell. Constit. 123. p. 353. Basil. 1561.]

[8 adeoque ex, Lat. and so with.]

[9 This was Jethro's direction.]   [10 Ad ipsum populum, Lat.]

[11 beatus Titus, Lat.]

he might do privately as he thought good, not having the advice and consent of the churches. Wherefore they sin not at all, that, shaking off the yoke and tyranny of the bishops of Rome for good and reasonable causes, do recover that ancient right granted by Christ to the churches.

Neither makes it any great matter, whether discreet men chosen of the church, or the whole church itself, do ordain fit ministers; and that either by voices[1], either by lots, or after some certain necessary[2] and holy manner; for in these things godly men will not move contention, so that all things be done holily and in order. But I will not here rip up the crafts, deceits, practices, and grievous wars, taken in hand for this right of ordaining, with shedding of much blood, spoilings, and lamentable burnings of countries. The histories of the acts of Henry the IV. and V., and also of the affairs of the Frederiches[4], do most evidently witness, how impudently and abominably the popes of Rome, with their sworn friends the bishops, have behaved themselves. Peradventure I shall have occasion to speak of this matter elsewhere more at large.

Master Bullinger hath written more largely of this matter elsewhere in these words: "Because amongst the tumults and factions of the people nothing was done according to the prescript of God's word, but all things done upon affections, whereby the worst were ordained instead of the best; to the end that this might not be, and that the best, the learnedest, and the godliest ministers might be appointed unto churches, the whole right of choosing them was granted unto bishops, &c." And a little after: "Wherefore if any (of the bishops) do well use this right or authority to the edifying of the church, it is very well. But if any of them do abuse it through tyranny, let them either be brought into good order by the godly magistrate, or else let the right or authority to appoint ministers be put from them[3]."

What manner of men are to be ordained ministers.
Now we will declare, what manner of men it behoveth to ordain ministers: truly not whoso lust, but the most choicest men of sound religion, furnished with all kind of sciences, exercised in the scriptures, cunning in the mystery of faith and religion[5], strong and constant, earnest, painful, diligent, faithful, watchful, modest, of a holy and approved conver-

[1 suffragia, Lat.]   [2 commoda, Lat.]
[3 These extracts from Bullinger's treatise De Episcop. Instit. et Funct. cap. 7, fol. 99, are not given in edd. 1577 and 1584; nor in the folio Latin ed. of the Decades, Tiguri, 1552; but they are found in the London ed. of the Latin, 8vo.—See above, p. 111.]
[4 See Foxe, Acts and Mon. Vol. II. pp. 125, &c. 174, &c. 190, &c. 455, &c. Lond. 1837; and Tytler's Elements of Gen. Hist. Part II. Sect. 14 and 16.]
[5 tenentes mysterium fidei, Lat.]

sation, lest through their corruption of life and scant good name and fame the whole ministry become vile, and that which with wholesome doctrine they build up their wicked life do pull down again.   We will rehearse the rule of the apostle, fully comprehending all things pertaining to this matter: "Thou shalt ordain elders, or bishops," saith he, Tit. i. "if any be blameless, the husband of one wife, having faithful children, which are not slandered of riot, neither are disobedient; for if a man cannot rule his own house, how shall he 1 Tim. iii. care for the church of God? For a bishop must be blameless, as the steward of God; (for it is required in the disposers, 1 Cor. iv. that a man be found faithful;) not froward, not angry, no striker, but gentle[6], not given to wine, not covetous, not given to filthy lucre, but harborous, one that loveth goodness, watchful, sober, righteous, godly, temperate, modest, apt to teach, holding fast the faithful word which is according to doctrine, that he may be able both to exhort in wholesome doctrine, and to improve[7] them that say against it, and to stop their mouths: no young scholar, lest he, being puffed up, fall into the condemnation of the devil.   He must also have a good report of them that are without, lest he fall into the rebuke and snare of the devil."   All these are the words of the apostle, recited out of the 1st Epistle to Timothy, and in his epistle to Titus.

Wherefore exact judgment and great diligence shall be Censure and examination. very needful in this case, to discuss all the points of doctrine and life.   I say there shall be needful of a strait trial of life and perfect examination of learning: for this is not a matter of small weight; the whole safety of the church hangeth hereupon.   If any unworthy and unlearned be ordained, the whole church for the most part is neglected, led astray, and overthrown.   But we do not mean a childlike and scholarlike examination; but a grave and strait examination of knowledge in the scripture and the true interpretation thereof, of the charge of a pastor, of the mysteries of sound faith, and of other such like points.   And that the elders in times past were very diligent in these things, it may appear by that which Ælius Lampridius, in the life of Alexander Severus, rehearseth; that it was the manner among the Christians to offer the names of their bishops to the whole church afore

[6 alienum a pugnis, Lat. omitted.]   [7 improve: convince.]

they were received, if happily any among the people would shew a reason that he were unworthy of such an office[1].

Whereupon Justinian the emperor, Const. 123 : " If in the time of ordination (saith he) any accuser stand up, and say he is unworthy to be ordained; let all things be deferred, and let examination and judgment first be had[2]." And here I will at this present recite the decree of the 4th council of Carthage upon this matter, which is after this sort : " When a bishop is to be ordained, let him be first examined, whether he be by nature wise, if he be able to teach, if he be temperate in behaviour, if chaste in life, if he be sober, if careful about his own business, if lowly, if courteous, if merciful, if learned, if instructed in the law of the Lord, if wary and careful in the sense and meaning of the scriptures, if exercised in the opinions of the church ; and above all things, if he teach the grounds of faith with substantial words (or perhaps, of less moment), that is to say, confirming that the Father, and the Son, and the Holy Ghost, are one God, and avouching the whole Godhead of the Trinity to be co-essential, and consubstantial, and co-eternal, and co-omnipotent ; if he acknowledge every person by himself in the Trinity to be perfect God, and the whole three persons one God ; if he believe the incarnation of God, not wrought in the Father, neither in the Holy Ghost, but in the Son only : so that he who was the Son in God the Father, the same should be made the son of man in the manhood of his mother ; very God of the Father, and very man of his mother, having flesh in the womb of his mother, and having in him a human and reasonable soul together of either nature, that is to say, God and man, one person, one Son, one Christ, one Lord, creator of all things, and the author, lord, and governor of all creatures, with the Father and the Holy Ghost ; who suffered a true suffering of his flesh, died with

[1 Ubi aliquos voluisset vel rectores provinciis dare, vel præpositos facere, . . . nomina eorum proponebat, hortans populum ut siquis haberet criminis, probaret. . . . dicebatque grave esse, quum id Christiani et Judæi facerent in prædicandis sacerdotibus qui ordinandi sunt, &c.—Æl. Lamprid. Vit. Alex. Sever. cap. 45. Hist. August. Scriptor. p. 570. Lugd. Bat. 1661.]

[2 Si quis adversus eum qui episcopus ordinandus est . . . accusationem instituat, suspendetur hujus ordinatio, atque prius . . . examinetur, &c.—Justin. Novell. Constit. 123, p. 354. Basil. 1561.]

the true death of his body, rose again with the true taking again of his flesh and a true taking again of his soul, wherein he shall come to judge the quick and the dead. He must also be asked, if he believe one and the selfsame author and Lord of the new and old Testament, that is to say, of the law, the prophets, and apostles; if the devil became evil, not by creation, but by choice. He must also be asked, if he believe the resurrection of this flesh which we bear, and none other; if he believe the judgment to come, and that every one shall receive, according to that they have done in the flesh, either punishments or rewards; if he forbid not marriage, if he condemn not bigamy or second marriage; if he condemn not the eating of flesh; if he have fellowship with penitent persons that are reconciled; if he believe that all sins in baptism are forgiven, as well original sin wherein we are born, as also those which we commit willingly; if he believe that none which are without the catholic church can be saved, &c. When he shall be examined upon all these points, and found fully instructed; then let him be ordained a bishop, with the consent of the clergy and laity, and by the assembly of the bishops of the whole province, and especially of the metropolitan[3]." This council is said to be celebrated in the year of

[3 Qui episcopus ordinandus est antea examinetur, si natura sit prudens, si docibilis, si moribus temperatus, si vita castus, si sobrius, si semper suis negotiis cavens, si humilis, si affabilis, si misericors, si literatus, si in lege Domini instructus, si in scripturarum sensibus cautus, si in dogmatibus ecclesiasticis exercitatus; et ante omnia, si fidei documenta verbis simplicibus (Bullinger wrote, verbis duplicibus, simplicibus forte) asserat, id est, Patrem et Filium et Spiritum sanctum unum Deum esse confirmans, totamque Trinitatis deitatem co-essentialem et consubstantialem et coæternalem et coomnipotentem prædicans; si singularem quamque in Trinitate personam plenum Deum (Bullinger read further, et totas tres personas unum Deum); si incarnationem divinam non in Patre neque in Spiritu Sancto factam, sed in Filio tantum credat; ut qui erat in divinitate Dei Patris Filius, ipse fieret in homine hominis matris filius; Deus verus ex Patre, homo verus ex matre, carnem ex matris visceribus habens, et animam humanam rationalem simul in eo ambæ (Bullinger read, utriusque) naturæ, id est, Deus et homo, una persona, unus Filius, unus Christus, unus Dominus, creator omnium quæ sunt, et auctor et dominus et rector cum Patre et Spiritu Sancto omnium creaturarum : qui passus sit vera carnis passione, mortuus vera corporis sui morte : resurrexit vera carnis suæ resurrectione (Bullinger read, receptione) et veræ

the Lord 400. But I do not rehearse these things to that end, as if I staid myself upon the decrees of councils and men; or as if I thought all things which pertain to true salvation and perfection were not contained in the holy scriptures; but to admonish our adversaries, that their manners and doings at this day do not only not agree with the examples and doctrines of the apostles, but not so much as with the decrees of the ancient writers: if happily they may enter into themselves, and, leaving the diverse doctrine of men, they may receive the most ancient tradition and the most infallible doctrine of the holy apostles.

How they that are called are to be ordained. I come now to the declaration of the last point; that is to say, after what manner they that be called are to be ordained. The apostles in their ordinations exhorted the church to fasting and prayer; and they that were called they placed and set in the sight of the church, and, laying their hands upon the heads of them that were ordained, they committed the churches

Acts xiii.
Acts i.
1 Tim. iv.
2 Tim. i. unto them. Of the laying on of hands I have spoken elsewhere[1]. It was a signification of the charge committed unto them. Neither is it read, that among the old fathers there was any other consecrating of pastors; as also all other things were simple and not sumptuous in the primitive and apostolic church. In the ages following ceremonies increased, but yet so that at the beginning to some they seemed not altogether

(Bullinger, vera) animæ resumptione, in qua veniet judicare vivos et mortuos. Quærendum etiam ab eo si novi et veteris testamenti, id est, legis et prophetarum et apostolorum unum eundemque credat auctorem et Deum; si diabolus non per conditionem sed per arbitrium factus sit malus. Quærendum etiam ab eo si credat hujus quam gestamus, et non alterius, carnis resurrectionem; si credat judicium futurum, et recepturos singulos, pro his quæ in carne gesserunt, vel pœnas, vel gloriam (Bullinger, prœmia); si nuptias non improbet, si secunda matrimonia non damnet; si carnium perceptionem non culpet; si pœnitentibus reconciliatis communicet; si in baptismo omnia peccata, id est, tam illud originale contractum, quam illa quæ voluntarie admissa sunt dimittantur; si extra ecclesiam catholicam nullus salvetur. Cum in his omnibus examinatus inventus fuerit plene instructus, tunc cum consensu clericorum et laicorum, et conventu totius provinciæ episcoporum, maximeque metropolitani vel auctoritate vel præsentia, ordinetur episcopus.—Concil. Carthag. IV. Labb. et Coss. Tom. II. col. 1198. Lut. Par. 1671. The date of this council is A. D. 398.]

[1 Vol. II. page 221.]

to have exceeded measure.   But to me that seemeth to be
overmuch, which at man's pleasure is added to God's institution.   And, I pray you, what need is there to patch men's
fancies and customs unto the institutions of the apostles?   Why
doth not the laying on of hands suffice thee, since it sufficed
the blessed apostles, who were far holier than thou, and more
skilful in heavenly matters?   There was afterward added oil;
there was also added the book of the gospels.   For after this
manner the fourth council of Carthage decreeth: "When a
bishop is ordained, let two bishops place and hold over his
head and shoulders the book of the gospels; and one pouring
upon him the blessing, let all the other bishops that are present touch his head with their hands[2]."   They of latter time
have added hereunto a pall.   But at this day there is no   A pall.
end of ceremonies; nay rather, of follies.   If any man do
diligently compare their ceremonies with the attire of Aaron
and the Jewish priests, he will swear the whole Aaronism is
brought again by them into the church; yea, that this is more
sumptuous[3] and burdensome; yea, and that contrary to the
doctrine of the gospel: that at this time I affirm not their
consecration to be both infamous, and fully stuffed with excess,
pride, and offence, and by that means to be intolerable.   There
is another thing to be noted; which is, that albeit among the
old fathers consecration increased by the multiplying of ceremonies, yet was it freely bestowed; neither was there anything
either in it, or in the whole church of Christ, set to sale.   But at
this day how dear palls are sold by that Romish Canaanite[4],
and with how great costs consecrations are made, it is a shame
even to speak.   Gregory, in the council at Rome, celebrated
in the time of Mauricius and Theodosius, among other things
thus decreeth: "Following," saith he, "the ancient rule of the   The pall was in old time
fathers, I ordain, that there be nothing at any time taken of   freely given.
ordinations, neither for the giving of the pall, nor for the delivery of the bulls.   For seeing that in ordaining of a bishop

[2 Episcopus cum ordinatur, duo episcopi ponant et teneant evan-
geliorum codicem super caput et cervicem ejus; et uno super eum
fundente benedictionem, reliqui omnes episcopi qui adsunt manibus
suis caput ejus tangant.—Concil. Carthag. IV. Labb. et Coss. Tom. II.
col. 1199.]

[3 instructiorem, Lat.]

[4 Cf. Vol. II. p. 45, note 7; and p. 153, n. 8.]

the high bishop layeth his hand upon him, and the minister readeth the lesson of the gospel, and the notary writeth the epistle of his confirmation ; as it becometh not the bishop to sell the hand he layeth on, so neither the minister nor the notary ought in the ordination, either the one to sell his voice, or the other his pen. But if any man shall presume to take any gain thereby, he shall be sure before the judgment-seat of Almighty God to undergo the sharp sentence due to so horrible an offence." Yet forthwith he addeth : " But if he that is ordained, not required, but of his own free will, only for favour's sake, will offer any thing, we grant he may[1]."

Why we receive not orders at the hands of popish bishops.

I have hitherto declared what manner of men, and after what sort, bishops or pastors must be ordained in the church of God. And albeit out of those things it may easily be gathered, why at this day we suffer not ourselves to be ordained of those who are called, and seem to themselves to be, the only lawful ordinaries; that is to say, such as in the Romish Church by continual succession descend from the apostles ; I will yet, if I can, declare the cause somewhat more plainly. Of the continual succession of bishops or pastors, and of the church, I have spoken elsewhere[2]; so that it were superfluous here to repeat and rip up the same again. I have also proved, that our churches are the true churches of God, though they agree not with the late upstart church of Rome. And it is evident, that true churches have power to ordain pastors, whether it be done by the voices of the whole church, or by the lawful judgment of such as are chosen by the church. Whereupon it consequently followeth, that they are lawfully

[1 Antiquam patrum regulam sequens, nihil unquam de ordinationibus accipiendum constituo, neque ex datione pallii, neque ex traditione chartarum.... Quia enim ordinando episcopo pontifex manum imponit, evangelii vero lectionem minister legit, confirmationis vero hujus epistolam notarius excipit; sicut pontificem manum non decet, quam imponit, vendere, ita minister vel notarius non debet in ordinatione ejus vocem suam vel calamum venundare.... Si quis aliquid commodi appellatione exigere vel petere præsumpserit, in districto omnipotentis Dei examine reatui subjacebit.... Is autem qui ordinatus fuerit, si non ... exactus ... offerre aliquid cuilibet ex clero gratiæ tantummodo causa voluerit, hoc accipi nullo modo prohibemus.—Decret. Gregor. I. Concil. Gen. stud. Labb. et Coss. Tom. v. col. 1587. Lut. Par. 1671.]

[2 See above, page 28.]

ordained which our, or rather which the churches of Christ,
do ordain.   And there are weighty causes, why the holy
churches of God do refuse to have their ministers ordained of
popish ordinaries.   For St Paul saith: "Though we, or an angel Gal. i.
from heaven, shall preach any other gospel unto you, than that
which we have preached unto you, let him be accursed."   But
these men preach another gospel, beside that which Paul
preached; which thing we will have to be understood as touching the sense (wherein there is more danger), and not as touching
the words: and therefore from heaven these men are stricken
with this curse or excommunication.   But who can abide to be
ordained of them that be stricken with a curse, or excommunicate?   Moreover, the chief thing in the ordination is the
doctrine of the gospel; seeing that to this end especially
ministers of the church are ordained, that they preach the
pure gospel of Christ unfeignedly unto the people, and without
mingling of man's traditions.   But this very thing they do
not only most straitly forbid them that are ordained, but also
they compel them to abjure by a certain kind of oath which
they offer unto them.   For they are bound by that wicked
oath, not unto Christ, but to the pope against Christ.   For,
among other things, thus they which are elected bishops take
their oath: "I, N. elected bishop of N., from this time forth The oath of
will be faithful and obedient to blessed Peter, and to the holy bishops.
apostolic church of Rome, and to our lord N. the pope, and to
his successors entering canonically.   The counsel, which they
shall commit unto me by themselves or messengers, or by
their letters, to their hinderance I will not willingly disclose to
any man.   I will be a helper unto them, to retain and defend
against all men the popedom of Rome and the royalties of St
Peter.   I will do my endeavour to keep, defend, increase, and
enlarge the rights, honours, privileges, and authority of the
church of Rome, of our lord the pope, and of his foresaid successors.   Neither will I be in counsel, practice, or
treaty, wherein shall be imagined against our lord the pope
himself, or the same church of Rome, any sinister or prejudicial matter to their persons, right, honour, state, or power.
And if I shall understand such things to be imagined or procured by any, I will hinder the same as much as lieth in me;
and with as much speed as conveniently I may, I will signify
the same to our said lord, or to some other, by whom it may

come to his knowledge. The rules of the holy fathers, the decrees, ordinances, sentences, dispositions, reservations, provisions, and commandments apostolical, I will observe with my whole might, and cause them to be observed of other. Heretics, schismatics, and rebels against our lord the pope, I will persecute, and to my ability fight against[1]." Since these men are sworn thus after this manner, who, I pray you, that is a faithful lover of Jesus Christ, of his church, of true faith, yea, and add thereunto, of the commonwealth, can abide to be ordained by such? There is no talk in their oath of the gospel, neither of our Lord Jesus[2] Christ himself. There is no mention of the holy scriptures; but of the rules and ordinances of the fathers there is most diligent mention. Peter is named; but not that apostle of Christ saying, "Silver and gold have I none;" but another, I know not who, having kingly dignity. Indeed, the apostolic church is named; but by

[1 Ego N. electus ecclesiæ N. ab hac hora in antea fidelis et obediens ero beato Petro apostolo, sanctæque Romanæ ecclesiæ, et domino nostro, domino N. papæ N. suisque successoribus canonice intrantibus... Consilium vero, quod mihi creditur sunt per se aut nuntios suos seu literas, ad eorum damnum, me sciente, nemini pandam. Papatum Romanum et regalia sancti Petri adjutor eis ero ad retinendum, et defendendum, salvo meo ordine, contra omnem hominem... Jura, honores, privilegia, et auctoritatem sanctæ Romanæ ecclesiæ, domini nostri papæ, et successorum prædictorum, conservare, defendere, augere, promovere curabo. Neque ero in consilio, vel facto seu tractatu, in quibus contra ipsum dominum, nostrum, vel eamdem Romanam ecclesiam, aliqua sinistra vel præjudicialia personarum, juris, honoris, status, et potestatis eorum machinentur. Et si talia a quibuscumque tractari. vel procurari novero, impediam hoc pro posse; et quanto citius potero, significabo eidem domino nostro, vel alteri, per quem possit ad ipsius notitiam pervenire. Regulas sanctorum patrum, decreta, ordinationes seu dispositiones, reservationes, provisiones, et mandata apostolica totis viribus observabo, et faciam ab aliis observari. Hæreticos, schismaticos, et rebelles eidem domino nostro, vel successoribus prædictis, pro posse persequar et impugnabo, &c.—Pontificale Roman. p. 63. Rom. 1818.—Among the Simler MSS. in the City Library at Zurich is a letter from Martin Micronius, dated London, 14 April, 1553, in which he inquires of Bullinger, whence he had taken this form of oath: for he says; "Extat forma quædam juramenti episcoporum, Lib. II. Decretal. de juramento, titul. 24. c. 4. Ego N. sed ea non per omnia respondet formæ a te perscriptæ."]

[2 Jesu, ed. 1577.]

and by, by interpretation, they add what manner of church they would have understood, and call it the papalty. This papalty, not the church of God; I say, the papalty, and the honours, privileges, and rights of the popedom, against all men; behold, they promise they will defend this against all men. For they acknowledge the pope to be their lord, against whom they will have nothing to be imagined; yea, if they may know that other do devise anything against the pope and popedom, they promise discovery thereof and faithful help. But I think not that any man can bind himself more straitly to one. Neither is it unknown, that those, whom they call heretics, are not enemies to the christian faith, nor teachers of opinions contrary to the scriptures, but rebels to the pope: they are, I say, they, who as they neglect the decrees and laws of the pope, and preach the scriptures only, so they give all the glory unto Christ, as to the only head and high priest of the church; and therefore they teach that the pope is neither the head, neither the high priest, of the church. But who, loving true godliness, can bind himself with such an oath? Who will renounce and forsake the friendship of Christ, and humble himself to become the bond-slave and footstool of the pope of Rome? To be short, who will desire to be ordained a minister of Christ and of his church at the hands of those that have done after this manner?

Here may be added, that in the consistory of Rome all things as touching holy orders are most corrupt; insomuch as scarce any small tokens of Christ's institution do appear. I will not rehearse at this present, that there are many new constitutions of men joined unto them; that in a manner there remaineth no voice of the church in the ordination of pastors; that there is no choice made of such as the church deputeth thereabouts. For the right of presentation, collation, and confirmation, being dispersed among many, with some is become even an heritage; so as both daws and half fools[3] may be made ministers or[4] bishops. And neither can I let this thing pass, that with them is lost that true examination and sharp pastoral discipline. Indeed, there remaineth examination, but altogether childish; in the which lightly they that are ordained are asked that which scholars in common schools are wont to

[3 fatui aut semimoriones, Lat.]
[4 ministers or, not in Lat.]

be demanded; whether one can read well, construe well, sing, and be cunning in their numbers? They cannot deny this thing; neither also this, that priests are ordained more to read, to sing, and say mass, than to govern the church with the word of God: whereby the more regard is had of the voice, that it be apt for singing, than of skilfulness or experience in the holy scriptures. But they think the matter is cunningly handled, if some skilful lawyer be preferred to the office of a pastor. For it seemeth for the most part to be more profitable, to plead cunningly in the court for the increase and maintenance of riches, than to preach well in the church for the winning of souls. What? do not we see men sent from the law, and out of the courts of kings and princes, to possess churches, fitter for anything else than to govern the churches of God? For ecclesiastical offices are begun to be counted as princes' donatives: whereupon they are also called benefices. The bishops of Rome themselves have bestowed priesthoods upon their cooks, ravenous[1] soldiers, barbers, and muletors: and this was far more honestly, than when they bestowed them upon bawds. A great many of priests thrust themselves into the holy ministry by violence and simony; which office nevertheless he neither could nor would execute well. And they, that are received by an honester title, are received through commendation and favour. Herein availeth much either affinity or kindred, and consanguinity. In all these there is a greater regard had of the belly than of the ministry: they provide better for those which are accounted priests and are no priests, than for the church of God and salvation of souls. But by this means all things go to wrack in the church, and the flock of God is oppressed with the weight and ruin of the shepherds.

Plurality of benefices.
Hereunto pertaineth the plurality (as they call it) of benefices. Some one, either soldier or curtisan, oftentimes rakes to himself, the pope offering it to him, half a dozen benefices or more; of which benefices they take no further care, but to receive the gain. For he never teacheth; nay, he is very seldom at his flock, unless it be when he sheareth them. In the mean time the Lord's flock is neglected, and perisheth: *Unlearned ministers and many benefices the spoil of the church.* for the vicars which are set over the flock by them, for the most part, are unlearned and hirelings. He that is content

[¹ cupediariis, Lat.]

with least wages is placed over the flock, what manner of one soever he be; and he seems to have learning enough, if he can read, sing, say mass, hear confessions, anoint, and read the gospel out of the book upon the Sunday. That which remaineth moreover to be done seemeth to them to be small matters.

I am ashamed and sorry to rehearse what a censure for reformation of manners remaineth in the church. The thing itself crieth, and experience witnesseth, that unworthy persons are not shut out from this holy ministry ; for without difference all are admitted; and as yet whoremongers, drunkards, dice-players, and men defiled, yea, overwhelmed with divers heinous crimes, are suffered in the ministry.

But lest they should seem to do nothing herein, the bishop asketh at giving of orders, " Who are worthy of honour?" and his chancellor, or the archdeacon [2], forthwith answereth the bishop, who before that time never saw or heard what manner of men they are of whom he beareth witness, " They are worthy [3]." Moreover, they use so many and such kinds of ceremonies in their consecration, that he that is studious of the truth of the gospel cannot receive them with a safe conscience. These causes, and other not unlike, make us, that we can so much less abide [4] to be ordained of the ordinaries or bishops of the Romish church.

The last point remaineth, which I purposed to declare in the beginning of this treatise ; which is [5], the office of the ministers that are ordained in the church. I can shew you in one word ; to govern the church of God, or to feed the flock of Christ. For Paul the apostle, speaking unto the pastors of Asia, saith : " Take heed unto yourselves, and to all the flock, over the which the Holy Ghost hath made you overseers, to rule (or feed) the church of God, which he hath purchased with his own blood." And the pastors do govern the church of God with God his word, or with wholesome doctrine, and

What the office is of those that are ordained in the church.

Acts xx.

[2 his chancellor or the archdeacon, not in Lat.]

[3 Pontifex interrogat, dicens: Scis illos dignos esse? Respondet archidiaconus, Quantam humana fragilitas nosse sinit, et scio, et testificor ipsos dignos esse ad hujus onus officii.—Pontificale Rom. p. 37. Rom. 1818.]

[4 quo minus sustineamus, Lat.: that we cannot abide.]

[5 What is, ed. 1577.]

with holy example of life. For St Paul saith again unto Timothy : " Be thou unto them that believe an ensample in word, in conversation, in love, in spirit, in faith, and in pureness." He writeth also the same unto Titus, ii. chap. But forsomuch as the papists do forge far other things of the office or function of bishops, and do confirm the same, as they also do their other trifles, by the authority or power of the keys ; as I said when I entreated of the power of the church[1]: I will therefore first of all speak somewhat (and that as much as I shall think to be sufficient for this matter) as touching the keys.

A key is an instrument very well known to all men, wherewith gates, doors, and chests, are either shut or opened. It is transferred from bodily things unto spiritual things ; and it is called the key of knowledge, and of the kingdom of heaven. For the Lord saith in the gospel of Luke : " Woe unto you, interpreters of the law : for ye have taken away the key of knowledge ; ye enter not in yourselves, and them that came in ye forbad." The same sentence St Matthew bringeth forth after this sort : " Woe unto you, scribes and Pharisees, hypocrites ! because ye shut up the kingdom of heaven before men : for ye yourselves go not in, neither suffer ye them that would enter to come in." Behold, that which Luke calleth, to " take away the key of knowledge," that Matthew expoundeth, " to shut heaven." The key therefore of knowledge is the instruction itself as concerning a blessed life, by what means we are made partakers thereof. He taketh away the key, which instructeth not the people of true blessedness ; or else is a hinderance, that other cannot instruct[2] them. Therefore the keys of the kingdom of heaven are nothing else but the ministry of preaching the gospel, or word of God, committed by God unto his ministers, to that end that every one may be taught which way leadeth unto heaven, and which way carrieth down unto hell. These keys the Lord promised to Peter, and in him to all the other apostles, when he said : " I will give thee the keys of the kingdom of heaven : and whatsoever thou shalt bind in earth, shall be bound in heaven ; and whatsoever thou shalt loose on earth, shall be loosed in heaven." Let us inquire, therefore, when the keys

Marginal notes: 1 Tim. iv. · Of the keys of the church. · Luke xi. · Matth. xxiii. · Matt. xvi.

[1 See above, p. 38.]
[2 recte instituant, Lat.: rightly instruct.]

were delivered to Peter and to the rest ? And the agreeable consent of all men is, that they were given in the day of the resurrection. But it is evident, the same day the ministry or function of preaching the gospel was committed to the apostles : whereby it followeth, that the keys are nothing else but the ministry of preaching the gospel among all nations. For this thing is declared unto the world ; that salvation purchased by Christ is communicated to them that believe, and that hell is open for the unbelievers.

But now let us hear the testimonies of the holy evangelists. John the apostle and evangelist saith : " The Lord came unto his John xx. disciples, and said, Peace be unto you ; as my Father hath sent me, so send I you. And when he had said that, he breathed on them, and said unto them, Receive the Holy Ghost : whose soever sins ye remit, they are remitted unto them ; and whose soever sins ye retain, they are retained." These sayings agree with the words whereby he promised the keys ; for there he said : " Whatsoever ye shall bind[3] in earth, shall be bound in heaven :" here he saith : " Whose soever sins ye retain, they are retained." There he said : " And whatsoever ye shall loose[4] in earth, shall be loosed in heaven :" here he saith : " Whose soever sins ye remit, they are remitted unto them." Wherefore, " to bind" is, " to retain sins ;" " to loose" is, " to remit sins." You will say, How do men remit sins, since it is written, that only God forgiveth sins ? Let other testimonies therefore of the other evangelists be adjoined, expressing that the same history was done in the day of his resurrection. Luke saith : " Then the Lord opened their understanding, Luke xxiv. that they might understand the scriptures ; and said unto them, Thus it is written, and thus it behoved Christ to suffer, and to rise again from the dead the third day ; and that repentance and remission of sins should be preached in his name among all nations." And Mark saith : " He appeared Mark xvi. unto them as they sat together[5], and reproved them of their unbelief and hardness of heart[6] ; and he said unto them, Go ye into all the world, and preach the gospel to every creature : he that shall believe and be baptized, shall be saved ; but he that will not believe, shall be damned." Therefore God only

[3 alligaveris, Lat. : thou shalt bind.]
[4 solveris, Lat. : thou shalt loose.]   [5 discumbentibus, Lat.]
[6 and hardness of heart, not in Lat.]

forgiveth sins to them that believe in the name of Christ, that
is to say, through[1] the merits and propitiation of Christ: but
that sins are forgiven, the ministers do assuredly declare by
the preaching of the gospel; and by that preaching do bind
and loose, remit and retain sins. The matter will be made
plainer by an example or two. St Peter, speaking unto the
Acts ii. citizens of Jerusalem : " Repent ye," saith he, " and let every
one of you be baptized in the name of Jesus Christ, for the
remission of sins; and ye shall receive the gift of the Holy
How the
apostles did
bind and
loose. Ghost." And so St Peter used the keys committed unto him
after this manner : he[2] looseth in earth, and remitteth sins
unto men, that is, promising to them that believe assured remission of sins through Christ; which message God hath
confirmed, giving remission of sins unto the faithful, as they
believed. Moreover, the keeper of the prison at Philippos,
Acts xvi. being amazed, saith to Silas and Paul : " Sirs, what must I do
to be saved ?" The apostles answered : " Believe on the Lord
Jesus, and thou shalt be saved, and thy whole household."
The apostles loosed him that was bound, and forgave him his
sins, by the keys, that is, by the preaching of the gospel:
which gospel since he believed in earth, the Lord judged him
to be loosed in heaven. These things are taken out of the
Acts of the Apostles. In the same Acts we read examples
Acts xiii. of the contrary in this manner. " The Jews, being filled with
indignation, spake against those things which were spoken
of Paul, and railed. But Paul and Barnabas waxed bold, and
said, It was necessary that the word of God should first have
been spoken to you : but seeing ye put it from you, and think
yourselves unworthy of everlasting life, lo, we turn to the
gentiles." Again, when the same Paul at Corinth had preached
Acts xviii. Christ to the Jews, and they resisted and reviled; " The
apostle shook his raiment, and said, Your blood be upon your
own heads : I am clean : from henceforth I will go unto the
gentiles." And so he did bind the unbelievers. And God
confirmed the preaching of Paul, because it proceeded from
God himself. And unless you put the proper and true key
into the lock, you shall never open it. The true and right
key is the pure word of God; the counterfeit and thievish
key is a doctrine and tradition of man, estranged from the
word of God. I think I have sufficiently proved by evident

[1 propter, Lat.: for and on account of.]   [2 Sic, Lat. So he.]

testimonies of the scripture, that the keys given to the apostles and pastors of the church, and so to the church itself, are nothing else than the ministry of teaching the church. For by the doctrine of the gospel, as it were with certain keys, the gate of the kingdom of heaven is opened, when a sure and ready mean and way is shewed to come to attain unto the participation of Christ and the joys of everlasting life by true faith. To the testimony of God man's record agreeth. For St John Chrysostom upon Matthew, chap. xxiii. : "The key," saith he, "is the word of the knowledge of the scriptures, by which the gate of truth is opened to men. And the key-bearers are the priests, to whom is committed the word of teaching and interpreting the scriptures[3]." Other testimonies of old interpreters of the scriptures, differing nothing from these of ours, for that I am desirous to be brief, I do not bring.

Since these things are thus, brethren, and are delivered unto us in the express scriptures, we will not therefore greatly pass[4] what the papists babble touching the power of the keys; and what offices, dignities, preferments, and I know not what other thing, and what authority of priests, they derive from thence. We have learned, not out of the words or opinions of men, but out of the manifest word of God, that the keys are the ministry of the preaching of the word of God; and that the keys are given to the apostles, and to their successors; that is to say, the office of preaching remission of sins, repentance, and life everlasting[5] is committed to them. Where- Whence doctrine is upon we now conclude this, that the chief office of a pastor of to be the church is, to use those very keys which the Lord hath fetched. delivered to his apostles, and no other; that is, to preach the only and pure word of God, and not to fetch any doctrine from any other place than out of the very word of God. For there is a perpetual and inviolable law at this day also laid upon our pastors, which we read was laid upon the most ancient governors of the church, the Lord himself witnessing in Malachi, and saying : "My covenant was with Levi of life Mal. ii.

[3 Clavicularii sunt sacerdotes, quibus creditum est verbum docendi et interpretandi scripturas. Clavis autem est verbum scientiæ scripturarum, per quam aperitur hominibus janua veritatis.—Chrysost. Op. Imperf. in Matth. Hom. XLIV. p. 186. Opp. Tom. VI. Par. 1724.]

[4 pass, care for : curabimus, Lat.]   [5 vita beata, Lat.]

and peace; and I gave him fear, and he feared me, and was afraid before my name. The law of truth was in his mouth, and there was no iniquity found in his lips; he walked with me in peace and equity, and turned many from their iniquity. For the priest's lips should preserve knowledge, and they should seek the law at his mouth: for he is the messenger of the Lord of hosts." Again, the Lord saith to Ezechiel: "Thou shalt hear the word at my mouth, and give them warning from me." In Jeremy the Lord saith: "The prophet that hath a dream, let him tell a dream; and he that hath my word, let him speak my word faithfully[1]." He expressly puts a difference between heavenly things and earthly[2] things; between those things which are of the word of God, and those that are feigned and chosen by man, which he willeth[3] to let pass as uncertain things, and as dreams. For he immediately addeth: "Is not my word as fire, saith the Lord, and like a hammer that breaketh the hard stone[4]?" And again: "Hear not the words of the prophets, that preach unto you and deceive you: truly, they teach you vanity; for they speak the meaning of their own heart, and not out of the mouth of the Lord." Therefore all the true prophets of God have this continually in their mouth: "Thus saith the Lord; The mouth of the Lord hath spoken it." And therefore they delivered unto the people nothing contrary unto the word of God. The old people had also the scripture; and the prophets were nothing else but interpreters of the law, applying the same to the place, time, matters, and persons. Also our Lord Jesus Christ saith oftentimes, that his doctrine is not his own, but the Father's: which thing if you understand literally and according to his words, I know not whether anything can be spoken more absurd. Therefore the Lord meaneth, that his doctrine is not of man, but of God. Doth not he send us continually to the writings of the law and the prophets, and confirmeth his own sayings by them? But Christ is the only teacher of religion, and master of life, appointed unto the universal church by God the Father. To this church he himself also sending teachers, and shewing them what they should deliver[5], saith: "Teach them to observe those things

Ezek. iii.

Jer. xxiii.

Matt. xxviii

[1 faithfully, not in Lat.]   [2 humana, Lat.]   [3 jubet, Lat.]
[4 petram, Lat.]   [5 ecclesiæ tradant, Lat.]

which I have commanded you." Also : "Go into the whole Mark xvi.
world, and preach the gospel to all creatures." But the apostle
Paul witnesseth, that the gospel was promised by the prophets Rom. i.
of God in the holy scriptures. And this doctrine received of
Christ the apostles delivered to the nations, adding nothing
unto it, taking nothing from it; and therewithal also they
expounded the ancient writings of the prophets : yet neither
in this matter trusting anything to their own wit, nor being
ruled by their own judgment. For the apostle Peter saith :
"As every man hath received the gift, even so minister the 1 Pet. iv.
same one to another, as good stewards of the manifold graces[6]
of God. If any man speak, let him talk as the words[7] of
God." Tertullian also in his book intituled *De Præscript.
Hæret.* (which I have also elsewhere rehearsed), expressly
saith : "It is not lawful for us in anything to rest upon our
own fancy or judgment, neither yet to be negligent markers
what any other man bringeth forth of his own brain. We
have the apostles of the Lord for authors; for not they themselves did choose anything which they might establish after
their own fancy ; and the doctrine which they received of
Christ they faithfully delivered to the nations. And therefore if even an angel from heaven should preach any otherwise, he shall be accursed at our hands[8]." Thus far he. We
have moreover shewed in our sermons of faith and of the
church, that faith dependeth upon the only word of God ;
and that it wholly stayeth upon the only word of God ; and
also that the churches of God are builded and preserved by
the word of God, and not by man's doctrine[9] : all which seem
to appertain to this matter.

Neither is it left to the bishops of the church of Christ, The bishops
as the popish pastors do falsely boast, to ordain new laws and mitted to
to broach new opinions. For the doctrine, which was de- laws.

[6 gratiæ, Lat.]   [7 sermones, Lat. and Vulg.]
[8 Nobis vero nihil ex nostro arbitrio inducere licet, sed nec eligere
quod aliquis de arbitrio suo induxerit. Apostolos Domini habemus
auctores, qui nec ipsi quicquam ex suo arbitrio, quod inducerent, ele-
gerunt: sed acceptam a Christo disciplinam fideliter nationibus adsig-
naverunt. Itaque etiamsi angelus de cœlis aliter evangelizaret, anathema diceretur a nobis.—Tertull. de Præs. Hær. cap. 6. ap. Scriptor.
Eccles. Opusc. ed. Routh. Vol. i. p. 126. Oxf. 1840.]
[9 See Vol. i. p. 93; and above, p. 26.]

livered to the apostles of Christ, is simply to be received of
the church, and simply and purely to be delivered of the
pastors to the church, which is the congregation of such as
believe the word of Christ. And who knoweth not, that it is
said by the prophet, "All men are liars; God only is true?"
And the church is the pillar and ground of truth, because as
it stayeth upon the truth of the scriptures, even so it publisheth none other doctrine than is delivered in the scriptures,
neither receiveth it being published. And who is he that
will challenge to himself the glory due unto God only? God
is the only lawgiver to all mankind, especially in those things
which pertain to religion and a blessed life. For Esay saith:
Isai. xxxiii. " The Lord is our judge, the Lord is our lawgiver, the Lord
is our king; and he himself shall be our Saviour." And St
James iv. James also saith: "There is one lawgiver, which is able to
save and to destroy." God challengeth this thing as proper
to himself, to rule those that are his with the laws of his
word, over whom he only hath authority of life and death.
Moreover, those laws cannot be godly, which presume to prescribe and teach faith and the service of God after their own
fancy. The doctrine concerning faith and the worship of
God, unless it be heavenly[1], is nothing less than that which
it is said to be. God only teacheth us what is true faith, and
what worship he delighteth in; and therefore in Matthew
Matth. xv. the Son of God pronounceth out of Esay: " In vain do they
worship me, teaching for doctrines the commandments of men."
Join hereunto also, that from the new constitutions of men
there springeth always up a wonderful neglecting, yea, and
contempt, of the word of God and of heavenly laws: for
through[2] our own traditions, as the Lord also saith in the
gospel, we go astray, and despise the commandments of God.

Now since it is manifest from whence the pastor or doctor
must fetch his doctrine, to wit, from no other place than out
of the scripture of the old and new Testament, which is the
infallible and undoubted word of God; and that therefore this
doctrine is certain and immutable[3]: there remaineth now
also something to be spoken of the manner of teaching, which
the teacher or pastor of the church ought to follow. And
here I will only briefly touch the short sum or effect of
matters.

[1 divina, Lat.]   [2 propter, Lat.]   [3 definitam, Lat.]

Afore all other things, therefore, it is required of pastors, *The scope or drift whereunto the pastors in the church should aim.* that continually they account that to be spoken unto them, which the apostle commanded to be often told to Archippus: "Take heed to the ministry that thou hast received in the *Col. iv.* Lord, that thou fulfil it." And moreover, that they never turn away their eyes from that lively picture of a good and evil shepherd, which Ezechiel, that famous prophet, setteth out after this manner: "Thus saith the Lord God, Woe be unto *Ezek. xxxiv.* the shepherds of Israel that feed themselves: should not the shepherds feed the flocks? Ye eat the fat; ye clothe you with the wool; ye kill them that are fed; but ye feed not the sheep: the weak have ye not strengthened, the sick have ye not healed, neither have ye bound up the broken, nor brought again that which was driven away, neither have ye sought that which was lost; but with cruelty and with rigour have ye ruled them." And again: "I will feed my sheep, saith the Lord God; I will seek that which was lost, and bring again that which was driven away, and will bind up that which was broken, and will strengthen the weak; but I will destroy the fat and the strong, and I will feed them with judgment." Hereby we gather, that it is the duty of a good pastor or shepherd to feed, and not to devour, the flock; to minister, not to exercise dominion; to seek the safety of his sheep, not his private gain; and also to seek out again the lost sheep, that is to say, to bring again such as cannot abide the truth, and wander in the darkness of errors, home to the church and unto the light of the truth; and to restore and bring back again the sheep that is driven or chased away, to wit, such as are separated from the fellowship of saints[4], or godly, for some private affection's sake; to heal or bind up such as are broken; for he meaneth the wounds of sins, which Jeremy also commandeth to heal: and to be short, to *Jer. viii. xxx.* strengthen the weak and feeble sheep, and not altogether to tread them under foot; and to bridle such sheep as be strong, that is to say, men flourishing in virtues, lest they be proud and puffed up with the gifts of God, and so fall away. But let him think, that these things cannot be performed but *Isai. xlii. viii.* through sound and continual teaching derived out of God his *Matt. xii. xix.* word.

The manner of teaching extendeth itself to public and

[4 the saints, ed. 1577.]

private doctrines. By public doctrine the pastor either cate-
chiseth, that is to say, instructeth, them that be younglings
in religion, or other which are grounded therein[1]. To the
younglings or ignorant sort he openeth the principles of true
religion. For catechesis, or the form of catechising, comprehendeth the grounds or principles of faith and christian
doctrine; to wit, the chief points of the covenant, the ten
commandments, the articles of faith or[2] Apostles' Creed, the
Lord's Prayer, and a brief exposition of the sacraments. The
ancient churches had catechisers[3] appointed properly to this
charge. And the Lord commendeth unto us, both in the old
Testament and in the new, with great earnestness the charge
of the youth; commanding us to instruct them both betimes,
and also diligently, in true religion. Moreover, he setteth
out great rewards and grievous punishments in that behalf.
Assuredly, no profit or fruit is to be looked for in the church
of those hearers, that are not perfectly instructed in the principles of religion by catechising: for they know not of what
thing the pastor in the church speaketh, when they hear the
covenant, the commandment, the law, grace, faith, prayer,
and the sacraments, to be named. Therefore if in anything,
then in this, ought greatest diligence to be used.

The doctrine, which appertaineth to the perfecter sort, is
specially occupied in the exposition of holy scripture. It
may appear out of the writings of the old bishops, that it was
the custom in that happy and most holy primitive church, to
expound unto the churches, not certain parcels of the canonical
books, neither some chosen places out of them, but the whole
books as well of the new Testament as of the old[4]: and in so
doing there came no small fruit unto the churches[5]. As at
this day also we see by experience, that churches cannot be
better instructed, nor more vehemently stirred up, than with
the words of God himself, and with the faithful interpretation
of the books of the gospel, the law, the prophets, and apostles.
Where, by the way, we give warning, that the interpretation

*Of the man-
ner of teach-
ing the
church.*

*The benefit
of catechis-
ing.*

*The interpre-
tation of the
scripture.*

[1 instituit publice vel catechemenos, vel perfectiores, Lat.]
[2 articles of faith or, not in Lat.]
[3 catechistas, Lat. Bingham, Book III. chap. 10.]
[4 So also 1584: but 1577, as the old.]
[5 See an incident in Zwingle's life. D'Aubigne's Hist. of Reform.
Book VIII. chap. 6.]

of the scriptures is not a liberty to feign what one lust, and
to wrest the scriptures which way one will; but a careful
comparing of the scripture[6], and a special gift of the Holy
Ghost; for St Peter saith: "No prophecy in the scripture 2 Pet. i. 20.
is of any private interpretation." Wherefore no man hath
power to interpret the scriptures after his own fantasy. Neither is that the best exposition which hath most favourers;
as if that were the best interpretation which hath the consent
of the greater multitude: for Arianism and Turcism would,
by many degrees[7], excel Christianism. That exposition is
best, which is not repugnant to faith and love, neither is
wrested to defend and spread abroad the glory and covetousness of men. But I have spoken of interpretation of the
scriptures in the second sermon of the first decade[8].

But unless the scripture be aptly applied, respect being Application
had of place, time, matter, and persons of every church; and ^of scripture.
to this end (which I also taught in the third sermon of this
decade[9]), that the church may be edified, not that the teacher
in the church may seem better learned or more eloquent; his
exposition of the canonical books of the scripture shall be
fruitless to the people. The Lord commendeth unto us the
wise steward, and saith: "Who is a faithful and wise steward, Luke xii.
whom his Lord hath made[10] ruler over his household, to give
them their portion of meat in due season?" and as followeth
in the xii. of Luke. St Paul also, writing to Timothy the
bishop, saith: "Study to shew thyself approved unto God, 2 Tim. ii.
a workman not to be ashamed, rightly dividing the word of
truth." Meat is unprofitable unless it be divided and cut
into parts. But here the householder knoweth what portions
he should give to every one in his family, not having regard
what delighteth every one, but what is most profitable for
every one. The same apostle, teaching that all the actions of a
preacher in the church ought to be directed to edification, saith :
"He that prophesieth, speaketh unto men to edifying, and to
exhortation, and to comfort." Therefore to the teaching of the
perfecter sort pertaineth, not only the exposition of the holy
scripture, but also a plain demonstration, and manifest as may

[6 scriptures, ed. 1577.]   [7 parasangis, Lat.]
[8 Rather, the Third Sermon. See Vol. I. p. 70, &c.]
[9 See above, p. 101.]   [10 constituet, Lat. : shall make.]

be, of the principles and grounds of Christianity[1]; and chiefly an evident doctrine of repentance and remission of sins in the name of Christ; and also a sharp rebuking to be used in due time, or a grave, but yet a wise, reproving of their faults. For the Lord, speaking to his apostles, saith : " Ye are the salt of the earth; if the salt become unsavoury, wherewith shall it be salted?"   Hereunto also pertaineth the confuting of errors and repressing of heresies, and the defence of sound doctrine. Paul saith, that the "mouths of vain talkers and seducers of minds must be stopped and sharply rebuked."   Neither is it enough simply to teach true religion, unless the teacher in the church, by often teaching, constantly urge, defend, and main- tain the same. Hereunto chiefly belong these words of Paul : "I charge" (or adjure) "thee therefore before God, and before the Lord Jesus Christ, which shall judge the quick and dead at his appearing and in his kingdom; preach the word, be instant in season and out of season, improve, rebuke, exhort, with long-suffering and doctrine. For the time will come, when they will not suffer wholesome doctrine; but, having their ears itching, shall after their own lusts get them a heap of teachers, and shall turn their ears from the truth, and shall be given unto fables.   But watch thou in all things, suffer adversity, do the work of an evangelist, make thy ministry fully known[2]." Therefore they need very often exhortations, that what the church by often and plain teaching understandeth either to be followed or to be avoided; the same she may, being stirred up and compelled by a fervent exhor- tation, either constantly follow or refuse.   And here it shall be needful for a preacher[3] to use long-sufferance, lest forthwith he cast away all hope, if he see not by and by such happy success as he wisheth for; and that some mighty and impu- dent adversaries obstinately strive against him.   For Paul saith : " The servants[4] of the Lord must not strive; but be gentle unto all men, apt to teach, suffering evil[5] with meek- ness, instructing them that are contrary-minded; if God at any time will give them repentance to the knowledge of the truth; and that they may come unto themselves again out of the snares of the devil, which are taken captive of him at his

Matt. v.

Tit. i.

2 Tim. iv.

2 Tim. ii.

[1 rerum Christianarum, Lat.]
[2 ad plenum probatum reddito, Lat. and Erasmus.]
[3 episcopo, Lat.]   [4 servum, Lat.]   [5 malos, Lat.]

will." There needeth, moreover, mild and quickening [6] comfort: for many are troubled, being tried with divers temptations; whom unless you faithfully comfort, they are overcome of Satan. These, and such other like, do pertain to the teaching of the perfecter sort.

Here I may also make mention of the care of the poor; *Care of the poor.* for this especially pertaineth to a minister [7] and to their public preaching, whereby he may continually provoke the richer sort to mercy, that they may be ready to distribute. The apostle Paul hath left us notable examples of this matter almost in all his epistles; but specially in the sixteenth chapter to the Romans, and in the first to the Corinthians, and also in the eighth and ninth chapter of the latter epistle to the Corinthians. St Peter, James, and John, commended very diligently to St Paul the care of the poor; as Paul himself rehearseth in the second chapter to the Galatians. And albeit Peter in some place refuse the office of distribution; yet herein he is altogether careful, that godly and faithful dis- *Acts vi.* posers may be appointed for the poor. Therefore the care of the poor pertaineth chiefly to the pastors, that they be not neglected, but tenderly cherished, as the members of Christ.

The private kind of teaching differeth nothing in the *Private kind of teaching.* thing itself from that public kind, but it is called private in respect of the learners. For some one cometh to the pastor, after the manner of Nicodemus, and desireth very familiarly to be instructed of him in things properly concerning himself. Besides that, this shepherd goeth privately and instructeth those, whom by evident tokens he hath learned by private conference may be more easily won unto Christ than by public preaching. Moreover, he privately admonisheth, and taketh heed in time, lest they that are more unadvised be deeplier plunged in evil. Hitherto pertaineth the visitation both of sick persons and prisoners, none of whom a faithful pastor neglecteth; but visiteth them so much the more diligently, as he perceiveth them more grievously tempted. For a good pastor is always watchful over the whole flock of Christ, for whom Satan layeth snares, ranging about, seeking whom he may devour. Him the pastor resisteth by prayer, admonitions, teaching, and exhortations. If so be that every church had such a pastor, which would

[6 vivida, Lat.]   [7 episcopum, Lat.]

not easily forsake the flock, how great fruit, I pray you,
should we hope for! Wherefore not without cause are we
commanded incessantly and earnestly to pray unto God, that
he would give faithful, wise, godly, and diligent pastors unto
his church.

Prayer for faithful pastors.

Thus have I hitherto spoken of the doctrine of bishops in
the church of God. And unless a bishop teach after this manner,
and do those things which are joined to teaching, he is unworthy
either of the name of a bishop, pastor, or doctor, howsoever
he pretend an apostolic title. For certain things are joined
to the doctrine of the church, which also are required of a
preacher of the gospel, and belong to his office; as are these, to
gather together an holy assembly, wherein he may preach,
conceive prayer¹, and minister the sacraments. But of these
things shall be spoken in their place.

What things are joined to teaching.

Now there resteth to be considered, how bishops may
govern the church of Christ with holy example of their life.
The Lord in the gospel saith to his apostles: " Ye are the
light of the world: a city that is set on a high hill cannot be
hid; neither do men light a candle, and put it under a bushel,
but on a candlestick, and it giveth light unto all that are in
the house. Let your light so shine before men, that they may
see your good works, and glorify your Father which is in
heaven." Wherefore pastors, not only in doctrine but in holy
life, do give light unto the church; which, beholding their life
agreeable to their doctrine, is herself also moved to practise
innocency of life. For the example of a good man much
prevaileth to the furthering of the love of virtues; and contrariwise the scripture witnesseth, that the corrupt example
of the sons of Heli, the chief rulers in religion, was very
available to corrupt the people. For the scripture saith:
" And the sin of the children of Heli was too abominable
before the face of the Lord, so that² the people began to
abhor the sacrifices of the Lord." For men, seeing the corrupt
life of the ministers of the church, begin somewhat to doubt
of the whole doctrine, crying: If the pastor thought those things
true which he teacheth unto us, he himself would not live so
dissolutely. Therefore such teachers are said to overthrow
that with their naughty life, which they have builded with

Of the holy and un-blameable life of bishops.
Matt. v.

1 Sam. ii.

[¹ oretur, Lat.]   [² quod, Lat. for.]

wholesome doctrine. Wherefore Paul requireth a bishop, or pastor of the people, which should be blameless; that is to say, which cannot rightly and worthily be reprehended of the faithful. For otherwise by how much every bishop shall be more sincere and upright, by so much more shall he be subject to slanders and reproaches of the wicked; the Lord himself foretelling the same in the gospel: "If they have called," saith Matt. x. he, "the Lord of the house Beelzebub, how much more shall they call them of his household!" And, "If they have per- John xv. secuted me, they will also persecute you." And again, "Blessed are ye, when men shall revile you, and persecute you, Matt. v. and lying shall say all manner of evil saying against you for my sake. Rejoice and be glad, for great is your reward in heaven." Therefore a pastor ought very carefully, and as much as in him is, to take heed that, both at home and abroad, he live a life worthy of himself and his calling. Let him live chastely, as well being single as married. Let temperance, soberness, thriftiness or good husbandry, hospitality, and other virtues, which I have before rehearsed out of the apostle, flourish in a bishop. Let him govern his own household wisely, and godlily instruct them; and so bridle them, that he give not occasion of offence to the church through riotousness or other misdeeds. For so also the apostle Paul hath commanded, who (framing again the exercises of a bishop) saith: "Till I come, give attendance to reading, to exhorta- 1 Tim. iv. tion, and doctrine." He requireth of Timothy a diligent reading, that is to say, a continual study, whereby he may more perfectly [3] exhort and teach. But Paul requireth of him that hath been brought up in the knowledge of the scriptures from a child, as elsewhere he writeth, a continual study of the scriptures [4]. How great diligence then doth the apostle require of them, who as they have not obtained so plentiful gifts of the Spirit as Timothy had, so they are not exercised in the scriptures from their infancy! Let a sort of them [5] therefore be ashamed of their unskilfulness: let them be ashamed of leisure not bestowed in study, and of their travelsome idleness. For as many read not anything at all, but continually live idly, and, as it were, rot away in idleness; so a number of

[3 evidentius, Lat.]   [4 of the scriptures, not in Lat.]
[5 multos, Lat.: sort, number, multitude. Becon's Works, ed. P. S.
Vol. I. p. 5. n, 2.]

innumerable others are busied in those things which nothing become bishops. Therefore the apostle saith[1]: "No man which goeth a warfare entangleth himself with the affairs of this life, that he may please him which hath chosen him to be a soldier." Here were a fit place to speak of stipends due unto pastors; but we will defer it to another place. But if bishops come abroad among the people at any time for business' sake, and be present in assemblies of honest men[2]; with no less care ought they to endeavour, lest either by deed or word, or by apparel, or company keeping, or finally, in the whole course of their life, they give any just occasion of offence to the church. Let there appear in pastors, in all places and at all times, holy uprightness, meet ripeness of judgment, honest behaviour, wisdom, modesty, humanity, humility, and authority worthy of God's ministers; but let the contrary vices and wicked misdeeds be far from them.

In these few words I think are contained those things, which other have handled at large, in treating of the discipline and behaviour of the clergy. For all ages understood, that a dissolute and loose life was evil in all degrees and kinds of men; but in the ministers of the church worse and most intolerable. For what can a minister of the church do in the church, whose authority is altogether lost? Authority therefore is requisite in pastors.

Of the want hereof many do complain; and, seeing it under foot, go about to rear it up again with I cannot tell what kind of props of titles and ceremonies. But authority is not gotten with such light and vain things. It is rather obtained by the grace of God, through the love of truth and uprightness of life; if happily God touch men's hearts, so as they understand, that God worketh his work in the church by his ministers as by his instruments; if they perceive that ministers do the work of the Lord with ferventness of spirit, and not coldly; not fearing anything in a good cause, no, not the wicked and mighty men of this world, but do resist them; and yet that they do nothing of hatred or malice, but do all things of a fatherly affection, with a good courage, constancy, and wisdom. Whereunto if there be joined, not an hypocritical, but a holy and upright life indeed, together with honest, modest,

Marginal notes:
2 Tim. ii.

Authority of pastors.

[1 rursus, Lat. omitted: again.]
[2 cœtibus hominum honestis, Lat.]

and comely behaviour[3], all wise men shall perceive, that there is sufficient authority thereby proved[4] to a godly minister.

I would not yet the Donatists, or anabaptists[5], should hereby claim any kind of defence or protection, were it never so small. They contend, that the ministry of the word and sacraments, executed by a minister whose life is unclean, becometh thereby of no value. But albeit a holy life be requisite in a minister, yet their ministry becometh not of no value through the minister's unhonest life, so his doctrine be sound and perfect. For the Lord in the gospel commandeth to hear them that teach in Moses' chair, but he forbiddeth to follow their doings; for they teach good things, but do them not. Of this matter I have spoken in the second sermon of this decade[6]. Nazianzen very properly saith: "The print of a seal is all one, whether it be graven in iron or in gold[7]." And it is one and the same gospel, it is one and the selfsame heavenly treasure sent of the Father, whether it be brought by a good messenger or a bad. But in the mean space the unhonest life of the ministers of the church ought not to be winked at, but to be chastened; and such as are past cure ought to be put out of the ministry, lest through their continual offence[8] they make the holy ministry infamous.

For the scarce good life of ministers good doctrine must not be rejected.

But many will say: Why handle you these things in public preaching? These things were to be told the ministers privately. I answer; that the very laws, which properly pertained to the priests, were in times past communicated to the magistrates and governors of the people, and read before the people themselves. Moreover it is manifest, that Christ our Lord handled those things in public sermons, which properly pertained to the doctors and pastors of the people. Hereunto may be added, that St Paul, speaking of elders or ministers[9], saith: "Them that sin rebuke openly, that the rest also may fear."

1 Tim. v.

The holy scripture, with great diligence describing good

[3 mores suaves et jucundi, Lat.]   [4 paratum, Lat.: gained.]
[5 Mosheim. Eccles. Hist. Book II. Cent. 4. part 2. chap. v. § 8. Vol. I. p. 379. ed. Soames. Bullinger. adv. Anabapt. Lib. III. cap. 7.]
[6 See above, p. 56.]
[7 Ἔστω χρυσὸς, ἔστω σίδηρος, δακτύλιοι δὲ ἀμφότεροι, καὶ τὴν αὐτὴν ἐγκεχαράχθωσαν εἰκόνα βασιλικήν.—Greg. Naz. Orat. XL. cap. 26. p. 713. Tom. I. Par. 1778.]
[8 offendiculo, Lat.]   [9 or ministers, not in Lat.]

and faithful shepherds and teachers, with no less faithfulness
and diligence doth paint out the false teachers and false
shepherds or wolves[1], to the end all men[2] may know them,
and take heed of them.   These things are everywhere to be
seen in the writings of the prophets and apostles; yet singular
places, if any man would know, are to be seen, Deut. xiii.
and xviii., Isai. lvi., Jeremy xxiii., Ezechiel xxxiv., Daniel xi.,
Matthew vii. and xxiii. The epistles of Paul in describing and
confuting of them are very plentiful; and St Peter in overthrowing of such men spendeth a great part of his latter epistle.

The testimonies and examples of the same prophets and
apostles do shew, that godly ministers and faithful pastors shall
be vexed with all kinds of afflictions and persecutions.   Yet
the very same nevertheless do witness evidently, that the
ministry shall never be utterly oppressed, but that the ministers shall continually have the victory, yea, even when they
are slain.   For the Lord always giveth ministers unto his
church, who, though they be tried as gold is in the fire, yet
they overcome through him which hath overcome the world
and the prince of the world.   The last times shall be very
wicked, as we read the times of Noe and Loth were: but as
then also, in that uttermost corruption, those two most excellent
men, with a few other singular men in all godliness and true
worshippers of God, are read to have flourished and done
their duty; even so, unto the very end of the world, the
ministry of the word shall also endure; and worthy doctors
and pastors shall flourish, striving against and persecuting all
ungodliness and looseness of life.   Let the enemies of the
truth cease to hope for the overthrow of the ministry and
ministers of the word of God. "I will," saith the Lord in the
gospel, "be with you always, even unto the end of the world."
He cannot lie who hath spoken this.   "He[3] shall consume
antichrist," saith the apostle, "with the spirit of his mouth;
and shall[4] abolish him with the brightness of his coming unto
judgment." There shall be therefore ministers in the church
and preachers, yea, in despite of the gates of hell, rage they
never so horribly, even unto the end of the world.

Hirelings.

2 Thess. ii.

[1 depastores, Bullinger's one word for "false shepherds or wolves."]
[2 omnibus sanctis, Lat. : all the saints.]
[3 Idem, Lat. : The same.]
[4 quem mox abolebit, Lat. : yea, he shall shortly, &c.]

These things hitherto have I comprehended, as briefly as
I could, touching the ministry of the word, and the ministers
of the churches of Christ. But it is not in our power to frame
or give such pastors.   By the grace and goodness of God good
pastors are given, and the wicked are taken away.   Let us all
therefore call upon God, praying him to give us faithful and
godly ministers[5], whereby his name may be
always sanctified and the church of God
may be happily governed,
to the salvation of
all those that
believe.

OF THE FORM AND MANNER HOW TO PRAY TO GOD;
THAT IS, OF THE CALLING ON THE NAME OF
THE LORD: WHERE ALSO THE LORD'S
PRAYER IS EXPOUNDED; AND ALSO
SINGING, THANKSGIVING, AND
THE FORCE OF PRAYER,
IS ENTREATED.

THE FIFTH SERMON.

AFTER the ministry of the word of God in the church of
Christ handled, methinketh I have convenient place to entreat
of the prayer of the faithful, whereunto godly ministers never
leave to stir up the church.

The word prayer is very largely taken among writers,
and in daily use.   At this present we use it after the same
manner that David the prophet used it, saying: "Hear my
prayer, O God; and let my cry come unto thee." For prayer
is an humble and earnest laying forth of a faithful mind,
whereby we either ask good things at God's hands, or else
give him thanks for those things which we have received.
And[6] of prayer chiefly there are two parts; invocation or
asking, and thanksgiving.   By petition we lay open unto
God the requests and desires of our heart; beseeching him to
give us good things, and that he will turn from us evil things,
as may be to his glory and good pleasure, and according to

What prayer is.

The definition of prayer, and what be the parts thereof.

[5 episcopos, Lat.]   [6 Etenim, Lat. : For.]

our necessity. In invocation or petition we comprehend obsecration, which is a more vehement prayer; and also intercession, whereby we commend other men's matters to the Lord. For we offer prayers to the Lord our God, not only for ourselves, but also for our brethren, and for their manifold necessities; for them that are distressed with perils; for those that be sick; for them which suffer persecution, or are in a manner oppressed with other calamities and afflictions. Neither[1] do we exclude beseechings, whereby we earnestly desire evils to be turned away from ourselves or from others. There are also complaints, whereby the saints in their prayers do holily expostulate with God. Thanksgiving comprehendeth both divine praises; and also celebrateth with a joyful spirit God his noble power[2], and the benefits received at his hand. Hereunto is referred a great part of the Psalms: whereof part pertain to invocation or calling upon God; and some serve to teach or instruct, and some to declare or expound: whereof at this present there is no place to speak. Paul, the blessed apostle of Christ, acknowledging these parts of prayer, writing

Col. iv. to the Colossians, saith: "Continue in prayer, and watch in

Phil. iv. the same with thanksgiving." And to the Philippians: "Let your requests be shewed unto God, in prayer and supplication

1 Tim. ii. with giving of thanks." And again unto Timothy: "I exhort, therefore," saith Paul, "that first of all prayers, supplications, intercessions, and giving of thanks, be made for all men."

Kinds of prayers. Kinds of prayers are these. There is a private prayer of every faithful man; and there is also a public prayer of the whole church. Private prayer is made unto God by every faithful man, in what place soever, either in the house or without doors, in the closet of his heart and temple of his

Acts x.
1 Tim. ii. own body: for St Peter went up into the uppermost part of the house and prayed; St Paul saith, "I will therefore that the men pray everywhere, lifting up pure hands;" and Christ our Lord himself very often departed even out of the temple into the mount to pray. And in the gospel he saith:

Matt. vi. "When thou prayest, enter into thy chamber; and when thou hast shut thy door, pray to thy Father which is in secret."

Public prayer is that which is used of the church, which

[1 Ergo nec, Lat.]   [2 virtutes eximias, Lat.]

is made unto God in the holy assembly, according to the accustomed order of every church. Now the pastor's duty is, as Paul also admonisheth in the 1 Tim. ii., and we in the last sermon before this have rehearsed, to gather together, instruct, and preserve the assemblies, in which supplications or common prayers are made. And they are greatly to be blamed, who are more negligent in this behalf than becometh them; neither are they indeed to be suffered, which seldom or never teach diligently, and are cold in stirring up a desire in men, to pray. Men by nature are slow and slack in the study of religion, and therefore we have need of a sharp spur ; and the charge and office of stirring up, and provoking, is committed to the pastors of churches. The prophets somewhere cry : " Blow out the trumpet in Sion, assemble a congregation." For in Of holy assemblies. a holy congregation three things are chiefly used ; the teaching of the gospel, faithful prayers, and religious celebration or administration of the sacraments : and sometimes there is a collection made for the relieving of the poor and of the church. The holy scripture witnesseth, that these things are not instituted at the will and pleasure of man, but by the authority of God ; yea, and immediately after the first beginning of things ; and that they were also used of the most holy worshippers of God. Of those most ancient patriarchs, both which were first before the flood and which followed immediately after, there is no doubt ; since the scripture plainly witnesseth of Jacob himself, the nephew[3] of Abraham, that he Gen. xxxv. erected an altar in Bethel, whereunto he assembled his whole household, though it were exceeding great, and there offered sacrifice[4] unto God. In Moses' time by the law, in most evident commandments, he instituted holy assemblies : yea, in the ten commandments he diligently commandeth to sanctify Exod. xx. the sabbath-day; which also comprehendeth holy assemblies. The holy prophets of God do everywhere praise and commend the ecclesiastical assemblies of God's people. Neither did Christ our Lord disallow them, when he came in the flesh : for as in the most notable[5] assemblies and feasts he taught with great diligence ; even so he gathered and assembled together both the people and also his disciples, whom he specially commanded that they should not depart from Hierusalem, but Luke xxiv.

[3 nepote, Lat.: grandson.]
[4 cultum exhibuerit, Lat.]   [5 frequentissimis, Lat.]

Acts ii.
wait for the promise of the Father : which thing, when they were gathered together into an assembly and in prayer, we read in the Acts to have been performed. There also the assembly of the faithful is commended to us; as appeareth both in[1] the xi. and xiv. cap. of the 1 epist. of Paul to the Corinth. Those supplications, which the same Paul commandeth to be made for all them that are set in authority, are made chiefly in holy assemblies. Truly Pliny, an heathen author, writing to Trajanus the emperor, doth make very manifest mention of holy assemblies[2]. Holy assemblies had of old time very 1 Kings viii. excellent promises; as we may see in the prayer of Solomon, which is described unto you in the first book of the Kings, the viii. cap. And at this day the church of Christ hath promises nothing inferior to them; Christ our Lord saying : Matt. xviii. "I say unto you, that if two of you shall agree in earth as touching anything that they shall ask, it shall be done for them of my Father which is in heaven. For where two or three are gathered together in my name, there am I in the midst of them." Behold, the Lord himself is in the midst of the assemblies of saints; and where the Lord is, there is both plenty and the treasure of all good things. And therefore experience itself which we have of matters teacheth, that the supplications of the church are effectual; for the Lord heareth the prayers of the church, and delivereth from evil those whose safety the church commendeth unto him[3]. We have oftentimes had experience, that they which were in extreme danger have found very present help, even at the same instant wherein the congregation hath offered their prayers to the Lord. Moreover, the example moveth very many, otherwise hard-hearted and barbarous; for they see the devout godliness of the holy congregation, and the fervency of the faithful in assemblies, and are thereby moved; so that entering into themselves, they acknowledged that they are miserable, and desire to be partakers of this fellowship, ac- 1 Cor. xiv. cording to the saying of St Paul : "If therefore, when the

[1] Ibidem ... sicut et, &c. Lat. There also (i. e. in the Acts) ... as likewise in, &c.]

[2] Affirmabant (Christiani) quod essent soliti stato die ante lucem convenire; carmenque Christo, quasi Deo, dicere secum invicem, &c.—Plin. Ep. Lib. x. Ep. 97.]

[3] Domino, Lat. : to the Lord.]

whole church is come together in one, and all speak strange tongues[4], there come in they that are unlearned, or they which believe not; will they not say, that ye are out of your wits? But if all prophesy, and there come in one which believeth not, or one unlearned, he is rebuked of all men, and is judged of all. And so are the secrets of his heart made manifest; and so he will fall down on his face, and worship God[5], and say plainly, that God is in you indeed." With what confidence, therefore, and how shamefully, dare some set light by holy assemblies; and not only set light by them, but also scorn at them, as if they were assembled together without any profit at all? David in his banishment maketh complaint of nothing so much, as that he was compelled to wander in the wilderness, and was shut out from holy assemblies. For[6] he promiseth the Lord, he will enter into his holy congregation, if ever he be restored again. Verily, when the Lord saith in the gospel, "He which is of God heareth God's word;" it followeth, that they which love the congregation, wherein the word of God is preached, have the natural mark of the sons of God.

But because many do not only loathe holy assemblies, We must but also say that prayers are altogether superfluous, vain, pray. and unprofitable; before we proceed any further, we will shew that the godly must pray, and that the prayers of the faithful are both effectual, profitable, and[7] necessary. They say, All things are done by the providence of God, and therefore prayers are unprofitable; for that which God hath foreknown, that verily will he bring to pass after the manner of his foreknowledge, neither can it be hindered by prayers. But these men abuse the providence of God; for that out of it they gather that thing, which the holy scriptures do not teach them to gather. For in Deuteronomy, in express words, Moses hath left written: "The Lord had determined to de- Deut. ix. stroy you; therefore I made intercession unto the Lord, and I found favour." Jonas threateneth so certain destruction Jonah iii. iv. unto the Ninevites from the Lord, that he even foretold the number of days: but when the men of Nineveh believed the Lord, and repented, the Lord became favourable to them again; neither did he destroy them, when they repented.

[4 linguis, Lat.: *strange* not in Lat.]   [5 God, not in Lat.]
[6 Autem, Lat.: And.]   [7 adeoque, Lat.: and so.]

Moreover, Esay had spoken to Ezechias out of the mouth of
the Lord, " Thou shalt die, and not live :" but when the
king poured forth his prayers, even from the bottom of his
heart unto the Lord, God changed his sentence that he had
pronounced. For the Lord himself saith in Jeremy : " I will
speak suddenly against a nation or a kingdom, for to pluck it
up, and to root it out, and to destroy it[1] : but if this nation,
against whom I have pronounced, turn from their wickedness,
I will repent of the plague that I thought to bring upon
them," &c. Wherefore the prayers of the faithful are effectual,
staying the wrathful judgments of God, yea, and taking them
clean away.

For whereas they object again, That prayer is a declaration of things which we require of the Lord; and that God
foreknoweth all things; therefore that these[2] things are unprofitably and superfluously declared unto him, which he
already knoweth ; and so for that cause that prayer is unprofitable : it is confuted of Christ our Lord himself, who, when
he had plainly said, " Your heavenly Father knoweth what
things ye have need of, before ye ask of him ;" yet nevertheless, adding a form of prayer, he teacheth us to pray. In
another place he commandeth us and stirreth us up to pray
often : " Watch and pray," saith he, " lest you enter into
temptation." And Paul saith : " Rejoice always ; pray continually." In every place there are many precepts of this
kind. Neither do we declare our matters to him as to one
that knoweth them not; but we utter them to him that understandeth the desires of our heart, and do humble ourselves at
the feet of his majesty. We ask that of him which we know
we want; but yet of him certainly to be received, who is the
author of all goodness ; for we believe his sure and infallible
promises. In the meantime prayers are not superfluous, for
that the Lord would assuredly give that which we asked.
The Lord promised the delivery of his people, whereof the
godly doubted nothing at all : yet with incessant supplications
they prayed unto the Lord, crying, " Deliver us, O Lord our
God ;" neither did they think they laboured in vain. To
the anabaptists[3], pretending absolute pureness, and therefore,

Isai. xxxviii.

Jer. xviii.

Objection.

Matt. vi.

1 Thess. v.

Jer. xxix.

Anabaptists.

[[1] and to — destroy it, not in Lat.]
[[2] So also 1584; but 1577, those.]
[[3] See Vol. III. p. 66, note 2.]

being pure, neither can nor ought to pray, "Forgive us our debts," since there remain no debts, the most holy evangelist and apostle John answereth, and saith: "If we say we have no sin, we deceive ourselves, and the truth is not in us. If we acknowledge our sins, he is faithful and just to forgive us our sins, and to cleanse us from all unrighteousness. If we say that we have not sinned, we make him a liar, and his word is not in us." For as long as we live in this world, there remain remnants of sin to be washed away every moment by the grace of Christ. *1 John i.*

Moreover, whereas they object, it is written, "We know that God doth not hear sinners;" but we are all sinners, therefore God doth hear none of us, and so men's prayers are found to be unprofitable: we answer, that of sinners some are altogether ungodly and despisers of God: those God heareth not. There are again repentant men, and such as fear God; which nevertheless are sinners, and rightly so called, because of the remnants of sin: those God heareth. Which might be shewed by the examples of David, Manasses, Peter, the thief crucified with Christ, and many other; which were both sinners, and when they prayed were heard. *John ix.*

Therefore we say, that the prayers of the faithful are not only profitable and effectual, but also necessary unto men. For we are men, defiled with sin, destitute and void of all goodness. "Every good giving, and every perfit gift is from above, and cometh down from the Father of lights." He commandeth us to pray, and offereth to them that pray very large promises. Wherefore our fathers were both very often exercised, and very fervent, in prayer; by their example teaching us that prayers are necessary. The scripture also diligently and at large rehearseth, how great things by their prayers in very weighty affairs and dangers, yea, in matters most necessary, they obtained of our most true and most bountiful Lord and God. The apostles pray for the Holy Ghost, faith, and the increase of faith; and they receive their requests, not sparingly, but liberally, being made partakers of all manner graces of Christ. In the gospel the publican prayeth in the temple, and saith: "God, be merciful to me a sinner:" and he forthwith found the Lord merciful unto him. What and how great things Helias by his prayers obtained of the Lord, the holy history recordeth. And the blessed *Prayers are necessary.* *James i.* *Luke xviii.*

apostle James applieth his example unto us also, that we also in faith should call upon God: which I rehearse, lest any man should think that that pertaineth nothing unto us. Again, how much the faithful prayers of Moses, David, Josaphat, Ezechias, and other valiant men, prevailed in wars, in famines, in sickness, and in other exceeding great dangers, it were long to recite. These examples prove, that prayer is both always necessary unto men, and very effectual. For we

God is moved with prayers. plainly see that God is moved with the prayers of his faithful; for he is good and merciful, he loveth us, he took flesh, that he might be touched with feeling of our infirmities, lest we should be dismayed at him: he is true and faithful, performing those things faithfully which he promiseth. What? doth he not freely, liberally, and bountifully call all men unto him, offering himself wholly to them that call upon him in faith?

Why they that pray do not always receive that they ask. But in that they which pray do not always receive that which they ask, it doth not prove that prayer is altogether unprofitable; for it is oftentimes profitable for him that prayeth not to receive his requests. There are moreover many causes, for the which God either putteth off the things that are asked, or doth not grant them. There is a kind of men

Prov. xxi. which pray, of whom we read written: "He that stoppeth his ear at the cry of the poor, shall cry himself, and not be

Isai. i. heard." Again: "Though ye make many prayers, yet will I hear nothing at all, seeing your hands are full of blood."

Prov. i. So again in Solomon Wisdom crieth, testifying that she will not hear them that call on her, because they would not first hear her giving them warning in time. All these things in a manner are gathered from the person of them that pray: from the thing itself which they pray for, that which follow-

James iv. eth is derived. St James saith: "Ye ask and receive not, because ye ask amiss, even to consume it upon your lusts."

Matt. xx. For the Lord also, answering two even of his chosen[1] disciples which required the highest rooms[2] in the kingdom of Christ, saith: "Ye know not what ye ask." Furthermore, holy men when they ask holy and necessary things, or at the least not unjust or evil, which nevertheless they receive not of the Lord; they forthwith think, that God is a God of judgment and justice, and therefore that he will not immediately deliver

[1 alioqui selectis, Lat.: otherwise choice.]   [2 primatum, Lat.]

out of afflictions: yet desire they deliverance with continual prayers. "Whom the Lord loveth he chasteneth:" whom he chasteneth, he doth[3] not to this end, to destroy them; but "that they should not be condemned with the wicked world." For it is lawful in such distresses to pray with David, "Rebuke me not in thine anger, O Lord; neither chasten me in thy displeasure:" and with Jeremy, "Lord, correct me in judgment, not in fury:" and with Abacuch, "When thou art angry, remember thy mercy." The godly doubt nothing of the power and goodness of God to men-ward. That which God will, and which is profitable for the children of God, God can do. Innumerable examples of this thing the old and new Testament[4] doth afford us. Wherefore, when we are not delivered, when we obtain not our desires, it is most sure that God will have it so, and that it is profitable for us it should so be. By this means he heareth our prayers, when he heareth us; for our prayers tend to this end only, that it might go well with us. God, since he is only wise, knoweth what can profit and what can hurt us, and doth not give us that we ask; yet by not giving he in very deed granteth that which is good for us. Therefore the lawful prayer of the faithful is always effectual, and evermore obtaineth his purpose; the Lord granting to his that which he knoweth to be good.

Furthermore, the Lord deferreth to perform that which is asked, yea, and at sometime seemeth altogether to neglect our prayers: but he doth that by prolonging to try his, that he may make their faith the more fervent, and his gifts also more acceptable; which are so much the more joyfully received, by how much they are looked for by an ardent[5] desire. In this temptation let that saying of the prophet comfort us: "Can a woman forget her child, and not have compassion on the son of her own womb? Though they should[6] forget, yet will not I forget thee." For the church had said: "God hath forsaken me, and my Lord hath forgotten me."

Let us now consider, what manner of prayer that should be which he that calleth on God useth. That question cannot be better resolved, than by weighing the chiefest circumstances.

Margin notes: Prov. iii. Heb. xii. — Psal. xxxviii. — Why God deferreth to give that which he meaneth to give. — Isai. xlix. — Who is to be called upon of them that pray.

[3 corripit, Lat.: he doth chasten.]
[4 historia vetus et evangelica, Lat.]
[5 ardentiori, Lat.: more ardent.]   [6 poterit, Lat.: she may.]

First therefore let us consider, Who must be called upon of them that pray. None verily, but the one and only God. For three things are required of him which is prayed unto : first, that he hear the prayers of all the men in the whole world; that he pierce and exactly know their hearts ; yea, that he know more rightly and better all the desires of men than men themselves can utter them : secondly, that he be present everywhere, and have power over all things in heaven, in earth, and in hell ; which hath in his power all the ways and all the means to help : thirdly, that his will be exceeding good and ready prepared; that that which he can, he may also be willing to do. But these properties are found in God only. For God only searcheth the reins and the hearts : he only seeth and heareth all things : he only knoweth more perfectly those things which are within and without man, than man himself : he only is present in all places : he only is almighty : he only is wise : the will of God only embraceth man with most perfect goodness, and is always ready, and only procureth faithfully that which is profitable for man : therefore ought God only to be called upon. But who can attribute these properties, were it to the most chosen souls in heaven, without blasphemy and sacrilege ? Therefore the souls in heaven, living with God, are not to be called upon : especially since the scripture in plain words testifieth, that "Abraham and Jacob know us not ;" and commandeth us to call on God, and forbiddeth to communicate those things which are God's to creatures.. And, that we say nothing else ; to whom, I pray you, of all the saints or angels in heaven can we say without blushing, " Our Father, which art in heaven," and that which followeth in the Lord's prayer ? Let us therefore call upon God only, that heavenly Father, whom alone all the saints, or godly men, as many as have been in the church, have called upon.

Isai. lxiii.

By whom God the Father is called upon. But since no mortal man, how good soever[1] he seem to be, is worthy to come forth into the sight of the eternal and most holy God ; which thing all men with one voice confess : many indeed and divers patrons, intercessors, and advocates, are chosen and received of them that pray ; by whose intercession either they themselves might be brought to God, or their prayers presented unto God. Wherefore some have

[1 et sanctus, Lat. : omitted, and holy.]

chosen to themselves angels, other apostles, other the most
holy and among all other women that blessed virgin, the
mother of Christ[2]; other some have chosen other, as they
have put confidence in this man or that man: but they have
forged these things unto themselves out of the imagination[3]
of their own heart, and have not learned them at the mouth
of the Lord. The scripture, that only rule of truth, setteth
forth to us one mediator, intercessor, patron, and advocate, by
whom we may come unto God, and by whom we may present
our prayers unto the Lord. All the prayers of all men are
unpleasant and abominable, which are not made by Jesus
Christ. Neither doth true faith teach us[4] to forge and imagine another advocate for Christ, or some other with Christ,
in the sight of God; nor ourselves alone without our advocate
Christ to rush into the presence of God the Father. Here
true[5] Christians are separated from Jews, from Turks[6], yea,
and papists also. For they, despising[7] the Son of God, call
upon the Father only, without the mediation of Christ Jesus.
But the voice of God, by the gospel and his apostles, pronounceth against them. In the gospel we read the Lord
said: "The Father hath committed all judgment unto the John v.
Son, because that all men should honour the Son, even as
they honour the Father. He that honoureth not the Son,
the same honoureth not the Father which hath sent him."
And again: "I am the way, and the truth, and the life. No John xiv.
man cometh to the Father, but by me." And John, the
apostle and evangelist, saith: "Whosoever denieth the Son, 1 John ii.
the same hath not the Father." But these men do not
acknowledge Christ to be the only intercessor; but teach that
saints in his stead, or with him, ought to be called upon,
as patrons before God. But the same John[8], shewing an
advocate unto Christians, did not appoint himself; did not lay
before us saints instead of Christ, or them with Christ;
"but," saith he, "we have an advocate with God the Father,
Jesus Christ the righteous." Neither doth Paul shew us any
other in 1 Tim. ii. cap., and Heb. vii. cap. To the Ephesi. iii.

[2 of Christ, not in Lat.]   [3 arbitrio, Lat.]
[4 So also 1584; but 1577 *suffer* us, patitur, Lat.]
[5 true, not in Lat.]   [6 Mahumeticis, Lat.]
[7 So also ed. 1577; but 1584, despising of.]
[8 apostolus, Lat. omitted.]

Ephes. iii. "By Christ," saith he, "we have boldness and entrance with confidence by faith in him." Christ is sufficient for them that believe, as in whom alone the Father hath stored up all good things, commanding us to ask those things in him and by him through prayer. These things are sufficient for minds not desirous of contention. They that will, let them search further in the fifth sermon of the fourth decade[1].

What things provoke man to call upon God. I have told you, who is to be prayed unto or called upon of the godly worshippers of God; and by[2] whom: to wit, God alone, by[2] the only Son of God, our Lord Jesus Christ. Let us now see, what should stir up man to call upon God. Surely, the Spirit of our God principally; for prayer is rightly counted among the gifts of grace: for neither could we earnestly nor heartily call upon our God, unless we be stirred up and provoked thereunto by the Spirit of God. For albeit the commandment of God will us to pray, and present necessity and danger drive us, and the example of other allure us to pray; yet all these things would do nothing, unless the Spirit enforce our minds unto his will, and guide and keep us in prayer. Therefore, though there be many causes concurring which move men to prayer, yet the chief original of prayer is the Holy Ghost; to whose motion and government, in the entrance of all prayers, whosoever pray with any fruit do beg with an holy preface. To this pertain these words of the holy apostle: "The Spirit also," saith he, "helpeth our infirmities;

Rom. viii. for we know not what to pray as we ought; but the Spirit itself maketh requests for us with sighs which cannot be expressed. But he which searcheth the hearts knoweth what is the meaning of the Spirit; for he maketh requests for the saints according to the will of God." Indeed, the Spirit of God is said to make intercession; not that he in very deed prayeth and groaneth; but because he stirreth up our minds to pray and to sigh, and bringeth to pass that, according to the pleasure of God, we should make intercession or pray for the saints, that is to say, for ourselves.

With what abilities he must be furnished which cometh to pray unto God. But let us consider, with what abilities he must be furnished, which cometh of purpose to pray unto God. First, it is necessary that he lay aside all opinion of his own worthiness and righteousness; that he acknowledge himself to be a sinner, and to stand in need of all good things; and so let

[1 See Vol. III. p. 212, &c.] [2 per, Lat.: through.]

him yield himself unto the mere mercy of God, desiring of the
same to be filled with all things that are good. For that great
prophet of God, Daniel, saith : " We do not present our pray- Dan. ix.
ers before thee in our own righteousness, but in thy manifold
mercies." Also you read the like prayers offered unto God,
Psalm lxxix.; for the people of the Lord cry : " Help us, O
Lord of our salvation, for the glory of thy name : deliver us,
and be merciful unto our sins, for thy name's sake. Remember
not our sins of old ; make haste, and let thy mercy deliver
us." In the new Testament, the Pharisee in Luke, trusting Luke xviii.
in his own righteousness, is put by, and cast off from the
Lord ; but the publican, freely confessing his sins and craving
mercy of God, is heard and justified. For unless we acknowledge our nakedness, weakness, and poverty, who, I pray
you, will pray unto God ? " For not they that be strong,
but they that be sick, have need of the physician." And
the Lord in the gospel saith : " Ask, and ye shall receive ; Matt. vii.
knock, and it shall be opened unto you ; seek, and ye shall
find." He therefore that is commanded to ask, that he may
receive, hath not as yet that he asketh ; he that knocketh,
by knocking signifieth that he standeth without doors ; and
he which seeketh, hath lost that which yet he seeketh for.
We therefore, being shut out from the joys of paradise, by
prayer do seek and ask for that which we have lost and have
not. Therefore, whereas David and Ezechias and other
saints of God in prayer do allege their own righteousness, for
which they seem worthily to require to be heard ; truly they
regard not their own worthiness, but rather the truth of
God. He hath promised, that he will hear them that worship
him ; therefore the godly say : Behold, we are thy worshippers;
therefore it is meet thou shouldest not neglect us, but deliver
us. In the meanwhile, in other places they speak in such
sort of their righteousness, that we cannot doubt that in their
prayers they made mention of their righteousness with a
certain measure and limitation. " Enter not into judgment
with thy servant," saith David ; " for in thy sight shall no
man living be justified," &c.

Furthermore, and that which is the chief of all ; it is Faith is
needful that they which pray must have a true and fervent chiefly need-
faith. Let the doctrine of faith, therefore, in the matter of that pray.
prayer, shew us light as the morning-star ; and with an assured

hope to obtain of God the thing which is asked, let him that prayeth make his petition. "Let him ask in faith," saith

James i. St James[1], "nothing wavering: for he that wavereth is like a wave of the sea, tost of the wind, and carried with violence. Neither let that man think that he shall receive anything of the Lord." And[2] Paul also saith: "How shall they call upon him, on whom they have not believed?" I have spoken of faith in the fourth sermon of the first decade. But to the end that faith may increase in just measure, and flourish and continue stable; we must labour in the promises and examples from every place gathered together. We will

Psal. l. recite a few. In the book of Psalms we read: "Offer unto God thanksgiving, and pay thy vows unto the most Highest."

Psal. cxlv. And: "Call upon me in the day of trouble, and I will deliver thee, and thou shalt glorify me." Again: "The Lord is nigh unto all that call upon him, unto all such as call upon him in truth (or faithfully). He will fulfil the desire of them that fear him: he will also hear their cry, and will save them."

Isai. lxv. Again, in Esay, the Lord saith: "And it shall come to pass, that before they call, I will answer them; and while they are but yet thinking how to speak[3], I will hear them." In

Matt. vii. Matthew the Lord saith: "Ask, and it shall be given you; seek, and ye shall find; knock, and it shall be opened unto you. For whosoever asketh receiveth, and whosoever seeketh findeth, and to him that knocketh it shall be opened," &c. In

Matt. xxi. the same gospel the Lord saith: "And all things whatsoever ye shall ask in prayer, believing, ye shall receive it[4]." In the

Mark xi. xi. of Mark the same sentence is thus alleged: "Whatsoever," saith he, "ye desire, when ye pray, believe that ye shall have it, and it shall be done unto you." Again, in the gospel

John xiv. according to St John the Lord saith: "Whatsoever ye shall

John xvi. ask in my name, that will I do." Again: "Verily, verily, I say unto you, Whatsoever ye shall ask the Father in my name, he will give it you. Ask, and ye shall receive." David frameth an argument of the example of the fathers,

Psal. xxii. and saith: "Our fathers hoped in thee, they trusted in thee, and thou didst deliver them; they called upon thee, and they

[1 apostolus, Lat.: omitted.]   [2 Nam, Lat.: For.]
[3 So Coverdale, 1535; but Lat. adhuc illis loquentibus: while they are yet speaking.]
[4 So also 1584; but 1577 omits it.]

were helped; they did put their trust in thee, and were not
confounded:" for thereupon he gathereth, that he also shall
not be forsaken of the Lord. In the history of the gospel
are very many examples to be seen, which exceedingly confirm
and establish the faith of the godly.

But since faith is not a vain imagination, but an effectual Let the life of him that
power, working by the Holy Ghost all kind of good works, prayeth be answerable
(though they neither trust unto these, neither think in con- to his faith.
sideration of them to be heard;) yet nevertheless such sinners
as are faithful do not impudently, and without repentance,
trust to their own wits[5], dealing only in words with the Lord;
but they join a holy life with prayers. For Salomon saith:
"He that turneth his ear from hearing the law, his[6] prayer Prov. xxviii.
shall be abominable." And the Lord saith in Esay: "Though Isai. i.
ye make many prayers, yet will I hear nothing at all, seeing
your hands are full of blood." Of such impenitent persons
we understand that in the gospel: "God heareth not sinners." John ix.
But that more is; the saints shall obtain nothing, if they continue prayer for such; for Jeremy, praying earnestly for his
people otherwise being obstinately wicked, heareth: "Thou Jer. vii.
shalt not pray for this people; thou shalt neither give thanks
nor bid prayer for them[7]; make thou no intercession for them;
for in no wise will I hear thee. Seest thou not what they do
in the cities of Juda? The children gather sticks, the fathers
kindle the fire, the women knead the dough to make cakes for
the queen of heaven. They pour out[8] drink-offerings unto
strange gods, to provoke me unto wrath." After the same
manner saith the Lord in Ezechiel: "If I send a pestilence Ezek. xiv.
into this land, and if[9] Noe, Job, and Daniel, were[10] therein," (or
in the midst of it,) "as truly as I live, saith the Lord God,
they shall deliver neither son nor daughter, but save their
own souls in their righteousness." Wherefore it followeth,
that the supplications of unrepentant men and impudently

[5 ingenio indulgent, Lat.: rather, give loose to their lusts.]

[6 etiam, Lat.: even his, &c.]

[7 neque attollas pro illis clamorem et deprecationem, Lat.: but
the Vulgate, nec assumas pro eis laudem et orationem; and Coverdale,
1535, as above.]

[8 et ut, Lat.: and to pour out, &c.]

[9 tres viri, Lat. omitted: the three men.]

[10 steterint, Lat.: stood.]

persevering in their sins, though they cry without ceasing, "Help us, O God, our Saviour; deliver us, O Lord; we beseech thee to hear us," are altogether fruitless; for they desire to be preserved, that they might take their further pleasure and commit wickedness. And though God give us freely those things which we ask, yet it is necessary, that an affection or desire to live well do accompany so great benefits received at the hands of God: for here we ought most diligently to take heed, that we think not we shall be heard for our virtues' sake, but for the mere mercy of God in Christ Jesus[1].

Our minds must be lifted up to heavenly things.

Moreover, whosoever desireth to have his prayers to be acceptable unto God, let him lift up his mind from earthly things unto heavenly things. Touching that thing the blessed martyr of Christ, Cyprian, eloquently[2] and holily entreating, saith: "When we stand occupied in prayer, we must with our whole heart watch, and be diligent in prayer. Let all worldly and fleshly thoughts depart; neither let the mind think upon anything else at that time than only that which it prayeth. Let thy breast be shut against the adversary, and let it be open to God only; neither let it suffer the enemy of God to enter into it in the time of prayer. For he oftentimes stealeth upon us, and entereth in; and, subtilly deceiving us, turneth away our prayers from God, that we may have one thing in our heart, and another thing in our mouth. But not the sound of the voice, but the mind and sense, ought to pray unto God with an unfeigned affection[3]." Thus far he.

But that the mind of him that prayeth may be lifted up from earthly things unto heavenly things, that is chiefly the work of the spirit of true faith, the stedfastness of hope, and the fervent love of God; if also we have in remembrance the dreadful majesty of God, before whose eyes we stand pray-

[1 So also 1584; but 1577, Jesu.]   [2 eleganter, Lat.]
[3 Quando autem stamus ad orationem, fratres dilectissimi, vigilare et incumbere ad preces toto corde debemus. Cogitatio omnis carnalis et secularis abscedat, nec quidquam tunc animus quam id solum cogitet quod precatur.... Claudatur contra adversarium pectus, et soli Deo pateat, nec ad se hostem Dei tempore orationis adire patiatur: obrepit enim frequenter et penetrat, et subtiliter fallens preces nostras a Deo avocat, ut aliud habeamus in corde, et aliud in voce, quando intentione sincera Dominum debeat non vocis sonus, sed animus et sensus orare.—Cyprian. de Orat. Domin. Opp. p. 152. Oxon. 1682.]

ing.   Him all the creatures in heaven and earth do worship
and reverence; thousand thousands of angels serve him.   Let
us think with ourselves, how profitable and necessary things
we ask of God, without which we cannot be happy.   Let us,
moreover, remove from us all those things, which either detain
and keep us in this world, or pull us back unto earthly things;
of which sort are these, slothfulness, covetousness, and surfeiting, and, to be short, all other sins like unto these: and
contrariwise, let us apply ourselves to watchfulness, soberness,
gentleness, and liberality.   Surely the scripture almost everywhere joineth unto prayer fasting and mercy; for these
virtues make us more cheerful and ready to pray through
faith.   Daniel saith: " I turned my face unto the Lord God, Dan. ix.
and sought⁴ him by prayer and supplication, with fasting,
sackcloth, and ashes."   Neither unlike to this do Jonas and
Joel teach.   Yea, in the gospel and writings of the apostles we
everywhere hear: "Watch; be fervent in prayer; be sober."
For, the belly being full, either no prayers at all, or else fat
and unwieldy prayers, are made.   Whereof we read that
St Augustine said: " Wilt thou have thy prayer fly up unto
God? make it two wings, fasting and alms-deeds⁵." For in the
Acts of the Apostles the angel of the Lord saith to Cornelius,
the centurion: "Thy prayers and thine alms-deeds are had in Acts x.
remembrance in the sight of God."

   And surely God requireth of us fervent prayer; but it Let prayer
proceed from
cannot choose but be cold, which is not inflamed with charity. love.
Therefore they that be cruel, and unwilling to forgive their
brethren their trespasses, and do still retain hatred toward
their brethren, cannot pray before God, who saith: " And Mark xi.
when ye stand praying, forgive, if ye have ought against any
man; that your Father also which is in heaven may forgive
you your trespasses." And again: "If ye forgive men their Matt. vi.
trespasses, your heavenly Father shall also forgive you: but
if ye forgive not men their trespasses, no more shall your
heavenly Father forgive you your trespasses." And in another
place he saith: "Therefore if thou bring thy gift unto the Matt. v.
altar, and there rememberest that thy brother hath ought

[⁴ ut rogarem, Lat. : to seek.]
[⁵ Vis orationem tuam volare ad Deum? Fac illi duas alas, jeju-
nium et eleemosynam.—August. Enarrat. in Psalm. xlii. 8. Opp.
Tom. viii. fol. 81. col. 4. Par. 1531.]

against thee, leave there thy gift before the altar, and go thy way; first be reconciled to thy brother, and then come and offer thy gift:" for otherwise all thy gifts shall not be acceptable unto God.   Let us therefore willingly forgive, and let us love and do good unto our neighbours; so our prayers shall pierce the heavens.

We must not pray with the mouth only, but with the heart.   Agreeable unto this is, that we pray not only with the mouth or voice, but with the mind and inward affection of the heart, and with the spirit and fervency.   There was no voice heard of Moses, neither of Anna, the mother of Samuel, when they prayed; but most earnestly in spirit they cried unto God: who also heard, and led him safely with all the people of Israel through the Red sea, out of the most bloody hands of the Egyptians; and her which afore was barren he made fruitful.   And contrariwise we read that the Lord in the gospel out of Esay

Matt. xv.   alleged these words against the Pharisees: " This people draweth nigh unto me with their mouth, and honoureth me with their lips, howbeit their heart is far from me: but in vain do they worship me, teaching doctrines precepts of men."   There-

Cor. xiv.   fore aptly said Paul: " I will pray with the spirit, and will pray with the understanding also;" where he calleth the lively breath and voice of man "spirit[1]."   By these heavenly testimonies their prayers are condemned, who, with a marvellous rolling[2] and swiftness of the tongue, in a short space babble many words, and those maimed and curtailed, uttering words without sense; for their mind in the meanwhile is otherwise occupied.   No other desire is there felt of them, unless happily this seem a desire, in that they pant and blow, hasting to make an end of praying.   Among which kind of men monks and priests are chief, who pray for money and for their hire ; that is, sell a thing of nought for a great price unto the mad people. Not that prayers are vain of themselves, but because, being used after that manner, they become vain.   Of these

Matt. xxiii.   men the Lord pronounceth in the gospel: "Woe be unto you, scribes and Pharisees, hypocrites; for ye devour widows' houses, and that under a pretence of long prayer; therefore ye shall receive the greater damnation."   I know what those[3] sophisters[4] do here bring forth and allege for the defence of prayers said for reward or stipend; but in few words I give

[1 See Vol. III. p. 298.]   [2 volubilitate, Lat.]
[3 So also 1584; but 1577, *these.*]   [4 logodædali, Lat.]

them this knot to loose. These men, that pray in this sort, either have faith and charity, or else they have not: if they have, they pray without reward, for charity's sake; if they have not, their prayers are of no effect: and therefore with a false shew they deceive the ignorant people, paying their money for lawful prayers, whereas they requite them with unlawful; and if they were lawful, yet were they neither to be sold or bought.

This is also required of him that prayeth; that he desire not things unworthy for God to grant, nor require those things that are contrary to the laws of God. For St John the apostle saith, "If we ask anything according to his will, he heareth us:" therefore when we ask things unworthy for God to grant, he heareth us not. Moreover, always and in all our prayers our will and our desires ought to be obedient to God and his will. Therefore let no man go about wickedly to tie God to certain circumstances; let no man prescribe unto God at what time, in what place, or after what manner, he shall bring to pass anything that he will do. God, who is only wise, knoweth when it is time to help. He is also both faithful and omnipotent, and able indeed to do greater things than either we can ask or understand; which thing we also read that Paul hath said. Therefore, not without cause is that most honest widow, Judith, very angry with Osias the priest, because he appointed a set number of days unto God; which being ended, he should deliver, or otherwise they would give up the city. For Judith saith: "What manner of sentence is this, whereunto Osias hath consented; to deliver this city unto the Assyrians, if within five days there come not succour for us? And who are ye that tempt the Lord? This is not a sentence like to obtain mercy, but rather to provoke wrath and kindle displeasure. You have set the mercy of God a time, and have appointed him a day after your own phantasy. But forasmuch as the Lord is patient, let us so much the rather repent, and crave pardon at his hands, by pouring out of tears." Therefore David is read to have spoken most godly, being in extreme danger: "If I shall find favour in the eyes of the Lord, he will bring me again; but if he say to me, I have no lust to thee; behold, here am I; let him do with me what seemeth good in his eyes."

And now also long continuance is very needful in prayers.

Margin notes:
We must require nothing that is unworthy for God to grant, and contrary to his laws. 1 John v.

Judith viii.

2 Sam. xv.

We must continue in prayer.

"Ask," saith the Lord in the gospel, "and it shall be given you; seek, and ye shall find; knock, and it shall be opened unto you." And by this heaping together of words, he often remembereth us[1] of continuance in prayer. "Ask," saith he, earnestly and constantly, as they do which require things whereof they stand in need; "seek," as they are wont, that search for things that are hidden and precious; "knock," as they are wont, who with earnest desire covet to come in to their friend. For all these sayings do not only signify a desire, but also a continual study to obtain things required. In the gospel according to St Luke, the Lord put forth a parable tending "to this end, that we ought always to pray, and 1 Thess. v. never to be wearied." For Paul also saith: "Rejoice alway; pray continually; in all things give thanks." Yet let no man think, that by these words of the Lord and the apostle the error of the heretics Psallini, or Euchitæ[2], is confirmed. They did nothing else but pray. The Lord commandeth to pray always; that is to say, as often as we conveniently may, at all times and in all places, to be of an upright heart toward God[3] in all things, which should always wait for good things at God's hand, and give him thanks for benefits received; which should also continually ask favour of him. Such an endeavour is commended unto us in Anna, the daughter of Phanuel, of Luke i. whom Luke maketh mention, that she "departed not from the temple, but night and day served the Lord with fastings and prayers." Not that she did nothing else, having no regard to her body, nor did at any time eat, drink, or sleep; but because that was her continual and chiefest business. For at this day, speaking after the same manner, we say that the husbandman doth labour without ceasing, and the student read night and day; when as yet all men understand, that by this kind of speech is signified a continual and exceeding great diligence in work and reading. The woman of Syrophœnissa, in Matt. chapter xv. sheweth unto us a notable example of unwearied continuance in prayer or invocation. But if so be God seem to neglect us, or to defer our requests longer than

[1 inculcavit, Lat.]

[2 Mosheim, Eccles. Hist. Book II. cent. 4. part 2. chap. 5. § 24. Vol. I. p. 409, note 5, ed. Soames. Bullinger. adv. Anabapt. Lib. I. cap. 12.]

[3 erecto ad Deum corde, Lat.: a heart raised unto God.]

is meet, let us always remember what the prophet hath said: Habak. ii.
" Yet a little while, and he that shall come will come, and ^{Heb. x.} will not tarry ;" and, " The just shall live by faith," &c.

Here[4] it shall be very easy to shew the time of prayer, whereof inquiry is made; to wit, when we ought to pray. We When we ought therefore privately to pray always ; for continually ^{must pray.} while we live there is divers and manifold matter offered unto us to pray. Pray therefore as oft as the Spirit moveth thee, and as often as necessity itself or matter provoketh thee to pray. Yet let nothing here be of constraint; let all things proceed from a willing and free spirit. But public prayers are restrained to time; for there are set and fore-appointed hours to pray. Set hours are those certain times received of the church, wherein in the morning or evening the whole congregation assembleth together, to hear the word of God, to pray, and to receive the sacraments. That the ancient churches, which were in times past, did not meet together in an holy assembly all at one time and the selfsame hours, Socrates in his history beareth witness ; and in this diversity there is no danger[5]. Let it be left to the discretion of the churches to come together[6] unto the service of God, when it shall seem most necessary, comely, meet, and profitable unto themselves. Moreover, fore-appointed hours of prayer are those which are set or forewarned for a certain time by the church for present necessity's sake. In dangerous times, and in weighty affairs, the holy apostles appointed prayers and fastings ; which thing also at this day is lawful, without superstition, and with just moderation. And that this is a most ancient ordinance, it appeareth out of these words of the prophet Joel : Joel ii. " Blow the trumpet in Sion, sanctify a fast, call a solemn assembly, gather the people together," &c. Doth not the apostle command man and wife privately to separate them-1 Cor. vii. selves for a time, and to abstain from their lawful delights, that prayer in necessity may be the more fervent ?

And now also it will not be hard to judge of the place of Of the place prayer ; for as at all times privately, so also in all places, I ^{of prayer.} have said in the beginning of this sermon, that holy men may pray. For the true prayer of holy men is not tied to any

[4 Ex his, Lat. : Hence.]
[5 Socratis Hist. Eccles. Lib. v. cap. 22.]
[6 Conveniant ecclesiæ, Lat. : let the churches come together.]

place, neither is it judged better in one place than in another; for the goodness or worthiness of the prayer is not esteemed by the place, but by the mind of him that prayeth. For the John iv. Lord in the gospel saith : " The hour will come, and now is, when the true worshippers shall worship the Father in spirit

To pray in the chamber. and in truth, &c." But they are in no wise to be passed over in this place, who are persuaded that the godly may pray in no other place but at home in their chamber; to the confirmation whereof they wrest these words of our Saviour :

Matt. vi. " But thou, when thou prayest, enter into thy chamber ; and when thou hast shut thy door, pray to thy Father, which is in secret; and thy Father, which seeth in secret, shall reward thee openly." But these words have an *antithesis*, or contrary sentence, to that which goeth afore. For there went before : " And when thou prayest, thou shalt not be[1] as the hypocrites are ; for they love to stand praying[2] in the synagogues, and in the corners of the streets, that they may be seen of men." Against this immediately he opposeth : " But thou, when thou prayest, enter into thy chamber." And as in reproving the abuse of prayer, he did not properly condemn the place, but rather spake figuratively after this manner, The Pharisees, with their prayers which they make in the streets, do hunt after praise and commendation of the people ; so on the contrary part, making mention of a chamber, he meant not that the place of itself maketh the prayer either better or worse ; but he taught by a figurative speech, that we ought to pray with an upright mind, and most free from hunting after the praise of men. For he that prayeth with a mind not troubled with affections, having regard only unto God, he prayeth in his chamber, whether he pray in the church or in the street. For otherwise, the Lord prayed with his disciples in the temple, in the city, in the field, and wheresoever occasion was offered. Also it followeth : " And the Father, which seeth thee in secret, shall reward thee openly ;" that is to say, the Father, who alloweth the mind that is not proud, but humble and free from ambition, will reward thee openly. But public prayers are used in the church or assembly of saints ; which if any man despise, saying that prayer ought not to be tied to any place, I cannot think him worthy

[1 cum oraveritis, non eritis, Lat.]   [2 stantes orare, Lat.]

the name of a Christian, since he shamefully abuseth christian liberty. Finally, of assemblies I have spoken before[3]: we will peradventure speak more in the last sermon of this decade.

Here cometh also to be handled the gesture of those that pray. But let all riot, all pride, all immoderate trimming of the body, be far from them that shall come into the church of Christ to pray. He should seem filthily to have scorned the godly magistrate, whosoever he were, that, in coming to crave pardon for his fault, would lay aside his mourning weeds; and, putting on white apparel, proudly appear before the assembly of grave and godly senators. Such a one might be judged worthy, not only to be denied of his request, but also to be cast into prison. And who will deny, that they more shamefully mock God, who, coming into the church to ask pardon, being oppressed with the burden of their sins, and yet in that place to be so far off from being humble, that they rather appear before the presence of God and his saints having their bodies so attired, as they thereby both provoke the wrath of God anew against them, and do grievously offend the most godly that are in the church? Wherefore Paul at large teacheth, that modesty, comely and humble behaviour, is to be used in the church. The place is to be seen in the xi. chapter of the first epistle to the Corinthians. That which remaineth of this matter the blessed martyr of Christ, Cyprian, comprehendeth in these words: " Let the words and prayers of such as pray be orderly governed, keeping modesty and shamefacedness. Let us think we stand in the sight of God. God his eyes must be delighted both in the gesture of our body, and manner of our words; for as it is the part of an impudent person to use clamorous shouts in praying; so, contrariwise, it beseems a shamefaced person to pray with modest prayers[4]."

The gesture of them that pray.

Some foolishly imagine, that prayer is made either better or worse by the gesture of our bodies. Therefore let them hear St Augustine, Lib. ii. *ad Simplicianum, Quæst.* 4, saying:

[3 See Vol. i. p. 261. Vol. ii. p. 263.]

[4 Sit autem orantibus sermo et precatio cum disciplina, quietem continens et pudorem. Cogitemus nos sub conspectu Dei stare; placendum est divinis oculis et habitu corporis et modo vocis. Nam ut impudentis est clamoribus strepere, ita contra congruit verecundo modestis precibus orare.—Cyprian. de Orat. Domin. Opp. p. 140. Oxon. 1682.]

"It skilleth not, after what sort our bodies be placed, so that
the mind, being present with God, do bring her purpose to
pass. For we both pray standing, as it is written, 'The
publican stood afar off;' and kneeling, as we read in the
Acts of the Apostles; and sitting, as did David and Elias.
And unless he might pray lying, it should not have been
written in the Psalms, 'Every night wash I my bed.' For
when any man seeketh to pray, he placeth the members of
his body after such a manner as it shall seem most meet to
him for the time to stir up his devotion. But when prayer is
not sought, but an appetite or desire to prayer is offered;
when anything cometh on the sudden into our mind, whereby
we are devoutly moved to pray with sighs that cannot be
uttered; after what manner soever it findeth a man, doubtless,
prayer is not to be deferred, until we have sought in what
place we may sit, or where we may stand or kneel down[1]."
Tertullian, making mention of the behaviour of the Christians
of his time when they prayed, in his Apology against the
Gentiles, saith: "We Christians are all of us evermore
praying for all men, looking up into heaven, with our hands
spread abroad, because we are harmless; we are bare-headed,
because we are not ashamed; to be short, we need none to
put us in remembrance, because we pray from the heart[2]."
Where, notwithstanding, we must chiefly have in our remem-

[1 Quibus admonemur exemplis, non esse præscriptum quomodo
corpus constituatur ad orandum, dummodo animus Deo præsens per-
agat intentionem suam.   Nam et stantes oramus, sicut scriptum est,
Publicanus autem de longinquo stabat; et fixis genubus, sicut in
Actis Apostolorum legimus; et sedentes, sicut, ecce, David et Helias.
Nisi autem jacentes oraremus, non scriptum esset in Psalmis, Lavabo
per singulas noctes lectum meum. . . . Cum enim quisque orationem
quærit, collocat membra sicut ei occurrerit, accommodata pro tempore positi corporis ad movendum affectum.   Cum autem non quæritur, sed infertur appetitus orandi, hoc est, cum aliquid repente venit in
mentem, quo supplicandi moveatur affectus gemitibus inenarrabilibus;
quocunque modo invenerit hominem, non est utique differenda oratio,
ut quæramus quo sedeamus, aut ubi stemus, aut ubi prosternamur.—
August. Opp. Tom. IV. fol. 139. col. 3. Par. 1531.]

[2 Illuc sursum suspicientes Christiani manibus expansis, quia
innocuis, capite nudo, quia non erubescimus, denique sine monitore,
quia de pectore oramus.   Precantes sumus omnes semper pro omnibus imperatoribus, &c.—Tertul. Apol. adv. Gentes. cap. 30. ed. Semler. Tom. V. p. 63.]

brance the doctrine of our Saviour in the gospel, saying:
"When thou prayest, thou shalt not be as the hypocrites are;
for they love to pray standing in the synagogues and in the
corners of the streets, that they may be seen of men. Verily,
I say unto you, they have their reward." For above all
things we must beware, that we neither pray privately nor
publicly to this end, neither yet fashion the gesture of our
body, to get the vain praise of the people, that we may seem
to be renowned and accounted holy before men: it sufficeth
that we please God, and be allowed by his judgment.

In the discourse of prayer, no man will say that it is the
smallest thing, to know what you ought to pray, what thing
you should ask of God, or for whom you should pray. Here
are to be considered the persons and things. Persons are
either public or private. Public persons are bishops, teachers,
magistrates, and all set in authority. For these men the
writings of the prophets, evangelists, and apostles, give commandment to pray. Paul more than once requireth intercessions to be made by the church unto the Lord for him,
that he might be delivered from disordered and froward men;
and that he might freely preach the gospel, as it became him
to preach it. The same Paul commandeth us to pray for all
those that be set in authority, "that we may lead a quiet and
peaceable life in all godliness and honesty." Private persons are
our parents, wife, children, kinsfolk, allies, neighbours, citizens,
friends, enemies, sick persons, captives, such as are afflicted,
and, to be short, all that are nigh about us, whose health and
safety nature and Christian charity willeth by prayers to
commend unto God; and whereof there are also testimonies and
examples in the scripture. But the things we should pray
for are those good things that are to be desired; whereof
some are heavenly, spiritual, or eternal; and other earthly,
corporal, or temporal. Moreover, some things verily are common, other some again are private: those things that are
common pertain to the whole church and commonwealth;
neither belong they to a few, as do private things. And
spiritual things are chiefly reckoned to be these; faith, hope,
charity, perseverance, and that whole company of all manner
virtues, the profit and safety of the church, forgiveness of
sins, and life everlasting. Among the which not unfitly are
reckoned the gifts of understanding, the liberal sciences, well

What we must ask or pray for of God.

Ephes. vi.
2 Thess. iii.
1 Tim. ii.

ordered schools, faithful teachers, godly magistrates, and up-right laws. Corporal things are, a peaceable commonwealth, strong and valiant armies for war, health, strength, and come-liness of body, abundance or sufficient wealth, the safe pros-perity of wife and children, the protection and defence of friends and citizens, peace, a good name, and other things which are of this kind. But no man is ignorant, that we ought to have a greater care of spiritual things than corporal things, and principally to desire heavenly things. And in corporal things there is also a choice to be used; that the profit of the commonwealth be preferred before our own private gain. For the commonwealth continuing in safety, the citizens may also be safe; and so long as schools and universities, or places of learning, be maintained, there is hope that the commonwealth shall never be destitute of wise and upright governors. There are also in temporal goods some better than other some: those things that are best, therefore, the saints or godly men do chiefly require of the Lord; and nevertheless those which are of less value they understand to come from him, and therefore they ask them also of the Lord. They that are but meanly exercised in the scriptures affirm, that it is not lawful in prayer to ask corporal goods of the Lord; but they are confuted by many examples of the scripture. For not only the patriarchs and prophets, but also the apostles of Christ, asked temporal goods of the Lord; as defence against their enemies, a good report, and other things necessary for the body. Which thing we shall learn anon by the form of prayer which the Lord him-self hath taught us, diligently shewing us what we should ask.

This also cometh in question, In what tongue prayer must be made? They that affirm that privately and publicly we must pray in Latin, seem in my judgment to be out of their wits, unless they speak of such as are skilful in the Latin tongue. For since we must pray, not only with mouth and voice, but also with heart and mind; how, I pray you, shall he pray with heart and mind, who useth a language he understandeth not? Indeed, he uttereth godly words, but he knoweth not what he saith. For it cometh all to one reckoning, to pray never a whit or not at all, and to babble out words which are not understood. Let every nation there-fore pray in that language, which it understandeth best and

Marginal notes:

It is lawful to ask cor-poral goods of the Lord.

In what tongue we must pray.

most familiarly. And no less madness is it in public assemblies to use a strange language: which thing also hath been the root of the greatest evils in the church. Whatsoever the priests that were ordained of God, and the prophets which were sent from him, spake[1] or rehearsed to the people of old time in the church, they did not speak or recite them in the Chaldean, Indian, or Persian, but in the Hebrew tongue, that is, in their vulgar and mother-tongue. They wrote also books in their vulgar tongue. Christ our Lord, together with his apostles, used the vulgar tongue. He furnished the apostles with the gift of tongues, that they might speak to every nation; and forsomuch as in that age the Greek tongue of all other was most plentiful and common, the apostles wrote not in the Hebrew tongue, but in the vulgar Greek tongue. Truly, it behoveth that those things, that are done in the public church for the holy assemblies' sake, should be understood of all men; for otherwise in vain should so many men be assembled together. Whereby it is clearer than the daylight, that they, that have brought in strange tongues into the church of God, have troubled all things, have quenched the ferventness of men's minds, yea, and[2] have banished out of the church both prayer itself and the use of prayer, and all the fruit and profit that should come of things done in the church. And truly, the Roman and[3] Latin prince hath brought this Latin abomination into the church of God. He crieth out, that it is wickedly done, if Germany, England, France, Poland, and Hungary[4], do use, both in prayer and other kind of service in the church, not the Roman or Latin tongue, but Dutch or[5] German speech, English, French, Polonish, or the Hungarian language. St Paul, once handling[6] this controversy, saith in plain words: "If I pray in a strange tongue[7], my spirit or voice prayeth, but my understanding is without fruit. What is it then? I will pray with the spirit, but I will pray with the understanding also. I will sing with the spirit, but I will sing with the understanding also. Else, when thou blessest with the spirit, how shall he that occupieth the room of the unlearned say

1 Cor. xiv.

[1 egerunt, Lat. : did.] [2 adeoque, Lat. : and so.]
[3 Roman and, not in Lat.] [4 Pannonia, Lat.]
[5 Dutch or, not in Lat.] [6 dirimens, Lat. : deciding.]
[7 lingua, Lat. : strange, not in Lat.]

Amen at thy giving of thanks, seeing he knoweth not what thou sayest? Thou verily givest thanks well[1], but the other is not edified. I thank my God, I speak languages more than you all: yet had I rather in the church to speak five words with mine understanding, that I might also instruct others, than ten thousand words in a strange tongue." And truly, this very place doth Justinian the emperor cite *In Novell. Const.* 123, where he straitly commandeth bishops and ministers, not secretly, but with a loud voice which might be heard of the people, to recite the holy oblation and prayers used in holy baptism, to the intent, that thereby the minds of the hearers might be stirred up with greater devotion to set forth the praises of God[2]. Moreover, it is evident that Gregory himself, who is called the Great, spake to the citizens[3] in the city of Rome in their country language: which thing he himself witnesseth in the preface of his commentary upon Ezechiel to Marianus the bishop[4]. Of the Greek bishops, no man is ignorant that they had their whole service in their churches in their own native language, and have left their writings unto us in the same tongue. We might therefore worthily be judged mad and void of understanding, if we also in the administration of divine service in the church use not our own language; since so many and so excellent examples, both of most famous churches, and of most singular bishops and governors of the church, have gone before us; that I speak not again of the most express and manifest doctrine of St Paul the apostle.

Of singing in the church.

This place now requireth, that I speak somewhat of singing in the church, and of canonical hours. But let no

[1 Well, not in Lat.]

[2 Πρὸς τούτοις κελεύομεν πάντας ἐπισκόπους τε καὶ πρεσβυτέρους μὴ κατὰ τὸ σεσιωπημένον, ἀλλὰ μετὰ φωνῆς τῷ πιστοτάτῳ λαῷ ἐξακουομένης τὴν θείαν προσκομιδὴν καὶ τὴν ἐπὶ τῷ ἁγίῳ βαπτίσματι προσευχὴν ποιεῖσθαι, πρὸς τὸ κἀντεῦθεν τὰς τῶν ἀκουόντων ψυχὰς εἰς πλείονα κατάνυξιν καὶ τὴν πρὸς τὸν Δεσπότην Θεὸν διανίστασθαι δοξολογίαν. Οὕτως γὰρ ὁ θεῖος ἀπόστολος διδάσκει, λέγων ἐν τῇ πρὸς Κορινθίους πρώτῃ ἐπιστολῇ, &c.— Corp. Jur. Civil. Auth. Coll. IX. Tit. XX. Novell. CXXXVII. 6. Tom. II. pp. 196, 7. Amst. 1663.]

[3 So also 1584; but 1577 his citizens, suis civibus, Lat.]

[4 Homilias, quæ in beatum Ezechielem prophetam, ita ut coram populo loquebar, exceptæ sunt, &c.—Gregor. Pap. Homil. in Ezech. Præf. Tom. I. p. 1173. Par. 1705.]

man think, that prayers sung with man's voice are more acceptable unto God, than if they were plainly spoken or uttered; for God is neither allured with the sweetness of man's voice, neither is he offended, though prayer[5] be uttered in a hoarse or base sound. Prayer is commended for faith and godliness of mind, and not for any outward shew. Those outward things are rather used, as means to stir us up; albeit even they also take little effect, unless the Spirit of God do inflame our hearts. Neither can any man deny, but that the custom of singing is very ancient; for the holy scripture 2 Chron. witnesseth, that the Levites in the ancient church, long before xxix. the coming of Christ, did sing; yea, and that they did sing at the commandment of God. And again; I think no man can deny, that the same cunning[6] kind of music, brought into the church of God by David, was both accounted among the ceremonies, and that the same was abolished together with the temple and the ceremonies. We read not of our Lord Jesus Christ, who is the true Messias and full perfection of the law, that he sung in any place, either in the temple or without the temple; or that anywhere he taught his disciples to sing, or commanded them to ordain singing in the churches. For that which is read in Matthew and Mark, (Καὶ ὑμνή- Matt. xxvi. σαντες ἐξῆλθον εἰς τὸ ὄρος τῶν ἐλαιῶν, which may be Mark xiv. Englished, "And when they had sung an hymn, or psalm, they went out into the mount of Olives,") is such a kind of saying, as doth not necessarily force us to understand, that the Lord sang with his disciples; for a hymn, which is the praise due unto God, may be humbly uttered without quavering[7] of the voice. Truly, the old translation in both places, as well in Matthew as in Mark, constantly interpreteth it: *Et hymno dicto exierunt in montem Olivarum;* that is to say: " When they had said a hymn, they went out into the mount of Olives." Erasmus, in Matthew, hath translated it, *Et cum hymnum cecinissent;* "When they had sung an hymn:" but translating Mark, he saith, *Et cum hymnum dixissent;* "When they had said an hymn:" but in either place is read, ὑμνήσαντες. And ὑμνέω signifieth, to praise, or to set forth one's praise; which both by singing, and also without singing, hath been accustomed to be done.

[5 So also 1584; but 1577 prayers.]   [6 operosam, Lat.]
[7 modulatione, Lat.]

And albeit we neither read, that the Lord himself commanded singing to his apostles, neither that they ordained singing in the church; neither yet do read in the Acts of the Apostles, that they themselves did sing in holy assemblies; yet

Paul rebuked not them that sung. Paul did not rebuke the church at Corinth, which began to sing, either of her own accord, or by a certain imitation of the old church; because he saw their manner of singing differed much from the old. He therefore suffered singing of psalms; but, in the mean time, he preferred before it prophecy, or the office of preaching: and he also required of them that did sing, both a measure to be kept, and also that it should be done with understanding; without which, doubtless, both prayer and singing is not only unprofitable, but also hurtful.

1 Cor. xiv. "I will pray with the spirit," saith the apostle, "and will pray with the understanding also. I will sing with the spirit, and will sing with the understanding also." Neither do I know, that in any place else the apostle maketh mention of singing in holy assemblies; unless we list to apply that hither, which Paul hath left written in the iii. to the Colossians; though that may seem to be a private institution. For that which he hath left written in the epistle[1] to the Ephesians in

Eph. v. these words, "Be not drunken with wine, wherein is excess; but be fulfilled with the Spirit; speaking unto yourselves in psalms, and hymns, and spiritual songs, singing and making melody to the Lord in your hearts; giving thanks always for all things unto God, even the Father, in the name of our Lord Jesus Christ;" what manner of saying it is, it is easily judged by the occasion and order of the words. For he speaketh nothing of the public singing accustomed to be used in the church, but of the private manner of singing; for he had respect unto riotous banquets, where, for the most part, were used to be sung, of such as were well tippled, songs which were not very honest. "Be ye not, therefore, drunk with wine," saith the apostle, lest ye sing songs that are scarce honest; but rather, if ye list to sing, sing psalms and spiritual songs. Whereunto this also may be added; that even in those kinds of songs, he requireth rather the song of the heart than the warbling of the voice; so far off is it that he at any time alloweth uncomely shriekings, either public or private. Albeit, the sense and meaning shall be more simple

[1 So also 1584; but 1577, his epistle.]

and plain, if we understand *in corde*, which signifieth "in the heart," to be spoken in that place instead of "joyfully," or[2] "from the heart." Wherefore no man can or ought to disallow moderate and godly singing of psalms, whether it be publicly used in holy assemblies, or at home in private houses. And truly you shall find many testimonies in the ecclesiastical history written by Eusebius and Sozomenus, declaring that The manner of the the eastern churches, even immediately after the time of the ancient sing-
ing in the apostles, did use to sing psalms and hymns unto Christ our church. Lord[3]. Ye shall also find this, that by certain decrees of councils it was ordained, that no other thing should either be read or sung in holy assemblies but only the canonical scripture[4]. For even betimes there began neither a mean to be kept in the church, neither the canonical scripture only to be used, for that certain men intermeddled their own songs.

Yet here, dearly beloved, I thought good to put you in What man-
ner of sing- mind of two excellent things concerning this matter. The first ing was in
old time used. of them is, that the singing of the ancient church was a far other kind of singing than that which at this day is used. For Erasmus Roter. doth rightly judge, that the singing used in the ancient churches was no other than a distinct and measured pronunciation, such as at this day in some places is used in pronouncing of the Psalms, the Gospel, and the Lord's Prayer[5]. Truly Pliny, the lieutenant[6] in Asia, by diligent search or examination of matters found out, that the Christians at certain appointed times met together before day, and sung a psalm together among themselves unto Christ their God. The place of Pliny is to be seen in the 10. book of his Epistles to Trajanus the emperor[7]. Also Rabanus Maurus, *lib. Instit. Cler.* 2. cap. 48. saith: "The primitive church did so

[2 joyfully or, not in Lat.]
[3 Euseb. Hist. Eccles. Lib. III. cap. 33. v. cap. 28. VII. cap. 30. Sozomen. Hist. Eccles. Lib. III. cap. 16. VIII. 8.]
[4 Ὅτι οὐ δεῖ ἰδιωτικοὺς ψαλμοὺς λέγεσθαι ἐν τῇ ἐκκλησίᾳ, οὐδὲ ἀκανόνιστα βίβλια, ἀλλὰ μόνα τὰ κανονικὰ τῆς καινῆς καὶ παλαιᾶς διαθήκης.— Can. 59. Concil. Laod. Labb. et Coss. Tom. I. col. 1507. Item placuit, ut præter scripturas canonicas nihil in ecclesia legatur sub nomine divinarum scripturarum.—Can. 47. Concil. Carthag. III. Labb. et Coss. Tom. II. col. 1177. Lut. Par. 1671.]
[5 Erasm. Annot. in 1 Cor. xiv. 26. Opp. Tom. VI. col. 731. Lugd. Bat. 1705.]
[6 proconsul, Lat.]   [7 See above, p. 166.]

[BULLINGER, IV.]   13

sing, that with a little altering of the voice it made him that
sang to be heard the further; so that the singing was more
like loud reading than song[1]." These things he borrowed out
of the 33. chap. of St Augustine's 10. book of Confessions;
who in that one place plainly confesseth, that he doth sin when
he is more delighted with the sweetness of the voices than
with the sense of the words; and therefore desireth, that all
the melodious tunes of sweet songs, wherewith the Psalter of
David is replenished, might be removed from his ears and the
hearing of the church. For it seemed to be more safe, which
he remembered he had often heard concerning Athanasius,
bishop of Alexandria; who with so little straining of the voice
made the reader of the psalm to utter it, that he rather
seemed to read than to sing[2].

Song was always free, but not universally used.

The last of the things I said I would put you in mind
of is, that singing, howsoever it be an ancient institution,
nevertheless was never universal, and of necessity thrust
upon the churches; but it was free, neither was it always
used in all churches. Whereunto may be added that which
Sozomenus witnesseth, that those churches which did sing
used not the very same kinds of prayers, or psalms, or
reading[3], or the very same time[4]. Socrates also, in the
5. book of his history, chap. 22. saith: "To be short, in all countries, everywhere, you shall not find two churches, which in
all points agree together in prayer[5]." And that it was long

[1 Primitiva ecclesia ita psallebat, ut modico flexu vocis faceret
resonare psallentem, ita ut pronuncianti vicinior esset quam canenti.—
Raban. Maur. de Instit. Cler. Lib. II. cap. 48. Opp. Tom. VI. p. 28.
Col. Agrip. 1626.]

[2 Valde interdum, ut melos omne cantilenarum suavium quibus
Davidicum Psalterium frequentatur ab auribus meis removeri velim
atque ipsius ecclesiæ; tutiusque mihi videtur quod de Alexandrino
episcopo Athanasio sæpe mihi dictum commemini, qui tam modico
flexu vocis faciebat sonare lectorem psalmi, ut pronuntianti vicinior
esset quam canenti.... Tamen, cum mihi accidit ut me amplius can-
tus quam res quæ canitur moveat, pœnaliter me peccare confiteor, et
tunc mallem non audire cantantem.—August. Confess. Lib. X. cap.
33. Opp. Tom. I. fol. 38. col. 4. Par. 1531.]

[3 So also 1584; but 1577, readings.]

[4 Καὶ εὐχαῖς καὶ ψαλμῳδίαις ταῖς αὐταῖς ἢ ἀναγνώσμασι, κατὰ τὸν αὐτὸν
καιρὸν, οὐ πάντας κεχρημένους εὑρεῖν ἐστίν.—Sozomen. Hist. Eccles. Lib.
VII. cap. 19. p. 308. Cantab. 1720.]

[5 Καθόλου μέντοι πανταχοῦ καὶ παρὰ πάσαις θρησκείαις τῶν εὐχῶν οὐκ

ere the western churches received melody, or the custom of
singing, it appeareth even by the testimony of Augustine; who,
in his 9. book of Confess. chapter 7. rehearseth, that Ambrose,
being oppressed with the snares and persecutions of Justina,
the Arian empress, ordained that hymns and psalms should be
sung according to the custom of the east parts; since which
time the custom of singing hath been retained and also received of other parts of the world[6]. Nevertheless, before the
western churches received the order of singing, they were
esteemed of all them of the east to be true churches; neither
came it into any man's brain, that therefore they were heretical and schismatical churches, or not rightly governed,
because they were destitute of song or melody. No man
gathered, The eastern churches sing, the western do not so;
therefore they are no churches.

If this uprightness and liberty had remained safe and ^{Agreement in singing in the church.} unaltered[7]; that is to say, if, according to that ancient use of
singing, nothing had been sung but canonical scriptures; if it
had been still in the liberty of the churches to sing or not to
sing; truly at this day there should be no controversy in the
church about singing in the church. For those churches,
which should use singing after the ancient manner practised
in singing, would sing the word of God and the praises of
God only; neither would they think that in this point they
surpassed other churches, neither would they condemn those
churches that sang not at all; whereas also these would not
despise them that used soberly and godlily to sing. For if
godly men persevere in the study of godliness, and in daily[8]
prayers; though they sing not, yet remain they nevertheless
the sons of God. Neither yet doth all singing and in every
place edify; neither are all churches fit to sing. Doth not
Rabanus say, in the same place that I even now cited, "For

ἔστιν εὑρεῖν συμφωνούσας ἀλλήλαις δύο ἐπὶ τὸ αὐτό.—Socrat. Hist. Eccles.
Lib. v. cap. 22. p. 297. Cantab. 1720.]

[6 Annus erat, aut non multo amplius, cum Justina Valentiniani
regis pueri mater hominem tuum Ambrosium persequeretur hæresis
suæ causa, qua fuerat seducta ab Arianis. . . . Tunc hymni et psalmi ut
canerentur secundum morem orientalium partium. . . . institutum est;
et ex illo in hodiernum retentum, multis jam ac pene omnibus gregi-
bus tuis et per cetera orbis imitantibus.—August. Confess. Lib. ix.
cap. 7. Opp. Tom. i. fol. 33. col. 3.]

[7 intemerata, Lat.]   [8 assiduis, Lat.]

fleshly-minded men's sake, and not for such as are guided by the Spirit, the custom of singing is instituted in the church; that they, that are not moved by words, may be allured with the sweetness of the melody, &c.[1]"

But the singing, about which there is controversy at this day, is not that ancient singing; but, that more is, both in matter and tune for the most part it is clean contrary to the old.

Gregory's singing. The common sort call it Gregory's singing; doubtless not of that great Gregory, who seemeth not to have been very friendly to singing; as it appeareth by his constitution, which is read in the Registry, in the fifth part thereof, cap. 44[2]: we shall therefore seem to judge more truly, if we refer it to Gregory the fifth, which is said to have been enthronized[3] about the year of our Lord 995, and moreover to have used the help of I know not who, one Robertus Carnotensis[4]. Yet there are some which ascribe it to Vitalianus, some to Gelasius[5]. It irketh me to rehearse what Durandus hath patched together of this matter in his *Rat. Divin.* lib. v.; for I little weigh it.

What things are to be discommended in the use of singing in the church. There are many things in this kind of singing to be discommended. For first of all, many things, yea, the most, are sung contrary to true godliness; neither are all things that are sung taken out of the holy scriptures, but out of I know not what kind of legends, and out of the traditions of men. And those things which are sung out of the scriptures are for the most part so wrested and corrupted, that there remaineth no part of the heavenly sense or meaning. Creatures and dead men are called upon. Moreover, this kind of singing is commanded; and they sing not of their own accord or good will, but upon constraint: yea, they sing for money, and to the end that they may get an ecclesiastical benefice, as they term it. Only clerks hired for that purpose do now-

---

[1 Propter carnales in ecclesia, non propter spirituales, consuetudo cantandi est instituta, ut qui verbis non compunguntur, suavitate modulaminis moveantur.—Raban. Maur. de Instit. Cler. Opp. Tom. VI. p. 28.]

[2 The reference is to Gregor. Regist. Epistol. Lib. IV. Indict. 13. Ep. 44, which contains a decree of a synod at Rome, ut sacri altaris ministri cantare non debeant, &c.—Opp. Tom. III. p. 143. Rom. 1591. Bullinger de Episc. Instit. et Funct. cap. 6. fol. 87. Tigur. 1538.]

[3 sedisse, Lat.]   [4 Platina de Vitis Pontif. in Greg. V.]

[5 Polydor. Vergil. de rer. invent. Lib. VI. cap. 2.]

a-days sing; not the whole church of Christ, as in time past hath been accustomed. Neither is there any end or measure in their singing; they sing day and night. And to this foolish and ungodly kind of singing, as to a heavenly or meritorious work, there is more attributed than true faith doth allow. A man may well say, that it is that much babbling, which the Lord in Matthew forbiddeth and condemneth as an heathenish superstition. They sing moreover in a strange tongue, which few do understand; and that without any profit at all to the church. There is heard a long sound, quavered[6], and strained to and fro, backward and forward, whereof a man cannot understand one word[7]. Oftentimes the singers strive among themselves for the excellency of voices; whereby it cometh to pass, that the whole church ringeth with an hoarse kind of yelling, and through the strife that riseth about their voices the hearers little understand what is sung. I say nothing at this present of their music which they call figurative, and of their musical instruments, all which are contained in a manner in their organs, as they term them. I say nothing of their dirges, or prayers for the dead: of which I have also entreated in another place[8]. But these, and such other like, so occupied the whole time of divine service in the church, that very little or none was left for true prayers, and for the holy and heavenly preaching of the word of God. Therefore for most just causes they that believe the gospel do neither use such singing, neither suffer it in the church of God. And they seem to deal very devoutly, and in like manner most wisely, which bestow the best part of the time, or even the very whole time, of ecclesiastical assemblies in fervent and quiet[9] prayers, and in the wholesome preaching of the word of God, omitting that singing: especially since it is a hard thing so to limit or restrain singing, which otherwise is tolerable, lest at some time it exceed and go beyond the appointed bounds.

Furthermore, that our ancient predecessors had certain Of canonical and appointed hours, wherein they prayed both privately in hours. their houses and publicly in assemblies, all the holy scripture

[6 suspensus, Lat.]
[7 sine verbis significantibus, Lat.]　　　[8 See Vol. III. p. 395.]
[9 tranquillis, Lat.]

witnesseth in many places. David more than once in his Psalms saith, that he will go unto the Lord in the morning and evening. Daniel prayed unto the Lord at three several hours or times of the day. Again, David saith: " Seven times in a day do I praise thee ;" but by seven times he understandeth many times. For so elsewhere we read written : " I will smite you for your sins seven times ;" and again : " The just man falleth seven times, and riseth up again ;" and also : " If thy brother sin seven times in a day, and turn seven times in a day unto thee," &c. Seven times therefore in divers places, as also in this of David, is put for many times. And Christ our Lord hath tied the private prayers of the faithful (as we have also told you before[1]) neither to place, nor yet to time : he hath not taken away public prayers; for he is the Lord, not of confusion, but of order : but his disciples, when they were in the land of Jury[2], did themselves also observe the accustomed hours of praying which that nation kept, at liberty, not of necessity, and specially for the assembly's sake. For Peter and John go up into the temple at the ninth hour of prayer. In the day of Pentecost all the saints with one accord were gathered together, and received the Holy Ghost, at the third hour of the day. And it is also read, that Peter privately went up into the upper part of the house about the sixth hour. The temple being destroyed, and the Jews scattered abroad, the churches gathered out of the gentiles did not observe like hours of gatherings together[3], or of assemblies; but at their own liberty, as to every church it seemed most meet and convenient. Of which diversity truly the ecclesiastical history also maketh mention; yet for the most part there were hours in the morning and evening used for assemblies. St Hierome, in his epitaph upon Paula, expounding not the rite or order of the universal church, what it should do in holy assemblies, but what the companies of solitary virgins are wont to do of their own accord, saith : " In the morning, at three, six, and nine of the clock, at evening, at midnight, they did sing the Psalter by order. Only upon the Sunday they went unto the church,

Marginal notes:
Dan. vi.
Lev. xxvi.
Prov. xxiv.
Luke xvii.
Acts iii.
Acts ii.
Trip. lib. ix. cap. 39.

[1 Vol. II. p. 264; and above, p. 183.]
[2 cum agerent in gente Judaica, Lat.]
[3 collectarum, Lat.]

near unto the which they dwelt[4]," &c. So it pertaineth to
private institution, which of the same sort is read written to
Læta, touching the institution of her daughter[5] ; and to De-
metriades, *De Custodienda Virginitate*[6].

And truly, the greater or more famous and solemn
churches (which at this day they call cathedral, to wit, of
cathedra, a chair, or of the order of prophets teaching or
professing there ; as some time the church of Antioch, Corinth,
Alexandria, and such like, seemed to have been), at certain
hours, to wit, in the morning, at noon, yea, at evening also,
assembled to expound or discuss the holy canonical scriptures.
The foundations of that observation seem to be laid in the
church of the Corinthians ; of which the apostle abundantly
witnesseth, 1 Cor. xiv. chapter. Eusebius, in the fifth book of
his ecclesiastical history and ninth chapter, making mention
of an ecclesiastical school at Alexandria, saith : "From a long
time the doctrine and exercise of the holy scriptures flourished
among them : which custom also continueth even to our time ;
which we have heard also to be instituted by men mighty in
eloquence, and in the study of the holy scriptures[7];" to wit,
after the example of the Corinthian church. Some marks[8] of
this most wholesome rite or custom appeared sometime in the
occidental or west church, as it is to be gathered out of the
writings of St Ambrose and Augustine. But truly in these
very times, and in the times immediately following, when all

[4 Mane, hora tertia, sexta, nona, vespere, noctis medio, per ordinem psalterium cantabant (virgines in monasteriis Paulæ). . . . Die
tantum dominico ad ecclesiam procedebant, ex cujus habitabant latere
&c.—Hieron. Ep. 86. ad Eustoch. Epitaph. Paulæ matris. Opp. Tom.
IV. par. 2. col. 682. Par. 1706.]

[5 — virgo veterana. . . . assuescat (illam) exemplo ad orationes et
psalmos nocte consurgere ; mane hymnos canere, tertia, sexta, nona
hora stare, &c.—Hieron. Ep. 57. ad Lætam de Instit. filiæ. Ibid.
col. 595.]

[6 Præter psalmorum et orationis ordinem, quod tibi hora tertia,
sexta, nona, et vesperum, media nocte et mane semper est exercendum,
&c.—Hieron. Ep. 97. ad Demetriadem de Servanda Virginitate, ibid.
col. 793.]

[7 — ἐξ ἀρχαίου ἔθους διδασκαλείου τῶν ἱερῶν λόγων παρ᾽ αὐτοῖς συνε-
στῶτος, ὃ καὶ εἰς ἡμᾶς παρατείνεται, καὶ πρὸς τῶν ἐν λόγῳ καὶ τῇ περὶ τὰ
θεῖα σπουδῇ δυνατῶν συγκροτεῖσθαι παρειλήφαμεν.—Euseb. Hist. Eccles.
Lib. v. cap. 10. Tom. I. p. 336. ed. Burton.]

[8 vestigia, Lat.]

nations in a manner were together by the ears with perpetual
wars ; and when the Roman empire, in revengement of the blood
of Christ, of his holy apostles and martyrs, according to the
prophecy of Daniel and St John the apostle and evangelist,
was torn in pieces, and made a prey for all people[1]; the
Goths or Germans rushing upon them on this side, the
Huns and other barbarous soldiers on the other side assaulting Rome sharply[2]; the best schools were spoiled, goodly
libraries were burned, honest and good studies perished :
whereupon were given unto the churches doctors or teachers
most unlike unto the ancient doctors and teachers, who were
not furnished with that ability, that they could deal in the
holy scriptures with such dexterity and fruitfulness as their
predecessors.   In this disorder and downfal, lest nothing
should remain of the canonical scriptures[3] untouched, it is
evident, that there rose up men not altogether negligent of
the canonical doctrine, who divided the whole canonical scripture after such a sort into parts, and for the whole course of
the year, that they might once in a year read over the whole
bible, and the psalter oftener, yea, even every sevennight[4].
They used the Psalms instead of prayers, to which, as times
increased, many other prayers also were joined.   And lest
the very reading of the scriptures should seem to want all
exposition, the readings, lectures, or homilies of the fathers
were thereunto added at the length : not that the priests[5]
should read them secretly to themselves, (as at this day in a
manner they are wont to do,) or that they should with a
post-haste reading mumble them up instead of matins[6]; but
that they should throughly handle them in the open church,
as an exercise before the people, to the edification of the
church[7]:—that I may not now rehearse that this rite was
not received of all men, so far off is it from being strictly
commanded.   Of which thing there remain some tokens or

[1 See Vol. II. p. 109.]
[2 in cervicem Romæ involantibus, Lat.: cf. Isai. xi. 14.]
[3 tractationis canonicarum scripturarum, Lat.]
[4 See Preface to Common Prayer, Concerning the Service of the
Church.]
[5 soli, Lat. omitted: alone.]
[6 precum loco, Lat. : prayers, not matins.]
[7 Bingham, Antiq. Book xiv. chap. 4. § 22.]

proofs, *In Distinct.* 15. *Sancta Rom.*[8] Furthermore, of
reading the canonical scriptures those hours wherein they
were read seemed to be named canonical[9]; as also canons[10]
are so called, of studying and reading the canonical scriptures.
But at what time this was done, and who were the doers
thereof, it is not certainly known. Some do attribute some
part hereof to Hierome, other some to Damasus, and some to
Pelagius, the second of that name; other some also to Gelasius
and Gregory[11].

And because homilies and lectures not a few were said[12]
to be Beda's, and other doctors' of later times[13]; finally, for
that many other things are read in those hourly prayers[14],
which savour never a whit of antiquity; truly, as it is an
institution patched up diversly and at sundry times, so is
it far more new than the papists think or take it to be.
Neither are there some wanting which affirm, that, at the request of Carolus Magnus, Paulus Diaconus or monk of Cassina, and monk Isuard, ordained and delivered to the church
selected or chosen lessons, those especially which concern the
saints and are accustomed to be read in these hours[15]. But
howsoever the matter standeth, most certain it is, that those
hours at this day commanded, and called canonical, are the
invention of man and not of God, and ragged or[16] rotten
relics or shadows of the old law[17]. Whereunto beside, that
there are many fables, toys, and follies annexed, it cannot be
denied. Truly, at this day there appeareth such a mingle-
mangle or hoch-potch, that it seemeth utterly unworthy either
to be used or suffered any longer in the church of Christ;
unless we had rather, that care were taken for the bellies of
some than for the good state and welfare of the whole church.
Of which thus much thus far.

It remaineth, in the last place, to discuss how we must *How we must pray.*

[8 Sancta Romana ecclesia post illas veteris testamenti et novi
scripturas.... etiam has suscipi non prohibet, &c.—Gratian. Decret.
par. I. Distinct. 15. cap. 3.]
[9 Bingham, Book VII. chap. 3. § 17.]
[10 Canonici, Lat. : Bingham, Book I. chap. 5. § 10.]
[11 Polydor. Vergil. de rer. invent. Lib. VI. cap. 2.]
[12 So ed. 1584; but 1577, are said.]
[13 So ed. 1584; but 1577, time.]   [14 precibus horariis, Lat.]
[15 Magd. Centur. Cent. VIII. cap. 10. coll. 473-475. Basil. 1624.]
[16 So ed. 1584; but 1577, and.]   [17 veteris prophetiæ, Lat.]

pray; what words, or what form of prayer, we must use. Truly, there are many forms of prayer; but none better than that which our Lord, the only-beloved Son of God the Father, hath delivered. Neither is there a more certain form, as comprehending in few words all in all. In this summary he hath prescribed what is worthy of him, what is acceptable to him, what is necessary for us, and, to be short, what he is willing to grant. Whereupon St Cyprian, expounding the Lord's Prayer, among other things saith: " He that made us to live, the same hath taught us also to pray; even of the same his bountifulness, whereby he hath vouchsafed both to give and to bestow all other things whatsoever: that when we speak with the Father in that prayer and supplication which the Son hath taught us, we may be the more easily or readily heard, and may truly and spiritually worship him. For what prayer can be more spiritual, than that which is given unto us of Christ, from whom also the Holy Ghost is sent unto us? What prayer before the Father more true, than that of the Son, proceeding out of his mouth, who is truth itself? So that to pray otherwise than he hath taught is not only ignorance, but also offence, since he himself hath set down and said: ' Ye cast aside the commandment of God to stablish your own tradition.' Therefore, dearly beloved brethren, let us pray as God our master hath taught us. It is a friendly and familiar prayer, to call upon God in such manner as he hath taught us, and when that the prayer of Christ cometh to his ears. Let the Father acknowledge the words of his Son, when we pray. He that dwelleth within the heart, let him also be in the tongue. And since we have him our advocate with the Father for our sins, when we, being sinners, ask pardon for our offences, let us utter the words of our advocate. For since he saith, 'Whatsoever ye shall ask the Father in my name, he will give it you;' how much more effectually do we obtain that which we ask in the name of Christ, if we ask it in his prayer [1]!" Thus far he.

[1 Qui fecit vivere, docuit et orare; benignitate ea scilicet qua et cetera dare et conferre dignatus est, ut cum prece et oratione, quam Filius docuit, apud Patrem loquimur, facilius audiamur; ... ut ... vere et spiritaliter adoremus. Quæ enim potest esse magis spiritalis oratio, quam quæ a Christo nobis data est, a quo nobis et Spiritus Sanctus missus est? Quæ vera magis apud Patrem precatio, quam quæ a Filio,

From hence ariseth a question, Whether we be so tied to Whether we be tied to the the words of the Lord's Prayer, that we may not pray in words of the Lord's other words at all? I answer, That the Lord would not so prayer. tie us to his[2] words set down and conceived, as though it were not lawful to use other words or another form; but he set forth unto us certain universal things, unto the which we might refer all our prayers. For Augustine also to Proba, *de Orando Deo*, Of praying unto God, sheweth, that there is nothing in any place in the holy scriptures prayed for, which is not comprehended in the Lord's Prayer. "For," saith he, "if you run over and through all the words of all holy prayers, you shall find nothing which this prayer of the Lord doth not comprehend and contain." To which words he addeth immediately: "So that it is free to use such and such words in praying, howbeit to say the same things; but to speak other things it is not free[3]." Most warily therefore and wisely do they, who refer all their prayers unto the Lord's Prayer, unto the which they attribute the chief and principal place; and keeping it continually in their mind, do meditate thereupon, and exercise themselves therein.

There is wont also another question to be asked, What What it needeth to need there is to express and open our desires in words unto express our desires unto God, since he already knoweth all things? We told you God in words. anon after the beginning of this sermon, that our prayer is

qui est veritas, de ejus ore prolata est? Ut aliter orare quam docuit, non ignorantia sola sit, sed et culpa; quando ipse posuerit et dixerit, Rejicitis mandatum Dei ut traditionem vestram statuatis. Oremus itaque, frates dilectissimi, sicut magister Deus docuit. Amica et familiaris oratio est, Deum de suo rogare, ad aures ejus ascendere Christi oratione (Bullinger read, orationem). Agnoscat Pater Filii sui verba, cum precem facimus; qui habitat intus in pectore, ipse sit et in voce; et cum ipsum habeamus apud Patrem advocatum pro peccatis nostris, quando peccatores pro delictis nostris petimus, advocati nostri verba promamus. Nam cum dicit, Quia quodcunque petierimus a Patre in nomine ejus dabit nobis, quanto efficacius impetramus quod petimus in Christi nomine, si petamus ipsius oratione!—Cypr. de Orat. Domin. Opp. p. 140. Oxon. 1682.]

[2 his, not in Lat.]

[3 Si per omnia precationum sanctarum verba discurras . . . nihil invenies quod non ista dominica contineat et concludat oratio. Unde liberum est aliis atque aliis verbis eadem tamen in orando dicere, sed non debet esse liberum alia dicere.—August. Opp. Tom. ii. fol. 121. col. 2. Par. 1531.]

an humbling of ourselves before the majesty of God. Whereunto, moreover, we add this: we do not express and open
our desires unto God, as though he knew them not; or that
we would teach him being ignorant; or that we would entreat
and get God's favour with our curious, laboursome, and eloquent[1] prayer : but for our own sakes we use words, wherewith to stir up ourselves.   And to this end also[2] the most
holy men of God are read, in the Psalms and holy histories,
to have declared their desires largely unto the Lord. "We
are not," saith St Hierome, "declarers, but cravers. For it is
one thing to declare a thing to him that is ignorant, and another thing to crave a thing of him that knoweth : in that, it
is a declaration; in this, a duty : there we faithfully declare;
here lamentably beseech[3]." And St Augustine saith: "Words
are needful for us, wherewith we may be moved, and diligently
consider what we should ask ; not wherewith we should believe
that the Lord is either taught or entreated[4]."

How lip-
labour or
much bab-
bling is for-
bidden.

Wherefore, when the Lord forbad much babbling or vain
lip-labour in prayer, he did not simply tie the prayer of the
faithful unto a few and short sum of words: but he forbiddeth
us, after the manner of ethnics, to pour out many words
without wit, reason, meaning, and understanding; and so
finally to think, that we shall be heard for our much babbling
sake, and often repeating of prayers ; as at this day they do
falsely think, which say a certain number of prayers, which
they call Rosaries of prayers[5]. For the Lord addeth : "They

[1 eleganti, Lat.]

[2 So also ed. 1584; but 1577, all : sanctissimi quique, Lat.]

[3 — breviter respondendum est, nos non narratores esse, sed
rogatores. Aliud est enim narrare ignoranti, aliud scientem petere.
In illo judicium est, in hoc obsequium: ibi fideliter indicamus, hic
miserabiliter obsecramus.—Hieron. Comment. in Matth. cap. 6. Opp.
Tom. IV. col. 20. Par. 1706.]

[4 Nobis verba necessaria sunt, quibus commoveamur et inspiciamus quid petamus; non quibus Dominum seu docendum seu flecten-
dum esse credamus.—August. Ep. 121. ad Probam. Opp. Tom. II.
fol. 121. col. 1. Par. 1531.]

[5 et rosaria contexentes, Lat. The bead-roll, by which the private
devotions of multitudes in the church of Rome are reckoned, was made
up of tens of smaller beads, having a bead of a larger size between each
decade. In the *Rosary*, properly so called, there were five of these
decades : and the *Ave Maria* was repeated fifty times, the *Pater Noster*
five times, and the *Credo* once.]

think they shall be heard for their much babbling sake."
St Augustine maketh difference between babbling much, and
praying much. " To babble much," saith he, " is in praying
to make many superfluous words in a necessary matter. But
to pray much, is to call unto him whom we pray unto with
a long and godly stirring up of the heart. For this business,
for the most part, is accomplished more with sighings than
with speakings." And anon : " It is not wicked and fruitless,
when we have leisure, to pray the longer ; for it is written
of our Lord himself, that he spent the whole night in prayer,
and prayed a long time. Wherein what did he else, but give
us an example[6]?" Thus far he. And if it be a hard matter
for any man to pray long and continually, he may break off
his prayer : howbeit he must to it again, and oftentimes
renew the same afresh ; for such short speaking in prayer is
praiseworthy. And, that we may make an end of this place ;
let no man think, that in praying he declareth our affairs unto
God as not knowing them : let no man think, that he is heard
for his setting forth, and even for his laboursome and exact
setting forth, and that oftentimes repeated, and with most
earnest outcries instilled or poured into the ears of God : let
no man think, that his prayer must stand upon a certain
number ; that is to say, that *Paternosters* must be numbered
up to our God as not having a good memory, and to a Lord
ill to be trusted, upon corals and beads, put together upon a
lace[7], serving (as it were) to make a reckoning or accompt[8].

And because I have said, which all godly men also
throughout the whole world confess, that a most perfect platform of praying is delivered unto us in the Lord's Prayer by
our Lord Jesus Christ himself; it remaineth, that we cite word

[6 Multum loqui est in orando rem necessariam superfluis agere
verbis. Multum autem precari est ad eum quem precamur diuturna
et pia cordis excitatione pulsare. Nam plerumque hoc negotium
plus gemitibus quam sermonibus agitur ... cum diu orare vacat ...
non est improbum nec inutile ... Nam et de ipso Domino scriptum
est, quod pernoctaverit in orando, et quod prolixius oraverit : ubi quid
aliud quam nobis præbebat exemplum ?—August. Ep. 121. ad Probam. Opp. Tom. ii. fol. 121. col. 1.]

[7 upon a lace, not in Lat.]

[8 Etenim talia non citra fœdissimam superstitionem fiunt, Lat.
omitted. For such things are not done but with most abominable
superstition.]

for word that most holy form of praying, orderly made with most divine words even by the mouth of the Lord, as Matthew the apostle hath left it recorded unto us; and then to expound the same as briefly and plainly as may be, to the intent that every one may the better understand what he prayeth, and feel a more effectual working inwardly. Of that most heavenly prayer this is the form:

O our Father, which art in heaven; hallowed be thy name. Thy kingdom come. Thy will be done, as well in earth, as it is in heaven. Give us this day our daily bread. And forgive us our trespasses*, as we forgive them that trespass against us †. And lead us not into temptation, but deliver us from evil. Amen.

* Or debts.

† Or our debtors.

The Lord's Prayer divided.

This most holy prayer of our Lord Jesus Christ, our saviour, our doctor or teacher, and highest priest, delivered to the catholic church to be a catholic form or rule to pray unto God, is wont to be divided into a little preface, and six petitions. Some reckon seven. Some say, that the three former petitions serve chiefly to the spreading abroad of God's glory; the three latter concern the care of ourselves, and ask those things that are needful for us. But they seem in manner all[1] to contain both.

The little preface is this: "O our Father, which art in heaven." By this we call upon God; and, dedicating ourselves unto him, we commit ourselves wholly unto his protection and mercy. And every word hath his high mysteries; for our Lord would have us rather pray with understanding than with words. These therefore do admonish us, and suffice to be thought upon. But the mind, being instructed with the Holy Ghost, which I told you is needful before all things to them that pray, and being lifted up to the beholding of God and of heavenly things, doth devoutly and ardently meditate these things.

Father.

And truly the word, "Father," putteth us in mind of many things together. For first, it teacheth us, that all our prayers ought to be[2] offered to none other than to him, which is a father; that is to say, that only God is to be called upon, and not another for him, or another with him. For our God and Father is one, the fulness and sufficiency of all good things,

[1 plerœque, Lat.]   [2 So also ed. 1584; but 1577, are to be.]

in whom only the faithful are acquieted and do rest, and without whom[3] they seek nothing that is truly good. And verily this prayer can be offered to no creature. For to which of the angels, or the saints, canst thou say without sacrilege: " O our Father, which art in heaven ?" &c.

Furthermore this word Father teaches us, through whom we should call upon this Father; not by the mediation or by the mouths of saints, but by Jesus Christ our Lord; through whom only we are made the sons of God, who were otherwise by birth and by nature the children of wrath. Who, I pray you, durst come forth before the presence of the most high and everlasting God, and call him " Father," and himself " son," unless the Father in his beloved and natural Son had adopted us the sons of grace ? Therefore, when we say, " Father," we speak from the mouth of the Son, who hath taught us so to pray, and by whom we be promoted into this dignity; that it needeth nothing at all to add the name of Christ, and to say, We pray thee, O heavenly Father, for Christ's sake; since in the first word, " Father," we comprehend the whole mystery of the Son of God and our redemption. For insomuch as he is our Father, we are his sons, and that by the merit of Christ: therefore we call upon the Father, and so call him through Christ; that I may not now repeat, that we pray so from the mouth of Christ. Moreover, this sweet and favourable word, " Father," disburdens us clean of all distrust of heart; for we call him " Father," not so much in consideration of his creating of all things, as for his singular and fatherly good-will toward us. Whereupon, though he be Lord God, and indeed a great Lord, and an Almighty God; yet when we pray, we attribute none of these names unto him; but call him Father, because indeed he wisheth us well, loveth us, taketh care and charge over us, and, having pity upon us, is desirous, yea, of his own accord and good-will toward us, to store and heap upon us all good things whatsoever. Hitherto appertain the testimonies of the prophets, especially that of David : " The Lord is full of compassion and mercy, slow to anger, and of great kindness. He will not alway chide, neither keep his anger for ever. He hath not dealt with us after our sins, nor rewarded us according to our iniquities. For as high as the heaven is above the earth, so great is his

The Lord's prayer offered to the Father by Christ.

Ps. clii.

[3 extra quem, Lat.; out of whom.]

mercy toward them that fear him. As far as the east is from the west, so far hath he removed our sins from us. As a father hath compassion on his children, so hath the Lord compassion on them that fear him. For he knoweth whereof we be made, he remembereth that we are but dust." A very excellent example of this thing is to be seen in the gospel after St Luke; where the loving father is painted out with wonderful affections receiving into favour again that prodigal son and waster of his wealth.

Luke xv.

Hereunto is added this word " Our ;" which putteth us in mind of two things. For first, it is a small matter to acknowledge God to be the God and Father of all, or to be the God and Father of others, unless we also believe that he is our Father; unless we dedicate and yield ourselves wholly into his faith and protection, as of our Father, who wisheth well unto us, loveth us, hath a care over us, at no time and place neglecteth us. For unless we do so believe, neither with faith nor with the love of God is our prayer commended, and therefore not a whit acceptable unto God. But that that best and greatest God is our God, we do understand as well by his manifold benefits, as also especially by the mystery of our redemption through Christ: of which thing we have spoken elsewhere[1]. Furthermore, since he bad us pray, " Our Father," and not "My Father;" straightway, upon the very beginning, he requireth love of us. For his will is, that we should not only have care of our own salvation, but of the salvation of all other men. For we are all the members of one body; whereupon each several one prayeth not severally for themselves, but every one for the safety of all the members and also the whole body. Touching that matter I spake before, when I entreated of the manner of praying unto God[2].

Our.

There is by and by added, " Which art in heaven ;" not that God is shut up in heaven as in a prison. Solomon, the happiest and wisest king of all, confuting that error long agone, said : " If the heavens of heavens are not able to contain thee, how much less this house !" To which words I think that may be annexed, which Stephen alleged in the Acts of the Apostles out of Esay concerning the same thing. He is therefore said to be in heaven, because his divine majesty, and power, and glory, shineth most of all in the

Which art in heaven.

1 Kings viii.

Acts vii.

[1 Vol. i. p. 125.]   [2 See above, p. 179.]

heavens : for in the whole course of nature there is nothing
more glorious, nothing more beautiful, than the heavens.
Moreover, the Father exhibiteth and giveth himself unto us
to be enjoyed in the heavens. Heaven is the country common
to us all, where we believe that God and our Father doth
dwell, and where we worship God and our Father; albeit we
believe that he is in every place, and always present with all.
For as heaven compasseth and covereth all things, and is everywhere distant from the earth by even spaces; so the presence
of his Majesty also doth fail us in no place. We have heaven
everywhere in our sight; we are everywhere in the sight of
God. But beside this, by mention made of heaven we are
put in mind of our duty, and our wretchedness. It is our duty,
to be lifted up in our minds, by praying, into heaven, and to
forget earthly things; and more to be delighted with that
heavenly Father and country than with this earthly prison
and exile : it is our wretchedness, that being banished out of
that country for our sins, and wandering[3] in this earth, we
are subject to divers calamities; and therefore, being constrained by necessity, we never cease crying unto the Father.
But first of all[4], saying, " Which art in heaven," we make a
difference between the Father whom we call upon, saying,
"our," and our earthly father; attributing almightiness unto
him. He surely, that is called upon and ought to hear, must
know all, see all, and hear all; yea, and more too, will and be
able to do all. Therefore to his good-will to us-ward, which
in these words, " Our Father," we have expressed, we do
now join knowledge of all things, and power to do all
things, adding, " Which art in heaven." By these words the
faith of them that pray is stirred up and confirmed.

Now there do follow in order six petitions. The first is, Hallowed be
" Hallowed be thy name." We have called God our Father, thy name.
and ourselves his sons. But it is the part of sons to honour
or glorify their father; and therefore immediately upon the
beginning we desire, that the name of the Lord God, and our
Father, might be sanctified or hallowed. That truly is holy
and undefiled always in itself; neither is it made any whit
the better or the worse by us. Whereupon we pray, that
that which is and remaineth holy in itself should be acknowledged of us to be such, and always sanctified of us.

[3 reptantes, Lat.]   [4 in primis, Lat.: especially.]

The name of God.

A name is the definition of anything whatsoever; and names are invented to make a difference of one thing from another, whereby they might be known among themselves. But God is infinite and unmeasurable; moreover, he is one: therefore he hath not a name whereby to be defined; he needeth not a name whereby to be discerned from other gods. Therefore those names, that are attributed unto him in the scriptures, are attributed for our infirmity; to the end that by some reason and comparison we might understand some things that are spoken of him that is unmeasurable and infinite. Therefore the name of God, in very deed, is God himself, with all his majesty and glory.

To sanctify, or hallow.

To "sanctify," or "hallow," otherwhiles signifieth, to separate things from a profane unto an holy use. In this place it signifieth to magnify, to praise, and to glorify. We desire therefore, that God himself, who of his own nature is a good, holy, and for ever blessed, gentle, bountiful, and a merciful, Father, might as he is in himself be acknowledged and magnified of all us; that all nations, leaving their error[1] and heresies, might consecrate themselves in truth to this one only Father and God; that all things which defile the name of the Lord, of which sort are wicked deceits or practices, ungodliness, epicurism, an unclean life, and especially corrupt and antichristian doctrine, may be taken away; that, being enlightened, we might sanctify or hallow the name of the Lord.

Wherefore in this petition we desire the Holy Ghost, the very only author itself of all true sanctification; we pray for true faith in God by Christ throughout the whole world; we pray for holy thoughts and a pure life, wherewith we might glorify the name of the Lord; which is done, while every one doeth his own duty; while Satan, the author of all uncleanness, is cast out; while corrupt doctrine is taken away, and deceit ceaseth; while the filthiness of the world is banished. This petition the most excellent king and prophet David setteth forth in these words: "God be merciful unto us, and bless us, shew us the light of his countenance, and be merciful unto us[2]; that thy way may be known[3] upon earth, thy saving health among all nations. Let the people praise thee, O God;

[1 erroribus, Lat.]   [2 benedicat nobis, Lat.]
[3 ut cognoscamus, Lat. and Vulgate. That we maye knowe, Coverdale, 1535.]

yea, let all the people praise thee :" and as followeth in the
threescore and seventh psalm. To this belongeth the whole
prayer of our Saviour, described by St John in the xvii.
chapter of his gospel.

The second petition is, "Thy kingdom come;" for the name of God and our Father cannot be sanctified or hallowed unless he reign in us. There is one kingdom of God, another of the devil. Furthermore, one kingdom of God is said to be of glory, and another rightly of grace. The kingdom of glory is not of this world, but of another world. The kingdom of grace is the kingdom of Christ in this world; wherein Christ reigneth by the Holy Spirit in his faithful ones, which of their own accord submit themselves unto him to be governed, saying and doing those things which beautify and beseem Christians. The devil also[4] reigneth in the children of unbelief, which yield themselves unto him to be governed according to his ungodliness and wickedness; doing those things which are not only delightful to the flesh, but which turn to the reproach of God's majesty ; whom after this life, by the just judgment of God, the devil, the king of the ungodly, catcheth unto hell, into the kingdom of death and judgment, there continually to burn. Moreover, the earthly kingdom, which princes of this world govern, is called either the kingdom of God, or the kingdom of the devil, even as it shall fashion and frame itself to one of the twain. All these things we do knit up in few words, because we have more plentifully entreated of them in another place[5]. Wherefore we pray in this second petition, that Christ might reign and live in us, and we in him ; that the kingdom of Christ might be spread abroad, and enlarged, and prevail through the whole world; that doctors or teachers, and ecclesiastical magistrates, finally, that princes also, yea, and schools too, and whosoever may further the kingdom of Christ, being anointed and watered with his graces, may flourish, overcome, and triumph. Furthermore, we pray that the kingdom of the devil and antichrist may be broken and vanquished, lest it hurt and annoy the saints ; that with the kingdom of the devil all ungodliness may be dashed and trodden under foot : to be short, that all the weapons and armour of antichristianism may be broken into shivers, and come to nought. Lastly, we pray in this second petition, that, after

Thy kingdom come.

[4 vero, Lat.: but.]   [5 See Decade iv. Serm. 7.]

14—2

we have sailed out of the tempestuous gulf[1] of this world, we might be received and gathered unto Christ and all the saints, into the everlasting kingdom of glory. For as we desire the kingdom of God to come unto us, and God to reign in us; so we pray to come or to be received into his kingdom, and to live for ever with him most holily.

Thy will be done.

The third petition is: "Thy will be done, as well in earth as it is in heaven." God reigneth not in us, unless we be obedient unto him; therefore after his kingdom, we desire the grace of perfect obedience. For we desire not that God do what he will; for continually God's will is done, albeit we never pray for it, and though we wrestle and strive against it with all our might. For the prophet saith: "Our God is in heaven; he hath done whatsoever pleased him in heaven and in earth." We ask, therefore, that what he will, the same he may make us both to will and to do[2]. For his will is always good; but our will, through the corruption of sin, is evil. Therefore we pray him to be present with us with his grace, that our will may be regenerated and framed to the good will of God, that of its own accord it yield itself to the Holy Ghost to be framed; that his grace will that which he inspireth[3]; that he finish in us that which he hath well begun; give us, moreover, strength and patience hereunto; that, as well in prosperity as in adversity, we may acknowledge the will of God[4], lest we will anything of ourselves, and swell and be puffed up in prosperity, in adversity also faint and perish; but that we may apply ourselves in all things, and through all things, to be governed by his will; to wit, after this manner to submit our will to his will: furthermore, if we ask anything contrary to his will, that he would not grant it, but rather pardon our foolishness, and weaken our will, which is not good for us; to instruct and teach us in his good will, to the end we may doubt nothing that this is always to be followed, that this is always good, and that this worketh all things for our commodity and benefit.

Psal. cxv.

[1 Euripo, Lat. See Erasmi Adag. Chiliad. p. 345. Hanov. 1617; *inconstantiæ*.]

[2 semper, Lat. omitted: at all times.]

[3 The German translation more correctly renders this sentence:— That it (i. e. our will) by the grace of the Holy Ghost may will that which he inspireth into it.]

[4 bonam, Lat. omitted: to be good.]

In this point the faithful feel a very great battle in them- selves; Paul witnessing and saying: " The flesh lusteth against the Spirit, and the Spirit against the flesh. And these two are at mutual enmity between themselves, that what things ye would that ye cannot do." Therefore we desire not any kind of framing our will to God's will, but we add: " As well in earth, as it is in heaven;" that is, Grant, O Father, that thy will may be done in us earthly men, as it is done in thy saints[5], the blessed spirits. These do not strive against thy most holy will in heaven; but, being in one mind[6], they only will that which thou wilt, yea rather, in this one thing they are blessed and happy, that they agree and acquiet[7] themselves in thy will. Truly, it is not the least part of felicity or happiness in earth, to will that God willeth; it is the greatest unhappiness, not to will that which God willeth. And this, truly, by in- finite examples might be declared. I will allege only one, and that common too. Some one is grievously sick, and feel- eth pains and torments scarce tolerable[8]; but he in the mean time acknowledgeth, that he suffereth these things by the com- mandment and will of God, his most good, bountiful, and just Father, who wisheth him well, and hath sent this grievous calamity for his salvation and for his own glory. Doth not he, in the midst of his torments, by submitting himself to the will of God feel refreshing? And that which seemed most sharp and most bitter to man, by this voluntary and free submission he maketh it delightful and most sweet. Again; another is sick, vexed not with a very great disease; but this man doth not acknowledge this sickness to be laid upon him by the good will of God; yea, rather thinketh that God knoweth not the disease, that God doth not care for the disease: therefore he referreth it unto divers and sundry causes, and imagineth and seeketh divers means to heal it. And in these things he is wonderfully vexed and afflicted; and yet, by striving so against the will of God, he feeleth no refreshing or comfort at all. What therefore doth he else, nilling[9] that which God willeth, than (which they are wont to do), by ill means avoiding evil, double the same? Wherefore

[5 cœlitibus tuis, Lat.: in thy heavenly ones.]
[6 So also ed. 1584; but 1577, of one mind.]
[7 acquiescunt, Lat.]　　　　　[8 tolerabilia homini, Lat.]
[9 nolens, Lat.; not willing.]

the foundation of all happiness is faithful obedience, whereby we fully submit ourselves and whatsoever else unto us belongeth to the good will of God. And therefore in this greatest petition we pray unto the Father, that he would give us regeneration or newness of heart[1], true obedience, persevering patience, and a mind always and in all things agreeing with and obeying God.

Bread.

The fourth petition is such : " Give us this day our daily bread." For the will of God cannot be done in us, unless we be nourished and strengthened with the bread of God. Bread, among the Hebricians, signifieth all kind of meats, and the preserving or sustenance of the substance of man. Whereupon we read it said in the prophet[2] : " I will break the staff of bread." But man consisteth of two substances, the soul and body. The soul is the spirit ; the body is made of earth and other elements. Therefore it is preserved with two kinds of bread, spiritual and corporal. The spiritual meat of the soul, whereby it is preserved in life, is the very word of God, proceeding out of the mouth of God ; the Lord out of the law

Matt. iv.
Deut. viii.

repeating, and saying: " Man liveth not by bread only, but by every word that cometh out of the mouth of God." And for because this only setteth forth unto the faithful the eternal and incarnate Word of God, I mean, the very Son of God ; we rightly acknowledge him to be.the meat of the soul, yea, the meat of a whole faithful man. For he himself witnesseth, that he is " the bread that came down from heaven ; of which they that eat shall not die," but have life everlasting. Corporal bread consisteth of elements, and is earthly, and comprehendeth meat, drink, raiment, prosperous health of body, maintenance, to be short, the safety and good estate of man's life.

Ours.

And this bread truly we call ours ; not that it is not the gift and benefit of God, but because it is appointed for us, and pertaineth to our preservation, and is necessary for us. Yet

Daily.

in the mean season, when we call it daily, or ἐπιούσιον, that is to say, for the morrow, we signify, that it is the most excellentest of all, which only can sustain and preserve our substance, as much as is sufficient and as long as it is meet, and altogether after the same manner and order which is needful : for we said afore, that it is not our part to prescribe unto God a manner of doing or giving. To this also pertain

[1 mentis, Lat.]   [2 prophetis, Lat.]

these words following, "Give us this day:" for it belongeth Give only unto God to give; neither agreeth this petition to any creature. David saith : "All things wait upon thee, that thou mayest give them meat in due season. When thou givest them, they gather it; when thou openest thy hand, all things are filled with good." Again : "The eyes of all things do look upon thee, O Lord, and thou givest them meat in due season; thou openest thy hand, and fillest with thy blessing every living creature." Now we pray, "Give us," not, "Give me;" Us. which putteth us in mind again both of brotherly love and unity : for we ought not only to seek our own, but also to pray for the safety and preservation of all other men. The word, "this day," appointeth us a measure. For this we say : This day. Suffice thou us, O Lord, daily and every moment with as much as is needful and enough for us, which thou thyself only knowest best of all. For we are admonished by the way, that we should not burn with immoderate desire of transitory things; and that we should not lavish them out riotously when we have them, losing both our goods and our souls. And therefore that wise man is read to have said : "Two things Prov. xxx. have I required of thee; deny me them not before I die. Remove far from me vanity and lies; give me neither poverty nor riches; only feed me with food convenient for me: lest peradventure being full, I should deny thee, and say, Who is the Lord ? or being oppressed with poverty, fall to stealing, and forswear the name of my God." Therefore, in this fourth petition, we yield ourselves wholly into the care and tuition of God the Father, and commit ourselves to his providence ; that he, which only is able to save us, might feed, defend, and save us. For unless he pour his blessing upon us, unless he give us strength by those things that are means pertaining to our sustentation and maintenance, all things are of no force. We pray for the happy course of the word of God; for the pastors of the church themselves; for the maintainers of the commonweal ; for the safety of the church and commonweal. We crave that the bountiful Father would supply all wants, and give whatsoever things are necessary for the sustentation both of the body and the soul.

Furthermore, lest any should think himself unworthy of And forgive the daily bread, because it is due to children and not to us. dogs ; and therefore should pray the slowlier, and with a more slender courage; the Lord, preventing[1] this carefulness of the godly, addeth the fifth petition, which is this: "And forgive us our debts, as we forgive our debtors." In these words we ask forgiveness of our sins. And, that we may obtain forgiveness of our sins, it is needful that we confess ourselves to be sinners; for unless we do this, how shall we pray that our sins should be forgiven us? Truly, all the saints use this order of praying; therefore all of them acknowledge themselves to be sinners. For there remain relics, yea, even in the regenerate and most holy men, which daily burst out into evil thoughts, evil sayings and doings, yea, and oftentimes into heinous offences. But whatsoever faults and sins ours be; first, truly we confess them humbly to God the Father, and afterward pray him to forgive them. We call our sins "debts," God himself so teaching, because we are indebted for the punishment (as the price) of them unto God. And he forgiveth our debts, when he taketh not deserved punishment of us; so judging of us as if we were nothing indebted unto him. For the allusion is made to corporal debts: which if the creditor forgive the debtor, he hath no further power to cast in prison, or to punish him which was his debtor. Therefore, not only the fault is forgiven unto us, but the punishment also. Neither do we make any words of our merits unto the Father; but we say, "Remit, or forgive, us our debts." By the word remission, is meant a free forgiveness of sins; for he forgiveth us, because we are not able to pay. Whereupon we read in the gospel: "When the debtors were not able to pay, he forgave them both their debts." The like are set down in the eighteenth chapter of Matthew. Therefore by no merits[2] of ours, by no satisfaction of ours, but by the bountifulness of God through Christ, we pray that all our sins may be forgiven us. Neither do the saints here doubt of the certainty of forgiveness; for the Lord saith in the gospel: "Whatsoever ye ask in my name, believing, ye shall receive it." They therefore that pray in faith, doubt not that their sins are forgiven them for Christ's sake; for so also we confess in our creed: "I believe the forgiveness of sins."

We add forthwith hereunto: "As we forgive our debtors." Not that we should think, through our forgiveness, that we

Margin notes: Our debts. | Luke vii. | As we forgive our debtors.

[1 præoccupans, Lat.]
[2 So also ed. 1584; but 1577, merit; merito nostro, Lat.]

deserve or obtain forgiveness of our sins; for otherwise the reason of remission were not certain. For he that either bringeth or doth any thing, for which thing's sake sin is taken away; or he that satisfieth for sin; to him nothing is forgiven, but rather recompensed as a desert. Therefore, for other causes these things seem to be added. First, forasmuch as we be careful for forgiveness, of which many doubt, the Lord's will is to comfort our infirmity by adding this as it were a sign, whereby we might understand, that so surely our sins are forgiven us of God, as we are sure we have remitted and forgiven other their offences, wherewith they have offended us. Furthermore, his will was to drive out of us all old grudge, hatred, and malice; and to drive into us the study and desire of love and charity; and to admonish us of our duty, that, if as yet there did stick in our minds any part of old enmities, we may know, that it ought altogether to be laid aside and cast out of our stomach; yea, and that even now we must call upon the Lord to move our hearts, that we may be able to do it. Surely, we do hardly[3] lay down old injuries and offences. But it is meet, that we forgive our brethren lesser faults, which have obtained pardon of very great sins of our most gracious Father: unless, happily, we list to take trial of his fortune, who, in the parable of the gospel, had himself proof of the great bountifulness and liberality of the Lord in forgiving him, he in the meanwhile being fierce and cruel toward his brother, in exacting of him a very small and trifling debt. The parable is very well known in the eighteenth chapter of St Matthew.

The sixth and last petition is: "And lead us not into temptation, but deliver us from evil;" for sin is never so forgiven, that there remaineth not concupiscence in the flesh, which temptations stir up, and lead into divers kinds of sins. And these are of divers sorts. For first, God tempteth us, when he biddeth us do any thing whereby to prove us, as when he bad Abraham to offer up his son; or else, when he sendeth adversity upon us, that with the fire of temptation he may both fine[4] our faith, and cleanse away the dross of our misdeeds. These temptations of God tend to the salvation of the faithful. Wherefore we do not simply pray, not to be tempted: for the temptation of God is profitable. For that

And lead us not into, &c.

[3 graviter, Lat.]   [4 exerceat, Lat.]

James i. man is said to be blessed, which suffereth temptation: "for when he is tried, he shall receive the crown of life." We pray also[1], that we be not led into temptation: for the devil likewise tempteth; we are tempted of the world, and of our flesh. There are temptations on our right hand and on our left; tending to this end, to overthrow us, to drown us in the bottomless pit of our sins, and thereby to destroy us: when that is done, we are not only tempted, but we are led into and also entrapped in temptation. Such a petition therefore wo do make: If it please thee, O heavenly Father, to exercise us with thy wholesome temptations, we beseech thee grant that we may be found tried[2]: and suffer us not to be led by a devilish and wicked temptation; that, leaving thee, and being made bond-slaves to our enemy, and drowned in the gulf of wickednesses, we be caught and kept of him in evil, sin, and in our own destruction. For now we add the contrary clause, which also expoundeth the former; which, as

But deliver us from evil. other say, is the seventh petition: "But deliver us from evil;" ἀπὸ τοῦ πονηροῦ; I say, from that evil, to wit, from Satan, who elsewhere is called a tempter. Deliver us from Satan, and from all evils which he sendeth: deliver us from snares, crafty practices, deceivings; from war, famine, captivity, plague; from all those things which are evil, hurtful, and dangerous. Those things that are such our heavenly Father knoweth very well, to whom we say here: "Give us healthful and good things; take away from us those things which thou knowest to be hurtful and evil."

And so, briefly we conclude the Lord's Prayer, adding
Amen. moreover, "Amen." That confirmation and giving of assent is read to have been common and usual of old; as it is to see in Deut. xxvii., Nehem. viii., 1 Cor. xiv. The same in the beginning[3] doth express our desire; for we confess that we desire those things heartily which we pray for. Besides that, it declareth the certainty of our faith; as if we should say, I believe assuredly, that these things are granted unto me of God: for "Amen" is as much as if one should say,
* Which is commonly translated, Verily, verily. "So be it." And the Lord in the gospel oftentimes saith*, "Amen, Amen, I said unto you;" that is, of a certainty I tell

[1 Petimus autem, Lat.: But we pray.]
[2 probati, Lat.: approved.]
[3 principio, Lat.: in the first place.]

you the truth: or, I utter and pronounce unto you the undoubted truth. And so the faithful, after they have offered
prayers unto God, having their minds pacified, do now joyfully
wait for the gifts of the Lord.

Furthermore, some do place before the word, "Amen,"
immediately after the rehearsal of these words, "But deliver us *For thine is*
from evil," "For thine is the kingdom, and the power, and the *power, and*
glory, for ever. Amen." But Erasmus Roterod., in his anno- *ever.*
tations upon the new Testament, witnesseth, that those words
are not found in any old Latin copy; but are found added
in all Greek copies, howbeit not expounded of any of the interpreters, but of Chrysostom only and his follower Theophy-
lact; and that therefore they seemed unto him to be added
unto the Lord's Prayer, as some have added these unto the
Psalms: "Glory be to the Father, to the Son," &c. The same
Erasmus immediately adjoineth: "Wherefore there is no
cause why Laurentius Valla should stomach the matter, that
a good part of the Lord's Prayer was curtailed. Their rashness was rather to be reproved, who feared not to so heavenly
a prayer to patch their own toys. For I may call them toys,
in comparison of that which God hath taught, whatsoever
hath proceeded from men; especially if that which men have
added and put to, be compared with Christ the author of
prayer[4]." Neither did Erasmus only doubt of this addition;
for the Spanish copy, which they call *Codex Complutensis*,
hath: "That it seemeth more credible, that these words are
not a part of the Lord's prayer, as a member of the whole;
but put in through the fault of some certain writers, or
printers." In the same book is by and bye added: "And

[4 Hanc coronidem in omnibus Græcorum exemplaribus adjectam
comperio... verum quando nec in ullis Latinorum exemplaribus
ascriptum visitur, nec exponitur ab Hieronymo, aut ullo prorsus
interpretum præter Chrysostomum et hujus abbreviatorem recentem
Theophylactum, apparet ex solenni consuetudine... additum... Con-
simili studio adjectum est in fine Psalmorum, Gloria Patri. Proinde
non est cur Laurentius Valla stomachetur bonam precationis dominicæ partem fuisse decurtatam. Magis taxanda fuerat illorum teme-
ritas, qui non veriti sint tam divinæ precationi suas nugas assuere.
Nugas enim jure dixerim ad divinam doctrinam quicquid ab hominibus profectum fuerit; præsertim si quod ab hominibus annexum
sit, ad Christum auctorem conferatur.—Erasm. Annot. in Matt. loc.
cit. p. 31, 32. Basil. 1522.]

albeit St Chrysostom in his Commentaries upon Matt., Homil. xx., do expound these words, as if they were of the text; yet it is conjectured to be more true, that even in his time the first originals in his[1] treatise were corrupted: whereupon none of the Latins, no, not of the ancient interpreters or entreaters thereof, is read to have made any mention of these words[2]." And surely this is truly said. For the most diligent interpreters, which have taken in hand each of them word for word to expound the Lord's Prayer, as were St Cyprian, Hierome, and Augustine, of this addition have not spoken so much as one word.

Thus much have I spoken hitherto of the Lord's Prayer, and of calling upon God's name; of which Salomon, the wisest that ever was, most truly pronounceth: "The name of the Lord is a strong tower; the righteous runneth unto it, and is exalted[3];" that is, he standeth and is preserved in a safe, or in a high place, out of the reach of any weapon.

We will say somewhat (as we have done of this) of thanksgiving, another kind of prayer. And though the same also be comprehended in the Lord's Prayer, (for it comprehendeth all things belonging to true prayer, therefore it containeth thanksgiving also;) yet, after the expounding of that, I also would entreat of this by itself, lest by mingling of things there rise a confusion or disorder in our minds. And truly the Lord requireth thanksgiving of us: of which thing there are extant in the holy scriptures arguments not a few. For how many praises, rejoicings, and thanksgivings, are read in the Psalms, written and left both of David and of other prophets! And in the law also the Lord instituted a peculiar kind of oblation and sacrifice, which we have said is called the Eucharist, or the sacrifice of thanksgiving[4]. What thing else

Prov. xviii. (margin)

Of thanksgiving. (margin)

[1 So also ed. 1584; but 1577, this.]

[2 Magis credibile videtur quod ista verba non sint de integritate orationis dominicæ; sed quod vitio aliquorum scriptorum fuerunt hic inserta... Et licet beatus Chrysostomus in suis commentariis super Matthæum hom. 20. exponat ista verba tanquam si essent de textu; verisimilius tamen præsumitur jam suis temporibus originalia in isto passu fuisse corrupta; ex quo nullus Latinorum etiam ex antiquissimis interpretibus sive tractatoribus legatur de his verbis aliquam fecisse mentionem.—Nov. Test. Compluten. Matth. cap. vi.]

[3 Safe, Auth. Ver.; set aloft, Marg.]

[4 See Vol. II. p. 203.]

was the supper of the Passover, but a thanksgiving for the deliverance out of the Egyptian captivity? Surely, our Lord Jesus Christ, both instituting a remembrance of all his benefits and specially of the redemption purchased by his death, and knitting up all sacrifices in brevity, delivered the Eucharist, or sacrament of thanksgiving, to his church; as we will declare in place convenient, and have partly shewed in our former sermons[5]. Mankind in prosperity is all upon lustiness and jollity, and seldomtimes thinketh with himself, from whence prosperity cometh: so he doth not set by those spiritual mysteries and benefits so much as otherwise he ought. But they seem to be swine, and not men, which do not only not set by the benefits of God as they ought, but do moreover contemn them, and tread them under feet. The heavy judgment of God doth tarry for them.

Furthermore, the sacrifice of praise and thanksgiving is due to God only: for he is the only giver and author of all good things; though in the meanwhile he use the means and ministry of men and other creatures. Some prince sendeth unto thee a most royal gift; and that by a courtier not of the lowest degree, but a most chosen man: yet to him, nevertheless, though he be a nobleman, thou givest not thanks, but to the prince from whom the gift came: howbeit, in the mean while, thou dost honestly confess, that the courtier herein bestowed his labour for thy sake. But he had not bestowed it, unless his prince had so commanded: and so the whole benefit at the length redoundeth unto the prince himself, even unto him alone. And as all our invocation or calling upon God is acceptable unto God the Father through Jesus Christ our Lord; so no thanksgiving of ours is acceptable unto God, unless it be offered through Jesus Christ: for hitherto pertaineth the mystery of the altar of incense, whereof mention is made in the ceremonies of the law[6]. But the apostle also saith: "Give thanks always for all things unto God the Father[7] in the name of our Lord Jesus Christ." And again he saith: "By him we offer sacrifice of praise always to God, that is, the fruit of lips confessing his name."

But that we may be thankful for all the benefits of God, and offer continual thanksgiving unto God; it is needful first, to

We owe thanksgiving only to God.

Thanks are to be given to God through Christ.

Ephes. v.

Heb. xiii.

The benefits of God must be acknowledged

[5 See Vol. II. p. 269.]   [6 Vol. II. p. 157.]
[7 So also ed. 1584; but 1577, and the Father; et Patri, Lat.]

acknowledge, and well to weigh with ourselves, the benefits of God; for these being not yet known, or rightly weighed, our mind is not set on fire to give God thanks for his benefits. And these are indeed diverse, yea, they are infinite: for they are private and public, general and special, spiritual and corporal, temporal and eternal, ecclesiastical and political, singular and excellent. But who can reckon up all their kinds and parts? God created, beautified, garnished, and made this world fruitful for man. To the ministry of this he severally appointeth angelical spirits, whom he had created ministers for himself. He giveth us souls and bodies, which he furnisheth and storeth with infinite gifts and abilities; and, that which far passeth all other benefits, he loosed man, being entangled in sin; he delivered him, being a bond-slave to the devil. For the Son of God setteth us free into the liberty of the sons of God; by dying, he quickeneth; by shedding his blood, he purgeth and cleanseth[1]; he also giveth us his Spirit, whereby we may be guided and preserved in this banishment, until we be received into that our everlasting and true country. They that consider these things with a true faith cannot choose but be rapt into the praise and setting forth of God's goodness, and into a wondering at a thing doubtless to be marvelled at; that the gracious and mighty God hath such a special care of men, than whom this earth hath nothing either more wretched or miserable.

How the godly give thanks unto God.

Psal. viii.

2 Sam. iv.

Here the saints of God are destitute of words, neither have they words meet enough for this so great a matter. David crieth: "O Lord our God, how wonderful is thy name in all the world; for that thou hast set thy glory above the heavens;" and as it followeth[2] in the eighth psalm. And again the same: "Who am I, O Lord God, and what is the house of my father, that thou hast brought me hitherto (or so advanced me)? And what can David say further unto thee? for thou, Lord God, knowest thy servant;" and so forth, as followeth in the 2. book of Samuel, chap. vii. The same David hath set down a most notable form of blessing, or praising, or giving thanks unto God, in the ciii. Psalm, which beginneth thus: "Bless the Lord, O my soul; and all that is within me, bless his holy name. Bless the Lord, O my soul,

[1 expiat, Lat.]
[2 So also ed. 1584; but 1577, as followeth.]

and forget not all his benefits; who forgiveth all thy wickedness;" and so forth.   But what need any more words?   The
Lord's Prayer may be a most perfect form of praising God,
and giving thanks to God for all his benefits, and serve
in stead of many.   For as the preface and all the petitions do
call unto our remembrance, and absolutely set forth unto us,
God's greatest benefits most liberally bestowed upon us, and
also upon all other: so if we consider that it is our duty to
give thanks to God for every one of these, and by and bye
begin, even at the beginning of the Lord's Prayer, to weigh
this chiefly with ourselves, that God the Father, of his unspeakable mercy to us-ward, hath adopted us miserable sinners into the number of sons, by whom he will be sanctified,
and in whom he will reign, and at the last also translate unto
his everlasting kingdom; that I may speak nothing of other
petitions; what plentiful matter of praising God and giving
thanks unto him shall be ministered!   But these things are
better and more rightly understood by good, godly, and devout
exercise, than by precepts, though never so diligent.

And the Lord doth so much esteem this thanksgiving, Thanks-
offered unto him with true humility of mind, and also faith, giving a sacrifice.
that he receiveth it and counteth it for a most acceptable
sacrifice.   Of this thing there is very often mention in the
old Testament; as when it is said: "Whosoever offereth me Psal. l.
thanks and praise, he honoureth me.   I will not reprove thee
because of thy sacrifices.   I will take no bullocks out of thy
house, nor goats out of thy folds[3].   Offer unto God the sacrifice of praise, and pay thy vows unto the most Highest; and
call upon me in the day of trouble; I will hear thee (and[4]
deliver thee), and thou shalt glorify me."   Again: "I will offer Psal. cxvi.
unto thee the sacrifice of thanksgiving, and I will call upon
the name of the Lord."   And Oseas also saith: "Take these[5] Hos. xiv.
words with you, and turn ye to the Lord, and say unto him,
O forgive us all our sins, and receive us graciously, (Nim
recht fur gut); and then will we offer the calves of our lips
unto thee."   After which manner Malachi also hath left
written: "I have no pleasure in you, saith the Lord of hosts; Mal. i.
neither will I receive an offering at your hand.   For from
the rising of the sun unto the going down of the same my

[3 nor—folds, not in Lat.]   [4 hear thee and, not in Lat.]
[5 these, not in Lat.]

name is great among the gentiles; and in every place incense
and a pure offering shall be offered to my name : for my name
is great among the gentiles, saith the Lord of hosts." Furthermore[1], this pure offering all the old interpreters with
great consent, Irenæus chiefly and Tertullian, do interpret
Eucharistia, that is to say, praises and thanksgivings, and
prayer proceeding from a pure heart and a good conscience
and an unfeigned faith[2]. Truly, for no other cause have the
ancient fathers called the Eucharist, or mystical supper of
Christ, a sacrifice, than for that in it praise and thanksgiving
is offered unto God : for the apostle Paul sheweth, that Christ
was once offered, and that he cannot be offered often or any
more.

Of the force or virtue of prayer.

For great is the worthiness, power, and virtue, not only
of praise or thanksgiving, but also of prayer wholly; I mean,
of invocation also itself. Whereof although I have already
spoken somewhat[3], where I declared that our prayers are
effectual, yet do I add these few words. The saints truly had
a most ardent desire of praying, because of the wonderful
force of prayer. For, that I may say nothing of those most
ancient fathers before and anon after the flood; did not Abraham pray, when he received the promises ? and as often as he
changed his dwelling, did not he call upon God ? At his
prayer king Abimelech is delivered from death; and barrenness, which the Lord, being displeased, laid upon his house, is
cured. Jacob poured forth most ardent prayers unto God,
and received of him[4] inestimable benefits. In Exodus, Moses
prayeth, not once, but often; and taketh away the plagues from
the Egyptians, which the Lord by his just judgment had
brought upon them. At the prayer of Moses the Amalechites
turn their backs; and, when he ceased or left off, the Israelites fled away. Again, when the fire of the Lord devoured
the utmost parts of the tents of Israel, they cried unto Moses;
and Moses again cried unto the Lord : and suddenly the fire
that devoured them was consumed[5]. Again, the people mur-

[1 Ceterum, Lat. But.]

[2 Irenæus contra Hæres. Lib. iv. cap. 17. § 6, p. 249. Par. 1710.
Tertullian. adv. Marcion. Lib. iii. cap. 22, Lib. iv. cap. 1. Adv.
Judæos. cap. 5.]

[3 See Vol. iii. p. 206.]

[4 a Deo, Lat.]   [5 absorptus est, Lat.]

mured against the Lord, and vengeance is prepared; but Moses by mild and continual prayer quencheth the wrath of God; for it is said unto him: "I have let them go according to thy word." Anon after, when the people began afresh to murmur against Moses and Aaron, and that the vengeance of God had already consumed fourteen thousand and seven hundred men, Aaron, at the commandment of Moses, burneth incense, and standing between the dead and those that were living, howbeit near and appointed to death, he pleadeth for and obtaineth pardon by prayers. Innumerable other of this kind are read of Moses. Josue, Moses' successor, by prayers made the course of the sun and moon so long to stay, until he had revenged himself upon his enemies. Anna, without any voice heard, by prayer putteth from her the reproach of barrenness, and forthwith is made a fruitful mother of very many children. Samuel, the most godly son of godly Anna, by prayer vanquisheth the Philistines; and suddenly, in the time of harvest, raised up a mighty tempest of thunders and rain. We do also read things not unlike of Helias. Jonas in like manner prayed in the whale's belly, and was cast on the shore safe. Josaphat and Ezechias, most religious kings, by prayers poured forth unto God by faith, do triumph over their most puissant enemies. Nehemias asked nothing of his king before he had first prayed to the Lord of heaven; therefore he obtained all things. The most valiant and man-like stomached Judith by prayer overthrew and slew Holophernes, the most proud enemy of God's people, and the terror of all nations. And as Daniel brought all his affairs to pass by prayers unto God; so Hester took a deed in hand that was necessary for God's people, and with three days' fasting and daily[6] prayers bringeth it to an happy end. In the most blessed and most desired birth of our Lord Jesus, companies of angels are heard singing praises together unto God. What, and did not our Lord, when his life was in extreme danger, betake himself to prayer; and by and bye heard the voice of an angel comforting him? The apostles, together with the rest of the church, pray with one accord about the third hour of the day, and anon they received[7] the Holy Ghost. And when the apostles were in dangers, the

[6 assiduis, Lat.]
[7 So also ed. 1584: but 1577, receive; accipiunt, Lat.]

[BULLINGER, IV.]

15

church crieth suppliantly for God's help, and presently without delay findeth succour : they receive much liberty to speak, and work very great signs and miracles among the people. Peter by an angel of God is brought out of a very strong and fenced prison. What should I speak of Paul and Silas praying and praising the Lord in prison? Is it not read, that the foundations of the prison were all shaken with an earthquake, and by that occasion the keeper of the prison was turned unto God? Examples of which sort truly I could bring innumerable, but that I am persuaded that to the godly these are sufficient. And faithful men do not attribute these forces, effects, or virtues, to prayer, as to a work of ours, but as proceeding from faith; and so to God himself, which promiseth these things, and performeth them to the faithful. For the judgment of Paul touching these is known, in the xi. to the Hebrews; and that all glory is due to
one God : who vouchsafe so to illumi-
nate all our minds, that our
prayer may always
please him.
Amen.

OF SIGNS, AND THE MANNER[1] OF SIGNS; OF SACRA-MENTAL SIGNS: WHAT A SACRAMENT IS; OF WHOM, FOR WHAT CAUSES, AND HOW MANY SACRAMENTS WERE INSTITUTED OF CHRIST FOR THE CHRISTIAN CHURCH; OF WHAT THINGS THEY DO CONSIST; HOW THESE ARE CONSECRATED; HOW THE SIGN AND THE THING SIGNIFIED IN THE SACRAMENTS ARE EITHER JOINED TOGETHER OR DISTINGUISHED; AND OF THE KIND OF SPEECHES USED IN THE SACRAMENTS.

THE SIXTH SERMON.

THE treatise upon the sacraments remaineth, which we heard is joined to the word of God and prayer[2]. But in speaking of sacraments, delivered by Christ our king and high-priest, and received and lawfully used of his holy and

[1 ratione, Lat.]   [2 orationibus, Lat.]

catholic church, I will, by God's grace and assistance[3], observe this order; first, we entreat of them generally, and then particularly or severally. And here beforehand I will determine upon the certain signification of a sign or sacrament, wherein, if I shall be somewhat long or tedious[4], I crave pardon, dearly beloved, therefore; for I hope it shall not be altogether fruitless.

Signum, a sign, the Latin writers call a token[5], a representing, a mark and shew of something that hath signification[6]. So say Tully[7] and Fabius. Fabius saith: "Some call *signum*, σημεῖον, though some term it *indicium;* other some *vestigium*, a mark or token whereby a thing is understood, as slaughter by blood[8]." St Aurelius Augustine, the famous ecclesiastical writer, cap. 4, *De Magistro*, saith: "We generally call all those things signs, which signify somewhat; where also we find words to be[9]." Again, Lib. ii. *De Doctrina Christiana*, cap. 1, he saith: "A sign is a thing beside the semblance which it layeth before our senses, making of itself something to come into our mind or thought; as by seeing smoke, we believe there is fire[10]." {.marginal} A sign.

The said Aurelius Augustine doth divide signs into signs natural and signs given. "Natural he calleth those which, without any will or affection to signify, beside themselves make something else to be known, as is smoke signifying fire; for smoke hath not any will in itself to signify. Signs given are those which all living creatures do give one to another, to declare as well as they can the affections of their mind, or any thing which they conceive, mean, or understand." And signs given he divideth again by the senses. For some belong to the eyes; as the ensigns or banners of captains, moving of the {.marginal} Division of signs out St Augustine.

[3 ipso Domino inspirante, Lat.]
[4 or tedious, not in Lat.]   [5 notam, Lat.]
[6 vestigium et indicium rei significantis, Lat.]
[7 Cicero de Invent. Lib. I. cap. 30.]
[8 Fabius Instit. Lib. V. cap. 9.]
[9 Dicimus ea signa universaliter omnia, quæ significant aliquid; ubi etiam verba esse invenimus.—August. de Magistro, cap. 4. Opp. Tom. I. fol. 116, col. 2. Par. 1531.]
[10 Signum est res præter speciem quam ingerit sensibus, aliud aliquid ex se faciens in cogitationem venire: sicut...fumo viso ignem subesse cognoscimus.—Id. de Doctr. Christ. Lib. II. cap. 1. Opp. Tom. III. fol. 5, col. 3.]

hands, and all the members. Some again belong to the ears; as the trumpet and other instruments of music, yea, and words themselves, which are chief and principal among men, when they intend to make their meaning known. Unto smelling he referreth that sweet savour of ointment mentioned in the gospel, whereby it pleaseth the Lord to signify somewhat. To the taste he referreth the supper of the Lord; for, saith he, " by the taking of the sacrament of his body and blood he gave or made a sign of his will." He addeth also an example of touching: " and when the woman by touching the hem of his vesture is made whole, that is not a sign of nothing, but signifieth somewhat[1]." In this manner hath St Augustine entreated of the kinds and differences of signs.

Other also, whose opinion doth not much[2] differ from his, distinguish signs according to the order of times. For of signs, say they, some are of things present, some of things past, and some of things to come. They think them signs of things present, which signify those things to be present which are signified: as the ivy-garland hanging for a sign doth give us to understand, that there is wine to be sold where it is hanged up. The signs which our master Christ wrought did signify, that the Messias, and the kingdom of God promised by the prophets, was come. Under signs past they comprise all tombs, monuments of the dead, and those stones pitched of

Marginal notes: John xii. · Mark xiv. · Matt. ix. · Signs distinguished according to their times. · Matt. xii.

[1 Signorum igitur alia sunt naturalia, alia data. Naturalia sunt quæ sine voluntate atque ullo appetitu significandi præter se aliquid aliud ex se cognosci faciunt... Data vero signa sunt ea quæ sibi quæcunque viventia invicem dant ad demonstrandos quantum possunt motus animi sui vel sensa aut intellecta quælibet... Signorum igitur quibus inter se homines sua sensa communicant, quædam pertinent ad oculorum sensum, pleraque ad aurium, paucissima ad ceteros sensus. ...Et quidam motus manuum pleraque significant; et histriones omnium membrorum motibus dant signa quædam scientibus... Et vexilla draconesque militares per oculos insinuant voluntatem ducum ...Et tuba et tibia et cithara dant plerumque ... significantem sonum. Sed omnia signa verbis comparata paucissima sunt: verba enim prorsus inter homines obtinuerunt principatum significandi... Et odore unguenti Dominus, quo perfusi sunt pedes ejus, signum aliquod dedit. Et sacramento corporis et sanguinis sui prægustato, significavit quod voluit. Et cum mulier, tangendo fimbriam vestimenti ejus, salva facta est, nonnihil significat.—August. ibid. cap. 3, fol. 5, col. 3.]

[2 nihil, Lat.: nothing.]

Josue in the midst of Jordan, signifying to them which came Josh. iv.
after what was done in times before. The fleece did give to Judg. vi.
Gideon a sign of things to come; that is to say, a sign of
the victory which he should have over his enemies.

But these signs, being well considered and not neglected[3], Of signs, some are may more amply and plainly be divided into other signs, given of men, other whereof some are given of men, and some ordained of God some ordained of himself. Signs or tokens are given of men, whereby they God. shew and signify something, and by which[4] also they keep
something in memory among men, or do as it were seal up
that which they would have certain and sure. After this Signs given of men. manner is every description or picture demonstrative called
a sign; for in Ezechiel, chap. iv., Hierusalem, which was Ezek. iv.
portrayed in a tile[5], is called a sign. They also in ancient
time termed the images of the dead signs, because by those
images they would renew afresh the memory of them whose
signs they were called, and keep them in remembrance, as if
they were alive[6]. Yea, and the holy scripture calleth idols
signs; as it appeareth in Esay, cap. xlv., and the 2. Paralip.
xxxiii.[7] So stones being set or laid to mark out anything,
as landmarks, and all tombs and monuments, are signs.
Rahab of Hierico said to the Israelites[8]: "Give me a sign
by oath[9], that you will shew mercy to me; and they gave
her a rope to hang out[10] of her window." Behold, the rope
was a sign of their faith and truth, wherewith they did, as
we would say[11], seal themselves surely and without all dissimulation, to take diligent heed that Rahab should not be
destroyed. We Zwicers[12] term such signs, given or received
in confirmation of faith and truth, *wortzeichen*, because they
are added to the words, and do as it were seal them; and
wahrzeichen also, because by them we do as it were give
witness, that in good faith, and without all fraud or guile, we
will perform that indeed which we promised in word.

[3 expensis nec rejectis illis quidem, poterunt signa, &c. Lat.
These (definitions) being well considered, and not rejected, signs, &c.]

[4 So also ed. 1584; but 1577, by the which.]

[5 in a tile, not in Lat.]   [6 superstitem quasi retinere, Lat.]

[7 2 Chron. xxxiii. 7. Vulg.   In Isai. XLV. 20, Bullinger seems to
have mistaken lignum for signum.]

[8 ad exploratores Israelitas, Lat.: to the spies of Israel.]

[9 signum veritatis, Lat.]   [10 suspensum, Lat.]

[11 So also ed. 1584; but 1577, as ye would say.]

[12 Germani, Lat.: Swiss.]

The diversity of signs given of man. Now these kinds of signs are of divers sorts. For some are mute or dumb, and pertain to the sense of the eyes; of which sort are the standards used in war, crosses[1], banners, flaming fires, whereof mention is made, Numbers ii., Psalm [Ps. lxxiv. 4] lxxiii. &c. Neither is any man able to reckon up all of this sort: for ever and anon new come in, as pleaseth men. Matt. xx. Judas gave a sign unto his company: "Whomsoever," saith he, "I shall kiss, that same is he: take[2] him." The joining of right hands, which pertaineth to the sense of feeling, is a sign of faithfulness, help, and fellowship; yea, it is the dumb Gal. ii. sign[3], which sign Paul calleth "the right hand[4] of fellowship." Hitherto belong divers movings and gestures. Some of them are pertaining to the voice, which are conceived[5] by hearing, and are uttered by man's voice, or by the sound of things which have no life. By man's voice are uttered words, whistling, and whatsoever other things are of this kind; whereunto watch-words uttered by the voice may be added, as Judg. xii. Schiboleth in the xii. chapter of the Judges. Moreover, voices without life are they which are made by trumpets, flutes, horns, guns, drums, by ringing of bells and sounding instruments; which also extend very far and largely.

Signs given of God. Now signs are given of God to this end, to teach and admonish us of things to come, or of things past: either that they may after a sort lay before the eyes of the beholders, and represent in a certain likeness, the things themselves whereof they are signs; or else that they may, as it were[6], seal the promises and words of God with some visible ceremony celebrated of men by God's institution: to be short, that they might exercise our faith, and gather together those which are scattered into one assembly or company. And these are not all of one sort, but do much differ between themselves. The diversity of signs given by God. For some have their beginning of natural causes, and yet nevertheless are given as signs of God, to put us in mind of things, or to renew his promises[7], and to teach men things that have been done; of which kind is the rainbow, mentioned

[1 fasciæ, Lat. omitted: bundles.]   [2 tenete, Lat.]
[3 So also ed. 1584; but 1577, a dumb sign.]
[4 signum, Lat.]
[5 percipiuntur, Lat.]
[6 as it were, not in Lat.]
[7 so also ed. 1584; but 1577, to put us in mind of things past, or &c.: quæ præteritas res, aut etiam promissiones renovent, Lat.]

by Moses, Gen. ix. For when the flood ceased, that[8] God
made a new league with Noah, and ordained the rainbow for
a sign of his covenant, he made it not anew; but being made
long afore, and appearing by natural causes, by a new institution he consecrated it, to the intent it might cause us[9] to call to
our[9] remembrance the flood, and as it were to renew the promise of God, that is to say, that it should never come to pass
again, that the earth should be drowned with water. Now[10]
this sign hath not any ceremony ordained, whereby it might
be celebrated among men; neither doth it gather us together
into the society of any body or fellowship: but this sign is
referred chiefly to God, saying: "I will set my rainbow in the
clouds[11], that when I see it, I may remember the everlasting
covenant made between me and you." Not much unlike to *Signs and wonders.*
this are signs and wonders; signs, I say, in the sun, the moon, *Luke xxi.*
and the stars, which do forewarn men[12] of destruction and
calamities to come, unless by repentance they amend: but
neither have these any ceremony ordained, to celebrate the
remembrance of them, or to gather us together, &c. Again, *Miraculous signs.*
there be other signs altogether miraculous, not natural, though
there be natural things[13] in them; of which sort Gideon's fleece
is, and the shadow of the sun going back in the dial of king *Isai. xxxviii.*
Ezechias. These signs, as we read them to have been once
shewed, so by no institution are they commanded to be followed, or for some certain end to be celebrated. To Ezechias[14]
they were given at that time, to signify and witness the victory
which he should have against his enemies, and the recovery
of his health. Altogether and merely marvellous are those
things which, in the last of Mark, by our Lord Jesus Christ
are called signs, gifts, and means of healing, and speaking
with tongues[15], given unto and bestowed upon men, not by any
power of man or virtue of healing in him, but by the power
and virtue of Christ only. Those signs declared unto men,
that that was the true and undoubted preaching of the gospel,

[8 dum, Lat.] [9 us, our, not in Lat.]
[10 Interim, Lat.]
[11 Erit arcus in nube, Lat. Gen. ix. 15, 16.]
[12 cœlitus, Lat. omitted: from heaven.]
[13 naturalia quædam concurrant, Lat.]
[14 To Ezechias, not in Lat.]
[15 So also ed. 1584; but 1577, gifts, I mean, of healing, and &c.:
beneficia, inquam, sanitatis et linguarum, Lat.]

whereby Christ is declared to be Lord of all, Lord of life and
death, of Satan, and of hell also itself. For now when
through the name of Christ the dead do rise, and diseases being driven out go their way; by these very signs it is proved,
that that is true which is said, that Christ is Lord of all things.
So the wonders which Moses and Aaron wrought in Egypt,
Exod. iv., are called in the scripture signs; for they were
witnesses both of God's lawful sending, and tokens of his
mighty power to be executed against Egypt: but neither had
these any ceremony, neither gathered together into any society.

Signs para-
digmatical,
or for ex-
ample.

Now also we read, that some signs are paradigmatical,
that is[1], used indeed of men, but not without God's commandment, that these also may be said to be signs from God. Those
be altogether free[2] from miracles; and indeed not only fetched
from natural things, but also from things mere common and

Jer. xxvii.
xix. xxviii.

usual, as were the bands, pitcher, and chains of the holy prophet Jeremy; whereby, being willed of God so to do, he laid[3]
before them those things in a certain evident form and figure,
I mean, in a visible sign to be seen with men's eyes, which by
his preaching he prophesied should fall upon them[4]. The
like we may see in Ezech. the xviith. and xxivth. chap. These
signs paradigmatical, or for example, are in some things like
to those exercises of rhetoric, called *chriæ activæ;* yea, rather
they are certain mixed *chriæ,* so termed, for that they consist
partly in words and partly in deeds[5]. Aphthonius defineth an
active *chria,* "to be that which declareth and plainly sheweth a thing by action, deed, or gesture: as when Pythagoras
was demanded, how long man's life lasted; he for a while
stood still, that they might look upon him; but anon he shrunk
away, and withdrew himself out of their sight[6]: after that
manner and action signifying, that man's life is but short and
momentany[7]." But in the scripture for the most part are set
down *chriæ*[8] consisting of word and deed; as when Christ

[1 that is, not in Lat.]   [2 aliena, Lat.]
[3 voluit subjicere, Lat.]   [4 res sermone copiose expositas, Lat.]
[5 so termed—in deeds, the Translator's addition.]
[6 a conspectu hominum, Lat.]
[7 Τῆς χρείας τὸ μέν ἐστι λογικόν· τὸ δὲ πρακτικόν· τὸ δὲ μικτόν....
Πρακτικὸν δὲ, τὸ πρᾶξιν σημαῖνον· οἷον Πυθαγόρας ἐρωτηθεὶς πόσος ἂν
εἴη τῶν ἀνθρώπων ὁ βίος, βραχύ τι φανεὶς ἀπεκρύψατο, μέτρον τοῦ βίου
τὴν θέαν ποιούμενος.—Aphthon. Progymnas. p. 3. Genev. 1569.]
[8 chriæ mixtæ, Lat.]

took a child[9], and set him in the midst of his disciples, and
spake these words: "Verily I say unto you, Except ye shall　Matt. xviii.
turn, and become as little children, ye shall not enter into the
kingdom of heaven." But these actions or signs have not the
institution and commandment of God, charging us to renew
this very action by solemn celebrating the same. Neverthe-　Sacramental
less, sacramental signs have some affinity with these, namely,　signs are severed from other signs
baptism and the Lord's supper; for they are given unto us　with which they have
from above, and are taken from natural things, without any　many things common.
miracle; yea, they are instituted under the form of natural
and sensible things, and in such things as are very common, water, bread, and wine. This they have common with
other signs given of God, in that they renew things past,
and shadow out things to come, and by a sign[10] do represent
things signified. They differ peculiarly from other signs, in
that they have ceremonies joined with the commandment of
God[11], which ceremonies he[12] hath commanded his church to
solemnize. And this also is peculiar to them, that, being seals
of God's promises, they couple us visibly to God and to all
the saints; and they are dedicated to the most holy mysteries
of God in Christ. Of these I will entreat more largely and
diligently hereafter.

　　The sacramental signs of Christ and of Christ his church,　Sacrament.
namely, which Christ our Lord hath delivered to his church,
and which his church hath received of him and do lawfully
use[13], the same are called of Latin writers by the name of
"sacraments." But the word is not found in the whole scripture, saving that it is read to be used of interpreters[14]. Howbeit, the word "sign" is oft in the scriptures, and, that which
helpeth for our purpose, is most significantly set down in Gen.
xvii. and Rom. iv. In the meanwhile we do not reject the
Latin word *sacramentum*, a sacrament, as lightly regarding it;
neither yet, rejecting it, do we forge or devise a new. I like
well enough of the word sacrament, so it be used lawfully.

[9 So also ed. 1584; but 1577, a little child.]
[10 similitudine, Lat.]　　　　　　　[11 of God, not in Lat.]
[12 ipse Dominus, Lat. : the Lord himself.]
[13 religiosissime custodit, Lat. : doth most religiously keep.]
[14 In the Vulgate it is used both in the Old and New Testament
for a *secret* and *mystery*. See Fulke's Defence of Translat. ed. P. S.
p. 493.]

St Augustine, in his fifth epistle to Marcellinus, saith : "It were too long to dispute of the diversity of signs, which, when they pertain to holy things, are termed sacraments[1]." From whence doubtless sprang the common definition or description, "a sacrament is a sign of an holy thing[2]:" which as it cannot be rejected, so there is none but seeth, that in it the nature of the thing is not fully comprehended or expressed; neither is it separated from those things which also are holy signs. There is another definition therefore brought forth and used, which

What a sacrament is. is indeed more perfect than the other: "a sacrament is a visible sign of an invisible grace[3]." But because this also doth not in all points express the nature of the thing, this definition following seemeth unto many more allowable, which is after this manner : "Sacraments are ceremonies, wherewith God exerciseth his people, first to stir up, increase, and maintain their faith; then, to the end to testify before men his religion[4]." This is a true and right definition. But what if you define a sacrament somewhat more fully and largely in this manner ? "Sacraments are holy actions, consisting of words or promises of the gospel, or[5] of prescript rites or ceremonies, given[6] for this end to the church of God from heaven, to be witnesses and seals of the preaching of the gospel, to exercise and try faith, and by earthly and visible things to represent and set before our eyes the deep mysteries of God; to be short[7], to gather together a visible[8] church or congregation, and to admonish them of their duty." This definition truly is

---

[1 Nimis autem longum est convenienter disputare de varietate signorum, quæ cum ad res divinas pertinent sacramenta appellantur. —August. Ep. v. ad Marcellin. Opp. Tom. II. fol. 3, col. 4. Par. 1531.]

[2 Sacramentum est sacræ rei signum.—Lombard. Sentent. Lib. IV. dist. 1. B. fol. 304. Par. 1575.]

[3 Sacramentum est invisibilis gratiæ visibilis forma.—August. ap. Decret. Grat. par. III. de Consecr. dist. 2. can. 32. p. 2373. Par. 1583.]

[4 ... dicere merito possis sacramenta hujusmodi ceremonias esse quibus exercere vult populum suum Deus ad fidem intus primum fovendam, excitandam, confirmandam; deinde testandam apud homines religionem.—Calvin. Instit. Lib. IV. cap. 14. § 19. Opp. Tom. IX. p. 347. Amstel. 1667.]

[5 et, Lat.: and.]   [6 divinitus, Lat.: from God.]

[7 denique, Lat.: and lastly.]

[8 visibiliter, Lat. : in a visible manner.]

far fet[9], large, and manifold; a definition, I say, gathered of many parts: but we mean to go to it simply and plainly, and to lay forth the whole matter before your eyes to be seen; then will we make manifest every part thereof, and confirm the same with testimonies of scripture.

Now that I may fully[10] entreat of the names that are given to this thing; I find that Latin writers call sacrament an oath, or a religious bond; because it was not done (as I think) thoroughly and to the proof without certain ceremonies. M. Varro, in his second book *De Lingua Latina*, declaring what it is to contend with an oath, saith: "The plaintiff and the defendant each of them in some things gaged down at the place, appointed for that purpose, five hundred pieces of silver, and also in other things a set number of ounces; so that he which recovered in judgment should have his gage again, but he which was cast should forfeit it to the treasury[11]." Since therefore by intermeddling of holy things[12], through partaking of the sacraments, we are bound to God and to all the saints, as it were by obligation; and that God himself also, by the testimony of the sacraments, hath, as it were by an oath, bound himself to us; it appeareth that the name of sacrament is very aptly and properly applied to our signs. We read also in Latin writers of an oath that soldiers used to take; for it was not lawful for them to fight, unless they were put to ther oath and sworn. They took a solemn oath, having one to recite the form of the oath to them word by word, (as Vegetius saith in his book *De Re Militari*[13],) that they would stoutly and readily do whatsoever their captain commanded them, and that they would never forsake the field in the defence of the commonweal of Rome. They had a donation given unto each of them, as it were a pledge or

Sacrament taken for an oath.

Soldiers oath.

[9] longe petita, Lat.]   [10] plenius, Lat.: more fully.]
[11] Ea pecunia quæ in judicium venit in litibus, sacramentum a sacro. Qui petebat, et qui inficiabatur de aliis rebus, uterque quingentos æris ad pontem deponebant, de aliis rebus item certo alio legitimo numero assium. Qui judicio vicerat, suum sacramentum a sacro auferebat, victi ad ærarium redibat.—Varro. de Ling. Lat. Lib. IV.]
[12] sacris interpositis, Lat.]
[13] Jurant autem milites, omnia se strenue facturos quæ præceperit imperator, nunquam deserturos (militiam) nec mortem recusaturos pro Romana republica.—Veget. de Re Milit. Lib. II. cap. 5.]

earnest; they gave up their name to be enrolled; and were marked, that they might be known from other soldiers[1]. Now because we by our sacraments, specially by baptism, are received and enrolled to be Christ's soldiers; and by receiving the sacraments do profess and witness ourselves to be under Christ our captain's banner[2]; therefore not amiss, nor without reason, are the signs of Christ and his church called sacraments. In the mean while I will not stoutly stand in contention, that the word sacrament was for that cause chiefly attributed of them in ancient time to these our signs[3]. For Erasmus Rot., a man very well seen in the tongues, and thoroughly tried in old and ancient writers[4], none better, in *Cathe. sua Symb.* v., saith: "They which speak most exquisitely call *sacramentum* an oath or bond, confirmed by the authority of God and reverence of religion. But our elders used this word to express that which the Greeks call a mystery; which a man may call a religious secret, because the common people were excluded from meddling with them[5]." Thus far he. Therefore the old writers[6] did call those signs sacraments, instead of mysteries[7].

What a mystery is. For the selfsame signs are called of the Greeks[8] μυστήρια, mysteries, which the Latin writers for the most part interpret, holy and religious secrets; holy secrets, I say, from the celebration of which secrets[9] the profane common people were excluded and debarred. For Cælius in *Lectio. Antiqui.* supposeth, that they are called mysteries, ὅτι δεῖ μύσαντας τηρεῖν ἔνδον, because it behoved them which hid them, or which ministered them, to keep them close, and to shew them

[1 signabantur notis, is all that Bullinger says.]
[2 esse Christi milites, Lat.]   [3 sacris signis, Lat.]
[4 in sacris vetustisque scriptoribus, Lat. : in sacred and ancient writers.]
[5 Qui exactius locuti sunt, sacramentum appellant jusjurandum, aut obligationem, numinis ac religionis interventu confirmatam. At majores nostri vocem eam accommodarunt ad significandum id quod Græci dicunt *mysterium*, quod *religiosum arcanum* possis dicere ... quia ab his tractandis secludebatur vulgus.—Erasm. Symboli Catech. 5. Opp. Tom. v. col. 1175. Lugd. Bat. 1704.]
[6 ecclesiasticis, Lat. omitted : of the church.]
[7 quasi mysteria, Lat. : as it were mysteries.]
[8 a scriptoribus ecclesiasticis Græcis, Lat.]
[9 ut modo dictum, Lat. omitted : as was just said.]

to no common person[10]. Whereupon mysteries may be well called separated and holy secrets, known to them only which were ordained for that purpose[11], and to be celebrated only of saints or holy men. Yet it may seem, that μυστήριον is derived of μύστης and μύω, as ἀποδυτήριον of ἀπὸ and δύω, that the etymon thereof with the Greeks may be of no more force than *testamentum* among the Latins, which is a witness-bearing of the mind: although I am not ignorant what some also do reason in this case. [12]Sacraments therefore[13] are called mysteries, because in a dark speech[14] they hide other things which are more holy. And Paul willingly useth this word in his epistles. And why this word was attributed to the holy signs of the christian church, there is a plain reason; for these things are only known to the faithful, and are hid from those that are profane and unholy[15]. And surely the preaching of the gospel itself is called, "The mystery of the king- Matt. xiii. dom of God," to teach us, that, the unclean being shut out, it is revealed to the only children of God. For our chief inter- Eph. iii. preter of mysteries[16] saith: "Cast not your pearls before swine, Matt. vii. neither give that which is holy unto dogs." And Paul: "If our gospel lie hid as yet," saith he, "it is hid in them which are lost, in whom the god of this world hath blinded the minds of them that believe not," 2 Cor. iv.

Furthermore, many of the Greek doctors of the church What a sym-have called our sacraments σύμβολα, *symbola*, which word is bol is. also received and used very often of the Latins. It is derived of συμβάλλω, that is to say, *confero*, to confer or compare together; for by comparing one thing with another symbols are made apparent and rightly perceived. *Symbolum* therefore signifieth a sign which hath relation to some other thing, as we said of the standard, &c. And truly, among the Grecians in old time the use of symbols or signs was divers; for in their sacrifices[17] they had their symbols, signs (I say)

[10] Dicta mysteria quod ea δεῖ μύσαντας τηρεῖν ἔνδον, hoc est, occludentes oportet intus custodire, nec cuiquam explicare.—Ludov. Cælii Rhodig. Lect. Antiq. Lib. xvi. p. 596. Basil. 1542.]
[11] solis initiatis cognita, Lat.]   [12] Certe, Lat. : Indeed.]
[13] therefore, not in Lat.]   [14] involucro, Lat. : under a cover.]
[15] excluduntque prophanos, Lat.]
[16] mystagogus ille noster, Lat.]
[17] in sacris, Lat. : in their sacred rites.]

allegorically meaning something; as in the sacrifices of Bacchus a sieve was their symbol or sign, and the same they carried about when they were well tippled[1]; thereby signifying, that such as be drunken are blabs, and can keep nothing in secret. What if I can prove, that opinions of men[2], containing somewhat of deep understanding by an allegory or dark speech, are called[3] symbols? For Pythagoras his symbols are well enough known. So mystical divinity began to be called symbolical, because it was inwrapped in more hid and secret mysteries. So that is mystical[4], which is darkly uttered and in manner of a riddle, having in it a far more contrary[5] meaning than by words it seemeth to offer. Again, the gift and token of faith and truth, which by mutual consent passeth between the bride and the bridegroom, whereby it is not lawful for them to shrink or go back from their word, promise, or covenant, is called a symbol. Furthermore, to soldiers also, serving under one and the same banner, symbols or badges were given. Unto certain confederate cities, in like manner, and joined together in league of friendship, to the end that they might go safely to the bordering cities and to those which took parts with them, symbols or mutual signs[6] were given, that is to say, tokens; which being shewed and seen, they gave each other gentle and courteous entertainment[7], as to their league-fellows, companions, and singular friends. The ancient writers therefore hereupon have applied this word symbol to our sacraments, because they represent and shew unto us the exceeding great and deep mysteries of God: they are allegorical and enigmatical, hard and dark to understand; because[8] the Lord himself by the institution of his sacraments hath bound himself unto us, and we again by the partaking of them do bind ourselves to him and to all the saints, testifying and openly professing to fight stoutly and valiantly under the Lord's banner. Moreover, these holy

[1 quod circumferebant bacchantes, Lat.]
[2 sententiæ, Lat.: sayings.]   [3 dici cœperunt, Lat.]
[4 symbolicum, Lat.]
[5 So also ed. 1584; but 1577, a far contrary.]
[6 tesseræ, Lat.]
[7 intelligebant offerentem humaniter esse tractandum, Lat.: they understood that they were to give courteous treatment to those who presented them.]
[8 quod denique, Lat.: and lastly because.]

symbols and signs[9] do admonish and put us in mind of brotherly love and concord, and that we remember to love them most entirely and with all our heart, as God's children and our brethren, which are communicants or partakers with us of the same table, and are washed clean by the same baptism.

Thus much concerning sacraments: what they are, by what names they are called, and why they are so called, let it be sufficient that we have briefly noted.

Setting aside all other things, it seemeth necessary first of all to declare and shew, who was the author of the sacraments, and for what causes they were instituted. All men in a manner confess, that God alone is[10] the author of sacraments, and not men, nor yet the church itself. An odd man there is[11] among the schoolmen, which teacheth the church this lesson; to wit, that she should remember she is no lady or mistress over the sacrament[12], but a servant or minister ; and that she hath no more power or authority to institute any form of a sacrament[12] than she hath to abrogate any law of God[13]. Aquinas also, part. iii. quæst. 46. articulo 2. saith : "He instituteth, or is the author of a thing, which giveth it force and virtue : but the virtue and power of the sacraments cometh from God alone ; therefore God alone is of power to institute or make sacraments[14]." And indeed, God alone is of power to institute the true service and worship: but sacraments belong to his service and worship; therefore God alone doth institute sacraments. If any one in the old Testament had offered sacrifice which God commanded not, or offered it not after that manner that God willed it to be offered, it was not only nothing available unto him, but also his offence in so doing was rewarded with most terrible and fearful punishment. Who knoweth not, that the sons of Aaron, for offering strange fire, were horribly burnt and scorched up with fire which fell down from heaven? Such sacrifices therefore dis-

Only God is the author of sacraments.

Isai. lxvi.

Levit. x.

[9 So also ed. 1584; but 1577, or signs.]
[10 posse, Lat. : can be.]
[11 Est enim qui, Lat. : For there is one.]
[12 So also ed. 1584; but 1577, sacraments.]
[13 The editor has not been able to verify this reference.]
[14 Ille instituit aliquid, qui dat ei robur et virtutem ;... sed virtus sacramenti est a solo Deo... ergo solus Deus potest instituere sacramentum.—Aquinas Summa Theol. par. iii. quæst. 64. p. 133. Col. Agrip. 1622.]

please God, as profane or unholy; neither deserve they to
be called lawful sacraments, which have not God himself for
their author.   Hereunto is added[1], that sacraments are testimonies, and as it were seals, of God's good-will and favour
toward us.   And who, I pray you, can better, more uprightly,
or more assuredly bear witness of God's good-will[2] to us-ward,
than God himself?   In nowise deserveth that to be called or
counted the seal of God, whereto he neither set his hand, nor
printed it with his own mark[3]; yea, it is a counterfeit seal,
because it cometh not from God, and yet in the mean time
beareth a shew outwardly of the name of God.   In this
behalf is read that saying of St Augustine, which is in every
man's mouth: "The word is added to the element, and there
is made a sacrament[4]:" whereby we gather, that in the institution of sacraments the word of God obtaineth principal
place, and hath most ado; the word, I say, of God, not the
word of men, nor yet of the church: whereupon it followeth[5],
that the sign ought to have his proceeding even from God
himself, and not from any manner of men, be they never so
many, be they never so clerklike or learned, be they never so
harmless and holy of life: of[6] that now there can be no other
author of sacraments than God himself alone.

Sacraments are to be received as it were at the hands of Christ.

As we do receive the word of salvation and grace, so it
is needful also that we receive the signs of grace.   Although
the word of God be preached unto us by men, yet we receive
it not as the word of man, but as the word of God, according

1 Thess. ii.

to the saying[7] of the apostle: "When ye had received the
word of God which ye heard of us[8], ye received it not as the
word of men, but (as it is in deed) the word of God."   It is
behoveful for us to have respect to the first author thereof,

Mark xvi.
Matt. xxviii.

who when he sent abroad his disciples, said: "Go into the
whole world, and preach the gospel to all creatures, teaching
them to observe whatsoever I have commanded you; and

[1 His accedit, Lat.]   [2 rather, of God's will.]
[3 quod ab ipso Deo non est appensum, aut impressum, Lat.]
[4 Accedit verbum ad elementum, et fit sacramentum.—August.
Expos. in Evang. Joan. Tract. LXXX. Opp. Tom. IX. fol. 91. col. 2.
Par. 1531.]
[5 denuo, Lat.: again.]
[6 A misprint in all the editions for, so that.]
[7 So also ed. 1584; but 1577, that saying.]
[8 See above, p. 95, note 12.]

baptizing them in the name of the Father, and of the Son, and of the Holy Ghost." "He that heareth you heareth me ; Luke x. and he which despiseth you despiseth me." And therefore, albeit by the hands of men the sacraments are ministered, yet are they not received of the godly and religious as proceeding from men, but as it were from the hand of God himself, the first and principal author of the same. To this belongeth the question which Christ our Lord asked in the gospel, saying : " The baptism of John, was it from heaven or Matt. xxi. of men ?" Truly John, who did baptize, was a man ; but in that he baptized, he baptized according to God's institution and ordinance : and therefore the baptism of John was from heaven, though the water wherewith he baptized flowed out of the bottomless depth into the river Jordan[9], and John himself conversant on the earth. To this also notably agreeth that which Paul saith[10] : " That which I delivered unto you 1 Cor. xi. I received of the Lord." Therefore, although St Paul were a man, yea, and a sinner too, yet that which he delivered to the church, he did not deliver it as from himself, or as any invention of man, but as Christ hath delivered[11] the same ; so that it is not his, or man's, but[12] Christ's tradition, a divine and heavenly tradition. Besides this, our high priest and everlasting bishop worketh even at this day in his church; whose ministry they execute, that is, at whose commandment they baptize, and according to whose institution they, which are the stewards or disposers of the mysteries of God, minister the holy sacraments of the Lord's supper[13]. The institution therefore of the sacraments[14] must be acknowledged[15] of us to be the very work of God. And thus far touching the author of sacraments.

Peter Lombard, in his Sentences, reckoneth up three causes Why sacraments were instituted ; that is to say, why spiritual instituted unto us in and heavenly things were delivered and committed[16] unto us visible things. under visible signs, forms, and ceremonies : the first of which is so cold and weak, that I am loath to move it to memory.

[9 in alveo Jordanis, Lat.]   [10 diserte, Lat.: in express words.]
[11 So also ed. 1584; but 1577, had delivered.]
[12 not his, or man's, but, not in Lat.]
[13 sacrum exhibent convivium, Lat. : sacraments of the Lord's, not in Lat.]
[14 The institution of the sacraments, not in Lat.]
[15 ingenue, Lat. omitted : candidly.]   [16 commendatæ, Lat.]

16

He placeth merit in that, that by God's government and direction (as he affirmeth) man seeketh salvation in things baser and inferior to himself. Unto the which he addeth this afterward; although not in them, yet in God through them he seeketh salvation: which also unadvisedly enough he hath uttered, and not sufficiently considered. The other two causes, to wit, that sacraments were invented and ordained under visible signs for our instruction and exercise, seem not altogether absurd or disagreeing from reason[1].

The truest and most proper cause, why sacraments be instituted under visible signs, seemeth partly to be God's goodness, and partly also man's weakness. For very hardly do we reach unto the knowledge of heavenly things, if, without visible form[2], as they be in their own nature pure and excellent, they be laid before our eyes: but they are better and more easily understood, if they be represented unto us under the figure of earthly things, that is to say, under signs familiarly known unto us. As therefore our bountiful and gracious Lord did covertly and darkly, nay rather, evidently and notably, set before us to view[3] the kingdom of God in parables or dark speeches; even so by signs it pleased him to lay before our eyes, after a sort, the very same thing, and to point out the same unto us, as it were painted in a table; to renew it afresh, and by lively representation to maintain the remembrance of the same among us. This cause doth John Chrysostom allow, as a chief and proper cause; who in his eighty and three homily upon Matthew saith: "The Lord hath delivered unto us nothing that is unsensible[4]. The things indeed are sensible, howbeit they have altogether a spiritual understanding or meaning. So baptism is ministered under a sensible element, namely water; but that which is wrought thereby, that is to say, regeneration and the new birth,

Chrysostom touching the cause of sacraments.

John iii.

[1 Triplici de causa sacramenta instituta sunt; propter humiliationem, eruditionem, exercitationem. Propter humiliationem quidem, ut dum homo insensibilibus rebus, quæ natura infra ipsum sunt, ex præcepto Creatoris se reverendo subjicit, ex hac humilitate et obedientia Deo magis placeat et apud eum mereatur; cujus imperio salutem quærit in inferioribus se, etsi non ab illis, sed per illa a Deo.—Lombard. Sentent. Lib. iv. dist. 1. B. fol. 305. Par. 1575.]

[2 involucro aliquo, Lat.]

[3 parabolis obtexit, imo illustravit ornavitque, Lat.]

[4 So also ed. 1584; but 1577, sensible.]

doth spiritually enter into the mind. For if thou wert a bodiless creature, he would have delivered unto thee all these gifts bare, naked, and bodiless, according to thy nature : but since thou hast a reasonable soul coupled and joined to thy body, therefore hath he delivered unto thee in sensible signs and substances those things, which are perceived with a spiritual understanding[5]." Which I do not allege [to] this end, as if I would take the testimony of man for my stay; but because I see St John Chrysostom his speech according to the manner observed and used in the scripture. For who knoweth not, that the scripture is full of parables, similitudes, allegories, and figurative speeches, which the Holy Ghost useth, not for his own, but for our sakes? The talk which Christ had in the gospel with Nicodemus touching heavenly regeneration is very well known; where he by hidden and covert kind of speeches of air, wind, and water, &c. reasoneth, saying : "If I have told you of earthly things, and ye believe not; how will you believe, if I shall tell you of heavenly things?" He calleth "earthly things" that his doctrine of heavenly regeneration or new birth figured to us under earthly signs of water and the spirit, or of air and the wind; and by "heavenly things" he meaneth that selfsame doctrine of heavenly regeneration nakedly delivered to Nicodemus without any imagination, without similitude or sensible signs. The Lord therefore signifieth hereby, that men do more easily conceive and understand the doctrine of heavenly things, when it is shadowed out under some dark and covert sign of earthly things[6], than when it is nakedly and spiritually indeed delivered : that by comparing together of things not much unlike, it may appear that the sacraments were for none other cause found out or instituted[7] than for demonstration sake, to wit, that the heavenly things might become more familiar and plain unto us.

John iii.

[5] Οὐδὲν γὰρ αἰσθητὸν παρέδωκεν ἡμῖν ὁ Χριστός· ἀλλ' αἰσθητοῖς μὲν πράγμασι, πάντα δὲ νοητά. Οὕτω γὰρ καὶ ἐν τῷ βαπτίσματι δι' αἰσθητοῦ μὲν πράγματος γίνεται τοῦ ὕδατος τὸ δῶρον, νοητὸν δὲ τὸ ἀποτελούμενον, ἡ γέννησις καὶ ἡ ἀναγέννησις, ἤτουν ἀνακαίνισις. Εἰ μὲν γὰρ ἀσώματος εἶ, γυμνὰ ἂν αὐτά σοι τὰ ἀσώματα παρέδωκε δῶρα· ἐπεὶ δὲ σώματι συμπέπλεκται ἡ ψυχή, ἐν αἰσθητοῖς τὰ νοητά σοι παραδίδωσι.—Chrysost. Hom. in Matth. LXXXII. (al. LXXXIII.) Opp. Tom. VII. p. 787. Par. 1727.]
[6] involucro aliquo, Lat. : of earthly things, not in Lat.]
[7] divinitus, Lat. omitted : by God.]

16—2

In which thing we have to mark the analogy, which is a certain aptness, proportion, or (as Cicero termeth it) a convenience[1], or fit agreement of things, I say, known by their signs; that if they be slightly[2] passed over without this analogy, the reason of a sacrament cannot be fully and perfectly understood : but this analogy, being diligently discussed and observed to the full, offereth to the beholder, without any labour at all, the very ἀναγωγή, that is to say, the hidden and secret meaning of a sacrament[3]. We will, when we come to entreat of these things, do what we can to make them manifest by examples.

The Lord is to be praised for instituting sacraments.

Whosoever therefore shall throughly weigh the institution[4] of sacraments, he cannot choose but extol with praises the exceeding great goodness of the Lord, who doth not only open unto us miserable men the mysteries of his kingdom, but hath a singular care of man's infirmity; whereby he, framing himself to our capacity, doth after a sort stut and stammer with us, whilst he, having respect to our dulness and the weakness of our wit, doth as it were clothe and cover heavenly mysteries with earthly symbols or signs; thereby most plainly and pithily opening them unto us, and laying them before our eyes evidently to be beheld.

The wisdom of God shineth in the institution of the sacraments.

In this same institution of the sacraments we have cause to extol and praise the wisdom of God; if so be we take in hand[5] to compare great and small things together. For this custom is received as a law throughout the world, that all the wisest men, when they had occasion to speak of high mysteries of wisdom, they did not by words only, but by signs and words together, commend them to their hearers; to the end that the two most noble senses in man, to wit, hearing and seeing, might be both at once vehemently moved, and forcibly provoked to the consideration of the same. The volumes of heathenish philosophers are full of examples. What say you to the Jews, God's old and ancient people? Did not God himself shew among them very many such kind of examples ?

Again, as in making leagues, or in confirming promises in

[1 Ὁμολογία is what Cicero explains by convenientia, de Fin. Lib. III. cap. 6.]

[2 Rather, it be.]   [3 of a sacrament, not in Lat.]
[4 hanc inventionem, Lat.]
[5 rather, it is permitted us : licet, Lat.]

earnest and weighty matters, men use signs or tokens of truth, The manner of making leagues or covenants. to win credit to their words and promises; even so the Lord, doing after the manner of men[6], hath added signs of his faithfulness and truth in his[7] everlasting covenant and promises of life; the sacraments, I mean, wherewith he sealeth his promises and the very doctrine of his gospel. Neither is this rare or strange unto him. Men swear even by the Lord himself, when they would make other believe certainly, and in no case to mistrust the truth of their promises: yea[8], it is read in the holy scriptures, that the Lord himself took an oath and sware by his own self, when he meant "most abundantly to shew to the heirs of the promises," as the apostle saith, "the stableness of his counsel." Moreover, it was the accustomed manner among them of old, as they were making their league or covenant, to take a beast, and to divide him in pieces, and each of them to pass through and between the pieces so divided; testifying by that ceremony, that they would yield themselves so to be divided and cut in pieces, if they did not stedfastly stand to that which they promised in their league or covenant. After the same manner the Lord, making or Gen. xv. renewing a league with Abraham, which Moses describeth at large in the xv. of Genesis, he commandeth him to take an heifer, a she-goat, and a ram, each of them three years old, and to divide them in the midst, and to lay every piece one over against another; which when Abraham had done, the Lord himself, in the likeness of a smoking furnace or firebrand, went between the said pieces, that thereby Abraham might know, that the land of Canaan should of a certainty be given to him, and to his seed to possess; and that all things which he had promised in that league should be brought to pass. Since therefore the good and true Lord is always like unto himself, and frameth himself after the same manner now to this[9] church, as we said he did then; what wonder or strange thing is it, I pray you, that he hath left unto us also at this day, under visible things, signs and seals of his grace and mysteries[10] of the kingdom of God? And hitherto have we

[6 hac quoque in re, Lat. omitted: in this matter also.]
[7 So also ed. 1584: but 1577, to his; fœderi, Lat.]
[8 ergo, Lat.: therefore.]
[9 So also ed. 1584; but 1577, to his: suæ, Lat.]
[10 et mysteriorum, Lat.: and of the mysteries.]

entreated of the chief causes of sacraments, for the which they were instituted.

The number
of sacra-
ments. Touching the kind and number of sacraments, which hath the next place to that which went before; there are divers opinions among the writers, specially of later time. For among the old and ancient this question, as an undoubted and well-known perfect principle, drew quickly to an end. But he which shall diligently search the scriptures shall find, that they of the old Testament had sacraments after one kind, and they of the new Testament[1] sacraments after another kind. The sacraments of the people under the old Testament were circumcision and the paschal lamb, to which were added sacrifices; whereof I have abundantly spoken in the third decade and the sixth sermon[2]. In like manner the sacraments of the people under the new Testament, that is to say, of Christians, by the writings of the apostles, are two in number; "baptism," and "the supper of the Lord." But Peter Lombard reckoneth seven, baptism, penance, the supper of the Lord, confirmation, extreme unction, orders, and matrimony[3]. Him followeth the whole rabblement of interpreters and rout of schoolmen. But all the ancient doctors of the church for the most part do reckon up two principal sacraments; among whom Tertullian, in his first and fourth book *Contra Marcionem,* and in his book *De Corona Militis,* very plainly maketh mention but of two only, that is to say, baptism, and the Eucharist or supper of the Lord[4]. And Augustine also, Lib. III. *De Doctr. Christiana,* cap. ix. saith: "The Lord hath not overburdened us with signs; but the Lord himself and the doctrine of the apostles have left unto us certain few things instead of many, and those most easy to be done, most reverend to be understood, most pure to be observed; as is baptism, and the celebration of the body and blood of the Lord[5]." And again to Januarius, *Epist.* cxviii.

[1 ac populi, Lat. omitted: and people.]

[2 Vol. II. page 178, &c.]

[3 Sacramenta novæ legis ... sunt, baptismus, confirmatio, panis benedictio, id est, eucharistia, pœnitentia, unctio extrema, ordo, conjugium.—Lombard. Sentent. Lib. IV. dist. 2. A. fol. 306. Par. 1575.]

[4 Tertull. adv. Marcion. Lib. I. cap. 28. IV. cap. 38. De Coron. Mil. cap. 3.]

[5 Hoc vero tempore, posteaquam resurrectione Domini nostri Jesu Christi manifestissimum indicium nostræ libertatis illuxit, nec

he saith: "He hath knit and tied together the fellowship of a new people with sacraments in number very few, observing[6] very easy, in signification very excellent: as is baptism, consecrated in the name of the Trinity; and the partaking of Christ's body and blood; and whatsoever thing else is commended unto us in the canonical scriptures: except those things wherewith the servitude of the old people was burdened, according to the agreeableness of their hearts and the time of the prophets[7]; which are read in the five books of Moses[8]." Where by the way is to be marked, that he saith not, "And whatsoever things else are commended unto us in the canonical scriptures;" but, "And whatsoever thing else," &c.: which plainly proveth, that he speaketh not of sacraments, but of certain observations both used and received of the church, as the words of Augustine which follow do declare. Howbeit, I confess without dissimulation, that the same Augustine elsewhere maketh mention of the sacrament of orders[9]: where, nevertheless, this seemeth unto me to be also considered, that the selfsame author giveth the name of sacraments to anointing, and to prophecy, and to prayer, and to certain other of this sort[10], as well as he doth to orders; and

eorum quidem signorum quæ jam intelligimus operatione gravi onerati sumus: sed quædam pauca pro multis, eademque factu facillima, et intellectu augustissima, et observatione castissima, ipse Dominus et apostolica tradidit disciplina; sicuti est baptismi sacramentum et celebratio corporis et sanguinis Domini.—August. de Doct. Christ. Lib. III. cap. 9. Opp. Tom. III. fol. 11. col. 3. Par. 1531.]

[6 So also ed. 1584; but 1577, *in* observing.]

[7 So also ed. 1584; but 1577, Except those ceremonies, which through the hardness of their heart and the time of the prophets made the bondage of the old people more grievous.]

[8 Sacramentis numero paucissimis, observatione facillimis, significatione præstantissimis, societatem novi populi colligavit; sicuti est baptismus Trinitatis nomine consecratus, communicatio corporis et sanguinis ipsius, et si quid aliud in scripturis canonicis commendatur, exceptis iis quæ servitutem populi veteris, pro congruentia cordis illorum et prophetici temporis, onerabant, quæ in quinque libris Moysi leguntur.—August. Ep. CXVIII. Januario. Opp. Tom. II. fol. 108. col. 2.]

[9 Sacramentum ordinationis.—Id. de Bono Conjug. cap.24. Opp. Tom. VI.]

[10 August. de Bono Conjug. cap. 18. Contra litt. Petil. Lib. II. cap. 104. Hom. 83. de Diversis. De Peccat. Merit. Lib. II. cap. 26. Sentent. Excerp. 335. St. Hilary speaks of the sacrament of prayer, in Matth. cap. V. 1.]

now and then among them ho reckoneth up the sacraments of the scripture[1]: so that we may easily see, that in his works the word "sacrament" is now used one way, and sometimes another. For he calleth these sacraments, because, being holy, they came from the Holy Ghost; and because they be holy institutions of God, observed of all that be holy: but yet so, that these differ from those sacraments which are holy actions consisting of words and ceremonies, and which gather together into one fellowship the partakers thereof. But Rabanus Maurus also, bishop of Mentz[2], a diligent reader of Augustine's works, *Lib. De Instit. Cleric.* cap. xxiv. saith: "Baptism and unction, and the body and blood, are sacraments; which for this reason are called sacraments, because, under a covert of corporal things, the power of God worketh more secretly our salvation signified by these[3] sacraments: whereupon also, for their secret and holy virtues, they are called sacraments[4]." This Rabanus Maurus was famous about the year of the Lord eight hundred and thirty; so that even by this we may gather, that the ancient apostolic church had no more than two sacraments. I make no mention here of Ambrose; although he, in his books of sacraments, numbereth not so many as the company of schoolmen do: because some of those works, set forth in his name, are not received of all learned men as of his own doing[5]. So I little force the authority of the works of Dionysius, which of what price and estimation they be among learned and good men, it is not needful to declare[6]. But howsoever the case standeth, the holy scripture, the only and infallible rule of life and of all things which are to be done in the church, commendeth baptism and the Lord's supper unto us, as solemn institutions and sacraments

[1 August. de Ver. Relig. cap. 17. Enarrat. inPsalm. xciii.]

[2 He was archbishop of Mentz from A. D. 847—857. Mosheim, E. H. ed. Soames. Vol. ii. p. 195. n. 6. Lond. 1845.]

[3 So also ed. 1584; but 1577, *those.*]

[4 Sunt autem sacramenta baptismus et chrisma, corpus et sanguis: quæ ob id sacramenta dicuntur, quia sub tegumento corporalium rerum virtus divina secretius salutem eorundem sacramentorum operatur; unde et a secretis virtutibus vel sacris sacramenta dicuntur. —Rab. Mauri. de Instit. Cler. Lib. i. cap. 24. Opp. Tom. vi. p. 8. Col. Agrip. 1626.]

[5 See James's Corruption of Scripture, Councils, and Fathers. Part i. treat. 45, &c.]

[6 See Vol. iii. p. 137, note 9.]

of Christ. Those two are therefore sufficient for us; so that
we need not be moved, whatsoever at any time the subtle
invention of man's busy brain bring against or beside these
twain. For why? God never gave power to any[7] to institute
sacraments.

In the meanwhile, we do not contemn the wholesome rites
and healthful institutions of God, nor yet the religious observations of the church of Christ. We have declared elsewhere[8] touching penance and ecclesiastical order[9]. Of the
residue, which latter writers do authorise[10] for sacraments, we
will speak in their convenient place. So have we also elsewhere, so far forth as we thought requisite, entreated of the
likeness and difference of sacraments of the people of the old
and new Testament[11]. *Wholesome rites of the church are not contemned.*

Now let us see in what things sacraments consist. By the
testimony of the scripture and of all the godly men, they consist in two things; to wit, in the sign and the thing signified,
in the word and the rite, in the promise of the gospel and in
the ceremony, in the outward thing and the inward, in the
earthly thing, I say, and the heavenly; and, as Irenæus
the martyr of Christ witnesseth[12], in the visible thing and invisible, in the sensible thing and the intelligible. For hereunto belongeth that which St John Chrysostom upon Matthew
saith: οὐδὲν γὰρ αἰσθητὸν παρέδωκεν ἡμῖν ὁ Χριστὸς, ἀλλ'
αἰσθητὰ μὲν τὰ πράγματα, πάντα δὲ νοητά: "Christ delivereth nothing unto us that is sensible but under visible things; the
outward things are sensible, but yet all spiritual[13]." But he
calleth those things αἰσθητὰ, sensible, which are perceived by
the outward senses, as by seeing, hearing, tasting, and touching;
but those things he calleth νοητά, intelligible or mental, which
are perceived by the mind, the understanding, consideration,
discourse or reasoning of the mind, not of the flesh, but of
faith. *In his book against heresies.*

[7 Rather, to it.]
[8 quid sentiamus et doceamus, Lat. omitted: what we think and
teach.]
[9 See Vol. III. p. 90; and above, pp. 104, &c.]
[10 venditant, Lat.]   [11 Vol. II. page 293.]
[12 — e re, inquam, terrena et cœlesti, ut habet martyr Christi
Irenæus, Lat.—εὐχαριστία, ἐκ δύο πραγμάτων συνεστηκυῖα, ἐπιγείου τε
καὶ οὐρανίου.—Iren. Adv. Hæres. Lib. IV. cap. 34. p. 327. Oxon. 1702.]
[13 See quotation, above, p. 243, note 7.]

Sacraments
consist of the
sign and the
thing sig-
nified.
Mark i.
By the testimony of the scriptures this thing shall be made manifest[1]. The Lord saith to his disciples in the gospel: " Go into the whole world, and preach the gospel to all creatures; and he which shall believe and be baptized shall be saved. Ye shall baptize in the name of the Father, and of the Son, and of the Holy Ghost." The same[2] saith of John Baptist: " John baptized in the wilderness, preaching the baptism of repentance for the remission of sins." So also St

Acts ii.
Luke witnesseth, that St Peter said to the Israelites : " Repent ye, and be baptized every one of you in the name of Jesus Christ, for the remission of sins, and ye shall receive the gift of the Holy Ghost." Therefore in baptism, water, or sprinkling of water in the name of the Father, and of the Son, and of the Holy Ghost, and all that which is done of the church, is a sign, rite, ceremony, and outward thing, earthly and sensible, lying open and made plain to the senses : but remission of sins, partaking of (everlasting) life, fellowship with Christ and his members, and gifts of the Holy Ghost, which are given unto us by the grace of God through faith in Christ Jesus, is the thing signified, the inward and heavenly thing, and that intelligible thing which is not perceived but by a faithful mind. After the same manner the scripture, bearing witness also of the supper of the Lord, which is the other sa-

Matt. xxvi.
Luke xxii.
crament of the church, saith: " The Lord Jesus when he had taken bread, he gave thanks, and brake it, and gave it to his disciples, and said, Take ye, eat ye ; this is my body which is given for you. Likewise he took the cup, and gave it to them, saying, Drink ye all of this; for this is my blood of the new testament, which is shed for many for the remission of sins. Do this in remembrance of me." Now therefore all that action which is done of the church[3] after the example of Christ our high-priest, (I mean, breaking of bread, the distribution thereof, yea, and the banquet or receiving of bread and wine,) is the sign, rite, ceremony, and the outward or earthly thing, and also that self-same sensible thing which lieth open before the senses: but the intelligible thing and thing signified, the inward and heavenly thing, is the very body of Christ given for us, and his blood shed for the remission of sins, and our redemp-

[1 illustrior, Lat.]
[2 Eadem scriptura evangelica, Lat.]
[3 in cœna Domini, Lat. omitted : in the Lord's Supper.]

tion and fellowship which we have with Christ and all the saints, yea, which he chiefly hath with us.

By these things it shall be easy to determine certainly of the names or terms now given to the sacraments[4]. For they are called external or outward signs, because they are corporal or bodily, entering outwardly into those senses whereby they be perceived. Contrariwise, we call the things[5] signified inward things; not that the things lie hid included in the signs, but because they are perceived by the inward faculties, or motions of the mind, wrought[6] in men by the Spirit of God. So also those signs are termed both earthly and visible, because they consist of things taken from the earth, that is to wit, of water, bread, and wine; and because they are manifestly seen in these likenesses[7]. To be short, the things signified are called heavenly and invisible, because the fruit of them is heavenly, and because they are discerned with the eyes of the mind or of faith, not of the body. For otherwise the same[8] body and blood of our Lord Jesus Christ, which in the supper are represented to the faithful by the form of bread and wine, are not of their own proper nature heavenly or invisible; for the body of our Lord, touching his substance and nature, is consubstantial or of the same substance that our bodies are of. Now the same is called heavenly, for his deliverance from corruption and infirmity, or else because it is clarified; not by reason of the bringing to nought or laying aside of his own nature[9]. The same body of his own nature is visible, not invisible, resident in heaven; howbeit it is seen of the godly celebrating the supper, not with the eyes of the body, but with the eyes of the mind or soul: therefore in respect of us it is called invisible, which of itself is not invisible.

Now the word in the sacraments is called, and is indeed, a witnessing of God's will, and a remembrance and renewing of the benefits and promises of God; yea, and it is the institution and commandment of God, which sheweth the author of the sacrament with the manner and end of the same. For the word in baptism is the very same that even now we have recited: "Go ye into all the world," &c. In the supper of

Signs external and inward things.

Signs earthly and visible, things heavenly and invisible.

The word and rite.

[4 huic negotio, Lat.]   [5 thing, ed. 1577.]
[6 concessis, Lat.]   [7 in his speciebus, Lat.]
[8 ipsum, Lat.: the very.]   [9 See Vol. I. pp. 143 and 173.]

the Lord this is the word of God: "Jesus took bread," &c. And the rite, custom, and manner, how to celebrate the supper[1], is to be sought out of the example of the Lord going before in the holy action, wherein we comprehend both prayers and those things which are recited out of the word of Christ. For as he brake bread and divided it, and in like manner the cup; so likewise, with holy imitation and sacramental rite, we follow the same in this[2] holy action. As he gave thanks, so also we do give thanks. We by certain prayers in baptism[3] do request the assistance and grace of the Lord; we recite certain places out of the gospel, which we know to be requisite in the administration of baptism[4]; and we are wont to do the same also in the celebration of the Lord's supper. But it is not my intention at this present to speak largely and exactly of the rites of the sacrament[5]; which notwithstanding we hold to be best, that are taken out of the holy scripture, and do not exceed[6]: of which shall be spoken in their place.

Promise and ceremony. Some instead of "the word" do put "promise;" and instead of "rite," "ceremony." And truly in the word "ceremony" I see no danger at all, if by ceremony be understood the outward comeliness[7] and rite, which the Lord himself hath commended to us by his example, and left to be used in the celebration. And in very deed, sacramental signs are not simple or bare signs, but ceremonies or religious actions. So also there seemeth to be no danger in the word "promise;" so that by promise we understand the preaching of the gospel, and the commemoration or remembrance of God's promises, which we often use in the preaching of the gospel and celebration of the sacraments[8]; that is to say, that God doth receive us into his fellowship for Christ his sake through faith, doth wash away our sins, endueth us with divers graces; that Christ was given for our sins, shed his blood to take away the sins of all faithful. For in celebrating of baptism we use these words of the Lord: "Suffer little children to come unto me; for unto such belongeth the kingdom of heaven," &c. In the cele-

---

[1 how—supper, not in Lat.]　　　　[2 this, not in Lat.]
[3 super baptizandos, Lat.]
[4 quos ad negotium baptismi pertinere credimus, Lat.]
[5 Sacramentorum, Lat.]　　　　[6 modum non excedant, Lat.]
[7 cultus, Lat.]
[8 recitantes, Lat. omitted: rehearsing them.]

bration of the banquet of God's holy children, we use these holy words of our Lord: "And after supper Jesus took bread, and after he had given thanks he brake it, and gave it to them, saying, Take ye, eat ye: this is my body which is given for you. This is my blood, which is shed for you for the remission of sins: this do in the remembrance of me[9]," &c. For those remembrances and rehearsals are promises of the gospel, promising forgiveness of sins to the believers, shewing that the Lord's body is given for them, and his blood shed for them; which faith verily is the only and undoubted mean to obtain life and salvation. Christ is the strength and substance of the sacraments, by whom only they are effectual, and without whom they are of no power, virtue, or effect.

But if any man by "promise" do understand "covenant," whereby the Lord doth singularly bind, or, as you would say, tie himself to the signs, in which or with which he would be present bodily, essentially, and really; therein he saith more than he can shew or prove by the scriptures. For in no place hath Christ promised to be present corporally, that is, with his true body, in the signs, or with the signs: otherwise I am not ignorant, how God appeared sometimes to our fathers under a bodily figure, that is, in some visible form or shape; as when he shewed himself to Jacob, which was named Israel, leaning on a ladder, and to Moses[10] in the hole of a rock, as it were in a glass. But these do not properly pertain to this purpose, where we entreat of the corporal presence of Christ, and of the sacramental signs. But because many wrest these words of the Lord, "This is my body, this is my blood," to prove a corporal presence of the Lord's body in the supper; I answer, that those words of the Lord are not roughly[11] to be expounded according to the letter, as though bread and wine were the body and blood of Christ substantially and corporally, but mystically and sacramentally: so that the body and blood of Christ do abide in their substance and nature, and in their place, I mean, in some certain place of heaven; but the bread and wine are a sign or sacrament, a witness or sealing, and a lively[12] memory of his body given and his

[9 See Miscell. Tigur. theil. III. pp. 139—150, Zurich. 1724, where the Order of Baptism and of the Communion is given.]

[10 constituto, Lat. omitted: placed.] [11 rigide, Lat.]

[12 celebris, Lat.]

blood shed for us. But of this thing in place convenient we will entreat more at large.

By these things which we have spoken of it[1], it appeareth sufficiently how sacraments consist of two things, the sign and the thing signified, of the word of God and the rite or holy ceremony.

There are some, notwithstanding, which think there is such force graffed of God into the words, that, if they be pronounced over the signs, they sanctify, change, and in a manner bring with them or make present the things signified, and plant or include them within the signs, or at the least join them with the signs. For hereupon are these kind of speeches heard: That the water of baptism by the virtue of the words doth regenerate; and that, by the efficacy of the words, the bread itself and the wine in the supper are made the natural flesh and blood of the Lord. But the sacraments of Christ and his church do consist of the word and the sign. But it seemeth that we must diligently search out what must be understood by "the word."

What is understood by "the word" in the sacraments

I said even now, that "the word" in the sacraments was a witness-bearing of God's will, and the commandment of God itself, or institution of God, which declareth unto us the author, manner, and end of a sacrament. By this word, I say, and commandment of God, by this will and institution of God, the sacraments are sanctified: not that the words are so pronounced of the ministers, as they are read afore to be recited of the Lord himself, or delivered by his apostles; but because God so would, so did, and commanded his apostles[2] to do. For whatsoever God doth, or commandeth to do, is sanctified by the very commandment or deed of God. For all things which he hath done are exceeding good; therefore these things, which he commandeth to do, cannot choose but be holy, because he is holy and the only sanctifier. Wherefore by the nature, will, deed, and commandment of God, and not by the pronunciation of any words, are the sacraments sanctified. To which will of God[3], that it may be applied unto man and do him good, the faithful obedience of men is

---

[1 So also ed. 1584; but 1577, which we have spoken of; ex iis quæ diximus, Lat.]

[2 his apostles, not in Lat.]

[3 Cui, Lat.—will of God, not in Lat.]

necessarily required; which altogether should make us put our trust and confidence in the mercy and power of God, who[4] in no wise should despise or cast behind us the institution of God, although it seem in outward appearance base and contemptible. This will appear more plainly in the example of 2 Kings v. Naham[5], the captain of the king of Syria his band. He heard of the prophet, undoubtedly at the Lord's commandment, that he should wash himself seven times in Jordan: for so it should come to pass, that he should be cleansed from his leprosy. Here thou dost hear the word, the will (I say) and commandment of God; but thou dost not hear that any words were rehearsed either over Jordan or over Naaman, or that any words were prescribed of the prophet to Naaman that he should rehearse[6], whereby (forsooth) there[7] be any force of purifying or cleansing given to the water. Naaman by faith obeyeth the commandment of God, and is cleansed from his leprosy; not by his own merit, or by the benefit of the water of Jordan, but by the power of God and faithful obedience. Lepers also in the gospel, and that not a few, are cleansed by the power and will of Christ, and through faith, and not by[8] pronouncing or speaking of words. The Lord indeed said, " I will, be thou clean:" but if any man at this Matt. viii. day should have recited the same words a hundred times over any leper, he should have prevailed nothing. Whereby it is manifest, that to words there is no force given of working health, if they be pronounced.

The apostles indeed said to the sick, feeble, and lame, In the name " In the name of the Lord Jesus, arise and walk;" and they of the Lord rose up and were healed[9]; but they were not healed by the the feeble are healed. benefit of the words, but by the name, by the power (I mean) Acts iii. and virtue of Christ. For Peter, which said unto the lame man in Hierusalem, " In the name of Jesus Christ of Nazareth, arise and walk," said in the midst of the council of Hierusalem : " If[10] we this day be examined of the deed done to the Acts iv. sick man, by what means he is made whole, be it known

[4 quæ denique, Lat.: which lastly.]
[5 So also ed. 1584; but 1577, Naaman.]
[6 So also ed. 1584; but 1577, repeat.]
[7 So also ed. 1584; but 1577, might be.]
[8 ulla, Lat. omitted: any.]
[9 Rather, being healed, they rose up.]   [10 If, not in Lat.]

unto you all, in[1] the name of Jesus Christ of Nazareth this man standeth here whole." And to the same people he saith[2] : " And his name, through faith in his name, hath made this man sound, whom ye see and know; and the faith which is by him hath given to this man health." Beside these, we read in the Acts of the Apostles, that the sons of one Scæva a priest, being exorcists or conjurers, did call on the name of the Lord Jesus over them that had evil spirits; but these were so far off from giving place to their exorcisms and conjurings, that they ran on them and overcame them, so that they had much ado to escape alive[3]. Where it is most apparent, that those exorcists used the same form almost in their enchantments, which the apostle[4] used ; for in the name of the Lord Jesus they proved[5] to cast out the foul spirit. But sith they[6] were not able so to do, who cannot see and perceive, that the words pronounced do prevail nothing at all? Neither is that any let or hinderance at all, that those exorcists were without faith; for this is a thing very well known and received of all men, that sacraments are no less effectual when they are ministered by wicked ministers, than when they are ministered by the best ministers.

But here is objected against us this saying of the apostle : " Christ gave himself for the church to sanctify it, cleansing it[7] in the fountain of water by the word," or, in the word. Behold, say they, men are cleansed by the water of baptism, which by the word hath the force of sanctifying put into it : therefore it must needs be, that words have force to sanctify. But I will confute them by an evident demonstration, that the apostle did not so mean as they suppose.

The apostle prescribeth unto married Christians their duty: to the more plain and pithier setting forth whereof, he useth the example of Christ and his church, commending that exceeding love which Christ beareth toward his church; wherewith being inflamed, he gave himself for it, to this end, to

(Margin: Acts xix.)

(Margin: The place of Paul in the fifth to the Ephesians is expounded.)

[1 So also ed. 1584; but 1577, that in.]
[2 Rather, to the people the same (apostle) saith.]
[3 illos fere ad mortem usque mulctarint, Lat.]
[4 apostoli, Lat.: the apostles.]
[5 tentabant, Lat.: they tried.]
[6 So also ed. 1584, but 1577, these.]
[7 mundatam, Lat.: being cleansed.]

make it to himself a pure[8] and glorious spouse. Where, by
the way, he setteth down the manner of purging; for the
Lord Jesus himself, saith he, hath cleansed it: for it is
only Christ's office to purge and to cleanse. Now the manner of purging followeth: "In the fountain of water by the
word:" which, because it is briefly spoken, hath in it some
obscurity. He maketh mention of two things, which the Lord
useth to cleanse those that be his, "the fountain of water,"
and "the word." "The fountain of water" is baptism, which
is the outward action and witness-bearing of the inward purifying or cleansing, wrought by the grace and Spirit of God,
as the apostle saith: "According to his mercy he saved us by Tit. iii.
the fountain of regeneration and renewing of the Holy Ghost;
which he shed upon us richly, through Jesus Christ our
Saviour." For he addeth, in way of interpretation, "and
renewing of the Holy Ghost," whereof the fountain of water is
a sign. Moreover, "the word" is the very preaching of the
gospel, testifying that, by the grace and mercy of (God) the
Father, his only Son was given unto us; who, being given for
our sins, maketh them that believe in him heirs of eternal
life. So that now these words of Paul to the Ephesians, the
fifth chapter, do very well agree with this commandment of
the Lord mentioned in St Mark: "Go into all-the whole world,
and preach the gospel to all creatures: he which shall believe
and be baptized, shall be saved," &c. For by these words
also the Lord shadoweth out unto us the manner and means
of our salvation, that it is he only which purgeth us by faith:
yet in the mean while he willeth the believers to be signed
with baptism; and that it should be preached openly in the
world, that it is he which pardoneth sins, yea, and which freely
giveth everlasting life. But what do all these things, I
pray you, make for their purpose, who will prove by those
words of Paul, that there is force and virtue in the words to
sanctify baptism? These words of the Lord spoken to his
apostles do yet make our matter more manifest. "Now are John xv.
ye clean," saith he, "through the word which I have spoken
unto you." Shall we say here, that through the words which
Christ rehearsed the disciples of Christ were made clean?
What then needed he the next day to have been crucified and
to have died? What, to the end that he might purchase

[8 purgatam, Lat.]

17

power¹ unto the words? Therefore all boasting in the force
of words shall be clean taken away². Doth not faith and
godliness tell us, "by the word of the Lord" we should
rather understand this which is declared by the preaching of
the Lord; that is, the death and redemption of Christ, whereby because they believed it they are cleansed? For in
another place he saith, "purifying their hearts by faith."
Wherefore they err in that, because they do not rightly
judge of the word or speech. For the Lord speaketh of the
word preached and believed; and they understand him of the
word pronounced, as though being pronounced it had force
from the Lord to sanctify. St Augustine also maketh for us;
who in his 80th treatise upon John saith: "From whence
cometh so great virtue and power unto the water, that it
should touch the body and wash the heart, but through the
working of the word; not because it is spoken or pronounced,
but because it is believed? For in the word itself, the sound
passing away is one thing, and the virtue which remaineth is
another thing. 'This is the word of faith which we preach,'
saith the apostle; 'because if thou shalt confess with thy mouth
that Jesus is the Lord, and believe with thy heart that God
hath raised him from the dead, thou shalt be saved. For
with the heart man believeth unto righteousness, and with
the mouth confession is made unto salvation.' Whereupon we
read in the Acts of the Apostles, 'purifying (or cleansing) their
hearts by faith.' And St Peter in his epistle saith: 'So also
baptism saveth us; not the putting away of the filth of the
flesh, but in that a good conscience maketh request to God³.'
This is the word of faith which we preach, wherewith undoubtedly baptism is also consecrated, that it may have power
to cleanse. For Christ with us the vine, with his Father the
husbandman, hath loved his church, and gave himself for it.
Read the apostle, and mark what he addeth, saying: 'that he
might sanctify it, cleansing it by the fountain of water in the
word.' In vain therefore should cleansing be attributed to a
frail and vading element, unless this were added, 'in the word⁴.'"

Rom. x.
Acts xv.

[¹ illam potestatem, Lat.: that power.]
[² Rather, In that case all the glory will be given to the words:
Omnis itaque gloria verbis porro vindicabitur, Lat.]
[³ So the Geneva Version, 1557.]
[⁴ Unde ista tanta virtus aquæ, ut corpus tangat et cor abluat, nisi

And so forth; for thus far I have recited St Augustine's words: not that I stay myself upon man's testimony, or that I would have any man to urge the same, or that I am content to be ruled by the witness of man; but because in these words he hath gathered together some testimonies out of the scripture, bearing witness of the word; whereby we may understand, that the word of faith preached, and not the word spoken or pronounced, ought to be received. This word, I say, doth truly cleanse; that is to say, the grace of Christ only doth purify, to the which both the word and faith are directed; and for that cause he said expressly, "Not because it is spoken, but because it is believed." Anon after he saith: "The word of faith which we preach." Furthermore he saith: "By the word of faith baptism is consecrated, that it might have power to cleanse." Which what is it else than if he had said, the very substance of faith maketh baptism effectual? For it followeth: "For cleansing in vain should be attributed to the vading and corruptible element, unless were added, 'in the word.'"

Now if a man do consider the mysteries of the saints or holy men in old time, he shall not find in the celebration of circumcision, the feast of the passover, and sacrifices, any words to have been spoken or pronounced, whereby they were formed, and as it were created, sacraments, and were made effectual. To which belongeth this, that John Baptist did not only baptize the common people without respect of person, but the Lord Jesus himself also in the water of Jordan; no

The words spoken do not form and make sacraments effectual.

faciente verbo? Non quia dicitur, sed quia creditur. Nam et in ipso verbo aliud est sonus transiens, aliud virtus manens. Hoc est verbum fidei quod prædicamus, ait apostolus; quia si confessus fueris in ore tuo quia Dominus est Jesus, et credideris in corde tuo quia illum suscitavit a mortuis, salvus eris: corde enim creditur ad justitiam, ore autem confessio fit ad salutem. Unde in Actibus apostolorum legimus, Fide mundans corda eorum. Et in epistola sua beatus Petrus, Sic et nos, inquit, baptisma salvos facit, non carnis depositio sordium, sed conscientiæ bonæ interrogatio. Hoc est verbum fidei quod prædicamus, quo sine dubio, ut mundare possit, consecratur et baptismus. Christus quippe nobiscum vitis, cum Patre agricola, dilexit ecclesiam, et semetipsum tradidit pro ea. Lege apostolum, et vide quid adjungat; ut eam sanctificaret, ait, mundans eam lavacro aquæ in verbo. Mundatio igitur nequaquam fluxo et labili tribueretur elemento, nisi adderetur, In verbo.—August. Expos. in Evan. Joan. Tract. LXXX. Opp. Tom. IX. fol. 91, col. 2. Par. 1531.]

17—2

words in the mean while being pronounced, whereby he called
and drew down the heavenly grace over or upon the water of
baptism. Again, whiles Christ our high bishop did institute his
supper in the gospel, he commanded nothing to be spoken or
pronounced, by virtue of which speech or pronunciation the
elements might either be changed, or the things signified,
being drawn down from heaven, should be present with or
joined to the signs: but what the Lord hath simply done, and
what his will was we should do, after what manner and to
what end he instituted his supper, the evangelists have declared. We read in no place that the Lord said, As often as
ye speak or pronounce these my words, "This is my body,
This is my blood," it shall come to pass by the virtue of my
words, that the substance of the sign shall be made void; and
that in the same prick of time, wherein the words are spoken, it
shall begin to be the true body and the true blood of the Lord,
under the forms or likenesses of bread and wine; or that the
forms or likenesses and the truth of the sign remaining, it
shall begin at once, with the bread and wine, to be the very
body and blood of Christ. Wherefore, in the pronouncing or
speaking of the words of the Lord in the supper, there is no
power or virtue either to call down the things signified, or to
change the things present[1]. These imaginations do rather
seem more to maintain superstition than religion; as though
the words, pronounced according to the form conceived, had
power to call down out of heaven, to bring from one place to
another, to restore health, to draw to, to put from, or to
transform or change. St Augustine reckoneth up among superstitious vanities those things which for remedies of diseases
are tied or fastened about the body; which also physic maketh
no account of; whether it be in charming[2], or in certain signs
called characters, or in hanging certain things about some part
of the body. The place is to be seen *Cap.* 20, *Li. De Doct.
Christ.* 2.[3] Chrysostom[4], being very angry with them that

[1 the things signified, the things present, not in Lat.]
[2 So also ed. 1584; but 1577, charmings.]
[3 Ad hoc genus (superstitiosorum) pertinent omnes etiam ligaturæ
atque remedia, quæ medicorum quoque disciplina condemnat, sive in
præcantationibus, sive in quibusdam notis, quas characteres vocant,
sive in quibusdam rebus suspendendis, &c.—August. Opp. Tom. III.
fol. 7, col. 4. Par. 1531.]
[4 So also ed. 1584; but 1577, and Chrysost.]

hang the written gospel about their neck, hath these words upon Matt. xxiii. ch.: "Wherein consisteth the force or power of the gospel? In the form and figure of the letters, or in the understanding of the meaning and sense of the same? If in the form of letters, thou dost well to hang it about thy neck: but if in the understanding of the meaning, it is better they were laid up in thy heart[5]." Thus saith he. But there is the same reason of the figures, and of the pronunciation of the letters or words of the gospel; for as the figure of the letters is of power to do nothing, even so is there no force or virtue either in the pronunciation or sound of words. Pliny, an heathenish writer, allegeth many heathenish examples, wherein he declareth that words are effectual; but yet, among other things which he bringeth, he hath this: "It is a question," saith he, "whether words or enchanting speeches are of any force: but every one that is wise is so far from believing it, that even man by man they utterly deny it." The place is to be seen Lib. xxviii. cap. 2.[6] But most worthily is the true word of God itself preferred before all these, the which by Moses, Deut. xviii. with great severity forbiddeth and condemneth all kind of superstitions and enchantments.

I know what the adversaries will here object unto me; namely, that it is a blessing or consecration, and not a superstition, which they use. Besides this, they bring many examples out of the scripture, set down in their canonical decrees, whereby very foolish[7] and most unaptly doubtless they go about to prove, that by blessing or consecration (as they say) the natures of the things are changed; whereupon they also gather, that the bread by the words of blessing or consecrating is turned into flesh. Their examples are these and of this sort: the water flowing out of the rock, after it was

Whether by blessing the natures of things are changed.

Numb. xx.
Exod. vii.
John ii.
Exod. xv.
Exod. vii.

[5] Ubi est virtus evangelii, in figuris literarum, an in intellectu sensuum? Si in figuris, bene circa collum suspendis; si in intellectu, ergo melius in corde posita prosunt.—Chrysost. Op. Imperf. in Matth. Hom. xliii. Tom. vi. p. clxxxiv. Par. 1724.]

[6] Ex homine remediorum primum maximæ quæstionis, et semper incertæ est, valentne aliquid verba... carminum? Quod si verum est, homini acceptum ferri oportere conveniet. Sed viritim sapientissimi cujusque respuit fides.—Plin. Nat. Hist. Lib. xxviii. cap. 2.]

[7] So also ed. 1584; but 1577, foolishly.]

smitten with Aaron's rod[1]; the river Nilus turned into blood; the water at the marriage in Cana of Galilee turned into wine; the bitter waters of Marath changed into sweet water; and Moses his rod turned into a serpent. But, I beseech you, what make these to the Lord's supper, wherewith they have no manner of similitude or likeness? So that this must needs be an unapt[2] comparison[3] and a doltish which they make: The river Nilus was turned into blood, therefore the bread is turned into flesh: the water at the marriage in Cana was changed into wine, therefore the wine in the Lord's supper is changed into the blood of Christ. For while that the water gushed out of the rock when it was smitten, while the river Nilus was turned into blood, while the water of the marriage was changed into wine, while the bitter waters of Marath became sweet, while Moses' rod was turned into a serpent; the water truly, the blood, the wine, the sweet water, and the serpent, so turned and changed, were not under the form or likeness of those things which they were before; neither were they at once that which they were before, and that which they were then made: but the water of Nilus was very blood, not water and blood together; neither was there invisible blood under the visible form of water. And so stands the case also in the other examples. Therefore they do nothing agree with the sacramental signs; but are so far from being like them, that they are altogether unlike them. Moreover, who can well tell by what pronunciation of words Moses made water burst out of the hard rock, turned the river Nilus into blood, changed the bitter waters into sweet? Who knoweth what form also of words the Lord used, when he changed water into wine? Therefore very fitly[4] do they apply these examples to their blessing or consecration, changing the natures of things; since it cannot be shewed what manner blessings the saints or holy men used. Likewise we read not that Moses and Joshua pronounced any words of blessing, whereby they divided the channel of the Erithian[5] sea and the river

[1 with Aaron's rod, not in Lat.]
[2 So also ed. 1584; but 1577, a very unapt: ineptissima, Lat.]
[3 collectio, Lat.: inference.]
[4 So also ed. 1584; but 1577, unfitly: ineptissime, Lat]
[5 Erythræi, Lat.]

Jordan. Eliseus is read to have uttered no words of blessing, 2 Kings vi. when he made the axe to swim, and reached it out of the water by the helve. In all these things the power of God The omnipotency of did work; but we must not imagine what we list to proceed God. from it. For it is weakness, and not power, which is repugnant to justice, and taketh things in hand which are contrary to God's truth; but the mighty works of God are of such sort, that any man may understand and manifestly see, that they are such as they are said to be. The Lord said, "Let there Gen. i. be light; and there was light." Such a kind of light, I mean, which was both called light, and, according to the nature of light, gave light: it was not called or made light, which was light indeed, and yet gave not light: as the bread is called the body of Christ, which yet hath not so much as one jot of the body of Christ.

Furthermore, this word "blessing" in no place in the scrip- Of the word "blessing." tures is so used as they would make us believe. To bless, in the scriptures, is to thank, to praise, to salute, to bid farewell, to speak well of any, to wish well, to rejoice, highly to extol, to give thanks for a good turn, to increase, to enrich, to multiply, or to make fruitful. I could, if need were, bring examples to prove each of them. But a man shall nowhere read, that to bless is as much as to turn the natures of things by the words of God, or otherwise by good words and prayers after a set manner pronounced. We read, say they, in the gospel, that the Lord took bread and blessed: yea, and Paul also calleth the bread and cup by that name, to wit, "The 1 Cor. x. bread and cup of blessing;" the bread and cup, undoubtedly, of consecration, by which consecration the substance of the signs is miraculously changed. I answer, That the words both of the gospel and of the apostle are wrongfully wrested to that sense, which never came into the mind of the Lord or his apostles. For to declare the meaning of that place in the gospel: To bless is not with the gesture of the hand to make the sign of the cross, or to lay one's mouth to the bread and cup, and in a low voice to whisper out the set syllables of the words of consecration; but to sing praises to God, or to give thanks[6] for his benefits bestowed on us.

That which I have said I will confirm by the authority of the evangelists and apostles; for the apostles and evan-

[6 So also ed. 1584; but 1577, give him thanks.]

Thanks-
giving and
blessing.

gelists use the word of blessing or thanksgiving indifferently. For where Mark hath εὐλογήσας, that is to say, "blessing," Matthew, Luke, and Paul have εὐχαριστήσας, that is to say, "giving thanks;" which word Mark also using a little after writeth: "And when he had took the cup," εὐχαριστήσας, that is, "when he had given thanks, he gave to them[1]." To bless therefore is, as the apostles themselves do interpret it, to give thanks, since that they put the one for the other. The diligent reader may see them[2] also in that place of Paul, which is 1 Cor. x. cap.; which place we will fully and wholly entreat of in that which followeth. Our adversaries therefore have not as yet proved out of the scriptures, that to bless is as much as to change the things; or that by words, pronunciation or reciting of words, the things themselves signified are brought to, or made present[3]. The ancient writers, truly, made mention of a mystical blessing, but in a far other sense than these consecrators. Of true consecration we will speak anon; and will confute also in another place whatsoever things they have brought concerning blessing or consecrating of baptism. Now we will make an end of that which we began.

Words of themselves were instituted of God to this end, to signify; and by signifying to bear witness, and to admonish: neither have they beside any hidden force to change the natures of things, or to cause the things themselves to be corporally present; neither do we read that holy men ever used them after this manner: therefore they sin and deceive men, which otherwise use them than they were instituted.

For what
purpose
words are in-
stituted, and
of what force
they are.

Aurel. Augustine acknowledgeth[4] the very same thing, who in his *Enchiridion ad Laurent. Capit.* 22, saith: "And verily words to this purpose are instituted, not that men should deceive one another by them, but by the which one might make another to know his meaning: therefore to use words unto deceit, and not to that end whereunto they were ordained, is sin[5]." The same Aurelius Augustinus, gathering a

---

[1 Mark xiv. 22; Matth. xxvi. 26; Luke xxii. 19; 1 Cor. xi. 24. Bullinger borrows here from Erasm. Annot. in Marc. xiv. 22.]

[2 So also ed. 1584; but 1577, the same: idipsum, Lat.]

[3 Rather, or by words, &c., to bring or make present, &c.]

[4 So also ed. 1584; but 1577, acknowledged: agnovit, Lat.]

[5 Et utique verba propterea sunt instituta, non per quæ se invicem homines fallant, sed per quæ in alterius quisque notitiam cogitationes

sum of his whole book intituled *De Magistro*, asketh this
question: "But now I would have thee tell me, what thy opinion
is of all this that I have spoken unto thee?" Which by and by
he answereth: "I have learned being admonished by the[6] words,
that a man is taught no other thing by words than to learn;
and that it is a very small matter, that by speech or talk we
know partly what he thinketh that speaketh: but whether
the words which he spake were true, that teacheth he only,
who admonished that he dwelt in the heart when the other
spake with the tongue[7]." Thus much he in the last chapter
of his book *De Magistro*. To this purpose pertain the words
of Solomon the wise, in the book of the Preacher, saying:
"The words of the wise are like pricks, and nails that go
through of the authors of gatherings, which are given of one
shepherd[8]." Where we willingly acknowledge, that there is
a great force in eloquence and prayers of the just[10]; as the
Grecians signified by that Hercules of Gallia, also Cicero
very plentifully hath declared the same Lib. I. *De Oratore:*
but that which they do forge and imagine of Pitho, or Suada,
or Suadela, the lady and mistress of eloquence[11], that verily
do we attribute to the Holy Ghost, which doth both give grace
to the speaker, and prepareth and stirreth up the minds of
the hearers. By these things it is manifest unto all men, I
think, that it is a new forgery of man, and not a doctrine of
Oracle, to say, that in the celebration of the sacraments there
is such force graffed in the words recited, that they turn and
change the things, or make the things signified to be present,

Eccles. xii.
Authors of
gatherings,
he calleth
wise men,
because they
gather the
saying of the
wiser sort of
men in their
books[9].

suas perferat. Verbis igitur uti ad fallaciam, non ad quod instituta
sunt, peccatum est.—August. Enchirid. cap. 22, Opp. Tom. III. fol. 34.
col. 3. Par. 1531.]

[6 So also ed. 1584; but 1577, thy.]

[7 Sed mihi jam dicas velim, quid de hoc toto meo sermone
sentias. .... AD. Ego vero didici admonitione verborum tuorum, nihil
aliud verbis, quam admoneri hominem ut discat, et perparum esse
quod per locutionem aliquanta cogitatio loquentis apparet: utrum autem
vera dicantur, eum docere solum, qui se intus habitare cum foris loque-
retur admonuit.—Aug. de Magistro. cap. 14, Opp. Tom. I. fol. 120. col. 1.]

[8 Velut clavi plantati inter folia collectitia, tradita ab uno pastore,
Lat. and Bibl. Lat. Tigur. 1544.]

[9 The translator's explanation.]

[10 Rather, and a perfect speech: orationi justæ, Lat.]

[11 the lady—eloquence, not in Lat.]

and either put on or join them with the signs. But we will shew hereafter, that the signs are not changed or mingled with the things signified, but that both of them do remain still in their own nature and property. It shall be sufficient, if we attribute that to the words which the scripture doth attribute; to wit, the office of signifying and admonishing, of moving and stirring up, which they have from God. For they do defile and blemish the words of God, which deck them with strange and falsified titles.

How the power of almighty God is attributed to the word.
We acknowledge indeed, that all the power of almighty God is attributed to the word of God: but who seeth not, that that is spoken and meant of the everlasting Son of God, who in[1] the scripture is called the Word of God? Who is such a dorhead[2], that cannot rightly distinguish between the everlasting Word of God, which is the Son of God, the second person in the reverend Trinity, and the word rehearsed, spoken, or pronounced by man? The everlasting Word of God remaineth in his own substance and nature a creator, and not a creature: it is not mingled, it is not graffed or incorporated into man's voice. The word which proceedeth from man is a creature, not a creator, and remaineth still a creature; for it is a sound which passeth away: nevertheless it is[3] a virtue which (still) remaineth, if it be sincere and not adulterate, and received by faith. For so it preserveth; yet not of his own proper virtue or power, or because it is pronounced by man: but through his power or virtue which revealed the word, who is true, and therefore preserveth those things which by his word he promiseth to preserve[4]; so that now indeed God himself doth preserve, who said that by his word he would preserve those that believe. The word therefore, which God hath revealed unto us by his servants the prophets and by his chosen apostles, is not, neither is called, the word of God, as if the sound of syllables, words, and voices, are of their own nature the word of God; that very same, I mean, which of his own substance[5] is the Son of God: but because the revelation of the word was made from God in the Holy Ghost through the word or wisdom of God. Wherefore although

[1 Misprinted in all the editions, wherein: qui in, Lat.]
[2 See Vol. II. p. 332, n. 1.]
[3 Fit, Lat.: it becomes.]   [4 to preserve, not in Lat.]
[5 of his substance, ed. 1577.]

the original be of God and not of man, yet the words which the prophets and apostles uttered are man's words, neither can they do anything else but give signification; with the which, notwithstanding, I would not have the due force of the external word of God to be lifted up above that which is meet and comely, and those things imputed to the literal word which is proper to God[6]. I acknowledge all those things, which with a sound understanding or judgment are attributed to the word of God. But of this thing I have elsewhere discoursed more at large[7].

But now some will say: If by reciting the words of God sacraments are not sanctified or consecrated, from whence then have they this, that they be and are called sacraments, or holy signs? Is the consecration vain and of no force? Surely, vain and of no force is that consecration which the papists have feigned. But of consecration or true sanctification I have spoken in the beginning of this chapter, which now I will set forth a little plainer and more abundantly. The holy scriptures, when they make mention of holy things, they use very often this Hebrew word קדשׁ, which the Greek interpreters commonly have translated by ἁγιάζω, the Latins by *Sanctifico, Consecro,* and *Initio*. The use of this word reacheth very far: for it signifieth to sanctify, to offer unto God, to purify or cleanse, and to justify; also to sever or put apart, and to separate, to separate (I mean) from profane use, and to dedicate them to holy things; to call a thing by some name, to apply, and to appoint. Therefore we say, that to consecrate, in this place, is no other thing but to sanctify, to dedicate to God, and after a fashion to separate, or of a thing profane to make an holy thing. But who doth this? or he which doth it, by what means or instrument, I pray you, doth he it? Who, I beseech you, consecrateth, or holieth? is it God? or is it man? Verily, God, and not man. For God instituting anything, and testifying and declaring by his word what he hath instituted and to what end, of his own holy, just, and good will, by his own only institution, I say, without

[marginal note: Of true sanctification or consecration.]

[6 Rather; by which statement meanwhile I would not disparage the due force of the external word of God. Quibus interim nolo externi verbi Dei vim justam elevatam, Lat. The latter half of the sentence is the translator's addition.]

[7 Decade I. Serm. 1.]

any other mean, he consecrateth the thing which he himself hath already instituted. For as he is holy, just, and good, so whatsoever he commandeth is holy, just, and good; and man, understanding by the word of God that God hath instituted anything to a holy, just, and good use, accepteth, receiveth, and useth that institution for holy, good, and just. Therefore man doth not by uttering certain words consecrate and make holy the institution. And because he believeth that all the institutions of God are holy and good, therefore he also celebrateth this institution of God, even as God hath ordained, and giveth God thanks, depending altogether upon God and the rule of his word[1]. Of this manner of sanctification the apostle speaking in another certain place saith:

1 Tim. iv. "Now the Spirit speaketh evidently, that in the latter times there shall rise deceivers, forbidding to marry, and commanding to abstain from meats, which God hath created to be received with thanksgiving of them which believe and know the truth. For every creature of God is good, and nothing to be refused, if it be received with thanksgiving: for it is sanctified by the word of God and prayer." Lo, he saith, "meat is sanctified by the word of God and prayer." But the word of God is in this place (as Paul the apostle expoundeth it) a testimony of the scripture and will of God, whereby we are taught, that all things which God hath made are exceeding good, and that they are clean, and not unclean, which God hath created for to be eaten and for our use.

Acts x. In the Acts St Peter heareth, "Arise, Peter, slay, and eat;" for he saw in a vision before him all living creatures of the earth and the air. "Peter answered, Not so, Lord; for I have never eaten anything that is common or unclean." Therefore he heard again: "What God hath cleansed, that call thou not common." But where, I pray you, did he make them clean? When he made and gave them for the use of man. To the word is annexed prayer, not a charming or an enchantment, but a faithful thanksgiving. For the apostle more than once or twice maketh mention of thanksgiving, that by the general word, that is to say, prayer, no other thing might be understood than the special word, I mean, thanksgiving; for prayer is (as a man would say) to invo-

[1] Of the world, edd. 1584 and 1587, by misprint: verbi ejus, Lat.]

cation and giving of thanks, as the root to the branches[2]. Therefore saith he, the meat is holy, because God, who is good, hath made and appointed the same for the use of man ; and also because it is received of man with faith and thanksgiving. For meat is not holy and good to many men, not through any fault in the meat, which is always the good creature of God ; but in them is the fault, which acknowledge not by faith the benefits of God, or which abuse them, and glut themselves contrary to the word of the Lord. Even so standeth the case with the matter of sanctification, which we must also apply to the sacraments. God, of his own good will, and for the commodity of men, ordained sacraments. He chose unto himself, out of his good creatures, water, bread, and wine ; and, appointing them to some certain end, he laid a platform, and commanded us to use and celebrate them. Now therefore, by the commandment and choice of God, the water, bread, and wine, are consecrated, and he signeth them with his word, and declareth that he will have them counted for sacraments, and sheweth the manner how he will have them celebrated : so that the consecration of sacraments is made through the will, institution, choice, or commandment of God, and seal of his word. Wherefore water, bread, and wine, used after a common manner, or not so as they are chosen and instituted of God, the word of God is as it were slandered[3], and they are altogether common and profane ; but being only used according to the choice or commandment of God holily, and the word or sign being added, they begin to be sacraments, which they were not afore. The same substance remaineth in them still, which they had before ; but they are instituted to another end and use, for they are sealed with the word and commandment of God, and therefore are hallowed. Whereunto may also be added their holy use, by a true faith setting forth the benefit of our redemption, and giving of thanks[4] by faithful prayers to our bountiful Redeemer.

How our sacraments are consecrated.

[2 veluti genus ad has species, Lat.]

[3 insculpta quodammodo nota verbi, Lat. The German translation renders this sentence : And (when) the word is not added to them as a sign, then they are, &c. Compare below, They are sealed with the word of God : Lat. habent nunc notam verbi Dei impressam.]

[4 Rather, the holy use of those who by a true faith set forth, &c. give thanks, &c.]

To this purpose we may fetch examples of civil government, wherein some things, for certain new causes adjoined, having their substance remaining still, are now made that which before they were not. For silver or gold, being not yet coined with the magistrate's mark, is nothing else but silver and gold: but if, by the commandment of the magistrate, a new form be added by a print, it is made money, which it was not before, although it be the very same substance which it was before. Wax, before it be sealed, is common and usual wax; but when, by the king's will and commandment, that which is engraven in the king's seal is printed in the wax, and is set to evidences and letters patents, by and by it is so esteemed, that whoso shall deface the sealed evidences[1] is attached as guilty of treason. Whereby I trust you see plainly, that the true sanctification or consecration of sacraments doth consist in the will and institution of God, in a certain end and holy use of the same, which are declared unto us in the word; of the which peradventure I have spoken more at large than some may think needful. But the godly reader will pardon me this my tediousness, since my desire is to open all things faithfully, diligently, and at large.

Now that I have defended the lawful use of the word, and declared the virtue of it, and opened unto you, as occasion served, the true sanctification or consecration of sacraments, I will return to that where I left. And because I taught, that sacraments consist of two parts, the sign and the thing signified, it remaineth to shew, that those two parts retain their natures distinguished, not communicating properties; by declaration whereof, both to those things which go before and to those which follow, yea, and to the whole substance of the sacrament, a wonderful light without doubt shall appear. But of communicating of the names or terms I will speak in their convenient place.

The sign and the thing signified do retain their several natures in the sacraments. That each part retaineth their natures distinguished, without communicating or mingling of properties, it is to be seen hereby; that many be partakers of the sign, and yet are barred from the thing signified[2]. But if the natures of the parts were united or naturally knit together, it must needs be then, that those which be partakers of the signs must be par-

[1 aut cerum, Lat. omitted: or the wax.]
[2 cum re significata nihil commune habent.]

takers also of the thing signified. Examples of scripture, as they are ready, so are they evident. For Simon Magus, in the Acts of the Apostles, received the sign, and was baptized: but of the thing signified he had not neither received so much as one iota. And Judas Iscariot, a cruel and faithless traitor of his master, did likewise eat the bread of the Lord, but he did not eat bread the Lord[3]; otherwise he had lived happy, just, and blessed for ever: for " he which eateth me, saith the Lord himself, shall never die :" but Judas died everlastingly; therefore he did not eat that food of life.

The wicked are not partakers of the thing signified in the sacraments.

To these evident testimonies of scripture I will now add also certain of St Augustine's pertaining to that purpose, who in his treatise upon John xxvi. saith: " We receive this day visible meat: but the sacrament is one thing, and the virtue of the sacrament is another. How many do receive of the things upon the altar, and when they have received it do die! Whereupon the apostle saith, ' He eateth and drinketh his own damnation.' Was not the morsel poison, which the Lord gave unto Judas? and yet he received it, and after he had received it, the enemy entered into him; not because that was evil which he received, but because he, being evil, did receive that good thing unworthily." And immediately after he saith: " The sacrament of the thing, that is, of the knitting together of the body and blood of Christ, is received at the Lord's table, of some unto life, of other some to destruction: but the thing itself, whereof it is a sacrament, is received of all men unto life, of none to destruction, whosoever shall be partakers thereof." And again he saith: " He which dwelleth not in Christ, nor Christ in him, without doubt he neither eateth his flesh, nor drinketh his blood spiritually ; although carnally and visibly he chaw with his teeth the sacrament of the body and blood of Christ: but he doth rather eat and drink the sacrament of so great a thing to his own damnation[4]." And so

[3 Illi (apostoli) manducabant panem Dominum, ille (Judas) panem Domini contra Dominum.—August. in Evang. Joan. Tract. LIX. Opp. Tom. IX.]

[4 Nam et nos hodie accepimus visibilem cibum: sed aliud est sacramentum, aliud est virtus sacramenti. Quam multi de altari accipiunt, et moriuntur, et accipiendo moriuntur! Unde dicit Apostolus, Judicium sibi manducat et bibit. Nonne buccella dominica

forth.   He hath the like words in his book *De Civit. Dei*[1],
xxi. 25. cap.   And in his book *De Doctr. Christ.* iii. cap. 9.
he sheweth, that "in the conjunction of natures there had
need to be a distinction, lest we should stick too much upon
the outward sign[2]."

Now we come to the proofs of the scripture.   The apostle
witnesseth in the 1 Cor. x. cap. that "all our fathers were
baptized, and did all eat of one spiritual meat, and did all
drink of one manner of spiritual drink; but the Lord in many
of them had no delight:" whereas, if they had eaten that
spiritual meat and drunk that spiritual drink spiritually by
faith, undoubtedly the Lord had delighted in them.   "For
without faith," as he himself saith, "it is impossible to please
God:" therefore with them that have faith God is well
pleased.   Wherefore our fathers truly were partakers of visible sacraments, but they were destitute of invisible grace:
whereby it followeth, that the sign and the thing signified do
retain their natures not confounded or mingled, but distinguished and separated.   Besides this, the words of the gospel
have some affinity, or at the least some likeness, with sacramental signs; otherwise, the words are preferred far before
the signs, the apostle saying, "that he was sent to preach,
and not to baptize."   But many hear with their outward ears
the word of the Lord, who for all that, because they are void

The affinity of the word of God and sacraments.

venenum fuit Judæ? Et tamen accepit, et cum accepit in eum inimicus intravit: non quia malum accepit, sed quia bonum male malus
accepit.... Hujus rei sacramentum, id est, unitatis corporis et sanguinis Christi .... de mensa dominica sumitur, quibusdam ad vitam,
quibusdam ad exitium: res vero ipsa, cujus et sacramentum est, omni
homini ad vitam, nulli ad exitium, quicunque ejus particeps fuerit....
Qui non manet in Christo et in quo non manet Christus proculdubio
nec manducat spiritaliter carnem ejus, nec bibit ejus sanguinem, licet
carnaliter et visibiliter premat dentibus sacramentum corporis et sanguinis Christi; sed magis tantæ rei sacramentum ad judicium sibi
manducat et bibit.—August. in Evang. Joan. Tract. xxvi. Opp. Tom. ix.
fol. 47, coll. 2. 4. Par. 1531.]

[1 On this chapter archbishop Cranmer has written in the margin
of his copy of Augustine's works now in the British Museum: "Impii
apostatæ non manducant corpus Christi manducantes sacramentum."
—Aug. Opp. Tom. v. fol. 293. col. 2.]

[2 Ut autem literam sequi et signa pro rebus quæ iis significantur
accipere servilis infirmitatis est; ita inutiliter signa interpretari male
vagantis erroris est.—Id. de Doct. Christ. Opp. Tom. iii. fol. 11, col. 3.

of faith, are also without the inward fruit of the word; Paul saying yet again: "For to us was the gospel preached, as Heb. iv. well as unto them; but the word which they heard did not profit them, because it was not coupled with faith." For so it cometh to pass, that many receive the visible sacraments, and yet are not partakers of the invisible grace, which by faith only is received. Whereupon yet again it followeth, that the sign is not confounded with the thing signified, but both of them do retain their substance and nature distinguished. What, and doth not the scripture expressly and pithily make a difference between the outward ministry of man, and God the inward worker and giver of spiritual gifts? For John Baptist saith: "I baptize you with water, but he Matt. iii. (Christ) shall baptize you with the holy Ghost." Wherewith agreeth that saying of Peter: "Baptism saveth us, not the 1 Pet. iii. putting away of the filth of the flesh, but in that a good conscience maketh request to God[3]."

To this now pertaineth that evident testimony of St Augustine, which is read, iii. *Quæst. lib. in Levit.* Quæst. 83. in these words: "We must diligently consider, as often as he saith, 'I the Lord which sanctify him,' that he speaketh of the priest; when he also spake this to Moses, 'and thou shalt sanctify him.' How therefore doth both Moses and God also sanctify? For Moses doth not sanctify for the Lord; but Moses doth sanctify in the visible sacraments by his ministry, and the Lord by invisible grace by his Holy Spirit, where the whole fruit of visible sacraments also is. For without this sanctification of invisible grace what profit have we by visible sacraments[4]?" Thus far Augustine. As John Baptist made distinction between his own ministry in baptism and the power of Christ, even so maketh he distinction between the

The scripture maketh difference between the ministry of man and the operation of the Spirit.

[3 See above, p. 259, n. 3.]

[4 Animadvertendum est quoties dicit, Ego Dominus qui sanctifico eum, loqui de sacerdote; cum hoc etiam Moysi dixerit, Et sanctificabis eum. Quomodo ergo et Moyses sanctificat et Dominus? Non enim Moyses pro Domino; sed Moyses visibilibus sacramentis per ministerium suum, Dominus autem invisibili gratia per Spiritum Sanctum: ubi est totus fructus etiam visibilium sacramentorum. Nam sine ista sanctificatione invisibilis gratiæ visibilia sacramenta quid prosunt? —August. Quæst. super Levit. Lib. III. cap. 84. Opp. Tom. IV. fol. 49. col. 1. Par. 1531.]

[BULLINGER, IV.]

18

ministry of preaching and the drawing of the spiritual[1]
John iii. [2] teacher : " I am," saith he, " the voice of a crier in the wilderness, Make straight the way of the Lord." And again : " He
that cometh from an high is above all ; he that is of the earth
is earthly, and speaketh of the earth ; he that cometh from
heaven is above all ; and what he hath seen and heard, that
he testifieth," &c. St Paul also agreeing thereunto saith :
1 Cor. iii. " Who is Paul, what is Apollos, but ministers by whom
ye believed, even as the Lord gave to every man? I have
planted, Apollos watered ; but God gave the increase. So
that neither is he that planteth anything, neither he that
watereth ; but God that giveth the increase." Albeit the
comparison of ministers with the signs agree not altogether
and in every part (which I told you before), because ministers
are fellow-labourers with Christ according to their office ; but
the signs which are without life are not so, unless κατ᾽ ἐξοχὴν
we translate unto them that which is the ministers' : yet by
other proofs I suppose it to be made plain, that the sign and
thing signified do retain their natures distinguished in the
sacraments.

The opinion
of the papists
touching
transubstan-
tiation is
confuted.
These things do specially disprove and convince those, who
are persuaded of that papistical transubstantiation of bread
and wine into the substance of the body and blood of Christ ;
for these men utterly deny that the bread and wine, being
consecrated in the mysteries, do remain in their own substances. For they contend that the[3] substances (of bread
and wine) are annihilated and turned into the very body and
blood of the Lord ; so that after the consecration the accidents
of bread and wine do remain, and no part of the substance
thereof at all. For they say, that the Lord in express words
pronounced over the bread and wine, " This is my body, this
is my blood ;" and that the Lord can easily bring to pass, by
his own omnipotency, that that which he said may be as he
said. For proof whereof they allege these and such like
places[4] ; that the Lord, forsooth, fashioned man out of the clay
of the earth, and by and by of the rib of man made woman,
and also turned Lot's wife into a pillar of salt ; and therefore
that he by the self-same his power can make of bread his

[1 interni, Lat.: inward.]   [2 Joan. i. and iii. capite, Lat.]
[3 So also ed. 1584 : but 1577, these : has, Lat.]
[4 similia non pauca, Lat. : like instances not a few.]

body, and of wine his blood. And these truly are their bulwarks. But we in another place have plentifully disputed of the meaning of the Lord's words, " This is my body ;" so that it is superfluous to make long repetition of them. I have also told you, that of the omnipotency of God we must not gather and determine whatsoever cometh into our brain; and also that God's power doth nothing against truth, neither against itself; and that no godly man ought to take that in hand, under pretence of the power of God, which is repugnant to the plain scriptures and the articles of the catholic faith[5].

Now it is evident and plain, that after consecration there remaineth in the sacrament the substance of bread and wine; and herein we need no other witnesses than our very senses, which perceive, see, taste, and feel, no other thing than bread and wine. But while clay was turned into a man's body, the rib into a woman, and Lot's wife into a pillar of salt, they were not, as the sacrament of the supper[6], that which they were before, neither did there appear unto the senses any iota of the clay, of the rib, of Lot's wife. Very foolishly, therefore, and unaptly are these examples applied to the mystery[7] of the Lord's supper, wherewith they nothing agree: which thing also we touched before[8].

The gospel, very diligently describing the most holy institution of the Lord's supper and the manner thereof, maketh no mention of miraculous transubstantiation[9]; but calleth the bread and wine, which the Lord took and distributed to his disciples, and which they also received, by the names of bread and wine, as well after the words of consecration (as they term it) were spoken, as also before consecration. Doth not the Lord in the xxvi. chap. of Matt. call the wine, being consecrated, not wine only, but the fruit of the vine, after a more vehement and significative[10] kind of speech, lest any should be ignorant that the wine was wine indeed, and so remained? In Mark we read this of the cup: " And he took the cup, [Mark xiv.] and when he had given thanks, he gave to them, and they[11]

That bread and wine remain in their substances after consecration.

[5 See Vol. I. page 90; and above, p. 263.]
[6 altaris, Lat.]
[7 negotio, Lat.]
[8 See above, p. 272.]
[9 conversionis, Lat.]
[10 emphatico, is Bullinger's *one* word.]
[11 omnes, Lat. omitted : all.]

drank of it; and he said unto them, This is my blood of the
new Testament," &c. Lo, they drank all (saith he) of the
cup before the words of consecration (as they term it) were
spoken; therefore they drank wine. Now if so be they
answer, that this place of the evangelist is to be expounded
by the figure *hysteron proteron*, that is, when any thing is
declared out of order preposterously [1], then admit they tropes
and figures in the celebration of the supper; which, notwithstanding, they have contended ought simply to be understood
without the help of tropes or figures. But Paul also, the
apostle, in the 1 Cor. chap. x. calleth the bread of the Lord,
being now in very holy use, and (that I may so say) consecrated, by the name of bread. And in the 1 Cor. xi. chap.
the third time he calleth it bread. To this appertaineth [2],
that the Acts of the Apostles do testify [3], how that the
churches [4] of the apostles do call the whole mystical action
the breaking of bread, not the breaking of his body or distribution of his blood. It is manifest therefore, that the substance of bread and wine in the sacrament of the Lord's supper do remain in their own nature, and that transubstantiation
is a sophistical imagination.

Whether the bread and wine for their former sub-stance are so called after consecration. This also is a sophistical and a notable papistical forgery [5],
in that they say that the bread and wine, consecrated in the
supper, is therefore called of the apostles [6] bread and wine,
because they were bread and wine before. For that is now
done, which is read in Exodus to have been done in times
past, where Aaron's rod is said to devour the enchanters' rods,
which nevertheless then were not rods, but serpents; but now
they are named rods, because they were rods before they
were so changed, which now are serpents, and not rods. But
again; who doth not see this example hath no similitude or
likeness with the bread and wine of the Lord? For the rod
truly was called a rod; but in the meanwhile it was, and
seemed plainly to be, not now a rod, but a serpent: but the
bread is called bread, neither doth it appear to be anything
else but bread. Here is no form of flesh seen, as was seen
there the form of a serpent. Beside this; the rod is said to

[1 This explanation is the Translator's.]   [2 His accedit, Lat.]
[3 Act. ii. and xx. marg. Lat.]
[4 So also ed. 1584: but 1577, *church: ab apostolica ecclesia*, Lat.]
[5 forgery, not in Lat.]   [6 in literis apostolicis, Lat.]

be turned into a serpent, and is shewed for a wonder or miracle; but ye shall read in no place that the bread was turned into flesh by any miracle: but a sacrament is instituted, which indeed loseth the name and nature of a sacrament, when, the substance of the sign being annihilated and made void, nothing remaineth there but the thing signified; for that which they triflingly say of accidents miraculously subsisting without their subject, and remaining instead of a sign[7], is to no purpose. If we should go about to boast of our dreams for miracles, there will be nothing so absurd and foolish which we shall not colour with our fancies and lies. What if this word transubstantiation doth manifestly prove, that this whole trifling toy is not fetched from the simple and plain doctrine of the apostles, but from the subtle school of quarrelling[8] sophisters? But the apostle Paul giveth us in charge Col. ii. 1 Tim. vi. to beware both of philosophy and strangeness[9] of words; though at this present we do not only entreat of new words, but also of new matter and new doctrine, contrary in all points to the apostles'. For this doctrine of transubstantiation is clean contrary both to the doctrine of the apostles and evangelists touching the true incarnation of our Lord, and the true nature and property of his human body, and also the true raising up again of our bodies. For they are constrained[10] to forge many things altogether miraculous; as of the invisible body of Christ, and of the subtle body of Christ piercing by his subtlety through the gate and the stone[11], I mean, that which covered his sepulchre; or the Lord's very body being altogether and[12] at one time in many places and filling all things; and other innumerable, which are of this stamp, absurd and wicked. Now also Joan. Scotus, a subtle doctor, in his work, *Sentent. Distinct.* II. *Lib.* 4. *quæst.* 3, saith[13]: That the article of transubstantiation is neither expressed

[7 So also ed. 1584: but 1577, *the* sign.]
[8 quarrelling, not in Lat.]   [9 novitatibus, Lat.]
[10 hic, Lat. omitted: in this place.]
[11 per corpus januæ et lapidis, Lat.]
[12 Rather, of the Lord's body, being a true body, and yet in the meanwhile, &c.]
[13 Dicendum quod ecclesia declaravit istum intellectum esse de veritate fidei in illo symbolo edito sub Innocent. III. in concilio Lateranensi, *Firmiter credimus*, &c. . . . ubi explicite ponitur veritas aliquorum credendorum, magis explicite quam habebatur in symbolo

in the creed of the apostles, neither in those creeds of the ancient fathers; but that it was brought in and invented of **The council of Lateran was in the year of the Lord 1215.** the church (so saith he, meaning the Romish church,) under Innocentius the third, in the council of Lateran. Whereby we gather, that the doctrine of transubstantiation is of late time and newly start up; the history whereof we have elsewhere more largely compiled[1]. But by this that I have said I think it plainly and effectually enough declared, that the signs are not mingled with the things signified, or changed into them; but that each of them remain in their several natures.

But albeit either of the parts without mixture do retain their own nature, yet those two agree in one sacrament; and being joined together and not divided, do make one perfect and lawful sacrament. For water alone, both privately and ordinarily sprinkled, is no sacrament, unless it be applied and used according to the institution of Christ. Purifying also, or washing away of sins, and the engrafting or receiving into the league and fellowship of God and all saints, of itself is no sacrament, unless there be also a sprinkling of water in the name of the blessed Trinity. In like manner, it is no sacrament, if we eat bread in a common assembly, and drink wine of the self-same cup after the common manner; neither is it a sacrament, if through a faithful remembrance thou consider that the Lord's body was betrayed for thee, and his blood shed for thee, for the which also thou givest thanks; but so far forth as they are all mysteries of God and our salvation, they are generally termed[2] sacraments, that is, secret and spiritual mysteries of God and our salvation. For in a perfect and lawful sacrament there must needs go together both the holy action, corporal or sensible, and the spiritual celebration thereof[3] for the which this sacramental action was invented and put in practice.

Of the sacramental union. But here some move many and divers questions touching the sacramental union, whether it be personal, real, or rational. I, because I see nothing of this matter doubtfully[4]

apostolorum, vel Athanasii, vel Niceni.—Duns Scot. Sentent. Lib. IV. dist. 11. quæst. 3. Opp. Tom. VIII. p. 618. Lugd. 1639.]

[1 De Origine Erroris circa Cœnam et Miss. Pap. cap. x.]

[2 Rather; excepting in so far as all mysteries, &c. are in a general way termed, &c.]

[3 i. e. of that thing.]   [4 anxie, Lat.]

delivered of the apostles, and that the thing, being plain
of itself, by such manner of sophistications is made dark,
doubtful, difficult, and obscure; simply and plainly say, that
the sign and the thing signified are joined together in the
sacraments by God's institution, by faithful contemplation
and use; to be short, in signification and likeness of the
things: but I utterly deny, that those two are naturally united
together, so that the sign in the sacrament beginneth to be
that which the thing signified is in his own substance and
nature: I deny, that the thing signified is joined corporally
with the sign, so that the sign remaineth still in his own substance and nature, and yet nevertheless, in the mean time,
hath the thing signified corporally joined unto it; that thereby
whosoever is partaker of the sign, should be also by the sign
or with the sign partaker of the thing itself. The reason
why I do so constantly deny that, appeareth, I think, sufficiently by those examples which I have hitherto declared,
and which hereafter shall be declared.

Furthermore, I say that the sign and the thing signified
are coupled together by God's[5] institution, because he which
instituted the sacrament of baptism and the supper, instituted
it not to this end, that with water we might wash away
the filth of the body, as the custom is to do by daily use of
baths; neither that we should take our fill of the bread and
wine: but that under visible signs he might commend unto us
the mysteries of our redemption and his grace, and, to be
short, of our salvation, by[6] representing them to renew them,
and by sealing them to confirm them. My saying is, that
they are coupled together in a faithful contemplation, because
they which partake the sacraments religiously do not fasten
their eyes on sensible things only, but rather on things insensible, signified, and heavenly; so that the faithful have in
themselves both twain coupled together, which otherwise in
the sign or with the sign are knit together with no bond.
For corporally and sensibly they receive the signs, but spiritually they possess, comprehend, renew, and exercise the
things signified. In signification and likeness of the things,
I say, they are coupled together, because the sign is a token
of the thing signified: and unless signs have likeness with
those things whereof they are signs, then would they be no

It is declared, how in sacraments the signs and the things signi-fied are joined to-gether.

[5 God's, not in Lat.]   [6 and by, Lat.]

signs. They have therefore most apt and very near affinity between themselves. For as water washeth away the filth of the body; as bread and wine satisfieth and maketh merry the heart of man; even so by the grace of God the people of God are purified; even so the body and blood of the Lord, which was given for us, being apprehended by faith, doth both satisfy and make merry the whole man, that he may yield himself wholly unto thanksgiving, and obedient to God-ward. I would speak here more largely of the analogy, or of the sign and thing signified, but that I see I may do the same hereafter in place more convenient. But I think I shall not need any more places out of the scripture, to open these things more evidently; since they follow of their own accord upon that which we have hitherto by testimonies of scriptures confirmed, and will hereafter more at large confirm.

Signs borrow the names of things signified.

Moreover, in respect of the likeness of the sign and the thing signified, the name of the one is given to the other[1], as I will prove by most evident testimonies of scripture. In

Circumcision.

Genesis xvii. the Lord saith thus to Abraham: "Thou shalt keep my covenant therefore, both thou and thy seed after thee in their generations. This is my covenant, which ye shall keep between me and you; every man-child among you shall be circumcised. Ye shall circumcise the flesh of your foreskin, and it shall be a token of the covenant between me and you." The mouth of the Lord hath spoken this. Who will gainsay the word of God? The word of God calleth circumcision a covenant; therefore the name of the thing signified is given to the sign. For in very deed circumcision is not the covenant itself; for the covenant is the bargain and agreement between God and men, which hath certain conditions and articles. Wherefore afterward, by interpretation, the same circumcision is called "a token of the covenant." And who will find fault with this interpretation of God? The signs therefore, yea, God being the interpreter, take the names of the things signified.

The paschal lamb.

So you may read in the twelfth chapter of Exodus: "Ye shall eat the lamb in haste, for it is the Lord's passover." Again: "And the blood shall be unto you a sign in the houses wherein you are," &c. And again: "This day shall

[1 aut nomina rerum ipsis signis, Lat. omitted: or the names of the things are given to the signs themselves.]

be unto you a remembrance," &c. What can be spoken more
plainly, than that the lamb is called the passover? But what
is the proper meaning of the passover? Let us give ear to
the Lord, here again expounding himself, and saying: " I will
pass through the land of Egypt this same night, and will
smite all the first-born of Egypt, from man to beast; and
when I shall see the blood (of the lamb), I will pass over
you, and the plague shall not be upon you to destroy you."
Behold, the Passover, God himself so interpreting it, is that
passing over, whereby the angel of God, passing over the
houses of the Israelites which were marked with the blood of
the lamb, spared the[2] first-born, and slew the first-born of
the Egyptians. If thou art ignorant what and what manner
of lamb it was, listen again to the Lord instructing thee, and
saying: " In the tenth day of this month, every man take
unto him a lamb according to the household; and let your
lamb be without blemish, a male of a year old, which ye shall
take out from among the sheep and from among the goats."
And here the lamb is plainly called the Passover. And who
doth not see, that the lamb is not the Passover? Yet because
it is a sign or remembrance of the Passover, as the mouth of
the Lord saith, surely it taketh the name of the Passover or
passing by.

Again, you read in the nineteenth of Numbers: " Thus ^Sacrifices.^
spake the Lord unto Moses: Speak unto the children of Israel,
that they bring thee a red cow[3] without blemish, and ye shall
give her unto Eleazar the priest, that he may bring her
without the host, and cause her to be slain before his face[4],
and to be burnt whole; and a man that is clean shall gather
up the ashes of the cow, and lay them without the host in
a clean place; and it shall be kept for the multitude of the
children of Israel[5] for a water of separation (or sprinkling);
for it is sin." Mark again the manner of the speaking of
the scripture. A heifer or cow is sin, that is, a sacrifice for
sin; as Christ is said to be made sin for us, that for (or by) ^Rom. viii.^
sin[6] he might condemn sin; which is, that by the only oblation[7]

[2 So also ed. 1584: but 1577, their: ipsorum, Lat.]
[3 buculam, Lat.]   [4 ubi sacrificet, Lat.]
[5 ab ecclesia Israelitica, Lat.]
[6 de peccato, Lat. See Vol. II. p. 256, n. 5.]
[7 So also ed. 1584: but 1577, *one* oblation: unica hostia, Lat.]

of his body he might cleanse and purge us from sin. Hitherto also belongeth that which the apostle, speaking of sacrifices

Heb. x. unto the Hebrews, saith : " But in these sacrifices there is mention made of sins every year ; for it is not possible that the blood of bulls and goats should take away sins." As often therefore as sacrifices, as heifers, goats, bulls, and lambs, are called sanctifications, cleansings, or sins, the signs take the

Zech. iii. names of the things signified. For these were certain types and figures of the priest which was to come and of Christ[1],

Isai. liii. upon whom all our sins are laid ; for he truly is " the Lamb of God, which taketh away the sins of the world."

Now we are come also to the sacraments of the new Testament, whose signs also bear the names of the things sig-

1 Pet. i. nified. For Peter saith, Acts ii. : " Let every one of you be baptized in the name of Jesus Christ, for the remission of sins." And Paul also in the Acts of the Apostles heareth :

Baptism.
Acts xxii. " Arise, and be baptized, and wash away thy sins by calling on the name of the Lord." Therefore truly baptism is called a cleansing, or washing away of sins. And Peter also else-

[1 Pet. iii.] where saith : " Baptism saveth you, not that thereby the filth of the flesh is put away, but in that a good conscience

Cor. vi. maketh request unto God[2]." And Paul also saith : " Ye are washed, ye are sanctified, ye are justified, in the name of the Lord Jesus, and by the Spirit of our God." Therefore the due and right comparing of the[3] places between themselves doth manifestly prove, that to the sign of baptism, which is water, is given the name of the thing signified.

The supper
of the Lord. After the same manner is it to be seen in the institution[4] of the Lord's supper, òr Eucharist. The bread is called the body of Christ, and the wine the blood of Christ. But since the right faith believeth, that the true body of Christ, ascended out of this world, liveth and is now in heaven, and that the Lord returneth no more into this world until he come in the clouds of heaven to judge the quick and the dead ; every man understandeth, that to the sign, to wit, bread and wine, the names of the things themselves, to wit, the body and blood of Christ, are given through the communicating of names.

[1 venturi sacerdotis et hostiæ Christi, Lat.]
[2 See above, p. 274.]
[3 So also ed. 1584: but 1577, these : horum, Lat.]
[4 habet et negotium, Lat.]

Many other speeches used in the scripture and in our Sacramental and figu-
daily talk are not much unlike to the speeches used in the rative speeches.
sacrament. We read that Christ is, and is called, a lion, a
lamb, a shepherd, a vine, a door, a way, a ladder, the day,
the light, the sun, the water, the bread, a spring, and a rock :
which if at this day any should roughly[5] urge, contending
that Christ is a lamb indeed, a door in substance, a natural
vine, or such like; who, I pray you, could abide him so reasoning? We would hiss and drive out from among us such a one,
as a mad man, and a perverter of God's oracles. We read
indeed, "And that rock was Christ:" in the meantime it is
to be considered what should follow. For if that rock really
and in very deed had been Christ, none of them that drank
of that rock had been reprobates; for they are acceptable
unto God which are partakers of Christ. "But in many of
them, that drank of the rock, the Lord had no delight; for
they were slain in the wilderness." Therefore they which drank
of the rock, which was Christ, were not made partakers of
Christ. Therefore the rock was not Christ really and in very The manner of speech
deed. We also seeing the standards of kings, princes, and which we use.
cities, we call the signs by the names of the kings, princes,
and cities : for we say, This is the king of France, This is
the prince of Germany, This is Tigure[6], This is Berne. So if
we see the marriage-ring, or the image of any prince, we
call it the faith and troth of wedlock, or man and wife; yea,
and we say by the image, This is the prince. For matrons,
shewing their wedding-ring, say, This is my husband : when
we shew to any man the picture or image of the duke of
Saxony, we say, This is the duke of Saxony. If any should
go[7] obstinately to affirm, that the sign in very deed is the
thing signified, because it beareth the name thereof; would
not all men cry out, that such a one were without wit or
reason, and that he were to be abhorred by all means as an
obstinate brawler?

Those therefore that are skilful in the things understand
that that is and hath been catholic, received of all men, and
also sound, which we shewed even now at large ; to wit, that
the signs do borrow the names of the things, and not turn
into the things (which they signify). And therefore the ancient

[5] rigide, Lat.]   [6] Zurich.]
[7] So also ed. 1584: but 1577, go on : pergeret, Lat.]

The ancient
fathers
moved no
contentions
about the
sacraments.
fathers moved no strife nor contentions about the sacraments, as are at this day among us. For as they did beautify the signs with the names of the things (signified), so did they acknowledge the kind of speech; neither did they roughly urge the words, as though the very signs were really and corporally that selfsame thing which they signified. Therefore this canon or rule is so often repeated and beaten upon by Aurelius Augustine, "That the signs do take or borrow the names of things signified[1]." By the same canon or rule he maketh plain certain dark places; of which thing we will now set down some testimonies. In his *Epist.* 23. *ad Bonifacium, de Parvulorum Baptismate*, he saith : " If sacraments had not some likeness with those things whereof they are sacraments, no doubt they were no sacraments; for of this likeness, for the most part, they take the names of the things themselves. As also the apostle, speaking of baptism, saith, 'We are buried with Christ by baptism into his death.' He doth not say, we signify the burial; but he doth flatly say, 'we are buried.' Therefore he called the sacrament of so great a thing no otherwise but by the name of the selfsame thing[2]." And in *Tract. super Joan.* 63: " When the unclean person is gone, all which remain are clean. Such a like thing shall there be, when the world, being overcome of Christ, shall pass away, and there shall no unclean person remain among the people of God; when, the tares being separated from the wheat, the just shall shine like the sun in the kingdom of their Father. The Lord foreseeing this would come to pass, and now witnessing that it was signified, when Judas fell away as tares separated, the holy apostles remaining as wheat, he saith, ' Now is the Son of man glorified;' as if he had said, Behold what shall be when I am glorified, where there shall be no wicked person, and where no good man shall perish. For he

[1 Solet res quæ significat ejus rei nomine quam significat nuncupari.—August. Quæst. super Levit. LVII.]

[2 Si sacramenta quandam similitudinem earum rerum, quarum sacramenta sunt, non haberent, omnino sacramenta non essent: ex hac autem similitudine plerumque etiam ipsarum rerum nomina accipiunt... Sicut de ipso baptismo apostolus, Consepulti, inquit, sumus Christo per baptismum in mortem. Non ait sepulturam significamus, sed prorsus ait, Consepulti sumus. Sacramentum ergo tantæ rei non nisi ejusdem rei vocabulo nuncupavit.—Id. Epist. XXIII. ad Bonifac. Opp. Tom. II. fol. 18. col. 4. Par. 1531.]

saith not thus, Now is the glorying of the Son of man signified ;
but he saith, ' Now is the Son of man glorified.' As it is not
said, The rock signified Christ ; but, ' The rock was Christ :' It is not said,
the rock sig-
neither is it said, The good seed signifieth the children of the nifieth, but,
"the rock is
kingdom, but he saith, ' The good seed, these are the children Christ."
of the kingdom ; and the tares, the children of the wicked.'
As the scripture therefore is wont to speak, calling the things
which signify as the things that are signified, even so spake
the Lord, saying, 'Now is the Son of man glorified,' after that
wicked (Judas) was separated, and, his holy apostles remaining
with him, his glorification was signified, when, the wicked being
divided, he shall remain eternally with the saints[3]." The same
Aurelius Augustine, in his epistle to Evodius 102, saith : " The
sound of the voice, and the bodily shape of a dove, and cloven
tongues like unto fire, which came upon every one of them ;
as those things in mount Sina, which were done after a
most fearful manner ; and as that pillar of the cloud by day,
and that pillar of fire by night ; were ordained and set for
some operation which they signified. Herein we must specially take heed of this ; that none be persuaded or believe,
that the nature and substance of the Father, or of the Son,
or of the Holy Ghost, is changeable, or may be turned :
neither let any man be moved for that sometime the thing

[3 Exeunte immundo omnes mundi remanserunt . . . . tale aliquid
erit cum victus a Christo transierit hic mundus, et nemo in populo
Christi remanebit immundus ; cum zizaniis a tritico separatis justi
fulgebunt sicut sol in regno Patris eorum. Hoc futurum prævidens
Dominus, et nunc significatum esse contestans, discedente Juda tanquam zizaniis separatis, remanentibus tanquam tritico apostolis sanctis, Nunc, inquit, clarificatus est Filius hominis : tanquam diceret,
Ecce in illa clarificatione mea quid erit, ubi malorum nullus erit, ubi
bonorum nullus perit ! Sic autem non est dictum, Nunc significata
est clarificatio Filii hominis : sed dictum est, Nunc clarificatus est
Filius hominis ; quemadmodum non est dictum, Petra significabat
Christum, sed, Petra erat Christus : nec dictum est, Bonum semen
significabat filios regni . . . . sed dictum est, Bonum semen hi sunt
filii regni, zizania autem filii maligni. Sicut ergo solet loqui scriptura, res significantes tanquam illas quæ significantur appellans ; ita
locutus est Dominus dicens, Nunc clarificatus est Filius hominis,
posteaquam separato inde nequissimo, et secum remanentibus sanctis,
significata est glorificatio ejus, quando separatis iniquis manebit in
æternitate cum sanctis.—August. in Evang. Joan. Tract. LXIII. Opp.
Tom. IX. fol. 84. col. 3.]

which signifieth taketh the name of that thing which it signifieth. The Holy Ghost is said to descend and remain upon him in the bodily shape of a dove. For so also is the rock Christ, because it signifieth Christ[1]."

Their error, which will not have sacramental speeches expounded sacramentally. By these examples alleged out of the scripture it is plain, that the signs do borrow the names of the things, and not their natures and substances. Whereupon it is undoubtedly true, that they err as far as heaven is wide, which are persuaded, that the sacramental speeches are not to be expounded as figurative and borrowed, but most properly and literally; so that by that means the water, bread, and wine, are not now signs and tokens only of regeneration, and of the body of Christ given and of his blood shed for us; but regeneration itself, and the very substantial body and blood of our Lord Jesus. For being of this opinion, they are offensive unto the common manner both of speaking and interpreting used in all ages; they are also repugnant to true faith, yea, and to common sense. Whereby it cometh to pass, that by their confounding of the sign with the thing signified they bring in a servile weakness, and (that I may use St Augustine's words) " a carnal bondage." For he, Li. iii. *de Doct. Chr.* ca. 9, entreating of the sacraments of Christians, saith : " The Lord himself, and the apostles in their doctrine, have left us few things instead of many ; and those most easy to be done, most reverend in understanding, and most pure in observing; as is baptism, and the celebration of the body and blood of the Lord : which sacraments every man when he receiveth, being instructed, acknowledgeth whereunto they are referred, that we should not worship them with carnal servitude or bondage, but rather with spiritual freedom or liberty. And as to follow the letter, and to take the signs instead of the things which are signified

[1 Sonitus ille vocis et columbæ species corporalis, et linguæ divisæ velut ignis, qui insedit super unumquemque eorum, sicut illa in monte Syna quæ terribili specie facta sunt, et sicut columna illa nubis per diem et flammæ per noctem, significativa operatione acta atque transacta sunt. Illud in his maxime cavendum est, ne cuiquam Dei natura vel Patris, vel Filii, vel Spiritus Sancti commutabilis et convertibilis esse credatur. Nec moveat quod aliquando res quæ significat nomen ejus rei quam significat accipit. Spiritus Sanctus dictus est corporali specie tanquam columba descendisse et mansisse super eum. Sic enim et petra Christus, quia significat Christum.— August. Epist. CII. ad Evod. Opp. Tom. II. fol. 89. col. 1.]

by them, is a point of servile weakness; so to expound the signs unprofitably is a point of evil-wandering error[2]." And yet he speaketh more plainly, chap. 5 : " First of all you must beware, lest you take a figurative speech according to the letter. For to this agreeth that which the apostle saith : ' The letter killeth, but the spirit giveth life.' For when that which is figuratively spoken is taken as though it were spoken properly, it is carnally understanded. Neither is there anything that may more agreeably be termed the death of the soul, than when that wherein we excel beasts, which is understanding or knowledge, is made subject to the flesh by following the letter. For he that followeth the letter, understandeth words translated or borrowed, as proper or natural ; neither doth he refer that which is signified by a proper word to another signification : but if (for an example) he shall hear mention of the sabbath, he understandeth it no otherwise but as one day of the seven which by continual course come and go. And when he heareth mention made of sacrifice, it will not out of his head, but that this is meant of that which was wont to be done about offering of beasts and fruits of the earth. To be short, this is the miserable bondage of the soul, to take the signs for the things themselves, and not to be able to lift up the eyes of the mind above the bodily creature for the obtaining of everlasting light[3]." Thus far Augustine. By these

Marginal note: Carnal bondage and servile weakness

[2 Pauca pro multis, eaque factu facillima et intellectu augustissima et observatione castissima, ipse Dominus et apostolica tradidit disciplina : sicuti est baptismi sacramentum et celebratio corporis et sanguinis Domini : quæ unusquisque cum percipit, quo referantur imbutus agnoscit, ut ea non carnali servitute sed spiritali potius libertate veneretur. Ut autem literam sequi, et signa pro rebus quæ iis significantur accipere, servilis infirmitatis est ; ita inutiliter signa interpretari, male vagantis erroris est.—Id. de Doct. Christ. Lib. III. cap. 9. Opp. Tom. III. fol. 11. col. 4.]

[3 In principio cavendum est, ne figuratam locutionem ad literam accipias. Et ad hoc enim pertinet quod ait apostolus, Litera occidit, spiritus autem vivificat. Cum enim figurate dictum sic accipitur tanquam proprie dictum sit, carnaliter sapitur. Neque ulla mors animæ congruentius appellatur, quam cum id etiam quod in ea bestias antecellit, hoc est, intelligentia, carni subjicitur sequendo literam. Qui enim sequitur literam, translata verba sicut propria tenet ; neque illud quod proprio verbo significatur refert ad aliam significationem : sed si sabbatum audierit, verbi gratia, non intelligit nisi

words of Augustine we do gather, that they reverence the
sacraments by spiritual liberty, which neither stick to the
letter, neither worship and reverence the visible things and
elements, as water, bread, and wine, instead of the things signified; but being rather admonished and stirred up by the
signs, they are lifted up in their minds to behold the things
signified.

How a figu-
rative speech
is to be re-
ceived and
acknow-
ledged.   This same Augustine, in the same book, chapter 15,
teaching when and after what manner a trope or figure is to
be received or acknowledged, saith: " In figurative speeches
this manner of rule shall be kept; that so long you view with
diligent consideration what is read, until the interpretation
come unto the rule of charity.   For if it be not repugnant to
charity, think not that it is a figurative speech[1]."   And yet
more plainly he addeth in the 16. chapter following: " If it
be an imperative speech, either forbidding any heinous offence
or wicked deed, or commanding any profitable or good deed, it
is no figurative speech: but if it command any wicked deed,
or forbid any deed of charity, then it is figurative. ' Except
ye eat the flesh of the Son of Man, and drink his blood, ye
have no life in you.'   He seemeth to command some horrible
offence or wicked deed; therefore it is a figurative speech,
commanding us to communicate with the passion of Christ, and
comfortably and profitably to lay up in our remembrance, that
his flesh was crucified and wounded for us.   The scripture
saith, ' If thine enemy hunger, feed him.'   Here no man doubteth but he commandeth well-doing; but that which followeth,
' for in so doing thou shalt heap coals of fire upon his head,'
a man would think that a wicked and evil deed were
commanded: therefore doubt not but that it is figuratively

unum diem de septem, qui continuo volumine repetuntur; et cum
audierit sacrificium, non excedit cogitatione illud quod fieri de vic-
timis pecorum terrenisque fructibus solet.   Ea demum est mise-
rabilis animæ servitus, signa pro rebus accipere, et supra creaturam
corpoream oculum mentis ad hauriendum æternum lumen levare non
posse.—August. ibid. cap. 5. Opp. Tom. III. fol. 11. col. 2.]
    [1 Servabitur in locutionibus figuratis regula hujusmodi; ut tam
diu versetur diligenti consideratione quod legitur, donec ad regnum
caritatis interpretatio perducatur.   Si autem hoc jam proprie sonat,
nulla putetur figurata locutio.—Id. ibid. cap. 15. fol. 12. col. 2.]

spoken[2]." And so forth. All these things do convince their error, which interpret sacramental speeches as proper, and reject all figures and tropes, especially in the institution of the supper.

Nevertheless, I am not ignorant what they set against this last testimony of St Augustine ; that the words of our Saviour, in the sixth of John, do make nothing to the interpretation of the ministration of the sacrament ; and therefore that the place of St Augustine doth nothing agree to our purpose. But it is manifest, that in the same book St Augustine disputeth of signs and of the sacramental speeches. And that is manifest also by many other places out of St Augustine, that he often alleged these words of our Saviour, out of the sixth of John, to expound the celebration of the supper. But why do they nothing pertain to the celebration of the supper ? Doth he speak of one body in the supper, and of another in the sixth chapter of John ? Shall we believe that the Lord had and hath two bodies ? Our Lord Jesus hath but one body, the which as it profiteth nothing being eaten corporally according to St John, vi. chapter ; even so that body, being corporally eaten, doth nothing avail according to St Matthew, xxvi. chapter. But this matter we have elsewhere handled[3].

And of as little force is this unsavoury objection of theirs ; which is, that the consequence is false when we argue thus : Circumcision is the covenant, the lamb is the passover, sacrifices are sins and sanctifications or cleansings, are sacramental speeches, mystical and figurative ; therefore this also, " This is my body," is a mystical and figurative speech. For since

The words of our Saviour in the vi. of John do make much for the interpretation of the words of the supper.

To argue from the sacraments of the old Testament to ours of the new.

[2 Si præceptiva locutio est, aut flagitium aut facinus vetans, aut utilitatem aut beneficentiam jubens, non est figurata: si autem flagitium aut facinus videtur jubere, aut utilitatem aut beneficentiam vetare, figurata est. Nisi manducaveritis, inquit, carnem Filii hominis et sanguinem biberitis, non habebitis vitam in vobis. Facinus vel flagitium videtur jubere ; figura est ergo, præcipiens passioni Domini esse communicandum, et suaviter atque utiliter recondendum in memoria, quod pro nobis caro ejus crucifixa et vulnerata sit. Ait scriptura, Si esurierit inimicus tuus, ciba illum.... Hic nullo dubitante beneficentiam præcipit. Sed quod sequitur, Hoc enim faciens carbones ignis congeres super caput ejus, malevolentiæ facinus putes juberi ; ne igitur dubitaveris figurate dictum.—August. ibid. cap. 16. fol. 12. col. 1.]

[3 De Orig. Error. circa Cœn. et Miss. Pap. cap. 16.]

in sacraments there is the like reason, why may we not frame arguments from the one to the other? And that sacraments have the like reason, it is received of all them which acknowledge the truth aright; and it shall be proved hereafter to the full. But if it be not lawful to reason from the sacraments of the old Testament, and by them after a certain comparison to interpret ours, and by ours to make them plain; truly then the apostle did not well, who by a false consequent by comparison we read to have argued from their sacraments unto ours, in the 1 Corinth. x. and to the Coloss. ii. chapter. But now we return to our purpose.

We may use sacramental speeches.

That we may yet at length make an end of this place; they are sacramental and figurative speeches, when we read and hear that the bread is the body of Christ, and the wine the blood of Christ; and that they do eat and drink the body and blood of Christ, which eat and drink the sacrament of the body and blood of the Lord; also that they are purged from their sins and regenerated into a new life, which are baptized in the name of Christ; and that baptism is the washing away of[1] our sins. And after this manner speaketh the scripture, and this form of speech kept the old doctors of the church; whom for so doing none that is wise doth dispraise: neither can one discommend any man which speaketh after this manner, so that he also abide in the same sincerity wherein it is manifest that those holy men of God did walk. For as they did willingly and simply use those speeches, so did they not roughly and rigorously strain the letter and speeches: they did interpret them in such sort, that none was so unskilful but that he might understand, that the signs were not the thing itself which they signified, but that the signs do take the names of the things; therefore they used words significatively, sacramentally, mystically, and figuratively.

Sacramental speeches are to be expounded.

Now whereas some will not have the sacramental speeches to be expounded, as though, being not expounded, they were of more authority, majesty, and worthiness; this draweth after it a sore danger, and giveth a most grievous offence, and is repugnant to the rule of the apostles, to sound reason, and to the custom of them of old. For when these kind of speeches are set forth and uttered to the simple sort, being not expounded; to wit, "That bread is the body of Christ; When

[1 So also ed. 1584: but 1577, all: omnium, Lat.]

thou drinkest the wine of the Lord, thou drinkest the very blood of the Lord; Baptism saveth us," &c.; what other thing, I pray you, is set forth, than a snare of carnal bondage, and a most dangerous offence of idolatry? Many words need not in this matter, since experience doth abundantly enough set forth in this place what hath been done, and what at this day is done[2].

The rule of the apostles commandeth the divine oracles to be expounded in the church, and to lay forth all the mysteries of the scripture, that they may be soundly understanded, as we may see 1 Corinth. xiv. And reason itself teacheth us, that the mind of man is little or nothing moved, if the things themselves be not understood. What fruit therefore shall the simple sort receive by the sacraments, unto whom the meaning of the sacraments hath not been opened? Better therefore did the ancient fathers, not only in expounding all the mysteries of the kingdom of God, and especially the sacraments; but in teaching also that they ought to be expounded: which although it be made plain enough by those things which go before, yet will I add two examples out of St Augustine touching this matter. He, cap. 6. *De Catechisandis Rudibus*, saith: "Let the new christian man be taught concerning the sacraments, that they be visible signs of heavenly things, and that invisible things are to be honoured in them; neither that the sign, after it is blessed and sanctified, is so to be taken as it is daily used. It must also be told him what that speech signifies which he heareth; and what thing is given in the sign, whereof it is a representation. Moreover, upon this occasion he must be taught, that if he hear any thing even in the scriptures that soundeth carnally, although he understand it not; yet to believe that some spiritual thing is signified thereby, which belongeth to holy manners and to the life to come[3]." And as followeth. The same Augustine, Lib. iv. *De Doctr. Chri.* cap. 8. doth utterly forbid the doctors and

[2 Rather, Experience, (that is,) what has happened, and what is daily happening, abundantly illustrate this point.]

[3 De sacramento quod accepit, cum ei bene commendatum fuerit, signacula quidem rerum divinarum esse visibilia, sed res ipsas invisibiles in eis honorari; nec sic habendam esse illam speciem benedictione sanctificatam quemadmodum habetur in usu quolibet: dicendum etiam quid significet et sermo ille quem audivit, quid in illo condatur,

teachers of the church, not to think that they ought therefore
to speak obscurely of the mysteries of the scripture, because
they see that these things are delivered somewhat intricately
and darkly in the scripture; but he rather requireth light
and plainness in them. If any man desire to hear his words,
they are these: " If we fetch examples of the manner of speaking out of the writings of our canonical authors and doctors
which are easily understood, yet we ought not to think that
we should follow them also in those speeches wherein they
have used a profitable and wholesome obscurity, to exercise,
and as it were to quicken, the readers' minds, and to take
away loathsomeness, and to stir up the studies of the willing
learners, and also to make the minds of the wicked zealous,
that they may either be turned to godliness, or else excluded
from the mysteries. For so they spake, that those which
came after them, and could understand and rightly expound them, might reveal a second grace unlike to the
former, but yet ensuing in the church of God. Therefore
they which expound them ought not so to speak, as if
they by the like authority would offer themselves to be
expounded: but in all their kind of speeches, first let them
labour chiefly and first of all to be understanded, with as
plain kind of speaking as they can, that he be very dull
and slow witted which doth not understand; or at the least
let not the fault of the hardness and subtilty of the things,
which we go about to open and declare, be in our own
speech, whereby that which we speak should be somewhat
longer in understanding[1]." Thus far Augustine. And let this
that I have hitherto said of sacramental speeches be sufficient.
The Lord be praised. Amen.

(Bullinger read, condonatur) cujus illa res similitudinem gerit.
Deinde monendus est ex hac occasione, ut si quid etiam in scripturis
audiat, quod carnaliter sonet, etiamsi non intelligit, credat tamen
spirituale aliquid significari, quod ad sanctos mores futuramque vitam
pertineat.—August. de Catech. Rud. cap. 26. Opp. Tom. IV. fol. 208.
col. 3.]

[1 Quapropter et eloquentes quidem non solum sapientes canonicos
nostros auctores doctoresque fateamur tali eloquentia usos, quali personis ejusmodi congruebat. Sed nos etsi de literis eorum, quæ sine
difficultate intelliguntur, nonnulla sumimus elocutionis exempla,
nequaquam tamen putare debemus imitandos eos nobis esse in iis
quæ ad exercendas et elimandas quodammodo mentes legentium, et

THAT WE MUST REASON REVERENTLY OF SACRAMENTS;
THAT THEY DO NOT GIVE GRACE[2], NEITHER HAVE
GRACE INCLUDED IN THEM. AGAIN, WHAT THE VIRTUE
AND LAWFUL END AND USE OF SACRAMENTS IS.
THAT THEY PROFIT NOT WITHOUT FAITH;
THAT THEY ARE NOT[3] SUPERFLUOUS TO
THE FAITHFUL; AND THAT THEY DO
NOT DEPEND UPON THE WORTHI-
NESS OR UNWORTHINESS
OF THE MINISTER.

THE SEVENTH SERMON.

YESTERDAY, dearly beloved, I told you what a sacrament was; who was the author of them, and for what cause[4] sacraments were instituted; of what things they consist, that is to say, of the sign and the thing signified. I told you also what a sign is and what the thing signified, and by what names they are termed; how they are consecrated; that the sign is not mingled with the thing signified, but that both of them remain in their own nature and property of nature; that the sign is not taken away or miraculously turned, neither that the thing signified is so joined with the same[5], that whosoever is partaker of the one, is partaker also of the other. To be short, I declared how and after what manner the sign and the thing signified are coupled together, to make a full,

A brief rehearsal of such points as he entreated upon in his former sermon.

ad rumpenda fastidia atque acuenda studia discere volentium, zelandos quoque sive ut ad pietatem convertantur, sive ut a mysteriis secludantur, animos impiorum, utili ac salubri obscuritate dixerunt. Sic quippe illi locuti sunt ut posteriores, qui eos recte intelligerent et exponerent, alteram gratiam, disparem quidem veruntamen subsequentem, in Dei ecclesia reperirent. Non ergo expositores eorum ita loqui debent, tanquam se ipsi exponendos simili auctoritate proponant: sed in omnibus sermonibus suis primitus ac maxime ut intelligantur elaborent ea quantum possunt perspicuitate dicendi, ut aut multum tardus sit qui non intelligat, aut in rerum quas explicare atque ostendere volumus difficultate ac subtilitate, non in nostra locutione, sit causa quo minus tardiusve quod dicimus possit intelligi.
—Id. de Doct. Christ. Lib. IV. cap. 8. Opp. Tom. III. fol. 16. col. 3.]
　[2 per se, Lat. omitted: of themselves.]
　[3 So ed. 1577: but edd. 1584 and 1587 omit *not:* non esse supervacanea, Lat.]
　[4 So also ed. 1584; but 1577, causes: quas ob causas, Lat.]
　[5 So also ed. 1584: but 1577, with the sign; cum hoc, Lat.]

perfect, and lawful sacrament; where also I entreated of sacramental speeches. Now therefore it remaineth, that I also consequently speak of the nature, virtue, and efficacy of sacraments, and of those things which are joined and of affinity with them: for so the order which I used in my division requireth.

Touching the virtue and nature of sacraments, that is to say, what they work in man, writers have disputed diversely and plentifully. It seemeth unto me, that reverence must be used in this disputation, and that heed must be taken that I do not incline either to the right hand or to the left; that is, that I do not attribute too much unto them, to the derogating of the doctrine of[1] the evangelists and apostles; neither that I should diminish or take from them, to mine own damnation, that which the scripture, the word of God, doth attribute unto them. But we shall plentifully give great praise and glory to the ordinances of God, if we shall say that of them which the Spirit of God hath set down in the holy scriptures: to be willing to attribute more unto them, is not only an error in man, but a great fault which bringeth death and horrible destruction. This is declared unto us in the holy scripture by examples most worthy of remembrance. The ark of the covenant, given by Moses to the people of Israel, was a witness of God's presence among the people, and of the league and friendship between God and man. For in these words God made a league with the people: " I will make my dwelling-place among them, and walk among them; and I will be their God, and they shall be my people." Of the ordinance and agreement the ark itself was called, " The Lord God of hosts, sitting between the cherubims;" as we may see, 2 Sam. vi. and in the book of the Chronicles. It was also called, " The ark of the covenant of the Lord." For[2] when the prophets of God did attribute these things to the sacrament of God, they both thought and spake plentifully and reverently enough of the sacrament of God; but when the ignorant and malicious priests, and the people corrupted by them, did attribute far greater things to the ark or sacrament of God, what, I pray you, came to pass? Give ear first what they attributed to the ark: " The elders of Israel said, Wherefore hath the Lord

We must use reverence in disputing of sacraments.

The ark of the covenant.

[Lev. xxvi. 2.]

To attribute too much to sacraments.

[1 So also ed. 1584: but 1577, from.]
[2 Autem, Lat. : But.]

cast us down this day before the Philistines? Let us fetch the
ark of the covenant of the Lord out of Silo unto us, that,
when it cometh among us, it may save us out of the hands
of our enemies." You have heard what they attributed to
the ark. Now give ear what they did. "So the people sent *It is a great sin not to*
into Silo, and brought from thence the ark of the covenant of *attribute so much unto*
the Lord of hosts, which sitteth between the cherubims. And *the sacra-ments as the*
it came to pass, that when the ark of the covenant of the Lord *scripture doth attri-*
came into the host, all Israel shouted out a mighty shout, so *bute.*
that the earth rang again. And when the Philistines heard
the noise of the shout, they said, What meaneth the sound of
this mighty shout? And they understood that the ark of the
Lord was come into the host. And the Philistines cried, Woe
be unto us! God is come into the host. Who shall deliver
us out of the hands of those mighty gods, that smote the
Egyptians?" But hearken now what happened; and how
God did declare that the ark was not God, as it was called
and counted of the unskilful in holy things; and how he
punished the sins of the people[3], because they attributed too
much to the sacrament. It followeth therefore: "And the
Philistines fought; and Israel was smitten down, and fled every
man into his tent; and there was an exceeding great slaughter;
for there were overthrown of Israel thirty thousand footmen;
beside that, also, the ark of God was taken, and the two sons
of Heli were slain." All these things are read in the first
book of Sam. iv. cap. Again, when the sacrament of God was
unreverently handled of the swinish Philistines, they were
smitten with a loathsome and deadly plague. They did boast
that their gods and the religion of the Philistines had overcome the God and the religion of the Israelites; but the gods
of the Philistines fell down and are broken in pieces, and their
heathenish religion is confounded. What, and did not the
Israelites perish with a more grievous plague than before,
when they lightly handled, and, contrary to the law of God,
Numb. iv., looked into the sacrament brought back by the
Philistines into Bethsames? " For the Lord smote fifty thousand threescore and ten men." 1 Sam. vi. When Moses did
negligently defer the circumcising of his children, he fell into
great danger. The Sichimites, for receiving circumcision rashly,
were destroyed[4]. And Simeon and Levi, for profaning

[3 So also ed. 1584; but 1577, his people : populi sui, Lat.]
[4 So also ed. 1584; but 1577, are destroyed : delentur, Lat.]

the sacrament, are cursed of their father. Genesis xlix. To
this that agreeth which the apostle saith of them which celebrate the supper unworthily: "For this cause many are
weak and sick among you, and many sleep." Hitherto also
belongeth the example of Oza, a man not altogether evil,
which touched this same sacrament, that was not lawful for
him to do. Wherefore the Lord stroke him with a sudden
death; and that not privately in the tabernacle, but in the
sight of all the people. Of the which deed of God David
also speaking in the congregation and church of the Israelites,
saith to the Levites: "The Lord hath chosen the Levites to
bear the ark of the Lord" (and not that kine shall draw it in a
new cart); "therefore see that ye be holy, that ye may bring
in the ark of the Lord God of Israel unto the place which I
have prepared for it. For because ye did not this at the
first, our Lord God hath made a rent among us; for that we
sought him not as the fashion ought to be." And it followeth
immediately: "The priests and Levites sanctified themselves
to fetch the ark of the Lord God of Israel. And the children
and Levites[1] bare the ark of God upon their shoulders with
staves, as Moses commanded, according to the word of the
Lord." All these things are to be seen in the first of the
Chronicles, cap. xv. Whereby we gather, that the Lord will
none of our good meanings or intents, and pompous cele-
brations in celebrating the sacraments: but that he only requireth, that we should so judge and speak of the sacraments,
as he judgeth and speaketh by his word; and that we should
so use and celebrate them, as he himself hath instituted and
celebrated them. Therefore he sufficiently setteth forth the
dignity of sacraments, who attributeth that unto them which
God himself in the holy scriptures vouchsafeth to give them.

Let us therefore first of all search out of what dignity[2]
sacraments have been for the most part in our time, that
thereby we may the better understand what is to be attributed, and what is not to be attributed, unto them. The common sort of priests and monks have taught, that the sacraments
of the new law are not only signs of grace, but together also
causes of grace, that is, which have power to give grace. For
they say, that they are as instruments, pipes, and certain con-

Marginal notes:
[1 Cor. xi. 30.]

Numb.iv.

It is taught
that sacra-
ments give
grace.

[1 So also ed. 1584; but 1577, of the Levites: filii Levitarum, Lat.]
[2 quid tributum sit, Lat.]

duits of Christ's passion, by which the grace of Christ is conveyed and poured into us; but that the signs of the old Testament, given to the fathers, were signs only, and not causes of
grace also; which have force to signify, but not to give grace.

They seem truly to have sucked that error out of St *Augustine taught not that sacraments give grace.*
Augustine's words wrongfully understood. For he writeth upon
the 73. Psalm thus: "The sacraments of the new law are
more wholesome and happy than they of the old law, because
they promise, these give[3]." But St Augustine meant to say
no other thing, than that which in another place he speaketh
after this manner: "The sacraments of the old law did foreshew that Christ should come, but ours do shew that he is
come[4]." For also against Faustus, Lib. XIX. cap. 14, he
calleth the sacraments of the old law "promises of things to
be performed; but our sacraments, tokens of things that are
already performed[5]." Wherefore upon the 73. Psalm he
saith: "The sacraments of the old law are given to signify
the very thing; but ours do witness that it is given, and signifieth that it is present[6]." I confess that he saith more than
once, that our sacraments are more comfortable and effectual[7];
but he said that by no other reason, than for that, the Messias
being already revealed and given unto us in the new Testament, our sacraments[8] are more perfit, more lightsome, and
more beautiful: for Christ hath brought all signs to an end;
wherefore ours have a more full signification, and after a
sort are the more lively. But if Augustine had been alto-

[3 Sacramenta novi testamenti dant salutem, sacramenta veteris
testamenti promiserunt salvatorem.... Mutata sunt sacramenta;
facta sunt faciliora, pauciora, salubriora, feliciora.—August. Opp.
Tom. VIII. fol. 167. col. 4. Par. 1531.]

[4 Lex enim et prophetæ usque ad Joannem Baptistam sacramenta
habebant prænunciantia rem futuram; nostri vero temporis sacramenta
venisse contestantur quod illa venturum essa prædicabant.—August.
contra Lit. Petil. Lib. II. cap. 37. Opp. Tom. VII. fol. 24. col. 2.]

[5 — illæ fuerint promissiones rerum complendarum, hæc sunt
indicia completarum.—Id. con. Faust. Opp. Tom. VI. fol. 72. col. 2.]

[6 The Translator has here mistaken Bullinger's meaning. The
correct rendering is: "Wherefore on Psal. 73. Augustine uses *give*
for *testify that it is given*, or *signify that it is exhibited*." See quotation above.]

[7 See above, note 4; and August. con. Faust. Lib. XIX. cap. 23.
Alia (sacramenta) sunt instituta virtute majora, utilitate meliora, &c.]

[8 omnia nostra, Lat. : sacraments, not in Lat.]

gether of that opinion which these men do favour and follow, would not godliness itself persuade us to forsake the authority of men, and cleave to the word of truth?

Of the like-
ness and dif-
ference of
the sacra-
ments of the
old and new
Testament.
Let us see therefore what may be gathered out of the word of truth, that is, out of the canonical scriptures, touching the likeness and difference of the sacraments of the old and new Testament. This we hold for a certainty out of the scriptures, that there is but one everlasting and unchangeable God and Lord of either Church; that there is but one faith in him through Christ of either church; that there is but one way laid down in either church to attain to the promises of salvation: to be short, that there is but one church of the only living God, gathered together out of either people, both of the Jews and Gentiles[1]. I think there needeth no large confirmation of these things out of the scripture, because in the eighth decade and third sermon I have handled them at the full. Now that I have fortified and confirmed these things before by the writings of the apostles, thus I conclude, not of mine own brain, but by the authority of God: They which always have one everlasting and unchangeable God, one way of salvation set forth for all in Christ from the beginning, one faith, one church, one baptism, the same spiritual meat and drink; they cannot choose but have the selfsame sacraments, as touching their substance. But the Jews and Christians have one God, one faith, one way of salvation, which is by Christ; to be short, one church: therefore have they also the selfsame sacraments, saving that ours are given under other signs, and for that through the revelation of the Sun of righteousness, I mean Christ, are made more lightsome and manifest. I say further, that the scripture witnesseth that the sacraments of the old Testament and ours are of the same force, insomuch that Paul calleth them circumcised which are baptized, and them baptized which are circumcised. And he also teacheth, that our fathers did eat that spiritual meat which we eat, and drank of that spiritual drink, that is, the rock. But anon he addeth: "And that rock was Christ." The words of the apostle are well known, and are read in the 1 Cor. x. The same apostle, in the second chapter to the Colossians, saith: "In Christ ye are complete (or made perfit); in whom also ye are circumcised with circumcision made

[1 both of — Gentiles, not in Lat.]

without hands, by putting off the body of the flesh, subject to sin[2], by the circumcision of Christ; buried with him in baptism," &c. What, I pray you, can be spoken more plainly? "Circumcision made without hands," is the circumcision of Christians, which is baptism. But in the former place of Paul to the Corinthians we must mark (as elsewhere I put you in mind[3],) that to be baptized into Moses is not the same that it is to be baptized into Christ. For to be baptized into Moses is all one as if he had said, to be baptized by Moses, or through the ministry of Moses. For it is manifest that Moses brought the people to God, which were only committed to his charge[4].

In many places in Aurel. August. ye shall read the like, howsoever our adversaries do father upon Augustine this difference between the sacraments of the old law and ours, of their own bringing in. For he, Lib. II. *Cont. Literas Petil.* cap. 27, saith : " The sacraments of the Jews were in outward tokens diverse from ours, but in the things signified they were equal and all one[5]." Also *Tract. in Joan.* 26. upon this place, " He is the bread which came down from heaven," he saith : " Manna did signify this bread; the altar of God signified this bread. Those were sacraments. In signs they are diverse, but in the thing signified equal[6]." The like words thou mayest read, Lib. XIX. *Contra Faustum Manicheum*, cap. 13, 16, 17.[7] And again, *Tract. in Joan.* 45 : " Before the coming of our Lord Jesus Christ, when he came basely in the flesh, there were just and righteous men, who did so believe in him then that was to come, as we do believe in him now that is come. The times were changed, but so was not faith[8];" and so

[margin note: Augustine teacheth that the sacraments of the Jews and ours are all one.]

[2] peccatorum, Lat. : of the sins, as in Auth. Ver.]

[3] See Vol. II. page 293.]

[4] Rather, brought the people committed to his charge to God only : unice Deo adduxisse, Lat.]

[5] The chapter is 37; and Bullinger has given (in a sentence formed on the next quotation) the sentiment, and not the express words, of Augustine in the place.]

[6] Hic est panis qui de cœlo descendit. Hunc panem significavit manna : hunc panem significavit altare Dei. Sacramenta illa fuerunt. In signis diversa sunt, sed in re quæ significatur paria sunt.—August. in Evan. Joan. tract. XXVI. Opp. Tom. IX. fol. 47. col. 2.]

[7] Id. Opp. Tom. VI. fol. 72, &c.]

[8] Ante adventum Domini nostri Jesu Christi, quo humilis venit in carne, præcesserunt justi, sic in eum credentes venturum quomodo

forth. And anon : " In divers signs is all one faith ; so in divers signs as in divers words, because words change their sounds by times, and truly words are nothing but signs. For in that they signify, they are words : take away the signification from the word, and it is a vain noise. Therefore all words are significations. Did not these that ministered those signs in the old law, believe those things which we now believe were prophesied before and[1] by them ? No doubt they did believe them; but they believed they should come, and we that they are come[2]." Also upon the 77. Psalm : " The same meat and drink (saith he) had they in the[3] sacraments, which we have in ours ; but in signification the same, not in likeness. For the selfsame Christ was figured to them in the rock, but manifested to us in the flesh. But with them all God was not well pleased. All verily did eat one spiritual meat, and drank one spiritual drink; that is, which signified some spiritual thing : but in all of them God had no delight. And whereas the sacraments were common to all, yet grace was not common to all, which is the pith of the sacraments. As even now at this day, faith is revealed which then was hid ; the fountain of regeneration is common to all, which are baptized in the name of the Father, and of the Son, and of the Holy Ghost; but the inward grace, whereof they are sacraments, whereby the members of Christ with their head are born anew, is not common to all[4]." Thus far Augustine ; who

nos credimus in eum qui venit. Tempora variata sunt, non fides.—Id. in Evang. Joan. Tract. XLV. Opp. Tom. IX. fol. 68. col. 4.]

[1 So also ed. 1584: but 1577, *beforehand.*]

[2 In signis diversis eadem fides, sic in signis diversis quomodo in verbis diversis; quia verba sonos mutant per tempora, et utique nihil aliud sunt verba quam signa. Significando enim verba sunt; tolle significationem verbo, strepitus inanis est. Significata sunt ergo omnia. Nunquid non' eadem credebant per quos hæc signa ministrabantur, per quos eadem quæ credimus prophetata prænunciabantur? Utique credebant, sed illa ventura esse, nos autem venisse.—Id. ibid. fol. 68. col. 4.]

[3 So also ed. 1584: but 1577, their.]

[4 Idem in mysterio cibus et potus illorum qui noster, sed significatione idem, non specie: quia idem ipse Christus illis in petra figuratus, nobis in carne manifestatus est. Sed non, inquit, in omnibus illis beneplacitum est Deo. Omnes quidem eundem cibum spiritalem manducaverunt, et eundem potum spiritalem biberunt, id est, spiritale aliquid significantem: sed non in omnibus illis bene-

teacheth, that their signs or sacraments are not unequal or
unlike, which have the same faith and religion; but that all
the difference that is resteth in the diversity of the time;
otherwise they differ not.

Now that I have made an end of the similitude and difference of the sacraments of the old and new Testament, and
that by occasion of a received opinion that the sacraments
of the new law do confer or give grace of themselves; let us
also consider what manner of thing the same is.

And first; touching the word "grace," I will give you Grace, what
these few things to note. Grace is the favour and good-will of $^{it is.}$
God, wherewith God the Father embraceth us for Christ's
sake, purifieth, justifieth, and endueth us with his good[5] gifts,
and saveth us. For the writings of the apostles do plainly
call that (grace), whereby we are saved, and justified, or made
righteous[6], by faith in Jesus Christ. Of this grace it is written:
"I make not the grace of God of no effect; for if righteous- [Gal. ii. 21.]
ness come by the law, then Christ died in vain." Of this
grace it is written: "Christ unto us[7] is become unprofitable: [Gal. v. 4.]
as many as are justified by the law are fallen from grace."
Of this grace it is written: "If it come of grace, then is it not [Rom. xi 6.]
of works; for else grace now is no more grace." What, is
not the Son of God himself called "the grace and gift of
God?" John iv. and Titus ii. cap.

Now to confer grace[8], what is it else than to give, or
frankly and freely to bestow something on a man which he
had not before? Therefore, if the sacraments do give grace
to the receivers of them, then truly they give those things
which they signify to them which had them not, I mean,
Christ with all his gifts; that is to say, they make them

placitum est Deo....Et cum essent omnia communia sacramenta,
non communis erat omnibus gratia, quæ sacramentorum virtus est.
Sicut et nunc jam revelata fides, quæ tunc velabatur, omnibus in
nomine Patris et Filii et Spiritus Sancti baptizatis commune est lavacrum regenerationis, sed ipsa gratia cujus ipsa sunt sacramenta, qua
membra corporis Christi cum suo capite regenerata sunt, non communis est omnibus.—Id. in Psal. LXXVII. Enarr. Opp. Tom. VIII.
fol. 177. col. 4.]
[5 good, not in Lat.]
[6 or made righteous, the Translator's addition.]
[7 vobis, Lat.]
[8 grace, not in Lat.]

pleasant and acceptable unto God, they justify and save, yea, and that of themselves ; insomuch as they are said to have received virtue to sanctify from the passion of Christ, and not to signify only or to help, to commend or to further[1]. Yea, and they also attribute the receiving of grace to our work, whereby we receive the sacrament. But how contrary this doctrine is to the truth of his[2] holy prophets and apostles, I will now declare.

Sacraments do not confer or give grace.

It was an old error among the Jews, that sacraments did justify. Hereof cometh it, that the holy prophets of God, reasoning and rebuking the people of God committed to their charge, yet savouring of false opinions, cried, that their labour which they bestowed upon their ceremonies and sacrifices was in vain ; and that God is delighted with faithful obedience, with faith, I say, charity, innocency, and also with true godliness. Among whom Jeremy saith : " Thus saith the Lord of hosts, the God of Israel, Heap up your burnt-offerings with your sacrifices, and eat the flesh : for when I brought your fathers out of Egypt, I spake no word unto them of burnt-offerings and sacrifices ; but this I commanded them, saying, Hearken and obey my voice, and I will be your God, and ye shall be my people; so that ye walk in all the ways which I have commanded you, that ye may prosper." The like place is in Esay, the first chapter. The Lord hath not despised, neither have his holy prophets contemned, all sacrifices in general, since he himself instituted them by Moses ; but they sought to suppress and beat down that false opinion and vain confidence which they had in sacrifices. It is a vain confidence and a false opinion, to believe and think that sacrifices of themselves, and for our works' sake, do make us acceptable unto God ; for faith maketh us acceptable unto God by the Messias. And the Lord did not institute sacraments or sacrifices, that, being offered, they might give grace, or justify us ; but to be witnesses of the grace of God ; and that by them his people might be kept, and drawn[3] in due order, from idols and heathenish worshippings, and led to Christ the high priest and only sacrifice (or oblation) for the whole world. For they were certain schoolings or exercises,

Jer. vii.

Isai. i.

[1 gratiam, Lat. omitted : grace.]
[2 his, not in ed. 1584 : but 1577, the holy.]
[3 Rather, might be kept in due order, or drawn, &c.]

as Paul proveth, saying: "The law was our schoolmaster
unto Christ, that we should be justified through faith; but
after that faith is come, we are no longer under a schoolmaster." Therefore the sacrifices of the old law[4] did not
give grace to them that sacrificed, neither wrought they their
justification; but were tokens and testimonies, that God doth
sanctify and justify by and through the sacrifice appointed
before all worlds[5], the Messias, I mean; to faith in whom they
did, as it were a certain schoolmaster by guiding us, bring us.

And truly, when the apostles preached the pure and The error in
the apostolic
sound doctrine of the gospel, that by the only grace of God church.
in Christ the faithful are saved, this ancient error of their
elders had taken such deep root in the minds of the Jews,
that even they which had received Christ stood nevertheless
in contention, that Christ was not able fully to sanctify and
justify without the help of the Jewish sacrifices. Against
whom the apostles, disputing with great gravity and invincible
power of the Spirit, did plainly prove that a Christian, without any observations of the ceremonial law, or help of any
works, even by the only mere and free[6] grace and mercy
of God in Christ[7], is sanctified, purified, justified, and saved:
which undoubtedly is the helm (as commonly is said) and stern
of the evangelists' and apostles' doctrine; which whoso denieth,
he hath no part doubtless in the inheritance of Christ and Acts xv.
his gospel. Neither is it obscure or doubtful, which even now
I have set forth in these few words; for who is ignorant
of that memorial[8] dissension between the chief apostles of
Christ, Paul and Barnabas, kindled against those which
taught, "Except the Christians were circumcised after the
manner of Moses, they could in no wise be saved?" Against
whom Peter maketh this conclusion: "That our hearts are
purified by faith; and that we which believe[9] shall be saved
by the grace of our Lord Jesus Christ."

True it is, that the adversaries would bring back again That grace is
given freely
that which the apostles abrogated and took away; but in the and received
by faith.

[4 veterum, Lat.: of the ancients.]
[5 omnibus seculis destinatam, Lat.]
[6 sive gratuita, Lat. omitted: or gratuitous.]
[7 Rather, grace of God, or mercy through Christ, &c.]
[8 So also ed. 1584: but 1577, memorable: memorabilem, Lat.]
[9 Rather, they which believe.]

meanwhile this is also undoubtedly true, that the apostles with no other forcible engine more strongly battered (as it were) and beat down flat to the ground their adversaries' bulwark in defence of sacraments that purify, than with this: "That we which believe[1] shall be saved by the grace of our Lord Jesus Christ." And whereas in every place almost they add, "Not by the law, not by ceremonies or other[2] ritual observations;" do we think that they will admit sacraments to the partaking of such power and virtue, seeing they be comprehended under rites and ceremonies, and so accounted[3]? Christian faith doth attribute the grace of God, remission of sins, sanctification and justification, fully and wholly to the free mercy of God, and to the merit of Christ's passion; yea, in such sort doth christian faith attribute these spiritual benefits unto it[4], that beside it nothing at all is admitted to take part with it. Therefore whereas Lombard saith, "That sacraments have received power to confer or give grace by the merit of the passion of Christ[5];" it is of his own forging. For as Christ giveth not his glory to any, either saint or mortal man, much less to a creature without life; even so he that believeth to be fully justified by the death and resurrection of the Lord, seeketh no further grace and[6] righteousness in any other thing than in Christ only, upon whom he stayeth, whom also by faith he feeleth in his heart or mind already to exercise his force by the Holy Ghost. For hereunto pertain those things[7] in the gospel:

Luke vii.
John iv.

"Go in peace, thy faith hath saved thee:" and also: "He which drinketh of this water shall thirst again; but whosoever shall drink of that water which I shall give him, shall never thirst, &c." To this pertaineth the saying of Paul also:

Rom. v.

"Therefore being justified by faith, we are at peace with God through our Lord Jesus Christ: by whom also we had an entrance by faith unto this grace wherein we stand, and rejoice in hope of the glory of God."

Their fantasy, which feign a general and special faith, is here confuted.

I am not ignorant of the crafty sleights of some, who

[1 Rather, they which believe.]   [2 ullis, Lat. : any.]
[3 and so accounted, the Translator's addition.]
[4 Rather, and so attributes, that, &c.]
[5 Ex ipsius (Christi) morte et passione virtutem sortita sunt (sacramenta.) Lombard. Sentent. Lib. III. dist. 2. B. fol. 307. Par. 1575.]
[6 aut, Lat. : or.]   [7 So also ed. 1584: but 1577, sayings.]

imagine there is a certain general and also a special faith. The general faith they call that whereby we believe, that we are truly justified by the death and resurrection of Christ: but that they call a special faith, whereby we believe that by the sacraments and by our own works the gifts of God are applied particularly to every one of us one by one. But to what purpose was it, being in a land where they might be fed with manna, to look back to the pottage-pots and (unsavoury) leeks of Egypt? What, I pray you, have Christians to do with the distinctions of subtle sophisters? Or how will they prove this distinction of theirs unto us? Verily, there is but one faith; and the same is no other in the use of the sacraments than it is without the use of them. Without the use of them we believe that we are sanctified by the death and resurrection of Christ. In baptism and the Lord's supper we practise no other faith, than whereby we believe that we are purged from our sins by the grace and mercy of Christ; and that by his body given for us, and his blood shed for us, we are redeemed from death, and become heirs of eternal life. Not the sacraments, but faith through the Holy Ghost, applieth these things unto us: which thing all the writings of the apostles do witness, but[8] such feigned glosses do obscure and darken. To be short; there is one God and Saviour of all, one salvation, one redemption and purging, one faith whereby we receive salvation offered unto us of God in Christ through the Holy Ghost. The same is declared or preached unto us in the word by the minister, and is represented and sealed by the sacraments.

And now, who knoweth not that Paul, the apostle, in all his writings only laboureth to prove, that those that believe are justified by faith in the Lord Jesus, and not by any works? Again, who is ignorant, that the receiving and celebration of sacraments are also counted among our works? Whereunto I will add this, that sacraments give not that which they have not themselves: but they have not grace, and righteousness, and heavenly gifts; therefore they do not give them.

But hence springeth up another disputation for us to handle: Whether the grace of God and a certain heavenly power be put in or included in the sacraments, and as it *Whether the grace of God be contained in the sacraments.*

[8 Rather, which, i.e. which writings of the apostles.]

were contained in them, so that from them it might be conveyed into the receivers? The whole rabble of priests and monks, as well in word as in deed, have bewrayed themselves, that they think that in the bare signs there is heavenly grace included, yea, and that God himself is comprehended in them. From no other fountain sprang their careful disputations concerning that the mouse eateth, when it eateth the sacrament of the body of Christ. Pope Innocent, *Libro quarto, De Sacramento altaris, Capite undecimo,* saith: "Miraculously doth the substance of bread return again; not that bread which was turned into flesh; but it cometh to pass, that instead of it other bread is miraculously created, which bread is eaten[1]," &c. Behold, here is certain witty and miraculous kind of divinity. I pass over of purpose many other which are of this kind.

And hereunto[2], that by crossings and certain secret words, gestures, and breathings, they consecrate the water of baptism; all which things they beautify with the name of blessing. And among other things they sing thus: "God, by the secret mixture of his light, make fruitful this water prepared to regenerate men withal; that, being sanctified and born again of the immaculate womb of the heavenly fountain, it may come forth a new creature. Let this holy and innocent creature be free from all the assaults of the adversary. Let him not entrap it in his snare. Let it become a living fountain, a regenerating water, a purifying river; that all that are dipped in this wholesome laver, the Holy Ghost working in them, may attain to the excellency of perfect purification. Wherefore, O thou creature of water, I bless (or conjure) thee, by the living God, by the true God, by the holy God, by the God which in the beginning separated thee by his word from the dry land," &c. Again breathing thrice on the water, he

These are sung in the Easter holy days at their consecration of baptism[3].

[1 — miraculose revertitur (substantia panis), cum ipsum ibi desinit esse; non quod illa panis substantia revertatur, quæ transivit in carnem; sed quod ejus loco alius miraculose creatur, quamvis hujus accidentia sine subjecto possunt sic corrodi, sicut edi.—Innocent. Pap. III. Myster. Missæ. Lib. IV. cap. 11. The title of the chapter is, Quid etiam a mure comedatur, cum sacramentum corroditur. Opp. Tom. I. p. 380. col. 1575.]

[2 An error in all the editions for, Add hereunto. Adde his, Lat.]

[3 The water to be used in baptism is blessed, in the church of Rome, on holy Saturday.]

forthwith uttereth these words: "Thou, O Lord, bless with thy word these waters which make request unto thee, that beside their natural cleanness which in washing they may give to our bodies, they may also be effectual to purify our souls." Then the priest taketh a burning wax candle, and putteth it thrice in the water consecrated to baptism, saying: "Let the power of the Holy Ghost come down into this plentiful fountain." He addeth: "And let it make the whole substance of this water fruitful with the fruit of regeneration[4]." And so forth.

All these things they understand and expound to be spoken simply and without tropes or figures; which evidently enough declareth what these men attribute to holy or consecrated water, and how they think that in the signs the holy things themselves are contained. About this matter Bonaventura hath wonderfully busied himself, who in his writing, *In* 4. *Magistri Distinct. Quest.* 3. among other things at the length saith: "We must not say by any means that grace is contained substantially in the sacraments, as water in a vessel, or as a medicine in a box; yea, to understand it so, it is erroneous. But they are said to contain grace, in that they signify grace; and because, unless there be a want on the part of the receiver, grace is always given in them: so that ye must understand that grace is in the soul, and not in the visible signs. For this cause they are called also vessels of grace. They may be also called vessels after another manner; because, as that which is in a vessel is no part of it,

Bonaventura saith that grace is not contained in the sacraments.

[4 Qui hanc aquam regenerandis hominibus præparatam arcana sui (Bullinger read, sua) luminis admixtione fœcundet; ut sanctificatione concepta, ab immaculato divini fontis utero in novam renata creaturam progenies cœlestis (Bullinger has omitted these two words) emergat ... non insidiando circumvolet (contrariæ virtutis admixtio). ...Sit hæc sancta et innocens creatura, libera ab omni impugnatoris incursu...sit fons vivus, aqua regenerans, unda purificans. Ut omnes hoc lavacro salutifero diluendi, operante in eis Spiritu Sancto, perfectæ purgationis indulgentiam consequantur. Unde benedico te, creatura aquæ, per Deum vivum, per Deum verum, per Deum sanctum, per Deum qui te in principio verbo separavit ab arida, &c..... Halat (sacerdos) ter in aquam ... dicens, Tu has simplices aquas tuo ore benedicito; ut præter naturalem emundationem quam lavandis possunt adhibere corporibus, sint etiam purificandis mentibus efficaces. Hic sacerdos paululum demittat (cereum) in aquam, et dicit, Descendat in_hanc plenitudinem fontis virtus Spiritus Sancti,...totamque hujus aquæ substantiam regenerandi fœcundet effectu.—Brev. Rom.]

neither cometh of it, and yet nevertheless is drawn out of it ; so grace cometh neither of nor by the sacraments, but springeth from the eternal fountain, and is drawn out from thence by the soul in the sacraments. And as a man, when he would have liquor, goeth straight to the vessel ; so he that seeketh after the liquor of grace, and hath it not, must have recourse to the sacraments[1]." Thus far Bonaventura, who rightly referred grace unto God, the fountain of all good things. I would he had also more purely and simply set down the rest.

The seat of the grace of God.

He also said[2] truly, that the soul of man was the seat and[3] receptacle of grace and of the gifts of God, and not things without sense. For the holy scripture teacheth everywhere, that the mind of man, not any element, or whatsoever is forged by man's device, is the mansion-place of the grace of God ; and that it is not to be sought for, or worshipped, as

1 Kings viii.

included in any insensible thing. "If the heaven of heavens," saith Solomon, "be not able to contain thee, how should then this house do it, that I have builded ?" Whereunto the most

Acts vii.

constant martyr of Christ, Stephen, alluding, saith : "He that is highest of all dwelleth not in temples made with hands, as saith the prophet : Heaven is my seat, and earth is my footstool. What house will ye build for me ? saith the Lord ; or which is the place of my rest ? Hath not my hand made all these things ?" Which that great apostle of Christ,

Acts xvii.

Paul, following, saith : "God that made the world and all that are in it, seeing that he is Lord of heaven and earth, dwelleth not in temples made with hands ; neither is wor-

[1 Non est aliquo modo dicendum, quod gratia contineatur in ipsis sacramentis essentialiter, tamquam aqua in vase, vel medicina in pyxide ; imo hoc intelligere est erroneum. Sed dicuntur continere gratiam, quia ipsam significant, et quia, nisi ibi sit defectus ex parte suscipientis, in ipsis gratia semper confertur, ita intelligendo quod gratia sit in animo, non in signis visibilibus. Pro tanto etiam dicuntur vasa gratiæ. Possunt etiam dici vasa alia ratione : quia sicut quod est in vase, non est de ipso nec ex ipso, sed tamen ab ipso hauritur ; sic gratia non est a sacramentis, nec de sacramentis, sed oritur a fonte æterno, et ab illo hauritur ab ipsa anima in ipsis sacramentis : et sicut quis recurrit ad vas, cum requirit liquorem ; sic quærenti liquorem gratiæ et non habenti recurrendum est ad ipsa sacramenta. —Bonavent. Sentent. Lib. iv. Dist. i. Quæst. 3. Opp. Tom. v. p. 7. Mogunt. 1609.]

[2 sensit, Lat. : understood.]   [3 seu, Lat. : or.]

shipped with men's hands, as though he needed of anything, seeing he himself giveth to all life, and breath, and all things, &c." Whereupon Christ himself in the gospel speaketh more expressly: "The hour cometh, when ye shall neither in this John iv. mountain, neither at Hierusalem, worship the Father. But the hour cometh, and now is, when the true worshippers shall worship the Father in spirit and truth." The faithful therefore do lift up the eyes of their mind from earthly and visible things unto heavenly : whereupon our godly forefathers, when they celebrated the Lord's Supper, heard that saying repeated or sung unto them, most agreeable to such holy mysteries, "Lift up your hearts:" all the people answered[4] together, "We lift them up unto the Lord." Doth not the very gross absurdity of the thing plainly prove, that grace is not contained in the signs? For if by grace you understand the favour and good-will of God, if pardon and forgiveness of sin, cleansing, I say, and justifying of the believers ; if, finally, the gifts and graces of the Spirit ; what, I pray you, can be imagined more absurd and senseless, than that such excellent things should be kept inclosed in water, bread, and wine? The signs, truly, have no need of grace, nor any pardon and forgiveness of sins. To what purpose, then, should grace be contained within sacraments? What profit, I pray you, will redound unto men? Or who knoweth not, that all the institutions of God were ordained for the commodity of man? Or shall we say, that grace is therefore kept included within the sacraments, that from thence it might be conveyed unto us[5] by channels? But the scripture speaketh not after that manner. For grace, as hath been often now repeated, is the favour and good-will of God ; whereby he himself, not by sensible matters, but of his own accord and through his power and might, is brought unto us. These things are spiritual, and therefore are brought to pass by the gift and mediation of the Holy Ghost. God is joined unto us by his Spirit ; and we are coupled to him by faith, through the gift of the Holy Ghost: which thing in the writings of the evangelists and apostles is everywhere to be seen.

Moreover, the words of the canon of the council of Nice are not to be understood after such a gross and rude manner: *The canon of the Nicene council touching baptism.*

[4 So also ed. 1584: but 1577, answering : respondente, Lat.]
[5 tanquam, Lat. omitted: as though.]

"Our baptism is not to be considered with the bodily eyes, but with the eyes of the mind. Thou seest water; weigh the heavenly force which lieth hid in the water, &c.[1]" For it is a sacramental speech, which truly every body at that time understood; as also at this day[2] it is no new nor hard kind of speaking to say, that in the seal there is faith and truth, in a marriage-ring the faith and love of wedlock, in a sceptre and crown the king's authority. For no man is so foolish, that by reason of the kind of speeches he will affirm, that the things themselves are contained and inclosed in the signs: every man knoweth this kind and manner of speech[3].

The apostles baptized in water not consecrated. To this matter also appertaineth, that John the Baptist baptized in the river Jordan; and that the apostles also themselves baptized with water neither consecrated nor prepared with any enchantments, breathings, or crossings[4], that it might receive the grace of God into it, and make them that are baptized partakers thereof. The Æthiopian, in the Acts of the Apostles, saw a fountain, not mingled with oil, neither consecrated with any holy charms, neither moreover prepared with any breathings or putting in of wax-candles nor pictures of crosses; yet nevertheless he said to Philip the apostle: "See, here is water; what doth let me to be baptized?" But Philip required faith of him in the Lord Jesus; and upon his confession he forthwith baptized him; no consecration of the fountain first provided for, by the which forsooth he might call down the grace of the Holy Ghost and the power of regeneration into the water; and forthwith might apply it to the purifying of the Æthiopian.

To include grace in the sacraments causeth idolatry. And if so be we proceed to include the grace of God within the elements, and the things themselves within the signs by the which they are represented; who seeth not with how great danger we shall do the same, especially among the simple sort? For unto those we shall give occasion of idolatry, and to cleave unto the visible signs; of whom also they

[1 Τὸ βάπτισμα ἡμῶν οὐ τοῖς αἰσθητοῖς ὀφθαλμοῖς κατανοητέον, ἀλλὰ τοῖς νοεροῖς· ὕδωρ ὁρᾷς, νόησον τὴν ἐν τοῖς ὕδασι κρυπτομένην τοῦ Θεοῦ δύναμιν.—Gelas. Hist. Concil. Nic. Labb. et Coss. Tom. II. col. 233. Lut. Par. 1671.]
[2 to us, ed. 1577: but omitted also in 1584: nobis Lat.]
[3 et consuetudinem, Lat. omitted: and practice.]
[4 characteribus, Lat.]

will require and ask that which ought to be asked of God,
the author of all goodness, with minds lifted up into heaven. For whereas it is objected, that by a certain heavenly
covenant it is so appointed by God, that sacraments should
have grace in themselves, and should from themselves, as by
pipes, convey abroad the water of grace unto those that are
thirsty; that is alleged without warrant of the scripture,
and is repugnant unto true religion: as by those things
which have hitherto been handled and disputed of doth, as
we think, sufficiently appear; whereunto also we add this.

The holy and elect people of God are not then first
of all partakers of the first[5] grace of God and heavenly gifts,
when they receive the sacraments; for they enjoy the
things before they be partakers of the signs. For it is plainly
declared unto us, that Abraham our father was justified before he was circumcised. And who gathereth[6] thereby, that
justification was not exhibited and given unto him by the
sacrament of circumcision; but rather, that that righteousness, which he by faith before possessed, was by the sacrament[7] sealed and confirmed unto him? And moreover, who
will not thereof gather, that we, which are the sons of Abraham, are after no other manner justified than it appeareth that
our father was justified; and that our sacraments work no
further in us than they did in him? especially since the
nature of the sacraments of the people of the old Testament
and ours is all one. Whereof I will speak a little afterward
more at large, when I expound the place of the apostle in the
fourth to the Romans.

The godly are first justified into favour, and received before they be made par-takers of the sacraments.

The eunuch, of whom I spake even now out of the Acts, as
he journeyed and saw water, he said to Philip: " See, here is Acts viii.
water; what letteth me to be baptized? Philip said unto him;
If thou believest with all thy heart, thou mayest. And he
answered and said, I believe that Jesus Christ is the Son of
God." Afterward immediately it followeth: " And they went
down both into the water, and he baptized him." The eunuch
(saith the evangelist) believed with all his heart, that is to
say, truly and without dissimulation. Now let us see what

[5 the first, not in Lat.]
[6 An error in all the editions for, *gathereth not*: quis non colligat,
Lat.]
[7 by the sacrament, not in Lat.]

the scripture saith concerning such a faith. St John, the
apostle and evangelist, saith : "Whosoever believeth that
Jesus is Christ, is born of God." He again saith : "Whosoever confesseth that Jesus is the Son of God, in him dwelleth
God, and he in God." Also Paul, that elect vessel and
doctor of the Gentiles, saith : "If thou shalt knowledge with
thy mouth the Lord Jesus, and shalt believe in thine heart
that God raised him from the dead, thou shalt be saved."
And again, St John saith in his epistle : "He that believeth
on the Son of God hath the witness in himself. And this is
the record, how that God hath given unto us eternal life, and
this life is in his Son. He that hath the Son hath life, and
he that hath not the Son hath not life." Briefly, of all these
things this we gather : the eunuch believed before he received baptism ; therefore, before he received baptism he was
born of God, in whom he dwelled, and God in him ; he was
just and acceptable [in] the sight of God ; and moreover, he
had also life in himself ; and therefore the baptism which followed did not give that to the eunuch which he had before ;
but it became unto him a testimony of the truth, and a seal of
the righteousness which came by faith[1] ; and therewithal to
assure unto him[2] the continuance and increase of God his[3]
gifts.

After the same manner we read of Cornelius the centurion in the same Acts of the Apostles ; that he, believing the
preaching of the apostle Peter, received the Holy Ghost also
in a visible shape, as the apostles did at Hierusalem in the day
of Pentecost ; and that Peter, when he knew that thing, said :
"Can any man forbid water, that these should not be baptized,
which have received the Holy Ghost as well as we ?" Forasmuch therefore as Cornelius with his household received the
Holy Ghost before they were baptized, it is manifest, that he
did not obtain the Holy Ghost as given first by baptism, or
with baptism. Again, we read in the Acts of the Apostles :
"They that gladly received the word of Peter were baptized." Therefore before they were baptized of Peter, they
had obtained the grace of God through faith.

For[4] why, I pray you, do we baptize our infants ? Is it

Margin notes:
1 John iv.
1 John iv.
Rom. x.
1 John v.
Acts xiii.
Acts ii.

[1 justitiæ fidei, Lat.]
[2 Rather render, for a continuation, &c.]
[3 God his, not in Lat.]   [4 Aut cur, Lat. : Or why.]

because they believe with their heart and confess with their mouth? I think not. Do we not therefore baptize them, because God hath commanded them to be brought unto him? because he hath promised, that he will be our God, and the God of our seed after us? to be short, because we believe that God, of his mere grace and mercy, in the blood of Jesus Christ, hath cleansed and adopted them, and appointed them to be heirs of eternal life? We therefore, baptizing infants for these causes, do abundantly testify, that there is not first given unto them in baptism, but that there is sealed and confirmed which they had before.

Let us also join unto these things a testimony of the Supper of the Lord. The apostle, teaching how the godly should prepare themselves to come to the Lord's table, saith: " Let a man prove himself, and so let him eat of this bread and drink 1 Cor. xi. of this cup." But to examine or prove signifieth to search, as much as lieth in man, the heart, or mind, and through diligent inquisition to sift one's conscience. And God is said to prove our hearts. And the same apostle willeth us " to prove what is the good and acceptable will of God." But this proof cannot be without knowledge and judgment; Rom. xii. and the knowledge and judgment of Christians is faith: therefore whosoever proveth himself before he come to the supper hath faith ; if he hath faith, then he wanteth not those things that are coupled with faith ; and therefore in the supper those heavenly benefits are not first received, but thanks are given for those that are received[5]. I have hereby shewed and proved, I suppose, that sacraments do not confer grace.

They object, I know well enough, against these things, (who are persuaded that sacraments give grace, and contain To evacuate the sacra- included within them the things signified,) that we do evacuate ments, and and make of none effect the sacraments ; and that we teach of a lie. that the faithful receive in them, or by them, nothing but bare water, and bare bread and wine ; and that by that means God by us is accused of falsehood and lying.

We briefly answer: If they set void or empty things (as I may so say) against full things, so as they be void or empty which have not the things themselves included in them; truly,

[5 pro acceptis, Lat. : for them as received.]

I had rather confess them to be void than full. But if they call them void or empty, and mean profane or unholy things, that is to say, which differ nothing from profane signs; if by bare they understand things of no force; we openly profess, that we have sacraments which are holy, and not profane; effectual, and not without force; garnished from above, not naked; and therefore full, not void or empty. For they are holy things and not profane, because they are instituted of God, and for godly men, not for profane persons. They are effectual, and not without force: for in the church with the godly and faithful they work the same effect and end whereunto they are ordained[1] of God; whereof more hereafter. They are also worthily said to be beautified and adorned by God, and not bare things, which have the word of God itself, wherewith they are most beautifully adorned. And therefore also they are full, and not empty sacraments, because they have those things which make a perfect sacrament.

Sacraments are holy, and not profane things. We will repeat here the parables, or similitudes (which above also, entreating of consecration, for the most part we did allege), to the intent to give more clear light unto this treatise. All the while that wax, for confirmation and witness' sake, is not hanged on letters patents or other public instruments, it is common, void, and bare wax; that is to say, nothing else but wax: but when it is sealed and fastened to those public instruments, it is now neither void nor bare wax; for it is called the testimony of the truth[2]. The arms of a prince or of any commonwealth, if it be painted in a window or on a wall, it is a bare sign: but if the same be fastened to writings or set to letters, there is great difference between this and the other. For now it declareth and witnesseth the will of the prince, or commonwealth; therefore it hath this estimation among all men, that whoso defaceth it, or, contrary to the will of the prince and commonweal, doth set it to any other charter, is reputed guilty of counterfeiting and of high treason. A stone, when as yet it is not set for a mark or bound of fields, it is a bare and void, that is to say, a common stone, which to tread under foot, or to remove out of his place, is no offence: but being set to part the

[1 So also ed. 1584: but 1577, were ordained.]
[2 Rather, and the truth: et veritas, Lat.]

bounds of fields, it is no more a bare and void[3] stone, but a witness of lawful division and just possession; which to move out of his place is accounted an heinous offence. And therefore water, bread, and wine, without the institution and use of the sacrament, are nothing else but water, bread, and wine: but being used in the celebration of the sacrament, they differ very far from that they were before; and are sacraments signed of Christ by his word, ordained[4] for the salvation of the faithful.

Therefore they that are partakers of the sacraments do not receive nothing, as these say, unless the institution of God be to be esteemed as nothing. He instituted sacraments to be testimonies of his grace, and seals of the truth of his promises: which thing I will anon declare more at large. Therefore, as God is true and cannot lie, so the seals of his promises are most true. He hath promised that he will be ours, and that in Christ he will communicate himself unto us with all his gifts: he therefore of a certainty sheweth himself such an one, and doth communicate himself unto us; although he do it not now first of all when we receive the sacraments, as if he should pour out of himself[5] into us by them, as it were by conduit pipes, and were included in them as in vessels. For immediately upon the beginning of the world he promised his grace unto us; as soon as we first believed, he began to shew himself such an one unto us, and doth shew himself more and more through the whole course of life[6]: we receive him and comprehend him spiritually and by faith. Therefore, when we are partakers of the sacraments, he proceedeth to communicate himself unto us after a special manner, that is to say, proper unto sacraments; and so we, which before were made partakers of Christ, do continue and strengthen that communion or fellowship spiritually and by faith in the celebration of the sacraments, outwardly sealing the same unto ourselves by the signs[7].

Now, who will hereafter say, that they which think thus of the sacraments, and are by this faith partakers of them,

[3 So also ed.1584: but 1577, a void or bare: vacuus aut nudus,Lat.]
[4 So also ed. 1584: but 1577, and ordained: et instituta, Lat.]
[5 Rather, pour out himself.]
[6 So also ed. 1584: but 1577, our life.]
[7 Rather, the signs sealing the same unto us by things sensible.]

have nothing but empty shews, and receive nothing in them; albeit we neither include grace in the signs, neither derive it from them? But if any man have any other opinion of God and his ordinances, that shall no more be falsehood in God[1], or accuse him of untruth, than if any one should charge a just man with a lie, because he performeth not that which he looked for; when in the meantime this man promised not the thing which he looked for; but he, through his corrupt and false opinion, hath dreamed that it was promised unto him. And thus far by occasion I have shewed what agreement and difference there is between the sacraments of the old and new Testament, and that our sacraments do neither confer nor contain grace.

Now we return to that which we began; I mean, to the principal ground of this disputation: that, forasmuch as we have taught what they do not work, so now at length we may set down what they work in very deed; that is to say, expounding what is the power, end, and lawful use of the sacrament[2], whereunto they are ordained of God. We handled indeed the place of the causes why they were instituted in the beginning of the sixth sermon. But now I will add other things which pertain to this purpose, and entreat of each thing by itself more fully and at large.

Sacraments are witnesses of the truth.

The chief end of sacraments is this; that they are testimonies to confirm the truth, by which the Lord in his church even visibly doth testify, that the things now uttered by preaching of the gospel, and by the promises assured to the faithful from the beginning of the world, are in every point so brought to pass, and are so certainly true, as they are declared and promised in the word of truth. Even so baptism is the heavenly and public witness in the church of Christ, whereby the Lord testifieth, that it is he which receiveth men freely into favour, and which cleanseth from all blemishes, and, to be short, maketh us partakers and heirs of all his goodness. For after the same manner circumcision in times past was a public and heavenly testimony, that it is God that purgeth and adopteth us[3]. For therefore Moses saith, Deut. xxx.: "The Lord thy God will circumcise thine heart, and the heart of thy seed, that thou mayest love the Lord thy God

[1 Deo fraudi fuerit, Lat.]
[2 sacramentorum, Lat.]   [3 us, not in Lat.]

with all thy heart," &c. After the selfsame manner the
Lord himself, instituting the holy supper in his church, by the
present signs doth openly bear witness, that his body was
certainly given for us, and his blood truly shed for the remission of our sins; that he also is that living food, that feedeth
us to eternal life. Wherefore we read in Chrysostom his
83rd Homily upon Matthew these words: "As in the old
law, so in the same manner hath he here left with us a
memory of the mysteries, stopping and bridling hereby the
mouths of heretics. For when they say, Whereby appeareth
it that Christ was offered? and many other mysteries; then
we, alleging these things, do thereby stop their mouths. For
if Jesus be not dead, whose representation or sign is this sacrifice[4]?" Thus far he. You perceive, I suppose, how this
writer doth bring against heretics the sacrament[5] of the supper for the testimony of truth, that is to say, of the Lord's
true death. Wherefore as the gospel is called a witness, and
the preachers of the gospel witnesses; even so we call sacraments witnesses of the same truth, which, though they be dumb,
yet nevertheless are visible; after which name[6] St Augustine
calleth them "visible words[7]." For the preaching of the
gospel, consisting of words heard with the ears, is a speaking
witness; but sacraments, which consist of signs and are seen
with the eyes, are speechless witnesses, and, as it were, remnants and remembrances of the preaching of the gospel.

The gospel is a witness.

Yea, sacraments were instituted by God to that end, that
they might visibly confirm[8] unto us the ready good will of God
toward us, and also[9] the preaching of the gospel, and all the
promises of life and salvation; and that they should be, as it
were, seals set and fixed to the gospel and promises made by
God, which might testify and confirm that faith in Christ is

Sacraments do visibly confirm the good will of God to us-ward.

[4 Ὥσπερ οὖν ἐπὶ τῶν Ἰουδαίων, οὕτω καὶ ἐνταῦθα τῆς εὐεργεσίας
ἐγκατέδησε τὸ μνημόσυνον τῷ μυστηρίῳ· κἀντεῦθεν ἐμφράττων τῶν αἱρε-
τικῶν τὰ στόματα· ὅταν γὰρ λέγωσι, πόθεν δῆλον ὅτι ἐτύθη ὁ Χριστός;
μετὰ τῶν ἄλλων, καὶ ἀπὸ τῶν μυστηρίων αὐτοὺς ἐπιστομίζομεν. Εἰ γὰρ
μὴ ἀπέθανεν ὁ Ἰησοῦς, τίνος σύμβολα τὰ τελούμενα;—Chrysost. Hom. in
Matth. LXXXII. (al. LXXXIII.) Tom. VII. p. 783. Par. 1727.)

[5 symbolum, Lat.]　　[6 quo nomine, Lat.: on which account.]

[7 Quid sunt aliud quæque corporalia sacramenta, nisi quædam
quasi verba visibilia?—Aug. contra Faust. Man. Lib. XIX. cap. 16. Opp.
Tom. VI. fol. 72. col. 3. Par. 1531.]

[8 obsignent, Lat.]　　　　　　[9 adeoque, Lat.: and so.]

true righteousness.   That which I have said I will confirm
by the writings of the apostles.   But I taught a little before,
that there is all one ground of the sacraments of the old
Testament and of the new, a few things only excepted; so
that now by very good right, by the comparing of both together we may estimate and utter what the force[1] and use
of our sacraments is.   Paul therefore to the Romans, fourth

Rom. iv.

chapter, saith : " We say that faith was imputed to Abraham
for righteousness.   How was it then imputed ?   When he was
circumcised, or when he was uncircumcised ?   Not when he
was circumcised, but when he was uncircumcised : after he received the sign of circumcision, as the seal of the righteousness
of the faith which he had when he was uncircumcised, that he
should be the father of all them that believe, not being circumcised, that righteousness might be imputed unto them also ;
and the father of circumcision, not unto them only which are
of the circumcised, but unto them also that walk in the steps
of the faith of our father Abraham, which he had when he
was uncircumcised."   All these are Paul's words.   Among
which, first of all, some words are meet[2] to be expounded: then
we must seek after the sense and meaning of the apostle's
words : and last of all we must apply them to our purpose
touching the sacrament.

Sacraments
are seals, and
whereunto
seals do
serve.

The apostle here useth two words, that is to say, the
sign and the seal.   *Signum*, the word sign, is more general
and stretcheth very far ; but a seal[3] is a word that properly
belongeth unto sacraments, which are seals and confirmations.
For all signs seal not ; for some by signification only do
accomplish their duty ; but σφραγίζειν properly is, to seal
for assurance and confirmation sake of faith or credit : wherefore σφραγίς is a seal which is set to, to keep and confirm our faith and promise, and to be without all danger of
deceit.   And here, as elsewhere very often, the Lord doth imitate the manner of men.   For we men are wont, by setting to
our seals, to confirm our writings, covenants, and faithful promises, which we before had made by word.   And that this
hath always been the cause of the instituting and use of seals,
appeareth plainly by these testimonies of the scriptures.   When
the children of Israel under Ezra made a covenant with the

[1 finem, Lat. omitted: end.]
[2 videntur, Lat.]   [3 σφραγίς, omitted.]

Lord, by and by they set down their covenant in writing, and
seal the writing, to be a testimony of the truth; as in Nehem.
the ix. chap. And Hag. the ii. chapter thou mayest read: "I ^{Neh. ix.}
will take thee to my servant⁴, Zorobabel, thou son of Sala-
thiel," saith the Lord, "and will make thee as a sign or sealing ring; for I have chosen thee." As if he had said; All men
shall certainly learn, that in the son of Salathiel the continuance of the posterity of the Messias doth consist and remain⁵.
Thus writeth Jeremy, chap. xxii.: "As surely as I live, saith ^{Jer. xxii.}
the Lord, if Chonenias, the son of Jehoakim, king of Juda, were
the signet or seal on my right hand, yet will I pluck thee
thence." Which is as much as if he had said; Though thou
were he in whom I will keep my promises, yet shalt thou be
led captive into Babylon. To this agreeth that of Matthew
written of the Jews: "So they went, and made the sepulchre ^{Matth. xxvii.}
sure, and sealed the stone;" without doubt, against deceitful
practices; "they appointed a watch⁶." It appeareth therefore
by these testimonies whereto the use of seals serveth.

These things being thus declared, let us now diligently ^{The place of Paul,}
search out the counsel and meaning of the apostle's words. ^{Rom. iv. is expounded:}
Paul sheweth, that justification happeneth unto men by the ^{'And he received a sign}
power and virtue of no works, of no ceremonies or sacra- ^{of the circumcision,'}
ments, but by the only merit⁷ of Christ through faith. To ^{&c.}
prove this, he bringeth the example of Abraham, of whom the
scripture hath pronounced: "Abraham believed God, and it
was imputed unto him for righteousness." Thence he gathereth,
that Abraham was justified by faith; yea, that that was imputed unto him for righteousness. Where both by the word
or force of imputation, and by the whole sentence of Moses,
he doth most strongly reason, shewing that through grace
righteousness is imputed by faith. Whereunto he joineth
also a testimony out of David touching righteousness by
imputation. I handled that place in the first sermon of the
fourth decade⁸. Then he returneth again to the example of
Abraham, and applieth to his purpose that place alleged out of
Genesis, weighing the circumstances of the manner and time

[⁴ Rather, O my servant: serve mi, Lat.]
[⁵ propaganda Messiæ posteritas, Lat.]
[⁶ Rather, appointing also a watch.]
[⁷ beneficio, Lat.]
[⁸ See Vol. III. page 44, &c.]

of his justification[1], and saith: "How was it then imputed?
when he was circumcised, or when he was uncircumcised?
Not when he was circumcised, but when he was uncircumcised." Which things, verily, are plainer than that they
require any exposition. But because the Jew might object;
Why then, the institution and use of circumcision was of no
force, but void, unprofitable, and vain; for if Abraham
were justified before he was circumcised, what could circumcision profit him further? and if it brought nothing, surely
it was superfluous and unprofitable: Paul, preventing that
objection, maketh answer: "And he received," saith he, "the
sign of circumcision, as the seal of the righteousness of faith,
&c." Circumcision, saith he, was neither void nor unprofitable. For albeit it justify not, neither cleanse, nor apply the
gifts of God; yet it followeth not therefore that there is no
further use of it: for it hath another end. For he received
the sign of circumcision for a certain seal of the righteousness of faith; that is to say, God instituted circumcision, that
it should be a seal to ratify and confirm, yea, and also[2] visibly
to testify, that faith is righteousness, and that men are justified
through faith; I say, in such sort as faith is also imputed
unto them for righteousness, as it was imputed unto Abraham. For it followeth: "That he might be the father of all
that believe, though they be not circumcised, that righteousness might be imputed unto them also;" and so forth. And
although these things be more clear than the daylight, yet I
will endeavour further to open the same by a parable. For
suppose that a king, of his favour and mere liberality, would
entertain[3] some servant into his court, yea, and[2] make him
partaker of all his goods; and moreover would extend this
benefit unto the children and posterity also of him whom he
had adopted; and would immediately command, that that
covenant[4], privilege, and favour, granted by lively words,
should also be put in writing, which he might confirm by
setting to his seal; to the end that might be to his posterity
a sure testimony against all gainsayers, that the same favour
and adoption doth pertain to them also, and that the prince
would continue his good and favourable kindness unto the
posterity of him whom he had adopted, if they also continue

The matter is made plain by a parable.

[1 of his justification, not in Lat.]   [2 adeoque, Lat.: and so.]
[3 recipere, Lat.]   [4 transactio, Lat.]

faithful unto their prince. For even after the same manner Almighty God, the King of kings, and most bountiful of all princes, freely and not by any merit of ours going before, chooseth Abraham, upon whom he bestoweth innumerable benefits, and unto whom he offereth a covenant and participation of all goodness; and not unto him only, but to all his posterity also, saying: "I, the Almighty[5] God, will be thy God, and the God of thy seed after thee; I will bless thee and thy seed; and in thy seed shall all the nations of the earth be blessed." He sanctified also this privilege, confirming it with an oath; and by and by commandeth to deliver the same unto their children, as it were from hand to hand, instead of writing; and afterward willeth his servants the prophets to set it down in writing; and last of all he himself, by instituting circumcision, now as it were setting to his seal to the letters patents, or charter, would have it confirmed and ratified to them that should come after, to the end they might certainly know that that also pertained unto them.

Where notwithstanding it seemeth this must not be dissembled of us, that sacraments have a greater and more effectual force than any sealed charters can have. For privileges, which princes give, are written in parchment, and their seals are set to parchment written; but God imprinteth his seal into the very bodies of those that are his. For he caused circumcision to be on the privy member of man, whereby issue is raised, increased, and continued; that, as a mark printed in the very bodies, it might more than seal and witness, that the blessing and partaking of all good things pertaineth to the circumcised, if they abide faithful to the Lord God entered into league with men. And therefore very significantly is circumcision called of Paul, not "the seal of righteousness," but, "the seal of righteousness of faith;" that is, a ratifying and assurance that faith is righteousness, that it is faith whereby we are justified, that righteousness is due to them that believe, that God assuredly will bless the faithful and impute faith unto them for righteousness, as he also imputed faith unto Abraham.

Sacraments have a more effectual force than any sealed charters.

Now since sacraments have the like reason, we may apply these things to our sacraments. Christ therefore, the

How baptism sealeth.

[5 omnisufficientia, Lat. See Vol. III. page 135.]

anointed of the Lord, after he had by guiltless[1] and undeserved death redeemed the world from the power of Satan, and being now ready to ascend into heaven to the Father, he

Mark xvi. called his disciples about him, and said: " Go into the whole world, and preach the gospel to all creatures; he that shall believe and be baptized, &c." The preaching of the gospel doth lay open and abroad the great, the precious, the healthful, the lively, the bountiful, the royal, and divine privilege, that of the children of the devil we are made the children of God, the heirs (I say) of God, and joint-heirs with Christ, who by the shedding of his blood hath purchased for us this inestimable salvation. From this grace of God none is excluded, but he which through disobedience, by his own corruption and fault, doth exclude himself. For touching the children and infants of the believers, the Lord in the gospel pronounceth,

Mark x. saying: " Suffer the young children to come unto me, and forbid them not; for of such is the kingdom of God." And

Matth. xviii. again: " Verily I say unto you, Except ye turn, and become as little children, ye shall not enter into the kingdom of heaven. Who shall receive such a little child in my name, receiveth me. Take heed that ye despise not one of these little ones; for I say unto you, that in heaven their angels do always behold the face of my Father which is in heaven." Neither is it likely, now Christ is come, that God is more unmerciful than he was before he came into the world. But then he said: " I will be thy God, and the God of thy seed after thee." That therefore is now of more force, since the Lord is come to seek and save that which was lost; and, to be short, to pour forth most liberally his grace and good gifts upon all flesh. Wherefore that royal, ample, and divine privilege, is first by the very preaching of our Lord Christ, and then by the doctrine of his apostles, revealed unto the world; and afterward, the Lord so commanding, the same privilege was set down of the apostles and evangelists in writing. Now, the Lord himself added this sacrament[2], as a sign and seal, unto his preaching and to the scripture, ordaining baptism in the place of circumcision, the which, because it was a bloody thing and, to conclude[3], a sign of the

[1 So also ed. 1584: but 1577, his guiltless.]
[2 Rather, a sacrament.]
[3 denique, Lat.]

blessed seed which was to come, which then was revealed, ought to be abrogated. And baptism itself also, succeeding circumcision, is also a seal of the righteousness of faith, an evidence and sealed charter [4], that God doth assuredly cleanse us and make us heirs of eternal life; and that the whole grace of baptism [5] pertaineth to them that are baptized, if they stand stedfast in true faith.

But thou wilt say, the infants of Christians, which are to be baptized, believe not. I grant. No more did the infants of the Jews believe; which nevertheless were circumcised, and were in league with God, and made partakers of all good gifts: so that true godliness biddeth us attribute the same to our infants. When the offspring of the Jews waxed in age and did wickedly transgress, they fell from the covenant of God. So likewise the infants of the Christians, when they come to age and commit wickedness, do fall from the grace of the gospel: yet are they received again by faithful repentance into the same grace from whence they fell.

Infants which believe not are baptized.

But to our purpose. Baptism, the seal of the righteousness of faith, is not set to parchment, or to the writing of the gospel; but it is applied to the very bodies of the children of God, and is as it were marked and imprinted in them. For we are wholly dipped with our bodies, or wholly sprinkled with the water of baptism: which truly is a visible sealing, confirming that the true God is our God, which sanctifieth and purifieth; and that purification, and every good gift of God, is due unto us as the heirs of God. And to the setting forth of this matter pertaineth that evident place of Paul, which in the Epistle to the Galatians is thus read: "For ye are all the children of God by faith in Christ Jesus. For all ye that are baptized have put on Christ." And so forth.

The supper of the Lord hath the like reason, which also is a seal of the righteousness of faith. For the Son of God died; he by his death redeemed the believers; also his body and blood is our meat and drink unto eternal life. And truly, this singular and excellent privilege, given unto the faithful, is declared and set down in writing by the apostles: but it is consecrated and sealed of the Lord himself by the sacrament of his body and blood; whereby he sealeth us an assurance,

How the Lord's supper is a seal of the righteousness of faith.

[4 Rather, and charter, sealing that, &c.]
[5 Rather, of the gospel: evangelii, Lat.]

21—2

that we are justified by faith in the death of Christ, and that all the good gifts of Christ are communicated unto us, and that we are fed and strengthened by Christ. Moreover, that the sealing might be the more lively, he setteth not the seal to written parchment, but it is brought and also given to be eaten of our bodies; that we might have a witness within ourselves, that Christ with all his gifts is wholly ours, if we persevere in

John vi. faith. For the Lord himself in the gospel saith: "He that eateth me shall live by the means of me." But he eateth which believeth. For in the same place the Lord saith: "I am the bread of life; he that cometh to me shall not hunger, and he that believeth in me shall never thirst."

Hereby we gather the sum of the whole matter; that the sacraments do seal up the promises of God and the gospel; and that therefore so often mention is made in the church of evidences or letters patents, or charters, and seals of the preaching of the gospel and the promises of God; and that the whole mystery of our salvation is renewed and continued, as oft as those actions, instituted of God, (I mean sacraments,) are celebrated in the church.

Hitherto I think doth that belong, which the faithful minister of Christ, Zuinglius, upon the sacraments hath de-

Zuinglius of the sacraments, which certify and bear witness. livered in these words: "Sacraments bear witness of a thing that hath been done. For all laws, customs, and ordinances, do shew their authors and beginnings. Therefore baptism, since it setteth forth in signification the death and resurrection of Christ, it must needs be that those things were done indeed[1]." These words are to be found *In Expositione Fidei ad Regem Christianum.* The same Zuinglius, *ad Principes Germaniæ contra Eggium,* saith: "When that nobleman, taking his journey into a far country, distributing bread and wine, did far more lively and peculiarly give himself unto us, when he said, ' This is my body,' than if he had said, This is a token or sign of my body; although he took away his natural body and carried it into heaven. Yet nevertheless by these words, in that appertaineth to faith and grace, he giveth him-

[1 Testimonium rei gestæ præbent (sacramenta). Universæ enim leges, mores, ac instituta, auctores suos initiaque prædicant. Baptismus ergo cum Christi mortem ac resurrectionem significando prædicat, eas vere gestas esse oportet.—Zuingl. Christ. Fid. præd. Expos. Opp. Tom. II. fol. 555. Tigur.]

self wholly, as if he had said : Now I go to die for you, and
after a while will wholly depart from hence; but I will not
have you doubt of my love and care to you-ward.　How
much soever I am, I am altogether yours.　In witness whereof,
I commend unto you a sign of this my betraying and testament, to the intent you might maintain the memory of me
and of my benefits : that when ye see this bread and this cup
ministered unto you in the supper of my remembrance, ye
may be no otherwise mindful of me, that is, that I delivered
up myself for you, than if you should see me with your eyes
face to face, as ye now see me both to eat with you, and by
and bye shall see me to be led from you to die for you[2]."
Hitherto I have recited Zuinglius his words, and anon I will
rehearse other words of his again : not that I stay myself upon
them, or upon any testimonies of man ; but that it may be
made manifest, that this man did not (as some have falsely
thought) contemn the sacraments.

　　In the meanwhile, we acknowledge these testimonies of The Holy
the holy scripture : "And God it is which stablisheth us properly
with you in Christ, and hath anointed us : which hath also seal.
sealed us, and hath given the earnest of the Spirit in our
hearts." 2 Cor. i.　And also : "After ye believed, ye were
sealed with the holy Spirit of promise, which is the earnest
of our inheritance, unto the redemption of the purchased possession, unto the praise of his glory." Ephes. i. verse 13.　And
again : "Grieve not the holy Spirit of God, by whom ye are
sealed unto the day of redemption." Ephes. iv.

[2 Sic in eucharistia, cum homo ille nobilis abiturus esset in
regionem longinquam, panem ac vinum præbens, longe vividius ac
peculiarius sese nobis dabat cum diceret, Hoc est corpus meum, quam
si dixisset, Hoc est symbolum corporis mei: etiamsi naturale corpus
suum ablaturus ac cœlo illaturus esset.　Nihilo tamen minus sese
totum, quod ad fidem et gratiam pertinet, his verbis donat, quasi
diceret, Nunc in mortem pro vobis eo, paulo post ex integro hinc
migraturus.　At nolo de amore et cura in vos mea ambigatis.　Totus
vester sum, quantus quantus sum.　In cujus rci testimonium, hujus
meæ traditionis ac testamenti symbolum vobis commendo, quo memoriam mei meorumque beneficiorum excitetis; ut cum vobis hunc
panem et hunc calicem exhiberi videatis in memorali cœna, non aliter
sitis mei memores, quod scilicet me pro vobis tradiderim, quam si
videritis me coram, quemadmodum nunc videtis, et vobiscum convivari,
et mox ad supplicium pro vobis a vobis rapi.—Id. ibid. Tom. II. fol.
549.]

We acknowledge the truth of God to be sufficiently sound, true, and certain of itself; neither can we from elsewhere have a better confirmation than out of it[1]. For if[2] our mind be not confirmed on every side, it wavereth. God therefore frameth himself according to our weakness, and by his sacraments, as much as may be, doth as it were uphold us; yet so, that we refer all the benefit of our confirmation to the Spirit itself and to his operation, rather than to the element. Wherefore, as we attribute confirmation to doctrine and to teachers, even so do we sealing to the sacraments. We read in the Acts of the Apostles, chapter xiv. and xviii.: "The apostles returned and strengthened the disciples' souls again, and exhorted them to continue in the faith." Again, in the first to the Thess. iii.: "We have sent (saith Paul) Timotheus, our brother and minister of God, to confirm or stablish you, and to comfort you concerning your faith." Nevertheless, unless the inward force of the Spirit do draw and quicken the hearts of the hearers, the outward persuasion of the teacher, though it be never so forcible and vehement, shall nothing avail: but if the Holy Spirit do shew forth his might, and work with the word of the preacher, the souls of the hearers are most mightily strengthened. And so it standeth with the mystery of the sacrament. For if the inward anointing and sealing of the Holy Ghost be wanting, the outward action will be counted but a toy to the unbelievers, neither worketh the sealing of the sacraments anything at all; but when faith, the gift of the Holy Ghost, goeth before, the sealing of the sacraments is very strong and sure. Some also have said very well: If our minds be destitute of the Holy Ghost, the sacraments do no more profit us, than it doth a blind man to look upon the bright beams of the sun. But if our eyes be opened through the illumination of the Spirit, they are wonderfully delighted with the heavenly sight of the sacraments[3]. And Zuinglius, in *Libello ad Principes Germaniæ*, saith: "It doth not offend us, though all those things which the Holy Ghost worketh be referred to the external sacrament, as long as we understand them to be spoken figuratively, as the fathers spake[4]." Thus saith he.

[1 ex seipsa, Lat.]   [2 Rather, But if. Nisi vero, Lat.]
[3 Calvin. Instit. Lib. IV. cap. 14. § 9. Opp. Tom. IX. p. 344. Amstel. 1667.]
[4 Nos non offendit, ut etiamsi universa quæ Spiritus operatur

And although sacraments seal not the promises to the *The sacraments seal nothing to the unbelievers.* unbelievers, because they mistrust them; yet nevertheless the sacraments were instituted of God that they might seal. The wicked and ungodly person receiveth not the doctrine of the gospel; yet no man therefore doth gather, that this doctrine was not instituted of God to teach. Some one there is that will not give credit to a sealed charter; yet doth it not therefore follow, that the sealed charter serveth not to assure or confirm one's faith. Therefore since the doctrine of the gospel worketh nothing in him that is obstinate and rebellious; since the sacraments do nothing move him that is profane and unholy, neither profit the wicked by any manner means; that cometh not to pass through him that did institute them, or through the word and sacraments[5], but through the default of the unbeliever. In the meantime, of themselves they are instituted to profit and to seal, and to have their holy use and end in the holy. And thus much have I said of the principal virtue of sacraments; that they be testimonies of God's truth and of his good will toward us, and are seals of all the promises of the gospel; sealing and assuring us that faith is righteousness, and that all the good gifts of Christ pertain to them that believe.

There is also another end and use of sacramental signs; *Sacraments represent things.* that is to say, that they signify, and in signifying do represent: which were superfluous to prove by many testimonies, since it is most manifest to all men, at least by that which we spake before. Now to signify is to shew, and by signs and tokens to declare and point out any thing. But to represent doth not signify (as some dream) to bring, to give, or make that now again corporally present which sometime was taken away; but to resemble it in likeness and by a certain imitation, and to call it back again to mind, and to set it as it were before our eyes. For we say that a son doth represent or resemble his father, when after a sort he expresseth his father in favour and likeness of manners; so that he which seeth him may verily think, that he seeth his father as it were present.

And after this manner do sacraments stir up and help our *Sacraments do stir up and help faith.*

externo sacramento referantur, dummodo symbolice dicta, quomodo patres locuti sunt, intelligamus.—Zuing. Opp. Tom. II. fol. 549.]

[5 Rather, by any fault of him, &c. or of the word and sacraments.]

faith, while we see outwardly before our eyes that which stirreth up the mind, worketh in us[1] and warneth us of our
duty : yea, that very thing, which we awhile before comprehended in our mind, is now after a sort visibly offered to our
senses, in a similitude, parable, type, or figure, to be viewed
and weighed in our mind, that mutually they might help one
another.   The similitude, therefore, or analogy of the sign to
the thing signified is here by the way to be considered.

Of the ana-
logy in bap-
tism.

I told you before[2], that analogy is an aptness, proportion,
and a certain convenience of the sign to the thing signified, so
that this may be seen in that as in a looking-glass. The matter shall be made manifest by examples.

The bountiful and gracious Lord of his mere mercy receiveth mankind into the partaking of all his good gifts and
graces, and adopteth the faithful, that now they be not only
joined in league with God, but also the children of God; which
thing by the holy action of baptism, being instead of the sign
or the very sign itself, is most evidently by representation laid
before the eyes of all men.   For the minister of God standeth
at the holy font, to whom the infant is offered to be baptized ;
whom he receiveth and baptizeth into the name, or in the
name, of the Father, and of the Son, and of the Holy Ghost:
for we may find both "into the name," and " in the name."
So that[3] to be baptized "into the name of the Lord," is to be
sealed into his virtue and power (for the name of the Lord
signifieth power), into the favour, mercy, and protection of
God ; yea, to be graffed, and as it were to be fastened, to be
dedicated, and to be incorporated into God.   To be baptized
"in the name of the Lord," is by the commandment or
authority of God to be baptized; I mean, by the commission
or appointment of God the Father, the Son, and the Holy
Ghost, to be received into the company of the children of
God, and to be counted of God's household ; that they which
are baptized are, and be called, Christians, and be named
with the name of God, being called the children of God the
Father, &c.   His speech therefore doth somewhat resemble
that which we read elsewhere, that " the name of God was
called upon over some one[4];" which is in a manner as if we

[1 excitat, Lat.]

[2 See above, page 244.]

[3 Porro, Lat.: Furthermore.]

[4 See Vol. III. page 205.]

should say, that one is called by the name of God, that is, to be called "the servant and son of God." They therefore which before by grace invisibly are received of God into the society of God, those selfsame are visibly now by baptism admitted[5] into the selfsame household of God by the minister of God, and therefore at that time also receive their name[6], that they may always remember that in baptism they gave up their names to Christ, and in like manner also received a name. After this manner, by a most apt analogy, the very sign resembleth the thing signified. To be short, baptism is done by water; and water in men's matters hath a double use: for it cleanseth filth, and, as it were, reneweth man; also it quencheth thirst, and cooleth him that is in a heat. So also it representeth the grace of God, when it cleanseth[7] his faithful ones from their sins, regenerateth and refresheth us with his Spirit. Beside this, the minister of Christ sprinkleth, or rather poureth in[8], water; or, being dipped, taketh them out of the water: whereby it is signified, that God very bountifully bestoweth his gifts upon his faithful ones; it signifieth also that we are buried with Christ into his death, and are raised again with him into newness of life. Pharaoh was drowned in the gulf of the Red sea, but the people of God passed through it safe. For our old Adam must be drowned and extinguished; but our new Adam day by day must be quickened, and rise up again (out of the water). Therefore is the mortification and vivification of Christians very excellently represented by baptism.

To give and take names in baptism.

Now in the Lord's supper bread and wine represent the very body and blood of Christ. The reason hereof is this. As bread nourisheth and strengtheneth man, and giveth him ability to labour; so the body of Christ, eaten by faith, feedeth and satisfieth the soul of man, and furnisheth the whole man to all duties of godliness. As wine is drink to the thirsty, and maketh merry the hearts of men; so the blood of our Lord Jesus, drunken by faith, doth quench the thirst of the burning conscience, and filleth the hearts of the faithful with unspeakable joy. But[9] in the action of the supper the bread of the Lord is broken, the wine is poured out. For

Of the analogy in the supper.

[5 inscribuntur, Lat.]   [6 a name: their, not in Lat.]
[7 Rather, he cleanseth.]   [8 Rather, poureth on.]
[9 Rather, Therefore. Ergo, Lat.]

the body of our Saviour was broken, that is, by all means afflicted, and his blood gushed and flowed plentifully out of his gaping wounds. And we ourselves truly do break with our own hands the bread of the Lord; for we ourselves are in fault that he was torn and tormented. Our sins wounded him, and we ourselves crucified him; that is to say, he was crucified for us, that by his death he might deliver us from death. Furthermore, we take the bread into our hands, we likewise take the cup into our hands, because he said, " Take ye, eat ye ; take ye, and divide it among you." Neither do we lay them aside or hide them, neither do we[1] give them forthwith to others : but when we have received them, we eat and drink them, swallowing them down into our bodies; then afterward, we do communicate and offer them to other. For they, which lawfully celebrate the Lord's supper, do not only believe that Christ suffered, or that he suffereth, for other and not for them ; but they believe that Christ suffered for themselves ; they believe that Christ doth, and as it were, hath already communicated all his gifts most liberally unto them. Therefore, as the sustenance of bread and wine, passing into the bowels, is changed into the substance of man's body ; even so Christ, being eaten of the godly by faith, is united unto them by his Spirit; so that they are one with Christ, and he one with them. And as meat plentifully prepared, daintily dressed, and only seen upon the table, doth not asswage hunger; so, if thou hear Christ reverently[2] preached unto thee, and dost not believe that Christ with all his good gifts is thine, neither the word though reverently preached, nor yet the board though abundantly stored, do profit thee anything. And it maketh much to the reconciling, renewing, and maintaining of friendship, that we are all partakers of one bread, that we offer bread to our brethren, and that we drink of the cup which we receive at our brethren's hand. For upon no other cause the ancient fathers seem to call the supper

Synaxis, communion.

synaxis, a communion. But of that we will speak somewhat elsewhere. And this much have I brought for example sake touching the analogy of the sign and thing signified, and would say more, but that I trust to them that be diligent this is sufficient; for I have ministered occasion to think upon, and to find out more and greater things.

[1 modo, Lat. omitted : only.]   [2 magnifico, Lat.]

By this short treatise touching the analogy I think it is How the sacraments do stir up faith. plain, that[3] sacraments stir up and help the faith of the godly. For whiles our mind comprehendeth and considereth the benefits of God, Christ his blessing, our redemption, and other his good gifts; while it enjoyeth them with great pleasure of the spirit; whiles in them it is glad and rejoiceth; sacraments are now also outwardly given, which do visibly represent those things to our eyes, and as it were make them to enter into all our senses[4], which the mind inwardly comprehendeth, considereth, and meditateth upon. For because the whole action, which consisteth of the words and the rite or ceremony, is counted with the sign; our eyes see the signs and all things which are done in the whole action of the signs; all which do as it were speak: our ears hear the words and institutions of Christ: yea, our very touching and tasting, they also do feel and perceive how sweet and good the Lord is: so that now the whole man, as it were both body and soul, caught up into heaven, doth feel and perceive that his faith is stirred up and holpen, and, to be short, that the fruit of faith in Christ is passing sweet and comfortable. All these things have place in them that believe. In them that believe not the signs remain, as they are, without life. Therefore these things are brought to pass by the virtue or power of faith and of the Spirit working in the lawful use of the sacraments: without faith and the Holy Ghost they are not felt or perceived.

There is not unlike efficacy or force also in the preaching The efficacy or force in the preaching of God's word. of the word of God. For when this word by parables, by examples, and by description, is set forth to the hearers, if the Spirit and faith shine in their mind, by these they seem not only to hear things expounded, but to see them with their eyes. In consideration whereof I think Paul said: "O foolish Galatians, who hath bewitched you, that ye should not believe the truth; to whom Jesus Christ was described[5] before your eyes, and among you crucified?" For it is certain, that Christ was nowhere either described[6] or crucified among the Galatians. He speaketh therefore of his plainness of preaching the word, whereby things indeed are shewed; but

[3 Rather, how, in what way: quomodo, Lat.]
[4 Rather, which meeting our eyes, and so likewise all our senses, visibly represent those things, which the mind, &c.]
[5 depictus, Lat.: Erasmus' rendering.]　　　　[6 pictum, Lat.]

yet with such force and efficacy, as if they were in a manner
laid before their eyes. There is the same reason also in
sacraments, which for that cause were called of them of old
" visible words."

Zuinglius of the sacraments upholding faith. Of these things in this manner entreateth Zuinglius in
his book *Ad Principes Germaniæ contra Eggium*, saying :
" Doth not a faithful man desire, when he feeleth his faith to
fall[1], to be upholden and restored to his place? And where
in the whole world shall he hope to find that more conveniently, than in the very actions of the sacraments, so much
as belongeth to all sensible things? For let it be, that all
creatures allure and provoke us to the contemplation or beholding of God's majesty; yet all that their allurement or
provoking is dumb: but in the sacraments there is a lively
provoking and speaking allurement. For the Lord speaketh,
and the elements also speak ; and they speak and persuade
that to our senses, which the word and Spirit speaketh to our
mind. Howbeit, hitherto all these visible things are nothing,
unless the sanctification of the Spirit go before[2]." These
things he handleth more at large, first in his annotations upon
the 27. cap. of Jeremy[3]; and afterward, *In Expositione Fidei
ad regem Christianum*[4].

Furthermore, we read that St Augustine, disputing against
the Manichees, *Lib.* XIX. *contra Faustum, cap.* 11, said :
"Men cannot be gathered together into any name of religion,
either true or false, unless they be knit together in some
fellowship of visible signs or sacraments, &c.[5]" We acknow-

---

[1 So also ed. 1584: but 1577, like to fall.]

[2 Nonne cupit (fidelis), ubi fidem labi senserit, fulciri et in locum
restitui ? Id autem ubi gentium commodius, quam in ipsa sacramentorum actione inventurum sperare poterit, quantum ad omnia
sensibilia attinet ? Esto enim, omnes creaturæ invitent nos ad numinis contemplationem; at omnis ea invitatio muta est: in sacramentis vero viva et loquens est invitatio. Loquitur enim Dominus,
loquuntur et elementa : atque idem loquuntur et suadent sensibus,
quod menti sermo et Spiritus. Adhuc tamen hæc visibilia omnia
nihil sunt, ni invisibilis sanctificatio Spiritus præcedat.—Zuing. Opp.
Tom. II. fol. 547. Tigur.]

[3 Ibid. Tom. III. fol. 363.]   [4 Ibid. Tom. II. fol. 551.]

[5 In nullum autem nomen religionis seu verum seu falsum coagu-
lari homines possunt, nisi aliquo signaculorum vel sacramentorum
visibilium consortio colligentur.—August. contra Faust. Opp. Tom. VI.
fol. 72. col. 1. Par. 1531.]

ledge this opinion of St Augustine, fetched from the scriptures, doth teach[6] touching the sacraments, that we by them are gathered and knit together into the unity of the body of Christ, and are separated from all other religions, fellowships, and assemblies : and more too we are bound by them, as by an oath, to the true worship of one God, and unto one sincere religion; to the which we openly profess that we agree and give our consent with all them that are partakers of the sacraments.   Where this chiefly is to be marked; that the gathering or knitting together into the unity of the body of Christ hath a double respect.   For either we are joined with A conjunction with Christ, that he is in us, and we live in him ; or else we are Christ and with the coupled with all the members of Christ, to wit, with Christ's church. faithful servants, I mean, with the catholic church itself. Furthermore, we are knit together with Christ in spirit and faith.   But we are joined to the church, or to the members of Christ, by the unity of faith and of the Spirit, and by the bond of charity.   All which verily are the inward gifts of the Spirit, which freely are bestowed on us by the Lord only, not by any creatures, not by any elements. Sacraments therefore do visibly graff us into the fellowship of Christ and his saints, who were invisibly graffed by his grace before we were partakers of the sacraments : but by receiving of the sacraments, we do now open and make manifest of whose body we should be[7], and are, members; the Lord with his signs or marks by his minister also visibly marking us for his own household, and for his own people.   Which thing by the scriptures we will more fully open and make manifest.

They who in time past, by the force of the covenant, by By sacraments we are the grace, mercy, and promise of God, were the people of visibly gathered to-God, were by circumcision visibly gathered together into one gether into one religion, church, and knit together into one body.   For the apostle and distinguished from St Paul saith unto the Ephesians : " Wherefore remember, Eph. ii. that ye being in time passed gentiles in the flesh, called un-circumcision of them which are called circumcision in the flesh made with hands; that at that time, I say, ye were without Christ, and were aliants from the commonwealth of Israel, and strangers from the covenant of promise, &c." Whereby

[6 So also ed. 1584: but 1577, rightly, We acknowledging this opinion, &c. do teach touching, &c.]

[7 So also ed. 1584: but 1577, we would be : esse velimus, Lat.]

it is also easily understood, how the Jews by circumcision were distinguished from other religions and fellowships, and that circumcision in another place for this cause is put for them that are circumcised, and why the name of uncircumcised was reproachful: for those that were uncircumcised were counted for ungodly and unclean persons, that had no fellowship, nor part, or inheritance, with God and his saints. Of baptism, which was ordained in the stead of circumcision, something is spoken in my former sermons. And also the apostle setteth it out most plainly: "As the body," saith he, "is one, and hath many members, and all the members of the body, which is one, though they be many, yet are but one body; even so is Christ. For by one Spirit are we all baptized into one body, whether we be Jews or Gentiles, whether we be bond or free; and have been all made to drink into one Spirit." We are therefore knit together by the sacrament of baptism into the unity of the body of Christ; so that to have broken this bond, and to yield ourselves into another fellowship of religion and brotherhood, may worthily be called sacrilege and treason. Hereunto the apostle seemed to have respect when he asked the Corinthians: "Are ye not baptized into the name of Christ?" declaring thereby, that they which are baptized into the name of Christ have openly sworn and bound their faith before the church of Christ, so that now they neither can nor ought to rejoice in any other name than in the name of Christ, into whose household they are received by baptism. So, I say, we are separated by baptism from all other religions, and are only consecrated to christian religion.

He hath the like place in all points touching the supper of the Lord, 1 Corinth. chap. x. For when the apostle would declare to the Corinthians, that it is a thing far from all godliness, unseemly, yea, and sacrilegious, that Christians should eat in the idols' temples things offered to idols, and be partakers of the gentiles' sacrifices, reasoning from the manner and nature of the sacrament of the Lord's supper, he saith: "Fly from idolatry; I speak as unto them that have understanding; judge ye what I say. The cup of blessing which we bless, is it not the communion of the blood of Christ? The bread which we break, is it not the communion of the body of Christ? For we that are many are one bread, and one body, because we are all partakers of one bread. Behold Israel

Marginal notes:
Phil. iii.
Rom. xv.
1 Cor. xii.

The place of Paul, i. Cor. x. The bread which we break, &c. is expounded.

which is after the flesh; are not they which eat of the sacrifices partakers of the altar? What say I then? That the idol is any thing? or that that which is sacrificed unto idols is any thing? Nay, but rather this I say, that those things which the gentiles sacrifice, they sacrifice to devils, and not to God; and I would not that ye should have fellowship with the devils. Ye cannot drink the cup of the Lord, and the cup of the devils. Ye cannot be partakers of the Lord's table, and of the table of devils, &c." For all this is Paul's saying; which since it serveth notably to our purpose and is very plain, I will but briefly run over it.

First, he layeth down the state and scope of the matter, whereunto he immediately directeth his whole discourse. "Flee," saith he, "idolatry." And he meaneth by the word, "idolatry," whatsoever pertaineth to idolatry, especially the eating of meat offered to idols. But if you know not what *idolothytum* is (which word he there useth[1]), understand that it is a Greek word, which Paul useth in this case; and it signifieth a thing sacrificed to an idol, or a thing publicly in sacrifice consecrated to an idol. And it was the manner of the Corinthians to sacrifice at the altars of their gods in idol-houses, that is to say, in their idol-temples, and to call Christians unto those their sacrifices: and they, when they came, sat and ate of that which was offered unto idols, eating without difference with the idolaters, thinking they might have done that without any fault at all; because by the bright shining of the gospel it appeared, that neither the idol, neither that god whom the idol represented, and therefore also the things themselves that were offered to idols, were nothing else but vain names and things of no price or estimation. But Paul, disputing against these from the eighth chap. unto the eleventh, teacheth, that it is far wide from Christianity to be partakers of the gentiles' sacrifices, and saith: I will speak unto you as unto them that have discretion; that, after I have shadowed out unto you which way to walk, you by the sharpness of your wit may understand what is true and what is false, and, to be short, which way you must incline. And then he scattereth certain grounds of arguments, which they afterward discussing might by their diligence polish and make perfect. They, saith he, that are partakers of the supper of the Lord

[1 The parenthesis is the Translator's.]

(in which the bread of the Lord is broken, and the cup of the Lord is drunken) are of the same communion, fellowship, or body with the Lord. For κοινωνία, which word Paul useth here, and which interpreters have translated communion or partaking (though fellowship is better than partaking; as in the Dutch translation "Gemeind" is better than "Gemeind-chafft[1]"), is not taken actively (as I may so say), for the distributing, giving, or reaching out Christ's body by the minister; but passively, for the fellowship and society, for the body, I say, of the church: as when the church is called a communion, that is, an assembly, a gathering together and society of saints or godly Christians[2]. Furthermore, the church is called κοινωνία, or a communion, of the body and blood of Christ, because it is redeemed by the body and blood of Christ, and, being partaker of Christ, liveth by him. For he liveth in the godly Christians, communicating unto them all his good gifts of life. And that the partakers of the supper of the Lord are the body and[3] communion of Christ, he declareth by a reason which followeth, saying: "Because we, that are many, are one bread and one body." Whereunto by and bye he addeth another more evident reason, for interpretation's sake, saying: "For we are all partakers of one bread." In that we are partakers of one bread, saith he, we do openly testify that we are partakers of the same body with Christ and all his saints: in which words he hath a notable respect to the analogy. "For as by uniting together of many grains," as Cyprian saith, "is made one bread or one loaf; as of many clusters of grapes one wine is pressed out: so out of many members groweth up and is made the body of the Church, which is the body of Christ[4]."

Now in the words of Paul these things offer themselves unto us to be marked. First, for that now he calleth that a

[1 Luther's Version has gemeinschafft.]
[2 or godly Christians, the Translator's addition.]
[3 So also ed. 1584: but 1577, or: aut, Lat.]
[4 Nam quando Dominus corpus suum panem vocat de multorum granorum adunatione congestum, populum nostrum, quem portabat, indicat adunatum: et quando sanguinem suum vinum appellat, de botris atque acinis plurimis expressum atque in unum coactum, gregem item nostrum significat, commixtione adunatæ multitudinis copulatum. —Cyprian. Opp. Ep. LXIX. p. 182.]

multitude, or many, by a word expressing his mind better, which before he named a communion. A communion therefore is nothing else but a multitude or congregation. For he said, "The bread is the partaking of the body of Christ:" but now he saith, "We being many are one bread, one body." "We being many," saith he; that is, all we which are a multitude and a congregation or church, redeemed by the body of Christ (which was) given, and by his blood (which was) shed for us. Afterwards he saith, "We being many are one body:" he doth not say, are made one body. For we are not first graffed into the body of Christ (as we have often repeated already) by partaking of the sacraments; but we, which were before engraffed by grace invisibly, are now also visibly consecrated. Again, by the like reason of sacraments, or by an example of the scripture taken from the sacraments of the people of the old Testament, he sheweth, that the partakers of the sacraments are one body, both with him to whom they offer, and with them with whom they offer, or with whom they eat of things offered to idols. "Behold," saith he, "the Israelites, which offer sacrifices after the flesh. Are not they that eat the sacrifices κοινωνοὶ, that is to say, communicants, fellows, or partakers of the things[5] of the temple or of the altar?" For under the word, of the things of the temple or of the altar (θυσιαστήριον is his word), he comprehendeth whatsoever doth belong to the worship and religion of the God of the Jews; so that the sense or meaning may be this: Are not all they one body, one communion, one people, both with the God of Israel and with his people, which eat of the sacrifices offered to the God of Israel by the Israelitish people? As if he had said: There is none that is ignorant of it, or that can deny it, since it is confessed and manifest among all men. By these things he leaveth to the Corinthians of their own accord thus much to be gathered: Therefore they, that are partakers of the sacraments of the Gentiles, are one body and one fellowship with the gods of the Gentiles and the Gentiles which do sacrifice. Now by the figure *occupatio* (which is, when in answering we prevent an objection that may be made[6]) he placeth these words between: "What say I then? That the idol is anything? Or, that that which is offered in sacri-

[5 of the things, not in Lat.]
[6 This parenthetical explanation is the Translator's.]

They are
the members
of the devil
that are par-
takers of
unlawful
sacraments.
fice to idols is any thing[1]?" Whereunto by and bye he addeth : " But this I say[2], that the things, which the Gentiles offer in sacrifice, they offer to devils[3], and not to God." Hereupon he might lawfully have inferred : Therefore, if you continue to be partakers of things offered to idols, ye shall verily be one body and one fellowship both with the devil himself and all his members. But because this might have been taken of many to have been bitterly[4] spoken, he addeth another saying somewhat more mild and gentle, and saith : " And I would not that ye should be κοινωνοὶ," that is, " communicants, or partakers, and have fellowship with devils." After which words, by comparing the contrary parts, he bringeth in the sum of the whole matter, to which he directed all his reasons, and saith : " Ye cannot drink the cup of the Lord, and the cup of devils: ye cannot be partakers of the Lord's table, and of the table of devils." And so forth. The sacraments therefore do separate us from all other worshippings and religions, and do bind and consecrate, yea, and also as it were make us of the same body with one true God and sincere Christian religion ; because we, being partakers of them, do openly profess that we be the members of Jesus Christ: which no man that is well in his wits will take, and make them the members of fornication and of idols.

Zuinglius of
binding sa-
craments,
&c.
That which Zuinglius, that learned man, hath *In Expositione fidei Christianæ ad Regem Christianum*, is not impertinent to this purpose. " Sacraments," saith he, " are instead of an oath. For *sacramentum* with the Latins is used also for an oath. For they that use one and the self-same sacraments are one peculiar nation, and an holy sworn congregation ; they are knit together into one body and into one people; whom whoso betrayeth shall perish. Therefore the people of Christ, since by eating his body sacramentally they are knit into one body ; now he that is faithless, and yet dare be so bold as to make himself one of this society or fellowship, betrayeth the body of Christ, as well in the head as in the members, &c.[5]" Thus far he.

[1 Rather, But I do not say this because the idol is worth any thing, or that which is offered in sacrifice to an idol has any divine majesty about it.]   [2 sentio, Lat.]
[3 diabolo, Lat.]   [4 acerbius, Lat.: too bitterly.]
[5 Septima sacramentorum vis est, quod vice jusjurandi sunt.

By this it is easy to understand, that sacraments put us **Sacraments put the faithful in mind of their duty.** in mind of our duty: especially if we mark in the writings of the apostle[6] how considering the manner of sacraments the apostles frame their exhortations. Where again the analogy being considered, it hath very much light and force in it. Trees are pruned, and all that which is dry, barren, and superfluous in them is cut away. And so by circumcision, they that were circumcised were put in mind to cut away with the knife of the Spirit whatsoever grew up in the flesh[7] against the law of God. Hereunto had Moses respect when he said in Deut. : " Circumcise therefore the foreskin of your heart, **Deut. x.** and be no more stiff-necked." Whom Jeremy following in the iv. chap. saith : " Be ye circumcised in the Lord[8], and cut **Jer. iv.** away the foreskin of your hearts," &c. Those things, which the apostle hath taught touching the celebration of the passover, are more plain than that they need here to be rehearsed; and I have already entreated of them at large in the sixth sermon of my third decade. The very same apostle, in his epistle to the Romans, saith : " Know ye not, that all we, **Rom. vi.** which have been baptized into Jesus Christ, have been baptized into his death ? We are buried then with him by baptism into his death ; that likewise as Christ was raised up from the dead by the glory of the Father, even so we should walk in newness of life," &c. So we are put in mind by the mystery of baptism to renounce and forsake Satan and the world, to mortify and subdue the flesh, and to bury the old Adam, that the new man may rise up again in us through Christ. Furthermore, the supper of the Lord doth admonish us of brotherly love and charity, and of the unity that we have with all the members of Christ. It warneth us also of purity and sincerity in faith, that, because we have openly professed that we

Nam et sacramentum Latinis pro jurejurando usurpatur. Qui enim unis eisdemque sacramentis utuntur, una eademque gens ac sancta quædam conjuratio fiunt ; in unum corpus, inque populum unum coeunt: quem qui prodit, perjurus est. Populus ergo Christi cum ejus corpus sacramentaliter edendo in unum corpus conjungitur, jam qui perfidus est, attamen sese huic societati audet insinuare, corpus Christi prodit tam in capite quam in membris.—Zuingl. Christ. Fid. Expos. Opp. Tom. ii. fol. 556.]

[6 apostolorum, Lat. : the apostles.]
[7 ex carne, Lat.: from the flesh.]
[8 Domino, Lat. : to the Lord.]

are united to Christ and to all his members, we should have a special care and regard, that we be not found faithless and untrue to our Lord Christ and his church; that we should not defile ourselves with foreign and strange sacrifices. We are also admonished of thankfulness, to magnify the grace of God who hath redeemed us, according to that saying: "As often as ye shall eat of this bread, and drink of this cup, ye shall shew forth his death[1] until he come."

1 Cor. xi.

Thus far have I entreated of the force, the end, and the effect of sacraments; unto the which I have, as I think, attributed no more nor no less than I ought, that is, as much as may be proved out of the scripture to be due unto them. They are the institutions of Christ; therefore they care not for counterfeit and strange praises. They have praise sufficient, if they have those praises, which he that instituted them, namely God, and Christ Jesus, the high priest of the catholic church, vouchsafed to attribute unto them.

That the sacraments profit nothing without faith.

Now, because there is mention made very oft of faith in this whole book, I will further shew also that without faith sacraments profit nothing; and again, that to those which receive them by faith they are not superfluous or vain: for this seemeth as yet to belong to the full exposition and consideration of sacraments. That sacraments without faith profit not, it is easily proved. For it is said, that sacraments are seals of the preaching of the gospel, and things appertaining to the same. For[2] if the preaching of the gospel be heard without faith, it doth not only profit nothing unto life, but it turneth rather unto judgment, (to him that heareth); the Lord himself bearing witness, and saying: "If any man hear my words, and believe not, I judge him not; for I came not to judge the world, but to save the world. The word that I have spoken, the same shall judge him in the last day." To that saying of the Lord agreeth this of the apostle: "For unto us was the gospel preached, as well as unto the fathers: but the word which they heard did not profit them, because it was not coupled with faith to them that heard[3]." Who now is such a dorhead which cannot gather, that sacraments without faith are unprofitable; especially since the same apostle saith,

John xii.

Heb. iv.

[1 So also ed. 1584: but 1577, the Lord's death: mortem Domini, Lat.]

[2 Cæterum, Lat.: But.]   [3 Erasmus' Version.]

"Whosoever shall eat this bread, and drink this cup of the 1 Cor. xi.
Lord unworthily, shall be guilty of the body and blood of the
Lord?" But all our worthiness before God doth consist in faith;
the same apostle yet again witnessing out of the prophet, "The Rom. i.
just shall live by faith:" and, "By faith the elders (or Heb. xi.
fathers) obtained a good report." Whereunto also belongeth
that which is read in the gospel: "They which were bidden Matt. xxii.
were not worthy:" whereupon it followeth, that worthiness
consisteth in faithful obedience. Hereunto also may be referred (I think) those examples, whereof mention hath been
made more than once already before: "All our fathers were 1 Cor. x.
baptized, and did all eat of one spiritual meat; but in many
of them God had no delight." And Paul again saith:
"Without faith it is impossible to please God:" therefore Heb. xi.
without faith sacraments profit nothing. The examples of
Simon Magus and Judas the traitor are very well known; of
which one was baptized, the other admitted to the supper,
and yet had no fruit of the sacraments, because they wanted
true faith.

To these pithy and divine testimonies of God we will now Augustine
add some places of St Augustine. Out of his nineteenth book doth teach
against Faustus, and twelfth chapter: "Peter saith, 'Bap- that sacra-
tism saveth us;' and lest they should think the visible sacra- ceived with-
ment were sufficient, by which they had the form of godliness, out faith are
and through their evil manners, by living lewdly and despe- to the re-
rately, should deny the power thereof, by and bye he addeth: ceivers.
'Not the putting away of the filth of the flesh, but in that a
good conscience maketh request to God[4].'" Again, Lib. ii.
Contra Literas Petiliani, cap. 7, he saith: "They are not
therefore to be thought to be in the body of Christ, which
is the church or congregation, because they are corporally
partakers of his sacraments. For they in such are also holy;
but to them that use and receive them unworthily they shall
be forcible to their greater judgment. For they are not in
that society of Christ's church, which in the members of Christ,

[4 Sic et vos, inquit (apostolus Petrus), simili forma baptisma
salvos facit. Et ne sibi sufficere putarent visibile sacramentum, per
quod habebant formam pietatis, et per malos mores perdite vivendo
virtutem ejus abnegarent, continuo subjecit, Non carnis depositio
sordium, sed conscientiæ bonæ interrogatio.—August. contra Faust.
Opp. Tom. vi. fol. 72. col. 1. Par. 1531.]

by being knit together and touching one another, do grow into the fulness of God. For that church is builded on a rock; as saith the Lord, ' Upon this rock will I build my church :' but they build on the sand ; as the Lord also saith, ' He that heareth my words and doth them not, I will liken him to a foolish man¹.' " And again in his treatise upon John xiii. : " The syllables of Christ's name and his sacraments profit nothing, where the faith of Christ is resisted. For faith in Christ and his sacraments is, to believe in him which justifieth the ungodly, to believe in the Mediator, without whose intercession we are not reconciled unto God². " Thus far Augustine.

Sacraments depend not on our worthiness or unworthiness.

An objection is made : If sacraments do nothing profit without our faith, then they depend on our worthiness or unworthiness ; so that they are not perfect³. I answer : That among the wicked and unbelievers sacraments, verily, of themselves are sufficiently ratified and confirmed by the institution of God ; neither dependeth their perfectness upon the condition and state of the partakers, that they are either better among the good, or worse among the bad. For that remaineth perfect and sound which the Lord hath instituted, and retaineth his institution always good, howsoever men Rom. iii. vary and are faithless. For the apostle saith : " Shall their unbelief make the faith of God without effect ? God forbid. Yea, let God be true, and every man a liar." But I have

[¹ Nec ideo putandi sunt esse in Christi corpore, quod est ecclesia, quia sacramentorum ejus corporaliter participes fiunt. Illa enim et in talibus sancta sunt, et eis indigne tractantibus et sumentibus ad majus judicium valebunt. Ipsi autem non sunt in illa ecclesiæ Christi compage, quæ in membris Christi per connexum et contactum crescit in incrementum Dei. Illa quippe ecclesia in petra est; sicut Dominus dicit, Super hanc petram ædificabo ecclesiam meam: illi autem in arena ædificant; sicut idem Dominus dicit, Qui audit verba mea, et non facit ea, similabo eum viro stulto.—August. cont. Lit. Petil. Lib. II. cap. 108. Opp. Tom. VII. fol. 34. col. 3.]

[² Non aliquid prosunt syllabæ nominis Christi et sacramenta Christi, ubi resistitur fidei Christi. Fides autem Christi est credere in eum, qui justificat impium; credere in mediatorem, sine quo interposito non reconciliamur Deo.—August. in Evang. Joan. Tract. LIII. Opp. Tom. IX. fol. 79. col. 3.]

[³ inter malos et infideles, Lat.: among the wicked and unbelievers. The Translator inserts the words in the next sentence.]

touched this matter also somewhat before. Yet, because it is one thing to offer, and another thing to receive; God verily offereth of his goodness his bountiful gifts unto men to this end, to profit and to save them, and to make them whole, as the physician doth by ministering physic to his patient ; but because that foolish and mad man doth not acknowledge the benefit, as the sick patient which refuseth physic being ministered, the benefit which is offered doth no more profit the one, than physic not received doth good to the other ; not through the default of him that offereth the benefit, or of him which ministereth physic, but through the folly of him which refuseth and will none of it. After this manner disputeth St Augustine also of this matter. For Lib. iii. *De Baptismo cont. Donat.* cap. 14, he saith : " It skilleth not, when the perfectness and holiness of the sacrament is in handling, what he believeth, and what manner of faith he hath, that receiveth the sacrament. Verily, it availeth very much to the way of salvation, but for the question of the sacrament it maketh no matter[4]." Also *Contra Literas Petiliani*, Lib. ii. cap. 47, he saith : " Remember, that the lewd life and corrupt manners of evil men do nothing hinder the sacraments of God, to make them not holy at all, or less holy; but that to the ungodly they are a testimony of their damnation, and not a furtherance of their salvation[5]." He also, *Tract. in Joan.* 26, saith : " If thou receive the sacrament carnally, it ceaseth not to be spiritual; but to thee it is not so[6]."

As easily is that objection confuted, that baptism profiteth not infants, if we still say that sacraments without faith profit

Of baptism of infants.

[4 Nec interest, cum de sacramenti integritate et sanctitate tractatur, quid credat, et quali fide imbutus sit ille qui accipit sacramentum : interest quidem plurimum ad salutis viam, sed ad sacramenti quæstionem nihil interest.—August. de Baptismo contra Donatist. Lib. III. cap. 14. Opp. Tom. VII. fol. 83. col. 2.]

[5 Memento sacramentis Dei nihil obesse mores malorum hominum, quo illa vel omnino non sint, vel minus sancta sint : sed ipsis malis hominibus, ut hæc habeant ad testimonium damnationis, non ad adjutorium sanitatis.—Id. contra Lit. Petiliani, Lib. II. cap. 47. Opp. Tom VII. fol. 25. col. 4.]

[6 Quid est, Spiritus et vita sunt ? Spiritaliter intelligenda sunt. Intellexisti spiritaliter ? Spiritus et vita sunt. Intellexisti carnaliter? Etiam sic illa spiritus et vita sunt, sed tibi non sunt.—Id. in Evang. Joan. Tract. XXVII. Opp. Tom. IX. fol. 48. col. 3.]

not; for infants have no faith. Thus they babble. We answer first, That the baptism of infants is grounded upon the free mercy and grace of God, who saith: " I will be thy God, and the God of thy seed;" and again: " Suffer children to come unto me; for of such is the kingdom of God," &c. Infants therefore are numbered and counted of the Lord himself among the faithful; so that baptism is due unto them, as far forth as it is due unto the faithful. For by the imputation of God infants are faithful; whereunto pertaineth this saying of our Saviour: " He that shall offend one of these little ones that believe in me," &c. For he manifestly calleth " little ones " believing; for imputation's sake, doubtless, not for confession, which by no means as yet is in little ones. To this also may be added, that the father of the infant doth therefore desire to have his child signed with the mark of the people of God, to wit, baptism, because he believeth the promises of God, that is, that his infant is of the household of God; therefore there is faith in the baptism of infants. But the father doth not believe. Be it so; yet that is no hinderance to the infant; for in the faith of the church he is brought to be baptized. The church, verily, believeth that infants ought to be brought to the Lord; the church believeth that they are of the household and people of God: therefore she commandeth them to be partakers of the mysteries. So that again, in the baptism of infants a man may find faith. Hereunto doth St Augustine add this, saying, Lib. i. *De Peccatorum Meritis et Remissione,* cap. 19: " Wherefore infants are rightly called faithful, because they after a sort do confess their faith by the words of them that bear them[1]." He reasoneth more touching this matter in his epistle to Boniface, which is in order the three and twentieth[2], where he that desireth may find more.

But all these things, say they, prove not that infants have faith of their own; for the faith of their parents, of their bearers, or the faith of the church, is another's faith, and not theirs. Be it so. Yet most certain is that saying, that the Lord counteth infants among his, that is, among the faithful; so that now they are not only baptized in another's faith, but in their own, that is to say, which it pleaseth the

[1 — recte fideles vocantur (parvuli), quoniam fidem per verba gestantium quodammodo profitentur.—Id. Opp. Tom. VII. fol. 136. col. 4.]
[2 Id. Opp. Tom. II. fol. 17, &c.]

Lord to impute unto them. Furthermore, that is not another's, which is common to the self-same body: but infants are in the very same body of the church, whereby that which is the church's is their own, and not another's. Neither can any man easily tell what motions of the Holy Spirit infants have beside, &c. For insomuch as they are of God, they have the Spirit of God; "and whoso have not, they are not Rom. viii. of God," Rom. viii.

As they decline too much to the left hand, which are That sacraments are persuaded that sacraments, yea, without faith, do profit the not superfluous or receivers; so they go too far wide on the right hand, who void to them think that the sacraments are superfluous to them that have that have faith. Faith, say they, doth fully acquit us; so that after we have faith sacraments can increase nothing in us: therefore it must needs be that they are unprofitable. Such in times past are the heretics Messaliani read to have been, who were both called *Euchitæ*[3], and ἐνθουσιασταί, that is, divine men, forsooth, and inspired of God; for they did contend that the faithful, after they had received the Holy Ghost, had need of no sacraments. But these men are very injurious even to God himself; who instituted not his sacraments for the faithful without great cause, neither unprofitably. And, "Verily, Abraham believed God, and it was reckoned unto him for righteousness, and he was counted the friend of God," just and holy, not being void doubtless of the Holy Ghost: but he also "received circumcision, the seal of the righteousness of faith which was before he was circumcised." It is said to the same Abraham: "Every man-child, whose Gen. xvii. foreskin shall not be circumcised, shall be cut off from my people, because he hath broken my covenant." Truly, the angel of the Lord is ready to kill Moses, because he delayed Exod. iv. circumcision in his children longer than was lawful, either by his own negligence, or through the fault of his Madianitish wife. What, shall there be found any more righteous and holy than the Son of God, as he which, having received the fulness of the Spirit, poureth plentifully of the same into his members? He himself being the head, yet he came to John Baptist, and requireth to be baptized of him in Jordan. And when he refused, and said, "I have need to be baptized of Matt. iii.

[3 Mosheim. E. H. Book II. Cent. IV. part 2. chap. 5. § 24. Vol. I. p. 409. note 5, ed. Soames. See also above, page 94, note 6.]

thee, and comest thou to me?" he heareth : "Suffer it to be
so now ; for thus it becometh us to fulfil all righteousness."
Certainly righteousness giveth to every man that which is
his own. Faith therefore, which is the righteousness of Christians, giveth glory to God; and believeth, that he being wonderful wise doth will well unto men ; and therefore that he
hath instituted nothing unprofitably, but all things for the
salvation of his faithful ones. A faithful man therefore useth
all the institutions of God without any reasoning or gainsaying. Neither is there any here, I think, that will say,
that this deed of Christ pertaineth nothing to him, whereby
undoubtedly he laid before us an example to follow. Yea,
that which he himself did, he willed other also to do, when
he sent his disciples forth, and said : "Go into the whole
world, and preach the gospel to all creatures; baptizing them
in the name of the Father," &c. "He which shall believe
and be baptized shall be saved." Where truly he joineth together both faith and baptism ; which to abide upon[1] he would
not have done, if sacraments were superfluous there, where
faith is. Whereby it manifestly appeareth, that they are
wrong as far as heaven is wide, which think that sacraments
are indifferent, that is to say, a thing put to our own will
and choice, either to use or not to use. For as we have
heard already a flat commandment concerning baptism ; so
the Lord, instituting and celebrating the supper, saith : "Do
this in the remembrance of me." He therefore that despiseth
these commandments of God, I see not how he can have faith,
whereby he should be invisibly sanctified. Hitherto belongeth
now that which the faithful prince of Æthiopia confesseth,
that he believed with all his heart in the Lord Jesus ; yet
nevertheless, as soon as he saw water, he said : "Behold,
here is water; what letteth me to be baptized?" He doth
not say, I believe with all my heart, and I feel that I am
justified and cleansed; why then should I be washed with
water, having no filth remaining? Therefore, wheresoever
true faith is, there sacraments are not contemned or refused,
but more desired. For Cornelius the centurion also, after
he had received the Holy Ghost, doth not gainsay Peter,
who said : "Can any man forbid water, that these should not
be baptized, which have received the Holy Ghost as well as

Sacraments are indifferent.

[1 So all the editions; haud dubie, Lat.]

we?" Peter was a faithful preacher of the gospel, a skilful teacher of the truth; therefore he deceiveth no man: and he teacheth us by his own deed, that faith doth then specially provoke us to be partakers of the sacraments, when it is true in the faithful. To whom Paul, his fellow-minister, agreeth, saying: "Let every one prove himself, and then let him eat of this bread, and drink of this cup:" but that proving is made by faith. Therefore not faith, but unthankfulness[2], doth contemptuously reject the sacraments.

Truly I am not ignorant, that very many without the use of visible sacraments have been sanctified, and at this day also are sanctified: but none of those despised or contemned them. They were not partakers of the sacraments, being thereunto driven by necessity; as there be at this day some that are held captives under the tyranny of antichrist and the Turk, and for the time believe with their whole heart in the Lord Jesus. Therefore the examples of these or such like are no defence for them which may receive the sacraments, if they regard[3] the ordinances of God, and set so much by them as of duty they should do. I will note here, for the singular benefit of the readers, St Augustine's disputation, because it maketh notably for our purpose. He, *Quæst. lib. in Levit.* iii. cap. 84. saith: "It is demanded not without cause, whether invisible sanctification do profit nothing without visible sacraments, wherewith a man is visibly sanctified? which without doubt is absurd. For more tolerably it may be said, that this sanctification is not without them, than that it doth not profit, if it be without them; since in sanctification all their profit consisteth. But we must also weigh this; how it is rightly said, that without the sacraments sanctification cannot be. For visible baptism did nothing profit Simon Magus, to whom invisible sanctification was wanting: but because this invisible sanctification profited them that had it, in like manner they which were baptized received also the visible sacraments. And yet neither is it shewed, where Moses himself was sanctified with visible sacrifices or oil, who notwithstanding did visibly sanctify the priests: but who dare deny that he was invisibly sanctified, whose grace was so great, surpassing, and excellent? This also may be said of John Baptist. For he was first a baptizer, before he was seen to be

Many are sanctified without visible sacraments.

[2 perfida, Lat.]   [3 So also ed. 1584; but 1577, regarded.]

baptized: whereupon we can deny by no means that he was sanctified; yet we do not find that that was visibly wrought in him before he came to the ministry of baptizing. This also may be verified of the thief crucified with Christ, to whom the Lord said, as he hung with him on the cross, 'To-day shalt thou be with me in Paradise.' For he could not have been partaker of so great felicity, unless he had been invisibly sanctified. Whereby we gather, that invisible sanctification hath been present with some, and profited them, without the visible sacraments; and that visible sanctification, which is wrought by visible sacraments, may be present without this invisible sanctification, but yet may not profit us. Yet nevertheless, the visible sacrament is not therefore to be contemned; for the contemner thereof can by no means be invisibly sanctified. Hereof it is that Cornelius and they that were with him, when they did now appear to be invisibly sanctified by the Holy Ghost poured into them, yet notwithstanding they are baptized: neither is visible sanctification, which had invisible sanctification going before it, counted superfluous[1]." Thus far he.

[1 Merito quæritur, utrum etiam ista invisibilis sanctificatio sine visibilibus sacramentis, quibus visibiliter homo sanctificatur, pariter nihil prosit? Quod utique absurdum est. Tolerabilius enim quisque dixerit, sine illis istam non esse, quam si fuerit non prodesse; cum in ista sit omnis utilitas illorum. Sed etiam hoc, quod sine illis ista esse non possit, quomodo recte dicatur intuendum est. Nihil quippe profuit Simoni Mago visibilis baptismus, cui sanctificatio invisibilis defuit: sed quibus ista invisibilis, quoniam affuit, profuit, etiam visibilia sacramenta perceperant similiter baptizati. Nec tamen Moyses, qui visibiliter sacerdotes sanctificabat, ubi fuerit ipse ipsis sacrificiis vel oleo sanctificatus ostenditur: invisibiliter vero sanctificatum negare quis audeat, cujus tanta gratia præeminebat? Hoc et de Joanne Baptista dici potest. Prius enim baptizator quam baptizatus apparuit; unde eum sanctificatum nequaquam negare possumus: id tamen in eo factum visibiliter non invenimus antequam ad ministerium baptizandi veniret. Hoc et de latrone illo, cui secum crucifixo Dominus ait, Hodie mecum eris in paradiso. Neque enim sine sanctificatione invisibili tanta felicitate donatus est. Proinde colligitur, invisibilem sanctificationem quibusdam affuisse atque profuisse sine visibilibus sacramentis: ... visibilem vero sanctificationem, quæ fieret per visibilia sacramenta, sine ista invisibili posse adesse, non posse prodesse. Nec tamen ideo sacramentum visibile contemnendum est. Nam contemptor ejus invisibiliter sanctificari nullo modo potest. Hinc est, quod Cornelius et qui cum eo erant, cum jam visibiliter infuso sancto spiritu sanctificati apparerent, baptizati sunt tamen, nec superflua judicata est

With this disputation another question also hath some Cyprian's error touching the sacrament of baptism. affinity or likeness; which is, Whether sacraments depend upon the worthiness of the ministers, and whether they be hindered in their force by the unworthiness of the ministers? Cyprian more than in one place doth contend, " That they cannot baptize[2] which want the Holy Ghost[3]:" which error springeth hereupon, for that he attributeth too much to the ministry of baptism. He doth think that men are purified or cleansed by baptism : so that thereby he doth gather, that an unclean person cannot purify or cleanse, and therefore not baptize; and that the baptism of an unclean person is not baptism: from whence he deriveth anabaptism, or rebaptizing. But if that holy man had rightly and religiously distinguished between power and ministry, between the sign and the thing signified, between the outward and inward sanctification; he had undoubtedly understood, that we are invisibly sanctified by the mere grace of God, and that this inward sanctification is outwardly by the ministry represented and sealed. There he might have understood, that sealed evidences may be published as well by an evil minister as by a good. God's sacraments are[4] to be referred to God, the author of them; who is faithful and true in all his ordinances, how false and faithless soever men be. Although Judas were a thief, yet he preached and baptized ; whose doctrine and baptism was as well the doctrine and baptism of Christ, as was Peter's and Andrew's, James' and John's. And touching the perfectness and pureness both of the doctrine and baptism done by the ministry of Judas; no man ever doubted, as though they were never taught or baptized whom he taught and baptized, who in the mean while is called of the Lord himself, not a devilish man, but a very devil. For he John vi. baptized not in his own name, but in the name of Christ; preached not his own, but the doctrine of Christ. To conclude; the Lord of his goodness, for his truth's sake and not for Judas' sake, wrought in the faithful; which working of

visibilis sanctificatio, quam invisibilis jam præcesserat.—August. Quæst. super Levit. Lib. III. cap. 84. Opp. Tom. IV. fol. 49. col. 1.]

[2 So ed. 1577; the other edd. they cannot be baptized: eos baptizare non posse, Lat.]

[3 See especially Cyprian. Ep. LXX. p. 189, &c.]

[4 Rather, The sacraments are God's, and are, &c.]

his another's ungraciousness and maliciousness could not hinder, as at this day verily it hindereth not a whit. Truly, we must do what we can to have holy and unblameable ministers, so far forth as by our care and diligence we are able to procure and bring to pass: yea, let us deprive and disgrace them, whom we shall find to behave themselves unworthy of their function: but in the mean time, let us not doubt at all of the pureness of the sacraments, which they while they were in their office ministered unto us, that is to say, after the same manner and form as the Lord instituted. And verily, as the faithful do not fasten their minds on the elements, so neither do they on the ministers. They in all things look only up to God the author of all goodness, and to the end of those things which the Lord ordained.

St Augustine hath handled this matter very diligently, excellently well applying to these things very effectual arguments; whose words I will set down, Lib. III. *Contra Donatist. de Baptismo* 3, cap. 10. "The water is not unholy," saith he, "or defiled, over which the name of the Lord is called on, though it be called on of unholy and unclean persons; because neither the creature itself, nor yet the name, is unclean. And the baptism of Christ, consecrated with the words of the gospel, is holy, both by them that are unclean and in them that are unclean, though they be defiled and unclean; because his holiness cannot be polluted, and in his sacraments a divine power is present, either to the salvation of them that use them well, or to the condemnation of them that use them ill. Doth the light of the sun, or of a candle, when it shineth through a filthy sink, gather no uncleanness from thence; and can the baptism of Christ be polluted with any man's wickedness? For if we apply our minds unto the very visible things under which sacraments are delivered, who knoweth not that they are corruptible? But if we ascend unto that which is figured by them, who seeth not that they be incorruptible; though men by whom it is ministered according to their deservings are either rewarded or punished[1]?" And so

[1] Non est aqua profana et adultera, super quam nomen Dei invocatur, etiamsi a profanis et adulteris invocetur: quia nec ipsa creatura, nec ipsum nomen adulterum est; baptismus vero Christi, verbis evangelicis consecratus et per adulteros et in adulteris, sanctus est, quamvis illi sint impudici et immundi; quia ipsa ejus sanc-

forth. I could allege many examples of this kind, if I thought
them necessary. For I think that by them it is largely
and plainly enough declared, that the perfectness
and pureness of the sacraments are not to be
esteemed by the worthiness or unworthiness of the ministers, but by
the truth of God who did
institute them. To him
be glory, power and
dominion, for ever
and ever.
Amen.

OF HOLY BAPTISM; WHAT IT IS; BY WHOM, AND WHEN
IT WAS INSTITUTED, AND THAT THERE IS BUT ONE
BAPTISM OF WATER. OF THE BAPTISM OF FIRE. OF
THE RITE OR CEREMONY OF BAPTISM; HOW, OF WHOM,
AND TO WHOM IT MUST BE MINISTERED. OF BAP-
TISM BY MIDWIVES; AND OF INFANTS DYING
WITHOUT BAPTISM. OF THE BAPTISM OF
INFANTS. AGAINST ANABAPTISM OR
RE-BAPTIZING; AND OF THE
POWER OR EFFICACY
OF BAPTISM.

THE EIGHTH SERMON.

Now I have to entreat particularly of holy baptism, and
of the holy supper of the Lord; which may be done so much
the more briefly, as we have largely spoken already of sacraments in general. Christ our Lord open your minds, and
guide my tongue unto the glory and praise of his blessed
name for ever!

titas pollui non potest, et sacramento suo divina virtus assistit, sive
ad salutem bene utentium, sive ad perniciem male utentium. An
vero solis vel etiam lucernæ lux, cum per cœnosa diffunditur, nihil inde
sordium contrahit, et baptismus Christi potest cujusquam sceleribus
inquinari? Si enim ad ipsas res visibiles, quibus sacramenta tractantur,
animum conferamus, quis nesciat eas esse corruptibiles? Si autem ad
id quod per illas agitur, quis non videat non posse corrumpi; quamvis
homines per quos agitur pro suis moribus vel prœmia percipiant vel
pœnas luant?—August. contra Donatist. Lib. III. cap. 10. Opp. Tom.
VII. fol. 83. col. 1.]

Baptism.

Baptism is a word fetched from the Greeks, who use both these words *baptismus* and *baptisma*, (both which signify baptism), as the Latins also do; and baptism is a dipping, which word Tertullian willingly useth[1]. For βάπτω signifieth to dip or dip in; and βαπτίζω, to plunge or put far in. Whereupon also, to baptize, is used for to plunge in, to wash away, or to cleanse; and baptizings in the scriptures are put for washings and purifyings, as it appeareth in St Mark, the seventh chapter, and in Paul to the Hebrews, the ninth chapter. To be baptized with the same baptism, is proverbially spoken of him that is partaker of the self-same danger or misfortune[2]; and to be baptized with blood, is to be imbued with blood.

What baptism is.

They define baptism, for the most part, to be a token or recognizance of our cleansing, yea, of our enrolling[3], whereby we are received into the church to be of the number of God's children. But we, describing the nature of baptism more at large, do say; that it is an holy action instituted of God, and consisting of the word of God and the holy rite or ceremony whereby the people of God are dipped in the water in the name of the Lord: to be short, whereby the Lord himself doth represent and seal unto us our purifying or cleansing, gathereth us into one body, and putteth the baptized in mind of their duty.

In this description of baptism these things seem chiefly to be considered: Who did institute baptism: of what things it consisteth: whether it be simple, but one and the self-same[4], or drawn into many parts: what rite or ceremony of baptizing is delivered (to the church): what the end and force of baptism is.

Who instituted baptism.

It was no man that did institute the sacrament of baptism, but God himself; though by man it took the name[5], that is to say, by John it was ministered, who of it was called the Baptist. That we might understand this, the evangelists in many places have confirmed that the calling of John was

[1 intinctio. Tertull. de Pœnitentia, capp. 2. 6. Tom. iv. pp. 38, 47. ed. Semler. Hal. Mag. 1824.]

[2 Erasmi. Adag. Chiliad. p. 478. *mali retaliatio.* Han. 1617.]

[3 initiationis, Lat.]

[4 but—self-same, Translator's paraphrase and addition.]

[5 it took the name, not in Lat.]

from heaven; for thereby we may gather, that his ministry was from heaven[6]. Doth not he say himself in express words: "He which sent me to baptize with water, the same *John i.* said unto me, Upon whomsoever thou shalt see the Holy Ghost," &c.? Also our Lord in the gospel, arguing that the baptism of John was not from men but from God, he demandeth of the Pharisees: "The baptism of John, whence was it, from *Matt. xx.* heaven, or of men?" Wherefore the godly, yea even at this day, do receive baptism as it were at the hands of God himself, though they be baptized through the ministry of men. For the Lord, establishing[7] his institutions by his Spirit, worketh salvation in the elect. So that it must needs follow, that the virtue or efficacy of baptism is not hindered by an evil minister: whereof hath been already elsewhere[8], and hereafter shall be spoken.

At that time truly baptism was instituted and began at *When baptism was instituted.* St John the apostle[9], when he began to preach openly that the time was fulfilled, and that Christ was exhibited and given to the world. But the signs of things to come or of things which should be revealed, the thing itself being present, do no more remain, but ought to be changed into other signs. And circumcision was a sign of the blessed seed which was to come; I mean, of the Messias himself, which, by the shedding of his blood, should bestow his blessing upon the whole world. Therefore when he was come and should forthwith shed forth his blood, it was needful that circumcision should be changed into baptism. Whereof shall be spoken hereafter.

Now baptism consisteth of the sign and of the thing *Of what things baptism consisteth.* signified; of the word or promise of God and of the holy rite or ceremony. The sign is the outward action, that is, the sprinkling of water in the name[10] of the Father and of the Son and of the Holy Ghost, with the calling upon of the name of God. The promise or word of God is, "baptizing them:" "He that shall believe and be baptized shall be

[6 divinum, Lat.: of God.]   [7 assistens, Lat.]
[8 See above, pp. 343. 350.]
[9 Eo tempore vero institutus est a Deo, et incœptus a beato Joanne baptismus, &c. Lat. *by God*, is omitted; and *the apostle* is added (wrongly) by the Translator.]
[10 in nomen, Lat.: into the name.]

saved." And so forth. Whereof we have spoken abundantly enough in the sixth sermon.

One only baptism.

Many in the old time have distinguished between the baptism of John, and the baptism of Christ and his apostles[1]. For some of them deny that forgiveness of sins was comprehended in the baptism of John: but if we diligently view and weigh the doctrine of the holy scripture, we shall find, that the baptism of John and Christ and his apostles is one and the self-same. Certainly, the doctrine of John, of Christ, and his apostles, is one and the self-same everywhere; for they all with one mouth do preach the gospel, and by it repentance and the remission of sins in the name of Christ. Let him that will confer those things which John the Evangelist writeth of the doctrine of John Baptist in the first and third chapter, and that which Luke writes, in the four and twentieth chapter of his gospel and in the Acts of the Apostles, of the doctrine of Christ and his apostles; and he will say, that all their doctrine is one and the self-same. But to their doctrine is baptism set to, as a seal to an evidence. Who therefore believeth, that there are divers seals of their doctrine, or divers baptisms[2]? St John baptized with water: the Lord commended no other element to his disciples than water; neither baptized they any otherwise than with water.

The baptism of John, of Christ, and of the apostles, is one and the self-same.

Acts xix.

They themselves baptized into Christ, into repentance and remission of sins: but St Mark writeth of John Baptist: "John baptized in the wilderness, preaching the baptism of repentance for the remission of sins." And St Paul, speaking of the doctrine and baptism of John, saith: "John baptized with the baptism of repentance, saying unto the people, that they should believe on him which should come after him, that is, on Jesus Christ." By these testimonies who cannot gather, that the baptism of John and of Christ is altogether the very same?—unless this peradventure seem to any man to bring some difference, that John baptized in him that was to come and should be revealed, but the apostles into him that was already revealed. But I see not how so little space

[1 Tertull. de Baptism. cap. x. August. Vincentio, Epist. 48. De Baptism. contr. Donat. Lib. v. capp. 9—15. Chrysost. Homil. in Matt. xiv.]

[2 ejusdam doctrinæ diversa esse sigilla vel baptismata, Lat.: that there are different seals or baptisms of the same doctrine.]

of time can bring any difference, especially since John spake so much, from the beginning of his preaching, of him which should be revealed[3]: for immediately he did both point him out present with his finger, and he bare witness that he was present and revealed, and that he should come no more or be revealed. Hereunto is added, that Christ was baptized with no other than with the baptism of John. For if John's baptism were another baptism beside the baptism of the church of Christ, it would follow, that neither Christ was baptized with our baptism, neither we in the baptism of Christ. But Christ did sanctify with his body the baptism of John, and did vouchsafe to be baptized with us into the same fellowship; so that we at this day are also baptized, not with the baptism of John, but of Christ, who by John instituted baptism, and he himself consecrated the same. Wherefore Christ in Matthew, xxviii. cap., and in Mark, the xvi. cap., doth not abrogate the baptism which John began; he doth not institute a new, but commandeth to continue and to minister the same to them that believe: "In the name of the Father, and of the Son, and of the Holy Ghost."

Now whereas John saith himself, "I baptize with water, but he shall baptize you with the Holy Ghost:" he maketh not difference between his own baptism of water and Christ's baptism; but he attributeth somewhat more unto Christ, wherein no man or minister (for they did err which in time past baptized with fire) had part with him; but he alone giveth the baptism of fire, that is, the singular gifts of the Holy Ghost; but first of all, the use of tongues under the form of fire. For so this matter is expounded in the Acts; first by the Lord Christ himself, then by experience in the church. For the Lord saith: "Depart not from Hierusalem, but wait for the promise of the Father, whereof, saith he, ye have heard of me. For John truly baptized with water; but ye shall be baptized with the Holy Ghost after these few days." And consequently, upon the day of Pentecost they were baptized with the baptism of Christ; not with water again, but were all filled with the Holy Ghost; cloven tongues, as it were fiery, sitting upon each one of their heads; and they began to speak with other tongues. In the Acts, the citi-

Of the baptism of Christ, which is also the baptism of fire.

Acts i.

Acts viii.

[3 testimoniumque exhibuit præsenti et revelato, non venturo amplius aut revelando, Lat.]

zens of Samaria are baptized of Philip with the baptism of Christ in water lawfully and fully : but the very same afterward are baptized with the peculiar baptism of Christ, while by the laying on of hands by Peter and John they receive the Holy Ghost. Not that hitherto they were altogether void of the gift of the Holy Ghost (for how could they believe without the Holy Ghost?); but for that they were baptized with the visible baptism of fire beside, and received the gift of tongues and other excellent graces. As it is also read of Cornelius, who verily, being first baptized with fire, I mean, with the peculiar baptism of Christ, spake with tongues, and afterward was baptized with water. Contrariwise, those twelve disciples at Ephesus were first fully baptized with the baptism of John, and with the baptism of the water of the christian church or congregation; and afterward, Paul the apostle laying his hands on them, they are baptized, not with water again, but with fire; Luke bearing witness, and saying : " The Holy Ghost came upon them, and they spake with tongues and prophesied."

But this baptism of fire, and the visible ministration of the gifts, ceased together with miracles ; neither at this day is it usual or common in the church : but the baptism of water remaineth, which is one and the self-same, whether it be ministered by the hands of John or of the apostles, or by divers hands of the ministers of the church ; for divers hands make not divers baptisms. Wherefore we rightly believe, that there is but one only and simple baptism of the faithful in all ages. For Paul in express words saith: "There is one Lord, one faith, one baptism, and one God and Father of all." Whereunto also tendeth this saying of the same apostle: " I thank God that I baptized none of you, but Crispus and Gaius; lest any should say that I had baptized in mine own name." Upon this apostolic truth the reverend fathers of the council of Constantinople are read to have made this confession in their creed : " I believe one baptism for the remission of sins[1]." For there is but one church only, one body, one head, and one king, prince, and high priest of the catholic church.

Now I am come to expound the rite or ceremony of baptism. It was simple and but one from the beginning, and not

Marginal notes:
Acts x.
Acts xix.
Ephes. iv.
1 Cor. i.
Of the rite or ceremony of baptism.

[1 Vol. I. pp. 16, 17.]

chargeable or burdenous to the church through immoderate ceremonies. John baptized in Ænon beside Salem, because John iii. much water was there; and he baptized in the name of Christ. So did the apostles likewise. Whereby it remaineth for an undoubted truth, that the very best form of baptizing is that which is done by water, in the name of the Father and of the Son and of the Holy Ghost; for so the Lord commanded in the xxviii. of Matthew. Do you ask how it cometh to pass, that Luke in the Acts maketh mention that Peter and Paul baptized in the name of the Lord, and expresseth not that they baptized in the name of the Father and of the Son and of the Holy Ghost? I answer, that under the name of the Lord the mystery of the Trinity is comprehended. For when the Lord said, "I and the Father are one," he which is baptized in the Lord[2] is also baptized into the Father, and so in like manner into the Holy Ghost which is not divided from them; for verily they have one and the self-same Spirit. For truly Luke saith, that they were baptized of the apostles in the name of the Lord, whom the apostles baptized according to the Lord's institution. Some say Christ is the accomplishment or fulfilling, and the proper object, of baptism: wherefore it is no marvel, that the apostles baptized into the name of the Lord, who nevertheless were commanded to baptize in the name of the Father and of the Son and of the Holy Ghost; for all the mysteries of baptism are laid forth unto us in the only Son of God.

Truly we say both, "To baptize into the name of the Lord," and "To baptize in the name of the Lord." The use of speaking after the first manner is read in the xxviii. of Matthew, and in Luke, Acts the xix.; for both have εἰς τὸ ὄνομα, *In nomen*, "into the name." And also[3] Tertullian interpreteth it, *contra Praxeam*, saying: "He commanded that we should be baptized into the Father and the Son[4]," &c. The latter manner doth the same Luke use in the Acts, x. and ii., saying, ἐν τῷ ὀνόματι, and ἐπὶ τῷ ὀνόματι, that is, "In the name." Moreover, what it is to baptize into the name, or What it is to baptize in the name of the Lord. in the name, of the Lord, I told you in the last sermon next

[2 in Dominum, Lat.: into the Lord, ed. 1577.]
[3 ita interpretatur, Lat. And so also, ed. 1577.]
[4 Novissime mandans (Christus) ut tinguerent (discipuli) in Patrem et Filium et Spiritum Sanctum.—Tertull. adv. Prax. cap. 26. Tom. II. p. 199. ed. Semler. Hal. Magd. 1824.]

before this[1]; that it is, to be enrolled into God's household, that he which is baptized may now receive the name of God and be called the son of God, yea, and be as it were registered into the roll of the children of God, citizens of the kingdom of heaven. Whereupon we have also names given us in baptism, that, as often as we hear ourselves named, we may remember our baptism and the mysteries thereof. Neither is it a new thing or strange from the scriptures, that names are given us in baptism; for so it was used also in circumcision, which is to be seen in Luke, ii. chapter[2].

Furthermore the question is asked, Whether we ought to baptize with these bare words, " I baptize thee in the name of the Father and of the Son and of the Holy Ghost;" or whether it be lawful to add or join something else? I think we ought to answer, That it is the servant's duty to add nothing to his Lord's institution, but diligently to keep that which he hath delivered; yea, and advisedly to mark what in baptism the Lord himself and his apostles did, and holily to imitate the same; that in the church of God, as Paul hath commanded, all things may be done decently and in good order. But after that most holy form of baptism[3] set down and delivered, we see two things in holy baptism and in the use thereof to be observed. For first, the apostles, and they that were with the apostles, did teach very significantly of the promises of God and faith in Christ; which is apparent in the Acts of the Apostles. It is lawful therefore, in the action or ministration of baptism, to recite the promises of God, to rehearse the belief, and require faith, either of them that are to be baptized, being of perfect age, or else of them which bring the infants to be baptized. Moreover, when the Lord was baptized of John Baptist in Jordan, he prayed; which thing Luke in his gospel reporteth of him in the history of the gospel. It is lawful therefore in the use of baptism to pray, and solemnly to call upon the name of the Lord. At the first the prayers were moderate and short, not of a great length and tedious; in process of time there was no measure kept, not only in tedious blessings, but also in divers ceremonies which they that came after added there-

1 Cor. xiv.

Luke iii.

[1 See page 255.]   [2 See Vol. ii. p. 179.]
[3 of baptizing, ed. 1577.]

unto; of the which it shall not seem altogether unprofitable
to rehearse somewhat out of the old doctors.

Tertullian, in his book *De Corona Militis*, saith: "When Ceremonies added in
we go to the font, there, and also a little before in the church, times past to baptism.
the bishop laying his hand on us, we do confess that we forsake
the devil, his pomps, and all his angels. Then are we thrice
dipped in the water, not" (some leave out 'not') "answering any
thing more than the Lord hath set down in the gospel. When
we be taken out of the font, we taste of milk and honey
mingled together; and from that time we abstain from daily
washing by the space of a whole week[4]." We hear in this
an utter denying or renouncing, a third dipping, a tasting of
milk and honey, and after baptism an abstinence from bathing
by a week's space. In his first book against Marcion he maketh
mention also of oil[5]. Truly, milk is meet for children, unto
whom also they that be of perfect age, being baptized, are
likened. Beside this, in the old Testament there is often
mention made of the land of promise flowing with milk and
honey. Those things were first offered to be tasted of them
that are baptized, to give them to understand, that, Christ
Jesus being their captain, and having passed over Jordan,
they might by an infallible hope have[6] an inheritance in the
land of promise.

St Hierome witnesseth that wine was mingled with milk,
and saith, *Com. Lib.* 15. *ad Isaiam:* "The Lord provoketh
us not only to buy wine, but milk also; which signifieth the
innocency of infants: which type and custom is even unto
this day kept in the west churches, to give to them that are
born anew in Christ wine and milk[7]." At this day neither of

[4 .... aquam adituri, ibidem, sed et aliquanto prius in ecclesia sub
antistitis manu contestamur nos renuntiare diabolo et pompæ et angelis ejus. Dehinc ter mergitamur amplius aliquid respondentes quam
Dominus in evangelio determinavit. Inde suscepti, lactis et mellis
concordiam prægustamus: exque ea die lavacro quotidiano per totam
hebdomadam abstinemus.—Tertull. de Coron. Mil. cap. 3. ed. Semler. Tom. IV. p. 293. Hal. Magd. 1824.]

[5 Sed ille quidem (Dominus) usque nunc nec aquam reprobavit
creatoris, qua suos abluit; nec oleum, quo suos unguit, &c.—Id. adv.
Marcion. Lib. I. cap. 14. Tom. I. p. 21.]

[6 esse repositos, Lat.]

[7 .... ut non solum vinum emamus (provocans), sed et lac, quod
significat innocentiam parvulorum: qui mos ac typus in occidentis

them both is given to infants, no, not of them which will seem to be zealous maintainers of the old ceremonies. They believe in the meanwhile, that their omitting of these ceremonies is without sin, and needeth no satisfaction. Now also we may gather out of the sixth book of Augustine *De Bap. Contra Donat.* cap. 24. that they used divers and what prayers they thought good about baptism[1]. The same Augustine *Contra Pelag. et Celest.* Lib. ii. cap. 40. saith : " In baptizing of children they first conjure and blow away all contrary power : which also the infants, by the words of them that bear them, do answer that they renounce[2]." This ceremony he mentioneth also *Libro Primo de Nup. et Concup. ad Valer.* cap. 20. and *Libro* ii. cap. 18.[3] It is said in the ecclesiastical decrees, that the holy church throughout the whole world used that ceremony[4]. Again, Augustine, *In Epistola ad Bonifa.* 43. saith, that the godfathers do answer for the faith of the children, and confess their faith. " We ask them," saith he, " which offer the infants, and say, Believeth he in God? (who, being of that age, knoweth not whether there be a God or no.) They answer, He believeth ;

ecclesiis hodie usque servatur ; ut renatis in Christo vinum lacque tribuatur.—Hieron. Comment. in Isai. Proph. cap. LV. Lib. XV. Opp. Tom. III. col. 401. Par. 1693—1706.]

[1 Si non sanctificatur aqua, cum aliqua erroris verba per imperitiam precator effundit, &c. Multorum enim preces emendantur quotidie, si doctioribus fuerint recitatæ, et multo in eis reperiuntur contra catholicam fidem, &c.—August. de Baptis. contra Donat. Lib. VI. cap. 25. Opp. Tom. VII. fol. 95. col. 4.]

[2 — prius exorcizatur in eis (parvulis) et exsufflatur potestas contraria ; cui etiam verbis eorum a quibus portantur sese renunciare respondent.—Id. de Peccat. Orig. contra Pelag. et Celest. Lib. II. cap. 40. Opp. Tom. VII. fol. 166. col. 1.]

[3 In veritate itaque, non in falsitate potestas diabolica exorcizatur in parvulis, eique renunciant.—Id. de Nupt. et Concup. ad Valerium. Lib. I. cap. 20. Opp. Tom. VII. fol. 169. col. 1. Omnes baptizandi infantuli non ob aliud exsufflantur, nisi ut ab eis princeps mundi mittatur foras.—Ibid. Lib. II. cap. 18. fol. 174. col. 1.]

[4 Illud etiam quod circa baptizandos in universo mundo sancta ecclesia uniformiter agit, non otioso contemplamur intuitu : cum sive parvuli sive juvenes ad regenerationis veniunt sacramentum, non prius fontem vitæ adeant quam exorcismis et exsufflationibus clericorum spiritus ab eis immundus abigatur.—De Eccles. Dogm. cap. 31. ap. August. Opp. Tom. III. fol. 43. col. 2.]

and so they answer unto every question which is asked[5]."
The same Augustine, in his book *de Trinitate*. 15. cap. 26,
maketh mention also of oil, wherewith they that were baptized were anointed[6].

Rabanus Maurus, bishop of Mentz, a long time following
after Augustine[7], reckoneth up many more ceremonies of
baptism. For he, *Libro de Institutione Cleri*. i. cap. 27,
saith : " They are marked in the forehead and heart with the
cross in baptism, that the devil, seeing that mark, may know
that that sheep is not of his fold. Also consecrated salt is
put into the child's mouth, that, being seasoned with the
salt of wisdom, he may be free from the stink of wickedness,
and rot no more with the worms of sin. His ears and nostrils are touched with spittle, saying the word, *Ephatha*, used
of our Saviour, being thereunto added, that by the virtue of
Christ, the high priest, his ears may be opened to receive the
knowledge of God, and to hear the will and commandments of
God. Then the child is blessed, and his breast anointed
with holy oil, that no reliques of the enemy may lurk and
remain in him. After this, in the name of the holy Trinity
he is baptized, being dipped thrice in the water." And in his
28. chapter : " And being baptized, he immediately is signed
in the forehead with the chrism, with a prayer together following, that he may be made an inheritor of the kingdom of
Christ, and of Christ may be called a Christian." And in the
29. chapter : " After baptism there is delivered to the
Christian a white garment, signifying pureness and innocency[8]." Also for this cause were the baptized clothed with

[5] Interrogamus enim eos a quibus offeruntur (parvuli) et dicimus,
Credit in Deum? de illa ætate, quæ utrum sit Deus ignorat. Respon-
dent, Credit: et ad cetera sic respondetur singula quæ geruntur.—
August. Ep. 23. Bonifacio, Opp. Tom. II. fol. 18. col. 3.]

[6 — dono gratiæ, quod visibili significatur unguento quo baptizatos
ungit ecclesia.—Id. de Trinit. Lib. xv. cap. 26. Opp. Tom. III. fol. 101.
col. 2.]

[7 See above, page 248, note 2.]

[8 — signatur ipse homo signaculo sanctæ crucis tam in fronte
quam in corde, ut ipse apostata diabolus, in vase suo pristino suæ
interemptionis cognoscens signum, jam sibi deinceps sciat illud esse
alienum.... Tunc datur ei sal benedictum in os, ut per sal typicum,
sapientiæ sale conditus, fætore careat iniquitatis, et nec a vermibus
peccatorum ultra putrefiat..... Postea tanguntur ei nares et aures

white garments, that they might now remember that they were set free, and of servants and bondslaves of the devil made the freemen of Christ Jesus. Moreover, white colour in times past was consecrated to victories and triumphs: whereby it may seem, that the white garment was therefore given to them that were baptized, that they might be mindful, that whiles they live here on earth they must continually fight, and overcome in Christ; for the life of man is a warfare upon earth. And certainly, whereas offerings also began to be given to the baptized by the godfathers, that seemeth to have been borrowed from warfare. For by the offering or earnest (which we Switzers call *Die ynbindeten*[1]) he that is baptized is warned of his faith given in baptism, always to be mindful what a captain he forsook, and into what garrison he was entertained, wherein he must keep his faith given to the new captain Christ.

Many other things of this kind, which I find among writers of this latter age, I willingly pass over, lest I should seem to abuse your patience and gentleness. And who perceiveth not, yea, that at this day other of this kind innumerable new devices are added[2] to baptism? Therefore the safest and surest way is to build upon the first foundations of the blessed apostles. For if antiquity seem to bolster up the last[3] invented ceremonies, who dare deny, that the authority of the apostles doth excel it many ways? For the apostles were

cum saliva, et dicitur ei illud verbum evangelicum . . . . . Epheta, quod est, adaperire . . . . . ut per salivam typicam sacerdotis et tactum sapientia et virtus divina salutem ejusdem catechumeni operetur; ut aperiantur ei nares ad accipiendum odorem notitiæ Dei, ut aperiantur illi aures ad audiendum mandata Dei. Deinde benedictione sacerdotali munitur, ut ad sacrum baptismum cum fide accepta custodiatur. Ungetur illius tunc pectus de oleo sanctificato cum invocatione sanctæ Trinitatis, ut nullæ reliquiæ latentes inimici in eo resideant. Cap. 27. —et sic in nomine sanctæ Trinitatis trina submersione baptizatur . . . . postquam . . . . . statim signatur in cerebro a presbytero cum sacro chrismate, sequente simul et oratione, ut regni Christi particeps fiat, et a Christo Christianus possit vocari. Cap. 28. Post baptismum traditur Christiano vestis candida, designans innocentiam et puritatem, &c.—Rabani Mauri de Instit. Cler. Lib. I. Opp. Tom. VI. Col. Agrip. 1626.]

[1 presents made to a godchild at the christening.]
[2 posse, Lat.: can be.]
[3 So also ed. 1584: but 1577, these last.]

before them all which have lastly[4] invented and delivered
those manifold ceremonies to be used in baptism.

This also cometh in question, Whether we ought to
baptize with bare fair water, or with consecrated water; and
why the Lord commanded to baptize with water. St Cyprian, *Epist.* Lib. I. Epist. 12, saith; "The water ought to be
cleansed and sanctified before of the priest, to wash away the
sins of the man that is baptized[5]." But the examples and
testimonies of the holy scripture do more prevail with me
than the authority of Cyprian, or any other man, whatsoever
it be. This good man of God was also deceived in another
place about the mystery of baptism[6]; so that we must read
his writings with judgment. The scripture telleth us that John
Baptist, and the apostles and faithful disciples of Christ, baptized with water not consecrated. For what can be spoken or
read more plain, than that "John baptized in Jordan;" yea,
that Christ himself and his apostles also baptized in the river
Jordan? Where or how did the apostles consecrate the water
of baptism in the Acts of the Apostles? Philip, when the
eunuch shewed him water as they journeyed, he baptized him
out of that pure and clear fountain. Beside this, I have declared in the sermon next going before, how little pureness
is in common form of baptism, whereby the font is consecrated. But if any man think that we ought to baptize with
consecrated or holy water, and by consecrated do neither
understand anointed or prepared with crosses[7] or sanctified
with charms, but chosen to holy uses, I would stand in contention with him never a whit. For the water of baptism in
very deed is holy, not in respect of the words rehearsed, or
by crosses and other signs made; but because God hath instituted it, and in respect of the holy use and prayers of the
godly. Of which matter I spake not long ago, when I entreated of the sanctification or consecration of the sacraments.
And Christ commanded his disciples to baptize with water

Marginal notes: Whether we ought to baptize with water not consecrated.

Marginal note: Why the Lord commanded to baptize with water.

[4 posterius, Lat.: in later times.]

[5 Oportet ergo mundari et sanctificari aquam prius a sacerdote,
ut possit baptismo suo peccata hominis qui baptizatur abluere.—
Cyprian. Epist. LXX. Opp. p. 190. Oxon.]

[6 Bullinger doubtless refers to the sentiments of Cyprian on the
re-baptizing of those who had been baptized by heretics.]

[7 characteribus, Lat.]

for divers causes. For types or figures went before baptism in water; as the flood, as the Red sea through which the people of Israel passed, as divers cleansings and set washings mentioned in the law. Neither do the apostles of Christ dissemble those things. For Peter saith, that Noe was saved in the water of the flood, but the wicked drowned in the water. Paul affirmeth, that all our fathers were baptized by Moses in the cloud and in the sea. Therefore mortification and vivification is prefigured. And truly, the principal badge of the new Testament is baptism, witnessing that full remission of sins is brought unto us by Christ. And the holy prophets of God, by the mouth of the Lord foreshewing and promising this, have willingly shadowed out this inestimable benefit by water: therefore baptism must be ministered in water. This also served notably to represent the mystery: of which matter I have spoken in my last sermon[1], when I entreated of the analogy or likeness of signs. And for these causes chiefly baptism ought to be ministered in this, and not in any other element.

1 Pet. iii.

1 Cor. x.

Whether once or thrice the infant ought to be dipped in the water. There is contention also about this, Whether once or thrice he that is baptized ought to be dipped or sprinkled with water. Truly, the apostles have not curiously commanded anything in this behalf; so that it is free either to sprinkle or to dip. Sprinkling seemeth to have been used of the old fathers: for honesty and shamefacedness forbiddeth to uncover the body; and also the (weak) state of infants for the most part cannot away with dipping, since sprinkling also doth as much as dipping. And it standeth in the choice of him that ministereth baptism, to sprinkle him either once or thrice, after the custom of the church whereof he is minister. Tertullian, *contra Praxeam*, saith: "The Lord commanded to baptize into the Father, and into the Son, and into the Holy Ghost. Not into one: for we are baptized not once but thrice, at each name into each person[2]." And Gregory, answering Leonard the bishop, saith: "A diverse custom hindereth nothing the holy church, so that it be done in one faith. We by thrice

[1 See above, p. 327.]

[2 Novissime mandans (Dominus) ut tinguerent in Patrem et Filium et Spiritum Sanctum, non in unum; nam nec semel, sed ter, ad singula nomina in personas singulas tinguimur.—Tertull. adv. Prax. cap. 26.]

dipping do signify the mystery of Christ's lying in the grave three days[3]." Again, the reverend fathers in the fourth council held at Toledo do allow but one dipping in baptism, and then add immediately this reason : "And lest any should doubt of the mystery of this sacrament, why we allow but one dipping, he may see therein our death and resurrection. For the dipping into the water is as it were the going down into the grave; and the coming up again out of the water is the rising again out of the grave. Also he may perceive, that therein is shewed the unity of the Godhead, and the Trinity of the persons. The unity is figured, when we dip once; the Trinity, when we baptize in the name of the Father and of the Son and of the Holy Ghost[4]." This I do not allege to stay myself upon man's testimony[5]; but by man's testimony to shew, that it is free to follow that which serveth most to the edifying of the church.

Also there is a question moved touching the place of baptism : Whether it be not lawful to baptize in any other place than in the church. I say, that the church is consecrated to ministries and the worship of God, and therefore that comeliness itself requireth to baptize openly in the church. But if necessity will not permit this, the baptism of Christ is tied to no place; for we hear that Philip baptized out of the fountain in the broad field. Yet let us take heed, that we make not necessity a pretence for our lewd affections; but let all things in the church be clean which pertain unto baptism. Let all superfluity be laid aside; let all filth and uncleanness be banished; let all things (as saith the apostle) be done honestly and in order.

Of the place of baptism.

[3 — in una fide nihil officit sanctæ ecclesiæ consuetudo diversa. Nos autem quod tertio mergimus, triduanæ sepulturæ sacramenta signamus.—Greg. M. Lib. I. Indict. IX. Epist. 43. Opp. Tom. II. col. 532. Par. 1705.]

[4 Et ne forte cuique sit dubium hujus simpli mysterium sacramenti, videat in eo mortem et resurrectionem Christi significari: nam in aquis mersio quasi in infernum descensio est, et rursus ab aquis emersio resurrectio est. Item videat in eo unitatem Divinitatis et Trinitatem personarum ostendi: unitatem, dum semel immergimus; Trinitatem, dum nomine Patris et Filii et Spiritus Sancti baptizamus. —Concil. Toletan. IV. can. 5. (A. D. 633) Labb. et Coss. Tom. V. col. 1706.]

[5 So also ed. 1584: but 1577, testimonies.]

Touching the time, there is no law prescribed of the Lord: that is left free to the judgment of the godly. They that believed the preaching of St Peter at Hierusalem in the day of Pentecost, the eunuch also whom Philip baptized, and Cornelius the centurion likewise, finally, Paul the apostle at Damascus, yea, and Lydia the purple-seller, a religious or devout woman, and the keeper of the prison, they of Philippos also[1], and other faithful men or women, as soon as they had tasted of the gifts and graces of Christ and believed his word, forthwith they desired to be baptized: they did not foade it off[2] till another next time. Wherefore they do very well, which neither in themselves nor in their families do linger in receiving baptism. The delaying of circumcision in his children fell not out well unto Moses. As therefore we grant, that the time of the baptism[3] is free, so it ought to be our duty to take heed that we abuse not our liberty; being always mindful of these words spoken by God: "The uncircumcised man-child, in whose flesh the foreskin is not circumcised, that soul shall be cut off from his people, because he hath broken my covenant." But we are not ignorant that baptism came into the place of circumcision. Therefore the omitting of baptism is not free. There were some in the time of Cyprian which held opinion, that baptism ought to be received on the eighth day, after the manner of circumcision. But Cyprian, and the sixty-six bishops and elders that were with him in the council, ordained the contrary; to wit, that every one without any delay should receive baptism, and procure the same speedily in their family. That place is extant, *Epist.* Lib. iii., Epist. viii.[4] Furthermore, Socrates the

[1 custos carceris Philippici, Lat.: the keeper of the prison at Philippi also, and other, &c.]

[2 Vol. ii. p. 38, note 3.]

[3 So also ed. 1584: but 1577, of baptism.]

[4 Cyprianus, et ceteri collegæ qui in concilio affuerant numero 66, Fido fratri, Salutem. . . . Quantum vero ad causam infantium pertinet, quos dixisti intra secundum vel tertium diem, quo nati sint, constitutos, baptizari non oportere ; et considerandum esse legem circumcisionis antiquæ, ut intra octavum diem eum qui natus est baptizandum et sanctificandum non putares: longe aliud in concilio nostro omnibus visum est . . . . universi potius judicavimus, nulli hominum nato misericordiam Dei et gratiam denegandum.—Cyprian. Epist. LXIV. Opp. p. 158. ed. Oxon.]

historiographer, Lib. v. ca. 22, saith : " I know also another
custom in Thessaly, according to the which they baptize
only on the days of Easter. Whereby it cometh to pass,
that, saving a very small number, they die unbaptized[5]." But
after a certain time there was a law made, that the infants of
the faithful should not be baptized but at the feasts of
Easter and Whitsuntide. They excepted the time of necessity.
We may read this in *Decret. Syricii Pont. in Isidore;* and
in the epistles of Pope Leo unto the bishop of Campania and
Sicilia, which in order are reckoned to be fifty-seven and
sixty-two[6]. But the things that moved them hereunto are
such as may be easily disproved and overthrown. Truly,
from the beginning the time of baptism was not so limited.
Nevertheless, that law of baptizing the faithful at the feast of
Easter and Pentecost was renewed by Pipine, Charles, Lodo-
vick, and Lothar, French kings, and was spread far as their
dominions reached far[7]. Many things are sung in the service
of the papists at the time of Easter and Whitsuntide, which
are not understood but by this law and custom. At the
length it grew out of use, and the faithful were baptized as
occasion and opportunity first served.

This is also in controversy, Who ought to baptize, and
what the baptizer worketh ? Of the last I will speak first.

The baptizer giveth visibly the sacrament of regeneration, What the
baptizer
and a testimony of the remission of sins ; but the Lord by his worketh.
Spirit doth invisibly regenerate, and forgiveth sins, and sealeth

[5 Καὶ ἄλλο δὲ ἔθος ἐν Θεσσαλίᾳ οἶδα γινόμενον. Ἐν ταῖς ἡμέραις
τοῦ πάσχα μόνον βαπτίζουσι· διὸ σφόδρα πλὴν ὀλίγων οἱ λοιποὶ μὴ βαπ-
τισθέντες ἀποθνήσκουσιν.—Socrat. H. E. Lib. v. cap. 22. p. 297. Cantab. 1720.]

[6 — sola temeritate præsumitur, ut passim .... plebes baptismi
mysterium consequantur: cum hoc sibi privilegium et apud nos et
apud omnes ecclesias dominicum specialiter cum Pentecoste sua
pascha defendat .... infantibus .... vel his, quibus in qualibet necessitate opus fuerit sacri unda baptismatis, omni volumus celeritate suc-
curri.—Siricii Papæ ad Himerium Tarracon. Epist. Labb. et Coss.
Tom. II. col. 1018. Leonis I. Papæ ad universos episcopos per Sici-
liam constitutos. Epist. ibid. Tom. III. col. 1299. These authorities
are quoted Gratian. Decret. par. III. de Consecrat. dist. 4. can. 11—17.]

[7 See Concil. Matiscon. II. Labb. et Coss. Tom. v. col. 981. Mogunt. Tom. VII. col. 1242. Parisiens. VI. Tom. VII. col. 1603. Wor-
matiens. Tom. VIII. col. 945.]

the regeneration. John and the apostles baptize with water: Christ baptizeth with the Holy Ghost; not only with the visible sign of fire and the gift of tongues, but even he only giveth all spiritual gifts. Which thing the ancient fathers that they might expressly declare, did diligently distinguish between power and ministry. For Augustine, Tract. in John v. saith: "It is one thing to baptize in way of ministry, another thing to baptize by power. Our Lord Jesus Christ could, if he had would, have given power to any one servant to give his baptism, as in his stead; and could translate or remove from himself power to baptize, and place it in one of his servants, and give as great force to baptism being translated or removed into his servant, as it should have being given by the Lord. He would not do so for this purpose; that the hope of them which were baptized should hang on him, of whom they acknowledge themselves to be baptized. He would not therefore that a servant should settle his hope in a servant. And therefore cried the apostle, when he saw men willing to put their hope and trust in him: ' Was Paul crucified for you? Or were ye baptized in the name of Paul?' Paul therefore baptized as a minister, not as the power itself; but the Lord baptized as the power." And again: "John Baptist learned by the dove, 'Upon whomsoever thou shalt see the Spirit descending, like unto a dove, and tarry still upon him, the same is he which baptizeth with the Holy Ghost.' Therefore, O dove, let not deceivers seduce thee, which say, We baptize. O dove, acknowledge what the dove taught: ' The same is he which baptizeth with the Holy Ghost.' By the dove it is known that it is he; and dost thou think that thou art baptized by his power, by whose ministry thou art baptized? If thou be of that mind, thou art not yet in the body of the dove; and if thou be not in the body of the dove, it is no marvel because thou hast not simplicity; for simplicity especially is figured by the dove. John learned by the simplicity of the dove, that this is he which baptizeth with the Holy Ghost[1]." Thus far he.

John i.

True simplicity.

[1 Aliud est baptizare per ministerium, aliud baptizare per potestatem . . . . Potuit autem Dominus noster Jesus Christus, si vellet, dare potestatem alicui servo suo, ut daret baptismum suum tanquam vice sua, et transferret a se baptizandi potestatem, et constitueret in aliquo servo suo, et tantam vim daret baptismo translato

Furthermore, the minister of the church, being lawfully Who should baptize. ordained, ought to baptize. The Donatists contend, that none can baptize but he which is pure and holy. They boldly avouched, that that baptism was fruitless and void of effect, which a lewd-living minister, or defiled with wicked vices, did administer. Against these Augustine gravely disputed, and convinced them by the truth of the scripture. He in his 166. epistle saith : " See how perversely and wickedly that is spoken, which ye are wont to say : Because[2] if he be a good man, he sanctifieth him whom he baptizeth ; but if he be an evil man, and he not know so much which is baptized, then God sanctifieth him. If this be true, then men ought rather to wish to be baptized of ministers unknown to be evil, than of them which are known to be good, that they may rather be sanctified of God than of man. But far from us be this madness. Why then do we not speak truth and are rightly wise : Because[2] that grace belongeth alway to God, and the sacrament is his, and the ministry only committed unto man ; who if he be good, he cleaveth to God, and worketh with God ; but if he be evil, God worketh by him the visible form of the sacrament, but he himself giveth the invisible grace? Herein let us all be wise, and let there be no schisms or divisions among us[3]." The same Augustine, in his third book *contra*

in servum, quantam vim haberet baptismus datus a Domino. Hoc noluit ideo, ut in illo spes esset baptizatorum, a quo se baptizatos agnoscerent. Noluit ergo servum ponere spem in servo. Ideoque clamabat apostolus, cum videret homines volentes ponere spem in seipso, Nunquid Paulus pro vobis crucifixus est? aut in nomine Pauli baptizati estis? Baptizavit ergo Paulus tanquam minister, non tanquam ipsa potestas : baptizavit autem Dominus tanquam potestas ... Super quem videris Spiritum descendentem, sicut columbam, et manentem super eum, hic est qui baptizat Spiritu Sancto. Non ergo te decipiant, O columba, seductores qui dicunt, Nos baptizamus. Columba, agnosce quid docuit columba, Hic est qui baptizat in Spiritu Sancto. Per columbam discitur, quia hic est ; et tu ejus potestate putas te baptizari cujus ministerio baptizaris? Si tu hoc putas, nondum es in corpore columbæ ; et si non es in corpore columbæ, non mirandum, quia simplicitatem non habes : simplicitas enim maxime per columbam demonstratur. Quare per simplicitatem columbæ didicit Joannes, quia hic est qui baptizat in Spiritu Sancto.—August. in Evang. Joan. Tract. v. Opp. Tom. IX. fol. 9. col. 2. and 4. Par. 1531.]

[2 Rather, that.]

[3 Videte quam perverse et impie dicatur quod dicere soletis ; quia

Literas Petiliani[1], cap. 49, doth plentifully set forth the same matter. And because we have also handled the same thing in the end of our former sermon next before this, it is needless to speak one thing twice.

Whether midwives may baptize. Here is a question objected unto us, touching the baptism of midwives; Whether women midwives upon the point of necessity, that is, when the infant is in jeopardy to die before he come to be baptized at the hands of the ecclesiastical minister, ought and may baptize? We answer, that baptism is a sacrament of the church, and that women are forbidden to minister in the church; therefore that they neither can nor ought to baptize, as they are by no means permitted to teach. 1 Tim. ii. The laws of the apostle are well known. " But I suffer not a woman," saith Paul, " to teach, neither to usurp authority over the man, but to be in silence." The same law is repeated of the same apostle, the first to the Corinthians and fourteenth chapter, and is confirmed by God's law. Man's testimonies agree with God's. For Tertullian, in his book *De Velandis Virginibus*, saith: " It is not permitted unto a woman to speak in the church, much less to teach or to baptize, nor to offer; neither to take to herself the execution of any man's office, much less the priest's[2]." This also is read repeated in the fourth council of Carthage[3], where also Aurelius Augustine is said to have been present. Epiphanius, bishop of Salome[4] in

si bonus sit homo, ipse sanctificat eum quem baptizat; si autem malus sit, et nesciat ille qui baptizatur, tunc Deus sanctificat. Hoc si verum est, optare ergo debent homines ut a malis ignoratis baptizentur potius quam a notis bonis, ut magis a Deo quam ab homine possint sanctificari. Sed absit a nobis ista dementia. Quare ergo non verum dicimus et recte sapimus, quia semper Dei est illa gratia et Dei sacramentum; hominis autem solum ministerium: qui si bonus est, adhæret Deo et operatur cum Deo; si autem malus est, operatur per illum Deus visibilem sacramenti formam, ipse autem donat invisibilem gratiam. Hoc sapiamus omnes, et non sint in nobis schismata.— Aug. Epist. 166. Opp. Tom. ii. fol. 146. col. 3. Par. 1531.]

[1 Id. Opp. Tom. vii. fol. 40. col. 3.]

[2 Non permittitur mulieri in ecclesia loqui; sed nec docere, nec tinguere, nec offerre, nec ullius virilis muneris, ne duo (alii, nedum) sacerdotalis officii sortem sibi vendicarent.—Tertull. de Virg. Veland. cap. 9. Tom. iii. p. 15. ed Semler. Hal. Mag. 1829.]

[3 Mulier baptizare non præsumat.—Concil. Carthag. iv. can. 100. Labb. et Coss. Tom. ii. col. 1207.]

[4 Salaminæ, Lat. : Salamis.]

Cypres, disputing against divers heresies and confuting Marcion, saith : " He also giveth women leave and licence to baptize[5]." He saith as much of the Quintilian and Peputian heretics[6]. He also, reasoning against the heretics Collyridiani, saith : " If women were commanded to sacrifice unto God, or to execute any regular thing in the church, then Mary ought rather to do sacrifice in the new Testament, which was made worthy to carry in her own arms the King of all kings, the heavenly God, the Son of God; whose womb was made a temple and dwelling for the dispensation of the Lord in the flesh, being prepared for that purpose through the bountifulness and marvellous mystery of God. But it did not so please God. But neither was it committed or granted unto her to baptize; otherwise her Son might have been rather baptized of her than of John." The same author addeth : " And truly there is in the church an order of women-ministers called women-deacons; but not permitted to sacrifice, neither to attempt anything, but for reverence sake of women-kind, or for the hour of bathing, or visiting, or for affection and travel[7]."

Whereas they object the example of Sephora the Madianite, wife of Moses, which circumcised her son[8] in the time of necessity ; that doth establish no common law : as the particular example of Delbora maketh not all women judges.

Sephora circumciseth.

[5 Δίδωσι καὶ (Μαρκίων) ἐπιτροπὴν γυναιξὶ βάπτισμα διδόναι.—Epiphan. adv. Hæres. Lib. I. hær. xxii. vel xlii. Opp. Tom. i. p. 305. Par. 1622.]

[6 Τὴν ἀδελφὴν τοῦ Μωϋσέως ὡς προφῆτιδα λέγουσιν, εἰς μαρτυρίαν τῶν παρ' αὐτοῖς καθισταμένων γυναικῶν ἐν Κλήρῳ.—Epiph. adv. Hær. Lib. ii. hær. xxix. sive xlix. p. 418.]

[7 Εἰ ἱερατεύειν γυναῖκες Θεῷ προσετάσσοντο, ἢ κανονικόν τι ἐργάζεσθαι ἐν ἐκκλησίᾳ, ἔδει μᾶλλον αὐτὴν τὴν Μαρίαν ἱερατείαν ἐπιτελέσαι ἐν καινῇ διαθήκῃ, τὴν καταξιωθεῖσαν ἐν κόλποις ἰδίοις ὑποδέξασθαι τὸν παμβασιλέα Θεὸν ἐπουράνιον, Υἱὸν τοῦ Θεοῦ, ἧς ἡ μήτρα ναὸς γενομένη καὶ κατοικητήριον εἰς τὴν τοῦ Κυρίου ἔνσαρκον οἰκονομίαν κατὰ φιλανθρωπίαν Θεοῦ, καὶ ἔκπληκτον μυστήριον ἡτοιμάσθη. Ἀλλ' οὐκ εὐδόκησεν· ἀλλ' οὐδὲ βάπτισμα διδόναι πεπίστευται· ἐπεὶ ἠδύνατο ὁ Χριστὸς μᾶλλον παρ' αὐτῆς βαπτισθῆναι, ἤπερ παρὰ Ἰωάννου... Καὶ ὅτι μὲν Διακονισσῶν τάγμα ἐστιν εἰς τὴν ἐκκλησίαν, ἀλλ' οὐχὶ εἰς τὸ ἱερατεύειν, οὐδέ τι ἐπιχειρεῖν ἐπιτρέπειν, ἕνεκεν δὲ σεμνότητος τοῦ γυναικαίου γένους, ἢ δι' ὥραν λουτροῦ, ἢ ἐπισκέψεως πάθους, η πόνου, &c.—Id. Lib. iii. hær. lix. sive lxxix. Opp. Tom. i. p. 1060.]

[8 So also ed. 1584: but ed. 1577, their son.]

For there are many peculiar things done in the scripture, out of which if any man shall go about to draw general things and common laws, he shall bring in absurdities innumerable. What if Moses in the same place doth only describe the deed of his wife, moved thereunto by anger and displeasure, and not for religion's sake, to perform the ministry unto God? For she, grudging[1] against her husband, yea, and against God, took the foreskin of her son which was cut away, and cast it at his father her husband's feet, not without reproach, saying : "A bloody husband art thou unto me." As if you should say : *Ich habb woll ein bluotigman an dirr*[2]. And though the angel was appeased with Moses, because he seemed to allow the deed of the woman as well pleasing God; yet that is more to be imputed to the mercy of God, rather than to the righteousness of the woman's deed. It did grievously displease God, that David had slain Urias, and moreover had taken Beerseba to himself to wife; yet of his goodness and singular mercy he vouchsafed to call Salomon, who was born of Beersabe, by this name, Jedidia, because the Lord loved him. So the gracious Lord is also reconciled with Moses, who either by his own negligence, or through the fault of his Madianitish wife, lingered circumcision in the body of her son against the law longer than was meet; and is content with, and taketh in good part, the circumcision, which the woman performed rather of indignation than for religion : yet he will not that after her, as a perfect example, other women should circumcise.

But, you say, by baptism ministered by a woman the peril of death or eternal damnation was to be prevented, into which the infant falleth if he depart this world without baptism. My answer is : When the infant, being newly delivered out of his mother's womb, departeth with too too speedy death, so that the parents cannot, though they would never so fain, bring him to be baptized of the minister of the church, this pinch of necessity truly is not to the damnation or death of the infant; because he, being received into the covenant by the grace of God, is delivered from death through the blood of the Son of God. We are not destitute of testimonies of scripture duly serving in this behalf. In the law it was not lawful

Exod. iv.

2 Sam. xii.

Of salvation of infants departing without baptism.

[1 impotenter obstrepens, Lat.]
[2 A full bloody husband have I in thee! Luther's rendering is: Du bist mir ein blutbräutigam.]

to circumcise an infant before the eighth day ; but it is certain, that very many departed out of this world before the eighth day : yet in the meanwhile, if any man-child had departed the third or fourth day after his birth, no condemnation was imputed unto him. For otherwise David, a very sound man in religion, and one that loved his children dearly, and one very desirous of the salvation of his household, when his child was dead which was begotten and born unto him of Beersabe, could not have shewed himself so cheerful to his courtiers; to whom among other things he said, that he should go unto the dead child, to wit, into the land of the living. If it were no danger unto women-children to die uncircumcised (for they without circumcision were saved), neither verily shall it be damnable for men-children being not baptized to die at the point of necessity ; for we have oftentimes said, that holy baptism entered and took the place of circumcision. Hitherto pertain the testimonies out of the law and the prophets. In the law the Lord protesteth more than once, that he hath a most certain care and regard of infants. In Jonas he expressly professeth, that he hath a consideration and a respect of those that are not yet come to the years of discretion : for the Lord spared the most famous city of Ninive partly for their sakes.

Thou sayest, These testimonies of the old Testament pertain nothing to us, which live under the new Testament. I answer; That God, after the coming of Christ in the flesh, is not more rigorous unto us than he was before Christ's coming. For if it were so, what should we say else, but that Christ came not to fulfil, but to weaken and abolish the promises of God ? since that in times past among them of old the grace and the promise were effectual in necessity without the sign ; but now among us, being without the sign, they begin to be void and of no force.

Wherefore I, trusting to God's mercy and his truth and undoubted promise[3], believe that infants, departing out of this world by too too timely[4] death, before they can be baptized, are saved by the mere mercy of God, in the power of his truth and promise through Christ, who saith in the gospel: " Suffer little ones to come unto me ; for of such is the king- Mark x.

[3 So also ed. 1584: but ed. 1577, true and undoubted promise; veraci et indubitatæ promissioni, Lat.]

[4 præpropera, Lat.]

dom of God:" again: "It is not the will of my Father which is in heaven, that one of these little ones should perish." For verily God, who cannot lie, hath said: "I am thy God, and the God of thy seed after thee." Whereupon St Paul also affirmeth, that they are born holy which are begotten of holy parents: not that of flesh and blood any holy thing is born; for "that which is born of the flesh is flesh:" but because that holiness and separation from the common seed of men is of promise, and by the right of the covenant. For we are all by nature and natural birth born the sons of wrath, death, and damnation; but Paul attributeth a special privilege to the children of the faithful, wherewith by the grace of God they which by nature were unclean are purified. So the same apostle in another place doth gather holy branches of an holy root; and again elsewhere saith: "If by the sin of one many be dead, much more the grace of God, and the gift of grace, which is by one man Jesus Christ, hath abounded unto many." And therefore Augustine doubted not to say: "As all which die, die no otherwise but in Adam; even so all that are made alive, are not made alive but in Christ. And upon this whosoever shall say unto us, that any in the resurrection of the dead can be made alive otherwise than in Christ, he is to be abhorred and detested as a common plague of the christian faith[1]." *Ad Hiero. epi.* 28.

They object, By this means the use of baptism is made void and quite taken away; yea, Pelagianism is sprung up again, which with so great travail St Augustine, with many other learned and holy men, beat down and kept under. He

falsely spake that said: "The soul, whose foreskin is not circumcised, shall be cut off from his people, because he hath broken my covenant." He falsely spake that said: "Verily, verily, I say unto you, Except a man be born of water and of the Spirit, he cannot enter into the kingdom of God." For if these sayings be true, and children not baptized, truly the sequel is, that they dying without baptism are not saved. I answer, That I weaken holy baptism by no means, much

[1 Sicut omnes qui moriuntur, non nisi in Adam moriuntur, ita omnes qui vivificabuntur, non nisi in Christo vivificabuntur. Ac per hoc quisquis nobis dixerit quenquam in resurrectione mortuorum vivificari posse nisi in Christo, tanquam pestis communis fidei detestandus est. —August. Epist. 28. Opp. Tom. II. fol. 21. col. 2. Par. 1531.]

less take it quite away, when I defend that infants upon the pinch of necessity, not being guilty of the contempt of God or wicked negligence, are not damned though they die unbaptized. For so salvation should be tied to the sign, and the promise of God should be made void; as though that alone without the sign upon the point of necessity were vain, and could work nothing: as if the hand of God were shortened, and bound as it were to the sign. For otherwise I teach by all means, that infants are to be baptized, and that baptism is not to be delayed negligently, or to be put off maliciously. But in the meantime, if by too too speedy death they depart unbaptized, I exhort and charge, that a good hope and confidence be had in the truth and mercy of the Lord, who promiseth in the law and the gospel, that he is the God of young infants, and that his will is that not so much as one of his little ones should perish.

With Pelagius and Pelagians we have nothing to do: neither are we ignorant what St Augustine hath written unto Hierome, Epist. 28, in this behalf. "Whosoever shall say," saith he, "that infants which leave this life, not having been partakers of Christ his sacrament of baptism, are quickened and made alive in him, this man doubtless doth set himself both against the preaching of the apostles, and condemneth the whole church; where for this cause they make haste, and run with their children to have them baptized, for that without doubt they believe, that by no means otherwise they could be made alive in Christ[2]." And against the Pelagians, Epist. 106: "The apostolical seat, dealing against Pelagius, accurseth them which said that infants unbaptized have life everlasting[3]." The same Augustine, Lib. I. *De Ani. &c.* cap. 9, to Renatus, disputeth against Vincentius Victor, who granteth[4]

The Pelagians deny the baptism of infants, and why.

[2 Quisquis dixerit quod in Christo vivificabuntur etiam parvuli, qui sine sacramenti ejus participatione de vita exeunt, hic profecto et contra apostolicam prædicationem venit, et totam condemnat ecclesiam, ubi propterea cum baptizandis parvulis festinatur et curritur, quia sine dubio creditur aliter eos in Christo vivificari omnino non posse.—Id. ibid.]

[3 — contra apostolicæ sedis auctoritatem (disputabit), ubi de hac ipsa re cum ageretur, hoc testimonium adhibitum est evangelicum, ne parvuli non baptizati vitam posse habere credantur.—Aug. Ep. 106. Opp. Tom. II. fol. 95. col. 1.]

[4 So ed. 1584: but ed. 1577, granted.]

that infants are inthralled to original sin, and yet nevertheless are saved though they be not baptized. Against whom
he bringeth forth this saying of our Saviour: "Except a
man be born of water and of the Spirit, he cannot enter into
the kingdom of God[1]." But we, which condemn both Pelagius
and Pelagians, do affirm both those things which they deny;
to wit, that infants are born in original sin, and therefore
that the sanctification of Christ is necessary unto them, without which they are not saved. Again we defend and maintain, that the same infants ought to be baptized, if it be
possible, though by the right of the covenant they belong to
the body of Christ and are sanctified by the blood of Christ.
Pelagius taught, that infants ought not to be baptized; for that,
he held opinion, they are without all fault, or any sin, blame,
and offence. That wicked and ungodly man therefore did
not acknowledge either our own corruption, or the benefit
which God hath performed by, in, and through Christ. Yet
canst thou find neither of these in our assertion and doctrine;
wherefore we take no part with the Pelagians. St Augustine,
in that selfsame epistle unto St Hierome, expressly saith:
"Thou art none of them which say, that there is no guilt
drawn from Adam, from which the infant should be washed
by baptism[2]." And against Julian also, Lib. I. cap. 2,[3] he
proveth by the sentences of the holy fathers, that infants
have original sin[4]; and thereupon gathereth, that therefore
infants ought to be baptized, because they have sin. For the
Pelagians gathered clean contrary: They have no sin, therefore they are not to be baptized. For the council of Carthage
writeth thus to Innocent: "The Pelagians deny that infants
are to be baptized: for these, say they, perished not, neither is
there anything to be saved; because there is nothing in them
that is corrupt or wicked, &c.[5]" But we, insomuch as we

[1 Aug. Opp.Tom. VII. fol. 236. col. 1.]
[2 Non es ex illis qui modo nova quædam garrire cœperunt,
dicentes nullum reatum esse ex Adam tractum, qui per baptismum in
infante solvatur.—Aug. Ep. 28. Opp. Tom. II. fol. 20. col. 1.]
[3 The title of this chapter is, Testimonia Doctorum de Peccato
Originali.—August. Opp. Tom. VII. fol. 193.]
[4 astruit originale peccatum, Lat.: proveth original sin: that
infants have, not in Lat.]
[5 Parvulos etiam propter salutem ... baptizandos negant ... Quia,

believe that infants are born in sin, yea, and that they are both born the children of wrath, and are corrupt and wicked; moreover, because we believe that the Son of God was born without sin of a pure virgin, to fulfil and confirm God's promises, which do not shut out infants from salvation, but let them in as joint partners in the league; therefore we hold and defend that they are to be baptized. And therefore this reason gathered of Augustine we cannot simply allow: "Out of the fellowship of Christ no man cometh unto life: but by baptism we are joined as members into the body of Christ, and have fellowship with him. Therefore infants which are not to be baptized[6] are without the fellowship of Christ, and therefore are condemned[7]." For as we deny not, that we are graffed into the body of Christ by partaking of the sacraments (as we declared in our last sermon of sacraments, next and immediately going before this); so we have elsewhere shewed, and that too oftentimes already very largely, that the first beginning of our uniting or fellowship with Christ is not wrought by the sacraments; but that the same uniting or fellowship, which was founded and grounded upon the promise, and by the grace of God through the Holy Ghost was communicated unto us and ours, yea, before the use of the sacraments, is continued and sealed unto us by the participation or receiving of the sacraments. Although therefore an infant die without baptism, and being shut out by necessity from having fellowship with Christ[8], so that he be neither partaker nor yet sealed by the visible sign of the covenant; yet he is not altogether an aliant or stranger from Christ, to whom he is fastened with the spiritual knot of the covenant, by the virtue whereof he is saved.

Lib. iii. De pec. mer. et remiss. cap. 4.

inquiunt, isti non perierant, nec est quod in eis salvetur . . . quia nihil est in eis vitiatum.—Labb. et Coss. Tom. II. col. 1535.]

[6 infantes non baptizati, Lat.: infants which are not baptized.]

[7 Quid autem apertius tot tantisque testimoniis divinorum eloquiorum, quibus dilucidissime apparet, nec præter Christi societatem ad vitam salutemque æternam posse quenquam hominum pervenire, nec divino judicio posse aliquem injuste damnari . . . unde sit consequens, ut quamvis nihil agitur aliud cum parvuli baptizantur nisi ut incorporentur ecclesiæ, id est, Christi corpori membrisque socientur, manifestum sit eos ad damnationem nisi hoc eis collatum fuerit pertinere.—Aug. de Pecc. Mer. et Remis. Lib. III. cap. 4. Opp. Tom. VII. fol. 148. col. 2.]

[8 from having—with Christ, not in Lat.]

The exposition of the place, "The soul of the uncircumcised shall be cut off."

The place of Gen. xvii., alleged of cutting off the uncircumcised from the people of God, in consideration of the time, it fitly agreeth to those that are of perfect age and well grown in years, and not to babes or infants; which thing is seen in Moses, whom the angel of the Lord, for neglecting circumcision, or for delaying it longer than was lawful, would have slain[1], as he testifieth of himself: neither am I ignorant that certain old interpretators[2] refer that not to Moses, but to Eleazar the son of Moses. But the very course of the history and the circumstances of the same do sufficiently prove, that the danger lay on the father's, and not on the son's neck. What if a reason be added in the words of the law, which by no means agreeth to infants? "Therefore shall the uncircumcised perish," saith he, "because he hath broken my covenant." So that if we consider that circumcision in the very same place was commanded not only to infants, but to such as were of perfect age, as to Abraham, Ismael, and others desiring visibly to be joined into the fellowship of God; we are not to marvel that destruction is threatened to the disobedient. For if any man at this day understand and know the Lord's ordinance comprehended in his words[3], "He which shall believe and be baptized shall be saved," will yet nevertheless not be baptized, but boasteth that faith is sufficient for him unto salvation, that baptism is superfluous; he hath despised the ordinance of God, and is condemned for a rebel and an enemy[4] to God.

The exposition of the place, "Except a man be born of water, &c." John iii.

Furthermore, that place of John iii. is not to be understood of the outward sign of the holy baptism[5], but simply of the inward and most spiritual regeneration of the Holy Spirit; which when Nicodemus understood not perfectly, the Lord figured and made the same manifest unto him by parables of water and of the spirit, that is to say, of the wind or the air, by elements very base and familiar. For by and bye he addeth: "That which is born of the flesh is flesh," &c.: again, "The wind bloweth where it lusteth," &c.; which must needs be meant of the air; for the other part of the comparison followeth: "So is every one that is born of the Spirit."

[1 invadit, Lat.]
[2 Tertullian adv. Jud. cap. 3. Augustin. Quæst. in Exod. § 11.]
[3 So ed. 1584: but ed. 1577, these his words; his ejus verbis, Lat.]
[4 non amico, Lat. omitted: and for one who is not a friend.]
[5 So also ed. 1584: but ed. 1577, of holy baptism.]

Furthermore he addeth : " If I tell you of earthly things, and ye believe not; how will you believe, if I tell you of heavenly things?" But the argument which he put forth was not altogether earthly ; for this is the argument of his whole disputation : " Except a man be born from above[6] he cannot see the kingdom of God:" that is to say, unless a man be renewed, and as it were born again by the Spirit of God, which is given from above, that is to say, poured into him from heaven, he cannot be saved. The doctrine is altogether heavenly; but the means whereby he delivered, declared, and set forth this heavenly doctrine, is earthly. For by things taken from the earth he shadowed out to man, being gross of understanding and earthly, a spiritual and heavenly thing, and laid it open as it were even to the view of his eyes. As by water and air oftentimes the qualities of bodies are changed, and as the effect and working of water and the air in bodies is marvellous; in like manner is the working of the Holy Ghost in the soul of man, which it changeth, purifieth, and quickeneth, &c. For so the Lord himself afterward (which I told you even now) expoundeth another parable of the Spirit. And because all old writers, for the most part, by water have understood sacramental water, that is to say, holy baptism, we also receive this interpretation. For we willingly grant that baptism is necessary to salvation, as well in such as are of perfect age as also in babes or infants, so that necessity constrain not the contrary. For otherwise, if we go forward stubbornly with St Augustine to condemn infants by this place, truly we shall be compelled also to condemn even those that are baptized, if they depart this life without partaking of the body and blood of Christ. For St Augustine, being infected with the like error, defendeth that the sacrament of the Lord's supper ought to be put into the infants' mouth, or else they are in danger of death and damnation[8], because it is written : " Except ye eat the flesh of the Son of man, and drink his

De peccatorum meritis et remissione, Lib. i. cap. 20.7

John vi.

[6] e supernis, Erasmus's rendering : and Auth. Ver. marg.]

[7] The title of the chapter is, Eucharistia etiam infantibus necessaria ut baptismus.—August. Opp. Tom. VII. fol. 136. col. 4. Par. 1531.]

[8] de vita periclitaturis, Lat.: or else they are brought into danger as to life.]

blood, ye have no life in you." Therefore after this same order he placeth these two sentences: "Except a man be born of water and of the Spirit, he cannot see the kingdom of God;" and, "Except ye eat the flesh of the Son of man," &c. So that if thou persist obstinately in St Augustine's sentence, verily thou wilt condemn the whole church at this day, which denieth the partaking of the Lord's supper unto infants. But if in this thing there be admitted a convenient interpretation, why are ye so rigorous and obstinate in another and the like place and cause not disagreeable?

What will you say, if in this opinion Augustine doth not satisfy, no, not himself in all and every point? To a layman he thinketh it venial sin, if he baptize in time of necessity. He cannot tell whether it be godlily spoken, that baptism ministered by a layman ought to be iterated or done again[1]. But how much better and safer had it been, letting the necessity of baptism pass, which hath no lawful causes, to hold opinion that infants, if they be not prevented by death, ought to be baptized of the minister of the church, in the church, their parents procuring it as opportunity first serveth; and that too too speedy and sudden death (which we call the pinch of necessity) is no let or hinderance to salvation to them which are not yet brought to be baptized? The same Augustine trembleth and is afraid to determine of the punishment of damned infants for not being baptized; neither knoweth truly what he might certainly say. In his first book, *De Anim. &c.*, cap. 9, he saith: "Let no man promise to infants unbaptized as it were a middle place of rest or felicity, whatsoever it be, or wheresoever it be, between hell and the kingdom of heaven[2]." But that sentence is, for the most part, received of all men; whereupon also the infants are buried in the churchyard in a certain middle place between the profane

[1 Et si laicus aliqua percuntis dederit (baptismum) necessitate compulsus ... nescio an pie quisquam dixerit esse repetendum. Nulla enim cogente necessitate si fiat, alieni muneris usurpatio est: si autem necessitas urgeat, aut nullum, aut veniale delictum est.— August. cont. Ep. Parmen. Lib. II. cap. 13. Opp. Tom. VII. fol. 9. col. 3.]

[2 Non baptizatis parvulis nemo promittat inter damnationem regnumque cœlorum quietis vel felicitatis cujuslibet atque ubilibet quasi medium locum.—Id. de Anim. et ejus Orig. Lib. I. cap. 9. Opp. Tom. VII. fol. 236. col. 1.]

and holy ground[3]. And again the same Aug. *contra Juli-anum Pelagianum*, Lib. v. cap. 8, writeth: "That those infants of all other shall come in the easiest damnation." And immediately he addeth: "Which of what manner and how great it shall be, although I cannot describe, yet I dare not say that it were better for them to be as no body than to be there[4]." And again, in his epistle to St Hierome, 28, he saith: "When I come to determine of the punishments of little infants, believe me, I am driven into narrow straits, neither find I anything at all to answer[5]." Here also may that be added which he disputeth upon, Lib. iv. *contra Donatist.* cap. 22 and 23, touching the thief which was crucified with Christ, among other things saying: "That then baptism is fulfilled invisibly, when not the contempt of religion, but the point of necessity, excludeth and shutteth out from visible baptism[6]." Why then should we not believe also, that in infants departing by too too timely death, baptism is invisibly performed, since that not contempt of religion, but the extremity of necessity which cannot be avoided, excludeth and debarreth them from visible baptism? And since very many at this day do grant, that any man of perfect age without baptism in the point of necessity may be saved, so that he have a desire of baptism; why then may not the godly desires of the parents acquit the infants now newly born from guiltiness? But this much hitherto.

Touching this also, who are to be baptized, both in time past and our age there hath been bitter jarring. Pelagius in time past denied that infants ought to be baptized, which we

Who are to be baptized.

[3 in cœmiterio innocentum, Lat.: omitted.]

[4 Quis dubitaverit parvulos non baptizatos, qui solum habent originale peccatum nec ullis propriis aggravantur, in damnatione omnium levissima futuros? Quæ qualis et quanta erit, quamvis definire non possum, non tamen audeo dicere, quod eis ut nulli essent quam ut ibi essent potius expediret.—Aug. contra Julian. Pelag. Lib. v. cap. 8. Opp. Tom. VII. fol. 213. col. 2.]

[5 Cum ad pœnas ventum est parvulorum, magnis, mihi crede, coarctor angustiis, nec quid respondeam prorsus invenio.—Id. Epist. XXVIII. Opp. Tom. II. fol. 21. col. 4.]

[6 Tunc impletur (baptismus) invisibiliter, cum mysterium baptismi non contemptus religionis, sed articulus necessitatis excludit.—Aug. de Baptismo contra Donat. Lib. IV. cap. 22. Opp. Tom. VII. fol. 88. col. 3. Par. 1531.]

heard even now.   Before Pelagius' time, Auxentius Arianus, with his sectaries, denied that they are to be baptized[1].   Some in the time of St Bernard denied the same, as we may gather out of his writings[2].   The anabaptists at this day, a kind of men raised up of Satan to destroy the gospel, deny it likewise[3].   But the catholic truth, which is delivered unto us in the holy scriptures, doth simply pronounce, that all they are to be baptized whom God acknowledgeth for his people, and giveth sentence that they are partakers of purification or sanctification or remission of sins.   For in all this treatise concerning the sacraments I have already and do now shew, that baptism is a badge or cognisance of the people of God, and an assured token of our purification by Christ.   Therefore since the young babes and infants of the faithful are in the number or reckoning of God's people, and partakers of the promise touching the purification through Christ; it followeth of necessity, that they are as well to be baptized, as they that be of perfect age which profess the christian faith.

Who be the people of God.   But there is a busy disputation begun, Who be the people of God, and partakers of remission of sins by Christ?   So that the disputation is touching the secret election of God, and other hard questions depending on this thing.   But briefly and simply we can rid our hands of this.   We say, that the people of God are acknowledged either by men's confession of the christian faith, or else by the bountiful promise of God.   By men's confession; for we acknowledge them to be the children of God, who, being now grown to perfect age, do openly confess the true God, that God is their God, and that Jesus Christ is their Saviour.   But that confession is either unfeignedly or hypocritically made: unfeignedly, as when St Peter saith, "Thou art Christ, the Son of the living God;" when the eunuch saith, "I believe that Jesus Christ is the Son of God:" but hypocritically, as when Simon Magus in the Acts of the Apostles saith, that he believeth in Jesus Christ. But whether a man believe unfeignedly or hypocritically,

[1 See Examinations, &c. of Archdeacon Philpot, ed. Park. Soc. pp. 274, &c. where much is borrowed, word for word, from this sermon of Bullinger's.]

[2 Bernard. in Cantic. Serm. LXVI. § 9. Tom. IV. col. 3071. Epist. 241. Tom. I. col. 506. ed. Par. 1839.]

[3 Bulling. adv. Anabapt. Lib. VI. cap. 2.]

when he maketh open confession of his faith in Christ, (the secrets of the heart God only seeth; for he only is rightly believed to be the searcher of men's hearts,) it belongeth not to us, if he make a right confession, to separate or cast him away from the people of God. For Philip did not cast off or put back Simon Magus; but upon his confession received him for a faithful man, and baptized him as a faithful man, though he in very deed, and before God, were an hypocrite. In the first sermon of this decade[4] we declared, that hypocrites also are reckoned in the church, till time they be revealed. But concerning remission of sins, those only among them that be of perfect age do obtain it, which unfeignedly believe: which in another place is often shewed. St Peter said to Simon Magus, though he were baptized, "Thou hast neither part nor fellow- Acts viii. ship in this business, because thy heart is not right in the sight of God."

Furthermore, by the free and bountiful promise of God, not only by the confession of men, we esteem and acknowledge the people of God. For to whomsoever the Lord promiseth that he will be their God, and whomsoever he receiveth and acknowledgeth for his, those no man without an horrible offence may exclude from the number of the faithful. And God promiseth, that he will not only be the God of them that confess him, but of infants also; he promiseth to them his grace and remission of sins. Who therefore, gainsaying the Lord of all things, will yet deny that infants belong to God, are his, and that they are made partakers of purification through Christ? And that God acknowledgeth infants for his and sanctifieth them, by the very sum of the covenant it is manifest. "I will make my covenant between me and Gen. xvii thee," saith the Lord unto Abraham, "and thy seed after thee in their generations, by an everlasting covenant; that I may be God unto thee, and to thy seed after thee." There is added circumcision, a sign of sanctification, whereof I spake abundantly, when according to order I entreated of circumcision[5]. Neither is there any cause why any man should fear, that with circumcision and the ceremonies of the law the promise is abrogated, and that by the coming of Christ the covenant is broken and annihilated. For we said even now,

[4 See above, p. 12.]
[5 Vol. II. pp. 171—182.]

that Christ came to fulfil the promises of God, and not to break them. And therefore the Lord in the gospel speaketh of infants, that is to say, which have not as yet confessed the faith, and saith : " Suffer little children to come unto me, and forbid them not; for of such is the kingdom of God." And though it be said " of such," and not " of those;" yet no man is so ignorant, but understandeth, there is a likeness between those things which are compared between themselves. Therefore if the kingdom of God belongeth unto them that are of perfect age, because they are become like little children ; surely it followeth of necessity, that the inheritance of the kingdom of heaven belongeth also to infants or little children. For it followeth in the gospel : " Whosoever shall not receive the kingdom of God as a little child, he shall in no wise enter therein." Therefore it behoveth the heirs of the kingdom of God to be first infants or little children. And who knoweth not, that no man, unless he be sanctified and purified, shall enter into the kingdom of heaven ? Children enter into the kingdom of God: therefore they are purified, to wit, by the grace of God. For by their nature and birth they are unclean, and sinners; but for Christ's sake they are purified, who said, " That he came to seek and save that which was lost." Paul also expressly testifieth, that " by the sin of one, Adam, sin came on all men unto condemnation ; and that by the righteousness[1] of one, Christ, good came upon all men to the righteousness[1] of life." Therefore it is certain, that infants are partakers of purification and remission of sins through Christ, albeit they do not confess remission of sins. What, doth not the Lord say in the gospel, " It is not the will of your Father which is in heaven, that one of these little ones should perish ?" Again: " He that shall receive such a young child in my name, receiveth me; but he that shall offend one of these little ones that believe in me, it were better that a millstone were hanged about his neck," &c. See therefore and " take heed, that ye despise not one of these little ones : for I say unto you, that their angels in heaven do always behold the face of my Father which is in heaven." Behold, what could be more manifestly spoken ? It is not the will of my heavenly Father, that infants should perish. Therefore he receiveth them freely into grace and favour, though they have

Rom. v.

[1 justificationem, Lat.]

not yet confessed. Moreover, he that receiveth such a little
one, to wit, as he himself set in the midst of them, for Christ's
sake, he is said to receive Christ himself. Lo, he attributeth
to the receivers of infants that which he promised to the
receivers of the prophets. He addeth: "But he which shall Infants con-
fessing or be-
lieving.
offend one of these little ones that believe in me." He mani-
festly calleth the little ones, not yet able to confess, believers,
because he reputeth them of his grace for believers. Neither
is this any wonder or strange thing, since God, yea to them
that are of perfect age, imputeth faith for righteousness. For
in all points righteousness, acceptation, or sanctification, is
free and imputative, that the glory of his grace might be
praised. Furthermore, his will is that little ones should not be
despised, much less to be cast out among [2] the number of the
saints. Yea, he doth affirm that angels are given unto them
to be their keepers, who though they be ministers of God's
majesty, yet the selfsame are given and granted to little children to be their guard: so that hereby [3] we may judge what
great store the Lord setteth by infants, and learn not to wipe
them out of the score of God's people, to whom the inheritance of life is due. We attribute nothing here to the birth
which is after the flesh, but all things to the grace and promise of God. Now it is evident by all the [4] testimonies,
that as well the infants of the faithful are to be baptized, as
also those that are of perfect age, confessing the faith.

Now on the contrary part the anabaptists do contend, that By what ar-
guments the
anabaptists
teach that
infants ought
not to be
baptized.
none is to be baptized, but he alone which both is able to be
taught, and to believe, yea, and make confession of his faith
also. And for confirmation of this thing they bring these
sayings of our Saviour: out of St Matthew, "Go ye therefore, and teach all nations, baptizing them in the name of the
Father," &c.: out of Mark, "Go ye into the whole world,
and preach the gospel to all creatures: he which shall believe
and be baptized, shall be saved," &c. Behold, say they,
teaching goeth before baptism; therefore they that are not
able to be taught ought not to be baptized. Furthermore,
to believe goeth before, and to baptize followeth after: infants
do not believe, therefore they are not to be baptized. Upon
all these they heap up out of the Acts of the Apostles ex-

[2] e numero, Lat.: from among.]   [3] vel inde, Lat.: hereby also.]
[4] So also ed. 1584: but ed. 1577, all these: ex his omnibus, Lat.]

amples, which prove that the faithful, that is to say, they that
confess the faith, were baptized of the apostles. They reckon
up also the newly-instructed Christians[1] of the old time, to
whom, say they, there had been no place given, if they had
baptized infants. I answer : If the order of the words make
any thing in this matter, we also have in a readiness to serve

Matt. xxviii. our turn. For in Mark thus we read : "John baptized in the
desert, preaching the baptism of repentance ; " in which place
we see, that to baptize goeth before, to preach followeth after.
Yea, I will shew also that that place, which they allege out
of Matthew for themselves, maketh also for us. For Matthew's
words be these : "All power is given unto me both in heaven
and in earth," saith the Lord. "Go therefore," and μαθή-
τευσατε, that is to say, discipulate, (that I may so speak ;)
that is, make ye me disciples, or gather together all nations.
Yea, he teacheth them also the way and means how to gather
disciples unto him out of all nations, or all nations, by
baptizing and teaching them. By baptizing and preaching
ye shall gather me together a church. And he setteth out
both of them severally one after another, sweetly and shortly,
saying : "Baptizing them in the name of the Father and of the
Son and of the Holy Ghost; teaching them to observe all
things which I have commanded you." Now therefore baptism
goeth before teaching. But we do not thereby gather, that
those nations, which never heard anything before of God and
the Son of God and the Holy Ghost, are to be baptized;
neither would the apostles have borne that : but we allege
these things, to declare upon how fickle a foundation the
anabaptists do build. And we simply say, that it is not true
which these men imagine, that the Lord commanded his
apostles to baptize them only whom they taught. Neither
doth he here point out who are to be baptized in the whole
world[2]; but he speaketh of them that are of perfect age, and
of laying the first foundations of faith and of the church
among the gentiles, being rude as yet and ignorant altogether
in religion. They that are of perfect age are able to hear
preaching or teaching: infants are not so. They that are
of perfect age are able to believe and confess: infants are
not so. Therefore he speaketh nothing here of infants. Yet

[1 catechumenos, Lat.]
[2 in universum, Lat. : in all instances.]

therefore they are not debarred from baptism. It is a general law, " He which doth not labour, let him not eat;" but who is so cruel and unnatural to think, that therefore infants are to be famished to death ? The Lord, when true religion began to be spread abroad, sent his apostles into all nations, unto them which both were ignorant of God and strangers from the testaments of God. Truly, it behoved them not first to baptize, and afterward to teach; but first to teach, and then to baptize. If at this day we should go to convert or turn the Turks to the faith of Christ, first truly we should teach them, afterward baptize the servants of Christ and those that would yield themselves into his subjection. So the Lord himself in times past also first renewed his covenant with Abraham himself, and instituted circumcision for a seal of the covenant; and after that Abraham was circumcised. But he himself, when he understood that infants also were partakers in the covenant, and that circumcision was the seal of the covenant, he afterward did not only circumcise Ismael, being thirteen years of age, and all that were born in his own house, but infants also, among whom we reckon Isaac also. Even so the faithful which were turned by the preaching of the gospel from gentilism, and confessing were baptized; when they understood that their infants were counted among the people of God, and that baptism was the badge of God's people, they caused also their infants to be baptized. As therefore it is written of Abraham, he circumcised all the men-children in his house; so we oftentimes read in the Acts and writings of the apostles, that, after the master of the house is turned, the whole family is baptized.

But as concerning the newly-instructed Christians, they came in the old time from the Gentiles daily unto the church, whom these did instruct in the principles of faith, being ignorant therein, and afterward baptized them. But the ancient fathers themselves nevertheless baptized also the infants of the faithful; which anon we will declare.

Neither do they lawfully gather, when they conclude in this sort: He which shall believe, and be baptized, shall be saved; infants do not believe; therefore they are not to be baptized. For again, it is certain that it is spoken of them that be of perfect age, as in Matthew. And because he requireth faith and confession of faith of those that are of perfect age, it doth not follow thereupon that he requireth the same of infants. For he accounteth these as his own of his mere grace and free promise, without their confession. So that of the contrary part we do thus reason : They that believe are to be baptized : (which the very adversaries also do confess:) infants do believe ; for God reckoneth them in the number of the faithful, which I have afore manifestly proved : therefore infants are to be baptized.

Infants understand not the mystery of baptism. They object, that infants understand not the mystery of baptism ; and therefore, that it is not only repugnant to religion, but to common sense and reason, to baptize infants ; for to baptize an infant is to baptize a log, since neither of them hath the use of reason. But these filthy knaves let their tongues run at random against the very majesty of God. God commanded to circumcise the infants ; and circumcision containeth high mysteries, which infants understand not. But hath God ordained anything against reason and common sense ? Go, ye false knaves, go with your blasphemies to the place which you deserve ! It. is a most filthy deed, yea, and more than barbarous, in that ye compare infants to logs ; for what great store God setteth by infants, we taught you already before out of the gospel. But men, which now begin to have the use of sound reason, are diligently and earnestly to be taught and admonished to remember they are baptized, and to endeavour, by calling on the name of the Lord, in all points to be answerable in life and conversation to their promise and profession. For[1] Abraham instructed his son Isaac, and all the holy fathers their children.

That the baptism of infants is of God, and that the apostles baptized infants. But letting pass these brainsick, frantic, and foul-mouthed railers, who (as we have heard) never want words to wrangle, though we have had never so much, never so often, and never so earnest conference with them[2] ; let us proceed to declare in a few but yet manifest arguments, that infants are to be baptized, and that the apostles of Christ our Lord have baptized infants. The Lord commanded to baptize all nations,

[1 So also ed. 1584 : but ed. 1577, For so. Ita vero, Lat.]
[2 Bullinger had many conferences with anabaptists during his pastorate at Bremgarten ; and in the years 1525, 1527, 1531, and 1532, public disputations with them were specially held in Zurich, Basle, Berne, and other neighbouring towns.—Bulling. adv. Anabap. Lib. i. capp. 5—7.]

and therefore infants; for they are comprehended under the word of "all nations." Again, whomsoever God reckoneth among the faithful are faithful: for Peter in a vision heareth: "That which God hath cleansed call not thou common or Acts x. unclean." God reckoneth infants among the faithful; therefore they are faithful: except we had rather resist God, and seem to be stronger than he. And now we count it out of all controversy, that the apostles of Christ baptized them, whom Christ commanded to baptize: but he commanded to baptize the faithful; therefore the apostles baptized infants.

The gospel is greater than baptism: for Paul saith, 1 Cor. i. "The Lord sent me to preach the gospel, and not to baptize." Not that he did absolutely deny that he was not sent to baptize, but because he preferred doctrine; for the Lord commended them both to his apostles. Furthermore, in the gospel children are received of God, and not refused: who then, unless he be willingly obstinate, can debar them from the less? In sacraments the thing signified and the sign are considered. The thing signified is the excellenter; from that infants are not debarred. Who, then, will deny them the sign? Truly, the holy sacraments of God are more esteemed by the word than the sign. By the word we gather, that women are not excluded from the supper of the Lord. Although therefore we read not that they were in the first institution, and set at the first table of the Lord, neither that there is any express law which commandeth us to admit them to the supper; yet nevertheless, without fear or doubt, by a perfect argument[3] we admit them.

St Peter could not deny them the baptism of water, to whom he saw the Holy Ghost to be given, which is an assured token of God's people; for he saith in the Acts of the Apostles: "Can any man forbid water, that these should not be baptized, which have received the Holy Ghost as well as we?" Wherefore the holy apostle Peter denied not baptism to infants. For he knew assuredly, even by the doctrine of his Lord and Master (that I may speak nothing now of the everlasting covenant of God), that the kingdom of heaven is of infants. No man is received into the kingdom of heaven, unless he be the friend of God; and these are not destitute of the Spirit of God: "For he which hath not the Spirit of Rom. viii.

[3 ex syllogismo, Lat.]

Christ, the same is none of his." Children are God's; therefore they have the Spirit of God. Therefore, if they have received the Holy Ghost, as well as we; if they be accounted among the people of God, as well as we that be grown in age; who, I pray you, can forbid these to be baptized with water in the name of the Lord? At the first the apostles murmured, being then not sufficiently instructed, against them that brought infants unto the Lord. But the Lord rebuked them, and said: "Suffer little children to come unto me." Why then do not the rebellious anabaptists obey the commandment of the Lord? For what other thing do they at this day, which bring children unto baptism, than that which they in times past did, which brought infants unto the Lord? And the Lord received them, laid his hands on them, and blessed them; and, to be short, by words and gestures he notably signified, that children are the people of God, and most acceptable to God. But why then by the same means, say they, did he not baptize them? Because it is written, that "Jesus himself did not baptize, but his disciples." Now[1] since of the thing itself it is so plainly determined, why as yet do we contend about the sign? Hitherto good men are satisfied; but contentious persons go on to busy themselves with questions.

John iv.

Beside this, circumcision among the old people of God was given to infants; therefore baptism ought to be given to infants among the new people; for baptism succeeded in the place of circumcision. For St Paul saith: "By Christ ye are circumcised with circumcision made without hands, by putting off the body of the flesh subject to sin[2], by the circumcision of Christ; buried with him in baptism." Lo, Paul calleth baptism the circumcision of Christians, "made without hands;" not that water is not ministered by hands, but in that no man henceforth is circumcised with hands, the mystery of circumcision remaining nevertheless in the faithful. Neither shalt thou read any of the old interpreters of the church which have not confessed, that baptism came instead of circumcision. Yea, the likeness and similitude of both of them do shew a manifest succession.

Col. ii.

To that which I have said I join this. The servants of God have always been careful to give the signs to them for

[1 Præterea, Lat.: And besides.]
[2 corpus peccatorum carnis, Lat., and Erasmus.]

whom they were ordained. For, that I may pass over all
other; did not Josua diligently provide, that the people should Josh. v.
be circumcised afore they entered into the land of promise?
And since the apostles, the preachers to the whole world, have
been the faithful servants of Jesus Christ, who hereafter may
doubt that they baptized infants, since baptism came into the
place of circumcision?

Undoubtedly the apostles of Christ framed all their doings
unto the types and figures of the old Testament: therefore it
is certain, that they framed baptism also, and therefore that
they baptized infants, because they were in the figure of baptism; for the people of Israel went through both the Red sea
and the river Jordan with their children. And although they be
not always expressed, as neither women are in the holy scriptures; yet they are comprehended and understood by them.

To this appertaineth that which is clearly set down in
the scriptures, that the apostles baptized whole houses or
families. In houses first of all children are comprehended, as
the greatest and most beautiful part of the house. So then the
apostles baptized children or little ones, and not only them that
are of perfect age. And that a house especially comprehendeth
infants or little ones, it may be declared very easily. And
first out of the place of Genesis xvii. which even very now I
alleged. Next, in that Joseph sent for Jacob his father with
his whole house out of the land of Canaan into the land of
Egypt, lest his house should have perished with hunger.
There are many places of this kind in the law and the prophets, and in the whole scripture. But be it, that there were
no infants in those houses (which thing these janglers object)
which the apostles baptized; yet nevertheless they do pertain
unto the house, and are counted of it; so that if they had
been in the house, without doubt they had baptized them.
Whereas therefore they contend, that they were not baptized
in those families or houses; truly, I say that the fault was
neither in the children, as though they had been unworthy
of baptism, neither in the apostles, as though they were not
wont to baptize infants; but in that, because they were not
present: for if they had been present, they had been baptized. For why? the apostles baptized whole houses, unto
which children belong.

Now I can shew by the writings of the old doctors, that The baptism
of infants baptism of infants hath continued from the apostles' time even unto us; neither was it ordained by any councils, or by the decrees of any pope, or other men; but instituted and delivered of the apostles out of the scriptures. Origen, Lib. *Enarrat. in Epist. Pauli ad Rom. v.* expounding the vi. chap. saith: "That the church of Christ received of the apostles themselves baptizing of infants[1]." St Hierome maketh mention of the baptizing of infants, Lib. iii. *Contra Pelagianos*[2], and in his epistle to Læta[3]. St Augustine citeth the place of Chrysostom, nay, being cited of Julian, chap. ii.[4] He also unto Hierome, Epist. 28, saith: "St Cyprian, making no new decree, but most stedfastly keeping the faith of the church, was of this opinion with certain of his fellow-bishops, that the new-born child might rightly be baptized[5]." The place of Cyprian is to be seen in *Epi. ad Fidum;* as also I declared before, when I spake of the time of baptism[6]. The same Augustine against the Donatists, Lib. iv. cap. 23 and 24, boldly affirmeth, that "baptizing of children was not fetched from the authority of men, or of councils, but from the tradition or doctrine of the apostles[7]." Cyril, Lib. *in Levit. viii.* both approveth the baptizing of children[8], and condemneth the

[1] Ecclesia ab apostolis traditionem suscepit etiam parvulis baptismum dare.—Origen. Comment. in Ep. ad Rom. Lib. v. Opp. Tom. iv. p. 565. Par. 1759.]

[2] Critob. Dic, quæso, et me omni libera quæstione, quare infantuli baptizentur?—Hieron. adv. Pelag. Dial. Lib. iii. Opp. Tom. iv. par. 2. col. 545. Par. 1704.]

[3] Nisi forte æstimas Christianorum filios, si baptisma non acceperint, &c.—Id. Epist. ad Lætam, lvii. Opp. Tom. iv. par. 2. col. 593.]

[4] So also ed. 1584: but ed. 1577, nay, being cited of Julian he expoundeth it, Lib. i. contra Julian. cap. 2. Imo a Juliano citatum illustrat lib. contra Julian. i, cap. 2. Lat.—Aug. Opp. Tom. vii. fol. 195. col. 1. Par. 1531.]

[5] Beatus quidem Cyprianus non aliquod decretum condens novum, sed ecclesiæ fidem firmissimam servans, ... mox natum rite baptizari posse, cum suis quibusdam coepiscopis censuit.—Id. Ep. xxviii. Opp. Tom. ii. fol. 21. col. 3.]

[6] See above, page 365.]

[7] — quod universa tenet ecclesia, nec conciliis institutum, sed semper retentum est, non nisi auctoritate apostolica traditum rectissime creditur.—Aug. de Bap. contra Donat. Lib. iv. cap. 24. Opp. Tom. vii. fol. 88. col. 3.]

[8] — quid causæ sit, cum baptisma ecclesia observatur, etiam

iterating of baptism [9]. Which thing I do not allege to this end, to build the baptizing of children upon man's witness; but to teach that man's testimonies agree with the testimonies of God, and that the truth of antiquities is on our part, lies and new forgeries on the shameless anabaptists' side, who feign that baptizing of children was commanded by the pope.

Now I think it not labour lost to speak somewhat of ana- baptism. In the time that Decius and Gallus Cæsar were emperors, there arose a question in the parts of Africa of re-baptizing heretics. And St Cyprian and the rest of the bishops, being assembled together in the council of Carthage, liked well of anabaptism. But Cornelius, bishop of Rome, in very deed an holy and learned man, and a martyr also, together with the other [10] bishops of Italy, misliked the same. For they would that heretics, after they had renounced their wicked opinions and made their confession touching the right opinion, should be cleansed by the only laying on of hands. Ye may read this in Eusebius, Ecclesiastical History, Lib. vii. There is also extant a treatise of that matter in the Ecclesiastical Decrees, cap. 52. [11] But we must understand, that St Cyprian affirmed nothing obstinately in this cause. For in the end of his epistle to Jubaianus he writeth: " These things have I briefly sent unto you in writing, after our mean capacity, most dear brother, commanding no man to follow them, neither preventing any man's opinion; but that every bishop, having liberty of his own judgment, may do what he thinketh best [12]."

After that time both the Arians and Donatists did rebaptize. Touching the Arians historiographers write, and especially Sozomenus, Lib. vi. [13] Ecclesiastical writers do touch the same thing also elsewhere in their works. Against the

The history of ana-baptism.

parvulis baptismum dari &c.—Cyril. Alexand. Comment. in Levit. Lib. VIII. fol. 33. Par. 1514.]

[9 Id. de Adorat. in Spirit. et Ver. Lib. VI. Opp. Tom. I. p. 176. Par. 1638.]

[10 multis, Lat. : many.]

[11 Qui sint habendi pro baptizatis.—Aug. de Eccles. Dogmat. 52. Opp. Tom. III. fol. 44. col. 1. Par. 1531.]

[12 Hæc tibi breviter pro nostra mediocritate rescripsimus, frater carissime, nemini præscribentes aut præjudicantes, quo minus unusquisque episcoporum quod putat faciat, habens arbitrii sui liberam potestatem.—Cyprian. Jubaiano. Ep. LXXIII. p. 210. Oxon.]

[13 Sozom. H. E. p. 227. Cantab. 1720.]

Donatists St Augustine with other learned men disputed. There is also an imperial law made by Honorius and Theodosius, that holy baptism should not be iterated. Justin. Cæs. hath published the same *In Cod.* Lib. i. Tit. 6, in these words :

" If any minister of the catholic church be detected to have rebaptized any, let both him which committed the unappeaseable offence (if at least by age he be punishable), and he also that is won and persuaded thereunto, suffer punishment of death[1]." Moreover, Valentin., Valens, and Gratianus, give in charge to Florianus, superintendent of Asia, in these words : " That same minister which by unlawful usage shall iterate holy baptism, we account him unworthy of an ecclesiastical function. For we condemn their error, which tread under foot the precepts of the apostles; and having obtained the sacraments in Christ's name, they purify not again by a second baptism, but defile and deflower them under the name of cleansing[2]." Thus far they.

And verily they which rebaptize and are rebaptized, they both defile the name of God, which was called on over the baptized in the former baptism, and cast from them the institution of God as vain and vicious. Christ is read to be baptized but once. The apostles were not baptized twice. All the saints of God are baptized only but once. Yea, those which Judas baptized once are not read to be baptized again of a worthier minister ; for in my last sermon I shewed, that the pureness of the sacraments dependeth not upon the worthiness or unworthiness of the minister. Neither can you read that any in the old time were twice circumcised, no, not they which were manifestly known to be circumcised of idolatrous priests before the reign of Ezechias and Josias : but they were not baptized[3] into

[1 Impp. Honorius et Theodosius A. A. Anthemio P. P. Si quis rebaptizare quempiam de ministris catholicæ sectæ fuerit detectus, una cum eo qui piaculare crimen commisit, (si tamen criminis per ætatem capax sit,) et hic cui persuasum sit, ultimo supplicio percellatur.—Justinian. Cod. Lib. I. tit. 6. II. p. 88. Lugd. 1551.]

[2 Impp. Valentin. Valens, et Gratian. A. A. A. ad Florianum, vicarium Asiæ. Antistitem, qui sanctitatem baptismatis illicita usurpatione geminaverit, sacerdotio indignum esse censemus. Eorum enim condemnamus errorem, qui apostolorum præcepta calcantes, christiani nominis sacramenta sortitos alio rursus baptismato non purificant, sed incestant lavacri nomine polluentes.—Ibid. p. 87.]

[3 Rather, but not into, &c. : they were baptized, not in Lat.]

idolatry, but into the covenant of the Lord God; whereof I have admonished you elsewhere. Therefore it is an horrible offence to iterate the ceremony of baptism, and it is without example. Neither in this matter is there any necessity: for to what end is it to baptize again, when as baptism once given is sufficient for the whole course of a man's life? Beside this; since anabaptism is nothing else but a confederacy, conspiracy, and a certain linking together by one mark into a new and seditious, or at the least superstitious, company, into a new and schismatical church, and into a new and strange kind of doctrine, and as contrary as can be to the doctrine of Christ and his apostles; truly it is no marvel, that the obstinate anabaptists are kept under and punished by common laws. For otherwise these things are damnable, and not to be dissembled or suffered of a christian magistrate.

But the anabaptists presently object unto us these two places. The first out of the fifth chapter of Josua, where we read in these words: " Make thee sharp knives (of stone), and go to again, and circumcise the children of Israel the second time." Behold, the second time they could not be circumcised, say they, unless they had been also circumcised before. I answer: To circumcise the second time, or to do a thing once again, doth not signify to do that which was done before. For when the foreskin was once cut off, how could it be cut off again? Therefore that which was left undone for a certain space is now again renewed, and is said to be done the second time. So that the second time is not applied to them that would be circumcised[4], but unto the very time wherein they that were uncircumcised should be circumcised. For they were first solemnly circumcised in Egypt, before they did eat the passover. Now, entering into the land of Canaan, they are the second time solemnly circumcised, which hitherto by reason of the wilderness and journeying were not circumcised. And so it followeth immediately in the same chapter, that all the males that came out of Egypt died in the wilderness, and that their sons were uncircumcised; so that now it was expedient that they should be circumcised, as their fathers were before them. Therefore the anabaptists in this testimony of the law have no defence at all.

The latter testimony to maintain anabaptism, or rebaptizing,

The places alleged to prove anabaptism are confuted. Josh. v.

The twelve men of

[4 So also ed. 1584: but ed. 1577, should be circumcised.]

Ephesus not rebaptized.
they bring out of the xix. chapter of the Acts; where they say that those twelve men of Ephesus were once baptized by Apollos with the baptism of water, and with that of John's likewise; but the very same afterward are rebaptized of Paul in the name of Christ. I answer, that those twelve men were not baptized again of Paul with water ; they were once baptized with water, which was sufficient for them. But neither could Paul minister another baptism of water than that of John's. For I taught and evidently proved, anon after the beginning of this sermon, that the baptism of water ministered by John, Christ, and his apo-

Acts viii.
stles, is one and the selfsame. There I declared, that the baptism of fire, or of the Spirit, is peculiar and proper to Christ. Those men therefore of Ephesus were baptized with the baptism of water, as the Samaritans were by Philip; but they were not as yet fully instructed of the baptism of fire, neither were they baptized with fire : yea, they confess they know not whether there be any such baptism, that is, whether there be an Holy Ghost which in the visible form of fire should come down upon men. For they could not be altogether ignorant that there was a Holy Ghost, without whom undoubtedly they had not believed, yea, in whom they had believed if they had rightly believed. Therefore they were only ignorant of that baptism of fire. As therefore Peter and John laid their hands on the Samaritans, and they forthwith received the Holy Ghost; so Paul layeth hands on the men of Ephesus,

Acts xix.
and they receive the Holy Ghost. For Luke saith : " When they heard these things, they were baptized in the name of the Lord Jesus." And lest any man should understand this of the baptism of water, by and bye he addeth the manner thereof, and a plain exposition, saying : " And when Paul had laid his hands on them, the Holy Ghost came upon them." This, I say, he called baptizing in the name of the Lord Jesus; for it followeth : " And they spake with tongues, and prophesied." And this always hath been the fruit and effect of the baptism of fire in the primitive church, as I declared anon after the beginning of this sermon. Wherefore the anabaptists have no testimony out of the scriptures for their anabaptism, or rebaptizing. So that all that will gather their wits about them do plainly see, that they are to be forsaken and shunned of all good men. But we have sufficiently disputed against them, as it seemeth. Now we go forward to expound those things that

remain to be opened touching baptism, which are not the last and of least account.

Now that we are come to entreat of the virtue and efficacy Of the force of baptism. of baptism, we will follow that order which we shadowed out in the description of baptism; knitting up at least the particulars[1], because in the general consideration of sacraments we have spoken largely of them. Yet nevertheless, it is good first of all to know, what the adversaries of the church have sometime thought touching the force of baptism.

The Manichees baptized none of their sect; for they taught, that baptism did avail the receivers nothing to salvation[2]. The Seleucians, who are called also Hermiani, did likewise set baptism at nought[3]. The Messalians, which be called Euchetes, or prayer-makers, (as I have shewed in the end of my former sermon,) and the Enthusiastes, inspired, I say, by some heavenly power, nay rather by some hellish[4] fury, are persuaded that baptism neither profiteth nor hindereth any man. For so they did attribute all means of salvation to the inward working of the Spirit, yea, to man's prayers, insomuch that they loathed and abhorred all outward helps, yea, and doctrine also, as unprofitable and without force. Which Theodoret in his Ecclesiastical History, Lib. IV. cap. 11, rehearseth of them[5].

But the holy scripture teacheth, that we are washed clean from our sins by baptism; for baptism is a sign, a testimony and sealing, of our cleansing. For God verily hath promised sanctification to his church, and he for his truth's sake purifieth his church from all sins by his grace through the blood of his Son, and regenerateth and cleanseth it by his Spirit; which cleansing is sealed in us by baptism, which we receive:

[1 perstringentes saltem singula, Lat. : at least touching lightly on the several parts.]

[2 Baptismum in aqua nihil cuiquam perhibent (Manichæi) salutis afferre, nec quemquam eorum quos decipiunt baptizandum putant.—Aug. de Hær. Opp. Tom. VI. fol. 5. col. 3. Par. 1531.]

[3 Seleuciani vel Hermiani . . . baptismum in aqua non accipiunt —Id. ibid. fol. 6. col. 2.]

[4 hellish, not in Lat.]

[5 — μηδεμίαν μὲν ἐκ τοῦ θείου βαπτίσματος ὠφέλειαν τοῖς ἀξιουμένοις γίνεσθαι, &c.—Theodoret. H. E. Lib. IV. cap. 11. p. 162. Cantab. See also Epiphan. adv. Hæres. hær. LXVIII. sive LXXX. Tom. I. pp. 1067, &c. Par. 1622.]

and thereof is it called in the scriptures cleansing, and remission of sins, purifying, new birth, regeneration, and the
laver or fountain of regeneration: as circumcision is called the
covenant; and sacrifices, sins and sanctifications.   For we
read in the gospel according to St Mark: "John baptized in
the desert, preaching the baptism of repentance, for the remission of sins."   The same also is mentioned in Luke.   In
the gospel of John, the third chapter, baptism is called purifying.   In the Acts of the Apostles, Peter saith to the people
which demanded what they should do: "Repent ye, and let
every one of you be baptized in the name of Jesus Christ, for
the remission of sins."   Ananias also saith to Paul: "Arise,
and be baptized, and wash away thy sins, in calling on the
name of the Lord."   And now Paul himself saith: "Christ
loved the church, and gave himself for it, to sanctify it, when
he had cleansed it, in the fountain of water in the word."
Wherefore the promise, yea, the truth of sanctification and
free remission of sins, is written and engraven in our bodies
when we are baptized.   For God by his Spirit, through the
blood of his Son, hath newly regenerated and purged again
our souls, and even now doth regenerate and purge them.

And baptism is sufficient and effectual for the whole life
of man; yea, and reacheth and is referred to all the sins of
all them that are baptized.   For the promise of God is true.
The seal of the promise is true, not deceivable.   The power
of Christ is ever effectual throughly to cleanse and wash
away all the sins of them that be his.   How often therefore
soever we have sinned in our life-time, let us call into our
remembrance the mystery of holy baptism; wherewith for the
whole course of our life we are washed[1], that we might
know, and not doubt, that our sins are forgiven us of the
same God and our Lord, yea, and by the blood of Christ,
into whom by baptism once we are graffed, that he might
always work salvation in us, even till we be received out of
misery into glory.   Neither is there any doubt, that Abraham
in his whole life had continually in his mind[2] the mystery of
circumcision, and rested in God and the seed promised unto
him.   Yet I think that that ought diligently to be marked,
which St Augustine pithily and plainly hath often cited[3]:

Side notes:
We are baptized into the remission of sins.
Mark i.
Luke iii.
John iii.
Acts ii.
Acts xxii.
Ephes. v.
Baptism is effectual for man's whole life.

[1 semel, Lat. omitted: once.]   [2 exercuerit, Lat.: practised.]
[3 inculcavit, Lat.: insisted on.]

" That our sins are forgiven, or purged, in baptism, not that they are no more in us, (for as long as we live concupiscence beareth sway, and always breedeth and bringeth forth in us somewhat like itself;) but that they should not be imputed unto us : neither that we may not sin[4], but that it should not be hurtful for us to have or had sinned, that our sins may be remitted when they are committed, and not suffered to be continued[5]." *De Fide et Operib.* cap. 20. And also many more of this kind Gratian reciteth *Distinct.* iv. *de Consecrat.*[6]

Beside that, by baptism we are gathered together into the fellowship of the people of God. Whereupon of some it is called the first sign or entry into Christianity[7], by the which an entrance into the church lieth open unto us. Not that before we did not belong to the church : for whosoever is of Christ, partaker of the promises of God and of his eternal covenant, belongeth unto the church. Baptism therefore is a visible sign and testimony of our ingraffing into the body of Christ ; and it is rightly called a planting, incorporating, or ingraffing into the body of Christ. For I said in the general discourse of sacraments, that we first by baptism were joined with Christ, and afterward with all the members of Christ, our brethren. For Paul saith : " All ye that are baptized **Gal. iii.** have put on Christ." But to put on Christ is to be made one with him, and as it were to be joined and incorporated in him, that he may live in us and we in him. For he only by his Spirit regenerateth and reneweth us, and most liberally enricheth us with all manner good gifts; which the same apostle in another place expresseth in these words : " God **Tit. iii.** saved us by the fountain of regeneration[8], and renewing of the Holy Ghost, which he shed on us richly through Jesus Christ

Marginal notes: By baptism we are gathered together to be the people of God.

[4 nec ut peccare liceat, Lat.: neither that we may take licence to sin.]

[5 — a mortuis operibus agant pœnitentiam (baptizandi), omniumque se omnino præteritorum remissionem in baptismo accepturos esse non dubitent: nec ut peccare liceat, sed ut peccasse non noceat, ut sit factis remissio, non permissio faciendi.—Aug. de Fid. et Oper. cap. 20. Opp. Tom. IV. fol. 17. col. 2. Par. 1531.]

[6 Dist. IV. col. 1986. Taurin. 1620.]

[7 initiale vel initiationis signum, Lat.: into Christianity, not in Lat.]

[8 So also ed. 1584: but ed. 1577, the regeneration.]

Luke iii. our Saviour." Yea, and therefore Christ our Lord is baptized in our baptism, to declare that he is our brother, and we joint-heirs with him. Very well therefore said St Augustine: "That baptism is thus far forceable, that we, being baptized, are incorporated into Christ and counted his members[1]." The same Augustine calleth baptism "the sacrament of christian fellowship[2]." For we are gathered again visibly by baptism to the unity[3] of one body with all the faithful, as many as 1 Cor. xii. have been, are, and shall be. For Paul also saith: "By Baptism serveth for our confession. one Spirit we are all baptized into one body." And it followeth hereby, that baptism serveth for our confession, and is rightly called the token of christian religion. For it is a badge or cognisance, whereby we witness and profess that we consent and are linked into christian religion. We confess that we by nature are sinners and unclean, but sanctified by the grace of God through Christ. For if we were clean by nature, what needed we then any cleansing? But now since we are cleansed, who doubteth of the truth of God? Therefore when we receive baptism, we truly and freely confess both our sin wherein we were born, and also free forgiveness of sins.

Lastly, the remembrance and consideration of the mystery of baptism putteth us in mind of the duties of Christianity and[4] godliness; that is to say, all our life long to weigh diligently with ourselves, of whose body we be made members, to deny ourselves and this world, to mortify our flesh with the concupiscences of the same, and to be buried with Christ into his death, that we may rise again in newness of life, and live innocently; to love our brethren as our members, with whom by baptism we are knit together into one body; to remain in the bond of concord and in the unity of the church, not to follow strange religions; being mindful that we are baptized into Christ, to whom alone we are consecrated, and far separated and divided from all other gods, worships, or religions, and, to be short, from all heresies. Let us think also that we

[1 See quotation above, page 377, note 7.]
[2 — qui (parvuli) post gravissimos cruciatus sine sacramento christianæ societatis expirant, &c.—Aug. de Nat. et Orig. Anima. Epist. xxviii. Hieronym. Opp. Tom. ii. fol. 21. col. 2.]
[3 So also ed. 1584: but ed. 1577, into the unity.]
[4 christianity and, not in Lat.]

must constantly and valiantly fight against Satan[5]. As often therefore as we remember we are baptized with Christ's baptism, so often are these things put into our minds, and we admonished of our duty. But the apostle handleth this matter more at large in the sixth chapter of his epistle to the Romans; where he expressly maketh mention, that we by baptism are made the grafts of Christ, that is to say, that we might grow out of him as branches out of the vine, and feel in our minds and bodies both the death and resurrection of Christ.

For since we are endued with the Spirit of Christ
which worketh in us, our body verily
dieth daily, but our spirit liveth
and rejoiceth in Christ. To
whom be glory for
ever and ever.
Amen.

¶ OF THE LORD'S HOLY SUPPER; WHAT IT IS, BY WHOM, WHEN, AND FOR WHOM IT WAS INSTITUTED; AFTER WHAT SORT, WHEN, AND HOW OFT IT IS TO BE CELE-BRATED, AND OF THE ENDS THEREOF. OF THE TRUE MEANING OF THE WORDS OF THE SUPPER, "THIS IS MY BODY." OF THE PRESENCE OF CHRIST IN THE SUPPER. OF THE TRUE EATING OF CHRIST'S BODY. OF THE WORTHY AND UNWORTHY EATERS THEREOF: AND HOW EVERY MAN OUGHT TO PREPARE HIM-SELF UNTO THE LORD'S SUPPER.

THE NINTH SERMON.

UNTO the holy baptism of our Lord Christ is coupled the sacrament of the body and blood of our Lord, which we call the Lord's supper: for those whom the Lord hath re-generated with the laver of regeneration, those doth he also feed with his spiritual food, and nourisheth them unto eternal life. Wherefore it followeth necessarily that we entreat next of the holy supper of the Lord.

[5 and the whole kingdom of Satan, ed. 1577: omitted also in ed. 1584: et universum Satanæ regnum, Lat.]

Sundry names of the Lord's supper.   This hath many names, even as hath the feast of passover, and is instituted in the place thereof. In old time it was called[1], The passing over, or, the Lord's passover; which was indeed a memorial of the passover, also a remembrance, sign, solemnity, a festival or holy day, a meeting together, or an holy assembly, an observation or worshipping[2], a ceremony and sacrifice of passover, a sacrifice or offering, of which we have spoken in place convenient[3]. This is called by St Paul the apostle "the Lord's supper[4]," because this ceremony was instituted by the Lord in his last supper, and because therein is offered

The Lord's table. unto us the spiritual banquet[5]. The same Paul termeth it "the Lord's table," and that doubtless for none other causes.

Communion. By the same Paul it is also called the communion; not so much for that we have communion or fellowship with Christ, and he with us, as that we being many are one bread and

Breaking of bread. one body, which do partake of the same bread. Luke calleth it "breaking of bread," naming the whole by a part. And it is evident, that our forefathers of old gave not unto the receivers of the Lord's supper a morsel, but that they brake

A memorial of the Lord's passion. the bread amongst themselves. In time past firm leagues were performed by breaking of bread. It is called also a memorial and remembrance of the Lord's passion; for the

A thanksgiving. Lord said: "Do this in the remembrance of me." It is named a thanksgiving, because when we celebrate the Lord's supper, we thank him for all his benefits, and especially for his death,

A sacrament. by the which we are redeemed. It is called also a token and a mystery, and a sacrament of the body and blood of the Lord. Our forefathers did term it by this word, synaxis.

Synaxis. Synaxis is a joining together, a knitting, a closing, or an agreement. For the church is joined and united unto Christ in the holy supper by a most strait league: and to conclude, the members themselves are therewith joined very fast toge-

An assembly. ther. Furthermore, it is called an assembly of saints, an holy company, and a gathering together; for in the old

[1 More correctly; even as the feast of the passover, into the place whereof it is instituted, was called, &c.]

[2 So also ed. 1584: but 1577, of worshipping: cultus observatio, Lat.]

[3 See Vol. II. page 178, &c.]

[4 Rather, the Lord's supper is so called, &c.]

[5 Rather, because it is prepared for us as a spiritual banquet.]

time it was never customably celebrated but in the common assembly of the church; which is plainly to be proved by the words of the apostle, 1 Corinth. xi. To conclude, we shall offend nothing at all, if we call the supper of our Lord the testament and will of God and of our Lord; for herein A testament. shalt thou find all things belonging to a full and perfect testament: for Christ is the testator; all faithful Christians are appointed heirs; the legacy is the forgiveness of sins and life everlasting, obtained by the body of Christ (which was) given, and his blood (which was) shed. The letters or table of this testament or will be the words of the Lord's supper, witnessing as it were by a public writing, that Christ is the food and life of the faithful; the order and doing thereof is as it were the seal. Wherefore, even as we do call that a testament which hath letters sealed, containing a testament both by writing and sealing; so the Lord himself did call his supper a testament; for, " this cup," said he, " is the new testament in my blood." For otherwise the new testament is not the remission of sins[6]: which thing Jeremy the prophet doth plainly testify in the xxxi. chapter, and Paul to the Hebrews, in the viii. chapter. This holy mystery hath divers other names; but these for the most part are chiefest and most commonly used. Of the other names we will speak elsewhere.

They do define (for the most part) the Lord's supper to What the Lord's supper is. be a spiritual banquet, wherewith the Lord doth both keep his death in remembrance, and also feedeth his people unto life (everlasting). But let me set down a more large description thereof unto you. The supper of the Lord is an holy action instituted unto the church from God, wherein the Lord, by the setting of bread and wine before us at the banquet, doth certify unto us his promise and communion, and sheweth unto us his gifts, and layeth them before our senses; gathereth them[7] together into one body visibly, and, to be short, will have his death kept of the faithful in remembrance; and admonisheth us of our duty, and especially of praise and thanksgiving.

[6 A mistake in all the editions for, The new Testament is the remission of sins: alioqui enim testamentum novum est peccatorum remissio, Lat.]

[7 them, not in Lat.]

The supper
of the Lord
is an holy
action.

First we say, that the supper of the Lord is an action or deed. For the Lord, when he made his supper, did give thanks unto God; he brake bread and gave the cup, and said, " Do this in the remembrance of me." Again, it cannot be every action. For at the table, where we eat meat, we also give thanks unto God, we break bread and give the cup: but it is an holy action, because it is from God and instituted unto the church. Wherefore it far differeth from our ordinary meat-suppers; as well for that it is specially instituted by the Son of God unto the church, as also because it hath the word of God and the peculiar example of Christ. Therefore St Paul, making a difference between this and common eating, saith : " If any man hunger, let him eat at home; lest that ye come together to your condemnation." And again : " Have ye not houses to eat and drink in ?" As though he might say, This supper is mystical. Again, what manner of action it is, it doth forthwith appear by that which followeth; where the Lord, by the setting of bread and wine before us at the banquet, doth assure us of his promise and communion, &c. This supper therefore hath his peculiar limits; of the which although I spake when I entreated generally of the virtue of the sacraments, yet will I repeat certain of them that make most for this purpose, when I shall draw toward an end of this sermon.

[1 Cor xi.
34, 22.]

Who is the
author of
the supper.

But concerning the description[1] of this supper, these things are chiefly to be considered and declared. First, who did institute it, and who is the true author and maker[2] of the Lord's supper. Not any man, but the very Son of God himself, the wisdom of the Father, very God and man: so that we come not to the table of men, although a man being the minister be the chiefest there ; neither do we receive holy signs at the hands of the minister only, but also at the hand of our Lord himself[3], whose guests we are if we be faithful. He hath consecrated the supper for us, and doth yet consecrate it by his holy word, his will, and his power: of which matter we spake before. And because the faithful understand and know these things, they sit down to the holy

[1 Rather, this description : hanc descriptionem, Lat.]
[2 hospes, Lat.: host.]
[3 accumbentes ad mensam Christi Domini nostri, Lat. omitted: seeing we sit down at the table of Christ our Lord.]

and heavenly banquet with Christ, being wholly occupied in heavenly things both in mind and soul.

He instituted the supper the same night that he was betrayed; and the next night by his death and blood-shedding he confirmed the new testament. For so soon as he had eaten the figurative lamb with his disciples, and had plainly told them that from that time forwards that ceremony should not be used, the supper was established in the place of that which was abolished; that, like as the bloody lamb did signify that Christ should suffer, even so the bread which is without blood witnesseth that Christ, who is the bread of life, is already baked upon the cross, and hath suffered, and made the food of all believers[4]. Wherefore that night was worthy to be observed and celebrated, and that last supper is full of mysteries. For we commonly most of all account of the words and deeds of our dearest friends, which they use a little before their death. Wherefore as all Christ's doings are beloved and precious unto us, so[5] ought this his last supper to be most dearly beloved and precious in our sight. *When the supper was instituted.*

The supper consisteth of the word and manner, promise and ceremony. The word is this; that Christ is preached to have been given up to death for our sins, and that he shed his blood for the remission of our sins. Promise is made unto all that believe, that their offences shall be forgiven. The same thing is also expressed by the manner. The manner is diligently set down in writing by St Matthew, Mark, and Luke; whom St Paul following hath nothing at all varied from them. The words therefore, dearly beloved, as they be gathered out of these four into one text, I will recite unto you: "The same night, in the evening wherein he was betrayed, the Lord came with the twelve; and when it was time, he sat down, and the twelve with him. And while they were eating, Jesus took bread; and when he had given thanks, he brake it, and gave it unto his disciples, saying, Take, and eat; this is my body which is given for you (or broken). Do this in the remembrance of me. Likewise taking the cup (after he had supped), he gave thanks, and delivered it unto them saying: Take ye this, and divide it among you; drink ye all thereof. And they drank all thereof. *Whereof it consisteth.* *The words of the supper.*

[4 So ed. 1584: but ed. 1577, for all believers.]
[5 *merito*, Lat. omitted: deservedly.]

And he said unto them, This is my blood, which is of the new Testament, which is shed for many for the remission of their sins. This cup is the new Testament in my blood (which is shed for you). This do, as oft as you shall drink it, in the remembrance of me. Verily I say unto you, that I will not drink henceforth of the fruit of the vine, until that day come that I drink it new with you in my Father's kingdom." These are, word for word, the solemn and most holy words of the Lord spoken at his last supper.

After what manner the supper was celebrated and instituted. The high bishop of the catholic church, Christ our Lord, celebrated his supper with his disciples in like sort, as we have now seen and heard, without all pomp, simply, plainly, and sparingly. He took away the over-busy ceremony of the law, appointing another, very easy to be gotten and nothing sumptuous. Most things appertaining to the law were troublesome, and all belonging to the gospel easy and nothing sumptuous. The Lord sitteth down with his twelve disciples: whereby we learn, that first of all there must a company be gathered together, which must celebrate the supper. In his assembly these things doth the Lord. First of all, he preacheth most diligently unto his disciples, of those things especially which concern the mystery of his passion and of our redemption. But wheresoever is the preaching and hearing of the word of God or of the gospel of Christ, there are also groanings and vows or prayers of the faithful: wherefore they that intend to celebrate the supper of the Lord, before all thing, according to the example and institution of the high bishop Christ our Lord, they do most diligently hear the preaching of the gospel, and also pray most earnestly. Afterward he took bread; and the Lord blessed it and brake it; moreover, he gave unto his disciples, and bade them eat. Anon he parted the cup among them, commanding them all to drink thereof. And thereupon he plainly and expressly commanded, saying, " Do this;" to wit, as you have seen me do. Wherefore the disciples did eat the bread, and drank all of the cup. Therefore they that celebrate the Lord's supper lawfully, do one unto another break, distribute, and eat the Lord's bread, which they receive at the hands of Christ's ministers; and likewise distribute and drink all of the Lord's cup, which they receive at the hands of Christ's ministers. And like as the high bishop Christ bade them do it in remembrance of him, so they that celebrate the Lord's supper remember the death of Christ and all his benefits. Moreover, as the Lord hath gone before us in his example, in giving thanks to God the Father; so likewise do the faithful make an end with this holy mystery with giving of thanks, praising his goodness and mercy, because he is good, and his mercy endureth for ever. This is the most simple and best manner of the Lord's supper, which the apostles receiving of Christ[1] delivered to be observed of all nations.

Wherefore, when this question is asked, Whether it be lawful to sup after another rite or manner; whether it be lawful to add or diminish anything from the manner left and delivered, or to change anything therein; whether the supper of the Lord ought only to be celebrated after the manner already delivered, and not after any other;—there is no small folly and rashness, yea, rather great ungodliness, therein bewrayed. For to what end serveth the most simple, most plain, best, and perfectest form of the supper, delivered of the Lord himself and received of his apostles, if we devise another? Who, I pray you, shall deliver a better than the Son of God himself, the high priest of the catholic church, hath already delivered? Or who, I beseech you, that is well in his wits, shall either add or diminish anything to the ordinance[2] of God? Who dare be so bold as to change that which is delivered by the everlasting wisdom of God? All the sayings and doings of Christ are most perfect: therefore the form also of the Lord's supper is a most perfect form of a right singular and excellent ordinance or institution. The rites or ceremonies of celebrating the sacraments of the old Testament were most perfect; so delivered from the first institution of them, that nothing was added to them nor taken from them by such as were religious, no, not many years after. For Ezechias the king celebrated the passover; so likewise did Josias celebrate the same; but not after any other rite or manner than was delivered from Moses. The fathers circumcised their infants; but not after any other manner nor any other rite than was first instituted[3]. In times past whoso had not sacrificed in the same place and according to the same

(marginal notes:) Whether it be lawful to add anything to the rite, &c.

(marginal notes:) Levit. xvii. Lev. x. 1 Sam. ix. Numb. v.

[1 a Domino Christo, Lat.]
[2 So also ed. 1584: but ed. 1577, ordinances: institutis, Lat.]
[3 tradito, Lat.]

manner which God commanded by Moses, was by the law accused of murder. Nadab and Abihu are smitten with lightning from heaven for bringing strange fire into the tabernacle. Oza is smitten with sudden death, for that the ark of the Lord of hosts was not handled in such sort as was by the law commanded. And therefore that manner of celebrating the Lord's supper, as it was by the Lord instituted and delivered to the church by the apostles, is to be observed with great religion: unless we will believe, that the institutions and manners of celebrating our sacraments are more unperfect than theirs of old time; and that God the Father doth now-a-days less regard the profanation or the religious observation of his Son's institution, than these of Moses and the fathers[1] in old time. But Paul, the vessel of election, knowing Christ's institution to be most perfect, and that the same ought to be kept still in the church simply and without any addition, saith to the Corinthians: "I received that of the Lord, which I have also delivered unto you." For he thought it an heinous offence, to deliver any other thing to the church than that which he had received of the Lord. Let us therefore with great religion hold that fast which is delivered unto us by the Lord and the apostles. But the apostle delivered none other thing to the Corinthians, yea, many years after the Lord's ascension into heaven, than that which was faithfully set down unto us in writing by the holy apostles and evangelists, St Matthew, Mark, and Luke.

Cor. xi.

How in old time it hath been celebrated in the church. Certainly it is well known, how that certain hundred years after the death of the apostles this simple manner of celebrating the Lord's supper was held in the church. For the pastor or minister of the church, after that he had preached the gospel, and given public thanks unto God in open[2] prayer, then came he forth into the midst of the holy assembly. Before the face of the people stood a table furnished with bread and wine, behind the which the minister standing blessed the people, saying, "The Lord be with you." The people answered, "And with thy spirit." Then replied the minister, "Lift up your hearts;" admonishing the congregation, that the holy mysteries shall be celebrated, and therefore that they must lift up their minds from visible things

[1 So also ed. 1584; but ed. 1577, forefathers.]
[2 prævia oratione, Lat. : in prayer going before.]

unto invisible. The people answered : "We lift them up unto
the Lord." Afterwards, exhorting the whole company to
give thanks, he cried aloud : "Let us give thanks unto the
Lord our God." The congregation answered, "It is meet
and right so to do." Then proceeded the minister, saying :
"It is very meet and right, our bounden duty, and behooveful
for us," (turning himself then to the Lord,) "that we give
thanks always, and in all places unto thee, Lord, holy Father,
almighty and everlasting God; through Christ our Lord; who
the day before that he suffered his passion took bread, gave
thanks, brake it, and gave it to his disciples;" with the residue,
as followeth in the gospel. These things being repeated out
of the gospel, the minister proceeded further, saying : "Let
us pray : being admonished by wholesome precepts, and instructed by divine institution, we are emboldened to say, Our
Father, which art in heaven, &c." After the rehearsal of the
holy mysteries[3], the people received the holy mysteries and
did communicate together; and after they had given thanks
and praised God, they were dismissed. And of this form
there remain certain footsteps in the writings of the ancient
fathers to be seen, to wit, in St Cyprian, St Augustine, and
others. But consequently in latter times the prayers, bless- The per-
ings, and the ceremonies, grew to be very great. Moreover the Lord's
Christ's institution was changed, and turned into a strange changed.
use; and in fine the mass was patched together, in which
appeareth but small antiquity. But touching these matters I
have entreated very largely in another place[4], and you yourselves are very well seen in this point. We, which defend and
hold that the institution of our Lord Christ which is delivered
unto us by the apostles is most pure and perfect, do nothing
regard neither what any man, nor at what time any bishop,
hath added this or that to the holy rite, or else hath taken
away or changed; but rather what he, who is before and
above all, did first himself, and commanded to be done. If
the authority of him that did institute, if learning and holiness,
if antiquity may be of force, then the victory is ours, who
have Christ on our side with the best chosen company of the

[3 So also ed. 1584; but 1577, of the Lord's prayer : orationem
Dominicam, Lat.]

[4 De Origine Erroris circa Cœnam Domini Sacram et Missam
Papisticam, cap. vii. Tigur. 1539.]

apostles; for from these we have what we celebrate; and that which we hold, that all godly men ought to celebrate.

Why it was instituted in the form of bread and wine. But why the Lord instituted this mystery under the form of bread and wine, it is evident. For bread comforteth, and wine maketh glad, the heart of man; which I also touched, where I entreated of the proportion and agreement[1] of the sacraments. Moreover, our fathers in the figure of manna did eat bread, which rained down from heaven. Also in their sacrifices gratulatory and of thanksgiving, and in their drink-offerings, they used bread and wine. But there hath sprung a great contention concerning the substance of the Lord's supper; some holding opinion, that it ought to be celebrated with unleavened bread, and others, with such as is leavened.

Whether the bread ought to be leavened or unleavened. But among our forefathers of old there was about these no such contention; for the church[2] used both indifferently as them pleased. It may seem, that at the first supper the Lord used unleavened bread at the table, according to the ancient manner of celebrating the passover; whereupon many churches used unleavened bread[3], who notwithstanding condemned not them of heresy which used leavened bread. The pope[4] and his adherents, conceiving no small displeasure hereat[5], hath deeply accursed the Greek church for so trifling a matter. But the Artotyrites were upon some just cause condemned by the ancient fathers; of whom Epiphanius[6] maketh mention between the Pepuzianes and the Priscillians, setting bread and cheese upon the table in their celebrating, contrary to Christ's institution.

Whether water is to be mingled with the wine. It is furthermore disputed upon, whether unmingled wine, or delayed[7] with water, is by the faithful to be used at the supper. Cyprian the martyr holdeth opinion, that in this

---

[1 analogia, Bullinger's one word. See above, pp. 244. 280.]

[2 ecclesiæ, Lat.: the churches.]

[3 See Bingham. Antiq. Book xv. chap. 2. § 5.]

[4 Autem, Lat. omitted: But the pope.]

[5 Rather, not without much scandal; non levi scandalo, Lat.]

[6 Κυιντιλλιανοὶ δὲ πάλιν, οἱ καὶ Πεπουζιανοὶ καλούμενοι, Ἀρτοτυρῖται τε καὶ Πρισκιλλιανοὶ λεγόμενοι, &c. Ἀρτοτυρίτας δὲ αὐτοὺς καλοῦσιν ἀπὸ τοῦ ἐν τοῖς αὐτῶν μυστηρίοις ἐπιτιθέντας ἄρτον καὶ τυρὸν, καὶ οὕτως ποιεῖν τὰ αὐτῶν μυστήρια.—Epiphan. adv. Hæres. Lib. ii. xxix. sive xlix. Opp. Tom. i. p. 417. Par. 1622.]

[7 softened; dilutum, Lat.]

mystery[8] the wine ought not to be unmingled, but delayed with water, and so to be offered, that is to say, drunken by the faithful. For thus he hath written: "Because Christ hath borne us all, who also bare our sins, we may perceive that in the water the people is to be understood; in the wine, the blood of Christ is to be understood. For when water is mingled with the wine in the cup, the people is united unto Christ; and the multitude of the believers is coupled and joined unto him in whom they believed. And thus in blessing the Lord's cup, only water may not be offered, neither in like sort may wine only. For if any man offer only wine, the blood of Christ beginneth to be without us; but if it be water only, then doth the multitude begin to be without Christ. But when they are both mingled together, and are joined with a confused mixture betwixt them, then is there an heavenly and spiritual sacrament wrought[9]." By these words truly doth St Cyprian shew unto us a good mystery. But why do we seek to be wiser than Christ, and to mingle together[10] more mysteries than we have received of him? The holy scripture maketh mention of no water, but rather reporteth that the Lord used nought else but mere wine. For the Lord saith: "Verily I say unto you, that henceforth I will drink no more of the fruit of the vine." For he plainly[11] said not, the wine, but, "the fruit of the vine," that herein we should make no manner of mingling. But what if that holy martyr of God himself, St Cyprian, hath laboured by all the means he might to shew, that that only is to be followed of the faithful in celebrating of the Lord's supper, which they have received of our Lord Christ himself? And forasmuch as that testimony doth make much to all this our treatise

[8 propter mysterium, Lat.: by reason of a mystery.]

[9 Quia nos omnes portabat Christus, qui et peccata nostra portabat, videmus in aqua populum intelligi, in vino vero ostendi sanguinem Christi. Quando autem in calice vino aqua miscetur, Christo populus adunatur, et credentium plebs ei in quem credidit copulatur et conjungitur.... Sic autem in sanctificando calice Domini offerri aqua sola non potest, quomodo nec vinum solum potest. Nam si vinum tantum quis offerat, sanguis Christi incipit esse sine nobis: si vero aqua sit sola, plebs incipit esse sine Christo. Quando autem utrumque miscetur, et adunatione confusa sibi invicem copulatur, tunc sacramentum spiritale et cœleste perficitur.—Cyprian. Epist. LXIII. Opp. p. 154. Oxon.]

[10 comminisci, Lat: to devise.]   [11 significanter, Lat.]

concerning Christ's supper, to be celebrated according to the words of the gospel, I will recite it word for word out of the second epistle of the 3rd book of his Epistles. "We must not," saith he, "depart in any respect from the doctrine of the gospel; and those things that our Master taught and did himself, the scholars also ought to observe and do. The blessed apostle in another place speaketh more constantly and stoutly, saying, 'I marvel that you are so soon changed from him that called you to grace unto another gospel: which is nothing else; but there be some that trouble you, and go about to overthrow the gospel of Christ. Howbeit, if we ourselves, or an angel from heaven, do preach unto you any other thing than that we have taught, let him be accursed. As I have said before, so say I now again, If any man preach any other thing unto you than that which you have received, let him be accursed.' Since, therefore, neither the apostle himself, neither an angel from heaven, can preach or teach otherwise than Christ himself once hath taught and his apostles have preached; I much marvel from whence this custom hath grown, that, contrary to the doctrine of the gospel and the apostles, in some places water is offered in the Lord's cup, which being taken alone cannot express the Lord's blood." And again: "There is no cause, dearly beloved brother, that any man should think that the custom of certain men is to be followed, if there be any that heretofore have supposed that water alone is to be offered in the Lord's cup. For it must be demanded of them, whom they have followed herein. For if in the sacrifice, which is Christ, none is to be followed but Christ; doubtless then ought we to hearken unto and to do after that which Christ hath done and commanded to be done, since he himself saith in his gospel: 'If you do that which I command you to do, I will call you no longer servants, but friends.' And that Christ alone should be heard, the Father himself also witnesseth from heaven, saying, 'This is my well-beloved Son, in whom I have delight: hear him.' Wherefore if only Christ is to be heard, we ought not to regard what any other before us hath thought meet for us to do, but what Christ did first who is before all other. Neither ought we in any case to follow the custom of men, but the truth of God; considering what the Lord speaketh by the prophet Esay, saying, 'They worship me in vain, teach-

ing the commandments and doctrine of men.' And again
the Lord repeating the selfsame words in the gospel saith:
'Ye set God's commandments aside, to establish your own
traditions.' And in another place he saith: 'He that shall
break any one of the least of these commandments, and shall
on this sort teach men, shall be accounted least in the kingdom of heaven.' But if it be not lawful to break the least
of the commandments of God, how much more heinous is it
to break things so great, so weighty, and so much belonging
to the Lord's passion and the sacrament of our redemption;
or else to change it into any other order by man's traditions,
than is instituted by God[1]?" And so forth as followeth.

[1 Ab evangelicis præceptis omnino recedendum non esse, et eadem
quæ magister docuit et fecit discipulos quoque observare et facere
debere, constantius et fortius alio in loco beatus apostolus docet,
dicens: Miror quod sic tam cito demutamini ab eo, qui vos vocavit ad
gratiam, ad aliud evangelium; quod non est aliud, nisi sunt aliqui qui
vos turbant et volunt convertere evangelium Christi. Sed licet nos
aut angelus de cœlo aliter annunciet præterquam quod annunciavimus
vobis, anathema sit. Sicut prædiximus, et nunc iterum dico, Si
quis vobis annunciaverit præterquam quod accepistis, anathema sit.
Cum ergo neque ipse apostolus, neque angelus de cœlo annunciare
possit aliter aut docere præterquam quod semel Christus docuit et
apostoli ejus annunciaverunt, miror satis unde hoc usurpatum sit, ut
contra evangelicam et apostolicam disciplinam quibusdam in locis
aqua offeratur in dominico calice, quæ sola Christi sanguinem non
possit exprimere. . . . Non est, frater carissime, quod aliquis existimet
sequendam esse quorundam consuetudinem, si qui in præteritum in
calice Dominico aquam solam offerendam putaverint. Quærendum est
enim, ipsi quem sint secuti; nam si in sacrificio quod Christus obtu-
lerit (Bullinger read, est) non nisi Christus sequendus est, utique id
nos obaudire et facere oportet quod Christus fecit et quod faciendum
esse mandavit; quando ipse in evangelio dicat, Si feceritis quod mando
vobis, jam non dico vos servos, sed amicos. Et quod Christus debeat
solus audiri, Pater etiam de cœlo contestatur, dicens, Hic est Filius
dilectissimus, in quo bene sensi: ipsum audite. Quare si solus Christus
audiendus est, non debemus attendere quid alius ante nos faciendum
putaverit; sed quid qui ante omnes est Christus prior fecerit. Neque
enim hominis consuetudinem sequi oportet, sed Dei veritatem, cum
per Isaiam prophetam Deus loquatur et dicat, Sine causa autem colunt
me, mandata et doctrinas hominum docentes; et iterum Dominus
in evangelio hoc idem repetat, dicens, Rejicitis mandatum Dei ut traditionem vestram statuatis. Sed et alio in loco ponit et dicit, Qui
solverit unum ex mandatis istis minimis, et sic docuerit homines,
minimus vocabitur in regno cœlorum. Quod si nec minima de man-

There is no man can deny but that these things are of authority, even against the author himself. For neither by the scriptures, nor by the example of Christ, can it be proved that water was mingled with the wine at the supper. As for the authorities and testimonies which the author allegeth, every man may perceive how little they make to the purpose, yea, that they be wrested from their natural meaning. The gospel plainly pronounceth, that the Lord drank of the fruit of the vine unto his disciples. And as often as Paul maketh mention of the cup, yet teacheth he in no place that water was mingled with the wine, or that it ought to be mingled with it. Wherefore these water-men, that is to say, they that use water only in celebrating the Lord's supper, are justly condemned: such as the Marcionites and Tatians[1] were. Howbeit it is an indifferent matter, whether you use red wine or white in the supper.

Of both kinds to be given and received in the supper. Again, why did not the Lord deliver the sacrament of the supper unto us under one form of bread or wine only, but rather under both kinds? The doctors of the church by one consent suppose this to be the cause; for that he would signify, or rather testify, unto us that he took both soul and flesh upon him, and gave the same for us, and also hath delivered our souls and flesh from everlasting destruction. For although there be two kinds, yet do they make but one sacrament, and they may not be separated. Neither is their opinion of judgment to be allowed of, who of their own private or rather sacrilegious authority do corrupt the institution of Christ; offering to the lay people which do communicate the one kind only of bread, and granting to priests both kinds, and so challenging both kinds to themselves only[2]. But Paul the apostle received the authority from the Lord himself, to admit all the faithful people of Christ unto the Lord's cup: and therefore let these bold fellows consider, from whom they have received commandment to put back the laity, and to forbid them the cup, which by the Lord our God is granted unto

datis Dominicis licet solvere, quanto magis tam magna, tam grandia, tam ad ipsum Dominicæ passionis et nostræ redemptionis sacramentum pertinentia fas non est infringere, aut in aliud, quam quod divinitus institutum sit, humana traditione mutare!—Cyprian. Epist. LXIII. Opp. pp. 152, 155. Oxon.]

[1 See Mosheim. E. H. Book I. cent. 2. part 2. chap. 5. § 7 and 9.]
[2 solis his, Lat.: to these (i. e. the priests) only.]

them. For Christ in plain words, and as it were by the spirit of prophecy, foreseeing what should come to pass in the church, said not of the bread, "Eat ye all of this;" but when he took the cup he added, "Drink ye all of this." St Mark also adjoineth hereunto, not without deep judgment[3], "And they drank all thereof." Hereunto also appertaineth that which the Lord speaketh in St Luke : "Take this, and divide it among you." St Paul the apostle, having a special regard unto this excellent and plain institution of Christ, three or four times joineth the cup to the bread, saying : "As often as you shall eat of this bread, and drink of this cup, you shall express the Lord's death." Again: "Whosoever eateth of this bread, or drinketh of the Lord's cup unworthily, he shall be guilty of the body and blood of the Lord." And again he saith : "Let a man examine himself, and then let him eat of the bread, and drink of the cup." Again : "Whoso eateth and drinketh unworthily," &c. These testimonies are manifold, and worthy absolutely to be believed; and unto which all traditions of all men whatsoever should give place. The Lord hath instituted the cup of the supper unto all the faithful; wherefore the apostles exhibited the same unto all the faithful. For if the sacrament of the blood of Christ were given to the apostles only, surely then the thing itself, to wit, the remission of sins, which is obtained through Christ's blood, belongeth only to the apostles. Howbeit the Lord saith plainly : "This is the blood of the new Testament, which is shed for many for the remission of sins." It is also in other places of the scripture manifestly set down, that Christ's blood was shed for the remission of the sins of all the faithful. Wherefore if the laity be capable of the thing, how much more of the sign? Now if our adversaries proceed further and say, that the apostles only sat at the supper, (who represented the figure of the priests,) and that the use of the cup was granted unto them only, and not to be granted unto other, but to such only as were present at the first supper ; then do we demand of them, by what authority they give the Lord's bread to the laity, or by what right they do admit simple women unto the Lord's supper ? since it is manifest that neither the one nor the other (according unto their speaking in this matter) sat at the Lord's table. And in this point

[3 non sine gravi causa, Lat.]

they, being taken tardy, can go no further. But they object the danger of the cup; which if it be given unto all without exception, it would come to pass, through the folly and negligence of men, there might some great offence be committed in letting it fall, or pouring it on the floor: as who should say, The eternal providence hath not foreseen so great an offence, which these wise men do well perceive now at length in the end of the world, and do amend that wherein the Son of God did amiss. For they cry out, that one kind is enough for the lay people, forasmuch as by a necessary coherence it followeth, that where the body of Christ is, there is his blood also; and thus must it then follow, that the one kind is instituted in vain. But the Lord distinctly first offered the bread, and afterward the cup; and the Lord instituted nothing in vain: therefore both kinds, since the Lord hath so commanded, ought to be parted among all the faithful; which as many as have read the writings of the ancient fathers will report was observed ever before, even almost unto the time of the council of Constance[1]: of whom many[2] have not been afraid to say, that the dividing of this sacrament after this manner could not be done without sacrilege.

Of the consecration of the bread and wine. The matter and substance of the supper being declared, there is lightly some question moved concerning the form, or of the consecration of the bread and wine. But forasmuch as I have entreated hereof in the general consideration of the sacraments[3], there is no cause why I should, with loathsomeness to the hearers, repeat the self-same thing again. We do not acknowledge any transubstantiation to be made by force of words or characters; but we affirm, that the bread and wine remain as they are in their own substances, but that there is added unto them the institution, will, and word of Christ, and so become a sacrament, and so differ much from common bread and wine, as we have said in place convenient.

Whether there must be one chief dealer in the action of the supper. Consequently ensueth the question touching this point: Who should administer the supper: that is to say, whether

[1 A.D. 1414.]

[2 nonnulli, Lat. Gelasius. Decret. Gratian. Decr. Tert. Pars De Consecr. Dist. II. Can. 12. col. 1918. See also Cyprian, Serm. de Lapsis.]

[3 See above, page 267.]

any one of the congregation ought to be chief in the celebrating of the supper: then, who the same should be? Surely,
the thing itself requireth, and nature also commandeth, that
everything be done decently and in good order: and religion
requireth that all things appertaining to the supper be done
according to Christ's example. But he was the chief dealer
in the supper: and he likewise hath appointed ministers of
the church, by whom he will have the sacraments to be
administered. Wherefore, like as every man doth not baptize, but the lawful minister of the church; so appertaineth it
not unto every man to prepare and minister the holy supper,
but to the minister which is ordained by God. Herein now
we disprove the papistical doctrine, which alloweth of private
masses, and teacheth that the priest offereth up the body and
blood of our Lord for the standers by; and that by the mass
he applieth the merit of redemption unto them that with
devotion come to that sacrifice. For as there is no one word
of the Lord extant, that commandeth the priests to sacrifice,
or privately to apply the supper for others, or that promiseth
anything unto them that stand by and look on it; (for he
saith, "Do this; eat ye and drink ye all in the remembrance
of me;" he saith not, Look upon the priests only while they
be eating and drinking for you;) so Christ is not bodily
present in the bread and wine; he is joined unto our hearts
and minds by his Spirit; for it were of none effect[4] that he
remained in the bread. And if he were present there indeed,
yet could he not be sacrificed, both for that he hath offered
up himself once upon the cross, neither can the most worthy
and only-begotten Son of God be offered up again to God
the Father by a sinful man: as also for that there is no need
for him to offer again. For St Paul saith: "Christ, being one Heb. x.
only sacrifice offered up for sin, sitteth for ever at the right
hand of God, looking for that which is yet to come, until his
enemies be made his footstool. For by one oblation he hath
made them for ever perfect that are sanctified." And again
he saith: "Where as is full remission of sins, there is no
more oblation for sin." But we have full remission of sin
by the death which Christ once suffered: therefore there is
no sacrifice in the church for sin[5]. Indeed, the church doth

[4 So also ed. 1584: but ed. 1577, to none effect.]
[5 amplius, Lat. omitted: any more.]

27

celebrate the memorial of the sacrifice which was once perfectly finished upon the cross; but the church doth not offer up sacrifice any more, either with blood or without blood. Praise and thanksgiving are a most acceptable sacrifice to the Lord: the same the minister offereth not for others, but with others. Here now therefore we ascribe none other thing to the minister but the ministry; that he be the president or chief dealer to recite the prayers in the celebration of the supper; and after the holy prelection and the pronouncing of the solemn words let him, after the example of Christ, begin to break the Lord's bread and distribute his cup, and let him receive also the sacrament for himself, as the other faithful people do, as companion of the faith; and when the communion is done, let him end the holy action with thanksgiving and some holy exhortation.

Of the place where the supper is to be celebrated. Concerning the place where the supper is to be celebrated, I find no contention hath been amongst the most ancient ministers of the church. It is read how that our Lord Jesus used the hall of a certain private man's house. *Acts xx.* And also the apostle Paul both preached and brake bread at Troas in a certain dining-place. The ancient church, which ensued immediately after the death of the apostles, almost unto the time of Constantine the great, had none or very few large and public churches; for it was scarce lawful or safe in so troublesome a time for the Christians to creep abroad. In the meantime they used very honest places, in the which they met together in holy assemblies, having places of prayer. At this present there seemeth no place to be more worthy or more commodious to celebrate the holy supper in, than that which is appointed for doctrine and prayer. For so have we learned of St Paul, 1 Cor. chap. xi. Howbeit, if tyrannical power will not suffer us to have a church, what shall let us but that we may reverently celebrate the supper in honest private houses?

Of the Lord's altar or table. Touching the holy instruments belonging to the supper, the matter also requireth to speak something in this place. In the time that the apostles lived, they supped at tables set forth and furnished for the purpose; they knew no fixed altars builded of stone, which are more fit to make fire upon and to burn beasts on for a sacrifice[1]. A removing table

[1 for a sacrifice, not in Lat.]

agreeth better with the example of Christ. Notwithstanding, we condemn not standing altars, so that they serve only to the lawful use of the supper. St Paul, in the first to the Corinthians, calleth the altars of ethnicks tables; so that we need not to marvel that the ancient fathers termed our tables altars. For it is an easy matter to fall from the one to the other; and it should seem, that they alluded unto the only altar of the tabernacle of God. In old time the tables were covered with some fair cloth, with some linen table-cloth, or towel; from whence perhaps were borrowed those things which are called corporals[2]. As for that outward bravery and worldly trimming, it was not then used on the altars of Christians. We read how it is forbidden by the law, that there must no altar be builded of hewn stone; by which proviso all cost and bravery in religion is forbidden.

Thus it is manifest, that in the ancient times there were no precious nor costly vessels used at the supper. For like as Christ and the apostles taught, that frugality should be used in all places, condemning superfluity, and beating into us the contempt of gold and silver ; so in those holy mysteries they have not overthrown that doctrine of theirs, or given occasion of excess. After long persecution, when peace was restored to the church, then began the custom to celebrate in the church with vessels of gold and silver. But then also there were some, that brought the same again to his old frugality and simplicity. Chrysostom cried out (as I have also declared in another place[3]), that in receiving the Lord's supper we ought to have golden minds, not golden vessels[4]. And St Ambrose saith: " The sacraments require not gold, neither are those things pleasant in gold which are not bought with gold. The ornaments[5] of the sacraments is the redemption of captives[6]." St Hierome commends St Exuperius, bishop of

Of vessels belonging to the Lord's supper.

[2 Fine linen cloths, on which the host is laid in the Romish churches.]

[3 De Origine Erroris circa Cœnam Domini Sacram et Missam Papisticam, cap. VI. fol. 207. Tigur. 1539.]

[4 — μηδὲ νομίζωμεν ἀρκεῖν ἡμῖν εἰς σωτηρίαν, εἰ... ποτήριον χρυσοῦν καὶ λιθοκόλλητον προσενέγκωμεν τῇ τραπέζῃ ... τὴν ψυχὴν προσένεγκε... ταύτην χρυσῆν ποίησον.—Chrysost. in Matth. Hom. L. Opp. Tom. VII. p. 518.]

[5 So also ed. 1584; but ed. 1577, ornament.]

[6 Aurum sacramenta non quærunt, nec in auro placent, quæ auro

Toledo[1], who carried the Lord's body in a basket of wicker and the blood in a glass, and had expelled covetousness out of the church[2]. And truly that canon of the Triburean council, which is yet extant in the pope's decrees, forbidding that no priest should minister this holy mystery in wooden vessels, doth prove sufficiently, that certain churches, more than eight hundred years since Christ's passion, used to drink the blood of Christ in wooden vessels: wherefore wooden cups in the supper be of all most ancient. Bonifacius the archbishop, (which example although I have alleged elsewhere, yet am I enforced to repeat it here again, for that it agreeth so fitly with this present matter,) being asked long since, Whether it were lawful to minister the sacraments in vessels of wood, answered: "In old times," saith he, "golden priests used wooden cups; but now contrariwise, wooden priests use golden cups[3]." But if any man bring vessels made of any other stuff, without excess and superstition, I would not greatly strive with him, so that he will also acknowledge that they do not offend which use the wooden. For as touching the form and matter of the cups, all are free and lawful for the faithful church to use.

What garment is to be worn at the supper. Look more of this matter in epist. added at the end of this book[4].

Moreover, it is evident that the Lord in the first supper, yea, and the apostles also in celebrating the same supper, used their own usual and decent apparel. And therefore it is not disagreeable from the first institution, if the minister come unto the Lord's table covered with his own garment, so that it be

non emuntur. Ornatus sacramentorum redemptio captivorum est.— Ambros. de Officiis, Lib. I. cap. 28. Opp. Tom. IV. col. 61. Par. 1615.]

[1 Rather, Toulouse; Tolosanum, Lat.]

[2 Sanctus Exuperius Tolosæ episcopus ... corpus Domini canistro vimineo, sanguinem portat in vitro. Qui avaritiam ejecit e templo.— Hieron. Epist. ad Rustic. xcv. Opp. Tom. IV. par. 2. col. 778. Par. 1693 —1706.]

[3 Vasa, in quibus sacrosancta conficiuntur mysteria, calices sunt et pateræ: de quibus Bonifacius, martyr et episcopus, interrogatus, si liceret in vasculis ligneis sacramenta conficere, respondit: Quondam sacerdotes aurei ligneis calicibus utebantur: nunc e contrario, lignei sacerdotes aureis utuntur calicibus.—Gratian. Decret. par. III. de Consecrat. Dist. I. can. 44. col. 1900. Taurin. 1620. Labb. et Coss. Concil. Triburiens. can. 18. Tom. IX. col. 450.]

[4 This reference, which was introduced into ed. 1587, is to the joint letter of Bullinger and Gualther (Zurich Letters, 1st Series. Append. Let. III.) which was added to that edition of the translated Decades.—See title-page, Vol. I.—A similar reference is inserted in

comely and honest. Surely the communicants do wear on them their own usual apparel. We must take heed then that there creep in no superstition[5]. Our forefathers, as it seemed, did wear a cloke cast over their common garments; which they did not after the example of Christ or the apostles, but according to man's tradition. At the length that stuff, which is used at this day, was taken up according to the imitation of the priest's garments of the old law, and appointed to be worn by the ministers that would celebrate the supper. Neither doth Innocentius, the 3d of that name, dissemble this matter in the iv. chap. and 4 book of his work, De Sac. Altar. Mysterio[6]. As for us, we have learned of late[7], that all Levitical matters are not only put away, but not to be brought again into the church by any. Forasmuch therefore as we remain in the light of the gospel, and not in the shadow of the law, we do upon good cause reject that Levitical massing apparel.

I have also declared in another place[8], that it hath been the manner in old time[9], that every nation hath used their own native and vulgar tongue[10] in ministering the sacraments. Of the gestures which the ministers do use in celebrating the Lord's supper, we can say none other thing out of the gospel than what we have learned: "The Lord took the bread, blessed it, brake it, distributed it," &c. If the minister do follow these things, he needs not to be careful of other gestures. Those which at this day are by the invention of men received into the celebration of the mass, are so far off from giving any majesty to the mysteries, that they bring them rather the more into contempt. I will say nothing else that may seem more grievous.

What tongue is to be used.

What gestures.

the margin of the *London* edition of the Latin Decades by Henry Middleton.]

[5 hic, Lat. omitted: in this matter.]

[6 Sciendum quod non omnes antiquæ legis consuetudines abjecit ecclesia, sed quasdam provida consideratione retinuit. ... Adhuc habet .... vestes, et vasa, et pontifices, et Levitas.—Innocent. Pap. III. Myster. Miss. Lib. iv. cap. 4. Opp. Tom. i. p. 376. col. 1575. Cf. Zurich Letters, p. 158. A.]

[7 See Vol. ii. page 255.]

[8 De Origine Erroris circa Cœnam, &c. cap. vi. fol. 208.]

[9 ab antiquo, Lat.]

[10 et omnibus intelligibili, Lat. omitted: and that which all could understand.]

Of taking it in the hands. The matter is indifferent, whether the church take the supper sitting down, or going to the table; whether a man take the holy mysteries in his own hand, or receive it into his mouth at the hands of him that ministereth. It is most agreeable with the first simplicity and institution of the supper, to sit, and to receive the sacraments in a man's own hands of him that ministereth; and afterwards to break it, eat it, and to divide it unto others. For as the Lord sat at table with his disciples, so he reached forth the mysteries, saying: "Take, and divide it among you." Moreover, as there is more quietness and less stir in sitting at the supper, while the ministers carry the holy mysteries about the congregation; so it is well known by histories of antiquity, that the sacrament hath been delivered into the hands of the communicants. It is mere superstition and repugnant to the doctrine of the apostles, to scrape the hands of the lay people that have touched the holy sacrament of the supper. Why do they not also by the same law scrape the lips, tongue, and jaws of the communicants?

The remnants of the supper. Of these things before handled springeth another question: What is to be thought of the remnants and leavings of the Lord's supper; and whether there ought any part of it to be reserved; and whether that which is reserved or shut up ought to be adored? This question seemeth to have no godliness at all in it, but to be altogether superstitious and very hurtful. For who knoweth not, that bread and wine, out of the holy and lawful use appointed, are not a sacrament? Shall we proceed to demand with these sophisters, what that is which the mouse gnaweth when he gnaweth the Lord's bread? Whether to be shut up and adored. These questions are most unworthy to be demanded, and to be raked up in holy oblivion. Touching the shutting up of the sacrament, the Lord teacheth us not one word in the gospel, much less of worshipping it. "Take," saith he, "eat, and divide it among you." He saith not, Lay it up, and worship it; for the true worshippers worship the Father in spirit and truth. Moreover, we read how the Lord hath plainly said in the gospel: "If they say unto you, Behold, where he is in the desert, go not forth; behold, where he is in the innermost parts of the house, do not believe." He setteth down the cause of this his commandment: "For like as the lightning goeth forth of the east, and appeareth in the west, so shall the coming of the Son of man be." The coming again of the Son of man[1], saith he, shall be glorious and not obscure; neither shall he come again but to judge both the quick and the dead. And therefore St Paul the apostle, Col. iii. teaching us true religion, willeth us to worship Christ, not upon the earth, but with our minds lifted unto heaven, where he sitteth at the right hand of his Father. And who will be so frantic, I beseech you, to worship the holy sign for the holy thing itself? It appeareth by the decrees made of late, that these things were invented by man's device : for it is certain, that the feast of Christ's body, commonly called *Corpus Christi*, was instituted but of late years under pope Urban, in the year of our Lord, 1264 ; as it may appear in Clement, the iii. book, title 16, the chapter beginning, *Si Dominum*[2].

It remaineth, that we discuss the question concerning the time of celebrating the Lord's supper, and what season is meetest for the same, the morning or evening; whether we ought to sup together; whether we must receive it fasting, or when we have dined; also, how often we must celebrate the supper, once, or often, or seldom. It is evidently enough known, that Christ sat down at the table with his disciples in the evening ; but it followeth not hereof, that the supper cannot be rightly celebrated at any other time but at evening. The Lord, upon occasion of the feast of the passover, and because he should be betrayed that night, did both eat the supper that evening with his disciples, and instituted also the supper for us. Notwithstanding, he left the liberty to remove this mystery unto the morning ; for that when we be sober, then are we most meet to deal in all matters, specially in religion, for which we be then fitter than when our bellies be full of good cheer. Wherefore this banquet requireth fasting and empty guests ; but yet not so fasting, that a man may not taste of somewhat aforehand for his health's sake ; for St Paul saith : "If any man be hungry, let him eat at home." The same apostle also will not have any other feast to be received together with the Lord's mystical supper. And therefore we say, that we ought not to receive that with other meat. Tertullian writeth, that Christians have used oftentimes to eat

What time to be celebrated.

[1 in mundum, Lat, omitted : into the world.]
[2 Corpus Jur. Can. Clement. Lib. iii. tit. 16. coll. 240, &c. Lugd. 1624. See Jewel's Works, ed. Park. Soc. Vol. i. p. 516.]

other meat with it; which kind of supper, as he writeth, was called ἀγάπη, that is to say, mutual love or charity, borrowing the name from love[1]: for that there the poor were refreshed with the feasting of the richer sort. Howbeit, provision of meat, drink, and other necessaries, might well enough be made for them without the church. Paul will not permit, that in one place both public feasts should be made, and also the mystical supper of the Lord celebrated.

How often to be celebrated. Furthermore, how many times in a year the faithful ought to receive this sacrament of the Lord's supper, the apostles have given forth no commandment, but have left it indifferent unto every church's discretion. For what is more plain than that which St Paul hath said : "As often as you shall eat of this bread, and drink of this cup, you shall declare the Lord's death until he come?" For the Lord (as the same apostle setteth it down), first commanding, said : "Do this, as oft as you shall drink it, in remembrance of me." Howbeit, let no man think, that the celebration of the Lord's supper is left so freely unto him, that he need never to receive it ; for that were no lawful liberty, but most unlawful licentiousness. They that celebrate the supper of the Lord upon certain and ordinary times of the year, would not have it brought into contempt or loathed by reason of the daily frequenting. For they have some consideration of their own people ; and they would have the supper to be celebrated worthily, and that the people may have a desire unto it. But they that celebrate it very oft, they suppose it an unmeet thing, that good things, by often frequenting them, should be despised : for the better the thing is, the oftener, say they, it is to be used. Both these sorts desire to serve the Lord, and would have that to be done to great and good effect, which the Lord hath left free. Between these, if St Augustine be made umpire[2] and judge, doubtless he would pronounce none other judgment, than that which he hath already pronounced of the same cause, writing unto Januarius, and saying : "He shall best decide this strife between them, who so advised them especially to abide in the peace of Christ; and that every man do that which according to his faith he is persuaded to be good and godly. For neither

[1] Tertull. Apolog. cap. 39. Opp. Tom. v. p 75. ed. Semler. Hal. Mag. 1828.]

[2] hodie, Lat. omitted: at this day.]

of them dishonoureth the body and blood of our Lord. Only that meat must not be contemned[3]."

Now for whom this holy supper is instituted, and to whom it is to be ministered, we have also to consider. It seemeth, that it is instituted and to be given unto all faithful christian people, of what sex soever, men and women, high and low. Wherefore so great a mystery is not to be cast unto swine and dogs, to be contemned and trodden under foot. Before it be ministered, all men are earnestly and effectually to be admonished unto whom this meat appertaineth, namely, to them that acknowledge their sins, that are sorry for their faults, and believe in Christ; all are to be admonished, that every man descending into himself do prove himself, and afterward so eat of this holy bread and drink of this holy drink, that he eat not and drink not thereof unworthily unto his condemnation. But after this severe admonition, if any approach unto the table and sit down, and by their sitting down do as it were openly profess, both that they are, and also desire to remain, true worshippers of Christ, by whom they trust to have remission of their sins; surely such are not to be put back by the ministers, neither are the holy mysteries to be denied them. For the Lord himself, who is the searcher of hearts, severely, diligently, plainly, and in many words in his last supper, before he distributed the mysteries, admonished Judas, being an hypocrite, a thief, a traitor, a murderer, yea, a parricide, a blasphemer, and a forsaker of his master; but being admonished, when notwithstanding he departed not from the table, but tarried among the saints, the Lord did not violently put him away, nor bade him openly to depart, neither withheld he the Lord's bread from him, but gave it unto him as he did unto others, although he knew assuredly what he was: which thing the ministers of the church do not always so certainly know of them that sit down at the table. Neither did the Lord offend any whit at all in so doing, neither did he cast that which was holy to the dogs. For the Lord warned him diligently of all matters, whereof he

For whom the supper is instituted.

[3 Rectius inter eos fortasse quisquam dirimit litem qui moneat præcipue in Christi pace permaneant; faciat autem unusquisque quod secundum fidem suam pie credat esse faciendum. Neuter enim eorum exhonorat corpus et sanguinem Domini......Contemptum solum non vult cibus ille.—Aug. Ep. cxviii. Opp. Tom. ii. fol. 108. col. 3.]

was to be warned; and he, hearing and understanding them all, remaineth notwithstanding among the saints, vaunteth himself for one of the faithful, not for an hog, and as one of the faithful taketh part of the bread and of the cup. By which hypocrisy, notwithstanding, he provoked the heavy judgment of God against him; even as also at this day this holy meat and this holy drink turneth to the destruction both of the body and soul of all hypocrites. Neither did the presence of the hypocrite at the Lord's supper defile the other faithful disciples of Christ which sat at the table: like as neither at this day are the faithful polluted, although they see many hypocrites sit down at the table with them; for they sup not with them as with hypocrites, but as it were with the faithful. In the meanwhile, the hypocrite hurteth himself, and not others; he falleth and perisheth to his own destruction, he eateth and drinketh his own damnation; but the faithful liveth by his own faith: of which thing we have entreated in other sermons[1].

The supper was not instituted for infants.

And although that infants are reputed to be of the church and in the number of the faithful, yet are they not capable of the supper. In this point the ancient fathers shamefully erred: which I have also noted in the sermon of Baptism[2]. Infants are not deprived of everlasting life, although they depart out of this world without receiving this mystical meat. This was instituted for them that are of lawful years, and not for infants. "Let a man examine himself," saith the apostle, "and let him so eat of the bread, and drink of the cup." And the Lord saith: "Do this in the remembrance of me." And again: "Shew forth the Lord's death until he come." All which sayings take place in people of lawful years, not in infants. Our children must be diligently instructed from their infancy, that they may rightly understand those mysteries, and frequent them; which thing the Lord commanded the children of Israel, saying: "If your children shall say unto you, What manner of worshipping is this? you shall answer, It is the sacrifice of the Lord's passover, who passed over the houses of the children of Israel, when he stroke the Egyptians and delivered our houses." Surely we must not shew ourselves to be more slack in informing our children than they were, since we have received a more noble benefit than they have.

[1 See Vol. I. page 103; and above, page 13.]
[2 See above, page 379.]

Of like nature unto this question are these other: Whether the supper be to be celebrated privately for every cause or necessity? whether it be to be carried unto the sick and those that keep their beds? whether it be to be applied to the dead, that is to say, to be offered for the dead, to obtain rest for them? Touching these matters, I know what is commonly said and done. There happeneth some pestilence, famine, war, or tempest, and by and by the supper is commanded to be celebrated, that as it were by this sacrifice[3] the present calamity may be taken away. Again, there is one sick; another perisheth with hunger, and afflicted for want of all manner of necessaries; the same requireth of the priest to have the Lord's supper ministered unto him, that thereby the disease may be cured as by a most present and approved remedy, and his hunger and poverty released. But this is not the due celebration of the supper, but a filthy profanation thereof. For the Lord hath not instituted it to be a cleansing sacrifice against all calamities, whereby he would be pleased; but to be a memorial of his death, and a dutiful thanksgiving. For when we be at the supper, we offer nothing unto him for which he should be favourable unto us, and turn away such an evil from us, and give us such a good thing as we desire of him; but we give thanks for the benefits which we have received. It is lawful otherwise for them that are oppressed with troubles, to offer up their vows (that is to say, their prayers) to the Lord; but it is not lawful to convert his holy mysteries to any other purpose than he hath appointed. Neither have we any examples to prove, that any holy man[4] did ever use the Lord's supper to any such end as these men do. The children of Israel received the feast of the Paschal Lamb in remembrance of their deliverance out of Egypt, and that they should continue thankful unto so beneficial a Lord: how great an offence had they committed, if they had so oftentimes eaten their banquet as, being oppressed with calamities, they desired to be delivered, and desired it by doing that deed! They received the ark of the covenant from the Lord in token of his divine presence and assured help; but when, contrary to the end whereunto it was appointed, they bare it into the camp,

[3 expiatione, Lat.]
[4 So also ed. 1584; but ed. 1577, men: viros, Lat.]

to the intent they might obtain the victory thereby, they themselves were put to flight and slain, and the ark carried away by the Philistines into captivity.

The supper not to be celebrated at home or privately, for the sick nor whole. Again; if the Lord's supper be a public holy feast of the whole church gathered together in one, in the which there ought to be breaking, distributing, eating and drinking, and thereby the communion of the body and blood of Christ be declared and sealed; it followeth, that the Lord's supper ought not to be ordained neither for any in health or sickness, neither for any lying sick in his bed or at the point of death, be it either[1] privately at home, or openly[2] at church: neither can the godly require the Lord's supper unto any such private uses. For the institution of Christ our Lord must not be altered by any human authority or custom. Verily, St Paul requireth a public assembly of the church and a general meeting for the due celebrating of the supper. "When you meet together therefore in one place, this is not to take the supper of the Lord," that is to say, "ye do not eat the Lord's supper." The reason is, "For every one, when they should eat, taketh his own supper, &c." Wherefore he will not that anything be done therein privately. Likewise in the same place he saith, that they meet together and eat the Lord's supper to their own damnation, which make haste to the supper, not tarrying for the congregation until they do all meet, and they eat and drink together. For he saith: "Wherefore, my brethren, when you meet to eat and drink, tarry one for another (if any man be hungry, let him eat at home, to wit, that he be not constrained[3] to eat before the residue), that ye meet not together to your condemnation." Wherefore the Lord's supper is not a private, but a public supper, to be given to no man privately. And forasmuch as that assembly is not public or general, when four or five do communicate with the sick; their saying is nothing which say, that the supper may be ordained for the sick, if so be that others do sup with them[4]. Moreover, who will deny that the example of Christ and the apostles is perpetually to be

---

[1 Rather, privately, be it either, &c.]

[2 openly, not in Lat.]

[3 propter famem, Lat. omitted: because of hunger.]

[4 See Original Letters, ed. Park. Soc. p. 123. See also Zurich Letters, 2nd Series, p. 358.]

followed[5]?   But it is evident enough, that Christ celebrated his supper in a common dining place, having gathered the church unto him, as well as it might at that time be gathered. St Paul saith, that in that point he followed the example of the Lord, and that he hath delivered no other thing to the church than that which he received of the Lord.   Neither read we in any place of the scriptures, that the other apostles of Christ carried the sacrament to the sick, and that they ordained the holy supper privately for every one to appease his tentation.   But all the apostles command us in every place to confirm and strengthen the sick and afflicted conscience[6] with the Lord's word: they teach us also to succour the distressed with diligent prayer.   St James hath diligently set James v. down in writing, how the faithful shall behave themselves towards the sick and them that are departing out of this world: but as touching the celebrating or carrying the sacrament unto them, he speaketh not one word.   Neither is it likely, that the apostles, the most faithful doctors of the church, would dissemble the matter, if so be they had thought that it had appertained chiefly to our salvation.   They have warned us often of things of far less importance.   And certain it is, that they have taught the church all things that belong to true godliness and salvation: but as for this matter, they have not mentioned one word of it.

They object out of the Acts of the Apostles this authority: "And breaking bread from house to house, they ate meat Acts ii. together with gladness and singleness of heart, praising God." But that place is to be understood of the bodily and nourishing meat, not of the mystical food; for it followeth: "They received meat or sustenance together." And therefore, as it is read in the lviii. chapter of Esay, to break bread is as much to say as to feed, and so it signifieth here also.   For the richer sort gave food to the poorer, which they did with a cheerful, not with a sorrowful heart; and they that received the benefit praised God.   But if any man do stubbornly contend, that the apostles did sup in private houses, we answer, that it maketh nothing to the present matter of the sick, and of private communion; for, as I have said before, at that time they used private houses instead of churches.

[5 hic, Lat. omitted: in this matter.]
[6 Rather, and the troubled in conscience.]

And therefore they supped in private houses, not to feed the sick with the bread of the sacrament, but because the universal church of that place was gathered together in them: as it appeareth in the xx. chapter of the Acts; as the manner is in persecutions.

They object, moreover, that the ancient fathers sent the sacrament unto them that were bound in prison, and to them that were departing, to feed on upon the way. But I have declared in place elsewhere[1], wherefore the ancient fathers did so. Hereunto also we add, that man's custom cannot prejudice the word of God. The blessed martyr Irenæus writeth, that the bishops of Rome were wont to send the sacrament to other bishops which came to Rome from other places, in token of concord and agreement[2]. But that custom was not used by all bishops, neither is it used in the church at this present. Hereof it followeth, that many things were used by the ancient fathers (as that whereof we spake before, which was, in giving the sacraments to infants), which notwithstanding are no law unto us. Good men also at this day may suffer a private supper, for a time, for them that do not yet understand the full use of the supper. But who will gather hereof, that every man ought of duty to do that which is permitted unto some upon sufferance? But if we continue contentiously to affirm it to be a relief for us in our travel[3], it will grow to this, (which we have seen received already certain hundred years ago,) that there shall be hope and confidence put in the receiving of the sacrament, as though that in respect thereof we were acceptable unto God, and when we depart out of this life we should fly straightways up into heaven, but without receiving the sacrament be thrown directly down to hell. There must also needs arise sundry other errors. Neither is there any necessity to constrain us to minister the sacrament to the sick. For as prisoners are absent from receiving the Lord's supper without danger of salvation, so likewise are the sick and those that are ready to die. For being nevertheless by perfect faith gathered to the body of Christ, and although they be absent in body yet being in mind present with the congregation, they be also made partakers of all spi-

[1 De Origine Erroris circa Cœnam, &c. cap. iv. fol. 198.]
[2 Euseb. Hist. Eccles. Lib. v. cap. 24.]
[3 asserere viaticum illud, Lat.]

ritual good things[4]. And it is sufficient for them, that as long
as they have been in health they have been always present at
the holy mysteries. The feast of passover was not celebrated Deut. xvi.
everywhere, but at Hierusalem only, in one place. But how
many were there, think we, that by reason of their bodily
health impaired with sickness, and for old age, could not travel to Hierusalem from so large and wide a kingdom? And
although no man brought them home a piece of the paschal
lamb in their pockets, notwithstanding they did communicate with the whole church of Israel. And who doubteth but
that by the coming of Christ the condition of the Christians is
not impaired[5]?

Our Lord Christ did not institute his mystical supper for The sacrament not to
the dead, but for the living only: wherefore it is not to be be offered for
the dead.
celebrated for the dead, and to be applied to their redemption. They that die without faith immediately fall under
the judgment of damnation; but they that are dead in
Christ are already joined unto the company of the elders,
and stand before the Lamb, singing Hallelujah for evermore.
For I have declared in my sermon of the soul[6], that the
salvation of the faithful souls, which are departed by corporal
death, is most undoubted. And where some object, that the
ancient fathers have made mention of offering for the dead,
we suppose that it appertaineth not unto us. For we believe
the canonical scriptures without contradiction: we believe not
the fathers further than they can prove their own sayings
by the canonical scriptures; neither would they have themselves otherwise believed. And therefore if the fathers think,
that the supper is a sacrifice, and that it is to be offered to
procure rest to the souls departed; we do not receive that
opinion, as not agreeing with the canonical scriptures, which
teach that the Lord instituted not his supper for that purpose,
and therefore by such abuse of the supper God is rather
displeased than pleased: yea, that there is no work of man,
be it never so good, much less if it be against God's word,
that can sanctify, since that prerogative belongeth only to
the merit of the Son of God: and moreover, that the souls
departed are not in any such state in that other world, that

[4] ecclesiæ, Lat. omitted: of the church.]
[5] So also ed. 1584; but ed. 1577, is made better? Minime factam
esse deteriorem? Lat.]
[6] See Vol. III. page 404, &c.]

they can or ought to be holpen by any works in this world.
But if the ancient fathers by oblation or offering do understand the sacrifice of praise or thanksgiving; we will not strive
against them but that there may be made oblations for the
dead, that is to say, that thanks be given to God and his
goodness praised, who hath called out of this miserable world
such as were endued with true faith, and hath joined them
unto the companies of angels and all the blessed saints in
that everlasting kingdom of all joy and felicity.   But surely
there is no truth nor godliness that willeth us to celebrate the
supper for the dead.

Sacrifices of two sorts, of expiation and confession.   And we make a distinction in sacrifice or oblation.   For
there is a sacrifice of expiation, and there is a sacrifice of con-
fession or praise.   The sacrifice of expiation is offered to
cleanse or purge sins, and also for satisfaction for sins.   This
cannot be accomplished without death and blood: as St Paul
the apostle sheweth plainly in the ix. chapter to the Hebrews.
The sacrifice of Christ was such a one (the figures of which
were all the sacrifices of all the holy fathers of the old Testament); who, being both priest and sacrifice, offered up himself
once to God the Father, while he suffered upon the cross,
and, shedding his most innocent blood, there gave up the
ghost.   The supper at this day is no such sacrifice, but a
commemoration of the death or of the sacrifice once offered
upon the cross.   For neither ought or can Christ be sacrificed
again, who, being once offered, is sufficient to cleanse all the
sins of all ages.   Why then should he be sacrificed again?
Neither can the Son of God be sacrificed by any man, since
that for the same cause he offered up himself once to God, as
being a priest for ever after the order of Melchisedech.   Therefore the minister of the church doth not in the church
sacrifice the body and blood of Christ in the supper for the
living; but together with the whole church doth celebrate the
remembrance of the sacrifice which was once offered upon the
cross.   Of which, as I have said elsewhere[1], the supper may
also be called a sacrifice, because it is a sacrament or sign
of the sacrifice which was once offered by Christ, as Augustine
also hath left written[2].

[1 De origine Erroris circa Cœnam, &c. Lib. IV. fol. 199.]
[2 Nonne semel immolatus est Christus in seipso? Et tamen in
sacramento ... populis immolatur. ... Si enim sacramenta, &c.—See
quotation above, p. 284. note 2.]

The sacrifice of confession is of praise and thanksgiving, which we offer to God for the redemption and benefits of God freely bestowed upon his church. And since we offer the same always unto God in prayer, but chiefly when we are joined in the sacrament of the eucharist or celebrating the supper, therefore the ancient fathers called it a sacrifice, because in the same we give thanks unto God for our deliverance from death, and for the inheritance of everlasting life which is given unto us. And that this sacrifice is generally offered by the universal church in celebrating the supper, and not by the minister of the church alone, for those that live in the church, we told you before.

Now forasmuch as we have hitherto discussed certain *Of the ends of the Lord's* circumstances or questions, which are wont to be moved about *supper.* the Lord's supper, so far forth as the necessity of the matter seemed to require, and as much as our small ability was able to perform; it remaineth, that we descend further to declare for what cause the Lord's supper was by the Lord instituted: which place truly is not rashly reckoned among the chiefest. For we made mention of the same immediately upon the beginning of this sermon. For the Lord, by setting bread and wine before us in the holy banquet, would have his promise and communion testified unto us, and his gifts represented unto us, and made manifest to our senses; and would also gather us visibly into one body, and retain the memory of his death in the hearts of the faithful; and finally, put us in mind of our duty, chiefly of praise and thanksgiving. All these things have we severally expounded, having discoursed upon them at large in the general consideration and treatise of the sacraments: and therefore at this present we will do no more but touch them briefly for memory's sake, meaning to handle those things somewhat more largely which shall by occasion arise as they are entreated upon.

But [by] this word communion I mean, the society, con- *The Lord witnesseth* junction, or partaking of the Lord Christ, by the which through *unto us his promise and* his Spirit he doth wholly knit and join himself to us, and we *communion.* are made partakers of him by faith, and are coupled unto him: so that, being by him delivered from sin and death, we may live in him, being made heirs of everlasting life; and that he may live in us and be wholly ours, as we be wholly his. Neither do we say that the communion of the Lord's body and blood is anything else. For by his body which was delivered over to death for us, and by his blood which was shed for the remission of our sins, it is come to pass, that we, being purged from our sins, are made his members; and he now quickeneth us and sustaineth us, as food which giveth life: whereupon we are also said to eat and drink him as the meat and drink of life. The promise therefore, whereof we made mention even now, is none other than the word of God, which declareth unto us that life is in Christ only: for Christ delivered his body to the death, and shed his blood, for the remission of sins, that we, believing in him, may have life everlasting. But this promise and communion of Christ is not now first of all given in the supper, or by the supper. For the Lord our God, immediately after the creation of the world, promised life and remission of sins unto Adam and his seed through Christ; and afterward reneweth[1] the same promise with Noe, Abraham, Moses, and David, and the other fathers. And that the fathers did communicate with Christ and were partakers of his goodness, Paul the apostle, with the whole scripture, is a witness. But this so great goodness happened not to the fathers only. For the promise was made unto us also, and the communion of Christ was conveyed unto us, and is conveyed particularly unto every one of us in holy baptism, and also in the manifest preaching of the gospel. Moreover, we receive the same by faith, by which we are joined to Christ, and are made his members. Therefore, as we are not void and without Christ before the supper, but are quickened by him and made his members or partners; so in the very action or celebration of the supper the promise is renewed unto us, and we renew and continue that fellowship which we have in Christ[2] by the body and blood of Christ spiritually, truly participating his life and all his good gifts through faith. And by this means we eat the Lord's body, and drink his blood. Moreover, the Lord doth visibly declare and seal unto us that spiritual communion and promise of life, made through Christ, by visible signs, to wit, the banquet of bread and wine, joined to his word or promise; namely, that it is a[3] quickening bread and drink; and that we (having

[1 So also ed. 1584: but ed. 1577, renewed: renovavit, Lat.]

[2 So also ed. 1584: but ed. 1577, with Christ: communionem Christi in qua sumus, Lat.]

[3 So also ed. 1584: but ed. 1577, that *he* is the: se esse, Lat.]

received the signs by faith and obedience) being thereto
sealed, do take upon us the promise and communion of Christ[4],
by imprinting or transferring into our bodies the seal or
sacrament of the body and blood of Christ.   Of which thing
the apostle hath also entreated in the first Corinthians, cap. x. ;
and also to the Romans, cap. iv. : and we also have said more
thereof in the general treatise of the sacraments.

But before I entreat further of the other ends[5] of the
supper, consisting in the description thereof; I will recite what
other some allege of the promise and communion of Christ.
They condemn our doctrine as heretical.   For they contend,
that the Lord promised that he would give unto the faithful
his very body and blood, to be eaten and drunken under the
form of bread and wine ; therefore it must by all means, and
without all contradiction, be believed, that the bread is the
Lord's natural body, and the wine his blood; and that these
ought to be eaten and drunken, not only spiritually, but also
corporally, unto life everlasting.   And that Christ is bodily
present in the supper, and that the bread is his body and
the wine his blood, thus they prove : That which the Lord
speaketh cannot be false, for he is the truth itself; but he
saith, that the bread is his body, and the wine his blood; therefore the bread and wine of the sacrament are verily, really,
and essentially the body and blood of Christ.   Which truth,
they say, must simply be believed, although reason itself, the
whole world, all senses, and nature itself, be against it.   We
answer : That indeed all things are very true which the Lord
hath spoken, who is truth itself; but in that sense which he
himself said and understood, not in that meaning which we
will enforce upon his words.   Wherefore before all things we
must search out the true sense of the Lord's words in the
supper, " This is my body," " This is my blood, &c."

These men cry out, saying, that the Lord's words ought
to be expounded simply, and according to the letter ; for
they are the words of a testament; and that permitteth not
his words to be expounded[6] by a trope or figure.   But we

[marginal note: Opinion of bodily presence confuted.]

[marginal note: Of the true understanding of the Lord's words : " This is my body."]

[4 Rather: And we, having received, &c., bear the promise and
communion of Christ sealed upon us, &c.]

[5 So also ed. 1584 : but ed. 1577, of other ends.]

[6 So also ed. 1584 : but ed. 1577, and the same would not have his
words to be taken &c. : hoc non admittere, Lat.]

say, that all the evangelical and apostolical books are numbered under the title[1] of the testament; and therefore throughout all and every place of the scripture nothing must be corrupted, nothing added, nothing diminished[2], unless we will be subject to the curse of God[3]. And yet we are also constrained to confess, that there be infinite sentences in the holy scriptures, which if we will proceed to expound simply according to the letter, we shall overthrow the whole scripture and the true faith, or we shall seem to charge the scriptures with lies and contradiction[4]. I will bring forth one or two examples of this sort. The evangelist St John writeth: "The Word became flesh." Now if we will cleave to the very words, then must we say that God was changed into man. But forasmuch as this sense is contrary to the faith and the scriptures; for God is immutable: and Christ is true God and man, and therefore without all mixture or conversion of natures[5], but remaining still in their own properties: and so do[6] we admit that[7] exposition which declareth that the Word took flesh, and that God was made man. And this sense is not against scripture; for Paul saith, that the Son of God in no sort[8] took upon him the nature of angels, but the seed of Abraham. Moreover[9], the catholic fathers, together with the apostle, do expound this word *est*, by this word *assumpsit*, took upon him; whereof Theodoret hath entreated at large in his *Polymorphus, Dialog.* i.[10] Again, the Lord saith in the same John: "The Father is greater than I." We should enforce an inequality upon the holy Trinity[11], if we

[1 So also ed. 1584: but ed. 1577, the name.]

[2 So also ed. 1584: but ed. 1577, taken away: detrahendum, Lat.]

[3 So also ed. 1584: but ed. 1577, omits *of God:* maledictioni Dei, Lat.]

[4 So also ed. 1584: but ed. 1577, to go about to reprove the scriptures of lies or contradiction: videbimur arguere, Lat.]

[5 So also ed. 1584: but ed. 1577, perfect God and man, without all mingling or converting of natures.]

[6 and so do, should be omitted.]

[7 So also ed. 1584: but ed. 1577, this.]

[8 So also ed. 1584: but ed. 1577, never: nuspiam, Lat.]

[9 So also ed. 1584: but ed. 1577, And therefore: Proinde, Lat.]

[10 Theodoret. Eranist. seu Polymorph. Dial. I. Opp. Tom. IV. p. 13. Par. 1642—84.]

[11 So also ed. 1584: but ed. 1577, make an inequality in adoring the Trinity: inæqualitatem adorandæ Trinitati obtrudemus, Lat.]

should contend that the Lord's words are simply to be understood, without interpretation. But by conference of other
places and[12] taking advice of faith, we say that the Son is
equal with the Father touching his divinity, but inferior unto
him in respect of his humanity; according to that saying of
the prophet, which is alleged by the apostle to that purpose:
" Thou hast made him little inferior to the angels." We read
in the gospel, that Christ our Lord had brethren, and that
St John the apostle was called the son of Mary, and Mary
called the mother of John. But who, unless he were infected
with the heresy of Helvidius[13], will stand herein, that these
places are to be expounded according to the letter?—specially
since other places of the scripture do manifestly prove, that
they were called brethren which indeed were brothers' and
sisters' children, cousin germans, kinsmen, or near of blood.
Also the circumstances of the place in the xix. cap. of St John
prove, that Mary was committed to John as a mother to her
son. Wherefore if they have a desire still to wrangle, as
hitherto at their own pleasures we have by proof found them
to do, crying out, and reiterating in their cries[14], " This is my
body, This is my blood; This is, This is, This is, This is; Is,
Is, Is;" we will also repeat: " The word was made, was
made, was made flesh: The Father is, is, is greater than I:
Christ hath brethren; I say, he hath brethren, he hath brethren. The scripture hath so. The truth saith so." But
tell me now, what commodity shall there redound to the
church by these troublesome and odious outcries and most
froward contentions? How shall the hearers be edified?
How shall the glory of God be enlarged? How shall the
truth be set forth? Necessity therefore constraineth us to
confess, that in some places we must forsake the letter, but
not the sense; and that sense is to be allowed which faith
itself, with other places of scripture conferred with it, and
finally, the circumstances of the place, the first being compared
with the last, do yield as it were of their own accord. How- When to
beit, we also cry out and repeat again and again, that we depart from
the letter.

[12 So also ed. 1584: but ed 1577, omits *and*: et, Lat.]
[13 Helvid ianiexorti ab Helvidio ita virginitati Mariæ contradicunt,
ut eam post Christum alios etiam filios de utero suo Joseph peperisse
contendant.—August. de Hæres. Opp. Tom. VI. fol. 7. Par. 1531.]
[14 So also ed. 1584: but cd. 1577, and in crying to repeat.]

ought not without great cause to go from the simplicity of the word. But when as the absurdity, not of reason, but of piety, and the repugnancy of the scriptures, and contrariety to the articles of our faith, do enforce us; then we say, affirm, and contend, that it is godly, yea, necessary, to depart from the letter and from the simplicity of the words. And that these places[1], which we alleged even now, do constrain us to depart from the letter in these words of the Lord, " This is my body, This is my blood," we will prove by most sound arguments taken out of the scriptures, when I have first briefly declared the true and ancient sense and meaning of those usual and solemn words.

The ancient exposition of the words of the supper: "This is my body."

The Lord, sitting at the self-same table with his disciples, reached the bread unto them with his own hand. And he, having only one true, human, and natural body, with the very same body of his delivered bread unto his disciples, and not a body either of any other man's, or that of his own. Neither doth that trouble us, which St Augustine reciteth of David, in expounding the xxxiii. Psalm, " And he was borne in his own hands;" whereunto he addeth immediately: " Who is borne in his own hands ? A man may be borne in the hands of other men, but none can be borne in his own. This is therefore meant of David, not of Christ. For Christ was borne in his own hands, when as, commending his very body unto them, he said, ' This is my body:' for that body was borne in his own hands[2]." For by these words St Augustine doth not feign, that Christ hath two human bodies; but he meaneth, that the human body bare in his hands the sacramental body, that is to say, the bread which is the sacrament of the true body; for he speaketh plainly, saying : " He, commending his body, bare that body in his own hands." For in the second sermon, almost in the same words being but a little changed, he saith : " How was he borne in his own hands ? For when he had commended his body

[1 illa ipsa, Lat.: those considerations.]

[2 Et ferebatur in manibus suis. . . Quis enim portatur in manibus suis? Manibus aliorum potest portari homo ; manibus suis nemo portatur. Quomodo intelligatur in ipso David secundum literam non invenimus, in Christo autem invenimus. Ferebatur enim Christus in manibus suis, quando commendans ipsum corpus suum ait, Hoc est corpus meum. Ferebat enim illud corpus in manibus suis.—Aug. Enarrat. in Psal. xxxiii. Opp. Tom. VIII. fol. 49. col. 1. Par. 1531.]

and blood, he took that in his hands which the faithful know; and after a sort he bare himself, when he said, This is my body[3]." By which words he manifestly declared, that he meant not that Christ in his natural body delivered his natural body to his disciples; but that which the faithful do know, to wit, the sacrament or mystery. For it followeth: "And he bare himself after a sort (I pray you, mark this saying, after a sort), when he said, This is my body." Wherefore those solemn words, "This is my body, which is broken for you;" and likewise, "This is my blood, which is shed for you;" can have none other sense than this: This is a commemoration, memorial, or remembrance, sign or sacrament, of my body which is given for you; This cup, or rather the wine in the cup, signifieth or representeth unto you my blood which was once shed for you. For there followeth in the Lord's solemn words that which notably confirmeth this meaning: "Do this in the remembrance of me." As if he should say: Now am I present with you, before your eyes; I shall die and ascend up into heaven, and then shall this holy bread and wine be a memorial or token of my body and blood given and shed[4] for you. Then break the bread and eat it, distribute the cup and drink it; and do this in the remembrance of me, praising my benefits bestowed on you in redeeming you and giving you life.

Although this interpretation be most slanderously reviled and become abominable in the sight of many, yet is it manifest to be the true, proper, and most ancient interpretation of all other. Tertullian, Lib. IV. contra Mart., saith: "Christ, taking the bread, and distributing it to his disciples, made it his body, in saying, 'This is my body,' that is to say, the figure of my body[5]." Hierome upon St Matthew's gospel saith: "That, like as in the prefiguring of Christ Melchisedech the priest of Almighty God had done, in bringing forth bread and

[3 Quomodo ferebatur in manibus suis? Quia cum commendaret ipsum corpus suum et sanguinem suum, accepit in manus suas quod norunt fideles; et ipse se portabat quodammodo cum diceret, Hoc est corpus meum.—Id. ibid. fol. 49. col. 2.]

[4 Rather, of my body given, and of my blood shed.]

[5 Acceptum panem et distributum discipulis corpus suum illum fecit (Christus), Hoc est corpus meum dicendo; id est, figura corporis mei.—Tertull. adv. Marcion. Lib. IV. cap. 40. Opp. Tom. I. p. 305. Hal. Mag. 1827. ed. Semler.]

wine, so he might represent the truth of his body[1]." Chrysostom also in his 83. homily upon Matthew : " If Jesus be not dead (saith he), whose token and sign is this sacrifice[2]?" Ambrose upon the first to the Corinthians, cap. xi. : " Because we be delivered by the Lord's death," saith he, " being mindful thereof, in eating and drinking we do signify the flesh and the blood which were offered for us[3]." Au. Augustine also in many places heapeth up many speeches like to this same kind of speech : " The blood is the soul, The rock was Christ," and, " This is my body." Let us hear then what he saith of these speeches, that we may understand what he thinketh of the true interpretation of this text, " This is my body." In the 3rd book of Questions, in the 57. question upon Leviticus, he saith : " It remaineth that that be called the soul, which signifieth the soul; for the thing that signifieth is wont to be called by the name of that thing which it signifieth ; as it is written, ' The seven ears of wheat are seven years ;' he said not, Do signify seven years; and, 'Seven oxen are seven years ;' and many such like. In like sort it is said : ' The rock was Christ.' He said not, The rock signifieth Christ; but as though it were so indeed, which is not the same in substance, but by signification. So likewise the blood, because through a certain vital substance it signifieth the soul, in the sacraments is called the soul[4]." Thus far he. The same Augustine also against Adimantus, cap. 12, saith :

[1 — assumit (Christus) panem . . . ut, quomodo in præfiguratione ejus Melchisedec, summi Dei sacerdos, panem et vinum afferens, fecerat, ipse quoque veritatem sui corporis et sanguinis repræsentaret. —Hieron. Comment. in Matth. cap. xxvi. Lib. iv. Opp. Tom. iv. par. 1. col. 128. Par. 1693—1706.]

[2 See quotation above, page 317, note 4.]

[3 Quia morte Domini liberati sumus, hujus rei memores in edendo et potando carnem et sanguinem, quæ pro nobis oblata sunt, significamus.—Ambros. in 1 Cor. xi. p. 183. Opp. Tom. iii. col. 1616. But these commentaries are not genuine.]

[4 Restat itaque . . . ut illud appelletur anima, quod significat animam. Solet autem res quæ significat ejus rei nomine quam significat nuncupari: sicut scriptum est, Septem spicæ septem anni sunt. Non enim dixit, Septem annos significant. Et, Septem boves septem anni sunt. Et multa hujusmodi. Hinc est quod dictum est, Petra erat Christus. Non enim dixit, Petra significat Christum ; sed tanquam hoc esset quod utique per substantiam non hoc erat, sed per significationem. Sic et sanguis, quoniam propter vitalem quandam corpu-

" So is blood the soul, like as the rock was Christ." And again in the same place he saith: "I may also expound, that that precept of the blood and soul of the beast &c. consisteth in the sign. For the Lord doubted not to say, 'This is my body,' when he gave the sign of his body[5]." Thus much Augustine. There is no fool so doltish that will say[6], that these words of Augustine are dark or doubtful. Who so list may add hereunto that which the same author hath plainly written concerning figurative speech, *Libro* II. *Contra Advers. Legis. cap.* 2.[7]

But let us leave off to cite men's testimonies concerning the proper and most ancient exposition of Christ's words, "This is my body." Let us rather proceed to allege sound arguments out of the scriptures, as we promised to do, thereby to prove that we must sometime of necessity depart from the letter, and that Christ's words are accordingly, as I have said, to be expounded by a figure. *A demonstration of the figurative words of the supper: "This is my body."*

First, it is evident that the Lord at this present instituted a sacrament: whereby it is manifest, that the Lord spake after the same manner as he is wont to speak[8] in other places of the scripture concerning sacraments; as when he saith, that circumcision is the Lord's covenant; the lamb, the Lord's passover; that sacrifices are sins and sanctifications; baptism, the water of regeneration. But we declared in the sixth sermon of this decade, that all these kinds of speeches remain to be expounded. This saying or speech therefore is to be expounded: "This is my body," "This is my blood:" because it is sacramental. For it received[9] the common interpretation,

lentiam animam significat, in sacramentis anima dictus est.—Aug. Quæst. sup. Levit. LVII. Opp. Tom. IV. fol. 47. col. 3. Par. 1531.]

[5 Sic est sanguis anima, quomodo petra erat Christus. . . . Possum etiam interpretari præceptum illud in signo esse positum. Non enim Dominus dubitavit dicere, Hoc est corpus meum, cum signum daret corporis sui.—Id. con. Adimant. cap. 12. Opp. Tom. VI. fol. 39. col. 2.]

[6 Ne Choræbus dixerit.—See Erasmi Adag. Chil. p. 404. Hanov. 1617. in *stupidos.*]

[7 Atque in omnibus sanctis scripturis secundum sanæ fidei regulam figurate dictum vel factum si quid exponitur, de quibuslibet rebus et verbis quæ sacris paginis continentur, expositio illa ducatur, non aspernanter, sed sapienter audiamus.—Aug. contr. Adv. Leg. et Proph. Lib. II. cap. 9. Opp. Tom. VI. fol. 130. col. 4.]

[8 Rather, as the scripture is wont to speak.]

[9 Admittit autem, Lat.]

which most truly and for certainty was used and received by the catholic church ever since the time of the apostles; yea, and ever since the time of the patriarchs until this day : to wit, that signs do receive the terms and names of those things that are signified; so that thereby they receive no part of their substance, but do still continue and remain in their own proper nature.

For this cause it cometh to pass[1], that our Lord Christ, in the gospel written by St Luke, did join the banquet of the passover with this our Lord's supper, in such sort that he substituted this in the place of the other; that it should not seem strange if he had said in this our supper, "This is my body;" for in the solemnising of the feast of passover it is thus said, "The lamb is the Lord's passover." Which kind of speech was not dark to be understood by the apostles, who understood that this lamb was a remembrance of the passage once past. By that means also they understood, that the Lord's bread, given unto them by the Lord, is a remembrance of his body. For in other matters of much less weight they diligently questioned and inquired of the Lord touching the proper sense and signification of the words; but of these words they never once doubted or asked any question : for all sacramental speeches were to the holy fathers very well known.

Moreover, if we continue to understand the words of the supper simply, according to the letter; it followeth, that the Lord hath delivered unto us his body and blood corporally to be received. And, I pray you, to what end should he deliver them, but that we, receiving them corporally, might live? But the universal canonical scripture teacheth, that our life or salvation, and our justification, consisteth in faith only, which we repose in the body which was given and the blood shed for us (which is the spiritual eating), not in any work of ours, much less in the bodily eating of Christ's body; which he sheweth in another place to be nothing available. Then, since there is but one means, and that most simple, whereby to obtain life and justification, to wit, by faith only, not by the work of our eating; neither is the scripture repugnant to itself; surely the Lord hath not instituted any such work of eating : and therefore the solemn words of the supper do admit some other exposition.

[[1] Huc accedit, Lat. : Add to this.]

If the bread were the Lord's true and natural body, it must needs follow, that even the wicked, being partakers of this bread, should eat Christ's body, and that verily his flesh should be meat to feed the belly; since they that eat it[2] lack both minds[3] and faith. But all holy men abhor that thought as absurd and most unworthy; of which matter I will entreat more hereafter. Therefore the saying of Christ, "This is my body," admitteth an exposition.

The whole universal canonical scripture witnesseth, that our Lord Jesus Christ took a body of the undefiled virgin, consubstantial in all points unto our bodies, that is to say, an human body; yea, that he was made like unto us in all respects, except sin. Now it is manifest, that he spake of his true sensible body when he saith, "This is my body;" for he addeth, "Which is broken or given for you." But the true, natural, sensible, or human body was delivered and died for us. But this appeareth not in the bread, or under the bread. Wherefore the Lord's words must be expounded.

Surely, if it had been the Lord's will to make his body of bread and his blood of wine, according to the power whereby he made all things with his word; as soon as ever he had said, "This is my body," the bread had been the body of Christ, and that very body whereof he spake, mortal, passible, to be felt and seen. For "he spake the word, and they were made; he commanded, and they were created." He said, "Let there be light," and light was made; and such kind of light as might be perceived and did shine. But in the supper we see nothing in Christ's hands but bread, no body. And therefore it was not our Saviour's meaning by these words, "This is my body," to create or make his body of the bread: for if he had meant so to do, surely it had been done.

Neither is there any cause why they should here, as it were, casting their mists before our eyes[4], and apply their coloured interpretation unto a rotten construction, using words, "unspeakably, supernaturally, invisibly, not qualitively, not quantively, not as in a place[5]." For by these terms they, intending in the meanwhile to bring some other thing to pass, do

[2 that eat it, not in Lat.]   [3 mente, Lat.]
[4 Rather, scattering mists abroad, throw them before us.]
[5 Aquinas, Sum. Tot. Theol. par. III. quæst. 57. Tom. VIII. p. 218. Col. Agrip. 1639. Lomb. Sentent. Lib. IV. dist. 10. p. 310. Lugd. 1570.]

by the wonderful judgment of God quite subvert and overthrow all that is their own. For if this their mystery be unspeakable, why then do they use these terms, " essentially, substantially, really, corporally ?" For they that speak so, do utter truly and set down the manner of his presence. If the bread be supernaturally the body of Christ, why then do they add "naturally?" And if the bread be Christ's body invisibly, then can it not be corporally, neither can it be a true body, whose property is to be visible. Who would not laugh, if he should hear that fire burnt and gave no heat, and that light did shine and gave no light? If he be not present in quality, quantity, and as in a place, then is he not corporally present. For, I pray you, are not qualities, quantities, and place, belonging to the body? Hearken what Augustine saith unto Dardanus touching the presence of God: " Take," saith he, " space of place from bodies, and they shall be nowhere; and because they shall be nowhere, they shall not be at all. Take the bodies themselves from the qualities of bodies, and they shall be nowhere; and therefore it must needs be they cannot be at all[1]." Let not us therefore rob or spoil the Lord's body of the properties thereof, and so deny the truth of his body. Again, that we bring not so many contraries[2] and absurd things into one and the same opinion, we interpret the words of the Lord, " This is my body," This is a memorial or remembrance of my body ; or else, This signifieth my body.

Moreover, if this word *est*, " is," be to be understood substantively in the Lord's words, " This is my body," it followeth then, that the bread is changed into Christ's body. But that this is not so, all our senses do witness ; the very substance remaining, not only the accidents of the bread. It is necessary therefore that our adversaries do understand, that in this, with this, or under this, is Christ's body. But so are they gone from the simplicity of the Lord's words, who said, " This is my body ;" and not, Under this is my body.

Again, if we be so tied to the words above recited, that upon pain of sacrilege we may not start from them an hair's breadth; I beseech you then, how durst Luke and Paul recite the words which belong to the cup far otherwise than Matthew and Mark? For these two do set down the words be-

[1 See the quotation, Vol. III. page 265, note 2.]
[2 So also ed. 1584: but ed. 1577, contrary.]

longing to the cup in this sort: "This is my blood which is of the new Testament, which is shed for many for the remission of their sins." But they two recite them thus: "This cup being the new Testament through my blood, which is shed for you;" and, "This cup is the new Testament in my blood." But shall we think, that there is no difference between the blood of Christ and the new Testament? St Paul defineth the new Testament, after Jeremy, to be a full remission of all sins; and the self-same saith, that this remission of sins is obtained through the blood of Christ. But who will so impudently contend as will dare to affirm, that the very cup, or the wine in the cup, is really and substantially the remission of sins? What cause is there, if we hold on and stick precisely to the letter, why we should be forced to confess that the cup, not the wine, nor the drink, is either the blood of Christ, either the new Testament, or the remission of sins? For the Lord saith not, This wine, but, "This cup." Howbeit in this place, to avoid absurdity, we willingly admit a trope: wherefore then are we not indifferent[3] in a matter of equal importance? Therefore, like as the cup, or the wine, is the testament, or remission of sins; so likewise the cup, or the wine, is Christ's blood, and in like manner also the bread is Christ's body. But the cup is not substantially the remission of sins or blood, but the sacrament of Christ's blood, whereby the new testament was dedicated, and full remission of sins obtained for us: therefore the bread is the body of Christ, because it is the sacrament of the body of Christ.

Surely it is a strong and firm argument that we have brought forth: and of no less force and strength, we hope, is that behind, which we will now bring forth. The Lord at the celebrating of the holy supper saith: "Do ye this in remembrance of me." These words do not import, that we would[4] determine them to be really present whom we ought to remember; for who shall be said to remember those things which he beholdeth before him in presence? But we must go[5] from the simple signification of remembrance or

[3 sumus iniquiores, Lat.: are we more rigid.]
[4 So also ed. 1584 : but ed. 1577, should.]
[5 So also ed. 1584: but ed. 1777, not go: Non debemus recedere, Lat.]

memory, specially since Paul saith: "Declare the Lord's death until he come." For thus we gather thereby: He whose remembrance is repeated until he come or return, he surely is not counted to be present, but is looked for to come: therefore the Lord's body which was given for us, the remembrance whereof is celebrated in the mystical supper, is not present, but is looked for to come.

John xvi.   Now those places, touching Christ's leaving the world and departing hence, do not simply admit the interpretation of the words of the supper. "It is expedient for you," saith he, "that I depart: for if I go not away, the Comforter shall not come unto you; but if I depart from you, then will I send him unto you." Also: "I went from the Father, and came into the world: again, I leave the world and go to the Father." And again: "And henceforth I am not in the world; but these are in the world, and I come unto thee." These sayings truly are repugnant: That he went hence; That he is no longer in the world; That he left the world; and, That his natural body is in the world, and that verily it is given and received really and substantially in the supper. Neither is it lawful figuratively to interpret the testimonies which are brought forth of St John's gospel concerning Christ's departure; for the apostles do confess, that the Lord spake plainly or simply, without any parable. Insomuch therefore as the apostles do testify, that this speech of the Lord was simple and simply pronounced, it is needful that those other words which are contrary unto these, " This is my body," be expounded by a figure, that the scripture be not repugnant to itself.

Moreover, those places, which bear record that Christ's body after the resurrection was circumscribed by place, seen and felt, which also do make a difference between Christ's body clarified and the angelical spirits (where, by the way, we may see that here is no place left for the device of the definitive mean[1]), do not admit the bare interpretation of the

Mark xvi.   solemn words of the Lord. The angels say: "He is risen, he is not here. Behold the place where they laid him." Also:
"He shall go before you into Galilee; there shall you see

Luke xxiv.   him." And again he himself saith to his disciples: "Feel me, and see: a spirit hath not flesh and bones, as you see me

[1 modi definitivi, Lat.]

have." These sayings of[2] the clarified body (which is that which ascended, and sitteth at the right hand of the Father) repugn wholly with ubiquity or being in every place, and the insensibility of Christ's body : which notwithstanding must needs be granted, if we proceed to enforce the real presence of Christ's body out of the words of the supper simply understood. Wherefore[3] belongeth that which the apostle, disputing of the resurrection of the dead, saith : " If the dead do not 1 Cor. xv. rise, neither is Christ risen ;" but, " Christ is risen, being the firstfruits of them that sleep ;" and therefore shall we rise also. Wherefore, by our own bodies being raised again it appeareth, what manner of body Christ's glorious body was, or is, whereunto our bodies are made like. But our bodies shall be true bodies, consisting of sinews, veins, flesh, skin, and bones, visible, not invisible, and remaining in some certain place in heaven, not everywhere : whereupon it followeth, that the Lord's body is not invisible and everywhere. But if any man think that to be no good argument, which is fet[4] from our raised bodies to the Lord's raised body, or contrariwise, let him accuse St Paul, who hath taught us this by his 1 Cor. xv. example. Therefore the catholic and right ancient faith constraineth[5] to expound the words of the supper by a trope or figure.

Finally, when as the Capernaites had heard the Lord dispute touching the eating of his body and drinking of his blood, and did think and imagine of a carnal eating and drinking, he said that he would ascend into heaven : to wit, that they should not think on the eating of his natural body, since in the selfsame body he would ascend into heaven. Neither is there left here any place for the new and frivolous device of certain men[6], which feign that to ascend into heaven is nothing else than to lay down the weak state and condition thereof, and to receive a supernatural. For St Luke, whom To ascend into heaven. altogether we must rather believe than such subtle devices or

[2 de, Lat.: concerning.]
[3 So also ed. 1584: but ed. 1577, Whereunto : Quibus accedit, Lat.]
[4 Fet: fetched.]
[5 So ed. 1584: but ed. 1577, constraineth us.]
[6 Bullinger refers to the interpretation of Brentius and his followers.]

rather follies, saith that the Lord was lifted up on high, and carried up into heaven from the sight of his disciples : moreover, that his body was received by a cloud ; and that his disciples looked up into heaven after him, until they heard the angels say unto them, that he would return again in the very same manner altogether as they saw him depart away. But who knoweth not, that he shall come again in the clouds of heaven ? Therefore heaven, into which the Lord ascended, is the name of a place, not of a state or condition. Also in the gospel he promiseth us a place with himself, saying : " If I go to prepare you a place, I will come again, and take you unto me ; that where I am, there you may be also." Yea, he laid down all the conditions and infirmities of a mortal body in his resurrection ; so that he had no need to lay them down at his ascension.

Acts i.

John xiv.

I suppose that there is none of the faithful that will deny, that the Lord instituted nothing to us in vain, or without some singular and special commodity to us. But when the Lord said in the gospel, that his flesh being corporally eaten availed nothing ; where he speaketh of none other body than of that very same, whereof he spake in the words of the supper, to wit, which he gave for us ; it followeth without all contradiction, that the Lord delivered nothing unto us in the supper but that would profit us. But he should have delivered that which would not have profited us, if he had given us his body to be eaten corporally. It is evident therefore, that it is very necessary the words of the supper should be expounded.

Matt. xxiv.

Hereunto belongeth the notable prophecy and manifest commandment of our Lord Jesus Christ, saying in the gospel : " Then if they shall say unto you, Lo, here is Christ, or there is Christ, do not believe. For there shall arise false Christs and false prophets, and they shall work great signs and wonders, so that if it were possible, the very elect shall be brought into error. Behold, I have told you before. If therefore they shall say unto you, Behold, where he is in the wilderness; go not forth. Behold, where he is in the innermost parts of the house," (in the closets or coffers, I say ; for this word, ἐν ταμείοις, signifieth the most secret and innermost parts of all the house, wherein we use to lay up those things which we would have safest kept, which in Dutch we

call *Schryn, schloss, und ghalt*,) " do not believe. For like as
the lightning goeth out of the east, and appeareth even unto
the west, so shall the coming of the Son of man be." But
although this place is used to be expounded by many of the
calamities of the Jews, yet that cannot be denied, which
St Hierome also himself confesseth, that in the same likewise
the destiny of all the world is prophesied of, even unto the
end thereof[1]. Wherefore this place, which we have alleged,
is concluded with the saying concerning Christ's last coming
into the world at the day of judgment. And moreover it
cannot be denied, that the Lord doth absolutely condemn
that doctrine that defendeth, that Christ remaineth or is present, in divers places of the world, in boxes or close places:
which not only the books of the teachers of transubstantiation
are seen to do, but also tabernacles which are erected unto
Christ's body[2] (which they call meat-tents[3]), also chapels with
famous temples and monasteries. In all and every one of
these places, I say, they shew us Christ, saying, " Lo, here is
Christ, and there is Christ; behold the bread of angels.
Christ is wholly in all these sacrifices, and he is fully and
wholly in every part of them, even in such sort as he was
when he was born of the virgin Mary, and hung upon the
cross." Which thing they by and by confirm by miracles and
wonders; they also set it forth with circumstance of words,
saying, that so great mysteries are not to be inquired of, but
simply to be believed; and that these things were wrought
unspeakably and invisibly by the omnipotency of God.
Neither did the Lord dissemble how much this error should
increase. There shall be such plenty, such great numbers of
people that receive this error, and running after Christ into
the deserts and innermost places of the houses, that the very
elect shall be in danger. But in the mean while, in so great

[1 — discipuli interrogant tria : quo tempore Jerusalem destruenda
sit; quo venturus Christus; quo consummatio seculi futura sit.—
Hieron. Comment. in Matth. xxiv. Lib. IV. Opp. Tom. IV. par. 1. col.
114. Par. 1704.]

[2 quæ ubique locorum cernuntur, Lat. omitted: which are to be
seen in all places.]

[3 ciboria, Lat. The tabernacle (called by modern writers the
ciborium) was a sort of turret or cabinet on the upper surface of the
altar, containing the *pyx* in which the consecrated hosts were reserved.
—Hart's Eccles. Records, p. 230.]

peril and danger of things what doth Christ teach his elect to
do? Immediately he addeth: "Do not believe." What,
do not believe that Christ is here or there upon earth, in the
wilderness, or in the innermost parts of the house, or even in
the midst of the cities, or in the fields? He addeth moreover:
"Go not forth." Follow not the multitude, which by distance
of place seeketh for Christ, as if he were yet conversant upon
the earth. Therefore now, if so be the whole world, and all
the councils in the world, all the kings and princes, yea, if all
the angels and saints, should command us to believe that
Christ is here or there corporally, yet the commandment of
our only Redeemer Jesus Christ, the Son of God, the Father
of wisdom[1], by whom all things were made, who forbiddeth
us to believe the same, ought to be of that authority among
all the godly, that they may know that they must not believe
as creatures command them, but as the Creator hath commanded them. Yea moreover, the Lord vouchsafeth in this
very same place of the gospel to give us a reason of his doctrine. For why must we not believe that Christ is conversant
or bodily present upon the earth, but invisibly? Because,
like as the lightning goeth forth of the east and appeareth in
the west, so shall the coming of the Son of man be. Which
is as much as if he had said: The Son of God came once
humbly into the earth, to redeem us through his humility and
death on the cross; which thing being finished, he forsook the
earth, and ascended into heaven, and sitteth on the right
hand of the Father: from thence he shall not return into these
our regions but to judgment. But then shall he appear
glorious, noble, to be seen of all men, as it were the most
clear sun, yea, rather like a lightning, right terrible to all the
wicked. And therefore there is no cause why, from the time
of his ascension until his coming to judgment, we should look
for him to come invisibly, and to remain with us corporally
present. St Hierome, expounding the same place, saith: "This
also must be said, that the second coming of our Saviour shall
not be shewed in humility as before, but in glory. It were a
foolish part therefore to seek him in a little corner, or in
some secret place, who is the light of the whole world[2]."

[1 Rather, the wisdom of the Father.]

[2 Hoc quoque dicendum, quod secundus Salvatoris adventus non
in humilitate, ut prius, sed in gloria demonstrandus est. Stultum est

Thus far he. But lest I may seem to stay myself upon some human authority, I will rehearse that which St Paul teacheth us in his epistle to the Hebrews, saying: "Christ Heb. ix. appeared once before the end of the world, to put away sin by offering up of himself. And forasmuch as it is appointed to men once to die, and after this cometh the judgment: even so Christ, being once offered up to take away the sins of many, shall the second time be seen of them without sin, who look for him to their salvation." Because therefore our Lord came once into the world he was once offered up, but he shall come again, or the second time, at the end of the world, truly he cometh not again every day into the world. And because he hath forbidden us to believe, if any man should shew him present here or there unto us in this world; ³it must needs follow, that he may be shewed present here or there, yea, in all places where the sacrament of thanksgiving is celebrated, if we will understand the words of the supper according to the letter; therefore it followeth without all contradiction, by conference of places, that the words of the Lord's supper ought not to be expounded according to the letter.

I think herewith I have satisfied such as be not of contentious disposition; for undoubtedly their meaning is⁴, that we should speak of the sacraments sacramentally, and that sacramental speeches ought to be expounded sacramentally. Besides that, we ought to believe nothing that is repugnant to the rule of belief. But by⁵ the miracles and omnipotency of God, brought forth and alleged in this place for the setting out and persuading of an evil matter, they do no good at all after so many and manifest arguments of truth. Miracles Miracles and the omni-
are joined unto the word, as it were seals; which thing the potency of God.
Lord God himself testifieth in St Mark. If then they be repugnant to the word, and affirm that which the word altogether denieth, who will not perceive them to be of that

itaque eum in parvo loco vel abscondito quærere, qui totius mundi lumen sit.—Hieron. Comment. in Matth. Lib. iv. Opp. Tom. iv. par. 1. col. 116.]

[³ autem, Lat. omitted: but.]

[⁴ intelligunt, Lat.: they understand.]

[⁵ So also ed. 1584: but ed. 1577, omits by: miracula &c. nihil probant, Lat.]

kind of miracles, whereof the apostle speaketh in the second chapter of the second epistle to the Thessalonians, and whereof we have heard now that the Lord gave us warning in the gospel, that we should in no case believe them? The Lord can do all things, but therefore he doth not all things[1]. The prophet saith : " Whatsoever the Lord would do, that he did, both in heaven and in earth." Moreover, he will not do such things as are contrary to his word and his faith; therefore he cannot do that he will not do. Theodoretus, in his third dialogue intituled *Polymorphus*, saith : " The Lord God will do nothing that is not in him of his own nature; but he can do whatever he will; but he will do such things as are fit and agreeing to his nature. Therefore sith God of his own nature is true, he cannot do that which is contrary to his word[2]." Other sound writers do add : Not that he cannot do all things, but that he will not do that which is contrary to his nature, and because it doth not become him to do against himself.

Of Christ's presence in the supper. In the mean season I do expressly profess, that I condemn not or flatly am against all manner of Christ's presence in the church, and in the action also of the supper; for I am flat against that bodily presence of Christ in the bread, which the papists defend and enforce upon the church of God. But I confess and acknowledge with open mouth and sincere heart that spiritual, divine, and quickening presence of our Lord Christ, both in the supper and also out of the supper, whereby he continueth to pour himself into us, not by signs lacking life, but by his Holy Spirit, to make us partakers of all his good graces, to justify, quicken, nourish, sustain, and satisfy us : which presence we do also feel in ourselves through faith, by the which we are both sustained, nourished, and satisfied. For Christ is the head of his church, and we have fellowship with him. But how should a living body be without his head? How should we be partakers of Christ, if we should not feel him present, yea, living and working in us?

[1 See Vol. I. page 91.]

[2 Ἐραν. Οὐδὲν ἀδύνατον τῷ παντοδυνάμῳ Θεῷ. Ὀρθ. Διὰ τί; Ἐραν. Ἐπειδήπερ οὐ βούλεται. Ὀρθ. Τοῦ δὴ χάριν οὐ βούλεται; Ἐραν. Ἐπειδὴ τῆς φύσεως ἐκείνης τὸ ἁμαρτάνειν ἀλλότριον, &c.—Theodoret. Dial. III. Impatibilis. Opp. Tom. IV. p. 122. Par. 1642.]

But of these matters we have also entreated more at large in place convenient[3].

Some there are, I know well enough, who otherwise are not injurious to the truth, which gainsay these things, crying out, that by this reason the manner of Christ's presence in the supper is not fully enough expressed, especially since he himself also hath said elsewhere, " Behold, I am with you con- Matt. xxviii. tinually unto the world's end." I, saith he, wholly, not my power or divinity, not my spirit, nor my strength. Moreover, it is a hazard lest we should seem to tear Christ in pieces, seeing that he cannot be wholly with us, unless he be present with us as well in body as in divinity. But we wonder what is in their heads. Do they not understand, that the Lord in that divine talk, spoken both in the very supper and also immediately after the supper, did beat upon nothing so much as that very same thing against which they set shoulder[4]; to wit, that Christ would be absent in body, but present in spirit; and that this presence would be more profitable to the church than his bodily presence? Do they not also understand, wherefore he took flesh, and was nailed on the cross; that is to say, what the effect and use is of Christ's body, to wit, that the sacrifice of his body being once offered for us upon the earth, he might carry the same up into heaven, in token that both our bodies and souls after our death shall through his merit be also carried thither? Therefore, after that the Lord's body had fulfilled on earth that which it came to fulfil, there is no cause why it should do anything else upon earth. He now sitteth, and ought to sit, at the right hand of the Father, that he may draw all us thither unto him. If there be any that doth not yet fully believe that which we say, let him read the doctrine of St Paul the apostle in the ninth and tenth chapters of his epistle to the Hebrews. Let him also read the fourteenth and sixteenth chapters of St John's gospel. But if it be a pleasure to them to hale at the gable of contention[5], and to stick precisely as well to these words of the Lord, " I am with you unto the world's end," as to these, " This is my body, This is my blood," let them then expound to me these holy testimonies of the holy scripture. Paul saith that Christ dwelleth in our

[3 See Decade IV. Serm. 8.]   [4 impugnant, Lat.]
[5 contentionis funem trahere, Lat.]

hearts, and that Christ liveth in him, and he in Christ. The Lord saith to the thief: "This day shalt thou be with me in paradise." And the evangelist saith of the Lord being dead: "They laid him into the sepulchre." The scripture saith not, they laid flesh and bones into the sepulchre; but, they laid him into the sepulchre. The Lord said not to the thief, Thy soul shall be with my spirit, or soul, in paradise; but, "Verily I say unto thee, this day shalt thou be with me in paradise." Neither doth St Paul say, that Christ's Spirit and life doth live in him, or dwell in our hearts; but he saith simply, that Christ doth dwell in our hearts. But who is so foolish and given to contention, that for these words and places of the scripture will contend, that Christ's divinity was buried with his body, that Christ's body was with his soul that same day in paradise in which either of them departed this life, that Christ's body together with his Spirit dwelleth in the hearts of the faithful, and liveth in Paul, and that Paul liveth in Christ's flesh? All men do willingly admit the catholic sense of the catholic church, gathered out of the word of God, namely, that Christ in his Spirit is present in his church even to the world's end, but absent in body; and that the thief's soul was that day present in paradise with Christ's soul, not with his body. So judgeth it also of the residue. But if any man mistrust mine interpretation, let him hear St Augustine in his treatise upon John, saying thus: "He speaketh of the presence of his body, when he saith, 'The poor you shall always have with you, but me shall you not have always.' For in respect of his majesty, of his providence, and of his unspeakable grace, is that fulfilled which he spake, 'Behold, I am with you always, even to the world's end.' But in respect of the flesh which the Word took upon it, in respect that he was born of the virgin, that he was taken by the Jews, that he was nailed to the cross, that he was taken down from the cross, that he was wound in a sheet, that he was laid into the sepulchre, that he was manifested in the resurrection, 'you shall not have me with you always.' And why so? Because he was conversant, as touching his bodily presence, forty days with his disciples; and they accompanying him, but not following him, he ascended into heaven, and is not here; for there he 'sitteth at the right hand of the Father:' and he is here; for he is not gone hence in respect of the presence of his majesty[1]." Thus far St Augustine.

But if they yet proceed, not regarding all this that we have said, to urge that saying of the Lord out of Matthew, "Behold, I, even I, I say, am, μεθ' ὑμῶν, with you;" we will also object against them this saying of the Lord, and the same out of the gospel: "It is expedient for you that I (lo, here they have also this word 'I') do depart:" we object also against them this testimony of the angels out of Luke: "This Jesus, which is taken up, ἀφ' ὑμῶν, from you into heaven, &c." They shall be at length constrained, whether they will or no, to reconcile such places as seem to be repugnant, and to admit the general understanding which we have alleged and defended hitherto.

Neither is there here any danger of dividing Christ; neither divide we Christ's person with Nestorius, since we defend the propriety of both natures in Christ against the Eutychians. While Christ our Lord in body was yet conversant upon the earth, he himself witnesseth in the gospel, that nevertheless he was[2] also in the heavens. And indeed Christ, who was both God and man all at one time, was then in heaven, when he was crucified and conversant upon earth, although his body was not crucified in the heavens. But as Christ divided not himself, although, being in heaven, he was notwithstanding conversant and crucified in body upon earth, not in heaven; so neither do we divide Christ, who is both God and man,

Christ is not divided.

[1 Pauperes semper habebitis vobiscum, me autem non semper habebitis. Accipiant et hoc boni, sed non sint solliciti: loquebatur enim de præsentia corporis sui. Nam secundum majestatem suam, secundum providentiam, secundum ineffabilem . . . gratiam impletur quod ab eo dictum est, Ecce ego vobiscum sum omnibus diebus usque ad consummationem seculi. Secundum carnem vero quam Verbum assumpsit, secundum id quod de virgine natus est, secundum id quod a Judæis comprehensus est, quod ligno confixus, (Bullinger read, affixus) quod de cruce depositus, quod linteis involutus, quod in sepulchro conditus, quod in resurrectione manifestatus, non semper habebitis me vobiscum. Quare? Quoniam conversatus est secundum corporis præsentiam quadraginta diebus cum discipulis suis, et eis deducentibus videndo, non sequendo, ascendit in cœlum ; et non est hic, ibi enim sedet ad dexteram Patris : et hic est, non enim recessit præsentia majestatis.—Aug. in Evan. Joan. Tract. L. Opp. Tom. IX. fol. 76. col. 3. Par. 1531.]

[2 fuisse aut esse, Lat.: was or is. See John iii. 13.]

although we say he is present with us when we celebrate the supper, and that we communicate with him; yet nevertheless we affirm, that in his body he remaineth in heaven, where he sitteth at the right hand of the Father; and so let us keep ourselves within the compass of the scripture. Of this matter I have reasoned at large, where I have entreated of one person and of both natures in Christ unpermixed[1].

Hitherto have I spoken of the natural meaning of the words of the Lord's supper as briefly and plainly as possibly I could. Touching the place of Paul in the first to the Corinthians, chap. x. "The cup of blessing which we bless, &c.," with such other texts which are alleged to prove bodily presence, I shall not need to use many words; for we have handled that place already once or twice.

Of the true eating of Christ's body.   It remaineth therefore that we examine and weigh what they deliver unto us touching the eating of Christ's body, and also what the canonical scriptures do teach to be thought of that eating. What, say they, the Lord hath promised, the same most surely and fully he performeth. They add: But he promised that he would give us his true body and very blood to be eaten and drunken in the form of bread and wine unto everlasting life. They gather, Therefore he hath given his very body and blood to the faithful, under the form of bread and wine, for meat and drink to everlasting life: whereupon it must be eaten[2] corporally, as it is corporal. To the confirmation whereof they allege the Lord's words, as they are written in the vi. chapter of John's gospel. We answer: God most perfectly and fully performeth that which he hath promised. But we add, that he performeth not according to that meaning that we devise, but as his word truly importeth. We *How Christ hath given his flesh unto us for bread, that is to say, to be meat for us.* must therefore see first of all in what sense the Lord promised to give his flesh for bread, and his blood for drink to the faithful; and next, how we ought to eat[3] his flesh, and how to drink his blood. These things truly, which the Lord promiseth here, are well nigh[4] allegories and parables. The Lord promiseth that he will give us his flesh for bread or meat, and his blood for drink. But because meat and drink are ordained

[1 See Decade IV. Serm. 6.]
[2 *talem omnino qualis est*, Lat. omitted: every way so as it is.]
[3 Rather, how we eat: *quomodo edamus*, Lat.]
[4 So also ed. 1584: but ed. 1577, all: *prope omnia*, Lat.]

and given unto men to preserve their bodily life, and the Lord in the vi. chapter of John speaketh not of the life of the body but of the soul, there is a passage made from bodily things to spiritual things. When therefore the Lord promised, that he would give us his flesh for bread or meat and his blood for drink, what other thing did he promise us, than that he would give his body to the death, and shed his blood for the remission of sins? For by the death of Christ we are, as it were by meat, preserved and delivered from death. By Christ's blood we are washed from sin, and our souls are as it were with drink spiritually drunken. Therefore the Lord speaketh nothing here of the bread of the Lord's supper, neither doth he promise that at the supper he will make of bread his flesh, or that he would give his body in form of bread. Then let this mine exposition of Christ's words, concerning the giving of Christ's body or flesh in the form of bread, &c. be false and feigned, unless I confirm the same by the words of Christ.

The Lord said in the gospel: "Seek for the meat that perisheth not, but remaineth to life everlasting, which the Son of man shall give unto you." A little after by interpretation he addeth: " And the bread which I will give unto you is my flesh, which I will give for the life of the world." I said that I would give you bread or meat, (for this word "bread" is, after the Hebrew manner, used by the Lord for meat and all manner of sustenance;) but saith he: This bread or this meat is my flesh, and therefore I promise to give you my flesh, when I promise to give you the bread of life. Here hast thou expressly to understand, that the Lord by bread did not mean bodily bread, or the bread of the supper. But how doth he promise to give his flesh for bread, that is to say, to be meat for us, or to quicken us? The Lord repeateth this word, " I will give;" and saith, " Which I will give for the life of the world." I will give it, that is to say, even to the death, that through my death I may quicken you. By dying therefore my flesh shall feed, that is to say, shall quicken. Thus much concerning the promise of his flesh for bread. Hereafter followeth of the eating thereof.

Like as the holy scripture setteth down in every place, without trope or allegory, that we are made partakers of Christ's death, or of his body which was given for the world

How Christ's body is eaten and his blood drunken.

unto life, through faith; so also in this present place, by a
trope or allegory, he biddeth us to eat and drink the flesh and
blood of Christ unto everlasting life. Therefore to eat Christ's
flesh and drink his blood is nothing else but to believe that
Christ's body was given for us, and his blood shed for us to
the remission of sins; and consequently, that we remain in
Christ, and have Christ remaining in us. For the faith,
whereof we spake, is not only an imagination or thought concerning things past and exceeding our capacity; but a most
certain assurance, and a feeling of heavenly things received
within us, to our great commodity. For therefore not only
faith, but also the virtue and force of faith, is by the Lord
signified in John by the allegory both of eating and drinking.
Meat passeth not into the substance of our body without delight: so also by faith, through a great desire of the spirit,
we are joined with Christ, that he may live in us, and we may
live in Christ, and be partakers of all his good gifts. This is
the spiritual eating of Christ, who never thought, no, not so
much as once dreamed in this place, of the gross and bodily eating, which is indeed unprofitable. But forasmuch as the whole
point of the controversy consisteth in these words of eating
and drinking the flesh and blood of the Lord, they interpreting
the same words bodily and we spiritually, it seemeth good to
be shewed, that by the words of eating and drinking the Lord
meant no other thing than to believe, and consequently to
abide in Christ, and to have Christ abiding in us. We will
therefore, by conference of places of the scripture, bring forth
six evident testimonies in confirmation of our assertion.

1.   "I am," saith the Lord, "that bread of life: whoso cometh
to me shall not hunger, and whoso believeth in me shall not
thirst for ever." But who will deny, that there is relation between to eat and not to hunger, to drink and not to thirst?
Because therefore the Lord said, "He shall not hunger," he
should first have said, "Whoso eateth me:" but he rather
used the word of coming, and said, "Whoso cometh to me
shall not hunger." To eat therefore is to come, and to come
is to eat. And what it is to come to him, he expoundeth immediately, saying: "Whosoever hath heard from the Father,
and hath learned, he it is that cometh to me;" that is to say,
receiveth me, and believeth in me. For Paul also saith:
Heb. xi.   "Whosoever will come to God must believe." These testi-

monies without contradiction do prove, that to eat is nothing else but to believe. Yet that followeth which is more manifest: "And whoso believeth in me shall never thirst." And whoso drinketh shall not thirst[1]. Therefore " to drink," he hath put for " to believe[2]." Therefore to drink is to believe; for faith satisfieth and pacifieth our minds. Here they have an answer that make this objection, Whether the Lord himself had not words whereby he might declare his mind, if so be by eating and drinking he had meant believing? They have, I say, an open testimony whereby he useth the one for the other.

Again, in the same treatise the Lord saith: " Whoso eateth my flesh, and drinketh my blood, hath everlasting life; and I will raise him at the latter day." And again in the same treatise he saith: " This is the will of him that sent me, that whosoever shall see the Son, and believe in him, may have everlasting life; and I will raise him at the latter day." Lo, here thou hast again these words, to eat Christ's flesh, to drink his blood, and to believe in Christ, all in one sense.

2.

Again, the Lord saith: " I am the lively bread which came down from heaven." And again he saith: " Verily I say unto you, he that believeth in me hath life everlasting. Whosoever shall eat of this bread shall live for ever." Then to eat Christ, and to believe in Christ, are all one.

3.

And again he saith: " Whoso eateth my flesh, and drinketh my blood, abideth in me, and I in him." Moreover, John in his canonical epistle saith: " Whosoever shall confess," that is to say, shall believe, " that Jesus is the Son of God, God abideth in him, and he in God."

4.
1 John iv.

Again: " Verily, verily, I say unto you, Unless you eat the flesh of the Son of man, and drink his blood, you can have no life in you." And the same Lord saith also in the viii. chapter of John: " If you do not believe that I am he, ye shall die in your sins." And again: " Verily, verily, I say unto you, whoso keepeth my sayings, he shall never see death."

5.

Again the Lord saith: " Like as the living Father hath sent me, and I live by means of the Father ; so likewise, who-

6.

[1 Rather, Whoso drinketh does not thirst: Qui bibit non sitit, Lat.]
[2 Rather, therefore for, to drink, he has put, to believe: pro bibere ergo reposuit credere, Lat.]

so eateth me shall also live by means of me." And John in the v. chapter saith: "Like as the Father hath light[1] in himself, so hath he given to the Son to have life in himself." And likewise in his canonical epistle he saith: "Whoso believeth in the Son of God hath a testimony in himself." And, "Whoso hath the Son hath life."

Unto these most evident testimonies of God we will now join the testimonies of men, which do say the very same, that to eat Christ is nothing else but to believe in Christ and to abide in Christ. St Augustine in his 25th treatise upon John, expounding these words of the Lord, saith: "This is the work of God, that you should believe in him whom he sent:" as he left written: "This is therefore to eat the meat that perisheth not, but which remaineth unto everlasting life. Why then dost thou prepare thy teeth and thy belly? Believe, and thou hast eaten[2]." The same again, in his 26th treatise, saith: "To believe in him, this is to eat the bread of life. Whoso believeth in him eateth invisibly and is filled, because he is born invisible." And again in the same treatise he saith: "This is to eat that meat and drink that drink, to abide in Christ and to have Christ abiding in him; and by this means whoso abideth not in Christ, and in whom Christ doth not abide, doubtless, he neither eateth spiritually his flesh," &c.[3] The same Augustine, *Lib. de Doctrina Christiana*, *cap.* 16, shewing when a figurative speech is to be

[1 So also ed. 1584: but ed. 1577, life.]

[2 Hoc est opus Dei, ut credatis in eum quem misit ille. Hoc est ergo manducare cibum, non qui perit, sed qui permanet in vitam æternam. Ut quid paras dentes et ventrem? Crede, et manducasti. —Aug. in Evang. Joan. Tract. xxv. Opp. Tom. ix. fol. 45. col. 2. Par. 1531.]

[3 Credere in eum hoc est manducare panem vivum. Qui credit in eum, manducat, invisibiliter saginatur, quia invisibiliter renascitur. ...Hoc est manducare illam escam, et illum bibere potum, in Christo manere et illum manentem in se habere. Ac per hoc qui non manet in Christo, et in quo non manet Christus, proculdubio nec manducat spiritaliter carnem ejus, nec bibit ejus sanguinem, licet carnaliter et visibiliter premat dentibus sacramentum corporis et sanguinis Christi: sed magis tantæ rei sacramentum ad judicium sibi manducat et bibit, quia immundus præsumpsit ad Christi accedere sacramenta, quæ aliquis non digne sumit, nisi qui mundus est. De quibus dicitur, Beati mundi corde, quoniam ipsi Deum videbunt.—Id. in Evang. Joan. Tract. xxvi. Opp. Tom. ix. fol. 46. col. 3. et fol. 47. col. 4.]

admitted and when not, saith : " If it be an enjoining speech, or forbidding some heinous offence or trespass, or commanding some profit or good deed to be done, it is not figurative. But if it seem to command some heinous offence or trespass, or to forbid some profit or good deed, then is it figurative. ' Unless you eat the flesh of the Son of man, and drink his blood, you can have no life in you;' this seemeth to command an heinous offence and trespass : therefore it is figurative, willing us to be partakers of the Lord's passion, and sweetly and profitably to keep in memory, that his flesh was crucified and wounded for us[4]." Thus said Augustine, who doubtless set down not only his own meaning herein, but also the meaning of the whole catholic church which was at that time. Let our adversaries therefore take heed what they do, who will drive all the faithful to this wickedness and offence, to wit, that we should corporally eat Christ's body.

The flesh profiteth nothing.

Furthermore, hereunto is to be added that which by reason of the perspicuity and plainness thereof doth almost surpass all that we have alleged before, which the Lord himself answered to those that wondered or rather murmured, saying : " How can he give us that his flesh to eat ?" after that he had declared the sum of the true faith. " Doth this offend you, saith he, that I said I would give you bread which came from heaven, even my flesh, to be meat to all believers ?" I suppose that offence shall take no just place, when you shall see me ascend into heaven, from whence I came down unto you, and where I was with my Father before all beginning. Then shall ye perceive by my divine ascension that I am the heavenly bread, the natural Son of God, and the life of the world : ye shall perceive, moreover, that my flesh is not to be eaten bodily, and to be consumed and torn in morsels, but is carried up into heaven for a pledge of the salvation of mankind. And shortly after this he saith further : " It is the spirit that quickeneth ; the flesh availeth nothing." And yet more manifestly he speaketh : "The words which I speak unto you are spirit and life." Certain it is that Christ's flesh availeth very much, and is more profitable to the world than any tongue, yea, the most eloquent, can express. Yea, the Lord hath warned us beforehand, that we shall have no life unless we eat his flesh. Then

[4 See quotation above, page 289, note 2.]

doth the Lord deny that his flesh availeth us anything at all, if so be it be eaten as the Capernaites understood, that is to say, bodily. For being bodily eaten it availeth nothing, but being spiritually eaten it quickeneth: and the Lord hath plainly professed, that he spake of the spiritual eating, in which consisteth life.

These things being declared and confirmed after this manner, we gather such things into a short summary, wherein we think sufficient answer is made unto our adversaries' objection. The proposition is true, which holdeth, that the Lord doth certainly perform that which he hath promised. But the second proposition is false, which saith, that the Lord by his words in the sixth chapter of John by bread meant the material bread of the sacrament, and that he promised that he would convert the same into his flesh. For by bread he meant not the material bread of the sacrament, but meat to live withal, according to the propriety of the Hebrew tongue; yea, his very flesh, which was delivered to the death, to be meat, I say, that we might live through Christ's death. Thus therefore should the argument have been framed: That which God promiseth he performeth: but he promiseth that he will give us his flesh for bread, that is to say, to be meat and life for us: therefore hath he given his flesh to be meat, that is to say, he hath given over himself to the death, that by his death we might live. Which being so, surely the meat whereof the Lord speaketh is no bodily meat, although the Lord himself have a true, human, and natural body, of like substance to ours, but spiritual: not that the flesh is converted into the spirit, but for that it ought to be received spiritually, not bodily. But it is eaten spiritually, by faith, not with the bodily mouth. For as chewing or eating maketh us partakers of the meat, so are we made partakers of the body and the blood of Christ through faith.

The Lord's words in John vi. are fitly to be applied to the matter of the supper. But thou wilt say: How cometh it to pass, that seeing bread, whereof mention is made in the vi. chapter of John, doth not signify the bread of the supper, that almost all the doctors, interpreters, and ministers of the church, do apply these words to the Lord's supper? I answer, That these words of the Lord may be applied to the matter of the Lord's supper for other causes, although the bread signify not the bread of the sacrament. Yea, I confess that these words of the Lord, of the

eating his flesh and drinking his blood, do bring great light
to the matter of the Lord's supper. St Augustine, *Lib. de
Consensu Evangelistarum tertio, capite primo*, saith : "John
said nothing in this place (John the xiii.) of the body and
blood of the Lord, but plainly witnesseth, that the Lord hath
spoken more at large thereof in another place[1]." This much
saith he, speaking undoubtedly of the vi. of John. Since
therefore it is one and the self-same[2] body of our Lord,
whereof he speaketh in both places, in the vi. of St John and
the xxvi. of Matthew ; and the self-same is said in both places
to have been delivered to the death for us, or for our life;
and likewise, because there is but one means to be partaker of
Christ, which is, by faith in his body which was delivered and
his blood shed ; and finally, because it is the catholic or universal and undoubted doctrine, that Christ's flesh being bodily
eaten availeth nothing : surely the things before written in the
vi. chapter of John are agreeable and do fully open the matter
of the Lord's supper. And to the intent that this yet may
be the better understood, I will recite what testimonies have
been always alleged in the church out of the holy scriptures
concerning the two kinds of eating of Christ. Christ's body
is eaten and his blood drunken spiritually ; it is also eaten and
drunken sacramentally. The spiritual manner [is] accomplished by faith, whereby being united to Christ, we be
made partakers of all his goodness. The sacramental manner
is only performed in celebrating the Lord's supper. The
spiritual eating is perpetual unto the godly, because faith is
to them perpetual. They communicate with Christ both
without the supper and in the supper ; and by it they do
more increase and continue their new beginnings, as we have
also shewed before : and now, by adjoining of the holy action,
all things are done more manifestly and plainly. As for the
unbelievers and hypocrites, with their captain Judas, they
never communicate with Christ, neither before the supper, nor
in the supper, nor after the supper, inasmuch as they continue

Of two kinds of eating the Lord's supper.

[1 Joannes de corpore et sanguine Domini hoc loco nihil dixit, sed
plane alibi multo uberius hinc Dominum locutum esse testatur.—Aug.
de Cons. Evang. Lib. III. cap. 1. Opp. Tom. IV. fol. 100. col. 3. Par.
1531.]

[2 So also ed. 1584: but ed. 1577, flesh and the same, &c.: una
atque eadem caro et idem corpus, &c., Lat.]

in their unbelief; but they [partake[1]] of the Lord's sacraments to their own judgment and condemnation.

The third kind of eating.   I know here what some do teach, and how they devise a certain third kind of eating Christ, which is neither spiritual nor yet sacramental, but altogether compounded of sacramental and corporal. For they hold opinion also, that the true and natural body of Christ is received bodily by the unbelievers in the forms of the sacrament. Howbeit, it shall easily appear by certain sound arguments of the scripture, that this is but a device of man; which arguments we will apply to the traitor Judas, that by this one example all the godly[2] may learn what they eat and drink at the Lord's supper; for that, the judgment which is made of the head being revealed unto us, it shall be easier for us to pronounce of the members.

That Judas was present at the Lord's supper.   Some truly do make a doubt, whether Judas were present at the supper, when the Lord distributed the holy mysteries; among whom is St Hilary[3]. Howbeit, the evangelical history saith plainly, that the Lord sat down to meat with the twelve; yea, Luke so handled his narration, that we cannot doubt but that Judas did communicate of the mysteries with the rest of the apostles; which St Augustine also avoucheth, *Libro de Consensu Evangelistarum tertio, capitulo primo*[4]; and likewise in the 62. treatise upon John[5], and upon the x. Psalm[6], and in his 163. epistle[7]. Yea, moreover, Aquinas also, answering in this point to St Hilary, approveth the same with

What Judas received of the Lord at the supper.   us, *Parte tertia Quæsti. 81. Art. 2.*[8] Now therefore [it] being manifest, that Judas was at supper with the rest of the apostles, it seemeth needful that it were known, what he received of the Lord. He received the sacrament of Christ's body, as the other disciples did; but because he had not faith,

---

[1 All the editions omit this word : participant, Lat.]

[2 An error in all the editions for, "the ungodly:" impii, Lat.]

[3 Post quæ Judas proditor indicatur, sine quo pascha conficitur : dignus enim æternorum sacramentorum communione non fuerat.— Hilar. Comment. in Matth. cap. 30. Opp. col. 740. Par. 1693.]

[4 Aug. Opp. Tom. IV. fol. 100. col. 4. Par. 1531.]

[5 Opp. Tom. IX. fol. 84. col. 1.]

[6 Opp. Tom. VIII. fol. 16. col. 1.]

[7 Opp. Tom. II. fol. 143. col. 3.]

[8 Aquinas, Summa Theol. par. III. quæst. 81. art. 2. p. 186. Col. Agrip. 1622.]

as the other had, he partaked not of Christ, neither did he
eat and drink the Lord's body and blood. For as many as
eat the Lord's body and drink his blood, do not hunger nor
thirst; for they dwell in Christ, and Christ in them; they are
Christ's members; and they never die. The contrary altogether
appeareth in Judas and all his fellows. Wherefore the unbelievers do neither eat the Lord's body nor drink his blood.
Moreover, it is out of all doubt, that there is no agreement 2 Cor. vi.
between Christ and Belial; for this hath the apostle pronounced out of the general consent of the scriptures. But
Judas is by Christ himself called Satan; therefore Judas did
not communicate with Christ. Now if we will contend absolutely, that Judas did eat the Lord's body; truly we shall be
constrained wickedly to affirm, that it is not only an unprofitable, but also an hurtful meat; howbeit, godliness teacheth
us, that Christ is a wholesome meat always to all them that
eat him truly. St Augustine also denieth that Judas did eat
the Lord's body or drink his blood. In the 59th Treatise upon
St John, "The apostles," saith he, "did eat the bread which
was the Lord, but Judas did eat the Lord's bread against the
Lord. They did eat life, but he punishment[9]." Again in the
26th treatise: "Whoso dwelleth not in Christ nor Christ in him,
doubtless he neither eateth his flesh spiritually, nor drinketh
his blood: although carnally and visibly he break in his teeth
the sacrament of the body and blood of Christ; but he rather
eateth and drinketh the sacrament of so great a matter to his
condemnation, &c.[10]" The like also, and almost plainer, doth
he write in the 21st book and 25th chapter, *De Civitate Dei*[11].

Against these they object the authority of Paul, saying,
That they which eat unworthily are not guilty of the bread
and cup which they have eaten and drunken of, but of the
Lord's body and blood; and also, that they do eat and drink
their own damnation, for that they make no difference of the
Lord's body: whereby it followeth necessarily, that they have

[9 Illi manducabant panem Dominum; ille panem Domini contra
Dominum. Illi vitam, ille poenam.—Aug. in Evang. Joan. LIX. Opp.
Tom. IX. fol. 82. col. 4.]

[10 See quotation above, page 460, note 3.]

[11 Non dicendum eum manducare corpus Christi, qui in corpore
Christi non est.—Aug. de Civit. Dei, Lib. XXI. cap. 25. Opp. Tom. V.
fol. 292. col. 4.]

eaten and drunken the Lord's body unworthily, and not only the sacraments of the body and blood of Christ. We answer, that Paul saith thus in plain words: "Whosoever eateth of this bread and drinketh of the Lord's cup, &c." Mark this: he saith, "Whoso eateth this bread and drinketh of this cup unworthily;" he saith not, Whoso eateth the flesh and drinketh the blood unworthily. For they which eat the Lord are not without faith, and Christ dwelleth in them and

How the unbelievers are made guilty of Christ's body and blood. John xiii. Matt. xxv.

they in him. If thou yet marvel, how the unbelievers can be guilty of the Lord's body and blood, being eaten but sacramentally; learn this out of other places of the scripture. The Lord saith in John: "Verily, verily, I say unto you, He that receiveth whomsoever I shall send, receiveth me; and whoso receiveth me, receiveth him that sent me." Wherefore, whoso receiveth not an apostle, trespasseth not against the apostle, but against God himself, although in the meanwhile he hath not seen God, nor will not seem to have repelled him. We read, how the Judge will say to them that are on his left hand: "Depart from me, you wicked, into everlasting fire: for I was hungry; and you gave me no meat: I was thirsty, and you gave me no drink, &c." But hearken now, how the reprobate will make exceptions against this sentence of the Judge. "Lord, when did we see thee hungry or thirsty, and ministered not unto thee?" Then hear again what the Judge will answer: "Verily I say unto you, in that ye did it not to one of the least of these, ye did it not to me." Wherefore, like as he that sinneth against a minister or a beggar, sinneth against Christ himself, although in the meanwhile he hath not hurt Christ's person in any point; so is he also guilty of the body and blood of Christ, whosoever receiveth the sacrament of the body and blood of Christ unworthily, although in the mean season he have not received the very body and blood of the Lord. Paul saith in another place,

Heb. vi.

that revolters do crucify again unto themselves the Son of God. He also denieth in another place by all manner of means, that it is possible for Christ to be crucified or to die any more. Therefore Christ cannot be crucified again by the apostates or revolters; howbeit their shameful falling away from him is so esteemed of, as if they had crucified the Son of God. Although, therefore, the wicked do not eat the Lord's very body nor drink his blood, nevertheless they are guilty of betraying the Lord's body and blood as far as in them lieth. If a rebel tread under his foot the seal or letters of the prince or magistrate, although he touch not the magistrate himself nor tread him under his foot, yet is he said to have trodden the magistrate under his foot; and is accused not for hurting the seal or defiling the letters, but he is charged of treason, and accused for treading the prince under his feet. What marvel, then, if we hear it said, that they which do eat the Lord's bread unworthily, are guilty of the body and blood of Christ? For the bread and the mystical cup are a sacrament and seal of it.

Hitherto have we disputed of the eating of the body of Christ, and of drinking of his blood, handling every one point thereof with as much brevity as we could. Now we go to knit up the other ends of the Lord's supper, being placed in the description of the supper. We said, that the supper was instituted by the Lord, that it might represent visibly the gifts of God unto the church, and lay them forth before the eyes of all men. But we have learned by the whole discourse of this matter, that Christ himself is a most full and rich treasure of all the gifts of God; as namely from whom, being delivered for us unto death, we have all things belonging to life, remission of sins and life everlasting. Since these things be invisible and gotten by faith, they be also visibly, that is to say, by sacraments, represented almost unto all the senses, to the sight, to hearing, to tasting, and to feeling; to the intent, that man, being wholly therewith moved both in body and soul, may celebrate this most comfortable mystery with great rejoicing in heart. Hereunto now appertaineth that analogy, whereof I have spoken before in the seventh sermon of this decade[1], whereby I would have these things to be better learned.

Furthermore, we have said, that the supper was instituted of the Lord, that he might visibly gather together into one body all his members, which were in a manner[2] dispersed throughout all parts of the world. Whereupon we have said, that the holy men somewhere else did call the supper a league or confederacy. We are knit invisibly with Christ and all his members by unity of faith and participation of one Spirit; but in the supper we are joined together even by a visible

Of the other ends of the Lord's supper.

[1 See above, page 328.]   [2 Rather, otherwise: alioqui, Lat.]

conjunction. For now not by words, but by deeds also, but by mystery, but by sacrament, we are very nearly knit and joined together, opening and declaring to all men, by celebrating the supper, that we are also of the number of them that believe that they are redeemed by Christ, and that they are Christ's members and people. But we bind ourselves together unto Christ and the church, both that we will keep the sincere faith, and promising that we will use good deeds and charity towards all men. Look for more touching this matter in the seventh sermon of this decade[1]. Hereupon truly did St Paul prove, that it was not lawful for them which receive together at the Lord's table to eat of meat offered to idols, and to take part of profane sacrifices. Which thing if at this day many would rightly weigh and consider, they would not seem to be seen so busy in strange and foreign sacrifices.

We said also, that the Lord instituted the supper, that thereby he might keep his death in memory, so that it should never be blotted out with oblivion. For Christ's death is the summary of all God's benefits. He would have us therefore to keep in memory the benefit of his incarnation, passion, redemption, and of his love. And although the remembrance of a thing that is past be celebrated, to wit, of his death, yet the same belongeth greatly unto us, and quickeneth us. Neither must we think that this is the least end; for there is none so diligently expressed as this is. For the Lord repeateth this saying : " Do this in remembrance of me." But that holy rite or holy action, being joined with the word or with the preaching of Christ's death and the redemption of mankind, how marvellously doth it renew from time to time that benefit, and suffereth it not to be forgotten !

Last of all we said, that the supper was ordained of the Lord, that thereby we might be admonished of our duty, praise and thanksgiving. It is our duty to be sincere in the faith of Christ, and to embrace all our brethren with christian charity for the Lord's sake, and to beware that we defile not our bodies with the filth of the world, since we be cleansed with the blood of Christ. Paul the apostle saith : " So often as ye shall eat of this bread, and drink of the Lord's cup, declare the Lord's death until he come." But to declare the Lord's death is to praise the goodness of God, and to give

[1 See above, page 333.]

thanks for our redemption obtained through his death; for the apostle Peter saith: "Ye are a chosen generation, a royal 1 Pet. ii. priesthood, an holy nation, a people set at liberty[2], that ye should shew forth virtues of him that hath called you out of darkness into his marvellous light." But hereof we have spoken also in another place[3].

Thus much I thought good in few words to repeat touching the ends of the supper, which every godly man being instructed by the Holy Ghost doth diligently consider. I would now let you go, dearly beloved brethren, but that I see it will be a common commodity to teach in few words, how every one should prepare himself to the Lord's supper, that he come not to it unworthily. But it were not lost labour first Of worthily of all to search out, who do worthily or unworthily eat and thily eating drink of the Lord's bread and cup. There is no man that the Lord's can deny, that there are degrees in our worthiness and unworthiness, if he rightly examine the judgments of God, and, looking narrowly into the nature of our religion, is able to give judgment thereof. The chiefest degree of unworthiness is, to come to the holy mysteries of faith without faith. He cometh worthily, that cometh with faith; unworthily, he that cometh without faith. Such are said to be works worthy of repentance in the gospel, as are penitent works, or seemly for such as profess repentance[4]. But what is more beseeming, more meet and just, than that he who is to celebrate the Lord's supper do believe that he is redeemed by Christ's death, who was offered up as a price for the whole world, and that for that cause is desirous to give thanks to Christ his Redeemer? Contrariwise, what is more unseemly and unjust, than to receive that pledge of Christ's body, and in the meanwhile to have no communion or fellowship with Christ; to come to thanksgiving, and yet not to give thanks from the bottom of his heart? For what uniteth us to Christ, or what maketh us partakers of all his benefits, and therewith also to be thankful, but faith? What doth separate us from Christ, and spoileth us of all his gifts, and maketh us most loathsome, but unbelief? Therefore faith or unbelief maketh us partakers of the Lord's table worthily or unworthily. Paul the apostle, in the

[2 populus acquisitionis, Lat.]   [3 See Vol. iii. p. 288.]

[4 Rather, for such as are penitent, or for the profession of repentance: pœnitentes vel pœnitentiam professam decentia, Lat.]

Acts xiii.

Acts, saith to the Jews, who through unbelief did reject or set at nought the preaching of the gospel: "The word of God ought first to be preached unto you; but because you reject it, and judge yourselves unworthy of everlasting life, behold, we turn unto the Gentiles." How did the Jews pronounce against themselves, that they were unworthy of everlasting life, and like judges gave sentence against themselves? In setting themselves against God's word through unbelief, neither apprehending Christ by faith, who is the life and righteousness of the world. Wherefore the chief and greatest portion of our worthiness and unworthiness is and consisteth in faith or unbe-Acts xv. lief. St Peter witnesseth, that our hearts are purified by faith: true faith therefore is the cleanness of Christians. Whereupon St Augustine saith: "The unbeliever eateth not the flesh of Christ spiritually, but rather eateth and drinketh the sacrament of so great a thing to his own condemnation; because being unclean he hath presumed to come to Christ's sacraments; which no man receiveth worthily but he that is clean: of whom it is said, 'Blessed be the clean in heart; for they shall see God,' &c.[1]"

Moreover, they eat and drink of the Lord's supper unworthily, who, although they be not destitute of faith, yet by their abusing of it do pervert the right institution of the Lord. Such seemeth to have been the error of the church of Corinth, which mingled the private and profane with the ecclesiastical and mystical banquet, and did put no difference between the Lord's bread, which is called Christ's body, and common meat. For Paul saith: "Whoso eateth and drinketh unworthily, he eateth and drinketh his own damnation, making To make difference of the Lord's body. no difference of the Lord's body." Therefore, to make no difference of the Lord's body, is unworthily to eat the Lord's bread and to drink of his cup. For this word διακρίνειν, to judge or to make a difference, is to weigh and consider of a matter exactly with judgment to the uttermost of a man's power, to judge of it, and make a difference[2] between that and all other things. Furthermore, the Lord's body is not only that spiritual body of the Lord, to wit, the church of the faithful, but that very body which the Lord took of the virgin, and offered up for our redemption, and that now sitteth at the

[1 See quotation above, page 460, note 3.]
[2 ita ut decet, Lat. omitted: as is proper.]

right hand of the Father. To be short, the bread of the sacrament in the supper is the Lord's body; it is, I say, the sacrament of the true body which was given for us. Whosoever, therefore, putteth no difference between this, the Lord's mystical bread, and profane meat, but cometh to Christ's table as he would to a table of common and gross meat, and acknowledgeth not that this heavenly meat differeth far from other human meat, neither cometh after that sort as the Lord hath instituted, but followeth his own reason; surely he maketh no difference of the Lord's body, but eateth and drinketh his own damnation. Paul again expoundeth himself, saying : "Therefore, my brethren, when ye come together to eat, tarry one for another, that ye meet not to condemnation." Whoso therefore preventeth[3] the public supper by eating his own private supper, that is to say, whoso suppeth not as the Lord hath appointed, the same eateth and drinketh unworthily. For before, unworthy eaters and drinkers are said to eat and drink their own damnation; and here, they are said to meet together to their condemnation that make haste to the supper, not tarrying for their brethren; and they make no difference of the Lord's body. St Augustine in his 62nd treatise upon John saith : "The apostle speaketh of those which received the Lord's body without difference and carelessly, as if it had been any other kind of meat whatsoever. Here therefore, if he be reproved which maketh no difference of the Lord's body, that is to say, doth not discern the Lord's body from other meats, how then should not Judas be damned, who came to the Lord's table feigning that he was a friend, but was an enemy[4]," &c.? How much more grievously do they seem to sin at this day, who, perverting the lawful and first use that was instituted by the Lord, do stablish their own abuse with great contention, yea, and grievously persecute them that cry out against it and will not receive it !

Furthermore, since by experience we find every day

[3 præoccupat, Lat.]
[4 De his erat sermo, cum hoc apostolus diceret, qui Domini corpus velut alium cibum quemlibet indiscrete negligenterque sumebant. Hic ergo si corripitur, qui non dijudicat, id est, non discernit a ceteris cibis Dominicum corpus, quomodo non damnatur, qui ad ejus mensam fingens amicum accedit inimicus?—Aug. in Evang. Joan. Tract. LXII. Opp. Tom. IX. fol. 83. col. 4. Par. 1531.]

that there are many things wanting unto our faith, by means whereof divers vices spring up among us, whereof our unworthiness is the lightest or least of all[1], which the Lord of his grace may easily wash away, and almost wipeth away by sending his cross upon us, not imputing such infirmities to us to our condemnation. For the apostle in another place saith, that "there is no condemnation for them which are graffed into Christ Jesus, and walk not after the flesh, but after the Spirit."

The punishment of those that eat unworthily. Neither with equal punishment doth our most just Lord punish these sundry sorts of unworthiness. Let us therefore see what the blessed apostle teacheth us concerning the punishment of those that eat unworthily. Therefore he saith: "Whoso eateth this bread, or drinketh of the Lord's cup unworthily, the same shall be guilty of the Lord's body and blood." By which words verily he meaneth that chief and most foul unworthiness of all other, to wit, unbelief. For he is guilty of the Lord's body and blood, to whom the fault of the Lord's death is imputed, that is to say, to whom Christ's death becometh death, and not life: as it also happened unto them, who through unbelief and wickedness did crucify Christ; for unto them Christ's blood seemed profane, as it had been the blood of some beast, murderer, or wicked person, as being worthily shed for his offences. And, I pray you, what else doth he think than that Christ's blood is profane, who believeth not that the same was shed for the sins of the world? And yet he dareth take part of the Lord's supper, that he may worthily be said to be guilty of the Lord's body and blood. It is a very great offence, to eat the Lord's bread and to drink of his cup unworthily, through unbelief: which thing by the example of Judas is laid before our eyes. He believed not in the Lord Jesus, yea, he invented how to deliver him into the hands of thieves and murderers; yet nevertheless he sat down to meat and took part of the Lord's supper: therefore in the end the devil worthily challenged *John xiii.* him wholly unto him. For St John witnesseth, that about

[1 Rather, whence proceeds our unworthiness, yet it is the lightest of all; (—that is, of all kinds of unworthiness) being such as the Lord of his grace easily washes away, &c. The Latin original is obscure; but this is evidently Bullinger's meaning. Haller in his German version understands the sentence in the same manner.]

the end of the supper the devil entered into Judas: not that
he was not in him before that he came to the supper, (for he Luke xxii.
had begun before to dwell in him, and to stir him forward;)
but for that, after so many admonitions of our Lord Christ,
and after that, he had profaned the mysteries of Christ, and
as it were trodden them under foot, he wholly entered into
him, and fully possessed him.

The same apostle Paul threateneth damnation to them
that make no difference of the Lord's body, who are placed,
as it were, in another degree of unworthiness, saying: "For
whoso eateth and drinketh unworthily, eateth and drinketh
his own damnation." The reason hereof he setteth down in
this sentence, to wit, why we ought not rashly and carelessly
to come to the Lord's table, for that we approach then to our
condemnation. But condemnation or judgment is the pain or
punishment which the Lord layeth upon his faithful people
when they sin, not in another world truly, as he doth upon
the unbelievers, but in this world. For it followeth in the
words of the apostle, which ministereth unto us the same
sense: "For this cause many are weak and feeble among
you, and many sleep. For if we had judged ourselves, we
should not have been judged. But when we are judged, we
are corrected by the Lord, that we should not be condemned
with the world." The apostle plainly distinguisheth between
the unworthy eaters that are subject to God's correction, and
worldly men, that is to say, unbelievers, whose punishment
the Lord deferreth to that other world. But upon his faithful people, who yet offend through negligence, and come to
the supper not sufficiently instructed, he layeth divers and
sundry afflictions, as pestilence, famine, sickness, and such like,
to shake off their drowsiness. For it followeth: "If we had
judged ourselves," that is, if we ourselves had restrained
our vices, and separated ourselves from evil, "we had not
been judged," that is to say, punished and corrected. For
immediately he addeth: "But when we are judged, we are
chastised of the Lord." To be judged therefore is to be
chastised. But hereby we learn, from whence there do flow
so many mischiefs into the church, to wit, by the unworthy
use of the Lord's supper.

But some man will answer here, If the matter be so, it How we should pre-
were better wholly to abstain from the Lord's supper. But pare our-

selves to the
Lord's sup-
per.

if any abstain wholly, he also thereby sinneth against the Lord, and that grievously. For he setteth at nought the Lord's commandment, who saith, "Do this;" yea, he setteth at nought both the Lord's death and all the gifts of God. Wherefore he hath not escaped danger, who hath omitted to celebrate the supper : which thing also we have said before. Thou must go another way to work, if thou desire to avoid both danger and sin. Hear the counsel of Paul, very compendiously saying : "Let a man examine himself, and so let him eat of that bread, and drink of that cup." And we must mark, that in this examination he sendeth no man to another, but every man to himself. The papists bid thee, "Go to an auricular confessor," there to confess thyself, to receive absolution, and to make satisfaction for thy sins according to the form that is commanded thee ; and so they bid thee, as sufficiently cleansed, to go to the Lord's table. But Paul, the doctor of the Gentiles and the vessel of election, speaketh not a word of those things, but saith simply : "Let a man examine himself, and so let him eat of that bread, and drink of that cup." For like as God is the searcher of the hearts, and requireth the affection of the mind, and hateth hypocrisy ; so none knoweth what is in the heart of man, or what affections we bear to God-ward, but we ourselves do. Therefore he willeth us ourselves to examine everything in ourselves ; that is to say, he willeth every man to descend into himself, and to examine himself. This examination cannot be made without faith and the light of God's word. But the faithful man, having the light of God's word shining before him, and faith extending[1] her force and power, inquireth of himself, whether he doth acknowledge all his sins which he hath manifoldly committed against God, and whether he be sorry for them being committed ; and whether with sincere faith of heart he believe that Christ hath washed away and forgiven all his sins ; and whether he confess freely with his mouth, as he believeth in his heart, that life and salvation consisteth in Jesus Christ only, and in none other; and whether he have determined with himself to die in this confession ; and whether he mean diligently and earnestly to apply himself to innocency and holiness of life ; and whether he be ready to love and help all the members of Christ's body, of whom he is also a

[1 exerente, Lat.: putting forth.]

member, and be ready to spend his life for them, according to the example of Christ; and whether he have remitted or pardoned all anger and enmity; and whether he be desirous to call to mind Christ's passion and the whole mystery of our redemption, and to give thanks to God for our redemption, and for all other gifts of God already received and to be received. This is the right examining, which agreeth with the receiving of the mystical supper; and when we have done so, we may, in humbleness and fear of the Lord and with gladness[2], approach to the supper of our Lord Christ.

But here the faithful do tremble, who are as it were privy to their own imperfection and infirmity; for they do not find these things to be so perfect in their minds, as otherwise they know a just perfection requireth. Satan cometh, and he casteth in many and great stays, to the intent he may draw us back from the celebration of the supper. Therefore we say, if any man suppose that none is to be admitted to the supper but he that is purged from all sin and infirmity, surely he shall drive away and exclude all men, how many soever live in this world; nay, he shall altogether deprive them of the Lord's supper, as not to be any longer for sinful men but for angels. We must remember, that this examination resteth within his own bounds, and that God here also, as everywhere else, doth use this[3] clemency and mercy towards us. He knoweth our weakness and corruption, and with us can bear our infirmities. The Israelites under king Ezechias, being not fully cleansed, took part of the paschal lamb; but the king prayed, and said: "The Lord, who is good, will have mercy upon all men that with all their heart seek after the God of the fathers, and will not impute it unto them that they are not sanctified." And hereunto is added in the holy history, in 2 Chron. xxx. chap.: "And the Lord heard Ezechias, and he was pleased with the people." The worthiness, which is inquired for by exact examination, is no absolute perfection, but a will and mind instructed by God, which humbly acknowledgeth its own unworthiness, and therefore humbly prayeth for increase of faith and charity, and[4] all perfection in Christ only. At that first supper the apostles were Christ's guests,

A comfort for afflicted consciences.

[2 Rather, although in humbleness, &c. yet with gladness.]
[3 An error in all the editions for *his:* sua, Lat.]
[4 requirit, Lat. omitted: seeks.]

and among these was Judas; but because he lacked faith and was a traitor, yea, a murderer, he was made guilty of the body and blood of the Lord. The other apostles were also sinners themselves, but not wicked; they believed in Christ; they loved Christ, and one of them loved another like brethren: therefore they did not eat of the Lord's supper unworthily, as Judas did; although in the meantime at the same table they shewed tokens of great imperfection. For Peter, not without great contempt and reproach of his brethren, preferreth himself before them all. Moreover, they contend among themselves for honour, which of them should seem to be greater than another. I will not now recite, that, straightway after they arose from the table, they shamefully forsook their master and ran away, and many ways behaved themselves unworthily: but all these things were easily washed away, for that faith had taken very deep root within them.

Matt. xxvi.
Luke xxii.

Neither will I here stick to recite word for word the comfort of Master John Calvin, a godly and learned man, who with great commendation teacheth in the church at this day, my fellow-minister and most well-beloved and dear brother, which he hath set down for the afflicted in this case. "Let us call to remembrance," saith he, "that this holy banquet is a medicine for the sick, a comfort for the sinful, a largess to the poor; which to the whole, righteous, and rich, if there could any such be found, would bring small vantage. For seeing that in this banquet Christ is given unto us to be eaten, we understand that without him we faint, fail, and are forsaken. Moreover, seeing he is given to us to be our life, we understand that without him we are but dead. Wherefore this is the greatest and only worthiness which we can give unto God, if we lay before him our own vileness and unworthiness, that through his mercy he may make us worthy of himself; if we despair in ourselves, that we may be comforted in him; if we humble ourselves, that we may be lifted up by him; if we accuse ourselves, that we may be justified by him. Moreover, if we attain unto that unity which he commendeth unto us in the supper; and, like as he maketh us all to dwell in him, so that we may wish likewise that there were one soul, one heart, and one tongue in us all; if we well weigh and meditate these things, then shall these thoughts never trouble us: We that are naked and destitute of all goodness, we that are stained with spots of sin, we that are half dead, how should we worthily eat the Lord's body? Let us rather think, that we being poor do come to a plentiful giver, we that are sick come to a physician, we that are sinful come to a Saviour; that the worthiness, which is commanded by God, consisteth in faith chiefly, which reposeth all in God and nothing in ourselves: secondly, in charity; and such charity, as it is sufficient if we offer it unto God unperfect, that he may increase it to the better, seeing we cannot perform it absolute as it ought to be[1]." Thus far he.

Thus much have I said hitherto of the most holy supper of our Lord Jesus Christ, the most excellent and wholesome sacrament of Christians; for which even from the very beginning, and while the apostles were yet living, Satan, the most deadly enemy to our salvation, lying in wait, hath gone about to overthrow by many corruptions and defilings; from which being now for a time faithfully cleansed, yet doth he not so leave it, but intermingles and throws an heap of contentions into it, being made unto the church the token of a covenant

[1 Meminerimus has sacras epulas ægrotis esse pharmacum, peccatoribus solatium, pauperibus largitionem: quæ sanis, justis, et divitibus, si qui reperiri possent, nullum afferrent operæ pretium. Nam cum in illis Christus nobis in cibum detur, intelligimus nos sine ipso tabescere, liqui, deficere. Deinde cum in vitam detur, intelligimus nos sine ipso in nobis plane mortuos esse. Quare ea est dignitas, quam unam et optimam afferre Deo possumus, si nostram ei vilitatem et (ut ita loquar) indignitatem offeramus, ut sua misericordia nos se dignos faciat; si animos in nobis despondeamus, ut nos in ipso consolemur; si nos humiliemus, ut ab ipso erigamur; si nos accusemus, ut ab ipso justificemur. Præterea, si ad eam, quam in sua cœna nobis commendat, unitatem adspiremus; et quemadmodum nos omnes unum in seipso esse facit, ita unam omnium animam, cor unum, linguam unam nobis omnibus optemus; hæc si perpensa et meditata habuerimus, nunquam nos illæ cogitationes perturbabunt: Nos bonorum omnium egeni et nudi, nos peccatorum sordibus inquinati, nos semimortui, quomodo corpus Domini digne manducaremus? Magis cogitabimus, nos pauperes venire ad benignum largitorem; ægros, ad medicum; peccatores, ad salvatorem: dignitatem illam, quæ a Deo mandatur, fide præcipue constare; quæ omnia in Deo, nihil in nobis reponit; deinde caritate, et ea quidem ipsa, quam Deo imperfectam offerre satis est, ut ipsam in melius augeat, quando præstari solida non potest.—Calvin. Instit. Christ. Rel. cap. XI. p. 341. Argent. 1539. *Second Edition.*]

never to be broken[1]. Whereupon the thing itself and our salvation requireth, that we be circumspect, and give no place to the tempter; but agreeing altogether in Christ, and being joined into one body by faithful celebrating of the supper, we may love one another, and give everlasting thanks to our Redeemer and Lord Christ; to whom be praise and glory now and for ever. Amen. Amen.

¶ OF CERTAIN INSTITUTIONS OF THE CHURCH OF GOD. OF SCHOOLS. OF ECCLESIASTICAL GOODS, AND THE USE AND ABUSE OF THE SAME. OF CHURCHES AND HOLY INSTRUMENTS OF CHRISTIANS. OF THE ADMONITION AND CORRECTION OF THE MINISTERS OF THE CHURCH, AND OF THE WHOLE CHURCH. OF MATRIMONY. OF WIDOWS. OF VIRGINS. OF MONKS. WHAT THE CHURCH OF CHRIST DETERMINETH CONCERNING THE SICK; AND OF FUNERALS AND BURIALS.

THE TENTH SERMON.

THERE remain certain things, but a few truly, which are to be expounded unto you, dearly beloved; the which partly appertain to the institution of the ecclesiastical ministry and preservation thereof; there are partly certain peculiar ordinances of the church, which the church cannot want. Whereof in this last sermon of this Decade, so far as the Lord shall give me grace to speak, I intend as briefly as I can to entreat.

The Lord hath not burdened his church with infinite laws. First of all, we must know that the Lord our God hath not burdened his church with over many laws and institutions; but hath set down a few easily to be numbered, and those not costly, nor intricate, nor long, but profitable, simple, plain, and short. In time past, when as under the law the Lord appointed unto the people a costly and sumptuous worshipping of him, notwithstanding all things therein were certain, numerable, and moderate; neither would he have anything added to, or taken from it, at the pleasure of men, or to be otherwise used than he had appointed. Who then will

[1 Rather, he ceases not to cast it in the way and to bring it in, as a kind of ball of contentions, though it is to the church a token of a covenant never to be broken.]

think, that, after the abrogating of the law, the Lord would deliver unto the church of his new people a sumptuous and an infinite discipline? Wherefore it is partly the covetousness of the pastors and estates of the church, and partly the monstrous superstition of the common people, that hath made everything so sumptuous and infinite in the church. Let us stick unto this, that the Lord our God hath instituted in his church but very few things, and such as are necessary; and therefore we ought all to endeavour, that the church be not over-burdened with traditions and institutions which proceeded not from God himself. The church of God is gorgeously enough decked and furnished, if she retain and keep the institutions of her God and Lord.

The chief and principal points of the godliness of the church of God are, the sincere teaching of the law and the prophets, of Christ and the apostles; faithful prayer offered unto her only God through Christ alone; a religious and lawful administration and receiving of Christ's sacraments; whereof we have entreated hitherto through five decades. Hereunto belongeth charity also, which is a communicating of riches, or well-doing; whereof we have said somewhat already in the first decade[2], and will say somewhat else in this sermon. Neither doth Luke in the Acts make mention of any other things, describing what manner of church the faithful primitive church of Christ was, being founded by the apostles, and what were the principal points thereof. "They were continuing," saith he, "in the doctrine of the apostles, and in communicating, and in breaking of bread, and in prayer." Under these few points all godliness is comprised. *The chiefest points of true godliness in the church.* *Acts ii.*

Unto the ecclesiastical ministry are joined these that follow. Christian schools have the first place, which bring forth a plentiful increase of prophets or ministers of the church. All nations, unless they were altogether barbarous, have understood, that without schools no kingdoms or commonweals can happily be maintained. And therefore not only Moses in the book of Genesis[3], but also Strabo in the xvii. book of his Geography, reporteth how that among the Egyptians were instituted most famous colleges for priests and philosophers. *Of schools.*

[2 Sermon 10.]
[3 Bullinger seems to refer to Gen. xlvii. 22. See his treatise De Episcop. Instit. et Funct. cap. iii. fol. 74. Tigur. 1538.]

Histories also make mention, that the most noble men of all the world travelled into Egypt to obtain wisdom; in which number Plato also is said to be the first of the chief and principal among the philosophers[1]. Neither is it unadvisedly written in the book of the Kings, that Salomon excelled the wise men of the Egyptians in wisdom. And not only the Egyptians, but also the Palestines, a nation more famous for wars than for learning, are said to have had their priests, of whom they asked counsel in matters of doubt, as writeth [1 Sam. vi. 2.] Samuel in his holy history. And Daniel also witnesseth, that the Babylonians had most famous schools; as also had the Medes and Persians, from whence sprang forth their Magi, I would say, wise men, notable in all parts of philosophy. I need not to speak anything of the Greeks and Romans; since there is no man but knoweth their most famous city of Athens, which is so much spoken of by all learned men, and also the goodly colleges of their priests and soothsayers. But, omitting foreign examples, let us allege our own, or such as are ecclesiastical.

God, who gave unto his people a most absolute form of an happy commonweal and kingdom, distributed schools through forty and eight towns of the realm. Those towns, by reason of the philosophing Levites, were called Levitical. For he had consecrated all the Levitical tribe unto the priesthood and to studies; not for that it was not also lawful for gentlemen of other tribes to study philosophy or wisdom; but because the Levites were peculiarly appointed unto holy studies[2]: for it is evident that Esay and Daniel, two of the most bright lights of them that prophesied, were of the tribe of Juda. Other tribes also have brought forth men right singular in all kind of knowledge. And those towns likewise were called Levitical and priestly, not that priests only dwelt in them, but because they had synagogues in them. But at the tabernacle in Silo, and specially in the city of Jerusalem, there was a school surpassing all other, and in manner of Governors of an university, as they call them now-a-days. And the same schools. holy history witnesseth, that most famous men had the govern-1 Sam. x. 2 Kings ii. and iv. cap. ment of those schools. For we read in Rama that Samuel,

[1 philosophorum Alpha, Lat.—Erasm. Adag. Chili. Dignitatis. p. 188. Hanov. 1617.]

[2 See Vol. I. pp. 334, &c. and Vol. II. pp. 133, 143.]

who was the very chiefest in all wisdom, godliness, and learning, was governor and principal of Naioth, that is to say, the burse[3] (as they term it) or college of prophets. Helias and Heliseus, the most clear lights of the church of Israel, were rulers over the school of Hierico and Gilgal. That naughty Jeroboam did pull down the schools, and trod under foot the order of the priests, and placed without all choice some that were of the refuse of the people in their places. But the men of God, Helias and Heliseus, knew well, that without schools the sound doctrine could not flourish or be preserved; and therefore they applied themselves wholly to the renewing of schools. And when lawful tributes were denied them, being by wicked princes bestowed upon flatterers and bellies, that is to say, priests of the idols of calves and of Baal; yet it came to pass by the goodness of the Lord, that some good men bestowed somewhat upon such as were desirous of learning, who, holding themselves contented with a mean living, behaved themselves valiantly in that most corrupt age. But those notable men, those wise men and prophets, who had the government over schools, were called fathers; whereupon also their disciples and scholars were termed the sons of the prophets. Amos and Jeremy call them Nazarites[4]. For saith Amos : " I am no prophet, neither the son of a prophet;" to Amos vii. wit, not brought up in the knowledge of liberal arts. And the same man saith again: " I have raised up of your sons Amos ii. for prophets, and of your young men for Nazarites." But Jeremy commendeth also the manner of them that studied, which in his Lamentations he bewaileth to be altogether [Lam. iv. 8.] perished in the captivity. Furthermore, they are called the sons of the prophets, for the affection which they bare towards their schoolmasters, as if they had been their parents, and for their obedience and daily study towards them. But how much the more noble and wise the princes were, so much the more diligence they employed in repairing schools, and restoring ecclesiastical order[5] : which a man may see, not in David and Salomon only, but also in Josaphat and Ezechias and Josias, who were most virtuous and most happy princes. In the captivity and after the captivity of Babylon the Lord's people was dispersed and scattered into many kingdoms far

[3 bursæ, Lat.]   [4 See Vol. II. p. 207.]
[5 So also ed. 1584: but ed. 1577, orders: ordinibus, Lat.]

and wide; but whithersoever they were carried, they erected
schools or synagogues; and when the city of Jerusalem was
restored, then they often came unto the same. For therefore
the Acts of the Apostles make mention, that at what time St

Acts xv. Paul preached the word of God among the Gentiles, he went
into the synagogues and taught. And St James the apostle
saith : "Moses of old time hath in every city them that
preach him in the synagogues;" where he speaketh not of
the cities of Judea and Galilee, but of the cities of the Gentiles, in Syria, Cilicia, and Asia. But that which we read in the
Acts doth shew, that they, being dispersed and scattered abroad,

Acts ii. did sometime come unto the holy city of Jerusalem. "There
were dwelling at Jerusalem certain Jews, religious men, of all
nations that are under heaven." And that also, which St
Paul reciteth of himself, confirmeth the same; that, being born

Acts xxii. free in the city of Tharsus, he travelled to Jerusalem unto
Gamaliel's feet, that is to say, to the intent to hear the instruction and to be a scholar under Gamaliel. So likewise we

Acts vi. read, that at Jerusalem there were colleges or synagogues of
the Libertines, Cyrenians, Alexandrines, Cilicians, and Asians.
This use of schools continued until Christ's time, yea, and
after his ascension into the heavens, almost until the destruction
of the city; although in the meantime it may appear to have
been sundry times depraved.

*Christ and
his apostles
do institute
schools.* Christ also, the Son of God, our king and high bishop, he
himself instituted the most famous school of all other, calling thereunto the twelve apostles and the seventy disciples;
chosen men, I say, to the number of fourscore and two. Yea,
the apostles themselves drew unto them very many disciples;
and first of all[1] St Paul, the most chosen instrument of God to
convert the Gentiles, is read to have had in his company
Sopater of Berrhœ, Luke of Antioch, Mark of Jerusalem,
Barnabas, Sylva or Sylvanus, Caius and Timothy, Aristarchus
and Secundus, Tychicus and Trophimus, Titus and Linus,
Crescens and Epaphras, Archippus and Philemon, Epaphro-
ditus and Artemas, and many other. He hath also commended most diligently unto good men the studious and the
ministers of the churches, exhorting all men unto liberality,

Titus iii. that they may want nothing. And writing unto Titus : "Bring
diligently," saith he, "Zenas the lawyer and Apollo upon

[1 imprimis, Lat.: more especially.]

their way, that they may want nothing." Moreover, it may
be gathered by plain and manifest proofs out of the thirteenth
chapter of the Acts, that there was a very famous, and that
an apostolic, school at Antioch in Syria. Eusebius also of
Cesarea abundantly witnesseth, what noble schools were at
Alexandria in Egypt, and in other renowned churches[2]; and
we have also declared the same more at large, when time
served, in a book which we have written of the institution of
bishops[3]. But in process of time, when all things appertaining
to the church began to decline to the worse, ecclesiastical
schools also degenerated into abbeys or into colleges of canons
and monks.

But of all these things, whereof we have spoken, I think
it not unknown unto any man, that schools do principally belong to the preservation of the church, and the maintenance of
the holy ministry; in which schools good arts might be exercised, very profitable for the furtherance of the study of the
holy scriptures: of which sort chiefest of all are the studies
and knowledge of holy tongues, of logic, natural philosophy,
and the mathematics; and these moderately known, and directed unto the certain scope and end of godliness. For a
man may sometime find wits worn and waxed old in divers
arts and disciplines, howbeit not once meddling or inured with
holy exercises and studies. But I would to God that the
wicked, being too much glutted with profane study, would also
leave to contemn holy scriptures as things plain barbarous.
A man also may find some wits so busied in the study of the
mathematics, that they are more meet to be masters of buildings, than governors or pastors of churches. Yea, they are
so far crept into the study of astronomy and the astronomer's
heaven, that they quite forget the blessed[4] heaven, which is
the seat of the blessed saints, anything to pertain unto them;
and that they should be[5] sufficiently happy, if they can but once
attain unto the knowledge of the motion of the visible heaven,
and to the course of the stars. As for those that meddle
overmuch with the study of philosophy, and the trifles of logic,

*Schools ap-
pertain to
the preserva-
tion of the
ministry.*

[2 Euseb. Hist. Eccles. Lib. v. cap. 10; and Lib. vi. cap. 30; and
Lib. vii. cap. 32.]
[3 De Episcop. Instit. &c. cap. viii. p. 102. Tigur. 1538.]
[4 verum cœlum, Lat.: the true heaven.]
[5 So also ed. 1584: but ed. 1577, shall be.]

31—2

and the rules of rhetoric, [and that] never attain unto any end, nor earnestly think upon the bestowing of their travails to the edifying of the church; commonly they become contentious and brawling disputers for the most part, and arrogant controllers: unto whom nothing seemeth to be neatly and aptly enough either spoken or done of others, but that which is tempered, and as it were tuned, to their great conceiving heads, and so agreeing with prescript rules, that they swerve not therefrom, no, not so much as a hair's breadth. These men snarl[1] and entangle all things with their doltish disputations, puffing out nothing else but quarrelling controversies, taking upon them most arrogantly to judge all men's doings and sayings whatsoever; yea, though they be good and tolerable, they snap at them, and maliciously cavil against them, being rather vain babblers than philosophers, yea, the very plagues of schools and churches; who spit out the poison of debates, contentions, variances, strifes, and divisions, at and into the church. Against these St Paul the apostle to Timothy seemeth to speak: for, after he had briefly set down the sum of sound doctrine, he addeth thereupon: "This teach and exhort. Whosoever teacheth otherwise, and holdeth not himself contented with the healthful word of our Lord Jesus Christ, and the doctrine which is according unto godliness, he is puffed up, knowing nothing, but spending his time about questions and contention in words; whereof groweth hatred, strife, slander, evil suspicions, vain conflicts of men corrupt in heart and destitute of the truth, which suppose gain to be godliness. Avoid the company of such."

1 Tim. vi.

Truly, it never went well with the church, when learned and studious men, forsaking the plainness and pureness of the word of God, turned their eyes another way, and aimed not at the word of God alone. They in ancient time[2] did not contemn the word of God: but in the meanwhile they attributed more to traditions than was convenient. But by that means they both gave occasion unto errors, and confirmed such abuses as were already brought in. Certain years past and gone, Gratian and Lombard[3], with other ecclesiastical

The corruption of schools.

[1 snarl, embarrass, twist.—Johnson.]
[2 Rather, Of the ancients some: ex veteribus quidam, Lat.]
[3 Gratian completed his *Decretum* A. D. 1151. Peter Lombard, author of *The Sentences*, died A. D. 1164.]

writers, went about to make an agreement of opinions, and to gather together a perfect and certain sum of divinity. But thereby they did not only carry the schools away from the scriptures, but also intruded strange doctrines into the church. After these there followed Alexander, Albertus, and Thomas[4], who not only depended upon those Sentences and commended them unto others, but also endeavoured to mingle philosophy with divinity, and to couch[5] them together into one body. And hereof it came to pass, that we had so many ways and sects, so many puddles crawling full of frogs, so many schools, so many abbeys, so many sophisters. And if at this day likewise we continue unhappily to couple philosophy with the holy scriptures, and superstitiously call them into disputation, and to call them unto examination by human rules, or to the handling by arts; then shall we also corrupt them in the schools, perverting the integrity[6] of the apostolic doctrine, to the great detriment of the church. In the meanwhile, certain it is, that good arts and learning do make much unto perspicuity and plainness, but moderately and religiously applied with judgment, so that the scriptures may have the upper hand, and all other arts obey the same.

Wherefore let pure godliness be taught in ecclesiastical schools, yea, let godliness be the end of all our studies. At the first let the studious be diligently taught the catechism, and let them never rest until such time as they have learned it perfectly, and made it familiar unto themselves: then let this young-begun godliness be daily increased with lectures and holy sermons: let the writings of the holy evangelists and apostles be always read unto them, that they may become perfect in them in due season: let them also commodiously learn the tongues and good arts, and let them be exercised in writing and reasoning. But above all, let dissoluteness and wantonness be banished out of the godly-instituted and christian schools. Let discipline, yea, though it be somewhat sharp, flourish. For if youth be corrupted in the schools

The true end of schools.

Discipline in schools.

[4 Alexander Hales, called *The Irrefragable Doctor*, died A.D. 1245. Albertus Magnus, died A. D. 1280. Thomas Aquinas, called *The Angelic Doctor*, died A.D. 1274.]

[5 to couch, to include, to lay close to another. Johnson: redigere, Lat.]

[6 Rather, we also shall corrupt in schools the integrity, &c.]

and grow up in that corruption, what, I pray you, shall we look for at their hands, when they be set in authority over the church? Let us not believe that they will be the salt of the church, who as they are most dissolute and blockish, so can they not abide sharpness in other. Shall we think that they will become lights of the church, who do themselves hate the light, and are delighted in darkness and in the works of darkness? Wherefore, that which the sons of Heli were in the church of Israel, the same shall be and are the corrupt sons of the prophets in the church of Christ. They therefore shall likewise perish with the people which are committed unto them. And therefore now-a-days there is great offence committed through too much lenity in the schools; a mischief which will never be washed away. For a man shall come into many schools, where he shall think he seeth so many soldiers and ruffians, no[1] scholars and students, whom they commonly call clerks. Neither their fare, neither their apparel, neither their manners, neither their words, neither their deeds, declare them to be of any good disposition, honest, or studious. I know, that much is to be ascribed unto our unhappy and most dissolute age, in which the stubborn and rebellious will not hearken to the counsel of the elders; and again I know, that there are great offences committed through the negligence and fond gentleness of them that are in authority. But forasmuch as the welfare of the church consisteth of schools well ordered, we ought all of us to use great diligence, that in this behalf there may no offence be committed through our carelessness and negligence. This much have I said concerning ecclesiastical schools, in as few words as might[2] conveniently: of which I have entreated more at large in my book of the institution of bishops[3].

Of ecclesi-
astical goods.
Furthermore, to the end that schools with the whole ministry may be maintained, together with all holy buildings and ecclesiastical charges, there needeth to be some good wealth and ability correspondent. This place therefore admonisheth us to say somewhat concerning ecclesiastical goods[4]. God, in that commonwealth which he would have to excel all

---

[1 So also ed. 1584: but ed. 1577, not.]
[2 So also ed. 1584: but ed. 1577, as I might.]
[3 De Episcop. Instit. &c. capp. IV., VIII., and XVIII.]
[4 See Zurich Letters. Second Series, Let. XCVIII. p. 242.]

other as best furnished with all things necessary, appointed standing fees to be paid unto the holy ministry of the common charge, to wit, the tithes, the first-fruits, and sundry other kinds of offerings[5]. These things are in the law expressed by Moses, the man of God, in many words: who nothing feared lest for handling of that matter he should be accused of greedy desire or covetousness; for those things which God commanded him to declare plainly to the people, he uttered unto them faithfully. Yea, the law of nature commandeth to reward him that taketh pain, and to maintain common charges by common contribution. And those revenues or tributes, that were publicly gathered, were not bestowed but to public uses; for they were partly given to the ministers for their ministry and service, partly they were disbursed upon public buildings and holy charges, and part was employed to the relief of the poor. And although by the new Testament the Levitical law with the whole priesthood be abrogated; notwithstanding it is certain, that the same universal law, which commandeth that public charges should be levied by public contributions, is not abolished. For we read that our Lord Jesus Christ, although he lived not of the tenths and revenues of the priests, yet lived he of the contributions of the godly, (for he executed a public function;) and, sending his disciples abroad to preach, expressly saith unto them: "I would not have you to be careful for food and apparel; for the labourer is worthy of his hire." Wherefore the primitive church, which the apostles have gathered to Christ, bestowed their houses, lands, and money, for the preservation of the ministry and other things necessary for the church. The priests and Levites at that time possessed the holy revenues, not giving one iota to the apostolic church, which rather they wished might starve for hunger; but the godly and faithful people knew very well, that earthly substance and riches were very necessary for the preservation of the church. For God hath appointed men, and not angels, to be ministers of the church; and hath recommended poor men unto the church to stand in his stead. But they, as men are wont to do, lack and are destitute of many things: wherefore good men, through the motion of the Holy Ghost, do contribute together and bestow money, houses, lands, and other goods, whereby both the

The church of the new Testament hath goods and revenues.

Luke viii.

Matt. x.

Acts iv.

[5 See Vol. II. page 143.]

poor, and also the holy ministry, may be maintained. And hereupon also it is evident, that the church of the people of the new Testament had, ever since the time of Christ and the apostles, goods and possessions publicly gathered and received; and also laid out and bestowed them again for public and common commodity.

How in old time the church-goods were bestowed.

Gregory, the first of that name, bishop of Rome, saith, that it was the custom in his time, and also before his time, that there ought to be four portions or parts of the church of God[1]; one for the bishop and his family, another for the clergy, the third for the poor, and the fourth for the repairing of churches[2]. But there are a great many that say, that a bishop ought not to receive wages of the church. Let us therefore examine what Christ and his apostles do teach us touching that matter. Christ our Lord, who never committed any unjust thing, received, as it is read, maintenance from such women as he taught, who "ministered unto him of their substance." He also sending his disciples abroad, and willing them not to be careful for meat and drink and raiment, saith

Ministers of churches ought to be rewarded.

further: "The labourer is worthy of his hire." The Lord judgeth it to be worthy, meet, and right, to minister necessaries unto preachers. Wherefore they do no unworthy deed, which receive wages, thereby to provide necessaries for themselves and their family; yea, he compareth preachers not to idle bellies, not to them that eat freely of other men's bread, neither to beggars, but to labourers. For as the Lord setteth down in the law, how that it is a great offence to deny labourers their hire; even so their offence is not small, that suffer

Matt. x.

such as are faithful feeders of the flock to perish and decay through need. For in another place the Lord speaketh to his disciples, saying, "Ye have freely received it, and therefore give it freely:" but he speaketh of the gift of working miracles, and of the benefit of health to be bestowed upon the sick, diseased, and oppressed; for thus it is written: "Heal the

[1 ex bonis ecclesiasticis, Lat.]

[2 Mos autem sedis apostolicæ est ordinatis episcopis præcepta tradere, ut in omni stipendio, quod accedit, quatuor debeant fieri portiones: una, videlicet, episcopo et familiæ propter hospitalitatem atque susceptionem, alia clero, tertia pauperibus, quarta ecclesiis reparandis.—Gregor. Epist. ap. Bed. Hist. Eccles. Vol. ii. p. 108. ed. Giles. Lond. 1843.]

sick, cleanse the leprous, raise the dead, cast out devils." And to these words he added this saying: "Ye have received it freely, and therefore bestow it freely." Therefore though the apostles received reward of them to whom they preached, yet never any man read that ever they took anything for the gift of healing, which they received in the Lord's name. Like as Heliseus would not take anything at all, though it were freely offered him by Naaman the Syrian captain, for that by his counsel he was healed of the leprosy; yet the self-same Heliseus refused not the gift of the man that came unto him [2 Kings iv. 42.] from Baal-salisa. Out of the self-same gospel of Christ our Lord ministers have to learn, to what use they ought to put the wages they have of the church. For what time the Lord commanded Judas, who carried the purse, to depart, John x iii. the residue of the disciples thought, that he had been commanded to go and buy such necessaries as should serve for the holy day, or else to bestow something on the poor. Therefore it is plain, that the Lord used with the stipend which he received to provide necessaries for him and his, and also to give alms thereof. Mark well then, that the ministers of the church may provide things necessary for their living, function, and maintenance of their household, of the wages they receive of the church. Again, they may also of the same wages give alms unto the poor, even as it were of their own goods truly gotten. For the Lord saith plainly in the law, that the sacrifice of the Levites, made of tithes and other oblations or holy revenues, shall be as acceptable unto him, as their sacrifice that offer anything out of their own chest, store, or possessions. Truly, if a labourer do offer unto God anything of his hire or wages, that is to say, if he give unto the poor, doth it not seem a very acceptable sacrifice unto God? Very acceptable then is the alms that the minister of the church doth bestow, proceeding of the wages of the holy ministry. Put the case, a labourer in building a church receiveth his wages of the church-goods; should a man therefore say, that the labourer took an alms, and that one alms ought not to be given out of another? He received wages for his work; for he did labour; therefore he giveth alms of his wages, and of his own lawful and proper goods. Wherefore then should the minister of the church seem to live by alms, and that he ought not to give alms of alms, who notwithstanding doth labour for his wages, and therefore receiveth the reward of his work as a labourer doth, unto whom the Lord himself compareth the minister? [1] If any man be so far past honesty to think so, he shall hear not what I say, but what Paul the apostle saith: "If we sow unto you spiritual things, is it a great matter if we mow your carnal things?" And again: "Such elders as govern well are worthy of double honour, and chiefly that travail in preaching and teaching. For the scripture saith, Thou shalt not muzzle the mouth of the ox treading out the corn. And, The labourer is worthy of his hire." Behold, therefore, the apostle doth not think that that inestimable goodness of the ministry can by any means be recompensed with a vile thing, I mean, with earthly wages. Again, "They that labour," saith he: they that labour, say I, not they, saith he, that loiter in teaching. These doth he compare unto an ox, that is a toiling beast, and a thrasher out of corn[2]; and also to a labouring man. That whereof I do so greatly warn you is, that because in this our wicked and unthankful world certain men, nay, rather monsters most unthankful, are to be found out, that are persuaded that ministers do nothing at all, yea, even such as most faithfully do their duty; for they cry out, saying, They eat their bread as beggars do, and it costeth them nought[3]. By which name and infamy they terrify many fine wits, and make them to forsake the study of good learning and divinity, so that they utterly abhor the ministry, as it were a thing most beggarly and unhonest; for in such sort the devil can devise to enlarge his kingdom, abusing, or rather fitly using to his purpose, our ingratitude and malice. But why do they not suffer themselves to be numbered with Christ and the holy apostles, who were fed and maintained by the church's stipend, than to be reckoned up among those unthankful and proud people, who have scraped and gathered all their goods together for the most part by usury and other wicked means? or at the least, if

1 Cor. ix.
1 Tim. v.

[1 An vero dicet aliquis, ministrum ecclesiæ, suo fungentem munere fideliter, nihil laborare? Lat. omitted: But will any man say, that the minister of the church, when he does his duty faithfully, labours not at all?]

[2 et trituranti quidem, Lat.: and that when he is treading out the corn.]

[3 Bulling. adv. Anabapt. Lib. iii. cap. 9.]

they have not gotten their goods by sinister means, they have received them through the liberality and mere goodness of God, for the which they never sweat or took pains?

St Paul proveth by strong and many arguments the right to receive a stipend for the holy ministry. " Have we not," 1 Cor. ix. saith he, " power and authority to eat and drink, or may we not carry about with us a woman sister?" For he meaneth the lawfulness and authority to receive anything necessary for himself, his wife, and his whole household. And for that he asketh a question, he sheweth what he meaneth [4], that thereby he may declare a plain truth and equity amongst all men; and thereto addeth examples, not of every man severally, but of all generally, and specially of the chiefest apostles of Christ, and of them that were kin unto Christ by blood, saying: " Even as the other apostles, and brothers of our Lord, and Cephas?" And who is that Cephas but Peter? To this Cephas the Lord said in the first chapter of St John: " Thou shalt be called Cephas; which, if a man interpret it, signifieth a stone." But Peter also was so sirnamed of a rock, to the intent the interpretation of the name may always fall upon the same [5]. And who, I pray you, are the Lord's brethren, but John and James, and James the brother of Judas, and Judas and Simon, the brethren of James? All these, saith St Paul, lived of the stipend [6] they had, being gathered of the common assembly of the church. Unto these examples he addeth other also like unto them, commonly put in practice. " Who," saith he, " doth go to war at his own costs and charges? Or who planteth a vineyard, and eateth not of the fruit thereof? Or who feedeth a flock, and eateth not of the milk thereof?" Surely he bringeth forth these similitudes very finely, and properly applied unto them and not unto any other [7]. For the ministers of the church are sometimes called soldiers or vineyard-keepers, sometimes husbandmen and shepherds. And who, I pray you, is so far from reason, that he would deny unto soldiers, husbandmen, and shepherds, meat and clothing, for the pains they take in warfare, husbandry, and about cat-

The apostles received wages.

Mark vi.

[4 Rather, And he speaketh what he meaneth by a question.]
[5 ut in idem semper recidat etymon nominis, Lat.]
[6 So also ed. 1584: but ed. 1577, a stipend.]
[7 Rather, Surely he bringeth forth these similitudes very finely, and most properly (brings forth) these, and not others.]

tle ?   The true-hearted men therefore, and such as are of an indifferent judgment, do acknowledge, that the ministers of the church may live by the ecclesiastical ministry.   But lest that any should object, that these human parables and similitudes, taken from the common use, do prove nothing in an ecclesiastical cause, he addeth presently : " Do I speak these things according to man ?   Doth not the law say also the same ? For it is written in the law of Moses, Thou shalt not muzzle the ox that treadeth out the corn." As though he should say : I have in a readiness, for the confirmation of our right, not only human similitudes, but also testimonies of the holy scripture. And he allegeth a place out of the xxv. chapter of Deuteronomy, concerning the nourishing of labouring oxen.   Again, lest any man should say that place is not to be understood of preachers, but simply of oxen, he addeth : " Doth God take care for oxen ?   Or doth not he speak it altogether for our sakes ?   Doubtless he hath written it for our sakes, that he which plougheth may plough in hope, and he that thresheth in hope may be partaker of his hope." The Lord, said he, in his law would provide for us. For he would have the equality gathered by a certain syllogism or kind of argument, after this or such like manner : If the Lord provided for beasts and cattle, and would have consideration to be had of them, how much more of men !   It were truly a very unjust thing, that an husbandman should labour with his ox without hope, that is to say, in vain, and without commodity.   Therefore were it also a most unjust thing for the minister to exercise ecclesiastical husbandry in the church without hope or due stipend.   Moreover, where it is again objected here against, that unto the spiritual ministry belongeth no corporal but a spiritual reward, the apostle answereth : " If we sow unto you spiritual things, is it a great matter if we reap your temporal things ?"   He therefore thinketh, that the Corinthians give nothing when they give their temporal things, namely if they be compared with eternal good things, which the ministers do bring by teaching.   For look, how far the soul excelleth the body, by so much more are spiritual things better than temporal.   The apostle also concealeth an evident argument in these words, where he admonisheth, that it is meet that he that soweth should also reap.   In this point also is great inequality, in that the ministers sow the better, and reap the worse. Because men set light by God and the divine ministry, therefore they think that the ministers do nothing. St Paul again confirmeth his own right by the example of others, saying: " If others be partakers of the power towards you, why rather are not we ?" For seeing none had taken more pains among the Corinthians than St Paul, no man was more worthy of reward. Moreover, he confirmeth his right by the example, commandment, and ordinance of the Lord, saying: " Know ye not, that they which take pains in the holy things, do eat of the holy things ; and they that minister at the altar, are partakers of the altar ? Even so hath the Lord ordained, that they that do preach the gospel should live of the gospel." Where hath the Lord ordained this ? Forsooth, when he said in the gospel, that "the labourer is worthy of his hire." But I judge this especially to be observed, which the apostle speaketh in plain words ; that the Lord instituted his ordinance concerning the maintenance of the ministers of the church unto the imitation of the ancient laws of the Jewish people. Hereof we gather, that we miss not much the mark, if in this and such like cases we do not utterly reject the ancient institutions of the fathers.

But in that St Paul the apostle used not his authority as he might have done, it maketh nothing against these things : for one question is of the deed, and another of the right of the thing. In very deed he took nothing of the Corinthians for divers causes, yet notwithstanding he took of other churches. Neither received he any thing of the church of Thessalonica. Yet for all that this doing[1] is not prejudicial to the equity of the right ; for he saith unto the Corinthians : " I have robbed other churches, having received wages of them, to the intent I might do you service. And when I was with you and wanted, I was not burdensome unto any man ; for the things that were lacking unto me were given me by the brethren that came from Macedonia." And unto the Thessalonians he saith : " We behaved not ourselves inordinately amongst you, neither did we take our bread for nothing ; but with labour and pain both night and day doing our work, to the intent we would not be a burden unto any of you. Not

St Paul received no wages.

2 Cor. xi.

2 Thess. iii.

[1 So also ed. 1584: but ed. 1577, this his doing: hoc factum suum, Lat.]

that it is not lawful for us to do it; but because we would set
down ourselves as a pattern for you to follow after." And
1 Thess. v. again the same St Paul saith unto the Thessalonians: "I beseech you, that you acknowledge them that labour among you,
and are over you in the Lord, and admonish you; that you
have them in singular love through love for their work sake.
Be at peace with them[1]." Let so much therefore of the
church-goods, as is sufficient, be given unto the ministers and
teachers, so far forth as honest necessity requireth. And thus
much have we spoken concerning the proportion[2] that is due
unto pastors.

Students to be maintained by wages of the church. In times past the second part of ecclesiastical goods was
allotted unto clerks. And clerks are the harvest of pastors,
studious of divinity, and wholly disposed to the holy ministry.
And forasmuch as these have dedicated themselves and all
that they have wholly to the church and the ministry thereof,
it is most fit that they should be nourished and maintained
by the costs of the church. But it is convenient they be
nourished meanly[3], who ought to be an example of mean and
thrifty living to other; for to be brought up delicately doth
nothing agree with the ministries of the church. And therefore Amos found fault that the Nazarites drank wine; for that
he meant, that drunkards did not maintain the church, but
utterly destroy it. Of which matter we spake in another
place[4]. Moreover, it is fit that due portions be paid to
priests, schoolmasters, scholars[5], and to all other ecclesiastical
persons whatsoever.

The poor to be relieved by the church-goods. Finally, the third part of ecclesiastical goods are appointed
for the poor. And there are divers sorts of poor folk; as
widows, pupils, orphans, and infants cast out (whose parents
are not known[6]), also they that are worn with old age and
spent with diseases. There are infinite kinds of diseases,
whereof the most grievous are these: leprosy, fury, and madness, the French pox, or the scab of India or Naples, the

[1 Rather, as Bullinger here divides the words, Be at peace with
them for their work's sake.—Cf. Vol. I. page 284, note 1.]

[2 So also ed. 1584: but ed. 1577, portion: portione, Lat.]

[3 frugaliter, Lat.]   [4 See Vol. II. page 207.]

[5 professoribus, Lat.]

[6 The parenthesis is the Translator's.]

palsy, the gout, and a great many more. There are not only poor men born within the land, but also strangers that are banished their country and home for righteousness' sake and for the word of God. There are other who are not yet come to extreme poverty, but are even now ready to fall into it, so that, if they be not holpen a little with ready money, they by and bye come to be kept by the church-box. Again, there are some that are consumed by imprisonment, by wars, by great floods of waters, by fire, and divers other mishaps, as by hail, frosts, and other storms and distemperatures of the air. Of all whose health and safeguard the Lord willed us to be mindful whereas he saith, that whatsoever we bestow upon the poor, we bestow it upon him. Therefore if we despise and regard not the poor, without all doubt we despise and neglect even our Lord God himself in the poor. We ought of duty to succour the poor of our own good will by counsel, comfort, medicines, cures[7], money, meat, drink, clothes, lodgings, succouring, and by any means else that we may, and in all such matters and cases as they shall have need of our help. If so be the church-goods are not suf- *The poor not to be de-* ficient to perform all this at the full, then let the abundance of *frauded of their portion.* all other good faithful people supply their want. But if there be goods sufficient in store laid up, which have been in times past contributed by the liberality of the godly, which notwithstanding through negligence or wickedness of the governors are taken away, so that the necessity of the poor cannot thereby be succoured; for that cause truly most sharp tempests of infelicities are poured forth both upon commonwealths and kingdoms. For why? they are very sharply punished, which do not give unto the poor of their own private goods, if they be able : with how much more grievous calamities may we think they shall be plagued, which wickedly, sacrilegiously, and forcibly take away to their own private uses those riches, which were given by others to the common use of the poor ! He that hath this world's substance, and *1 John iii.* seeth his brother want, and shutteth up his affection from him, is cruel; therefore he that taketh from the poor[8] that which is already given them, is more cruel, and committeth

[7 cura, Lat.: care.]
[8 sibi, Lat. omitted: for himself.]

sacrilege. It is read, that the Sodomites with their fellow-cities were burned[1], because they strengthened not the hand of the poor, but rather weakened it. The Moabites and Chaananites are destroyed for disdaining strangers, and for having no care of the poor. But why do we fetch examples so far off? Why do we not call to mind the last sentence of the high Judge, uttered from his heavenly judgment-seat which is stablished in the clouds, pronounced in this manner: "Come, ye blessed children of my Father, possess the kingdom which was prepared for you from the beginning of the world. I have been hungry, and you have given me meat: I have been a-thirsty[2], and you have given me drink: I was a stranger, and you harboured me: I was naked, and you clothed me: I was sick, and you visited me: I was in prison, and you came unto me." The evangelist also addeth that which agreeth very much to our purpose: "Then shall the just answer, and say, Lord, when saw we thee hungry, and gave thee meat? thirsty, and gave thee drink? When saw we thee harbourless, and lodged thee? or naked, and clothed thee? Or when saw we thee sick or in prison, and came unto thee? The King answering shall say unto them, Verily I say unto you, In that you did it unto one of the least of these my brethren, you did it unto me. Then shall he say also unto them that are on his left hand[3]: Depart from me, ye cursed, into everlasting fire, which is prepared for the devil and his angels. For I was hungry, and you gave me no meat: I was thirsty, and you gave me no drink: I was a stranger, and you harboured me not: I was naked, and you clothed me not: I was sick and in prison, and you visited me not. Then shall they answer, and say unto him, Lord, when saw we thee hungry, or thirsty, or a stranger, or naked, or sick, or in prison, and ministered not unto thee? Then shall he answer them, saying, Verily I say unto you, Inasmuch as you did it not unto one of the least of these, neither did you it unto me." It followeth after[4]: "And they shall go

[1] So also ed. 1584: but ed. 1577, were drowned: subversi, Lat.]
[2] So also ed. 1584: but ed. 1577, athirst.]
[3] So also ed. 1584: but ed. 1577, at the left hand: a sinistris, Lat.]
[4] ergo, Lat. omitted: therefore.]

into everlasting punishment, but the righteous into everlasting life." The Lord also[5] in another place in the gospel, substituting the poor in his stead, saith: "Ye have the poor with Mark xiv. you always, and when ye will, ye may do them good; but me ye shall not have always." And therefore we read, that the primitive church was careful in providing for the poor, even to the working of miracles[6].

St Paul in all places commendeth the poor to the church of God: he made collections for the poor almost in all churches; and the blessings[7], which he had gathered, he distributed with great judgment, faith, and diligence; as it will appear almost in all his epistles, specially in the xv. to the Romans, in the first to the Corinthians the sixteenth chapter, in the second to the Corinthians the eighth and ninth chapters; and to the Galatians: "While we have time," saith he, "let us do good Gal. vi. towards all men, especially towards the household of faith." In the first epistle to Timothy he warneth, that there be con- 1 Tim. v. sideration had who should be holpen, and who not to be holpen. In the same epistle he giveth charge to Timothy and to all the bishops, how to deal with the richer sort in the church, saying: "Command them that are rich in this world, 1 Tim. vi. that they be not high-minded, neither put their trust in uncertain riches, but in the living God, who giveth us all things abundantly to enjoy; that they may do good, that they may be rich in good works, that they may be ready to give, and bestow willingly, laying up unto themselves a good foundation against the time to come, that they may take hold of life everlasting." And unto the Hebrews: "To do good and Heb. xiii. to distribute forget not: for with such sacrifice God is pleased." Wherefore riches were gathered even in the time of the apostles to succour the necessity of the poor withal. Deacons were appointed by the church as providers and stewards: among whom those first deacons were most famous, of whom the Acts of the Apostles make mention, and also the notable Acts vi. martyr of Christ, Laurence[8]. And the writings of the ancient fathers do testify, that with those ecclesiastical goods prisoners

[5] qui ascensurus erat in cœlos, Lat. omitted: being about to ascend into heaven.]
[6] Rather, even to a miraculous extent: ad miraculum usque,Lat.]
[7] benedictionem, Lat.: 2 Cor. ix. 5. Marg. Auth. Ver.]
[8] See Vol. iii. page 106.]

32

were redeemed out of captivity; poor maidens of lawful years married[1]; finally, hospitals, almories, spittals, harbours, hostels, and nurseries, were builded, namely to entertain poor travellers, for the maintenance of the poor that were born in that country, for the relief of the sick and diseased, for the necessity of old men, and for the honest bringing up of pupils and orphans[2]. Concerning these matters there are yet extant certain imperial laws.

Reformation of churches to be made.

Wherefore in reforming of churches very diligent heed must be taken, that there be no offence committed in this behalf through oversight or of purpose; that the poor be not defrauded; and that in taking away one abuse we bring not in many. If there be plenty of goods, let them be kept: if there be none, let them be gathered of the rich. Then let the state of the poor be searched, and what every man needeth most, or how provision may best be made for every one: which being known, let that which is meet and necessary for every one be done speedily, gently[3], and diligently. If then any of the common goods remain, let them be kept against such calamities as may ensue. Let nothing be consumed unprofitably or ungodlily. Again, let not the treasure of the poor unhappily be detained from them by fraud[4] and to the increasing of their poverty. For there may be like offence committed on both sides; for on each side the poor are defrauded of their goods. Touching liberality, we have entreated in another place in these our decades[5]: and of providing for the poor, in other of our works[6]. And Lewis Vives hath written very well of relieving the poor[7].

Holy buildings.

The fourth and last part of the goods of the church ap-

[1 dotatas, Lat.]

[2 Xenodochia, Ptochotrophia, Nosocomya, Gerontocomia, Brephotrophia, et Orphanotrophia.—Cf. Vol. i. page 286, note 3; and Vol. ii. page 281, note 8.]

[3 benigne, Lat.]

[4 Rather; let no evil treasure be heaped together by defrauding of the poor, &c.]

[5 See Vol. ii. page 58, &c.]

[6 De Episcop. Instit. &c. cap. ix. fol. 113. Tig. 1538.]

[7 John Ludovicus Vives, born at Valentia in Spain, A.D. 1492, died A.D. 1537 (or 1541). He published a treatise, De Subventione Pauperum, in two books, A.D. 1526 —Opp. Tom. ii. p. 889, &c. Basil. 1555. Mosheim. E. H. Vol. iii. p. 52. ed. Soames.]

pertaineth unto holy buildings, as churches, schools, and houses belonging to churches and schools. Churches, which because of the companies gathered together in them are also called congregations[8], are the houses of the Lord our God. Not that God, whom the wide compass of the heavens cannot comprehend, doth dwell in such manner of houses; but because the congregation and people of God meet together in those houses to worship and perform due honour unto God, to hear the word of God, to receive the Lord's sacraments, and to pray for the assistance and presence of God. Churches therefore are very necessary for the church and people of God. Touching holy assemblies, I have said somewhat in the disputations of prayer[9].

Temples of Christians.

And although that at the commandment of God Moses builded a moveable church, and afterward the most wise king Solomon founded a standing church not without great cost; notwithstanding, we must not think therefore, that God liketh of such great charges after that he had sent Christ and fulfilled the figures. For as before the law was made it is not to be found, that the patriarchs did ever build any minsters and[10] great churches; even so after the disannulling of the law in the church of Christ, a mean and sparing cleanliness pleaseth God best. For God misliketh that foolish and mad kind of buildings, not much unlike to that unwise building of Babylon[11], enterprising to set up the top of the tower above the clouds. For God liketh not the riotousness of churches, who without all riot doth gather his church together from out all the parts of the world; which church also he hath taught both sparingness and the contempt of all riot. A church is large and big enough, if it be sufficient to receive all that belong unto it; for the place is provided for men, and not for God. But above all things, let that place be clean and holy. A church is hallowed or consecrated, not (as some do superstitiously think) with the rehearsing of certain words, or making signs and characters, or with oil, or purging fire; but with the will of God and his commandment, bidding us to assemble and come together, promising his presence amongst us; and also, it is hallowed by the holy use of it. For in the tem-

[8 ecclesiæ, Lat.]   [9 See above, page 184.]
[10 So also ed. 1584: but ed. 1577, or: basilicas, Bullinger's one word.]
[11 furori Babylonico, Lat.: Babylonish madness.]

ple the holy church of God is gathered together; the true
and most blessed word of God is also declared in the temple;
the holy sacraments of God are received in the temple; and
also in the temple prayers are poured forth to God, which are
most acceptable unto him. Verily, the place of itself is nothing
holy; but because these holy things are done in that place, in
respect that they are done there, the place itself is called
holy. Therefore not without great cause ought all profanation and filthiness be far from the holy temple of the Lord.
The senator's court or seat of judgment is accounted so holy
a thing, that whosoever either in word or deed used himself
unreverently towards it should be accused of treason. And
yet in this court the senators only are gathered and assembled together, to hear the matters of suitors in things transitory, that shall pass away and perish. By how much the
more then ought reverence to be given unto temples, into the
which the children of God do come to worship him, to hear
the true word of God, and to receive his holy sacraments!
And therefore, as we hate and abandon all superstition in temples, so we love not the profanation of them; yea, rather I say,
we cannot abide it. Neither have we leisure at this time
about the consideration of temples, to rehearse and search out
open and plain superstitions[1]; of which matter we have
spoken in another place[2].

Toward what part of the world we must pray.

I find it a matter of controversy among the fathers of old
time, to what part of the world we ought to turn when we
pray. Socrates, the historiographer, in his fifth book, cap. 22,
speaking of the most ancient apostolic church of the whole
world at Antioch, saith: "At Antioch, which is in Syria, the
church is set contrary to other; for the altar looketh not towards the east, but towards the west[3]." It may be they did
imitate the fashion of the old people in building and setting
their tabernacle, and in the fashion of their temple; for they
worshipped God turning towards the west, without doubt be-

[1 Rather, to rehearse and discuss all the manifest superstitions
about the consideration of temples.]

[2 De Episcop. Instit. cap. IX. fol. 115. Tig. 1538. De Origine
Erroris, Lib. I. cap. 21. fol. 102. Tig. 1539.]

[3 Ἐν Ἀντιοχείᾳ δὲ τῆς Συρίας ἡ ἐκκλησία ἀντίστροφον ἔχει τὴν θέαν·
οὐ γὰρ πρὸς ἀνατολὰς τὸ θυσιαστήριον, ἀλλὰ πρὸς δύσιν ὁρᾷ.—Socrat.
H. E. Lib. V. cap. 22. p. 297. Cantab.]

cause of the coming of Christ in the latter time and at the
end of the world.   Otherwise it is commonly used, that men
worship with their faces towards the east.   But in all these
matters, so there be no superstition, dissension, licentiousness,
and offence, a man may do what him lusteth.

But there ought no temple to be built for the worshipping *Churches not*
of saints.   For unto God only, to whom all honour and wor- *to be builded to saints.*
ship is due, we ought to build churches; which thing we are
taught by the examples of ancient fathers, and the determination of the whole scripture.   The heathenish idolaters built
temples unto creatures, sinning against the true and eternal
God in committing a grievous offence.   St Augustine, in his
book *De Civitate Dei*, saith plainly : " We build not temples
unto our martyrs[4]."   And again in his first book against
Maximinus, a bishop of the Arians : " If we should," saith he,
" build a church of timber and stones unto some excellent holy
angel, should we not be accursed by the truth of Christ and
the church of God ; because we should do that service unto
a creature, that is due only to God ?   Therefore, if we should
commit sacrilege in making a temple to every creature whatsoever ; how may it be that God is not true, unto whom we
make no temple, but we ourselves are a temple for him[5] ?"
Thus much saith he.   Again[6], they are to be counted liars,
who affirm, that temples were built by certain religious men in
the worship of the apostles, while they were alive.   Of which
matter we have spoken in times past, as we have both against
the riotousness of the church and the unprofitable expenses
thereof, in the first book intituled *De Origine Erroris*, the
21 chap.

Instruments belonging to the church ought to be holy, *Holy instru-*
clean, and void of all riot[7], and far from any kind of super- *ments.*
stition.   The instruments be these: an holy seat or pulpit, in
the which the minister may teach and preach; convenient
seats for the congregation ; a font ready to baptize infants in[8],
and the Lord's table, with such things as are necessary there-

[4 Nec tamen nos eisdem martyribus templa. . . . constituimus.—
Aug. de Civit. Dei, Lib. VIII. cap. 27. Opp. Tom. v. fol. 107. col. 2.
Par. 1531.]
[5 See the quotation, Vol. III. page 348, note 3.]
[6 Proinde, Lat.: Therefore.]   [7 luxu, Lat.]
[8 Rather, to baptize the faithful in : baptizandis fidelibus, Lat.]

to, as water, bread, wine, books, candles, baskets, and cups. These at some times were all of gold ; but good and godly bishops have oftentimes molten them, and therewithal delivered prisoners out of captivity, and fed such as were like to perish for hunger[1]. Many examples of this sort have I gathered in my book of the Institution of Bishops, the ix. chapter. As for candles, whereof we made mention even now, sure it is, that the ancient fathers used them in the churches to drive away the darkness of the night, as it appeareth in the twentieth chapter of the Acts of the Apostles. But it is a foolish matter and nothing religious, to use lights in the worshipping of God. Lactantius crieth out : " Shall we judge him to be well in his wits, which offereth the light of a burning wax-candle, or a taper, for a present to the author and giver of light ? He requireth other manner of light at our hands, and that not smoky, but clear and bright, to wit, the light of the mind[2]." But a man may commonly see, in these days, a great part of the worshipping of God to be reposed in the offering of candles ; which thing is clean against the manifest truth.

Amongst other instruments of the church bells are reckoned up ; which at these days are unto us, as in old time trumpets were unto the people of God: for they serve to call the congregation together, and they are numbered among tokens and warnings. About bells there is a wonderful superstition. They are christened by bishops ; and it is thought, that they have power to put away any great tempest. In the old time men were stirred up to prayer by the ringing of them, what time any sore tempest did rise ; but now the very ringing of bells, by reason of their consecration, seemeth to have a peculiar kind of virtue in it. Who can but marvel and be astonied at this extreme blindness ? Moreover, they use bells to bewail the dead. All which things are superstitious, and utterly to be contemned[3].

Forsomuch as the true use of the church-goods con-

[1 See Vol. II. page 45.]

[2 Num igitur mentis suæ compos putandus est, qui auctori et datori luminis candelarum ac cerarum lumen offert pro munere? Aliud vero ille a nobis exigit lumen, et quidem non fumidum, sed (ut ait poeta) liquidum atque clarum, mentis scilicet.—Lactant. de Vero Cultu, Lib. VI. cap. 2. p. 545. Lugd. Bat. 1660.]

[3 Cf. Early Writings of Bp Hooper, ed. Park. Soc. p. 197.]

sisteth in those things which we reckoned up before; it followeth, that the abuse thereof must needs be in the contraries, whether we do offend in one kind or in many. Justice and *Abuse of the church-goods.* equity is to be kept in these, as well as in all other things. We ought not to take from one man and give to another; but we must give unto every one that which is his own. Therefore we may not take anything from the poor, and give it to the ministers of the church: neither is their portion and necessaries to be taken from them, that the poor may live thereof. The holy scripture giveth one portion of the church-goods to the ministers of the church : and the same church[4] willeth us to give unto the poor their part. Therefore if bishops or ministers of the church do challenge unto themselves all the church-goods, and give not unto the poor their parts due unto them, they defile themselves with sacrilege. If the ministers do not challenge unto themselves all the goods of the church, and yet do take unjustly more than either it becometh them, or than need requireth, or otherwise than the decree of God and the apostles doth allow ; or else if they spend unthriftily that portion due unto them; they grievously offend. But they sin greatly, yea, most horribly, if they waste the goods of the poor in hunting, dicing, drinking and rioting, whore-hunting, or else in warfare; and in the meantime have no regard of the church[5], neither care what is done there or how[6]. But if a just and good portion fall unto the poor, perhaps there will be a fault in this point, in the steward or almoner, through favour or hatred, that they that have most need shall have nothing, and the least worthy shall have most; then in this case there is also great offence committed through filthy abuse. But of all abuses that seemeth to be the shamefullest, which is now-a-days almost commonly used. We bestow great costs and charges upon stones and stocks, that is to say, upon idols void of all understanding ; but there is no regard had unto the poor, who are the perfect images of God. Which kind of madness is heathenish and extreme folly. But forsomuch as other have already very largely spoken of the abuse of the church-goods, and we also have set down certain matters concerning the same elsewhere[7], I will for this time make an end of speaking thereof.

[4 Rather, the same scripture.]
[5 ædificia sacra, Lat.]   [6 See Vol. II. page 44.]
[7 De Episcop. Instit. &c. cap. 19. fol. 163. Tig. 1538.]

Holy time.

I would also now entreat of the holy time; which treatise is altogether like that of the holy place, whereof we disputed elsewhere: but that we have also discoursed thereof in the expounding of the Ten Commandments[1]. This only I do add at this present time; that there ought to be no odious contention in the church concerning that matter, but that in this and other such like cases discipline with charity is constantly to be observed. For it behoveth us to be mindful of the most pernicious contention about the keeping of Easter, which with much danger and great detriment much and long time troubled the churches of the east and west[2]; and beware in any case that through contention there be not a gap left open unto Satan to enter in. It were profitable in mine opinion, both in this case and in such like, to remember the counsel which St Augustine giveth: that that which is enjoined us, and is neither against faith nor good manners, is to be accounted indifferent, and to be observed according to the society of them with whom we live. In the 118. epistle, to Januarius[3].

Discipline and correction of ministers.

Unto the holy ministry belongeth also discipline and correction of the ministers. How necessary this is, it may be gathered by these words of our Lord Christ: "You are the salt of the earth. If the salt have lost her saltness, what shall be salted therewith[4]? It is good for nothing else, but to be thrown out of the doors, and to be trod under foot of men." I know there be some that do boast themselves of certain privileges, whereby they are exempted from all discipline. But they are deceived; for the Lord hath made all the ministers of his church subject unto discipline. Whoso therefore will be exempted from discipline are not Christ's ministers. Or who, I pray you, will say, that he is free from discipline, whom the Lord would have altogether subject and bound unto it? Against the commandment of God there is no pope's law, no privilege of king or emperor, of force; for no man can abrogate the decree of the high God: and the

[1 Decade II. Serm. IV.]
[2 Euseb. Hist. Eccles. Lib. v. cap. 24. See Vol. I. p. 433. n. 4.]
[3 Quod neque contra fidem, neque contra bonos mores injungitur, indifferenter est habendum, et pro eorum inter quos vivitur societate servandum est.—Aug. Ep. cxviii. Opp. Tom. II. fol. 108. col. 2. Par. 1531.]
[4 quo salietur, Lat. But Tyndale, 1534, and Cranmer, 1539, render the words as the translator here.]

Lord commandeth, to warn and correct every brother that doth amiss. Therefore would he have us also sharply to admonish the ministers of the churches, that are negligent and go astray. Truly, he himself did often and very sharply reprove the whole order of the priests of the church of Hierusalem. Heli the Lord's priest is ill reported of in the holy scripture, for that he bridled not his sons, being priests, with sharper discipline. We read how the prophets of the Lord blamed very bitterly all the colleges of priests, and the high priests also. Examples are to be found in every place throughout the holy history, and in the writings of the prophets. Yea, St Paul reproved the most holy apostle St Peter at Gal. iii. Antioch in Syria, in the sight of the whole congregation, for that he taught not directly[5] according to the prescript rule of the gospel. And to be short, Christ himself, in the revelation which was made to St John the apostle, doth very sharply admonish and reprove the angels, that is to say, the ministers of the churches. Again, St Paul the apostle saith : "Against 1 Tim. v. an elder receive no accusation, but under two or three witnesses. But those that do offend reprove before the whole congregation, that the other may stand in fear." There are extant also in the scriptures many notable examples of most holy princes, who by their laws have restrained even the chiefest ministers of the churches, and have thrust down from their chairs and degrees such as did not well discharge their duties[6]. Yea, very necessity itself and the good estate of the people of God requireth, that the naughty ministers of churches be deposed. And better it were that a few evil ministers were troubled, than so many congregations brought into danger of body and soul. For the churches and congregations are utterly destroyed through the negligence and ungodliness of wicked pastors. Therefore let them be deposed with speed.

But to the end that the ministers of churches might the Of synods. better and the more easily be kept in their function and calling, the ancient fathers in the old time solemnly held convocations of the clergy once or twice in a year, applying the same as remedies to the diseases of the ministers. And that I may not bring anything here far fet, I will recite unto you, dearly beloved, what is read in the Imperial Constitutions of

[5 non recto pede incederet, Lat.]   [6 Cf. Vol. I. page 331.]

the emperor Justinian, commanding after this manner : " The ancient fathers solemnly held convocations of the clergy twice a year in every province, that such things as are grown up may there be examined, and amended by competent correction. Which hitherto not being observed, it seemeth now to be needful to bring it to [the] right way. And forasmuch as we ourselves, by reason of this negligence, have found many to be entrapped with sundry errors and sins, we command them all, that in all provinces every year, either in the months of July or September, one synod be holden, and that the priests meet together, either at the patriarch's or the bishop's, and that there matters of faith be handled, and also of canonical questions, and of the administration of ecclesiastical things, or of reproveable life, or other matters which require correction. These things being thus observed, the laity also shall reap much profit concerning the true faith and honest life, and amendment of themselves to the better." Immediately after he addeth these words : " Moreover, we command the lieutenants of the provinces, if they see this to be negligently looked unto, that they urge the bishops to assemble synods. But if they perceive them to seek delays and to be negligent herein, let them certify us thereof, that we may proceed with due correction against such lingerers[1]." Thus much have I

[1] Ἐπειδὴ δὲ τὸ τοῖς κανόσιν εἰρημένον περὶ τῶν συνόδων τῶν ὁσιωτάτων ἐπισκόπων, τῶν ὀφειλουσῶν καθ' ἑκάστην ἐπαρχίαν γίνεσθαι, μέχρι τοῦ νῦν μὴ παραφυλαχθὲν, τῶν ἀναγκαιοτάτων ἐστὶν ἐπανορθῶσαι. Οἱ μὲν οὖν ἅγιοι ἀπόστολοι καὶ οἱ πατέρες ὥρισαν δεύτερον ἔτους ἑκάστου γίνεσθαι συνόδους τῶν ὁσιωτάτων ἱερέων ἤτοι ἐπισκόπων ἐν ἑκάστῃ ἐπαρχίᾳ, καὶ τὰ ἀναφυόμενα ἐξετάζεσθαι, καὶ τῆς προσηκούσης ἀξιοῦσθαι διορθώσεως· τουτέστι μίαν μὲν τῇ τετάρτῃ ἑβδομάδι τῆς ἁγίας Πεντηκοστῆς, τὴν δὲ ἄλλην κατὰ τὸν Ὀκτώβριον μῆνα. Ἡμεῖς δὲ εὑρόντες ὡς ἐκ τῆς τοιαύτης ἀμελείας πολλοῖς καὶ διαφόροις ἁμαρτήμασι περιεβλήθησαν, κελεύομεν πᾶσι τρόποις μίαν σύνοδον γίνεσθαι καθ' ἕκαστον ἔτος ἐν ἑκάστῃ ἐπαρχίᾳ, ἢ τῷ Ἰουνίῳ ἢ τῷ Σεπτεμβρίῳ μηνί· καὶ συνιέναι παρὰ μὲν τοῖς μακαριωτάτοις πατριάρχαις ἐκείνους τοὺς παρὰ αὐτῶν μὲν χειροτονουμένους . . . . . ἐφ' ᾧ τὰς κινουμένας αἰτίας, ἢ τὰ παρά τινων προσαγγελλόμενα (ἢ προφάσει πίστεως, ἢ κανονικῶν ζητήσεων, ἢ διοικήσεως ἐκκλησιαστικῶν πραγμάτων . . . . . ἢ περὶ κατεγνωσμένου βίου, ἢ καὶ ἄλλων τινῶν δεομένων ἐπανορθώσεως) κινεῖσθαί τε καὶ προσηκόντως ἐξετάζεσθαι . . . . . Τούτων γὰρ οὕτω φυλαττομένων καὶ οἱ λαϊκοὶ πολλῆς ἐντεῦθεν περί τε τὴν ὀρθὴν πίστιν καὶ τὸν σεμνὸν βίον προκοπῆς τε καὶ ἐπανορθώσεως ἀξιωθήσονται . . . . Κελεύομεν δὲ καὶ τοὺς τῶν ἐπαρχιῶν ἄρχοντας, εἴπερ ἀμελούμενόν τι τῶν παρ' ἡμῖν νομοθετηθέντων ἴδοιεν, πρῶτον μὲν κατεπείγειν τοὺς μητροπολίτας καὶ τοὺς ἄλλους ἐπισκόπους

reported out of the Cæsarial decree. Therefore let bishops take heed, that in this behalf there be no fault committed through their negligence; and if they forget their duty, let the magistrate beware that he wink not at their sluggishness, to the destruction of the whole church and all the ministers of Christ[2]. There creep in continually many vices, for that the disposition of the flesh is very corrupt. Unless therefore there be admonition in the church and correction continually put in use, those things which we think to be most firm shall fall to decay and perish sooner than we suppose.

Like as the Lord would have the transgressing ministers of the churches privately to be admonished and corrected, so doth he extend the commodity of the same admonition and correction to the whole church. And therefore the ancient church had an holy senate of elders, which diligently warned them that transgressed in the church, corrected them sharply, yea, and excluded them out of the ecclesiastical fellowship, namely if they perceived that there was no hope of amendment to be looked for in them. But in the latter times the popes and bishops tyrannically taking that kind of punishment into their hands, and exercising it sacrilegiously, contrary to the first institution, have turned an wholesome medicine into an hurtful poison, making it abominable both to the good and bad. St Paul, teaching that this kind of punishment was permitted by the Lord to restrain the licentiousness of many[3], saith: "I have decreed, that he which hath committed this offence, when you be gathered together, in the name of our Lord Jesus Christ and my spirit with you, together with the power of our Lord Jesus Christ, be delivered to Satan to the destruction of the flesh, that the spirit may be saved in the day of the Lord Jesus." Lo, this is the power

Marginal note: Ecclesiastical admonition and correction.

Marginal note: 2 Cor. v.

τὰς εἰρημένας συνόδους ποιεῖσθαι ....εἰ δὲ ἀναβαλλομένους αὐτοὺς ἴδοιεν, τηνικαῦτα μηνύειν ἡμῖν, πρὸς τὸ ἐξ ἡμῶν τὴν προσήκουσαν διόρθωσιν προϊέναι.—Justinian. Novell. Constit. 137. p. 365. H. Stephan. 1558.]

[2 Sicubi vero exolevit salubre celebrandi synodos institutum, revocetur, et justa cum gravitate reparetur ad ministerii conservationem incolumitatemque ecclesiarum, Lat. omitted: But if in any quarter the wholesome ordinance of holding synods has grown out of use, let it be brought back, and with due solemnity renewed, for the preservation of the ministry and welfare of the churches.]

[3 Rather, that this revengement was not granted by God to the licentiousness of a few.]

and revengement of the elders of the church[1]. The means is, the destruction of the flesh: the end is, the safety of the spirit, or the saving of a faithful man. For the same apostle to the Thessalonians hath these words: "If there be any man," saith he, " that obeyeth not our words, signify to me of him by an epistle, and see that ye have nothing to do with him, that he may be ashamed. Neither will I you to account him as an enemy, but warn him as a brother." The same apostle also, plainly shewing in another place who ought to be punished by the ecclesiastical sword, not such as be offenders through weakness of the flesh, or good men being adjudged for heretics of the bishops only or their company about them, or poor men for not paying their duty to their ordinary or their official[2], but wicked doers, and pernicious men: "If any man," saith he, " that is called a brother, be a whore-hunter, or a covetous person, or an idolater, or a slanderer, or a drunkard, or a thief, with such see that ye eat not." St Augustine doth admit moderation in giving punishment; and then especially, when through punishment not the edifying, but the destruction of the church is to be feared[3]. Which fear might perhaps seem either vain, or else too much, if the same apostle, who commanded the incestuous adulterer to be delivered to Satan, had not said in the latter epistle to the Corinthians: " I fear, that when I come, I shall not find you such ones as I would; and shall mourn for many that offended before, and have not repented themselves of their uncleanness, and of their whoring and wantonness they have used," &c. Truly, he threateneth them hardly, that he will not spare them : but because he perceived, that it did rather tend to the utter destruction and overthrow of the church, than to the gathering together and increase thereof, if (as he did the adulterer) he should deliver them unto Satan, he used moderation therein, according to God's commandment: " Suffer both of them to grow, lest that while ye pluck up the cockle, ye also pull up the wheat by the roots." It is necessary therefore, that holy judgment be used, lest offence be committed either by too much favour, or by too much extremity. Moreover, let speedy

Marginal notes: 2 Thess. iii. · 2 Cor. xii. · Matt. xiii.

[1 ecclesiæ seniorumque in ecclesia, Lat.]
[2 officiali aut vicario in spiritualibus, Lat.]
[3 Aug. de Sermone Domini in Monte, Lib. i. Opp. Tom. iv. fol. 251. col. 1. Par. 1531.]

reconciliation be of force among such as be repentant. St
Paul saith: "It is sufficient to such a man, that he be thus 1 Cor. ii.
blamed or chidden." St Peter, who shamefully denied the
Lord, doth hear of women, in the day of the resurrection,
the gospel preached by angels.

Moreover, we have shewed that there is a magistrate in
the church, and authority to execute the sword upon evil-
doers; and a magistrate, which doth judge and exercise the
sword, and notwithstanding is reckoned up among the true
members of the church; yea, and that a magistrate is very
necessary for the church in respect of his office: as it is set
down in our 7. and 8. sermon of the second Decade.

The special institutions and ordinances, which God hath Of christian
appointed in the church, are these that follow. And truly, matrimony.
amongst all the ordinances of the church, wedlock is not to be
accounted least; which if it be well used, it bringeth forth a
great company of good fruits in the church; but if it be not
well ordered, it breedeth a number of offences and deadly
mischiefs in the church. For they judge uprightly which say,
that that church is most holy and best assembled, which is
gathered together from out of many houses well ordered:
again, out of many wicked houses a wicked church is assembled. God therefore in his holy word doth diligently appoint
couples, and garnisheth wedlock very beautifully. But it is
not our purpose at this present to set forth the praise of
matrimony. For it sufficeth to know, that God himself is the
author of wedlock, and that he instituted it first in Paradise:
and he did it to this end, that man might live well and pleasantly with a fellow; to conclude, he first coupled them, man
and woman together, and being coupled he blessed them: and
that the most holy friends of God, the patriarchs, princes,
prophets, kings, bishops, wise men, and priests, lived in this
kind of life. Whereof perhaps St Paul said: "Wedlock is Heb. xiii.
honourable amongst all men, and the bed undefiled." He in
another place calleth the doctrine that forbiddeth wedlock,
"The doctrine of devils." For it is evidently known, that 1 Tim. iv.
Christ's disciples and the apostles were married men; neither
did they put away their wives, when they took upon them
the office of preaching, though some most shamefully feign
that they did.

It is notable, that the apostle requireth at the hands of a

1 Tim. v.
Tit. i.

1 Cor. ix.

bishop or an elder, to be the husband of one wife; and that in another place he plainly saith, that it is lawful to carry about a christian wife, being in the calling of the apostleship: and he challengeth it both to himself and also to Barnabas. What shall I say moreover, that it was pronounced in the council of Nice, to wit, that to lie with a man's own wife is chastity[1]? For St Paul had said before: "Let every man

1 Cor. vii.

Heb. xiii.

have his own wife, to avoid fornication." And, "The bed of wedlock is undefiled." Again: "If a virgin marry, she offendeth not." Wherefore we judge that papistical doctrine, which forbiddeth marriage unto ministers, to be such as the blessed apostle St Paul termed to be the doctrine of devils. The very papists themselves, who have not as yet put all shamefacedness away, will confess[2] it with us. For if we judge the tree by the fruits, I pray you, what fruits of single life[3] may we recite? What filthiness, what bawdry, what adulteries, what fornications, what ravishings, what incests and heinous copulations may we rehearse? Who at this day liveth more unchaste or dishonest, than the rabble of priests and monks do? For as they have no care or regard to obey God's word and his laws, and to glorify God with their holy life in chaste wedlock; even so hath God, through the desire of their hearts, given them up unto all uncleanness, that their bodies may be stained with reproach.

Contracts of marriage to be soberly made.

But first of all, the holy scripture diligently teacheth all men to have a special care, that they contract matrimony devoutly, holily, soberly, wisely, lawfully, and in the fear of God; and that no evil disposition of covetousness, desire of promotion, or fleshly lust, may lead and provoke them; and that wedlock be not entered into otherwise than either the laws of man or of God[4] will permit. And in this place we must consider of the degrees of consanguinity and affinity, of public honesty, of the reverence of blood, of offence towards other, and that no man take unto wife a heathen woman or one that is of a contrary religion; for we are expressly for-

2 Cor. vi.

bidden to yoke ourselves with the unbelievers. Again, we are taught to enter into the knot of wedlock lawfully, godlily,

[1 See quotation, Vol. i. p. 401. n. 6.]
[2 coguntur fateri, Lat.]
[3 cœlibatus illius, Lat.: of that single life.]
[4 Rather, the laws, that is, either scripture, or the law of charity.]

and holily, with prayer and the receipt of godly blessings in the temple of the Lord, both in the sight and with the prayer of the whole congregation; and to beware, that in any case we be not stained in this point with all profanation of the filthy world.   Neither be we ignorant in this case also, that men of this world are commonly wont to celebrate their weddings more fit for the devil than God[5], with rioting, pride, surfeiting, drunkenness, and all kind of wantonness.   Moreover, we are taught to dwell with our wives according to knowledge, 1 Pet. iii. moderation, patience, faith, and love; and also to bring up our children virtuously and honestly, and them also to place and bestow, when time requireth, in holy wedlock.

But if for adultery, or some other matter more heinous Divorcements. than that, necessity[6] forceth to break wedlock, yet in this case the church will do nothing unadvisedly.   For she hath her judges, who will judge[7] in matters and causes of matrimony according to right and equity, or rather according to God's laws and the rule of honesty.   The holy apostle would not have the faithful to contend and stand in law in the court of 1 Cor. vi. the unfaithful: wherefore he exhorted them, to take umpires to make agreements friendly betwixt them that were in contention.   But in causes and matters of matrimony there are far greater matters, that forbid the parties that sue or be sued to come before unbelieving judges: therefore the church of God hath very well appointed a court to try matters of matrimony.   But because we spake of wedlock in the tenth sermon of the second Decade, and also have set forth sometime a book specially concerning the same[8], I have knit up this matter in these few words touching christian wedlock.

The church of God hath widows in it, but such as the Of widows. apostle of Christ doth describe in this sort, saying: "She that is a widow, and a lone woman indeed, trusteth in God, and continueth in prayer and supplication night and day.   But she that liveth in pleasures and delights, is dead though she be alive."   The same Paul doth will the younger sort to marry, to get children, and to govern the house, neither to give any

[5 Rather, to the devil, and not to God.]
[6 ipsa inevitabilis necessitas, Lat.]
[7 Rather, who must judge.]
[8 See Works of Becon, ed. Park. Soc. Vol. I. p. 29. n. 2, and Biograph. Mem. of Bullinger, p. xviii. n. 26.]

occasion at all for the enemy to speak evil of them. The place
is evident in the first epistle of St Paul to Timothy, the fifth
chapter.

Of virgins.   The church also hath virgins. These be careful only for
those things that long unto the Lord, and are true virgins,
without all deceit or hypocrisy. Paul saith : " A virgin careth
for that that belongeth to God, that she may be holy both in
body and spirit." There are many that rule and govern their
bodies, but not their minds : God requireth both, and especially of the mind. It is an easy matter to deceive men, but
we cannot by any means deceive God. St Paul, in the first
epistle to the Corinths, the seventh chapter, setteth forth the
praise of virginity ; and by comparing a virgin to a married
wife, he sheweth how great the goodness of virginity is. Notwithstanding, it is lawful for virgins to marry, if they will; which
thing the same apostle plainly sheweth in the self-same place
of scripture. Unto this testimony of God the testimony of
man also is agreeable. For Cyprian, with his fellow-bishops
and elders, making answer to a question demanded by Pomponius, saith : " Dost thou desire, that we should write unto
thee what we think of those virgins, who, after that they once
determined to continue their state continently and stedfastly,
are found to have lain and continued in the same bed with
men ? Concerning which thing, because thou dost desire to
know our judgment, thou shalt understand, that we do not
depart from the traditions and ordinances of the gospel and
the apostles, whereby we should so much the less strongly and
stoutly provide for our brethren and sisters, and that ecclesiastical discipline should be kept by all means for their profit
and safety." And it followeth : " But if through faith they
have vowed unto Christ, and continue chastely and shamefacedly
without leasing, let them stedfastly and stoutly look for the
reward of virginity : but if they will not or cannot continue,
it is better that they marry, than to fall into the fire of their
delights and pleasures[1]." And so forth. St Augustine, dis-

[1 Cyprianus ... cum presbyteris qui præsentes aderant, Pomponio
fratri ; salutem ... Literas misisti ... desiderans ut tibi rescriberemus
quid nobis de iis virginibus videatur, quæ cum in statu suo esse et
continentiam firmiter tenere decreverint, detectæ sint postea in eodem
lecto pariter mansisse cum masculis ? ... Circa quam rem quoniam
consilium nostrum desiderasti, scias nos ab evangelicis et apo-

puting of the words of the apostle, "Having the greater 1 Tim.
damnation, because they brake their first promise and faith,"
ascribeth not this damnation to the marriage following, but to
the inconstancy going before.   "Such are damned," saith he, De Bono Vi-
duitatis,
"not because they entered into the bond and promise of wed- cap. 9.
lock, but because they brake the first promise made of continency and chastity." And a little after that, he addeth these
words: "They therefore that say such marriages are no marriages indeed, but rather adulteries, it seemeth to me that
they speak foolishly and without consideration². " And this
much he. I understand that by this word "condemnation,"
or "judgment³," is meant by the apostle "reprehension ;"
which we Switzers term, "Ein auzrichten oder nachred⁴:" for
they be evil spoken of by many, for that they have broken
their first faith, that is to say, they have broken the promise
of continency. Wherefore the apostle thinketh it much better
for young women to match themselves in marriage, than to set
down to themselves such an order of life, from the which,
although necessity forceth them thereunto, they cannot depart
without reprehension of men.   But in that place he speaketh
not of virgins, but of widows.   St Cyprian speaketh simply of
virgins.

Monks and nuns were altogether unknown in the primitive Of monasteries and
church of Christ and the apostles. The latter ages had monks, monks.
but not such as are now-a-days, which are their own rule and
law, whose monasteries abound in all filthiness and uncleanness.   Which, though we should hold our peace, yet to be
true, truth itself and experience will sufficiently declare.   And

stolicis traditionibus non recedere, quo minus fratribus et sororibus
nostris constanter et fortiter consulatur, et per omnes utilitatis et
salutis vias ecclesiastica disciplina servetur .... Quod si ex fide se
Christo dicaverunt, pudice et caste, sine ulla fabula, perseverent, ita
fortes et stabiles præmium virginitatis expectent: si autem perseverare
nolunt, vel non possunt, melius est ut nubant, quam in ignem delictis
(Bullinger read, deliciis) suis cadant.—Cyprian. Epist. iv. Opp. p. 7.
Oxon.]

[² Damnantur tales, non quia conjugalem fidem posterius inierunt,
sed quia continentiæ primam fidem irritam fecerunt... Proinde qui
dicunt talium nuptias non esse nuptias, sed potius adulteria, non mihi
videntur satis acute ac diligenter considerare quid dicant.—Aug. de
Bono Viduitat. cap. 9. Opp. Tom. iv. fol. 229. col. 4. Par. 1531.]

[³ κρῖμα, Bulling. Lat.]   [⁴ calumny or slander.]

those that seem to be governed by more severe discipline are
defiled with hypocrisy ; I will say none other thing. Touching
the first monks, they dwelt not in cities, neither intermeddled
themselves with worldly affairs. We have declared in another
place[1], how that a writer of the middle age, being made an
abbot, required that he might leave off from being a clerk;
for that no man could well be both a monk and a clerk, since
the one is an impediment to the other. Then lived they not
of the common revenues of the church, but of the travail of
their own hand, as the lay people do. St Hierome, disputing of
the original of monks, in the life of Paulus, hath thus written :
" Among many it hath oftentimes been called into question,
Who first began chiefly to dwell in the wilderness of the
monks ? Some, fetching the matter somewhat far off, begin
to reckon from Helias the holy prophet, and St John: of whom
Helias seemeth to us to have been more than a monk, and
that St John began to prophesy before he was born. But
others (in which opinion the most part of all people do commonly agree) affirm, that St Antony was the first beginner of
that order ; which in part is true. For he was not only the
first, but also the motioner of all others thereunto. Amathas
and Macarius, St Antony's scholars, whereof the first buried
his master's body, do now affirm, that one Paulus Thebius was
the first beginner of that way ; which thing we also confirm,
not only in name, but also in opinion." And anon he addeth,
that Paulus, forsaking the city, being thereto enforced for fear
of torments under the persecutors Decius and Valerianus,
departed into the wilderness, where he found a cave, and lay
hid therein until he was found out by St Antony[2]. The

[1 See above, page 113, note 5.]
[2 Inter multos sæpe dubitatum est, a quo potissimum monachorum
eremus habitari cœpta sit. Quidam enim altius repetentes, a beato
Elia et Johanne sumsere principium : quorum et Elias plus nobis
videtur fuisse quam monachus ; et Johannes ante prophetare cœpisse
quam natus sit. Alii autem, in quam opinionem vulgus omne consentit, asserunt Antonium hujus propositi caput ; quod ex parte verum
est. Non enim tam ipse ante omnes fuit, quam ab eo omnium
incitata sunt studia. Amathas vero et Macarius, discipuli Antonii, e
quibus superior magistri corpus sepelivit, etiam nunc affirmant Paulum
quendam Thebæum principem istius rei fuisse, non nominis: quam
opinionem nos quoque probamus .... Sub Decio et Valeriano persecutoribus .... quum persecutionis procella detonaret, in villam re-

emperors Decius and Valerianus governed the empire about the year of the Lord 260 ; but it is said that St Antony died, when he was an hundred and five years old, in the year of our Lord 360. St Augustine, who in his 80. epistle to Hesychius witnesseth of his own time, how that he lived in the year of our Lord 420 [3], (but Eutropius and Beda report, how that he died in the year of our Lord 430; [4]) in the thirty and one chapter of the manners of the catholic church, reciting the manners and institutions of the monks in his time, reporteth such things as are very far from the orders and institutions of our monks now-a-days [5]. In the time of Justinian the emperor, who made certain laws of monks and monasteries, there lived one Benet, whom many of the monks now-a-days do call father, whose life I will recite unto you out of Trittenheymius [6], who died about fifty years since, to the intent you may understand what power and dignity they obtained in process of time, who at the beginning were contemned and of none authority. " Benet, abbot of Cassina," saith he, " first founder, beginner, and governor, of the monks in the west, wrote in eloquent style and with grave judgment the rule for monks, in one book which beginneth, ' Give ear, O my son, to my precepts, &c.;' and it containeth threescore and thirteen chapters. He died in the year of our Lord 542. But Marianus Scotus supposeth, that he died in the year of our Lord 601, in the last year of the emperor Maurice [7]." He writeth also of twenty

motiorem et secretiorem secessit (Paulus) . . . . ad montium deserta confugiens. . . tandem reperit saxeum montem ; ad cujus radicem haud procul erat grandis spelunca, quæ lapide claudebatur. . . . Igitur adamato habitaculo, omnem ibidem in orationibus et solitudine duxit ætatem.—Hieron. Vita S. Pauli Eremitæ. Opp. Tom. IV. par. 2. coll. 69, 70. Par. 1706.]

[3 a nativitate autem Domini hodie computantur anni ferme quadringenti viginti.—August. Ep. LXXX. Hesych. Opp. Tom. II. fol. 69. col. 4. Par. 1531.]

[4 Eutropius de Gestis Roman. Lib. XIV. p. 183. Basil. 1532. Beda de Temp. Ratione. Opp. Vol. VI. p. 317. ed. Giles. Lond. 1843. Augustine died 28 August. A.D. 430, aged 76 years.—Mosheim, E. H. Vol. I. p. 338, note 2. ed. Soames.]

[5 Aug. Opp. Tom. I. fol. 161. col. 4.]

[6 John Trithemius, or de Trittenheim, a celebrated abbot of the Benedictine order, was born at Trittenheim in the diocese of Treves, A.D. 1462, and died 1516.—Mosheim, E. H. Vol. III. p. 50. ed. Soames.]

[7 Benedictus dux et princeps monachorum, ac regularis vitæ insti-

orders of monks that were under Benet's rule[1]. Of St Benet's
order there have been eighteen popes in the see of Rome,
cardinals above two hundred, archbishops in divers churches
to the number of one thousand six hundred, bishops almost
four thousand[2], famous abbots, who excelled in life, doctrine,
and writings, fifteen thousand seven hundred, of such as are
canonized fifteen thousand six hundred[3]. And, that I may
not recite many other orders of monks, it is known, that the
mendicant monks and friars, being the faithful, diligent, and
valiant Roman champions of the pope and the spiritual monarchy[4], were confirmed by Honorius about the year of our
Lord 1222.[5]

Hereby I would declare nothing else but only that all men
should understand, that monkery was devised by man's invention, not delivered unto the church of Christ by the apostles; and
that at the first it seemed to be tolerable, but afterward became
altogether intolerable. How unprofitable it is to the commonwealth, experience itself teacheth. And whosoever knoweth not
that it is quite repugnant to true religion, knoweth nothing. They

tutor magnificus, patria Nursensis . . . sacrum ordinem nostrum primus
in monte Cassino incepit, anno videlicet Domini 520. . . . Hic scripsit
regulam monachorum omni discretione præcipuam, sermone luculen-
tam. . . . Moritur, ut volunt quidam, anno Domini quingentesimo
quadragesimo secundo . . . . Sed Marianus Scotus . . . . aliter sentit,
dicens eum obiisse anno Domini sexcentesimo primo.—Trithem. de
Viris Illustr. ord. S. Benedicti. Lib. II. cap. 1. Opp. p. 29. Mogunt.
1605.]

[1 Militant sub ejus (Benedicti) regula multi ordines monachorum,
&c.—Ibid. Lib. I. cap. 3. p. 19.]

[2 De hoc sacratissimo Benedicti ordine fuerunt sanctæ Romanæ
et universalis ecclesiæ summi pontifices decem et octo . . . Cardinales
quoque . . . centum octoginta quatuor; . . . Archiepiscopi . . . in diversis
mundi partibus . . . . . mille quingenti sexaginta quatuor. Episcopi
. . . tria millia quingenti duodecim.—Ibid. cap. 5. p. 20.]

[3 de ordine divi patris Benedicti plus quam 15000 sancti et
catalogo divorum inserti, abbates, monachi et moniales, numerantur.
—Ibid. Lib. III. cap. 337. p. 114. Sunt qui scribunt ex hac monas-
tica religione nostra sanctorum catalogo insertos tam viros quam moniales, quindecim millia sexcentos.—Ibid. Serm. I. p. 531.]

[4 ut vocant, Lat. omitted: as it is called.]

[5 The Carmelites, a subdivision of the Mendicant Friars, were
placed by Honorius III. A.D. 1226, among the approved orders in the
western church.—Mosheim, E. H. Book III. cent. XIII. par. 2. chap. 2.
§ 22.]

feign, that it is meritorious before God, and the state of perfection. But who seeth not how repugnant it is to Christ's merit, and to the sincere doctrine of the gospel? What godliness or necessity is it that moveth us, after that we have wholly betaken ourselves to one God in baptism, to betake ourselves also and to make our vows to saints, and to bind ourselves by religion of an oath to the observing of their rules? True religion forbiddeth us to vow ourselves to saints, or by any means to depend in way of religion upon them. True religion forbiddeth us to choose us any other fathers or masters. True religion forbiddeth us to devise new manners of worshippings or new religions, or to receive them that are devised by others. The example of Jeroboam and his fellows maketh us afeard. True religion forbiddeth us to swear by the names of other gods. Religion referreth[6] us to one God by faith and obedience. Superstition breaketh this band, and admitteth creatures. St Paul to the Corinthians saith: " Every one of you 1 Cor. iii. saith, I am Paul's, I am Apollo's, I am Cephas', and I am Christ's. Is Christ divided? was Paul crucified for you? or were you baptized in the name of Paul?" Behold, Christ is our Redeemer and our Master. The faith of Christ hath made us one body. By baptism we are baptized into one body, that we might be called Christians, not Petrines or Paulines. St Paul would not suffer that Christians should take their name of the apostles: how much less would he abide that at this day some should be called Benedictines, some Franciscans, some Dominicans[7]? We are the Lord's inheritance and possession ; it is not lawful for us to bind ourselves to the service of men. But who so bind themselves, they tear in sunder the unity of Christ's body, they profane the cross and baptism of Christ. The apostle saith plainly : " Is Christ divided? was Paul crucified for you? or were you baptized in the name of Paul?" And therefore although they be commonly called spiritual persons, yet are they nothing less than spiritual. For the apostle saith: " When one of you saith, I am Paul's, and I Apollo's, are ye not carnal?" To what end is it, after the receiving of the gospel of Christ Jesus and the doctrine of the apostles, which contain and deliver unto us all godliness, to invent new rules? For truly, when they had

[6 religet, Lat.   See Vol. i. p. 233. n. 5 : and Vol. iii. p. 231.]
[7 Cf. Vol. iii. p. 295.]

once found out certain peculiar laws and means of living, they separated themselves from the common sort of Christians in all outward manner of living, in their behaviour, and in all their apparel, to the intent that by that means they might make evident to all men, that they would live apart as it were from that common, lay, and imperfect church, to live more holily, perfectly, and spiritually. But how well the same hath framed or doth frame with them[1], the whole world speaketh it at this day.

Of monastical vows.   The vows which they vow are most foolish. They vow chastity, which they have not. Chastity is the gift of God, and it is not incident to all men. And St Paul saith : " Whoso cannot live continently, let him marry : for it is better to marry than to burn." Generally he said, " to burn," whether it were in a vow, or out of a vow. Neither is it lawful, that a human vow and which was foolishly taken in hand and vowed should prejudice the law of God. What manner of poverty it is which is in abbeys, experience itself teacheth. They put off poverty, when they put off their common garments : and with their cowl they put on great riches ; for monks, a thing which in the old time would have seemed a strange and monstrous matter, are made princes. The common sort of them live idly, and eat their bread freely and for nought, against the apostle's rule in the 2 epistle to the Thessalonians, chap. iii., where such be also accursed. They forsake their parents and kinsfolk, whom by the law of God they are bound to serve and obey, and betake themselves unto strange men, by whom they are enforced to infinite superstitions. And they which are thus freely set at liberty to[2] their parents, either they are set at liberty through superstition, or to the intent they may have all the days of their life wherewithal to lie and riot in idleness. So that it is evident, that such put on the cowl for their belly's sake, not for any religion. What obedience is that, which is quite contrary to the obedience which is revealed by the word of God? When the magistrate commanded[3] them to sustain and bear public burdens with the residue of the faithful, they be evermore free and exempted.

[1 quomodo id eis cesserit et cedat, Lat.]
[2 So also ed. 1584: but ed. 1577, by their parents: qui sponte a parentibus manumittuntur, Lat.]
[3 jubet, Lat.]

In old time ministers of strange religions had, under the kings of Judah, princely privileges and customs confirmed by prescription of long time; but forasmuch as their ministry was not allowed by the word of God[4], but was rather repugnant to the word of God, they were not ungodly neither unjustly nor sacrilegiously broken and dissolved by holy kings.

Who can well abide to hear their excuse, who, being admonished to do penance for the sins which they have committed, make this exception; that by virtue of their oath they are referred[5] to their monkish order, so that with safe conscience they cannot depart from the same? For it is evident, that the oath, which they pretend, is altogether a rash oath; which is not to be performed, as I have declared in the third sermon of the second Decade[6]. What, I pray you, can a bond, which is made by man without God, yea, rather against the word of God, bind one unto, specially being made unwisely or unadvisedly[7]? If the cross of Christ be of so great virtue, that it hath released us from the curse unto which we were all subject; how much more shall it deliver us from outward bonds, wherewith we were entrapped, not by God, but otherwise through the folly or wickedness of men or craft of the devil! The apostle St Paul crieth out: "Ye were bought for 1 Cor. vii. a price; become not the servants of men." But if happily, through the malice of men or our own folly[8] we become servants, the godly must endeavour that through true faith and obedience they may be restored to the liberty of the children of God. Verily, the gospel is preached unto us, to the intent we should be delivered from all unjust captivity, and serve God in spirit and truth.

Moreover, where some object, that it were good and convenient that all monasteries throughout the whole world were reformed and brought back to the first simplicity; we answer, how that in this our unhappy age it were in vain, yea, plain folly, to hope for it. They cannot be reduced to the ancient simplicity, neither will the princes and monks suffer such reformation to be made: for then they know, that they must

[4 divina comprobatione, Lat.]
[5 religari, Lat.: are bound.]   [6 Vol. i. page 250.]
[7 Rather, either unadvisedly, or knowingly made: vel imprudenter vel scienter, Lat.]
[8 inertia, Lat.]

depart not only with much of their profits, honours, and pleasures, but with all together[1]. Howbeit, they had rather that the whole world were together by the ears, than they would deliver up to God his kingdom, which they have hitherto enjoyed. But admit this thing were easy enough to accomplish; who shall persuade us, that if abbeys were reformed according to the ancient institution, that in this our age they should be as well or better governed than they were in the old time? We see what beginning they had, how they have gone forward, and how increased. We see what hypocrisy, ambition and covetousness, pleasure and idleness, could do, and to what point all things are come. Do we think that men's desires at this day will be more moderate? Do we think that discipline shall now be less corrupted by us and our posterity, than it was by our forefathers? Yea, we are constrained not to hope for the better but to fear the worse, who every day do experiment that which is worse than other; for we live in the dregs of the world and in the very latter end of all ages, wherein the dragon of the bottomless pit, through the malice and ungodliness of men, hath gotten to himself great power and force, to disturb and corrupt all things that are in the whole world. Howbeit, in so great perils this comforteth us not a little, which is written in the word of truth, that for the elect's sake those days shall be shortened; and that he shall be loosed for a short time, and then anon be cast into the lake that burneth with fire and brimstone. Moreover, if we will make a just reformation, we must needs go to the fountains themselves. But in the primitive church we read of nothing set down in the doctrine of Christ and his apostles concerning[2] monkery; and thereby we understand, that it is not necessary for the church; yea, we have learned by experience that it is noisome and hurtful to the church. Wherefore true reformation persuadeth us altogether to abrogate monkery: not rejecting or neglecting in the mean season such as do repent, whom the wickedness of the time hath made unprofitable both for themselves and others; but gently to receive them into the care and alms of the church.

[1 Rather, that together with their profits, &c., many, nay, all things depart.]

[2 Rather, in the primitive church, in the doctrine, &c. we read of nothing set down concerning, &c.]

Thus much hitherto have we said by occasion, and as it were by the way, concerning monkery, which we have declared to have had no place in the primitive church of Christ and his apostles. Let us therefore return to other necessary institutions of the church.

Likewise the faithful church of Christ useth discipline about the sick and such as are departing out of this life. There come about them neighbours and brethren, and every one for his part sheweth the duties of love and charity : they relieve the needy with their goods, and, if the sick be not needy, then do they shew other duties of good-will. There cometh also the minister of the church, who, in comforting the sick person, prepareth him to die, by making first his confession of sins to God ; which he pronounceth out of the word of God to be forgiven, if he do stedfastly believe. He requireth of him also that he forgive, and be in love and charity with all men, and that he keep no old grudge or malice in his heart. After this, some public prayer is made to God by the sick person, and by those that are about the party that is at the point of death. He is also admonished of sundry things; he is confirmed in the faith ; he is called to patience ; he is instructed according as his goods and everything else requireth ; and he is taught that, at his departing out of this world, he commend his soul into the hands of God the Father, according to the doctrine and example of our Redeemer, who at the very point of death cried aloud, saying, " Father, into thy hands I commend my spirit."

How the church dealeth with the sick.

This discipline have we learned of the apostles of our Lord Christ. For the apostle St James saith : " If any be sick among you, let him send for the elders of the church; and let him[3] pray over him, anointing him with oil in the name of the Lord. And the prayer which is made in faith shall deliver the sick ; and the Lord shall raise him up again. And if he be in sin[4], they shall be forgiven him. Confess your sins one of you to another, and pray one for another, that you may be safe ; for the hearty prayer of the just is of great force," &c. This is the apostolic discipline. But if you say unto me, Where is the oil ? I answer ; That in St James the apostle's time, and certain ages after, there remained yet

James v.

Anointing with oil.

[3 So also ed. 1584: but ed. 1577, *them :* orent, Lat.]
[4 peccatis, Lat.]

in the church the miraculous gift of healing the sick. Of this we read in St Mark's gospel: "And the disciples, going forth, preached the gospel, that they might repent; and they cast out many devils, and they anointed many with oil that were sick, and healed them." And again in the same place saith: "Moreover, these signs shall follow them that believe. In my name they shall cast out devils," &c. And anon he saith: "They shall lay their hands upon the sick, and they shall be healed." And because this benefit remained yet in the church, St James biddeth us use oil[1]; and to use it in the name of the Lord, as the Lord had commanded. But seeing that gift is now ceased in the church, and we find by experience that oil doth no good to the sick; according to the time, and as our duty bindeth us, we do the best we can to assuage and cure the diseases of the sick by medicines most convenient for the sickness, being applied in the name of Christ.

Last annoiling.

I know how by this testimony of the apostle the papists go about to set out and commend their extreme unction, or last annoiling: but they labour in vain. [2]But, to let pass that St James speaketh nothing of the hallowed oil; and that they do not admit this medicine but in very extremity, where St James commandeth to anoint every one that is sick; how, I pray you, can they defend out of St James' words that which the priest demandeth of the sick person: "Dost thou believe, that the Lord will hear our prayers for the merits' sake and prayers of the saints?" The sick man answering, "I do believe;" he then saith, "Let us therefore pray to God and his saints." Or where, I beseech you, hath St James, or any other apostle of Christ, taught that which they bring in their anointing: "In the name of the Father, and of the Son, and of the Holy Ghost, I anoint thee with holy oil, that by this anointing thou mayest receive full remission of thy sins[3]?" What scripture,

[1 apud ægros, Lat. omitted: in the case of the sick.]
[2 Enim, Lat.: For.]
[3 Deinde hortetur (parochus) infirmum ... ut speret Christum Dominum nostrum pro sua immensa clementia sibi fore propitium, et merito ejus sanctissimæ passionis et per intercessionem beatæ Mariæ et omnium sanctorum se vitam æternam consecuturum .... Dum ipse unctionis sacramentum administrat ... dicat: In nomine Patris et Filii et Spiritus Sancti, extinguatur in te omnis virtus diaboli per impo-

I pray you, teacheth us, that full remission of sins is obtained by that anointing? These things are done manifestly against the principal article of our religion, which teacheth, that we are purged from all our sins only by the blood of Christ, and that most fully. To him only is the glory due, not to the oil, nor to any creature in the whole world.

Moreover, the church of Christ doth not reject[4] the bodies of the dead, as if it were a dead dog: for it acknowledgeth, that their bodies have been the temples of the Holy Ghost, which hath dwelt in them; it acknowledgeth, that they are buried in hope of resurrection and glory of life everlasting. Wherefore the church doth in most reverent manner take the bodies, windeth them in a sheet, and covereth them very decently; and being put into the coffin carefully, carrieth them unto the place of burial, or church-yard, the near friends, neighbours, and brethren following after, and accompanying the corse. While the body is set down and laid in the earth, there are public prayers made by them that brought the corse. For they give thanks unto God, for that he hath called the party deceased out of this world in the true faith; and they pray also, that it may please the Lord to take them likewise unto him speedily, being lightened with the true faith. Moreover, the name of the dead brother or sister is recited in the public assembly of the church with honour; and all the people are put in mind of their own destiny, and speedily to prepare themselves to die. And after this manner we read in the scriptures, that the ancient fathers buried their dead, yea, the most holy of them. We read nothing of canonizing, of worshipping of relics, of months' and[5] years' minds[6] for the dead, which are offered to the end the souls of the departed should be delivered from the pains of purgatory. There be certain burials described unto us in the old Testament, as the burial of Abraham, Sara, Isaac, Jacob, and Joseph, Aaron, Marie, Josua, Samuel, and David, &c.; and in the new Testament of John Baptist, and Stephen: but they were all

Of funerals and burials.

sitionem manuum nostrarum. . . . Per istam sanctam unctionem et suam piissimam misericordiam indulgeat tibi Dominus quidquid per visum deliquisti, &c. &c.—Ritual. Rom.]

[4 abjicit, Lat.]

[5 months' and, not in Lat.]

[6 et oblationibus, Lat. omitted: and of offerings.]

sparing, and without all manner of superstition[1]. In that Joseph's bones were carried forth, they were carried in a mystery, that the Israelites might gather thereof that they should be brought into the land of promise. Whereunto also that belongeth, that the patriarchs chose a burial[2] in Hebron. Otherwise, the place availeth nothing, to purchase the better or worse speed[3] to the body that is buried in it. We must think that the place, by reason of the bodies of the saints and holy men which are there buried, is after a manner sanctified, or at the least wise called holy: not that the bodies do get any holiness or safety by the ground. Therefore, unless it seem good otherwise to the divine providence of God, the saints would gladly lie with their ancestors in the self-same place of burial. But if it please God otherwise, they acknowledge that they are notwithstanding received into the same earth without any exception; and that they are not separated from their ancestors by distance of place. Wherefore there is no superstition in the church of God about burials and graves; but how much there was in the time of popery, no man can declare in few words.

The church hath no need of the legal instruction. These be the necessary institutions of the church of God, and are by the faithful religiously observed without superstition, to edification: as for other matters, which are only devised by the invention of man, the godly nothing weigh them. I know what things may here be objected; That, forsooth, the ancient people of the old Testament had sundry and manifold rites and ceremonies instituted of God by his prophets, because being rude they had need of such instruction[4]; but since the common sort of Christians are also more rude than is to be wished, so many sundry and diverse ceremonies were devised by the ancient fathers not without the motion of the Spirit, which they must also obey. I answer, That this is no true nor sound reason, whereby the weak in faith may receive commodity; for surely then would not the apostles of Christ have said nothing thereof. Moreover, experience teacheth that the state and condition of the weak and simple is such, that the more ceremonies are left unto them, the more their minds are diversely[5] disposed, and are less united to Christ, to whom alone all things are to be ascribed: for it pleased

[1 Cf. Vol. III. page 399.]   [2 unam sepulturam, Lat.]
[3 sortem, Lat.]   [4 pædagogia, Lat.]   [5 in diversa, Lat.]

the Father that all fulness should dwell in him, and to heap together in him[6] all things appertaining to our life and salvation. Yea, the divine wisdom of God hath taken away that whole external discipline and instruction, setting a difference between us and them. We should therefore proceed to bring again Judaism, if we should not leave off to multiply and heap together rites and ceremonies, according to the manner of the old church. For in old time those ceremonies were had in use[7], although they were not infinite, but comprised within a certain number. At this present there is no use nor place for them in the church. Neither do we want most grave authority to prove the same. The apostles and elders in a great ^Acts xv. assembly meet together at Hierusalem at a council; where the apostle[8] plainly telleth them, that they tempt the Lord in going about to lay the yoke of the law upon the free necks of the Christians. There is also a synodal epistle written, wherein by one consent they testify, that it hath seemed good to the Holy Ghost and them, to lay none other burden upon the church of Christ than that which they recite in few words; to the intent thereby it may be evident[9], that the doctrine of the gospel is sufficient for the church without the ceremonies of the law. If he would not then have the rites, which in old time were by God instituted, to be joined to the gospel; how much less ought we at this present to couple therewith the inventions of men! Unto which, moreover, is wickedly ascribed either the preparation to the grace and worshipping of God; or part of our salvation; that we may say no less at this day than St Paul said long ago: "After that you have known ^Gal. iv. God, how chanceth it that ye return again to weak and beggarly elements, which you would begin to serve anew? Ye observe days and months, times and years. I am afeard lest I have taken pains about you in vain." Unto all these things this is also to be added, that this instruction of ceremonies, whereof they speak, belongeth to the worshipping of God; but we are forbidden to devise unto ourselves any strange

[6 ut compendio, Lat. omitted: as in a summary. See Vol. i. p. 156.]

[7 Rather, had their use: habuerunt suum usum, Lat.]

[8 Petrus, Lat. omitted: Peter.]

[9 ut vel inde inclarescat, Lat.: So that even from this it appears most clearly.]

worshipping : we are forbidden also to put to or take away anything from the institution or word of God. Wherefore the church of God neither ordaineth nor receiveth of any other such constitutions. Of which matter we have also spoken somewhat before, where as we entreated of the abrogating of the law and of christian liberty [1].

I trust that in these fifty sermons I have, as shortly and conveniently as might be, comprehended the whole matter of faith, godliness or true religion, and also the church. That which I do often repeat in all my sermons and my books, that do I also again repeat in this place; that the learned may with my good-will and thanks gather and embrace better things out of the scriptures [2]. Unto the Lord our God, the everlasting [3] Fountain of all goodness, be praise and glory, through our Lord Jesus Christ. Amen.

[1 Decade III. Sermons 8, 9.]

[2 Rather, that being taught better things out of the scriptures, I will with good-will and thanksgivings embrace the better.]

[3 inexhausto, Lat.]

APPENDIX.

APPENDIX I.

[1] TO THE MOST ILLUSTRIOUS PRINCE AND LORD, HENRY
GREY, MARQUIS OF DORSET, BARON FERRERS, OF
GROBY, HARRINGTON, BONVILLE AND ASTLY; ONE
OF THE PRIVY COUNCIL OF HIS MOST SERENE
MAJESTY, THE KING, AND OF THE FAMOUS
KINGDOM OF ENGLAND; HENRY BULLIN-
GER WISHETH GRACE AND PEACE
FROM GOD THE FATHER
THROUGH OUR LORD
JESUS CHRIST [2].

Upon no other topic, I suppose, can I more fitly discourse with
you, most illustrious prince, than of the safety of the English church,
and so of the maintenance of the weal of the whole noble kingdom: seeing that, in the providence of Almighty God, you have
been made of the most sacred council of the king's serene majesty
and of the famous kingdom of England[3]; and on this account it
is your most especial duty to understand and tend the public safety
of the kingdom.

Without all controversy, then, he is thoroughly informed of the
main point of this safety, who knows whence proceeds the destruction of kingdoms. And certainly there exists no more deadly plague
to kingdoms than that which the corruption of true religion engen-
ders; for nowhere do empires find a more splendid good than in
pure religion, or in religion reformed after it has been corrupted.
And this good the famous kingdom of England now in part enjoys,
while, in reforming the church, it both calls back and restores the
ancient purity of religion, and casts off and takes out of the midst
of it those new abuses, errors, and superstitions, which we have seen
rooted therein during the lapse of several ages. He therefore will
doubtless be a disturber of so great felicity, and will inflict an un-
appreciable injury on the whole kingdom, whosoever places obstacles
in the way of that your most happy and pious design. But there

[1 This dedication is omitted in the English translation of Bullinger's Decades.
It formed the preface to the fifth and last Decade. Portions of it had been translated and published in 1566, in a small work entitled: "The judgement of the
Reverend Father Master Henry Bullinger, pastor of the church of Zurich, in
certeyne matters of religion, beinge in controversy in many countreys, even
where as the gospel is taught." These portions have been adopted in this translation by the Editor; and a star marks the beginning and end of them.]
[2 On this dedication see Orig. Lett. ed. Park. Soc. pp. 3, 7, 77, 82, 90, 393,
399, 406, 409, 434.]
[3 See Orig. Lett. p. 675.]

has come forth lately a bull[4], fixing the assembling on the first of
May of the so-called General Council at Trent; and as many as are
serious in looking for a reformation of the church by its means,
there may be found possibly among yourselves also, as indeed are to
be met with in all places, those who think that we ought to wait
for that reformation, and that meanwhile all attempts at reformation
should be stayed. And so this summoning of a council and this
expectation of a reformation may disturb your happy estate, and
delay or impede the work which has been well begun. It will be
your part, therefore, most illustrious prince, and that of all the
other most sacred nobles of the kingdom, to look diligently, and to
be watchful, that there arise no hurt from this quarter, as to
Christ's holy church, so to your most famous kingdom : while for my
part I will shew by valid reasons, and even, as it is said, to the eyes
of men, that this hope of a reformation is the vainest of all vanities.

This council the pope has appointed for no other object than to
prop up ancient error and superstition, and to overturn the reformations begun in Germany, England, Denmark, and other nations
of Christendom; in a word, to suppress pure or sincere evangelical
truth. And on this detection of its design all godly persons in the
church of Christ will be satisfied that their duty is to go forward,
both in the reforms that have been begun, and in all other duties of
godliness; and not to wait for that reformation, which all the pious
will find soon to be either none at all, or, if any, certainly no legitimate reformation. For it is indeed no general and free council,
which these men summon; but the same which was once commenced at Trent[5], and is now to be continued there, and to be re-
sumed at that point at which it stood before the death of Pope
Paul, the third of that name[6]; all whose statutes or decrees also,
put forth in matters of the council, are confirmed[7]. But it is more
than once declared expressly in public documents issued under this
Paul, that the council was appointed for the extirpation of heresies[8].
And the same Paul accused and condemned of heresy all us who
profess the gospel, and demand a reformation agreeable with the
word of God, and teach that Christ Jesus, and not the pope,—nay,
Christ Jesus alone,—is the Head, Pastor, and Chief-priest of the
Catholic church. Wherefore, inasmuch as the council is appointed
for the extirpation of heresies, and they are accounted heretics who

[4 Pope Julius III. published this bull Nov. 14, 1550.]
[5 On Dec. 13, 1545.]   [6 He died Nov. 10, 1549.]
[7 — quas (literas prædecessoris nostri) cum omnibus et singulis in eis con-
tentis clausulis et decretis in suo robore permanere volumus atque decernimus, et,
quatenus opus sit, innovamus.—Bull. Resump. Concil. Trid. sub Jul. III.]
[8 — ad exstirpationem hæresum.—Can. Concil. Trid. p. 15. Lips. 1837.]

demand and undertake a reformation agreeable with the word of God; who sees not, that the council is not summoned to reform the churches, but for the extinction of the reformations that have been begun?

Besides, there are called unto this council, not learned and pious, prudent and holy, men out of every nation under heaven; but they only who are by oath bound to the pope. For so run the words of indiction: "We call together all out of all places, as well our venerable brethren the patriarchs, archbishops, bishops, and our well-beloved sons the abbots, as singular others who have the power conceded to them by right or privilege of sitting and giving judgment in general councils; commanding them by virtue of the oath they have taken to us and this holy see, and in consideration of holy obedience, that they be present in their own persons[1]." So clear is it who are called to the council, and are, as it were, the fathers, assessors, and judges therein. And what can be expected from persons so bound by oath to the pope and the church of Rome, but that they can do nothing else but what the former wills, and what pertains to the safety of the latter? For the bishops and heads of the church of Rome bind themselves to the pope by an oath of this form: "I will be helper to keep and defend the Roman papacy, and royalties of St Peter, against every man. I will be careful to preserve, defend, increase, and further the rights, honours, privileges, and authority of the church of Rome, of our lord the pope, and of his successors: neither will I be of any counsel, act, or treaty, whereby ought adverse to our lord or the church of Rome, or to the prejudice of their persons, right, honour, state, and power, shall be devised. And if I shall know such things to be undertaken by any one, I will hinder them to the utmost of my ability. The rules of the holy fathers, the decrees, ordinances, judgments, dispositions, reservations, provisions, and apostolical mandates, with all my power I will observe, and cause to be observed by others. Heretics, schismatics, and rebels against our lord, I will persecute and fight against with all my might[2]." Thus, I say, these men have sworn. And therefore what, I pray, can we hope that they, who come to a council bound by such an oath, will pronounce in a point of religion which is in con-

[1 Omnes omnibus ex locis tam venerabiles fratres nostros patriarchas, archiepiscopos, episcopos, et dilectos filios abbates, quam alios quoscunque, quibus jure aut privilegio in conciliis generalibus residendi et sententias in eis dicendi permissa potestas est; requirentes, hortantes, admonentes ac nihilominus eis vi jusjurandi quod nobis et huic sanctæ sedi præstiterunt, ac sanctæ virtute obedientia, ut ipsimet.....adesse—debeant.—Bull. Indict. Conc. Trident. p. 11. Lips. 1837.]

[2 See Decade v. Serm. iv. p. 141.]

troversy? Verily, fools, nay impious, should we be, to surrender to the determination of these men the churches which Christ has redeemed with his blood! For we know already, and, as it were, hold in our hands, what they would pronounce:—namely, whatever makes for the propagation, vindicating, and upholding of the papacy, and for the subversion of our religion which rests on the word of Christ, the Son of God.

Furthermore, if all the decrees of pope Paul, and whatever he has defined already in matters of the council, ought to be ratified; then also those seven sessions[3], or the decrees of the sessions that have been now published, must be confirmed. But these furnish us with manifold proofs, that that council was not appointed to search into and illustrate the truth by the scriptures, or to make a lawful reformation of the church; but to establish the error, abuses, and superstition of the church of Rome; nay, to hinder right and holy reformations. For to mention a few only out of many things. In Session IV. Decree I. they pronounce thus: "The most sacred, holy, œcumenical and general council of Trent, lawfully assembled in the Holy Spirit, following the examples of the orthodox fathers, doth receive and reverence with equal affection of piety and veneration all the books as well of the old as of the new Testament, and also the unwritten traditions pertaining both to faith and manners, as though they had been dictated either from Christ by word of mouth, or from the Holy Spirit, and preserved in the catholic church by continual succession[4]." And then they add upon these words a catalogue of the canonical books; among which, notwithstanding, they introduce ecclesiastical writings which are not canonical[5]. Afterwards they strike with an anathema all who contemn traditions, and who do not receive all those books as canonical; and declare that the council will chiefly use those witnesses and sanctions in establishing doctrines and reforming manners in the church[6]. In the same session they reject all other translations, and obtrude upon

[3 In the sessions 8—12 no decrees were passed, nor canons ratified: only the council was prorogued.]

[4 Sacrosancta œcumenica et generalis Tridentina synodus, in Spiritu Sancto legitime congregata...orthodoxorum Patrum exempla secuta, omnes libros tam veteris quam novi Testamenti...nec non traditiones ipsas, tum ad fidem, tum ad mores pertinentes, tanquam vel ore tenus a Christo, vel a Spiritu Sancto dictatas, et continua successione in ecclesia catholica conservatas, pari pietatis affectu ac reverentia suscipit et veneratur.—Can. Concil. Trid. p. 19.]

[5 Sacrorum vero librorum indicem huic decreto adscribendum censuit (Trident. synodus)...Sunt vero infra scripti: Testamenti veteris...Tobias, Judith,... Sapientia, Ecclesiasticus...duo Macchabæorum, primus et secundus.—Ibid.]

[6 Si quis libros ipsos...pro sacris et canonicis non susceperit, et traditiones prædictas sciens et prudens contempserit, anathema sit. Omnes itaque intelli-

the church, as an authentic book, the received Latin version of the Bible. *And as touching the meaning of holy scripture, they do openly condemn every exposition that agreeth not with the sense which the holy mother church hath holden and doth hold, and with the universal consent of the fathers; for they say that it belongeth unto the church to judge of the true sense and interpretation of [the] scriptures[1]. But in these matters I give you warning to mark and diligently to examine four things. The first is, that they receive not only the canonical scriptures, whereby they may determine of the truth and falsehood of religion; but, beside the scripture, they join also unwritten things, or traditions not written, but kept in the church by continual succession. The second is, that they mix with canonical books other that are not canonical; and yet, for all that, they do curse them that receive them not as canonical books. The third is, that they thrust upon the church for that authentical book the common translation of the Bible in Latin. The fourth is, that they allow no other sense of the scripture but it that the mother-church alloweth. It appeareth evidently of these things what they do seek in the foresaid[2] council.

If that these fathers would have the matters of religion that are in controversy lawfully to be decided with scripture alone, what need men to join traditions that are not written? As who [should] say, the scripture of God were not sufficient to make a perfit reformation without traditions that are unwritten. But they do know well enough, that the chief points of popery can be proved with no expressed scripture, or with reasons deducted out of the scripture: therefore they feign unwritten matters, or traditions that were never written, whereby they may clout up and supply fitly that which they see they want in the scripture, and cannot be proved thereby. For, these traditions being kept safe, even their most foolish absurdities may be kept safe also. For as oft as they shall be disappointed for lack of the authority of scripture, they will run back unto the feigned device of their traditions. They will make it a tradition to pray for the dead. Another tradition shall be the wifeless state of ministers [of the church]. They will make also a tradition of the

gant...quibus potissimum testimoniis ac præsidiis in confirmandis dogmatibus et instaurandis in ecclesia moribus sit usura (synodus Trid.)—Ibid. p. 20.]

[1 Insuper eadem sacrosancta synodus...statuit et declarat, ut hæc ipsa vetus et vulgata editio (sacrorum librorum)...pro authentica habeatur...Præterea...decernit, ut nemo...contra eum sensum, quem tenuit et tenet sancta mater ecclesia, cujus est judicare de vero sensu et interpretatione scripturarum sanctarum, aut etiam contra unanimem consensum patrum ipsam scripturam sacram interpretari audeat. —Ibid.]

[2 indicto, Lat.]

mass. The use of images in temples or churches[3] must also be a tradition. To be short, whatsoever the old[4] church of Rome hath hitherto agreeably[5] kept shall be a tradition, although it be neither found, nor painted, nor written anywhere in any book canonical; yea, although it be quite contrary to the scripture. And so that shall be a tradition what they list.

The Jews also did brag in times past of their traditions, which they call [called] the traditions of the fathers. But Christ said unto them[6]: "Why do ye break the commandment of God for your traditions[7]?" And afterward he doth shew, that they are contrary unto his[8] by an example brought forth of their traditions, and compared by setting one against another by[9] the word of God. And then he said afterwards: "Ye have made void the commandment of God for your traditions. Esay [the prophet[10]] prophesied well of you, saying, Hypocrites[11], This people draw near unto me and honour me with their mouth and lips, but their heart is far from me. But they worship me in vain, teaching doctrines of men." Therefore, whilst we can prove that their traditions which they call *living* be contrary to the written word [of God], I pray you then, who will deny but that they be refused and condemned of Christ with the traditions of the Jews? Let them set forth, therefore, those their traditions, which they receive even as reverently as the scripture; for then it shall easily appear, by the likeness or by the contrariety, what came from the apostles, and what is privily conveyed in under their names. For this is without all doubt, that the apostles of God delivered nothing by their lively word of mouth that was contrary to their writings, which they delivered afterwards to their posterity that came after them. Wherefore that cannot be apostolic at all, which is contrary to the writings of the apostles.*

The maintainers of unwritten traditions object, The apostles themselves have made mention in their writings of traditions not written. But we say, that the apostles spake not of such traditions as they intend. St Luke witnesses, that he brought together in his written history of the gospel those things which they, who were eye-witnesses, had "delivered[12]:"—lo! he says, "delivered." So that what had once been a lively tradition of the apostles is now by St Luke transferred into letters and writing. Nay, St Paul, comprehending the sum and substance of Christian doctrine, says: "I

[3 or churches, not in Lat.]   [4 mis-translation, for *whole*: tota, Lat.]
[5 concorditer, Lat.]
[6 they heard from our Saviour: so Lat.]   [7 Matt. xv. 3.]
[8 unto this: illas cum hoc (præcepto) pugnare, Lat.]
[9 with: cum, Lat.]   [10 Not in Lat.]
[11 Rather, of you hypocrites, saying.]   [12 Luke i. 2.]

delivered unto you first of all that which I also received, how that Christ died for our sins according to the scriptures¹." Lo! the apostle combines lively tradition with writing, so that now the writing contains what was before his tradition. The same [apostle] again, in the epistle to the Corinthians making mention of tradition in the matter of the Lord's supper, immediately collects in writing and explains what that tradition was. And although he adds just after, " And the rest will I set in order when I come²;" yet he then spake of discipline, and of appointing and keeping up that which was decent in church-assemblies. For indeed it was not possible that he could deliver anything else about the supper of the Lord but what he had delivered already, unless he would contradict himself. The same apostle to the Thessalonians says: " Therefore, brethren, stand fast, and hold the traditions which ye have been taught." But he adds immediately, by way of explanation, " Whether by word or our epistle³." Consequently the tradition of the apostles is contained in the word and epistles of Paul. The word of Paul is the lively preaching of the gospel, which he repeated and renewed in his epistles. Furthermore, Paul's word of the gospel is read also very fully described by the other apostles: for Paul preached none other gospel than did the rest of Christ's apostles.

Nay, and what more is: Paul himself avouches, that he preached the gospel of Christ; and in that preaching delivered nothing beyond that which the law and the prophets had taught. But *who can deny but [that] the writings of Moses and the prophets are fully perfit? Therefore the canonical scriptures [which are the new Testament and the old⁴] are enough for us; which as they contain the lively traditions necessary for godliness, so they are sufficiently furnished to teach, to reprove, or to reform; and finally, to teach whereby the worshipper of God may be perfit, and made ready unto every good work : * as Paul himself declares in those very words which I have just recited⁵. Wherefore because the fathers of the council of Trent are not content to be referred to the canonical scriptures alone, and to prove or reprove all things by their means; but mingle with them beside traditions, and with consummate iniquity, or rather impiety, place them on an equality with the scriptures, equalling, that is, human with divine things, they clearly betray what it is they seek by the council which has been called; namely, not to draw forth and affirm the truth in sincerity out of the canonical scriptures, but to defend and confirm long-established errors :—

[¹ 1 Cor. xv. 3.]   [² 1 Cor. xi. 23, 34.]   [³ 2 Thess. ii. 15.]
[⁴ This parenthesis is the Translator's addition.]
[⁵ 2 Tim. iii. 16, 17.]

an object which those feigned traditions marvellously serve to accomplish.

*These [things] that I have written now of traditions are enough for them that know the truth. But, that provision may be made for them that set too much by traditions, and say that it is most unrighteous to despise generally all the traditions of the fathers; we make a plain difference amongst the old traditions of the fathers. For to begin withal: I do see Irenæus and Tertullian, disputing against heretics, call the abridgment or rule of the apostolic doctrine, yea, and also the symbol of the apostles (called now the creed[6]), though it were not set out[7] in the same words yet in the same sentences, A tradition of the apostles[8]. But who is there but he knoweth, that that tradition was fet out even of the very midst of the scriptures, and that it may be proved with infinite witnesses of scriptures? Therefore there is none of us that refuseth any such tradition, because there is none of us that despise the authority of the scriptures, teaching us openly and plenteously to believe as that universal tradition against all heresies and heretics hath holden and taught. Furthermore, the old fathers have in some places traditions historical; as is that tradition that is in some place written of John the apostle, which fled out of the bath when as Cerinthus entered into it[9]. But when as these and such like of the same kind are neither contrary unto godliness, neither do sow any superstition, godly men do not abhor from them; yet for all that they give not like authority unto them as they do unto the story of the gospel. Furthermore, there are other traditions, not of that universal rule of the faith or of the other chapters[10] pertaining thereunto, which are set out, and are not altogether historical, but propounded and set forth of opinions, doctrines, and certain rites: of which order they are which they rehearse amongst other, that men should pray for them that are departed, and virgins should have veils, or should be consecrated to perpetual virginity, and be shut up in monasteries, &c. But how little these do agree with apostolic scripture, I have sufficiently declared in another place[11]. They bring forth[12] also certain other traditions, that by the discussing of them it may appear[13], how

[6 Rather, the symbol which we at this day call the apostles'.]
[7 Rather, though they give it not, &c.: redditum, Lat.]
[8 Tertull. de Præscrip. adv. Hær. cap. 20. Irenæus adv. Hær. Lib. iii. cap. 4. See above, Vol. i. p. 28.]
[9 Euseb. H. E. Lib. iv. cap. xiv.]   [10 capitibus, Lat.]
[11 Alibi abunde est demonstratum, Lat.: Bullinger does not necessarily refer to his own writings; yet see Bulling. De Script. sanct. auth. &c. Lib. i. cap. 13.]
[12 A mistake for, I will bring forth: proferam, Lat.]
[13 to all men, omitted : omnibus, Lat.]

perilous a thing it is to receive and allow even those traditions which the most ancient writers do greatly regard, and commend highly unto the church.

Irenæus against the Valentinians, the second book and the XL. chapter, speaketh thus of our Lord. "Therefore he was not far," saith he, "from L. years; and therefore they said unto him, Thou art not L. year old as yet, and hast thou seen Abraham[1]?" And he stablisheth this his opinion by apostolic traditions in the chapter that goeth before, and saith : " He declineth [now] from the XL. or L. year[2], which our Lord having did teach, as the gospel and all the old fathers bear witness, which met together with John, the disciple of our Lord[3], and say that John did deliver them that tradition; for he abode with them until the time of Trajan, and some of them did not only see John, but also other apostles, and heard the same things of them, and they bear witness of such a report[4]." These things, word for word, did that old writer leave, which is numbered to be amongst the eldest : but if we receive and allow that tradition, there shall follow a marvellous confusion of times, though I talk of no other matters. For if our Lord was near hand[5] the fiftieth year of his age (let us grant XLVIII.), it shall follow, that Christ preached xviii. years ; whereas it is sufficiently known, that he began his preaching about the xv. year of Tiberius Cæsar, which was the xxx. year of the Lord : neither do they follow any other account, so many as do reckon the times of Christ. Therefore after the lively tradition of the apostles, which Irenæus followeth very earnestly, Christ should have died, risen again, and ascended into heaven, and have sent the Holy Ghost unto his disciples the vii. or viii. of [the empire of] Claudius Cæsar. But the order of the story of the gospel is contrary unto this reckoning, and also the Acts of the Apostles ; which make mention of Claudius, where as [where] Paul the apostle's matters are entreated, at which time a great dearth and hunger did grievously vex the whole world[6]. Wherefore it is out of all

---

[1] Quinquaginta annos nondum habes, et Abraham vidisti ? Hoc autem con-sequenter dicitur ei, qui jam XL. annos excessit, quinquagesimum autem annum nondum attigit, non tamen multum a quinquagesimo anno absistit.—Irenæus adv. Hær. Lib. II. cap. 40. p. 162. ed. Grabe. Oxon. 1702.]

[2 toward an older age, Lat. omitted.]   [3 in Asia, Lat. omitted.]

[4 — a quadragesimo autem et quinquagesimo anno (Jesus) declinat jam in ætatem seniorem : quam habens Dominus noster docebat, sicut evangelium et omnes seniores testantur, qui in Asia apud Joannem discipulum Domini conve-nerunt, id ipsum tradidisse eis Joannem. Permansit autem cum eis usque ad Trajani tempora. Quidam autem eorum non solum Joannem, sed et alios apo-stolos viderunt, et hæc eadem ab ipsis audierunt, et testantur de hujusmodi rela-tione. —Irenæi adv. Hæres. Lib. II. cap. 39. p. 161. ed. Grabe.]

[5 fere attigit, Lat.]   [6 Acts xi. 28.]

doubt, that the tradition [of the blessed Irenæus], which he fathered upon the apostles of Christ the Lord, doth shamefully beguile men. [But] who can, after such a foul error is spied, believe afterwards those living traditions, though they have the witness even of the most ancient writers? It is likely that he did seek this tradition of Papias of Hieropolis, a disciple of the apostles: for even as Papias greatly regarded living traditions, wherewith men say that he was greatly delighted, [so he] had Irenæus, Apollinarius, and certain other[7], for the reverence of antiquity, the followers of his error of the Millenarians, whose first foundation he laid. And in the mean time the height [high] learned man, Eusebius, bishop of the church of Cæsarea, doth not greatly regard his judgment; for in the third book of his Ecclesiastical History, and the xxxix. chapter, he doth write in express words, that Papias wrote some fables[8]. Why should we therefore be blamed, if we either unwillingly, or not at all, receive those living traditions?

Beside these that I have rehearsed before, this is also to be added: that the notable great strife that rose between the churches of the east and west, concerning the keeping of Easter, sprung up of those lively traditions; wherefore I have [we have] good cause to suspect them. For when as the priests of the west judged that the tradition of Peter and Paul the apostles, concerning keeping of Easter, ought not to be despised, and the Asians did hold that they followed the tradition of St John, there rose up a very hot and sharp contention between the east and the west; insomuch that Victor, a minister of the church of Rome, was not afraid to curse and excommunicate them of Asia; for the which doing he was [in turn] sharply reproved of the [blessed] martyr Irenæus. Moreover, there was found a notable historiographer, called Socrates, who did interpret[9] to speak openly against both the traditions concerning celebrating of Easter, both it of the east and also the west. For after that he had brought forth certain places of scripture, he concluded at the length, that the apostles delivered no tradition to the church concerning the celebration of Easter. If any man require his words they are these: "Neither the apostle, neither the gospels, lay any yoke of bondage upon them which come to the preaching;* but men severally in their own places celebrated the festival of Easter and other feast-days after a certain practice, for the remission of labours

[7 Lactantium, Lat. Lactantius: and certain others, not in Lat.]

[8 Καὶ ἄλλα δὲ ὁ αὐτὸς [ὁ Παπίας] ὡς ἐκ παραδόσεως ἀγράφου εἰς αὐτὸν ἥκοντα παρατέθειται, ξένας τέ τινας παραβολὰς τοῦ Σωτῆρος καὶ διδασκαλίας αὐτοῦ, καί τινα ἄλλα μυθικώτερα... Σφόδρα γάρ τοι σμικρὸς ὢν τὸν νοῦν, &c.— Euseb. H. E. Lib. III. cap. 39. ed. Burton.]

[9 who dared: ausus est, Lat.]

and remembrance of the passion which bringeth salvation, just as pleased them. Neither has our Saviour or his apostles ordained this feast by any commandment to be observed by us; neither do the gospel or the apostles threaten us with any penalty or punishment, as the law of Moses did the Jews." And a little after: "It seems to me, that as many other things in various places passed into custom, so did likewise the festival of Easter, because, as I have said, no apostle appointed anything concerning it[1]," &c. These words are found in his histories, lib. v. cap. 22. This writer therefore contradicted traditions openly, and was charged neither with sacrilege nor heresy for it.* What then should hinder us, but that we [at this day] may speak against such traditions that [as] are contrary unto the scripture? These [things] being so, [and so] plain that they cannot be denied even of our enemies, we will not suffer us [ourselves] to be drawn away [by any means] from the undoubted and sure scripture unto those uncertain [I know not what] traditions. Surely, if those fathers of the council of Trent were sincere, and had a hot zeal to set out the truth clearly and to help the church, doubtless they would suffer themselves and all their doings to be judged of that best and greatest God, and of his most true word. But because they refuse to do that, and set out certain fabulous traditions, they have openly declared unto all the world what help and strength they trust to have for the maintenance of their cause of [out of] the holy scripture.*

Now, that they mix up uncanonical books with the canonical; as the books of the Maccabees, of Tobias, and others, which by other men are called ecclesiastical, or at the least, not canonical; this they do to the same end, that they make traditions equal to the scriptures of God. For they hope to supply out of them that which they see the true canonical books have wanting. For, to say nothing of other particulars; out of the second book of the Maccabees they hope to shew, that it is a wholesome thing to pray and offer for the dead, to be absolved from sins[2]: they hope to prove

[1] Οὐδαμοῦ τοίνυν ὁ ἀπόστολος, οὐδὲ τὰ εὐαγγέλια, ζυγὸν δουλείας τοῖς τῷ κηρύγματι προσελθοῦσιν ἐπέθηκαν·...ὅθεν ἐπειδὴ φιλοῦσι τὰς ἑορτὰς οἱ ἄνθρωποι, διὰ τὸ ἀνίεσθαι τῶν πόνων ἐν αὐταῖς, ἕκαστοι κατὰ χώρας, ὡς ἐβουλήθησαν, τὴν μνήμην τοῦ Σωτηριώδους πάθους ἐξ ἔθους τινὸς ἐπετέλεσαν. Οὐ γὰρ νόμῳ τοῦτο παραφυλάττειν ὁ Σωτὴρ ἢ οἱ ἀπόστολοι ἡμῖν παρήγγειλαν· οὐδὲ καταδίκην ἢ τιμωρίαν ἢ κατάραν, ὡς ὁ Μωϋσέως νόμος τοῖς Ἰουδαίοις, καὶ ἡμῖν τὰ εὐαγγέλια ἢ οἱ ἀπόστολοι διηπείλησαν...Ἐμοὶ δὲ φαίνεται, ὅτι ὥσπερ ἄλλα πολλὰ κατὰ χώρας συνήθειαν ἔλαβεν, οὕτω καὶ ἡ τοῦ Πάσχα ἑορτὴ παρ᾽ ἑκάστοις ἐκ συνηθείας τινὸς ἰδιάζουσαν ἔσχε τὴν παρατήρησιν, διὰ τὸ μηδένα τῶν ἀποστόλων, ὡς ἔφην, μηδενὶ νενομοθετηκέναι περὶ αὐτῆς.—Socrat. Hist. Eccles. Lib. v. cap. 22, p. 292. Cantab. 1720.]

[2] 2 Maccab. xii. 43—45. See Vol. III. p. 396.]

that the prayers of saints in heaven are presented unto God in
behalf of them that are alive in the earth. Whereas, meanwhile,
in the ancient church, among the most faithful and holy ministers
of the churches, the second book of the Maccabees and other books
of the like kind were never accounted among those that are canonical. I am not ignorant indeed that in this instance these men
betake themselves to the patronage of St Augustine, who in his
treatise *De Doct. Christ.*, book II. chap. 8, numbers among the
canonical books, not only those ecclesiastical books, but also the
second book of the Maccabees[3]. But if we consult histories and
the records of the ancients, it will be found that only in the age of
Augustine, in the third council of Carthage, which is said to have
been held in the consulship of Cæsarius and Atticus, when Honorius
and Arcadius were emperors, about the year of our Lord 400 or
399,[4] was it received into the number of canonical, or rather of
ecclesiastical books[5]. Nor does St Augustine conceal this fact:
for in his book *De Civit. Dei*, book XVIII. chap. 36,[6] and in his
treatise against the epistle of Gaudentius, book II. chap. 23,[7] he
states, that the books of the Maccabees were not included in the
canon by the ancients; although he adds, that "it is not without
profit that they have been received, provided only they be read
soberly." Lo, he says, "Provided they be read soberly." And
elsewhere he says, that he "holds them canonical because of the
great and wonderful sufferings of certain martyrs." Now all this
establishes my opinion given above; and chiefly the further saying
of the same writer, that not everything set forth in that book is to
be allowed, unless it be fully tried and compared with the other
scriptures. For in another place also he teaches, that the books

[3 Totus autem canon scripturarum...his libris continetur. Quinque Moyseos
...Sunt aliæ tanquam ex diverso ordine...sicut est Job, et Tobias, et Hester, et
Judith, et Machabeorum libri duo, &c.—Aug. de Doct. Christ. Lib. II. cap. 8.
Opp. Tom. III. fol. 6. col. 2. Par. 1531.]

[4 Anno Christi 397.—Labb. et Coss. Tom. II. col. 1165. Lut. Par. 1671.]

[5 Sunt canonicæ scripturæ Genesis, &c....Tobias, Judith,...Machabæorum
libri duo.—Ibid. can. 47. p. 1177. But see Cosin's Scholastical Hist. of Can. § 82.]

[6 — quorum (principium) supputatio temporum, non in scripturis sanctis quæ
canonicæ appellantur, sed in aliis invenitur: in quibus sunt et Machabæorum
libri, quos non Judæi, sed ecclesia pro canonicis habet propter quorundam
martyrum passiones vehementes atque mirabiles.—Aug. de Civit. Dei, Lib. XVIII.
cap. 36. Opp. Tom. V. fol. 244. col. 3.]

[7 Hanc quidem scripturam, quæ appellatur Macchabæorum, non habent
Judæi sicut legem et prophetas et psalmos.....sed recepta est ab ecclesia non
inutiliter, si sobrie legatur vel audiatur, maxime propter illos Macchabæos, qui
pro Dei lege, sicut veri martyres, a persecutoribus tam indigna atque horrenda
perpessi sunt.—Id. contra Gaudent. Ep. Lib. II. cap. 23. Opp. Tom. VII. fol.
73. col. 4.]

which are received by all are to be preferred to those which are not received by some churches[1]. But we are able to prove, that the books of the Maccabees were never received as canonical by the most ancient and distinguished churches of the east. Melito, bishop of Sardis, who flourished not many years after the death of the apostles, about the year of our Lord 173, under the emperor Antony Verus[2], unto whom also he presented a defence of our faith, recites no other books of the old Testament as canonical but those which Jerome in his prologue, Galeatus[3], gives a list of, leaving out all that are called ecclesiastical. He says also, that he had travelled as far as the East, where the beginning of our preaching had its rise, and where all things occurred which we read in scripture, that there he might search out with diligence all that related to the truth and certainty of the canonical books; and that he there found that precise number[4]. After Melito, Origen also recounts no more books of the old Testament than twenty-two[5]. So likewise St Jerome, not so much in his prologue, Galeatus, as in his epistle to Paulinus concerning all the books of scripture, acknowledges those twenty-two books as canonical; and says that the rest are to be excluded from the canon[6]. The same author, in his prologue to the Proverbs of Solomon, having spoken of the book called the Wisdom of Solomon and Ecclesiasticus, adds: "As therefore the church reads indeed the books of Judith and Tobias and the Maccabees, but does not receive them among the canonical scriptures; so likewise she reads these two books for the edification of the people, but not to establish the authority of ecclesiastical doctrines[7]."

[1 — Tenebit igitur (solertissimus indagator) hunc modum in scripturis ca-nonicis, ut eas, quæ ab omnibus accipiuntur ecclesiis catholicis, præponat eis quas quædam non accipiunt.—Id. de Doct. Christ. Lib. II. cap. 8.]

[2 Marcus Aurelius Antoninus Verus was emperor of Rome from A. D. 161 to 180.]

[3 Hieron. Opp. Tom. I. fol. 317. Par. 1693.]

[4 Ἀνελθὼν οὖν εἰς τὴν ἀνατολὴν, καὶ ἕως τοῦ τόπου γενόμενος ἔνθα ἐκηρύχθη καὶ ἐπράχθη, καὶ ἀκριβῶς μαθὼν τὰ τῆς παλαιᾶς διαθήκης βιβλία, ὑποτάξας ἔπεμψά σοι· ὧν ἐστι τὰ ὀνόματα· Μωϋσέως πέντε· Γένεσις, Ἔξοδος, Ἀριθμοὶ, Λευιτικὸν, Δευτερονόμιον, Ἰησοῦς Ναυῆ, Κριταὶ, Ῥοὺθ, Βασιλειῶν τέσσαρα, Παραλειπομένων δύο, Ψαλμῶν Δαβὶδ, Σολόμωνος Παροιμίαι, ἢ καὶ Σοφία, Ἐκκλησιαστὴς, Ἄσμα ἀσμάτων, Ἰὼβ, Προφητῶν, Ἡσαΐου, Ἱερεμίου· τῶν Δώδεκα ἐν μονοβίβλῳ· Δανιὴλ, Ἰεζεκιὴλ, Ἔσδρας.—B. Melitonis Frag. apud Reliq. Sacr. Tom. I. pp. 119, 110. Oxon. 1846.]

[5 Οὐκ ἀγνοητέον δ' εἶναι τὰς ἐνδιαθήκους βίβλους, ὡς Ἑβραῖοι παραδιδόασιν, δύο καὶ εἴκοσι.—Origen. ap. Euseb. H. E. Lib. VI. cap. 25.]

[6 Hieron. Epist. L. Opp. Tom. IV. Par. 1706.]

[7 Sicut ergo Judith et Tobiæ et Machabæorum libros legit quidem ecclesia, sed inter canonicas scripturas non recipit ; sic et hæc duo volumina (Ecclesiasticus et Sapientia Salomonis) legat ad ædificationem plebis non ad auctoritatem ecclesias-

In the same way we think St Augustine reckoned the second book of the Maccabees among those which are canonical; meaning that it was an ecclesiastical book, but had not like authority with those that are truly and from of old in the canon. Nor could St Jerome be ignorant of the decree of the council of Carthage, seeing that he is said by many writers to have died about the year of our Lord 422.[8] Of the same tendency is the reckoning of Ruffinus of Aquileia, in his Exposition of the Apostles' Creed: for he recounts neither more, nor any other, books of the old Testament than those we have mentioned above. And among other words he says: " These are the books of the old Testament, which, according to the tradition of our elders, are believed to have been inspired by the Holy Spirit himself, and have been handed down to the churches of Christ." And a little after the same author says: " But it is to be known, that there are other books beside, which have been called by our ancestors not canonical, but ecclesiastical; such as the Wisdom of Solomon, Ecclesiasticus, and the books of Tobias, and Judith, and the Maccabees: all which they were content should be read in the churches, but not brought forward to confirm out of them the authority of the faith[9]." Thus he. So then it appears, that we have upon our side the primitive church and all antiquity, which the fathers of the council of Trent strike with their curse because they anathematize us also. For as we do not reject the ecclesiastical books; so agreeably with the old church we contend, that either the truth or falsity of our religion is to be proved or disproved out of the canonical books alone, and appeal to none but the canonical scriptures. Unto which since our adversaries refuse to submit all their doctrines, turning their eyes away to other shadowy defences, it is manifest of what sort their cause is, and what it is they seek by a council called together on such conditions as we have described.

But again : No person, who is well in his senses, condemns and rejects the vulgate Latin version of the Bible altogether : but we all

ticorum dogmatum confirmandam.—Hieron. Proleg. in libros Salomonis. Opp. Tom. I. fol. 939. Par. 1693.]

[8 Jerome is said to have died on the 30th of September, A. D. 420, aged ninety years.—Mosheim, E. H. Vol. I. p. 337, note, ed. Soames.]

[9 Et ideo quæ sunt novi ac veteris instrumenti volumina, quæ secundum majorum traditionem per ipsum Spiritum Sanctum inspirata creduntur, et ecclesiis Christi tradita, competens videtur...sicut ex patrum monumentis accepimus, designare......Sciendum tamen est, quod et alii libri sunt qui non canonici, sed ecclesiastici a majoribus appellati sunt; ut est Sapientia Salomonis......Ecclesiasticus......libellus Tobiæ, et Judith, et Maccabæorum libri :......quæ omnia legi quidem in ecclesiis voluerunt, non tamen proferri ad auctoritatem ex his fidei confirmandam.—Ruffin. Expos. Symb. Apostol. p. 26. Cypriani Opp. Oxon. 1682.]

cry out, that in places that are doubtful, or controverted, or obscurely translated, or corrupted, recourse must be had to the Hebrew and Greek originals; because the authentic book is that which is written in either Hebrew or Greek: for neither the prophets nor the apostles wrote in Latin, but the latter in Greek and the former in Hebrew. And in this instance we demand nothing unjustifiable, and more than what the papists themselves have previously allowed. For in the *Decrees, Distinct.* 9, this Canon is read: "The correctness of the old books is to be tried by the Hebrew volumes, as the correctness of the new must be ruled by the Greek language[1]:" words borrowed out of an epistle of St Augustine's, which he wrote to St Jerome. The same Augustine, in his treatise against Faustus the Manichee, book xi. chap. 2, says: "If a question turn on the fidelity of copies, as in some are diversities of sentences, few however and well known to students in the scriptures, either our doubt must be resolved by codices in other countries, from which the doctrine itself emanated; or if the codices themselves vary, the more in number must be preferred to the fewer, or the older to the more modern; and if doubtful variations yet remain, the earlier language, and that from which the translation was made, must be consulted[2]," &c. Again, the same writer in his treatise *De Doct. Christ.*, book ii. chap. 11, says: "The Latins want two other languages also, that they may attain the knowledge of the scriptures of God; namely, the Hebrew and the Greek: that reference may be made to the first texts, whenever the endless variations of the Latin cause a doubt." Again: "They who translated the scriptures out of Hebrew into Greek may be counted up; but not so they who rendered them into Latin. For in the first times of the faith every man, as he obtained a copy of the Greek text, and seemed to himself to possess some measure of skill in both languages, presumed to make a translation[3]." And in the

[1 Ut veterum librorum fides de Hebræis voluminibus examinanda est, ita novorum Græci sermonis normam desiderat.—Decret. Gratian. distinct. ix. can. 6. Par. 1583.]

[2 Ita si de fide exemplarium quæstio verteretur, sicut in nonnullis, quæ et paucæ sunt et sacrarum literarum studiosis notissimæ sententiarum varietates, vel ex aliarum regionum codicibus, unde ipsa doctrina commeavit, nostra dubitatio dijudicaretur: vel si ibi quoque codices variarent, plures paucioribus, aut vetustiores recentioribus præferrentur. Et si adhuc esset incerta varietas, præcedens lingua, et illud interpretatum est, consuleretur.—Aug. contra Faust. Manich. Lib. xi. cap. 2. Opp. Tom. vi. fol. 51. col. 3. Par. 1531.]

[3 Latinæ linguæ homines et duabus aliis (linguis) ad scripturarum divinarum cognitionem habent opus, Hebræa scilicet et Græca, ut ad exemplaria præcedentia recurratur, si quam dubitationem attulerit Latinorum interpretum infinita varietas...Qui enim scripturas ex Hebræa lingua in Græcam verterunt linguam numerari possunt; Latini autem interpretes nullo modo. Ut enim cuique primis fidei temporibus in manus venit codex Græcus, et aliquantulum facultatis sibimet

twelfth chapter of the same book he adds, speaking of the variety of
translations : " Which thing indeed has rather assisted than hindered
understanding, provided only readers be not negligent: for the examination of a larger number of copies has often served to clear up
some doubtful passages[4]." Now when the fathers of the council of
Trent with one decree lay aside all this, and against all antiquity
and sound reason obtrude upon us the Latin version as an authentic
book, we see manifestly again what is to be looked for from them,
unless we are smitten with blindness. And indeed the fourth canon,
which they have put forth concerning the exposition of scripture,
even should we have learned nothing from those going before, will
alone of itself be able to testify fully, that these men, ere they met
together, had resolved with consummate wickedness to seize to
themselves beforehand most assured victory and the greatest security,
that so they might never seem to change or in ever so slight a degree
to miss their aim. For they condemn all expositions which agree
not with the opinion that holy mother church has held and holds,
and which contradict the unanimous interpretation of the fathers.
For so long as this decree stands, nothing however plain shall be
brought forward out of the scriptures that is against popish doctrines and superstitious ceremonies, but they will be able to evade it
by one word, saying, " The church understands not so." Again,
however foully themselves shall distort and corrupt any passage of
scripture, they will forthwith be able to apply their salve, saying:
" The church understands it so, and some of the fathers have so
explained it." Thus, they will bring forth in support of the pope's
supremacy, " Thou art Peter;" and, " Upon this rock I will build
my church ;" " Thou shalt be called Cephas;" " Feed my lambs."
And should any one desire to sift these passages lawfully, by means
of a sober comparison of scripture with scripture, and to search for
the genuine sense of them, he will be told immediately, that the
church and the fathers expound them of the pope; and therefore
that he must understand them of the pope, and of his principality,
(as they call it.) More instances of this kind I would produce, if
I thought they were wanted.

But from these extracts, that I have made out of the decrees of
the council of Trent, I feel sure it appears more clear than the light,
to what end chiefly the pope has called that council : namely, not

---

utriusque linguæ habere videbatur, ausus est interpretari.—Aug. de Doct. Christ.
Lib. ii. cap. 11. Opp. Tom. iii. fol. 6. col. 3. Par. 1531.]

[4 Quæ quidem res plus adjuvit intelligentiam quam impedivit, si modo
legentes non sint negligentes. Nam nonnullas obscuriores sententias plurium
codicum sæpe manifestavit inspectio.—Aug. ibid.]

that the truth might be drawn forth and illustrated from the scriptures, but that scripture itself might be degraded, and serve those men's dignity, honours, and wealth, and the maintenance and establishment of superstition; not that churches might be reformed, but that those churches, which have begun to emerge, might be reduced to their former condition of deformity.

And therefore, whereas, through God's singular grace, the light of Christ has shone upon the famous realm of England, do not you turn back your eyes from that light, which whosoever follows walks "not in darkness, but has the light of life[1]." Go forward, go forward, under the guidance of Christ, in reforming what needs to be reformed! It will be no sin, although you never again reconcile yourselves to that late upstart church of Rome. I give place here to no wrong spirit : for I have proved by invincible arguments, in the beginning of this my fifth decade, that we must needs come out of her altogether, and consecrate ourselves to Christ only and to the true church of Christ.

This decade I inscribe and dedicate to your piety, most illustrious Prince, as to a vigorous maintainer of real godliness; nothing doubting but you will take upon yourself the faithful patronage of these my studies; especially after you shall have read them with diligence, and discover that I have advanced nothing without the authority of scripture and contrary to true piety, but everything from the scriptures of God and in defence of the true religion. For I desire that not the smallest weight should be granted to myself and my writings, unless I justify all my statements with express scriptures and solid reasons fetched out of the scripture. And although your piety needs none of my teaching, seeing that it is well enough instructed in true religion, and is surrounded with most learned and godly men on all sides, of whom master Robert Skinner and master Andrew Wullock[2], very excellent individuals, are none of the least; yet do I entertain the hope, that these labours of mine will be pleasing to you, and that you will take in good part my dedication which has proceeded from a good mind: for truly I seek in it nothing else than the public weal; that is, that the kingdom of God's Son, which has begun to flourish anew in these our times, when the terrible judgment of the Son of God is close at hand and already knocking at our doors, may spread abroad far and wide, as well among you in the famous realm of England, as everywhere else in the earth.

Other men indeed in their epistles of dedication celebrate his praises, to whom they inscribe their books: but knowing full well that you care for no such applause, and require no such commenda-

[1 John viii. 12.]   [2 See Orig. Lett. pp. 401, 407, 409, 422.]

tions, because your virtue is otherwise sufficiently distinguished, and yourself also labour day by day to increase it with modesty and humility; I have made it my aim rather in my epistle to exhort your piety, as diligently as I am able, to outdo yourself in the most excellent pursuit and increase of virtues. Whatever things are in men worthy to be praised, all are the gifts of our Lord God. The Lord gave you the mind to discern, that while it is justly esteemed a great favour to be sprung from the royal line[3], it is a far greater and nobler distinction to be called, and to be truly, a son of God, and a joint-heir with Christ Jesus, God's Son. As then you enjoy, by the grace of God, this highest nobility, look to it that you keep it even unto the end by a diligent following after godliness; look to it that you cleave constantly to Christ the Redeemer, and further his glory; look to it that, out of the faith which you keep unto the King of everlasting glory, you continue to be faithful also to the King's most serene majesty and to the whole of the famous realm of England, your most dear father-land. Hitherto have you been to strangers (whom the Lord has especially commended to our regards) a defence and refuge; and, in one word, the tower and pattern of studious and learned men. Go on to be the same! So shall you obtain, not a perishing but an everlasting glory in this world and in the world to come.

Be pleased, I beseech you, to deliver my commendations to that high-minded champion, lord John Dudley, earl of Warwick[4], a nobleman every way most eminent; on whom I pray every blessing may descend, and to whom I present all my duty.

The Lord Jesus, the supreme and only Sovereign of the universe, the King of kings and Lord of lords, preserve in safety your most serene king and all the whole famous realm of England; also the counsellors of the realm, most faithful and wise, and yourself also, most gentle prince!

Zurich in Switzerland. The month of March. 1551.[5]

[3] Henry Grey, marquis of Dorset, married Frances, daughter of Charles Brandon, duke of Suffolk, by Mary Tudor, sister of Henry VIII.—See Orig. Lett. p. 399, note 2.]

[4] See Orig. Lett. pp. 407, 409, 422.]

[5] For the reception of this letter and decade, see Orig. Lett. ṗp. 3, 7, 277, 279, 428, 429, 436, 498, 574.]

APPENDIX II.

[1] TO THE MOST ILLUSTRIOUS MEN, MASTERS RODOLPH GUALTER, PETER SIMLER, JOHN STUMPHIUS, JOHN BLU- MEN[2], JOHN SEILER, HADRIAN HOSPINIAN[3], NICHOLAS SCHNEIDER[4], AND JOHN HUGO, DEANS OR ARCHPRESBY- TERS[5]; AND TO ALL THE MINISTERS OF CHRIST AND OF THE CHURCHES OF THE CLASSES[6] OF THE ZÜRICH- SEE, FREYAMT, STEIN, WINTERTHUR, ELGG, WE- RIKON, AND REGENSPERG, IN THE TERRI- TORY OF ZURICH; HIS REVEREND AND VERY BELOVED FELLOW-MINISTERS AND BRETHREN; GREETING.

IF any other age has furnished a fruitful subject for discourse, this time present of ours furnishes the most fruitful; for what happens and what threatens Christendom at this day, is too evident to require many words to declare it. The just Lord is angry at our sins, and punishes them also; nay, he is preparing far heavier calamities to pour out on the heads of the impenitent. Our duty is then to watch for the Lord's flock, and on the approach of the sword to give timely warning to all the sheep committed to our trust, that the blood of those who perish be not required at our hands. Me- thinks, therefore, I shall do a profitable work, if I talk with you, reverend fellow-ministers and most dear brethren, of the right dis- charge of our duty in this dangerous age, and of the sure method whereby we may piously appease the anger of God provoked by our sins. I know with whom I speak; even with men, who are per- fectly skilled in the things of God. I shall therefore study to be brief.

The sins of men must be set forth and accused.   That the most righteous Lord is angry at the sins of men, is beyond a doubt: and it follows therefore, that to wash away sins is the only way of appeasing the divine wrath. But sins are not washed away without being acknowledged first, and afterward put away by faith and repentance. Wherefore, if we desire according to our office that anger and severe punishments be taken off from the Lord's flock, we must of necessity shew and accuse the sins of men, and also teach faith and enforce repentance. For the Lord by Ezekiel says: " Wilt thou judge, son of man, wilt thou judge the bloody city ? Shew her all her abominations, and say, O city, that sheddest blood in the midst of her, that her time may come; and

---

[1 This dedication also is omitted in the English translation. It was prefixed to the original edition of Decades I. and II.]

[2 Florus, Lat.]   [3 Wirt. Germ.]
[4 Sarctorius, Lat.]   [5 See above, page 117.]
[6 Classium, Lat. Haller translates the word, *Capiteln*.]

maketh idols against herself, to defile herself! Thou art become guilty in thy blood that thou hast shed, and hast defiled thyself in thine idols which thou hast made; and thou hast caused thy days to draw near: therefore I will deliver thee unto the heathen. Behold thy princes, every one was to their power to shed blood. In thee have they set light by father and mother. They have dealt by reproach with the stranger that is in the midst of thee. In thee have they vexed the fatherless and the widow. Thou hast despised mine holy things, and hast profaned my sabbaths. In thee were men of deceit to shed blood: and in thee they eat upon the mountains; and in thee they go about the wickedness they have thought on. In thee have they discovered their father's nakedness; in thee have they humbled her that was set apart for pollution; and every one hath committed abomination with his neighbour's wife, and every one hath lewdly defiled his daughter-in-law; every one in thee hath humbled his sister, his father's daughter. In thee have they taken gifts to shed blood; thou hast taken usury and increase; and thou hast greedily gained of thy neighbour by extortion, and hast forgotten me, saith the Lord God. And behold, I have clapped my hands at thy covetousness which thou hast practised, and at thy blood which hath been in the midst of thee. And canst thou prevail in the day that I shall arise against thee? I will scatter thee among the heathen, and disperse thee in the countries, and will make an end of thy filthiness which is in thee[7]." Thus far have I quoted word for word, brethren, out of Ezekiel; and the more freely, because these verses present us with a certain general form not of reproving sins only, but of judging also what sins God most especially hates and would have rebuked very sharply. For again and again must we take heed, lest as blind guides we strain out a gnat and swallow a camel; I mean, lest we tarry on small errors and faults, blaming and chasing away them, and pass by, without once touching them, enormous crimes and wickednesses.

Wherefore this passage of Ezekiel shews, and other places of holy scripture declare also, what crimes are most of all to be abhorred; namely, those which directly tend to subvert the glory of God, to oppress justice and holiness, and to cast aside charity. I am aware that these awful crimes do not reign, God be thanked! nor are found in every several church. Different churches have different disorders. Nor is it beneficial to set before a people these horrible crimes, if they be not found among them. But the part of a wise pastor is, to consider diligently what is adapted for each church, what is proper for it, useful, and necessary; and to insist upon that.

, [7 Ezek. xxii. 1-15.]

But things that are not condemned by the judgment of God in the scriptures, and that do not militate against the points above mentioned, those we ought not to attack; for they sin grievously who condemn as sins what God has not condemned. "Woe unto them," says Isaiah, the beloved of God, "that call evil good, and good evil; that put darkness for light, and light for darkness; that put bitter for sweet, and sweet for bitter." In this matter then nothing may be done by us after our own mind, but we must judge and do rather after the commandment of God. Yet must we take heed that we do not, like some persons, palliate sins; but, as the proverb has it, call a spade a spade, and a fig a fig, and speak with plainness, though withal soberly and modestly. Far from us be also the gall of bitterness and the depraved affection of the flesh; far from us be an unruly tongue; far be banter, unclean words, and abusiveness; lest we be thought to transgress the bounds of decency, and to be possessed with the lust of evil-speaking, rather than to burn with zeal for God, and truth, and righteousness. Let it appear to impartial hearers, that we reprove with the feeling of a father, and assail sinners of mankind from a desire to save and not to destroy them; that we attack the crime and not the person of the criminal. For in the case of the ministers of God's word freedom of speech in the church is honesty of heart, and not the ungoverned passion of one possessed and disordered with envy. Neither are all things lawful for ministers, neither are all things expedient. And therefore no good man can approve the wanton boldness and the abusive evil temper of some, who think they have not fulfilled their duty, unless they have poured forth and emptied out upon their unfortunate hearers whole cart-loads of abuse without all measure and discrimination. The examples of the prophets give no support to such ravings as these; and they are wrongly applied, because circumstances are overlooked. Let the rebuke or fault-finding of the ministers of the truth be prudent rather than daring; sober and well-weighed, and not light and loose: let it glow not with passion, but with fervency of spirit; let it be chaste, modest, and holily tempered with a just severity, and come down upon the guilty individual and hold him fast rather by matter-of-fact plainness, transparency, and majesty, than pierce by profusion of ill words: I mean, wound the guilty conscience by a lively setting forth of sin, and by exposing the foulness or enormity of bad deeds, rather than exasperate it by scoffings and impure quips. And certain is it, men are deeply moved, whenever they are brought to understand clearly, that the things they go about are directed against God, and tend to the destruction of their body and the eternal ruin of their soul.

Isai. v.

The way of accusing sins.

Still in vain and fruitlessly shall we have attacked sin, if we do *Sins must be acknow-* not at the same time urge faith and repentance. When he has been *ledged and confessed.* provoked, God is not appeased by a few ceremonies and commonplace acts, which are trifling and brought to us by human tradition. "In vain do they worship me," saith the Lord, "teaching for doctrines the commandments of men[1]." Nay, the Lord is highly indignant, when we persist in seeking reconciliation with him by some absurd worshipping of God. For he cries by Jeremiah: "Amend your ways and your doings, and I will cause you to dwell in this place. But behold, ye trust in lying words that cannot profit. Will ye steal, murder, and commit adultery, and swear falsely, and walk after other gods, and come and stand before me in this house, which is called by my name, and say, We are delivered to do all these abominations? Is this house which is called by my name become a den of robbers in your eyes[2]?" Wherefore let us lay aside false doctrine, and learn from God's word what kind of conversion pleases him, and what is true repentance and faith.

When sins have been rebuked sharply by the ministers of God's *Dan. ix.* word; then the word of truth requires of godly hearers, that they acknowledge with the heart the sins that have been laid to their charge, and which they have practised against God's law; and confess them to the omniscient and omnipotent God, unto whom all hearts be open, and ascribe all glory unto God who is true and righteous, but unto themselves lying, wickedness, and confusion of face. For the apostle and evangelist St John says: "If we say that we have no sin, we deceive ourselves; we make God a liar, and the truth is not in us[3]." In Jeremiah we read also: "Wherefore makest thou thy way good, when it is evil? Thou sayest, I am innocent: but I will judge thee. Is not the blood of the poor found in thy skirts[4]?" And in the gospel the Lord says: "If ye were blind, ye should have no sin. But now ye say, We see; therefore your sin remaineth[5]." Before all things then acknowledgment and confession of sins is indispensable. This goes before humiliation in the sight of God.

For whoso acknowledges his sins and confesses them to God from *Need of hu-miliation* the heart, he must humble himself before God. He groans, mourns, *and sorrow.* yea, draws sighs even from his breast. He is ashamed, that so often and in such unworthy ways he has offended his most indulgent Father; and he casts himself on that account in the dust at the Lord's feet. In this manner the woman in the city, which was a sinner, came to our Lord as he sat at meat; and Peter, when

[1 Matt. xv. 9.]   [2 Jer. vii. 3, 8-11.]   [3 John i. 8-10.]
[4 Jer. ii. 33-35.]   [5 John ix. 41.]

he had denied his Lord, went out from the palace of the high-priest; and prostrated themselves before the Lord, and shed tears in great abundance. David cries: "Thine arrows stick fast in me, and thy hand presseth me sore. There is no soundness in my flesh, because of thine anger; neither is there any rest in my bones, because of my sin. For mine iniquities have gone over mine head: as an heavy burden they are too heavy for me. I declare mine iniquity, and am sorry for my sin. My soul also is sore vexed. I am weary with my groaning: all the night make I my bed to swim, I water it with my tears[1]." In these terms he expresses the intense grief which was wrought in him, and which proceeded from the acknowledgment of his sins: and he has left unto us in them a true pattern of true repentance.

We must believe that our sins are forgiven for Christ's sake. However, to acknowledge and confess our sins, and to humble ourselves in the sight of the Lord, and to be sorry, will not suffice, unless we believe also that all our sins are forgiven us for Christ's sake. For Judas greatly grieved, because he had betrayed Christ; he heartily confessed his sin, saying, "I have sinned in that I have betrayed the innocent blood:" nay, he brought again into the temple the price of blood[2], which he had received from those robbers. But because he had no true faith in the Lord Jesus, his sorrow and confession availed nothing. We must before all things therefore teach and enforce faith: that faith, I mean, by which penitents believe that their sins are forgiven them freely for Christ's sake. But this is a truth, which we must establish and prove by manifest promises of God and undoubted examples: for the apostle witnesseth, "Faith cometh by hearing, and hearing by the word of God[3]." Nay, by so much the more is it needful to do this, and to prove this point with all diligence, by how much the more violently the minds of believers are assaulted on this head.

I will not allege testimonies out of the law and the prophets, (although they exist there in large abundance,) but only from the writings of the evangelists and apostles, which teach with one accord that unto them that believe sins are forgiven freely for Christ's sake. The Baptist, our Lord's forerunner, points the finger to the

John i. Lord Jesus Christ himself, and cries: "Behold the Lamb of God, which taketh away the sin of the world." For the apostle John has

1 John i. ii. said: "The blood of the Son of God cleanseth us from all sin. For he is the propitiation for our sins; and not for ours only, but also for the sins of the whole world." Nay, the Lord Jesus himself tes-

John iii. tifies of these things, and says: "As Moses lifted up the serpent in

[1 Psal. xxxviii. 2-4, 18; vi. 3, 6.]
[2 Matt. xxvii. 3-5.]
[3 Rom. x. 17.]

the wilderness, even so must the Son of man be lifted up; that whosoever believeth in him should not perish, but have eternal life." The apostle Paul bears witness also, and says: "This is a faithful 1 Tim. i. saying, and worthy of all acceptation, that Christ Jesus came into the world to save sinners." For Peter said also: "To Christ give Acts x. all the prophets witness, that through his name whosoever believeth in him shall receive remission of sins." Examples also of the free forgiveness of sins and acceptance into favour to those who believe in Christ, or are penitent, the scripture, and more especially the gospels, present us with without number. Of this sort are the cases of Matthew, Zaccheus, the woman which was a sinner, Peter, Paul, the dying thief on the cross, and many more. These things, there-fore, let the faithful minister of Christ enforce in the church without ceasing, that no one may be swallowed up with sorrow, and stricken with conscience of sins, and pine away, and despair, and be lost. Let every one believe, that the heavenly Father is appeased toward him for the sake of the death, and righteousness, and redemption that is by Christ. For thus by faith only[4] is peace and tranquillity vouchsafed to troubled consciences.

And yet the faith, which believeth that our heavenly Father is Faith stirreth appeased toward us for the sake of Christ, and will not any more ers. up to pray-punish us for the sins we have committed—the faith which calms our spirits and tranquillises our consciences—removes not all anxiety out of our bosoms, nor introduces a torpid slothfulness, but rather stirs us up to prayers and all godly duties. Abraham believed God; but he did not on that account cease to pray: nay, the more surely he believed that he should receive the divine promises, the more fervently did he pray. David doubted not in the least that he should have of the Lord the thing he had promised him: yet not-withstanding he prayed without ceasing. Wherefore the people must carefully be instructed by us, not to give over pouring out supplications and prayers before the Lord, that he would have mercy upon us for Christ's sake, and turn away his anger from us, and give and increase in us true faith, and ever rule us with his Spirit, and in a word deliver us from all evils both of our soul and body, and grant us peace and safety; and that to our princes and magistrates he would vouchsafe wisdom, prudence, courage, justice, and happiness. But in all these prayers the people must be care-ful, that they call on none other than God the Father alone through his well-beloved and only Son, our Lord Jesus Christ; that so they may not pray without faith and charity. For he that wavereth in his faith may not think that he shall receive anything. And he

[4 sola fide, Lat.]

that bringeth his gift to the altar must first be reconciled to his brother, and then let him offer his gift. And let all be kept in the practice of prayer by that word of our Lord's in the gospel: "Ask, and it shall be given you; seek, and ye shall find; knock, and it shall be opened unto you. For every one that asketh receiveth; and he that seeketh findeth; and to him that knocketh it shall be opened. Or what man is there of you, whom if his son ask bread, will he give him a stone? Or if he ask a fish, will he give him a serpent? If ye then, being evil, know how to give good gifts unto your children, how much more shall your Father which is in heaven give good things to them that ask him[1]!"

Furthermore, we must live holily, righteously, and unblameably. Holy Jeremiah, however, although he prayed at times for the Lord's people fervently and continually, yet heard from the Lord this word: "Pray not thou for this people, neither lift up cry nor prayer for them, neither make intercession to me: for I will not hear thee. Seest thou not what they do in the city and in the field? The children gather wood, and the fathers kindle the fire, and the women knead their dough, to make cakes to the queen of heaven, and to pour out drink-offerings unto other gods, that they may provoke me to anger[2]." Wherefore no one will think, that the wrath of the Lord can be appeased with prayers only, however long or many, if yet we go on to provoke it daily by iniquities. Let us urge the people committed to our charge therefore, while they pray earnestly and without ceasing, to amend their evil manners also; that is, to lay aside covetousness, usury, pride, incest, adulteries, fornication, luxury, drunkenness, surfeiting, blasphemies, slandering, idolatry, superstition, ungodliness, anger, envy, wrong and venal judgment, blood-shedding, unjust and mercenary warfare[3], and oppression and contempt of the poor; and to serve God in Christ with doing good, liberality, humility, modesty, chastity, continence, sobriety, fastings, blessing, thanksgiving, religion, godliness, tenderness, benevolence, judgment and justice, vindicating and care of the poor, faith, hope, charity, love of our country, obedience and heart[4], patience, and all other virtues. For most truly has Solomon, the wisest of men, said: "He that turneth away his ear from hearing the law, even his prayer shall be abomination[5]." Yet should we do all which is commanded us, still let us say, as the Lord has taught us in the gospel: "We are unprofitable servants; we have done that which was our duty to do[6]:" believing however, that for the sake of Christ and for the

[1 Matt. vii. 7-11.] [2 Jer. vii. 16-18.]
[3 See Vol. I. page 277, note 5.] [4 spiritu, Lat.]
[5 Prov. xxviii. 9.] [6 Luke xvii. 10.]

merits of Christ, and not for our own sake or our merits, we are pleasant and acceptable unto God the Father.

Finally, in addition to all this we need long-suffering, patience, and a hope stedfast and unmoved by all dangers which come about us, that our faith may not fail, and that we may never waver in our hope, or place our confidence in things that perish. Let that excellent saying of the Lord by Isaiah be before the eyes of all therefore: "In sitting still and rest shall ye be saved; in quietness and in confidence shall be your strength: and ye would not. But ye said, No; for we will flee upon horses: therefore shall ye flee," and your trust shall perish "as a breach ready to fall." Here is the place then, to tear away from men and to break up all the defences whereon this world is commonly prone to lean, that they may be stript and made destitute of every thing, and hang upon heaven alone. Still, let them not despise the means and instruments that are allowed, or even commanded, or not forbidden of God; but only not attribute more to them than piety allows, nor trust in them altogether by themselves. For "except the Lord keep the city, the watchman waketh but in vain[7]." Except the Lord supply strength and counsel to the senate, however otherwise most wise; or to the army, though it be most strong and well appointed; it perishes in the twinkling of an eye, it is thrown into confusion, and scattered like dust before the wind. Wonderfully applicable to this subject is the prophecy of Obadiah: for with remarkable comprehensiveness he shews, of how little avail those things would be in which the Edomites trusted;— places fortified by nature and art, wisdom, riches, treaties, and most experienced soldiers. And by Jeremiah also the Lord says: "Let not the wise man glory in his wisdom, neither let the mighty man glory in his might, let not the rich man glory in his riches: but let him that glorieth glory in this, that he understandeth and knoweth me, that I am the Lord, which exercise loving-kindness, judgment, and righteousness, in the earth; for in these things I delight, saith the Lord."

And now, briefly to sum up what I have discoursed of with you, reverend and most dear fellow-ministers and brethren:— We have learnt by all that has been said, that God, when he is provoked by our sins, cannot otherwise be appeased than by our acknowledging every one of us and confessing our sins, which the word of God has brought home to us, and which we have committed against God our Father; by our humbling ourselves, and sorrowing before our God with all our heart; by our not yielding to despair on account of our sins, but believing without doubt that they are

Margin notes: There is need of patience and unmoved hope. Isai. xxx. Jer. ix. The sum of all.

[7 Psal. cxxvii. 1.]

done away entirely and forgiven us, not for our sake or merits, but for the sake of Jesus Christ our Lord, the Saviour of the whole world, upon whom the heavenly Father laid all the sins of the world, for which the same Son of God made satisfaction upon the cross; finally, by continuing in supplication and prayer without ceasing, and serving the God, who hath redeemed us, and whose we are altogether, with true repentance and worthy fruits of repentance, with a stedfast hope, with love unfeigned, with kindness, benevolence, righteousness, holiness, patience, and innocence.

Isai. liii.

This method is most sure.   That this is the only way of escaping the evils that hang over our heads; this the only method of appeasing the wrath of God; the scripture of both testaments bears witness in every part. God had decreed to overthrow the people of Nineveh, and provided that that overthrow should be proclaimed to the Ninevites by the most illustrious prophet Jonah. He appointed also a space of forty days, after which the city should fall. But when the people of Nineveh believed God, and repented, and cried unto the Lord with continual prayer, God spared the penitents and saved them. Nay, did not the Jews require, with impious and sacrilegious clamours, that Jesus Christ, the Son of God, the Saviour of the world, should be crucified? And yet Peter cries and teaches, that such great wickedness as that may be done away with true faith and faithful repentance. Let us then not doubt, brethren, concerning a truth which is established by so many and such manifest testimonies.

Acts v.

Of God's decree against sinners.   I know what some persons object against this statement:—that it is vain to enforce repentance, for it can profit nothing, because of the sentence which God has pronounced, and because of God's immutable decree, by which he has determined to cut us off for our sins. But if we examine the scripture more closely, that speaks not of God's decree so harshly. For in Jeremiah we read these words: "At what instant I shall speak concerning a nation, and concerning a kingdom, to pluck up, and to pull down, and to destroy it; if that nation, against whom I have pronounced, turn from their evil, I will repent of the evil that I thought to do unto them." And a most apposite example I brought even now out of the prophet Jonah, in the instance of the Ninevites, against whom sentence of destruction was uttered, but was recalled immediately on the repentance of the people of Nineveh. For the sentence of overthrow was delivered with this condition, if they abode in impenitence. A like passage is found in Deut. ix. For Moses says: "I fell down before the Lord forty days and forty nights, because the Lord had said he would destroy you. I prayed therefore to the Lord, and his anger was appeased." Wherefore let not the decree of God, which he has

Jer. xviii.

pronounced against sinners, deter any one from repentance, or from importunate prayer; for just as that decree is immutable against the ungodly, so it stands not at all in the way of penitents.

But again: should any one find an objection in the sins of our fathers, Ezekiel has replied already in his eighteenth chapter. For he sternly rebukes the parable, which some also in his time cast in the way of repentance, saying: "The fathers have eaten sour grapes, and the children's teeth are set on edge." And after a long disputation he concludes at last: "The soul that sinneth it shall die. The son shall not bear the iniquity of the father; neither shall the father bear the iniquity of the son. The righteousness of the righteous shall be upon him; and the wickedness of the wicked shall be upon him." *The sins of fathers hurt not penitents.*

I know all do not repent of the sins they have committed. But shall the repentance of believers be on that account unprofitable? Rather, we read in not a few cases, that many sinners have been spared for the sake of a very few good and righteous persons. Besides, the Lord by Isaiah says expressly: "Say ye to the righteous, that it shall be well with him; for they shall eat the fruit of their doings. Woe unto the wicked! it shall be ill with him; for the reward of his hands shall be given him[1]." Righteous Lot is led by angels out of the city of Sodom, and the wicked city with all its inhabitants is consumed by fire from heaven. Hezekiah, the faithful king, is delivered from the danger that threatened him, and out of the hand of the Assyrians, who were about to assault the city; and Shebna, the scribe, perishes shamefully[2]. King Zedekiah is taken, and led away into captivity; and Jeremiah is saved from death, and receives his liberty. Most truly therefore said St Peter: "The Lord knoweth how to deliver the godly out of temptations, and to reserve the unjust unto the day of judgment to be punished[3]." Therefore, let us stedfastly cultivate virtues, for our labour shall not be in vain. If the Lord visits the earth with some common calamity on account of sins and flagrant iniquities, he will nevertheless not forget them that fear him and call upon his name, although they may be involved in like evils with the ungodly, and seem to share the same end as the wicked. *The repentance of believers is not vain.*

But certain it is that a kingdom or commonweath, which repents not and is impious and refractory, cannot long endure. Nay, even the preaching of the gospel shall not profit such despisers of God and of the divine laws. For again the Lord says by Jeremiah: "At what instant I shall speak concerning a nation, and concerning a kingdom, to build and to plant it; if it do evil in my sight, that it *The impenitent perish.*

[1 Isai. iii. 10, 11.]   [2 Isai. xxii. 15-19.]   [3 2 Pet. ii. 9.]

obey not my voice, then I will repent of the good wherewith I said I would benefit them." Still let no one forthwith despair, when he sees a people, that is inclined to wickedness, rush on from sin to sin : but if you see many breaking forth in their obstinate love of iniquity, harden your heart also, and all the more oppose yourself to them with zealous desire of that which is just and true. For in such a case we must remember the words of the apostle, where he says:

2 Tim. ii. " The servant of the Lord must be gentle unto all men, apt to teach, patient, in meekness instructing those that oppose themselves ; if God peradventure will give them repentance to the acknowledging of the truth; and that they may recover themselves out of the snare of the devil, who are taken captive by him at his will." And truly, great are the rewards set before us, brethren, if we be faithful and earnest; as on the other hand horrible punishment with everlasting shame is prepared for the unfaithful and slothful. Let us therefore

Matt. xxiv. " watch and pray." Let this doctrine of our Lord Jesus Christ be always before our eyes : " Who then is a faithful and wise servant, whom his lord hath made ruler over his household, to give them meat in due season ? Blessed is that servant, whom his lord, when he cometh, shall find so doing. Verily I say unto you, that he shall make him ruler over all his goods. But and if that evil servant shall say in his heart, My lord delayeth his coming; and shall begin to smite his fellow-servants, and to eat and drink with the drunken ; the lord of that servant shall come in a day when he looketh not for him, and in an hour that he is not aware of, and shall cut him asunder, and appoint him his portion with the hypocrites : there shall be weeping and gnashing of teeth." Let these things, I say, be ever before our eyes and minds: and let us pray that God will grant us his principal Spirit [1], and increase it in us day by day; so that by his inspiration and guidance we may discharge the office, which the Lord has assigned us, faithfully and very fruitfully.

These sermons truly I have written, that I might bestow my labours upon you, assist your own studies, or even stimulate each one of you to think and find out more ; but not that every one should use them word for word in the church confided to his care. For selection and judgment is needed, that we may not speak to our own church what is foreign to it, or little profitable and necessary for it. Let the wise pastor consider well of what kind are the morals of the people of his charge, and what things are most requisite for them, and so set them before them, having regard always to edification, true faith, piety, charity, and innocence. For we must both

[¹ See Vol. ii. page 147, note 6.]

teach and admonish, that the church over which it hath pleased the Lord to set us may be godly and holy. Certain forms of sermons, therefore, I put forth, by which I desire also to gratify those who have for many years asked this of me. And in all these, and with regard to all points, I would have that most just rule of the apostle to prevail with all readers: "Prove all things; hold fast that which is good[2]." Nor am I much affected by the slanders of those who cry out, that such sermons make the brethren idle; as was the case formerly when the sermons of Discipulus[3] and Pelbart[4] were read. For I have on my side the example of the greatest luminaries in the church: I mean, the most eminent bishops in the church, who themselves also wrote sermons and homilies to the great profit of the church. The idle are always idle, even though nothing at all be written.

Before these sermons I have set the oldest creeds, as well of the most ancient councils in the church, as of the most orthodox fathers or bishops; to no other end than to shew, that our doctrine and faith, which has among many at this day a very ill name and is most unjustly accused of heresy, is agreeable with the doctrine of the apostles, and of the primitive church, which from the beginning delivered nothing to be believed and taught but what we believe and teach in our churches at this day. Innocent, the third of that name, was the first to presume to add more articles than the ancient creeds of the christian faith set forth. His creed is found in the Decretals, cap. *Firmiter credimus*[5]. He occupied the see of Rome about the year of our Lord 1215; and published his creed at the Lateran council.

But ye, brethren, inasmuch as you know whom you have believed, and that the doctrine of our faith is christian, apostolical, catholic, orthodox, and true, the ancient and undoubted faith and doctrine, continue stedfast in holding it and teaching it! Truth ever conquers: it may be pressed, but it cannot be oppressed. The truth of the Lord, says the prophet, abideth for ever. And the Lord in the gospel says: "The gates of hell shall not prevail against it;" that is, against the church that is placed on the rock, which Peter confessed when he said, "Thou art Christ, the Son of the living

[2 1 Thess. v. 21.]

[3 John Herolt, of the order of Dominicans, was commonly called *Discipulus*, because, as himself says, he compiled his published sermons, "collecti ex diversis sanctorum dictis et ex pluribus libris, non per modum magistri, sed per modum *discipuli*." They are commended (ed. Nuremb. 1520) as "opus perutile simplicibus curam animarum gerentibus."]

[4 Pelbartus Osvaldus, an Hungarian Franciscan, who flourished A.D. 1501, and wrote many sermons.—Mosheim, E. H. Vol. III. p. 52. ed. Soames.]

[5 Decretal. Gregor. Pap. IX. Lib. I. tit. 1. p. 7. Par. 1585. See Vol. III. p. 82.]

God;" and concerning which Paul disputed and said, "That rock was Christ." "For other foundation can no man lay than that is laid, which is Christ Jesus[1]." For the Holy Spirit also foretold by the prophets: "Behold, I lay in Zion for a foundation a stone, a corner stone, elect, precious: and he that believeth on him shall not be confounded[2]." Upon this foundation therefore, Christ Jesus, who elsewhere is called "the foundation of the prophets and apostles[3]," let us settle the people or churches committed to our charge: that so, according to the doctrine of St Peter, the teacher of our church, we also, "as lively stones, may be built up a spiritual house, an holy priesthood, to offer up spiritual sacrifices, acceptable to God by Jesus Christ our Lord[4]." This if we do faithfully, the Lord will never leave us: for whether we live or die, the Lord will be our rock, reward, life, and recompence.

Receive then these my labours with indulgence, and take them in good part. They come forth under the name of you all, whom from my heart I love, and whom I desire faithfully to serve. Farewell; and be ever mindful of these words of the apostle: "Take heed to the ministry which ye have received of the Lord, that ye fulfil it[5]."

Your brother and fellow-minister,
With all his heart,
HENRY BULLINGER.

Zurich, 1 March, 1549.

[1 Matt. xvi. 18. 1 Cor. x. 4 ; iii. 11.]   [2 Isai. xxviii. 16.]
[3 Eph. ii. 20.]   [4 1 Pet. ii. 5.]
[5 Col. iv. 17.]

INDEX

OF SUBJECTS AND PERSONS.

The former number marks the Volume, the latter the page.

INDEX

OF VARIOUS WRITERS QUOTED AND REFERRED TO.

ERRATA.

VOLUME I.

Page 17, line 13, for *prophets : in* read *prophets in.* See below, p. 158.
  „ 22, „ 28, „ *in* read *is.*
  „ 110, „ 6, „ 2 „ 11.
  „ 148, note 2, „ *lib.* „ *Epist. LVII.*

VOLUME III.

Page 131, note 3, for *spiritalibus* read *spiratilibus.*
  „ 352, line 7, „ *Job* read *Joh.*

VOLUME IV.

Page xvi. line 28, for *numeros* read *nummos.*
  „ xxx. „ 18, „ *Nov.* 1   „ *Nov.* 10.
  „ 273, note 3, „ 259 read 258.
  „ 275, „ 8, „ 272 „ 262.
  „ 282, „ 2, „ 274 „ 273.
  „ 392, „ 6, „ 365 „ 366.

DELENDA.

VOLUME IV.

Page xxviii, line 14, dele *them.*

ADDENDA.

VOLUME I.

Page 10, note 2. Non videtur prætereundum, quod Eusebius hasce epistolas (i. e. Dionysii) *catholicas* vocet: forte, quia in ecclesiis piorum solitæ sint legi, sicut Clementis.—Centuriat. Magd. Cent. II. cap. 10.
  „ 13, „ 4. See page 56.
  „ 51, „ 7. Bullinger adopts Erasmus' suggestion of *Polyhistor*, instead of philoïstoros, in his edition of Jerome's Works, Tom. IV. Col. 4. Par. 1533.
  „ 58, line 23. See Bulling. adv. Anabapt. Lib. II. fol. 74.
  „ 67, „ 8. die : concidat, Lat.
  „ 70, note 2. See also Bulling. adv. Anabapt. Lib. III. cap. 11, fol. 114.
  „ 158, „ 5. Cap. 10.
  „ 202, „ 1. Lib. IV. cap. 31.
  „ 214, „ 3. Lib. III. cap. 4.
  „ 252, line 1. Bullinger has quoted from Lombard. Sentent. Lib. III. dist. 39.
  „ 418, „ 8. meddling : commixtio, Lat.

VOLUME II.

Page 106, note 2. See also Bulling. von der verfolgung, &c. Chap. 13, p. 47, and Homil. in Jesaiam, fol. 93 a.
  „ 217, line 19. See Zurich Letters, B. p. 243.
  „ 360, note 2. quæst. 2.
  „ 380, „ 2. See also Contra Adv. Leg. et Proph. Lib. I. cap. 24.
  „ 385, line 14. This is Calvin's definition in the 2nd edition of his Institutes. Argent. 1539.
  „ 406, note 1, line 13. Lib. I. cap. 23.
  „ 425, „ 8, „ 3. Cap. 4.

VOLUME III.

Page 135, line 17. Extracted from Galatinus, De Arcanis Cathol. Veritat. Lib. II. cap. 17.
„ 194, note 3. The philosopher was Anaxagoras. Lactant. Lib. III. cap. 9.
„ 242, See Zurich Letters, A. p. 30.
„ 245, line 37. The definition is Augustine's, Contra Maxim. Lib. II. cap. 5.
„ 329, note 4, line 1. cap. 3.
„ „ „ „ „ 2. Lib. I. cap. 6.
„ 337, „ 3, „ 7. cap. 11.
„ 375, „ 2, „ 4. cap. 14.

VOLUME IV.

Page viii. line 15. See Vol. III. p. 57.
„ xiii. note 18. See Zurich Letters, A. p. 127. n. 2.
„ xx. Numb. 38. Quære. Is not this the book, in an English translation, mentioned by the Martyr, Philpot? See Examinations, &c. of Archdeacon Philpot, ed. P. S. pp. xix. xx.; and see also p. 382, note 1, of this volume.
„ xxii. line 26. See Zurich Letters, A. p. 26.
„ xxviii. „ 30. Of these "Orders" at least six original or contemporary copies are known to exist: viz. 1. Mr. Fisher's copy in his epitome of the Acts of Convocation: (Wilkins' Concil. Vol. IV. pp. 321, 322. Cardwell's Synodal. Vol. II. pp. 562—564.) 2. The copy in the State-paper Office. 3. The copy in Abp. Whitgift's Register at Lambeth. 4. A copy made for Abp. Whitgift by his private secretary, Mr. Murgatroid, (Lambeth Library, MSS. 178. fol. 64.) 5. A copy in Bp. Cox's Register at Ely, (ff. 317. b. 318. a.) where also they are stated to have been "sent down by his Lord's Grace of Canterbury in August, 1587." And 6, a copy in the British Museum, (Cotton. MSS. Cleopatra, F. II. ff. 275, 276,) written on a folio sheet, which has been cross-folded in the usual form for registry deposit, and endorsed in the original hand,—" Orders for the better increase of learning in the inferior sorte of Ministers, Secundo Decemb. 1586. Not established by Synodall authoritye, but thought convenient to put in execution by Ordinary Authoritye, and till further order shall be provided by Authoritye of hir Ma'ty and the Synode.—Registratur. fol. 97."

Even previous, however, to the introduction of these "Orders" into the Upper House of Convocation, it appears by the Records of the Diocese of London preserved in St Paul's, that in the summer of 1586, an "Order was sent forth by my L. Grace of Cant. for th' exercise of the unlerneder sorte of the Ministery;" and that on the 5 day of August, Edward Stanhope, Chancellor of that diocese, directed the Archdeacon's Registrar to make a copy.

For all this additional information, the Editor is indebted to the obliging kindness of the Rev. G. C. Gorham.
„ 63, „ 23. See August. De Util. Cred. cap. 1.
„ 67, note 8, line 2. cap. 5.
„ 125, „ 7, „ 5. Lib. I.
„ „ „ 8, „ 5. Lib. II.
„ 126, „ 1, „ 10. Lib. I.
„ 247, „ 9, „ 2. Also De Baptismo contra Donat. Lib. I. cap. 1.
„ 397, line 13. See pp. 94. n. 6. and 345. n. 3.
„ 409, „ 21. See Cyprian. De Orat. Dom. and August. De Bono Persev. cap. 13.

SELECTED BIBLIOGRAPHY
George Ella

Catalogs
Herkenrath, E., *Heinrich Bullinger Werke, Beschreibendes Verzeichnis der Litaratur über Heinrich Bullinger*, TVZ, 1977.

Staedke, J., *Heinrich Bullinger Werke, Beschreibendes Verzeichnis der gedruckten Werke von Heinrich Bullinger*, TVZ, 1972.

Primary sixteenth century sources used
Bächtold, Hans Ulrich and Henrich, Rainer (eds), *Heinrich Bullinger Werke, Briefe des Jahres 1539*, TVZ, 2002.

Bächtold, Hans Ulrich and Henrich, Rainer (eds), *Heinrich Bullinger Werke, Briefe des Jahres 1540*, TVZ, 2003.

Bächtold, Hans Ulrich, *Heinrich Bullinger vor dem Rat, Zur Gestalltung und Verwaltung des Züricher Staatswesens in den Jahren 1531-1775*, Bern-Frankfurt a. M., 1982.

Blanke, Fritz, *Zwingli Hauptschriften*, only vols 1,2,3,4,7,9,11 issued, Zwingli-Verlag, Zürich, 1940-48.

Bromiley, G. W. (ed), *Zwingli and Bullinger*, The Library of Christian Classics, Vol. XXIV, SCM Press, 1953.

Bucer, Martin, *Common Places of Martin Bucer* (ed. and trans. by D. F. Wright), The Sutton Courtenay Press, 1972.

Bullinger, Heinrich, *Der Widertöufferen ursprung fürgang Secten wäsen etc.*, 1561 facsimile, Zentralantiquariat der Deutschen Demokratischen Republik, Leipzig, 1975.

Calvin, Jean, *Calvin-Studienausgabe I.1., Band I, Reformatorische Anfänge (1533-1541)*, hrsg. Eberhard Busch et al., Neukirchener Verlag, 1994.

Calvin, Johannes, *Unterricht in der christlichen Religion: Institutio Christianae Religionis* (trans. Otto Weber), Neukirchener Verlag, 1986.

Calvin, John, *Calvin's Commentaries*, The Library of Christian Classics, Vol. XXIII, SCM, 1958.

Calvin, John, *Institutes of the Christian Religion*, (2 vols.), Eerdmans, 1979.

Calvin, John, *Theological Treatises*, The Library of Christian Classics, Vol. XXII, SCM, 1954.

Calvin, John, *Works*, Ages Digital Library, John Calvin Collection, CD, Rio, Wisconsin, 2000.

Cardwell, Edward, *Documentary Annals of the Reformed Church of England*, (2 vols.), 1844.

Christoffel, R., *Huldrich Zwingli: Leben und Ausgewählte Schriften*, Elberfeld, 1857.

Clemen, O., (ed.), *Luthers Briefe an seine Käthe*, Berlin, 1929.

Cochrane, Arthur (ed.), *Reformed Copnfessions of the Sixteenth Century*, SCM, 1966.

Duke, Alastair (trans. And ed.), *Calvinism in Europe 1540-1610: A Collection of Documents*, Manchester University Press, 1997.

Franz, Johann Friedrich, *Merkwürdige Züge aus den Leben des Zürcherischen Antistes Heinrich Bullinger, nebst dessen Reiseinstruktion und Briefen an seinen ältesten Sohn Heinrich, auf den Lehranstalten zu Strassburg und Wittenberg*, Bern, 1828.

Gäbler, Ulrich and Zsindely, E. (eds), *Heinrich Bullinger Werke, Briefe der Jahre 1524-1531*, TVZ, 1974.

Gee, Henry and Hardy, William John, *Documents Illustrative of English Church History*, Macmillan, 1910.

Harder, Leland (ed.), *The Sources of Swiss Anabaptism: The Grebel Letters and Related Documents*, Herald Press, 1985.

Held, Friedrich (ed.), *Dr. Martin Luthers Vorreden zur Heiligen Schrift*, Heilbronn, undated.

Hillerbrand, H. J., *The Reformation in its Own Words*, SCM, 1964.

Melanchthon, Philipp, *Loci Communes 1521*, Lateinisch-Deutsch, übers. Horst Georg Pöhlman, Gütersloher Verlagshaus, 1993.

Metzger, Wolfgang (ed.), *Martin Luther: Ausgewählte Werke* (6 vols.), Calver Verlag, 1930.

Parker Society, *Decades*, 4 vols., 1849.

Parker Society, *Original Letters Relative to the English Reformation, 1537-1558*, 2 Vols., 1847.

Parker Society, *Zürich Letters*, First Series, 1558-1579, 1842.

Parker Society, *Zürich Letters*, Second Series, 1558-1602, 1845.

Parker, T.H.L. (ed.) *English Reformers*, The Library of Christian Classics, Vol. XXVI, SCM, 1966.

Pestalozzi, Carl, *Heinrich Bullinger. Leben und ausgewählte Schriften*, Eberfeld, 1858.

Schirrmacher, Friedrich Wilhelm (ed.), *Briefe und Akten zum Marburger Religionsgespräch (1529) und zum Augsburger Reichstag (1530)*, VKW, Bonn, 2003.

Spitz, Lewis W., et al., *The Protestant Reformation: Major Documents*, CPH, St Louis, 1997.

Stotz, P. (trans. and ed.) *Heinrich Bullinger Werke*, Studiorum ratio: Studienanleitung, Teil Band 2, Einleitung, Kommentar, Register, TVZ, 1987.

Stotz, P. (trans. and ed.), *Heinrich Bullinger Werke, Studiorum ratio: Studienanleitung*, Teil Band 1, Text und Uebersetzung, TVZ, 1987.

Vom Berg, H. G. and Hausammann S. (eds), *Heinrich Bullinger Werke, Exegetische Schriften aus den Jahren 1525-1526*, TVZ, 1983.

Vom Berg, H. G. et al (eds), *Heinrich Bullinger Werke, Unveröffentlichte Werke der Kappeler Zeit*. Theologica, TVZ, 1991.

Wartenberg, Günther (ed.), *Martin Luther Briefe*, Leipzig, 1983.

Whitaker, E. C. (ed.), *Martin Bucer and the Book of Common Prayer*. Censura; De Ordinatione Legitima, Mayhew-McCrimmon Ltd, 1974.

Biographies and Critical Historical Evaluations

Anrich, Gustav, *Martin Bucer*, Strassburg, 1914.

Atkinson, James, *Martin Luther and the Birth of Protestantism*, Penguin Books, 1968.

Bächtold, Hans Ulrich, *Heinrich Bullinger*, Historisches Lexicon der Schweiz, Institute für schweizerische Reformationsgeschichte, 2003.

Bachtolf, Hans Ulrich, *Heinrich Bullinger vor dem Rat, Zur Gestalltung und Verwaltung des Züricher Staatswesens in den Jahren 1531-1775*, Bern-Frankfurt a. M., 1982.

Bevan, Frances, *The Life of William Farel*, Alfred Holness, Glasgow, undated.

Blanke, Fritz and Leuschner, Immanuel, *Heinrich Bullinger: Vater der reformierten Kirche*, Theologischer Verlag Zürich, 1990.

Blanke, Fritz, *Der Junge Bullinger*, Zürich, 1942.

Bouvier, André, *Henri Bullinger, Réformateur et conseiller oecuménique*, Zürich-Neuchâtel, 1940.

Bromiley, G.W., *Thomas Cranmer*, Church Book Room Press, 1956.

Büsser, Fritz, *Die Prophezei: Humanismus und Reformation in Zürich*, Züricher Beiträge zur Reformationsgeschichte, Verlag Peter Lang, 1994.

Büsser, Fritz, *Heinrich Bullinger (1504-1575): Leben, Werk und Wirkung*, Band I, TVZ, 2004.

Campi, Emidio (ed.), *Heinrich Bullinger und seiner Zeit: Eine Vorlesungsreihe*, TVZ, 2004.

Choisy, Eugene, *L'État Chrétien Calviniste A Genève*, Genève and Paris, undated, ca 1900.

Collette, Charles Hastings, *The Life, Times, and Writings of Thomas Cranmer, D.D.*, London, 1887.

Ella, G. M., *The Troublemakers at Frankfurt: A Vindication of the English Reformation*, Go Publications, 2003.

Ella, G. M., *Mountain Movers*, Go Publications, 1999.

Ella G. M., *More Mountain Movers*, Go Publications, 2005.

Evangelisches Kirchenlexikon, Vol. I, A-G, Göttingen, 1956. See entry under Bullinger, Johann Heinrich.

Fast, Heinold, *Heinrich Bullinger und die Täufer*, Mennonitischen Geschichtsverein e. V., Weierhof (Pfalz), 1959.

Friedrich, Reinhold, *Martin Bucer - Fanatiker der Einheit?*, VKW, Bonn, 2002.

Gäbler, Ulrich, *Huldrych Zwingli: His Life and Work*, Fortress Press, 1986.

Gloede, Günter, *Calvin: Weg und Werk*, Leipzig, 1953.

Hollweg, Heinrich, *Bullingers Hausbuch*, Neukirchen, 1956.

Kendall, R.T., *Calvin and English Calvinism to 1649*, Paternoster Press, 1997.

Koenigsberger, H. G. and Mosse, George L., *Europe in the Sixteenth Century*, Longman, 1972.

Köhler, Walter, *Huldrych Zwingli*, Leipzig, 1943.

Krahn, Cornelius, *Dutch Anabaptism*, Herald Press, 1981.

Kraijewski, Ekkehard, *Leben und Sterben des Züricher Täuferführers Felix Manz*, Oncken Verlag, 1962.

Lang, August, *Zwingli und Calvin*, Bielefeld and Leipzig, 1913.

Lee, Frederick George, *The Church under Queen Elizabeth*, 2 vols, London, 1880.

Lindsay, T. M., *Luther and the German Reformation*, Edinburgh, 1900.

Locher, Gottfried W., *Die evangelische Stellung der Reformatoren zum öffentlichen Leben*, Zwingli Verlag, 1950.

Locher, Gottfried W., *Huldrych Zwingli und Karl V. Das Vorwort zur Fidei Ratio, 1530*, Theologische Zeitschrift der Universität Basel, Jahrgang 46, 1990, pp. 205-218.

Locher, Gottfried W., *Huldrych Zwingli in Neuer Sicht: Zehn Beiträge zur Theologie der Züricher Reformation*, Zwingli Verlag, 1969.

MacCulloch, Diarmaid, *Thomas Cranmer*, Yale University Press, 1996.

McGrath, Alister E, *Johann Calvin*, Benziger, 1991.

McGrath, Alister E., *Reformation Thought: An Introduction*, Basil Blackwell, 1988.

McGrath, Patrick, *Papists and Puritans under Elizabeth I*, London, 1967.

Middleton, Erasmus, *Biographia Evangelica* (4 vols), Bullinger's biography in vol. II, Subscription, 1784.

Müller, Patrik, *Heinrich Bullinger: Reformator, Kirchenpolitiker*, Historiker, TVZ, 2004.

Oberman, Heiko A., *Luther: Mensch Zwischen Gott und Teufel*, dtv, 1986.

Pesch, Otto Hermann, *Hinführung zu Luther*, Matthias Grünewald, 1982.

Prestwich, Menna (ed), *International Calvinism 1541-1715*, Clarendon Press, 1986.

Schirrmacher, Thomas (Hg.), *Anwalt der Liebe – Martin Bucer als Theologe und Seelsorger*, VKW, 2001.

Schraepler, Horst W., *Die rechtliche Behandlung der Täufer in der deutschen Schweiz, Südwestdeutschland und Hessen 1525-1618*, Tübingen, 1957.

Staedtke, Joachim, *Johannes Calvin: Erkentnis und Gestaltung*, Göttingen, 1969.

Stephens, W.P. (ed.), *The Bible, the Reformation and the Church: Essays in Honour of James Atkinson*, Sheffield Academic Press, 1995.

Stupperich, Robert, *Melanchthon: The Enigma of the Reformation*, Lutterworth Press, 1966.

Suts, Johannes, *Heinrich Bullinger: Der Retter der Züricher Reformation*, Zürich, 1915.

Tulloch, John, *Luther and Other Leaders of the Reformation*, William Blackwood and Sons, 1883.

Van Campen, M., *Martin Bucer en vergeten reformator*, Boekcentrum, 1991.

Van der Zwaag, K., *Afwachten of verwachten? De toe-eigening des heils in historisch en theologisch perspectif*, Uitgeverij Groen/Heerenveen, 2003.

Von, Schulthess-Rechberg, *Heinrich Bullinger der Nachfolger Zwinglis*, Halle, 1904.

Warfield, Benjamin B., "On the Literary History of the Institutes," *Works*, Vol. V, Baker Book House, 1981.

Specific Theological Studies

Adam, Gottfried, *Der Streit um die Prädestination im ausgehenden 16. Jahrhundert*, Neukirchener Verlag, 1970.

Baker, Joseph Wayne, *Heinrich Bullinger and the Covenant. The Other Reformed Tradition*. Athens (Ohio), 1980.

Battles, Ford Lewis (ed. and trans.), *John Calvin's Institutes of the Christian Religion*, 1536 Edition, Eerdmans, 1995.

Battles, Ford Lewis, *Analysis of the Institutes of the Christian Religion*, Baker Book House, 1989.

Beeke, Joel R., *Puritan Reformed Spirituality*, Reformation Heritage Books, 2004.

Cochrane, Arthur C. (ed.), *Reformed Confessions of the 16th Century*, SCM, 1966.

Cunningham, William, *Historical Theology*, 2 vols, Edinburgh, 1870.

Cunningham, William, *The Reformers and the Theology of the Reformation*, BOTT, 1979.

Davies, Horton, *Worship and Theology in England*, (3 vols.), Eerdmans, 1996.

Gordon, Bruce and Campi, Emido (eds), *Architect of Reformation: An Introduction to Heinrich Bullinger, 1504-1575*. Baker Academic, 2004.

Green, E. Tyrrell, *The Thirty-Nine Articles and the Age of the*

Reformation: An Historical and Doctrinal Exposition in the Light of Contemporary Documents, London, 1896.

Krabbendam, Henry, *Sovereignty and Responsibility: The Pelagian-Augustinian Controversy in Philosophical and Global Perspective*, VKW, Bonn, 2002.

Locher, Gottfried, W., *Grundzüge der Theologie Huldrych Zwinglis im Vergleich mit derjenigen Martin Luthers und Johannes Calvins*, Zwingliana, Zürich, Sonderdruck aus den Zwingliana, Heft 7 und 8, 1967.

Opitz, Peter, *Heinrich Bullinger als Theologe: Eine Studie zu den 'Dekaden,'* TVZ , 2004.

Schaff, Philip, *The Creeds of Christendom*, 3 vols., Baker, 1996.

Venema, Cornelis P., *Heinrich Bullinger and the Doctrine of Predestination*, Baker Academic, 2002.

Walser, Peter, *Die Prädestination bei Heinrich Bullinger im Zusammenhang mit siner Gotteslehre*, Zürich, 1957.

General Works on the English and Continental Reformations

Blunt, John Henry, *The Reformation of the Church of England*, 2 vols, Rivington's, 1882.

Bornkamm, *Das Jahrhundert der Reformation*, Göttingen, 1966.

Brieger, Theodor, *Die Reformation: Ein Stück aus Deutschlands Weltgeschichte*, Verlag Ulstein, 1913.

D'Aubigné, J. H. Merle, *History of the Reformation of the Sixteenth Century*, Edinburgh, 1854.

D'Aubigné, J. H. Merle, *Reformationen in Europa på Calvins Tid*, 2 vols., Stockholm, 1874.

D'Aubigné, J. H. Merle, *The Reformation in England*, Vol. II, BOTT, 1963.

Dickens, A. G., *Reformation and Society in Sixteenth-Century Europe*, Thames and Hudson, 1966.

Dickens, A.G., *The English Reformation*, B.T. Badsford Ltd, 1965.

Froude, James Antony, *History of England* (12 vols.), New York, 1969.

Gairdner, James, *History of the English Church in the Sixteenth Century*, Macmillan & Co., 1904.

Green, V. H. H., *Renaissance and Reformation: A Survey of*

European History between 1450 and 1660, Edward Arnold, 1969.

Janse, W., *Grenzeloos gereformeerd*, Vreije Universiteit Amsterdam, 2004.

Kidd, B.J., *The Continental Reformation*, Rivingtons, 1925.

Lindburg, Carter, *The European Reformations*, Blackwell, 1996.

Lindsey, T. M., *History of the Reformation*, vol. 2, In Lands Beyond Germany, Edinburgh, 1951.

MacCulloch, Diarmaid, *Reformation: Europe's House Divided 1490-1700*, Penguin, 2004.

Milner, Joseph and Isaac; Haweis, Thomas, *The History of the Church of Christ*, Thomas Nelson, undated.

Miles, Charles Popham, *The Voice of the Glorious Reformation*, London, 1844.

Moeller, Wilhelm, *History of the Christian Church*, Vol. III, Reformation and Counter-Reformation 1517-1648, London, 1893.

Murdock, James (ed.), *Mosheim's Institutes of Ecclesiastical History*, Ward, Lock & Co., 1848.

Oberman, Heiko A., *Die Reformation*, Vandenhoeck und Ruprecht, 1986.

Oberman, Heiko A., *The Dawn of the Reformation*, T. & T. Clark, 1986.

Oberman, Heiko A., *Werden und Wertung der Reformation*, J.C.B Mohr, 1995.

Overton, John Henry, *The Church in England*, 2 vols, London, 1897.

Pflugk-Harttung, Julius von, et al, *Im Morgenrot der Reformation*, Hersfeld, 1912.

Pill, David H., *The English Reformation 1529-58*, University of London Press, 1973.

Schmidt, Kurt Dietrich, *Kirchengeschichte*, Göttingen, 1967.

Scribner, Bob, et al, *The Reformation in National Context*, CUP, 1994.

Scott, John, *The History of the Church of Christ*, 3 vols, L. B. Seeley and Sons, 1826.

Seebass, Gottfried, *Die Reformation und ihre Ausenseiter*, Göttingen, 1997.

Smedley, Edward, *History of the Reformed Religion in France*, vol. 1, London, 1832.

Stupperich, Robert, *Geschichte der Reformation*, dtv, 1967.

Thulin, Oskar et al, *Reformation in Europa*, Berlin, 1967.

Von Ranke, Leopold, *Deutsche Geschichte im Zeitalter der Reformation*, Bertelsmann, undated.

Von Ranke, Leopold, *History of the Reformation in Germany*, London, 1905.

Wengler, J., *Die dritte Reformation*, Oncken Verlag, 1963.

Journal, Magazine, Webpage, and Newspaper Articles

Beeke, Joel R., "Election and Reprobation: Calvin on Equal Ultimacy," *BOT Magazine*, Issue 489, June 2004, pp. 8-19.

Bühler, Peter, "Der Abendmahlsstreit der Reformatoren und seine aktuellen Implikationen," *Theologische Zeitschrift*, Basel, 35. Jahrgang, 1979, pp. 228-241.

Campi, Emidio, "Ein Leben für die Reformation," *Neue Züricher Zeitung*, 17 July, 2004, 08:46, also NZZ Online.

Ella, G. M., "Henry Bullinger," *New Focus*, Part I, Vol. 7, No. 01, Part II, Vol. 7, No. 02, 2002 and Zürich University website, www.unizh.ch.

Ella, G. M., "Henry Bullinger (1504-1575), Shepherd of the Churches," *The Banner of Sovereign Grace Truth*, Grand Rapids, Vol 12, No. 5, May-June 2004.

Ella, G. M., "Martin Bucer: Moderator of the Reformation," *New Focus*, Vol. 6, No. 4, Dec.-Jan. 2002.

Engammare, Max, "Calvin: A Prophet without a Prophecy, Church History: Studies in Christianity and Culture," *The American Society of Church History*, Year 1998, pp. 643-661.

Faber, Eva-Maria, "Zur Frage der Prädestination in der Theologie Johannes Calvins," *Theologische Zeitschrift der Universität Basel*, Jahrgang 56, 2000, pp. 50-68.

Kohls, Ernst-Wilhelm, "Martin Bucer als Anhänger Luthers," *Theologishe Zeitschrift*, Basle, 33. Jahrgang, 1977, pp. 210-218.

Naphy, William G., "Calvin's Letters. Reflections on their usefulness in Studying Genevan History," *Archiv für Reformationsgeschichte*, Jahrgang 86, pp. 67-89.

Müller, Bernd, "Bildersturm: ein Ausstellungskatalog und ein

Sammelband," *Archiv für Reformationsgeschichte*, Jahrgang 93, pp. 391-396.

Pine, Leonard, "Heinrich Bullinger: The Common Shepherd of All Christian Churches," Zürich University website, www. unizh.ch

Rabe, Horst, "Zur Entstehung des Augsburger Interims 1547-48," *Archiv für Reformationsgeschichte*, Jahrgang 94, pp. 6-104.

Schmid, Peter, "Heinrich Bullinger – zum 500 Geburtstag – neu zu entdecken," *Livenry*, Ch., 25.01.2005.

Sladeczek, Franz-Josef, "Die goetze in miner herren chilchen sind gerumpt!, Ein Beitrag zur Berner Reformationsgeschichte," *Theologishe Zeitschrift*, Basel, 44. Jahrgang, 1988, pp. 289-311.

Wilcox, Peter, "The Lectures of John Calvin and the Nature of his Audience," *Archiv für Reformationsgeschichte*, Jahrgang 87, pp. 136-48.